Guide

AA Lifestyle Guides

Please contact
Advertisement Sales: advertisingsales@theaa.com
Editorial Department: lifestyleguides@theaa.com

Typeset by Servis Filmsetting Ltd, Stockport
Printed in Italy by Printer Trento SRL, Trento

This directory is compiled by AA Lifestyle Guides; managed in the Librios Information Management System and generated by the AA establishment database system.

AA Restaurant Guide edited by Andrew Turvil, assisted by Fiona Griffiths

Restaurant descriptions have been contributed by the following team of writers: Fiona Griffiths, David Hancock, Hugh Morgan, Mike Pedley, Carina Simon, Allen Stidwill, Stuart Taylor, Andrew Turvil

Published by AA Publishing, a trading name of AA M[...]
Fanum House, Basing View, Basingstoke, Hampshir[...]
Registered number 06112600.

A CIP catalogue for this book is available from the B[...]
ISBN: 978-0-7495-7363-8
A04886

Maps prepared by the
Mapping Services Department
of AA Publishing.

Maps © AA Media Limited 2012.

Contains Ordnance Survey data
© Crown copyright and database right 2012.

 Land & This is based upon Crown
Property Copyright and is reproduced
Services. with the permission of Land &
Property Services under delegated authority from the
Controller of Her Majesty's Stationery Office.

© Crown copyright and database rights 2012
Licence number 100,363.
Permit number 110095

 Ordnance Republic of Ireland mapping based
Survey on © Ordnance Survey Ireland/
Ireland Government of Ireland Copyright
Ireland's National Mapping Agency
Permit number MP000611

Information on National Parks in England provided by the Countryside Agency (Natural England).

Information on National Parks in Scotland provided by Scottish Natural Heritage.

Information on National Parks in Wales provided by The Countryside Council for Wales.

Contents

How to Use the Guide

1 MAP REFERENCE

The atlas section is at the back of the Guide. The map page number is followed by the National Grid Reference. To find a location, read the first figure horizontally and the second figure vertically within the lettered square. For Central London and Greater London, there is a 13-page map section starting on page 233.

2 PLACE NAME

Restaurants are listed in country and county order, then by town and then alphabetically within the town. There is an index by restaurant at the back of the book and a similar one for the Central & Greater London sections on page 229.

3 RESTAURANT NAME

4 ⚙ THE AA ROSETTE AWARD

Entries have been awarded one or more Rosettes, up to a maximum of five. See page 7.

5 FOOD STYLE

Food style of the restaurant is followed by a short summary statement.

6 PHOTOGRAPHS

Restaurants are invited to enhance their entry with up to two photographs.

7 CHEF(S) AND OWNER(S)

The names of the chef(s) and owner(s) are as up-to-date as possible at the time of going to press, but changes in personnel often occur, and may affect both the style and quality of the restaurant.

8 PRICES

Prices are for fixed lunch (2 courses) and dinner (3 courses) and à la carte dishes. Service charge information (see also opposite). Note: Prices quoted are a guide only, and are subject to change.

---

2 COGGESHALL   Map 7 TL82 **1**

3 **Baumann's Brasserie**

4 ⚙⚙ French, European V **18**

5

6

Gutsy cooking in buzzy brasserie

☎ 01376 561453
4-6 Stoneham St CO6 1TT
e-mail: food@baumannsbrasserie.co.uk
web: www.baumannsbrasserie.co.uk **17**

10 dir: A12 from Chelmsford, exit at Kelvedon into Coggeshall. Restaurant in centre opposite clock tower

Chef-patron Mark Baumann's buzzy brasserie in a 16th-century timbered house is still thriving a quarter of a century after it was launched by his then boss, Peter Langan, of Langan's Brasserie renown. The formula of serving inventively-reworked French and British dishes is clearly a winner, since a strong following of loyal locals have grown up with its continental-style pavement tables. Inside, the place is a true one-off, resembling a **16** bijou art gallery decorated with antique linen-clothed tables, and there's always a sense of fun to set the mood. Its no-nonsense plats du jour and daily-changing menus are driven by the seasons rather than the winds of culinary fashion, so you might start out with a hot-smoked salmon crumpet with fennel and olive carpaccio, followed by braised ox cheeks with mushrooms and bacon, and celeriac purée. The cooking remains robustly appealing all the way through to desserts such as salted caramel chocolate sponge with custard and home-made marmalade.

7 **Chef** Mark Baumann, John Ranfield **Owner** Baumann's Brasserie Ltd **Times** 12-2/7-9.30 Closed 2 wks Jan, Mon-Tue **Prices** Fixed L 2 course £16, Fixed D 3 course £25, Starter £5-£9, Main £17-£23, Dessert £6.95, Service optional **Wines** 20 bottles over £20, 24 bottles under £20, **14** 11 by glass **Notes** Fixed L plat du jour daily, Fish menu daily, Sunday L, Vegetarian menu **Seats** 80 **15**
12 **Children** Portions **Parking** Opposite

8   **9**   **11**   **13**

---

9 NOTES

Additional information e.g. availability of vegetarian dishes, civil weddings, air conditioning etc.

10 DIRECTIONS

Directions are given if supplied.

11 PARKING DETAILS

On-site parking is listed if applicable, then nearby parking.

12 CHILDREN

Menu, portions, age restrictions etc.

13 NUMBER OF SEATS

Number of seats in the restaurant, followed by private dining room (Pr/dining room).

14 NUMBER OF WINES

Number of wines under and over £20, and available by the glass.

15 DAILY OPENING AND CLOSING TIMES

Daily opening and closing times, the days of the week it is closed and seasonal closures. Note that opening times are liable to change without notice. It is wise to telephone in advance.

16 DESCRIPTION

Description of the restaurant and the food.

17 E-MAIL ADDRESS AND WEBSITE

18 VEGETARIAN MENU

V Indicates a vegetarian menu. Restaurants with some vegetarian dishes available are indicated under Notes.

19 NOTABLE WINE LIST

🍷 Indicates notable wine list (See p22-23).

20 LOCAL AND REGIONAL PRODUCE

🥬 Indicates the use of local and regional produce. More than 50% of the restaurant food ingredients are produced within a 50-mile radius. Suppliers are mentioned by name on the menu.

All establishments take major credit cards, except where we have specified otherwise.

All information is correct at the time of printing but may change without notice. Details of opening times and prices may be omitted from an entry when the establishment has not supplied us with up-to-date information. This is indicated where the establishment name is shown in *italics*.

Service Charge

We ask restaurants the following questions about service charge (their responses appear under Prices in each entry):
- Is service included in the meal price, with no further charge added or expected?
- Is service optional – charge not automatically added to bill?
- Is service charge compulsory, and what percentage?
- Is there a service charge for larger groups, minimum number in group, and what percentage?

Many establishments automatically add service charge to the bill but tell the customer it is optional.

Smoking Regulations

From July 2007 smoking was banned in all enclosed public places in the United Kingdom and Ireland. A hotel or guest accommodation proprietor can designate one or more bedrooms with ventilation systems where the occupants can smoke, but communal areas must be smoke-free. Communal areas include the interior bars and restaurants in pubs and inns.

Facilities for Disabled Guests

The Equality Act 2010 provides legal rights for disabled people including access to goods, services and facilities, and means that service providers may have to consider making adjustments to their premises. For more information about the Act see www.direct.gov.uk/en/DisabledPeople/ RightsAndObligations/DisabilityRights/ DG_4001068 or www.equalities.gov.uk.

The establishments in this guide should be aware of their obligations under the Act. We recommend that you phone in advance to ensure that the establishment you have chosen has appropriate facilities.

Website Addresses

Where website addresses are included they have been supplied and specified by the respective establishment. Such websites are not under the control of AA Media Limited and as such AA Media Limited has no control over them and will not accept any responsibility or liability in respect of any and all matters whatsoever relating to such websites including access, content, material and functionality. By including the addresses of third-party websites the AA does not intend to solicit business or offer any security to any person in any country, directly or indirectly.

Restaurant Insurance

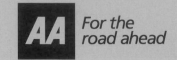

We could **save you £££'s** on your insurance.

Our fantastic Restaurant Insurance Package includes the following:

- ✔ Buildings and Contents, including frozen foods, wines & spirits
- ✔ Generous seasonal increases in stock cover
- ✔ Public Liability & Employers Liability
- ✔ Loss of Licence
- ✔ Business Interruption covered
- ✔ Money with personal accident & assault benefits
- ✔ Plus much more all tailored to your business

Call us on
0800 107 9791

How the AA Assesses for Rosette Awards

The AA's Rosette award scheme was the first nationwide scheme for assessing the quality of food served by restaurants and hotels. The Rosette scheme is an award, not a classification, and although there is necessarily an element of subjectivity when it comes to assessing taste, we aim for a consistent approach throughout the UK. Our awards are made solely on the basis of a meal visit or visits by one or more of our hotel and restaurant Inspectors, who have an unrivalled breadth and depth of experience in assessing quality. They award Rosettes annually on a rising scale of one to five.

So what makes a restaurant worthy of a Rosette Award?

For our Inspectors, the top and bottom line is the food. The taste of a dish is what counts, and whether it successfully delivers to the diner the promise of the menu. A restaurant is only as good as its worst meal. Although presentation and competent service should be appropriate to the style of the restaurant and the quality of the food, they cannot affect the Rosette assessment as such, either up or down. The summaries below indicate what our Inspectors look for, but are intended only as guidelines. The AA is constantly reviewing its award criteria, and competition usually results in an all-round improvement in standards, so it becomes increasingly difficult for restaurants to reach award level. For more detailed Rosette criteria, please visit theAA.com.

⚘ One Rosette
- Excellent restaurants that stand out in their local area
- Food prepared with care, understanding and skill
- Good quality ingredients

Around 50% of restaurants have one Rosette.

⚘⚘ Two Rosettes
- The best local restaurants
- Higher standards
- Better consistency
- Greater precision apparent in the cooking
- Obvious attention to the quality and selection of ingredients

About 40% of restaurants have two Rosettes.

⚘⚘⚘ Three Rosettes
- Outstanding restaurants demanding recognition well beyond local area
- Selection and sympathetic treatment of highest quality ingredients
- Timing, seasoning and judgement of flavour combinations consistent
- Excellent intelligent service and a well-chosen wine list

Around 10% of restaurants have three Rosettes.

⚘⚘⚘⚘ Four Rosettes
Dishes demonstrate:
- intense ambition
- a passion for excellence
- superb technical skills
- remarkable consistency
- appreciation of culinary traditions combined with desire for exploration and improvement
- Cooking demands national recognition

Twenty-seven restaurants have four Rosettes.

⚘⚘⚘⚘⚘ Five Rosettes
- Cooking stands comparison with the best in the world
- Highly individual
- Breathtaking culinary skills
- Setting the standards to which others aspire
- Knowledgeable and distinctive wine list

Nine restaurants have five Rosettes.

The walls are coming down

Coming of Age

By ANDREW TURVIL

Welcome to the twentieth edition of the AA Restaurant Guide.

A lot has happened in the world since we published our first edition. Recessions have come and gone, and come back again with a vengeance. The internet is now hard wired into our way of life. Mobile phones turned out to be more than just an annoying buzzy sound from the next table. And there's no doubt a time-travelling restaurant customer jumping those 20 years in an instant might be rather baffled when presented with the wine list on an iPad (yes, it's happening), raise an eyebrow at the sight of ice cream and pannacotta among the first courses, and be confounded by the array of vegetables in the desserts. And they've no need to complain if there's dust or ash on their plate...there it is on the menu in black and white. Things really have changed.

Menus don't read the same as they did. When the first edition of The Restaurant Guide came out in the early 1990s, the name of the farm from whence came the lamb you're tucking into didn't get a mention. But now...there it is along with the breed of animal. They tell you if the scallops were brought to the surface by hand. Today's menus give us information. Previously we seemed happy in the knowledge that the loin of lamb 'nestled' amongst its accompanying vegetables, or that the sea bass was 'napped' in its accompanying saffron sauce. The flowery adverb is (thankfully) a dying art form.

And the best change of all: The UK is no longer an international byword for rubbish food. The tide started to turn some time ago, and just as the technology landscape has changed over the past two decades, so too has the world of food. The restaurants have changed, our expectations have changed, and standards have risen across the board.

What led to this quiet and hungry revolution?

Switched On

In May 2012 the BBC announced that children's TV was being shifted permanently onto its digital channels. No more are *The Clangers*' spiritual descendants to be found on BBC1 and 2. What will you find filling your screen instead? A whole larder of cookery and foodie shows, that's what.

Ready Steady Cook first aired in 1994 and a love affair with chefs was born. Apparently chefs had personalities...who knew? There was Happy, Grumpy, Doc, Bashful...erm...Angry, et al. A new career emerged...that of celebrity chef. Sure there'd been chefs on TV before, but not in these numbers.

The previous food-focused output on TV was somewhat parochial, with the honourable exception of Mr Floyd, with programmes such as the BBC's *Food and Drink* and the early *Masterchef* presenting a rather stuffy image of food culture. With *Ready Steady Cook*... cooking went main stream: food as entertainment, as fun.

Producers sought out the next big thing – and an angle – *Two Fat Ladies* (1996), *Rhodes Around Britain* (1994), and then in 1999, *The Naked Chef*, one Mr Jamie Oliver. Chefs were household names.

Today programmes such as *The Great British Menu* continue to make a competition out of professional chefs' naturally competitive instincts – they still have to suffer the indignity of the pregnant pause...and the winner is... ... ... – but the best of these shows give real insight into the work of the very best chefs in the country. They reveal the acute technical skill required to cook at the top level, what it takes to develop a dish and execute it perfectly - perhaps cooking isn't so easy after all! Like a magician betraying the secrets of the Magic Circle, the TV chef is by turns revealing the trade secrets and inspiring a generation. These programmes fuelled the public's interest in the subject, and they're one hell of a recruitment drive.

Newspaper coverage has increased and foodie magazines fill the shelves.

Professional chefs even advertise supermarkets on TV. Making entertainers out of chefs gave them a platform to inform and educate the public. Their passion has rubbed off on many of us. And by revealing their personalities, the public can relate to them – they're no longer just cooks, but little stars in the kitchen, like it or not.

New Wave

One of the biggest changes over the last 20 years is the rise of new Asian cooking. You didn't find the word Pan-Asian in the first-edition of this guide. Chinese was Chinese, Thai was Thai, the cooking of Asian food in the UK was generic stuff.

The wind of change had arrived in the form of places like Chutney Mary, which took the flavours of the sub-continent and served up something a little more outré. 'Only time will tell if this initially fashionable restaurant will flourish', we wrote. Little did we know that in only a few years time the Asian restaurants would be amongst the hottest around (and that wasn't down to the chilli).

Wagamama opened its doors in 1992 and we queued around the block to sit at communal tables. This wasn't ground-breaking food – certainly not if you'd been to Tokyo – but it was a change to a more authentic and low-key style of Japanese eating (up to that point Japanese restaurants were all high-end, expense account sushi joints).

When The Sugar Club opened in 1996 and Nobu in 1997, the zinging flavours of Asia had never been more cool. The latter's black cod in miso was an epoch-defining dish, overflowing with umami before we even knew what umami was (the enigmatic fifth taste after sweet, sour, salty and bitter). The appeal was obvious. Flavours were fresh and vibrant,

"...the nation's desire to explore the flavours of the world continues."

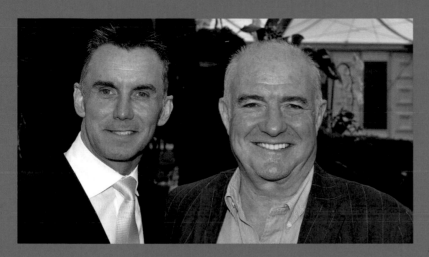

Gary Rhodes and Rick Stein - flying the flag for British food

the atmosphere cool and confident. This was fun. Not particularly cheap, but fun.

Tamarind opened in 1994 and was amongst the vanguard of the new Indian cooking, and in this guide you'll find Indian restaurants from Brighton to Edinburgh that are a million miles from the curry and lager brigade.

These dynamic changes to the style and substance of Asian cooking in the UK over the last 20 years have permeated through to the non-Asian restaurants, too, with Asian flavours giving a welcome injection of spice to many a menu, so you're just as likely to find ponzu perking up your fish as you are black butter and capers.

The journey of discovery isn't over either. These days it is the authentic cooking of South and Central America that is grabbing the headlines. The UK has always drawn inspiration from around the world and whereas the imperial flag has been lowered, pretty much, the nation's desire to explore the flavours of the world continues, now with a more authentic ring to it.

Land of hogweed and garlic

If you were blindfolded and dropped somewhere in France it wouldn't take long to work out roughly where you were if you could get your hands on a menu from a local restaurant (and you'd removed that blindfold). Whether you're in Brittany or Provence, Burgundy or Périgord, it's pretty obvious from what's on the menu. Here 20 years ago? Not a chance. Now? Well, more and more so in the restaurants that feature in this guide. Chances are, of course, the first menu you'd get hold of in the UK would come from a chain restaurant, the same from Penzance to Aberdeen, but regional identity, a local flavour, a sense of place, is a passion of many of the chefs whose restaurants appear within these pages. And they're serious about it. And it is one of the great strides forward in the UK restaurant scene over the last 20 years.

Gary Rhodes was amongst the first to fight the corner for long ignored British preparations, including bringing the faggot back into the fold (and there are a lot of faggot dishes in this edition of the Guide by the way). There were places in

our first edition which flew the flag for rustic British dishes, but it was mostly generic stuff with little or no regional identity. Flagging up the produce on a menu as local is now a major selling point.

The likes of Rick Stein in Padstow had always made a virtue of the locality, what with the quayside just across the water, the Scots made good use of their amazing shellfish, and the Welsh would let you know the lamb hadn't come from half way around the world. But today regional identity is becoming a broad and tangible thing. Local and regional produce is not just fashionable, it is what most chefs like to use. At last we are seeing the beginnings of an appreciation of what is on our doorstep. And don't go thinking those Asian-run restaurants don't have an understanding of regionalism either, for a good many of them seek out top British ingredients. For in the UK the idea of regionalism is not a list of ye olde local recipes, but rather taking the best of what the surrounding land and sea has to offer.

Many British consumers take care to enquire about the provenance of what they eat, be it sustainability or animal welfare friendly, organic or seasonal. The top chefs have always sought the very best, and still do, but now increasingly the public expect it as well. The growth of Farmers' Markets and even the premium food brands in supermarkets show consumers' enthusiasm for food that tastes of something. Those that can afford it at least.

But there's free food out there too if you know where to look! Foraging has gone from a niche activity undertaken by a few mavericks with a penchant for mushrooms to a must-do method of sourcing for any self-respecting, high achieving, 21st-century chef. And with good reason too. What better way is there to bring the seasons and a taste of your environment onto the plate? Whether it is sea purslane, hogweed or alexanders, more and more restaurants are serving up the wild ingredients that are abundant in our fields and woodlands, shores and hedgerows.

Eating inn

If what we eat has evolved over the last 20 years, where we eat it has changed too. All hail the British pub.

Let's not get carried away, chances are if you pop into your typical village inn you're going to find some pretty average food sourced from catering suppliers. Not every pub serves good fresh food cooked on the premises by any means. They don't all have to serve food at all of course, but some of those that do, do it very well indeed. The pub has in the life of this Guide become a serious contender when it comes to choosing somewhere to eat.

The Hand & Flowers, Marlow

Serious chefs don't think twice about running pubs these days, whereas 20 years ago it seemed like a punt. Take a look at the entries from the Royal Oak in Paley Street or the Hand & Flowers in Marlow if you want to see what the pub can serve up these days.

And why not? The more relaxed environment suits the 21st-century customer, where eating out need not be a big formal occasion. Some might complain that too many pubs have become restaurants, and there is indeed a line that some have crossed where they can no longer really be classed as pubs, but with so many pubs closing and remaining boarded up or converted to houses, the gastro-pub has saved many an inn from being lost forever.

The best of them combine the authentic rusticity and charm of the pub with a passion for real food. It can be a dynamic combination. And they will be around for a long time.

This relaxed attitude towards the eating environment has rubbed off on many restaurants, too. Fiona Griffiths writes (see page 24) about the ever-increasing informality in the top-end fine-dining restaurants. But despite this you will still find establishments in this Guide which expect men to wear jackets and ties; something which we try to mention in the text so you're forewarned.

Now the science bit

Molecular gastronomy. It's not a popular term among chefs. Bit too clinical I guess. Whatever we choose to call it, though, the approach of applying the laws of science to how we prepare our food has led to the biggest change in haute cuisine for a generation.

Heston Blumenthal gives us his perspective (see page 32) and it was his personal desire to question what is happening in the pan, why things are done in a particular way, and how we can use this knowledge to move things forward, that has led to so many of the advances over the last few years. He and chefs like Ferran Adria in Spain, and Paul Kitching and John Campbell here in the UK, were among the first to experiment with new cooking techniques and creative, unusual flavour combinations.

This does not debunk the past. It builds on the past and has quite possibly prevented fine dining in this country from withering away forever. French classical ways are not ignored, rather they are the springboard from which this great leap forward has been made.

Twenty years ago the top restaurants in our Guide were arguably too bound by the ways of French classical cooking, but this new way of thinking has opened up a whole world of possibilities, and given the top chefs the confidence to find their own way.

Dinner at a top-end restaurant can still be a refined and formal occasion if you wish to seek out one of its practitioners, with solicitous service and precise, classical cooking, but it can also be a rollercoaster ride of new flavours and spectacular presentations.

The greatest strength of the UK restaurant scene is its diversity: posh or scruffy, old or new...vive la différence, or horses for courses as we should probably say.

Legacy

There were four restaurants in Birmingham featured in our first edition, 9 in 2013. For a start that is a 125% increase, but, more importantly, three of those restaurants hold three Rosettes, which means they are... well...seriously good.

It is true to say London reigns supreme in its sheer number of culinary hotspots compared with the rest of the country - with its vast population that is perhaps no surprise – but today the top restaurants are reasonably spread around the country. Edinburgh had seven entries in the first AA Restaurant Guide, today it has 38. That's a 440% increase! And it has eight restaurants with three Rosettes or more.

There are first-class restaurants all over the country. It used to be the case that young chefs were drawn to the capital like moths to a lightbulb, but finally there is a sense that a good career can be gained, a name made, without resorting to a London life.

The brothers Roux, Raymond Blanc, Pierre Koffmann, Nico Ladenis and Marco Pierre White were the top dogs in the Guide 20 years ago. They'd already made their reputations, staked their claims to culinary greatness. And what we are experiencing today is the

Marco Pierre White – trots on the menu?

legacy of those great chefs - those who passed through their kitchens. It is many of the men and women who worked with these great chefs, who learned what it takes to cook at the highest level, that are leading the British culinary charge today.

The restaurant landscape of today owes a great debt to these chefs whose own obsessions for perfection have been passed down the line to the next generation. And so it continues.

The next 20 years

There are many important issues facing our food culture over the next 20 years and subjects like how to feed the planet

and get food to the starving millions dwarfs any discussion of fashions and fads in the UK restaurant industry. But anything that leads to a greater understanding of food, a greater respect for the fruits of the land and the sea, has to be a good thing.

The restaurants listed in this edition of the Guide are those places that are passionate about real food. About fresh ingredients. About eating things when they are at their best. Whether they like to experiment or keep things simple, they have a vested interest in sustainability and quality. You can't make a silk purse out of a sow's ear, but you can make a very nice beignet.

This year's AA Chefs' Chef Award goes to the legendary Pierre Koffmann

Pierre Koffmann

A love of rugby first brought Pierre Koffmann to London, but it is his achievements in the culinary world that have kept him here for over 40 years. This year his peers have recognised his phenomenal contribution to the nation's gastronomy, which saw La Tante Claire become a beacon of haute cuisine, second to none among UK restaurants.

Born and brought up in Tarbes in south-west France, not far from Lourdes, Koffmann left school early and found himself at catering college. This three years of training, combined with a love of the food of his native Gascony gained from his mother and grandmother, set him on a path to become one of the UK's top restaurateurs.

Arriving in London at the beginning of the 1970s, he never intended to stay (just to watch that game of rugby at Twickenham), but a job at Le Gavroche saw him promoted up the ranks very quickly. When Michel Roux opened the Waterside Inn, such was the talent of this young Frenchman, Koffmann was the man he turned to to become head chef, a position he held for five years.

Then in 1977, Koffmann and his wife Annie opened La Tante Claire in Royal Hospital Road, Chelsea, and the accolades came, as did the customers, packing out the restaurant night after night. Koffmann's cooking combined the flavoursome country dishes of Gascony with the refinement of classic French haute cuisine to deliver superlative food.

...a craftsman who delights in sending out first-class food.

Pierre Koffmann is a chef who likes to be at the stove, a craftsman who delights in sending out first-class food. A pussycat he is not. But those who worked with him at La Tante Claire have gone away with an understanding of what it takes to achieve the very best, and many of today's kitchens are staffed by people educated and inspired by him.

Following the sad passing of Annie in 1996, it was only a couple of years before the great days in Royal Hospital Road came to an end. A foray into the Berkeley Hotel kept the Tante Claire name alive for a few more years before retirement beckoned.

Those who know him best were doubtless unsurprised that 'retirement' only lasted a few years. First it was a pop-up restaurant on the roof of Selfridges, then in 2010 Koffmann's at the Berkeley Hotel opened to a resounding hurrah from Britain's foodies. Taking inspiration once again from the cooking of south-western France, Koffmann's serves expertly crafted brasserie-style dishes in a charmingly relaxed space, and there's even an open kitchen so you can see the master at work.

On The Menu

Foie gras chaud, pain de épice et pomme
Hot foie gras with gingerbread and apple

Bar sauvage, légumes racines et citron confit
Wild sea bass with lemon confit
and root vegetables

Ouef à la neige caramelise
Caramelised floating islands

PREVIOUS WINNERS

Chris and Jeff Galvin
Galvin La Chapelle,
London E1
page 254

Michael Caines
Gidleigh Park, Chagford,
Devon
page 131

Andrew Fairlie
Andrew Fairlie @ Gleneagles,
Scotland
page 600

Germain Schwab
Winteringham Fields
(former chef), Lincolnshire

Raymond Blanc
Le Manoir aux Quat' Saisons,
Great Milton, Oxfordshire
page 399

Shaun Hill
Walnut Tree Inn,
Abergavenny,
Monmouthshire, Wales
page 631

Heston Blumenthal
The Fat Duck, Bray,
Berkshire
page 53

Jean-Christophe Novelli

Gordon Ramsay
Restaurant Gordon Ramsay,
London SW3
page 296

Rick Stein
The Seafood Restaurant,
Padstow, Cornwall
page 94

Marco Pierre White

Kevin Viner

Philip Howard
The Square,
London W1
page 339

Marcus Wareing
Marcus Wareing at
The Berkeley, London SW1
page 283

Martin Wishart
Restaurant Martin Wishart,
Leith, Edinburgh
page 572

AA Lifetime Achievement Award 2012-2013

Antonio CARLUCCIO

Few chefs have done so much to champion Italian food and wine to the British people as Antonio Carluccio.

Now well into his 70s, Carluccio - with his distinctive gruff voice and wild crop of white hair - is often rightly referred to as the Godfather of Italian gastronomy.

Born in 1937 on the Amalfi Coast in the south of Italy, he grew up in the wooded Piedmont region in the north-west and it was here, at the age of seven and encouraged by his father, that Carluccio began his lifelong love of hunting and collecting wild mushrooms.

In 1958, at the age of 21, he began to cook simple pasta suppers for himself and his flatmate on a two-ring stove in Vienna, and from that moment his passion for the traditional foods of his mother country was sealed.

After time spent living in Germany Carluccio moved to London in 1975 and, while learning English, traded as a wine merchant importing Italian wines.

He became the manager of Terence Conran's Neal Street Restaurant in Covent Garden in 1981, taking over as owner in 1989.

In 1991, together with his then wife Priscilla (Conran's sister), he opened a deli named Carluccio's next to the restaurant, later expanding it into a wholesale business in 1994.

In 1998 the first Carluccio's Caffè - a combined authentic Italian restaurant with integrated food shop - was launched in Market Place, London. The concept was so successful it quickly expanded into a chain, initially in the south-east and then right across the UK.

Carluccio sold the Carluccio's Caffe business - which now totals over 57 sites in the UK - in 2010 (the Neal Street Restaurant closed in 2006) but still continues to work with the chain as a consultant,

helping with menu development and chef training.

In 1983 Carluccio made his first appearance on BBC2 talking about Mediterranean food, and at the same time was asked to write his first book, *An Invitation to Italian Cooking*.

Subsequently he has written 13 books and made numerous television programmes including the hugely popular *Antonio Carluccio's Northern Italian Feast* and *Southern Italian Feast*.

In 2011 his travels around Italy with friend and fellow chef Gennaro Contaldo were filmed for the BBC2 series *Two Greedy Italians*.

Carluccio is certainly no stranger to receiving awards: in 1998 he was awarded the Commendatore OMRI by the President of Italy for services to Italian gastronomy, the equivalent of a British knighthood, while in 2007 he received an honorary OBE.

AA Restaurants of the Year

Potential Restaurants of the Year are nominated by our team of full-time Inspectors based on their routine visits. In selecting a Restaurant of the Year, we look for somewhere that is exceptional in its chosen area of the market. Whilst the Rosette awards are based on the quality of the food alone, Restaurant of the Year takes into account all aspects of the experience.

ENGLAND

THE CHURCH GREEN BRITISH GRILL ❀❀
LYMM, CHESHIRE
Page 86

The year 2012 marked a change in direction for celebrated chef Aiden Byrne's Cheshire restaurant: out went the fine-dining set-up which previously held three AA Rosettes, to be replaced by a more simplified 'British grill', with steaks cooked on the Inka grill (an enclosed barbecue) the big draw. This more informal approach is right in line with the times, and yet it doesn't mean you get any less of a quality experience, for Byrne is a highly talented chef who honed his skills in some top kitchens (Tom Aikens, Pied à Terre and The Dorchester amongst them). Against a stylish backdrop of bare brickwork, natural wood, leather seating and neutral hues – and with Byrne's partner Sarah looking after things out front – you can expect wonderful local and seasonal ingredients to show up in homely classics like steak and kidney pudding, beef hotpot, sausages and mash, and potted Lancashire shrimps, along with those exemplary 28-day dry-aged steaks, seared over coconut husk charcoal, and served, perhaps, with bonbons of bone marrow and stilton, beef dripping chips and béarnaise sauce.

LONDON

DINNER BY HESTON BLUMENTHAL ❀❀❀
LONDON, SW1
Page 281

Heston's first venture outside the Berkshire village of Bray – in the swanky Mandarin Oriental hotel, no less – has quickly become one of the hottest tickets in town. Quite the opposite from the molecular goings-on at The Fat Duck, the menu represents an exploration of our culinary heritage, featuring dishes unearthed by Heston from as far back as 500 years. Executive chef Ashley Palmer-Watts heads up the operation in the kitchen, which is fully enclosed in glass so you can watch all the action (including whole pineapples turning on the clockwork rotisserie). The buzzy, upscale dining room has views over Hyde Park and is decked out with darkwood tables, lots of leather and light fittings resembling jelly moulds. An approximate date is ascribed to the origins of each dish, as in the signature 'meat fruit' (c1500) which looks like a mandarin, but is full of rich, smooth chicken liver parfait. Main courses sound equally intriguing, such as (c.1670) powdered duck breast with smoked confit fennel and umbles, or roast halibut (c.1830) with leaf chicory and cockle ketchup.

SCOTLAND

ROGANO

GLASGOW

Page 582

Rogano is no young upstart in the café quarter of Glasgow that is Exchange Place – it's been open for business since 1935, when the Cunard liner Queen Mary was being built on the Clyde. The art-deco styling brings a sense of bygone sophistication to the restaurant, a vision of grand living reinforced by the presence of buckets of chilled champagne. The service approach is reassuringly formal and the kitchen, while definably modern in its orientation, manages to imbue most dishes with a sense of occasion. A partnership of scallops with bacon-wrapped black pudding in shallot-dressed watercress is handled with delicacy, but delivers big flavours, while the haggis comes with foie gras and a potato rösti, with a dressing of red onion marmalade. Fish dishes are generous in their scope, taking in grilled sea bass with a smoked haddock fishcake in mussel and saffron cream, while a main course of rabbit offers moist and tender meat, wrapped in Parma ham, accompanied by earthy beech mushrooms and a sweet garlic jus.

WALES

SOSBAN RESTAURANT

LLANELLI, CARMARTHENSHIRE

Page 621

The Victorian building that once provided hydraulic power for Llanelli's docks has been revitalised as an industrial-chic powerhouse on the local gastronomic scene. The 90-foot-high castellated stone tower is a local landmark, which makes it easy enough to find; once inside, the setting is certainly impressive with walls of arched glass windows looking out to sea, Welsh slate floors, and classy bare wooden tables beneath the exposed industrial skeleton of the heritage building. At work inside an open-to-view kitchen, the team at the stoves turns out a French-accented brasserie-style repertoire with a broad appeal and maximum input from local suppliers and producers all over Wales. A signature starter of crab lasagne shows the unfussy style, followed by hearty crowd-pleasers along the lines of breast and confit leg of Barbary duck with Puy lentils and red wine sauce, or braised Brecon venison with red cabbage and celeriac purée. To finish, the Welsh cheeseboard is hard to overlook, otherwise prune and Armagnac parfait makes a grown-up pudding.

AA Wine Awards

The AA Wine Award

The annual AA wine award, sponsored again by T&W Wines, attracted a huge response from our AA recognised restaurants with over 1,000 wine lists submitted for judging. Three national winners were chosen – L'Etranger, London, England; Castle Terrace, Edinburgh, Scotland; and The Felin Fach Griffin, Brecon, Wales. L'Etranger was also selected as the Overall Winner of the wine award for the UK, with a member of their wine team set to enjoy the prize of an all-expenses-paid trip to Willi Opitz's vineyards at Illmitz in Austria's Burgenland.

All 2,000 Rosetted restaurants in last year's guide were invited to submit their wine lists. From these the panel selected a shortlist of around 250 establishments who are highlighted in the guide with the Notable Wine List symbol ▲.

The shortlisted establishments were asked to choose wines from their list (within a budget of £70 per bottle) to accompany a menu designed by last year's winner The Bell at Skenfrith in Wales.

The final judging panel included Simon Numphud, AA Hotel Services Manager, William Hutchings, proprietor of The Bell at Skenfrith, and Trevor Hughes, Managing Director of T&W Wines (our sponsor). The judges' comments are shown under the award winners on the opposite page.

Other wine lists that stood out in the final judging included Terroirs, London, The Chester Grosvenor, Chester, and Ellenborough Park, Cheltenham.

Notable Wine Lists

What makes a wine list notable?
We are looking for high-quality wines, with diversity across grapes and/or countries and style, the best individual growers and vintages. The list should be well presented, ideally with some helpful notes and, to reflect the demand from diners, a good choice of wines by the glass.

What disappoints the judges are spelling errors, wines under incorrect regions or styles, split vintages (which are still far too common), lazy purchasing (all wines from a country from just one grower or negociant) and confusing layouts. Sadly, many restaurants still do not pay much attention to wine, resulting in ill considered lists.

To reach the final shortlist, we look for a real passion for wine, which should come across to the customer, a fair pricing policy (depending on the style of the restaurant), an interesting coverage (not necessarily a large list), which might include areas of specialism, perhaps a particular wine area, sherries or larger formats such as magnums.

The AA Wine Awards are sponsored by T&W Wines Ltd, 5 Station Way, Brandon, Suffolk, IP27 0BH. Tel: 01842 814414
email: contact@tw-wines.com web: www.tw-wines.com

L'Etranger – Winning Wine Selection

Menu	Wine selection
Canapés	Philippe Gonet, Blanc de Blanc "Le Mesnil sur Oger" NV
Starter – Foie gras crème brûlée with cherry compôte, pistachio crumble and truffle brioche	Riesling Felsner Rohrendorfer, Gebling, Austria 2006
Fish course – Butter-poached lobster lasagne, shellfish and cardamom bisque, summer flowers	Macon Verze Domaine Leflaive 2008
Main course – Gower salt marsh lamb, smoked garlic and potato purée, aubergine caviar, Moroccan-spiced sweetbread and a lamb jus	Beaujolais Village "Le Rang de Merle", Jean Claude Lapalu 2003
Cheese – Welsh soft blue perl las cheese with a peach pickle	Ramos Pinto 10 years tawny port
Dessert – Floating islands with wild strawberries, cornflowers and a tonka bean ice anglaise	Château La Tout Blanche Sauternes 1989
Coffee and chocolates	Bas Armagnac Château de Lacaze 1982

WINNER FOR ENGLAND AND OVERALL WINNER

L'ETRANGER ⊚⊚

LONDON SW7 Page 302

WINNER FOR SCOTLAND

CASTLE TERRACE ⊚⊚⊚

EDINBURGH Page 562

WINNER FOR WALES

THE FELIN FACH GRIFFIN ⊚⊚

BRECON Page 638

Japan meets France in this silkily minimalist South Kensington restaurant. It's an intimate and somewhat sophisticated space of soothing lilacs and greys against wooden flooring with lots of fresh flowers. Service is on the ball and combinations are well thought through and attractively presented on the plate. The wine list – put together by restaurant director Ibi Issolah in partnership with the head sommelier – is a fine piece of work. It encompasses no less than 1,600 bins from countries as diverse as Japan and Turkey, yet with more established wine-producing regions also well represented, particularly France, Italy, Australia and America. Much thought is given to selecting wines that complement the cooking of head chef Jerome Tauvron.

Judges' comments: A top-drawer, serious wine list that's difficult to put down. The depth of vintages is outstanding, and the pricing policy – with a price match guarantee if the same wine is found cheaper elsewhere in London – is highly commendable.

Chef-patron Dominic Jack perfected his craft across the Channel before coming home to set up Castle Terrace in collaboration with his friend Tom Kitchin of The Kitchin in Leith. The two restaurants share the 'from nature to plate' mantra printed on the carte, as well as elegant and precise cooking and a passion verging on obsession for seasonal Scottish ingredients. It is all perfectly judged and delivered with high-level technical skills, and the cooking is done justice by an intelligently composed wine list featuring top quality wines from almost every wine-producing country in the world. The list touches all bases, offering a variety of styles, and includes a wide-ranging selection of dessert wines.

Judges' comments: Impressive, well chosen list that is extremely well laid out and presented. Interesting selection of wines by the glass and nice to see a page of half bottles. Good diversity of selections that are both balanced and quality driven.

Although the Griffin treats its real ales with due respect, the level of refinement in this country inn in a tiny Brecon village places it more in the category of a restaurant than a pub. With its chintz-free interior of deep sofas, warming Aga, painted stone walls and floors of wood and Welsh slate, it's a welcoming place that won't turn up its nose if you pitch up with the dog after a walk on the hills. Much of what appears on the plate comes from the organically certified kitchen garden. The wine list is full of lesser-known and very affordable choices from select suppliers, with up to 20 wines available by the glass and carafe.

Judges' comments: A beautifully laid out list full of quality choices offered by the glass and carafe, plus a good list of sherries. Good pricing and a clear commitment from all the team to promoting and understanding wine.

Head chef James Golding gets down with it in the
kitchen garden at The Pig in Brockenhurst, Hampshire

fun dining

Does the term 'fine-dining' conjure up images of waiters dressed in penguin suits, hushed dining rooms, tables draped in white linen laden with sparkling silver and glassware, and tiny portions at not-so-tiny prices? Well, the world of fine-dining is changing - it's shaking off its stuffy image and going all informal, as Fiona Griffiths discovers...

It's a weekday lunchtime at Tom Aikens Restaurant in Chelsea and, glancing around the room, I do a quick tally of the number of people I can see wearing jeans: I count 10 in total, half of whom are staff.

Make no mistake, this is a restaurant at the pinnacle of gastronomy, holder of the ultimate five AA Rosettes (an accolade shared by only nine restaurants in this guide), but stuffy and formal it ain't.

It hasn't always been this way. From the day chef Tom Aikens opened his eponymous restaurant in 2003 until the summer of 2011, it was fine-dining in the stereotypical sense: all plush carpets, white tablecloths with black under-cloths, cover plates, fine silverware, plain white porcelain, black lacquered chairs, and front-of-house staff dressed in traditional black and white.

But then Aikens decided it was high time for a change: he closed the restaurant in July 2011 and over the ensuing six months every last bit of its original décor was stripped out to be replaced by a minimalist, contemporary look dominated by wood and other natural materials, with not a starched linen tablecloth in sight.

"A lot of customers were saying that the way the restaurant was with the carpet and the table settings and the uniforms, it just wasn't relaxing; it made the staff very formal and stiff," explains Aikens.

"I felt that having the staff in more informal clothes was really key to making us stand apart. It also helps the staff feel more relaxed and gives them a bit more of an identity, rather than just being a robot in a black and white uniform"

Understated luxury at the new-look Tom Aikens Restaurant in Chelsea

"It was definitely in a time warp considering how dining out has evolved in the last few years: if you look at the majority of new restaurants, they're casual eateries - there are no traditional fine-dining restaurants opening."

The new look is certainly in keeping with modern design trends and is far more "low key" than before, but that doesn't mean it has lost anything of its luxury feel.

Instead it's an understated type of luxury, thanks in large part to Aikens' travels around Europe looking for unusual crockery and glassware from artisan producers, now used to great effect to showcase his stunning food (he was determined to move right away from the ubiquitous white plates).

The furniture too - bespoke hand-made oak chairs and tables sourced from Turkey - are of palpable high quality as well as being extremely comfortable.

Aikens says: "I've gone for a much more simple look but it's still very high-end - you can tell that the furniture is super-luxury and you can just see the attention to detail in the glassware, the plates, and the unusual vases on the tables that look like they're going to fall over but don't."

The pricing structure has been simplified, too, to make things easier for diners: all the menus are set-price, including a stupendous value set lunch at £29 for three courses.

"I've never really liked it when everything is individually priced because

it's just extra hassle for people to have to start adding up at dinner," says Aikens.

And simplicity was the watchword again when it came to replacing staff uniforms.

Aikens recalls interviewing for new front-of-house staff and, "99 per cent [of the candidates] were wearing black and white, having come straight from work".

"That just goes to show how formal a lot of the fine-dining restaurants are," he says.

"I felt that having the staff in more informal clothes was really key to making us stand apart. It also helps the staff feel more relaxed and gives them a bit more of an identity, rather than just being a robot in a black and white uniform.

"From the customer's point of view, too, they're faced with someone who's

Above: Loch Duart salmon at Pollen Street Social

Below: The dessert bar at Pollen Street Social

approachable rather than someone wearing formal restaurant wear."

So what has the feedback been like from Aikens' regulars?

"People have commented on how nice it is to be in a restaurant serving high-end food but without the high-end service style and with a more informal feel," says Aikens.

"There will always be a place for formal fine-dining - Le Gavroche, for instance, is an institution in the way we all understand gastronomy to be, and it's still really nice to go to places like that that are very good at what they do.

"But I think people are eating out more and more and if you want to twist a customer's arm to come back on a regular basis, having a relaxed setting for them is absolutely vital."

Aikens is by no means the first high-flying UK chef to go for a more informal approach.

Jason Atherton went down a similar route when he left Gordon Ramsay's Maze and opened his own restaurant, Pollen Street Social, in Mayfair in April 2011.

He wanted to offer the same level of food that won him four AA Rosettes at Maze, but in a much more relaxed and sociable environment.

Atherton explains: "I used my wife as a barometer - every time I asked her where she wanted to go for dinner she'd say, 'don't take any offence, but can we go somewhere with a bit of atmosphere?'

"When you get to four or five Rosettes it normally means a particular type of restaurant, and that's exactly the sort of place she didn't want to go to."

So in Pollen Street Social - which has been awarded four Rosettes in this year's guide - Atherton has created a contemporary bistro serving serious food

"The biggest compliment I can get is when a customer leaves here and says, 'wow, that was so much fun'…"

but with a relaxed, informal feel, where flexibility is key.

You can order from the a la carte, go for some sharing plates, or simply sit up at the dessert bar - the first of its kind in the UK - and tuck into a mouthwatering pud (or two, or four).

You can wear what you like, the staff, although smartly dressed in uniforms typical of a French bistro, are friendly and approachable, and you can watch Jason and his team at work in a glass-walled theatre kitchen, while soaking up the buzzing atmosphere.

The restaurant's relaxed, flexible ethos is summed up rather nicely by its name, as Atherton explains.

"The name comes from my northern roots, because my aunts and uncles used to spend all their time down the social, playing snooker and seeing their friends.

"I came to London as a teenager without a pound in my pocket, worked my way up through some of the best kitchens, and now I have my own restaurant in Mayfair and I thought how cool it would be to call it a social club:

you can have a pint of beer in the bar, you can sit at the dessert bar and have a cup of tea and a macaroon, you can even have desserts to start and starters after.

"I think that's what the new generation of restaurant diners want, that kind of flexibility."

And Atherton is mindful of the fact that to be a proper social club the restaurant needs to be inclusive and accessible, hence the set lunch menu is only £25 for three courses ("we don't scrimp on ingredients one bit"), and the wine list offers 30-40 bottles for under £30.

It's a strategy that has really paid off, with Pollen Street Social now full for every service, including Monday lunchtimes when there's a waiting list for tables.

"There are lots of amazing chefs out there who are struggling to fill their restaurants on a Monday lunch, and maybe that's because the ambience and the service they offer aren't want people want these days," says Atherton.

"The biggest compliment I can get is when a customer leaves here and says,

'wow, that was so much fun'. To me that means we've achieved what we set out to do."

'Fun' isn't a word that would have summed up Whitley Ridge Hotel in the New Forest, Hampshire, in the past, but today - after a total transformation at the hands of Hotel du Vin co-founder Robin Hutson - it's a totally different story.

Whitley Ridge has gone from being a traditional country house hotel with a rather stuffy French restaurant holding three AA Rosettes, to a laid-back 26-room hotel called 'The Pig', proudly holding two AA Rosettes.

"It was a bit serious and a bit gourmet and pretentious before," says Hutson.

"The quality of the food was good but there were three people having lunch. Today we're full all the time for lunch and dinner and all the rooms are full."

Hutson actually prefers to term The Pig (the name was chosen to send out a message of complete transformation) a "restaurant with rooms" rather than a hotel, as the main draw is its new restaurant in a light and airy greenhouse-

"… it's simplicity that always stands the test of time"

style extension, where chef James Golding's menu is built entirely around what's growing in the redeveloped kitchen garden.

The menu changes daily - sometimes twice a day in the summer - and is designed to offer diners complete freedom, as Hutson explains: "We have a lot of small dishes and large dishes, so you don't feel you've got to have three courses. If you want to come in and have a starter-size salad and a glass of wine you can, and you won't feel awkward about that."

He adds: "While before almost everyone who came here was a pensioner, the age group has dropped by 20 years.

"We used to average about 35 covers a day and during February [2012] we did 135 covers a day."

Some of the old customers are still coming, although some have taken a while to get used to Golding's light and simple cooking style, let alone the new staff "uniform" of pink shirts, blue jeans and aprons, and the clothless wooden tables with mismatched old chairs.

As for Golding, he's very happy with his two AA Rosettes and isn't looking for a return to three.

"I'm a firm believer in cooking what you like to cook and cooking with what you have around you," he says.

"Simplicity is the route we've gone down and it's simplicity that always stands the test of time."

Above: Chewton Glen

Not far down the road at the five red-star Chewton Glen hotel in New Milton, they've gone through a similar process of 'deformalisation' (as some in the industry are calling it).

Gone is the traditional fixed price menu (formerly £67.50 for three courses, including canapes, amuse-bouche and coffee), and in its place is a flexible carte of individually priced dishes.

Head chef Andrew du Bourg explains: "Previously, people would be staying for a weekend and just have one meal here because they didn't want to have a heavy three courses two nights on the trot.

"The way the menu is now, you can have three courses one night and then just go straight for a grill and a dessert the next. The customer is boss as to how they order."

For those who still want to splash out, a five-course tasting menu is available for £79.50, while for those with more modest means there's a daily set lunch menu at £25 for three courses.

The restaurant, which holds three AA Rosettes, has also undergone a major makeover to create a much more modern, metropolitan look, and is spread over five rooms including two conservatories.

The changes are all aimed at making it more accessible and "less of a special occasion only venue" - and so far they seem to have paid off: in February 2012 (eight months after the relaunch) covers were up by 300 on the same month the previous year, while the hotel's capture rate (guests who are now dining in-house throughout their stay) has jumped from 78 to 86 per cent.

Managing director Andrew Stembridge says: "We realised we needed to create a one-size-fits-all restaurant with different spaces each with a different feel, and a range of menu items at different price points.

"I think it's a necessary evolution in country-house-hotel dining – we've certainly had a lot of fellow hoteliers coming in to see what we've done."

Above: Thrilling food at Roganic

fine-dining unleashed

Gastronomic experiences can happen anywhere these days - be it in a park, an empty warehouse or an old power station - thanks to the rise of the 'pop-up' restaurant.

There can't be a better demonstration of the 'deformalisation' of fine-dining than these temporary restaurants, which have been literally 'popping up' all over the place and are often run by renowned chefs.

Simon Rogan and Pierre Koffmann are two such legendary chefs who have brought their food to a wider audience in the makeshift, casual environment of a pop-up.

For Koffmann, who ran his pop-up at the end of 2009, the setting was a marquee on the roof of Selfridge's in London's Oxford Street.

The French chef had been absent from the capital's restaurant scene for 10 years when he was asked by the store to operate the pop-up for a week. It was such a success - and Koffmann enjoyed his return to the stoves so much - that it turned into a two-month project and led to him opening Koffmann's in Knightsbridge (three AA Rosettes) the following summer.

"During those two months we did 3,200 covers from basically an army kitchen," recalls Koffmann.

"Coming back after 10 years of retirement, I was really surprised by the number of young people who came to eat - people in their 20s who had never eaten my food before but had heard what I do."

When Simon Rogan decided to open his two-year "extended pop-up", Roganic, in a vacant restaurant in Marylebone, it was for two reasons: to give people in the south a chance to experience his cooking without having to travel to Cumbria (to five-Rosette L'Enclume); and to give him a chance to test the London market without a big investment.

So far it's worked well on both fronts, according to Rogan, who has picked up three Rosettes for Roganic in this year's guide.

"The diners certainly aren't coming for the lavish surroundings - with a pop-up it's about the food first and then the atmosphere, as it's got that slightly underground feel," says Rogan.

"We've been thinking for a while about doing something in London but were worried about spending lots of money that could potentially be lost.

"We haven't spent a massive amount on Roganic, and as a pop-up if it doesn't work we can just close the doors and walk away."

So, keep your eyes peeled and your ears open: you never know when a top chef might pop up in your neighbourhood.

Chef Heston Blumenthal, The Fat Duck, Bray

MODERN BRITISH cuisine

by Heston Blumenthal

Cuisine owes a lot to the French Revolution. Before the 1790s, restaurants barely existed anywhere. If you were on the road, you might eat in a café, tavern or inn for sustenance, but that was about all. Dining out simply wasn't done.

The Revolution changed this. As noble families either fled the country or lost their heads to a contraption not unlike a giant mandolin, many of the professional chefs who worked for them suddenly found themselves unemployed. Restaurants took on these chefs and were transformed by their culinary creativity. The foundations of haute cuisine were laid, and French cooking never looked back, developing a formidable and authoritative range of dishes and techniques.

When I first started to cook I was in thrall to this magnificent tradition. After all, the *coup de foudre* that made me want to become a chef in the first place was eating in a three-star restaurant in the south of France, amid the buzz of cicadas, the sun's warmth on my skin,

and the scents of lavender and roast lamb. And so when I first opened a restaurant in 1995, my only ambition was to offer a menu of bistro classics – haricot blanc soup, petit salé of duck, crème brûlée and triple-cooked chips (the very first recipe I created). I had no game plan or philosophy beyond this. I certainly didn't set out to shake things up.

It was circumstances – and my curiosity – that got the better of me. I had set up the Fat Duck in what had previously been a ramshackle pub with a dubious clientele. It had no grand view or lavender or cicadas. I soon realised that if I wanted diners to enjoy the kind of full-on sensory magic I'd experienced in France, I was going to have to somehow produce it at the table. Moreover, since the minuscule kitchen at the Fat Duck was completely unsuited to the demands of the catering business (its gas pipes too feeble to heat any more than a modest-sized pan of water, making even the simple task of simmering virtually impossible), I was forced to explore ways of outflanking its technological shortcomings.

That's how I got into science. I reasoned that if I understood exactly what was happening at a technical level during cooking, then maybe it would help me to overcome the drawbacks of my kitchen – and perhaps give me ideas I could use to produce dishes that triggered all of the senses. I met up with a handful of scientists, peppered them with questions and got excited by the answers. But even then I had little idea of how thinking scientifically would change the way I cooked and even the way I looked at food.

After that first moment of inspiration in France in 1982, I had immersed myself in the French repertoire, respectfully cooking the classics over and over, never questioning the techniques, even

> **"The more a chef makes a dish appeal not just to the tongue but to the senses of sight, smell, touch and even sound, the more powerful, emotional and delicious it is."**

when recipes appeared to contradict one another. Then, three years later, I read in Harold McGee's brilliant *On Food & Cooking* that, despite what dozens of recipes had told me over the years, searing doesn't in fact 'seal' meat at all. That's when I stopped taking kitchen lore for granted and started asking questions. (That's how I came up with the technique for triple-cooked chips, for example:

Below: Quail jelly truffle toast & oak film strip

by asking myself exactly why chips go soggy.) And so when I started talking to scientists and looking into their methods, I was further encouraged along this path, because science constantly asks *Why not?* Nothing is taken for granted until it's proven. A scientist develops an idea then tests it rigorously to see whether it works. Applying the same spirit of inquiry to cuisine opened up all sorts of avenues to me: even the most fundamental kitchen truths were open to question. Did an ice-cream base have to be heated to 85°C? Were oats suitable only for breakfast? Why couldn't meat be cooked at a temperature that would prevent it drying out, and could it be carved in a way that would make it more tender? Why do we like some foods but not others? What, in fact, actually *is* taste?

The answers to such questions led to the creation of snail porridge, scrambled-egg ice cream, low-temperature cooking techniques and 'cooking' with nitrogen, orange and beetroot jelly, pine sherbet fountain, and much more besides. Examining food in such a technical way, for example, made me more convinced than ever that eating is a multisensory experience. The more a chef makes a dish appeal not just to the tongue but to the senses of sight, smell, touch and even sound, the more powerful, emotional and delicious it is. This has become a very deliberate part of my approach to recipe development, whether it's taking something familiar, like a scotch egg, and accentuating the lovely crisp crunch of the breadcrumbed exterior, followed by the ooze of a perfectly soft-boiled egg at the centre, or creating something completely new, like the 'Sound of the Sea', which captures the looks, smells and sounds of the meeting point between sea and shore – the briny tang, the call of the gull, the froth of the ebbing surf – and often transports diners to their own, intensely personal and emotional, seaside memories.

As a result of these kinds of developments, in the last decade or so the British culinary landscape has changed beyond recognition, and chefs have begun to re-evaluate what makes cuisine 'modern'. A few years ago Harold McGee and I (with the support of Ferran Adria and Thomas Keller) tried to do exactly that, and came up with a document called 'Statement on the New Cookery', which was subsequently published in the *Observer*. As far as we were concerned, modern cuisine ultimately drew its strength and identity from four simple principles: first, we should embrace the opportunities offered by global communications. Chefs have access to ideas, to ingredients, to techniques as never before. We should be making full use of this privileged access to strive for excellence and reach new creative heights in cooking.

Second, the push for innovation mustn't blind us to the value of tradition. The springboard for creativity is a centuries-old heritage forged by hundreds of

generations of dedicated cooks. Cooking is about evolution not revolution. It's only by understanding the tradition of cuisine and mastering its techniques that a chef can take food in a meaningful new direction. Culinary history is a rich source of inspiration. In the last decade or so, I've spent as much of my research time with ancient, leather-bound cookery manuscripts as I have with vacuum centrifuges and liquid nitrogen, and some amazing recipes have come out of this, like Meat Fruit, Powdered Duck Breast and Tipsy Cake. The French originally nicknamed us 'Les Rosbifs' not because they thought that's all we ate but because they admired our skill with the rotisserie. Somewhere along the line we Brits forgot that we once had a great culinary reputation. Regaining that self-respect is, I think, part of what has brought our cuisine alive again.

Third, we mustn't lose sight of the fact that, for all its sophistication, modern technology and scientific developments (be it a vacuum centrifuge, low-sweetness sugar substitute or liquid nitrogen) are still just a means to an end: a tool in the chef's arsenal, alongside knives, pans and strainers. We should be open to any piece of technology or scientific breakthrough that helps us to achieve new, different and better dishes. But modern cuisine shouldn't draw on novelty for its own sake. (I've attended plenty of cooking demos that presented technically breath-taking techniques but produced food that tasted disappointing.)

Fourth, since we have come to understand just how profoundly eating is bound up with our senses and our emotions – how our perception of flavour is influenced by our minds as much as our mouths – we can now see cooking in more wide-ranging and

inclusive terms, drawing on all kinds of disciplines – science, psychology, theatre, architecture, industrial design, script-writing, music and even, say, magicians and sound engineers – in order to realise its full potential.

In the end, the real legacy, it seems to me, of the revolution that has taken place in cooking in Britain over the last few years is how it has broken down the barriers of cuisine. Even as recently as five years ago, refined British cooking was still essentially an adaptation of classic French tradition and techniques. Now, however, I see a real pride in British dishes and a newfound enthusiasm and respect for our own food history. It seems as though, for the first time in a long time, we have a real sense of our own culinary identity. This is the foundation stone of any great cooking culture, and it's going to be very exciting to be part of it, and to see it develop.

FARMHOUSE TOUCH –
AT HOME WITH THE PRESENT,
INSPIRED BY THE PAST.

The captivating charm of Farmhouse Touch makes any occasion a special occasion. Relaxed, informal and designed for the way we live today. Mix and match the white and Blueflowers versions to express your individuality, or combine with Farmhouse Touch cutlery and glassware to create a perfect sense of home.

Villeroy & Boch
1748

Villeroy & Boch are proud to present the AA Hospitality Awards. Quality and inspiration are the defining qualities of a great restaurant. They are also the values that have made Villeroy & Boch, with its tradition of innovation dating back to 1748, the leading tableware brand in Europe.

Our distinctive and original designs have consistently set the pace for others to follow and provide the perfect setting chosen by many of the world's leading chefs to frame their award-winning creations.

Villeroy & Boch offer a wide range of stunning designs to suit any lifestyle and décor, and create the perfect ambience for successful entertaining and stylish family living. Discover the exciting range of Villeroy & Boch designs in our stores and save 10% off your total bill.

LONDON:
Harrods, Knightsbridge, Tel: 020 7824 8566
Selfridges & Co, Oxford Street, Tel: 020 7493 8455
House of Fraser: Oxford Street, Tel: 020 7493 7293,
House of Fraser, Croydon, Tel: 020 8688 7263
Allders, Croydon, Tel: 020 8686 0757
Bentalls, Kingston, Tel: 020 8547 2974
SOUTH:
Beales, Bournemouth, Tel: 01202 314417
House of Fraser, Guildford, Tel: 01483 303413,
House of Fraser, Bristol, Tel: 0117 376 3557
House of Fraser, Plymouth, Tel: 01752 251903
House of Fraser, Bluewater, Tel: 01322 423154
House of Fraser, Camberley, Tel: 01276 24900
House of Fraser, Chichester, Tel: 0844 800 3716
House of Fraser, Maidstone, Tel: 01622 609405
Hoopers, Tunbridge Wells, Tel: 01892 553274
Beales, Worthing, Tel: 01903 236294
EAST:
House of Fraser, Lakeside, Tel: 01708 869658
House of Fraser, Norwich, Tel: 01603 607030
Jarrold's The Store, Norwich, Tel: 01603 765217
WEST:
House of Fraser, Bath, Tel: 01225 334484
House of Fraser, Cheltenham, Tel: 01242 253603
House of Fraser, High Wycombe, Tel: 01494 474693
Camp Hopson, Newbury, Tel: 01635 551049
House of Fraser, Reading, Tel: 0118 959 2090
MIDLANDS:
House of Fraser, Solihull, Tel: 0121 704 4320
House of Fraser, Leamington Spa, Tel: 01926 470339
House of Fraser, Wolverhampton, Tel: 01902 399822
House of Fraser, Birmingham, Tel: 0121 236 7473
NORTH:
Beales, Kendal, Tel: 01539 739043
Fenwick, Newcastle, Tel: 0191 230 3652
Selfridges & Co, Manchester, Tel: 0161 746 9592
House of Fraser, Hull, Tel: 01482 213483
House of Fraser, Leeds, Tel: 01132 470903
House of Fraser, Manchester, Tel: 0161 834 1839
House of Fraser, Darlington, Tel: 01325 389256
House of Fraser, Gateshead, Tel: 0191 460 1992
House of Fraser, Meadowhall, Sheffield, Tel: 0114 2568697
House of Fraser, Middlesbrough, Tel: 01642 245270

WALES:
House of Fraser, Cardiff, Tel: 029 2039 8336
SCOTLAND:
Jenners, Edinburgh, Tel: 0131 260 2243
House of Fraser, Glasgow, Tel: 0141 221 7346

UK OUTLETS:
Bicester Village, Oxfordshire, Tel: 01869 324646
Boundary Mill Outlet, Colne, Tel: 01282 856200
Boundary Mill Outlet, Newcastle upon Tyne, Tel: 0191 297 2420
Braintree, Essex, Tel: 01376 528800
Gloucester Quays Design Outlet, Gloucester, Tel: 01452 521253
Gunwharf Quays, Portsmouth, Tel: 02392 851600
Factory Outlet, London, Southfields, Tel: 020 8875 6006
Clarks Village, Street, Somerset, Tel: 01458 448983
House of Fraser Outlet, Swindon, Tel: 01793 490036
House of Fraser Outlet, Leicester, Tel: 0116 261 9752

IRELAND
NORTH:
House of Fraser, Belfast, Tel: 0289 0245099
SOUTH:
Arnotts, Dublin, Tel: 00 353 1 872 9771
Brown Thomas, Cork, Tel: 00 353 214 251002
Brown Thomas, Limerick, Tel: 00 353 61 417222
House of Fraser, Dundrum, Tel: 00 353 1 296 2627
OUTLET: Kildare Village, Tel: 00 353 4 553 5788

Members of the AA receive **10% off** when shopping online using this link:

www.theaa.com/rewards

In addition Members of the AA also receive **10% off** full price products in the stores listed on presentation of an AA membership card at the till.

(These discounts are valid until 30 June 2012.)

UK & Ireland customer services line: **0208 871 0011**
line is open Monday-Friday 9am-5pm

email: customerservices@villeroy-boch.co.uk
web: www.villeroy-boch.co.uk

Villeroy & Boch
1748

The Top Ten Per Cent

Each year all the restaurants in the AA Restaurant Guide are awarded a specially commissioned plate that marks their achievement in gaining one or more AA Rosettes. The plates represent a partnership between the AA and Villeroy & Boch – two quality brands working together to recognise high standards in restaurant cooking.

Restaurants awarded three, four or five AA Rosettes represent the Top Ten Per Cent of the restaurants in this Guide. The pages that follow list those establishments that have attained this special status.

5 ROSETTES

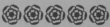

LONDON

Marcus Wareing at The Berkeley
The Berkeley, Wilton Place, Knightsbridge, SW1
020 7235 1200

Tom Aikens
43 Elystan Street, SW3
020 7584 2003

Hibiscus
29 Maddox Street, Mayfair, W1
020 7629 2999

Sketch (Lecture Room & Library)
9 Conduit Street, W1
0870 777 4488

ENGLAND

BERKSHIRE
The Fat Duck
High Street, BRAY, SL6 2AQ
01628 580333

CUMBRIA
L'Enclume
Cavendish Street, CARTMEL, LA11 6PZ
01539 536362

NOTTINGHAMSHIRE
Restaurant Sat Bains with Rooms
Lenton Lane, NOTTINGHAM, NG7 2SA
0115 986 6566

OXFORDSHIRE
Le Manoir aux Quat' Saisons
GREAT MILTON, OX44 7PD
01844 278881

SURREY
Michael Wignall at The Latymer
Pennyhill Park Hotel & Spa, London Road, BAGSHOT, GU19 5EU
01276 471774

4 ROSETTES

LONDON

Seven Park Place by William Drabble
St James Hotel & Club, 7-8 Park Place, SW1
020 7316 1600

Restaurant Gordon Ramsay
68 Royal Hospital Road, SW3
020 7352 4441

Hélène Darroze at The Connaught
Carlos Place, W1
020 3147 7200

Pied à Terre
34 Charlotte Street, W1
020 7636 1178

Pollen Street Social
8-10 Pollen Street, W1
020 7290 7600

The Square
6-10 Bruton Street, W1
020 7495 7100

LONDON, GREATER

Chapter One
Farnborough Common, Locksbottom, BROMLEY, BR6 8NF
01689 854848

ENGLAND

BERKSHIRE
The Waterside Inn
Ferry Road, BRAY, SL6 2AT
01628 620691

BRISTOL
Casamia Restaurant
38 High Street, WESTBURY-ON-TRYM, BS9 3D2
0117 959 28840

BUCKINGHAMSHIRE
Adam Simmonds at Danesfield House
Henley Road, MARLOW, SL7 2EY
01628 891010

CAMBRIDGESHIRE
Midsummer House
Midsummer Common, CAMBRIDGE, CB4 1HA
01223 369299

CHESHIRE
Simon Radley at The Chester Grosvenor
Chester Grosvenor Hotel & Spa, Eastgate, CHESTER, CH1 1LT
01244 324024

DEVON
Gidleigh Park
CHAGFORD, TQ13 8HH
01647 432367

GLOUCESTERSHIRE
Le Champignon Sauvage
24 Suffolk Road, CHELTENHAM, GL50 2AQ
01242 573449

LANCASHIRE
Northcote
Northcote Road, LANGHO, BB6 8BE
01254 240555

RUTLAND
Hambleton Hall
Hambleton, OAKHAM,
LE15 8TH
01572 756991

SUSSEX, WEST
The Pass at South
Lodge Hotel
LOWER BEEDING,
RH13 6PS
01403 891711

WILTSHIRE
Whatley Manor
Easton Grey,
MALMESBURY,
SN16 0RB
01666 822888

YORKSHIRE, NORTH
The Devonshire Arms
Country House Hotel
& Spa
BOLTON ABBEY,
BD23 6AJ
01756 718111

JERSEY
Ocean Restaurant
at the Atlantic Hotel
Le Mont de la Pulente,
ST BRELADE, JE3 8HE
01534 744101

Bohemia Restaurant
The Club Hotel & Spa,
Green Street, ST HELIER,
JE2 4UH
01534 880588

SCOTLAND
CITY OF EDINBURGH
The Kitchin
78 Commercial Quay,
Leith, EDINBURGH,
EH6 6LX
0131 555 1755

Restaurant Martin Wishart
54 The Shore, Leith,
EDINBURGH, EH6 6RA
0131 553 3557

HIGHLAND
Boath House
Auldearn, NAIRN,
IV12 5TE
01667 454896

PERTH & KINROSS
Andrew Fairlie @
Gleneagles
AUCHTERARDER,
PH3 1NF
01764 694267

SOUTH AYRSHIRE
Glenapp Castle
BALLANTRAE,
KA26 0NZ
01465 831212

REPUBLIC OF IRELAND
DUBLIN
Restaurant Patrick
Guilbaud
Merrion Hotel, 21 Upper
Merrion Street, DUBLIN
01 676 4192

3 ROSETTES

LONDON
E1
Galvin La Chapelle
35 Spital Square
020 7299 0400

E2
Viajante
Patriot Square
020 7871 0461

EC1
Club Gascon
57 West Smithfield
020 7796 0600

EC2
1901 Restaurant
ANdAZ London,
40 Liverpool Street
020 7618 7000

Rhodes Twenty Four
Tower 42, Old Broad Street
020 7877 7703

NW1
Odette's Restaurant
& Bar
130 Regent's Park Road
020 7586 8569

SW1
Apsleys at
The Lanesborough
Hyde Park Corner
020 7259 5599

Dinner by
Heston Blumenthal
Mandarin Oriental
Hyde Park,
66 Knightsbridge
020 7201 3833

Thirty Six by Nigel
Mendham at Dukes London
35 St James's Place
020 7491 4840

Koffmann's
The Berkeley, Wilton Place
020 7235 1010

Nahm
The Halkin Hotel,
Halkin Street
020 7333 1234

One-O-One
Sheraton Park Tower,
101 Knightsbridge
020 7290 7101

Pétrus
1 Kinnerton Street,
Knightsbridge
020 7592 1609

The Rib Room
Jumeirah Carlton
Tower Hotel,
Cadogan Place
020 7858 7250

Roux at Parliament Square
RICS Parliament Square
020 7334 3737

Zafferano
15 Lowndes Street
020 7235 5800

SW3
Rasoi Restaurant
10 Lincoln Street
020 7225 1881

SW4
Trinity Restaurant
4 The Polygon,
Clapham Old Town
020 7622 1199

SW17
Chez Bruce
2 Bellevue Road,
Wandsworth Common
020 8672 0114

W1
Alain Ducasse at
The Dorchester
53 Park Lane
020 7629 8866

3 ROSETTES

W1 CONTINUED

**Alyn Williams at
The Westbury**
Bond Street,
Mayfair
020 7078 9579

Arbutus Restaurant
63-64 Frith Street
020 7734 4545

L'Autre Pied
5-7 Blandford Street
020 7486 9696

Corrigan's Mayfair
28 Upper Grosvenor Street
020 7499 9943

CUT at 45 Park Lane
Mayfair
020 7493 4545

Dabbous
39 Whitfield St
020 7323 1544

**Galvin at Windows
Restaurant & Bar**
London Hilton on Park
Lane, Park Lane
020 7208 4021

Gauthier Soho
21 Romilly Street
020 7494 3111

Le Gavroche Restaurant
43 Upper Brook Street
020 7408 0881

**Gordon Ramsay
at Claridge's**
Brook Street
020 7499 0099

Hakkasan Mayfair
17 Bruton Street
020 7907 1888

Locanda Locatelli
8 Seymour Street
020 7935 9088

Maze
London Marriott Hotel
Grosvenor Square,
10-13 Grosvenor Square
020 7107 0000

Murano
20 Queen Street
020 7592 1222

Roganic
19 Blandford Street,
Marylebone
020 7486 0380

Rhodes W1 Restaurant
Great Cumberland Place
020 7616 5930

The Ritz Restaurant
150 Piccadilly
020 7493 8181

Roka
37 Charlotte Street
020 7580 6464

Sketch (The Gallery)
9 Conduit Street
0870 777 4488

Texture Restaurant
34 Portman Street
020 7224 0028

Theo Randall
InterContinental London,
1 Hamilton Place,
Hyde Park Corner
020 7318 8747

Umu
14-16 Bruton Place
020 7499 8881

Wild Honey
12 Saint George Street
020 7758 9160

W4
La Trompette
5-7 Devonshire Road,
Chiswick
020 8747 1836

W6
The River Café
Thames Wharf,
Rainville Road
020 7386 4200

W8
Kitchen W8
11-13 Abingdon Road,
Kensington
020 7937 0120

**Launceston Place
Restaurant**
1a Launceston Place
020 7937 6912

Min Jiang
Royal Garden Hotel,
2-24 Kensington
High Street
020 7361 1988

W11
The Ledbury
127 Ledbury Road,
Notting Hill
020 7792 9090

WC1
Pearl Restaurant & Bar
Renaissance Chancery
Court, 252 High Holborn
020 7829 7000

WC2
L'Atelier de Joël Robuchon
13-15 West Street
020 7010 8600

Clos Maggiore
33 King Street,
Covent Garden
020 7379 9696

LONDON, GREATER

The Glasshouse
14 Station Road,
KEW, TW9 3PZ
020 8940 6777

Bingham
61-63 Petersham Road,
RICHMOND-UPON-
THAMES, TW10 6UT
020 8940 0902

ENGLAND

BEDFORDSHIRE
Paris House Restaurant
Woburn Park, WOBURN,
MK17 9QP
01525 290692

BERKSHIRE
Royal Oak at Paley Street
MAIDENHEAD, SL6 3JN
01628 620541

The Vineyard at Stockcross
Stockcross, NEWBURY,
RG20 8JU
01635 528770

L'ortolan
Church Lane, SHINFIELD,
RG2 9BY
01189 888 500

BUCKINGHAMSHIRE
**Aubergine at
The Compleat Angler**
Macdonald
Compleat Angler,
Marlow Bridge,
MARLOW, SL7 1RG
01628 484444

The Hand & Flowers
126 West Street,
MARLOW, SL7 2BP
01628 482277

Stoke Place
STOKE POGES,
SL2 4HT
01753 534790

CAMBRIDGESHIRE
Restaurant Alimentum
152-154 Hills Road,
CAMBRIDGE,
CB2 8PB
01223 413000

CHESHIRE
The Alderley Restaurant
Alderley Edge Hotel
Macclesfield Road,
ALDERLEY EDGE,
SK9 7BJ
01625 583033

**CORNWALL &
ISLES OF SCILLY**
Hell Bay
BRYHER, Isles of Scilly,
TR23 0PR
01720 422947

The Seafood Restaurant
Riverside, PADSTOW,
PL28 8BY
01841 532700

Driftwood
Rosevine, PORTSCATHO,
TR2 5EW
01872 580644

Restaurant Nathan Outlaw
The St Enodoc Hotel,
ROCK, PL27 6LA
01208 863394

Hotel Tresanton
Lower Castle Road,
ST MAWES, TR2 5DR
01326 270055

CUMBRIA
Hipping Hall
Cowan Bridge,
KIRKBY LONSDALE,
LA6 2JJ
015242 71187

**Rampsbeck
Country House Hotel**
WATERMILLOCK,
CA11 0LP
017684 86442

Gilpin Hotel & Lake House
Crook Road,
WINDERMERE,
LA23 3NE
015394 88818

**Holbeck Ghyll Country
House Hotel**
Holbeck Lane,
WINDERMERE,
LA23 1LU
015394 32375

DERBYSHIRE
Fischer's Baslow Hall
Calver Road, BASLOW,
DE45 1RR
01246 583259

**East Lodge Country
House Hotel**
ROWSLEY, DE4 2EF
01629 734474

The Peacock at Rowsley
Bakewell Road
ROWSLEY, DE4 2EB
01629 733518

DEVON
The Old Inn
DREWSTEIGNTON,
EX6 6QR
01647 281276

**The Elephant
Restaurant & Brasserie**
3/4 Beacon Terrace,
TORQUAY, TQ1 2BH
01803 200044

DORSET
Sienna Restaurant
36 High West Street,
DORCHESTER,
DT1 1UP
01305 250022

**Summer Lodge
Country House Hotel**
EVERSHOT, DT2 0JR
01935 482000

CO DURHAM
**Kenny Atkinson at
The Orangery**
Rockliffe Hall,
Hurworth on Tees,
DARLINGTON,
DL2 2DU
01325 729999

GLOUCESTERSHIRE
Ellenborough Park
Southam Road,
CHELTENHAM,
GL52 3NH
01242 545454

Lords of the Manor
UPPER SLAUGHTER,
Cheltenham, GL54 2JD
01451 820243

Cotswolds88 Hotel
Kemps Lane,
PAINSWICK, GL6 6YB
01452 813688

5 North Street
5 North Street,
WINCHCOMBE,
GL54 5LH
01242 604566

GREATER MANCHESTER
The Saddleworth Hotel
Huddersfield Road,
DELPH, OL3 5LX
01457 871888

HAMPSHIRE
The Montagu Arms Hotel
Palace Lane,
BEAULIEU, SO42 7ZL
01590 612324

36 on the Quay
47 South Street,
EMSWORTH, PO10 7EG
01243 375592

**The Dining Room
at Lime Wood**
Beaulieu Road,
LYNDHURST, SO43 7FZ
023 8028 2944

Chewton Glen Hotel & Spa
Christchurch Road,
NEW MILTON,
BH25 6QS
01425 275341

JSW
20 Dragon Street,
PETERSFIELD, GU31 4JJ
01730 262030

**Avenue Restaurant at
Lainston House Hotel**
Sparsholt, WINCHESTER,
SO21 2LT
01962 863588

HERTFORDSHIRE
Colette's at The Grove
Chandler's Cross,
RICKMANSWORTH,
WD3 4TG
01923 807807

Auberge du Lac
Brocket Hall Estate,
WELWYN, AL8 7XG
01707 368888

KENT
The West House
28 High Street,
BIDDENDEN,
TN27 8AH
01580 291341

Apicius
23 Stone Street,
CRANBROOK,
TN17 3HF
01580 714666

Thackeray's
TUNBRIDGE WELLS,
TN1 1EA
01892 511921

LINCOLNSHIRE
Harry's Place
17 High Street,
Great Gonerby,
GRANTHAM,
NG31 8JS
01476 561780

MERSEYSIDE
Fraiche
11 Rose Mount, Oxton
Village, BIRKENHEAD,
CH43 5SG
0151 652 2914

Stewart Warner at Hillbark
Royden Park,
FRANKBY, CH48 1NP
0151 625 2400

The Lawns Restaurant
Thornton Hall Hotel,
Neston Road, THORNTON
HOUGH, CH63 1JF
0151 336 3938

NORFOLK
Morston Hall
Morston, Holt,
BLAKENEY, NR25 7AA
01263 741041

3 ROSETTES

NORFOLK CONTINUED

The Neptune Restaurant with Rooms
85 Old Hunstanton Road,
HUNSTANTON,
PE36 6HZ
01485 532122

Roger Hickman's Restaurant
78 Upper St Giles Street,
NORWICH, NR2 1AB
01603 633522

OXFORDSHIRE
Orwells
Shiplake Row, Binfield
Heath, HENLEY-ON-
THAMES, RG9 4DP
0118 940 3673

SHROPSHIRE
La Bécasse
17 Corve Street,
LUDLOW, SY8 1DA
01584 872325

Fishmore Hall
Fishmore Road,
LUDLOW, SY8 3DP
01584 875148

SOMERSET
Bath Priory Hotel, Restaurant & Spa
Weston Road, BATH,
BA1 2XT
01225 331922

The Olive Tree at The Queensberry Hotel
4-7 Russell Street,
BATH, BA1 2QF
01225 447928

Little Barwick House
Barwick Village,
YEOVIL, BA22 9TD
01935 423902

SUFFOLK
The Bildeston Crown
104 High Street,
BILDESTON, IP7 7EB
01449 740510

Tuddenham Mill
High Street, Tuddenham
St Mary, NEWMARKET,
IP28 6SQ
01638 713552

SURREY
The Oak Room at Great Fosters
Stroude Road, EGHAM,
TW20 9UR
01784 433822

Drake's Restaurant
The Clock House,
High Street, RIPLEY,
GU23 6AQ
01483 224777

SUSSEX, WEST
Ockenden Manor
Ockenden Lane,
CUCKFIELD, RH17 5LD
01444 416111

Gravetye Manor Hotel
Vowells Lane, West
Hoathly, EAST
GRINSTEAD, RH19 4LJ
01342 810567

TYNE & WEAR
Jesmond Dene House
Jesmond Dene Road,
NEWCASTLE UPON
TYNE, NE2 2EY
0191 212 3000

WARWICKSHIRE
Mallory Court Hotel
Harbury Lane,
Bishop's Tachbrook,
ROYAL LEAMINGTON
SPA, CV33 9QB
01926 330214

WEST MIDLANDS
Loves Restaurant
The Glasshouse,
Canal Square,
Browning Street,
BIRMINGHAM,
B16 8FL
0121 454 5151

Purnell's
55 Cornwall Street,
BIRMINGHAM,
B3 2DH
0121 212 9799

Simpsons
20 Highfield Road,
Edgbaston,
BIRMINGHAM,
B15 3DU
0121 454 3434

WIGHT, ISLE OF
The Hambrough
Hambrough Road,
VENTNOR,
PO38 1SQ
01983 856333

WILTSHIRE
The Bybrook at the Manor
CASTLE COMBE,
SN14 7HR
01249 782206

The Park restaurant
Lucknam Park,
COLERNE,
SN14 8AZ
01225 742777

The Harrow at Little Bedwyn
LITTLE BEDWYN,
SN8 3JP
01672 870871

YORKSHIRE, NORTH
Feversham Arms Hotel & Verbena Spa
1-8 High Street,
HELMSLEY, YO62 5AG
01439 770766

Samuel's at Swinton Park
MASHAM, Ripon,
HG4 4JH
01765 680900

The Black Swan at Oldstead
OLDSTEAD, YO61 4BL
01347 868387

Judges Country House Hotel
Kirklevington, YARM,
TS15 9LW
01642 789000

YORKSHIRE, WEST
Box Tree Restaurant
35-37 Church Street,
ILKLEY, LS29 9DR
01943 608484

Anthony's Restaurant
19 Boar Lane,
LEEDS, LS1 6EA
0113 245 5922

JERSEY
Grand Jersey
The Esplanade,
ST HELIER, JE4 8WD
01534 722301

Longueville Manor Hotel
ST SAVIOUR, JE2 7WF
01534 725501

SCOTLAND
ABERDEENSHIRE
Darroch Learg Hotel
Braemar Road,
BALLATER, AB35 5UX
013397 55443

The Green Inn
9 Victoria Road,
BALLATER, AB35 5QQ
013397 55701

ANGUS
Gordon's
Main Street,
INVERKEILOR,
DD11 5RN

ARGYLL & BUTE
Isle of Eriska
Benderloch, By Oban,
ERISKA, PA37 1SD
01631 720371

The Ardanaiseig Hotel
KILCHRENAN,
Taynuilt, PA35 1HE
01866 833333

Airds Hotel & Restaurant
PORT APPIN, PA38 4DF
01631 730236

DUMFRIES & GALLOWAY
Knockinaam Lodge
PORTPATRICK,
DG9 9AD
01776 810471

EDINBURGH
Castle Terrace Restaurant
33-35 Castle Terrace,
EDINBURGH,
EH1 2EL
0131 229 1222

Mark Greenaway at No.12 Picardy Place
12 Picardy Place,
EDINBURGH, EH1 3JT
0131 557 0952

Norton House Hotel & Spa
Ingliston, EDINBURGH,
EH28 8LX
0131 333 1275

Number One, The Balmoral
Princes Street,
EDINBURGH,
EH2 2EQ
0131 557 6727

Plumed Horse
50-54 Henderson Street,
Leith, EDINBURGH,
EH6 6DE
0131 554 5556

21212
3 Royal Terrace,
EDINBURGH, EH7 5AB
0131 523 1030

GLASGOW
Hotel du Vin at One Devonshire Gardens
1 Devonshire Gardens,
GLASGOW, G12 0UX
0141 339 2001

FIFE
The Cellar
24 East Green,
ANSTRUTHER, KY10 3AA
01333 310378

The Peat Inn
PEAT INN, KY15 5LH
01334 840 206

Road Hole Restaurant
Old Course Hotel Golf
Resort & Spa,
ST ANDREWS,
KY16 9SP
01334 474371

Rocca Grill
Macdonald Rusacks Hotel
The Links, ST ANDREWS,
KY16 9JQ
0844 879 9136

HIGHLAND
Inverlochy Castle Hotel
Torlundy, FORT WILLIAM,
PH33 6SN
01397 702177

The Cross at Kingussie
Tweed Mill Brae,
Ardbroilach Road,
KINGUSSIE, PH21 ILB
01540 661166

The Torridon Restaurant
TORRIDON, IV22 2EY
01445 791242

SCOTTISH BORDERS
Cringletie House
Edinburgh Road,
PEEBLES, EH45 8PL
01721 725750

SOUTH AYRSHIRE
Lochgreen House Hotel
Monktonhill Road,
Southwood,
TROON, KA10 7EN
01292 313343

The James Miller Room
Turnberry Resort
Scotland, Maidens Road,
TURNBERRY,
KA26 9LT
01655 331000

STIRLING
Roman Camp Country House Hotel
CALLANDER,
FK17 8BG
01877 330003

WEST DUNBARTONSHIRE
Martin Wishart at Loch Lomond
Cameron House on
Loch Lomond,
BALLOCH,
G83 8QZ
01389 722504

SCOTTISH ISLANDS

Kinloch Lodge
Sleat, ISLE ORNSAY,
IV43 8QY
01471 833214

The Three Chimneys
COLBOST, Isle of Skye
IV55 8ZT
01470 511258

Ullinish Country Lodge
STRUAN, Isle of Skye,
IV56 8FD
01470 572214

WALES

CEREDIGION
Ynyshir Hall
EGLWYSFACH,
Machynlleth, SY20 8TA
01654 781209

CONWY
Tan-y-Foel Country House
Capel Garmon,
BETWS-Y-COED,
LL26 0RE
01690 710507

Bodysgallen Hall and Spa
LLANDUDNO, LL30 1RS
01492 584466

MONMOUTHSHIRE
The Walnut Tree
Llandewi Skirrid,
ABERGAVENNY,
NP7 8AW
01873 852797

The Crown at Whitebrook
WHITEBROOK,
NP25 4TX
01600 860254

NEWPORT
Terry M at the Celtic Manor Resort
Coldra Woods,
NEWPORT, NP18 1HQ
01633 410262

NORTHERN IRELAND

BELFAST
Deanes Restaurant
36-40 Howard Street,
BELFAST, BT1 6PF
028 9033 1144

REPUBLIC OF IRELAND

CO CLARE
Gregans Castle
BALLYVAUGHAN
065 7077005

CO KILKENNY
The Lady Helen Restaurant
Mount Juliet Hotel,
THOMASTOWN
056 7773000

CO MONAGHAN
The Restaurant at Nuremore
CARRICKMACROSS
042 9661438

CO WATERFORD
The House
The Cliff House Hotel,
ARDMORE
024 87800

England

Little Langdale, Lake District National Park, Cumbria

BEDFORDSHIRE

BEDFORD
Map 12 TL04

The Bedford Swan

@@ Modern British V

18th-century hotel with modish cooking and a charming riverside position

☎ 01234 346565
The Embankment MK40 1RW
e-mail: info@bedfordswanhotel.co.uk
dir: M1 junct 13, take A421 following signs to city centre (one way system). Turn left to The Embankment, car park on left after Swan statue

A multi-million-pound facelift in recent years has brought the Georgian Bedford Swan hotel up to speed with the 21st century in fine style. The period elegance of its oak panels, ornate plasterwork and bare stone walls now sits happily with contemporary colours and textures - a style that works well in the brasserie-like River Room restaurant. The setting is certainly impressive - its bow windows overlook the River Ouse, or on fine days you can sit out on the embankment terrace to explore a menu of uncomplicated modern dishes. A starter of quail breast with pistachio and quail pithivier, sun-blushed grapes, and Madeira jus shows a keen eye for clever flavour pairing, while main course delivers another well-balanced success with a pavé of smoked salmon teamed with coriander and shrimp velouté. A lemon and lime meringue makes a great finish.

Chef Jason Buck **Owner** BDL **Times** 12-3/6-10 **Prices** Food prices not confirmed for 2013. Please telephone for details **Wines** 23 bottles over £20, 15 bottles under £20, 6 by glass **Notes** Sunday L, Vegetarian menu, Dress restrictions, Smart casual, Civ Wed 100 **Seats** 90, Pr/dining room 20 **Children** Portions, Menu **Parking** 90

BOLNHURST
Map 12 TL05

The Plough at Bolnhurst

@ Modern British 🍷NOTABLE 🖐

Classy modern menu in Tudor pub

☎ 01234 376274
Kimbolton Rd MK44 2EX
e-mail: theplough@bolnhurst.com
dir: A14/A421 onto B660 for approx 5m to Bolnhurst village

This whitewashed 15th-century country inn has period charm in spades - doughty Tudor beams and timbers, tiny windows, and welcoming open fires in its cosy bars. So the contemporary restaurant in an expansive, light-bathed room comes as a striking contrast. Fizzing with life at lunchtime - when chalkboards suggest ideas such as deep-fried whitebait with tartare sauce and lemon, or local Dexter steak pie with Savoy cabbage and duck fat roast potatoes - the mood segues into a more intimate,

candlelit vibe in the evening. Top-class local produce is translated into big-flavoured modern dishes on a daily-changing menu that could open with pan-fried pigeon breast with beetroot purée, pancetta, trompette mushrooms and juniper, and follow with corn-fed Goosnargh duck breast with turnip gratin, roast shallots and Armagnac sauce. Awaiting at the end, perhaps cider and apple mousse with caramelised apple tart and caramel ice cream.

Chef Martin Lee **Owner** Martin Lee, Jayne Lee, Michael Moscrop **Times** 12-2/6.30-9.30 Closed 27 Dec-14 Jan, Mon, D Sun **Prices** Fixed L 3 course £15-£19, Fixed D 3 course £19, Starter £4.50-£7.95, Main £15.50-£17.95, Dessert £6.50-£7.25, Service optional **Wines** 80 bottles over £20, 42 bottles under £20, 12 by glass **Notes** Sunday L, Vegetarian available **Seats** 96, Pr/dining room 38 **Children** Portions **Parking** 30

FLITWICK
Map 11 TL03

Menzies Flitwick Manor

@ Modern, Traditional

Georgian manor house with confident kitchen

☎ 01525 712242
Church Rd MK45 1AE
e-mail: steven.essex@menzieshotels.co.uk
dir: M1 junct 12, follow Flitwick after 1m turn left into Church Rd. Manor 200 yds on left

The manor is a Georgian gem dating back to the 17th century and is reached down a long drive through rolling parkland. In true country-house style, it comes with a full complement of antiques, oil paintings, and oriental rugs on oak parquet floors, while the restaurant also fits the bill with its traditional look and lovely views over the terrace and peaceful gardens. Classic dishes are given a modern spin on a well-thought-out repertoire, opening with seared scallops with carrot and raisin salsa and pea cream, ahead of beef sirloin with rösti potato, baby vegetables and red wine jus, or sea bream with leek and bacon tart and saffron foam, and mango soufflé with vanilla anglaise and mango compôte.

Chef James Bryars **Owner** Menzies Hotels plc **Times** 12-3/7-10 **Prices** Food prices not confirmed for 2013. Please telephone for details **Wines** 48 bottles over £20, 6 by glass **Notes** Vegetarian available, Civ Wed 60 **Seats** 50, Pr/dining room 20 **Children** Portions **Parking** 60

LUTON
Map 6 TL02

Adam's Brasserie

@ Modern British

Brasserie cooking in the smartened up stables at Luton Hoo

☎ 01582 734437 & 698888
Luton Hoo Hotel, Golf and Spa, The Mansion House LU1 3TQ
e-mail: reservations@lutonhoo.co.uk
dir: M1 junct 10A, 3rd exit to A1081 towards Harpenden/St Albans. Hotel less than a mile on left

Part of the fabulous Luton Hoo estate, complete with golf course, wonderful gardens, a luxurious hotel, spa, and elegant fine-dining restaurant (see entry for the Wernher Restaurant), Adam's Brasserie is yet another string to their bow. Situated in the former stables, now the country club, the high-ceilinged and many-windowed room is adorned with pictures of movie stars who have filmed on the estate over the years, and serves up a pleasing array of brasserie-style dishes. That amounts to meats from the grill (Casterbridge beef sirloin, for example), herb-crusted fillet of cod, and butternut squash ravioli. Start with pan-seared scallops with a black pudding bonbon or home-smoked fillet of trout (smoked in Jasmine tea and thyme), and finish with a traditional rice pudding, or caramelised pear Pavlova.

Chef Kevin Clark **Owner** Elite Hotels **Times** 12-3/6-10 Closed D Sun **Prices** Starter £6-£8.95, Main £15-£21, Dessert £6.75-£7.75, Service optional, Groups min 6 service 10% **Wines** 38 bottles over £20, 6 bottles under £20, 8 by glass **Notes** Sunday L, Vegetarian available, Civ Wed 120 **Seats** 90 **Children** Portions, Menu **Parking** 100

Best Western Menzies Strathmore Hotel

@ Modern British

Smart cooking in a contemporary setting

☎ 01582 734199
Arndale Centre LU1 2TR
e-mail: strathmore@menzieshotels.co.uk
dir: Exit M1 junct 10a towards town centre, adjacent to Arndale Centre car park

Well placed in the heart of Luton overlooking St George Square, this smart hotel has recently been refurbished in contemporary style and offers a health club and spa facilities. A huge wall of glass makes the brasserie-style restaurant a luminous space, and its unclothed wooden tables and secluded booths upholstered in rich tones of red, orange and brown all add up to a stylish modern look. The kitchen has broad appeal with its unfussy repertoire of comfort-oriented, up-to-date ideas. You might start with pressed ham hock terrine served with piccalilli and crusty bread, then follow with a fashionable trio of pork - pressed belly, pig's cheek and loin - teamed with potato purée, Savoy cabbage and sea salt crackling,

Save on Hotels. Book at **theAA.com/hotel**

BEDFORDSHIRE 47 **ENGLAND**

or sea bream fillet with saffron broth, new potatoes, spinach and snow peas. Finish with chocolate orange fondant with vanilla ice cream.

Times 12-3/7-9.45

Wernher Restaurant

◎◎ Modern European NOTABLE WINE LIST

Magnificent country estate with modern cooking

☎ 01582 734437
Luton Hoo Hotel, Golf and Spa, The Mansion House
LU1 3TQ
e-mail: reservations@lutonhoo.com
web: www.lutonhoo.com
dir: M1 junct 10A, 3rd exit to A1081 towards Harpenden/ St Albans. Hotel less than a mile on left

The 'Hoo' in question is actually an old Saxon word for the spur of a hill. Straddling the counties of Hertfordshire and Bedfordshire, Luton Hoo is a striking and rather stately house with impeccable credentials: Robert Adam and Sir Robert 'British Museum' Smirke are responsible for the magnificent façade, 'Capability' Brown sorted out the gardens, and Elite Hotels have provided every comfort for the 21st-century visitor. There's a golf course, spa facilities, splendidly handsome rooms and a restaurant which is done-out in a lavish, elegant manner, with marble panelling, ornate chandeliers, opulent fabrics and immaculately dressed tables. The menu is based around well-sourced produce and follows a modish path. Start, perhaps, with crispy goats' cheese with braised rocket, tomato, pine nut and red onion sauce, before the likes of roast rack of lamb with beetroot pommes purée, sautéed kale, roast baby turnips and thyme jus, and, to finish, warm roasted fig tart with orange ice cream and crème anglaise. Adam's Brasserie (see entry) offers an alternative.

Werner Restaurant

Chef Kevin Clark **Owner** Elite Hotels **Times** 12.30-2/7-10 Closed Mon-Tue **Prices** Fixed L 2 course £25-£58.50, Fixed D 3 course £42.50-£63.50, Service optional, Groups min 6 service 10% **Wines** 352 bottles over £20, 13 by glass **Notes** Sunday L, Vegetarian available, Dress restrictions, Jacket or tie, Civ Wed 120 **Seats** 80, Pr/ dining room 280 **Children** Portions, Menu **Parking** 316

WOBURN	**Map 11 SP93**

The Inn at Woburn

◎◎ Modern British, French

High-impact Anglo-French cooking on the Woburn estate

☎ 01525 290441
George St MK17 9PX
e-mail: inn@woburn.co.uk
web: www.woburn.co.uk/inn
dir: 5 mins from M1 junct 13. Follow signs to Woburn. Inn in town centre at x-rds, parking to rear via Park St

If watching the big cats feeding at the Woburn Abbey estate's safari park has brought on an appetite, head for

the Georgian coaching inn where chef Olivier Bertho delivers refined Anglo-French cooking in a smart country-house setting. The venue is rather posher than its 'inn' title suggests; Olivier's restaurant is furnished with clubby buttoned leather seating at bare wooden tables, displays of lilies in blue-and-white Chinese vases, and gilt mirrors on neutral cream and mushroom-hued walls. The food is a labour-intensive take on the modern French idiom - grilled scallops with pea purée, beetroot coulis and chervil oil is one way to start, before turning to something like an assiette of pork with cider jus, comprising belly pork with red cabbage, pork fillet on colcannon with apple jam, and mini meatballs with sage and tomato coulis. Leave room for a multi-faceted dessert such as an 'assiette du verger' (orchard assiette) involving tarte Tatin, blackberry pannacotta and vanilla crème brûlée.

The Inn at Woburn

Chef Olivier Bertho **Owner** Bedford Estates
Times 12-2/6.30-9.30 **Prices** Fixed L 2 course £13.75, Fixed D 3 course £26.65-£37.15, Starter £5.20-£9.95, Main £14.50-£18.85, Dessert £6.95-£8.35, Service optional **Wines** 25 bottles over £20, 12 bottles under £20, 18 by glass **Notes** Sunday L, Vegetarian available, Civ Wed 60 **Seats** 40, Pr/dining room 90 **Children** Portions, Menu **Parking** 80

See advert on page 48

Paris House Restaurant

◎◎◎ *– see page 48*

continued

Paris House Restaurant

WOBURN   Map 11 SP93

British, French V

Creative reinventions of old restaurant classics in a transplanted mock-Tudor house

☎ 01525 290692
London Rd, Woburn Park MK17 9QP
e-mail: info@parishouse.co.uk
web: www.parishouse.co.uk
dir: M1 junct 13. From Woburn take A4012 Hockliffe, 1m out of Woburn village on left

Why Paris? Because the house was built on the Quai d'Orsay in 1878 as part of an exhibition that represented the architectural styles of 28 nations. Britain's entry was this Elizabethan timbered building in the Cheshire style. Why Woburn? Because the then Duke of Bedford liked it so much that he had it dismantled and reassembled in the landscaped grounds of Woburn Park for his compatriots to enjoy. Dukes could do things like that then. Adorned with modern artworks and with a smart monochrome dining room, the place is now a member of Alan Murchison's 10 in 8 Fine Dining group, and comes with the obligatory chef's table for those who like to keep an eye on the kitchen. The vogue for blending old and new techniques is explored in thorough-going fashion, with contemporary takes on ham, egg and pineapple, steak and chips, prawn cocktails and banana splits like you've never seen them before. These are fun dishes, evidence of an enlivening culinary intelligence, but not all the nostalgia is British. A terrine of foie gras and Medjool dates with pain d'épice and hazelnuts is a melt-in-the-mouth homage to French classicism, while a main course of Kentucky fried veal-breads offers calves' sweetbread in crisp batter with corn purée, de-cobbed corn nibs, morels and green tomato for something altogether more Stateside. A take on millionaire's shortbread involves layering the biscuit base with caramel ganache and chocolate, plus marshmallow, honeycomb and gold leaf, accompanied by a vanilla milkshake. Even the appetisers, and the orange jelly and chocolate mousse cornet pre-dessert, display the same level of entertaining ingenuity.

Chef Phil Fanning **Owner** Alan Murchison
Times 12-2/6.30-9 Closed Mon, L Tue, D Sun & 26 Dec-8 Jan **Prices** Fixed L 2 course £25, Fixed D 3 course £67, Service added but optional 12.5% **Wines** 80 bottles over £20, 8 by glass **Notes** ALC 2 course £54, 3 course £67, Gourmand menu 8 or 10 course, Sunday L, Vegetarian menu, Dress restrictions, Smart casual **Seats** 37, Pr/dining room 14 **Children** Portions, Menu **Parking** 24

WYBOSTON   Map 12 TL15

Wyboston Lakes Hotel

🏵 British, International

Cosmopolitan eating by a lake

☎ 0333 700 7667
Great North Rd MK44 3BA
e-mail: restaurant@wybostonlakes.co.uk
web: www.wybostonlakes.co.uk
dir: Off A1/A428, follow brown Cambridge signs.
Wyboston Lakes Hotel on right, marked by flags

Pitched squarely at the business conferencing and golfing markets (it has its own course), the modern Wyboston Lakes Hotel sits in 350 acres of countryside perfect for clearing out your head when the day's work is done. The Waterfront Restaurant lives up to its name, as it sits beside the lake, and has large picture windows to open up that view, plus a terrace for outdoors dining on fine days. The kitchen deals in simple concepts that take their inspiration from a global perspective, starting with an impressive pavé of home-smoked salmon and a salmon fishcake served with cucumber and fennel salad and sauce remoulade. A well-balanced main course delivers roast breast of lamb with red chard, parsnip dauphinoise, sweet potato purée and red wine jus, then it is over to seasonal summer strawberries to do their stuff in a modern dessert of strawberry Daiquiri with clotted cream pannacotta and honeycomb.

Chef Fergus Martin **Times** 12-2.30/6.30-9.30
Closed Xmas & New Year, L Mon **Prices** Food prices not confirmed for 2013. Please telephone for details
Notes Sunday L, Vegetarian available, Civ Wed 130
Seats 90, Pr/dining room 24 **Children** Portions
Parking 100

BERKSHIRE

ASCOT   Map 6 SU96

The Barn at Coworth

🏵 British

Converted barn serving well-judged English dishes

☎ 01344 876600
Blacknest Rd SL5 7SE
e-mail: restaurants.CPA@dorchestercollection.com
dir: M25 junct 13 onto A30 to Sunningdale. Hotel on left

A rather slick barn conversion, with stone floors, a fireplace and wooden tables and bench seating, is one of the informal dining venues at Coworth Park (see separate entry for the fine-dining option). A wall of windows looks over a terrace, used for outdoor eating in summer, and upstairs is a bar with country views. 'Comfort food' is The Barn's own description of its style, although the cooking displays more ambition than that would suggest. Potted trout with horseradish and watercress, and roast beetroot with goats' cheese and caramelised onions are typical starters, with main courses like shepherd's pie of lamb shoulder with confit root vegetables, and Cornish seafood casserole with parsley sauce.

Chef Brian Hughson **Owner** Dorchester Collection
Times 12.30-2.45/6-9.30 **Prices** Fixed L 3 course £29.95-£60, Service added but optional 12.5% **Wines** 50 bottles over £20, 13 by glass **Notes** ALC 3 course £60, Sunday L, Vegetarian available, Civ Wed 300 **Seats** 55
Children Portions, Menu **Parking** 100

See advert on page 51

Bluebells Restaurant & Garden Bar

🏵🏵 Modern, International

Smart setting for contemporary cooking

☎ 01344 622722
Shrubbs Hill, London Rd SL5 0LE
e-mail: info@bluebells-restaurant.co.uk
dir: From M25 junct 13, A30 towards Bagshot. Restaurant between Wentworth & Sunningdale

You wouldn't know it from the slick interior, but a 300-year-old building is at the heart of this stylish contemporary restaurant. Bluebells was conceived with a high-end clientele from nearby Ascot and Windsor in mind, so a designer makeover has transformed the interior with a glossy magazine look - gauzy voile curtains divide the open-plan space into bar, main restaurant and conservatory areas without reducing the sense of wide-open space, while exposed brick, darkwood floors, white-leather seats and a muted olive colour scheme give the place a highly-polished feel. Smartly engineered dishes offer a light touch, like a dainty trio of crab cakes dressed in a fresh sweet chilli sauce. Next, flavours, colours and textures all combine perfectly in a dish of slow-braised belly pork with apple and cider foam, red onion marmalade and bubble-and-squeak. Creative and confident to the end, the curtain comes down on a ginger-

infused winter fruit pudding with home-made honeycomb ice cream coated in crushed pistachios.

Chef Adam Turley **Owner** John Rampello
Times 12-2.30/6.30-9.45 Closed 25-26 Dec, 1-11 Jan, BHs, Mon, D Sun **Prices** Fixed L 2 course £15, Starter £8.50-£16, Main £17-£28.50, Dessert £7.80-£8.95, Service added but optional 10% **Wines** 76 bottles over £20, 13 bottles under £20, 12 by glass **Notes** Sunday L, Vegetarian available, Dress restrictions, Smart casual **Seats** 90, Pr/dining room 14 **Children** Portions, Menu **Parking** 100

Hyperion at Macdonald Berystede Hotel & Spa

🏵 Modern European

Victorian hotel handy for the races

☎ 01344 623311 & 0844 8799 104
Bagshot Rd, Sunninghill SL5 9JH
e-mail: general.berystede@macdonald-hotels.co.uk
dir: M3 junct 3/A30, A322 then left onto B3020 to Ascot or M25 junct 13, follow signs for Bagshot. At Sunningdale turn right onto A330

Minutes from Royal Ascot and Windsor, in the glorious Thames Valley, the smartly refurbished Berystede occupies an impressive Victorian mansion and has state-of-the-art leisure facilities as well as the elegant Hyperion restaurant. The attractive dining room overlooking the roof terrace takes its name from a well-known Derby racehorse and features tables set neatly with good crockery and cutlery and fresh orchids. Good quality ingredients are highlighted in simple modern European dishes such as smoked fish terrine with basil and horseradish remoulade and a caper, shallot and tomato dressing, followed by venison saddle and venison pie with braised red cabbage, potato fondant and honey-glazed winter vegetables, and something like mandarin parfait with dark chocolate sauce for dessert.

Times 12.30-2/7-9.45 Closed L Sat

Restaurant Coworth Park

Rosettes not confirmed at time of going to press – see page 50

See advert on page 51

Restaurant Coworth Park

Rosettes not confirmed at time of going to press

ASCOT   Map 6 SU96

Contemporary cooking in a luxury hotel with high-flying chef

☎ 01344 876600
Blacknest Rd SL5 7SE
e-mail: restaurants.CPA@
dorchestercollection.com
web: www.coworthpark.com
dir: M25 junct 13 onto A30 to
Sunningdale. Hotel on left

This country cousin to the West End's
glittering Dorchester Hotel is no less
impressive than its big-city counterpart.
The elegant Manor House is surrounded
by 240 acres of luxuriant Berkshire
countryside for a start, and boasts the
Queen as a neighbour (Windsor Great
Park is next door). The Coworth Park
Equestrian Centre is available for
guests - a game of polo anyone? -
there's a spa, and the place can put on
a very swanky event - planning on
getting married anytime soon? There's
an awful lot going on here with the
eating options running to the modish
Spatisserie located in the spa, a
converted barn has a bistro-dining vibe
(The Barn - see entry), the swish
Drawing Room in the main house offers
all-day dining and afternoon tea, a
swanky bar with a terrace overlooks the
croquet lawn and sunken gardens, and
then there's the fine-dining option, the
Restaurant, for which a new executive
chef has been recruited as we go to

print. The main event takes place in a
splendid series of rooms with fine
Georgian proportions done out in warm
autumnal shades with a centrepiece
artwork of shimmering leaves and twigs
dominating the ceiling, and impeccably
dressed tables throughout. The cooking
has been at the sharp end of
contemporary thinking, with the à la
carte supported by a Best of British
menu available midweek for lunch and
in the evening during the week. You
might kick off with seared foie gras
partnered with caramelised pears,
spiced bread and toasted brioche,
before a line-caught Cornish sea bass
with roast violet artichokes, parsley
gnocchi, crayfish and cauliflower purée,
ending with a creative dessert such as
mango parfait with coconut rice, black
olive caramel, peanut brittle and vanilla
dressing.

Chef Brian Hughson **Owner** Dorchester
Collection **Times** 12.30-3/6.30-9.30
Closed Mon, D Sun **Prices** Fixed L 2
course £25-£35, Starter £6.50-£12.50,
Main £14.50-£26.50, Dessert £7.25-
£9.50, Service added but optional
12.5% **Wines** 580 bottles over £20, 18
by glass **Notes** Sunday L, Vegetarian
available, Dress restrictions, Smart
casual, Civ Wed 300 **Seats** 70, Pr/dining
room 14 **Children** Portions, Menu
Parking 100

Save on Hotels. Book at **theAA.com/hotel**

BERKSHIRE 51 ENGLAND

The scent of crushed herbs. A sense of warmth. A moment to savour. A taste of the season.
The best of British. The Barn.

Contact us on +44 (0)1344 876 600, email restaurants.CPA@dorchestercollection.com or visit coworthpark.com

THE COUNTRY HOUSE HOTEL THAT REWRITES THE RULES

COWORTH · PARK
ASCOT

Dorchester *Collection*

The Dorchester	The Beverly Hills Hotel	Le Meurice	Hôtel Plaza Athénée	Hotel Principe di Savoia	Hotel Bel-Air	Coworth Park	45 Park Lane	Le Richemond
LONDON	BEVERLY HILLS	PARIS	PARIS	MILAN	LOS ANGELES	ASCOT	LONDON	GENEVA

BRACKNELL
Map 5 SU86

Coppid Beech

◉ European, Pacific Rim

Alpine atmosphere and modern food by the Thames

☎ 01344 303333
John Nike Way RG12 8TF
e-mail: sales@coppidbeech.com
web: www.coppidbeech.com
dir: M4 junct 10 take Wokingham/Bracknell onto A329. In 2m take B3408 to Binfield at rdbt. Hotel 200yds on right

You may think that the Thames Valley is not known for its skiing and Alpine chalets, but that is because you haven't yet discovered the Coppid Beech Hotel. The smart modern hotel not only has the look of a Swiss chalet, but there's the chance to strap on the planks too as there's a dry-ski slope, an ice rink and toboggan run in the complex. With an appetite suitably sharpened by the year-round winter sports, move on to Rowans, the hotel's upscale dining option. It is an eye-catching space, with plush drapes and linen-clothed tables beneath a soaring timbered ceiling hung with crystal chandelier as a backdrop to a menu that covers a fair amount of modern European territory. Start with wood pigeon en croûte served with beetroot carpaccio, and orange and beetroot jus, followed by sirloin steak with mushrooms, parsnip purée, garlic spinach and marchand de vin sauce. Finish with a Thai-influenced coconut pannacotta with sweet-and-sour pineapple, and basil jelly.

Chef Paul Zolik **Owner** Nike Group Hotels Ltd
Times 12-2/7-9.45 Closed L Sat, D Thu **Prices** Fixed L 2 course fr £18, Fixed D 3 course fr £25.50, Starter £6-£13, Main £16-£25, Dessert £5.25-£8.95, Service optional **Wines** 48 bottles over £20, 9 bottles under £20, 20 by glass **Notes** Sunday L, Vegetarian available, Dress restrictions, Smart casual, Civ Wed 300 **Seats** 120, Pr/dining room 20 **Children** Portions, Menu **Parking** 350

BRAY
Map 6 SU97

Caldesi in Campagna

◉◉ Traditional Italian **NEW**

Refined Italian eatery in Bray

☎ 01628 788500
Old Mill Ln SL6 2BG
e-mail: campagna@caldesi.com
dir: M4 junct 8/9, at rdbt exit A308 Bray/Windsor. Continue for 0.5m, left B3028 Bray village, right Old Mill Lane, rest in 400yds on right

As if to prove that nobody in Bray need be stuck for somewhere to eat out, yet another fine-dining venue springs up, this one a two-handed operation from Italian chef Giancarlo Caldesi and his wife Katie, a food writer specialising in Italy. The restaurant is in a small white house on the outskirts of the village, the refined but simple décor extending to beige tones, parquet flooring, a brick fireplace and quality tableware. There's bar seating too, as well as an outdoor area, and when the Berkshire sun comes out, you might just fancy you were in Tuscany. The more so as Caldesi's cooking pulls off that very 21st-century trick of using British (mainly local) sustainable ingredients to give a convincing impression of the food of somewhere else entirely. The carpaccio is made from Scotch beef, and comes properly dressed with shaved parmesan, rocket, rosemary and balsamic, gaining true succulence from its being served warm. Squid is slow-cooked to tenderness and married with tomatoes and chilli for a fine crostini topping, and the home-made pasta that encases sea bass in ravioli, or tangles up clams, garlic and chilli in spaghetti, is the real thing. Fish cookery is spot-on, the timing of a piece of fried stone bass flawless, while meat might be classic saltimbocca Romana, or Barbary duck breast crusted in pink peppercorns with mashed potato in red grape sauce.

Chef Gregorio Piazza **Owner** Giancarlo Caldesi
Times 12-2.30/6-10.30 Closed Xmas for approx 5 days, Mon, D Sun **Prices** Fixed L 2 course fr £15.50, Starter £9.50-£12.50, Main £14-£25, Dessert £6.95-£13.50, Service added but optional 12.5% **Wines** 96 bottles over £20, 2 bottles under £20, 13 by glass **Notes** Sunday L, Vegetarian available, Dress restrictions, **Seats** 50 **Children** Portions, Menu **Parking** 8

The Crown

◉ Modern British 🍷

16th-century inn in the hands of Heston

☎ 01628 621936
High St SL6 2AH
dir: M4 junct 8/9, follow signs for Maidenhead Central, left towards Windsor, right to Bray

The 16th-century Crown is a real charmer, with beams in the low ceilings, leaded windows, lots of little nooks and crannies, and a bar for drinkers. There's no hint that it's owned by Heston Blumenthal, but it is, along with The Hinds Head (see entry). The food is straightforward

British gastro-pub stuff, albeit of a consistently high standard using impeccable ingredients. Favourite pub staples are brought off with aplomb, among them pork pie (home-made, of course) with piccalilli and pickles, fish and chips, and suet, steak and ale pie with mash. Elsewhere, look for seasonal specials - perhaps variations on Jerusalem artichoke (as soup, or as a purée with fillet of hake and curly kale) - and, a curiosity nowadays, cheese fondue. Cheeses are resolutely British, and puddings like apple and cranberry crumble, or sticky toffee are of the old school.

Chef Nick Galer **Owner** Heston Blumenthal
Times 12-2.30/6-9.30 Closed 25 Dec **Prices** Fixed L 2 course fr £12, Starter £4.50-£8.25, Main £12.50-£23.50, Dessert £5.50, Service added but optional 12.5% **Wines** 24 bottles over £20, 4 bottles under £20, 18 by glass **Notes** Sunday L, Vegetarian available **Seats** 40, Pr/dining room 12 **Parking**

The Fat Duck

◉◉◉◉◉ – **see opposite**

Hinds Head

◉◉ British 🎖

Heston's modern take on old-English hearty fare

☎ 01628 626151
High St SL6 2AB
e-mail: info@hindsheadbray.com
dir: M4 junct 8/9, at rdbt take exit to Maidenhead Central, next rdbt take exit Bray & Windsor, after 0.5m take B3028 to Bray

One of Heston Blumenthal's three Bray outposts (see entries for The Fat Duck and The Crown) is a traditional inn dating from the 15th century, complete with oak panelling and beams, open fires, comfortable leather-look seats and a child-friendly, casual atmosphere. There's none of Heston's molecular gastronomy here; rather, the intention is to revive the traditions of hostelry dining, keeping things simple and straightforward, with dishes defined by bold, upfront flavours. Chicken liver parfait is a textbook example, and other starters could be snail hash (from an 1884 recipe, says the menu), and a salad of beetroot, goats' curd, orange and pumpkin seeds. Quality and timings are never in doubt, seen in roast fillet of cod with celeriac purée, sultanas and salt cod, a winning combination, and veal chop with cabbage and onions and classic sauce Reform. Desserts recreate some long-forgotten dishes: try rhubarb and custard quaking pudding, or wassailing caramelised butter loaf with apple and Pomona.

Chef Kevin Love **Owner** Hinds Head Ltd
Times 12-2.30/6.30-9.30 Closed 25-26 Dec, D 1 Jan, BH's, Sun **Prices** Starter £7.50-£11.75, Main £16.95-£29.50, Dessert £7.95-£9.50, Service added but optional 12.5% **Wines** 69 bottles over £20, 5 bottles under £20, 13 by glass **Notes** Tasting menu available 7 course, with 24 hr notice, Sunday L, Vegetarian available **Seats** 100, Pr/dining room 22 **Children** Portions, Menu **Parking** 40

Save on Hotels. Book at **theAA.com/hotel**

BERKSHIRE 53 **ENGLAND**

The Fat Duck

BRAY Map 6 SU97

Modern British NOTABLE WINE LIST

Snail porridge and other culinary wizardry

☎ 01628 580333
High St SL6 2AQ
dir: M4 junct 8/9 (Maidenhead) take A308 towards Windsor, turn left into Bray. Restaurant in centre of village on right

Welcome to Hestonworld. The entrance fee is £180 these days, which sounds like an awful lot of loot in austerity Britain, but the 14-course tasting menu delivers an experience that stays with you for life, and that surely has to be worth splashing out for. Sure, there are more egalitarian ways to sample Mr B's products - Bray's high street pubs, the Hinds Head and The Crown (see entries), offer a more wallet-friendly route, for starters, and there's the rather more pricy heritage-inspired gastronomy at Dinner by Heston Blumenthal (see entry) if you're up for a blowout in a five-star gaff in swanky Knightsbridge. But when all is said and done, The Fat Duck is where it all started in 1995, and there is an undeniable allure to eating in a venue lauded repeatedly as 'the world's best restaurant', an accolade which puts the FD on every foodie's 'must do before I die' wish list. Self-taught Blumenthal has always taken a questioning, iconoclastic approach to his craft, and while international fame and TV stardom

means you won't find the man with his sleeves rolled up at the stoves every day, he could well be across the road in the 'laboratory' kitchen, experimenting, developing and perfecting new dishes to keep the creative genius driving the operation on the boil. Anyone who has seen Heston (for he is now counted among the select côterie of chefs who go by one name) on the telly would find a stuffy temple to gastronomy hard to reconcile with his sense of fun, and while the restaurant is certainly a looker with its well-designed contemporary style, it's a relaxed, non-reverential sort of place. The menu evolves gently, always playing the old hits - snail porridge with Iberico Bellota ham and shaved fennel is a fixture - whilst revisiting the back catalogue and reworking favourite themes. Every sense is involved - smell, taste, sight are taken as read, even touch, although we're not great fondlers of our food in the UK - but it's not often that sound comes into the conception of a dish: the 'Sound of the Sea' is an essential element of the 'multi-sensory perception' ethos, heightening the pleasure of a superb fish composition ('sand' tapioca, crispy-fried eels, fish foam, seaweed, and pieces of kingfish, halibut and mackerel) by throwing an iPod housed in a shell playing crashing wave sounds into the mix. The strange science gets under way with nitro-poached aperitifs - vodka and lime sour, gin and tonic or Campari soda - in the form of a meringue-like mousse poached in liquid nitrogen at -196 degrees C that

dissolves with whizz-bang flavour fireworks on the tongue. There's a bit of cross-pollination between The Fat Duck and Heston's 'Dinner' operation at the Mandarin Oriental Hyde Park too, which is evident in dishes of yore that venture back into the past and are flagged up with their approximate date of origin: the 'Mad Hatter's Tea Party' (c.1850) is a piece of pure theatre from the zanier end of the spectrum, delivering 'mock turtle soup' with an edible gold leaf watch that dissolves into the dish, while taffety tart (c1660) is a delightful Restoration-era sweetie involving caramelised apple, fennel, rose and candied lemon. Dishes that play things relatively straight also deliver knockout combinations of taste and texture: roast foie gras with rhubarb, braised konbu and crab biscuit, or Anjou pigeon with a silky blood pudding, risotto of spelt and umbles (or offal, as we know it today). Part of the experience aims to achieve the Proustian trick of evoking the past, so be prepared (if you're old enough) for memories of the '70s - T.Rex, flares and platform shoes - as you tackle the 'BFG' - a remarkable deconstruction of a Black Forest gâteau.

Chef Heston Blumenthal, Jonny Lake **Owner** Fat Duck Ltd **Times** 12-2/7-9 Closed 2 wks at Xmas, Sun-Mon **Prices** Food prices not confirmed for 2013. Please telephone for details **Wines** 500 bottles over £20, 13 by glass **Notes** Tasting menu only, Vegetarian available **Seats** 40 **Children** Portions **Parking** Two village car parks

Waterside Inn

French ⚜ NOTABLE WINE LIST

A truly gastronomic experience right beside the river

☎ 01628 620691
Ferry Rd SL6 2AT
e-mail: reservations@waterside-inn. co.uk
dir: M4 junct 8/9, A308 (Windsor) then B3028 to Bray. Restaurant clearly signed

The 'water' in question is the Thames, and the restaurant has been sitting right beside it since the early 1970s. It may not be far from here to London, or the M4 and Heathrow, but when you're sitting on the terrace gazing out to the river and watching the swans and the boats going about their business, you could easily be miles away from anywhere. If the weather allows you can even head out onto the water and join them - The Waterside has its very own little electric boat that guests can hire. Pre-dinner drinks on the terrace are a great way to begin, before proceeding into the classically elegant restaurant with its wall of windows facing the river. If the make-up of a good restaurant is 50% great food and 50% great service, then The Waterside Inn is a truly magnificent restaurant. In fact, without wishing to be harsh on Alain Roux - who took over the kitchen from his father Michel in 2002 - the impeccable service

is at least as memorable as the food. The front-of-house team, led by Diego Masciaga, are masters at what they do, managing to spot a guest's every need and be at their side in an instant to assist, but without the guest ever noticing their presence. It's quite a trick. And then there's the food: Alain's style is a pleasing mixture of classic French haute cuisine combined with more modern ideas. There are dishes on the menu that have been there since day one - the grilled rabbit fillets on a celeriac fondant with Armagnac sauce and glazed chestnuts will never go out of fashion (the rabbit wonderfully tender and infused with a chargrilled flavour, contrasting brilliantly with an accompanying single ravioli stuffed with braised meat and rabbit kidneys). The kitchen faithfully follows the seasons, and so a spring starter could be a light and fresh-tasting courgette flower filled with wild mushrooms and accompanied by spring vegetables tossed in warm olive oil with chopped truffle. Singing with equally fresh, vibrant flavours is the flaked Devon crab and marinated sea bass on a delicate carrot jelly lightly infused with ginger, and finished with some Oscietra caviar. Amongst main courses, the poached fillets of Dover sole flavoured with tarragon, crayfish tails, morels and a 'vin jaune' sauce is an old-school dish which still delights to this day. At dessert stage, the traditional French patisserie skills on display in a vanilla

flavoured millefeuille served with strawberries in melba sauce and a mascarpone ice cream are second-to-none (and the same can be said of the wonderful array of petits fours). Prices are by no means cheap here - that dessert alone will set you back £28.50, while the most inexpensive way of experiencing Monsieur Roux's cuisine is via the 'menu gastronomique' at £58 for three courses. But a meal at The Waterside is certainly one you'll remember for all the right reasons for many years to come.

Chef Alain Roux **Owner** Alain Roux **Times** 12-2/7-10 Closed Mon-Tue **Prices** Fixed L 2 course £42.50, Fixed D 4 course £147.50, Starter £29.50-£52, Main £49.50-£69, Dessert £29-£39.50, Service included **Wines** 650 bottles over £20, 14 by glass **Notes** Sunday L, Vegetarian available, Dress restrictions, Smart casual, Civ Wed 70 **Seats** 75, Pr/dining room 8 **Children** Menu **Parking** 20

Save on Hotels. Book at **theAA.com/hotel**

BERKSHIRE 55 ENGLAND

BRAY continued

The Riverside Brasserie

◉◉ Modern European

Accomplished cooking by the Thames

☎ 01628 780553
Bray Marina, Monkey Island Ln SL6 2EB
e-mail: info@riversidebrasserie.co.uk
web: www.riversidebrasserie.co.uk
dir: Off A308, signed Bray Marina

Aptly named to be sure, this simple café-like building can be found tucked away beside the Thames in Bray Marina, and is the perfect spot if you're in the market for an alfresco meal - the waterside decked terrace is great. The smart interior makes the most of the setting, too, and, with a relaxed atmosphere and an open-to-view kitchen, it's a charming setting for some straightforward yet skilfully cooked brasserie food. Potted rabbit with piccalilli makes a full-flavoured starter, and might appear alongside crispy pork salad with lemon and fennel. Main-course ingredients are generally treated simply to bring flavours to the fore; Romney Marsh lamb rump, say, with Sicilian pesto, or plaice with braised fennel, chorizo and saffron. Desserts can range from lavender pannacotta with passionfruit to sticky toffee pudding with carrot sauce.

Times 12-2.30/7-9.30 Closed Mon-Thu (Oct-Mar), L Fri (Oct-Mar)

Waterside Inn

◉◉◉◉ – see opposite

CHIEVELEY	Map 5 SU47

The Crab at Chieveley

◉◉ Modern British V

Fine seafood dining in a rustic village setting

☎ 01635 247550
Wantage Rd RG20 8UE
e-mail: info@crabatchieveley.com
web: www.crabatchieveley.com
dir: M4 junct 13, towards Chieveley. Left into School Rd, right at T-junct, 0.5m on right. Follow brown tourist signs

An upmarket country restaurant with boutique rooms in the verdant, but landlocked, Berkshire Downs might not be the first place that comes to mind when you're in the mood for splendid seafood, but The Crab certainly delivers the goods. Inside the cosy beamed dining rooms, the piscine theme is pursued with seafaring paraphernalia - fishing nets, shells, and curios - and vibrant artwork crowds the walls. Supplies of fish are delivered daily from Devon and Cornwall and the kitchen treats it all simply, and with spot-on timing. Naturally, there's crab - perhaps paired with lobster in a creamy bisque starter, or starring thermidor-style, or with garlic or lemon butter in a main course. Elsewhere, there could be monkfish Wellington with Parma ham and Madeira jus, or steamed sea bass with scallop and brown shrimp mousse, and orange and fennel salad. Nor are meat-eaters sidelined: venison loin with braised red cabbage and celeriac could appear, while the sweet of tooth are assuaged by rum baba with Chantilly cream.

Chef Dave Horridge, John Mackee **Owner** Andrew Hughes **Times** 12-2.30/6-9.30 Closed D 25 Dec **Prices** Fixed L 2 course £15.95, Fixed D 3 course £19.95, Starter £6.50-£12.50, Main £14.50-£39, Dessert £6-£8.50, Service added but optional 10% **Wines** 150 bottles over £20, 10 bottles under £20, 15 by glass **Notes** Sunday L, Vegetarian menu **Seats** 120, Pr/dining room 30 **Children** Portions **Parking** 80

COOKHAM — Map 6 SU88

Malik's

◎◎ Indian

Upmarket Indian cooking in a converted old inn

☎ 01628 532914 & 520085
High St SL6 9SF
web: www.maliks.co.uk
dir: M4 junct 7, take A4 towards Maidenhead, 2m

Malik's looks nothing like your average Indian restaurant. For a start, it's in a creeper-covered old coaching inn, and, within, wall panelling, beams, a log fire and a bar back up the impression of an English country pub. The cooking, too, is a cut above the average, with a long and varied menu embracing old friends like chicken dansak and prawn dopiaza as well as less familiar dishes, such as starters of alkrashma (sliced egg and spicy minced lamb), and marrechi ponir (deep-fried breadcrumbed chilli stuffed with cheese). Among main courses, seafood gets distinctive treatments: soft-shelled crunchy crabs on aromatic sauce, pan-fried pomfret with spicy fried garnishes, and Goan-style monkfish in coconut milk. Elsewhere there's a choice of poultry and lamb, from slices of duck roasted in lemon sauce with chillies, to lamb with lentils, ginger and garlic. As ever, vegetarian dishes get a good showing, and among the list of desserts is creamy rice pudding hinting of cardamom and saffron served with coconut.

Chef Malik Ahmed, Shapon Miah **Owner** Malik Ahmed **Times** 12-2.30/6-11 Closed 25-26 Dec, L Eid festival **Prices** Fixed L 2 course fr £12, Fixed D 3 course fr £30, Tasting menu fr £45, Starter £4-£8, Main £8-£16, Dessert £4-£6, Service added but optional 10% **Wines** 44 bottles over £20, 6 bottles under £20, 7 by glass **Notes** Tasting menu bookable in advance, Vegetarian available, Dress restrictions, Smart dress **Seats** 70, Pr/dining room 30 **Children** Portions **Parking** 26

See advert on page 55

FRILSHAM — Map 5 SU57

The Pot Kiln

◎◎ Traditional British, European ◎

Robust country cooking in rural inn

☎ 01635 201366
RG18 0XX
e-mail: info@potkiln.org
dir: From Yattendon follow Pot Kiln signs, cross over motorway. Continue for 0.25m pub on right

People come to this rural red-brick inn for a drink in the bar as well as for a meal in the relaxed restaurant, with its open fire and plain wooden tables. The pub grows its own vegetables and salads, fish is delivered daily, and what game, particularly venison, isn't shot by Mike Robinson is provided by a local supplier. Dishes are marked out by their robust flavours: belly pork with bean cassoulet and crackling, pan-fried salmon fillet with chorizo and clam broth, and braised lamb leg with fennel and sweetbreads are typical of main courses. You could start with crayfish bisque, or sweet-and-sour ox tongue with crispy pork cheeks, and end with an unusual pudding like pears poached in red wine and cinnamon with thyme ice cream and walnut crumble.

Chef Mike Robinson **Owner** Mike & Katie Robinson **Times** 12-2.30/7-9.30 Closed 25 Dec, Tue, D Sun **Prices** Food prices not confirmed for 2013. Please telephone for details **Wines** 51 bottles over £20, 8 bottles under £20, 6 by glass **Notes** Sunday L, Vegetarian available **Seats** 48 **Children** Portions **Parking** 70

HUNGERFORD — Map 5 SU36

The Bear Hotel

◎ Modern European

Contemporary cooking in an updated coaching inn

☎ 01488 682512
41 Charnham St RG17 0EL
e-mail: info@thebearhotelhungerford.co.uk
dir: M4 junct 14, follow A338/Hungerford signs. 3m to T-junct turn right onto A4 over 2 rdbts. Hotel 500yds on left

Located on the A4 as it brushes past the northern edge of town, this ancient coaching inn has its origins in the 15th century, as testified by the vast open fireplace in the lounge and the striking black beams in the restaurant. This soothing room, with its plain white walls hung with vibrant artwork, and upholstered chairs at tables set with crisp cloths and highly polished cutlery, is the setting too for some bright modern cooking. For starters there may be Thai-spiced fish broth or chilli-spiced duck spring rolls served with minted yoghurt and pickled ginger dressing. Among the main courses, expect pan-fried turbot with crab and saffron risotto, or calves' liver with butterbean mash, spring cabbage and sage butter, with a pudding along the lines of rhubarb and stem ginger crème brûlée.

Chef Philip Wild **Owner** The Bear Hungerford Ltd **Times** 12-3/7-9.30 Closed D Sun, BHs **Prices** Starter £3.95-£9.95, Main £10.50-£19.95, Dessert £5.25-£8.95, Service included **Wines** 18 bottles over £20, 13 bottles under £20, 11 by glass **Notes** Sunday L, Vegetarian available, Civ Wed 80 **Seats** 50, Pr/dining room 18 **Children** Portions **Parking** 60

Littlecote House Hotel

◎ Modern British

Modern eating in an historic house

☎ 01488 682509
Chilton Foliat RG17 0SU
dir: From A4 Hungerford, follow brown signs

The house as it stands today may date back to the 16th century, but the history of this site stretches even further into the past. Within the grounds is a beautiful Roman mosaic and the remains of what was clearly a substantial Roman settlement. The house itself is where Henry VIII was first introduced to his third wife Jane Seymour, and Cromwell's soldiers were billeted here in the Civil War. No prizes for guessing where the restaurant - Oliver's Bistro - gets its name from then. The kitchen's output brings things squarely into the 21st century, and the menus are firmly rooted in British seasonal produce. Begin, perhaps, with hand-picked Devon crab with pancetta and a quail's egg, moving on to baby Great Farm chicken with langoustines and a vegetable medley. Save room for the banana and peanut butter mousse with peanut brittle.

Chef Matthew Davies **Owner** Warner Leisure Hotels **Times** 6.30-9 Closed Mon, L all week **Prices** Fixed L 2 course £24.95, Service optional **Wines** 33 bottles over £20, 7 bottles under £20, 3 by glass **Notes** Vegetarian available, Civ Wed 60 **Seats** 40, Pr/dining room 8 **Parking** 200

HURLEY — Map 5 SU88

Black Boys Inn

◎◎ French

Modern French cooking in a Chilterns village

☎ 01628 824212
Henley Rd SL6 5NQ
e-mail: info@blackboysinn.co.uk
dir: M40 junct 4, A404 towards Henley, then A4130. Restaurant 3m from Henley-on-Thames & Maidenhead

This 16th-century coaching inn got its name from Charles II's clandestine visit in 1651 after the Battle of Worcester: it was the fond moniker given him by his soldiers because of his swarthy complexion. Today, a modern gloss adds a degree of sophistication to the oak beams, polished floors and unclothed tables, while the kitchen's style suits the environment to a T, its roots based firmly in French provincial cooking. Thus, mussels marinière may be followed by goose confit accompanied by Alsace-style apple and red cabbage flavoured with Calvados. There can be a welcome contemporary pitch to dishes too, seen in a salad of smoked eel, beetroot and apple with wasabi

Save on Hotels. Book at theAA.com/hotel

BERKSHIRE 57 **ENGLAND**

crème fraîche, and roast duck breast flavoured with lime in Armagnac sauce. Desserts are prepared with care, whether homely apple and plum crumble with custard or Sicilian-style lemon posset.

Chef Adrian Bannister **Owner** Adrian & Helen Bannister **Times** 12-2/7-9 Closed D Sun **Prices** Fixed L 2 course £12.50, Starter £5.50-£11.50, Main £15.95-£22.50, Dessert £5.50-£6.50, Service optional **Wines** 105 bottles over £20, 6 bottles under £20, 32 by glass **Notes** Carte du jour 2 course £12.50, 3 course £16, Sunday L, Vegetarian available **Seats** 45, Pr/dining room 12 **Children** Portions **Parking** 45

The Olde Bell Inn

Modern British

Classy, creative cooking in a smartly revamped coaching inn

☎ 01628 825881
High St SL6 5LX
e-mail: oldebellreception@coachinginn.co.uk
dir: M4 junct 8/9 follow signs for Henley. At rdbt take A4130 to Hurley, turn right to Hurley Village, 800yds on right

A 12th-century coaching inn with bags of original features it certainly is, but the 'olde' sits well alongside the more fashionable at the Bell, with a sympathetic modern facelift that delivers a good deal of designer chic. The restaurant looks rather smart with its muted colours and wooden floors, while a mix of table and seating styles (from broad-oak tables to booth-style seating around the walls) delivers a relaxed, upbeat vibe. The cooking matches the surroundings, built on classical foundations but showcasing a modern approach with plenty of flair and imagination. Fresh local, seasonal produce and flavour drive the appealing roster; perhaps stuffed saddle of rabbit teamed with crosnes (Chinese artichoke), chanterelle and parsnip dauphinoise, or perhaps roast flounder with shallot purée, English asparagus, sea vegetables and confit garlic. To finish, expect the likes of treacle tart, clotted cream and raisin caramel. A separate bar menu, large garden and smart bedrooms put the icing on the cake.

Times 12.30-2.30/6-10 Closed Xmas, New Year, D Sun

Red Lyon

Modern British

Good honest pub cooking in a whitewashed country inn

☎ 01628 823558
Henley Rd SL6 5LH
e-mail: info@redlyon.co.uk
web: www.redlyon.co.uk
dir: M4 junct 8/9 onto A4130, restaurant on left after Burchetts Green rdbt. Adjacent to Temple Golf Club

A whitewashed country pub not far from Henley, the Red Lyon hails from a time when clean-lined, minimalist design was a twinkle in nobody's eye. The interiors are a heart-warming, higgledy-piggledy array of rough brickwork, beams and rustic furniture, but there is also a pretty garden for clement days. Deli boards for sharing may well appeal if you're not in the market for the three course approach, but if you are, expect the likes of ham hock terrine with apple and cinnamon purée, pollock fillet with lemon crushed potatoes and baby gems in citrus and honey dressing, and sticky toffee pudding with vanilla ice cream to finish. A 'proper menu for little people' should keep the kids happy too.

Chef Simon Pitney-Baxter **Owner** Simon Pitney-Baxter, David Thompson **Times** 12-2.30/6-9.30 Closed D 25-26 & 31 Dec **Prices** Fixed L 2 course £14.70-£24, Fixed D 3 course £19.65-£30.95, Starter £4.75-£6.95, Main £9.95-£17.50, Dessert £4.95-£6.50, Service optional, Groups min 10 service 10% **Wines** 18 bottles over £20, 13 bottles under £20, 11 by glass **Notes** Sunday L, Vegetarian available **Seats** 70, Pr/dining room 35 **Children** Portions, Menu **Parking** 60

LAMBOURN Map 5 SU37

The Hare Restaurant and Bar

Modern British

Flavour-packed modern cooking in horseracing country

☎ 01488 71386
Ermin St RG17 7SD
e-mail: cuisine@theharerestaurant.co.uk
dir: M4 junct 14, A338 towards Wantage, left onto B4000 towards Lambourn, restaurant 3m on left

The Hare has come a long way since it was a simple village inn: the operation now comprises a stylish bar and restaurant with four separate dining areas, including a garden room. The interior looks the part with its slate

floors, exposed beams, chunky wooden tables, squishy sofas by an open fire, and an eclectic array of artwork with 'for sale' stickers on the walls. 2012 saw new broom Jamie Hodson move in to drive the kitchen's output forward; he comes fresh from stints in the Ramsay and Marco empires, so you can expect punchy, flavour-driven contemporary dishes along the lines of pear and onion marmalade tarte Tatin matched with roquefort pannacotta, caramelised pecans and chicory salad, followed by pan-fried venison loin with a steamed venison suet pudding, roast salsify, Jerusalem artichoke purée and red wine jus. To finish, dark chocolate fondant is studded with honeycomb for extra textural interest, and served with white chocolate sorbet.

Chef Jamie Hodson **Owner** John Kirby **Times** 12-2/7-9.30 **Prices** Food prices not confirmed for 2013. Please telephone for details **Wines** 70 bottles over £20, 6 bottles under £20, 6 by glass **Notes** Lounge menu available all day, Vegetarian available, Dress restrictions, Smart casual **Seats** 75, Pr/dining room 30 **Children** Portions **Parking** 30

MAIDENHEAD Map 6 SU88

Boulters Riverside Brasserie

Modern British

Modern brasserie dining by the river

☎ 01628 621291
Boulters Lock Island SL6 8PE
e-mail: info@boultersrestaurant.co.uk

Expect knock-your-socks-off views at this buzzy, contemporary brasserie overlooking Boulters Lock, where the Thames wends its way lazily towards Maidenhead Bridge. But with nothing but a wall of glass between darkwood tables and the water, the ground-floor fine-dining brasserie is not all location over substance: quality local produce and fashionable, well-executed brasserie dishes (underpinned by a classical theme) also hit the spot. Take pan-fried Cornish hake teamed with bacon boulangère potatoes, choucroute and a juniper butter sauce, or a passionfruit soufflé dessert partnered by banana ice cream and hot chocolate sauce. Upstairs the quality and views continue in the all-day Terrace Bar, serving the likes of cod and chips, Caesar salad and linguini bolognese.

Chef Daniel Woodhouse **Owner** The Dennis Family **Times** 12-2.45/6.30-9.30 Closed Mon, D Sun **Prices** Fixed L 2 course £15.95, Tasting menu £35, Starter £6.95-£9.50, Main £14.95-£23.50, Dessert £6.95-£9.95, Service added but optional 12.5% **Wines** 110 bottles over £20, 15 bottles under £20, 22 by glass **Notes** Sunday L, Vegetarian available, Air con **Seats** 70, Pr/dining room 12 **Children** Portions, Menu **Parking** 20

The Royal Oak Paley Street

Modern British | NOTABLE WINE LIST

First-class modern British cooking in a spruced up country pub

☎ 01628 620541
Paley St, Littlefield Green SL6 3JN
e-mail: info@theroyaloakpaleystreet.com
web: www.theroyaloakpaleystreet.com
dir: M4 junct 8/9. Take A308 towards Maidenhead Central, then A330 to Ascot. After 2m, turn right onto B3024 to Twyford. Second pub on left

There isn't an awful lot to the village of Paley Street, save for a couple of pubs and a few houses. But one of those pubs - The Royal Oak - has really put this tiny settlement on the map. The white-painted inn, which dates back to the 17th century, is these days owned by Nick Parkinson, son of former chat show host Sir Michael, which explains the black-and-white photographs of various celebs on the walls and the generally spruced up, country-chic look of the place. Indeed, it's immaculate inside and out, whilst all of its original features remain intact, including beamed ceilings, wooden floors, exposed brickwork and the old bar for those who simply want to pop in for a pint. In the winter a wood-burning stove keeps things cosy, while in the warmer months you can dine outside on the lovely, flower-decorated terrace, with its giant umbrellas giving shade. Head chef Dominic Chapman knows a thing or two about how to bring the best out of tip-top British produce (mostly locally sourced) without ever taking it too far and losing an ingredient's natural flavour. He faithfully follows the seasons and tweaks the menu every day to ensure everything that goes onto the plate is as good as it can possibly be. So a May lunch might begin (after making your way through a basket of fabulous, just-out-the-oven breads) with a creamy but not overly rich new season garlic soup, the flavour intense but not overpowering, served with an equally punchy anchovy toast. Main course could be a sea-fresh piece of Scottish halibut, roasted to perfection and served with samphire, cockles and mussels. Super-sweet Gariguette strawberries with buttermilk cream and hazelnut biscuits is a light and refreshing dessert that heralds the start of summer. There's an extensive wine list, too, with plenty by the glass and carafe.

Chef Dominic Chapman **Owner** Nick Parkinson **Times** 12-2.30/6-9.30 Closed D Sun **Prices** Fixed L 2 course £25, Fixed D 3 course £25-£30, Starter £8-£12.95, Main £19.50-£30, Dessert £8.50-£10.50, Service added but optional 12.5% **Wines** 350 bottles over £20, 30 bottles under £20, 20 by glass **Notes** Fixed D menu available Mon-Thu, L Mon-Sat, Sunday L, Vegetarian available **Seats** 50 **Parking** 70

MAIDENHEAD *continued*

Fredrick's Hotel Restaurant Spa

◉◉ Modern British, French

All-round quality in spa hotel

☎ 01628 581000
Shoppenhangers Rd SL6 2PZ
e-mail: reservations@fredricks-hotel.co.uk
web: www.fredricks-hotel.co.uk
dir: From M4 junct 8/9 take A404(M), then turning (junct 9A) for Cox Green/White Waltham. Left on to Shoppenhangers Rd, restaurant 400 mtrs on right

Fredrick's is a luxury hotel, in well-manicured grounds, with pool and spa treatments on tap. Classy decoration and furnishings give the place an air of indulgence, helped along by solicitous and professional staff. The restaurant is a grand room, complete with chandeliers and crisply set tables. The kitchen works around a contemporary take on established principles, partnering well-timed langoustines with crisp belly pork and serving them with white cabbage salad and butternut squash purée, for example. Top-end ingredients are used to good effect - lobster tortellini with apple purée, lobster jelly and shellfish foam, say, and main-course halibut fillet given the bourguignon treatment - but the team is just as happy with humbler ham hock, pressed and accompanied by pear and saffron chutney, and calling on local supply lines for seasonal game. Fruit is used compellingly in puddings: an assiette on a theme of apple, or orange cake with lime and honeycomb parfait and grapefruit pannacotta.

Chef Craig Smith **Owner** R Takhar **Times** 12-2.30/7-9.30 Closed 23-27 Dec **Prices** Fixed L 2 course £12-£15, Fixed D 3 course £40-£58, Starter £9-£15, Main £22-£33, Dessert £10, Service optional **Wines** All bottles over £20, 10 bottles under £20, 7 by glass **Notes** Sunday L, Vegetarian available, Dress restrictions, Smart casual, Civ Wed 100 **Seats** 60, Pr/dining room 140 **Children** Portions **Parking** 90

The Royal Oak Paley Street

◉◉◉ *— see opposite*

— see opposite

NEWBURY   **Map 5 SU46**

Donnington Valley Hotel & Spa

◉◉ Modern British 🍷NOTABLE WINE LIST 🌸

Engaging modern cooking in a golfing and spa hotel

☎ 01635 551199
Old Oxford Rd, Donnington RG14 3AG
e-mail: general@donningtonvalley.co.uk
dir: M4 junct 13, A34 towards Newbury. Take immediate left signed Donnington Hotel. At rdbt take right, at 3rd rdbt take left, follow road for 2m, hotel on right

The Wine Press restaurant at Donnington Valley - a modern hotel with golf course, spa and conference facilities - is filled with light during the day thanks to large windows along one wall, while in the evening the lighting is pitched to create a warm and intimate atmosphere. It's a pleasant, relaxing space on two levels, with artwork and flowers providing splashes of colour against the neutral shades of the décor. The kitchen's consistently high technical standards can be seen in such main courses as plainly grilled Dover sole with baked tomato and courgettes, and pan-fried pheasant breast with rosemary fondant potatoes, roast shallots and leeks. Flavours are well considered: a starter of pan-fried scallops is partnered by pancetta, black pudding, and pea purée, and ham hock and foie gras terrine by beetroot chutney. A sense of adventure can be detected in some puddings - lime cheesecake parfait with lime and celery ice cream, coriander and ginger syrup and pickled celery, for instance - or stick to crêpe Suzette.

Chef Kelvin Johnson **Owner** Sir Peter Michael **Times** 12-2/7-10 **Prices** Fixed L 2 course £18, Fixed D 3 course £28, Starter £8-£12, Main £17-£26, Dessert £8, Service optional **Wines** 292 bottles over £20, 25 bottles under £20, 21 by glass **Notes** Sunday L, Vegetarian available, Dress restrictions, Smart casual, Civ Wed 160 **Seats** 120, Pr/dining room 130 **Children** Portions, Menu **Parking** 150

The Vineyard at Stockcross

◉◉◉

NEWBURY   **Map 5 SU46**

Modern French V 🍷NOTABLE WINE LIST

Alluringly confident modern French cuisine

☎ 01635 528770
Stockcross RG20 8JU
e-mail: general@the-vineyard.co.uk
dir: From M4 take A34 towards Newbury, exit at 3rd junct for Speen. Right at rdbt then right again at 2nd rdbt

There's no vineyard at The Vineyard, although the five-star hotel is in itself a celebration of the world of wine and gastronomy. Named in honour of owner Sir Peter Michael's world-class Californian winery, the operation is luxurious to the n-th degree, offering the full-works spa and business conferencing package, plus putting on swanky weddings. But even if none of the above is on your agenda, chef Daniel Galmiche's contemporary French cooking should have you hot-footing it to the classy contemporary restaurant, where a sweeping staircase with a balustrade fashioned as if it were a coiling grapevine connects the two levels; it is a thoroughly refined space of mellow tones splashed with eye-catching art, and well-spaced tables turned out in their best whites, tended by an unstuffy front-of-house team who make sure everything ticks over just as it should. Galmiche's French pedigree naturally underpins the output, delivering electrifying marriages of Mediterranean and Asian-accented flavour and texture without recourse to gimmickry. An elegant terrine of rabbit and parsley opens proceedings in the company of onion marmalade and white bean salad. Next up, pan-roasted monkfish wrapped in pancetta avoids the all-too-common pitfall of oversaltiness, and is perfectly matched by braised fennel, carrot and clementine purée, and citrus jus - nothing flashy, just mature restraint at work. For dessert, blackberry parfait shares a plate with Earl Grey rice pudding, and sesame and nougatine biscuit. Wine-wise, you'd need a lifetime and a lottery win to take the epic list to its outer reaches - the statistics say it all: in the cellar are 30,000 bottles, priced from £20 to £20,000, of which 100 or so are available by the glass.

Chef Daniel Galmiche **Owner** Sir Peter Michael **Times** 12-2/7-9.30 **Prices** Tasting menu £40-£79, Service optional **Wines** 30,000 bottles over £20, 60 bottles under £20, 120 by glass **Notes** ALC 2/3 course £62/£72, Tasting menu 5/7 course, Sunday L, Vegetarian menu, Civ Wed 120 **Seats** 86, Pr/dining room 120 **Children** Portions, Menu **Parking** 100

NEWBURY *continued*

Newbury Manor Hotel

◎◎ Modern European

Romantic waterside setting for classically-inspired cooking

☎ 01635 528838
London Rd RG14 2BY
e-mail: enquiries@newbury-manor-hotel.co.uk
web: www.riverbarrestaurant.co.uk
dir: M4 junct 13, A34 Newbury, A4 Thatcham, 0.5m on right

The Riverbar Restaurant lives up to the name as it is housed in an old mill with floor-to-ceiling windows overlooking the tranquil pool at the confluence of the Kennet and Lambourn Rivers, where the iridescent flash of a kingfisher is a frequent sight. In fact, the whole package at the fabulous Georgian Newbury Manor is pretty enticing, with its nine acres of woodlands and water meadows to work up an appetite on a deer-spotting stroll before heading for the Riverbar to take on the kitchen's well-thought-out menus of seasonally-driven dishes. Local produce is the foundation of flavour-led ideas such as hearty Scotch broth with country bread, or pigeon breast with beetroot and horseradish risotto, and devilled jus, while among main courses you might find pan-fried brill teamed with wild mushroom and crème fraîche tortellini, or crispy pork belly with apple and celeriac gratin, teriyaki prawns, spinach and rosemary jus.

Chef Jan Papcun **Owner** Heritage Properties & Hotels **Times** 12-2.30/6-10 **Prices** Fixed L 2 course £14.95, Fixed D 3 course £19, Starter £6.50-£8.50, Main £12.95-£19.95, Dessert £6.50-£8.50, Service optional **Wines** 29 bottles over £20, 15 bottles under £20, 12 by glass **Notes** Sunday L, Vegetarian available, Civ Wed 160 **Seats** 48, Pr/dining room 160 **Children** Portions **Parking** 80

The Vineyard at Stockcross

◎◎◎ *— see page 59*

PANGBOURNE Map 5 SU67

The Elephant at Pangbourne

◎ Modern British 🌱

Contemporary cooking in a colonial setting

☎ 0118 984 2244
Church Rd RG8 7AR
e-mail: reception@elephanthotel.co.uk
dir: A4 Theale/Newbury, right at 2nd rdbt signed Pangbourne. Hotel on left

Prepare to enjoy the opulence of the former British Empire at this smart boutique hotel in Pangbourne, beside the River Thames. Throughout, handcrafted Indian furniture and fabrics set the scene - be it in the more casual BaBar bistro or Christoph's stylish fine-dining restaurant. There's an enclosed garden, if the weather lives up to the theme. The menu sometimes harks back to the UK's colonial past with the use of the accordant spicing, but it's broadly modish European in focus; start, perhaps, with pecan, chicken and pork pâté served with rustic bread, apple juice and jelly before poppadom-encrusted coley with Bombay potatoes and sweet curry sauce, and finish with an Elephant knickerbocker glory or bitter chocolate parfait with rosewater and cardamom ice cream.

Chef Chris Ayres **Owner** Hillbrooke Hotels **Times** 12-2.30/7-9 **Prices** Fixed L 2 course fr £12.95, Starter £5.50-£9, Main £11.95-£22, Dessert £6, Service optional **Wines** 23 bottles over £20, 6 bottles under £20, 8 by glass **Notes** Sunday L, Vegetarian available, Civ Wed 100 **Seats** 40, Pr/dining room 77 **Children** Portions, Menu **Parking** 15

READING Map 5 SU77

Cerise Restaurant at The Forbury Hotel

◎◎ Modern British

Bold brasserie cooking in a striking hotel restaurant

☎ 0118 952 7770
26 The Forbury RG1 3EJ
e-mail: reception@theforburyhotel.co.uk

The Forbury is a handsome townhouse boutique hotel done out in striking, sexy, sybaritic style. As a style statement it is hard to beat: there is something eye-catching at every turn, from modern artworks liberally spread throughout, to bold contemporary fabrics and wallpapers, and a remarkable Italian chandelier with 86,000 glass beads running from top to bottom of the building in the lift shaft. Not to be outfaced by all this, the Cerise Restaurant is a contemporary split-level space, with squiggly cherry-red stripes along the walls, wooden floors and bare wood tables divided by etched glass screens; on warm days you can eat in the secret garden in the shade of a pomegranate tree. Modern brasserie-style dishes keep step with the seasons, starting with a rich pot of confit duck leg rillettes with sweet shallot jam and toasted brioche, ahead of pan-seared fillet of John Dory with spring onion, coriander and lemon couscous. Meatier ideas could see home-smoked

---

saddle of venison teamed with parsnip purée and venison sauce, while desserts get creative with the likes of a honeycomb, Kahlua and bitter chocolate ice cream sandwich.

Chef Michael Parke **Times** 12-3/5-10.30 **Prices** Fixed L 2 course £15, Fixed D 3 course £15-£20, Starter £6.50-£11.50, Main £14-£26.50, Dessert £8.50-£10.50, Service optional **Wines** 77 bottles over £20, 2 bottles under £20, 11 by glass **Notes** Fixed D available 5-7pm, Sunday L, Vegetarian available, Civ Wed 50 **Seats** 72, Pr/dining room 35 **Children** Portions, Menu **Parking** 18

Crowne Plaza Reading

◎◎ Modern British

Well-judged modern cooking by the Thames

☎ 0118 925 9988
Caversham Bridge, Richfield Av RG1 8BD
e-mail: info@cp-reading.co.uk
dir: M4 junct 11, take the Inner Distribution Rd to Caversham

The Reading branch of the Crowne Plaza chain sits right on the Thames, a location that its contemporary Acqua Restaurant exploits to the full with its expansive riverside terrace and watery views from the stylish open plan space within. The kitchen takes a suitably modern line: fresh, well-sourced materials lay a secure foundation, and clear flavours and attractive presentation secure the deal. A first-class terrine of duck confit and foie gras is served inventively with camomile-infused sea salt, and peach and golden grape purée, ahead of monkfish fillet, which is rolled in herbs, wrapped in Serrano ham, and matched with smoked garlic and vanilla risotto. Flavours are well combined through to dessert which partners lemon and Cointreau tart with vanilla ice cream and lemongrass foam.

Times 12-2.30/6.30

Forbury's Restaurant

◎◎ French, European ⓦ

Refined, confident cooking in smartly contemporary venue

☎ 0118 957 4044
1 Forbury Square RG1 3BB
e-mail: forburys@btconnect.com
dir: In town centre, opposite Forbury Gardens

If this stylish modern restaurant feels more big-city cool than Reading central - with its floor-to-ceiling windows overlooking swanky Forbury Square - it will come as no surprise to hear that the striking glass office block in which it is located was designed by the same architect who created Canary Wharf. Smartly decked out in an appropriately modish manner, Forbury's comes with large canvases of modern art, leather chairs, rich colours and linen-clad tables. There's a buzzy wine bar area and large fair-weather terrace to cover all bases. The kitchen delivers a progressive take on the classic French theme, with reliance on fresh quality produce, clean flavours and creative presentation. Expect pan-roasted Barbury duck

Save on Hotels. Book at **theAA.com/hotel**

BERKSHIRE 61 **ENGLAND**

breast teamed with a cassoulet of Puy lentils and sprout tops, or wild sea bass fillet with fricassée of truffled potatoes, broad beans and chanterelle mushrooms. To finish, there might be a warm Amedei chocolate fondant with pistachio ice cream.

Chef David George **Owner** Xavier Le-Bellego **Times** 12-2.15/6-10 Closed 26-28 Dec, 1-2 Jan, Sun **Prices** Fixed L 2 course fr £12.95, Fixed D 3 course £23, Tasting menu £59, Starter £6.50-£13.50, Main £14-£26, Dessert £7-£9.50, Service optional, Groups min 4 service 12.5% **Wines** 145 bottles over £20, 9 bottles under £20, 11 by glass **Notes** Tasting menu 6 course, Early bird D 3 course £20, Vegetarian available **Seats** 80, Pr/dining room 16 **Children** Portions **Parking** 40

Malmaison Reading

🏵 Modern European

Contemporary brasserie dining in rejuvenated former Great Western Railway hotel

☎ 0118 956 2300 & 956 2302
Great Western House, 18-20 Station Rd RG1 1JX
e-mail: reading@malmaison.com
dir: Next to Reading station

Transformed by Malmaison into a funky modern hotel, the former Great Western Railway Hotel successfully combines contemporary boutique chic style without losing sight of its history as a grand railway hotel. Railway memorabilia is spread liberally around its public areas to remind guests of the Victorian romance of the golden age of steam. The restaurant is a moodily low-lit den, done out with exposed red-brick walls, industrial ducting overhead, black floor tiles underfoot, and theatrical lighting to give the sepulchral ambience of a nightclub. The thrust and impetus of the menu remains true to the modern brasserie idiom, using top-class local materials in a repertoire that might lead off with tuna carpaccio with avocado and pickled cucumber, then progress to salmon fishcake with spinach and parsley sauce, or rib of beef with béarnaise.

Times 12-2.30/6-10.30 Closed L Sat

Millennium Madejski Hotel Reading

🏵🏵 British, International V

Modern British menu at the Madejski Stadium

☎ 0118 925 3500
Madejski Stadium RG2 0FL
e-mail: sales.reading@millenniumhotels.co.uk
dir: 1m N from M4 junct 11. 2m S from Reading town centre

The glass-fronted contemporary hotel is part of the Madejski Stadium complex, home to both Reading FC and London Irish rugby club. From the twisted branches in huge red planters in the lobby to the streamlined restaurant, Cilantro, that takes its name from the American word for 'coriander', not to mention the gleaming chrome champagne bar, it's clear that cons were never modder, and modernity stalks the menus too. A blue goats' cheese soufflé with Granny Smith sorbet might be the way in to an entrée such as roast Telmara duck breast with Savoy and pancetta, or whole shelled lobster with a bonbon of potato brandade and macaroni cheese. After a dessert such as warm pistachio cake with dark chocolate mousse and cherry sorbet, it may be time for a match.

Chef Denzil Newton **Owner** Madejski Hotel Co **Times** 7-10 Closed 25 Dec, 1 Jan, BHs, Sun-Mon, L all week **Wines** 64 bottles over £20, 36 bottles under £20, 12 by glass **Notes** Gourmand menu 7 course £47, Vegetarian menu, Dress restrictions, Smart casual **Seats** 55, Pr/dining room 12 **Children** Portions **Parking** 100

L'ortolan

SHINFIELD   **Map 5 SU76**

Modern French V 📖 NOTABLE WINE LIST

Breathlessly contemporary excellence in a Berkshire village

☎ 0118 988 8500
Church Ln RG2 9BY
e-mail: info@lortolan.com
web: www.lortolan.com
dir: From M4 junct 11 take A33 towards Basingstoke. At 1st lights turn left, after garage turn left, 1m turn right at Six Bells pub. Restaurant 1st left (follow tourist signs)

The red-brick 17th-century former vicarage with conservatory extension stands in a village near Reading, a mere five minutes from the M4, if you're travelling out from London. It's a lavishly appointed place, with deep carpets, ornamental light fittings and Riedel glassware to elevate the tone, and has been home to some of Britain's culinary movers and shakers over the decades. Alan Murchison's present-day

tenure incorporates the place into a network of fine-dining venues that extends from Shropshire to Devon, and is concerned to inculcate these skills in the rising generation. It's breathlessly contemporary food in its styling, with jellies, pannacottas and purées popping up all over, and salt in at least one of the puddings. A serving of crab two ways, impressive flakes of white meat alongside a luxurious custard of the brown, are juxtaposed with a variety of passionfruit items - jelly, juice and meringues - for a complex, bold and memorable creation. A main course of Goosnargh duck offers chunks of breast with a crunchy pastilla of the leg meat, and accompaniments of turnip and pear, once again appearing in textural and seasoning variations, from razor-sharp pickles to silky-smooth purées. Fish might be a pavé of skate in a cockle and brown shrimp nage, accompanied by watercress pannacotta. Visual jokes add levity to the occasion, as when a pre-dessert of coconut espuma with mango purée in it is fashioned to look like a fried egg. Variations of sugar at dessert brings together a muscovado sponge, a lump of delicious honeycomb, wibbly-wobbly crème caramel, and a Muscovado version of Scottish tablet, all gaining a touch of bite from lemongrass ice cream.

Chef Alan Murchison, Nick Chappell **Owner** Newfee Ltd **Times** 12-2/7-9 Closed 2 wks Xmas-New Year, Sun-Mon **Prices** Food prices not confirmed for 2013. Please telephone for details **Wines** 400 bottles over £20, 1 bottle under £20, 11 by glass **Notes** Tasting menu 7 or 10 course, Chef's table availble, Vegetarian menu, Dress restrictions, Smart casual, Civ Wed 62 **Seats** 62, Pr/dining room 22 **Children** Portions **Parking** 62

READING *continued*

Mya Lacarte

◉ Modern British

Carefully-sourced British produce on the high street

☎ 0118 946 3400
5 Prospect St, Caversham RG4 8JB
e-mail: eat@myalacarte.co.uk
dir: M4 junct 10, continue onto A3290/A4 signed
Caversham. At Crown Plaza Hotel continue over
Caversham Bridge, restaurant 3rd left

Though the name might seem somewhat left field, Mya
Lacarte - a relaxed, unpretentious outfit set on a busy
road in central Caversham - shows itself to be a
restaurant with an environmental conscience. Keeping air
miles low is just one commitment, the kitchen dealing in
fresh British produce and local wherever possible (Tadley
rabbit, Hampshire beef fillet, Watlington pork, et al). The
décor has a clean-lined contemporary look, with oak
flooring and close-set burnished-wood tables, while the
seasonal-changing menu offers Brit dishes with a
corresponding modern twist. Take a duo of Ashampstead
venison teamed with butternut squash and thyme purée,
haggis dumplings and chocolate jus, or perhaps a
populist rich chocolate brownie cake dessert, given its
Mya Lacarte spin with an accompaniment of mint white
chocolate ice cream and beetroot marshmallows.

Chef Matt Hynes **Owner** Matthew Siadatan
Times 12-3/5-10.30 Closed 25-26 Dec, 1 Jan, D Sun
Prices Food prices not confirmed for 2013. Please
telephone for details **Wines** 14 bottles over £20,
10 bottles under £20, 10 by glass **Notes** Sunday L,
Vegetarian available, Dress restrictions, Smart casual
Seats 35, Pr/dining room 12 **Children** Portions
Parking NCP

SHINFIELD   Map 5 SU76

L'ortolan

◉◉◉ – *see page 61*

SONNING   Map 5 SU77

The French Horn

◉◉ British, French **V**

Classical French dining on the Thames

☎ 0118 969 2204
RG4 6TN
e-mail: info@thefrenchhorn.co.uk
dir: From Reading take A4 E to Sonning. Follow B478
through village over bridge, hotel on right, car park on
left

The cooking at The French Horn may not be at the cutting
edge of culinary trends, but you know you'll be treated to
the delights of timeless Gallic gastronomy in an idyllic,
quintessentially English Thames-side setting. The elegant
glass-fronted dining room revels in old-school refinement,
and opens onto a waterfront terrace where manicured

lawns give way to ancient willows dipping their fronds
into the river. As you sip a glass of fizz, you might catch a
waft of the signature dish - caneton rôti à l'anglaise -
that's spit-roast duck en anglais, which turns fragrantly
above the fire, and comes to table with apple purée, sage
stuffing and rich duck jus. Otherwise, you might start
with pan-fried foie gras with caramelised pear and
blackcurrant sauce, followed by pheasant casserole, and
bow out French-style with crêpes Suzette, or do things the
British way with bread-and-butter pudding and custard.

Chef J Diaga **Owner** Emmanuel family
Times 12-2.30/7-10 Closed 1-4 Jan **Prices** Fixed L 2
course £19.50, Fixed D 3 course £26.50, Starter £8.10-
£19, Main £16.95-£37.45, Dessert £8.10-£11.80, Service
included **Wines** 450 bottles over £20, 14 by glass
Notes Sunday L, Vegetarian menu, Dress restrictions, No
shorts or sleeveless shirts **Seats** 70, Pr/dining room 24
Children Portions **Parking** 40

STREATLEY   Map 5 SU58

The Swan at Streatley

◉◉ Modern European ⬥

**Historic Thames-side setting for creative contemporary
cooking**

☎ 01491 878800
High St RG8 9HR
e-mail: sales@swan-at-streatley.co.uk
web: www.swanatstreatley.co.uk
dir: Follow A329 from Pangbourne, on entering Streatley
turn right at lights. Hotel on left before bridge

Legend has it that Jerome K Jerome wrote *Three Men in a
Boat* in the 17th-century Swan at Streatley, thus
spawning a healthy local income from the tourist dollar
and yen (and perhaps yuan, these days). Aficionados can
sleep in the suite named after the writer, and even if you
couldn't care a fig for literary connections, the idyllic
Thames-side views of weeping willows dipping their
fronds into the river are reason enough to take a seat in
Cygnetures restaurant. The setting is minimal - snow
white walls hung with nautically-themed images - while
the kitchen deals in modern cooking underscored by
classic French ideas. Raw materials are top-class,
whether it is Berkshire wood pigeon showcased in a
starter with the likes of salsify, beetroot and Paris brown
mushrooms, or a main course that matches fillet of sea
bass with ox cheek, endives and olive beignet. To finish,
there might be passionfruit soufflé with guava coulis.

Chef Christopher Prow **Owner** Nike Group Hotels
Times 12-2/7-10 **Prices** Fixed L 2 course £13.95, Fixed D
3 course £26.95, Starter £6.95-£12.95, Main £11.50-
£26.95, Dessert £6.95-£11, Service optional
Wines 40 bottles over £20, 8 bottles under £20, 21 by
glass **Notes** Tasting menu on request, Sunday L,
Vegetarian available, Dress restrictions, Smart casual,
Civ Wed 130 **Seats** 70, Pr/dining room 130
Children Portions **Parking** 130

WINDSOR   Map 6 SU97

Mercure Castle Hotel

◉◉ Modern British ⬥

Bright modern cooking by the castle

☎ 0870 4008300 & 01753 851577
18 High St SL4 1LJ
e-mail: h6618@accor.com
dir: M25 junct 13 take A308 towards town centre then
onto B470 to High St. M4 junct 6 towards A332, at rdbt
first exit into Clarence Rd, left at lights to High St

You get a ringside seat for the Changing of the Guard at
Windsor Castle at this 16th-century coaching inn in the
heart of Windsor. The place is rather more than a simple
inn these days, of course - kitted out with bare darkwood
tables and contemporary hues of aubergine and grey,
Restaurant Eighteen sports a clean-cut 21st-century look
that matches its imaginative, French-influenced modern
menu. The kitchen sends out well-balanced and clear-
flavoured dishes and has the confidence to try out
interesting combinations - perhaps flavouring a
pannacotta with stilton and rosemary and serving it with
roast figs, caramelised walnuts and sherry-like vin de
curé vinegar. Main course might run to a modish duo of
spring lamb - roast rack and confit shoulder teamed with
sautéed samphire, butternut purée, celeriac fondant and
roast shallots - and to finish, perhaps rhubarb parfait
with poached rhubarb crumble, and strawberry
consommé.

Chef Gregory Watts **Owner** Mercure Hotels
Times 12-2.30/6.30-9.45 **Prices** Fixed L 2 course £14-
£19, Fixed D 3 course £20-£25, Starter £6-£10, Main
£15-£21, Dessert £6-£10, Service optional
Wines 67 bottles over £20, 22 bottles under £20, 14 by
glass **Notes** Sunday L, Dress restrictions, Smart casual,
Civ Wed 80 **Seats** 60, Pr/dining room 300
Children Portions, Menu **Parking** 112

BRISTOL

BRISTOL   Map 4 ST57

The Avon Gorge Hotel

◉ Modern British ⬥

**Stylish modern café with majestic views over iconic
bridge**

☎ 0117 973 8955
Sion Hill, Clifton BS8 4LD
e-mail: rooms@theavongorge.com
dir: From S: M5 junct 19, A369 to Clifton Toll, over
suspension bridge, 1st right into Sion Hill. From N: M5
junct 18A, A4 to Bristol, under suspension bridge, follow
signs to bridge, exit Sion Hill

The Clifton area has to be the most photogenic part of the
city, and with its location overlooking the famous
suspension bridge, the Avon Gorge Hotel has the money
shot. Built towards the end of the 19th century, the grand
old dame of a building has a sweeping semi-circular
terrace built to take in the magnificent view; rest assured,

though, the vista is still pretty tasty if you've got a table indoors. The décor in the Bridge Café is sensibly restrained - there's no point competing with the view - and with lots of natural wood and light, it's a pleasingly contemporary space. On the menu is an equally unfussy range of modish brasserie-style dishes, from venison carpaccio with pickled vegetables to slow-roasted onion and gruyère tart, followed by home-made burger or braised lamb shank with root vegetable dauphinoise and port sauce.

Chef Rowen Babe **Owner** Swire Hotels **Times** 12-6/6-10 **Prices** Fixed L 2 course £9.95, Starter £5.25-£8.50, Main £9.95-£16.95, Dessert £5.25-£6.95, Service added but optional **Wines** 20 bottles over £20, 8 bottles under £20, 12 by glass **Notes** Sunday L, Vegetarian available, Civ Wed 100 **Seats** 50, Pr/dining room 20 **Children** Portions, Menu **Parking** 25

Bell's Diner

◉◉ Modern European

Ambitious food in one-time grocery shop

☎ 0117 924 0357
1-3 York Rd, Montpellier BS6 5QB
e-mail: info@bellsdiner.com
web: www.bellsdiner.com
dir: From centre of Bristol follow A38, turn right at Stokes Croft lights then 1st left

The unassuming grocer's shop frontage in a Bohemian area of Bristol gives nothing away. First impressions are of an easygoing neighbourhood restaurant with an idiosyncratic approach to interior design - polished wooden floors, and an eclectic mix of old flour bags in the window, coffee pots and wine bottles sprinkled about. And if the designation of 'diner' implies fast-food Americana, think again: with chef-patron Christopher Wicks at the helm, the maverick approach also extends to what leaves the kitchen - Bell's serves genuinely creative modern European food, conjured from excellent local ingredients. Adventurous flavour combinations are there from the off - Orkney Bay scallops are served with fennel risotto, blobs of zingy lemon purée, and slashes of liquorice. Next out, local organic beef turns up with deep-fried croquettes of bone marrow, and the well-balanced flavours of tarragon, parsley, artichoke and Pink Fir potatoes. A dessert involving toasted hay custard tart, beer-flavoured granité, toasted walnuts, and coffee ice cream is another eclectic-sounding dish that works a treat on the plate.

Chef Christopher Wicks, Alex Collings **Owner** Christopher Wicks **Times** 12-2/7-10 Closed 24-30 Dec, Sun, L Mon & Sat **Prices** Tasting menu £49.50, Starter £7.50-£10.50, Main £14.50-£22.50, Dessert £7-£8.50, Service added but optional 10% **Wines** 181 bottles over £20, 3 bottles under £20, 15 by glass **Notes** Tasting menu 8 course, wine flight 6 glasses £34.50, Vegetarian available **Seats** 60 **Children** Portions **Parking** On street

Berkeley Square Hotel

◉ British

Contemporary art hotel with modish cooking

☎ 0117 921 0455
15 Berkeley Square, Clifton BS8 1HB
e-mail: berkeley@cliftonhotels.com
dir: M32 follow Clifton signs. 1st left at lights by Wills Memorial Tower (University) into Berkeley Sq

There's a new head chef at the stoves at this self-styled art hotel's restaurant overlooking Georgian Berkeley Square. Inside, wooden tables are laid with flickering candles, original artworks hang on the walls (bare-brick or blood red), and in daylight hours all-comers can gaze out over the Square through the generously proportioned Georgian windows. The new man gives local produce a good showing on the menu, which reveals classical foundations and a creative streak. Roast scallops come in a fashionable-sounding partnership with braised ham hock, celeriac and chicken jus, before line-caught St Ives sea bass with langoustines, cucumber and vanilla consommé, or an 8oz sirloin with triple-cooked chips. A pear workout - poached, sorbet, crisps and soup - is a fine finish.

Times 12-3/6-10.30 Closed L Sun-Mon

Best Western Henbury Lodge Hotel

◉◉ Modern British ◉

Charming Georgian country-house hotel near Bristol

☎ 0117 950 2615
Station Rd, Henbury BS10 7QQ
e-mail: info@henburyhotel.com
dir: M5 junct 17/A4018 towards city centre, 3rd rdbt right into Crow Ln. At end turn right, hotel 200mtrs on right

This elegant small hotel fashioned from a Georgian mansion is a country house in the city, stylishly made over with a pared-back contemporary look. The Blaise Restaurant sports a light and airy décor involving creamy yellow walls hung with gilt-framed mirrors, wooden floors, toffee-brown leather chairs at bare blond-wood tables, and French doors leading out to a terrace in the pretty walled garden. The kitchen makes the most of local ingredients and seasonal produce in its straightforward modern ideas, as in a tasty starter of potted ham served with hot toast and home-made crab apple jelly. Main course is a well-matched trio of guinea fowl breast with caramelised apples and cider cream sauce, or there could be roasted cod with creamed Savoy cabbage, and mustard and parsley sauce. Finish with a dark chocolate and orange mousse with cinnamon shortbread.

Chef Paul Bullard **Owner** Tim & Rosalind Forester **Times** 7-10 Closed Xmas-New Year, Sun, L all week **Prices** Fixed D 3 course £24.95-£29.95, Service optional, Groups min 6 service 10% **Wines** 2 bottles over £20, 14 bottles under £20, 14 by glass **Notes** Vegetarian available **Seats** 22, Pr/dining room 12 **Children** Portions **Parking** 20

Bordeaux Quay

◉ Modern European ◉

Modern warehouse conversion covering all bases on the Bristol waterfront

☎ 0117 943 1200
V-Shed, Canons Way BS1 5UH
e-mail: info@bordeaux-quay.co.uk
dir: Canons Rd off the A4, beyond Millennium Square car park

The converted warehouse is named after the stretch of city waterfront on which it stands, so called because it once stored imported Sauternes. Lighter bar options and an all-day brasserie are on the ground floor, while the main restaurant, with its industrial ducting and smart, breezy décor, is upstairs. There's a cookery school in there too. Modern European stylings are the name of the game. Cornish crab gratin topped with gruyère is garnished with pink grapefruit for an appealing starter. At main course, salmon en croûte comes with a white wine sauce, or go for ballottine of chicken breast with preserved lemon, creamed cabbage and pommes Anna. An inventive way with rhubarb sees a portion of poached surmounting a layer of set rice pudding flavoured with the same, on a base of firm pistachio parfait.

Chef Alex Murray **Owner** Alex & Luke Murray **Times** 12.30-3/6-10 Closed Mon, L Tue-Sat, D Sun **Prices** Fixed L 2 course fr £17.50, Fixed D 3 course fr £28.50, Starter £4.50-£9.50, Main £12.50-£24.50, Dessert £5.50-£8.50, Service added but optional 10% **Wines** 140 bottles over £20, 20 bottles under £20, 30 by glass **Notes** Sunday L, Vegetarian available **Seats** Pr/dining room 28 **Children** Portions, Menu **Parking** Millennium Square

The Bristol Marriott Royal

◉ Modern

Modern brasserie food in a magnificent Victorian hotel

☎ 0117 925 5100
College Green BS1 5TA
e-mail: bristol.royal@marriotthotels.co.uk
dir: Next to cathedral by College Green

The Bristol Marriott has certainly grabbed pole position in the city centre, next to the cathedral and the historic waterfront, with a statue of Queen Victoria standing in profile to the grandiose Empire-era pomp of its Victorian façade. The Palm Court restaurant is the centrepiece, a sandstone-walled dining room done in shades of spring green and sunny yellow. The West Country's fine produce is showcased in a menu of uncomplicated modern

continued

BRISTOL *continued*

brasserie dishes, kicking off with tried-and-true combos such as Gloucestershire Old Spot ham hock terrine with piccalilli, followed by prime Devon beef or yellowfin tuna steaks from the grill, or a hearty surf and turf partnership of baked cod with braised oxtail, razor clam beignet and red wine reduction. End with fine West Country cheeses or something sweet such as tangerine posset with orange jelly and marmalade granita.

Times Closed Sun

Casamia Restaurant

◉◉◉◉ *– see opposite*

Culinaria

◉◉ Traditional British, Mediterranean

First-rate bistro cooking

☎ 0117 973 7999
1 Chandos Rd, Redland BS6 6PG

Nothing much changes at Culinaria, and why should it? The Markwicks have established a winning formula at their popular neighbourhood-style restaurant. A pine floor and unclothed wooden tables provide the backdrop for what they describe as 'traditional bistro food', which translates into a modern British style with an emphasis on the Mediterranean. Provençale fish soup with rouille and aïoli might precede a whole grouse roast in the traditional English style, or watercress soup before venison lasagne. Ingredients are well sourced with an eye to the seasons, combinations are often beguiling - witness a starter of squid braised in red wine served with leeks, orange and chilli - and desserts can be as memorable as plum and frangipane tart with the kitchen's own cherry ice cream, or St-Emilion au chocolat.

Chef Stephen Markwick **Owner** Stephen & Judy Markwick **Times** 12-2/6-9 Closed Xmas, New Year, BHs, 4 wks during year, Sun-Wed **Prices** Fixed L 2 course £15.50, Starter £7.50-£8.95, Main £13.50-£19, Dessert £6.25-£6.95, Service optional **Wines** 13 bottles over £20, 20 bottles under £20, 6 by glass **Notes** Early D menu 2 course £17, 3 course £21.50 6-6.45pm, Vegetarian available **Seats** 30 **Children** Portions **Parking** On street

Glass Boat Restaurant

◉ Modern French

Well-sourced, appealing dishes served on the water

☎ 0117 929 0704
Welsh Back BS1 4SB
e-mail: bookings@glassboat.co.uk
dir: Moored below Bristol Bridge in the old centre of Bristol

Given the name, you might feel shortchanged if it wasn't, but it is...a boat with lots of glass giving views over the water. Having once earned its crust along the waterways of the Severn Estuary, the old 1920s barge, moored up in the docks in heart of the city, has been converted to a decidedly handsome and contemporary-feeling restaurant. The European-accented cooking (Anglo-French mostly) matches the mood of the setting, blending traditional favourites with the occasional contemporary spin, and making use of fine regional produce. Start with potted shrimps on toast or maybe the simplicity of some rock oysters will appeal. Next up, perhaps braised rabbit with mustard sauce, or fish pie. Blood orange cake with Chantilly cream may bring things to a close before disembarkation.

Chef Freddy Bird, Charlie Hurrell **Owner** Arne Ringer **Times** 12-2.30/5.30-10.30 Closed 24-26 Dec, 1-10 Jan, L Mon, D Sun **Prices** Fixed D 3 course fr £20, Starter £5.50-£8, Main £15.50-£28.50, Dessert £5.50-£6.50, Service optional, Groups min 8 service 12.5% **Wines** 40 bottles over £20, 4 bottles under £20, 7 by glass **Notes** Early bird 2 course £15, 3 course £20 Mon-Sat 5.30-7pm, Sunday L, Vegetarian available, Civ Wed 100 **Seats** 120, Pr/dining room 40 **Children** Portions, Menu **Parking** NCP Queen Charlotte St

Goldbrick House

◉◉ Modern British ▮NOTABLE WINE LIST

Mod Brit cooking in a multi-purpose city-centre venue

☎ 0117 945 1950
69 Park St BS1 5PB
e-mail: info@goldbrickhouse.co.uk
dir: M32, follow signs for city centre. Left side of Park St, going up the hill towards museum

Goldbrick House is a multi-tasking sort of operation in the heart of Bristol. Housed in a pair of stylishly converted Georgian townhouses, it's a buzzy place where you could breeze into the all-day café/bar for anything from eggs Benedict for breakfast, to pan-fried lamb burger with chips and tzatziki for lunch or dinner. Otherwise, head upstairs for a glass of fizz in the champagne and cocktail bar, and push on into the stylish contemporary restaurant, where there are keenly-priced early-evening menus to set you up for a concert at nearby St George's Hall, a set menu with five choices at each stage, or the

full-on carte which majors in unpretentious modern ideas. Venison ragù with pappardelle and shaved pecorino, perhaps, or mussel and pancetta chowder with chives to set the ball rolling, then steamed duck leg pudding with Creedy Carver duck breast, braised chard and orange jus, or if you're in the mood for fish, monkfish scampi with chunky chips, mustard cress and radish salad, pepper ketchup and lemon mayo. Round things off with honey and thyme crème brûlée with lavender, rosewater and lemon shortbreads.

Chef Matthew Peryer **Owner** Dougal Templeton, Alex Reilley, Mike Bennett **Times** noon-10.30 Closed 25-26 Dec, 1 Jan, Sun **Prices** Fixed L 2 course £10-£15, Fixed D 3 course fr £26, Starter £4.95-£10.95, Main £12.95-£21.95, Dessert £4.95-£8.95, Service added but optional 10% **Wines** 36 bottles over £20, 20 bottles under £20, 12 by glass **Notes** Early D menu 6-7pm, Vegetarian available, Civ Wed 90 **Seats** 180, Pr/dining room 40 **Children** Portions, Menu **Parking** On street, NCP

Hotel du Vin Bristol

◉ Modern European ▮NOTABLE WINE LIST ✍

Bristol outpost delivering great wine and brasserie classics

☎ 0117 925 5577
The Sugar House, Narrow Lewins Mead BS1 2NU
e-mail: info.bristol@hotelduvin.com
dir: From M4 junct 19, M32 into Bristol. At rdbt take 1st exit & follow main road to next rdbt. Turn onto other side of carriageway, hotel 200yds on right

This branch of the well-known boutique chain comes housed in a Grade II listed 18th-century restored sugarhouse close to the rejuvenated waterfront and has all the expected HdV-style branding. Its buzzy, shabby-chic French-themed bistro and bar are at its heart, decked out in relaxed, white-linen-free mode, with well-worn floorboards and colourful posters, prints and empty bottle displays celebrating the importance of viniculture here - the wine list is outstanding. The modern brasserie menu complements the theme; a seasonal roster of straightforward, clean-cut classics that celebrate local produce; thus onglet steak comes with the classic accompaniment of pommes frites and Café de Paris butter to the more modish cod served with saffron potatoes, scallops and cherry tomato broth, while desserts serve up apple tarte Tatin and crème brûlée.

Chef Marcus Lang **Owner** MWB **Times** 12-2.30/6-10.30 **Prices** Fixed L 2 course fr £12.95, Starter £4.95-£9.50, Main £9.50-£23.50, Dessert £4.95-£9.50, Service added but optional 10% **Wines** 400 bottles over £20, 15 bottles under £20, 20 by glass **Notes** Pre-theatre D 2 main course for price of 1 until 7.30pm, Sunday L, Vegetarian available, Civ Wed 60 **Seats** 85, Pr/dining room 72 **Children** Portions, Menu **Parking** 8, NCP Rupert St

Casamia Restaurant

Modern

Exciting progressive cooking following the seasons

☎ 0117 959 2884
38 High St, Westbury Village, Westbury-on-Trym BS9 3DZ
e-mail: info@casamiarestaurant.co.uk
dir: Close to Westbury College Gatehouse

With its tiled floor and whitewashed walls, Casamia has the homespun look of a local trattoria, but as spring 2012 arrived, so came Seasons Casamia, with its seasonal decorative touches (changing again in summer, autumn and winter) and even greater focus on produce in the prime of its life. Jonray and Peter Sanchez-Iglesias's cooking is of the experimental cutting-edge European school, ultra-modern, progressive, bold, but never too overwrought, seen in a starter of beetroot 'risotto' made with barley, topped with sweet caramelised barley cut by the sharpness of yoghurt and pickled fennel. Ideas can be artfully presented - scrambled duck egg is stuffed with smoked duck and served in an eggshell presented in an egg box (complete with straw), the whole lot topped with thyme foam - while soft, flavourful pig's cheek comes with celery root and a side jar of apple jelly and dice. Ingredients, often imported, are of the first order, and experimentation pays off: salmon fillet is slowly poached in olive oil to produce melt-in-the-mouth texture, the dish balanced by a swipe of cauliflower purée, capers and sea salt, and creamy pine nut pannacotta comes with intense lemon sorbet, with dry ice poured over at the table for the dramatic all-round experience of sight, taste and aroma. If roast rump of lamb, onion, garlic family, mint sauce sounds a little tame, think again! With lamb as tender as can be, a cannelloni (of leek rather than pasta) filled with delicious garlickness, and a little pot of stunning mint sauce, this dish is anything but homely. Upstairs is a recently opened state-of-the-art kitchen and demonstration room.

Chef Peter & Jonray Sanchez-Iglesias
Owner Paco & Susan Sanchez-Iglesias
Times 12.30-1.45/7-9 Closed Sun-Mon, L Tue-Fri **Prices** Tasting menu £45-£88, Service optional, Groups min 6 service 12.5% **Wines** 30 bottles over £20, 8 bottles under £20, 20 by glass
Notes Tasting menu 5, 8 or 11 course, Vegetarian available, Dress restrictions, Smart casual **Seats** 40 **Parking** On street

BRISTOL *continued*

Juniper

@ Modern **NEW**

Intimate neighbourhood place with satisfying bistro fare

☎ 0117 942 1744 & 07717 277 490
21 Cotham Road South BS6 5TZ
e-mail: enq@juniperrestaurant.co.uk

The engagingly intimate neighbourhood bistro in the Cotham district has a hard to miss royal blue frontage, and is run with loquacious charm for a clientele largely formed of tables for two. A seasonally changing menu of modern bistro food keeps the emphasis on the comfort factor, and utilises some fine raw materials to that end. Dishes are often substantially proportioned, from a starter like smoked haddock and salmon fishcake with creamy parmesan-seasoned spinach and dill sauce, to mains such as a trio of Somerset pork - tenderloin, crackled belly and faggot - with garlicky dauphinoise and a reduction of pork juices and sage, or roast sea-bass with a crispy prawn dumpling and crushed potatoes. A main-course trio might be succeeded by a dessert duo of chocolate fudge brownies and chocolate and Baileys mousse, served with honeycomb ice cream.

Times 6.30-12 Closed 26-30 Dec, L all week

No.4 Clifton Village

@ Modern European

Flavour-focused cooking in Clifton

☎ 0117 970 6869
Rodney Hotel, 4 Rodney Place, Clifton BS8 4HY
e-mail: bookings@no4cliftonvillage.co.uk
dir: M5 junct 19, follow signs across Clifton Bridge. At mini rdbt turn onto Clifton Down Rd. Hotel 150yds on right

Within the stylish Georgian townhouse that is the Rodney Hotel, No. 4 restaurant comes fashionably kitted out in a clean-cut contemporary manner whilst making the most of its original features. There are huge sash windows, ornate ceilings and oak floorboards for a start, with the promise of a table in the secluded garden when the weather allows. It's a dinner-only operation dealing in good quality seasonal produce from the abundant local larder; the small kitchen's intelligently compact menu allows flavours to shine in dishes with a refreshingly simple take on modern classics. An opener chicken liver parfait, for example, with red onion marmalade and home-made focaccia, followed by rump of lamb teamed with minted crushed potatoes, sautéed leeks, green beans and a rich jus. Desserts follow suit with pannacotta and home-made shortbread or chocolate tart.

Chef David Jones **Owner** Hilary Lawson **Times** 6-10 Closed Xmas, Sun, L all week **Prices** Fixed D 3 course £19.99-£25.99, Starter £4.50-£6.95, Main £12.50-£18.50, Dessert £5.50-£5.95, Service added but optional 10% **Wines** 8 bottles over £20, 7 bottles under £20, 5 by glass **Notes** Vegetarian available **Seats** 35, Pr/dining room 42 **Children** Portions

The Pump House

@@ Modern British **NEW** 🏆 🕭

Thriving dockside pub-restaurant with serious approach to food

☎ 0117 927 2229
Merchants Rd, Hotwells BS8 4PZ
e-mail: info@the-pumphouse.com
web: www.the-pumphouse.com
dir: A4 Clevedon to city centre, left before swing bridge

The Victorians gave many of their industrial buildings rather more architectural appeal than was strictly necessary for their original purposes - in this case, a hydraulic pumping station. Down on the dock, chef-proprietor Toby Gritten has made great use of the scale of the building and the position by the water to create a pub and restaurant of vim and vigour. You can eat downstairs in the pub part of the operation (or outside by the water's edge) or head upstairs for a little more refinement and a little less hubbub. There's a good deal of regional produce on the menu and a steady hand in the kitchen turning out dishes of genuine appeal. Cornish crab is wrapped up cannelloni-style in thin slices of grapefruit, and served with apple textures (sorbet and crisp) and curried granola to start. Main-course Cornish hake is paired with Creedy Carver chicken wings, salsify and crown prince (a squash) purée. Desserts are no less creative - 'citrus', for example, consists of a lime posset, lemon sherbet, orange curd and grapefruit sorbet.

Chef Toby Gritten, Jamie Tubb **Owner** Toby Gritten & Dan Obern **Times** 12-3/6.30-9.30 Closed 25 Dec, Mon, D Sun **Prices** Fixed L 2 course £17.50, Fixed D 3 course £20, Tasting menu £45, Starter fr £5, Main £14-£20, Dessert £5-£8, Service added but optional **Wines** 109 bottles over £20, 15 bottles under £20, 14 by glass **Notes** Tasting menu 8 course, must be ordered by whole table, Sunday L, Vegetarian available **Seats** 50 **Children** Portions **Parking** 20

riverstation

@ Modern European

Buzzy riverside setting and modish brasserie food

☎ 0117 914 4434 & 914 5560
The Grove BS1 4RB
e-mail: relax@riverstation.co.uk
dir: On the dock side in central Bristol

As the name suggests, this cool, contemporary glass-fronted city venue (once a river police station) is set on the waterfront and has cracking views. Split over two levels, downstairs is a relaxed café-bar, upstairs the restaurant, and both have terraces overlooking the water. The restaurant's modish brasserie roster of dishes is based around local, seasonal produce, and everything - from bread to chutney and ice cream - is made in-house. Classic Mediterranean fish soup comes with the anticipated croûtons and rouille, and main courses extend to the likes of pan-fried stone bass fillet served with black-eyed bean purée, plantain fritters and mango salsa. Finish with pear and almond frangipane tart and Seville orange curd cream. Good value fixed-price lunches are a bonus.

Chef Peter Taylor & Toru Yanada **Owner** J Payne & P Taylor **Times** 12-2.30/6-10.30 Closed 24-26 Dec, D Sun (except BH) **Prices** Fixed L 2 course fr £12.75, Fixed D 3 course fr £18.50, Starter £6.50-£10.50, Main £14-£19.75, Dessert £4.50-£6.50, Service optional, Groups min 8 service 10% **Wines** 56 bottles over £20, 4 bottles under £20, 12 by glass **Notes** Pre-theatre £9 Mon-Fri 6-7.15pm, Fixed D 2/3 course Mon-Fri, Sunday L, Vegetarian available, Civ Wed 130 **Seats** 120, Pr/dining room 26 **Children** Portions, Menu **Parking** Pay & display, meter parking opposite

The Rockfish Grill & Seafood Market

@ Mediterranean, Seafood

Vibrant fish bistro and seafood market

☎ 0117 973 7384
128 Whiteladies Rd, Clifton BS8 2RS
e-mail: enquiries@rockfishgrill.co.uk
dir: From city centre follow signs for Clifton, restaurant half way along Whiteladies Rd

Brainchild of Mitch Tonks, fishmonger, chef and champion of all things piscine (with a sister venue in Dartmouth - see entry), Rockfish is a lively Clifton-based seafood bistro with an easygoing, café-style vibe. There are pictures of fish and fishermen on the walls, pale deck-like floorboards, shelves stacked with wine, and the buzz of an open kitchen. Great supply lines to the south coast fishing ports (especially Brixham) deliver sea-fresh daily landings that are more often than not simply chargrilled without any unnecessary fiddling about. Start with razor clams grilled with garlic and parsley, then move on to roast hake with clams and green sauce, or grilled whole sea bass to share, served with rosemary and olive oil. Check out the seafood market next door.

Times 12-2.30/6-10.30 Closed 25 Dec, 1 Jan, Mon, D Sun

Second Floor Restaurant

◉◉ Modern European 🍷

Bags of style and plenty of substance

☎ 0117 961 8898
Harvey Nichols, 27 Philadelphia St, Quakers Friars BS1 3BZ
e-mail: Reception.Bristol@harveynichols.com

The second floor in question is in a coolly modernist building that houses the Bristol outpost of the Harvey Nichols brand. That means only one thing: a mix of designer clothes, fabulous food market, glamorous bar with a decidedly jet-set vibe, and a restaurant that delivers refined brasserie-style cooking in a chic and rather classy setting. The young service team keep their feet on the ground. The menu is broadly modish European in scope, with excellent British ingredients and plenty of creative thinking. Thus Cornish blue cheese-enriched arancini is served with spiced beetroot and raspberry purée and fennel pickle, and main-course fillet of cod comes with seared squid, braised chick peas and chorizo spiced up with harissa in a bourride sauce. Provençal olive oil brings its natural fruitiness to a chocolate mousse, served with a fennel seed biscuit, and the wine list is a peach.

Chef Louise McCrimmon **Owner** Harvey Nichols Restaurants Ltd **Times** 12-3/6-10 Closed 25 Dec, Etr Sun, D Sun-Mon **Prices** Fixed L 2 course £15.50, Fixed D 3 course £19, Starter £6-£9.50, Main £12-£24, Dessert £5-£6.50, Service added but optional 10% **Wines** 320 bottles over £20, 4 bottles under £20, 16 by glass
Notes Vegetarian available **Seats** 60, Pr/dining room 10 **Children** Portions, Menu **Parking** NCP/Cabot Circus multi

BUCKINGHAMSHIRE

AMERSHAM   Map 6 SU99

The Artichoke

◉◉ Modern European

Creative, locally-driven cooking

☎ 01494 726611
9 Market Square, Old Amersham HP7 0DF
e-mail: info@artichokerestaurant.co.uk
dir: M40 junct 2. 1m from Amersham New Town

Forced to shut after a fire in the neighbouring premises in 2008, when The Artichoke reopened 18 months later it quickly got back to form. Positioned on the market square of the lovely old town, the Grade II listed building retains many original features such as open fireplaces and oak beams, but meets contemporary expectations with its artworks, designer chairs and walnut tables. Somewhat ironically, husband-and-wife-team Laurie and Jacqueline Gear expanded The Artichoke into that fire-damaged neighbouring property and now have a state of the art open kitchen to show for it, plus a private dining room. Chef Laurie spent time at highly feted Noma in the months after the fire and he's keener than ever these days on foraging and sourcing locally, and his cooking shows bags of ambition (which is matched by his culinary skills). Start with red wine-braised English snails with crisp pig's tail, mild garlic purée and young garlic shoots, then follow on with poached fillet of brill with white onion and cider mousse, girolles, chicken wafer, stuffing crumb, sea beet, orange and bay leaf dressing. Flavours are well judged at dessert stage, too: carrot cake with passionfruit curd, macerated carrots, almond and chocolate crumb, coriander cress, orange and passionfruit sorbet, for example.

Chef Laurie Gear, Ben Jenkins **Owner** Laurie & Jacqueline Gear **Times** 12-3/6.30-11 Closed 1 wk Xmas, 1 wk Apr, Sun-Mon **Prices** Fixed L 2 course £21.50, Fixed D 3 course £45, Tasting menu £65, Starter £9.50-£13, Main £19.50-£22, Dessert £6.50-£8.50, Service added but optional 12.5% **Wines** 150 bottles over £20, 5 bottles under £20, 11 by glass **Notes** Tasting menu 7 course, wine flight £48, Vegetarian available **Seats** 48, Pr/dining room 16 **Children** Portions **Parking** On street, nearby car park

Gilbey's Restaurant

◉ Modern British

Imaginative modern cooking in a former school building

☎ 01494 /27242
1 Market Square HP7 0DF
e-mail: oldamersham@gilbeygroup.com
dir: M40 junct 2, A355 exit Beaconsfield/Amersham

Gilbey's Old Amersham restaurant occupies a former grammar school building dating from the 17th century, and serves its local clientele as a textbook reliable neighbourhood bistro. There are low ceilings, wood flooring and cheerful art on sky-blue walls to create an ambience of stylish, intimate rusticity, while the friendly staff help foster a congenial, upbeat vibe. The kitchen makes a virtue of simplicity, working an intelligent vein of appealing modern British ideas that bring together spiced pickled red mullet with red pepper bavarois and black olive tapenade toast, or pork and pink peppercorn terrine with cider jelly, and leek vinaigrette. The same inventive streak partners herb-crusted Scottish cod with caramelised onion fregola, spiced aubergine and tomato compôte, or roast loin of lamb with a mini shepherd's pie, mint-crushed peas and redcurrant sauce. To finish, a zippy lemon tart is served to good effect with pistachio ice cream.

Chef Adam Whitlock **Owner** Michael, Bill, Caroline & Linda Gilbey **Times** 12-2.15/6.45-10 Closed 24-29 Dec, 1 Jan **Prices** Fixed L 2 course £18.50, Fixed D 3 course £24, Starter £6.25-£10.50, Main £14.75-£23.50, Dessert £3.25-£7.55, Service added but optional 12.5% **Wines** 26 bottles over £20, 3 bottles under £20, 10 by glass **Notes** Sunday L, Vegetarian available, Air con **Seats** 50, Pr/dining room 12 **Children** Portions **Parking** On street & car park

AYLESBURY   Map 11 SP81

Hartwell House Hotel, Restaurant & Spa

◉◉ British, French 🍷

Majestic country house with refined cooking

☎ 01296 747444
Oxford Rd HP17 8NR
e-mail: info@hartwell-house.com
dir: 2m SW of Aylesbury on A418 (Oxford road)

Owned by the National Trust and for five years in the 19th century home to the exiled pretender to the French throne, Louis XVIII, Hartwell is a grand stately home with impeccable credentials. It certainly looks the part with its Jacobean and Georgian façade and magnificent 90 acres of grounds to explore, and inside the scale of the rooms, period details and elegant furnishings push all the right buttons. The dining room is a formal, traditional space, with smart table settings and views over manicured gardens. Daniel Richardson seeks out high quality produce, much of it from the local area, and delivers dishes based on sound classical technique with a contemporary light touch and an eye for presentation. To start, crispy fillet of mackerel comes in a salad with capsicum, cherry tomatoes and a powerful tapenade, followed by roasted breast and leg of duck (Aylesbury, of course) with dauphinoise, chard and cherry sauce, and, to finish, peach tarte Tatin is paired with a fabulous cracked pepper ice cream and basil syrup.

Chef Daniel Richardson **Owner** Historic House Hotels/National Trust **Times** 12.30-1.45/7.30-9.45 **Prices** Fixed L 3 course fr £23.75, Fixed D 3 course fr £27, Starter £8.95-£13.95, Main £21-£29.95, Dessert £7.75-£10.50, Service included **Wines** 325 bottles over £20, 15 by glass **Notes** Tasting menus available, Sunday L, Vegetarian available, Dress restrictions, Smart casual, No jeans, tracksuits/trainers, Civ Wed 60 **Seats** 56, Pr/dining room 36 **Children** Portions **Parking** 50

BEACONSFIELD — Map 6 SU99

Crazy Bear Beaconsfield

◉ British

Bright modern menus in flamboyant setting

☎ 01494 673086

75 Wycombe End, Old Town HP9 1LX

e-mail: enquiries@crazybear-beaconsfield.co.uk

dir: M40 junct 2, 3rd exit from rdbt, next rdbt 1st exit. Over 2 mini-rdbts, on right

The shell of the coaching inn may date from the 15th century, but internally it's been given a flamboyant, even eccentric look, the English-themed restaurant (there are other eating options) featuring chequerboard-patterned cloth walls, chandeliers, cream bench seating, and low light levels. It's a fun, lively place, with a menu that covers a lot of ground, with starters of tuna sashimi with salade Niçoise, steak tartare, and grilled lobster. A global tilt can be detected among main courses too, so tiger prawns 'pil pil', served with Caesar salad, may appear alongside properly timed pan-fried fillet of halibut with crab bisque and a herby potato cake. Finish with classic crêpe Suzette or remain native with English trifle with sloe gin sabayon.

Times 12-12

The Jolly Cricketers

◉ Modern British **NEW**

Cracking village inn with food to match

☎ 01494 676308

24 Chalfont Rd, Seer Green HP9 2YG

e-mail: jacl.baker@virgin.net

dir: M40 junct 2, take A355 N, at rdbt 1st exit onto A40, next rdbt 2nd exit onto A355, turn right into Longbottom Ln, turn left into School Ln & continue into Chalfont Rd

This is just the sort of traditional country pub you love to come across: overlooking the church, it is truly the heart of the pretty village of Seer Green, beloved of the locals and welcoming to strangers, whether they have two or four legs, as this is a genuinely dog-friendly place. Low ceilings and splendid real ales add to the all-round conviviality, and the kitchen team cook to please their market with an unpretentious contemporary repertoire. A classic combo of seared scallops and black pudding gets an exotic lift from aniseed foam and silky smooth carrot and cardamom purée; next up, no-one could be immune to the charms of main courses such as roasted grey leg partridge with braised red cabbage, chestnut and caramelised apple. At the end, warm vanilla rice pudding with pear, prune and Armagnac ice cream goes down a treat too.

Chef Gerd Greaves **Owner** A Baker & C Lillitou **Times** 12-6.30-9 Closed 2 wks Jan, Mon, D Sun **Prices** Starter £6-£13, Main £13-£21, Dessert £6-£10.50, Service optional, Groups min 6 service 10% **Wines** 40+ bottles over £20, 15 bottles under £20, 16 by glass **Notes** Sunday L, Vegetarian available **Seats** 36 **Children** Portions, Menu **Parking** 10, On street

BLETCHLEY — Map 11 SP83

The Crooked Billet

◉ Modern British

Thatched country pub with city-smart menu

☎ 01908 373936

2 Westbrook End, Newton Longville MK17 0DF

e-mail: john@thebillet.co.uk

web: www.thebillet.co.uk

dir: M1 junct 14 follow A421 towards Buckingham. Turn left at Bottledump rdbt to Newton Longville. Restaurant on right on entering village

Although very much a traditional pub with plenty of rustic charm, real ale at the bar and a grand, bench-filled lawn for fine weather drinking, the 17th-century thatched Billet is also a serious pub-restaurant and one that offers a jaw-dropping 200 wines by the glass. The inglenook fireplace isn't merely decorative, but is used for smoking bacon, and an aromatic ambience is likely to greet you on arrival. A menu that wouldn't raise eyebrows in a chic city brasserie is full of appeal, perhaps kicking off with confit duck, chicken liver and foie gras parfait with orange and onion marmalade, and continuing with pan-fried hake with spiced potato, courgette and onion beignet and a creamy mussel and ginger broth. To finish, try the sticky toffee and banana pudding. Lighter set lunch dishes may include salmon with black linguini, olives, wilted spinach and lemon cream.

Times 12-2/7-10 Closed 27-28 Dec, L Mon, D Sun

BUCKINGHAM — Map 11 SP63

Villiers Hotel Restaurant & Bar

◉◉ Modern British

Updated coaching inn with well-judged cooking

☎ 01280 822444

3 Castle St MK18 1BS

e-mail: reservations@villiershotels.com

dir: Town centre - Castle Street is to the right of Town Hall near main square

In the centre of historic Buckingham, the Villiers is a classic coaching inn with over 400 years of history under its belt. It shows its venerable age in the bar with flagstone floors, oak panelling and open fires, but things take a more contemporary turn in the restaurant, where a smart modern look suits the cooking. Seekers of value should head straight for the market menus which propose simple contemporary ideas along the lines of Scotch duck egg with pea and herb vinaigrette and celeriac remoulade, followed by navarin of lamb with creamed potatoes and green beans. Comfort also informs the main menu, which might start out with a heart-warming combination of pan-fried pigeon breast with confit beetroot, watercress and honey mustard dressing, then progress to roast duck suprême with celeriac purée, braised red cabbage, and duck and potato cake, or roast sea bass with wild garlic creamed potatoes, crisp roast broccoli and red wine sauce. Dessert ideas such as sticky date and Guinness pudding with blackcurrant ice cream and Guinness syrup are hard to pass by.

Chef Paul Stopps **Owner** Oxfordshire Hotels Ltd **Times** 12-2.30/6-9.30 **Prices** Fixed L 2 course £11.95-£16.95, Fixed D 3 course £20.95-£23.95, Service optional, Groups min 6 service 10% **Wines** 22 bottles over £20, 25 bottles under £20, 13 by glass **Notes** Sunday L, Vegetarian available, Civ Wed 150 **Seats** 70, Pr/dining room 150 **Children** Portions **Parking** 52

Save on Hotels. Book at **theAA.com/hotel**

BUCKINGHAMSHIRE 69 **ENGLAND**

Burnham Beeches Hotel

@ Modern British, European

Confident cooking in an early Georgian hotel

☎ 0844 736 8603 & 01628 600150
Burnham Beeches, Grove Rd SL1 8DP
e-mail: burnhambeeches@corushotels.com
web: www.corushotels.com
dir: off A355, via Farnham Royal rdbt

An early Georgian house in 10 acres of grounds, the corporately owned Burnham Beeches stands in a rural spot sufficiently tranquil to have inspired Thomas Gray to have composed his celebrated Elegy here. He is honoured in the name of Grays Restaurant, a pair of interlinked rooms, one panelled, with views over the attractive gardens. The kitchen turns out a confident version of modern British food, adding a portion of grilled gilt head bream to Niçoise salad in citrus dressing to start, and then garnishing rump of lamb with cumin-spiked couscous and chargrilled veg. Finish with rhubarb and apple crumble with ginger ice cream and vanilla sauce.

Chef Rafal Wysocki **Owner** Corus Hotels
Times 12-2/7-9.30 **Prices** Starter £5.50-£8.50, Main £15-£25, Dessert £6.50-£8 **Wines** 19 bottles over £20, 2 bottles under £20, 8 by glass **Notes** Sunday L, Vegetarian available, Dress restrictions, Smart casual, Civ Wed 160 **Seats** 70, Pr/dining room 120 **Children** Portions, Menu **Parking** 150

The Grovefield House Hotel

@@ Traditional, Mediterranean

Classic cooking with a twist in an Edwardian country-house hotel

☎ 01628 603131
Taplow Common Rd SL1 8LP
e-mail: info.grovefield@classiclodges.co.uk
dir: From M4 left on A4 towards Maidenhead. Next rdbt turn right under railway bridge. Straight over mini rdbt, garage on right. Continue for 1.5m, hotel on right

Built on the beery fortune of London brewer John Fuller (creator of the masterpiece that is London Pride) as a country bolt-hole near to Windsor, Edwardian Grovefield House is looking rather spruce after a £2m contemporary facelift. With fabulous views over the grounds as a backdrop, the classy Hamilton's Restaurant is at the heart of culinary matters. Dishes follow the seasons and

draw on well-sourced ingredients in a style that is essentially classic country house but with a modern sensibility, thus you might open with roasted vegetable Wellington with garlic purée and basil crisps, then proceed to a main course that teams pan-fried fillet of pollock with seafood fricassée and saffron sauce. Carnivores might find satisfaction in an unfussy pairing of braised blade of beef with mash and glazed vegetables, while puddings aim at all-round satisfaction with the likes of hot chocolate fondant with vanilla ice cream.

Times 12-2.30/7-9.30 Closed L Sat

The Bedford Arms Hotel

@ Modern International

Hotel restaurant with confident cooking

☎ 01923 283301
WD3 6EQ
e-mail: contact@bedfordarms.co.uk
dir: M25 junct 18/A404 towards Amersham, after 2m follow signs on right for hotel

Peacefully set in its own grounds, The Bedford Arms was converted to a hotel in the late 1930s. Leaded bay windows in the oak-panelled restaurant, where an elaborate fireplace catches the eye, look over the gardens. The menu displays the occasional international touch - prawn tempura with mooli and carrot salad and ponzu sauce, say - but otherwise doesn't roam too far from Europe, with seasonality to the fore. Pan-fried scallops with sauce vierge and samphire, and pistachio-crusted goats' cheese with roast figs and watercress may show up among starters, followed by the likes of roast rack of lamb with pea and mint purée and lamb jus, or pan-fried salmon fillet with grilled asparagus and tomato and saffron chutney. A dedicated pastry chef is responsible for puddings like pear Tatin.

Chef Christopher Cloonan **Owner** Arthur & Celia Rickett
Times 12-2.30/7-9.30 Closed 26 Dec-5 Jan, D Sun
Prices Starter £5.50-£9.50, Main £14.50-£24.50, Dessert £5.50-£6.50, Service optional, Groups min 6 service 10% **Wines** 22 bottles over £20, 19 bottles under £20, 10 by glass **Notes** Tasting menu available, Sunday L, Vegetarian available, Dress restrictions, Smart casual, Civ Wed 55 **Seats** 55, Pr/dining room 24 **Children** Portions **Parking** 55

The Unicorn

@@ British

The kind of pub every village should have

☎ 01296 681261
12 High St LU7 0LQ
e-mail: theunicornpub@btconnect.com
web: www.theunicornpub.co.uk
dir: 2m N of A418 (between Aylesbury & Leighton Buzzard). In village centre

The welcome is warm and sincere, the menu chock-full of the sort of unfussy modern pub food that makes you want a bit of everything, and the 17th-century interior is replete with low beams, open fires, homely mismatched wooden furniture, and old pictures of village life on the walls. The place is the hub of local life too, selling home-made bread, milk, wine, butter, stamps and Cublington greetings cards. And the food lives up to its promise, whether it is a cooked breakfast on Saturday mornings, coffee and afternoon tea with home-made cakes throughout the week - which is rather nice out in the lovely garden - or a doorstop sandwich and a pint of real ale. If you want to put the kitchen through its paces properly, go for the full three-courses: smoked wood pigeon and chicory salad with apple chutney and toasted pumpkin seeds to start, then slow-roast pork belly with mash, braised red cabbage, and sage and cider jus. Wrap it all up with toffee and date pudding with clotted cream and toffee sauce.

Chef Christopher George **Owner** Mr S D George
Times 12-2.30/7-9 Closed D Sun (Pre bookings only)
Prices Food prices not confirmed for 2013. Please telephone for details **Wines** 8 bottles over £20, 15 bottles under £20, 8 by glass **Notes** Vegetarian available **Seats** 60, Pr/dining room 20 **Children** Portions, Menu **Parking** 20

Adam Simmonds at Danesfield House

MARLOW   Map 5 SU88

Modern European  NOTABLE WINE LIST

Impressive Thames-side hotel with highly skilled modern cooking

☎ 01628 891010
Henley Rd SL7 2EY
e-mail: reservations@danesfieldhouse.co.uk
web: www.danesfieldhouse.co.uk
dir: M4 junct 4/A404 to Marlow. Follow signs to Medmenham and Henley. Hotel is 3m outside Marlow

Victorian magnates usually went in for the red-brick Hammer Horror look for their stately piles, but the heir to the Sunlight soap fortune took his inspiration from the Italian Renaissance when he rebuilt Danesfield House. With its crenallated façade of snowy-white local rock-chalk surveying 65 acres of primped and topiaried Thames-side gardens, it's a memorable sight, and since it started a new career as a top-flight country-house hotel in the 1990s, its grandiose oak-panelled interiors are open to anyone with the urge to splurge on treating themselves to the full Monty package of spa pampering and fine dining. The latter takes place in a contemporary setting of limed oak panelling designed by Anouska Hempel, which makes an appropriate showcase for the gastronomically-erudite, modern cooking of Adam Simmonds. This is a chef who likes to deploy the full arsenal

of modern day culinary wizardry - there's a penchant for low-temperature and sous-vide techniques, supported by a battalion of espumas, foams and jellies to keep the entertainment factor ticking over. But that's not to say that the cooking is a case of style over substance: his ideas are imaginative and fun, without ever losing the plot. Nothing is done at the expense of flavours and textures, which dazzle from the off in a 'Mojito' amuse-bouche that nails the rum, mint and lime essences of the celebrated Cuban cocktail in layers of jelly, granita and foam, setting the palate tingling in anticipation of the next dish - a starter that partners confit foie gras of impeccable quality with smooth William Pear compôte, walnut purée, and rocket. At main course stage, pork fillet is cooked sous-vide for maximum delicacy of flavour, and matched with plump Scottish langoustines, salt-baked turnip and turnip purée, finely-sliced discs of kohlrabi, and trompette mushrooms. Fish might get a more speculative treatment involving pan-fried fillet of brill with parmesan macaroni, salt-baked celeriac, and Granny Smith apple. A pre-dessert brings yoghurt espuma with blackberry sorbet and gel as an attention-grabbing preamble to a banana and caramel soufflé served in a copper pan with salted caramel ice cream scooped out at the table; otherwise, you might head off-piste into the realms of goats' curd mousse with

taupinière (a nutty, tangy goats' cheese) and fig purée, fig granita and pistachios. The compendious wine list has helpful suggestions for seasonal choices by the glass, as well as useful notes on how each region's bottles will work with food.

Chef Adam Simmonds
Times 12-2/7-9.30 Closed 18 Aug-2 Sep, 23 Dec-7 Jan, BHs, Sun-Mon, L Tue-Wed **Prices** Fixed L 2 course fr £50, Fixed D 3 course fr £65, Tasting menu £82, Service added but optional 12.5%
Wines 350 bottles over £20, 14 by glass
Notes Tasting menu 7 course, Vegetarian available, Dress restrictions, Smart casual, Civ Wed 30 **Seats** 24, Pr/dining room 14 **Children** Portions **Parking** 100

Save on Hotels. Book at **theAA.com/hotel**

BUCKINGHAMSHIRE 71 ENGLAND

GREAT MISSENDEN
Map 6 SP80

Nags Head Inn

British, French

Charming pub offering well-cooked Anglo-French food

☎ 01494 862200 & 862945
London Rd HP16 0DG
e-mail: goodfood@nagsheadbucks.com
web: www.nagsheadbucks.com
dir: N from Amersham on A413 signed Great Missenden, left at Chiltern Hospital into London Rd (1m S of Great Missenden)

There's nothing knackered or tired about this Nag; the 15th-century red-brick hostelry - set in the rolling Chilterns - comes sporting a modern makeover that has fashioned it into a stylish foodie pub with rooms serving creative Anglo-French cooking. At heart though, it's still a quaint, intimate old inn, inviting enough to have tempted various Prime Ministers to call in for a pint on their way to Chequers. And, thanks to erstwhile regular Roald Dahl, it appeared in the film of his children's book *Fantastic Mr Fox*, while colourful artworks on the walls are based on Dahl characters. You can certainly see its appeal: a fire blazes away in the inglenook beneath ancient oak beams in the small bar, while the equally cosy restaurant areas on either side are all carpeted comfort. Fresh organic produce - local where possible - drives the kitchen's accomplished output; take sea bream fillet with sour apple-pickled cockles served with cider vinegar white butter, and perhaps a warm apple and rhubarb tart finale.

Chef Alan Bell, Howard Gale, Claude Paillet **Owner** Alvin, Adam & Sally Michaels **Times** 12-11 Closed 25 Dec **Prices** Fixed L 2 course £15, Fixed D 3 course £20, Starter £5.95-£13.95, Main £12.95-£24.95, Dessert £4.75-£6.95, Service optional, Groups min 6 service 10% **Wines** 80 bottles over £20, 28 bottles under £20, 12 by glass **Notes** Sunday L, Vegetarian available, Dress restrictions, Smart casual **Seats** 60 **Children** Portions **Parking** 35

LONG CRENDON
Map 5 SP60

The Angel Restaurant

Modern European V

Confident cooking in 16th-century coaching inn

☎ 01844 208268
47 Bicester Rd HP18 9EE
e-mail: info@angelrestaurant.co.uk
dir: M40 junct 7, beside B4011, 2m NW of Thame

The Angel may sound like a pub, and does indeed have a bar serving real ales with comfy leather sofas around an open fire, but food is the main thing these days. Inside it has the chic good looks of a switched-on 21st-century restaurant, blending age-old wattle-and-daub walls, gnarled timbers, and slate floors with funky fabrics and scrubbed pine tables. Whether you eat in the cosy bar, luminous conservatory, or outdoors on the heated terrace, expect up-to-date ideas shot through with Mediterranean or Asian inspiration. The coast may be some way off, but daily deliveries of fish keep the kitchen well-supplied with the materials for specials - crispy fillet of sea bass on chargrilled Mediterranean vegetables with sweet chilli and basil dressing, perhaps. Elsewhere there may be a trio of Sandy Lane pork - a fillet wrapped in Parma ham, cider-glazed belly and braised cheek with potato purée, roast baby fennel, and morel sauce. Remember to leave space for afters as it would be a shame to miss out on warm treacle tart with butterscotch sauce and honeycomb ice cream.

Chef Trevor Bosch **Owner** Trevor & Annie Bosch **Times** 12-2.30/7-9.30 Closed D Sun **Prices** Fixed L 2 course £14.95, Fixed D 3 course £24.95, Starter £5.25-£8.50, Main £16.25-£29.50, Dessert £6.95, Service optional, Groups min 8 service 10% **Wines** 58 bottles over £20, 29 bottles under £20, 12 by glass **Notes** Sunday L, Vegetarian menu **Seats** 75, Pr/dining room 14 **Children** Portions **Parking** 30

MARLOW
Map 5 SU88

Adam Simmonds at Danesfield House

– see opposite

Aubergine at the Compleat Angler

– see below

Aubergine at the Compleat Angler

MARLOW
Map 5 SU88

Modern European

Waterside restaurant with sharp, contemporary cooking

☎ 0844 879 9128 & 01628 405405
Macdonald Compleat Angler, Marlow Bridge SL7 1RG
e-mail: aubergineca@londonfinediningroup.com
web: www.auberginemarlow.com
dir: M4 junct 8/9 or M40 junct 4. A404 to rdbt, take Bisham exit, 1m to Marlow Bridge, hotel on right

Back in the day, the original Chelsea Aubergine was a hotbed of culinary achievement where Mr Ramsay earned his spurs. It is now called 11 Park Walk, but the brand lives on, and has moved out to a country life in the stockbroker belt on the banks of the River Thames next to Marlow Weir. Housed in the upscale Macdonald Compleat Angler, the décor has a few nods to the eggplant theme - hues of purple and olive, and motifs on the chargers and silverware - but the theme is not overplayed. It is all impeccably chic and chimes seamlessly with the timeless English location and chef Miles Nixon's intelligently-conceived modern European ideas. Don't expect any pushing of the culinary envelope here: tradition is embedded in daily roasts served from the silver carving trolley. But the kitchen's output is driven by seasonality and extracting the best from top-drawer ingredients, whether it is luxurious native lobster matched with bonbons and purée of cauliflower, and lobster butter, or a more humble chicken liver parfait with a port reduction. Main courses bring saddle of venison with red cabbage, pumpkin fondant and braised chestnuts, or aged fillet of beef with garlic mash, and truffle and Madeira jus. To finish, desserts maintain the high-flying tone with an assemblage of Pear William bavarois, marzipan, pear sorbet and almond milk foam.

Chef Miles Nixon **Owner** London Fine Dining Group **Times** 12-2.30/7-10.30 **Prices** Fixed L 2 course £23, Fixed D 3 course £50, Service added but optional 12.5% **Wines** 50+ bottles over £20, 4 bottles under £20, 6 by glass **Notes** Gourmand menu 5 course from £55 (with cheese £65), Sunday L, Vegetarian available, Dress restrictions, Smart casual **Seats** 49 **Children** Portions **Parking** 100

The Hand & Flowers

British, European 🌶

Stellar cooking in charmingly unpretentious setting

☎ 01628 482277
126 West St SL7 2BP
e-mail: reservations@
thehandandflowers.co.uk
web: www.thehandandflowers.co.uk
dir: M40 junct 4/M4 junct 8/9 follow
A404 to Marlow

The tripartite of seriously good food, unpretentious service and confidently unaffected décor is a rare beast indeed. Tom and Beth Kerridge had the confidence to go their own way and have been rewarded with a shower of praise and a packed restaurant. It's a winning formula. To pull it off, though, it helps if the person at the stoves has Tom's divertingly skilful abilities. The H&F still looks like a cheerful local with its hanging baskets and pebble-dashed façade, whilst inside maintains the rustic finish - this is no hollowed out gastro-pub. A closer inspection reveals the attention to detail: the carefully-chosen warm neutrality of the colour palette, the leather chairs and banquettes, and the quality of the crockery and glassware. And then there's the menu. The kitchen takes high quality, mostly British ingredients and produces dishes that are by equal turns straightforward and sophisticated.

The fine produce is not overworked, but neither is there any lack of invention and creativity; everything looks fabulous on the plate (which may be a wooden board or a coloured bowl) and flavours sing out from start to finish. Devilled whitebait with Marie Rose sauce is a fun amuse to get you in the mood, plus there's excellent home-made bread before a first-course parsley soup, say, silky smooth and punchy of flavour, studded with smoked eel and bacon and topped with a parmesan tortellini of genuine refinement. Next up, spiced sea bream is of exceptional quality, with smoky aubergine, sea aster and a side-serving of excellent dhal and coconutty moilee sauce, or go for the star of the BBC's *Great British Menu* 2011: roast hog with salt-baked potatoes and apple sauce (it's for two, so you'll need a friend). Glazed Cox's apple tart with rose water ice cream or English blueberry soufflé with blueberry sorbet and mint sauce ensure the difficult choices continue through to dessert. Service is thoroughly charming.

Chef Tom Kerridge **Owner** Tom & Beth Kerridge **Times** 12-2.30/6.30-9.30 Closed 24-26 Dec, D Sun, 1 Jan **Prices** Starter £8.50-£13, Main £22.50-£32, Dessert £9-£11, Service optional, Groups min 6 service 10% **Wines** 100 bottles over £20, 1 bottle under £20, 13 by glass **Notes** Sunday L, Vegetarian available **Seats** 50 **Children** Portions **Parking** 20

Save on Hotels. Book at **theAA.com/hotel**

BUCKINGHAMSHIRE 73 ENGLAND

MARLOW *continued*

Bowaters

◎◎ Modern British

Modern British food served in a charming Thames-side setting

☎ 0844 879 9128 & 01628 405406
Macdonald Compleat Angler, Marlow Bridge SL7 1RG
e-mail: compleatangler@macdonald-hotels.co.uk
dir: M4 junct 8/9 or M40 junct 4. A404 to rdbt, take Bisham exit, 1m to Marlow Bridge, hotel on right

Fabulously located on the banks of the River Thames overlooking the rushing water at Marlow Weir, the handsome Georgian Compleat Angler Hotel was named after the famous angler Izaak Walton. It's hard to imagine a more charming spot on a summer's evening, with tables laid on the riverside lawn, flickering candles reflected on the water, a view of Marlow church, and the distant thunder of that aforementioned weir. If the weather isn't up to it, the suave setting of Bowaters restaurant won't disappoint, where classic pastel shades meet contemporary style - and you get those watery views come rain or shine. The kitchen delivers an intelligent menu of accessible contemporary dishes with clearly defined flavours presented with a distinct wow factor. Seared scallops might appear in a trio with pancetta and a warm chicory and asparagus salad, followed by tender medallions of veal with deep earthy flavoured sweetbreads and a well-reduced Madeira sauce, and a deliciously moist almond tart with sweet rhubarb and a zesty yoghurt sorbet. Aubergine (see entry) is the hotel's other restaurant option.

Times 12.30-2/7-10 Closed D Sun

Crowne Plaza Marlow

◎ Modern British

Lake-view dining in the Buckinghamshire countryside

☎ 01628 496800
Field House Ln SL7 1GJ
e-mail: reservations@crowneplazamarlow.co.uk
dir: A404 exit to Marlow, left at mini rdbt, left into Field House Lane

The Marlow branch of Crowne Plaza has five acres of Buckinghamshire to itself, and is sited next to a splendid lake, which makes for restful views on light evenings. In the Glaze restaurant, raspberry-coloured banquettes and darkwood tables without coverings offer a bold, contemporary look. Consistently popular dishes include the starter of smoked chicken risotto balls with yellow pepper coulis; well-crackled pork belly with caramelised apple, little rösti of potato and sage and a thick jus given consistency with apple purée; and firmly set strawberry pannacotta with strawberry and balsamic salsa. Friendly, attentive service rises above the corporate norm.

Chef Stuart Hine **Owner** BDL Hotels **Times** 6.30-10 **Prices** Food prices not confirmed for 2013. Please telephone for details **Wines** 26 bottles over £20, 11 by glass **Notes** Vegetarian available, Civ Wed 400 **Seats** 150 **Children** Portions, Menu **Parking** 300

The Hand & Flowers

◎◎◎ – *see opposite*

The Vanilla Pod

◎◎ British, French V

Intelligently constructed dishes in central townhouse

☎ 01628 898101
31 West St SL7 2LS
e-mail: contact@thevanillapod.co.uk
dir: From M4 junct 8/9 or M40 junct 4 take A404, A4155 to Marlow. From Henley take A4155

The Vanilla Pod is a charming little restaurant where dimmed lighting and the buzz of conversation add to the intimate feel of the place. Walls are a warm cream, tables are well dressed, and service is clued-up. The kitchen superimposes modern British tastes on classic French lines, so a terrine of ham hock and chicken with prunes may precede fillet of lamb with lentils and Madeira jus, and it pulls off some robust flavour combinations: earthy girolles and the aniseed kick of fennel confit for lemon sole in a herb crust, coffee-infused celeriac for slowly cooked duck breast, while the eponymous vanilla pod goes into a jus for lightly seared scallops with shallots in red wine. Vanilla and olive breads have been applauded, and puddings could run to rich, light chocolate and orange fondant with none other than vanilla ice cream.

Chef Michael Macdonald **Owner** Michael & Stephanie Macdonald **Times** 12-2/7-10 Closed 24 Dec-3 Jan, Sun-Mon **Prices** Fixed L 2 course £15.50, Tasting menu £55, Service optional, Groups min 10 service 12.5% **Wines** 102 bottles over £20, 3 bottles under £20, 10 by glass **Notes** Alc 3 course £45, Tasting menu 8 course, Vegetarian menu, Dress restrictions, Smart casual **Seats** 28, Pr/dining room 8 **Parking** West Street car park

MILTON KEYNES Map 11 SP83

Mercure Parkside Hotel

◎ Modern British NEW

Modernised traditional dishes in a boutique hotel

☎ 01908 661919
Newport Rd, Woughton on the Green MK6 3LR
e-mail: h6627-gm@accor.com
web: www.mercure.com
dir: M1 junct 14, A509 towards Milton Keynes. 2nd exit on H6 follow signs to Woughton on the Green

Set in the Ouzel Valley Park, and yet only a short hop from the hurly-burly of Milton Keynes, the Grade II listed, white-painted building has been stylishly made over inside to give it a boutique hotel feel. Simply laid bare-wood tables and framed pictures set the tone in the dining room, where a menu of confidently rendered brasserie favourites is offered. Sea trout smoked over Earl Grey and rosemary, served with horseradish mayonnaise, is an aromatically compelling starter, and might precede Gressingham duck breast with honey-roasted chicory and plums, or chargrilled tuna with roasted vine tomatoes and chips in the skins. If deconstructed puddings are your thing, try the apple pie, which arrives as a hollowed-out baked apple filled with the cooked fruit, alongside a slice of crisp sweet pastry, with an accompanying jug of very fine vanilla custard.

Times 12-2/6.30-9.30 Closed D Sun

STOKE POGES Map 6 SU98

Humphry's at Stoke Park

◎◎ British, European

Fashionable British cooking in a grand country club

☎ 01753 717171 & 717176
Park Rd SL2 4PG
e-mail: info@stokepark.com
web: www.stokepark.com
dir: M4 junct 6 or M40 junct 2, take A355 towards Slough, then B416. Stoke Park in 1.25m on right

Stoke Park is a vision from another era, a snow-white 18th-century confection designed by George III's architect James Wyatt. If the old pile looks familiar that's perhaps due to its long career as a film set in movies ranging from Bond classics to *Bridget Jones's Diary*. It became the UK's first country club back in Edwardian times and now trades as a full-dress hotel and country club with all of the expected golf, tennis, spa and gym diversions. Plenty to work up a keen appetite, then, for a session in Humphry's restaurant, which plays its part with fancy wall coverings, huge windows and mirrors, and linen-swathed tables. Broadly modern British in its thinking, the cooking offers up-to-date ideas along the lines of pan-fried scallops with celeriac purée, crispy pancetta, port reduction and caviar, followed by pan-fried pavé of halibut with a leek, butternut squash and sorrel risotto, marinated artichokes and crispy leeks. A modishly deconstructed 'Snickers' - milk chocolate and peanut

continued

STOKE POGES *continued*

mousse, salted chocolate caramel, caramel foam, and peanut tuile - is a typical finale.

Humphry's at Stoke Park

Chef Chris Wheeler **Owner** Roger King
Times 12-2.30/7-10 Closed 24-26 Dec, 1st wk Jan
Prices Fixed L 2 course £25, Fixed D 3 course £48-£52.50, Starter £9.50-£16.50, Main £17.50-£28.50, Dessert £9-£12.50, Service added but optional 12.5%
Wines 64 bottles over £20, 8 by glass **Notes** ALC L only, Vegetarian available, Dress restrictions, Smart casual, no trainers or T-shirts, Civ Wed 120, Air con **Seats** 50, Pr/dining room 120 **Children** Portions **Parking** 400

See advert opposite

Stoke Place

❀❀❀ *– see below*

Berry's at Taplow House Hotel

❀❀ Modern British

Intelligent British cooking in an eye-catching Georgian mansion

☎ 01628 670056
Berry Hill SL6 0DA
e-mail: reception@taplowhouse.com
web: www.taplowhouse.com
dir: M4 junct 7 towards Maidenhead, at lights follow signs to Berry Hill

You don't have to be an architecture anorak to be struck by the crenallated red-brick and white-stucco façade of this Georgian house on the Berks-Bucks border, and its gardens are equally out of the ordinary, with their centuries-old tulip trees and Cedar of Lebanon. In Berry's restaurant, tall French windows are framed with heavy, swagged drapes and a crystal chandelier hangs above plush traditional table settings. The food, however, has taken a contemporary country-house route, using great ingredients in intelligent combinations, with plenty of European accents, as in a starter that matches poussin and foie gras terrine with prune purée and grape dressing. Next out, a very fine slab of pan-fried turbot shares a plate with Parisienne potatoes, confit cherry tomatoes, and broccoli with artichoke cream. To wrap things up, there's a banana tarte Tatin with rum and raisin ice cream.

Berry's at Taplow House Hotel

Times 12-2/7-9.30 Closed L Sat

Stoke Place

Modern European ⬟NOTABLE WINE LIST 🍴

Rural idyll with stunning 21st-century cooking

☎ 01753 534790
Stoke Green SL2 4HT
e-mail: enquiries@stokeplace.co.uk
dir: M4 junct 6, A355, right at 1st lights to A4 Bath Rd. At 1st rdbt take 2nd exit onto Stoke Rd. B416 to Stoke Green. Hotel 200mtrs on right

With its grandly elegant William and Mary façade and 26 acres of grounds landscaped by the great 'Capability' Brown, Stoke Place has an awful lot going for it. And that's before you take into consideration the smart, boutique-style makeover of the interior and the fact that chef Craig van der Meer is serving up some seriously good contemporary European food in the Garden Room restaurant. There are lovely views of the eponymous grounds from the restaurant, which is a pleasingly unbuttoned space with a rustic-chic simplicity about it (no starched linen tablecloths here), and on the menu well-sourced materials are turned into smart modern food showing bags of invention and precise execution. To start, a superb piece of monkfish cheek stars in an impressive dish with vibrant avocado purée, chorizo 'dust', a perfectly cooked scallop and Royal Beluski caviar. Among main courses, rolled belly comes with crushed paprika potatoes, apple and almond purée, almond pannacotta and Madeira jus, while among fish options might be pan-fried gurnard with creamed lentils, butternut squash, quenelles of delicious banana chutney and a nicely judged light curry foam. To finish, the creativity and technical skills of the kitchen are on display once again, perhaps with an Amaretto mousse with coffee 'air sheet', milk chocolate feuillantine and green tea ice cream.

Chef Craig van der Meer **Owner** Dhillon Hotels
Times 12-2.30/7-9.30 Closed 24 Dec-9 Jan, L Sun
Prices Fixed L 2 course £18-£35, Fixed D 3 course fr £45, Tasting menu £55, Service added but optional 12.5%
Wines 266 bottles over £20, 5 bottles under £20, 14 by glass **Notes** Tasting menu 5 course, Sunday L, Vegetarian available, Dress restrictions, Smart casual, Civ Wed 120 **Seats** 24, Pr/dining room 14 **Parking** 120

'Star Quality'
HELLO! MAGAZINE

Humphry's.

AN INNOVATIVE TAKE ON BRITISH CUISINE…

Celebrated Chef Chris Wheeler invites you to indulge your tastebuds at Humphry's, Stoke Park's award winning restaurant.

Open to all, Humphry's allows you to enjoy 'an experience you want to relive again and again' *(At Home with Marco Pierre White).*

Named in the 'Top 20 Best out of Town Restaurants' by Harpers and Queen magazine. Humphry's innovative take on Modern British Cuisine and enviable wine list provide an unforgettable treat, all set within the sumptuous, romantic surroundings of Stoke Park's Georgian mansion.

Open daily for lunch and dinner.
To make a reservation please call 01753 71 71 71 www.stokepark.com

TAPLOW *continued*

The Terrace Dining Room, Cliveden

@@ Modern, Traditional

Fine dining in a stunning country house setting

☎ 01628 668561
Cliveden Estate SL6 0JF
e-mail: info@clivedenhouse.co.uk
dir: M4 junct 7, A4 towards Maidenhead, 1.5m, onto B476 towards Taplow. 2.5m hotel on left

They don't come much more stately than Cliveden, the grandest of English stately homes. The Italianate pile has played host to almost every British monarch since George I: it's no wonder its walls just seem to ooze history. Today it's in the care of the National Trust and as well as its 376 acres of parkland and gardens overlooking the Thames being open to the public, the house itself is run as a hotel. The elegant Terrace Dining Room, with its fine artworks, is bathed in natural light and looks out through French windows over the parterre and gardens towards the river. The menu here is rooted in French classicism, but with plenty of modern flourishes and a faithfulness to seasonality of ingredients. Wild garlic soup with a truffle-cream-filled pastry bun, or smoked lamb carpaccio with Caesar cream and pickled spring vegetables might kick off proceedings, before poached John Dory with a saffron potato mousseline, or spring poussin with bread sauce purée, sweet potato fondant and lemon thyme jus. Finish with a vanilla crème brûlée with rhubarb purée and rhubarb sorbet.

Times noon-2.30/7-9.30 **Prices** Fixed L 3 course £28-£50, Fixed D 3 course £60, Tasting menu £75 **Notes** Tasting menu 7 course, Dress restrictions, Smart casual

WOOBURN COMMON   Map 6 SU98

Chequers Inn

@ British, French

Chilterns coaching inn with impressive modern British food

☎ 01628 529575
Kiln Ln HP10 0JQ
e-mail: info@chequers-inn.com
dir: M40 junct 2, A40 through Beaconsfield Old Town towards High Wycombe. 2m from town left into Broad Ln. Inn 2.5m on left

The oak beams and bare stone walls are proof that the Chequers has been around since the 17th century, but the inn now takes a modern approach to keep its 21st-century customers happy. It is still the heart of a pretty Chilterns village with its chatty bar serving well-kept ales, but there's also a natty-looking contemporary lounge with chocolate leather sofas, and a thoroughly modern restaurant done out with wooden floors, fancy silver-framed wall mirrors and high-backed leather chairs at linen-clothed tables. The food is an imaginative assortment of up-to-date ideas influenced by classical themes - tea-smoked duck with sweetcorn custard, baby chard and pomegranate dressing, perhaps, followed by a

three-way serving of venison comprising pan-fried loin, suet pudding and home-made sausage teamed with sweet potato and tonka bean purée, and juniper jus. Finish with a classic tarte Tatin with vanilla ice cream and cinnamon custard.

Chef Pascal Lemoine **Owner** PJ Roehrig
Times 12-2.30/7-9.30 Closed D 25 Dec, 1 Jan
Prices Fixed L 2 course £13.95-£22.95, Fixed D 3 course £25.95-£28.95, Starter £6.95-£10.50, Main £14.95-£23.95, Dessert £6.95-£8.50, Service optional
Wines 36 bottles over £20, 25 bottles under £20, 11 by glass **Notes** Sunday L, Vegetarian available **Seats** 60, Pr/dining room 60 **Children** Portions **Parking** 50

CAMBRIDGESHIRE

CAMBRIDGE   Map 12 TL45

Best Western Cambridge Quy Mill Hotel

@@ Modern European 🌿

Confident cooking in a former watermill

☎ 01223 293383
Church Rd, Stow-Cum-Quy CB25 9AF
e-mail: info@cambridgequymill.co.uk
web: www.cambridgequymill.co.uk
dir: exit A14 at junct 35, E of Cambridge, onto B1102 for 50yds. Entrance opposite church

At the heart of this extended contemporary hotel and health club complex set in 11 acres of riverside meadows, is the original watermill, which was built in 1830. Situated in the miller's house, and overlooking the waterwheel and mill race, the recently refurbished Mill House restaurant makes the most of this feature, while putting on a distinctly modern designer look. It is a friendly, upbeat venue, with a background soundtrack of jazz, cosy and candlelit at night, and with views over the garden. The menu proudly lists local East Anglian suppliers whose produce forms the foundations of an accessible modern European repertoire. Suffolk crab with sea purslane, risotto, cucumber and lime is one way to start, or there might be local rabbit teamed with langoustines, trompette mushrooms, chicory, walnut and rosemary. Main courses might include a luxurious pairing of sea trout and lobster with samphire and young carrots, while meatier fare runs to slabs of locally-bred Angus and Limousin beef from the grill. Inventive desserts could turn up an acorn pannacotta with maple cake, pear, and toffee popcorn.

Best Western Cambridge Quy Mill Hotel

Chef Gregg Thorne **Owner** David Munro
Times 12-2.30/6.30-9.45 Closed 24-31 Dec **Prices** Fixed L 2 course £12.50, Fixed D 3 course £28, Starter £6-£9, Main £12-£29, Dessert £6.50-£9, Service optional, Groups min 8 service 10% **Wines** 55 bottles over £20, 13 bottles under £20, 27 by glass **Notes** Complimentary canapés & amuse bouche with all ALC, Sunday L, Vegetarian available, Dress restrictions, Smart dress/smart casual - no shorts (men), Civ Wed 80 **Seats** 48, Pr/dining room 80 **Children** Portions, Menu **Parking** 90

See advert opposite

Hotel du Vin & Bistro Cambridge

@ French 🍷

Classic French bistro cooking in an old university building

☎ 01223 227330
15-19 Trumpington St CB2 1QA
e-mail: info.cambridge@hotelduvin.com
dir: M11 junct 11 Cambridge S, pass Trumpington Park & Ride on left. Hotel 2m on right after double rdbt

The Cambridge branch of HdV is in a former university building in the centre of the city, very near the Fitzwilliam Museum. With its brick-walled bar and open-plan bistro dining, complete with on-view kitchen and unclothed tables, it fits squarely into the niche Francophilia that the group has made all its own. French onion soup and moules frites are on the way to go, but there is also a more trendy beetroot and goats' cheese salad to start, with duck confit and Lyonnaise garnish to follow. The grill works overtime to produce great steaks, burgers and rack of lamb, and it all rounds off with lemon tart, rum baba or crêpe Suzette. The wine list, as at all the group's hotels, is worthy of your serious attention.

Chef Jonathan Dean **Owner** MWB **Times** 12-2/6-10 **Prices** Starter £4.95-£10.95, Main £11.50-£23.95, Dessert £6.95, Service added but optional 10% **Wines** 25 by glass **Notes** Sunday L, Vegetarian available **Seats** 76, Pr/dining room 24 **Children** Portions **Parking** Valet parking service

Save on Hotels. Book at **theAA.com/hotel**

CAMBRIDGESHIRE 77 ENGLAND

Hotel Felix

◎◎ Modern British

Intricate modern cooking in a boutique hotel

☎ 01223 277977
Whitehouse Ln, Huntingdon Rd CB3 0LX
e-mail: help@hotelfelix.co.uk
web: www.hotelfelix.co.uk
dir: M11 junct 13. From A1 N take A14 turn onto A1307.
At City of Cambridge sign turn left into Whitehouse Ln

A bow-fronted Victorian villa is the setting for a rather
distinctive boutique hotel, in which the battleship-grey
interiors are offset with splashes of abstract-art colour,
and outdoor tables on a terrace overlooking the attractive
gardens make the most of the punting weather.
Contemporary brasserie cooking is the draw in Graffiti,
where braised shoulder of mutton might be a starter
portion, served with chargrilled aubergine and red pepper
jam. Main courses resound to French and Italian notes,
either for salt hake with petits pois and violet potatoes
Parisienne, or poached ballottine of local rabbit wrapped
in coppa, with walnut gnocchi, prune purée and
Armagnac cream. The flavours of these busy dishes ring
clearly and harmoniously through them, and the
momentum is maintained in desserts such as lemon
polenta cake, served warm with plum compôte and
Margarita crème fraîche.

Chef Tom Stewart **Owner** Jeremy Cassel
Times 12-2/6.30-10 **Prices** Fixed L 2 course £14.50,
Starter £5.75-£9.95, Main £15-£21, Dessert £6.25-£7.50,
Service added but optional 10% **Wines** 45 bottles over
£20, 3 bottles under £20, 19 by glass **Notes** Vegetarian
available **Seats** 45, Pr/dining room 60 **Children** Portions,
Menu **Parking** 90

Menzies Cambridge Hotel & Golf Club

◎ Modern, International

Well-rendered brasserie dishes in a golfing hotel

☎ 01954 249988
Bar Hill CB23 8EU
e-mail: cambridge@menzieshotels.co.uk
dir: M11 N & S to A14 follow signs for Huntingdon. A14
turn off B1050 Bar Hill, hotel 1st exit on rdbt

A short drive away from the centre of the historic
precincts of the academics' city, the modern Cambridge
branch of the Menzies hotel chain makes a splendid base
with its relaxed 200-acre rural setting and requisite
offering of beauty treatments and 18-hole championship
golf course. The smart Brasserie is an expansive, open-
plan space with mezzanine floors lit by an atrium-style
roof, and done out in a clean-lined contemporary style
favouring lots of bare wood. A crisply efficient front-of-
house team dishes up a please-all repertoire of modern
brasserie cooking - perhaps game terrine with kumquats
and Madeira jelly to start, then Parma ham-wrapped
monkfish served with violet potatoes and saffron cream,
or a classic mixed grill and triple-cooked chips sizzling
from the chargrill. Desserts stick to the classic territory of
Trinity burnt cream, or apple tarte Tatin and ice cream.

Chef Kevin Jackman **Owner** Menzies Hotels
Times 1-2.30/7-9.30 Closed L Sat (by appt only)
Prices Food prices not confirmed for 2013. Please
telephone for details **Wines** 27 bottles over £20,
10 bottles under £20, 11 by glass **Notes** Sunday L,
Vegetarian available, Dress restrictions, Smart, Civ Wed
180 **Seats** 170, Pr/dining room 50 **Children** Portions,
Menu **Parking** 200

Midsummer House

◎◎◎◎ **– see page 78**

Restaurant Alimentum

◎◎◎ **– see page 79**

Restaurant 22

◎ Modern European

Modish cooking in charming little venue

☎ 01223 351880
22 Chesterton Rd CB4 3AX
e-mail: enquiries@restaurant22.co.uk
dir: M11 junct 13 towards Cambridge, turn left at rdbt
onto Chesterton Rd

As the name implies, look out for that number 22 - with a
cream frontage and green door and shutters - to track
down this converted Victorian townhouse restaurant on
Chesterton Road. Inside, the small dining room is set out
with close-up, white-linen-decked tables, decorated with
flickering candles. The cooking keeps things sensibly
simple too, but with an appealing contemporary European
sheen. Salted-cod croquettes, perhaps, with lamb's
lettuce, garlic and caper berry aïoli, or white bean and
thyme soup with garlic croûtons to start. Next up on the
fixed price menu is a sorbet, followed by main-courses
such as pan-fried pork cutlet teamed with potato rösti,
creamed leeks, porcini mushrooms and sage. To finish,
the flavours of the Med are laid bare in a dish of
clementine and polenta cake with Limoncello cream.

Chef Mr Kipping **Owner** Mr A & Mrs S Tommaso
Times 7-9.45 Closed 25 Dec & New Year, Sun-Mon, L all
week **Prices** Fixed D 4 course £32.95, Service optional
Wines 40 bottles over £20, 30 bottles under £20, 6 by
glass **Notes** Vegetarian available **Seats** 26, Pr/dining
room 14 **Children** Portions **Parking** On street

Midsummer House

CAMBRIDGE Map 12 TL45

Modern British NOTABLE WINE LIST

Compelling contemporary cooking

☎ 01223 369299
Midsummer Common CB4 1HA
e-mail: reservations@
midsummerhouse.co.uk
web: www.midsummerhouse.co.uk
dir: Park in Pretoria Rd, then walk
across footbridge. Restaurant on left

Whatever your business in the city - something to do with the university, hi-tech industry, tourism, or your team is playing Cambridge United away (less likely that one admittedly) - it is worth knowing there's a stunning, world-class restaurant up the road. Not every city in this country has one by any means. It's in a lovely part of Cambridge by the River Cam, beside a green where cattle freely roam, and all is seemingly well with the world. Daniel Clifford is a prodigious talent and it has been his mission since 1998 to put Midsummer House on the map. He's received a lot of praise in that time, won plenty of plaudits, (including a winner's place on the BBC's *Great British Menu* in 2012) but continues to drive the business forward with a remarkable amount of energy. The Victorian villa in a walled garden, the river running by, is in a truly delightful spot, and inside is as open-plan as it can be without the roof falling in; it's contemporary without being over-bearing, smart without being precious. The attention to detail here is evident from the off, with a mostly French service team who don't miss a beat and cooking that raises the roof. It begins with canapés in the bar - top-quality olives, gougères and Bloody Mary sorbet, maybe - before moving to the restaurant, done out in calming neutral tones, which extends into a conservatory (newly extended in 2012). Next up, the amuse-bouche confirms the intensity of the work ethic here: a fabulous piece of smoked haddock with a silky smooth Vichyssoise velouté topped with a perfectly cooked soft-boiled quail's egg. There are a few menus to choose from, the Taste of Midsummer being the show stopper, ably supported by the Classic Menu and Taste of the Market; whichever way you go, creative contemporary cooking of the highest order awaits, with visual impact on the plate and flavour and texture contrasts measured to the nth degree. Pressed terrine of chicken and mushroom is a well-crafted first course, with moist chicken, tender garlic and earthy mushrooms, topped with a super-thin piece of crispy chicken skin, plus sorrel essence, intensely flavoured mushroom purée and a perfectly cooked confit chicken leg. The produce is of supreme quality, not least a piece of cod, cooked to delectable translucence, served with caramelised celeriac, buttered spinach and a deeply satisfying Madeira sauce, or the superb pork that is slow-roasted and comes with a fabulous black pudding and apple purée and a potato cylinder filled with unctuous confit pork and apple and shallot foam (amongst other things). The technical virtuosity is confirmed once again with the arrival of a pistachio soufflé and chocolate sorbet. The wine list is a fine piece of work, too.

Chef Daniel Clifford **Owner** Midsummer House Ltd **Times** 12-1.45/7-9.30 Closed 2 wks Xmas, Sun-Mon, L Tue **Prices** Fixed L 3 course £40-£60, Fixed D 3 course £40-£60, Service added but optional 12.5% **Wines** 900 bottles over £20, 12 by glass **Notes** Fixed D 3 course Tue-Thu, 6 course Tue-Sat £75-£95, Vegetarian available **Seats** 45, Pr/ dining room 16 **Children** Portions **Parking** On street

Restaurant Alimentum

Modern European **NOTABLE WINE LIST**

Strong ethical principles and classy, contemporary cooking

☎ 01223 413000
152-154 Hills Rd CB2 8PB
e-mail: reservations@
restaurantalimentum.co.uk
web: www.restaurantalimentum.co.uk
dir: Opposite Cambridge Leisure Park

A short journey from the centre of the city, near the leisure park, Mark Poynton's restaurant, with its Latin name and designer good-looks, serves up creative food in the modern manner. That means lots of bold ideas and cutting-edge cooking techniques. It all takes place in a space given a bit of contemporary swagger with smoked glass, shimmering black-lacquered tables, red padded walls above leather banquettes and windows looking into the heart and soul of the place - the kitchen. The service team plays their part with a good deal of polish, and there's live music (a singer and accompanying pianist) on Friday and Saturday evenings to reinforce that special occasion vibe. Poynton puts ethics and sustainability at the top of the agenda when it comes to sourcing his ingredients, while the fixed-price lunch and early-evening menu evolves on a weekly basis to ensure everything is at its best (there's a carte and

tasting menus as well). This may well be perky modish cooking, but there is belief and confidence in classical thinking on show too, so nothing jars or confuses. Things kick off with canapés such as smoked paprika and houmous macaroon and salt and vinegar popcorn, before excellent breads such as milk loaf and sage and onion turn up. Menu descriptions are brief, thus from the carte comes 'mackerel', with cucumber, sesame seeds and avocado, followed by 'beef' (sirloin and cheek with onion ash, red onion and carrot). Everything looks beautiful on the plate; witness a sea trout starter from the lunch menu, the superb quality fish perfectly cooked and served in a salad with fennel, grapes, leeks and topped with a black olive crumb, followed by a boned and stuffed chicken leg served with carrots in various forms and a horseradish-flavoured pommes purée. To finish, cheesecake is flavoured with lemon and thyme and accompanying candied ginger which packs quite a punch. The wine list gives a good showing to organic and biodynamic growers.

Chef Mark Poynton **Owner** Mark Poynton **Times** 12-2.30/6-10 Closed 24-30 Dec, BHs, L 31 Dec, D Sun **Prices** Fixed L 2 course £16.50-£19.50, Tasting menu £65, Starter £12.50, Main £22.50, Dessert £10, Service added but optional 12.5% **Wines** 188 bottles over £20, 2 bottles under £20, 16 by glass **Notes** ALC fixed 2 course £32, 3 course

£45, Tasting menu 7 course, Sunday L, Vegetarian available **Seats** 62, Pr/dining room 34 **Children** Portions **Parking** NCP Cambridge Leisure Centre (3 min walk)

CAMBRIDGE *continued*

The Rupert Brooke

◉ Modern British **NEW** ◐

High-calibre pub cooking in Rupert Brooke's Grantchester

☎ 01223 840295
2-4 Broadway, Grantchester CB3 9NQ
e-mail: info@therupertbrooke.com
dir: M11 junct 12, follow signs to Granchester

Rupert Brooke immortalised the village in his poem *The Old Vicarage, Grantchester*, so it's probably not wise to ask 'And is there honey still for tea?' at this charming inn. A raftered ceiling creates a rustic look, but the bar, broken up into several areas, has a modern sheen, with highly polished floors and tabletops. Seared scallops with lardons, celeriac fondant, samphire, roast garlic and tarragon butter is about as complicated as things can get here, the kitchen generally producing unpretentious, straightforward dishes of clear flavours. Chicken and pork liver pâté with chutney, or an impeccable gruyère soufflé may be followed by tender pink roast duck breast on a berry jus, served with rösti and sugar snaps. Flexibility means that pub classics like fish and chips, and sausage and mash, are not forgotten, and to finish there may be moist, chocolatey brownie with berry compôte and vanilla milkshake.

Chef Harry Dyer **Owner** Matthew Knight **Times** 12-3/6-9 Closed 25 Dec **Prices** Starter £5-£8, Main £11-£18, Dessert £5-£8, Groups min 5 service 10% **Wines** 9 bottles over £20, 14 bottles under £20, 10 by glass **Notes** Sunday L, Vegetarian available **Seats** 65 **Children** Portions, Menu **Parking** 20

| DUXFORD | Map 12 TL44 |

Duxford Lodge Hotel

◉ British, European

Confident cooking in historic country house

☎ 01223 836444
Ickleton Rd CB22 4RT
e-mail: admin@duxfordlodgehotel.co.uk
dir: M11 junct 10, onto A505 to Duxford. 1st right at rdbt, hotel 0.75m on left

Just a few minutes from the famous airfield and its museum, Edwardian Duxford Lodge is steeped in wartime history, having played host in the 1940s to stars and bigwigs such as Bing Crosby, Churchill and Douglas Bader. Le Paradis restaurant is a soothing, pastel-hued venue where crisp white linen, comfy chairs and smartly turned-out staff add an old-style charm to proceedings. The European-influenced food maintains a healthy attachment to familiar ideas - chicken liver and foie gras pâté for example, followed by loin of pork with black pudding mash, and apple and cider jus, or a seared fillet of sea bass with sun-blushed tomatoes, fennel gremolata and Provençal herbs to add a touch of southern sunshine. To finish, there are comforting old friends such as sticky toffee pudding with toffee sauce.

Chef Phillip Low **Owner** Mr Hemant Amin
Times 12-2/7-9.30 Closed 24 Dec-2 Jan, L Mon, Fri- Sat **Prices** Fixed L 2 course fr £14.95, Starter £5-£7, Main £15-£20, Dessert £5-£8, Service optional
Wines 12 bottles over £20, 10 bottles under £20, 6 by glass **Notes** Sunday L, Vegetarian available, Dress restrictions, Smart casual, Civ Wed 45 **Seats** 45, Pr/dining room 24 **Children** Portions **Parking** 30

| ELY | Map 12 TL58 |

The Anchor Inn

◉ Modern British

Creative cooking in rural East Anglian inn

☎ 01353 778537
Bury Ln, Sutton Gault, Sutton CB6 2BD
e-mail: anchorinn@popmail.bta.com
web: www.anchor-inn-restaurant.co.uk
dir: Signed off B1381 in Sutton village, 7m W of Ely via A142

Deep in Fen country, this marshland oasis is protected from the New Bedford River by a veritable rampart of earthworks. The low, brick-built 17th-century pub has been spared a boutique makeover: the cosy, low-beamed bar and adjoining dining rooms ooze charm and character - wonky tiled floors, dark oak-panelled walls, scrubbed pine tables and chairs, and roaring fires when winter is knocking at the door. You're in East Anglia, so the region's excellent ingredients, including produce from local allotments, are what turn up on the plate, brought together in intelligent, intuitive combinations with a clear eye to the sunnier climes of Europe. The menu sparkles with good ideas - Anchor-cured gravad lax with horseradish pannacotta, while mains might include Telmara duck breast with spicy sweet potato wedges and an apricot and ginger beer sauce. Finish with baby lemon meringue with lemon sorbet and chocolate and lemon cup.

Times 12-3.30/7-11

| HINXTON | Map 12 TL44 |

The Red Lion Inn

◉ Modern British ◐

Impeccably modern cookery in a spacious country inn

☎ 01799 530601
32 High St CB10 1QY
e-mail: info@redlionhinxton.co.uk
dir: M11 junct 10, at rdbt take A505 continue to A1301 signed Saffron Walden/Hinxton for 0.75m & follow signs for Hinxton

With its low ceilings, comfy Chesterfields and oak rafters, The Red Lion has the balance right, being simultaneously a good country pub with guest rooms, as well as a spacious and welcoming eatery. The kitchen specialises in gently contemporary cookery, bringing French and Italian accents to bear on quality local produce. Smoked haddock and spring onion risotto topped with a poached egg and a parmesan crisp, followed by tournedos Rossini

with foie gras, or best end of lamb with leek and potato gratin and courgette purée in rosemary jus, are the name of the game. Daily specials are chalked up on the board, and a wide choice of desserts covers all bases, from the comfort of bread-and-butter pudding to the tang of tangerine and star anise Tatin with clotted cream ice cream.

Chef Chris Woodward **Owner** Alex Clarke
Times 12-2/6.30-9 **Prices** Starter £4.50-£11, Main £9.50-£26, Dessert £2.50-£8, Service optional, Groups min 8 service 10% **Wines** 25 bottles over £20, 15 bottles under £20, 12 by glass **Notes** Tasting menus available, pudding club, Sunday L, Vegetarian available **Seats** 60 **Children** Portions **Parking** 43

| HUNTINGDON | Map 12 TL27 |

The Old Bridge Hotel

◉◉ Modern British ⏺ NOTABLE WINE LIST

Distinctive cooking and exceptional wines

☎ 01480 424300
1 High St PE29 3TQ
e-mail: oldbridge@huntsbridge.co.uk
dir: From A14 or A1 follow Huntingdon signs. Hotel visible from inner ring road

The handsome, ivy-covered, 18th-century Old Bridge is all things to all men: a combination of townhouse hotel, bustling inn and destination restaurant, with people here for a coffee, a pint of real ale, a glass of champagne or a full gourmet evening. There's plenty to entice and enjoy on a menu that shows a kitchen taking a pretty global approach, from a crab starter, accompanied by fennel, radicchio and pomegranate salad, to a main course of slow-cooked lamb shoulder, tender and full of flavour, with roast pepper couscous, spinach, olives and salsa verde. Dishes are carefully planned with flavours in mind, from bresaola with rocket, radish, parmesan and balsamic to pan-fried wild sea bass with spinach and cockle, mussel and potato chowder. Flexibility means you could pop in for just traditional cod and chips, and then be tempted to stay on for one of the irresistible puddings like chocolate délice with salted caramel and barley ice cream.

Chef James Claydon **Owner** J Hoskins **Times** 12-2/6.30-10 **Prices** Fixed L 2 course fr £14.95, Starter £6.95-£9.95, Main £13.95-£29.50, Dessert £6.90-£8.95, Service optional **Wines** 350 bottles over £20, 45 bottles under £20, 35 by glass **Notes** Sunday L, Vegetarian available, Civ Wed 80 **Seats** 100, Pr/dining room 60 **Children** Portions, Menu **Parking** 60

KEYSTON   Map 11 TL07

Pheasant Inn

◉◉ Modern British ▮NOTABLE

Interesting modern menus in charming old thatched inn

☎ 01832 710241
Loop Rd PE28 0RE
e-mail: info@thepheasant-keyston.co.uk
dir: 0.5m off A14, clearly signed, 10m W of Huntingdon, 14m E of Kettering

With its thatched roof and location in a sleepy farming village, this looks like a quintessential English inn, an impression not dispelled by a choice of real ales, oak beams, large open fires and simple wooden furniture. The quality of the cooking lifts the place well above the pub grub average, the wide-ranging, modern menu kicking off with a soup - celeriac and apple, say - or bresaola with beetroot, watercress and horseradish, before pink, tender fillet of lamb Wellington accompanied by sweetbreads, parsnip purée and sprout tops, or pan-fried sea trout with shrimp butter and an unusual turnip gratin. Even old favourites can be given a contemporary spin, with venison burger served with goats' cheese and beetroot relish, and rhubarb compôte accompanying vanilla pannacotta.

Chef Simon Cadge **Owner** John Hoskins
Times 12-2/6.30-9.30 Closed 2-15 Jan, Mon, D Sun
Prices Fixed L 2 course £14.95, Starter £5.95-£8.95, Main £11.95-£25, Dessert £5.95-£8.95, Service optional **Wines** 60 bottles over £20, 20 bottles under £20, 12 by glass **Notes** Sunday L, Vegetarian available **Seats** 80, Pr/dining room 30 **Children** Portions **Parking** 40

LITTLE WILBRAHAM   Map 12 TL55

Hole in the Wall

◉ Modern British

Classic country inn with sound seasonal cooking

☎ 01223 812282
2 High St CB21 5JY
dir: A14 junct 35. A11 exit at The Wilbrahams

The name comes from a long-gone beer collection system whereby farm labourers collected their refilled jugs and barrels on the way home from work, but nowadays Alex Rushmer and Ben Maude attract custom to their heavily-beamed 15th-century inn with rather more substantial fare. Inside, it is the archetypal country pub: logs crackling in inglenook fireplaces, low beams garlanded with hopbines, and scrubbed pine tables squeezed in elbow-to-elbow to feed into the convivial ambience. The kitchen aims for full-flavoured cooking wrought with an eye to local supplies and seasonality, which is reflected on the specials board and monthly menus. Heart-warming winter offerings could see roasted bone marrow served with pickled shallots and parsley, or duck liver brûlée with pineapple and passionfruit preceding venison loin with parsnip, haggis fritters, port sauce and coffee. Desserts mine a similar fortifying vein - perhaps warm

treacle tart with locally-milled oats and raspberry ripple ice cream.

Chef Alex Rushmer **Owner** Alex Rushmer & Ben Maude
Times 12-2/7-9 Closed 2 wks Jan, Mon, L Tue, D Sun
Prices Fixed L 2 course fr £14, Starter £5-£12, Main £11-£20, Dessert £6-£9, Service optional **Wines** 82 bottles over £20, 16 bottles under £20, 15 by glass **Notes** Sunday L, Vegetarian available **Seats** 75, Pr/dining room 40 **Children** Portions **Parking** 30

PETERBOROUGH   Map 12 TL19

Best Western Orton Hall Hotel

◉ Modern British

Grand old building with well-crafted menu

☎ 01733 391111
The Village, Orton Longueville PE2 7DN
e-mail: reception@ortonhall.co.uk
web: www.bw-ortonhall.co.uk
dir: off A605 E, opposite Orton Mere

The history of the house built in this spot goes back to the 11th century, but the main part of today's structure is a stripling by comparison, built as it was in 1835. It's an impressive complex of buildings set in a 20-acre estate, which includes some specimen trees, and there's a decidedly traditional feel on the inside too. The Huntly Restaurant has plenty of period detailing, rich fabrics and smartly dressed tables. The menu sets a nice balance, offering pigeon and vegetable broth alongside spiced dry-cooked mackerel crostini among first courses, and pan-roasted fillet of Lincolnshire beef with onion and thyme purée and grain mustard butter, or baked tilapia with garlic mash and sweet peppers among mains. The stables has been converted into an inn, and the old library is the hotel's lounge bar.

Chef Kevin Wood **Owner** Abacus Hotels
Times 12.30-2/7-9.30 Closed 25 Dec, L Mon-Sat
Prices Fixed D 3 course fr £30, Service optional **Wines** 23 bottles over £20, 42 bottles under £20, 6 by glass **Notes** Sunday L, Vegetarian available, Civ Wed 90 **Seats** 34, Pr/dining room 40 **Parking** 200

Bull Hotel

◉ Modern European **NEW**

Modernised classic dishes in a 17th-century coaching inn

☎ 01733 561364
Westgate PE1 1RB
e-mail: rooms@bull-hotel-peterborough.com
dir: Off A1, follow city centre signs. Hotel opposite Queensgate Shopping Centre. Car park on Broadway adjacent to library

The 17th-century Bull Hotel is in the Westgate area of town, where most of Peterborough's business and entertaining goes on. It's a characterful building that was once a coaching inn, and has at its heart a contemporary brasserie in muted pale colours with unclothed tables and a pleasingly informal air. Modern

spins on classic dishes are the favoured theme, though the classic dishes themselves may hail from far and wide. Smoked duck breast with a salad of spring onions, chilli and ginger in toasted sesame dressing kicks things off in Oriental style, and might be followed by lamb Wellington with pea mousse in shallot gravy, or sea bream on crab and chilli linguine in vegetable broth. Banish any thought of winter colds with a honey-and-lemon hot toddy, served as an accompaniment to lemon posset and gingerbread cake.

Chef Jason Ingram **Owner** Peel Hotels plc
Times 12-2/6.30-9.45 **Prices** Fixed D 3 course £19.50, Starter £6.50-£8.50, Main £14-£21.50, Dessert £6-£8 **Notes** Sunday L, Vegetarian available, Dress restrictions, Smart casual, Civ Wed 100 **Seats** 80, Pr/dining room 200 **Children** Portions **Parking** 100

ST NEOTS   Map 12 TL16

The George Hotel & Brasserie

◉◉ Modern British

Popular brasserie with well-judged dishes

☎ 01480 812300
High St, Buckden PE19 5XA
e-mail: mail@thegeorgebuckden.com
web: www.thegeorgebuckden.com
dir: Off A1, S of junct with A14

The George, with its distinctive frontage of timbering and columns, was originally a coaching inn and today combines a boutique hotel with a wine bar and brasserie-style restaurant (as well as a ladies' fashion shop). The Italian chef brings more than a hint of his homeland to the menus, from crayfish lasagne with white wine and basil velouté to properly roasted partridge with boar lardo, pearl barley orzotto, glazed beetroot and horseradish crème fraîche, a dish of great flavour combinations. Otherwise the menu combines a modern British approach with a classical perspective and an eye on the seasons: tempura squid with harissa and spring onion sauce, sirloin steak with Café de Paris butter, then vanilla crème brûlée, or grenadine-poached rhubarb with meringue and rhubarb sorbet.

Chef José Graziosi **Owner** Richard & Anne Furbank
Times 12-2.30/7-9.30 **Prices** Fixed L 2 course £15-£18, Starter £5.50-£9.50, Main £11.95-£24.95, Dessert £5.50-£7.50, Service optional **Wines** 75 bottles over £20, 14 bottles under £20, 18 by glass **Notes** Sunday L, Vegetarian available, Dress restrictions, Smart casual, Civ Wed 60 **Seats** 60, Pr/dining room 30 **Children** Portions **Parking** 25

STILTON
Map 12 TL18

Bell Inn Hotel

◉ British, French **V** ✋

Modish cooking in rambling old coaching inn

☎ 01733 241066
Great North Rd PE7 3RA
e-mail: reception@thebellstilton.co.uk
dir: A1(M) junct 16, follow Stilton signs. Hotel in village centre

Dick Turpin used to pop into this rambling mellow-stone old coaching inn, and no doubt he'd recognise the fireplaces and rustic beams if he walked in today. The first-floor restaurant might look familiar to him too, with its vaulted ceiling and impressive wooden staircase leading to a gallery. The menus are more cutting edge and cosmopolitan than the surroundings would suggest, though, with seared scallops appearing with black pudding, cauliflower purée and garlic sauce, and a main course of saffron-poached salmon fillet accompanied by herby lemon risotto and a trio of beetroot. The kitchen is led by the seasons, so expect game in winter - perhaps roast breast of guinea fowl with rocket and potato croquettes, tempura broccoli and redcurrant jus - and it comes as no surprise to see no fewer than six stiltons alongside desserts of chocolate tart with pistachio ice cream, or the creative-sounding coconut and lime risotto with chocolate sorbet.

Chef Robin Devonshire **Owner** Mr Liam McGivern
Times 12-2/7-9.30 Closed 25 Dec, 31 Dec, L Mon-Sat, D Sun **Prices** Fixed D 3 course £29.50-£37.35, Service optional **Wines** 30 bottles over £20, 30 bottles under £20, 8 by glass **Notes** Sunday L, Vegetarian menu, Dress restrictions, Smart casual, Civ Wed 100 **Seats** 60, Pr/dining room 20 **Children** Portions, Menu **Parking** 30

WANSFORD
Map 12 TL02

Orchards Restaurant at the Haycock Hotel

◉ British

Informal conservatory restaurant with appealing British cooking

☎ 01780 782223 & 781124
London Rd PE8 6JA
e-mail: linda.nicholson@thehaycock.co.uk
dir: In village centre accessible from A1/A47 intersection

The Haycock, a celebrated 17th-century coaching inn, is set in attractive grounds beside the River Nene. A familiar and welcoming sight for A1 travellers, it combines history and character and is now a popular business and leisure hotel. Public rooms are cosy with a log fire in the lounge, a quiet, comfortable library and a convivial bar. By contrast, Orchards is a relaxed, brasserie-style restaurant in the airy conservatory beyond the bar. Cooking focuses on grills and makes good use of local produce, with key suppliers listed on the menu. Tuck into chicken liver parfait with fruit chutney, followed by grilled lemon sole with capers and parsley butter, or a range of steak

dishes, perhaps rib-eye steak with peppercorn sauce, with sticky toffee pudding for dessert.

Times 12-2.30/6.30-9.30 Closed D Sun, 24 & 31 Dec

WISBECH
Map 12 TF40

The Crown Lodge Hotel

◉ Modern, Traditional ✋

All-comers' hotel menu in a converted car showroom

☎ 01945 773391
Downham Rd, Outwell PE14 8SE
e-mail: office@thecrownlodgehotel.co.uk
dir: 5m SE of Wisbech on A1122, 1m from junct with A1101, towards Downham Market

On the banks of Welle Creek at Outwell, just outside Wisbech, The Crown Lodge is a modern hotel that utilises what were the expansive spaces of a car showroom to resplendent effect. An open-plan bar, lounge and restaurant allows plenty of breathing space, and looks smart and modern. It's a popular local venue, and a glance at the all-encompassing menu, which ranges from light snacks to brasserie dishes of big appeal, reveals why. A salad of goats' cheese and beetroot dressed in red wine vinegar and walnut oil is one modish way to start, three scallops with minted pea purée and hollandaise another. Main course could be mozzarella-glazed gammon steak with a sun-dried tomato and olive salad, or lemon- and thyme-crusted salmon on creamy spinach with asparagus, while comfort is assured at the finishing line in the form of a warm chocolate brownie, offset by raspberry sorbet.

Chef Mick Castell **Owner** Mr W J Moore
Times 12-2.30/6-10 Closed 25-26 Dec, 1 Jan
Prices Starter £5-£8, Main £7-£24, Dessert £5-£6, Service optional **Wines** 58 bottles over £20, 13 bottles under £20, 12 by glass **Notes** Sunday L, Vegetarian available, Dress restrictions, Smart casual **Seats** 40, Pr/dining room 100 **Children** Portions, Menu **Parking** 50

CHESHIRE

ALDERLEY EDGE
Map 16 SJ87

The Alderley Restaurant

◉◉◉ – *see opposite*

BROXTON
Map 15 SJ45

Carden Park Hotel

◉ Modern British

Contemporary British cooking in a modern golfing hotel

☎ 01829 731000
CH3 9DQ
e-mail: reservations.carden@devere-hotels.com
dir: A41 signed Whitchurch to Chester, at Broxton rdbt turn on to A534 towards Wrexham. After 2m turn into Carden Park Estate

Part of the De Vere group, Carden Park is a massively-extended and redeveloped mock-Tudor extravaganza lost

among 1,000 acres of rolling green Cheshire countryside encompassing its own vineyard, two championship golf courses, a glitzy spa with 20 treatment rooms, and the expansive, split-level Redmonds Restaurant. In a smart modern setting of unclothed dark mahogany tables, leather armchairs and smart wicker chairs, choose from similarly contemporary ideas kicking off with the likes of terrine of haddock and smoked trout with leeks and shallots, served with dill crème fraîche and lemon dressing, ahead of an ambitious main course involving braised belly pork with chilli vegetable pickle, spiced plums, pork samosa, wasabi potato, carrot purée and oil.

Chef Graham Tinsley MBE **Owner** Carden Park Hotel LLP
Times 12.30-2.30/7-10 Closed L Mon-Sat, D Sun
Prices Food prices not confirmed for 2013. Please telephone for details **Wines** 114 bottles over £20, 5 bottles under £20, 15 by glass **Notes** Sunday L, Vegetarian available, Dress restrictions, Smart casual, no jeans or T-shirts, Civ Wed 400 **Seats** 300, Pr/dining room 80 **Children** Portions, Menu **Parking** 500

CHESTER
Map 15 SJ46

La Brasserie at The Chester Grosvenor

◉◉ Modern, European

Refined French-based brasserie cooking at the Grosvenor

☎ 01244 324024
Eastgate CH1 1LT
e-mail: restaurants@chestergrosvenor.co.uk
dir: A56 follow signs for city centre hotels. On Eastgate St next to the Eastgate clock Northgate St

La Brasserie is the more casual eating option at this local landmark hotel. Owned by the wealthiest Brit on the block, the Duke of Westminster, there was enough cash in the pot to pay for a revamp which has installed a Josper Grill burning sustainable Kentish coppice wood in the kitchen. In homage to classic Parisian brasseries, the staff bustle about in long aprons, and the setting is all mirrors and brass light fittings, black leather chairs and sleek granite tables beneath a hand-painted glass skylight. The kitchen looks to France for most of its ideas, but is not above rubbing shoulders with Italian and British concepts, so you might progress from potato ravioli with Barolo snails, parsley and bacon to Josper-grilled Welsh Black fillet steak with onion chips, scorched tomato, mushroom and béarnaise sauce, or Gressingham duck breast with leg meat pudding and sour plums. Spiced nougat glacé with quince and toasted pain d'épice is typical of the refined desserts.

Chef Simon Radley, John Retallick **Owner** Grosvenor - Duke of Westminster **Times** 12-10.30 Closed 25-26 Dec **Prices** Food prices not confirmed for 2013. Please telephone for details **Wines** 40 bottles over £20, 5 bottles under £20, 11 by glass **Notes** Vegetarian available **Seats** 80, Pr/dining room 250 **Children** Portions, Menu **Parking** 250, NCP attached to hotel

Save on Hotels. Book at **theAA.com/hotel**

CHESHIRE 83 ENGLAND

The Alderley Restaurant

ALDERLEY EDGE Map 16 SJ87

Modern, Traditional British V

Dynamic modern British cooking amid the Cheshire smart set

☎ 01625 583033
Alderley Edge Hotel, Macclesfield Rd SK9 7BJ
e-mail: reception@alderleyedgehotel.com
dir: A538 to Alderley Edge, then B5087 Macclesfield Rd

The Victorian captain of industry who picked out this spot to build his family home back in 1850 had a keen eye, but not even he could have predicted the village would become quite so desirable. The Edge, as the hotel is known, looks down through wooded slopes to the village which has become popular with affluent north-westerners and a footballer or two or three. The sylvan view from the conservatory dining room of The Alderley Restaurant is positively calming, and the service team do their level best to maintain the sense of harmony. By contrast, what turns up on the plate fizzes with creativity and reflects the very best of what might be regarded as modern British cooking. Plenty of fabulous local, regional and nationally renowned ingredients are used, and cooking techniques tend towards the à la mode. There's a six-course tasting menu, naturally, plus fixed-price lunch and market menus in support of the carte. All of the anticipated incidentals are present and correct - excellent canapés for example - and everything looks (as well as tastes) beautiful. First-course carpaccio of maple-cured pork neck with textures of new season apple and crackling 'popcorn' is a shining example of how to elevate a simple dish to something much more exciting, whilst maximum flavour is wrought from main-course Dunham Massey wood pigeon, cooked sous-vide and served with superb sloe gin and damson gel and charred breakfast radish. To finish, hot banana soufflé rises to the occasion perfectly, served with Cluizel chocolate ice cream (Cluizel being a top Parisian chocolatier). Do also give due consideration to the excellent English cheeses (Bertelin Blue and Mrs Bourne's mature Cheshire among them, perhaps), which come with Harrogate fruitcake, home-made biscuits and chutneys.

Chef Chris Holland **Owner** J W Lees (Brewers) Ltd **Times** 12-2/7-10 Closed 1 Jan, L 31 Dec, D 25-26 Dec **Prices** Fixed L 2 course £19.95, Fixed D 3 course £34.50, Tasting menu £58.50-£91.50, Starter £11.75-£12.50, Main £23.50-£23.80, Dessert £10.50, Service optional **Wines** 300 bottles over £20, 19 bottles under £20, 16 by glass **Notes** Sunday L, Vegetarian menu, Dress restrictions, Smart casual, Civ Wed 150 **Seats** 80, Pr/dining room 130 **Children** Portions, Menu **Parking** 82

CHESTER *continued*

Grosvenor Pulford Hotel & Spa

◎ Italian, European **NEW**

The flavours of Italy in a smart hotel

☎ 01244 570560
Wrexham Rd, Pulford CH4 9DG
e-mail: enquiries@grosvenorpulfordhotel.co.uk
dir: M53/A55 at junct signed A483 Chester/Wrexham &
North Wales. Left onto B5445, hotel 2m on right

The Grosvenor Pulford, in its own grounds a five-minute
drive from the city centre, is a luxury hotel, with Ciro's
brasserie at its heart. It's a remarkable room, light and
airy, with stucco paintwork, Romanesque arches and
murals. What's on offer is Italy's cuisine, with some other
influences along the way, all using fresh seasonal
produce. Terrine de prosciutto turns out to be pressed
game terrine with celeriac purée and mulled pear, or go
for twice-baked cheese soufflé with pickled beetroot and
rocket. Main courses show a kitchen on its game - well-
timed seared sea bass fillet and scallops with crisp basil
and spinach, tournedos Rossini, and pollo arrosto with
crisp pancetta and red wine sauce - as do desserts of
apple and cinnamon soufflé with a mini toffee apple.

Chef Leigh Myers **Owner** Harold & Susan Nelson
Times 12-2/6-9.30 Closed L Sat **Prices** Starter £5.10-
£9.95, Main £9.10-£28, Dessert £6.25, Service optional
Wines 21 bottles over £20, 12 bottles under £20, 10 by
glass **Notes** Sunday L, Vegetarian available, Civ Wed 250
Seats 120, Pr/dining room 200 **Children** Portions, Menu
Parking 200

Oddfellows

◎ Modern British

Skilful cooking in idiosyncratic hotel

☎ 01244 400001
20 Lower Bridge St CH1 1RS
e-mail: reception@oddfellows.biz

One whole wall in the restaurant at this Georgian hotel is
a window looking over 'Bedouin tents' outside; bare
wooden tables are set with candles and quality fittings,
staff dressed in black are friendly and knowledgeable,
and music beats out gently. The menu offers around half
a dozen choices at each course, the scope taking in ham
hock ballottine with home-made piccalilli, or smoked
salmon with beetroot, apple jelly and horseradish, then
roast fillet of cod, beautifully cooked, wrapped in Parma

ham served with flavourful mussel velouté and herby
crushed potatoes. Meat main courses are as well
handled: neck of lamb is flavoured with garlic, orange
and rosemary, slowly roasted and served with potatoes en
cocotte and creamed leeks. Presentation throughout is
slick, as seen in banana Tatin with walnut foam and
honey ice cream.

Chef Richard Allen **Owner** Oddfellows **Times** 12-3/5-10
Prices Food prices not confirmed for 2013. Please
telephone for details **Wines** 37 bottles over £20,
12 bottles under £20, 22 by glass **Notes** Vegetarian
available, Civ Wed 60 **Seats** 50, Pr/dining room 65
Children Portions, Menu **Parking** Pepper Street

Rowton Hall Country House Hotel

◎ British ◎

Classic menus in a Georgian manor

☎ 01244 335262
Whitchurch Rd, Rowton CH3 6AD
e-mail: reception@rowtonhallhotelandspa.co.uk
dir: M56 junct 12, A56 to Chester. At rdbt left onto A41
towards Whitchurch. Approx 1m, follow hotel signs

Just a couple of miles outside Chester's city walls,
Georgian Rowton Hall sits in eight acres of splendid
gardens. It still has all of the grand Adam fireplaces, oak
panelling and carved central staircase you would expect
in a house of this vintage, as well as a swanky health
and beauty spa to take care of the pampering angle. The
fetching blend of period elegance and restrained
contemporary style continues in the Langdale restaurant
with Lloyd Loom seating at linen-clothed tables on
wooden floors. The kitchen continues to deal in
straightforward dishes, offering among starters crab
ravioli with spinach and horseradish foam, and mains
that can be as classic as rib-eye steak with Pont-Neuf
potatoes, field mushrooms, watercress and horseradish
butter, or monkfish wrapped in Parma ham with Puy
lentils and buttered spinach. Puddings have the soothing
familiarity of apple crumble and sauce anglaise, or
vanilla crème brûlée with a sablé biscuit.

Chef Matthew Hulmes **Owner** Mr & Mrs Wigginton
Times 12-2/7-9.30 **Prices** Fixed L 3 course £13-£26,
Fixed D 3 course £19.95-£26.50, Starter £3.25-£7.95,
Main £9.95-£25, Dessert £4.50-£7.95, Service optional
Notes Sunday L, Vegetarian available, Dress restrictions,
Casually elegant, Civ Wed 170 **Seats** 70, Pr/dining room
120 **Children** Portions, Menu **Parking** 200

Simon Radley at The Chester Grosvenor

◎◎◎◎ – *see opposite*

– *see opposite*

CREWE Map 15 SJ75

Crewe Hall

◎ Modern European

Contemporary brasserie in a 17th-century stately home

☎ 01270 253333 & 259319
Weston Rd CW1 6UZ
e-mail: crewehall@qhotels.co.uk
dir: M6 junct 16 follow A500 to Crewe. Last exit at rdbt
onto A5020. 1st exit next rdbt to Crewe. Crewe Hall
150yds on right

Segueing from Jacobean architecture to 21st-century
design, Crewe Hall is a striking Grade I listed stately
home with period features in abundance. Have a drink in
the revolving bar before heading to the modern Brasserie
with its open-plan kitchen and classy modern European
repertoire based on good quality ingredients. A well-
executed confit of duck and pistachio terrine with quince
and cranberry chutney and rocket leaves makes for a
confident start, followed by haunch of venison with a
beetroot gratin and gingerbread sauce. Finish with
rhubarb and custard pannacotta.

Times All day

KNUTSFORD Map 15 SJ77

Cottons Hotel & Spa

◎ Modern British

Broadly appealing menus in modern surroundings

☎ 01565 650333
Manchester Rd WA16 0SU
e-mail: cottons@shirehotels.com
dir: On A50, 1m from M6 junct 19

Cottons is a large, modern hotel with extensive facilities,
including a restaurant that occupies two split-level
rooms, smartly decorated along clean cut contemporary
lines. Formal but friendly staff make recommendations as
they hand out menus and also inform guests about the
daily specials. The seasonally-changing carte offers
much to appeal, from well-timed, tender seared scallops
with pea purée and crisp pancetta, to roast rump of lamb
(served pink, as requested) with salsa verde and crushed
new potatoes. Gluten-free dishes are highlighted - among
them perhaps scallops and salmon with samphire and
saffron risotto - while puddings might run to crème
brûlée, or summer berry meringue sundae.

Times 12.15-2/7-9.30 Closed L Sat-Sun & BHs

Save on Hotels. Book at **theAA.com/hotel**

CHESHIRE 85 ENGLAND

Simon Radley at The Chester Grosvenor

CHESTER   Map 15 SJ46

Modern French V NOTABLE WINE LIST

Cooking of grand excitement at the north-west's premier address

☎ 01244 324024 & 895618
Chester Grosvenor & Spa, Eastgate CH1 1LT
e-mail: hotel@chestergrosvenor.co.uk
dir: A56 follow signs for city centre hotels. On Eastgate St next to the Eastgate clock

The Grosvenor is something of an architectural hodge-podge to look at, its mix of stone and brick façades surmounted by Tudor-style timbering. It stands within Chester's Roman walls, next to the city's landmark, the Eastgate Clock, and has been through several manifestations since its inception as an Elizabethan inn. Reinvented as The Grosvenor in the Victorian era, there can be few who don't know that today it houses what is surely the north-west's most opulent dining experience. Where others might have gone a-wandering, Simon Radley has kept the faith here over the years, and has turned the dining room from somewhere merely very good into a place of grand excitement. He has achieved this with a style of cooking that works with the grain of contemporary British philosophy, yet retains an exploratory edge that produces one revelation after another. The tasting menu remains the ideal, but any of its dishes may be taken individually too. A pairing of pork jowl and sea-fresh scallop strewn with fruit tabbouleh is a bravura opener, but the ante is soon raised when a superb avocado pannacotta, garnished with lobster and crab, turns up. A tribute to Burgundy brings together a garlicky snail, a huge garlicky cep mushroom, a wing of translucently pearly skate, and parsley purée of exhilarating intensity. Just as you imagine that each dish couldn't be topped, another arrives to make you think again, as when a serving of wild mallard, its fat beautifully rendered, comes with crunchy cherry granola, rich liver truffle and a scattering of winter berries. Radley firmly resists any temptation to take his foot off the gas at dessert stage, producing a technically astonishing Manjari chocolate cream, offset with burnt orange and mandarin accompaniments, or there may be a sublime Italianate sponge cake made with Chantenay carrots and Sicilian olive oil, its traditional toppings transfigured into a walnut croquant and cream cheese sorbet.

Chef Simon Radley, Ray Booker
Owner Grosvenor - Duke of Westminster
Times 6.30-9.30 Closed 25 Dec, 1 wk Jan, Sun-Mon, L all week (except Dec)
Prices Fixed D 3 course £69-£69, Tasting menu £90, Service added but optional 12.5%, Groups min service %
Wines 620 bottles over £20, 5 bottles under £20, 15 by glass **Notes** Tasting menu 8 course, Vegetarian menu, Dress restrictions, Smart dress, no shorts or sportswear, Civ Wed 250 **Seats** 45, Pr/dining room 240 **Parking** Car park attached to hotel (£10 24hrs)

KNUTSFORD *continued*

Mere Court Hotel & Conference Centre

🏵 Mediterranean, Modern British

Arts and Crafts style and accomplished modern cooking

☎ 01565 831000
Warrington Rd, Mere WA16 0RW
e-mail: sales@merecourt.co.uk
web: www.merecourt.co.uk
dir: A50, 1m W of junct with A556, on right

Mere Court, built in 1903, is a perfect example of the Arts and Crafts style, seen internally in wood carving, metalwork and stained glass. The Arboreum Restaurant is a fine room with beams, panelling, a stone fireplace and views over the lake. The kitchen focuses on the repertory of modern British dishes, turning out ham hock terrine with piccalilli purée and pork crackling, and pan-fried chicken breast with parsley risotto, fennel purée, truffled vinaigrette and beetroot crisps. But it shows flexibility too, so before beef Rossini may come tempura prawns with authentic Thai green sauce, or duck spring roll, with white chocolate pannacotta with basil ice cream to round things off.

Owner Mr Chawla **Times** 12-2/7-9.30 **Prices** Starter £5.95-£7.95, Main £11.50-£19.95, Dessert £6.50-£7.50, Service included **Wines** 35 bottles over £20, 15 bottles under £20, 4 by glass **Notes** Sunday L, Vegetarian available, Dress restrictions, Smart casual **Seats** 40, Pr/dining room 150 **Children** Portions, Menu **Parking** 150

LYMM Map 15 SJ68

RESTAURANT OF THE YEAR FOR ENGLAND

The Church Green British Grill

🏵🏵 Modern British

A class act in a refurbished village pub

☎ 01925 752068
Higher Ln WA13 0AP
dir: M6 junct 20 follow signs for Lymm on B5158 after 1.5m right at T-junct onto A56 towards Altrincham, on right after 0.5m

Aiden Byrne is a modern media-savvy British chef par excellence. Having made his bones in A-list kitchens - Tom Aikens, Pied à Terre, and the Grill at the Dorchester,

among others - he has become a well-known face on the telly, written a cookbook and set up on his own account in The Church Green, a stylishly reinvented old pub in a Cheshire village. Inside is the bare brickwork, natural wood, leather seating and neutral hues you'd expect in a contemporary gastro set-up, and his partner Sarah presides over a switched-on front-of-house team. Byrne stays in touch with the zeitgeist, so in order to chime with the prevailing mood of belt-tightening austerity, he reined in the culinary concept from fine dining to a 'British Grill' with a simplified, more everyman appeal in 2012. Be assured, though, that the same uncompromising approach to sourcing the finest local and seasonal ingredients still drives the operation. There are homely classics - steak and kidney pudding, beef hotpot, sausages and mash - or potted Lancashire shrimps, a traditional dish brought bang up to date by adding nutmeg mayonnaise, toasted sourdough bread and apple and watercress salad to the deal. Seared over coconut husk charcoal on the Inka grill, 28-day dry-aged steaks sourced from small Cheshire farms are exemplary, as witnessed in a perfectly-timed and well-rested rib-eye with bonbons of bone marrow and stilton, beef dripping chips and béarnaise sauce. For those wanting to dig deeper into Byrne's culinary capacities, take a bunch of pals for the four-course 'Great British' menu, which must be shared by the whole table.

Times 12-3/6-9.30 Closed 25 Dec

NANTWICH Map 15 SJ65

Rookery Hall Hotel & Spa

🏵🏵 Modern British

Modern country-house cooking in parkland-set hotel

☎ 0845 0727 533
Main Rd, Worleston CW5 6DQ
e-mail: rookeryhall@handpicked.co.uk
dir: B5074 off 4th rdbt, on Nantwich by-pass. Hotel 1.5m on right

Dating from 1816, this grand mansion combines all the amenities of a modern hotel with the sumptuous panelled interiors of yesteryear, its restaurant a splendid room, with chandeliers in the corniced ceiling, and high-backed seats at crisp-clothed tables. The kitchen works around the modern country-house idiom, its technical skills evident in such starters as breast of wood pigeon on a bubble-and-squeak cake with cider cream, and onion soufflé with matching velouté and pungent herb salad. Produce is of a high quality - Holker Estate red deer, Herdwick mutton (cannon with slow-cooked breast and a shallot Tatin, for instance), and fish from Cornwall, the last seen in a labour-intensive main course of sea bass with smoked haddock rösti, chorizo, roast fennel and vanilla hollandaise. Fruit is often mobilised in desserts: a theme on rhubarb, say, or orange, or a prettily presented, tangy raspberry cheesecake with lemon and ginger ice cream.

Chef Mark Walker **Owner** Hand Picked Hotels
Times 12-2/7-9.30 Closed L Sat **Prices** Food prices not confirmed for 2013. Please telephone for details **Wines** 160 bottles over £20, 20 bottles under £20, 16 by

glass **Notes** Sunday L, Vegetarian available, Dress restrictions, Smart casual, no jeans or trainers, Civ Wed 200 **Seats** 90, Pr/dining room 150 **Children** Portions, Menu **Parking** 100

PECKFORTON Map 15 SJ55

1851 Restaurant at Peckforton Castle

🏵🏵 Modern British, French 🏵

Conceptual-art cookery in a Victorian medieval fortress

☎ 01829 260930
Stonehouse Ln CW6 9TN
e-mail: info@peckfortoncastle.co.uk
dir: 15m from Chester, situated near Tarporley

The castle, we are asked to note, is not to be thought of as pastiche in any way. It is a real medieval fortress, constructed to withstand besieging hordes, that just happens to have been built for a Victorian peer of the realm. The date of its completion is celebrated in the name of the restaurant, just the place to repair to after a morning's consorting with Peckforton's resident birds of prey. This vaulted stone fastness feels as secure as a nuclear bomb-shelter, and was once the private quarters of its owner. Deep-pile carpets and thick napery add to the sense of stolidity, but the cooking is the chink in the armour by which the modern world breaks in. And how. A list of dishes with titles like conceptual artworks may include Orange Duck Inside Out (whipped Jaffa parfait, cured ginger and pain d'épice accompany orange-stuffed confit in a bold starter), and Porcine Top to Bottom, incorporating slow-cooked ventrèche, roast trotter and caramelised head compression with Granny Smith 'bits'. If this approach feels likely to bring you out in a caramelised head compression, let it be said that the precision-engineering of the food works to good effect, and the prime materials are impeccable. And to finish, Muscovado caramel pannacotta comes with textural variations of banana, including a crunchy fritter.

Chef Mark Ellis **Owner** Naylor Family **Times** 12-9/6-9 Closed L Mon-Sat **Prices** Fixed L 2 course £19.95, Fixed D 3 course £24.95-£39, Service optional **Wines** 40 bottles over £20, 12 bottles under £20, 9 by glass **Notes** Sunday L, Vegetarian available, Dress restrictions, Smart casual, no trainers **Seats** 60, Pr/dining room 165 **Children** Portions, Menu **Parking** 100

PUDDINGTON Map 15 SJ37

Macdonald Craxton Wood

🏵🏵 Modern British

Smart British cooking and top-notch ingredients

☎ 0151 347 4000 & 0844 879 9038
Parkgate Rd, Ledsham CH66 9PB
e-mail: info@craxton.macdonald-hotels.co.uk
dir: from M6 take M56 towards N Wales, then A5117/A540 to Hoylake. Hotel on left 200yds past lights

The eponymous woodland is 27 acres of leafy grounds that surround this traditional hotel, which now sports a

Save on Hotels. Book at **theAA.com/hotel**

CHESHIRE 87 ENGLAND

new restaurant backed by a starry chef - the Aiden Byrne British Grill. The style is smart and understated as suggested by the 'grill' tag, so slate and grey tones, photos on the walls pointing up the direction of the menu (lots of local agricultural scenes and farm animals aplenty), and bare tables. The efficient service team is smartly turned out in long aprons. There are plenty of classics on the menu (fish and chips the trad way), a Josper Grill to max out the flavours in the steaks (and lamb and duck), plus sharing platters and well-judged main courses such as slow-cooked pork belly with exemplary crackling, thyme mash, roasted apple and broccoli. Top quality ingredients shine through in dishes presented in a fashionable manner - think slate bread boards and a richly flavoured chicken liver parfait served in a jar, alongside toasted brioche, truffle Madeira jelly and sweet onion marmalade. The ideas are straightforward enough, but the level of technical skill on display is high. Rice pudding mousse with raspberries and cream makes a highly satisfying finish.

Times 6-9.30 Closed L all week

SANDIWAY
Map 15 SJ67

Nunsmere Hall Country House Hotel

◉◉ British, European ☺

Accomplished modern cooking in plush restaurant

☎ 01606 889100
Tarporley Rd, Oakmere CW8 2ES
e-mail: reservations@nunsmere.co.uk
dir: M6 junct 18, A54 to Chester, at x-rds with A49 turn left towards Tarporley, hotel 2m on left

Dating from the turn of the last century, this mansion is surrounded on three sides by a 60-acre lake. It's now a luxury country-house hotel, its Crystal Restaurant, which overlooks the south-facing terrace and sunken Italian garden, a room of distinction, with yards of fabrics everywhere, an intricate ceiling, gilt-framed mirrors and a wooden floor topped by a rug. The kitchen sources materials conscientiously and corrals them into well-conceived dishes that are never unnecessarily fussy. Start off with potted shrimps with potato salad and pickled cucumber, or a subtly flavoured warm salad of baby leeks, chorizo, parmesan and a soft-boiled egg drizzled with truffle oil, before a gutsy main course like slowly braised shin of beef served with horseradish mash and bourguignon-style sauce. Lemon sole is cooked with pinpoint accuracy and comes with a light truffle and parsley butter served with spring onion mash and French-style beans, and to crown proceedings may be a prettily presented dessert like dark chocolate mousse with chocolate sponge, cherry sorbet and jelly, and sour cream parfait.

Chef Craig Malone **Owner** Prima Hotels
Times 12-2/7-9.30 **Prices** Fixed L 2 course fr £16.95, Fixed D 3 course fr £34.50, Service added but optional 12.5% **Wines** 140 bottles over £20, 3 bottles under £20, 15 by glass **Notes** Tasting menu available, Sunday L, Vegetarian available, Dress restrictions, No jeans, trainers or shorts, Civ Wed 80 **Seats** 60, Pr/dining room 80 **Children** Portions, Menu **Parking** 80

TARPORLEY
Map 15 SJ56

Macdonald Portal Hotel Golf & Spa

◉◉ Modern British

Sophisticated country-club setting for classic cuisine

☎ 0844 879 9082
Cobbiers Cross Ln CW6 0DJ
e-mail: general.portal@macdonald-hotels.co.uk
dir: Off A49 in village of Tarporley

With three courses spread around its expansive acreages of rolling Cheshire countryside, it is odds-on that most guests are up for a spot of golf at this upscale contemporary hotel, and those not bearing a weighty bag of clubs will no doubt be heading for some serious pampering in the glossy spa. Named after the 12th century Earl of Chester who built nearby Beeston Castle, the classy Ranulf Restaurant has a clubby feel thanks to a butch décor of sleek contemporary wall panelling, tobacco-hued leather banquettes and bare darkwood tables, softened by romantic candlelight in the evening. The kitchen sources its materials well, and has the sense not to faff around with them, offering among starters Stornoway black pudding with caramelised apple and bacon salad, or fishcakes with caper mayonnaise. Main courses continue the theme of tried-and-true classics - Scottish sirloin or rib-eye steaks sizzling from the grill, or pan-fried fillet of wild sea bass with new potatoes and seasonal greens. Puds are equally comforting - perhaps Eton Mess or a straight-up crème brûlée.

Chef Kevin Hay **Owner** Macdonald Hotels **Times** 6-9.30 Closed L all week **Prices** Fixed D 3 course £31, Starter £5-£7.95, Main £10.50-£19, Dessert £5.50-£7.50, Service optional **Wines** 59 bottles over £20, 6 bottles under £20, 19 by glass **Notes** Early bird available before 7pm, Sunday L, Vegetarian available, Dress restrictions, Smart casual, Civ Wed 250 **Seats** 100, Pr/dining room 45 **Children** Portions, Menu **Parking** 200

WARMINGHAM
Map 15 SJ76

The Bear's Paw

◉ Modern European **NEW**

Refined gastro-pub cooking near Crewe

☎ 01270 526317
School Ln CW11 3QN
e-mail: info@thebearspaw.co.uk
web: www.thebearspaw.co.uk
dir: M6 junct 17, A534, A533 signed Middlewich & Northwich. Continue on A533, left into Mill Ln, left into Warmingham Ln. Right into Plant Ln, left into Green Ln

In a village just outside Crewe, The Bear's Paw is a large inn with a stylish open-plan layout and lots of wood: floor, panelling, bare tables. Candles, flowers and prints on the walls add character, and there's a lounge area with tub leather-look chairs and a log fire. The menus are conventional enough, with few surprises, but the kitchen sources the best materials it can find, free-range whenever possible, and treats them with integrity. Pan-fried calves' liver, with bacon, creamy mash and onion gravy, is given a lift from deep-fried haggis, and there may be baked hake fillet with samphire, tomato ragout and paprika-spiced potato. Some dishes can be ordered as a starter or a main - salmon and smoked haddock fishcake with tartare sauce, for instance - and to finish there may be a copybook example of vanilla crème brûlée.

Chef Mark Brooks **Owner** Harold & Susan Nelson
Times 12-9.30 **Prices** Starter £4.75-£8.95, Main £9.95-£23.95, Dessert £4.25-£9.95, Service optional **Wines** 26 bottles over £20, 16 bottles under £20, 10 by glass **Notes** Sunday L, Vegetarian available **Seats** 150 **Children** Portions, Menu **Parking** 75

WILMSLOW Map 16 SJ88

Stanneylands Hotel

◎◎ Modern British

Well-executed British food in smart country hotel

☎ 01625 525225
Stanneylands Rd SK9 4EY
e-mail: sales@stanneylandshotel.co.uk
dir: from M56 at airport turn off, follow signs to
Wilmslow. Left into Station Rd, onto Stanneylands Rd.
Hotel on right

From its humble origins in the 18th century as a
farmhouse, Stanneylands has ascended the social ladder
to trade as a relaxing country hotel handy for Manchester
airport and for forays into the city centre. With its oak
panelling and well-drilled, professional staff, the
restaurant makes an intimate setting for a well-
conceived repertoire of modern ideas appealing to classic
culinary sensibilities. Ham hock and parsley terrine with
home-made piccalilli is a guaranteed crowd pleaser - as
long as it is done well - and this example hits all the
right notes. Next up, seared venison tenderloin with
caramelised shallots, curly kale, Vichy carrots and
Madeira jus delivers a fine depth of flavours; to finish,
warm cherry Bakewell tart with clotted cream could
hardly do more to oblige.

Chef Richard Maun **Owner** Mr L Walshe
Times 12-2.30/7-9.45 **Prices** Food prices not confirmed
for 2013. Please telephone for details **Wines** 102 bottles
over £20, 4 bottles under £20, 15 by glass **Notes** Tasting
menu available, Vegetarian available, Dress restrictions,
Smart casual, Civ Wed 120 **Seats** 60, Pr/dining room 120
Children Portions, Menu **Parking** 110

CORNWALL & ISLES OF SCILLY

BODMIN Map 2 SX06

Trehellas House Hotel & Restaurant

◎ Modern European V

**Cornish produce put to good effect in converted
courthouse**

☎ 01208 72700
Washaway PL30 3AD
e-mail: enquiries@trehellashouse.co.uk
dir: Take A389 from Bodmin towards Wadebridge. Hotel
on right 0.5m beyond road to Camelford

Trehellas House has worn a few hats over the years since
it was built in the early 18th century: initially an inn that
also served as the local court house (trials must have
been entertaining after a few flagons of ale...), then a
farm, and a pub once more in the '70s. Nowadays it has
traded up to a country-house hotel with an appealing
restaurant, where low beams and slate-flagged floors set
the scene for punchy modern cooking. Effective dishes
are delivered without undue fuss, and Cornish produce is
at the heart of it all. Start with partridge and juniper
casserole with peppercorn rice and parsnip crisps,
followed by St Ives Bay sea bass with ginger, lemon and

pepper linguine and mussel cream. Artisan Cornish
cheeses are hard to resist, but the incurably sweet of
tooth might finish with sticky toffee pudding with toffee
sauce and clotted cream.

Chef Tim Parsons **Owner** Alistair & Debra Hunter
Times 12-2/6.30-9 **Prices** Fixed L 2 course fr £11.95,
Starter £6-£10, Main £12-£22, Dessert £6-£8, Service
included **Wines** 7 bottles over £20, 24 bottles under £20,
6 by glass **Notes** Sunday L, Vegetarian menu **Seats** 40
Children Portions, Menu **Parking** 25

BOSCASTLE Map 2 SX09

The Wellington Hotel

◎ Modern British **NEW**

Stylish modern cooking in popular fishing village

☎ 01840 250202
The Harbour PL35 0AQ
e-mail: info@wellingtonhotelboscastle.com
dir: A30, A395 at Davidstowe follow Boscastle signs.
B3266 to village. Right into Old Rd

Overlooking the small harbour of the fishing village, this
former coaching inn, with a ground-floor bar and upstairs
restaurant, dates from the 16th century, making it one of
the oldest in the county. It got its name from the Iron
Duke, so it's no surprise that the restaurant is called The
Waterloo. On offer is a slab of ideas in the familiar
modern style of crab salad with peas, apple and vanilla,
and a main course of monkfish with oxtail, butternut
squash and curried bisque. Herbs and vegetables come
from the hotel garden, fish from the harbour, and meat
from local farms - spring lamb, say, with cauliflower,
pickled pears and liquorice - and the kitchen does a fair
bit of foraging, flavouring pannacotta with gorse flowers
and serving it with banana and popcorn ice cream.

Chef Isaac Robb **Owner** Cornish Coastal Hotels Ltd
Times 6.30-9.30 Closed L all week, D Tue **Prices** Food
prices not confirmed for 2013. Please telephone for
details **Wines** 25 bottles over £20, 25 bottles under £20,
10 by glass **Notes** Vegetarian available **Seats** 35, Pr/
dining room 28 **Children** Portions, Menu **Parking** 15

BUDE Map 2 SS20

The Castle Restaurant

◎ Modern European

Wharfside castle with good, honest fare

☎ 01288 350543
The Wharf EX23 8LG
e-mail: enquiries@thecastlerestaurantbude.co.uk
web: www.thecastlerestaurantbude.co.uk
dir: From A39 into Bude at mini-rdbt go straight ahead
along The Crescent. Then 1st right to The Castle Heritage
Centre. Restaurant within centre

Bude Castle is now an arts and heritage centre and also
houses this small, busy restaurant, which has more the
feel of a bistro, with lots of bare wood, compactly spaced
tables and efficient, chatty staff. The menu hints of a
bistro too, taking in as it does tasty ham hock terrine with
onion jam, crispy duck confit with truffled jus, mash and
broad beans, and crème brûlée, although there's also a
tasting menu if you want to spread your wings, ranging
from fried scallops with cauliflower purée and curry oil,
and rump of beef with salt beef cottage pie and greens.
Produce is judiciously sourced, from a beautifully fresh
portion of hake in beer batter with sauce gribiche and
chips, to a platter of local cheeses.

Chef Kit Davis **Owner** Kit Davis **Times** 12-2.30/6-9.30
Closed D Sun **Prices** Fixed L 2 course £12.50, Starter
£5.50-£7.50, Main £14.50-£18.50, Dessert £5.50-£6.50,
Service optional **Wines** 4 bottles over £20, 15 bottles
under £20, 7 by glass **Notes** Tasting menu available,
Sunday L, Vegetarian available, Civ Wed 100 **Seats** 40,
Pr/dining room 60 **Children** Portions, Menu
Parking Parking nearby

CALLINGTON   Map 3 SX36

Langmans Restaurant

◎◎ Modern British ◔

Pedigree local produce on a six-course tasting menu

☎ 01579 384933
3 Church St PL17 7RE
e-mail: dine@langmansrestaurant.co.uk
dir: From the direction of Plymouth into town centre, left at lights and second right into Church St

The Butterys have carved out a glittering reputation for themselves at their highly singular restaurant in this pleasant market town, drawing custom in from Plymouth and beyond. Hung about with work by local artists, and driven by produce from local growers and farmers, it's a distinctively regional operation, and distinctive too in that the format is a six-course tasting menu for all. Most of this is table d'hôte, perhaps opening with a portion of 36-hour pork belly with a strip of crunchy crackling and Cox's apple purée. A soup could be rich and silky butternut squash topped with a halved scallop, before the fish course, a serving of beautifully timed brill with salsify and oyster mushrooms in a creamy sauce. Meat may well offer a choice, maybe chump of lamb sauced with red wine and star anise, or truffled beef sirloin, with a showboat of wonderful vegetables. Pause for some West Country cheeses, and then set about the dessert trio, served on a compartmented glass plate - chocolate tart, passionfruit and chocolate tower, and rhubarb and ginger cheesecake, served with variously complementary ice creams.

Chef Anton Buttery **Owner** Anton & Gail Buttery
Times 7.30 Closed Sun-Wed, L all week **Prices** Tasting menu £37.50, Service optional **Wines** 50 bottles over £20, 34 bottles under £20, 11 by glass **Notes** Tasting menu 6 course, Vegetarian available, Dress restrictions, Smart casual preferred **Seats** 24 **Parking** Town centre car park

FALMOUTH   Map 2 SW83

Falmouth Hotel

◎ Modern British **NEW** V

Victorian coastal hotel with confident cooking

☎ 01326 312671
Castle Beach TR11 4NZ
e-mail: reservations@falmouthhotel.com
dir: A30 to Truro then A390 to Falmouth. Follow signs for beaches, hotel on seafront near Pendennis Castle

The Victorian Grande Dame of Falmouth's coastline stands in a commanding position overlooking Pendennis Castle, the sandy beaches and the sea. In case the splendid view out of the window isn't enough, model ships and maritime pictures remind you of the port's seagoing heritage in the Trelawney dining room, where the kitchen draws on fine Cornish and West Country produce for its repertoire of modern dishes. Expect Cornish seafood terrine with lemon and dill crème fraîche, followed by pan-fried cutlets and braised shoulder of lamb with rosemary mash, sweet red cabbage and broad

bean jus. Given the location, you may be in the mood for fish - perhaps red wine-poached brill fillet with wild mushroom risotto, sautéed salsify, and Merlot. Local cheeses or bitter lemon tart with orange marmalade and Cornish clotted cream provide a satisfying finish.

Chef Mark Aldred **Owner** Richardson Hotels of Distinction
Times 12-2/6.45-8.45 **Prices** Fixed D 3 course £26, Starter £4-£9, Service optional **Wines** 21 bottles over £20, 29 bottles under £20, 7 by glass **Notes** Sunday L, Vegetarian menu **Seats** 150, Pr/dining room 40 **Children** Portions, Menu **Parking** 65

The Greenbank Hotel

◎ Modern British

Wide sea views and a strong line in seafood

☎ 01326 312440
Harbourside TR11 2SR
e-mail: sales@greenbank-hotel.co.uk
dir: Approaching Falmouth from Penryn, take left along North Parade. Follow sign to Falmouth Marina and Greenbank Hotel

The hotel is right on the water of the Fal Estuary, with a large terrace and wrap-around windows in the restaurant giving wide-angled harbour views. This is a pleasant room, with a relaxed vibe, slat-backed chairs with padded seats at decently spaced tables, and a menu that focuses, but not exclusively so, on seafood, with good materials sourced locally. There's variety aplenty too, with starters ranging from the luxury of lobster and crab cocktail with a shot of Bloody Mary to Thai-style fishcakes with miso dip and pickled ginger. Creditable main courses have included well-timed black bream with asparagus, red peppers, white bean purée and pea shoots, and slow-roast pork belly with soba noodles, hot-and-sour broth, and pak choi cooked with peanuts. Among enterprising puddings might be elderflower and lemon posset, served with sea buckthorn sorbet and vanilla-flavoured apricots.

Times 12-2/7-9.15

The Royal Duchy Hotel

◎◎ Modern International

Simple modern dishes overlooking Falmouth Bay

☎ 01326 313042
Cliff Rd TR11 4NX
e-mail: info@royalduchy.co.uk
web: www.brend-hotels.co.uk
dir: on Cliff Rd, along Falmouth seafront

The grandiose grey Royal Duchy Hotel sits proudly between the town and the beach, gazing imperiously across the bay towards Pendennis Castle. Inside is a classic example of seaside splendour, with a light, expansive dining room done in vibrant plum enjoying those maritime views. Book a table on the terrace itself for the ultimate in summer-evening dining. The food is largely simple and modern, with some appealing combinations. Start with beetroot-cured salmon with marinated baby vegetables and micro-herbs, and then choose from the likes of glazed duck leg with pear purée in date and grape jus, or wild mushroom fricassée with spinach and baby onions. Rounding things off might be lemon mousse with kalamansi ice cream and chocolate syrup, or a plate of West Country cheeses.

Chef John Mijatovic **Owner** Brend Hotel Group
Times 12.30-2/6-9 Closed L Mon-Sat **Prices** Food prices not confirmed for 2013. Please telephone for details **Wines** 16 by glass **Notes** Sunday L, Vegetarian available, Dress restrictions, Smart casual, Civ Wed 150 **Seats** 100, Pr/dining room 24 **Children** Portions, Menu **Parking** 40

The Fowey Hotel

⊛ Modern European V

Modern European food with calming harbour views

☎ 01726 832551
The Esplanade PL23 1HX
e-mail: info@thefoweyhotel.co.uk
web: www.richardsonhotels.co.uk
dir: A30 to Okehampton, continue to Bodmin. Then B3269
to Fowey for 1m, on right bend left junct then right into
Dagands Rd. Hotel 200mtrs on left

Fowey is the sort of Cornish town whose narrow streets of
crooked houses and shops tumbling towards the River
Fowey estuary make it great simply to amble around. If
you fancy making a pitstop to dine on excellent local
produce, including fish and seafood landed fresh
practically on the doorstep, keep an eye out for the
handsome Victorian hotel lording it from its perch amid
landscaped gardens with lovely panoramic views across
the water to Polruan village. Its dining room basks in
those splendid watery vistas, while the kitchen delivers
an upbeat repertoire of simple classic combinations that
seek to soothe rather then challenge the palate. Expect
pan-seared mackerel with carrot salad and sauce vierge,
ahead of roast monkfish with smoked haddock brandade,
braised red cabbage, broad beans, and mint jus, and
wind things up with the comfort of steamed orange
sponge pudding with crème anglaise.

Chef Mark Griffiths **Owner** Keith Richardson
Times 12-3/6.30-9 **Prices** Fixed D 3 course £35, Service
optional **Wines** 50 bottles over £20, 13 bottles under £20,
15 by glass **Notes** Sunday L, Vegetarian menu, Dress
restrictions, Smart casual, no torn denim, trainers,
shorts, Civ Wed 70 **Seats** 60, Pr/dining room 24
Children Portions, Menu **Parking** 20

Cormorant Hotel & Restaurant

⊛⊛ Modern British

Appealing Cornish cooking with glorious river views

☎ 01726 833426
PL23 1LL
e-mail: relax@cormoranthotel.co.uk
dir: A390 onto B3269 signed Fowey. In 3m left to Golant,
through village to end of road, hotel on right

Perched on the Fowey estuary, with glorious views over
the river from a decked outdoor seating area as well as
the ground-floor dining room, the Cormorant represents
the distilled essence of Cornwall. Well-spaced linen-clad
tables and a bare floor help the bright, airy feel indoors,
as do the properly informed staff. The kitchen doesn't
attempt anything too showy, but the team cooks
confidently within itself to produce fresh, appealing
dishes based on fine prime materials. A fillet of mackerel
arrives with braised fennel and brown shrimps in an
assertive orange syrup, while mains move on to braised
shoulder and seared cutlet of local lamb, served with
good dauphinoise and two textures of peas - crushed and
puréed. An enterprising fish dish might be seared salmon
with saffron pineapple in chicken jus with purple
sprouting broccoli, and desserts make the most of
appetising fruit combinations, as in caramelised lemon
tart with lime posset, kiwi sorbet and passionfruit coulis.

Chef Martin Adams **Owner** Mrs Mary Tozer
Times 12-2/6.30-9.30 Closed L Nov-Feb **Prices** Starter
£6-£11, Main £14-£22, Dessert £6-£10, Service optional,
Groups min 7 service 12% **Wines** 41 bottles over £20,
30 bottles under £20, 6 by glass **Notes** Tasting menu,
incl vegetarian 6 course, Vegetarian available, Dress
restrictions, Smart casual, no shorts **Seats** 30
Children Portions **Parking** 20

New Yard Restaurant

⊛⊛ Modern British ⊛

Quality local produce and confident modern cooking

☎ 01326 221595
Trelowarren Estate, Mawgan TR12 6AF
e-mail: kirsty.newyardrestaurant@trelowarren.com
web: www.trelowarren.com
dir: 5m from Helston

Trelowarren, on the Lizard Peninsula, is a working estate
of 1,000 acres, plus tourist accommodation, and The New
Yard is at its heart. It's been converted from the coach
house, the old arched doorways now windows looking over
the courtyard with its olive trees in giant pots. Almost 90
per cent of the kitchen's produce comes from within a 10-
mile radius, with vegetables, herbs, fruit and game from
the estate itself, the last appearing as a main course of
roast pheasant wrapped in pancetta. The kitchen tends to
keep things simple, and there's a strong comfort factor to
its output: pork belly with braised red cabbage and
celeriac, for instance, or spicy monkfish tail with
cauliflower, lentils and curry oil. More voguish ideas are
equally well handled, seen in starters of crab tortellini
with fennel and apple salad, and curd cheese and
beetroot salad. At dessert stage, a theme on lemon
(posset, cake, tart and sorbet) might fight for attention
with warm chocolate mousse.

Chef Olly Jackson **Owner** Sir Ferrers Vyvyan
Times 12-2/7-9 Closed Mon (mid Sep-Whitsun), D Sun
Prices Fixed L 2 course £20, Fixed D 3 course £27, Starter
£6.50-£10, Main £15-£21, Dessert £6.50-£7.50, Service
optional **Wines** 55 bottles over £20, 7 bottles under £20,
6 by glass **Notes** Sunday L, Vegetarian available, Dress
restrictions, Smart casual **Seats** 50 **Children** Portions
Parking 20

LIZARD   Map 2 SW71

Housel Bay Hotel & Restaurant

◉ Modern British V ✪

Modern British cooking on the Cornish coast

☎ 01326 290417 & 290917
Housel Cove TR12 7PG
e-mail: info@houselbay.com
dir: A30 from Exeter, exit Truro and take A34/A394 to
Helston & A3083 to Lizard

The Victorians who built Housel Bay Hotel weren't scared
of a bit of hard work: the substantial pile was literally
carved out of stone taken from the clifftop on which it
stands. The site was chosen by local bigwigs keen to
attract visitors to the area when the very concept of
tourism was in its infancy, and boy did they choose a
cracker of a spot, lording it over the eponymous bay with
views across the Lizard Peninsula to its lighthouse.
Whether you're after a pitstop along the South West
Coastal Path or turning up the easy way by car along the
country lanes, the place offers a friendly welcome and
up-to-date dining in a bright and breezy restaurant with
bare darkwood floors and sage-green walls hung liberally
with wartime memorabilia. With the Atlantic crashing on
the rocks below, thoughts turn inevitably to seafood,
which may be present in the shape of pan-seared
scallops teamed creatively with peppered sour apple
salad, young radishes, and caviar vinaigrette, followed by
slow-roasted fillet of John Dory with creamed colcannon
mash, samphire, and clam and buttermilk ragoût.
Otherwise, meatier appetites might be assuaged by roast
rack of lamb with lemon-glazed sweetbreads, stuffed
rösti, wilted spinach and mint.

Chef Raimonds Eiemelis **Owner** Mr & Mrs Mesropians
Times 12-2.30/7-9.30 Closed Jan **Prices** Fixed L 2 course
£19-£26.45, Fixed D 3 course £29.45-£36.95, Service
optional **Wines** 7 bottles over £20, 31 bottles under £20,
12 by glass **Notes** ALC 2 course £27, 3 course £32,
Sunday L, Vegetarian menu, Dress restrictions, Smart
Casual **Seats** 70 **Children** Portions **Parking** 25

LOOE   Map 2 SX25

Barclay House

◉◉ Modern British V ✪

Coastal cuisine with exquisite sea views

☎ 01503 262929
St Martin's Rd PL13 1LP
e-mail: info@barclayhouse.co.uk
dir: 1st house on left on entering Looe from A38

Colourful artworks and blond-wood seats at crisp linen-
clad tables set a bright tone in the dining room of Barclay
House, a snow-white country villa perched on the sylvan
hillsides above Looe harbour. Those keen on keeping food
miles to an absolute minimum will be heartened to learn
that the fish and seafood comes fresh off the day boats
down on the quayside, and the kitchen has Cornish
produce as an abiding theme in its light and punchy
cooking. On the seafood front, dishes range from Looe

Bay scallops with pea purée, chorizo and organic
watercress, to Fowey River mussels steamed in Cornish
Orchards cider with shallots, garlic, thyme and cream,
while West Country meat could be represented by local
duck breast with truffled mash, braised red cabbage, and
red wine and blackberry jus. The deep comfort of a
saffron bread-and-butter pudding becomes more
indulgent still with the addition of a dollop of Cornish
clotted cream, and there's a Cornish cheeseboard too,
served with onion marmalade.

Chef Joe Sardari **Owner** Malcolm, Graham & Gill Brooks
Times 7-9 Closed Sun, L all week (except by arrangement)
Prices Fixed D 4 course £32-£45, Tasting menu £39,
Service added but optional 10% **Wines** 34 bottles over
£20, 11 bottles under £20, 11 by glass **Notes** Tasting
menu 6 course, Vegetarian menu, Dress restrictions,
Smart casual, Civ Wed 70 **Seats** 60 **Children** Portions,
Menu **Parking** 25

Trelaske Hotel & Restaurant

◉◉ Modern British ✪

Local produce in verdant Cornwall

☎ 01503 262159
Polperro Rd PL13 2JS
e-mail: info@trelaske.co.uk
dir: B252 signed Looe. Over Looe bridge signed Polperro.
1.9m, hotel signed on right

Run with great charm by hands-on owners, this lovely
small-scale hideaway sits in four acres of woodland and
pretty, well-tended gardens between Looe and Polperro.
Chef-proprietor Ross Lewin is clearly a man who likes to
go his own way - self-taught and, to a certain degree,
self-sufficient thanks to harvests of fruit, vegetables and
herbs grown in the hotel's own poly tunnels, he delivers
an accomplished modern British repertoire, built on
Cornish materials. Fish fresh from the Looe day boats
stars in dishes such as cod fillet with cauliflower
couscous and lemon sauce, while Cornish Black pork loin
is matched with vanilla mash, hog's pudding and glazed
pear. Staying with the local terroir, you could wind
proceedings up with Cornish cheeses, crackers and
home-made chutney, or go for the comforts of spotted
dick with pouring cream

Chef Ross Lewin **Owner** Ross Lewin & Hazel Billington
Times 12-2/7-9 Closed 22-26 Dec, L Mon-Sat
Prices Fixed D 3 course £30, Service optional
Wines 16 bottles over £20, 18 bottles under £20, 8 by
glass **Notes** Sunday L, Vegetarian available, Dress
restrictions, Smart casual, no shorts **Seats** 40
Children Portions **Parking** 60

LOSTWITHIEL   Map 2 SX15

Asquiths Restaurant

◉◉ Modern British NEW ✪

Minimal fuss, maximum flavours

☎ 01208 871714
19 North St PL22 0EF
e-mail: info@asquithsrestaurant.co.uk
dir: Opposite St Bartholomews church

Opposite the medieval church in Lostwithiel, there's a
serenity about Asquiths that is wholly inviting. The smart
interior is monochrome, except for works by Penzance
artist Steve Slimm on the exposed stone walls, and staff
are easygoing but nevertheless on the ball. A serious
restaurant, then, but not one that takes itself so seriously
as to be intimidating. Food-wise, there are no smoke and
mirrors here, just well-sourced, cleverly-conceived and
skilfully-cooked modern dishes. Cornish credentials are
evident throughout, from the beers and wines to the duck
livers that appear with a creamy sage and mushroom
sauce and potato gnocchi to open proceedings. Next up,
crispy-skinned black bream is matched with buttered
spinach, crab and chilli potato cake and a well-made
citrus beurre blanc, or there might be slow-cooked belly
and faggot of local pork with potato purée, white beans
and grain mustard. This is confident, mature cooking that
shows its final flourish of class with a pannacotta with
Monbazillac jelly, raspberry sorbet, and biscotti crumbs.

Chef Graham Cuthbertson **Owner** Graham & Sally
Cuthbertson **Times** 7-9 Closed Sun-Mon, L all week
Prices Starter £5.50-£7, Main £12-£16, Dessert £5.50-
£7, Service optional **Wines** 6 bottles over £20, 21 bottles
under £20, 4 by glass **Notes** Vegetarian available
Seats 30, Pr/dining room 10 **Children** Portions
Parking Car park at rear

MARAZION   Map 2 SW53

Mount Haven Hotel & Restaurant

◉◉ Modern British

Accomplished modern cooking in family-run hotel

☎ 01736 710249
Turnpike Rd TR17 0DQ
e-mail: reception@mounthaven.co.uk
dir: From centre of Marazion, up hill E, hotel 400yds on
right

A few miles east of Penzance, this smartly revamped
19th-century coach house has stunning views of St
Michael's Mount, which can be appreciated through the
large windows of the lounge or, even better, from the
terrace. It's a small, family-run hotel, with the restaurant
at its heart, serving up some unfussy cooking that brings
together influences from Britain and mainland Europe
with the occasional touch from Asia. Scallops in a starter
are classically accompanied by beurre noisette and
capers, or there may be belly pork with roast pears and
celeriac. Fish, from Newlyn, and local meat are carefully
treated: a fillet of haddock, of pinpoint accuracy, served

continued

MARAZION *continued*

with tempura prawns and chowder, for instance, and venison steak, cooked rare, with red cabbage, cauliflower fritters and chocolate jus. Puddings come up trumps in the shape of pineapple cannelloni and sorbet with coconut rice pudding.

Chef James Morris **Owner** Orange & Mike Trevillion **Times** 12–2.30/6.30-10.30 Closed mid Dec-mid Feb **Prices** Fixed L 2 course £12.50-£15, Fixed D 3 course £27.50-£38.50, Starter £6-£8.50, Main £15.50-£23, Dessert £6.50-£7.50, Service optional **Wines** 27 bottles over £20, 16 bottles under £20, 7 by glass **Notes** Sunday L, Vegetarian available, Dress restrictions, Smart casual **Seats** 38 **Children** Portions, Menu **Parking** 30

MAWGAN PORTH — Map 2 SW86

The Scarlet Hotel

@ @ Modern European V

Confident contemporary cooking and wonderful sea views

☎ 01637 861800
Tredragon Rd TR8 4DQ
e-mail: stay@scarlethotel.co.uk
web: www.scarlethotel.co.uk
dir: A39, A30 towards Truro. At Trekenning rdbt take A3059, follow Newquay Airport signs. Right after garage signed St Mawgan & Airport. Right after airport, right at T-junct signed Padstow (B3276). At Mawgan Porth left. Hotel 250yds on left

Huge windows opening on to the terrace, with wonderful views of the beach, sea and headland, dominate the restaurant at this modern hotel, which was built along eco-friendly lines. The kitchen's larder has been 'grown, reared, caught or foraged to taste as it should', according to the hotel, and indeed dishes are praiseworthy for the freshness of the ingredients and the clear flavour combinations. Langoustine consommé with tortellini and pickled celery is straight out of today's cookery school, and could be followed by the more orthodox lamb rump with rosemary jus, fondant potato and broccoli, or you might start with venison terrine with toast and pears poached in red wine and move on to grilled plaice in a crab and herb crust, accompanied by garlic-flavoured spinach, beetroot and mash. Vegetarians are properly catered for, and desserts have the wow factor, among them ginger pannacotta with sea buckthorn sorbet and micro shoots.

Chef Tom Hunter **Owner** Red Hotels Ltd **Times** 12.30-2.15/7-9.30 Closed 3 Jan-2 Feb **Prices** Fixed L 2 course £18, Fixed D 3 course £42.50, Service optional **Wines** 89 bottles over £20, 2 bottles under £20, 46 by glass **Notes** Sunday L, Vegetarian menu, Civ Wed 74 **Seats** 70, Pr/dining room 20 **Parking** 37, In village

MAWNAN SMITH — Map 2 SW72

Budock Vean - The Hotel on the River

@ Traditional British V ©

Well-crafted dishes served up near the coast

☎ 01326 252100
TR11 5LG
e-mail: relax@budockvean.co.uk
dir: from A39 follow tourist signs to Trebah Gardens. 0.5m to hotel

Cornwall's balmy climes allow Budock Vean to sit in 65 fabulous acres of organically-managed subtropical gardens on the Helford River. Country-house tradition holds sway in the expansive restaurant, where the chefs source the best local, seasonal produce they can get their hands on to create menus of straightforward ideas embracing pan-seared Falmouth Bay scallops with shallot purée, orange and watercress, ahead of best end of locally-reared lamb with root vegetables, Savoy cabbage, garlic and mint mash, and redcurrant and thyme jus. Fish could turn up as baked suprême of hake with a Serrano ham crust, Parmentier potatoes, green beans and butter sauce, while desserts take refuge in the homely comfort of orange marmalade sponge pudding with Cornish vanilla ice cream.

Chef Darren Kelly **Owner** Barlow Family **Times** 12–2.30/7.30-9 Closed 3 wks Jan **Prices** Fixed L 3 course £19.95, Fixed D 4 course £39.95, Starter £8.95-£19.95, Main £16.60-£35, Dessert £6.75, Service optional **Wines** 84 bottles over £20, 15 bottles under £20, 8 by glass **Notes** Sunday L, Vegetarian menu, Dress restrictions, Jacket & tie (ex school hols) **Seats** 100, Pr/dining room 40 **Children** Portions, Menu **Parking** 100

MOUSEHOLE — Map 2 SW42

The Cornish Range Restaurant with Rooms

@ Modern British ©

Locally-caught seafood in a charming village restaurant

☎ 01736 731488
6 Chapel St TR19 6SB
e-mail: info@cornishrange.co.uk
dir: From Penzance 3m S to Mousehole, via Newlyn. Follow road to far side of harbour

Squirrelled away down one of Mousehole's skinny back lanes (leave your car at the outskirts of the village) this delightful stone-built restaurant with rooms is rooted deep in local fishing heritage, since it was once a factory for salting and packing the local pilchard catch. And as

Newlyn is just up the road, prime fish and seafood still drives the activity here, albeit in a more sophisticated manner. Inside, the feel is homely but smart, with scrubbed pine tables and colourful local art on the walls. Hard at it in the open-to-view kitchen, Keith Terry cooks confident, forthright dishes with robust flavours, opening with the likes of grilled mackerel fillets with seared scallops, Serrano ham and horseradish cream, followed by baked hake fillet with monkfish in prosciutto, braised Puy lentils and herb pesto or, for die-hard carnivores, a chargrilled rib-eye steak with tomato and garlic confit, wild mushroom gratin and balsamic glaze.

Chef Keith Terry **Owner** Chad James & Keith Terry **Times** 10–2.15/5.30-9.30 Closed L winter **Prices** Fixed D 2 course £17.50, Starter £3.95-£7.95, Main £11.50-£22.50, Dessert £5.95, Service optional **Wines** 13 bottles over £20, 19 bottles under £20, 6 by glass **Notes** Vegetarian available **Seats** 42 **Children** Portions, Menu **Parking** Harbour car park

MULLION — Map 2 SW61

Mullion Cove Hotel

@ Modern British ©

Clifftop hotel serving up skilfully cooked modish food

☎ 01326 240328
TR12 7EP
e-mail: enquiries@mullion-cove.co.uk
dir: A3083 towards The Lizard. Through Mullion towards Mullion Cove. Hotel in approx 1m

The sizeable white hotel is high on the cliffs above Mullion Cove, looking over miles of coastline - it's some location. It's on the coast path too and surrounded by National Trust land. The large, comfortable lounges look over the cove out to sea, and The Atlantic Restaurant fully merits its name. The menu changes daily, depending on what's good, with the kitchen focusing on the modern British style, producing starters like seared scallops and black pudding on sweet potato purée, and ballottine of duck confit and wild mushrooms with apple chutney. Main courses bring on some appetising combinations, too, without overloading dishes: roast pork fillet stuffed with black pudding in mustard sauce, say, served with dauphinoise potatoes and Savoy cabbage, or baked whole plaice (local, of course) with caper and shallot dressing, accompanied by fennel and citrus risotto and kale. Puddings might deliver blueberry cheesecake, or orange crème brûlée.

Chef Lee Brooking **Owner** Matthew Grose **Times** 12–2/7-8.45 Closed L Mon-Sat **Prices** Food prices not confirmed for 2013. Please telephone for details **Wines** 40 bottles over £20, 19 bottles under £20, 12 by glass **Notes** Sunday L, Vegetarian available, Dress restrictions, Jackets req for men **Seats** 60 **Children** Portions, Menu **Parking** 45

PADSTOW
Map 2 SW97

Margot's

◉ British

Intimate little bistro serving up simple food with a smile

☎ 01841 533441
11 Duke St PL28 8AB
e-mail: bazbeachdog@aol.com

There are only nine tables at this charming little French-style bistro just a stone's throw from Padstow harbour, so it's worth booking ahead if you don't want to miss out on the fuss-free, feel-good cooking of chef-patron Adrian Oliver. Against a nautical-style backdrop of blue and white décor with local marine themed artworks, dinner might start with crab and fennel soup with dill and cream, or Cornish smoked duck breast with pea shoots, parsnip crisps and a balsamic reduction - both prepared using top-notch local ingredients. Cornish lamb cutlets with roast new potatoes and rosemary sauce, and cod fillet roasted with garlic anchovies and parsley with herb mash, might feature among mains, with something rich and comforting like sticky toffee pudding with butterscotch sauce and cream to finish.

Times 12-2/7-9 Closed Nov, Jan, Sun-Mon

The Metropole

◉ Modern British

Harbourside restaurant with an assured team in the kitchen

☎ 01841 532486
Station Rd PL28 8DB
e-mail: reservations@the-metropole.co.uk
dir: M5/A30 past Launceston, follow signs for Wadebridge and N Cornwall. Then take A39 and follow signs for Padstow

'The Met' to its friends is just about Padstow's most imposing building, a Victorian grande dame that is a local landmark. From its lofty perch on a hill above town it looks across the estuary to the comings and goings of the local fishing boats, so window seats are much in demand in the dignified traditional surroundings of the Harbour Restaurant. Thanks to a certain Mr Stein, Padstow has become foodie central in this part of Cornwall, and chef Adam Warne, a Cornishman through and through, is not about to let the side down, particularly when the rich local bounty of land and sea turns up practically on his doorstep. His sure-footed cooking has a lightness of touch that delivers clear, crisp flavours, as witnessed in a starter of pollock with cauliflower, onion bhaji and curry emulsion. Next up, Cornish pork is the star, its belly, cheek and crackling teamed with celeriac and apple, buttered Savoy cabbage and the roasting juices. To finish, treacle tart with custard is a nursery classic that is too good to pass up.

Chef Adam Warne **Owner** Richardson Hotels Ltd
Times 6.30-9 Closed L Mon-Sat **Prices** Fixed D 2 course £24.95, Fixed D 4 course £29.95, Starter £4-£11, Main £8-£25, Dessert £4-£7, Service included **Wines** 14 bottles over £20, 10 bottles under £20, 9 by glass **Notes** Sunday L, Vegetarian available, Dress restrictions, Smart casual **Seats** 70, Pr/dining room 30 **Children** Portions, Menu **Parking** 50

Paul Ainsworth at No. 6

◉◉ Modern British V ♨

Confident cooking in smart townhouse

☎ 01841 532093
6 Middle St PL28 8AP
e-mail: enquiries@number6inpadstow.co.uk
dir: A30 follow signs for Wadebridge then sign to Padstow

Having represented the South West in the BBC's *Great British Menu* (and reaching the final), Paul Ainsworth's profile is on the rise. You might even say he'd put Padstow on the map, if it wasn't already on it. But TV shows aside, this old Georgian townhouse restaurant hits all the right buttons, from its smart contemporary good looks to its relaxed vibe and classily modish food. Paul has worked with many of the great and the good in the capital and it shows in his slick and creative dishes, which reveal a classical soul and an inventive streak. Quail comes with smoked mushrooms on toast and a gribiche dressing among first courses, or go for barbecued mackerel with celeriac remoulade, Parma ham and cucumber. Main-course Jimmy Butler pork roll comes with turnips, Bramley apples and a trotter sauce, and to finish, there's 'a trip to the fairground' (for two), which is Paul's dish off the telly.

Chef Paul Ainsworth **Owner** Paul Ainsworth
Times 12-2/6-10 Closed 24-26 Dec, 7-31 Jan, Mon **Prices** Fixed D 3 course fr £17, Starter £9-£11, Main £19-£24, Dessert £7-£11, Service optional **Wines** 76 bottles over £20, 7 bottles under £20, 16 by glass **Notes** Tasting menu available, Vegetarian menu **Seats** 40, Pr/dining room 22 **Children** Portions **Parking** Harbour car park and on street

St Petroc's Hotel and Bistro

◉ French, Mediterranean

Rick Stein's lively seafood bistro

☎ 01841 532700
4 New St PL28 8EA
e-mail: reservations@rickstein.com
dir: Follow one-way around harbour, 1st left, establishment 100yds on right

In the fifth-oldest building in Padstow, Rick Stein's bistro has bare wooden tables, white walls hung with bold artwork, and a courtyard and garden for alfresco dining. The focus, as expected, is on seafood in various guises, although there are a few token meat dishes in the shape of pan-fried chicken breast with black pudding, and steaks. Plainly grilled lemon sole with béarnaise, or bourride of brill, salt cod and red mullet take centre stage, preceded perhaps by crab tart with garlic, tomato and tarragon, or smoked trout with horseradish cream. For dessert, expect something like pannacotta with vanilla-poached rhubarb.

Chef Paul Harwood, David Sharland **Owner** R & J Stein **Times** 12-2/7-10 Closed 25-26 Dec, 1 May, D 24 Dec **Prices** Fixed L 2 course £15, Starter £6.90-£7.95, Main £14.50-£25.50, Dessert £4.80-£6.50, Service optional **Wines** 21 bottles over £20, 1 bottle under £20, 12 by glass **Notes** Fixed L menu & Sun L only available in winter, Sunday L, Vegetarian available **Seats** 54 **Children** Portions, Menu **Parking** Car park

The Seafood Restaurant

◉◉◉ – see page 94

PENZANCE
Map 2 SW43

The Coldstreamer Inn

◉ Modern British NEW

Modern Cornish cooking at a village hostelry

☎ 01736 362072
Gulval TR18 3BB
e-mail: info@coldsteamer-penzance.co.uk
dir: 1m NE of Penzance on B3311, right turn into School Ln in Gulval, opposite church

Once the New Inn, the pub was renamed after WWII in honour of a son of its then owners, a Coldstream Guardsman who had died on active service. Standing across from the church, it's very much the local hostelry of the little village of Gulval, only a mile or so from Penzance. A reassuringly rustic ambience has been allowed to prevail, with a bare wood floor and pine tables in the separate dining area. In the evenings, candles are lit and a contented babble rises from the room. What's contenting them is the modern Cornish cooking of Tom Penhaul, which is based on Newlyn fish, locally grown fresh produce and meat from a Penzance butchor. A breast of pigeon has been a modish starter for a while now, and appears here in tenderly pink guise under a welter of hazelnuts, orange and sorrel. That may be followed by a well-crisped and forthrightly seasoned fillet of black bream, dressed in lemon oil and partnered by asparagus and rainbow chard risotto, while meats take in roast sirloin with a flat mushroom, kale and béarnaise.

Chef Tom Penhaul **Owner** Richard Tubb **Times** 12-3/6-9 Closed 25 Dec **Prices** Food prices not confirmed for 2013. Please telephone for details **Wines** 26 bottles over £20, 16 bottles under £20, 7 by glass **Notes** Sunday L, Vegetarian available **Seats** 40 **Children** Portions, Menu **Parking** Village square

PENZANCE continued

Harris's Restaurant

◉ Modern European

Clearly focused, unfussy food just off the high street

☎ 01736 364408
46 New St TR18 2LZ
e-mail: contact@harrissrestaurant.co.uk
dir: Located down narrow cobbled street opposite Lloyds TSB & the Humphry Davy statue

Harris's is an unshowy, reassuringly traditional restaurant with wooden floors, clothed tables, and an engaging atmosphere generated in part by unflappable and friendly service. The emphasis is on seafood, carefully and unfussily prepared, from a simple starter of smoked salmon with white crabmeat, or grilled scallops with herb dressing, to accurately timed roast John Dory with pesto, or a whole lobster in buttery lemon sauce. For meat-eaters there's gutsy duck terrine with green tomato chutney, followed by noisettes of local lamb with rosemary sauce and fennel purée, and a meal could be capped off by iced lemon soufflé in a dark chocolate case.

Chef Roger Harris **Owner** Roger & Anne Harris
Times 12-2/7-9.30 Closed 3 wks winter, 25-26 Dec,

1 Jan, Sun (also Mon in winter), L Mon **Prices** Starter £8.50-£10.50, Main £15.95-£32.50, Dessert £7.50-£9.50, Service added but optional 10% **Wines** 34 bottles over £20, 8 bottles under £20, 6 by glass **Notes** Vegetarian available, Dress restrictions, Smart casual **Seats** 40, Pr/ dining room 20 **Parking** On street, local car park

The Hotel Penzance

◉◉ Modern British V

Splendid cooking and sea views

☎ 01736 366890 & 363117
Britons Hill TR18 3AE
e-mail: table@thebaypenzance.co.uk
dir: from A30 pass heliport on right, left at next rdbt for town centre. 3rd right onto Britons Hill. Restaurant on right

The Bay Restaurant in the Hotel Penzance is a light and relaxed room, with a bar at one end, unclothed tables, artwork on the walls, and views over rooftops to Mount's Bay. Staff are friendly, polite and on the ball - which it has to be, with four menus to cope with: one for vegans, a tasting menu, one devoted to shellfish (24 hours' notice required), taking in lobster thermidor with new potatoes, and fruits de mer, and the main event. The last

showcases local produce, and the cooking is assured and uncluttered. Among starters, smoked eel is served with buckwheat blinis and an apple and fennel compôte, and pan-fried rabbit loin with salsify, wild mushrooms, a fried quail's egg and Calvados jus. Fish is a strong suit, judging by a thick fillet of crisp-skinned grilled red mullet accompanied by cauliflower purée and diced beetroot and beetroot foam. Meat-eaters could opt for belly pork fillet and hogs pudding with an apple and cider reduction, and dessert is often the star of the show: maybe fig frangipane tart with fig purée and star anise and honey ice cream.

Chef Ben Reeve **Owner** Yvonne & Stephen Hill
Times 11-6.30/6.30-9 Closed 1st 2 wks Jan, L Sat
Prices Fixed L 2 course fr £11.50, Fixed D 3 course fr £32, Service optional, Groups min 8 service 10%
Wines 15 bottles over £20, 16 bottles under £20, 12 by glass **Notes** Tasting menu 9 course, vegan menu available, Sunday L, Vegetarian menu, Dress restrictions, Smart casual, no shorts, Civ Wed 60 **Seats** 60, Pr/dining room 12 **Children** Portions, Menu **Parking** 12, On street

The Seafood Restaurant

| **PADSTOW** | Map 2 SW97 |

Traditional, International Seafood V ▲NOTABLE WINE LIST

The Stein flagship

☎ 01841 532700
Riverside PL28 8BY
e-mail: reservations@rickstein.com
dir: Follow signs for town centre. Restaurant on left of riverside

The Stein brand needs no introduction and its mothership venue still keeps Padstow firmly on the map. The quayside location embodies the basic premise of taking the catch straight from where it is landed in through the kitchen door to be treated simply - no foams, fussing or trickery here - an approach that will always have an eager audience. The restaurant is an expansive, bustling space of blond wood, white walls, colourful splashes of

contemporary art, and tables dressed in their best linen, spread around a central seafood bar where you can watch the brigade assembling those celebrated platters of super-fresh crustaceans. The global influences of Stein's many TV travel cookery programmes have tended to be reflected in the menu - a rustic Spanish-accented starter of seared Cornish hand-dived scallops matched with Ibérico ham with pimenton and Pardina lentils, being a case in point. Essentially, though, the culinary ethos remains true to its roots, avoiding fads and fashions and sticking to the business of dishing up seafood of exemplary quality and freshness in an unbuttoned and buzzy ambience. A roast tronçon of turbot with hollandaise sauce typifies the unvarnished style, and it sits alongside the ever-popular monkfish vindaloo with pilau rice, puri bread, raita and kachumber salad.

Chef Stephane Delourme, David Sharland **Owner** R & J Stein **Times** 12-2/7-10 Closed 25-26 Dec, 1 May, D 24 Dec **Prices** Fixed L 3 course £29.95, Starter £12.50-£23, Main £18-£47.50, Dessert £8.90-£9.20, Service optional **Wines** 200+ bottles over £20, 1 bottle under £20, 22 by glass **Notes** Vegetarian menu **Seats** 120
Children Portions, Menu **Parking** Pay & display opposite

The Navy Inn

⊛ Modern British 🍷

Traditional seaside pub punching well above its weight

☎ 01736 333232
Lower Queen St TR18 4DE
e-mail: keir@navyinn.co.uk
web: www.navyinn.co.uk
dir: In town centre, follow Chapel St for 50yds, right into Queen St to end

Just off the Promenade, The Navy is very much a traditional pub, as opposed to a pub with an aspirational dining room. Expect plenty of local cheer, no airs (but one or two graces, where they matter), and a kitchen that punches well above its weight. A plethora of fish is on offer, as is only right with Newlyn just around the corner, and the team shows good technical understanding in getting the best out of it. A serving of crab dressed in lemon and coriander, with tomato jam and avocado purée, gets things off to a bracing start, and may be followed by sharply seasoned cod with baby spinach in a fish velouté, or chargrilled pollock with mussel stew and silverskin onions. If it's meat you're after, look to peppered pork fillet with sweet potato purée in lemon and coriander dressing. Desserts can get a little way-out on occasion, as in basil pannacotta with pineapple sorbet, candied mango and a sesame and poppy seed wafer, and there are good West Country cheeses, served with home-made apricot chutney.

Chef Keir Meikle, Jay Orrey **Owner** Keir Meikle
Times 12-10 Closed 26 Dec **Prices** Food prices not confirmed for 2013. Please telephone for details
Wines 15 bottles over £20, 14 bottles under £20, 11 by glass **Notes** Sunday L, Vegetarian available **Seats** 54
Children Portions, Menu **Parking** Free parking on promenade

---

PERRANUTHNOE   Map 2 SW52

The Victoria Inn

⊛ Modern British 🍷

Top-notch ingredients in lovely village inn

☎ 01736 710309
TR20 9NP
e-mail: enquiries@victoriainn-penzance.co.uk
dir: A30 to Penzance, A394 to Helston. After 2m turn right into Perranuthnoe, pub is on right on entering the village

Good beaches and lovely pubs are not quite 10-a-penny in Cornwall, but the county has more than its fair share. And Perranuthnoe has a couple of crackers. The beach is a draw for holiday-makers, whilst The Victoria Inn attracts anyone who knows a good thing when they see it It is still an unspoilt pub with all the natural west-country charm you'd hope for, with real ales on tap and a lack of pretension all round, whilst Stewart Eddy's straight-up, clearly focused cooking elevates the place still further. Whether you eat in the bar or the marginally more formal dining area, you'll get fine, fresh regional produce and clear-headed food. There's Cornish crab, of course, but this time with warm garlic toast, pickled fennel and herb salad and aïoli; next up, perhaps slow-roasted Primrose Herd belly of pork, or wild mushroom and local vegetable risotto with Lyburn cheese. Valrhona dark chocolate and espresso mousse with Cornish sea salt and caramel sauce and coffee ice cream reveals the chef's experience under the tutelage of the great and the good.

Chef Stewart Eddy **Owner** Stewart & Anna Eddy
Times 12-2/6.30-9 Closed 25-26 Dec, 1 Jan, Mon (off season), D Sun **Prices** Starter £4.95-£7.95, Main £9.95-£17.25, Dessert £5.75-£8.75, Service optional
Wines 21 bottles over £20, 21 bottles under £20, 8 by glass **Notes** Vegetarian available **Seats** 60
Children Portions, Menu **Parking** 10, On street

PORTHLEVEN   Map 2 SW62

Kota Restaurant with Rooms

⊛ British, Pacific Rim 🍷

Asian-influenced modern British cooking by the sea

☎ 01326 562407
Harbour Head TR13 9JA
e-mail: kota@btconnect.com
dir: B3304 from Helston into Porthleven, Kota on harbour head opposite slipway

Chef-proprietor Jude Kereama has Maori, Chinese and Malaysian blood in his veins, so you can expect vibrant pacific rim fusion cooking in his relaxed bistro in an 18th-century corn mill on Porthleven harbour. In such a setting, local fish naturally plays a starring role (Kota is Maori for shellfish, by the way): exciting and inventive dishes see Far-Eastern flavours colliding creatively with tastes from elsewhere - so you could start with Falmouth Bay oysters au naturel with shallot vinegar, or take them tempura-battered with wasabi tartare, while Cornish mussels could arrive with tamarind, chilli and coconut broth. The good ideas keep coming: pan-fried hake with

prawn and green pea risotto, samphire and a rich bisque sauce hits all the right notes, and if you're in a meaty mood, the likes of Cornish sirloin steak teamed with a beef and mushroom pie, spinach, horseradish mash and watercress purée will satisfy. Finish with a millefeuille of rhubarb parfait with green apple sorbet.

Chef Jude Kereama **Owner** Jude & Jane Kereama
Times 5.30-9 Closed 25 Dec, Jan, Sun (also Mon off season), L all week **Prices** Fixed D 2 course £15, Starter £5.75-£8.95, Main £11.75-£21, Dessert £6.25-£6.95, Service optional, Groups min 6 service 10%
Wines 30 bottles over £20, 23 bottles under £20, 13 by glass **Notes** Fixed D 2 course, Tasting menu available (pre-order), Vegetarian available **Seats** 40
Children Portions, Menu **Parking** On street

PORTLOE   Map 2 SW93

The Lugger Hotel

⊛ European 🍷

Enterprising cooking by the harbour

☎ 01872 501322
TR2 5RD
e-mail: reservations.lugger@ohiml.com
dir: A390 to Truro, B3287 to Tregony, A3078 (St Mawes Rd), left for Veryan, left for Portloe

Dating from the 16th century, now a luxury hotel, The Lugger overlooks the sea and tiny harbour of this picturesque Roseland Peninsula village, with a terrace outside the smart restaurant for summer dining. Local ingredients are the kitchen's linchpin, particularly seafood, which might appear as moules marinière, or crab salad, followed by cod fillet with caper and lemon butter. Elsewhere, look for contemporary treatments of maple-glazed pork belly with a scallop and cauliflower cream, and pigeon with beetroot and pomegranate salad, then pheasant breast with basil polenta, dried tomatoes and game chips, and saddle of venison with bitter chocolate jus, spinach and dauphinoise potatoes. Cornish cheeses are alternatives to puddings like orange pannacotta with poached rhubarb.

Chef Jonathan Domé **Owner** Oxford Hotels & Inns
Times 12.30-2.30/7-9 **Prices** Tasting menu £75, Starter £6.90-£12, Main £13.90-£20.50, Dessert fr £7.50, Service optional **Wines** 8 by glass **Notes** Tasting menu 6 course including wines, Sunday L, Vegetarian available, Civ Wed 43 **Seats** 45 **Parking** 25

PORTSCATHO   Map 2 SW83

Driftwood

⊛⊛⊛ – *see page 96*

ROCK   Map 2 SW97

Restaurant Nathan Outlaw

⊛⊛⊛ – *see page 96*

Driftwood

Map 2 SW83

Modern European

Accomplished cooking in a stunning coastal setting

☎ 01872 580644
Rosevine TR2 5EW
e-mail: info@driftwoodhotel.co.uk
web: www.driftwoodhotel.co.uk
dir: 5m from St Mawes off the A3078, signposted Rosevine

This chic contemporary bolt-hole encapsulates the very essence of Cornwall on its clifftop perch above the crashing waves – a location that comes into its own on the decking terrace at aperitif time. There are uplifting views over the jagged coastline of Gerrans Bay, and indoors, a quietly stylish affluent Cape Cod beachcomber chic is evident in the pared-back contemporary décor.

Understated, is the word that sums up the muted neutral shades, pale wood floor, and expanses of whiteness – and the word applies equally to the kitchen's culinary aesthetic. Head chef Chris Eden is a Cornishman whose regional pride leads him to hunt down the best ingredients his home territory can offer and bring it together in intelligently-designed compositions. The food aims high and hits the mark with a well-constructed dish of poached ray wing, crisp belly pork, celeriac purée, apple and shallot rings. Next up, a main course of loin, kofta and pie of venison with Savoy cabbage, carrot and orange and juniper crumb is packed with interest, while elegant desserts could deliver spiced pineapple carpaccio with toasted coconut marshmallow, and lemongrass and lime sorbet. Unobtrusive and efficient service is well-matched to the serenity of the setting.

Chef Christopher Eden **Owner** Paul & Fiona Robinson **Times** 12-2/7-9.30 Closed early Dec-early Feb, L all week (ex Thu-Sat, Jun-Sep) **Prices** Fixed D 3 course £46, Service optional **Wines** 50 bottles over £20, 2 bottles under £20, 6 by glass **Notes** Tasting menu available summer, Vegetarian available **Seats** 34 **Parking** 20

Restaurant Nathan Outlaw

Map 2 SW97

Modern British, Seafood V

Inspired seafood tasting menus in a modern hotel

☎ 01208 863394 & 862737
The St Enodoc Hotel PL27 6LA
e-mail: mail@nathan-outlaw.co.uk
dir: M5/A30/A39 to Wadebridge. B3314 to Rock

The village of Rock sits alongside the River Camel, a sleepy haven from the madding crowd, which on a clear day can be seen cramming Padstow across the estuary. A sense of refuge is the predominant tone at the St Enodoc Hotel, where spare contemporary design is enlivened by striped upholstery, brightly painted furniture and bold artworks that reflect the surrounding landscape. Nathan Outlaw, who may be said to have invented Rock, offers two routes to happiness here: one is the Seafood & Grill,

where a menu of straightforward fish and shellfish options, plus steaks and chicken, is served, the other the self-named destination restaurant with its lengthy and now legendary tasting menus. Take a dear friend, ideally someone with whom you haven't caught up for ages. It's going to take a while. The drill is five fish dishes, cheese and two desserts. If that sounds a bit much, you could skip cheese (although you'd be missing some fine local artisan specimens in all textures and colours). In fact, the main dishes are so precisely weighted, and the pace of output so precisely timed, that there is nothing daunting about the experience, and rather a lot that is purely sensational. The freshest fish, cooked or cured with nerveless accuracy, will remind you all over again what it is you love about seafood. Nor are the preparations especially avante-garde, but are based on sound culinary tradition. Start with a scallop, not seared and sitting on cauliflower purée, but slivered into a tartare with fines herbes. That leads into a portion of pin-sharp soused mackerel with Jerusalem artichoke, then a combination of

the much-underrated lemon sole with cucumber in lemon and oyster sauce, before the more robust presentations follow. Cod is lightly salted and accompanied by mushrooms and hazelnuts, while sea bass with crab, celeriac and apple takes centre stage. The lighter of two sweet things may be something like rhubarb and custard cream, before the main dessert arrives, perhaps a small portion of treacle tart with quince jam and orange yoghurt sorbet. Every one of these dishes can be paired with a small glass of an appropriate wine match. This will add substantially to the bill, but the choices - from Japanese Koshu through Australian Gewürztraminer to Uruguayan Albariño - are never less than hugely interesting.

Chef Nathan Outlaw **Owner** Nathan Outlaw **Times** 7-9 Closed Xmas, Jan, Sun-Mon, L all week **Prices** Tasting menu £85-£155, Service added but optional 12.5% **Wines** 200+ bottles over £20, 15 by glass **Notes** Tasting menu 8 course (with wine £155), Veg tasting menu, Vegetarian menu, Dress restrictions, Smart casual **Seats** 20 **Parking** 30

Save on Hotels. Book at **theAA.com/hotel**

CORNWALL & ISLES OF SCILLY 97 ENGLAND

ST AGNES
Map 2 SW75

Rose-in-Vale Hotel

◉ Traditional & Modern British ⬮

Peaceful setting for appealing dishes

☎ 01872 562202
Mithian TR5 0QD
e-mail: reception@rose-in-vale-hotel.co.uk
dir: Take A30 S towards Redruth. At Chiverton Cross rdbt take B3277 signed St Agnes. In 500mtrs turn at tourist info sign for Rose-in-Vale. Into Mithian, right at Miners Arms, down hill

A handsome 18th-century property, the Rose-in-Vale is a stylish country-house hotel in a secluded wooded valley near the coast, with bay windows in the Valley Restaurant looking over terraces and gardens. The kitchen is a hive of activity, changing the menus daily and making everything in-house, and there's evidence of plenty of skill and ambition behind its output. Its fresh and lively approach can be seen in starters like clam, cockle and cider broth with apple and shallot croûtes, and main courses of seared hake fillet topped with crabmeat in a herb crust served on rösti with tomato salsa, and ham-wrapped roast poussin on greens with a ballottine of leg and chicken and root vegetable consommé. Inventive puddings can run to beetroot cake served with rich chocolate mousse and fennel-flavoured ice cream.

Chef Colin Hankins, Michael Parker **Owner** James & Sara Evans **Times** 12-2/7-9 Closed 2 wks Jan, L Mon-Wed (winter) **Prices** Fixed L 2 course £8-£40, Fixed D 3 course £50, Starter £3-£7.50, Main £7.50-£25, Dessert £3-£4.00, Service optional **Wines** 14 bottles over £20, 25 bottles under £20, 7 by glass **Notes** Sunday L, Vegetarian available, Dress restrictions, Smart dress, Civ Wed 80 **Seats** 80, Pr/dining room 12 **Children** Portions **Parking** 50

ST AUSTELL
Map 2 SX05

Austell's

◉◉ Modern British ⬮

Classy modern cooking by a Cornish beach

☎ 01726 813888
10 Beach Rd PL25 3PH
e-mail: brett@austells.net
dir: From A390 towards Par, 0.5m after Charlestown rdbt at 2nd lights turn right. Left at rdbt. Restaurant 600yds on right

The beach at Carlyon Bay is man-made, the product of a diversion of the River Sandy in the Victorian era. Hedged about with golf courses, with the South-West Coast path running along the cliff, it's an atmospheric locality, so much so that Alison Moyet once made a video for one of her hits here. The Eden Project is not more than 20 minutes away, which makes Austell's a choice destination for the end of a perfect day. A concise menu of modern Cornish cooking delivers some classy touches, from the bistro favourite of chicken liver parfait served with spicy pineapple pickle, to the cured and roasted salmon with spiced lentils and herbed crème fraîche, among starters, and mains such as braised shin of excellent local beef, served with puréed celeriac and roast veg. Fish cookery is generous and hearty, partnering roast gurnard with mussels, cockles and saffron aïoli, or sea bream with brown shrimps and baby leeks. Dark chocolate fondant with raspberry ice cream and a honeycomb tuile is a fine finish.

Chef Martin Adams **Owner** J & S Camborne-Paynter **Times** 7-10 Closed 25-26 Dec, 1-15 Jan, Mon, L all week **Prices** Fixed D 3 course £24.00, Service optional **Wines** 38 bottles over £20, 5 bottles under £20, 7 by glass **Notes** Vegetarian available **Seats** 48 **Children** Portions **Parking** 30

Boscundle Manor Country House Hotel

◉ Modern British

Local sourcing at 18th-century manor house

☎ 01726 813557
Tregrehan PL25 3RL
e-mail: reservations@boscundlemanor.co.uk
dir: 2m E on A390, 200yds on road signed Tregrehan

On a hillside just outside St Austell, this small, tastefully refurbished 18th-century manor house is peacefully set in secluded grounds. Candles and low lighting, fresh flowers in tall vases, gleaming glasses, comfortable high-backed chairs, and a gold and red theme create an intimate atmosphere in the elegant dining room. In this classic country-house setting expect a seasonally-changing fixed-price menu that brims with local produce and offers traditional British cooking with some modern twists. From a typical summer menu, perhaps start with wild mushroom risotto with a parmesan crisp, then follow with pan-fried John Dory with garlic mash and asparagus velouté, or rib-eye steak with béarnaise. Round off with coconut rice pudding with diced mango, or pannacotta with rhubarb compôte.

Times 6.45-8.45

The Cornwall Hotel, Spa & Estate

◉ Modern British

Smart manor house setting for ambitious, modern cooking

☎ 01726 874050
Pentewan Rd, Tregorrick PL26 7AB
e-mail: enquiries@thecornwall.com
dir: A391 to St Austell then B3273 towards Mevagissey. Hotel approx 0.5m on right

Set in 43 acres of Victorian parkland, this luxurious hotel is accompanied by a spa and woodland holiday homes. In the old White House part of the hotel - once a private mansion - sits the Arboretum restaurant but there's also Acorns Brasserie for lighter meals and the Parkland Terrace with views over the Pentewan Valley making it a fine spot for a pre-dinner cocktail. The Arboretum restaurant is formally but unfussily dressed in neutral tones with large tables and stylish paintings in black and gilt frames above the original fireplaces. The kitchen is led by what's in season and the fruits of the local area figure prominently among the modern British output. Cannelloni of wild Cornish rabbit, for example, comes with wild mushroom salsa and carrot soup, followed by pan-roasted fillet of local bream with globe artichoke and truffle risotto, sautéed broccoli and parmesan. Puds are as inventive as crisp croquettes of vanilla rice pudding with spiced apple compôte and vanilla ice cream.

Chef Brett Camborne-Paynter **Owner** Rudrum Holdings **Times** 12.30-2.30/6.30-9.30 **Prices** Food prices not confirmed for 2013. Please telephone for details **Notes** Sunday L, Vegetarian available, Dress restrictions, Smart casual, Civ Wed 60 **Seats** 38, Pr/dining room 16 **Children** Portions, Menu **Parking** 100

ST IVES   Map 2 SW54

Carbis Bay Hotel

Mediterranean

Contemporary cooking and panoramic views

☎ 01736 795311
Carbis Bay TR26 2NP
e-mail: info@carbisbayhotel.co.uk
web: www.carbisbayhotel.co.uk
dir: A3074, through Lelant. 1m, at Carbis Bay 30yds
before lights turn right into Porthrepta Rd to sea & hotel

Dating from the late 19th century, the family-run Carbis
Bay Hotel has stunning views over the eponymous waters
from its lofty position. The panoramic view can also be
appreciated from the Sands restaurant, a spacious,
traditionally decorated room, where the menus are
evidence of a kitchen working in the modern vein, with
starters encompassing battered haloumi on minted pea
purée with beetroot and balsamic dressing, and duck and
bean sprout spring roll with hoisin dipping sauce. The
same broad sweep of styles is seen in main courses of
honey-glazed duck breast with an orange and Cointreau
sauce accompanied by patatas bravas and asparagus,
and well-timed fried cod served on parmesan mash with
creamed leeks and a Noilly Prat reduction. Crème brûlée
is a classical rendition, flavoured with Baileys and
garnished with raspberries.

Chef Paul John Massey **Owner** Messrs M W & S P Baker
Times 12-3/6-9 Closed 3 wks Jan **Prices** Fixed L 2 course

£10.95-£14.95, Starter £6-£8, Main £16-£20, Dessert
£6-£8, Service optional **Wines** 28 bottles over £20,
20 bottles under £20, 12 by glass **Notes** Sunday L,
Vegetarian available, Dress restrictions, Smart casual,
Civ Wed 150 **Seats** 150, Pr/dining room 40
Children Portions, Menu **Parking** 100

Garrack Hotel & Restaurant

Modern British

Inventive cooking and stunning views

☎ 01736 796199 & 792910
Burthallan Ln, Higher Ayr TR26 3AA
e-mail: reception@garrack.com
dir: Exit A30 for St Ives, then from B3311 follow brown
signs for Tate Gallery, then brown Garrack signs

From its lofty position high above the tourist crowds of the
town centre, this ivy-clad granite hotel's show-stopping
views over Porthmeor beach and the Atlantic are a diner's
dream-ticket. The unstuffy, light-and-airy restaurant's
simple design blends traditional and contemporary
elements to allow those stunning vistas pride of place,
while menus likewise demonstrate a kitchen making the
most of Cornwall's natural resources in accomplished
modern dishes of creativity and ambition. Seafood rightly
scores high in the billing; perhaps seared fillets of red
mullet teamed with pea risotto, tapenade of black olives
and wilted spinach, while from the land, perhaps another
dish with a sunny-climes influence like pan-roasted
breast of free-range chicken with chorizo, root vegetable

and white bean stew with saffron aïoli. To finish, vanilla
pannacotta with forced rhubarb, red berry reduction and
fresh strawberries fits the bill.

Times 12.30-2/6-9 Closed 5 days Xmas, L Mon-Sat

Porthminster Beach Restaurant

Modern Mediterranean V

Seafood-led fusion cookery on the beach at St Ives

☎ 01736 795352
TR26 2EB
e-mail: pminster@btconnect.com
dir: On Porthminster Beach, beneath the St Ives Railway
Station

They got there early and bagged themselves a prime spot
on the beach at St Ives, beneath the towering eminence
of Porthminster Point, the better to look out over the
crashing waves breaking on spotless sands. It's a classic
contemporary seafood venue, with chilled-out staff, the
tiled interior opening onto outdoor decking, where you
might sit and set about a dish of crisp-fried salt-and-
spice squid with citrus miso under the Cornish sun. An
Australian chef ensures there's a lot of knowledgeable
fusion thinking going on, as in a main course of baked
pollock with smoked pancetta, celeriac, almonds, salsa
verde, a razor clam and truffled parcel of egg yolk. Or go
with the much simpler crab linguine with Fowey mussels,
dressed in chilli, garlic, parsley and lemon. There are
good vegetarian dishes too, and sweet treats such as

Hotel Tresanton

ST MAWES   Map 2 SW83

British, Mediterranean

Bright modern cooking in super-stylish seafront hotel

☎ 01326 270055
27 Lower Castle Rd TR2 5DR
e-mail: info@tresanton.com
dir: On the waterfront in town centre

The Hotel Tresanton has played its part in transforming
the reputation of Cornwall from a bucket-and-spade
holiday destination to something a little less parochial.
That's not to look down on traditional holidays - indeed
this hotel is extremely family-friendly: there are family
suites and a playroom, for example. It's just a lot more
chi-chi than in the old days. Entering via a discreet
road-level entrance, a few steps up the hillside reveals
the smart boutique hotel, fashioned from a cluster of

cottages, sitting at different levels above the St Mawes
waterfront (there are lovely unbroken views towards
Falmouth). The design by Olga Polizzi seems to fit the bill
perfectly, with its jaunty nautical stylishness and
Mediterranean-inspired luminosity. The restaurant, with
its vanilla-painted tongue-and-groove walls, and blue
seats at pristine, white linen-clad tables on mosaic-tiled
floors, is a delightful setting for the sparkily confident
modern British and Mediterranean-inspired cooking. A
summer minestrone soup with pecorino might get the ball
rolling, or steamed Cornish mussels with spiced tomato,
white beans and coriander. Next up, Terras Farm duck
with cannellini beans, wild mushrooms and rainbow
chard, or St Mawes lobster with chips and basil
mayonnaise. Regional produce features strongly on the
menu, including in a dessert of clotted cream tart with
strawberry ice cream, and West Country cheeses served
with pressed fig, chutney and celery.

Chef Paul Wadham **Owner** Olga Polizzi
Times 12-2.30/7-9.30 Closed 2 wks Jan **Prices** Fixed L 2
course fr £26.50, Fixed D 3 course fr £43.50, Service
optional **Wines** 114 bottles over £20, 8 by glass
Notes Sunday L, Vegetarian available, Civ Wed 45
Seats 60, Pr/dining room 45 **Children** Menu **Parking** 30

coconut rice pudding with mandarin sorbet, mango and peanut brittle.

Chef M Smith **Owner** Jim Woolcock, David Fox, Roger & Tim Symons, M Smith **Times** 12-3.30/6 Closed 25 Dec, Mon (Winter) **Prices** Starter £6-£10, Main £15-£24, Dessert £6-£10, Service optional **Wines** 13 bottles over £20, 15 bottles under £20, 9 by glass **Notes** Vegetarian menu **Seats** 60 **Children** Portions **Parking** 300yds (railway station)

The Queens

◎ Modern British **NEW** ◎

Purposeful pub cooking near the harbour

☎ 01736 796468
2 High St TR26 1RR
e-mail: info@queenshotelstives.com
dir: A3074 to town centre. With station on right, down hill to High St

The catering side of the operation may have been taken up a gear with refurbishment in 2011, but this is still pre-eminently a local pub, and a friendly and welcoming one at that. A short stroll from the harbour, it's a granite-fronted Georgian building, with a pleasing ambience of unclothed tables, sofas and bare floorboards inside. The short menu is chalked up on boards, and the approach is nice and relaxed. That said, the cooking has a real sense of purpose and drive these days, with straightforward dishes cooked and presented with simple flair. Good husbanding of leftovers results in a starter of massively enjoyable pork bubble-and-squeak with seared hog's pudding and a poached egg, while the right attention to detail produces a piece of crisp-skinned, moist-fleshed stone bass for main, served with a fondue dressing of mussels, tomato and saffron. A generous pairing of meats might furnish a leg of confit duck with guinea fowl, alongside roots and Puy lentils, and heritage puddings such as apple crumble with vanilla ice cream are bound to please.

Chef Matt Perry **Owner** Neythan Hayes
Times 12.30-2.30/6.30-9 Closed 25 Dec, Mon (Nov-Mar), D Sun **Prices** Fixed L 2 course £10, Starter £3.50-£6, Main £6-£15, Dessert £3-£4, Service optional **Wines** 2 bottles over £20, 10 bottles under £20, 12 by glass **Notes** Sunday L, Vegetarian available **Seats** 50 **Children** Portions, Menu **Parking** Station car park

---

ST MAWES   Map 2 SW83

Hotel Tresanton

◎◎◎ – *see opposite*

Idle Rocks Hotel

◎◎ Modern British

Modern cuisine in picturesque fishing port

☎ 01326 270771
Harbourside TR2 5AN
e-mail: reception@idlerocks.co.uk
dir: From St Austell A390 towards Truro, left onto B3287 signed Tregony, through Tregony, left at T-junct onto A3078, hotel on left on waterfront

Idle Rocks perches on the harbour wall at St Mawes, so it's impossible to get any closer to the sea without putting your swimming costume on. The aptly-named Water's Edge restaurant makes the most of its location with a split-level layout that ensures every table gets the harbour view through floor-to-ceiling picture windows, while the nearness of the sand and sea is evoked with a shipshape décor of curvy balustrades, pale wood panelling and glowing hues of gold and blue. Head chef Stephen Marsh is passionate about Cornish produce and is kept well supplied by Cornish meat producers, foragers who bring in nature's bounty, and local crab and lobster boats, whose catch is showcased on a modern brasserie-style menu. Start with a full-flavoured pairing of roasted monkfish and slow-braised oxtail with girolles and onions, then follow that with something like pan-seared Cornish beef fillet with fondant potato, wild garlic soufflé, watercress and truffles, or a whole plaice roasted in the oven and served with Parisienne potatoes and seasonal vegetables. When the sun is out, and the waves lap against the wall, the waterside terrace is an unbeatable spot.

Chef Stephen Marsh **Owner** E K Richardson
Times 12-2.30/6.30-9 Closed Xmas, New Year
Prices Food prices not confirmed for 2013. Please telephone for details **Wines** 42 bottles over £20, 8 bottles under £20, 11 by glass **Notes** Vegetarian available, Dress restrictions, Smart casual **Seats** 70 **Children** Portions **Parking** 5

ST MELLION   Map 3 SX36

St Mellion International

◎◎ Modern International

Confident modish cooking in top-notch Cornish golf resort

☎ 01579 351351
PL12 6SD
e-mail: stmellion@crown-golf.co.uk
dir: On A388 about 4m N of Saltash

The 450-acre estate that makes up the St Mellion resort includes the Jack Nicklaus Signature golf course amongst its wealth of top-notch facilities. With a great spa, fitness club and conference rooms, there's no shortage of things to do, but do make time to eat at An Boesti (which means 'The Restaurant' in Cornish), for it is no after-thought. A smart and formal dining room in the modern hotel is the setting for some ambitious contemporary cooking. Mi-cuit salmon, tomato and anchovy dressing and black olive tapenade shows a light touch among first courses, or go for rabbit lasagna. Among main courses venison might be cooked sous-vide, showing this kitchen is up to speed with culinary goings-on, served alongside celeriac purée, red cabbage and blackberries. Well-chosen ingredients bring a local flavour to proceedings, including the Cornish cheese trolley, which offers a good regional selection served with home-made chutney. To finish with a touch of exoticism, go for pineapple parcels with coconut sorbet, honey jelly and mango salsa.

Chef Kevin Hartley **Owner** Crown Golf **Times** 6.30-9.30 Closed Xmas, New Year, Mon-Tue (off season), L all week **Prices** Fixed D 3 course £32.50-£42.50, Service optional **Wines** 120 bottles over £20, 10 bottles under £20, 7 by glass **Notes** Sunday L, Vegetarian available, Dress restrictions, Smart casual, Civ Wed 300 **Seats** 60 **Children** Portions **Parking** 750

SALTASH   Map 3 SX45

China Fleet Country Club

◎ Modern British

Modern flavours in a converted farmhouse

☎ 01752 854661 & 848668
PL12 6LJ
e-mail: thefarmhouse@china-fleet.co.uk
dir: A38 towards Plymouth/Saltash. Cross Tamar Bridge, take slip road before tunnel. Right at lights, 1st right follow signs, 0.5m

The Farm House restaurant occupies the former farmhouse within the hotel complex at the China Fleet Country Club, which also comprises a golf course and extensive leisure facilities. Expect a relaxed atmosphere, an elegant, stylish décor and pleasant and engaging service. Unpretentious, well-balanced dishes are presented with care and soundly cooked using good local ingredients. You could start with a simple but effective pigeon salad with black pudding and cauliflower purée, and proceed to a well constructed roast cod with

continued

SALTASH *continued*

boulangère potatoes and shrimp butter. Children have a separate menu, and puddings might run to apple tarte Tatin with caramel sauce and vanilla ice cream.

Times 12-2/5-9.30 Closed 24 Dec-New Year, L Mon-Sat, D Sun

TALLAND BAY　　　　　　　　Map 2 SX25

Talland Bay Hotel

◎◎ Modern

Coastal views and imaginative cooking

☎ 01503 272667
PL13 2JB
e-mail: info@tallandbayhotel.co.uk
dir: Signed from x-rds on A387 between Looe & Polperro

Dating back around 400 years, this charming whitewashed hotel is set about 150 feet above sea level in a quiet rural location between Looe and Polperro, just a few hundred yards from the beach. Inside there's lots of swagger - the style is decidedly contemporary with copious natty artworks - whilst the oak-panelled restaurant benefits from huge picture-windows opening out onto a terrace area with fab views across the bay. Local ingredients, particularly seafood, abound in imaginative dishes cooked with much flair and a lightness of touch. Expect the likes of Gevrik goats' cheese mousse with apricot and walnut bread and walnut dressing, followed by main-course seared Cornish seafood with new potatoes, smoked tomatoes, fennel céviche, olive tapenade and spiced fish velouté. Great local cheeses vie for attention alongside puds such as burnt cinnamon custard, apple doughnut and hazelnut tuile.

Chef David Tunnicliffe **Owner** Vanessa Rees
Times 12.30-2.30/6.30-9.30 Closed L Mon-Sat (Oct-mid Apr) **Prices** Fixed L 2 course £15.95, Fixed D 3 course £38, Service optional **Wines** 50 bottles over £20, 12 by glass **Notes** Sunday L, Vegetarian available, Civ Wed 70 **Seats** 40 **Children** Portions, Menu **Parking** 20

TRURO　　　　　　　　　　Map 2 SW84

Bustophers Bar Bistro

◎ Modern British

Locally popular neighbourhood bistro with imaginative cooking

☎ 01872 279029
62 Lemon St TR1 2PN
e-mail: info@bustophersbarbistro.com
dir: Located on right, past Plaza Cinema up the hill

The backbone of the bustling, friendly ambience on display at this appealing neighbourhood bistro is the strong local following it enjoys - about-towners quaffing Sauvignon Blanc, couples and young business types. The open-plan kitchen helps to add vivacity too, and outdoor tables are on hand to make the most of the Cornish summer. Local materials inform the modern bistro cooking, opening a meal with a little pan of potted Primrose Herd rare-breed pig's cheek with pea custard and gentle horseradish cream, and following up with pan-roasted parmesan-crusted hake and Cornish prawns in mixed pepper and fennel ragout. The slates and Kilner jars may seem gimmicky but as seen in a dessert of tiramisù with superb mascarpone ice cream and a quenelle of rum truffle made with Havana Club, the results can certainly impress.

Times 12-2.30/5.30-9.30 Closed 25-26 Dec, 1 Jan

Indaba Fish

◎ Modern British, Seafood **NEW** 🌼

Modish seafood dishes in the city centre

☎ 01872 274700
Tabernacle St TR1 2EJ
e-mail: eating@indabafish.co.uk
dir: 100yds off Lemon Quay

On a quiet street, Indaba Fish is a buzzy restaurant with wooden floors and tables, high ceilings, banquettes and brown and cream leather-look seats, and some 'fish shoal' lampshades reflecting the seafood credentials of the place. Flavourful dishes with a pleasing lack of pretension are what to expect from a kitchen clearly in its element working in a variety of styles. Start with razor clams cooked with ginger, spring onions, chilli and soy, or prawn and squid escabèche with noodles. Crabs are chosen from a tank, and the whole of the kitchen's arsenal has been determined with quality in mind: tip-top monkfish tail, for instance, fried in vanilla flour served with spicy clams, butternut squash, peppers and coconut, or roast loin of cod with a gratin of mussels, pancetta, leeks and spinach. There are a couple of meat dishes, and to finish might be rich chocolate and honeycomb tart with raspberry coulis.

Chef Robert Duncan **Owner** Stephen Shepherd
Times 12-2.30/5.30-9.30 Closed Sun **Prices** Fixed D 3 course £16.95, Starter £5-£8, Main £10-£44, Dessert £5-£7, Service optional, Groups min 10 service 10% **Wines** 20 bottles over £20, 9 bottles under £20, 12 by glass **Notes** ALC D only, alt ALC offered L main £7-12, dessert £5-£7, Vegetarian available **Seats** 40, Pr/dining room 24 **Children** Portions **Parking** Car park opposite

---

Probus Lamplighter Restaurant

◎◎ Modern British

Charming village restaurant with a local flavour

☎ 01726 882453
Fore St, Probus TR2 4JL
e-mail: maireadvogel@aol.com
dir: 5m from Truro on A390 towards St Austell

Chef-patron Robert Vogel used to be head chef on the QE2, where he got his sea legs and learned a thing or two about fancy presentation. His family-run restaurant, tucked away in Probus village, between St Austell and Truro, is in a 300-year-old former farmhouse with bags of period features (oak beams, roaring log fires), plus a charming country vibe. The food is unpretentious, seasonal stuff, with top West Country produce put to good use in satisfying modern British dishes. Start with a light and fluffy Cornish blue cheese soufflé with poached pears and walnut dressing, moving on to herb-crusted best end of Trudgian Farm lamb with a rolled, braised shoulder, dauphine potatoes and Merlot jus, or fillet of brill with herbed potatoes and saffron sauce. Finish with a chocolate tart paired with bourbon ice cream.

Chef Robert Vogel **Owner** Robert & Mairead Vogel
Times 7-10 Closed Sun-Mon, L all week **Prices** Fixed D 3 course £29.90, Starter £5.50-£9.50, Main £14.95-£25, Dessert £6-£7.50 **Wines** 16 bottles over £20, 17 bottles under £20, 7 by glass **Notes** Vegetarian available, Dress restrictions, Smart casual **Seats** 32, Pr/dining room 8 **Children** Portions **Parking** On street & car park

---

Tabb's

◎◎ Modern British 🌼

Contemporary dining championing local produce

☎ 01872 262110
85 Kenwyn St TR1 3BZ
e-mail: n.tabb@virgin.net
dir: Down hill past train station, right at mini rdbt, 200yds on left

Since Nigel Tabb set out his stall in a completely renovated town pub in 2005, the gastronomes of Truro have beaten a path to his door. The seductive mood of stylish intimacy created by black slate floors, lilac walls, and high-backed cream and lilac leather chairs is part of the attraction, but it is the kitchen's trademarks - bold

Save on Hotels. Book at **theAA.com/hotel**

CORNWALL & ISLES OF SCILLY 101 ENGLAND

Mediterranean-infused flavours and excellent seasonal Cornish ingredients - that make the real impact. Things stay lively and inventive, all the way from a smoked haddock soup pepped up with chilli and Devon Blue relish, to main courses that might see slow-roasted belly of pork partnered with star anise gravy, chick pea hash and red pepper oil. Desserts are also a strong suit - perhaps tonka bean pannacotta with strawberry and black pepper sorbet. No short cuts are taken here: it is all made in-house, from scratch, from breads to the chocolates that round things off with coffee (Nigel is an expert chocolatier).

Chef Nigel Tabb **Owner** Nigel Tabb **Times** 12-2/6.30-9.30 Closed 25 Dec, 1 Jan, 1 wk Jan, Sun-Mon, L Sat **Prices** Fixed L 2 course £19.50, Fixed D 3 course £29.50-£38.50, Starter £7.25-£10.50, Main £14.75-£20.50, Dessert £7.50, Service optional **Wines** 34 bottles over £20, 9 bottles under £20, 15 by glass **Notes** Vegetarian available **Seats** 30 **Children** Portions **Parking** 200yds

VERYAN   Map 2 SW93

Nare Hotel

@ Traditional British 🍷

Traditional cooking with panoramic views of the south Cornish coast

☎ 01872 501111
Carne Beach TR2 5PF
e-mail: stay@narehotel.co.uk
dir: from Tregony follow A3078 for approx 1.5m. Left at Veryan sign, through village towards sea & hotel

Settings like this are few and far between: the Nare Hotel perches above a secluded sandy beach on the Roseland Peninsula with nothing to intrude on spectacular views across Gerrans Bay. The Dining Room takes full advantage of this unforgettable spot with huge expanses of glass on three sides, while staff glide unobtrusively between linen-clothed tables. Tradition is the watchword in this venue, bringing a classic silver service five-course table d'hôte affair each evening, with hors d'oeuvre and sweet trolleys trundled out to start and finish proceedings. Naturally, the kitchen isn't planning to scare any horses, relying instead on high calibre produce cooked simply and accurately for its effect. Warm wood pigeon with black pudding and caramelised apple sets the ball rolling, while main course delivers caramelised shallots, pancetta, ceps, celeriac and potato purée as the accompaniment to a splendid pan-fried fillet of brill. The less formal dining option is The Quarterdeck - see entry.

Chef Richard James **Owner** T G H Ashworth **Times** 12.30-2.30/7.30-10 Closed L Mon-Sat **Wines** 300 bottles over £20, 200 bottles under £20, 18 by glass **Notes** Fixed D 5 course £49.50, Sunday L, Vegetarian available, Dress restrictions, Jacket and tie **Seats** 75 **Children** Portions, Menu **Parking** 70

The Quarterdeck at the Nare

@@ Modern British 🍷

Superb local produce, creative cooking and fab sea views

☎ 01872 500000
Carne Beach TR2 5PF
e-mail: stay@narehotel.co.uk
dir: From Tregony follow A3078 for approx 1.5m. Left at Veryan sign, through village towards sea & hotel

Overlooking a heavenly sandy beach, the Nare Hotel has much to recommend it, including a brace of excellent restaurants. The Quarterdeck has its own entrance and a different, more unbuttoned vibe to its sister venue, the Dining Room (see entry). The view is worth going out of your way for, and you get it whether you're out on the idyllic terrace breathing in the salty air, or indoors on a typically severe English summer's day, taking it all in through vast full-length windows in a yachtie-themed setting of polished teak, gingham seats and square rails. The kitchen ensures that peerless piscine produce from the local waters gets star billing in its confident modern dishes - perhaps seared scallops partnered with parsnip purée and truffled mushrooms, then John Dory with cider and thyme mussels, roast garlic and chive mash. Local meat fans will be pleased to learn that the prime protein hasn't clocked up many food miles either - loin of venison is served with butternut squash purée, girolles and potato gnocchi, while two could sign up to a rib of Heligan beef, and wrap things up with Valrhona chocolate fondant, rum ice cream and white chocolate sauce.

Chef Richard James **Owner** Toby Ashworth **Times** 12.30-2.30/7-9.30 Closed 25 Dec, D 31 Dec **Prices** Starter £6.50-£9, Main £13-£39, Dessert £6.50-£9, Service optional **Wines** 300 bottles over £20, 200 bottles under £20, 18 by glass **Notes** Vegetarian available, Dress restrictions, Smart casual after 7pm **Seats** 60 **Children** Portions, Menu **Parking** 60

WATERGATE BAY   Map 2 SW86

Fifteen Cornwall

@ Italian 🍷

Italian sunshine by the Cornish surf

☎ 01637 861000
On The Beach TR8 4AA
e-mail: restaurant@fifteencornwall.co.uk
dir: M5 to Exeter & join A30 westbound. Exit Highgate Hill junct, following signs to airport and at T-junct after airport, turn left & follow road to Watergate Bay

Chances are you've heard of the laudable objective behind Jamie Oliver's Fifteen Foundation, and here it is in full swing: young people given a chance to shine, and shine they do. The location is rather special: right on the beach, looking out over the surf, floor to ceiling glass giving everyone a view, and the décor is modish simplicity at its best. The cooking is Italian, Jamie stylee, which means first-rate ingredients (plenty of local stuff too) and unfussy preparations. Start, perhaps, with antipasti to share, or go for celeriac and roasted garlic soup with almond gremolata, before the likes of Primrose Herd pork shoulder with bianco perla polenta, cavolo nero and rosemary and anchovy dressing. It might be more expensive than you think, so check out the prices first if you're on a budget.

Chef Andy Appleton **Owner** Cornwall Foundation of Promise **Times** 12-2.30/6.15-9.45 **Prices** Fixed L 3 course £28, Tasting menu fr £60, Starter £7.75-£13.95, Main £14.50-£26.95, Dessert £6.40-£7.95, Service optional **Wines** 119 bottles over £20, 4 bottles under £20, 13 by glass **Notes** Tasting menu D 5 course, Vegetarian available **Seats** 100, Pr/dining room 12 **Children** Portions, Menu **Parking** In front of restaurant & on site P&D

ZENNOR   Map 2 SW43

The Gurnard's Head

@ Modern 🍷NOTABLE WINE LIST

Flavourful modern cooking on the north Cornish coast

☎ 01736 796928
Treen TR26 3DE
e-mail: enquiries@gurnardshead.co.uk
dir: 6m W of St Ives by B3306

This yellow-painted inn is in a superb spot overlooking the rocky promontory it takes its name from, with the coast path nearby. It's a laid-back sort of place, colourfully decorated, with a fire in the flagstone-floored bar and a dining room off it. The cooking gives the impression that a strong sense of integrity is at work, with nothing too elaborate or fancy, just intelligently handled raw materials, seen in plaice fillets with vermouth, grape and tarragon sauce and new potatoes, and braised beef with colcannon, celeriac, and mushroom ravioli. Among starters, roast quail is interestingly partnered by squid ink risotto, and seared scallops familiarly by black pudding with sweetcorn cream and apple, and to end might be an unusual peanut parfait with chocolate sorbet.

Times 12-2.30/6.30-9.30 Closed 24-25 Dec

SCILLY, ISLES OF

BRYHER
Map 2 SV81

Hell Bay

◎◎◎ – see below

TRESCO
Map 2 SV81

New Inn

◎ Modern, Traditional

Simple and direct cooking at a welcoming Scillies inn

☎ 01720 422849 & 422867
TR24 0QQ
e-mail: newinn@tresco.co.uk
dir: Ferry or helicopter from Penzance; 250yds from harbour (private island, contact hotel for details)

A popular venue for Tresco walkers, the New Inn is reliably full of banter and bonhomie, with eating spread across the main bar, the residents' dining room and a pavilion. It all feels reassuringly lived-in, and outdoor eating in the garden with sea views (it's only a short hop back from the waterfront) is a real treat, as is getting bedded in here on a rough winter's night. Scilly crab and baby leek tart blends its fine components into a soufflé-like filling, garnished with dressed leaves, and could be followed by seared venison steak with braised red cabbage, fine beans and truffle-oiled mash, a simple, direct and uncluttered way of presenting a great piece of meat. Finish with enjoyably bitter chocolate and pecan brownie, served hot with vanilla ice cream.

Chef Alex Smith **Owner** Mr Robert Dorrien-Smith **Times** 12-2/6.30-9 **Prices** Starter £6-£8, Main £10-£20, Dessert £5-£6, Service optional **Wines** 17 bottles over £20, 13 bottles under £20, 11 by glass **Notes** Sunday L, Vegetarian available **Seats** 30 **Children** Portions, Menu **Parking** Car free Island

CUMBRIA

ALSTON
Map 18 NY74

Lovelady Shield Country House Hotel

◎◎ Modern British **NEW**

Refined modern dining in intimate country house

☎ 01434 381203
CA9 3LF
e-mail: enquiries@lovelady.co.uk
web: www.lovelady.co.uk
dir: 2m E of Alston, signed off A689 at junct with B6294

This intimate Georgian country house with an impossibly romantic name is hidden away in three acres of secretive gardens on the River Nent in the wild North Pennine countryside. Inside, it has the feel of a posh private house: its traditionally decorated lounge is warmed by a log fire, and hands-on owners add that personal touch.

Dining takes place in an elegant pastel-hued room with well-spaced linen-clothed tables immaculately laid with silverware and crockery bearing the house's image, and the seasonal menus deal in intelligently-conceived classic British dishes. Head chef Barrie Garton has been at the stoves of Lovelady Shield for over 20 years, so has deeply-rooted supply lines to the best regional producers, whose peerless ingredients form the bedrock of the contemporary repertoire. Expect starters along the lines of confit salmon fillet partnered with salmon jelly and roe, and honey and soy vinaigrette; next come mains such as seared loin and braised belly of lamb with pommes purées, spinach, girolles and garden rosemary jus. Desserts are equally refined affairs - perhaps dark chocolate mousse with coconut (as jelly, ice cream and macaroon), Piña Colada foam, and lime syrup.

Chef Barrie Garton **Owner** Peter & Marie Haynes **Times** 12-2/7-8.30 Closed L Mon-Sat **Prices** Fixed D 3 course £32, Tasting menu £55, Service optional **Wines** 100 bottles over £20, 12 bottles under £20, 11 by glass **Notes** Tasting menu available, Sunday L, Vegetarian available, Dress restrictions, No shorts, Civ Wed 100 **Seats** 30 **Children** Portions, Menu **Parking** 20

Hell Bay

BRYHER
Map 2 SV81

Modern British **V**

Blistering cooking in island hideaway

☎ 01720 422947
TR23 0PR
e-mail: contactus@hellbay.co.uk
dir: Helicopter from Penzance to Tresco, St Mary's. Plane from Southampton, Bristol, Exeter, Newquay or Land's End

The journey to the isles heightens expectations, involving as it does a final ferry ride from St Mary's or Tresco to reach Bryher, which has little other than stunning rugged beauty and crystal-clear seas. The hotel itself has a serene feeling of calmness, a true place at which, to use that old cliché, to get away from it all. Large windows in the restaurant look over tussocks of windswept grasses to the rock-strewn shore and the sea; it's a simply decorated room, predominantly in blue and fawn, with plain wooden tables and a pitched wooden ceiling with rafters. Richard Kearsley is a supremely confident and talented chef, whose cooking is quite complex but flavours are nonetheless uncluttered and well balanced. A typical starter from the short menu is a trio of seafood: a chunk of battered cod on pea purée, a sweet-tasting scallop on parsnip purée, and a crab cake on wilted spinach, each successful on its own but working well together. Another one might see ballottine of rabbit confit with piquant pickled carrots and radishes and sharp orange purée spiked with star anise. A favoured device among main courses is to apply a different cooking medium to different cuts of the same meat, so braised and then roast shoulder of lamb might be plated with roast loin and served with butternut squash fondant, spiced lentils and rosemary-infused jus. A fish alternative might be roast fillet of monkfish with crab risotto sauced with lemongrass and ginger. Attention to detail is manifest throughout a meal from canapés and breads to desserts of a copybook fig tarte Tatin with liquorice ripple ice cream, or tiramisù.

Chef Richard Kearsley **Owner** Tresco Estate **Times** 12-2/7-9.30 Closed 2 Nov-17 Mar **Prices** Fixed D 3 course £37.50, Service optional **Wines** 44 bottles over £20, 2 bottles under £20, 16 by glass **Notes** Vegetarian menu, Dress restrictions, Smart casual **Seats** 70, Pr/dining room 12 **Children** Portions

Save on Hotels. Book at theAA.com/hotel

CUMBRIA 103 **ENGLAND**

AMBLESIDE
Map 18 NY30

Drunken Duck Inn

◉◉ Modern British ✿

Superb local produce and contemporary seasonal cooking

☎ 015394 36347
Barngates LA22 0NG
e-mail: info@drunkenduckinn.co.uk
web: www.drunkenduckinn.co.uk
dir: Take A591 from Kendal, follow signs for Hawkshead (from Ambleside), in 2.5m sign for inn on right, 1m up hill

High above Lake Windermere, with breathtaking views of the fells, the inn is a combination of bar, restaurant and hotel. There may be the usual ceiling beams and wooden floors, but this is a slick, classy operation without any hint of chintz. The lunch menu, with orders placed at the bar, is a pretty impressive listing (think cheese soufflé, sirloin steak with béarnaise and fries, Cullen skink with pancetta and a poached egg), while the evening carte ups the ante. An amuse-bouche of perhaps pea and mint soup raises expectations before the arrival of a well-conceived, tasty starter of, say, lamb fillet on a dollop of mash surrounded by cockles and samphire in a tomato and tarragon jus, or crab ravioli in shellfish bisque. Main courses are along the lines of contemporary brasserie-style dishes, from ox cheek braised in red wine served with mash and bourguignon sauce, to crisp-skinned, succulent sea bass with a selection of accurately cooked vegetables. To finish, try Manchester tart with vanilla ice cream.

Chef Jonny Watson **Owner** Stephanie Barton
Times 12-4/6.30-9 Closed 25 Dec **Prices** Starter £4.75-£9.95, Main £12.95-£27.50, Dessert £6.50-£7, Service optional **Wines** 200 bottles over £20, 26 bottles under £20, 26 by glass **Notes** Vegetarian available **Seats** 52 **Children** Portions **Parking** 40

The Log House

◉ Modern Mediterranean

Eclectic cooking in a Norwegian log house

☎ 015394 31077
Lake Rd LA22 0DN
e-mail: info@loghouse.co.uk
dir: M6 junct 36. Situated on A591 on left, just beyond garden centre

Local artist Alfred Heaton Cooper imported The Log House in the late 19th century and rebuilt it halfway between the town centre and the shore of Lake Windermere. It's a real eye-catcher, and refurbishments over the years have brought it up to a stylish and modern - and popular - restaurant. The kitchen has a flexible outlook, turning its hands to chermoula-spiced mussels as well as goats' cheese in puff pastry on beetroot chutney with toasted walnut vinaigrette. Main courses demonstrate similar diversity: chargrilled beef fillet served in a blue cheese and herb crust with pancetta, rösti and red wine jus; and gazpacho dressing giving a kick to grilled sea bass on

watercress and crab with sautéed potatoes. Finish with rich mocha mousse topped with meringue.

Times 5-9.30 Closed 7 Jan-7 Feb, Mon, L all week

Rothay Manor

◉ Traditional British Ⅴ

Accurate cooking in a well-established hotel

☎ 015394 33605
Rothay Bridge LA22 0EH
e-mail: hotel@rothaymanor.co.uk
web: www.rothaymanor.co.uk
dir: In Ambleside follow signs for Coniston (A593). Manor 0.25m SW of Ambleside opposite rugby pitch

Rothay Manor has the sense of deep-seated tradition that comes from being run by the same family for 45 years. The Regency manor was built in 1822 by a Liverpool shipping merchant and is close by Ambleside, yet cushioned from its bustle by an acre of lovingly maintained grounds. The restaurant goes for time-honoured Lakeland charm: candlelit mahogany tables are laid with crystal, china, silver and linen napkins, and tended by correctly formal but unstuffy staff. Flexibility has crept into the five-course dinner format, allowing diners to choose as many dishes as they are happy to take on; going for three courses from the gently-modernised country-house cooking, you might kick off with stilton, apricot and walnut pâté with home-made oat biscuits, then progress to Holker Hall wild mallard braised with damson gin, and served with juniper berry jus, braised red cabbage, and rosemary potatoes. At the end, choose between local cheeses or vanilla pannacotta with a compôte of rum-soaked raisins, and hazelnut ice cream.

Chef Jane Binns **Owner** Nigel Nixon **Times** 12.30-1.45/7-9 Closed 3-20 Jan, L 1 Jan, D 25 Dec **Prices** Fixed D 3 course £39.50, Service optional **Wines** 78 bottles over £20, 20 bottles under £20, 10 by glass **Notes** ALC L only, Sunday L, Vegetarian menu, Dress restrictions, Smart casual **Seats** 65, Pr/dining room 34 **Children** Portions, Menu **Parking** 35

Waterhead Hotel

◉ Modern British

Modern British cooking by Lake Windermere

☎ 015394 32566
Lake Rd LA22 0ER
e-mail: waterhead@englishlakes.co.uk
dir: A591 into Ambleside, hotel opposite Waterhead Pier

The splendid Lakeland landscapes sweeping across Windermere have been immortalised in the poems and paintings of Tennyson and Turner, and the Waterhead sits in pole position to ponder the pulchritude of it all, just a short stroll from the bustle of Ambleside. The view from the restaurant is timeless, but the venue itself sports a thoroughly modern boutique look to go with its up-to-date menus of classic and contemporary ideas. Local Cumbrian materials are of course to the fore - herb-crusted pork belly, perhaps, stuffed with home-made black pudding and served with Bramley apple purée, or a platter of Cartmel Valley smoked meats, followed by braised blade of beef with fondant potato, glazed root vegetables and red wine jus. There are chargrilled Cumbrian steaks too, and for pudding, something like treacle tart with butterscotch sauce and vanilla ice cream.

Chef Andrew Caulfield **Owner** English Lakes Hotels
Times 11.30-7/7-9.30 Closed Xmas, New Year (only open to residents), L Mon-Sat **Prices** Fixed D 3 course £22.50, Starter £5.50-£9.95, Main £12.95-£25, Dessert £6.25-£14, Service optional **Wines** 38 bottles over £20, 29 bottles under £20, 12 by glass **Notes** Vegetarian available, Civ Wed 80 **Seats** 70 **Children** Portions, Menu **Parking** 50, Nearby pay & display

APPLEBY-IN-WESTMORLAND
Map 18 NY62

Appleby Manor Country House Hotel

◉ Modern British Ⅴ ✿

Peaceful rural views and modern country-house cooking

☎ 017683 51571
Roman Rd CA16 6JB
e-mail: reception@applebymanor.co.uk
dir: M6 junct 40/A66 towards Brough. Take Appleby turn, then immediately right. Continue for 0.5m

This Victorian sandstone country-house hotel was sited in such a way that all the public rooms, including the oak-panelled restaurant and the conservatory extension, have unparalleled views over Appleby Castle and the Eden Valley towards the fells of the Lake District. The kitchen makes good use of local ingredients and generally follows a well-tried route: pan-fried calves' liver, for instance, with truffled celeriac purée, caramelised onions and crispy bacon, followed by Lancashire hotpot, or pan-fried Goosnargh duck breast with orange sauce, bubble-and-squeak and onion tarte Tatin. Fashionable and exotic touches are sometimes introduced, adding shrimp foam to seared scallops with pea purée, say, stir-fried Asian vegetables and hot-and-sour prawn soup to grilled

continued

APPLEBY-IN-WESTMORLAND *continued*

mackerel, and chocolate and chilli ice cream to an assiette of chocolate to finish, or go for the familiarity of sticky toffee pudding.

Chef Chris Thompson **Owner** Dunbobbin family **Times** 12-2/7-9 Closed 24-26 Dec **Prices** Fixed L 2 course fr £16.95, Starter £4.95-£10, Main £14.95-£20, Dessert £4.95-£7.50, Service optional **Wines** 45 bottles over £20, 15 bottles under £20, 10 by glass **Notes** Sunday L, Vegetarian menu, Dress restrictions, Smart casual, Civ Wed 100 **Seats** 100, Pr/dining room 20 **Children** Menu **Parking** 60

BARROW-IN-FURNESS Map 18 SD26

Clarence House Country Hotel & Restaurant

◉◉ British, International

Modern British versatility in an orangery setting

☎ 01229 462508
Skelgate, Dalton-in-Furness LA15 8BQ
e-mail: enquiries@clarencehouse-hotel.co.uk

The white-fronted hotel in Dalton-in-Furness, not far from Barrow, is perfectly poised between sandy beaches and the lush green acres of Lakeland. A dining room designed like an orangery, with windows on three sides, affords covetable views over the St Thomas Valley, and terrace tables make the best of the sun. The menus are defined by that resourcefully versatile reach that has come to be the hallmark of the modern British idiom, offering Chinese-style slow-roasted duck in plum sauce with cashews and pomegranate to start, or a tian of Cornish crab set in avocado, tomato and basil. For main, there may be grilled salmon garnished with crisp pancetta and a pea and mint risotto, or roast chump of Cumbrian lamb with provençal accompaniments of aubergine, confit peppers and tapenade. A grill section offers various steaks and chops with a choice of sauces. Friday night is carvery night.

Times 12-4/7-9

BASSENTHWAITE Map 18 NY23

Armathwaite Hall

◉ British, French V 🍃

Discreetly modernised country-house cooking with views of the Cumbrian hills

☎ 017687 76551
CA12 4RE
e-mail: reservations@armathwaite-hall.com
dir: From M6 junct 40/A66 to Keswick then A591 towards Carlisle. Continue for 7m and turn left at Castle Inn

The handsome crenallated Lakeland house looks exactly the sort of location in which you might expect to find Miss Marple pottering with intent, were it not for the fact that nothing seems to disturb the sylvan tranquillity. Views of the Cumbrian hills from the stolid windows of the

elegantly panelled dining room will lift the spirits on sunny days and light evenings, and the formally attentive staff know what they are about. All in all, it makes a contenting setting for the discreetly modernised country-house cooking on offer. A fixed-price dinner menu may proceed from ham hock terrine with pea shoots and mustard-dressed saladings, to mains like the creative spin on fish and chips - lemon sole in potato and shallot batter with puréed broccoli and sweet potato chips - or venison loin with poached pear in a caramelised sauce of redcurrant, orange and port. Finish with lemon syllabub, garnished with orange-almond biscotti and lemon sorbet.

Chef Kevin Dowling **Owner** Graves Family **Times** 12.30-1.45/7.30-9 **Prices** Fixed L 2 course £16.95, Service optional **Wines** 46 bottles over £20, 34 bottles under £20, 6 by glass **Notes** Fixed D 5 course £45.95, Sunday L, Vegetarian menu, Dress restrictions, Smart casual, no jeans/T-shirts/trainers **Seats** 80 **Children** Portions **Parking** 100

The Pheasant

◉ Modern British

Charming period coaching inn with clearly focused, seasonal menu

☎ 017687 76234
CA13 9YE
e-mail: info@the-pheasant.co.uk
web: www.the-pheasant.co.uk
dir: M6 junct 40, take A66 (Keswick and North Lakes). Continue past Keswick and head for Cockermouth. Signed from A66

With period charm to spare, The Pheasant is in a peaceful spot near Bassenthwaite Lake. A coaching inn since the 16th century, a gently contemporary restaurant is now part of the package, but rest assured the wonderfully atmospheric bar still dispenses local ales, and there's also a bistro if you're after something a little less formal. The Fell Restaurant is imbued with a pleasing understated refinement, with wood-panelled walls, upholstered chairs, linen-clad tables and smartly dressed staff (donning pheasant emblazoned ties) who maintain the air of civility. Good local produce shines through in nicely presented seasonal British dishes such as ham hock terrine with piccalilli purée and celeriac remoulade, followed by slow-cooked loin of Holker Hall venison with parsnip confit, buttered cabbage, thyme gnocchi and chocolate-scented jus.

Times 12-1.30/7-9 Closed 25 Dec

BORROWDALE Map 18 NY21

Leathes Head Hotel

◉ Modern British **NEW**

Traditional country-house cooking and lovely views

☎ 017687 77247
CA12 5UY
e-mail: reservations@leatheshead.co.uk
dir: 3.75m S of Keswick on B5289, set back on the left

A warm welcome awaits visitors to this small family-run hotel in the heart of the beautiful Borrowdale Valley. The Leathes Head was originally built in Edwardian times as a gentleman's residence, and is full of original features in its 11 bedrooms and its traditionally decorated public rooms, including the intimate restaurant. Here, with views of the two-and-a-half acres of gardens and the unspoilt fells beyond, you can enjoy some traditional, country-house-hotel cooking based on plenty of locally-sourced ingredients. Cream of butternut squash soup with cumin and herb croûtons might kick things off, with poached haddock with seasonal vegetables and Lancashire brown shrimps and prawns in a bisque sauce to follow. Black Forest chocolate pot with Bakewell tart ice cream and Amaretto is an ambitious but altogether winning dessert.

Times 7.30-8.15 Closed mid Nov-mid Feb

BRAITHWAITE Map 18 NY22

The Cottage in the Wood

◉◉ Modern European V

Relaxing rural surroundings for some original modern dishes

☎ 017687 78409
Whinlatter Forest CA12 5TW
e-mail: relax@thecottageinthewood.co.uk
dir: M6 junct 40, A66 signed Keswick. 1m after Keswick take B5292 signed Braithwaite, hotel in 2m

The name's a bit of a giveaway: the former coaching inn, dating from the 17th century, is at the heart of the Whinlatter Forest. The Mountain View restaurant is aptly named too, its conservatory-type windows giving wonderful views of the surrounding forest and Skiddaw range. The kitchen sources all its materials locally (herbs and mushrooms may be foraged from the forest), and uses them to produce some innovative dishes. Accurately roasted fillet of turbot with cauliflower, shrimps, sorrel, and curry and Sauternes velouté turns out to be a successful starter, its flavours working well together. Other combinations are just as winning, from pressed pig's head and crisp ear served with remoulade, pickled apple and a quail's egg, to braised and glazed shin of beef accompanied by wild mushroom ravioli, braised endive and celeriac purée. Breads are all made in-house, and desserts may include a simply presented pear and almond friand with a matching iced parfait and sorbet.

Chef Ryan Blackburn **Owner** Liam & Kath Berney **Times** 12.30-2.30/6-9 Closed Jan, Mon, D Sun

Save on Hotels. Book at **theAA.com/hotel**

CUMBRIA 105 **ENGLAND**

Prices Fixed D 3 course fr £36, Service included, Groups min 8 service 10% **Wines** 23 bottles over £20, 20 bottles under £20, 6 by glass **Notes** Fixed D 5 course £52, Sunday L, Vegetarian menu **Seats** 36 **Children** Portions **Parking** 16

BRAMPTON   Map 21 NY56

Farlam Hall Hotel

◎◎ Modern & Traditional British V

- -

Traditional cooking with relaxing pastoral views

☎ 016977 46234
Hallbankgate CA8 2NG
e-mail: farlam@relaischateaux.com
dir: On A689, 2.5m SE of Brampton (not in Farlam village)

Farlam Hall has been around since the 16th century, but owes most of its current splendour to a wealthy Victorian industrialist who created the glorious gardens and the old-school grandeur of its interiors. The same family have run Farlam for over 30 years, so you can expect well-polished service and an air of continuity. The dining room is well-lit by floor-to-ceiling windows overlooking the ornamental lake, and tables are formally turned-out with gleaming crystal and silver on starched linen, but there is no other presence of starch, least of all in the delightfully relaxed service. A daily-changing menu offers classic English country-house cooking with subtle modern tweaks - perhaps smoked and fresh salmon fishcake with buttered leeks and cream, dill and white wine sauce, followed by tenderloin of local Cumbrian pork wrapped in air-dried ham matched with apple mashed potato, apple sauce tartlet and Calvados sauce. Well-kept English cheeses intervene before time-honoured puddings such as glazed lemon tart with fruit coulis.

Chef Barry Quinion **Owner** Quinion family **Times** 8-8.30 Closed 24-30 Dec, 4-15 Jan, L all week **Prices** Fixed D 4 course fr £45, Service optional **Wines** 37 bottles over £20, 12 by glass **Notes** Vegetarian menu, Dress restrictions, Smart casual, no shorts, Civ Wed 40 **Seats** 40, Pr/dining room 20 **Children** Portions **Parking** 25

CARLISLE   Map 18 NY35

Crown Hotel

◎ Modern British

- -

Modern British cooking in a country conservatory

☎ 01228 561888
Station Rd, Wetheral CA4 8ES
e-mail: info@crownhotelwetheral.co.uk
web: www.crownhotelwetheral.co.uk

Just off the A69, outside Carlisle, the peaceful village of Wetheral is home to this attractive country hotel in its own gardens, views of which are on offer all round in the raftered conservatory restaurant. Unclothed darkwood tables and friendly service indicate the laidback approach, and the food is at the gentler end of the modern British spectrum. Producing black pudding in-house is a commendable venture, and a thick slice of it might turn up with spicy chorizo and salad, garnished with mustard mayonnaise, as a hearty starter. Roast lamb rump comes with grain mustard mash and confit root vegetables, a main course that delivers tender, flavourful meat and a robust jus. Fish may be fried trout with wilted greens, pesto mash and lemon butter. For pudding, you may be tempted by the northern classic Cumberland rum nicky, a concoction of dried fruits in ginger and rum, fashioned here into a tart and served with clotted cream.

Chef Paul Taylor **Owner** David Byers
Times 12-2.30/7-9.30 Closed L Sat **Prices** Food prices not confirmed for 2013. Please telephone for details
Notes Sunday L, Vegetarian available, Civ Wed 120
Seats 80, Pr/dining room 120 **Children** Portions, Menu
Parking 70

CARTMEL   Map 18 SD37

Aynsome Manor Hotel

◎ British ♨

- -

Long-standing Lakeland hotel with comfortingly traditional approach

☎ 015395 36653
LA11 6HH
e-mail: aynsomemanor@btconnect.com
dir: M6 junct 36, A590 signed Barrow-in-Furness towards Cartmel. Left at end of road, hotel before village

With origins dating back to the 16th century, today's Aynsome - set in attractive gardens looking out across the fells towards Cartmel's impressive Norman priory - deals in good old Lakeland country-house hospitality. Nowhere more so perhaps than in the elegant, oak-panelled and ornate-ceilinged Georgian restaurant, which bathes in those pastoral views and offers the perfect setting in which to savour the well-balanced five-course dinner menu. Intelligently simple British cooking is admirably conjured from quality local, seasonal produce; main-course roast chump of Lakeland lamb accompanied by Puy lentils, shallots and a rosemary and red wine jus, for example, or pan-fried fillet of red bream glazed with watercress pesto and served with courgette spaghetti.

Chef Gordon Topp **Owner** Christopher Varley **Times** 7-8.30 Closed 25-26 Dec, 2-28 Jan, L Mon-Sat, D Sun (ex residents) **Prices** Fixed D 3 course £28-£29, Service optional **Wines** 25 bottles over £20, 60 bottles under £20, 6 by glass **Notes** Sunday L, Vegetarian available, Dress restrictions, Smart dress **Seats** 28 **Children** Portions, Menu **Parking** 20

L'Enclume

◎◎◎◎◎ – *see page 106*

L'Enclume

CARTMEL
Map 18 SD37

Modern British V ⬥NOTABLE WINE LIST 🦢

Beautifully crafted food with flavour as king

☎ 015395 36362
Cavendish St LA11 6PZ
e-mail: info@lenclume.co.uk
web: www.lenclume.co.uk
dir: Follow signs for A590 W, turn left for Cartmel before Newby Bridge

Simon Rogan and Penny Tapsell's restaurant with rooms in the pretty village of Cartmel is one of the brightest lights in the UK's dining firmament. The 700-year-old one-time forge has been transformed with a tasteful, naturalistic touch into a charmingly peaceful place, but it is just one of the irons in the fire, which includes an organic farm down the road from whence come boundless vegetables, fruits, flowers and herbs (and more recently livestock too), a research and development premises, a dozen or so attractive bedrooms and suites in the main building and around the village, a second restaurant down the road (Rogan & Company, see entry) and a London outpost that is spreading the word to the capital city (see entry for Roganic). For such a high-flying restaurant, there's a pleasing unpretentiousness to the place, with lots of natural surfaces and original features alongside modish artworks and well designed fixtures and fittings. The

service team - including the admirably switched-on sommelier - keep things moving with seemingly effortless efficiency and charm, and with the multiple-dish format of the menu, they have got their work cut out. At the heart of everything, the very foundation of what Simon Rogan's food is all about... is ingredients. Hence the farm. For many years now, Rogan has been using some of the less commonly seen fruits (and veg) of this land, and with the capacity to grow them for himself, the provenance, freshness and quality of produce served up to his customers is second to none. And what isn't grown is foraged or sourced with diligence. Combine that passion with a curious mind, a creative imagination and a seriously perfectionist streak, and what appears on the plate is truly stunning. Modern cooking techniques are used, but never at the expense of flavour. Flavour is king around here. The menu follows the tasting route, from eight to 12 courses, and if that sounds like a lot of food, rest assured it is judged to a tee. An amuse-bouche of oyster macaroon with an oyster and apple jelly, and bread rolls made with organic flour, make a first impression that immediately puts one at ease - this is going to be great, and great it is. Beetroot and mozzarella, celery and dill delivers powerful flavours, judged to perfection, while marinated scallops - fresh as a daisy - with toasted seeds, red cabbage and wild sorrel looks

spectacular on the plate and shows real precision in the execution. Sea asters are a native plant little seen at UK tables and here they're served with Bessy Beck trout, varne leeks and a trout roe sauce, and vintage summer vegetables (preserved for winter eating) star alongside delicious Randolph's Lop suckling pig. The technical virtuosity of dishes is staggering at times and the visual impact never waivers. Coniston oatmeal, stout ice cream with liquorice and sea buckthorn bursts with appealing flavours, with the steady hand at the tiller ensuring no one thing overpowers the other. It will come as no surprise that the wines are sourced with the same passion and attention to detail.

Chef Simon Rogan **Owner** Simon Rogan, Penny Tapsell **Times** 12-1.30/6.30-9.30 Closed L Mon-Tue **Prices** Fixed L 3 course £25, Tasting menu £69-£89, Service optional, Groups min 8 service 10% **Wines** 356 bottles over £20, 4 bottles under £20, 10 by glass **Notes** Tasting menu L 8 course D 12 course, Vegetarian menu **Seats** 50, Pr/dining room 10 **Parking** 7, On street

Save on Hotels. Book at **theAA.com/hotel**

CUMBRIA 107 **ENGLAND**

CARTMEL *continued*

Rogan & Company Restaurant

◉◉ Modern British

Locally-based innovative cooking from the Cartmel maestro

☎ 015395 35917
The Square LA11 6QD
e-mail: reservations@roganandcompany.co.uk
dir: From M6 junct 36 follow signs for A590. Turn off at sign for Cartmel village

A short walk from Simon Rogan's nerve-centre of L'Enclume (see entry), his second restaurant in picturesque Cartmel is in an old beamed house, full of nooks and crannies, by the riverside. A recent refurbishment has worked to an autumnal palette of terracotta, browns and reds, with rapturous Lakeland views adorning the walls. Local farms (including Rogan's own) and orchards supply many of the kitchen materials, and foraged items are nearly always a feature, as Louie Lawrence interprets the Rogan style with fidelity and flair. Confit Goosnargh duck legs are texturally spot-on, bedded on sautéed diced Jerusalem artichoke, the whole thing scented with tarragon oil, for an impressive kick-off. Main courses raise the stakes for the likes of golden-crusted lemon sole partnered with lobster ravioli, garnished with crisp-fried leeks and sauced with a rich lobster cream, or Gloucesterhire Old Spot pork belly cooked in mead, with Brussels sprouts and salsify. A meltingly opulent hot chocolate fondant, served with bright white chocolate sorbet, is full of impressive concentration, or there may be spiced pineapple tart with coconut ice cream.

Chef Simon Rogan, Louie Lawrence **Owner** Simon Rogan, Penny Tapsell **Times** 12-2.30/6.30-9 Closed Mon-Tue **Prices** Food prices not confirmed for 2013. Please telephone for details **Wines** 19 bottles over £20, 15 bottles under £20, 9 by glass **Notes** Vegetarian available **Seats** 50, Pr/dining room 10 **Children** Portions **Parking** On street

---

The Punchbowl Inn at Crosthwaite

Map 18 SD49

◉◉ Modern British ⭐

Smartly updated inn with carefully crafted, appealing dishes

☎ 015395 68237
Lyth Valley LA8 8HR
e-mail: info@the-punchbowl.co.uk
web: www.the-punchbowl.co.uk
dir: A590 then A5074 signed Bowness/Crosthwaite. Inn within 3m on right

The whitewashed old inn, in a stunning rural spot at the heart of the Lyth Valley, is a stylish place indeed, always busy, with a slate-topped bar and a restaurant with a polished oak floor, leather chairs and a stone fireplace. The same menu is served throughout, the carefully composed dishes based on fine Lakeland produce. Seared scallops are served with a ball of black pudding and apple purée, a drizzle of caramel adding a welcome touch of sweetness, and garlicky potato soup is jazzed up by slices of chorizo. Main courses are no less appreciated: slow-cooked rolled pork belly with a tasty faggot, creamy mash and Savoy cabbage with bacon, say, and well-timed roast loin of cod with leek and bacon chowder and sweetcorn purée. Ambition extends into puddings too: witness chocolate mousse not just with raspberry sorbet but with popping candy and elderflower foam.

Chef Scott Fairweather **Owner** Richard Rose **Times** 12-6/6-9.30 **Prices** Fixed L 2 course fr £12.95, Starter £4.50-£7.95, Main £10.95-£19.95, Dessert £5.45-£5.95, Service optional, Groups min 10 service 10% **Wines** 58 bottles over £20, 15 bottles under £20, 14 by glass **Notes** Sunday L, Vegetarian available, Civ Wed 60 **Seats** 50, Pr/dining room 16 **Children** Portions, Menu **Parking** 40

ELTERWATER **Map 18 NY30**

Purdeys at the Langdale Hotel & Spa

◉◉ Modern, Traditional British

Well-crafted, modish cooking in a rustic setting

☎ 015394 37302 & 38080
The Langdale Estate LA22 9JD
e-mail: purdeys@langdale.co.uk
web: www.langdale.co.uk
dir: M6 junct 36, A591 or M6 junct 40, A66, B5322, A591

Part of the 35-acre Langdale Estate, Purdeys is a spacious, rustically styled restaurant, with bare stone walls, a raftered roof and wooden tables and chairs; an original cannon is a talking point, and there are views of a working waterwheel outside. The menus are in the modern British mode, with some input evident from far beyond these shores. Forward-looking starters might be along the lines of seared scallops with crispy veal sweetbreads sauced with salsa verde, and roast wood pigeon in a port reduction with textures of cauliflower. Ingredients are well chosen and compositions convincing: Morecambe Bay shrimp risotto to accompany accurately timed pollock fillet, served with salsify and a faddish vanilla foam, and rump of fell lamb, spiced Moroccan-style and accompanied by couscous and tomato confit. Puddings may include rhubarb cheesecake with vanilla-poached fruit and gingerbread ice cream.

Times 6.30-9.30 Closed L ex groups - booking essential

GLENRIDDING Map 18 NY31

The Inn on the Lake

◉ Modern European V ♨

Modern cooking on the shore of Ullswater

☎ 017684 82444
CA11 0PE
e-mail: innonthelake@lakedistricthotels.net
dir: M6 junct 40, A66 Keswick, A592 Windermere

Set in 15 acres of mature grounds on the shore of Ullswater, the hotel has undergone a refurbishment that has brought dramatic splashes of lilac and violet to the public rooms, though there still isn't anything to rival the wonderful prospect from the appositely named Lake View restaurant. A fixed-price menu of modern European food takes in salmon tartare and sautéed scallop with a mini-Scotch egg and beetroot carpaccio, rump of lamb with sticky red cabbage, carrot and swede purée and roast roots, or a generous fish assiette comprised of sea bass, curried monkfish and John Dory in leek and saffron broth. Finish with chocolate parfait, served with black cherry and rum compôte.

Chef Fraser Soutar **Owner** Charles & Kit Graves
Times 12-2/7-9 **Prices** Fixed L 2 course £16.50, Fixed D 2 course £25.95, Fixed D 4 course £36.95, Starter £6.95-£8.95, Main £17.95-£22.95, Dessert £6.95-£8.95, Service optional **Wines** 38 bottles over £20, 12 bottles under £20, 8 by glass **Notes** Sunday L, Vegetarian menu, Dress restrictions, Smart casual, Civ Wed 110 **Seats** 100, Pr/dining room 40 **Children** Portions, Menu **Parking** 100

GRANGE-OVER-SANDS Map 18 SD47

Clare House

◉ Modern British

Wonderful views and modern country-house cooking

☎ 015395 33026
Park Rd LA11 7HQ
e-mail: info@clarehousehotel.co.uk
dir: Off A590 onto B5277, through Lindale into Grange, keep left, hotel 0.5m on left past Crown Hill & St Paul's Church

This elegant Victorian country house stands in well-maintained gardens leading down to the expansive waters of Grange-over-Sands. The restaurant is split into two nicely done out rooms with artwork hung on the modern wallpaper and clothed and unclothed tables set with fresh flowers. The kitchen team turns out a happy blend of modern and traditional dishes, on a well-judged carte (not too long, not too short) and based on a good amount of local ingredients. On the five-course evening menu - served in one sitting at 6.45 - you might find a twice-baked cheese soufflé, the final baking with cream and gruyère, and main courses such as hearty roast tenderloin and belly of pork with grain mustard and parsley mash, purple sprouting broccoli, apple sauce, crackling and herb jus. To finish, lemon posset with spiced summer berries and East Yorkshire sugar cakes fits the bill.

Chef Andrew Read, Mark Johnston **Owner** Mr & Mrs D S Read **Times** 12-2.30/6.45-7.15 **Closed** Dec-Apr **Wines** 7 bottles over £20, 19 bottles under £20, 3 by glass **Notes** Fixed D 5 course £36, Light L menu Mon-Sat, Sunday L, Vegetarian available **Seats** 36 **Children** Portions **Parking** 16

GRASMERE Map 18 NY30

Macdonald Swan Hotel

◉ Traditional British

Good honest cooking in modernised Lakeland inn

☎ 0844 879 9120
LA22 9RF
e-mail: sales/oldengland@macdonald-hotels.co.uk
dir: M6 junct 36, A591 towards Kendal, A590 to Keswick through Ambleside. Hotel on right on entering village

Built as a coaching inn in 1650, the Swan Hotel is one of the Lake District's oldest. Delightfully positioned at the foot of the rolling Lakeland hills, it's just down the road from Wordsworth's home, Dove Cottage, and he even mentioned the place in his poem, 'The Waggoner' (spot the inspiration for the restaurant's name) though it's smartened up considerably in the intervening years. Work up an appetite fell walking or canoeing, then, in the winter, cosy up by a roaring log fire in Walker's Bar before moving into the candlelit Waggoner's Restaurant with its duck-egg blue walls and jazzy straight-backed chairs. Expect hearty dishes such as potted lamb's liver with Cumberland jelly and toasted brioche, and main-course outdoor-reared pork mixed grill (loin chop, braised rib, Macleod & Macleod black pudding, sausage) with roast potatoes, shallots and apple sauce.

Chef Robert Ryan **Owner** Macdonald Hotels & Resorts
Times 12.30-3.30/6-9 **Closed** L Mon-Sat **Prices** Starter £5.80-£6.95, Main £9.95-£18.95, Dessert £5.50-£7.25, Service optional **Wines** 22 bottles over £20, 6 bottles under £20, 12 by glass **Notes** Sunday L, Vegetarian available, Dress restrictions, Smart casual, no trainers or T-shirts, Civ Wed 70 **Seats** 60, Pr/dining room 20 **Children** Portions, Menu **Parking** 60

Oak Bank Hotel

◉◉ Modern British ♨

Stylish modern cooking in Lakeland country house

☎ 015394 35217
Broadgate LA22 9TA
e-mail: info@lakedistricthotel.co.uk
dir: N'bound: M6 junct 36 onto A591 to Windermere, Ambleside, then Grasmere. S'bound: M6 junct 40 onto A66 to Keswick, A591 to Grasmere

Go for a stroll through the well-tended gardens running down to the River Rother at this Victorian hotel before relaxing over a drink in front of the log fire in the lounge. Then make your way into the conservatory restaurant, its elegance uplifted by redecoration. Dinner, of two to four courses, might kick off with salt-cod cream with crackling and pea textures (purée, parfait and shoots), bringing the taste buds to life before something like

accurately roasted scallops on piquillo pepper salsa, the plate dotted with triangles of air-dried ham and romesco crumbs. The kitchen is painstaking about sourcing locally and has a good eye for presentation, evident in a main course of Holker Estate partridge, roast breast, braised leg and pithivier strategically plated with dauphinoise, swede purée and fondant, and sauced with game jus. Turbot poached in red wine, with potato purée and a fricassée of baby gem, mushrooms and salsify, might be an alternative, and the meal might end with a memorable theme on chocolate and orange.

Chef John Cook **Owner** Glynis & Simon Wood
Times 6.30-8.30 **Closed** 24-26 Dec, Jan (ex last wknd), L all week **Prices** Fixed D 3 course £29.50-£36.25, Service optional, Groups min 6 service 10% **Wines** 23 bottles over £20, 19 bottles under £20, 6 by glass **Notes** Vegetarian available, Dress restrictions, Smart casual **Seats** 32 **Children** Portions **Parking** 14

Rothay Garden Hotel & Restaurant

◉◉ Modern European V ♨

Well-balanced modern dishes in a chintz-free conservatory

☎ 015394 35334
Broadgate LA22 9RJ
e-mail: stay@rothaygarden.com
web: www.rothaygarden.com
dir: From N M6 junct 40, A66 to Keswick, then S on A591 to Grasmere. From S M6 junct 36 take A591 through Windermere/Ambleside to Grasmere. At N end of village adjacent to park

On the edge of Grasmere, the refurbished hotel sits in a couple of acres of riverside gardens, with the panoramic sweep of the Lakeland fells as background. Chintzophobes need have no fear; dining goes on in a thoroughly modern conservatory-style room with bare floor and smartly clothed tables, with restful views of the gardens all around. Andrew Burton has the balance right between country-hotel and modern edge in his cooking, offering a savoury Charlotte of spring onion and tomato, along with a seared scallop and crab, with rouille dressing and wilted spinach to start. Next up could be sautéed guinea fowl breast in sherry cream sauce, with ravioli of sun-blushed tomato and feta, as well as wild mushrooms and asparagus, before the finishing flourish sees Cassis coulis trickled into a black treacle soufflé, or a medley of orange and lemon flavours applied to posset, mousse and sablé.

Chef Andrew Burton **Owner** Chris Carss
Times 12-1.45/7-9.30 **Prices** Food prices not confirmed for 2013. Please telephone for details **Wines** 160 bottles over £20, 12 by glass **Notes** Vegetarian menu, Dress restrictions, Smart casual **Seats** 65 **Children** Portions **Parking** 35

Wordsworth Hotel & Spa

◎◎ Modern British ✪

Creative country-house cooking in the heart of the Lakes

☎ 015394 35592
LA22 9SW
e-mail: enquiry@thewordsworthhotel.co.uk
dir: Off A591 centre of village adjacent to St Oswald's Church

Built in 1870 as the hunting lodge for the Earl of Cadogan, this historic hotel is ideally situated in the heart of the Lake District. The classic country house has been brought up-to-date with contemporary touches and facilities, including a spa. It's not hard to see why Wordsworth was so inspired by the scenery that he put pen to paper. The hotel is set in two acres of riverside gardens with stunning views of Grasmere Vale and the mountains all around. In the Signature restaurant overlooking the village, neutral colours set off deep red and purple velvet chairs, making it a good choice for romantic assignations or special occasions. Local Cumbrian ingredients are used imaginatively in signature dishes such as Bessy Beck smoked trout fritters with tomato and saffron dressing, followed by Lyth Valley lamb saddle and shoulder served with root vegetable gratin, swede, purple sprouting broccoli, rosemary scented lamb jus. For pudding it's got to be textures of Yorkshire rhubarb with goats' milk, celery and Grasmere gingerbread.

Chef Jaid Smallman **Owner** Iain & Jackie Garside
Times 12.30-2/6.30-9.30 **Prices** Starter £4.95-£11.95, Main £14-£25, Dessert £4.95-£8.95 **Wines** 50 bottles over £20, 51 bottles under £20, 10 by glass **Notes** Sunday L, Vegetarian available, Dress restrictions, Smart casual, Civ Wed 100 **Seats** 65, Pr/dining room 18 **Children** Portions, Menu **Parking** 50

HOWTOWN   **Map 18 NY41**

Sharrow Bay Country House Hotel

◎◎ British, International Ⅴ ◢ NOTABLE WINE LIST ☜

Classically-based cuisine by the majestic tranquillity of Ullswater

☎ 017684 86301
Sharrow Bay CA10 2LZ
e-mail: info@sharrowbay.co.uk
dir: M6 junct 40. From Pooley Bridge right fork by church towards Howtown. Right at x-rds, follow lakeside road for 2m

If any view is guaranteed to bring out the landscape artist or poet manqué in you, it ought to be the majestic, tranquil prospect over Ullswater enjoyed by Sharrow Bay. The hotel is a venerable old trooper of the country-house movement. At its heart is the defiantly unreconstructed dining room, a place of heavily draped comfort, all pink flounce and cultivated, flawlessly courteous service. The format is still a single sitting for lunch and dinner, with a wide range of choice and classically based cuisine that flies the flag proudly for Cumbrian produce. A trio of seafood makes a compendious opener, offering dressed crab, a seared scallop and lobster tortellini, before the intermediate courses, the first a soup or fish dish (salmon with prawn risotto, perhaps), the second a citrus sorbet. Main course might be best end of Herdwick lamb, or fillet of Matterdale venison, the latter appearing with braised red cabbage, apple and raisins, puréed roast butternut squash, and a strong sauce founded on brandy and port. Some new-fangled thinking - orange polenta cake with blood orange jelly and Cointreau mascarpone cream inveigles itself among the traditional likes of nougat glacé and toffee pudding for dessert, and then there are fine British cheeses to bring down the curtain.

Chef Colin Akrigg, Mark Teasdale **Owner** Sharrow Bay Ltd **Times** 1-8 **Prices** Food prices not confirmed for 2013. Please telephone for details **Wines** 708 bottles over £20, 38 bottles under £20, 19 by glass **Notes** Sunday L, Vegetarian menu, Dress restrictions, Smart casual **Seats** 55, Pr/dining room 40 **Parking** 30

IREBY   **Map 18 NY23**

Overwater Hall

◎◎ Modern British

Creative modish cooking in splendid Georgian country-house hotel

☎ 017687 76566
CA7 1HH
e-mail: welcome@overwaterhall.co.uk
dir: A591 at Castle Inn take road towards Ireby. After 2m turn right at sign

A fine Georgian house with a stately facade, Overwater Hall was ripe for conversion to a hotel (which happened in the late 1960s), and it has been under the same private ownership since 1992. Nowadays, it is a splendidly handsome country house replete with winding driveway and 18 acres of pretty gardens and woodland, and a décor rich with elegant, traditional charms. The dining room is appropriately formal with the tables sharply dressed with white linen and fresh flowers. The kitchen follows four-course tradition, with a fish course such as fillet of hake in a creamy sauce with prawns and fresh herbs following a starter of a whole quail pan-fried with orange and thyme on a smoked bacon rösti with honey-glazed shallots and hedgerow jus. There's a good deal of regional produce on the menu, and lots of flavours on the plate: main-course pan-fried saddle of venison comes with beetroot purée, pithivier of pheasant and wild mushrooms, potato and pancetta terrine, and damson jus.

Times 12.30-2.30/7-8.30 Closed 1st 2 wks Jan, L Mon

KENDAL   **Map 18 SD59**

Best Western Castle Green Hotel in Kendal

◎◎ Modern British

Well-crafted dishes in a smart modern hotel

☎ 01539 734000
Castle Green Ln LA9 6RG
e-mail: reception@castlegreen.co.uk
web: www.castlegreen.co.uk
dir: M6 junct 37, A684 towards Kendal. Hotel on right in 5m

Set in 14 acres of gardens and woodland overlooking Kendal Castle and the fells, the Castle Green Hotel is a tranquil Lakeland hideaway. Vast picture windows allow you to take in the views in the smartly contemporary Greenhouse Restaurant, where the kitchen brigade set about their business with serious intent behind a 'theatre window'. Cumbrian ingredients are proudly trumpeted on a menu that keeps abreast of current trends, offering up ham hock and confit chicken terrine with raisin purée and piccalilli vegetables to set the ball rolling, then roasted brill teamed with Jerusalem artichokes, spinach, Cumbrian pancetta and Cumberland mustard. Finish with a nicely gooey chocolate fondant with white chocolate ice cream or artisan local cheeses. If you want to really put the kitchen through its paces, there's a keenly-priced five-course tasting menu.

Times 12-2/6-10

KESWICK — Map 18 NY22

Dale Head Hall Lakeside Hotel

Modern British

Tried-and-true country-house cooking in Lakeland seclusion

☎ 017687 72478
Lake Thirlmere CA12 4TN
e-mail: onthelakeside@daleheadhall.co.uk
dir: 5m from Keswick on A591

Dale Head Hall sits in a truly splendid location with Helvellyn rising from the back garden and Lake Thirlmere lapping at the foot of the lawned front garden. The thoroughly traditional Lakeland hideaway feels no need to inflict a modern makeover on itself, sticking instead to comforting chintz, while the kitchen takes a similarly tried-and-tested route with its classic country-house repertoire. Four-course dinners unfold in a relaxed ambience, opening with something like Parma ham-wrapped pork terrine with raisin dressing, then moving on via soup or sorbet to a main course of either fish or meat - pan-fried Borrowdale trout with hongroise potatoes and prawn paella sauce, say, if you opt for the former. Awaiting at the end, perhaps treacle and pecan tart with nutmeg cream.

Times 6.45-8.45 Closed Jan, L all week

Highfield Hotel

Modern European

Locally-led cooking and stunning views in the Lakes

☎ 017687 72508
The Heads CA12 5ER
e-mail: info@highfieldkeswick.co.uk
dir: M6 junct 40, A66, 2nd exit at rdbt. Left to T-junct, left again. Right at mini-rdbt. Take 4th right

In prime position for gazing out upon Derwent Water and across the fells, Highfield is a sympathetically restored slate-built Victorian country house just a few minutes hike from Keswick's beating heart. A contemporary revamp sits comfortably with the period splendour so as not to detract from those magnificent views showcased through bay windows. The restaurant - consisting of three areas - puts locally-sourced materials at the centre of things, with a chef who is admirably keen to support the local farming economy. A visually striking naturally-smoked haddock, crab and langoustine tart might get things underway, followed by tender, flavourful roast breast of guinea fowl, stuffed with chestnut and orange, and wrapped in locally-smoked pancetta. Pear frangipane tart - perfect pastry again - is accompanied by a nicely judged rosemary ice cream.

Chef Gus Cleghorn **Owner** Howard & Caroline Speck
Times 6.30-8.30 Closed Jan-early Feb, L all week
Prices Fixed D 2 course £29.50, Fixed D 4 course £37.50,
Service optional **Wines** 34 bottles over £20, 28 bottles
under £20, 8 by glass **Notes** Pre-theatre menu available,
Vegetarian available, Dress restrictions, Smart casual
Seats 40 **Children** Portions **Parking** 20

Morrels

Modern British

Relaxed contemporary dining

☎ 017687 72666
34 Lake Rd CA12 5DQ
e-mail: info@morrels.co.uk
dir: Between the market square & the Keswick Theatre by the Lake

Bang in the centre of Keswick between the market and the Theatre by the Lake, the exterior of Morrels may have the look of a classic Lakeland stone-built townhouse, but the stripped-out contemporary interior is a slice of metropolitan style that wouldn't look out of place in a big city. It is a slick act, all pine floors, bare wooden tables, chocolate and cream high-backed chairs, etched glass screens and an eclectic modern menu to match. The kitchen takes its inspiration from around the world, and pulls it all together in simple, contemporary ideas such as pan-fried scallops with chorizo and sweet potato purée, which you might follow with slow-roast pork belly with black mash, apple sauce, crackling and gravy, or steamed sea bass fillet with fennel, tomato and dill ragoût. Friendly staff and a laid-back modern soundtrack make for an easygoing ambience.

Times 5.30 Closed Mon, L all week

Swinside Lodge Country House Hotel

Modern British

Enticing table d'hôte menu near Derwentwater's edge

☎ 017687 72948
Grange Rd, Newlands CA12 5UE
e-mail: info@swinsidelodge-hotel.co.uk
dir: M6 junct 40, A66, left at Portinscale. Follow to Grange for 2m ignoring signs to Swinside & Newlands Valley

There is simply no excuse for not coming to dinner with a well-honed appetite at Swinside Lodge. The trim, whitewashed Georgian house lies at the foot of Catbells, just a five-minute stroll from the shore of Derwentwater, and evocatively-named fells - Skiddaw, Blencathra, and Causey Pike - crowd all around, beckoning you to pull on the boots to get the view from the top. Lakeland tradition holds sway at the dinner table: a four-course table d'hôte format, with a choice at pudding stage, and the option to squeeze in a cheese course. Menus change daily and with the seasons, thus a winter spread opens with galantine of pheasant and venison with pickled red cabbage, prune and brandy jelly, then on via soup (carrot and ginger with cumin yoghurt) to baked salmon with smoked salmon and cucumber, celeriac, fennel and spinach in a white wine and tarragon sauce. Dessert is an orange polenta sponge pudding with Grand Marnier sauce and mascarpone.

Times 7.30-10.30 Closed 20-26 Dec, L all week

KIRKBY LONSDALE — Map 18 SD67

Hipping Hall

– see opposite

The Sun Inn

Modern British V

Friendly old inn with a local flavour

☎ 015242 71965
6 Market St LA6 2AU
e-mail: email@sun-inn.info
dir: From A65 follow signs to town centre. Inn on main street

The Sun, dating from the 17th century, is a warm and characterful inn with the expected flagstone and oak floors, beams and log fires, while its restaurant has a modern feel, with bright fabrics and chairs made by Gillows of Lancaster. You can eat here or in the bar, and there are a number of options, from the 'Posh Nosher's' menu and lunchtime favourites like sausages and mash. Throughout, dishes are carefully composed making maximum use of local produce. Expect potted crab with roast garlic and dill mayonnaise, or beetroot Tatin with celeriac remoulade, then slow-roast shoulder of Lune lamb with rosemary and redcurrant jus, or fried sea bream fillets with crayfish sauce, finishing with something trad like rhubarb crumble.

Chef Charlotte Norfolk **Owner** Lucy & Mark Fuller
Times 12-2.30/6.30-9 Closed L Mon **Prices** Fixed D 4
course £25.95-£31.95, Starter £4.50-£6.95, Main £13.95-
£21.50, Dessert £4.25-£6.95, Service optional
Wines 8 bottles over £20, 23 bottles under £20, 7 by
glass **Notes** Sunday L, Vegetarian menu **Seats** 36
Children Portions, Menu **Parking** On street & nearby car
park

Save on Hotels. Book at **theAA.com/hotel**

CUMBRIA 111 ENGLAND

The Plough Inn Lupton

⊛ Modern British **NEW**

Smart contemporary refurb and smart contemporary cooking

☎ 015395 67700
Cow Brow LA6 1PJ
e-mail: info@theploughinnatlupton.co.uk
dir: M6 junct 36 onto A65 signed Kirkby Lonsdale

Bought by the team behind the Punch Bowl Inn (see entry, Crosthwaite) and given a major facelift, The Plough is now a modern restaurant with rustic features which the locals still hold dear. Wooden flooring through the open plan bar and dining area matches farmhouse-style tables, some with large, leather tub chairs. A log burning stove, oak beams, antique furniture and rustic wine caves add further character. Friendly, well-informed staff make this a great place to kick back, whilst the team in the kitchen uses good quality produce in dishes inspired by the global larder. Thus lamb koftas might come pointed up by cauliflower purée and spiced caramel, before a main course such as salmon and prawn bake with buttered greens. Classic lemon tart paired with cherry sorbet is a fine and tangy finale.

Chef Mark Swanton **Owner** Richard Rose **Times** 12-9
Prices Starter £2.25-£3.95, Main £9.95-£19.95, Dessert £4.25-£5.75, Service optional, Groups min 15 service

10% **Wines** 49 bottles over £20, 17 bottles under £20, 14 by glass **Notes** Sunday L, Vegetarian available **Seats** 120, Pr/dining room 8 **Children** Portions, Menu

Ees Wyke Country House

⊛ Modern, Traditional

Confident country-house cooking in elegant Georgian hotel

☎ 015394 36393
LA22 0JZ
e-mail: mail@eeswyke.co.uk
web: www.eeswyke.co.uk
dir: On B5285 on W side of village

A Georgian house above Esthwaite Water, with glorious fell views, Ees Wyke was at one time Beatrix Potter's holiday home before she bought Hill Top and moved to the village. It's now a comfortable, and comforting, country-house hotel, with dinner served in the dining room overlooking the lake. In typical Lakeland style, everyone takes their seats simultaneously for a daily-changing, five-course menu with a couple of choices per course. Good local sourcing is clear, and the kitchen combines classical ideas with gently modern notions, devising well-balanced meals. Start with seared scallops with balsamic dressing before broccoli and onion quiche, then go on to the main course: pink pan-fried noisettes of lamb with a wine jus hinting of mint and garlic, or gilt head bream fillets grilled with pancetta, thyme and oregano. Puddings might be a toss-up between sticky toffee sponge and pears poached in Muscat with honey and cinnamon, before a choice of local cheeses.

Chef Richard Lee **Owner** Richard & Margaret Lee
Times 7.30 **Wines** 39 bottles over £20, 19 bottles under £20, 5 by glass **Notes** Fixed D 5 course £35, Vegetarian available **Seats** 16 **Parking** 12

Hipping Hall

Modern British V ⊛

Smart contemporary cooking in stylish country-house hotel

☎ 015242 71187
Cowan Bridge LA6 2JJ
e-mail: info@hippinghall.com
dir: 8.5m E of M6 junct 36 on A65

The name references the stepping stones which allowed travellers back in the day to cross the beck that runs past this fine old house. It began life as a blacksmith's; upgrading to the rather handsome house we see today began in the 17th century after a rather fortuitous wedding. It makes a fine country-house hotel on a pleasingly grand scale (nine bedrooms) and blends the best of the building's original character with smart contemporary furniture and period pictures. The restaurant makes a feature of the minstrels' gallery, plus a fabulous fireplace, and with the ceiling opened to the rafters, it is grand without being overbearing. Tables are modishly dressed in readiness for the smart, vibrant contemporary cooking of Kiwi Brent Hulena. The short (or focused if you prefer) fixed-priced menu, supported by a multi-course menu gourmand, delivers high quality north-western produce cooked in a smart contemporary manner, underpinned with sound classical thinking. Braised pig's cheek, for example, comes with a crisp piece of belly which packs a powerful porcine punch and delivers a welcome textural contrast, plus parsnip purée and a perfectly cooked hen's egg yolk. The technical proficiency and clear-headed thinking continues in a main-course dish of halibut with spot-on seasoning and accompanying cockles, chive gnocchi and fresh peas, and a playfully named dessert, 'rhubarb, rhubarb, rhubarb', which is indeed a trio (poached, sorbet and jelly), served with tonka bean ice cream.

Chef Brent Hulena **Owner** Andrew Wildsmith
Times 12-2/7-9.30 Closed L Mon-Fri **Prices** Fixed L 3 course £29.50, Fixed D 4 course £49.50, Tasting menu £65, Service optional **Wines** 70+ bottles over £20, 10 by glass **Notes** Tasting menu 7 course, Sunday L, Vegetarian menu, Civ Wed 45 **Seats** 26 **Children** Portions **Parking** 20

NEWBY BRIDGE — Map 18 SD38

Lakeside Hotel

◎◎ Modern British

Lakeside dining with a choice of restaurants

☎ 015395 30001
Lakeside LA12 8AT
e-mail: sales@lakesidehotel.co.uk
web: www.lakesidehotel.co.uk
dir: M6 junct 36 follow A590 to Newby Bridge, straight over rdbt, right over bridge. Hotel within 1m

Originally a simple 17th-century coaching inn, the Lakeside Hotel has spread its wings to cater for the influx of visitors who want a piece of its splendid setting and a spot of me-time in the spa. Embraced by thickly-wooded hills and overlooking nothing but the boats nodding at anchor on Lake Windermere, the Lakeside Hotel certainly delivers on the promise. Luckily, the building's expansion has not been at the expense of its period charm - there are cosy lounges and snug traditional bars for an aperitif, before you head for the more formal oak-panelled Lakeview restaurant. Local produce forms the backbone of the modern British menu, which might kick off by putting up bacon jelly, creamed cabbage and pancetta crisp as the supporting cast for pigeon breast, then follow with pan-fried sea bass, crab ravioli, langoustine foam and lentils. Desserts show a similar propensity for delivering varied textures - perhaps an assemblage of chocolate mocha parfait, pannacotta, passionfruit mousse and white chocolate gel.

Times 12.30-2.30/6.45-9.30 Closed 23 Dec-15 Jan

Whitewater Hotel

◎ Modern, Traditional British

Appealing dishes in an old riverside mill

☎ 015395 31133
The Lakeland Village LA12 8PX
e-mail: enquiries@whitewater-hotel.co.uk
web: www.whitewater-hotel.co.uk
dir: M6 junct 36 follow signs for A590 Barrow, 1m through Newby Bridge. Right at sign for Lakeland Village, hotel on left

Tucked away in thickly-wooded Lake District seclusion, this hotel and leisure club is housed in Lakeland Village in an eye-catching conversion of the historic Backbarrow cotton mill. Its appropriately-named Riverside Restaurant is a smart space with rough slate walls, high-backed leather chairs and neatly turned-out tables overlooking the fast-flowing River Leven, a relaxed setting for the kitchen's repertoire of uncomplicated modern British dishes. One look at the menu tells you that they are proud of local produce - fillet of Cumbrian beef, for example, teamed with wild mushrooms, seasonal vegetables, Madeira and summer truffle sauce. Elsewhere, you might find sea bass with pea risotto, white asparagus, Wabberthwaite ham, and watercress sauce, and to finish, perhaps orange and rosemary pudding with caramelised oranges and vanilla custard.

Times 12-2/7-9 Closed L Mon-Sat

See advert opposite

PENRITH — Map 18 NY53

North Lakes Hotel & Spa

◎ Modern British ◐

Cumbrian spa hotel with modish menu

☎ 01768 868111
Ullswater Rd CA11 8QT
e-mail: nlakes@shirehotels.com
dir: M6 junct 40 at junct with A66

Within the modern North Lakes Hotel & Spa - with the said leisure facilities a major part of its appeal - is the Martindale Restaurant. With its high ceiling open to the rafters, wooden beams and large open fires, it's an unassumingly smart space for some gently contemporary brasserie-style dishes. There's plenty of regional flavour on the menu - Yorkshire Fettle cheese (made from ewes' milk), for example, crumbled onto a 'tarte Tatin' of baked figs and red onion - alongside some globally-inspired flavours such as tempura tiger prawns with chilli dipping sauce. Fellside lamb shank is cooked for four hours and comes in a main course with braised tomato and herb couscous, and, to finish, a farmhouse parkin pudding comes with treacle sauce and clotted cream.

Chef Mr Doug Hargeaves **Owner** Shire Hotels Ltd **Times** 12.15-1.45/7-9.15 **Prices** Food prices not confirmed for 2013. Please telephone for details **Wines** 41 bottles over £20, 17 bottles under £20, 14 by glass **Notes** Sunday L, Vegetarian available, Dress restrictions, Smart casual, Civ Wed 150 **Seats** 112 **Children** Portions, Menu **Parking** 120

SEASCALE — Map 18 NY00

Cumbrian Lodge

◎ British, Mediterranean ◐

Eclectic cooking in small Victorian hotel

☎ 019467 27309
58 Gosforth Rd CA20 1JG
e-mail: cumbrianlodge@btconnect.com
dir: From A595 onto B5344, hotel on left after 2m

Built as a family home in 1874, Cumbrian Lodge was converted into a hotel as recently as 1999. Subsequent improvements and upgrading have given the interior a contemporary gloss, with the restaurant featuring posters of jazz musicians on plain walls. The kitchen chooses its materials carefully and roams where'er it will for inspiration, producing starters of meatballs in tomato and oregano sauce with linguine, or chicken liver and mushroom pâté with Cumberland sauce, and main courses of salmon fillet in a sun-dried tomato crust accompanied by pak choi and a citrusy soy sauce, and pink and tender pan-fried duck breast with orange and chilli sauce, sautéed potatoes and green beans. Finish with something like white chocolate cheesecake with fruit compôte.

Chef A Carnall **Owner** David J Morgan **Times** 6.30-9.30 Closed Xmas, New Year, BHs, Sun, L all week **Prices** Starter £5.95-£8.95, Main £10.95-£22.95, Dessert £4.95-£6.95, Service optional **Wines** 17 bottles over £20, 19 bottles under £20, 15 by glass **Notes** Vegetarian available **Seats** 32 **Parking** 17

Save on Hotels. Book at theAA.com/hotel

CUMBRIA 113 ENGLAND

THE WHITEWATER HOTEL
SPA & LEISURE CLUB

The Ultimate Rural Retreat and Health club in the Lakes. This vibrant, chic Hotel is the perfect retreat to relax and unwind. Great Gym membership offers and treatments are all available at the Cascades Leisure Club.

OUR FABULOUS FACILITIES INCLUDE

- Fully Equipped Gymnasium
- Feature shower
- Arabian Mud Rasul
- Whale bone massaging chairs
- Outdoor hot tub
- Aromatherapy Hamam
- Indoor heated pool
- Weights room
- Exercise Studio
- Sauna.
- Jacuzzi Whirlpool
- Residential Spa Breaks
- Day and half Spa packages are available
- Group Bookings
- Dip and Dine offers and mid week treatment offers!
- Squash Court

GIFT
VOUCHERS
are available
and Elémis products can now be purchased in our Spa.

Lakeland Village · Newby Bridge
Cumbria · LA12 8PX · UK
Tel: +44 (0) 15395 31133
Fax: +44 (0) 15395 31881
enquiries@whitewater-hotel.co.uk
www.whitewater-hotel.co.uk

AA
★★★★

Whitewater
HOTEL & LEISURE CLUB

Rampsbeck Country House Hotel

Modern British

Smart modern cooking in a refined lakeside setting

☎ 017684 86442
CA11 0LP
e-mail: enquiries@rampsbeck.co.uk
web: www.rampsbeck.co.uk
dir: M6 junct 40, A592 to Ullswater, T-junct turn right at lake's edge. Hotel 1.25m

If Lakeland views are your thing, the inspirational views across Ullswater and the fells crowding the skyline should set the pulse racing. Rampsbeck is the tranquil country hideaway par excellence, combining 18 acres of splendid grounds where you can wander down to the hotel's own lake shore, with a traditionally cosseting 18th-century house replete with antiques, grand marble fireplaces and ornate ceilings. The elegant dining room does nothing to jar the nerves, while staff deliver polished service in an ambience of calm, well-practiced professionalism. Chef Andrew McGeorge has headed up the kitchen brigade for long enough to have the culinary operation firing on all cylinders, with local materials providing the backbone of a modern repertoire that looks to the French classics for its spiritual inspiration. Spiced poached pear with seared duck foie gras, duck confit and cinnamon jus is a marriage

made in heaven showing great vision and a feel for flavour and textural combinations. Main course brings more luxury in a tried-and-true composition involving roast fillet of local beef with sautéed veal sweetbreads, shallot confit, potato galette, foie gras, and Madeira jus; fish is also handled with aplomb in the likes of roast fillet of turbot with sautéed potatoes, salsify, langoustines, and red wine and shallot dressing. Only the finest Valrhona chocolate will do as the basis for a textbook fondant teamed with candied hazelnut, pistachio ice cream and praline crunch. All the peripherals - breads, canapés, amuses and petit fours - make an impact, while wines are a noteworthy cast by the bottle and glass.

Chef Andrew McGeorge
Owner Blackshaw Hotels Ltd
Times 12-1.45/7-9 **Prices** Fixed L 2 course fr £28, Fixed D 3 course fr £54.50, Service optional **Wines** 107 bottles over £20, 15 bottles under £20, 11 by glass **Notes** Sunday L, Vegetarian available, Dress restrictions, Smart casual, no shorts, Civ Wed 60 **Seats** 40, Pr/dining room 15 **Children** Portions **Parking** 30

Save on Hotels. Book at **theAA.com/hotel**

CUMBRIA 115 **ENGLAND**

TEBAY
Map 18 NY60

Westmorland Hotel

◎ Modern British

Modern country cooking minutes from the M6

☎ 015396 24351
Orton CA10 3SB
e-mail: reservations@westmorlandhotel.com
dir: Signed from Westmorland Services between M6
junct 38 & 39 north & southbound

The Tebay service station in the far northern reaches of
the M6 would not seem the most promising place to come
upon an oasis of quality gastronomy, yet the presence of
the motorway fades as you draw up at the Westmorland,
and dramatic views of the Howgill fells take over. The
split-level restaurant is an inviting venue done out with
oak tables, wicker chairs and Harris tweed, and looks
over a stream where ducks quack at you from the other
side of the full-length glass windows. At the heart of the
enterprise is produce such as Herdwick lamb and
Galloway beef from the hotel's own farm a few miles
away (don't worry, a farm shop is at hand for take-away
goodies). The kitchen works in a contemporary brasserie-
style vein, delivering ideas such as home-smoked
Cumbrian meats with carrot and orange chutney, followed
by hay-roasted shoulder of mutton (from the farm, of
course) with roasted root vegetables, and port and
redcurrant sauce.

Chef Phil Fazakerley **Owner** Westmorland Ltd
Times 6.30-9 Closed L all week **Prices** Starter £5.25-
£6.95, Main £14.50-£21.50, Service optional
Wines 11 bottles over £20, 25 bottles under £20, 13 by
glass **Notes** Set menus can be provided for pre-booked
groups, Vegetarian available, Dress restrictions, Smart
casual, Civ Wed 120 **Seats** 80, Pr/dining room 40
Children Portions, Menu **Parking** 60

TEMPLE SOWERBY
Map 18 NY62

Temple Sowerby House Hotel & Restaurant

◎◎ Modern British ♨

**Imaginative modern cooking in an intimate country-
house hotel**

☎ 017683 61578
CA10 1RZ
e-mail: stay@templesowerby.com
dir: 7m from M6 junct 40, midway between Penrith &
Appleby, in village centre

Dating back to 1727, this cosy country-house hotel is in a
particularly tranquil position close to Ullswater, opposite
the village green with the Pennine Fells in the distance.
Hardcore walkers and less strenuously inclined sightseers
can warm up next to the real fires in the winter, or chill-
out in the pretty walled garden in the summer. The team
in the kitchen clearly take great pride in using tip-top
local produce on the inventive modish British menu.
Beetroot three ways is a fashionable opener - pickled, set
consommé and mousse - served with warm Fine Fettle
(Yorkshire's answer to feta cheese) and salted walnuts.
Next up, perhaps roast breast of Cumbrian chicken with
crisp bacon, sautéed lettuce, warm mayonnaise and
chicken juices, finishing with a tasting of Yorkshire
rhubarb (parfait, sorbet, doughnuts, poached and
sherbet), or 'Liquorice Allsorts' of dark aniseed cake,
orange icing, mandarin sorbet, orange curd and Liquorice
Allsorts marshmallows.

Chef Ashley Whittaker **Owner** Paul & Julie Evans
Times 7-9 Closed 8 days Xmas, L all week **Prices** Fixed D
3 course £39.50, Service optional **Wines** 39 bottles over
£20, 2 bottles under £20, 7 by glass **Notes** Vegetarian
available, Dress restrictions, Smart casual preferred, Civ
Wed 40 **Seats** 24, Pr/dining room 24 **Parking** 20

WATERMILLOCK
Map 18 NY42

Macdonald Leeming House

◎ Modern British

**Ambitious country-house cooking on the shores of
Ullswater**

☎ 0870 400 8131
CA11 0JJ
e-mail: leeminghouse@macdonald-hotels.co.uk
dir: M6 junct 40, continue on A66 signed Keswick. At rdbt
follow A592 towards Ullswater, at T-junct turn right, hotel
3m on left

This 200-year-old Lakeland manor certainly knows how to
capitalise on its splendid location on the edge of
Ullswater, offering fishing rights to the rod and line
brigade, and making sure that the tables by the French
windows of the Regency Restaurant bask in glorious
views of the lake. Leeming House takes a traditional
approach to the grande-luxe country-house dining
experience: a polished front-of-house team deliver
correctly formal service, while the kitchen delivers gently

modern ideas along the lines of goats' cheese fondue
teamed with beetroot in the form of jelly, mousse and
caviar. Main courses major in grilled rib-eye and sirloin of
Scottish beef, or there might be grilled wild sea bass with
creamed potato, broccoli and salsa verde.

Times 12-2/6.30-9

Rampsbeck Country House Hotel

◎◎◎ – *see opposite*

WINDERMERE
Map 18 SD49

The Beech Hill Hotel

◎ Modern British V

Modern cooking on Windermere

☎ 015394 42137
Newby Bridge Rd LA23 3LR
e-mail: reservations@beechhillhotel.co.uk
dir: M6 junct 36, A591 to Windermere. Left onto A592
towards Newby Bridge. Hotel 4m from Bowness-on-
Windermere

On the shore of Windermere, Beech Hill naturally has
wonderful views over the waters to the fells beyond, and
diners can enjoy the vista from the restaurant, a large
and smartly kitted-out room, where the menus offer an
appealing range of dishes, the kitchen clearly in touch
with contemporary tastes. Salmon and watercress
fishcake with a poached egg and chive hollandaise might
appear next to another starter of more unorthodox grilled
smoked wood pigeon with a stir-fry of sprouts, lentils and
bacon, and among main courses roast local chicken
breast with dauphinoise, mushrooms and tarragon might
compete for your attention alongside tender, moist loin of
venison in prosciutto with a broth of pearl barley, apples
and celeriac. Fish is not overlooked - perhaps fillet of sea
bass with pea hash, fennel tempura and tartare sauce -
and puddings could extend to raspberry Alaska.

Chef Christopher Davies **Owner** Mr F Richardson
Times 7-9 Closed L all week, D 25 Dec **Prices** Fixed D 3
course £32.95, Service optional **Wines** 47 bottles over
£20, 35 bottles under £20, 8 by glass **Notes** Fixed D 5
course £37.95, Vegetarian menu, Dress restrictions,
Smart casual, no denim or trainers, Civ Wed 120
Seats 130, Pr/dining room 90 **Children** Portions, Menu
Parking 60

Gilpin Hotel & Lake House

Modern British V

Smart, contemporary cooking in fabulous family-run hotel

☎ 015394 88818
Crook Rd LA23 3NE
e-mail: hotel@gilpinlodge.co.uk
web: www.gilpinlodge.co.uk
dir: M6 junct 36 take A590/A591 to rdbt N of Kendal, then B5284 for 5m

The idea of a Lakeland house conjures up a particular image in one's mind and the Gilpin Hotel exceeds all expectations - the handsome white-painted building is surrounded by soaring mature trees (22 acres of grounds in all), and is the very definition of a peaceful (and luxurious) getaway. Owned and run by the Cunliffe family since 1988, the house has been turned into a hotel of considerable charm, void of country chintz, with the original features of the house, built in 1901, and well-chosen furniture and decoration giving it a classy, Arts and Crafts-style feel. There is also a Lake House a few miles down the road which gives six more bedrooms, a lakeside vista, spa and a complimentary chauffeur service up to the hotel for dinner. You're spoiled for choice here: whether you go for drinks and canapés in the plush lounge, the gently modish champagne bar or the pretty terrace, and then there's the four dining rooms which make up the restaurant, each with a slightly different feel, but each deliciously appealing with tables dressed up in anticipation for what follows. And what follows is some well-crafted, contemporary cooking based on first-class produce, a good deal of which is from the local area. Begin with a rabbit carpaccio, marinated in juniper and served with hazelnuts and smoked salt, aged gruyère, sorrel, rocket, rapeseed and apple, a creative and elevated interpretation of a classic dish. Next up, perhaps Isle of Gigha halibut with cockles and sea herbs and wild garlic mayonnaise, or a fashionable pairing of scorched veal sweetbreads with golden cauliflower, parmesan potato, carrot brittle and Pedro Ximenez sauce. The pre-starter and pre-dessert all up the ante, while desserts show no less invention and smart combinations of flavours: spiced palm sugar mousse, for example, with lychee and gingerbread. The wine list is a serious piece of work, too, with recommendations given for each dish on the menu.

Chef Phil Cubin **Owner** Cunliffe family **Times** 12-2/6.30-9.15 **Prices** Fixed L 3 course £30-£35, Starter £6-£11, Main £12-£22, Dessert £7.50-£8.50, Service optional **Wines** 235 bottles over £20, 14 by glass **Notes** Fixed D 5 course £58.50, ALC L only, Sunday L, Vegetarian menu, Dress restrictions, Smart Casual **Seats** 60, Pr/dining room 20 **Parking** 40

Save on Hotels. Book at theAA.com/hotel

CUMBRIA 117 ENGLAND

WINDERMERE *continued*

Cedar Manor Hotel & Restaurant

 Modern British

Soothing Lakeland hotel restaurant with impressive cooking

☎ 015394 43192
Ambleside Rd LA23 1AX
e-mail: info@cedarmanor.co.uk
dir: From A591 follow signs to Windermere. Hotel on left just beyond St Mary's Church at bottom of hill

This one-time gentleman's residence lies on the outskirts of Windermere in mature walled gardens, where the 200-year-old cedar that gives the place its name takes centre stage. Dinners here are a soothing affair: the candlelit restaurant looks smart with its high-backed leather chairs and crisp linen, while chef Roger Pergl-Wilson has established a strong local following for food that impresses with its classic culinary sensibilities and well-defined flavours. Ingredients are sourced carefully, and an eye is always kept on the calendar, thus an early spring menu might begin with venison terrine with juniper and pistachio, and progress to slow-cooked belly pork, which is cider-braised and honey-glazed and served with mustard mash. The chef's travels are reflected in forays into exotica, such as Cambodian marinated beef served with lime and black pepper dipping sauce and spicy potato wedges. At the end, local cheeses from a fine supplier in Kendal make a savoury alternative to the likes of nutmeg custard with cardamom doughnuts and raspberry jam sorbet.

Chef Roger Pergl-Wilson **Owner** Caroline & Jonathan Kaye **Times** 6.30-8.30 Closed Xmas & 6-25 Jan, L all week **Prices** Fixed D 3 course £39.95-£42.95, Service optional **Wines** 14 bottles over £20, 16 bottles under £20, 7 by glass **Notes** Vegetarian available, Dress restrictions, Smart casual, no mountain wear **Seats** 22, Pr/dining room 10 **Children** Portions **Parking** 12

Gilpin Hotel & Lake House

◉◉◉ – *see opposite*

The Hideaway at Windermere

◉◉ Modern British

Accomplished seasonal cooking in Lakeland getaway

☎ 015394 43070
Phoenix Way LA23 1DB
e-mail: eatandstay@thehideawayatwindermere.co.uk
dir: M6 junct 36/A5391. Pass sign to Windermere Village, then take 2nd left into Phoenix Way. Restaurant on right

Not quite hidden but certainly in a quiet pocket of Windermere, The Hideaway is a Victorian restaurant with rooms, with a pair of smartly decked-out candlelit dining rooms. Simply cooked seasonal, regional produce is the kitchen's strength, seen most noticeably in starters like potted shrimps with watercress and a crumpet, and asparagus with a crisp duck egg and hollandaise. Among main courses, the conventional pairing of roast rump of lamb with red wine sauce, served with crushed Jersey Royals and roast root vegetables, could appear alongside pan-fried fillets of grey mullet accompanied by tomato beurre blanc, braised fennel, samphire and saffron new potatoes. At the end might come rhubarb three ways (poached, crumble and jelly), or espresso crème brûlée.

Chef Richard Gornall **Owner** Richard & Lisa Gornall **Times** 6.30-11 Closed Jan, L all week, D Mon-Tue **Prices** Service optional, Groups min 10 service 10% **Wines** 10 bottles over £20, 20 bottles under £20, 3 by glass **Notes** Fixed D 5 course £36, Vegetarian available, Dress restrictions, Smart casual, no sportswear or trainers **Seats** 30, Pr/dining room 12 **Parking** 15

Holbeck Ghyll Country House Hotel

◉◉◉ – *see below*

Holbeck Ghyll Country House Hotel

◉◉◉

| WINDERMERE | Map 18 SD49 |

Modern British V

Breathtaking views and classy cooking

☎ 015394 32375
Holbeck Ln LA23 1LU
e-mail: stay@holbeckghyll.com
web: www.holbeckghyll.com
dir: 3m N of Windermere on A591, right into Holbeck Lane (signed Troutbeck), hotel 0.5m on left

With a starring role in Steve Coogan and Rob Brydon's *The Trip*, Holbeck Ghyll is no supporting player when it comes to dining in the Lakes. The approach down the driveway will win you over - the view across Lake Windermere to the peaks of Scafell Pike, Coniston Old Man and the Langdale Pikes is something to behold. And the house itself is rather a gem, with its Arts and Crafts credentials plain for all to see. All in all, it is a magnificent spot for a country-house hotel. Inside all is plush, elegant and rather luxurious, from the bedrooms to the public rooms, and the restaurant with its fabulous Lakeland vista. Chef David McLaughlin has been leading from the front for over a decade and has taken the food to exalted heights, building on a supply line of superb local growers and producers. There are solid classical foundations to what appears on the plate, but not without a bit of contemporary vitality, and always presented with genuine craft. First-courses of salad of warm Scottish langoustines with lobster and celeriac remoulade, and terrine of confit duck, pear and foie gras with toasted brioche, show the style. There is precision and focus in each dish. Next up, roasted brill with braised gem and cider foam, or best end of Cumbrian lamb with Puy lentils, swede purée and haggis beignets. And to finish, a chocolate plate includes soufflé, délice and tart, served with an astutely judged orange sorbet.

Chef David McLaughlin **Times** 12.30-2/7-9.30 **Prices** Fixed L 2 course £30-£41, Fixed D 3 course £65-£78, Service optional **Wines** 264 bottles over £20, 19 bottles under £20, 15 by glass **Notes** Sunday L, Vegetarian menu, Dress restrictions, Smart casual, Civ Wed 60 **Seats** 50, Pr/dining room 20 **Children** Portions, Menu **Parking** 50

WINDERMERE *continued*

Jerichos

◉◉ Modern British

Inventive cooking in a busy evening-only restaurant

☎ 015394 42522 & 45026
College Rd LA23 1BX
e-mail: info@jerichos.co.uk
dir: M6 junct 36. A591 to Windermere. 2nd left towards Windermere then 1st right onto College Rd. Restaurant 300mtrs on right

Jerichos is a thoroughly modern town-centre restaurant with rooms in a Victorian building, sporting a clean-cut look of white walls, pine floors, and black leather seats at bare wooden tables. The vibe is contemporary and relaxed, while the sourcing of materials, spot-on presentation and evident technical skills shows a confident hand in the kitchen, working always with the seasons. A summer dinner starts with a vibrant fresh pea and garden herb risotto with crispy pancetta and goats' cheese. At main course stage, a pan-fried fillet of lemon sole arrives on butter-glazed samphire, along with Jersey potatoes with spinach and lemon dressing, Avruga caviar and crispy potato, with each element adding to the overall composition. Creativity doesn't flag in a finale of salted dark chocolate and almond butter mousse with home-made nutmeg ice cream.

Chef Chris Blaydes, Tim Dalzell **Owner** Chris & Jo Blaydes
Times 7-9.30 Closed 1st wk Nov, 24-26 Dec, last wk Dec, 1 Jan, last 3 wks Jan, Mon & Thu, L all week
Prices Starter £4.50-£9.50, Main £16.25-£24.95, Dessert £6.90-£8, Service optional, Groups min 6 service 10%
Wines 49 bottles over £20, 7 bottles under £20, 8 by glass **Notes** Vegetarian available **Seats** 28
Children Portions **Parking** 13

Lindeth Howe Country House Hotel & Restaurant

◉◉ Modern British

Confident modern cooking chez Beatrix Potter

☎ 015394 45759
Lindeth Dr, Longtail Hill LA23 3JF
e-mail: hotel@lindeth-howe.co.uk
dir: 1m S of Bowness onto B5284, signed Kendal and Lancaster. Hotel 2nd driveway on right

Classic country-house hotels are 10 a penny in Lakeland, but Lindeth Howe is the only one that can say that it was once home to Beatrix Potter, who wrote *The Tale of Timmy Tiptoes* and *The Tale of Pigling Bland* here. The handsome half-timbered house sits in a painterly landscape, overlooking Lake Windermere and the mountains beyond - a vista which can be contemplated at leisure in the dining room. It is an old-school, civilised space where French chef Marc Guibert cooks in the modern British idiom, always keeping a keen eye on local provenance and seasonality. If you are enamoured of the trio format as a way of working a culinary theme, one menu is constructed specifically along these lines with, say, a riff

on Cumbrian beef as a main event comprising seared fillet with truffle mash, marrow with celeriac, and a mini Guinness, steak and oyster pudding with a red wine reduction. Otherwise, you might start with roast wood pigeon and its confit leg served with caramelised crosnes and pomegranate vinaigrette, and finish with a Pear William soufflé with white wine-poached pear and bitter chocolate sauce.

Chef Marc Guibert **Owner** Lakeinvest Ltd
Times 12-2.30/6.30-9 **Wines** 29 bottles over £20, 37 bottles under £20, 8 by glass **Notes** Fixed D 5 course £42.50-£48.50, Trilogy menu £48, Sunday L, Vegetarian available, Dress restrictions, Smart casual, no jeans or sleeveless T-shirts **Seats** 70, Pr/dining room 20
Children Portions, Menu **Parking** 50

Linthwaite House Hotel & Restaurant

◉◉ Modern British V 🍷NOTABLE WINE LIST 🌳

Lovely views and first-rate cooking

☎ 015394 88600
Crook Rd LA23 3JA
e-mail: stay@linthwaite.com
dir: A591 towards The Lakes for 8m to large rdbt, take 1st exit (B5284), 6m, hotel on left. 1m past Windermere golf club

Built as a private residence back in Edwardian times, this black-and-white property has stunning views over Lake Windermere and the fells from its hilltop location. The whole place has a traditional feel, with richly furnished lounges with an open fire and deep sofas for pre-dinner drinks, and an elegant restaurant. The kitchen makes good use of local materials, listing suppliers on the menu, and turns out uncomplicated, well-balanced dishes, among them pressed ham hock with piccalilli and toasted brioche, and roast scallops with black pudding and Xeres jus. Meat is handled confidently: impressively timed roast rump of lamb with potato and pumpkin gratin and merguez sausage, and rare loin of venison with a simple caramelised onion tart and juniper jus. Roast sea bass fillet with a broth of vegetables, saffron and brown shrimps is a typical fish dish, and incidentals like bread hit the mark too, as do puddings such as the clear, clean flavours of raspberry parfait with lemon curd sponge and almond foam, beautifully presented on a slate.

Chef Chris O'Callaghan **Owner** Mike Bevans
Times 12.30-2/6.45-9.30 Closed Xmas & New Year (ex residents), **Prices** Fixed L 2 course fr £14.95, Fixed D 4 course fr £52, Service optional **Wines** 180 bottles over £20, 8 bottles under £20, 14 by glass **Notes** Sunday L, Vegetarian menu, Dress restrictions, Smart casual, Civ Wed 60 **Seats** 64, Pr/dining room 16 **Children** Portions, Menu **Parking** 40

Macdonald Old England Hotel & Spa

◉◉ Traditional British, European

Stylish modern dining and stunning lake views

☎ 0844 879 9144
23 Church St, Bowness LA23 3DF
e-mail: sales.oldengland@macdonald-hotels.co.uk
web: www.macdonaldhotels.co.uk
dir: Through Windermere to Bowness, straight across at mini-rdbt. Hotel behind church on right

Fabulous views of Windermere are the crowning glory of this sprawling hotel complex on the shores of the iconic lake. At the heart of the operation is a handsome stone-built Victorian mansion, but recent years have seen a glitzy spa and leisure club grafted on, while the Number 23 Church Street Restaurant is the place to head for prime local produce served to a backdrop of fabulous views across the lake through a sweep of floor-to-ceiling picture windows. The cooking walks the line between classic crowd pleasers - top-grade steaks, lamb cutlets or fish from the grill, for example - and more up-to-date ideas along the lines of pan-fried scallops matched with pearl barley and cockle risotto, and cauliflower purée, followed by pan-fried fillet of pork with apple and sage rissole, and a Calvados and apple reduction. Bringing up the rear, perhaps pear strudel with pear sorbet and perry jelly.

Chef Nick Martin **Owner** Macdonald Hotels & Resorts
Times 6.30-9.30 Closed L all week **Prices** Food prices not confirmed for 2013. Please telephone for details
Wines 76 bottles over £20, 6 bottles under £20, 18 by glass **Notes** Vegetarian available, Dress restrictions, Smart casual jacket preferred, no denim/vests **Seats** 170, Pr/dining room 60 **Children** Portions, Menu **Parking** 100

Miller Howe Hotel & Restaurant

◉◉ Modern British V 🍷NOTABLE WINE LIST 🌳

Accomplished modern cooking with heavenly views over Windermere

☎ 015394 42536
Rayrigg Rd LA23 1EY
e-mail: info@millerhowe.com
dir: M6 junct 36. Follow the A591 bypass for Kendal. Enter Windermere, continue to mini rdbt, take left onto A592. Miller Howe is 0.25m on right

From its elevated perch on a sylvan hillside, this Lakeland Arts and Crafts classic basks in cinematic views over Lake Windermere towards Langdale Pikes. The interior is as plushly sumptuous as anyone could reasonably demand, and dining takes place in a luminous split-level dining room done out with classy sage-green fabrics and white linen-clad tables; a wall of glass ensures that everyone gets to watch the sun set over the lake at dinner. Having worked with Raymond Blanc at Le Manoir aux Quat' Saisons, chef Andrew Beaton's technical skills are well honed, and he uses them to deliver an elegant take on the modern British idiom, getting underway with the full-on flavours of roast sea bass with Thai-spiced crab, smoked red pepper, passionfruit and brown butter,

Save on Hotels. Book at theAA.com/hotel

CUMBRIA – DERBYSHIRE 119 ENGLAND

followed by confit guinea fowl leg teamed with red onion marmalade, sauté potato, chestnut mushrooms and cider jus. Dessert is a modish deconstruction of banoffee pie, with the elements presented as iced toffee parfait, caramelised bananas, banana sorbet and toffee sauce.

Chef Andrew Beaton **Owner** Martin & Helen Ainscough **Times** 12.30-1.45/6.45-8.45 Closed 2 wks Jan **Prices** Fixed L 3 course £25, Fixed D 4 course £45, Tasting menu £55, Starter £12-£16, Main £23-£29, Dessert £12-£16, Service optional **Wines** 100 bottles over £20, 10 bottles under £20, 12 by glass **Notes** Sunday L, Vegetarian menu, Dress restrictions, Smart casual **Seats** 80, Pr/dining room 30 **Children** Portions **Parking** 40

The Samling

@@ Modern British V 🔖 🖐

Contemporary luxe in a white-fronted Lakeland hotel

☎ 015394 31922
Ambleside Rd LA23 1LR
e-mail: info@thesamlinghotel.co.uk
dir: M6 junct 36, A591 through Windermere towards Ambleside. 2m. 300yds past Low Wood Water Sports Centre just after sharp bend turn right into hotel entrance

Built in the 1780s overlooking the north-eastern shore of Lake Windermere, when William Wordsworth was but a nipper, The Samling is these days a hotel of some distinction and class, one of those places that gets the blend of traditional elegance and contemporary swagger spot on. With 67 acres of grounds and woodlands to explore, it's not just for indoor types, but it is tempting to stay inside all day and kick back in the elegant public rooms adorned with well-chosen furniture and contemporary works of art. The two dining rooms maintain the classically cool vibe of the rest of the house, with well-spaced tables dressed for fine dining. There is evidence of sound classic technique among the team in the kitchen, plus bags of smart contemporary ideas. Leek velouté with apple espuma and crumble is an amuse-bouche to set the pulses racing, before a quail starter including braised leg, pain d'épice, black pepper poached rhubarb and burnt orange. The produce is first-rate throughout. New season wild halibut might come with braised shin of beef, sugar-smoked clams, cauliflower and sherry caramel, and a taste of apples from The Samling orchard includes the fruit in a pie, candied, sorbet, cider and toffee crab apple.

Times 12-1.30/7-9.30 **Prices** Fixed L 3 course £35, Fixed D 3 course £60, Tasting menu £65, Service optional **Wines** 260+ bottles over £20, 22 by glass **Notes** Tasting menu 7 course, Sunday L, Vegetarian menu, Dress restrictions, Smart casual **Seats** 22, Pr/dining room 8 **Children** Portions, Menu **Parking** 20

Storrs Hall Hotel

@@ Modern British V

Accomplished, imaginative cuisine in luxurious country surroundings

☎ 015394 47111
Storrs Park LA23 3LG
e-mail: storrshall@englishlakes.co.uk
web: www.englishlakes.co.uk
dir: on A592 2m S of Bowness, on Newby Bridge road

The setting may be a classically elegant Georgian mansion in a bucolic setting on the shores of Lake Windermere, but the kitchen at Storrs Hall is thoroughly up to speed with contemporary culinary ideas. Framed by immaculately landscaped gardens looking across the lake to the wild fells, the luxurious country-house hotel's interior conforms to Lakeland tradition - opulently sprinkled with antiques, oil paintings and plush furnishings; there's a bit of recycled seaside heritage, too, in the ornate solid oak and intricate glass bar, which was salvaged from Blackpool Tower. Basking in those world-class views across the gardens and lake, the formal Terrace dining room is the setting for the kitchen's ambitious contemporary creations. Start, perhaps, with the luxury of pan-seared foie gras with quince purée, gingerbread, roasted chestnuts and five spice jus, then move on to poached pork fillet with pancetta and apricot stuffing, crushed celeriac and pickled pear purée. Stay the course for an inventive finish such as butternut squash bavarois with cinnamon doughnuts, stem ginger ice cream, and vanilla espuma.

Chef Luke Woodend **Owner** English Lakes Hotels **Times** 12.30-2/7-9 **Prices** Fixed L 3 course £19.75-£22.75, Fixed D 3 course fr £43.50, Service included **Wines** 151 bottles over £20, 4 bottles under £20, 6 by glass **Notes** Tasting menu & themed evenings available, theatre L, Sunday L, Vegetarian menu, Dress restrictions, Smart casual, no jeans or trainers, Civ Wed 90 **Seats** 82, Pr/dining room 40 **Children** Portions **Parking** 50

DERBYSHIRE

ASHBOURNE   Map 10 SK14

Callow Hall

@@ Traditional British

Classic British cuisine in Peak District country-house hotel

☎ 01335 300900
Mappleton Rd, Mappleton DE6 2AA
e-mail: info@callowhall.co.uk
dir: A515 through Ashbourne towards Buxton, left at Bowling Green pub, then 1st right

Callow Hall is family-run again after it changed hands just before Christmas 2011. Ownership is just about all that has changed though - after all, what's not to like about this quintessentially English Victorian country-house retreat in 44 acres of woodlands and gardens on the edge of the Peak District National Park, overlooking the Dove Valley and Bentley Brook? Its ivy-festooned walls enfold an old-school set up of antiques, opulent fabrics, fancy plasterwork and oak panels galore, and the vibe in the elegant dining room isn't about to rock that particular boat. A sure-footed kitchen team still does things the old way, smoking and curing meats and fish in-house and doing all of its own baking. The result is country-house cooking in the classic mould; dinner starts with a textbook lobster bisque served with crème fraîche and chives, and a little skewer of tiger prawns and scallops, then moves via an intermediate course - gilt head bream with tomato and black olive tapenade - to mains, perhaps boned roast quail with home-made sausage stuffing, kale, cranberry and apple and rich game jus. To close the show, warm raspberry and blueberry frangipane tart comes with an exemplary vanilla ice cream.

Chef Anthony Spencer **Owner** Elyzian Hospitality **Times** 12-1.45/7.15-9 **Prices** Fixed L 2 course £20, Fixed D 4 course £40, Starter £7.25-£11, Main £17.95-£24, Dessert £8.95, Service optional **Wines** 65 bottles over £20, 6 by glass **Notes** Sunday L, Vegetarian available, Dress restrictions, Smart casual, no jeans, Civ Wed 40 **Seats** 70, Pr/dining room 40 **Children** Portions **Parking** 15

ASHBOURNE *continued*

The Dining Room

◉◉ Modern European

Imaginative menus in a Jacobean house

☎ 01335 300666
33 St John St DE6 1GP
dir: On A52 (Derby to Leek road)

Pete and Laura Dale's pint-sized restaurant works to a stunningly simple winning formula. A Jacobean house complete with its original beams and fireplace is the setting for six tables, where diners are offered a table-d'hôte menu of locally-sourced and foraged produce, subjected to traditional methods like smoking, air-drying, curing and baking. Even the butter is churned in-house. The five courses of weekday nights expand majestically to eight on Saturdays, for food that is imaginative and full of character. Shimeji mushrooms with Jerusalem artichoke and pearl barley precedes a more obviously classic dish such as smoked Ross-shire salmon with Avruga, sour cream, potato and chives, before the stops are pulled out for a main course like free-range chicken cooked sous-vide with lemon, grains of paradise and Douglas fir pine. Dessert could be a Yorkshired-up version of crema catalana with Wakefield rhubarb, adorned with flavours of almond, orange and rose. The great British cheeses are worth the extra.

Chef Peter Dale **Owner** Peter & Laura Dale **Times** 7 Closed 2 wks end Dec, 1 wk over Shrove Tue, 1 wk Sep, Sun-Mon, L all week **Prices** Food prices not confirmed for 2013. Please telephone for details **Wines** 51 bottles over £20, 3 by glass **Notes** Tasting menu 5 course wkday D, 8 course Sat D, Vegetarian available, Dress restrictions, Smart casual **Seats** 16 **Parking** On street opposite restaurant (evening)

ASHFORD-IN-THE-WATER Map 16 SK16

Riverside House Hotel

◉◉ Modern British 🏆

Intelligent cooking in a tranquil country-house hotel

☎ 01629 814275
Fennel St DE45 1QF
e-mail: riversidehouse@enta.net
dir: off A6 (Bakewell/Buxton road) 2m from Bakewell, hotel at end of main street

This creeper-covered Georgian property has all the attributes you could wish for in a country-house hotel: a riverside setting in the Peak District, lovely gardens and, inside, log fires in the comfortable lounges, and a choice of dining rooms, each furnished with antiques and rich fabrics. The kitchen's output is based on sound techniques and depends on quality local produce, and it eschews over-elaboration in favour of undiluted flavours and balance. Thus, local pork cutlet is chargrilled and served with an apple sausage and cheddar mash, and pan-fried halibut with crayfish and potato chowder. Such simplicity can belie the skill and thought behind each dish, as in starters of a risotto of sun-blush tomatoes

and smoked aubergine, or shellfish and pasta broth accompanied by a crab and couscous croquette. Puddings can seem busy in comparison, often made up of three components: perhaps rhubarb crumble, brûlée and ice cream.

Chef John Whelan **Owner** Penelope Thornton **Times** 12-2/7-9.30 **Prices** Fixed L 2 course £10, Fixed D 3 course £45, Service optional **Wines** All bottles over £20, 32 by glass **Notes** Sunday L, Vegetarian available, Dress restrictions, Smart dress, Civ Wed 32 **Seats** 40, Pr/dining room 32 **Children** Portions **Parking** 25

BAKEWELL Map 16 SK26

Monsal Head Hotel

◉ Modern British 🍴

Crowd-pleasing food and spectacular views

☎ 01629 640250
Monsal Head DE45 1NL
e-mail: enquiries@monsalhead.com

With its dream-ticket location in the heart of the Peak District National Park overlooking Monsal Dale, this lovely little country hotel has bags of atmosphere. Its rustic, flagstoned Stable Bar is a characterful spot, stocked with an array of real ales and chalkboards displaying food of the hearty variety, while the spacious Longstone Restaurant, smartly kitted out with cream walls, wooden tables, chairs and floors, ups the ante. Braised beef with home-smoked garlic mash, glazed shallots, Chantenay carrots, parsnip crisps and a rich red wine and wild mushroom jus, for example, or fillet of Channel sea bass teamed with wilted spinach, spaghetti, mussels and a saffron cream sauce. Desserts have a nursery ring; think sticky-toffee-pudding or home-made rhubarb trifle.

Chef Rob Cochran, Adrian Billings, Jason Kendra **Owner** Penelope Thornton Hotels **Times** 12-7.30-9.30 Closed 25 Dec ex pre-booked **Prices** Starter £3-£7, Main £8-£16, Dessert £3-£7, Service optional **Wines** 23 bottles over £20, 29 bottles under £20, 16 by glass **Notes** Sunday L, Vegetarian available **Seats** 50 **Children** Portions, Menu **Parking** 20

Piedaniel's

◉ Traditional French

French bistro dishes with an air of contemporary chic

☎ 01629 812687
Bath St DE45 1BX
dir: From Bakewell rdbt in town centre take A6 Buxton exit. 1st right into Bath St (one-way)

The stone-built timbered look suggests a traditional country inn, but this appealing venue has an air of contemporary chic about it indoors, with smartly dressed tables, whitewashed stone walls and splashes of spring green in the décor. The order of the day is bistro dishes that reliably deliver to their specifications, starting perhaps with saffron-scented mussel soup, or scallops and tiger prawns provençale, and bringing out the big guns at main-course stage, when best end of lamb is

served in its cooking juices with basil couscous and tomato confit, or chicken is swathed in smoked Black Forest ham and served with ratatouille sauce. Finish up with a wodge of chocolate truffle torte with raspberry sorbet.

Chef E Piedaniel **Owner** E & C Piedaniel **Times** 12-2/7-10 Closed Xmas & New Year, 2 wks Jan, 2 wks Aug, Mon, D Sun **Prices** Fixed L 2 course £13, Fixed D 3 course £15, Starter £6-£9.50, Main £16-£20, Dessert £6, Service included **Wines** 6 bottles over £20, 23 bottles under £20, 10 by glass **Notes** Sunday L, Vegetarian available **Seats** 50, Pr/dining room 16 **Children** Portions **Parking** Town centre

BASLOW Map 16 SK27

Cavendish Hotel

◉◉ Modern British V

Confident cooking in historic coaching inn

☎ 01246 582311
Church Ln DE45 1SP
e-mail: info@cavendish-hotel.net
dir: M1 junct 29 follow signs for Chesterfield. From Chesterfield take A619 to Bakewell, Chatsworth & Baslow

In case you need a reminder that the Duke and Duchess of Devonshire had a hands-on input into the design of the Cavendish Hotel, check out the antiques and original artworks. The house sits in handsome Derbyshire countryside on the borders of the Chatsworth Estate and is a thoroughbred example of serene elegance and quiet good taste. Done out in cool light turquoise and soothing silvery grey, the formal Gallery Restaurant dresses its tables in fine white linen, and its impeccably courteous staff in smart black and whites. The kitchen marries excellent local supplies with impressive technique to come up with vibrant dishes that are big on flavour. Foie gras parfait is delivered with sherry vinegar, rhubarb, pain d'épice and pistachios, while Hancock's beef might appear as a duo of slow-roasted shoulder and carpaccio, with beetroot, horseradish snow, blue cheese bonbons, and a bone marrow veal reduction. Apple tarte Tatin gets a nice twist with the addition of star anise ice cream and mulled cider.

Chef Mike Thompson **Owner** Chatsworth Estates **Times** 12-2.30/6.30-10 Closed D 25 Dec **Prices** Fixed L 2 course £35, Fixed D 3 course £45, Service added 5% **Wines** 41 bottles over £20, 9 bottles under £20, 11 by glass **Notes** Sunday L, Vegetarian menu, Dress restrictions, No trainers, T-shirts or jeans **Seats** 50, Pr/dining room 18 **Children** Portions **Parking** 40

Fischer's Baslow Hall

◉◉◉ — *see opposite*

Save on Hotels. Book at **theAA.com/hotel**

DERBYSHIRE 121 ENGLAND

Fischer's Baslow Hall

Modern European V ✍

Bold, creative cooking in an elegant country house

☎ 01246 583259
Calver Rd DE45 1RR
e-mail: reservations@fischers-baslowhall.co.uk
dir: From Baslow on A623 towards Calver. Hotel on right

At the distance of only a short potter from the fringes of the Chatsworth Estate, Baslow Hall is a sandy-coloured gritstone Edwardian country house in the style of a 17th-century manor. The Fischers bought it in 1988, and set about turning it into an elegant restaurant with rooms, complete with manicured lawns, handsome interiors and a prevailing mood of relaxed hospitality. Staff know how to dispense the old-fashioned courtesies without making you feel you've stepped into a parallel universe, and in Rupert Rowley, the Hall has a formidably gifted chef. One of the hallmarks of his output is that he is prepared to experiment with technique while not subverting the inherent character of the fine local materials with which he works. The Taste of Britain menus aim to celebrate whatever's in season 'from the peaks of Derbyshire to the coastlines'. Local ingredients may include root veg grown in the kitchen garden and rosehips

picked from the hedgerows, as well as St Petersburg stout brewed in Bakewell. Dishes tease and tantalise in the menu specs: start with crab and Bloody Mary cannelloni with Henderson's relish, crab ice cream, pickled cucumber, and lime and lemongrass snow. These are brave and bold dishes, but underpinned by a sound sense of what works together, and an understanding that we're all ready for a little more textural challenge in the purée era. Toasted granola adds snap and crackle to a main course of sea bass, in which the purée itself rings out with startling flavours of mandarin and star anise. Roast saddle of rabbit comes with Iberico ham and gnocchi made with Yorkshire Blue, while dry-aged sirloin is given a much more classical Burgundian treatment, with sauté potatoes, snails and ceps, garlic, herb butter and red wine. More crunch, this time flavoured with black sesame, arrives at dessert stage, in the company of black treacle sponge, yuzu caramel and banana and crème fraîche sorbet.

Chef Rupert Rowley, Craig Skinner
Owner Mr & Mrs M Fischer
Times 12-1.30/7-8.30 Closed 25-26 Dec, 31 Dec **Prices** Fixed L 2 course fr £28.50, Fixed D 3 course fr £72, Service optional **Wines** 134 bottles over £20, 5 by glass **Notes** Sunday L, Vegetarian menu, Dress restrictions, Smart casual, no jeans, sweatshirts, trainers, Civ Wed 38 **Seats** 55, Pr/dining room 20 **Children** Portions **Parking** 20

BASLOW *continued*

Rowley's Restaurant & Bar

◎◎ Modern British

Polished modern cooking in a former village pub

☎ 01246 583880
Church Ln DE45 1RY
e-mail: info@rowleysrestaurant.co.uk
web: www.rowleysrestaurant.co.uk
dir: A619/A623 signed Chatsworth, Baslow edge of Chatsworth Estate

Max and Susan Fischer (of Fischer's Baslow Hall fame - see entry) and head chef Rupert Rowley are the team behind the transformation of the former Prince of Wales pub in the pretty Derbyshire Peaks village of Baslow, which now does business as a cheerful contemporary restaurant operation. Whether you prefer the casual vibe of the stone-flagged bar, the area with views of the busy kitchen team at work, or the expansive Gallery room with its soothing hues of aubergine and cream, you can expect well-thought-out ideas that tweak classic dishes into the more inventive realms of goats' cheese terrine partnered with soused beetroot, toasted pine nuts and balsamic vinaigrette, or pan-fried black pudding sausage with champ potatoes, crispy air-dried ham and a soft poached hen's egg. Next out, slow-cooked blade of beef could appear in the company of caramelised onion risotto, 'poor man's parmesan', charred spring onions, and a glaze of stout and black treacle. The full-flavoured approach extends to desserts, which might include warm Yorkshire Parkin with spiced custard and banana ice cream. A changing cast of beers from local Peak District breweries adds to the appeal.

Chef Rupert Rowley, Craig Skinner **Owner** Susan & Max Fischer, Rupert Rowley **Times** 12-2.30/5.30-9 Closed 26 Dec, D Sun **Prices** Fixed L 2 course £18.50, Fixed D 3 course fr £28, Service optional **Wines** 24 bottles over £20, 7 bottles under £20, 8 by glass **Notes** Sunday L, Vegetarian available **Seats** 64, Pr/dining room 24 **Children** Portions, Menu **Parking** 17, On street

The Devonshire Arms at Beeley

◎◎ Modern British ✋

Accomplished cooking in an up-to-date country inn

☎ 01629 733259
Devonshire Square DE4 2NR
e-mail: enquiries@devonshirebeeley.co.uk
dir: 6m N of Matlock & 5m E of Bakewell, located off B6012

Set in a charming little village on the Chatsworth Estate, The Devonshire Arms looks for all it's worth the quintessential mellow-stone English country inn. Inside, though, that is not the whole story. The expected classic look of the cosy bar with oak beams, exposed-stone walls and wood-burning fires leads on to a light, modishly-styled brasserie extension rich with bold colours, tub dining chairs and vibrant modern artwork. The estate's produce rightly figures prominently on a repertoire that keeps things intelligently straightforward and seasonal. Start with warm scallop and cockle salad dressed in basil oil, or rabbit and mushroom tortellini with carrot and orange purée. There are classic pub dishes such as bangers (courtesy of one Mr Hancock) served with mash and red wine and onion gravy, or more the more modish tempura skate wing with Russian salad, lobster sauce and duck ham. To finish, Mrs Hill's (the chef's mum) lemon tart with sweet Chantilly cream is a fixture. There's a flexible approach here, with the same menu taken in the bar.

Chef Alan Hill **Owner** Duke of Devonshire **Times** 12-3/6-9.30 **Prices** Fixed L 2 course £14.95, Starter £4.50-£7.50, Main £10.50-£16.50, Dessert £4.95-£6.50, Service optional **Wines** 120 bottles over £20, 30 bottles under £20, 20 by glass **Notes** Sunday L, Vegetarian available **Seats** 60 **Children** Portions **Parking** 30

The Samuel Fox Country Inn

◎◎ Modern British

Accomplished modern cooking in an informal ex-pub

☎ 01433 621562
Stretfield Rd S33 9JT
e-mail: thesamuelfox@hotmail.co.uk
dir: M1 junct 29, A617 towards Chesterfield, onto A619 towards A623 Chapel-en-le-Frith. B6049 for Bradwell, restaurant located on left

Its refurb a few years ago has given the Samuel Fox (named after the local man who invented the folding umbrella) a fresh, modern style, with its open-plan layout, wicker chairs, wooden tables, fresh flowers and stunning views of the Peak District. The kitchen is diligent about sourcing locally whenever it can and takes a modern, fairly cosmopolitan approach to its output. A strong element of invention runs through starters, among which have appeared pan-fried mackerel fillet with crisp pancetta, sweetcorn purée and pickled kohlrabi, and

steamed rabbit and suet pudding with red cabbage and cauliflower purée. If main courses seem more mainstream - perfectly cooked, tender grilled chicken breast with mustard-flavoured crushed new potatoes and thyme jus, or smoked haddock and clam chowder with a poached egg - puddings can be an innovative bunch, from lemon meringue pie with white chocolate custard and raspberry sorbet to pain perdu with spiced winter fruits and prune and Armagnac ice cream.

Chef Charlie Curran **Owner** Bakewell Developments **Times** 12-2.30/6-9.30 Closed D 25 Dec **Prices** Fixed L 2 course £10, Starter £4.50-£6.75, Main £11.95-£17.50, Dessert £4.25-£5.75, Service optional **Wines** 24 bottles over £20, 26 bottles under £20, 14 by glass **Notes** Sunday L, Vegetarian available **Seats** 50 **Children** Portions, Menu **Parking** 15

Breadsall Priory Marriott Hotel & Country Club

◎ Traditional

Honest British cooking in historical property

☎ 01332 832235
Moor Rd DE7 6DL
dir: M1 junct 25, A52 to Derby, then follow Chesterfield signs. Right at 1st rdbt, left at next. A608 to Heanor Rd. In 3m left then left again

In 300 acres that include two golf courses, Breadsall Priory is a handsome building with its roots in the 13th century. An archway in the Priory Restaurant, a beamed room with leaded windows looking out on to the grounds, was part of the original property. The menu doesn't stray too far beyond these shores, and the kitchen delivers admirably straightforward and uncluttered starters, among them perhaps ham hock terrine with piccalilli, and seared scallops with celeriac purée and pickled apple. Main courses show the same sort of restraint, teaming well-timed fillet of bream with chive tagliolini and creamed leeks, and roast guinea fowl with port jus. Grilled steaks, with a choice of sauces, are popular choices, and comforting puddings have included steamed chocolate sponge.

Owner Royal Bank of Scotland **Times** 7-10 Closed Mon, L Tue-Sat **Prices** Food prices not confirmed for 2013. Please telephone for details **Wines** 32 bottles over £20, 3 bottles under £20, 10 by glass **Notes** Sunday L, Dress restrictions, Smart casual, Civ Wed 90 **Seats** 90, Pr/dining room 40 **Children** Portions **Parking** 300

BUXTON
Map 16 SK07

Best Western Lee Wood Hotel

◉ Traditional & Modern British

Modern brasserie cooking (with nostalgic classics) in a Georgian manor house

☎ 01298 23002

The Park SK17 6TQ

e-mail: reservations@leewoodhotel.co.uk

dir: M1 junct 24, A50 towards Ashbourne, A515 to Buxton. From Buxton town centre follow A5004 Long Hill to Whaley Bridge. Hotel approx 200mtrs beyond University of Derby campus

A handsome Georgian manor-house hotel in the famously charming Derbyshire spa town, Lee Wood does a roaring trade in country weddings. The expansive conservatory-style Elements dining room overlooks the gardens, and comes with a patio for aperitifs. Expect modern British brasserie cooking as the order of the day, starting with the likes of a terrine of belly pork, black pudding and apricots, served with green apple purée and pork scratchings, as a prelude to baked monkfish with a fricassée of ceps and Puy lentils, or smoked rump and roast rack of lamb with puréed carrot and confit potatoes. A small nostalgia section provides steak-and-ale pie or fish and chips, and there's fruit crumble and custard to finish, if the modernism of chestnut honey tart with yoghurt ice cream and granola isn't your bag.

Chef Rian Skidmore **Owner** Mr J C Millican **Times** 12-2/5.30-9.15 Closed 24-25 Dec **Prices** Fixed L 2 course £25-£30, Fixed D 3 course £28.95-£38, Starter £5-£8.25, Main £11.50-£21.95, Dessert £4.25-£6.25, Service optional **Wines** 30 bottles over £20, 9 bottles under £20, 6 by glass **Notes** Pre-theatre menu available from 5.30, Sunday L, Vegetarian available, Civ Wed 175 **Seats** 50, Pr/dining room 12 **Children** Portions, Menu **Parking** 30

CHESTERFIELD
Map 16 SK37

Casa Hotel

◉ Spanish, Mediterranean V

Classic Spanish food in a dramatic 21st-century hotel

☎ 01246 245990

Lockoford Ln S41 7JB

e-mail: cocina@casahotels.co.uk

dir: M1 junct 29 to A617 Chesterfield/A61 Sheffield, 1st exit at rdbt, hotel on left

Rising phoenix-like from a derelict site, Casa Hotel is the new kid on Chesterfield's historic townscape, joining the famous twisty spire of St Mary's and All Saints Church. Part of the town's redevelopment strategy, the award-winning architecture is a postmodern masterpiece of asymmetrical blocks, woven through with an imaginative Spanish-style thread, as the name might hint. An impeccably contemporary interior works a glitzy look, all marble floors, quirky artworks and nightclubby lighting, while the expansive first-floor Cocina restaurant is reduced cleverly into more intimate portions using swirly-patterned voile curtains, slatted wood sections and

wooden wine walls; as you might expect in this sleek space, a vast glass panel opens the kitchen to view. Get into the Latin mood with a few tapas, perhaps calamari tempura, or prawns sautéed in garlic, parsley and olive oil, before moving on to mains such as twice-cooked belly pork teamed with crushed new potatoes, tart apple purée and red wine jus. A Josper charcoal oven from Barcelona adds extra Iberian authenticity to prime slabs of steak, or a taster plate of organic lamb from the hotel's own Walton Lodge Farm, comprising roast saddle, grilled rack and confit shoulder.

Chef Andrew Wilson **Owner** Steve Perez **Times** 12-2/6-10 Closed L Sat, D Sun **Prices** Fixed L 2 course £11.50, Fixed D 3 course £17.50, Starter £2-£6, Main £12-£28, Dessert £5-£7, Service optional **Wines** 28 bottles over £20, 12 bottles under £20, 12 by glass **Notes** Early bird menu available D 6-7pm Mon-Fri, Sunday L, Vegetarian menu, Dress restrictions, Smart casual, Civ Wed 280 **Seats** 100, Pr/dining room 200 **Children** Portions **Parking** 200

CLOWNE
Map 16 SK47

Hotel Van Dyk

◉ Modern British V

Boutique Georgian hotel with fine modern cooking

☎ 01246 810219

Worksop Rd S43 4TD

e-mail: info@hotelvandyk.co.uk

dir: M1 junct 30, towards Worksop, at rdbt 1st exit, next rdbt straight over. Through lights, hotel 100yds on right

This boutique hotel, a grand Grade II listed building, has two eating options, The Bowden being the fine-dining venue, a splendid room with panelled walls, luxurious fabrics, chandeliers and a self-playing baby grand. The kitchen hits a few international notes, steaming mussels and clams in a starter with coconut, lemongrass and chilli and serving them with wild rice salad, and marinating rump of lamb and plating it with vegetable tagine, spicy apricot chutney and tzatziki dressing. Smoked duck breast might come with pancetta and cherry compôte, followed by beef bourguignon, or roast halibut fillet accompanied by saffron fondant potatoes, broccoli, sorrel purée and lemon beurre blanc.

Chef Mr Sam Booler **Owner** Gail & Peter Eyre **Times** 12-9.30 Closed Mon-Tue **Prices** Food prices not confirmed for 2013. Please telephone for details **Wines** 29 bottles over £20, 17 bottles under £20, 13 by glass **Notes** Sunday L, Vegetarian menu, Dress restrictions, Smart casual, no T-shirts or sportswear, Civ Wed 150 **Seats** 89, Pr/dining room 16 **Children** Portions, Menu **Parking** 80

DARLEY ABBEY
Map 11 SK33

Darleys Restaurant

◉◉ Modern British V ♨

Modern British cooking by the water's edge

☎ 01332 364987

Haslams Ln DE22 1DZ

e-mail: info@darleys.com

web: www.darleys.com

dir: A6 N from Derby (Duffield road). Right in 1m into Mileash Ln, to Old Lane, right, over bridge. Restaurant on right

This converted silk mill on the banks of the River Derwent - rather appropriately once a mill workers' canteen - is a fab location on fair-weather days with its smart decked terrace overlooking the weir. The interior is bang up-to-date, so shades of darkwood, chocolate and toffee are joined by vibrant fabrics giving splashes of colour. Likewise, the kitchen takes a modern approach to the cooking, driven by quality local and seasonal produce. A soundly-priced lunch menu might feature braised lamb shoulder with colcannon potato cake, while dinner cranks up the ante serving up smoked haddock chowder with cauliflower bhaji, followed by a trio of pork accompanied by root vegetable terrine and cider sauce. Baby meringues with broken shortbread and Daiquiri curd and sorbet makes for a stylish finale. Plenty of the inside tables benefit from the watery views.

Chef Jonathan Hobson, Mark Hadfield **Owner** Jonathan & Kathryn Hobson **Times** 12-2/7-9.30 Closed BHs, 1st 2 wks Jan, D Sun **Prices** Fixed L 2 course fr £18.95, Starter £7.60-£8.50, Main £19.20-£21.50, Dessert £7.05-£7.70, Service optional **Wines** 59 bottles over £20, 39 bottles under £20, 15 by glass **Notes** Sunday L, Vegetarian menu **Seats** 70 **Children** Portions **Parking** 12

Masa Restaurant

◉◉ Modern British **V**

Modern classic brasserie dishes in a converted Wesleyan chapel

☎ 01332 203345
The Old Chapel, Brook St DE1 3PF
e-mail: enquiries@masarestaurantwinebar.com
dir: 8m from M1 junct 25. Brook St off inner ring road near BBC Radio Derby

A stone chapel of the Wesleyan persuasion is the converted home to Masa, a city-centre venue that comprises a bustling ground-floor bar with a galleried restaurant divided into a number of different levels. Modern classic brasserie dishes contribute to the urban cool of the place, and staff make impressively short work of all the steps to bring them to you. Expect seared scallops with cauliflower purée, or ham hock and chicken terrine with piccalilli, to start, followed by beef fillet and dauphinoise, or sea bass with crushed new potatoes, roasted Mediterranean veg and basil oil. The ideas may not be exactly cutting edge, but they are rendered with convincing panache and with palpably good prime materials. Finish with lemon tart, served with vanilla ice cream and raspberry coulis.

Chef David Humphreys **Owner** Didar & Paula Dalkic **Times** 12-2/6-9.30 Closed Mon-Tue **Prices** Fixed L 2 course £15.50, Fixed D 3 course £25-£25, Starter £5-£8.50, Main £12.50-£21.50, Dessert £5.95-£7.45, Service optional, Groups min 8 service 10% **Wines** 44 bottles over £20, 11 bottles under £20, 11 by glass **Notes** Tasting menu 5 course, Sunday L, Vegetarian menu, Dress restrictions, Smart casual, black tie when specified, Civ Wed 100 **Seats** 120 **Children** Portions **Parking** On street (pay & display), Car park Brook St

The Chequers Inn

◉ Traditional, European ☝

Homely country inn in the Peak District

☎ 01433 630231
S32 3ZJ
e-mail: info@chequers-froggatt.com
dir: On A625 between Sheffield & Bakewell, 0.75m from Calver

Originally four 18th-century cottages, The Chequers stands above Calver Bridge on the steep banks of Froggatt Edge. Follow a visit to nearby Chatsworth House, or end an invigorating moorland ramble, with a meal at this traditional inn, which offers good pub food and comfortable accommodation. Look to the printed menu for a good choice of pub favourites (local sausages, mash and gravy, hot roast beef sandwiches) or, for something more modern and adventurous, order from the specials board, perhaps confit duck leg with roasted plums followed by seafood risotto with saffron, or pork shoulder with parsley mash and apple and vanilla compôte. Décor

has the homely feel of a country cottage, with simple wooden furniture, bare boards, pine dressers and rag-washed yellow walls.

Chef Graham Mitchell **Owner** Jonathan & Joanne Tindall **Times** 12-2.30/6-9.30 Closed 25 Dec **Prices** Starter £6.50-£7.50, Main £12.50-£17.50, Dessert £5.75-£6.75, Service optional **Wines** 14 bottles over £20, 23 bottles under £20, 10 by glass **Notes** Sunday L, Vegetarian available **Seats** 90 **Children** Portions, Menu **Parking** 50

The Maynard

◉◉ Modern British

Glorious views, a dash of boutique style and contemporary cooking

☎ 01433 630321
Main Rd S32 2HE
e-mail: info@themaynard.co.uk
dir: M1/A619 into Chesterfield, onto Baslow, A623 to Calver right into Grindleford

The glorious rolling Peak District opens up in front of this rather grand old house, now a decidedly swish boutique hotel. Needless to say, a drink on the terrace is a particularly good idea when the sun is up, laying bare a spectacularly green and pleasant vista, but indoors is no less eye-catching. With clever use of bold colours and artworks, and a mix of textures and materials, the lounge has a good deal of contemporary swagger, whilst the restaurant is done out with hand-painted murals, classy blue tones and smartly dressed tables. The cooking is equally of the moment, with plenty of regional flavours and bags of good ideas. Start, perhaps, with a confit duck and smoked chicken terrine, the luscious richness perfectly cut with rhubarb and pear chutney, or a vibrant Thai hot-and-sour broth with garlicky tiger prawns. Next up, breast of guinea fowl is roasted and comes with creamed Savoy cabbage, butternut squash and potato fondant, while oven-baked sea trout is accompanied by dauphinoise and a chive and caviar cream sauce. To finish, warm chocolate tart comes in a happy union with a red berry sorbet.

Chef Ben Hickinson **Owner** Jane Hitchman **Times** 12-2/7-9 Closed L Sat **Prices** Food prices not confirmed for 2013. Please telephone for details **Wines** 6 bottles over £20, 8 bottles under £20, 4 by glass **Notes** Sunday L, Vegetarian available, Civ Wed 140 **Seats** 50, Pr/dining room 140 **Children** Portions, Menu **Parking** 60

The Shoulder at Hardstoft

◉◉ Modern British **NEW** ☺

Food-driven pub with passion for local produce

☎ 01246 850276
Deep Ln S45 8AF
e-mail: info@thefamousshoulder.co.uk
dir: Follow signs to Hardwick Hall, take 1st right after turning off B6039

This one-time down-at-heel village boozer has been given a 'more-gastro-than-pub' contemporary makeover. Stone-built and 300-years old, the re-branded Shoulder is essentially a pub and restaurant with rooms, though still with a friendly, relaxed attitude. The restaurant itself is a light, clean-lined space of pale-wood floors and tables, fashionable high-back seating and red, cream or boldly papered walls. There's a snug bar, real fires and leather sofas to chill-out on, while the aroma of home-baked loaves (for sale on the bar) heightens anticipation and displays the kitchen's passion for local, home-made, home-smoked and home-grown produce. The cooking takes a modern, precise approach without being too showy: shoulder and loin venison Wellington, perhaps, with foie gras, braised red cabbage, baby leeks and smoked garlic jus. To finish, vanilla crème brûlée, shortbread and freeze-dried raspberries hits the spot. A bar menu is also available, but you can eat whatever you want wherever you want.

Chef Simon Johnson **Owner** Simon Johnson **Times** 12 Closed D Sun **Prices** Food prices not confirmed for 2013. Please telephone for details **Wines** 11 bottles over £20, 16 bottles under £20, 8 by glass **Notes** Sunday L, Vegetarian available **Seats** 60, Pr/dining room 12 **Children** Portions, Menu **Parking** 50

The Mill Wheel

◉ Modern British **NEW**

Locally-based cooking in a 17th-century mill

☎ 01283 550335
Ticknall Rd DE11 7AS
e-mail: info@themillwheel.co.uk
web: www.themillwheel.co.uk
dir: M42 junct 2, A511 to Woodville, left onto A514 towards Derby to Hartshorne

An inn only since the 1980s, The Mill Wheel is a converted 17th-century mill, still full of period detail in its stone walls, beamed ceilings and - most majestically of all - the original water-powered wheel, turning sedately in the midst of the bar which has been designed around it. Real ales and comfortable leather sofas are the plus points, and upstairs is a beamed restaurant, done in uncluttered modern style with contemporary artworks and light wooden furniture. Assiduously sourced local produce informs the modern British menus, which take in the likes of a trio of smoked fish with salmon keta and orange salad to start, followed by a pork duo - tenderloin and

Save on Hotels. Book at **theAA.com/hotel**

DERBYSHIRE 125 **ENGLAND**

smoked belly - accompanied by crushed sage potatoes, wild mushrooms and Calvados cream, or sea bass with smoked bacon and peas. An excellent, chunky bread-and-butter pudding with plenty of crème anglaise is the star finale. Pudding Table nights once a month offer a fixed-price three-course dinner with as many puddings as you feel you deserve.

Chef Russel Burridge **Owner** Colin & Jackie Brown **Times** 12-2.15/6-9.15 **Prices** Starter £3.95-£7.45, Main £7.95-£22.95, Dessert £4.95-£5, Service optional **Wines** 1 bottle over £20, 15 bottles under £20, 10 by glass **Notes** Champagne breakfast 4 course £19.95, Sunday L, Vegetarian available, Air con **Seats** 52 **Children** Portions, Menu

---

HATHERSAGE Map 16 SK28

George Hotel

🏵🏵 Modern British 🕭

Well-considered flavours in a 500-year-old former coaching inn

☎ 01433 650436
Main Rd S32 1BB
e-mail: info@george-hotel.net
dir: In village centre on junction of A625/B6001

This 500-year-old Peak District coaching inn comes with all the low beams, open fires, stone walls and bare wooden floors that one might expect in an inn mentioned by Charlotte Brontë in *Jane Eyre*. But times change and the inn has morphed into a rather stylish hotel and restaurant, overlaid with a cool, contemporary décor involving funky fabrics and modish patterned wallpapers. The cooking takes a similarly on-trend route, taking as its bedrock top-class materials from local suppliers, and doing it all the hard way, making breads, pastries and ice creams in-house. When summer peas are in season, they appear in an inventive combo of pea pannacotta, tempura crayfish tails, pea shoot salad and thermidor mayonnaise, while a winter main course could see steamed chestnut and venison pudding partnered with roasted root vegetables, juniper sauce and parsnip crisps. Whatever the time of year, treacle tart with vanilla sauce, banana and clotted cream ice cream and caramelised walnuts makes a stonking finish.

Chef Helen Heywood **Owner** Eric Marsh **Times** 12-2.30/7-10 Closed D 25 Dec **Prices** Fixed L 2 course £29.25, Fixed D 3 course £36.50, Service included **Wines** 39 bottles over £20, 8 bottles under £20, 10 by glass **Notes** Early bird menu Mon-Fri 6.30-7.30pm, Sunday L, Vegetarian available, Dress restrictions, Smart casual, no T-shirts or trainers, Civ Wed 70 **Seats** 45, Pr/dining room 70 **Children** Portions **Parking** 45

The Plough Inn

🏵 Modern British

Peak District riverside inn with Mediterranean-accented cooking

☎ 01433 650319
Leadmill Bridge S32 1BA
e-mail: sales@theploughinn-hathersage.co.uk
web: www.theploughinn-hathersage.co.uk
dir: 1m SE of Hathersage on B6001. Over bridge, 150yds beyond at Leadmill

The Tudor inn on the River Derwent exudes a sense of country-pub tradition, from the tartan carpeting in the bar, the open fires and the informal dining area with its pub furniture. The same menu is served throughout the place, and is comprised of modern British specials with a Mediterranean accent. Flash fried whitebait with lime and coriander mayo, butternut squash, goats' cheese and sage risotto, and spatchcocked poussin marinated in lemon and oregano with Greek salad are what to expect. Go east for a fish dish such as seaweed-battered red mullet with bok choy in black bean sauce, and back home again for original Bakewell pudding with poached blueberries and custard.

Times 11.30-2.30/6.30-9.30 Closed 25 Dec

HIGHAM Map 16 SK35

Santo's Higham Farm Hotel

🏵 Modern International 🕭

Pleasingly unfussy oooking in the lush Amber Valley

☎ 01773 833812
Main Rd DE55 6EH
e-mail: reception@santoshighamfarm.co.uk
web: www.santoshighamfarm.co.uk
dir: M1 junct 28, A38 towards Derby, then A61 to Higham, left onto B6013

This 15th-century farmstead has evolved over the years into a rambling small-scale hotel run with sincere charm by hands-on owner Santo Cusimano. It is a hideaway made for hiking through Derbyshire's wild landscapes, and even if you're not up to taking on the great outdoors, armchair ramblers can bask in uplifting views over the Amber Valley. The comfy candlelit dining room is done out in a reassuringly traditional way with linen-clad tables, and the food is equally unpretentious, comforting stuff wrought from well-chosen local ingredients. Expect Italian-inspired ideas along the lines of pheasant meatballs with tomato sauce and parmesan crisp, followed by classic combinations such as goose fillet with cranberry relish, fondant potato, braised chicory and port jus, or daube of beef with root vegetables and red wine sauce. Finish with white chocolate pannacotta served with a spiced apple samosa.

Chef Lee Sanderson **Owner** Santo Cusimano **Times** 12-3/7-9.30 Closed BHs, L Mon-Sat, D Sun **Prices** Starter £4.50-£7.50, Main £12.50-£21, Dessert £4.50-£6.50, Service added but optional 5% **Wines** 26 bottles over £20, 23 bottles under £20, 3 by glass **Notes** Sunday L, Vegetarian available, Dress restrictions, Smart casual, Civ Wed 100 **Seats** 50, Pr/dining room 34 **Children** Portions **Parking** 100

HOPE
Map 16 SK18

Losehill House Hotel & Spa

◉◉ Modern British V ☺

Glorious Peak District views and contemporary country-house cooking

☎ 01433 621219
Lose Hill Ln, Edale Rd S33 6AF
e-mail: info@losehillhouse.co.uk
dir: A6187 into Hope. Take turn opposite church into Edale Rd. 1m, left & follow signs to hotel

Losehill House, in the Arts and Crafts style, was originally built as a walking hostel, which accounts for its fantastic Peak District location. Meals are served in the Orangery Restaurant, a light, contemporary room with comfortable upholstered chairs and views of sheep-grazed fields. Dishes are put together creatively and are generally straightforward and uncluttered, taking in perfectly cooked lamb fillet with a mini shepherd's pie and crispy shoulder together with carrots and cauliflower cheese, or fillet of sea bass set off by tarragon foam with seasonal asparagus and broad beans. Starters are brought off successfully too, judging by tender monkfish cheek with prosciutto, aubergine purée and sultana dressing, and a meal might end with honey (from local bees) crème brûlée with summery gooseberry and elderflower sorbet, or a theme on rhubarb.

Chef Darren Goodwin **Owner** Paul & Kathryn Roden **Times** 12-2.30/6.30-9 **Prices** Fixed L 2 course £14.50-£28.50, Fixed D 3 course £35-£38.50, Service optional **Wines** 20 bottles over £20, 10 bottles under £20, 6 by glass **Notes** Taste of Losehill 8 course £50, Sunday L, Vegetarian menu, Civ Wed 80 **Seats** 50, Pr/dining room 12 **Children** Portions **Parking** 20

MATLOCK
Map 16 SK35

The Red House Country Hotel

◉ Traditional British ☺

Simple country cooking in a fine Victorian house

☎ 01629 734854
Old Rd, Darley Dale DE4 2ER
e-mail: enquiries@theredhousecountryhotel.co.uk
dir: off A6 onto Old Rd signed Carriage Museum, 2.5m N of Matlock

The Manchester architect who built his country bolt-hole in 1891 chose a great spot: splendid views down the Derwent Valley extend beyond its well-kept grounds, and the interior of this charming small country-house hotel has retained heaps of period charm. The light and airy dining room looks thoroughly elegant with its white linen and gleaming silverware, and friendly, switched-on staff do their bit in making things run smoothly. The kitchen takes an admirably straightforward path through classic ideas, taking fine local produce as its starting point, and avoiding over-elaboration, thus Scottish herring fillets

might be marinated in Madeira and served with a simple tomato salsa, while main course venison steak is marinated, coated in cracked peppercorns, then oven baked and served with red wine and balsamic sauce.

Chef Wesley Smith **Owner** David & Kate Gardiner **Times** 7-8.30 Closed 25-29 Dec, 1st 2 wks Jan, L all week, D Sun-Mon **Prices** Fixed D 4 course £29-£32.50, Service optional **Wines** 11 bottles over £20, 14 bottles under £20, 7 by glass **Notes** Vegetarian available, Dress restrictions, Smart casual **Seats** 24 **Parking** 15

Stones Restaurant

◉◉ Modern British

Basement venue with creative modern menu

☎ 01629 56061
1c Dale Rd DE4 3LT
e-mail: info@stones-restaurant.co.uk

On a sunny day the garden terrace perched above the River Derwent is hard to beat, but this being Derbyshire's Peak District, you may well find yourself indoors. And that is no hardship at all, since Stones' intimate basement is a sophisticated brasserie-style venue done out with warm, earthy tones of chocolate, toffee and cream, and textures of bare wood and exposed brickwork. The food also merits serious attention, as the kitchen delivers well-balanced renditions of contemporary British dishes - parsley and sweetcorn risotto with chicken wings and crisp chicken skin might be the prelude to a seldom-seen pairing of wood pigeon breast with slow-cooked pork belly, roasted vegetables and butternut squash purée. Well-executed desserts could offer chocolate terrine pointed up with salted caramel ice cream and caramelised banana.

Times 12-2/6-9 Closed 26 Dec, 1 Jan, Mon, L Tue-Sat, D Sun

MELBOURNE
Map 11 SK32

The Bay Tree

◉◉ Modern British

Modish cooking in a tranquil market town

☎ 01332 863358
4 Potter St DE73 8HW
e-mail: enquiries@baytreerestaurant.co.uk
dir: From M1(N) junct 23A or junct 24 (S) take A453 to Isley Walton, turn right & follow signs to Melbourne town centre.

The charming market town of Melbourne has a gem of a local restaurant in The Bay Tree. And it's a restaurant that takes inspiration from far beyond the Derbyshire countryside - chef Rex Howell has drawn on his experience around the world, especially the Far East, to deliver his style of modern British cooking. There is nothing to scare the horses, though, and flavour combinations are well judged. Cornish crab salad comes

with avocado and pickled kohlrabi, for example, or go for Keralan-style green mango and king prawn curry with a spicy home-made tomato chutney. The butternut squash purée that accompanies a rack of English lamb is flavoured with cumin, and star anise infuses the sauce accompanying line-caught sea bass. The village has an old-world feel, but inside The Bay Tree there's a soothing contemporary shimmer and pleasing absence of country chintz.

Chef Rex Howell **Owner** R W Howell & V A Talbott **Times** 10.30-3/6.30-10.30 Closed 25 Dec, 31 Dec, BHs, Mon-Tue, D Sun **Prices** Fixed L 2 course £22.50, Fixed D 3 course £35, Starter £5.50-£11.95, Main £15.50-£24.50, Dessert £7.50, Service added 10% **Wines** 50 bottles over £20, 13 bottles under £20, 6 by glass **Notes** Sunday L, Vegetarian available, Dress restrictions, Smart casual **Seats** 60 **Children** Portions **Parking** On street

MORLEY
Map 11 SK34

The Morley Hayes Hotel

◉ Modern British

Modern-classic cooking on a converted farm estate

☎ 01332 780480
Main Rd DE7 6DG
e-mail: enquiries@morleyhayes.com
dir: 4m N of Derby on A608

Morley Hayes near Derby has been a farm estate and an orphanage in its time, but has been run as a family hotel since the 1980s. The Dovecote, its principal dining room, is to be found on the raftered first floor of a separate former farm building, overlooking the golf course and surrounding countryside. The cooking is as trend-conscious as can be, with many modern-classic dishes and some novel ideas in evidence. King prawn ravioli with a seared scallop in lemongrass sauce may whet the appetite for Gressingham duck breast with bok choy, radishes, honey-roast carrots and a pastilla of the leg meat. Finish with rhubarb jelly and sorbet, served with buttermilk pannacotta, or else they'll happily deconstruct a Black Forest gâteau for you.

Chef Nigel Stuart **Owner** Robert & Andrew Allsop/Morley Hayes Leisure Ltd **Times** 12-2/7-9.30 Closed 27 Dec, 1 Jan, L Sat, Mon **Prices** Fixed L 2 course £16.95, Fixed D 3 course £19.95, Starter £6.25-£9.95, Main £16.95-£26, Dessert £6.10, Service optional **Wines** 25 bottles over £20, 15 bottles under £20, 12 by glass **Notes** Sunday L, Vegetarian available, Dress restrictions, Smart casual, Civ Wed 80 **Seats** 100, Pr/dining room 24 **Children** Portions, Menu **Parking** 250

Save on Hotels. Book at **theAA.com/hotel**

DERBYSHIRE 127 ENGLAND

East Lodge Country House Hotel

ROWSLEY Map 16 SK26

Modern British 🏵

Modern British cooking in the Peak District

☎ 01629 734474
DE4 2EF
e-mail: info@eastlodge.com
dir: On A6, 5m from Matlock & 3m from Bakewell, at junct with B6012

This one-time hunting lodge within the Peak District National Park has a more elevated position on the social scale these days - as a delightful and thoroughly charming country-house hotel. The 10 acres of grounds only add to its appeal, with landscape gardens to explore, whilst the interior has plenty of traditional character and comforts to soothe in fair weather and in foul. The restaurant - intimate in scale but big on ambition - is a major part of the draw here, with chef Simon Bradley serving up some classy and confident dishes in the intimate dining room. There's a chef's table, too, giving the opportunity to see all the action up close and personal, with its own tasting menu on offer. Wherever you choose to sit, you can expect modern food with up-to-date cooking techniques to the fore, and fine Derbyshire produce at its core. A first course preserved cod mousse comes with seared scallops and contrasting textures of carrot and cauliflower, and main-course beef is seared on the plancha and served with celeriac, horseradish mayonnaise and bone marrow. Desserts show a keen eye for innovation, too, such as in a damson sorbet with sweet pickled beetroot, damson paste, a salad of blackberries and oranges, thyme croquant, goats' curd and red wine syrup. Excellent breads and an array of delightful petits fours maintain the high standard from start to finish.

Chef Simon Bradley **Owner** Elyzian Hospitality Ltd **Times** 12-2/7-9.30 **Prices** Fixed L 2 course £20, Fixed D 3 course £35, Tasting menu £55, Service optional **Notes** Tasting menu 6 course, Chef's table 8 course £65, Vegetarian available, Dress restrictions, Smart casual, no jeans or trainers, Civ Wed 150 **Seats** 80, Pr/dining room 72 **Children** Portions, Menu **Parking** 40

The Peacock at Rowsley

ROWSLEY Map 16 SK26

Modern British V 🏵

Confident cooking in a stylish Peak District hotel

☎ 01629 733518
Bakewell Rd DE4 2EB
e-mail: reception@thepeacockatrowsley.com
web: www.thepeacockatrowsley.com
dir: A6, 3m before Bakewell, 6m from Matlock towards Bakewell

Under the same aristocratic ownership as nearby Haddon Hall in the heart of the Peak District, the mellow stone dower house dates from the 1640s, but looks rather more contemporary indoors after a facelift courtesy of Paris-based designer India Mahdavi, who did The Connaught's last makeover. The result is an opulent contemporary hotel with a luxurious, dark and sexy dining room done out with burgundy walls, taupe and claret tartan carpet, unclothed oak tables laid with leather mats and classy glassware, and leaded windows looking into the garden; staff clad in black bistro-style aprons know their business too, multi-tasking through food and wine service and tending unobtrusively throughout proceedings. Head chef Dan Smith's time in Tom Aikens's kitchen shows in his precise, technical dexterity, use of top-class produce, quirky spins of presentation and off-the-wall combinations here and there. After amuse-bouche in the bar - Comté cheese and onion soup, and cured trout with fennel and avocado purée - things get properly underway with a starter of duck liver ballottine with confit rabbit, prunes, walnuts and crisp radish. Main course sees faultless turbot matched with sticky oxtail, salt-baked celeriac, buttery pommes Maxim, and trompette mushrooms. To finish, there's a virtuoso assemblage of blood orange parfait with rhubarb, which is given a thorough workout - as jellied purée, poached, sauce, and with tapioca - and served with gingerbread croûtons.

Chef Daniel Smith **Owner** Rutland Hotels **Times** 12-2/7-9 Closed D 24-26 Dec **Prices** Fixed L 3 course £25.75-£27.50, Starter £6.50-£12.50, Main £28-£32.50, Dessert £7.95-£8.95, Service optional **Wines** 44 bottles over £20, 8 bottles under £20, 15 by glass **Notes** Vegetarian menu, Civ Wed 20 **Seats** 40, Pr/dining room 20 **Children** Portions, Menu **Parking** 25

RISLEY
Map 11 SK43

Risley Hall

◉ European

Modern cooking in a venerable Saxon manor

☎ 0115 939 9000
Derby Rd DE72 3SS
e-mail: enquiries@risleyhall.com
dir: M1 junct 25, Sandiacre exit into Bostock Ln. Left at lights, hotel on left in 0.25m

Risley Hall is a splendid creeper-clad Saxon house dating from the 11th century with a magnificent baronial hall that might count as a relatively recent addition, being a mere five centuries or so years old. As a country-house retreat, it delivers all the indulgences you could reasonably ask for, including 10 acres of landscaped grounds to roam in, spa treatments to de-stress the bones, and good, straightforward modern cooking based on local and seasonal ingredients in Abbey's Restaurant. Expect starters such as pan-fried scallops with fried quail's egg, black pudding, and beetroot purée, followed by mains that might see pork belly sharing a plate with celeriac and apple purée, pommes Anna, and cider and sage sauce. Desserts keep things simple with, say, lemon tart with passionfruit sorbet.

Times 12-6.30/7-10.30

ROWSLEY
Map 16 SK26

East Lodge Country House Hotel

◉◉◉ – see page 127

The Peacock at Rowsley

◉◉◉ – see page 127

DEVON

ASHBURTON
Map 3 SX77

Agaric

◉ Modern British ✪

Well-judged menu in engaging restaurant with rooms

☎ 01364 654478
30 North St TQ13 7QD
e-mail: eat@agaricrestaurant.co.uk
dir: Opposite town hall. Ashburton off A38 between Exeter & Plymouth

Behind the shop-front is a small, friendly and relaxing restaurant, well established on the Ashburton foodie trail, with rustic-style wooden tables, a wood-burner, and a few cabinets displaying the restaurant's range of products on sale. Nick Coiley is passionate about all things local, including home-grown garden produce, and is a confident, skilful cook, turning out starters of an unusual terrine of smoked cod, potato, leeks and saffron, and a warm salad of pigeon breast, bacon, celeriac and beetroot. Expect no bells, whistles or gimmicks among

main courses, which tend to be well composed with clearly defined flavours: roast loin of lamb, served rare, in a herb crust, say, accompanied by a softly grilled kidney in mustardy butter, a notable spinach and tapenade soufflé, and a jug of jus. Fish is as well judged as the rest, seen in grilled turbot steak with sorrel mayonnaise and grilled fennel, and first-class desserts have included hot chocolate soufflé.

Chef Nick Coiley **Owner** Mr N Coiley & Mrs S Coiley
Times 12-2/7-9.30 Closed 2 wks Aug, Xmas, 1 wk Jan, Sun-Tue, L Sat **Prices** Fixed L 2 course £15.95, Starter £5.95-£9.50, Main £15.95-£22.50, Dessert £6.95-£9.50, Service optional **Wines** 16 bottles over £20, 9 bottles under £20, 6 by glass **Notes** Vegetarian available **Seats** 30 **Children** Portions **Parking** Car park opposite

ASHWATER
Map 3 SX39

Blagdon Manor Restaurant With Rooms

◉◉ Modern British V ✪

Confident cooking in charming Devon longhouse

☎ 01409 211224
EX21 5DF
e-mail: stay@blagdon.com
web: www.blagdon.com
dir: From A388 towards Holsworthy, 2m N of Chapman's Well take 2nd right towards Ashwater. Next right by Blagdon Lodge. Hotel 2nd on right

In 20 acres, with country views towards Dartmoor, the manor dates from the 17th century, with oak beams, slate flagstones, large stone fireplaces, and, outside, a well to further prove it. It's comfortable rather than grand, with a friendly, relaxing atmosphere, good-natured, helpful staff, and a bright, cheery conservatory restaurant. The kitchen marshals the best produce from the locality and puts a modern gloss on a fairly traditional repertory. Galantine of guinea fowl and duck, with discs of black pudding, soft-centred quail's eggs and girolles, the plate dotted with gooseberry dressing, is typical of the effort that goes into starters. Main courses can be as robust as braised shin of beef with oxtail suet pudding and wild mushrooms, and as refined as poached fillet of turbot, moist and fresh, in a light champagne and chive sauce, served with artfully arranged vegetables. The same care is evident in desserts like lemon posset with a lemon curd doughnut.

Chef Stephen Morey **Owner** Stephen & Liz Morey
Times 12-2/7-9 Closed Jan, Mon-Tue, L Wed-Sat
Prices Fixed D 3 course £45, Service optional
Wines 22 bottles over £20, 6 bottles under £20, 7 by

glass **Notes** Sunday L, Vegetarian menu, Dress restrictions, Smart casual **Seats** 28, Pr/dining room 16 **Parking** 12

AXMINSTER
Map 4 SY29

Fairwater Head Hotel

◉ Modern British ✪

Straightforward brasserie cooking on the Jurassic Coast

☎ 01297 678349
Hawkchurch EX13 5TX
e-mail: info@fairwaterheadhotel.co.uk
dir: A358 into Broom Lane at Tytherleigh, follow signs to Hawkchurch & hotel

Four miles outside Axminster, the hotel stands on the Jurassic Coast, England's first ever designated World Heritage Site. In a stripped-wood ambience, the creatively spelt Greenfields Brazzerie does what it says on the tin, offering un-mucked about classic dishes presented efficiently and with flair. Vulscombe goats' cheese terrine with apple and nut salad utilises one of modern Devon's premier dairy products, while mains go in for braised daube of beef with horseradish mash in red wine jus, or simple grilled plaice in chive butter. The generous dessert choice runs from Eton Mess with winter berries to apple and sultana crumble with ice cream and custard.

Chef Jeremy Woollven **Owner** Adam & Carrie Southwell
Times 12-2/7-9 Closed Jan, L Mon-Tue, Thu-Fri
Prices Fixed L 2 course fr £12, Starter £4.75-£6.50, Main £11.50-£23, Dessert £5-£7.50, Service optional
Wines 33 bottles over £20, 27 bottles under £20, 12 by glass **Notes** Sunday L, Vegetarian available, Dress restrictions, Smart casual, Civ Wed 65 **Seats** 60, Pr/dining room 18 **Children** Portions, Menu **Parking** 40

BAMPTON
Map 3 SS92

The Quarrymans Rest

◉ Modern British ✪

Well-judged modern cooking at a welcoming village pub

☎ 01398 331480
Briton St EX16 9LN
e-mail: paul@thequarrymans.co.uk
dir: M5 junct 27 towards Tiverton on A361, at rdbt turn right signed Bampton. At next rdbt take 2nd exit signed Bampton, on right

The wild tracts of Exmoor are close by, and it's a short drive to the north and south coasts of Devon, so you can expect fish fresh from the Brixham day boats and prime West Country produce with minimal food miles at The Quarrymans. Paul and Donna Berry run their 250-year-old village inn with relaxed, hands-on charm, fostering a chatty, reassuringly unpretentious vibe throughout. An ever-changing specials board takes advantage of whatever's good and in season, and Paul delivers it all without unnecessary fuss, making his own soused herrings to serve with pickled cucumber, or chicken liver parfait to go with quince jelly. At main course stage, rump of Exmoor lamb could be served on a caramelised onion tarte Tatin, while wild sea bass fillet comes simply with bubble-and-squeak, leek sauce, and purple sprouting broccoli.

Chef Paul Berry **Owner** Paul & Donna Berry **Times** 12-2/6-9.30 Closed 25-26 Dec, D Sun **Prices** Starter £4.50-£9, Main £10.95-£19, Dessert £6, Service optional **Notes** Vegetarian available **Seats** 40 **Children** Portions **Parking** 6

BEESANDS   Map 3 SX84

The Cricket Inn

◉ Modern British

Quaint seaside inn serving tip-top seafood and more besides

☎ 01548 580215
TQ7 2EN
e-mail: enquiries@thecricketinn.com
dir: From Kingsbridge follow A379 towards Dartmouth, at Stokenham mini-rdbt turn right for Beesands

When the crabs, lobster and scallops are hauled in from the sea in front of where you're sitting, you know you're in for a treat. But that's not to say that this gem of an inn on the shingly beach of Start Bay neglects the bounty of the land, which turns up in the shape of locally-reared lamb chop served with cabbage, smoked bacon and black pudding mash. Smartly refurbished, The Cricket Inn still hangs on to its quaint traditional fishing inn character with old photos of Beesands village and fishing paraphernalia in the bar, while the airy restaurant extension is done out in a pared-back New England style. Those diver-caught scallops from the bay might be delivered with shiitake mushrooms, cauliflower purée, and crispy Parma ham, while lemon sole of the same provenance could turn up simply with lemon and chive butter, or there may be brill with a crab and ginger reduction and deep-fried angel hair noodles.

Chef Scott Simon **Owner** Nigel & Rachel Heath **Times** 12-3/6-9 **Prices** Food prices not confirmed for 2013. Please telephone for details **Wines** 8 bottles over £20, 19 bottles under £20, 14 by glass **Notes** Vegetarian available **Seats** 65, Pr/dining room 40 **Children** Portions, Menu **Parking** 30

BIDEFORD   Map 3 SS42

Yeoldon Country House Hotel

◉ British

Nostalgic cooking by the Torridge estuary

☎ 01237 474400
Durrant Ln, Northam EX39 2RL
e-mail: yeoldonhouse@aol.com
dir: A39 from Barnstaple over River Torridge Bridge. At rdbt right onto A386 towards Northam, then 3rd right into Durrant Lane

Newspaper cuttings and pictures from times gone by adorn the walls of the dining room at the Steeles' Victorian hotel, which also enjoys sweeping views of the Torridge estuary. Brian runs an industrious kitchen, often single-handedly, producing well-crafted food that has a nostalgic feel to it, and is none the worse for that. Chicken liver and cranberry terrine comes with an intensely flavoured onion marmalade, and could be followed by a generous portion of bracingly fresh baked cod with an old-school white wine and saffron cream sauce incorporating finely chopped fennel. Meats include fine West Country lamb chump on parsnip and horseradish mash, with traditional redcurrant and rosemary, while the pudding vote goes once more to the treacle and ginger tart, served with excellent ginger ice cream.

Chef Brian Steele **Owner** Brian & Jennifer Steele **Times** 7-8 Closed Xmas, Sun, L all week **Prices** Fixed D 3 course fr £35, Service included **Wines** 14 bottles over £20, 20 bottles under £20, 6 by glass **Notes** Vegetarian available, Dress restrictions, Smart casual, Civ Wed 60 **Seats** 30 **Children** Portions **Parking** 30

BRIXHAM   Map 3 SX95

Quayside Hotel

◉ Modern British

A strong line in seafood in popular harbour hotel

☎ 01803 855751
41-49 King St TQ5 9TJ
e-mail: reservations@quayside.co.uk
dir: From Exeter take A380 towards Torquay, then A3022 to Brixham

The well-established hotel, carved out of six fishermen's cottages, wears its name with pride, as it has great views over the harbour and bay. Windows in the restaurant, a

nicely decorated low-ceilinged, candlelit room, look over the quay too. With the fish market so near, the kitchen naturally makes the most of locally landed seafood, sometimes giving it an exotic spin: crab tian with apple salsa, a samosa and red wine syrup, say, followed by seared monkfish fillet on spicy lentils accompanied by tempura prawns and sautéed pak choi. Other treatments are just as effective: oysters with raspberry vinaigrette, and poached turbot with mussels and tarragon-flavoured leeks. Meat might appear in the shape of Moroccan-style lamb on couscous with courgette fritters and orange jus, and among puddings may be vanilla pannacotta with pineapple salsa.

Chef Andy Sewell **Owner** Mr & Mrs C F Bowring **Times** 6.30-9.30 Closed L all week **Prices** Food prices not confirmed for 2013. Please telephone for details **Wines** 5 bottles over £20, 27 bottles under £20, 10 by glass **Notes** Vegetarian available, Dress restrictions, Smart casual preferred **Seats** 40, Pr/dining room 18 **Children** Portions, Menu **Parking** 30

BURRINGTON   Map 3 SS61

Northcote Manor

◉◉ Modern British V 🍷 ⚘

Tranquil country-house setting and well-sourced modern British food

☎ 01769 560501
EX37 9LZ
e-mail: rest@northcotemanor.co.uk
dir: M5 junct 27 towards Barnstaple. Left at rdbt to South Molton. Follow A377, right at T-junct to Barnstaple. Entrance after 3m, opposite Portsmouth Arms railway station and pub. (NB do not enter Burrington village)

The 18th-century manor house used to be a Benedictine monastery and it maintains a sense of peacefulness today that the monks may well have appreciated. The 20 acres of sweeping lawns and patio overlooking the Japanese Garden offer plenty of opportunities for reflection, but a cream tea in the sunshine offers a more immediate form of gratification. In keeping with the unfettered elegance of it all, the stylishly understated restaurant serves up a daily-changing menu which pledges to use local ingredients wherever possible. So you might find medallions of Cornish cod in a light soda water and beer batter with crisp potatoes, lemon crème fraîche and pea purée, then move on to breast of Crediton Aylesbury duckling with gratin potatoes, wilted baby spinach, oven-baked fig and red wine gravy. Finish with an unctuous dark chocolate fondant with caramelised banana, white chocolate ice cream and hot chocolate drink.

Chef Richie Herkes **Owner** J Pierre Mifsud **Times** 12-2/7-9 **Prices** Fixed L 2 course £10.50, Starter £12, Main £22, Dessert £11, Service optional **Wines** 87 bottles over £20, 9 bottles under £20, 10 by glass **Notes** Sunday L, Vegetarian menu, Dress restrictions, Smart casual preferred, no jeans, Civ Wed 80 **Seats** 34, Pr/dining room 50 **Children** Portions, Menu **Parking** 30

CHAGFORD   Map 3 SX78

Gidleigh Park

◉◉◉◉ – *see opposite*

Mill End Hotel and Restaurant

◉◉ Modern British

Good modern cooking in a relaxed riverside setting

☎ 01647 432282
TQ13 8JN
e-mail: mike@millendhotel.com
dir: From A30 turn on to A382. Establishment on right before Chagford turning

Dating from the 15th century, this former water mill lies in a secluded valley on the edge of Dartmoor, with the River Teign running past the foot of the garden. Perfect then, for hiking, biking and fishing - after all, the small-scale country house comes with its own six mile-stretch of on-site angling. Indoors, the original water wheel is still in fine fettle, and plans are afoot to have it paying its way once more by generating power for the hotel; for now it provides a deeply-calming slosh as you dine in the spacious sage green dining room. In keeping with the unpretentious vibe, no-one is trying to make any incongruous statements in the kitchen - an experienced hand knows where to get hold of the finest local ingredients and treat them with the lightest of touch to produce fuss-free, refined modern dishes. Start, perhaps, with terrine of local venison with Cumberland sauce, and follow that with roast belly pork with plum compôte, dauphinoise potatoes, port wine sauce and crackling. Go for a savoury finish with a selection of West Country cheeses, or seek the comfort of pear and almond tart with home-made pear ice cream.

Chef Wayne Pearson **Owner** Sue & Peter Davies **Times** 12-2.30/7-9.30 Closed 1st 3 wks Jan **Prices** Fixed L 2 course £12-£20, Fixed D 3 course £39.50, Service optional, Groups min 8 service 10% **Wines** 41 bottles over £20, 16 bottles under £20, 7 by glass **Notes** Sunday L, Vegetarian available, Civ Wed 100 **Seats** 32 **Parking** 30

22 Mill Street Restaurant & Rooms

◉◉ Modern British V ⏱

Lively modern cooking in Dartmoor village

☎ 01647 432244
22 Mill St TQ13 8AW
e-mail: info@22millst.com
web: www.22millst.com
dir: A382/B3206 enter village into main square, Mill St is on the right

Just off the main street of this pretty Dartmoor village, 22 Mill Street combines contemporary décor with a country-house feel, with well-spaced wooden tables on oak floorboards and whitewashed walls hung with paintings. The kitchen embraces the classical and contemporary British styles of cooking, and calls on the best West Country products it can find. Goats' cheese mousse with beetroot and piccalilli vegetables makes a thoroughly modern starter, equalled by langoustines with black pudding, Jerusalem artichoke and roast garlic. Main courses can be richly flavoured: witness braised ox cheek and tail with sprout tops, gnocchi and root vegetables, and ras el hanout, cauliflower 'textures' and chick peas as accompaniments for pan-fried fillet of brill. Desserts can pile on the flavours too, seen in candy beetroot parfait with chocolate mousse, orange and honeycomb.

Owner Evision Group **Times** 12-4/6.30-10 Closed 2 wks Jan, Mon **Prices** Fixed L 2 course £16.95-£19.95, Fixed D 3 course £42-£49, Service optional **Wines** 50 bottles over £20, 10 bottles under £20, 8 by glass **Notes** Tasting menu 5 course, Sunday L, Vegetarian menu, Civ Wed 30 **Seats** 28, Pr/dining room 14 **Children** Portions **Parking** On street

DARTMOUTH   Map 3 SX85

Dart Marina Hotel & Spa

◉◉ Modern British V

Confident modern cooking in contemporary riverside hotel

☎ 01803 832580
The Dart Marina Hotel, Sandquay Rd TQ6 9PH
e-mail: info@dartmarinahotel.com
dir: A3122 from Totnes to Dartmouth. Follow road which becomes College Way, before Higher Ferry. Hotel sharp left in Sandquay Rd

The fine-dining option at the smart, modern waterfront Dart Marina Hotel, the aptly named River Restaurant

(extended in 2012), comes with full-drop windows and terrace for fab views over the marina and the River Dart's waterborne action. Unsurprisingly, it's a big hit with the yachting fraternity, but all-comers will appreciate its relaxed, modish charms and the good contemporary British food on offer. The team in the kitchen duly follow the seasons and seek out some of South Devon's excellent produce. Fish from the day-boats might include sea bass, the fillet served up with red kale, new potatoes, crayfish tails, broccoli and a white wine sauce, and, from the land, a Blackawton lamb 'plate' (herb-crusted cutlet, cannon and shepherd's pie) accompanied by glazed carrots and a Madeira sauce. To finish, perhaps classic tiramisù or lemon tart.

Chef Tom Woods **Owner** Richard Seton **Times** 12-2/6-9 Closed L Mon-Sat **Prices** Fixed D 3 course £37.50, Service optional **Wines** 45 bottles over £20, 15 bottles under £20, 12 by glass **Notes** Sunday L, Vegetarian menu, Dress restrictions, Smart casual **Seats** 80 **Children** Portions, Menu **Parking** 100

Jan and Freddies Brasserie

◉◉ Modern British ⏱

Smart modern brasserie in historic town centre

☎ 01803 832491
10 Fairfax Place TQ6 9AD
e-mail: info@janandfreddiesbrasserie.co.uk
dir: Fairfax Place runs parallel to South Embankment. Restaurant faces Hawley Rd

Right in the heart of the town, this unpretentious place has a contemporary finish and takes a thoroughly up-to-date approach to life. Stuck in the past it ain't. With its mood lighting and lack of starch (which means no linen tablecloths either), it's an egalitarian space for some smart, gently modernised trad cooking. Chef Richard Hilson used to work at Gidleigh Park (see entry) so knows a thing or two about getting the best out of ingredients (a good deal of which are local), and his unfussy approach wins plaudits. Start with salmon and prawn fishcakes (rolled in panko breadcrumbs), or steamed local River Teign mussels, before the catch of the day or steamed suet steak and kidney pudding with pea and parsley mash and a rich beef gravy. If a sweet finish is on the cards, expect the likes of orange and lemon posset with a shortbread biscuit, or Belgian style waffles with real maple syrup.

Chef Richard Hilson **Owner** Jan & Freddie Clarke **Times** 12.30-2/6.30-9 Closed Xmas, Sun, L Mon **Prices** Starter £5.50-£7.50, Main £13.95-£22.95, Dessert £5.50-£6.50, Service optional **Wines** 16 bottles over £20, 22 bottles under £20, 10 by glass **Notes** Vegetarian available **Seats** 40 **Children** Portions **Parking** On street

Save on Hotels. Book at **theAA.com/hotel**

DEVON 131 ENGLAND

Gidleigh Park

CHAGFORD   Map 3 SX78

Modern European V   NOTABLE WINE LIST

Culinary refinement in a Dartmoor setting to match

☎ 01647 432367
TQ13 8HH
e-mail: gidleighpark@gidleigh.co.uk
dir: From Chagford Sq turn right at Lloyds TSB into Mill St, after 150yds right fork, across x-rds into Holy St. Restaurant 1.5m

Gidleigh Park only counts as being in Chagford if you overlook the couple of miles of country, then private road, between it and the north Dartmoor village. It's a fabulous 1920s mock-timbered repro job built in the Arts and Crafts era, and lacks for nothing inside, where the furnishings and decorations are of an other-worldly refinement. Lingering on the terrace, from which the grounds fall away to the lawns and tennis court and River Teign below, is a most agreeable way to start the experience (if you're only here to eat), and the sense of fastidious correctness maintained by staff represents the best kind of old-school approach. Immaculate place settings, oak panelling and tasteful lithographs do the rest. This is the flagship of the formidable fleet of culinary operations now mustered by Michael Caines MBE, whose commitment to regional produce is a sine qua non wherever he sets up

shop. Fish from the Devon coasts, game from Dartmoor and fresh produce from Gidleigh's own kitchen garden are the mainstays of menus that take a contemporary approach to British and European culinary traditions, while insisting that fine food is first and foremost a treat, not the occasion for a cerebral exercise in denaturing. Witness a first-course tartlet piled with quail, smoked bacon, black truffle, wild mushrooms, onion confit and quail eggs, sauced with a light quail jus. Everything feels as though it belongs with everything else, the final result adding up to a composition made in heaven (and Devon). A seafood starter might see langoustines in cannelloni, served with braised fennel and a brace of sauces, vierge and shellfish. The Brixham boats supply a pairing of turbot and scallops as a main course, with leeks and wild mushrooms in chive butter, or there could be rose veal with truffled celeriac purée, a raviolo of the sweetbread and a fragrant sauce based on Gewürztraminer. Desserts, so often the occasion for vegetables and salt to make their appearances these days, instead remind you what the appeal once was in the likes of featherlight prune and Armagnac soufflé, hot apple tart with vanilla ice cream and cider sauce, or a triple-toned trio of chocolate offerings - a mousse of dark, ice cream of white, and a parfait of milk with hazelnuts.

Chef Michael Caines MBE
Owner Andrew and Christina Brownsword **Times** 12-2/7-9.45
Prices Fixed L 2 course £40, Tasting menu £115-£125, Starter £20-£30, Main £45-£55, Dessert £15-£20, Service optional **Wines** 1300 bottles over £20, 11 by glass **Notes** Tasting menu 5 & 8 course, Vegetarian menu, Dress restrictions, Shirt with collar, no jeans or sportswear **Seats** 52, Pr/dining room 22 **Children** Portions, Menu **Parking** 45

DARTMOUTH *continued*

The Seahorse

◉◉ Mediterranean, Seafood

Dynamic waterfront venue from a fish maestro

☎ 01803 835147
5 South Embankment TQ6 9BH
e-mail: enquiries@seahorserestaurant.co.uk

There's something about Dartmouth that always puts you in the mood for fish - perhaps it's the River Dart running by, or the knowledge that Brixham's trawler fleet is just up the road. Luckily, Mitch Tonks's seafood-based empire is at hand with this elegant bistro-style outpost to bring Brixham's catch to your plate, while casting its net wider to haul in langoustines, sea urchins and razor clams that aren't caught locally. It's a buzzy venue with an open-to-view kitchen and the slightly bohemian look of an old-school French bistro with its button-backed mustard leather banquettes, darkwood tables and floors and wall of wine bottles. The daily-changing menu, however, has strong Italophile leanings, and as soon as you cast an eye over it you can see that you're safe in the hands of chefs who love to eat: a stew of carpetshell clams with sherry and peas, or scallops roasted in the shell with garlic and port are typical starters, then there could be turbot steak with hollandaise, or grilled Dover sole with salsa limone. Meat addicts are not sent home hungry either, if rib of beef roasted on the bone over charcoal with rosemary and red wine is up for grabs.

Chef Mat Prowse, Mitch Tonks **Owner** Mat Prowse, Mitch Tonks **Times** 12-3/6-10 Closed 25 Dec,1 Jan, Mon, L Tue, D Sun **Prices** Food prices not confirmed for 2013. Please telephone for details **Wines** 109 bottles over £20, 14 bottles under £20, 6 by glass **Notes** Vegetarian available **Seats** 40 **Children** Portions **Parking** On street

---

DREWSTEIGNTON   Map 3 SX79

The Old Inn

◉◉◉ — *see below*

EGGESFORD   Map 3 SS61

Fox & Hounds Country Hotel

◉ British ♥

Tip-top local ingredients cooked without fuss

☎ 01769 580345
EX18 7JZ
e-mail: relax@foxandhoundshotel.co.uk
dir: M5 junct 27, A361 towards Tiverton. B3137 signed Witheridge. After Nomansland follow signs to Eggesford Station, hotel in 50mtrs

The traditional country name is an apt one for this hotel on the River Taw. Rural pursuits are all around - fishing is on the doorstep, rough shooting on the surrounding hills, or you could simply hike the Tarka Trail through Eggesford Forest and spot deer, woodpeckers and otters on the river. The Fox & Hounds has been spruced up for contemporary tastes, although the bar takes pride in its original beer engines dispensing local ales, and the dog-friendly ethos means Rover can warm himself by the fire. Eat here if you like - it's the same menu as in the restaurant, which means uncomplicated British classics in a hearty West Country vein, brimming with local ingredients. Ham hock terrine with pear chutney might set the ball rolling, then mignons and braised belly of locally-reared pork turn up in the company of caramelised apples and crushed potatoes. And for pud, baked Alaska flavoured with coconut rum, or go for the West Country cheeseboard.

Chef Alex Pallatt **Owner** Nick & Tara Culverhouse **Times** 12-2.30/6.30-9 **Prices** Fixed D 3 course £25-£27.50, Starter £5.25-£8.25, Main £10.95-£17.25, Dessert £5.50, Service optional **Wines** 23 bottles under £20, 8 by glass **Notes** Sunday L, Vegetarian available, Civ Wed 120 **Seats** 60, Pr/dining room 120 **Children** Portions, Menu **Parking** 100

The Old Inn

DREWSTEIGNTON   Map 3 SX79

French **NEW**

Intelligent, flavour-packed cooking of verve and vigour

☎ 01647 281276
EX6 6QR
e-mail: enquiries@old-inn.co.uk

Chef-patron Duncan Walker clearly has a thing about Dartmoor: he moved from the north-east 25 years ago to work with Shaun Hill at Gidleigh Park, and never looked back. After a brief rest from the stoves, he's now back in this chocolate box village on the fringes of the moor doing what he does so well - extracting the maximum amount of flavour from the region's top-class produce. The venue is a whitewashed, 17th-century cottagey restaurant with a trio of bedrooms and a deliciously unpretentious atmosphere - there's a cosy lounge with squashy sofas by a woodburner and a pair of retrievers to welcome guests; elsewhere, its bare oak tables, claret and sage green walls hung with eclectic art all look smart and inviting, but refreshingly free from chichi designer touches. With just 17 diners to attend to, the cooking is truly extraordinary. Walker is one of those rare talents who can achieve big flavours from just about any ingredient he lays his hands on, whether it's a humble vegetable or a luxurious lobe of foie gras, which, incidentally, is likely to come sautéed and matched with figs caramelised in port and Sauternes. Turbo-charged flavours are all very well, but here they are tempered by sensitivity and a confidence in matching ingredients that is the culinary equivalent of having perfect pitch. A simple-sounding plate of crab is typically understated, and delivers a head-spinningly rich crab bisque, a spicy crab fritter, crab ravioli and risotto. Main course brings a whole calves' sweetbread perfectly caramelised and partnered by oxtail wrapped in smoked bacon, and salsify served as buttered spears and crisp beignets. Fish gets equally robust treatment - perhaps pairing grilled turbot fillet with smoked haddock tortellini and chives. Quality is unwavering all the way through to desserts - and here's a tip: Walker is the soufflé king, so wind things up with a prune and Armagnac version with burnt honey ice cream to remind yourself why this old stager has such a timeless appeal in the hands of someone who unfailingly gets it right.

Chef Duncan Walker **Owner** Duncan Walker **Times** Closed L all week, D Sun-Tue (tables available for 6 to 10 by arrangement) **Prices** Food prices not confirmed for 2013. Please telephone for details **Seats** 17 **Parking**

EXETER   Map 3 SX99

Barton Cross Hotel & Restaurant

Traditional British, French V

Reliably good food in thatched hotel

☎ 01392 841245 & 841584
Huxham, Stoke Canon EX5 4EJ
e-mail: bartonxhuxham@aol.com
dir: 0.5m off A396 at Stoke Canon, 3m N of Exeter

In the Exe Valley four miles from the city centre, Barton Cross has been converted from a thatched longhouse, its restaurant showing signs of its age in an inglenook, cob walls, beams and an impressive gallery under a raftered ceiling. The kitchen deals in Anglo-European cooking with some polish, turning out chicken liver parfait with orange chutney alongside smoked salmon risotto spiked with dill and lemon, followed by beef fillet with oxtail cottage pie and port-based gravy, and well-timed fillet of sea bass with tangerine butter and chargrilled fennel. The occasional idea surfaces from further afield - pan-fried monkfish with coconut and curry sauce, say - and enterprising desserts have run to chocolate tart with marmalade and whisky ice cream.

Chef Nicholas Beattie **Owner** Brian Hamilton **Times** 12.30-2.30/6.30-11.30 Closed L Mon-Thu **Prices** Fixed D 3 course £25.50-£29.50, Starter £5.50-£7.50, Main £14.50-£18.50, Dessert £6.50, Service optional **Wines** 49 bottles over £20, 52 bottles under £20, 10 by glass **Notes** Sunday L, Vegetarian menu, Dress restrictions, Smart casual **Seats** 50, Pr/dining room 26 **Children** Portions, Menu **Parking** 50

The Olive Tree Restaurant at the Queens Court Hotel

Modern British

Confident, creative cooking in a townhouse hotel

☎ 01392 272709
Queens Court Hotel, 6-8 Bystock Ter EX4 4HY
e-mail: enquiries@queenscourt-hotel.co.uk
web: www.queenscourt-hotel.co.uk
dir: Exit dual carriageway at junct 30 onto B5132 (Topsham Rd) towards city centre. Hotel 200yds from Central Station

There is much to enjoy at this restaurant in a townhouse hotel on a quiet, leafy square just a short stroll from the city centre. The pared-back monochrome décor - black leather high-backed chairs at linen-clad tables and snow-white walls - has a certain gloss thanks to contemporary chandeliers and Venetian masks on the walls - a nod, perhaps, to the Mediterranean warmth that informs the modern cooking on offer. Sound sourcing lends substance to the whole operation, backed by the kitchen brigade's thoughtful approach and sound technical ability to pull off ideas such as boudin of rabbit mousseline and poached garlic served with lightly-spiced pickled red cabbage and a port reduction. Local roots are celebrated via a herb-crusted rack of West Country lamb, partnered with a slow-braised lamb shank faggot with Lyonnaise potatoes and carrot purée, while creative desserts run to a tiramisù-inspired coffee and mascarpone mousse-filled chocolate macaroon served with miniature jellies and espresso syrup.

Chef Darren Knockton **Owner** C F & B H Bowring **Times** 12-2/6.30-9.30 Closed Xmas, New Year, L Sun **Prices** Starter £7.95-£8.95, Main £17.95-£23, Dessert £6.50-£7.50, Service optional **Wines** 8 bottles over £20, 23 bottles under £20, 10 by glass **Notes** Tasting menu available, Vegetarian available, Dress restrictions, Smart casual preferred, Civ Wed 60 **Seats** 28, Pr/dining room 16 **Children** Portions **Parking** Public car park in front of hotel

EXMOUTH   Map 3 SY08

Les Saveurs

Modern European, Seafood

French fish cookery near the Exe estuary

☎ 01395 269459
9 Tower St EX8 1NT
e-mail: lessaveurs@yahoo.co.uk
dir: A376 to Exmouth, left at rdbt. Right at next rdbt onto one way system Rolle St. Tower St on right

With a skilled and sensitive French craftsman at work in the kitchen, it's no surprise to see the menu opening with a classic rich fish soup with rouille, grated emmental, and garlic croûtons at this family-run fish restaurant tucked down a little lane just a stone's throw from the sandy beach. Let your nose lead the way to the delicious wafts from the stock pot, which emanate from a delightfully romantic space done out with exposed brick walls, distressed-effect chairs and snow-white linen, and pile into a pot of Exmouth mussels marinières, followed perhaps by Lyme Bay turbot fillet with champagne sauce and mash, or gilt head bream with foraged nettle sauce and samphire. Meat eaters are sorted out by the likes of roast lamb rump with wild mushroom and Madeira sauce and gratin dauphinoise. End with a classic tarte Tatin, crème brûlée, or crêpes Suzette done with authentic French flair.

Chef Olivier Guyard-Mulkerrin **Owner** Olivier & Sheila Guyard-Mulkerrin **Times** 7-10.30 Closed Nov-Apr advance bookings only, Sun-Mon, ex by special arrangement, L all week **Prices** Starter £6.50-£7.95, Main £16.50-£17.95, Dessert £6.25-£7.95, Service optional, Groups min 6 service 10% **Wines** 15 bottles over £20, 11 bottles under £20, 4 by glass **Notes** Vegetarian available, Dress restrictions, Smart casual **Seats** 30, Pr/dining room 36 **Parking** On street/council offices

HAYTOR VALE   Map 3 SX77

Rock Inn

British

Simple, honest food at a traditional Dartmoor inn

☎ 01364 661305 & 661556
TQ13 9XP
e-mail: reservations@rockinn.co.uk
dir: From A38 at Drum Bridges, onto A382 to Bovey Tracey. In 2m take B3387 towards Haytor for 3.5m, follow brown signs

The 18th-century Rock Inn is a haven of civility and good cheer amid the wild, wind-blasted tors of Dartmoor - the sort of place you should factor in to a day's hiking or car touring in the area. Run by the same family for nigh on 30 years, it's still a proper pub with oak furniture, gleaming brasses and locally-brewed real ales in the bar, and the all-round feelgood factor that comes from roaring log fires, cosy nooks and romantically candlelit tables. The food is simple, effective and flavour-packed, with a good showing of local produce on a menu that gives due credit to suppliers of the principal component of each main course - perhaps pan-fried wild sea bass from Brixham partnered by chorizo risotto and tomato pesto, or for fans of local meat, pan-roasted rump of lamb with fine beans, rosemary fondant potato, beetroot purée and red wine sauce. At the end, West Country cheeses are mighty tempting, or you could go for a vanilla pannacotta with rhubarb compôte and shortbread.

Chef Sophie Collier, Mark Tribble **Owner** Mr C Graves **Times** 12-2.15/6.30-9 Closed 25-26 Dec **Prices** Fixed L 2 course fr £12, Fixed D 3 course fr £24, Starter £6.95-£8.95, Main £10.95-£27.95, Dessert £4.95-£6.95, Service optional, Groups min 6 service 10% **Wines** 44 bottles over £20, 18 bottles under £20, 11 by glass **Notes** Sunday L, Vegetarian available, Dress restrictions, No shorts (pm only) **Seats** 75, Pr/dining room 20 **Children** Portions, Menu **Parking** 25

HONITON — Map 4 ST10

The Holt Bar & Restaurant

◉ Modern British

Buzzy pub-restaurant with a local flavour

☎ 01404 47707
178 High St EX14 1LA
e-mail: enquiries@theholt-honiton.com
dir: At west end of High St

When you're in Honiton, track down The Holt for its lively, youthful energy, relaxed rustic vibe and confidently-cooked, imaginative modern dishes made from excellent local ingredients. The food may be well up to gastro standards, but the place hasn't turned its back on its roots: it's a great place to drop in for a pint too, as it is owned by the local independent Otter Brewery who proudly display a battery of their fine ales at the bar. The excellent sourcing policy extends to smoking fish and meats in-house, with salad leaves and veg grown up at the brewery. Culinary credentials duly established, you might start with smoked pork tenderloin pointed up with pineapple relish, black pudding and polenta toast, and proceed to seared lamb rump with sweetbreads, colcannon mash, maple-glazed onions and mint jus. Don't skip puddings such as hazelnut and caramel parfait with spiced walnut shortbread.

Times 12-2/7-10 Closed 25-26 Dec, Sun-Mon

Monkton Court

◉◉ Modern British

Well-judged modern British food in a Devon vicarage

☎ 01404 42309
Monkton EX14 9QH
e-mail: enquiries@monktoncourthotel.co.uk
dir: 2m E A30

Just off the A30 outside Honiton, Monkton Court is a former vicarage that radiates a tangible sense of the past. The Mary Magdalene Church it once served stands nearby, and features a stained-glass window by Burne-Jones, paid for by one of the Court's Victorian owners. A spacious, light-filled dining room with high-backed chairs and simple table appointments is in the modern idiom, a refreshing setting for the undoubted culinary dazzlements to come. The kitchen turns out the sort of dishes that have customers reaching for their phones to photograph them, but the aesthetics are nonetheless in the service of accuracy and clarity of seasoning and timing. This is finely detailed food, as may be seen from a starter of seared king scallops bathed in orange beurre blanc with a fennel-crumbed pannacotta and pickled beetroot; every element sensitively handled. Blackdown Hills lamb is celebrated in a trinity of treatments - sautéed loin, a spring roll of braised shoulder and breaded sweetbreads - alongside spring onion mash, baby leeks and a judiciously balanced port jus. A proper baked cheesecake sidesteps gelatinous sweetness to incorporate gentle lemon flavours and fat sultanas, and is offset by intense lemon ice cream.

Times 12-2.30/6.30-9.30

ILFRACOMBE — Map 3 SS54

11 The Quay

◉ Modern, Traditional

Brasserie cooking in a restaurant decorated by Damien Hirst

☎ 01271 868090 & 868091
11 The Quay EX34 9EQ
e-mail: info@11thequay.com
dir: Follow signs for harbour and pier car park. Restaurant on left before car park

The Hirst name is enough to draw attention to 11 The Quay, although its handsome red-brick and stone façade would be an inviting prospect even without the promise of the artist's work on the walls within. Forget formaldehyde-marinated sharks and shock tactics though - the pieces up in the Atlantic Room restaurant and the Harbourside space are more along the nostalgic lines of children's seashell friezes, and will do nothing to dent your appetite for the straightforward modern brasserie food on offer. Seated beneath the Atlantic Room's ceiling, which arches like the hull of an upturned boat, and with ocean views as a backdrop, a plate of Lundy Island crab claws with chilli mayonnaise is an apt choice among starters, or foie gras with Seville marmalade and toasted brioche might tempt. Next up, a rib-eye of Exmoor Angus steak with goose fat chips and béarnaise is a classic trio done just right, before a textbook crème brûlée ends things on another faultless note.

Owner Simon Browne & Damien Hirst **Times** 12-2.30/6-9 Closed Mon & Tue (Nov-Mar), D Sun **Prices** Food prices not confirmed for 2013. Please telephone for details **Notes** Sunday L, Vegetarian available **Seats** 32, Pr/dining room 26 **Children** Portions **Parking** Pier car park 100yds

Sandy Cove Hotel

◉ Modern British **NEW**

Simple cooking, local produce, views to die for

☎ 01271 882243
Old Coast Rd, Combe Martin Bay EX34 9SR
e-mail: info@sandycove-hotel.co.uk
dir: A339 to Combe Martin, through village towards Ilfracombe for approx 1m. Turn right just over brow of hill marked Sandy Cove

With its huge picture windows, the restaurant in this lovely family-run hotel makes the most of the magnificent views of the rugged North Devon coast and the rolling hills of Exmoor. On a fine day, things get better still when you can eat out on the sea decks overlooking the cove, and what's on your plate comes from the waves and fields of the landscape all around. There are no extravagant combinations or elaborate presentations here, just unpretentious, unchallenging ideas from a kitchen that has the confidence to bring splendid ingredients together in harmonious combinations and let them speak for themselves. Seared wood pigeon breast is matched with bubble-and-squeak, beetroot purée and a poached quail's egg, ahead of duck breast with braised fennel, orange and thyme carrots, dauphinoise potato

and red wine sauce, and for pudding there's vanilla pannacotta with fruit compôte and clotted cream.

Chef Debbie Meaden **Owner** Dawn Ten-Bokkel **Times** 12-2/6.30-9 **Prices** Fixed D 3 course £30, Starter £4.95, Main £16.95-£19.95, Dessert £5.95, Service optional **Wines** 11 bottles over £20, 20 bottles under £20, 3 by glass **Notes** Sunday L, Vegetarian available, Dress restrictions, Smart casual, Civ Wed 200 **Seats** 150, Pr/dining room 30 **Children** Portions, Menu **Parking** 50

ILSINGTON — Map 3 SX77

Ilsington Country House Hotel

◉◉ Modern European

Great Dartmoor views and confident cooking

☎ 01364 661452
TQ13 9RR
e-mail: hotel@ilsington.co.uk
web: www.ilsington.co.uk
dir: A38 to Plymouth, exit at Bovey Tracey. 3rd exit from rdbt to Ilsington, then 1st right, hotel on right in 3m

Ilsington presses all the right classy country-house buttons; a Dartmoor bolt-hole set in 10 acres of grounds that includes a health club and spa pool. The large airy restaurant maintains the theme, its floor-to-ceiling picture windows offering cracking views across to Haytor Rocks and beyond from well-dressed tables. The kitchen goes the extra mile in its quest for quality ingredients, including using their own eggs, foraging for wild herbs in the grounds and curing fish and meats in their own smokehouse. Otherwise, quality locally-sourced produce forms the basis of the modern approach here, underpinned by a classical French theme. Take seared rump of lamb served with confit shoulder, sweetbreads and a rosemary sauce, for instance, or fillet of sea bream with spring onion and tomato crushed potatoes, root vegetable nage and Avruga caviar chive oil. Finish with lime leaf pannacotta teamed with port braised plum and lemongrass gel.

Chef Mike O'Donnell **Owner** Hassell family **Times** 12-2/6.30-9 **Prices** Fixed D 3 course £36-£42, Service included **Wines** 31 bottles over £20, 40 bottles under £20, 9 by glass **Notes** Sunday L, Vegetarian available, Dress restrictions, Shirt with a collar (smart casual) no shorts, Civ Wed 100 **Seats** 75, Pr/dining room 70 **Children** Portions **Parking** 60

Save on Hotels. Book at **theAA.com/hotel**

DEVON 135 **ENGLAND**

KNOWSTONE Map 3 SS82

The Masons Arms

◉◉ Modern British

Strong contemporary cooking in the lush western countryside

☎ 01398 341231
EX36 4RY
e-mail: enqs@masonarmsdevon.co.uk
dir: Signed from A361, turn right once in Knowstone

A genuinely delightful thatched medieval country inn that maintains strong links to excellent local growers and suppliers, The Masons also manages to retain the atmosphere of a village pub. Deep in the lush countryside on the border between Devon and Somerset, it is surrounded by rolling hills, and is full of cheer on winter evenings when the fire crackles, and in summer too for an outdoor meal. The celestial ceiling mural in the dining room has to be seen to be believed. Mark Dodson once cooked under Michel Roux at Bray (see entry, Waterside Inn, Berkshire), which might explain the flair and precision evident in the dishes here. Good strong contemporary thinking informs a starter of wood pigeon breasts, flash-fried and tender, accompanied by puréed beetroot and pine nuts in blueberry jus, while the main-course pairing of local beef fillet and oxtail in its truffled, Madeira-rich juices continues to be a triumph of timing and seasoning. Fish could be something almost as robust, perhaps sea bass alongside Jerusalem artichoke purée, butter beans and flageolets with smoked garlic in red wine jus, and dessert closes things with a fitting flourish in the form of lemon mascarpone mousse with passionfruit syrup, or an apple trio with Granny Smith sorbet.

Chef Mark Dodson **Owner** Mark & Sarah Dodson
Times 12-2/7-9 Closed 1st wk Jan, Mon, D Sun
Prices Starter £8.75-£12.50, Main £18-£24.50, Dessert £7.50-£9, Service optional **Wines** 30 bottles over £20, 12 bottles under £20, 9 by glass **Notes** Sunday L, Vegetarian available **Seats** 28 **Children** Portions **Parking** 10

LEWDOWN Map 3 SX48

Lewtrenchard Manor

Rosettes not confirmed at time of going to press – see below

LIFTON Map 3 SX38

Arundell Arms

◉◉ Modern British **V** ✑

Assured cooking in an 18th-century coaching inn

☎ 01566 784666
Fore St PL16 0AA
e-mail: reservations@arundellarms.com
web: www.arundellarms.com
dir: Just off A30 in Lifton, 3m E of Launceston

After a hard day's hunting, shooting or fishing (the inn has 20 miles of fly-fishing rights on the Tamar), the Arundell Arms will welcome you with open arms and the comfy, classically chintzy embrace of squashy sofas, antiques and log fires. It's an elegant and sophisticated place, where you don't need to turn up in a waxed Barbour jacket and Hunter wellies to feel welcome. In the stylishly decorated restaurant, as you'd hope, there's game in season and fish from the river, while well-chosen local suppliers feature prominently on a menu that champions fabulous West Country produce. The cooking takes an unmistakably modern line that might see braised pork cheeks paired with spinach, apple and vanilla purée, smoked bacon, and cider sauce as a starter, with perhaps a ragoût of John Dory and monkfish with lentils, Pernod, leeks and pea shoots to follow. Desserts could run to blood orange parfait with coffee ice cream and marinated oranges.

Lewtrenchard Manor

Rosettes not confirmed at time of going to press

LEWDOWN Map 3 SX48

Modern British

Majestic old manor with exemplary modern food

☎ 01566 783222
EX20 4PN
e-mail: info@lewtrenchard.co.uk
dir: Take A30 signed Okehampton from M5 junct 31. 25m, exit at Sourton Cross. Follow signs to Lewdown, then Lewtrenchard

With a name-check in the Domesday Book, there's been a residence on this spot for a goodly while, and today's house has Jacobean credentials going back to the early 1600s. And what a magnificent manor house it is too. If that isn't enough historic backstory, it is worth mentioning that the Reverend Sabine Baring-Gould penned *Onward Christian Soldiers* while resident in the house. A perfect spot, then, for the country-house treatment which has served up a luxurious retreat in a lush valley on the fringes of Dartmoor. All the hoped for charms of the building remain – oak panels, stained-glass windows, ornate plasterworks – but it remains a switched-on sort of place, set up for satisfying the needs of the 21st-century sybarite. Chef John Hooker makes good use of regional supply lines (and the walled kitchen garden) to deliver bright modern dishes; start with black bream with braised cos and 'potted crab', followed by roast loin of venison with glazed pig's cheek, pommes Anna and truffle, finishing with baked cheesecake, blood orange, lime curd and mint. If the exclusivity of the chef's table concept appeals, the Purple Carrot private dining room provides an interactive experience with the chefs via a wall of split-screen TVs.

Chef John Hooker **Times** 12-1.30/7-9 **Prices** Service optional **Wines** 119 bottles over £20, 13 by glass **Notes** Fixed L 4 course £24, 5 course D £49.50, Sunday L, Vegetarian available, Dress restrictions, Smart casual, Civ Wed 100 **Seats** 45, Pr/dining room 22 **Children** Portions, Menu **Parking** 40

LIFTON *continued*

Chef Steven Pidgeon **Owner** Anne Voss-Bark
Times 12.30-2.30/7.30-10 **Prices** Food prices not
confirmed for 2013. Please telephone for details
Wines 37 bottles over £20, 3 bottles under £20, 7 by
glass **Notes** Sunday L, Vegetarian menu, Dress
restrictions, Smart casual, Civ Wed 80 **Seats** 70, Pr/
dining room 24 **Children** Portions, Menu **Parking** 70

Tinhay Mill Guest House and Restaurant

☸ British, French **V** 🖐

**Traditional atmosphere and well-crafted food in
revamped 15th-century mill**

☎ 01566 784201
Tinhay PL16 0AJ
e-mail: tinhay.mill@talk21.com
dir: From M5 take A30 towards Okehampton/Launceston.
Lifton off A30 on left. Follow brown tourist signs.
Restaurant at bottom of village near river

Emblazoned on the masthead of the menu of this
restaurant with rooms is the phrase 'Where time stands
still', and there is indeed an element of unchanging
tradition in 15th-century Tinhay Mill's whitewashed walls,
oak beams and crackling log fires. Its popularity with
locals and peripatetic gourmets is due in no small way to
the hands-on charm of owners Margaret and Paul Wilson.
Margaret has been cooking all her life and insists on the
best of the local larder as the basis for her honest, well-
crafted Anglo-French cooking. It is all made in-house,
starting with cracked green pepper bread straight from
the oven to go with a faultless cream of celeriac soup.
Main course delivers a choux bun filled with super-fresh
monkfish, scallops and king prawns and white wine,
chive and saffron sauce. To finish, there's ginger
pannacotta with fresh pineapple, citrus syrup and
coconut biscuits.

Chef Margaret Wilson **Owner** Mr P & Mrs M Wilson
Times 7-9.30 Closed 4 wks Xmas & New Year, 3 wks Feb
& Mar, Sun & Mon (ex residents), L all week **Prices** Fixed
D 3 course £35.50, Starter £5.75-£9.50, Main £16.50-
£24.50, Dessert £5.75-£8.75, Service optional, Groups
min 8 service 10% **Wines** 15 bottles over £20, 8 bottles
under £20, 4 by glass **Notes** Vegetarian menu, Dress
restrictions, Smart casual, no T-shirts, trainers or shorts
Seats 24, Pr/dining room 24 **Parking** 10

Dartmoor Inn

☸☸ Modern British

**Passionate cooking in a charmingly restored coaching
inn**

☎ 01822 820221
EX20 4AY
e-mail: info@dartmoorinn.com
web: www.dartmoorinn.com
dir: On A386 (Tavistock to Okehampton road)

Since taking over this 16th-century roadside inn on the
edge of the moor in 1998, Karen and Philip Burgess have
put heart and soul into restoring the place. The interior
still has the cosy feel of a venerable hostelry, but
lightened up with a contemporary country-chic style that
references Scandinavia and New England. There are real
ales on tap and a fire blazing away in the cold months in
the smartly rustic bar, plus a menu of pub classics done
right - home-made pork pie and piccalilli, or coq au vin
with garlic croûtons - while the main eating action, takes
place in a lovely collection of intimate interconnecting
spaces where tables are laid with sparkling glassware
and linen cloths. Chef Philip is an experienced hand who
has forged links with local producers to ensure his larder
is stocked with the finest materials, and it shows in the
big flavours and generosity of spirit you'll find in dishes
such as pork cheeks with potato purée and star anise
sauce, followed by pan-fried lamb's kidneys with bacon
and herb butter, or a fish casserole served with leek
ragoût and saffron sauce. Puddings stay in the comfort
zone for the likes of prune and almond tart with vanilla
ice cream.

Times 12-2.15/6.30-9.30 Closed Mon, D Sun

Rising Sun Hotel

☸ British, French

Confident cooking in historic one-time smugglers inn

☎ 01598 753223
Harbourside EX35 6EG
e-mail: reception@risingsunlynmouth.co.uk
dir: M5 junct 23 (Minehead). Take A39 to Lynmouth.
Opposite the harbour

The 14th-century Rising Sun occupies pole position on
Lynmouth's harbourfront and has a fair bit of history
under its belt, taking in tales of smugglers, the poet
Percy Bysshe Shelley's ill-fated honeymoon, and R D
Blackmore settling in to pen parts of *Lorna Doone* - or so
it is said. On a sunny day, you can't miss it - look for the
scrum of drinkers spilling out of the low-beamed bar of
the picture-perfect thatched inn. Candlelit and oak
panelled, the dining room certainly fulfils the romantic
brief, while the kitchen deals in confidently-cooked,
inventive ideas, often based on the lobster and fish that
are landed at the door, and meat and game that come
the short distance from Exmoor. Crab with sweet pepper
and mascarpone tortellini is the sort of thing to expect,
followed by slow-cooked belly pork with Pommery mustard
mash and spinach, or a whole grilled sea bass with
tarator (a tzatziki-style sauce of yoghurt, garlic and dill),
fennel and new potatoes.

Times 7-9 Closed L all week

Lynton Cottage Hotel

☸☸ Modern British **V** 🖐

Classy cooking and majestic views

☎ 01598 752342
North Walk EX35 6ED
e-mail: enquiries@lynton-cottage.co.uk
web: www.lynton-cottage.co.uk
dir: M5 junct 27, follow A361 towards Barnstaple. Follow
signs to Lynton A39. In Lynton turn right at church. Hotel
on right

This 'cottage' is more of a pocket-sized country house
than the cutesy shoebox that the name implies, and to
say it has a good view is equally wide of the mark: the
panorama that unfurls from its perch on the clifftops

Save on Hotels. Book at **theAA.com/hotel**

DEVON 137 **ENGLAND**

above the Valley of the Rocks for once truly merits the epithet 'jaw-dropping' as it sweeps across the ragged, densely wooded North Devon coastline above Lynmouth. The restaurant has a comforting, homely charm and an unstuffy informal ambience, but to be honest there could be a troupe of rollerskating polar bears serving, and diners would still find it hard to tear their eyes away from those views. When it arrives, the food makes you sit up and pay attention: this is seriously skilled cooking that nails the subtle interplay of taste and texture, and adds a modern flourish to traditional pairings. Diver-caught scallops could arrive crusted with macadamia nut, and matched with carrot purée and citrus beurre blanc, while mains run to fillet of Gloucestershire Old Spot pork rolled in Asian spices and served with belly meat, sage and onion potato bonbons and a duo of pork sauce. Desserts are no mere afterthought either - perhaps a raspberry millefeuille crafted with home-made puff pastry teamed with white chocolate powder and raspberry sorbet.

Chef Paul Ruttledge **Owner** David Mowlem, Heather Biancardi **Times** 7-9 Closed Dec-mid Jan, L all week **Prices** Food prices not confirmed for 2013. Please telephone for details **Wines** 9 bottles over £20, 15 bottles under £20, 4 by glass **Notes** Vegetarian menu **Seats** 30 **Children** Portions **Parking** 18

NEWTON POPPLEFORD Map 3 SY08

Moores' Restaurant & Rooms

◉◉ Modern British **V** 🕙

Charming village restaurant with well-crafted dishes on the menu

☎ 01395 568100
6 Greenbank, High St EX10 0EB
e-mail: info.moores@btconnect.com
dir: On A3052 in village centre

Jonathan and Kate Moore's restaurant with rooms is well placed for those exploring the fabulous East Devon coastline, and with the ever-present husband-and-wife-team in charge, there's no hint of corporate blandness here. In the centre of the village, all is nicely understated on the inside, with prints on the walls and linen cloths on the neatly laid tables. In the kitchen, Jonathan cooks in a broadly modern British manner and doesn't try to overturn culinary convention, choosing to allow the produce, much of it from the local area, to shine. Thus you might start with a creamy smoked haddock and pea risotto, before moving on to grilled fillet of red mullet with scallop and crab tartlet and wilted baby leaves. Combinations are well thought through and balanced correctly (as seen in a dark chocolate fondant with stem ginger ice cream), breads are home-made, and Kate is a charming and professional presence out front.

Chef Jonathan Moore **Owner** Jonathan & Kate Moore **Times** 12-1.30/7-9.30 Closed 1st 2 wks in Jan, BHs, Mon, D Sun **Prices** Fixed L 2 course £15.95, Fixed D 3 course £24-£28.50, Service optional **Wines** 22 bottles over £20, 15 bottles under £20, 6 by glass **Notes** Sunday L, Vegetarian menu **Seats** 32, Pr/dining room 12 **Children** Portions **Parking** On street

---

PLYMOUTH Map 3 SX45

Artillery Tower Restaurant

◉ Modern British 🕙

Confident cooking in historic maritime building

☎ 01752 257610
Firestone Bay, Durnford St PL1 3QR
dir: 1m from city centre & rail station

With the waves lapping at the base of the 15th-century Firestone Bay gunnery tower on Plymouth's seafront, Peter and Debbie Constable's atmospheric restaurant makes an inviting prospect for straightforward modern food based on materials from within a 30-mile radius. Inside three-foot-thick exposed stone walls, the setting is a circular, softly-lit space, with sturdy walnut ceilings and bare tables - a simple look that is reflected in the unfussy repertoire. Safe in the knowledge that you're in the hands of a kitchen that does things the hard way - making its own stocks, bread, pastries, pasta and chocolate - start, perhaps, with roast monkfish with lentils and curry sauce, then follow that with something rich and hearty like roast squab pigeon with foie gras, or loin and shoulder of lamb with rosemary and garlic.

Chef Peter Constable **Owner** Peter & Debbie Constable **Times** 12-2.15/7-9.30 Closed Xmas, New Year, Sun-Mon, L Sat **Prices** Fixed D 3 course £35-£45, Starter £5-£12, Main £15-£25, Dessert £6-£10, Service optional, Groups min 8 service 6% **Wines** 20 bottles over £20, 4 bottles under £20, 6 by glass **Notes** Vegetarian available **Seats** 26, Pr/dining room 16 **Children** Portions **Parking** 20, (Evening only)

Barbican Kitchen

◉ Modern **V** 🕙

Convincing brasserie food at former gin distillery

☎ 01752 604448
Plymouth Gin Distillery, 60 Southside St PL1 2LQ
e-mail: info@barbicankitchen.com
dir: On Barbican, 5 mins walk from Bretonside bus station

Wooden floors, unclothed tables, brightly coloured banquettes and a touch of industrial-chic create a chilled-out vibe here. Cheery and helpful staff and modern, straightforward, fairly priced food, all cooked to a consistently high standard, brings in the crowds. Salads, burgers and chargrilled steaks are all possibilities, but there are also starters of ham hock

---

terrine with piccalilli, and seared scallops with chorizo, before John Dory fillets and prawns in white wine sauce with parmesan mash and spinach, and honey-glazed roast duck breast with potato gratin. Vegetarians and vegans have separate menus, and puddings hit the spot in the shape of apple and cinnamon crumble with vanilla ice cream. The Tanner brothers also own Tanners (see entry).

Chef Chris Skantleberry, C & J Tanner **Owner** Christopher & James Tanner **Times** 12-3/5-10 Closed 25-26 & 31 Dec **Prices** Fixed L 2 course fr £10.95, Fixed D 3 course fr £14.95, Starter £3.95-£8.95, Main £8.95-£19.95, Dessert £5.50-£5.75, Service included **Wines** 16 bottles over £20, 22 bottles under £20, 13 by glass **Notes** Fixed 2/3 course L menu also available pre-theatre, Sunday L, Vegetarian menu **Seats** 80 **Children** Portions, Menu **Parking** Drakes Circus, Guildhall

---

Duke of Cornwall Hotel

◉ Modern British, European **V**

Modern cooking in a Victorian hotel

☎ 01752 275850 & 275855
Millbay Rd PL1 3LG
e-mail: enquiries@thedukeofcornwall.co.uk
dir: City centre, follow signs 'Pavilions', hotel road is opposite

The Duke of Cornwall has been a landmark building in Plymouth since 1863. It certainly stands out from the crowd with its Victorian gothic architecture, while inside it's all oak panels, elaborate ceiling roses and sparkling chandeliers in generously proportioned public rooms. The elegant, traditionally-furnished dining room is the setting for some modern cooking with a European flavour, with menus founded in the best of West Country produce from land and sea. Mini Scotch eggs with smoked salmon and spicy roast red pepper purée might get the ball rolling, followed by pork fillet with pommes purée, crisp pancetta and a red wine and pork jus. Desserts range from a richly indulgent dark chocolate truffle terrine with Crème de Menthe crème anglaise, to a lemon and mascarpone slice with red berry compôte.

Chef Darren Kester **Owner** W Combstock, J Morcom **Times** 7-10 Closed 26-31 Dec, L all week **Prices** Food prices not confirmed for 2013. Please telephone for details **Wines** 50% bottles over £20, 50% bottles under £20, 8 by glass **Notes** Vegetarian menu, Dress restrictions, Smart casual, Civ Wed 200 **Seats** 80, Pr/dining room 30 **Children** Portions, Menu **Parking** 40, Also on streeet

PLYMOUTH *continued*

Langdon Court Boutique Hotel & Restaurant

◉ French, International V

Accomplished modern food in a Tudor mansion

☎ 01752 862358
Down Thomas PL9 0DY
e-mail: info@langdoncourt.com
dir: From A379 at Elburton, follow brown tourist signs

With a rich and varied history, there's a real sense of the past around every corner of this magnificent Grade II listed Tudor manor. Set in 10 acres of mature grounds, it's upscale enough to have been home to Henry VIII's last wife, Katherine Parr. The restaurant is a light, appealingly modern space, yet elegant and rather romantic to boot, where white walls are hung with framed mirrors and discreet floral prints, and both tables and floor are uncovered, while a crackling log fire roars in the grate. Here, some well-executed modern cookery (underpinned by a classical French theme) is fashioned from fresh local produce without fuss; duck and foie gras terrine, for example, served with red onion compôte to open proceedings, and perhaps locally-caught halibut served with saffron potatoes, confit tomatoes and a champagne beurre blanc to follow.

Chef Erwan Bouhris **Owner** Emma & Geoffrey Ede
Times 12-3.30/6.30-10 Closed L Mon (Jan-Mar)
Prices Fixed L 2 course £15.95, Fixed D 3 course £35.95, Starter £6.75-£7.50, Main £17.95-£19.95, Dessert £5.95-£6.25, Service included **Wines** 4 bottles over £20, 3 bottles under £20, 7 by glass **Notes** Sunday L, Vegetarian menu, Dress restrictions, Civ Wed 100 **Seats** 36, Pr/dining room 1000 **Children** Portions **Parking** 50

Tanners Restaurant

◉◉ Modern European V ⓰ NOTABLE WINE LIST 🍷

Cooking of our time in an historic building

☎ 01752 252001
Prysten House, Finewell St PL1 2AE
e-mail: enquiries@tannersrestaurant.com
dir: Town centre. Behind St Andrew's Church on Royal Parade

The remarkable medieval building, behind St Andrew's Church in the heart of the city, is one of the oldest in Plymouth, but the restaurant it now houses is as switched-on as they come. Tanners is a stylish blend of ancient beams and stone walls hung with contemporary art, and smart modern claret leather high-backed chairs at unclothed wooden tables, while the food on the plate is aimed squarely at 21st-century palates. The emphasis is firmly on Devon's larder, in a repertoire embracing dishes such as Devon crab cannelloni with coriander and chilli, squid ink and coconut broth, followed by roast loin of Bodmin venison with a hazelnut and cocoa crust, red sauerkraut and pear, and maple-glazed parsnips. Local fish fans will be heartened to see seared fillet of brill partnered, perhaps, with buttered leeks, fennel pollen, cockles, chervil and vermouth, and to finish there are artisan cheeses, or tempting creations like dark chocolate moelleux with persimmon sorbet.

Chef Martyn Compton, C&J Tanner **Owner** Christopher & James Tanner **Times** 12-2.30/7-9.30 Closed 25, 31 Dec, 1st wk Jan, Sun-Mon **Prices** Fixed L 2 course fr £14, Fixed D 3 course fr £20, Starter £7.50-£9.95, Main £13.95-£24.95, Dessert £7.50-£8.95, Service optional, Groups min 8 service 10% **Wines** 40 bottles over £20, 20 bottles under £20, 8 by glass **Notes** Tasting menu 6 course, Vegetarian menu, Dress restrictions, Smart casual preferred, no trainers **Seats** 45, Pr/dining room 26 **Children** Portions **Parking** On street, church car park next to restaurant

---

ROCKBEARE Map 3 SY09

The Jack In The Green Inn

◉◉ Modern British V 🐾

Fabulous Devon pub with creative, confident cooking

☎ 01404 822240
EX5 2EE
e-mail: info@jackinthegreen.uk.com
web: www.jackinthegreen.uk.com
dir: 3m E of M5 junct 29 on old A30

Passionate foodie Paul Parnell has been the driving force behind this thriving roadside pub-restaurant for 20 years now and he shows no sign of flagging. Equally passionate and key to the success of 'The Jack' is long-serving chef Matthew Mason, whose innovative modern British menus brim with local seasonal ingredients. He has a great relationship with local farmers and artisan producers and the excellent value 'Totally Devon' meal experience champions the best. Presentation is simple as opposed to elaborate, letting the flavours of the top-notch produce shine through. Typically, tuck into a smooth chicken liver parfait with gingerbread and confit orange, followed by a beautifully cooked rack and braised shoulder of Whimple

lamb with tomato fondue and herb salad. A delicate elderflower pannacotta with gooseberries and sorrel ice cream could make the perfect finale. In addition, you'll find some cracking pub dishes, perhaps braised beef with stilton and mash and a local cheese ploughman's, carefully chosen wines and West Country ales - all served in a warren of cosy dining rooms and the newly refurbished bar and lounge.

The Jack In The Green Inn

Chef Matthew Mason **Owner** Paul Parnell
Times 12-2/6-9.30 Closed 25 Dec-5 Jan **Prices** Fixed L 2 course £20, Fixed D 3 course £25.75, Starter £6.95-£9.50, Main £14.95-£27.50, Dessert £6.50-£8.50, Service optional **Wines** 60 bottles over £20, 40 bottles under £20, 12 by glass **Notes** Tasting menu available, Sunday L, Vegetarian menu, Dress restrictions, Smart casual **Seats** 80, Pr/dining room 60 **Children** Portions, Menu **Parking** 120

SALCOMBE Map 3 SX73

Soar Mill Cove Hotel

◉◉ Modern British

High standards and sea views

☎ 01548 561566
Soar Mill Cove, Marlborough TQ7 3DS
e-mail: info@soarmillcove.co.uk
dir: A381 to Salcombe, through village follow signs to sea

There used to be a grain mill on this site, nowadays the only remnant is in the name of this modern low-slung hotel and the cove it's been built on, looking over the sandy beach and the waves. Floor-to-ceiling windows in the comfortable restaurant have those wonderful sea views. The kitchen utilises West Country produce, much of it organic, on its daily-changing menu, and with Salcombe just around the corner, fish naturally pops up often, perhaps roast monkfish wrapped in Serrano ham served with red wine sauce and wild mushrooms. Typical starters are smooth duck mousse with caramelised plums and toasted brioche, and clams steamed with chorizo, shallots and white wine. Sunday lunch is a bit of an event, with a whole roast lamb carved in the restaurant; at other times expect tried-and-trusted roast chicken breast in a light mustard sauce with wild mushrooms and potatoes sautéed with garlic.

Chef I Macdonald **Owner** Mr & Mrs K Makepeace & family
Times 10.30-5/7.15-9 Closed Jan, L all week **Prices** Fixed D 3 course £29, Service optional **Wines** 40 bottles over £20, 11 bottles under £20, 4 by glass **Notes** Vegetarian

Save on Hotels. Book at **theAA.com/hotel**

DEVON 139 **ENGLAND**

available, Civ Wed 150 **Seats** 60 **Children** Portions, Menu **Parking** 25

Tides Reach Hotel

◎ Modern British 🌐

Stunning seaside setting for good British food

☎ 01548 843466
South Sands TQ8 8LJ
e-mail: enquire@tidesreach.com
dir: Take cliff road towards sea and Bolt Head

This relaxed family-run hotel in Devon's splendid South Hams certainly lives up to its name: when the tide is in, the waves are practically lapping at the doorstep. The salty air and seaside vibes are enough to conjure up a healthy appetite for the kitchen's uncomplicated cooking, served to uplifting views of the idyllic South Sands cove in Salcombe Estuary through sweeping picture windows in the Garden Room restaurant. The provenance of superb West Country ingredients is painstakingly annotated on a menu that kicks off with smoked eel with an entertaining trio of onion preparations - marmalade, purée and pickles. Next out, gurnard fillet arrives with chive beurre blanc, stir-fried purple sprouting broccoli, leeks and smoked bacon, and sauté potatoes. At the end, perhaps a Sachertorte-inspired sponge with Grand Marnier chocolate cream, and cranberry compôte and sorbet.

Chef Finn Ibsen **Owner** Edwards family **Times** 7-9 Closed Dec-Jan, L all week **Prices** Fixed D 2 course £22.50-£25, Fixed D 4 course £34.50, Service included **Wines** 90 bottles over £20, 14 bottles under £20, 6 by glass **Notes** Vegetarian available, Dress restrictions, Smart casual, no jeans or T-shirts **Seats** 80 **Parking** 80

SAUNTON
Map 3 SS43

Saunton Sands Hotel

◎ Modern, Traditional **NEW** V 🌐

Assured local cooking beside a North Devon beach

☎ 01271 890212
EX33 1LQ
e-mail: reservations@sauntonsands.com
dir: Exit A361 at Braunton, signed Croyde B3231, hotel 2m on left

If the North Devon beach location evokes a flicker of déjà vu, it may be because you recognise it from the video for Robbie Williams' 'Angels' - or the cover of Pink Floyd's 'A Momentary Lapse of Reason' for older readers. The white art deco-ish hotel sits on an eminence, gazing loftily over the sand dunes out to the Atlantic and the UNESCO biosphere that is Braunton Burrows. A smart clientele rolls up here for poolside lounging and spa pampering, and not least for Ian Worley's assured southwestern cooking. Original ideas abound, from a starter of smoked haddock carpaccio with quail's egg arancini, trompettes and curried mayonnaise, to the Exmoor venison with three styles of parsnip, chestnuts and bitter chocolate. More mainstream dishes - chicken liver and foie gras parfait, Lancashire hotpot with pickled red cabbage - are rendered with imaginative aplomb too. Chocolate

Bakewell tart has fine buttery pastry, and is nicely cut with praline ice cream and a clutch of rum-soaked raisins.

Chef I Worley, D Turland **Owner** Brend Hotels **Times** 12.30-2/7-9.30 **Prices** Fixed L 2 course £19.95, Fixed D 3 course £37, Service optional **Wines** 80 bottles over £20, 15 bottles under £20, 15 by glass **Notes** Sunday L, Vegetarian menu, Dress restrictions, Smart, jacket & tie preferred, no sportswear, Civ Wed 200, Air con **Seats** 200, Pr/dining room 20 **Children** Portions **Parking** 140

SHALDON
Map 3 SX97

ODE

◎◎ Modern British 🌐

Top-quality local and organic produce in coastal village

☎ 01626 873977
21 Fore St TQ14 0DE
e-mail: info@odetruefood.co.uk
dir: Cross bridge from Teignmouth then 1st left into Fore St

After a career globetrotting around the kitchens of the world, Tim and Clare Bougel, are now intent that travel should be as minimal as possible - at least where local produce is concerned. ODE is a discreet little venue with a loud-and-proud commitment to green credentials. The three-storey Georgian townhouse was made over using environmentally-friendly materials, and nothing gets through the door unless it is line-caught, traditionally-reared or organically grown - except of course, the customers. The result is a vibrant modern British repertoire, cooked with subtlety and intelligence. A parfait of Duckaller Farm pork with crisp bread, and port and red onion compôte opens with a fine chorus of flavours and textures, then slow-cooked haunch of Haldon fallow deer arrives in the good honest company of English cabbage, bacon and glazed shallots. For pudding, treacle tart with lemon verbena cream hits just the right note.

Chef Tim Bouget **Owner** Tim & Clare Bouget **Times** 7-9.30 Closed 25 Dec, BHs, Sun-Tue, L all week **Prices** Starter £6.50-£9.50, Main £17-£22, Dessert £7-£10, Service optional, Groups min 6 service 10% **Wines** 15 bottles over £20, 8 bottles under £20, 5 by glass **Notes** Vegetarian available **Seats** 24 **Parking** Car park 3 mins walk

SIDMOUTH
Map 3 SY18

Riviera Hotel

◎ Modern British

Seafront restaurant with a local flavour

☎ 01395 515201
The Esplanade EX10 8AY
e-mail: enquiries@hotelriviera.co.uk
web: www.hotelriviera.co.uk
dir: From M5 junct 30 take A3052 to Sidmouth. Situated in centre of The Esplanade

In a prime seafront location, the bay-fronted Hotel Riviera is a classic slice of Regency elegance from the days when ladies and gentlemen paraded along Sidmouth's prom, attracted, perhaps, by the cachet of holidaying in a place favoured by royalty and literati. When the sun plays ball, the restaurant terrace is a glorious spot, with its views over Lyme Bay; indoors, a traditionally elegant dining room is the setting for the kitchen's locally-based modern British cooking. Try ham hock and flageolet bean terrine with pineapple crisps, and pineapple and chilli compôte to begin, followed perhaps by seared spiced salmon with pepper couscous, rösti potatoes, spring onion crème fraîche and caviar.

Chef Matthew Weaver **Owner** Peter Wharton **Times** 12.30-2/7-9 **Prices** Starter £10.50-£14, Main £16-£32, Dessert £6.50-£10.50, Service optional **Wines** 76 bottles over £20, 6 by glass **Notes** Fixed L 5 course £29.50, Fixed D 6 course £41.50, Sunday L, Vegetarian available **Seats** 85, Pr/dining room 65 **Children** Portions, Menu **Parking** 26

The Salty Monk

◎◎ Modern British V 🌐

Gentle modern British food in a former salthouse

☎ 01395 513174
Church St, Sidford EX10 9QP
e-mail: saltymonk@btconnect.com
dir: From M5 junct 30 take A3052 to Sidmouth, or from Honiton take A375 to Sidmouth, 200yds on right opposite church in village

The salinity of the said monk refers to the building's one-time incarnation as a 16th-century storage facility for the salt the monks traded at Exeter Cathedral. Modern times have transformed it into a perfectly relaxing restaurant with rooms with a lovely garden. A gentle colour scheme of deep pink and cream works wonders in the light, spacious dining room, where an equally gentle version of modern British food is the order of the day. Andy Witheridge caters more conscientiously than most for special diets of various kinds. Lyme Bay crab tart with a bisque sauce, or salmon and sole mousse with smoked salmon on lemon butter, are the seafoody ways to start. Main-course meats might find calves' liver paired with a game faggot on onion marmalade sauce, or beef medallion accompanied by a suet pie of stroganoff on red wine and shallot sauce. Homely puddings include

continued

SIDMOUTH *continued*

steamed marmalade sponge, lemon tart, or a duo of chocolate brownie and wine-poached pear.

Chef Annette & Andy Witheridge, Scott Horn **Owner** Annette & Andy Witheridge **Times** 12-1.30/6.30-9.30 Closed 1 wk Nov, L Mon-Wed **Prices** Fixed L 2 course fr £25.50, Fixed D 3 course fr £42.50, Starter fr £7.95, Main fr £25.50, Dessert fr £7.95, Service optional, Groups min 8 service 10% **Wines** 60 bottles over £20, 9 bottles under £20, 10 by glass **Notes** Tasting menu 8 course Fri-Sat, Sunday L, Vegetarian menu, Dress restrictions, Smart casual **Seats** 45, Pr/dining room 14 **Children** Portions **Parking** 20

Victoria Hotel

@ Traditional

Turn-of-the-century splendour beside the sea

☎ 01395 512651 **The Esplanade EX10 8RY** **e-mail:** reservations@victoriahotel.co.uk **dir:** At western end of The Esplanade

Standing proud in five acres of landscaped grounds at the end of Sidmouth's gorgeous Georgian esplanade, the handsome Victoria basks in sweeping views of the cliff-bracketed bay. Old-school tradition reigns within, from the high ceilings and ornate plasterwork, down to the dress code requiring gentlemen to turn up in jacket and tie at dinner, when a pianist or chamber orchestra provides the soundtrack. Expect straightforward cooking that aims to soothe rather than to challenge diners, and local materials as the bedrock of the output, starting with a silky smooth chicken liver parfait teamed with spiced fruit chutney and toasted brioche, ahead of loin of lamb with dauphinoise potatoes, petits pois with Parma ham, and minted jus. Apple tarte Tatin ends on an aptly classic note.

Times 1-2/7-9

SOUTH BRENT   Map 3 SX66

Glazebrook House Hotel & Restaurant

@ British

Unfussy, consistent cooking in a Dartmoor country house

☎ 01364 73322 **TQ10 9JE** **e-mail:** enquiries@glazebrookhouse.com **dir:** From A38, between Ivybridge & Buckfastleigh exit at South Brent, follow hotel signs

A small-scale country house that was once home to a Georgian gentleman of some substance makes a relaxed and intimate setting for a family-run hotel. On the southern fringe of Dartmoor, it sits in four acres, and its owners, the Cashmores, run the place with charm. Their chef has been with them a good many years, and achieves an impressive level of consistency for unfussy

food that uses the pick of southwestern produce. A voguish salad features warm baby beetroot with excellent goats' cheese and walnuts, and may be followed by carefully timed fillet of well-hung local venison in a shiny, deeply flavoured red wine reduction. Properly made tarte Tatin is a dependably satisfying dessert.

Chef David Merriman **Owner** Dave & Caroline Cashmore **Times** 7-9 Closed 2 wks Jan, 1 wk Aug, Sun, L all week **Prices** Fixed D 3 course fr £19.50, Starter £4.50-£6.50, Main £16.50-£20.50, Dessert £4.50-£5.95, Service optional **Wines** 5 bottles over £20, 16 bottles under £20, 7 by glass **Notes** Vegetarian available, Civ Wed 80 **Seats** 60, Pr/dining room 12 **Children** Portions **Parking** 40

STRETE   Map 3 SX84

The Laughing Monk

@ Modern British

Top-notch local produce cooked with care and attention

☎ 01803 770639 **Totnes Rd TQ6 0RN** **e-mail:** thelaughingmonk@btconnect.com **dir:** A38 & follow signs towards Dartmouth, 700yds past Dartmouth Golf Club take right turn to Strete. Restaurant on left just past church

Book-ended by the heavenly South Hams beaches of Blackpool Sands and Slapton, this Victorian school house was given a pared-back modern look - local art, bare wooden floors and tables, and sections of exposed stone wall - when Ben and Jackie Handley took over in 2008. It all makes a fitting backdrop for Ben's no-nonsense cooking, which delivers feisty dishes of ingredient-driven modern food. It helps, of course that this part of the world is blessed with outstanding locally-landed and reared produce, and the seafood doesn't come any fresher than the hand-dived Start Bay scallops that might come with butternut squash purée and crispy pancetta, or the John Dory that is pan-fried and served with smoked salmon potato cake, warm vegetable salad and vine tomato dressing. Meat eaters can sink their teeth into Dartmoor-bred, 28-day aged Devon Ruby Red sirloin from the chargrill, and for pudding there could be Bakewell tart with Devon clotted cream and raspberry sauce.

Chef Ben Handley **Owner** Ben & Jackie Handley **Times** 6.30-9 Closed Xmas, Jan, Sun, L all week **Wines** 5 bottles over £20, 16 bottles under £20, 5 by glass **Notes** Early supper menu available Mon-Sat, Vegetarian available **Seats** 60 **Parking** 4, On street

TAVISTOCK   Map 3 SX47

Bedford Hotel

@ Modern British

Contemporary menus in a comfortable old hotel

☎ 01822 613221 **1 Plymouth Rd PL19 8BB** **e-mail:** enquiries@bedford-hotel.co.uk **dir:** M5 junct 31, A30 (Launceston/Okehampton). Then A386 to Tavistock, follow town centre signs. Hotel opposite church

The Bedford, built by the ducal family who give it its name, is unmistakable, with its Gothic-style castellated façade. Its restaurant is special too, with moulded ceilings, panelled walls and candlelight. The menu is very much of the 21st century, though, with pan-fried duck breast with caramelised onion and fig tart and raisin jus followed by roast salmon fillet with a brown shrimp, lime and chilli beurre blanc, accompanied by buttered greens and rösti. Local produce is put to good use: River Exe mussels, served with leek and shallot ragout and parsley tagliatelle, then fillet of Devon beef, with thyme jus, oxtail ravioli, roast beetroot and dauphinoise potatoes, and, to finish, West Country cheeses are an alternative to something like treacle tart with raspberry coulis.

Chef Matt Carder **Owner** Warm Welcome Hotels **Times** 12-2.30/7-9.30 Closed L Mon-Sat **Prices** Fixed L 2 course fr £15.95, Fixed D 3 course fr £29.95, Service optional **Wines** 5 bottles over £20, 12 bottles under £20, 6 by glass **Notes** Sunday L, Vegetarian available, Dress restrictions, Smart casual, no jeans **Seats** 55, Pr/dining room 24 **Children** Portions, Menu **Parking** 48

The Horn of Plenty

@@ Modern British

Confident contemporary cooking and glorious valley views

☎ 01822 832528 **PL19 8JD** **e-mail:** enquiries@thehornofplenty.co.uk **web:** www.thehornofplenty.co.uk **dir:** From Tavistock take A390 W for 3m. Right at Gulworthy Cross. In 400yds turn left, hotel in 400yds on right

There are fabulous views across the Tamar Valley from The Horn of Plenty and picture windows in the restaurant frame the very best of them. Built for the Duke of Bedford's mine captain, this country-house hotel stands in five acres of wild orchards and gardens, including a kitchen garden which gives more ammunition to the chef when it comes to keeping things local and seasonal. Scott Paton arrived in 2011 and is serving up some bright, contemporary dishes from carefully-sourced ingredients. Start, perhaps, with a warm pork belly with pickled pears and hazelnut mayonnaise, or a perfectly cooked piece of cod with white bean and bacon chowder, moving on to main-course best-end of local lamb with a Mediterranean-inspired smoked aubergine purée, ratatouille and tapenade jus. Lemon sponge with lemon curd and spiced rum and raisin ice cream is a fine end to a meal.

Chef Scott Paton **Owner** Julie Leivers & Damien Pease **Times** 12-4/7-12 **Prices** Fixed L 2 course £19.50, Fixed D 3 course £49.50, Service optional, Groups min 10 service 10% **Wines** 55 bottles over £20, 3 bottles under £20, 12 by glass **Notes** Tasting menu available, Sunday L, Vegetarian available, Dress restrictions, Smart casual, smart Sat D, Civ Wed 80 **Seats** 60, Pr/dining room 14 **Children** Portions, Menu **Parking** 20, On street

The Library @ Browns

◉◉ Modern British **NEW** V

Accomplished contemporary cooking in smart boutique hotel

☎ 01822 618686
80 West St PL19 8AQ
e-mail: info@brownsdevon.com
web: www.brownsdevon.com
dir: B3250 onto A386 to Tavistock

Dating from the 17th century, the old girl still boasts open fires, oak beams, exposed stone and slate flags, although a makeover gives a contemporary sheen. Dining takes place in The Library, a small and intimate room with soft music, polished oak tables, vivid artwork and an eponymous wall of books. The kitchen hits the spot with modern British and classic dishes, with flavour as king and an eye for presentation. Start with tender, moist quail on a bed of Jerusalem artichoke risotto, with a scattering of girolles and hazelnuts adding depth, while home-made haggis adds a further dimension to a main course of Dartmoor venison paired with bubble-and-squeak and honey-roast roots. West Country produce plays a starring role throughout. Cornish gurnard might appear with mussel and clam chowder, before the likes of local pork with black pudding, bacon, apple, mustard sauce and Savoy cabbage, and, to finish, crème brûlée is a classic. Chocoholics can get their fix with the 'everything chocolatey'.

Owner Evision Group **Times** 12-3/7-10.30 **Prices** Fixed L 2 course £18-£29, Fixed D 3 course £39-£48, Starter £6-£10, Main £18-£29, Dessert £6-£12 **Wines** 15 bottles over £20, 15 bottles under £20, 14 by glass **Notes** Vegetarian menu, Civ Wed 200 **Seats** 40, Pr/dining room 30 **Children** Portions, Menu **Parking** On street

---

THURLESTONE   Map 3 SX64

Thurlestone Hotel

◉ Modern, Traditional British 🍃

Stunning sea views and well-judged cooking

☎ 01548 560382
TQ7 3NN
e-mail: enquiries@thurlestone.co.uk
dir: A38 take A384 into Totnes, A381 towards Kingsbridge, onto A379 towards Churchstow, onto B3197 turn into lane signed to Thurlestone

The location - a delicious coastal hotspot near Salcombe - would be reason enough to visit this part of the world, but the Thurlestone Hotel's 19 acres of subtropical gardens overlooking the sea and cliffs makes this a location to savour. That splendid panorama of the coastline across Bigbury Bay can be appreciated at leisure in the elegant Margaret Amelia restaurant, since floor-to-ceiling picture windows mean it stays as a backdrop throughout proceedings. The kitchen deals in well-conceived modern British dishes wrought from excellent local produce - South Devon crab, perhaps, which might share a plate with avocado pannacotta, tomato jelly and basil shoots, while mains run from chargrilled fillet steak with oxtail ravioli and horseradish hollandaise to herb-crusted hake with spinach, saffron mash and lobster butter sauce. Dessert could be a chocolate and orange torte with hazelnut ice cream.

Chef Hugh Miller **Owner** Grose family **Times** 12.30-2.30/7.30-9 Closed 4-20 Jan, L Mon-Sat **Prices** Fixed D 4 course £38.50, Service optional **Wines** 113 bottles over £20, 40 bottles under £20, 8 by glass **Notes** Fish tasting menu, Sunday L, Vegetarian available, Dress restrictions, Jacket, Civ Wed 150 **Seats** 150, Pr/dining room 150 **Children** Portions, Menu **Parking** 120

TORQUAY   Map 3 SX96

The Elephant Restaurant and Brasserie

◉◉◉ – *see page 142*

Grand Hotel

◉ Modern European 🍃

Fine local ingredients and sea views

☎ 01803 296677
Torbay Rd TQ2 6NT
e-mail: reservations@grandtorquay.co.uk
dir: M5 junct 31, follow signs for Torquay. At the Penn Inn rdbt follow signs for seafront

On the splendid sweep of Torquay's seafront stands this majestic Edwardian hotel with the regal air of a grande dame from a bygone era. Agatha Christie used to spend her hols here, and it doesn't take much imagination to conjure images of tea dances and grand balls in its stately lounges and public rooms. The Gainsborough restaurant is the fine dining venue, built on an epic scale and with splendid views of the English Riviera coastline

---

to mull over, while solicitous staff keep things ticking along smoothly. The kitchen team aims to please all comers with a modern European menu covering a lot of ground: duck parfait with caramelised apricots, perhaps, then mains such as local brill with broad beans, peas and pancetta, Parmentier potatoes and shellfish bisque, and to finish, caramelised apple terrine with Calvados semi-fredo, cinnamon beignets and ice cream, and butterscotch sauce.

Chef Richard Hunt **Owner** Keith Richardson **Times** 12.30-3/6.30-9.30 Closed L Mon-Sat **Prices** Fixed D 3 course £29-£35, Service included **Wines** 36 bottles over £20, 5 bottles under £20, 11 by glass **Notes** Sunday L, Vegetarian available, Dress restrictions, Smart casual, Civ Wed 100 **Seats** 160, Pr/dining room 40 **Children** Portions, Menu **Parking** 30, Station car park opposite

---

TOTNES   Map 3 SX86

Riverford Organic Field Kitchen

◉ Modern British 🍃

Vegetables take a starring role at organic Devon farm

☎ 01803 762074
Riverford TQ11 0JU
e-mail: fieldkitchen@riverford.co.uk
dir: From A38 Buckfastleigh, take A384 to Totnes. Turn off to Landscove & Woolston Green & follow signs to Riverford Organics

As the name suggests, this is no place for high heels and designer suits, with Riverford (the renowned supplier of organically grown fruit and veg) offering a homely, communal, refectory-style dining experience at its farm restaurant just outside Totnes. There's just one sitting for lunch and dinner and you share tables (and food) with your fellow diners, while chef Jane Baxter deals in whatever's seasonal and picked from the fields that day at her open-to-view kitchen. As such there's no menu, rather each table is given one main meat dish and around six creative veg dishes to share - vegetables are king here. It's a two-course affair, so expect to go straight into mains such as slow-roast lamb shoulder with salsa verde, plus a whole array of veggie side-plates, perhaps taking in Swiss chard and anchovy gratin and red cabbage with blue cheese and walnuts. Steamed marmalade sponge or sticky toffee pudding end things comfort style.

Chef Jane Baxter **Owner** Guy Watson **Times** 1-3/7.30-11.30 Closed Mon (winter), D Tue-Thu (winter) **Prices** Fixed L 2 course £19.95, Fixed D 3 course £26, Service optional **Wines** 6 bottles over £20, 11 bottles under £20, 6 by glass **Notes** Sunday L, Vegetarian available **Seats** 64 **Children** Portions **Parking** 30

TWO BRIDGES
Map 3 SX67

Two Bridges Hotel

Modern British V

Scenic moorland spot with fine-dining approach

☎ 01822 892300
PL20 6SW
e-mail: enquiries@twobridges.co.uk
dir: 8m from Tavistock on B3357, hotel at junct with B3312

In the heart of Dartmoor, this cosy, welcoming and quintessentially English hotel sits in 60 acres of grounds beside the two bridges on the River Dart that give the place its name. Inside, you probably won't have the heart to evict the purring cat from its favourite fireside seat, so find another spot in the cosseting bar and lounge for a pre-dinner drink before moving into the restaurant, where oak panelling is hung with hunting pictures, tables are draped with linen and the views are sublime. The kitchen works with the seasons and local producers to deliver its well-thought-out menus, so you might start with confit duck leg with red onion marmalade and Parma ham, move on to pork tenderloin with champ potatoes, bok choy, and apple and vanilla purée, and finish with dark chocolate fondant with griottine cherries and chocolate ice cream.

Owner Warm Welcome Hotels **Times** 12-2/6.30-9.30 **Prices** Food prices not confirmed for 2013. Please telephone for details **Wines** 6 bottles over £20, 12 bottles under £20, 6 by glass **Notes** Vegetarian menu, Dress restrictions, Smart casual, No jeans, Civ Wed 150 **Seats** 85 **Children** Portions, Menu **Parking** 150

WOODBURY
Map 3 SY08

Woodbury Park Hotel & Golf Club

British

Ambitious modern cooking with golf and classic racing cars laid on

☎ 01395 233382 & 234735
Woodbury Castle EX5 1JJ
e-mail: enquiries@woodburypark.co.uk
dir: M5 junct 30, take A376/A3052 towards Sidmouth, turn right opposite Halfway Inn onto B3180 towards Budleigh Salterton to Woodbury Common, hotel signed on right

After tearing around a race track in a Formula One car, former owner of Woodbury Park Nigel Mansell used to wind down on a golf course, so this swish country-house hotel neatly combines both subjects with its own PGA Championship course and the one-time champion's collection of classic racing cars. The Atrium restaurant trumpets Devon's fine produce in a stylish contemporary setting. Local materials from within a 50-mile radius turn up one way or another in an uncomplicated repertoire of modern ideas, kicking off, perhaps, with a tried-and-true duo of seared scallops and crispy pork belly with watercress and cider vinaigrette, followed by chargrilled rib-eye and fillet cuts of Devon steak with oxtail pudding, Pont-Neuf potatoes and peppercorn butter. Desserts offer the likes of peach clafoutis with home-made lemongrass ice cream.

Chef Matthew Pickett **Owner** Sue & Robin Hawkins **Times** 12.30-2.30/6.30-9.30 Closed L Mon-Sat, D 31 Dec **Prices** Starter £6-£9, Main £14.50-£22.50, Dessert £6, Service optional **Wines** 38 bottles over £20, 19 bottles under £20, 10 by glass **Notes** Sunday L, Vegetarian available, Dress restrictions, Smart casual, Civ Wed 150 **Seats** 120, Pr/dining room 180 **Children** Portions **Parking** 350

WOOLACOMBE
Map 3 SS44

Watermeet Hotel

Traditional British

Straightforward, unfussy cooking and memorable sea views

☎ 01271 870333
Mortehoe EX34 7EB
e-mail: info@watersmeethotel.co.uk
dir: M5 junct 27. Follow A361 to Woolacombe, right at beach car park, 300yds on right

In a fantastic coastal location, this refined and elegant hotel serves up an unfussy, daily-changing menu in a restaurant where there are no dud seats when it comes to

The Elephant Restaurant and Brasserie

TORQUAY
Map 3 SX96

Modern British

Thrilling modern British cookery overlooking the marina

☎ 01803 200044
3-4 Beacon Ter TQ1 2BH
e-mail: info@elephantrestaurant.co.uk
dir: Follow signs for Living Coast, restaurant opposite

A pair of converted Georgian townhouses overlooking the harbour and marina are home to Simon Hulstone's supremely accomplished contemporary restaurant. The two floors offer the twin poles of today's dining, with simpler brasserie fare in the expansive ground-floor space, while The Room upstairs opens in the evenings for half the year to offer a full-throttle version of modern British cookery, using local and wild ingredients in a style that fuses classic technique and up-to-the-minute thrills in equal measure. A six-course tasting menu, with optional wines, offers the pick of the carte, perhaps opening with a selection of beet varieties - candy, golden and Cheltenham - and Vulscombe goats' cheese, garnished with elderflower and tansy. Something as apparently pubby as smoked mackerel and horseradish pâté with pickled cucumber is lifted out of the ordinary by the quality of materials and an accompaniment like dashi-stock jelly, while main courses aim high but don't neglect the comfort factor, as in a double-bill of braised cheek and crisp belly of pork, with celeriac purée and roasted button onions. The pastoral note from wild ingredients is sounded even in desserts such as lemon verbena cream with Cassis sorbet. In The Brasserie, a revelation of a Scotch egg, its soft-poached centre still runny, bedded on grain mustard mayonnaise, is a fine curtain-raiser, while sweet trips down memory lane include floating islands and crème caramel.

Chef Simon Hulstone **Owner** Peter Morgan, Simon Hulstone **Times** 7-9.30 Closed 1st 2wks Jan, Sun-Mon, L all week **Prices** Fixed D 3 course £49.50, Service added but optional 10% **Wines** 43 bottles over £20, 10 bottles under £20, 8 by glass **Notes** Tasting menu available, Vegetarian available **Seats** 24 **Parking** Opposite restaurant

Save on Hotels. Book at theAA.com/hotel

DEVON – DORSET 143 ENGLAND

sea views. West-facing, so ideal for catching sunsets over dinner, the traditionally-decorated room has a light and bright feel, and service is reassuringly old school. On the menu might be pressed ham hock with apples, honey and cloves, followed by fillet of turbot with spicy fried scallops, tomato and white wine, finishing off with a simple as it comes pudding such as fresh strawberries with clotted cream.

Times 12-2/7-9

DORSET

BEAMINSTER
Map 4 ST40

BridgeHouse

◎◎ Modern International 🕙

Up-to-date cooking in a 13th-century building

☎ 01308 862200
3 Prout Bridge DT8 3AY
e-mail: enquiries@bridge-house.co.uk
web: www.beaminsterbrasserie.co.uk
dir: From A303 take A356 towards Dorchester. Turn right onto A3066, 200mtrs down hill from town centre

The 700-year-old stone-built BridgeHouse was originally a home to priests, and while there's no lack of old-world charm, sympathetic renovation has brought modern-day style to the hotel. The restaurant (the Beaminster Brasserie) comes in three distinct areas: a more formal panelled and candlelit main room with an Adam fireplace and intimate ambience, a lighter, modern conservatory and canvassed-over terrace overlooking the walled garden. The kitchen's creative modern cooking is inspired by the abundant local larder and comes with a nod to France and sunnier climes, as well as the occasional influence from even further afield. Crispy Lyme Bay hake fillet is served with tiger prawn and squid paella, and lobster, broad bean and pea bisque, or Creedy Carver chicken tikka saag with tandoori leg, crispy liver, peshwari rice, crispy skin and cucumber raita. Desserts extend to pineapple tarte Tatin or dark chocolate fondant.

BridgeHouse

Chef Mr Stephen Pielesz **Owner** Mark and Joanna Donovan **Times** 12-2.30/6.30-9.30 **Prices** Fixed L 2 course fr £19.50, Fixed D 3 course £27.50-£41.50, Starter £6.50-£10.50, Main £14.50-£21.50, Dessert £6.50-£9.50, Service added but optional 10% **Wines** 82 bottles over £20, 8 bottles under £20, 12 by glass **Notes** Sunday L, Vegetarian available, Civ Wed 40 **Seats** 50, Pr/dining room 30 **Children** Portions, Menu **Parking** 20

The Wild Garlic

◎◎ Modern British V 🕙

Careful sourcing and considered cooking from *MasterChef* winner

☎ 01308 861446
4 The Square DT8 3AS
e-mail: mail@thewildgarlic.co.uk
web: www.thewildgarlic.co.uk
dir: From A303, exit A3066 Crewkerne and follow signs for Bridport. Restaurant in Town Sq.

A few years on from the PR boost conferred by winning BBC's *MasterChef* in 2009, Mat Follas continues to pull in the punters at his unpretentious restaurant in a 16th-century toll house on Beaminster's bustling main square. Inside, a chilled-out ambience reigns in a smartly rustic setting of rough-hewn solid oak tables on wooden floors, white and sage-green half-panelled walls and chalkboards announcing the day's offerings. Follas's cooking is engagingly straightforward stuff: there is no doubting the quality or freshness of the supplies sourced from local artisan producers and foragers, and the treatments are not over-ambitious: pigeon breast with pear purée and parsnip crisp, perhaps, followed by 12-hour triple-cooked pork belly with sweet potato and crackling, and bitter chocolate fondant with vanilla ice cream and walnut brittle to close the show.

Chef Mat Follas **Owner** Mat & Amanda Follas
Times 12-2/7-11 Closed BHs, Sun-Tue **Prices** Fixed L 2 course £14, Starter £6-£9, Main £15-£24, Dessert £6-£7,

Service optional, Groups min 10 service 10% **Wines** 18 bottles over £20, 5 bottles under £20, 11 by glass **Notes** Vegetarian menu **Seats** 40 **Children** Portions **Parking** Car park at front of building

BOURNEMOUTH
Map 5 SZ09

Best Western The Connaught Hotel

◎◎ Modern British

Gentle modern British cooking in fashionable Bournemouth

☎ 01202 298020
30 West Hill Rd, West Cliff BH2 5PH
e-mail: reception@theconnaught.co.uk
web: www.theconnaught.co.uk
dir: Follow Town Centre West & BIC signs

Bournemouth is in vogue. Its glorious sandy beaches were declared among the best in Europe by the EU in 2012, and it has gradually shaken off its image as a sedate resort of the venerable, and put on a new suit of fashionable clothes. That said, it still does old-school elegance well, as may be witnessed at The Connaught, which gazes imperiously out over those aforesaid beaches from the eminence of the West Cliff. The smart Blakes dining room is done in café crème, and offers a congenial version of the modern British idiom, with no alarming combos to cause palpitations. Start with cured seared salmon in an aïoli salad of fennel, radish and caviar, and then follow on with Creedy Carver duck breast with three-cheese potato gratin and Savoy cabbage, in a sauce of morels and red wine. After which, it's surely worth a 15-minute pause to await a hot banana soufflé, served with matching ice cream and chocolate sauce.

Chef David Hutcheson **Owner** Franklyn Hotels Ltd **Times** 6.30-9 Closed L all week (private lunches by arrangement) **Prices** Fixed D 3 course £25, Starter £5.50-£8.50, Main £14-£24.75, Dessert £5.50-£8.95, Service optional **Wines** 27 bottles over £20, 21 bottles under £20,

continued

BOURNEMOUTH *continued*

15 by glass **Notes** Pre-theatre menu available must pre-book, Vegetarian available, Dress restrictions, Smart casual, no jeans, T-shirts or mobiles, Civ Wed 120 **Seats** 80, Pr/dining room 16 **Children** Menu **Parking** 66

Bournemouth Highcliff Marriott Hotel

◉◉ Modern British

Smart cooking in a Victorian clifftop hotel gone cool

☎ 01202 557702
St Michael's Rd, West Cliff BH2 5DU
e-mail: reservations.bournemouth@marriotthotels.co.uk
dir: Take A338 dual carriageway through Bournemouth, then follow signs for International Centre to West Cliff Rd, then 2nd right

The aptly-titled Highcliff Marriott Hotel lords it from its perch on Bournemouth's West Cliff, basking in views across the resort and its Blue Flag beaches. Externally, the place is still a snow-white grande dame of Victorian vintage, but once inside, it is clear that the chintz has been well and truly chucked. Right in tune with the new image, the Highcliff Grill is looking pretty slick with its modern brasserie-style décor involving bare darkwood tables and funky cherry and lime green seating. The cooking plays a straight bat: contemporary, but sticking to the unfussy grill concept with a mix of modern and classic dishes built on well-sourced materials. Chicken liver and Madeira parfait with pear chutney and pickled walnuts is a tried-and-true starter done right, then grilled fillet of sea trout appears in the company of a fluffy potato crêpe, intense beetroot confit, curly kale and chervil hollandaise. Awaiting at the end is a textbook melting centre within a chocolate fondant teamed with chocolate ice cream and a crunchy praline.

Chef Matthew Budden **Owner** Marriott Hotels
Times 1-3/6-9.30 Closed L Mon-Sat **Prices** Fixed L 3 course £21.50, Starter £7-£11.50, Main £15-£28.50, Dessert £6-£8.50, Service included **Wines** 43 bottles over £20, 1 bottle under £20, 13 by glass **Notes** Sunday L, Vegetarian available, Dress restrictions, Smart casual, Civ Wed 215 **Seats** 80, Pr/dining room 14 **Children** Portions, Menu **Parking** 100

The Chine

◉ Modern British, European 🍴

Seaside hotel with sumptuous gardens

☎ 01202 396234
Boscombe Spa Rd BH5 1AX
e-mail: reservations@chinehotel.co.uk
web: www.chinehotel.co.uk
dir: From M27, A31, A338 follow signs to Boscombe Pier. Boscombe Spa Rd is off Christchurch Rd near Boscombe Gardens

A majestic slice of Victoriana, The Chine hotel sits in three acres of mature gardens with a path leading down to the promenade and glorious sandy beaches. Expect heaps of period style in the dining room, where stained-glass windows and burnished wood panelling set the tone, and tables are thoughtfully arranged so that everyone gets a piece of that view over Poole Bay through the huge picture windows. The kitchen keeps things simple and straightforward, aiming to comfort rather than challenge with its tried-and-true combinations of top-class, locally-sourced ingredients. You might start with something as unreconstructed as a pint of shell-on prawns with Marie Rose sauce and brown bread, then move on to beer-battered haddock with triple-cooked chips, mushy peas and tartare sauce, and end with Normandy apple tart with cider sorbet and cinnamon syrup.

Chef Claudio Nortarbartolo **Owner** Brownsea Haven Properties Ltd **Times** 12.30-2/7-9 Closed L Sat **Prices** Food prices not confirmed for 2013. Please telephone for details **Wines** 21 bottles over £20, 8 bottles under £20, 10 by glass **Notes** Vegetarian available, Dress

restrictions, No jeans, T-shirts or trainers at D, Civ Wed 120 **Seats** 150, Pr/dining room 120 **Children** Portions, Menu **Parking** 55

Crab at Bournemouth

◉◉ Seafood **NEW**

Imaginative ways with seafood near the pier

☎ 01202 203601
Exeter Rd BH2 5AJ
e-mail: info@crabatbournemouth.com
dir: Follow signs to B.I.C, restaurant opposite

Opposite Bournemouth International Centre, moments from the pier, The Crab, like its sister in Chieveley (see entry, Berkshire), is a seafood restaurant, and, if the name isn't enough, fishy plates on the chunky darkwood tables and piscine shapes in the wrought-iron room dividers are reminders. Daily deliveries from the West Country mean everything is spankingly fresh, timings are accurate, and glazes, sauces and broths add further interest to dishes. Classics like moules marinière and lobster thermidor jostle for attention among more contemporary choices: seared scallops with black pudding, or prawn and pork dumpling, presented in a steamer with a teriyaki dipping sauce, followed by a meaty chunk of cod with a brown shrimp and mussel broth, served with saffron potatoes and spinach, or John Dory fillets with macaroni cheese and lobster bisque. Meat-eaters are not entirely overlooked, and desserts can be as inventive as apple cheesecake with caramel ice cream.

Chef Dave Horridge **Owner** Julie Savage
Times 12-2.30/5.30-10 **Prices** Fixed L 2 course £15.95, Fixed D 3 course £19.95, Starter £5.95-£15, Main £14.50-£39.95, Dessert £4.95-£6.50, Groups min 6 service 10% **Wines** 42 bottles over £20, 10 bottles under £20, 15 by glass **Notes** Sunday L, Vegetarian available, Dress restrictions, Smart casual **Seats** 80 **Children** Portions, Menu **Parking** B.I.C

Cumberland Hotel

◉◉ British **NEW**

Hip contemporary dining in an art-deco hotel

☎ 01202 290722 & 556529
27 East Overcliff Dr BH1 3AF
e-mail: kwood@cumberlandbournemouth.co.uk
dir: A35 towards East Cliff & beaches, right onto Holdenhurst Rd, straight over 2 rdbts, left at junct to East Overcliff Drive, hotel on seafront

Overlooking the sea on Bournemouth's East Cliff, the Cumberland is a bright-white temple to art-deco architecture that brings a touch of Miami Beach style to the English seaside with its palm-lined poolside terrace. Recently made over with a loud-and-proud funky contemporary style to appeal to a vibrant crowd, the Ventana Brasserie is the focus of culinary endeavours, serving a roll-call of unfussy crowd-pleasing modern dishes wrought from local materials. Start with duck liver pâté with crispy smoked bacon, piccalilli and granary

Save on Hotels. Book at **theAA.com/hotel**

DORSET 145 ENGLAND

toast rubbed with English mustard, before moving into the well-trodden territory of steaks and burgers from the grill, or monkfish with red pepper coulis and stir-fried vegetables. To finish, almond and raspberry tiramisù offers a creative take on an old favourite.

Chef Mateusz Nowatkowski **Owner** Kevin Wood **Times** 12-6/6-10 **Prices** Starter £4.95-£12.95, Main £10.45-£20.95, Service optional, Groups min 6 service 10% **Wines** 18 bottles over £20, 22 bottles under £20, 9 by glass **Notes** Sunday L, Vegetarian available, Dress restrictions, Smart casual, Civ Wed 90 **Seats** 90, Pr/dining room 40 **Children** Menu **Parking** 55, On street

Hermitage Hotel

⊛ Modern British

Seafront hotel with good, honest food

☎ 01202 557363
Exeter Rd BH2 5AH
e-mail: info@hermitage-hotel.co.uk
web: www.hermitage-hotel.co.uk
dir: Follow A338 (Ringwood-Bournemouth) & signs to pier, beach & BIC. Hotel directly opposite

The Hermitage sits centre-stage in Bournemouth, opposite the splendid pier and the promenade running alongside the town's celebrated golden beaches, and lies a handily short stroll from the Pavilion Theatre and whatever is going down in the Bournemouth International Centre. The old girl has been smartly refurbished and still has a sense of majesty in the high-ceilinged dining room with its grand decorative fireplaces. The cooking here ploughs a crowd-pleasing furrow, delivering uncomplicated ideas along the lines of a retro prawn and crayfish cocktail with Marie Rose sauce to start, then classic steaks or braised lamb shank with creamed potato, crispy pancetta, green beans and rosemary and redcurrant sauce. End with dark chocolate fondant with vanilla ice cream and chocolate sauce.

Times 6-9 Closed L Mon-Sat

Menzies Carlton Hotel

⊛ Traditional British **NEW**

Sea views and classical cooking

☎ 01202 552011
East Overcliff BH1 3DN
e-mail: carlton@menzieshotels.co.uk
dir: M3/M27, follow A338 (Bournemouth). Follow signs to town centre and East Overcliff. Hotel is on the seafront

This traditional hotel makes the most of its spectacular location on Bournemouth's East Cliff. The dining room has fab views over the outdoor pool and decking area to the sea beyond, and when the sun shines you might even forget you're in the UK. In Frederick's restaurant, with its high ceilings adorned with chandeliers and swag drapes, a formal dress code applies, which certainly helps maintain that sense of grandeur. Unfussy, classical food is what to expect; smoked haddock and chive ravioli, for example, with a mussel and vegetable broth, or chicken, basil and mint terrine with home-made chutney. Next up,

best end of English lamb is served pink with goats' cheese glazed dauphinoise potatoes and seasonal greens, with chocolate and coffee layer mousse with roasted hazelnut ganache a star turn for dessert.

Times 12.30-7

The Print Room & Ink Bar & Brasserie

⊛⊛ Classic Brasserie

Cosmopolitan menu in a magnificent art-deco venue

☎ 01202 789669
Richmond Hill BH2 6HH
e-mail: info@theprintroom-bournemouth.co.uk
web: www.theprintroom-bournemouth.co.uk
dir: Just off town centre in Daily Echo newspaper building

Arising in 1932 as the offices of local paper, *The Daily Echo*, this corner site is a magnificent piece of Depression-defying art-deco hubris. While much of Britain does its best to defy depression once again, it feels like a fitting venue for a seaside resort that has shaken off its postwar dowdiness and is living in the now. The Ink Bar opens first thing for breakfasts; The Print Room, where the presses once roared, now provides the maplewood booths and Swarovski chandeliers for an all-day brasserie operation. The menu speaks several languages in the modern way, offering pork samosa with pickled apple purée or moules marinière to start, and then monkfish and lentil red curry or vegetable couscous with fried haloumi to follow. In between are some unmistakable modern British offerings, of the likes of pink-seared fillet of New Forest venison with goats' cheese gnocchi, long-stem broccoli and port sauce. Finish with blueberry cheesecake, served with a sorbet of Dorset cider.

Chef Ian Gibbs **Owner** Print Room Dorset Ltd **Times** 12-3/6-11 Closed D Sun **Prices** Fixed L 2 course fr £12, Fixed D 3 course £22-£35, Starter £4.50-£9, Main £7.50-£18.95, Dessert £4.95-£8.50, Service optional, Groups min 10 service 10% **Wines** 30 bottles over £20, 15 bottles under £20, 12 by glass **Notes** Pre-theatre

menu available, Sunday L, Vegetarian available **Seats** 120, Pr/dining room 22 **Children** Portions, Menu **Parking** NCP - 100yds

West Beach

⊛⊛ Modern, Seafood

Sophisticated seafood dishes on the beach

☎ 01202 587785
Pier Approach BH2 5AA
e-mail: enquiry@west-beach.co.uk
web: www.west-beach.co.uk
dir: 100yds W of the pier

For a seafood restaurant, West Beach couldn't have a better location: it's almost on the beach, with a fabulous decked terrace and great views. It's a friendly place with clued-up staff, done out in pastels and light woods, and with an open-plan kitchen. Some meat and vegetarian dishes are on the menu, but it would be churlish to arrive here and pass up on the spankingly fresh seafood. A few preparations are pulled out of the classical repertoire - moules marinière, lobster thermidor - but in general the kitchen leaves no modern culinary stone unturned, giving hake the bourguignon treatment and serving it with spinach and mash, and partnering pan-fried John Dory with ham hock ballottine and emulsion and accompanying it with braised baby gem, celeriac and fondant potato. You could start with accurately pan-fried scallops, served with carrot purée and couscous, pickled raisins and coriander, go on to fish pie, and finish with a dessert from the short list: perhaps plum trifle.

Chef Nick Hewitt **Owner** Andrew Price **Times** 12-3.30/6-10 Closed 25 Dec, D 26 Dec, 1 Jan
continued

BOURNEMOUTH *continued*

Prices Starter £5.50-£10, Main £12.50-£79.95, Dessert £4.50-£9.50, Service optional, Groups min 10 service 10% **Wines** 37 bottles over £20, 10 bottles under £20, 11 by glass **Notes** Tasting & pre-theatre menus available, Sunday L, Vegetarian available, Dress restrictions, No bare feet or bikinis **Seats** 90 **Children** Portions, Menu **Parking** NCP 2 mins

BRIDPORT   Map 4 SY49

Riverside Restaurant

◎ Seafood, International ◎

The pick of local seafood in a waterside setting

☎ 01308 422011
West Bay DT6 4EZ
e-mail: neilriverside@hotmail.com
web: thefishrestaurant-westbay.co.uk
dir: A35 Bridport ring road, turn to West Bay at Crown rdbt

Lonnie Donegan was top of the pops with 'My Old Man's a Dustman' when the Watson family set up shop in their unaffected restaurant. Over half a century later, it is still going great guns and has never deviated from its prime directive: serving generous, fuss-free dishes of fish and seafood fresh off the local Lyme Bay boats. With water all around, the setting is retro beachcomber-chic, with hues of lavender blue and pale wood tables, and the kitchen's approach admirably uncheffy and to the point - what appears at the table depends on what the boats have brought in: deep-fried squid with saffron aïoli needs no further adornment, as is the case with Portland crab and sweetcorn chowder. Next up, there are whole fish grilled on the bone, platters of shellfish, or the daily specials may offer grilled brill with a celeriac, coriander and horseradish remoulade.

Chef N Larcombe, A Shaw, B Streak **Owner** Mr & Mrs A Watson **Times** 12-2.30/6.30-9 Closed 30 Nov-12 Feb, Mon (ex BHs), D Sun **Prices** Fixed L 2 course £19.55, Starter £4.95-£9.95, Main £12.95-£25, Dessert £4.95-£6.95, Service optional, Groups min 7 service 10% **Wines** 35 bottles over £20, 25 bottles under £20, 10 by glass **Notes** Sunday L, Vegetarian available **Seats** 80, Pr/dining room 30 **Children** Portions, Menu **Parking** Public car park 40 mtrs

CHRISTCHURCH   Map 5 SZ19

Captain's Club Hotel

◎◎ Modern European

Contemporary spa hotel with appealing riverside restaurant

☎ 01202 475111
Wick Ferry, Wick Ln BH23 1HU
e-mail: enquiries@captainsclubhotel.com
dir: Hotel just off Christchurch High St, towards Christchurch Quay

Right on Christchurch Quay, this eye-catching modern hotel isn't just of interest to the boating fraternity. The views over the River Stour may well excite those of a nautical persuasion, but the hotel has much to offer all comers, not least some modish eating in its Tides Restaurant. With floor-to ceiling windows, live music in the piano bar, plus a large terrace to further endorse that Riviera vibe, there is a lot of 21st-century va-va-voom hereabouts. From a menu that thinks local and regional, start, perhaps, with a classic steak tartare made with Devon beef, or go for something with more fashionable leanings such as seared scallops with crisp pork belly, cauliflower purée, golden raisin and hazelnut dressing. Among main courses there are the traditional comforts of half a roasted free-range chicken with watercress, game chips and bread sauce, or the more à la mode smoked haddock and coconut risotto, with crispy poached egg and curry oil.

Chef Andrew Gault **Owner** Platinum One Hotels Ltd **Times** 12-2.30/7-10 **Prices** Fixed L 2 course fr £16, Fixed D 3 course fr £28, Starter £6-£12, Main £12-£22, Dessert £6-£12, Service optional **Wines** 118 bottles over £20, 10 bottles under £20, 12 by glass **Notes** Sunday L, Vegetarian available, Civ Wed 80 **Seats** 72, Pr/dining room 44 **Children** Portions, Menu **Parking** 41

Christchurch Harbour Restaurant

◎◎ British, French

Lovely sea views and accomplished modern cooking

☎ 01202 483434
95 Mudeford BH23 3NT
e-mail: martin-neil.robinson@harbourhotels.co.uk
dir: A35/A337 to Highcliffe. Right at rdbt, hotel & restaurant 1.5m on left

The restaurant and terrace at this 18th-century hotel, a Grade II listed building, have spectacular views across

Mudeford Quay to Hengistbury Head. It's been decorated in neutral shades, perhaps so attention is not diverted from the seascape outside or from the well-presented food. The seasonally-changing menus celebrate the produce of Dorset's pastures and daily-landed seafood, the latter seen as plainly grilled lemon sole served simply with buttered vegetables and herbed new potatoes. The kitchen generally takes a straightforward approach without mucking about with its ingredients, and what it does it does well. Starters have included haddock and cheddar soufflé with white wine sauce, and ham hock with piccalilli, and main courses bring on seared calves' liver with mash and Savoy cabbage, and, in summer, pork chops with dauphinoise and new season's peas and broad beans. Finish with homely apple and pear crumble with custard, or sticky toffee pudding.

Chef Loic Gratadoux **Owner** Harbour Hotels Group **Times** 12-2/7-9 **Prices** Fixed L 2 course £14.50-£24.50, Fixed D 3 course £28, Starter £7.50-£11.50, Main £16.50-£26.50, Dessert £7-£9.50, Service optional **Wines** 44 bottles over £20, 18 bottles under £20, 9 by glass **Notes** Sunday L, Vegetarian available, Dress restrictions, Smart casual **Seats** 90, Pr/dining room 20 **Children** Menu **Parking** 100

Crooked Beam Restaurant

◎ Modern British

Friendly, family-run restaurant with well-judged menu

☎ 01202 499362
Jumpers Corner, 2 The Grove BH23 2HA
e-mail: info@crookedbeam.co.uk
web: www.crookedbeam.co.uk
dir: Situated on corner of Barrack Road A35 and The Grove

A fixture on the Christchurch dining scene for a good few years now, the Crooked Beam is a charming, family-run restaurant in a 300-year old character building, complete with a conservatory extension. Chef Simon Hallam - who runs the restaurant with wife Vicki - serves up no-nonsense food using good quality ingredients, with the menus full of crowd-pleasers. Take, for instance, a starter of chicken liver and pistachio pâté with a warm plum chutney and toasted brioche, or Thai salmon fishcakes with a chilli salsa. For the main event you might choose the 8oz hand-made beef burger or honey-glazed pork tenderloin, while for dessert there could be vanilla crème brûlée with a berry compôte, or lemon cheesecake with raspberry sorbet. The market menu is particularly good value, while traditional roast lunches are a hit on Sundays.

Chef Simon Hallam **Owner** Simon & Vicki Hallam **Times** 12-2/7-11 Closed Mon, L Sat, D Sun **Prices** Food prices not confirmed for 2013. Please telephone for details **Wines** 4 bottles over £20, 28 bottles under £20, 6 by glass **Notes** Sunday L, Vegetarian available, Dress restrictions, Smart casual **Seats** 80, Pr/dining room 20 **Children** Portions **Parking** 10, On street

Save on Hotels. Book at **theAA.com/hotel**

DORSET 147 **ENGLAND**

The Jetty

◉◉ Modern British ☙

Sleek modish venue with sharp, unfussy contemporary cooking

☎ 01202 400950
95 Mudeford BH23 3NT
e-mail: dine@thejetty.co.uk
dir: A35/A337 to Highcliffe. Right at rdbt, hotel & restaurant 1.5m on left

It is always reassuring to eat within sight of where your food is coming from, and The Jetty, in the grounds of the swish Christchurch Harbour Hotel, looks across the bay to Mudeford Quay where the kitchen's fish and seafood is landed. The venue is a memorable spot - a clean-cut, contemporary Baufritz-designed carbon-neutral waterside pavilion of wood and glass, so that you get the views whatever the weather. Directing the culinary action is local food hero Alex Aitken, who sources sustainably and treats his peerless materials with due respect, which means simply and without superfluous faffing about. A charcoal-fired Josper oven helps too when it comes to searing those flavours in at high temperature. Naturally, fish and seafood plays a key part in the repertoire - a potted trio of Mudeford crab, mackerel, and Poole Bay shrimps to start, perhaps, then cod fillet with Weymouth scallops, mashed potato, leeks, and bacon cream sauce. For meat fans there might be rare saddle of New Forest venison with local haggis, red wine-poached pear and caramelised walnuts, and to finish, hot passionfruit soufflé and sauce. The hotel also has its own two-Rosetted restaurant (see entry).

Chef Alex Aitken **Owner** Christchurch Restaurants Ltd
Times 12-2.30/6-10 **Prices** Fixed L 2 course fr £17.95, Fixed D 3 course fr £21.95, Tasting menu £49.50, Starter £5.95-£11.95, Main £15.95-£28.50, Dessert £5.25-£7.95, Service added but optional 10% **Wines** 50 bottles over £20, 7 bottles under £20, 24 by glass **Notes** Sunday L, Vegetarian available **Seats** 70 **Children** Portions **Parking** 40

The Lord Bute & Restaurant

◉ British, European

Well-heeled surroundings for local ingredients

☎ 01425 278884
179-185 Lymington Rd, Highcliffe BH23 4JS
e-mail: mail@lordbute.co.uk
dir: Follow A337 to Lymington, opposite St Mark's churchyard in Highcliffe

Set above the beach, the hotel dates from the 18th century; parts of the property used to be the entrance lodges to Highcliffe Castle. Nowadays the restaurant is a delightful, elegant room with an orangery extension, its walls hung with paintings, with plenty of space between tables, and attentive and swift service. Using organic, GM-free local produce, the kitchen has assembled a crowd-pleasing menu, from New Forest asparagus topped

with a poached egg and mustard and chive hollandaise, or light foie gras parfait with apple and apricot chutney, to well-timed, tender rump of Romsey lamb with shepherd's pie and redcurrant and mint sauce, or grilled local sea bass fillet with caper and brown shrimp butter. Among a half-dozen or so desserts may be iced praline parfait with butterscotch sauce and clotted cream.

Chef Kevin Brown **Owner** S Box & G Payne
Times 12-2/7-9.30 Closed Mon, L Sat, D Sun **Prices** Fixed L 2 course fr £14.95, Fixed D 3 course fr £32.95, Service optional **Wines** 28 bottles over £20, 32 bottles under £20, 6 by glass **Notes** Sunday L, Vegetarian available, Dress restrictions, Smart casual, no jeans or T-shirts **Seats** 95 **Children** Portions **Parking** 50

Splinters Restaurant

◉◉ Modern International

Superior cooking in lively neighbourhood restaurant

☎ 01202 483454
12 Church St BH23 1BW
e-mail: eating@splinters.uk.com
web: www.splinters.uk.com
dir: Directly in front of Priory gates

Evidently taking its name from the splinters carpenters suffered as they installed booth seating, this restaurant, on a cobbled street leading to the Priory, consists of a bar-lounge where canapés are served and a series of appealing dining rooms. The balanced menus generally include an interesting vegetarian main course - perhaps wild mushroom risotto with glazed goats' cheese - as well as fish and meat options: well-timed fillet of beef with roast shallots, dauphinoise and wild mushroom jus, say, and super-fresh seared sea bass fillet with chive butter and crushed new potatoes. Starters can vary from chicken liver parfait with orange marmalade to a more ambitious plate of gravad lax, smoked salmon and crayfish tails with beetroot purée and a salad of cucumber, capers and lemon. The kitchen's industry in making everything on the premises reaps rewards not least in puddings like lemon tart.

Chef Paul Putt **Owner** Paul & Agnes Putt
Times 11-2/6.30-10 Closed 26 Dec, 1-10 Jan, Sun-Mon **Prices** Fixed L 2 course fr £13.50, Fixed D 3 course fr £26.50, Service optional, Groups min 8 service 10% **Wines** 105 bottles over £20, 37 bottles under £20, 5 by glass **Notes** ALC 2 course £31.95, 3 course £38.95, Vegetarian available, Dress restrictions, Smart casual **Seats** 42, Pr/dining room 30 **Children** Portions **Parking** Priory car park

---

CORFE CASTLE   Map 4 SY98

Mortons House Hotel

◉◉ Traditional & Modern British

Enjoyable eating in Elizabethan building

☎ 01929 480988
East St BH20 5EE
e-mail: stay@mortonshouse.co.uk
dir: In village centre on A351

It did no harm to curry favour with the royals back in Tudor times, and the family who built Mortons House went so far as to build their home in the shape of an 'E' in honour of Elizabeth I. Now it operates as an intimate and easygoing family-run hotel with an elegant classically-styled restaurant that sits well with the venerable building. The cooking is rooted in classical ideas, and is based on impeccable sourcing and a flavour-driven philosophy that embraces modern concepts. Smoked ham hock, rabbit and foie gras terrine with raisin purée and truffled walnut brioche is a typical opener, while main courses could delight fans of local meat with a Dorset fillet steak with dauphinoise potatoes, wild mushrooms, baby artichoke and truffle jus, or seek inspiration from far-off shores in the form of Moroccan spiced lamb fillet teamed with breaded smoked tongue, aubergine purée, couscous, spinach, and cucumber and mint yoghurt. If you have someone to share with, sign up for a pear tarte Tatin for two with crunchy pistachio ice cream.

Chef Ed Firth **Owner** Mrs Woods, Mr & Mrs Clayton
Times 12-1.45/7-9 **Prices** Starter £7-£8, Main £21.50-£25, Dessert £7-£9, Service optional, Groups min 20 service 10% **Wines** 40 bottles over £20, 5 bottles under £20, 4 by glass **Notes** Sunday L, Vegetarian available, Dress restrictions, Smart casual preferred, Civ Wed 60 **Seats** 60, Pr/dining room 22 **Children** Portions, Menu **Parking** 40

Sienna

DORCHESTER   Map 4 SY69

Modern British

Small is beautiful on Dorchester's high street

☎ 01305 250022
36 High West St DT1 1UP
e-mail: browns@siennarestaurant.co.uk
dir: Near top of town rdbt in Dorchester

In the decade since they opened their doors on Dorchester's high street, Russell and Elena Brown have established their small restaurant's place firmly among the A-listers of the Dorset dining scene. Sienna proves that size doesn't always matter, and in this case, its pocket-sized interior is a positive advantage, as it means that with less than twenty lucky diners to cater for, the husband-and-wife-team can ensure that every aspect of the food and service punches above its weight. Elena's

calm professionalism out front feeds into the ambience of refined and relaxed intimacy in the quietly stylish contemporary dining room, where solid ash tables are set against hues of ochre and cream and colourful splashes of artwork. In the engine room, Russell cooks with intelligence and an innate feel for what works well with what, backed by the requisite technical skills to pull it all off; there's no chasing after ephemeral fads and fashions here, just a deft hand that wrings full-on flavours from the finest seasonal materials. In this era of austerity, bargain hunters should turn up for lunch menus offering stonking value for cooking at this level, but it's worth digging deeper for dinner and tasting menus composed with more complex, insightful combinations. Slow-cooked pork and apple terrine served with sweet onion relish and wafer-thin crispy prosciutto is an exemplary dish, while main course sees pinkly-yielding roast loin of Dorset lamb sharing a plate with a lamb sausage roll, Jerusalem artichoke velouté and thyme jus. The cooking continues to show its class at dessert stage, bringing together

saffron-poached pear with pistachio and marzipan cake, and rich honeycomb ice cream. In tune with the whole operation, the wine list is small but perfectly formed, and full of global delights.

Chef Russell Brown **Owner** Russell & Elena Brown **Times** 12.30-2/7-9 Closed 2 wks Feb/Mar, 2 wks Sep/Oct, Sun-Mon, L Tue **Prices** Fixed L 2 course £25.50, Fixed D 3 course £43, Service optional **Wines** 33 bottles over £20, 6 bottles under £20, 7 by glass **Notes** Tasting menu 6 course, Vegetarian available **Seats** 15 **Parking** On street, top of town car park

Summer Lodge Country House Hotel, Restaurant & Spa

EVERSHOT   Map 4 ST50

Modern British

Assured modern cooking in peaceful surroundings

☎ 01935 482000
Fore St DT2 0JR
e-mail: summerlodge@rchmail.com
web: www.summerlodgehotel.com
dir: 1m W of A37 halfway between Dorchester & Yeovil

In a pretty village, within four acres of manicured grounds, this listed Georgian country-house retreat has an indoor pool, jacuzzi, spa and gym - all very helpful for losing a few pounds. Luxuriously done out, the hotel gives off a feeling of relaxed grandeur without being oppressive or intimidating, helped by approachable, practised staff. Meals are served in the conservatory and the rather busily decorated dining room, where an amuse-bouche of perhaps chanterelle with mushroom foam sets the tone for what follows. Steven

Titman's menus are streaked with invention, and he certainly stocks up on quality produce. Foie gras terrine with poached rhubarb flavoured with sloe gin may be first up, offered alongside pheasant Scotch egg with black pudding, bacon and an apple and cider dressing, both typically straightforward and uncluttered. A signature dish of roast loin of local lamb and a shepherd's pie of the shoulder, served with Savoy cabbage and rosemary jus, impresses with its superb timing and delicious flavours. Another main course sees sea bass fillets teamed with new potato and horseradish gratin, spinach purée and a dressing of beetroot and clams, and the chef is not afraid to use exotic flavours when he feels the ingredients can take them - soy-infused loin of venison accompanied by Szechuan pepper jus, for instance. Technical skills are abundantly clear, manifestly so in crisp, buttery frangipane pastry for blueberry pie with crème fraîche ice cream.

Chef Steven Titman **Owner** Mrs Bea Tollman **Times** 12-2.30/7-9.30 **Prices** Fixed L 2 course £22, Fixed D 3 course £40, Tasting menu £78-£200, Starter

£17.50-£19, Main £20-£28, Dessert £11-£13, Service optional, Groups min 12 service 12.5% **Wines** 1100 bottles over £20, 15 bottles under £20, 25 by glass **Notes** Tasting menu 8 course available with/out wines, Sunday L, Vegetarian available, Dress restrictions, No shorts, T-shirts or sandals, Jackets pref, Civ Wed 40 **Seats** 60, Pr/dining room 20 **Children** Portions, Menu **Parking** 60

Save on Hotels. Book at **theAA.com/hotel**

DORSET 149 ENGLAND

DORCHESTER
Map 4 SY69

Sienna

◉◉◉ – *see opposite*

EVERSHOT
Map 4 ST50

The Acorn Inn

◉ British 🍷

Modern gastro-pub fare in Hardy country

☎ 01935 83228
28 Fore St DT2 0JW
e-mail: stay@acorn-inn.co.uk
web: www.acorn-inn.co.uk
dir: From A37 between Yeovil & Dorchester, follow
Evershot & Holywell signs, 0.5m to inn

In a pretty village at the heart of Hardy's Wessex, this
16th-century coaching inn is a gem, with a warm and
welcoming bar (low ceiling, open fire, brick walls and its
own snacky menu) and a stylishly cottagey restaurant
with local artwork, antiques and Persian rugs.
Scrupulously sourced ingredients bring on locally-smoked
venison with classic celeriac remoulade, and Dorset
cheddar and walnut soufflé with thyme butter and celery
cream. Main courses cover a range of flavours, from
chicken, mushroom and tarragon pie with spring onion
mash, to a winter hotpot of venison served with
caramelised onions and braised red cabbage. Fish might
appear as pan-fried hake fillet with salsa verde, and
among puddings may be almond tart with a poached
pear and vanilla ice cream.

Chef Christopher Smith **Owner** Red Carnation Hotels
Times 12-2/7-9 **Prices** Starter £4.95-£7.95, Main
£12.40-£19.95, Dessert £2-£6.95, Service optional
Wines 29 bottles over £20, 7 bottles under £20, 8 by
glass **Notes** Sunday L, Vegetarian available **Seats** 45, Pr/
dining room 35 **Children** Portions **Parking** 40

Summer Lodge Country House Hotel, Restaurant & Spa

◉◉◉ – *see opposite*

LYME REGIS
Map 4 SY39

The Mariners

◉ International 🍷

Updated old coaching inn with consistently interesting food

☎ 01297 442753
Silver St DT7 3HS
e-mail: enquiries@hotellymeregis.co.uk
dir: S onto B3261 from A35, on left opposite right turn to
the Cobb

Dating from the 17th century, this low-slung pink former
coaching inn has been made over, its restaurant now a
neat room with a wooden floor, wall lights and wooden
tables. Local seafood turns up among starters, perhaps
roast scallops with celeriac purée and rocket; otherwise
there may be smoked duck salad with onion relish and a
balsamic reduction. Vegetables and sauces are well-
considered additions to the central element of main
courses, so roast hake fillet comes with spinach and
potato curry, cucumber crème fraîche and parsley oil, and
chargrilled medallions of beef fillet with truffled mash,
baby vegetables and port jus. Puddings are not
neglected, among them perhaps plum and apple crumble
with custard and vanilla ice cream.

Chef Richard Reddaway, Steve Rainey **Owner** Jerry
Ramsdale **Times** 12-2/6.30-9 Closed D 25 Dec
Prices Fixed L 2 course £12-£18.95, Fixed D 3 course
£24.95-£29.95, Starter £4.95-£7.95, Main £11.95-
£24.95, Dessert £5-£13.50 **Wines** 25 bottles over £20,
19 bottles under £20, 7 by glass **Notes** Sunday L,
Vegetarian available **Seats** 36 **Children** Portions, Menu
Parking 20

MAIDEN NEWTON
Map 4 SY59

Le Petit Canard

◉ Modern British, French

Honest, accomplished cooking in pretty village restaurant

☎ 01300 320536
Dorchester Rd DT2 0BE
e-mail: craigs@le-petit-canard.co.uk
web: www.le-petit-canard.co.uk
dir: In centre of Maiden Newton, 8m W of Dorchester

Gerry and Cathy Craig's homely cottage restaurant has a
loyal following of local gastronomes, and its name not
only sums up the proportions and wholesome appeal of
the place, but also spotlights the cross-Channel
undercurrent that runs through the cooking. Inside, its
350 years are revealed in ancient low beams and exposed
stone walls, and a soothing pastel colour scheme feeds
into the traditional cosiness of the ambience. Cathy is an
ever-smiling presence out front, while back in the
kitchen, Gerry takes regional ingredients as his building
blocks and handles them with sensitivity in modern
Anglo-French ideas spiked here and there with more
exotic influences. Dorset crab risotto with spring onions,
parmesan and coriander is always a good bet, and might
be followed by slow-roasted pork belly with crackling and
cider gravy. End with dark chocolate and Amaretto
mousse torte.

Chef Gerry Craig **Owner** Mr & Mrs G Craig **Times** 12-2/7-9
Closed Mon, L all week (ex 1st & 3rd Sun in month), D
Sun **Prices** Fixed D 3 course £33-£36, Service optional
Wines 21 bottles over £20, 10 bottles under £20, 6 by
glass **Notes** Vegetarian available, Dress restrictions,
Smart casual preferred **Seats** 28 **Parking** On street/
village car park

POOLE

Map 4 SZ09

Harbour Heights

◎◎ Modern British ☝

Modern bistro with unbeatable harbour views

☎ 01202 707272
73 Haven Rd, Sandbanks BH13 7LW
e-mail: enquiries@harbourheights.net
web: www.fjbhotels.co.uk
dir: From A338 follow signs to Sandbanks, restaurant on left past Canford Cliffs

An art deco cracker built in the 1920's with widescreen views over Poole Harbour, Brownsea Island and the Purbecks from its hilltop perch, the Harbour Heights has a Riviera flavour. The expansive teak-decked alfresco terrace is the place to take it all in when the sun shines, but a 21st-century boutique facelift (this is Sandbanks after all) makes the glossy open-plan bistro an equally inviting prospect when the weather forces you to enjoy the vista through its sweep of floor-to-ceiling picture windows. The menu is peppered with enticing seasonal ideas built with top-quality local ingredients - check out the fresh fish counter, laden with the day's catch from Poole Quay to tease those taste buds, then start with seared scallops teamed, perhaps, with Jerusalem artichoke purée and black truffle. Next up, there could be baked skate wing with clams, home-made saffron linguine, brown butter, herb and black olive sauce, and awaiting at the end, something like hot chocolate praline fondant with griottines and Frangelico jelly, and white chocolate ice cream.

Chef Clyde Hollett **Owner** FJB Hotels
Times 12-2.30/7-9.30 **Prices** Starter £6.50-£13, Main £14-£45, Dessert £6-£10, Service optional
Wines 113 bottles over £20, 6 bottles under £20, 11 by glass **Notes** Chef's table, Sunday L, Vegetarian available, Dress restrictions, Smart casual **Seats** 90, Pr/dining room 100 **Children** Portions, Menu **Parking** 50

The Haven

◎◎ Modern British V ☝

Delightful Poole Bay views and confident modern cooking

☎ 01202 707333
161 Banks Rd, Sandbanks BH13 7QL
e-mail: reservations@havenhotel.co.uk
web: www.havenhotel.co.uk
dir: Follow signs to Sandbanks Peninsula; hotel next to Swanage ferry departure point

On sunny days, with views across the waves and waterborne action from tables on the terrace of the water's-edge La Roche restaurant, there's a real touch of the Riviera. The stylish art-deco era hotel itself - once the home of radio pioneer Guglielmo Marconi - sits at the southernmost tip of the Sandbanks strip and overlooks the sweep of Poole Bay. Inside, the brasserie-style restaurant's tiered tables make the best of the views too, while two large fish tanks continue the watery theme. Likewise, the sharp, French-influenced menu makes the most of the local larder, especially (given the location) sea-fresh locally-landed fish and shellfish. Pan-fried cod fillet might be served with cod cakes, brandade and a mussel sauce, South Coast native lobster is grilled or served thermidor-style, or for meat-lovers, perhaps rump of lamb with fondant potato, ratatouille and shallot purée. Finish with baked vanilla cheesecake with textures of apple and blackberries.

Chef Jason Hornbuckle **Owner** Mr J Butterworth
Times 12-2.30/7-9.30 **Prices** Fixed L 2 course fr £22.50, Fixed D 3 course fr £29.50, Starter £8.25-£12.95, Main £25.25-£28.95, Dessert £9.50-£12.95, Service optional
Wines 67 bottles over £20, 5 bottles under £20, 11 by glass **Notes** Sunday L, Vegetarian menu, Dress restrictions, No shorts or beach wear, Civ Wed 99 **Seats** 80, Pr/dining room 156 **Children** Portions, Menu **Parking** 90

Hotel du Vin Poole

◎ Modern British, French

Bistro cooking in an elegant Georgian house

☎ 01202 685666
Mansion House, Thames St BH15 1JN
dir: A350 into town centre follow signs to Channel Ferry/ Poole Quay, left at bridge, 1st left is Thames St

Another location, another special building for the boutique hotel chain. Formerly the Mansion House off the Old Quay, it's a lovely Virginia-creeper-clad Georgian house with smart bar, wine cellar and wine-tasting room, plus the trademark open-plan bistro. Like the others, it's an informal place to eat with plenty for oenophiles to admire in the décor and get stuck into on the impressive, French-orientated wine list. A dining terrace is a big attraction in the warmer months. The cooking is mostly French, classic bistro-style, featuring plenty of excellent regional produce. Salad of sliced Dorset veal, for example, could be the place to start before chicken Dijonnaise, or pan-fried fillet of sea bass and tiger prawns provençale.

Times 12.30-2/6-10

The Rising Sun

◎◎ Traditional & Modern British

Skilful cooking in popular gastro-pub

☎ 01202 771246 & 01202 471858
1 Dear Hay Ln BH15 1NZ
e-mail: paul@risingsunpoole.co.uk
dir: From A349, take A350 signed Poole

More gastro than pub, The Rising Sun delivers a winning formula, where a modish lounge-bar decked out with tub chairs, sofas and black leather banquettes and wooden tables, is joined by a more intimate restaurant with real fires and carpeted neatness. And there's a sunny-day patio too. Though laid-back it may be, The Rising Sun takes its food seriously, with an accomplished kitchen giving classic gastro-pub food a modern spin conjured from top-notch local produce. Thus roasted fillet of cod is teamed with baked crushed new potatoes and a micro salad of semi-dried tomatoes, broad beans and sakura cresses and courgette crisps, while a surf and turf option, such as slow-roast belly of pork, might arrive with sautéed shell-on langoustines, garlic and rosemary rösti, wild mushroom and rocket salad, and apple purée. From the grill comes steak with all the trimmings.

Chef Phil Etheridge **Owner** Dick Goemaat
Times 12-2.30/6-9.30 Closed 25-26 Dec, 1 Jan, Sun
Prices Fixed L 2 course £12.95, Fixed D 3 course £17.95, Starter £4.95-£9.95, Main £11.50-£25, Dessert £5-£6.50, Service optional, Groups min 8 service 10%
Wines 15 bottles over £20, 16 bottles under £20, 14 by glass **Notes** Fixed L not always available please check, Vegetarian available, Dress restrictions, Smart casual **Seats** 65, Pr/dining room 15 **Children** Portions **Parking** Car park opposite

Save on Hotels. Book at **theAA.com/hotel**

DORSET 151 **ENGLAND**

The Sandbanks

Mediterranean, European

Unfussy bistro dishes with bracing marine views

☎ 01202 707377 & 709884
15 Banks Rd, Sandbanks BH13 7PS
e-mail: reservations@sandbankshotel.co.uk
web: www.fjbhotels.co.uk
dir: From Poole or Bournemouth, follow signs to
Sandbanks Peninsula. Hotel on left along peninsula

Seven miles of Blue Flag beach on the doorstep and
splendid views across Poole Bay mean that this upscale
seaside hotel will always be a magnet for summer's day
dining, particularly when alfresco eating on the
beachfront terrace is on the cards. Whether you're indoors
in the relaxed octagonal brasserie, or out on the terrace,
there's a real jet-set Riviera buzz to the place and a
simple menu of appropriately contemporary
Mediterranean-accented dishes. You might get going
with in-house-smoked and marinated salmon with crab,
brown shrimp, prawns and lemongrass dressing, then
proceed to rump of local lamb with seasonal vegetables
and gratin dauphinoise, and wind proceedings up with
chocolate crème brûlée with almond biscuits.

Times 12-3/6-10 Closed Mon-Tue, D Sun

The Bluefish Restaurant

Modern

Well-judged cooking next to Chesil Beach

☎ 01305 822991
15-17a Chiswell DT5 1AN
e-mail: thebluefish@tesco.net
dir: Take A354 by Chesil Bank, off Victoria Square in
Portland, over rdbt towards Chesil Beach, next to 72hr
free car park

On the Isle of Portland, next to Chesil Beach, The Bluefish
is an easygoing, relaxed and child-friendly restaurant
with stone walls and a mishmash of chairs at plain
wooden tables, with popular outdoor seating under
parasols. It's the sort of place that people return to again
and again, drawn by the atmosphere and the quality of
the cooking. The Anglo-European, modern menu might
kick off with split-pea and ham soup with a duck egg and
go on to beef broth with pasta and vegetables. Fish and
shellfish are expertly cooked, turning up in palate-
pleasing combinations: perhaps pan-fried local scallops
with sweetcorn purée, black pudding and orange butter,
followed by sea bass fillet poached in olive oil with
Serrano ham, faggots, beetroot and port sauce. Desserts
are no less appealing, from lemon posset with berries to
chocolate fondant with poached cherries and lemon curd.

Chef Luciano Da Silva **Owner** Jo Da Silva **Times** 12-3/7-9
Closed Xmas, Mon-Tue, L Wed-Fri, D Sun (in winter)
Prices Fixed L 2 course £11.50, Starter £6.95-£12.50,
Main £14.50-£19.50, Dessert £6.95, Service added but

optional 10%, Groups min 8 service 10% **Wines** 2 bottles
over £20, 12 bottles under £20, 9 by glass **Notes** Sunday
L, Vegetarian available **Seats** 45 **Children** Portions
Parking 72-hr free car park

Three Horseshoes Inn

British **NEW**

Proper pub, proper pub food

☎ 01308 485328
DT6 3TF
e-mail: threehorseshoespowerstock@live.co.uk
dir: 3m from Bridport. Powerstock signed off A3066
Bridport to Beaminster

You wouldn't normally go out of your way for Scotch eggs
and burgers, but this classic Dorset village inn has
elevated pubby classics to a higher plane - that burger
being made of Dorset veal and bone marrow, and teamed
with barbecue pulled short rib, celeriac slaw and triple-
cooked chips. But first, serpentine, skinny lanes have to
be negotiated before you arrive to a warm greeting and a
fine pint of Palmers ale in the convivial bar - take a table
here if you prefer the cheerful country pub vibe, or move
through to the cosy restaurant decorated with works (for
sale) by local artists, or on fine days, head outside for
valley views from the terrace and lovely garden. The
kitchen is driven by an enthusiasm for local produce and
working with the seasons, and lines up a cast of ideas
we'd all like to see in our local: wild boar Scotch egg (a
quail's egg, that is) with a venison sausage roll, crispy
pig's ears and pickles is a starter that should be on every
pub's menu, while mains bring on a proper pub pie - a
deep, pastry-topped dish of beef chunks in a rich sauce
of Guinness and oysters, served with clotted cream mash,
and honey-roasted parsnips and carrots.

Chef Karl Bashford **Owner** Mr K Bashford, Ms Prekopova
Times 12-2.30/6.30-9.30 Closed L Mon **Prices** Starter
£6-£9, Main £10-£20, Dessert £8, Service optional
Wines 3 bottles over £20, 10 bottles under £20, 8 by
glass **Notes** Sunday L, Vegetarian available **Seats** 60
Children Portions, Menu **Parking** 20

Best Western Royal Chase Hotel

Modern British

Nicely unfussy cooking in Thomas Hardy country

☎ 01747 853355
Salisbury Rd SP7 8DB
e-mail: reception@theroyalchasehotel.co.uk
web: www.theroyalchasehotel.co.uk
dir: Close to rdbt junct with A350 & A30 (avoid town
centre)

Formerly a 17th-century monastery, the Best Western
Royal Chase is housed in beautiful tree-lined grounds
close to the centre of Shaftesbury. Its tucked-away
location adds a soothing sense of calm, and the friendly
local service team don't burst the bubble. In the Byzant
restaurant, the kitchen turns out unfussy dishes such as
forestière terrine with home-made chutney, Dorset
leaves and home-baked bread, followed perhaps by the likes of
pan-fried fillet of sea bass with dauphinoise potatoes,
shellfish bisque and samphire, and for dessert, chocolate
cheesecake with pistachio ice cream. If you've got the
kids in tow, check out their special menu in the family-
orientated country bar.

Chef Stephen Bant **Owner** Travel West Inns
Times 12-2/7-9.30 **Prices** Starter £4.25-£7.95, Main
£7.50-£15.95, Dessert £4.95-£5.50, Service optional
Wines 8 bottles over £20, 11 bottles under £20, 6 by
glass **Notes** Sunday L, Vegetarian available, Civ Wed 70
Seats 49, Pr/dining room 150 **Children** Portions, Menu
Parking 101

SHAFTESBURY *continued*

La Fleur de Lys Restaurant with Rooms

◉◉ Modern French

Former girls' school turned smart restaurant with rooms

☎ 01747 853717
Bleke St SP7 8AW
e-mail: info@lafleurdelys.co.uk
web: www.lafleurdelys.co.uk
dir: Junct A350/A30

With over twenty years under their belt, the owners of this welcoming restaurant with rooms in the heart of Shaftesbury have evolved a polished act that keeps the loyal regulars knocking at their door. The feel inside is homely and traditional - there's a comfy lounge with squidgy sofas to sink into for a pre-dinner drink, and the dining room is a plushly kitted-out space with linen-clothed tables and smart glassware and cutlery. As the name may hint, modern French cooking is the deal here, based on top-class local supplies brought together in confident, ambitious combinations starting, typically, along the lines of pan-fried breast of quail and duck liver with celeriac purée, and asparagus tips in truffle sauce. Main courses run to grilled Dover sole with langoustines, baby leeks, and light caviar sauce, or roast breast of Creedy Carver duck with broad beans, spring onions and passionfruit sauce. Finally, hot lime soufflé might arrive with dark chocolate ice cream and lime sauce.

Times 12-2.30/7-10.30 Closed 3 wks Jan, L Mon-Tue, D Sun

The Grange at Oborne

◉◉ Modern British ♨

Pleasing contemporary ideas in a rural setting

☎ 01935 813463
Oborne DT9 4LA
e-mail: reception@thegrange.co.uk
dir: From A30 turn left at sign & follow road through village to hotel

This 200-year-old manor built of Purbeck stone in a tiny hamlet near Sherborne does brisk business as a country-house hotel with a nice line in weddings these days. The romantic candlelit restaurant seems tailor-made for such occasions, as it looks through graceful Georgian windows over a fountain and gardens which are floodlit at night.

The kitchen goes in for a modernised style of country cooking perfectly in keeping with the surroundings, with the boxes ticked for seasonality and regional sourcing. Start with venison terrine, its gamey richness tamed by kumquat jam, then follow with fillet of beef served with a cottage pie, roasted banana shallot purée, glazed carrots and truffle jus. Desserts end on a high with a fresh apricot and almond tarte Tatin balanced by a zesty peach and mango sorbet.

Chef Nick Holt **Owner** Mr & Mrs K E Mathews
Times 12-1.30/7-9 **Prices** Fixed L 2 course fr £21, Fixed D 3 course fr £35, Service optional **Wines** 31 bottles over £20, 13 bottles under £20, 7 by glass **Notes** Sunday L, Vegetarian available, Dress restrictions, Smart casual, Civ Wed 120 **Seats** 30, Pr/dining room 120 **Children** Portions, Menu **Parking** 50

The Green

◉◉ Modern British ♨

Period building serving up stylish modern cooking

☎ 01935 813821
3 The Green DT9 3HY
e-mail: info@greenrestaurant.co.uk
dir: A30 towards Milborne Port, at top of Greenhill turn right at mini rdbt. Restaurant located on the left

There's not actually a green here anymore, but let's not quibble - the reason to come to this inviting stone-built Grade II listed building is to sample its straightforward yet intelligent modern cooking. Inside it is a buzzy little venue, bursting with character thanks to heavy beams, wooden floors and antique wooden tables and chairs, and service is genial and unfussy. A dedication to local produce is trumpeted in the '30-mile radius' menu, so you can expect that what leaves the kitchen is a celebration of the local hills and coast, starting with a corker of a soup - cappuccino of celeriac with shredded curly kale and Dorset partridge breast. Next up, local lamb is casseroled with a rich red wine and rosemary sauce and served simply with mustard mash and cabbage. Pudding presses seasonal fruits into service as a trio of tastes and textures - blackberry ice cream, damson jelly and elderberry pannacotta.

Chef Michael Rust **Owner** Michael & Judith Rust
Times 12-2/7-9 Closed Sun-Mon **Prices** Starter £5-£7.25, Main £9.50-£17.50, Dessert £6.95, Service optional, Groups min 8 service 10% **Wines** 30 bottles over £20, 12 bottles under £20, 10 by glass **Notes** Tasting menu 8 course available, Vegetarian available **Seats** 40, Pr/dining room 30 **Parking** On street, car park

The Greyhound Inn

◉ British **NEW**

Popular village inn with good, unfussy cooking

☎ 01300 341303
26 High St DT2 9PD
e-mail: info@dorsetgreyhound.co.uk

This relaxed 17th-century inn is still a proper boozer with hand-pulled real ales, but good wines and contemporary cooking are equally part of the equation these days. The Greyhound lies in a postcard-pretty Dorset village in verdant Thomas Hardy country, and its easy-on-the-eye good looks take in a flagstoned bar buzzing with convivial banter, exposed stone and brick walls, and a glassed over well where coachmen once hauled water for their horses. The kitchen keeps things simple, leaving the quality of top-notch local materials to do the talking. Seafood fresh from the Dorset coast has the opening shout - Weymouth squid sliced and sautéed with spicy chorizo, shallots and lemon. Main course could be as forthright as a local rib-eye steak with hand-cut chips, field mushrooms and béarnaise sauce, or fish fans could go for wild sea bass tempura with pea purée, chips and sauce gribiche. Honey and ginger cheesecake with vanilla ice cream keeps things squarely in the comfort zone.

Chef Lou Jones **Owner** Martin Frizell **Times** 12-2/6.30-9 Closed D Sun **Prices** Food prices not confirmed for 2013. Please telephone for details **Wines** 11 bottles over £20, 23 bottles under £20 **Notes** Sunday L, Vegetarian available **Seats** 60, Pr/dining room 30 **Children** Portions, Menu **Parking** 20

Kemps Country House

◉ Traditional, International

Simple but effective cooking in a Dorset country house

☎ 0845 8620315 & 01929 462563
East Stoke BH20 6AL
e-mail: info@kempscountryhouse.co.uk
dir: A352 between Wareham & Wool

Kemps is a commodious country house in a south-facing position looking over the Frome Valley towards the Purbeck Hills, a particularly picturesque slice of Dorset (and handy for the local Monkey World, primate-fans). The prettily decorated white dining room with its net curtained ceiling makes a relaxing venue for the brasserie-style cooking the place trades in. Start with a painstakingly constructed parcel of duck confit in filo pastry with dressed leaves, before considering a shank of local lamb, served with roast honeyed root veg, creamy mash and redcurrant jus, or battered cod with chips and mushy peas. It's simple, but effective, hearty food, concluding perhaps with chocolate and raspberry tart, served with densely rich clotted cream ice cream.

Times 12-3/6.30-9.30

Les Bouviers Restaurant with Rooms

⊛⊛ French ⚑ NOTABLE WINE LIST

Francophile cooking in an elegant restaurant with rooms

☎ 01202 889555
Arrowsmith Rd, Canford Magna BH21 3BD
e-mail: info@lesbouviers.co.uk
dir: 1.5m S of Wimborne on A349, turn left onto A341. In 1m turn right into Arrowsmith Rd. 300yds, 2nd property on right

James Coward is now confidently embarked on a third decade running Les Bouviers, which moved to its current site a few years ago, offering half-a-dozen guest rooms as well as a smartly appointed restaurant in shades of red and gold. The feel of being invited to dine in a private home results in a particularly congenial atmosphere, but the culinary standards are some way above the domestic, not least in the breadth of choice. France is the premier amour, as is evident in classic bouillabaisse with garlic rouille to start, with breast of guinea fowl and foie gras-stuffed ballottine on braised red cabbage following on. Other influences are woven carefully into the mix too, though, perhaps for a starter of smoked haddock and butternut squash risotto with truffle oil, or peppered monkfish with pickled veg, chillied peppers and pimento oil. A host of signature desserts awaits for the grand finale, including mango, apricot and thyme crème brûlée with Earl Grey granité, or the classic lemon tart with saffron ice cream.

Chef James Coward **Owner** James & Kate Coward **Times** 12-2.15/7-9.30 Closed D Sun **Prices** Fixed L 2 course £16.95-£18.95, Fixed D 3 course £31.95-£33.95, Tasting menu £53-£68, Service optional, Groups min 7 service 10% **Wines** 100+ bottles over £20, 100+ bottles under £20, 24 by glass **Notes** ALC 2 course £39, Tasting menu 7 course with/without wine, Sunday L, Vegetarian available, Dress restrictions, No ripped jeans or shorts, Civ Wed 120 **Seats** 50, Pr/dining room 120 **Children** Portions, Menu **Parking** 50

Number 9

⊛⊛ Modern British **NEW** ✍

Bags of charm and well-sourced produce close to the theatre

☎ 01202 887557
West Borough BH21 1LT
e-mail: no9wimborne@aol.com
dir: 150 yds from The Square before Tivoli Theatre, on West Borough

Just off the market square and a couple of doors down from the town's Tivoli Theatre, Number 9 occupies a Grade II listed building full of charm and character. It looks inviting with its natural, neutral colour scheme both inside and out, and its side terrace for alfresco drinks and dining when the weather allows (there's also a small walled garden at the back), and you can stop off for tea and home-made cake, coffee and morning pastries, a

light snack or a full-blown meal. Lunchtime brings forth the likes of steamed Cornish rope-grown mussels in a white wine, garlic and cream sauce with fries, spot-on fish and chips, and hot- and cold-smoked salmon, artichoke and chicory tagliatelle. In the evenings, chef Greg Etheridge cranks things up a notch or two, turning out the likes of braised shin of beef sausage roll to start, followed by baked fillet of trout and clams with Parmentier potatoes, English asparagus, dandelion leaf, pea tops, pea crème fraîche and crisp wild garlic. The menu changes with the seasons, March, for example, bringing forth a dessert of poached rhubarb and custard millefeuille.

Chef Greg Etheridge **Owner** Roy & Linda Tazzyman **Times** 12-2.30/6-9.30 Closed Xmas, BH Mon, D Mon **Prices** Fixed D 3 course £25-£30, Starter £5.95-£9.95, Main £12.95-£21.95, Dessert £5.95-£8.50, Service optional, Groups min 8 service 10% **Wines** 9 by glass **Notes** Pre-theatre menu available, Vegetarian available **Seats** 50 **Children** Portions, Menu **Parking** On street

Crab House Café

⊛ British, Seafood

The freshest seafood in a laid-back beach hut

☎ 01305 788867
Ferrymans Way, Portland Rd DT4 9YU
e-mail: info@crabhousecafe.co.uk
web: www.crabhousecafe.co.uk
dir: A354 along Westwey once onto Portland Rd continue for just under a mile, at rdbt take 2nd exit for restaurant

Take a seat under a frilly pink parasol outside the beachcomber-style wooden shack and gaze across Chesil Beach to the Portland oyster beds, and you know you're in for a treat. The vibe is totally relaxed - it needs to be when you're about to get down and dirty with bib, hammer and claw crackers to attack super-fresh crabs and shellfish. What's on the menu changes twice a day, driven by whatever the local boats have brought in. It's all kept simple and unpretentious, with starters such as Singapore-style squid and mussels steamed in white wine, garlic, lemon and thyme cream. For mains, the piscine pleasures might run from steamed turbot steak with curried sweet potato and chick peas, to red mullet with cumin seeds, coriander and fresh pineapple salsa, or a whole roasted sea bass with lemon, thyme and rosemary.

Crab House Café

Chef Nigel Bloxham, Adam Foster **Owner** Nigel Bloxham **Times** 12-2/6-9 Closed mid Dec-Jan, Mon-Tue (except 8 wks in summer), D Sun (Oct-Apr) **Prices** Starter £3.95-£12, Main £11.95, Dessert £3.95-£9.90, Service optional, Groups min 8 service 8% **Wines** 36 bottles over £20, 20 bottles under £20, 16 by glass **Notes** Sunday L, Vegetarian available **Seats** 40 **Children** Portions **Parking** 40

CO DURHAM

The Morritt Arms Hotel

⊛ British, International **NEW**

Historic country house with flavoursome cooking

☎ 01833 627232
Greta Bridge DL12 9SE
e-mail: relax@themorritt.co.uk
dir: 3m S of Barnard Castle off A66. 9m W of Scotch Corner from A1 (Darlington)

Named after a local artist, Major Morritt, whose paintings hang in the hotel, this 18th-century coaching inn turned country-house hotel has a long history of feeding travellers well before sending them on their way. Nowadays, the restaurant's dark oak panelling and herringbone parquet floors have been jollied up with a gently contemporary look involving lively artwork, silk window blinds and moody lighting; it all adds up to an amenable setting for good French-inspired cooking that straddles the border between the classics and more modern ideas. Pan-fried mackerel is pointed up with rhubarb, toasted seeds and pea purée, and there's plenty of generosity and flavour in a main course of braised lamb neck fillet with sweet potato, wild mushrooms, and butternut squash purée. Dessert ends on a high note with a rich dark chocolate tart with white chocolate ice cream and an espresso shot poured affogato-style on top.

Chef Lee Stainthorpe **Owner** B A Johnson & P J Phillips **Times** 12-3/6-9 **Prices** Fixed L 3 course £18, Starter £5-£8, Main £14-£20, Dessert £6-£8, Service optional **Wines** 85 bottles over £20, 18 bottles under £20, 18 by glass **Notes** Fixed L Sun only, Sunday L, Vegetarian available, Dress restrictions, Smart, No shorts, T-shirts, flip flops, Civ Wed 200 **Seats** 60, Pr/dining room 24 **Children** Portions, Menu **Parking** 30

BILLINGHAM

Map 19 NZ42

Wynyard Hall Hotel

◉◉ Modern British V ✋

Boldly original cooking in a palatial Victorian hall

☎ 01740 644811
Wynyard Village TS22 5NF
e-mail: enq@wynyardhall.co.uk
dir: A19 onto A1027 towards Stockton. At rdbt 3rd exit B1274 (Junction Rd). At next rdbt 3rd exit onto A177 (Durham Rd). Right onto Wynyard Rd signed Wolviston. Left into estate at gatehouse

If you're expecting a modest little manor house, think again. Wynyard is halfway to Versailles in scale, a colossal Victorian pile that shouts opulence from the golden gates through which you enter to the gilded interiors, with their glass-fronted display cases, fabulous oil portraits and the jaw-droppingly lavish dining room, where some tables have sofa seating. In such surroundings, the food can struggle to make an impression, but Alan O'Kane is no shrinking violet, and cooks to a boldly original template. Openers on the fixed-price dinner menus take in trout mi-cuit in celery and apple velouté, and a pairing of scallops and smoked duck with baby artichoke and carrot barigoule, before the main dishes up the ante. An Indian approach lends curry-spiced sea bass its distinctiveness, coming as it does with a cauliflower bhaji, golden sultanas and cumin velouté, with Israeli couscous to set the compass dial spinning, or there may be saddle of local lamb with cannelloni of potato and Brillat-Savarin. Variations of chocolate and mint allow pâtisserie skills to take wing, although a slice of vanilla cheesecake is rather outshouted by its high-octane pineapple sorbet.

Chef Alan O'Kane **Owner** Allison Antonopoulos
Times 12-3/7-9.30 **Prices** Fixed L 3 course £19-£25, Fixed D 3 course £23-£55, Service optional
Wines 68 bottles over £20, 5 bottles under £20, 10 by glass **Notes** Sunday L, Vegetarian menu, Dress restrictions, Smart casual, Civ Wed 250 **Seats** 80, Pr/dining room 30 **Children** Portions, Menu **Parking** 200

DARLINGTON

Map 19 NZ21

Best Western Walworth Castle Hotel

◉ Modern British

Contemporary cooking in 12th-century castle hotel

☎ 01325 485470
Walworth DL2 2LY
e-mail: enquiries@walworthcastle.co.uk
dir: A1 junct 58, follow A68 Corbridge for 1m. At rdbt keep left for 1m

There's always a sense of occasion when you get to dine in an authentic castle, and Walworth Castle is the real deal, a 12th-century fortress in 18 acres of lawned gardens and woodlands in the Tees Valley. But if you're expecting the full medieval banqueting schtick, think again: Hansard's restaurant has been stylishly refurbished to the extent that you have to look hard to spot any traces of the 16th-century room's origins amid the unclothed darkwood tables and slatted, high-backed wooden chairs, burnished hardwood floors and designer wallpapers. The kitchen has also evolved from the roast beef of Old England (although this classic is actually served here with Yorkshire pudding, pink peppercorn potatoes and glazed turnips) and delivers a repertoire of unchallenging contemporary ideas. The menu name-checks local suppliers, and might begin with Whitby crab cakes with tartare sauce, followed by roast belly pork with Bramley apple compôte, sage potato meat loaf, and buttered cabbage.

Times 6-9.30

Headlam Hall

◉ British, French ✋

Country mansion with contemporary menu

☎ 01325 730238
Headlam, Gainford DL2 3HA
e-mail: admin@headlamhall.co.uk
dir: 8m W of Darlington off A67

Dating from the 17th century, Headlam Hall is an upmarket manor house hotel with a ritzy spa grafted seamlessly on to keep 21st-century sybarites happy. The views from the grand old house are of rolling countryside and the grounds are extensive enough to encompass a nine-hole golf course. When it comes to dining, the space is split between the more traditional country-house feel of the elegant Panelled Room, and the more contemporary Orangery. The kitchen allies sound technique with thorough use of local produce in its European-accented menus. A pressed terrine of ham hock, parsley, sage and hazelnuts comes well-presented with apple purée and toasted brioche, ahead of seared fillet of sea bass with sautéed new potatoes, wilted spinach, peas, prawns and lemon butter. In honour of the season, there's cherry pannacotta with summer fruits and home-made shortbread to finish.

Chef David Hunter **Owner** J H Robinson
Times 12-2.30/7-9.30 Closed 25-26 Dec **Prices** Food prices not confirmed for 2013. Please telephone for details **Wines** 35 bottles over £20, 20 bottles under £20, 10 by glass **Notes** Vegetarian available, Dress restrictions, Smart casual, no shorts or T-shirts, Civ Wed 120 **Seats** 70, Pr/dining room 30 **Children** Portions, Menu **Parking** 80

Kenny Atkinson at The Orangery

◉◉◉ – see opposite

See advert below

Save on Hotels. Book at **theAA.com/hotel**

CO DURHAM 155 ENGLAND

Kenny Atkinson at The Orangery

Modern British **V** 🍴

Stellar cooking in a unique setting

☎ 01325 729999
**Rockliffe Hall, Rockliffe Park,
Hurworth-on-Tees DL2 2DU**
web: www.rockliffehall.com
dir: A1(M) junct 57, A66 (M), A66
towards Darlington, A167, through
Hurworth-on-Tees. In Croft-on-Tees left
into Hurworth Rd, follow signs

Built for the Backhouse family, co-
founders of Barclays Bank, Rockliffe
Hall is an impressively triple-gabled
mansion surrounded by parkland in a
curve of the River Tees, its Orangery
originally used for cultivating trees and
shrubs that can still be seen in the
grounds. Nowadays it's an imposing
space with wrought-iron pillars, painted
gold, supporting a glass roof, a superb
room in which to savour Kenny
Atkinson's refined modern British
cooking. The three set menus (plus the
same number for vegetarians) have to
be ordered by the whole table, so no
squabbling please. Once rapprochement
is reached, diners are in for quite a
culinary experience. Start with the
clean-tasting flavours of accurately
cooked mackerel fillets with
gooseberries, lemon and mustard, or
crab risotto with sautéed scallops and
asparagus, and go on to a superbly
composed dish of braised and pressed

pig's head accompanied by sautéed
langoustines, smoked eel beignets and
sharply hot apple and horseradish.
Ingredients from the top end of the
quality spectrum are the norm - wild
North Sea turbot with sautéed veal
sweetbreads and truffle, accompanied
by baby leeks and Jerusalem artichoke
risotto, for instance - but lesser cuts
can move a dish up to a higher plane:
duck hearts, for example, the star of a
main course of Goosnargh duck leg
confit with purple-sprouting broccoli,
mushrooms and pine nuts. Presentation
is outstanding, seen at its best in
puddings like high-powered dark
chocolate terrine with strawberries and
colourful candied rose petals.

Chef Kenny Atkinson **Owner** Rockliffe
Hall **Times** 6.30-9.30 Closed L all week,
D Sun-Mon **Prices** Tasting menu
£69.50-£85, Service optional **Wines** 385
bottles over £20, 14 by glass
Notes Market menu 3 course £49.50,
Tasting menus 6/7/10 course,
Vegetarian menu, Dress restrictions,
Smart attire, collared shirts/jackets for
men, Civ Wed 100 **Seats** 65, Pr/dining
room 20 **Children** Portions **Parking** 200

DURHAM
Map 19 NZ24

Best Western Honest Lawyer Hotel

Modern European **NEW** V

Something for everybody in a modern city hotel

☎ 0191 378 3780
Croxdale Bridge, Croxdale DH1 3SP
e-mail: enquiries@honestlawyerhotel.com
dir: A1 junct 61

Now there's a name that appears to be tempting us towards a sardonic chuckle. The hotel is a cleanly designed modern corporate hotel, its guest rooms mostly in a separate building round a courtyard, and with a small, low-ceilinged but pleasant restaurant, Bailey's, done in cheering hues of purple and pink. The menu makes a good fist of pleasing everybody, whether you're in the market for modern brasserie cooking, obliging comfort food or global-larder fare. Thai-spiced seared scallops with smoked bacon and mange-tout is a generous portion of garlicky, spicy shellfish. Main courses pack a lot in, as in the ragout of ham, peas and carrots that comes with chicken and black pudding pie, parsley mash and fried quail eggs. Fishcakes of salmon, haddock and crab with lemon mayonnaise and chips offers something simpler. Stimulating contrasts of sweet and bitter are the hallmarks of an orange-chocolate fondant with marmalade ice cream and milk chocolate sauce.

Chef Harry Bailie **Owner** John Sanderson **Times** 11-9.30 **Prices** Starter £4.50-£7.95, Main £12.50-£18.95, Dessert £5-£6, Service included **Notes** Sunday L, Vegetarian menu **Seats** 50, Pr/dining room 30 **Children** Portions, Menu **Parking** 150

Bistro 21

Modern British

Upbeat bistro cooking in a former farmhouse

☎ 0191 384 4354
Aykley Heads House, Aykley Heads DH1 5TS
e-mail: admin@bistrotwentyone.co.uk
dir: Off B6532 from Durham centre, pass County Hall on right & Dryburn Hospital on left. Turn right at double rdbt into Aykley Heads

From the outside, the bistro has a cottagey look, a feeling of rusticity extending inside via stone floors, bare brick walls and low ceilings, although a central atrium adds a more modern touch. There's something reassuringly familiar about the menu, featuring as it does calves' liver with bacon, and a chunk of perfectly timed grilled cod with tartare sauce, chips and crushed peas, although the appeal is broadened by the likes of starters of Asian-style duck breast dressed with honey and mustard served with bean sprouts, and jasmine-cured salmon with watermelon and cucumber, and a main course like chicken breast with Moroccan-style couscous and lemon crème fraîche. Puddings are an enticing slate, from knickerbocker glory to steamed ginger sponge with rhubarb compôte and custard.

Chef Gareth Lambert **Owner** Terence Laybourne **Times** 12-2/6-10.30 Closed 25 Dec, 1 Jan, BHs, Sun **Prices** Fixed L 2 course £15.50, Fixed D 3 course £19.50, Starter £5.50-£11.20, Main £12-£27, Dessert £5.50-£8.20, Service added but optional 10% **Wines** 24 bottles over £20, 10 bottles under £20, 9 by glass **Notes** Early D menu available, Vegetarian available **Seats** 55, Pr/dining room 20 **Children** Portions **Parking** 11

HUTTON MAGNA
Map 19 NZ11

The Oak Tree Inn

Modern British

Confident, creative cooking in a converted village inn

☎ 01833 627371
DL11 7HH
e-mail: claireross67@hotmail.com
dir: 7m W on A66 from Scotch Corner

Locals still prop up the bar at this traditional inn in a quiet little village, but the majority of people come from further afield to dine. It's easy to see what the attractions are: beams and panelled walls, an open fire, and, in the dining room, wooden tables and high-backed leather-look seats on a red carpet, and an informal atmosphere. The menus change according to availability and quality, so roast pheasant may appear in season, accompanied by sticky red cabbage, bacon, apple, and parsnip purée. Ideas are sophisticated and modern, so cheddar and mushroom rarebit comes with roast fillet of beef and crushed new potatoes, and chorizo and steamed mussels with crisp-skinned fillet of sea bass and new potatoes. Starters are no less compelling, among them perhaps beetroot and goats' cheese tart with olives and tomato, while invention doesn't flag in desserts like passionfruit crème brûlée.

Chef Alastair Ross **Owner** Alastair & Claire Ross **Times** 6.30-9.30 Closed 24-27 & 31 Dec, 1-2 Jan, Mon, L all week **Prices** Starter £5.50-£8.50, Main £18.50-£22.50, Dessert £4.50-£6.50, Service optional **Wines** 36 bottles over £20, 13 bottles under £20, 8 by glass **Notes** Vegetarian dishes for children by prior arrangement **Seats** 20, Pr/dining room 20 **Children** Portions **Parking** 3, On street

REDWORTH
Map 19 NZ22

Redworth Hall Hotel

Modern British **NEW**

Fine dining at imposing Jacobean hotel

☎ 01388 770600
DL5 6NL
dir: From A1(M) junct 58 take A68 towards Corbridge. At 1st rdbt take A6072 towards Bishop Auckland. At next rdbt take 2nd exit (A6072). Hotel on left

Surrounded by 150 acres of woodland, Redworth Hall was built on a palatial scale in 1693. Sympathetic modernisation has retained some original features, such as the magnificent baronial hall and an ornate spiral stone staircase, while Restaurant 1744 is a spacious room with nicely upholstered chairs, a large fireplace and friendly staff. The enterprising menu may open with crispy oriental duck salad with sesame and hoisin dressing, but the choice is generally more Euro-centric, running from gravad lax with beetroot and orange salad to braised belly pork with thyme jus, parsnip purée and rösti, or baked cod in a tapenade crust with mussel and tomato linguine. Grilled steaks are popular, served with a straightforward sauce, and to finish might come the exotic flavours of coconut pannacotta with mango, ginger and chilli sorbet.

Chef Richard Chilver **Times** 12-2/6.30-9.30 Closed 25 Dec **Prices** Starter £5-£7, Main £18.50-£23, Dessert £5-£9, Service optional **Wines** 46 bottles over £20, 6 bottles under £20, 13 by glass **Notes** Sunday L, Vegetarian available, Civ Wed 200 **Seats** 140, Pr/dining room 20 **Children** Portions, Menu **Parking** 150

ROMALDKIRK
Map 19 NY92

Rose & Crown Hotel

Traditional British

Seasonal cooking in a traditional rural setting

☎ 01833 650213
DL12 9EB
e-mail: hotel@rose-and-crown.co.uk
web: www.rose-and-crown.co.uk
dir: 6m NW of Barnard Castle on B6277

Rubbing shoulders with a doughty Saxon church known as the Cathedral of the Dale, and bracketed by three village greens, the stone-built 18th-century Rose & Crown is a haven of sybaritic pleasures among the fells and meadows of remote Teesdale. Chris and Alison Davy nailed their names above the door over two decades ago and have things sorted to a T: there's fine hand-pulled ale to quaff by the crackling log fire in the bar, and a rather classy oak-panelled and candlelit dining room, where Chris Davy's four-course dinner menus are built on local, seasonal produce and inspired by neatly-dovetailed classic and contemporary trends. Smoked wood pigeon with chicory and hazelnut salad and red wine dressing shows the style, then comes soup - cauliflower and smoked cheese, perhaps - before a main course showcasing pork in the shape of roast fillet, confit belly, and black pudding with root vegetable mash, stick beans, diced potatoes and bone jus. North Country cheeses or something sticky such as warm apricot and ginger pudding with vanilla ice cream close the show.

Chef Chris Davy, Andrew Lee **Owner** Mr & Mrs C Davy **Times** 12-1.30/7.30-9 Closed Xmas, L Mon-Sat **Prices** Fixed L 3 course £21.95, Fixed D 4 course £35-£42, Service optional **Wines** 46 bottles over £20, 20 bottles under £20, 14 by glass **Notes** Sunday L, Vegetarian available **Seats** 24 **Children** Portions **Parking** 24

Save on Hotels. Book at **theAA.com/hotel**

CO DURHAM – ESSEX 157 ENGLAND

SEDGEFIELD   Map 19 NZ32

Best Western Hardwick Hall Hotel

◉ Modern British **V**

Bistro-style restaurant in parkland hotel

☎ 01740 620253
TS21 2EH
e-mail: info@hardwickhallhotel.co.uk
dir: Off A1(M) junct 60 towards Sedgefield, left at 1st
rdbt, hotel 400mtrs on left

Hardwick Hall, just off the A1(M) but within a country
park, has at its heart an 18th-century property built by a
wealthy businessman, but renovations and extensions
have turned it into a top-end hotel. The Rib Room,
downstairs, is the main dining venue, full of nooks and
crannies and leather-look seating. It concentrates on
steaks, on view in a meat locker, ranging from six-ounce
fillet ('perfect for a lady', they say) to massive 20-ounce
rib-eye (perfect for a trencherman perhaps). Otherwise,
the kitchen sets to with Thai-spiced fishcakes with chilli
sauce and coriander pesto, or twice-baked spinach and
gruyère soufflé, and main courses of herb-marinated
lamb rump with mint jus and potato gratin, and grilled
halibut fillet with tartare sauce.

Chef Michael Glover **Owner** Ramside Estates **Times** 6-10
Closed L all week **Prices** Starter £4.95-£11.95, Main
£11.95-£29.95, Dessert £5.95-£7.95, Service optional
Wines 64 bottles over £20, 20 bottles under £20, 12 by
glass **Notes** Sunday L, Vegetarian menu, Dress
restrictions, Smart casual, Civ Wed 200 **Seats** 90, Pr/
dining room 15 **Children** Portions, Menu **Parking** 350

ESSEX

BRENTWOOD   Map 6 TQ59

Marygreen Manor

◉◉ Modern European **V** 🍷NOTABLE WINE LIST

Enterprising modern food in a Tudor mansion

☎ 01277 225252
London Rd CM14 4NR
e-mail: info@marygreenmanor.co.uk
dir: M25 junct 28, onto A1023 over 2 sets of lights, hotel
on right

The endearingly asymmetrical timbered Tudor mansion
was once the home of one Henry Roper, a manservant of
Catherine of Aragon. Nice work if you could get it. It
retains much of the panelling, oak beams and ornate
ceilings of the 16th century, and has been gently eased
into the modern hotel trade with sensitivity and class. An
attractive courtyard garden makes a fine venue for sunny
days, and you can bet the log fire will have been lit to
cheer the scene in winter's chill. The Tudors dining room
is a sight for sore eyes, with its heavy beams, helical
stanchions of weathered oak and chairs with Gothic-
arched backs, but the cooking doesn't restrict itself to
any English yesteryear. Start with a dish of English
garden snails and French bulots (the kind that look like
whelks), girolles, baby squid and confit garlic, a

something-for-everyone assemblage of good things,
which may be succeeded by locally-reared roebuck with
variations on beetroot (pickled, puréed and sorbet).
Dessert could be jasmine tea chiboust with passionfruit
ice cream.

Chef Mr Majid Bourote **Owner** Mr S Bhattessa
Times 12.30-2.30/7.15-10.15 Closed L Mon, D Sun & BHs
Prices Fixed L 2 course fr £18, Fixed D 3 course fr £24,
Tasting menu £48, Starter £7.50-£12.50, Main £21.50-
£32, Dessert £7.50, Service added but optional 12%
Wines 80 bottles over £20, 21 bottles under £20, 7 by
glass **Notes** Tasting menu 6 course, Sunday L, Vegetarian
menu, Dress restrictions, Smart casual, no jeans or
trainers, Civ Wed 60 **Seats** 80, Pr/dining room 85
Children Portions **Parking** 100

CHELMSFORD   Map 6 TL70

County Hotel

◉ Modern European

British and Mediterranean flavours in town-centre hotel

☎ 01245 455700
29 Rainsford Rd CM1 2PZ
e-mail: kloftus@countyhotelgroup.co.uk
dir: Off Chelmsford ring road close to town centre and
A12 junct 18

A conveniently short stroll from the railway station and
town centre, the County Hotel is done out in a cheery
modern style, as typified in the County Kitchen restaurant,
where oak floors and leather seats in summery pastel
hues of mustard, mint and tangerine add colour to
neutral contemporary décor. Uncomplicated modern
European cooking using local materials is the kitchen's
stock in trade, starting along the lines of venison and
confit pheasant terrine with celeriac remoulade and
toasted walnut bread; mains might bring fillet steak with
potato rösti, butternut squash purée, curly kale and red
wine jus, or a burst of Mediterranean warmth in the form
of Ligurian fish stew. For dessert, there could be dark
chocolate fondant with clotted cream ice cream.

Chef Wayne Browning **Owner** Michael & Ginny Austin
Times 12-2.30/6-10 Closed L Sat **Prices** Fixed L 2 course
£16.95-£21.95, Fixed D 3 course £21.95-£29.95, Starter
£4.95-£7.95, Main £11.95-£21.95, Dessert £4.50-£5.50
Wines 40 bottles over £20, 6 bottles under £20, 6 by
glass **Notes** Pre-theatre menu available, Sunday L,
Vegetarian available, Civ Wed 80 **Seats** 64, Pr/dining
room 135 **Children** Portions, Menu **Parking** 70

COGGESHALL   Map 7 TL82

Baumann's Brasserie

◉◉ French, European **V**

Gutsy cooking in buzzy brasserie

☎ 01376 561453
4-6 Stoneham St CO6 1TT
e-mail: food@baumannsbrasserie.co.uk
web: www.baumannsbrasserie.co.uk
dir: A12 from Chelmsford, exit at Kelvedon into
Coggeshall. Restaurant in centre opposite clock tower

Chef-patron Mark Baumann's buzzy brasserie in a 16th-
century timbered house is still thriving a quarter of a
century after it was launched by his then boss, Peter
Langan, of Langan's Brasserie renown. The formula of
serving inventively-reworked French and British dishes is
clearly a winner, since a strong following of loyal locals
have grown up with its continental-style pavement
tables. Inside, the place is a true one-off, resembling a
bijou art gallery decorated with antique linen-clothed
tables, and there's always a sense of fun to set the mood.
Its no-nonsense plats du jour and daily-changing menus
are driven by the seasons rather than the winds of
culinary fashion, so you might start out with a hot-
smoked salmon crumpet with fennel and olive carpaccio,
followed by braised ox cheeks with mushrooms and
bacon, and celeriac purée. The cooking remains robustly
appealing all the way through to desserts such as salted
caramel chocolate sponge with custard and home-made
marmalade.

Chef Mark Baumann, John Ranfield **Owner** Baumann's
Brasserie Ltd **Times** 12-2/7-9.30 Closed 2 wks Jan, Mon-
Tue **Prices** Fixed L 2 course £16, Fixed D 3 course £25,
Starter £5-£9, Main £17-£23, Dessert £6.95, Service
optional **Wines** 20 bottles over £20, 24 bottles under £20,
11 by glass **Notes** Fixed L plat du jour daily, Fish menu
daily, Sunday L, Vegetarian menu **Seats** 80
Children Portions **Parking** Opposite

COLCHESTER — Map 13 TL92

The North Hill Hotel

◉ Modern British

Well-prepared food in popular, modern-day hotel bistro

☎ 01206 574001
51 North Hill CO1 1PY
e-mail: info@northhillhotel.com
web: www.northhillhotel.com
dir: Follow signs for town centre. Up North Hill, hotel on right

You can't get too funky with the exterior of a Grade II listed Georgian building in the heart of historic Colchester, but North Hill's sunny yellow-painted façade offers a gentle foretaste of its stylishly made-over contemporary interior. The whole place works a breezy, de-cluttered look, while vibrant and swirly artwork feeds into the modish style of the Green Room bistro. An easygoing vibe completes the setting for the kitchen's upbeat modern cooking. Driven by well-sourced local ingredients and unfussy execution, the menu might open with haggis Scotch egg with kohlrabi remoulade and crispy capers, then move on to baked pork fillet Wellington with apple, gruyère cheese and thyme stuffing, watercress, and wholegrain mustard cream sauce. For dessert, there could be a classic custard and nutmeg tart sharpened up with vanilla roasted rhubarb and home-made stem ginger ice cream.

Chef John Riddleston **Owner** Rob Brown
Times 12-2.30/6-9.30 **Prices** Starter £4.50-£6.25, Main £9.95-£16.50, Dessert £4.50-£5.25, Service optional
Wines 22 bottles over £20, 21 bottles under £20, 14 by glass **Notes** Sunday L, Vegetarian available **Seats** 45, Pr/dining room 30 **Children** Portions **Parking** NCP opposite

Stoke by Nayland Hotel, Golf & Spa

◉ Modern British V ☺

Complex contemporary cooking overlooking the golf

☎ 01206 262836
Keepers Ln, Leavenheath CO6 4PZ
e-mail: winston.wright@stokebynayland.com
dir: From A134, pass through the village of Nayland, ignoring signs to Stoke-By-Nayland. Continue on A134, shortly after Hare & Hounds turn right on to B1068 signed Stoke by Nayland Golf Club. In approx 1.5m right

Set in 300 acres of rolling landscapes that would have had Constable running for his easel, this golf-centric resort and spa hotel has a brace of 18-hole courses, as well as all the requisite pampering and de-stressing therapies. In the Lakes Restaurant, a wall of floor-to-ceiling sliding glass doors makes sure that the action on the fairways is never out of sight, and on balmy days it all opens onto an outdoor terrace. The menus show a kitchen with a clear fondness for carefully-sourced British ingredients that it deploys in a broad-minded European-influenced repertoire, from starters taking in an intriguing combination of oriental salmon 'pastrami' with a wasabi wafer, sake vinegar, grapefruit and radish, through to labour-intensive mains that might see pan-seared Scottish scallops sharing a plate with artichoke and roe risotto, chive pannacotta, chicken crackling and vanilla.

Chef Alan Paton **Owner** The Boxford Group
Times 12.30-2.30/6.30-10 **Prices** Fixed L 2 course £15.95-£24.50, Fixed D 3 course £26, Starter £4.95-£8.50, Main £11-£17.50, Dessert £5.25-£6.75, Service optional **Wines** 20 bottles over £20, 20 bottles under £20, 12 by glass **Notes** Sunday L, Vegetarian menu, Civ Wed 100 **Seats** 90, Pr/dining room 60 **Children** Portions **Parking** 200

DEDHAM — Map 13 TM03

milsoms

◉ Modern International ☺

Global food in a contemporary setting

☎ 01206 322795
Stratford Rd CO7 6HN
e-mail: milsoms@milsomhotels.com
web: www.milsomhotels.com
dir: 7m N of Colchester, just off A12

There's no booking at milsoms contemporary brasserie and bar, serving food all day in the village of Dedham. It's a set-up that's served them so well, they've now replicated it at Kesgrave Hall near Ipswich (see entry, Suffolk). The rustic and airy split-level restaurant has scrubbed pine tables, wooden floors and colourful artwork and gets its buzz from the 'engine room', or open-plan kitchen, plus the happy hum of contented diners, of course. The terrace is cushioned from the extremes of the weather by a huge sail and is a lovely spot in the warmer months. Expect crowd-pleasing brasserie-style dishes (sometimes influenced by more exotic climes) along the lines of rabbit schnitzel with sauerkraut, poached egg, caper and anchovy butter, or blackened 'Essex bird' chicken breast with tabouleh, aubergine and Greek yoghurt and harissa. Finish with triple chocolate brownie

with butterscotch sauce, crushed pecan nuts and vanilla ice cream.

Chef Sarah Norman, Ben Rush **Owner** Milsom family
Times 12-9.30 **Prices** Starter £5.50-£9.95, Main £9.95-£24.50, Dessert £5.95-£6.95, Service optional
Wines 78 bottles over £20, 12 bottles under £20, 25 by glass **Notes** Sunday L, Vegetarian available **Seats** 80, Pr/dining room 30 **Children** Portions, Menu **Parking** 80

The Sun Inn

◉ Modern British, Italian ⓘ ☺

A taste of Italy in a village inn

☎ 01206 323351
High St CO7 6DF
e-mail: office@thesuninndedham.com
dir: In village centre opposite church

In the heart of the pretty village, this 15th-century inn is a real treat, with its mixture of period features, open fires, great service from smiling, helpful staff, and cooking that's a cut above average: simple, seasonal food, technically accomplished, with Italy the main focus. Start with pheasant ravioli in thyme and lemon butter, or the crisp flavours of smoked haddock carpaccio with fennel and rocket. Game shows up in season - roast breast and braised leg of guinea fowl with baked polenta and salsa rossa, say - or go for lemon sole wrapped in speck served with radicchio with capers, and potato purée. Finish with properly made saffron pannacotta with rhubarb.

Chef Ugo Simonelli **Owner** Piers Baker
Times 12-2.30/6.30-9.30 **Closed** 25-26 Dec **Prices** Fixed L 2 course £12.50, Fixed D 3 course £15.50, Starter £5-£7, Main £9.50-£18, Dessert £1.50-£7.50, Service optional **Wines** 50 bottles over £20, 30 bottles under £20, 20 by glass **Notes** Sunday L, Vegetarian available **Seats** 70 **Children** Portions, Menu **Parking** 15

Le Talbooth

◎◎ Modern ▮MUTABLE ✍

Seasonal cooking in a sublime setting by the Stour

☎ 01206 323150
Gun Hill CO7 6HN
e-mail: talbooth@milsomhotels.com
web: www.milsomhotels.com
dir: 6m from Colchester follow signs from A12 to Stratford St Mary, restaurant on the left before village

The setting is quintessentially English - trout jumping in the River Stour alongside a former toll house dating from Tudor times that oozes period character. And whatever the weather throws at you, alfresco dining is on the cards thanks to an impressive sail canopy above the waterside terrace. The Milsom family have run this East Anglian stalwart for over half a century, so the whole operation ticks over with well-drilled precision; inside, the look is slick and contemporary, and the kitchen stays abreast of culinary trends while keeping an eye to the seasons and the local larder. Expect the likes of roast rack and confit leg of rabbit with celeriac remoulade, truffle and walnuts, followed by an upscale surf and turf combo of turbot with Dingly Dell pork belly, palourde clams and carrot consommé; local meat fans could find Dedham Vale beef Rossini, served with rösti potato, spinach and Madeira jus. To finish, perhaps an orange and lemon soufflé with Madagascan vanilla ice cream and Cointreau.

Chef Ian Rhodes, Zack Deakins **Owner** Milsom family
Times 12-2/6.30-9 Closed D Sun (Oct-Apr) **Prices** Fixed L 2 course £23.25, Starter £8-£13.25, Main £18-£31, Dessert £7.95-£9.25, Service included **Wines** 250+ bottles over £20, 15 bottles under £20, 19 by glass **Notes** Sunday L, Vegetarian available, Dress restrictions, Smart casual, No jeans, Civ Wed 50 **Seats** 80, Pr/dining room 34 **Children** Portions, Menu **Parking** 50

GREAT TOTHAM　　　　　Map 7 TL81

The Willow Room

◎◎ Modern British ✍

Accomplished cooking in contemporary gastro-pub

☎ 01621 893385 & 894020
The Bull at Great Totham, 2 Maldon Rd CM9 8NH
e-mail: reservations@thewillowroom.co.uk

The Willow Room is the fine-dining option at The Bull - a 16th-century inn that's more gastro than pub with a modern-day makeover for a 21st-century clientele. It now delivers something of a triple whammy, combining a dinky snug bar (where you can grab a pint and watch the footie) to a stylishly modernised bar offering pub staples (Hereford beef burger with onion purée, crisp pancetta, smoked applewood, onion rings and fries), while the Willow Room pulls out all the stops. Here the kitchen keeps things up to date yet intelligently simple and clean-cut allowing quality local and seasonal produce to shine in punchy-flavoured dishes. Seared calves' liver, for example, is partnered with bubble-and-squeak croquettes, smoked bacon, curly kale, crisp shallots and a red wine jus, while a hot chocolate mousse might get the Willow Room treatment with an accompaniment of salted caramel ripple ice cream and honeycomb.

Chef Mark Blake **Owner** David Milne
Times 12-2.30/7-9.30 Closed Mon-Tue **Prices** Fixed D 2 course fr £14.90, Starter £4.50-£8.50, Main £12.95-£22.50, Dessert £3-£6.50, Service optional, Groups min 8 service 10% **Notes** Sunday L, Vegetarian available, Dress restrictions, Smart casual, Air con **Seats** 75, Pr/dining room 20 **Children** Portions, Menu

---

GREAT YELDHAM　　　　　Map 13 TL73

The White Hart

◎◎ British, European ✍

Characterful old inn with skilful contemporary cooking

☎ 01787 237250
Poole St CO9 4HJ
e-mail: mjwmason@yahoo.co.uk
dir: On A1017, between Halstead & Haverhill

The black and white timbered Tudor frontage of The White Hart dates from 1505, and is the very image of romantic Olde England - perhaps that is why so many guests are here for the business of tying the knot. Inside there is historic charm in spades: oak panelling, inglenooks piled with logs, leaded windows, burnished oak tables and head-grazing beams. The kitchen team has moved things up a gear or two in the past year or so, cooking with intelligence and precision to deliver flavour-driven modern British dishes. Provenance is taken very seriously too - the operation has also scaled up its efforts to produce more home-grown materials, taking on a nearby field to grow herbs and veg, and it has set up its own beehives. The fruits of this culinary dedication are clear in a starter of Yeldham rabbit loin matched enterprisingly with wild mushroom and feta cheese ravioli, sweetcorn purée, crisp chicken skins and tarragon. Next up, a first-class piece of wild sea bass sits alongside a smoked haddock and salmon fish pie, scallop, poached quail's egg, apple foam, and bacon and haddock sauce; a choc-fest finale of chocolate fondant, délice, white chocolate and Kahlua ice cream and peanut caramel is also right on the money.

Chef Mr Wu Zhenjang, D Borowy **Owner** Matthew Mason
Times noon-mdnt Closed Mon, L Tue, D 25 Dec
Prices Starter £7.50-£12.95, Main £16.95-£24.95, Dessert £5.95-£10.95, Service optional, Groups min 7 service 10% **Wines** 40 bottles over £20, 17 bottles under £20, 8 by glass **Notes** Fixed L & D 4 course £25.95, 5 course £36.50, Sunday L, Vegetarian available, Dress restrictions, Smart casual, Civ Wed 200 **Seats** 44, Pr/dining room 200 **Children** Portions, Menu **Parking** 50

HARWICH
Map 13 TM23

The Pier at Harwich

◎◎ Modern British, Seafood ◎

Harbourside views and a delightfully fishy menu

☎ 01255 241212
The Quay CO12 3HH
e-mail: pier@milsomhotels.com
web: www.milsomhotels.com
dir: A12 to Colchester then A120 to Harwich Quay

This hotel and restaurant, housed in two historic buildings right on Harwich's quayside, is part of the Milsom family empire. Inside, the theme is nautical and nowhere more so than the first floor Harbourside Restaurant. Take a drink at the polished pewter bar before enjoying views over the Stour and Orwell estuaries as you eat at linen-clad tables. Head chef (formerly at sister restaurant Le Talbooth; see entry, Dedham) Tom Bushell's menus focus on seafood - well you would too if you could see the day's catch being landed from the pier just opposite the hotel. Diver-caught scallops come with cucumber seeds and gremolata, pan-fried halibut supreme is paired with oxtail ravioli and parsley root purée, and apple tarte Tatin is served with Earl Grey tea ice cream. Downstairs, the all-day Ha'penny Bistro is more informal.

Chef Tom Bushell **Owner** Milsom family
Times 12-2/6-9.30 Closed 25 & 31 Dec (bookings only),
Prices Fixed L 2 course £20, Starter £7.95-£13.75, Main £16-£39, Dessert £7.25, Service optional
Wines 92 bottles over £20, 8 bottles under £20, 16 by glass **Notes** Sunday L, Vegetarian available, Civ Wed 50
Seats 80, Pr/dining room 16 **Children** Portions, Menu

MANNINGTREE
Map 13 TM13

The Mistley Thorn

◎◎ Modern ◎

Convincing Cal-Ital style on the Stour Estuary

☎ 01206 392821
High St, Mistley CO11 1HE
e-mail: info@mistleythorn.co.uk
dir: From A12 take A137 for Manningtree & Mistley

A combined bar and restaurant with rooms, The Mistley Thorn is directly opposite the swan basin designed by Robert Adam. It was built as a coaching inn in 1723, but the bistro-style restaurant has a modern look. Seafood gets a good airing on the imaginative, daily-changing menus, from lobster with garlic mayonnaise, to grilled lemon sole with ginger butter. Good local ingredients are handled with skill, and a love of Italian cooking is evident throughout, seen in a plate of superior charcuterie (salamis, prosciutto and bresaola), venison carpaccio with fricò (fried cheese), and fritto misto di mare. Sauces and accompaniments are well considered adjuncts to the main event: salsa verde for roast skate wing, say, plum and red wine sauce for seared duck breast, and tomato, orange and coriander sauce for seared fillet of brill. Some puddings have a French accent - crème brûlée, St-Emilion au chocolat - but then there's also affogato, with Sherri's Mom's cheesecake highlighting chef-patron Sherri Singleton's Californian origins.

Chef Sherri Singleton, Karl Burnside **Owner** Sherri Singleton, David McKay **Times** 12-2.30/6.30-9.30 **Prices** Fixed L 2 course £10.95-£14.95, Starter £4.95-£7.95, Main £9.95-£17.95, Dessert £5.25-£5.95, Service optional, Groups min 8 service 10% **Wines** 30 bottles over £20, 12 bottles under £20, 17 by glass **Notes** Sunday L, Vegetarian available **Seats** 75, Pr/dining room 28 **Children** Portions, Menu **Parking** 7

STOCK
Map 6 TQ69

The Hoop

◎ Modern British **NEW**

Assured modern cooking in an old pub

☎ 01277 841137
High St CM4 9BD
e-mail: thehoopstock@yahoo.co.uk
dir: A12 Billericay Galleywold junct, on B1007

Over 450 years old, The Hoop is on two levels, a ground-floor bar dispensing real ales, with a small fireplace and the real ambience of a country pub, and the upstairs Oak Room restaurant, with a beamed ceiling, bare wooden tables and prints on the walls. The lively menu focuses on modern British flavours, which translates into starters of ham knuckle and guinea fowl terrine with pickled vegetables, and seared scallops with a salt-cod beignet and cauliflower purée. Dishes are well composed so individual components add up to a satisfying whole: a well-timed fillet of John Dory on creamed potatoes surrounded by a ragout of tomato and plump mussels, and pork belly and fillet with a sauce of caramel, vanilla

and apple served with pancetta, roast shallots and a potato croquette.

Chef Phil Utz **Owner** Michelle Corrigan **Times** 12-2.30/6-9 Closed Mon, Beer festival wk, D Sun **Prices** Fixed L 2 course £17-£20, Fixed D 3 course £30-£50, Starter £5-£9, Main £15-£25, Dessert £5-£10 **Wines** 52 bottles over £20, 11 bottles under £20, 14 by glass **Notes** Seasonal tasting menu available, Sunday L, Vegetarian available **Seats** 40 **Children** Portions

TENDRING
Map 7 TM12

The Fat Goose

◎ Modern British ◎

Rustic cooking in a charming old pub

☎ 01255 870060
Heath Rd CO16 0BX
e-mail: eat@fat-goose.co.uk
dir: A120 to Horsley Cross, follow B1035 to Tendring/Thorpe-le-Soken. 1.5 m on right

Five years on from its top-to-toe revamp, the Goose is still hitting all the right notes for switched-on, comfort-oriented dining. Slate floors, high barn-like wooden beams, and chunky wooden chairs and tables set a suitably rustic tone for punchy food with a big heart. The chef-proprietor believes in doing things the slow way with no corners cut, so everything from stocks to bread is made from scratch, in-house, using local produce, and it is all priced to put an extra smile on your face. The menu is packed with the sort of dishes you want to eat: twice-baked ham and gruyère soufflé with a cheese and chive glaze ahead of roast rump of new season lamb with gratin dauphinoise, confit shallots, roast garlic and rosemary jus, or a posh burger made from Sandringham Estate venison on caramelised onion focaccia, served with blue cheese, redcurrant and shallot chutney, Adnams-cured bacon and Pont-Neuf potatoes. Slacken the belt, and end with apple and sultana steamed pudding with cinnamon crème anglaise and Calvados ice cream.

Chef Philip Hambrook-Moore **Owner** Philip Hambrook-Moore **Times** 12-2.30/6.30-9.30 Closed Mon **Prices** Fixed L 2 course fr £10, Fixed D 3 course fr £12.50, Starter £5-£8.50, Main £11-£22, Dessert £4.50-£8.50, Service optional, Groups min 8 service 10% **Wines** 34 bottles over £20, 17 bottles under £20, 17 by glass **Notes** Tasting menu available for groups 6-8, Sunday L, Vegetarian available **Seats** 100, Pr/dining room 50 **Children** Portions, Menu **Parking** 50

TOLLESHUNT KNIGHTS   Map 7 TL91

Crowne Plaza Resort Colchester - Five Lakes

◉ Modern British

Modern British brasserie cooking in a multi-resourced hotel

☎ 01621 868888
Colchester Rd CM9 8HX
e-mail: enquiries@cpcolchester.co.uk
dir: M25 junct 28, then on A12. At Kelvedon take B1024 then B1023 to Tolleshunt Knights, clearly marked by brown tourist signs

Following a multi-million-pound refurbishment at this resort hotel - with its two 18-hole golf courses, country club and swish spa - the spacious main restaurant has been re-branded 'Brasserie 1'. In tune with its relaxed, contemporary outlook, the kitchen's classic British comfort food - with emphasis on quality ingredients and freshness - fits the bill to a tee. Expect the likes of a fillet of sea bass teamed with pesto and lemon barley risotto, watercress and a parmesan tuile, or loin of local pork served with mustard mash and a cider sauce, while a range of steaks (21-day dry-aged rib-eye, maybe, with vine tomatoes, flat mushrooms, thick chips and Café de Paris butter) are a perennial favourite. Finish with a warm Bakewell tart and raspberry ripple ice cream.

Chef James Parsons **Owner** Mr A Bejerano **Times** 7-10 Closed 26, 31 Dec, 1 Jan, Sun-Mon **Prices** Food prices not confirmed for 2013. Please telephone for details **Wines** 63 bottles over £20, 18 bottles under £20, 7 by glass **Notes** Sunday L, Vegetarian available, Civ Wed 250 **Seats** 80 **Children** Portions, Menu **Parking** 550

GLOUCESTERSHIRE

ALMONDSBURY   Map 4 ST68

Aztec Hotel & Spa

◉ Modern British ✿

Eclectic modern menu in a vibrant room

☎ 01454 201090
Aztec West BS32 4TS
e-mail: quarterjacks@shirehotels.com
dir: M5 junct 16/A38 towards city centre, hotel 200mtrs on right

Taking its name from an iconic Bristol clock, the large, fashionable Quarter Jacks Restaurant at the modern Aztec Hotel & Spa scores high on the cool stakes. A thoroughly contemporary affair it may be, but it has managed to incorporate recycled Jacobean timbers into its Nordic-styling. The high-vaulted ceiling, big rustic stone fireplace, polished wooden floors, leather seating and eye-catching modern abstract art certainly make a strong impression. The vibe is relaxed and unstuffy, a bit like the food, which takes good regional produce and deals with it in an uncomplicated, crowd-pleasing manner. Grilled venison sausages might be partnered with mash and pickled red cabbage, or go for the more modish pan-seared sea bass fillets with brown shrimp and saffron risotto. Desserts can be as comforting as sticky toffee pudding or apple and blackberry crumble.

Chef Mike Riordan **Owner** Shire Hotels
Times 12.30-2/7.9.30 Closed L Sat, D 25-26 Dec **Prices** Fixed L 2 course £13.95, Fixed D 3 course £21-£24.50, Starter £6.50-£8.75, Main £12.50-£23.75, Dessert £3.50-£6.75, Service optional **Wines** 25 bottles over £20, 10 bottles under £20, 12 by glass **Notes** Sunday L, Vegetarian available, Civ Wed 160 **Seats** 80, Pr/dining room 40 **Children** Portions, Menu **Parking** 200

ALVESTON   Map 4 ST68

Alveston House Hotel

◉ Modern European

Georgian country house with good seasonal cooking

☎ 01454 415050
Davids Ln BS35 2LA
e-mail: info@alvestonhousehotel.co.uk
dir: On A38, 3.5m N of M4/M5 interchange. M5 junct 16 N'bound or junct 14 S'bound

Whitewashed and Georgian on the outside, yet revamped in a clean-cut contemporary style inside, Alveston House Hotel sits in lovely walled gardens near to Bristol. A secluded walled garden is just the spot for alfresco aperitifs before settling into the soothing caramel and cream hued setting of Carriages restaurant for seasonally-changing menus which make the most of fine regionally-sourced produce. Simple, trustworthy combinations set the tone - perhaps smoked haddock and salmon fishcakes with lemon and dill mayonnaise, followed by honey-glazed rump of lamb with aubergine

and anchovy confit, or pan-fried sea bass fillet on a bed of spinach with mushroom and tarragon sauce. End indulgently with chocolate, rum and raisin fondant with honeycomb ice cream.

Chef Ben Halliday **Owner** Julie Camm
Times 12-1.45/7-9.30 **Prices** Fixed D 3 course £25, Starter £5.75-£7.95, Main £14.75-£23.50, Dessert £5.75-£7.25, Service optional **Wines** 18 bottles over £20, 18 bottles under £20, 5 by glass **Notes** Vegetarian available, Civ Wed 75 **Seats** 75, Pr/dining room 40 **Children** Portions, Menu **Parking** 60

ARLINGHAM   Map 4 SO71

The Old Passage Inn

◉◉ Seafood

Exemplary fish and seafood cookery on the River Severn

☎ 01452 740547
Passage Rd GL2 7JR
e-mail: oldpassage@btconnect.com
web: www.theoldpassage.com
dir: M5 junct 13/A38 towards Bristol, 2nd right to Frampton-on-Severn, over canal, bear left, follow to river

The riverside setting of The Old Passage is nothing less than sublime, with the River Severn flowing by and the thickly-wooded hillsides of the Forest of Dean as a backdrop. The bottle-green building sits where an ancient ford crossed the river, and now trades as a modern restaurant with rooms; done out with the colourful hues of the Mediterranean inside, there's also a garden terrace for taking in the glory of the location on fine days. The kitchen deals almost exclusively in fish and seafood brought in from ports in Pembrokeshire and Cornwall, with tanks to keep crustaceans and shellfish fighting fit until it is time for them to line up in seafood platters. Otherwise, scallop thermidor with spinach and creamy sherry sauce is a good way to start, followed perhaps by roast herb-crusted brill with seasonal vegetables and cockles and clams, or a slab of halibut with hollandaise, samphire and new potatoes. Meat might get a solitary look-in in the shape of local beef sirloin with the classic

continued

ARLINGHAM *continued*

accompaniments of balsamic cherry tomatoes, mushrooms, hand cut chips and béarnaise sauce.

The Old Passage Inn

Times 12-2/7-9.30 Closed 25-26 Dec, Mon, D Sun, Tue-Wed Jan-Feb

Barnsley House

◎◎ Modern European

Refined cooking in beautiful Cotswold setting

☎ 01285 740000
Barnsley GL7 5EE
e-mail: info@barnsleyhouse.com
web: www.barnsleyhouse.com
dir: 4m N of Cirencester on B4425 between Cirencester & Burford

If you can't tell a Muscade pumpkin from a Red Brunswick onion, the specialist vegetables that turn up on the menu of the Potager Restaurant could well extend your culinary vocabulary. Rosemary Verey's celebrated garden is key to the popularity of Barnsley House, framing the old Cotswold-stone manor in delightful grounds, as well as supplying the chefs with super-fresh produce. The 17th-century house itself is no slouch either: the upscale hotel has been reworked with an immaculately tasteful boutique look; there's a spa too, and even a small cinema to complete the high-end package. The Potager Restaurant (French for 'kitchen garden') is a floaty, soft-focus space in neutral shades of white and cream with large windows and French doors through which to soak

up the garden view. The cooking works within a broadly modern British idiom, with Italian accents - vincisgrassi (baked pasta with Parma ham, porcini and truffles) is something of a signature; elsewhere, there might be confit leg of Great Farm chicken with wild mushrooms, or Sicilian lobster salad with lemon mayonnaise. For dessert, perhaps Russet apple croustade with vanilla ice cream. The Village Pub opposite is under the same ownership (see entry).

Chef Graham Grafton **Owner** Calcot Health and Leisure **Times** 12-2.30/7-9.30 **Prices** Fixed L 2 course £21, Starter £6-£9, Main £12.50-£29, Dessert £8-£9, Service included **Wines** 95 bottles over £20, 7 bottles under £20, 10 by glass **Notes** Sunday L, Vegetarian available, Dress restrictions, Smart casual preferred, Civ Wed 120 **Seats** 40, Pr/dining room 14 **Children** Portions, Menu **Parking** 25

The Village Pub

◎ Modern British

Cotswold inn with deserved reputation for good food

☎ 01285 740421
GL7 5EF
e-mail: info@thevillagepub.co.uk
dir: 4m from Cirencester, on B4425 to Bibury

The name sounds simple, but this particular village pub is a posh country-chic affair aimed at a moneyed Cotswolds audience. You can still drop in for a pint - there are locally-produced real ales - but it is the wide-ranging menus of unfussy contemporary cooking that are on most people's minds. A stylish rustic boutique blend of flagstone and oak floors, bare beams and open fireplaces, antiques, oil paintings, cosy window settles and polished candlelit tables makes the quintet of dining rooms an attractive proposition. Dishes keep a keen eye on the seasons and draw on the best local supplies, which might mean locally-smoked sea trout paired with beetroot, horseradish and spring onions, followed by grilled lamb steak with butternut squash mash, roast red pepper, and tomato and chilli salsa, and the comfort of sticky toffee pudding with vanilla ice cream as a finale. The pub is part of the stable that owns boutique Barnsley House, just up the road, and classy Calcot Manor (see entries).

Times 12-2.30/7-9.30

Bibury Court

◎◎ Modern British

Confident modern cooking in stunning country-house hotel

☎ 01285 740337
GL7 5NT
e-mail: info@biburycourt.com
web: www.biburycourt.com
dir: On B4425 between Cirencester & Burford; hotel behind church

This is the very image of green-and-pleasant England: a handsome, mellow stone Jacobean mansion secreted away in six acres of grounds beside the River Coln, on the fringes of a chocolate-box Cotswold village. Inside, however, Bibury Court has stayed in step with many of its posh Cotswolds neighbours and overlaid the cosy log fires, flagstone floors and wood panelling of the classic country-house idiom with a stylish contemporary designer makeover. The classy Oak Room restaurant makes a splash with its hand-made embroidered silk wall hangings, or you could dine in the new English oak conservatory - whichever you go for, expect menus that read rather like a shopping list offering dishes with a modern British sensibility. To start, Cotswold chicken liver parfait might be matched with hazelnut, orange, fig and brioche; next out, main courses could bring sauté potatoes, root vegetables and redcurrant sauce as the accompaniments to a two-way serving (shoulder and cutlet) of Bibury lamb, while pheasant Kiev comes with bubble-and-squeak, baby leeks and garlic foam.

Times 12-2/7-9

Save on Hotels. Book at theAA.com/hotel

GLOUCESTERSHIRE 163 ENGLAND

Swan Hotel

◉ Traditional British, European

Appealing cooking in a Cotswold idyll

☎ 01285 740695
GL7 5NW
e-mail: info@swanhotel.co.uk
web: www.cotswold-inns-hotels.co.uk/swan
dir: 9m S of Burford A40 onto B4425. 6m N of Cirencester A4179 onto B4425. In town centre by bridge

A thoroughly relaxing country experience is on offer at the Bibury Swan, a Cotswold retreat in an idyllic setting. The Gallery dining room is so named in acknowledgement of the display of pony pictures by a Dartmoor artist. Logs are stacked against the wall, tables are properly clothed, and there's a pleasant buzz of bonhomie about the place. The menu invites you to 'commence' with something like sea trout escabèche, pickled cucumber and saffron aïoli, and then 'continue' with chargrilled sirloin and dauphinoise with béarnaise, or a whole baked lemon sole with olive beurre blanc. You'll then want to 'complete' the experience with honey and hazelnut tart, served with vanilla ice cream and caramel sauce.

Chef Gordon Reynolds **Owner** Mr & Mrs Horton
Times 7-9.30 Closed L Mon-Sat **Prices** Fixed D 3 course £35, Service added but optional 10% **Notes** Sunday L, Vegetarian available, Dress restrictions, Smart casual, Civ Wed 100 **Seats** 60, Pr/dining room 10
Children Portions **Parking** 15, On street

BOURTON-ON-THE-WATER   Map 10 SP12

The Dial House Hotel & Restaurant

◉◉ Modern

Rousing cooking in the Cotswolds

☎ 01451 822244
The Chestnuts, High St GL54 2AN
e-mail: info@dialhousehotel.com
dir: Just off A429

In a picture-postcard (and mega-touristy) Cotswolds village, this mellow stone house dates from the late 17th century, with large stone fireplaces as reminders of its

antiquity. It's a comfortable place, more homely than grand, with two small dining rooms. The kitchen seeks out the best produce it can find, much of it locally, and uses it inspirationally: a starter of langoustine cannelloni, with mousse and chunks of flesh, for instance, accompanied by moist and flaky pig's cheek and parsley root purée. Techniques are spot on, and imaginative, confidently handled combinations extend to main courses - poached fillet of brill, of superb quality, in truffled butter, served with battered sea aster, oxtail, ceps and salsify - or there may be a more prosaic-sounding assiette of suckling pig with apple and onion. Dishes are artfully presented - vegetables in stacks, sauces dribbled - while a perfectly set caramel soufflé comes in a copper pan on a marble slab, cut open at table, vanilla ice cream added, then hot chocolate sauce poured over.

Times 12-2/6.30 9.30 Closed L Mon-Tue (winter only)

CHARINGWORTH   Map 10 SP13

Charingworth Manor

◉ French, Mediterranean V

Charming country-house hotel with unfussy contemporary cooking

☎ 01386 593555
GL55 6NS
e-mail: gm.charingworthmanor@classiclodges.co.uk
web: www.classiclodges.co.uk
dir: M40 exit at signs for A429/Stow. Follow signs for Moreton-in-Marsh. From Chipping Camden follow signs for Charingworth Manor

Part of the Cotswolds landscape for 700 years, and with the sort of looks that have graced many a wedding album, the honey-coloured stones of Charingworth Manor speak of unchanging tradition. Yet the interior is a surprisingly winsome blend of old and new, pulling together venerable flagstones, vast fireplaces and medieval decorated beams with sexy modern fabrics and designer touches. In the fine-dining John Greville Restaurant, candlelight sets off the low-beamed intimacy of the setting to perfection, while the kitchen takes a straightforward approach with seasonal Gloucestershire goodies. At dinner, you could start with pan-fried duck foie gras teamed with quince compôte and Madeira, then follow with roast rump of Oxford lamb with fondant potato, butternut squash purée and rosemary jus. End with a classic lemon tart with crème fraîche.

Chef Chris Lelliott **Owner** Classic Lodges
Times 12-2.30/7-10 **Prices** Fixed L 2 course fr £14.95, Fixed D 3 course fr £39.95, Service optional
Wines 84 bottles over £20, 12 bottles under £20, 10 by glass **Notes** Fixed D 4 course, Vegetarian menu, Dress restrictions, Smart dress, Civ Wed 85 **Seats** 44, Pr/dining room 50 **Children** Portions, Menu **Parking** 100

CHELTENHAM   Map 10 SO92

Le Champignon Sauvage

◉◉◉◉ – *see page 164*

The Curry Corner

◉ Bangladeshi **NEW** 🍴

Upmarket Bangladeshi gastronomy

☎ 01242 528449
133 Fairview Rd GL52 2EX
e-mail: info@thecurrycorner.com
dir: From A40 turn right into Hewlett Rd, at mini-rdbt turn left

In a residential street a short distance from the centre of town (on a corner as you might imagine), The Curry Corner brings the flavours of Bangladesh to Cheltenham. The spacious dining room, with its contemporary décor, has distinctive Indian carvings and sari bolsters against a backdrop of ruby-red wall coverings and tapestries, while downstairs is a lounge bar. The kitchen, run by father and daughter Shamsul and Monrusha Krori, imports from Bangladesh and the sub-continent, seeks out produce from Cotswolds farms and makes its own bread, and has assembled a broad ranging menu running from street snacks like roshun gusht luchi (tender lamb with garlic and coriander wrapped in fennel pastry) to tandoor pineapple with vanilla ice cream. In between might come spicy crab samosa, tandoor-smoked chicken breast marinated in yoghurt, garlic and mustard, tandoori monkfish, beautifully cooked, in a well-balanced creamy saffron curry sauce, and the signature dish of raan gusht: 16-spiced lamb shank masala served with Bengal-style mashed potato.

Chef Shamsul Krori, Monrusha Krori **Owner** Shamsul & Saleha Krori **Times** 12-2/5.30-11.30 Closed Mon (some BHs open), L Fri **Prices** Fixed L 2 course fr £20, Fixed D 3 course £30-£39, Starter £5.50-£12, Main £12.95-£26, Dessert £7.50, Service added but optional 12.5%
Wines 41 bottles over £20, 10 bottles under £20, 7 by glass **Notes** Pre-theatre set menu 2 course £20 5.30-6.30 except Fri-Sat, Sunday L, Vegetarian available **Seats** 54, Pr/dining room 40 **Children** Menu **Parking** On street

Le Champignon Sauvage

Modern British

Refined, intelligent cooking from Cheltenham's long-stayer

☎ 01242 573449
24-28 Suffolk Rd GL50 2AQ
e-mail: mail@lechampignonsauvage.co.uk
dir: S of town centre, on A40, near Cheltenham College

Notching up 25 years in 2012, David and Helen Everitt-Matthias's restaurant in a charming part of the town opened the same year Marco Pierre White opened Harveys, as the film *Wall Street* was showing in cinemas and Margaret Thatcher was getting re-elected for her third term in office. To show such dedication and commitment is remarkable, and the reward comes in the form of the accolades lauded on the place over the years. With an extension into next door, a new kitchen a few years back, and cookery books on the shelves of all good bookshops, plus cooking that has moved with the times (or even led from the front), complacency has never been an issue. The interior has never been cutting edge, preferring a more rarified serenity, with a rich blue carpet, neutral tones on the walls, vivid contemporary artworks, and formally dressed tables adorned with fresh flowers. Helen deals with the front-of-house with charm and efficiency, keeping it all ticking along at a measured and reassuring pace, whilst David is to be found in the kitchen, for he is a thoroughly hands-on kind of chef. An amuse-bouche such as field mushroom soup with truffle foam might get the ball rolling, the seasoning on the money, before first-course diver-caught scallops with a miso glaze, turnip and verjus cream and toasted sesame purée. This is cooking of acute technical dexterity with classical French foundations, a real sense of place (or terroir), and plenty of modish ideas. Sautéed and braised brisket of beef, for example, is served with a fork and spoon (the knife not needed to cut through this tender meat), teamed with caramelised onion risotto and onion ash oil, whilst main-course partridge might come with woodruff-roasted parsnips, black pudding purée and wild baby figs. David is a keen forager and what he can't source by his own hand from the earth is judiciously bought. To finish, warm banana cake with beurre noisette ice cream and peanut croquant might round off a winter lunch. The excellent wine list has French leanings with starting prices that won't scare the horses.

Times 12.30-1.30/7.30-8.30 Closed 10 days Xmas, 3 wks Jun, Sun-Mon

Save on Hotels. Book at theAA.com/hotel

GLOUCESTERSHIRE 165 ENGLAND

CHELTENHAM *continued*

The Daffodil

◉ British, European

Brasserie dining in a magnificent converted art deco cinema

☎ 01242 700055
18-20 Suffolk Pde, Montpellier GL50 2AE
e-mail: eat@thedaffodil.com
dir: S of town centre, just off Suffolk Rd, near Cheltenham Boys' College

Wow factor is not in short supply at this stately relic from the era when cinemas were truly palatial. The art deco movie house dates from 1922, and after a glamorous makeover it now makes a magnificent open-plan dining space; period posters, vending machines and original projectors all still in place, and an elegant staircase sweeps up to the mezzanine bar. Where once you might have been riveted by a black-and-white classic, there is now the cheffy action in an open-to-view kitchen to entertain, supplemented by live jazz on the half-moon-shaped stage. Food-wise, the deal is brasserie-style dining on modern European dishes that cover all the bases from salmon and pollock fishcakes with wilted spinach and hollandaise sauce or warm Double Gloucester soufflé with chive and truffle oil dressing, through to slow-roasted pork belly with Savoy cabbage, champ mash, apple sauce and roasting juices. The ace in the hole is a Josper charcoal grill, from which might come roasted lamb chump with charred ratatouille and fondant potato, or sizzling slabs of beef with béarnaise. The curtain comes down with the likes of dark chocolate pavé with orange jelly and pistachio wafer.

Chef Mark Davidson **Owner** Mark Stephens & James McAlpine **Times** 12-2.30/6-10 Closed 25-26 Dec, 1-7 Jan, Sun **Prices** Fixed L 2 course £13.50, Fixed D 3 course £15.50, Starter £4.50-£10.50, Main £12.95-£23.95, Dessert £5.95, Service added but optional 10% **Wines** 44 bottles over £20, 11 bottles under £20, 14 by glass **Notes** Fixed price menu Mon-Sat until 7.30pm, Bar menu all day, Vegetarian available, Civ Wed 100 **Seats** 140 **Children** Portions, Menu **Parking** On street, NCP

Ellenborough Park

◉◉◉ — *see below*

The Greenway Hotel & Spa

◉◉ Modern British, French V

Vibrant modern cooking in the Cotswolds

☎ 01242 862550
Shurdington Rd GL51 4UG
e-mail: info@thegreenway.co.uk
dir: 3m S of Cheltenham on A46 (Stroud) & through Shurdington

A 16th-century Elizabethan manor house of mellow Cotswolds stone draped in ivy; eight acres of fabulous landscaped grounds with green-and-pleasant views of the rolling hills; an upscale interior filled with the historic charm of grand stone fireplaces and arches, wooden floors, and antiques. The Greenway certainly has a lot to offer. On the food front there's the stylish Orchard Brasserie, or contemporary country-house dining with views of the sunken garden and lily pond in the oak-panelled Garden Restaurant. The kitchen takes an appealing contemporary European approach, perhaps serving roast breast and confit leg of quail with beetroot carpaccio to get things started, then quince purée, dauphinoise potato and thyme jus as the accompaniments to twice-cooked belly and pan-fried loin of pork. Fishy ideas could see sea bass matched with braised fennel, smoked eel, and red wine jus, while lime parfait with marinated cherries, goats' curd, and passionfruit sorbet could close the show.

Chef Robin Dudley **Owner** Sir Peter Rigby **Times** 12-2.30/7-9.30 **Prices** Fixed L 2 course fr £15, Fixed D 3 course £29.50-£45, Service optional **Wines** 100+ bottles over £20, 7 bottles under £20, 11 by glass **Notes** ALC 3 course £45, Sunday L, Vegetarian menu, Dress restrictions, Smart casual **Seats** 56, Pr/dining room 22 **Children** Portions, Menu

Ellenborough Park

CHELTENHAM　　　　　　　Map 10 SO92

Modern British ▒WINE LIST **NEW**

Stunning manor-house hotel with dynamic cooking and a luxurious finish

☎ 01242 545454
Southam Rd GL52 3NH
dir: A46 right after 3m onto B4079, merges with A435, 4m, over 3 rdbts onto Southam Lane, right onto Old Rd, right onto B4632, hotel on right

Ellenborough Park is a very stately house indeed, standing in rolling parkland next to the Cheltenham racecourse, with grandly proportioned features brimming with fine period details. Add to that a swanky spa, 21st-century business facilities, smart bedrooms, and two restaurants, and it's easy to see the appeal of this new, top-end addition to the Gloucestershire scene. The dining options include a brasserie and the main event, the fine-dining Beaufort Dining Room, where head chef David Kelman deals in carefully-crafted, refined and classically-based ideas, with plenty of contemporary vivacity and sparkle. It all takes place in a magnificent room, with stained glass adding splashes of colour to the windows and original, ornately carved oak panels on the walls, looked over by a confident and charming team. The attention to detail in the kitchen's output is evident from the off with top-notch canapés (ham hock with pickled carrot, perhaps) and first-course pan-fried scallops, cooked to glistening perfection, in a well judged dish with parsnip purée, apple jelly and a curried shallot and carrot dressing. Next up, perhaps a pink and tender pan-fried breast of Creedy Carver duck partnered with a potato fondant and thyme-roasted root vegetables, or Chateaubriand carved at the table, or the more modish 62°-cooked loin of Gloucestershire Old Spot accompanied by the cheek slowly braised, Savoy cabbage, lentils and a sage and onion potato bonbon. To finish, Valrhona 70% cocoa chocolate is used in a spot-on fondant, which oozes in all the right places, served with chocolate crémeux and cocoa nibs ice cream. The 500-strong wine list is a serious piece of work, with excellent global coverage, and there's a good team on hand to help you make the best of it.

Chef David Kelman **Times** Closed Mon, D Sun **Prices** Food prices not confirmed for 2013. Please telephone for details **Parking**

CHELTENHAM *continued*

Hotel du Vin Cheltenham

◉ British, European ✆

Classic bistro dining in popular boutique hotel

☎ 01242 588450
Parabola Rd GL50 3AQ
e-mail: info.cheltenham@hotelduvin.com
dir: M5 junct 11, follow signs for city centre. At rdbt opposite Morgan Estate Agents take 2nd left, 200mtrs to Parabola Rd

Centred around a show-stopping spiral staircase and wine glass chandelier, this outpost of the HdV chain comes located in the fashionable Montpellier district of town. Decked out in trademark style, the lively bistro (with outstanding wine list) comes with well-trodden floorboards, wooden tables and black leather upholstered chairs and banquettes, while wine-themed artwork adorns walls and shelves and windowsills are brimful of bottle displays. Alfresco eating on the large terrace is a boon in fair weather, while the pewter-topped bar inside is a hit day and night. The simple, sharp, bistro cooking - based on local produce from name-checked producers - looks south for inspiration; think gilt head bream with lemon potatoes, braised chicory and chive beurre blanc, or lamb neck fillet served with Mediterranean vegetables, and, from the daily specials list, perhaps beef bourguignon and mash.

Chef Paul Mottram **Owner** MWB **Times** 12-2/6.30-10.30 **Prices** Starter £5.75-£10.50, Main £12.50-£26.75, Dessert £6.95-£9.50, Service added but optional 10% **Wines** 450 bottles over £20, 20 bottles under £20, 20 by glass **Notes** Sunday L, Vegetarian available **Seats** 92, Pr/dining room 32 **Children** Portions, Menu **Parking** 23

Lumière

◉◉ Modern British **NEW V** ✆

Resourceful, innovative cooking from a new Cheltenham star

☎ 01242 222200
Clarence Pde GL50 3PA
e-mail: info@lumiere.cc
dir: Town centre, near bus station

Keep your eyes peeled to find Lumière. The discreet narrow frontage with its one window might easily be missed. Inside is a vision of serene elegance, a mauve and creamy-white room that extends to a glass panel at the back, through which the kitchen activity can be glimpsed. Helen Aubrey presides over front-of-house in a professional yet friendly manner, while her partner Jon Howe cooks. Having trained under the likes of Heston Blumenthal and John Campbell, he comes with something of a CV, and the results are apparent from the minute the canapés arrive - a beetroot and apple macaroon with cream cheese, for example. The cooking is full of modern Britain's resourcefulness and innovation, producing a starter of local oxtail faggot with celeriac purée, wine-poached balled pear and a jus based on stout ale, accompanied by a side-serving of two Kiev-style beignets

of bone marrow, filled with herb butter. An equally convincing main course brings on a voguish pair of wings - skate and chicken - alongside a couple of langoustines, trompettes, and chunks of salsify poached in red wine to look like rhubarb. The actual thing turns up in various manifestations at dessert, when poached batons, dried strips, sorbet quenelles, and a hibiscus- and ginger-scented trifle make a dazzling array. There's a new star in Cheltenham's firmament.

Chef Jon Howe **Owner** Jon Howe & Helen Aubrey **Times** 12-1.30/7-9 Closed 2 wks winter, 2 wks summer, Sun-Mon, L Tue **Prices** Fixed L 2 course £22, Fixed D 3 course £47, Tasting menu £47-£60, Groups min 7 service 10% **Wines** 75 bottles over £20, 2 bottles under £20, 7 by glass **Notes** Tasting menu 5 or 7 course, Vegetarian menu **Seats** 25 **Parking** On street

Monty's Brasserie

◉◉ Modern British

Smart brasserie cooking in stylish Grade II listed hotel

☎ 01242 227678
George Hotel, 41 St Georges Rd GL50 3DZ
e-mail: info@montysbraz.co.uk
dir: M5 junct 11, follow signs to town centre. At lights (TGI Fridays) turn left onto Gloucester Rd. Straight on, at lights turn right, Monty's 0.75m on left

The George delivers all the Regency style one hopes for in Cheltenham - Grade II listed no less, so plenty of period details inside and out, and grand Georgian proportions. There's a cocktail bar in the basement with a decidedly contemporary sheen, and in fact the whole place is done out with a good degree of finesse. Monty's matches the modish tone with its brasserie good looks - lots of darkwood, smart lighting - and a lively carte, backed with daily specials, and based on good quality ingredients. Start with a classic moules marinière done well, or chicken liver and black truffle parfait, before a main course such as Cotswold beef Wellington, or loin of monkfish wrapped in Serrano ham with confit grelot onions, creamed potatoes, carrot purée, creamed potatoes and a thyme and red wine sauce. The acute technical abilities of the team in the kitchen are on display again at dessert stage in the form of an excellent tiramisù cheesecake.

Chef Renark Cousins **Owner** Jeremy Shaw **Times** 12-2/6-10 Closed 25-26 Dec **Prices** Fixed L 2 course £12.50, Fixed D 3 course £15, Starter £7-£10, Main £15-£24, Dessert £5-£8, Service added but optional 10% **Wines** 32 bottles over £20, 11 bottles under £20, 7 by glass **Notes** Fixed D available 6-7pm, Sunday L, Vegetarian available **Seats** 40, Pr/dining room 32 **Children** Portions, Menu **Parking** 30

The Kings Hotel

◉◉ Modern British

Georgian Cotswold townhouse with energetic brasserie cooking

☎ 01386 840256
The Square, High St GL55 6AW
e-mail: info@kingscampden.co.uk
dir: In centre of town square

Occupying a prime site in Chipping Campden central, The Kings is a classic Georgian townhouse of Cotswold stone. The temptation to kit the place out in layers of flowery flounce has been heroically resisted, in favour of an informal modern brasserie look in the restaurant, where unclothed tables, chunky candle-stands and a flagged floor reflect the up-to-date approach. That's also reflected in the cooking, which takes an energetic line with combinations, and offsets some familiar modern dishes with newer thinking. Start with a duck pastilla accompanied by celeriac remoulade, cherries and apple, or seared scallops with a black pudding beignet and fennel purée. Mains incorporate quality prime materials, such as corn-fed chicken breast with a polenta cake, chorizo, peppers and pesto, and the grand finale might be pear and butterscotch cheesecake with apple sorbet.

Chef Gareth Rufus **Owner** Sir Peter Rigby **Times** 12-2.30/6.30-9.30 **Prices** Fixed D 3 course £29.50-£35, Service optional **Wines** 47 bottles over £20, 13 bottles under £20, 10 by glass **Notes** Sunday L, Vegetarian available, Civ Wed 65 **Seats** 45, Pr/dining room 20 **Children** Portions, Menu **Parking** 12

Seagrave Arms

◉ Modern British ✆

Local ingredients at a beautifully sited Georgian inn

☎ 01386 840192
Friday St, Weston-Sub-Edge GL55 6QH
e-mail: info@seagravearms.co.uk
dir: A44 Oxford/Evesham, exit Broadway & follow B4632 towards Stratford-upon-Avon

A Georgian Cotswold country inn between Chipping Campden and Broadway, the Seagrave is a Grade II listed building that looks out over some of the lushest scenery in England. The kitchen sources assiduously from local farms and suppliers, bakes its own bread, and makes its own chutneys and ice creams. Daily specials and fish dishes are chalked up on the blackboard, to supplement the likes of grilled herring with stewed white beans in shellfish sauce, roast chicken breast with chicken and leek 'cannelloni' in a sauce of Rioja, and banana cake with salt caramel, rum and raisin ice cream and peanut crumble. Local cheeses come with apple chutney.

Chef Kevin Harris **Owner** Kevin & Sue Davies **Times** 12-3/6-10 Closed 2nd wk Jan, Mon **Prices** Starter £6.25-£7.95, Main £11.95-£18.95, Dessert £5.95-£8.95, Service optional **Wines** 7 bottles over £20, 7 bottles under £20, 9 by glass **Notes** Sunday L, Vegetarian available

Save on Hotels. Book at **theAA.com/hotel**

GLOUCESTERSHIRE 167 **ENGLAND**

Seats 36, Pr/dining room 14 **Children** Portions **Parking** 14

Three Ways House

◉ Modern British

Well-conceived dishes at the home of the Pudding Club

☎ 01386 438429
Chapel Ln, Mickleton GL55 6SB
e-mail: reception@puddingclub.com
dir: On B4632, in village centre

Let us begin at the end, with a warning that Three Ways House is the Cotswolds seat of the Pudding Club, so skipping dessert just won't do. However, there's plenty to take in here before hove into view. The Victorian building has heaps of period charm, although the restaurant sports a more contemporary, eclectic look with good use of mirrors to boost the feeling of space. As you might expect, the cooking is punchy, big-hearted British stuff, with a flag-waving dedication to local raw materials balanced by a multi-cultural approach to flavour combinations. Thus a starter tian of crab and red pepper with a mango and lime salsa does not have an especially Gloucestershire ring about it, while main course brings things closer to home with a juniper-crusted loin of venison with curly kale and port wine jus. And so to pudding which could be a selection of steamed puds with lashings of custard, or a heretical plate of British cheeses.

Chef Mark Rowlandson **Owner** Simon Coombe, Peter Henderson **Times** 12-2.30/7-9.30 Closed L Mon-Sat **Prices** Fixed L 2 course £21.50, Fixed D 3 course £37-£40, Service included **Wines** 40 bottles over £20, 10 bottles under £20, 13 by glass **Notes** Sunday L, Vegetarian available, Civ Wed 80 **Seats** 80, Pr/dining room 70 **Children** Portions, Menu **Parking** 37, On street

---
CIRENCESTER Map 5 SP00

Hare & Hounds

◉ Modern British

Excellent home-cooking in a traditional Cotswold pub

☎ 01285 720288
Foss Cross GL54 4NN
e-mail: stay@hareandhoundsinn.com
web: www.hareandhoundsinn.com
dir: On A429 (Stow road), 6m from Cirencester

The mellow Cotswold-stone Hare & Hounds is somewhat of a landmark building in this neck of the woods, standing beside the ancient Roman Fosse Way at Foss Cross. You can well imagine travellers stopping off here in days gone by on long, cross-country journeys (the Fosse Way was originally built to link Exeter with Lincoln), and in that respect little has changed today. Original flagstone floors and fireplaces with built-in bread ovens provide a character backdrop to the accomplished cooking of chef-patron Gerry Ragosa (the lovely orangery and the garden provide alternative dining areas), who makes everything in-house, including the bread and ice cream. Start with salt beef and carrot terrine with home-

made piccalilli, before tucking into grilled fillet of plaice with prawns and rice noodles and a Malaysian sauce, with a richly indulgent chocolate and pecan tart with crème anglaise to finish.

Times 12-3/6-10 Closed Xmas, New Year, BHs

Jesse's Bistro

◉ Modern British **NEW** 🍷

Appealing bistro food down a cobbled alley

☎ 01285 641497 & 07932 150720
14 Blackjack St GL7 2AA
e-mail: info@jessesbistro.co.uk
web: www.jessesbistro.co.uk
dir: In town centre between the parish church & Roman Museum, behind Jesse Smith the Butchers

The bistro is to be found in a converted stable down a little cobbled alley in the centre of town, behind a butcher's shop of the same name. The exposed stone walls, wrought-iron fitments and beams of the interior, which is divided into three spaces, provide a characterful backdrop, and there's a small mezzanine area for group bookings. A compact courtyard opens on fine days. An Anglo-French approach to the bistro ethic brings on simple dishes that are carefully presented and deliver plenty of flavour. Ham, duck and foie gras terrine with red onion marmalade and toasted date bread is a typical starter, or the idiom may be stretched to encompass panko-crumbed soft-shelled crab with glass noodle salad in teriyaki-style soy dressing. The quality and proportions of a main-course serving of well-timed sea bass with buttered spinach and puréed fennel in basil and lime oil are impressive, while the slow-braised pork belly comes with a glazed apple tart.

Chef Paul Driver-Dickenson, David Witnall, Andrew Parffrey **Owner** Watermoor Meat Supply **Times** 12-3/7-10 Closed Xmas, Sun, D Mon **Prices** Starter £6-£13, Main £12.50-£32, Dessert £5.50-£9.50, Service optional, Groups min 8 service 10% **Wines** 60 bottles over £20,

3 bottles under £20, 15 by glass **Notes** Vegetarian available, Dress restrictions, Smart casual preferred **Seats** 55, Pr/dining room 12 **Children** Portions **Parking** Old station car park

---
CLEARWELL Map 4 SO50

Tudor Farmhouse Hotel & Restaurant

◉◉ Modern British

Clear modern flavours in an ancient ex-farmhouse

☎ 01594 833046
High St GL16 8JS
e-mail: info@tudorfarmhousehotel.co.uk
web: www.tudorfarmhousehotel.co.uk
dir: Off A4136 onto B4228, through Coleford, turn right into Clearwell, hotel on right just before War Memorial Cross

In a sleepy village deep in the Forest of Dean, this converted farmhouse restaurant, as the name suggests, has inglenooks, wood panelling, venerable beams and exposed stone walls to attest to its origins, but what comes out of the kitchen these days is far from stuck in the past. Driven by seasonal and local ingredients, the menus are full of fresh, modern ideas, among which you might find a terrine of confit chicken, shiitaki mushrooms and pancetta, served with raisin purée, while main courses run to braised shoulder of locally-farmed lamb with poached apple, carrot purée and red wine jus. To finish, head for chestnut and maple tart with vanilla mascarpone cream and orange caramel syrup. This is genuine, unaffected cooking and it's all backed by personable staff who provide efficient, friendly service.

Times 12-2/7-9 Closed 24-27 Dec

The Wyndham Arms Hotel

◉ Modern British 🍷

Polished gastro-pub fare in old village inn

☎ 01594 833666
GL16 8JT
e-mail: stay@thewyndhamhotel.co.uk
dir: Exit B4228. Hotel in village centre on B4231

Clearwell is a picturesque village near Offa's Dyke Path between the Wye Valley and the Forest of Dean, and this characterful old inn is at its centre. Local ales and cider are dispensed in the rustic-style bar, and meals are served in the stone-walled, vaulted restaurant. The pub

continued

CLEARWELL *continued*

keeps Gloucestershire Old Spot pigs (and sells its own takeaway sausages and burgers), which turn up in pork and ham hock terrine, and as roast loin with apple and potato mash and cider cream. Elsewhere, starters can take in home-smoked duck breast with raspberry vinaigrette, or sardine escabèche in a salad with crayfish and citrus dressing, with pubby main courses like grilled gammon steak with fried eggs and chips, or more classically orientated pan-fried fillet of sea bass with barigoule sauce and saffron-flavoured potatoes.

Chef Steve Jenkins **Owner** Nigel & Pauline Stanley **Times** 12-2/6.30-9 Closed 1st wk Jan, L some days in winter, D some Sun **Prices** Starter £5-£7.50, Main £9.50-£19.50, Dessert £5-£7.50, Service optional, Groups min 8 service 5% **Wines** 3 bottles over £20, 10 bottles under £20, 10 by glass **Notes** Sunday L, Vegetarian available, Civ Wed 60 **Seats** 50, Pr/dining room 24 **Children** Portions **Parking** 30

COLN ST ALDWYNS   Map 5 SP10

The New Inn at Coln

◉◉ Traditional & Modern British

Tranquil country inn with appealingly modish menu

☎ 01285 750651
GL7 5AN
dir: 8m E of Cirencester, between Bibury & Fairford

The scene is one of a quintessentially English hideaway: a creeper-clad, honey-coloured stone inn, with a delicious little garden and terrace dotted with tables and parasols overlooking verdant fields. Inside, the place is gastro through and through: rugs and flagstone floors, inglenooks and beams are overlaid with slick modern design touches, while the kitchen pleases all comers with a menu that runs from grills to pub classics, and mighty tempting sandwiches - how about a rib-eye steak ciabatta with melted Shropshire Blue and shallot marmalade? At dinner, things are ramped up to take in intelligently-conceived modern ideas along the lines of seared scallops with bacon, black pudding, redcurrants and chorizo oil, followed by Gloucestershire Old Spot pork belly with fondant potato, confit Savoy cabbage and celeriac, and thyme jus. At the end, splendid local cheeses are well worth a punt, or you could bow out with tempura-battered apple fritters with black pepper ice cream.

Chef Darren Bartlett **Owner** Hillbrooke Hotels **Times** 12.30-2.30/7-9 **Prices** Starter £5.95-£8.95, Main £9.95-£18.95, Dessert £5.95-£6.95, Service optional **Wines** 30 bottles over £20, 6 bottles under £20, 8 by glass **Notes** Vegetarian available **Seats** 40 **Children** Portions, Menu **Parking** 25

CORSE LAWN   Map 10 SO83

Corse Lawn House Hotel

◉◉◉ British, French V 🔘

Opulent setting for classic cooking

☎ 01452 780771
GL19 4LZ
e-mail: enquiries@corselawn.com
dir: 5m SW of Tewkesbury on B4211, in village centre

A red-brick Grade II listed Queen Anne building with a coach wash out front (yes, it was for washing down a coach and its four horses back in the day but since turned into an ornamental pond), Corse Lawn has been in the hands of the Hine family for more than 30 years. It's a smart and fairly formal environment and one is expected to dress accordingly in the elegantly done-out dining room. Local ingredients play a starring role on a menu that steers clear of froths and foams in favour of carefully considered combinations and clearly defined flavours, and the kitchen is very happy to turn its hand to game and offal preparations. Hereford snails might appear with herbs, garlic and flageolets, pan-fried calves' brains with caper butter sauce and olive crushed potatoes, and a whole roast flounder is served on the bone with a beurre noisette. To finish, banana tempura with coconut ice cream competes for your attention with the cheese trolley. A separate vegetarian menu is no afterthought.

Chef Andrew Poole, Martin Kinahan **Owner** Hine family **Times** 12-2/7-9.30 Closed 24-26 Dec **Prices** Fixed L 2 course £15-£22.50, Fixed D 3 course £20-£33.50, Starter £5.95-£12.95, Main £14.95-£22.95, Dessert £5.95-£7.95, Service optional **Wines** 400 bottles over £20, 39 bottles under £20, 10 by glass **Notes** Sunday L, Vegetarian menu, Civ Wed 70 **Seats** 50, Pr/dining room 28 **Children** Portions, Menu **Parking** 60

DAYLESFORD   Map 10 SP22

Daylesford Farm Cafe

◉ Modern British 🔘

Organic produce cooked with flair in converted barn

☎ 01608 731700
GL56 0YG
e-mail: thefarm@daylesfordorganic.com
dir: From Cheltenham take A40 & A436 through Stow-on-the-Wold, follow signs to Daylesford farmshop

A comfortable and welcoming café, evocative of a farmhouse kitchen, in a converted barn is only part of the complex of retailers here, which include a greengrocer, butcher, baker, wine shop and much more - even a spa. The farm is totally organic, as is the produce on sale, as well as all the ingredients delivered each day to the café's kitchen, so dishes are not just bursting with seasonal flavours but have impeccable ethical credentials too. Start with warm crab on toast, or hot salt beef with roast beet salad and a mustardy dressing, and progress to a salad or something more substantial like roast mackerel with salsa verde, wilted greens and new potatoes, or lamb from the farm in a hotpot with spelt,

accompanied by spring greens. If everything sounds too wholesome, pig out on chocolate nemesis with vanilla cream.

Chef Gaven Fuller **Owner** Carole Bamford **Times** 12-3/7-9.30 Closed 25-26 Dec, 1 Jan **Prices** Starter £5.95-£9.95, Main £9.95-£16.95, Dessert £4.50-£5.95, Service added but optional 10% **Wines** 9 bottles over £20, 3 bottles under £20, 9 by glass **Notes** Vegetarian available **Seats** 75 **Children** Portions **Parking** 100

EBRINGTON   Map 10 SP14

The Ebrington Arms

◉◉ Modern British

Village inn with great food

☎ 01386 593223
GL55 6NH
e-mail: reservations@ebringtonarms.co.uk
dir: From Chipping Campden take B4035 towards Shipston-on-Stour, left to Ebrington

This gem of a 17th-century village inn - tucked away in green-and-pleasant Cotswold countryside - brims with the genuine charm and character of a proper old-style pub, and is justly revered by its locals who huddle around its small bar. Cotswold-stone walls, oak beams and big open fireplaces are all present and correct, as are real ales on tap. The restaurant continues the rustic-chic theme, decked out with old darkwood tables, while the kitchen turns up the gas with a decidedly modern approach based around quality local seasonal produce and something of a nod to sunnier climes. From a spring menu might come rack of top quality new season Cotswold lamb served with provençale vegetables and confit tomato tapenade, or perhaps a classic bouillabaisse (monkfish, red mullet, king prawns and sea bass with rouille and croûtes), while a cleverly presented rhubarb and custard tart with ginger ice cream might provide the finale.

Times 12-2.30/6.30-9.30 Closed 25 Dec, D Sun

GLOUCESTER   Map 10 SO81

The Wharf House Restaurant with Rooms

◉ British, European 🔘

Broadly appealing cooking in a former lockhouse by the Severn

☎ 01452 332900
Over Waterside, Over GL2 8DB
e-mail: enquiries@thewharfhouse.co.uk
dir: From Over rdbt take A40 westbound to Ross-on-Wye, 1st right in 50 yds

Owned by the Herefordshire & Gloucestershire Canal Trust, profits from this restaurant with rooms by the River Severn go towards the upkeep of 34 miles of canals in the two counties. It really comes into its own when the weather allows for eating on the terrace overlooking the water, but it's a pleasant space if you're dining indoors, with its wooden tables, parquet floor and fashionably neutral colour palette. The menu suits the relaxed and informal setting, offering a large choice of well-prepared and unfussy dishes. Start with a tart filled with leeks and stilton, or a salad enriched with crab and mango salsa, before main-course rainbow trout with tangy tomato chutney, or a rack of Herefordshire lamb with leek and potato dauphinoise and rich honey and rosemary sauce.

Chef David Penny **Owner** H & G Canal Trust **Times** 12-6 Closed 25 Dec-4 Jan, D 24 Dec **Prices** Starter £5.59-£7.99, Main £8.99-£18.99, Dessert £4.99-£12.99, Service optional, Groups min 6 service 10% **Wines** 33 bottles over £20, 15 bottles under £20, 6 by glass **Notes** Sunday L, Vegetarian available, Dress restrictions, Smart casual **Seats** 40 **Children** Portions **Parking** 32

LOWER SLAUGHTER　　　　　　Map 10 SP12

Lower Slaughter Manor

@@ Modern British

Smart manor house with confident modern cooking

☎ 01451 820456
GL54 2HP
e-mail: info@lowerslaughter.co.uk
dir: Off A429, signed 'The Slaughters'. 0.5m into village on right

With its mellow Cotswold-stone façade, Lower Slaughter is a manor house of impeccable credentials, built by a master stone mason back in the 1650s. The house has been gently added to through the centuries but remains a mightily handsome property, now a chic country-house hotel. The combination of charming period features and elegant furnishings and decoration is a winning one. The Sixteen58 Restaurant cuts a well-dressed contemporary dash, with its chocolate-brown silk walls, Murano glass chandeliers and candlelit tables dressed in their best whites, and is the setting for some modish cooking under the auspices of chef Andrew Birch. Start with a fine piece of foie gras counterpointed with a blood orange purée, braised chicory and spiced walnuts, then move on to main-course roasted fillet of cod with a timbale of ratte potatoes flecked with crab meat. Carrot cake is a deconstructed version, served with orange and mascarpone cream, walnut crunch and golden raisin purée.

Times 12.15-2/6.30-10

MORETON-IN-MARSH　　　　　　Map 10 SP23

Manor House Hotel

@@ Modern British V

Classy, modern cooking in a 16th-century gem

☎ 01608 650501
High St GL56 0LJ
e-mail: info@manorhousehotel.info
web: www.cotswold-inns-hotels.co.uk/manor
dir: Off A429 at south end of town

In a happy blend of old and new, period character rubs along nicely with aesthetics in tune with contemporary tastes in this mellow yellow Cotswold-stone classic. The Manor House comes from blue-blooded stock: Henry VIII bequeathed the house to the Dean and Chapter of Westminster in 1539, and the trencherman royal would no doubt give the kitchen's output the seal of approval. Highly-refined country-house cooking in the modern British mould is the name of the game in the Mulberry Restaurant. Escabèche of Brixham monkfish appears with smoked salmon mousse and wafer thin shards of pancetta to create a well-conceived opener, while mains go down the inventive route of partnering tenderloin and braised shoulder of pork with Madeira-poached apple, black pudding crumble, leeks and a soft quail's egg. Popping candy injects a note of frivolity to an entertaining rosemary pannacotta with pineapple salsa and piña colada sorbet.

Chef Nick Orr **Owner** Michael & Pamela Horton **Times** 12-2.30/7-9.30 **Prices** Fixed L 3 course £19.95, Fixed D 4 course £39, Service added but optional 10% **Wines** 53 bottles over £20, 26 bottles under £20, 8 by glass **Notes** Tasting menu 8 course, Sunday L, Vegetarian menu, Dress restrictions, Smart casual, no jeans, shorts or trainers, Civ Wed 120 **Seats** 55, Pr/dining room 120 **Children** Portions **Parking** 32

Redesdale Arms

@ British

Relaxed dining in historic Cotswold inn

☎ 01608 650308
High St GL56 0AW
e-mail: info@redesdalearms.com
dir: On A429, 0.5m from rail station

This fine old Cotswold-stone inn has been a part of the bustling, picture-postcard-pretty Moreton scene for

centuries, today offering a classy fusion of old and modern. It successfully blends venerable wood panelling, oak floorboards and exposed stone walls with a relaxed contemporary style, using tobacco-hued sofas, modern art and muted colour schemes. Dinner is served in the modern brasserie-styled rear conservatory, with its please-all menus conjured from quality, local and seasonal produce with simplicity and flavour to the fore. Take an opener of warm Cotswold goats' cheese and caramelised red onion tartlet with dressed leaves and balsamic and port wine syrup, and to follow, perhaps pan-seared Cornish sea bass fillet with sautéed potatoes, wilted spinach and a caviar and lemon butter sauce. To close, Greek yoghurt pannacotta with winter berry compôte.

Times 12-2.30/6.30-9

White Hart Royal Hotel

@ Modern British **NEW**

Enterprising cooking in a Cotswold coaching inn

☎ 01608 650731
High St GL56 0BA
e-mail: whr@bpcmail.co.uk
dir: In town centre

The 17th-century former coaching inn of Cotswold stone looks a picture in summer when festooned with hanging baskets. It stands in the centre of this delightful market town at the top of the Evenlode Valley, the quintessence of pastoral England. Since everywhere built in this era has to have sheltered either Cromwell or Charles I at some point, be it noted that the King holed up here for a night after the battle of Marston Moor in 1644. A pair of lounges, a flagstoned snug with original inglenook and the courtyard restaurant, which includes tables en plein air for the sunny days, come as standard. After a starter of 'Soup of the Moment', or a tri-coloured stack of Marie Rose prawns, crab salad and avocado mousse, the main courses try out some enterprising ideas, such as Balinese-style fish (red snapper, king prawn and catfish) wrapped in a banana leaf, served with lemongrass and coconut broth and saffron rice. Impressively tender lamb is two lumps of rump seared on all sides, accompanied by silky-smooth minted pea purée in red wine and rosemary reduction. Recline into the comfort-zone at the end with the likes of steamed lemon and honey pudding.

Chef Dewa Anggarayasa **Owner** Bulldog Hotel Group Ltd **Times** 11-3/6-10 **Prices** Starter £4.95-£6.95, Main £9.95-£17.95, Dessert £3.95-£6.95, Service optional **Wines** 16 bottles over £20, 23 bottles under £20, 11 by glass **Notes** Sunday L, Vegetarian available **Seats** 44, Pr/dining room 12 **Children** Portions **Parking** 6, On street

NAILSWORTH
Map 4 ST89

The Wild Garlic Restaurant

@@ Modern British V ⚘

Imaginative modern cooking in former blacksmith's

☎ 01453 832615
3 Cossack Square GL6 0DB
e-mail: info@wild-garlic.co.uk
dir: M4 junct 18. A46 towards Stroud. Enter Nailsworth, turn left at rdbt and then an immediate left. Restaurant opposite Britannia Pub

This sweet, small-yet-perfectly-formed modern restaurant is a stylish, relaxed place with enthusiastic staff to match. Chef-prop Matthew Beardshall's kitchen takes an admirable hands-on approach making everything in-house, from organic bread and pasta to sorbets and ice cream, while the concise brasserie-style menu changes monthly to reflect seasonality and make the very best use of the regional larder. On a late spring menu, expect simplicity and flavour from the likes of a fillet of South Coast turbot teamed with a slow-roast tomato salad and samphire, or perhaps Cotswold white chicken Kiev served with wild garlic butter (wild garlic rightly making an appearance on the plate; it's abundant in the area), plus potato, smoked bacon and watercress salad. To finish, maybe rhubarb and custard with champagne and poached rhubarb jelly and almond tuile.

Chef Matthew Beardshall **Owner** Matthew Beardshall **Times** 12-2.30/7-9.30 Closed 1st 2 wks Jan, Mon-Tue, L Wed, D Sun **Prices** Tasting menu £42.50, Starter £3.95-£9.95, Main £9.95-£21.95, Dessert £4.25-£6.95, Service optional, Groups min 7 service 10% **Wines** 40 bottles over £20, 9 bottles under £20, 10 by glass **Notes** Tasting menu 6 course, Sunday L, Vegetarian menu **Seats** 42 **Children** Portions, Menu **Parking** NCP, parking on street

NETHER WESTCOTE
Map 10 SP22

The Feathered Nest Inn

@@ Modern British ⚜ NOTABLE WINE LIST

A gem of a country pub in the Cotswolds

☎ 01993 833030
OX7 6SD
e-mail: info@thefeatherednestinn.co.uk
web: www.thefeatherednestinn.co.uk
dir: On A424 between Burford & Stow-on-the-Wold, signposted

After new owners lavished an upmarket facelift on this 17th-century malthouse in a lovely Cotswold village between Stow-on-the-Wold and Burford, it has come storming onto the local foodie scene with all guns blazing. Inside, there is the stylish blend of ancient character and contemporary sharpness you'd expect of a switched-on modern pub, and the garden looking over rolling green-and-pleasant countryside is a delight. All of this is unquestionably lovely, but it is the kitchen's high-achieving efforts that have the punters beating a path to the relaxed dining areas. Menus nicely in tune with today's sensibilities support local produce, and bristle with good, honest ideas such as hand-dived scallops with ham hock, home-made black pudding, and apple salad to start, while mains take in game in season - local wild venison, perhaps, matched with cabbage and bacon, pickled russet apple, and chocolate and juniper sauce - or fish, in the shape of Cornish stone bass with chorizo and clam chowder. Desserts are equally well-considered ideas such as chocolate and mint torte with caramelised custard and mint oil.

Chef Kuba Winkowski **Owner** Tony Timmer **Times** 12-2.30/6.30-9.30 Closed 25 Dec, Mon, D Sun **Prices** Food prices not confirmed for 2013. Please telephone for details **Wines** 145 bottles over £20, 19 bottles under £20, 18 by glass **Notes** Sunday L, Vegetarian available, Civ Wed 200 **Seats** 60, Pr/dining room 16 **Children** Portions, Menu **Parking** 45

NEWENT
Map 10 SO72

Three Choirs Vineyards

@@ Modern British, European

Award-winning vineyard with seriously good food

☎ 01531 890223
GL18 1LS
e-mail: ts@threechoirs.com
dir: 2m N of Newent on B4215, follow brown tourist signs

The next time you hanker after a break amid vineyards combed across rolling hillsides, forget Burgundy and Tuscany and set the GPS for deepest Gloucestershire. Once at the award-winning Three Choirs estate, you can discuss the merits of local terroir, south- versus west-facing slopes and all that, while sipping on a glass of Britain's finest on the vine-festooned terrace of the converted farmhouse. Since the UK climate can't quite match that of the Rhône Valley, it might be wise to dine indoors in the Vineyard Restaurant, an airy contemporary space with darkwood tables and high-backed leather chairs looking through large windows across the estate. The kitchen also works with the local terroir in sourcing materials for its uncomplicated, flavour-driven dishes, as seen in an Asian-accented starter involving crisp cubes of breaded pork belly teamed with crunchy Chinese cabbage and ginger dressing. Main course reverts to a more typical European idiom, delivering Madgetts Farm duck breast with parsnip purée, duck fat potato, and parsnip crisps. To finish, there's a delicate cherry and Amaretto cheesecake with bitter chocolate sorbet.

Chef Sarah Louking **Owner** Three Choirs Vineyards Ltd **Times** 12-2/7-9 Closed Xmas, New Year **Prices** Fixed L 2 course £22.50, Fixed D 3 course £37.50, Starter £5-£11, Main £11-£19, Dessert £5.50-£8.50, Service optional, Groups min 10 service 10% **Wines** 20 bottles over £20, 34 bottles under £20, 12 by glass **Notes** Sunday L, Vegetarian available **Seats** 50, Pr/dining room 20 **Children** Portions, Menu **Parking** 50

PAINSWICK
Map 4 SO80

Cotswolds88 Hotel

@@@ – see opposite

Save on Hotels. Book at **theAA.com/hotel**

GLOUCESTERSHIRE 171 ENGLAND

Cotswolds88 Hotel

Modern British

Imaginative modern British cooking in a hip boutique hotel

☎ 01452 813688
Kemps Ln GL6 6YB
e-mail: reservations@cotswolds88hotel.com
web: www.cotswolds88hotel.com
dir: M4 junct 15, follow A419 past Swindon & Cirencester to Stroud. Turn off to Painswick

Whilst the rather grand Cotswold-stone exterior makes a reassuringly traditional first impression, what lies behind the timeless façade is a myriad of bold designer flourishes and a cornucopia of luxuriant furnishings. This is a boutique hotel and no mistake. The dining room goes for a black, white and red theme, and stripes - lots of stripes - whilst the crisp white linen-clad, smartly laid tables reflect the serious intent that lurks behind the playfulness of the décor. A canapé of miniature fish and chips shows that a bit of fun is not out of the question, but notice the fabulous quality of the fish. The Eighty Eight Room is chef Lee Scott's domain and he turns out confident modern dishes that showcase his acute technical skills. Caramelised veal sweetbreads, for example, come with a cassonade of Herefordshire snails, roast garlic and parsley velouté in a first course which is

rich and earthy but light and full of flavour. Next up, perhaps wild Cornish sea bass - a beautiful piece of fish, cooked to a tee - with chorizo and squid 'bolognaise', followed by 88 apple pie mousse with green apple sorbet. There's a tasting menu if you want to push the boat out, and the terrace serves up some delectable views over the Cotswold Hills.

Chef Lee Scott **Owner** Mr & Mr Harris **Times** 12-2.30/6.30-10 Closed 1 wk Jan **Prices** Tasting menu £74.95, Service added but optional 12.5% **Wines** 149 bottles over £20, 21 bottles under £20, 10 by glass **Notes** Tasting menu 7 course, Sunday L, Vegetarian available, Civ Wed 80 **Seats** 42, Pr/dining room 14 **Parking** 17, Public car park

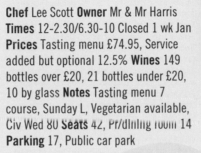

PAXFORD
Map 10 SP13

Churchill Arms
◎◎ ⊛ Traditional

Classy cooking in a civilised dining pub

☎ 01386 594000
GL55 6XH
e-mail: info@thechurchillarms.com
dir: A429 from The Fosse, then A44 to Bourton-on-the-Hill. Turn right at end of village to Paxford via Blockley

On the face of it the Churchill Arms looks like many another Cotswolds pub, a mellow stone building dating from the 18th century, with its complement of inglenook and ceiling beams and an informal, relaxed atmosphere. What marks it out is not just its setting in a pretty village surrounded by lovely walking country but the quality of the cooking. The daily-changing menus are written on boards and may open with robustly flavoured roast tomato and red onion soup with pesto and cheese croûtes, or cheese soufflé with spring onion cream and tomatoes dressed with balsamic. Most ingredients are sourced locally - rump of lamb, say, served plainly (and appreciated for it) with creamed Savoy cabbage and mash - with fish coming from Cornwall: grilled sea bass sauced with salsa verde, accompanied by samphire, wild mushrooms and crushed potatoes, for instance. Pubby classics like fish and chips are fixtures, and puddings are old favourites like Eton Mess and pannacotta with poached rhubarb.

Chef Jamie Forman **Owner** Richard Shore
Times 12-2/6.30-9 Closed 25 Dec **Prices** Starter £5-£8, Main £11-£18, Dessert £5-£7.50, Service optional, Groups min 10 service 10% **Wines** 14 bottles over £20, 14 bottles under £20, 9 by glass **Notes** Vegetarian available **Seats** 56 **Children** Portions, Menu **Parking** On street

SOUTH CERNEY
Map 5 SU09

The Old Boathouse
⊛ Modern British

All-day brasserie cooking in a water-park

☎ 01285 864111 & 864000
Cotswold Water Park, Four Pillars Hotel, Lake 6, Spine Road East GL7 5FP
e-mail: oldboathouse@four-pillars.co.uk
dir: M4 junct 15/A419 to Cirencester, turn onto B4696 & follow signs for Cotswold Water Park Information Centre

Perched on the edge of Lake six in the grounds of the Cotswold Water Park, an aquatic concept hotel in the Four Pillars group, The Old Boathouse is styled as a family pub. It looks much fresher and airier than many a hostelry, with sky-blue colour scheme, light wood and an overturned boat suspended in the rafters. The kitchen offers the lot, from breakfasts of smoked salmon and scrambled eggs, through sandwich and deli-board lunches, afternoon tea, and a modernised brasserie-style menu containing masses of choice in the evenings. Potted crab with lemon crème fraîche, roast lamb rump

with dauphinoise in Madeira jus, and red pepper Tatin with glazed baby veg in pepper coulis are what to expect, with the satisfaction of treacle tart, apple sorbet and coffee syrup to round it all off.

Chef Daniel Driscoll **Owner** Four Pillars Hotels
Times 11-10 **Prices** Food prices not confirmed for 2013. Please telephone for details **Wines** 7 bottles over £20, 12 bottles under £20, 14 by glass **Notes** Sunday L, Vegetarian available **Seats** 110 **Children** Portions, Menu **Parking** 300

STOW-ON-THE-WOLD
Map 11 SP12

Fosse Manor
◎◎ ⊛ Modern British

Smart country-house hotel with a local flavour

☎ 01451 830354
GL54 1JX
e-mail: enquiries@fossemanor.co.uk
dir: From Stow-on-the-Wold take A429 S for 1m

The classic Cotswolds honey-stone, creeper-clad exterior of this former rectory looks like it conceals a scene of country-house chintz, but inside the picture is one of pared-back, neutral-hued contemporary style. You'll find Fosse Manor on the fringes of Stow-on-the-Wold in five acres of idyllic grounds and gardens that provide the backdrop to dining in the smart restaurant. The kitchen too, has stayed in touch with current trends, serving up appealing menus of uncomplicated modern British ideas built on top-grade local produce. A terrine of local game, duck and foie gras with pear chutney might be one way to start, while main course could showcase Lighthorn lamb in a trio of rump, sweetbread and hotpot, served with tomato and basil, and red wine sauce. At the end, local cheeses are always a good bet, or you could bow out sweetly with dark chocolate torte with vanilla ice cream and cherries in Kirsch.

Times 12-2/7-9

The King's Head Inn
⊛ British

Refined pub fare in an atmospheric village inn

☎ 01608 658365
The Green, Bledington OX7 6XQ
e-mail: info@kingsheadinn.net
dir: On B4450, 4m from Stow-on-the-Wold

The King's Head is a textbook example of a switched-on village pub. The scene is idyllic: honey-hued Cotswold houses huddle around the village green where ducks and bantams play in a trickling brook; inside are wobbly flagstone floors, log fires and head-skimming beams. A commendable balance is struck between food and drink - the place is still the village boozer serving a fine pint of Hook Norton, while the cooking is a definite notch or two above your average pub. A menu in the modern British mould showcases local free-range and organic materials, starting with super-fresh grilled sardines with fennel, mint and chilli, then perhaps an Aberdeen Angus steak

reared on the family farm, or roast haunch of Cotswold venison with mash, green beans and beetroot jus.

Times 12-2/7-9.30 Closed 25-26 Dec

Number Four at Stow Hotel & Restaurant
◎◎ ⊛ British, European

Stylish modern restaurant serving imaginative food

☎ 01451 830297
Fosseway GL54 1JX
e-mail: reservations@hotelnumberfour.co.uk
dir: Situated on A424 Burford Road, at junction with A429

A building dating from the 17th century is home to this stylish boutique hotel in the heart of the Cotswolds. Number Four is one of those places that gets everything pitch perfect, from the opulent contemporary look, to the sort of prescient service that anticipates guests' needs, and, in the oldest part of the house, light and modern cooking in the characterful beamed and painted wood-panelled Cutler's Restaurant. Head chef Brian Cutler uses local, seasonal produce from a well-chosen network of suppliers to good effect in well-executed dishes. Salad of Cornish crab and smoked salmon, or chicory tarte Tatin with blue cheese and artichoke might open proceedings, while mains extend to well-conceived pairings of flavour and texture - medallions of Cotswold venison with walnut spätzle, or suprême of sea bass with scallop cannelloni, say. Finish with something like strawberry parfait with marshmallow.

Chef Brian Cutler **Owner** Caroline & Patricia Losel
Times 12-2/7-9 **Prices** Fixed L 2 course £14.50, Starter £6-£10.50, Main £14.50-£22, Dessert £6.50-£8.50, Service optional **Wines** 25 bottles over £20, 7 bottles under £20, 10 by glass **Notes** Sunday L, Vegetarian available, Air con **Seats** 50, Pr/dining room 40 **Children** Portions, Menu **Parking** 50

The Old Butcher's
◎◎ ⊛ Modern British

Appealing modern British cooking in informal surroundings

☎ 01451 831700
Park St GL54 1AQ
e-mail: info@theoldbutchers.com

The only hint that Peter and Louise Robinson's clean-cut modern brasserie was once a butcher's shop lies in a perusal of the menu: here are big-hitting carnivorous ingredients - pig's head terrine, crispy calves' brains, ox tongue and cheeks - which show a kitchen that subscribes to the nose-to-tail eating ethos. Otherwise, the setting has a sharp cosmopolitan look with banquettes, bare wooden tables, artworks on white walls; pavement terrace tables bring a further hit of continental style to the Cotswold market town. The vibe is casual and chatty, the service suitably unbuttoned, yet on the ball, and the ingredients-led repertoire reliably delivers no-nonsense ideas with gutsy flavours, starting, perhaps,

Save on Hotels. Book at **theAA.com/hotel**

GLOUCESTERSHIRE 173 **ENGLAND**

with Cornish scallops, oxtail and red wine sauce, or warm smoked eel with beetroot, horseradish and watercress. Mains might see Hinchwick partridge matched with bread sauce and Armagnac gravy, while chocolate and almond pudding with chocolate sauce and praline parfait is a typical finale.

Chef Peter Robinson **Owner** Louise & Peter Robinson **Times** 12-2.30/6-9.30 Closed 1 wk in May & Oct, Mon, D Sun **Prices** Starter £6.50-£9.50, Main £14.50-£25, Dessert £5-£7.50, Service optional **Wines** 55 bottles over £20, 19 bottles under £20, 14 by glass **Notes** Sunday L, Vegetarian available **Seats** 45 **Children** Portions **Parking** On street

Wyck Hill House Hotel & Spa

◎◎ Modern British

Modern British food in beautiful surroundings

☎ 01451 831936
Burford Rd GL54 1HY
e-mail: info.wyckhillhouse@bespokehotels.com
dir: A429 for Cirencester, pass through 2 sets of traffic lights in Stow-on-the-Wold, at 3rd set of lights bear left signed Burford, then A424 signed Stow-on-the-Wold, hotel 7m on left

Wyck Hill House is a place to pamper yourself in: apart from its 100 acres of fabulous grounds with green-and-pleasant views over the folds of the Cotswold Hills and Windrush Valley, there are chic antique-strewn lounges, an oak-panelled bar, and a glitzy spa. In the classy restaurant, floor-to-ceiling French windows let light flood in on a setting of cream-painted tongue and groove walls, and plushly-upholstered seats at white-linen tables on bare boards - a suitably elegant backdrop for meals with a contemporary British tone and a fondness for regional produce. You might set out with wild rabbit terrine with chanterelles, parsley root purée, and warm chestnut and cider jelly, then proceed to pan-roasted venison with smoked potato purée, parsnip fondant, braised red cabbage and game jus. To end, beetroot purée, and dark chocolate and chilli put a radical spin on the Baked Alaska theme.

Chef Mark Jane **Owner** Bespoke Hotels
Times 12.30-2/7-9.30 **Prices** Fixed L 2 course £15.95, Fixed D 3 course £39, Service optional **Wines** 30 bottles over £20, 4 bottles under £20, 4 by glass **Notes** Sunday L, Vegetarian available, Civ Wed 120 **Seats** 50, Pr/dining room 120 **Children** Portions, Menu **Parking** 120

STROUD   **Map 4 SO80**

Burleigh Court Hotel

◎◎ British, European

Grand old house, confident cooking

☎ 01453 883804
Burleigh, Minchinhampton GL5 2PF
e-mail: burleighcourt@aol.com
dir: 2.5m SE of Stroud, off A419

Guests at this Cotswold stone manor house have none other than Clough Williams-Ellis of Portmeirion fame to thank for the superb view of the Golden Valley, since he designed its terraced gardens in the 1930s to provide a perfect viewing platform to take it all in. Built at the outset of the 19th century, Burleigh Court is every inch the classic English country-house retreat: an oak-panelled lounge bar is the venue for a snifter before dinner in the formal, old-school elegance of the dining room. The kitchen revisits classical ideas with a modern eye, using top-drawer ingredients together with home-grown seasonal herbs and veg. It's a straightforward way of doing things that produces accomplished partnerships all the way: a twice-baked goats' cheese soufflé with roasted pears, pine nuts and rocket, ahead of sautéed Cornish mullet and scallops with spring onion and herb potato, creamed leeks, and lemon and dill dressing. To close the show, a summer assiette of lime brings on rose and lime jelly, lime curd tart, and iced lime parfait.

Chef Adrian Jarrad **Owner** Louise Noble **Times** 12-2/7-9 Closed 24-26 Dec **Prices** Fixed L 2 course fr £20, Starter £6-£13.50, Main £15.95-£25.95, Dessert £7.25-£9.95, Service optional **Wines** 50 bottles over £20, 7 bottles under £20, 8 by glass **Notes** Sunday L, Vegetarian available, Civ Wed 50 **Seats** 34, Pr/dining room 18 **Children** Portions, Menu **Parking** 28

TETBURY   **Map 4 ST89**

Calcot Manor

◎◎ Modern British

Charming 14th-century Cotswold retreat with vibrant modern cuisine

☎ 01666 890391
Calcot GL8 8YJ
e-mail: reception@calcotmanor.co.uk
web: www.calcotmanor.co.uk
dir: M4 junct 18, A46 towards Stroud. At x-roads junct with A4135 turn right, then 1st left

Calcot Manor has traded up to the Premier League in the 700 years since it began life as a lowly farmhouse. Nowadays it is a decidedly glossy design-led, boutique-style country hotel kitted out in contemporary rustic-chic finery, and offers the full-dress pampering package: luxurious rooms pitched squarely at style-conscious sybarites, and a state-of-the-art spa to de-stress body and mind before treating the palate to a workout in the chic Conservatory Restaurant. Local suppliers furnish the kitchen's needs for its modern British output, while the sunny cuisines of the Mediterranean provide spiritual inspiration. Tagliatelle of organic beef shin with spinach, black olives and sage is a typical starter, then the wood-fired oven adds an authentic earthy edge to proceedings in main courses such as roasted monkfish with Asian slaw, noodles and dressing, or marinated wood-roasted beef fillet on the bone teamed with French bean and artichoke salad, roast shallots, goose fat chips, and black peppercorn hollandaise.

Chef Michael Croft **Owner** Richard Ball (MD)
Times 12-2/7-9.30 **Prices** Fixed L 2 course £22-£24.50, Fixed D 3 course £27-£29.50, Starter £8.50-£15.95, Main £19-£32, Dessert £8.75, Service optional **Wines** 2 bottles under £20, 14 by glass **Notes** Sunday L, Vegetarian available, Civ Wed 100 **Seats** 100, Pr/dining room 16 **Children** Portions, Menu **Parking** 150

TETBURY *continued*

Hare & Hounds Hotel

◉◉ Modern British V

Charming Cotswold hotel with confident team in the kitchen

☎ 01666 881000
Westonbirt GL8 8QL
e-mail: reception@hareandhoundshotel.com
web: www.cotswold-inns-hotels.co.uk
dir: 2.5m SW of Tetbury on A433

The name might be pubby, but this Hare & Hounds is a classy Cotswolds country hotel that started off as a farmhouse built in 1928 to put up an Indian maharaja and his entourage who were playing at the neighbouring Beaufort Polo Club. Fully refurbished, it is now a luxurious amalgam of period features and contemporary chic, as typified in the striking Beaufort Restaurant where a vaulted hammer-beamed ceiling, stone mullioned windows and saffron-coloured walls form the backdrop to the kitchen's skilful modern British take on classical French cooking. A carefully-sourced menu might get underway creatively with a composition of foie gras crème brûlée with poached rhubarb, exotic fruit, and chicken jus vinaigrette, then continue by partnering boudin noir-stuffed saddle of rabbit with rabbit leg terrine, fondant potato, Dijon soubise, purée, wild mushrooms and Marsala jus. Otherwise, you might consider a fish dish - perhaps pan-fried wild sea bass with spring onion risotto, Jerusalem artichoke purée, roast salsify, and vanilla cream sauce - then wrap things up with a labour-intensive deconstruction of carrot cake, comprising orange and cardamom cake, sweet potato and orange purée, carrot parfait and sorbet, and cinnamon macaroons.

Chef Paul Hudson **Owner** Cotswold Inns & Hotels Ltd
Times 7-9.30 Closed L Mon-Sat **Prices** Food prices not confirmed for 2013. Please telephone for details
Wines 25 bottles over £20, 6 bottles under £20, 6 by glass **Notes** Tasting menu 8 course, Sunday L, Vegetarian menu, Dress restrictions, Smart casual, Civ Wed 120
Seats 60, Pr/dining room 10 **Children** Portions
Parking 40

Ronnie's of Thornbury

◉◉ Modern European 🍷

Modern European cooking in a 17th-century schoolhouse

☎ 01454 411137
11 St Mary St BS35 2AB
e-mail: info@ronnies-restaurant.co.uk

Hidden away in an unlikely location in the town's shopping precinct, Ronnie's became an instant hit with locals when it opened in 2007, and it's easy to see why: whether you pop in for brunch or dinner, the vibe is easygoing, and the modern European cooking keeps things local, seasonal and to the point. The 17th-century building wears its contemporary look well: stone walls, beamed ceilings, wooden floors and neutral hues are pointed up by paintings and photos by West Country artists. Ronnie Faulkner's team will send you away happy, whether you turn up to kick start the day with coffee and eggs Benedict, or round it off with intelligent, precisely-cooked dinner ideas such as cassoulet with confit duck and a fashionable quail's Scotch egg, followed by roasted pork loin matched with a pork and apricot pie, butternut squash, caramelised apple and pork crackling. For pudding, there may be almond sponge with ginger and rhubarb pannacotta, or you could go for a savoury finish with the splendid array of English artisan cheeses.

Lords of the Manor

Modern British 🍷 🌱

Accomplished modern cooking in a Cotswold manor house

☎ 01451 820243
GL54 2JD
e-mail: reservations@lordsofthemanor.com
dir: Follow signs towards The Slaughters 2m W of A429. Hotel on right in centre of Upper Slaughter

The timeless honey stone exterior of this 17th-century manor house is the very picture of green-and-pleasant English loveliness that turns up in rom-com film sets. If that's not enough to tempt you, the classy package includes eight acres of landscaped gardens and parkland bordered by the River Eye, and a vibrant contemporary décor worthy of a glossy interior design magazine - the sort of looks that have funky fabrics and sexy splashes of colour alongside antiques, grand fireplaces and mullioned windows and leave hoteliers with a bill for £1.5 million. The restaurant favours a demure country kitchen-esque décor in pastel greens and creams, while staff classically attired in black and white keep it all ticking over with unobtrusive professionalism. Matthew Weedon's cooking excites with its subtly-nuanced flavours and textures, all underpinned with a thorough grounding in French classical techniques. It is clear from the outset - perhaps grilled breast of mallard with pork belly and apple pastilla, beetroot, and fig purée - that there's an inventive spirit propelling the kitchen's efforts. Mains can have a thoroughly British feel when roasted rib of Longhorn rare breed beef is partnered earthily with braised oxtail, chervil root, Hereford snails, caramelised salsify and red wine sauce, while other combinations - line-caught Cornish sea bass with caramelised cauliflower, roasted diver-caught scallops, star anise and red wine sauce, and shellfish cream, say - speak of sunnier climes. Desserts also flaunt technical proficiency with the likes of prune and Armagnac soufflé served with Earl Grey mousse, and prune and Armagnac ice cream. A hefty wine list runs to many hundreds of bins, and a savvy sommelier is on hand to match either glasses or bottles to the food.

Chef Matt Weedon **Owner** Empire Ventures
Times 12-2.30/7-9.30 Closed L Mon-Sat **Prices** Fixed D 3 course fr £65, Service added 10% **Wines** 700+ bottles over £20, 10 bottles under £20, 15 by glass **Notes** Tasting menu 7/10 course available, Sunday L, Vegetarian available, Dress restrictions, Smart casual, no trainers or jeans, Civ Wed 80 **Seats** 50, Pr/dining room 30
Children Portions, Menu **Parking** 40

Save on Hotels. Book at **theAA.com/hotel**

GLOUCESTERSHIRE 175 ENGLAND

Chef Ron Faulkner & George Kostka **Owner** Ron Faulkner **Times** 12-3/6.30-10.30 Closed 25-26 Dec, 1 Jan, Mon, D Sun **Prices** Fixed L 2 course fr £13, Fixed D 3 course fr £22, Tasting menu fr £30, Starter £6-£11, Main £13-£32, Dessert £6.50-£9.50, Service added but optional 10%, Groups min 7 service 10% **Wines** 101 bottles over £20, 20 bottles under £20, 16 by glass **Notes** Fish tasting menu available Fri, Sunday L, Vegetarian available **Seats** 68 **Children** Portions **Parking** Car park

Thornbury Castle

◉◉ Modern British

Modern cuisine served up in a genuine Tudor castle

☎ 01454 281182
Castle St BS35 1HH
e-mail: info@thornburycastle.co.uk
dir: M5 junct 16, N on A38. 4m to lights, turn left. Follow brown historic castle signs. Restaurant behind St Mary's church

Henry VIII and his second wife Anne Boleyn stayed at Thornbury Castle during the early 1500s, and Queen Mary I lived here for many years, so you could say the place has a lot of history. These days it's the only Tudor castle in England to be run as a hotel, and anyone is welcome - particularly families with children (it's part of Luxury Family Hotels). Step inside the heavy oak doors and you'll find everything you might expect from a 500-year old castle: roaring log fires, wood panelled walls, winding stone staircases, suits of armour, tapestries, the lot. The restaurant retains a sense of period grandeur but the service isn't remotely stuffy or overbearing. The menu offers a good mix of the traditional and the more contemporary, with ingredients sourced locally, including herbs and vegetables from the garden, and check out the vintages from the castle's own vineyard. A spring meal might begin with ravioli of Everleigh Farm pheasant egg with sautéed English asparagus, pancetta and parmesan dressing, moving on to herb-crusted neck fillet of

Wiltshire lamb with baby artichoke, boulangère potato, celeriac and rosemary jus.

Times 11.45-2/7-9

UPPER SLAUGHTER Map 10 SP12

Lords of the Manor

◉◉◉ — see opposite

WICK Map 4 ST77

Oakwood at Tracy Park Golf & Country Club

◉◉ Modern British

Simply presented dishes in a posh country club

☎ 0117 937 1800
Bath Rd BS30 5RN
e-mail: info@tracypark.co.uk
web: www.tracypark.co.uk
dir: Just off A420

Tracy Park is an extensive golf hotel and country club not far from Bath, boasting acres of lush parkland and a château-style dining room, the Oakwood. Here, a wood-burning oven steals the show, and the candelit evening ambience is properly soothing and intimate. Dishes are simply presented, making much use of local produce in season, with breads made in-house. A bowl of rich, well-seasoned onion and cider soup with mini-loaves straight from the oven is a blessing on a winter menu, and may be followed by chargrilled chicken breast with black pudding mash and red wine sauce. Top it all off with a trendy chocolate brownie dessert, served with honeycomb ice cream and raspberry coulis. Lighter snacks are served in the main bar and lounge.

Times 12-2.30/7-9.30 Closed L Mon-Sat

WINCHCOMBE Map 10 SP02

5 North Street

◉◉◉ — see page 176

Wesley House

◉◉ Modern European

Gently modish cooking in an atmospheric medieval house

☎ 01242 602366
High St GL54 5LJ
e-mail: enquiries@wesleyhouse.co.uk
web: www.wesleyhouse.co.uk
dir: In centre of Winchcombe

Named after the Methodist preacher who stayed here in the 18th century, Wesley House is a characterfully sagging half-timbered 15th-century house. After a stylish facelift, the dining room is a winning blend of bare stone walls, beamed ceilings, and a clean-cut modern look involving high-tech, colour-changing mood lighting and trademark designer displays of flowers. Confident modern European cooking is the kitchen's thing, delivering big, well-defined flavours from cracking seasonal produce. A typical dinner might get going with a layered terrine of foie gras, duck confit and wood pigeon with pear and

continued

5 North Street

WINCHCOMBE   Map 10 SP02

Modern European V

Confidently intricate cooking in charming old property

☎ 01242 604566
GL54 5LH
e-mail: marcusashenford@yahoo.co.uk
web: www.5northstreet.com
dir: 7m from Cheltenham

Just off the main street, 5 North Street is a 450-year-old bow-fronted, half-timbered building with, inside, two tiny interconnecting dining rooms, all beams, red-painted walls and highly polished dark tables. It may look cosy and rustic, but Marcus Ashenford's cooking is most definitely of our times, working as he does around modern Anglo-European ideas. A range of three-course set-price menus operates at dinner, with no choice (although mixing between them is possible), with lunch altogether more straightforward. Dishes can be complex: a starter of duck confit is served on a disc of Morteau sausage, on a base of mushy peas with apple chutney, accompanied by a salad of pine nuts and deep-fried sage leaves in a sweet-and-sour dressing, a deeply resonant combination of flavours and textures, seen also in another starter of poached and chilled trout and scallops with creamed celeriac and beetroot and orange salad. Timings and seasonings are precisely considered, and materials

are of the first order: roast turbot fillet, for instance, topped with tomato confit, garnished with sautéed potatoes and warm piccalilli, the plate embellished with tapenade and deep-fried garlic. Meat is handled with confidence too, loin of venison sauced with jus infused with lapsang souchong, served with caramelised pear and honey-roast root vegetables. An acute sense of balance pulls together the various components of a dish with satisfying results - witness a dessert of caramelised pineapple with bay-infused rice pudding, Guinness ice cream and a beetroot tuile - although more basic ideas are also appreciated: soft, rich chocolate brownie, for instance, topped with a scoop of banana ice cream.

Chef Marcus Ashenford **Owner** Marcus & Kate Ashenford **Times** 12.30-1.30/7-9 Closed 1st 2 wks Jan, 1 wk Aug, Mon, L Tue, D Sun **Prices** Fixed L 2 course £23, Fixed D 3 course £39-£49, Starter £10-£13, Main £20-£24, Dessert £8-£11, Service optional **Wines** 60 bottles over £20, 12 bottles under £20, 6 by glass **Notes** Gourmet menu 7/10 course, Sunday L, Vegetarian menu **Seats** 26 **Children** Portions **Parking** On street, pay & display

WINCHCOMBE continued

raisin compôte and roasted pain d'épice, while mains run to roast medallion of Scottish beef and bone marrow with horseradish mash, roasted seasonal vegetables, and red wine and bayleaf jus. Puddings aim straight at the comfort zone with the likes of apple and Medjool date strudel with apple sauce, and vanilla and Calvados cream.

Wesley House

Chef Cedrik Rullier **Owner** Matthew Brown
Times 12-2/7-9 Closed D Sun **Prices** Fixed L 2 course fr £12.95, Fixed D 3 course fr £24.95, Starter £5.50-£7.95, Main £18.50-£29.50, Service optional **Wines** 65 bottles over £20, 20 bottles under £20, 15 by glass **Notes** Sunday L, Vegetarian available, Civ Wed 70 **Seats** 70, Pr/dining room 24 **Children** Portions **Parking** In the square

See advert on page 175

Wesley House Wine Bar & Grill

🌸 European

Trend-setting brasserie next door to Wesley House

☎ 01242 602366
High St GL54 5LJ
e-mail: enquiries@wesleyhouse.co.uk
web: www.wesleyhouse.co.uk
dir: In the centre of Winchcombe

The funked-up sibling of venerable Wesley House's fine-dining restaurant (see entry) comes with plenty of cool contemporary attitude, thanks to its mirrorballs, purple lighting, and zebra-skin bar-stools. This unbuttoned side of the operation is the place to head for when lighter, more switched-on dining and a more up-tempo vibe is what's needed, although the same high standards still apply when it comes to sourcing top-quality materials for its repertoire of modern brasserie dishes. Start with something like oak-roast salmon with pickled cucumber and horseradish cream, followed by confit duck with butter bean casserole and cherry sauce, or pan-fried pollock with creamy Savoy cabbage with smoked salmon and crushed potato. It is all simple and delicious stuff, all the way to desserts such as vanilla and honeycomb parfait with caramelised banana.

Chef Cedrik Rullier **Owner** Matthew Brown
Times 12-2/6-10 Closed 25-26 Dec, 1 Jan, Sun-Mon
Prices Fixed L 2 course £10.50, Starter £5-£6.50, Main £9.50-£19.95, Service optional **Wines** 8 bottles over £20, 12 bottles under £20, 18 by glass **Notes** Vegetarian available, Civ Wed 70 **Seats** 50 **Children** Portions

GREATER MANCHESTER

BOLTON   Map 15 SD70

Egerton House Hotel

🌸 Modern British 🌿

Well-tuned English cuisine

☎ 01204 307171
Blackburn Rd BL7 9PL
e-mail: sales@egertonhouse-hotel.co.uk
web: www.egertonhouse-hotel.co.uk
dir: M61, A666 (Bolton road), pass ASDA on right. Hotel 2m on just past war memorial on right

A handsome country mansion built by a Victorian textile baron, Egerton House sits in gorgeous landscaped gardens on the fringes of the Lancashire hills - a peaceful retreat that is equally handy for business in Bolton. It offers a nice balance of country-house comfort and contemporary style; with its polished pine floors, claret-hued walls hung with gilt-framed pictures, and bare darkwood tables, the dining room makes a sharp modern setting for cooking that adds intelligent touches to traditional pairings. That might translate as smoked Applewood cheese soufflé with celery and apple salad to open, then roast pork tenderloin with spring bean cassoulet and mashed potato. Round things off with the nursery comfort of steamed syrup sponge pudding and custard.

Owner Jan Hampton **Times** 12-3/7-11 Closed BHs, L Mon-Sat, D Sun **Prices** Fixed L 2 course £18.95-£25, Fixed D 3 course £35-£40, Starter £7.95-£11.95, Main £15.95-£27, Dessert £6.95-£9.95, Service optional **Wines** 21 bottles

over £20, 10 bottles under £20, 5 by glass **Notes** Sunday L, Vegetarian available, Civ Wed 130 **Seats** 50, Pr/dining room 120 **Children** Portions, Menu **Parking** 90

See advert on page 178

DELPH   Map 16 SD90

The Saddleworth Hotel

🌸🌸🌸 – see page 179

MANCHESTER   Map 16 SJ89

The Dining Rooms @ Worsley Park

🌸 Modern British 🌿

Accomplished cooking on country club estate

☎ 0161 975 2000
Walkden Rd, Worsley M28 2QT
e-mail: anna.collier@marriotthotels.com
dir: M60 junct 13, over 1st rdbt take A575. Hotel 400yds on left

This country club and hotel is on a 200-acre estate (once the Duke of Bridgewater's) that includes an 18-hole golf course, yet it is only seven miles from the centre of Manchester. The Dining Rooms - three of them - are decorated in contemporary style, an appropriate backdrop for some ambitious modern cooking that might include starters of pan-fried sea trout with black pudding, spinach and mustard dressing, and smoked bacon and artichoke tart with pea purée and shoots. The Bolton Abbey Estate is the source of beef and lamb - perhaps well-timed rump with chunky chips and watercress - with plenty of variety in other main courses: game pie with sweet potato mash and buttered greens, say. Cheeses are all from the north-west, and puddings may extend to rhubarb and custard parfait.

Chef Sean Kelly **Owner** Marriott Hotels **Times** 6.30-10 **Prices** Fixed D 3 course fr £30, Starter £5.50-£11.50, Main £14.50-£24, Dessert £6-£9, Service optional **Wines** 40 bottles over £20, 27 bottles under £20, 20 by glass **Notes** Sunday L, Vegetarian available, Civ Wed 180 **Seats** 140, Pr/dining room 14 **Children** Portions, Menu **Parking** 250

Greens

🌸 Modern Vegetarian

Veggie Mancunian star

☎ 0161 434 4259
43 Lapwing Ln, West Didsbury M20 2NT
e-mail: simoncgreens@aol.com
dir: Between Burton Rd & Palatine Rd

Greens has grown in reputation and size since it opened back in 1990 in its trendy Didsbury base, in part down to TV chef and co-owner Simon Rimmer's media profile. It's a relaxed modern brasserie-style outfit; a fashionable confection of darkwood tables and chairs, wooden floor, leather banquettes and a feature wall of bold-patterned

continued

MANCHESTER *continued*

wallpaper. The modern vegetarian food comes with verve and vigour to match the on-cue surroundings, taking inspiration from the global larder in simply presented dishes with flavour to the fore. Thus homely Cheshire cheese and sage sausages might come with bubble-and-squeak, beer gravy and tomato chutney, or perhaps an Asian-influenced Indian-spiced chick pea parcel with spinach and sweet potato served with yellow mustard seed and tomato sauce. To finish, there's lemon tart with raspberry sauce.

Times 12-2/5.30-10.30 Closed BHs, L Mon

Harvey Nichols Second Floor Restaurant

◎◎ Modern European **V**

Chic department store with trendy modish cooking

☎ 0161 828 8898
21 New Cathedral St M1 1AD
e-mail: secondfloor.reservations@harveynichols.com
dir: Just off Deansgate, town centre. 5 min walk from Victoria Station, on Exchange Sq

Manchester city centre's outpost of the much-loved brand houses a striking restaurant in-keeping with the city's industrial image. Round metal spiked chairs, girders, tiled flooring, black walls and grey table cloths with white covers meet expectations. The large windows bring the bustling landscape in, and there's also a chance to watch the landmark big wheel turn. Business types make up a large part of the lunchtime clientele, but all-comers get to tuck into unfussy, imaginative modern European food. Flavours sing out in the likes of crisp oxtail salad with roast garlic, onion jam and pickled mushroom, followed by stone bass with fennel risotto, artichoke, chard and lemon dressing. Puddings are equally voguish; beetroot parfait with yoghurt mousse, chocolate soil and pickled blackberries, perhaps, or popcorn pannacotta with maple syrup jelly and caramel mousse.

Chef Sam Everett, Matthew Horsfield **Owner** Harvey Nichols **Times** 12-3/6-9.30 Closed 25-27 Dec, Etr Sun, D Sun-Mon **Wines** 100+ bottles over £20, 30 bottles under £20, 20 by glass **Notes** Menu Gourmand 6 course £55, Vegetarian menu **Seats** 50 **Children** Portions, Menu **Parking** NCP under store opposite

Lowry Hotel

◎◎ Modern British

Super-stylish hotel with talent in the kitchen

☎ 0161 827 4000 & 827 4041
50 Dearmans Place, Chapel Wharf, Salford M3 5LH
e-mail: hostess@roccofortehotels.com
dir: M6 junct 19, A556/M56/A5103 for 4.5m. At rdbt take A57(M) to lights, right onto Water St. Left to New Quay St/Trinity Way. At 1st lights right onto Chapel St for hotel

The River Irwell which flows past the five-star Lowry marks the boundary between Manchester and Salford, and the heart of the city is just a stroll away on the other side of the landmark Trinity Bridge. With its acres of glimmering glass, the hotel makes a bold statement - this place is big, glamorous and classy, and with its River Restaurant, it has a dining venue to match. The position by the river means the terrace is a hotspot when the north-western weather is kind, but the immaculate dining room is a hit year-round. It is all calming contemporary neutrality inside, with white linen tablecloths and smart duck-egg blue leather chairs, and the service style is slick and polished. The menu draws inspiration from a broadly modish European template, so you might get a bit of autumnal Mediterranean sunshine in the form of a salad of roasted pumpkin with ricotta, sage and beurre noisette, followed by a bit of northern charm in the form of lamb noisette with Lancashire hotpot, wild mushrooms and Shrewsbury sauce (a port and redcurrant jelly combo).

Chef Ryan Murphy **Owner** Sir Rocco Forte & family **Times** 12-2.30/6-10.30 **Prices** Fixed L 2 course fr £15, Fixed D 3 course £19.95, Starter £6.50-£13.50, Main £10.50-£24.50, Dessert £5.50-£9.50, Service added but optional 10% **Wines** 100 bottles over £20, 10 bottles under £20, 12 by glass **Notes** Sunday L, Vegetarian available, Civ Wed 400 **Seats** 85, Pr/dining room 20 **Children** Portions, Menu **Parking** 100, RCP

The Saddleworth Hotel

DELPH   Map 16 SD90

Modern European 🍴

Inventive contemporary cuisine in estate-set hotel

☎ 01457 871888
Huddersfield Rd OL3 5LX
e-mail: enquiries@thesaddleworthhotel.
co.uk
web: www.thesaddleworthhotel.co.uk
dir: A62, located between A6052 & A670

The Saddleworth is surrounded by landscaped gardens and woodland within the Castleshaw Valley yet is just 10 minutes from Oldham and half an hour from Manchester. The restaurant here makes quite an impression, with comfortable leather seats and black linen on tables set with glittering crystal and silverware. Meals begin impressively with an amuse-bouche of, perhaps, lamb hotpot, an immediate sign of the high levels of skill and ambition. Chef Anthony Byrom doesn't skimp on his ingredients, adding truffle to a starter of seared scallops with Jerusalem artichoke purée, and is fond of using wild plants and fungi, seen in a deeply flavoured soup of St George's mushrooms, for instance, and the accompaniments of jack-by-the-hedge, monk's beard and turnip tops for pig's trotters. What distinguishes the cooking is its accuracy, balance and seasonality, such as main courses of saddle of rabbit with a selection of autumn

vegetables, and wild sea bass fillet with chicory, fennel purée and caviar. The kitchen's labours are appreciated in the home straight too: Lancashire cheese with quince jelly and tangy chutney, an alternative to a masterly pudding such as apple and Calvados parfait with apple milk custard and almond sponge.

Chef Anthony Byrom **Owner** A J Baker **Times** 12-2/7-9.30 **Prices** Starter fr £13, Main fr £24, Dessert fr £10, Service optional **Wines** 100+ bottles over £20, 3 bottles under £20, 7 by glass **Notes** Tasting menu 12 course, Vegetarian available, Dress restrictions, Smart casual, Civ Wed 400 **Seats** 30, Pr/dining room 6 **Children** Portions **Parking** 200

MANCHESTER *continued*

Macdonald Manchester Hotel

Modern British, Scottish

Traditional Scottish food in the middle of Manchester

☎ 0161 272 3200
London Rd M1 2PG
e-mail: general.manchester@macdonald-hotels.co.uk
dir: Opposite Piccadilly Station

Hard by Piccadilly Station, the Macdonald Manchester is a tower-block hotel in the modern style. A re-conceptualisation of the eating options has imbued the informal dining room with a Scottish vibe, so Highland business visitors needn't feel all at sea. John Ross Jr of Aberdeen supplies the smoked fish platters - salmon, trout and mackerel with horseradish cream - which are a good place to start, while haggis, neeps and tatties in whisky sauce comes in two sizes. For mains, grilled meats with various sauces, including one made with Dunsyre Blue, are done on the Josper charcoal grill, or you might opt for fried halibut with new potatoes and seasonal greens. Scottish desserts are conspicuous by their absence, but sticky toffee pudding and New York cheesecake won't lack for takers.

Chef Stuart Duff **Owner** Macdonald Hotels **Times** 5-10 Closed L all week **Prices** Food prices not confirmed for 2013. Please telephone for details **Wines** 20+ bottles over £20, 2 bottles under £20, 13 by glass **Notes** Vegetarian available **Seats** 140 **Children** Portions, Menu **Parking** 85, Fee for parking

Malmaison Manchester

Modern International

Broadly appealing menus in chic city-centre hotel

☎ 0161 278 1000
1-3 Piccadilly M1 1LZ
e-mail: manchester@malmaison.com
dir: From M56 follow signs to Manchester, then to Piccadilly

An old linen warehouse formed the infrastructure for Manchester's Malmaison, a cool, hip hotel, its laid-back restaurant furnished with red leather-look banquettes and funky tables. The menu is a good match for the place, with ideas picked up from around the globe, the Josper grill turning out steaks, lamb cutlets, barbecue ribs, and so on. Elsewhere, look for mutton masala with saffron rice and raita, Thai-style vegetable, miso and noodle soup, or salmon fishcake with spinach and parsley sauce, preceded by the likes of chicken liver and foie gras parfait with grape chutney, or corn chowder, and followed by Valrhona chocolate tart.

Chef Varda Hlavsa **Owner** Malmaison Limited **Times** 12-2.30/6-11 **Prices** Fixed L 2 course £16.95-£67.50, Starter £4.95-£7.50, Main £12-£60, Dessert £5.95, Service added but optional 10% **Wines** 173 bottles over £20, 19 bottles under £20, 21 by glass **Notes** Sunday L, Vegetarian available **Seats** 85, Pr/dining room 10 **Children** Portions **Parking** NCP 100 mtrs

The Midland

British, French

Grand luxe Franglais in the city centre

☎ 0161 236 3333
Peter St M60 2DS
e-mail: midlandsales@qhotels.co.uk
dir: M602 junct 3, follow Manchester Central Convention Complex signs, hotel opposite

The Midland hotel in the centre of Manchester is something of a local legend for traditional grand luxe. You have all the city-centre action on the doorstep, and it's a relatively straightforward journey from here to Old Trafford. The French dining room experience pours on the glitz, with tableside flambéing going on under the chandeliers, and the cooking speaks the gastronomic French lingo d'autretemps with a distinct Mancunian accent. So a breast and leg of quail come with 'breakfast flavours' to start, while a fish finger and salad cream are the accoutrements of a mackerel starter. The menu credits Reg as the provider of a duck, its breast and leg cuts accompanied by its foie gras, rhubarb and granola, or there may be sea bass in bouillabaisse with provençale garnishes. Manchester tart parfait is a regional reinvention, or share an assiette of French desserts with your companion.

Chef Paul Beckley **Owner** QHotels **Times** 7-11 Closed BHs, Sun-Mon, L all week **Prices** Fixed D 3 course £35, Starter £9.95-£14.95, Main £23.95-£32.95, Dessert £7.95, Service optional **Wines** 69 bottles over £20, 13 by glass **Notes** Dress restrictions, Smart casual, no sportswear, Civ Wed 80 **Seats** 55 **Children** Portions **Parking** NCP behind hotel

Room Manchester

Modern British

Confident city brasserie fare with plenty of twist

☎ 0161 839 2005
81 King St M2 4AH
e-mail: jamie@roomrestaurants.com

Booking is essential at the Room, so much of a red-hot venue has it become in the bustling heart of the city. A door attendant conducts you to reception, and then you move on up to the first-floor, where music thrums, a cocktail barman works flat-out, and the polished service runs on rails. Classic retro brasserie fare, given today's de rigueur 'twist', is what to expect, and dishes exude confidence and flair. Crispy duck pancakes come with smoked meat, rhubarb and pickled ginger (see, that's what they mean by a twist), while that trendy appetiser, the no-longer-humble Scotch egg, is made with rare-breed pork, along with black pudding and crispy egg. A chunky steak-and-ale pie for main course is fashioned from Longhorn beef and Old Tom ale with ceps, or let's twist again for 'posh fish and chips', which comprises sea bass and cod cheek with curry sauce à la chip-shop. Finish with lemon meringue pie and gin-and-tonic sorbet, or Valrhona chocolate fudge cake with honeycomb.

Chef Peter Taylor, Nick Dawson **Owner** Phillip Barker **Times** 12-2.45/5.30-10 Closed 24-26 Dec, BHs, Sun **Prices** Fixed L 2 course £14, Fixed D 3 course fr £19, Starter £5.75-£8.25, Main £12.50-£21.50, Dessert £5.50-£14, Service added but optional 10% **Wines** 48 bottles over £20, 14 bottles under £20, 17 by glass **Notes** Fixed menu L, D 2/3 course includes glass wine, Vegetarian available, Dress restrictions, No hats, Air con **Seats** 56, Pr/dining room 56 **Children** Portions, Menu **Parking** NCP 200 yds

Sweet Mandarin

Chinese **V**

A vibrant modern setting for fab Chinese food

☎ 0161 832 8848
19 Copperas St M4 1HS
e-mail: lisa@sweetmandarin.com

On a standout glass-fronted corner site opposite the old Smithfield market, Sweet Mandarin is run by three sisters whose USP is that they produce home-style 'fresh, healthy and authentic' Chinese food that stands out from the norm. Inside, the décor goes for a modern de-cluttered look with a nod to traditions in the customary red napkins and lanterns. Quoting their grandmother as a major influence, the ladies send out a mix of classics, as well as more contemporary fusion ideas, all built on a sound basis of quality ingredients. Family heritage recipes take in Mabel's claypot chicken, cooked with ginger, spring onions, mushrooms, and the special ingredient - a Chinese sausage called lap cheung. Seafood makes a good showing too, in the likes of sizzling scallops or 'firecracker' prawns, heated up with a kung pao sauce of chilli, garlic and peanuts.

Chef Lisa Tse **Owner** Helen Tse **Times** 5-11 Closed 25-26 Dec, Mon, L all week **Prices** Fixed D 2 course £20-£35, Starter £3.50-£10.50, Main £9.95-£16.95, Dessert £3-£4.95, Service added 10% **Wines** 3 bottles over £20, 12 bottles under £20, 7 by glass **Notes** Vegetarian menu **Seats** 85 **Children** Portions **Parking** Shudehill car park

MANCHESTER AIRPORT   Map 15 SJ88

Etrop Grange Hotel

Modern British

Georgian elegance and modern cooking a stone's throw from the airport

☎ 0161 499 0500
Thorley Ln M90 4EG
e-mail: foh@etrophotel.co.uk
dir: Off M56 junct 5. Follow signs to Terminal 2, take 1st left (Thorley Ln), 200yds on right

Etrop Grange sits right beside Manchester Airport, but it's got a lot more going for it than just a stopover hotel for those jetting off abroad. It's a splendid Georgian, Grade II listed mansion in lovely secluded grounds, traditionally furnished throughout with chandeliers, heavy drapes and original fireplaces. The light and airy WineGlass Restaurant overlooks a courtyard garden, and the ambitious kitchen team turn out a thoroughly modern menu which may begin with salmon cooked at 42.5 degrees C, with passionfruit, smoked salmon and beetroot, followed by pan-fried rump of lamb with broccoli, soft herbs and heart, and a coconut brûlée with banana, raspberry and rum to round things off.

Times 12-2/6.30-9.30

OLDHAM   Map 16 SD90

The White Hart Inn

Modern British **V**

Modern British cooking in a traditional Lancashire inn

☎ 01457 872566

51 Stockport Rd, Lydgate OL4 4JJ
e-mail: bookings@thewhitehart.co.uk
dir: M62 junct 20, A627, continue to end of bypass, then A669 to Saddleworth. Enter Lydgate turn right onto Stockport Rd. White Hart Inn 50yds on left

The centre of Oldham is not far off, but when you're ensconced in this cosy old coaching inn on the fringes of the wild moors, the city feels a long way away. Real fires and fine local ales add a glow of conviviality to the Tap Room, although eating is the core business these days, whether you go for the brasserie menu, which is also served in the rustic Barn Room, or trade up to the more contemporary-styled restaurant. The food is good, hearty unpretentious stuff - Morteau sausage and Puy lentil casserole followed by braised beef in red wine with smoked mash and glazed carrots, perhaps, from the brasserie menu, while the restaurant menu might propose foie gras two ways with pear sorbet and hazelnuts, then loin of local venison with turnip gratin, quince and chanterelles. Make sure to leave room for pudding, which could be rhubarb crumble soufflé with thyme and ginger ice cream, or pannacotta with Armagnac-poached Agen prunes.

Chef Mike Shaw **Owner** Charles Brierley
Times 12-2.30/6-9.30 Closed 26 Dec, 1 Jan, L Mon-Sat, D Tue & Sun **Prices** Fixed L 2 course £13.50, Starter £7-£9.50, Main £16-£25.50, Dessert £6-£9.80, Service optional **Notes** Tasting menu available, Sunday L, Vegetarian menu, Civ Wed 180 **Seats** 50, Pr/dining room 32 **Children** Portions, Menu **Parking** 75

PRESTWICH   Map 15 SD80

Aumbry

British **V**

Innovative cooking in friendly and relaxed restaurant

☎ 0161 798 5841

2 Church Ln M25 1AJ
e-mail: enquiries@aumbryrestaurant.co.uk
dir: M60 junct 17, A56 signed Manchester/Prestwich. Turn right into Church Ln

Aumbry (the name for a small cupboard in the wall of a church) is a compact restaurant in two knocked-together red-brick Victorian cottages with a cobbled frontage.

Dishes may sound simple, but the thought and workmanship behind them are impressive. Slow-cooked Ringley pork, black peas, vinegar and apple turns up melt-in-the-mouth meat, served with contrastingly crisp crackling, smooth apple purée and perfectly cooked peas topped with vinegar-filled battered teardrops. Quality is high and timings just so, seen in roast wild turbot with robustly flavoured smoked eel pudding, tender deep-fried frog's leg, parsley root purée and verjuice. Starters show the same sort of mixings and matchings: black pudding Scotch eggs (rich and runny quail's eggs) served on tomato ketchup and mushroom relish, or home-smoked mackerel with poached rhubarb and a smear of mustard cream. Beetroot and chocolate cakes prove to be a successful combination, served with beetroot-flavoured marshmallow, honey, hazelnuts, caraway and pollen.

Chef Laurence Tottingham, Mary-Ellen McTague
Owner Laurence Tottingham, Mary-Ellen McTague
Times 12-2.30/6-9.30 Closed Xmas, 1st week Jan, Sun-Mon, L Tue-Thu **Prices** Fixed L 2 course £18, Fixed D 4 course £35, Starter £8-£9, Main £16-£26, Dessert £8-£11, Service optional, Groups min 6 service 10% **Wines** 105 bottles over £20, 3 bottles under £20, 15 by glass **Notes** Fixed D 5 course Tue, 6,9 course Sat £45-£60, Sunday L, Vegetarian menu **Seats** 34 **Children** Portions, Menu **Parking** On street

---

ROCHDALE   Map 16 SD81

Nutters

Modern British **V** NOTABLE WINE LIST

Gifted chef creatively cooking with Lancashire ingredients

☎ 01706 650167

Edenfield Rd, Norden OL12 7TT
e-mail: enquiries@nuttersrestaurant.com
dir: From Rochdale take A680 signed Blackburn. Edenfield Rd on right on leaving Norden

Andrew Nutter is no shy and retiring wallflower and his restaurant (family owned and run) in a rather grand 18th-century manor house in six acres of well-cared for parkland, does not want for personality either. The restaurant with its stone arches and high ceilings has bags of vitality and is the setting for some fine cooking with some excellent regional produce. There's no lack of fun and personality in the food, either, but first and foremost this is technically impressive and enjoyable stuff. Each dish is stamped with Nutter's personality and his take on classical and contemporary cooking, thus crispy Dingley Dell pork and apple beignets with bacon bits and golden delicious salsa might kick things off, before corn-fed chicken supreme with wild herb stuffing, potato 'hush puppy' and a yellow pepper and shallot dressing. For pudding, there is much fun to be had too; warm treacle tart, perhaps, served with baby Baileys profiteroles and rum and raisin ice cream. A vegetarian menu ensures everyone can come out to play, and there's a 'surprise' six-course gourmet menu if you're up for the adventure.

Chef Andrew Nutter **Owner** Mr A Nutter, Mr R Nutter, Mrs K J Nutter **Times** 12-2/6.30-9.30 Closed 1-2 days after

both Xmas & New Year, Mon **Prices** Fixed L 2 course fr £13.95, Starter £4.80-£9.50, Main £14.80-£23, Dessert £3.95-£7.80, Service optional, Groups min 8 service 10% **Wines** 176 bottles over £20, 19 bottles under £20, 9 by glass **Notes** Gourmet menu 6 course £40, Sunday L, Vegetarian menu, Dress restrictions, Smart casual, Civ Wed 120 **Seats** 143, Pr/dining room 30 **Children** Portions, Menu **Parking** 100

The Peacock Room

Modern British

Luxe art-deco look and smart modish food

☎ 01706 368591

Crimble Hotel, Crimble Ln, Bamford OL11 4AD
e-mail: crimble@thedeckersgroup.com
web: www.thedeckersgroup.com
dir: M62 junct 20 follow signs for Blackburn, left onto B6222 (Bury road) contine for 1m Crimble Lane on left

Within the Crimble Hotel, dating from the 17th century, the ornate Peacock Room restaurant makes a powerful visual statement with its art-deco styling recalling the days of the great ocean liners. Indeed the opulent chandeliers hail from a cruise ship and sit nicely with the lush furnishings, swag curtains, gold effect cornicing, mirrored ceiling and tables dressed in their best whites. Outside the eponymous peacocks strut their stuff in the grounds. The passion in the kitchen shines through in contemporary British dishes such as hand-dived scallops with a caper and angelica purée, cauliflower and raisin dressing, or an aesthetically pleasing main-course Texal lamb four ways, served with roasted pumkin, roasted seeds, chervil root fondants and rosemary jus. Among fish main courses might be fillet of halibut with roast garlic risotto, pak choi, soused cherry tomatoes and golden tomato vierge, and among desserts perhaps a Manchester tart with raspberry sorbet.

Chef Robert Walker **Owner** The Deckers Hospitality Group **Times** 12-2.30/6.30-10 Closed Mon-Tue, L Sat, D Sun **Prices** Fixed L 2 course fr £13.50, Fixed D 3 course fr £19.50, Starter £5-£9.55, Main £15.95-£23.95, Dessert £4.50-£7.90, Service optional **Wines** 80 bottles over £20, 14 bottles under £20, 6 by glass **Notes** Sunday L, Vegetarian available, Dress restrictions, No tracksuits or trainers, Civ Wed 100 **Seats** 80 **Children** Portions, Menu

Macdonald Kilhey Court Hotel

◉ Modern British

Peaceful garden views and sound cooking

☎ 01257 472100
Chorley Rd, Standish WN1 2XN
e-mail: general.kilheycourt@macdonald-hotels.co.uk
dir: M6 junct 27, through village of Standish. Take
B5239, left onto A5106, hotel on right

The hotel dates from 1884, when it was built by a local
brewer, and its Laureate Restaurant occupies a large
conservatory on three levels, its atmosphere relaxed and
informal, overlooking the hotel's grounds. The kitchen
puts fresh seasonal produce to good effect in such tried-
and-trusted classics as Stornoway black pudding with
caramelised apple and bacon salad, or shrimp cocktail
with Marie Rose sauce, then coq au vin, steaks from the
grill or pan-fried fillet of sea bass with seasonal
vegetables. Vegetarians can go for pumpkin ravioli with
sage butter, and to finish, we're all in it together with
Eton Mess and crème brûlée.

Chef Dean Finch **Owner** Macdonald Hotels
Times 12.30-2.30/6.30-9.30 Closed L Sat **Prices** Fixed D
3 course fr £22.50, Starter £4.50-£6.95, Main £12.95-
£24.95, Dessert £5.50-£7.50, Service optional
Wines 24 bottles over £20, 16 bottles under £20, 13 by
glass **Notes** Sunday L, Vegetarian available **Seats** 80, Pr/
dining room 22 **Children** Portions, Menu **Parking** 300

Wrightington Hotel

◉ Modern International

Unfussy cooking and top-notch leisure facilities

☎ 01257 425803
Moss Ln, Wrightington WN6 9PB
e-mail: info@bennettsrestaurant.com
dir: M6 junct 27, 0.25m W, hotel on right after church

The leisure and conference facilities place the modern
Wrightington Hotel firmly on the local map, with its
location close to the M6 (albeit in a quiet countryside
setting) delivering a steady flow of business customers
and pleasure seekers. Bennett's Restaurant is a large
open-plan space with darkwood tables, warm colours and
a menu that includes a section called 'Lancashire
Classics'. Duck liver parfait with brandied sultanas,
tomato chutney and brioche gets the ball rolling, with an
individual hotpot with carrot and swede purée flying the
regional flag. Finish with a warm melting Belgium
chocolate pudding.

Times 6.30-9.30 Closed Sun, L all week

The Anchor Inn

◉◉ Traditional British ◐

Unspoilt country inn with a British (and sometimes Italian) flavour

☎ 01420 23261
Lower Froyle GU34 4NA
e-mail: info@anchorinnatlowerfroyle.co.uk
dir: From A31, turn off to Bentley

Dating back to the 16th century, The Anchor is a
picturesque country inn in Lower Froyle, close to Alton.
Open fireplaces and low beams are what to expect, plus a
slate of smart bedrooms all named after war poets.
Classical furnishings spruce up the restaurant, where
pictures recalling the history of this country take pride of
place. This is country pursuit territory, so you might work
up an appetite with a bit of fly fishing and shooting
before cosying up for some impressive British (ish) food.
Local, seasonal ingredients crop up on the menu which
incorporates some Italian influences and balances the
flavours very well indeed. You might start with haricot
beans on toast with chorizo, rocket and parmesan, then
move on to Ryland lamb loin with roast beetroot and
mash, flageolet bean and lamb shoulder crumble, and
finish with sticky date pudding with fudge sauce and
clotted cream.

Chef Kevin Chandler **Owner** The Millers Collection
Times 12-2.30/6.30-9.30 Closed 25 Dec, D 26 Dec, 1 Jan
Prices Food prices not confirmed for 2013. Please
telephone for details **Wines** 35 bottles over £20, 6 bottles
under £20, 9 by glass **Notes** Vegetarian available, Civ
Wed 60 **Seats** 70, Pr/dining room 20 **Children** Portions,
Menu **Parking** 36

Esseborne Manor

◉◉ Modern British, European

Timeless country-house setting for updated classics

☎ 01264 736444
Hurstbourne Tarrant SP11 0ER
e-mail: info@esseborne-manor.co.uk
dir: Halfway between Andover & Newbury on A343, just
1m N of Hurstbourne Tarrant

In curvaceous countryside high above the beautiful
Bourne Valley, Esseborne Manor is a pleasantly intimate
and comfortingly traditional take on the country house
idiom. The Victorian house has the feel of a private home,
albeit a rather plush and handsomely decorated one, with
an opulent dining room where walls are hung with red
and gold fabric, and immaculately-laid tables look
through large sash windows to the gardens. A herb
garden plays its part in furnishing the kitchen's needs,
together with quality materials sourced largely from
Hampshire and Berkshire. The cooking tacks an
ambitious modern course through a European-accented

repertoire of classic flavour combinations. Expect starters
along the lines of cauliflower soup with parmesan foam,
while main course delivers crisp belly, stuffed fillet and
breaded cheek of local pork, sage polenta chips and pear.

Chef Dennis Janssen **Owner** Ian Hamilton
Times 12-2/7-9.30 **Prices** Fixed L 2 course £15-£21,
Fixed D 3 course £25-£31, Service optional
Wines 82 bottles over £20, 23 bottles under £20, 12 by
glass **Notes** Fixed menu with wine available 2/3/4 course
£29-£43, Sunday L, Vegetarian available, Dress
restrictions, Smart dress, Civ Wed 100 **Seats** 35, Pr/
dining room 80 **Children** Portions **Parking** 40

Pebble Beach

◉ French, Mediterranean

Stunning views and simply prepared, quality ingredients

☎ 01425 627777
Marine Dr BH25 7DZ
e-mail: mail@pebblebeach-uk.com
dir: Follow A35 from Southampton onto A337 to New
Milton, turn left onto Barton Court Av to clifftop

Fish and seafood dominate proceedings at this popular
modern bar and brasserie - alongside sweeping views
across Christchurch Bay to the Isle of Wight from its
clifftop perch. Inside, it's a buzzy, split-level open-plan
affair, with full-drop windows, wrought-iron railings and
even a baby grand piano. High stools feature at the oyster
bar, catching all the open-kitchen action, while the
expansive alfresco terrace makes the most of those
horizon views. But it's not all location and aesthetics over
substance here, with the kitchen's accomplished output -
under chef Pierre Chevillard - underpinned by a French
theme. Shellfish come by platter or perhaps a whole local
lobster thermidor, while pan-fried turbot might be teamed
with celeriac purée, salsify, mushrooms and lardons and
a red wine sauce. Otherwise, meat options could take in
lamb rump with ratatouille gratin and boulangère
potatoes.

Chef Pierre Chevillard **Owner** Michael Caddy
Times 11-2.30/6-11 Closed D 25 Dec, 1 Jan **Prices** Fixed
L 2 course £24.90-£26.50, Fixed D 3 course £31.50-
£31.90, Starter £5.70-£11.20, Main £7.90-£45.20,
Dessert £6.95-£17.90, Service optional, Groups min 10
service 10% **Wines** 78 bottles over £20, 16 bottles under
£20, 16 by glass **Notes** Sunday L, Vegetarian available,
Dress restrictions, Smart casual, no beach wear **Seats** 90,
Pr/dining room 8 **Children** Portions **Parking** 20

BASINGSTOKE   Map 5 SU65

Apollo Hotel

◉ International

Smart and stylish modern hotel dining

☎ 01256 796700
Aldermaston Roundabout RG24 9NU
e-mail: admin@apollo-hotels.com
dir: From M3 junct 6 follow ring road N & signs for Aldermaston/Newbury. Then follow A340 (Aldermaston) signs, at rdbt take 5th exit onto Popley Way. Hotel entrance 1st left

Handy for the M3, doing business, or whatever brings you to the Basingstoke area, the luxurious modern Apollo Hotel also offers gastronomic satisfaction in its fine-dining Vespers restaurant. It is a clean-lined contemporary space furnished with curvaceous wood and leather chairs at linen-clothed tables, neutral tones, and vibrant modern abstract art to inject a note of contrasting colour. In case the name isn't enough of a clue, it is a dinner-only venue, where the kitchen delivers a please-all repertoire of inventive modern dishes. Smoked lamb loin with feta cheese, green bean salad and raspberry dressing could give way to fillet steak with smoked garlic béarnaise, thyme-roasted potatoes and oxtail jus. After that, apple pannacotta with cinnamon doughnut and butterscotch sauce might provide a satisfying finish.

Times 12-3/7-11 Closed BHs, 1 Jan, L Mon-Sat

Audleys Wood Hotel

◉◉ Modern British **NEW** ☙

Local ingredients cooked with flair

☎ 01256 817555
Alton Rd RG25 2JT
e-mail: thesimondsroom.audleyswood@handpickedhotels.co.uk
dir: M3 junct 6. From Basingstoke take A339 towards Alton, hotel on right

As its name might hint, Audleys Wood Hotel is surrounded by woodland, but the Victorian country house also comes with its own seven acres of well-kept grounds, and the all-round appeal of an upmarket operation run with style and thoroughly contemporary levels of service. The fine-dining Simonds Room provides an impressive setting with a contemporary sheen to go with its period oak panelling - recycled, so it is said, from Tewkesbury Abbey. A Gallic undercurrent drifts through the modern English cooking, but that said, local Hampshire ingredients are the kitchen's building blocks and they are handled with seasonal sensitivity and technical aplomb. Go for the 'Taste of Hampshire' menu, and the exact provenance of the principal components is spelled out in detail. There's no lack of creativity either: confit rainbow trout might start things off in the company of quinoa, celeriac, and sea urchin and cumin velouté, while mains could see noisette of new season lamb partnered by pea cannelloni, fricassée of sweetbreads and cockles, and beans. Fishy ideas might run to roast turbot with ratte potatoes, crab and spring onion beignets, samphire, and oyster and

sorrel velouté, while desserts such as New Forest rhubarb and custard stick with the local theme.

Chef Adam Fargin **Owner** Hand Picked Hotels **Times** 7-9 Closed Sun-Mon, L all week **Prices** Fixed D 3 course fr £45, Tasting menu £65-£95, Service optional **Wines** 150 bottles over £20, 10 by glass **Notes** Vegetarian available **Seats** 20, Pr/dining room 40 **Parking** 52

Basingstoke Country Hotel

◉ Modern European **NEW**

Good simple cooking in country hotel

☎ 01256 764161
Scures Hill, Nately Scures, Hook RG27 9JS
e-mail: basingstokecountry.reception@pumahotels.co.uk
dir: On A30 between Nateley Scures & Hook

Close to the M3 and connections to London, this inviting modern hotel and country club sits in four acres of grounds in a pleasant woodland setting in rural Hampshire. When you're done getting fit and pampered in the health club and beauty spa, the split-level Scures Brasserie is the place to head for straightforward modern comfort cooking. For the traditionally minded, there are rump steaks, Cumberland sausage and tuna loin sizzling from the grill, or you might take home-made game and prune terrine with apple chutney as an opener, then move on to a homely slow-cooked blade of beef with herb dumpling, bubble-and-squeak and curly kale, or pan-roasted sea bass with seared scallop, salsify, gnocchi and chive velouté. Puddings wind up on a similarly soothing note with the likes of apple tarte Tatin with Madagascan vanilla ice cream.

Chef Corrie Barnard **Owner** Paramount Hotels (Basingstoke) Ltd **Times** 7-10 Closed 23-27 Dec, L all week **Prices** Fixed D 3 course £21.50-£30.50, Service optional **Wines** 33 bottles over £20, 14 bottles under £20, 12 by glass **Notes** Vegetarian available, Dress restrictions, Smart casual, no shorts, Civ Wed 120 **Seats** 85 **Children** Portions, Menu **Parking** 200

Oakley Hall Hotel

◉ Modern British ☙

Modern brasserie cooking with Jane Austen connections

☎ 01256 783350
Rectory Rd, Oakley RG23 7EL
e-mail: enquiries@oakleyhall-park.com
dir: M3 junct 7, follow Basingstoke signs. In 500yds before lights turn left onto A30 towards Oakley, immediately right onto unclass road towards Oakley. In 3m left at T-junct into Rectory Rd. Left onto B3400. Hotel signed 1st on left

Built in 1795, and extended in the 19th century, Oakley Hall certainly doesn't lack for grandeur or literary associations, since it was once owned by friends of Jane Austen, who lived in a nearby village. In keeping with modern trends, the Winchester Restaurant has been made over with banquette seating, wall mirrors and unclothed tables - a city-slicker contemporary brasserie

look that sits well with the kitchen's clearly focused output. You might start luxuriously with lobster ravioli in smoked salmon and tomato broth, then proceed with rack of lamb with Anna potatoes and rosemary sauce, and wrap it all up in fine style with a trio of apple tarte Tatin, pear crumble and cinnamon-crusted vanilla ice cream.

Chef Graham Weston **Owner** Jon Huxford **Times** 12-2/7-9.30 **Prices** Starter £6.25-£7.95, Main £19.50-£24.95, Dessert £6.50-£8.50, Service included **Wines** 20 bottles over £20, 4 bottles under £20, 8 by glass **Notes** Sunday L, Vegetarian available, Dress restrictions, Smart, no jeans or T-shirts, Civ Wed 100, Air con **Seats** 40, Pr/dining room 200 **Children** Portions, Menu **Parking** 100

BAUGHURST   Map 5 SU56

The Wellington Arms

◉◉ Modern British ☙

Good pub food crafted from the most local of local produce

☎ 0118 982 0110
Baughurst Rd RG26 5LP
e-mail: hello@thewellingtonarms.com
dir: M4 junct 12 follow Newbury signs on A4. At rdbt left signed Aldermaston. Through Aldermaston. Up hill, at 2nd rdbt 2nd exit signed Baughurst, left at T-junct, pub 1m on left

The only problem you may encounter at this small-but-perfectly-formed pub is actually getting a table in the first place, such is its popularity with local foodies. Simon Page and Jason King are passionate about provenance, and it shows from top to bottom of the menu: in the garden and paddock behind The Wellington are Tamworth pigs, rare-breed Longwool sheep, chickens (150 of them) and bees, as well as vegetables and herbs for the pot. The ambience within is more cosy pub than modish gastro-pub, with a low beamed ceiling, tiled floor, chunky oak tables, and chalkboard menus updated every day, and wiped off as dishes run out. At its most intensely seasonal, a summer meal might get going with home-grown pumpkin flowers stuffed with ricotta, parmesan and lemon zest and served with salad leaves from the pub's polytunnel, then move on to barbecued leg of Hampshire Downs lamb with smashed chick peas, coriander and baba ganoush, or a fine piece of Cornish skate with capers, flat leaf parsley, brown butter and sautéed greens. Don't pass on afters, as there may be sticky toffee pudding with lashings of toffee sauce and clotted cream.

Chef Jason King **Owner** Simon Page & Jason King **Times** 12-2.30/6.30-9.30 Closed D Sun **Prices** Fixed L 2 course fr £15.75, Service added but optional 10% **Wines** 51 bottles over £20, 8 bottles under £20, 9 by glass **Notes** Sunday L, Vegetarian available **Seats** 34, Pr/dining room 20 **Children** Portions **Parking** 25

BEAULIEU   Map 5 SU30

Beaulieu Hotel

◉ Modern, Traditional

Contemporary British cooking at a New Forest country house

☎ 023 8029 3344
Beaulieu Rd SO42 7YQ
e-mail: beaulieu@newforesthotels.co.uk
dir: On B3056 between Lyndhurst & Beaulieu. Near Beaulieu Road railway station

A former coaching inn standing on open heathland in the New Forest, the Beaulieu Hotel is just the place for an escape to landscapes where wild ponies outnumber the hikers. There's no lack of grandeur in the smart country-house interiors, while the cream and lemon-panelled Exbury dining room is a handsome space with French windows opening onto the patio where you can dine alfresco overlooking the landscaped gardens when the weather plays ball. A well thought-out menu delivers up-to-date compositions built on the eminently sound foundations of well-sourced local ingredients, thus Hampshire pigeon breast might share a plate with blue cheese dauphinoise and pear, ahead of a three-way presentation of local free-range pork, comprising belly, tenderloin and hock with apple purée. Desserts take the classic route of crème brûlée, or apple tarte Tatin with Bramley apple sorbet.

Times 7-9 Closed L all week

The Master Builders at Bucklers Hard

◉ British

Modern Brit cooking with shipbuilding history to boot

☎ 01590 616253
Bucklers Hard SO42 7XB
e-mail: res@themasterbuilders.co.uk
dir: From M27 junct 2 follow signs to Beaulieu. Turn left onto B3056, then 1st left, hotel in 2m

This smartly spruced-up 18th-century hotel sits on Lord Montagu's Beaulieu estate at the end of the tiny village high street of Bucklers Hard. The Master Builder in question is not of the white van-driving variety, but rather the famous shipbuilder Henry Adams who created several of Nelson's ships right here on the River Beaulieu at the edge of the grounds. Turn up for lunch and the same menu is served in both the pubby Yachtsman bar and the more upmarket, bistro-style main restaurant, while dinner in the latter ups the ante to offer a menu with a clear undertow of modern British culinary ideas. Expect plenty of local fish and seafood in the guise of Lymington crab mayonnaise with pink grapefruit, hazelnuts and basil, followed by scallops with pork belly, black pudding and pea purée, and cider and apples. For carnivores, the contenders might include a simple rib-eye with béarnaise, watercress and chips.

Times 12-2.30/7-9

The Montagu Arms Hotel

◉◉◉ – see below

Monty's Inn

◉ British, Mediterranean

Classic English favourites at the Montagu Arms

☎ 01590 614986 & 612324
Palace Ln SO42 7ZL
e-mail: reservations@montaguarmshotel.co.uk
dir: M27 junct 2, follow signs to Beaulieu

Monty's Inn seems very happy in its own skin. It is part of the smart 17th-century Montagu Arms Hotel so it goes for a clubby look involving wood-panelled walls, wooden floors and unclothed tables - all in all, the feel of a posh country pub - and it serves hearty, unpretentious food that doesn't try to punch above its weight. A crowd-pleasing menu opens with the likes of smoked ham hock terrine with piccalilli and toast before moving on to slow-cooked pork belly with braised red cabbage and mustard mash. The coast isn't too far off, so fish is well represented by Ringwood Brewery beer-battered haddock with sea salt and black pepper chips and fresh pea purée, or seared sea bass with creamed Savoy cabbage, smoked bacon sauté potatoes and red wine jus. Afters such as sticky toffee pudding with toffee sauce and

The Montagu Arms Hotel

BEAULIEU   Map 5 SU30

Modern French V

Luxurious comforts and ambitious modern cooking

☎ 01590 612324
Palace Ln SO42 7ZL
e-mail: reservations@montaguarmshotel.co.uk
dir: From M27 junct 2 take A326 & B3054 for Beaulieu

The Montagu Arms has some history behind it, as it was built in 1742, with original features like oak panelling and open fireplaces still in place, and its formal Terrace Restaurant overlooks the attractive gardens. Matthew Tomkinson is evangelical about local produce, picking vegetables and herbs from the hotel garden, and sourcing fish and meat from within the New Forest. To them he adds his own ultra-modern spin, producing exciting starters like wild mushroom and Madeira consommé with

tarragon gnocchi, pickled mushrooms, braised game and confit tomatoes, and succulent pork belly with sautéed squid and roast pumpkin, toasted peanuts adding some bite. There's a lot going on, certainly, but flavours and textures are well judged. A nicely grilled turbot fillet might turn up among main courses, attractively presented with glazed wild mushrooms and salsify, truffled lettuce and rosemary velouté, or go for Wellington-style wild mallard with Morteau sausage, sweet-and-sour cabbage, and crab-apple jelly. Mr Tomkinson's a busy man, compiling a separate vegetarian menu, a tasting menu and making labour-intensive desserts like cherry soufflé with clotted cream ice cream and dark chocolate sauce.

Chef Matthew Tomkinson **Owner** Greenclose Ltd, Mr Leach **Times** 12-2.30/7-9.30 Closed Mon, L Tue **Prices** Fixed L 2 course £19, Fixed D 3 course £65, Tasting menu £80, Service optional **Wines** 200+ bottles over £20, 12 by glass **Notes** Sunday L, Vegetarian menu, Dress restrictions, Smart casual **Seats** 60, Pr/dining room 32 **Children** Portions **Parking** 45

Save on Hotels. Book at **theAA.com/hotel**

HAMPSHIRE 185 ENGLAND

peanut butter ice cream occupy the same comforting territory. See also the entry below on the opposite page.

Chef Robert McClean **Owner** Mr J Leach
Times 12-2.30/6.30-9.30 **Prices** Starter £5.50-£7.50, Main £11.50-£18.95, Dessert £5.50-£6, Service optional **Wines** 12 bottles over £20, 10 bottles under £20, 8 by glass **Notes** Sunday L, Vegetarian available **Seats** 45 **Children** Portions, Menu **Parking** 45

BOTLEY — Map 5 SU51

Macdonald Botley Park, Golf & Country Club

◉ Modern British, European

Simple, honest cooking in relaxed hotel

☎ 01489 780888
Winchester Rd, Boorley Green SO32 2UA
e-mail: botleypark@macdonald-hotels.co.uk
dir: M27 junct 7, A334 towards Botley. At 1st rdbt left, past M&S store, over the next 5 mini rdbts. At 6th mini rdbt turn right. In 0.5m hotel on left

Botley Park is a sprawling modern country hotel in 176 acres of landscaped grounds just a short hop from Southampton Airport and the M3. When you have worked up an appetite on its 18-hole championship golf course and steamed away the stress in the spa, the Winchester Restaurant offers a smart contemporary setting for an uncomplicated repertoire of unpretentious cooking. Expect well-sourced, high-quality ingredients in starters such as Stornoway black pudding with caramelised apple and bacon salad, followed by a prime slab of Scottish steak from the grill, or slow roasted shoulder of lamb with boulangère potatoes and ratatouille. End with the comfort of fig sponge pudding with walnut praline and crème anglaise.

Chef Robert Quehan **Owner** Macdonald Hotels Group
Times 12.30-2.30/7-9.45 Closed L Sat **Prices** Fixed D 3 course £29.50, Service added but optional 12.5% **Wines** 48 bottles over £20, 20 bottles under £20, 14 by glass **Notes** Sunday L, Vegetarian available, Civ Wed 250 **Seats** 70, Pr/dining room 250 **Children** Portions, Menu **Parking** 200

BRANSGORE — Map 5 SZ19

The Three Tuns

◉◉ British, European 🍃

Appealingly varied menu in a traditional thatched inn

☎ 01425 672232
Ringwood Rd BH23 8JH
e-mail: threetunsinn@btconnect.com
web: www.threetunsinn.com
dir: On A35 at junct for Walkford/Highcliffe follow Bransgore signs, 1.5m, restaurant on left

The weather might help you decide: is it a drink in the oak-beamed snug bar or out on the terrace surrounded by mature trees? This traditional 17th-century thatched inn has bags of character and country charm, and a long menu that can doubtless meet your needs whatever the time of day; there's a good showing of regional ingredients, too. Whether you're on the look-out for a thick-cut sandwich, light salad, something traditional like fish and chips, or the more modish winter squash risotto, the kitchen can sort you out. There's also the likes of calves' liver with apple, bacon and mash, alongside pan-fried Mudeford sea bass with roast chervil root, porcini mushrooms, shaved fennel, truffle, red wine zabaglione, New Forest mushroom dust and dauphinoise potatoes, and puddings run from quince turnover with maple pear and crème fraîche to New Forest ice creams and sorbets.

Chef Colin Nash **Owner** Nigel Glenister
Times 12-2.15/6.30-9.15 Closed 25-26 Dec, D 31 Dec **Prices** Starter £4.95-£9, Main £9.95-£22.95, Dessert £6-£8.95, Service optional **Wines** 2 bottles over £20, 21 bottles under £20, 11 by glass **Notes** Sunday L, Vegetarian available, Dress restrictions, Smart casual **Seats** 60, Pr/dining room 50 **Children** Portions **Parking** 50

BROCKENHURST — Map 5 SU30

Balmer Lawn Hotel

◉ Modern British

Fine dining at grand New Forest hotel

☎ 01590 623116 & 625725
Lyndhurst Rd SO42 7ZB
e-mail: info@balmerlawnhotel.com
dir: Take A337 towards Brockenhurst, hotel on left after 'Welcome to Brockenhurst' sign

The privately-owned Balmer Lawn is a large pavilion-style Victorian hunting lodge turned country hotel in a charming position in the New Forest. With hunting off the agenda, it's all about pampering or business these days, with its spa, sports and conference facilities. The hotel's Beresford's restaurant is the fine-dining option, situated in a room of grand proportions done-out in an understated contemporary style. That kind of goes for the food, too, which runs from carrot and orange soup to sautéed langoustines with pickled apple purée and cured ham among starters, and from a steak from the grill to pan-fried halibut with Jerusalem artichoke purée and morel sauce among mains. Finish with chocolate fondant, or, if you want to have your cake and eat it, go for the assiette of desserts.

Chef Jim Wright **Owner** Mr C Wilson
Times 12.30-2.30/7-9.30 **Prices** Fixed L 2 course £14.95, Fixed D 3 course £25-£46, Tasting menu £50-£85, Starter £5-£10, Main £15-£28, Dessert £5-£8, Service added but optional 10%, Groups min 10 service 12.5% **Wines** 36 bottles over £20, 10 bottles under £20, 9 by glass **Notes** Tasting menu 8 course, 2 for 1 L Mon-Fri, Sunday L, Vegetarian available, Dress restrictions, Smart casual, no jeans or trainers, Civ Wed 120 **Seats** 80, Pr/dining room 100 **Children** Portions, Menu **Parking** 100

BROCKENHURST *continued*

Careys Manor Hotel

◉◉ Modern British **V** ✪

Local produce used to good effect in the New Forest

☎ 01590 623551

Lyndhurst Rd SO42 7RH

e-mail: stay@careysmanor.com

dir: M27 junct 2, follow Fawley/A326 signs. Continue over 3 rdbts, at 4th rdbt right lane signed Lyndhurst/A35. Follow A337 (Lymington/Brockenhurst)

Hidden away in the depths of the New Forest, Careys Manor soothes away its guests' stresses with a top-drawer spa complex that fuses eastern and western treatments and philosophies. The same multicultural approach applies to its gastronomy: the Zen Garden restaurant deals in Thai cooking, while the Blaireau bistro serves French cuisine. Top of the shop, however, is the fine-dining Manor Restaurant, which goes for an inventive cocktail of modern British ideas brought together by a kitchen that sets great store by local, free-range and organic materials - Hampshire beef, for example, which is turned into home-cured bresaola and served with Jerusalem artichoke purée and parmesan crisps. The New Forest is well-placed for supplies from either land or sea, so the latter might furnish pan-roasted cod with a crab and spring onion cake, spiced beetroot purée, caramelised salsify and saffron foam, while dry land could come up with slow-cooked haunch of venison on braised red cabbage with parsnip purée, venison pudding and hickory-smoked sauce.

Chef Chris Wheeldon **Owner** Greenclose Ltd **Times** 7-10 Closed L all week **Prices** Starter £7-£12, Main £13-£25, Dessert £7-£12, Service optional **Wines** 70 bottles over £20, 24 bottles under £20, 8 by glass **Notes** Tasting menu available D Fri-Sat, Vegetarian menu, Dress restrictions, Smart casual, no jeans, shorts or trainers, Civ Wed 100 **Seats** 80, Pr/dining room 100 **Children** Portions **Parking** 100

The Pig

◉◉ British ✪

Relaxed vibe and genuinely local food

☎ 01590 622354

Beaulieu Rd SO42 7QL

e-mail: info@thepighotel.com

web: www.thepighotel.co.uk

dir: M27 junct 2, follow A326 Lyndhurst, then A337 Brockenhurst onto B3055 Beaulieu Road. 1m on left up private road

In the heart of the New Forest, a mile from Brockenhurst, this boutique-style hotel is a country house with a difference. You won't find any luxe interior design here, instead it goes for an appealing rusticity, smart (make no mistake), but relaxed and unpretentious. There's lots of recycled furniture and muted colours, squashy chairs in the sitting rooms, and a restaurant, the Country Kitchen, which extends into a wonderful conservatory. The staff are in tune, dressed in jeans and striped butchers' aprons, button-down pink Oxfords and converse trainers. The constantly evolving menu is driven by what's ready from the walled kitchen garden, and what foraged ingredients turn up on the doorstep. Headed the '25 mile menu', expect the likes of potted wild New Forest rabbit with piccalilli and pickled duck egg, or the pie@the pig - a Hampshire game pie with crushed new potatoes. And for pudding, perhaps steamed prune sponge with Amaretto syrup and Dorset crème fraîche.

Chef James Golding **Owner** Robin Hutson **Times** 12-2.30/6.30-9.30 **Prices** Starter £6-£8, Main £12-£23, Dessert £7, Service added but optional 12.5% **Wines** 76 bottles over £20, 8 bottles under £20, 10 by glass **Notes** Sunday L, Vegetarian available **Seats** 85, Pr/dining room 14 **Children** Portions, Menu

Rhinefield House Hotel

◉◉ Traditional & Modern British ✪

Modern takes on classic dishes in an eye-popping Victorian mansion

☎ 01590 622922

Rhinefield Rd SO42 7QB

e-mail: rhinefieldhouse@handpicked.co.uk

web: www.handpickedhotels.co.uk/rhinefieldhouse

dir: M27 junct, A337 to Lyndhurst, then A35 W towards Christchurch. 3.5m, left at sign for Rhinefield House. Hotel 1.5m on right

The Walker-Munros, a pair of enterprising newlyweds, had Rhinefield built to their eye-popping specifications in the year of Queen Victoria's golden jubilee. It's a hubristic amalgam of Tudor and Gothic references, scarcely more so than in the frieze of the doomed Spanish Armada carved from a four-foot-thick oak block, which dominates the dining room. The place was also once a boys' boarding school. Lucky boys. The menus don't quite attempt to match the surroundings for decadent glam, but essay instead a capable tour of modern British methods, based on much quality local produce. Pastrami salmon is an interesting idea that comes kitted out with a salad of pickled shallots, radishes and parsley jelly, and may be the prelude to a textbook rump steak in chasseur dressing with a potato rösti in red wine jus. Finish with plum frangipane tart with a compôte of the fruit, rhubarb sorbet and ginger essence.

Chef Norman Mackenzie **Owner** Hand Picked Hotels Ltd **Times** 12-5/7-10 **Prices** Fixed L 2 course fr £16, Fixed D 3 course fr £36, Starter £8-£15, Main £17-£27, Dessert £9-£14, Service optional **Wines** 100+ bottles over £20, 2 bottles under £20, 18 by glass **Notes** Sunday L, Vegetarian available, Dress restrictions, Smart casual preferred, Civ Wed 130 **Seats** 58, Pr/dining room 12 **Children** Portions, Menu **Parking** 150

BROOK Map 5 SU21

The Bell Inn

@ Modern English

New Forest setting for brasserie-style cooking

☎ 023 8081 2214
SO43 7HE
e-mail: bell@bramshaw.co.uk
web: www.bellinnbramshaw.co.uk
dir: M27 junct 1 onto B3079, hotel 1.5m on right

Squirrelled away in the heart of the New Forest and part-owned by the Bramshaw Golf Club, The Bell is a handsome Georgian hotel and something of a '19th hole' for golf enthusiasts. A traditional vibe and original features grace the cosy bar, while the Oak Room restaurant aims for a more modern style, blending period character with a smart contemporary look. The kitchen takes a serious approach to keeping things local - much of the produce comes from the New Forest and game from their own estate, while fish is caught by day-boats on the coast nearby. Wherever you choose to sit, the accomplished brasserie-style output pleases all; think slow-cooked lamb rump served with gratin potatoes and ratatouille to a selection of steaks from the grill, or from the sea, a fillet of Lymington sea bass with mussel and clam chowder.

Times 7-9.30 Closed L all week

BURLEY Map 5 SU20

Moorhill House

@ Traditional

Well-thought-through dishes in Edwardian country house

☎ 01425 403285
BH24 4AG
e-mail: moorhill@newforesthotels.co.uk
dir: Exit A31 signed Burley Drive, through village, turn right opposite cricket pitch

Approached via a long driveway through landscaped grounds (spot the New Forest ponies and deer), Moorhill House is a comfortable country-house hotel dating from the Edwardian period. Within is a lounge with an open fire, a panelled bar and a restaurant opening on to a patio. The kitchen is clearly in touch with what its patrons want, with a menu of appealing dishes: duck confit with apple, apricot and thyme chutney, say, or sautéed wild mushrooms with tarragon cream, followed by pan-fried duck breast with red wine jus, onion marmalade, dauphinoise and roast root vegetables. Culinary know-how is evident throughout, fillet of bream grilled just so, for example, partnered by lemon and prawn butter, sautéed leeks and Parisienne potatoes. Finish with sticky toffee pudding with banana ice cream.

Chef Ben Cartwright **Owner** New Forest Hotels
Times 12-2/7-9 Closed L Mon-Sat **Prices** Starter £4.50-£6, Main £15.50-£20, Dessert £5-£8, Service optional
Wines 19 bottles over £20, 19 bottles under £20, 8 by glass **Notes** Sunday L, Vegetarian available, Dress restrictions, Smart casual, Civ Wed 90 **Seats** 60, Pr/dining room 40 **Children** Portions, Menu **Parking** 50

CADNAM Map 5 SZ21

Bartley Lodge

@ British

Elegant surroundings for country-house cooking

☎ 023 8081 2248
Lyndhurst Rd SO40 2NR
e-mail: bartley@newforesthotels.co.uk
web: www.newforesthotels.co.uk
dir: M27 junct 1, A337, follow signs for Lyndhurst. Hotel on left

Part of the small family of New Forest Hotels, Bartley Lodge conforms to the group's format of country retreats tucked away in the forested tracts of Hampshire. A long drive meanders through landscaped grounds to the door of the 18th-century hunting lodge, which has been extensively made-over and spruced-up in recent years whilst leaving its ample period character intact. Housed in the original library, the Crystal Restaurant (named presumably after the elegant centrepiece chandelier) is a spacious, high-ceilinged room done out in Wedgwood blue and gold - a setting that sits well with the repertoire of straightforward country-house cooking. Duck liver parfait with red onion marmalade is a trusty starter, while main course delivers lamb two ways - rare roasted and slow-braised - served with dauphinoise potatoes and red cabbage. At dessert, a classic vanilla crème brûlée comes with lavender and crab apple jelly and lime shortbread.

Chef John Lightfoot **Owner** New Forest Hotels plc
Times 12-2/7-9 Closed L Mon-Sat **Prices** Starter £5-£9.50, Main £15-£20, Dessert £5-£7, Service optional
Wines 19 bottles over £20, 19 bottles under £20, 8 by glass **Notes** Sunday L, Vegetarian available, Dress restrictions, Smart casual, Civ Wed 80 **Seats** 60 **Children** Portions, Menu **Parking** 90

DENMEAD Map 5 SU61

Barnard's Restaurant

@ Modern British

Friendly neighbourhood restaurant

☎ 023 9225 7788
Hambledon Rd PO7 6NU
e-mail: mail@barnardsrestaurant.co.uk
dir: A3M junct 3, B2150 into Denmead. Opposite church

Sitting opposite the parish church in a tranquil Hampshire village, David and Sandie Barnard's small-but-perfectly-formed restaurant and wine bar is a long-running favourite on the local foodie scene. It owes its longevity to their hands-on, upbeat charm and friendliness, and, of course, David's simple, effective approach, hauling in local ingredients and sending it all out with the minimum of fuss. Expect unclothed darkwood tables and exposed brick walls lined with bright prints in

the two cosy dining rooms, and on the plate, perhaps home-made pork rillettes with dill pickle and toasted ciabatta, followed by fillet of bream with roast asparagus, egg noodles, and lime and chilli dressing. Meatier appetites might be assuaged by lamb hotpot served with rosemary and garlic-roasted courgettes and tomatoes, while crowd-pleasing puddings take in Eton Mess, and coffee cream-filled profiteroles with chocolate sauce.

Chef David & Sandie Barnard **Owner** Mr & Mrs D Barnard
Times 12-2/6.45-9 Closed 25-26 Dec, New Year, Sun-Mon, D Tue **Prices** Fixed L 2 course £14.95-£18.50, Fixed D 3 course £19.95-£27.95, Starter £5.40-£7.95, Main £13.50-£26, Dessert £5.50-£7.95, Service optional
Wines 8 bottles over £20, 20 bottles under £20, 8 by glass **Notes** Vegetarian available **Seats** 40, Pr/dining room 34 **Children** Portions **Parking** 3, Car park opposite

DOGMERSFIELD Map 5 SU75

Four Seasons Hotel Hampshire

@@ Modern French, European V 🌱

Creative cooking in a grand Georgian manor

☎ 01252 853000
Dogmersfield Park, Chalky Ln RG27 8TD
e-mail: reservations.ham@fourseasons.com
dir: M3 junct 5 onto A287 Farnham. After 1.5m take left to Dogmersfield, hotel 0.6m on left

Part of the luxurious Four Seasons chain, this hotel is every inch the grand red-brick Georgian mansion, framed in the expansive acreages of the Dogmersfield Estate. In keeping with the upscale brand's house style, you can expect to be treated like royalty and pampered to within an inch of your life amid a period setting of grand staircases, intricate plasterwork and glitzy chandeliers overlaid with slick contemporary design touches. The Seasons restaurant is the top-end eating option, a glossy modern venue flooded with light through French windows overlooking the estate. The kitchen takes a thoroughly modern view of things, deploying peerless Hampshire materials in creative ideas, thus the tried-and-true duo of scallops and black pudding is teamed with in-house-cured pancetta, celery root cream and a compôte of apples from the hotel's orchard. Next up, Hyden Park duck appears as pan-seared breast and confit leg flavoured with five spice, and served with a vibrant parsley purée. To finish, buffalo milk pannacotta comes with blackberries foraged from the hotel grounds.

Chef Cyrille Pannier **Owner** Four Seasons Hotels & Resorts
Times 6-10.30 Closed Mon, L Tue-Sat, D Sun
Wines 167 bottles over £20, 17 by glass **Notes** Fixed D 5 course £55, Sunday L, Vegetarian menu, Dress restrictions, Smart casual **Seats** 100, Pr/dining room 24 **Children** Portions, Menu **Parking** 100

Bakers Arms

British, Mediterranean

Well-rendered pub dishes and local ales in a Hampshire village

☎ 01489 877533
High St SO32 3PA
e-mail: adam@thebakersarmsdroxford.com
dir: Off A32

The Bakers is a pillar of its local Meon Valley community, sourcing Hampshire supplies for its kitchen, and feeding and watering a local clientele with impressive professionalism. The Bowman brewery only being a mile distant, expect to find its pedigree ales in the bar. Cheery, efficient staff serve well-rendered pub dishes in the informal dining room, with blackboard specials always worth a punt. Meaty salads - black pudding and chorizo, pigeon breast and bacon - might be the curtain-raiser for a satisfying fish dish such as hake with couscous, smoked garlic rouille and caper butter, or go for a flavourful pasta dish like roasted squash, walnut and sage linguine with Lyburn Gold, a semi-soft artisan cow's-milk cheese from Wiltshire. Pear and apple crumble and custard rounds things off a treat.

Chef Richard Harrison, Adam Cordery **Owner** Adam & Anna Cordery **Times** 11.45-3/6-11 Closed Mon, D Sun **Prices** Fixed L 2 course £13, Fixed D 2 course £13, Starter £5.50-£7.50, Main £10.95-£17.95, Dessert £5.50, Service optional, Groups min 8 service 10% **Wines** 10 bottles under £20, 9 by glass **Notes** Sunday L, Vegetarian available **Seats** 35 **Children** Portions **Parking** 30

Fat Olives

British, Mediterranean

Locally-inspired modern cooking near the quay

☎ 01243 377914
30 South St PO10 7EH
e-mail: info@fatolives.co.uk
dir: In town centre, 1st right after Emsworth Square, 100yds towards the Quay. Restaurant on left with public car park opposite

Refurbishment has given a touch of contemporary comfort to this 17th-century fisherman's cottage about 25 yards from the quay. The kitchen remains as enthusiastic as ever, its building blocks supplies from the surrounding area, and cooking everything on the premises from delicious bread to peanut butter ice cream (to accompany caramel mousse and a chocolate brownie). The menu is a slate of modern, successful ideas, from smoked trout, leek and potato terrine in a cress emulsion, or pig's head balanced by apple purée and slaw, to roast gurnard with a buttery sauce of sage and verjuice, served with cippolini onions and butternut squash, or the full-on flavours of roast pork loin with a black pudding faggot and quince and trotter sauce.

Chef Lawrence Murphy **Owner** Lawrence & Julia Murphy **Times** 12-2/7-9 Closed 1 wk Xmas, 1 wk Mar, 2 wks Jun, Sun-Mon **Prices** Fixed L 2 course £17.75, Starter £5.95-£8.95, Main £14.95-£29, Dessert £6.25, Service optional, Groups min 8 service 10% **Wines** 44 bottles over £20, 5 bottles under £20, 8 by glass **Notes** Sat L no min age for children, Vegetarian available **Seats** 25 **Parking** Opposite restaurant

36 on the Quay

⊕⊕⊕ – **see below**

Solent Hotel & Spa

British, European

Accomplished cooking and countryside views

☎ 01489 880000
Rookery Av, Whiteley PO15 7AJ
e-mail: solent@shirehotels.com
dir: M27 junct 9, hotel on Solent Business Park

Stone floors, timber beams and open fires all add up to a feeling of cosy well-being at this smart modern hotel tucked away in mature woods and ancient meadowland bracketed by the coastal buzz of Southampton and

---

36 on the Quay

Modern British

Superlative cooking on Chichester Harbour

☎ 01243 375592 & 372257
47 South St PO10 7EG
e-mail: info@36onthequay.com
dir: Last building on right in South St, which runs from square in centre of Emsworth

In a fishing village on Chichester Harbour, 36 is a four-square property with a cottagey dining room done out in pastel shades. It's long been a destination restaurant, people drawn by Ramon Farthing's reputation for assured, sophisticated, modern cooking. The deal is a set-price menu with extras (a pre-dessert like lemon posset with lime jelly, say: always much appreciated), starting with perhaps three ways with smoked haddock (Cullen skink, omelette Arnold Bennett, and poached in milk, Florentine-style), before moving on to another trio - this time roast beef fillet, of superb quality, gently braised heel and sliced calves' liver, with a light beef reduction accompanied by artichoke purée and confit potatoes. If dishes can seem complicated and labour-intensive, an eye is kept on the ball so that clearly defined flavours work well together rather than fight each other. Seared scallops, for instance, are served in fragrant dashi soup with mushrooms, accompanied by daikon cress and a crisp vegetable salad, and fish, ever a strength, might bring on red mullet fillets with steamed langoustine and leek cannelloni and a langoustine broth. Presentation is a delight, even in a deconstructed take on apple pie with vanilla ice cream.

Chef Ramon Farthing **Owner** Ramon & Karen Farthing **Times** 12-2/7-10 Closed 1st 2/3 wks Jan, 1 wk end May & Oct, 25-26 Dec, Sun-Mon **Prices** Fixed L 2 course fr £22.95, Fixed D 3 course fr £55, Tasting menu fr £70, Service optional **Wines** 15 bottles over £20, 10 bottles under £20, 7 by glass **Notes** Tasting menu for complete tables only Sun-Thu, Dress restrictions, Smart casual, no shorts **Seats** 45, Pr/dining room 12 **Children** Portions **Parking** Car park nearby

Save on Hotels. Book at theAA.com/hotel

HAMPSHIRE 189 ENGLAND

Portsmouth. The relaxed Terrace Restaurant is a cosseting, low-lit setting with a crackling fireplace, or when the weather plays ball there's the eponymous terrace for dining alfresco with views over the meadows. Enviably positioned for tapping into the bounty of Hampshire's coast and rolling hinterland, the kitchen delivers easygoing menus of crowd-pleasing modern ideas - tiger prawn tempura with sweet chilli sauce and lime, for example, ahead of pan-seared sea bass teamed with brown shrimps and saffron risotto. Puddings land in the comfortable territory of rhubarb and stem ginger crumble with custard.

Chef Peter Williams **Owner** Shire Hotels
Times 12.15-2/7-9.30 Closed L Sat **Prices** Fixed L 2 course fr £16.50, Fixed D 3 course fr £19.95, Starter £6.50-£8.75, Main £14-£21.50, Dessert £6.70, Service optional **Wines** 44 bottles over £20, 17 bottles under £20, 15 by glass **Notes** Sunday L, Vegetarian available, Dress restrictions, No T-shirts, Civ Wed 160 **Seats** 130, Pr/dining room 40 **Children** Portions, Menu **Parking** 200

FARNBOROUGH — Map 5 SU85

Aviator

◉ Modern European

Modern cuisine in sleek surroundings

☎ 01252 555890
Farnborough Rd GU14 6EL
e-mail: brasserie@aviatorfarnborough.co.uk
dir: A325 to Aldershot, continue for 3m. Hotel on right

Aficionados of blingy wrist-candy may spot that this glossy contemporary bolt-hole overlooking Farnborough's airfield is owned by the TAG group of Aviator watch fame, and comes fully laden with the brand's high-end aspirations. In case the name isn't enough of a hint, flying machines are the theme in a sleek futuristic building designed to look like a huge propeller. This is, quite literally, a jet-set world: private planes and uniformed flight crew come and go, flying in their well-heeled and corporate clients, so the sleek contemporary brasserie aims straight at an unashamedly luxurious ambience involving banquettes and cream leather seats, darkwood tables and monochrome pictures of screen legends. Happily, the kitchen feels no need to fly in its supplies, looking instead to local farms, butchers, and day boats from the Sussex and Kent coast to supply the backbone for its intelligent modern European menus. Blackmoor Farm venison cottage pie with truffled potato espuma is a typical opener, while mains turn the focus on prime Hampshire beef, or crisp local pork belly served with braised cheek, curly kale, champ and caramelised apple purée.

Chef Mr Andrew Donovan **Owner** TAG
Times 12-2.30/6-10.30 **Prices** Fixed L 2 course £18, Starter £5.95-£10.95, Main £14.95-£31.50, Dessert £6-£8.50, Service optional **Notes** Tasting menu available, Sunday L, Vegetarian available, Civ Wed 90 **Children** Portions **Parking** 169

HAMBLE-LE-RICE — Map 5 SU40

The Bugle

◉ Modern British ⊙

Contemporary food in lovingly-restored riverside inn

☎ 023 8045 3000
High St SO31 4HA
e-mail: manager@buglehamble.co.uk
dir: M27 junct 8 to Hamble-Le-Rice. In village follow signs to foreshore

With its textbook rustic interior of bare-brick walls, doughty timbers, flagstone and wooden floors, oak slab bar, and warming wood-burning stove, it's hard to believe that this historic waterside pub was once in line for demolition. Luckily, a campaign by villagers rescued the place, and English Heritage pitched in to oversee its restoration and put this well-loved inn firmly back at the heart of local life. Casual 'small plates' such as pork and chorizo sausage rolls or warm home-made scotch egg with celery salt give a taste of what's on offer. The menu is peppered with classic pub grub done right - local ale battered fish with triple-cooked chips, crushed peas and tartare sauce, as well as beef shin and Bowman Ale puff pastry pie with mash; elsewhere there could be slow-roasted pork belly teamed with celeriac gratin, spiced pear, and perry gravy. It's hard to pass by the local artisan cheeses, but the incurably sweet of tooth could head for bread-and-butter pudding with real custard. On a fine day, tuck in out on the terrace to a picturesque backdrop of boats nodding at anchor on the River Hamble.

Chef Jim Hayward, Rickard Gutaffsson **Owner** Ideal Leisure Ltd **Times** 12-2.30/6-9.30 Closed 25 Dec, **Prices** Starter £5-£10, Main £9-£17, Dessert £5-£10, Service optional **Wines** 10 bottles over £20, 10 bottles under £20, 9 by glass **Notes** Sunday L, Vegetarian available **Seats** 28, Pr/dining room 12 **Children** Portions, Menu **Parking** Foreshore car park 50 yds

HAYLING ISLAND — Map 5 SU70

Langstone Hotel

◉◉ Modern British

Accomplished cooking in modern conference hotel

☎ 023 9246 5011
Northney Rd PO11 0NQ
e-mail: info@langstonehotel.co.uk
dir: From A27 signed Havant/Hayling Island follow A3023 across roadbridge onto Hayling Island & take sharp left on leaving bridge

With views overlooking the salt marsh flats and Langstone Harbour, this modern hotel's Brasserie Restaurant - incorporating a circular design, large windows and an alfresco terrace - makes the best of its watery location. It's a popular address whatever the weather with a relaxed, airy contemporary vibe (neutral tones of beige and brown, unclothed tables and friendly service), while the kitchen follows up with some well-dressed modern Brit food conjured from well-sourced local produce. Expect seared sea bream with parsnip purée and fricassée of cockles and mussels, for example, or belly pork teamed with a sage rösti, crushed peas, apple jelly and Madeira jus. There's comfort food such as grilled sausages, pea champ and onion gravy for the traditionalists, while among the creative desserts might be coffee crème brûlée with mascarpone foam and cinnamon doughnuts.

Chef Duncan Wilson **Owner** BDL Hotels
Times 12.30-2/6.30-9.30 **Prices** Starter £6-£10, Main £15.50-£19.50, Dessert £6.95-£7.95, Service optional **Wines** 27 bottles over £20, 8 bottles under £20, 7 by glass **Notes** Sunday L, Vegetarian available **Seats** 120, Pr/dining room 120 **Children** Portions, Menu **Parking** 132

HIGHCLERE — Map 5 SU45

The Yew Tree Inn

◉ Traditional British

Smart dining pub close to Highclere Castle

☎ 01635 253360
Hollington Cross, Andover Rd RG20 9SE
e-mail: info@theyewtree.net
dir: M4 junct 13, A34 S, 4th junct on left signed Highclere/Wash Common, turn right towards Andover A343, Yew Tree Inn on right

This 17th-century whitewashed inn near to Highclere Castle in a well-heeled part of Hampshire is these days a posh dining pub and looks the part with low-beamed ceilings and log fires to foster a cosy vibe, and a clean-lined 21st-century sheen to its décor. It delivers solid renditions of hearty dishes that are designed to comfort rather than challenge, and it is all constructed on the solid foundations of meticulously-sourced ingredients, many of which travel no more than 30 miles. Expect coarse pork pâté with candied walnuts ahead of roast haunch of venison with braised red cabbage and caramelised plums, and treacle tart with vanilla ice cream for afters.

Times 12-2.30/6-9.30

The Dining Room at Lime Wood

LYNDHURST   Map 5 SU30

British, Italian **V** NOTABLE WINE LIST

Country-house cooking based on impeccable local produce

☎ 023 8028 7167 & 8028 7177
Beaulieu Rd SO43 7FZ
e-mail: info@limewood.co.uk
web: www.limewood.co.uk
dir: A35 through Ashurst for 4m, then left in Lyndhurst signed Beaulieu, 1m to hotel

Lime Wood was presumably pretty impressive on its establishment as a hunting lodge in the 13th century, but has certainly come a long way since then. During the Regency period, it became a grand country house and, in its modern incarnation, has been treated to the bells-and-whistles design job, including interiors by the much sought-after David Collins. At one time, a country-house hotel might be supplied from markets far and wide, but localism is all these days, and Lime Wood plays a particularly assiduous part in that movement, maintaining supply lines with many growers in the vicinity, so that farm produce picked first thing in the morning is on the menu at lunchtime. New Forest foraging furnishes some of the provender too. The results are seen in hugely accomplished cooking, served in a variety of different settings, with the elegant Dining Room the jewel in the crown. Here, you might feast on barbecued local leeks with slow-roast organic beets, cocoa nibs and spiced bread to begin, or on a fascinating combination of butter-roasted langoustine with caramelised chicory, grapefruit and salted pistachios. Shellfish from the Dorset coast might appear in a main-course pasta dish with roast artichoke, tomato, capers and olives, while regional meats include New House Estate venison, and Mr Elton's new season lamb, the confit loin served with mustard-crusted tongue, sweetbreads and crosnes. A riot of seasonal fruit can be expected to turn up on the dessert menu at the appropriate times of the year, but so perhaps may something surprising like parsnip tart with brown bread ice cream.

Chef Luke Holder **Owner** Lime Wood Group **Times** 12.30-2.30/7-10 Closed L Mon **Prices** Fixed L 2 course £21, Starter £7-£22, Main £10-£35, Dessert £8-£11, Service added but optional 12.5% **Wines** 7 bottles under £20, 16 by glass **Notes** Tasting & sharing menu on request, Sunday L, Vegetarian menu, Civ Wed 80 **Seats** 64, Pr/dining room 20 **Children** Portions, Menu **Parking**

Save on Hotels. Book at theAA.com/hotel

HAMPSHIRE 191 **ENGLAND**

LYMINGTON Map 5 SZ39

Stanwell House Hotel

◉◉ Modern European

Bright, modish cooking in boutique hotel

☎ 01590 677123
14-15 High St SO41 9AA
e-mail: enquiries@stanwellhouse.com
dir: M27 junct 1, follow signs to Lyndhurst into Lymington centre & High Street

A classy boutique operation close by Lymington's quay on the edge of the New Forest, Stanwell House occupies a Georgian coaching inn that was once a finishing school for young ladies, and now delivers refinement in a more edible form. Two dining venues - Seafood at Stanwell House and The Bistro - take advantage of excellent Hampshire produce: as its name suggests, the former deals in fishy tapas and piscine pleasures such as seared fillet of brill with shellfish velouté, poached scallops and tomato and basil, or monkfish in Parma ham with squid ink risotto, pickled lemon, and saffron aïoli, while The Bistro's four menus work a more wide-ranging remit of contemporary European dishes in a glossy, modern space overlooking the inviting terrace. Here, you might start with haggis ravioli with braised cabbage, whisky foam and veal jus, and follow with steaks from the grill, or cheek, loin and belly of pork with pickled carrots, haricot beans and orange oil.

Times 12-3/6-10

LYNDHURST Map 5 SU30

The Dining Room at Lime Wood

◉◉◉ – *see opposite*

The Glasshouse

◉◉ Modern British

Contemporary-style restaurant with well-judged cooking

☎ 023 8028 6129
Best Western Forest Lodge, Pikes Hill, Romsey Rd SO43 7AS
e-mail: enquiries@theglasshousedining.co.uk
web: www.theglasshousedining.co.uk
dir: M27 junct 1, A337 towards Lyndhurst. In village, with police station & courts on right, take 1st right into Pikes Hill

A former dower house built in the Georgian period, this hotel has been given a thoroughly modern look inside, the restaurant with a dramatic décor of black and gold, with striking artwork on the walls. The kitchen prides itself on sourcing ingredients locally and pays due respect to

seasonality, so haunch of venison might appear, accompanied by game jus, confit garlic, creamed potatoes and a selection of vegetables. The menus offer plenty of variety, from chicken tikka with pickled cucumber, mango and an onion bhaji, to confit duck with plum sauce and jelly, spring onions, cucumber and a poppadom. Fish is not overlooked - pavé of haddock is poached in red wine and accompanied by crushed new potatoes, roast mooli and beans - and in colder months the kitchen might put winter fruits into a crumble and serve it with juniper pannacotta and clotted cream ice cream.

Chef Richard Turner **Owner** New Forest Hotels
Times 12-2/7-9.30 Closed Mon, D Sun **Prices** Starter £6-£9, Main £17.50-£20, Dessert £6.50-£7.50, Service optional **Wines** 41 bottles over £20, 30 bottles under £20, 8 by glass **Notes** Sunday L, Vegetarian available, Dress restrictions, Smart dress, Civ Wed 90 **Seats** 40, Pr/dining room 10 **Parking** 60

MICHELDEVER Map 5 SU53

The Dove Inn

◉ Traditional British **NEW**

Traditional pub grub with a modern spin

☎ 01962 774288
Andover Rd SO21 3AU
e-mail: info@the-dove-inn.co.uk
dir: just off the main A33 London to Winchester road

Just off the A33, The Dove Inn bar and restaurant with rooms is the sister property of the Running Horse Inn at Littleton, near Winchester (see entry). A pint of real ale at the bar by a roaring fire is reason enough to visit, but it would be a mistake not to get stuck into the smart menu of pub classics brought bang up-to-date. An intriguing-sounding baked mushroom and Rosary goats' cheesecake with toasted ciabatta and hazelnut dressed salad delivers on flavour, while a cleverly deconstructed beef, ale and mushroom pie is a great dish which even comes with an accompanying shot-glass of real ale. Standards remain high in the pudding department too; dark chocolate brownie, perhaps, served with vanilla ice cream.

Chef Mike Gray **Owner** Kim Gottlieb **Times** 12-2/6.30-9
Prices Food prices not confirmed for 2013. Please telephone for details **Wines** 22 bottles over £20, 12 bottles under £20, 12 by glass **Notes** Sunday L, Vegetarian available **Seats** 50, Pr/dining room 40 **Children** Portions, Menu **Parking** 20

NEW MILTON Map 5 SZ29

Chewton Glen Hotel & Spa

◉◉◉ – *see page 192*

OLD BURGHCLERE Map 5 SU45

The Dew Pond Restaurant

◉ British, European

Country restaurant with fine views and modern cooking

☎ 01635 278408
RG20 9LH
dir: Newbury A34 South, exit Tothill. Follow signs for Highclere Castle, pass castle entrance on right, down hill & turn left signed Old Burghclere & Kingsclere, restaurant on right hand side in approx 0.25 miles

It would take strong resolve to eat rabbit at this idyllic country restaurant in a pair of converted 16th-century drover's cottages looking across the eponymous dew pond to Watership Down and Highclere Castle. Naturally, the setting is at its most memorable on a sunny day, eating out on the raised decking terrace, but if the weather won't play ball, the two cosy dining rooms exude the comforting warmth of ancient oak beams, calming pastel shades and colourful artwork. Chef-patron Keith Marshall has no truck with fads and fashions, preferring to rely on solid technical ability applied to splendid local produce, delivered in thoughtful compositions, so fillet of sea bream might get the Provençal treatment with mussels, ratatouille, basil oil and tapenade, while saddle of local wild roe deer comes with chestnuts, roasted root vegetables, field mushrooms and a port wine sauce. Go out on a high note with something like caramel parfait with Bramley apple purée, apple sorbet and Calvados syrup.

Chef Keith Marshall **Owner** Keith Marshall **Times** 7-9.30 Closed 2 wks Xmas & New Year, 2 wks Aug, Sun-Mon, L served by appointment only **Prices** Fixed D 3 course £34-£45, Service optional, Groups min 8 service 10%
Wines 70 bottles over £20, 35 bottles under £20, 12 by glass **Notes** Vegetarian available **Seats** 45, Pr/dining room 30 **Children** Portions **Parking** 20

Chewton Glen Hotel & Spa

Modern British V

Classy cooking in luxury country-house hotel

☎ 01425 275341
Christchurch Rd BH25 6QS
e-mail: reservations@chewtonglen.com
web: www.chewtonglen.com
dir: Off A35 (Lyndhurst) turn right through Walkford, 4th left into Chewton Farm Rd

The 18th-century red-brick mansion never fails to impress. Within a walk of the sea, it is set in 130 acres that include a helipad and a garden providing the kitchen with vegetables, herbs and soft fruit; leisure facilities, including a fabulous spa, are outstanding, and there's also a kids' club. Staff are approachable, friendly and professional, adding to the enjoyment of eating in the luxuriously appointed Vetiver restaurant without detracting from a sense of occasion. Seafood is a strong point, from crab with apple and celeriac remoulade, to a main-course platter of fruits de mer. The cooking is based on prime ingredients, and a solid grounding in the classical repertoire is evident: emmental soufflé, Dover sole meunière, and beef Wellington, for instance. Daily trolley specials are popular - rack of pork, say, or roast monkfish tail - with the kitchen elsewhere plucking ideas

from around the world: tagliatelle alle vongole, or tuna tartare with wasabi crème fraîche, followed by lamb tagine with couscous and harissa, Thai-style lobster curry, or Sardinian fish stew. Desserts, listed with a recommended wine by the glass, have ranged from classic egg custard tart with clove ice cream to ginger and lemongrass crème caramel with poached pears.

Chef Andrew Du Bourg, Luke Matthews **Owner** Chewton Glen Hotels Ltd **Times** 12-2.30/6-10 **Prices** Fixed L 2 course £20, Tasting menu £79.50, Starter fr £8.50, Main £19.50-£68.50, Dessert £7.50-£12.50, Service added but optional 10% **Wines** 750 bottles over £20, 11 by glass **Notes** Tasting menu 5 course, Sunday L, Vegetarian menu, Civ Wed 100 **Seats** 164, Pr/dining room 50 **Children** Portions, Menu **Parking** 150

Save on Hotels. Book at **theAA.com/hotel**

HAMPSHIRE 193 **ENGLAND**

The White Horse

◉ Traditional & Modern British **NEW**

Modern pub grub done right

☎ 01962 712830
Main Rd SO21 2EQ
e-mail: manager@whitehorseotterbourne.co.uk
dir: M3 junct 12

The team behind the White Star in Southampton and the Bugle in Hamble (see entries) have scored a hat trick with the classy refurbishment of this neglected village boozer. Now sporting a classic modern dining pub look of bare wood and quarry-tiled floors, beams, cheerful heritage hues, and mismatched vintage tables, the place has an easygoing family-friendly vibe and the sort of no-nonsense contemporary food you want to eat. The kitchen works in tandem with local producers, whose splendid materials are served up in chicken liver parfait with rhubarb and ginger chutney and toasted soda bread, followed by ale-battered pollock with triple-cooked chips, crushed peas with mint, and tartare sauce. Local meat fans might find a Hampshire free-range steak burger with smoked paprika ketchup, or roast rump and rolled shoulder of lamb with fondant potato, wild garlic purée and port jus. Puddings take a similarly hearty path -

perhaps warm ginger parkin with oatmeal ice cream and sticky ginger sauce.

Chef Emma Berriman **Owner** Chris Lidgitt
Times 12-2.30/6-9.30 **Prices** Starter £4-£7, Main £10-£16.50, Dessert £5.50, Service optional, Groups min 8 service 10% **Wines** 27 bottles over £20, 8 bottles under £20, 10 by glass **Notes** Sunday L, Vegetarian available **Seats** 90 **Children** Portions, Menu **Parking** 25

Annie Jones Restaurant

◉ Modern European

Contemporary cooking in an inviting venue near the station

☎ 01730 262728
10a Lavant St GU32 3EW
e-mail: info@anniejones.co.uk
dir: From A3 into town centre, following Winchester direction. Restaurant is in Lavant St (the road leading to rail station)

Look for the discreet sign that picks out the converted shop premises of this town-centre restaurant near the railway station. Inside goes for a richly inviting look, with burgundy walls, black seating and coffee-coloured cloths,

and there's also a patio for outdoor dining. What's on offer is modern European cooking with notable imaginative panache, delivering king prawn linguine with garlic and chilli, topped with shellfish foam, to start, then sea bass with bacon, braised baby gem, ceps and peas, or honey-roast duck breast with couscous and a pastilla of dates and duck confit. Dessert brings on pistachio and olive oil cake with a cherry samosa and vanilla ice cream, or a classic tarte Tatin with cream.

Chef Steven Ranson **Owner** Steven Ranson, Jon Blake
Times 12-2/6-late Closed Mon, L Tue, D Sun **Prices** Fixed L 2 course £15.95, Fixed D 3 course £35, Service added 12% **Wines** 16 bottles over £20, 11 bottles under £20, 6 by glass **Notes** Tasting menu 7 course, early bird Tue-Thu 6-7.30pm, Sunday L, Vegetarian available **Seats** 32 **Children** Portions **Parking** On street or Swan Street car park

JSW

◉◉◉ – see below

JSW

Modern British **V** ⬩NOTABLE WINE LIST

Dynamic contemporary cooking

☎ 01730 262030
20 Dragon St GU31 4JJ
e-mail: jsw.restaurant@btconnect.com
dir: A3 to town centre, follow one-way system to College St which becomes Dragon St, restaurant on left

Jake Saul Watkins - the man behind the initials - was born in Hampshire and is a hands-on kind of chef-patron. He's been in Petersfield for a dozen years or so, and in this smartly revamped old coaching inn since 2006. You wouldn't know it was an old coaching inn particularly, with its impeccable white-painted period façade, and once inside this restaurant with rooms (three rather charming ones with well-chosen contemporary

furnishings) you'll find lots of exposed oak beams, neutral colour tones, well-spaced, well-dressed tables, and a professional, up-to-the-mark service team. There's a terrace out back and, wherever you sit, you won't be hurried off your table for it's yours for as long as it takes. It is evident from the off that this is a kitchen that does not miss a beat, baking the excellent bread on the premises (a treat at breakfast, too, if you're staying over), and sourcing its produce with due diligence. What turns up on the plate is clearly-focused and refined stuff, but not overworked to the point of exhaustion, with the flavours nicely balanced. Duck ravioli with duck ham, crispy yolk and foie gras croûtons might compete for your attention with warm salmon with pickled vegetables and salted apple purée among first courses, with main-courses delivering the likes of turbot with artichoke risotto, truffle, oak and sorrel, or beef fillet served up with its slow-cooked cheek, with smoked carrot purée and bone marrow. There is bags of creativity and craft on show here, with each dish delivering on its promise -

flavours and textures are spot on. To finish, hazelnut macaroon, white chocolate and Muscovado, or tropical fruit cheesecake with coconut are sweet options, with the cheeses selected from artisan English producers. The fixed-price carte is supported by an excellent value set lunch and midweek dinner menu, plus there's a tasting menu, with choice of wine flights. And to cap it all off, the wine list is a serious piece of work.

Chef Jake Watkins **Owner** Jake Watkins
Times 12-1.30/7-9.30 Closed 2 wks Jan & summer, Sun-Mon **Prices** Fixed L 2 course £17.50-£29.50, Fixed D 3 course £32.50-£48, Tasting menu £42.50-£65, Service added but optional 10%, Groups min 10 service 10% **Wines** 721 bottles over £20, 6 bottles under £20, 9 by glass **Notes** Tasting menu L/D 5 or 7 course, Vegetarian menu **Seats** 58, Pr/dining room 18 **Children** Portions **Parking** 19

PETERSFIELD *continued*

Langrish House

◉◉ Modern British ✦

Vigorous modern British cooking at a New Forest house with a past

☎ 01730 266941
Langrish GU32 1RN
e-mail: frontdesk@langrishhouse.co.uk
dir: A3 onto A272 towards Winchester. Hotel signed, 2.5m on left

Langrish House's singular place in English history is assured. In the 17th century, when it was built, it became a repository for Royalist prisoners during the Civil War (they were put to work digging the vaults), while one of the forebears of the present generation of Talbot-Ponsonbys was a thoroughgoing eccentric, revered as the Emperor Frederick by the family, in whose ironic honour an imperial crest was designed, on display in the dining room named after him to this day. The culinary style would once have been thought as eccentric as Frederick, but is these days recognisable as a vigorous expression of the modern British idiom. Expect to start, perhaps, with black tiger prawns on a risotto of preserved lemon and chorizo in beurre noisette, before moving on to pork tenderloin with twice-baked cauliflower strudel, glazed beetroot, plum and vanilla jam and curry oil, before coming to rest with passionfruit pannacotta, cheesecake ice cream and pine nut brittle.

Chef Peter Buckman **Owner** Mr & Mrs Talbot-Ponsonby **Times** 12-2/7-9.30 Closed 1-17 Jan **Prices** Fixed L 2 course fr £18.95, Fixed D 3 course fr £37.95, Service added but optional 12.5% **Wines** 44 bottles over £20, 3 bottles under £20, 12 by glass **Notes** Sunday L, Vegetarian available, Dress restrictions, Smart casual, Civ Wed 80 **Seats** 24, Pr/dining room 80 **Children** Portions **Parking** 100

The Thomas Lord

◉◉ Modern British ✦

Best of British food in relaxed village pub

☎ 01730 829244
High St, West Meon GU32 1LN
dir: M3 junct 9, A272 towards Petersfield, right at x-rds onto A32, 1st left

The Thomas Lord's kitchen genuinely aims for 100% Britishness in its materials. Named after the founder of Lord's Cricket Ground, who lies in the nearby churchyard, it is a proper pub too: local ales are good, and no-one turns up their nose at visiting canines, who are welcomed with a pat and a biscuit. The place has a shabby-chic charm, kitted out with lived-in furniture and open fires, an individual identity that is mercifully free of designer trickery. Menus of simple British ideas are built from the ground up - everything is made in-house, the garden supplies seasonal goodies, and the vast majority of materials come from small-scale local producers and farmers. Expect dressed Portland crab with watercress and chilli dressing, followed by Marwell Manor Farm rib-

eye steak with bone marrow butter, baked mushrooms and proper chips, or pan-fried whole plaice with garlic and herb butter. Finish with apple and toasted oat crumble with custard, or British (what else?) cheeses with Hampshire chutneys.

Chef Gareth Longhurst **Owner** Richard Taylor **Times** 12-2/7-9 Closed 25 Dec, Mon, D Sun **Prices** Fixed L 2 course £9.95, Fixed D 2 course £9.95, Starter £6.50-£9.50, Main £12.95-£20.50, Dessert £4-£6, Service optional, Groups min 8 service 12.5% **Wines** 18 bottles over £20, 7 bottles under £20, 7 by glass **Notes** Sunday L, Vegetarian available **Seats** 70 **Children** Portions **Parking** 20

PORTSMOUTH & SOUTHSEA   Map 5 SU60

Portsmouth Marriott Hotel

◉ Modern, Seafood

Seafood-led menu in a characterful hotel restaurant

☎ 0870 400 7285
Southampton Rd PO6 4SH
dir: M27 junct 12, keep left to lights, turn left. Hotel on left

Not far from the historic Naval Dockyards, the Spinnaker Tower and the outlet shopping at Gunwharf Quays, the Marriott is an anonymous-looking office block of a hotel that boasts a much more characterful dining room in the shape of the Sealevel Restaurant and Lounge. Done in bold primary colours, with intimate curved booths as well as elbow-to-elbow bar-seating, it features a seafood-led menu offering grilled tiger prawns doused in garlic and lemon butter, sea bass with butternut squash and sage risotto, and generous fish stews in tomato and fennel broth. Meats from the grill are the alternative, and meals conclude with the likes of apple crumble or a chocolate array of brownies, ice cream and sauce.

Chef Jaap Schep **Times** 12-3/6.30-10 **Prices** Fixed L 2 course fr £12.95, Service optional **Wines** 41 bottles over £20, 21 by glass **Notes** Sunday L, Vegetarian available **Seats** 70 **Children** Portions, Menu **Parking** 196

Restaurant 27

◉◉ Modern European

Confident modern cooking near the sea

☎ 023 9287 6272
27a South Pde PO5 2JF
e-mail: info@restaurant27.com
dir: M27 junct 12, take M275 to A3, follow A288 South Parade, left Burgoyne Rd

The trim white building on a street corner site just back from Southsea seafront has been a restaurant since the '60s when the Fab Four dropped by to dine. In its current guise as Restaurant 27 the place still moves with the times, sporting a cool minimal look involving discreet blocks of modern art and bare darkwood tables in a low-key ambience. The kitchen keeps a similarly switched-on approach to its work: ingredients are well chosen, in tune with the seasons and brought together in innovative

combinations using modern techniques. Sensibly concise, the menu proposes four choices at each stage - say, marinated foie gras teamed with passionfruit, chorizo and brioche, ahead of 30-hour-cooked belly of pork with rhubarb, aubergine and rosemary. A fine cheese board is an alternative to poached Braeburn apple, paired enterprisingly with gorgonzola ice cream and figs. It is all artfully presented and well-briefed staff are able to expound on the details of the tight-lipped menu.

Chef Kevin Bingham, Dominic Gower, Matt Wain, Annie Smith **Owner** Kevin & Sophie Bingham **Times** 12-2.30/7-9.30 Closed Xmas, New Year, Mon-Tue, L Wed-Sat, D Sun **Prices** Fixed L 3 course fr £27, Fixed D 3 course fr £40, Tasting menu £35, Service optional **Wines** 49 bottles over £20, 2 bottles under £20, 14 by glass **Notes** Tasting menu 7 course Wed-Thu, Sunday L, Vegetarian available **Seats** 34 **Children** Portions **Parking** On street

ROMSEY   Map 5 SU32

The Three Tuns

◉ Modern British **NEW**

Neighbourhood local with a good pedigree

☎ 01704 512639
58 Middlebridge St SO51 8HL
e-mail: manager@the3tunsromsey.co.uk

Something of a Romsey best-kept secret, the century's old Three Tuns comes hidden from the town-centre crowds among the old cottages of Middlebridge Street and retains an endearing local atmosphere. It has pedigree though, taken on by the team behind Winchester's Chesil Rectory restaurant (see entry), but admirably hasn't gone the restro-pub route. Sympathetic remodelling rides in tandem with the kitchen's simple, accomplished, cleanly flavoured food that impresses without being too flashy. So there are warming winter fires, dark beams and timbers and slate floors, while the dining area has a well-groomed country feel, with polished-wood furniture, mustard-coloured and exposed brick walls and antler-style chandeliers. Eat where you fancy - restaurant, bustling bar or small terrace - and order from the traditional menu hewn from local seasonal produce. There are classics such as Hampshire beef, mushroom, horseradish and ale pie, blackboard specials like whole baked John Dory with seasonal greens and caper beurre noisette, and desserts might include dark chocolate tart with blood orange sorbet.

Chef Andrew Freeman, Damian Brown **Owner** M Dodd, D Brown, I Longhorn **Times** 12-2.30/6-9 **Prices** Starter £4.95-£6.95, Main £9.95-£18.95, Dessert £4.95-£6.95 **Notes** Sunday L, Vegetarian available **Seats** 35 **Children** Portions, Menu **Parking** On street

Save on Hotels. Book at **theAA.com/hotel**

HAMPSHIRE 195 ENGLAND

The White Horse Hotel & Brasserie

◉◉ Modern British, International

Modern British classics in an ancient coaching inn

☎ 01794 512431
19 Market Place SO51 8ZJ
e-mail: reservations@silkhshotels.com
web: www.silkhotels.com

Established as a coaching inn 600 years ago, The White Horse is plumb in the middle of the charming market town of Romsey. Retaining much of its period detail, it offers a boldly decorated bar where orders are taken, as well as a plush dining room with smartly clothed tables. The cooking style is all about modern British classics, delivered with considerable panache. Seared scallops sit on their now canonical cauliflower purée, given texture with crisp-fried shallots and a deeper note of seasoning with curry oil. Duck three ways (breast, confit leg and foie gras) seems the best of all worlds, with its accurately cooked meat and liver, unified with a well-judged white wine jus of orange and grape, while satisfaction is assured in the sticky department with Jamaica gingerbread chocolate fondant, served with caramelised banana ice cream.

Chef Chris Rock **Owner** Mr Nuttall **Times** 7-3/6-10 **Prices** Fixed L 2 course fr £14, Fixed D 3 course fr £16.50, Starter £4.95-£8.50, Main £7.95-£24, Dessert £5.25-£6.25, Service optional **Wines** 34 bottles over £20, 16 bottles under £20, 11 by glass **Notes** Sunday L, Vegetarian available, Dress restrictions, Smart casual, Civ Wed 65 **Seats** 85, Pr/dining room 40 **Children** Menu **Parking** Car park nearby

---

ROTHERWICK Map 5 SU75

Tylney Hall Hotel

◉◉ Modern British 🍃

Modern country-house eating in a plush Victorian mansion

☎ 01256 764881
Ridge Ln RG27 9AZ
e-mail: sales@tylneyhall.com
web: www.tylneyhall.com
dir: M3 junct 5, A287 to Basingstoke, over junct with A30, over rail bridge, towards Newnham. Right at Newnham Green. Hotel 1m on left

When you're up for spoiling yourself with the whole country-house hotel, fine-dining schtick, Tylney Hall should fit the stately bill. Its 66 acres of glorious parkland include gardens designed by Gertrude Jekyll, woodland trails, waterfalls and lakes. And the Grade II listed Victorian red-brick pile is pretty fine, too, with its oak panelling, rococo plasterwork, and spectacular ceiling imported from a Florentine palazzo in the Italian Lounge. In such surroundings, classical country-house dining is perhaps to be expected, and what we have here in the Oak Room restaurant is the full-dress, jacket-and-tie version, in a setting involving oak panels, a domed ceiling, and opulent swagged drapes - all accompanied by a tinkling grand piano. What arrives on the plate is a gently updated take on the classics, underpinned by a clear focus on top-class ingredients. Chicken ballottine is served with the contrasting crunch of crispy chorizo and chicken scratchings, then pan-fried fillet of cod is partnered by a risotto of lovely sweet crayfish and crispy onion rings. To finish, there's a textbook treacle tart with caramel sauce and clotted cream ice cream, and it's all punctuated by a bountiful supply of beautifully-crafted nibbles.

Chef Stephen Hine **Owner** Elite Hotels
Times 12.30-2/7-10 **Prices** Fixed L 2 course fr £19.50, Fixed D 3 course fr £39.50, Starter fr £13.50, Main fr £25,

Dessert fr £11, Service optional **Wines** 350 bottles over £20, 2 bottles under £20, 10 by glass **Notes** Bill of Fayre menu 3 course £46, Sunday L, Vegetarian available, Dress restrictions, Jacket & tie at D, no jeans Fri-Sat, Civ Wed 120 **Seats** 80, Pr/dining room 120 **Children** Portions, Menu **Parking** 150

SHEDFIELD Map 5 SU51

Marriott Meon Valley Hotel & Country Club

◉ Modern British

Modern leisure hotel with appealing contemporary menu

☎ 01329 836826
Sandy Ln SO32 2HQ
dir: M27 junct 7 take A334 towards Wickham & Botley, continue past Botley and vineyard, hotel on left in 1m

Within the modern Meon Valley Marriott Hotel & Country Club, which as you might expect from the name excels in health, leisure and golf facilities, the smart Broadstreet restaurant is a beacon of civility. It all stands in 225 acres of beautiful grounds, just a short hop from the motorway. In the restaurant, smartly dressed staff are on the ball and the unfussy, gently modish food hits the spot. Start with ham hock and parsley terrine with apple and cider chutney and toasted brioche, before moving on to grilled leg of lamb steak with dauphinoise potatoes, chilli-roasted butternut squash, wilted spinach and rosemary jus. Two cheeses from the county (served with quince jelly and fig and raisin bread) is an alternative to a sweet such as iced lemon meringue parfait with mango coulis.

Times 6.30-9.30 Closed Mon, L Tue-Sat, D Sun

SOUTHAMPTON Map 5 SU41

Legacy Botleigh Grange Hotel & Spa

◉ Traditional British, Modern European V

Fine dining in a sylvan setting

☎ 0844 411 9050
Grange Rd, Botley SO30 2GA
e-mail: res-botleighgrange@legacy-hotels.co.uk
dir: On A334, 1m from M27 junct 7

Surrounded by 25 acres of grounds that include two lakes, yet only a mile from the M27, the Grange is a turreted Victorian pile complete with an Italianate clock tower. Dinner is taken in the spacious, elegant restaurant under a glass-domed ceiling. The menu changes monthly, and the kitchen makes as much as possible of local materials: a chargrilled fillet of Hampshire beef, for instance, served with sautéed shallots, wild mushrooms and red wine jus. Dishes tend to be modern European workings, so expect goats' cheese pannacotta with beetroot salad, or pork rillette with pickles, then spiced lamb with a herby tomato sauce and roast vegetables. Lemon and lime posset is a fine, tangy finale.

continued

SOUTHAMPTON *continued*

Chef Stephen Lewis **Owner** David K Plumpton
Times 12.30-2.30/7-9.30 **Prices** Fixed D 3 course £26.95,
Starter £5.45-£6.95, Main £11.50-£16, Dessert £5.25,
Service optional **Wines** 33 bottles over £20, 5 bottles
under £20, 7 by glass **Notes** Sunday L, Vegetarian menu,
Dress restrictions, Smart casual, Civ Wed 200 **Seats** 80,
Pr/dining room 350 **Children** Portions, Menu **Parking** 300

Mercure Southampton Centre Dolphin Hotel

◉ Modern International ◔

Historic hotel with crowd-pleasing menu

☎ 023 8038 6460
34-35 High St SO14 2HN
e-mail: H7876@accor.com
dir: A33 follow signs for Docks & Old Town/IOW ferry, at
ferry terminal turn right into High Street, hotel 400yds up
on the left hand side

Formerly a 17th-century coaching inn boasting the likes
of Jane Austen, Queen Victoria and Admiral Nelson among
its former guests, several million pounds and a takeover
from the Mercure chain later, this is a striking and
characterful place to stay and to eat. In the Signature
Restaurant, contemporary tones abound and it all looks
suitably modish and unstuffy - darkwood tables, plenty of
period character, and a menu that doesn't stray far from
traditional, brasserie-style comforts. Baked ramekin of
Hampshire pear with stilton cream and watercress salad
might precede steak and kidney pie, half a roast poussin
with bubble-and-squeak and bread sauce, or a
Casterbridge steak from the grill.

Chef Tibor Suli **Owner** Longrose Buccleuch
Times 12-2.30/7-9.45 **Prices** Starter £4.95-£9.95, Main
£9.95-£25, Dessert £4.95-£8.95, Service included
Wines 22 bottles over £20, 11 bottles under £20, 12 by
glass **Notes** Vegetarian available, Civ Wed 120, Air con
Seats 80 **Children** Portions, Menu **Parking** 80

White Star Tavern, Dining and Rooms

◉◉ British ◔

Seasonal local cooking amid ocean-liner décor

☎ 023 8082 1990
28 Oxford St SO14 3DJ
e-mail: reservations@whitestartavern.co.uk
dir: M3 junct 14 onto A33, towards Ocean Village

Housed in an old shipping line hotel once owned by the
White Star Line (forever associated with a certain
RMS *Titanic*) this buzzy gastro-pub and restaurant
celebrates Southampton's maritime heritage with rooms
that pay homage to the bygone era of great ocean-liners.
After an aperitif in the lively bar, head for the smart
banquette seating in the wood-floored and panelled
dining rooms, where contemporary brasserie-style dishes
featuring plenty of Hampshire produce offer the likes of
braised duck meat Scotch egg with bacon bits and sherry
vinaigrette as a prelude to loin of New Forest venison with

thyme polenta, spinach, mushrooms, and pomegranate
dressing. Day boat fish might be battered (with local ale
in the mix) and served with triple-cooked chips, mushy
peas and tartare sauce, while splendid local cheeses
offer a savoury alternative to baked rhubarb crumble
cheesecake with stem ginger ice cream.

Chef Stewart Hellsten **Owner** Matthew Boyle
Times 12-2.30/6-9.30 Closed 25-26 Dec **Prices** Starter
£4-£9, Main £10-£22, Dessert £5-£6, Service optional,
Groups min 6 service 10% **Wines** 22 bottles over £20,
10 bottles under £20, 9 by glass **Notes** Sunday L,
Vegetarian available **Seats** 40, Pr/dining room 10
Children Portions **Parking** On street or 2 car parks nearby

STOCKBRIDGE Map 5 SU33

The Greyhound Inn

◉◉ Modern British ◔

15th-century pub by the River Test

☎ 01264 810833
31 High St SO20 6EY
e-mail: enquiries@thegreyhound.info
dir: 9m NW of Winchester, 8m S of Andover. Off A303

The unassuming pubby exterior of the 15th-century
Greyhound opens into a stylish interior awash with period
character - there are low oak beams, wonky floors, an old
butcher's block, open fires and woodburners - although
the vibe these days is more of an easygoing restaurant
with rooms than a pint-and-pie local. The beautiful
garden sits on the banks of the River Test (angler's can
dangle their flies into the inn's private double-banked
stretch of it) making an idyllic setting for drinks and
dining on the patio, while the restaurant is done out
smartly with scrubbed wood tables, polished wooden
floors, and sage green walls. The kitchen keeps things
simple, but the results are still far from rustic, with daily
blackboard specials to bolster the seasonally-changing
menu. Expect the likes of crispy confit of lamb's belly with
pan-fried smoked eel, maple-glazed celeriac, green apple
purée and pickled fennel, followed by braised shin of
Hampshire beef with oxtail ravioli, root vegetables,
tarragon and oxtail consommé, and roasted bone marrow.
Desserts might run to caramelised millefeuille of spiced
pear with liquorice ice cream.

Chef Alan Havghie **Owner** Tim Fiducia **Times** 12-2/7-9
Closed 25-26 Dec, 31 Dec, 1 Jan, D Sun **Prices** Starter
£7-£11.95, Main £11.50-£20.50, Dessert £4.50-£8.95
Wines 60 bottles over £20, 10 bottles under £20, 8 by
glass **Notes** Sunday L, Vegetarian available **Seats** 52, Pr/
dining room 20 **Children** Portions **Parking** 20

Peat Spade Inn

◉ Traditional & Modern British

Sound modern dishes by the River Test

☎ 01264 810612
Longstock SO20 6DR
e-mail: info@peatspadeinn.co.uk
dir: 1.5m N of Stockbridge on A3057

The brick-built inn on a bank of the River Test is a
country-sports paradise, with fly-fishing and game-
shooting in the vicinity. The neighbouring Leckford Estate
supplies seasonal game, the beef is from cattle reared on
the local water meadows, and the wild mushrooms will
have been gathered in the New Forest. Sound modern
thinking informs dishes such as a starting breast of wood
pigeon with Stornoway black pudding, chicken liver
parfait and a well-dressed salad of mixed leaves, while
mains might offer Test trout with pan-roasted beetroot,
watercress and horseradish cream, or sensational calves'
liver with bacon and mustard mash. Texturally comforting
desserts such as dark chocolate fondant with white
chocolate ice cream, or Cambridge burnt cream with
poached winter fruits, will see you to bed happy.

Chef Tracy Levett **Owner** Miller's Collection
Times 12-2.30/6.30-9.30 Closed 25 Dec **Prices** Starter
£5.50-£9.50, Main £10.50-£19.50, Dessert £6, Service
optional, Groups min 10 service 10% **Wines** 39 bottles
over £20, 7 bottles under £20, 9 by glass **Notes** Sunday L,
Vegetarian available **Seats** 45, Pr/dining room 20
Children Portions **Parking** 25

WICKHAM Map 5 SU51

Old House Hotel & Restaurant

◉◉ Modern British

Inventive cooking in a chic Georgian bolt-hole

☎ 01329 833049
The Square PO17 5JG
e-mail: enquiries@oldhousehotel.co.uk
web: www.oldhousehotel.co.uk
dir: In centre of Wickham, 2m N of Fareham at junct of
A32 & B2177

The creeper and wisteria-festooned Georgian façade of
Old House Hotel on Wickham's gorgeous village square is
a deceptively unchanging front for an operation that has
moved with the times. The interior brings together chic
contemporary style with period character that runs to
timbers salvaged from an American warship captured by

Save on Hotels. Book at **theAA.com/hotel**

HAMPSHIRE 197 **ENGLAND**

the English during the American Civil War in the garden room, which is one of three dining areas; others include a classy clean-cut modern space enlivened by colourful art, or there's a light-flooded conservatory as a relaxed setting for the kitchen's modern output. Local produce is enthusiastically championed and brought to the table in engaging ideas - pan-seared scallops with honey tarragon jelly, pickled apple and smoked paprika caramel, say, then Moroccan grilled monkfish with crispy celeriac, tomato and olive sauce, and lime dressing. Desserts are no less inventive, perhaps a trio of hot chocolate fondant, honey parfait, and white chocolate and lemon mousse.

Chef Daniel Crook **Owner** Mr J R Guess **Times** 12-2.30/7-9.30 Closed D Sun **Prices** Fixed L 2 course fr £14.95, Starter £6.50-£10.95, Main £15.95-£25, Dessert £6.75 £8.75, Service optional, Groups min 8 service 10% **Wines** 73 bottles over £20, 11 bottles under £20, 14 by glass **Notes** Tasting menu available, Sunday L, Vegetarian available, Dress restrictions, Smart casual, Civ Wed 50 **Seats** 85, Pr/dining room 14 **Children** Portions **Parking** 12, Street parking

---

WINCHESTER   Map 5 SU42

Avenue Restaurant at Lainston House Hotel

◉◉◉ – *see below*

The Black Rat

◉◉ Modern British

Former pub serving up seriously good food

☎ 01962 844465 & 841531
88 Chesil St SO23 0HX
e-mail: reservations@theblackrat.co.uk
dir: M3 junct 9/A31 towards Winchester & Bar End until T-junct. Turn right at traffic lights, restaurant 600yds on left

For some, The Black Rat may simply be a white-fronted old pub that you pass by on your way out of the city. But to those in the know, it's actually a great little restaurant in a former 18th century pub serving up modern British cuisine. Step inside and you'll find it's full of character with its original wood floors strewn with old rugs, beams, exposed brickwork, open fires and chunky bleached wood tables with mismatched old wooden chairs. The dining area is spread over two rooms, the larger of which is split level, and there are only a handful of tables, lending the place a cosy, intimate feel (and resulting in a need to book especially at weekends). High quality, seasonal and largely locally-sourced ingredients (including vegetables from the restaurant's own allotment) are put to good use in an imaginative menu which may run from a vivid green and vibrantly fresh-tasting wild garlic velouté with pied bleu mushrooms and whipped ricotta to start, to braised hare pie - the hare from just up the road at Alresford - served with crushed Jersey Royals and spring vegetables.

Chef Chris Bailey **Owner** David Nicholson **Times** 12-2.15/7-9.30 Closed 2 wks Etr, 2 wks Xmas & New Year, 2 wks Oct/Nov, L Mon-Fri **Prices** Fixed L 2 course £22.95, Starter £7-£9.50, Main £18-£22, Dessert £7-£8.50, Service optional, Groups min 10 service 10% **Wines** 40 bottles over £20, 18 bottles under £20, 6 by glass **Notes** Fixed L Sat-Sun only, Sunday L, Vegetarian available **Seats** 40, Pr/dining room 16 **Parking** Car park opposite

The Chesil Rectory

◉◉ Modern British

Modern cooking in the city's oldest house

☎ 01962 851555
1 Chesil St SO23 0HU
e-mail: enquiries@chesilrectory.co.uk
dir: S from King Alfred's statue at bottom of The Broadway, cross small bridge, turn right, restaurant on left, just off mini rdbt

A beautiful half-timbered building dating back to 1450, The Chesil Rectory is the oldest house in Winchester. It has been home to a restaurant in various guises for a good many years, the modish British cooking contrasting rather nicely with the ancient surroundings. From the street you enter through an extremely low door - the first of many original features - to be greeted in the cooler

continued

Avenue Restaurant at Lainston House Hotel

WINCHESTER   Map 5 SU42

Modern British V 🍷 🌿

Enterprising contemporary cooking in a charming 17th-century house

☎ 01962 776088
Woodman Ln, Sparsholt SO21 2LT
e-mail: enquiries@lainstonhouse.com
dir: B3049 Stockbridge road

Built as a royal hunting lodge in the 17th century, Lainston House is a charming property, tastefully extended over the past 30 years into a luxury hotel. The restaurant, a traditionally styled, carpeted room, its panelled walls hung with paintings, gets its name from its spectacular views of the mile-long avenue of limes in the hotel's 63 acres of parkland. Whenever possible, all the produce used in the kitchen comes from within a

25-mile radius (producers are listed on the menu); they also grow their own vegetables, fruit and herbs and rear pigs: perhaps served as a main course of slowly braised belly with apple, Dijonnaise potato, and swede. Andy MacKenzie assembles compact but varied menus and cooks more or less in the contemporary British style, serving marinated mackerel with beetroot jelly and honeyed wasabi dressing, and a main course of poached cod fillet with mussels, Jerusalem artichoke, and smoked potato foam. Slow-cooked ox cheek, on potato and horseradish emulsion, topped with a quenelle of red onion and potato sticks, the plate dotted with cep purée - impressive for its depth of flavours, accuracy and attractive presentation - may be followed by another well-conceived dish of wild sea bass fillet with crab pearls and clams. Finish with an inventive dessert such as pain perdu with truffle ice cream, lime sabayon and a sweet bacon crisp.

Chef Andy MacKenzie, Phil Yeomans **Owner** Exclusive Hotels **Times** 12-2/7-10 **Prices** Fixed L 2 course £22, Fixed D 3 course £55, Tasting menu £70-£120, Service added but optional 10% **Wines** 200 bottles over £20, 200 by glass **Notes** Sunday L, Vegetarian menu, Dress restrictions, Smart casual, Civ Wed 120 **Seats** 60, Pr/dining room 120 **Children** Portions, Menu **Parking** 200

WINCHESTER *continued*

months by a roaring log fire. You can eat here or upstairs where a log-burner warms the room. Whether you choose up or down, expect a brilliantly preserved interior of solid oak beams, low ceilings, wooden floors and leaded windows. The menu draws heavily on local, seasonal produce and serves up pleasingly straightforward dishes such as grilled mackerel with forced rhubarb and horseradish crème fraîche, followed by roast rump of lamb with cream layered potatoes, young vegetables and rosemary and garlic sauce.

Chef Damian Brown **Owner** Mark Dodd, Damian Brown, Iain Longhorn **Times** 12-2.20/6-9.30 Closed 1 wk Xmas, BH Mons **Prices** Fixed L 2 course £15.95, Fixed D 3 course £19.95, Starter £4.95-£10.50, Main £13-£20, Dessert £6.50, Service optional, Groups min 10 service 10% **Wines** 50+ bottles over £20, 4 bottles under £20, 9 by glass **Notes** Set menu Mon-Sat 12-2.20, 6-7, Sun 6-9, Vegetarian available **Seats** 75, Pr/dining room 14 **Children** Portions **Parking** NCP Chesil St adjacent

---

Hotel du Vin Winchester

◉◉ Traditional British, French ⚑

Bustling bistro and great wines in Georgian townhouse hotel

☎ 01962 841414
14 Southgate St SO23 9EF
e-mail: info@winchester.hotelduvin.co.uk
dir: M3 junct 11, follow signs to Winchester town centre, located on left

The Winchester branch is where the HdV brand got started with a formula that goes like this: take a characterful old building (in this case an elegant early-Georgian townhouse near the cathedral), add upmarket, style-driven bedrooms, and a wine-themed, retro-French-style bistro serving simple but well-prepared contemporary brasserie-style classics built from top-class local materials. Et voilà, as the French say. It's a lively space, done out with lots of wood - bare floorboards, burnished wooden tables - and wine-related memorabilia to go with an eager-to-please menu that might offer dressed crab with walnut toast as an opening gambit, then move on to duck confit with Puy lentils, or roast cod with buttered leeks and salsa verde. Tarte au citron or crêpes Suzette are desserts as beret-wearingly Gallic as the bulk of the excellent wine list.

Times 12-1.45/7-10

Running Horse Inn

◉◉ Traditional, International

Innovative cooking in upgraded inn

☎ 01962 880218
88 Main Rd, Littleton SO22 6QS
e-mail: runninghorseinn@btconnect.com
dir: B3049 out of Winchester 1.5m, turn right into Littleton after 1m, Running Horse on right

Three miles from the centre of Winchester, The Running Horse combines the functions of bar, restaurant and

small hotel. It's a relaxed and informal sort of place, with the restaurant featuring modern art on battleship-grey walls, and wicker-back chairs at plain wooden tables. Fresh, seasonal food that's big on flavours is what to expect here. Roast pigeon breast, with a black pudding fritter, beetroot purée, confit garlic and thyme jus, has been an impressive starter, or there might be a trio of ravioli (trout, crab and crayfish) with pea purée and bisque foam. Timings are accurate - witness pink, moist, flavourful roast rack of lamb, served with braised neck along with pea and mint pannacotta and rosemary and garlic gratin - and even complicated dishes seem to work: poached fillets of plaice are rolled in spinach and served with shellfish sauce, shrimp and cucumber jelly, vanilla potato purée and roast tomatoes. Stick to a simple dessert like espresso crème brûlée with Amaretto cream.

Chef Paul Down **Owner** Light Post Ltd **Times** 12-2/6-9.30 **Prices** Starter £4.95-£7.95, Main £9.95-£23, Dessert £4.95-£6.95, Service optional, Groups min 6 service 10% **Wines** 13 bottles over £20, 13 bottles under £20, 14 by glass **Notes** Sunday L, Vegetarian available **Seats** 50 **Children** Portions, Menu **Parking** 40

The Winchester Hotel

◉ Modern European

Contemporary brasserie fare in a modern hotel

☎ 01962 709988
Worthy Ln SO23 7AB
e-mail: info@thewinchesterhotel.co.uk
dir: A33 then A3047, hotel 1m on right

Smack in the centre of Winchester, Hutton's Brasserie at The Winchester Hotel comes with a glossy interior of polished floorboards, darkwood tables, creamy leather chairs and banquettes, and chillout music in the background. Switched-on staff look the part, and the kitchen delivers a crowd-pleasing repertoire of classic and modern European ideas. A terrine of rabbit, ham hock and morels with apricot chutney might kick off proceedings, followed by venison medallions with garlic mash, buttered purple broccoli, and port wine jus, or baked fillet of red snapper with broad beans, peppers and lemon dressing. Bringing up the rear, there might be dark chocolate crème brûlée with walnut biscotti.

Chef Neil Dore **Owner** Quantum Hotels Ltd **Times** 12.30-2/7-9.30 **Prices** Food prices not confirmed for 2013. Please telephone for details **Wines** 15 bottles over £20, 25 bottles under £20, 9 by glass **Notes** Sunday L, Vegetarian available, Dress restrictions, Smart casual, Civ Wed 150 **Seats** 80, Pr/dining room 40 **Children** Portions, Menu **Parking** 70

HEREFORDSHIRE

HEREFORD
Map 10 SO53

Castle House

◉◉ Modern British ♖

Classy townhouse hotel with innovative style of cooking

☎ 01432 356321
Castle St HR1 2NW
e-mail: info@castlehse.co.uk
web: www.castlehse.co.uk
dir: City centre, follow signs to Castle House Hotel

It might be in the city centre, hard by the cathedral, but Castle House has a peaceful setting, its restaurant looking over gardens to the Wye. This is a comfortable room, with vivid artworks on pastel-green walls and candles on the tables. The kitchen makes good use of local suppliers, and comes up with some bright, modern ideas, pairing crisp pork belly with scallops, sweetcorn purée and chilli jam, and grilled Cornish mackerel with a trio of gooseberries (fruit, jam and jelly). Sound techniques and an eye for presentation are clear in main courses: perhaps accurately cooked loin of lamb set atop little gems and peas and mint-infused braised shoulder, with fondant potato, or roast grey mullet with clams, shrimps, fennel and broad bean tartare. To finish, expect something equally labour-intensive: perhaps lavender crème brûlée, with raspberry Pavlova to one side and three tiny quenelles of lime and honey pickle adding contrasting sharpness.

Chef Claire Nicholls **Owner** David Watkins **Times** 12-2/6.30-9.30 **Prices** Tasting menu £50, Starter £5-£9, Main £12-£24, Dessert £7-£8, Service optional **Wines** 77 bottles over £20, 20 bottles under £20, 9 by glass **Notes** Tasting menu 7 course, Sunday L, Vegetarian available, Civ Wed 50 **Seats** 30 **Children** Portions **Parking** 12

Save on Hotels. Book at **theAA.com/hotel**

HEREFORDSHIRE 199 **ENGLAND**

Holme Lacy House Hotel

◉◉ Modern British

Fine dining in a fine country-house setting

☎ 01432 870870
Holme Lacy HR2 6LP
dir: B4399 at Holme Lacy, take lane opposite college.
Hotel 500mtrs on right

Looking for a restorative break from the rat race? Well,
this Grade I listed Georgian mansion set in 20 acres of
parkland in the idyllic Wye Valley near to Hereford should
fit the bill. And Holme Lacy House Hotel lives up to its
promise on the inside too, with a sweeping central
staircase and all the fancy ceilings and acreages of oak
panelling you'd expect in a building of this pedigree. The
fine-dining Orchard Restaurant stays true to the style
while moving its culinary efforts gently into the modern
world using top-grade local materials in fine-tuned
classic partnerships. Glazed belly of Gloucestershire Old
Spot served with roasted scallop, carrot and cumin, wild
mushrooms and pancetta might open proceedings, ahead
of Wye Valley beef partnered with leeks, confit shallot,
sticky oxtail tortellini and thyme jus. Sound technical
skills are a hallmark all the way through to a finale of
pineapple tarte Tatin with chocolate and chilli ice and
caramel sauce.

Chef Gary Wheeler **Owner** Bourne Leisure **Times** 6-9
Closed L all week **Prices** Fixed D 3 course fr £39.50,
Service optional **Wines** 25 bottles over £20, 7 bottles
under £20, 9 by glass **Notes** Vegetarian available, Dress
restrictions, Smart casual **Seats** 50 **Parking** 200

KINGTON   Map 9 SO25

The Stagg Inn and Restaurant

◉◉ Modern British V 🍽️ 🖐️

First-class gastro-pub in rural Herefordshire

☎ 01544 230221
Titley HR5 3RL
e-mail: reservations@thestagg.co.uk
dir: Between Kington & Presteigne on B4335

Whitewashed and handsome from the outside and
comfortably rustic within, The Stagg stands in tiny Titley
amid unspoilt Welsh border country. Here the Marches are
a treasure-trove of fine raw ingredients, put to best use
by the Roux-trained chef-patron Steve Reynolds. His
passion for food may have put this rural local on the
culinary map but it's still very much the local pub, with
jolly, pint-drinking farmers and walkers filling the homely,
pine-furnished bar. His short daily menus bristle with
local produce, from estate game to sausages, faggots
and chorizo from their own pigs, and fresh fruits and
vegetables from the kitchen garden. Expect to find gutsy
modern British dishes, cooked with an assured, yet
restrained touch, allowing key flavours to shine through.
Perhaps kick off with a full-flavoured crabcake served
with watercress and a vibrant tartare sauce. Follow with
a succulent, accurately cooked chicken breast,
accompanied by girolles, spinach, creamy dauphinoise
and tomato purée, then round off with a light and silky

honey pannacotta with Marsala baked figs, or a plate of
impressive local cheeses.

Chef S Reynolds, M Handley **Owner** Steve & Nicola
Reynolds **Times** 12-2/6.30-9 Closed 1st 2wks Nov, 2 wks
Jan-Feb, Mon, D Sun **Prices** Starter £6-£10, Main £17-
£24, Dessert £4.75-£7, Service optional **Wines** 52 bottles
over £20, 23 bottles under £20, 8 by glass **Notes** Sunday
L, Vegetarian menu **Seats** 70, Pr/dining room 30
Children Portions, Menu **Parking** 22

LEDBURY   Map 10 SO73

Feathers Hotel

◉ Modern British 🍽️

Confident contemporary cooking in half-timbered inn

☎ 01531 635266
High St HR8 1DS
e-mail: mary@feathers-ledbury.co.uk
dir: M50 junct 2. Ledbury on A449/A438/A417. Hotel on
main street

The heavily timbered Tudor building in a prime site on the
High Street was at one time a coaching inn and is now a
classy, efficiently run hotel. Fuggles Brasserie is the main
eating venue, named after a variety of hops, a profusion
of which hang from the ceiling beams. The cooking shows
a high level of confidence and expertise, seen in starters
like bream fillet with caponata and crisp pancetta, and a
salad of goats' cheese glazed in smoked paprika with
chorizo and tomatoes. Influences from beyond the
European framework are evident in some main courses -
Thai green curry of monkfish with limed basmati rice, say
- while others can be reassuringly familiar, among them
roast breast of guinea fowl with sautéed leeks, cabbage
and a potato cake. Imaginative puddings may include
prune and almond tart with caramelised apple cream.

Chef Susan Isaacs **Owner** David Elliston
Times 12-2/7-9.30 **Prices** Fixed D 3 course £23.50,
Starter £5.95-£7.95, Main £14-£21.50, Dessert £6.25-
£6.50, Service added but optional 10% **Wines** 89 bottles
over £20, 42 bottles under £20, 12 by glass **Notes** Sunday
L, Vegetarian available, Civ Wed 120 **Seats** 55, Pr/dining
room 60 **Children** Portions **Parking** 30

LEINTWARDINE   Map 9 SO47

The Lion

◉ Modern British **NEW** 🍽️

Modern British dishes in an idyllic English inn

☎ 01547 540203 & 540747
High St SY7 0JZ
e-mail: enquiries@thelionleintwardine.co.uk
web: www.thelionleintwardine.co.uk
dir: On A4113. At bottom of High Street by bridge

Set beside the River Teme in a peaceful Herefordshire
hamlet, The Lion is a sensitively restored village local
with a patio area looking over extensive gardens, and
riverside tables under the trees. An English idyll, it was
once the local of Sir Banastre Tarleton, who distinguished
himself controversially in the American War of
Independence, albeit on the losing side. The bare
floorboards, leather sofas and beams make all the right
noises within, and Jason Hodnett offers a polished
repertoire of modern British dishes for your perusal. A
pressed terrine of Devon crab and smoked langoustine
has good flavour, and is accompanied by a light
watercress pannacotta and baby pear, while prime
materials are in evidence in a pairing of best end and
herbed breast of spring lamb, which comes with beech
mushrooms and mash, or there could be a bracing early
summer risotto of green beans, peas and red mint, served
with gremolata, lemon yoghurt and pecorino. Modern
menus would be lost without their 'textures', here
manifesting as doughnut, mousse, ice cream and sherbet
sprinkle, composed of different apple varieties.

Chef Jason Hodnett **Owner** Mr & Mrs W Watkins
Times 12-2/7-9.30 Closed 25 Dec **Wines** 43 bottles over
£20, 17 bottles under £20, 15 by glass **Notes** Sunday L,
Vegetarian available, Dress restrictions, Smart casual
Seats 50, Pr/dining room 20 **Children** Portions, Menu
Parking 20

See advert on page 200

THE LION

LEINTWARDINE
BAR, RESTAURANT & ROOMS

Set in the picturesque village of Leintwardine, this stunning country restaurant with rooms is the perfect place to unwind, enjoy a drink or dinner, or stay the night in an excellent position for exploring Herefordshire, South Shropshire and the Welsh Marches.

Specialising in modern British cuisine using fine local seasonal ingredients, excellent wines and local ales.

The Lion, High Street, Leintwardine, Shropshire, SY7 0JZ | *Telephone:* 01547 540203
www.thelionleintwardine.co.uk | *Email:* enquiries@thelionleintwardine.co.uk | *FB:* lionleintwardine

The Chase Hotel

◉ British, European

Georgian country-house hotel with modish restaurant

☎ 01989 763161
Gloucester Rd HR9 5LH
e-mail: res@chasehotel.co.uk
dir: M50 junct 4 onto A449. Take A40 towards Gloucester, turn right at rdbt into Ross-on-Wye. Hotel on left 0.25m

Every bit the contemporary dining room, Harry's - set in a large Georgian mansion which is the Chase Hotel (with 11 acres of grounds) - is named after the owner's grandson. Shades of cream, tan and black, modern furnishings and silk drapes blend quite happily with the room's original features - high ceilings, ornate plaster covings and tall windows included. Fresh, quality local ingredients drive the kitchen's equally modern roster of dishes, with things like slow-roasted lamb shank (with a mixed bean cassoulet) lining up alongside those with a nod to sunnier climes, perhaps cod fillet saltimbocca (served on creamed potatoes with a chorizo and paprika Mediterranean sauce). Desserts follow suit, with the ubiquitous Brit sticky toffee pudding favourite strutting its stuff alongside a classic tiramisù or tarte Tatin.

Chef Richard Birchall **Owner** Camanoe Estates Ltd **Times** 12-2/7-10 Closed 24-27 Dec **Prices** Fixed L 2 course £15.50, Fixed D 3 course £27.50-£35, Starter £5.50-£9.50, Main £16-£22, Dessert £5.50-£8.50, Service included **Wines** 27 bottles over £20, 15 bottles under £20, 13 by glass **Notes** Sunday L, Vegetarian available, Civ Wed 150 **Seats** 70, Pr/dining room 300 **Children** Portions, Menu **Parking** 75

Glewstone Court Country House Hotel & Restaurant

◉ Modern British, French ✪

West Country produce in an attractive Wye Valley Georgian hotel

☎ 01989 770367
Glewstone HR9 6AW
e-mail: glewstone@aol.com
web: www.glewstonecourt.com
dir: From Ross Market Place take A40/A49 (Monmouth/ Hereford) over Wilton Bridge. At rdbt left onto A40 (Monmouth/S Wales), after 1m turn right for Glewstone. Hotel 0.5m on left

Set in lovely gardens in the Wye Valley, just three miles from Ross-on-Wye and with views of the Forest of Dean, Glewstone Court is a friendly, family-run Georgian country house. The elegant house has preserved many period features, not least a fine curving Regency staircase, while the candlelit dining room goes for a gently-updated style offset by fancy plasterwork cornicing and crystal chandeliers. This is the right spot for sourcing the fine bounty of the Marches - Welsh lamb, Gloucester pork, and Hereford beef, which might be put to good use as pan-fried strips of steak with lemongrass, chilli and garlic in a Thai-spiced salad. Next, Abergavenny venison turns up with honeyed figs and sloe gin jus, before a dreamy honey pannacotta with raspberry confit wraps things up in fine style.

Chef Christine Reeve-Tucker, Tom Piper **Owner** C & W Reeve-Tucker **Times** 12-2/7-10 Closed 25-27 Dec **Prices** Food prices not confirmed for 2013. Please telephone for details **Wines** 23 bottles over £20, 19 bottles under £20, 8 by glass **Notes** Sunday L, Vegetarian available, Dress restrictions, No baseball caps, Civ Wed 72 **Seats** 36, Pr/dining room 40 **Children** Portions, Menu **Parking** 28

Orles Barn

◉◉ Modern British ✪

Confident modern cooking in smart restaurant with rooms

☎ 01989 562155
Wilton HR9 6AE
e-mail: reservations@orles-barn.co.uk
dir: A49/A40 rdbt outside Ross-on-Wye, take slip road between petrol station & A40 to Monmouth. 100yds on left

The setting for this restaurant with rooms on the outskirts of Ross-on-Wye is a red-brick building whose oldest parts date from the 14th and 17th centuries. In the restaurant, sage-green walls, country-kitchen heritage hues of cream and beige, and swathes of white linen shrouding tables and high-backed chairs all gel together for an understated boutique style. Head chef Dan Wall is a local Hereford boy who likes to keep things fresh, seasonal, and locally sourced, with farmers, growers and suppliers given due credit on the menu. A repertoire of big-hearted flavours delivers starters such as locally-shot pigeon with asparagus and walnut pesto tart, or wild garlic and potato soup with garlic crisps, while mains might see seared loin and faggot of locally-shot venison with sweet onion tart, sauté potatoes and curly kale sitting alongside seared line-caught sea bass with razor clam gratin and nettle risotto. End with baked Alaska with marinated cherries and brown bread ice cream.

Chef Dan Wall **Owner** Richard & Kelly Bailey **Times** 12.30-2/6.30-9 **Prices** Starter £6-£11, Main £13-£24, Dessert £7-£9, Service optional **Wines** 28 bottles over £20, 14 bottles under £20, 7 by glass **Notes** Tasting menu 7 course, Sunday L, Vegetarian available, Civ Wed 100 **Seats** 40, Pr/dining room 12 **Children** Portions **Parking** 22

ROSS-ON-WYE *continued*

Wilton Court Restaurant with Rooms

◉◉ Modern British ◉

Skilful modern cooking in a riverside setting

☎ 01989 562569
Wilton Ln HR9 6AQ
e-mail: info@wiltoncourthotel.com
web: www. wiltoncourthotel.com
dir: M50 junct 4 onto A40 towards Monmouth at 3rd rdbt turn left signed Ross-on-Wye then take 1st right, hotel on right

Stone-mullioned windows and ancient oak beams are proof of red-brick Wilton Court's Elizabethan pedigree. Yet this small-scale restaurant with rooms in an idyllic location on the banks of the River Wye is no brooding relic from the Tudor age: it has all been lightened up to suit contemporary aesthetics, particularly in the luminous Mulberry Restaurant, where a light-flooded conservatory extension furnished with Lloyd Loom tables and chairs overlooks the 300-year-old tree that gives the place its name. The kitchen takes a modern British view of things and name-checks local suppliers on a menu that goes from starters like seared king prawns with horseradish croûtons and chive cream to mains such as garlic and rosemary-marinated loin of local lamb with rösti potato, pea purée and rosemary jus, or venison haunch steak with celeriac purée, pickled walnut and red wine jus. Proceedings stick by the local terroir to the end, with Weston's cider pannacotta with apple crisp and lemon sorbet, or superb artisan cheeses from Herefordshire and Gloucestershire.

Chef Martyn Williams **Owner** Roger & Helen Wynn **Times** 12-2.15/7-9 **Prices** Fixed L 2 course fr £14.95, Fixed D 3 course fr £32.50, Tasting menu £52.50, Starter £6.25-£8.95, Main £16.50-£22.50, Dessert £6.95-£7.50, Service optional **Wines** 23 bottles over £20, 15 bottles under £20, 8 by glass **Notes** Tasting menu 7 course (complete tables only), Sunday L, Vegetarian available, Dress restrictions, Smart casual preferred **Seats** 40, Pr/dining room 12 **Children** Portions, Menu **Parking** 25

Butchers Arms

◉◉ Modern European ◉

Period Herefordshire pub with excellent food

☎ 01432 860281
HR1 4RF
e-mail: food@butchersarmswoolhope.com
dir: 0.5m out of village, on Ledbury road

When so many pubs have gone gastro and sidelined drinkers, it is heartening to see that this classic Herefordshire pub has its priorities right: it is still very much the village local with a central bar serving local beer, cider and perry. The Butchers is just the sort of half-timbered inn you'd hope to come across when messing about in Herefordshire: heavily beamed, festooned with hopbines, and kitted out with chunky rustic tables and a pair of log fires, the setting is one you want to linger in to take on the daily-changing menu of flavour-driven modern dishes. Chef-proprietor Stephen Bull is a man who is heroically striving for maximum seasonal and local output - this is down-to-earth cooking, taking in the likes of wild rabbit rillettes with rabbit jelly, and orange and hazelnut salad, or hot smoked haddock custard with rocket cream. Proper pies run to a chicken version with leeks, mushrooms and wild garlic in cream cheese pastry, or there could be pheasant breast wrapped in prosciutto and served with pheasant ravioli, creamed leeks and chestnuts. Leave room for hearty rib-sticking puddings like warm ginger cake with treacle toffee ice cream.

Chef Stephen Bull **Owner** Stephen & Annie Bull **Times** 12-2.15/6.30-9 Closed Mon (except BHs), D Sun **Prices** Starter £4.50-£7.50, Main £10.50-£17, Dessert £5.50, Service optional **Notes** Sunday L, Vegetarian available **Seats** 60, Pr/dining room 24 **Children** Portions **Parking** 40

The Gatsby

◉ Modern European

Modish menus in a converted 1930s cinema

☎ 01442 870403
97 High St HP4 2DG
e-mail: thegatsby@live.co.uk
web: www.thegatsby.net
dir: M25 junct 20/A41 to Aylesbury in 3m take left turn to Berkhamsted following town signs. Restaurant on left on entering High St

The fabulously restored Rex Cinema is a classic slice of curvy 1930s art deco that has embraced a second career as an on-trend 21st-century brasserie since it opened its doors in 2005. The interior references the golden age of the movies with its nostalgia-fest of black and white photos, original fluted pillars and fancy cornicing, but it all blends seamlessly with contemporary darkwood tables and high-backed cream and toffee-hued leather seats. The mood is busy and the open-to-view kitchen lays bare the engine room where the crowd-pleasing repertoire of classic and modern ideas takes shape. Tortellini of confit rabbit with carrot purée and bacon and tarragon foam is one way to start, while mains run to fillet of sea bass with fennel and spring onion risotto and spinach coulis, or beef bourguignon with celeriac creamed potatoes and parsnip crisps. Desserts could take in Granny Smith tarte fine with Calvados crème fraîche.

Chef Matthew Salt **Owner** Nick Pembroke **Times** 12-2.30/5.30-10.30 Closed 25-26 Dec **Prices** Fixed L 2 course fr £14.95, Fixed D 3 course fr £20.90, Starter £6.95-£9.95, Main £16.25-£25.95, Dessert fr £7.95, Service optional, Groups min 6 service 12.5% **Wines** 33 bottles over £20, 13 bottles under £20, 14 by glass **Notes** Pre cinema menu Mon-Sat 12-2.30 & 5.30-6.30, Sunday L, Vegetarian available, Dress restrictions, Smart casual **Seats** 65 **Children** Portions **Parking** 10

DATCHWORTH — Map 6 TL21

The Tilbury

◉ Modern British V 🕐

Proper village pub serving up well-sourced, carefully-cooked food

☎ 01438 815550
1 Watton Rd SG3 6TB
e-mail: info@thetilbury.co.uk
web: www.thetilbury.co.uk
dir: A1(M) junct 7, A602 signed Ware & Hertford. At Bragbury End right into Bragbury Lane to Datchworth

Paul Bloxham is a flag-waving supporter of regional and seasonal British food, and if he can serve it up in a smartly renovated pub, so much the better. Known for his TV appearances, Bloxham has plenty of energy left over for pulling tired old boozers up by their bootstraps (the buildings, that is, rather than the clientele) and that is exactly what he has done here in the village of Datchworth. The Tilbury goes for a shabby-chic look with darkwood flooring and tables and bold slabs of colour on the walls, and the vibe is laid-back: a switched-on, food-oriented modern pub, in other words. Food miles are kept to a minimum, but that doesn't preclude shellfish from Scotland and Welsh salt marsh lamb from appearing on the menu, since quality first and foremost is what drives the kitchen's output. Wild boar and quail make an inviting duo for posh Scotch eggs, served with Guinness and mango ketchup, while mains span everything from roast rump of Herdwick mutton with braised white onion, spinach and capers, to steamed Norfolk mussels in saffron, leek and perry cream with chips. Pudding could be a trendy prune and Armagnac sandwich with rice pudding ice cream.

Chef Paul Bloxham, Ben Crick **Owner** Paul Bloxham & Paul Andrews **Times** 12-3/6-late Closed 1 Jan, some BHs, D Sun **Prices** Fixed L 2 course fr £13.95, Fixed D 3 course fr £17.95, Starter £4-£13, Main £11-£25, Dessert £5-£9, Service optional, Groups min 6 service 10% **Wines** 16 bottles over £20, 16 bottles under £20, 32 by glass **Notes** Sunday L, Vegetarian menu **Seats** 70, Pr/dining room 14 **Children** Portions, Menu **Parking** 40

FLAUNDEN — Map 6 TL00

Bricklayers Arms

◉ British, French **NEW**

Traditional country inn with well-crafted Anglo-French cooking

☎ 01442 833322 & 831722
Black Robin Ln, Hogpits Bottom HP3 0PH
e-mail: goodfood@bricklayersarms.com
web: www.bricklayersarms.com
dir: M25 junct 20, A451 towards Chipperfield. Into Dunny Ln, 1st right into Flaunden Ln. 1m on single track

An assemblage of three 18th-century cottages that once housed a blacksmith's forge and a butcher's is now a country inn, surrounded by rolling English acres and the walking country of the Chess Valley. Inside is as rustic as you like, with low ceilings, oak beams and a log fire in winter, and there are tables on the terrace and dotted around the garden for when the sun shines on Hertfordshire. Anglo-French food based on plenty of local produce is the name of the game, and dishes are carefully crafted and attractively presented. Start with lightly battered king scallops with stir-fried seafood and spicy tomato coulis, or a signature selection of smoked fish with lemon coriander butter. A potato-topped pie is a familiar enough sight in a country inn, but not perhaps one incorporating partridge, pheasant and venison in red wine and game stock. Sticky toffee pudding or apple and rhubarb tart turn the comfort factor up to max. A splendid wine list and fine selection of local ales completes a thoroughly cheering picture.

Chef Claude Paillet **Owner** Alvin & Sally Michaels
Times 12-2.30/6.30-9.30 Closed 25 Dec **Prices** Fixed L 2

course £15, Fixed D 3 course £20, Starter £5.95-£13.95, Main £12.95-£24.95, Dessert £4.75-£6.95, Service optional, Groups min 6 service 10% **Wines** 18 bottles under £20, 110 by glass **Notes** Sunday L, Vegetarian available **Seats** 95, Pr/dining room 50 **Children** Portions **Parking** 40

HATFIELD — Map 6 TL20

Beales Hotel

◉◉ Modern British 🕐

Contemporary architecture and vibrant contemporary cooking

☎ 01707 288500 & 288518
Comet Way AL10 9NG
e-mail: outsidein@bealeshotels.co.uk
dir: On A1001 opposite Galleria Shopping Mall - follow signs for Galleria

The striking modernist design has the look of a Scandinavian art gallery, all smoked glass panels suspended within a cage of cedarwood and steel girders, but this is actually the Hatfield outpost of the Beales Hotels group. Well done for picking up on the art reference, though, since the place really does house a substantial collection of contemporary art from the University of Hertfordshire. The Outsidein Restaurant follows the theme of funky Nordic-style minimalism, using designer ceiling lights above darkwood tables, groovy fabrics on seats and sofas, and pale wood all around on the walls and floors. Thankfully the operation is not a case of style over substance, since creative ideas and bags of flavour emanate from the kitchen. Tried-and-true combos such as pan-fried scallops with cauliflower purée, chorizo and pancetta crisp aren't going to set the world on fire, but are executed with the skill required to tease out all the flavours and textures. A main course of venison Wellington with swede rösti, chestnut purée and honey jus hits all the right autumnal notes, and a finale of pear frangipane tart is matched effectively with honey soup and caramel.

Chef Diego Granada **Owner** Beales Ltd
Times 12-2.30/6-10 **Prices** Fixed L 2 course £20.50-£31.50, Fixed D 3 course £27-£40, Starter £7-£10, Main £13.50-£21.50, Dessert £6.50-£8.50, Service optional, Groups min 8 service 12.5% **Wines** 48 bottles over £20, 15 bottles under £20, 11 by glass **Notes** Vegetarian available, Civ Wed 300 **Seats** 60, Pr/dining room 300 **Children** Portions, Menu **Parking** 126

HEMEL HEMPSTEAD — Map 6 TL00

The Bobsleigh Hotel

🏵 British, European

British grill classics in a soothing rural setting

☎ 01442 833276

Hempstead Rd, Bovingdon HP3 0DS
e-mail: bobsleigh@macdonald-hotels.co.uk
dir: M1 junct 8, A414 signed Hemel Hempstead. At Plough Rdbt follow railway station signs. Pass rail station on left, straight on at rdbt, under 2 bridges. Left onto B4505 (Box Lane) signed Chesham. Hotel 1.5m on left

The hotel gets its name from a former owner's son - Tony Nash Jr - a gold medalist in the 1964 Winter Olympics. Lucky he wasn't an exponent of the skeleton bob. This fine old hotel stands in landscaped gardens and although close to Heathrow and Luton airports, plus the motorway network, you wouldn't know it when you're here. The light and airy Garden Room restaurant has a great service team, plus a terrace that comes into its own in the warmer months. The unfussy British grill menu sticks to simple combinations and does not throw the baby out with the bathwater; expect the likes of potted roast chicken and piccalilli, followed by 8oz rib-eye steak and wild mushroom gratin. Staying true to the theme, desserts run to lemon curd tart and sticky toffee pudding.

Chef Tracy White **Owner** Macdonald Hotels
Times 12.30-2/6.30-9.30 Closed BHs, L Sat, D Sun

Prices Starter £3.95-£5.95, Main £8-£14, Dessert £4.95-£6.95, Service optional **Wines** 33 bottles over £20, 6 bottles under £20, 16 by glass **Notes** Sunday L, Vegetarian available, Civ Wed 70 **Seats** 40, Pr/dining room 22 **Children** Portions, Menu **Parking** 60

HITCHIN — Map 12 TL12

Redcoats Farmhouse Hotel

🏵 Traditional European

Vibrant flavours in an ancient former farmhouse

☎ 01438 729500

Redcoats Green SG4 7JR
e-mail: sales@redcoats.co.uk
dir: A602 to Wymondley. Turn left to Redcoats Green. At top of hill straight over at junct

The same family have lived in this charming 15th-century farmhouse in four acres of pleasant countryside for over a century, and they are proud to share its delights with guests. Redcoats is a warm, welcoming and homely place with a light-flooded conservatory dining room looking over the grounds providing an airy summery vibe to the kitchen's full-flavoured seasonal cooking. A classic winter main course of partridge served with watercress, game chips and game gravy is bookended by a starter of pan-seared wasabi crabcakes with lime and sweet chilli dressing, and an inventive finale of bay leaf-infused crème brûlée pointed up with greengage coulis and gingersnap biscuit.

Chef Scott Liversedge **Owner** Mr P Butterfield & Mrs J Gainsford **Times** 12-6.30 Closed 1 wk after Xmas, BH Mons, D Sun **Prices** Fixed L 2 course £18-£22, Fixed D 3 course £30, Starter £7.50-£12, Main £20-£30, Service optional, Groups min 8 service 10% **Wines** 114 bottles over £20, 45 bottles under £20, 11 by glass **Notes** Sunday L, Vegetarian available, Dress restrictions, Smart casual, No jeans or T-shirts, Civ Wed 80 **Seats** 70, Pr/dining room 24 **Children** Portions **Parking** 30

RICKMANSWORTH — Map 6 TQ09

Colette's at The Grove

🏵🏵🏵 – *see below*

The Stables Restaurant at The Grove

🏵 Modern British **NEW**

Creative modern cooking in George Stubbs' favourite stables

☎ 01923 807807 & 296015

Chandler's Cross WD3 4TG
e-mail: restaurants@thegrove.co.uk
dir: M25 junct 19, A411 towards Watford. Hotel on right

The former stable block was illustrious enough in its day to have brought Britain's foremost equine painter George Stubbs here in search of his models. It now forms the restaurant of a country house reinvented as The Grove hotel, and is an informal, raftered dining space with

Colette's at The Grove

RICKMANSWORTH — Map 6 TQ09

Modern British

Creative modern cooking on a country estate not far from London

☎ 01923 807807

Chandler's Cross WD3 4TG
e-mail: info@thegrove.co.uk
dir: M25 junct 19, follow signs to Watford. At 1st large rdbt take 3rd exit. 5m, entrance on right

The extended and rather grand Georgian house feels a world away from the hurly-burly of central London, but it is within the M25, and it's easy to see why it has attracted numerous prime ministers and even Queen Victoria over the years. Today's incarnation is as a luxurious country estate with all the necessary accoutrements to satisfy the 21st-century visitor; that

means a championship golf course, indulgent spa, sharp old-meets-new décor, and a range of dining options. Among the latter, Colette's is the shining star, a neutrally-toned space with vivid contemporary artworks and plushly laid tables, and a menu packed with appealing, modish dishes based on high quality produce, some of which comes from the hotel's own walled garden. This is a kitchen - led by Russell Bateman - up-to-speed with cutting-edge culinary goings on, but also with a keen eye on balance within each dish. Hand-dived Scottish scallops, for example, cooked to perfect golden caramelisation, come creatively partnered with peanuts, radish and lime - a dish that gets sweetness, textural contrast and acidity just right. Next up, perhaps a rib of dry-aged beef with vintage onions, horseradish, water cress, Pink Fir potatoes and red wine jus, or another complex construction of Scottish partridge with Alsace bacon, girolles, bread sauce and bourguignon jus. Everything looks spectacular on the plate and attention to detail runs right the way through to desserts: blood

orange parfait and curd, maybe, with burnt meringue and whipped cream, or hot chocolate cake served with a Manjari chocolate and lime ice cream and lime gel. There's a tasting menu if you want to splash out, and the wine list is certainly worth a moment or two of your time. See entry above for The Stables, an alternative dining option at The Grove.

Chef Russell Bateman **Owner** Ralph Trustees Ltd
Times 7-10 Closed Sun-Mon (ex BHs), L all week
Prices Fixed D 3 course £65, Tasting menu £80, Service optional **Wines** 300 bottles over £20, 24 by glass **Notes** Tasting menu 11 course, market menu £45 Tue-Thu, Vegetarian available, Civ Wed 500 **Seats** 40, Pr/dining room 24 **Children** Portions **Parking** 500

Save on Hotels. Book at theAA.com/hotel

HERTFORDSHIRE 205 ENGLAND

open-to-view kitchen, complete with wood-burning oven for pizzas and a chargrill for the steaks. Starters draw inspiration from dessert ideas, such as poached pear with blue cheese and walnuts in ginger dressing, or goats' cheese cheesecake with hazelnut base, garnished with roasted figs. Mains might take in a duo of lamb - best end and shoulder - with hotpot potatoes and roots, or fillets of lemon sole with cavolo nero in Jerusalem artichoke butter. Substantial puddings include treacle tart and clotted cream, simply but classically rendered. Colette's (see entry) is the fine-dining option at The Grove.

Chef Christakis Mouyiassi **Times** 12-3/6-9.30 Closed 25 & 31 Dec, **Prices** Starter £7.20-£10.50, Main £9-£25, Dessert £6-£9.50, Service optional **Wines** 32 bottles over £20, 3 bottles under £20, 10 by glass **Notes** Sunday L, Vegetarian available **Seats** 120, Pr/dining room 16 **Children** Portions, Menu

---

ST ALBANS

Map 6 TL10

Chez Mumtaj

◉◉ French, Asian

French-Asian fusion in opulent surroundings

☎ 01727 800033
Centurian House, 136-142 London Rd AL1 1PQ
e-mail: info@chezmumtaj.com
web: www.chezmumtaj.com

What's in a name? Well this one says it all in two words: modern Franco-Asian cuisine is the deal at Chez Mumtaj, and the décor takes its cue from a gentlemen's club with mahogany panelled walls, glass screens etched with a regimental-style coat of arms, and cream leather banquettes. The kitchen team serves up a wide-ranging, eclectic repertoire that travels as extensively as a gap-year backpacker through the cuisines of southeast Asia

and Europe, bringing it all together with classic French cooking techniques. Expect to see pan-seared spice-crusted Scottish scallops teamed with sautéed wild mushrooms and shallots, almond, cardamom, and saffron cappuccino foam, ahead of main-course hybrids involving 28-day-aged rib-eye beef crusted with sumac and pepper, and partnered with herb butter, potato fondant, Madeira cardamom glaze, ceps, spinach, celeriac purée and veal jus.

Chez Mumtaj

Chef Chad Rahman **Owner** Chad Rahman **Times** 12-2.30/6-11 Closed 25 Dec, Mon **Prices** Food prices not confirmed for 2013. Please telephone for details **Wines** 27 bottles over £20, 18 bottles under £20, 14 by glass **Notes** Tasting & early bird D menus available, Sunday L, Vegetarian available, Dress restrictions, Smart casual **Seats** 100, Pr/dining room 16 **Parking** On street & car park nearby

See advert below

ST ALBANS continued

St Michael's Manor

◉◉ Modern British

Classically-based cooking in a Tudor manor

☎ 01727 864444
Fishpool St AL3 4RY
e-mail: reservations@stmichaelsmanor.com
web: www.stmichaelsmanor.com
dir: At Tudor Tavern in High St into George St. After abbey & school on left, road continues onto Fishpool St. Hotel 1m on left

An Elizabethan manor house not far from the cathedral and the city centre, St Michael's sits in five acres of well-kept grounds with a lake at the centre. The lake lends its name to the conservatory dining room, from which it looks a picture on balmy days, and where attentively professional service and classically-based cooking add to the sense of contentment. One or two modish touches crop up, as in the unexpected raspberry powder that has been wafted over a dish of smoked venison carpaccio and horseradish cream, but otherwise combinations are tried-and-true, such as the pairing of lemon sole and langoustine that comes with baby fennel and braised shallots in pea sauce, or herb-crusted rack of lamb. A Black Forest Pavlova for afters mixes two old favourites, and comes tricked out with cinnamon and Cognac jelly.

Chef Mr Daniel Park **Owner** Sheila Newling-Ward
Times 12-2/7-9.30 Closed L 31 Dec, D 25 Dec
Prices Fixed L 2 course £17, Starter £7.50-£9, Main £17-£25, Dessert £8.50, Service added but optional 12.5%
Wines 42 bottles over £20, 10 bottles under £20, 11 by glass **Notes** Sunday L, Vegetarian available, Dress restrictions, Smart casual **Seats** 120, Pr/dining room 24
Children Portions, Menu **Parking** 60

TRING
Map 6 SP91

Pendley Manor

◉◉ Modern British

Handsome manor house with modern cooking

☎ 01442 891891
Cow Ln HP23 5QY
e-mail: sales@pendley-manor.co.uk
dir: M25 junct 20, A41 (Tring exit). At rdbt follow Berkhamsted/London signs. 1st left signed Tring Station & Pendley Manor

Although Pendley's history stretches back a thousand years and gets a mention in the Domesday Book, the current incarnation is part Victorian neo-Tudor, built in 1872 after a fire destroyed the original, and part modern annexe, built to extend significantly its events and conference capacity. The Victorian section offers period grandeur in spades, particularly in the Oak Restaurant where oak flooring, lofty ceilings, colourful patterned wallpaper, and swagged-back drapes at vast bay windows make for an imposing setting. The refined cooking avoids risk taking in favour of well-tried mainstream ideas: a starter of seared yellowfin tuna with spiced crab, scallop fritter and guacamole saffron mayonnaise is convincing and well executed, while excellent Cornish lamb - a cutlet and 12-hour-braised shoulder, to be precise - is teamed to equally good effect with wild mushroom mousse, confit garlic, and pea purée with thyme jus. Finally, chocolate fondant releases a rich melting centre just as it should, to mingle with pistachio ice cream and crunchy meringue.

Chef Martin White **Owner** Craydawn Pendley Manor
Times 12.30-2.30/7-9.30 Closed L Sat **Prices** Fixed L 3 course £22.50, Starter £8.50-£11.25, Main £18.75-£32, Dessert £7.50-£9, Service optional **Wines** 40 bottles over £20, 5 bottles under £20, 8 by glass **Notes** Fixed D 2 course £27, Sunday L, Vegetarian available, Dress restrictions, Smart casual, Civ Wed 180 **Seats** 75, Pr/dining room 200 **Children** Portions, Menu **Parking** 150

WARE
Map 6 TL31

Marriott Hanbury Manor Hotel

◉◉ French, Mediterranean V

Creative cooking in a Jacobean manor house

☎ 01920 487722
SG12 0SD
e-mail: wendy.traynor@marriotthotels.com
dir: From M25 junct 25, take A10 towards Cambridge, for 12m. Leave A10 Wadesmill/Thundridge/Ware. Right at rdbt, hotel on left

This fabulous Jacobean stately home in 200 acres of Hertfordshire with delightful walled gardens trades as an upmarket golf and country club. Inside, the requisite period features are all present and correct - acres of oak panelling, tapestries and oil paintings in grandly-proportioned rooms - and when the day's conferencing, golfing and spa pampering activities are over, head for the formal fine-dining restaurant where ornate plasterwork, white-painted wall panels, gilt-framed portraits and a magnificent fireplace set a refined tone. Look up to the signs picked out in gold leaf on the barrel-vaulted ceiling, and you'll see why it gets the name of Zodiac. The kitchen deals in inventive, modern dishes with impeccable production values - perhaps a pressing of duck rillettes and foie gras with apples from the Hanbury estate and toasted brioche to start, then John Dory with braised baby gem lettuce, pancetta potato, and saffron emulsion. Finish with an orange and bitter chocolate dome with blood orange sorbet and olive oil cake.

Chef Gopi Chandran **Owner** Marriott International
Times 12-2.30/7-10.30 Closed Mon-Tue, L Wed-Sat, D Sun **Prices** Fixed D 3 course £49-£55, Service added but optional 10% **Wines** 50+ bottles over £20, 2 bottles under £20, 3 by glass **Notes** Sunday L, Vegetarian menu, Dress restrictions, Smart dress, No jeans or trainers, Civ Wed 120 **Seats** 50, Pr/dining room 25 **Parking** 200

WELWYN
Map 6 TL21

Auberge du Lac

◉◉◉ – see opposite

Save on Hotels. Book at **theAA.com/hotel**

HERTFORDSHIRE 207 **ENGLAND**

Auberge du Lac

WELWYN Map 6 TL21

French, European **V** NOTABLE WINE LIST

Refined and modish cooking in a lakeside hunting lodge

☎ 01707 368888
Brocket Hall Estate, Brocket Rd AL8 7XG
e-mail: auberge@brocket-hall.co.uk
web: www.brocket-hall.co.uk
dir: A1(M) junct 4, B653 to Wheathampstead. In Brocket Ln take 2nd gate entry to Brocket Hall

The Hertfordshire countryside may not have inspired great British poets (although George Bernard Shaw did live down the road), but it has never looked so charmingly, soothingly English as when seated at a table in this lodge on the Brocket Estate. With the stately Brocket Hall in the distance and the eponymous lake to the fore, Auberge du Lac is a fine setting indeed, and yesterday's hunting lodge is today's fine-dining champion. Even the passing golfers don't ruin the scene (the Brocket Estate includes a top-notch course). To describe the building as a former hunting lodge does not do it justice: the red-brick 18th-century structure has the look of a small country mansion and inside it retains original character alongside a suitably smart demeanor, appropriate for what is to follow. And what follows is some seriously well-crafted, creative and dynamic modern food. With a foot firmly in French classicism, this is a kitchen, led by Phil Thompson, which has grown in confidence over the years and produces dishes where superb produce, acute technical ability and an eye for contemporary modes combine with spectacular success. Attention to detail is evident from the start (superb breads and top-end service) to the finish (first-rate espresso). First-course veal sweetbreads are soft and succulent, alongside well-judged kohlrabi, broccoli, ventrèche bacon and toasted granola - excellent balance of flavours and textures. There is refinement and balance in main-course roast breast of Devon duck, too, with accompanying bitter orange marmalade, marjoram, sweet shallot purée, oca tuber, and duck heart and crispy tongue. There's a lightness of touch in the white chocolate and Roquefort mousse that comes with poached pear and an olive oil and pear sorbet - a memorable finale it makes too. The wine list is a real gem and the sommelier is on hand to lead you to some genuine treasures.

Chef Phil Thompson **Owner** CCA International **Times** 12-2.30/7-9.30 Closed 27 Dec-14 Jan, Sun-Mon **Prices** Fixed L 3 course fr £29.50, Fixed D 3 course fr £60, Tasting menu £69.50, Service added but optional 10% **Wines** 750 bottles over £20, 14 by glass **Notes** ALC fixed 3 course £60, Tasting menu 6 course, Vegetarian menu, Dress restrictions, No jeans or trainers, Civ Wed 62 **Seats** 70, Pr/dining room 32 **Children** Portions, Menu **Parking** 50

WELWYN *continued*

The Restaurant at Tewin Bury Farm

◉◉ Modern British

Up-to-the-minute modern cookery in 500 acres of Hertfordshire farmland

☎ 01438 717793
AL6 0JB
e-mail: restaurant@tewinbury.co.uk
web: www.tewinbury.co.uk
dir: A1M junct 6 (signposted Welwyn Garden City), 1st exit A1000. 0.25m to B1000 Hertford Rd. Hotel on left

Although this is still a working farm in the best part of 500 acres of lush Hertfordshire countryside with the dinky River Mimram threading through, the Williams family diversified to set up lovely guest rooms and a restaurant in the complex of converted barns. The results are light, contemporary - almost Scandinavian - in the use of pale natural oak for tables and chairs, flooring, and rough-hewn rafters. Logs are stacked ready for use in the wood-fired oven, which lies at the heart of the kitchen's output of sunny, French-accented contemporary dishes. Vegetables, herbs and trout are produced on the farm, while other materials are kept as local as possible. Well-judged ideas such as lime-marinated mackerel with black olive caramel, hazelnut and green beans lead on to mains of Hertfordshire beef fillet with bone marrow dumplings, sweet garlic purée, wilted sorrel, ale foam and beef jus. The switched-on creativity continues through to desserts, which could bring warm carrot cake with cream cheese mousse, cinnamon ice cream and caramelised walnuts.

Times 12-2.30/6.30-9.30

The Waggoners

◉ French

Authentic French cooking in lovely village inn

☎ 01707 324241
Brickwall Close, Ayot Green AL6 9AA
e-mail: laurent@thewaggoners.co.uk
web: www.thewaggoners.co.uk
dir: A1(M) junct 6 to B197, right into Ayot and 1st left Brickwall Close

The bi-lingual menu is a clue to what's going on in the kitchen of this smartly revamped 17th-century coaching inn: hands-on French owners Laurent and Aude Brydniak have injected a hit of Gallic flair into the quintessentially English setting. Ancient blackened beams, an inglenook fireplace, and walls festooned with copper pans and pewter mugs make for a cosy space, and cheery staff add a pleasant tone to proceedings. The menu is packed with well-executed classics to bring a smile to Francophile foodies - there could be foie gras ballottine with apricot and peach purée or frogs' legs sautéed with garlic and parsley butter, then a pause for a palate-cleansing trou normand - apple, rosemary and honey granita with Calvados - before mushroom and rosemary-stuffed roast leg of lamb with parsnip mash, asparagus and Marsala jus. Dessert could be a French fancy such as a praline chiboust cream-filled Paris-Brest cake served with Grand Marnier ice cream.

Chef Pierre Kolabukoff **Owner** Laurent & Aude Brydniak **Times** 12-2.30/6.30-9 **Prices** Fixed L 2 course fr £13.95, Fixed D 3 course £25, Starter £5.12-£12, Main £12-£18.50, Dessert £5.95-£7, Service optional, Groups min 6 service 10% **Wines** 49 bottles over £20, 14 bottles under £20, 22 by glass **Notes** Sunday L, Vegetarian available, Dress restrictions, Smart casual **Seats** 65, Pr/dining room 35 **Children** Portions **Parking** 70

The White Hart Hotel

◉ British **NEW** ✧

Pub cooking with panache in an old coaching inn

☎ 01438 715353
2 Prospect Place AL6 9EN
e-mail: bookings@whitehearthotel.net
dir: A1(M) junct 6, follow signs to Welwyn shops

A 17th-century coaching-inn in a thriving Hertfordshire village ticks all the boxes for bucolic charm. The flagstone floors, brick fireplace and uneven beams inside tell a venerable story, but the modernisation job in the décor

---

has resulted in an elegant look to the dining room, with deep violet walls and quality table settings. An upbeat, friendly air pervades, and the place is understandably popular with locals who lunch, as well as travelling custom motoring over for a relaxing dinner. Pub stalwarts are rendered with some panache, from hearty carrot and coriander soup with croûtons, venison with pearl barley and dumplings, and a rather sophisticated rhubarb syllabub, and there are enterprising fish specialities too, such as baked cod in clam and bacon chowder.

Chef Alex Hart **Owner** Piers Lyon **Times** 12-2.30/6.30-9.30 **Prices** Fixed L 2 course £16.95-£18.95, Fixed D 3 course £19.95-£21.95, Starter £5.95-£9.50, Main £10.95-£21.95, Dessert £6.95, Service optional **Wines** 20 bottles over £20, 12 bottles under £20, 10 by glass **Notes** Sunday L, Vegetarian available **Seats** 44, Pr/dining room 40 **Children** Portions, Menu

---

The Fox

◉ Modern British ✧

Creative cooking in a smart local pub

☎ 01462 480233
SG6 2AE
e-mail: info@foxatwillian.co.uk
dir: A1(M) junct 9 towards Letchworth, 1st left to Willian, The Fox 0.5m on left

The stylish Fox may have a proper pubby locals' bar with a fine array of well-kept real ales, but a cursory glance over the menu reveals the heart of a gastro-pub serving food that goes way beyond pub grub staples. The smartly contemporary open-plan dining room looks the part too with its original artwork and glazed atrium ceiling. Under the same ownership as The White Horse in Brancaster Staithe (see entry), the kitchen has good supply lines to fish and seafood from the Norfolk coast, so oysters fresh from the beds next to its seaside sibling might get things going, or if you prefer the kitchen to do some work, there could be pan-roasted wood pigeon breast with wilted baby gem lettuce, butter bean purée and red wine jus. Things continue in a similar French-accented contemporary mode with mains such as pan-roasted loin of Wood Hall Estate venison with confit garlic purée, celeriac fondant, buttered kale and chocolate jus. An apple-themed finale might bring a trio of tarte Tatin, Aspall cider jelly, and apple crumble ice cream.

Chef Chris Jones **Owner** Clifford Nye **Times** 12-2/6.45-9.15 Closed D Sun **Prices** Starter £4.95-£9.95, Main £11.50-£18.95, Dessert £6-£7.95, Service added but optional 10% **Wines** 35 bottles over £20, 5 bottles under £20, 14 by glass **Notes** Sunday L, Vegetarian available **Seats** 70 **Children** Portions **Parking** 40

Save on Hotels. Book at **theAA.com/hotel**

KENT 209 **ENGLAND**

KENT

ASHFORD
Map 7 TR04

Eastwell Manor

British, French

Creative, classical cooking in a grand manor house

☎ 01233 213000
Eastwell Park, Boughton Lees TN25 4HR
e-mail: enquiries@eastwellmanor.co.uk
web: www.eastwellmanor.co.uk
dir: From M20 junct 9 take 1st left (Trinity Rd). Through 4 rdbts to lights. Left onto A251 signed Faversham. 0.5m to sign for Boughton Aluph, 200yds to hotel

Eastwell Manor is about as stately and blue-blooded as anyone could reasonably ask of a country-house hotel. With a pedigree dating back to Norman times, it has 62 acres of landscaped and manicured grounds, and an interior fully loaded with magnificent plasterwork, carved oak panelling, baronial fireplaces and antiques at every turn. The restaurant is none too shabby either, holding its own with the grandeur of high ceilings, a walk-in fireplace and leaded mullioned windows looking over the gardens, while service is of the formal style that sees staff wearing white gloves. The kitchen, however, has its feet firmly in the contemporary world of blow-torched mackerel served with a trio of beetroot, or you might start with a more trad terrine of ham hock with sweet apple purée, then proceed to pan-seared chicken suprême with fondant potato and red wine jus. Finish with citrus pannacotta matched with raspberry sorbet.

Chef Neil Wiggins **Owner** Turrloo Parrett
Times 12-2.30/7-10 **Prices** Fixed L 2 course £15.50-£19.50, Fixed D 3 course £26.50, Service added but optional 10% **Wines** 158 bottles over £20, 4 bottles under £20, 20 by glass **Notes** Gourmet Champagne evenings, Sunday L, Vegetarian available, Dress restrictions, Smart collared shirt D, no denim/sportswear, Civ Wed 250 **Seats** 80, Pr/dining room 80 **Children** Portions **Parking** 120

The Wife of Bath Restaurant with Rooms

Modern British

Intimate, stylish village restaurant with accomplished cooking

☎ 01233 812232
4 Upper Bridge St, Wye TN25 5AF
e-mail: relax@thewifeofbath.com
dir: 4m NE of Ashford. M20 junct 9, A28 for Canterbury, 3m right to Wye

This stylish small restaurant with rooms brings a touch of contemporary class to the pretty medieval Kentish village of Wye. On the accommodation side, the rooms deliver a high comfort factor if you fancy slackening off the belt and staying over in order to put the kitchen team through its paces. The ambience is laid-back and intimate, while fashionable patterned wallpaper, modern art and linen-clothed tables add up to a fresh, uncluttered setting. The kitchen doesn't labour the point, but the lion's share of its ingredients come from local Kentish producers, and are brought together in well-conceived dishes showing plenty of flair and imagination, resulting in some off-the-wall combinations - smoked duck delivered with a whisky and tobacco-infused vinaigrette, for example. Grilled hake arrives wearing a gruyère crust, and matched with a punchy crayfish velouté, spiced broccoli, and smooth mash, while dessert brings down the curtain with an enterprising combination of roasted sesame seed and orange parfait, orange liquid gel, and a shredded marmalade garnish.

Chef Robert Hymers **Owner** Rupert & Victoria Reeves
Times 12-2.30/6.30-9.30 Closed 25 Dec, Mon, L Tue, D Sun **Prices** Food prices not confirmed for 2013. Please telephone for details **Wines** 50 bottles over £20, 19 bottles under £20, 11 by glass **Notes** Sunday L, Vegetarian available **Seats** 45 **Children** Portions, Menu **Parking** 12

AYLESFORD
Map 6 TQ75

Hengist Restaurant

Modern European V

Polished cooking in sophisticated setting

☎ 01622 719273
7-9 High St ME20 7AX
e-mail: restaurant@hengistrestaurant.co.uk
dir: M20 junct 5 & 6, follow signs to Aylesford

History buffs might be interested to note that Hengist is named after the man who invaded across the Medway with his brother Horsa in AD 449 and rewarded themselves with the titles of Kings of Kent. But enough of history. Within the 16th-century building, oak beams, brick and stonework are juxtaposed with a rather decadent Paul Smith-designed contemporary look involving chocolate suede walls, smoked glass and twinkling chandeliers. Under the guidance of Richard Phillips (see entry for Thackeray's, Tunbridge Wells) the kitchen deals in modern French ideas underpinned by well-sourced local produce, inventive combinations and punctilious attention to detail. Pistachio-wrapped foie gras with Sauternes jelly, celeriac purée and Kentish cherries shows the refined style, while main courses could deliver Barolo-poached wild sea bass partnered inventively with creamed cauliflower salad, buttered girolles, caper raisin dressing and cauliflower velouté. The same high-gloss values continue to the end in an exquisite modern take on cheesecake, flavoured with citrus and vanilla and served with raspberries, lemon meringue and mint ice cream.

Chef Richard Phillips, Jon Baldork **Owner** Richard Phillips & Paul Smith **Times** 12-2.30/6.30-10 Closed 26 Dec & 1 Jan, Mon, D Sun **Prices** Fixed L 2 course £12.95, Fixed D 3 course £25.50, Tasting menu £48-£65, Starter £4.95-£10.95, Main £17.25-£22, Dessert £4.95-£7.95, Service added but optional 12.5% **Wines** 64 bottles over £20, 6 bottles under £20, 27 by glass **Notes** Fixed L Tue-Sun, D Tue-Thu, Tasting menu 7 course, Sunday L, Vegetarian menu, Dress restrictions, Smart casual, no jeans or trainers **Seats** 70, Pr/dining room 18 **Children** Portions **Parking** Free car park nearby

BEARSTED — Map 7 TQ85

Soufflé Restaurant

◉ Modern European

Charming village setting for modish cooking

☎ 01622 737065
31 The Green ME14 4DN
e-mail: soufflerestaurant@hotmail.co.uk
web: www.soufflerestaurant.net
dir: M20 junct 7 follow Maidstone signs, bear left towards Bearsted straight over at rdbt, towards Bearsted Green at next mini-rdbt, continue for approx 1.5m to the green. Restaurant on left, turn left just before Soufflé sign & park at rear of restaurant

With its lovely location on Bearsted's pretty village green, you're already off to a flying start at this charming 16th-century timbered cottage restaurant - especially when fine weather lets you dine out on the front terrace. Inside, the old-world charm is bolstered further still by gnarled, head-skimming timbers, bare brickwork, and a crackling winter log fire. Add in the lure of creative cooking that puts a modern spin on classic ideas, and has impeccably-sourced ingredients at the centre of things, and it's no wonder Nick Evenden's place is a long-running stalwart of the local dining scene. Expect pan-fried scallops served on a ham and parsley terrine with pea purée and mustard foam, followed by roast saddle of rabbit wrapped in pancetta and stuffed with black pudding, and to finish, perhaps a rhubarb-fest involving crème brûlée, compôte and sorbet.

Chef Nick Evenden **Owner** Nick & Karen Evenden
Times 12-2.30/7-10 Closed Mon, L Sat, D Sun
Prices Fixed L 2 course fr £14.50, Fixed D 3 course fr £25,

Starter £7.50-£11, Main £19-£22.50, Dessert £7.50-£8.50, Service optional **Wines** 40 bottles over £20, 3 bottles under £20, 7 by glass **Notes** Sunday L, Vegetarian available **Seats** 40, Pr/dining room 25 **Children** Portions **Parking** 12, On street

BIDDENDEN — Map 7 TQ83

The West House

◉◉◉ – see opposite

BOUGHTON MONCHELSEA — Map 7 TQ75

The Mulberry Tree

◉◉ Modern British

Serious cooking in Kent countryside setting

☎ 01622 749082 & 741058
Hermitage Ln ME17 4DA
e-mail: info@themulberrytreekent.co.uk
dir: B2163 turn into Wierton Rd straight over x-rds, 1st left East Hall Hill

If you're expecting a typical weatherboarded and tile-hung Kentish hostelry, the clean-lined modern building may come as a surprise in the time-warp bucolic setting of Boughton Monchelsea. The former pub has been reinvented as a stylish and relaxed contemporary bar and restaurant done out with leather sofas on wooden floors, set against a warm colour scheme and boldly-patterned designer wallpapers. It is all clearly abreast of current trends, as is the team in the kitchen who send out daily-changing menus of well-tuned modern British food with a European accent. Having supply lines to the 'Garden of England's' finest ingredients would keep many a kitchen happy, but here they go the whole nine yards, raising their own turkeys and Kentish Middle White pigs in the field at the back and cultivating a productive kitchen garden. Roasted brill with chargrilled potato, braised leek, and smoked bacon and cockle vinaigrette, and rump of lamb with broad beans, wild garlic and dauphinoise potatoes are typical mains, and you might follow that with spiced ginger pannacotta with caramelised pear and pear macaroon.

Times 12-2/6.30-9.30 Closed 26 Dec, Mon, D Sun

BRANDS HATCH — Map 6 TQ56

Brandshatch Place Hotel & Spa

◉◉ Modern British

Grand location for modern British food

☎ 01474 875000
Brands Hatch Rd, Fawkham DA3 8NQ
e-mail: brandshatchplace@handpicked.co.uk
dir: M25 junct 3/A20 West Kingsdown. Left at paddock entrance/Fawkham Green sign. 3rd left signed Fawkham Rd. Hotel 500mtrs on right

The Brands Hatch name is immediately synonymous worldwide with the high-octane thrills of the motor racing circuit, but the nearby luxury hotel that shares its name

may be new to many. Originally built by the Duke of Norfolk, the red-brick Georgian manor is these days an elegant country-house with a smart spa and on-song restaurant. Its stylish, understated elegance fits the bill, with views of the garden from smartly dressed tables, and seasonal regional produce from the abundant Kentish larder on the menu. Start, perhaps with a terrine made from confit duck leg, partnered with pear pickle, before moving on to lamb rump with an onion tarte Tatin, green olive purée and roasted vine cherry tomatoes, or pan-fried black bream with crushed parsley and caper new potatoes and a mussel and tomato butter sauce. To finish, go for dark chocolate fondant with mascarpone ice cream.

Chef Carl Smith **Owner** Hand Picked Hotels
Times 12-2/7-9.30 **Prices** Fixed D 3 course £36, Service optional **Wines** 103 bottles over £20, 2 bottles under £20, 18 by glass **Notes** Sunday L, Vegetarian available, Civ Wed 70 **Seats** 60, Pr/dining room 110 **Children** Portions, Menu **Parking** 100

CANTERBURY — Map 7 TR15

The Dove Inn

◉ British, French ◔

Refreshingly simple modern country-pub cooking

☎ 01227 751360
Plum Pudding Ln, Dargate ME13 9HB
e-mail: doveatdargate@hotmail.com
dir: 6m NW of Canterbury. A299 Thanet Way, turn off at Lychgate service station

A Georgian country pub with an expansive garden, not far from Canterbury and Faversham, The Dove is popular with walkers as well as those fancying a drive out from the towns. The unvarnished wood tables and brick fireplace set a rustic tone, and there is a similar simplicity about the cooking. Modern classic dishes such as scallops and black pudding with parsnip purée, Torbay sole with almonds and capers, and Marsh lamb shoulder with black cabbage and pearl barley offer plenty of substance and flavour. Modish presentations see rectangular plates and Kilner jars brought into play, but there's nothing pretentious about the dishes on offer. Finish with cinnamon rice pudding and apricot compôte, or a good local cheese selection.

Chef Phillip MacGregor **Owner** Phillip & Sarah MacGregor **Times** 12-2.30/7-9 Closed Mon, D Sun, Tue **Prices** Fixed L 2 course fr £19, Starter £5-£9.50, Main £13-£19, Dessert £5-£7, Service added but optional 10%, Groups min 6 service 10% **Wines** 6 bottles over £20, 15 bottles under £20, 12 by glass **Notes** Sunday L, Vegetarian available **Seats** 26 **Children** Portions **Parking** 15, On street

Save on Hotels. Book at **theAA.com/hotel**

KENT 211 ENGLAND

The West House

BIDDENDEN Map 7 TQ83

Modern European 🌸

Self-assured cooking in a delightful setting

☎ 01580 291341
28 High St TN27 8AH
e-mail: thewesthouse@btconnect.com
dir: Junct of A262 & A274. 14m S of Maidstone

Chef-patron Graham Garrett's public profile has expanded seriously after numerous TV appearances in recent years, but the limelight hasn't gone to his head - it's still business as usual at The West House, the high-flying restaurant that he runs with his wife and son in a Wealden village. The 16th-century Flemish weaver's cottage is a quintessentially Kentish setting: beefy oak beams and an inglenook are set against a classily-understated contemporary décor that makes no fuss about itself - darkwood tables on bare floorboards, buttery leather seats and food-oriented art on plain white walls. Garrett learned his craft in the kitchens of such luminaries as Nico Ladenis and Richard Corrigan, so you can be sure that his cooking is muscular, contemporary stuff that aims to nail big, clearly-defined flavours. The ruthlessly seasonal approach stocks the larder with impeccable local materials that are brought together with finesse, careful balance of texture and flavour, deploying the full arsenal of modern, cutting-edge cooking methods and techniques to ensure that each ingredient is shown off to its best advantage. The menu eschews purple prose, opting for concise descriptions that offer little elucidation - Irish coffee and doughnuts sounds an unlikely starter, but what arrives is a feisty pea soup with ham cream, bacon, and parmesan doughnuts. Next up, a splendid fillet of grilled hake is matched with cauliflower purée, raisins soaked in Pedro Ximénez sherry, and Ibérico ham dressing; meat is given similarly robust treatment, perhaps partnering slow-cooked beef cheeks with parsnip purée and truffle sauce. At dessert, there's a clever riff on the classic combination of rhubarb and custard that delivers a textbook vanilla crème brûlée with zingy Yorkshire rhubarb and rhubarb sorbet, or you might go for a modish deconstruction of a Crunchie bar involving white chocolate honeycomb parfait and dark chocolate sorbet

Chef Graham Garrett **Owner** Jackie Hewitt & Graham Garrett **Times** 12-2/7-9.30 Closed 25 Dec-1 Jan, Mon, L Sat, D Sun **Prices** Food prices not confirmed for 2013. Please telephone for details **Wines** 46 bottles over £20, 20 bottles under £20, 15 by glass **Seats** 32 **Children** Portions **Parking** 7

Apicius

CRANBROOK Map 7 TQ73

Modern European 🌸

Imaginative star quality in a small high-street venue

☎ 01580 714666
23 Stone St TN17 3HF
dir: In town centre, opposite Barclays Bank, 50yds from church

It may seem a little incongruous to find a shrine to the Roman cookery writer Apicius on the high street of an unassuming town in Kent, but here we are, and Cranbrook can feel jolly grateful for it. Framed menus emphasise the point that culinary researches are taken seriously here, while the original artworks on cream walls lighten the tone, and large picture-windows keep you abreast of Cranbrook goings-on. There aren't too many covers, so it's as well not to turn up on spec, especially given the star quality in evidence in Tim Johnson's highly skilled contemporary cuisine, which uses quality produce in imaginative and often astonishing ways. Pannacottas crop up for starters quite as much as at dessert these days, and here's one made with ceps, full of deep, rich earthiness, and counterpointed by the sharper flavours of an endive salad, creamy Jerusalem artichokes and roast almonds. This cooking isn't about complexity for its own sake, as witness a main course of steamed brill that comes in a simple but expressive mussel broth along with spring vegetables, or slow-roast shoulder of Kentish pork with traditional accompaniments of prunes and apple purée, as well as a little braised fennel and Sarladaise potatoes. A vegetarian dish, on the other hand, is a study in robust richness, with roast artichoke hearts, shallots, leeks and tomatoes in truffled linguine. Dessert stage keeps up the verve and vigour, when zesty lemon meringue comes with a fragrant sablé biscuit, lemon cream, Cassis sorbet and piquant strawberry chutney.

Chef Timothy Johnson **Owner** Timothy Johnson, Faith Hawkins **Times** 12-2/7-9 Closed 2 wks Xmas/New Year, 2 wks summer, Mon-Tue, L Sat, D Sun **Prices** Fixed L 2 course fr £28, Fixed D 3 course fr £40, Service added but optional 12.5% **Wines** 26 bottles over £20, 5 bottles under £20, 10 by glass **Notes** Vegetarian available, Air con **Seats** 30 **Parking** Public car park at rear

CANTERBURY *continued*

The Goods Shed Restaurant

@ British ℭ

Innovative cooking next to a thriving farmers' market

☎ 01227 459153
Station Road West CT2 8AN
e-mail: restaurant@thegoodsshed.co.uk
dir: Adjacent to Canterbury West train station

What better amenity for a thriving local farmers' market to boast than an on-site restaurant, cooking some of that day's freshest and best (so that you don't have to, perhaps)? The former railway shed next to Canterbury West station features an open kitchen where you can see the brigade at work, and all staff are sufficiently well-versed in the produce to stop and have a chat, if they've time, about what they're cooking and serving. That might well be pork, chestnut and prune terrine with apple chutney, or leek and Shropshire Blue tart with hazelnuts, to start, and then venison haunch with lentils, bacon and chocolate vinegar to follow on. A treat to round things off comes in the form of dark chocolate and rosemary fondant with blood orange sorbet.

Chef Rafael Lopez **Owner** Rafael Lopez **Times** 12-2.30/6-mdnt Closed 25 Dec, 1 Jan, Mon, D Sun **Prices** Starter £6-£9, Main £12-£20, Dessert £6.50, Service optional **Wines** 22 bottles over £20, 11 bottles under £20, 8 by glass **Notes** Sunday L, Vegetarian available **Seats** 80 **Children** Portions **Parking** 40

The Granville

@ Modern European

A serious attitude to cooking in a village gastro-pub

☎ 01227 700402
Street End, Lower Hardres CT4 7AL
dir: On B2068 in the village of Lower Hardres, about 3m from Canterbury city centre

The Granville is the sister pub to The Sportsman in Seasalter near Whitstable (see entry), so you can rely on the kitchen having an eye for, and supply lines to, the best produce in the area. Despite the serious foodie focus and the modern de-cluttered look, it's still properly pubby in the bar, while the restaurant area has a circular open fire as its centrepiece, and hangs local artwork and chalkboards displaying the daily-changing dishes on its walls. A quick glance shows some appealing, no-nonsense ideas: cauliflower and parmesan soup, or smoked salmon tart with beetroot relish may figure among starters, while mains run to roast pork belly with crackling and apple sauce, and locally-farmed leg of lamb with potato gratin and mint sauce. Puddings follow the crowd-pleasing path with the likes of tiramisù with marinated cherries.

Times 12-2/6.45-9 Closed 26 Dec, 1 Jan, Mon, D Sun

CRANBROOK Map 7 TQ73

Apicius

@@@ – *see page 211*

DARTFORD Map 6 TQ57

Rowhill Grange Hotel & Utopia Spa

@@ Modern European V

Soothing modernised dishes in Kentish rural tranquillity

☎ 01322 615136
DA2 7QH
e-mail: admin@rowhillgrange.com
dir: M25 junct 3, take B2173 towards Swanley, then B258 towards Hextable. Straight on at 3 rdbts. Hotel 1.5m on left

A Georgian house set in acres of trimly manicured grounds, complete with a duck-dotted lake, Rowhill has the virtue of rural tranquillity going for it. Its newly styled principal dining room, RG's, is a gently lit space done in mother-of-pearl shades, with quality table linen and modern artworks. The kitchen works to today's best-practice watchwords of seasonality and regionality and modernising takes on bastions of culinary tradition. Thus, green pea soup comes garnished with a poached egg and truffle oil, or smoked salmon with a pickled cucumber salad, for starters. Mains go in for soothing textures and classic combinations, as when butter-poached south coast lobster is served on linguine with spinach and beetroot purée, or poached and grilled chicken is supported by truffled potatoes and peas and broad beans with pancetta. A slate of grill options for mixing and matching with sauces is a popular feature.

Chef Luke Davis **Owner** Peter & Deborah Hinchcliffe **Times** 12-2.30/7-9 **Prices** Starter £7.50-£12.50, Main £17.50-£29, Dessert £7.50-£9, Service added but optional 12.5% **Wines** 91 bottles over £20, 11 by glass **Notes** Sunday L, Vegetarian menu, Dress restrictions, No sportswear, Civ Wed 150 **Seats** 100 **Children** Portions, Menu **Parking** 300

DEAL Map 7 TR35

Dunkerleys Hotel & Restaurant

@@ Modern British

Fresh seafood on the seafront

☎ 01304 375016
19 Beach St CT14 7AH
e-mail: ddunkerley@btconnect.com
web: www.dunkerleys.co.uk
dir: Turn off A2 onto A258 to Deal - situated 100yds before Deal Pier

With the sea just across the road from this well-established family-run hotel restaurant on Deal's beachfront, fish and seafood is quite rightly the star turn on the menu. The overall feel is relaxed, homely and unpretentious, with the feeling of continuity that comes with owners Ian and Linda Dunkerley having run the show for a quarter of a century. There are lived-in leather armchairs to slump into for aperitifs in the bar before taking a seat in the bistro-style restaurant. The kitchen works within a broadly modern British idiom, keeping things simple, fresh and local with the likes of seared scallops with pea purée and pancetta, followed by a whole grilled Sandwich Bay Dover sole with parsley butter, or a half-lobster with Deal potatoes, thermidor sauce and courgette and chorizo spaghetti. It's not all about fish though: rump of Kentish lamb could appear with seasonal vegetables, gratin potato and a red wine reduction, and awaiting at the end, perhaps coconut pannacotta with black pepper caramel and Malibu-infused ice.

Chef Ian Dunkerley, Josh Hackett **Owner** Ian Dunkerley & Linda Dunkerley **Times** 12-2.30/7-9.30 Closed Mon, D Sun

Save on Hotels. Book at **theAA.com/hotel**

KENT 213 **ENGLAND**

Prices Fixed L 2 course £11.95-£14.95, Fixed D 3 course £28.50-£38.50, Service optional **Wines** 41 bottles over £20, 43 bottles under £20, 12 by glass **Notes** Sunday L, Vegetarian available, Dress restrictions, Smart casual preferred **Seats** 50 **Children** Portions **Parking** Public car park adjacent

---

DOVER Map 7 TR34

The Marquis at Alkham

◉◉ Modern British **V** 🕭

Boutique chic and creative cooking in attractive Kent village

☎ 01304 873410

Alkham Valley Rd, Alkham CT15 7DF

e-mail: reception@themarquisatalkham.co.uk

dir: M20 continue to A2. Take A260 exit & turn on to the Alkham Valley Rd

Set in a delightful Kent Downs village in the rolling hinterland between Dover and Folkestone, this former village boozer has been reinvented as an upscale restaurant with rooms. Views over the luscious Alkham Valley from the lovely garden terrace are part of the lure, and should you want to hole up and give the whole sybaritic contemporary cuisine and wine package a thorough workout, the chic designer bedrooms are straight from a glossy interiors magazine. A glass of bubbly from the nearby Chalksole Estate vineyard makes a fitting preamble to Charlie Lakin's cooking, which hits the spot with its creative flair and emphasis on splendid Kentish produce, including a penchant for fashionably foraged ingredients. A starter matching crisp pig's head and trotter with piccalilli, fried quail's eggs and 'creeping Charlie' (a type of edible ivy) ticks all of the on-trend boxes for fashionably earthy touches. Next up, Alkham Valley mutton is teamed with pearl barley, few-flowered leek (similar to ramsons), and pickled red cabbage for more of those full-throttle flavours, or you might prefer to tone things down a bit with a fishy idea such as brill fillet with black trompette mushrooms, purple sprouting broccoli and turnips. To finish, Hopdaemon ale cake is matched with Granny Smith apple sorbet and crisps, and ice cream made with mature Ashmore cheese from Canterbury.

Chef Charles Lakin **Owner** Tony Marsden & Hugh Oxborrow **Times** 12-2.30/6.30-9 Closed L Mon **Prices** Fixed L 2 course £17.50-£22.50, Fixed D 3 course fr £25, Starter £8-£9.50, Main £22-£26.50, Dessert £8-£9.50, Service optional, Groups min 10 service 10% **Wines** 260 bottles over £20, 14 bottles under £20, 14 by glass **Notes** Tasting menu available, Sunday L, Vegetarian menu, Civ Wed 55 **Seats** 60, Pr/dining room 20 **Children** Portions **Parking** 26

Wallett's Court Country House Hotel & Spa

◉◉ Modern British

Creative cooking in historic manor

☎ 01304 852424

Westcliffe, St Margaret's-at-Cliffe CT15 6EW

e-mail: dine@wallettscourt.com

dir: M2/A2 or M20/A20, follow signs for Deal (A258), 1st right for St-Margaret's-at-Cliffe. Restaurant 1m on right

The unassuming whitewashed exterior of this family-run country-house hotel hides a 17th-century Jacobean manor, but if staying in a room built of ancient bricks and mortar is too prosaic for your tastes, you could go 'glamping' in a Navajo tipi in the lovely grounds instead. At dinner, though, it's back to the past among the oak beams, inglenook fireplaces and candlelit tables of the romantic restaurant, where the modern British idiom gets a workout to produce dishes based on carefully-sourced materials from Kent and Sussex. The kitchen keeps things straightforward, setting off along the lines of Kentish rabbit terrine with tarragon emulsion and toasted sourdough bread, followed, perhaps, by a 40-day-matured sirloin of Sussex Red beef with roasted salsify, girolles, pommes purées and Madeira jus. In winter, there may be Christmas pudding soufflé with mulled wine sorbet and brandy sauce to wrap things up.

Chef Ryan Tasker **Owner** Gavin Oakley **Times** 12-2.30/7-9 Closed 25-26 Dec, L Mon-Sat (ex group bookings 10+) **Prices** Fixed L 2 course £16.95, Fixed D 3 course £39.95, Service optional **Wines** 46 bottles over £20, 2 bottles under £20, 17 by glass **Notes** Tasting menu on request, Sunday L, Vegetarian available, Dress restrictions, Smart casual, Civ Wed 40 **Seats** 60, Pr/dining room 40 **Children** Portions, Menu **Parking** 50

The White Cliffs Hotel

◉ Modern British

A warm welcome and ethically-sourced ingredients

☎ 01304 852229

High St, St Margaret's-at-Cliffe CT15 6AT

e-mail: mail@thewhitecliffs.com

dir: From M2/M20 follow signs for Deal onto A258. 1st right for St Margaret's-at-Cliffe & after 2m take right at T-junct. Opposite church in village centre

Close to the port terminal in Dover, The White Cliffs dates way back to the 16th century and is a traditional weather-boarded inn with an easygoing restaurant. The hotel's allotment provides a great bounty of vegetables and many other ingredients are sourced locally (with sustainability and organic as watchwords). In the oak-beamed Bay Restaurant, you might start with Golden Cross goats' cheese and Kentish cobnut fritter with roasted baby beet salad, moving on to Goan fish curry (containing local white fish and prawns) flavoured with coriander, coconut and ginger, or maybe the less esoteric fish and 'real proper chips'. Interesting desserts include Twinings 1706 tea crème brûlée and gingernut ice cream, and English rose buttermilk pudding with hot rhubarb compôte.

Chef Andrew Butcher **Owner** Gavin Oakley **Times** 12-2/7-9 Closed L Mon **Prices** Starter £4.95-£7.50, Main £7.95-£18.95, Dessert £2.95-£8.95, Service optional, Groups min 6 service 10% **Wines** 14 bottles over £20, 16 bottles under £20, 6 by glass **Notes** Sunday L, Vegetarian available **Seats** 50 **Children** Portions, Menu **Parking** 20, Village car park

---

EDENBRIDGE Map 6 TQ44

Haxted Mill Restaurant

◉ Modern French, Mediterranean

Popular dishes in a country inn with waterwheel

☎ 01732 862914

Haxted Rd TN8 6PU

e-mail: david@haxtedmill.co.uk

dir: M25 junct 6, A22 towards East Grinstead. Through Blindley Heath, after Texaco garage left at lights, in 1m 1st left after Red Barn PH. 2m to Haxted Mill

They were grinding grain for flour here until just after the Great War, but the watermill is still fully functional, and quite an education to behold. The restaurant is housed in the stables with their steeply sloping beamed ceilings, and also on a pair of terraces under sunshades. Should you wish to defy the elements on cooler evenings, the staff will provide shawls for draping yourself in. A populist menu of international brasserie classics might guide you from sautéed squid with chorizo, tomato and peppers, through roast rack of lamb with minted veg, or salmon marinated in soy sauce and maple syrup, to the final satisfaction of chocolate profiteroles with vanilla ice cream.

Chef David Peek **Owner** David & Linda Peek **Times** 12-2/7-9 Closed 23 Dec-1 Apr, Mon, D Sun **Prices** Fixed L 2 course £18, Fixed D 3 course £24, Starter £6-£13.95, Main £14.95-£25, Dessert £6-£7, Service added but optional 10% **Wines** 30 bottles over £20, 7 bottles under £20, 16 by glass **Notes** Fixed D not available Sat eve, Sunday L, Vegetarian available, Dress restrictions, Smart casual **Seats** 52 **Parking** 100

Read's Restaurant

◎◎ Modern British ⓘ NOTABLE WINE LIST ⌂

Refined modern British cooking in an elegant Georgian manor

☎ 01795 535344

Macknade Manor, Canterbury Rd ME13 8XE
e-mail: enquiries@reads.com
dir: From M2 junct 6 follow A251 towards Faversham. At T-junct with A2 (Canterbury road) turn right. Hotel 0.5m on right

The Pitchfords' Georgian manor house has long been a Kentish destination for those in the know. Set in lush grounds, from which emerge much of the fresh produce used in the kitchen, it feels like a pleasingly remote country retreat, and is run with the kind of friendly, grown-up affability we hope to find in such places. Read's was doing modern British cooking before many others had cottoned on to it, the dishes kept reasonably simple, for all that the menu descriptions might look long-winded. Potted Whitstable crab with baby gem and rustic toast is made to an old regional recipe, or there may be salmon ballottine with fennel marmalade, sweet-and-sour cucumber and horseradish crème fraîche. Excellent local lamb might be the roast loin, served with a fricassée of shallots, broad beans and tomato, while halibut fillet arrives on a bed of deeply coloured red wine risotto. A 15-minute wait for dessert is amply rewarded with a prune and Armagnac soufflé, served with vanilla ice cream and buttery shortbread. A stunning wine list completes the picture.

Chef David Pitchford, Simon McNamara **Owner** David & Rona Pitchford **Times** 12-2.30/7-10 Closed BHs, Sun-Mon **Prices** Fixed L 3 course £25, Fixed D 3 course £58, Tasting menu £56, Service optional **Wines** 250 bottles over £20, 12 bottles under £20, 18 by glass **Notes** Tasting menu 7 course, Vegetarian available, Dress restrictions, Smart casual, Civ Wed 60 **Seats** 50, Pr/dining room 30 **Children** Portions **Parking** 30

Rocksalt Restaurant

◎◎ Modern British NEW ⌂

Splendid seafood in slick harbourfront venue

☎ 01303 212070 & 884633

4-5 Fish Market CT19 6AA
e-mail: info@rocksaltfolkestone.co.uk
dir: M20 junct 13, follow A259 Folkestone Harbour, then left to Fish Market

A stylish glass and timber apparition smack on the harbourside, Rocksalt is a million miles from the prosaic shop frontages all around. Newly opened in 2011, this is a sleek design-led operation that would not look out of place in the capital: a luxurious interior of lime-washed oak floors, soft leather banquettes, and dark timber tables looks through a wall of glass over a cantilevered decking terrace to the docks, and beyond - as far as France on a good day. Under the culinary direction of Mark Sargeant (once a grandee in the Ramsay empire) the concept here is to take the finest Kentish ingredients and subject them to minimal intervention in order to let the quality do the talking. Folkestone's days as a cross-Channel port may be mothballed, but the trawlers still ply their trade, and their catch will be on Rocksalt's menu as soon as it is landed - local mackerel gets zing from a citrus and spice marinade and is served simply with crisp carrot and fennel, while the spanking freshness of poached sea bass shines out in partnership with samphire from the white cliffs of Dover and a light fish cream sauce. Kentish salt marsh lamb rump cooked in the wood-fired Josper oven and served with rosemary sauce is a worthy meat option. Puddings might gain extra interest from unusual ingredients, as in a cold chocolate and sea buckthorn fondant.

Chef Simon Dyer **Owner** Mark Sargeant, Josh De Haan **Times** 12-3/6.30-10 **Prices** Fixed L 2 course £15.50, Fixed D 3 course £18.50, Starter £5.75-£12.50, Main £10.50-£28.50, Dessert £5-£7.50, Service added but optional 12.5% **Wines** 55 bottles over £20, 11 bottles under £20, 14 by glass **Notes** Sunday L, Vegetarian available, Dress restrictions, Smart casual **Seats** 100, Pr/dining room 24 **Children** Portions, Menu **Parking** On street, pay & display car park

Le Petit Poisson

◎ Modern British

Fish, glorious fish

☎ 01227 361199
Pier Approach, Central Pde CT6 5JN
e-mail: mail@lepetitpoisson.co.uk
dir: On Herne Bay seafront by old pier

The former ticket office for Herne Bay's old pier is now a thriving seafront eatery, with a sunny alfresco terrace for summer dining and great views out to sea. Expect a friendly and relaxed vibe, simple whitewashed walls, stone floors, basic unclothed tables, and a charming seaside feel to the décor. As its name suggests, fresh fish and shellfish, all landed by Kentish day boats, is the focus of the kitchen, with chalkboards listing the day's catch. The kitchen knows not to mess around with its ingredients, so refreshingly simple dishes kick off with seared scallops with cauliflower purée and black pudding, followed by whole grilled Dover sole with brown shrimp butter, or braised brill with lemon and capers. Puddings might include spiced cheesecake with baked apple and butterscotch.

Chef Allan Ford & Andy Lowe **Owner** Philip Guy & Valerie Kersten **Times** 12-2.30/6.30-9 Closed Mon (ex BHs), Tue (after BHs), D Sun **Prices** Starter £5.50-£7.95, Main £10.10-£16.25, Dessert £3.75-£5.75, Service optional **Wines** 8 bottles over £20, 25 bottles under £20, 20 by glass **Notes** Vegetarian available **Seats** 50 **Children** Portions **Parking** On street

Chilston Park Hotel

◎◎ Modern British ⌂

Splendid Georgian mansion with elegant restaurant

☎ 01622 859803
Sandway ME17 2BE
e-mail: chilstonpark@handpicked.co.uk
dir: M20 junct 8

Chilston has gone the way of many a Georgian country house and opened its doors to the public as an upscale hotel. Set in 22 acres of gorgeous landscaped gardens and parkland, the house is a full-on stately home brimful of period antiques (it was once owned by the authors of Miller's Antiques guide) and oil paintings, and enough ornate plasterwork ceilings, regal fireplaces and crystal chandeliers that the place could easily earn a full-time living as a set for bodice-and-breeches period dramas. The cosseted mood continues in the elegant Venetian-style Culpeper's restaurant, where a French-accented contemporary country-house repertoire starts out inventively with an artichoke and shallot tarte Tatin with rosemary and mascarpone ice cream, followed by pancetta-wrapped monkfish with chorizo and fine bean risotto and fresh parmesan. Desserts also show plenty of flair and complexity with a well-made roast hazelnut soufflé served with milk chocolate ganache and hazelnut nougatine.

Chef Gareth Brown **Owner** Hand Picked Hotels **Times** 12-2/7-9.30 Closed L Sat **Prices** Fixed L 2 course £13.95, Fixed D 3 course £32.50, Starter £8.50-£10.50, Main £28.50-£35, Service optional **Wines** 90 bottles over £20, 1 bottle under £20, 18 by glass **Notes** Seasonal fixed Gourmet menu available, Sunday L, Vegetarian available, Dress restrictions, Smart casual, Civ Wed 100 **Seats** 54, Pr/dining room 12 **Children** Portions, Menu **Parking** 100

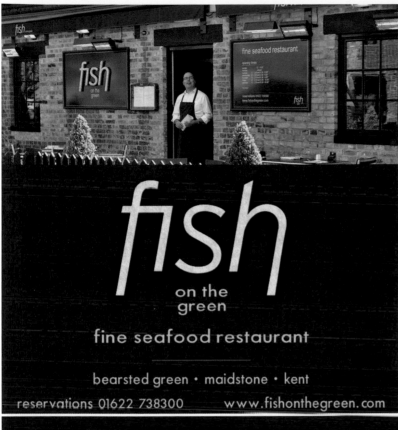

fish
on the green

fine seafood restaurant

bearsted green • maidstone • kent

reservations 01622 738300   www.fishonthegreen.com

  We are proud to announce that we have been awarded an AA ROSETTE and a recommendation in the Michelin Guide and the AA Restaurant Guide.

Fish on the Green has now established itself as one of the top 'fine' seafood restaurants in Kent, having been entered into the Michelin Guide and gaining its first rosette and still striving to set new standards in fresh seafood.

Fish on the Green is part of the attracttive setting that makes up 'one of the prettiest village greens in England', formerly a stable block near to the original coaching inn, The Oak on the Green. The entire building has been completely renovated to provide a simple, stylish, yet unassuming dining room with a small pre-dinner drinks bar, that complements the style of service and food offering.

Naturally the menu reflects the culture of the restaurant with 'trawler fresh' fish and shellfish and the finest quality ancillary ingredients, the most superb local salad and farm produce, not to mention the Kentish Limousin beef or Romney Marsh lamb etc, all prepared in a skilled, yet simple, unpretentious and often exhilarating manner.

FULL A LA CARTE MENU ALWAYS AVAILABLE

MAIDSTONE — Map 7 TQ75

Fish on the Green

⊚ Seafood

Refreshingly simple fish and seafood in a Kentish village

☎ 01622 738300
Church Ln, Bearsted Green ME14 4EJ
web: www.fishonthegreen.com
dir: N of A20 on village green

The venue was once the stable-block for the inn next door, in a tranquil location in Bearsted, a village east of Maidstone. Fishing-related artworks set the tone for the maritime menu, which offers the bounty of the seas in refreshingly straightforward culinary formats. Baked spiced crab with wholemeal toast, or steamed mussels in leeks, bacon and cider, are among the possible curtain-raisers for whole grilled lemon sole with brown shrimp and mace butter, or halibut with wilted spinach and chive hollandaise. If you're not into fish, a main course such as slow-roast pork belly with winter greens and pancetta, apple purée and thyme jus should fit the bill. Finish with rhubarb and ginger crumble, served with clotted cream.

Chef Peter Baldwin **Owner** Alexander Bensley
Times 12-2.30/6.30-10 Closed Xmas, Mon (some), D Sun (some) **Prices** Fixed L 2 course £14.95, Starter £5.25-£10.50, Main £15.95-£26.95, Dessert £6.25, Service optional **Wines** 13 bottles over £20, 11 bottles under £20, 7 by glass **Notes** Vegetarian available, Air con **Seats** 50 **Children** Portions **Parking** 50

See advert on page 215

MARGATE — Map 7 TR37

The Ambrette

⊚ Modern Indian NEW V

Modern Anglo-Indian food in a growing southeastern chain

☎ 01843 231504
44 King St CT9 1QE
e-mail: info@theambrette.co.uk
dir: A299/A28, left into Hawley St B2055. Restaurant on right corner King St

Dev Biswal has cannily spotted a gap in the culinary market, and moved to fill it with a steadily growing southeastern empire. This isn't modern Indian food as such; it's 'modern British with Indian influences'. There's a branch in Rye, and another planned in Canterbury. The Margate Ambrette is a light, breezy venue with chunky wood tables, minimally adorned walls and engagingly informative service. A strong aesthetic sense informs the presentations of dishes that both look good and deliver a panoply of upstanding flavours. Start with a grilled fillet of claresse (a freshwater member of the European catfish family) crusted in black pepper, coriander and sesame, or aromatically spiced calves' liver in Madeira jus. Kentish pork loin in a fennel and cinnamon coat comes with Goan-style garlic and vinegar sauce, with aubergine and chick pea timbale and basmati, or opt for stir-fried crab done in mustard oil, cinnamon and cardamom. Vegetarian specials and side-orders bring bright, spicy flavours to humble ingredients.

Chef Dev Biswal **Owner** Dev Biswal
Times 11.30-2.30/5.30-9.30 Closed 25-26 Dec, Mon **Prices** Fixed L 2 course £14.95, Tasting menu £35-£50, Starter £3.50-£5.95, Main £8.95-£15.95, Dessert £3.95-£8.95, Service added but optional 12.5% **Wines** 7 bottles over £20, 12 bottles under £20, 11 by glass **Notes** Pre-theatre menu 2, 3 course 6.30 & after 9pm, Sunday L, Vegetarian menu, Dress restrictions, Smart casual **Seats** 52 **Children** Portions **Parking** 10

ROCHESTER — Map 6 TQ76

Topes Restaurant

⊚⊚ Modern British ⓒ

An atmospheric gem in historic Rochester

☎ 01634 845270
60 High St ME1 1JY
e-mail: julie.small@btconnect.com
web: www.topesrestaurant.com
dir: M2 junct 1, through Strood High St over Medway Bridge, turn right at Northgate onto High St

Born again Dickens fans might like to know that the 15th-century building which houses Topes gets a name check in his last novel, *The Mystery of Edwin Drood*. The gnarled beams and narrow stairs climbing to the kitchen and dining room certainly have a Dickensian feel, but the interior has had a nip here and a tuck there to give it a more contemporary look. The mood is relaxed and chef-proprietor Chris Small's cooking taps into the current appetite for ingredients-led, unpretentious dishes with forthright flavours. Excellent Kentish produce underpins a gutsy starter of wild rabbit and pork terrine teamed with rabbit rillettes, pickled walnuts and grape chutney, before main course sees wood pigeon breasts sharing a plate with black pudding and bacon forestière and butternut squash purée. To finish, a British cheeseboard fights it out with the likes of bread-and-butter pudding with crème anglaise, caramelised pineapple and butterscotch ice cream.

Chef Chris Small **Owner** Chris & Julie Small
Times 12-2.30/6.30-9 Closed Mon-Tue, D Sun
Prices Fixed L 2 course £16, Fixed D 3 course £22, Starter £5.50-£8, Main £12.50-£17.50, Dessert £5.50-£8, Service optional **Wines** 15 bottles over £20, 25 bottles under £20, 6 by glass **Notes** Sunday L, Vegetarian available **Seats** 55, Pr/dining room 16 **Children** Portions, Menu **Parking** Public car park

SEVENOAKS   Map 6 TQ55

Gavin Gregg Restaurant

◎◎ Modern British, European ✍

Popular high street operation with hands-on owners

☎ 01732 456373
28-30 High St TN13 1HX
web: www.gavingreggrestaurant.com
dir: 1m from Sevenoaks train station. 500yds from top of town centre towards Tonbridge on left

Now into its 12th year, the 17th-century timbered house on the high street has become a stalwart of the foodie scene in the Sevenoaks area. Inside, the décor is simplicity itself: head-skimming black beams juxtaposed with cream and bright-orange-painted walls, and the restaurant's twirly 'g' logo displayed prominently in the windows. Gavin Gregg heads a team of four serving up supremely confident modern dishes with great clarity, depth and balance of flavour. Starters could get straight down to a display of technique, drawing the contrasts from Loch Duart salmon ballotine done three ways - slow-poached, vodka-cured and smoked - with potato and chive salad and caviar. Main course brings pan-seared honeyed duck breast with confit duck leg pithivier, celeriac purée, buttered leeks and Savoy cabbage, and boulangère potatoes; to finish, fine ingredients are again in evidence in an intense chocolate and honey cheesecake served with caramelised hazelnuts, and honey and yoghurt ice cream. If you're after top value, the fixed price menus are hard to beat.

Chef Gavin Gregg **Owner** Gavin & Lucinda Gregg **Times** 12-2/6.30-9.30 Closed Mon, D Sun **Prices** Fixed L 2 course £14-£16.50, Fixed D 3 course £20-£22.50, Tasting menu £45-£60, Starter £5-£7.50, Main £14-£22, Dessert £6-£10, Service added 10% **Wines** 34 bottles over £20, 16 bottles under £20, 9 by glass **Notes** Tasting menu 7 course Fri & Sat (with wine £60), Sunday L, Vegetarian available **Seats** 80, Pr/dining room 32 **Children** Portions **Parking** Town centre

SISSINGHURST   Map 7 TQ73

Rankins Restaurant

◎ Modern British

Appealing bistro-style dishes with a local flavour

☎ 01580 713964
The Street TN17 2JH
e-mail: rankins@btconnect.com
dir: Village centre, on A262

Just up the road from the celebrated Sissinghurst Castle Gardens, Hugh and Leonora Rankin's white clapboard restaurant on the high street is the setting for uncomplicated, soundly-cooked British bistro-style food. The Rankins have run their classic cottagey operation for over 25 years, so have well-established supply lines to the finest materials to be had in the Kent and Sussex area - fish landed in Rye and Hastings, and lamb from Romney Marsh, for example - which appears in an eclectic array of dishes that follow the calendar and score with their honest simplicity. For starters, there could be smoked haddock baked in a pot with creamy lemon sauce and glazed with cheddar cheese, while main courses could run to roast duck confit served with red wine sauce and green lentils, sharpened with redcurrant jelly and orange zest. To finish, perhaps coffee fudge pudding with coffee ice cream.

Chef Hugh Rankin **Owner** Hugh & Leonora Rankin **Times** 12.30-2/7.30-9 Closed BHs, Mon-Tue, L Wed-Sat, D Sun **Prices** Fixed L 2 course £27.50, Fixed D 3 course £32.50, Service optional, Groups min 20 service 10% **Wines** 11 bottles over £20, 9 bottles under £20, 2 by glass **Notes** Sunday L, Vegetarian available, Dress restrictions, Smart casual **Seats** 25 **Children** Portions **Parking** On street

SITTINGBOURNE   Map 7 TQ96

Hempstead House Country Hotel

◎ Traditional European

Classical cooking in a charming Victorian hotel

☎ 01795 428020
London Rd, Bapchild ME9 9PP
e-mail: info@hempsteadhouse.co.uk
web: www.hempsteadhouse.co.uk
dir: 1.5m from town centre on A2 towards Canterbury

The Lake family who built the original Hempstead House in 1850 and had its four acres of mature landscaped gardens to themselves until it became a country-house hotel and spa in 1990 are honoured in the name of its restaurant. The conservatory-style space has a plush look that reflects the old house's Victorian character, involving swagged drapes, plasterwork ceilings, crystal chandeliers and swanky tables laid with fine china, silver and glassware. The kitchen steers an accessible course that is clearly rooted in French classics, starting out with the likes of pan-seared pigeon breast with roasted leeks, wild mushrooms and tarragon butter, followed by brill fillet teamed with braised fennel, saffron pommes dauphinoise and anchovy sauce. Desserts run to caramel and apple bavarois with apple sorbet and bitter apple compôte.

Chef Paul Field, Peter Gilbey **Owner** Mr & Mrs A J Holdstock **Times** 12-2.30/7-10 Closed D Sun (non residents) **Prices** Fixed L 2 course £12-£14.50, Fixed D 3 course £27.50, Starter £5.95-£8.50, Main £16.50-£21.95, Dessert £7.50, Service optional **Wines** 30 bottles over £20, 25 bottles under £20, 4 by glass **Notes** Sunday L, Vegetarian available, Dress restrictions, Smart casual, Civ Wed 150 **Seats** 70, Pr/dining room 30 **Children** Portions, Menu **Parking** 200

TENTERDEN   Map 7 TQ83

Number 75 Dining Room & Wine Bar

◎ Modern, International NEW ✍

Vibrant High Street venue serving Kentish produce

☎ 01580 762075
75 High St TN30 6BB
e-mail: info@number75.com
dir: Located High St, next door to Ladbrokes

The best of Kentish produce is at the heart of things in this relaxed modern operation on Tenterden's tree-lined High Street. It's a buzzy place with a simple, uncluttered décor of white walls hung with pieces by local artists; staff are eager-to-please, and the accessible, seasonally-driven menu of unpretentious dishes has an everyman appeal. When it is asparagus time of year, you'll find it here, grilled and served in a classic combo with a crispy poached duck egg and hollandaise sauce. Popular demand keeps the signature main course as a fixture, and it's easy to see why: an indulgently moist and flavoursome piece of belly pork and crackling is partnered by seared scallops, black pudding and Bramley apple croquette, fennel purée, and honey and sage jus. For pudding, excellent pastrywork distinguishes a chocolate, pear and ginger tart with home-made vanilla ice cream.

Chef Tyrone Power, Matthew Howe **Owner** Tyrone & Elizabeth Power **Times** 12-2.30/6-10 Closed Mon, D Sun **Prices** Fixed L 2 course £14.95, Starter £5.95-£7.50, Main £12.95-£19.95, Dessert £5.95-£6.95, Groups min 7 service 10% **Wines** 24 bottles over £20, 12 bottles under £20, 10 by glass **Notes** Sunday L, Vegetarian available **Seats** 90 **Children** Menu **Parking** Highbury Lane

The Brew House

◉ Modern European

Smart modish cooking in an ultra-modern boutique hotel

☎ 01892 520587
1 Warwick Park TN2 5TA
e-mail: reception@brewhousehotel.com
dir: A267, 1st left onto Warwick Park, hotel immediately on left

In the historic Pantiles quarter of town, this former 18th-century brewery has been given the full-works makeover into an über-hip boutique hotel and restaurant. You might need to go Italian and wear shades indoors for the minimalist all-white look lit by funky fluorescent tube chandeliers, although the Barbarella vibe brings blocks of purple or cerise-painted wall, and splashes of vibrantly-coloured art. The kitchen mines a broadly modern European vein whilst sourcing its materials from as close to home as possible. A well-made roasted butternut squash risotto with wild rocket and aged parmesan gets things going, ahead of crispy-skinned confit of duck leg served with a silky butter bean purée and Savoy cabbage. For pudding, hot chocolate fondant comes with praline ice cream.

Chef Andrew Giles **Owner** Kevin Spencer **Times** 12-10 **Prices** Food prices not confirmed for 2013. Please telephone for details **Wines** 36 bottles over £20, 9 bottles under £20, 14 by glass **Notes** Sunday L, Vegetarian available **Seats** 80, Pr/dining room 120 **Children** Portions, Menu **Parking** On street

Hotel du Vin Tunbridge Wells

◉ French, British ♨ ☙

Simple French brasserie cooking with views of the vineyard

☎ 01892 526455
Crescent Rd TN1 2LY
e-mail: reception.tunbridgewells@hotelduvin.com
dir: Follow town centre to main junct of Mount Pleasant Rd & Crescent Rd/Church Rd. Hotel 150yds on right just past Phillips House

The Tunbridge Wells arm of HdV is a Georgian house with commanding views from the back, where outdoor tables come into play in summer, over Calverley Park and the hotel's own vineyard. That last feature is a fitting accoutrement to a hospitality group where wine and food have always been the principal driver. Simple French brasserie fare founded on local materials is the name of the game, offering cod and salmon fishcakes with sauce gribiche, then roast lamb rump with pea purée, or whole lemon sole meunière, with the likes of crème brûlée to finish. The wine list is worth spending time over, an inspired international cruise round the modern vinous landscape with good choice by the glass.

Chef Daniel McGarey **Owner** Hotel du Vin Ltd **Times** 12-2/7-10.30 **Prices** Food prices not confirmed for

2013. Please telephone for details **Wines** 700 bottles over £20, 50 bottles under £20, 16 by glass **Notes** Pre-theatre meal offer on selected nights, Vegetarian available, Civ Wed 84 **Seats** 80, Pr/dining room 84 **Children** Portions, Menu **Parking** 30, NCP

Montrose Restaurant

◉ Modern European Ⓥ ☙

Smart seasonal cooking in stylish setting

☎ 01892 513161
15a Church Rd, Southborough TN4 0RX
e-mail: bookings@montroserestaurant.co.uk
dir: M25 junct 5 to A21. Exit A21 Tunbridge Wells/Tonbridge, to Southborough. Restaurant located on the right after the cricket green

Behind a stirring late-Victorian façade, the Montrose makes no less of an impact on the inside: swish black chandeliers, black clothed tables and lavishly upholstered chairs combine to give the space a sense of occasion. The kitchen keeps it simple with good quality, locally-sourced ingredients the star of the show in its modish output. You might encounter braised rabbit ravioli with caramelised shallots, carrot crisps and jus, followed by supreme of guinea fowl stuffed with brie and apple, prosciutto ham, balsamic sauce and pomme mousseline, and bring down the curtain with a liquorice and Pernod parfait served with lime syrup. Wine is a big deal here - the co-owner is a dedicated oenophile and it shows in an interesting list.

Chef Richard Hards **Owner** Richard Hards **Times** 12-2.30/6.30-late Closed D Sun **Prices** Food prices not confirmed for 2013. Please telephone for details **Wines** 60 bottles over £20, 3 bottles under £20, 24 by glass **Notes** Sunday L, Vegetarian menu, Dress restrictions, Smart casual **Seats** 40, Pr/dining room 18 **Parking** On street

The Spa Hotel

◉ Modern, Traditional British

Country-house dining beneath crystal chandeliers

☎ 01892 520331
Mount Ephraim TN4 8XJ
e-mail: reservations@spahotel.co.uk
dir: On A264 leaving Tunbridge Wells towards East Grinstead

The anonymous writer of angry letters to the press known as 'Angry of Tunbridge Wells' might like to head for the grand Spa Hotel and chill for a while. The Georgian mansion sits in 14 acres of fabulous grounds on the edge of town and has been welcoming paying guests since the late-Victorian vogue for taking the waters. But now we're in the 21st century, and the grand interiors have been reworked with a healthy dollop of boutique style to go with its period elegance. The Regency-style Chandelier Restaurant gets its name for an obvious reason that we need not spell out here, with those fancy light fittings dangling from lofty ornate ceilings above panelled walls painted Wedgwood blue and white, the look completed

with caramel high-backed seats and crisp white napery. On the menu are classically-based ideas built with a fair input from fine local produce, starting, perhaps, with a roulade of smoked salmon, cream cheese and crayfish with horseradish jelly, before a more modern three-way serving of Gloucestershire Old Spot pork comprising fillet, belly, and black pudding pork sausage teamed with pancetta mash, Savoy cabbage, wild mushrooms and apples. Happy of Tunbridge Wells.

Chef Steve Cole **Owner** Scragg Hotels Ltd **Times** 12.30-2/7-9.30 Closed L Sat **Prices** Food prices not confirmed for 2013. Please telephone for details **Wines** 69 bottles over £20, 29 bottles under £20, 8 by glass **Notes** Vegetarian available, Dress restrictions, Smart casual, No jeans or T-shirts **Seats** 80, Pr/dining room 200 **Children** Portions, Menu **Parking** 150

Thackeray's

◉◉◉ – *see opposite*

The Swan

◉◉ Modern British ☙

Mix of modern and traditional cooking in a contemporary Kentish inn

☎ 01732 521910
35 Swan St ME19 6JU
e-mail: info@loveswan.co.uk
dir: M20 junct 4 follow signs for West Malling, left into Swan St. Approx 200yds on left

A cursory glance shows a classic Kentish high street inn, but take a peek in The Swan's 'secret garden' in summer, and the urban-cool outdoor lounge look of Philippe Starck furniture, rugs, lanterns and chimeneas reveals that this slick operation has travelled a long way from its origins as a 15th-century coaching inn. Inside, a top-to-toe facelift has transformed The Swan into a sleek 21st-century bird, all stainless steel, granite and wood, funky modern artworks and mirrors beneath the original oak beams of its stylish bars and main brasserie, and it is all kept ticking over by clued-up staff. Thankfully, it's not a case of style over substance here: the kitchen deploys ingredients from Kentish producers in a menu that delivers thoroughly modern food with big-city flavours. Expect South Downs rabbit and leek terrine with piccalilli, or Rye Bay scallops with confit bacon, fennel and harissa, followed by rump and sweetbreads of salt marsh lamb teamed with artichokes and shallot purée. For afters, how about a trio of cherry trifle, custard tart and rice pudding?

Chef Scott Goss **Owner** Swan Brasserie Ltd **Times** 12-10 **Prices** Fixed L 2 course £14.50, Starter £6-£10.40, Main £11.80-£22, Dessert £5-£7, Service added but optional 12.5% **Wines** 57 bottles over £20, 10 bottles under £20, 12 by glass **Notes** Fixed menu 2 course 5.30-7pm, Sunday L, Vegetarian available, Dress restrictions, Smart casual, Civ Wed 100 **Seats** 90, Pr/dining room 20 **Children** Portions, Menu **Parking** Long-stay car park

Save on Hotels. Book at **theAA.com/hotel**

KENT 219 ENGLAND

WHITSTABLE
Map 7 TR16

Crab & Winkle Seafood Restaurant

 British Seafood

Local seafood right on the harbour

☎ 01227 779377
South Quay, The Harbour CT5 1AB
e-mail: info@seafood-restaurant-uk.com
dir: M2, exit at Whitstable, through town to harbour

As far back as 1930 the tourists were piling into Whitstable for fresh fish and seafood; in fact, the train that brought them from Canterbury - one of the world's first steam passenger railways, incidentally - was nicknamed the 'Crab and Winkle Line'. Nowadays you would have to hike or bike it along the trail of the disused railway to arrive at the eponymous seafood restaurant, which is on the first floor above the fish market on Whitstable harbour. The perfect spot, then, for the kitchen to get hold of the sparkling fresh supplies straight from the quayside as they are landed each day by the local fishing boats below. Inside, wooden booths and white walls hung with local art give the wooden building a light and bright Mediterranean flavour, or for perfect summer's day dining, there are balcony tables perched outdoors above the harbour. Fish and shellfish this fresh doesn't need any messing about: get things rolling with platters of oysters, winkles, cockles, whelks, prawns and hot-smoked salmon, and follow that with something like mussels and chips or grilled skate wing with caper butter and new potatoes.

Times 11.30-9.30 Closed 25 Dec, Mon (Nov-Apr), D Sun (Nov-Apr), 26 Dec, 1 Jan

The Sportsman

 Modern British

Spanking-fresh produce and clear flavours in splendid isolation on the coast

☎ 01227 273370
Faversham Rd, Seasalter CT5 4BP
e-mail: contact@thesportsmanseasalter.co.uk
dir: On coast road between Whitstable & Faversham, 3.5m W of Whitstable

Although we're in lush Kent, this foodie pub on the Seasalter marshes outside Whitstable has a remote feel, with the windswept beach out front and flat marshy meadows behind. This simplicity finds its reflection in the stripped-out woody décor within, and chef-patron Steve Harris's idiosyncratic, no-nonsense approach to his craft. The local sourcing policy here is far more than mere lip service, as the bulk of the materials come from local farms, and fish and shellfish come from Whitstable and Hythe; the dedication to authentic flavours even extends as far as the kitchen churning its own butter. There are two menus: chalked up on the boards are daily menus of whatever is good and in season, and there's also a tasting menu. Dishes are described minimally, but that belies the big flavours and the sound technical skills needed to distill their essence onto the plate. Seafood illustrates what the kitchen can accomplish: whether it's slip sole grilled with seaweed butter to start, or main courses such as turbot fillet braised in sherry-like vin jaune with pork belly, or gurnard with bouillabaisse sauce and green olive tapenade, flavours are emphatic, and timings spot-on. Meat dishes score highly too: the farm that supplies the pork belly served simply with apple sauce can be seen from the pub, while ideas such as dark chocolate mousse with salted caramel and milk sorbet turn up at pudding time.

Times 12-2/7-9 Closed 25-26 Dec, 1 Jan, Mon, D Sun

Thackeray's

TUNBRIDGE WELLS (ROYAL)
Map 6 TQ53

Modern French V

Classy modern French cooking at former home of a great Briton

☎ 01892 511921
85 London Rd TN1 1EA
e-mail: reservations@thackerays-restaurant.co.uk
web: www.thackerays-restaurant.co.uk
dir: A21/A26, towards Tunbridge Wells. On left 500yds after the Kent & Sussex Hospital

Victorian author William Makepeace Thackeray would not recognise the radically-reworked interior of the white-painted clapboard 18th-century Kentish villa he called home: the dark oak floors and high ceilings are fixtures, but the two dining rooms are most definitely boutique these days, done out in subtle hues of cream and honey, and autumnal leaf-patterned wallpaper. For alfresco eating, the serene Japanese terrace is an equally stylish spot, and a heated canopy means you don't need to turn up in thermal survival kit. Chef-proprietor Richard Phillips brings a superstar CV to the equation, having worked with the Roux brothers at Le Gavroche, and Marco Pierre White in Premier League London venues, and is himself no stranger to the world of TV. But what counts is what he can accomplish in the kitchen, and that is an unquestionably high-achieving take on modern French cooking wrought from the superb materials to be had from the hills and coastlines of Kent and Sussex. Pan-fried fillet of south coast brill teamed with haddock brandade, roast cucumber, cockle and cucumber ketchup is typical of the emphatic flavours and well-considered constructions here. Likewise an inventive main course of Kentish venison, which turns up as hot smoked and roasted loin, and a pie of braised shoulder, served with sautéed chestnuts, ventrèche bacon and Portobello mushrooms, beetroot and roasting juices. To finish, lemon meringue pie paired with fennel ice cream and limoncello jelly is a clever variation on a traditional theme.

Chef Richard Phillips, Christopher Bower, Daniel Hatton **Owner** Richard Phillips, Paul Smith **Times** 12-2.30/6.30-10.30 Closed Mon, D Sun **Prices** Food prices not confirmed for 2013. Please telephone for details **Wines** 113 bottles over £20, 4 bottles under £20, 23 by glass **Notes** Sunday L, Vegetarian menu, Dress restrictions, Smart casual **Seats** 70, Pr/dining room 16 **Children** Portions **Parking** On street in evening, NCP

The Bull

🏵 Modern British 🍷

Contemporary cooking in old village inn

☎ 01732 789800
Bull Ln TN15 7RF
e-mail: info@thebullhotel.com
web: www.thebullhotel.com
dir: In centre of village

The Bull, a pub in a peaceful village on the North Downs Way (and just off the M20), has a bit of a past. It dates back to the 14th century, and pilgrims to Canterbury would have stopped here; more recently it was a source of solace for Second World War pilots from nearby airfields. It's still a haven, with a popular bar and a beamed restaurant with two wood-burners. The cooking has more cutting edge than might be expected in a village inn; starters of beetroot-cured gravad lax, or smoked pigeon breast with apple and celeriac remoulade might be followed by sea bass fillet with pancetta and a tarragon and langoustine sauce. Meats are from local farms - pork chop, say, served with a fried duck egg, black pudding and baby vegetables - and puddings such as champagne syllabub are a highlight.

Chef James Hawkes, David Evans **Owner** Martin Deadman **Times** 12-2.30/6-9.30 **Prices** Food prices not confirmed for 2013. Please telephone for details **Wines** 74 bottles over £20, 18 bottles under £20, 9 by glass **Notes** Sunday L, Vegetarian available **Seats** Pr/dining room 12 **Children** Portions **Parking** 18

The Clog & Billycock

🏵 Traditional British 🍷

Unpretentious pub with great local flavour

☎ 01254 201163
Billinge End Rd, Pleasington BB2 6QB
e-mail: enquiries@theclogandbillycock.com
web: www.theclogandbillycock.com
dir: M6 junct 29/M65 junct 3. Follow signs to Pleasington

From the same stable as The Highwayman in Burrow and the Three Fishes at Mitton (see entries), The Clog & Billycock is named after the favourite attire of a landlord a century or so ago (a billycock is a bowler hat). Inside, log-burning fires await in winter and there's a decent patio garden for warmer times of year. The menu is overseen by co-owner Nigel Haworth (see entry for Northcote) and championing local suppliers is very much his thing (they're duly credited on the menu); some of these 'regional food heroes' also appear in black and white photos on the wall and on place mats on the wooden tables. Local Daniel Thwaites ales are on tap, while the seasonal menu might take you from Ashcroft's deep-fried cauliflower fritters with curried mayonnaise, via warm Morecambe Bay shrimps with mace butter and toasted English muffin, to a Lancashire hotpot with heather-reared Lonk lamb, potatoes, and pickled red cabbage. Finish with a pineapple upside-down cake served with a lime syllabub.

Chef Richard Upton **Owner** Nigel Haworth, Craig Bancroft **Times** 12-2/5.30-8.30 Closed Xmas **Prices** Starter £4.75-£8, Main £9.50-£19.50, Dessert £5, Service optional **Wines** 22 bottles over £20, 17 bottles under £20, 5 by glass **Notes** Sunday L, Vegetarian available **Seats** 130 **Children** Portions, Menu **Parking** 75

See advert opposite

The Millstone at Mellor

🏵🏵 Modern British 🍷

Fine Lancashire produce in a smart village inn

☎ 01254 813333
Church Ln, Mellor BB2 7JR
e-mail: info@millstonehotel.co.uk
dir: 4m from M6 junct 31 follow signs for Blackburn. Mellor is on right 1m after 1st set of lights

It's always a treat to find an inn that puts equal importance on food and drink - such is The Millstone. This Ribble Valley local serves a fine pint of Thwaites, the renowned Lancashire brewing company, the founding-father of which is buried in the cemetery next door. And if you really want to sample the beers, go for the 'Thoroughly Thirds', which is a taster board of three different ales. And the wine list ain't no slouch either. There is a rustic handsomeness to the bar and eating areas, but rough and ready it most certainly is not. Chef-patron Anson Bolton is passionate about produce and the provenance of what turns up on the plate is never in doubt. There are pub classics (Bowland steak, kidney and Thwaites' Wainwright's ale suet pudding), deli boards (local cheeses among them), steaks cooked on the grill, and seasonally-changing dishes such as grilled Middlewhite pork cutlet with black pudding rösti, pork scratching and apple purée. Start with baked goats' cheese on buttered crumpet and finish with baked ginger parkin with cinnamon ice cream and treacle sauce.

Chef Anson Bolton **Owner** Shire Hotels Ltd **Times** 12-9.30 Closed D 25-26 Dec, 1 Jan **Prices** Starter £4.50-£8, Main £9.95-£23.95, Dessert £4.95-£7.45, Service optional **Wines** 55 bottles over £20, 30 bottles under £20, 9 by glass **Notes** Vegetarian available **Seats** 90, Pr/dining room 20 **Children** Portions, Menu **Parking** 45, Also on street

THE CLOG
& BILLYCOCK
AT PLEASINGTON

Award-winning food.
Fresh local ingredients.
The perfect local pub.

Following a £1.3 million refurbishment, this rural retreat – only minutes from the centre of Blackburn – opened to rave reviews and has since built a delicious, award-winning reputation for championing 'food with roots'...Lancashire classics with a contemporary twist.

- New Seasonal Menu and new Wine List
- Produce sourced from our local food heroes
- Traditional Lancashire dishes, with a delicious twist ...inspired by Michelin Star chef Nigel Haworth
- Selection of great Lancashire cask ales and fine wines

- Healthy and nutritional Kids' Menu and new Kids' activities too
- Glorious landscaped terraces for alfresco dining
- Crackling log fires in the winter months

PUB OPENING TIMES
Monday - Saturday 12 noon - 11.00pm , Sunday 12 noon - 10.30pm

FOOD SERVED
Lunch	Mon - Sat Noon - 2.00pm, Sun Noon - 8.00pm
Afternoon Bites	Mon - Sat 2.00pm - 5.30pm
Dinner	Mon - Thur 5.30pm - 8.30pm, Fri & Sat 5.30pm - 9.00pm, Sun Noon - 8.00pm
Bank Holidays	Open all day Noon - 8.00pm for food *Food service times indicate the last order times.*

VIEW OUR WEBSITE FOR TODAY'S MENUS

Less than 7 miles from junction 31, M6
less than 5 miles from junction 3, M65
and less than 7 miles from junction 9, M61

 Join us on Facebook and Twitter facebook.com/RibbleValleyInns twitter.com/RVIpubs

The Clog & Billycock • Billinge End Road Pleasington • Blackburn Lancashire • BB2 6QB
tel 01254 201163 www.theclogandbillycock.com

THE HIGHWAYMAN AT NETHER BURROW

AWARD-WINNING FOOD. FRESH LOCAL INGREDIENTS. THE PERFECT LOCAL PUB.

If you like food that's bursting with local flavour and tradition, you'll love The Highwayman. From 'Pub Newcomer of the Year' to 'County Dining Pub of the Year', RVI's landmark pub has picked up award after award since re-opening just 4 years ago.

- New Seasonal Menu and new Wine List
- Produce sourced from our local food heroes
- Classic regional dishes, with a contemporary twist
  ...inspired by Michelin Star chef Nigel Haworth
- Selection of great Lancashire cask ales and fine wines

- Healthy and nutritional Kids' Menu and new Kids' activities too
- Glorious landscaped terraces for alfresco dining
- Crackling log fires in the winter months

PUB OPENING TIMES
Tuesday - Saturday 12 noon - 11.00pm , Sunday 12 noon - 10.30pm

FOOD SERVED

Lunch	Tues - Sat Noon - 2.00pm, Sun Noon - 8.00pm
Afternoon Bites	Tues - Sat 2.00pm - 5.30pm
Dinner	Tues - Thur 5.30pm - 8.30pm, Fri & Sat 5.30pm - 9.00pm, Sun Noon - 8.00pm
Bank Holidays	Open all day Noon - 8.00pm for food
	Food service times indicate the last order times.

VIEW OUR WEBSITE FOR TODAY'S MENUS

THE HIGHWAYMAN
A Ribble Valley Inn

Less than 8 miles from junction 36 on the M6

Join us on Facebook and Twitter facebook.com/RibbleValleyInns twitter.com/RVIpubs **f**

The Highwayman, Burrow, Kirkby Lonsdale, Lancashire LA6 2RJ
Tel 01524 273 338 Email enquiries@highwaymaninn.co.uk www.highwaymaninn.co.uk

Save on Hotels. Book at theAA.com/hotel

LANCASHIRE 223 ENGLAND

Jali Fine Indian Dining

◉ Indian

Vibrant Indian spicing by the seafront

☎ 01253 622223
Best Western Carlton Hotel, 286 North Promenade FY1 2EZ
e-mail: blackpool@jalirestaurants.co.uk
dir: M6 junct 32/M55 follow signs for North Shore. Between Blackpool Tower & Gynn Sq

Set in a prime location on Blackpool's seafront, Jali - situated in the traditional-looking Best Western Carlton Hotel - brings some well-judged Indian dining to the self-styled Playground of the North. The smart dining room offers a nod to its Indian roots through authentic artefacts, staff in traditional costume and a backing track of Indian music. The cooking is likewise given a modern spin; expect achari fish tikka and nawabi fish curry standing alongside the more trad lamb bhuna and chicken saag. The fact the restaurant holds the world record for the tallest poppadom tower is surely the icing on the cake.

Chef Kasi Shanmugastin, Khagaraj Kandel, Kuldeep & Sanjeev Nanda **Owner** Ablecrest Ltd **Times** 6-10 Closed 25-26 Dec, Sun (except BH wknds), 19-26 Dec, L all week **Prices** Fixed D 3 course £12.95-£19.95, Starter £4.75-£6.75, Main £8.25-£10.95, Dessert £3.95-£4.50, Service added but optional 10% **Wines** 6 bottles over £20, 16 bottles under £20, 4 by glass **Notes** Vegetarian available, Dress restrictions, No shorts, Civ Wed 90 **Seats** 100, Pr/dining room 18 **Children** Portions, Menu

The Highwayman

◉ Traditional British ⌾

Regional cooking in a restored country inn

☎ 01524 273338
LA6 2RJ
e-mail: enquiries@highwaymaninn.co.uk
web: www.highwaymaninn.co.uk
dir: Off A683

If you're a fan of Nigel Haworth and Craig Bancroft's other pubs serving good food with a local flavour (see entries for the Clog & Billycock and The Three Fishes), you might have a sense of déjà vu here. And that's a good thing. The gently revamped pub has simple wooden

tables, roaring fires and black and white photos of the much valued suppliers on the walls, and it's a popular place; rock up to the till to order the satisfying regional food. Mrs Kirkham's Lancashire cheese crops up on toast, served with Sillfield Farm streaky bacon and Worcestershire sauce, while a main course dish might be slow-cooked leg of Goosnargh duckling with spiced lentils, mint yoghurt and fondant leeks, with elderflower syllabub and jelly and Grasmere gingerbread to finish.

Chef Colin McKevitt **Owner** Nigel Haworth & Craig Bancroft **Times** 12-2/5.30-8.30 Closed 25 Dec, Mon (ex BHs) **Prices** Starter £4.75-£8, Main £9.50-£19.50, Dessert £5, Service optional **Wines** 20 bottles over £20, 17 bottles under £20, 4 by glass **Notes** Sunday L, Vegetarian available **Seats** 120 **Children** Portions, Menu **Parking** 45

See advert opposite

The Red Cat

◉◉ Modern British V ⌾

Intelligent modern British cooking in relaxed setting

☎ 01257 263966
114 Blackburn Rd, Whittle-le-Woods PR6 8LL
e-mail: enquiries@theredcat.co.uk
dir: M61 junct 8 signed Wheelton, left off A674

Look out for the red cat motif etched into a large glass panel by the door in this former farmhouse, turned local pub, turned restaurant, just outside Chorley. Neutral tones complement the modern look with the lounge and interconnecting dining rooms divided by glass panels, and wooden tables are elegantly set with candles. It's a popular place, with its smart look and relaxed feel, but they come for the food, which is unfussy yet refined, imaginatively presented, and based on tip-top local Lancashire produce. Fleetwood smoked haddock, for example, comes with crushed peas, and mussel and herb velouté, and fillet of Bowland beef with bourguignon garnish, crushed thyme potatoes and seared foie gras. For dessert, lemon curd pannacotta is paired with rhubarb milkshake.

Chef Chris Rawlinson **Owner** Chris & Mike Rawlinson **Times** 12-2/6-mdnt Closed Mon-Tue, D Sun **Prices** Fixed L 2 course £15, Fixed D 3 course £22.50, Tasting menu £55, Starter £6.95-£9.95, Main £17.95-£25.95, Dessert £6.95-£7.95, Service added but optional 10% **Wines** 39 bottles over £20, 18 bottles under £20, 9 by glass **Notes** Tasting menu 5 course, Sunday L, Vegetarian menu **Seats** 50 **Children** Portions **Parking** 100

Stirk House Hotel

◉ Traditional & Modern ⌾

Modern Lancashire cooking in a Tudor manor

☎ 01200 445581
BB7 4LJ
e-mail: reservations@stirkhouse.co.uk
dir: M6 junct 32, W of village, on A59. Hotel 0.5m on left

The weathered stone exterior of 16th-century Stirk House, set amid majestic scenery in the heart of the Ribble Valley, promises a degree of old-world charm that the interiors and the friendly approach of staff impressively fulfill. An ornate ceiling and statement fireplace are the main decorative features of the dining room, and the cooking offers a modern take on exalted Lancashire tradition. Start with duck leg confit hash served with barbecue sauce and a fried egg, ahead of carefully timed plaice, warm potted brown shrimps and sprouting broccoli, and round things off with a meringue dessert incorporating roasted rhubarb and custard, or a duo of Lancashire and Blacksticks Blue cheeses with fruity chutney.

Chef Chris Dobson **Owner** Paul Caddy **Times** 12.30-2.30/7-9 Closed Xmas **Prices** Food prices not confirmed for 2013. Please telephone for details **Wines** 20 bottles over £20, 17 bottles under £20, 9 by glass **Notes** Sunday L, Vegetarian available, Civ Wed 95, Air con **Seats** 40, Pr/dining room 50 **Children** Portions, Menu **Parking** 300

Northcote

◉◉◉◉ – *see page 224*

Northcote

Modern British V   🍷NOTABLE WINE LIST 👌

The heart and soul of Lancashire

☎ 01254 240555
Northcote Rd BB6 8BE
e-mail: reception@northcote.com
web: www.northcote.com
dir: M6 junct 31, 9m to Northcote. Follow Clitheroe (A59) signs. Hotel on left before rdbt

Rather modestly dubbed a restaurant with rooms by Nigel Haworth and Craig Bancroft, their grand red-brick Victorian pile has been championing home-grown, local and regional produce in exemplary fashion since 1984. Perched on the edge of the Ribble Valley, it's a lovely location with beauty spots aplenty nearby. With a trio of successful gastro-pubs on the team too - The Three Fishes in Mitton, The Clog and Billycock in Pleasington and The Highwayman Inn in Burrow - the grass does not grow under their feet. Here in Langho all is soothing luxury with an eye for detail, and 21st-century expectations met when it comes to interior design; local art remains on-message on the walls, the colours recall nature, and, in the restaurant, tables are impeccably presented and serve up lovely views of the grounds. The bar areas and lounges for pre- and post-prandial drinks are jolly nice places to spend time; they advise rocking up 30 minutes before your dining reservation

to make the best of it. The true magic of this partnership comes into play when Bancroft's superb 300-bin wine list is seen in conjunction with the menu, the kitchen headed up by the extremely capable and ever-passionate head chef Lisa Allen (protégé and chip off the old block). The choice of menus covers all bases, from tasting and gourmet menus with fabulous wine flights (veggie versions available too), à la carte and, quite frankly, cheap as hotpot seasonal lunch menu. Although the style is honest, simple and direct, everything makes an impact; first-class ingredients help but so too does the high level of technical skill and refined presentation. Everything from the canapés to the simple but exceptional petits fours shows attention to detail, craft and skill. Celeriac soup with pickled celeriac and Jabugo ham is a first course with real depth of flavour and balance, with pickling again used to good effect in a dish with pickled mushrooms combining with a coddled free-range Bowland egg, Périgord truffle and bread shards - this is rustic yet refined cooking at its best. Slow-cooked English veal cheek comes with its sweetbread, fennel and Seville orange marmalade and buttery potatoes, and for dessert, cross the border for a carpaccio of Yorkshire rhubarb, ginger parfait, blood orange and basil.

Chef Nigel Haworth, Lisa Allen **Owner** Nigel Haworth, Craig Bancroft **Times** 12-2/7-9.30 Closed 25 Dec, 1 Jan L, Food & Wine Festival **Prices** Fixed L 3 course £26, Tasting menu £85, Starter £9-£15, Main £27-£30, Dessert £9.50-£12, Service added but optional 10% **Wines** 300 bottles over £20, 9 bottles under £20, 6 by glass **Notes** Fixed D 5 course £58, Sunday L, Vegetarian menu, Dress restrictions, No jeans or trainers **Seats** 70, Pr/dining room 36 **Children** Portions, Menu **Parking** 60

Save on Hotels. Book at **theAA.com/hotel**

LANCASHIRE 225 ENGLAND

LYTHAM ST ANNES   Map 18 SD32

Clifton Arms Hotel

British

Modern British cooking on the seafront

☎ 01253 739898
West Beach FY8 5QJ
e-mail: welcome@cliftonarms-lytham.com
dir: On A584 along seafront

The Clifton Arms, a Grade II listed red-brick hotel, is in a prime spot on the seafront, and its restaurant has tab sea views. White-clothed tables are correctly set, candles are lit in the evening, and smartly dressed staff are formal but friendly. The kitchen makes the most of its location, buying Bowland beef - the fillet, perhaps, accompanied by blade braised with root vegetables served with creamed potatoes - Goosnargh chicken, and fish from Fleetwood, and it has created a menu along modern lines of seared scallops with crisp pork belly, cauliflower purée, and five-spice jus, and roast cannon of lamb served with tomato and basil butter and chargrilled vegetables. Cheeses are all from Lancashire, and treacle tart with berry compôte and vanilla ice cream may be among desserts.

Chef Dean Piavani **Owner** David Webb
Times 12-2.30/6.30-9 **Prices** Fixed D 3 course £25-£28.50, Starter £5-£12.50, Main £12.95-£29, Dessert £5.50-£8.50, Service optional **Wines** 55 bottles over £20, 19 bottles under £20, 10 by glass **Notes** Sunday L, Vegetarian available, Civ Wed 100 **Seats** 60, Pr/dining room 140 **Children** Portions **Parking** 50

Greens Bistro

Modern British

Charming basement bistro with Lancashire cooking

☎ 01253 789990
3-9 St Andrews Road South, St Annes-on-Sea FY8 1SX
e-mail: info@greensbistro.co.uk
dir: Just off St Annes Sq

Just off St Annes Square, Greens is an intimate, low-ceilinged basement venue offering a degree of rustic charm a short way down the coast from Blackpool. With its various little hideaway nooks and alcoves, it's definitely the place to bring your loved one, and the Websters are practised hosts, Anna front of house and Paul in the kitchen. The bill of fare is an unashamedly Lancashire version of modern bistro food, with many reliable local ingredients on parade. Singleton's Lancashire cheese and bacon tart with a green salad is a good start, while Goosnargh duck leg may appear confit-fashion, with honey-roasted parsnips and its own gravy. Ribble sea bass is a possible fish option, served with rösti potato and creamed leeks, and homely puddings include Bramley apple crumble with cinnamon ice cream.

Chef Paul Webster **Owner** Paul & Anna Webster
Times 6-10 Closed 25 Dec, BHs, 2 wks Jan, 1 wk summer, Sun Mon, L all week **Prices** Food prices not confirmed for 2013. Please telephone for details **Wines** 7 bottles over

£20, 15 bottles under £20, 7 by glass **Notes** Vegetarian available **Seats** 38 **Children** Portions **Parking** On street

PRESTON   Map 18 SD52

The Pines Hotel

Traditional British

Classy cooking in charming hotel

☎ 01772 338551
570 Preston Rd, Clayton-Le-Woods PR6 7ED
e-mail: mail@thepineshotel.co.uk
web: www.thepineshotel.co.uk
dir: M6 junct 28/29 off A6 & S of B5256

Sticklers for tradition will find much to love at The Pines Hotel. Owned and managed by Betty Duffin for nigh-on half a century, it is this deep-rooted personal touch that makes the hotel a sincerely friendly place that stands out from the corporate crowd. Originally a Victorian cotton mill owner's residence, it is set in four acres of lovely landscaped gardens and mature woodland, and has been extended to cope with the brisk trade in weddings and conferences. If you can't find something that appeals on the truly compendious menu in the Haworth Restaurant you must be a difficult person to please. A hearty starter partners wood pigeon breast with confit pork belly, Lancashire black pudding, shallot purée and game jus, while mains could deliver roast breast and braised leg of guinea fowl in tomato, bacon and chestnut sauce with dauphinoise potatoes and root vegetable purée.

Chef Ryan Greene **Owner** Betty Duffin
Times 12-2.30/6-9.30 **Prices** Fixed L 2 course fr £12.50, Fixed D 3 course fr £16.50, Starter £4.90-£9.25, Main £11.50-£28, Dessert £5.25-£7, Service optional **Wines** 22 bottles over £20, 25 bottles under £20, 7 by glass **Notes** Sunday L, Vegetarian available, Dress restrictions, No jeans, T-shirts/trainers, cabaret evenings, Civ Wed 250 **Seats** 95, Pr/dining room 46 **Children** Portions, Menu **Parking** 150

See advert on page 226

THORNTON   Map 18 SD34

Twelve Restaurant and Lounge Bar

Modern British

Lancastrian cooking in contemporary setting next to a windmill

☎ 01253 821212
Marsh Mill Village, Marsh Mill-in-Wyre, Fleetwood Road North FY5 4JZ
e-mail: info@twelve-restaurant.co.uk
web: www.twelve-restaurant.co.uk
dir: A585 follow signs for Marsh Mill Complex. Turn right into Victoria Rd East, entrance 0.5m on left

Right next to a working windmill in Thornton Cleveleys (yes, they've got one), Twelve is a stripped-down contemporary eatery that wouldn't look out of place in a city-centre redevelopment. Stark clean lines frame the interior styling, where Pop Art montages, vermilion walls and cubist bar stools make a statement. Lancastrian cooking with flourishes of Français is the business, ranging from starters such as pig's head croquette with Puy lentils and apple purée to mains along the lines of roast breast and confit leg of guinea fowl with parsnip purée, or fried cod with fennel vierge and mini-fondant potatoes. Threesomes are popular, whether for cuts of beef, bits of lamb, or the local cheese selection, but desserts may go one better, with four in one under the distinctly vernacular rubric of 'Banana Butty'.

Chef Paul Moss **Owner** Paul Moss & Caroline Upton
Times 12-3/6.30-12 Closed 1st 2 wks Jan, Mon, L Tue-Sat **Prices** Fixed L 3 course £16.95, Fixed D 3 course £19.90-£27.50, Starter £5.95-£13.25, Main £14.95-£26, Dessert

continued

ROSETTE AWARD

AA Rosette Award for Culinary Excellence

THE
Pines

HOTEL & ROSETTE RESTAURANT

The Pines Hotel is independently owned and has been in the same family since 1963. Over the years the Victorian Cotton Mill owners' house has been extensively extended. His once billiard room is now, some might say, the best 300 seat function room in the North West.

The hotel restaurant, "Haworth's" (the owners maiden name), has enjoyed the accolade of being awarded the acclaimed AA Rosette since 2003.

The menu is of classic English style which is in keeping with the style & décor of the restaurant. All produce is sourced locally except the meat, which is from Donald Russell in Aberdeenshire, Scotland who supplies premium meats to some of the finest restaurants and hotels across the globe.

The menu includes Scallops, Dover Sole, Venison and Chateaubriand. To complete your meal the Assiette of Desserts is a mouth watering must have.

In such beautiful & comfortable surroundings, a meal at The Pines is always a memorable occasion.

The Pines Hotel & Haworth Restaurant
570 Preston Road, Clayton-le-Woods, Chorley, Lancashire PR6 7ED
T: 01772 338551 | E: mail@thepineshotel.co.uk | W: www.thepineshotel.co.uk

THORNTON *continued*

£5.95-£8.95, Service optional **Wines** 53 bottles over £20, 22 bottles under £20, 12 by glass **Notes** Sunday L, Vegetarian available **Seats** 90 **Children** Portions **Parking** 150

See advert below

WHALLEY   Map 18 SD73

The Freemasons at Wiswell

◉◉ Modern British **NEW**

Seriously skilful cooking in village gastro-pub

☎ 01254 822218

8 Vicarage Fold, Wiswell BB7 9DF

e-mail: steve@freemasonswiswell.co.uk

dir: A59, located on the edge of Whalley village near Clitheroe

Funny handshakes and rolled-up trouser legs are not required to gain admission to this rustic country gastro-pub, although it might take you some time to track it down in the narrow back streets of the chocolate-box village of Wiswell. Inside are flagstoned floors, antique rugs and furniture, and huntin' shootin' fishin'-themed paintings on heritage-hued walls, while the kitchen works to an ethos that aims to satisfy rather than push the culinary envelope. Chef-patron Steven Smith knows his onions and has strong supply lines to local suppliers, having worked in some of the North's top kitchens before going solo, and sends out inventive, technically-accomplished dishes that use Granny Smith apple jelly, smoked almonds and tandoori-spiced brown butter to point up the sweetness of pleasingly plump scallops. There is plenty of fun and perfect balance of taste and textures in the whimsically-named 'Anna's Happy Trotters', which sees roast loin of pork teamed with black pudding purée, gammon, poached pineapple, a breaded quail's egg, and a pork pie sauce that nails the essence of that particular delicacy. Pudding takes its title from the legendary chocolatier Michel Cluizel, whose peerless products are at the heart of a dark chocolate cone filled with passionfruit mousse, served with passionfruit sorbet and banana tart.

Chef Steven Smith **Owner** Steven Smith **Times** 12-2.30/5.30-9.30 Closed 2 Jan for 2 wks, Mon **Prices** Fixed L 3 course fr £15.95, Tasting menu £55, Starter £7.95-£15.95, Main £15.95-£29.95, Dessert £7.95-£9.95, Service optional **Wines** 200 bottles over £20, 2 bottles under £20, 30 by glass **Notes** Fixed L 3 course seasonal menu also offered early supper, Sunday L, Vegetarian available **Seats** 70, Pr/dining room 12 **Children** Portions **Parking** In village

The Three Fishes

◉ Traditional British 🍃

Refined traditional food in a rural pub

☎ 01254 826888

Mitton Rd, Mitton BB7 9PQ

e-mail: enquiries@thethreefishes.com

web: www.thethreefishes.com

dir: M6 junct 31, A59 to Clitheroe. Follow Whalley signs, B6246, 2m

The Three Fishes has the sort of look you'd hope for in a 400-year-old inn in a tiny village: stone walls, rugs on a slate floor, log fires, upholstered benches and wooden tables, and better still, it is part of the group run by Nigel Haworth and Craig Bancroft of Northcote fame (see entry). The kitchen is dedicated to supporting 'local food heroes' and building on Lancashire's culinary traditions. A high level of integrity is evident here; dishes tend to be

continued

THE THREE FISHES AT MITTON

AWARD-WINNING FOOD.
FRESH LOCAL INGREDIENTS.
THE PERFECT LOCAL PUB.

Now a legend in these parts, this 400 year old pub was the first Ribble Valley Inn to open and launched the idea of creating traditional regional classics, but with an inspired and contemporary twist...landing an impressive catch of top national awards in the process!

- New Seasonal Menu and new Wine List
- Produce sourced from our local food heroes
- Classic Lancashire dishes, with a contemporary twist ...inspired by Michelin Star chef Nigel Haworth
- Selection of Yorkshire & Lancashire cask ales and fine wines

- Healthy and nutritional Kids' Menu and new Kids' activities too
- Landscaped gardens for alfresco summer dining
- Crackling log fires in the winter months

PUB OPENING TIMES
Monday - Saturday 12 noon - 11.00pm , Sunday 12 noon - 10.30pm

FOOD SERVED
Lunch	Mon - Sat Noon - 2.00pm, Sun Noon - 8.00pm
Afternoon Bites	Mon - Sat 2.00pm - 5.30pm
Dinner	Mon - Thur 5.30pm - 8.30pm, Fri & Sat 5.30pm - 9.00pm, Sun Noon - 8.00pm
Bank Holidays	Open all day Noon - 8.00pm for food Food service times indicate the last order times.

VIEW OUR WEBSITE FOR TODAY'S MENUS

THE THREE FISHES
A RIBBLE VALLEY INN

Less than 15 miles from junction 31 on the M6
Less than 8 miles from junction 7 on the M65

Join us on Facebook and Twitter facebook.com/RibbleValleyInns twitter.com/RVIpubs

THE THREE FISHES • MITTON ROAD • MITTON NR WHALLEY • LANCASHIRE BB7 9PQ
TEL 01254 826888 FAX 01254 826026 WWW.THETHREEFISHES.COM

WHALLEY *continued*

uncomplicated, flavours clear, presentation attractive. Bury black pudding with onion relish and mustard or treacle-cured salmon with pikelets may precede fish pie, Lancashire hotpot, or a chargrilled steak. A trio of 'European classics' includes daube de boeuf, and desserts are unabashedly English, from parkin to moreish sticky toffee pudding.

The Three Fishes

Chef Andy McCarthy **Owner** Craig Bancroft & Nigel Haworth **Times** 12-2/5.30-8.30 Closed 25 Dec **Prices** Fixed L 2 course £11.50, Fixed D 3 course £15, Starter £4.75-£8, Main £9-£17, Dessert £5-£5.50, Service optional **Wines** 20 bottles over £20, 16 bottles under £20, 5 by glass **Notes** Fixed L & D 2 or 3 course Mon-Thu only, Sunday L, Vegetarian available **Seats** 140 **Children** Portions, Menu **Parking** 70

See advert opposite

WHITEWELL   Map 18 SD64

The Inn at Whitewell

Modern British

Traditional rural inn with a local flavour

☎ 01200 448222
Forest of Bowland, Clitheroe BB7 3AT
e-mail: reception@innatwhitewell.com
dir: From S M6 junct 31 Longridge follow Whitewell signs. From N M6 junct 33 follow Trough of Bowland & Whitewell signs

This rural 16th-century inn overlooking the River Hodder has bags of appeal. The Forest of Bowland along the valley makes for quite a view for a start, while stone floors, old beams, roaring fires and antique furniture are all you might hope for within. Take a seat wherever the mood takes you, be it in the informal bar area with wooden tables or the plusher main restaurant complete with linen tablecloths and smart table settings. Local ingredients make a good showing on the menu; start perhaps with seared scallops with grilled black pudding, minted pea purée, smoked bacon lardons and a watercress dressing, before moving on to roast rack of Burholme Lonk lamb cooked with cumin, tomatoes and garlic. Puddings take the comfort route - banoffee pie with dark chocolate, for example.

Chef Jamie Cadman **Owner** Charles Bowman **Times** 12-2/7.30-9.30 **Prices** Food prices not confirmed for 2013. Please telephone for details **Wines** 120 bottles over £20, 60 bottles under £20, 20 by glass

Notes Vegetarian available, Civ Wed 80 **Seats** 60, Pr/dining room 20 **Children** Portions **Parking** 70

WRIGHTINGTON   Map 15 SD51

The Mulberry Tree

Modern British

Lancashire gastro-pub with unfussy cooking

☎ 01257 451400
Wrightington Bar WN6 9SE
e-mail: info@themulberrytree.info
dir: 4m from Wigan. From M6 junct 27 towards Parbold, right after motorway exit, by BP garage into Mossy Lea Rd. On right after 2m

Originally built as a wheelwrights in 1832, The Mulberry Tree is handily situated close to the M6 in a peaceful Lancashire village. It's a convivial place to eat sure enough, with a decidedly gastro-pub vibe going on; there's a busy bar and a trad restaurant with white painted walls hung with copper pans, red flowery carpet and clothed tables. The expansive menu of crowd-pleasers shows broad global influences with a decent showing of local produce. Start perhaps with sautéed Loch Fyne scallops served with Bury black pudding and pea purée, following on with something from the 'Lancashire classics' section such as a trio of Green's butcher's pork sausages (Lancashire cheese, Branston pickle and black pudding) with creamed potatoes, roast gravy and seasonal vegetables.

Times 12-2.30/6-9.30 Closed 26 Dec, 1 Jan

LEICESTERSHIRE

BELTON   Map 11 SK42

The Queen's Head

British

Modern gastro-pub with broad appeal

☎ 01530 222359
2 Long St LE12 9TP
e-mail: enquiries@thequeenshead.org
web: www.thequeenshead.org
dir: Located just off B5324 between Loughborough and Ashby-de-la-Zouch

In a pretty little village, The Queen's Head has been given an up-to-the-minute look, with furniture to match the décor: leather sofas in the bar and modern wooden tables and chairs in the dining areas, with contemporary artwork on the walls, and the ambience throughout is casual and relaxed. Pub stalwarts like shepherd's and fish pies, served with seasonal vegetables, and beefburger with chips have their fans, judging by the numbers of contented diners, and you can eat very well from the rest of the appealing menu, which eschews the normal three-course format in favour of small and large dishes: salmon and prawn fishcake with salsa and tartare sauce, crisp pork belly with black pudding, apple and mash, and pan-fried scallops with chorizo, pickled apple and watercress.

Times 12-2.30/6-9.30 Closed 25-26 Dec, L Sun

CASTLE DONINGTON

For restaurant details see East Midlands Airport

EAST MIDLANDS AIRPORT   Map 11 SK42

Best Western Premier Yew Lodge Hotel & Spa

British

Peaceful country hotel with creative cooking

☎ 01509 672518
Packington Hill DE74 2DF
e-mail: info@yewlodgehotel.co.uk
dir: M1 junct 24. Follow signs to Loughborough & Kegworth on A6. On entering village, 1st right, after 400yds hotel on right

Although it sits just minutes from the motorway network and East Midlands airport, the Yew Lodge Hotel is a surprisingly peaceful hideaway. The split-level bistro-style Orchard Restaurant is tended by smartly-uniformed and welcoming staff who play their part in ensuring the place is as well-supported by locals as it is by hotel diners. The skilled kitchen takes classic ideas and adds a contemporary spin here and there, perhaps surprise ingredients such as white chocolate and champagne added to a classic pairing of seared scallops and black pudding, or the sharpness of radish, carrot and citrus to cut the richness of a hay-smoked salmon cheesecake. Mains could bring on pork Wellington with pig's cheek, apple and wild mushrooms, or fish, in the shape of turbot fillet with mussels, curry, coriander, onion and garlic. Dessert could be a playful 'Night at the Movies' assemblage of popcorn, Oreo biscuit, Cola, candyfloss, caramel and retro sweets.

Chef Trevor Bearder **Owner** Pick Family **Times** 12-2/6.30-9.30 Closed L Sat **Prices** Fixed L 2 course £12.95, Fixed D 3 course £29.80-£35.40, Starter £6.25-£7.50, Main £16.95-£19.95, Dessert £5.95-£7.95, Service optional **Wines** 3 bottles over £20, 27 bottles under £20, 10 by glass **Notes** Sunday L, Vegetarian available, Dress restrictions, Smart casual, Civ Wed 250 **Seats** 90, Pr/dining room 20 **Children** Portions, Menu **Parking** 188

The Priest House Hotel

◉◉ Modern British V

Fine dining in historic house

☎ 0845 072 7502
Kings Mills, Castle Donington DE74 2RR
e-mail: thepriesthouse@handpicked.co.uk
dir: M1 junct 24, onto A50, take 1st slip road signed
Castle Donington. Right at lights, hotel in 2m

The area is well known for its high-octane car racing or
rock concerts in the nearby Donington Park, but this
historic house - now contemporary country-house hotel -
on the banks of the Trent, offers a more tranquil retreat.
At its culinary heart, a classy fine-dining restaurant
blends stylish modernity (leather banquettes, white linen
and contemporary art) with heavy beams and exposed
stone walls. The kitchen's up-to-date cooking -
underpinned by classic technique - fits with the
surroundings, fashioned from quality produce, including
beef, pork and lamb from the Chatsworth Estate. Expect
the likes of pan-fried black bream accompanied by
roasted garlic and parsley risotto with a port reduction,
while that Chatsworth House beef could be partnered
with root vegetables, wild mushroom and red wine sauce.
A cheffy 'trio of apple' (tarte Tatin, trifle and apple pie ice
cream) brings you across the finish line.

Chef Paul Soczowka **Owner** Hand Picked Hotels
Times 12-2.30/7-9.30 Closed L Sat, D Sun
Wines 125 bottles over £20, 31 by glass **Notes** Fine
Dining Seasonal Menu £39, Sunday L, Vegetarian menu,
Civ Wed 120 **Seats** 34, Pr/dining room 100
Children Portions, Menu **Parking** 100

HINCKLEY
Map 11 SP49

Sketchley Grange Hotel

◉◉ British, European

Sound modern British cooking in a spa retreat

☎ 01455 251133
Sketchley Ln, Burbage LE10 3HU
e-mail: reservations@sketchleygrange.co.uk
dir: From M69 junct 1 take B4109 (Hinckley). Straight on
1st rdbt, left at 2nd rdbt & immediately right into
Sketchley Lane. Hotel at end of lane

Just inside Leicestershire, right on the border with
Worcestershire, Sketchley Grange is a mock-Tudor country
house which has been extended and upgraded over the
years to create a luxurious hotel with a range of top-notch
facilities. There are lovely grounds to explore, a spa to
relax in, and a choice of restaurants including The Dining
Room - an elegant and intimate setting in which to enjoy
some contemporary fine-dining. You might start with
chilli and coriander beef carpaccio with horseradish and
cornichon, then follow with steamed fillet of wild sea
bass partnered with seared scallops, parsley potatoes,
leeks, sun-dried tomatoes and a langoustine and basil
cream. Chocoholics will rejoice in the 'tasting of
chocolate' - a combination of a milk chocolate

pannacotta, dark chocolate brownie and a scoop of white
chocolate and basil ice cream.

Times 7-9.30 Closed Mon, L Tue-Sat, D Sun

KEGWORTH

For restaurant details see East Midlands Airport

KIBWORTH
Map 11 SP69

Firenze Restaurant

◉◉ Italian NEW

Ambitious Italian cooking in the town centre

☎ 0116 2796260
9 Station St LE8 0LN
e-mail: info@firenze.co.uk
dir: On A6 between Leicester & Market Harborough

Formerly a musical instrument shop, Lino and Sarah
Poli's Italian restaurant is a low-ceilinged, comfortable
place done in violet and cream, with a pine floor and an
air of breezy informality. They have built up a tenacious
local following for a repertoire of traditional and modern
Mediterranean dishes. Linen-dressed tables decorated
with coloured stones form a smart backdrop for such
seasonally inspired offerings as prawn and courgette
pappardelle in saffron sauce, and beetroot and goats'
cheese ravioli. Unusual ingredients suggest a desire to
push the boundaries, as when slivers of deep-fried pig's
tail turn up with peppery scallops and puréed peas. If
you've skipped an intermediate pasta course, you could
still get your fill in mains such as roast quail with
sausage tortellini, served with forthrightly seasoned
polenta, while a new spin on the familiar pear in red wine
sees that fruit poached in brown butter, and
accompanied by rich chocolate ice cream, powdered dried
raspberries and popcorn. Italian-style breads come with a
selection of oils, vinegars and tapenade.

Chef Lino Poli & Max Faulkner **Owner** Lino & Sarah Poli
Times 12-2.30/7-10.30 Closed 4/5 days at Xmas, Sun-
Mon **Prices** Fixed L 2 course fr £17.50, Fixed D 3 course fr
£22.50, Starter £6.25-£8.50, Main £16-£20, Dessert £7-
£9.75, Service optional **Wines** 51 bottles over £20,
12 bottles under £20, 11 by glass **Notes** Tasting menu 5,
6 or 7 course by arrangement, Vegetarian available
Seats 60 **Children** Portions **Parking** On street, car park
nearby

LEICESTER
Map 11 SK50

Hotel Maiyango

◉ Modern European ◔

Fab décor and smart modern European cooking

☎ 0116 251 8898
13-21 St Nicholas Place LE1 4LD
e-mail: reservations@maiyango.com
web: www.maiyango.com
dir: M1 junct 21, A5460 for 3.5m. Turn right onto A47
round St Nicholas Circle onto St Nicholas Place

With its rooftop cocktail bar and new Deli Kitchen, this
city centre boutique hotel has got it all going on. The
décor is Moroccan and Middle Eastern inspired, so expect
sumptuous fabrics in cushions and drapes, lanterns and
darkwood tables, charcoal- and tangerine-coloured seats,
not forgetting some eclectic world beats while you eat.
Modern European cuisine is on the menu and the kitchen
takes it commitment to sourcing locally seriously; fresh
produce comes daily from the community allotment three
miles away and the flour used in their bread is milled in
nearby Claybrooke Magna. Tuck into smoked guinea fowl,
ham hock and apple terrine with watercress, pickled
radish and toasted brioche, then seared sea bass with
shellfish foam, saffron linguini, creamed peppers and
capers, winding up with mocha fondant with salted
caramel ice cream.

Chef Phillip Sharpe **Owner** Aatin Anadkat
Times 12.30-2.30/6.30-9.45 Closed 25 Dec, 1 Jan, L Sun
Prices Fixed L 2 course £16.50-£18.50, Fixed D 3 course
£29-£35, Service optional, Groups min 6 service 10%
Wines 46 bottles over £20, 16 bottles under £20, 12 by
glass **Notes** Tasting & pre-theatre menus available,
Vegetarian available **Seats** 55, Pr/dining room 80
Children Portions **Parking** NCP

LONG WHATTON
Map 11 SK42

The Royal Oak

◉ Modern British ◔

**Skilful modern cooking in a smartly modernised village
inn**

☎ 01509 843694
26 The Green LE12 5DB
e-mail: enquiries@theroyaloaklongwhatton.co.uk

Once a run-down old village boozer, The Royal Oak has
turned around its fortunes with a complete facelift. It is
now the sort of place where you can spend a night in one
of the classy new bedrooms after giving the eating and
drinking side of the operation a thorough workout. The
kitchen sticks to a tried-and-true formula: local produce
is the name of the game and it appears in an appealing
repertoire of modern British dishes. Game terrine of
partridge, pheasant and duck with chestnut purée,
clementine marmalade and toasted brioche is one way to
start, while an assiette of pork - loin stuffed with
apricots, slow-roasted belly, black pudding fritter and
crackling served with sage and pancetta potatoes, mulled
red cabbage and a cider reduction - makes a tempting

case for main course. End with Bakewell tart with clotted cream.

Chef James & Charles Upton, Shaun McDonnell **Owner** Alex & Chris Astwood **Times** 12-2.30/5.30-9.30 Closed D Sun **Prices** Fixed L 2 course £13.50, Fixed D 3 course £27, Starter £4.50-£7.50, Main £9.95-£22, Dessert £5.50-£6.75, Service optional **Wines** 14 bottles over £20, 17 bottles under £20, 9 by glass **Notes** Early doors menu Mon-Fri 5.30-6.30, Sunday L, Vegetarian available **Seats** 45 **Children** Portions **Parking** 30

MELTON MOWBRAY   Map 11 SK71

Stapleford Park

◉◉ Modern French, British ⚑

Fine dining amid the splendour of 'Capability' Brown parkland

☎ 01572 787000 & 787019
Stapleford LE14 2EF
e-mail: reservations@stapleford.co.uk
dir: A1 to Colsterworth onto B676, signed Melton Mowbray. In approx 9m turn left to Stapleford

Set in 500 acres of 'Capability' Brown-designed parkland, Stapleford is a truly stately home that trades as a full-works country-house hotel, replete with all of the spa, pampering and championship golf diversions you would expect in a house of this standing. The old pile has been around since the 14th century, but what we're seeing today is a hybrid of Georgian and Victorian styles, courtesy of a beer magnate who tacked on a huge wing, which is home to the Grinling Gibbons Restaurant, an extravaganza of luminous pastel-hued panelling, fine plasterwork and crystal chandeliers, named after the Victorian master woodcarver who did the amazing mantelpiece. It is an aptly opulent setting for classically-rooted modern cooking of serious intent, with luxury ingredients setting the tone in a starter of foie gras, salted caramel pear and Sauternes jelly. Main course capitalises on quality local produce with slow-cooked belly and braised cheek of pork with butternut gratin and purée and spice jus, then dessert deconstructs carrot cake with an assemblage of light sponge surrounded by carrot jelly, cream cheese sorbet and walnut parfait.

Times 11.30-2.30/7-9.30 Closed exclusive use days, D Sun-Tue

NORTH KILWORTH   Map 11 SP68

Kilworth House Hotel & Theatre

◉◉ Modern British **V**

Modern country-house cooking in a luxury hotel

☎ 01858 880058
Lutterworth Rd LE17 6JE
e-mail: info@kilworthhouse.co.uk
dir: A4304 towards Market Harborough, after Walcote, hotel 1.5m on right

Period authenticity runs through this Italianate 19th-century mansion thanks to a top-to-toe restoration

overseen by the eagle eyes of English Heritage. Only two families lived in it for 120 years before it became an upmarket country-house hotel in the noughties with all the plush style, fittings and furniture befitting a hotel of this standing (including, these days, an open-air theatre in the grounds). If you want to see what the chefs can do, the Wordsworth Restaurant is the fine-dining venue, a truly remarkable confection of stained-glass windows, rich red patterned wallpaper and burnished antique tables beneath a lanterned dome of elaborate plasterwork and twinkling chandeliers; in short, the sort of place you feel that best bib and tucker is required. The scene thus set, what's on the menu is classic country-house cooking brought gently up to date - seared scallops with spiced tomato relish and parsnip purée, for example, while at main course duck is served three ways as breast, confit and rillettes, with pommes Anna, pickled cabbage and orange. If you're in the market for fish, consider brill with sweet potato and coconut curry and red lentil salsa.

Chef Carl Dovey **Owner** Mr & Mrs Mackay
Times 12-3/7-9.30 Closed L Sun-Tue **Prices** Fixed D 3 course fr £40, Starter £8-£15, Main £15-£25, Dessert £8-£12, Service optional **Wines** 49 bottles over £20, 12 bottles under £20, 10 by glass **Notes** Theatre menu in season 3 course £28, Vegetarian menu, Dress restrictions, No jeans or trainers, Civ Wed 150 **Seats** 70, Pr/dining room 130 **Children** Portions, Menu **Parking** 140

WOODHOUSE EAVES   Map 11 SK51

The Woodhouse

◉◉ Modern British

Vibrant cooking in stylish village restaurant

☎ 01509 890318
43 Maplewell Rd, Woodhouse Eaves LE12 8RG
e-mail: info@thewoodhouse.co.uk
web: www.thewoodhouse.co.uk
dir: M1 junct 23 towards Loughborough, right into Nanpantan Rd, left into Beacon Rd, right in Main St & again into Maplewell Rd

A little village near Leicester seems an unlikely spot in which to find this thoroughly up-to-the-minute-looking restaurant, its striking red walls hung with modern art, with upholstered dining chairs at properly set tables. The cooking can be pretty racy too. How about foie gras with rhubarb tapioca, smoked rhubarb, dehydrated honey cake, duck liver macaroon, walnuts and dandelion? Such dishes sound laboured, but a thoughtful, professional chef manages to pull them together into a pleasing whole. Other starters can seem calmer in comparison: for

instance, crispy pork belly served with confit egg yolk, black pudding and caper berries. Main courses show a painstaking amount of workmanship and skill, with spring lamb appearing four ways - belly, neck, cannon and cured - with parmesan gnocchi, watercress and baby onions. The same sense of enthusiastic experimentation creeps into desserts as well: try chocolate fondant with popcorn ice cream and caramel jelly.

Chef Paul Leary **Owner** Paul Leary **Times** 12-3/6.30-12 Closed BHs, Mon, L Sat, D Sun **Prices** Fixed L 2 course £15.95, Fixed D 2 course £21.95, Tasting menu £65, Service optional **Wines** 130 bottles over £20, 4 bottles under £20, 8 by glass **Notes** Fixed ALC 3 course £37.50, Sunday L **Seats** 50, Pr/dining room 40 **Children** Portions **Parking** 15

LINCOLNSHIRE

GRANTHAM   Map 11 SK93

Harry's Place

◉◉◉ – *see page 232*

HORNCASTLE   Map 17 TF26

Magpies Restaurant with Rooms

◉◉ British, European ✿

Creative modern cooking in Lincolnshire Wolds

☎ 01507 527004
73 East St LN9 6AA
dir: 0.5m from town centre on A158 towards Skegness

In a row of 200-year-old black and cream cottages, Magpies has a warm and relaxing air, created by a colour scheme of honey and russet and by friendly and attentive service. The kitchen's well placed to pick up the best Lincolnshire agricultural produce and uses it in a modern British repertory, epitomised by such main courses as loin of lamb with cauliflower roasted with walnuts, served with fig and mustard seed tart, and a rib-sticking winter dish of braised oxtail with creamy mash and glazed root vegetables. Fish is well timed and treated imaginatively - fillet of cod is studded with pancetta and garlic and sauced with rhubarb and star anise - and dishes can have multi layers of ingredients and flavours, seen in starters of crab with lime mayonnaise, crayfish tortellini, and scallops with lemongrass sauce, or guinea fowl and ham hock terrine with a salad of beetroot, radish, and goats' cheese. Puddings can bring together myriads of flavours: try warm rice pudding with blood orange sorbet and blood oranges in cardamom caramel syrup.

Chef Andrew Gilbert **Owner** Caroline Gilbert **Times** 12-2/7-9.30 Closed 27 Dec, 1st wk Jan, Mon-Tue, L Sat **Prices** Fixed L 2 course £20, Fixed D 3 course £42, Service optional **Wines** 62 bottles over £20, 50 bottles under £20, 6 by glass **Notes** Sunday L, Vegetarian available, Dress restrictions, Smart casual **Seats** 34 **Children** Portions **Parking** On street

HOUGH-ON-THE-HILL   Map 11 SK94

The Brownlow Arms

◉ British

Well-judged menu in a smart village inn

☎ 01400 250234
High Rd NG32 2AZ
e-mail: armsinn@yahoo.co.uk
dir: Take A607 (Grantham to Sleaford road). Hough-on-the-Hill signed from Barkston

A 17th-century country inn, formerly owned by Lord Brownlow funnily enough, in a picturesque Lincolnshire village, today's incarnation feels like a country-house hotel as much as anything else. The bar stocks local ales and an open fire warms up the old oak beams, while in the dining room tapestry-backed chairs and polished wooden tables set the scene. On warmer days the landscaped terrace comes into its own. With a good showing of local produce, the dishes on offer are given a bit of a contemporary polish, so you might start with pork belly and mixed fruit terrine with pistachios and spiced plum chutney, followed by fillet of turbot with braised fennel, olive oil, orange and aged balsamic dressing, with hot plum tarte Tatin and Mirabelle plum sorbet for dessert.

Chef Oliver Snell **Owner** Paul & Lorraine Willoughby
Times 12-3/6.30-9.30 Closed 25-26 Dec, Mon, L Tue-Sat, D Sun **Prices** Food prices not confirmed for 2013. Please telephone for details **Wines** 4 bottles over £20, 4 bottles under £20, 5 by glass **Notes** Vegetarian available **Seats** 80, Pr/dining room 26 **Parking** 26, On street

LINCOLN   Map 17 SK97

Branston Hall Hotel

◉◉ Modern British Ⅴ

Complex modern British food with lake and parkland views

☎ 01522 793305
Lincoln Rd, Branston Park, Branston LN4 1PD
e-mail: info@branstonhall.com
web: www.branstonhall.com
dir: On B1188, 3m S of Lincoln. In village, hotel drive opposite village hall

Branston Hall is an exuberant Victorian country house, with decorative gables and pinnacle chimneys reaching for the stars. Eighty-eight acres of mature parkland do wonders for the feeling of gracious living the place exudes, and it serves its purpose as a retreat hotel in the Lincolnshire countryside with great aplomb. The Lakeside dining room is a restful place, with views over the park to the said stretch of water, and it majors in today's unmistakable culinary style of mingled classical and modern. An appetising array of flavours is assembled in a terrine of rabbit, pistachios and sultanas, accompanied by pickled carrots and Agen prunes. The same may be said of complex but well-balanced main courses such as a double-act of cep-crusted monkfish and sticky salt beef, served with pease pudding and clams, while desserts sing something simpler in the key of liquorice parfait or almond tart.

Branston Hall Hotel

Chef Miles Collins **Owner** Southsprings Ltd
Times 12-2/7-9.30 **Prices** Food prices not confirmed for 2013. Please telephone for details **Wines** 17 bottles over £20, 36 bottles under £20, 14 by glass **Notes** Sunday L, Vegetarian menu, Dress restrictions, Smart casual, no jeans, T-shirts or trainers, Civ Wed 120 **Seats** 75, Pr/dining room 28 **Children** Portions **Parking** 75

See advert opposite

Harry's Place

GRANTHAM   Map 11 SK93

Modern French

Outstanding quality in a restaurant built for ten

☎ 01476 561780
17 High St, Great Gonerby NG31 8JS
dir: 1.5m NW of Grantham on B1174

There's always a waiting list at Harry's Place for two very good reasons: the first is the inspirational cooking of chef-patron Harry Hallam; the second is the fact that a maximum of ten lucky diners are treated to it at each sitting. First impressions are of a very pleasant Georgian house - a former farmhouse and wheelwright's to be precise - sitting modestly behind tall trees. In fact, the place is so unassuming that you could pass right by without realising that Harry and Caroline Hallam's bijou operation is one of Britain's outstanding foodie addresses. Inside, the set-up is equally domestic in scale and ambience: Caroline runs front-of-house single-handedly and with easygoing conviviality in a simple-yet-elegant dining room in which hues of deep red and apple-green predominate, while Harry takes care of business behind the scenes as he has done for the best part of a quarter of a century. The formula is simple enough, but as we all know, the devil is in the detail. Top-class materials are provided by a well-established network of trusted suppliers, and they are brought together with razor-sharp classical French technique and an unerring eye for balance in flavour and texture. The hand-written menu proposes just two choices at each of three courses (sensible given the small scale of the set-up, and it also helps keep a tight rein on quality control) - perhaps escalopes of Norfolk sea trout with a sauce of Sauternes, chives and shallots to start, or a soup, say, fresh tomato and pesto. Sticking with fish for main course, monkfish fillet could arrive lightly-sautéed and matched with white wine, Pernod, basil and coriander sauce, while the meaty alternative could bring local Aberdeen Angus beef fillet with horseradish mayonnaise and sauced with red wine, Armagnac, rosemary, sage and thyme. Vibrant desserts are simplicity itself: caramel mousse brûlée with wild blackberries.

Chef Harry Hallam **Owner** Harry & Caroline Hallam
Times 12.30-3/7-8.30 Closed 2 wks from 25 Dec, Sun-Mon **Prices** Starter £9.50-£18.50, Main £37.50-£39, Dessert £8, Service optional **Wines** All bottles over £20, 4 by glass **Notes** Vegetarian meal on request at time of booking, Vegetarian available **Seats** 10 **Children** Portions **Parking** 4

Welcome to
Branston Hall Hotel
the ultimate Country House Hotel retreat!

This is the perfect place to relax, unwind and enjoy the beautiful Lincolnshire countryside. Explore the city of Lincoln which is a 5 minute drive from this oasis of tranquility.

Our facilities include

- 51 Good sized bedrooms.
- Fine Dining at the AA 2 rosette, elegant Lakeside Restaurant.
- Sunday Lunch & Afternoon tea.
- Parklands indoor swimming pool and fitness Suite.
- Weddings & Private Dining Suites.

- Six Conference rooms with great day rates and residential packages.
- Dip and Dine promotions.
- Simpsons Spa and Spa Breaks.
- Great mid week and weekend Break offers.
- Gift vouchers are available to be used with any of the hotel facilities.

For reservations or further information visit

www.branstonhall.com
or call (01522) 793305

BRANSTON HALL
HOTEL

Branston, Lincoln, LN4 1PD
T: 01522 793305 - F: 01522 790734
info@branstonhall.com
www.branstonhall.com

**CHECK OUT OUR
SPA BREAKS
PACKAGES
ON OUR WEBSITE!**

LINCOLN *continued*

The Lincoln Hotel

◉ Modern British V ✋

Modern brasserie cooking in the uphill quarter

☎ 01522 520348
Eastgate LN2 1PN
e-mail: vandrews@thelincolnhotel.com

The hotel is situated in the historic uphill part of the city, where it enjoys great views of the medieval cathedral, once the tallest building in the world. Bold colour blocks of raspberry, purple and blue defy the beige mindset to create uplifting interiors, though you may be hard pushed to spot any green in the principal restaurant, The Green Room. What you will spot is some confidently handled modern brasserie food founded on big bold flavours. Crisp local pork belly with celeriac and apple remoulade might be the foreword to mains such as sea bass with garlicky potato Anna and tomato and fennel confit, or steak-and-ale pudding with pancetta and mash. The house dessert pairing relieves you of any need to choose between lemon tart and chocolate brownie.

Chef James Maulgue **Owner** Christopher Nevile, Lady Arnold **Times** 6-9.30 Closed Sun-Mon, L all week **Prices** Fixed D 3 course £15-£32, Starter £4-£7, Main £7-£18, Dessert £4-£7, Service optional **Notes** Vegetarian menu, Air con **Seats** 30, Pr/dining room 12 **Children** Portions, Menu

The Old Bakery

◉◉ Modern British ✋

Smart former bakery with local ingredients to the fore

☎ 01522 576057
26-28 Burton Rd LN1 3LB
e-mail: enquiries@theold-bakery.co.uk
dir: From A46 follow directions for Lincoln North then follow brown signs for The Historic Centre

Close to Lincoln Cathedral, this former bakery turned restaurant with rooms is a charmingly rustic place, partly thanks to plenty of surviving period features, and note there's now a fabulous deli from which you can take home all sorts of goodies. The restaurant still has the old ovens in situ (now defunct), plus the original hand-operated wooden mixing vat has been split and made into bench seating, with the rustic-chic dining rooms extending into a conservatory-style garden room. The passionate Italian chef-patron and his small kitchen team deliver clearly flavoured, carefully crafted dishes based on local, seasonal Lincolnshire produce. The weekly-changing menu brings together contemporary British and Italian ideas, so after tucking into home-made foccacia presented in white bags as per a bakery, you can tuck into Eden Farm organic roasted butternut squash and garlic soup with sherry-braised onion crostino and crème fraîche jelly. And for main course Peter Lundgren slow-roasted Gloucestershire Old Spot baby pig might come with stir-fried garlic potato, cinnamon-braised apple and red cabbage, and smoked pancetta cream.

Chef Ivano de Serio **Owner** Alan & Lynn Ritson, Tracey & Ivano de Serio **Times** 12-2.30/7-9.30 Closed 26 Dec, 1 Jan, Mon, D Sun **Prices** Fixed L 2 course £12.50, Starter £5.95-£10.50, Main £13.95-£24.50, Dessert £5.50-£7.50, Service optional **Wines** 37 bottles over £20, 38 bottles under £20, 9 by glass **Notes** Tasting menu 7 or 10 course, Sunday L, Vegetarian available, Dress restrictions, Smart casual **Seats** 85, Pr/dining room 15 **Children** Portions **Parking** On street, public car park 20mtrs

Washingborough Hall Hotel

◉ Modern British

Modern cooking in Georgian country house

☎ 01522 790340
Church Hill, Washingborough LN4 1BE
e-mail: enquiries@washingboroughhall.com
dir: B1190 into Washingborough. Right at rdbt, hotel 500yds on left

Washingborough Hall is a haven of civility: a delightful Georgian manor house earning its living as a switched-on small-scale country-house hotel at the heart of a sleepy Lincolnshire village. Its three acres of glorious grounds aren't just for show - a garden provides herbs for the kitchen, which turns out an enticing line in unaffected modern cooking. The Dining Room restaurant exudes quietly understated class with its restrained heritage colours, unclothed tables, pale wooden floors, ornate marble fireplace and floor-to-ceiling Georgian windows overlooking the garden. The hoped-for Lincolnshire ingredients turn up in inventive contemporary ideas that respect the seasons and aim to soothe rather than challenge; expect starters along the lines of pig's cheek croquette with pineapple salsa salad and wild garlic mayonnaise, followed by rack of local lamb in a Moroccan-inspired casserole with apricot couscous and curly kale.

Chef Dan Wallis **Owner** Mr E & Mrs L Herring **Times** 12-2/6.30-9 **Prices** Food prices not confirmed for 2013. Please telephone for details **Wines** 34 bottles over £20, 16 bottles under £20, 12 by glass **Notes** Alfresco summer menu 2,3 course 12-7pm, Vegetarian available, Dress restrictions, Smart casual **Seats** 50, Pr/dining room 50 **Children** Portions **Parking** 40

Brackenborough Hotel

◉ Modern British ✋

Relaxed bistro dining in rural Lincolnshire

☎ 01507 609169
Cordeaux Corner, Brackenborough LN11 0SZ
e-mail: reception@brackenborough.co.uk
web: www.oakridgehotels.co.uk
dir: Hotel located on main A16 Louth to Grimsby Rd

Formerly part of an arable farm, this red-brick hotel with conference facilities is located in the idyllic Lincolnshire Wolds surrounded by beautifully maintained lawns and gardens with fabulous views over the surrounding countryside. The bistro bar is a swish modish-looking space, with a high vaulted ceiling and contemporary furniture giving it a decidedly 21st-century finish. Working closely with Lincolnshire suppliers, the kitchen delivers a long menu of modern brasserie stuff, with something for everyone. Start with ham hock terrine with piccalilli and mustard cress, following on with main-course honey-roasted duck breast served with a Thai red curry risotto and chargrilled spring onions. For dessert, chocolate brownie crème brûlée with a home-made shortbread biscuit is suitably à la mode.

Chef Tony Greenland **Owner** Ashley Lidgard **Times** 11.30-9.30 **Prices** Fixed L 2 course £9.95-£10.95, Fixed D 3 course £19.95-£29, Starter £4.50-£7.50, Main £9.95-£19.95, Dessert £4.95-£5.75, Service optional **Wines** 42 bottles over £20, 24 bottles under £20, 12 by glass **Notes** Fixed D 2 people/2 course with bottle of wine £33, Sunday L, Vegetarian available, Civ Wed 100 **Seats** 78, Pr/dining room 120 **Children** Portions, Menu **Parking** 80

The Advocate Arms

◉ Modern European **NEW** ✋

Creative ideas in a town-centre restaurant with rooms

☎ 01673 842364
2 Queen St LN8 3EH
e-mail: info@advocatearms.co.uk
dir: Located just off Market Place, High Street

It sounds like a pub, but this handsome 18th-century building in the heart of Market Rasen has been reinvented as a contemporary restaurant with rooms serving a nice line in quietly inventive modern cooking.

Save on Hotels. Book at theAA.com/hotel

LINCOLNSHIRE 235 ENGLAND

The place makes an ideal base if you're in town for the gee gees, as the famous racecourse is just a few minutes drive away, and whether you've lost your shirt or are popping a cork to celebrate a winning streak, commiseration and celebration are on offer in the relaxed and convivial bar and dining rooms. It is a popular venue, where locals pop in for a pint and something toothsome from the bar menu, or you could put the kitchen through its paces with something more involved, such as pan-seared scallops with curried cauliflower purée, squid ink dressing and coconut dust. After that, there might be pork tenderloin medallions teamed with belly pork mousse, breaded black pudding, apple purée, and pork jus flavoured with bayleaf and capers.

Chef Matthew Horsefield **Owner** Darren Lince **Times** 7am–9.30pm Closed D Sun **Prices** Fixed L 2 course £13.95–£19.95, Fixed D 3 course £15.95–£24.95, Starter £4.50–£8.95, Main £9.95–£27.95, Dessert £4.50–£5.95, Service optional **Wines** 24 bottles over £20, 19 bottles under £20, 12 by glass **Notes** Sunday L, Vegetarian available **Seats** 65, Pr/dining room 16 **Children** Portions, Menu **Parking** 6, Short walk

---

SCUNTHORPE — Map 17 SE81

Forest Pines Hotel & Golf Resort

Modern British

Sustainable seafood in a country-house hotel

☎ 01652 650770
Ermine St, Broughton DN20 0AQ
e-mail: forestpines@qhotels.co.uk
dir: From M180 junct 4, travel towards Scunthorpe on A18. Continue straight over rdbt, hotel is situated on left

Say the name 'Grimsby' and the port's fishing heritage immediately springs to mind. The fine-dining restaurant at the swish Forest Pines Hotel & Golf Resort a few miles inland in the North Lincolnshire countryside is called Eighteen57 in honour of the year Grimsby's main fish dock opened. Its interior follows a snazzy piscine theme involving blue mosaic-tiled walls, and pictures, reliefs and murals to celebrate the maritime world. Naturally, local fish and seafood feature prominently, but by no means exclusively, on an enticing modern repertoire produced by a kitchen that has an eye to sustainability in its sourcing policy. Scarborough crabcakes with lemon and chive crème fraîche are a good way to start, followed by line-caught Brixham sea bass with mussel, crab and scampi risotto. As fish is tricky to incorporate into pudding, how about a straightforward vanilla crème brûlée with chocolate chip cookie?

Chef Paul Montgomery **Owner** Q Hotels **Times** 6.30–10 Closed Sun-Mon, L all week **Prices** Tasting menu £39, Starter £5.50–£10.75, Main £15.75–£32.50, Dessert £6.50–£8.75, Service included **Wines** 59 bottles over £20, 7 by glass **Notes** Tasting menu 6 course, Sunday L, Vegetarian available, Dress restrictions, Smart casual, no ripped jeans **Seats** 70 **Children** Menu **Parking** 400

SLEAFORD — Map 12 TF04

The Bustard Inn & Restaurant

Modern British, International

Sensitively refurbished old inn in peaceful village

☎ 01529 488250
44 Main St, South Rauceby NG34 8QG
e-mail: info@thebustardinn.co.uk
dir: A17 from Newark, turn right after B6403 to Ancaster. A153 from Grantham, after Wilsford, turn left for South Rauceby

The local community lost its original boozer when it was demolished in the 19th century to make way for a new entrance to the Rauceby Hall estate, and it got this Victorian inn as its replacement in 1860. Now smartly revitalised with a contemporary country-chic look involving a pared-back décor of dove-grey painted chairs on a flagstone floor, and a solid oak bar, The Bustard now puts food at the heart of the operation. Exposed stone walls, ancient timbers and an ornate oriel window are its original features, which combine with solid ash tables and tapestry chairs in a smart, relaxed setting for modern cooking with its feet on the ground and its roots in local, seasonal ingredients. Start out along the lines of pan-fried scallops with butternut squash purée and chorizo, then move on to loin of Belton Park venison teamed with potato gratin, carrot purée, blackberries and chestnuts, and wrap things up with a Lincolnshire plum bread-and-butter pudding with vanilla ice cream.

Chef Phil Lowe **Owner** Alan & Liz Hewitt **Times** 12-2.30/6-9.30 Closed 1 Jan, Mon, D Sun **Prices** Fixed L 2 course £18.10, Starter £5.50–£13.95, Main £13.50–£25.95, Dessert £5.75–£8.90, Service optional **Wines** 38 bottles over £20, 12 bottles under £20, 12 by glass **Notes** Sunday L, Vegetarian available, Civ Wed 60 **Seats** 66, Pr/dining room 12 **Children** Portions, Menu **Parking** 18, On street

---

STAMFORD — Map 11 TF00

The Bull & Swan at Burghley

Traditional British

Fuss-free classics in historic inn

☎ 01780 766412
St Martins PE9 2LJ
e-mail: enquiries@thebullandswan.co.uk

The 17th-century Bull & Swan has a colourful history involving a drinking club for a bunch of gentlemen reprobates who called themselves the Honourable Order of Little Bedlam and made it their business to quaff local ales, feast on the Burghley Estate and local area's finest morsels, and generally behave badly. The clientele is less lively these days, but the eating and drinking business is still in full swing in a stylishly reworked interior done out with darkwood floors and tables and caramel-hued leather chairs. Local produce is firmly at the heart of the kitchen's output, which eschews faddish foams and jellies and puts its faith in classic rib-sticking ideas along the lines of Grasmere Farm faggots with sauté

potatoes and tomato and garlic sauce, or local pork and apricot sausages with creamy mash and caramelised red cabbage. Elsewhere, there are sharing slates of local fish and meat, and a winter-season game menu majoring in pheasant broth with sherry-infused prunes and leeks, ahead of stuffed saddle of rabbit with mushroom duxelle.

Chef Phil Kent **Owner** Hillbrooke Hotels **Times** 12-2.30/6-9 **Prices** Fixed L 2 course £12.95, Starter £5.50–£9.50, Main £11–£19.50, Dessert £7–£8.50, Service optional **Wines** 15 bottles over £20, 3 bottles under £20, 8 by glass **Notes** Sunday L, Vegetarian available **Seats** 40 **Children** Portions, Menu **Parking** 7

The George of Stamford

Traditional British

Historical institution treasured for its traditional values and cooking

☎ 01780 750750
71 St Martins PE9 2LB
e-mail: reservations@georgehotelofstamford.com
web: www.georgehotelofstamford.com
dir: From A1(N of Peterborough) turn onto B1081 signed Stamford and Burghley House. Follow road to 1st set of lights, hotel on left

It is not often that you can sup a pint in a place where pilgrims and knights of the Holy Sepulchre stopped off on the journey to Jerusalem, but not many inns come with The George's thousand years of history. The Great North Road no longer has the same importance as the days when 40 coaches stopped here each day, but you can still tap into something of the feel of bygone times in the splendid oak-panelled restaurant. There is still a nostalgic adherence to old ways here: roast sirloin of English beef is carved on a trolley at your table, and a straight-up grilled Dover sole is expertly de-boned. Modernists are kept happy too with the likes of confit leg of wood pigeon with cep risotto and espresso jus, followed by a fashionable trio of lamb - seared cutlet, confit shoulder and a little shepherd's pie with spinach purée and roast garlic. Things rewind to a traditional ending when trolleys of cheeses and desserts are wheeled out.

Chef Chris Pitman, Paul Reseigh **Owner** Lawrence Hoskins **Times** 12.30-2.30/7.30-10.30 **Prices** Fixed L 2 course fr £23.50, Starter £6.95–£18.50, Main £14.85–£39.95, Service optional **Wines** 136 bottles over £20, 2 bottles under £20, 19 by glass **Notes** Walk in L menu, Sunday L, Vegetarian available, Dress restrictions, Jacket or tie, no jeans or sportswear, Civ Wed 50 **Seats** 90, Pr/dining room 40 **Children** Portions **Parking** 110

STAMFORD *continued*

Jim's Yard

◉ British, European V ▮ NOTABLE WINE LIST

Bistro cooking in a conservatory restaurant

☎ 01780 756080
3 Ironmonger St PE9 1PL
e-mail: jim@jimsyard.biz

As its name might hint, Jim's Yard is secreted away in two dinky knocked-together cottages in a hidden courtyard in Stamford's historic centre. The luminous dining room opens into a conservatory area with café-style tables and an alfresco terrace in a pretty walled garden; upstairs is a contemporary loft-style space of bare stone walls hung with black-and-white photos of old Stamford. Throughout, the vibe is relaxed and family-run, and the cooking is in the classic bistro mould, starting with a terrine of confit chicken and chorizo wrapped in Parma ham, followed, perhaps, by fillet of sea bream with saffron potatoes, spinach, and mussel butter sauce. End on a resolutely Gallic note with a pukka tarte Tatin with vanilla ice cream.

Chef James Ramsay **Owner** James & Sharon Trevor **Times** 12-2.30/6.30-9.30 Closed 24 Dec 2 wks, last wk Jul-1st wk Aug, Sun-Mon **Prices** Fixed L 2 course £14.50, Fixed D 3 course £19.50, Starter £5-£9, Main £12-£20, Dessert £5-£7, Service optional **Wines** 56 bottles over £20, 28 bottles under £20, 13 by glass **Notes** Vegetarian menu **Seats** 55, Pr/dining room 14 **Children** Portions **Parking** Broad St

The William Cecil

◉ Modern British **NEW**

Confident cooking within the Burghley Estate

☎ 01780 750070
High St PE9 2LG
e-mail: enquiries@thewilliamcecil.co.uk
dir: Exit A1 signed Stamford & Burghley Park. Continue & hotel 1st building on right on entering town

Re-opening after a complete refurbishment in summer 2011, this handsome old hotel on the Burghley Estate successfully melds old and new. In the restaurant, split into two areas using screening, the panelling has been painted a lighter shade to make it less oppressive and in-line with the overall feeling of modernity, while antique looking dark oak tables and chairs retain the period feel. The expansive alfresco area is a great spot when the weather is kind. On the menu, fillet carpaccio with capers, parmesan, rocket and 12-year-old balsamic is a suitably straight-up beginning, before the likes of pan-fried halibut with baby gem lettuce, persillade potatoes, shallot rings and red wine sauce, and to finish, perhaps the sunny flavours of passionfruit and lemon posset with fresh pineapple and mango sorbet.

Owner Hillbrooke Hotels Ltd **Times** 12-3/6-9 **Prices** Fixed L 2 course £16.95-£18.95, Starter £6.75-£10, Main £15-£25, Dessert £7-£9, Service optional **Wines** 18 bottles over £20, 7 bottles under £20, 10 by glass **Notes** 'Speedy Cecil' guarantees 2 or 3 course served in 1 hour, Sunday L, Vegetarian available, Civ Wed 100 **Seats** 72, Pr/dining room 100 **Children** Portions **Parking** 70

Winteringham Fields

◉◉ Modern British, European ▮ NOTABLE WINE LIST

Ambitious cooking in luxurious restaurant with rooms

☎ 01724 733096
1 Silver St DN15 9PF
e-mail: reception@winteringhamfields.co.uk
web: www.winteringhamfields.co.uk
dir: Village centre, off A1077, 4m S of Humber Bridge

This opulent contemporary restaurant with rooms in a stylishly-restored 16th-century manor house feels appealingly lost in the depths of Lincolnshire, yet the Humber Bridge is visible in the distance. The plush, richly-coloured restaurant is a place in which to spoil yourself: a stained-glass dome shelters a cossetting space; chairs are well padded, curtains are swagged back and waiters glide between immaculately-laid tables. It all adds up to a class act where food is taken seriously. Chef-patron Colin McGurran - whom you may recognise as a winner on BBC2's *Great British Menu* in 2012 - cooks with great attention to detail, delivering ambitious modern European ideas wrought from high quality local produce (much grown seasonally in the garden). Yorkshire quail escabèche is teamed with confit leg, quail's egg kebab, and pickled and puréed carrots, ahead of superb fillet of brill with chorizo couscous, bouillabaisse sauce and a vibrant salad of courgettes, peppers and green beans. Dessert delivers a classic crème brûlée with red fruits and brandy snaps.

Chef Colin McGurran **Owner** Colin McGurran **Times** 12-1.30/7-9 Closed 2 wks Xmas, last 2 wks Aug, Sun-Mon **Prices** Fixed L 3 course fr £39.95, Fixed D 3 course fr £59, Service optional **Wines** 200 bottles over £20, 20 by glass **Notes** Menu surprise 10 course £79, Vegetarian available, Dress restrictions, Smart dress preferred, Civ Wed 55 **Seats** 60, Pr/dining room 12 **Children** Portions **Parking** 20

London

London Eye

Index of London Restaurants

This index shows rosetted restaurants in London in alphabetical order, followed by their postcodes and map references. Page numbers precede each entry.

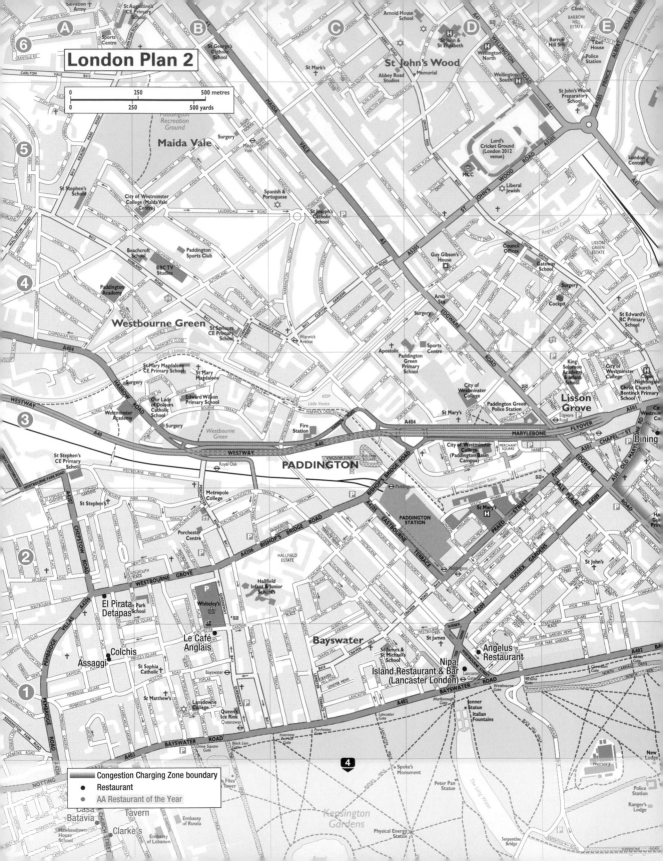

London Plan 2

Maida Vale

Westbourne Green

PADDINGTON

Bayswater

Lisson Grove

St John's Wood

0 250 500 metres
0 250 500 yards

Paddington Recreation Ground

St Augustine's CE Primary School
Salvation Army
Sports Centre
St George's Catholic School
St Mark's
Arnold House School
Abbey Road Studios
St John's Wood Memorial
St John & St Elizabeth
Wellington North
Wellington South
Barrow Hill Sch
Clinic
Barrow Hill Estate
Tibet House
Police Station
St John's Wood Preparatory School
St Joseph's Catholic School
Surgery
Spanish & Portuguese
Lord's Cricket Ground (London 2012 venue)
MCC
Liberal Jewish
London Central
Beachcroft School
BBC TV Studios
Paddington Sports Club
City of Westminster College (Maida Vale Centre)
Paddington Academy
St Stephen's School
Guy Gibson's House
Council Offices
Gateway School
Surgery
Cockpit
St Edward's RC Primary School
St Saviour's CE Primary School
St Mary Magdalene CE Primary School
St Mary Magdalene
Our Lady of Dolours Catholic School
Edward Wilson Primary School
Westbourne Academy
Surgery
Warwick Avenue
Little Venice
Apostolic
Paddington Green Primary School
Sports Centre
City of Westminster College
St Mary's
Paddington Green Police Station
King Solomon Academy Gateway School
City of Westminster College
Capit
Christ Church Bentinck Primary
St Stephen's CE Primary School
Westway
Fire Station
Westbourne Green
Marylebone Flyover
Dining
Metropole College
Royal Oak
Porchester Centre
City of Westminster College (Paddington Basin Campus)
Merchant Square
Paddington Basin
St Mary's
Paddington Station
St Mary's
St John's
Hallfield Estate
Hallfield Infant & Junior Schools
Whiteley's
St James & St Michael's School
St James
El Pirata Detapas
Le Café Anglais
Colchis
Assaggi
St Sophia Catholic
Lansdowne College
Baywater
Nipa
Island Restaurant & Bar (Lancaster London)
Angelus Restaurant
Jenner Statue
Italian Fountains
Queen's Ice Rink Queensway
St Matthew's
New Lodge
Nursery
Casa Batavia
Tavern
Clarke's
Hawkesdown House School
Embassy of Russia
Embassy of Lebanon
Kensington Gardens
Physical Energy Statue
Speke's Monument
Peter Pan Statue
Files Tower
Serpentine Bridge
The Long Water
Police Station
Ranger's Lodge
Block Lion Gate
Marlborough Gate
Inverness Terrace Gate
Lancaster Gate

Congestion Charging Zone boundary
● **Restaurant**
● **AA Restaurant of the Year**

London Plan 3

London Plan 4

St Matthew's
Landsowne College
Queen's Ice Rink Queensway

Notting Hill Gate

Kensington Place
Embassy Slovak Republic
The Mall Tavern
Casa Batavia
Hawkesdown House School
Clarke's
Embassy of Nepal
Embassy of Russia
Embassy of Lebanon

Time Flies Clock Tower

Inverness Terrace Garden

Italian Fountains
Jenner Statue
Nursery
New Lodge

Police Station

Ranger's Lodge

Kensington Gardens

Speke's Monument
Peter Pan Statue
The Long Water

Serpentine Bridge

The Serpentine

Romanian Embassy

Kensington Palace

Kensington Palace Green

Physical Energy Statue

Serpentine Gallery

Isis Statue

The Lido

Diana, Princess of Wales Memorial Fountain

Israel Embassy
Fire Station
Min Jiang, Park Terrace Restaurant (Royal Garden)
St Govor's Well
Round Pond
Bandstand
Mount Gate
Bowling Green
Tennis Courts

Kensington & Chelsea Town Hall
St Mary Abbots
Zaika
St Mary Abbots CE Primary School
KENSINGTON
The Milestone Hotel
High Street Kensington
Baglioni Hotel
HYDE PARK GATE
KENSINGTON ROAD
KENSINGTON GORE
Albert Memorial
KENSINGTON ROAD
KENSINGTON
Royal College of Art
Royal Albert Hall
Royal Geographical Society
Knightsbridge

Babylon
Heythrop College
Kitchen W8
Thomas's Day School
St Alban's Grove
Launceston Place Restaurant
L'Etranger
Chantry Square
Hansom Cab
Superstore
Cromwell
Health Centre
Baden Powell House
Millennium Bailey's Hotel London Kensington

Royal College of Music
Imperial College London
Imperial College London
Imperial College London
Science
Darwin Centre
Natural History
Victoria & Albert
Royal College of Art
The Oratory
Nozo
Bromp
Racine
Police Station
Cassis Bistro

CROMWELL
Institute Français
ROAD
Gloucester Road
Bombay Brasserie
South Kensington
Our Lady of Victories RC Primary School
Lycée Français
Bibendum
Marlborough Primary School
Police Station

New Lotus Garden
Police Station
EARL'S COURT STATION
Earl's Court
WEST CROMWELL ROAD
CROMWELL ROAD
A4

Tom Aikens
Royal Marsden
Le Colombier
Royal Marsden
Tom's Kitchen
St Luke's
Royal Brompton & Harefield

Cambio de Tercio
Capote Y Toros
Bousfield Primary School
St Cuthbert & St Matthias CE Primary School
Earls Court Exhibition Centre (London 2012 venue)
EARL'S COURT
St Luke's

OLD BROMPTON ROAD
FULHAM ROAD
Royal Cancer
CHELSEA
Glebe Hampshire School
Register Office
Fire Station
Sports Centre

WEST BROMPTON STATION
Redcliffe Gardens
Serviте RC Primary School
Chelsea & Westminster
Park Walk Primary School
Sushinho
Le Colombier

West Brompton
Sushinho
Eight Over Eight
Carlyle's House

Ambulance Station
Brompton Cemetery
Chelsea & Westminster
KING'S ROAD

0	250	500 metres
0	250	500 yards

Fulham Primary

A   **B**   **C**   **D**   **E**

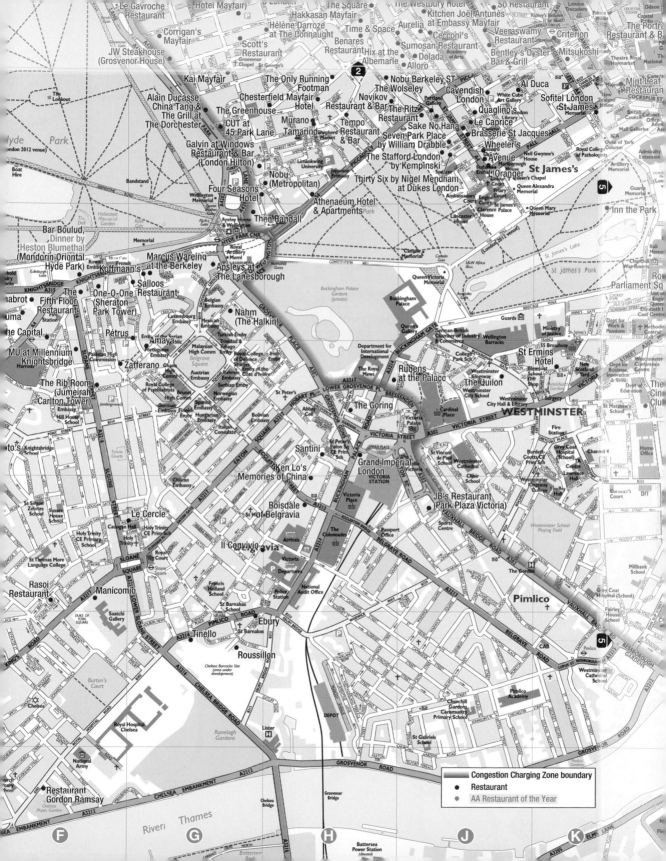

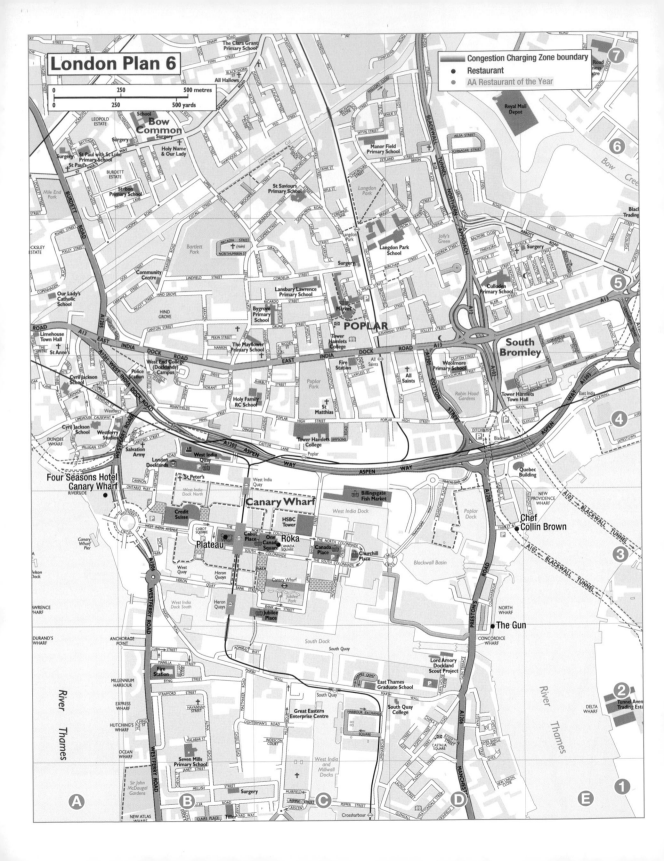

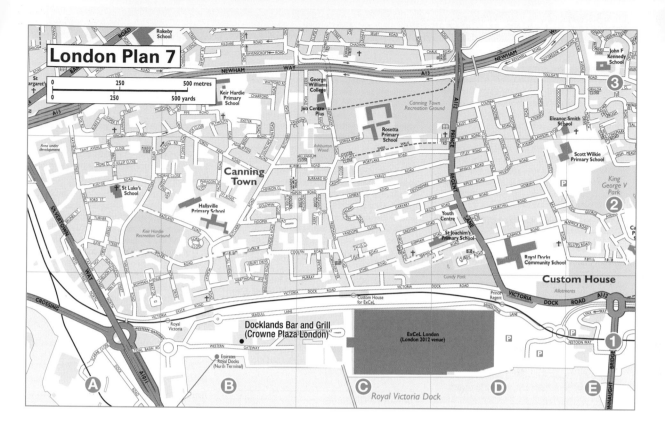

London Plan 7

LONDON

Greater London Plans 1-7, pages 242-253. (Small scale maps 6 & 7 at back of Guide.) Restaurants are listed below in postal district order, commencing East, then North, South and West, with a brief indication of the area covered. Detailed plans 2-7 show the locations of restaurants with AA Rosette Awards within the Central London postal districts. If you do not know the postal district of the restaurant you want, please refer to the index preceding the street plans for the entry and map pages. The plan reference for each restaurant also appears within its directory entry.

LONDON E1

Café Spice Namasté   PLAN 3 J1

◉ Indian

Vibrant modern Indian cooking in Whitechapel

☎ 020 7488 9242
16 Prescot St E1 8AZ
e-mail: binay@cafespice.co.uk
dir: Nearest station: Tower Gateway (DLR), Aldgate, Tower Hill. Walking distance from Tower Hill

'Namasté' means 'gracious hello' in Hindi, and this large, colourful Whitechapel restaurant is certainly a welcoming place. Contemporary Indian cuisine is the thing, with standards seldom slipping, and the kitchen making good use of the best seasonal British produce. Order a starter platter, a set meal or the tasting menu, including wine; alternatively, start with something like beetroot and coconut samosa, or fiery-hot Goan-style squid, and progress to seared scallops (from Cornwall) on garlic-spiked spinach in a light korma sauce, and venison (from Denham Estate) tikka aflatoon, flavoured with star anise and fennel. Picking from the tapas menu is a good way to try the full range, from vegetable samosa to lightly marinated partridge and pheasant roulade.

Chef Cyrus Todiwala **Owner** Cyrus & Pervin Todiwala **Times** 12-3/6.15-10.30 Closed Xmas, BHs, Sun, L Sat **Prices** Starter £5.55-£10.50, Main £13.95-£18.25, Dessert £7.25-£9.75, Service added but optional 12.5% **Wines** 17 bottles over £20, 6 bottles under £20, 7 by glass **Notes** Tasting menu available, Vegetarian available, Dress restrictions, Smart casual **Seats** 120 **Children** Portions **Parking** On street; NCP

Galvin Café a Vin   PLAN 3 H3

◉◉ French, Italian

Impressive brasserie-style cooking and a lively atmosphere

☎ 020 7299 0404
35 Spital Square E1 6DY
e-mail: info@galvinrestaurants.com
dir: Nearest station: Liverpool St. Close to Spitalfields Market, 5 min walk from Liverpool St Station

The revamped Spitalfields Market area is home to two Galvin brothers restaurants, the fine-dining Galvin La Chapelle (see entry) and this thriving, buzzy and informal

café-style eatery. Both can be found in the revitalized St Botolph's Hall, with the café occupying a swish new extension to its grander sibling. There are bare wooden tables and a lively vibe, and you can sit and eat at the vast pewter bar, but the look and feel of the place is very contemporary and smart. An open kitchen adds a touch of theatre to the upbeat atmosphere, from which David Stafford delivers rustic and hearty French and Italian inspired dishes, alongside a few brasserie classics, all simply presented and freshly prepared from first-class ingredients. The daily menu may offer brawn terrine with piccalilli and steak tartare with sourdough toast for starters. For main course, maybe braised shin of beef with lardons and roast shallots, or a pizza topped with potato, artichoke, fontina cheese and rosemary straight from the wood oven. Leave room for a classic tarte Tatin with vanilla ice cream. The lunchtime and early evening fixed-price menu is a steal.

Chef Chris & Jeff Galvin, David Stafford **Owner** Chris & Jeff Galvin **Times** 12-3/6-10.30 Closed 25-26 Dec, 1 Jan, D 24 Dec **Prices** Fixed L 2 course fr £14.95, Fixed D 2 course fr £14.95, Starter £6-£9, Main £11-£15, Dessert £5.50-£6.50, Service added but optional 12.5% **Wines** 43 bottles over £20, 2 bottles under £20, 10 by glass **Notes** Fixed D 6-7pm, all day menu available, Sunday L, Vegetarian available, Air con **Seats** 47 **Children** Portions **Parking** On street

Galvin La Chapelle   PLAN 3 H3

◉◉◉ — **see opposite**

The Luxe   PLAN 3 J3

◉ Modern British

All-day brasserie dining in a Victorian market building

☎ 020 7101 1751
109 Commercial St E1 6BG
e-mail: reservations@theluxe.co.uk
dir: Nearest station: Liverpool Street

Most bases are covered in this multi-purpose eatery and music venue, starting in the basement with music and cabaret, moving on up through the all-day café-bar on the buzzy ground floor, to the main restaurant on the first floor. Built in the 1880s, the building shows its heritage with a skeleton of steel girders, exposed brickwork and wooden floors, and you dine at bare wooden tables sandwiched between the long marble counter of an open kitchen and the half-moon windows. Simple modern brasserie dishes are the order of the day, kicking off with something like smoked eel, sauté potatoes, pancetta and cheese sauce. The prime attraction at main course stage is slabs of 28-day, dry-aged Devon-bred beef cooked on the wood-fired oven and served simply with béarnaise. If you're not up for the red meat action, there may be pollock with samphire and beurre blanc.

Times 12-3/6-11

Marco Pierre White   PLAN 3 H3
Steak & Alehouse

◉ Modern European

Quality City steakhouse in bright basement setting

☎ 020 7247 5050
East India House, 109-117 Middlesex St E1 7JF
e-mail: info@mpwsteakandalehouse.org
dir: Nearest station: Liverpool Street

This roll-out brand offers a brasserie-style roster of dishes with timeless English appeal and plenty of ideas from France and Italy. Thus Brit classics like York ham with home-made piccalilli meet tuna steak provençale or wild halibut à la Sicilienne. Meat is the mainstay, with Scottish steaks (from fillet to top-drawer Chateaubriand for two - with the usual choice of sauces) to the likes of calves' liver and dry-cured bacon. Expect well-sourced ingredients and cooking that's not too showy, but factor-in necessary side order veg, while desserts tend to stay on the nursery slopes (Eton Mess to sticky toffee pudding). The basement setting - hidden away from the Bishopsgate mayhem - is a light, clean-cut space, decked out with wooden flooring, red leather chairs, white linen-clad tables and walls lined with JAK cartoons (Mail on Sunday fame). Throw in well-selected wines and good cocktails and all bases are covered.

Times 12-3/5.30-10 Closed BHs, 25 Dec, 1 Jan, Sun, L Sat

St John Bread & Wine   PLAN 3 J3

◉ British

Gutsy British cooking in Spitalfields

☎ 020 3301 8069
94-96 Commercial St E1 6LZ
e-mail: reservations@stjohnbreadandwine.com
dir: Nearest station: Liverpool Street/Aldgate East

Across the street from Spitalfields Market, this younger, smaller sister of St John (see entry) concentrates, like the original, on seasonal, indigenous produce and promotes the concept of 'the whole beast', so crispy pig's skin (with chicory and mustard) or ox heart (with celeriac) are as likely to feature as prime cuts. There's little distinction between starters and main courses, so sharing is encouraged. The kitchen takes a no-nonsense approach, turning out straightforward dishes strong on flavour. Start with, or share, pigeon with pickled red cabbage or smoked sprats with horseradish, and proceed to faggots with turnip and black cabbage or black bream with green sauce. Breads are exceptional, and British desserts make an impact: perhaps rhubarb Eton Mess or bread pudding.

Chef Lee Tiernan **Owner** Trevor Gulliver & Fergus Henderson **Times** 9am-11pm Closed 24 Dec-1 Jan, BH, **Prices** Starter £4.50-£8.90, Main £12.90-£17.50, Dessert £6.50-£7.10, Service optional, Groups min 6 service 12.5% **Wines** 85 bottles over £20, 12 by glass **Notes** Vegetarian available **Seats** 60 **Parking** On street

Save on Hotels. Book at **theAA.com/hotel**

LONDON, CENTRAL (E1) 255 **ENGLAND**

Super Tuscan
PLAN 3 H3

◉ Italian **NEW**

An authentic enoteca in Spitalfields

☎ 020 7247 8717
8A Artillery Passage E1 7LJ
e-mail: info@supertuscan.co.uk
dir: Nearest station: Liverpool Street. 5 min walk from
Liverpool Street Station, Bishopsgate exit

An unassuming entrance leads into a parquet-floored
restaurant with brown banquettes along one wall, plain
wooden chairs, some booths, and tall stools at a long bar,
the sort of functional interior, like many enotecas, that
doesn't distract attention from the gutsy Italian food on
offer here - or from the intelligently chosen Italian wines.
Start with 'sample-sized portions', to use menu-speak:
arancini di prosciutto (fried rice balls stuffed with ham,
parmesan and béchamel) or polpette di vitello (veal
meatballs poached in stock with peas and potatoes), or
go for an antipasti platter of assorted meats or regional
cheeses for sharing, and proceed to a classic Tuscan dish
of chargrilled sausages with fennel seeds. Ingredients,
sourced from Italy, are used in authentic Italian recipes,
and dishes are big on flavour. Finish with ricotta-stuffed
doughnuts with a scoop of outstanding ice cream.

Chef Maurizio Sgroi, Rita Piscitello **Owner** Nick Grossi
Times 12-3/5.30-10 Closed Xmas, New Year, Sat-Sun
Prices Starter £3-£4.50, Main £8-£20, Dessert £5-£6.50,
Service optional **Wines** 39 bottles over £20, 7 bottles
under £20, 11 by glass **Notes** Vegetarian available
Seats 30 **Children** Portions

Les Trois Garçons
PLAN 3 J4

◉◉ French

Theatrical surroundings for some smart fine dining

☎ 020 7613 1924
1 Club Row, Shoreditch E1 6JX
e-mail: info@lestroisgarcons.com
web: www.lestroisgarcons.com
dir: Nearest station: Liverpool Street. From station, follow
Bishopsgate towards Shoreditch High St. Right after
bridge onto Bethnal Green Rd. Restaurant on left

This was a Victorian pub before the trois garçons got
their hands on it and did it up in high camp style:
handbags and chandeliers hang from the ceiling, stuffed
animals wear costume jewellery, and there's much more
besides. However tables are smartly dressed, staff are
well groomed and service is attentive. The French-
inspired cooking is rather more down to earth than the
surroundings. Start with a luxury entrée of foie gras - cold
with apple and plum chutney, hot with plum tart - and go
on to Chateaubriand with béarnaise, truffled broccoli,
balsamic onions and pommes purée. The style may be
classically-based, but the kitchen moves with the times
too, serving Dorset snails with shallots, chilli and garlic
on a bed of braised beef and onions, and seared scallops
with parmesan polenta, fennel sauce and wild
mushrooms. Finish with a classic crème brûlée.

Chef Michael Chan **Owner** Stefan Karlson, Hassan
Abdullah, Michel Lassere **Times** 12-2.30/6-9.30
Closed Xmas, New Year, L Sat, D Sun **Prices** Fixed L 2
course £17.50-£40.50, Fixed D 3 course fr £47, Service
added but optional 12.5% **Wines** 50+ bottles over £20,
11 by glass **Notes** Vegetarian available **Seats** 65, Pr/
dining room 10 **Parking** On street

Galvin La Chapelle

French 🍷NOTABLE WINE LIST

French style and Victorian pomp in the City

☎ 020 7299 0400
St. Botolph's Hall, 35 Spital Square E1 6DY
e-mail: info@galvinrestaurants.com
dir: Nearest station: Liverpool Street. Close to Old
Spitalfields Market

The third edition in the ever-expanding story of the Galvin
brothers' rise to fame and gastronomic glory, La Chapelle
certainly causes a sharp intake of breath once the
bowler-hatted doorman admits you inside and you take in
the brown marble pillars soaring up to the vaulted ceiling
of Victorian St Botolph's school hall. It has wow factor in
spades with its glamorous buzz, swagged curtains, plush
brown leather seating and white linen tables, and a
mezzanine level called The Gallery from where you can
look down on the other diners. The cooking conforms to
the Galvin template, that is to say based on the modern
French idiom, but expanded out to encompass some
distinctly contemporary British ideas. The produce that
underpins it all is second to none, if not always native, as
in the gold-standard Landaise foie gras that is pointed
up by poached Yorkshire rhubarb, pain d'épice and stem
ginger. Other richly appealing flavour combinations could
take in lasagne of Dorset crab with cauliflower velouté,
then move on to roast rump of Scottish beef with glazed
oxtail, truffled pommes purée and Hermitage jus (fans of
the iconic Rhône red take note that the place has a
breathtaking collection of Hermitage la Chapelle with
prices to match). Fish is handled with equal precision
and flair - perhaps a pavé of Cornish sea bass with an
étuvée of leeks, red wine salsify, chorizo and brown
shrimps. End with the house's exemplary take on apple
tarte Tatin with crème fraîche, or a Valrhona chocolate
fondant with honeycomb and tonka bean ice cream.

Chef Chris & Jeff Galvin **Owner** Chris Galvin, Jeff Galvin,
Ken Sanker **Times** 12-2.30/6-10.30 Closed 25-26 Dec, 1
Jan, D 24 Dec **Prices** Fixed L 3 course fr £26.50, Fixed D 3
course fr £29.50, Starter £10.50-£16.50, Main £22.50-
£35, Dessert £8.50-£10.50, Service added but optional
12.5% **Wines** 330 bottles over £20, 2 bottles under £20,
21 by glass **Notes** Menu gourmand £70 (with matching
wine £110), Sunday L, Vegetarian available **Seats** 110, Pr/
dining room 16 **Children** Portions **Parking** On street, NCP

LONDON E1 *continued*

Wapping Food
PLAN 1 F3

◉ Modern International

Gutsy mod-European cooking in an old pumping station

☎ 020 7680 2080
Wapping Hydraulic, Power Station, Wapping Wall E1W 3SG
dir: Nearest station: Shadwell DLR, Wapping. Between Wapping Wall & King Edward VII Memorial Park, parallel to the river opposite the Prospect of Whitby

As settings go, an old hydraulic pumping station certainly counts as one of the more unusual. But that's exactly what you get at Wapping Food, the restaurant within the Wapping Project arts and entertainment centre in London's East End. The high-ceilinged restaurant, with its distinctly industrial look of bare-brick walls, girders and old machinery dotted about amongst the tables, manages to be both cheerfully informal by day and atmospheric at night. Settle into a designer chair and tuck into modern European food from a menu that changes twice daily (accompanied by wines from an all-Aussie list). Start with Spanish octopus céviche or English asparagus with pistachio sauce, moving on to brill steamed on the bone over wild dill with Amalfi lemon confit and mammole artichoke, or lamb shoulder cooked in red chillies, coconut and tamarind with violetta aubergine and rice.

Chef Matthew Young **Owner** Women's Playhouse Trust **Times** 12-3/6.30-11 Closed 24 Dec-3 Jan, BHs, D Sun **Prices** Fixed L 3 course £37.50-£53.50, Fixed D 3 course £37.50-£53.50, Starter £6-£12, Main £15-£21, Dessert £5-£7.50, Service added but optional 12.5% **Wines** 120 bottles over £20, 4 bottles under £20, 20 by glass **Notes** Sunday L, Vegetarian available **Seats** 150 **Children** Portions **Parking** 20

Whitechapel Gallery Dining Room
PLAN 3 J3

◉◉ Modern British

Forthright flavours at the go-ahead gallery

☎ 020 7522 7896
77-82 Whitechapel High St E1 7QX
e-mail: dining@whitechapelgallery.org
dir: Nearest station: Aldgate East

The Whitechapel Gallery Dining Room is a good place in which to recharge batteries after taking in an exhibition. A modern-looking restaurant of bare blond-wood tables, rectangular mirrors hung vertically, some leather-look banquettes, and big windows overlooking the street, it looks the part. Angela Hartnett, of Murano (see entry), is the consultant, her commitment to fresh seasonal produce and a bias towards Italy evident on the short, daily-changing menu. There's no distinction between courses, dishes being either small or larger, giving diners the flexibility to share, have a quick bite or a full meal.

Among the former may be veal meatballs in herby tomato sauce, salt-cod croquettes with saffron aïoli, or crab with toasted sourdough. Bigger plates are marked out by simplicity and honest, upfront flavours - herb-crusted sea trout with caponata, perhaps - whilst puddings such as rhubarb fool end things on a high.

Chef Emma Duggan **Owner** Whitechapel Gallery **Times** 12-2.30/6-11 Closed 24 Dec-2 Jan, Mon, D Sun & Tue **Prices** Fixed L 2 course £22, Fixed D 3 course £28, Starter £4.50-£8, Main £10.50-£20, Dessert £4.50-£5.50, Service added but optional 12.5% **Wines** 11 bottles over £20, 8 bottles under £20, 7 by glass **Notes** Sunday L, Vegetarian available **Seats** 36, Pr/dining room 14 **Children** Portions **Parking** On street

LONDON E2

Brawn
PLAN 3 K5

◉◉ Traditional European

Smart, honest cooking in trendy East London

☎ 020 7729 5692
49 Columbia Rd E2 7RG
e-mail: enquiries@brawn.co
dir: Nearest station: Liverpool St, Bethnal Green. From Liverpool Street, follow Shoreditch High St, right Hackney Rd, right Columbia Rd

On the Columbia Road - of flower market fame - this sister of Terroirs (see entry) is a vibrant place with quirky

Viajante

LONDON E2
PLAN 1 G4

Modern V

Cutting-edge cooking in Bethnal Green

☎ 020 7871 0461
Patriot Square, Bethnal Green E2 9NF
e-mail: info@viajante.co.uk
dir: Nearest station: Bethnal Green. Entrance Cambridge Heath Road

'We are young and restless, driven by emotions and inspired by a long journey of discoveries in food,' so says chef-patron Nuno Mendes. It matters not if you are old and relaxed, but it is probably best, if you're planning on coming here, that you are up for discoveries in food. For this is avante-garde, thrillingly creative stuff. Located in the old town hall in Bethnal Green, now a swish boutique hotel, Viajante looks good with its light wood and pale

blue hues, cloth-less tables, local contemporary artworks on the walls and an open-to-view kitchen that is so 'open' as to practically be in the room. Mendes has travelled a fair bit from his native Portugal, as you might have gathered, working in the US and undertaking a stint at the legendary El Bulli, and today he has very much developed his own style of creative and bold cooking. The deal is three, six, nine or 12 courses (the three being at lunch only, the 12 at dinner only) with recommended wines if you so wish. Presentation is never less than interesting, sometimes very beautiful indeed, and there is much to enjoy on this journey (viajante, if you haven't gathered, means journey). Scallops with radish and liquorice might kick off the 12-course menu, followed by roasted celeriac with home-made ricotta and lemon and thyme, then razor clams with turnips and chicken crumbs. Cutting-edge cooking techniques and interesting combinations of flavours mean everything goes by in a whirl of excitement, one after the other, something new, something exhilarating. Turbot with duck heart, beetroot

and toasted milk, maybe, or frozen pear with cider and pecans (yes, that last one is a dessert). So, come along for the ride if you're up for it.

Chef Nuno Mendes **Owner** Nuno Mendes, Peng Lah **Times** 12-2/6-9.30 Closed BHs, L Mon-Thu **Prices** Fixed D 3 course £28-£46, Service added but optional 12.5% **Wines** 130 bottles over £20, 14 by glass **Notes** Tasting menu 3,6 or 9 course L, 6,9, or 12 course D, Sunday L, Vegetarian menu **Seats** 40, Pr/dining room 16 **Parking** On street

artwork, a definite buzz, and fabulously hearty food. The broadly European-focused daily-changing menu (particularly France and Italy) is straightforward enough - and that's the genius of it. Top-notch produce is served without a jot of flim-flam (as Boris might say), and our piggie friends get their own section on the menu. Thus pork rillettes or a selection of charcuterie may get the ball rolling, plus there's the likes of potted brown shrimps and toast; foie gras and confit shallots; snails and polenta; or oxtail and kidney ravioli and hispi cabbage. It's advisable to linger long enough to sample chocolate ganache with crème anglaise and praline. Cheeses and sourdough bread hail from East London and the wine list focuses on sustainable, biodynamic and organic varieties.

Chef Owen Kenworthy **Owner** Ed Wilson, Oli Barker **Times** 12-3/6-11 Closed Xmas, New Year, BHs, L Mon-Wed, D Sun **Prices** Starter £5-£8, Main £8-£15, Dessert £5-£6, Service added but optional 12.5% **Wines** 142 bottles over £20, 9 bottles under £20, 12 by glass **Notes** Sunday L, Vegetarian available, Air con **Seats** 70 **Parking** On street

Viajante
PLAN 1 G4

◉◉◉ – see opposite

LONDON E9

The Empress
PLAN 1 G4

◉ Modern British **NEW**

Laid-back crowd-pleaser with simple, feisty dishes

☎ 020 8533 5123
130 Lauriston Rd, Victoria Park E9 7LH
dir: Nearest station: Cambridge Heath, Mile End. A10 S towards Dalston, left Hackney Rd, then right onto A107, left into Old Ford Rd and left again into Grove Rd

With the generous proportions of a Victorian pub and the white walls, bare brickwork, claret Chesterfield banquettes, modern art and canteen-like simplicity of an on-trend contemporary urban eatery, The Empress slots right into the easygoing vibe of its Victoria Park neighbourhood. The kitchen brigade is led by Hackney resident Elliott Lidstone who comes hot-foot from the high-achieving L'ortolan (see entry), and while there's none of that high-falutin' stuff going on here, the emphasis is still firmly on quality produce cooked with care and skill. The simple approach delivers retro ham croquettes, which doesn't sound like it will get your motor running, but they are well-made, creamy and crunchy, or there are similar offerings along the lines of pig's ears, or crab on toast, which you could treat as either bar snacks or nibbly starters. A brace of roasted quails on top of chargrilled spring salad shares the stage with snails and bone marrow and wild garlic, or there might be rainbow trout with Jersey Royals and braised lettuce. End with ginger pannacotta with rhubarb or chocolate mousse with peanut brittle and lime.

Chef Elliott Lidstone **Owner** Michael Buurman **Times** 12-3.30/6-10.15 Closed 25-26 Dec, L Mon (ex BHs) **Prices** Starter £4.75-£7, Main £11-£29, Dessert £2-£5.50, Service optional, Groups min 5 service 12.5% **Wines** 56 bottles over £20, 8 bottles under £20, 17 by glass **Notes** Sunday L, Vegetarian available **Seats** 49 **Children** Portions **Parking** On street

LONDON E14

Chef Collin Brown
PLAN 6 D3

◉ Caribbean

Caribbean flavours in Docklands

☎ 020 7515 8177
2 Yabsley St E14 9RG
e-mail: info@chefcollinbrown.com
dir: Nearest station: Blackwall

A couple of paces from the river, Chef Collin Brown is a smart, modern restaurant, with parquet floors, large windows, atmospheric lighting and neatly clothed tables. The man himself was born in Jamaica and brings the tastes of the Caribbean to this pocket of town. Starters run from homely red kidney bean soup with dumplings to the opulence of grilled lobster marinated in coconut cream, with main courses of tender jerk chicken breast, deep-fried snapper in brown stewing sauce, and a gutsy dish of oxtail braised with butter beans and peppers served with rice and peas. Finish with mango and passionfruit cheesecake with summer berries.

Chef Collin Brown **Owner** Collin Brown **Times** 5-11.30 Closed Xmas, New Year, L all week **Prices** Fixed D 2 course £21-£27.50, Service added 12.5% **Wines** 16 bottles over £20, 8 bottles under £20, 7 by glass **Notes** Vegetarian available, Dress restrictions, Smart casual **Seats** 50 **Children** Portions **Parking** On street

Four Seasons Hotel London at Canary Wharf
PLAN 6 A3

◉ Modern Italian

Sophisticated Italian cooking in a smart Docklands hotel

☎ 020 7510 1999
46 Westferry Circus, Canary Wharf E14 8RS
dir: Nearest station: Canary Wharf. Just off Westferry Circus rdbt

The Quadrato restaurant of the Four Seasons' Canary Wharf branch sits among the Docklands forest of concrete and glass skyscrapers, yet looks across the river from its secluded Thames-side gardens, which are a real plus for alfresco eating on fine days. The dining room goes for a butch city-slicker look of dark wood, leather and crisply dressed tables, while the chefs in the glass-partitioned

kitchen turn out accomplished modern Italian cuisine. Kick off with seared scallops wrapped in pancetta, and if you're not up for the full four-course format of tradition, pasta such as shell-shaped cavatelli with crab meat, lemon and thyme. The cast of secondi takes in beef fillet with thyme and a ragù of smoked aubergine, shallots and mushrooms, or grilled tuna loin with asparagus, olives, capers and tomato concasse. The splendid array of artisan Italian cheeses is hard to sidestep, but the incurably sweet of tooth could end with an updated take on tiramisù, served with coffee crumble and Amaretto jelly.

Chef Moreno Casaccia **Owner** Four Seasons Hotels and Resorts **Times** 12-3/6-10.30 **Prices** Starter £8-£16, Main £12-£30, Dessert £7, Service optional, Groups min 6 service 12.5% **Wines** 130 bottles over £20, 29 by glass **Notes** Sunday L, Vegetarian available, Civ Wed 200 **Seats** 90 **Children** Portions, Menu **Parking** 26

The Gun
PLAN 6 D2

◉ Modern British

Vivacious gastro-pub food in a historic Docklands setting

☎ 020 7515 5222
27 Coldharbour E14 9NS
e-mail: info@thegundocklands.com
dir: Nearest station: South Quay DLR, Canary Wharf. A12/A13 exit A1206. From South Quay DLR, E down Marsh Wall to mini rdbt, turn left, over bridge, 1st right

Brilliant riverside views across the Thames to the O2 Arena from the terrace are part of the attraction at this buzzy Docklands gastro-pub. The name is a nod to the bygone industrial era, when iron foundries turned out cannon for the 18th- and 19th-century fleets to ensure that Britannia stayed ruling the waves. The place has been around in one form or another for 250 years, and has the darkly moody vibe of a smugglers den with its hardwood floors, hues of charcoal and burgundy red, and clubby Chesterfield seating. Nowadays, it combines history and atmosphere with gusty British food - crisp calves' brain with sauce gribiche, ahead of stuffed rabbit leg with mushrooms, gnocchi, and mustard and tarragon sauce. If you've still room, finish with black treacle and ginger cake with orange custard.

Chef Mark Fines **Owner** Tom & Ed Martin **Times** 12-3/6-10.30 Closed 25-26 Dec **Prices** Starter £6-£9.50, Main £14-£28, Dessert £5.50-£9.50, Service added but optional 12.5% **Wines** 125 bottles over £20, 5 bottles under £20, 23 by glass **Notes** Sunday L, Vegetarian available **Seats** 40, Pr/dining room 22 **Children** Portions, Menu **Parking** On street, NCP

LONDON E14 *continued*

Plateau
PLAN 6 B3

◉◉ Modern French ▲

Sophisticated, contemporary fine dining in futuristic landscape

☎ 020 7715 7100
4th Floor, Canada Place, Canada Square, Canary Wharf E14 5ER
e-mail: plateaureservations@danddlondon.com
web: www.plateau-restaurant.co.uk
dir: Nearest station: Canary Wharf DLR/Tube. Facing Canary Wharf Tower and Canada Square Park

There are show-stopping views over Canary Wharf's high-rise cityscape from the aptly named Plateau - a sleek, glass-and-steel roof-top restaurant set four floors up above the shopping mall. The long, lightdrenched space is divided into two zones by a central theatre-style kitchen, each with its own bar and outdoor terrace. The hip Bar & Grill (cocktails and brasserie menu) is up first, while the restaurant on the other side is calmer and more sophisticated. The design mixes retro styling with warm, restrained neutral tones in the restaurant; think funky white plastic 'tulip' swivel dining chairs and curvy upholstered banquettes, white marble-topped tables, huge arching stainless-steel floor lamps, stunning flower arrangements and changing art displays. But it's not all style over substance here, the ambitious, light, well-dressed modern European cooking - underpinned by a classic French theme - shows real pedigree, driven by quality seasonal materials. Take a duo of fine-tuned signature dishes from the carte: English parsley risotto with sauté of snails, garlic butter and red wine jus, and main-course honey-spiced Goosnargh duck with braised endive and port-marinated radish. Desserts keep up the style count, perhaps organic lemon posset with kalamansi crush and jelly, while the wine list is one of distinction.

Chef Allan Pickett **Owner** D & D London **Times** 12-3/6-10 Closed 25-26 Dec, 1 Jan, BHs, Sun, L Sat **Prices** Fixed L 2 course £22-£25, Fixed D 2 course £22-£25, Starter £6.50-£14.50, Main £16-£32.50, Dessert £5-£9.50, Service added but optional 12.5% **Wines** 400 bottles over £20, 5 bottles under £20, 20 by glass **Notes** Gourmand menu available, Vegetarian available, Dress restrictions, Smart casual, Civ Wed 100 **Seats** 90, Pr/dining room 25 **Children** Menu **Parking** 200

Roka
PLAN 6 C3

◉◉ Japanese ▲

Top-flight Japanese cooking in Canary Wharf

☎ 020 7636 5228
1st Floor, 40 Canada Square E14 5FW
e-mail: info@rokarestaurant.com
dir: Nearest station: Canary Wharf. 5 min walk from Canary Wharf tube

The four elements are the inspiration for the interior design of Roka's Canary Wharf outpost (see also Roka W1), which seems to mean a lot of polished wood, soft lighting from cleverly positioned spots, and green and mustard-yellow seating. Steering a course through the menu is a cinch even for those unfamiliar with Japanese cuisine, as it's divided into categories: amazingly fresh sashimi and nigiri, tempura and fried, robata meat, and so on. The chef's sashimi selection is a good way to start, although there are no courses as such and dishes are served in waves when ready. Prawn tempura, and cabbage spiked with chilli and garlic might arrive with robata dishes like cedar-roast baby chicken with chilli, garlic and lemon, Korean-spiced lamb cutlets, and asparagus with soy and sesame. Bankers on bonuses could go for the premium tasting menu or splash out even more on marinated black cod, Wagyu rib-eye and a beautifully presented dessert platter.

Chef Cristian Bravaccini **Owner** Rainer Becker, Arjun Waney **Times** 12-3/5.30-11 Closed 25 Dec **Wines** 148 bottles over £20, 14 by glass **Notes** Average price L/D £50-£60, Sat L £22-£25, Sun brunch £42, Vegetarian available, Dress restrictions, Smart casual **Seats** 99 **Children** Portions, Menu

LONDON E16

Docklands Bar and Grill
PLAN 7 B1

◉ Modern British ✿

Bistro-style dining in contemporary, business-savvy hotel

☎ 020 7055 2000
Crowne Plaza London Docklands, Royal Victoria Dock, Western Gateway E16 1AL
e-mail: sales@crowneplazadocklands.co.uk
dir: Nearest station: DLR Royal Victoria. A1020 towards ExCeL West, hotel on left 400mtrs before ExCeL

Overlooking the Royal Victoria Dock, and handily placed in the thick of the action close to the ExCel, Canary Wharf and City Airport, this upmarket contemporary hotel is geared to the cut and thrust of Docklands business life. Start in the sleek contemporary bar with a glass of prosecco, then hit the restaurant where wooden floors, tables and high-backed chairs all add up to a city-slicker look, with a wide-screen Docklands backdrop to absorb through floor-to-ceiling windows. The kitchen keeps things on message: simple, fresh and modern ideas, starting with a crowd-pleasing duck terrine with plum dressing and toasted rustic bread, followed by pancetta-wrapped chicken with herb mash, Savoy cabbage and

white wine sauce. Finish with a classic lemon tart with crème fraîche.

Chef Brian Henry **Owner** BDL Hotels **Times** 12.30-2/5.30-10.30 **Prices** Starter £3.75-£6.25, Main £7.25-£25, Dessert £5.50, Service added but optional 12.5% **Wines** 26 bottles over £20, 9 by glass **Notes** Vegetarian available **Seats** 132, Pr/dining room 48 **Children** Portions, Menu **Parking** 70

LONDON EC1

Bistrot Bruno Loubet
PLAN 3 E4

◉◉ French

Superior bistro cookery in a Clerkenwell boutique hotel

☎ 020 7324 4444
The Zetter Hotel, St John's Square, 86-89 Clerkenwell Rd EC1M 5RJ
e-mail: info@thezetter.com
web: www.bistrotbrunoloubet.com
dir: Nearest station: Farringdon. From west A401, Clerkenwell Rd A5201. Hotel 200mtrs on left

Toss a coin in the air in Clerkenwell and it's practically bound to land these days on somewhere decent to eat. Hard by Smithfield meat market, The Zetter is a corner-site boutique warehouse hotel that just happens to boast the celebrated French chef eponymously behind this Bistrot among its prize draws. Water is pumped from an old well beneath the building for purifying and bottling, and you won't find much of that going on in London. The menu, meanwhile, isn't some ironic recasting of the concept, but really does offer a repertoire of appealing bistro dishes - snails and meatballs, chicken ballottine, bouillabaisse, vegetable tagine with garlic bread. The cooking is overlaid with the Loubet lustre, so that great intensity is conjured out of pairings such as sardine escabèche with piquillo pepper mousse, followed by breaded confit lamb shoulder on smoked aubergine purée. There are one or two bold desserts, such as olive oil and star anise pannacotta, but many will find it hard to resist the old-world charm of an immaculately rendered apple tarte fine, served with cinnamon ice cream and crème fraîche.

Chef Bruno Loubet **Owner** Bruno Loubet, Michael Benyan, Mark Sainsbury **Times** 12-2.30/6-10.30 Closed 26 Dec, D 25 Dec **Prices** Fixed L 2 course £19, Tasting menu £60, Starter £7-£8.50, Main £16.50-£20, Dessert £6-£6.50, Service added but optional 12.5% **Wines** 83 bottles over £20, 5 bottles under £20, 17 by glass **Notes** Sunday L, Vegetarian available **Seats** 90, Pr/dining room 40 **Children** Portions **Parking** NCP

The Bleeding Heart
PLAN 3 D3

⊛ Modern French ⚑ NOTABLE WINE LIST

Discreet and romantic Hatton Garden favourite

☎ 020 7242 2056
Bleeding Heart Yard, off Greville St EC1N 8SJ
e-mail: bookings@bleedingheart.co.uk
dir: Nearest station: Farringdon. Turn right out of
Farringdon Station onto Cowcross St, continue along
Greville St for 50mtrs. Turn left into Bleeding Heart Yard

Secreted away in a rather Dickensian cobbled courtyard,
this bastion of French cooking has bags of character and
atmosphere; its name recalls the macabre murder of
society beauty Lady Elizabeth Hatton, killed by her jealous
lover back in the 17th century. The cellar restaurant itself
has charm by the bucket-load; a trio of intimate,
romantic, warmly toned subterranean rooms, with low-
beamed ceilings, panelling, fireplaces and wine-themed
prints. White linen, burgundy leather seating and slick
Gallic service up the ante for some modish,
unapologetically French fare: think roast rump of Suffolk
Blackface lamb teamed with caramelised root vegetables,
pommes mousseline and rosemary jus to a classic finish
of warm chocolate fondant with orange ice cream. A
serious wine list impresses, including bottles from their
own Hawkes Bay estate, while all carte dishes come with
recommendations by the glass.

Chef Julian Marshall **Owner** Robert & Robyn Wilson
Times 12-3/6-10.30 Closed Xmas & New Year (10 days),
Sat-Sun (Bistro open Sat) **Prices** Food prices not
confirmed for 2013. Please telephone for details
Wines 274 bottles over £20, 2 bottles under £20, 23 by
glass **Notes** Vegetarian available, Dress restrictions,
Smart casual **Seats** 110, Pr/dining room 40 **Parking** 20
evening only, NCP nearby

Le Café du Marché
PLAN 3 E3

⊛ French

**Rustic, Gallic cooking in a classically converted
warehouse**

☎ 020 7608 1609
Charterhouse Mews, Charterhouse Square EC1M 6AH
dir: Nearest station: Barbican

When the urge for Gallic gastronomy strikes, head down a
cobbled alley off Charterhouse Square for this authentic
slice of France. The place drips classic cross-Channel
style with its bare-brick walls, French posters, jazz
pianist and candlelit starched linen-dressed tables set in
a rustic-chic converted Victorian warehouse. The scene
thus set, you can expect unreconstructed French
provincial dishes on an uncomplicated two- or three-
course fixed price menu - honest, peasant cooking that
has stood the test of time, starting with fish soup or
grilled lamb's tongues with sauce gribiche, and
progressing to a côte de boeuf with béarnaise sauce for
two, or duck confit en croûte with Savoy cabbage and

Agen prunes. Finish with the bavarois du jour, or the
splendid selection of French cheeses.

Chef Simon Cottard **Owner** Anna Graham-Wood
Times 12-2.30/6-10 Closed Xmas, New Year, Etr, BHs,
Sun, L Sat **Prices** Food prices not confirmed for 2013.
Please telephone for details **Notes** Vegetarian available
Seats 120, Pr/dining room 65 **Children** Portions
Parking Next door (small charge)

Cicada
PLAN 3 E4

⊛ Pan-Asian

Authentic pan-Asian cooking in trendy Clerkenwell

☎ 020 7608 1550
132-136 St John St EC1V 4JT
e-mail: cicada@rickerrestaurants.com
dir: Nearest station: Farringdon

Will Ricker's first outlet (see also entries for E&O, Eight
Over Eight and XO) has had a bit of a refurb, but it
remains a popular, fun place, people drawn by its
reasonably priced pan-Asian cooking. The kitchen
assiduously sources authentic Eastern ingredients and
turns out convincing renditions, from dim sum - pumpkin
and spinach gyoza, say, or chicken siu mai - to whole sea
bream chargrilled with garlic and chilli. Dishes like
tempura soft-shelled crab, a plate of sashimi, Wagyu
beef with sesame and shallots, and chicken phad thai all
share the billing, in grazing-size portions, attractively
presented, to encourage experimentation. Sticky coconut
rice with banana and vanilla may be the real thing, but
Western chocolate pudding may be harder to resist.

Times 12-3/6-11

Club Gascon
PLAN 3 E3

⊛⊛⊛ – see page 260

Le Comptoir Gascon
PLAN 3 E3

⊛ Traditional French

Gutsy French dishes by Smithfield Market

☎ 020 7608 0851
61-63 Charterhouse St EC1M 6HJ
e-mail: info@comptoirgascon.com
dir: Nearest station: Farringdon, Barbican, St Paul's,
Chancery Ln

The casual, bustling, petite bistro-deli sibling of
heavyweight Club Gascon (see entry), Comptoir deals in
the gutsy food of southwest France. The feel is one of true
cuisine terroir, with simple market-driven cooking and
full-on flavours: duck confit and garbure béarnaise, for
example, or a traditional Toulousain cassoulet. Lighter
things might include crispy squid Basquaise with garlic
and mixed herbs, while desserts - like lemon tart or a
classic chocolate fondant - keep things simple yet show
acute technical ability in their making. The décor fits the

bill with its modern-rustic vibe; exposed brickwork and
ducting, dinky elbow-to-elbow wooden tables, small
velour-covered chairs and copious wines tantalizing from
their cabinets. The fixed-price blackboard lunch menu
offers good value, while the miniscule deli counter - with
displays of breads, conserves, pastries and the like -
offers supplies to takeaway. Well-selected wines are from
southwest France... where else?

Owner Vincent Labeyrie, Pascal Aussignac
Times 12-2.30/7-10 Closed 25 Dec-1 Jan, BHs, Sun-Mon
Prices Fixed L 2 course £12-£22, Fixed D 3 course £19-
£29, Starter £6-£8.50, Main £8.50-£14, Dessert £3.50-
£5.50, Service added but optional 12.5%
Wines 27 bottles over £20, 3 bottles under £20, 11 by
glass **Notes** Vegetarian available **Seats** 32
Children Portions

Hix Oyster & Chop House
PLAN 3 E3

⊛ Modern British V

No-nonsense British cooking in chilled-out Clerkenwell

☎ 020 7017 1930
36-37 Greenhill Rents, Cowcross St EC1M 6BN
e-mail: chophouse@restaurantetcltd.co.uk
dir: Nearest station: Farringdon. Turn left out of
underground station (approx 1min walk)

A wooden floor, white-tiled walls, visible pipes, revolving
overhead fans, and tightly packed tables ready and
waiting with ketchup and vinegar bottles, all create an
unfussy, roughcast sort of atmosphere at Mark Hix's
buzzy Clerkenwell restaurant. The kitchen takes an
equally straightforward, no-nonsense approach to its
output, turning out steaks, fish fingers with mushy peas
and chips, and beef flank and oyster pie. As well as the
expected oysters, starters may take in tender and full-
flavoured veal dumpling wrapped in cawl and served with
bashed neeps, a fine example of winter comfort food, and
squid with ink-cooked spelt. Go out on a high with an
excellent chocolate and orange sponge with orange
sorbet, while for the impecunious there's credit crunch
ice cream with hot chocolate sauce.

Chef Martin Sweeney **Owner** Mark Hix **Times** 12-11
Closed BHs, L Sat **Prices** Fixed L 2 course £17.50, Fixed D
3 course £22.50, Starter £5.75-£16, Main £14.50-£36,
Dessert £2-£9.50, Service added but optional 12.5%
Wines 17 by glass **Notes** D served from 5.30pm, Sunday
L, Vegetarian menu **Seats** 65 **Children** Portions
Parking On street (meters)

LONDON EC1 *continued*

Malmaison Charterhouse Square PLAN 3 E3

@@ French, European ©

Boutique hotel with a chic brasserie

☎ 020 7012 3700

18-21 Charterhouse Square, Clerkenwell EC1M 6AH
e-mail: athwaites@malmaison.com
dir: Nearest station: Barbican

With Smithfield meat market practically on the doorstep, there's no difficulty for the London Mal's kitchen to lay its hands on slabs of prime protein. Tucked discreetly away in a cobbled courtyard off Charterhouse Square, the slick basement brasserie caters to all-comers, whether it's city slickers doing deals over a grilled rib-eye with bone marrow, or lunch to refuel after a hit of retail therapy and pampering. The chic setting conforms to the Malmaison house style: intimate tables for two are tucked into secretive alcoves, amid sexy contemporary boudoir textures of velvet, bare wood and exposed brickwork, and hues of purple and burgundy. In tune with the Moulin Rouge vibe, classic French-accented brasserie dishes built on top-quality ingredients are the thing here. Expect the likes of braised oxtail with smoked and crispy polenta, followed by something gamey - pan-fried partridge with cauliflower purée, Savoy cabbage and tarragon jus, say.

Elsewhere there are comfort classics such as Toulouse sausages with caramelised onion and red wine jus, and for fish fans, perhaps roast monkfish with fines herbes, cream of haricot blanc and trompette de mort mushrooms. Stay with the French theme and finish with a crème brûlée.

Chef John Woodward **Owner** Malmaison Hotels **Times** 12-2.30/6-10.30 Closed 23-28 Dec, L Sat **Prices** Starter £4.95-£8.50, Main £12.95-£22.50, Dessert £3.95-£8.50, Service added but optional 12.5% **Wines** 200 bottles over £20, 6 bottles under £20, 21 by glass **Notes** Sunday L, Vegetarian available **Seats** 70, Pr/dining room 12 **Children** Portions, Menu **Parking** Smithfield Market 200m

The Modern Pantry PLAN 3 E4

@@ Modern ▮ NOTABLE WINE LIST

Inspired fusion cooking in trendy Clerkenwell

☎ 020 7553 9210

47-48 St John's Square, Clerkenwell EC1V 4JJ
e-mail: enquiries@themodernpantry.co.uk
dir: Nearest station: Farringdon, Barbican

Kiwi chef Anna Hansen has been at the vanguard of fusion food (with Peter Gordon at the Sugar Club and then Providores, see entry) and, here at her own venture, the innovation continues. The fashionable conversion of two listed Georgian townhouses on St John's Square splits between an airy, modish café (and traiteur) on the ground floor and a coolly smart first-floor restaurant. Light and sleek, the restaurant combines heritage features with clean contemporary design to deliver an intimate, relaxed backdrop for a vivid culinary journey. Anna takes her influences from the global larder, delivering inspired combinations and contrasting flavours. Menus challenge three-course convention with in-vogue tapas-sized small plates, backpacking from okra, feta and turmeric fritters with blackcurrant compôte and Greek yoghurt to salmon sashimi with green tea and kalamansi lime dressing, tomatillo and shiso cress. Main courses run to grilled tamarind-marinated onglet steak with moi moi and kalamata mash and cavolo nero. Breakfast (and, at weekends, brunch) keep the blue-chip crowd and happy locals on-side.

Chef Anna Hansen **Owner** Anna Hansen **Times** 12-10.30 **Prices** Fixed L 2 course £20, Starter £4.50-£9.70, Main £15.50-£22.50, Dessert £6-£8.50, Service added but optional 12.5% **Wines** 75 bottles over £20, 2 bottles under £20, 15 by glass **Notes** Pre-theatre D & Tasting menu available, Sunday L, Vegetarian available **Seats** 110, Pr/dining room 60 **Children** Portions **Parking** On street (meter)

Club Gascon

LONDON EC1 PLAN 3 E3

Modern French V ▮ NOTABLE WINE LIST

Compelling regional French cooking and a chic interior

☎ 020 7796 0600

57 West Smithfields EC1A 9DS
e-mail: info@clubgascon.com
dir: Nearest station: Barbican, Farringdon

Hard by Smithfield market you'll find this shrine to southwestern French cookery delivered like you've never seen it before. Step beyond the grey façade of what was once the Lyons Teahouse, and you enter a world of marble walls and large flower arrangements (done by the chef, but more of his creativity later), with jazzy piano music in the air and enthusiastic staff who nip up ladders to access top-shelf wines behind the bar. The wine list is a thing of beauty, by the way, and the head sommelier is on sparkling form to see you through the 400-plus varieties from the South West region. Pascal Aussignac shows fierce pride in sourcing ingredients direct from the region, and his love for treading untrodden ground and playing with flavours makes for some seriously good eating. Artistic presentation leaves an impression whether you go for the stonkingly good value lunch menu, 'dejeuner club', 'le marche' seasonal tasting menus (with wine pairings), or the carte. Under headings such as 'la route du sel', expect superb flavour combinations borne of great creativity. Venison carpaccio with sea urchin sauce, crisps and cauliflower, perhaps, or an exotic surf and turf combo in the form of langoustine and squid plancha with saffron pearls and pig's trotter cake, or maybe squab pigeon on vine shoots embers, confit roots and fruits and violet dip. Regional French cheeses are paired with something sweet (Roquefort with cinnamon doughnut, white chocolate and Cognac jelly), with desserts running to turrón with sweet foie gras, Baileys meringues and passionfruit.

Chef Pascal Aussignac **Owner** P Aussignac & V Labeyrie **Times** 12-2/7-10 Closed Xmas, New Year, BHs, Sun, L Sat **Prices** Fixed L 3 course £25, Starter £10-£16, Main £20-£23, Dessert £10, Service added but optional 12.5% **Wines** 140 bottles over £20, 15 by glass **Notes** Fixed D 5 course £55, Vegetarian menu, Dress restrictions, Smart casual **Seats** 40 **Children** Portions **Parking** NCP opposite restaurant

Morgan M
PLAN 3 E3

◉◉ Modern French V

French master moves to the City

☎ 020 7609 3560
50 Long Ln, Barbican EC1A 9EJ
dir: Nearest station: Barbican, Farringdon. Opposite Smithfield Market, left out of Barbican Tube, 2 mins walk

Islington house prices are doubtless robust enough to survive the loss, but Morgan Meunier's departure from the borough will have saddened the hearts of a good many locals. The City is the beneficiary, for Monsieur M has moved just around the corner from the Barbican, opposite Smithfield Market. And very smart it looks too, with its olive-green frontage and etched glass windows. Inside, there's a decidedly natural quality to the chosen colour palette, with patterned wallpaper and natural wood floors to match. Wherever he pitches up, Morgan's food will garner a following, built as it is on robust French foundations and a good deal of craft and endeavour. His cooking is a harmonious meeting of modern refinement and seasonally-led classicism. Ravioli of snails in Chablis, for example, is rich with earthy flavours, topped with garlic froth and finished with red wine jus, while main-course pavé of halibut comes with wild mushroom tempura that gets the light batter just right and packs a wonderful punch. To finish, tarte paysanne is a skillfully constructed dessert, with an accompanying olive oil and lime ice cream, and all the high-class incidentals such as amuse-bouche, pre-dessert and excellent bread (served with wonderful butter) only add to the whole experience.

Chef M Meunier, S Soulard **Owner** Morgan Meunier **Times** 12-2.30/6-10.30 Closed 24-30 Dec, Sun, L Sat **Prices** Fixed L 2 course fr £21.50, Fixed D 3 course fr £25.50, Tasting menu £50, Starter £9.50-£14.50, Main £21.50-£28.50, Dessert £9.50, Service added but optional 12.5% **Wines** 140 bottles over £20, 2 bottles under £20, 13 by glass **Notes** Tasting menu 6 course, veg £46, Grazing tasting dishes, Vegetarian menu, Dress restrictions, Smart casual **Seats** 59 **Children** Portions **Parking** Long Lane

Moro
PLAN 3 D4

◉◉ Islamic, Mediterranean ⬥NOTABLE WINE LIST

Vibrant home of Moorish food

☎ 020 7833 8336
34-36 Exmouth Market EC1R 4QE
e-mail: info@moro.co.uk
dir: Nearest station: Farringdon, Angel. 5 mins walk from Sadler's Wells theatre, between Farringdon Road and Rosebery Avenue

It may have celebrated its 15th birthday in 2012, but the energetic Moro still has bags of contemporary verve and vigour; Sam and Samantha Clark's Moorish food (from the eastern Mediterranean via North Africa to southern Spain) proves ever popular. The inventive, daily-changing menus deliver vibrant, colourful dishes of generosity and big flavours: wood-roasted chicken with sweet-and-sour

aubergine salad, pomegranate, mint and braised chard, for example, or charcoal-grilled lamb served with caramelised marrow, lemon, farika and yoghurt. Desserts - like grilled peaches with raspberries and labneh - keep things fresh and simple. Tapas is served pretty much all day at its zinc-topped bar, while a corking list of sherries and Iberian wines fit the mood. The room is a hard-surfaced, white-linen-free space (floorboards, café-style chairs or wall banquettes, tightly packed tables and plain walls and pillars), which means noise levels are on the high side, but that's all part of the fun. There are alfresco tables, too, plus a dinky, casual, sibling tapas operation (Morito) next door.

Chef Samuel & Samantha Clark **Owner** Mr & Mrs S Clark & Mark Sainsbury **Times** 12.30-2.30/6-10.30 Closed Xmas, New Year, BHs, D Sun **Prices** Starter £6.50-£9.50, Main £15.50-£19.50, Dessert £6-£7.50, Service added but optional 12.5% **Wines** 76 bottles over £20, 6 bottles under £20, 12 by glass **Notes** Private dining L only, Sunday L, Vegetarian available, Civ Wed 70 **Seats** 90, Pr/dining room 20 **Children** Portions **Parking** NCP Farringdon Rd

North Road
PLAN 3 E3

◉◉ Modern European

Exciting new Nordic cooking in bustling Clerkenwell

☎ 020 3217 0033
69-73 Saint John St EC1M 4AN
e-mail: contact@nrrestaurant.com
dir: Nearest station: Barbican, Farringdon

There's a good deal of cool Scandinavian style to Danish chef-patron Christoffer Hruskova's smartly understated Clerkenwell restaurant. The soothingly minimalist interior - neutral tones, parquet flooring, well-designed seating and simplistic line drawings - meets expectations in a series of interlinking rooms with an open-to-view glass kitchen. But the innovative, dynamic new Nordic cooking is full of surprise, reflecting the new wave that has Rene Redzepi of Copenhagen's Noma as its leading light. Hruskova's light modern approach applies of-the-moment kitchen technique to quality British-only produce - you won't find chocolate or olive oil used as they're not indigenous to these shores. Creative flavour combos and cutting-edge presentation are all in the mix; a first-course dish of Galloway beef cheeks, perhaps, with verbena and pear and Jerusalem artichokes, followed by Norfolk venison and smoked bone marrow with beetroot textures and wild sorrel. Among fish main courses Scottish halibut comes with salsify, burnt onions and Alexander shoots, and for dessert, millet porridge comes with toasted ice cream, crumble and linseed nougat. As you might expect, there is a tasting menu.

Chef Christoffer Hruskova **Owner** Christoffer Hruskova **Times** 12-2.30/6-10.30 Closed Xmas, BHs, Sun, L Sat **Prices** Starter £8.50-£9.50, Main £18-£24, Dessert £7-£9, Service added but optional **Notes** Vegetarian available **Seats** 62, Pr/dining room 22 **Parking** On street, Smithfield NCP

St John
PLAN 3 E3

◉◉ British

Nose-to-tail eating at its best

☎ 020 3301 8069
26 St John St EC1M 4AY
e-mail: reservations@stjohnrestaurant.com
dir: Nearest station: Farringdon. 100yds from Smithfield Market, northside

Fergus Henderson and Trevor Gulliver pioneered the vogue for 'nose-to-tail' eating for adventurous, un-squeamish foodies when they set up St John in a former smokehouse up the road from Smithfield market in 1994. Since then, the concept has expanded a lot of minds and turned diners on to less-common cuts of meat and the bits that might once have been ignored. Now firmly entrenched on London's dining scene (and with two sister venues - St John Bread & Wine and the St John Hotel), the place has become something of a rite of passage for anyone claiming foodie credentials. A skinny staircase leads up from the ground-floor bar and bakery to the dining room, where the utilitarian look remains the same: canteen-style tables covered with paper tablecloths, white walls, staff dressed in long aprons, and an open-to-view kitchen to feed in to the buzz. On the food front, others have aped the style, but few come close to achieving St John's unvarnished, honest simplicity. The tight-lipped menu takes advantage of what's good each day, updating dishes between 'lunch and supper', so while roast bone marrow with parsley salad is a fixture, you might encounter any, or none, of the following: crispy pig skin and dandelion; rabbit offal and radishes; lamb tongues, butter beans and green sauce; or grilled ox heart, carrots and horseradish. It's not all aimed at carnivores either - there could be turbot, chips and tartare sauce, and veggies get a look in with the likes of beetroot, boiled egg and spinach.

Chef Christopher Gillard **Owner** T Gulliver & F Henderson **Times** 12-3/6-11 Closed Xmas, New Year, BHs, L Sat, D Sun **Prices** Starter £6.30-£11.50, Main £13.80-£18.90, Dessert £6.80-£8, Service added but optional, Groups min 6 service 12.5% **Wines** 15 by glass **Notes** Feasting menu groups 10 or more, Vegetarian available **Seats** 110, Pr/dining room 18 **Parking** Meters in street

LONDON EC1 *continued*

Smiths of Smithfield, Top Floor

PLAN 3 E3

◉◉ Modern British

Terrific London views, a buzzy vibe and spot-on ingredients

☎ 020 7251 7950

(Top Floor), 67-77 Charterhouse St EC1M 6HJ
e-mail: reservations@smithsofsmithfield.co.uk
dir: Nearest station: Farringdon, Barbican, Chancery Lane. Opposite Smithfield Market

From the top floor of this Grade II listed former meat warehouse by Smithfield Market the views across to St Paul's are mightily impressive. Up here is the most refined restaurant of the bunch - Top Floor - but it's still a relaxed place with floor-to-ceiling windows to catch that view. Wherever you eat - breakfast or brunch or alcoholic milkshakes at ground-floor level, or the dining room on the second floor - clued-up staff pitch the balance of banter and knowledgeable efficiency just right. With the market just opposite, you'd expect top quality produce on the menu and SOS absolutely delivers, particularly on rare breed meats. Up on the Top Floor a flavoursome shellfish risotto and tempura soft-shelled crab is a nicely judged first course, followed perhaps by duck breast with bok choy, mango, chilli and star anise sauce. Almond sponge with poached Cox's Orange Pippin apple and toffee sauce is a fine finale.

Times 12-3.30/6.30-12 Closed 25-26 Dec, 1 Jan, L Sat, D Sun

LONDON EC2

L'Anima

PLAN 3 H4

◉◉ Italian

A contemporary take on regional Italian cooking

☎ 020 7422 7000

1 Snowden St, Broadgate West EC2A 2DQ
e-mail: info@lanima.co.uk
dir: Nearest station: Liverpool Street

L'Anima has the sort of über-cool, contemporary style that could have been airlifted from style-conscious Milan, all white seats, brownish porphyry walls and floor-to-ceiling windows, with a lightwood floor and a chic bar at one end. The kitchen delivers contemporary versions of traditional Italian regional dishes, from malloreddus (hand-made eggless pasta, flavoured with saffron, typical of Sardinia) with clams, salted mullet roe and tomatoes to Sicilian-style rabbit. Authentic Italian ingredients are carefully sourced, or made in-house, treatments are generally straightforward so flavours are clearly defined, and presentation is unfussy and all the better for it. A meal could start with simple crab linguine, go on to slow-roast belly pork sauced with honey, paprika and spices, with a dessert like zeppola (deep-fried choux pastry filled with lemon cream) to crown it all.

Chef Francesco Mazzei **Owner** Francesco Mazzei
Times 11.45-3/5.30-11 Closed BHs, Sun, L Sat
Prices Fixed L 2 course £24.50, Tasting menu £50, Starter £9.50-£23.50, Main £13-£36, Dessert £7-£15, Service added but optional 12.5% **Wines** 240 bottles over £20, 5 bottles under £20, 18 by glass **Notes** Tasting menu 5 course Mon-Sat, Fixed L Mon-Fri until 7pm, Vegetarian available **Seats** 120, Pr/dining room 15
Children Portions **Parking** On street

Boisdale of Bishopsgate

PLAN 3 H3

◉ Traditional British

Cooking showcasing Scotland's best produce

☎ 020 7283 1763

Swedeland Court, 202 Bishopsgate EC2M 4NR
e-mail: manager@boisdale-city.co.uk
dir: Nearest station: Liverpool Street. Opposite Liverpool St station

In a narrow alley near Petticoat Lane market, Boisdale's City branch (see also Boisdale of Belgravia) occupies a subtly lit vaulted basement, its vivid red-painted walls hung with a plethora of photographs and prints, with booth seating, upright timbers, and, to underline its Scottish credentials, a tartan carpet; there's also a champagne and oyster bar. The cooking is founded on thoroughbred Scottish meats and seafood, starters including various ways with smoked salmon - perhaps as céviche with pea and avocado purée - the range broadened by the likes of a haggis Scotch egg with piccalilli, and crab with lobster jelly, horseradish and fennel cream. Main courses tend to be safe bets: prime steaks with béarnaise or foie gras and truffle shavings, along with Dover sole meunière with Jersey Royals and spinach, or Hebridean mutton with confit potato, smoked onion purée, and spring greens with pickled raisins.

Chef Neil Churchill **Owner** Ranald Macdonald
Times 11-3/6-9 Closed Xmas, 31 Dec, BHs, Sat-Sun
Prices Food prices not confirmed for 2013. Please telephone for details **Wines** 117 bottles over £20, 3 bottles under £20, 21 by glass **Notes** Vegetarian available, Dress restrictions, Smart casual **Seats** 100
Parking Middlesex St

Bonds

PLAN 3 G2

◉◉ Modern British, European

Well-crafted, modish cooking in an old City banking hall

☎ 020 7657 8088 & 7657 8090

Threadneedles, 5 Threadneedle St EC2R 8AY
e-mail: bonds@theetoncollection.co.uk
dir: Nearest station: Bank. Bank Tube station exit 3, follow Threadneedle St for 200m, then cross Finch Lane, entrance on right

Housed in a former City banking hall, the Threadneedles Hotel is unsurprisingly right in the heart of the financial district, and it makes a pretty fine setting for some ambitious, ingredient-led cooking in its Bonds restaurant. Close to many iconic London landmarks - St Paul's

Cathedral, the Gherkin and the Bank of England - this premises has a crack at making an impression, too, and with its soaring ceiling, stained-glass dome dating back to 1856, pillars aplenty and American walnut walls against marble floors, it does a pretty good job. Stephen Smith's technical modern European cooking is the main attraction, though. Begin with a tian of Dorset crab, avocado and apple, served with tarragon mayonnaise and tomato vinaigrette, then move onto confit and roast coquelet with potato and thyme rösti, curly kale, button onions, Alsace smoked bacon and poultry jus. Standards don't slip at dessert stage either: peanut butter parfait with chocolate brownie, butterscotch base, chocolate ganache and pomegranate jelly cubes, for example.

Chef Stephen Smith **Owner** Westmont Hospitality Group
Times 12-2.30/6-10 Closed BHs, Sat-Sun **Prices** Fixed L 2 course £19.95-£24.95, Fixed D 3 course £19.95-£25.95, Starter £7.25-£13.75, Main £13.75-£30.75, Dessert £7.50-£10.25, Service added but optional 12.5%
Wines 100 bottles over £20, 3 bottles under £20, 14 by glass **Notes** Vegetarian available, Dress restrictions, Smart casual **Seats** 80, Pr/dining room 16
Children Portions **Parking** NCP Finsbury Sq

Catch Restaurant

PLAN 3 H3

◉ Modern European, Seafood

Fresh fish, shellfish and champagne in chic City hotel

☎ 020 7618 7200

ANdAZ London, 40 Liverpool St EC2M 7QN
e-mail: london.restres@andaz.com
dir: Nearest station: Liverpool Street. On corner of Liverpool St & Bishopsgate, attached to Liverpool St station

Catch reels in the City suits and high heels to sample its seafood and champagne in the über-trendy ANdAZ Hotel. The horseshoe-shaped champagne bar (with separate bar menu) is a smart see-and-be-seen spot, while the adjoining dining room's Victorian glamour - stunning stained-glass windows, marble columns and staircase - sets a more sedate tone with white-linen-clad tables. Watch as the chefs effortlessly open-up fresh shellfish and glistening crustaceans from a splendid tiered display. The kitchen adds contemporary flourish to classic dishes without over-complicating flavours, using quality sustainable produce and supporting small-scale fishermen. There are six types of oysters available, while main courses such as line-caught Cornish sea bass might be teamed with rope-grown mussels, samphire risotto and bouillabaisse jus. Traditionalists aren't forgotten either, with classics like fish and chips (served with English watercress and tartare sauce) having their place too.

Chef Martin Scholz **Owner** Hyatt Int **Times** 12-2.30/6-10 Closed Xmas, New Year, BHs, Sat-Sun **Prices** Fixed L 2 course fr £20, Fixed D 3 course fr £25, Starter £7-£16, Main £13-£34, Dessert £7-£11, Service added but optional 12.5% **Wines** 100+ bottles over £20, 20 by glass **Notes** Vegetarian available **Seats** 50 **Parking** NCP London Wall St

Cinnamon Kitchen PLAN 3 H3

@@ Modern Indian

Modern Indian cuisine in former warehouse

☎ 020 7626 5000 & 7397 9611
9 Devonshire Square EC2M 4YL
e-mail: info@cinnamon-kitchen.com
dir: Nearest station: Liverpool St. Follow New St (off Bishopsgate) into Devonshire Sq

The younger sister of Cinnamon Club (see entry) is, appropriately enough, in what used to be the East India Company's spice warehouse, some features of which remain in a large, buzzy space with polished wooden tables and leather-look chairs; there's a sleek bar serving cocktails and a terrace for outdoor eating, too. The philosophy is straightforward: to fuse the seasonings and spices of the sub-continent with native produce and traditions to create modern, innovative dishes, resulting in starters like a Bengali-style vegetable cake with beetroot and raisins, and charred pork ribs in a hot-and-sweet glaze. The cooking is marked out by a lack of frills and fuss - although dishes make a visual impact, with blobs and drizzles of this and that - well-judged use of spices and careful timing. The full-on flavour of caramelised ox cheek in date and apricot sauce is in marked contrast to the subtlety of prawns stir-fried with Tanjore spices, while Rajasthani-style roast deer comes with stir-fried mushrooms.

Times 12-3.30/6-10.30 Closed 25-26 Dec, 1 Jan, some BHs, Sun, L Sat

Coq d'Argent PLAN 3 G2

@@ French **NEW**

Traditional French food and rooftop views

☎ 0171 3955 000
1 Poultry EC2R 8EJ
e-mail: coqdargent.co.uk
dir: Nearest station: Bank

With what must be some of the best rooftop views in central London, Coq d'Argent is a smart contemporary setting for some confident French cooking. Divided into a brasserie (food at lunchtimes, lively bar in the evening) and a restaurant with a reception area in between, both have terraces which are a big pull when the sun shines on the City. The restaurant has tables dressed up for serious dining and service which matches the formality without ever taking itself too seriously. Both menus are printed in French with English translations; from the restaurant menu you might kick off with a foie gras parfait with pear and ginger relish, before moving on to baked stone bass with fennel, courgette, tomato and saffron casserole. Desserts to send you home (or back to work) happy include apple tart with roasted cardamom ice cream, and frozen passionfruit and vanilla vacherin.

Chef Mickael Weiss **Times** 11.30-3/6-10 **Prices** Fixed L 2 course £26, Fixed D 3 course £30, Service added but optional 12.5% **Notes** Sunday L

Eyre Brothers PLAN 3 H4

@@ Spanish, Portuguese

Big, enticing Iberian flavours in the City

☎ 020 7613 5346
70 Leonard St EC2A 4QX
e-mail: eyrebros@btconnect.com
dir: Nearest station: Old Street Exit 4

Doing its authentic Iberian thing in the City's northern hinterland since 2001, this modern, urban-cool outfit rather slips under the radar of its West-End counterparts. David Eyre's cooking draws inspiration from across the Iberian Peninsula, with full-on flavours created from top-notch produce treated with integrity and skill. Take an opener of Viscaya salted anchovies on grilled bread teamed with pimentos de piquillo, black olives, capers and a soft-boiled egg to evoke those sun-drench flavours, or a big-hearted signature main course of grilled fillet of acorn-fed Ibérica pig (marinated with smoked paprika, thyme and garlic) delivered with patatas pobres (oven potatoes with green peppers, onions, garlic and white wine). Tapas are served at the all-day bar, while well-matched Spanish and Portuguese wines patriotically take their cue from the cuisine. It's a stylish place without trying too hard, with full-drop windows, classy wood veneer and brown leather banquettes and matching chairs, while a hip backing track of jazz music and friendly service keeping it humming along nicely.

Chef Dave Eyre, Joao Cleto **Owner** Eyre Bros Restaurants Ltd **Times** 12-3/6.30-11 Closed Xmas-New Year, BHs, Sun, L Sat **Prices** Food prices not confirmed for 2013. Please telephone for details **Wines** 50 bottles over £20, 7 bottles under £20, 14 by glass **Notes** Vegetarian available **Seats** 100 **Parking** On street

Manicomio, City PLAN 3 F2

@ Modern Italian

Modern glass-fronted building and equally modern Italian food

☎ 020 7726 5010
Gutter Ln EC2V 8AS
e-mail: gutterlane@manicomio.co.uk
dir: Nearest station: St Paul's. Just off Cheapside

The Norman Foster-designed three storey, glass-fronted building offers something different as you go up the floors, starting at the casual ground-floor café (open from breakfast), heading up to the first-floor restaurant, and peaking with the Roundhouse cocktail lounge and private party space. It's as slick inside as out, making it popular with the district's bright young things. Gutsy modern Italian food combines well-sourced, home-grown produce with Italian imports. Antipasti might include grilled cuttlefish with black farro, roasted peppers and tomato dust, then move on to roast Devon duckling with salsify purée, rhubarb and Swiss chard, or sautéed Sicilian red prawns and Veraci clams with fregola, chilli and courgettes. If the artisan Italian cheese board doesn't tempt, perhaps jasmine tea crème brûlée will. The 100-plus bin wine list caters for all pockets.

Chef Tom Salt **Owner** Andrew & Ninai Zarach **Times** 12-3/6-10 Closed 1 wk Xmas, Sat-Sun **Prices** Starter £8-£11, Main £13.50-£29.50, Dessert £5.50-£10.50, Service added but optional 12.5% **Wines** 124 bottles over £20, 2 bottles under £20, 14 by glass **Notes** Vegetarian available **Seats** 95, Pr/dining room 60 **Children** Portions

Miyako PLAN 3 H3

@ Japanese

Authentic Japanese cooking and buzzy atmosphere

☎ 020 7618 7100
ANdAZ London, 40 Liverpool St EC2M 7QN
e-mail: london.restres@andaz.com
dir: Nearest station: Liverpool Street. On corner of Liverpool St & Bishopsgate

As the name announces, this is the Japanese dining option of the sprawling ANdAZ hotel, though it has a stand-alone feel with its own street entrance. A design-led affair, it's effortlessly cool and modern, with a clean-lined, low-lit, minimalist feel of bamboo-panelled walls and black lacquered tables and chairs. The bustling sushi bar counter upfront services the City suits who pile in for lunch (and queue for take-out bento boxes), while beyond the dining room has a slightly calmer atmosphere. The menu deals in a wide range of authentic Japanese cooking; from sashimi (scallop or squid) to hand-rolled sushi (eel and avocado) and tempura (prawn or vegetable), while salmon teriyaki or specials like sea bass goma ankake (deep-fried with a sesame seed crust and vegetable sauce) come as larger plates.

Chef Sueharu Hamaue **Owner** Hyatt **Times** 12-2.15/6-10 Closed Xmas, New Year, Sun, L Sat **Prices** Starter £3-£7, Main £16-£28, Dessert £7-£11, Service added but optional 12.5% **Wines** 11+ bottles over £20, 9 by glass **Notes** Vegetarian available **Seats** 30 **Parking** NCP London Wall

1901 Restaurant PLAN 3 H3

@@@ – see page 264

Rhodes Twenty Four PLAN 3 H2

@@@ – see page 264

1901 Restaurant

LONDON EC2   **PLAN 3 H3**

British ⬧NOTABLE WINE LIST

21st-century style and classy, contemporary cooking

☎ 020 7618 7000
ANdAZ London, 40 Liverpool St EC2M 7QN
e-mail: london.restres@andaz.com
dir: Nearest station: Liverpool Street. On corner of Liverpool St & Bishopsgate

Despite its name, this restaurant (one of five within the ANdAZ London) is certainly no blast from the past. The grand Victorian building of red-brick unites traditional features such as soaring classical pillars with a decidedly funky wow-factor, and its 'floating' marble champagne bar is unsurprisingly popular with the local clientele and dominates the entrance to the 1901 Restaurant. Originally the hotel's ballroom, it has a beautiful glass vaulted dome ceiling which was protected during the Second World War by being wrapped in mattresses and blankets. There's an upbeat atmosphere helped along by music and the enthusiasm of the casually dressed (and knowledgeable) staff. The food lives up to this trendy setting, the kitchen turning out skillfully cooked dishes which show an enthusiasm for exploring flavour and texture combos. British produce is at the heart of it all. A thoroughly modish first course sees scallops (perfectly cooked) combined with chicken wings, sweetcorn purée and balsamic sauce, followed by beautifully cooked venison with a cobnut crust, Granny Smith apple and red wine purée and creamed salsify. A mini lemon meringue pie is accompanied by British berries and a refined yet intense basil sorbet. The cheese trolley is consigned to history and replaced by a cheese and wine tasting table. The wine list is certainly worth a visit with some real classics at the top end sitting alongside excellent value bottles; all are enthusiastically described by the sommelier and dedicated wine team.

Chef Michael Kreiling **Owner** Hyatt
Times 12-2.30/6.30-10 Closed Xmas, New Year, BHs, Sun, L Sat **Prices** Fixed L 2 course fr £19, Fixed D 3 course fr £29, Tasting menu £60, Starter £10-£15, Main £16-£28, Dessert £7-£11, Service added but optional 12.5% **Wines** 500 bottles over £20, 50 by glass **Notes** Tasting menu 6 course, Vegetarian available **Seats** 100 **Parking** NCP London Wall

Rhodes Twenty Four

LONDON EC2   **PLAN 3 H2**

British

Exceptional cooking above the City

☎ 020 7877 7703
Tower 42, 25 Old Broad St EC2N 1HQ
e-mail: reservations@rhodes24.co.uk
dir: Nearest station: Bank, Liverpool Street

It is all very much in the name; Gary Rhodes' city outpost (delivering the man's trademark reinvigorated British-style dishes) is 24 floors up above the capital's skyline in what is still familiarly referred to as the NatWest Tower - now Tower 42. Once through airport-style security, a high-speed lift whisks you skyward for show-stopping views from the heart of corporate money-land. The dining room's curved floor-to-ceiling windows make the most of the cityscape - day or night - with banquette seating on the back wall sitting on a raised tier so everyone gets a gander. The neutral colour scheme - dark greens or cream leather seating, hazel carpet and white linen - doesn't compete for your attention, but the well-crafted food most certainly does. The menu champions Rhodes' love affair with British food via some gutsy ingredients, with punchy flavours to the fore, and presentation adding a bit of theatre of its own. A starter of slow-braised ox cheek pie, for example, might come with mash and smoked eel in a parsley liquor, the latter arriving in a separate mini-pan that's added to the dish at the table. Fish is a strength too; witness a fillet of red mullet delivered on wilted greens with its separate mini-pan of citrus squid risotto and jug of delicious mullet gravy. Traditionalists could go for a main course such as steamed mutton and onion pudding with buttered carrots, or a bread-and-butter pudding dessert, while poached rhubarb with toasted marshmallow meringue, rhubarb sorbet and warm vanilla custard offers a more modish alternative. Peripherals such as bread, amuse-bouche and petits fours (fabulous passionfruit marshmallow, perhaps) keep standards sky-high to the end. The slick service and comprehensive wine list complete the picture, but it's worth mentioning that cocktails in the bar (with those views) are a bit of a treat.

Chef Gary Rhodes **Owner** Compass Group
Times 12-2.30/6-9.15 Closed Xmas, New Year, BHs, Sat-Sun **Prices** Tasting menu £75-£105, Starter £9.80-£17.80, Main £18.50-£31.50, Dessert £9.45-£13.75, Service added but optional 12.5% **Wines** 310 bottles over £20, 14 by glass **Notes** Tasting menu 5 course (£105 with wine), Vegetarian available, Dress restrictions, Smart casual, no shorts **Seats** 75, Pr/dining room 30

Save on Hotels. Book at **theAA.com/hotel**

LONDON, CENTRAL (EC3) 265 **ENGLAND**

LONDON EC3

Apex City of London Hotel
PLAN 3 H1

Modern European

Smart European flavours in a swanky City hotel

☎ 020 7977 9580 & 0845 365 0002
1 Seething Ln EC3N 4AX
e-mail: addendum@apexhotels.co.uk
dir: Nearest station: Tower Hill. Follow Lower Thames St, left onto Trinity Square, left into Muscovy St, right into Seething Ln, opposite Seething Ln gardens

Thanks to its location smack bang in the middle of the Square Mile, Addendum (in the Apex City of London Hotel) is a big hit with those who work around these here parts. It's a contemporary-looking space with soft lighting, sleek furniture and smartly laid tables setting the scene for some smart modern European cooking. Kick off with an old favourite such as London Particular soup (pea and bacon) served with parsley cream and garlic croûtons, following on with fillet of sustainable pollock with cabbage, lentils and red wine sauce, or breast of corn-fed chicken with mushrooms, tarragon and garlic mash. The wine list has a good range by the glass.

Chef Darren Thomas **Owner** Norman Springford
Times 12-2.30/6-10 **Prices** Fixed D 3 course fr £19.50, Starter £5.20-£7.25, Main £12.50-£19.50, Dessert £4.50-£6.50, Service added but optional 12.5%
Wines 41 bottles over £20, 2 bottles under £20
Notes Sunday L, Vegetarian available **Seats** 40
Children Portions **Parking** Car park in Lower Thames St

Caravaggio
PLAN 3 H2

Modern Italian

Smart City Italian in former banking hall

☎ 020 7626 6206
107-112 Leadenhall St EC3A 4DP
e-mail: caravaggio@etruscarestaurants.com
dir: Nearest station: Aldgate, Fenchurch St. Close to Leadenhall Market & the Lloyds building

The ornate high ceilings, splendid art-deco light fittings, and a grand staircase sweeping up to a mezzanine gallery certainly add a touch of class to this smart Square Mile Italian in a revamped banking hall. The décor has a retro feel recalling the days of luxurious ocean liners, a theme that finds its reflection in the eclectic mix of classic and contemporary regional Italian cooking. Alongside standard fare such as saffron risotto with fresh seafood, and grilled rib-eye of Argentinian beef with hand-cut chips and béarnaise, there are some interesting options: home-made chestnut maccheroncini with turnip tops and fresh tomato, followed by roasted loin of venison with cavolo nero, potato gratin and cranberry jus. Desserts follow the theme with a panettone tiramisù, or you could go for a savoury finish: mature pecorino sheeps' cheese and a shot of venerable grappa. The vibe is buzzy and service is as slick as the lunchtime City suits.

Chef Faliero Lenta **Owner** Enzo & Piero Quaradeghini
Times 12-3/6.30-10 Closed Xmas, BHs, Sat-Sun
Prices Fixed L 2 course £16.50, Fixed D 2 course £16.50, Starter £6.50-£11, Main £12.70-£25, Dessert £5.80-£7, Service added but optional 12.5% **Wines** 124 bottles over £20, 2 bottles under £20, 12 by glass **Notes** Vegetarian available, Dress restrictions, Smart casual **Seats** 150 **Parking** On street

Chamberlains Restaurant
PLAN 3 H2

Modern British, Seafood

Super-fresh fish in the heart of the City

☎ 020 7648 8690
23-25 Leadenhall Market EC3V 1LR
e-mail: info@chamberlains.org
dir: Nearest station: Bank, Monument

Long-established Billingsgate fishmongers Chamberlain and Thelwell are behind this classy City venture, so no surprises that fish and seafood are its main stock in trade. Spread over three floors and sitting pretty amid the Victorian splendour of Leadenhall Market, Chamberlains buzzes with the power-lunch crowd. There's an all-weather front terrace (beneath the market's glazed roof), while inside huge windows give views over the action from the lively brasserie-like ground floor and mezzanine balcony. Blond-wood floors, red seating, white linen and subtle nautical references keep things light and breezily fashionable. Upstairs there's a more formal room, and a 'chill-out' bar (with a separate menu) hides in the vaulted basement. Sea-fresh seafood is what to expect, with provenance and sourcing rightly to the fore. The menu mixes classics (lobster thermidor or skate wing with brown nut butter) with more modern thinking (wild sea bass with braised oxtail, endive and hazelnut dressing). Some dishes are simply cooked without frills, others a little more intricate, and there's a few meat options too (assiette of lamb, for instance).

Chef Andrew Jones **Owner** Chamberlain & Thelwell
Times 12-9.30 Closed Xmas, New Year & BHs, Sat-Sun
Prices Food prices not confirmed for 2013. Please telephone for details **Wines** 60 bottles over £20, 10 bottles under £20, 8 by glass **Notes** Vegetarian available **Seats** 150, Pr/dining room 65 **Children** Portions

Prism Brasserie and Bar
PLAN 3 H2

Modern European

Accomplished brasserie cooking in the City

☎ 020 7256 3888
147 Leadenhall St EC3V 4QT
e-mail: prism.events@harveynichols.com
web: www.harveynichols.com
dir: Nearest station: Bank, Monument. Take exit 4 from Bank tube station, 5 mins walk

The grand surroundings of the former Bank of New York bring a touch of style and class to this fashionable Harvey Nichols' heart-of-the-City outpost. Soaring Doric columns and lofty decorative ceilings sit alongside fashionable red leather chairs, white-clothed tables, striking flower displays and mood artwork to deliver a touch of colour to the dining quarter's lunching bankers and brokers. The large bar area comes with low-slung matching seating and a baby grand piano that hints at more relaxed evening service. The versatile brasserie menu covers all the bases, with the kitchen's fresh, clean-flavoured, modern approach driven by top-notch produce, including ingredients from their own rooftop kitchen garden. Pot-roasted duck breast, for example, served with forestière potatoes, steamed curly kale and pan juices, or from the grill, 50-day dry-aged Longhorn rib-eye. For dessert, perhaps prune and almond tart served with prune and Armagnac ice cream.

Chef Daniel Sherlock **Owner** Harvey Nichols
Times 11.30-3/6-10 Closed Xmas, BHs, Sat-Sun
Prices Fixed L 2 course £25.50, Fixed D 3 course £29.50, Starter £8.95-£13.50, Main £16.95-£27.95, Dessert £6.50, Service added but optional 12.5%
Wines 67 bottles over £20, 12 by glass **Notes** Vegetarian available, Civ Wed 150 **Seats** 120, Pr/dining room 40 **Children** Portions **Parking** On street & NCP

LONDON EC3 *continued*

Restaurant Sauterelle

PLAN 3 G2

@@ Modern European V

Confident contemporary cooking in landmark building

☎ 020 7618 2483
The Royal Exchange EC3V 3LR
e-mail: pierrem@danddlondon.com
web: www.restaurantsauterelle.com
dir: Nearest station: Bank. Exit 3. In heart of business centre

Dining up on the mezzanine floor of the historic Royal Exchange certainly adds plenty of wow factor to proceedings at glossy Sauterelle. Sitting beneath glazed arches peering down on an inner courtyard glistening with boutiques and jewellers, and surrounded by expense account Square Milers, a more glammed-up setting is harder to imagine; the vibe is suitably chic, service is slickly professional, and the cooking inspired by modern European thinking. Robin Gill has paid his dues in stellar kitchens and delivers fashionably-dressed dishes of well-judged, full-throttle flavours, starting typically with apple wood-smoked eel matched with beetroot, horseradish, wild sorrel, white radish and parsley. The robust approach could bring 28-day-aged Aberdeen Angus beef fillet with smoked potato purée, red wine, wild mushrooms and bone marrow, but the kitchen can also turn its hand to lemon sole with razor clams, cockles, brown crab and lettuce sauce. Desserts such as white chocolate mousse with blood orange sorbet and cardamom meringue also bring refined combinations of taste and texture.

Chef Robin Gill **Owner** D & D London **Times** 12-2.30/6-10 Closed BHs, Sat-Sun **Prices** Fixed L 2 course fr £20, Fixed D 3 course fr £23.50, Tasting menu fr £48, Starter £7.50-£14, Main £18-£31, Dessert £7.50-£10.50, Service added but optional 12.5% **Wines** 134 bottles over £20, 2 bottles under £20, 14 by glass **Notes** Fixed D 5 course £35, Tasting menu D 7 course, Vegetarian menu **Seats** 66, Pr/dining room 26 **Children** Portions **Parking** Bell Wharf Lane, Finsbury Sq, Shoe Lane

LONDON EC4

Barbecoa

PLAN 3 F2

@ Modern

Jamie's bbq joint

☎ 020 3005 8555
20 New Change Passage EC4M 9AG
dir: Nearest station: St Paul's. Opposite St Paul's Cathedral

Expect a buzzy, vibrant atmosphere, a stylishly cool interior, stunning views of St Paul's Cathedral, and some top-notch meat at Jamie Oliver and Adam Perry Lang's barbecue steakhouse in the City. Cooking by fire, smoke and charcoal is the central theme here, which means robata grills, tandoor ovens and Texan smokers among other bits of snazzy kit. The flames and smoke from the semi-open kitchen add a touch of theatre in the first-floor restaurant, where floor-to-ceiling windows offer great views of the cathedral. The meat comes directly from the farm and is prepared in the downstairs butchery, with beef being hung on-site for five to eleven weeks. Tuck into a plate of Lyme Bay crab with avocado, chervil and tomato before the main event, perhaps lamb chops from the wood oven, served with butter beans and Swiss chard, or dry-aged sirloin steak from the grill with a cep and rosemary cream.

Chef Jamie Oliver, Adam Perry Lang, Sebastian La Rocca **Owner** Jamie Oliver, Adam Perry Lang **Times** 11.30-11 **Prices** Starter £8-£11, Main £16-£33, Dessert £9-£11 **Wines** 8 by glass **Notes** Vegetarian available, Air con **Seats** 220, Pr/dining room 30 **Children** Portions

Bread Street Kitchen

PLAN 3 F2

@@ Modern European **NEW**

Vibrant, city-cool brasserie from the Gordon Ramsay stable

☎ 020 3030 4050
10 Bread St EC4M 9AJ
e-mail: info@breadstreetkitchen.com
dir: Nearest station: Mansion House

From Gordon Ramsay Holdings comes Bread Street Kitchen, an ambitious, 230-cover, two-floored space at the One New Change shopping mall in the City. It's an open-all-day joint, rather cool, with a high-octane, industrial warehouse look - very New York with a pinch of art deco. And, at a reputed cost of £5m, it's a good job it looks good. With gantries, creative lighting (dangling retro-glass lampshades and an army of angle poises), black-and-white floor tiles and leather banquettes, BSK makes an impression. The first-floor level is a long, large-windowed room with an open theatre kitchen stretching its length, while above there's an eye-catching balconied wine gallery. The kitchen turns-out quick-fire dishes from a lengthy all-day roster (including breakfast weekdays); take salmon céviche with ruby grapefruit, jalapeño, lime and coriander from the 'raw bar', perhaps slow-roasted Dingle Dell pork belly with spiced apple sauce from the 'wood stone' oven, or Herdwick mutton and potato pie (with Worcestershire sauce) from the 'hot kitchen'. Do factor-in the necessity for side orders and some very light portioning, though good cocktails, global wines and an army of staff keep things on track.

Chef Erion Karaj **Owner** Gordon Ramsay Holdings **Times** 11-3/5.30-11 **Prices** Food prices not confirmed for 2013. Please telephone for details **Wines** 180 bottles over £20, 2 bottles under £20 **Notes** Late L menu available Mon-Sat 3-5.30pm, Vegetarian available, Dress restrictions, Casual **Seats** 275 **Children** Portions, Menu

The Chancery

PLAN 3 D2

@@ Modern British, French ©

Smart brasserie-style food in the City

☎ 020 7831 4000
9 Cursitor St EC4A 1LL
e-mail: reservations@thechancery.co.uk
dir: Nearest station: Chancery Lane. Situated between High Holborn and Fleet St, just off Chancery Ln

This intimate city brasserie is a favourite with the district's legal folk. Recently refurbished, there are two dining rooms on the ground floor and an even cosier basement space. It's understated inside and out with a slick interior - what they term a 'Manhatten-esque appeal' - plus lots of artworks to catch the eye. Mediterranean-led food with the occasional foray to Asia hits the spot and the kitchen delivers on bold flavour combinations. Start with an ethereal sounding tomato cloud with parmesan tuile, bois boudrin sauce, tomato coulis and pesto, then move onto Barbary duck breast with honey-glazed confit leg, oriental salad and spiced jus. Inventive desserts run to chocolate and black olive tart with rosemary ice cream, or blood orange crème brûlée with a sangria sorbet.

Chef Stephen Englefield **Owner** Zak Jones **Times** 12-2.30/6-10.30 Closed Xmas, Sun, L Sat **Prices** Fixed L 2 course £28.50, Fixed D 3 course £35, Tasting menu £45-£65, Service added but optional 12.5% **Wines** 4 bottles over £20, 2 bottles under £20, 3 by glass **Notes** Tasting menu 6 course, Vegetarian available **Seats** 70, Pr/dining room 40 **Children** Portions **Parking** On street

Chinese Cricket Club

PLAN 3 E1

@ Chinese

Smart setting for confident Chinese cooking

☎ 020 7438 8051
Crowne Plaza London - The City, 19 New Bridge St EC4V 6DB
e-mail: loncy.ccc@ihg.com
dir: Nearest station: Temple, St Paul's, Blackfriars. Opposite Blackfriars underground (exit 8)

In the Crowne Plaza, which also houses Refettorio (see entry), this primarily Szechuan restaurant is named in honour of the Chinese National Cricket team. The rather handsome, contemporary neutral space is decorated with Chinese calligraphy prints on the walls, and smartly turned-out staff have good knowledge of a menu with a mix of modern and traditional ideas (with a European influence cropping up among desserts). Start perhaps with 'hot and numbing' chicken or the excellent soft-shelled crab with chilli mayonnaise, then move on to dry-fried lamb with cumin (succulent and flavoursome), and finish with a hot chocolate fondant with Szechuan pepper cream. Good dim sum options and a tasting and vegetarian menu add to the appeal.

Times 12-2.30/6-10 Closed Xmas & Etr, L 10 Jan

Lutyens Restaurant
PLAN 3 E2

@@ French 🍷NATIONALE WINE LIST

Smart brasserie-style food à la Conran

☎ 020 7583 8385
85 Fleet St EC4Y 1AE
e-mail: info@lutyens-restaurant.com
dir: Nearest station: Chancery Lane, St Pauls, Blackfriars. Adjacent to St Bride's Church

In the former Reuters building on Fleet Street, this Prescott & Conran owned joint bears all the hallmarks of a classic Conran restaurant. As well as the modern and minimalist main restaurant, you'll find a charcuterie counter and shellfish bar, plus a members club. Formally attired waiting staff ensure all goes swimmingly within, and the menu compris (available evenings too) is particularly great value. There's a decidedly French bent to the menu, with brasserie style classics built on tip-top produce. Kick off with oysters or fish soup with rouille and gruyère and follow on with double lamb chop with rosemary and anchovy butter. Brie de Meaux and tomato chutney competes with red wine pear and cinnamon ice cream in the final showdown. A small outside dining area in St Bride's Passage is now open all-day, and on Fridays there's a special offer on fish, chips and champagne.

Times 12-3/5.30-10 Closed Xmas & BHs, Sat-Sun

Refettorio
PLAN 3 E1

@ Italian

Italian refectory dining in the City

☎ 020 7438 8052 & 7438 8055
Crowne Plaza London - The City, 19 New Bridge St EC4V 6DB
e-mail: loncy.refettorio@ihg.com
dir: Nearest station: Blackfriars. On New Bridge St, opposite Blackfriars underground (exit 8)

The Edwardian Crowne Plaza hotel in the City plays host to Refettorio, a slick Italian restaurant under the Giorgio Locatelli banner. The central communal table gives the place its name, but you can choose to sit at regular tables if you wish. The said tables are dark wood and clothless, and the décor, like the cooking, is unfussy but a little bit classy. Menu descriptions are bilingual. Start perhaps with pan-fried scallops with a leek and chick pea purée and a sweet-and-sour sauce, before a pasta dish (maybe spaghettini with octopus, tomato, chilli and garlic), and a secondi such as pork chop with braised black cabbage, chestnut and pork sauce. Finish with a classic tiramisù or a plum tart made with puff pastry.

Chef Alessandro Bay **Owner** Crowne Plaza
Times 12-2.30/6-10.30 Closed Xmas, 24-30 Jan, Etr & BHs, Sun, L Sat **Prices** Fixed L 3 course £25-£50, Fixed D 3 course £25-£35, Starter £5.75-£14.50, Main £12-£24, Dessert £6.50-£9.50, Service added but optional 12.5% **Wines** 60 bottles over £20, 4 bottles under £20, 12 by glass **Notes** Pre-theatre D menu £25, Bi-monthly seasonal menu from £35, Vegetarian available, Dress restrictions, Smart casual **Seats** 100, Pr/dining room 33 **Children** Portions **Parking** NCP - Queen Victoria St

28-50 Wine Workshop & Kitchen
PLAN 3 D2

@@ French, European

Serious about wine, serious about food

☎ 020 7242 8877
140 Fetter Ln EC4A 1BT
e-mail: info@2850.co.uk
dir: Nearest station: Chancery Lane. At the bottom of Fetter Ln, close to the corner of Fleet St

The digits in its name refer to the latitude range, north and south of the equator, within which the world's vineyards are planted - thus announcing this relaxed venture (from the team behind Texture - see entry) is serious about wine. It's an on-trend subterranean venue decked out in an olive and cobalt colour scheme, with wine the theme at every turn (displays of bottles, pictures, corks and boxes). Well-trodden floorboards, exposed brick and artfully placed mirrors add to the unbuttoned vibe, while service is a hit and not just for its wine knowledge. The food is straightforward, French bistro-inspired stuff, with the focus firmly on quality produce and fresh flavours. Thus onglet with chips and choron sauce sits alongside gilt head bream with aubergine purée, grilled courgette and olive oil vinaigrette. Kick off with charcuterie for two or goats' cheese salad, and finish with apple and almond cake partnered with salt caramel ice cream and Calvados anglaise. And then there are the eminently fairly priced, well-chosen wines, with some 30 served by 75ml and 125ml glass, 250ml carafe and bottle, or simply go for a pre-selected flight. There's a second branch in Marylebone.

Chef Paul Walsh **Owner** Xavier Rousset, Agnar Sverrisson **Times** 12-2.30/6-9.30 Closed Xmas, New Year, BHs, Sat-Sun **Prices** Fixed L 2 course fr £15.95, Starter £6-£7.50, Main £14.50-£16.95, Dessert £6-£8.50, Service added but optional 12.5% **Wines** 70 bottles over £20, 2 bottles under £20, 30 by glass **Notes** Air con **Seats** 60, Pr/dining room 12 **Parking** NCP

Vanilla Black
PLAN 3 D2

@@ Modern Vegetarian **NEW** V

Classy vegetarian cookery in a hidden London location

☎ 020 7242 2622
17-18 Tooks Court EC4A 1LB
e-mail: vanillablack@btconnect.com
dir: Nearest station: Chancery Lane. Exit 4 from Chancery Lane tube station. 2nd left into Chancery Ln, left into Cursitor St, left into Tooks Court

Andrew Dargue and Donna Conroy's upscale vegetarian restaurant is to be found in an almost hidden location down a side street near Chancery Lane, but the venue itself is expansive and spacious, its clean modern design overlaid with echoes of art deco. There's a good deal of excitement around British vegetarian gastronomy these days, and here's why: interesting, innovative dishes that combine high-quality ingredients, up-to-the-minute technique and a sound approach to texture and flavour

contrasts. A brace of Yukon Gold potato cakes start a meal off boldly, gaining plenty of savoury depth from their garnishes of smoked mayonnaise, pickled cucumber ketchup, vinegar dust and crisps. On offer for main may be something strongly redolent of bracing seaside air - seared seaweed, cabbage and pickled potatoes, with soda bread sauce and seaside veg. If something cheesy appeals, try a winning combination of celery pannacotta and blue wensleydale profiteroles, with charred celery and carrots in a precisely and distinctively flavoured apple sauce. The inventiveness doesn't stop there - how about white chocolate and cep tart with a cornflake cake, picpoul wine sorbet and fried tarragon?

Chef Andrew Dargue **Owner** Andrew Dargue & Donna Conroy **Times** 12-2.30/6-10 Closed 2wks Xmas & New Year, BH Mons, Sun, L Sat **Prices** Fixed L 2 course £18.50, Fixed D 3 course £32.50, Starter £8.75, Main £15, Dessert £8.75, Service added but optional 12.5% **Wines** 35 bottles over £20, 6 bottles under £20, 10 by glass **Notes** Vegetarian menu **Seats** 45 **Children** Portions **Parking** On street (metered) or NCP

The White Swan Pub & Dining Room
PLAN 3 D3

@ Modern British

Swish gastro-pub in the City

☎ 020 7242 9696
108 Fetter Ln EC4A 1ES
e-mail: info@thewhiteswanlondon.com
dir: Nearest station: Chancery Lane. Fetter Lane runs parallel with Chancery Lane

This rather handsome sister pub to The Gun (see entry) is the kind of place where you can pull up a stool in the bar and sip on a pint of real ale and eat some classy bar food (braised Yorkshire rabbit leg, for example), or head upstairs for a little more refinement in the form of smart leather-look chairs and linen-clad tables. Expect smart, seasonal food that is based on well-judged combinations of tip-top produce, including a daily specials board. Choose from the likes of chargrilled Norfolk asparagus served with Dorset crab and Irish white pudding, or a rustic pork terrine with pear, apple and raisin chutney to start, and then move on to roast fillet of Cornish brill with ox cheek ravioli, braised gem, sprouting broccoli and red wine jus.

Times 12-3/6-10 Closed Xmas, New Year, BHs, Sat-Sun (except private parties)

LONDON N1

Almeida Restaurant
PLAN 1 F4

◉◉ French

Honest French cooking opposite the theatre

☎ 020 7354 4777
30 Almeida St, Islington N1 1AD
e-mail: almeida-reservations@danddlondon.com
dir: Nearest station: Angel, Highbury & Islington. Turn right from station, along Upper St, past church

A little walk from the hustle and bustle of Islington's busy centre rewards with good honest French food in a contemporary setting. The eponymous theatre is opposite. In the airy room, dressed in fashionable contemporary neutrality, large windows look out onto the street where parasols are set along the pavement for eating outside in the warmer months. White linen tablecloths adorn the tables at the back of the space, whilst up front is a tad less formal; both areas, though, hum with a heartfelt Gallic bonhomie. The food carries its French allegiances lightly, with some standout seasonal British ingredients taking centre stage. Cornish crab ravioli comes with buttered lettuce and beurre blanc in a well-crafted first course, followed by Denham Estate venison à la bourguignon with gratin dauphinoise which is brim full of flavour. Finish with a textbook crème brûlée à la vanille and a warm madeleine.

Times 12-2.30/5.30-11 Closed 26 Dec, 1 Jan, L Mon, D Sun

The Drapers Arms
PLAN 1 F4

◉ British

Skilful cooking in smart neighbourhood pub

☎ 020 7619 0348
44 Barnsbury St N1 1ER
e-mail: info@thedrapersarms.com
dir: Nearest station: Highbury & Islington/Angel. Just off Upper St, situated between Angel/Highbury & Islington tube stations, opposite town hall

A proper neighbourhood pub, The Drapers Arms gets its gastro balance just right. The vibrant green-painted bar revels in its free-of-tie status, so you'll find real ales and a bite to eat, or you can head upstairs to the slightly more restaurant dining room (complete with a chandelier). The confident cooking sensibly errs on the straightforward side, so you might find surf clams with cider and lovage, or pork and veal brain terrine with cornichons and toast, before pearl barley and beetroot risotto, mint and goats' curd, or confit pork belly with chick peas, tomatoes and Swiss chard. Hot chocolate pudding with honeycomb ice cream will send you home happy. The regionally-focused wine list includes 500ml carafes.

Times 12-3.30/6-10

Fifteen London – The Restaurant
PLAN 3 G5

◉◉ Modern Italian

Authentic Italian food and a good cause

☎ 020 3375 1515
15 Westland Place N1 7LP
dir: Nearest station: Old Street. Exit 1 from Old Street tube station, walk up City Rd, opposite Moorfields Eye Hospital

Housed over two floors of a converted warehouse in Shoreditch, Jamie Oliver's charitable venture is a cool place to eat some authentic Italian food and contribute to a good cause at the same time. The name harks back to the original 15 apprentices in 2002 (yes, that long ago!) and the restaurant has continued to take an annual influx of unemployed and under-qualified local young people and train them up. There have been some fantastic success stories but even without knowing how worthy it is, it's still a place that can hold its own food-wise. The ground floor trattoria has an open kitchen, bar and canteen-style seating while in the basement, the restaurant proper has a sleek, contemporary feel - think white industrial-style tiling, silver metal panelling on the walls, bare wooden tables and aluminum chairs. Authentic, regional Italian cooking is created using UK suppliers on the main. Presentation is on the rustic side in starters like bruschetta of first of the season broad beans, with burrata and chilli mint dressing, or a pasta dish of pappardelle with a rich oxtail ragu, Amalfi lemon, flat leaf parsley and parmesan, and a main-course slow-cooked Cumbrian pork with a dry porcini, heritage potato and fennel stew, wild rocket and salsa verde.

Times 12-2.45/6.30-9.30 Closed 25 Dec, 1 Jan, L 26 Dec

Frederick's Restaurant
PLAN 1 F4

◉ Modern European

Long-standing Islington favourite

☎ 020 7359 2888
106-110 Islington High St, Camden Passage, Islington N1 8EG
e-mail: dine@fredericks.co.uk
dir: Nearest station: Angel. From underground 2 mins walk to Camden Passage. Restaurant among the antique shops

Right in the heart of Islington, tucked away amid the antique shops of Camden Passage, Frederick's (family-run since 1969) is a bit of a Tardis. There's a happy buzz inside, where modern artworks hang on exposed brick walls, and tables are laid with linen cloths, plus there's a walled terrace with a lofty glass roof, and tables outside overlooking the garden for when the London weather delivers. Good quality British seasonal produce is the thing, given some broadly modish European treatments, and presented without frills or fuss. Pan-fried scallops come in fashionable partnership with textures of parsnip (purée, carpaccio and crisps), with main course bringing forth the likes of pan-fried venison with potato rösti and

creamed spinach, and to finish, lemon brûlée and madeleines.

Chef Adam Hilliard **Owner** Louis Segal
Times 12-2.30/5.45-11.30 Closed Xmas, New Year, BHs, Sun (ex functions) **Prices** Fixed L 2 course fr £15.50, Fixed D 3 course fr £19, Dessert £6.50-£9.50, Service added but optional 12.5% **Wines** 100 bottles over £20, 40 bottles under £20, 35 by glass **Notes** Vegetarian available **Seats** 150, Pr/dining room 30 **Children** Portions, Menu **Parking** NCP Business Design Centre

Trullo
PLAN 1 F4

◉◉ Italian

Fine Italian cooking in a bustling setting

☎ 020 7226 2733
300-302 St Paul's Rd N1 2LH
e-mail: enquiries@trullorestaurant.com
dir: Nearest station: Highbury & Islington

Hidden away amongst a jumble of shops - look for the black awning - just off Highbury Corner, Trullo is a cracking little place, a vibrant, friendly and affordable Italian restaurant serving top-notch food. The simply adorned interior has darkwood floors, dimmed low-hanging lamps, and paper covers on closely set wooden tables, providing a rustic and bustling setting for tucking into some honest Italian cooking. Expect good seasonal ingredients, great pasta, good use of the wood-burning oven, and a pleasing daily menu that bristles with hearty and very authentic dishes. Kick off with pappardelle with beef shin ragoût, follow with skate wing on mixed wilted greens with brown crab meat, or pork chop with potato, trevise and anchovy sauce. Cheeses are Italian, and patriotic puddings may include Amalfi lemon and polenta cake. Fantastic wines and excellent service complete the picture.

Chef Tim Siadatan **Owner** Jordan Frieda, Tim Siadatan **Times** 12.30-2.30/6.30-10.30 Closed 25 Dec-3 Jan, L Mon-Fri, D Sun **Prices** Starter £5-£9, Main £14-£19, Dessert £4.50-£6.50, Service optional, Groups min 7 service 12.5% **Wines** 28 bottles over £20, 7 bottles under £20, 9 by glass **Notes** Large table menus available £25-£45, Sunday L, Vegetarian available **Seats** 40, Pr/dining room 35 **Children** Portions **Parking** On street

LONDON NW1

La Collina
PLAN 1 E4

◉ Italian

A taste of Italy in pretty Primrose Hill

☎ 020 7483 0192
17 Princess Rd, Chalk Farm NW1 8JR
e-mail: info@lacollinarestaurant.co.uk
dir: Nearest station: Chalk Farm, Camden Town

La Collina is an authentic-feeling Italian local for the boho-chic denizens of Primrose Hill. The smart gun-metal-coloured frontage looks of the moment, but inside there's an unfettered simplicity to the spaces (traditional prints on white walls, for example), with a ground-floor room and a pint-sized room below (accessed via a spiral staircase), where you can watch the culinary action at the open kitchen, to choose from. The walled garden out back is the hot-seat when the weather is warm. The homespun regional Italian cooking keeps things equally simple, with quality, ingredient-led dishes offering a mix of tradition and more modish thinking. Take home-made ravioli filled with scamorza cheese and sun-dried tomatoes and calves' liver Venetian style served with pan-fried polenta, while the all-Italian wines and friendly Latin service add to its appeal.

Chef Diana Rinaldo **Owner** Patrick Oberto, Diana Rinaldo **Times** 12-3/6-11 Closed Xmas wk, L Mon **Prices** Food prices not confirmed for 2013. Please telephone for details **Notes** Vegetarian available, Dress restrictions, Smart casual **Seats** 40 **Children** Portions **Parking** Free after 6pm & weekends

The Gilbert Scott   PLAN 3 B5

◉◉ British **NEW** V

Nostalgic cooking that trumpets the best of British

☎ 020 7278 3888
Renaissance St Pancras Hotel, Euston Rd NW1 2AR
dir: Nearest station: St Pancras. On Euston Rd at front of St Pancras Station

The rebirth of what was once the Midland Grand Hotel in St Pancras station has not lacked for media attention in the last couple of years, and if you want to see what the whole shebang looks like after £200 million, give or take, pull up a chair in The Gilbert Scott restaurant. GS himself was the Victorian architect who oversaw the building of the whole Gothic-revival fantasy pile, and he would surely have felt at home with both the clubby grandeur of the cavernous dining room's soaring plasterwork ceilings, gilt mirrors and claret-hued, buttoned banquettes, and Marcus Wareing's nostalgic take on the heritage cooking of old time England. The menu covers a lot of ground and makes for a good read with intriguing listings such as Dorset snail and chicken pie, soles in coffins, and 'tweed kettle'. What turns up on the plate is all very appealing, starting with nettle and watercress soup with confit egg yolk and crème fraîche, followed by rump and breast of Cumbrian spring lamb teamed with broad beans and minted yoghurt. For pudding, it's playtime with a quirkily entertaining orange marmalade Jaffa cake with Earl Grey ice cream.

Chef Oliver Wilson **Owner** Marcus Wareing **Times** 12-3/5.30-11 **Prices** Fixed L 2 course fr £22, Fixed D 3 course fr £27, Starter £8-£13.50, Main £15.50-£28, Dessert £6-£8.50, Service added but optional 12.5% **Wines** 200 bottles over £20, 14 by glass **Notes** Express menu 2 course £22, 3 course £27, Sunday L, Vegetarian menu **Seats** 110, Pr/dining room 14 **Parking** 12, NCP St Pancras

Gilgamesh Restaurant Lounge   PLAN 1 E4

◉ Pan-Asian

Pan-Asian dishes in a psychedelic re-creation of ancient Babylon (in Camden)

☎ 020 7482 5757 & 7428 4922
The Stables Market, Chalk Farm Rd NW1 8AH
e-mail: reservations@gilgameshbar.com
dir: Nearest station: Chalk Farm, Camden Town. Stables Market on Chalk Farm Rd, next to Camden Lock

Scholars of the eponymous ancient Mesopotamian epic will spot the reference to the legendary excesses of Babylon in this one-off venue in Camden's Stables Market. And the vast, high-octane venue certainly wasn't built on a shoestring: murals worthy of a Babylonian palace cover the walls, every surface is carved, inlaid with mother-of-pearl and lapis lazuli or upholstered in riotous fabrics, while nightclub-esque psychedelic lighting floods over the whole scene. Food-wise, a pan-Asian repertoire takes an eclectic path through everything from sushi prepared by Japanese chefs, via Chinese dim sum, to fusion ideas such as plum miso Chilean sea bass in hoba leaf, or the more familiar territory of spiced lamb with Japanese mushrooms, or Malaysian beef Penang with coconut rice. Desserts such as chocolate and lemongrass brûlée with exotic fruit sorbet toe the fusion line.

Chef Ian Pengelley **Times** 12-2.30/6-mdnt **Prices** Food prices not confirmed for 2013. Please telephone for details **Wines** 51 bottles over £20, 2 bottles under £20, 11 by glass **Notes** Vegetarian available, Dress restrictions, Smart casual (Smart for club) **Seats** 240, Pr/dining room 90 **Parking** Supermarket car park

Karpo   PLAN 3 B5

◉ British, European **NEW** ◔

Funky all-day restaurant with a crowd-pleasing menu

☎ 020 7843 2221
23-27 Euston Rd, St Pancras NW1 2SD
e-mail: info@karpo.co.uk
dir: Nearest station: King's Cross, St Pancras

You shouldn't have any difficulty finding Karpo - just look for the multi-coloured graffiti-art mural spanning the entire side of an old building (part of which is occupied by Barclays bank) just opposite St Pancras International station. It's certainly an interesting looking place from the outside, and that theme continues inside with its mixture of modern furnishings, colourful artworks, a 'living wall' of plants, and a mezzanine level with balcony railings reminiscent of scaffolding and wire mesh. There's a mixture of canteen-style benches and smaller, individual tables, plus counter dining and an open kitchen at one end. Altogether it's a relaxed, easygoing kind of place, with friendly staff and food available all day, from breakfast through brunch to afternoon tea. The daily-changing carte takes an international path, offering the likes of an authentic gazpacho on an early summer evening, or smoked eel with Finnish bread and

horseradish, followed, perhaps, by turbot (super-fresh), clams and samphire, or tender and flavour-packed braised beef with coconut, ginger and lemongrass. All of the herbs and some vegetables used by head chef Daniel Taylor are grown on a nearby roof, and everything on the menu is made in-house.

Chef Daniel Taylor **Times** 12-11 **Prices** Fixed L 2 course fr £20, Fixed D 3 course fr £30, Starter £4-£9, Main £12, Dessert £5-£6.50, Service added but optional 12.5% **Wines** 75 bottles over £20, 7 bottles under £20 **Notes** Sunday L, Vegetarian available **Seats** 140, Pr/dining room 36 **Children** Portions **Parking** On street

Meliá White House   PLAN 2 H4

◉◉ Spanish, Mediterranean

Ambitious Spanish cooking in an art-deco hotel

☎ 020 7391 3000
Albany St, Regent's Park NW1 3UP
e-mail: melia.white.house@solmelia.com
dir: Nearest station: Great Portland St, Regent's Park, Warren St. Opposite Gt Portland St underground station

Close to Regent's Park, and an easy stroll from Oxford street, the Iberian-owned art-deco hotel pays homage to its national cuisine in the elegant fine-dining Spanish restaurant, L'Albufera. It is a glossy space, all polished wooden floors, black-clothed tables and cream upholstered chairs as a backdrop to vibrant cooking that straddles both traditional and modern Spanish schools. Materials are sourced from the homeland for maximum authenticity, so Serrano ham is carved from a trolley, and there are tapas dishes - crab croquettes, or cod tongues in pilpil sauce with shiitaki mushrooms, say - if that's the route you want to take, otherwise you might start with in-house-smoked sea trout with marinated baby beetroot and citrus dressing, then move on to slow-cooked turbot in a crab crust with fondant potatoes and fennel consommé. For dessert, a mojito could be deconstructed as brown rum parfait with mint sorbet and lime foam, or finish instead with exemplary Spanish cheeses served with figs and tarragon oil.

Chef Gines Lorente Barcelona **Owner** Melia White House (Biosphere Hotel Co) **Times** 7-10.30 Closed Sun, BHs, L all week **Prices** Fixed D 3 course fr £30, Tasting menu £30, Starter £7-£19.50, Main £14-£22, Dessert £6.50-£9.50, Service added but optional 12.5% **Wines** 44 bottles over £20, 12 by glass **Notes** Buffet L only available daily in The Place, Vegetarian available, Dress restrictions, Smart casual, Civ Wed 180, Air con **Seats** 62, Pr/dining room 12 **Children** Portions, Menu **Parking** On street

LONDON NW1 *continued*

Odette's Restaurant & Bar PLAN 1 E4

⚫⚫⚫ – *see below*

St Pancras Grand PLAN 3 B6

⚫ British

British classics in the international terminus

☎ 020 7870 9900
St Pancras International NW1 9QP
e-mail: stpg@searcys.co.uk
dir: Nearest station: King's Cross St Pancras

Part of the lavishly and lovingly restored station, St Pancras Grand, on the upper level, is a large space in art-deco style, with banquettes and some original features like an old railway clock. The menu reads like a roll call of classical British stalwarts, from dressed crab to steak and kidney pudding, and Scotch egg, served with curried mayonnaise, to fish pie with buttered leeks (Tuesday's special). Quality is high in terms both of produce and cooking skills, and combinations are judiciously considered, so pan-fried wood pigeon is teamed with roast root vegetables, and sea bass fillet with a crispy fried oyster, hollandaise and purple-sprouting broccoli.

Times 11-mdnt

Sardo Canale PLAN 1 E4

⚫ Italian

Regent's Canal setting for authentic Sardinian food

☎ 020 7722 2800
42 Gloucester Av NW1 8JD
e-mail: info@sardocanale.com
dir: Nearest station: Chalk Farm, Camden Town. 5 mins walk along the Regent's Canal from Camden Market

Younger sibling to Sardo in Fitzrovia (see entry), Sardo Canale is in a lovely spot by a canal between Camden Market and Primrose Hill. The listed building, the vaults of which were once a thoroughfare for horses, is the setting for rustic Sardinian dishes with a touch of modernism. The slate-floored dining room is a chic place to sample this kind of food (especially the pretty courtyard complete with 300-year old olive tree); shut your eyes and pretend you're in the Med. Tucking into baby octopus in a white wine and gently spicy tomato sauce and roasted pine kernels will help keep up the illusion, too, followed by home-made rocket tagliatelli with grey mullet, cherry tomatoes, basil and the island's speciality, bottarga. Calves' liver is cooked in balsamic vinegar and served with sautéed peppers and potatoes, and pudding might be semi-fredo of the day.

Times 12-3/6-11 Closed 25-26 Dec, Mon (ex BHs)

The Winter Garden PLAN 2 F3

⚫⚫ British, Mediterranean

Classical cooking under a soaring glass roof

☎ 020 7631 8000 & 7631 8230
The Landmark London, 222 Marylebone Rd NW1 6JQ
e-mail: restaurants.reservation@thelandmark.co.uk
web: www.wintergarden-london.com
dir: Nearest station: Marylebone. M25/A40 follow signs for West End. Continue along Marylebone Rd for 300 mtrs. Restaurant on left

The Landmark Hotel started off life in the late 1800s as a grand railway hotel and has been stylishly and

---

Odette's Restaurant & Bar

LONDON NW1 PLAN 1 E4

Modern British V

Smart neighbourhood restaurant with classy, confident cooking

☎ 020 7586 8569
130 Regent's Park Rd NW1 8XL
e-mail: info@odettesprimrosehill.com
dir: Nearest station: Chalk Farm

Among the upmarket shops and cafés in chi chi Primrose Hill, Odette's has been a star turn since opening its doors in 1978. And under the auspices of Welshman Bryn Williams, it remains a force to be reckoned with on the London dining scene (and remains much loved by locals). A few tables out front give the place a decidedly Parisian air; a feeling not dispelled by the interior with its charming retro-chic look of bold floral wallpaper, rich

leather chairs and smartly dressed, linen-clad tables. There's a seductive bar, too, with its cosy alcoves, and a patio garden. Williams wears his Welsh heritage with pride, cooking in a broadly contemporary British manner, where produce is king and allowed to shine. There are bar nibbles (deep-fried whitebait with curried mayonnaise, perhaps) if you're just after something light, plus good value set lunch and early evening menus. It's all pretty good value to be fair, including the tasting menus (an excellent vegetarian version, too). From the à la carte you might start with a well judged dish of roasted wood pigeon with foie gras, pickled cherries, chocolate and vanilla salt - each flavour and texture contributing to a thrilling whole. Everything looks beautiful on the plate and high technical proficiency is evident throughout. The regulars won't stand for the removal of the dish cooked for the Queen's 80th (perfectly cooked roasted turbot with braised oxtail, cockles and samphire), or go for braised Welsh beef with mashed potato and onion and parsley

salad. To finish, blackberry soufflé with vanilla ice cream shows how to nail an oft-feared technique.

Chef Bryn Williams **Owner** Bryn Williams
Times 12-2.30/6-10.30 Closed 25-26 Dec, 1 Jan
Prices Fixed L 2 course £17, Fixed D 3 course £25, Starter £7-£12, Main £16-£25, Dessert £8-£12, Service added but optional 12.5% **Wines** 58 bottles over £20, 4 bottles under £20, 16 by glass **Notes** Fixed D 2/3 course 6-7pm, Tasting/Vegetarian menu 6 course, Vegetarian menu **Seats** 70, Pr/dining room 25 **Children** Portions **Parking** On street

expensively restored. The Winter Garden has the prime spot: right in the middle of the grand atrium which goes up and up (through eight storeys to be precise) to the glass roof. It's like being outdoors, really. Adding to the sense of occasion, a pianist can be heard tinkling away amid the palm trees. Classical-minded dishes hit the spot, and it's worth checking out the luxurious Sunday champagne brunch if you're in the mood to spoil yourself. From the carte you might begin with Cornish crab lasagne and chive butter sauce, or a topical Queen's Jubilee kedgeree. Next up, rack of Cotswold lamb comes with a herb crust, aubergine and roasted red peppers, and rosemary sauce, while Dover Sole is served off the bone with lemon, parsley and brown shrimps. Finish with a chocolate délice, orange, kumquats, salted caramel and Cointreau ice cream.

Times 11.30-3/6-10.45

LONDON NW3

Manna
PLAN 1 E4

◉ International Vegetarian, Vegan V

Long-running neighbourhood vegetarian in leafy Primrose Hill

☎ 020 7722 8028
4 Erskine Rd, Primrose Hill NW3 3AJ
e-mail: geninfo@manna.com
dir: Nearest station: Chalk Farm. 500 mtrs from underground station

Perhaps it's not altogether surprising that Manna - a '60s veggie/vegan trailblazer - should be tucked away down a side street off fashionable Primrose Hill's main drag, not a million miles from Camden. Manna has moved with the times and these days serves up smart-looking, creative dishes based on high quality ingredients to a well-heeled crowd. The menu takes inspiration from around the globe, backpacking its way from starters like spiced jerk tofu, plantain and sweet potato kebabs to mains like enchilada casserole, root vegetable tagine or organic bangers (fennel and pumpkin seed) and mash. The understated, modish, natural-toned décor suits dressing up or down, with wooden floors and furniture given a touch of pizzazz with elegant wallpaper featuring silhouetted trees and birds and branch-themed ceiling lights. Add to this a relaxed mood, friendly service and organic, biodynamic and vegan wines, and it's easy to see why Manna is sill going strong.

Owner R Swallow, S Hague **Times** 12-3/6.30-11 Closed Xmas & New Year, Mon, L Tue-Fri **Prices** Food prices not confirmed for 2013. Please telephone for details **Wines** 20 bottles over £20, 8 bottles under £20, 8 by glass **Notes** Vegetarian menu **Seats** 50 **Children** Portions **Parking** On street

XO
PLAN 1 E4

◉ Pan-Asian

Asian variety act in well-heeled Belsize Park

☎ 020 7433 0888
29 Belsize Ln NW3 5AS
e-mail: xo@rickerrestaurants.com
dir: Nearest station: Swiss Cottage/Belsize Park. From Havistock Hill, right into Ornan Rd (before BP garage). Restaurant on right

The Belsize Park branch of Will Ricker's stable of pace-setting bar-restaurant hangouts looks sleek and slick in minimal monochrome with low-slung lime-green booth seating and mirror-lined walls which help the local in-crowd keep tabs on who's checking out who. The menu roams Asia as widely as a gap-year backpacker, and it is all cooked with care and flair. After Asian-infused cocktails at the bar, you might sample the kitchen's wares via the dim sum department - roast pumpkin and spinach gyoza or chilli salt squid, say - then move on to grilled black cod with sweet miso or steamed sea bass with green tea soba noodles. If you're out of your depth with the Asian terminology, the menu offers a useful glossary of what's what, and to finish, more prosaic comforts in the form of banoffee pie or sticky toffee pudding await.

Chef Tom Cajone **Owner** Will Ricker **Times** 12-3/6-11 Closed 25-26 Dec & 1 Jan **Prices** Fixed L 2 course £12, Starter £3.50-£9.25, Main £8.50-£36, Dessert £4.50-£6, Service added but optional 12.5% **Wines** 60 bottles over £20, 1 bottle under £20, 14 by glass **Notes** Sunday L, Vegetarian available **Seats** 92, Pr/dining room 22 **Children** Portions, Menu **Parking** On street

LONDON NW4

Hendon Hall Hotel
PLAN 1 D5

◉◉ British, European

Historic North London mansion with contemporary cooking

☎ 020 8203 3341 & 8457 2502
Ashley Ln, Hendon NW4 1HF
e-mail: hendonhall@handpicked.co.uk
dir: Nearest station: Hendon Central. M1 junct 2. A406. Right at lights into Parson St. Next right into Ashley Lane, Hendon Hall on right

This North London 16th-century mansion with terraced gardens became a hotel in 1911 and retains a host of period features blended with the occasional modern touch here and there. The fine dining Garrick Restaurant makes for an impressive setting; modern art hangs on the walls and smart red chairs and formally-laid tables

complete the up-market picture. A wine cellar with an iron gate is a nice effect inside, whilst the terrace is a warm-weather hit. The menu has modish sensibilities, delivering the likes of pan-fried scallops with glazed chicken wing, peanut butter purée and coconut, followed by tenderloin of pork with the slow-cooked belly and cheek, plus wild garlic, sage and onion gnocchi. The modernity and creative thinking continues at dessert stage too; set lime custard, for example, with lemon and lime jelly, lemon sorbet and pine nut praline.

Times 12-2.30/7-10

LONDON SE1

The Anchor & Hope
PLAN 5 E5

◉◉ British

Thrilling gastro-pub with big-hearted cooking

☎ 020 7928 9898
36 The Cut SE1 8LP
e-mail: anchorandhope@btconnect.com
dir: Nearest station: Southwark, Waterloo. On left approaching from Waterloo Rd towards Blackfriars Rd, just past Young Vic Theatre

The Anchor & Hope is a high octane gastro-pub, and whatever your personal opinion on the use of that particular term, this one still looks and feels like a pub, and the food is fabulous (you can't book to eat - except for Sunday lunch - so expect to turn up and wait in the bar). The hard-edged, no-frills interior comes with elbow-to-elbow, mismatched wooden furniture, rough and ready floorboards, and an open kitchen manned by a gaggle of chefs. A heavy curtain screens the dedicated dining area from the animated bar. The food suits the mood of the place: hearty, unpretentious, with dishes hewn from quality seasonal ingredients on a menu that changes each session. There's no truck with three-course formality or flowery descriptions here; foie gras and pickled cherries or duck hearts on toast might kick things off, followed by salt beef and Russian salad, or you could share a slow-roast veal shin with chopped spinach (for three, apparently). Puds stay on-theme, perhaps a big-hearted cherry and almond tart, while ales are well-kept and Euro-centric wines are downed in no-nonsense tumblers. There are some tables outside on the pavement too.

Chef Jonathon Jones **Owner** Robert Shaw, Mike Belben, Jonathon Jones, Harry Lester **Times** 12-2.30/6-10.30 Closed BHs, 25 Dec-1 Jan, 2 wks Aug, L Mon, D Sun **Prices** Starter £5-£9, Main £10.80-£24, Dessert £3.60-£6, Service optional **Wines** 25 bottles over £20, 26 bottles under £20, 13 by glass **Notes** Sunday L, Vegetarian available **Seats** 58 **Parking** On street

LONDON SE1 *continued*

Brigade

PLAN 5 H6

@ British NEW ✿

Turning up the heat in an old fire station

☎ 0844 346 1225

The Fire Station, 139 Tooley St SE1 2HZ
e-mail: info@thebrigade.co.uk
dir: Nearest station: London Bridge. Between station &
Tower Bridge

Brigade isn't only so-called because of its location in an
old fire station. The name also references the brigade in
the kitchen as they're mostly apprentices who have been
at risk of homelessness or have lived on the streets, and
are on a six-month chef training scheme aimed at giving
them the skills, qualifications and confidence to turn
their lives around. The scheme is being run in conjunction
with Southwark College and the Beyond Food Foundation
charity, founded by Brigade chef-patron Simon Boyle. The
restaurant has a contemporary look with leather high-
backed chairs and banquettes, and black lacquered
tables, and the lively atmosphere is helped along by the
sounds, sights and smells of the centrally positioned
open kitchen (grab a seat at the counter if you want to be
really close to the action). The menu is broadly modern
British, using plenty of top-notch seasonal, British
ingredients. Hand-dived Scottish scallops with beetroot
and chilli risotto is one way to start, perhaps followed by
one of the best burgers in town, made from rump steak
and with shredded oxtail sitting on top.

Chef Simon Boyle **Owner** Simon Boyle
Times 12-3/5.30-10 Closed Sun, L Sat **Prices** Starter
£4.95-£13.50, Main £8.95-£20.95, Dessert £4.95-£10.95,
Service added but optional 12.5% **Wines** 45 bottles over
£20, 4 bottles under £20, 18 by glass **Notes** Deposit £10
per person req for groups over 10, Vegetarian available
Seats 89, Pr/dining room 45 **Children** Portions

Canteen Royal Festival Hall

PLAN 5 C6

@ British

Traditional British cooking in the Royal Festival Hall

☎ 0845 686 1122

**Royal Festival Hall, Southbank Centre, Belvedere Rd
SE1 8XX**
e-mail: rfh@canteen.co.uk
dir: Nearest station: Waterloo

One of a five-strong group, the Canteen concept suits the
billing here at RFH, the kitchen putting-out an all-day
roster of traditionally-focused Brit food with a touch of
modern-day panache. On the lower level at the rear of the
building, this South Bank outlet fairly rocks at prime
times. Fairly-priced, well-sourced, seasonal ingredients,
handled with refreshing simplicity is the thing, and
flexibility means you can call by when you're passing for
all-day breakfast, tea and cake, a quick bite like a fish
finger sandwich, or push the boat out with cod, chips and
tartare sauce to shepherd's pie, or a daily-changing roast
(perhaps Sussex lamb rump with mint sauce). It's a large
contemporary space, high on decibels and decked-out
with pale-wood tables and booth-like lime green
banquette seating, complete with a bar down one side
and an open kitchen on the other. There's a large terrace,
too.

Times 8-11 Closed 25 Dec

Cantina del Ponte

PLAN 5 J6

@ Italian

Relaxed Italian dining by the Thames

☎ 020 7403 5403

The Butlers Wharf Building, 36c Shad Thames SE1 2YE
e-mail: cantinareservations@danddlondon.com
web: www.cantina.co.uk
dir: Nearest station: Tower Hill, London Bridge. SE side of
Tower Bridge, on river front

Fantastic riverfront views of Tower Bridge are part of the
pull at this contemporary Italian trattoria, as is the sunny
day vibe when you get a little hit of the Med on its heated
and canopy-sheltered Thames-side terrace. Inside, a
huge Italian market mural adds to the Latin mood in a
venue that's as sharp-looking as an Italian suit. The
cooking is simple, crowd-pleasing stuff, and considering
the riverside location, the menu is remarkably good value,
as is the wine list, a well-chosen all-Italian affair with
plenty of choice by the glass and 500ml carafe. There's
nothing to scare the horses here, just pasta classics like
seafood spaghetti and tortelloni with ricotta, spinach,
butter and sage sauce, or mains such as swordfish stew
with cherry tomatoes, garlic, capers and olive oil; for the
die-hard carnivore, perhaps a rib-eye with balsamic glaze
and Borretane onions.

Owner D and D London **Times** 12-3/6-11
Closed 24-26 Dec, L 31 Dec **Prices** Fixed L 2 course fr
£12.50, Fixed D 3 course fr £22.95, Service optional,
Groups min 8 service 12.5% **Wines** 33 bottles over £20,
5 bottles under £20, 11 by glass **Notes** Sunday L,
Vegetarian available **Seats** 110 **Children** Portions
Parking NCP Gainsford St

Cantina Vinopolis   PLAN 5 F6

◎ Mediterranean ♦ NATIONAL WINE LIST

Dining underneath the arches at the South Bank's wine emporium

☎ 020 7940 8333
1 Bank End SE1 9BU
e-mail: cantina@vinopolis.co.uk
dir: Nearest station: London Bridge. 5 min walk from London Bridge on Bankside, between Southwark Cathedral & Shakespeare's Globe Theatre

The soaring arches of a Victorian railway viaduct near London Bridge Station make an impressive cathedral-like space for worshipping the grape in its multifarious forms. Part of the Vinopolis complex, Cantina is the place to head for Mediterranean-accented dining in a modish setting of oak tables and leather banquettes beneath cavernous vaulted brick ceilings, with the rumble of overhead trains as an evocative soundtrack. It's run by staff who are passionate about food and wine, and in case you had forgotten that this is a temple to good wines, there are displays of bottles and a splendid list to jog the memory. Expect straight-talking ideas along the lines of duck foie gras terrine with home-made bread, followed by pheasant served with potato fondant, braised black cabbage, green lentils and vegetable stew, or if you fancy fish, perhaps lemon sole with spinach, new potatoes, capers and passionfruit marinière. Stay with the wine theme and treat yourself to a glass of something sticky to go with prune and almond tart served with vanilla ice cream.

Chef Moges A Wolde **Owner** Claudio Pulze
Times 12-3/6-10.30 Closed Xmas, BHs, Sun, L Mon-Wed
Prices Fixed L 2 course fr £25.95, Starter £6.50-£9.50, Main £14.50-£22.50, Dessert £5.50-£7.50, Service added but optional 12.5% **Wines** 193 bottles over £20, 16 bottles under £20, 50 by glass **Notes** Vegetarian available, Dress restrictions, Smart casual **Seats** 200, Pr/dining room 100 **Children** Portions **Parking** On street

Chino Latino London   PLAN 5 G5

◎◎ Modern Pan-Asian

East Asian food and western cocktails in a South Bank hotel

☎ 020 7769 2500
Park Plaza Riverbank London, 18 Albert Embankment SE1 7TJ
e-mail: london@chinolatino.co.uk
web: www.chinolatino.co.uk
dir: Nearest station: Vauxhall. Between Vauxhall & Lambeth bridge

Latino cocktails and a Pan-Asian menu is the thing at this hot-spot on the South Bank. Part of an international franchise - with branches in the UK and Germany - it scores high in the cool stakes: all cream leather and darkwood set to a backdrop of striking ruby-coloured glass panels, back-lit cocktail bar and a sushi station with a busy chorus of chefs. The fashionable Pan-Asian menu - where fish and seafood make a strong showing - comes highlighted with signature dishes, plus there's a trio of tasting options. Expect dim sum of chicken sui mai with foie gras and shiitake mushrooms to tempura of stuffed red chilli and soft-shelled crab. Among main courses monkfish tail with yuzu kusho dressing and yuzu jelly, black cod with miso, and pork belly with shiso apple cider and popcorn crackling show the style. Sharp cocktails and a good range of sake stay true to the theme.

Chef Werner Seebach **Owner** Park Plaza Hotels
Times 12-2.30/6-10.30 Closed 1 Jan, L Sat-Sun
Prices Fixed D 2 course £45, Fixed D 4 course £35-£50, Tasting menu £35-£50, Starter £4.50-£17.50, Main £16.50-£35, Dessert £6.75-£15.25, Service added but

optional 12.5% **Wines** 45 bottles over £20, 9 bottles under £20, 12 by glass **Notes** Three tasting menus available, Vegetarian available, Dress restrictions, Smart casual, no sportswear or fancy dress **Seats** 85 **Children** Portions **Parking** 60

See advert opposite

Gregg's Table   PLAN 5 H4

◎ Modern British **NEW**

Fun comfort eating courtesy of Gregg Wallace

☎ 020 7378 2450
Bermondsey Square Hotel, Bermondsey Square, Tower Bridge Rd SE1 3UN
e-mail: gm@bermondseysquarehotel.co.uk
dir: Nearest station: London Bridge, Borough, Bermondsey. From station exit towards Guys Hospital, left into Saint Thomas St, 200mtrs right into Bermondsey St, 400mtrs cross Abbey St into Bermondsey Sq

Just past a lovely pewter-topped bar in the Bermondsey Hotel, Gregg's Table (that's Wallace of *MasterChef* fame) has displays of hallowed foodie artifacts such as Oxo Cube boxes and tins of Spam, but the place is not entirely stuck in the past. The expansive room has a New England feel as much as anything else, with boarded walls and pillars painted in appealing pastel shades, plus an open-to-view kitchen in the modern manner. As you might expect from something associated with Mr W, it is an unstarchy, relaxed kind of place. The British cooking is simple and honest and on the comforting side, with a few old favourites reinvented for our times. Start with a well-balanced mulligatawny soup with flaked chicken, lentils and onion bhaji, or poshed-up mushroom vol-au-vents incorporating wild mushrooms and cep velouté. If you can resist lamb chops with dauphinoise, shallot purée and juniper jus, you might go for the smoked haddock soufflé with spinach, poached egg and purple sprouting broccoli. Tart of the day - lemon, perhaps, served with pistachio sorbet - or cheese with Carrs (savoury biscuits) will send you away happy. Cooking doesn't get ... well, you know.

Times 8am-11pm **Prices** Food prices not confirmed for 2013. Please telephone for details

LONDON SE1 *continued*

Magdalen
PLAN 5 H6

◎◎ British, European

Reassuringly focused cooking by London Bridge

☎ 020 7403 1342
152 Tooley St SE1 2TU
e-mail: info@magdalenrestaurant.co.uk
web: www.magdalenrestaurant.co.uk
dir: Nearest station: London Bridge. 5 min walk from London Bridge exit. Restaurant 300yds on right opposite Unicorn Theatre

Magdalen is run by a husband-and-wife-team with fine CVs (The Fat Duck and the Mandarin Oriental to name but two previous employers) and a passion for clear-headed, flavourful food. In the thriving London Bridge setting, their restaurant is an unfussy space, on the smart side of casual (or the casual side of smart) with its richly coloured walls, wooden floor, contemporary artworks and tables laid with white linen cloths. With the provenance of the produce to the fore, whether best of British or quality European imports, the menu is packed full of food you want to eat, cooked without fuss. Kick off with crisp fried pig's head and gribiche, or nettle soup with goats' curd toast, then follow on with roast diver-caught scallops with lentils, broad beans and wild garlic, or grilled veal's heart served with potato cake, watercress and béarnaise. East India sherry and raisin ice cream or excellent cheeses bring things to a close.

Chef James Faulks, Emma Faulks, David Abbott **Owner** Roger Faulks & James Faulks **Times** 12-2.30/6.30-10 Closed Xmas, BHs, Sun, L Sat **Prices** Fixed L 2 course fr £15.50, Starter £7-£12.50, Main £13.50-£21, Dessert £5.50-£6.50, Service added but optional 12.5% **Wines** 76 bottles over £20, 2 bottles under £20, 12 by glass **Notes** Vegetarian available **Seats** 90, Pr/dining room 30 **Parking** On street

The Oxo Tower Restaurant
PLAN 3 D1

◎◎ Modern European V

Captivating views and modish food

☎ 020 7803 3888
8th Floor, Oxo Tower Wharf, Barge House St SE1 9PH
e-mail: oxo.reservations@harveynichols.com
web: www.harveynichols.com
dir: Nearest station: Blackfriars, Waterloo, Southwark. Between Blackfriars & Waterloo Bridge on the South Bank

The view is 24-carat gold. Up on the eighth-floor of the old Oxo building, this bar, brasserie and restaurant combo overlooks the river and St Paul's Cathedral, a position which never ceases to impress, day or night. A table on the outdoor terrace is a prized possession indeed (when the weather's right, of course), but it's impressive enough from behind the vast wall of glass. The contemporary cooking in the restaurant matches the modish neutrality of the décor, whilst the white linen on the tables and the well turned-out staff are a reminder that the restaurant is no afterthought. Lobster tempura served alongside a well-flavoured consommé and daikon and wasabi salad demonstrates the kitchen is not beyond a bit of globe-trotting, but the cooking is more broadly focused on European preparations. Monkfish, for example, with smoked ham hock croquettes and quince and vanilla purée, or South Devon fillet of beef with pickled girolles, truffle mash and Madeira sauce. To finish, you'll need a friend to join you for the Bramley apple soufflé with Calvados ice cream, and do allow some time to peruse the wine list.

Chef Jeremy Bloor **Owner** Harvey Nichols & Co Ltd **Times** 12-3/6-11.30 Closed 25 Dec, D 24 Dec **Prices** Fixed L 3 course £35, Starter £13.50-£22, Main £21.50-£35, Dessert £7.50-£9.50, Service added but optional 12.5% **Wines** 660 bottles over £20, 19 bottles under £20, 14 by glass **Notes** Sunday L, Vegetarian menu, Civ Wed 300 **Seats** 250 **Children** Portions, Menu **Parking** On street, NCP

Park Plaza County Hall
PLAN 5 C5

◎ Modern British

Modish cooking in the grand old County Hall building

☎ 020 7021 1919 & 7021 1800
1 Addington St SE1 7RY
e-mail: oldavid@pphe.com
dir: Nearest station: Waterloo

Close to the South Bank's attractions, London Eye et al, the Park Plaza County Hall is a behemoth of nearly 400 state-of-the-art rooms and is also home to the stylish Spectrum restaurant. Located on the mezzanine floor overlooking the ground floor bar, it's a minimalist space with unclothed white tables and cream leather chairs, moody lighting that changes colour, and some pieces of modern art. The broadly modern British repertoire of dishes is supported by daily specials; start with potted hot-smoked salmon and crab with caper butter with rye and caraway toast, then move on to roast saddle of rabbit with white onion soubise and wild watercress and hazelnut salad. Leave room for the County Hall special: chocolate fondant with chocolate cardamom jelly and space dust ice cream.

Times 5.30-10.30 Closed L all week

Le Pont de la Tour
PLAN 5 J6

◎◎ Modern French ▲

Great views and assured French cooking

☎ 020 7403 8403
The Butlers Wharf Building, 36d Shad Thames SE1 2YE
e-mail: lepontres@danddlondon.com
web: www.lepontdelatour.co.uk
dir: Nearest station: Tower Hill, London Bridge. SE of Tower Bridge

There's a touch of Riviera-style about Le Pont on sunny days, with its planter-lined terrace, but the view is 24-carat London - Tower Bridge (floodlit at night) and the cityscape beyond. Accessed through the more informal Bar and Grill, the restaurant has large windows (catch those views even if you're indoors) and mirrored pillars, and comes decked out with white linen-clad tables, soothing pastel shades and walls lined with caricaturist Sem prints. The fruits of the sea are a strong suit here and luxury ingredients come thick and fast; caviar, oysters or a salad of poached lobster are good ways of getting the ball rolling, for example. The assured cooking is underpinned by classic French influence but given a light, creative modern touch and well-dressed presentation. Main courses run to grilled whole lobster (with leaf spinach and sauce choron) and Chateaubriand (with frites and sauce béarnaise), while an assiette of English strawberries might provide a summery finish. Service is slick and professional and friendly enough, but prices (including many menu supplements) are on the high side. The wine list is an absolute corker.

Times 12-3/6-11

Roast PLAN 5 G6

Traditional British

Great British produce overlooking Borough Market

☎ 0845 034 7300
The Floral Hall, Borough Market, Stoney St SE1 1TL
e-mail: info@roast-restaurant.com
web: www.roast-restaurant.com
dir: Nearest station: London Bridge

The distinctive setting - perched above colourful Borough Market - is a real showstopper. The first-floor conservatory-like restaurant - with its centrepiece floral portico from Covent Garden - is a cool, contemporary confection with open-to-view kitchen and bar. By day there's the hubbub of the market below (it's open for breakfast, too), while in the evenings there are knockout views of floodlit St Paul's alongside the bright lights of the capital's newest tower block, the Shard, while trains arriving at London Bridge station seem almost to gatecrash proceedings. This is no place for faddish cooking, with menus designed to show-off quality home-grown produce (sourcing and provenance are king here) via simple, robust, traditional Brit dishes. Take roast Hampshire pheasant served with sherry-glazed parsnips and chestnuts, or pan-fried fillet of Cornish hake with surf clams and seashore vegetables. Daily roasts might feature rare-breed suckling pig, while puddings hit the mark from apple crumble to sticky date pudding.

Chef Marcus Verberne **Owner** Iqbal Wahhab
Times 12-3/5.30-11 Closed 25-26 Dec, 1 Jan **Prices** Fixed L 3 course £28-£32, Fixed D 3 course £28, Service added but optional 12.5% **Wines** 100 bottles over £20, 6 bottles under £20, 10 by glass **Notes** Tasting menu with matching wines, Sunday L, Vegetarian available **Seats** 120 **Children** Portions, Menu

RSJ, The Restaurant on the South Bank PLAN 5 D6

Modern European

Pleasingly unfussy food and notable Loire wines

☎ 020 7928 4554
33 Coin St SE1 9NR
e-mail: tom.king@rsj.uk.com
dir: Nearest station: Waterloo. Towards Waterloo Bridge & the IMAX cinema. At rdbt, right into Stamford St. RSJ on the corner of Coin St, 2nd right

RSJ's proximity to the National Theatre and other delights of the ever-improving South Bank makes it a big hit with culture vultures stopping by for the pre- and post-theatre menus. The wine list is a big draw too, or so it should be, with its focus on the Loire; many of the wines are organic and have been selected by the owner who's been visiting France for 'research purposes' for over 30 years. In the kitchen, simple food is elevated by intelligent flavour combinations and sound cooking in the likes of Essex ham hock with oxtail and foie gras terrine, served with piccalilli, or a main-course braised pork belly with honey-glazed celeriac, parsnips, butternut squash, poached apple and sage jus. Finish with a pear and hazelnut tart with home-made honey ice cream.

Times 12-2.30/5.30-11.30 Closed Xmas, 1 Jan, Sun, L Sat

Zucca PLAN 5 H4

Italian

Compelling new-wave Italian cooking

☎ 020 7378 6809
184 Bermondsey St SE1 3TQ
e-mail: kitchen@zuccalondon.com
dir: Nearest station: London Bridge. Five minutes' walk from London Bridge tube. At the Long Lane end of Bermondsey St

On a Bermondsey side street, this glass-fronted restaurant has a minimalist feel, quite in keeping with the new-wave Italian cooking on offer, with its white walls, broken up by some abstracts, white formica-type tables and white chairs, and an open-to-view kitchen behind a bar. The menu changes daily, depending on availability, and the freshest of ingredients are simply cooked to bring out clear, undiluted flavours. Lardo and game crostini, pesce crudo, and tripe, tomato and guanciale are the sort of vibrantly tasting starters to expect. Grilling and roasting seem to bring out the best of main courses, among which have been roast skate with cime di rapa and chick peas, and grilled calves' liver with lentils, catalogna and salsa verde, although pork shoulder gets slowly cooked and served with porcini mushrooms and polenta.

Chef Sam Harris **Owner** Sam Harris
Times 12.30-3/6.30-10 Closed 25 Dec, 1 Jan, Etr, Mon, D Sun **Prices** Starter £3.95-£5.95, Main £10-£16, Dessert £4-£5.50, Service optional **Wines** 150 bottles over £20

Notes Vegetarian available **Seats** 64, Pr/dining room 10 **Children** Portions **Parking** On street

Bella Vista Cucina Italiana PLAN 1 H3

Italian **NEW**

Italian classics in vibrant setting

☎ 020 8318 1143
3/5 Montpelier Vale, Blackheath SE3 0TA
dir: Nearest station: Blackheath

Blackheath Village's Bella Vista is a lot of fun, a taste of Italy as a jaded copywriter might say. That 'vista' is over Blackheath Village, all the street action clearly visible through the floor-to-ceiling windows to the front. It looks pretty tasty inside with a contemporary-rustic-chic vibe going on, some exposed brick, darkwood tables, and some authentic Italian foodie products on shelves to bring a touch of 'cucina' to proceedings. The menu is devised by Piero Marenghi and the place is from the same stable as Chapters All Day Dining (see entry) and the high-flying Chapter One (see entry). So what's on the menu? You might start with some fabulous burrata cheese with basil pesto and cherry tomatoes, or the more substantial fritto misto, and pasta and risottos are a good bet too (pappardelle with new season lamb ragu, maybe, or wild mushroom risotto). Main-courses bring forth the likes of tagliata (sliced rib-eye with soft polenta, pine nuts, raisin and truffle sauce), and to finish, vanilla pannacotta with blood oranges and biscotti.

Chef Alex Tyndall **Times** 12-3/6-11 **Prices** Food prices not confirmed for 2013. Please telephone for details

Chapters All Day Dining PLAN 1 H3

Modern British

Blackheath Village eatery buzzing all day long

☎ 020 8333 2666
43-45 Montpelier Vale, Blackheath Village SE3 0TJ
e-mail: chapters@chaptersrestaurants.co.uk
web: www.chaptersrestaurants.com
dir: Nearest station: Blackheath. 5 mins from Blackheath Village train station

Chapters was rewritten to move on from the fine dining concept taken by its sibling restaurant Chapter One in Bromley (see entry), and takes a more flexible approach, covering all bases from breakfast to brunch to morning

continued

LONDON SE3 *continued*

coffee to brasserie classics at lunch and dinner. It all suits the casual mood of trendy Blackheath Village, as does the unbuttoned décor of wooden floors, bare brickwork and banquette seating. The crowd-pleasing all-day menu delivers the likes of braised pork belly terrine with Jazz apple purée and Waldorf salad, followed by daube of beef with sweet potato purée and Savoy cabbage, or something fishy along the lines of smoked haddock fishcake with creamed spinach and beurre blanc. For card-carrying carnivores, there are slabs of pedigree protein - Herefordshire rib-eye, or Kentish double Barnsley lamb chops - cooked on the charcoal-fired Josper grill. Finish on a sweet note with Valrhona chocolate fondant with crème anglaise and banana sorbet.

Chef Simon Cotterill **Owner** Selective Restaurants Group **Times** 8am-11pm Closed 2-4 Jan **Prices** Starter £4.85-£9.95, Main £9.45-£24.50, Dessert £4.25-£7.10, Service added but optional 12.5% **Wines** 40 bottles over £20, 11 bottles under £20, 15 by glass **Notes** Sunday L, Vegetarian available **Seats** 100 **Children** Portions, Menu **Parking** Car park by station

---

LONDON SE22

Franklins

PLAN 1 F2

◉ British ✪

Hearty British cooking in Lordship Lane

☎ 020 8299 9598
157 Lordship Ln, East Dulwich SE22 8HX
e-mail: info@franklinsrestaurant.com
dir: Nearest station: East Dulwich. 0.5m S from East Dulwich Station via Dog Kennel Hill & Lordship Ln

British produce is celebrated zealously at Franklins, an exemplary neighbourhood operation that combines the virtues of a pubby bar and a buzzy brick-walled bistro at the rear. The place takes an unbuttoned, no-frills approach, producing food from the more visceral end of the modern British spectrum in a tiny open kitchen behind a glass screen. Provenance is key here, and the chefs are lucky to share the same supply lines as those that keep the Franklins farm shop next door stocked with a cornucopia of Kentish fruit and vegetables, rare-breed meats, English artisan cheeses, and sustainably-caught fish from Cornish day boats. Ox heart with chicory, capers and seed mustard, or smoked eel with potatoes, cornichons and dill are typically punchy starters, while mains deal in equally unpretentious concepts - rabbit cooked in cider with button onions and turnips, perhaps, or a retro-Brit idea such as veal kidneys with pease pudding. Leave room for puddings such as custard tart

and red wine or burnt cream, and if it's top value you're after, look to the daily set lunch menu.

Chef Ralf Witting **Owner** Tim Sheehan & Rodney Franklin **Times** 12-12 Closed 25-26, 31 Dec, 1 Jan **Prices** Fixed L 2 course fr £13.95, Fixed D 3 course fr £32.50, Starter £5-£9, Main £11-£21, Dessert £5-£6, Service optional, Groups min 6 service 10% **Wines** 23 bottles over £20, 13 bottles under £20, 10 by glass **Notes** Sunday L, Vegetarian available **Seats** 42, Pr/dining room 24 **Children** Portions **Parking** Bawdale Road

---

The Palmerston

PLAN 1 F2

◉ Modern European ✪

Quality eating and drinking in a proper Dulwich pub

☎ 020 8693 1629
91 Lordship Ln, East Dulwich SE22 8EP
e-mail: info@thepalmerston.net
dir: Nearest station: East Dulwich. 2m from Clapham, 0.5m from Dulwich Village, 10min walk from East Dulwich station

A made-over corner boozer in Dulwich is the setting for this switched-on gastro-pub. Darkwood abounds in its wall panelling and tables, and there are mosaic and terracotta floors to take in as you ponder a splendid selection of beers and wines. Food-wise, a modern European menu offers some confidently-produced and appealing cooking from a kitchen that is at home in the

world of rabbit and green olive ravioli served with Savoy cabbage and thyme broth, and venison tartare with home-made walnut bread. Mains could bring forth roast saddle of Cumbrian lamb with braised Puy lentils, pancetta, salsa verde and radicchio, or a bouillabaisse of cod and gurnard with saffron potatoes, French beans and rouille. Rib-sticking desserts run to the likes of steamed fig pudding with brandy butter.

Chef Jamie Younger **Owner** Jamie Younger, Paul Rigby, Remi Olajoyegbe **Times** 12-2.30/7-midnight Closed 25-26 Dec, 1 Jan **Prices** Fixed L 2 course fr £13, Starter £6.50-£9.50, Main £12.50-£19, Dessert £3-£3.50, Service added but optional 10% **Wines** 40 bottles over £20, 40 bottles under £20, 30 by glass **Notes** Light menu available daily 3-6pm, Sunday L, Vegetarian available **Seats** 70 **Children** Portions **Parking** On street

LONDON SE23

Babur   PLAN 1 G2

◎◎ Modern Indian

Modern Indian cuisine in a cool brasserie setting

☎ 020 8291 2400
119 Brockley Rise, Forest Hill SE23 1JP
e-mail: mail@babur.info
web: www.babur.info
dir: Nearest station: Honor Oak Park. Turn left from Honor Oak Park station, continue for 150mtrs to first lights, right again for 100mtrs along Brockley Rise

The simple, stylish décor of this contemporary Indian makes quite an impact: there are American walnut tables, blue limestone floors, chocolate brown banquettes, exposed brick walls and industrial ducting, and eye-catching suede and leather triptychs as well as a textile kalamkari painted with intricate Sanskrit text. Luckily, this is not a case of style over substance, as the kitchen delivers an out-of-the-ordinary repertoire of contemporary, creative ideas that borrow freely from eastern and western culinary modes. Tamarind-glazed quail breast roasted in the tandoor and served with bubble-and-squeak leg meat is not a starter you are likely to have encountered before, nor is ostrich, which is clove-smoked and marinated in Rajasthani spices. Moving along to main course, how about rabbit, pot-roasted in rabbit broth, mustard and ginger, and served with garlic roti, or steamed, spice-crusted shoulder of lamb marinated for 100 hours in a spicy Punjabi masala, served with beetroot khichdi and lamb jus? End with an Indo-Scottish cranachan - made with Indian Amrut malt

whisky and buffalo milk. Helpful wine suggestions make tricky food pairing easier.

Babur

Chef Praveen Kumar Gupta **Owner** Babur 1998 Ltd **Times** 12-2.30/6-11.30 Closed 26 Dec, L 27 Dec, D 25 Dec **Prices** Starter £6.75-£8.50, Main £11.95-£16.95, Dessert £4.25-£5.25, Service optional **Wines** 17 bottles over £20, 17 bottles under £20, 14 by glass **Notes** Tasting menu available Jul-Aug, Sunday L, Vegetarian available, Air con **Seats** 72 **Parking** 15, On street

See advert opposite

LONDON SW1

Al Duca   PLAN 4 J6

◎ Modern Italian

Buzzy, fairly priced Italian in St James's

☎ 020 7839 3090
4-5 Duke of York St SW1Y 6LA
e-mail: alduca@btconnect.com
dir: Nearest station: Green Park. 5 mins walk from station towards Piccadilly. Right into St James's, left into Jermyn St. Duke of York St halfway along on right

There's always a lively hubbub in this eternally popular St James's restaurant. The glass frontage rolls back for alfresco eating on fine days, while the modern interior is done out invitingly in Italian tones of olive, terracotta and stone, with mosaic tiles and oak furniture; efficient service by smartly turned-out, knowledgeable and attentive staff feeds into the upbeat vibe. Considering the postcode, prices are sensible too. The kitchen plays it straight down the line, sending out uncomplicated classic Italian dishes - well-timed tagliolini with fresh crab, white wine, sweet chilli and garlic, before chargrilled sea bass fillet with spinach and balsamic. Tiramisù is one of those acid tests of an Italian meal, and the version served here passes with flying colours.

Chef Giovanni Andolfi **Owner** Cuisine Collection, Claudio Pulze **Times** 12-11 Closed Xmas, New Year, BHs, Sun **Prices** Fixed L 2 course £23.50, Fixed D 3 course £28, Service added but optional 12.5% **Wines** 118 bottles over £20, 10 bottles under £20, 13 by glass **Notes** Pre & post theatre menu 2 course £16.50, 3 course £19, Vegetarian available, Dress restrictions, Smart casual **Seats** 56 **Children** Portions **Parking** Jermyn St, Duke St

Amaya   PLAN 4 G4

◎◎ Indian

Fine Indian cuisine with plenty of kitchen theatre

☎ 020 7823 1166
Halkin Arcade, Motcomb St SW1X 8JT
e-mail: amaya@realindianfood.com
dir: Nearest station: Knightsbridge

Amaya certainly has seductive style in spades. Located in Knightsbridge's glossy Halkin Arcade, it is as well-dressed as its customers: by day, light floods in through a glazed atrium roof; at night, textures of black granite, rosewood and leather are set against white walls splashed with bold modern artwork, plus there's the added culinary drama of chefs doing their thing in an impressive open kitchen. The cooking takes a three-pronged approach using traditional methods - the clay tandoor oven, sigri (a grill with a coal flame) and tawa (a thick iron hot-plate). Food arrives as and when it is ready, rather than in the conventional starter/main course format, so be prepared to share and graze through a succession of ideas, taking in flash-grilled rock oysters with coconut and ginger moilee sauce, or griddled sea bass with a coconut and herb crust, and on via tandoori monkfish tikka and Punjabi chicken wing lollipops to boned tandoori quail.

Chef Karunesh Khanna **Owner** R Mathrani, N Panjabi **Times** 12.30-2.15/6.30-11.30 Closed D 25 Dec **Prices** Food prices not confirmed for 2013. Please telephone for details **Wines** 83 bottles over £20, 19 by glass **Notes** Fixed D 2 course, Vegetarian tasting menu, Vegetarian available **Seats** 99, Pr/dining room 14 **Parking** NCP

Apsleys at The Lanesborough PLAN 4 G5

◎◎◎ – *see page 278*

LONDON SW1 *continued*

Avenue
PLAN 4 J6

◉ Modern British

Buzzy, contemporary restaurant and bar

☎ 020 7321 2111
7-9 St James's St SW1A 1EE
e-mail: avenuereservations@danddlondon.com
web: www.theavenue-restaurant.co.uk
dir: Nearest station: Green Park. Turn right past The Ritz,
2nd turning into St James's St

There's an air of chic modern refinement at Avenue, with
its long bar, a predominantly plum and rust décor, some
banquettes at closely set clothed tables, and smartly clad
professional staff. It's a popular place, people drawn by
the appealing, largely modern British menu as much by
the atmosphere. Crab tart, given bite by an
accompanying fennel salad, can get a meal off to a flying
start, or there may be more robust-sounding braised pork
cheeks with Jerusalem artichokes and chanterelles. Fish
is handled well, judging by a fresh and moist fillet of sea
bass, with a golden crisp skin, sauced with orange beurre
blanc, served atop spring greens with pan-fried
cauliflower stalks. Meat-eaters could opt for chicken
breast intriguingly offset by bacon vinaigrette served with
pears and parsnips, and to finish there could be a classic
rendition of tarte Tatin with vanilla ice cream.

Times 12-3/5.45-11 Closed 25-26 Dec, 1 Jan, Sun, L Sat

Bar Boulud
PLAN 4 F5

◉◉ Modern French ⓵ NATIONAL WINE LIST

Classy bistro cooking from superstar chef

☎ 020 7201 3899
**Mandarin Oriental Hyde Park, 66 Knightsbridge
SW1X 7LA**
e-mail: barboulud@mohg.com
dir: Nearest station: Knightsbridge. Opposite Harvey
Nichols

Sister restaurant to internationally acclaimed chef Daniel
Boulud's New York outpost, if you want somewhere
fashionably glossy with a genuine buzz and a lesson in
stunning bistro food, this is the place to come. Housed in
the Mandarin Oriental in the heart of Knightsbridge, it's
not the place to linger over a long, slow meal - there's
usually a two-hour limit on tables - but what you get
instead is bags of Gallic atmosphere. Settle in with a
drink at the long zinc-topped bar before moving onto the
charcuterie counter overlooking the kitchen, or perhaps a
red leather banquette in one of the inter-connected dining
rooms. Wine plays a central role here, as evinced from
framed wine-stained muslins, duly labeled with the
vintage and used as decoration. Boulud's Lyonnaise
birthplace shines through in a big menu of elegantly
presented pâtés, terrines, charcuterie and platters of
seafood jazzed up by a New York state of mind. Start with
boudin blanc or truffled white sausage and mashed
potato, or terrine of duck, foie gras and figs with myrtle
liquor and chestnut compôte, before the DBGB 'piggie
burger', pairing of beef patty with barbecue pulled pork
and green chilli mayonnaise, or a rather more classic
roasted chicken breast with carrot pûrée, Swiss chard
and spiced cranberries. To finish, coupe peppermint - a
flourless sponge, hot chocolate sauce, mint ice cream
and chocolate sorbet - stands out alongside ile flottante
with caramel sauce, crème anglaise and apple sorbet.

Chef Dean Yasharian, Daniel Boulud **Owner** Daniel
Boulud **Times** 12-3/5-11 **Prices** Fixed L 3 course fr £23,
Fixed D 3 course fr £23, Starter £8-£14, Main £12-£28,
Dessert £6-£9, Service added but optional 12.5%
Wines 500 bottles over £20, 36 by glass **Notes** Sunday L,
Vegetarian available, Dress restrictions, Smart casual
Seats 168, Pr/dining room 20 **Children** Portions
Parking NCP Sloane St

Apsleys at The Lanesborough

LONDON SW1   PLAN 4 G5

Modern Italian

Outstanding Italian cooking in luxury hotel

☎ 020 7333 7254 & 7333 7645
The Lanesborough, Hyde Park Corner SW1X 7TA
e-mail: apsleys@lanesborough.com
dir: Nearest station: Hyde Park Corner

As befitting a world-class luxury hotel, Apsleys, named
after the Duke of Wellington's London home on the other
side of Hyde Park Corner, is an expensively opulent room
under its glass atrium, with plush multicoloured carpets,
a striking mural and the sort of seats you never want to
leave, while staff hover solicitously. The modern Italian
menus are devised by Heinz Beck, based at his own
restaurant in Rome but with an international reputation,
with Massimiliano Blasone in daily charge of running the
kitchen. Inevitably, there are luxuries for high rollers -
lobster with avocado and tomato, say, and foie gras
terrine, its richness nicely balanced but not eclipsed by
smoked apple and crunchy amaretti - but staff won't
blanch at an order for pumpkin soup either. Pasta is a
strong suit, whether spaghetti with langoustines and
crab or tortellini filled with tender, flavourful minced
game, served with pumpkin purée and parmesan cream.
Main courses are never too adventurous or racy, with
brilliant techniques applied to impeccable ingredients:
breadcrumbed Dover sole with ratatouille, roast suckling
pig, or beef fillet braised in red wine. End with a suitably
indulgent pudding like a chocolate dome, topped with
gold leaf, filled with layers of ice cream, surrounded by
various biscuity and chocolatey enhancements, with
sublime caramel sauce and a blob of ice cream.

Chef Heinz Beck, Massimiliano Blasone **Owner** St Regis
Hotels and Resorts **Times** 12.30-2.30/7-10.30
Prices Fixed L 2 course £25, Fixed D 3 course £45,
Tasting menu £65-£85, Starter £15.50, Main £29, Dessert
£12.50, Service added but optional 12.5% **Wines** all
bottles over £20, 27 by glass **Notes** Tasting menu 5 & 7
course, Vegetarian available, Dress restrictions, Smart
casual **Seats** 100, Pr/dining room 14 **Children** Portions,
Menu **Parking** 25

Boisdale of Belgravia

PLAN 4 H3

◉ British, Scottish

A bit of Scotland imported to London

☎ 020 7259 1257
15 Eccleston St SW1W 9LX
e-mail: info@boisdale.co.uk
dir: Nearest station: Victoria. Left along Buckingham Palace Rd, Eccleston St is 1st on right

A combination of jazz venue, bar and restaurant, Boisdale of Belgravia is spread over a number of rooms in a handsome townhouse, with a clubby décor and red walls hung with a profusion of pictures. As at its sibling in Bishopsgate (see entry), the cooking is built on fine Scottish produce, skilfully and accurately worked. Seared scallops with haggis and saffron mashed potatoes are a happy blend of flavours, an alternative to another starter of seasonal asparagus with a poached duck egg and truffle vinaigrette. Top-quality Aberdeenshire steaks with a choice of sauces may vie for attention with the luxury of grilled lobster with garlic and parsley butter, although a gutsy dish of sautéed lamb's sweetbreads and braised kidneys, served with mustard and tarragon sauce, mash, and Savoy cabbage mixed with bacon, may be an option too.

Times 12-3/7-11.15 Closed Xmas, New Year, Etr, BHs, D Sun

Brasserie Saint Jacques

PLAN 4 J6

◉ Traditional French

French brasserie in St James's

☎ 020 7930 1007
33 St James's St SW1A 1HD
e-mail: brasseriestjacques@btconnect.com
dir: Nearest station: Green Park

If you can't make it across the Channel, you could always try out this authentically Gallic brasserie in monied St James's. The look, and even the smell, is liable to bring memories flooding back, and the décor is evocative without resorting to too many clichés. High ceilings and old posters add a bit of old-school charm, while the staff do a briskly efficient job. The cooking is classic in the main, though there are some contemporary versions of old favourites. Start with fried smoked eel with beetroot, Granny Smith apples and horseradish cream, or garlic and parsley buttered snails with crunchy bread, then move on to seared scallops with a compôte of endive and smoked sausage and new potatoes, or fillet of sea bass with fennel, flambéed in Pernod right in front of you.

Times 12-2.30/6-10 Closed BHs, Sat-Sun

Le Caprice

PLAN 4 J6

◉ Modern British, European **V**

Renowned Mayfair favourite

☎ 020 7629 2239
Arlington House, Arlington St SW1A 1RJ
e-mail: reservation@le-caprice.co.uk
dir: Nearest station: Green Park. Arlington St runs beside The Ritz. Restaurant is at end

A 30th-anniversary refurb (September 2011) has kept the iconic revolving front doors at this glam Mayfair classic - tucked away behind The Ritz - with a terrace, cool bar, and sleek new floor and windows ringing the changes. The monochrome retro-cool '80s look remains, including its celebrated gallery of black-and-white David Bailey photographs. The much-loved simple classic dishes - like salmon fishcakes or Caprice burger - haven't gone anywhere either. Service is slick and professional, with the charm offensive commencing as soon as you enter through those doors. The please-all roster of reliable European-brasserie comfort dishes includes the likes of deep-fried fish with minted pea purée, chips and tartare, plus seasonal specials like whole grilled Cornish monkfish tail with béarnaise, or the more modish Thai-baked sea bass with fragrant rice. Nursery desserts (aka, lemon curd steamed sponge pudding) and a short afternoon menu (served 3-5.30pm) keep the fun rolling all day, and note the cover charge remains.

Chef Andy McLay **Owner** Caprice Holdings Ltd
Times 12-3/5.30-12 Closed 25-26 Dec, D 24 Dec
Prices Food prices not confirmed for 2013. Please telephone for details **Wines** 120 bottles over £20, 5 bottles under £20, 22 by glass **Notes** Pre & post theatre menus available, Sunday L, Vegetarian menu **Seats** 80 **Children** Portions **Parking** On street, NCP

Cavendish London

PLAN 4 J6

◉ British 🌱

Modern British food with nostalgia touches in a smart St James's hotel

☎ 020 7930 2111
81 Jermyn St SW1Y 6JF
e-mail: info@thecavendishlondon.com
dir: Nearest station: Green Park, Piccadilly. From Piccadilly, (pass The Ritz), 1st right into Dukes St before Fortnum & Mason

The stylish first-floor restaurant at the Cavendish is named after the scent that arises from the earth after a dry spell has been broken by the first rains (Petrichor). Striped upholstery and bright original paintings create a cheering atmosphere, as does the kitchen's wholesale commitment to sustainability. Modern British cooking, with some nostalgia touches that should go down well with the kinds of gents who buy their suits in these environs, is the name of the game. Egg and soldiers is a slow-cooked duck egg with toasted brioche fingers and hollandaise. Mains run from cider-cured trout with Anna potatoes in herb sauce to rack of Welsh lamb with minted broad beans in its own jus, and there's Bakewell tart with

cherry ice cream to finish. Either that, or cheeses from nearby Paxton and Whitfield.

Chef Nitin Padwal **Owner** Ellerman Investments Ltd
Times 12-2.30/5.30-10.30 Closed 25-26 Dec, 1 Jan, L Sat-Sun & BH Mon **Prices** Fixed L 2 course fr £15.50, Fixed D 3 course fr £19.50, Starter £6-£8.50, Main £14.50-£19.50, Dessert £6-£9.50, Service added but optional 12.5% **Wines** 34 bottles over £20, 2 bottles under £20, 10 by glass **Notes** Pre-theatre menu Sun-Thu 5.30-6.30, Fri-Sat 5-6.30pm, Vegetarian available **Seats** 80, Pr/dining room 70 **Children** Portions, Menu **Parking** 60, Secure on-site valet parking

Le Cercle

PLAN 4 G3

◉◉ Modern French

Modish basement restaurant serving up inspired modern French dishes

☎ 020 7901 9999
1 Wilbraham Place SW1X 9AE
e-mail: info@lecercle.co.uk
dir: Nearest station: Sloane Square. Just off Sloane St

From the same stable as Club Gascon (see entry), this stylish modern basement dining room close to Sloane Square is a lively place much of the day. The glamorous interior boasts a mezzanine lounge area with secluded booths where you can chillax with an inventive cocktail or two, and an equally cool restaurant with polished wood tables, smart leather seating and a glass-fronted wine cellar. Creative modern French grazing-style dishes are the order of the day, plus the occasional conventional French favourite alongside good-value set lunch, pre-theatre and 'Traditions' tasting menus. Clear flavours and stylish presentation characterise the likes of onglet tartare with smoked ketchup and mustard ice cream, baby squid ragoût with crab bisque, and among the larger plats, braised and seared venison with parsnip and white chocolate pulp and artichoke macaroons. Desserts are no less inventive: crème brûlée with raspberry and hibiscus sorbet, for example. A racy French wine list doesn't let standards slip.

Times 12-2.30/5.30-10.45 Closed Xmas, Sun-Mon

LONDON SW1 *continued*

Chabrot

PLAN 4 F5

◉◉ French ❖❖

Authentic French bistro in Knightsbridge

☎ 020 7225 2238
9 Knightsbridge Green SW1X 7QL
e-mail: info@chabrot.co.uk
dir: Nearest station: Knightsbridge

'Bistrot d'amis' heads up the menu, and indeed Chabrot
has the sort of friendly atmosphere typical of a bistro du
coin, helped along by characteristic bentwood chairs,
closely set tables covered by red and white cloths, and
friendly, informal service. The cooking is based on the
cuisine of southern France, the menu ranging from
grazing-sized plates of, for example, smoked herrings
with warm potato salad, or foie gras terrine with green
beans, to duck confit with a salad of potatoes, beans and
shallots. The kitchen puts tip-top French produce to good
effect: Brittany oysters with baby chorizo, andouille and
jambon de Bayonne in a platter of charcuterie, Périgord
truffle with poached Landais chicken breast, served with
vegetables, and, for two to share, Pyrenean lamb shoulder
roasted with spices, dried fruit and couscous. Wave the
tricolore at the end with prunes and Armagnac syrup.

Chef Thierry Laborde **Owner** Thierry Laborde, Pascal
Lavorel, Yann Chevris **Times** 12-3.30/6.30-11 Closed Sun
Prices Fixed D 3 course £21.50, Service added but
optional 12.5% **Wines** 130 bottles over £20, 4 bottles
under £20, 10 by glass **Notes** Fixed L 1 course £12.50
(wine £15.50 & dessert/coffee £17.50), Vegetarian
available, Air con **Seats** 65, Pr/dining room 20
Parking On street

The Cinnamon Club

PLAN 5 A4

◉◉ Modern Indian

Inventive Indian food in a grand listed building

☎ 020 7222 2555
**The Old Westminster Library, 30-32 Great Smith St
SW1P 3BU**
e-mail: info@cinnamonclub.com
dir: Nearest station: Westminster, St James Park. Take
exit 6, across Parliament Sq, pass Westminster Abbey on
left. 1st left into Great Smith St

Close to Westminster's finest (Abbey, School and
Parliament), the historic Grade II listed Old Westminster
Library makes for an appealing dining venue. It's
certainly a characterful setting, with a decidedly
gentlemen's clubby vibe, with some inspired modern
Indian dishes on the menu. High ceilings, skylights,
parquet floor, darkwood and contemporary seating all
play their part, but it is the gallery of books above the
main dining room that sticks in the mind. The star turn
here (attracting political types and Westminster suits) is
the innovative, high calibre contemporary Indian food,
which comes well-dressed and driven by top-notch
ingredients and balanced spicing. Spiced crusted sea
bass, for example, with chick pea salad, green mango
and coconut chutney to start, followed by clove-smoked
grouse breast teamed with pumpkin pickle and green
moong 'tadka'. The same attention to detail is lavished
on desserts, perhaps coriander and corn cake delivered
with coconut parfait and spiced ice cream. Tasting
menus, a good value fixed-price lunch, professional but
smiley service and a spice-friendly corker of a wine list
complete the picture. (See also entry for the Cinnamon
Kitchen.)

Chef Vivek Singh **Owner** Indian Restaurant Limited
Times 12-2.45/6-10.45 Closed BHs, L 25 Dec
Prices Fixed L 2 course £22, Fixed D 3 course £24,
Tasting menu £75-£150, Starter £8-£22, Main £16-£45,
Dessert £6-£9, Service added but optional 12.5%
Wines 300 bottles over £20, 20 by glass **Notes** Tasting
menu D 7 course, with paired wines £115-£150,
Vegetarian available, Dress restrictions, Smart casual,
Civ Wed 40 **Seats** 130, Pr/dining room 60
Parking Abingdon St

Dinner by Heston Blumenthal

RESTAURANT OF THE YEAR FOR LONDON	
LONDON SW1	PLAN 4 F5

British

Heston looking back to move forward

☎ 020 7201 3833
**Mandarin Oriental Hyde Park, 66 Knightsbridge
SW1X 7LA**
dir: Nearest station: Knightsbridge. Opposite Harvey
Nichols

Despite the name, you don't have to turn up in the evening to
get fed at Heston's operation in the swanky Mandarin Oriental
Hyde Park hotel: dinner was originally the word for the main
meal of the day, apparently, whenever you chose to eat it. So
what does the man who made snail porridge a household
name, and whose flagship in Bray gets voted one of the best
restaurants in the world, turn his hand to next? Well, in some
ways, what's on offer here is a polar opposite of the futuristic
food-boffin business that has elevated Mr B to the ranks of
chefs who go by just one name. His fascination with our
culinary heritage has always been eclipsed by the science
stuff, so this is his chance to travel back to the past and
delve into 500 years of historic British cooking. And, despite
the name once again, dinner is not actually by Heston, but led
instead by executive chef Ashley Palmer-Watts who developed
the menu with his Fat Duck mentor. The kitchen fashionably
takes centre stage - glassed-in but fully open to view, so you
can watch the action at the Josper grill and see whole
pineapples turning on the clockwork rotisserie. The room itself
is what you'd expect in the jet-set Knightsbridge postcode -
upscale, glossy and understated, with darkwood tables,
neutral tones, lots of leather and a fun, on-message detail in
the porcelain light fittings, which are modelled on antique
jelly moulds. Oh yes, there are exclusive views over Hyde Park
too, with tables on the terrace in predictably high demand.
Food anoraks will be pleased to see an approximate date
ascribed to the origins of each dish (spanning the years from
1390 to 1940, since you ask). Meat fruit (c1500) is the
signature dish and it plays with your head in the manner of a
Fat Duck idea: outside it's a mandarin, with life-like dimpled
peel, but cut it open and - drums roll and cymbals clash - it is
full of rich, smooth chicken liver parfait. Elsewhere though,
trickery gives way to heritage ideas treated with 21st-century
science to bring out pinpoint flavours and textural contrasts.
Main courses deliver intriguing prospects such as (c.1670)
powdered (ie salted) duck breast with smoked confit fennel
and umbles - minced offal in modern parlance - or roast
halibut (c.1830) with leaf chicory and cockle ketchup. If you're
wondering what the story is with those spit-roast pineapples,
they turn up in dessert with a Regency-era tipsy cake. Value
hunters should aim their sights at the set lunch, offering two
choices per course.

Chef Ashley Palmer-Watts **Owner** Mandarin Oriental Hyde
Park **Times** 12-2.30/6.30-10.30 **Prices** Food prices not
confirmed for 2013. Please telephone for details **Wines** 400
bottles over £20, 20 by glass **Notes** Vegetarian available,
Dress restrictions, Smart casual **Seats** 138, Pr/dining room 10
Parking Valet parking, NCP

Save on Hotels. Book at **theAA.com/hotel**

LONDON, CENTRAL (SW1) 281 **ENGLAND**

Corinthia Hotel London PLAN 5 B6

◉◉ Modern British **NEW**

Glamorous dining room and smart modern British cooking

☎ 020 7930 8181

Whitehall Place SW1A 2BD

e-mail: northallenquiry@corinthia.com

dir: Nearest station. Embankment/Charing Cross

Named for its location on the corner of Northumberland Avenue and Whitehall, the Corinthia Hotel's flagship Northall restaurant cuts a dash with its art-deco-style good looks, soaring ceiling, vast arched windows and glamorous fixtures and fittings. With rich tan-coloured seating, dark wood tables impeccably laid, and a service team who know their onions, this is a click and polished operation, serving up some classically-inspired cooking under the auspices of executive chef Garry Hollihead. The quality of the produce shines through in dishes such as potted shrimps with sweet pickled cucumber, brown bread and butter (a classic done well), or Herdwick lamb short loin chops cooked on the grill (beautifully pink and tender) and served with a béarnaise sauce. Farmers and producers are name-checked on the menu. To finish, rose, raspberry and lychee Pavlova and crystallized rose petals shows a keen ability to balance flavours. There's a daily market menu at lunch and early evening, plus a three-course Sunday lunch which includes a glass of champagne.

Times 12-3/5.30-11

Dinner by Heston Blumenthal PLAN 4 F5

◉◉◉ – see opposite

Ebury PLAN 4 G2

◉ British, French

Ever-popular bar-brasserie with eclectic menu

☎ 020 7730 6784

11 Pimlico Rd SW1W 8NA

e-mail: info@theebury.co.uk

dir: Nearest station: Sloane Sq, Victoria. From Sloane Sq Tube left into Holbein Place, left at intersection with Pimlico Rd. On corner of Pimlico Rd & Ranelagh Grove

The original team who established the Ebury's reputation for stylish bar-brasserie eating in the early noughties came back on the block in 2011, and after a healthy dose of TLC, the place is back on top form. The smart brasserie look still fits the bill for the Chelsea postcode, but the kitchen has lightened up its approach, bringing in Med-influenced marinades, olive oil, vinegar and citrus to add punch, rather than the old-school sauces of the past. Classic ideas kick off along the lines of chilli salt squid with lime, or burrata with tomato, black olives and basil, while mains run the gamut from salt-baked sea bass with braised artichokes, pickled carrots and basil, to pork belly confit with choucroute, Morteau sausage and sage. The new regime has also declared that Sunday is fun day,

with sage Bloody Marys and classic roasts on the menu, and DJs providing the soundtrack.

Chef James Holah **Owner** TLIC Ltd **Times** 12-3/6-10.30 Closed 24-27 Dec, BHs **Prices** Starter £6.50-£22, Main £12.50-£25, Dessert £5-£6.50, Service added but optional 15% **Wines** 110 bottles over £20, 6 bottles under £20, 8 by glass **Notes** Sunday L, Vegetarian available **Seats** 60, Pr/dining room 50 **Children** Portions **Parking** On street & NCP

The Fifth Floor Restaurant PLAN 4 F5

◉◉ Modern International ⟨NOTABLE WINE LIST⟩ 🍷

Market menus on the top floor at Harvey Nics

☎ 020 7235 5250

Harvey Nichols, 109-125 Knightsbridge SW1X 7RJ

e-mail: reception@harveynichols.com

web: www.harveynichols.com

dir: Nearest station: Knightsbridge, Hyde Park Corner. Entrance on Sloane St

The top floor at Harvey Nics is consecrated to food and wine in a big way, with a great retail operation, a café and the flagship restaurant, antecedent of all the various Fourth Floors and Second Floors boasted by branches of the glitzy department store around the country. Menus divided into Field, Farm and Sea are reminders that there is a world beyond Knightsbridge, and the Market menu offers seasonal specials along the lines of butternut squash soup with chive oil, crispy duck salad with curly endive, spring onions and plum sauce, hake 'tournedos' with choucroûte and Morteau in red wine fumet, and Tokaji parfait with soaked Agen prunes and sesame caramel. Afternoon tea is a superior version that offers the likes of Ortiz tuna mayonnaise on focaccia as a change from cucumber sandwiches. Breakfast with freshly squeezed juices and eggs Benedict starts at 8am.

Chef Jonas Karlsson **Owner** Harvey Nichols Ltd **Times** 12-3/6-11 Closed Xmas, Etr Sun, D Sun **Prices** Fixed L 2 course £20, Fixed D 3 course £25, Starter

£10.50-£14, Main £17.50-£31.50, Service added but optional 12.5% **Wines** 700 bottles over £20, 30 bottles under £20, 30 by glass **Notes** Sunday L, Vegetarian available **Seats** 120 **Children** Portions, Menu **Parking** On street, NCP Cadogan Place

The Goring PLAN 4 H4

◉◉ Traditional British

Refined, classical English cooking in a grand hotel

☎ 020 7396 9000

Beeston Place SW1W 0JW

e-mail: reception@thegoring.com

web: www.thegoring.com

dir: Nearest station: Victoria. From Victoria St turn left into Grosvenor Gdns, cross Buckingham Palace Rd, 75yds turn right into Beeston Place

A starring role in the royal wedding in 2011 (the Middletons stayed here, you might recall) was surely among the highlights of the Goring family's hundred-plus year tenure of this fine piece of Belgravia real estate. It remains one of London's most luxurious and alluringly English hotels. The lavishly done out restaurant suits the mood, with its grand Edwardian proportions, moulded plasterwork, bespoke Swarovski chandeliers and precisely laid tables, watched over by a skilled service team who work in a formal manner. From the trolley comes a roast at lunch, with perhaps a beef Wellington in the evening, and, from the carte, dishes that follow the British seasons and are based on top quality produce. Goosnargh duck leg might come in a terrine with pickled red cabbage, followed by Lincolnshire ham knuckle with egg pithivier, pea purée and English mustard sauce, or wild mushroom and leek tart with a leek sauce. It's back to the trolley for desserts and cheeses.

Chef Derek Quelch **Owner** Goring family **Times** 12.30-2.30/6-10 Closed L Sat **Prices** Service added but optional 12.5% **Wines** 400 bottles over £20, 13 by glass **Notes** Pre-theatre 2 course £35, Sunday L, Vegetarian available, Dress restrictions, Smart dress, Civ Wed 50 **Seats** 70, Pr/dining room 50 **Children** Portions, Menu **Parking** 7

LONDON SW1 *continued*

Grand Imperial, London
PLAN 4 H4

@@ Cantonese **NEW**

Vibrant Chinese cooking amid Victorian splendour

☎ 020 7821 8898
The Grosvenor, 101 Buckingham Palace Rd SW1W 0SJ
e-mail: reservations@grandimperiallondon.com
dir: Nearest station: Victoria. On junct with Terminus Place

Converted banks may be a little ten-a-penny these days, but converted railway stations are something else again, particularly when they used to be Victoria station. The Grosvenor Hotel sits beside the present-day rail terminus, and is a place of stolid 19th-century grandeur. In the days when rail passengers were treated to first-class dining rooms, what is now the Grand Imperial was it. Gorgeously remade as a Chinese restaurant, it naturally has all its marble columns and ceiling mouldings intact, but the space has been offset with paper screens, bonsai and orchids. The culinary style takes refined Hong Kong dining as its launchpad, and spreads its wings to encompass some beautifully rendered modern Chinese dishes as well as classics. Fish is a strong suit: steamed whole turbot with XO chilli sauce, freshwater eel steamed in rice wine, and sautéed brown crab with turnip in black pepper sauce are among the opulent offerings. Salt-and-pepper soft-shelled crab is properly crisp and singing with fantastically intense seasoning, while a Chinese

barbecue duo of honey-glazed pork loin and crisp-roasted duck bring fresh lustre to long-familiar items. A slate of healthy cuisine options includes stuffed bamboo with asparagus.

Times Noon-11 Closed 25-26 Dec, 1 Jan

Il Convivio
PLAN 4 G3

@@ Modern Italian

Modish Italian in smart Belgravia

☎ 020 7730 4099
143 Ebury St SW1W 9QN
e-mail: ilconvivio@etruscarestaurants.com
web: www.ilconvivio.co.uk
dir: Nearest station: Victoria, Sloane Square. 7 min walk from Victoria Station - corner of Ebury St and Elizabeth St

Named after Dante's poem which translates as 'a meeting over food and drink', Il Convivio offers creative

modern Italian food based on high quality ingredients. Entering the Georgian townhouse restaurant on moneyed Ebury Street, the feeling is one of light and space, thanks to a glass frontage, a skylight in the main restaurant and the conservatory out back with a fully retractable roof to cope with the UK's unpredictable seasons. A deep red wall amongst the white continues the theme with inscriptions of Dante's poems, while limestone-tiled floors, cedar wooden panels and white linen add to the romantic atmosphere. The large Italian wine list has plenty to choose from by the glass. Start with all the simplicity of beef carpaccio with celery and basil infused olive oil, before moving on to tagliatelle with Cornish crab, rocket and black olive, and a main course such as monkfish fillet wrapped in courgette and Parma ham, served with fennel and mint salad.

Il Convivio

Chef Jonathan Lees **Owner** Piero & Enzo Quaradeghini
Times 12-3.15/6.30-11.15 Closed Xmas, New Year, BHs, Sun **Prices** Fixed L 2 course £17.50, Fixed D 2 course

Koffmann's

@@@

LONDON SW1
PLAN 4 G5

French ⬥ NOTABLE WINE LIST

Top-grade regional French cooking from a virtuoso

☎ 020 7235 1010 & 7201 1665
The Berkeley, Wilton Place SW1X 7RL
e-mail: koffmanns@the-berkeley.co.uk
dir: Nearest station: Knightsbridge. 300mtrs from Hyde Park Corner along Knightsbridge

Pierre Koffmann's restaurant, with its colour scheme of green, brown and grey, and foodie prints on textured walls and crisply set tables, has a slick and professional French service team as if to underline the uncompromisingly French menu. The kitchen's attention to detail is remarkable, from an amuse-bouche such as caramelised onion tart, through sensational breads, to petits fours. Top-drawer ingredients are standard, with

classics from the great French traditions including foie gras terrine, lobster, mildly spiced and served with ratte potatoes, and rib of beef with béarnaise. But the generous brasserie-style menu is more focused on Koffmann's native south-west, seen in Gascony-style black pudding with cheese, onion and beetroot, and beef cheeks braised in red wine. A meal might open with smooth, deeply flavoured asparagus soup or the earthier flavours of duck and sweetbread pâté. Roast cod is a dazzling main course, the flesh translucent, the skin crisp, served with subtly spiced couscous and a rich, buttery tomato sauce with a kick of red pepper, while professional mastery has turned plainly roast chicken, served with parsley croûtons, into a memorable dish. Puddings are a delight, too, judging by a textbook version of floating islands, and pistachio soufflé with matching ice cream.

Chef Pierre Koffmann **Owner** Pierre Koffmann
Times 12-2.30/6-10.30 **Prices** Fixed L 2 course fr £21.50, Starter £9-£28, Main £22-£60, Dessert £8-£15, Service added but optional 12.5% **Wines** 220 bottles over £20, 25 by glass **Notes** Pre/post theatre menu 2 course £24, 3 course £28, Sunday L, Vegetarian available, Dress restrictions, Smart casual **Seats** 114, Pr/dining room 16 **Children** Portions **Parking** Knightsbridge car park

£23.50, Starter £8.50-£16.50, Main £14-£24, Dessert
£5.90-£10.50, Service added but optional 12.5%
Wines 146 bottles over £20, 2 bottles under £20, 12 by
glass **Notes** Vegetarian available, Dress restrictions,
Smart casual **Seats** 65, Pr/dining room 14 **Parking** On
street

Inn the Park   PLAN 5 A5

🏮 British

Good British cooking in St James's Park

☎ 020 7451 9999
St James's Park SW1A 2BJ
e-mail: reservations@innthepark.com
dir: Nearest station: St James's Park, Charing Cross,
Piccadilly. 200mtrs down The Mall towards Buckingham
Palace

With The Mall and Horseguards Parade close by, this
smart wooden building with floor-to-ceiling glass has
upped the ante as far as eating in a London park goes.
There's a distinctly Scandinavian feel to the structure,
but this is central London alright. A covered decked
terrace is the place to be when the weather allows, but
those windows ensure the lake and magnificent trees are
visible all year round. It's a café, too, with the restaurant
bit looking good with its comfy tubular chairs and
orange-topped tables. As if to confirm its contemporary
credentials, the kitchen is open to view. Expect good
British produce prepared with a pleasing
straightforwardness; grilled razor clams or crab salad
with pea shoots and mint might kick things off, followed
by green lentil, pea and toasted cashew burger, or honey-
glazed spring chicken with wild garlic stuffing.

Times 12-3.30/5.30-9.30

JB's Restaurant   PLAN 4 J3

🏮 Modern French, Mediterranean

Modern hotel brasserie dining

☎ 020 7769 9772 & 020 7769 9999
Park Plaza Victoria, 239 Vauxhall Bridge Rd SW1V 1EQ
e-mail: gfernando@pphe.com
dir: Nearest station: Victoria. 2 min walk from Apollo
Victoria Theatre

Well placed for London's history and heritage
and conveniently close to Victoria Station, the Park Plaza
is a smart modern hotel with stylish public areas. The
coffee bar is a popular daytime venue, and at cocktail
o'clock, the glossy bar is an inviting spot to linger a while
before moving on into JB's Restaurant. Staying with the
up-to-date theme, it has full-length windows for
watching the street bustle while you choose from a wide-
ranging menu of modern crowd pleasers. Ingredients are
well-sourced and treated without undue fuss starting,
perhaps, with grilled baby squid with lemon, parsley, red
pepper and chorizo, while mains may include roast pigeon
with grilled polenta, smoked pork belly and date sauce.
Finish with blackberry, limoncello and mascarpone trifle.

Times 6-10 Closed BHs, Sun, L all week

Ken Lo's Memories of China   PLAN 4 H3

🏮 Chinese

Smart Chinese cooking in Belgravia

☎ 020 7730 7734
65-69 Ebury St SW1W 0NZ
e-mail: memoriesofchina@btconnect.com
web: www.memories-of-china.co.uk
dir: Nearest station: Victoria. At junction of Ebury Street &
Eccleston St

Serving the well-heeled of Belgravia for some 30 years,
Ken Lo's is a smart, upmarket restaurant with a loyal
following. Chinese fabrics and red lanterns combine in a
room divided by sandalwood screens, looked over by a
slick service team. Authentic regional Chinese cooking is
the order of the day, with lots of classic dishes featured
in a range of set menus and on the mighty à la carte. You
might start with three-spiced squid, siu mai dumplings
or red oil-poached chicken dumplings, following on with a
soup (Shanghai fish and crabmeat, perhaps). Next up,
Peking quick-fried lamb with spring onion, Cantonese
beef in black bean sauce, or a clay pot dish such as
aubergine with minced prawns.

Chef Kam Po But **Owner** A-Z Restaurants
Times 12-2.30/6-11 Closed 25-26 Dec **Prices** Food prices
not confirmed for 2013. Please telephone for details
Wines 129 bottles over £20, 4 bottles under £20, 6 by
glass **Notes** Vegetarian available, Dress restrictions,
Smart casual **Seats** 120, Pr/dining room 20
Children Portions **Parking** On street

Koffmann's   PLAN 4 G5

🏵🏵🏵 – see opposite

Marcus Wareing at the Berkeley   PLAN 4 G5

🏵🏵🏵🏵🏵 – see page 284

Mint Leaf   PLAN 5 A6

🏮 Modern Indian

Upmarket Indian cooking in super-cool setting

☎ 020 7930 9020
Suffolk Place, Haymarket SW1Y 4HX
e-mail: reservations@mintleafrestaurant.com
web: www.mintleafrestaurant.com
dir: Nearest station: Piccadilly, Charing Cross. At the end
of Haymarket, on corner of Pall Mall & Suffolk Pl

Enter the canopied door from the street, descend the
stairs and make your way along the catwalk-style
walkway that splits the two sides of this voguishly
designed and furnished restaurant. Top-end Indian
cooking is the deal, with dishes sourced from all over the
sub-continent. Grilled chicken breast infused with lemon
served with spicy mint sauce, plump and succulent
prawns in a sweet-and-sour-style tomato sauce, and
accurately seared scallops with star anise and green
peppercorns show the style. Bite-sized pieces of lightly
smoked chicken come in a well-balanced, velvety sauce
of tomato and fenugreek leaves and incidentals like
breads get the thumbs up. Gulab jamon might be given
the brûlée treatment for pudding.

Chef Vishal Rane **Owner** Out of Africa Investments
Times 12-3/5.30-11 Closed 25-26 Dec, 1 Jan, L Sat-Sun
Prices Fixed L 2 course fr £13.95, Starter £6.50-£11,
Main £14.50-£22.50, Dessert fr £7.50, Service added but
optional 12.5% **Wines** 130 bottles over £20, 8 bottles
under £20, 12 by glass **Notes** Pre-theatre menu 5-7pm 2
course £13.95, 3 course £17.95, Vegetarian available,
Dress restrictions, Smart casual, no scruffy jeans or
trainers, Civ Wed 100 **Seats** 144, Pr/dining room 66
Children Portions **Parking** NCP, on street

Marcus Wareing at the Berkeley

LONDON SW1   **PLAN 4 G5**

Modern European V NOTABLE WINE LIST

Thrilling cooking from a hands-on super-chef

☎ 020 7235 1200
The Berkeley, Wilton Place, Knightsbridge SW1X 7RL
e-mail: marcuswareing@the-berkeley.co.uk
dir: Nearest station: Knightsbridge, Hyde Park Corner. 300mtrs from Hyde Park Corner along Knightsbridge

Arriving at The Berkeley you might well see limousines dropping off their charges as bodyguards watch the street for unwanted attention. There are doormen, too, who will usher you in the right direction for lunch or dinner chez Marcus, where the sense of occasion and cosseting five-star luxury continues, and five-Rosetted cooking of the very highest order awaits. The front-of-house team will put you at your ease and it's easy to relax in such a reassuringly comfortable space, where burgundy velvet panels adorn the walls, burnished leather covers the seats, and tables are dressed up in crisp white linen. It's a classical look, avoiding the clichés of contemporary restaurant design, low-lit to further add to the sense of intimacy, with tables generously spaced around the room to heighten the sense of exclusivity. That space between tables is needed as various trolleys work the room carrying perfectly ripened cheeses and brandies among their gastronomic cargoes. The menus run from fixed-price carte to gourmand and tasting menus, including a vegetarian version which is a beacon of high-end veggie eating, plus a set lunch menu that gives an opportunity to get a sense of the place at a very reasonable cost. Things get off to a flying start with canapés that demonstrate this kitchen's ability to get maximum flavour from its ingredients without getting bogged down in showboating: smoked cods' roe and toast, perhaps, and pork haslet with crackling and plum chutney. Orkney scallops in a first course are prime examples, plump and perfectly fresh, cooked lightly and partnered with grapes, kaffir lime and alexanders in a dish of divinely balanced flavours. Herdwick mutton in these hands is as tender as you'll find anywhere, served in a main course with supremely judged acidity and sweetness from the accompanying caper and raisin purée, plus char-grilled cabbage and a lightly spiced sauce. There are supplements on the fixed-price carte: 30 quid if you want to add Oscietra caviar to a dish of halibut and cockles. The classical technique on show is the surest of foundations for food that never loses its way, always impressing with its juxtapositions of flavours and dazzling presentations. A dessert of apple, crispy cinnamon pastry and apple jelly packs a fabulous punch of appleyness, the perfect balance of sweetness and tartness. With the superb breads supported by delicious brown butter (melted to nutty brownness, chilled over ice and mixed with some crème fraîche) and coffee that is about as good as it gets, Marcus Wareing's restaurant leaves no stone unturned in search of perfection, and that goes for the magnificent wine list and the impeccable service team, too.

Chef Marcus Wareing **Owner** Marcus Wareing Restaurants Ltd
Times 12-2.30/6-11 Closed 1 Jan, Sun, L Sat **Prices** Fixed L 2 course fr £30, Fixed D 3 course fr £80, Service added but optional 12.5% **Wines** 900 bottles over £20, 15 by glass **Notes** Fixed D 8,10 course £98, £120, Vegetarian menu, Dress restrictions, Smart - jacket preferred, No jeans/trainers **Seats** 70, Pr/dining room 16 **Children** Portions **Parking** NCP, on street

LONDON SW1 *continued*

Mitsukoshi   PLAN 2 K1

◉ Japanese

Friendly, traditional, Japanese department store restaurant

☎ 020 7930 0317
Dorland House, 14-20 Lower Regent St SW1Y 4PH
e-mail: restaurant@mitsukoshi.co.uk
web: www.mitsukoshi-restaurant.co.uk
dir: Nearest station: Piccadilly Circus. Piccadilly Circus, exit Lower Regent St, entry via Mitsukoshi department store lower ground floor

In the basement below the Mitsukoshi department store, just a short stroll from all the Piccadilly Circus mêlée, this authentic, traditional-style Japanese restaurant is much loved by Japanese tourists and expats. It comes with separate sushi and cocktail bars, while the main dining area - a few steps below - is a modish space, decked out with red carpet and black lacquered furniture with red-leather upholstery; pale-wood booth-like dividers break up the large space (though it's looking a tad tired these days). Authentic, polite and smiley service backs up an extensive carte of honest, traditional Japanese dishes, which include several set and fixed-priced options as well as sushi and sashimi. Expect king prawn tempura, grilled salmon with a spicy teriyaki sauce, or prime Scottish rib-eye steak with an onion soy dressing. For a touch of theatre, try the sukiyaki or shabu-shabu (hotpots) cooked in the pan at the table.

Times 12-2/6-10 Closed 25-26 Dec, 1 Jan, Etr

MU at Millennium Knightsbridge   PLAN 4 F4

◉ Mediterranean, European

Simple Italian dishes in fashion-conscious Knightsbridge

☎ 020 7201 6330
17 Sloane St, Knightsbridge SW1X 9NU
e-mail: reservations.knightsbridge@millenniumhotels.co.uk
dir: Nearest station: Knightsbridge, Victoria. 200yds from Knightsbridge Stn, near Harrods

The culinary orientation of MU continues to evolve almost as rapidly as the tides of fashion in haute couture, to which its hot-red interiors and style-conscious clientele continue to pay respectful homage. Asian tapas was once the theme, now supplanted by a menu of flat-out retro Italian dishes of almost provocative simplicity. Starters range from seafood salad and pancetta and pea risotto to Parma ham and melon, while the mains are listed only by their principal proteins: grilled fillet of salmon, roast belly of pork, fried sea bass. There are Scotch rib-eye steaks with chips and peppercorn sauce, if you will, and a couple of vegetarian offerings.

Chef Paul Knight **Owner** Millennium & Copthorne Hotels **Times** 12-2.30/5.30-10.30 Closed Sun-Mon, L Sat **Prices** Food prices not confirmed for 2013. Please telephone for details **Wines** 60 bottles over £20, 4 bottles under £20, 25 by glass **Notes** Vegetarian available **Seats** 90, Pr/dining room 50 **Children** Portions, Menu **Parking** 8, NCP Pavilion Rd

Nahm   PLAN 4 G5

◉◉◉ – *see below*

One-O-One   PLAN 4 F5

◉◉◉ – *see page 286*

Nahm

LONDON SW1   PLAN 4 G5

Traditional Thai V ▮NOTABLE WINE LIST

Top-class Thai cooking in a luxury hotel

☎ 020 7333 1234
The Halkin Hotel, 5 Halkin St, Belgravia SW1X 7DJ
e-mail: res@nahm.como.bz
web: www.halkin.como.bz
dir: Nearest station: Hyde Park Corner. Halkin Street just off Hyde Park Corner

The glossy Thai operation in the Halkin Hotel exudes a sheen of glamour that sits well with its blue-blooded Belgravia location; its sleek looks involving shimmering tones of gold and bronze, tan marble floors and warm wooden walls, state from the off that it is a far cry from the average Thai restaurant. The scene is a showcase for David Thompson's vibrant contemporary Thai cuisine, which is guaranteed to jolt jaded palates to attention with its exciting combinations of taste and texture. The menu may be unpronounceable to any other than a native Thai speaker, but its elements are all helpfully spelled out in translation. Sometimes the worthy concept of food miles has to be sacrificed on the altar of authenticity, so the whole edifice is built on the rock solid foundations of top-class materials brought in from Thailand. The flexible repertoire allows you to approach it in a pick and mix way, but perhaps the best plan is to follow the tradition of 'nahm arharn' and take a starter, then choose a dish from each of the five sections entitled salad, soup, relish, curry, and 'stir-fried, braised and steamed' dishes. Thus a dish of crispy noodles with prawns, pickled garlic, bean sprouts and coriander leads onto a langoustine salad with rambutans, lemongrass and toasted coconut. The soup stage is tender slices of roast duck in a punchy broth with crab and young coconut, and the relish is taken care of by minced prawns and pork simmered in coconut cream and teamed with fish cake and cucumber. Next out, minced quail stars in a red curry with ginger, green beans and Thai basil, and the final flourish is a sweet and crispy pork hock.

Chef David Thompson, Matthew Albert **Owner** Halkin Hotel Ltd **Times** 12-2.30/7-11 Closed 25 Dec & BHs, L Sat-Sun **Wines** 190 bottles over £20, 12 by glass **Notes** Traditional Nahm Arharn menu L £35, D £60, Vegetarian menu, Dress restrictions, Smart casual **Seats** 78, Pr/dining room 30 **Children** Portions **Parking** On street

One-O-One

LONDON SW1   PLAN 4 F5

French V ![NOTABLE WINE LIST]

A temple of seafood in a Knightsbridge hotel

☎ 020 7290 7101
Sheraton Park Tower, 101 Knightsbridge SW1X 7RN
e-mail: oneoone@luxurycollection.com
dir: Nearest station: Knightsbridge. E from station, just after Harvey Nichols, corner William St & Knightsbridge

You can rely on chef Pascal Proyart's immaculate sourcing policy to steer you clear of unwittingly eating endangered sealife: everything that turns up on your plate, whether farmed or line-caught, is from sustainable stocks and works around the different species' breeding seasons to avoid eating undersized or immature fish. The ethical issues thus neatly taken care of, you're free to relax and enjoy the luxurious sheen of the venue at the base of the Sheraton Park Tower in Knightsbridge, which is conceived to evoke the shape of a shucked oyster, right down to the seafood counter representing the pearl at its centre, and the colour palette of a sandy beach all around. Top-flight fish and seafood cooking such as this is all about spot-on timing and teasing out the subtleties of flavour, and with Proyart's razor-sharp modern French technique you can't put a foot wrong. The 'petits plats' offers a flexible format of small tasting dishes running from wild Norwegian red king crab with coconut vichyssoise and mango, lime and coriander tartare, to pan-fried turbot with saffron, pea and seafood risotto. If the trendy grazing approach isn't your bag, the carte offers standard-sized dishes, starting with the likes of pan-fried langoustines partnered luxuriously with duck foie gras, petit ravioli, hoisin froth and Peking duck consommé, with main courses such as wild Cornish sea bass cooked in basil oil with barigoule sauce, artichoke compôte, ratatouille and Provençal olive tapenade. There are meat dishes too, if you must - perhaps roast Gressingham duck breast with green peppercorn and lime sauce, apple compôte with verjus, and cider fondant potato. To finish, head for something like caramelised Granny Smith apple with Calvados and popcorn.

Chef Pascal Proyart **Owner** Starwood Hotels & Resorts **Times** 12-3/6.30-10 Closed 25 Dec, 1 Jan **Prices** Fixed L 2 course £17-£67, Fixed D 3 course £47.50-£76.50, Tasting menu £59-£89, Starter £11-£28, Main £27-£39, Dessert £9.50, Service optional, Groups min 15 service 12.5% **Wines** 160 bottles over £20, 8 by glass **Notes** Tasting menu 5 course, Sunday L, Vegetarian menu, Dress restrictions, Smart casual **Seats** 51, Pr/dining room 10 **Children** Portions, Menu

Pétrus

LONDON SW1   PLAN 4 G5

Modern French V ![NOTABLE WINE LIST]

High-achieving Ramsay kitchen in Knightsbridge

☎ 020 7592 1609
1 Kinnerton St, Knightsbridge SW1X 8EA
e-mail: petrus@gordonramsay.com
dir: Nearest station: Knightsbridge, Sloane Square

There's no shortage of high-end eating establishments in this part of the capital, but this Gordon Ramsay-run operation more than holds its own against the competition. It has plenty to offer, not least the divertingly confident modern French cooking of Sean Burbidge. It looks pretty swanky - de rigueur in this postcode - with the rather odd-shaped room given a decidedly luxe sheen with fashionable neutral tones, smart table settings, and a centre-piece wine cave showing off its enticing wares (it's an excellent wine list, by the way, as you might expect of a restaurant named after such a famous French château). The cooking hits the mark with the acute technical abilities of the kitchen team clear for all to see, the dishes looking a picture on the plate, and the quality of the produce ensuring all is well from the bottom up. Pan-fried fillet of red mullet might come in a first course with clams, coriander gnocchi and a lemongrass sauce, or go for three ways with Windsor Estate venison (served with shaved chestnuts and cider consommé). Main- courses have no less appeal: chargrilled lemon sole, perhaps, with compressed apple, celery, capers and apple velouté, or fillet of Casterbridge beef with braised ox tongue and ale sauce. To finish, a pistachio soufflé is sure to rise to the occasion, with its accompanying Guanaja chocolate sorbet. There are masterclasses available at the chef's table if you want to pick up a tip or two, plus a decent value set lunch menu.

Chef Sean Burbidge **Owner** Gordon Ramsay Holdings **Times** 12-2.30/6.30-10.30 Closed Sun **Prices** Fixed L 2 course £55, Fixed D 3 course fr £65, Service added but optional 12.5% **Wines** 800 bottles over £20, 12 by glass **Notes** Chef's menu 5 course £75, Vegetarian menu, Dress restrictions, No sportswear **Seats** 55, Pr/dining room 7 **Children** Portions **Parking** On street (free after 6.30)/NCP Park Towers

Save on Hotels. Book at **theAA.com/hotel**

LONDON, CENTRAL (SW1) 287 ENGLAND

LONDON SW1 *continued*

L'Oranger
PLAN 4 J6

◉◉ Modern French

Refined French cooking in an elegant room

☎ 020 7839 3774
5 St James's St SW1A 1EF
e-mail: loranger@londonfinedininggroup.com
web: www.loranger.co.uk
dir: Nearest station: Green Park. Access by car via Pall Mall

Its frontage is perhaps a little unassuming compared with L'Oranger's opulent interior, a softly carpeted room with comfortable banquettes and high-backed upholstered seats at correctly set tables, and abstract art on the walls. Formal service from smartly dressed French staff underpins the style of the operation. The cooking is resolutely French, focusing on the cuisine of Provence in particular. Dishes are notable for their simplicity, and accurate cooking bringing out vibrant, fresh flavours, as in a main course of tender, moist chicken breast casseroled with seasonal vegetables, a broth poured at table by a waiter, accompanied by croûtons smeared in foie gras mousse. Grilled swordfish fillet might come with grilled courgettes, sauce vierge and basil, and there's more waiter action when a velvety smooth velouté flavoured with chorizo is poured over a soft-boiled egg and its accompanying croûton. More technically challenging dishes are no less successful; a thin, crisp pastry base for light and airy chestnut soufflé, for example.

Chef Laurent Michel **Owner** A to Z Restaurants Ltd **Times** 12-2.45/6.30-10.45 Closed Xmas, Etr, BHs, Sun, L Sat **Prices** Food prices not confirmed for 2013. Please telephone for details **Wines** 290 bottles over £20, 4 bottles under £20, 12 by glass **Notes** Vegetarian available, Dress restrictions, Smart casual **Seats** 70, Pr/dining room 40 **Children** Portions **Parking** On street/NCP

Osteria Dell'Angolo
PLAN 5 A4

◉ Italian

Italian classics in the heart of Westminster

☎ 020 3268 1077
47 Marsham St SW1P 3DR
e-mail: osteriadell_angolo@btconnect.com
dir: Nearest station: St James's Park, Westminster. Located off Horseferry Rd

The kitchen of this contemporary Italian in the heart of Westminster near to the Houses of Parliament has its finger firmly on the regional pulse of Tuscan cuisine. After a glass of prosecco in the smart darkwood bar, take a seat in the dining room where butch burgundy leather contrasts with white linen and the Mediterranean warmth of a yellow and amber colour scheme. Well-sourced artisan produce from Italy and splendid true-Brit materials work together in dishes such as grilled Cornish

squid filled with Swiss chard, capers, pine kernels, stracciatella Pugliese cheese and black olives, while home-made gnocchi are stuffed with goats' cheese and served with wild mushrooms, pumpkin and sage sauce. Full-flavoured mains run to roast monkfish with osso buco sauce, sautéed radicchio, and toasted almond and red wine sauce, or grilled Galloway beef fillet with turnip tops and a timbale of borlotti beans and leeks.

Chef Massimiliano Vezzi **Owner** Claudio Pulze **Times** 12-3/6-10.30 Closed Xmas, New Year, BHs, Sun, L Sat **Prices** Fixed L 2 course £16.50, Starter £8-£11, Main £17-£24.50, Dessert £5.50, Service added but optional 12.5% **Wines** 180 bottles over £20, 2 bottles under £20, 4 by glass **Notes** Vegetarian available **Seats** 80, Pr/dining room 24 **Parking** 6

Pétrus
PLAN 4 G5

◉◉◉ – see opposite

Quaglino's
PLAN 4 J6

◉ French Brasserie

Classic venue serving classic brasserie menu

☎ 020 7930 6767
16 Bury St, St James's SW1Y 6AJ
e-mail: quaglinos@danddlondon.com
web: www.quaglinos.co.uk
dir: Nearest station: Green Park/Piccadilly Circus. Bury St is off Jermyn St

The art-deco theme prevails at this St James's stalwart, these days owned by the D&D group. Sweep dramatically down the impressive marble staircase, past tall vases of white gladioli, to the huge dining space, where some 250 diners can make for a tremendous buzz, aided by live music from the balcony above. Not in the business of re-inventing the wheel, the food is good, honest bistro-style fare in the hands now of former Quo Vadis chef, Jean-Philippe Patruno. Get stuck into well-executed classics such as dressed Cornish crab or bang bang chicken, and main courses like Dover sole or côte de veau, finishing off with baked Cox's apple with mincemeat and nutmeg ice cream, or lemon tart and raspberry coulis. The very good wine list includes a good range by the 50ml carafe.

Times 12-3/5.30-mdnt Closed 24-25 Dec, 1 Jan, L 31 Dec

The Quilon
PLAN 4 J4

◉◉ Indian

Sophisticated versions of the cuisine from India's south-west coast

☎ 020 7821 1899
41 Buckingham Gate SW1E 6AF
e-mail: info@quilonrestaurant.co.uk
web: www.quilon.co.uk
dir: Nearest station: St James's Park. Next to Crowne Plaza Hotel St James

A major refit has given a new bar to The Quilon, with its own short snacky menu along the lines of tamarind-glazed chicken wings and semolina chips with tomato and onion chutney. It's a smart restaurant, part of the Crowne Plaza, with its own entrance. Modern, upmarket versions of south-western Indian coastal cooking are the specialities, so seafood takes up a chunk of the menu, from chargrilled scallops with mango and chilli relish to subtly spiced baked black cod. The kitchen seeks out the appropriate spices and other ingredients and uses them unerringly to give dishes their authentic flavours. Lamb shank is slowly braised with freshly ground herbs, spices and chillies, roast quail legs are stuffed with minced meat mixed with chilli, ginger, brown onions and spices, served in mustard sauce, and lobster (available as both starter and main) is cooked with mango, ginger, kokum and curry leaves. Vegetables are as impressive as the rest of the package, and accompaniments like breads are up to snuff.

Chef Sriram Aylur **Owner** Taj International Hotels Limited **Times** 12-2.30/6-11 Closed 25 Dec **Prices** Fixed L 3 course £27-£45, Fixed D 3 course £43-£60, Starter £8.50-£10, Main £14-£28, Dessert fr £8, Service added but optional 12.5% **Wines** 129 bottles over £20, 16 by glass **Notes** Taster menu from £43, Sunday L, Vegetarian available, Dress restrictions, Smart casual **Seats** 90, Pr/dining room 16 **Children** Portions **Parking** On street, NCP

The Rib Room
PLAN 4 F4

◉◉◉ – see page 288

Roux at Parliament Square
PLAN 5 B5

◉◉◉ – see page 289

See advert on page 288

The Rib Room

LONDON SW1 PLAN 4 F4

British V 🕙

Great British beef and more at a top-end hotel

☎ 020 7858 7250 & 7858 7181
**Jumeirah Carlton Tower Hotel, Cadogan Place
SW1X 9PY**
e-mail: JCTinfo@jumeirah.com
dir: Nearest station: Knightsbridge. Follow road signs for
City Centre, towards Knightsbridge/Hyde Park/Sloane Sq,
then into Sloane St/Cadogan Place

The Rib Room, reached via the lobby of the Jumeirah
Carlton Tower, has a club-like feel, thanks to low ceilings
and a proliferation of dark wood, while attentive staff,
complete with sommelier, help create a slightly formal
atmosphere. The menu focuses on the best traditional
British cooking - raw materials are second to none - with
luxuries making an appearance, from lobster and Dover
sole to the eponymous rib of Casterbridge Angus beef,
perfectly timed and served with Yorkshire pudding. But
there's more to the menu than time-honoured classics,
and a sure hand in the kitchen in the form of Ian Rudge.
Start with hot-smoked wood pigeon with Scotch quail's
egg, damson jam, baby watercress, cauliflower and
hazelnuts - a perky salad indeed - or braised lamb neck
with marrowbone, garlic purée and parsley and carrot
caramel. Next up, fillet of sea bass with cod cheeks, leeks
and roast salsify, and saddle of pork with glazed beetroot,
Savoy cabbage and a deeply flavoured cider jus. Finish
with a perfectly executed apple crumble soufflé with a
custard sauce or farmhouse cheeses from Alsop and
Walker.

Chef Ian Rudge **Owner** Jumeirah
Times 12.30-2.45/7-10.45 **Prices** Fixed L 2 course £19,
Starter £8.50-£20, Main £21-£52, Dessert £8.50, Service
added but optional 15% **Wines** 17 by glass **Notes** Fixed
ALC D fr £28, British experience menu available, Sunday
L, Vegetarian menu, Dress restrictions, Smart casual
Seats 88, Pr/dining room 16 **Children** Portions, Menu
Parking 70

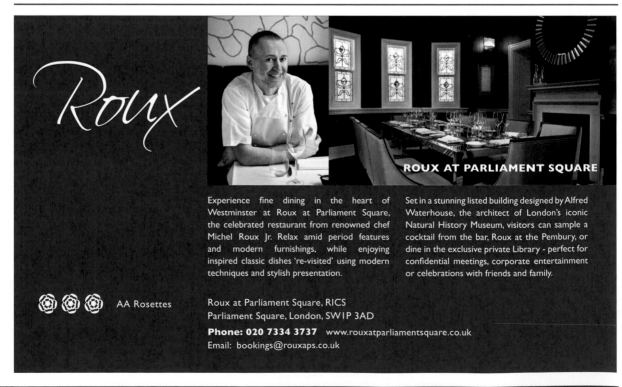

Roux at Parliament Square

Modern European

High-flying candidate on Parliament Square

☎ 020 7334 3737
Parliament Square SW1P 3AD
e-mail: roux@rics.org
web: www.rouxatparliamentsquare.co.uk/contact.aspx
dir: Nearest station: Westminster

The address may suggest a bastion of the British establishment, whilst the Roux name might imply a touch of classical refinement. But Roux at Parliament Square also has a decidedly contemporary sheen. Michel Roux jnr of Le Gavroche and *MasterChef* fame has a real winner up his sleeve here, a restaurant that might not hit the headlines on a regular basis, but is delivering some compellingly modern food, with head chef Toby Stuart cooking up a storm. There's a bar with big ideas in the cocktail department, and two dining rooms done out in soothing neutral tones with a restrained contemporary finish to the space (the original building was designed by the chap who built the British Museum). The service team does Monsieur Roux proud. A meal starts with a bang - fabulous breads and amuse-bouche set the bar high - before a first-course such as ballottine of Lincolnshire pork with mustard emulsion, pickled onions and smoked hock beignet. Technique is as sharp as a pin, flavours and textures perfectly judged, and it all looks beautiful on the plate. Main-course saddle of rabbit is stuffed with apple black pudding and comes with confit cabbage, macaroni and cider sauce, grilled fillet of Arctic char with an emulsion of sea vegetables and shellfish, plus Jersey Royals and white asparagus. To finish, poached Williams pear and almond sponge is lifted by the well-judged flavours of camomile and fennel. The wine list has all the verve and swagger of a Roux-inspired selection.

Chef Toby Stuart **Owner** Restaurant Associates **Times** 12-2/6.30-10 Closed Xmas, New Year, BHs, Sat-Sun **Prices** Fixed L 3 course £25, Starter £10-£16, Main £18-£26.50, Dessert £8-£14, Service added but optional 12.5% **Wines** 295 bottles over £20, 21 by glass **Notes** Vegetarian available, Dress restrictions, Smart casual **Seats** 56, Pr/dining room 10 **Children** Portions **Parking** NCP Semley Place

LONDON SW1 *continued*

The Royal Horseguards PLAN 5 B6

@@ Modern, Traditional British 🕮

Enterprising cooking near Whitehall

☎ 0871 376 9033 & 020 7451 9333
2 Whitehall Court SW1A 2EJ
e-mail: royalhorseguards@guoman.co.uk
dir: Nearest station: Embankment/Charing Cross. From
Trafalgar Sq take exit to Whitehall. Turn into Whitehall
Place then into Whitehall Court

Whitehall 1212 was once the telephone number of
Scotland Yard, a number dialled in many a black-and-
white noir thriller. The rozzers have moved house, but
their number lives on in One Twenty One Two, the
restaurant of this grand Thames-side hotel, an upmarket
address that is about as central as things get, not far
from the Houses of Parliament and Trafalgar Square. The
dapper restaurant comes kitted out with plushly-
upholstered crimson banquettes and seats, and linen-
clothed tables. In keeping with the updated décor, the
kitchen delivers appealing food in a gently modern vein,
while never losing sight of its French roots. Dinner starts
out creatively with smoked Goosnargh duck with poached
rhubarb, baby watercress and candied walnut. Sourcing
is of the highest order, as seen in a main course of oven-
seared organic salmon, sea trout and Dublin Bay prawns
with carrot purée and sauce Jacqueline, while a
distinguished dessert known as 'The Afternoon Tea'
brings things to a close - Earl Grey crème brûlée served
with mini fruit scones and honey crème fraîche.

Chef Ryan Matheson, Ben Purton **Owner** Guoman Hotels
Times 12-3/5.30-10 **Prices** Fixed L 2 course fr £15, Fixed
D 3 course fr £39, Tasting menu fr £75, Service added
but optional 12.5% **Wines** 200+ bottles over £20, 14 by
glass **Notes** Pre-theatre menu 2 course from £19, Sunday
L, Vegetarian available, Dress restrictions, Smart casual,
Civ Wed 250 **Seats** 75, Pr/dining room 30
Children Portions, Menu **Parking** NCP Trafalgar Sq

The Rubens at the Palace PLAN 4 H4

@@ Modern British

British food in a hotel with history

☎ 020 7834 6600
39 Buckingham Palace Rd SW1W 0PS
e-mail: bookrb@rchmail.com
web: www.redcarnationhotels.com
dir: Nearest station: Victoria. Opposite Royal Mews,
100mtrs from Buckingham Palace

The Rubens Hotel was originally built in the mews
opposite Buck House to put up debutantes in the days
when blue-blooded gels were presented to the world at
palace parties, and when all of that upstairs, downstairs
world was swept aside by World War II, it was taken over
by the Polish Resistance as their wartime HQ. These days
the clubby Library restaurant still has a whiff of bygone
times about it - there are plush armchairs upholstered
with heraldic designs, and tables swathed in crisp white
linen crisscrossed by red runners, as if flying the Cross of
St George. What leaves the kitchen, however, is stamped
firmly with the mark of the modern British idiom. The
menu might start out with a modish composition of
seared scallops with cauliflower purée, curry oil, piccalilli
and micro herbs, or keep things staunchly traditional by
serving smoked salmon carved at the table. A thoroughly
modern main course could see peppered tenderloin of
Gloucestershire Old Spot pork paired with white onion
tarte Tatin, pearl barley and pancetta risotto, sage jus
and spring greens, and to finish, perhaps an assiette of
lemon comprising lemon and polenta cake, lemon posset
and iced lemon parfait.

Chef Daniel Collins **Owner** Red Carnation Hotels
Times 7.30-10.30 Closed 24-27 Dec, L all week
Prices Fixed D 3 course £39.50, Starter £8-£14, Main
£18-£28, Dessert £8-£12, Service added but optional
12.5% **Wines** 60 bottles over £20, 12 by glass
Notes Vegetarian available, Dress restrictions, No shorts,
tracksuits or trainers **Seats** 30, Pr/dining room 50
Parking NCP at Victoria Coach Station

St Ermin's Hotel PLAN 4 K4

@ Modern European **NEW**

Super-funky hotel with modish menu

☎ 020 7222 7888
2 Caxton St, St James's Park, Westminster SW1H 0QW
e-mail: reservations@sterminshotel.co.uk
dir: Nearest station: Victoria, St James's Park

Following a £30 million makeover, it's easy for once to
see where the money went - the St Ermin's Hotel is a
divertingly impressive looking place. With its boutique
styling and jaw-dropping proportions, it's very much a
hotel of our times. The Caxton Grill fits the bill with its
contemporary finish - designer chairs, modish fabrics

and artworks, a feature wine cabinet, darkwood tables
(nary a tablecloth to be seen), and splashes of bold colour
amid the fashionable neutrality. Likewise the cooking has
a contemporary European spin, and there's a Josper Grill
to raise the bar when it comes to cooking the first-rate
meats (all the produce used is excellent here). Start with
squid ink ravioli (top-notch pasta) with West Country
crab and accompanying bisque, before tucking into a
steak from the grill: perfectly cooked sirloin with a
smoked béarnaise, perhaps, served with herb mash and
purple watercress.

Times 12-2/6-10.30 **Prices** Food prices not confirmed for
2013. Please telephone for details

Sake No Hana PLAN 4 J6

@@ Traditional Japanese

Sophisticated Japanese cooking in a smart part of town

☎ 020 7925 8988
23 Saint James's St SW1A 1HA
e-mail: reservations@sakenohana.com
dir: Nearest station: Green Park/Piccadilly Circus. From
Green Park Station, head towards Piccadilly Circus, first
right St James's St. Restaurant situated halfway down on
right

Pause for a drink, perhaps a Japanese whisky or Velvet
Haiku cocktail in the smart, contemporary bar before
riding the escalator to the sophisticated first floor modern
Japanese restaurant in well-to-do St James's. Here, large
windows, a wooden lattice-decorated ceiling and full-
length blinds to emulate sushi rolling mats make for an
authentic Japanese feel. Light wooden tables oiled with
tinted maple and light green leather banquettes are
tended by charmingly attentive staff, happy to talk you
through a menu which combines imported Japanese
produce and UK ingredients to good effect in traditional
and some fusion dishes. Wend your way through the
enticing menu starting perhaps with white miso soup
with wild mushrooms, or prawn and yam croquette with
dashi. Deep-fried tofu with white miso, served with red
miso and white miso with spinach, is a dish full of
flavour, whilst slow-poached beef is beautifully tender
and complemented by its accompanying light, creamy
mashed potato and yam with chestnuts, all set on a hoba
leaf over charcoal. Mandarin semi-fredo with spiced caramel and
roasted macadamia nuts makes for a fine fusion finale.
Or pull up a chair at the sushi bar for a less formal
experience.

Chef Daisuke Hayashi **Owner** Hakkasan Ltd
Times 12-2.30/6-11.30 Closed 24-25 Dec, Sun, L Sat
Prices Fixed L 2 course £23.50-£25, Fixed D 3 course
£65-£75, Starter £4-£23.50, Main £9.50-£24.50, Dessert
£8, Service added but optional 13% **Wines** 31 bottles
over £20, 7 by glass **Notes** Vegetarian available, Dress
restrictions, Smart casual **Seats** 100 **Parking** NCP

Seven Park Place by William Drabble

LONDON SW1   **PLAN 4 J6**

Modern French NOTABLE WINE LIST

Profoundly flavoured French-inspired dishes in a Mayfair hotel

☎ 020 7316 1600
St James's Hotel and Club, 7-8 Park Place SW1A 1LS
e-mail: info@stjameshotelandclub.com
dir: Nearest station: Green Park. Off St James's St

St James's is the kind of area where it does to be proper, where expectations are high, money does not seem to be in short supply, and a little exclusivity goes a long way. The St James's Hotel and Club fits right in, delivering a private members club, 60 well turned out bedrooms, and, in the form of Seven Park Place by William Drabble, a restaurant that is a star in its own right. The eponymous chef gets his name above the door, and rightly so, for he is a prodigious talent. The allocated space is rather swish, designed by the award winning Anna-Maria Jagdfeld: there are leafy motifs snaking across the walls, colours are rich browns, black and gold, artworks are individual pieces that certainly catch the eye, and the tables are correctly dressed and precisely laid. Drabble's cooking is divertingly contemporary but never seemingly overworked, everything looks fabulous on the plate, ingredients are of the highest order, and everything comes

together in perfect harmony. Thus a first course baked fillet of red mullet with garlic, parsley and mullet liver sauce has punchy flavours deftly handled, or go for seared foie gras with caramelised pear and ginger syrup. Next up, Barbon Fell venison with black pepper, beetroot and celeriac is another intelligent combination of textures and flavours, with a fish alternative partnering griddled fillets of John Dory with apples, mussels, celeriac and chives. Assiette of pork is a stunning combo of black pudding (rich yet delicate), tender head, stick trotters and crisp ears, served up with broad beans and truffles. The craft and control continues into dessert stage with the likes of lemon Charlotte, perfectly moist and packed with flavour, with accompanying poached rhubarb and passionfruit mousse, or dark chocolate mousse cake with raspberries. As you might expect at this level, the wine list does justice to the terrific food.

Chef William Drabble **Times** 12-2/7-10 Closed Sun-Mon **Prices** Fixed L 2 course fr £24.50, Fixed D 3 course fr £58, Service added but optional 12.5% **Wines** 8 by glass **Notes** Fixed 6 course Menu Gourmand £69, Vegetarian available, Civ Wed 40 **Seats** 34, Pr/dining room 40 **Parking** On street and NCP

LONDON SW1 *continued*

Salloos Restaurant
PLAN 4 G5

🏵 Pakistani

Pakistani cooking in Knightsbridge mews

☎ 020 7235 4444
62-64 Kinnerton St SW1X 8ER
dir: Nearest station: Knightsbridge. Kinnerton St is opposite Berkeley Hotel on Wilton Place

There's no trekking out to the suburbs to find Salloos: discreet and upmarket, this long-running family-run Pakistani restaurant has been doing its thing in a posh Knightsbridge mews house by the Berkeley Hotel since 1976. It has moved with the times in its intimate first-floor dining room, where delicate latticework, flame-red banquettes and lively art spice up the setting, and correctly courteous, old-school service completes a polished package. The Mughlai cuisine at Salloos springs no nouveau-fusion surprises on diners, sticking to pukka kebabs and plates of marinated meats sizzled in the tandoor. Order a day ahead for house specialities such as haleem akbari (shredded lamb cooked for a whole day with wheat germ, lentils and spices), or go for gurda masala (kidneys with hot spices), or veteran Punjabi favourites done right, such as palak gosht - lamb with spinach, fenugreek and ginger.

Chef Abdul Aziz **Owner** Mr & Mrs M Salahuddin
Times 12-3/7-11.45 Closed Xmas, Sun **Prices** Starter £7-£12.25, Main £15-£20, Dessert £6.50, Service added but optional 12.5% **Wines** 40 bottles over £20, 3 bottles under £20, 2 by glass **Notes** Vegetarian available **Seats** 65 **Parking** Meters, car park Kinnerton St

Santini Restaurant
PLAN 4 H4

🏵 Italian

Faithful Italian cooking in ritzy surroundings

☎ 020 7730 4094
29 Ebury St SW1W 0NZ
e-mail: santini@santinirestaurant.com
dir: Nearest station: Victoria. Take Lower Belgrave St off Buckingham Palace Rd. Restaurant on 1st corner on left

This long-running Belgravia restaurant continues to produce carefully crafted Italian food in a sophisticated, upmarket décor of subtle pastel and soft grey shades, marble floor, and comfortable seating. The straightforward, honest cooking is based on quality ingredients and flavours ring true. Carpaccio and spaghetti carbonara may come as no surprise, but there's also crab salad with pomegranate, mint and parsley. Main courses take in classics like breadcrumbed veal chop, calves' liver with crisp pancetta, and plainly grilled Dover sole, with things ending memorably with the indulgence of chocolate and vanilla cheesecake.

Chef Christian Gardin **Owner** Mr G Santin
Times 12-3/6-11 Closed Xmas, 1 Jan, Etr Sun-Mon, L Sat-Sun **Prices** Food prices not confirmed for 2013. Please telephone for details **Wines** all bottles over £20, 7 by glass **Notes** Vegetarian available, Dress restrictions, Smart casual **Seats** 65, Pr/dining room 30
Children Portions **Parking** Meters (no charge after 6.30pm)

Seven Park Place by William Drabble
PLAN 4 J6

🏵🏵🏵 – *see page 291*

Sofitel London St James
PLAN 4 K6

🏵 French, British

A touch of French style on Pall Mall

☎ 020 7968 2900
6 Waterloo Place SW1Y 4AN
e-mail: thebalcon.london@sofitel.com
dir: Nearest station: Piccadilly Circus. From Piccadilly right on to Haymarket, right on to Pall Mall, right on to Regent St & Waterloo Place

Following a swanky refit in the grand Parisian style, The Balcon restaurant sports its own charcuterie and champagne bars in its opulent ground-floor space, with double-height ceiling, grand columns and a show-stopping duo of matching spiral staircases leading up to the champagne balcony. The all-embracing menu fits the bill, full of Gallic swagger and a British flavour, too; from the 'rotisserie', perhaps rump of Devon rose lamb with juniper-infused jus and seaweed and garlic greens, or from the 'pan or grill' section, Cornish brill (on the bone) with butternut squash purée, brown shrimps and lilliput capers. There are salads such as sautéed chicken livers with walnuts, garlic croûtons and raspberry vinegar or charcuterie including game salami. Finish with red plum tarte Tatin with Poire William and clotted cream sorbet.

Chef Vincent Menager **Owner** Accor UK
Times 12-3/5.30-11 **Prices** Fixed L 2 course £15, Fixed D 3 course £20, Starter £7.50-£11.25, Main £19-£52, Dessert £6-£8, Service added but optional 12.5%
Wines 12 by glass **Notes** Vegetarian available **Seats** 100, Pr/dining room 16 **Children** Portions, Menu **Parking** NCP at Piccadilly

The Stafford London by Kempinski
PLAN 4 J6

🏵 Traditional British ⚑

Luxurious hotel dining in exclusive location

☎ 020 7493 0111
16-18 St James's Place SW1A 1NJ
e-mail: info@thelyttleton.com
web: www.thelyttleton.com
dir: Nearest station: Green Park

Tucked away in a discreet street behind Green Park, this genteel, newly refurbished hotel has the feel of a traditional country-house hotel in the heart of swanky St James's. Don't miss the famous American Bar, renowned for mixing a mean martini, then head for the now light and airy Lyttelton Restaurant, recently spruced up in ivory and grey, with contrasting floral fabrics, commissioned artwork and central chandelier. The dining experience remains classic British, the straightforward choice on the carte taking in rabbit loin and hash with chorizo and grain mustard, or grilled turbot with razor clams, lentils and parsley, with burnt Cambridge cream among the desserts.

Chef Brendan Fyldes **Owner** Dr A El Sharkawy
Times 12.30-2.30/6-10.30 **Prices** Fixed L 2 course fr £18.50, Starter £8.50-£28, Main £18.50-£38, Dessert £9.50-£12.50, Service added but optional 12.5%
Wines 340 bottles over £20, 6 by glass **Notes** Sunday L, Vegetarian available, Civ Wed 44 **Seats** 52, Pr/dining room 44 **Parking** NCP on Arlington Street

Thirty Six by Nigel Mendham at Dukes London
PLAN 4 J6

🏵🏵🏵 – *see opposite*

Thirty Six by Nigel Mendham at Dukes London

LONDON SW1   PLAN 4 J6

Modern British **NEW**

Refined contemporary cooking in luxe Mayfair hotel

☎ 020 7491 4840
35 36 St James's Place SW1A 1NY
e-mail: thirtysix@dukeshotel.com
dir: Nearest station: Green Park. From Pall Mall into St James's St. 2nd left into St James's Place. Hotel in courtyard on left

Dukes is a hotel with a decidedly luxe finish. A Mayfair institution, it wears its boutique label with pride, and provides the sort of glamorous, cosseting luxury you might hope for in this part of town. There's a fabulous bar (martinis a speciality), champagne lounge and a fine-dining restaurant named after its chef, Nigel Mendham; the 36 bit relates in part to its address and associations with the solar square of ancient Western tradition, and it's a favoured number in Chinese astrology too. All that good luck has resulted in a smart, dynamic dining room with eclectic artworks and high comfort levels. Mendham is not a chef who buys into every gadget that comes into fashion, preferring to craft his food in more traditional ways, but it is nevertheless contemporary and refined stuff. A first course fillet of mackerel, for example, is teamed with smoked eel, a silky smooth watercress purée and quail's eggs rolled in a light crispy crumb. Next up, braised beef is full of flavour, served with 'sticky cheek' cooked to unctuous perfection, and 'flavours of Burgundy' (crispy bacon, morels both sautéed and purée, and wild mushrooms), plus excellent mash and a glossy jus. To finish, 'dark chocolate' includes a fondant and accompanying pear pannacotta and tea gelée.

Chef Nigel Mendham **Times** 12-2.30/6-9.30 Closed L Mon, D Sun **Prices** Fixed L 2 course £21, Fixed D 3 course £60, Tasting menu £75, Service added but optional 12.5% **Wines** 60 bottles over £20, 13 by glass **Notes** Tasting menu 6 course, Sunday L, Vegetarian available, Dress restrictions, Smart casual, Civ Wed 80 **Seats** 36 **Children** Portions, Menu **Parking** Holiday Inn, Britannia car park

Zafferano

LONDON SW1   PLAN 4 F4

Modern Italian 🍷NOTABLE WINE LIST

Suave contemporary Italian restaurant

☎ 020 7235 5800
15 Lowndes St SW1X 9EY
e-mail: zafferano@londonfinedininggroup.com
web: www.zafferanorestaurant.com
dir: Nearest station: Knightsbridge. Located off Sloane St, behind Carlton Tower Hotel

Since Giorgio Locatelli opened Zafferano in 1995 it has stayed in the premier league of the country's upscale Italians. The man himself moved on long ago, but his dedication to superb ingredients as the starting point of everything that leaves the kitchen is still the bedrock of Zafferano's culinary credo. In the well-heeled environs of Knightsbridge you have to look the part, so the exposed brickwork, stripy fabrics and exuberant explosions of fresh flowers certainly speak of a high-toned, discreetly elegant sort of place. A class act, then, bolstered by staff who are real pros, smooth, charming and devoid of starchiness. On the menu, there is much that is familiar from the classic Italian lexicon, spiked judiciously with new-wave ideas to keep it all fresh and interesting, while the unimpeachable class of the raw materials raises the bar to a new level of lightness and definition. The Italian way of dining is worthy of emulation, so after a starter - say, Tuscan ham with celeriac and mustard fruits - don't dodge the pasta course, or you might pass on a seasonal star turn such as pheasant ravioli with rosemary. Seafood is a strong suit at main course stage - sea bass in a herb crust with vernaccia and green olives, perhaps; otherwise, meaty delights could include roasted venison loin with polenta and red wine sauce. Desserts such as a simple vanilla pannacotta with seasonal berries or cherry and almond tart with mascarpone are benchmarks by which others may be measured. A joyous wine list lines up quality bottles from top Italian producers next to little known gems.

Chef Andrew Needham, Michele Nargi **Owner** A-Z Restaurants-London Fine Dining Group **Times** 12-3/7-11 Closed 3 days Xmas **Prices** Food prices not confirmed for 2013. Please telephone for details **Wines** 500 bottles over £20, 2 bottles under £20, 8 by glass **Notes** Vegetarian available, Dress restrictions, Smart casual **Seats** 85, Pr/dining room 20 **Children** Portions **Parking** NCP behind restaurant

LONDON SW1 *continued*

Tinello
PLAN 4 G2

◉◉ Italian

Classy Italian cooking in elegant restaurant

☎ 020 7730 6327 & 3663
87 Pimlico Rd SW1W 8PH
e-mail: max@tinello.co.uk
dir: Nearest station: Sloane Square. From Sloane Square
tube station, down Holbein Place. Left at T-junct

Tinello is a stylish place with its trendy dining chairs and
brown banquettes at smartly set tables under dangling
copper lampshades. It makes a classy backdrop to
straightforward modern Italian cooking built around
prime ingredients. Antipasti (perhaps goats' cheese,
beetroot and pumpkin salad) or 'small eats' like deep-
fried squid are possibilities before skilfully made pasta:
spaghetti vongole, or pappardelle with hare ragù, say.
Don't expect gimmicks or fuss in main courses: steamed
lemon sole, beautifully timed, is accompanied by nothing
more than aubergine and basil sauce, a dish singing with
flavours, and pan-fried veal cutlet by vibrantly flavoured
fennel and lemon salad. Tiramisù seems to be a fixture
among desserts, or there may be light frangipane pear
tart with yoghurt ice cream.

Chef Federico Sali **Owner** Giorgio Locatelli
Times 12-2.30/6.15-10.30 Closed BH Mon, Sun
Prices Starter £1.95-£15.50, Main £11.50-£26, Dessert
£4.75-£8, Service optional, Groups min 8 service 12.5%
Wines 203 bottles over £20, 22 bottles under £20, 20 by
glass **Notes** Vegetarian available, Dress restrictions, Smart
casual **Seats** 75, Pr/dining room 25 **Children** Portions
Parking On street, single yellow from 6.30pm

Wheeler's
PLAN 4 J6

◉◉ Seafood

Seafood stalwart in St James's

☎ 020 7408 1440
72-73 St James's St SW1A 1PH
e-mail: info@wheelersrestaurant.org
dir: Nearest station: Green Park

If you're after a bit of spruced-up, old-school style and
some classic seafood dishes, this long-running restaurant
(opened in 1856) will sort you out. The fact it is co-owned
by Sir Rocco Forte and Marco Pierre White should give a
clue that there's a good deal of swagger and charm about
the place, too. This is traditional dining for the modern
age. Rich red walls are crammed with prints and
photographs, some of which are of a risqué nature (we're
talking scantily clad ladies), tables are dressed up in
white linen, and there's an art-deco sheen to the décor.
On the menu is classic seafood done right, simply turned
out, starting perhaps with a bisque of fresh crab Newburg,
or calamari fritti alla Romana and tartare sauce, followed
by wing of skate with winkles, jus à la Parisienne, or
tranche of cod à la Viennoise and sabayon of champagne.
British stouts, ales and ciders are the business, too.

Times 12-3/5.30-11 Closed Sun, L Sat

Zafferano
PLAN 4 F4

◉◉◉ – see page 293

LONDON SW3

Bibendum Restaurant
PLAN 4 E3

◉◉ British, French V 🍷 NOTABLE WINE LIST

Modern classics at a Chelsea institution

☎ 020 7581 5817
Michelin House, 81 Fulham Rd SW3 6RD
e-mail: reservations@bibendum.co.uk
web: www.bibendum.co.uk
dir: Nearest station: South Kensington. Left out of South
Kensington underground station on to Pelham St & walk
as far as lights

Climb the stairs to the first-floor restaurant and take one
of the comfortable seats at well-spaced tables amid the
crisp, sharp décor, with its Michelin Man theme, not least
his stained-glass depiction. Good-quality, honest modern
British and European cooking is what Bibendum excels
at, served with style by efficient staff. Seasonality plays
its part, fresh and tasty gazpacho appearing in summer,
a main course of roast quails in a foie gras croûte with
mushrooms and Madeira sauce in winter. The odd
interloper adds interest - say, tuna tataki with an Asian
herb salad and soy, lime and ginger dressing - among
popular fixtures such as deep-fried haddock and chips
with tartare sauce, and calves' liver and bacon. Breads
are excellent and puddings can be highlights: perhaps
vibrantly flavoured blueberry and elderflower jelly with
cherry compôte and crème Chantilly.

Chef Matthew Harris **Owner** Sir Terence Conran, Simon
Hopkinson, Michael Hamlyn **Times** 12-2.30/7-11
Closed 25-26 Dec, 1 Jan, D 24 Dec **Prices** Fixed L 2
course £26.50, Starter £10.75-£20, Main £18.50-£29.75,
Dessert £7.50-£11, Service added but optional 12.5%
Wines 530 bottles over £20, 2 bottles under £20, 14 by
glass **Notes** Sun D 3 courses £30, Sunday L, Vegetarian
menu **Seats** 80 **Children** Portions **Parking** On street

The Capital

*Rosettes not confirmed at time of going to press –
see opposite*

Cassis Bistro
PLAN 4 E4

◉◉ French 🍷 NOTABLE WINE LIST

**Modern French bistro with a good dose of
contemporary style**

☎ 020 7581 1101
232-236 Brompton Rd SW3 2BB
e-mail: reception@cassisbistro.co.uk
dir: Nearest station: Knightsbridge & South Kensington.
Opposite V&A

To call Cassis a 'bistro' is rather like saying an Aston
Martin is a shopping runabout: this is a solidly upmarket
rendition of the genre aimed at the denizens of
Knightsbridge and Kensington. The cosmopolitan venue
brings a touch of southern French flair to the Brompton
Road with its sunny-day roll-back doors and pavement
tables, and a glossy interior done out with striking in-
vogue artworks, moody lighting and a zinc-topped bar.
Chef David Escobar comes hot-foot from Lameloise in
Burgundy (one of France's top-flight restaurants outside
of Paris) and his colours are nailed to the mast with the
words cuisine de Provence atop the menu. Get in the
mood with a couple of petites bouchées - grazing nibbles
such as Mediterranean charcuterie or pissaladière -
before starters of sea bream carpaccio with marinated
courgette and Menton lemon. If you're longing for a taste
of the Med, bouillabaisse is a house signature that is
hard to ignore; alternatively, mains could be rabbit
fricassée à la provençale with rosemary potatoes, and to
finish, a trademark super-sized Grand Marnier and
orange soufflé.

Chef David Escobar **Owner** Marlon Abela **Times** 12-11
Closed 25 Dec **Prices** Fixed L 2 course £17, Starter £4-
£19, Main £15-£34, Dessert £6-£14, Service added but
optional 12.5% **Wines** over 650 bottles over £20, 1 bottle
under £20, 12 by glass **Notes** Vegetarian available, Air
con **Seats** 90 **Children** Portions **Parking** On street

Le Colombier
PLAN 4 D2

◉ French

Unfussy brasserie cooking just off the Fulham Road

☎ 020 7351 1155
145 Dovehouse St SW3 6LB
e-mail: lecolombier1998@aol.com
dir: Nearest station: South Kensington. Dovehouse St is
just off the Fulham Rd S of South Kensington
underground station

If you're looking for a hit of pure France without the need
to cross la Manche, head down to Chelsea, just off the
Fulham Road, where Le Colombier will satisfy your
cravings. The front conservatory is a lovely spot when the
weather is fine, but the décor inside is perfectly sunny all
year round; relaxing blue and cream tones, wooden
floorboards, and white linen-clad tables. The formal

service zips along nicely, making the place good for a working lunch. Expect classic French brasserie-style dishes; duck liver terrine, perhaps, served with fig jam and brioche, followed by grilled monkfish with wild rice and tomato and vermouth cream sauce. Desserts can be as classic as tarte Tatin and the all-French wine list has something for all pockets and preferences.

Chef Philippe Tamet **Owner** Didier Garnier
Times 12-3/6.30-10.30 **Prices** Fixed L 2 course fr £19.50, Starter £6.90-£14.50, Main £17.80-£35, Dessert £6.90-£7.90, Service added but optional 12.5%
Wines 200 bottles over £20, 12 bottles under £20, 10 by glass **Notes** Sunday L, Vegetarian available, Dress restrictions, Smart casual **Seats** 70, Pr/dining room 28 **Parking** Metered parking

Eight Over Eight
PLAN 4 D1

◉ Pan-Asian

Pan-Asian cooking in a cool, buzzy Chelsea favourite

☎ 020 7349 9934
392 King's Rd SW3 5UZ
e-mail: eightovereight@rickerrestaurants.com
dir: Nearest station: Sloane Sq, South Kensington

The ethnicity of the cuisine here is easy enough to work out, as the trend-central King's Road branch of Will Ricker's oriental fusion empire is named after the Chinese lucky number eight. The space is split between bar and restaurant and kitted out with an effortlessly cool and minimally chic décor. Well-conceived pan-Asian grazing is what the kitchen does here, and happily, the food is no mere afterthought to the socialising. Dim sum are a reliably good way to get going (perhaps nori-wrapped chicken dumplings, or prawn and black cod gyoza), before exploring the other categories of the menu. Sushi and sashimi take in luxury Wagyu beef sashimi or spicy tuna ura maki; elsewhere are a barbecued rack of ribs with black pepper sauce or a spicy prawn and pumpkin curry. Desserts draw their inspiration from closer to home - perhaps chocolate fondant with green tea ice cream. Switched-on, upbeat service, and an eye-catching cocktail list complete the picture.

Chef Alex Ziverts **Owner** Will Ricker **Times** 12-3/6-11 Closed 24-29 Dec, Etr **Prices** Starter £3.75-£14.50, Main £9.75-£36, Dessert £4.75-£6.50, Service added but optional 12.5% **Wines** 84 bottles over £20, 2 bottles under £20, 15 by glass **Notes** Sunday L, Vegetarian available **Seats** 95, Pr/dining room 18 **Children** Menu

Manicomio
PLAN 4 F3

◉ Italian

Bustling modern Italian just off Sloane Square

☎ 020 7730 3366
85 Duke of York Square, Chelsea SW3 4LY
e-mail: info@manicomio.co.uk
dir: Nearest station: Sloane Square. Duke of York Sq 100mtrs along King's Rd from Sloane Sq

Built as the military asylum of the Duke of York barracks, Manicomio presents a cool, calming image, with its planked floor, wall banquettes and vivid artwork. Contemporary Italian cooking is the draw, with many ingredients imported from the Motherland: perhaps speck d'Aosta in a starter with mozzarella and baby artichokes, and lentils from Umbria to accompany roast hake fillet, parsley pesto and spinach. The menu is evenly divided between fish and meat, the latter extending to chargrilled quail skewered with chicken livers on polenta with vin cotto sauce, followed by a winter main course of grilled sirloin with bone marrow, braised ox cheek and roast squash. Finish with tiramisù or maybe treacle and lemon tart.

Chef Tom Salt **Owner** Ninai & Andrew Zarach **Times** noon-3/6.30-10.30 Closed Xmas & New Year **Prices** Starter £8.75-£10, Main £13.50-£26.50, Dessert £4.50-£9.50, Service added but optional 12.5% **Wines** 64 bottles over £20, 2 bottles under £20, 18 by glass **Notes** Sunday L, Vegetarian available **Seats** 70, Pr/dining room 30 **Children** Portions **Parking** On street

The Capital

Rosettes not confirmed at time of going to press

LONDON SW3
PLAN 4 E3

British, French ⬩ NOTABLE WINE LIST

Chic landmark hotel, over 40 years young

☎ 020 7589 5171
22-24 Basil St, Knightsbridge SW3 1AT
e-mail: caprest@capitalhotel.co.uk
dir: Nearest station: Knightsbridge. Off Sloane St, beside Harrods

Run by the Levin family since it opened its doors in 1971, The Capital is one of those rare old-school establishments that goes about its business with quietly refined discretion, and is worthy of the five-star designation in every sense. The intimate townhouse occupies a top-drawer Knightsbridge address in a discreet little street just round the corner from Harrods, there's a liveried doorman to admit you to the opulent yet unshowy interior, and as we go to press a relaunch of the restaurant is planned, and a new chef is due to take command. Previously, the menu has offered a perfectly-timed, unctuously-textured starter of ravioli of duck foie gras with leeks and black truffle, followed by pink-roasted venison with poached pear, pan-fried potato terrine and roasted carrots, or pan-fried turbot with girolles, lardons, button onions and Jerusalem artichoke, and to finish, frozen Valrhona Tainori chocolate parfait with praline biscuits and caramelised walnuts.

Owner Mr D Levin **Times** 12-2.30/6.45-10.30 **Prices** Food prices not confirmed for 2013. Please telephone for details **Wines** All bottles over £20, 37 by glass **Notes** Sunday L, Vegetarian available, Dress restrictions, Smart casual **Seats** 35, Pr/dining room 24 **Parking** 10

LONDON SW3 *continued*

Nozomi

PLAN 4 E4

◉◉ Japanese

Contemporary Japanese cooking in slick setting

☎ 020 7838 1500 & 7838 0181
14-15 Beauchamp Place, Knightsbridge SW3 1NQ
e-mail: info@nozomi.co.uk
web: www.nozomi.co.uk
dir: Nearest station: Knightsbridge

Make your way through the fashionable cocktail bar at the front and into the restaurant behind, a dimly lit space with a décor of silver and black and where the music, more foreground than background, is intended to 'relax inhibitions'. Authentic contemporary Japanese cuisine is the deal, with the long menu covering a lot of ground. Start with a selection of sushi - anything from tuna, crab and sea bass - or choose from an extensive list of maki rolls and temaki, plus small dishes such as tofu steak with aubergine and miso. Not surprisingly in this postcode, luxuries are littered about, among them whole tempura lobster with ponzu and daikon, pan-fried foie gras marinated in whisky, and chargrilled Wagyu beef steaks, although the same attention to detail is evident throughout from black cod with pickled daikon to grilled lamb cutlets with mushrooms and yuzu-infused yoghurt, and pan-fried pork tenderloin and crispy ribs with grilled pear and soy.

Times 12-3/6.30-11.30 Closed L Mon

Racine

PLAN 4 E4

◉ Traditional French

An authentic French brasserie opposite Brompton Oratory

☎ 020 7584 4477
239 Brompton Rd SW3 2EP
e-mail: bonjour@racine.com
dir: Nearest station: Knightsbridge, South Kensington

When you long for the French bourgeois cooking of the neighbourhood bistros and brasseries of Paris and the elbow-to-elbow bouchons of Lyon, Racine comes up with the goods: this is timeless dining built on the solid foundations of diligently-sourced, seasonal produce. The look is spot-on too, with wooden floors, chocolate leather banquettes, wall mirrors, soft-focus lighting and an easygoing vibe, all kept ticking over by correctly courteous staff. Slacken your belt and be prepared for big-hearted, robust, gutsy cooking. Seared foie gras with caramelised apple and Calvados makes a classic opener, or you might go for a visceral plate of calf's brains with black butter and capers. Mains plough a similarly Gallic furrow - grilled rabbit with mustard sauce and smoked bacon, or veal kidneys with creamed Fourme d'Ambert cheese, Espelette pepper jus and pommes purée.

Chef Henry Harris **Owner** Henry Harris
Times 12-3/6-10.30 Closed 25 Dec **Prices** Fixed L 2 course £15.50, Fixed D 3 course £17.75, Starter £6.75-£14.75, Main £16.50-£28.50, Service added but optional 14.5% **Wines** 136 bottles over £20, 20 by glass
Notes Fixed D up to 7.30pm only, Vegetarian available
Seats 60 **Children** Portions

Rasoi Restaurant

PLAN 4 F3

◉◉◉ — *see below*

Restaurant Gordon Ramsay

PLAN 4 F1

◉◉◉◉ — *see opposite*

Rasoi Restaurant

LONDON SW3   PLAN 4 F3

Modern Indian V ⚡NOTABLE WINE LIST

The frontline of modern Indian cooking

☎ 020 7225 1881
10 Lincoln St SW3 2TS
e-mail: info@rasoirestaurant.co.uk
dir: Nearest station: Sloane Square. Near Peter Jones and Duke of York Sq

Down a smart little street off the King's Road, Vineet Bhatia's restaurant is at the cutting edge of modern Indian cooking. As if to further differentiate it from the crowd, there's a doorbell to be rung to gain access, and once inside it's all very chic - silk wall hangings, artefacts and antiques, with the heady aroma of eastern spices in the air. There are menus prestige and gourmand if you wish to submit to the chef's will, or go your own way off the fixed-price carte. Either way, you can expect thrillingly evocative, precise and refined cooking. A pre-starter gets the ball rolling with a show of the kitchen's mettle - tomato, lentil and chilli soup, perhaps, served in a shot glass - before a first-course of succulent grilled lamb chop with kheema-mattar timbale and a samosa filled with smoked cashews and goats' cheese. Dishes are beautifully presented, spicing is well judged and ingredients are high quality throughout. Main-course 'pot-enclosed' chicken - beautifully tender - is served with chilli rice and kachumber raita, whilst the vegetarian dishes are certainly no make-weights: spinach galouti with Punjabi chick peas and aubergine achari, for example. Desserts show serious intent, too, with evocative names such as Zaffran Bar and Chocomosa.

Chef Vineet Bhatia **Owner** Vineet & Rashima Bhatia
Times 12-2.30/6-10.30 Closed Xmas, New Year, BHs, L Sat **Prices** Fixed L 2 course £22-£27, Fixed D 3 course £59-£63, Tasting menu £167, Starter £18-£20, Main £24-£30, Dessert £10-£15, Service added but optional 12.5% **Wines** 250 bottles over £20, 4 bottles under £20, 10 by glass **Notes** Tasting menu 7 course incl wine, Sunday L, Vegetarian menu, Dress restrictions, Smart casual **Seats** 35, Pr/dining room 14 **Parking** On street

Save on Hotels. Book at **theAA.com/hotel**

LONDON 297 ENGLAND

Restaurant Gordon Ramsay

LONDON SW3   PLAN 4 F1

French, European V NOTABLE WINE LIST

The mothership of the Gordon Ramsay ompirc

☎ 020 7352 4441
68 Royal Hospital Rd SW3 4HP
e-mail: reservations@gordonramsay.com
dir: Nearest station: Sloane Square. At junct of Royal Hospital Road & Swan Walk

Mr Ramsay is not a man to let the grass grow, with the most recent openings including Bread Street Kitchen in the City (see entry), and a new venture in Montreal, and of course, the telly shows continue unabated. In an era of austerity-led belt tightening, globally-branded superchefs may seem a bit passé, but Ramsay Holdings still runs a dozen operations in London alone, although the man whose name is above the door of the Royal Hospital Road flagship leaves the work to protégée Clare Smyth and her team these days. And that task is to interpret the Ramsay take on classic French haute cuisine. Since it opened in 1998, this address has become one of London's gastronomic institutions. The place has the presence of an exclusive establishment with its 15 or so tables in a setting of quiet refinement - and the prices have always been at the vanguard of UK restaurant pricing

structure, to put it nicely. But this is not every-day eating, what you are paying for is clearly on display, from the quality of the cooking to the peerless service lead by maître d' Jean-Claude Breton. The food is not about showboating or pushing the envelope with outlandish propositions of taste and texture: what is on offer is top-level technical precision that delivers refinement and balance, and it is all veneered with a lightness and assurance of touch. By all means go for broke with the full-dress menu prestige, but the set lunch is a good entry level route, and a relatively affordable deal when you're eating at this level. In autumn, that means opening with pan-fried Isle of Skye scallops with peas, broad beans, quail's egg, crispy pancetta and baby gem lettuce. The sheer quality of the raw materials is again stunning in a main course that delivers the compelling flavour combinations of roasted fillet of turbot with coco beans, earthy girolles, fresh almonds, punchy Morteau sausage, fennel pollen, and a deeply intense chicken jus. The pace-setting standards continue through to a dessert of banoffee pie soufflé matched with banana and salted caramel crumble. The wine list offers mind-bending stuff from France and the world's top producers, with prices to match, but does not sideline those who want to drink on a more accessible level.

Chef Gordon Ramsay, Clare Smyth **Owner** Gordon Ramsay Holdings Ltd **Times** 12-2.30/6.30 11 Closcd 1 wk Xmas, Sat-Sun **Prices** Fixed L 3 course fr £45, Service added but optional 12.5% **Wines** 800+ bottles over £20, 18 by glass **Notes** ALC 3 course £95, Tasting menu 7 course, Vegetarian menu, Dress restrictions, Smart dress, no jeans, trainers or sportswear **Seats** 45 **Children** Portions **Parking**

Tom Aikens

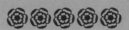

LONDON SW3   **PLAN 4 E3**

Modern European 🍷 NOTABLE WINE LIST 🐦

Culinary powerhouse with new chilled out look

☎ 020 7584 2003
43 Elystan St SW3 3NT
e-mail: info@tomaikens.co.uk
dir: Nearest station: South Kensington, Sloane Square. Off Fulham Rd (Brompton Rd end)

Talent will out, as the saying goes, and Tom Aikens, who has weathered a storm or two over his career, has relaunched his Chelsea restaurant and hit the ground not simply running, but rather gliding majestically like Paula Radcliffe in the home straight. The changes here are not simply cosmetic, they are emblematic of a shift in attitude towards a more unpretentious and relaxed approach to dining. This Chelsea address was never the epitome of old-school stuffiness, but now it is flying the flag for a contemporary kind of informality. With foodie quotes emblazoned on the walls, not a tablecloth in sight, and staff wearing the very best in smart-casual (jeans included), one might have assumed the cooking had been pared down, but as the five Rosettes above attest, that is most certainly not the case. The food here is creative, contemporary, refined, bold and stunningly beautiful to look at. The bread is pretty much perfect - four

superb rolls to choose from, served warm in a heated hessian bag and with three flavours of butter - and confirms the serious intent of the kitchen. The menu is a wee bit confusing at first glance, although the excellent staff are on hand to clarify when need be; there are options for two or three courses on the carte, six-, eight- or ten-course Taster Menus to choose from, plus an excellent value set lunch. Marinated hand-dived scallops demonstrates the acute sense of balance in Aikens' dishes, with the apple vinaigrette, lardo crudo and acidulated apple combining into a magnificent whole. Romney lamb melts like butter in the mouth, served with ewes' cheese, anchovy and confit garlic, while chorizo-baked cod comes with 24-hour squid and cod soup. Technical dexterity is displayed again at dessert stage, with Regent's Park honey (a superb piece of honeycomb), goats' curd, poppy seed glace and crisp fennel, or candied beetroot with yoghurt parfait, sweetened beets and port syrup. Everything from the stunning petits fours to the wine list, rather cleverly presented in old copies of wine encyclopedias (check out the amusing, and slightly risqué, cartoons), impresses for its attention to detail and downright joie de vivre.

Chef Tom Aikens **Owner** Tom Aikens Group Ltd **Times** 12-2.30/6.45-11 Closed 2 wks Xmas & New Year, Etr, BHs, Sun, L Sat **Prices** Fixed L 2 course fr £24, Service added but optional 12.5% **Wines** 250 bottles over £20, 10 by glass **Notes** Tasting menu L 6, D 8 course, ALC 2/3 course £40/£50, Vegetarian available **Seats** 54, Pr/dining room 10 **Children** Portions **Parking** Parking meters outside

Save on Hotels. Book at **theAA.com/hotel**

LONDON, CENTRAL (SW3 – SW4) 299 **ENGLAND**

LONDON SW3 *continued*

Sushinho
PLAN 4 D1

◉ Japanese, Brazilian

Japanese-Brazilian fusion in Chelsea

☎ 020 7349 7496

312-314 King's Rd, Chelsea SW3 5UH

e-mail: info@sushinho.com

dir: Nearest station: Sloane Sq. On N side of King's Rd, Between Old Church St & The Vale

The linguistically inclined might spot the conflation of Japanese and Brazilian sounds in the name of this trendy Chelsea venue - then wonder what the two cultures have to do with each other, gastronomically speaking. Well, Japanese immigration means that Rio and Sao Paolo are well supplied with fusion eateries serving classic Japanese food for purists, and hybrid South America-meets-Asia ideas for the more adventurous. Inside, the contemporary oriental look involves bare bricks, bamboo screens and shades of coffee and cream, and the cocktail list sums up the cross-cultural approach with a 'sakeirinha'. By all means stick with straight-up Japanese sushi and sashimi, as it is very good indeed, but it's not every day that you can go off-piste into the intriguing territory of Wagyu steak tartare with wasabi tobiko and fried plantain, or blackened butterfish with wasabi guacamole and daikon. Desserts conform to a more westernised aesthetic with the likes of citrus pannacotta with white sesame cake and grapefruit granita.

Chef Joni Viscardi **Owner** Oliver Girardet **Times** 12-3/6-10.30 Closed 25-26 Dec, 1 Jan, L Sun-Tue **Prices** Tasting menu fr £35, Starter £3.75-£16.50, Main £9.50-£25, Dessert £7-£9, Service added but optional 12.5% **Wines** 75 bottles over £20, 4 bottles under £20, 11 by glass **Notes** Tasting menu groups 8 or more, Vegetarian available **Seats** 110, Pr/dining room 12 **Parking** On street

Tom Aikens
PLAN 4 E3

◉◉◉◉◉ – *see opposite*

Tom's Kitchen
PLAN 4 E2

◉◉ British, French

First-class brasserie food from top-class chef

☎ 020 7349 0202

27 Cale St, South Kensington SW3 3QP

e-mail: info@tomskitchen.co.uk

dir: Nearest station: South Kensington, Sloane Square. Cale St (Parallel to Kings Rd), midway between Chelsea Green and St Luke's Church

Tom Aikens' informal all-day brasserie occupies a handsome Chelsea townhouse, just a few hundred yards from his eponymous five-Rosetted address. Covering three floors, it successfully combines a laid-back and lively atmosphere with a crowd-pleasing seasonal menu of rustic French brasserie dishes (with a goodly Britishness, too) that champion quality UK produce and are big on flavour. There's a laid-back bar on the first floor, private dining rooms upstairs, while downstairs is an urban-rustic brasserie, with chunky oak furniture, white-tiled walls and a buzzy elbow-to-elbow vibe boosted by the bustle of the chefs at work in an open-plan kitchen. Serving through from breakfast to dinner, you can kick-start the day with blueberry pancakes with maple syrup or a Rhug Estate sausage sandwich, and tuck into the likes of steamed mussels with dill, Pernod and fennel, duck confit and haricot bean cassoulet, fish pie, and lamb rump with green olives, lemon and basil polenta from the lunch/dinner menu. There's a second branch in Somerset House in the West End

Chef Tim Brindley, Tom Aikens **Owner** Tom Aikens **Times** 12-3/6-11 Closed 25-26 Dec, D 24 Dec **Prices** Starter £6-£18.50, Main £13.50-£31, Dessert £7, Service added but optional 12.5% **Wines** 55 bottles over £20, 3 bottles under £20, 16 by glass **Notes** Sunday L, Vegetarian available **Seats** 75, Pr/dining room 40 **Children** Portions **Parking** On street

Trinity Restaurant

LONDON SW4 PLAN 1 E2

British, French

Accomplished modern cooking in Clapham

☎ 020 7622 1199

4 The Polygon, Clapham SW4 0JG

e-mail: dine@trinityrestaurant.co.uk

dir: Nearest station: Clapham Common. 200 yds from underground left towards Common & follow road keeping Common on left. Restaurant far side of The Polygon (an island block of buildings) opposite the Sun pub

If only every neighbourhood had somewhere like Adam Byatt's Trinity, we would indeed be a nation of happy foodies. For now, we must content ourselves with envious glances in the direction of Clapham locals, who have this smart restaurant in the Polygon on the north side of the Common. Why head across town for the glitzy tables of the West End and City when pace-setting food is on the doorstep? Cane chairs line up at smartly dressed tables indoors, and when the sun does its job properly, windows open onto the pavement; for those who like to get up close and personal with the action, a chef's table can be booked. Helped by an innate feel for what works with what, Adam Byatt's extraordinary talent weaves interesting ingredients into inspired dishes, providing creative flavour combinations and delivering them in refined presentations. A starter delivers layers of moist chicken, firm artichoke and buttery foie gras in a superb terrine wrapped in prosciutto, and served with pickled apples and brioche, while buttered poached brill is brought together with crab tortellini and a delicate crab and ginger broth. Dessert is a subtly-textured rhubarb crumble soufflé with stem ginger ice cream, or could be a feisty variation on cheesecake, made with a rich and nutty vacherin cheese and teamed with quince and walnuts. What's more, you don't need to clench your teeth when the bill arrives, and the good-value approach extends to treated tap water provided free.

Chef Adam Byatt **Owner** Angus Jones & Adam Byatt **Times** 12.30-2.30/6.30-10.30 Closed 24-26 Dec, L Mon, D Sun **Prices** Food prices not confirmed for 2013. Please telephone for details **Wines** 244 bottles over £20, 6 bottles under £20, 14 by glass **Notes** Sunday L, Vegetarian available **Seats** 63, Pr/dining room 12 **Children** Portions **Parking** On street

Bistro Union
PLAN 1 E2

◉◉ Traditional British **NEW**

True-Brit food in neighbourhood bistro

☎ 020 7042 6400

40 Abbeville Rd, Clapham SW9 9NG

e-mail: eat@bistrounion.co.uk

dir: Nearest station: Clapham South. Left from Clapham South tube onto Clapham Common south side. Continue with park on left and take 4th right Narbonne Ave, Abbeville Rd directly ahead

Chef-proprietor Adam Byatt certainly seems comfortable in Clapham. His Trinity operation (see entry), which opened in 2006, has gone from strength to strength to be the top dog in the postcode, and it is now joined by this new, more informal neighbourhood venture. A simple, de-cluttered brasserie décor sits well with the local clientele in the trendy Abbeville enclave: there are stripped wood floors, chunky unclothed tables, and a central bar where you can perch on wooden stools with your cutlery and menu in individual drawers under the counter, perusing a bar menu of on-trend nibbles (pork scratchings, pickled quail's eggs, winkles and pickled shallots, to name but three) hand-written onto a roll of brown paper. The food is in the day-to-day hands of Karl Goward who comes from Fergus Henderson's St John Bread and Wine (see entry), so you can expect a no-nonsense approach with a nod to the 'nose-to-tail' eating style. What leaves the kitchen is creative, fun, and built with British-led ingredients - perhaps beer and onion soup with Welsh rarebit, or baked aubergine with cow's curd and mint to start, then more of the same butch, true-Brit ideas, along the lines of Cumberland toad in the hole with Guinness onions.

Chef Karl Goward, Adam Byatt **Owner** Adam Byatt **Times** 11-3/6-10 Closed D Sun **Prices** Starter £4-£12, Main £10-£16, Dessert £2-£5, Service added but optional 12.5% **Wines** 11 by glass **Notes** Sunday L, Vegetarian available **Children** Portions, Menu

Trinity Restaurant
PLAN 1 E2

◉◉◉ – *see page 299*

Tsunami
PLAN 1 F2

◉ Japanese ✪

Cool minimalism and Japanese fusion food

☎ 020 7978 1610

5-7 Voltaire Rd SW4 6DQ

e-mail: clapham@tsunamirestaurant.co.uk

dir: Nearest station: Clapham North. Off Clapham High Street

The Clapham branch of two Tsunami operations (the other is in Charlotte Street) is a big hit with those seeking a trendy locale and the mouth-filling flavours of Japanese fusion dining. The minimal club-like décor ticks all the right style boxes with its buzzy, brightly lit cocktail bar

serving warm and cold sakes, and an open-plan eating area done out with darkwood tables, sleek banquettes, huge mirrors, and funky modern art; the modish open-to-view kitchen gives everyone a good look at the chefs doing their stuff. It's a high-decibel, sociable place, so the menu obliges with dishes that are meant for sharing and grazing - classic sushi, tempura, sashimi as you'd expect, but the kitchen isn't scared to cross borders and send out roast duck and foie gras nigiri, or grilled scallops flambéed with whisky to get things going. Mains offer everything from hira unagi (grilled marinated eel with rice and pickles) to a rib-eye with exotic mushrooms and truffle sauce.

Chef Ken Sam **Owner** Ken Sam **Times** 12.30-3.30/5.30-11 Closed 24-26 Dec, 1 Jan, L Mon-Fri **Prices** Fixed L 2 course £15, Starter £3.50-£13.50, Main £7.90-£22.50, Dessert £3.95-£6.50, Service added but optional 12.5% **Wines** 28 bottles over £20, 4 bottles under £20, 11 by glass **Notes** Sunday L, Vegetarian available **Seats** 90 **Parking** On street

Cambio de Tercio
PLAN 4 C2

◉◉ Spanish

Contemporary Spanish cooking in fun, vibrant atmosphere

☎ 020 7244 8970

163 Old Brompton Rd SW5 0LJ

dir: Nearest station: Gloucester Road. Close to junction with Drayton Gardens

With sibling tapas bars Capote y Toros (see entry) almost next door and Tendido Cero opposite, this stretch of Old Brompton Road is indelibly Spanish. Now with a swanky new entrance bar (including a few extra tables and impressive new kitchen below), Cambio feels more expansive and less frenetic than previously, though it still comes decked out in its wonderful trademark throbbing colours with large flamboyant artworks. Floors are covered in cool black slate, closely set tables are laid with white linen, while black banquettes and chairs afford the comforts. The food is similarly colourful and well dressed and comes with a sparkling touch of innovation and flair; nibbles might include fried manchego 'lollipops', for example, while the carte flouts three-course convention for tapas-sized portions for sharing. Traditionalists might go for crispy Serrano ham croquettes, while signature tapas like eight-hour cooked semi-dry tomatoes with sweet Oloroso sherry and cured Cecina beef crank it up a little. There are more substantial plates, too, such as flame-grilled Presa Iberica teamed with smoked chorizo mash, figs and vinegar carame, with an 'all lemon dessert' consisting of an airy sponge, ice cream, custard and jelly.

Times 12-2.30/7-11.30 Closed 2 wks at Xmas, New Year

Capote y Toros
PLAN 4 C2

◉ Spanish **NEW**

Authentic tapas and fabulous range of sherries

☎ 020 7373 0567

157 Old Brompton Rd SW5 0LJ

e-mail: cambiodeterciogroup@btconnect.com

dir: Nearest station: South Kensington, Gloucester Road

Step into this pint-sized bodega on the Old Brompton Road and you're transported to a lively, sunny, neighbourhood bar in downtown Càdiz. It's another show-stopper from next-door-but-one big-brother outfit, Cambio de Tercio (see entry) and bills itself as a ham, tapas and sherry joint. Photos of matadors line one wall of the narrow, vibrant-coloured space, while Iberico hams hang from the ceiling above the tiny bar set amongst display racks of sherry and wine. There's a no booking policy, so catch a seat at the single row of modern pale-wood tables or perch on a high stool at the counter opposite and wait your turn over a glass of manzanilla. Sherry (a staggering 110 labels) is the thing, though all-Spanish wines roll out to 350 bins. Friendly, clued-up Spanish staff add to the fun, while the menu keeps things simple and accessible, offering first-class hams and charcuterie shipped in from southern Spain alongside traditional Andalucían tapas. Expect the likes of carpaccio of duck liver with Pedro Ximénez reduction; pork meatballs with Oloroso sherry sauce; Iberico pork with chorizo purée; and roasted codfish in a Sobrasada chorizo crust with courgette carpaccio. Olé!

Times 6-11.30 Closed Sun-Mon, L all week **Prices** Food prices not confirmed for 2013. Please telephone for details

New Lotus Garden
PLAN 4 B3

◉ Chinese **V**

Neighbourhood Chinese that really hits the spot

☎ 020 7244 8984

15 Kenway Rd SW5 0RP

e-mail: jiang.hubert@gmail.com

dir: Nearest station: Earl's Court

We could all do with a top-notch Chinese such as Hubert Jiang's welcoming little place in our neighbourhood. This is Chinese cooking as it should be done - precise, well-judged dishes of clean, clearly-defined flavours. You'll find it all on a quiet residential street close to Earl's Court, in a bijou room with maroon cloths on elbow-to-elbow tables, serving up a compendious repertoire of old favourites running from dim sum to Pekinese and Cantonese classics - soft-shelled crabs baked with garlic, salt and chilli, or crispy aromatic duck with wheaten pancakes to start, then sea bass steamed with ginger and spring onion, or twice-cooked belly pork with preserved vegetables. All the accompaniments like Fujian fried rice or Singapore noodles are top-class too.

Chef Hubert Jiang **Owner** Hubert Jiang **Times** 12-2.30/5-11.30 Closed 24-26 Dec, L Sat 2 wks **Prices** Fixed L 2 course £16.50-£27, Fixed D 3 course £16.50-£27, Starter £4-£15, Main £4-£12, Dessert £2-£4,

Service added but optional 10% **Wines** 6 bottles over £20, 15 bottles under £20, 2 by glass **Notes** Sunday L, Vegetarian menu **Seats** 40 **Children** Portions

LONDON SW6

Blue Elephant
PLAN 1 E3

@ Thai V

New home for old Thai favourite

☎ 020 7751 3111
The Boulevard, Imperial Wharf, Townmead Rd SW6 2UB
e-mail: london@blueelephant.com
dir: Nearest station: Imperial Wharf

There are Blue Elephants around the world, from Jakarta to Lyon, from Bahrain to Brussels, and now the London branch has a swanky new home in Imperial Wharf (not a million miles from its former home on Fulham Broadway). With a décor inspired by the Saran Rom palace in Bangkok, it looks pretty good in its new home, with wood-carvings, warm, sunny colours, some green foliage like the old days, and, in the Blue Bar, a model of the Royal Barge of Thailand. There's a fab terrace, too, overlooking the water. The menu has had a bit of a revamp with sections focusing on the Thai cooking of 'the past', 'today' and 'tomorrow'. From the old days comes khang khao phuak (minced prawn, chicken and sweet spices in a taro pastry case), or go for something new, such as main-course grilled wild catch tiger prawns, or red conger curry.

Chef Nooror Somany **Owner** Blue Elephant International Group **Times** 12-2.30/6-10.30 Closed 25-26 Dec, 1 Jan **Prices** Food prices not confirmed for 2013. Please telephone for details **Wines** 80 bottles over £20, 9 bottles under £20, 14 by glass **Notes** Sunday L, Vegetarian menu, Dress restrictions, Smart casual **Seats** 150, Pr/dining room 8 **Parking** Car park next to Imperial Wharf tube station

The Harwood Arms
PLAN 1 E3

@@ British

Supplier-led British cooking in smart gastro-pub

☎ 020 7386 1847
27 Walham Grove, Fulham SW6 1QR
e-mail: admin@harwoodarms.com
dir: Nearest station: Fulham Broadway. Located on the corner of Farm Lane & Walham Grove

On an unassuming backstreet in trendy Fulham, the stylish Harwood Arms is one of Britain's top gastro-pubs, all the more so as it remains true to its roots as a cracking community local - Tuesday night is quiz night, there's a raft of real ales on tap, and the overall vibe is relaxed and informal. With Brett Graham of The Ledbury (see entry) and The Pot Kiln's (see entry) Mike Robinson as owners, you've a right to have high expectations. And they are duly met. Inside you could almost forget you're in London with photos of outdoor country pursuits hung on grey and cream walls, and rustic wooden tables. On the menu, first class, carefully-sourced English produce is cooked with confidence; Berkshire rabbit faggots, for

example, with split peas, smoked bacon and pickled mushrooms is a robust way to start, before moving on to Gloucestershire Old Spot pork belly with root vegetable broth and ribs glazed in ginger beer, or wild sea bass with cauliflower, oat-crusted mussels and preserved lemon. And neither do desserts miss a beat: baked stem ginger custard with honeycomb ice cream is an unerringly satisfying finale.

Times 12-3/6.30-9.30 Closed 24-28 Dec, 1 Jan, L Mon

Marco
PLAN 1 E3

@@ Anglo-French

MPW brasserie-style dishes at Stamford Bridge

☎ 020 7915 2929
M&C Hotels At Chelsea FC, Stamford Bridge, Fulham Rd SW6 1HS
e-mail: info@marcorestaurant.org
dir: Nearest station: Fulham Broadway

Valet parking may seem a touch Hollywood for the UK, but it can come in quite handy in the streets around Chelsea's Stamford Bridge ground. Then again, if you inhabit the world of Roman Abramovich and Marco Pierre White, who have joined forces to set up this high-gloss operation, such services are likely par for the course. Although the Blues' supporters would no doubt appreciate the excellent range of ales on offer inside, this is a world a long, long way from the pies and hotdogs that fuel the footie fans: a chic décor brings together charcoal-grey walls, smoked mirrors, low-level lighting, and leather banquettes and velour seats at linen-swathed tables. On the culinary front, MPW's signature style of tried-and-tested French brasserie dishes is stamped all over the carte, and it is all driven by top-class ingredients, sharply-defined flavours and classy execution. Artichokes Barigoule à la Provençale sets out in fine Gallic style, then line-caught sea bass is served à la marinière with fresh clams; if you're in the market for meatier fare, there are steaks, grilled calves' liver with bacon, or roast rump of lamb à la Dijonnaise with gratin dauphinoise. The menu comes back across the Channel to end with English cheeses with quince jelly, or flag-waving puddings along the lines of Eton Mess or Cambridge burnt cream.

Chef Roger Pizey **Owner** Marco Pierre White & C.F.C **Times** 6-10.30 Closed 2 wks Jul-Aug, Sun-Mon, L all week **Prices** Starter £8.50-£16.50, Main £16.50-£36, Dessert £6.50-£7.50, Service added but optional 12.5% **Wines** 40 bottles over £20, 6 bottles under £20, 8 by glass **Notes** Vegetarian available **Seats** 70 **Children** Portions **Parking** 10

LONDON SW7

Baglioni Hotel
PLAN 4 C5

@ Modern Italian

Modern Italian cooking in swish hotel

☎ 020 7368 5700
60 Hyde Park Gate, Kensington Rd SW7 5BB
e-mail: brunello.london@baglionihotels.com
dir: Nearest station: Kensington High Street. Hotel entrance facing Hyde Park Gate & Kensington Palace

The Baglioni's Brunello restaurant is an open-plan bar-lounge and stylish dining room with plush seating, rich fabrics, chandeliers and charming and attentive staff, mostly Italian. Ingredients are diligently sought out, many from the motherland, to re-create the modern Italian cooking style, as in a richly flavoured starter of caponata and burrata cheese drizzled with olive oil, and smoked swordfish with exotic fruit salad in a grape reduction. Pasta dishes are given their due - perhaps pappardelle with veal ragù and broad beans - and main courses have included pink and succulent veal chop with creamy mash and sautéed spinach, and chargrilled prawns and squid with baby seasonal vegetables. There's a great range of home-made breads, and among dolci might be vanilla cheesecake with cherry sorbet.

Times 12-3/5.30-11

Bombay Brasserie
PLAN 4 C3

@@ Indian **NEW**

A taste of Mumbai near Gloucester Road

☎ 020 7370 4040
Courtfield Close, Courtfield Rd SW7 4UH
e-mail: info@bbrestaurant.co.uk
dir: Nearest station: Gloucester Road. Opposite tube station

For three decades the Bombay Brasserie has been offering a slice of Bombay (Mumbai) glamour to fans of authentic Indian cuisine. It's a restaurant on a grand scale, divided between two rooms, the first with a more traditional Raj-era look and feel (gold chandeliers, gilt-frame mirrors, plush patterned carpet, deep cushioned banquettes), and the second a vast conservatory with a much more contemporary and minimalist design (white and black tiled floor, black modern chairs). Mumbai is a melting pot of different cultures and hence its cuisine - and the menu here - takes its influences from India's many diverse regions and beyond. Much of the repertoire will sound familiar - seekh kebab, chicken tikka, lamb rogan josh, dal makhani - but this is no ordinary curry house: ingredients are top quality, spicing is precise, everything is cooked fresh to order using minimal fat, and presentation is refined. Malabari soft-shelled crab - fried in a light, crispy, subtly spiced batter - is a good way to start. Keep with the fishy theme at main course with the Goan halibut curry (chunks of fresh halibut simmered in a tangy coconut and red chilli sauce), and make sure you order one of the freshly-made, thin and light naan breads. The desserts are all made in-house too.

continued

LONDON SW7 *continued*

Chef Prahlad Hegde **Owner** Taj International Hotels
Times 12-3/6.30-11.30 Closed 25-26 Dec **Prices** Fixed L
3 course £22, Fixed D 3 course fr £43, Tasting menu £70,
Starter £6.50-£11.50, Main £16-£28.50, Dessert £6.50,
Service added but optional 10% **Wines** 40 bottles over
£20, 18 by glass **Notes** Fixed D 5 course £70, Tasting
menu on request, Sunday L, Vegetarian available, Dress
restrictions, Smart casual **Seats** 185, Pr/dining room 16
Parking Millennium Gloucester Hotel next door

WINNER OF THE WINE AWARD
FOR ENGLAND

L'Etranger   PLAN 4 C4

French, Japanese

A happy marriage between Japan and France

☎ 020 7584 1118 & 7823 9291
36 Gloucester Rd SW7 4QT
e-mail: etranger@etranger.co.uk
dir: Nearest station: Gloucester Road. 5 mins walk from
tube station at junct of Queens Gate Terrace and
Gloucester Rd

Japan meets France in this silkily minimalist South
Kensington restaurant. It's an intimate and somewhat
sophisticated space of soothing lilacs and greys against
wooden flooring with fresh flowers used as design
features. Service is on the ball and the superb wine list
(supported by a sommelier) is a fine piece of work. There
are some good bargains to be had on brunch, lunch and
early bird menus. Combinations are well thought through
and everything is attractively presented on the plate, with
the high quality of the produce a hallmark. Baked mussel
soup is topped with puff pastry, whilst tuna tataki comes
with foie gras and truffle ponzu jelly. Main course might
serve up slow-cooked guinea fowl with pancetta and leek
fondue served with morel sauce. There's a section on the
bilingual menus called Les Tartares, which might include
a scallop version with karasumi (Japanese bottarga).
Chocoholics will melt into L'Etranger's tasting plate -
Death by Chocolate - or go for banoffee pie with poached
kumquat compôte and toffee sauce.

Chef Jerome Tauvron **Owner** Ibi Issolah
Times 12-3/5.30-11 Closed 26-27 Dec **Prices** Fixed L 2
course fr £14.50, Fixed D 3 course fr £48, Starter £9.50-
£19.50, Main £15-£65, Dessert £7.50-£10.50, Service
added but optional 12.5% **Wines** 1000+ bottles over £20,
9 bottles under £20, 14 by glass **Notes** Degustation 5/6
course £65/£95, Early bird Mon-Fri 6-6.45pm, Sunday L,
Vegetarian available, Dress restrictions, Smart casual
Seats 64, Pr/dining room 20 **Children** Portions
Parking NCP

Millennium Bailey's Hotel   PLAN 4 C4
London Kensington

Italian

Italian cooking in smart townhouse hotel

☎ 020 7331 6308
140 Gloucester Rd SW7 4QH
e-mail: olives.baileys@millenniumhotels.co.uk
dir: Nearest station: Gloucester Road. Hotel opposite tube
station

The setting may be a blue-blooded, beautifully restored
Victorian townhouse in Kensington, but the language
changes to Italian in the Olives Restaurant. Waiting staff
bring an authentic Italian buzz to a modern setting of
bare darkwood tables and contemporary artwork on rich
blue walls, while an open kitchen adds a further dynamic
element to proceedings. A glass of prosecco in the stylish
bar should cement the feel-good mood before tucking into
a mix of classic and updated dishes all made with well-
sourced materials. Get going with excellent bread and
olive oil, then follow with risotto of wood pigeon and
artichokes, or venison ragoût with red wine and juniper
berries. Main courses offer classic osso buco Milanese
alongside oven-baked monkfish served with spelt and
olives in clam guazzetto. Check out the keenly-priced
lunch special and pre-theatre menus too.

Chef Davide Di Croce **Times** 12-5/5-10.30 **Prices** Fixed L
2 course £8.95-£14.95, Fixed D 3 course £17.95, Starter
£4.95-£9.95, Service added but optional 12.5% **Wines** 8
by glass **Notes** Pre-theatre 2/3 course £14.95/£17.95, inc
wine £22.50/£25.50, Sunday L, Vegetarian available
Seats 70 **Children** Portions

Zuma   PLAN 4 F5

Modern Japanese

Buzzy modern Japanese in fashionable Knightsbridge

☎ 020 7584 1010
5 Raphael St, Knightsbridge SW7 1DL
e-mail: info@zumarestaurant.com
dir: Nearest station: Knightsbridge. Brompton Rd west,
turn right into Lancelot Pl & follow road to right into
Raphael St

With a network of branches spanning the planet from
Miami to Hong Kong as well as Knightsbridge, Zuma is an
expanding global brand. Its aim is to spread the word on
the informal Japanese dining style, known as izakaya. The
venue uses all the contemporary textures of blond wood,
granite blocks, steel and glass you might expect in an
über-chic, minimally Zen-like setting, but the vibe is the
polar opposite of calm and relaxation when the crowds
turn up (often in chauffeur-driven Bentleys - it's that sort
of place) and fuel up on the 40 different types of sake in
the buzzing bar. It is certainly not a case of style over
substance: whether you are dining in the main restaurant
or at the open robata grill and sushi counter, the cooking
is defined by superb fresh ingredients, razor-sharp
flavours and magnificent presentations. The sushi is
exemplary, and you could go about things tapas-style and
graze through yellowtail sashimi with soy dashi, shallot

and crispy garlic, then seared beef with soy, ginger, lime
and coriander alongside pork skewers with yuzu mustard
miso. Desserts can be a weaker element of the Japanese
idiom, but a parfait-like caramelised chocolate saikoro
with cocoa crumble holds its own.

Chef Soon Lee Ong **Owner** Rainer Becker & Arjun Waney
Times 12-2.30/6-11 Closed 25 Dec **Prices** Tasting menu
£96, Service added but optional 15% **Wines** 270 bottles
over £20, 17 by glass **Notes** Tasting menu min 2 people,
Vegetarian available, Dress restrictions, Smart casual
Seats 175, Pr/dining room 14 **Parking** On street

LONDON SW8

Tom Ilic   PLAN 1 E3

Modern European

**Robust flavours from seasoned chef in downtown
Battersea**

☎ 020 7622 0555
123 Queenstown Rd SW8 3RH
e-mail: info@tomilic.com
dir: Nearest station: Clapham Common. Close to Clapham
Junct & Battersea Power Station

Though Tom Ilic's self-named shop-front restaurant may
have the look of a workaday neighbourhood bistro, savvy
locals and the capital's foodies know there's some smart
cooking going on here. Expect imaginative and gutsy
cooking with personality and full-on flavours served in
generous portions, and at reasonable prices, too. Tom's
trademark skill with meat, and, in particular, things
porcine, is on show. Consider carte signatures like a
starter of braised pig's cheek with chorizo (accompanied
by garlic mash and crackling) to a main-event
'degustation of pork' (with pickled white cabbage and
caramelised apple), while fish lovers are not ignored;
witness baked fillet of line-caught sea bass with tomato
fondue, crab and prawn tartlet. Fixed-price menus (lunch
and dinner) offer more cracking value - twice-baked
mature cheddar soufflé followed by baked fillet of salmon,
for example - while the atmosphere has a relaxed, white-
linen-free vibe, with modern art, leafy fronds and leather
chairs providing a contemporary sheen.

Times 12-2.30/6-10.30 Closed last wk Aug, Xmas, Mon, L
Tue, D Sun

LONDON SW10

Chutney Mary Restaurant   PLAN 1 E3

Indian

Stunning venue for Indian cooking that's a cut above

☎ 020 7351 3113
535 King's Rd, Chelsea SW10 0SZ
e-mail: chutneymary@realindianfood.com
dir: Nearest station: Fulham Broadway. On corner of
King's Rd and Lots Rd

This glamorous Chelsea Indian has been going strong for
more than two decades, and when you descend the
staircase from the reception and first set eyes on the

glittering spectacle that is the basement restaurant, you start to understand why. The place looks simply stunning, and the tricky decisions start before you've even looked at the menu: do you take a table in the opulently decorated split-level dining room, with its mirrored walls, rich orange hues, framed crystal-studded silk hangings and Raj-era sketches, or in the spacious conservatory, decked out greenhouse-style with trees and plants soaring towards the high ceiling? Wherever you sit, expect flickering candles on the linen-clad tables and friendly, professional service. The authentic Indian cooking is brought bang up-to-date with attractive, modern presentation, and the ingredients are top-notch. Start, perhaps, with tokri chaat, a crispy straw potato basket filled with traditional Indian street foods and topped with strained yoghurt and chutneys - a dish full of contrasts in texture, flavour and colour. Roast shoulder of tender lamb in a brown onion based sauce with fine green beans is a suitably modern take on a lamb curry. Round things off in a slightly more Western vein with a first-class coconut pannacotta with black cherry sorbet.

Chef Siddharth Krishna **Owner** R Mathrani, N Panjabi **Times** 12.30-3/6.30-11.30 Closed L Mon-Fri, D 25 Dec **Prices** Food prices not confirmed for 2013. Please telephone for details **Wines** 76 bottles over £20, 18 by glass **Notes** Sunday L, Vegetarian available, Civ Wed 110 **Seats** 110, Pr/dining room 24 **Children** Menu **Parking** Parking meters outside

The Painted Heron   PLAN 1 E3

◉◉ Modern Indian

First-rate modern Indian cooking near Battersea Bridge

☎ 020 7351 5232
112 Cheyne Walk SW10 0DJ
e-mail: thepaintedheron@btinternet.com
dir: Nearest station: South Kensington

This paragon of contemporary Indian cuisine has been up and running for a decade on the Chelsea embankment near Battersea Bridge, and continues to pour forth a wealth of innovative ideas to pique a foodie's interest. The sleek modern minimalism of the interior - contemporary artwork on plain white walls, pale wooden floors, black-lacquered chairs - mirrors the contemporary spin brought by an endlessly creative kitchen team to the culinary idiom of the sub-continent. Soft-shelled crab fried in sesame and chilli batter, or tandoor-grilled pheasant in tamarind are starter possibilities you don't often encounter on Indian menus, and mains continue in the same inventive mood, serving tandoori grouse in an east-meets-west fusion with chilli game chips and chick peas, or teaming roasted Dover sole with crab meat pilau rice and coconut curry. At the end, passionfruit mousse with fresh mango should cool down the consequences of mutton chops in a super-hot curry with naga chillies.

Chef Yogesh Datta **Owner** Charles Hill **Times** 12-3/6.30-11 Closed Xmas, Etr, L Sat **Prices** Tasting menu £45, Starter £7-£20, Main £15.50-£22.50, Dessert £4-£6, Service added but optional 12.5% **Wines** 25 bottles over £20, 14 bottles under £20, 20 by

glass **Notes** Tasting menu 6 course whole table & min 2 people, Sunday L **Seats** 70 **Children** Portions **Parking** On street

Wyndham Grand London Chelsea Harbour   PLAN 1 E3

◉ Traditional British, French

Marina dining in the heart of London

☎ 020 7823 3000
Chelsea Harbour SW10 0XG
dir: Nearest station: Fulham Broadway, Imperial Wharf. A4 to Earls Court Rd S towards river. Right into Kings Rd, left down Lots Rd. Chelsea Harbour in front

The high-gloss Wyndham Grand is pitched squarely at the jet-set crew who frequent Chelsea Harbour waterfront. The concept of the restaurant can change from one year to the next, but seems to be sticking with its incarnation as the Chelsea Riverside Brasserie for now. It is a glitzy space, naturally, filled with plush royal blue and cream seats at bare wooden tables, although a wall of windows inevitably focuses the attention on the alfresco terrace perched above the boats moored in the marina - a space that is in much demand when the sun decrees that outdoor dining season is open. The menu sticks to a simple modern style, opening with caramelised foie gras roulade with apple chutney and toasted brioche, and pursuing the brasserie theme with top-grade cuts of Scottish steak slapped on the grill and served with French fries and a classic béarnaise sauce. Lighter ideas could be Shetland mussels in a time-honoured garlic and white wine sauce, or organic salmon with crème fraîche potatoes, sautéed lentils and thyme jus. Conclude with a dainty pairing of elderflower and champagne mousse with pistachio ice cream and gooseberries.

Times 11.30-5.30/5.30-10.30 **Prices** Food prices not confirmed for 2013. Please telephone for details **Wines** 12 bottles over £20, 2 bottles under £20, 18 by glass **Notes** Vegetarian available **Seats** 105, Pr/dining room 12 **Children** Menu **Parking** NCP

LONDON SW11

The Butcher & Grill   PLAN 1 E3

◉ Modern British

A carnivore's delight in relaxed, modern warehouse-style setting

☎ 020 7924 3999
39-41 Parkgate Rd, Battersea SW11 4NP
e-mail: info@thebutcherandgrill.com
dir: Nearest station: Clapham Junction, Battersea

Vegetarians may have a thin time at this switched-on, all-day contemporary amalgam of butcher's shop, deli, coffee bar, and no-frills Grill restaurant near Battersea Park. The USP here is top-grade, ethically-reared meat and poultry, and it is all handled with skill and a complete absence of fuss. A brasserie-style menu majors in lamb burgers, Gloucestershire Old Spot pork chops,

onglet skirt steak à la Bordelaise flashed on the grill, and classics such as devilled kidneys on toast, steak tartare with a quail's egg, or main-course haunch of venison with parsnip purée, chestnuts, braised red cabbage and juniper berry jus. Non-carnivores get a look in too - there's the likes of Cornish salt and chilli squid with rocket and lemon, or crab on toast with crab mayonnaise. This foodie paradise lives in a laid-back warehouse setting with bare floorboards, modern wood furniture and monochrome photos of livestock, and a rear terrace overlooks a disused Thames wharf. There's a second branch in Wimbledon too.

Chef Michael Slowik **Owner** Dominic Ford **Times** 12-3/5.30-11 Closed 25-26 Dec, D Sun **Prices** Food prices not confirmed for 2013. Please telephone for details **Wines** 45 bottles over £20, 13 bottles under £20, 16 by glass **Notes** Sunday L, Vegetarian available **Seats** 64 **Children** Portions, Menu **Parking** On street

Entrée Restaurant and Bar   PLAN 1 E2

◉◉ Modern European

Buzzing neighbourhood restaurant and bar

☎ 020 7223 5147
2 Battersea Rise, Battersea SW11 1ED
e-mail: info@entreebattersea.co.uk
dir: Nearest station: Clapham Junction, Clapham Common. Just off the corner of Clapham Common, Battersea Rise at Lavender Walk

A casual, relaxed feel, a buzzy, lively atmosphere, live weekend jazz and a touch of theatre from an open kitchen all combine to make this unpretentious neighbourhood restaurant a real hit. Peruse the weekly-changing menu over pre-dinner drinks in the cocktail bar, then head upstairs to the intimate restaurant, where wooden floors, black leather banquettes and glowing candles on bare wooden tables set the laid-back tone. Thoughtfully presented modish dishes are built around top-notch British seasonal produce; start with the likes of pheasant and chestnut soup or chilled poached salmon with Jerusalem artichoke and broccoli salad. For main course there may be venison with braised red cabbage, fondant potato and sultana purée, or stone bass with squid ink purée, Swiss chard and seafood parcels, and to finish, chocolate cake with white chocolate mousse and caramel ice cream.

Chef James McDonald **Owner** Jayke Mangion, Gerry O'Keefe **Times** 12-4/6-10.30 Closed 1 wk Xmas, L Mon-Fri **Prices** Fixed L 2 course £18, Fixed D 3 course £24, Starter £6-£10, Main £14-£21.50, Dessert £3.50-£6, Service added but optional 12.5% **Wines** 32 bottles over £20, 4 bottles under £20, 8 by glass **Notes** Sunday L, Vegetarian available, Dress restrictions, Smart casual **Seats** 55 **Children** Portions **Parking** On street

LONDON SW11 *continued*

Ransome's Dock
PLAN 1 E3

◉◉ Modern British

Long-serving neighbourhood restaurant with canal views

☎ 020 7223 1611 & 7924 2462
35-37 Parkgate Rd, Battersea SW11 4NP
e-mail: chef@ransomesdock.co.uk
dir: Nearest station: Sloane Square, Clapham Junction. Between Albert Bridge & Battersea Bridge

Sitting alongside moored houseboats on a small canal leading to the Thames in Battersea, this relaxed neighbourhood restaurant and bar is an excellent all-day option. Owned by Martin and Vanessa Lam for over 20 years, the combination of charming location, warm, easygoing atmosphere, dynamic wine list and unpretentious, modish cooking remains a winner. Large windows serve up lovely views of the water and an outdoor terrace gets you even closer. Generous portions of hearty bistro-style dishes are what to expect, plus that superb award-winning wine list with plenty of interesting options, including a great selection of dessert wines. Start perhaps with warm Lincolnshire smoked eel fillets with buckwheat pancake and horseradish cream, then move on to Elizabeth David's spinach and ricotta gnocchi or English rose veal goulash with parsley dumplings. The kitchen shows its mettle with a fine warm chocolate and damson tart with crème fraîche.

Chef Martin & Vanessa Lam **Owner** Mr & Mrs M Lam **Times** 12-11 Closed Xmas, Aug BH, D Sun **Prices** Fixed L 2 course £16, Starter £5.50-£12.50, Main £11.50-£24, Dessert £5-£8.50, Service added but optional 12.5% **Wines** 360 bottles over £20, 22 bottles under £20, 20 by glass **Notes** Fixed L menu Mon-Fri until 7.30pm, Sunday L, Vegetarian available **Seats** 55 **Children** Portions **Parking** 20, Spaces in evenings & wknds only

LONDON SW12

Harrison's
PLAN 1 E2

◉ Modern British

Thriving neighbourhood brasserie with confident cooking

☎ 020 8675 6900
15-19 Bedford Hill, Balham SW12 9EX
e-mail: info@harrisonsbalham.co.uk
dir: Nearest station: Balham. Turn right from Balham High Rd opposite Waitrose, onto Bedford Hill. Restaurant on corner of Bedford Hill & Harberson Rd

This easygoing and suitably cool brasserie and bar is a winner with the Balham crowd (kids and all). Owner Sam Harrison (of big-brother Sam's Brasserie & Bar in Chiswick fame - see entry) is a one-time lieutenant of Rick Stein, and he's pitched this place just right. An oval-shaped metal-formed bar is a great centrepiece to the room, encircling an open kitchen on one side and drinks counter on the other; low-slung lightshades, banquettes and simple wooden furniture complete the modern good

looks, while staff are seemingly sunny natured. The cooking keeps things relatively straightforward with a pleasing roster of brasserie-style dishes but does not lack contemporary verve. The daily-changing carte is joined by fixed-price options, weekend breakfast and brunch, and bar and children's menus. Start with something as enticingly modish as prawn popcorn with Cajun aïoli and follow on with pan-seared sea bass with curried butternut squash purée, leeks and apple foam, or stick with a classic such as cheeseburger and fries. Inspiring cocktails and a fashionable wine list, with plenty by the glass and 500ml carafe, complete the picture.

Chef Peter Murray **Owner** Sam Harrison **Times** 12-mdnt Closed 24-27 Dec, L 28 Dec **Prices** Fixed L 2 course £13.50-£19.50, Fixed D 3 course £16.50, Starter £6.50-£9.75, Main £12.50-£20.50, Dessert £3.50-£8, Service added but optional 12.5% **Wines** 49 bottles over £20, 10 bottles under £20, 19 by glass **Notes** Fixed L Mon-Fri, D Sun-Thu, Sunday L, Vegetarian available **Seats** 80, Pr/dining room 40 **Children** Portions, Menu **Parking** On street

Lamberts
PLAN 1 E2

◉◉ Modern British

Smart, seasonal cooking in popular neighbourhood restaurant

☎ 020 8675 2233
2 Station Pde, Balham High Rd SW12 9AZ
e-mail: bookings@lambertsrestaurant.com
dir: Nearest station: Balham. Just S of Balham station on Balham High Rd

Just a few yards from the station, this deservedly popular neighbourhood restaurant cuts a dash on the bustling High Road. The long room comes fashionably decked out in neutral tones, with wood floors, unclothed tables and banquette wall seating set to a backdrop of subdued lighting and background music. The kitchen's innovative, assured approach and commitment to seasonality and small artisan producers puts it a cut above the rest. Expect light, modish, well-dressed and well balanced dishes, mixing updated favourites with more contemporary ideas. Herb-crusted lamb rump and braised shoulder, for example, comes with pearl barley, chard and girolles, or go for fillet of plaice with mash, spinach and shrimp butter. Desserts follow suit; perhaps a chocolate and orange trifle rubbing shoulders with pear, treacle and walnut tart. Fixed-price offers keep all happy.

Chef Ryan Lowery **Owner** Mr Joe Lambert **Times** 12.30-2.30/6-10 Closed 25 Dec, 1 Jan, BH's (except Good Fri), Mon, D Sun **Prices** Fixed L 2 course £17-£20, Fixed D 3 course £30-£32, Service added but optional 12.5% **Wines** 51 bottles over £20, 5 bottles under £20, 14 by glass **Notes** Sunday L, Vegetarian available **Seats** 50 **Children** Portions, Menu **Parking** On street

LONDON SW13

Sonny's Kitchen
PLAN 1 D3

◉◉ Modern

Consistently high standards in Barnes

☎ 020 8748 0393 & 8741 8451
94 Church Rd, Barnes SW13 0DQ
e-mail: manager@sonnyskitchen.co.uk
dir: Nearest station: Barnes. From Castelnau end of Church Rd on left by shops

In a terraced row of shops, Sonny's has gently morphed into Sonny's Kitchen, with long-time owner Rebecca Mascarenhas joining forces with Phil Howard as per their successful joint venture in Kensington, Kitchen W8 (see entry). 'Neighbourhood and beyond' is the mantra, which builds on the reputation of the original Sonny's 26 years down the line. The chef has worked at The Square and Maze and his seasonally changing modish European menu has bags of appeal. Start with gazpacho with sour cream ice cream and a mini salmon, avocado and coriander wrap, or ravioli of kid with wilted greens, raisins, walnuts and goat's cheese. Move onto pizza bianco with cured Wagyu beef with smoked ewe's curd, artichokes and rosemary, finishing with coupe SW13 (vanilla ice cream with hot chocolate foam, crumbled brownie, roasted macadamia nuts, popping honeycomb and hundreds and thousands). Exciting times in SW13.

Chef Alex Marks **Owner** Rebecca Mascarenhas, Phil Howard **Times** 10-4/6-11 Closed Xmas, New Year, D Sun **Prices** Food prices not confirmed for 2013. Please telephone for details **Wines** 57 bottles over £20, 12 bottles under £20, 20 by glass **Seats** 100 **Children** Portions **Parking** On street

LONDON SW14

The Depot Waterfront Brasserie
PLAN 1 D3

◉ Modern European

Popular, relaxed riverside brasserie

☎ 020 8878 9462
Tideway Yard, 125 Mortlake High St, Barnes SW14 8SN
e-mail: info@depotbrasserie.co.uk
dir: Nearest station: Barnes Bridge. Between Barnes Bridge & Mortlake stations

The local council almost demolished this Victorian site until local residents saved it back in the '80s; the smart Thames-side brasserie has now been a favourite hangout for Barnes residents for a quarter of a century. Sadly, there's no outdoor riverside terrace, but Thames-view tables in the dining room offer ample compensation, and there's a lovely alfresco patio in the sunny cobbled courtyard. Inside, you'll be greeted by a pleasant vibe and no standing on ceremony in the stylish bar; in the restaurant are banquettes, chunky unclothed tables and herringbone parquet floors. Expect simply conceived, Mediterranean-inflected ideas such as foie gras and chicken liver parfait with plum jam and toasted walnut and raisin bread to start, and among the main-course options, haunch of venison with celeriac purée, chanterelles and purple broccoli. Fixed-price menus offer the best value you're likely to find within toe-dipping distance of the Thames.

Chef Gary Knowles **Owner** Tideway Restaurants Ltd **Times** 12-3.30/6-10 **Prices** Fixed L 2 course £12.95, Fixed D 3 course £15.95, Starter £5-£8.50, Main £10.50-£19.95, Dessert £5.50-£7.95, Service added but optional 12.5% **Wines** 32 bottles over £20, 19 bottles under £20, 20 by glass **Notes** Sunday L, Vegetarian available **Seats** 120, Pr/dining room 60 **Children** Portions, Menu **Parking** Parking after 6.30pm & at wknds

<hr />

LONDON SW15

Cantinetta   PLAN 1 D2

@@ Italian

Real Italian cooking in stylish neighbourhood restaurant

☎ 020 8780 3131
162-164 Lower Richmond Rd SW15 1LY
e-mail: eat@cantinetta.co.uk
dir: Nearest station: Putney Bridge. On Lower Richmond Rd between Putney Bridge & Barnes

On a corner site, fronted by a large terrace for a spot of alfresco eating, Cantinetta occupies two opened-up rooms, where white walls hung with colourful artwork, wooden tables, fashionable chairs and the occasional banquette add up to a fetching interior. The modern Italian menu successfully transplants the genuine flavours of Italy to SW15, sometimes literally, with some ingredients flown over. Mozzarella with bottarga, puntarelle and anchovy dressing is a boldly tasting starter, as is bruschetta with Tuscan-style chicken livers, marinated tomatoes, and ricotta. Tip-top materials are cooked straightforwardly so flavours sing out; Venetian-style calves' liver, for example, served simply with soft polenta, parsley and lemon and accompanied by rosemary potatoes. Pasta runs to gnocchi with black truffle, butter and parmesan, say, or spaghetti with lobster and cherry tomatoes - and desserts include rhubarb pannacotta.

Times 12-2.30/6-11 Closed BHs, L Mon (Sep-Etr), D Sun (Sep-Etr)

<hr />

Enoteca Turi   PLAN 1 D2

@ Italian NOTABLE WINE LIST

Regional Italian food and wine in Putney

☎ 020 8785 4449
28 Putney High St SW15 1SQ
e-mail: enoteca@talktalk.net
web: www.enotecaturi.com
dir: Nearest station: Putney Bridge. Opposite Odeon Cinema near bridge

Behind an unassuming frontage on Putney High Street, the family-run Enoteca has been serving regional Italian cooking to eager south Londoners for over 20 years. Wine is given a top billing here, too - there's over 300 to get through from across Italy, plus every dish is given a by-the-glass pairing. Seasonality and a light modern touch are evident in regional dishes along the lines of smoked duck breast with confit leg, white cabbage salad, quince preserve with cumin straws, and slow-cooked feather blade of organic beef with ricotta filled paccheri pasta, red wine and tomato sauce. Finish with a torta caprese - Capri chocolate and almond cake with limoncello cream.

Chef Mr G Turi, Mr B Amodio **Owner** Mr G & Mrs P Turi **Times** 12-2.30/7-10.30 Closed 25-26 Dec, 1 Jan, Sun, L BHs **Prices** Fixed L 2 course fr £17.50, Fixed D 3 course fr £32.50, Starter £7.75-£11.50, Main £12.50-£26.50, Dessert £6.75-£7.25, Service added but optional 12.5% **Wines** 300 bottles over £20, 16 bottles under £20, 11 by glass **Notes** Vegetarian available, Dress restrictions, Smart casual **Seats** 85, Pr/dining room 18 **Children** Portions **Parking** Putney Exchange car park, on street

<hr />

LONDON SW17

Chez Bruce   PLAN 1 E2

@@@ – see below

<hr />

Chez Bruce

<hr />

LONDON SW17   PLAN 1 E2

Modern NOTABLE WINE LIST

Seriously good cooking without pretence

☎ 020 8672 0114
2 Bellevue Rd, Wandsworth Common SW17 7EG
e-mail: enquiries@chezbruce.co.uk
dir: Nearest station: Wandsworth Common/Balham

Bruce Poole's eponymous restaurant facing Wandsworth Common is the sort of place everyone dreams of having in their locality, and it certainly has the feel of a neighbourhood restaurant, special enough for an occasion but not in the least stuffy or pretentious. The broadly appealing menus are in the modern Anglo-French idiom, which means ideas are pulled in from across Europe and even further afield, depending on the desired effect: two deep-fried fishcakes, for instance, are spiked with chilli and served with mussels in a creamy curry sauce and a poached egg. Another triumphant starter is a modish salad of pig's head, beetroot, mustard, finely grated Comté cheese and crackling, and the same high degree of workmanship is clear in main courses too, seen in roast chicken breast served on a ballottine of leg meat with meaty tortellini, silky herb velouté, buttery salsify and a garnish of sautéed chanterelles, a deeply satisfying dish. Among fish options, creamy squid-ink risotto with tender chargrilled baby squid adds a whole new dimension to well-timed, crisp-skinned sea bass fillets, given an extra kick from florets of broccoli flavoured with garlic and chilli. Comforting puddings include light rum baba with roast pineapple and cream mixed with Muscovado, and crisp-based frangipane pear tart.

Chef Bruce Poole **Owner** Bruce Poole, Nigel Platts-Martin **Times** 12-2.30/6.30-10 Closed 24-26 Dec,1 Jan **Prices** Fixed L 2 course £23.50-£29.50, Fixed D 3 course £45, Service added but optional 12.5% **Wines** 750 bottles over £20, 2 bottles under £20, 18 by glass **Notes** Sunday L, Vegetarian available, Dress restrictions, Smart casual **Seats** 75, Pr/dining room 16 **Children** Portions **Parking** On street, station car park

LONDON SW19

Cannizaro House
PLAN 1 D1

◉◉ British, European ◉

Confident cooking in a parkland setting

☎ 020 8879 1464
West Side, Wimbledon Common SW19 4UE
e-mail: info@cannizarohouse.com
web: www.cannizarohouse.com
dir: Nearest station: Wimbledon. From A3 (London Rd) Tibbets Corner, take A219 (Parkside) right into Cannizaro Rd, then right into West Side

It's difficult to believe that this magnificent Georgian mansion has a London postcode, as it's surrounded by parkland within Wimbledon Common. The menu, served in the tastefully decorated restaurant looking over greenery, is in the modern European idiom, with the kitchen marshalling prime ingredients, mostly organic, such as Somerset lamb, Wiltshire pork and Loch Duart salmon. Dinner could open with a cold starter of carpaccio with shallots and capers, or butter-poached quail breast with spinach tortellini and onion consommé. Main courses can be multi-layered, the results never less than successful: roast fillet of cod with lemon orzo, confit tomato, clams and bottarga, say, or roast fillet of pork with a black sesame bonbon, poached pear, and vegetable galette. Desserts are no less creative, judging by crispy pistachio cannelloni with vanilla and olive oil sorbet.

Chef Christian George **Owner** Bridgehouse Hotels
Times 12-2.30/7-9.30 **Prices** Fixed L 2 course £24.50, Fixed D 3 course £29.50, Starter £8-£10, Main £19-£22, Dessert £7-£9.50, Service optional **Wines** 95 bottles over £20, 5 bottles under £20, 12 by glass **Notes** Sunday L, Vegetarian available, Dress restrictions, No shorts, Civ Wed 100 **Seats** 60, Pr/dining room 120 **Children** Portions, Menu **Parking** 55

The Fox & Grapes
PLAN 1 D2

◉ Traditional British

Pub food à la Claude Bosi

☎ 020 8619 1300
9 Camp Rd, Wimbledon SW19 4UN
e-mail: reservations@foxandgrapeswimbledon.co.uk
dir: Nearest station: Wimbledon

The kitchen at this high-flying gastro-pub on the edge of Wimbledon Common is fortunate to have its larder stocked by the top-notch network of suppliers built up by owner Claude Bosi of Mayfair restaurant Hibiscus fame (see entry). Following the vogue for top chefs to convert old-fashioned boozers into dining destinations, Bosi has opened up the Fox & Grapes' interior into a capacious open-plan space focused on a central island bar; the parquet floor and wood panelling have survived, and there are the chunky bare wooden tables and mismatched chairs you'd expect to see in a contemporary food-oriented pub. The short, regularly changing menu trumpets no-frills, seasonal dishes from Cornish razor clams in white wine sauce with broad beans, peas and

chorizo, to mains taking in brown ale-battered pollock and chips with mushy peas, and prime slabs of beef from the charcoal-fired Josper grill. For pudding, generous satisfaction might come in the shape of Granny Smith apple crumble with custard, or you could go for fine artisan English cheeses.

Chef Claude Bosi, Julian Ward **Owner** Claude Bosi
Times 12-3/6-9.30 Closed 25 Dec **Prices** Starter £6.50-£8, Main £9.50-£26.95, Service optional
Notes Vegetarian available **Seats** 90 **Children** Portions, Menu **Parking** On street

The Lambourne
PLAN 1 E1

◉ Modern European NEW

A buzz and bistro food in downtown Wimbledon

☎ 020 8545 8661
263 The Broadway, Wimbledon SW19 1SD
e-mail: info@lambournebarandgrill.com
dir: Nearest station: Wimbledon

At the less glam end of The Broadway, The Lambourne is a trendy address none the less, and it draws the crowds for its mix of vibrant bar and slick dining. You can sit in the high-ceilinged bar at blond-wood stools at high blond-wood tables (blond wood is a theme) and sip on a cocktail (cocktails are a theme), or head into the dining area which has a more intimate vibe with its slate floors and black banquettes and chairs. Wherever you sit, the decibels can be high and the please-all roster (including daily specials) remains the same - simple, well-executed, no-fuss bistro-style dishes at prices that won't alarm your financial advisor. Battered calamari with grilled lime and tartare sauce to start perhaps, then roasted lamb rump with marinated Mediterranean vegetables and olive tapenade, or pan-fried skate wing with wilted spinach, capers and parsley noisette. Beef from Smithfield Market is cooked simply on the grill and served with triple-cooked chips.

Times 12-5-11 Closed 25-26 Dec, 1 Jan, L Mon-Fri **Prices** Food prices not confirmed for 2013. Please telephone for details **Wines** 13 bottles over £20, 11 bottles under £20, 6 by glass **Notes** Pre-theatre menu available, Sunday L, Vegetarian available **Seats** 45 **Children** Portions, Menu **Parking** 22

The Lawn Bistro
PLAN 1 D2

◉◉ British, European NEW

Modern French pedigree in stylish neighbourhood bistro

☎ 020 8947 8278 & 8944 1031
67 High St, Wimbledon SW19 5EE
e-mail: info@thelawnbistro.co.uk
dir: Nearest station: Wimbledon

Well-heeled locals pack this modern French bistro in the heart of Wimbledon village, and it's not hard to see why: the setting has the charm you'd expect of a bourgeois neighbourhood venue, with its light oak flooring, unclothed wooden tables and olive-green leather-clad chairs and banquettes looking as sleek and chic as the

trendy boutiques all around, while the food, courtesy of head chef Ollie Couillaud, is a blend of rusticity and refinement that doesn't miss a beat. Staff turned out smartly in long aprons, white shirts and dark ties run a tight ship, serving up a repertoire that is Franco-centric, with occasional brushstrokes of British, Spanish and Italian. Seared scallops and black pudding are matched with apple purée and lentil and hazelnut vinaigrette in a gutsy starter, then main course partners a top-class breast of free-range chicken with white asparagus, spring cabbage, Jersey Royals and a bowl of frothy truffle velouté. To finish, the flavours and textures of a Valrhona chocolate and caramel pot with salted pistachio praline are a match made in heaven, or two could sign up for a retro baked Alaska, flambéed at the table.

Chef Ollie Couillaud **Owner** Ollie Couillaud, Akbar Ashurov
Times 12-2.30/6.30-10.30 Closed Xmas, 1 Jan, D Sun
Prices Fixed L 2 course £24.50-£40.50, Fixed D 3 course £34.50-£60, Service added but optional 12.5%
Wines 127 bottles over £20, 6 bottles under £20, 11 by glass **Notes** Early D menu £24.95-£26.95, Sunday L, Vegetarian available, Dress restrictions, Smart casual **Seats** 70, Pr/dining room 24 **Children** Portions

The Light House Restaurant
PLAN 1 D1

◉ British, International

Smashing suburban local serving modern bistro dishes

☎ 020 8944 6338
75-77 Ridgway, Wimbledon SW19 4ST
e-mail: info@lighthousewimbledon.com
dir: Nearest station: Wimbledon. From station right up Wimbledon Hill left at mini-rdbt onto Ridgway, restaurant on left

This upbeat, modern Wimbledon village favourite has kept the locals coming back for more for 13 years and shows no sign of falling out of favour. Pale woods and light-coloured walls hung with cheerful artworks make for a bright and breezy space whose contemporary feel is in-line with the friendly style of service. Appealing menus of fresh, modern-bistro style dishes are on offer, with plenty of sunny, Mediterranean flavours cooked up in the open kitchen. Start with duck liver and foie gras pâté with grape and apple chutney, move on to roast beef fillet with wilted spinach, chips and Café de Paris butter, and end with a white chocolate pannacotta with plums poached in Grand Marnier. A global wine list offers a decent selection by the glass and half bottle.

Chef Chris Casey **Owner** Mr Finch & Mr Taylor
Times 12-3/6-10.30 Closed 24-26 Dec, 1 Jan, D Sun
Prices Fixed L 2 course fr £13.95, Fixed D 3 course fr £25, Starter £5-£11.50, Main £12.50-£17.50, Dessert £5-£6, Service added but optional 12.5% **Wines** 63 bottles over £20, 14 bottles under £20, 16 by glass **Notes** Fixed D 3 course Mon-Thu, Sunday L, Vegetarian available **Seats** 80, Pr/dining room 14 **Children** Portions, Menu

Save on Hotels. Book at **theAA.com/hotel**

LONDON, CENTRAL (W1) 307 ENGLAND

LONDON W1

Alain Ducasse at The Dorchester

PLAN 4 G6

◉◉◉ – see below

Alloro

PLAN 2 J1

◉ Modern Italian

Upper-crust Italian off Piccadilly

☎ 020 7495 4768
19-20 Dover St W1S 4LU
e-mail: alloro@londonfinedininggroup.com
web: www.londonfinedininggroup.com
dir. Nearest station: Green Park. From station towards Piccadilly, Dover St is 2nd on left

Alloro has the sort of decoration and furnishings appropriate to this expensive part of town - papered walls, leather-look banquettes and dining chairs at formally laid tables, crisp napery and a marble floor - while the menu, in Italian with translations, brings the flavours of the warm South. Generally straightforward treatments are given to top-notch produce, often imported, bringing on effective starters like deep-fried tomatoes layered with creamy burrata cheese sprinkled with balsamic, or, in season, chargrilled asparagus with quails' eggs and summer truffle. Fish is well handled - chargrilled tuna steak, pink, as requested, with a simple tomato and rocket salad, say - and among meat main courses might be slowly cooked pork belly served with apple purée and pickled onion. Pasta is made in-house, and puddings might see mango doughnuts hinting of chilli served with pineapple consommé.

Times 12-2.30/7-10.30 Closed Xmas, 4 days Etr, BHs, Sun, L Sat

---

Alyn Williams at The Westbury

PLAN 2 H2

◉◉◉ – see page 308

Andrew Edmunds

PLAN 2 J1

◉ Modern European

Evergreen, rustic, Soho favourite

☎ 020 7437 5708
46 Lexington St, Soho W1F 0LW
dir: Nearest station: Oxford Circus

There's something almost Dickensian about this old townhouse on a Soho side street - with its dark, higgledy-piggledy tavern-esque atmosphere. There's been no 'contemporary makeover' here (and hurrah for that) and no-one can doubt its enduring popularity. Pint sized and bijou, the narrow ground floor and basement come decked out with old prints, tightly-packed paper-clothed tables and time-worn cottagey furniture. The kitchen takes an equally simple, honest approach, with seasonal, ingredient-led dishes on a daily-changing handwritten menu that has its feet firmly on the ground. Line-caught cod, for example, with new potatoes, spinach and tartare sauce or salt beef with roast potato wedges, dill pickle, mixed leaves and poached free-range egg, although the kitchen is equally comfortable with octopus carpaccio among possible first courses. There's plenty on the wine list to keep oenophiles interested.

Times 12.30-3/6-10.45 Closed Xmas, Etr

Alain Ducasse at The Dorchester

LONDON W1

PLAN 4 G6

Modern French **V**

Refined but uncomplicated Ducasserie at the Dorchester

☎ 020 7629 8866
The Dorchester, 53 Park Ln W1K 1QA
e-mail: alainducasse@thedorchester.com
dir: Nearest station: Hyde Park Corner, Marble Arch

The name Ducasse is celebrated across southern Europe, Tokyo, New York, the Caribbean and London, these glitzy international franchises being the high-end representatives of the Ducasse style. Having ascended to the top of the profession, the master becomes a kind of éminence grise, hovering unseen over proceedings in city venues where the moneyed crowds come to dine. Jocelyn Herland, incumbent at the Dorchester, interprets the Ducasse style in London. The interpretations happen in a monochrome room with frosted views of Park Lane, the predominant tone being a sort of dilute greenish-tan, perhaps echoing the first arrival of spring in the park opposite. The culinary style is as refined as you might expect, though perhaps not as convoluted, which allows the best dishes to make strong, simple, seasonal statements, and showcase some top-drawer produce. Openers include steamed langoustines with ravioli in spiced consommé, as well as the glorious game and foie gras terrine with pickled Muscat grapes. Fish dishes tend to the delicate, as when halibut is gently simmered in stock with squid, shellfish and celeriac, but are not above earthing up a serving of turbot with gnocchi and bacon. Meats go the whole hog, offering the rib and saddle of venison Grand-Veneur with accompaniments of pumpkin, beetroot and quince, and the grand finale could be a chocolate and hazelnut biscuit of sensational richness, or the refreshing quince and grapefruit tart with Earl Grey sorbet.

Chef Jocelyn Herland, Bruno Riou, Angelo Ercolano
Owner The Dorchester Collection
Times 12-1.30/6.30-9.30 Closed 26-30 Dec, 6-9 Apr, 2-5 Jun, 11 Aug-5 Sep, Sun-Mon, L Sat **Prices** Fixed L 3 course £55, Fixed D 3 course £85, Tasting menu £120, Service added but optional 12.5% **Wines** 700 bottles over £20, 16 by glass **Notes** Tasting menu 7 course, Fixed L inc wine & coffee, Vegetarian menu, Dress restrictions, Smart casual L, smart D. No jeans or trainers **Seats** 82, Pr/dining room 28 **Parking** 20

Alyn Williams at The Westbury

Modern European V

Innovation, top-flight skills and heaps of glamour

☎ 020 7078 9579
Bond St W1S 2YF
e-mail: alynwilliams@westburymayfair.com
dir: Nearest station: Oxford Circus, Piccadilly Circus,
Green Park

The Westbury - one of Mayfair's swankiest hotels - has
long been a magnet for a stellar international cast of
royals, movers and shakers, and glitterati. Within, all is
self-conscious glamour and opulence: the see-and-be-
seen Polo Bar flaunts art-deco-inspired Swarovski
chandeliers and a Fendi-designed look, and the
restaurant is designed to pull in the well-heeled shoppers
with its understated classy décor of softly burnished
wooden panels, huge mirrors, subtly-backlit alcoves, and
plushly-padded oatmeal-hued leather chairs at linen-
swathed tables. Formerly known as Artisan, the venue
now proudly wears the name of its high-flying head chef
above the door: after many years in the kitchens of
Gordon Ramsay and Marcus Wareing, Alyn Williams'
pedigree is unquestionable, and here he continues to lead
diners along the path of highly-refined, French-accented
contemporary cooking. Sparse menu descriptions intrigue
with their juxtapositions of ingredients, but these are all
intelligent, thought-provoking ideas realised with top-
flight technical skills. The luxury of foie gras is creatively
matched with liquorice and puréed and lightly-poached
sand carrots, while an audacious main course involving
grilled plaice, squid ink, ricotta, cubes of cuttlefish, a
puntarella salad (wild chicory dressed with anchovies,
garlic, vinegar and olive oil), and smoked lardo knows
exactly where it is going. To finish, there may be a modish
deconstruction of a 'walnut whip' served with
marshmallow and walnut ice cream. For high-rollers, the
chef will design a bespoke meal based around their wine
choices in a private dining room encased within the wine
cellar itself, which is, of course, stocked with bottles of
the highest calibre, and priced accordingly.

Chef Alyn Williams **Owner** Cola Holdings Ltd
Times 12-2.30/6.30-10.30 Closed 25-26 Dec, Sun, L Sat
Prices Fixed L 3 course £24, Fixed D 3 course £45,
Tasting menu £55, Service added but optional 12.5%
Wines 280 bottles over £20, 20 by glass **Notes** Fixed ALC
3 course £45, Tasting menu 7 course, Vegetarian menu,
Dress restrictions, Smart casual, Civ Wed 20 **Seats** 65,
Pr/dining room 20 **Children** Portions **Parking** 20

Arbutus Restaurant

Modern French

Seriously good French cooking in Soho

☎ 020 7734 4545
63-64 Frith St W1D 3JW
e-mail: info@arbutusrestaurant.co.uk
dir: Nearest station: Tottenham Court Road. Exit
Tottenham Court Road tube station, turn left into Oxford
St. Left onto Soho St, cross over or continue around Soho
Sq, restaurant is on Frith St 25mtrs on right

Anthony Demetre and Will Smith's restaurant close to
Soho Square marks that happy meeting place where
contemporary verve meets traditional spirit. The urban-
chic, gun-metal frontage looks the part, with good use of
natural tones and textures within the U-shaped room
(well-designed darkwood tables, leather-clad seating,
black and white photos, oak floor), and a marble-topped
bar and high tables with high stools by the entrance for
that most fashionable of activities - counter dining. With
all these hard surfaces, the noise can crank up at busy
times, but there's no doubting that it's a happy hum.
There's an unmistakable Gallic accent to the menu, with
top-notch ingredients, acute cooking skills, and more
than enough va-va-voom to elevate Arbutus to a higher
tier of London dining. Good value has always been the
watchword here, and with a reasonably-priced carte (by
today's standards), good value working lunch and pre-
theatre menus, such laudable ambition remains. Squid
and mackerel 'burger' bursts with flavour and freshness
in a first course with cockles and sea purslane, whilst
main-courses can be as earthy and traditional as pied et
paquets (a vast portion of lamb's tripe and trotters
served Marseilles-style), or as gently modish as Cornish
gurnard with butternut squash, mussel and hazelnut
salsa. The cooking is well judged, the balance of flavours
adroitly handled, not least at dessert stage, where a
classic Sicilian lemon tart has perfect sharpness, or in all
the sticky richness of tarte Tatin for two. The good ideas
and consideration of customers' needs extends to the
wine list, too, with just about all of the circa 50-strong
bins also available in 250ml carafes. Do try the siblings,
Wild Honey and Les Deux Salons (see entries).

Chef Anthony Demetre **Owner** Anthony Demetre, Will
Smith **Times** 12-2.30/5-11.30 Closed 25-26 Dec, 1 Jan
Prices Fixed D 3 course £17.95, Starter £7.95-£11.95,
Main £16.95-£19.50, Dessert £6.95-£7.95, Service added
but optional 12.5% **Wines** 40 bottles over £20, 6 bottles
under £20, 50 by glass **Notes** Pre-theatre D 5-7pm 2
£18.95, 3 course £20.95, Sunday L, Vegetarian available
Seats 75 **Children** Portions

Save on Hotels. Book at theAA.com/hotel

LONDON, CENTRAL (W1) 309 ENGLAND

LONDON W1 *continued*

Aqua Kyoto

PLAN 2 J2

◉◉ Japanese

Classy Japanese food in super-cool roof-top setting

☎ 020 7478 0540
240 Regent St W1B 3BR
e-mail: reservation@aqua-london.com
dir: Nearest station: Oxford Street. Opposite the London Palladium, just behind Regent St

From the smart lobby entrance, you're whisked by lift to the 5th floor and the über-chic world of Aqua. The super-sexy Spirit cocktail bar is up first; it's shared by twin restaurants Aqua Nueva (Spanish tapas - see entry) and this modern Japanese outfit, and covers the top floor of the former Dickins & Jones building. There's great rooftop views from the terrace, while, like everything else here, Kyoto's ultra-designed dining room shimmers with contemporary style and teems with beautiful people, especially in the evenings when it becomes a high-energy 'destination' (lunch is quieter). Moody black, red and gold complement the theatre of a sunken centrepiece sushi bar, charcoal grill and jaw-dropping lantern-style light fitting. It's not design over substance: the cooking deserves serious attention, while friendly staff are happy to advise on the menus. Visually striking, well-constructed dishes and top-drawer ingredients are the thing; take king crab tempura with crab miso, or perhaps twice-cooked crispy pork belly with langoustine and yuzu pepper to high-rolling Wagyu beef with garlic ponzu and grape icicles. Otherwise there's cracking sushi and sashimi, fashionable wines and super cocktails.

Times 12-3/6-11.15 Closed Sun

Aqua Nueva

PLAN 2 J2

◉◉ Spanish **NEW**

Über-cool roof-top destination for refined modern tapas

☎ 020 7478 0540
5th Floor, 240 Regent St W1B 3BR
e-mail: reservation@aqua-london.com
dir: Nearest station: Oxford Circus. Opposite London Palladium

The fifth-floor entrance to Aqua's contemporary Spanish restaurant, Nueva (see also entry for Aqua Kyoto), is via a long, low-lit catwalk-like corridor (from its trendy Spirit Bar) guarded by a brooding, illuminated, full-sized sculpture of a bull. The large, glitzy dining room and long tapas bar (with chefs at work) is hung with an eye-catching 'forest' of 15,000 turned wooden spindles. Top-drawer lighting, a funky backing track and high decibels confirm this as a thoroughly modern kind of experience. When the sun shines, the roof terrace comes into its own, with cocktails competing for your attention with the all-Iberian wines. In the evening it's a sexy, high-rolling destination for posh tapas and beautiful people, while lunch is markedly quieter (with a good value fixed-price menu). Graze on refined, well-dressed, contemporary Spanish dishes, with tapas plates at the bar or as

starters on the carte; Iberica ham croquettes, or Galician-style octopus with potatoes and spicy paprika, for example, with the larger plates running to marinated venison served with membrillo and a red fruit sauce. It all looks and tastes great, but doesn't come cheap.

Chef Alberto Hernandez **Owner** Aqua Restaurant Group
Times 12-3/6-11.30 Closed Xmas, New Year, BHs,
Prices Fixed L 2 course £16-£51, Fixed D 3 course
£23.50-£59, Starter £4-£22, Main £12-£29, Dessert
£7.50-£8, Service added but optional 12.5%
Wines 20 bottles over £20, 13 by glass **Notes** Vegetarian available, Dress restrictions, Smart casual, Civ Wed 100
Seats 160, Pr/dining room 16

Arbutus Restaurant

PLAN 2 K2

◉◉◉ – *see opposite*

Athenaeum Hotel & Apartments

PLAN 4 H6

◉◉ Modern British

Classy British cooking in a luxurious Mayfair hotel

☎ 020 7499 3464
116 Piccadilly W1J 7BJ
e-mail: info@athenaeumhotel.com
web: www.athenaeumhotel.com
dir: Nearest station: Hyde Park Corner, Green Park. On Piccadilly, overlooking Green Park

This classy Mayfair stalwart facing Green Park has a green face of its own in the form of the 'living wall', a vertical garden of lush foliage climbing 10 floors that makes it a local landmark. The interior is no less arresting, a stylish and discreet world of five-star sheen, with plenty to attract foodies - top-drawer afternoon tea, for starters, then there's a fascinating menu matching malts with artisan cheeses in the Whisky Bar, and the evening-only Pudding Parlour is paradise for fans of macaroons, tarts and proper puddings. And that's before you go for the main event in the glamorous restaurant, where plush curvaceous seating encloses glossy unclothed tables, and walls are hung with monochrome photos and even panels of mother-of-pearl buttons resembling shimmering fish scales. The kitchen deals in

confident, skilfully-crafted stuff where full-blooded taste matters more than chi-chi presentation - perhaps home-made Middlewhite pork and quail pie with tomato chutney and quail's eggs, while a hearty main course teams rump of lamb with dauphinoise potatoes, sautéed wild mushrooms, Savoy cabbage and thyme jus. To finish, it has to be Valrhona chocolate tart with salted caramel ice cream.

Chef David Marshall **Owner** Ralph Trustees Ltd
Times 12.30-2.30/5.30-10.30 **Prices** Food prices not confirmed for 2013. Please telephone for details
Wines 41 bottle over £20, 1 bottle under £20, 15 by glass
Notes All day dining menu 11am 11pm, Sunday L, Vegetarian available **Seats** 46, Pr/dining room 44
Children Portions, Menu **Parking** Close car park

Aurelia

PLAN 2 J1

◉◉ Contemporary Mediterranean **NEW**

Fashionable all-day dining inspired by the flavours of southern Europe

☎ 020 7409 1370
13-14 Cork St, Mayfair W1S 3NS
e-mail: info@aurelialondon.co.uk
dir: Nearest station: Piccadilly Circus, Green Park

The latest see-and-be-scene offering from the people behind La Petite Maison, Zuma and Roka (see entries), Aurelia is tucked away in the heart of Mayfair with pricing to match the postcode. Like its siblings, it's a class act though, serious about its food and wine and open all day from breakfast. The modern Mediterranean menu takes its inspiration from the route of the ancient Roman coastal road, Via Aurelia, reflecting the best of Italian, French and Spanish cuisines from Rome to Valencia. The fashionable sharing-plate concept delivers those sun-drenched flavours via a lengthy please-all roster. Kick off with charcuterie (jamon Iberica de Bellota, perhaps) or sobrasada (warm, spicy Mallorcan sausage with honey and walnut crostini), while pasta might include pappardelle with wild boar ragù. Larger plates - say veal cutlet Milanese or from the rotisserie, salt marsh lamb leg with anchovies and salmorigilio sauce - deliver the same skilful simplicity and quality produce. Set over two floors, the ground floor comes dominated by its bar, while in the more formal basement, the open kitchen takes centre stage.

Chef Alex Simone **Owner** Arjun Waney
Times 12-3/6-11.30 Closed Sun **Prices** Starter £5.50-£14, Main £14.50-£45, Dessert £6.50-£8, Service added but optional 12.5% **Wines** 200 bottles over £20, 12 by glass **Notes** Vegetarian available **Seats** 80 **Parking** On street

LONDON W1 *continued*

L'Autre Pied   PLAN 2 G3

®®® – *see below*

Avista   PLAN 2 G1

®® Italian

Authentic Italian cooking in Grosvenor Square

☎ 020 7596 3399 & 7629 9400
**Millennium Hotel Mayfair, 39 Grosvenor Square
W1K 2HP**
e-mail: reservations@avistarestaurant.com
dir: Nearest station: Bond Street. Located on the south
side of Grosvenor Sq, 5 min walk from Oxford St

When Michele Granziera wanted to move on from
Zafferano to set up on his own, only the best would do: as
a home to Avista, the Millennium Hotel fits the bill. It is
the very image of moneyed Mayfair elegance, although
the restaurant also has its own equally posh entrance on
Grosvenor Square. The high-gloss setting fits the swanky
postcode: marble floors, vast interstices between linen-
swathed tables, and soft-focus tones of ivory, honey and
beige. A granite-topped workstation where chefs primp
dishes in readiness for presentation adds a touch of
drama to the hushed refinement. Granziera cherry-picks
his way around the Italian repertoire, bringing together

rustic and contemporary ideas that are taken to higher
level by the sheer quality of the ingredients. In winter, a
robust fish stew of salmon, prawns and squid comes in
the hearty company of fregola and croûtons rubbed with
garlic and fresh parsley. Next up, a full-flavoured dish of
venison loin with roast polenta, quince, pears and red
wine jus, while fish could be represented by roast
monkfish with crispy Parma ham and celeriac purée.

Chef Michele Granziera **Owner** Millennium & Copthorne
Hotels **Times** 12-2.30/6-10.30 Closed 1 Jan, Sun, L Sat
Prices Fixed L 2 course £18, Fixed D 3 course £23.50,
Starter £10–£16.50, Main £11–£29, Dessert £4.20–
£10.80, Service added but optional 12.5%
Wines 130 bottles over £20, 12 by glass **Notes** Vegetarian
available **Seats** 75, Pr/dining room 12 **Children** Portions,
Menu **Parking** On street/NCP

Barrafina   PLAN 2 K2

® Spanish

Authentic casual tapas bar hitting the spot in Soho

☎ 020 7813 8016
54 Frith St W1D 4SL
e-mail: jose@barrafina.co.uk
dir: Nearest station: Tottenham Court Rd

Soho's homage to Catalonia takes the hugely appealing
form of this authentic and traditionally casual tapas bar.

An admirably democratic no-bookings policy means you
may be forced to sip a glass of Cava or a fine fino sherry
while you wait, but hey, life could be worse. Inside it is
not much more than a long L-shaped marble counter
lined with high bar stools in front of an open kitchen,
where the chefs whip up those little grazing plates in a
fun, buzzing vibe. Tapas stands or falls on the quality of
its raw materials, and here they are sourced impeccably
and treated with unfussy respect on a concise menu
bolstered by daily specials. There's top-grade charcuterie,
seafood - deep-fried soft-shelled crab or salt-cod fritters,
say, and old Iberian friends such as chorizo with potato,
and watercress and ham croquettes, or morcilla with
quail's eggs. For pudding there's classic crema Catalana
or Santiago tart, and to wash it all down, a cracking
choice of wines by the glass.

Chef Nieves Barragan **Owner** Sam & Eddie Hart
Times 12-3/5-11 Closed BHs **Prices** Food prices not
confirmed for 2013. Please telephone for details
Wines 28 bottles over £20, 2 bottles under £20, 28 by
glass **Notes** Sunday L, Vegetarian available **Seats** 23
Children Portions **Parking** On street

L'Autre Pied

Modern European V

**Compelling, creative cooking at Pied à Terre's stable
mate**

☎ 020 7486 9696
5-7 Blandford St, Marylebone Village W1U 3DB
e-mail: info@lautrepied.co.uk
dir: Nearest station: Bond St, Baker St

L'Autre Pied is just the sort of classy neighbourhood
restaurant we would all like on our manor. Just off
Marylebone High Street, in the heart of the well-heeled
and ever-fashionable 'village', the other Pied is a more
casual version of its elder sibling Pied à Terre in Fitzrovia
(see entry). It is a class act that has made its mark on its
own terms, drawing in a strong following for its
unpretentious, lively buzz, switched-on service and

stylish, French-inspired contemporary menus. Chef
Andrew McFadden took over the helm in June 2011 and
has streaked ahead with his cooking, which has the same
elegance and pedigree as the surroundings: an interior
that is effortlessly and unobtrusively modish - unclothed
rosewood tables, dark brown leather chairs, burgundy
leather banquettes, and backlit floral-patterned glass
panels and artily-textured flower motifs on the walls.
There are formulas to suit most moods and budgets - set
lunch and pre-theatre menus, carte, or a full-works
tasting menu (with the optional half-dozen wines
selected to match the dishes). Pan-fried scallops with
suckling pork belly is brought off with perfect balance
and a rare lightness of touch, pointed up with Roscoff
onions, toasted hazelnuts, and Jerusalem artichoke
velouté. Next up, roasted loin and leg of hare is matched
with carrot and star anise purée, Chantenay carrots and
pine nut jus, before a final flourish of creativity brings
things to a close with a glazed custard tart with
honeycomb, apple foam and pear sorbet. Nor are

vegetarians marginalised - there are three well-conceived
ideas at starter and main course stages.

Chef Andrew McFadden **Owner** Marcus Eaves, David
Moore **Times** 12-2.45/6-10.45 Closed 4 days Xmas, 1 Jan,
D Sun **Prices** Tasting menu £67.50, Starter £12–£15.50,
Main £25–£29, Dessert £8–£9, Service added but optional
12.5% **Wines** 10 by glass **Notes** Tasting menu 9 course,
Sunday L, Vegetarian menu **Seats** 53, Pr/dining room 15

Bar Trattoria Semplice   PLAN 2 H2

@ Italian

Reliable Italian cooking just off Oxford Street

☎ 020 7491 8638
22 Woodstock St W1C 2AR
dir: Nearest station: Bond Street

The more relaxed and casual sibling of Ristorante Semplice (see entry) is an uncluttered space of light wood furniture, red walls, candles on the tables and friendly staff. 'Semplice' describes the kitchen's output too: no-frills but spot-on cooking using quality ingredients. Pasta runs from tagliatelle with bolognese sauce to orecchiette with Italian sausage and broccoli, while the rest of the menu is a roll-call of the tried and tested. Carpaccio with rocket and parmesan, and deep-fried squid and courgettes with tartare sauce head up a carte that may go on to baby chicken diavola with sautéed new potatoes, or yellowfin tuna with caponata. Among familiar-sounding desserts may be pannacotta, perhaps flavoured with mango.

Times 12-3/6-11 Closed Xmas, New Year & BHs

Bellamy's   PLAN 2 H1

@ French

Classy brasserie just off Berkeley Square

☎ 020 7491 2727
18-18a Bruton Place W1J 6LY
e-mail: gavin@bellamysrestaurant.co.uk
dir: Nearest station: Green Park, Bond St. Off Berkeley Sq, parallel with Bruton St

A deli-cum-brasserie, Bellamy's has the sort of plush good looks of Mayfair rather than a Parisian brasserie du coin, with dark green banquettes, quality table settings and smartly dressed staff, helpful and knowledgeable, wearing white aprons. The cooking is that of a classic French brasserie, with the menu written in franglais ('guinea fowl aux morilles', for instance), and some dishes are decidedly deluxe - caviar with prices in three figures, or scrambled eggs with Périgord truffles, to a main course of poached lobster au gingembre. Treatments are generally straightforward, the kitchen driven by the quality of its materials, with humbler ingredients handled equally well: smoked eel mousse, or a salad of saucisson de Lyon, then venison sausages. Finish with rich chocolate cake.

Chef Stephane Pacoud **Owner** Gavin Rankin and Syndicate **Times** 12-3/7-10.30 Closed Xmas, New Year, BHs, Sun, L Sat **Prices** Fixed L 2 course £25, Fixed D 3 course £29.50, Starter £8-£24, Main £18-£28.50, Dessert £6.50, Service added but optional 12.5% **Wines** 62 bottles over £20, 16 by glass **Notes** Vegetarian available, Dress restrictions, No shorts for men **Seats** 70 **Children** Portions **Parking** On street, NCP

Benares Restaurant   PLAN 2 H1

@ Modern Indian V

Modern Indian at a buzzy Mayfair hotspot

☎ 020 7629 8886
12a Berkeley Square W1J 6BS
e-mail: reservations@benaresrestaurant.com
dir: Nearest station: Green Park. E along Piccadilly towards Regent St. Turn left into Berkeley St and continue straight to Berkeley Square

On oh-so refined Berkeley Square, Benares modern fine-dining restaurant offers a creative take on regional Indian cooking. Once past the doorman, you'll be escorted upstairs where smartly attired staff welcome with a salutation of 'Namaste'. There's a buzz to the place, more akin to a nightclub than a restaurant at times, but make no mistake, the food is serious stuff and if you really want to push the boat out, there's both a chef's table and sommelier's table - a glass-walled cellar dining room. Top-notch ingredients and careful spicing appear in the likes of Goan rechado-spiced mackerel with ginger and sesame chutney, Parsee salli and marinated pears, and a signature main course of spice-rubbed Romney Marsh lamb cannon with white aubergine purée and artichoke fritters.

Chef Atul Kochhar **Owner** Atul Kochhar
Times 12-2.30/5.30-11 Closed 23-26 Dec, L 27-31 Dec, Sat **Prices** Fixed L 3 course £30, Fixed D 3 course £30, Starter £13-£25, Main £26-£54, Dessert £8.50-£11, Service added but optional 12.5% **Wines** 100 bottles over £20, 17 by glass **Notes** Fixed D available until 6.30pm Tasting menu available, Sunday L, Vegetarian menu, Dress restrictions, Smart casual **Seats** 120, Pr/dining room 34

Bentley's Oyster Bar & Grill   PLAN 2 J1

@ Modern British, Seafood ⚫NOTABLE WINE LIST

Classic fish and seafood in a historic setting

☎ 020 7734 4756
11-15 Swallow St W1B 4DG
e-mail: reservations@bentleys.org
web: www.bentleys.org
dir: Nearest station: Piccadilly Circus. 2nd right after Piccadilly Circus, opposite St James Church

In 2005 Richard Corrigan took on the challenge of continuing the legacy of this grand old institution into the 21st century, and has scored a palpable hit. Bentley's has been around since 1916, occupying a Victorian Gothic building between Piccadilly and Regent Street done out with Arts and Crafts elegance - William Morris wall coverings, blue leather upholstery and wooden floors - a setting that still holds massive appeal for fish-loving foodies. Quality of produce is key here, whether you're eating bivalves in prime condition from Essex, Jersey or Galway at the marble counter of the oyster bar, or ensconced at one of the red-leather banquettes to take on lobster bisque with brandy cream, wild Cornish mussels or terrine of foie gras and smoked eel with sour apple and sorrel. Move upstairs to the Grill room, and the carte extends to main courses running from monkfish saltimbocca with morcilla, quince and black cabbage, to meatier fare such as roast saddle of rabbit with black pudding, polenta and mustard jus.

Chef Michael Lynch **Owner** Richard Corrigan
Times 12-3/6-11 Closed 25 Dec, 1 Jan, L Sat (Grill only) **Prices** Fixed L 3 course fr £24.95, Starter £8.95-£95, Main £19-£36, Dessert £4.50-£10.95, Service added but optional 12.5% **Wines** 150+ bottles over £20, 1 bottle under £20, 16 by glass **Notes** Pre-theatre 2 course £16.95, 3 course £19.95, Sunday L, Vegetarian available, Dress restrictions, Smart casual **Seats** 90, Pr/dining room 60 **Children** Menu **Parking** 10 yds away

LONDON W1 *continued*

Bocca di Lupo PLAN 2 K1

◎◎ Italian

Buzzy backstreet Italian serving up rustic regional cooking from the heart

☎ 020 7734 2223 & 7734 7128
12 Archer St W1D 7BB
e-mail: info@boccadilupo.com
web: www. boccadilupo.com
dir: Nearest station: Piccadilly Circus. Turn left off Shaftesbury Av into Gt Windmill St, then right into Archer St. Located behind the Lyric & Apollo theatres

Tucked away down a Soho side street, Bocca di Lupo is the very definition of a hidden gem. Step through the door to discover a lively, 'happening' restaurant, popular for pre- and post-theatre meals and everything in between. Perch at the marble-topped bar and graze on small sharing plates whilst watching the chefs in the open kitchen just an arm's length away, or take a seat at one of the tightly packed tables and soak up the sounds and the smells as you either go for the grazing and sharing approach, or a more conventional three courses - the daily-changing menu is all about flexibility. It feels like you could be in Milan and it is authentic Italian food from the regions that's on the menu: top-notch, seasonal ingredients are used to produce big, bold flavours in rustic dishes which are simply presented. Don't miss the 'pick and mix fried balls' - crispy, breadcrumb-coated rice balls with different fillings inside (perhaps squid ink, cuttlefish and pea, or tomato and basil with mozzarella), perfect for sharing - or the delightfully delicate gnudi (gnocchi) filled with sheep's milk ricotta and served with a rich lamb ragù. With their own gelateria across the road (Gelupo) it has to be ice cream for dessert: perhaps a brilliant take on profiteroles, with each textbook choux bun filled with a ball of ice cream (saffron, hazelnut, pistachio) and topped with chocolate sauce.

Chef Jacob Kenedy **Owner** Jacob Kenedy
Times 12.15-3.45/5.15-close Closed Xmas **Prices** Fixed L 2 course fr £50, Fixed D 3 course fr £90, Starter £7-£20, Main £7-£30, Dessert £7-£20, Service added but optional 12.5% **Notes** Sunday L, Vegetarian available **Seats** 65, Pr/dining room 32 **Children** Portions **Parking** NCP Brewer St

Cecconi's PLAN 2 J1

◎◎ Traditional Italian

Fine Italian cooking and bags of style

☎ 020 7434 1500
5a Burlington Gardens W1X 1LE
dir: Nearest station: Piccadilly Circus, Oxford Circus. Burlington Gdns between New Bond St and Savile Row

Tops for people watching and a magnet for the Mayfair beau monde, Cecconi's is a hot ticket indeed. The room has bags of style, with its black-and-white marble floor and central bar flanked by fashionable green leather high stools, with white linen-clad tables all around, and sassy blue velour Chesterfield banquettes to sink into. The service runs like clockwork and delivers the all-day menu with a good deal of charm. Whether you're up for breakfast or cichetti (Venetian tapas - chicken liver crostini, mushroom arancini and the like), to more substantial courses, it's all here without any three-course convention. Dishes of simply prepared Venetian-inspired food are the thing, driven by tip-top seasonal produce and clean flavours (albeit at Mayfair prices); expect calamari fritti and top-drawer pastas (pappardelle with lamb ragù), and veal milanese and pan-fried halibut with grilled asparagus and salsa verde.

Times 7-11.30 Closed Xmas, New Year

Chesterfield Mayfair Hotel PLAN 4 H6

◎◎ Traditional British

Cosseting luxury Mayfair style

☎ 020 7491 2622
35 Charles St, Mayfair W1J 5EB
e-mail: bookch@rchmail.com
web: www.chesterfieldmayfair.com
dir: Nearest station: Green Park. From N side exit station left & first left into Berkeley St. Continue to Berkeley Sq left towards Charles St

A well-established restaurant within a popular hotel, Butler's delivers well-judged, traditional fine dining. The Chesterfield Mayfair certainly ticks the 'elegant' box, with plenty of antiques and tactile materials maximising the luxe feel. The ground floor restaurant is suitably formal, with a daily carving trolley adding to the old-school charm of it all. There's a degree of comfort to the food, but the kitchen also spreads its wings a little. Hampshire ham hock, triple-cooked chips and a fried quail's egg is a modish starter (a poshed-up version of ham, egg and chips), followed perhaps by hickory-smoked spring chicken with Jersey Royals, morels, sweetbreads and garlic mayonnaise. Founder Bea Tollman's rice pudding with salted caramel and roasted nuts is a fine finish.

Chef Ben Kelliher **Owner** Red Carnation Hotels
Times 12-2.30/5.30-10 Closed L Sat **Prices** Fixed L 2 course £19.50, Fixed D 3 course £25.50, Starter £8.50-£17.50, Main £19.50-£39.50, Dessert £8.50-£12.50, Service added but optional 12.5% **Wines** 84 bottles over £20, 4 bottles under £20, 20 by glass **Notes** Pre-theatre menu available, Sunday L, Vegetarian available, Civ Wed 100 **Seats** 65, Pr/dining room 40 **Children** Portions, Menu **Parking** NCP 5 minutes

China Tang at The Dorchester PLAN 4 G6

◎◎ Classic Cantonese ⓘ NOTABLE WINE LIST

Glamorous Cantonese cooking in five-star Park Lane surroundings

☎ 020 7629 9988
53 Park Ln W1K 1QA
e-mail: reservations@chinatanglondon.co.uk
dir: Nearest station: Hyde Park Corner

The glittering opulence of The Dorchester's Chinese restaurant was conceived with the glamour of colonial-era Shanghai in mind. Chinoiserie is naturally the name of the game, set against a backdrop of contemporary fish-themed Asian art and fabulous art-deco mirrored columns. The cooking toes the classic Cantonese party line, although the sheer quality of the produce ramps up the menu of familiar dishes and dim sum to a higher plane. Naturally in this setting, luxuries are liberally sprinkled around but you don't have to break the bank - pork satay makes a punchy starter, then you might follow with salt-and-pepper squid, Peking duck or join the high rollers with braised abalone with oyster sauce. Desserts are not usually a strong point in cuisine of this ethnicity, so it is rewarding to end strongly with an inspired pairing of poached plums with Chinese almond mousse.

Chef Chong Choi Fong **Owner** Sir David Tang **Times** 12-12 Closed 25 Dec **Prices** Fixed L 2 course £23, Service added but optional 12.5% **Wines** 512 bottles over £20, 5 bottles under £20, 12 by glass **Notes** Set L £23 including glass wine 12-3.30pm, Vegetarian available, Dress restrictions, Smart casual **Seats** 120, Pr/dining room 80 **Children** Portions

Cielo PLAN 2 J1

◎◎ Modern Italian

Upbeat setting and good Italian food

☎ 020 7297 2893
3 New Burlington St W1S 2JF
e-mail: info@luxx-london.com
dir: Nearest station: Oxford Circus

Located in the heart of Mayfair, Cielo is a trendy and glamorous venue, successfully combining a contemporary Italian restaurant with a cool cocktail lounge and buzzy nightclub. So, if you fancy sipping a few cocktails before sitting down to a fairly late dinner (the kitchen doesn't start serving until 8pm) and then dancing the night away, then Cielo is the perfect place for you. The food is top-notch Italian, with head chef Claudio Illuminati serving up such well-constructed and imaginative dishes as linguini with lobster and tomato, duck breast with black cabbage and spiced pear, venison with pink pepper, milk polenta and trevisano radish, and sea bass with spinach, artichoke and parsley sauce, with vanilla and coffee pannacotta among the puddings. The place has a nightclubby vibe and there's also a retractable roof in the bar for summer cocktails under the stars.

Times 7-11 Closed 25 Dec, Sun-Mon, L all wk

C London
PLAN 2 H1

® ® Italian

Venetian elegance in Mayfair

☎ 020 7399 0500
25 Davies St W1E 3DE
e-mail: london@crestaurant.co.uk
dir: Nearest station: Bond Street

Hugely charismatic and beloved by the glitterati, C London (formerly Cipriani) is the sibling restaurant to the famous Harry's Bar in Venice. A modern glass frontage and revolving door leads to the large, swish dining room and small bar, where meeter-greeters commence the charm offensive. There's plenty of air-kissing and people watching, while a Bellini at either bar or table is almost a requisite. Impeccable art-deco style meets beautiful Murano glass chandeliers, while an army of white-

jacketed staff deliver slick service. The straightforward, classic Italian cooking - driven by top-notch ingredients - is the real deal. Think veal cannelloni or perhaps calves' liver with polenta, while the dessert 'selection of cakes' might include triple layer chocolate cake. Factor in a buzzy atmosphere, 15% service and high prices.

Times 12-3/6-11.45 Closed 25 Dec

Cocochan
PLAN 2 G2

® Chinese, Japanese

Pan-Asian fusion cooking in chic West End venue

☎ 020 7486 1000
38-40 James St, Marylebone W1U 1EU
e-mail: info@cocochan.co.uk
web: www.cocochan.co.uk
dir: Nearest station: Bond Street

When you need to take the weight off your feet after a session of retail therapy in Selfridge's and Oxford Street,

Cocochan delivers eye-catching modernism in the form of involving metallic and mirrored latticework on the walls, and pure white or black bamboo tables. On the culinary front, the kitchen sends out quality Pan-Asian fusion cuisine on a broad-ranging menu inspired by cultures as diverse as China, Korea, Japan, all the way to South-East Asian staples from Thailand, Vietnam and Indonesia, and throws up-to-date techniques such as sous-vide cooking as well as traditional steaming and grilling into the mix. You might graze your way into things via dim sum, say black cod and chilli bean dumplings, or Vietnamese seared beef salad with nuoc cham; elsewhere, Japanese sushi such as soft-shelled crab futo maki might catch the eye. More substantial mains could bring chargrilled Bulgogi strip loin with wasabi jus, or sea bass baked in a banana leaf with jungle sauce.

Chef Syarlef Fachri **Owner** Ilrag Darakjian **Times** noon-5/5-mdnt Closed 25 Dec, 1 Jan **Prices** Starter £3.50-£22.50, Main £11-£30, Dessert £4.50-£8, Service added but optional 12.5% **Wines** 51 bottles over £20, 10 by glass **Notes** Sharing menu group 10 £30-£65, Bento box L min £13.50, Sunday L, Vegetarian available **Seats** 80, Pr/dining room 35 **Parking** On street

Corrigan's Mayfair
PLAN 2 G1

® ® ® – see below

Corrigan's Mayfair

LONDON W1   **PLAN 2 G1**

Modern British, Irish V 🍷NOTABLE WINE LIST

Finely crafted gutsy cuisine in a (sort of) German hunting lodge

☎ 020 7499 9943
28 Upper Grosvenor St W1K 7EH
e-mail: reservations@corrigansmayfair.com
web: www.corrigansmayfair.com
dir: Nearest station: Marble Arch. Off Park Ln, main entrance via Upper Grosvenor St

Richard Corrigan's odyssey around central London in recent years has been one of the more productive trajectories of any among those we might fairly consider the big-name chefs. His winning formula has always been an honest-to-goodness gutsiness and robustness, allied to the techniques of haute cuisine, but producing a creative amalgam that doesn't just feel like the culinary version of slumming it. Humble everyday ingredients juxtaposed with top-drawer stuff has been a

signature, as has the desire, fainter now to be sure, to meld in Irish food traditions. In fact, a German hunting lodge is the imaginary mise en scène for the present Corrigan address, albeit one that has been airlifted to a spot just off Park Lane, and done out in handsome slate-grey with plenty of burnished mirrors and the crispest of table napery. Wild boar, feathered game and venison find their way plentifully on to the menus in season, and when it isn't the season, a meal might kick off with generously stuffed crab ravioli with monk's beard in a cardamom-scented crab sauce, or a serving of Spain's Teruel ham with apple and rhubarb jelly. Fish cookery has always been a strong suit of Corrigan's, as is seen in the earthiness of a main course of brill poached in red wine, garnished with chopped razor clam, mussels and shrimps, on a chunky underlay of cabbage, carrot and bacon, while meats add bone marrow and onion rings to slow-cooked beef short rib, or give roasted squab the currently fashionable Indian treatment, in this case a kind of rogan josh. Dessert can be ethereally light, perhaps a pear and lime panncotta with yoghurt sorbet, decorated with tiny profiteroles lashed together with caramel, or else get stuck into a wodge of warm carrot cake with walnuts and honey ice cream.

Chef Richard Corrigan, Chris McGowan **Owner** Richard Corrigan Restaurants Ltd **Times** 12-2.30/6-11 Closed 23-27 Dec, L Sat **Prices** Fixed L 3 course £27, Starter £9-£24, Main £23-£42, Dessert £9-£12, Service added but optional 12.5% **Wines** 400 bottles over £20, 4 bottles under £20, 12 by glass **Notes** Tasting menu 6 course, Chef's table available, Sunday L, Vegetarian menu, Dress restrictions, Smart casual **Seats** 85, Pr/dining room 30 **Children** Portions **Parking** On street

LONDON W1 *continued*

Criterion

PLAN 2 K1

Modern European **NEW**

Spectacularly impressive room with passionate team in the kitchen

☎ 020 7930 0488
224 Piccadilly W1J 9HP
e-mail: reservations@criterionrestaurant.com
dir: Nearest station: Piccadilly Circus. Next to Eros statue

The Criterion's unique interior never fails to impress with its magnificent Byzantine opulence: all soaring arches to high ceilings, mosaics, mirrors, gold and marble. The kitchen's a busy place, making bread and pasta (pappardelle with sautéed wild mushrooms, say), smoking fish - salmon and eel in a starter with horseradish mousse - and even churning its own butter. Treatments vary from roasting (rack of lamb with aubergine purée, fondant potato and carrots) to poaching (cod with brown shrimps and caviar accompanied by Jerusalem artichokes and spinach) and the results are appreciated for their accurate seasoning and timing. A grounding in the classical repertoire is evident too, from moules marinière to crème brûlée.

Chef Matthew Foxon **Owner** Mr I Sopromadze
Times 12-2.30/5.30-11.30 **Prices** Fixed L 2 course £19, Starter £8-£15.50, Main £18-£32, Dessert £8-£9.50, Service added but optional 12.5%, Groups min 11 service 12.5% **Wines** 150 bottles over £20, 13 by glass **Notes** Fixed 2,3 course also available 5.30-7pm & 10-11.30pm, Sunday L, Vegetarian available, Civ Wed 70 **Seats** 104 **Children** Portions **Parking** Brewer Street

CUT at 45 Park Lane

PLAN 4 G6

⊛⊛⊛ – *see opposite*

Dabbous

PLAN 4 G6

⊛⊛⊛ – *see opposite*

Degò

PLAN 2 J2

⊛⊛ Modern Italian

New-wave Italian cooking near Oxford Street

☎ 020 7636 2207
4 Great Portland St W1W 8QJ
e-mail: info@degowinebar.co.uk
web: www.degowinebar.co.uk
dir: Nearest station: Oxford Circus. From Oxford Circus Tube enter Great Portland St, then first right

Degò has been vividly designed around the theme of 'the power of red', to use the restaurant's own phrase, a décor that certainly adds a theatrical feel to this combination of wine bar (ground floor) and restaurant (basement) near the throng of Oxford Street. The kitchen re-creates dishes from around Italy in a modern, even new-wave style, marinating salmon in lavender and mint and serving it with broccoli and chive yoghurt, for instance.

Home-made pasta gets a strong showing - Vicenzan-style bigoli with duck ragù, say - and experimentation pays off, resulting in some unusual but successful combinations: duck breast glazed with red and black pepper, served with frangipane potatoes and beans, and partnering grilled sea bass fillet with fennel and caramel velouté and broccoli. If veal milanese with balsamic-dressed salad and grilled radicchio seems subdued in comparison, finish with an inspired pudding like dark chocolate ravioli with coconut, pineapple and rum sauce.

Chef Massimo Mioli **Owner** Massimo Mioli
Times 12-3.30/6-11.30 Closed Xmas, Etr, Sun
Prices Food prices not confirmed for 2013. Please telephone for details **Wines** 36 bottles over £20, 4 bottles under £20, 10 by glass **Notes** Pre-theatre & tasting menus available, Vegetarian available, Dress restrictions, Smart casual, Air con **Seats** 45, Pr/dining room 15 **Children** Portions

Dehesa

PLAN 2 J1

⊛ Spanish, Italian

First-rate tapas in Soho

☎ 020 7494 4170
25 Ganton St W1F 9BP
e-mail: info@dehesa.co.uk
dir: Nearest station: Oxford Circus. Close to station, half way along Carnaby St on corner of Ganton & Kingly St

Dehesa comes from the same stable as Salt Yard and Opera Tavern (see entries) and, like them, is a charcuterie and tapas bar dedicated to the cuisines of Spain and Italy. It's a small place and it's easy to see why it gets so busy: quality ingredients are handled professionally, following authentic recipes, to bring the flavours of those two countries to life in London. Bar snacks of house-cured duck breast, or jamón ibérico, with a glass of fino make pleasing partners, or select from the full list of unfussy hot and cold dishes. Venetian-style sardines with sautéed onions, sultanas and pine nuts, and piquant salt-cod croquettes with sauce romesco are among the fish options, with tender confit pork belly with rosemary-scented cannellini beans, and fried lamb cutlet with broad beans, chilli and mint among the meat. You might not need extra vegetables like patatas fritas, but leave room for tempting puddings like chocolate cake with cappuccino ice cream.

Chef Giancarlo Vatteroni **Owner** Simon Mullins, Sanja Morris **Times** 12-3/5-11 Closed 10 days (Xmas & New Year), D Sun, BHs **Prices** Food prices not confirmed for 2013. Please telephone for details **Wines** 59 bottles over £20, 4 bottles under £20, 11 by glass **Notes** Sunday L, Vegetarian available **Seats** 40, Pr/dining room 12 **Parking** NCP

Dinings

PLAN 2 E3

⊛⊛ Japanese, European

Pint-sized basement room doing dazzling Japanese tapas

☎ 020 7723 0666
22 Harcourt St W1H 4HH
dir: Nearest station: Edgware Rd

Since opening in 2007, Dinings has subtly morphed from a traditional izakaya restaurant to a more east-meets-west concept, in which little Japanese tapas dishes are overlaid with the influences of modern European cuisine. This has been one of Asian gastronomy's most productive strands in recent years, especially in London, where a city-chic clientele packs the pint-sized basement room here to be led through the hot, sour, sweet and savoury spectrum. The tapas tasters embrace a range from grilled aubergine in sweet miso to sizzling scallops in yuzu, garlic, chilli and soy, and chargrilled duck breast in shiso salsa and ponzu sauce, but if you're in the market for something more instantly substantial, there are Wagyu beef or rack of lamb with winter veg. European borrowings are in evidence in white fish carpaccio with fresh truffle, or the sushi roll that combines eel and foie gras. Sushi and sashimi themselves are spanking-fresh, and to conclude, tea-flavoured desserts are the way to go.

Chef Masaki Sugisaki, Ketjt Fuku **Owner** Tomonari Chiba, Masaki Sugisaki **Times** 12-2.30/6-10.30 Closed Xmas, 31 Dec-1 Jan, Sun, L Sat **Prices** Starter £3.80-£19.85, Main £9.20-£47.60, Dessert £4.50-£6.95, Service added but optional 11.5% **Wines** 25 bottles over £20, 1 bottle under £20, 8 by glass **Notes** Fixed L menu available, Vegetarian available **Seats** 28 **Parking** On street & NCP

Dolada

PLAN 2 J1

⊛⊛ Italian

New-wave Italian cooking in stylish Mayfair basement

☎ 020 7409 1011
13 Albemarle St W1S 4HJ
e-mail: manager@dolada.co.uk
dir: Nearest station: Green Park

Secreted away below the DKNY store opposite Browns Hotel, this smart Italian restaurant, formerly known as Mosaico, has frieze-style mirrors, burgundy leather banquettes, limestone floors and contemporary artwork and lighting to overcome its basement location. And it looks good. Chef-patron Riccardo da Pra comes from fine culinary stock - his family own the upscale Ristorante Albergo Dolada in the Veneto - and he's making a name for himself in London with his technically adroit modern cooking. Expect a succession of striking flavours and creatively presented dishes, based on first-class ingredients. A starter of aubergine and goats' cheese ravioli with almonds and tomatoes, for example, or Maltagliati pasta with hare ragù, while a 'Venetian tempura' (seafood, fish and vegetables) references the chef's time in Japan. It's a classy place with a fixed-price lunch offering a good value entry point.

Times 12-2.30/6.30-10.45 Closed Sun, L Sat, Xmas, Etr, BHs

CUT at 45 Park Lane

LONDON W1   **PLAN 4 G6**

Modern American **NEW**

Stunning steaks from Wolfgang Puck

☎ 020 7493 4545
45 Park Ln W1K 1BJ
e-mail: restaurants45L@dorchestercollection.com
dir: Nearest station: Hyde Park Corner. Park Lane, near
The Dorchester

If Wolfgang Puck is not yet a household name in the UK,
this Austrian chef and entrepreneur is a big fish in the
US, and it was Hollywood where he made his name,
helping to define Californian cuisine - you might have
heard of Spago. And now he runs a whole bunch of places
around the world, including several under the CUT
banner, but this is his first in Europe. CUT focuses on
prime beef. Given pride of place in the 45 Park Lane

hotel, needless to say it doesn't look like your typical
steakhouse (this is Park Lane after all); the long, narrow
room is done out with mellow wood panelling, rich leather
seating, striking modish chandeliers and shimmering
curtains, all in colours chosen from today's favoured
neutral and natural colour palette. There is much other
than beef on the menu and it's all good (as they say in
the US of A), so start, perhaps, with big eye tuna tartar
with wasabi aïoli and togarashi crisps, followed by
broiled (to use the American vernacular) miso-glazed
Scottish salmon with sautéed garlic spinach. But CUT is
about steak and they are very, very good: go for USDA
prime Black Angus perhaps, from Creekstone Farms in
Kansas (aged for 35 days), the rib-eye a superbly tender,
powerfully flavoured piece of beef (served with excellent
French fries and tempura onion rings); or Casterbridge
Angus from Devon; or push the boat out for Wagyu.
There's a range of cuts in the American style, plenty of
sauces to choose from (Argentinean chimichurri, for
example), and the attention to detail throughout extends

to excellent desserts such as banana cream pie. Note to
self: it is expensive

Chef David McIntyre **Owner** Dorchester Collection
Times 12-2.30/6-10.45 **Prices** Fixed L 3 course £55,
Starter £9-£23, Main £21-£86, Dessert £9.50, Service
added 12.5% **Wines** 600 bottles over £20, 25 by glass
Notes Sunday L, Vegetarian available, Dress restrictions,
Smart casual, Civ Wed 60 **Seats** 70 **Parking** Valet parking

Dabbous

LONDON W1   **PLAN 4 G6**

British **NEW**

Highly innovative cooking in Fitzrovia

☎ 020 7323 1544
39 Whitfield St, Fitzrovia W1T 2SF
dir: Nearest station: Goodge Street

One-time head chef of Texture (see entry), Ollie Dabbous's
first solo restaurant - just off Goodge Street - has hit the
ground running. Set over two floors with a basement bar
and small street-level dining room, it comes decked out
in voguish utilitarian, industrial style; we're talking
pared-back, designer-distress. That amounts to concrete,
bare brick, sheet metal, exposed piping, and closely-set
wooden tables and dangling light bulbs. The cooking
shows a light, fresh, modern approach, serving up
fashionable smaller plates of highly innovative, well-

dressed food. It is fine-tuned cooking driven by top-notch
seasonal produce, including lots of wild ingredients,
clean flavours, interesting combinations and lovely
textures and colours. But this is a chef who knows how
far to push the envelope - there's nothing over
complicated here, with flavours given room to breathe.
Cream and butter are used with a light touch and it all
comes at unintimidating prices. Excellent bread arrives in
a brown paper bag, before a dish of mixed alliums in a
wonderful chilled pine infusion. Next up, barbecued
Iberico pork appears in an inspired dish with savoury
acorn praline, turnip tops and home-made apple vinegar,
or go for charred salmon with elderflower, spring onions
and almonds. Iced lovage or chocolate and virgin
hazelnut oil ganache teamed with basil moss and sheep's
milk ice cream, maintain the creative energy to the end.
It's a popular place, so book well in advance.

Chef Ollie Dabbous **Times** 12-3/5.30-11.30 Closed Sun,
Mon **Prices** Fixed L 2 course £21, Starter £5-£8, Main
£12-£14, Dessert £4-£9

LONDON W1 *continued*

L'Escargot - The Ground Floor Restaurant
PLAN 3 A2

@@ British, French

Soho grandee delivering accomplished French bistro fare

☎ 020 7439 7474
48 Greek St W1D 4EF
e-mail: sales@lescargotrestaurant.co.uk
web: www.lescargotrestaurant.co.uk
dir: Nearest station: Tottenham Court Rd/Leicester Square

The legendary 'snail ' of Soho has been on the scene since 1927, and if that venerable pedigree isn't enough to impress you, the remarkable collection of signed art by the likes of Miró, Chagall, Warhol, Hockney and Matisse should seal the deal. The eternally buzzing ground-floor bistro of this classy townhouse interior was reworked by designer du jour David Collins for a retro look blending cut-glass mirrors and elegant art nouveau lighting with contemporary neutral tones. The kitchen keeps the extrovert crowd of Soho types happy with modishly tweaked French bistro cooking, while on-the-ball French-accented service sets a suitably Gallic tone for reinvented classic ideas along the lines of sautéed frogs' legs with truffle croquette, parsley velouté and garlic purée. Mains could take in roast guinea fowl à la forestière with baby leeks and tarragon velouté, or black bass fillet with Swiss chard, salsify purée and beurre blanc sauce. Bow out with a French finale - tarte au citron with lemon sorbet, or Valrhona chocolate fondant with milk ice cream.

Chef Danny MacGechan **Owner** Jimmy Lahoud
Times 12-2.30/5.30-11.30 Closed 25-26 Dec, 1 Jan, Sun, L Sat **Prices** Fixed L 2 course £15-£16.50, Fixed D 3 course £18-£19.50, Starter £7.50-£14, Main £14-£30, Dessert £7.50-£8, Service added but optional 12.5% **Wines** 275 bottles over £20, 6 bottles under £20, 8 by glass **Notes** Fixed D 2/3 course available pre-theatre only,

Vegetarian available **Seats** 80, Pr/dining room 60 **Children** Portions **Parking** NCP Chinatown, on street parking

Fino
PLAN 2 J3

@@ Spanish

Top-notch tapas in buzzy, chic basement

☎ 020 7813 8010
33 Charlotte St W1T 1RR
e-mail: info@finorestaurant.com
dir: Nearest station: Goodge St/Tottenham Court Rd. Entrance on Rathbone St

Down an anonymous side-street off trendy Charlotte Street lurks this vibrant, classy tapas restaurant with bags of appeal. It is a cavernous basement room, understatedly cool, and positively throbs with a happy hum when on full throttle. Grab a high stool at the long marble-topped bar fronting the semi-open kitchen, or sit on comfy leather banquettes or rattan-backed chairs at well-spaced pale-wood tables. Orchid displays and slick service add further polish. From twice daily-changing menus, the kitchen serves stellar tapas for grazing, blending the traditional and inventive with top-drawer ingredients. Thus ham croquettas and Spanish meat platters sit alongside seafood cooked on an authentic Spanish plancha (squid wrapped in pancetta with its ink), and among the selection of tortilla is a black pudding number. Seasonal specials could feature red mullet served with new potatoes and tapenade, while to finish is a signature almondy Santiago tart. Fine sherries and an all-Spanish wine list raise the bar still further, plus there's a stand-alone cocktail bar. (See also popular sibling Soho outfits Barrafina and Quo Vadis.)

Chef Nieves Barragan Mohacho **Owner** Sam & Eddie Hart **Times** 12-2.30/6-10.30 Closed Xmas, BHs, Sun, L Sat **Prices** Starter £6.50-£18.50, Main £9.50-£28, Dessert £4.50-£7.50, Service added but optional 12.5% **Wines** 118 bottles over £20, 7 bottles under £20, 9 by glass **Notes** Vegetarian available **Seats** 90 **Children** Portions

Four Seasons Hotel London
PLAN 4 G6

@@ Italian V

Innovative Italian cooking in red-and-black splendour

☎ 020 7499 0888
Hamilton Place, Park Ln W1J 7DR
e-mail: reservations.lon@fourseasons.com
dir: Nearest station: Green Park, Hyde Park Corner. Hamilton Place, just off Hyde Park Corner end of Park Lane

A dramatic reworking of the interior of the grand old Four Seasons by Hyde Park Corner in 2011 has given the place an unapologetically opulent look. The Amaranto concept comprises an interlinked bar, lounge and restaurant involving mirror-shined black marble flooring as a foil to deep-pile carpets, onyx and burnished darkwood tabletops, abstract artworks, and theatrical hues of blood-red and jet-black, as well as a light-flooded conservatory and alfresco terrace. The cooking offers a nuova cucina take on Italian dishes using authentic Italian ingredients driven by flavour combinations that are more in line with a contemporary idiom. Antipasti such as beef carpaccio with aged parmesan mousse, Jerusalem artichoke, almonds, celeriac, and green apple chutney show the style, before moving into the realms of black truffle ravioli with Tuscan pecorino sabayon or roast loin of venison with Swiss chard gratin and fontina cheese, celeriac foam, forest berries and dark chocolate-scented jus.

Chef Davide Degiovanni **Owner** Four Seasons Hotels & Resorts **Times** 12-2/6-10.30 **Prices** Fixed L 2 course £22-£30, Tasting menu £95, Starter £9-£15, Main £15-£30, Service added but optional 15% **Wines** 290 bottles over £20, 18 by glass **Notes** Tasting menu 6 course, Allegro £26, Pre-theatre D £19.50, Sunday L, Vegetarian menu, Civ Wed 500 **Seats** 82, Pr/dining room 8 **Children** Portions, Menu **Parking** 10

Galvin at Windows Restaurant & Bar
PLAN 4 G6

@@@ – *see opposite*

Galvin at Windows Restaurant & Bar

LONDON W1 PLAN 4 G6

French

Fabulous views with food to match

☎ 020 7208 4021
London Hilton on Park Ln, 22 Park Ln W1K 1BE
e-mail: reservations@galvinatwindows.com
dir: Nearest station: Green Park/Hyde Park Corner. On
Park Lane, opposite Hyde Park

The view from up on the 28th floor is the Koh-i-Noor
diamond of vistas - it doesn't get any better. And the
cleverly split-level space that makes up the Galvin
brothers' flagship restaurant guarantees no one leaves
feeling short changed. With more than a touch of art-
deco allure to the design, Windows has to be one of the
most glamorous addresses in town. The service rises to
the occasion - the impeccable and engaging team do not

miss a beat. André Garrett is a fine exponent of the Galvin
brothers' favoured style of modern French cooking, which
is refined without being overworked, creative without
being overwrought, and built on high quality ingredients.
Thus a risotto of wild mushrooms is spiked with pickled
walnuts and topped with a delightful aged pecorino
emulsion, and a touch of chocolate is added to the sauce
grand veneur which accompanies a stunning venison
saddle (from the South West of England), served with
smoked pommes purée, salt-baked beetroot and
guanciale (an un-smoked Italian bacon). Royal Gala
apples might get the tarte Tatin treatment amongst
desserts, or go for a Manjari chocolate ganache with
candy and popcorn ice cream. There's a menu
degustation (with optional wine flight) and a set lunch
with its own mini wine flight (two glasses, so more take
off and landing). If the bottle prices on the high-flying
wine list cause you to shiver, there's a decent selection by
the glass to see you through.

Chef André Garrett **Owner** Hilton International
Times 12-2.30/6-10.30 Closed BHs, 26 Dec, 9 Apr, 7 May,
L Sat, D Sun, 25 Dec **Prices** Fixed L 2 course fr £25, Fixed
D 3 course fr £65, Tasting menu £95, Service added but
optional 12.5% **Wines** 284 bottles over £20, 5 bottles
under £20, 31 by glass **Notes** Tasting menu 6 course,
Dégustation menu available, Sunday L, Vegetarian
available, Dress restrictions, Smart casual **Seats** 105
Children Portions, Menu **Parking** NCP

Gauthier Soho

LONDON W1 PLAN 3 A1

French V

French culinary flair in the heart of Soho

☎ 020 7494 3111
21 Romilly St W1D 5AF
e-mail: info@gauthiersoho.co.uk
dir: Nearest station: Leicester Square. Just off
Shaftesbury Avenue, off Dean Street

The change of neighbourhood from genteel Pimlico, where
he delivered polished Gallic flair at Roussillon, to lairy
Soho must have been a shock to the system, but Alexis
Gauthier has established a bastion of calm refinement in
a discreet Georgian townhouse. The need to ring the
doorbell to gain access confers a certain exclusivity, and
once inside, lofty ceilings, an ornate marble fireplace,
snow white walls and linen, and beige leather seats all

contribute to the impression of quiet, understated
elegance. It's all rather hushed, but that is no bad thing
in such an intimate space, and while service is slick and
well-coordinated, staff get quite a workout running up
and down stairs in this multi-level venue. Gauthier's
modus operandi is cooking by instinct and intuition,
learned under his mentor, the French super-chef Alain
Ducasse, and it is an approach that results in subtle
contemporary French dishes as impeccably designed and
executed as a Dior suit. There are various routes in to the
creative repertoire: a remarkably good value lunch and
pre-theatre menu, the full works tasting schtick,
including an inventive vegetable-based version, or a
flexible three, four or five-course format with three
choices at each stage. A wild garlic risotto with snails
and an intense chicken jus hits all the right notes, and
you might follow that with a fish course - wild sea bass
roasted in brown butter and partnered with toasted
salsify, sautéed Cos lettuce, and morel velouté - then
continue with a meaty idea such as braised shoulder and

pink cannon of Welsh lamb with chanterelles, braised
Swiss chard, pommes fondant, and lamb, lemon and
thyme jus. The signature dessert, a 'Golden Louis XV', is a
glossy chocolate dome filled with chocolate mousse on a
praline base. If such things prey on your mind, the menu
gives a calorie count for each dish, and the wine list is
packed with fascinating stuff with France, naturellment,
playing a starring rôle.

Chef Gerard Virolle, Alexis Gauthier **Owner** Alexis Gauthier
Times 12-2.30/5.30-10.30 Closed Xmas, BHs, Sun
Prices Fixed L 2 course fr £18, Fixed D 3 course fr £40,
Service added but optional 12.5%, Groups min 8 service
15% **Wines** 200+ bottles over £20, 2 bottles under £20,
20 by glass **Notes** ALC Fixed L/D menu, Vegetarian menu,
Dress restrictions, Smart casual, no trainers **Seats** 60, Pr/
dining room 32 **Children** Portions **Parking** On street, NCP
Chinatown

Le Gavroche Restaurant

LONDON W1   **PLAN 2 G1**

French 🌸 NOTABLE WINE LIST

Pure class from top to bottom

☎ 020 7408 0881
43 Upper Brook St W1K 7QR
e-mail: bookings@le-gavroche.com
dir: Nearest station: Marble Arch. From Park Lane into
Upper Brook St, restaurant on right

The Catherine Deneuve of the restaurant world, Le Gavroche
is a grande dame that may be getting on a bit, having been
a stalwart of the Mayfair celeb dining scene since 1967,
but still goes about its business with a style and flair that
many wannabes aspire to but never quite achieve. You
have to hit the rewind button to put this phenomenon in its
true context: in the swinging '60s, Le Gavroche was in the
vanguard of aspirational dining that introduced us to the
exoticism of top-end French haute cuisine when most of the
UK thought living the high life meant prawn cocktails and

steak and chips; over four decades on, its attractions have
stood the test of time. The street level bar is a timelessly
plush gaff for an aperitif before descending to the rich
green and red-hued basement dining room, which manages
to stay looking glamorous despite a lack of natural light.
The chances are that unless you're a card-carrying member
of the glitterati, you're probably here on a special occasion,
and the supremely professional front-of-house team won't
let you down with their courteous, well-informed
orchestration of proceedings. Michel Roux Jnr took over the
kitchen from his father and uncle in 1991, and while he
didn't rock the boat, the cooking isn't all Escoffier
preserved in aspic. There are lighter contemporary ideas
- roast scallops with pumpkin, almonds and wild
mushrooms, say, followed by John Dory with sweet turnip
purée, wild rice and chorizo sauce, and while the
competition plays with foams, gels, powders and dusts,
here you can still open with classics - the legendary soufflé
Suissesse, or émincé de veau, wafer thin Parma ham-style
cooked belly of veal, served with a rich and creamy goats'
cheese risotto. The menu is helpfully bilingual for those

who don't have fluent command of French culinary
terminology, so we learn that gratin de merlu à la Viennoise
is hake topped with butter-fried golden breadcrumbs and
served with a spot-on hollandaise sauce and brunoise of
vegetables. Meatier ideas run to roast saddle of rabbit with
crispy potato galette and parmesan. Desserts, such as
pineapple roasted with vanilla and rum and served with
white pepper ice cream, are defined by peerless technique,
and the wine list is in a league of its own for those with the
means to access its aristocratic bottles. Prices on the carte
are high, but the set lunch, including half a bottle of wine
per person is a good deal.

Chef Michel Roux Jnr **Owner** Le Gavroche Ltd
Times 12-2/6.30-11 Closed Xmas, New Year, BHs, Sun, L
Sat **Prices** Fixed L 3 course fr £53, Service added but
optional 12.5% **Wines** 2000 bottles over £20, 21 bottles
under £20, 20 by glass **Notes** Fixed L 3 course, Tasting
menu 8 course, Vegetarian available, Dress restrictions,
Smart casual, jacket req, no jeans/trainers **Seats** 60
Children Portions **Parking** NCP - Park Lane

Gordon Ramsay at Claridge's

LONDON W1   **PLAN 2 H1**

Modern, Traditional V 🌸 NOTABLE WINE LIST

Art-deco institution with classy, confident cooking

☎ 020 7499 0099
Brook St W1K 4HR
e-mail: reservations@gordonramsay.com
dir: Nearest station: Bond Street, Green Park

In a world that never stays still for long, Claridge's is a
bastion of unchanging glamour. But that's not to say it is
stuck in a Rule Britannia time warp: the flag of Gordon
Ramsay Holdings has flown above the hallowed portals of
its restaurant for over a decade, and while the opulence
of its original art-deco features remain unsullied, it was
subjected to a lavish reworking by New York designer and
architect Thierry Despont, using statement pagoda-like
lightshades, burgundy-hued chairs, etched glass panels

and gold and toffee hued walls to add 21st-century
pizzazz to the 1930s look. A regiment of well-drilled staff
add further polish to the upscale package you'd expect in
this sort of destination dining venue, while a crack
kitchen brigade delivers the consummate contemporary
cooking that is synonymous with the Ramsay brand.
Founded in French classicism and backed by top-level
technical knowhow applied to materials of peerless
quality, the results are never less than highly impressive.
If you're after value for money - yes vfm, in Claridge's -
the set lunch is a steal for cooking at this level, otherwise
an assault on the carte yields juicy langoustines wrapped
in wafer-thin ventrèche bacon and fresh sage leaf atop
Cornish crab and spring onion risotto, or perhaps the
luxury of sautéed scallops with cauliflower, champagne
and Sevruga caviar. Next out, roast breast and confit leg
of duck is deeply flavoured and matched with roasted red
onion and sauce soubise, while fish might show up in the
guise of pan-fried John Dory with pommes boulangère,
braised cucumber, confit garlic and pan juices. Puddings

can be as showy as dark chocolate with a honeycomb
sphere and milk chocolate sauce, or as homespun as
custard tart with champagne rhubarb ice cream. The
wine list promises excitement and outstanding producers
and vintages for those on good terms with the bank
manager.

Chef Luke Rayment **Owner** Gordon Ramsay Holdings Ltd
Times 12-2.45/5.45-11 **Prices** Fixed L 3 course fr £30,
Service added but optional 12.5% **Wines** 900 bottles over
£20 **Notes** ALC 3 course £70, Prestige 5 course £80,
Tasting menu L, Vegetarian menu, Dress restrictions,
Smart **Seats** 150 **Children** Portions **Parking** Mayfair NCP

Save on Hotels. Book at **theAA.com/hotel**

LONDON, CENTRAL (W1) 319 **ENGLAND**

LONDON W1 *continued*

Galvin Bistrot de Luxe
PLAN 2 G3

◎◎ French NOTABLE WINE LIST

Well-crafted French cooking in stylish bistro

☎ 020 7935 4007
66 Baker St W1U 7DJ
e-mail: reservations@galvinrestaurants.com
dir: Nearest station: Baker Street. 5 min walk from Baker St station, on left near Dorset St

The appeal of a Parisian-style bistro has never waned, judging by the success of the Galvin brothers' faithful re-creation on Baker Street. It certainly looks the part, with bentwood chairs and banquettes at crisply-clothed tables, ball lights, and attentive white-aproned staff adding to the bustle. The menu is pitched just right too offering exceptionally well-executed bistro classics of escargots bourguignon and steak tartare before crisp-skinned, rich duck confit, and daube de boeuf provençale. A fish option might be spot-on pavé of cod with leek and potato fondue and Avruga caviar. Some dishes come from beyond France's frontier - perhaps lamb tagine with harissa and couscous - but desserts return to the fold, among them tarte Tatin and orange soufflé with chocolate and Grand Marnier sauce.

Chef Chris Galvin, Luigi Vespero **Owner** Chris & Jeff Galvin, Ken Sanker **Times** 12-2.30/6-10.30 Closed 25-26 Dec, 1 Jan, D 24 Dec **Prices** Fixed L 3 course fr £19.50, Fixed D 3 course fr £21.50, Starter £7.50-£12.50, Main £15.50-£20, Dessert £6.50-£8.50, Service added but optional 12.5% **Wines** 163 bottles over £20, 3 bottles under £20, 18 by glass **Notes** Fixed D 3 course available 6-7pm, Sunday L, Vegetarian available **Seats** 106, Pr/dining room 22 **Children** Portions **Parking** On street, NCP

Gauthier Soho
PLAN 3 A1

◎◎◎ *– see page 317*

Le Gavroche Restaurant
PLAN 2 G1

◎◎◎ *– see opposite*

Goodman
PLAN 2 J1

◎ American NOTABLE WINE LIST ◎

Top-quality steaks in New York-style steakhouse

☎ 020 7499 3776
26 Maddox St W1S 1QH
e-mail: daniela@goodmanrestaurants.com
dir: Nearest station: Oxford Circus. From Oxford Circus to Piccadilly along Regent St, 3rd street on right

'We source, age and cut all of our steaks, and we currently buy from over 12 suppliers from the UK, USA, Canada and Australia,' proclaims this American-style steakhouse off Bond Street, its prices no doubt reflecting the food miles the meat has travelled. Porterhouse, T-bone, sirloin - you name the cut, you'll find it here, the finest-quality meat accurately grilled to the customer's specification, accompanied perhaps by béarnaise or stilton sauce. As this is Mayfair, expect lobster cocktail alongside other starters of seafood risotto, or carpaccio with basil, cress and parmesan, and expect to finish with cheesecake. It's a bustling place, decked out appropriately with lots of darkwood and brown leather-look seats.

Chef John Cadieux **Owner** Michail Zelman **Times** noon-10.30 Closed Xmas, New Year, BHs, Sun **Prices** Fixed L 2 course £17-£22, Starter £7-£16, Main £20-£40, Dessert £6.50, Service added 12.5% **Wines** 150 bottles over £20, 2 bottles under £20, 15 by glass **Seats** 95 **Parking** On street

Gordon Ramsay at Claridge's
PLAN 2 H1

◎◎◎ *– see opposite*

The Greenhouse
PLAN 4 H6

Rosettes not confirmed at time of going to press – see page 320

The Grill At The Dorchester
PLAN 4 G6

◎◎ Modern British V

Top quality at the world-class hotel

☎ 020 7629 8888
The Dorchester, Park Ln W1K 1QA
e-mail: restaurants.TDL@thedorchester.com
dir: Nearest station: Hyde Park Corner. Halfway along Park Ln between Hyde Park Corner & Marble Arch

Perhaps the Scottish décor is in homage to the hotel's original owners, but there it is: a profusion of tartan and kilted men staring out of murals. Perhaps it also serves to remind us of the provenance of some of the superb ingredients the kitchen buys: Angus beef, carved from a trolley at the table, smoked salmon and gravad lax (likewise), and Mull scallops in a broth of mussels, garlic, celeriac and ginger. Classics like grilled Dover sole, precisely timed, get fair billing, and elsewhere dishes are gently innovative, with the odd surprise creeping in: beef tartare with horseradish, semolina crackers, a duck egg and caviar, say, then lobster roasted in vanilla butter,

served with mayonnaise and a salad, or full-bodied pig's head roasted with cinnamon and honey. Daily lunch specials are a fixture - poached halibut on Tuesday, for instance - and among desserts might be orange tart with chocolate ice cream.

Chef Brian Hughson **Owner** Dorchester Collection **Times** 12.30-2.30/6.30-10.30 **Prices** Fixed L 2 course fr £23, Fixed D 3 course fr £35, Starter £16.50-£29, Main £19.50-£47.50, Dessert £12.50, Service added but optional 12.5% **Wines** 455 bottles over £20, 15 by glass **Notes** Sunday L, Vegetarian menu, Dress restrictions, Smart casual **Seats** 75 **Children** Portions, Menu **Parking** 20

Hakkasan
PLAN 2 K2

◎◎ Chinese NOTABLE WINE LIST

New-wave Chinese cooking in a see-and-be-seen basement setting

☎ 020 7927 7000
8 Hanway Place W1T 1HD
e-mail: reservation@hakkasan.com
dir: Nearest station: Tottenham Court Rd. From station take exit 2, then 1st left, 1st right, restaurant straight ahead

Hidden away in a secretive alley off Tottenham Court Road, Hakkasan has always been a magnet for the glitterati, thanks to its original founder Alan Yau, whose mission was to make Chinese food sexy and sophisticated. Hakkasan continues to raise the profile of Cantonese cuisine and make it worthy of serious attention within London's foodie fraternity. The ambience within is that of a louche basement nightclub, with sepulchral lighting and a high-decibel vibe courtesy of the cocktail bar. A creative menu of new-wave and classic dishes covers every imaginable base, and then some, from an exhaustive compendium of dim sum, to 'small eat' ideas such as lamb salad with spicy peanut dressing or fried soft-shelled crab with red chilli and curry leaves. Main dishes include spicy scallops with almonds, spring onion and ginger, and stewed organic pork belly with oysters. The cooking is good, the prices are high.

Chef Tong Chee Hwee **Owner** Tasameem **Times** 12-3/6-mdnt Closed 25 Dec **Prices** Fixed L 3 course £29-£118, Fixed D 3 course £50-£118, Starter £8-£21.50, Main £16-£61, Dessert £7.50-£13.50, Service added but optional 13% **Wines** 350 bottles over £20, 9 by glass **Notes** Sunday L, Vegetarian available, Dress restrictions, Smart elegant, no trainers or sportswear **Seats** 200 **Parking** Valet parking from 6pm, NCP Great Russell St

Hakkasan Mayfair
PLAN 2 H1

◎◎◎ *– see page 321*

The Greenhouse

Rosettes not confirmed at time of going to press

LONDON W1 **PLAN 4 H6**

French, European 🍷 **NOTABLE WINE LIST**

New shoots at an old favourite

☎ 020 7499 3331

27a Hay's Mews, Mayfair W1J 5NY
e-mail: reservations@
greenhouserestaurant.co.uk
web: www.greenhouserestaurant.co.uk
dir: Nearest station: Green Park, Bond
St. Behind Dorchester Hotel just off Hill
St

If it's your first time to The Greenhouse, you're best off leaving yourself a good few minutes to find it, as it's rather discreetly tucked away at the far end of a lovely mews, albeit right in the heart of Mayfair. The name comes from the delightful small garden, complete with box hedges, bay trees and little fountains, which you pass through on your way to the front door. Dining alfresco isn't an option but no matter - a darkwood floor, avocado-coloured banquettes, ivory walls and a stunning wall display of tree branches arranged in a filligree pattern make up the pleasing modern décor. A succession of top-class chefs (amongst them Brian Turner and Gary Rhodes) have headed up the kitchen at The Greenhouse over the decades, ensuring it's long been a fixture on the UK's culinary map. And now there's a new chapter beginning, with the departure of Antonin Bonnet (after six years at the helm) and the

arrival of fellow Frenchman - by way of the celebrated Spondi restaurant in Athens - Arnaud Bignon. Bignon is a chef who cooks from the heart, combining classical French techniques with contemporary ideas and not shying away from some out-of-the-ordinary flavour combinations at times. Start with Cornish crab with mint jelly, cauliflower, Granny Smith apple and curry spices, followed by modishly presented line-caught sea bass with a nori seaweed and potato cake, plus a fruity yuzu dressing and chlorophyll herbs. 'Passion fruit' has several smile-inducing elements arranged on a slate, including an intense passionfruit sorbet, tiny chocolate fondants, caramelised bananas and a chocolate crumble. The front-of-house team are on the ball as ever, and the proficient sommelier is on hand to help with the impressive wine list.

Times 12-3/6.45-11 Closed BHs, Sun, L
Sat

LONDON W1 *continued*

Haozhan   PLAN 3 A1

Modern Chinese **NEW**

Exciting oriental-western fusion food in Chinatown

☎ 020 7434 3838
8 Gerrard St W1D 5PJ
e-mail: info@haozhan.co.uk
dir: Nearest station: Trafalgar Square, Piccadilly Circus.
10 mins walk from nearest underground stations

It takes a lot to stand out amid the welter of eating opportunities in Chinatown, but Haozhan manages it, not least because, as Mandarin-speakers won't need reminding, the name translates as something like 'great place'. A refreshing ambience of pale green and dark surfaces, with a feature wall of illuminated green panels, gives some indication of the modernising intention; there are traditional Chinese dishes here, but contemporary technique and European and Pan-Asian influences create an inspired fusion. Attention to detail is paramount. Butter-battered squid with deep-fried curry leaves, is a barnstorming opener, the batter light and transparent, the dish singing with coriander and chilli, or how about cuttlefish stir-fried with aubergine, okra and cherry tomatoes in an Assam-style curry sauce? A bowl of roast duck in goji-berry noodle soup might tempt you to an intermediate course, before main dishes raise the excitement levels further, perhaps with Japanese-influenced wasabi prawns with tobiko (flying-fish roe) or the signature beef rib-eye.

Chef Weng Kong Wong **Owner** Jimmy Kong
Times 12-5/5-11.30 Closed 24-25 Dec **Prices** Fixed D 3 course £32-£40, Tasting menu fr £30, Starter £4.30-£29.50, Main £9.50-£41, Dessert £5.30-£7, Service added but optional 12.5% **Wines** 47 bottles over £20, 21 bottles under £20, 13 by glass **Notes** Tasting menu for 2, Pre-theatre menu from £16.50, Vegetarian available, Air con **Seats** 80, Pr/dining room 40 **Parking** China Town

Hélène Darroze at   PLAN 2 H1
The Connaught

⊛⊛⊛⊛ – *see page 322*

Hibiscus   PLAN 2 J1

⊛⊛⊛⊛⊛ – *see page 323*

Hix   PLAN 2 J1

⊛⊛ British **V**

A celebration of British ingredients

☎ 020 7292 3518
66-70 Brewer St W1F 9UP
e-mail: reservations@hixsoho.co.uk
dir: Nearest station: Piccadilly. Short walk from Piccadilly tube

You could easily pass by the giant wooden door on Soho's Brewer Street without ever knowing there's a bustling restaurant on the other side. The red neon 'HIX' sign leads the way, for this is one of Mark Hix's gaffs - the burgeoning empire now running to eight venues (seven in the capital). Here in Soho, the spacious dining room has an air of art-deco style about it, with reeded glass panels, white-tiled floor, mirrors, brown leather banquettes and a long silver-topped bar running the whole length of one wall. Colourful mobiles and neon signs by Hix's artist chums (including Damien Hirst and Tim Noble) hang from the high ceiling. No-nonsense, modern British cooking utilising excellent seasonal ingredients is what to expect, and first impressions are good, with a small loaf of hot sourdough bread brought to the table fresh from the oven. Spring herb soup with Ticklemore goats' cheese is a delightfully earthy starter, while herb roasted Loch Duart salmon and spring vegetable salad is as fresh as fresh can be. Yorkshire rhubarb pie, served hot with a great big dollop ot cold, creamy custard on top, makes a smile-inducing finish. For drinks (and small plates of simple food) check out Mark's Bar in the basement.

Chef Simon Hicks **Owner** Mark Hix/Restaurants Etc Ltd (Soho) **Times** 12-mdnt Closed 25-26 Dec, 1 Jan **Prices** Fixed L 2 course £17.50, Fixed D 3 course £22.50, Starter £7.25-£14.75, Main £16.50-£36, Dessert £2-£8.50, Service added but optional 12.5% **Wines** 160 bottles over £20, 3 bottles under £20, 26 by glass **Notes** Pre-theatre L/D menus available, Sunday L, Vegetarian menu, Air con **Seats** 80, Pr/dining room 10 **Children** Portions

Hakkasan Mayfair

⊛⊛⊛

LONDON W1   **PLAN 2 H1**

Chinese NOTABLE WINE LIST

Uptown sibling to celebrated über-cool Cantonese original

☎ 020 7907 1888 & 7355 7701
17 Bruton St W1J 6QB
e-mail: mayfairreservation@hakkasan.com
dir: Nearest station: Green Park. Just off Berkeley Square

The Hanway Place original has been a paragon of the London dining scene since 2001, arguably changing the way Chinese food is seen in the UK. The uptown sibling lacks none of the verve and excitement that captured our hearts more than a decade ago. A first-timer may well be won over by kicking off with a cocktail - The Hakka, perhaps - but the food is capable of leaving a lasting impression, too. The doorman, who ushers in arrivals, adds to the Mayfair vibe, and the décor of burnished wood, marble and leather, combined with the low-lighting (particularly in the basement dining room) gives a feeling of inscrutable luxury. Those familiar with the lexicon of Chinese menus will find some familiar dishes, but what is on offer here is a cut above in terms of quality of produce, inspiration and execution; sweet-and-sour Duke of Berkshire pork with pomegranate, for example, or roasted silver cod with champagne and Chinese honey. Dim sum is staggeringly good and luxury ingredients abound - Wagyu beef in a spicy Szechuan sauce, or Peking duck with Royal Beluga caviar (you'll have to give 24 hours notice for that one). Desserts can take a more Western standpoint, such as a Jivara chocolate and hazelnut bomb, which looks a treat on the plate and shows skill in its execution.

Chef Tong Chee Hwee, Seng Han Tan **Owner** Tasameem **Times** 12-3.15/6-11.15 Closed 24-25 Dec, L 26 Dec, 1 Jan **Prices** Fixed L 3 course £50-£130, Fixed D 3 course £65-£130, Starter £8-£21.50, Main £11-£418, Dessert £8.50-£13.50, Service added but optional 13% **Wines** 80 bottles over £20, 9 by glass **Notes** Afternoon tea available 3.15-5pm, Vegetarian available, Dress restrictions, Smart casual, no trainers, hats or sportswear, Air con **Seats** 197, Pr/dining room 14 **Parking** NCP

Hélène Darroze at The Connaught

LONDON W1　　　　　**PLAN 2 H1**

Modern French V

Stellar cooking from a French chef in a British institution

☎ 020 3147 7200
Carlos Place W1K 2AL
e-mail: creservations@the-connaught.co.uk
dir: Nearest station: Bond Street, Green Park. Between Grosvenor Sq and Berkeley Sq

Hélène Darroze arrived in the blue-blooded true-Brit bastion of the Connaught in 2008. A protégée of French super-chef Alain Ducasse, who encouraged her to swap the business suit for chef's whites, Hélène Darroze had already stamped her presence onto the Parisian gastronomic scene with her eponymous Left Bank restaurant, before crossing the Channel to re-orient the Connaught kitchen's compass. The regiment of front-of-house staff, too, has been drafted in almost exclusively from across the water, and works unflaggingly to achieve the impeccable correctness of tone and solicitous ministrations that inevitably come with this style of dining operation. Even the makeover that ushered in a more curvy, swirly, feminine touch to lighten the Connaught's clubby Edwardian panelling was orchestrated by Paris-based designer India Mahdavi. Five years on, the initial kerfuffle has died down, and Darroze's classically-based French cooking continues to wow with its high-flying refinement, impeccable ingredients and unfashionable use of good old butter and rich stocks to achieve an earthy, peasant-inspired depth of flavour. The chef has cooking in her DNA: hailing from the Landes region of southwest France, she is a fourth-generation chef, brought up with a deep-rooted respect for quality produce (the Darroze family produces its own Armagnac), and here all the luxurious ingredients anyone could reasonably ask for are marshalled in intelligent contemporary ideas. The multi-course approach may be hard on the wallet, but it has its impact from the off, setting out with a luxurious take on Catalan arroz negro, twinning humble black and creamy Carnaroli Acquarello rice with blue lobster, scallops, baby squid, Bayonne ham and Espelette peppers, ahead of duck foie gras from Darroze's home turf, which is delivered with contemporary swagger in a crème brûlée with green apple sorbet and peanut emulsion. Next up, the very British pleasures of grouse are subjected to unorthodox treatment, by roasting it pink then flambéeing it in hot duck fat, and delivering the duck-infused results with yet more Landais foie gras, mirabelle plums, parsnip, beetroot and an intensely-flavoured Mexican-style mole jus. Spot-on precision is key to the success of a dish involving pan-roasted red mullet, chicken wings, lomo Ibérico tenderloin, calamari, clams, Sardinian fregola, saffron paella jus, and chargrilled vegetables. Desserts hold true to form with a virtuoso workout uniting a finger of Valrhona's Madagascar Manjari chocolate with raspberry sorbet and galangal cream. The prices on the wine list reach the alarming levels you'd expect in the Connaught, so take a deep breath before diving into a listing of pedigree French and European heavyweights.

Chef Hélène Darroze **Owner** Maybourne Hotel Group **Times** 12-2.30/6.30-10.30 Closed 1 wk Jan, 2 wks Aug, Sun-Mon **Prices** Fixed L 3 course £35-£42, Fixed D 3 course £80, Service added but optional 12.5% **Wines** 1100 bottles over £20, 10 by glass **Notes** ALC Fixed menu £80, Signature menu 6, 9 course £92-£115, Vegetarian menu, Dress restrictions, Smart, no jeans or sportswear **Seats** 64, Pr/dining room 20 **Children** Portions **Parking** Valet parking

Hibiscus

LONDON W1
PLAN 2 J1

Modern French V NOTABLE WINE LIST

Avante-garde French cooking from a chef at the peak of his powers

☎ 020 7629 2999
29 Maddox St, Mayfair W1S 2PA
e-mail: enquiries@hibiscusrestaurant.
co.uk
dir: Nearest station: Oxford Circus

Here, in rather anonymous-looking premises just off Regent Street, Claude and Claire Bosi's Hibiscus is one of London's happiest fine-dining hotspots. The West End can so often be a Bermuda Triangle of reputations but the operation has gone from strength to strength. An air of confidence and refinement flows through the spacious and comfortable single room, which is kitted out in muted tones with a variety of textures and materials, with tables well spaced and service that flows unobtrusively. The menu format is unabashedly contemporary, in that it consists of a word-cloud of prime ingredients that vary according to the season. You check off anything you're not fond of, and then choose how many courses (three, six or eight) you feel up to, and Claude Bosi does the rest. (A more traditional lunch menu is offered for those who have offices to get back to or shops to hit.) The style is modern French, the dishes full of speculative combinations and thorough-going

avante-garderie, but it's a measure of a chef at the peak of his powers that it's possible to work your way through a long, relaxed evening, and not encounter anything that is less than stunningly successful. Isle of Skye scallops en céviche of immaculate texture and flavour are boldly teamed with sweet-and-sour wasabi and gariguette strawberries for a daring opener, which is then followed by a single spear of spring asparagus in burnt hay, brightly attended by orange and hazelnuts. Bosi has always had the chef's equivalent of perfect pitch with fish, as is seen in a serving of Cornish bream stuffed with morels, a superb construction that gains from its intelligent accompaniments of kaffir lime, tarragon and coffee. That could be followed by lightly oak-smoked lamb's sweetbreads, the smokiness a subtle, underlying flavour, offset with vividly intense sorrel and goats' cheese. That last component provides the subliminal link into the next course, slow-grilled kid with new season's garlic and lemon thyme, the meat beautifully timed to pink throughout, and a dish that scores highly for its suddenly being, after all the restless experimentation that has gone before, a moment of pure classicism, like Picasso abruptly taking a break from Cubism to draw a perfectly Leonardo-esque head. The principal dessert might bring asparagus back for a curtain-call, a cream of the white version with garnishing of black olive,

coconut and a sweet whey sorbet. Once you factor in all the appetisers and pre-desserts, petits fours and fantastic breads, the whole experience is truly spectacular.

Chef Claude Bosi **Owner** Claude & Claire Bosi **Times** 12-2.30/6.30-10 Closed 10 days Xmas, New Year, Sun, L Mon **Prices** Fixed L 2 course £29.50, Fixed D 3 course £80, Service added but optional 12.5% **Wines** 350 bottles over £20, 2 bottles under £20, 12 by glass **Notes** Tasting menu D only 3, 6 or 8 course, Vegetarian menu **Seats** 45, Pr/dining room 18 **Children** Portions **Parking** On street

LONDON W1 *continued*

Hix at the Albemarle

PLAN 2 J1

◉◉ Traditional British V ▲ NOTABLE WINE LIST

Traditionally-inspired British cooking with bold British artworks

☎ 020 7518 4004

Brown's Hotel, Albemarle St W1S 4BP

e-mail: thealbemarle@roccofortehotels.com

dir: Nearest station: Green Park. Off Piccadilly between Green Park station & Bond St

Located in Brown's Hotel, the Albemarle restaurant may bear Mark Hix's brand and have as its driving force his commitment to the best of British produce, but don't expect to see the man himself with his sleeves rolled up in the kitchen - that would be Lee Streeton. The Victorian dining room could never look staid with its remarkable collection of contemporary Brit art - Tracey Emin's pink neon 'I loved you more than I can love' and works by Cool Britannia names such as Bridget Riley and Rankin stand out in stark relief to the patrician oak panelling, plasterwork ceiling and white linen tables. But food, not art, is what we're here for, and a quick once-over of the extensive menu reveals the kitchen's belief in the virtues of traditional British food, whose provenance is naturally trumpeted loud and proud. A starter showcases Whitfield Estate partridge as both pan-seared breast and a rich pâté on toast with quince, while main course delivers a punchy combo of herb-baked Scottish razor clams with Bath pig chorizo. A smattering of long-lost or foraged ingredients offers intrigue to the menu, turning up at dessert stage in the form of a sea buckthorn berry cheesecake.

Chef Mark Hix, Lee Streeton Owner The Rocco Forte Hotels Times 12-3/5.30-11 Prices Fixed L 2 course £27.50, Fixed D 3 course £32.50, Starter £7.25-£16.75, Main £16.25-£36.50, Dessert £6.50-£12.50, Service added but optional 12.5% Wines 340 bottles over £20, 18 by glass Notes Pre-theatre bookings 5.30-7.30pm Mon-Sat, Sunday L, Vegetarian menu, Dress restrictions, Smart casual Seats 80, Pr/dining room 70 Children Menu Parking Valet/Burlington St

Iberica Marylebone

PLAN 2 H4

◉◉ Modern Spanish

A taste of Spain in the heart of Marylebone

☎ 020 7636 8650

195 Great Portland St W1W 5PS

e-mail: reservations@ibericalondon.co.uk

web: www.ibericalondon.co.uk

dir: Nearest station: Great Portland St, Regent's Park. Regent's Park end of Great Portland St

With its vast glass frontage looking out over Great Portland Street, Iberica serves up top-notch tapas and more in a busy, vibrant setting. If you manage to walk through the deli without getting waylaid by the stonkingly good artisan cheeses, hams, charcuterie and olive oils, there's a tapas bar where you can pull up a high stool (or take a seat at one of the surrounding tables), or head upstairs to the restaurant. Blond wood and lots of natural daylight (and romantic lighting in the evening) plus an extensive selection of over 40 tapas and pinchos with a focus on Asturias specialities are a big draw. Iberico hams are rightly revered here, or go for cooked dishes such as torto with caramelised onions, eggs and Cabrales cheese; fried artichokes and white asparagus with sea urchin aïoli; octopus gallega with potatoes and paprika; or the thoroughly modish fried chorizo lollipops with pear aïoli. There's a choice of paellas on Sundays. Desserts might take in 'a personal interpretation' of a traditional chocolate, vanilla and biscuit cake, and don't miss the impressive list of Spanish wines.

Chef Cesar Garcia & Nacho Manzano Owner Iberica Food & Culture Ltd Times 11am-11.30pm Closed 25-26 Dec, D Sun Prices Fixed L 2 course fr £15, Starter £5.30-£8.50, Main £6.90-£14.40, Dessert £3.80-£5, Service added but optional 12.5% Wines 42 bottles over £20, 4 bottles under £20, 25 by glass Notes Vegetarian available Seats 120, Pr/dining room 30

JW Steakhouse

PLAN 2 G1

◉ American

Carnivore heaven in top-end hotel grill

☎ 020 7499 6363 & 7399 8400

Grosvenor House, 86 Park Ln W1K 7TN

e-mail: info@jwsteakhouse.co.uk

web: www.jwsteakhouse.co.uk

dir: Nearest station: Marble Arch

The unlikely partnership of a steakhouse restaurant and the grand Grosvenor House Hotel, one of the plushest hotels in London, has been a roaring success, offering the authentic modern American grill experience and delivering some top-notch steaks. Chefs slap top-grade beef onto the flames and grill it; cuts, sauces, cooking temperatures and provenance of the beef are listed on a big blackboard. The gold-standard American USDA protein is flown across the pond, but there is an option to keep it British with grass-fed Aberdeen Angus beef. The setting for such unreconstructed carnivorous activity is suitably butch, with chocolate leather banquettes and seats and bare darkwood tables. There are old favourites along the lines of oysters, crabcakes, and spit-roasted chicken with lemon thyme sauce, too, but beef is the star here. Go for a hangar steak with béarnaise sauce and fries, or if you're really peckish, take on the 32-ounce rib-eye called the 'Tomahawk'.

Times 12-2.30/6-10.30

Kai Mayfair
PLAN 4 G6

◉◉ Chinese 🏆 NOTABLE WINE LIST

Vibrant Chinese cooking in opulent Mayfair setting

☎ 020 7493 8988
65 South Audley St W1K 2QU
e-mail: reservations@kaimayfair.co.uk
web: www.kaimayfair.co.uk
dir: Nearest station: Marble Arch. From Marble Arch station along Park Ln toward Hyde Park Cnr left after car showrooms into South St, continue to end & left into South Audley St. Restaurant on 20mtrs left

Spread over two floors, this swanky Chinese restaurant is decorated in red, gold and silver, with Chinese reliefs on the walls; tables are immaculately presented, seats are comfortable, and staff, friendly but relatively formal, are smartly attired. Kai aims to show the diversity of Chinese cuisine and the cooking is noted for its accurate timing, judicious use of spicing and seasoning, and its subtle combination of flavours and textures. Deep-fried soft-shelled crab, in a crisp batter with garlic, chilli and shallots, served with green mango julienne, and tender char siu with steamed pancakes and pickled cucumber can get a meal off to a flying start, followed perhaps by deep-fried prawns in a complex sauce of mandarin peel, yellow beans, soy, chilli, shallots, garlic and coriander, or tender marinated lamb cutlets with achar pickle. The menu opens with a page of desserts, showing how seriously they are taken here, and indeed 'mango, dragonfruit, coconut, sago', a combination of sorbet, mousse, jelly and foams, has been the crowning glory of a meal.

Chef Alex Chow **Owner** Bernard Yeoh
Times 12-2.15/6.30-10.45 Closed 25-26 Dec, 1 Jan
Prices Fixed L 3 course £27-£39, Starter £12-£85, Main £16-£75, Dessert £11, Service added but optional 12.5%
Wines 350 bottles over £20, 16 by glass **Notes** Fixed D 3 course £39 if matched with wine, available Sun L, Sunday L, Vegetarian available **Seats** 85, Pr/dining room 12
Parking Directly outside

Kitchen Joël Antunès at Embassy Mayfair
PLAN 2 J1

◉◉ French

A slice of Provençal cool in chic Mayfair

☎ 020 7494 5660
29 Old Burlington St W1S 3AN
e-mail: reservations@embassymayfair.com
dir: Nearest station: Green Park/Piccadilly Circus. Just off Burlington Gardens (between Bond St & Regent St)

Respected French chef Joël Antunès' venture brings the South of France to the Embassy Mayfair. The light, airily remodelled interiors at Kitchen JA are inspired by a touch of retro-Riviera glamour, which amounts to patterned limestone tiled floors, white and spearmint-coloured leather chairs and banquettes, white linen and a marble-topped bar. There's a large terrace out front to enhance further the Mediterranean vibe (sunshine not guaranteed). Like the décor, the food is inspired by the South of France, with Provence the lynchpin and classic dishes given a light, well-dressed modern touch and based on good quality produce. Thus salad Niçoise stands alongside Provençal marinated red peppers with capers and anchovy to start, followed by traditional coq au vin or steak au poivre. At dinner, there's a couple of sharing dishes (perhaps roast suckling pork shoulder with baked apple), and for dessert tarte Tatin (of course) might rub shoulders with sablé noisette with milk chocolate Chantilly.

Chef Joël Antunès **Owner** Mark Fuller, Dan Kapp, Jacobi Anstruther-Gough-Calthorp **Times** 12-2.30/6-11.30 Closed 25-26 Dec, 1 Jan, Good Fri L, Sun-Mon
Prices Fixed L 2 course fr £15, Starter £9-£15, Main £18-£32, Dessert £7-£9, Service added but optional 12.5%, Groups min 10 service 15% **Wines** 110 bottles over £20, 9 by glass **Notes** Pre theatre menu 2,3 course Tue-Fri £15-£19, Group menu £50, Vegetarian available, Dress restrictions, Smart casual, no trainers, smart jeans only
Seats 95 **Parking** NCP opposite restaurant

Locanda Locatelli

LONDON W1
PLAN 2 G2

Italian 🏆 NOTABLE WINE LIST ❦

Fabulous Italian cooking of daring simplicity

☎ 020 7935 9088
8 Seymour St W1H 7JZ
e-mail: info@locandalocatelli.com
dir: Nearest station: Marble Arch. Opposite Marylebone police station

When it comes to eating Italian in London, or indeed the UK, Giorgio Locatelli is l'uomo principale. It was way back in 1995 when Giorgio first made a splash at Zafferano, then opening his Locanda in 2002. Secreted just north of Oxford Street, in the Hyatt Regency Churchill Hotel, this is a swanky Mayfair address which warranted a makeover from no less than David Collins, and by jove it looks the part: there are burnished parquet floors, textured wooden walls, beige leather bucket chairs and booths that give an air of exclusivity to proceedings. The service team deserves special mention: this is without doubt some of the most charming service around, done without a jot of obsequious fawning, and leaving an impression for all the right reasons. Out of the kitchen comes Italian food of verve and style, with the high quality of the ingredients taking centre stage and the thoughtful simplicity of it all taking your breath away at times. The selection of breads on offer kicks things off as they mean to go on (stunning, really), before an antipasti such as wild chicory salad with capers, anchovy and chilli, or ox tongue with green sauce. Not going for a pasta dish would be a mistake (pappardelle with chicken livers and sage, perhaps), before a main course such as steamed hake with a sweet-and-sour sauce and braised fennel, or braised ox cheek with red wine and chocolate sauce. To finish, tiramisù, various ice creams and sorbets, a tart of the day or the likes of white chocolate soup with passionfruit jelly and pistachio ice cream are the alternative to Italian cheeses served with honey. The wine list must surely have more Barolos than anywhere else in the UK, plus loads of interesting regional selections.

Chef Giorgio Locatelli **Owner** Plaxy & Giorgio Locatelli
Times 12-3/6.45-11 Closed Xmas, BHs **Prices** Starter £9.50-£16.50, Main £13.50-£32.50, Dessert £6.50-£9.50, Service optional **Wines** 2 bottles under £20, 24 by glass
Notes Vegetarian available **Seats** 70, Pr/dining room 50
Children Portions **Parking** NCP adjacent, parking meters

LONDON W1 *continued*

Latium
PLAN 2 J3

@@ Italian

Authentic Italian cooking, ravioli a speciality

☎ 020 7323 9123
21 Berners St W1T 3LP
e-mail: info@latiumrestaurant.com
dir: Nearest station: Goodge St & Oxford Circus

Named after the southern Italian region of Lazio, chef-patron Maurizio Morelli's smart, intimate Italian in Fitzrovia serves up an authentic flavour of the region around Rome, as well as other seasonal things from elsewhere. Black leather banquettes set against neutral walls enlivened with pebble mosaics and arty Italian photography make for a slick backdrop to vibrant offerings such pappardelle with wild boar ragù, and a main course starring rabbit roasted with thyme, served with fried gorgonzola polenta, rabbit jus and black olives. Desserts might include chocolate and almond tart with Amaretto sauce. Ravioli fans will find it is a much-loved medium here and has its own menu of little parcels containing crab with rocket sauce, oxtail with celery sauce, all the way through to sweet versions filled with apple, pine kernels, raisin and vanilla sauce.

Times 12-3/6.30-10.30 Closed BHs, Sun, L Sat

Levant
PLAN 2 G2

@ Lebanese, Middle Eastern V

Lebanese cooking in Wigmore Street

☎ 020 7224 1111
Jason Court, 76 Wigmore St W1U 2SJ
e-mail: reservations@levant.co.uk
dir: Nearest station: Bond Street. From Bond St station, walk through St Christopher's Place, reach Wigmore St, restaurant across road

If the name doesn't convince you, then the décor of this basement restaurant certainly will: an Aladdin's cave of lanterns, candles, incense and eastern European music, with belly dancers cranking up the action. The cover charge pays for breads and crudités to nibble while choosing from the menu. Expect dips, unusual hot meze - Armenian sausage with tomatoes, say, or deep-fried squid with sumac, harissa and mayonnaise - and other starter-size portions of pastries like spicy lamb with pine nuts, or tabouleh. Not all dishes are meant for sharing, with main courses of roast fillet of sea bass with citrus-scented rice, vegetarian moussaka, and grilled chicken marinated in garlic, lemon and spices. Meals end with mint tea, poured from a height, with baklava and Turkish delight.

Chef David Jones **Owner** Tony Kitous **Times** 12-5/5-mdnt Closed 25-26 Dec **Prices** Fixed L 2 course £9.95, Fixed D 3 course £28-£50, Starter £5.25-£6.50, Main £13-£26, Dessert £4.50-£9.50, Service added but optional 12.5% **Wines** 4 bottles under £20, 13 by glass **Notes** Sunday L, Vegetarian menu, Dress restrictions, Smart casual **Seats** 150, Pr/dining room 12 **Parking** Welbeck St

Locanda Locatelli
PLAN 2 G2

@@@ — *see page 325*

The Mandeville Hotel
PLAN 2 G2

@@ Modern British **NEW**

Edwardian club-like dining in a Marylebone hotel

☎ 020 7935 5599
Mandeville Place W1U 2BE
e-mail: info@mandeville.co.uk
dir: Nearest station: Bond St/Baker St. 3 mins walk from Bond St station

A modern urban hotel in Marylebone, just north of Oxford Street, and handily positioned between the Wallace Collection and the Wigmore Hall if you're in town for classical pictures and music, The Mandeville is a stylish hotspot. The cool bar feels like somewhere to see and be seen, though its dining room, the Reform Social and Grill,

---

Maze

LONDON W1   PLAN 2 G1

French, Asian influence V

Thrilling contemporary cooking from the Gordon Ramsay stable

☎ 020 7107 0000
London Marriott Hotel, Grosvenor Square, 10-13 Grosvenor Square W1K 6JP
e-mail: maze@gordonramsay.com
dir: Nearest station: Bond Street

David Rockwell's minimalist design creates a relaxing vibe, its monochrome effect broken by predominantly yellow seats at generously spaced clothless tables, a series of hand-crafted screens evoking the sense of - guess what? - a maze, and a partially open-to-view kitchen. As it has been since the restaurant opened, the cooking is essentially modern French food with a strong

input from Asia - crab with wasabi, mango, chilli and pickled mooli is typical - in tasting-size dishes so you get a variety of flavours and textures. Dishes sound exciting and combinations are successful; four slices of sea bass céviche, for instance, are edged with nori and topped with blobs of avocado purée, accompanied by squares of cucumber jelly and passionfruit dressing, and carpaccio is partnered by galangal-infused celeriac and dressed with marrowbone vinaigrette. Top-end raw materials can be expected - a dumpling of lobster, langoustine and salmon, for instance, with kaffir lime leaf and aromatic broth - but more everyday ingredients are handled with the same high level of attention to detail. Marinated beetroot comes with goats' curd, pine nuts and red wine dressing, whilst tender, deeply flavoured braised blade of beef has its accompanying jus served separately, plus shimiji mushrooms and pommes purée sprinkled with togarishi spice (red pepper dust, apparently). Presentation is impressive, noticeably in involved puddings like layers of apple, rhubarb and shortbread

topped with custard and rhubarb ice cream, or a humorous version of peanut butter and jam sandwich with berry sorbet and crystallised peanuts.

Chef Tristin Farmer **Owner** Gordon Ramsay Holdings Ltd **Times** 12-2.30/6-10.30 **Prices** Starter £7-£11, Main £10.50-£14.50, Dessert £9.50-£12, Service added but optional 12.5% **Wines** 400 bottles over £20, 3 bottles under £20, 16 by glass **Notes** Fixed L 4 course £25, Chef menu D 7 course £70, Vegetarian menu, Dress restrictions, No sportswear or shorts **Seats** 108 **Children** Portions **Parking** On street

has had a makeover and now takes inspiration from Edwardian gentlemen's clubs, both in its design ambience and its yesteryear menu. A bowl of spring chicken broth with little dumplings is a good way to settle into a cold-weather lunch, if you don't fancy St George's mushrooms on toast, or a pheasant Scotch egg with celery salt and mayonnaise for dipping. Catch of the day might be plaice, served with Morecambe Bay shrimps in caper and parsley butter, or there are porterhouse steaks being thrown on the charcoal grill, for two to share, as well as lamb cutlets Reform with ham hock and wild garlic, or traditional mixed grills.

Chef Jens Ove Folkel **Times** 12-3/7-11 **Prices** Food prices not confirmed for 2013. Please telephone for details **Notes** Vegetarian available, Dress restrictions, Smart casual **Seats** 90, Pr/dining room 12 **Children** Portions **Parking** NCP nearby

Maze   PLAN 2 G1

◉◉◉ – *see opposite*

Maze Grill   PLAN 2 G1

◉◉ American ⚑NOTABLE WINE LIST

Where's the beef? It's on Grosvenor Square

☎ 020 7495 2211
London Marriott Hotel, Grosvenor Square, 10-13 Grosvenor Square W1K 6JP
e-mail: mazegrill@gordonramsay.com
dir: Nearest station: Bond St

Gordon Ramsay's Maze Grill is a New York-style grill restaurant offering a broad selection of different breeds and cuts of cow, in a café ambience with no coverings on tables or floor, looking out on Grosvenor Square. The beef is excellent indeed: Casterbridge grain-fed, Angus grass-fed and Creekstone American corn-fed, aged for three, four and five weeks respectively, supplemented by the ninth-grade Wagyu half-pound rib-eye at a gold-standard price. It's all cooked over coal, and then finished at a full-on 1,200 degrees F for that final seared coating. If you're not a meathead, relief is on hand in the form of crab linguini with chilli and coriander, or miso-glazed gilt head bream with edamame, pak choi, shiitakes and spring onions. End it all with a bitter chocolate brownie served with matching ice cream.

Chef Chris Whitmore **Owner** Gordon Ramsay Holdings Ltd **Times** 12-10.30 **Prices** Fixed L 2 course fr £21, Starter £7-£16.50, Main £15-£85, Dessert £9, Service added but optional 12.5% **Wines** 400 bottles over £20, 16 by glass **Notes** Early supper menu 2,3 course £21-£24 Sun-Thu until 6.30pm, Sunday L, Vegetarian available, Dress restrictions, No sportswear or shorts **Seats** 100, Pr/dining room 12 **Children** Portions, Menu

Mele e Pere   PLAN 2 J1

◉ Italian **NEW**

Rustic Italian food in modish surroundings

☎ 020 7096 2096
46 Brewer St, Soho W1F 9TF
e-mail: info@meleepere.co.uk
dir: Nearest station: Piccadilly Circus

The name means 'apples and pears', which explains why the plate glass window of this Soho Italian is full of Murano glass renditions of the fruits. You also have to descend the 'apples and pears' to reach the buzzy, modishly minimal basement restaurant - all chunky bleached wood tables lit by wall-mounted anglepoise lamps - a décor that perhaps prepares diners for the fact that this is not a comfort-food Italian serving the usual spag bol suspects. The chef-patron hails from northern Italy, and his repertoire takes the path of well-rendered rusticity, as typified in an unusual Italian take on a classic beef tartare accompanied by shaved parmesan and yellow Castelfranco radicchio. The concise menu continues with tagliatelle with rabbit and fresh peas, while mains run to sea bream with fregola and fennel, or pork belly with lentils and bean sprouts. Finish with a classic pannacotta or excellent Italian cheeses.

Chef A Mantovani **Owner** P Hughes, A Mantovani **Times** 12-11 Closed 25-26 Dec, 1 Jan, Sun **Prices** Fixed L 2 course £12.50-£15.50, Starter £5-£9, Main £12.50-£24, Dessert £5-£7, Service added but optional 12.5% **Wines** 40 bottles over £20, 8 bottles under £20, 16 by glass **Notes** Pre-theatre menu until 7pm £15.50-£17.50, Vegetarian available **Seats** 90 **Children** Portions **Parking** NCP

Mennula   PLAN 2 K3

◉◉ Modern Italian

Sicily brought to Fitzrovia

☎ 020 7636 2833 & 7637 3830
10 Charlotte St W1T 2LT
e-mail: santino@mennula.com
dir: Nearest station: Goodge Street/Tottenham Court Rd. 5 min walk from station

Charlotte Street has its fair share of restaurants, but head here for a taste of Sicily. It's a small, modern and warm place, with aubergine-coloured seating, a walnut floor and a stencil of an almond tree ('mennula' in Italian) on white walls. The kitchen has a firm foothold in Italian traditions, adding a Sicilian slant to its menus. Everything is made in-house, from commendable breads and pasta to tuma cheese, served warm as a starter on a bed of winter leaves accompanied by quince marmalade, a refreshingly simple and tasty dish. Another starter may

be a Sicilian salad of bottarga, orange, fennel and mint, then there's a run of pasta before the main event: the freshest of cod fillet in tempura with squash purée, tender spiced lentils and spicy chutney, or the full-on flavours of rabbit stuffed with sausage and pancetta in aubergine sauce with carrots, pine nuts and sultanas. What better way to finish than with a tasting platter of Sicilian desserts, among them semi-fredo and cassata siciliana?

Chef Santino Busciglio **Owner** Joe Martorana **Times** 12-3/6-11 Closed Xmas, BHs, L Sat-Sun **Prices** Fixed L 3 course £17.95, Starter £9.50-£13.50, Main £19.50-£36, Dessert £6.50-£12.50, Service added but optional 12.5% **Wines** 72 bottles over £20, 8 bottles under £20, 18 by glass **Notes** Fixed 5 course menu £59.95, Pre-theatre menu 3 course £17.95, Sunday L, Vegetarian available **Seats** 44, Pr/dining room 14 **Children** Portions **Parking** On street

Mews of Mayfair   PLAN 2 H1

◉ Modern British V ◉

High-flying cooking off Bond Street

☎ 020 7518 9388
10-11 Lancashire Court, New Bond St, Mayfair W1S 1EY
e-mail: info@mewsofmayfair.com
dir: Nearest station: Bond Street. Between Brook St & New Bond St. Opposite Dolce & Gabbana

Mews of Mayfair is indeed on a Mayfair mews, a narrow, cobbled one, a bit of a restaurant alley, just off Bond Street. It's on the first floor, above its popular cocktail bar, with a snappy white and cream décor and an equally snappy menu of fashionable, imaginative dishes. Starters have included crab with cucumber jelly, and pan-fried foie gras with poached pear and a kick of mango purée. The cooking is driven by seasonality, and main courses, where seafood is given equal rights to meat, make an impact without being gimmicky: oh-so-tender beef fillet with deeply-flavoured tarragon sauce, served simply with ceps, or sautéed prawns with samphire spiked with chilli and ginger. Finish with creamy crème brûlée or something fruitier like mango cheesecake with blackberry mousseline.

Chef Alan Marchetti **Owner** James Robson & Robert Nearn **Times** 12-4/6-12 Closed 25 Dec, D Sun **Prices** Fixed L 2 course fr £18.50, Fixed D 3 course fr £22, Starter £6.50-£13.50, Main £12.50-£28.50, Dessert £6.50, Service added but optional 12.5% **Wines** 30+ bottles over £20, 8 bottles under £20, 16 by glass **Notes** Sunday L, Vegetarian menu **Seats** 70, Pr/dining room 28 **Children** Portions, Menu **Parking** On street, NCP

LONDON W1 *continued*

The Montague

PLAN 2 F2

@@ Modern British **NEW**

☎ 020 7299 2037

Hyatt Regency London - The Churchill, 30 Portman Square W1H 7BH

e-mail: montague.hrlondon@hyatt.com

dir: Nearest station: Marble Arch. From Marble Arch rdbt, follow signs for Oxford Circus onto Oxford St. Left after 2nd lights into Portman St. Hotel on left

The presence of Locanda Locatelli in the hotel (with its own entrance; see entry) may well have put the Hyatt Regency on the map for foodies, but it also has The Montague restaurant up its sleeve. Once past the liveried doormen, the restaurant offers up views over Portman Square and it's a suitably smart setting, complete with open-plan kitchen, for some skilful British cooking. It's a pleasant spot for a champagne lunch or afternoon tea, too. Prawn cocktail is a decidedly upmarket version, the prawns poached in court-bouillon, or there might be thickly cut Foreman's traditionally smoked salmon loin served in the traditional manner. Main-courses bring forth the likes of Angus steaks (rib-eye maybe), or sea trout with whelks, samphire, tomato and saffron velouté. The kitchen continues to show its mettle at dessert stage with damson crumble with ginger ice cream.

Chef Carlos Teixeira **Owner** Hyatt Regency London-The Churchill **Times** 12-3/6-10.45 **Prices** Fixed L 2 course £22, Fixed D 3 course £29, Starter £7-£15, Main £17-£35, Dessert £9-£11, Service added but optional 12.5% **Wines** 100 bottles over £20, 12 by glass **Notes** Chef's Table 3,5 course £55-£75 incl wine, Sunday L, Vegetarian available, Dress restrictions, Smart casual, Civ Wed 140 **Seats** 60 **Children** Portions **Parking** 48

Murano

PLAN 4 H6

@@@ – *see below*

Nobu

PLAN 5 H6

@@ Japanese

Top-end Japanese dining and views over Hyde Park

☎ 020 7447 4747

Metropolitan London, 19 Old Park Ln W1K 1LB

e-mail: london@noburestaurants.com

dir: Nearest station: Hyde Park Corner, Green Park

The Nobu brand now spans the globe from the Bahamas to Beijing, and this venue on the first-floor of the Metropolitan Hotel overlooking Hyde Park was the first of its brace of London outposts. The pared-back décor of black banquettes, pale wood and stone hasn't dated since it opened in 1997, and has become something of a timeless classic. The same might be said of the Latino-Japanese fusion cooking, which revolutionised what diners expected from upscale Japanese dining by creatively applying a hit of South American fire to the subtle delicacy of Japanese food. Make no mistake, this is a slick, celeb-spotting Mayfair operation manned by clued-up staff who can talk the uninitiated through the alien terminology of sunomono, ponzu, or toban-yaki tataki, and politely remind you when it's time to leave your table to the next booking. Expect the traditional roll-call of sashimi and sushi, or the culinary fusion concept as typified by anti-cucho Peruvian-style tea-smoked lamb. Elsewhere, high-rollers can find Wagyu beef tartare with caviar, lobster tempura with creamy wasabi, or the unctuous overload of Wagyu and foie gras gyoza with spicy ponzu. Presentation is unfailingly exquisite, and meals might conclude with yoghurt mousse with Manuka honey ice cream, green apple compôte, and green tea and olive oil sponge.

Times 12-2.15/6-10.15

Murano

LONDON W1   PLAN 4 H6

Modern European, Italian influence V ⬧ NOTABLE WINE LIST

Italian inspiration in chic Mayfair

☎ 020 7495 1127

20-22 Queen St W1J 5PP

e-mail: muranorestaurant@angela-hartnett.com

dir: Nearest station: Green Park. Turn left from Piccadilly to Half Moon St, then left Curzon Street, right Queen Street

A scion of the Ramsay empire, Angela Hartnett definitively cut loose from the brand after taking over Murano in her own name in 2010. The whole operation oozes high-end Mayfair gloss all the way from its discreet frontage through to the interior, which is a symphony in grey and white involving floor-length tablecloths, fluted art deco-style columns, swirly mural panels, and specially-commissioned Murano glass light fittings as the only nod to the restaurant's name. A raised chef's table gives the privileged few a more direct look into the workings within the glass-fronted kitchen. Hartnett's Italian ancestry drives the thinking behind the cooking, although the business at the sharp end is left in the capable hands of head chef Diego Cardoso, who has a firm grasp of the subtleties of the contemporary Italian idiom and meets the gamut of contemporary expectations by offering a stupendous value fixed-price lunch menu, a carte, and a full-dress 'kitchen market' tasting menu. Start, perhaps, with razor clams teamed with linguine, chilli, garlic and artichoke, or octopus with braised new potatoes, peperonata, and smoked almonds. Main courses gain lustre through the pedigree of their components - impeccable sea bass and Scottish langoustines, say, pointed up with fennel purée and baby artichokes, while meatier ideas could see roast rack and braised shoulder of lamb sharing a plate with carrot and cumin purée. Desserts reveal more creative dexterity: lemon served as parfait and jelly with sesame meringue and thyme crumble, or rhubarb terrine with candied rhubarb, black pepper yoghurt and vanilla sablé. Italy, naturally, has a strong showing on the fabulous wine list, but the rest of the world gets a fair crack of the whip too.

Chef Diego Cardoso **Owner** Angela Hartnett **Times** 12-3/6.30-11 Closed 25-26 Dec, Sun **Prices** Fixed L 2 course £25-£50, Fixed D 3 course £65, Service added but optional 12.5% **Wines** 400 bottles over £20, 17 by glass **Notes** Kitchen market menu 5 course £80, Vegetarian menu **Seats** 46, Pr/dining room 12 **Children** Portions

Nobu Berkeley ST   PLAN 4 H6

@@ Japanese

Super-cool Mayfair hot-spot for great Japanese food

☎ 020 7290 9222
15 Berkeley St W1J 8DY
e-mail: berkeleyst@noburestaurants.com
dir: Nearest station: Green Park

This super-stylish outpost of the Nobu brand is a fixture among the A-listers on London's restaurant scene. Mayfair fashionistas flock in for the high energy buzz of the ground-floor bar, while the supremely cool restaurant upstairs sports a dramatic wintry woodland-themed décor by designer David Collins; black-clad staff play their part too, keeping the up-tempo vibe ticking over, and clued up enough to brief diners on the ins and outs of the menu. Nobu's key contribution to the London foodie scene was to revolutionise perceptions of what high-end Japanese dining could be, with its exploration of Latino-accented fusion cooking; it is a concept that continues to develop productively. For traditionalists, there's a sushi bar, as well as DIY dining where chefs supervise your efforts around a sunken hibachi table; otherwise, the lengthy menu opens with South American céviche alongside yellowtail sashimi with jalapeño and yuzu dressing, and runs the gamut from the ever-popular signature black cod with miso, to cabbage steak with truffles cooked in the wood oven or the luxurious attractions of lobster wasabi and Wagyu rump toban-yaki.

Chef Mark Edwards **Owner** Nobu Matsuhisa, Robert de Niro **Times** 12-2.15/6-1am Closed 25 Dec, BH Mon **Prices** Food prices not confirmed for 2013. Please telephone for details **Wines** 10 by glass **Notes** Vegetarian available **Seats** 120 **Parking** Mayfair NCP

NOPI   PLAN 2 J1

@ Mediterranean NEW

Vibrant Middle Eastern flavours Ottolenghi style

☎ 020 7494 9584
21-22 Warwick St W1B 5NE
e-mail: contact@nopi-restaurant.com
dir: Nearest station: Oxford Circus, Piccadilly Circus

NOPI (north of Piccadilly) is a brasserie on two levels, a more formal ground floor, with lots of marble and brass, and a basement with canteen-type tables and views into the kitchen. Owner Yotam Ottolenghi's cooking is based on the cuisine of the Middle East, with some input from other cultures, and dishes are meant to be shared. The menu is packed with interest, the food is full of zingy flavours, and if ingredients sound alien ask the staff to explain. Among vegetarian options have been shakshuka (North African braised eggs with pepper and tomato), burrata cheese with peach and fennel seeds, and chargrilled broccolini with skordalia and chilli oil, all demonstrating a masterly control of flavours. Meat and seafood hit the spot too: twice-cooked baby chicken with lemon myrtle oil and chilli sauce, and soft-shelled crab with nashi pear and pea shoots. Puddings are just as

vigorous: try kaffir lime with meringue, tapioca, and honey mango.

Chef Yotam Ottolenghi, Ramael Scully **Owner** Yotam Ottolenghi **Times** 12-2.45/5.30-10.15 Closed D Sun **Prices** Starter £8.50-£12.50, Dessert £3.50-£8, Service added 12.5% **Wines** 83 bottles over £20, 16 by glass **Notes** Pre-Theatre menu 2/3 course £21.50/£24.50, Vegetarian available, Dress restrictions, Smart casual **Seats** 100

Novikov Restaurant & Bar   PLAN 4 H6

@ Italian NEW

Jaw-dropping temple of Italian (and Asian) gastronomy

☎ 020 7399 4330
50a Berkeley St W1J 8HA
e-mail: reservations@novikovrestaurant.co.uk
dir: Nearest station: Green Park

Arkady Novikov is an internationally known Russian restaurant entrepreneur with the resources to realise grandiose projects. The present complex is on the scale of a biblical temple, incorporating a sleek lounge-bar lit like a nightclub, a ground-floor Asian restaurant and an Italian venue in the basement. Security-staff are on hand to ensure there are no sudden moves, and everywhere you look, there are shrines devoted to food and drink - mountains of oranges in wicker baskets, panniers of fresh produce in front of a long service counter, bottles of grappa crowded on to the top of a wine barrel. Once you get down to it, the Italian cooking is convincing, surprisingly rustic and honest, with some southern and Sardinian dishes for depth. Gossamer-thin slices of beef carpaccio with parmesan strips and rocket is the real deal, as is the asparagus salad with broad beans and Sardinian stone-dried red mullet bottarga. Calves' liver is top-drawer gear, lightly sautéed for melting texture, dressed in butter and sage.

Chef Arkady Novikov **Owner** Arkady Novikov **Times** noon-11pm **Prices** Food prices not confirmed for 2013. Please telephone for details

140 Park Lane Restaurant and Bar   PLAN 2 F1

@@ Modern British

Good, straightforward cooking in grand centrally-located hotel

☎ 020 7493 7000 & 647 5678
London Marriott Hotel, 140 Park Ln W1K 7AA
e-mail: mhrs.parklane@marriotthotels.com
dir: Nearest station: Marble Arch. From Hyde Park Corner, left A4202 Park Lane

The swanky Mayfair address comes with equally privileged views over Marble Arch and Hyde Park. Number 140 is the luxurious London Marriott Hotel Park Lane address, whose eponymous restaurant is done out with an irreproachably smart contemporary look, featuring an open-plan kitchen where the culinary focus is on grilling prime grain-fed beef and spanking-fresh, sustainably-

sourced fish and seafood. But if you are immune to the attractions of grilled lobster thermidor, or sharing a 30-oz rib of beef with your dining partner, there are menus of appealingly unfussy ideas opening with grilled diver scallops with pea purée, red pepper sauce and crisp bacon, while main courses could see salt marsh lamb shank teamed with mash, glazed apricots and lamb gravy. Finish with the deep comforts of sticky toffee pudding with butterscotch ice cream.

Chef Anshu Anghotra **Owner** London Marriott Hotel Park Lane **Times** 11-3/5.30-10.30 **Prices** Food prices not confirmed for 2013. Please telephone for details **Wines** 33 bottles over £20, 3 bottles under £20, 15 by glass **Notes** Sunday L, Vegetarian available, Air con **Seats** 76 **Children** Portions, Menu

The Only Running Footman   PLAN 4 H6

@ Modern British

Smart Mayfair pub with commitment to great food

☎ 020 7499 2988
5 Charles St, Mayfair W1J 5DF
e-mail: manager@therunningfootmanmayfair.com
dir: Nearest station: Green Park. Close to south end of Berkeley Sq

It looks like a pub, which indeed it is, but there's more than meets the eye to The Only Running Footman. The distinctive red-brick corner building in Mayfair has a ground-floor bar where you can have a drink and pick something off the all-day bar menu (from a sandwich to chargrilled Longhorn rib-eye steak), plus a smarter and quieter upstairs restaurant, where closely-packed tables are done-out in crisp white linen and all is a little more refined. (There's also a chef's table in a separate room which doubles up as a cookery school.) Upstairs you might start with sautéed Cornish squid and chorizo salad, followed by pan-fried sea bass with caramelised salsify and sauce vierge, finishing off with a berry Pavlova or cheeses from the Bath Cheese Company with pear chutney and pain aux fruits.

Chef Eddie Konadio **Owner** Barnaby Meredith **Times** 12-2.30/6.30-10 Closed D 25 Dec **Prices** Fixed L 2 course £25-£35, Fixed D 3 course £30-£40, Starter £5.50-£12.50, Main £12.25-£19.50, Dessert £4.95-£11.95, Service added but optional 12.5% **Wines** 76 bottles over £20, 7 bottles under £20, 12 by glass **Notes** Chef's table available £70, Sunday L, Vegetarian available **Seats** 30, Pr/dining room 40 **Children** Portions **Parking** On street

LONDON W1 *continued*

Orrery
PLAN 2 G3

◉◉ Modern European

Stylish, elegant restaurant above designer store

☎ 020 7616 8000
55-57 Marylebone High St W1U 5RB
e-mail: orreryreservation@danddlondon.com
web: www.orrery-restaurant.co.uk
dir: Nearest station: Baker St/Regent's Park. At north end of Marylebone High St

Above the (Terence) Conran store at the top of fashionable Marylebone High Street, the landmark Orrery is a class act indeed. It's an elegantly streamlined, contemporary and understated space, the linear dining room flooded by light from large arched windows and roof skylights, with a glass wine cellar at one end and intimate bar tucked away at the other. Service is a strength here, professional certainly, but engaging, with a sommelier to advise on the excellent wine list. The modern cooking is underpinned by classical French thinking, with a refined touch and plenty of good ideas. Expect top-notch produce, a hint of luxury and meticulous presentation in dishes such as fillet of turbot with white asparagus, morels, peas and champagne velouté, or rump of Kentish lamb à la provençale served with pommes dauphinoise and rosemary jus, while a Melanosporum black truffle risotto is teamed with soft herbs and parmesan. A good value lunch du jour, plus a roof terrace and street-level Epicerie are all bonuses.

Chef Igor Tymchyshyn **Owner** Conran Restaurants **Times** 12-2.30/6.30-10.30 **Prices** Food prices not confirmed for 2013. Please telephone for details **Wines** 960 bottles over £20, 2 bottles under £20, 18 by glass **Seats** 80 **Children** Portions **Parking** NCP, 170 Marylebone Rd

Ozer Restaurant
PLAN 2 H2

◉ Turkish, Middle Eastern, Mediterranean

Busy upmarket Turkish restaurant near the BBC

☎ 020 7323 0505
5 Langham Place W1B 3DG
e-mail: ozer@ozer.co.uk
dir: Nearest station: Oxford Circus. 2 min walk towards Upper Regent St

If you're in a rush, this upmarket Turkish restaurant promises 'drinks in 2 minutes, starters in 5 minutes'. But why hurry? There's plenty to enjoy at leisure on a wide-ranging menu which is keen to show that there's more to the Turkish idiom than meze followed by kebabs - although the usual suspects such as spicy crisp lamb's liver, grilled sucuk sausage, lamb köfte meatballs, and ali nazik - sautéed lamb fillet with smoked aubergine caviar, yoghurt and garlic - are all present and correct. Near the BBC, the contemporary space is done out with cream leather seats at white linen tables set against vibrant red walls, and the place is always heaving, kept on the boil by energetic, personable waiters. The extensive repertoire strays from straightforward Turkish cuisine to

include a wide range of Middle Eastern classics, as well as grilled steaks served with French fries, and Asian-accented seafood dishes including black cod with miso. Keeping it Turkish, finish with the house speciality 'Su Muhallebisi' - a confection of cubes of milk pudding, rose syrup, berries and nuts.

Chef Mustafa Guzen **Owner** Huseyin Ozer **Times** noon-11.30 **Prices** Fixed L 2 course £19.40, Fixed D 3 course fr £29.10, Starter £3.95-£12.45, Main £8.95-£24.90, Dessert £3.95-£5.95, Service added but optional 12.5% **Wines** 22 bottles over £20, 20 bottles under £20, 7 by glass **Notes** Fixed menu includes glass wine per person, Sunday L, Vegetarian available **Seats** 120 **Children** Portions **Parking** On street

Park Plaza Sherlock Holmes
PLAN 2 F3

◉ British, European

Modern grill near the home of Holmes

☎ 020 7486 6161
108 Baker St W1U 6LJ
e-mail: info@sherlockholmeshotel.com
dir: Nearest station: Baker Street. On Baker St, close to tube station

The Baker Street address is spot-on, but if you're expecting a hit of Edwardiana from an operation bearing the great fictional sleuth's name, think again: this is a thoroughly chic boutique-style hotel with the slickly contemporary Sherlock's Bar & Grill catering to modern European appetites. Cream leather seats at black-topped tables have a ringside view of the chefs toiling over grills in the open-to-view kitchen, delivering a menu built around the everyman appeal of traditional grills and dishes cooked in the wood burning oven. The latter could offer up a whole lemon sole served on the bone with shellfish butter, or free-range chicken marinated in thyme and garlic, while the chargrilled repertoire runs to garlicky lamb cutlets or wild sea bass with samphire and fennel butter. Bookending all of this, there might be wild nettle and stilton soup to start, and apple crumble to finish.

Chef Rachid Hammoum **Owner** Park Plaza Hotels **Times** 12-2.30/6-10.30 Closed D Sun, BHs **Prices** Fixed L 2 course £15, Starter £5-£12, Main £14-£20, Dessert £5.50-£7, Service added 12.5% **Wines** 16 bottles over £20, 10 bottles under £20, 10 by glass **Notes** Sunday L, Vegetarian available, Dress restrictions, Smart casual, Civ Wed 40 **Seats** 50, Pr/dining room 50 **Children** Portions, Menu **Parking** Chiltern St, NCP

Patterson's
PLAN 2 J1

◉◉ Modern British, European

Fine dining in family-run Mayfair restaurant

☎ 020 7499 1308
4 Mill St, Mayfair W1S 2AX
e-mail: info@pattersonsrestaurant.co.uk
dir: Nearest station: Oxford Circus. Located off Conduit St opposite Savile Row entrance

Operated with consummate professionalism and disarming charm by the Patterson family since 2003, this stylish restaurant is tucked away between New Bond Street and Oxford Street. The black marble and plate-glass façade exudes high gloss in keeping with the neighbourhood; oak flooring, brown leather high-backed chairs, abstract artwork, colourful fish tanks and electric-blue back-lit glass panels all add up to a swanky, contemporary setting. Chef-proprietor Raymond Patterson grew up in the fishing port of Eyemouth and knows good produce when he sees it; staying true to his roots, he sources fish, seafood and top-grade beef from Scotland, and subjects it to modern European treatments. A thorough grounding in classical technique is clear in intelligent partnerships of flavour and texture that might begin with smoked haddock soufflé with chive and white wine sauce, followed by corn-fed chicken with asparagus fritters, potato purée and truffle sauce. Among sophisticated desserts could be lemon tart with honeyed mascarpone cream.

Times 12-3/6-11 Closed 25-26 Dec, 1 Jan, Good Fri & Etr Mon, Sun, L Sat

La Petite Maison
PLAN 2 H1

◉◉ French, Mediterranean 🍷NOTABLE WINE LIST

The flavours of the Midi in Mayfair

☎ 020 7495 4774
54 Brooks Mews W1K 4EG
e-mail: info@lpmlondon.co.uk
dir: Nearest station: Bond St

Modelled on and named after its sister restaurant in Nice, the light, open-plan, sunny room does have a breezily Mediterranean vibe. The Riviera-cool look takes in creamy walls with large frosted-glass windows, an open-to-view kitchen and an uptempo, see-and-be-seen atmosphere. A battalion of skilful staff respond without hovering at closely-set tables, while the cooking shows a light modern touch, keeping things simple and fresh, driven by top-notch produce in a procession of skilfully delivered dishes designed for sharing. Starters like a salad of French beans with foie gras or carpaccio of sea bream with salsa verde, precede mains along the lines of turbot served with artichokes and chorizo, or perhaps slow-cooked duck leg with orange glaze. Factor in two-hour table time slots or you could miss out on a vanilla crème brûlée or warm fig tart finale.

Times 12-3/6-11 Closed 25-26 Dec

Pied à Terre

Modern French **V** NOTABLE WINE LIST

Refined and intelligent cooking in Fitzrovia

☎ 020 7636 1178
34 Charlotte St W1T 2NH
e-mail: info@pied-a-terre.co.uk
dir: Nearest station: Goodge Street. S of BT Tower and Goodge St

Its place secure on the list of the ten most important restaurants of its generation in London, Pied à Terre is of all of them still the least obtrusive. If we expect to process in state into a chandeliered hotel dining room, or to some expansively designered space in Mayfair, to find ourselves at the cutting edge, this place has always been there to confuse preconceptions. It's a modestly sized joint (albeit spread over three floors, with a roof garden growing herbs), not all that far from the West End, and yet keeping a serene distance from the hurly burly. The place has always been run, however, with the kind of personal attention you often don't get in the big-name addresses, and its culinary route, which is primarily why we're here of course, has been an unerring journey into excellence. Shane Osborn set the controls for the heart of the sun when he took over here many years ago, and has now bequeathed the stoves to the capable hands of Marcus Eaves, who steps up to the plate with

impressive continuity. The style remains a tantalising one: dishes that sound mcsmcrisingly complex in the descriptions, but that deliver a fully rounded composition of tastes, textures and seasonings on the plate, matching overall lightness with undeniable intensity. The eight-course taster, with its cheese and two dessert courses and the option of accompanying wine pairings, is one of the outstanding experiences of London gastronomy, but if you're essaying a more cautious way through the menu, there are still revelations aplenty. Sea bass is the base for a tartare with counterpointing elements of kohlrabi and rocket, and an apple and vanilla purée, or there may be a delicate raviolo filled with spiced pig brawn and crab in a broth of pickled daikon, shiso and kaffir lime. Main courses add further grace-notes to their principal ingredients, as when Anjou pigeon is poached in chocolate stout, and served with creamed Swiss chard, celeriac, apple and cinnamon, the sweet-spicy accompaniments offsetting the dark richness of the meat, while a productive pairing of guinea fowl breast and crayfish tails seems a flawless match, supported by globe artichoke purée in a truffled lemongrass jus. Another tough choice arrives in the form of the dessert menu, where black treacle parfait with star anise foam and chocolate streusel competes with pumpkin and nutmeg tart with orange purée and ginger jelly and ice cream. It

all comes with a voluminous list of well-served quality wines.

Chef Marcus Eaves **Owner** David Moore **Times** 12-2.45/6.15-11 Closed 2 wks Xmas & New Year, Sun, L Sat **Prices** Fixed L 2 course £27.50-£60, Tasting menu £99, Service added but optional 12.5% **Wines** 620 bottles over £20, 11 bottles under £20, 15 by glass **Notes** Tasting 10 course, L Plat du jour or ALC, Theatre D £39.50, Vegetarian menu **Seats** 40, Pr/dining room 12 **Parking** Cleveland St

LONDON W1 *continued*

Pied à Terre
PLAN 2 J3

◉◉◉ — *see page 331*

Plum Valley
PLAN 2 K1

◉ Chinese

Contemporary dining in Chinatown

☎ 020 7494 4366
20 Gerrard St W1D 6JQ
dir: Nearest station: Leicester Square

In the heart of Chinatown, Plum Valley is a good bet, with its stylish and contemporary black frontage and coolly minimalist interior design. Set across several floors, it looks good with its darkwood furnishings and subtle lighting. Traditional Cantonese dishes - mostly served in authentic cooking pots - are given a gently modern makeover, with some use of organic produce. There's a good range of dim sum (scallop har gau for example) with the main menu serving up the likes of salt and pepper squid or Singapore vermicelli with king prawns, and stir-fried chicken with shallots and black beans comes in one of those clay pots.

Times noon-mdnt

Pollen Street Social
PLAN 2 J2

◉◉◉◉ — *see opposite*

Polpetto
PLAN 2 K1

◉ Italian

Thrillingly unpretentious Venetian-style 'bacaro'

☎ 020 7734 1969
Upstairs at The French House, 49 Dean St W1D 5BG
e-mail: contact@frenchhousesoho.com
dir: Nearest station: Piccadilly Circus

Expect a Bohemian, shabby-chic feel and a relaxed, fun and unpretentious vibe at this pint-sized sibling to big brother Polpo (see entry). Squeezed into a tiny room above an iconic Soho pub, The French House, it has just 28 seats and a no-booking policy in the evenings, so tables come elbow-to-elbow on a first-come, winner-takes-all basis. But that's fine, in its egalitarian way. There are bare zinc-topped tables with brown-paper throw-away menus as placemats, dangling bare light bulbs and exposed brick and distressed cream walls. This high-decibel joint, like its big sister, takes inspiration from the Venetian 'bacaro' (wine bar) and deals in simple, gutsy Italian-style tapas called cichetti, which pack a punch with big flavours. Expect plate sharing, no-nonsense dishes such as spiced cuttlefish, baked cod with cucumber and chilli, or quail with roasted radish.

Times noon-3/5.30-11 Closed Sun & BHs

Polpo
PLAN 2 J1

◉◉ Italian

Bustling Venetian-style bacaro in Soho

☎ 020 7734 4479
41 Beak St W1F 9SB
dir: Nearest station: Piccadilly Circus

Fizzing like a glass of prosecco, Polpo offers a trendy take on the bacaros of Venice, delivering on-vogue Italian-style tapas (cichetti) in a fabulously casual, high-energy atmosphere. Though Canaletto, the great Venetian master, may once have lived in this building, the décor is unapologetically stripped-back and designer distressed - think old tiles and exposed-brick walls, floorboards, dangling light bulbs and crammed-in tables. The street-level dining room comes with mandatory high-stool bar-dining (up front) and an open kitchen (out back), while there's a campari bar in the basement. It's high-octane when the place gets rammed (a given) and you can't book ahead in the evenings (so expect to queue), but that's all part of the relaxed fun of it all. Brown-paper menus double as placemats, staff are youthful but clued-up, while the kitchen sends out quick-fire, small plates for sharing (with very affordable price tags). It's authentic, simple, full-on flavoured stuff; perhaps potato and parmesan croquettas and wild mushroom piadina to fritto misto and lamb chump served with caponata and basil. The flourless orange and almond cake shouldn't be missed, while wines aptly reflect the northern Italian region too, served in tumblers by glass, carafe and bottle. Part of a burgeoning family (see entry for Polpetto).

Chef Tom Oldroyd **Owner** Polpo Ltd **Times** 12-11 Closed 25 Dec-1 Jan, D Sun **Prices** Food prices not confirmed for 2013. Please telephone for details **Wines** 21 bottles over £20, 5 bottles under £20, 15 by glass **Notes** Vegetarian available **Seats** 60 **Children** Portions

The Providores and Tapa Room
PLAN 2 G3

◉◉ International 🍷NOTABLE WINE LIST

High-excitement fusion food in fashionable Marylebone

☎ 020 7935 6175
109 Marylebone High St W1U 4RX
e-mail: anyone@theprovidores.co.uk
dir: Nearest station: Bond St/Baker St/Regent's Park. From Bond St station cross Oxford St, down James St, into Thayer St then Marylebone High St

When it comes to top-notch fusion food with a southern-hemisphere spin, Kiwi Peter Gordon is the man, and he has been since serving up his highly inventive trademark cooking here on Marylebone High Street since 2001. Spread over two floors - an up-tempo, all-day, café-bar-style ground-floor Tapa Room (no bookings) and more grown-up (but still suitably chilled) restaurant upstairs - both are light and bright spaces, appealingly minimalist, with linen-clad tables and black leather banquettes the extent of the refinement in the restaurant. The creative cooking delivers all the colour and excitement required.

Dish descriptions come with their enthralling array of esoteric ingredients (all excellent quality), and everything seems to work very well together. Tuna carpaccio to kick things off, perhaps, delivered on wakame, samphire and shiso cress salad with crunchy Cornish squid, wasabi tobikko and olive oil jelly. Next up, roast Elwy Valley lamb cannon is served on oregano corn bread with butter bean purée, raisin dressing and a kalamata olive tapioca crisp, showing the kitchen is quite comfortable with the flavours of the Mediterranean too. A star-turn New Zealand wine list only adds to its appeal. (See entry for sister restaurant Kopapa in Covent Garden.)

Chef Peter Gordon **Owner** P Gordon, M McGrath **Times** 12-2.30/6-10 Closed 24 Dec-3 Jan, Etr Mon **Prices** Fixed D 3 course fr £47, Service added but optional 12.5% **Wines** 81 bottles over £20, 18 by glass **Notes** Fixed D 5 course £63, Tasting menu available 6 nights a week, Vegetarian available **Seats** 38 **Children** Portions

Quo Vadis
PLAN 2 K2

◉◉ Grill

Brasserie-style cooking at a Soho institution

☎ 020 7437 9585
26-29 Dean St W1D 3LL
e-mail: info@quovadissoho.co.uk
dir: Nearest station: Tottenham Court Road, Leicester Square

This glorious art deco gem was spruced up at the beginning of 2012 to bring in a lighter, more pared-back look in honour of the new broom in the kitchen, Jeremy Lee. Back-to-back tan leather banquettes divide up the space, and cream walls are hung with modern art in a setting that sits well with its original stained-glass windows, wall mirrors and wooden floors. Owned by restaurateur brothers Sam and Eddie Hart, who made their name with tapas joints Fino and Barrafina (see entries), the food here continues to plough a fairly classic brasserie-style furrow mixing simple modern comfort ideas with old school grills and braised dishes. After a cocktail or bubbles in the buzzy bar (which has its own nibbles menu) take a seat for seasonal delights - a taste of spring in a plate of tender squid with fennel, wild garlic and peas, followed by flawlessly-cooked brill with silky smooth olive oil mash pointed up with a punchy gremolata. At the end, almond tart with caramelised pear and vanilla ice cream is another hit.

Times 12-2.30/5.30-11 Closed 24-25 Dec, 1 Jan, BHs, Sun

Pollen Street Social

LONDON W1   PLAN 2 J2

Modern British V NOTABLE WINE LIST

Unerringly well executed modern cooking in West End star

☎ 020 7290 7600
8-10 Pollen St W1S 1NQ
e-mail: reservations@
pollenstreetsocial.com
dir: Nearest station: Oxford Circus. 2 min walk from Oxford Circus, off Regent Street, between Hanover Street and Maddox Street

It is rare for a restaurant to come storming onto the map with the panache and confidence of Jason Atherton's new venture, but not many chefs come with Atherton's astonishing culinary talent. Tucked in a Dickensian-sounding side road off Regent Street, Pollen Street Social is much more of-the-moment than somewhere the chef describes as a 'bistro'. The design is unshowy, neutral, yet still undeniably chic: wooden floors, stark walls with contemporary art, cool lighting and an open-to-view kitchen. Separate spaces show a switched-on focus on letting the customers do what they want: cocktails in the bar whilst grazing on properly good tapas (Dingley Dell pork cheeks with black pudding and beans, perhaps). In the main dining room, a flexible concept lets you create your own tasting menu, stick to the conventional three-course format, or go for the excellent value set lunch. There's even a 'dessert bar' for eating pudding right by the main action if that's what floats your boat - the key is that it's you who calls the shots. Dining here most definitely fits into the 'fine' category, but the vibe is the polar opposite of what that tag can imply: hushed tones and hovering waiters are out, thank you, and fun is definitely allowed. Atherton ran Ramsay's Maze (see entry) so is in the business of crafting high-calibre miniatures and taking a deconstructed approach to eating, so expect plenty of pace-setting invention and cheeky combinations of taste and texture. Cornish crab vinaigrette with Nashi pear, cauliflower sweet-and-sour dressing and peanut powder has got it all going on, while a more classic combo of Atlantic halibut 'Bourguignon' delivers immaculate fish with bacon, mushrooms, onion and red wine. Throw convention to the wind and finish off at the dessert bar with a simple yet intensely rich and bitter chocolate pavé with mango sorbet - or why not have two, and follow that with a traditional English goats' milk rice pudding with hay ice cream and lime jelly, because it's allowed here.

Chef Jason Atherton **Owner** Jason Atherton **Times** 12-2.45/6-10.45 Closed BHs, Sun **Prices** Fixed L 2 course £22, Tasting menu £69, Starter £10.50-£12.50, Main £24-£33, Dessert £7.50-£12, Service added but optional 12.5% **Wines** 19 by glass **Notes** Tasting menu 7 course, Vegetarian menu **Seats** 60, Pr/dining room 14 **Children** Portions **Parking** On street, car park Mayfair, Park Lane

Rhodes W1 Restaurant

LONDON W1   **PLAN 2 F2**

Modern European ⚑ NOTABLE WINE LIST

Striking cooking in glitzy hotel restaurant

☎ 020 7616 5930
**The Cumberland Hotel, Great Cumberland Place
W1H 7DL**
e-mail: restaurant@rhodesw1.com
dir: Nearest station: Marble Arch

There are no windows at Gary Rhodes' restaurant at The Cumberland (see also Rhodes W1 Brasserie), so the focus is very much on the design, which creates quite an impression, with crystal chandeliers, rich dark fabrics, and antique French chairs and ornate mirrors; a funky touch in the bar is chairs printed with the chef's recipes in his own handwriting. Not surprisingly for a man who helped reinvigorate British cooking (and reintroduced the faggot), dishes are based on fine native traditions, with a strong classical French influence at work too. Potted veal, presented in a small jar alongside a dollop of sauce gribiche and warm caper butter - a self-assembly job - is a superb starter, another one combining the deep, earthy flavours of pig's trotter and ham hock with pea velouté and a quail's egg. Forthright meaty flavours can be seen in main courses too - witness slow-cooked veal breast and sweetbreads, served with garlic mousse, artichoke and wild mushrooms - and dishes generally impress with their precise timings and well-judged combinations: perfectly roast fillet of pollock, for instance, with a tasty stew of clams, mussels and celery. If deconstructed lemon meringue pie, with blackberry and yoghurt, doesn't appeal, there's always perfectly risen raspberry soufflé, served with pieces of Bakewell tart and outstanding roast almond ice cream.

Chef Gary Rhodes, Paul Welburn **Owner** Gary Rhodes **Times** 12-2.15/7-10.15 Closed 1st 2 wks Aug, L Sat-Mon, D Sun-Mon **Prices** Fixed L 2 course £25.95, Fixed D 3 course £49.90, Service added but optional 12.5% **Wines** 250 bottles over £20, 13 by glass **Notes** Vegetarian available, Dress restrictions, Smart dress, no torn jeans, no trainers **Seats** 46, Pr/dining room 22 **Parking** NCP at Marble Arch

The Ritz Restaurant

LONDON W1   **PLAN 4 J6**

British V ⚑ NOTABLE WINE LIST

Memorable dining in historic grand London hotel

☎ 020 7300 2370
150 Piccadilly W1J 9BR
e-mail: ritzrestaurant@theritzlondon.com
dir: Nearest station: Green Park. 10 min walk from Piccadilly Circus or Hyde Park Corner, less from Green Park station

It would be a brave person indeed who tried to argue The Ritz wasn't the most famous hotel in the world. The big news is the art-deco style Rivoli Bar has recently relaxed its dress code, so gents can slip off their tie whilst eating caviar and sipping on a cocktail - a Rivoli 10, perhaps, to celebrate the bar's anniversary. Keep the tie handy, though, for when you enter the grand dining room. It is a magnificent room to be sure. With its floor-to-ceiling windows looking over Green Park, rich Louis XVI-inspired décor, plush, tactile furnishings and chandeliers reflecting off mirrored walls, it's an extravagantly opulent space. A palm court orchestra plays most nights if anything else should be needed to make the experience memorable. Tailcoat-clad waiters set the scene for theatrical dining with classic tableside service, which, while knowledgeable and skilful, is not at all stuffy. Harking back to the days of Escoffier, the menu explores the classical repertoire with many old favourites such as grilled Dover sole but has also embraced more up-to-the-minute techniques; dressed crab roll with avocado and Charantais melon might precede terrine of goose liver with rhubarb and walnuts, followed by a fish course such as brill with ceps purée and artichoke heart. Sound technique is evident in a meat course, too, with superb peppered venison loin with smoked sausage, pumpkin and cabbage. To finish, praline parfait and mandarin sorbet has a delightful balance of flavours, or go for some tableside magic in the form of crêpe Suzette (for two). The world-class wine list is explained, unsurprisingly, with aplomb.

Chef John T Williams MBE **Owner** The Ritz Hotel (London) Ltd **Times** 12.30-2/5.30-10 **Prices** Fixed L 3 course £45, Fixed D 3 course £50, Tasting menu £99-£160, Starter £18-£28, Main £36-£49, Dessert £17-£18, Service optional **Wines** 500+ bottles over £20, 19 by glass **Notes** Fixed D 5 course £65, 'Live at the Ritz' menu £95pp, Sunday L, Vegetarian menu, Dress restrictions, Jacket & tie required, no jeans or trainers **Seats** 90, Pr/dining room 60 **Children** Portions, Menu **Parking** NCP

LONDON W1 *continued*

The Red Fort
PLAN 2 K2

 Traditional Indian V

Authentic contemporary Indian in the heart of Soho

☎ 020 7437 2525
77 Dean St, Soho W1D 3SH
e-mail: info@redfort.co.uk
dir: Nearest station: Leicester Square, Tottenham Court Road. Walk N on Charing Cross Rd. At Cambridge Circus left into Shaftesbury Av. Dean St 2nd right

Opened in 1983 and named after the eponymous Delhi landmark (although it no longer has a red façade), this smart and stylish Indian restaurant was one of the first in London to introduce regional cooking presented in a modern fashion. Nearly 30 years on and it continues to create innovative dishes, the unique Mogul Court cooking successfully combining great British produce with authentic sub-continental flavours. From the open kitchen may come a starter of spiced and roasted minced Devon lamb skewers with mint and onion salad, followed by such main courses as grilled stone bass with mustard, coconut milk and a curry leaf sauce, accompanied by a vegetable side dish, perhaps stir-fried okra and asparagus with tomato, onion and sun-dried spices. Dine in the subterranean Akbar bar or in the long ground floor dining room, with walls adorned with authentic artefacts amid ornate Mogul arches.

Chef M A Rahman **Owner** Amin Ali **Times** 12-4/5.30-11.30 Closed 25 Dec, L Sat-Sun **Prices** Fixed L 2 course £14-£20, Fixed D 3 course £30-£50, Tasting menu £55, Starter £6-£10, Main £16-£36, Dessert £7-£12, Service added but optional 12.5% **Wines** 325 bottles over £20, 14 by glass **Notes** Tasting menu 4 course, Fixed pre-theatre D, Vegetarian menu, Dress restrictions, Smart casual **Seats** 84 **Parking** NCP

Rhodes W1 Brasserie
PLAN 2 F2

 Modern British

Smart, contemporary brasserie cooking

☎ 020 7616 5930
The Cumberland Hotel, Great Cumberland Place W1H 7DL
e-mail: brasserie@rhodesw1.com
dir: Nearest station: Marble Arch

The popular brasserie at The Cumberland (see also Rhodes W1 Restaurant) is a thoroughly up-to-date space of big, bold colours, muted lighting and a crowd-pleasing menu of modern reworkings of British and European dishes. Simple but effective starters have included a plate of charcuterie with pickles, and smoked salmon terrine with potato salad, the range broadened by a soup: perhaps parsley with a soft-poached egg and cheese croûtons. The chargrill is the source of most main courses: T-bone pork cutlet, say, or wild boar and apple sausages; otherwise there could be something as ambitious as pan-fried salmon fillet with cockle and saffron broth and spicy stir-fried cauliflower. Desserts tend to be as uncomplicated as the rest of the output, crème caramel among them.

Times 12-2.15/6-8

Rhodes W1 Restaurant
PLAN 2 F2

 – *see opposite*

The Riding House Café
PLAN 2 J3

 Modern British **NEW**

Buzzy all-day brasserie near Oxford Street

☎ 020 7927 0840
43-51 Great Titchfield St W1W 7PQ
e-mail: info@ridinghousecafe.co.uk
dir: Nearest station: Oxford Circus/Goodge St

If you're shopping on Oxford Street and looking for a pit-stop, then take a short diversion up Great Titchfield Street to The Riding House Café, where a fashionable all-day dining menu - everything from breakfasts to afternoon tea - is served in a lively, buzzing environment. Much more restaurant than café, The Riding House stands out from the crowd with its striking art-deco design (think large, 1930s-style windows all around, affording its diners great street views and plenty of light), whilst inside it is all parquet flooring and clubby wood panelling. You can perch on a swivel seat at the bar and watch the chefs at work or take an old wooden cinema seat at the long communal table to eat refectory-style; there are plenty of regular tables too if communal ain't your thing. Classic brasserie dishes are the order of the day at lunch and dinner: start with a couple of 'small plates', such as beautifully flavoured braised rabbit with soft polenta and parmesan, and crispy salt-cod fritters with red pepper aïoli, before tucking into a very fine fish and chips. The apple and sultana crumble for two with vanilla ice cream and custard is a very happy ending.

Chef Paul Daniel **Owner** Clive Watson, Adam White **Times** 12-3.30/6-10 Closed 25 Dec **Prices** Starter £3-£7, Main £10.50-£25, Dessert £5-£7.50, Service added but optional 12.5% **Wines** 70 bottles over £20, 6 bottles under £20, 20 by glass **Notes** Sunday L, Vegetarian available **Seats** 115, Pr/dining room 14 **Children** Portions, Menu **Parking** On street

Ristorante Semplice
PLAN 2 H2

 Italian

Elegant modern Italian a hop, skip and a jump from Oxford Street

☎ 020 7495 1509
10 Blenheim St W1S 1LJ
e-mail: info@ristorantesemplice.com
dir: Nearest station: Bond Street. Off New Bond Street, next to Bonhams

If you're shopping in Oxford Street and New Bond Street and fancy some sustenance of the sophisticated Italian kind, Ristorante Semplice, tucked away down a small side street near sister eatery Bar Trattoria Semplice (see entry), fits the bill. It may look expensive with its glamorous décor of piano-gloss rosewood panelling and gold textured walls, high-backed caramel and chocolate chairs and banquettes, and tables dressed in their finery, but you can still eat here for a snip at lunchtime if you go for the set menu (the à la carte is less of a bargain). The kitchen deals in modern Italian cooking based around superb ingredients, and shows a good deal of skill and creative flair. Start, perhaps, with a knock-out home-made tagliatelle with hare ragù and black cabbage, followed by super-fresh plaice fillets cooked Milanese style and served with roasted cauliflower and baby spinach leaves. It's well worth waiting the extra 12 minutes for the Domori chocolate fondant with a boozy grappa pannacotta, deeply rich chocolate sorbet and crunchy croûtons of spiced bread.

Chef Marco Torri **Owner** Marimo Roberto, Marco Torri **Times** 12-2.30/6.30-10.30 Closed Xmas, New Year, Sun, L Sat **Prices** Fixed L 2 course £23, Starter £12.25-£15.50, Main £23.25-£29, Dessert £8-£9.50, Service optional **Wines** 30 bottles over £20, 10 bottles under £20 **Notes** Tasting menu available D, Vegetarian available **Seats** 70, Pr/dining room 45 **Children** Portions

The Ritz Restaurant
PLAN 4 J6

 – *see opposite*

Roganic
PLAN 2 G3

 – *see page 336*

Roka
PLAN 2 J3

 – *see page 336*

Roganic

LONDON W1 | **PLAN 2 G3**

Modern British **NEW**

Super-chef Simon Rogan pops up in the capital

☎ 020 7486 0380
19 Blandford St, Marylebone W1U 3DH
e-mail: info@roganic.co.uk
dir: Nearest station: Baker St, Bond St, Regent's Park

The clock is ticking. Simon Rogan - holder of five Rosettes at his Cumbrian high-flying gaff, L'Enclume - has a two-year lease at his big city outpost, between Marylebone Road and Baker Street. 'Pop up' restaurant is the expression, but, hopefully, Mr Rogan's talents won't be lost to the capital. Watch this space. The temporary nature of the venue means every expense has not been thrown at it, but it's none the worse for that. With tightly packed bare tables and splashes of colour from vivid modern artworks, there is little distraction from what appears on the plate - and what appears on the plate is sometimes surprising, usually amazing to look at, and always good to eat. Rogan's trademark is to search out unusual or little used British ingredients, to create thrilling combinations and to always allow the produce to take centre stage. The menu takes the form of multiple courses, six or ten dishes, plus a three-course weekly-changing lunch. Seawater-cured mackerel, orache (a spinach-like leaf), broccoli and warm elderflower honey shows the way, with the beautiful piece of fish lifted by its superbly-judged accompaniments. Royal kidneys cooked in chicken fat, with peas, goats' curd and clam juice is an inspired combination, and fine technical proficiency is evident once again in a dish of rose veal cooked in buttermilk, with cobnuts, Savoy cabbage and mead sauce. With three immaculate rolls served warm alongside a dollop of butter placed on a Kentish stone, and desserts such as white chocolate sorbet with rapeseed, plum and meadowsweet, the creativity and high quality is maintained from start to finish.

Chef Simon Rogan, Andrew Tomlinson **Owner** Simon Rogan & Penny Tapsell **Times** 12-2.30/6-9 Closed Sun-Mon **Prices** Food prices not confirmed for 2013. Please telephone for details **Notes** Please note Fri-Sat full Roganic experience of 10 courses only offered

Roka

LONDON W1 | **PLAN 2 J3**

Japanese

Exquisite robata-grill cookery in London's Medialand

☎ 020 7580 6464
37 Charlotte St W1T 1RR
e-mail: info@rokarestaurant.com
dir: Nearest station: Goodge St, Tottenham Court Rd. 5 min walk from Goodge St

Roka ought to be given a place in the dictionary with a definition for 'effortlessly cool, contemporary Japanese dining'. With another London branch in Canary Wharf (and also owners of the popular Zuma in Knightsbridge - see entries), Roka has pedigree and is a high-energy outfit and byword for fashionable plate-sharing Japanese eating. It's a light-filled corner-sited venue, with full-drop glass doors that open out to create a semi-alfresco vibe on sunny days, while outside, pavement-side tables under awnings and patio heaters go the full hog. Exotic hardwoods catch the eye under a warehouse-like ceiling, while the thick grainy counter around the centrepiece Robata (charcoal) grill (with its busy chorus of chefs) offers a ringside seat. Elsewhere, closely-set modern pale-wood tables, wide oak floorboards and sage-green upholstered chairs fit with the organic, neutral colour palette. The robata-grilled items provide the main action, whether meat or poultry, as in konbu-smoked duck breast with kumquats and sharon fruit, or sparkling fresh fish, perhaps sea bass with yuzu-miso and ginger seaweed salad. Meanwhile, perennials like tempura (rock shrimp with zingy wasabi pea seasoning and chilli mayo), or sashimi (yellowtail with truffle dressing, mizuma and pickled vegetables) and maki rolls (crispy prawn, avocado and dark sweet soy) catch the eye too. Desserts do the East-West thing immaculately, perhaps spiced crème brûlée with Japanese black sugar ice cream. Downstairs in the basement is the Shochu Lounge.

Chef Hamish Brown **Owner** Rainer Becker, Arjun Waney **Times** 12-3.30/5.30-11.30 Closed 25 Dec **Prices** Food prices not confirmed for 2013. Please telephone for details **Wines** 152 bottles over £20, 13 by glass **Notes** Average cost L/D £50-£60, Vegetarian available, Dress restrictions, Smart casual **Seats** 88 **Children** Portions **Parking** On street, NCP in Brewers St

LONDON W1 *continued*

Roti Chai
PLAN 2 G2

◎◎ Modern Indian **NEW**

Vibrant Indian street-food close to Oxford Street

☎ 020 7408 0101
3 Portman Mews South W1H 6HS
e-mail: infowala@rotichai.com
dir: Nearest station: Bond Street/Marble Arch. Short walk from Selfridges & Oxford St

Just off Oxford Street, close to M&S and Selfridges, Roti Chai takes its inspiration from the street stalls, roadside and railway cafés of the India sub-continent and brings a breath of fresh air to the West End shopping frenzy. There's an all-day Street Kitchen on the ground floor with an up-tempo urban café vibe, while below there's a more stylish evenings-only Dining Room, with its design inspired by India's famous rail transport (think luggage racks on walls and train-carriage like banquette seating). Expect intense, vibrant, robust flavours wherever you sit: Street Kitchen dishes might feature chicken lollipops (Keralan-spiced chicken wings) or railway lamb curry (lamb and potato served with chapatis), while the Dining Room still turns-out small 'street' plates alongside larger-options with a regional theme; perhaps awadhi lamb korma (flavoured with rosewater and saffron) or paneer pasanda (a speciality of the Mogul courts).

Owner Rohit Chugh **Times** 12-11.45 **Prices** Starter £3.80-£5.80, Main £7.50-£8.50, Dessert £2.50-£6.50, Service added but optional 12.5% **Wines** 10 by glass **Notes** Special party menus available for larger groups, Vegetarian available **Seats** 75 **Parking** On street, 24hr car park nearby

Roux at The Landau
PLAN 2 H4

◎◎ British, French **V** ⌂NOTABLE WINE LIST

Skilful Roux cookery in a luxurious dining room

☎ 020 7965 0165
The Langham London, Portland Place W1B 1JA
e-mail: reservations@thelandau.com
dir: Nearest station: Oxford Circus. N end of Regent St, at Oxford Circus

The old-school elegance of the Langham has been gently worked on in today's neutral shades by the David Collins studio to make of the elliptically shaped Roux dining room a place of great comfort and refinement, adorned with horsey memorabilia. The place represents the return of a collaboration between one of London gastronomy's greats, Albert Roux, and his son, Michel, the vision executed by the capable hands of the youthful Chris King. What results is a style of contemporary French cuisine that nonetheless also feels very 'London'. Cornish squid with shaved cauliflower, seasoned with Meyer lemon and dill, is impressive in its simplicity, but starters also stretch to a pairing of spiced pork jowl and gambas a la plancha, served on marjoram-scented arrocina beans. North African modes inveigle a main course of aubergine roasted in zatar, with bulgur pilaf and harissa vinaigrette, while the chorizo is made in-house, to

accompany a roast Ibérico pork chop in thyme-spiked Suffolk cider sauce. As you near the finishing-line, you'll find the aromatic tendency still going strong in desserts such as arabica coffee mousseline with Kahlúa jelly and warm cinnamon doughnuts.

Chef Chris King **Owner** Langham Hotels International **Times** 12.30-2.30/5.30-10.30 Closed BHs, Sun, L Sat **Prices** Fixed L 2 course fr £32, Fixed D 3 course £39.50-£49.50, Tasting menu £80-£140, Starter £11-£17.50, Main £20-£45, Dessert £8.50-£9.75, Service added but optional 12.5% **Wines** 265 bottles over £20, 20 by glass **Notes** Veg tasting £70, incl wine £130, Vegetarian menu, Dress restrictions, Smart casual **Seats** 100, Pr/dining room 18 **Children** Portions, Menu **Parking** On street, NCP

Salt Yard
PLAN 2 J3

◎◎ Italian, Spanish

Top-notch tapas just off Tottenham Court Road

☎ 020 7637 0657
54 Goodge St W1T 4NA
e-mail: info@saltyard.co.uk
dir: Nearest station: Goodge St. Near Tottenham Court Rd

An appealingly casual vibe and jolly staff are just part of the attraction at this smart contemporary tapas bar in Fitzrovia. While the setting is fresh, unfussy, and veneered with un-showy elegance, its tapas repertoire is not quite as the Spanish would know it: the kitchen reworks the theme Salt Yard-style with a down-to-earth fusion of Spanish, Italian and British ingredients and ideas. Eating here could be as simple as a glass of wine with a plate of top-notch charcuterie, or a coffee and something sweet to punctuate a day in the shops. Taking a dish from each of the categories (divided into fish, meat and vegetable) you could graze your way through poached Cornish cod cheeks with ceps, pancetta, and butter beans, then a veggie plate of roasted porcini with Jerusalem artichoke purée, poached free-range egg, pine nuts and parsley, before finishing with grilled under-blade fillet of beef teamed with artichokes, black olives and piquillo salsa. Wine is essential to the tapas experience, and you will be impressed - possibly floored - by an array of sherries, wines from lesser known vineyards, dessert wines by the glass, and a fine arsenal of fiery grappa and Spanish brandies.

Chef Benjamin Tish, Andrew Clarke **Owner** Sanja Morris & Simon Mullins **Times** 12-3/5.30-11 Closed BHs, 10 days Xmas, Sun, L Sat **Prices** Food prices not confirmed for 2013. Please telephone for details **Wines** 63 bottles over £20, 4 bottles under £20, 12 by glass **Notes** Vegetarian available **Seats** 60 **Parking** NCP Cleveland St, meter parking Goodge Place

Sartoria
PLAN 2 J1

◎ Italian

Smart setting for modern Italian cooking

☎ 020 7534 7000 & 7534 7030
20 Savile Row W1S 3PR
e-mail: sartoriareservations@danddlondon.com
web: www.danddlondon.com
dir: Nearest station: Oxford Circus, Green Park, Piccadilly Circus. Oxford Circus exit 3, left down Regent St towards Piccadilly Circus, 5th right into New Burlington St, end of street on left

Named in honour of its location in the fine suiting and booting world of Savile Row (the name is also Italian for tailor's shop), Sartoria is an immaculately turned-out operation with a chic, Milanese inspired interior and switched-on, upbeat service from staff dressed to look the part. On the menu is an earthy, uncomplicated roll-out of creatively re-imagined modern Italian ideas. Antipasti could take the shape of capon broth with cappellacci 'Bishop's hat' ravioli, pumpkin and chestnut, while pasta dishes run to Piemontese ravioli with sheep's milk ricotta, spinach, walnuts and sage. Among main courses might be braised lamb shank with celeriac purée, or baked red mullet with spinach and gremolata, while the dolci department offers layered Amedei chocolate cake with passionfruit.

Times 12-3/5.30-11 Closed 24-26 Dec, 1-2 Jan, Sun (open for private parties only), L Sat

Scott's Restaurant
PLAN 2 G1

◎◎ British **V**

Bags of style and first-rate seafood

☎ 020 7495 7309
20 Mount St W1K 2HE
dir: Nearest station: Bond Street, Green Park. Just off Grosvenor Sq, between Berkeley Sq & Park Ln

Reinvigorated by Caprice Holdings back in 2007, this elegant and rather glitzy seafood restaurant is a Mayfair institution. It was once Ian Fleming's favourite hangout, and it's easy to imagine his iconic creation sipping a Vesper cocktail among the Bond girl lookalikes sitting at the onyx-topped central crustacea bar. Like the people-watching, the décor positively shimmers with glamorous art-deco style - sleek oak-panelling, leather seating, oak floors, marble mosaic, and large mirrors and big-impact modern British art. Super-fresh fish and seafood are given the lightest of treatments in skilful, clean-cut renditions of classics (Dover sole for example) to more adventurous offerings like roast monkfish with saffron potatoes and gremolata, and cod with crab risotto and monk's beard. It doesn't come cheap, but this is high quality stuff, and the slick service meets expectations.

Chef Dave McCarthy **Owner** Caprice Holdings Ltd **Times** 12-10.30 Closed 25-26 Dec, D 24 Dec **Prices** Starter £6.75-£17, Main £17.75-£42, Dessert £9.50-£9.75, Service added but optional 12.5% **Notes** Sunday L, Vegetarian menu, Dress restrictions, Smart casual **Seats** 120, Pr/dining room 40 **Children** Portions **Parking** NCP

Sketch (The Gallery)

Modern European ⚜ NOTABLE WINE LIST

Turner Prize-winning artist and exciting food

☎ 020 7659 4500
9 Conduit St W1S 2XG
e-mail: info@sketch.uk.com
web: www.sketch.uk.com
dir: Nearest station: Oxford Circus. 5 mins walk from station, take exit 3, along Regent St. Conduit St 4th on right

Whatever your point of view regarding cutting-edge food as art or craft, here at Sketch the artistic side of culinary endeavour is allowed to run rampant, Big-time. The Gallery is indeed a gallery and the concept is that different artists will take over the space every 18 months or so. Right now, as we go to press, it's Turner Prize-winning Martin Creed. Exciting stuff. The idea is that the space is an exhibition, an artwork and a restaurant. What you get is a kaleidoscope of colours and patterns, an amazing mix of vintage and starkly modern tables and chairs (no two pieces the same), with 96 types of marble zigzagging across the floor, and the staff also part of the display in their bold patterned shirts. So, what to eat? The brasserie-esque focus of the menu remains, but this is not your every-day sort of eating as you might imagine (and nor are the prices). Pierre Gagnaire is the creative spirit behind the menu

and this is compelling stuff, with an evident sense of fun combined with serious attention to detail - flavour, texture and visual appeal are measured to the nth degree. The fact that a sunset over the Nevada Desert is inspiration for a first-course 'Dundee Pinky' gives you some idea of what's going on here; that particular dish being a duck foie gras terrine with cauliflower purée, apple and beetroot. Next up, main-course scallops salpicon poached in mussel jus delivers perfect shellfish, succulent and fresh as a daisy, with avocado and galangal, or there's grilled pork belly with black pudding and colcannon. And for dessert? 'Big Mac' is, obviously, a lemongrass macaroon with a sweet wine jelly and confit grapefruit marmalade. Good food? You betcha! Art? Of course.

Chef Pierre Gagnaire, Herve Deville **Owner** Mourad Mazouz **Times** 6.30pm-2am Closed Sun, L all week **Prices** Starter £8-£28, Main £20-£29, Dessert £2-£10, Service added but optional 12.5% **Wines** 93 bottles over £20, 1 bottle under £20, 13 by glass **Notes** Vegetarian available, Dress restrictions, Smart casual, Civ Wed 650, Air con **Seats** 150 **Children** Portions, Menu **Parking** On street, NCP

LONDON W1 *continued*

Shogun, Millennium Hotel Mayfair   PLAN 2 G1

◉ Japanese

Authentic Japanese food in the heart of Mayfair

☎ 020 7629 9400

Grosvenor Square W1A 3AN

e-mail: reservations.mayfair@millenniumhotels.co.uk

dir: Nearest station: Bond Street, Green Park

Tucked away in the rear courtyard of the Millennium Hotel (an upscale Georgian mansion overlooking Grosvenor Square) on the corner of Adam's Row, Shogun delivers straight-up traditional Japanese food in a subterranean room with a faux-stone wine-cellar look accessorised with heritage features such as a life-size Samurai warrior statue, traditional prints and lanterns, and kyudo archery arrows dividing tables. The authentic repertoire can be accessed via a half-dozen set menus based on sashimi, tempura, or teriyaki main dishes of chicken, duck or Scottish sirloin. Otherwise, the carte runs to main courses along the lines of pork fried with ginger, deep-fried calamari, or grilled eel in teriyaki sauce. There's also a small sushi bar. Among the hotel's array of upmarket eating options, classy Italian cuisine is to be had in Avista (see entry) off the main foyer.

Times 6-11 Closed Mon, L all week

Sketch (The Gallery)   PLAN 2 J1

◉◉◉ *– see opposite*

Sketch (Lecture Room & Library)   PLAN 2 J1

◉◉◉◉◉ *– see page 340*

Sketch (The Parlour)   PLAN 2 J1

◉◉ Modern European

Art and eccentricity in Mayfair café and cocktail bar

☎ 020 7659 4500

9 Conduit St W1S 2XG

e-mail: info@sketch.uk.com

web: www.sketch.uk.com

dir: Nearest station: Oxford Circus/Green Park/Bond Street. From Oxford Circus, 5 min walk along Regent St, 4th turning on right

A larger-than-life collaboration between French super-chef Pierre Gagnaire and Mourad 'Momo' Mazouz, Sketch spreads its whimsical wings around various eating and drinking spaces in this arty, theatrical and totally glamorous Mayfair playpen. In descending order of fabulousness, the Lecture Room & Library, and the Gallery (see separate entries) each have their singular culinary and stylistic attractions for those whose pockets have the necessary depth, while the Parlour is the entry-level venue that serves as a funky place to see and be seen all day long through breakfasts, informal lunches, afternoon tea (with champers, why ever not?), before morphing into an evening cocktail bar (members only after 9). The one-off boudoir look involves an eccentric mishmash of Louis XV antique chairs, sofas and divans, crimson drapes and retro swirly designs. If you're doing lunch, the all day comfort food menu takes in everything from French and Spanish charcuterie to beef cheek bourguignon, or fishy ideas such as brandade with parmesan and salmon roe. Cake fiends will revel in chestnut gâteau or a hunk of something made with Agen prunes poached in red wine and spices, and blackcurrant marmalade.

Sketch (The Parlour)

Chef Herve Deville **Owner** Mourad Mazouz **Times** 12-10 Closed Sun **Prices** Starter £7.50-£16.50, Main £10-£17.50, Dessert £5.50, Service added but optional 12.5% **Wines** 12 bottles over £20, 12 by glass **Notes** Vegetarian available **Seats** 50 **Children** Portions **Parking** NCP Soho

So Restaurant   PLAN 2 J1

◉◉ Japanese

Modern Japanese with some top-notch European ingredients

☎ 020 7292 0767 & 7292 0760

3-4 Warwick St W1B 5LS

e-mail: info@sorestaurant.com

dir: Nearest station: Piccadilly Circus. Exit Piccadilly tube station via exit 1. Turn left along Glasshouse St. Restaurant next to The Warwick

Tucked away in Soho's hinterland just behind Piccadilly Circus, So is an unassuming but authentic, smart, modern Japanese. It spreads over two floors; a busy café-like ground floor with sushi bar and a more intimate, low-lit basement room. Laminate tables, an open-plan kitchen and a yobanyaki grill (where items are cooked over volcanic rocks imported from Mount Fuji) tick all the design boxes. The menu has a broad scope, from tempura (soft-shelled crab or squid), to sushi and sashimi, plus some European-inspired dishes; the kitchen makes good use of quality European produce, too, such as pan-fried foie gras served with Japanese mushrooms and teriyaki sauce, or half lobster meunière. There's fashionable stuff like black cod marinated in saikyo miso, too, plus good value West End lunch and bento box deals.

Times 12-3/5-10.30 Closed Xmas-New Year, Sun

The Square   PLAN 2 H1

◉◉◉◉ *– see page 341*

Sumosan Restaurant   PLAN 2 H1

◉◉ Japanese Fusion

Creative modern Japanese cooking

☎ 020 7495 5999

26B Albermarle St, Mayfair W1S 4HY

e-mail: info@sumosan.com

dir: Nearest station: Green Park. Between Dover St & Old Bond St

With a swanky Mayfair address - adjacent to Brown's Hotel and opposite The Royal Institute - Sumosan is a classy, fashionably modern Japanese restaurant with a clientele of international jet-setters and Mayfair beau monde, who come for some high-end Japanese grub. The décor is minimalist and neutrally toned, smart and contemporary, with pale-wood flooring, highly varnished wooden tables and designer lighting. The busy open kitchen puts-out precisely cooked and well-dressed dishes from tip-top ingredients with some Western influences. There's highly accomplished sushi and sashimi, plus an extensive menu that runs to black cod with miso, toro stuffed with foie gras, or lamb chops furikaki, and, from the teppan yaki, perhaps Wagyu beef with sweet potato purée. Head downstairs for pre-dinner cocktails in the bar, while a sommelier can guide you through the international wines and myriad of sake.

Chef Bubker Belkhit **Owner** Janina Wolkow **Times** 12-3/6-11.30 Closed 26 Dec, New Year, L Sat-Sun **Prices** Tasting menu £75, Starter £3.90-£23.50, Main £6.50-£65, Dessert £6.70-£14.90, Service added but optional 15% **Wines** 110 bottles over £20, 10 by glass **Notes** Fixed L 4, 7 course min £24.90, Tasting menu D 2 people, Vegetarian available, Dress restrictions, Smart casual **Seats** 100, Pr/dining room 32 **Parking** On street

Sketch (Lecture Room & Library)

LONDON W1   **PLAN 2 J1**

Modern European V ♨ NOTABLE WINE LIST

A unique and exciting dining experience

☎ 020 7659 4500
9 Conduit St W1S 2XG
e-mail: info@sketch.uk.com
web: www.sketch.uk.com
dir: Nearest station: Oxford Circus. 5 mins walk from station, take exit 3, along Regent St. Conduit St 4th on right

As an antidote to the 'greige' anonymity of identikit contemporary restaurants, Sketch is hard to beat. But first, you need to make sure you're in the right room. Despite its rather anonymous exterior, the building just off Regent Street has form as far as style is concerned, having previously been HQ to RIBA and Christian Dior, and is now home to several dining and drinking possibilities designed by Algerian-born restaurateur Mourad 'Momo' Mazouz: the buzzy, real-life art installation that is the ground floor Gallery brasserie (see entry), plus the Louis XV decadence of the Parlour (tea room by day, hyper-trendy bar by night - see entry), and a brace of bars for pre-dinner cocktails. We're dealing here with the top-end fine-dining Lecture Room & Library, which is up on the first floor. So, having made sure you're bound for the right venue, and spoken to the bank manager to ensure that the required funds are at hand to foot the bill, you enter an elegantly-proportioned Georgian space sexed-up with walls of studded leather, a

hallucinogenic palette of orange, candy pink and yellow, and regularly-changing works of art. The service team are certainly clued-up - they have to be when the menu lists items such as 'Perfume of the Earth' and 'Sea Garden No 10'. At first glance it all seems rather whimsical, but it is driven by the iconoclastic imagination of French super-chef Pierre Gagnaire, the consultant behind an array of mind-bending complexity that works in the real world thanks to unrivalled attention to detail and technical brilliance. The results are extraordinary: visually-stunning assemblages of flavour and texture, with a generous side order of theatre along the way. Such is the complexity of the dishes that we scarcely have space to describe them in detail on this page, but here goes: a Rapide lunch - a good way to dip a toe into what the kitchen is all about - begins with a succession of four dishes: super-fresh sea bream is marinated in kombu and delivered with the textural contrast of crunchy rice, a cleansing cucumber granité, and crispy borage flowers; then, black olive jelly, topped with an intense roasted red pepper velouté, crisp black olive soil, and chopped rose petals and mint; next comes a courgette flower filled with Paris mushrooms alongside tender parmesan gnocchi and mushroom velouté, and finally, a deeply-flavoured, silken soup of foie gras is poured over hibiscus sorbet and rhubarb. And that's just for starters. A simple (relatively-speaking...) main course brings together barely-cooked, sea-fresh mackerel with confit carrots, pearl barley, and a sublime saffron

bouillon, while the combination approach is back for a 'Pierre Gagnaire' dessert - in this case, a lemon and rose sorbet teamed with diced apple and rhubarb, and a raspberry tartlet with rose jelly and passionfruit velouté, which has all the required flavours singing out loud and in harmony. The wine list runs to 99 pages of excellence.

Chef Pierre Gagnaire, Jean Denis Le Bras **Owner** Mourad Mazouz
Times 12-2.30/6.30-11 Closed 18-29 Aug, 23-30 Dec, 1 Jan, BHs, Sun-Mon, L Sat **Prices** Starter £35-£45, Main £37-£55, Dessert £13-£25, Service added but optional 12.5% **Wines** 709 bottles over £20, 20 by glass **Notes** Tasting menu 8 course, Vegetarian tasting menu 7 course, Vegetarian menu **Seats** 50, Pr/dining room 24 **Children** Portions **Parking** NCP Soho, Cavendish Sq

Save on Hotels. Book at **theAA.com/hotel**

LONDON, CENTRAL (W1) 341 ENGLAND

The Square

Modern French V NOTABLE WINE LIST

Shining star in the heart of Mayfair

☎ 020 7495 7100
6-10 Bruton St, Mayfair W1J 6PU
e-mail: reception@squarerestaurant.com
dir: Nearest station: Bond Street, Green Park

There is often a tipping point on the route to success in the world of high-profile cheffery where doing non-stop telly work to promote the latest recipe book seems to become more of a priority than time spent at the pass. Philip Howard is one of the most talented chefs in the UK, but he has never gone down that particular path - sure, he's been on TV, but since he opened his high-flying Mayfair operation with Nigel Platts-Martin back in 1991, he has never lost touch with what the job is really about. 'I want The Square to be known for food that is as delicious as it can possibly be' he says, and judging by the crowds beating a path to his door, that goal can be considered as achieved. The venue is dressed to suit the W1 postcode: a frosted glass and polished stone frontage sets the correct tone of exclusivity, and once inside, striking abstract art on pearlescent walls, high-gloss parquet floors and widely-spaced tables clothed in crisp linen give off all the right messages to make it clear you're in a top-end set-up with serious intent. The front-of-house team are a bunch of real pros, highly efficient and clearly confident in dealing with the volume of diners that comes with such popularity. And so to the food. Ingredients - driven by the seasons and impeccably sourced - inspire Howard, and he has an innate sense of how to unite them in compositions that achieve faultless harmony of flavour. This is not cooking that is motivated by look-at-me complexity or technical wizardry for its own sake - although the classically-oriented skills that underpin the whole thing are second to none. Fixed-price lunch menus offer austerity-era value, beginning with exquisitely sweet and fresh langoustines atop a single gossamer-thin, perfectly-cooked raviolo filled with a farce of langoustine and shellfish mousse, pointed up with orange foam and fennel. Even on this entry-level menu, the sheer pedigree of the ingredients shines in a main course of roast rump of spring lamb with new season's onions, herb gnocchi and peas, highlighted with the saltiness of shaved parmesan and world-class saucing that is simply rammed with flavour. Desserts continue the kitchen's display of exceptional dexterity with a deconstructed tiramisù comprising excellent iced mascarpone cream, Marsala-soaked sponge and coffee cream, an ethereal tuile filled with light chocolate mousse, and swipes of salted caramel and rich chocolate sauces. It is all creative and visually entertaining enough to thrill from start to finish, and makes you resolve to save up and head back for the full-works tasting menu next time round. The tremendously knowledgeable sommelier will help you zoom in on the right bottle from a head-spinning list of classic French heavyweights, with a remarkable showing from Burgundy.

Chef Philip Howard **Owner** N Platts-Martin & Philip Howard
Times 12-2.30/6.30-10.30 Closed 24-26 Dec,1 Jan, L Sun, BHs **Prices** Fixed L 2 course fr £30, Fixed D 3 course £80, Service added but optional 12.5%
Wines 1400 bottles over £20, 14 by glass **Notes** ALC 2/3 course £65/£80, Vegetarian menu, Dress restrictions, Smart casual, jacket & tie preferred
Seats 75, Pr/dining room 18
Children Portions

LONDON W1 *continued*

Tamarind
PLAN 4 H6

@@ Indian

Classy, contemporary Indian cooking

☎ 020 7629 3561
20 Queen St, Mayfair W1J 5PR
e-mail: manager@tamarindrestaurant.com
web: www.tamarindrestaurant.com
dir: Nearest station: Green Park. Towards Hyde Park, take 4th right into Half Moon St to end (Curzon St). Turn left, 1st right into Queen St

Tamarind has been a hot ticket in the modern Indian fine-dining scene since the mid-90s. It may be in a basement, but this is Mayfair, so expect plenty of contemporary chic, with luxe hues of shimmering gold, bronze and silver and towering floral displays. Formally dressed staff and tables keep-up sophisticated appearances, while a window onto the kitchen offers a glimpse of the action beyond. It impresses from the off with the opening gambit of poppadoms and chutneys a cut above the norm. Chef Alfred Prasad's food is inspired by the rich Mogul traditions of the Indian north-west, using top-drawer ingredients enhanced by sensitive spicing. Good use is made of the tandoor. A light, thoroughbred approach sees conventional thinking (rogan josh or Hyderabadi shank) lining up alongside the more innovative; pan-fried sea bass, for example, with fine beans and raw mango in a 'warmly spiced' sauce of tomato, mustard, curry leaves and coconut. Carte prices are on the high side, but lunch is a steal, and well-matched wines show that the attention to detail here runs deep.

Chef Alfred Prasad **Owner** Indian Cuisine Ltd
Times 12-2.45/5.30-11 Closed 25-26 Dec, 1 Jan, L Sat
Prices Fixed L 2 course £18.50-£28, Fixed D 2 course £28, Fixed D 4 course £56-£68, Starter £6.95-£12.95, Main £17.95-£28, Dessert £7.50-£8.50, Service added but optional 12.5% **Wines** 100+ bottles over £20, 14 by glass **Notes** Pre-theatre D £28.50 5.30-7pm, Sunday L, Vegetarian available, Dress restrictions, No jeans or shorts **Seats** 90 **Parking** NCP

Tempo Restaurant & Bar
PLAN 4 H6

@@ Italian

Classy, friendly modern Italian

☎ 020 7629 2742
54 Curzon St W1J 8PG
e-mail: manager@tempomayfair.co.uk
dir: Nearest station: Green Park. South side of Curzon St, near the Berkeley Square end

This chic contemporary Italian is in the heart of Mayfair. Owner Henry Togna's impeccable hosting skills are a perfect foil to the light-touch contemporary design of the restaurant's two interconnecting rooms, done out classily with pale floorboards, vibrant blue velvet seating, vintage lighting, glass-topped tables, and mirrors and bright artwork. The kitchen keeps things simple, leaving excellent ingredients to their own devices in starters such as Scottish beef carpaccio with hazelnuts and parmesan, and pasta dishes like Dorset crab ravioli with prawns, basil and lime. Main courses run from pan-fried red mullet with sautéed cuttlefish, samphire, and tomato and balsamic dressing, to braised pork belly with crackling, celeriac purée and rhubarb. An alternative approach is to head for the cool first-floor bar for drinks, and order numerous small grazing plates of Cichetti - perhaps fried polenta with gorgonzola, spicy Calabrian pork sausage, or bruschetta topped with Sicilian fennel seed salami - from an all-day menu served in a splendid 19th-century room with a rococo revival wall and ceiling mouldings.

Chef Yoshi Yamada **Owner** Henry Togna **Times** 12-3/6-11 Closed Xmas, New Year, BHs, Sun, L Sat **Prices** Fixed L 2 course £21.50, Fixed D 3 course £21.50-£25, Starter £6.75-£13.50, Main £13.75-£26.50, Dessert £6-£7, Service added but optional 12.5% **Wines** 60 bottles over £20, 3 bottles under £20, 15 by glass **Notes** Fixed D 6-7pm, Vegetarian available, Dress restrictions, Smart casual **Seats** 55, Pr/dining room 24 **Children** Portions **Parking** On street, NCP

Texture Restaurant
PLAN 2 F2

@@@ – *see opposite*

Theo Randall
PLAN 4 G5

@@@ – *see opposite*

Time & Space
PLAN 2 H1

@ British, European

Modish cooking amid Britain's scientific heritage

☎ 020 7670 2956
21 Albemarle St, Mayfair, Green Park W1S 4BS
e-mail: timeandspace@ri.ac.uk
dir: Nearest station: Green Park. In the Royal Institution of Great Britain building, close to underground

A contemporary London eatery that occupies the former library of the venerable Royal Institution in the heart of Mayfair, where you will also find the absorbing Michael Faraday Science Museum. Explore Britain's scientific

heritage then relax over a meal at this sleek and modern restaurant, where old bookcases, glass cabinets displaying chemistry instruments, and a fine marble fireplace add an air of history and culture. Cooking is modern British and the menu offers a wide range of dishes, including some traditional favourites like London Pride battered fish and chips. Alternatively, try potted Severn and Wye smoked salmon, chicken liver parfait, cod in sweetcorn chowder with samphire, and Cambridge burnt cream for pudding. The predominantly French wine list has a good range by the glass.

Chef Xavier Nicolau Oliver **Owner** Elior **Times** 12-3 Closed 24 Dec-3 Jan, Sat-Sun, D all week **Prices** Starter £5-£12, Main £9-£25, Dessert £3.50-£8, Service added but optional 12.5% **Wines** 33 bottles over £20, 2 bottles under £20, 12 by glass **Notes** Vegetarian available, Dress restrictions, Smart casual **Seats** 50 **Children** Portions **Parking** Berkeley Square

Trishna
PLAN 2 G3

@@ Modern Indian V

The distinctive flavours of south-west India brought to Marylebone

☎ 020 7935 5624
15-17 Blandford St W1U 3DG
e-mail: info@trishnalondon.com
dir: Nearest station: Bond St/Baker St. S of Baker St station, along Baker St, 4th left after Marylebone Rd junct

Trishna's two small dining rooms are modern and minimalist in style, decorated in shades of blue and cream with wooden tables and chairs, pale oak flooring, and exposed bricks, with floor-to-ceiling windows opening on to the street in warm weather. This is where to head to for the coastal cuisine of south-west India, although the kitchen deploys British seasonal produce in its successful quest for authenticity. Dishes are designed to be shared, so diners can experience a mixture of flavours and styles. Lobster and shrimps with carom seeds, garlic and sweet chilli chutney, and broccoli and mushroom salad can precede the next wave: melt-in-the-mouth lamb, in a curry distinctively flavoured with cinnamon and coconut, crab with butter, pepper and garlic, and mixed seafood biryani. Vegetarians get a good deal, and desserts are taken seriously, among them light, well-made carrot halva topped with caramelised cashews with refreshing lychee sorbet.

Chef Karam Sethi **Owner** Karam Sethi
Times 12-2.45/6-10.45 Closed 24-29 Dec, 1 Jan
Prices Fixed L 2 course £15.50-£18.75, Fixed D 4 course £20, Starter £5.50-£13, Main £8-£20, Dessert £6.50, Service added but optional 12.5% **Wines** 160 bottles over £20, 2 bottles under £20, 20 by glass **Notes** Early eve menu 4 course, Fixed D 5,7 course £38.50-£47.50, Sunday L, Vegetarian menu **Seats** 65, Pr/dining room 12 **Parking** On street, NCP

Umu
PLAN 2 H1

@@@ – *see page 344*

Texture Restaurant

LONDON W1   **PLAN 2 F2**

Modern European V

Creative and dynamic cooking with Icelandic soul

☎ 020 7224 0028
Best Western Mostyn Hotel, 34 Portman St W1H 7BY
e-mail: info@texture-restaurant.co.uk
dir: Nearest station: Marble Arch, Bond St. On corner of
Seymour St & Portman St

A few years ago the mention of a chef's Scandinavian
heritage might have been met with indifference, but not
now - 'Scandinavian? Book me a table!' In this particular
instance we're talking about Agnar Sverrisson who hails
from Iceland, perhaps not everyone's first-off-the-top-off-
the-head Scandinavian country, but he is a chef of
considerable talent. And with his business partner and
whizz-kid sommelier, Xavier Rousset, they are making

quite a name for themselves. Here in the Best Western
Mostyn Hotel, a grand Georgian building just off Oxford
Street, is their swish Texture restaurant, but they also
have two 28-50 wine bars, one in the City (see entry), the
newest in Marylebone Lane. The partnership is built on
putting equal importance on food and wine, which here at
Texture means over 100 champagnes to choose from - the
champagne bar at the front is a seriously cool and
sophisticated spot - and a wine list that deserves more
than a moment of your time. The room is on a grand scale
with those high ceilings beloved of the Georgians, the
ornate plasterwork intact, large windows and polished
wooden floors, but as you might expect given the
Scandinavian connections, there's nothing stuffy about it
either (the darkwood tables remain unclothed, for
example). There is a lightness of touch in the cooking of
Agnar Sverrisson, which is partly down to the absence of
cream or butter among the savoury courses, but it's also
his creativity and talent at balancing flavours and, yes,
textures. There are some clearly Scandinavian influences

at work, but this is broadly modern European cooking;
start with Cornish king crab, for example, with Périgord
truffles, wild Icelandic herbs and Jerusalem artichokes,
followed by rib-eye of grain-fed beef with slow-cooked ox
cheek, horseradish and olive oil béarnaise, or Icelandic
lightly salted cod with barley risotto, prawns, grapefruit
and shellfish jus. For dessert there might be chocolate
and peanut cake with banana and peanut ice cream, and
do ask the sommelier for a suggestion if you want
something to sip as you tuck in.

Chef Agnar Sverrisson **Owner** Xavier Rousset & Agnar
Sverrisson **Times** 12-2.30/6.30-11 Closed 2 wks Xmas, 2
wks Aug, Sun-Mon **Prices** Fixed L 2 course £19.90,
Tasting menu £76, Starter £12.50-£26.50, Main £27.50-
£34.50, Dessert £9.80, Service added but optional 12.5%
Wines 450 bottles over £20, 14 by glass
Notes Scandinavian fish tasting menu £68, Vegetarian
menu, Dress restrictions, Smart casual **Seats** 52, Pr/
dining room 16 **Children** Portions **Parking** NCP Bryanston
St

Theo Randall

LONDON W1   **PLAN 4 G5**

Italian V

Exciting Italian cooking in landmark hotel

☎ 020 7318 8747
InterContinental London Park Lane, 1 Hamilton Place,
Hyde Park Corner W1J 7QY
e-mail: reservations@theorandall.com
dir: Nearest station: Hyde Park Corner, Green Park

In its prime position on Hyde Park Corner, the
InterContinental is a London landmark, and with Theo
Randall in the kitchen it's a culinary one as well. His
ground-floor restaurant, comfortable and inviting, has a
relaxed, easygoing feel (neutral walls hung with artwork
and mirrors), underpinned by good-natured, helpful staff.
The daily-changing menu of rustic Italian cooking is
inspired by Randall's regular trips to Italy and dictated by

what's available from the markets or flown in each day.
Dishes are remarkable for their distinct, fresh flavours,
with straightforward techniques making the very best of
them. A salad of crab, bottarga, fennel, dandelion,
radicchio and celery makes a zingingly tasty, simple
starter, and hand-made pastas are superb, among them
cappelletti filled with a rich mixture of veal, pancetta and
wild mushrooms. The wood-fired oven is a favoured
medium for main courses, among them perhaps precisely
timed, deeply flavoured guinea fowl stuffed with
prosciutto, mascarpone and thyme, or monkfish and
scallops on rosemary with parsley and capers. If orange
sorbet sounds pedestrian in comparison, go for prune,
almond and Armagnac tart with vanilla ice cream: the
pastry is A1.

Chef Theo Randall **Times** 12-3/6-11 Closed Xmas, New
Year, BHs, Sun, L Sat **Prices** Fixed L 2 course fr £27,
Fixed D 3 course fr £33, Tasting menu £65, Starter £11-
£24, Main £28-£38, Dessert £7-£15, Service added
12.5% **Notes** Sharing menu £55, Children's menu £8-
£16, Vegetarian menu **Seats** 124, Pr/dining room 24
Children Portions, Menu

Umu

Japanese **NOTABLE WINE LIST**

Contemporary Kyoto cuisine in a luxurious Mayfair cocoon

☎ 020 7499 8881
14-16 Bruton Place W1J 6LX
e-mail: reception@umurestaurant.com
web: www.umurestaurant.com
dir: Nearest station: Green Park, Bond St. Off Bruton St & Berkeley Sq

A touch of a button begins the Umu experience: the door slides back, and rather like entering a Bond villain's lair, you step from the hectic Mayfair street just off Berkeley Square into a moody, low-lit world of multi-course Japanese haute-cuisine dining. Kaiseki is the word for it, and the setting is a stylised contemporary interpretation of a traditional kaiseki house, a good-looking space filled with glossy darkwood pillars and tables, intricate screens and mirrors. A spot-lit central sushi island is the place to sit if you want to observe the chefs' expert knife skills close up. The menu offers helpful elucidation on the dishes, and staff are also expertly knowledgeable when helping you steer a course through the finer points of the Kyoto-influenced cuisine which is at the heart of the kitchen's output. A supremely skilled head chef, Yoshinori Ishii, is the man who drives it all forward, and he comes with a stellar pedigree, having fed

customers at A-list venues in Japan and New York, as well as movers and shakers at Japan's UN diplomatic missions in Geneva and New York. The eight-stage kaiseki tasting menu is the ideal way to set about things, taking in mukouzuke (sake-steamed abalone with sea jelly and tosazu), nimonowan (John Dory and turnip soup with home-made tofu, ginger and kumquat-musubi), hashiyasume (Icelandic sea urchin with foie gras custard and umadashi jelly), shizakana (wild mallard with Jibuni sauce and pumpkin purée) among a fascinating array of tastes, textures and seasonings. Desserts such as satsuma ice cream wrapped in mochi served with white chocolate mousse, frozen white ear mushroom and almond powder, are inventive fusions of culinary cultures. Sakes of all styles (warm, cold, sweet, sparkling) make for a unique listing of over 160 labels, while a Premier League wine list covers all bases if sake is not your thing.

Chef Yoshinori Ishii **Owner** Marlon Abela Restaurant Corporation
Times 12-2.30/6-11 Closed Xmas, New Year, BHs, Sun, L Sat **Prices** Fixed L 3 course £25-£50, Starter £6-£45, Main £18-£65, Dessert £8-£16, Service added but optional 12.5% **Wines** 800+ bottles over £20, 15 by glass **Notes** 8 course Kaiseki menu £100, Vegetarian available **Seats** 64, Pr/dining room 12 **Parking** On street, NCP Hanover Hill

LONDON W1 *continued*

Vasco & Piero's Pavilion Restaurant

PLAN 2 J2

◎◎ Modern Italian

Seasonal Umbrian cooking in hospitable Soho favourite

☎ 020 7437 8774
15 Poland St W1F 8QE
e-mail: eat@vascosfood.com
dir: Nearest station: Oxford Circus. From station right towards Tottenham Court Rd, 5min right into Poland St. Restaurant on corner of Great Marlborough St & Noel St

If you're after some authentic Italian cooking and atmosphere, V & P's intimate, family-run restaurant won't disappoint. It's been a firm favourite in Soho for over 40 years now. Both the sunny Mediterranean décor and food are suitably unpretentious and to the point, with the unfussy Umbrian cooking concentrating on good quality ingredients (often imported from Italy) and allowing the flavours to shine through. Seasonality is celebrated with gusto here, so expect great things in the truffle season, and the likes of spring lamb will feature when at its best. Pasta is made in-house and the menus change twice daily, with good value early menus for post-work or pre-theatre brigades. Hand-made sea bass tortellini with fresh tomato, zucchini, carrots and celery is a fine version indeed, while strips of calves' liver and onions with sautéed cabbage also hits the spot. Finish with panettone bread-and-butter pudding with grappa-soaked raisins.

Chef Vasco Matteucci **Owner** Tony Lopez, Paul Matteucci & Vasco Matteucci **Times** 12-3/5.30-10 Closed BHs, Sun, L Sat **Prices** Fixed L 2 course £15, Starter £5-£11.75, Main £15-£24.50, Dessert £6-£9.25, Service added but optional 12.5% **Wines** 40 bottles over £20, 6 bottles under £20, 4 by glass **Notes** Tasting menu on request, Pre-theatre D 2 course £19.50, Vegetarian available, Dress restrictions, No shorts **Seats** 50, Pr/dining room 36 **Children** Portions **Parking** NCP car park opposite

Veeraswamy Restaurant

PLAN 2 J1

◎ Indian

Reliable Indian cooking in long-established restaurant

☎ 020 7734 1401
Mezzanine Floor, Victory House, 99 Regent St W1B 4RS
e-mail: info@realindianfood.com
dir: Nearest station: Piccadilly Circus. Entrance near junct of Swallow St & Regent St, in Victory House

Veeraswamy opened its doors in 1926 and has been trading from the same premises ever since. The décor might have changed, but the turbans of the maharajas who frequented the restaurant are still on the walls and the silvered screens are still in place. Dishes are cooked to recipes that are true to their Indian roots, the kitchen uses good-quality raw materials, and the menu offers plenty of scope without being overly long. Monkfish tikka, and tandoor-baked venison with dates and tamarind are among the intriguing starters, and there's an option of sharing platters too. Among main courses, lamb biryani sounds familiar enough, and others include raan akbari (baked lamb shank), lobster curry with coconut and mango, and grilled sea bass marinated in mint and cumin.

Chef Uday Salunkhe **Owner** R Mathrani, C Panjabi & N Panjabi **Times** 12-2.30/5.30-11.30 **Prices** Fixed L 2 course £17.75-£27.50, Fixed D 4 course £45, Starter £6.75-£14.50, Main £17.50-£32, Dessert £7-£9, Service added but optional 12.5% **Wines** 90 bottles over £20, 18 by glass **Notes** Business L 2 course £27.50, ALC D only, Sunday L, Vegetarian available, Dress restrictions, Smart casual **Seats** 114, Pr/dining room 24 **Parking** On street after 8pm/wknds, NCP

Wild Honey

◉◉◉

| **LONDON W1** | **PLAN 2 H1** |

Modern European

Classy bistro cooking and great wine

☎ 020 7758 9160
12 Saint George St W1S 2FB
e-mail: info@wildhoneyrestaurant.co.uk
web: www.wildhoneyrestaurant.co.uk
dir: Nearest station: Oxford Circus, Bond St

Driven by the same team as its elder Soho sibling Arbutus (see entry), Wild Honey is still a pace-setter on the capital's gastronomic scene. And it is easy to see why: the joint may be in swanky Mayfair, but it puts on no airs and graces, and abides by the same ethos of serving up superb food at reasonable prices. Closely-packed tables certainly help keep prices down, but that in no way detracts from the upper-crust ambience, since the venue was a gentlemen's club in its former life, lined with all the darkwood panelling and ornate plasterwork anyone could reasonably ask for, and offset by colourful contemporary art. At the heart of the action is a centrepiece onyx-topped bar with stools, otherwise banquettes and intimate booths sort out the seating. Chef Anthony Demetre takes as his starting point the timeless idiom of French bistro cooking, to which he adds his own confident, intelligent spin, uniting lowly and lordly ingredients in flavour-packed combinations on a daily-changing menu. If you have an eye for a bargain, check out the lunch and theatre set menus, which are a bit of a steal considering the postcode. Crisp belly pork with Herefordshire snails and carrot purée is a typically to-the-point starter, while mains run from an authentique Marseille-style bouillabaisse, to line-caught sea bass with grilled artichokes, cavolo nero and bergamot; a pair of meat lovers could sign up for a grilled rib-eye of 28-day-aged beef with bone marrow gratin and January king cabbage. Wild honey ice cream with crushed honeycomb is hard to overlook at dessert, but you might be equally tempted along the path of cheeses from La Fromagerie. Adding to the Gallic vibe is a wine list of around 25 reds and 25 whites, all of which are available in 250ml carafes - a brilliant idea! The formula is clearly a winner, as there's a third member of the family - Les Deux Salons (see entry).

Chef Anthony Demetre **Owner** Anthony Demetre & Will Smith **Times** 12-2.30/6-11 Closed 25-26 Dec, 1 Jan **Prices** Fixed L 3 course £21.95, Starter £8.50-£12.50, Main £17.95-£22.95, Dessert £7.50-£7.95, Service added but optional 12.5% **Wines** 40 bottles over £20, 10 bottles under £20, 50 by glass **Notes** Pre-theatre D 5-7 pm £22.95, Sunday L, Vegetarian available **Seats** 65 **Children** Portions **Parking** On street

LONDON W1 *continued*

Verru Restaurant
PLAN 2 G3

◉◉ Modern European **NEW**

Inspired modern Baltic cooking in Marylebone village

☎ 020 7935 0858 & 07545 225171
69 Marylebone Ln W1U 2PH
e-mail: info@verru.co.uk
dir: Nearest station: Bond St, Baker St

Tucked just off Marylebone High Street, this pint-sized but perfectly formed restaurant delivers a delightful fusion of modern Baltic cooking, with Scandinavian and French overtones. Two small dining areas, one on street level and the other partially subterranean, deliver a smartly modish vibe with exposed brick and distressed glass blending with oak parquet flooring, pale-wood tables and leather seating in neutral-toned harmony. Oak wine racks and colourful photos of London life feature too, while well-pitched, friendly service negotiates the tight space and up-tempo atmosphere with aplomb. Chef-patron Andrei Lesment, who hails from Estonia, uses quality ingredients and cooks with a sure hand and a light modern touch. Kick off with an opener of Matjes herring and tartare with shaved fennel, pickled black radish and toasted Ryvita, and follow on with rump of lamb teamed with a samosa made from the shoulder meat, Jerusalem artichoke, spätzle, pine kernel, and bergamot preserve. Chocolate pavé with Kahlua syrup is a finely tuned finale. Keenly-priced daily-changing set lunch and early-evening menus bolster the carte.

Chef Andrei Lesment **Owner** Andrei Lesment
Times 12-3/6-10.30 **Prices** Fixed L 2 course £12.95, Fixed D 2 course £14.95, Starter £6.95-£8.95, Main £16.50-£21.50, Dessert £5.95, Service optional **Wines** 50 bottles over £20, 14 bottles under £20, 20 by glass **Notes** Pre-theatre menu daily 6-7pm £14.95, Sunday L, Vegetarian available **Seats** 26, Pr/dining room 8 **Children** Portions

Villandry
PLAN 2 H3

◉ French, European

Toothsome dishes at popular deli-cum-restaurant

☎ 020 7631 3131
170 Great Portland St W1W 5QB
e-mail: contactus@villandry.com
dir: Nearest station: Great Portland Street, Oxford Circus. Entrance at 91 Bolsover St, between Great Portland St tube station & Oxford Circus

Villandry is something of a culinary institution, combining as it does the functions of deli, pâtisserie, baker, café and restaurant. Flexibility means you can have a pastry - coffee and walnut, or beetroot and macadamia nut cake, say - with a coffee, a platter of cheeses with a glass of wine, or book a table in the light, modern restaurant, where crowds can crank up noise levels. Bright dishes of honest, unrefined flavours are the order of the day from the French- and Mediterranean-inspired kitchen. Salmon tartare, carpaccio with rocket and parmesan, and a salad of smoked duck, chicory and walnuts with beetroot

dressing are the sorts of vivid starters to expect, with main courses of spot-on roast chicken breast with asparagus, polenta and tomato vinaigrette, and chorizo-crusted hake fillet with spinach, white beans and tomatoes.

Times 12-3/6-10.30 Closed 25 Dec, Sun, BHs

Wild Honey
PLAN 2 H1

◉◉◉ *– see page 345*

The Wolseley
PLAN 4 J6

◉ European **V**

Bustling landmark brasserie stylishly serving all day

☎ 020 7499 6996
160 Piccadilly W1J 9EB
e-mail: reservations@thewolseley.com
dir: Nearest station: Green Park. 500mtrs from Green Park tube

Standing on the same glitzy strip of Piccadilly as The Ritz, The Wolseley is a landmark in its own right these days, and now has a sibling in Aldwych, The Delaunay (see entry). A café-restaurant in the 'grand European tradition', everything is on a grand scale. It's big on glamour, atmosphere and art-deco style, with towering arches and pillars, dramatic chandeliers and marble floors. It bustles with life and is high on decibels, while battalions of well-drilled staff and all-encompassing menus keep up the tempo whatever the time of day. Breakfast serves up a full English or kedgeree among its many choices, and café and afternoon tea rosters to see you through the period between lunch and dinner. Crowd-pleasing timeless brasserie classics fill the lengthy lunch and dinner carte; from salad Niçoise to moules frites, wiener Holstein or duck confit with sautéed ceps and ratte potatoes. To finish, perhaps treacle tart or crème brûlée.

Chef Lawrence Keogh, Marc Benzimra **Owner** Chris Corbin & Jeremy King **Times** 7am-mdnt Closed 25 Dec, Aug BH, D 24 Dec, 31 Dec **Prices** Starter £7-£24.75, Main £11.75-£32.75, Dessert £3.75-£8, Service added but optional 12.5% **Wines** 56 bottles over £20, 3 bottles under £20, 32 by glass **Notes** Sunday L, Vegetarian menu **Seats** 150, Pr/dining room 12 **Children** Portions **Parking** NCP Arlington St

Yauatcha
PLAN 2 J2

◉◉ Modern Chinese

Skilful dim sum in a trendy Soho address

☎ 020 7494 8888
15 Broadwick St W1F 0DL
e-mail: reservations@yauatcha.com
dir: Nearest station: Tottenham Court Rd/Piccadilly/Oxford Circus. On corner of Broadwick St & Berwick St

Eight years on this self-billed modern reinterpretation of the old Chinese teahouse is still as fashionable as ever, the basement still a sexy, moody place to hang out. They

come (and boy do they come) for the all-day grazing of dazzling dim sum, built on top quality ingredients and eye-catchingly presented. Traditional Cantonese favourites sit alongside more esoteric pairings on the long menu. How about cuttlefish cake with lotus root, chicken and prawn taro croquette or Szechuan seafood and tofu claypot with peanut? Desserts are very special, too, and pretty as a picture; lychee rose, chocolate, biscuit spheres and almonds, perhaps, or dark chocolate and orange compôte with orange cremeaux. Tea smoothies or unusual iced tea combinations (kumquat, mandarin juice and jasmine for example) sit alongside inventive cocktails.

Chef Tong Chee Hwee (Exec Chef) **Owner** Tasameem **Times** Noon-11.45 Closed 24-25 Dec **Prices** Food prices not confirmed for 2013. Please telephone for details **Wines** 80 bottles over £20, 2 bottles under £20, 11 by glass **Notes** Taster menu Mon-Fri 3-6.30pm for 2 people, Sunday L, Vegetarian available, Dress restrictions, Smart casual **Seats** 120 **Parking** Poland Street - 100 yds

YMing Restaurant
PLAN 3 A1

◉ Traditional Chinese **V**

Chinese regional specialities in theatreland

☎ 020 7734 2721
35-36 Greek St W1D 5DL
e-mail: cyming2000@blueyonder.co.uk
dir: Nearest station: Piccadilly Circus. From Piccadilly Circus station, head towards Palace Theatre along Shaftesbury Av

Christine Yau's Soho Chinese has a strong fan base built up over 20 years. It's smarter than many of the eateries in Chinatown's epicentre on the more frenetic side of Shaftesbury Avenue, and the helpful and friendly service also helps it stand out from the crowd. The blue colour scheme looks smart, while the kitchen supplies Cantonese staples, supported by an eclectic mix of regional dishes on a biblical carte. Flavours are full-throttle and it is all driven by fresh quality ingredients and an inclination towards lowering the calories with leaner cuts and light oils. On a tour of China, you might dip into authentic regional dishes such as Beijing fish soup, anise-scented Gansu duck or a lotus leaf-wrapped 'treasure chest' of seafood (scallops, squid, prawns and fish). There are the expected set menus, but even these offer something a little more interesting than the norm.

Chef Tony Li Xiaosham **Owner** Christine Yau **Times** noon-11.45 Closed 25-26 Dec, 1 Jan, Sun (ex Chinese New Year) **Prices** Food prices not confirmed for 2013. Please telephone for details **Wines** 21 bottles over £20, 11 bottles under £20, 8 by glass **Notes** Vegetarian menu, Dress restrictions, Smart casual **Seats** 60, Pr/dining room 25 **Parking** Chinatown car park

Save on Hotels. Book at theAA.com/hotel

LONDON, CENTRAL (W2) 347 **ENGLAND**

Angelus Restaurant
PLAN 2 D1

◉◉ Modern French

Classy French brasserie with modish cooking

☎ 020 7402 0083
4 Bathurst St W2 2SD
e-mail: info@angelusrestaurant.co.uk
dir: Nearest station: Lancaster Gate, Paddington Station. Opposite Royal Lancaster Hotel

Step inside this one-time Victorian pub tucked away behind Hyde Park stables and be transported to the French capital, as the feel and vibe of this intimate, Parisian-style brasserie is so authentic. Expect original dark wood panelling with striking art deco flashes, rustic wooden floors, red-leather banquettes, close-set tables and a boudoir bar and lounge. Plus, there's a French dominated wine list, all-day opening, hands-on service from experienced patron Thierry Tomasin - once head sommelier at Le Gavroche - and a lively neighbourhood atmosphere. The cooking is modern French, of course, underpinned by a classic theme, driven by quality ingredients and a light, well-dressed touch; thus a starter of confit duck and foie gras terrine with spiced prune purée, thyme and sea-salt toast might precede rump of salt marsh lamb with blanquette of shoulder and sweetbreads with seasonal vegetables, and passion fruit soufflé with white chocolate ice cream and blood orange sauce.

Chef Martin Nisbet **Owner** Thierry Tomasin **Times** 10am-11pm Closed 23 Dec-4 Jan **Prices** Fixed L 2 course fr £20, Service added but optional 12.5% **Wines** 800 bottles over £20, 11 bottles under £20, 4 by glass **Notes** Sunday L, Vegetarian available **Seats** 40, Pr/dining room 20 **Children** Portions **Parking** On street

Assaggi
PLAN 2 A1

◉◉ Italian

Simple Italian food in a room above a former pub

☎ 020 7792 5501
39 Chepstow Place W2 4TS
e-mail: nipi@assaggi.demon.co.uk
dir: Nearest station: Notting Hill Gate

The sparely decorated dining room above a one-time Notting Hill pub (now a restaurant) has long been a beacon for simply prepared Italian food with no pretensions to cutting-edge avante-gardismo. In a colourful room crammed with chunky tables, it's all about fresh antipasti and shellfish, flawlessly executed, lemony seafood risottos and well-made pasta dishes, and some appealing main-course proteins that deliver big on flavour and seasoning. Grilled sea bass, fried calves' liver and generous servings of fritto misto are what to expect, with side-orders of mashed potato, or tomato, rocket and basil. Finish with white chocolate mousse or caramelised apple tart. Service is often entirely Italian, as is the wine

list, which features many of the gems that Italy is normally so good at keeping to itself.

Chef Nino Sassu **Owner** Nino Sassu, Pietro Fraccari **Times** 12.30-2.30/7.30-11 Closed 2 wks Xmas, BHs, Sun **Prices** Food prices not confirmed for 2013. Please telephone for details **Wines** All bottles over £20, 6 by glass **Notes** Vegetarian available **Seats** 35 **Children** Portions

Le Café Anglais
PLAN 2 B1

◉ French

Classic brasserie cooking in a beautiful art-deco room

☎ 020 7221 1415
8 Porchester Gardens W2 4DB
e-mail: info@lecafeanglais.co.uk
dir: Nearest station: Bayswater, Queensway

As far as surprises are concerned, finding Le Café Anglais up on the first floor of Whiteley's shopping centre in Queensway is as pleasant as they come. Entering via the street or through the mall itself, Rowley Leigh's take on a French bistro (of the de luxe variety for sure) is brimful of art-deco style and even a touch of glamour. The open-plan kitchen ensures the place buzzes with life and energy, and the appealing smells drifting across the room make choosing what to order even harder. There are oysters (fines de Claire, perhaps), birds cooked on the rotisserie (pheasant with apples and sprout tops), and Thai green curry and steak and kidney pie to emphasise the egalitarian nature of the place. Cheeses are of course both English and French, and desserts might include a classic tarte Tatin or quince and sherry trifle.

Chef Rowley Leigh **Owner** Rowley Leigh & Charlie McVeigh **Times** 12-3.30/6.30-10.30 Closed 25-26 Dec, 1 Jan **Prices** Food prices not confirmed for 2013. Please telephone for details **Wines** 90 bottles over £20, 3 bottles under £20, 14 by glass **Notes** Sunday L, Vegetarian available **Seats** 120, Pr/dining room 26 **Children** Portions, Menu **Parking** 120

Colchis
PLAN 2 A1

◉ Georgian, European **NEW**

A taste of Georgia in trendy Notting Hill

☎ 020 7221 7620
39 Chepstow Place W2 4TS
e-mail: info@colchisrestaurant.co.uk
dir: Nearest station: Bayswater, Notting Hill Gate

A revamped pub below the well-known Italian restaurant Assaggi (see entry) is home to this newcomer exploring the food and wine of Georgia - that's the East European country, not the US state. It's a stylish, light, contemporary place with little to announce its Georgian influences until you view the menu. Up front is an all-day bar with feature wine wall display and brass-topped bar counter, plus a mix of low and high tables, chairs and banquettes. Colours are neutral, seat coverings leather,

suede and fabric, while quirky lighting catches the eye. The dining room (to the rear) follows the theme and colour palette, with the dinner carte delivering authentic staples like khinkali (Georgian dumplings with mince beef and pork, eaten by nibbling a small hole in one side then sucking out the warm broth before eating the filling) or lobio mchadit (black-eyed bean stew with corn cakes), to the more Western-inspired sea bass with grilled vegetables. The small plates and sharing platters are a hit, and the wine list includes some Georgian numbers.

Times noon-mdnt Closed Mon **Prices** Food prices not confirmed for 2013. Please telephone for details

El Pirata Detapas
PLAN 2 A2

◉ Modern Spanish

Classy, creative tapas

☎ 020 7727 5000
115 Westbourne Grove W2 4UP
e-mail: info@elpiratadetapas.co.uk
dir: Nearest station: Notting Hill Gate. Located junct Westbourne Grove & Hereford Rd

The long, sleek room done-out in cool darkwood neutrality is just the ticket for the denizens of Westbourne Grove and Notting Hill, while the spot on modish tapas delivers just the right amount of contemporary pizzazz. There are Iberian hams hanging in the basement to give it that authentic feel. The kitchen delivers a mix of sunny, traditional Spanish flavours and contemporary ideas; expect well-balanced flavours and smart presentation. Croquettes (Serrano ham, perhaps) and charcuterie and cheese selections are all of high quality, then there are paellas (seafood among them), and dishes such as wood pigeon with fig purée, red cabbage and red wine jus at the modern end of the spectrum. Reasonable prices and all-Spanish wines hit just the right note.

Chef Omar Allibhoy, Esperanza Mateos **Owner** Detapas Restaurant Ltd **Times** 12-3/6-11 Closed 25-26 Dec, 31 Dec, D 24 Dec **Prices** Fixed L 2 course £9.95-£12, Starter £4.25-£7, Main £11-£12.25, Dessert £4.50-£5, Service added but optional 12.5% **Wines** 90 bottles over £20, 3 bottles under £20, 15 by glass **Notes** Chef menu £25, Degustation menu £21, Vegetarian available, Air con **Seats** 90, Pr/dining room 30 **Children** Portions **Parking** Queensway

LONDON W2 *continued*

Island Restaurant & Bar — PLAN 2 D1

◉◉ Modern European

Unpretentious modern cooking with Hyde Park views

☎ 020 7551 6070
Lancaster London Hotel, Lancaster Ter W2 2TY
e-mail: eat@islandrestaurant.co.uk
dir: Nearest station: Lancaster Gate. Adjacent to
Lancaster Gate station, 5 min walk to Paddington Station

Outside, the sheer volume of traffic racing around
Lancaster Gate is quite jaw-dropping, but the bedlam
fades away as soon as you're inside this hybrid lounge-
bar-restaurant, which has its own entrance in the glossy
Lancaster London Hotel opposite Hyde Park. The vibe in
the sleek metropolitan-chic bar is distinctly chilled-out
and disconnected from the frenetic street scene: the
smart set sip cocktails and gaze at the park through full-
length plate glass windows as a prelude to dining on a
please-all menu of European-accented contemporary
classics. Good quality ingredients are delivered with a
pleasing lack of fuss and affectation, as in a starter of
pan-fried Atlantic scallops served with a marinated
artichoke and bacon salad, and artichoke purée. Main
course brings a well-balanced dish of slow-cooked pork
belly with butter beans and roasted peppers, and it all
ends happily with a light and buttery banoffee
cheesecake with a brandy snap.

Times 6.45am-10.30pm Closed Sun

Nipa — PLAN 2 D1

◉◉ Thai

Genuine Thai cuisine with park views

☎ 020 7551 6039
Lancaster London Hotel, Lancaster Ter W2 2TY
e-mail: nipa@lancasterlondon.com
dir: Nearest station: Lancaster Gate. Adjacent to
Lancaster Gate station, 5 min walk to Paddington Station

The authenticity of this smart Thai restaurant, situated in
the first-floor of the Thai-owned Lancaster London Hotel
in Bayswater, transports you to Bangkok and Nipa's sister
restaurant in the city's Landmark Hotel. Expect to be
surrounded by carved teak panelling, pukka Thai
artefacts, exuberant orchid displays, and Thai chefs and
waiting staff, the latter offering polished service. It's only
the view across Kensington Gardens and Hyde Park that
places you firmly in London. Naturally the food is very
authentic, with a team in the kitchen who know their way
around the fresh herbs and spices flown in from Thailand,
and the wide-ranging carte and set menus delivering
plenty of regional specialties. Start with spicy prawn soup
with lemongrass, chillies and lemon juice, and follow
with stir-fried chicken with chillies and basil leaves, or
pork with garlic and pepper.

Times 12-2/6.30-10.30 Closed Sun, L Sat

LONDON W4

High Road Brasserie — PLAN 1 D3

◉ European

Buzzy brasserie serving good, honest food all day

☎ 020 8742 7474
162 Chiswick High Rd W4 1PR
e-mail: cheila@highroadhouse.co.uk
dir: Nearest station: Turnham Green. Exit station, left
onto Turnham Green Terrace (B491). Left onto Chiswick
High Rd

Nick Jones's urban-chic and wonderfully authentic French
brasserie is easy to pick out on Chiswick's trendy High
Road - look for the typical brasserie frontage of French
windows and canopied pavement seats. Inside, pewter-
topped tables, leather banquettes, patchwork coloured
floor tiles and a marble bar give the place a very French
feel and just enough of a 21st-century sheen. The all-day
menu (breakfast and dinner and all the others in-
between) of European dishes fits the surroundings just
so. Simplicity and good quality ingredients are the key in
dishes like duck liver parfait with cornichons, and cod
with fine beans and Café de Paris butter, with classic
beef bourguignon regularly featuring on the plats du jour
choice. The wine list has a good global reach.

Times 7-mdnt

Restaurant Michael Nadra — PLAN 1 D3

◉◉ Modern European

Classy modish cooking in Chiswick

☎ 020 8742 0766
6/8 Elliott Rd, Chiswick W4 1PE
dir: Nearest station: Turnham Green

Whatever Michael Nadra does, the rave reviews and full
dining room quickly follow. After the storming success of
Fish Hook in Chiswick, he revamped the look, hung his
name above the door, and carried on with the business of
wowing the punters with his inventive contemporary food.
Elbow-to-elbow, glossy wooden tables, black leather
banquettes and chairs have taken the décor upmarket,
but the relaxed neighbourhood vibe is still in place. At the
business end is a kitchen tucked away in one corner,
where fine raw ingredients are subjected to skilful
treatments. Nadra knows his way around a fish, so ideas
such as roasted cod with chorizo and wild rocket salad,
Shetland mussels and home-made squid ink spaghetti,
or steamed bass and black tiger prawns partnered by
parsley, chestnut velouté, chilli and roasted garlic pearl
barley have to be tempting. On the 'turf' side of the
equation, however, the prospect of aged Scottish fillet
steak with braised cheeks, truffle mash, pied de mouton
mushrooms, spinach and red wine jus is an equally
tempting proposition. Whichever way you jump, finish
with a classic apple tarte Tatin with cinnamon and
Calvados ice cream.

Chef Michael Nadra **Owner** Michael Nadra
Times 12-2.30/6-10 Closed Xmas, 1 Jan **Prices** Fixed L 2
course £19.50-£29.50, Fixed D 3 course £34-£44, Service

added but optional 12.5% **Wines** 183 bottles over £20,
3 bottles under £20, 16 by glass **Notes** Tasting menu
available 6 course, Sunday L, Vegetarian available, Dress
restrictions, Smart casual **Seats** 55 **Children** Portions
Parking On street

Sam's Brasserie & Bar — PLAN 1 D3

◉ Modern European

All-day brasserie in a factory conversion

☎ 020 8987 0555
11 Barley Mow Passage, Chiswick W4 4PH
e-mail: info@samsbrasserie.co.uk
dir: Nearest station: Chiswick Park, Turnham Green.
Behind Chiswick High Rd, next to green, off Heathfield
Terrace

Tucked away off Chiswick High Road and occupying the
former Sanderson wallpaper factory, this popular
neighbourhood restaurant has a cosmopolitan, New York
loft-style edge. It's a large space, retaining girders,
pillars, exposed pipes and brick walls as style features,
and it comprises a mezzanine dining area at the front
and a semi-open kitchen at the back with a buzzy bar off
to one side. Menus have something to appeal to all
comers, from brunchers (smoked haddock and spinach
Benedict, anyone?) to evening diners. Clean-cut flavours
from quality ingredients are characteristic of such
starters as deep-fried squid with anchovy mayonnaise, or
tuna tartare with soy, honey and wasabi dressing, and in
mains of whole roast sea bass with tabouleh salad and
lemon and dill butter, or rack of salt marsh lamb with
rosemary jus.

Times 9am-10.30pm Closed 25-26 Dec

La Trompette — PLAN 1 D3

◉◉◉ – *see opposite*

Le Vacherin
PLAN 1 D3

◉ French

French classics in smart, relaxed neighbourhood bistro

☎ 020 8742 2121
76-77 South Pde W4 5LF
e-mail: info@levacherin.com
dir: Nearest station: Chiswick Park. From Chiswick Park tube station turn left, restaurant 400mtrs on left

In case you're not fluent in Gallic gastro-speak, Le Vacherin is named after a French Alpine cheese and a light-as-air dessert consisting of a meringue crust filled with Chantilly cream and fruit. The small neighbourhood bistro manages to transport you from a parade overlooking Chiswick Park to the authentique French mood, thanks to its décor of polished-wood floors, burgundy leather banquettes and mirror-friezes on cream walls hung with French-themed posters. The classic bourgeois cooking follows suit, delivering bistro staples such as Burgundy snails with garlic and parsley butter, and its signature dish (for two) - a whole baked Vacherin with almonds and truffles, pickles and Bayonne ham. There are modern tweaks too - perhaps Tamworth pork belly and clams to add interest to frogs' legs, followed by a whole roast John Dory with Seville orange, caper and tarragon dressing, or a robust assiette of hare, comprising pie, loin and faggot, served with stuffed

cabbage. A true Gallic finale comes in the shape of tarte Tatin with vanilla ice cream.

Chef Malcolm John **Owner** Malcolm & Donna John
Times 12-3/6-11 Closed 25 Dec, New Year & BHs, L Mon
Prices Fixed L 2 course £18.50, Starter £8-£13.50, Main £15-£22.50, Dessert £6.50-£9.50, Service added but optional 12.5% **Wines** 77 bottles over £20, 12 bottles under £20, 12 by glass **Notes** Steak & wine offer £9.95 Mon-Thu/Sun before 8pm, Sunday L, Vegetarian available **Seats** 72, Pr/dining room 36 **Children** Portions
Parking On street (metered)

LONDON W5

Crowne Plaza London - Ealing
PLAN 1 C4

◉ Modern European

Modern and heritage cooking in a smart Ealing hotel

☎ 020 8233 3278
Western Av, Hanger Ln, Ealing W5 1HG
e-mail: west5@cp-londonealing.co.uk
dir: Nearest station: Hanger Lane. A40 from central London towards M40. Exit at Ealing & North Circular A406 sign. At rdbt take 2nd exit signed A40. Hotel on left

The rather unprepossessing exterior of this former office building on the notorious Hanger Lane hides a

surprisingly modern and stylish interior. In the smart and contemporary West 5 Brasserie you'll find shiny black pillars, neatly laid, half-clothed tables, relaxed and informal service from efficient staff, and an interesting repertoire of modern European dishes. The wide-ranging choice takes in seared scallops with bisque reduction and pea purée for starters, followed by cannon of lamb with braised red cabbage and a mini Lancashire hotpot, or John Dory with sautéed saffron potatoes and white onion cream. Puddings may include rhubarb syllabub with ginger nut crumble and clotted cream.

Chef Ross Pilcher **Owner** Pedersen (Ealing) Ltd **Times** 12-9.45 Closed D 31 Dec **Prices** Fixed L 2 course £22.50, Fixed D 3 course £27.50, Starter £5.70-£9.95, Main £9.75-£18.75, Dessert £4.55-£6.99, Service optional **Wines** 19 bottles over £20, 10 bottles under £20, 9 by glass **Notes** Vegetarian available, Air con **Seats** 106, Pr/dining room 60 **Children** Portions, Menu **Parking** 82

La Trompette

LONDON W4　　　PLAN 1 D3

Modern European ⬤ NOTABLE WINE LIST

Assured modern French cooking in Chiswick

☎ 020 8747 1836
5-7 Devonshire Rd, Chiswick W4 2EU
e-mail: reception@latrompette.co.uk
dir: Nearest station: Turnham Green. From station follow Turnham Green Terrace to junct with Chiswick High Rd. Cross road & bear right. Devonshire Rd 2nd left

Behind a neatly trimmed hedge, La Trompette, in the same stable as Wandsworth's Chez Bruce and Kew's Glasshouse (see entries), is the kind of restaurant we'd all like on our patch. Despite its suburban location on a side street, this is more than just a neighbourhood haunt and is very much a destination restaurant in its own right. The cooking has its roots in France, drawing on

influences from the south and south-west particularly, and while there may be a degree of rusticity to it, it's neither clumsy nor prissy. Among impressive starters have been pheasant raviolo with mushroom and tarragon duxelle and a nicely restrained red wine sauce, and the more vigorous flavours of crab with saffron risotto croquettes, curried mayonnaise, mango and coriander. Main courses can bring on an accumulation of flavours, all adding to a satisfying whole: a moist fillet of sea bass, for instance, with Jerusalem artichoke purée, roast salsify and parsley root, the plate dotted with red wine vinaigrette, or roast chicken breast with thyme jus, tartiflette, green beans and spinach. Desserts run from classic crème brûlée to fruitier offerings like rhubarb with set custard and nut crumble, and griottine cherry tart with almond ice cream.

Chef Anthony Boyd **Owner** Nigel Platts-Martin, Bruce Poole **Times** 12-2.30/6.30-10.30 Closed 25-26 Dec, 1 Jan, **Prices** Fixed L 2 course £23.50-£27.50, Fixed D 3 course £42.50, Service added but optional 12.5% **Wines** 500 bottles over £20, 20 bottles under £20, 15 by glass **Notes** Early bird D menu Sun-Thu until 7.30pm 3 course £19.50, Sunday L, Vegetarian available **Seats** 72 **Children** Portions **Parking** On street

LONDON W6

Anglesea Arms
PLAN 1 D3

@ Modern British

Buzzing gastro-pub in Hammersmith 'village'

☎ 020 8749 1291

35 Wingate Rd, Ravenscourt Park W6 0UR
dir: Nearest station: Ravenscourt Park, Goldhawk Rd,
Hammersmith. From Ravenscourt Park tube, walk along
Ravenscourt Rd, turn left onto Paddenswick then right
onto Wellesley Rd

An elder statesman of the gastro-pub movement, the
Anglesea is the epitome of the genre and still shows a
clean pair of heels to many a young pretender. It remains
rightly popular, an up-tempo and fun place that rocks all
week long. The darker, clubbier front bar (with roaring
winter fire) gives way to a sky-lit extension with open
kitchen and daily-changing blackboard menu. There's no
truck with three-course formality, so tuck into big flavours
and smaller plates (devilled kidneys on toast to
chanterelles and cheddar tart) or larger classics like
moules, frites and mayo, while a nod to sunnier climes
sees dishes like linguine with cuttlefish nero. It's a
young-at-heart, upmarket kind of place, with a discerning
wine list (offering 20 by glass and carafe), while real ales
are on hand-pump.

Chef Matt Cranston **Owner** Michael Mann, Jill O' Sullivan
Times 12.30-2.45/7-10.30 Closed 25-27 Dec

Prices Starter £4.95-£9, Main £9-£18, Dessert £1.50-£5,
Service optional, Groups min 6 service 12.5%
Wines 70 bottles over £20, 6 bottles under £20, 25 by
glass **Notes** Sunday L, Vegetarian available **Seats** 70
Children Portions **Parking** On street, pay & display (free
at wknds)

The Gate
PLAN 1 D3

@ Modern Vegetarian V

Globally-inspired vegetarian cooking

☎ 020 8748 6932

51 Queen Caroline St, Hammersmith W6 9QL
e-mail: hammersmith@thegate.tv
dir: Nearest station: Hammersmith. From Hammersmith
Apollo Theatre, continue down right side for approx 40 yds

If you have never tried the delights of the vegetarian
cooking here before, get ready for a voyage of discovery at
this bohemian eatery in the converted studio of artist Sir
Frank Brangwyn. The minimally-furnished space sits
beneath a high loft-style vaulted ceiling and is lit by a
large window; when the weather plays ball, you can eat
out in a lovely walled garden. This is the sort of vibrant
cooking that easily dispels vegetarianism's lingering
image problems - there are no nut cutlet clichés here,
just fresh, first-class seasonal materials driving the
kitchen's output, starting out with ideas such as wasabi
potato cake stuffed with roasted shiitaki, ginger and
chilli, served with pickled vegetables, while mains might

run to a colourful risotto alla contadina, made with fava
beans, peas, French beans, courgettes, lemon, mint and
parsley, or aubergine teriyaki. Desserts return from the
globetrotting theme with the likes of hazelnut Eton Mess,
or rhubarb, pear and ginger crumble.

Chef Adrian Daniel, Mariusz Wegrodski **Owner** Adrian &
Michael Daniel **Times** 12-2.30/6-10.30
Closed 23 Dec-3 Jan, Good Fri & Etr Mon, Sun, L Sat
Prices Starter £5-£7.50, Main £10.50-£14.50, Dessert
£4.50-£6.50, Service added but optional 12.5%
Wines 35 bottles over £20, 9 bottles under £20, 12 by
glass **Notes** Vegetarian menu **Seats** 60 **Children** Portions
Parking On street

Novotel London West
PLAN 1 D3

@ Modern British **NEW**

Clearly-focused, unfussy cooking

☎ 020 8741 1555

1 Shortlands W6 8DR
e-mail: H0737@accor.com
dir: Nearest station: Hammersmith. M4 (A4) & A316
junct at Hogarth rdbt. Along Great West Rd, left for
Hammersmith before flyover. On Hammersmith Bridge Rd
to rdbt, take 5th exit. 1st left into Shortlands, 1st left to
hotel main entrance

Novotel London West's Artisan Grill puts provenance and
simplicity high on the agenda. Hues of burnt orange

The River Café

LONDON W6
PLAN 1 D3

Italian 🍷 NOTABLE WINE LIST

Unimpeachable produce and cooking to soothe the soul

☎ 020 7386 4200

Thames Wharf Studios, Rainville Rd W6 9HA
e-mail: info@rivercafe.co.uk
dir: Nearest station: Hammersmith. Restaurant in
converted warehouse. Entrance on S side of Rainville Rd
at junct with Bowfell Rd

The River Café opened in 1987, the year of Black Monday,
when global stock markets crashed and millions were
wiped off share values around the world (in the UK the
stock market fell over 26%). Plus ça change. Luckily,
though, not a great deal has changed at The River Café
over the last 25 years either, and that is because Rose
Gray and Ruth Rogers got everything so absolutely right

from the off. Time has moved on, of course, Rose sadly
passed away in 2010, but everything this place stands
for has stood the test of time. The appeal of the sleek,
minimalist interior, the enthusiasm of the contagiously
passionate staff and the commitment to superb produce,
naturally, carefully and unfussily prepared, has never
waivered. The dedication to all things Italian is well
documented, as is the fact that the experience doesn't
come cheap. Start with capesante in padella, with two
beautifully plump Scottish scallops (with corals intact),
perfectly accompanied by the flavours of sage and salted
anchovy, alongside grumolo rosso (baby radicchio) and
borlotti beans. Presentation is rustic and never fails to
lift the spirits. Maiale in tegame is deliciously tender
shoulder of lamb slow cooked in Chianti Rufina and red
wine vinegar, and served with soft polenta and cima di
rape. Finish with home-made ice creams (roasted
almond, perhaps), the legendary chocolate nemesis, or
some superbly kept cheeses. A thorough read of the wine
list will reveal some hidden Italian treasures, and

probably improve your knowledge of the geography of the
country.

Chef Joseph Trivelli, Ruth Rogers, Sian Owen **Owner** Ruth
Rogers **Times** 12.30-3/7-11 Closed 24 Dec-1 Jan, BHs, D
Sun **Prices** Food prices not confirmed for 2013. Please
telephone for details **Wines** 7 bottles over £20, 3 bottles
under £20, 17 by glass **Notes** Vegetarian available
Seats 130, Pr/dining room 18 **Children** Portions
Parking 29, Valet parking in eve & wknd, Pay & display

dominate the intimate, glass-fronted dining room with its contemporary vibe, while the relaxed and upbeat service style is entirely in keeping. Classic dishes might run from a duo of smoked duck and rillette with redcurrant and green pepper confit, and toasted brioche, to 25-day aged Hereford rib-eye steak with spinach and dauphinoise, or Kentish home-made chicken and mushroom pie. Finish with brioche and golden sultana butter pudding served warm with Amaretto anglaise. The hotel's Aroma Restaurant goes for a less formal buffet approach.

Chef Roy Thompson **Owner** Accor UK
Times 12-2.30/5.30-10.30 Closed L Sat-Sun
Prices Starter £3-£8, Main £14-£28, Dessert £7-£8, Service optional **Wines** 23 bottles over £20, 7 bottles under £20, 30 by glass **Notes** Vegetarian available **Seats** 42, Pr/dining room 10 **Children** Menu **Parking** 240

The River Café   PLAN 1 D3

◉◉◉ – see opposite

Sagar   PLAN 1 D3

◉ Vegetarian, Indian V

Authentic, good-value Indian vegetarian dishes

☎ 020 8741 8563
157 King St, Hammersmith W6 9JT
e-mail: info@gosagar.com
dir: Nearest station: Hammersmith. 10min from Hammersmith Tube

In a parade of shops on Hammersmith's main drag, Sagar is a popular hangout. The attraction? Good-value, accomplished and well-presented dishes from the vegetarian cuisine of southern India in an environment of pale wood, brass figurines and closely set tables. Starters range from bhaji to idli - rice dumplings steamed, then fried, with coconut chutney and tomato sauce - with main courses concentrating on dosa with a variety of fillings, the top of the range a lightly spiced paper paneer dosa, with home-made cottage cheese, potato, onion, carrot and peppers. There's a selection of uthappams (lentil pizzas) and curries, including kurma - vegetables in a creamy sauce - and from further afield a list of chowpati specials - street snacks from Mumbai. Those who can't decide could order a thali, which culminates with a dessert like rasmalai, a sponge milk pudding.

Chef Ramadas **Owner** S. Shurmielan
Times 12-3/5.30-10.45 Closed 25-26 Dec **Prices** Food prices not confirmed for 2013. Please telephone for details **Wines** 8 by glass **Notes** Vegetarian menu **Seats** 60 **Parking** On street

LONDON W8

Babylon   PLAN 4 B5

◉◉ Modern British

South London skyline views and modern British cooking

☎ 020 7368 3993
The Roof Gardens, 99 Kensington High St W8 5SA
e-mail: babylon@roofgardens.virgin.com
web: www.roofgardens.virgin.com
dir: Nearest station: High Street Kensington. From High St Kensington tube station, turn right, then right into Derry St. Restaurant on right

Owned by Richard Branson, Babylon is a sleek and modern dining venue framed by the lush greenery of the famous Roof Gardens one floor below. The glass-sided dining room has booths, white linen and vivid green décor, and does nothing to detract from the stunning views over the London skyline - best enjoyed from the decked terrace. The food is also worth a look. The modern British menu is driven by quality seasonal produce and the kitchen is not scared of using luxury ingredients nor of indulging in butter and cream in the saucing. Dishes remain relatively light, though, and are creatively presented. Kick off, perhaps, with hot smoked halibut with beetroot spaghetti and potato mousse, moving on to duck leg braised in red wine with walnut gnocchi, sprouting broccoli and Jerusalem artichokes. To finish, try the pistachio sponge with citrus mousse, raspberry glaze and mandarin ice cream.

Chef Ian Howard **Owner** Sir Richard Branson
Times 12-2.30/7-10.30 Closed Xmas, 1 Jan, between 25-31 Dec, D Sun **Prices** Fixed L 2 course £20, Fixed D 3 course £46.50, Starter £8-£15.50, Main £18-£32, Dessert £8-£12.50, Service added but optional 12.5% **Wines** all bottles over £20, 11 by glass **Notes** Sunday L, Vegetarian available, Civ Wed 120 **Seats** 120, Pr/dining room 12 **Children** Portions, Menu **Parking** NCP car park on Young St

Belvedere   PLAN 1 E3

◉◉ British, French

Modern brasserie-type dishes in Holland Park

☎ 020 7602 1238
Abbotsbury Rd, Holland House, Holland Park W8 6LU
e-mail: sales@belvedererestaurant.co.uk
web: www.belvedererestaurant.co.uk
dir: Nearest station: Holland Park. Off Abbotsbury Rd entrance to Holland Park

Dating from the 17th century, surrounded by lawns and a flower garden with a fountain, The Belvedere must have one of the most remarkable interiors in the capital; a spacious, high-ceilinged room with a parquet floor, a large mural of butterflies, images of Marilyn Monroe, shell-like lampshades and a marble staircase sweeping up to a mezzanine. The menu sticks mainly within the Anglo-French traditions, so expect caramelised pork belly with boudin noir and apple sauce, followed by halibut fillet baked in a herb crust with spinach and mustard sabayon. Ingredients are well chosen, and the kitchen puts out consistently accomplished dishes: smoked mackerel pâté with chicory and hazelnut dressing, for instance, then roast Goosnargh duck breast with duck hash, green beans and port jus, and an assiette of chocolate with raspberry coulis, or rhubarb and ginger mousse.

Chef Gary O'Sullivan **Owner** Jimmy Lahoud
Times 12-2.30/6-10.30 Closed 26 Dec, 1 Jan, D Sun
Prices Fixed L 2 course £15.95-£16.95, Starter £7.95-£13.95, Main £16.95-£25, Dessert £7.50-£9.50, Service added but optional 12.5%, Groups min 13 service 15% **Wines** 129 bottles over £20, 14 by glass **Notes** Wknd L menu 3 course £27.50, Sunday L, Vegetarian available, Dress restrictions, Smart casual **Seats** 90 **Children** Portions **Parking** Council car park

LONDON W8 *continued*

Casa Batavia
PLAN 4 A6

◉ Italian **NEW**

Modern Italian cooking in well-heeled Kensington

☎ 020 7221 9348
135 Kensington Church St W8 7LP
e-mail: info@casabatavia.com
dir: Nearest station: Notting Hill Gate

The unassuming looking Italian joint in Kensington is sister to a highly rated restaurant in Turin. A sleek monochrome look creates an impression of space and informality, with witty black-and-white line drawings lining the walls. The cooking is refreshingly honest, with much modern thinking in evidence, and plenty of top-drawer ingredients, even if the approach to menu specifications is fairly loose. A starter of baby squid and creamy mash comes with smoked bacon, as well as a garnish of crumbled pistachios. Main-course salmon with sautéed zucchini and red onion fritters offers beautifully timed fish and another nutty garnish, this time hazelnuts, while meats include pork fillet tonnato with marinated vegetables. Antipasti, pastas and risottos maintain the best Italian traditions, as does the honey- and hazelnut-topped pannacotta, its textbook fragility offset with a deeply rich chocolate sauce.

Times 12-3/6-11 Closed Xmas, New Year, Bank Hols, L Sat-Sun

Clarke's
PLAN 4 A6

◉◉ Modern British, Mediterranean ✋

Full-on flavours chez Sally

☎ 020 7221 9225
124 Kensington Church St W8 4BH
e-mail: restaurant@sallyclarke.com
dir: Nearest station: Notting Hill Gate. Turn right out of Notting Hill Gate & then right into Kensingtson Church St. Restaurant on left

Sally Clarke's eponymous restaurant is on two levels: a light-filled ground-floor room and a larger basement with an open-to-view kitchen. Her cooking is founded on the best, freshest produce available in the markets each day, which means the menu changes at each session, and focuses on the integrity of that produce. Vegetables, herbs and salad leaves are often brought from Sally's own garden, the last going into a typical, clear-tasting starter with mozzarella, pears and blood orange with citrus dressing, or a heartier one of rare roast duck breast and grilled heart with balsamic and beetroot dressing. Main-course meats and fish are often chargrilled or roasted to bring out the maximum flavour: a large veal chop, precisely grilled, for instance, with well-chosen vegetables, or roast monkfish tail with anchovy salsa verde, baked artichoke and desiree potatoes. Imaginative puddings could run to rhubarb trifle or chocolate tart, its pastry light and crisp.

Chef Sally Clarke **Owner** Sally Clarke
Times 12.30-2/6.30-10 Closed 8 days Xmas & New Year, D Sun **Prices** Starter £7.50-£12.50, Main £19.50-£25,

Dessert £7.50, Service added but optional 12.5% **Wines** 86 bottles over £20, 10 bottles under £20, 8 by glass **Notes** Vegetarian available **Seats** 80, Pr/dining room 40 **Parking** On street

Hansom Cab
PLAN 4 A4

◉◉ British **NEW**

Classy Kensington pub with celebrity connections

☎ 020 7938 3700
84 Earls Court Rd, Kensington W8 6EG
e-mail: info@thehansomcab.com
dir: Nearest station: Earl's Court, High St Kensington

This good-looking Victorian pub's smart exterior suggests there's a lot going on behind the front door. And, once you learn Piers Morgan is involved, and Marco Pierre White has a foot in the door, then you might get an idea of what to expect: from the frosted-glass windows to the big white marble-topped central bar, wood-panelled walls (covered in JAK cartoons), linen-clothed tables and relaxed but well-drilled service, this is one swanky Kensington boozer. British classics take centre stage on the menu (with plenty of European flavours too) delivering high-end comfort food from tip-top produce treated with respect. Start with steak tartare à l'américaine (with toasted sourdough), followed up by grilled tranche of halibut teamed with triple-cut chips and béarnaise, and to finish, Mr White's rice pudding with fresh raspberries. Real ales come on tap and the wine list is concise but as well-considered as everything else.

Chef Ryan Edge **Owner** Rupert Pughe-Morgan, Piers Morgan & T Gorst **Times** 12-2.30/6-10 **Prices** Starter £7.50-£16.50, Main £12.50-£29.50, Dessert £6.50, Service added but optional 12.5% **Wines** 53 bottles over £20, 3 bottles under £20, 15 by glass **Notes** Sunday L, Vegetarian available, Dress restrictions, Smart casual **Seats** 60 **Children** Portions **Parking** On street

Kensington Place
PLAN 4 A6

◉ British

Buzzy brasserie starring seafood

☎ 020 7727 3184
201-9 Kensington Church St W8 7LX
e-mail: kensingtonplace@danddlondon.com
web: www.kensingtonplace-restaurant.com
dir: Nearest station: Notting Hill Gate

KP, as this seminal outfit is affectionately known, is quite the lesson in reinvention; its recent 25th anniversary makeover, 'fish-brasserie' styling and change of chef have rejuvenated the place. New features, including a chequerboard-tiled floor, banquette seating and a large communal table, ring the changes, though the glass-fronted room still runs on the same high octane. The menu is focussed on seafood (note the adjoining wet fish shop), with the kitchen turning out classics like fish pie or moules marinière, while more modern thinking might see roast sea bass fillet served with herb gnocchi and brown shrimp velouté. A selection of market fish (at a price) come roasted, poached or grilled (and on the bone

where possible), while meat eaters might tuck into Hereford dry aged rib-eye. Breezy, informed service matches the upbeat mood.

Chef Daniel Loftin **Owner** D & D London
Times 12-3/6.30-10.30 Closed L Mon, D Sun **Prices** Fixed L 2 course £17, Starter £4.75-£9.75, Main £10.50-£28, Dessert £4.50-£6.50, Service added but optional 12.5% **Wines** 63 bottles over £20, 3 bottles under £20, 23 by glass **Notes** Sunday L, Vegetarian available **Seats** 110, Pr/dining room 40 **Children** Portions, Menu **Parking** On street

Kitchen W8
PLAN 4 A4

◉◉◉ – **see opposite**

Launceston Place Restaurant
PLAN 4 C4

◉◉◉ – **see opposite**

The Mall Tavern
PLAN 4 A6

◉◉ Traditional British **NEW**

Modern British and nostalgia cooking in a Victorian pub

☎ 020 7229 3374
71-73 Palace Gardens Ter, Notting Hill W8 4RU
e-mail: info@themalltavern.com
dir: Nearest station: Notting Hill Gate. Exit Notting Hill station towards KFC, right Palace Gardens Terrace

You'd feel very welcome at The Mall Tavern if you simply wanted a pint of cask ale, but it would be a real shame not to stop for a bite to eat too, given the pub's growing reputation for its mix of traditional and modern British cooking. Make no mistake, this is still a pub with a laidback feel, a proper bar and even a little beer garden at the back, but it's also a place doing seriously good food, with a touch of nostalgia to some dishes and a good dose of creative flair in evidence too from head chef Jesse Dunford Wood. The menu changes daily, although some dishes are fixtures, such as the home-smoked salmon with fresh warm soda bread, the chicken Kiev (an exemplary version) and the cow pie. Ingredients are British, in-season and wonderfully fresh; begin with roasted celeriac soup with almonds and Chegworth apples, followed by an exercise in textural contrasts: crispy duck egg with savoury bread pudding, radishes, turnips and tops. When it comes to dessert it has to be the Arctic roll selection - your choice of three slices from a range of six different flavours (perhaps After Eight, peanut butter & jelly, and cheesecake).

Chef Jesse Dunford Wood **Times** noon-10
Closed 24 Dec-2 Jan **Prices** Fixed L 2 course fr £10, Starter £3-£8.50, Main £9.50-£17, Dessert £3.50-£6, Service added but optional 12.5% **Wines** 29 bottles over £20, 8 bottles under £20, 17 by glass **Notes** Sunday L, Vegetarian available **Seats** 45, Pr/dining room 15 **Children** Portions

Kitchen W8

Modern British

Smart neighbourhood restaurant with a good pedigree

☎ 020 7937 0120
11-13 Abingdon Rd, Kensington W8 6AH
e-mail: info@kitchenw8.com
dir: Nearest station: High Street Kensington. From station left onto High St for 500mtrs & left into Abingdon Rd

Not every part of town has a neighbourhood restaurant like this in its midst, but then again this part of W8 isn't like every other neighbourhood. The aim of Philip Howard - he of The Square in Mayfair - and Rebecca Mascarenhas - she of Sonny's in Barnes - is to make the produce the star of the show and keep the prices down, and indeed the ingredients are carefully chosen and the cost is relatively competitive (this is W8 after all). It's a smart looking place, with a coolly inviting black-painted frontage suggesting all sorts of hidden pleasures within, where fashionably neutral colour tones await, plus modish artworks and tables dressed up in white linen cloths. The kitchen takes a less-is-more approach, not overworking the food and letting those splendid seasonal ingredients speak for themselves, but there's still a decidedly contemporary gloss to what arrives on the plate. A first-course ravioli of partridge is packed full of tender meat and melted onions, served with persillade of chestnut mushrooms, or there might be roast Orkney scallops with clementine purée, crushed pumpkin and chestnuts and pumpkin seeds. There is a good amount of French classical thinking going on (whole lemon sole with lemon, capers and parsley butter, for example), in a repertoire that is broadly modern British. Fillet of halibut might come with a purée of celeriac, ragoût of lentils, wild mushrooms and red wine jus, and, for dessert, bitter chocolate mousse with salted caramel ice cream, thyme purée and honeycomb. The set lunch is great value and the intelligent wine list has a good choice by the glass and 250ml carafe.

Chef Mark Kempson **Owner** Philip Howard & Rebecca Mascarenhas **Times** 12-2.30/6-10 Closed 25-26 Dec, BH's **Prices** Fixed L 2 course £17.50, Fixed D 3 course £24.50, Starter £8.95-£14.75, Main £18.50-£29.95, Dessert £5.95-£8, Service added but optional 12.5% **Wines** 95 bottles over £20, 6 bottles under £20, 14 by glass **Notes** Fixed D 6-7pm, Sunday L, Vegetarian available **Seats** 75 **Children** Portions **Parking** On street, NCP High St

Launceston Place Restaurant

Modern British

Creative and intelligent cooking in leafy Kensington

☎ 020 7937 6912
1a Launceston Place W8 5RL
e-mail: lpevents@danddlondon.com
web: www.launcestonplace-restaurant.co.uk
dir: Nearest station: Gloucester Road/High Street Kensington. Just south of Kensington Palace, 10 min walk from Royal Albert Hall

Launceston Place kicked off 2012 with a new head chef at the helm: Tim Allen was lured to the big city from the four-Rosette luxury of Whatley Manor in the Cotswolds (see entry) to this stylish venue in the discreetly posh neighbourhood of South Ken. The setting is an early Victorian townhouse reworked to create a moodily chic space in shades of charcoal grey and bitter chocolate - a rather masculine look that is offset by warm café crème leather banquettes, statement fibre optic chandeliers and walls hung with contemporary artworks. The new broom in the kitchen has got straight on with the business in hand, delivering classy, uncluttered cooking with head-spinning depth of flavour. A thrilling amuse-bouche of celeriac foam and hazelnut oil certainly grabs the attention and paves the way for superb roasted scallops with glazed pork belly, pointed up by the acid bite of apple jelly, matchsticks of fresh green apple and a smooth celeriac purée. Next out, timings are spot-on and textures carefully considered in a main course showcasing new season lamb in the shape of tender pink loin, rich braised shoulder, and velvety pan-fried sweetbreads matched with fresh peas, mi-cuit tomato and white wine lamb sauce infused with rosemary; for fish fanciers, the market menu might offer milk-poached cod fillet with English rarebit, cauliflower, poultry juices and salt-cod croquettes. Baked English custard tart is a signature finale, served with zingy poached rhubarb and apple sorbet; choccy addicts could reach Nirvana with a Valrhona chocolate soufflé with praline ganache and dark chocolate sorbet. The front-of-house team are firing on all cylinders and there's a seriously knowledgeable sommelier to reveal the depths of an exemplary wine list.

Chef Timothy Allen **Owner** D & D London **Times** 12-2.30/6-10.30 Closed Xmas, New Year, Etr, L Mon **Prices** Fixed L 2 course fr £19, Fixed D 3 course fr £46, Tasting menu £60, Service added but optional 12.5% **Wines** 87 bottles over £20, 5 bottles under £20, 13 by glass **Notes** Tasting menu 8 course, Early bird £38 (depart by 8pm), Sunday L, Vegetarian available **Seats** 60, Pr/dining room 10 **Children** Portions **Parking** Car park off Kensington High St

LONDON W8 *continued*

The Milestone Hotel PLAN 4 B5

◉◉ Modern British

Refined British cuisine in luxurious surroundings

☎ 020 7917 1000
1 Kensington Court W8 5DL
e-mail: bookms@rchmail.com
web: www.milestonehotel.com
dir: Nearest station: High St Kensington. From Warwick
Rd right into Kensington High St. Hotel 400yds past
Kensington tube

The Milestone offers a form of refined opulence that is
hard to beat in the nation's capital. The Grade II listed
building is handsome enough, imperiously occupying a
Kensington corner, whilst the interior is elegant,
sumptuous and thoroughly 5-star. If you're staying, you'll
get a butler to show you around and serve your every
need. But if you're just here to eat, you'll still get a taste
of the cosseting luxury available. Cheneston's Restaurant
is the domain of Kim Sjobakk, and together with his
team, he delivers food that lives up to the surroundings.
The room is well-endowed with original features, from
ornate cornicing to mullioned leaded windows, and
decorated with rich fabrics and warming colours. The à la
carte menu is supported by a seven-course tasting menu,
with the focus on tip-top British produce sourced with
evident care and attention. The cooking shows classical
foundations and a keen contemporary eye - not least in
the presentation - and more often than not a single
ingredient is delivered up in any number of ways on the
plate. Goosnargh duck, for example, comes in a main
course as succulent breast, the confit leg in a luscious
cannelloni, and perfectly timed liver, partnered with
salted grapes, Muscat gel, pistachio butter and a sherry
reduction. For dessert, peach crumble is served with a
brûlée custard, ginger and lemon balm. The service team
more than meet expectations in such a setting.

Chef Kim Sjobakk **Owner** Red Carnation Hotels
Times 12-3/5.30-11 **Prices** Fixed L 2 course fr £25, Fixed
D 3 course fr £29, Starter £10.50-£27.50, Main £18-£38,
Dessert £9-£12, Service added but optional 12.5%
Wines 250 bottles over £20, 12 by glass **Notes** Vegetarian
available, Dress restrictions, Smart casual **Seats** 30, Pr/
dining room 8 **Children** Portions, Menu **Parking** NCP
Young Street off Kensington High Street

Min Jiang PLAN 4 B5

◉◉◉ – *see opposite*

Park Terrace Restaurant PLAN 4 B5

◉◉ Modern British

**Sophisticated modern British overlooking Kensington
Gardens**

☎ 020 7361 0602
Royal Garden Hotel, 2-24 Kensington High St W8 4PT
e-mail: dining@royalgardenhotel.co.uk
web: www.royalgardenhotel.co.uk
dir: Nearest station: High Street Kensington. Adjacent to
Kensington Palace & Ga]rdens, within Royal Garden Hotel

With its leafy views over Kensington Gardens and Hyde
Park, the upscale Royal Garden Hotel's location takes
some beating as a central London base. That view is laid
before you through sweeping floor-to-ceiling picture
windows in the aptly-titled Park Terrace restaurant, the
more casual of the hotel's two dining venues (the other
being Min Jiang, up on the 10th floor - see separate
entry). Following a contemporary makeover, the venue is a
clean-lined and neutral-hued backdrop for uncomplicated
modern cooking courtesy of Steve Munkley, who is a
dedicated follower of all things British. Home-cured
Denham Estate venison might open proceedings, in
partnership with celeriac remoulade and beetroot
caponata, while mains take in ideas along the lines of
pan-roasted Cornish halibut with smoked garlic mash,
leek tart and clam chowder, or for meatier tastes, a cutlet
of free-range Blythburgh pork with bittersweet
caramelised plums, bubble-and-squeak cake and curly
kale. It is all executed with flair, and patriotism extends
to British cheeses with quince jelly and home-made
crackers, or sweet endings such as baked ruby plum
cobbler with brandy ice cream.

Chef Steve Munkley **Owner** Goodwood Group
Times 12-3/6-10.30 **Prices** Fixed L 2 course £15.50-
£17.50, Fixed D 3 course £35-£37, Service optional,
Groups min 8 service 10% **Wines** 74 bottles over £20, 13
by glass **Notes** Pre-theatre menu available daily, Sunday
L, Vegetarian available, Dress restrictions, Smart casual
Seats 90, Pr/dining room 40 **Children** Portions, Menu
Parking 160

Zaika PLAN 4 B5

◉◉ Indian V

New-wave Indian cooking in an opulent setting

☎ 020 7795 6533
1 Kensington High St W8 5NP
e-mail: reservations@zaika-restaurant.co.uk
dir: Nearest station: High Street Kensington. Opposite
Kensington Palace & Royal Garden Hotel

If all Britain's banks could be transformed into something
as elegant and heartwarming as Zaika, a lot of people
would be very happy. The interior styling of this
Kensington venue utilises the wide panelled space, with
its tall windows and sky-high carved ceiling, to its fullest
potential to create a vision of the India of times gone by.
A scent of joss sticks as you enter helps to orientate you,
and the layers of napery speak of old-school formality,
but the menu is a world away from your local tandoori.
Semolina-crusted goats' cheese with beetroot, chilli rye
naan, aubergine chutney, pomegranate and pea shoots is
a dazzling opening array, providing a dramatic curtain
raiser to the likes of tandoori guinea fowl with smoked
aubergine mash and fennel salad, or duck masala with
okra in juices infused with cloves and black cardamom. A
more mainstream route may produce a plate of lamb
morsels, including sheekh kebab and minty samosa,
followed by breast and leg of butter chicken with pulao
rice. Refreshing desserts include passionfruit and
Moscato d'Asti granité, or a two-tone layered creation of
silky chocolate, served with tea masala ice cream and
chocolate space dust that will blast your palate into orbit.

Chef Jasbinder Singh **Owner** Claudio Pulze
Times 12-2.45/6-10.45 Closed BHs, Xmas, New Year, L
Mon **Prices** Food prices not confirmed for 2013. Please
telephone for details **Wines** 500+ bottles over £20,
3 bottles under £20, 14 by glass **Notes** Tasting menu
(incl veg) 6 course, Gourmand 8 course £60, Vegetarian
menu, Dress restrictions, Smart casual preferred
Seats 84 **Children** Portions **Parking** On street

Min Jiang

LONDON W8   PLAN 4 B5

Chinese

Well-crafted modern Chinese cooking with 10th-floor views

☎ 020 7361 1988
Royal Garden Hotel, 2-24 Kensington High St W8 4PT
e-mail: reservations@minjiang.co.uk
web: www.minjiang.co.uk
dir: Nearest station: High Street Kensington. Adjacent to Kensington Palace & Gardens on 10th floor of Royal Garden Hotel

While impressive at lunch, the splendid views across the treetops of Hyde Park and Kensington Gardens, as seen from up on the 10th floor of the swanky Royal Garden Hotel, are less of a draw at dinner in this high-end destination dining Chinese. When night draws a veil over London's green lungs, attention turns inward at Min Jiang, where a scarlet-painted wall hung with black-and-white photos, and a collection of blue-and-white Chinese ceramics are set against a neutral décor of muted creams and darkwood. Contemporary Chinese cuisine is the name of the game here on a compendious menu majoring in Cantonese and Szechuan dishes. If you're up for the signature wood-fired Beijing duck, consider ordering in advance to avoid a 45-minute wait, and expect the bird to be served in a traditional multi-faceted

workout, starting with crispy duck skin dipped in sugar, and on through variations involving garlic paste with radish and Tientsin cabbage, and lettuce-wrapped spicy minced duck among others. Elsewhere, a platter of steamed dim sum might get you off the blocks, ahead of stir-fried tiger prawns served in spicy rice wine sauce, or something like wok-fried neck fillet of lamb in osmanthus soy sauce. Desserts are creative east-meets-west fusions such as cinnamon cheesecake with green tea ice cream, or chocolate-coated lychees with ginger parfait.

Chef Lan Chee Vooi **Owner** Goodwood Group **Times** 12-3/6-10.30 **Prices** Food prices not confirmed for 2013. Please telephone for details **Wines** 149 bottles over £20, 15 by glass **Notes** Vegetarian available, Dress restrictions, Smart casual **Seats** 100, Pr/dining room 20 **Parking** 160

LONDON W10

The Dock Kitchen
PLAN 1 D4

@ Fusion

Appealingly eclectic cooking beside the canal

☎ 020 8962 1610

Portobello Docks, 344/342 Ladbroke Grove W10 5BU
e-mail: reception@tomdixon.net
dir: Nearest station: Ladbroke Grove

Stevie Parle's former pop-up restaurant in Tom Dixon's furniture design gallery has gone from strength-to-strength since becoming a permanent fixture called The Dock Kitchen. Set in a new building smack beside the Grand Union Canal, the restaurant is a cool and contemporary dining space, with an open-to-view, glass-walled kitchen at its heart, and floor-to-ceiling glass on the water-facing side giving great canal views. Tom Dixon's furniture still gets a showing in the dining area, the wooden and metal tables un-clothed and accessorised with flowers and tea lights. Parle's cooking is influenced by his travels around the world, and so the menu offers an eclectic mix of dishes ranging from Middle Eastern to Italian to Indian. Norfolk cod roe on toast with raw peas, broad beans, dill and crème fraîche is typical of the simple approach, as is a main of hake roasted in white wine and herbs with samphire, lentils, Marinda tomatoes and mayonnaise.

Times 12-2.30/7-9.30

LONDON W11

E&O
PLAN 1 D4

@ Pan Asian

Stylish Pan-Asian grazing in Notting Hill

☎ 020 7229 5454

14 Blenheim Crescent, Notting Hill W11 1NN
e-mail: eando@rickerrestaurants.com
dir: Nearest station: Notting Hill Gate/Ladbroke Grove. From station turn right, at mini rdbt turn into Kensington Park Rd, restaurant 10min down hill

There's no sign of the Notting Hill crowd deserting this decade-old style-led Pan-Asian; the fashionable restaurant and bar still rocks. Its warm but minimalist décor - black-slatted or mirror-edge white walls, giant drum-like low-slung light shades, leather banquettes or black lacquered chairs and polished-wood floorboards - comes set to a throbbing backing track of up-tempo socialising and music. The booming bar up front adds further high-octane atmosphere, while a few pavement-side tables are a sunny day hot ticket. The menu's Pan-Asian sharing and grazing format may be familiar to many, but dishes display skill and colour and are conjured from quality ingredients. Expect dim sum (pork and ginger gow gee for example) sitting alongside sushi (scallop maki with chilli mayo) to classics like chicken

phad thai and spiced honey-roast duck. Desserts have a western ring, with the chocolate pudding a particular winner.

Chef Simon Treadway **Owner** Will Ricker **Times** 12-3/6-11 Closed 25-26 Dec, 1 Jan, Aug BH **Prices** Fixed L 3 course £19, Fixed D 3 course £45, Starter £3.75-£13, Main £10-£36, Dessert £3.50-£6, Service added but optional 12.5%, Groups min 10 service 15% **Wines** 61 bottles over £20, 2 bottles under £20, 15 by glass **Notes** Fixed price D available reserved private dining only, Sunday L, Vegetarian available **Seats** 86, Pr/dining room 18 **Children** Portions, Menu **Parking** On street

Edera
PLAN 1 D3

@ Modern Italian

Well-liked neighbourhood Italian in leafy Holland Park

☎ 020 7221 6090

148 Holland Park Av W11 4UE
e-mail: roberto@edera.co.uk
dir: Nearest station: Holland Park. Exit Holland Park tube, left Holland Park Ave A40

Decked out on tiered levels, with blond-wood floors, light walls hung with big mirrors and linen-dressed tables, this minimally-styled Holland Park eatery pulls in a well-heeled crowd for its fashionable Sardinian-accented Italian cooking. Pavement tables fill early on warm sunny days despite traffic passing close by. The kitchen certainly knows its stuff, keeping things simple and straightforward, allowing the excellent ingredients to speak for themselves. There is much that is familiar from the Italian mainland, bolstered by a daily specials list featuring the likes of chargrilled sea bream with courgettes and basil oil, and baked salted sea bass with potato salad, but the chef is Sardinian, so there might be spaghetti with grey mullet roe, and Sicilian cannoli for pudding.

Times 12-5/5-11 Closed 25-26 & 31 Dec

The Ledbury
PLAN 1 E4

@@@ – *see opposite*

Lonsdale
PLAN 1 E4

@ British, European

Trendy Notting Hill lounge bar dining

☎ 020 7727 4080

48 Lonsdale Rd W11 2DE
e-mail: info@thelonsdale.co.uk
dir: Nearest station: Notting Hill/Ladbroke Grove. Parallel to Westbourne Grove, between Portobello Rd & Ledbury Rd

Tucked away on a residential street, this hip Notting Hill/Westbourne Grove hangout is an up-tempo evenings-only affair. The lively front bar gets rammed on busy nights, with cocktails and fizz de rigueur before moving on to the equally funky lounge-style dining area behind. Red mock-croc, low-backed banquettes, darkwood tables, gold walls and a centrepiece light feature deliver a low-lit night-club vibe for a backing track of trendy music, youthful service and high decibels. The equally well-dressed but straightforward modish cooking is driven by quality ingredients and suits the mood; perhaps haunch of venison with juniper and chocolate sauce or pan-roasted sea bass with a fricassée of mussels, samphire and sorrel. Steaks from the Lake District (35-day hung) and starters such as black figs with Gervic goats' cheese fit the bill.

Chef Luke Keating **Owner** Tim Gardener **Times** 6-12 Closed 25-26 Dec, 1 Jan, Sun-Mon, L Tue-Sat **Prices** Fixed D 3 course £40, Starter £7-£15, Main £13-£40, Dessert £3-£7, Service added but optional 12.5% **Wines** 47 bottles over £20, 4 bottles under £20, 11 by glass **Notes** Vegetarian available **Seats** 80, Pr/dining room 40 **Parking** On street

Notting Hill Brasserie
PLAN 1 E3

@@ Modern French

Impressive cooking in stylish surroundings

☎ 020 7229 4481

92 Kensington Park Rd W11 2PN
e-mail: enquiries@nottinghillbrasserie.com
web: www.nottinghillbrasserie.com
dir: Nearest station: Notting Hill Gate. 3 mins walk from Notting Hill station, exit 3 & turn right

The word 'brasserie' is a bit of a litotes, as this is a swish modern restaurant, with a cocktail bar, spread over five rooms. The self-assured cooking is based on first-class materials, the kitchen working around a modern European repertory with Mediterranean influences. Ravioli of slow-cooked rabbit with wild mushrooms and parmesan has been a stunning starter, an alternative to a well-balanced dish of grilled artichokes with goats' curd, an egg beignet and truffle pesto. There's normally a decent selection of fish main courses - perhaps pan-fried red mullet fillet with herb gnocchi, pumpkin purée, chanterelles and chestnuts on a winter menu - and seasonal game gets an airing: perhaps well-timed roast partridge breast with nothing more than creamed cabbage and cheesy croquette potatoes. Puddings are up to snuff too, among them classics like rich cocoa bean crème brûlée with coffee ice cream.

Notting Hill Brasserie

Times 12-3/7-11 Closed 28-29 Aug, 28-30 Dec, L 31 Dec

LONDON W14

Cibo   PLAN 1 D3

 Italian

W14's Italian flagship

☎ 020 7371 2085
3 Russell Gardens W14 8EZ
e-mail: ciborestaurant@aol.com
dir: Nearest station: Olympia/Shepherds Bush. S of Shepherds Bush station, right off Holland Rd into Russell Gdns

In a parade of shops on a small side street off busy Holland Road, Cibo is a small and unpretentious restaurant, a destination for lovers of Italian food. A bar dominates the room, decoration is provided by nude reliefs, ornaments and ceramic pots, and Italian staff are knowledgeable and helpful. Bread - focaccia, carta di musica - and nibbles like olives are promising openers before starters along the lines of smooth polenta topped with a tomato-based ragù of fennel-infused luganega sausage, or crudo di tonno with capers. Pasta is the real thing - perhaps ravioli, cooked al dente, stuffed with smooth minced pheasant in wild mushroom sauce, a well-balanced dish - and the kitchen's care with quality ingredients, some imported, shines throughout, from whole sea bass plainly grilled with lemon and herbs, to pan-fried venison fillet served with agnolotti pasta filled with apple in venison sauce. Puddings are convincing renditions of the classics, from tiramisù to zabaglione.

Chef Piero Borrell **Owner** Gino Taddei
Times 12.15-3/6.15-11 Closed Xmas, Etr BHs, L Sat, D Sun **Prices** Fixed L 2 course fr £19.50, Starter £6-£11, Main £13-£24, Dessert £4.50-£7.50, Service added but optional 12.5% **Wines** 41 bottles over £20, 5 bottles under £20, 4 by glass **Notes** Sunday L, Vegetarian available **Seats** 50, Pr/dining room 14 **Children** Portions **Parking** On street

---

The Ledbury

❀ ❀ ❀

LONDON W11   PLAN 1 E4

British, French **V**

Tirelessly imaginative cooking in a Notting Hill high-flyer

☎ 020 7792 9090
127 Ledbury Rd W11 2AQ
e-mail: info@theledbury.com
dir: Nearest station: Westbourne Park/Notting Hill Gate. 5 min walk along Talbot Rd from Portobello Rd, on corner of Talbot Rd & Ledbury Rd

The exterior hits just the right note of intrigue. And indeed, venturing in unprepared, you would doubtless be surprised at the level of chic comfort in evidence, the leather seating, the mirrored wall that seems to expand the space, the parquet floors. Is that a cheese trolley? That said, there can be few who don't know by now that

The Ledbury has been one of the most extravagant success-stories of the past London decade. Brett Graham is a dedicated, talented, tirelessly imaginative exponent of the new cuisine, and has a ferociously focused team to produce it, the result being cooking of high accomplishment, without too much fuss or foam, and yet always looking visually striking and founded on great, impactful flavour. How can a bouquet of root veg (beetroot, carrot, parsnip, turnip and spud), baked in salt and herbs, be so unbelievably stunning? A hint of lardo di Colonnata, a dab of cep marmalade, some roasting juices all help, but you return to the sheer quality of the vegetables themselves. Every bit of a main-course serving of native lobster is treated with respect, the tail and claw-meat tender and flavourful, the accompaniments of natural yoghurt, croûtons and Indian-spiced brown butter playing their supplementary parts. Servings of cheek by jowl (they're not quite the same thing) of pork come with excellent crackling, black pudding and puréed carrot, the whole dish again subtly spiced. The old-fashioned things are done supremely well too, as in an elegantly risen passionfruit soufflé with Sauternes ice cream. From canapés (wafer-thin foie gras and plum tart) to petits fours (including clementine jelly and hazelnut sablé) and fantastic espresso, this is a kitchen on a mission to impress. Allow some of the budget, if you can, for exploring the exemplary wine list.

Chef Brett Graham **Owner** Nigel Platts-Martin, Brett Graham & Philip Howard **Times** 12-6.30 Closed 25 Dec, Aug BH, L Mon **Prices** Food prices not confirmed for 2013. Please telephone for details **Notes** Sunday L, Vegetarian menu **Seats** 50 **Parking** Talbot Rd (metered)

The Montague on the Gardens PLAN 3 B3

@ British 🕒

Stylish hotel bistro with modern comfort classics

☎ 020 7612 8416 & 7612 8412
15 Montague St, Bloomsbury WC1B 5BJ
e-mail: pbradley@rchmail.com
web: www.montaguehotel.com
dir: Nearest station: Russell Square/Holborn. Just off Russell Sq, 10 min from Covent Garden, adjacent to British Museum

A discreet brass name plaque and bowler-hatted doorman at the entrance announce that the chic boutique Montague on the Gardens hotel is a cut above the norm. In a tranquil corner of Bloomsbury by the British Museum, its Blue Door Bistro is an appropriately cosseting and elegant operation with well-oiled service, and clean-lined contemporary looks - leather director's chairs at linen-clad tables, mahogany panelling, and a wall frieze of Dickensian London. Uncomplicated, comfort-oriented classics are the kitchen's stock in trade, starting with a properly-made winter vegetable soup, ahead of a quirky take on cottage pie - made in this case with a rich filling of duck, and served with baby carrots and leeks. Otherwise you might splash out on a fillet of beef with wild mushroom and artichoke fricassée, fondant potato and Merlot jus, and wind things up with rice pudding with salted caramel sauce and candied mixed nuts.

Chef Martin Halls **Owner** Red Carnation Hotels **Times** 12.30-2.30/5.30-10.30 **Prices** Starter £5.50-£10, Main £12.50-£38, Dessert £5.50-£8.50, Service added but optional 12.5% **Wines** 70 bottles over £20, 15 by glass **Notes** Vegetarian available, Civ Wed 100 **Seats** 40, Pr/dining room 100 **Children** Portions, Menu **Parking** On street, Bloomsbury Sq

Paramount PLAN 3 A2

@ Modern European NEW

Amazing views and modern dining

☎ 020 7420 2900
Centre Point, 101-103 New Oxford St WC1A 1DD
e-mail: reservations@paramount.uk.net
dir: Nearest station: Tottenham Court Rd

Perhaps Paramount isn't so first-date friendly, as you're bound to spend too much time looking out of the window at the show-stopping London skyline. Set on the 32nd floor of Centre Point, the Monopoly board views are jaw-dropping, with the capital's landmarks at your feet. The retro-'60's décor looks a tad tired these days, but then nothing could compete with those views. Huge windows give views to one and all, while darkwood floors, funky-ish lime green upholstered seating and copper tables (matching its copper cocktail bar) are inlaid with black lacquered tops. The cooking's modern approach and presentation tries hard to keep the attention on the plate, with an appealing repertoire and sprinkling of luxury. Sea bass might come with dill gnocchi, fresh peas, broad beans, cucumber and caviar sauce, or roast squab teamed with foie gras tortellini, wild mushroom and truffle consommé. (A pre- or post-meal drink in the corridor-like, wrap-around champagne bar on the 33rd floor offers 360-degree views.) It's quieter at lunch, but weekend evenings rock!

Chef Colin Layfield **Owner** Pierre & Kathleen Condou **Times** 12-3/5.30-11 Closed Xmas, 1 Jan, D Sun **Prices** Food prices not confirmed for 2013. Please telephone for details **Wines** 1 bottle under £20, 10 by glass **Notes** Sunday L, Vegetarian available, Dress restrictions, Smart casual, Civ Wed 100 **Seats** Pr/dining room 30

Pearl Restaurant & Bar PLAN 3 C3

@@@ – see opposite

L'Atelier de Joël Robuchon PLAN 3 A2

@@@ – see opposite

Christopher's PLAN 3 C1

@ Contemporary American

A taste of the States in Covent Garden

☎ 020 7240 4222
18 Wellington St, Covent Garden WC2E 7DD
e-mail: reception@christophersgrill.com
dir: Nearest station: Embankment, Covent Garden. Just by Strand, overlooking Waterloo Bridge

Above the bar, the first-floor restaurant, reached via a sweeping stone staircase, is a large room with high ceilings, a fireplace, mirrors and some banquette seating.

It opened its doors in 1991 and has been trading in America's cuisine ever since, to some acclaim, judging by the crowds. Lobster and steaks (some imported from the USA), the latter cooked exactly to the customer's request and served with chips and perhaps peppercorn sauce, form a sizeable chunk of the menu, and elsewhere there may be baked halibut with parsley dressing, roast peppers and fennel, or slow-cooked belly pork with Boston baked beans, feta and celeriac slaw. The Stars and Stripes is represented by Caesar salad among starters, the range broadened by the likes of carpaccio, and goats' cheese soufflé, while bringing up the rear are New York-style cheesecake, and pecan maple tart with vanilla ice cream.

Times 12-3/5-11 Closed 24 Dec-2 Jan, 25-26 Dec, 1 Jan, D Sun

Cigalon PLAN 3 D2

@@ French, Mediterranean

Friendly, relaxed and classy Provençal paradise in legal land

☎ 020 7242 8373
115 Chancery Ln WC2A 1PP
e-mail: bookings@cigalon.co.uk
dir: Nearest station: Chancery Lane/Temple

Cigalon brings a hit of sun-drenched Provence to the dry and dusty Dickensian legal world of Chancery Lane, courtesy of some former Club Gascon folk who have decided to go it alone in the city's hinterland. A soundtrack of birdsong and cicadas ('cigale' in French) puts you in mind of a Marcel Pagnol film set, although the design aesthetic is distinctly contemporary in the luminous glass-ceilinged dining room, where stripy banquettes, silver bamboo, reed fences and curvy pastel lavender booths create a chic, feminine vibe. A fashionable open kitchen makes much use of the grill to evoke those open-air Mediterranean flavours in a repertoire of classic Provençal dishes that would be familiar to Jean de Florette himself - soupe au pistou, baked Provençal snails with wild garlic butter, wild boar and fennel terrine to kick start those memories of Riviera holidays, then perhaps grilled rack of lamb with basil purée and caponata before winding things up with a warm dark chocolate and Pastis tart with pear sorbet, or a pungent platter of goat and ewes' cheeses.

Chef Julien Carlon **Owner** Vincent Labeyrie **Times** 12-2.30/5.45-10 Closed Xmas, New Year, BHs, Sat-Sun **Prices** Fixed L 2 course fr £19.50, Fixed D 3 course fr £24.50, Starter £8-£13.50, Main £8.50-£21.50, Dessert £5.50-£8, Service added but optional 12.5% **Wines** 104 bottles over £20, 2 bottles under £20, 9 by glass **Notes** Vegetarian available, Dress restrictions, Smart casual **Seats** 60, Pr/dining room 8 **Children** Portions **Parking** On street

Clos Maggiore PLAN 3 B1

@@@ – see page 360

Pearl Restaurant & Bar

LONDON WC1   PLAN 3 C3

Modern French

Outstanding cooking in glamorously opulent surroundings

☎ 020 7829 7000
Renaissance London Chancery Court Hotel, 252 High Holborn WC1V 7EN
e-mail: info@pearl-restaurant.com
dir: Nearest station: Holborn. 200 mtrs from Holborn tube station

The palatial marble hall of the former Pearl Assurance building was just begging to be transformed into a glamorous restaurant, and the designers who were let loose to do their thing clearly thought, hey, why not take the 'Pearl' theme and run with it? Accordingly, the luminescent pearl-curtained bar is the place to start with

a glass of something interesting from the 40-odd wines available by the glass, before sliding into the Edwardian grandeur of the dining room, where walnut panels, strand-of-pearl chandeliers and all round slinkiness add up to a serious wow factor. Jun Tanaka may be known as a telly chef, but he doesn't let the media get in the way of his day job - presiding over the pass and ensuring that the culinary action is tightly choreographed. Having started out in the kitchens of the Roux family, Marco Pierre White and Nico Ladenis, his cooking is stamped indelibly with their modern French thumbprints, but he throws elements of Asian sensibility into the mix to create artful, delicate and intense dishes. 'Beef' gets off the mark with a haute treatment of bone marrow alongside onion confit, herb-crusted frogs' legs and watercress purée. Flavour profiles continue to entertain in a faux-rustic main course combining barbecued Iberico pork with crispy chick peas and chorizo, grilled octopus and paprika, or there might be wild sea bass with a red pepper crust teamed with courgette salad, smoked

anchovy vinaigrette and clam beignets. Inventiveness and technical skills hold strong all the way to a refined dessert comprising a chocolate and caramel dome, quenelles of peanut caramel and hazelnut ice cream and cigars of nutty biscuit. The service team are as slick as the setting demands, while the sommelier will lead you informatively through a superior showing of A-list wines.

Chef Jun Tanaka **Owner** Hotel Property Investors **Times** 12-2.30/6-10 Closed Dec, last 2 wks Aug, BHs, Sun, L Sat **Prices** Starter £11-£19.50, Main £16.50-£32, Dessert £8.50-£19, Service added but optional 12.5% **Wines** 390 bottles over £20, 40 by glass **Notes** Fixed L 1 course £19, D £32, D 5 course £70, Tasting menu, Vegetarian available, Dress restrictions, Smart casual, no trainers **Seats** 74, Pr/dining room 12 **Parking** NCP Drury Lane/on street after 6.30pm

L'Atelier de Joël Robuchon

LONDON WC2   PLAN 3 A2

French

Concept dining with a clubby feel from a French master-chef

☎ 020 7010 8600
13-15 West St WC2H 9NE
e-mail: info@joelrobuchon.co.uk
dir: Nearest station: Leicester Sq/Covent Gdn/Tottenham Court Rd. Left off Cambridge Circus & Shaftesbury Av

Big-name French chefs coming to London have sometimes opted to get ahead of the chasing pack by creating a clubby cachet. Gagnaire has done it at Sketch (see entry) and Joël Robuchon's Atelier works to something like the same template. Three floors of chic appeal to a gastronautical in-crowd, from Le Bar at the top, the checkerboard-patterned La Cuisine on the first

floor and, at ground level, L'Atelier itself, a black granite bar-counter with high red stools, where diners get the skinny on the kitchen action, and a dynamically interactive mood reigns. Staff know how to chat you through the menus, which consist in the main of light-bite Franco-Mediterranean mini-dishes with some Japanese umami for good measure. They do afternoon tea too, of all the old-fangled things. It could all feel like overpriced gimmickry at its most wrong, but Robuchon doesn't do wrong. A deep-flavoured, coarse-textured veal pâté in a properly jellied croûte, studded with foie gras and pistachio, is as canonical a version as you'll find anywhere, offset with a little pickled squash. We glide across to Sardinia for a portion of pearl-like fregola sarda cooked cleverly in the style of a risotto, topped with seared scallops, the whole thing hauntingly scented with black truffle. Steamed Arctic char is a less familiar fish, and gains drama from a jet-black squid-ink sauce, and there might be calves' sweetbreads with pine nuts and almonds on a leaf of Savoy cabbage. The Japanese

element surfaces in an impeccably airborne yuzu soufflé with banana toffee sorbet, and there are enough varieties of chocolate to keep a cocoahead happy. If niblets of a cuisine are not your thing, larger versions of the dishes can be ordered from the carte.

Chef Olivier Limousin **Owner** Bahia UK Ltd **Times** 12-3/5.30-10.30 Closed 25-26 Dec, 1 Jan **Prices** Fixed L 2 course fr £28, Service added but optional 12.5% **Wines** 250 bottles over £20, 10 bottles under £20, 26 by glass **Notes** Menu Decouvert £125, Pre-theatre 2/3/4 course, Vegetarian available, Dress restrictions, Smart casual **Seats** 43 **Children** Portions **Parking** Valet parking service

LONDON WC2 *continued*

The Delaunay

PLAN 3 C2

🏵 European **NEW** V

All day brasserie dining in the grand European tradition

☎ 020 7499 8558

55 Aldwych WC2B 4BB

e-mail: reservations@thedelaunay.com

dir: Nearest station: Covent Garden

If the Wolseley (see entry) is your bag, then you'll adore its Aldwych sibling. The Delaunay, like the ever-popular Piccadilly original, gets its inspiration from the grand café-restaurants of central Europe. The David Collins' design follows the same winning formula, as does the extensive all-day dining repertoire, though the Delaunay's swish interior has a rather warmer tone. Darkwood panelling, marble surfaces, green leather upholstered banquettes and chairs, linen-clothed tables, brass lighting and white-and-grey tiled floors set a classy tone, alongside a roomy bar-café area. It's an equally vibrant, glamorous spot, great for people watching and with slick, well-pitched service. And the show never stops; from breakfast and an all-day carte, plus afternoon tea, you can expect the likes of omelette Arnold Bennett, moules frites or croque monsieur to more substantial things such as roasted rump of lamb with spinach fregola or Wiener schnitzel. Not leaving room for desserts - like apple and marzipan strudel or baked vanilla cheesecake - would be a mistake. The Delaunay Counter - with separate entrance - offers a takeaway service, including fabulous patisserie.

Chef Lee Ward **Owner** Jeremy King, Chris Corbin **Times** 11.30-mdnt **Prices** Starter £5.75-£13.50, Main £11.75-£29.50, Dessert £1.50-£8, Service added 12.5% **Wines** 44 bottles over £20, 2 bottles under £20 **Notes** Sunday L, Vegetarian menu

---

Les Deux Salons

PLAN 3 B1

🏵🏵 French

Covent Garden's re-created Parisian brasserie

☎ 020 7420 2050

40-42 William IV St WC2N 4DD

e-mail: info@lesdeuxsalons.co.uk

dir: Nearest station: Charing Cross/Leicester Square. Near National Protrait Gallery & Trafalgar Sq

The third venture from Anthony Demetre and Will Smith (see Arbutus and Wild Honey), Les Deux Salons is about as authentic a French brasserie as you'll find short of hopping on Eurostar, with its banquettes, globe lights, mosaic marbled floors and bustling ambience. The menu encapsulates everything you could hope for in a modern brasserie, from leek tart, or jambon persillé, to robust main courses of accurately timed roast cod with onions, cabbage and bacon, or beef slowly braised in red wine with carrots. Seasonality plays its part, autumn bringing on pork cheeks with honey and sherry vinegar and root vegetables, and Wednesday's plat du jour may be lapin à la moutarde, Thursday's cassoulet. Puddings are as French as can be, among them Paris-Brest and glazed lemon tart.

Chef Craig Johnson **Owner** Will Smith & Anthony Demetre **Times** 12-5/5-11 Closed 25-26 Dec, 1 Jan **Prices** Service added 12.5% **Wines** 34 bottles over £20, 6 bottles under £20, 40 by glass **Notes** Pre-theatre menu 2, 3 course Mon-Sat £15.95-£17.95, Sunday L, Vegetarian available, Air con **Seats** 160, Pr/dining room 25 **Children** Portions **Parking** On street

---

Clos Maggiore

LONDON WC2

PLAN 3 B1

Modern French V

An intimate oasis in the heart of Covent Garden

☎ 020 7379 9696

33 King St, Covent Garden WC2E 8JD

e-mail: enquiries@closmaggiore.com

web: www.closmaggiore.com

dir: Nearest station: Covent Garden, Leicester Sq. 1 min walk from Covent Garden piazza & Royal Opera House

Romance is always in the air in this Covent Garden stalwart hidden away from the tourist hurly burly all around, and it would take a hard heart not to fall under the spell of the blossom-festooned bower that is the heart of Clos Maggiore. With its stone floor, elegantly dressed tables and retractable roof allowing you to gaze up at blue sky or twinkling stars, you could imagine yourself in a classy auberge in Provence or Tuscany. Of course, bagging a courtyard table takes serious advance planning, so if you have to settle for one of the other dining rooms, don't feel short-changed as the cosseted ambience of dark mahogany, an open fire and soft-focus lighting imparts a feel of Orient Express luxury. Modern French dishes are driven by high-quality ingredients and underpinned by Marcellin Marc's well-honed classical technique. Flavours and textures are expertly balanced in a starter of braised shoulder of Loire Valley rabbit with sweet-and-sour black radish and wholegrain mustard mousseline, followed by roast leg of corn-fed chicken stuffed with Morteau sausage with piperade and Burgundy snails. Non-meat-eaters are not sidelined either: slow-cooked Cornish cod 'rougaille' is accompanied by vermicelli and shellfish and a spicy kick from a creamy Iberico chorizo sauce, and there are well-conceived vegetarian dishes. To finish, whether you opt for tiramisù with coffee ice cream and Amaretto sauce or Braeburn apple gratin with rosemary ice cream, expect delicate and subtle flavours and beautiful presentation. A biblical wine list offers further temptations to linger in this romantic oasis.

Chef Marcellin Marc **Owner** Tyfoon Restaurants Ltd **Times** 12-2.30/5-11 Closed 24-25 Dec **Prices** Fixed L 2 course £15.50, Fixed D 3 course £19.50-£22.50, Tasting menu £59, Starter £6.90-£13.90, Main £17.50-£21.50, Dessert £6.90, Service added but optional 12.5% **Wines** 1800 bottles over £20, 6 bottles under £20, 21 by glass **Notes** Pre/post theatre menus Mon-Sat 5-6, Sun 5-10 & 10-11, Sunday L, Vegetarian menu, Dress restrictions, Smart casual **Seats** 70, Pr/dining room 23 **Children** Portions **Parking** On street, NCP

Great Queen Street
PLAN 3 B2

◉ British, European

Best of British at bustling gastro-pub

☎ 020 7242 0622

32 Great Queen St WC2B 5AA

e-mail: greatqueenstreet@googlemail.com

dir: Nearest station: Covent Garden, Holborn

Younger stablemate of Waterloo's Anchor & Hope (see entry), Great Queen Street rocks week long. The long pub-like room - with a bar down one side (set for bar dining) and an open kitchen at the back - comes decked out in dark red walls, while elbow-to-elbow wooden tables (constantly being turned) and mismatched chairs fit with its back-to-basics ethos and high-decibel atmosphere. Wines are served in tumblers and specials get chalked-up, while the twice-daily-changing menu deals in quality produce where seasonality, sourcing and provenance are king. Intelligently simple, unfussy Brit fare with gutsy, big flavours is the kitchen's preference. There's no three-course formality, with dishes laid out in ascending price order, so mix-and-match with smaller plates (pork terrine to cured sprats, salsify and creamed horseradish) or large dishes like smoked Gloucestershire Old Spot and choucroute or braised harc with polenta.

Chef Tom Norrington-Davies, Sam Hutchins **Owner** R Shaw, T Norrington-Davies, J Jones, M Belben **Times** 12-2.30/6-10.30 Closed last working day in Dec-1st working day in Jan, BHs, D Sun **Prices** Starter £4-£8, Main £10-£25, Dessert £3-£6, Service added but optional **Wines** 20 bottles over £20, 25 bottles under £20, 13 by glass **Notes** Sunday L, Vegetarian available **Seats** 70

Incognico
PLAN 3 A2

◉ French, Mediterranean

Handsome interior and vibrant Franco-Italian food

☎ 020 7836 8866

117 Shaftesbury Av, Cambridge Circus WC2H 8AD

e-mail: incognicorestaurant@gmail.com

dir: Nearest station: Leicester Sq. Off Cambridge Circus at crossing with Charing Cross Rd, opposite Palace Theatre

With the atmosphere and look of a quintessential French brasserie, classy Incognico is located just off Cambridge Circus amidst the hustle and bustle of Shaftesbury Avenue. A theatreland favourite, it has a cool and handsome, art deco-esque David Collins' designed interior, smartly decked out with burgundy leather banquettes and matching chairs, darkwood panelling, wooden floors, globe lighting, mirrors and tightly packed white-linen-clad tables. It certainly looks the part and the Franco-Italian inspired cooking fits the mood, taking an uncomplicated, well-presented light modern touch driven by quality produce. Calves' liver comes with sage butter and cauliflower purée, smoked haddock with colcannon, grain mustard butter sauce and poached egg, and to finish, the warm chocolate mousse or the strawberry cheesecake are sure to satisfy. Pre-theatre, lunch and monthly deals deliver pocket friendlier prices, while the dapper bar is perfect for a pre-theatre tipple.

Times 12-3/5-11 Closed 10 days Xmas, 4 days Etr, BHs, Sun

The Ivy
PLAN 3 A1

◉ British, International V

Ever-popular Theatreland legend

☎ 020 7836 4751

1-5 West St, Covent Garden WC2H 9NQ

dir: Nearest station: Leicester Square. Leicester Sq station exit 3 right, along Charing Cross Rd, 2nd right into Litchfield St. Restaurant entrance is around left hand corner on West St, opposite St Martin's Theatre

It still takes advance planning to get a table, but once inside all is comforting, woody, and rather dignified with its clubby oak panelling and green leather seating. The Ivy shows no sign of losing its lustre. Charming staff keep everything ticking along with a smile, despite the rapid turnover of tables throughout the day. The brasserie-style menu is dominated by ideas from the comforting end of the spectrum, hopping between staples such as shellfish bisque with Armagnac or salt-beef hash, to bang bang chicken, and main courses such as pan-fried sea bream with slow-braised peppers and wild garlic, or Bannockburn rib steak served on the bone. Desserts are such fun things as wild strawberry and prosecco jelly with ripple ice cream.

Chef Gary Lee **Owner** Caprice Holdings **Times** 12-3/5.30-12 Closed 25-26 Dec, 1 Jan, D 24 Dec **Prices** Fixed L 2 course fr £21.75, Starter £7.50-£15.75, Main £11-£34.50, Dessert £7-£8.25, Service added but optional 12.5% **Notes** Pre & post theatre menu available, Sunday L, Vegetarian menu, Dress restrictions, Smart casual **Seats** 100, Pr/dining room 60 **Children** Portions **Parking** NCP, on street

Jamie's Italian
PLAN 3 B1

◉ Italian NEW

Jamie does the West End

☎ 020 3326 6390

11 Upper St Martin's Ln, Covent Garden WC2H 9FB

dir: Nearest station: Leicester Square

In a prime position between Covent Garden and Leicester Square, Jamie Oliver's West End gaff (the group grows and grows) packs them in; avoid peak times to beat the queues. The place fairly buzzes from noon to midnight, the closely-set tables leading to quite a chorus. Jamie's hallmark Italian food is the name of the game, with good quality seasonal produce featuring in unfussy, fresh and vibrant dishes brimful with chilli, lemon and herby flavours. Pasta is made in-house and bread is baked twice daily in their artisan bakery next door. From the seasonal menu and chalkboard specials, perhaps kick off with carpaccio of braised octopus with olives, rocket and herbs, then follow with a tender, full-flavoured feather steak, flash-grilled with sage and prosciutto, and served with a spicy tomato, basil and chilli salsa and a side dish of excellent polenta chips flavoured with rosemary and parmesan. Finish with a text-book smooth, creamy and precisely-flavoured vanilla pannacotta with fruit compôte.

Times noon 11.30

J. Sheekey & J. Sheekey Oyster Bar
PLAN 3 B1

◉ Seafood

Renowned theatreland fish restaurant

☎ 020 7240 2565

St Martin's Court WC2N 4AL

dir: Nearest station: Leicester Square. Leave station by exit 1 left into Charing Cross Rd. St Martin's Court 2nd left

Very much London legend, this enduring and much-loved seafood restaurant in the heart of theatreland began life as a seafood stall in the 19th century. J Sheekey expanded the business into adjoining properties and it has been a haunt of the great and the good ever since, including theatrical types who ply their trade on the surrounding boards. Inside is a warren of snug wood-panelled dining rooms, plus a seafood and oyster bar, and a menu listing relatively straightforward fish and shellfish dishes prepared from superb quality raw ingredients. Start with a classic Catalan-inspired dish of razor clams with chorizo and broad beans, or a choice of oysters if you want to keep it simple, followed by a superb cod fillet on buttered leeks with meaty Isle of Mull mussels and wilted sea aster. A-listers might go for Beluga with blinis and sour cream (£195 for 30g), but everyone else can take comfort in a plum and almond tart.

Owner Caprice Holdings **Times** 12-12 Closed Xmas, D 24 Dec **Prices** Main £5.50-£12.75, Service added but optional 12.5% **Notes** Dress restrictions, Smart casual **Seats** 32 **Children** Portions **Parking** On street

LONDON WC2 *continued*

Kopapa
PLAN 3 B2

◉◉ Fusion

Culinary Covent Garden alchemy from a master of fusion cuisine

☎ 020 7240 6076
32-34 Monmouth St, Seven Dials, Covent Garden WC2H 9HA
e-mail: information@kopapa.co.uk
dir: Nearest station: Covent Garden

This relaxed, all-day restaurant and café from Kiwi chef and fusion king, Peter Gordon (see also entry for Providores), has a good vibe and smart, unbuttoned good looks (close-set tables, marble-topped bar, neutral tones and service set to cool). Menus, kicking off with breakfast and brunch, deliver Gordon's trademark fusion dishes following the now fashionably familiar, tapas-sized, small-plate format, plus platters of charcuterie and cheese, and larger, standard portions if sharing isn't your thing. Among those smaller plates, deep-fried Szechuan pepper and chilli-salted Cornish squid with smoked aïoli shows the style - bursting with flavour - while larger plates don't lack for interest either with the likes of Madras-marinated New Zealand lamb rump with Israeli couscous, samphire, tomato and tamarind and coriander relish. Dessert could be as punchy as black sesame brûlée with a lemongrass and ginger beignet and lychee sorbet, or banana tarte Tatin with sea salt caramel and rum-and-raisin labneh (Greek yoghurt).

Chef Peter Gordon, Selin Kiazim **Owner** Peter Gordon, Adam Willis, Brandon Allan, Michael McGrath **Times** 12-10.45 Closed 25-26 Dec **Prices** Food prices not confirmed for 2013. Please telephone for details **Wines** 32 bottles over £20, 6 bottles under £20 **Notes** Pre-theatre menu until 7pm Mon-Sat, Sun 9.30pm, Vegetarian available, Air con **Seats** 66 **Parking** On street

Kyashii
PLAN 3 B1

◉ Japanese

Creative Japanese food to share

☎ 020 7836 5211
4a Upper St Martin's Ln, Covent Garden WC2H 9NY
e-mail: info@kyashii.co.uk
dir: Nearest station: Covent Garden

Eye-catchingly trendy with its glass-fronted entrance and futuristically-styled interior, Kyashii is an über-cool contemporary Japanese restaurant close to Covent Garden and the West End theatres. Dazzling white seating, yellow neon and tropical blue fish tanks enhance the wow-factor; there are four dining areas with the same vibe, while the street-level room (the others are subterranean) has a sushi bar, and, on the mezzanine above, a hip lounge bar all sleek in black. The kitchen turns out some accomplished modern Japanese food, conjured from quality ingredients and designed for sharing. Crispy chilli soft-shelled crab comes with garlic, chilli and spring onion, and there's the likes of pan-fried sea bream with mushrooms and soy sauce and lamb smoked with green

tea and served with a moro miso (baby soya bean) sauce. There are cocktails, too.

Times 12-3/6-11

Massimo Restaurant & Oyster Bar
PLAN 5 B6

◉ Italian, Mediterranean **NEW**

A bit of grand Roman style in the West End

☎ 020 7998 0555
10 Northumberland Av WC2N 5AE
e-mail: information@massimo-restaurant.co.uk
dir: Nearest station: Embankment, Charing Cross. From Trafalgar Sq into Northumberland Av, restaurant 2 mins walk

With bags of attitude and style, Massimo Riccioli's Italian seafood restaurant and oyster bar certainly makes a grand impression. David Collins has kitted out the interior, so expect some smart designer flourishes amid the Victorian splendour of the room, not least the glorious gyroscope-esque light fittings hanging from the high ceiling, plus lots of dark brown leather, stripped pillars, striking modern artworks, and tables dressed in white linen. At the Oyster Bar you can tuck into Maldon, Loch Fyne, Irish Rock and Natives and accompany them with an oyster martini, or go the whole way in the dining room, starting perhaps with skate served with cabbage on a chestnut cream, or lobster salad. Among pasta might be lasagna made with mackerel and Jerusalem artichokes, and among secondi's red mullet comes with razor clams, tomatoes, oregano and black cabbage. A beautifully judged ginger crème brûlée with pear sorbet brings things to a close in fine style.

Owner CHI (Corinthia Hotels) **Times** 12-3/6-11 Closed Sun **Prices** Fixed L 2 course fr £21.50, Fixed D 3 course fr £23, Starter £9-£19, Main £14-£38, Dessert £8-£12, Service added but optional 12.5% **Wines** 130+ bottles over £20, 3 bottles under £20, 10 by glass **Notes** Pre-theatre 2 course £21.50, 3 course £23.00, Vegetarian available **Seats** 140, Pr/dining room 20 **Parking** Car park

Mon Plaisir
PLAN 3 B2

◉ Traditional French

A Francophile's delight in theatreland

☎ 020 7836 7243
19-21 Monmouth St WC2H 9DD
e-mail: monplaisirrestaurant@googlemail.com
web: www.monplaisir.co.uk
dir: Nearest station: Covent Garden/Leicester Square. Off Seven Dials

It is 'fashion police be dammed' at this cosily nostalgic veteran French restaurant. While the original front room has changed little since the '40s (with red and white checked cloths and wooden chairs), beyond a series of lighter, more modish areas (including a mezzanine-style loft and small bar) come decorated in French posters and paintings and quirky memorabilia. The place gets rammed with the pre- and post-theatre crowd, adding congenial buzz to French service and retro accordion music. The menu does safe and respectable French things and doesn't do impressions; take cuisine bourgeoise classics like foie gras parfait to snails in garlic and parsley butter or côte de boeuf, while scallops with pork belly and a pumpkin and ginger broth is as modish as it gets.

Chef Franck Raymond **Owner** Alain Lhermitte **Times** noon-11.15 Closed Xmas, New Year, BHs, Sun **Prices** Fixed L 2 course £12.95, Fixed D 3 course £14.95, Starter £5.95-£13.90, Main £17.50-£24.50, Dessert £4.95-£7.50, Service added but optional 12.5% **Wines** 70 bottles over £20, 19 bottles under £20, 13 by glass **Notes** Fixed D pre-theatre 2,3 course incl wine & coffee, Vegetarian available, Dress restrictions, Smart casual **Seats** 100, Pr/dining room 25 **Children** Portions

Save on Hotels. Book at theAA.com/hotel

LONDON, CENTRAL (WC2) 363 ENGLAND

The Opera Tavern
PLAN 3 C1

@@ Spanish, Italian

Knock your socks off Spanish and Italian tapas

☎ 020 7836 3680

23 Catherine St, Covent Garden WC2B 5JS
e-mail: info@operatavern.co.uk
dir: Nearest station: Covent Garden

The team behind two of London's most happening tapas operations - Dehesa and Salt Yard (see entries) - have scored a hat-trick with the Opera Tavern in the heart of Theatreland. As its name suggests, the setting is a made-over pub, whose ghost lives on in the buzzy downstairs bar, where you can drop in for everything from a glass of fizz with crispy pig's ears, to a mini Ibérico pork and foie gras burger from the grill. But it is upstairs that you'll find a more formal, voguish venue for a proper sit-down assault on the main menu at elbow-to-elbow darkwood tables beneath a gold leaf ceiling. Friendly, clued-up staff will steer you through the entertaining fusion of Spanish and Italian ideas, taking in platters of charcuterie and cheese, and tapas that run the gamut from wild sea bass céviche with shaved asparagus, basil sorbet, radish and sea purslane to pistachio-crusted gurnard with baby artichokes, blood orange and mint. And that's just the fish. If you're in a meaty frame of mind, there could be confit Gloucestershire Old Spot pork belly with rosemary-scented cannellini beans, or chargrilled beef underblade fillet with watercress purée, gorgonzola and Portobello mushrooms. Puddings such as dark chocolate ganache with beetroot ice cream and hazelnut crumble keep the inventive flair coming to the end.

Chef Jamie Thickett **Owner** Simon Mullins, Sonya Morris **Times** 12-3/5-11.30 Closed 25-26 Dec, some BHs, D Sun **Prices** Main £5-£10, Service added but optional 12.5% **Wines** 78 bottles over £20, 4 bottles under £20, 17 by glass **Notes** Fixed Tapas menus 3 course over 7 people £35-£40, Vegetarian available **Seats** 75

Orso
PLAN 3 C1

@ Modern Italian

Italian food in a lively basement

☎ 020 7240 5269

27 Wellington St WC2E 7DA
e-mail: info@orsorestaurant.co.uk
dir: Nearest station: Covent Garden. Between Exeter St & Tavistock St

While the street entrance could easily be missed, the clued-up crowds have been flocking downstairs to this relaxed, all-day Covent Garden Italian since the mid-'80s. The cavernous hide-away basement - once an orchid warehouse - buzzes with conversation and unstuffy, friendly quick-fire service, and is always busy pre-theatre. It's all endearingly rustic, charmingly authentic and classic Italian with a nod to the Milan of the '50s; from checked tablecloths to herringbone-patterned wood floors, white-tiled walls, pastel shades and black-and-white photos. In turn, crowd-pleasing menus are the drill, showcasing simple regional Italian cooking. All the usual pizza (roasted pepper, red onion, sun-dried tomato and mozzarella), and pasta (linguine with white crabmeat, garlic, parsley and cherry tomatoes) are here, otherwise expect roast halibut to arrive with tomatoes, black olives and new potatoes, and perhaps a pannacotta dessert with champagne rhubarb. A fixed-price pre-theatre option and all-Italian wines prove popular.

Chef Morph Abiose **Owner** Orso Restaurants Ltd **Times** noon-mdnt Closed 24-25 Dec, L Sun (Jul-Aug) **Prices** Fixed L 2 course £17-£20.50, Starter £6-£12.50, Main £10.50-£24, Dessert £6.50, Service added but optional 12.5% **Wines** 50 bottles over £20, 14 by glass **Notes** Pre-theatre D 2,3 course Mon-Sat £17-£19, until 7pm, Sunday L, Vegetarian available **Seats** 100 **Children** Portions, Menu **Parking** On street

The Portrait Restaurant & Bar
PLAN 3 A1

@ Modern British

Sleek, contemporary, buzzy dining with rooftop views

☎ 020 7312 2490

National Portrait Gallery, St Martins Place WC2H 0HE
e-mail: portrait.reservation@searcys.co.uk
dir: Nearest station: Leicester Square/Charing Cross

You get unparalleled views across Trafalgar Square and Westminster to the London Eye from this stylish contemporary restaurant perched on the top floor of the National Portrait Gallery. The view alone would be worth the visit, but the surroundings - red leather banquettes and blond-wood floors set against minimalist shades of grey, cream and black   are easy on the eye too, and of course there's the appealingly light and simple modern bistro-style food to consider. A starter of potted confit duck with rhubarb and apple relish might be followed by pork belly with pear, sultana and almond stuffing, mustard mash, spring greens and leeks and bacon, or smoked haddock fishcake with mustard sauce. Finish with a rhubarb and pear bread-and-butter pudding with vanilla custard.

Times 11.45-2.45/5.30-8.30 Closed 24-26 Dec, D Sun-Wed

The River Restaurant
PLAN 3 C1

@@ Modern French

Contemporary French cooking in iconic hotel

☎ 020 7836 4343

The Savoy, Strand WC2R 0EU
e-mail: savoy@fairmont.com
dir: Nearest station: Embankment/Covent Garden/Charing Cross. Halfway along The Strand between Trafalgar Sq & Aldwych

The Savoy's iconic art deco style was mercifully preserved during the hotel's long overhaul, and The River Restaurant is no exception, a luxurious setting with Thames views and plenty of correct, solicitous staff on hand. Perhaps surprisingly, given the context, the cooking is up to the minute, the kitchen turning out starters like pork belly with prawn carpaccio, cucumber and citrus dressing, and roast scallops with marinated pineapple, sauce vierge, honey and soy. Grandeur doesn't come cheap, and nor do the sort of top-end materials expected in a world-class hotel. Pan-fried turbot fillet, timed to the second, is teamed with poached oysters and served bravely with saffron-flavoured miso along with potato terrine and cucumber tagliatelle, and noisettes of lamb, served pink as ordered, come with a gratin of neck meat with well-judged watercress sauce, spinach and roast shallots. High levels of workmanship are never more apparent than in puddings like peanut brittle parfait with quince purée and port-laced blackberry sorbet.

Chef James Pane **Owner** Fairmont **Times** 12-2.30/5.30-10.30 **Prices** Fixed L 2 course £24.50-£28, Starter £9-£22, Main £22-£36, Dessert £11, Service added but optional **Notes** Escoffier tasting menu, Sun Jazz L, Vegetarian available, Dress restrictions, Smart casual, Civ Wed 400 **Seats** 90, Pr/dining room 12 **Children** Portions

Savoy Grill
PLAN 3 C1

@@ British, French V

A bedrock of classicism at a premier-league London address

☎ 020 7592 1600

1 Savoy Hill, Strand WC2R 0EU
e-mail: savoygrill@gordonramsay.com
dir: Nearest station: Charing Cross. Walk E through the riverside gardens to the hotel

From the Victorian literati to stars of the silent screen to the movers and shakers of today's business and politics, the Grill has always been a place to see and be seen. That seeing all goes on within the sacred confines of walnut panelling, art-deco mirrors and plush banquettes, beneath the glitter of chandeliers. The Savoy's recent makeover refreshed the Grill as a Premier League London restaurant space, and while the cuisine rests on a solid bedrock of Edwardian classicism, it doesn't feel in the least old-fashioned. What's that line about class never going out of style? The grills themselves, from the wood-fired oven, include 35-day, dry-aged beef in a plethora of cuts, lamb cutlets, pork chops, gammon steaks and sausages, but there are also roasts and braises that span the range from the elevated - thyme-roasted quail with Landes foie gras and horseradish mash in port jus - to the downright homeliness of a steak-and-ale pudding with onion sauce. It's all bookended by a good selection of hors d'oeuvres, including grilled kippers in lemon and parsley, and desserts that are unreconstructed because they haven't been deconstructed in the first place (rum baba with vanilla cream, for example). They've got some wines too, if you're up for pumping up the financial volume.

Chef Andy Cook **Owner** Gordon Ramsay Holdings Ltd **Times** 12-3/5.30-11 **Prices** Starter £7.50-£70, Main £12-£60, Dessert £5.50-£18, Service added but optional 12.5% **Wines** 180 bottles over £20 **Notes** Pre-theatre 2,3 course Mon-Fri, 5.30-6.45pm £20-£26, Sunday L, Vegetarian menu, Dress restrictions, Smart casual **Seats** 98, Pr/dining room 40

LONDON WC2 *continued*

Terroirs
PLAN 3 B1

@@ French 🍷

Top-rate produce and French provincial cooking

☎ 020 7036 0660

5 William IV St, Covent Garden WC2N 4DW
e-mail: enquiries@terroirswinebar.com
dir: Nearest station: Covent Garden/Charing Cross. Exit Charing Cross station turn right, along The Strand, first left onto William IV St

Terroirs is on two levels, with a wine bar on the ground floor, where you can get stuck into tapas-size dishes and a glass of wine, and a downstairs restaurant. But you can eat what you like where you like; it's that kind of place. The manifesto is clear: to promote 'artisan products that taste simply of their origins', and cooking them in the style of French provincial recipes with some input from Italy and Spain. Grilled fillets of red mullet with braised fennel and basil beurre blanc, and braised rabbit leg with red pepper and olive oil mash are among gutsily-flavoured main courses. You could start with a selection of fresh-tasting, top-quality charcuterie, ranging from salami to duck rillette, or pick your way through some of the compelling assemblies of 'small plates': perhaps ox tongue with potato salad, clams with ham, garlic and chilli, or smoked eel with endive, pickled walnuts and bacon. Cheeses, all French, are in tip-top condition, or there may be a simple pudding like floating islands.

Chef Ed Wilson **Owner** Ed Wilson, Oli Barker, Eric Nariod **Times** 12-11 Closed Xmas, Etr, Sun **Prices** Starter £6.50-£9, Main £14-£17, Dessert £6-£6.50, Service added but optional 12.5% **Wines** 160 bottles over £20, 14 bottles under £20, 14 by glass **Notes** Fixed 1 course L £10, Vegetarian available **Seats** 120 **Children** Portions

BARNET
Map 6 TQ29

Savoro Restaurant with Rooms

@ Modern European, British

Contemporary good looks and well-judged menu

☎ 020 8449 9888

206 High St EN5 5SZ
e-mail: savoro@savoro.co.uk
web: www.savoro.co.uk
dir: M25 junct 23 to A1081, continue to St Albans Rd, at lights turn left to A1000

Set back from Barnet's bustling high street, the traditional frontage of this snazzy neighbourhood restaurant with rooms belies its contemporary good looks. Done out in clean-cut fashionable manner, with neutral tones, etched glass screens, mirrors and cream tiled floors, it provides the perfect backdrop for the kitchen's modern approach. The cooking encompasses British classics with the flavours of the Med and Asia; begin with buffalo mozzarella salad or goats' cheese soufflé, for example, then follow up with chargrilled calves' liver teamed with smoked bacon, mash and onion gravy, or perhaps teriyaki roasted salmon or pan-seared halibut cooked with lemon and herbs. A range of steaks from the grill covers all the bases, while desserts continue the style with homespun Bakewell tart lining up alongside rhubarb and vanilla pannacotta.

Chef Jackson Lopes **Owner** Jack Antoni, Dino Paphiti **Times** 12-3/6-11 Closed 1 Jan, 1 wk New Year, D Sun **Prices** Fixed L 2 course £11.95-£14.95, Fixed D 2 course fr £26.95, Starter fr £6, Main fr £15.95, Dessert fr £6, Service added but optional 12% **Wines** 30 bottles over £20, 15 bottles under £20, 12 by glass **Notes** Early eve menu Mon-Thu 2 course £11.95, Sunday L, Vegetarian available **Seats** 68 **Children** Portions **Parking** 9

BROMLEY

Chapter One
PLAN 1 H1

@@@@ *– see opposite*

ENFIELD
Map 6 TQ39

Royal Chace Hotel

@ Modern British

Well-crafted, modish cooking with a countryside aspect

☎ 020 8884 8181

162 The Ridgeway EN2 8AR
e-mail: reservations@royalchacehotel.co.uk
dir: 3m from M25 junct 24, 1.5m to Enfield

Positioned in six acres of grounds in pretty open countryside, the Royal Chace does a good line in modern British food with all of the expected European influences along the way. Smart tables set with crisp white linen, light oak floors, and rich green and gold tones around the room make for a pleasing setting. The busy bar area positively buzzes, while a central glass-covered atrium gives plenty of natural light when the sun is up. The kitchen has a keen grasp of what works with what, serving up the likes of pressed Gloucestershire Old Spot ham and parsley wrapped in Parma ham with sauce gribriche, pea shoots and toasted brioche, followed by smoked fillet of salmon with pea purée, smoked salmon dauphinoise, truffle oil and mustard frills, finishing with ginger pannacotta, gooseberry jam and ginger biscuit.

Times 12-9.30/6.30-9.30

HADLEY WOOD
Map 6 TQ29

West Lodge Park Hotel

@ Modern British

Polished cooking in a parkland setting

☎ 020 8216 3900

Cockfosters Rd EN4 0PY
e-mail: westlodgepark@bealeshotels.co.uk
dir: On A111, 1m S of M25 junct 24

A white Regency-style mansion - surrounded by 35 acres that include an arboretum of over 800 tree species - is the imposing setting for this hotel restaurant. Refurbishment has delivered a modern spin to the dining room's original features; its name dedicated to the 17th-century portrait artist Mary Beale (with family connection to the owners), whose original work adorns the walls. There's plenty to enjoy about the modish British cooking, with use of fresh quality local produce and provenance clearly a driving force behind the menus. Seared Denham Estate venison steak, for example, comes with roasted parsnip, beetroot purée, potato rösti and liquorice jus, whilst monkfish medallions might be wrapped in Parma ham and served with rocket, black noodles and tomato and olive oil sauce. To finish, a classic Belgian chocolate soufflé with Grand Marnier anglaise fits the bill.

Chef Wayne Turner **Owner** Beales Ltd **Times** 12.30-2.30/7-9.30 **Prices** Fixed L 2 course £18-£23, Fixed D 3 course £28-£32, Starter £5-£13.50, Main £13-£26, Dessert £6-£8, Service optional, Groups min 12 service 12.5% **Wines** 51 bottles over £20, 24 bottles under £20, 7 by glass **Notes** Sunday L, Vegetarian available, Dress restrictions, Smart casual, jacket & tie recommended, Civ Wed 90 **Seats** 70, Pr/dining room 100 **Children** Portions **Parking** 75

Chapter One

BROMLEY
PLAN 1 H1

Modern European ☙ NOTABLE WINE LIST

Strikingly refined cooking in out-of-town hotspot

☎ 01689 854848
Farnborough Common, Locksbottom BR6 8NF
e-mail: info@chaptersrestaurants.com
web: www.chaptersrestaurants.com
dir: On A21, 3m from Bromley. From M25 junct 4 onto A21 for 5m

Where once carriages paused on the journey in and out of the capital to sustain the horses and passengers for the long ride ahead, Andrew McLeish has created a respite to satisfy the most cultured of 21st-century traveller - a world-class restaurant of style and verve lies within. The old Tudor house has smartened up very nicely indeed and the ambition (and matching achievement) of the kitchen means those within striking distance need not head up to the bright lights of central London to sample divertingly creative modern food. And indeed they come from far and wide to eat here. It may be situated on a busy road junction, but access is easy and parking ample, and once through the door it's easy to imagine oneself in the swankiest of uptown joints. The colour palette is the flavour of the day - coffee and cream - with some striking flashes of red bringing a warm glow, and tables dressed up for the business of fine dining. If you're debating whether to make the trip out here or eat closer to home, here are two things you might like to chew over: the service is really rather charming, professional without a doubt, but lacking any West End stuffiness, and the pricing is positively generous given the quality of the food on offer. And to the food. Andrew McLeish trained under Nico Ladenis and his finely tuned technique and appreciation of classical ways is at the core of the kitchen's output, but there is a creative mind at work here, with contemporary ideas and presentations bringing a high-end sparkle to the food. Start with a salad of smoked eel and pan-fried Cornish mackerel, with crisp vegetables and an apple and horseradish purée, or a compression of pig's head served up with a traditional accompaniment of cornichons and then dressed with a fabulously intense potato and truffle espuma, plus an apple jelly. The Josper grill gets a workout for a main-course USDA prime rib-eye steak (with twice-cooked chips and béarnaise sauce), while hake is partnered with a white onion purée and the well-judged earthiness of trompettes and pancetta. Presentations are impressive and flavours and textures measured to the nth degree: main-course poached and roasted guinea fowl, for example, with a delicious foie gras and trompette mousse, roast artichokes and richly flavoured guinea fowl jus. The mastery of flavours is revealed once again at dessert stage in the form of an orange blossom and yuzu jelly with accompanying mandarin sorbet and chilli mango salad. The wine list matches the ambition of this memorable establishment.

Chef Andrew McLeish **Owner** Selective Restaurants Group
Times 12-2.30/6.30-10.30 Closed 2-4 Jan **Prices** Fixed L 2 course fr £14.95, Fixed D 3 course fr £35.50, Tasting menu £50, Starter £4.50-£8.75, Main £14.95-£19, Dessert £4.50-£7.75, Service added but optional 12.5% **Wines** 14 bottles over £20, 12 bottles under £20, 11 by glass **Notes** Sunday L, Vegetarian available, Dress restrictions, No shorts, jeans or trainers **Seats** 120, Pr/dining room 55 **Children** Portions **Parking** 90

HARROW ON THE HILL

Incanto Restaurant

PLAN 1 B5

◉◉ Modern Italian ☙

Regional Italian cooking with a light modern touch

☎ 020 8426 6767
The Old Post Office, 41 High St HA1 3HT
e-mail: info@incanto.co.uk
web: www.incanto.co.uk

An old Victorian red-brick post office on the village green in Harrow on the Hill is the setting for this sleek modern Italian. Inside it is an expansive loft-like, split-level space with a soaring glass skylight, huge beams and bare darkwood tables on a pale wooden floor. The menu of southern Italian-inspired dishes eats as well as it reads, as it is all built on fresh produce combined creatively - ravioli filled with duck egg and matched with red onion purée, pancetta, wild mushrooms and black truffle, for example. Elsewhere, rump of Welsh Elwy Valley lamb could be served with a cannelloni of shoulder, beetroot Tatin and artichoke purée in a well-balanced idea, while monkfish arrives with a ragu of borlotti beans and shellfish, lime and roasted almond foam, and razor clam gremolata. Desserts keep the creative flow moving - perhaps banana parfait, cinnamon crumble, champagne jelly and mascarpone. Friendly, informed service and a deli-café for stocking up on authentic goodies to take home complete the picture.

Chef Quentin Dorangeville **Owner** David & Catherine Taylor **Times** 12-2.30/6.30-10.30 Closed 25-26 Dec, 1 Jan, Etr Sun, Mon, D Sun **Prices** Fixed L 2 course £17.95, Fixed D 3 course £23.95, Starter £6.95-£11.95, Main £15.50-£23.95, Dessert £7.25-£8.95, Service added but optional 12.5% **Wines** 84 bottles over £20, 7 bottles under £20, 12 by glass **Notes** Sunday L, Vegetarian available **Seats** 64, Pr/dining room 30 **Children** Portions **Parking** On street

HARROW WEALD

Grim's Dyke Hotel

PLAN 1 B5

◉◉ Modern British

Magnificent setting for modern British cooking

☎ 020 8385 3100
Old Redding HA3 6SH
e-mail: reservations@grimsdyke.com
dir: 3m from M1 between Harrow & Watford

Something of a shrine for Gilbert & Sullivan aficionados, this striking country retreat was Sir William Gilbert's country residence for 20 years. It was also a tuberculosis recovery centre, such is its recuperative setting in 40 acres of gardens and grounds. Gilbert's restaurant housed in the flamboyant old billiard room looks out over the croquet lawn and terrace. An inglenook fireplace, stone carvings and Gothic arches add plenty of personality, whilst the menu is largely dictated by what's growing in the garden. Simple modern British ideas are carried off with flair; grilled sardines might be paired with courgettes and lemon chutney, and home-made pork and prune meatballs with buttered leeks and mashed potatoes. Puddings are creative takes on old favourites, perhaps coffee crème brûlée or banoffee cheesecake.

Chef Daren Mason **Owner** Skerrits of Nottingham Holdings **Times** 12.30-2/7-9.30 Closed 24 Dec, 1 Jan, L Sat, D 25-26 Dec **Prices** Fixed L 2 course £12.95, Fixed D 3 course £16.95-£22, Starter £5.50-£10.50, Main £12.95-£23.50, Dessert £5.50-£8.50, Service optional **Wines** 70 bottles over £20, 10 bottles under £20, 10 by glass **Notes** Fixed menu D 5 course £27.50, Tasting menu 6 course Fri-Sat, Sunday L, Vegetarian available, Dress restrictions, No jeans or trainers (Fri-Sat), Civ Wed 60 **Seats** 60, Pr/dining room 88 **Children** Portions **Parking** 100

HEATHROW AIRPORT (LONDON)

London Heathrow Marriott Hotel

PLAN 1 A3

◉ Traditional Italian **NEW**

Tuscan-influenced cuisine at smart hotel

☎ 020 8990 1100
Bath Rd UB3 5AN
e-mail: mhrs.lhrhrguestbackup@marriotthotels.com
dir: M4 junct 4, follow signs for Heathrow Terminals 1 & 3. Left at rdbt onto A4 towards central London. Hotel 0.5m on left

Enlivened by the atmosphere and aromas of an open-to-view theatre kitchen, the intimate fine-dining option at this modern airport hotel offers simple Italian cooking and is justifiably popular, so booking is advisable. Modern and classical Italian food has its roots firmly set in Tuscany, with top-notch produce used to good effect to create hearty and rustic dishes where the main ingredient shines. From the seasonal menu, perhaps kick off with a light and subtly flavoured warm garlic and parmesan polenta cake with marinated peppers and rocket salad, then follow with pan-fried cod with sautéed spinach and an enjoyable prosecco and cream sauce. Leave room for a stunning vanilla pannacotta with a well-timed poached pear in a rich red wine sauce.

Chef Joe Beaver **Owner** Marriott International **Times** 6-10.30 Closed 23 Dec-4 Jan, L all week **Prices** Fixed D 3 course £39, Starter £8-£12.50, Main £18-£29, Dessert £7-£8.50, Service added but optional 12.5%, Groups min 6 service 12.5% **Wines** 27 bottles over £20, 13 by glass **Notes** Vegetarian available, Dress restrictions, Smart casual, no jeans, trainers or shorts, Civ Wed 414, Air con **Seats** 65 **Children** Portions, Menu **Parking** 280

KESTON

Map 6 TQ46

Lujon

◉◉ Modern European **NEW**

Exciting modern cooking comes to Keston

☎ 01689 855501
6 Comonside BR2 6BP
e-mail: info@lujon.co.uk
dir: M25 junct 4, follow A21 Bromley

Refurbishment has given a smart and contemporary feel to Lujon, with its oak floor, white walls hung with artwork, wooden tables dressed with fresh flowers, and a relaxed atmosphere, with attentive but unbuttoned staff. The restaurant has hit the ground running with its brand of

Save on Hotels. Book at **theAA.com/hotel**

GREATER LONDON 367 ENGLAND

creative contemporary cooking which delivers main courses such as venison loin and confit shoulder with chervil root and a crispy shepherd's pie, and mackerel with crab cream, pickled squid and purple broccoli. Quality ingredients are accurately cooked, bringing out fresh, clear flavours, seen in another successful main course of roast cod fillet topped with black truffles, accompanied by chargrilled leeks and artichoke purée. Humble pumpkin soup comes to life with the addition of crisp shards and tortellini of the vegetable, and a sense of adventure is seen in other starters such as oxtail with parsnip custard and oxtail tea. Puddings exemplify the kitchen's exhilarating approach to cooking; witness a chocolate case of mandarin parfait, the plate dotted with candied chestnuts, served with warm chocolate sauce.

Chef Andrew Jones **Owner** Angela Bell
Times 12-3/6.30-10 Closed Mon (excl BHs), D Sun
Prices Fixed L 2 course £14.50, Fixed D 3 course fr £23.95, Starter £5.95-£11.95, Main £13.95-£23.95, Dessert £6.95, Service added 12.5% **Wines** 31 bottles over £20, 6 bottles under £20, 10 by glass **Notes** Fixed L 2 course includes wine, D 3 course Tue-Fri, Sunday L, Vegetarian available, Civ Wed 60 **Seats** 48, Pr/dining room 32 **Children** Portions, Menu **Parking** Free car park 1min walk away

KEW

The Glasshouse
PLAN 1 C3

 — see below

PINNER

Friends Restaurant
PLAN 1 B5

Modern British

Heartwarming French bistro fare in an old timbered house

☎ 020 8866 0286
11 High St HA5 5PJ
e-mail: info@friendsrestaurant.co.uk
web: www.friendsrestaurant.co.uk
dir: In centre of Pinner, 2 mins walk from underground station

With its timbered façade, and low-ceilinged beamed interior, the 400-year-old house wouldn't look at all out of place in a Cotswold village. As it is, it stands on Pinner's High Street, and does a fine job of gracing that thoroughfare. The name is fair indication of the warmth

of the welcome, and what's on the menu is heartwarming traditional French bistro fare, enlivened with some modern combinations. Expect to start with crab and apple salad with marinated beetroot and sauce gribiche, before the high-rolling main courses offer stone bass with prawns in seafood bisque with saffron potatoes, or pot-roasted quail with a truffled mousse, seared foie gras and girolles. Proper floating islands come with crème anglaise and caramel sauce, as per the textbook.

Friends Restaurant

Chef Terry Farr **Owner** Terry Farr **Times** 12-3/6.30-10.30 Closed 25 Dec, BHs, Mon in summer, D Sun **Prices** Fixed L 2 course £21, Fixed D 3 course £35, Service added but optional 12.5% **Wines** 40 bottles over £20, 2 bottles under £20, 22 by glass **Notes** Pre-jazz season D 3 course (incl wine) £20 Oct-Apr from 6pm, Sunday L, Vegetarian available **Seats** 40, Pr/dining room 30 **Children** Portions **Parking** Nearby car parks

---

The Glasshouse

KEW
PLAN 1 C3

Modern International

French-based cooking of exemplary consistency

☎ 020 8940 6777
14 Station Pde TW9 3PZ
e-mail: info@glasshouserestaurant.co.uk
dir: Close to Kew Gardens underground station

The Glasshouse appears to have found the magic formula that keeps a restaurant constantly busy and at the forefront of local diners' affections. The recipe is not as hard as you might think to pull off - set-price menus of the kind of full-flavoured food that contemporary foodies want to tuck into, served in uncluttered contemporary surroundings by conscientious, clued-up staff - so one might wonder why more operations don't follow the lead of the owners Nigel Platts-Martin and Bruce Poole, the

team behind the equally in-vogue La Trompette in Chiswick, and Chez Bruce in Wandsworth (see entries). The name comes from the huge plate-glass windows that make it stand out in the parade of shops by Kew Gardens tube station, and make a luminous and easygoing setting for a cleverly-reworked repertoire of French classics with accents from Spain and Italy. Dishes make their impact without any need to resort to culinary flimflam - a starter uniting venison and black pudding turnover with Jerusalem artichoke purée and Madeira sauce shows the style, while mains could see roast wood pigeon served with a pastilla of leg, braised endive, quince purée and spinach, or sea bass matched with braised leeks, brown shrimps, gnocchi and vermouth velouté. Classic puddings - crème brûlée or apple tarte Tatin with crème fraîche ice cream, perhaps - also achieve a level of refinement that only comes with top-level technical ability.

Chef Daniel Mertl **Owner** Nigel Platts-Martin, Bruce Poole **Times** 12-2.30/6.30-10.30 Closed Xmas, New Year **Prices** Fixed L 2 course £23.50-£27.50, Fixed D 3 course fr £42.50, Service added but optional 12.5% **Wines** 413 bottles over £20, 3 bottles under £20, 14 by glass **Notes** Tasting menu available D Sun-Fri, Sunday L, Vegetarian available **Seats** 60 **Children** Portions **Parking** On street-metered

RICHMOND UPON THAMES

Bacco Restaurant Italiano PLAN 1 C2

◉ Italian

Smart and welcoming neighbourhood Italian

☎ 020 8332 0348
39-41 Kew Rd TW9 2NQ
e-mail: bookings@bacco-restaurant.co.uk
dir: A316 towards Richmond Station or town centre, 2 min walk from tube

This smart independent Italian next to the Orange Tree Theatre draws a loyal local crowd for its lively vibe and a personal approach that makes it stand out from the chains. For sunny days, there's a decked terrace out on the pavement, and when the weather's not on your side, two distinct dining areas take in a 'library' of all-Italian wines lining the wall on one side, and it is all done out in an up-to-date style with bare floorboards, colourful artwork, and convivial elbow-to-elbow tables. The kitchen sends out straightforward contemporary Italian ideas on a menu shorn of spag bol and pizzas, and it's all based on quality produce. Sticking to time-honoured Italian practice, start with beef carpaccio with rocket, shaved parmesan and fresh black truffle, ahead of a pasta course - home-made lobster ravioli with lobster bisque sauce, perhaps - then pan-seared duck breast with potato purée and orange sauce.

Chef Vincenzo Indelicato **Owner** Stefano Bergamin **Times** 12-2.30/5.45-11 Closed Xmas, New Year, BHs, Sun **Prices** Food prices not confirmed for 2013. Please telephone for details **Wines** 45 bottles over £20, 12 bottles under £20, 16 by glass **Notes** Vegetarian available, Dress restrictions, Smart casual, Air con **Seats** 50, Pr/dining room 27 **Children** Portions

Bingham PLAN 1 C2

◉◉◉ – see below

La Buvette PLAN 1 C2

◉ French, Mediterranean

Cheery bistro serving French classics - and more

☎ 020 8940 6264
6 Church Walk TW9 1SN
e-mail: info@labuvette.co.uk
dir: 3 mins from train station, opposite St Mary Magdalene Church, off the main High St

At one time the refectory of the next-door church, La Buvette brings some French bistro style to Richmond, with its café-type chairs and banquettes, pastel décor and cordial atmosphere. The kitchen is dedicated to a repertoire based on regional French cooking, although it's not afraid to cross borders when it wants to. The usual suspects include escargots de Bourgogne, moules

marinière with chips, and crème brûlée. Dishes are accomplished and flavours clear, seen in uncluttered main courses like braised salted ox tongue with roast beetroot and creamy mustard sauce, and fillet of grey mullet with ratatouille and sauce verte. The walled courtyard is a great place for alfresco dining.

Chef Buck Carter **Owner** Bruce Duckett **Times** 12-3/6-10 Closed 25-26 Dec, 1 Jan, Good Fri, Etr Sun **Prices** Fixed L 2 course £14.75, Fixed D 3 course £21, Starter £5-£12, Main £12-£19.50, Dessert £5-£7.75, Service added but optional 12.5% **Wines** 26 bottles over £20, 4 bottles under £20, 14 by glass **Notes** Sunday L, Vegetarian available **Seats** 50 **Children** Portions, Menu **Parking** NCP - Paradise Road

The Petersham Hotel PLAN 1 C2

◉◉ British, European V

Lovely Thames views and a varied modern menu

☎ 020 8939 1084 & 020 8940 7471
Nightingale Ln TW10 6UZ
e-mail: restaurant@petershamhotel.co.uk
dir: From Richmond Bridge rdbt A316 follow Ham & Petersham signs. Hotel in Nightingale Ln on left off Petersham Rd

An unmistakeable mansion in floridly Italianate Gothic style, The Petersham was built as a hotel and opened its doors in 1865. Don't miss a glimpse of the magnificent

Bingham

RICHMOND UPON THAMES PLAN 1 C2

Modern British V ⬛ NOTABLE WINE LIST

Instinctive, dynamic cooking by the river at Richmond

☎ 020 8940 0902
61-63 Petersham Rd TW10 6UT
e-mail: info@thebingham.co.uk
web: www.thebingham.co.uk
dir: On A307, near Richmond Bridge

Straight from the pages of an interiors magazine, the chic boutique Bingham overlooks the Thames and its towpath just a short and scenic stroll from the centre of Richmond - a serendipitous location that comes into its own in summer when you're dining out on the riverside terrace. Originally a pair of Georgian cottages that were later knocked together, the opulent dining rooms are a bijou boudoir vision of shimmering cream banquettes,

pale gold carpets, velvet-cushioned chairs and silk curtains, all lit with a soft-focus glow by vast teardrop chandeliers and cleverly-recessed lighting. Shay Cooper is a chef with ambition and he pulls together a repertoire of intriguing, intricate dishes, whose components may in some cases seem unlikely bedfellows, but not in these hands. His technical skills are more than up to scratch, and these are ideas to lift the spirits: roast Orkney scallops are matched with finely-chopped razor clam, squid and herbs, and delicate potato cubes in an aromatic seafood bisque, while main course delivers a tender three-cutlet rack of Casterbridge lamb with confit shoulder, braised Roscoff onions, glazed chicory, and an orange and thyme jus. Fish might come in a more left-field composition of roast halibut with smoked eel carbonara, compressed cucumber, parsley purée and cockle butter sauce. To finish, a superb deconstructed tiramisù comprising espresso ice cream, cocoa tuile and coffee crumble is a triumph.

Chef Shay Cooper **Owner** Ruth & Samantha Trinder **Times** 12-2.30/7-10 Closed D Sun **Prices** Fixed L 2 course fr £16, Fixed D 3 course fr £45, Starter fr £12, Main fr £25, Dessert fr £8, Service added but optional 12.5% **Wines** 300+ bottles over £20, 14 by glass **Notes** Tasting menu 8 course, Pre-theatre 2 course menu, Sunday L, Vegetarian menu, Civ Wed 90 **Seats** 50 **Children** Portions, Menu **Parking** 8, Town centre

Portland stone staircase winding its way up the building, with a painted ceiling and skylight at the top. Each table in the generously spaced restaurant, with its panelling and mirrors, has a wonderfully bucolic view over meadows to the Thames through full-length windows. High-quality ingredients form a solid base for the kitchen to work with on its seasonally-changing menus: lobster butter for potted shrimps with pickled cucumber, say, followed by Kiev-style chicken and foie gras, served with truffled haricot blanc purée and vin jaune. Classics like Dover sole meunière and grilled fillet steak with béarnaise put in an appearance alongside more modish ideas with no particular loyalty to any one cuisine: grilled ox tongue with pickled mushrooms and horseradish and parmesan toast, seared stone bass topped with olives, accompanied by a stew of octopus, chorizo, white beans and shallots, then apple galette with Calvados ice cream.

Chef Alex Bentley **Owner** The Petersham Hotel Ltd **Times** 12.15-2.15/7-9.45 Closed 25-26 Dec, 1 Jan, D 24 Dec **Prices** Fixed L 2 course fr £19.75, Starter £8.50-£14.50, Main £16-£34, Dessert £8, Service added but optional 12.5% **Wines** 137 bottles over £20, 18 by glass **Notes** Degustation menu 5 course £95, Sunday L, Vegetarian menu, Civ Wed 40 **Seats** 70, Pr/dining room 26 **Children** Portions, Menu **Parking** 60

Petersham Nurseries Café PLAN 1 C2

🌸 Modern

From garden centre to plate

☎ 020 8605 3627
Church Ln, Petersham Rd TW10 7AG
e-mail: cafe@petershamnurseries.com
dir: Adjacent to Richmond Park & Petersham Meadows. Best accessed on foot or bicycle along the river

Produce has always been king here, and so it continues following the departure of Skye Gyngell. The uniquely ramshackle glasshouse café in a garden centre is willfully down-to-earth, rustic, unfussy, shabby-chic, really rather basic. But it's all the more fun for that, although don't go thinking that means the food comes cheap. It's advisable to dress warm and dress down. Copious flowers and plants act as decoration and the Indonesian tables and chairs suit the mood. A good deal of the wonderful, seasonal produce is grown on site and turns up in rustic, well-crafted plates of food. Start with sea bass céviche with hazelnuts, mache, green chilli and datterini, then go for duck bistayeea - 'Morocco's celebrated sweet spiced pie' (the new chef has brought a flavour of North Africa to proceedings) - finishing with Pavlova with lemon posset and ginger caramel pears. Lunch is served six days a week and candlelit supper clubs run various evenings throughout the summer.

Times 12-2.45 Closed Etr Sun, 25 Dec, Mon-Tue, D all week

Richmond Hill Hotel PLAN 1 C2

🌸 Modern European

Riverside dining in Richmond

☎ 020 8939 0265
144-150 Richmond Hill TW10 6RW
e-mail: restaurant.richmondhill@foliohotels.com
dir: A316 for Richmond, hotel at top of Richmond Hill

The hotel, a Grade II listed building overlooking the Thames and Richmond Park, has a bar with comfortable leather sofas and chairs and a two-part restaurant, the first carpeted, the second with a wooden floor and a fireplace. A few influences from the East - Chinese ginger beef with coconut rice, or grilled salmon steak with teriyaki sauce, noodles and Asian greens - add some variety to the menu, which will otherwise be familiar enough, opening with carpaccio with a parmesan basket, and seared scallops with cauliflower purée and pancetta, and closing with crème brûlée, and sticky toffee pudding. In between might come pan-fried calves' liver and bacon with onion gravy and mash, or seared mackerel with grilled potatoes and salad.

Times 10.30am-10.30pm

The Barn Hotel PLAN 1 A5

🌸🌸 Modern French V

Creative French cooking in a period-rich boutique hotel

☎ 01895 636057
West End Rd HA4 6JB
e-mail: info@thebarnhotel.co.uk
web: www.thebarnhotel.co.uk
dir: A40 onto A4180 (Polish War Memorial) exit to Ruislip. 2m to hotel entrance at mini-rdbt before Ruislip tube station

This 17th-century farmhouse turned boutique hotel stands in three acres of landscaped grounds and combines old-world charm with all the mod cons. As well as an impressive 70-odd bedrooms, the intimate Jacobean Hawtrey's Restaurant is a major draw. Burnished mahogany panelled walls are hung with traditional artwork and chandeliers hang from the ceiling, while formal service, carefully laid tables and classical music all sit comfortably with the period details. Modern French food is on the menu, based on seasonal ingredients and presented with originality and flair. Start perhaps with lemon sole with zucchini fricassée, mussel

and saffron emulsion and crisp spinach, then move on to guinea fowl with a cannelloni of the leg, sweetcorn mousse, forest mushrooms, potato gâteau and foie gras mousse, and mango three ways (tart, brûlée and ice cream). There's a tasting menu too.

Chef Vic Ramana **Owner** Pantheon Hotels & Leisure **Times** 12-2.30/7-10.30 Closed L Sat, D Sun **Prices** Fixed L 2 course £13.95, Fixed D 3 course £29, Tasting menu £49.95, Starter £8.50-£12.50, Main £21-£28, Service added but optional 10% **Wines** 68 bottles over £20, 52 bottles under £20, 9 by glass **Notes** Sunday L, Vegetarian menu, Dress restrictions, Smart casual, Civ Wed 74 **Seats** 44, Pr/dining room 20 **Children** Portions, Menu **Parking** 50

The French Table PLAN 1 C1

🌸🌸 French, Mediterranean 🌶

Contemporary French dining in the suburbs

☎ 020 8399 2365
85 Maple Rd KT6 4AW
e-mail: enquiries@thefrenchtable.co.uk
dir: 5 min walk from Surbiton station, 1m from Kingston

As its name suggests, this smart-looking restaurant specialises in simple, modern French/Mediterranean cooking. Well established and located in a most unlikely of locations - in a modest parade of shops - it is deservedly popular. The refurbished interior has a somewhat modern and sophisticated look, with vibrant green banquette seating, a slate-tiled floor, wooden chairs at linen-clothed tables, and relaxed and buzzing atmosphere. The monthly-changing carte makes sound use of fresh seasonal produce and delivers simply presented dishes with good flavour combinations. A starter of hare, ham hock and foie gras terrine with Armagnac prunes may precede steamed halibut with Dorset clams, salsify fondue and lemon and parsley sauce. The dessert list runs to passionfruit tart with raspberry marshmallows and white chocolate ice cream.

Chef Eric Guignard, Frederic Duvac **Owner** Eric & Sarah Guignard **Times** 12-2.30/7-10.30 Closed 25-26 Dec, 1-3 Jan, Mon, D Sun **Prices** Fixed L 2 course £19.50, Tasting menu £45-£75, Starter £6.50-£9.80, Main £11.80-£19.20, Dessert £7-£10.50, Service added but optional 12.5% **Wines** 100 bottles over £20, 5 bottles under £20, 9 by glass **Notes** Tasting menu whole table only (with wine £75), Sunday L, Vegetarian available, Dress restrictions, Smart casual **Seats** 48, Pr/dining room 32 **Children** Portions **Parking** On street

Retro

PLAN 1 C1

◉◉ French V

French bistro with bags of style and provincial cooking

☎ 020 8977 2239
114-116 High St TW11 8JB
e-mail: retrobistrot@aim.com
dir: A313 Teddington High St

Out in the Teddington suburbs, this flamboyant, French bistro is all you could want from a neighbourhood eatery. Parisian café-style tables and chairs, banquettes and glamorous chandeliers are set against trendy patterned wallpaper, exposed brick walls and wooden floors in an eye-catchingly colourful, retro-chic interior, and the vibe is relaxed and convivial. Classic cuisine bourgeoise dishes are given a modern tweak to deliver the hoped-for robust, big-hearted flavours and generous portions, and it is all done at remarkably attractive prices. Quality seasonal ingredients drive the repertoire, which reads like poetry to the francophile foodie: snails in garlic butter or chicken liver parfait with Madeira jelly might lead on to cider-braised halibut with mussel and clam chowder and parsley foam, or a timeless Chateaubriand for two with béarnaise sauce, Pont-Neuf potatoes and French beans. By all means head for crème brûlée at the end, but expect it to be flavoured with lime leaf and lemongrass and accompanied by green tea ice cream.

Chef Andrew West **Owner** Vincent Gerbeau
Times 12-3.30/6.30-11 Closed Xmas, 1 Jan, BHs, Mon (open on request), D Sun **Prices** Fixed L 2 course £10.95, Fixed D 3 course £19.95-£22.50, Starter £6.20-£9.95, Main £11-£24.95, Dessert £6.30, Service added but optional 12.5% **Wines** 55 bottles over £20, 14 bottles under £20, 25 by glass **Notes** Fixed D 2/3 course min price applys Tue-Thu, max Fri-Sat, Sunday L, Vegetarian menu, Air con **Seats** 110, Pr/dining room 50 **Children** Portions **Parking** On street

A Cena

PLAN 1 C2

◉ Modern Italian

Accomplished Italian cooking near Richmond Bridge

☎ 020 8288 0108
418 Richmond Rd TW1 2EB
e-mail: acenarichmond@gmail.com
dir: 100 yds from Richmond Bridge

On the Twickenham side of Richmond Bridge, A Cena is an informal neighbourhood Italian restaurant done out in bistro style. The menus are bilingual, cooking treatments are generally not too complicated, and dishes are big on flavours. Sicilian-style mussels with fennel, tomato and a chick pea pancake, and pork meatballs with ricotta cooked in milk are among interesting starters. A few pasta dishes may run to spaghetti with prawns, chilli and rocket, and among main courses may be pan-fried hake fillet served with capers and green beans, or barbecued duck breast with apricot dressing and rosemary-roast

potatoes. All-Italian cheeses or chocolate and praline pannacotta are appropriate ways to finish.

Chef Nicola Parsons **Owner** Camilla & Tim Healy
Times 12-2.30/7-10.30 Closed Xmas & BHs, L Mon, D Sun **Prices** Fixed L 3 course £45, Starter £6.95-£12, Main £12.95-£23.50, Dessert £6-£9.50, Service optional, Groups min 6 service 12.5% **Wines** 80 bottles over £20, 9 bottles under £20, 12 by glass **Notes** Fixed L 3 course available pre-rugby match, Sunday L, Vegetarian available **Seats** 55 **Children** Portions **Parking** On street

MERSEYSIDE

BIRKENHEAD
Map 15 SJ38

Fraiche

◉◉◉ – see opposite

FRANKBY
Map 15 SJ28

Stewart Warner at Hillbark

◉◉◉ – see opposite

LIVERPOOL
Map 15 SJ39

The London Carriage Works

◉◉ Modern International ◐

Well-executed cooking in trendy hotel conversion

☎ 0151 705 2222
Hope Street Hotel, 40 Hope St L1 9DA
e-mail: eat@hopestreethotel.co.uk
web: www.thelondoncarriageworks.co.uk
dir: Follow cathedral & university signs on entering city, at the centre of Hope St between the two cathedrals

The Hope Street Hotel's restaurant gets its name from a sign uncovered during renovation: the property, built in the 1860s in the style of a Venetian palazzo, was once a coach and carriage works. The interior is now all stripped-down bare bricks and wooden floors, a trendy environment for some seriously ambitious cooking, with starters like fresh and smoked salmon with Avruga caviar, celeriac remoulade and caper vierge, followed by a trio of Herdwick lamb (confit shoulder, roast loin and fried liver), served with caramelised onions, a cabbage parcel and Puy lentils. Dishes make an impact with their well-considered combinations and good timings: witness beautifully cooked scallops and braised pork cheek with morcilla, cauliflower purée and raisin dressing, and duck

breast with chicory tarte Tatin, peas and lettuce with bacon, and pommes mousseline.

Chef Paul Askew **Owner** David Brewitt **Times** 12-3/5-10 Closed D 25 Dec **Prices** Food prices not confirmed for 2013. Please telephone for details **Wines** 180 bottles over £20, 9 bottles under £20, 18 by glass **Notes** Prix fixe menu, Pre theatre & tasting menus available, Sunday L, Vegetarian available, Dress restrictions, Smart casual, Civ Wed 70 **Seats** 100, Pr/dining room 50 **Children** Portions, Menu **Parking** On street, car park opposite

Malmaison Liverpool

◉ Modern British ◐

Modern brasserie food on the Princes Dock

☎ 0151 229 5000
7 William Jessop Way, Princes Dock L3 1QZ
e-mail: liverpool@malmaison.com
dir: Located on Princes Dock near the Liver Building

The Liverpool 'Mal' was the first purpose-built hotel in this innovative chain. It sits on the rejuvenated Princes Dock, in the company of the famous Liver Birds, whose flight from their perch would, as the myth has it, cause the Mersey to engulf the city (perish the thought). Inside looks as contemporary as can be, with a stripped-down, industrial-chic feel from exposed brickwork and fat pipes, and there is a de rigueur chef's table next to the kitchen. Modern brasserie food is the name of the game; smoked salmon rösti with horseradish cream, two cuts of Gloucestershire Old Spot pork with beetroot, parsnip and chorizo, and chocolate fondant with espresso ice cream would be one satisfying route through the menu.

Chef Adam Townsley **Owner** MWB **Times** 12-2/6.30-10.30 Closed L Sat **Prices** Starter £6.50-£7.95, Main £12.95-£26.95, Dessert £5.95, Service added but optional 10% **Wines** 70 bottles over £20, 40 bottles under £20, 12 by glass **Notes** Sunday L, Vegetarian available, Civ Wed 90 **Seats** 87, Pr/dining room 10 **Children** Portions **Parking** Car park by hotel

Save on Hotels. Book at **theAA.com/hotel**

MERSEYSIDE 371 ENGLAND

Fraiche

BIRKENHEAD
Map 15 SJ38

Modern French, European V NOTABLE WINE LIST

Stunning modern cooking on the Wirral peninsula

☎ 0151 652 2914
11 Rose Mount, Oxton CH43 5SG
e-mail: contact@restaurantfraiche.com
dir: M53 junct 3 towards Prenton. In 2m left towards Oxton. Fraiche on right

Marc Wilkinson is a chef who puts his heart and soul into his work. Everything about his restaurant in a conservation village shows vision, purpose and attention to detail. It's exceedingly personal. There are less than 20 covers when many more could be squeezed into the space - the customer, like the chef, can spread their wings. The natural colours chosen to decorate the room are inspired by the shoreline, by all accounts, which translates as a smart, unfussy neutrality that meets contemporary expectations. Wilkinson's cooking is at the sharp end, where innovative techniques and creative thinking combine to deliver some impressive and memorable dishes. A series of fixed-price, multi-course menus - 'elements', 'signature' and 'bespoke' - are joined by the mysterious 'black' menu, which is available to members The balance of flavours and textures in each dish is judged with a masterly hand, thus artichoke, white port, parmesan (as it appears on the menu) is a divine combination of artichoke cream, parmesan mousse and crisp, crunchy hazelnuts and a zingy port jelly. And that's just the appetiser. Cod loin, cep and beetroot (menu descriptions are brief) has a stellar piece of fish at its heart, and roasted venison loin comes with a divine butternut squash purée, caramelised salsify and a fabulous potato crisp. It all looks wonderful on the plate. Chocolate mousse is cleverly partnered with a sea buckthorn sorbet, pear and salted-chocolate soil in a winning dessert. With the bread coming in two courses, a small service team full of passion and knowledge of the menu, and a wine list that is both fairly priced and broad in scope, Marc Wilkinson's restaurant really is a breath of fraiche air.

Chef Marc Wilkinson **Owner** Marc Wilkinson
Times 12-1.30/7-9.30 Closed 25 Dec, 1 Jan, Mon-Tue, L Wed-Thu **Prices** Tasting menu £30-£58, Service optional **Wines** 270 bottles over £20, 24 bottles under £20, 6 by glass **Notes** Sunday L, Vegetarian menu **Seats** 16, Pr/dining room 20 **Children** Portions **Parking** On street

Stewart Warner at Hillbark

FRANKBY
Map 15 SJ28

Modern British **NEW** V ✋

Quirky, imaginative contemporary cooking in high-glitz Wirral surroundings

☎ 0151 625 2400
Hillbark Hotel and Spa, Royden Park CH48 1NP
e-mail: enquiries@hillbarkhotel.co.uk
dir: M53 junct 3, A552 (Upton), right onto A551 (Arrowe Park Rd). 0.6m at lights left into Arrowe Brook Rd. 0.5m on left

Built in the 1890s, Hillbark Hotel and Spa on the Wirral peninsula is one of the most eye-popping examples of Victorian Tudor pastiche in all England, a riot of timbering outside and panelling within. Crown Prince Wilhelm, the Kaiser's son, stayed here not long after it was finished and, green with envy, went home and had a replica built at Potsdam. Its 250 acres of parkland should give you plenty to do, and inside are spa facilities and a restaurant - the Dining Room - kitted out in full country-house fig. Floral fabrics line the walls, the chairs look fit to support the posteriors of nobility, and gilt-framed oil portraits gaze down on the chandelier-lit scene. Stewart Warner rises to the occasion, and then some, in these glitz-bound surrounds, with a style of ultra-contemporary food that's full of technical skill, inventive imagination and quirky humour. Oblong plates and slates deliver gatherings of ingredients in the modern manner, perhaps mousse and tartare of scallops with morel foam, crispy pata negra ham, and a beignet and purée of cauliflower, to start. A leg of hoisin pigeon, complete with claw, is wrapped in a spring roll, to accompany the breast marinated in sesame, ginger and soy, along with fried Chinese leaves and a bean sprout salad. Dover sole with fine fennel ragoût, squid tempura and risotto in squid ink sauce is a dramatically successful main course, as is a duck composition involving breast and foie gras, together with the yolk of its egg topped with shredded carrot, accompanied by other textures of carrot in all its possible colours, and a striking anise-charged sauce. These multi-component dishes work best when their various elements are combined, rather than approached discretely, as is also the case with the desserts, which might combine lemon curd parfait and popping candy, a basil doughnut, miniature meringues and basil jelly. The Cellar Restaurant and Hillbark Grill are also on site.

Chef Stewart Warner **Owner** Contessa Hotels
Times 12-2.30/7-10 Closed Sun-Mon **Prices** Food prices not confirmed for 2013. Please telephone for details **Wines** 599 bottles over £20, 1 bottle under £20, 600 by glass **Notes** Sunday L, Vegetarian menu, Dress restrictions, Smart dress, Civ Wed 200 **Seats** 36, Pr/dining room 18 **Children** Portions **Parking** 160

LIVERPOOL *continued*

60 Hope Street Restaurant

Modern British V

Confident modern cooking near the cathedrals

☎ 0151 707 6060
60 Hope St L1 9BZ
e-mail: info@60hopestreet.com
web: www.60hopestreet.com
dir: From M62 follow city centre signs, then brown tourist signs for cathedral. Hope St near cathedral

Number 60, in a Georgian townhouse not far from the Philharmonic Hall and the two cathedrals, is split in two: an informal downstairs bistro and a ground-floor restaurant of pale wood and walls hung with large mirrors. The kitchen takes its inspiration from the modern British and European repertories, seen in starters like scallops with smoked potato, red pepper and chorizo, and crisp duck confit and livers with raisins and hazelnut dressing. Quality ingredients are evident throughout: foie gras in a terrine with pain d'épice, followed by pan-fried wild sea bass, accurately timed, with smoked aubergine tapenade, Jerusalem artichoke crisps and anchovies on toast, or roast rib of Cumbrian beef with pommes Anna, garlicky spinach and Café de Paris butter. A fresh approach doesn't falter among puddings, pairing rhubarb ripple sorbet with egg custard tart, for instance.

Chef Damien Flynn **Owner** Colin & Gary Manning
Times 12-2.30/6-10.30 Closed 26 Dec, L Sat **Prices** Fixed L 2 course £16.95, Starter £6.95-£14.95, Main £13.95-£29.95, Dessert £6.95-£9.95, Service optional, Groups min 8 service 10% **Wines** 70 bottles over £20, 18 bottles under £20, 6 by glass **Notes** Pre-theatre Mon-Sat 5-7pm, Sunday L, Vegetarian menu, Civ Wed 50 **Seats** 90, Pr/dining room 40 **Children** Portions **Parking** On street

Spire

Modern British, European **NEW**

Contemporary bistro comforts

☎ 0151 734 5040
Number One Church Rd L15 9EA
e-mail: spirerestaurant@btinternet.com

The name might lead you to think that this relaxed modern bistro lies in the shadow of one of Liverpool's two cathedrals, but it is actually a cab ride away in the Wavertree area, right by the one-and-only Penny Lane. The trip out of the centre is amply rewarded though: the friendly neighbourhood bistro venue has an unbuttoned vibe and looks the part too, with its well-trodden floorboards, bare brick and white-painted walls hung with colourful abstract art, and unclothed wooden tables. The kitchen deals in simple contemporary brasserie-style classics with a Mediterranean slant - chicken liver parfait with elderflower jelly and toasted brioche, say, while mains deliver the comforts of braised belly pork with swede purée, crispy black pudding, baby carrots and apple sauce, or roast mustard and herb-crumbed chump of salt marsh lamb partnered with ratatouille, lemongrass and oregano, and baby carrots. Chocolatey puddings - white chocolate pannacotta with chocolate ice cream, perhaps - will win friends, but there might also be apple tarte Tatin with caramel and vanilla sauce.

Chef Matt Locke **Owner** Matt & Adam Locke
Times 12-1.45/6-9 Closed BH Mon, 2wks from 2 Jan, Sun, L Sat, Mon **Prices** Fixed L 2 course fr £10.95, Fixed D 3 course fr £17.95, Starter £4.50-£8.95, Main £13.95-£19.95, Dessert £6-£7.50, Service optional **Wines** 35 bottles over £20, 30 bottles under £20, 12 by glass **Notes** Vegetarian available, Dress restrictions, Smart casual **Seats** 70, Pr/dining room 40 **Children** Portions **Parking** On street, local pub car park with cctv

The Lawns Restaurant at Thornton Hall

THORNTON HOUGH	Map 15 SJ38

Modern European V

Historic country-house hotel with contemporary cooking

☎ 0151 336 3938
Neston Rd CH63 1JF
e-mail: reservations@thorntonhallhotel.com
dir: M53 junct 4 onto B5151 & B5136, follow brown tourist signs (approx 2.5m) to Thornton Hall Hotel

This impressive Victorian manor house has a contemporary finish these days which sits happily with the grand period proportions of the building, and includes a large spa and enough space to host conferences and weddings. And in the form of The Lawns it has a restaurant which delivers some smart, complex contemporary cooking. It all takes place in a handsome room - the hall's one-time billiard room no less - with carved and coffered mahogany ceiling, impressive plasterwork friezes, and impeccably dressed tables. There are plenty of top-notch regional ingredients on show in dishes which display decidedly modish leanings. Start, perhaps, with hand-dived scallops with parsnip purée, bacon and parsley, or seared foie gras with duck garbure and gingerbread. Cheshire lamb might star in a main course as wonderfully full-flavoured rump and breast (served in a pastilla), with onion purée, samphire and honeycomb, or go for pheasant cooked sous-vide and served with Jerusalem artichokes and chestnut purée. Among desserts pear délice with a bitter chocolate crumb and pistachio ice cream shows good balance of flavours.

Chef David Gillmore **Owner** The Thompson family
Times 12-2.30/7-9.30 Closed 1 Jan, **Prices** Fixed L 2 course fr £16.95, Fixed D 3 course fr £34, Starter £8-£16, Main £20-£28, Dessert £7-£10, Service optional **Wines** 36 bottles over £20, 11 bottles under £20, 10 by glass **Notes** Tasting menu available Mon-Sat, Sunday L, Vegetarian menu, Dress restrictions, Smart casual, no T-shirts or jeans, Civ Wed 70 **Seats** 45, Pr/dining room 24 **Children** Portions **Parking** 250

Save on Hotels. Book at **theAA.com/hotel**

MERSEYSIDE – NORFOLK 373 ENGLAND

PORT SUNLIGHT
Map 15 SJ38

Leverhulme Hotel

@@ Modern International **NEW** V 🕙

Aspirational cooking in art deco gem

☎ 0151 644 6655 & 644 5555
Central Rd CH62 5EZ
e-mail: richardfox@leverhulmehotel.co.uk
dir: From Chester: M53 junct 5, A41 (Birkenhead) in approx 4m left into Bolton Rd, on at rdbt, 0.1m right into Church Drive. 0.2m hotel on right. From Liverpool: A41 (Chester), 2.7m, 3rd exit at 3rd rdbt into Bolton Rd (follow directions as above)

The centrepiece of Port Sunlight Garden Village on the Wirral is this splendid art deco boutique hotel. Built originally as a cottage hospital for the soap factory workers on Lord Leverhulme's pioneering philanthropic estate, the hotel has had a sprinkle of contemporary magic to bring its snow-white interiors up to meet 21st-century expectations, with cutting-edge modern dining in a striking designer setting. The space is airy and expansive with high ceilings, mirrored screens, leather chairs at glass tables and funky art-deco style carpets. Classics and grills feature on the menu, but it is the chef's approach to deconstructing dishes that has earned a reputation for cooking that is sharp, confident, and even edgy in places. Mackerel is served with gooseberry, crunchy onion rings and pointed up with a tartare sauce-style teaming of shallots, capers and gherkin, while main course Moroccan lamb arrives in the company of apricots, aubergines, couscous and a deeply-flavoured jus.

Chef Richard Fox **Owner** Contessa Hotels
Times 12-2.30/6-10 **Prices** Food prices not confirmed for 2013. Please telephone for details **Wines** 186 bottles over £20, 3 bottles under £20, 166 by glass **Notes** Sunday L, Vegetarian menu, Dress restrictions, Smart casual, Civ Wed 240 **Seats** 60, Pr/dining room 20 **Children** Portions, Menu **Parking** 70

SOUTHPORT
Map 15 SD31

Bistrot Vérité

@ French

Traditional French cooking in Birkdale village

☎ 01704 564199
7 Liverpool Rd, Birkdale PR8 4AR

Marc Vérité's self-named bistro in Birkdale village flies the tricolor proudly for the old French culinary traditions, with the benefit that much of what he produces is based on prime Lancashire ingredients. Crammed-in tables, chalkboard menus and a friendly, breezy buzz characterise the operation, as does some accomplished cooking. A wooden board of hors d'oeuvres variés encompasses a generous range of hot and cold items, including a scallop with pickled veg, duck and game terrine, battered frogs' legs, a snail simmered in Pernod, a goats' cheese croquette, and more. Main-course wood pigeon served with foie gras and wild mushrooms sautéed in garlic and parsley is a richly satisfying dish,

and meals may end with a thickly caramelised classic crème brûlée.

Chef Marc Vérité **Owner** Marc & Michaela Vérité **Times** 12-1.30/5.30-late Closed 1 wk Feb & 1 wk Aug, Sun-Mon **Prices** Food prices not confirmed for 2013. Please telephone for details **Notes** Vegetarian available **Seats** 45 **Children** Portions **Parking** Birkdale station

Vincent Hotel

@@ Modern International

Boutique hotel with an Anglo-European-Asian flavour

☎ 01704 883800
98 Lord St PR8 1JR
e-mail: manager@thevincenthotel.com
dir: M58 junct 3, follow signs to Ormskirk & Southport

The luxuriously contemporary Vincent Hotel has fab bedrooms (including a posh penthouse suite) and its cool V-Café and Sushi Bar looks out onto the perennially popular Lord Street. It's done out in fashionable coffee tones, with teapots hanging from the ceiling, and a bustling open-to-view kitchen. The all-day menu is a mixed bag of ideas, some British, some European, some Asian, including a good range of sushi. So you might go for a light lunch of eggs Florentine or tuck into something more substantial such as sautéed squid (fresh as a daisy and perfectly cooked) with roasted pepper, chorizo and basil, or a flavoursome lamb rump with spring onion mashed potato and pea purée. Pineapple tarte Tatin is a study in rich, buttery loveliness. Or choose from the Japanese favourites including salads, sushi and sashimi platters.

Chef Andrew Carter **Owner** Paul Adams **Times** 7.30am-9.30pm **Prices** Fixed D 3 course fr £13.95, Starter £3.95-£8.95, Main £7.95-£25.95, Dessert £5.95-£8.50, Service optional, Groups min 10 service 10% **Wines** 28 bottles over £20, 10 bottles under £20, 5 by glass **Notes** Fixed D 3 course available Sun-Thu, Sunday L, Vegetarian available, Dress restrictions, Smart casual **Seats** 85, Pr/dining room 12 **Children** Portions **Parking** Valet parking

Warehouse Kitchen & Bar

@@ International

Cool warehouse setting and smart modish cooking

☎ 01704 544662
30 West St PR8 1QN
e-mail: info@warehousekitchenandbar.com
dir: M58 junct 3, then A570 Southport

The stylish New York-esque Warehouse has white linen-clad tables against the bare-brick walls in a light and airy space and, up the stairs, a chic bar. Co-owned these days by Liverpool footballer Steven Gerrard, this town centre venue has been going strong for 15 years, its modern international cooking, cool design and relaxed vibe proving popular with the locals. Typical dishes include Ribble Valley pork croquettes with sweet honey mustard, crackling salad and baby pickles, followed perhaps by a trio of Cumbrian beef - steak and ale pie, fillet and oxtail sauce - and finishing with Wakefield

rhubarb 'mayhem' - rhubarb Bakewell tart, tonka bean pannacotta and rhubarb sorbet.

Chef Mini Patel **Owner** Paul Adams, Steven Gerrard **Times** 12-2/5.30-10 Closed 26 Dec, 1 Jan, Sun **Prices** Fixed D 3 course £15.95, Starter £5.95-£9.95, Main £12.95-£26.95, Dessert £4.95-£8.50, Service optional, Groups min 8 service 10% **Wines** 59 bottles over £20, 10 bottles under £20, 9 by glass **Notes** Fixed D 2, 3 course Mon-Thu all evening, Fri-Sat 5.30-6.30pm, Vegetarian available **Seats** 95, Pr/dining room 20 **Children** Portions, Menu **Parking** On street

THORNTON HOUGH
Map 15 SJ38

The Lawns Restaurant at Thornton Hall

@@@ – *see opposite*

NORFOLK

ALBURGH
Map 13 TM28

The Dove Restaurant with Rooms

@@ Modern European

Classic cooking in charming restaurant with rooms

☎ 01986 788315
Holbrook IP20 0EP
e-mail: info@thedoverestaurant.co.uk
dir: On South Norfolk border between Harleston & Bungay, by A143, at junct of B1062

The owners have generated a French country auberge-style vibe in the pleasant Waveney Valley on the south Norfolk border. It's a traditional place sure enough, with a recent refurbishment giving the dining room a cheerful countrified appearance; think blond-wood floors, pretty flowery wallpaper and clothed tables. The lounge or large raised terrace are the weather-dependent options for pre- or post-prandial drinks. This is a truly family-run business having been in the hands of the Oberhoffers since 1980 (Robert is the fifth generation chef), with good local ingredients, unpretentiously prepared, the star of the show; thus you might start with soufflé Arnold Bennett (a perennial favourite), or go for cream of home-grown pumpkin soup, followed by roasted loin of Blythburgh pork with grain mustard, Savoy cabbage, celeriac and thyme gravy, with raspberry Pavlova bringing proceedings to a satisfying close.

Times 12-2/7-9 Closed Mon-Tue, L Wed-Sat, D Sun

Morston Hall

Modern British **V** 🍷 NOTABLE WINE LIST 🍃

Country charm and refined, intelligent cooking

☎ 01263 741041
Morston, Holt NR25 7AA
e-mail: reception@morstonhall.com
web: www.morstonhall.com
dir: On A149 (coast road) between Blakeney & Stiffkey

Part of the charm of Morston Hall is that it feels a world away from the rat race, amid the wide-open skies, endless beaches and chocolate-box villages of the North Norfolk coast. Tucked away in pretty gardens opposite Morston Quay, the flint-faced mansion has been around since Jacobean times, and comes with the requisite blackened beams, stone-flagged floors and roaring fires that you would hope to find in an intimate country hotel. But Morston is not all about period romance: thanks to Galton Blackiston's cooking, it has become a foodie destination in its own right. Blackiston trained in the Lake District, and his menus stick to the tradition of the country houses of that region - a daily-changing, no-choice format that runs in this case to six courses brimming with local ingredients. Expect refined classical technique and a lively showing of good ideas delivering powerful, clearly defined flavours, all the way through

starters such as ox tongue with beetroot purée, onion rings and thyme oil, to a fish course of, say, North Sea hake with sea purslane soup. Main course could bring on lightly-smoked Norfolk lamb matched with salt-baked celeriac, tomato jam and lamb jus, then there's a pause for a hit of grapefruit and champagne sorbet before a finale of classic apple tarte Tatin with English whisky ice cream.

Chef Galton Blackiston **Owner** T & G Blackiston **Times** 12.30-7.30 Closed 2 wks Jan, L Mon-Sat (ex party booking) **Prices** Fixed L 3 course £35, Fixed D 4 course £62-£65, Service optional **Wines** 298 bottles over £20, 8 bottles under £20, 15 by glass **Notes** Sunday L, Vegetarian menu, Dress restrictions, Smart casual **Seats** 50, Pr/dining room 26 **Children** Portions, Menu **Parking** 40

Save on Hotels. Book at **theAA.com/hotel**

NORFOLK 375 ENGLAND

BACTON
Map 13 TG33

The Keswick Hotel

◉ British **NEW**

Unpretentious dining in small and friendly seaside hotel

☎ 01692 650468
Walcott Rd NR12 0LS
e-mail: margaret@keswickhotelbacton.co.uk
dir: On B1159 coast road

Smack on the seafront in Bacton, this charming small hotel punches above its weight in culinary matters thanks to a kitchen that takes carefully-sourced seasonal and local materials - Cromer crab, Brancaster mussels, rare-breed meats - as the starting point for its vibrant modern cooking. No one is trying to reinvent the wheel here: expect simple, classic combinations in unpretentious but skilfully-cooked dishes, starting out at its most emphatically seasonal with a summery idea such as crab cake with wasabi mayonnaise, pea shoots and a salad of micro leaves and herbs. Next, crisp-skinned, pan-fried sea bass arrives with rösti, wilted spinach, chorizo and brown shrimp butter, and for pudding there's condensed milk pannacotta with strawberry coulis and fresh strawberries.

Chef Russell Moore **Owner** Russell & Margaret Moore
Times 12-3/6-9 Closed L Mon-Sat **Prices** Starter £4.95-£6.95, Main £9.95-£22.95, Dessert £4.50-£5.50, Service optional **Wines** 4 bottles over £20, 14 bottles under £20, 6 by glass **Notes** Sunday L, Vegetarian available, Air con **Seats** 60 **Children** Menu **Parking** 75

BARNHAM BROOM
Map 13 TG00

Barnham Broom Hotel, Golf & Restaurant

◉◉ Modern British, European

Contemporary cooking with golfing views

☎ 01603 759393
Honingham Rd NR9 4DD
e-mail: enquiry@barnhambroomhotel.co.uk
dir: A11/A47 towards Swaffham, follow brown tourist signs

A sprawling, golf-centric hotel in 250 acres of bucolic Norfolk, Barnham Broom offers the full-dress country club and spa package, plus fine dining to views of the golf-course action in Flints Restaurant. A top-to-toe facelift in recent years has kept the place looking sharp, while the kitchen continues to come up with the goods, sourcing top-grade produce as the foundations of its assured contemporary cooking. To start, you might fancy roast pigeon breast teamed with black pudding, confit potato and apple chutney, or a tried-and-true trio of pan-fried scallops, pork belly and butternut squash purée, while

mains could stretch from an eastern-accented dish of Moroccan-marinated chicken suprême with tabouleh, aubergine caviar and preserved lemons, to a homely roast rump of English lamb served with a mini shepherd's pie, glazed carrots and wilted spinach. Finish with treacle tart with brown bread ice cream and salted caramel.

Chef John Batchelor **Owner** Barnham Broom Hotel
Times 7-9.30 Closed L Mon-Sat **Prices** Fixed L 3 course £17.95-£20.95, Fixed D 3 course £28.95-£36.95, Service added but optional 10% **Wines** 29 bottles over £20, 19 bottles under £20, 14 by glass **Notes** Sunday L, Vegetarian available, Dress restrictions, Smart casual, no trainers, Civ Wed 150 **Seats** 90, Pr/dining room 50 **Children** Portions, Menu **Parking** 500

BLAKENEY
Map 13 TG04

The Blakeney Hotel

◉ Modern British **V**

Modern British cooking in a quayside hotel

☎ 01263 740797
The Quay NR25 7NE
e-mail: reception@blakeneyhotel.co.uk
dir: From A148 between Fakenham & Holt, take B1156 to Langham & Blakeney

The Blakeney's quayside terrace is one of North Norfolk's gems on a sunny day, with a big-sky panorama sweeping across the estuary and salt marshes to Blakeney Point, and the cries of wading birds providing a soulful soundtrack. When the weather forces you inside the lovely flint-faced hotel, the restaurant still has that view, and is a shipshape venue with an easygoing, friendly ambience. The kitchen is clearly on good terms with local suppliers, showing off their wares to great effect in uncomplicated modern ideas - local crab, perhaps, on Bloody Mary jelly with avocado, cucumber salad and basil oil, or you could take simplicity to its extreme and tuck into Brancaster oysters with raspberry shallot vinegar and lemon. Given the setting, fish is a good bet - try roasted fillet of halibut on horseradish mash with baby leeks, girolles and tarragon cream; meat is handled deftly too, though, in ideas such as a baby rack and slow-cooked shoulder of lamb with celeriac and potato gratin, fine beans, artichoke, and olive jus. Finally, the pudding trolley trundles in bearing comfort in the shape of warm spiced bread pudding with maple syrup.

Chef Martin Sewell **Owner** Michael Stannard
Times 12-2/6.30-9 **Prices** Food prices not confirmed for 2013. Please telephone for details **Wines** 63 bottles over £20, 38 bottles under £20, 16 by glass **Notes** ALC 3 course £29-£43.50, No high chairs after 6.45pm, Sunday L, Vegetarian menu, Dress restrictions, Smart casual for D **Seats** 100, Pr/dining room 80 **Children** Portions **Parking** 60

Morston Hall

◉◉◉ – *see opposite*

BRANCASTER STAITHE
Map 13 TF74

The White Horse

◉◉ Modern British ☺

Fine regional produce and marsh views

☎ 01485 210262
PE31 8BY
e-mail: reception@whitehorsebrancaster.co.uk
dir: On A149 (coast road) midway between Hunstanton & Wells-next-the-Sea

While this neat, traditional but much-extended inn comes with a big bolt-on conservatory restaurant and decked terrace, the real show-stopper here is its location on the North Norfolk coast, offering knock-your-socks-off-views over the tidal salt marshes. The brasserie-style dining room is a relaxed spot - all natural-wood tables and seascape tones - and takes in the vista, while the kitchen doesn't disappoint, bringing fashionable modernity to great regional produce. Given the location, marine life has its say; as well as Brancaster oysters (with shallot vinegar or tempura) or mussels (with white wine, garlic and cream), there's pan-fried sea bass fillet served with saffron potatoes, chargrilled leeks, ratatouille and tomato-butter sauce. But the menu makes the best of Norfolk's land larder, too; witness pan-roast Norfolk pheasant breast teamed with Brancaster braised vegetables, new potato fondant, sautéed kale and jus. There's a separate bar menu.

Chef Avrum Frankel **Owner** Clifford Nye
Times 12-2/6.30-9 **Prices** Starter £5.25-£7.95, Main £9.25-£21, Dessert £6.95, Service optional **Wines** 37 bottles over £20, 8 bottles under £20, 13 by glass **Notes** Sunday L, Vegetarian available **Seats** 100 **Children** Portions, Menu **Parking** 85

continued

BRUNDALL — Map 13 TG30

The Lavender House

◎◎ Modern British V ᕔ

Engaging cooking in a modernised thatched cottage

☎ 01603 712215
39 The Street NR13 5AA
e-mail: lavenderhouse39@aol.com
dir: A47 E, 4m from Norwich city centre

The exterior may be an archetypally English thatched 16th-century cottage, but the interior of Lavender House has been reworked with a pared-back modern look involving exposed brickwork, modern art, high-backed leather chairs and crisp linen-clad tables beneath its head-skimming oak-beamed ceilings. Chef-proprietor Richard Hughes is the driving force in the kitchen, running a cookery school as well as the main business of turning out what he defines as 'modern Norfolk' cuisine. This translates as plenty of local produce delivered in flavour-driven dishes - starting, perhaps, with Cley smokehouse salmon with cucumber, crème fraîche and treacle loaf, or a modish presentation of pig's head, involving terrine, cheeks, remoulade of tongue, crispy ear and capers. Main courses favour multi-cut presentations - lamb for example, might come in the shape of rack, breast and middle neck, accompanied by tomato, olive, basil and polenta. There are fine local cheeses to wrap things up on a savoury note, or desserts like prune and Armagnac ice cream with Earl Grey syrup and brandy snaps.

Chef Richard Hughes **Owner** Richard Hughes
Times 12-4/6.30-11 Closed Mon-Wed, L Thu-Sat, D Sun
Prices Tasting menu £55, Service optional
Wines 50 bottles over £20, 16 bottles under £20, 8 by glass **Notes** Fixed D £42.50, Willi Opitz Table, Sunday L, Vegetarian menu **Seats** 50, Pr/dining room 36
Children Portions **Parking** 16

BURNHAM MARKET — Map 13 TF84

Hoste Arms Hotel

◎◎ Modern British, Pacific Rim ⬛NOTABLE WINE LIST ᕔ

Assured cooking with a global reach in historic inn

☎ 01328 738777
The Green PE31 8HD
e-mail: reception@hostearms.co.uk
web: www.hostearms.co.uk
dir: 2m from A149 between Burnham & Wells

In business for three centuries since local lad Horatio Nelson was a Saturday morning regular, the Hoste Arms is a quality set-up catering to all comers, whether it is lucky Burnham Market locals dropping in for a pint, or urbane weekenders out to spoil themselves with a break in one of the sybaritic boutique-styled bedrooms. And taking full advantage of the rather splendid food and wine on offer in two handsome wood-panelled dining rooms, or one of the other intimate nooks and crannies, is a good plan. New (and local) owners took over in 2012. The kitchen deals in up-to-date ideas, sprinkled liberally with global influences, although the raw materials come from closer to home - the Norfolk coastline assiette (smoked salmon, Brancaster oysters done tempura-style, as well as steamed with white wine and parsley cream, teriyaki sea bass with wasabi crème fraîche, fish soup with brown shrimps) looks a particularly good way for two to start out, or go for the reliable combo of confit pork belly with sauté black pudding, served with apple purée, thyme fondant potatoes and roasted celeriac. Save room to finish with dark chocolate fondant with white chocolate sorbet and chocolate popping candy.

Chef Aaron Smith **Times** 12-2/6-9 Closed D 25 Dec
Prices Starter £5.50-£11, Main £13.50-£21.95, Dessert £6.95-£8.95, Service optional **Wines** 153 bottles over £20, 14 bottles under £20, 21 by glass **Notes** Sunday L, Vegetarian available, Dress restrictions, Smart casual
Seats 140, Pr/dining room 24 **Children** Menu **Parking** 45

CROMER — Map 13 TG24

See also **Sheringham**

Frazers, Sea Marge Hotel

◎◎ Modern British ᕔ

Appealing modern menus on the North Norfolk coast

☎ 01263 579579
16 High St, Overstrand NR27 0AB
e-mail: info@mackenziehotels.com
dir: A140 to Cromer, B1159 to Overstrand, 2nd left past Overstrand Church

Terraced lawns lead down to the coast path and beach from this 1908-built mansion. The property has been lovingly restored, with many original features retained, a notable one being a minstrels' gallery. It's a friendly and relaxing hotel, with professional, helpful staff serving in the restaurant. The menu, with around a handful of choices per course, is an appealing package of contemporary ideas, running from marinated wood pigeon with duck liver ravioli, parsnip purée and roast hazelnut dressing, to poached fillet of sea bass with a chowder of smoked haddock, brown shrimps and vegetables. Goats' cheese soufflé, served with apple and walnut salad, rises to the occasion, and may be followed by flavourful rump of local lamb with thyme jus and well-considered accompaniments of minted pea purée, smoked bacon mash and roast green beans. Puddings include a memorable chocolate torte with pineapple sorbet and peanut brittle.

Chef Rene Ilupar **Owner** Mr & Mrs Mackenzie
Times 12-9.30/6.30-9.30 **Prices** Food prices not confirmed for 2013. Please telephone for details
Wines 10 bottles over £20, 21 bottles under £20, 6 by glass **Notes** Sunday L, Vegetarian available, Dress restrictions, Smart casual **Seats** 80, Pr/dining room 40
Children Portions, Menu **Parking** 50

White Horse Overstrand

◎◎ Modern European

Great Norfolk produce cooked with flair

☎ 01263 579237
34 High St, Overstrand NR27 0AB
e-mail: enquiries@whitehorseoverstrand.co.uk
dir: From A140, before Cromer, turn right onto Mill Rd. At bottom turn right onto Station Rd. After 2m, bear left onto High St, White Horse Overstrand on left

The family-run Victorian inn in the village of Overstrand goes from strength to strength, with food occupying an ever-prominent place at the heart of the operation, whether it is glammed-up old favourites in the bar, themed grill, Spanish, or Italian nights, or vibrant modern dishes in the recently converted Barn restaurant. Large wrought-iron chandeliers hang from ceilings with original oak roof trusses above rustic Norfolk flint walls and solid oak tables in a clean-cut contemporary setting that suits the switched-on modern food. Top-class local and seasonal produce underpins the repertoire, whether it is a starter trio of Cromer crab remoulade, brown shrimp

Save on Hotels. Book at **theAA.com/hotel**

NORFOLK 377 ENGLAND

rillettes, and shallow-fried Cajun squid, or mains of pan-roast rump of Norfolk lamb with rösti potato, garden pea purée, sautéed baby leeks and lamb jus. Don't skip pudding, as bittersweet chocolate fondant with home-made coconut ice cream is a real treat.

Chef Nathan Boon **Owner** Darren Walsgrove **Times** 12-3/6-9.30 Closed D 25 Dec **Prices** Food prices not confirmed for 2013. Please telephone for details **Notes** Sunday L, Vegetarian available **Seats** 80, Pr/dining room 40 **Children** Portions, Menu **Parking** 6, On street

---

GREAT BIRCHAM
Map 13 TF73

The Kings Head Hotel

◉ Modern British **NEW**

Country-house hotel with a local flavour

☎ 01485 578265
PE31 6RJ
e-mail: info@thekingsheadhotel.co.uk

Dating back to Edwardian times, this family-run hotel has Royal Sandringham as a near neighbour, and combines traditional and contemporary trappings to good effect. Food is served throughout the main dining room and bar. It's a casual, fairly trendy operation with informal service that goes down well with the locals. Brown leather style place mats on unclothed tables and modern cutlery and glassware set the tone for the modern British repertoire, supported by some pub classics, and based on good Norfolk ingredients. Thus warm salad of grilled goats' cheese with honey, orange segments and beetroot might precede crispy beer-battered Atlantic cod fillet with mushy peas, hand cut chips and home-made tartare sauce. Individual treacle sponges with home-made vanilla custard hit the spot for dessert.

Chef Nicholas Parker **Owner** Charlie & Holly Campbell **Times** 12-2.30/6.30-9 **Prices** Starter £4.95-£6.95, Main £9.95-£30, Dessert £5.25-£6.95, Service optional **Wines** 46 bottles over £20, 28 bottles under £20, 14 by glass **Notes** Sunday L, Vegetarian available, Civ Wed 80 **Seats** 80, Pr/dining room 30 **Children** Portions, Menu **Parking** 25

GREAT YARMOUTH
Map 13 TG50

Andover House

◉◉ Modern British

Breezily contemporary cooking in a townhouse

☎ 01493 843490
28-30 Camperdown NR30 3JB
e-mail: info@andoverhouse.co.uk
dir: Opposite Wellington Pier, turn onto Shadingfield Close, right onto Kimberley Terrace, follow onto Camperdown. Property on left

The Victorian terraced house that was once an undistinguished B&B has been given a classic boutique refurb, and is now full of character. A monochrome dining room in blond wood retains some of its original features, but the overall feel is breezily contemporary, as is the seasonally-changing culinary repertoire, which borrows from east Asian and southern European tradition for productive fusion. Starting things off might be classic duck spring rolls or Greek salad, before tiger prawn linguine, citrus-drizzled salmon with slow-cooked tomatoes and capers, or grilled sirloin glazed in veal jus with a cornucopia of vegetables. Finish with mandarin and lemon cheesecake, served with walnut ice cream. The short wine list is a model of its kind, compact and cosmopolitan, with seven table wines available by the glass.

Chef Sandra Meirovica **Owner** Mr & Mrs Barry Armstrong **Times** 6-9.30 Closed Sun-Mon, L all week **Prices** Food prices not confirmed for 2013. Please telephone for details **Wines** 13 bottles over £20, 15 bottles under £20, 8 by glass **Notes** Vegetarian available **Seats** 37, Pr/dining room 18 **Parking** On street

---

Imperial Hotel

◉ Modern British 🍷

Contemporary cooking by the sea

☎ 01493 842000
North Dr NR30 1EQ
e-mail: reception@imperialhotel.co.uk
web: www.cafecrurestaurant.co.uk
dir: follow signs to seafront, turn left. Hotel opposite waterways

The grand old Imperial Hotel on Great Yarmouth's seafront has been providing generations of visitors with what they want, and in the 21st century that means the contemporary style of the made-over Café Cru Restaurant. It brings a younger vibe to the old girl's empire pomp with its city-slicker looks involving banquette seating, modish chrome lights resembling bunches of grapes, and palette of caramel, chocolate and cream. Daily-changing blackboard specials bolster a repertoire of unpretentious modern British dishes wrought from splendid local materials, while smart staff in black aprons lend a buzzy bistro vibe to proceedings. Local Morston mussels in white wine, garlic and parsley are a perennial favourite to start, then you might follow with roast cod matched with roasted artichokes, clams, and tomato, herb and flageolet bean casserole; those in the mood for meat could find braised ox cheek and mushroom suet pudding with swede and spring onion champ, crispy carrots and ox cheek jus, and to finish, a star anise crème brûlée with vanilla-poached pear.

Chef Simon Wainwright **Owner** Mr N L & Mrs A Mobbs **Times** 12-2/6.30-10 Closed 24-28 & 31 Dec, L Sat & Mon, D Sun **Prices** Starter £5-£8.50, Main £11-£25, Dessert £6-£9, Service optional **Wines** 25 bottles over £20, 68 bottles under £20, 12 by glass **Notes** Sunday L, Vegetarian available, Dress restrictions, Smart casual, No shorts or trainers, Civ Wed 140 **Seats** 60, Pr/dining room 140 **Children** Portions, Menu **Parking** 45

GRIMSTON
Map 12 TF72

Congham Hall Country House Hotel

◉◉ Modern British V

Creative cooking in charming Georgian house

☎ 01485 600250
Lynn Rd PE32 1AH
e-mail: info@conghamhallhotel.co.uk
dir: 6m NE of King's Lynn on A148, turn right towards Grimston. Hotel 2.5m on left (do not go to Congham)

With over 700 varieties of herbs fresh from the garden, there's no lack of inspiration to hand for the Congham chefs. In fact the kitchen gardens and orchards in the 30 acres of grounds surrounding this handsome Georgian manor house play an important part in providing seasonal salad leaves, fruit and vegetables for the kitchen, as well as free herbal aromatherapy as you wander the landscaped gardens and parkland. French windows lead onto a terrace from the elegant dining room, where tables are dressed in their best whites, ready to receive the fruits of Norfolk's impressive larder, including game from the Queen's Sandringham estate next door. The kitchen cuts no corners, doing everything from smoking fish to baking bread in-house. The menu isn't short on good ideas and intelligent flavour combinations either: quail breast appears with wild mushrooms, hazelnuts and sweet shallot purée, while a duo of local pheasant is matched with boulangère potatoes, Brussels sprouts and smoked bacon salad, and mulled wine jus. A boozy brace of malts with Binham Blue and roquefort cheeses makes a unique alternative to desserts such as poached orchard pear with pain perdu and chocolate sauce.

Chef Roma Dupont **Times** 12-2/7-9 **Prices** Fixed L 2 course £17.25, Fixed D 3 course £42.50, Service optional **Wines** 60 bottles over £20, 10 bottles under £20, 10 by glass **Notes** Gourmand menu L £36, D £71.50 (with wines £101.50), Sunday L, Vegetarian menu, Dress restrictions, Smart casual, Civ Wed 100 **Seats** 50, Pr/dining room 18 **Children** Portions, Menu **Parking** 50

HETHERSETT
Map 13 TG10

Park Farm Hotel

Modern British

Unfussy modern cooking in a spa hotel

☎ 01603 810264
NR9 3DL
e-mail: enq@parkfarm-hotel.co.uk
dir: 6m S of Norwich on B1172

The family-run hotel has been modified over the past half-century from a rather grand Georgian farmhouse into a modern spa hotel, still surrounded by 200 acres of open countryside not far from Norwich. A smart orangery-style restaurant overlooking the gardens is where the main dining action goes on, in an atmosphere of bright informality, enhanced by boldly coloured paintings. The kitchen does simple things extremely well, turning out a decent Niçoise salad with new potatoes, fine beans, olives and a poached egg, all dressed in good olive oil, followed perhaps by five-spice pork belly, slow-roasted and served with chilli and soy egg noodles with stir-fried veg, or skate with wild mushrooms in red wine jus. The tiramisù is reassuringly doused in espresso and Tia Maria for a very moreish finish.

Times 12-2/7-9.30

HOLKHAM
Map 13 TF84

The Victoria at Holkham

British, French

Charming old building by the Holkham Estate

☎ 01328 711008
Park Rd NR23 1RG
e-mail: victoria@holkham.co.uk
dir: 3m W of Wells-next-the-Sea on A149. 12m N of Fakenham

Housed in a lovely Norfolk flint building on the main coastal road adjacent to the beach and Holkham Estate, The Victoria has a rich history indeed. Decked out in colonial style, its intricate detailing and Rajasthani furniture give a clue as to when it was in its pomp. Today there's a range of dining options to hold your interest, from the main dining area with its generously spaced tables to a large conservatory and outside barbecue area (complete with canopy). There's a good chance what you eat will come from within a five-mile radius, so if it's not from the Holkham Estate itself it won't have travelled very far; fish, for example, comes daily from Cromer and Brancaster. Kick off with spicy crabcakes with coriander and mouli salad, and follow on with the more European-focused confit of duck leg with Savoy cabbage, dauphinoise potatoes and red wine jus. As it's co-owned by local brewery Adnams, expect good beers on tap alongside a decent wine list.

Times 12-2.30/7-9.30

HOLT
Map 13 TG03

Butlers Restaurant

Modern British

Popular all-day venue with deftly handled cooking

☎ 01263 710790
9 Appleyard NR25 6BN
e-mail: eat@butlersrestaurants.com
dir: Just off High Street, signed Appleyard

A cheery and unpretentious local bistro is what we all need in the neighbourhood, and this happy-go-lucky venue has been serving the community of Holt admirably since 2005. A glass roof and glazed doors let the light flood in, and it leads into a pretty courtyard, where slatted garden tables and a jungle of potted plants in the shade of a 200-year-old copper beech make for a delicious alfresco space. The food is just the ticket too, unpretentious, appealing, and with plenty of local produce, as in a starter of Weyborne crab salad with home-made mayonnaise and coriander salsa. Whether you fancy beer-battered haddock with skinny chips and home-made tartare sauce or pan-fried sea bass with Moroccan-spiced venus clam linguine, the kitchen can oblige, and you could wrap it up with a zesty lemon posset, or Norfolk cheeses with quince jelly and biscuits.

Chef Gareth Williams **Owner** Charles Butler
Times 12-3/6-9 Closed 25-26 Dec, Sun **Prices** Fixed L 2 course £11.50, Starter £5.25-£6.95, Main £10.95-£17.95, Dessert £5.95-£6.95, Service optional **Wines** 10 bottles over £20, 20 bottles under £20, 10 by glass **Notes** Monthly events with special menu, Vegetarian available **Seats** 50 **Children** Portions, Menu **Parking** On street (free after 6pm)

The Lawns Wine Bar

Modern European

Populist cooking in a Georgian townhouse

☎ 01263 713390
26 Station Rd NR25 6BS
e-mail: mail@lawnsatholt.co.uk
web: www.lawnsatholt.co.uk
dir: A148 (Cromer road). 0.25m from Holt rdbt, turn left, 400yds along Station Rd

Fresh, seasonal local produce and a relaxed, please-all, modern brasserie-style are at the heart of the appeal of this smart Georgian townhouse restaurant, bar and hotel in the centre of town. The fashionably decked-out restaurant (darkwood tables and leather high-backed chairs), smart bar area, bright conservatory and terrace overlooking the garden, provides plenty of choice to suit the mood (and the weather), and, wherever you choose to sit, the vibe is unbuttoned and friendly. The cooking keeps things relatively uncomplicated: beer-battered haddock and rib-eye steak sit alongside slow-cooked belly of pork with sage mash and braised Savoy cabbage with bacon, and the more globetrotting green Thai curry.

Chef Leon Brookes **Owner** Mr & Mrs Daniel Rees
Times 12-2/6-9 **Prices** Starter £4.95-£7.50, Main £10.25-£17.95, Dessert £5, Service optional **Wines** 6 bottles over £20, 29 bottles under £20, 9 by glass **Notes** Vegetarian available **Seats** 24 **Children** Portions **Parking** 18

Save on Hotels. Book at **theAA.com/hotel**

NORFOLK 379 **ENGLAND**

The Neptune Restaurant with Rooms

HUNSTANTON   Map 12 TF64

Modern European V

Outstanding cooking on the Norfolk coast

☎ 01485 532122
85 Old Hunstanton Rd PE36 6HZ
e-mail: reservations@theneptune.co.uk
dir: On A149

Take a cursory glance, and you might mistake The Neptune for a simple 18th-century, creeper-clad, red-brick coaching inn - which is what the building indeed is. But since Kevin and Jacki Mangeolles took over in 2007, it has morphed into a stylish small restaurant with rooms with a chilled-out ambience and food that aims high. Inside, it is a fresh, jaunty space, with a touch of New England beachcomber style in its white tongue-and-groove panels, Lloyd Loom furniture, photographs of the coast, and model boats to evoke the sea, which is, as it happens, just a pebble's skim away. A glance at the menu shows that this is pretty elaborate stuff for such an easygoing setting, but the components are all In place for seriously good food: Kevin brings a serious level of culinary knowhow to the job, and has supply lines to the best local produce, including shellfish from down the road in Thornham, and organic meat, fruit and veg from local farms. A starter of perfectly-timed pan-fried scallops gets the oriental treatment with pak choi, ginger and rice broth, or if you're up for something more bracing, there might be partridge with fig purée and a partridge and foie gras brioche sandwich. Next up, a well-conceived main course brings Gressingham duck breast contrasted with a crispy croquette of leg meat, pointed up enterprisingly with almond praline, creamy butternut squash purée, Savoy cabbage and dauphine potatoes. It all looks as pretty as a picture on the plate, through to a simple but flavour-driven dessert of poached Yorkshire rhubarb with mascarpone jelly, vanilla ice cream and caramel sauce. North Norfolk is clearly on the culinary map. Service, led by Jacki, is suitably relaxed but on the ball, and a well-chosen wine list rounds off an extremely appealing package that should have you punching the coordinates for the North Norfolk coast into the GPS.

Chef Kevin Mangeolles **Owner** Kevin & Jacki Mangeolles **Times** 12 2/7-9 Closed 2 wks Nov & Jan, Mon, L Tue-Sat (except by arrangement) **Prices** Fixed L 2 course £24.50-£27, Starter £12.95-£15.95, Main £22.50-£29, Dessert £10.50, Service optional **Wines** 89 bottles over £20, 8 bottles under £20, 14 by glass **Notes** Tasting menu available on request when booking, Sunday L, Vegetarian menu, Dress restrictions, Smart casual **Seats** 24 **Children** Portions **Parking** 6, On street

HUNSTANTON — Map 12 TF64

Caley Hall Hotel

◉ Modern British V ◎

Well-judged menu on the North Norfolk coast

☎ 01485 533486
Old Hunstanton Rd PE36 6HH
e-mail: mail@caleyhallhotel.co.uk
web: www.caleyhallhotel.co.uk
dir: located on A149, Old Hunstanton

The core of Caley Hall, a 10-minute walk from wide unspoiled beaches, is a 17th-century manor, with the restaurant in an attractive, spacious former stable block, with high-backed leather-look seats at wooden tables, a tartan-patterned carpet and a vaulted ceiling. The kitchen goes out of its way to find fresh local produce and puts together a short, interesting menu with a handful of dishes per course. One way to start is smooth cinnamon-coated chicken liver parfait with apple chutney, an alternative to crab tian with avocado mousse, grapefruit and citrus dressing. Fish might get an airing as marinated mackerel fillets with distinctively flavoured accompaniments of fennel and potato salad, tomato salsa and anchovy vinaigrette, and to finish, try treacle tart with rum sorbet and toffee sauce.

Chef Amos Burrows **Owner** Caley Hall Hotel Ltd
Times 12-6/6-9 Closed 17-28 Dec, 3-16 Jan,
Prices Starter £6-£8, Main £12-£19, Dessert £7, Service optional **Wines** 11 bottles over £20, 12 bottles under £20, 7 by glass **Notes** Sunday L, Vegetarian menu **Seats** 80 **Children** Portions, Menu **Parking** 50

See advert on page 379

The Neptune Restaurant with Rooms

◉◉◉ — *see page 379*

KING'S LYNN — Map 12 TF62

Bank House Hotel

◉ Modern British ◎

Quality brasserie cooking in historic townhouse

☎ 01553 660492
King's Staithe Square PE30 1RD
e-mail: info@thebankhouse.co.uk
dir: Follow signs to Old Town and onto quayside opposite Custom House, through floodgate, hotel on right

Stylishly revamped to inject a hit of eclectic modern boutique style, this Georgian townhouse hotel with a slick modern brasserie-style restaurant lies in the heart of King's Lynn's historical quarter, right on the River Ouse quayside. Bank House was once Gurney's bank in the 18th century (Gurney's was later absorbed by Barclays), and its former counting house rooms are now the venue for a bar serving a fine spread of local ales and excellent wines, and the dark wood-furnished dining rooms. The kitchen's precise, unpretentious modern brasserie dishes kick off with a well-made chicken liver pâté with toasted granary bread and red onion marmalade followed by roast rump of lamb with rösti potato, parsnip purée and mint salsa verde. Banoffee tartlet with Chantilly cream wraps things up nicely.

Chef Stuart Deuchars **Owner** Jeannette & Anthony Goodrich **Times** 12-2/6.30-9 **Prices** Starter £5.50-£7.50, Main £8.50-£16.50, Dessert £6, Service optional, Groups min 8 service 10% **Wines** 10 bottles over £20, 20 bottles under £20, 6 by glass **Notes** Pre/post theatre menu available on request, Sunday L, Vegetarian available **Seats** 60, Pr/dining room 40 **Children** Portions, Menu **Parking** 5, On quayside or Baker Lane car park

NORTH WALSHAM — Map 13 TG23

Beechwood Hotel

◉◉ Modern British ◎

Charming hotel with good local ingredients on the menu

☎ 01692 403231
20 Cromer Rd NR28 0HD
e-mail: info@beechwood-hotel.co.uk
web: www.beechwood-hotel.co.uk
dir: From Norwich on B1150, 13m to N Walsham. Left at lights, next right. Hotel 150mtrs on left

The lure of the North Norfolk coast is strong to those who know what it has to offer, and this refined, creeper-covered Georgian hotel is a good base to make the best of it. Agatha Christie was a regular visitor to the house when it was owned by family friends and some framed letters from the author in the hallway are a nice touch. Today's hotel is run with a good deal of charm and good will, and its restaurant endeavours to provide a local flavour with its commitment to sourcing produce as much as possible from within 10 miles. Thus the elegant and comfortable dining room is the setting for some well-crafted, contemporary cooking: a first-course slow-cooked belly pork, for example, with apple purée, celeriac, crackling wafer and pork reduction, followed by Lowestoft-landed cod with cannellini beans, mushroom and red pepper ragoût, and tagliatelle of spring vegetables and crispy leeks, or Phil Roofe's fillet of beef with curly kale, roast salsify, carrot purée, fondant potato and red wine jus.

Chef Steven Norgate **Owner** Don Birch & Lindsay Spalding **Times** 12-1.45/7-9 Closed L Mon-Sat **Prices** Fixed D 4 course £38, Service optional **Wines** 220 bottles over £20, 10 bottles under £20, 11 by glass **Notes** Sunday L, Vegetarian available, Dress restrictions, Smart casual **Seats** 60, Pr/dining room 20 **Children** Portions **Parking** 20

Save on Hotels. Book at **theAA.com/hotel**

NORFOLK 381 **ENGLAND**

NORWICH   Map 13 TG20

Best Western Annesley House Hotel

◉◉ Modern British, European 🍷

Georgian hotel serving up consistently good food

☎ 01603 624553
6 Newmarket Rd NR2 2LA
e-mail: annesleyhouse@bestwestern.co.uk
dir: On A11, close to city centre

Annesley House, just outside the city walls in three acres of peaceful grounds, was built in the 1830s and converted to a hotel 100 years later. The restaurant, with its black, cream and silver theme, is in a modern conservatory overlooking a water garden with a pond of koi carp. The kitchen gives a broadly pan-European style to its fine East Anglian larder, so in winter it might bring on roast breast of pheasant with braised seasonal vegetables, fondant potato and roast garlic. Another main course could be pan-fried halibut fillet with wild mushroom and mozzarella risotto, roast shallots and pea shoot salad, while starters are well-thought-out affairs, from warm smoked salmon topped with a poached quail's egg in lemon and caper dressing with a salad of fennel and tarragon, to carpaccio with beetroot purée, pickled girolles, and rocket salad dressed with balsamic. Puddings are worth saving room for, from prune and almond tart with Earl Grey ice cream and custard, to chocolate mousse with cherry compôte.

Chef Steven Watkin **Owner** Mr & Mrs D Reynolds **Times** 12-2/6-9 Closed Xmas & New Year, L Sun **Prices** Fixed L 2 course fr £18.95, Fixed D 3 course £26.25-£32.50, Starter £7.50, Main £22.50, Dessert £7.25, Service optional **Wines** 6 bottles over £20, 14 bottles under £20, 7 by glass **Notes** Pre-theatre menu available from 6pm by arrangement, Vegetarian available **Seats** 30 **Children** Portions **Parking** 29

Best Western George Hotel

◉ Modern British 🍷

Simple brasserie cooking at a family-run hotel

☎ 01603 617841
10 Arlington Ln, Newmarket Rd NR2 2DA
e-mail: reservations@georgehotel.co.uk
dir: From A11 follow city centre signs, becomes Newmarket Rd. Hotel on left

A short stroll from the city centre, behind the frosted-glass frontage of the George, a family-run Victorian hotel, is a contemporary brasserie with leather banquette seating, dark wood panelling and mirrors setting the tone, and an open-to-view grill bringing a touch of restaurant theatre. Friendly, uniformed staff deliver formal service, and the kitchen makes good use of fresh seasonal produce, as well as of that grill. Fried corn-fed chicken breast comes with roast herbed new potatoes and red onion in a strong Madeira jus, and among desserts, an indulgent version of tiramisù is all present and correct.

Chef Paul Branford **Owner** David Easter, Kingsley Place Hotels Ltd **Times** 12-2/6-10 **Prices** Fixed L 2 course £9.50, Starter £4.75-£6.50, Main £10.50-£22.50, Dessert £4.75-£5.75, Service optional **Wines** 3 bottles over £20, 23 bottles under £20, 10 by glass **Notes** Vegetarian available **Seats** 44, Pr/dining room 80 **Children** Portions, Menu **Parking** 40

Brasteds

◉◉ Modern European 🍷

Exciting cooking in a stylish barn conversion

☎ 01508 491112
Manor Farm Barns, Fox Rd, Framingham Pigot NR14 7PZ
e-mail: enquiries@brasteds.co.uk
dir: A11 onto A47 towards Great Yarmouth, then A146. After 0.5m turn right onto Fox Rd, 0.5m on left

Four miles from the city centre, in the privately owned village of Framingham Pigot, Brasteds is a combination of restaurant - a swish converted barn with beams in the vaulted ceiling, brick walls, an oak floor and cleverly angled spotlights - boutique B&B and wedding and event venue. A canny kitchen brigade assembles regularly-changing menus with the sort of über-modern ideas that would have left Mrs Beeton reaching for her smelling salts. How about cumin-roast scallops with Iberico ham, smoked eel and truffle vinaigrette, or a main course of roast venison tenderloin with pure cocoa, beetroot gel, peanut and vanilla crumble and blackcurrant espuma? Dishes are built on prime local produce and put together intelligently; expect potted salt beef with horseradish and apple, followed by steamed lemon sole fillets with a cockle and caper fricassée, prawn mousse and watercress puree, and a finale of 'the rhubarb five' - clafoutis, poached fruit, syrup, granita and jelly.

Chef Chris Busby, Martin Recchi **Owner** Nick Mills, Chris Busby & Michael Zouvani **Times** 12-2.30/7-10 Closed Sun-Wed, L Sat, Thu **Prices** Starter £7-£10.95, Main £18.50-£28, Dessert £8.50, Service optional **Wines** 133 bottles over £20, 6 bottles under £20, 8 by glass **Notes** Vegetarian available, Dress restrictions, Smart dress advisable **Seats** 40, Pr/dining room 16 **Children** Portions **Parking** 50

Brummells Seafood Restaurant

◉◉ International, Seafood

Venerable seafood restaurant in a 16th-century building

☎ 01603 625555
7 Magdalen St NR3 1LE
e-mail: brummell@brummells.co.uk
web: www.brummells.co.uk
dir: In city centre, 2 mins walk from Norwich Cathedral, 40yds from Colegate

In the oldest part of the city, Brummells shows its age with its beams, standing timbers and stone walls, candlelight adding a romantic glow to the rustic interior in the evening, and a log fire burning in winter. Seafood cooked to consistently high standards is the draw. Preparations vary from classics like skate wing pan-fried with black butter, lobster thermidor, or plainly grilled Dover sole, to the more adventurous: chargrilled yellowfin tuna, served pink, with curried fruit marmalade, or steamed sea bass fillets with prawn butter, ginger and leeks. Starters show the same broad sweep, from mussels with creamy white wine and garlic sauce, to blackened swordfish with citrus and mustard dressing. There are some meat dishes too, and to finish might be pear and nutmeg parfait with caramelised fruit.

Chef A Brummell, J O'Sullivan **Owner** A Brummell **Times** 12-flexible/6-flexible **Prices** Starter £2-£14, Main £18-£35, Dessert £6.50, Service optional, Groups min 7 service 10% **Wines** 78 bottles over £20, 6 bottles under £20, 6 by glass **Notes** Sunday L, Vegetarian available, Dress restrictions, Smart casual or jacket & tie **Seats** 25 **Children** Portions **Parking** On street after 6.30pm & Sun, Car park nearby

NORWICH *continued*

Elm Hill Brasserie

◉ French

French food and cathedral views

☎ 01603 624847
2 Elm Hill NR3 1HN
e-mail: elmhillbrasserie@gmail.com

Simple regional French food with Mediterranean influences is the name of the game at this relaxed brasserie on the corner of a medieval cobbled street not far from the castle and cathedral. It looks the part too - unpretentious, relaxed unstuffy - with a table in the window of the characterful old building giving a glimpse of the cathedral's spire. Local ingredients get a good showing - as indeed they might if this place was in a French city - and the unfussy cooking fits the bill. Kick off with escabèche of Norfolk mackerel with smoked mackerel mousse, moving on to slow-cooked breast of mutton with provencale-spiced marinade, rösti potato and baby spinach. A dessert of vanilla fudge wrapped in 70% cocoa chocolate, milk sorbet and almond brittle, or classic custard and nutmeg tart with fresh rhubarb sorbet, will send you home happy.

Times 12.30-2.30/5.45-10.30 Closed Xmas, Mon

The Maids Head Hotel

◉ Modern British

Courtyard dining in the heart of Norwich

☎ 01603 209955
Tombland NR3 1LB
web: www.maidsheadhotel.co.uk
dir: A147 to north of the city. At rdbt for A1151, signposted Wroxham, follow signs for Cathedral and Law Courts along Whitefriars. Hotel is approx 400 mtrs on right along Palace St

This smart covered courtyard restaurant serves up a brasserie-style menu in a great position next to the cathedral. It's in the Maids Head Hotel in a building made up of Tudor, Georgian and medieval parts, with the informal WinePress@Wensum restaurant occupying the space where once coach and horses would have pulled in;

it's now a fabulous space with a high, vaulted glass ceiling, terracotta flooring, and darkwood tables. A wine list with over 40 to choose from by the glass is part of the appeal, alongside the unfussy modern British menu of dishes such as kipper and marinated salmon club sandwich and lobster bisque to start, followed by guinea fowl (pan-fried breast and terrine of slow-cooked leg) with red chicory and pan juices, and lemon syrup polenta cake with rhubarb to finish.

Times 12-3/6-9.30

Marriott Sprowston Manor Hotel

◉ Modern British, European

Grand manor house serving modernised classics

☎ 01603 410871
Sprowston Park, Wroxham Rd NR7 8RP
e-mail: mhrs.nwigs.frontdesk@marriotthotels.com
dir: From A47 take Postwick exit onto Norwich outer ring road, then take A1151. Hotel approx 3m and signed

A red-brick, step-gabled manor house sheltered by ancient oaks on the outskirts of Norwich, Sprowston offers the full country-house package of golf, spa treatments, and a choice of eating in the tile-floored Zest Café, or the 1559 Restaurant, named in honour of the foundation of the original building. Menus eschew the full-dress rural-retreat style for informal brasserie food

Roger Hickman's Restaurant

NORWICH Map 13 TG20

Modern British **NEW**

Well-crafted contemporary cooking

☎ 01603 633522
79 Upper St Giles St NR2 1AB
e-mail: info@rogerhickmansrestaurant.com
dir: In city centre, from A147 at rdbt into Cleveland Rd, 1st left into Upper St Giles St

What used to be Adlard's, a mainstay of Norwich's gastronomic scene for many years, is now relaunched under the aegis of its erstwhile head chef. If that doesn't sound like too much of a gear-change, rest assured that, in terms of style and ambience at least, it isn't. The place still feels as intimate and relaxed as it ever did, with a lightwood floor, linen-clad tables, and cream and swirly dark green walls adorned with prints. Mr Hickman runs a

tight ship out back, producing virtually everything in-house, from breads to ice cream, and a year as a sous-chef with Tom Aikens (see entry, London) has refined the conception and presentation of dishes to a high order. A serving of crab in a shell of cucumber with smooth avocado purée, lemongrass mousse, tiny dried tomatoes and pea shoots brings new lustre to tried-and-true combinations. Excellent meats include a chump of lamb of fabulous tenderness, served on a bed of spinach, with pearl barley risotto and a deeply rich jus, while fish could be a pairing of roast sea bass and puréed sardines with confit tomatoes. Strawberry trifle with honeycomb is one of the lighter dessert offerings, or you may opt to get seriously stuck in with banana Tatin and salted caramel ice cream.

Chef Roger Hickman **Owner** Roger Hickman
Times 12-2.30/7-10 Closed 1 week Jan & Aug, Sun, Mon
Prices Fixed L 2 course fr £18, Fixed D 3 course fr £40, Tasting menu £35-£50, Service optional, Groups min 6 service 10% **Wines** 100 bottles over £20, 2 bottles under £20, 12 by glass **Notes** Tasting menu L min price, D max price, Vegetarian available, Air con **Seats** 40
Children Portions **Parking** On street & St Giles multi-storey

Save on Hotels. Book at **theAA.com/hotel**

NORFOLK 383 **ENGLAND**

and modern spins on British classics. Crabcakes with tartare sauce, or ham hock terrine with piccalilli, are the comfortingly familiar preludes to slow-cooked pork belly with haricots and mash, or cheddar-crusted fish pie. A grill section offers steaks, cutlets, burgers and surf and turf, as well as lemon sole with prawns and brown caper butter. Finish with knickerbocker glory.

Chef Mark Lutkin **Owner** Marriott International Inc **Times** 12.30-3/6.30-10 Closed L Mon-Sat **Prices** Starter £5.50-£11.50, Main £9-£24, Dessert £6.50, Service optional **Wines** 30 bottles over £20, 4 bottles under £20, 10 by glass **Notes** Sunday L, Vegetarian available, Dress restrictions, Smart casual, no shorts, Civ Wed 300 **Seats** 70, Pr/dining room 150 **Children** Portions, Menu **Parking** 170

The Old Rectory

◎◎ Modern British V ◎

Georgian rectory hotel with updated classical dishes

☎ 01603 700772

103 Yarmouth Rd, Thorpe St Andrew NR7 0HF
e-mail: enquiries@oldrectorynorwich.com
dir: From A47 southern bypass onto A1042 towards Norwich N & E. Left at mini rdbt onto A1242. After 0.3m through lights. Hotel 100mtrs on right

Two miles from the centre, overlooking the River Yare and Thorpe Marshes nature reserve, The Old Rectory is a three-storey Georgian property with an adjoining Victorian coach house. Guests can peruse the daily-changing menu from wing backs in front of a log fire in the drawing room before moving on to the restaurant. The cooking has its roots in the classical repertoire, but dishes are given a modern, often European spin. Well-timed baked cod fillet is served on salsa verde with crushed potatoes and a creamy vermouth, brown shrimp and leek sauce, and roast pork fillet comes with nutmeg mash, cider-braised Puy lentils and apple purée. The locality is scoured for good materials, Cromer crab going into a starter tart with Norfolk cheddar and spinach, with tahini dressing, and potted local rabbit and pork in another starter, served with radish and pea shoot salad and quince jam. Iced raspberry parfait, with poached rhubarb and wild blackberry sauce, stands out among desserts for its clean, fresh flavours.

Chef James Perry **Owner** Chris & Sally Entwistle **Times** 7-9 Closed Xmas, New Year, Sun, L all week **Prices** Fixed D 3 course £28-£35, Service optional **Wines** 14 bottles over £20, 8 bottles under £20, 5 by glass **Notes** Vegetarian menu **Seats** 18, Pr/dining room 16 **Children** Portions **Parking** 16

Roger Hickman's Restaurant

◎◎◎ – *see opposite*

St Benedicts Restaurant

◎ Modern British

Imaginative cooking in the heart of Norwich

☎ 01603 765377

9 St Benedicts St NR2 4PE
e-mail: jayne@rafflesrestaurants.co.uk
dir: Just off inner ring road. Turn right by Toys-R-Us, 2nd right into St Benedicts St. Restaurant on left by pedestrian crossing

St Benedicts cuts a dash in the city centre with its smart French bistro looks, all duck-egg-blue-painted tongue and groove-panelled walls, jazzy fabrics, blondwood floors and unclothed tables, and the place is no flash in the pan either, having been a stalwart of the Norwich dining scene for 20 years. Its evergreen success is down to straightforward cooking that stays in tune with the demand for feisty, clear-flavoured food built on seasonal, locally-sourced ingredients, and it delivers it all in an accessible, well-priced package. Get going with something like a double-baked cheese soufflé or pheasant sausage with Savoy cabbage and Puy lentils, then move on to sous-vide-cooked rabbit with pan-fried potato cake, curly kale and rosemary, and end with gooseberry and apple crumble with gooseberry ice cream.

Chef Nigel Raffles **Owner** Nigel & Jayne Raffles **Times** 12-2/7-10 Closed 25-31 Dec, Sun-Mon **Prices** Fixed L 2 course fr £8.95, Fixed D 3 course fr £17.95, Groups min 10 service 10% **Wines** 15 bottles over £20, 34 bottles under £20, 8 by glass **Notes** A L C 2 course £21.95, 3 course £25.95, Vegetarian available **Seats** 42, Pr/dining room 24 **Children** Portions **Parking** On street, Car parks nearby

St Giles House Hotel

◎◎ Modern British ◎

Classic and modern dishes in an architectural gem

☎ 01603 275180

41-45 St Giles St NR2 1JR
e-mail: reception@stgileshousehotel.com
web: www.stgileshousehotel.com
dir: A11 into central Norwich. Left at rdbt signed Chapelfield Shopping Centre. 3rd exit at next rdbt. Left onto St Giles St. Hotel on left

You could punctuate your perusal of Norwich city centre's retail opportunities with a pitstop in St Giles House for coffee, a massage, cocktails or something more gastronomically satisfying in the SGH Bistro. The grand Edwardian pile is worth a gander in its own right - beyond its magnificent pillared façade is a palatial interior of marble floors, oak panelling and elaborate plaster ceilings, all sharpened with a slick contemporary makeover. The art-deco bistro restaurant is a slick setting for the kitchen's appealing repertoire of uncomplicated modern dishes, as witnessed in a smooth and well-flavoured chicken liver parfait served with celeriac remoulade, tomato chutney and melba toast, ahead of pan-fried chicken breast teamed with a leek and wild mushroom pie, olive oil mash, sautéed baby carrots and Marsala sauce. To finish, there's peanut butter and chocolate parfait served with chocolate biscotti, peanut brittle and salted caramel sauce. Smartly turned-out in black, the front-of-house team are a polished act who keep everything running smoothly.

Chef Stewart Jefferson **Owner** Rachel Roofe **Times** 11-10 **Prices** Fixed L 2 course fr £17.50, Fixed D 3 course fr £32.50, Starter £5.50-£7.50, Main £13.50-£22, Dessert £5.50-£7.50, Service optional **Wines** 38 bottles over £20, 25 bottles under £20, 9 by glass **Notes** Sunday L, Vegetarian available **Seats** 50, Pr/dining room 48 **Children** Portions, Menu **Parking** 30

NORWICH *continued*

Stower Grange

◉ Modern British

Eclectic dining in a Norfolk rectory

☎ 01603 860210
40 School Rd, Drayton NR8 6EF
e-mail: enquiries@stowergrange.co.uk
web: www.stowergrange.co.uk
dir: Norwich ring road N to ASDA supermarket. Take
A1067 (Fakenham road) at Drayton, right at lights into
School Rd. Hotel 150yds on right

The creeper-covered former rectory a few miles out of
Norwich makes a relaxing rural retreat, and is decorated
in classic country-house style, with a dining room done in
restful pastel shades looking out through full-drop
windows on to the well-tended gardens. Menus offer a
broad range of choice, from the oriental mash-up that is
Thai-spiced duck with mango and chilli chutney and duck
wonton, to mains such as slow-cooked belly of Blythburgh
pork with sweet potato fondant, spiced chick peas and
preserved lemon purée, or roast hake with braised lentils,
salsa verde and wilted spinach. It's good to see sharper
flavours being celebrated in desserts like lemon sponge
with lemon curd sauce and gooseberry ice cream.

Chef Lee Parette **Owner** Richard & Jane Fannon
Times 12-2.30/6.30-9.30 Closed 26-30 Dec, D Sun
Prices Starter £5.50-£7.95, Main £14.50-£19.50, Dessert
£6.50, Service optional **Wines** 28 bottles over £20,
20 bottles under £20, 8 by glass **Notes** Sunday L,
Vegetarian available, Civ Wed 120 **Seats** 25, Pr/dining
room 100 **Children** Portions **Parking** 40

The Sugar Hut

◉ Thai

Good Thai cooking in the city centre

☎ 01603 766755
4 Opie St NR1 3DN
e-mail: lhongmo@hotmail.co.uk
dir: City centre next to Castle Meadow & Castle Mall car
park

The upbeat name says it all: The Sugar Hut has been
serving up palate-pulsing Thai food to an appreciative
audience at the heart of Norwich for a decade now, and
the thriving enterprise has spread its wings to
encompass a quartet of lively venues in the city. They
come from far and wide for its authentic vibe, colourful

deep blue and yellow décor peppered with exotic
artefacts, and a menu that really delivers on the tongue-
tingling, fragrant, sense stimulation of Thai cooking. Get
going with a classic hot-and-sour tom yam goong soup of
prawns with Thai herbs and fresh lime juice, then proceed
to rump steak stir-fried with chilli, garlic and holy basil,
or deep-fried sea bass with chilli sauce.

Chef Chartchai Fodsungnoen, Kiattisak Amphai
Owner Leelanooch Hongmo **Times** 12-2.30/6-10.30
Closed Sun **Prices** Food prices not confirmed for 2013.
Please telephone for details **Wines** 6 bottles over £20,
24 bottles under £20, 3 by glass **Notes** Vegetarian
available **Seats** 40 **Children** Portions **Parking** Castle Mall

Tatlers

◉ Modern British

Smart, modish cooking by the cathedral

☎ 01603 766670
21 Tombland NR3 1RF
e-mail: info@tatlersrestaurant.co.uk
dir: In city centre in Tombland. Next to Erpingham Gate by
Norwich Cathedral

A stalwart of the Norwich dining scene, you will find
Tatlers right by the medieval cathedral in the wonderfully
Gothic-sounding Tombland quarter. A substantial
Victorian townhouse is the setting for this assured
operation, which spreads its wings through a trio of
capacious rooms painted in heritage hues of sage green
and primrose yellow with colourful modern art, and
unclothed mismatched tables on bare wooden floors. The
kitchen's focus is on sourcing the best local materials
and treating them with simplicity to deliver unpretentious
contemporary dishes on good value set menus and a
more wide-ranging carte. The latter might begin with
pan-fried cod cheeks with parmesan polenta, chorizo,
and tomato and anchovy dressing, then move on to breast
and confit leg of local pheasant partnered by wholegrain
mash, beetroot ,mushrooms, baby onions, pancetta and
red wine jus. To finish, pear and Armagnac tarte Tatin
with lemongrass and ginger crème anglaise puts a novel
spin on a classic theme. There's a sister restaurant,
Butlers in Holt - see entry.

Chef Adam Bateman **Owner** Natasha & Christopher
Williams **Times** 12-2/6-9 Closed BHs, Sun **Prices** Fixed L
2 course £14.50, Fixed D 3 course £18.50, Starter £5.95-
£8.95, Main £8.95-£23.95, Dessert £5.75-£6.95, Service
optional, Groups min 6 service 10% **Wines** 47 bottles
over £20, 15 bottles under £20, 9 by glass
Notes Vegetarian available **Seats** 75, Pr/dining room 35
Children Portions **Parking** Law courts, Elm Hill, Colegate,
St Andrews

Thailand Restaurant

◉ Thai V

Traditional Thai cooking

☎ 01603 700444
9 Ring Rd, Thorpe St Andrew NR7 0XJ
e-mail: siamkidd@aol.com
dir: From Southern bypass, follow airport signs. Located
at top of hill past Sainsbury's

Formerly known as Thai Cuisine, this hugely popular
restaurant in a large white house near the ring road
remains a local favourite. It takes a conventional
approach, with staff attired in traditional costume,
pictures of Thai locations hung about, and a menu of
regal banqueting dishes from the classic cookbook.
Chicken satay is moist and tender and comes with sweet
chilli dip, while the beef mussaman curries offer
flavourful meat, slow-cooked in coconut cream, chillies,
cinnamon and shallots, and there are good sweet-sour
dishes with potato-flour batter. Mixed vegetables in
oyster sauce are a generous array, and the fried rice is
spot on.

Chef Anan Sirphas, Sampoin Jukjan **Owner** Richard &
Onuma Kidd **Times** 12-3/6-10 Closed 25 Dec, L Sat-Sun
Prices Fixed L 2 course fr £30, Fixed D 4 course fr £30,
Starter fr £5.95, Main fr £11.95, Dessert fr £5, Service
optional **Notes** Vegetarian menu, Dress restrictions,
Smart casual **Seats** 55 **Parking** 25

RINGSTEAD	Map 12 TF74

The Gin Trap Inn

◉ Modern British

Charming 17th-century inn turned gastro-pub

☎ 01485 525264
6 High St PE36 5JU
e-mail: thegintrap@hotmail.co.uk
dir: A149 from King's Lynn towards Hunstanton. After
15m turn right at Heacham for Ringstead

Bikers and hikers on the Roman Peddars Way footpath -
and anyone else passing through the tranquil village of
Ringstead just inland from the North Norfolk coast - will
find the 17th-century Gin Trap is an irresistible pitstop. It
balances all the virtues of a well-run pub: genuine
hospitality, local ales and good food, whether you go for
the rustic bar with its bare bricks, gnarled beams and
wood-burning stove in a walk-in fireplace, or the
candlelit, linen-clad tables of the smart restaurant and
conservatory. The kitchen is proud to buy its materials
from local farmers and producers, and shows off its
prowess with confidence. Beer-battered haddock with
mushy peas and home-made tartare sauce keeps things
pubby, but there's also smoked mackerel pâté with
beetroot and onion compôte, pea shoots and reduced
balsamic, ahead of seared venison loin with thyme
creamed potatoes, carrots and braised red cabbage.

Times 12-2/6-9

Save on Hotels. Book at theAA.com/hotel

NORFOLK 385 ENGLAND

SHERINGHAM — Map 13 TG14

Dales Country House Hotel

◎◎ British, European ✦

Smart modern cooking in rural Norfolk

☎ 01263 824555
Lodge Hill NR26 8TJ
e-mail: dales@mackenziehotels.com
dir: On B1157, 1m S of Sheringham. From A148 Cromer to Holt road, take turn at entrance to Sheringham Park. Hotel 0.5m on left

With the famed North Norfolk coast only a couple of miles away, and Humphry Repton's Sheringham Park gardens next door a riot of rhododendrons and azaleas in the season, the Dales Country House Hotel lacks for little in local attractions. Sitting in its own secluded grounds on the edge of the village, the step-gabled house has a cosseting feel within, where the oak panelling and inglenook in the Upchers dining room contribute to the timeless countryside feel. The cooking, wouldn't you know it, is rather more urban brasserie than the surroundings suggest, offering dishes that aim to stimulate with defined, intense flavours. Salmon marinated in five spice comes with beetroot, apple and a horseradish emulsion, while mains follow up with 28-day-aged rib-eye, served with a braised-beef hash cake, roasted roots and confit shallots. To ensure interest through to dessert, there's quince in the crème brûlée, while the chocolate fondant comes with a sweet shop array of peanut brittle, praline, and Snickers ice cream.

Chef Rene Ilupar **Owner** Mr & Mrs Mackenzie
Times 12-2/7-9.30 **Prices** Fixed L 2 course £14.95, Starter £5.95-£7.25, Main £12.50-£21, Dessert £3.50-£8.95, Service optional **Wines** 15 bottles over £20, 10 bottles under £20, 9 by glass **Notes** Sunday L, Vegetarian available, Dress restrictions, No shorts or sportswear **Seats** 70, Pr/dining room 40 **Children** Portions **Parking** 50

SNETTISHAM — Map 12 TF63

The Rose & Crown

◎ Modern British ✦

Bustling local with global dishes and British classics

☎ 01485 541382
Old Church Rd PE31 7LX
e-mail: info@roseandcrownsnettisham.co.uk
dir: From King's Lynn take A149 N towards Hunstanton. After 10m into Snettisham to village centre, then into Old Church Rd towards church. Hotel 100yds on left

Brim-full with period atmosphere, the 14th-century Rose & Crown is all rambling nooks and crannies, low beamed ceilings, wobbly floors and log fires, but it has brought in summery colours and a hint of beachcomber-chic style to keep step with the times. The kitchen has also shifted up a gear, serving time-honoured pub classics done right - beer-battered haddock with hand-cut chips, mushy peas and tartare sauce, or local bangers and mash with onion gravy. If you want to trade up to unfussy contemporary

ideas, expect to find hearty dishes that celebrate the Norfolk larder - perhaps Brancaster mussels marinière with crusty bread, or pork tenderloin with black pudding mousse, potato rösti, green beans, and apple purée. Finish with the comfort of sticky toffee pudding with butterscotch sauce and ginger ice cream.

Chef Jamie Clarke **Owner** Anthony & Jeanette Goodrich
Times 12-2/6.30-9 **Prices** Starter £5.50-£9, Main £8.50-£17.50, Dessert £6-£8, Service optional, Groups min 8 service 10% **Wines** 10 bottles over £20, 27 bottles under £20, 10 by glass **Notes** Sunday L, Vegetarian available **Seats** 160, Pr/dining room 30 **Children** Portions, Menu **Parking** 70

SWAFFHAM — Map 13 TF80

Best Western George Hotel

◎ Traditional British **V**

British cooking in a bright white coaching inn

☎ 01760 721238
Station Rd PE37 7LJ
e-mail: georgehotel@bestwestern.co.uk
dir: Located on main x-rds in Swaffham

Swaffham, as followers of Stephen Fry's country solicitor Peter Kingdom won't need informing, is where the ITV series is filmed, and the George is one of its landmarks, a 16th-century coaching inn done in blinding white. The dining room is kitted out in baby-blue, with elaborately swagged pink drapes, and makes an old-world backdrop for some gently tweaked traditional British cooking. Devilled whitebait or prawn cocktail opens proceedings, which may continue with breadcrumbed chicken in creamy brandy and peppercorn sauce, or bangers and mash with red onion gravy. Steaks from the grill with all the trimmings are an abidingly popular option.

Chef Pete Crundwell **Owner** David Easter
Times 12-2.30/6.30-9.30 Closed 25 Dec **Prices** Starter £3.95-£6.95, Main £8.75-£21.95, Dessert £3.95-£7.50, Service optional **Wines** 5 bottles over £20, 14 bottles under £20, 8 by glass **Notes** Vegetarian menu **Seats** 40, Pr/dining room 18 **Children** Portions, Menu **Parking** 80

THETFORD — Map 13 TL88

Elveden Café Restaurant

◎ Traditional British

Farm produce and enterprising cooking on the Elveden Estate

☎ 01842 898068
London Rd, Elveden IP24 3TQ
e-mail: steve.pillinger@elveden.com
dir: On A11 between Newmarket & Thetford, 800 mtrs from junct with B1106

The café-restaurant is part of a complex of shops, selling East Anglian and farm produce, in converted red-brick farm buildings on the 10,000-acre Elveden Estate. It's a stylish place, with a beamed vaulted ceiling, and plenty of outside seating, with a barbecue an attraction in

summer. Breakfast, sandwiches and afternoon tea are served as well as lunch, with a wide-ranging menu encompassing burger and chips, and seared scallops with smoked mackerel with watercress sauce and bacon jelly. Vegetables and meats are from the estate, and bread is made in-house (accompanying a home-made Scotch egg in a main-course ploughman's, for instance). Enterprising starters have included steamed mussels in a sweet pepper and chorizo sauce, and rich and tender potted pig's cheek topped with lightly spiced parsnip purée.

Chef Scott Taylor **Owner** The Earl of Iveagh
Times 9.30am-5pm Closed 25 Dec, D all week **Prices** Fixed L 2 course £16.50, Starter £5.95-£7.50, Main £10.50-£14.95, Dessert £4.95-£5.95, Service optional **Wines** 6 bottles under £20, 6 by glass **Notes** Fixed L 3 course £24.95-£36.95, Sunday L, Vegetarian available **Seats** 80 **Children** Portions, Menu **Parking** 200

THURSFORD — Map 13 TF93

The Old Forge Seafood Restaurant

◎ Seafood **V** ✦

Unpretentious seafood cookery in a 700-year-old inn

☎ 01328 878345
Fakenham Rd NR21 0BD
e-mail: sarah.goldspink@btconnect.com
dir: On A148

The building was once a staging-post on the pilgrimage route to Walsingham, and was enough of a local landmark to have been mentioned in The Pilgrim's Progress. A venerable ambience of stone floors and beams is as expected, and the cooking is an entirely unpretentious roll-call of fish and seafood favourites, built of course around the best the waters off North Norfolk have to offer. Morston mussels are served marinière, and it would be unthinkable not to see a dressed Cromer crab, or oysters from the Blakeney beds. Here they all are, to be followed perhaps by salmon in a creamy mustard sauce, or grilled marinated swordfish based on a Sicilian recipe. Groaning platters of fruits de mer will be the way to go for many.

Chef Colin Bowett **Owner** Colin & Sarah Bowett
Times 6.30-8.30 Closed Mon, BH, L all week, D Sun **Prices** Starter £4.50-£9.50, Main £12.50-£34, Dessert £3.95-£6.50, Service optional **Wines** 5 bottles over £20, 10 bottles under £20, 5 by glass **Notes** Opening times vary (phone to check), no late bkgs Jan-Feb, Vegetarian menu **Seats** 28 **Children** Portions **Parking** 12

TITCHWELL — Map 13 TF74

Titchwell Manor Hotel

◎◎ Modern European

Bold modern European cooking on the coast

☎ 01485 210221
PE31 8BB
e-mail: margaret@titchwellmanor.com
dir: On A149 (coast road) between Brancaster & Thornham

Revamped in a contemporary boutique style, Titchwell Manor started out as a Victorian farmhouse, but now does business as a rather chic country hotel. It sits in a lovely spot on North Norfolk's sandy coast, near the Titchwell Marsh bird sanctuary, and has been run by the Snaith family for a quarter of a century, with Eric Snaith directing the action at the stoves for a decade. Of the two dining areas, it is the sage-green Conservatory overlooking the walled garden that serves as a stage for his inventive dinner-only, seven-course tasting menus, which showcase splendid local produce, particularly fish and seafood - Brancaster lobster, say, in a hot and cold soup with saffron, then scallop sashimi with citrus, miso mayonnaise and coriander, while monkfish could be served with brown butter, lettuce, kohlrabi and chicken jus. Meat could crop up in the shape of an Aberdeen Angus rib-eye with oxtail and parsley root. Less ambitious ideas - oysters, potted crab, hearty pies, steaks, fish and chips with mushy peas - are to be found in the more casual Eating Rooms.

Chef Eric Snaith **Owner** Margaret & Ian Snaith **Times** 12-2.30/6-9.30 **Prices** Tasting menu £45, Starter £5-£11, Main £9-£25, Dessert £5-£10, Service optional, Groups min 8 service 10% **Wines** 27 bottles over £20, 25 bottles under £20, 9 by glass **Notes** Tasting menu 7 course Mon-Sat D, must book, Sunday L, Vegetarian available, Civ Wed 70 **Seats** 80 **Children** Portions, Menu **Parking** 50

WESTON LONGVILLE — Map 13 TG11

The Parson Woodforde

◎ Modern British **NEW** 🍸

Modishly conceived dishes in updated old inn

☎ 01603 881675
Church St NR9 5JU
e-mail: info@theparsonwoodforde.com
dir: W past Norwich on A47. At Easton rdbt A47 to Dereham, right onto Wood Ln. After 3m, establishment on left opposite church

This characterful old inn, with a plethora of red-brick pillars and exposed beams contrasting with stylish contemporary-style seats and sofas, is more gastro than pub these days, following a major refurb in 2010. There are real ales on tap, though, and a menu very much of the times: spinach and Wensleydale tart is accompanied by gingered sweet potato purée, rocket and raspberry vinegar, and a main course of pan-fried fillet of sea bass is served with potatoes crushed with coriander and lime, chilli oil and pea shoots. Shepherd's pie with suet dumplings, roast carrots and port jus is a starter - you didn't see that coming, did you?- followed perhaps by pan-fried red mullet fillet with a prawn and chive potato cake, horseradish sauce and a breadcrumbed poached egg. Finish with a spot on lemon posset.

Chef Nick Hare, David Smith **Owner** Dreamlink Ltd **Times** 12-2.30/6-9.30 Closed 25 Dec **Prices** Starter £5.50-£6.95, Main £12.95-£21.95, Dessert £5.25, Service optional **Wines** 25 bottles over £20, 30 bottles under £20, 9 by glass **Notes** Sunday L, Vegetarian available **Seats** 60 **Children** Portions, Menu **Parking** 60

WIVETON — Map 13 TG04

Wiveton Bell

◎ British, European 🍸

Modernised village inn serving the treasures of the sea

☎ 01263 740101
The Green, Blakeney Rd NR25 7TL
e-mail: enquiries@wivetonbell.co.uk
dir: 1m S of Blakeney on the Holt road

On the village green opposite the church, this 18th-century inn has gone gastro, but that's not to say you can't turn up in walking boots with the dog. Its venerable beams are all present and correct, but the look has been lightened up with cream walls, vibrant contemporary art, bare wooden tables and church pews. The cooking is just what you'd hope for: inventive but not fussy, and driven by seasonal local materials. Pan-roasted cod and caper fishcakes with a julienne of leeks, and dill and shallot cream sauce precedes classic Yetman's beer-battered haddock and chips with minted mushy peas and home-made tartare sauce, or for something more hearty, go for slow-cooked local pork belly with black pudding mash, Savoy cabbage and apple and cider jus.

Chef Jamie Murch **Owner** Berni Morritt & Sandy Butcher **Times** 12-2.15/6-9.15 Closed 25 Dec **Prices** Food prices not confirmed for 2013. Please telephone for details **Wines** 6 bottles over £20, 28 bottles under £20, 21 by glass **Notes** Vegetarian available **Seats** 60 **Children** Portions, Menu **Parking** 5, village green 50yds away

WYMONDHAM — Map 13 TG10

Number Twenty Four Restaurant

◎◎ Modern British

Relaxed dining and market fresh produce

☎ 01953 607750
24 Middleton St NR18 0AD
web: www.number24.co.uk
dir: Town centre opposite war memorial

A row of Grade II listed 18th-century cottages in the historic heart of Wymondham is the setting for this smart, family-run restaurant. The dining room is a period gem done out with linen-clothed, widely-spaced tables set against warm, soothing colours, and the vibe is good humoured and unstuffy. There is dedication to good old-fashioned hard work in the kitchen, where everything is cooked from scratch and in tune with the seasons and local larder. The menu keeps things admirably to the point and works within the modern British idiom to deliver the likes of a local game hotpot with Cognac, red wine and onion gravy, caramelised onion and pancetta, as a prelude to grilled sea bass fillets, which could be partnered by roasted fennel and tomato, and smoked haddock and crayfish chowder. To finish, give in to temptation and go for steamed syrup sponge with vanilla custard.

Chef Jonathan Griffin **Owner** Jonathan Griffin **Times** 12-2/7-9 Closed 26 Dec, 1 Jan, Mon, L Tue, D Sun **Prices** Fixed L 2 course fr £14.95, Fixed D 3 course fr £25.95 **Wines** 15 bottles over £20, 21 bottles under £20, 7 by glass **Notes** Sunday L, Vegetarian available, Dress restrictions, Smart casual, no shorts **Seats** 60, Pr/dining room 55 **Children** Portions **Parking** On street opposite, in town centre car park

Save on Hotels. Book at **theAA.com/hotel**

NORTHAMPTONSHIRE 387 **ENGLAND**

NORTHAMPTONSHIRE

DAVENTRY
Map 11 SP56

Fawsley Hall

◉◉ Modern British **V**

Assertive modern British cooking

☎ 01327 892000
Fawsley NN11 3BA
e-mail: info@fawsleyhall.com
dir: A361 S of Daventry, between Badby & Charwelton,
hotel signed (single track lane)

Plantagenets, Tudors and Georgians all had a go at
Fawsley Hall over the centuries, resulting in the beguiling
architectural mishmash we see before us. However mixed
the stylistic messages, it all screams 'grand', and the
interiors maintain the pace with oak panels, stone arches
and the fabulous Equilibrium dining room, with its
25-foot-high beamed ceiling and huge inglenook,
flagstone floor and flickering candlelight. That said, the
number of covers is kept low, so that a proper feeling of
intimacy pervades the place. Some culinary readjustment
has gone on recently and a boldly assertive modern
British line is once more being taken. An ingenious terrine
of pigeon and foie gras is presented in Battenberg
squares, while a bowl of deep-green parsley soup has its
homogeneous silkiness offset with little chunks of
smoked eel and a cloud of parmesan foam. A fish main
course offers turbot with Evesham asparagus and
Lyonnaise potatoes, together with a cucumber-wrapped
herby mousse and a rather predominating note of grain
mustard. Blythburgh pork belly is daringly paired with
lobster and chive mash and red cabbage, and then
dessert comes up with a slice of unmoulded burnt vanilla
custard, alongside poached rhubarb and strawberry
sorbet.

Chef Jon Rix **Owner** Bahram Holdings **Times** 7-9.30
Closed Xmas, Sun-Mon, L all week **Prices** Fixed D 3
course £59, Service added but optional 12.5%
Wines 160+ bottles over £20, 10 bottles under £20, 20 by
glass **Notes** Sunday L in Brasserie, Vegetarian menu,
Dress restrictions, Smart casual, Civ Wed 120 **Seats** 30,
Pr/dining room 20 **Parking** 140

EASTON-ON-THE-HILL
Map 11 TF00

The Exeter Arms

◉ Modern British

Smartly revamped old inn with contemporary cooking

☎ 01780 756321
21 Stamford Rd PE9 3NS
e-mail: reservations@theexeterarms.net
dir: From A43 enter village, inn 300yds on left

If you're keen on the ideology of local sourcing, this
spruced-up village inn should be up your street: the lion's
share of the lamb, beef and pork is reared at the owners'
family farm, while in the season you're never far from a
bunch of asparagus from the same source. Inside, it is
refurbished in an unpretentious blend of tradition -

exposed beams and stonework - and contemporary style,
while the smart Orangery dining area has doors that fold
back, opening it out to the walled courtyard. The cooking
has a suitably contemporary tone, serving seared scallops
with parsnip purée and chicken wings, or in-house
liquorice-cured salmon with potato salad and horseradish
dressing, ahead of local wood pigeon Wellington with
buttered mash, Savoy cabbage and jus. If you've room
left for a sweet finish, go for something like white
chocolate crème brûlée from the 'something naughty'
section.

Chef Simon Pollendine **Owner** Michael Thurlby, Sue Olver
Times 12-2.30/6-9.30 Closed D Sun **Prices** Starter £4.95-
£9.50, Main £11-£24.95, Dessert £4.95-£6.50, Service
optional **Wines** 34 bottles over £20, 17 bottles under £20,
20 by glass **Notes** Sunday L, Vegetarian available
Seats 80, Pr/dining room 24 **Children** Portions, Menu
Parking 30

FOTHERINGHAY
Map 12 TL09

The Falcon Inn

◉ British, European ⌣

Modish pub grub in an historic village

☎ 01832 226254
Main St PE8 5HZ
e-mail: info@thefalcon-inn.co.uk
web: www.thefalcon-inn.co.uk
dir: From A605 at Warmington follow signs to
Fotheringhay. Situated centre of village

Considering it is such a sleepy backwater these days,
Fotheringhay has a lively history as the birthplace of
Richard III and the place where Mary, Queen of Scots was
imprisoned in the castle. But put aside the history books
and schedule a pitstop at The Falcon Inn, a proper
welcoming village pub with crackling log fires, and a
smart conservatory restaurant overlooking the Church of
St Mary. Straightforward modern British dishes keep in
step with the seasons, so a spring meal might kick off
with seared scallops with pancetta, butternut squash
purée and mixed cress, ahead of line-caught sea bass
with lemon crushed new potatoes, baby vegetables and
salsa verde, with dark chocolate and raspberry tart with
white chocolate and Cointreau mousse to finish.

Chef Danny Marshall **Owner** Sally Facer
Times 12-2.15/6.15-9.15 Closed D Sun (Jan-Mar)
Prices Fixed L 2 course fr £12.95, Fixed D 3 course fr
£15.50, Starter £5.25-£8.50, Main £12.95-£23, Dessert
£5.25-£7.50, Service optional, Groups min 10 service
10% **Wines** 21 bottles over £20, 28 bottles under £20, 14

by glass **Notes** Pre-concert menu 3 course £15, Sunday L,
Vegetarian available **Seats** 45, Pr/dining room 30
Children Portions, Menu **Parking** 50

KETTERING
Map 11 SP87

Kettering Park Hotel & Spa

◉ Modern British

Hotel restaurant dishing up local ingredients

☎ 01536 416666
Kettering Parkway NN15 6XT
e-mail: kpark.reservations@shirehotels.com
dir: Off A14 junct 9 (M1 to A1 link road), hotel in Kettering
Venture Park

The restaurant of the upmarket, modern Kettering Park
spa hotel is a light-bathed, open-plan space with an
inviting mezzanine level and a smart, rather masculine
look involving contemporary darkwood tables and slatted
window blinds. But what sets Langberrys apart from the
corporate chains is the youthful team of genuinely
friendly and helpful staff who make it all tick along nicely
and helpfully point diners towards the daily specials
designed to showcase the region's produce. It is all
straightforward stuff and prepared without undue fuss:
warm pigeon breast and pancetta salad is served with
blackberry dressing and roasted hazelnuts, ahead of pan-
fried calves' liver with sweet-and-sour onions and creamy
mash. The simple approach concludes with the comfort of
a ginger parkin pudding with treacle sauce and clotted
cream.

Chef Jamie Mason **Owner** Shire Hotels
Times 12-1.45/7-9.30 Closed Xmas, New Year (ex
residents & pre-booked), L Mon-Sat **Prices** Fixed D 3
course £19.95-£24.95, Starter £5.50-£7.95, Main £12.95-
£22.50, Dessert £6.50, Service optional **Wines** 69 bottles
over £20, 5 bottles under £20, 15 by glass **Notes** Sunday
L, Vegetarian available, Dress restrictions, Smart dress,
Civ Wed 150 **Seats** 90, Pr/dining room 40
Children Portions, Menu **Parking** 200

KETTERING *continued*

Rushton Hall Hotel and Spa

◉ ◉ Modern British

Accomplished cooking in magnificent surroundings

☎ 01536 713001
Rushton NN14 1RR
e-mail: enquiries@rushtonhall.com
web: www.rushtonhall.com
dir: A14 junct 7, A43 to Corby then A6003 to Rushton, turn after bridge

There's a swish spa at Rushton Hall, but other than that, the graceful old pile is pretty well as Charles Dickens would have found it on the visits that led him to immortalise it as Haversham Hall in *Great Expectations*. Built in 1438, it ticks all the boxes for an historic country-house hotel: acres of parkland, Tudor and Jacobean features, and thanks to a Victorian makeover, baronial stone fireplaces, fancy plasterwork and stained glass, and a magnificent oak linenfold-panelled dining room. In the kitchen, however, we fast forward into the world of French-influenced, fine-tuned culinary endeavours, presented on a sparsely-described menu. Local duck might get an outing in an assiette delivering the meat in various treatments - smoked, parfait, terrine, and foie gras - while main course could take a similar route with Suffolk pork, partnering belly, cheek and black pudding with Puy lentils and apple. The thoroughly modern approach might extend to a finale of blood orange cannelloni with chocolate gel.

Chef Adrian Coulthard **Owner** Tom & Valerie Hazelton **Times** 12-2/7-9 Closed L Mon-Fri **Prices** Fixed L 2 course £20.50, Starter £8-£14, Main £19.50-£28, Dessert £9, Service optional **Wines** 83 bottles over £20, 4 bottles under £20, 12 by glass **Notes** Fixed L 2, 3 course only available Sat-Sun, Sunday L, Vegetarian available, Dress restrictions, Smart casual, Civ Wed 200 **Seats** 40, Pr/dining room 60 **Children** Menu **Parking** 140

The Queens Head Inn

◉ Modern British

Inviting riverside inn with treats from the grill

☎ 01780 784006
54 Station Rd PE8 6QB
e-mail: info@queensheadnassington.co.uk
dir: A1M N exit Wansford, follow signs to Yarwell & Nassington

The 200-year-old honey-hued stone inn on the banks of the River Nene looks like everyone's idea of a chocolate-box pretty village inn. There are all the requisite trappings - real ales on tap in a smart oak-floored and beamed bar - but these days it is a world apart from beer and dominos. The Queens Head has built a solid reputation for good food served in the rustic-chic restaurant. A charcoal-fired Josper Grill in the kitchen is a serious piece of kit that drives the cooking in the direction of unfussy meat and fish dishes sizzled to perfection on the flames. If you're up for some serious meat action, the steaks are impeccably sourced, and even extend to a rib-eye of Wagyu beef. Otherwise, you might take on slow-braised ox cheek ballottine with scorched Atlantic scallops, pickled ginger, wasabi pea purée and miso velouté, and finish with a novel take on trifle, made with plums, Jamaican ginger cake and grappa, vanilla custard and roasted almonds.

Chef Duncan Hooper **Owner** Complete Hotels Ltd **Times** 12-2/5.30-9.30 **Prices** Fixed L 2 course £12, Starter £4.50-£8.25, Main £10-£32.50, Dessert £5.45-£6, Service optional **Wines** 9 bottles over £20, 13 bottles under £20, 8 by glass **Notes** Sunday L, Vegetarian available **Seats** 40, Pr/dining room 70 **Children** Portions, Menu **Parking** 45

Oundle Mill

◉ ◉ Modern British V ✿

Confident cooking in comfortably converted mill

☎ 01832 272621
Barnwell Rd PE8 5PB
e-mail: info@oundlemill.co.uk
dir: Located just outside Oundle off A605

'Rustic chic' is the hotel's chosen descriptive term, and indeed a total makeover has brought a classy, upmarket style to the old mill. Original features have been retained, as seen in the restaurant's oak beams and standing timbers, stone walls, and glass panel in the oak floor giving a view of the mill race below. The kitchen is clearly in touch with the mores of the day and shows plenty of skill in its output, producing tempura black pudding with an egg, crisp shallots, bacon and devilled sauce before a main course of steamed plaice with prawns, herbed spätzle and lemongrass nage. It's just as happy with fishcakes with lemon mayonnaise, prawn cocktail, fish and chips, and, for two to share, roast chicken stuffed with sage and onions accompanied by roast potatoes,

winter greens, bread sauce, and roasting juices. Puddings conclude on an upbeat note, among them apple jelly and Calvados pannacotta with a cinnamon doughnut, and rice pudding with strawberry jam.

Chef Gavin Austin **Owner** Mark & Sarah Harrod **Times** 12-2.30/6.30-9.30 **Prices** Fixed L 2 course £12.50, Fixed D 3 course £20.50, Starter £3.50-£8.50, Main £12.50-£22.50, Dessert £4.50-£6.50, Service optional **Wines** 170 bottles over £20, 6 bottles under £20, 17 by glass **Notes** Sunday L, Vegetarian menu, Civ Wed 60 **Seats** 50, Pr/dining room 45 **Children** Portions, Menu **Parking** 60

Roade House Restaurant

◉ Modern French

Well loved village restaurant with rooms with well-judged menu

☎ 01604 863372
16 High St NN7 2NW
e-mail: info@roadehousehotel.co.uk
dir: M1 junct 15 (A508 Milton Keynes) to Roade, left at mini rdbt, 500yds on left

An enjoyable time is on the cards at this welcoming village restaurant with rooms, near to the M1 and the high-octane thrills of Silverstone race track. Blackened beams and a neutral contemporary look involving cream walls and bentwood seats at white-linen tables add up to a soothing setting in the dining room, while Chris Kewley is the man directing the action at the stoves. His unfussy, flavour-driven modern cooking delivers intelligent combinations of taste and texture - perhaps rabbit terrine with brioche, walnuts and pickled mushrooms, while mains could see breast and confit leg of wild duck sharing a plate with a luxurious slab of seared foie gras, red cabbage, and apple and Calvados sauce. Hearty puddings could bring Santiago almond cake with spiced pears and red wine fruit.

Chef Chris Kewley **Owner** Mr & Mrs C M Kewley **Times** 12-2/7-9.30 Closed 1 wk Xmas, BHs, L Sat, D Sun **Prices** Fixed L 2 course £20.50, Starter £5.75-£7.75, Main £14.75-£22, Dessert £6.50-£7.75, Service optional **Wines** 40 bottles over £20, 30 bottles under £20, 4 by glass **Notes** Sunday L, Vegetarian available, Dress restrictions, No shorts **Seats** 50, Pr/dining room 16 **Children** Portions **Parking** 20

TOWCESTER
Map 11 SP64

Vine House Hotel & Restaurant

◉◉ Modern British ✆

Rural setting and a local flavour

☎ 01327 811267
100 High St, Paulerspury NN12 7NA
e-mail: info@vinehousehotel.com
dir: 2m S of Towcester, just off A5

A lovingly restored 300-year-old limestone cottage in a winsome village is the setting for this perfectly charming small restaurant and hotel. Inside, the vibe is homely and easygoing with Julie Springett taking care of front of house, while husband Marcus works with first-rate local and seasonal ingredients to deliver daily-changing three course fixed-price menus. Choosing from three well-conceived ideas at each stage, plus a slate of artisan British cheeses at the end, you might get off the blocks with local black pudding with shallot cream and mustard pickle purée, and follow that with saddle of local lamb with salted butter crushed peas, potato terrine and salsa verde, or there might be line-caught cod with lemon, capers, shallots and croûtons. For afters, local Bramley apples go into a mousse, served enterprisingly with blue cheese and vanilla shortbread crumble. The romantic garden folly is a lovely spot for outdoor dining.

Chef Marcus Springett, K Kerley, J Bateman **Owner** Mr M & Mrs J Springett **Times** 12-1.30/6-9 Closed 1 wk winter, Sun, L Mon **Prices** Fixed L 2 course fr £27.50, Service added 12.5% **Wines** 47 bottles over £20, 26 bottles under £20, 2 by glass **Seats** 26, Pr/dining room 10 **Parking** 20

WHITTLEBURY
Map 11 SP64

Whittlebury Hall

◉◉◉ British, European

Contemporary fine dining and motor-racing

☎ 01327 857857
NN12 8QH
e-mail: reservations@whittleburyhall.co.uk
web: www.whittleburyhall.co.uk
dir: A43/A413 towards Buckingham, through Whittlebury, turn for hotel on right (signed)

The nearby goings-on at Silverstone inspire the catering thematics at this extensive spa hotel, where dining rooms called Astons, Bentleys and Murrays (after the voice of Formula One, Murray Walker) await the confirmed motorhead. The last is adorned with photos of the great man, alongside memorable quotes from his commentaries. There is some cooking going on too, as attested by the tableful of awards on display. It's contemporary stuff, as sleekly streamlined as a modern racing-car, and just as full of intricate engineering. A starter offers puffed wheat, pine nuts and truffle honey as textural foils to an artichoke custard, while mains furnish a serving of poached brill, wild mussels and sprouting broccoli with an underlay of sesame seed 'sand', or garnish 35-day dry-aged beef with the relatively classical accompaniments of ox tongue, onions and horseradish. Chocolate and banana mousse comes with banana jelly and hazelnuts.

Chef Craig Rose, Damyan Stefanov **Owner** Whittlebury Hall and Spa Ltd **Times** 7-9.30 Closed selected dates at Xmas, Sun-Mon, L all week **Prices** Food prices not confirmed for 2013. Please telephone for details **Notes** Tasting menu available, Sunday L, Vegetarian available, Dress restrictions, Smart casual, No jeans, trainers or shorts **Seats** 32, Pr/dining room 10 **Children** Portions, Menu **Parking** 460

NORTHUMBERLAND

BAMBURGH
Map 21 NU13

Grays Restaurant at Waren House Hotel

◉ Modern British

Local supplies for country-house cooking

☎ 01668 214581
Waren Mill NE70 7EE
e-mail: enquiries@warenhousehotel.co.uk
dir: Exit A1 on B1342, follow signs to Bamburgh. Hotel in 2m in village Waren Mill

Waren House has all the hallmarks of a country-house hotel, from the log fire at the entrance to the oil paintings in the traditionally furnished restaurant overlooking the grounds. The kitchen continues to use the best produce it can find in the area, and its cooking, in the modern British idiom, is of a high order, from the complexity of thyme-breaded saddle of rabbit with creamed stilton, pickled carrot, red chard and girolles in tarragogn jus to more straightforward cheese soufflé with beetroot chutney. Main courses can be busy too: steamed fillet of sea bass on parmesan and vermouth cream comes with ratatouille, citrus-steamed wild garlic, red chard and roast beetroot. Rum and chocolate fondant, its centre soft and oozing, is a good way to finish, topped with streusel and served with chocolate sorbet.

Times 6.30-8.30

Victoria Hotel

◉ Modern British **NEW**

Slick modish setting and unpretentious menu

☎ 01668 214431
Front St NE69 7BP
e-mail: enquiries@thevictoriahotelbamburgh.co.uk
dir: Turn off A1, N of Alnwick onto B1342, follow signs to Bamburgh. Hotel opposite village green

With its position on the village green and views over to the historic castle, the Victoria Hotel is in a plumb spot. The Baileys Bar & Restaurant consists of a number of dining areas, some under a glass atrium roof, with a decidedly modish sheen to the décor. There are trendy muted colour tones, some exposed stonework, nicely designed tables and chairs, and some small fabric-covered banquettes, plus Milburn's bar which is decorated with black-and white pictures of the Magpies (that's Newcastle United football team) — it's named in honour of the legendary Jackie Milburn. The menu goes in for egalitarian modern Britishness, so you might go from Thai fishcakes with cucumber relish and chilli jam to Black Sheep ale-battered North sea haddock with fat chips and mint-flavoured mushy peas, or locally-sourced 28-day aged Northumbrian beef (10oz rib-eye maybe) with a choice of traditional sauces.

Times 12-3/7-9

CHATHILL
Map 21 NU12

Doxford Hall Hotel & Spa

◉ Modern British V ✆

Modish treatments of local supplies

☎ 01665 589700
NE67 5DN
e-mail: info@doxfordhall.com
dir: 8m N of Alnwick just off A1, signed Christon Bank & Seahouses. B6347 then follow signs for Doxford

Built in 1818 in the classic porticoed Georgian mould, Doxford Hall's 10 acres of landscaped grounds (including a maze) are just part of its attraction. The small-scale country house is looking spruce after a revamp in 2010, with a huge stone fireplace, white linen, burnished wood panelling and full-length windows making for a luminous and elegant restaurant. The cooking fits the setting: a gently modernised approach with clear roots in the classics produces constructions with a wide appeal - slow-cooked pork terrine with home-made piccalilli and toasted brioche, for example, followed by slow-braised blade of beef with pancetta, roasted shallots, and parsnip purée. An assemblage of vanilla pannacotta, rhubarb jelly, vanilla custard and rhubarb compôte is a good way to finish.

Chef Paul Blakey **Owner** Robert Parker **Times** 12-2/7-10 **Prices** Fixed L 2 course £18.95, Starter £6.25-£8.50, Main £20.95-£24.50, Dessert £5.95-£13.95, Service optional **Wines** 45 bottles over £20, 11 bottles under £20, 16 by glass **Notes** Sunday L, Vegetarian menu, Dress restrictions, Smart casual **Seats** 60, Pr/dining room 200 **Children** Portions, Menu **Parking** 100

Tillmouth Park Country House Hotel

◉ Modern British

Traditional country-house cooking in imposing Victorian mansion

☎ 01890 882255
TD12 4UU
e-mail: reception@tillmouthpark.force9.co.uk
dir: A698, 3m E from Cornhill-on-Tweed

Built in 1882 as a family home, this splendid mansion is surrounded by 15 acres of landscaped grounds. Stained glass and panelled rooms are typical of a property of this type, while the lounge and dining room are filled with objets d'art, oil paintings and antlers. The kitchen prides itself on buying produce from within 20 miles or so, so expect pan-fried Eyemouth haddock rolled in oats with lemon and caper butter, and herb-crusted rump of Borders lamb with rosemary jus. The rest of the menu is by and large reassuringly familiar, with starters of pork belly confit with apple sauce, and prawn cocktail with Marie Rose sauce, and puddings like hot chocolate fondant with orange ice cream.

Chef Piotr Dziedzic **Owner** Tillmouth Park Partnership **Times** 7-9 Closed 26-28 Dec, Jan-Mar, L all week **Prices** Starter £4.95-£7.50, Main £11.50-£18.95, Dessert £5.50-£8.25, Service optional **Wines** 35 bottles over £20, 9 bottles under £20, 7 by glass **Notes** Vegetarian available, Dress restrictions, Smart casual, No jeans or shorts, Civ Wed 50 **Seats** 40, Pr/dining room 20 **Children** Portions **Parking** 50

Close House

◉◉ Modern British NEW

Vintage glamour and modern food

☎ 01661 852255
NE15 0HT
e-mail: reservations@closehouse.co.uk
web: www.closehouse.co.uk
dir: A1 N, A69 W. Follow B6528 at junct turn left, hotel signed

A boutique-style makeover has turned this 18th-century mansion into a sleekly modern venue that hits the spot for anyone with an interest in golf (there are two courses), getting hitched, or putting on the Ritz in the glamorous surroundings of the Argent d'Or restaurant. Wow factor is

certainly not lacking in the palatial venue's soaring plasterwork ceilings, grandly neo-classical fireplace, crystal chandeliers and shimmering silk drapes - even the seats at the well-spaced tables are sheathed in gold fabric. It makes an unapologetically glamorous setting for cooking that works within a broadly modern British idiom, with a nod to the classics. Menus change to take advantage of the seasons, so spring brings fat and flavoursome seared scallops with black olive salsa and red pepper dressing, followed by a trio of Northumberland lamb served as confit shoulder, herb-crusted loin and slow-cooked rump with potato bake. To finish, there's an eye-catching chocolate dome with an orange brûlée centre.

Close House

Chef Chris Delaney **Owner** Graham Wylie **Times** 12-2.30/7-9.30 **Prices** Fixed L 2 course £17.95-£19.95, Fixed D 3 course £33.50-£39.50, Tasting menu £60, Starter £5.95-£10.95, Main £16.50-£29.50, Dessert £6.95-£9.95, Service added but optional 10% **Wines** 122 bottles over £20, 6 by glass **Notes** Tasting menu 6 course must be taken by whole table, Sunday L, Vegetarian available, Dress restrictions, Smart casual preferred, Civ Wed 100 **Seats** Pr/dining room 100 **Children** Portions **Parking** 100

De Vere Slaley Hall

◉ Modern British

Old and new in a grand Northumbrian manor

☎ 01434 673350
Slaley NE47 0BX
e-mail: slaley.hall@devere-hotels.com
dir: A1 from S to A68. Follow signs for Slaley Hall. From N A69 to Corbridge then take A68 S and follow signs to Slaley Hall

One thousand acres of windswept Northumbrian moorland are the setting for the suitably grand Slaley Hall, a castellated edifice of colossal proportions, with flights of steps sweeping up majestically from the lawns. Inside is a bay-windowed dining room done in tasteful Edwardiana, with wing-backed chairs in claret upholstery, lit framed pictures and mirrors, and an air of unruffled calm. The cooking balances old and new: starters may be mussels in Chablis and cream, or ox cheek tortellini with beetroot purée, while mains offer a pair of you the chance to share a Chateaubriand, carved at table, and served with Pont-Neuf potatoes, béarnaise and Madeira jus. Sailfish isn't often seen - find it here

with a tempura prawn, cauliflower purée and a pea dressing for company - while desserts mobilise vivid fruit flavours for lemon tart with mango sorbet and passionfruit and mango salsa, or chilled rhubarb crumble with a cherry doughnut and blackcurrant sorbet.

Times 1-3/6.30-9.45 Closed Mon

Langley Castle Hotel

◉◉ Modern British

Modern classic cooking in a Plantagenet fortress

☎ 01434 688888
Langley on Tyne NE47 5LU
e-mail: manager@langleycastle.com
web: www.langleycastle.com
dir: From A69 S on A686 for 2m. Hotel on right

Langley Castle is the real deal, a perfectly preserved 14th-century Plantagenet fortress built during the long reign of Edward III. Ten acres of woodland estate and seven-foot thick crenallated walls should suffice to keep the modern world at arm's length, (although this is a venue much favoured by those in the business of tying the knot) and once inside you're treated to original stained glass, log fires and sumptuous furnishings in the splendid Josephine Restaurant. When it comes to the food, forget the medieval period - what leaves the kitchen here is pretty up-to-date stuff, delivered in four-course table d'hôte menus that could get under way with pan-roasted scallops with crisp air-dried ham, sweet-and-sour chicory, celeriac purée and truffle oil, then slot in a sorbet or soup before pushing on to baked cod, perhaps, served with shellfish and tomato risotto, crisp roast salsify, and parsley sauce. A pre-desserts intervenes before the real finale - which could be an unusual twice-baked red wine soufflé with spicy plum pie and cinnamon ice cream.

Chef Andy Smith **Owner** Dr S Madnick **Times** 12-2.30/7-9 **Prices** Fixed L 2 course fr £13.95, Fixed D 4 course £39.50-£42.50, Service optional **Wines** 19 bottles over £20, 20 bottles under £20, 7 by glass **Notes** Sunday L, Vegetarian available, Dress restrictions, Smart casual, Civ Wed 120 **Seats** 48 **Children** Portions, Menu **Parking** 57

LONGHORSLEY   Map 21 NZ19

Dobson Restaurant

◉◉ Modern British

Appealing cooking in a grand Georgian manor

☎ 01670 500000
Macdonald Linden Hall, Golf & Country Club NE65 8XF
e-mail: general.lindenhall@macdonald-hotels.co.uk
dir: 7m NW of Morpeth on A697 off A1

Linden Hall is a 19th-century manor house in 450 acres of Northumbrian parkland. Having thus established its grandiose credentials, it's important also to note that it's run by the Macdonald hotel group with relaxing hospitality. The claret-hued Dobson Restaurant is the principal culinary option, enjoying seductive views of the grounds through full-length windows, and offering carefully thought-out dishes with broad appeal. A starter combination of king prawns, scallops and pork belly is an assured exercise in surfing and turfing, gaining depth from a purée of curried parsnip. That may be the prelude to pan-roasted Scottish lamb, with shredded braised shoulder and dauphinoise in a thyme-scented jus, while pudding turns up a smooth chocolate délice and pistachio ice cream, strewn with candied pistachios.

Times 12-2/6.45-9.45 Closed L Mon-Sat

MATFEN   Map 21 NZ07

Matfen Hall

◉◉ British **V**

Modern British dishes in the library of an ancestral seat

☎ 01661 886500 & 886400
NE20 0RH
e-mail: info@matfenhall.com
dir: A69 signed Hexham, leave at Heddon-on-the-Wall. Then B6318, through Rudchester & Harlow Hill. Follow signs for right for Matfen

Ancestral home of the Blackett family, Matfen was opened as a luxury spa hotel in 1999, so all may now enjoy its 300 acres of parkland, its grand public rooms, and the majestic, book-lined library with its ornate mouldings, panelling and magnificent views, which forms the dining room. The kitchen explores the modern British repertoire for inspiring stalwarts such as smoked haddock and pea risotto, king scallops with black pudding, and main courses such as seared salmon on lemon-crushed potatoes in dill beurre blanc, or roasted beef fillet with thyme and garlic rösti and Jerusalem artichoke purée. Desserts bring on plenty of fruity creations, along the lines of lime cheesecake with mango sorbet and passionfruit jelly, or apple sponge with blueberry parfait and honeycomb.

Chef Will Rideau **Owner** Sir Hugh & Lady Blackett
Times 12-2.30/6.45-9.30 Closed L Mon-Sat **Prices** Fixed L 3 course £22.95, Starter £6.50-£10, Main £19.50-£26.95, Dessert £6.50-£7.95, Service optional
Wines 92 bottles over £20, 2 bottles under £20, 15 by glass **Notes** Sunday L, Vegetarian menu, Dress

restrictions, Smart casual, Civ Wed 120 **Seats** 66, Pr/dining room 28 **Children** Portions, Menu **Parking** 200

MORPETH   Map 21 NZ18

Eshott Hall

◉ British **NEW** ◉

Local flavours in grand old country house

☎ 01670 787454
Eshott NE65 9EN
e-mail: info@eshotthall.co.uk
dir: Eshott signed from A1. N of Morpeth

Eshott Hall has been around in one form or another since the 14th century, but the handsome wisteria-clad manor we see today dates mainly from Georgian times. It is the kind of unspoilt traditional country house that has been the backdrop to many a wedding party, but you don't have to be dewy-eyed newlyweds to stay here as the place makes a perfect bolt-hole for exploring the castles of Alnwick and Bamburgh, the Holy Island of Lindisfarne, and the wilds of Northumberland. The dining room goes for a traditionally elegant look with its fancy plasterwork, pastel-painted panelling and silver candlesticks on white linen tablecloths, while the kitchen has a good eye for fine local ingredients which it deploys in a menu taking in a mix of traditional and gently-updated dishes for the modernists. You might start with lobster from nearby Seahouses teamed with potatoes and pea soup, then follow with local estate beef fillet with pan haggerty (a local baked dish of layered potatoes, onions and cheese), Savoy cabbage, onion purée and pepper jus.

Chef Chris Wood **Owner** Rev. Robert Parker
Times 1-2.30/6-9.30 Closed private functions, L Mon-Sat **Prices** Starter £7-£10.50, Main £17-£26, Dessert £8-£10, Service optional **Wines** 19 bottles over £20, 14 bottles under £20, 4 by glass **Notes** Sunday L, Vegetarian available, Dress restrictions, Smart casual, Civ Wed 100 **Seats** 30, Pr/dining room 30 **Children** Portions, Menu **Parking** 60

WARENFORD   Map 21 NU12

The White Swan

◉ Modern British **NEW** ◉

Gastro-pub cooking up fine local produce

☎ 01668 213453
NE70 7HY
e-mail: dianecuthbert@yahoo.com
dir: 100yds E of A1, 10m N of Alnwick

Formerly an 18th-century coaching hostelry on the Great North Road, today The White Swan aims to meet modern-day expectations. The Dukes of Northumberland once owned the pub, and its windows and plasterwork still bear the family crest, while the traditional bar itself comes with all the hoped-for classic features - open log fire and thick stone walls included. The restaurant has a more contemporary style, but with appropriately rustic furniture, a wood-burning stove and a relaxed, friendly vibe. The kitchen follows the décor's theme, taking a

traditional approach with a modern spin, and fashioning dishes from the tip-top Northumberland larder - including their own rare-breed Saddleback pigs. Lamb is also supplied by the extended farming family and could make an appearance as saddle served with anna potatoes and ragout of lamb's kidneys, or go for sea bass with roasted Mediterranean vegetables and chilli pesto.

Chef Mark Poole **Owner** Andrew & Diane Hay
Times 12-2.30/6-9 **Prices** Starter £4.50-£8.95, Main £10.50-£21.95, Dessert £4.95, Service optional
Wines 13 bottles over £20, 19 bottles under £20, 10 by glass **Notes** Sunday L, Vegetarian available **Seats** 65, Pr/dining room 30 **Children** Menu **Parking** 50

NOTTINGHAMSHIRE

FARNDON   Map 17 SK75

Farndon Boathouse

◉ Modern European ◉

Up-to-date brasserie cooking in a riverside setting

☎ 01636 676578
Riverside NG24 3SX
e-mail: info@farndonboathouse.co.uk

The leafy banks of the meandering River Trent make an interesting contrast to the contemporary exposed ducting, industrial-style lighting, stone floors and glazed frontage of the stylish Boathouse. The kitchen is driven by the guiding principles of sourcing locally and seasonally, and using modern cooking techniques such as sous-vide to squeeze every molecule of flavour from the ingredients. Uncomplicated contemporary brasserie dishes run the gamut from starters such as in-house-smoked duck breast with marinated feta cheese, compressed melon and lamb's lettuce, and cashew crumb, to seared sea bass with home-made pesto and parmesan gnocchi, squash purée and roast tomatoes; meaty ideas are along the lines of pan-fried pheasant breast with potato terrine, crispy ham, confit garlic and peas and roasting juices. Finish with the home comforts of sticky toffee pudding with milk ice cream and caramel sauce.

Chef Steve Munn, Dan Garner **Owner** Dan Garner, Nathan Barton **Times** 12-2.30/6-9.30 **Prices** Fixed L 2 course fr £14.95, Fixed D 3 course £17.95-£28.50, Starter £5-£11, Main £10-£16.95, Dessert £6.25-£7.50, Service optional **Wines** 39 bottles over £20, 12 bottles under £20, 18 by glass **Notes** Early bird menu L & 6-7pm daily, Sunday L, Vegetarian available **Seats** 120 **Children** Portions, Menu **Parking** 18

GUNTHORPE · Map 11 SK64

Tom Browns Brasserie

◉◉ Modern International

Creative cooking in an old Victorian schoolhouse

☎ 0115 966 3642
The Old School House, Trentside NG14 7FB
e-mail: info@tombrowns.co.uk
web: www.tombrowns.co.uk
dir: A6097, Gunthorpe Bridge

The Brasserie was once a Victorian schoolhouse, though you wouldn't know it. Any lingering echo of chanted multiplication tables is entirely muted in the cool, neutral-toned, wood-floored interior, and its outdoor mezzanine deck has views over the River Trent. The cooking, which is impeccably modern British in its mostly studious un-Britishness, is a few cuts above the brasserie norm, with dishes that sound satisfyingly multi-layered in the menu specifications, and look smart and alluring on the plate. Pears poached in red wine have shunted up the billing these days, from desserts to starters, and here's one with honey-glazed pork belly and celeriac remoulade, an inspired mix of flavours. The smoked salmon may appear with horseradish soufflé, puréed broad beans, pea shoots and salsa verde for another original composition, before mains such as fried stone bass in chilli, soy and ginger dressing with baby corn, red peppers, shiitake mushrooms and - just to ensure the final meeting of east and west - mushroom gnocchi. Meats include fine Scottish steaks from the chargrill and pudding might be Bakewell tart and custard. Theme nights are staged throughout the year.

Chef Peter Kirk **Owner** Adam & Robin Perkins **Times** 12-2.30/6-9.30 Closed D 25-26 Dec **Prices** Fixed L 2 course fr £14.95, Fixed D 3 course £17.95-£30, Starter £5.50-£12.50, Main £13.95-£26, Dessert £6-£8, Service optional **Wines** 43 bottles over £20, 13 bottles under £20, 16 by glass **Notes** Early bird L 12-3pm, Fixed D 6-7pm, Sunday L, Vegetarian available, Dress restrictions, Smart casual **Seats** 100, Pr/dining room 20 **Children** Portions **Parking** 28, On street

LANGAR · Map 11 SK73

Langar Hall

◉◉ Modern British ◐

A unique country house with a local flavour

☎ 01949 860559
Church Ln NG13 9HG
e-mail: info@langarhall.co.uk
dir: Signed off A46 & A52 in Langar village centre (behind church)

It was never originally in the owner's game plan to run this handsome saffron-washed Victorian mansion as a hotel, but after dipping a toe into the water, she dived in with great enthusiasm and has infused the place with a one-off character. An avenue of lime trees runs past croquet lawns, a 12th-century church, and carp-filled medieval fishponds; inside, is an elegant scene of statues, crystal chandeliers, antiques and oil paintings, while dining takes place in a romantic marble-pillared dining room lit by silver candelabra, or in an airy conservatory. The kitchen's repertoire is built on ingredients from the garden, game from local estates and top-class stuff from local producers, and veers eclectically from simple classics - a twice-baked cheese soufflé, perhaps - to elaborate modern ideas, such as pan-fried brill with crème fraîche crushed new potatoes, braised fennel, brown shrimp and tarragon. Elsewhere, pig's cheek croquette might be partnered by smoked eel, salt-baked beetroot, pickled apple and mustard, while potato gnocchi, home-made ricotta, wild garlic and green olives could be the supporting cast for an assiette of Langar lamb.

Chef Gary Booth **Owner** Imogen Skirving **Times** 12-2/7-10 **Prices** Fixed L 2 course £18.50-£20, Fixed D 3 course £25-£30, Tasting menu £60, Starter £5-£12.50, Main £12.50-£25.50, Dessert £5-£10.50, Service added but optional 10% **Wines** 55 bottles over £20, 10 bottles under £20, 8 by glass **Notes** Tasting menu 7 course, Sunday L, Vegetarian available, Civ Wed 50 **Seats** 30, Pr/dining room 20 **Children** Portions **Parking** 40

MANSFIELD · Map 16 SK56

Lambs at the Market

◉ Modern British ◐

Smart family-run restaurant with local flavour

☎ 01623 424880
Cattle Market House, Nottingham Rd NG18 1BJ
e-mail: troylamb2003@yahoo.co.uk
dir: From Nottingham A60, left at St Marks Church, 100m on left

With its landmark pepperpot turret, the handsome red-brick Victorian building may still look like the tavern that once slaked the thirsts of the traders at the town's original cattle market, but inside it is another story. A thoroughly modern facelift has brought in darkwood tables, black and cream leather seats, and large artworks on its bare brick and aubergine-hued walls. The kitchen plays up to its market heritage by sourcing fine local and

seasonal materials as the foundations of its hearty modern British menu. Crispy breadcrumbed pork belly makes a robust starter with apple and mustard coleslaw and spiced crackling, while main course serves up Whitby Bay sea trout with new potatoes, fennel salad and summer vegetables. A frozen strawberry parfait with Pimm's-soaked strawberries and black pepper meringue makes a fitting fine-weather finale.

Chef Troy Lamb **Owner** Ted & Brenda Dubowski, Alison & Troy Lamb **Times** 12-2.30/5.30-9.30 Closed 25 Dec & 1 Jan, 1 wk Jan, 1 wk summer, L Mon **Prices** Starter £4.95-£8.95, Main £13-£22, Dessert £5.50-£8, Service added but optional 10%, Groups min 8 service 10% **Wines** 31 bottles over £20, 21 bottles under £20, 8 by glass **Notes** Tasting menu available, Early bird L & D available Tue-Fri, Sunday L, Vegetarian available **Seats** 56 **Children** Portions **Parking** 4, Public car park adjacent or on street

NEWARK-ON-TRENT · Map 17 SK75

The Grange Hotel

◉ Modern British

Classy cooking in a charming Victorian setting

☎ 01636 703399
73 London Rd NG24 1RZ
e-mail: info@grangenewark.co.uk
dir: From A1 follow signs to Balderton, hotel opposite Polish War Graves

The Grange is a traditionally-styled small Victorian hotel that's been sympathetically renovated. Its elegant high-ceilinged dining room, Cutlers, is an intimate, white-linen-clad space done out in rich gold, blue and red fabrics, with prints and glass-display cases of antique cutlery (hence the name) donning the walls. The refreshingly honest traditional Brit cooking comes with a modish spin, while admirably showcasing the best of local seasonal produce. There might be herb-crusted sea bass fillet with parsnip purée and lemon and dill sauce, or braised blade of beef with rich Guinness gravy, creamed potatoes and wild mushrooms. Puds hit the spot for nursery comforts: steamed treacle sponge or Eton Mess. In summer, dine outside in the so-named Victorian secret gardens.

Chef Tamas Lauko **Owner** Tom & Sandra Carr **Times** 12-2/6.30-9 Closed 23 Dec-4 Jan, L Mon-Sat, D Sun **Prices** Starter £5-£6.95, Main £12.95-£18.50, Dessert £5.95-£6.75, Service optional **Wines** 20 bottles over £20, 10 bottles under £20, 6 by glass **Notes** Sunday L, Vegetarian available **Seats** 40 **Children** Portions **Parking** 17

Save on Hotels. Book at **theAA.com/hotel**

NOTTINGHAMSHIRE 393 ENGLAND

NOTTINGHAM

Map 11 SK53

Cockliffe Country House

⚜ Modern European

Vibrant brasserie food in a peaceful country retreat

☎ 0115 968 0179
Burntstump Country Park, Burntstump Hill, Arnold NG5 8PQ
e-mail: enquiries@cockliffehouse.co.uk
web: www.cockliffehouse.co.uk
dir: M1 junct 27, follow signs to Hucknall (A611), then B6011, right at T-junct, follow signs for Cockliffe House

An architecturally interesting greystone country house, Cockliffe sits a little way off the A614 and a world away from the urban hurly-burly of central Nottingham. The dining room is all tasteful elegance with full-length drapes, oval gilt mirrors and crisply turned-out tables, but the cooking is much more vibrant modern brasserie-style than your typical country house. Expect an opener such as crispy king prawns with feta salad and tapenade to be followed by the likes of confit Gressingham duck with buttered greens, chilli cashews and roasted coconut, or pan-roasted swordfish on butter bean and chorizo stew with pepper purée. The generously wide choice continues into desserts, which major in old faves - lemon tart, crème brûlée, white chocolate cheesecake.

Chef Garth Sequeira **Owner** Dane & Jane Clarke
Times 6-9.30 Closed Sun, L all week **Prices** Fixed D 3 course fr £19.95, Starter £5.95-£9.50, Main £13.95-£25.95, Dessert £4.95-£8.50, Service optional, Groups min 8 service 10% **Wines** 25 bottles over £20, 14 bottles under £20, 11 by glass **Notes** Early evening menu Mon-Fri 6-7pm, Vegetarian available, Dress restrictions, Smart casual, Civ Wed 50 **Seats** 50, Pr/dining room 30 **Children** Portions **Parking** 50

Hart's Hotel and Restaurant

⚜⚜ Modern British V

Smart modish cooking from a skilled team

☎ 0115 988 1900
Standard Court, Park Row NG1 6GN
e-mail: ask@hartsnottingham.co.uk
dir: At junct of Park Row & Ropewalk, close to city centre

Opposite the smart boutique hotel of the same name, in Nottingham's old General Hospital, Hart's has a contemporary finish (smart, neutral colour tones, some booth seating and tables laid with white linen) and a menu which deals in first-class produce, handled with intelligence and respect. The attention to detail shown all round is no surprise given the connections to Hambleton Hall (see entry), including the wine list, which is compiled by Tim Hart. There are plenty of options here, from a great value set lunch, pre-theatre menu and a bespoke vegetarian menu which is a definite cut above the average. From the carte - with its sensible six or so choices per course - you might start with beetroot and walnut salad with goats' cheese beignets and compressed comice pear, which looks great on the plate and has well judged flavours and textures. Next up, perhaps rump of beef Diane with 'Koffman' cabbage, rösti potato, crispy beef marrow, watercress and shallots, or a whole roast turbot with hollandaise sauce. To finish, kaffir lime baked Alaska, citrus and passionfruit is one way to go, or try apple crumble in soufflé form, served with crème anglaise.

Chef Daniel Burridge **Owner** Tim Hart
Times 12-2/6-10.30 Closed 1 Jan, L 31 Dec, D 25-26 Dec
Prices Fixed L 2 course fr £14.95, Fixed D 3 course fr £26, Starter £5.50-£10.95, Main £15.50-£30, Dessert £5.75-£9.50, Service added but optional 12% **Wines** 57 bottles over £20, 23 bottles under £20, 6 by glass **Notes** Pre-theatre menu 3 course £18, Sunday L, Vegetarian menu **Seats** 80, Pr/dining room 100 **Children** Portions **Parking** 15

Restaurant Sat Bains with Rooms

⚜⚜⚜⚜⚜ – *see page 394*

Tonic

⚜⚜ Modern British

Cool, contemporary address with modish Med cooking

☎ 0115 941 4770
6B Chapel Quarter, Chapel Bar NG1 6JS
e-mail: info@tonic-online.co.uk
web: www.tonic-online.co.uk
dir: W of city centre at junct of Maid Marian Way & Upper Parliament St

You have to push on past the temptations of cocktails and grazing dishes in the two bars on the lower floors of this hip multi-level venue to reach Tonic's striking contemporary dining room up on the third floor. The place ticks all the cool and stylish boxes with its cinematic art installations, booth seating, chic swivel armchairs and moody pools of purple and scarlet lighting, while the open-plan kitchen adds its own culinary theatre to the buzzy vibe, serving up menus that trumpet uncomplicated contemporary ideas with strong Mediterranean leanings. You might kick off with roast scallops with lemon risotto, tomato fondue and coriander, then follow that with basil-crusted rack of lamb teamed with Parmentier potatoes, ratatouille, Kalamata olives and pesto. At the end, go for something like a play on strawberries and cream - iced strawberry mousse, vanilla mousseline and strawberry jelly.

Tonic

Chef Aaron Givon **Owner** The Brasserie Business Ltd
Times 12-3/6-10 Closed 25-26 Dec, 1 Jan, Sun
Prices Fixed L 2 course £13.95, Fixed D 3 course £16.95, Starter £6-£10, Main £13-£19, Dessert £7-£9, Service added but optional 10% **Wines** 28 bottles over £20, 18 bottles under £20, 7 by glass **Notes** Gourmet menu 6 course £29.50 last Thu mth, Pre-theatre menu, Vegetarian available, Air con **Seats** 90 **Children** Portions **Parking** NCP Mount St (5 min walk)

Restaurant Sat Bains with Rooms

NOTTINGHAM   Map 11 SK53

Modern British V   NOTABLE WINE LIST

Culinary alchemy by one of the UK's brightest stars

☎ 0115 986 6566
Lenton Ln, Trentside NG7 2SA
e-mail: info@restaurantsatbains.net
dir: M1 junct 24, A453 for approx 8m. Through Clifton, road divides into 3 - take middle lane signed 'Lenton Lane Industrial Estate', then 1st left, left again. Follow brown Restaurant Sat Bains sign

Considering this is one of the UK's Premier League dining destinations, the location in a converted Victorian farmhouse and outbuildings on an out-of-town industrial estate near a flyover, might not be what you're expecting. But you don't pitch up at Sat Bains' place to dwell on the scenery: the anticipation of world-class food tends to be foremost in the mind. On that front, you're in a very safe pair of hands: Sat Bains is an endless dynamo of innovation, keeping an ever-evolving repertoire of cutting edge ideas on the boil via a seven- or ten-course tasting menu format. Nor does the restaurant itself lack pizzazz: once inside you're in another world that could have been beamed down from Mayfair, with its polished stone floors, bare brickwork, frosted-glass panelling, immaculately turned-out tables and discreet classical music in the background. There's also the chef's table to get close up to the sharp end of proceedings - de rigueur these days for any operation performing at this level - as well as a table in the development kitchen, where your own chef takes you on your own journey of discovery. If you like to retain a certain control over what you eat, the 'Unique' concept allows you to choose online the components to make up your own bespoke tasting menu . The five taste receptors - salt, sweet, sour, bitter, umami - are allocated colour-coded dots which spell out in each dish just which parts of your taste buds are about to be tickled. The juxtaposition of unusual flavours and textures is evidently a passion, and while ideas are complex, there's no doubting the technical expertise needed to pull them off, and it can be taken as read that the raw materials are second to none. Scoring full marks on the *Great British Menu* is a great way to push your signature dish, which is sold separately to the multi-course menus: ham, peas and egg might sound like a prosaic school dinner, but this amalgam of slow-cooked duck egg with Iberico ham, fresh peas, pea shoots, and a remarkable pea and mint sorbet will knock your socks off. Embarking on the entry-level seven-course format, everything that is promised is delivered: a single scallop sits atop smooth piccalilli purée, with pork crackling deep-fried to resemble popcorn, while a perfectly balanced trio of crab meat, avocado purée and sea vegetables is taken to a higher level when staff - who are courteous and professional throughout - pour over a powerful peanut and crab bisque. And there's more to delight: outstanding braised mutton is teamed with shallot 'textures' (poached, puréed and deep-fried rings, since you ask), before 'The Crossover' sets up the palate for dessert by partnering buttermilk with shaved parmesan, mandarin purée and toasted pumpkin seeds in an ingenious play on savoury, sweet and sour elements. Of the two desserts, treacle sponge is the lightest version you'll ever eat, served with apple purée and parmesan crisps. Sommeliers are particularly deft at plucking bottles from the well-balanced wine list to match with the challenging combinations of flavour.

Chef Sat Bains **Owner** Sat Bains, Amanda Bains **Times** 7-8.30 Closed 2 wks Jan,1 wk May, 2 wks Aug, Sun-Mon, L all week **Prices** Food prices not confirmed for 2013. Please telephone for details **Wines** 120 bottles over £20, 6 bottles under £20, 30 by glass **Notes** Tasting menu 7, 10 course, Vegetarian menu **Seats** 34, Pr/dining room 14 **Parking** 22

NOTTINGHAM *continued*

World Service

◎◎ Modern British ⭐

Sharp cooking and idiosyncratic surroundings

☎ 0115 847 5587
Newdigate House, Castle Gate NG1 6AF
e-mail: info@worldservicerestaurant.com
web: www.worldservicerestaurant.com
dir: 200mtrs from city centre, 50mtrs from Nottingham Castle

World Service is housed in Newdigate House, built in 1675, but it has been given a contemporary look, and the main dining area is filled with Far Eastern artefacts: Buddha heads, Indonesian vases, a prancing horse statue, and the like. There's a hint of East meets West on the menus too, with starters embracing soft-shelled crab with Malaysian curry, but generally the cooking follows a Western route. Prime ingredients are the kitchen's stock-in-trade, as in a starter of foie gras, chicken, and ham hock terrine with celeriac remoulade and pickled pears, and dishes can be creative - roast Cornish red mullet with candied aubergine, confit pepper and chorizo, say, or slow-cooked Gloucestershire Old Spot pork belly and fillet with spicy aubergine purée, sweet braised baby onions and rösti. Banana soufflé with toffee ice cream is well worth the 15-minute wait.

Chef Jacque Ferreira **Owner** Daniel Lindsay, Phillip Morgan, Ashley Walter **Times** 12-2.15/7-10 Closed 25-26 Dec, 1-7 Jan, D Sun (except Dec & BH Sun) **Prices** Fixed L 2 course £14.50, Fixed D 3 course £26.50, Starter £5-£15.50, Main £15.95-£25.95, Dessert £6.50-£9.50, Service added but optional 12% **Wines** 170 bottles over £20, 34 bottles under £20, 17 by glass **Notes** Sunday L, Vegetarian available **Seats** 80, Pr/dining room 34 **Children** Portions, Menu **Parking** NCP

Thoresby Hall Hotel and Spa

◎◎ Modern British ✿

Well-judged menu in a grand Victorian pile

☎ 01623 821000 & 821033
Thoresby Park NG22 9WH
e-mail: thoresbyhall@bourne-leisure.co.uk

On the edge of ancient Sherwood Forest, Thoresby Hall is a magnificent Grade I listed Victorian mansion standing in 100 acres of grounds. Its ornate facade is a riot of balconies, turrets and gables, while inside it's a similar story of period grandeur - all panelled walls, original wooden floors, hanging tapestries and highly-decorated fireplaces. The Blue Room is the hotel's fine-dining option (there are two other restaurants), a well proportioned room with chandeliers hanging from the high ceilings, aqua-blue walls, formally-dressed tables and lovely views of the grounds. The modern British menu offers up the likes of ham hock and foie gras terrine with soused vegetables and toasted rye bread, followed by native hake with saffron braised mussels, new potatoes and seasonal greens. Dessert could be ginger cake with caramelised banana and salted peanut ice cream.

Chef Fritz Ronnebourg, Mark Maris **Owner** Warner Leisure **Times** 12-2/6.30-9 Closed Tue-Wed **Prices** Fixed L 2 course £16.95, Starter £5.75-£8.50, Main £16.50-£20, Dessert £5.75-£7.50, Service optional **Wines** 25 bottles over £20, 7 bottles under £20, 5 by glass **Notes** Sunday L, Vegetarian available, Dress restrictions, Smart casual **Seats** 70, Pr/dining room 70 **Parking** 140

OXFORDSHIRE

The Boar's Head

◎◎ British, French ✿

Fine dining in a country pub

☎ 01235 833254
Church St OX12 8QA
e-mail: info@boarsheadardington.co.uk
web: www.boarsheadardington.co.uk
dir: 2m E of Wantage on A417, next to village church

A half-timbered pub by the village church in a leafy Downland village, The Boar's Head has been pulling pints for over 150 years and has a genuine country local vibe. Its low doorway entrance gives a real feeling of stepping

---

back in time, yet the interior is surprisingly light and bright. Drop in for a light meal and pint in the bar or head for the restaurant with its sunny Mediterranean hued walls and eclectic mix of sturdy wooden furniture. The kitchen makes everything in-house, from bread to pasta and ice cream, and the daily-changing menu is driven by fresh seasonal produce, with fish something of a speciality. Tranche of Cornish cod, for example, with Niçoise and gazpacho, or perhaps breast of duck served with chorizo, rösti and port sauce. Finish with a Brit classic like a freshly made bread-and-butter pudding with vanilla ice cream.

Chef Bruce Buchan **Owner** Boar's Head (Ardington) Ltd **Times** 12-2/7-10 Closed D Sun **Prices** Fixed L 2 course fr £14.50, Starter £6.50-£10.50, Main £16.50-£23.50, Dessert £7.50, Service optional, Groups min 8 service 10% **Wines** 70 bottles over £20, 30 bottles under £20, 12 by glass **Notes** Gastronomic menu 6 course £39.50 available on request, Sunday L, Vegetarian available **Seats** 40, Pr/dining room 24 **Children** Portions **Parking** 20

Lambert Arms

◎ Modern British V

Charming old inn with confident team in the kitchen

☎ 0845 459 3736
London Rd OX49 5SB
e-mail: info@lambertarms.com
dir: M40 junct 6, at T-junct right towards Chinnor (B4009), back under motorway. 1st left to Postcombe/ Thame (A40)

A classic black-and-white timbered coaching inn on the outside, the Lambert Arms has been made over inside to appeal to 21st-century sensibilities. The location at the foot of the Chiltern Hills is timeless, despite its nearness to the M40, and the de-cluttered clean-lined contemporary look sits well with its period features and a simple, robust approach to dining. Classic pubby favourites such as home-made burgers and deep-fried whitebait with tartare sauce sit alongside main courses built with generosity and full flavours in mind - local sausages and creamy mash with fresh vegetables and onion gravy, or herb-crusted Barnsley chop with Lyonnaise potatoes, baby spinach and fresh tomato sauce, for example. To finish, there could be summer pudding served with Cornish clotted cream ice cream.

Owner Bespoke Hotels **Times** 12-2.30/6.30-9 **Prices** Fixed L 2 course £19.50-£24.50, Fixed D 3 course £24.50-£29.95, Starter £4.95-£9.95, Main £11.95-£19.50, Dessert £4.95-£5.95, Service optional **Wines** 24 bottles over £20, 7 bottles under £20, 12 by glass **Notes** Sunday L, Vegetarian menu, Dress restrictions, Smart casual, Civ Wed 100 **Seats** 46, Pr/dining room 60 **Children** Portions, Menu **Parking**

Map 11 SP44

Best Western Plus Wroxton House Hotel

◉ Modern British

Charming inn with well-judged menu

☎ 01295 730777
Silver St, Wroxton OX15 6QB
e-mail: reservations@wroxtonhousehotel.com
dir: From M40 junct 11 follow A422 (signed Banbury, then Wroxton). After 3m, hotel on right

Set in a picturesque village, the restaurant at the thatched Wroxton House Hotel is in the oldest part of the building dating from the mid-17th century. Comprising three contemporary-styled intimate rooms, expect bags of period country-house charm (oak beams, timbers and inglenook included) teamed with a 21st-century sheen. Likewise, the kitchen delivers an appealing roster of classic British dishes given a modern spin. Quality local produce shines in intelligently simple dishes like grilled stone bass served with black linguine, chorizo and parsley and a lemon butter sauce, or perhaps roast rump of lamb with spiced couscous, pea purée and a red wine jus. To finish, go for classic lemon tart or chocolate fondant.

Chef Steve Mason-Tucker **Owner** John & Gill Smith
Times 12-2/7-9 Closed L Mon-Sat **Prices** Fixed L 2 course £16, Fixed D 3 course £31, Service optional
Wines 19 bottles over £20, 18 bottles under £20, 10 by glass **Notes** Sunday L, Vegetarian available, Dress restrictions, Smart casual, Civ Wed 80 **Seats** 60, Pr/dining room 80 **Children** Portions, Menu **Parking** 70

Map 5 SP21

The Bay Tree Hotel

◉ Traditional British

Modern British pub food in an elegant Cotswold inn

☎ 01993 822791
Sheep St OX18 4LW
e-mail: info@baytreehotel.info
web: www.cotswold-inns-hotels.co.uk/baytree
dir: A40 or A361 to Burford. From High St turn into Sheep St, next to old market square. Hotel on right

A Cotswold country inn smothered in wisteria with flagstone floors and leaded windows overlooking a garden is an appealing prospect, and The Bay Tree fills the bill.

Candlelit in the evenings, and professionally run, the dining room is a cream-coloured space with high-backed chairs and cooking that takes a modern approach to its task. Accompanying cured salmon with excellent crab jelly and watercress cream works a treat, ahead of duck breast with the leg meat rolled in cannelloni, served with confit celeriac and braised, subtly spiced red cabbage. When rhubarb and custard got deconstructed, it got deconstructed for good, and here is a prime example, incorporating rhubarb jelly and custard mousse with almond crumble.

Chef Brian Andrews **Owner** Mr & Mrs Horton
Times 12-2/7-9.30 **Prices** Fixed L 2 course £12.95, Fixed D 3 course £31.95, Service added but optional 10%
Wines 40 bottles over £20, 23 bottles under £20, 5 by glass **Notes** Sunday L, Vegetarian available, Dress restrictions, Smart casual, Civ Wed 80 **Seats** 70, Pr/dining room 24 **Parking** 55

The Bull at Burford

◉◉ Modern French

Impressive cooking in a former coaching inn

☎ 01993 822220
105 High St OX18 4RG
e-mail: info@bullatburford.co.uk
web: www.bullatburford.co.uk
dir: On A40 between Cheltenham & Oxford, in town centre

The Bull started life as a coaching inn in 1610 so it comes as no surprise to learn that it has seen some high-profile visitors over the centuries - Lord Nelson and Charles II to name but two. After a thorough facelift it is looking up to snuff, with a classy restaurant featuring bare Cotswold-stone walls, age-blackened beams, original artwork, and butterscotch-hued, high-backed seats at linen-swathed tables. Chef Paul Scott brings a fine pedigree to the stoves and has quickly established The Bull on the local foodie map. A repertoire of modern French-influenced dishes shows serious ambition, starting with a multi-faceted plate of pan-seared scallops with confit pork belly, caramelised apple compôte, and a smoked haddock and potato purée. Next up, local beef gets a workout in an assiette of pan-seared fillet, oxtail ravioli and bone marrow boudin with horseradish pommes purée. Dessert too is a labour-intensive workout on a caramel theme, in the forms of parfait, mousse, crème caramel and banana caramel ice cream.

The Bull at Burford

Chef Paul Scott **Owner** Mr & Mrs J-M Lauzier
Times 12-2.30/7-9.30 **Prices** Fixed L 2 course £14.50, Starter £6.75-£9.50, Main £14-£23.50, Dessert £6.50-£9.25, Service optional **Wines** 95 bottles over £20, 15 bottles under £20, 10 by glass **Notes** Fixed L incl 125ml glass wine, Sunday L, Vegetarian available **Seats** 40, Pr/dining room 12 **Children** Portions, Menu **Parking** 6, On street

The Lamb Inn

◉◉ Modern British V ◉

Imaginative modern cooking in classic village inn

☎ 01993 823155
Sheep St OX18 4LR
e-mail: info@lambinn-burford.co.uk
web: www.cotswold-inns-hotels.co.uk/lamb
dir: Exit A40 into Burford, down hill, take 1st left into Sheep St, hotel last on right

The setting is as chocolate-box English as you could ask - a wisteria-clad Cotswold stone 15th-century inn just off pretty Burford's high street - and the upmarket interior pursues the theme with beamed ceilings, flagstone floors, open fires, antiques, copper and brass, and squashy sofas. Outside in the buzzy, stone-walled courtyard is the place to be on a fine day, and the classy restaurant is none too shabby either, with its fuchsia and ivory walls, luminous skylights and mullioned windows. The kitchen delivers dishes that are more contemporary than the setting suggests, showing bags of ideas, careful preparation and flourishes of adventure - a starter of scallop and langoustine with cauliflower purée and seaweed salad, for example, followed by pan-fried Gressingham duck breast with braised cabbage, creamed potato, and confit duck and orange tortellini. Desserts such as cinnamon-poached apple with sun-dried cranberry gratin and apple sorbet are a treat.

Chef Sean Ducie **Owner** Cotswold Inns & Hotels
Times 12-2.30/7-9.30 **Prices** Fixed L 2 course fr £20,

Save on Hotels. Book at **theAA.com/hotel**

OXFORDSHIRE 397 **ENGLAND**

Fixed D 3 course fr £39, Service added but optional 10%
Wines 90 bottles over £20, 10 bottles under £20, 12 by
glass **Notes** Tasting menu available, with Dégustation
wines, Sunday L, Vegetarian menu **Seats** 40
Children Portions **Parking** Care of The Bay Tree Hotel

CHECKENDON   Map 5 SU68

The Highwayman

◉ Traditional British

Nice mix of menus in a welcoming country local

☎ 01491 682020
Exlade St RG8 0UA
dir: Exlade St signed off A4074 (Reading/Wallingford
road), 0.4m

Tucked away in a secluded hamlet, overlooking open
fields on the edge of the wooded Chiltern Hills, this
rambling, whitewashed 17th-century inn is first and
foremost a cracking local with a pubby bar serving fine
ales (and some pretty good wines too). When it comes to
eating, there are various good-value options, such as
two-course specials, as well as a roll-call of pub classics
(rabbit and bacon pie for example). The principal menu,
though, trics out some successful dishes that draw
influences from near and far; start with cod and
crabcakes with garlic mayonnaise, before moving on to
braised beef brisket with horseradish mash, or roast
chicken with pearl barley, chestnuts, mash and thyme
jus. Round off with bread-and-butter pudding with ginger
cream or vanilla pannacotta with mixed berries.

Chef Paul Burrows **Owner** Mr Ken O'Shea
Times 12-2.30/6-10 Closed 26 Dec, 1 Jan, Mon, D Sun
Prices Food prices not confirmed for 2013. Please
telephone for details **Wines** 15 bottles over £20,
25 bottles under £20, 5 by glass **Notes** Vegetarian
available, Dress restrictions, No work clothes or vests
Seats 55, Pr/dining room 40 **Children** Portions, Menu
Parking 30

CHINNOR   Map 5 SP70

The Sir Charles Napier

◉◉ British, French ⚑NOTABLE WINE LIST

Compelling cooking in unique pub restaurant

☎ 01494 483011
Sprigg's Alley OX39 4BX
e-mail: info@sircharlesnapier.co.uk
web: www.sircharlesnapier.co.uk
dir: M40 junct 6, B4009 to Chinnor. Right at rdbt to
Sprigg's Alley

Deep in the Chilterns surrounded by beech woods, this
unique pub restaurant is a captivating place, with the
sort of décor that makes you feel immediately relaxed and
at home. There's a lovely shady terrace for summer and
huge log fires in winter. The kitchen is led by the seasons;
kick off with rabbit terrine with Earl Grey and prune purée
and pickled girolles, then move onto amazingly fresh
turbot with pumpkin gnocchi, braised celeriac,
chanterelles and parsley root purée. Top-drawer
ingredients (those mushrooms may have been gathered
in the woods, for instance) are brought together with
culinary good sense, partnering seared foie gras with
Calvados-poached apples, Cassis and brioche, and a
main course of local beef appearing as fillet, shin
pudding, and tongue croquette with salsify. Desserts are
worth exploring, among them toffee apple bavarois, and
prune and Armagnac soufflé with cranberry and ginger
sorbet.

Chef Chris Godfrey **Owner** Julie Griffiths
Times 12-3.30/6.30-10 Closed 25-27 Dec, Mon, D Sun
Prices Fixed L 2 course £15.50-£17.50, Fixed D 2 course
£15.50-£17.50, Starter £9.50-£15.50, Main £19.50-
£28.50, Dessert £8.50, Service added but optional 12.5%
Wines 200 bottles over £20, 23 bottles under £20, 9 by
glass **Notes** Tasting menu available, Sunday L,
Vegetarian available **Seats** 75, Pr/dining room 45
Children Portions, Menu **Parking** 60

CHIPPING NORTON   Map 10 SP32

The Kingham Plough

◉◉ Modern British ❀

Revamped pub with creative cooking

☎ 01608 658327
The Green, Kingham OX7 6YD
e-mail: book@thekinghamplough.co.uk
dir: From Chipping Norton take B4450 to Churchill, left at
T-junct signed Kingham. Plough on right

The old pub on the green of a classic postcard-picture
Cotswolds village is the very image of bucolic Britain, but
once inside the Plough sports a rather cool rustic-chic
look after a facelift in 2007. There are hessian-covered
stools at the bar, real ales and hearty bar food such as
Scotched quail's egg, venison sausage roll, and crispy
rabbit shoulder and caper salad to nibble at, but it is in
the informal - though upmarket - restaurant where chef
Emily Watkins plays out modish themes learnt from her
stint with Mr Blumenthal in The Fat Duck. The menu
spans the ages from traditional recipes to cleverly
reworked classics - an 'Irish stew' starter for example,
which marries slow-cooked mutton with carrot chutney,
warm heritage potato salad and shallot rings. Main
courses might bring on locally-farmed Tamworth pork loin
with hodge podge pudding sausage roll, January King
cabbage, carrots and cider jelly. Puddings stay in the
same territory of clever comfort cooking with rhubarb and
stem ginger meringue pie, and Cheltenham steamed
pudding with lemon ripple ice cream.

Chef Emily Watkins & Gareth Fulford **Owner** Emily & Miles
Lampson **Times** 12-2/7-8.45 Closed 25 Dec
Prices Starter £6-£9, Main £12-£20, Dessert £6-£8,
Service optional, Groups min 10 service 10%
Wines 41 bottles over £20, 4 bottles under £20, 7 by
glass **Notes** Sunday L, Vegetarian available **Seats** 74, Pr/
dining room 20 **Children** Portions, Menu **Parking** 30

CHIPPING NORTON *continued*

Wild Thyme Restaurant with Rooms

◉◉ Modern British **NEW** ☺

Contemporary style and modish cooking

☎ 01608 645060
10 New St OX7 5LJ
e-mail: enquiries@wildthymerestaurant.co.uk
dir: A44 Evesham, through Market Place. On left opposite Sainsbury's car park

The mood is relaxed and the food is bathed with Mediterranean warmth in this charming chic restaurant in well-heeled Chipping Norton. Black beams are all that attest to the age of the building, otherwise the scene is one of rustic modernity - bare wooden floors, exposed stone or whitewashed walls hung with modern art, and chunky country-style tables. The kitchen goes about its business with quiet confidence, sending out robust flavours and plenty of seasonal ingredients in a spring dinner that starts with a delightful, well-conceived dish comprising Wye Valley asparagus, Cornish crab, poached quail's egg, pink grapefruit and hollandaise sauce. Next up, herb ravioli, peas and broad beans, trompette mushrooms, confit garlic, crispy pancetta and Madeira velouté are the accompaniments to a poached and roasted breast of guinea fowl, and it all ends happily with banana parfait, caramelised banana, and figgy pudding.

Chef Nicholas Pullen **Owner** Nicholas Pullen, Sally Daniel **Times** 12-2/7-9 Closed Jan 2 wks, Spring 1 wk, Sun, L Mon **Prices** Fixed L 2 course £18, Fixed D 3 course fr £25, Starter £5.75-£11, Main £13-£22, Dessert £7.25-£8.50, Service optional **Wines** 32 bottles over £20, 8 bottles under £20, 11 by glass **Notes** Fixed D 2, 3 course only available mid week, Vegetarian available **Seats** 35, Pr/dining room 14 **Children** Portions **Parking** Public car park 3 min walk

DEDDINGTON   Map 11 SP43

Deddington Arms

◉ Modern British

Good country-pub fare in a 16th-century inn

☎ 01869 338364
Horsefair OX15 0SH
e-mail: deddarms@oxfordshire-hotels.co.uk
dir: From S: M40 junct 10/A43. 1st rdbt left to Aynho (B4100) & left to Deddington (B4031). From N: M40 junct 11 to hospital & Adderbury on A4260, then to Deddington

The black-and-white village inn dates back to the 16th century, and is full of beamed and fireplaced period allure, despite being sensitively modernised inside. A wood-burning stove occupies pride of place, and the requisite tone of friendly cheer pervades the flagstoned dining room. The cooking is good honest country-pub stuff. Appetising nibbles to start you off include houmous and flatbread, and then it's on to smoked salmon and dill roulade with watercress pesto, followed by braised lamb shank with creamy mash, or chicken breast done up in

Parma ham with creamed leeks. Dark chocolate and Cointreau pot with orange biscotti makes for a richly satisfying finish.

Chef Nick Porter **Owner** Oxfordshire Hotels Ltd **Times** 12-2.30/6-9.45 **Prices** Fixed L 2 course £11.95, Fixed D 3 course £20.95, Starter £6.30-£6.80, Main £13.50-£17.95, Dessert £6.65-£7.95, Service optional, Groups min 6 service 10% **Wines** 19 bottles over £20, 24 bottles under £20, 10 by glass **Notes** Vegetarian available **Seats** 60, Pr/dining room 30 **Children** Portions, Menu **Parking** 36

FARINGDON   Map 5 SU29

BW Sudbury House Hotel & Conference Centre

◉ Modern European **NEW**

Good hotel dining between Oxford and Swindon

☎ 01367 241272
London St SN7 8AA
e-mail: events@sudburyhouse.co.uk
dir: Off A420, signed Folly Hill

On the fringes of the Cotswolds and handy for the M4 and M40, this traditional hotel in nine acres of grounds has croquet and pitch and putt among its possible distractions, plus a large restaurant with pleasant views over the garden; order at the bar before heading on through to the dining room. There's plenty of clear-headed thinking going on in the kitchen, the good quality ingredients given room to shine. Tartlet of wild mushrooms and Oxford Blue cheese might come with confit of tomato, while main-course seared lamb's liver is served up with colcannon, caramelised shallots and a redcurrant and rosemary scented sauce.

Chef Clifford Burt **Owner** Best Western **Times** 11.30-2.30/6-9.15 **Prices** Fixed L 2 course fr £11.95, Starter fr £4.95, Main fr £11, Dessert fr £4.95, Service optional **Wines** 10 bottles over £20, 10 bottles under £20, 10 by glass **Notes** Sunday L, Vegetarian available **Seats** 80 **Children** Portions, Menu **Parking** 100

The Eagle

◉◉ Modern European **NEW** ☺

Accomplished cooking in revamped village inn

☎ 01367 241879
Little Coxwell SN7 7LW
e-mail: eaglelittlecoxwell@gmail.com
dir: A420, follow signs for 1m to Little Coxwell Village

Set in the peaceful village of Little Coxwell in lush countryside, The Eagle is a traditional country pub made over in the clean-cut contemporary vein that dictates that wooden tables will be chunky, unclothed and candlelit, and art will adorn the pastel-hued timbered walls. The ambience is relaxed, the ales are well kept, and, best of all, the food punches well above its weight. The modern European cooking here is the real McCoy, thanks to chef Marcel Nerpas who hails originally from Slovakia, and lifts the repertoire out of the tried-and-tested category

with inventive flavour combinations. A mighty fine terrine of Aylesbury duck, foie gras, pear and pistachio is teamed with cardamom-scented pear compôte, while mains deliver shredded confit leg and roasted breast of guinea fowl with saffron potatoes, winter root vegetables and a punchy, flavour-packed clear consommé served in a pouring jug. To finish, Valrhona chocolate is showcased in a line-up involving a dark chocolate brownie, iced milk chocolate mousse, white chocolate pannacotta and praline.

Chef Marcel Nerpas **Owner** Marcel Nerpas **Times** 12-2.30/5.30-11 Closed Mon, D Sun **Prices** Fixed L 2 course fr £12.50, Fixed D 3 course £24.50-£28.50, Starter £2.95-£5.95, Main £13.50-£16.50, Dessert £6-£7, Service optional **Wines** 13 bottles over £20, 20 bottles under £20, 8 by glass **Notes** Sunday L, Vegetarian available **Seats** 28 **Children** Portions, Menu **Parking** On street

The Trout at Tadpole Bridge

◉ Traditional British ☺

Classy pub grub in a traditional Thames-side inn

☎ 01367 870382
Buckland Marsh SN7 8RF
e-mail: info@troutinn.co.uk
dir: A420 Swindon to Oxford road, turn signed Bampton. Inn 2m on right

This historic inn on the River Thames is very much a traditional pub where diners mingle with locals and drinkers at the bar to reinforce that quintessential country-inn vibe. All the hoped for exposed beams, log fires and plain wooden tables are present and correct, too, while if the weather is fine, the large garden proves a favoured spot to watch waterborne life float by. Otherwise settle into the laid-back atmosphere inside for some intelligently straightforward, flavour-driven cooking based around seasonal produce and an emphasis on fish dishes, with the daily-changing specials board showing the catch of the day. Go for roasted cod with Welsh rarebit and Lyonnaise potatoes, perhaps, while meat-lovers might tuck into pan-fried calves' liver served with fondant potato, cauliflower purée and wild mushrooms. To finish, how about green fig croissant bread pudding served with crème anglaise?

Chef Pascal Clavaud **Owner** Helen & Gareth Pugh **Times** 12-2/7-9 Closed 25-26 Dec **Prices** Fixed L 2 course fr £12.50, Starter £4.95-£12, Main £10.95-£19.95, Dessert £5.95-£7.95, Service optional **Wines** 86 bottles over £20, 32 bottles under £20, 16 by glass **Notes** Sunday L, Vegetarian available **Seats** 50, Pr/dining room 40 **Children** Portions, Menu **Parking** 40

Save on Hotels. Book at **theAA.com/hotel**

OXFORDSHIRE 399 **ENGLAND**

Le Manoir aux Quat' Saisons

GREAT MILTON   Map 5 SP60

Modern French V ◊NOTABLE WINE LIST

Incroyable cooking in magnifique setting

☎ 01844 278881
Church Rd OX44 7PD
e-mail: lemanoir@blanc.co.uk
dir: M40 junct 7 follow A329 towards Wallingford. After 1m turn right, signed Great Milton and Le Manoir aux Quat' Saisons

If you're planning your first visit to dine chez Raymond, we can safely say you will not be disappointed. And that is first and foremost down to the fact that consistency is the name of the game here, that and excellence. Consistently excellent. Le Manoir aux Quat' Saisons has been awarded five Rosettes in all 20 editions of The AA Restaurant Guide, and hats off to Monsieur Blanc for that. We'll get to the food in a minute, for it is the food which has won the plaudits, but a visit to this peaceful and beautiful Oxfordshire manor house is a joy for so many reasons. They could probably charge an entrance fee to the gardens with its sculptures, well-stocked greenhouses, little bridges and Japanese tea garden, so do make some time for a wander if the weather and daylight allow. And then there is the service. Exemplary is a good word to describe the experience, from beginning to end, and it feels effortless at times,

the charm natural, the passion evident. Prices are high, but this is an experience to cherish, and to emphasise Blanc's egalitarian spirit, there's a children's menu that pays so much more than the usual lip service to the toleration of young people. The chef-patron and executive chef Gary Jones have never waivered from the belief that the quality of the produce is at the heart of every dish. Indeed, the organic kitchen garden here at Le Manoir was supplying the kitchen from the off, and these days it stretches for two acres and provides bountiful vegetables, fruits and herbs for the table (90 types of vegetable, no less, and 70 varieties of herbs). The food has evolved with the times, never chasing bandwagons or following fashions for the sake of it, but neither has it stood still. The French soul of the place still runs deep, everything looks stunning on the plate, flavour is king, and creative desires are nuanced by a subtle touch and clear-headed thinking. First-impressions count and the canapés positively spark with vitality - crab tart, vegetable fritter to name but two - and the bread...oh the bread. Eight different types of roll are offered up and difficult decisions must be made. The menu - à la carte, découverte and a variety of fixed-price, multi-course menus - are written in French with precise English translations, and there are further difficult decisions ahead. Perhaps the Cornish lobster will catch your eye,

packed into ravioli and partnered with a perfectly balanced ginger and lemongrass bisque, alongside baby artichokes, samphire and a scattering of edible petals. Among main courses, roasted new season grouse makes a perfect autumnal dinner, with cabbage and bacon, a well-judged blackberry jus and some fabulous bread sauce. Or try the braised Cornish turbot with oyster, scallop and Scottish girolles. The supreme technical proficiency and consummately judged flavour combinations continue with desserts, where a pear almondine and caramel croustillant comes with a ginger sauce and sorbet.

Chef Raymond Blanc, Gary Jones
Owner Mr R Blanc & OE Hotels
Times 12-2.30/7-10 **Prices** Starter £36-£38, Main £48, Service optional
Wines 1100 bottles over £20, 15 by glass **Notes** Fixed L 5 course Mon-Fri, 7 course daily, D 6/9 course daily, Vegetarian menu, Dress restrictions, No jeans, trainers or shorts, Civ Wed 50
Seats 100, Pr/dining room 50
Children Portions, Menu **Parking** 60

FYFIELD
Map 5 SU49

The White Hart
◉◉ Modern British 🍷

Confident cooking in a tranquil village inn

☎ 01865 390585
Main Rd OX13 5LW
e-mail: info@whitehart-fyfield.com
dir: A420 Oxford-Swindon, 7m S of Oxford A34

With layers deep in Reformation history, The White Hart is a former chantry house which was sold to St John's college in Oxford after the Dissolution (the inn lies but a few miles outside the city) and is still replete with a secret tunnel to Fyfield Manor, a minstrels' gallery, and enough timbers to build a galleon. Nowadays, the thriving inn bustles with diners drawn in by chef-proprietor Mark Chandler's appealing contemporary gastro-pub cooking. The impressive level of technical proficiency here is all the more remarkable considering Mark is a self-taught chef; he stocks his larder with fresh produce from the kitchen garden, bolstered by a sound network of local suppliers. Sharing boards of meze, antipasti or fish nibbles are one way to go about things, otherwise a three-course approach might get going with goats' cheese and lemon ravioli with pink peppercorns and basil, followed by roast rack of Cotswold lamb with lamb faggot, dauphinoise potatoes, peas and minted hollandaise, and for pudding, something like apple and Calvados mousse with cobnut praline.

Chef Mark Chandler **Owner** Kay & Mark Chandler **Times** 12-2.30/7-9.30 Closed Mon (ex BHs), D Sun **Prices** Fixed L 2 course fr £16, Starter £6-£9, Main £14-£20, Dessert £6-£7, Service optional, Groups min 8 service 10% **Wines** 44 bottles over £20, 8 bottles under £20, 11 by glass **Notes** Chef's tasting menu available on request, Sunday L, Vegetarian available **Seats** 65, Pr/dining room 32 **Children** Portions, Menu **Parking** 60

GORING
Map 5 SU68

The Leatherne Bottel
◉◉ British, French 🍷 NOTABLE WINE LIST

Inventive waterside dining

☎ 01491 872667
Bridle Way RG8 0HS
e-mail: leathernebottel@aol.com
web: www.leathernebottel.co.uk
dir: M4 junct 12 or M40 junct 6, signed from B4009 towards Wallingford

It is hard to imagine a finer setting for a sunny summer lunch than a table shaded by a lavender-hued parasol on the Thames-side terrace of the Bottel. If you like to turn heads, arrive by boat and tie up at the inn's quayside moorings before taking in the idyllic views of the river and Berkshire Downs. When the sun doesn't play ball, head indoors for an old-school cottagey setting splashed with colourful art, and creative modern European dishes with a nod here and there to the Pacific Rim, courtesy of head chef Julia Abbey, where cooking is framed by her years spent in New Zealand. She has no truck with foams or the current trend for foraged ingredients, preferring to go with her innate feel for how flavours work together, so starters could include tea-smoked tuna carpaccio with cucumber sorbet, pickled ginger salad and wasabi mayonnaise, while mains run to roast magret of duck teamed with rolled confit leg, glazed figs and turnip gratin; fish might turn up in the shape of spiced monkfish with a fricassée of seasonal vegetables and Marsala sauce. Desserts are a treat too - perhaps cardamom and rosewater pannacotta with honeycomb, and rhubarb compôte.

Chef Julia Abbey **Owner** Leatherne Bottle Ltd **Times** 12-2/7-9 Closed D Sun **Prices** Fixed L 2 course £15.95-£25.50, Fixed D 3 course £25.50, Starter £6.75-£16, Main £16-£28, Dessert £8.50, Service added 10% **Wines** 190 bottles over £20, 17 by glass **Notes** Tasting menus available, Sunday L, Vegetarian available **Seats** 45 **Children** Portions **Parking** 20

GREAT MILTON
Map 5 SP60

Le Manoir aux Quat' Saisons
◉◉◉◉◉ – *see page 399*

HENLEY-ON-THAMES
Map 5 SU78

Hotel du Vin Henley-on-Thames
◉◉ European 🍷

An old riverside brewery made over by HdV

☎ 01491 848400
New St RG9 2BP
e-mail: info.henley@hotelduvin.com
dir: M4 junct 8/9 signed High Wycombe, take 2nd exit and onto A404 in 2m. A4130 into Henley, over bridge, through lights, up Hart St, right onto Bell St, right onto New St, hotel on right

Moving on from beer to wine usually results in a monumental headache, but the results here are a delight. The HdV brand has plenty of previous with its trademark chic contemporary makeovers, in this case converting the Georgian red-brick buildings encircling the yard of the former Brakspear's brewery with the customary Gallic inspiration. A central island of black leather banquettes is surrounded by copies of famous paintings on buttery-hued, panelled walls, and a plethora of paraphernalia references the wine-related theme, making an amenable setting for good bistro food. Home-grown and local are the buzzwords of the chain's sourcing ethos, although we will allow them a bit of leeway in an excellent crab and saffron tart starter, since the Thames hereabouts is not known for its crustaceans. Next up, chorizo and shellfish bring great flavours to a take on paella twinned with perfectly-timed, crisp-skinned hake and a chicken drumstick. A Black Forest gâteau done properly wraps things up on a fashionably retro note.

Chef Oliver Stewart **Owner** MWB Group **Times** 12-2.30/6-10 **Prices** Starter £4.50, Main £13.50, Dessert fr £4.50, Service added but optional 10% **Wines** 700 bottles over £20, 30 bottles under £20, 16 by glass **Notes** Vegetarian available, Civ Wed 72 **Seats** 90, Pr/dining room 72 **Children** Portions, Menu **Parking**

Orwells
◉◉◉ – *see opposite*

Le Parisien Restaurant
◉◉ Modern French

Top-notch French chef in Henley-on-Thames bistro

☎ 01491 571115
50 Bell St RG9 2BG
e-mail: leparisien@live.co.uk
web: www.leparisienrestaurant.co.uk

Regardless of the giveaway name, from the outside Le Parisien looks like a typical French restaurant, the interior following suit with dark brown leather banquette seating, white-clothed tables, fresh flowers, plus some contemporary artwork from a local artists to give a flavour of the terroir. So far so bistro. Chef-patron Phillipe Brillant has a notable culinary pedigree having worked for Joel Robuchon in Paris and various other high profile restaurants globally, and his food is a cut above your typical bistro. Classical techniques are applied to good fresh produce to create well-defined French flavours; start with grilled sea bass with baby spinach and a champagne sauce, moving on to braised ox cheeks in red wine with bacon, carrots, baby leeks and creamy ratte mashed potatoes, or go for his own recipe duck confit served with flagolets beans and dauphinoise potatoes. Save room for pancakes served with an orange glaze, Kirsch-stewed black cherries and bourbon vanilla ice cream.

Times 12-2/6.30-9 Closed BHs, D Sun

KINGHAM   Map 10 SP22

The Mill House Hotel

◉ British, French

Cotswold setting for modern British cooking

☎ 01608 658188
OX7 6UH
e-mail: stay@millhousehotel.co.uk
dir: Just off B4450, between Chipping Norton & Stow-on-the-Wold. On southern outskirts of village

Now a delightful hotel, this converted flour mill has a history going back to the Domesday Book. The Mill Brook Restaurant's white-clothed, well-spaced tables make for a calm, elegant place to enjoy the menu of well-considered dishes. Start, perhaps with seared Cornish

scallops, cauliflower mash and basil oil, followed by braised leg and saddle of wild rabbit, with fondant potato and basil and tomato jus, or twice- baked stilton souffle with pak choi and a watercress and red pepper coulis. Finish with classic hot chocolate mousse.

Times 12-2/6.30-10

KINGSTON BAGPUIZE   Map 5 SU49

Fallowfield Hotel & Restaurant

◉◉ Modern British NEW V ☺

Contemporary British cooking in smart country hotel

☎ 01865 820416
Faringdon Rd OX13 5BH
e-mail: stay@fallowfields.com
dir: A34 (Oxford Ring Rd) take A420 towards Swindon. At junct with A415 left for 100yds then turn at mini rdbt. Hotel on left after 1m

This small country-house hotel has its roots in the 17th century, its restaurant nowadays smartly turned-out in shades of cream and gold, the room handsomely dressed, and benefitting from a wonderful outlook on lawns and paddocks. The kitchen has the enviable position of being able to monopolise meal and poultry from the owners' own farm and vegetables, herbs and fruit from the kitchen gardens and orchards. Rest assured other materials are equally well sourced: Cornish mackerel is

smoked and served as a starter with cucumber spaghetti, confit lemon and herb salad, and locally-shot pheasant goes into a terrine, served with pineapple chutney and pineapple jelly - a fine contrast of flavours and textures. Chutneys accompany some main courses too, one of banana with a tasting of home-reared pork served with pork jus and confit potato, or go for roast halibut with confit chicken wings, chicken jus, sauerkraut and braised shallots. Puddings keep up the high standards, from Amaretto crème brûlée to moist carrot cake with honey ice cream.

Chef Shaun Dickens **Owner** Anthony & Peta Lloyd **Times** 12-2.30/7-9.30 **Prices** Fixed L 2 course £20-£24, Tasting menu £69, Starter £7-£12, Main £15-£25, Dessert £7-£9, Service added but optional 12.5% **Wines** 70 bottles over £20, 10 bottles under £20, 10 by glass **Notes** Tasting menu 7 course must be taken by the whole table, Sunday L, Vegetarian menu, Dress restrictions, Smart casual, Civ Wed 100 **Seats** 42, Pr/dining room 14 **Children** Portions, Menu **Parking** 50

Orwells

HENLEY-ON-THAMES   Map 5 SU78

Modern British ☺

Dazzling, creative cooking in a 17th-century pub

☎ 0118 940 3673
Shiplake Row, Binfield Heath RG9 4DP
e-mail: eat@orwellsatshiplake.co.uk
dir: A4155 to Binfield Heath, take Plough Lane to Shiplake Row, restaurant on left

On Shiplake Row, five minutes' drive out of Henley, Orwells has gone from strength to dazzling strength since Ryan Simpson and Liam Trotman opened here in 2010. It looks like a lovely 17th-century country pub from the outside, and indeed the interior makeover has achieved the best of compromises between the expected period features - low beams and exposed stone walls - and a relaxed modern feel. There is an informal pub dining

area, and also a room known cryptically as the Room, which used to be consecrated exclusively to the Tasting Menu, until demand for that grew to the extent that it overspilled the Room, and became available throughout. An internal window affords views of the kitchen team at work in its conservatory, an unusual arrangement for some unusual and glitteringly accomplished cooking. Local farmers, foragers and fisherman are the mainstays of the operation, their wares celebrated on the multi-course taster menus. A fine piece of crisp-skinned sea bass opens proceedings, served with minted peas and pickled veg in spicy laksa noodle soup, and is pursued to the table by a seared Lyme Bay scallop, surrounded by a complex array of parsnip, seaweed, pak choi and a verjus sauce of sultanas and spring onion. These opening statements are full of textural and flavour contrasts, bravura dishes that deliver on all levels. Main course might be pan-roasted middle rump of Angus beef, its velvet texture underpinned by accompaniments of oxtail, marrow, smoked bacon, liquorice, aubergine and peanut.

Dessert brings a moist sponge pudding, topped with caramel and spiced with ras el hanout. With four different home-made breads to go at from the outset, the class of Orwells runs from top to bottom.

Chef Ryan Simpson & Liam Trotman **Owner** Ryan Simpson & Liam Trotman **Times** 11.30-3/6.30-9.30 Closed 2 wks beg Jan, 1 wk Apr, 2 wks beg Sep, Mon, D Sun **Prices** Fixed L 2 course £10, Starter £5-£13, Main £12.50-£24, Dessert £6.50-£8, Service optional **Wines** 102 bottles over £20, 6 bottles under £20, 13 by glass **Notes** Tasting menu available, Sunday L, Vegetarian available **Seats** 60, Pr/dining room 20 **Children** Portions **Parking** 40

| MILTON COMMON | Map 5 SP60 |

The Oxfordshire

◉ Modern British

Delightful views and gently modish cooking

☎ 01844 278300
Rycote Ln OX9 2PU
e-mail: info@theoxfordshire.com
dir: From S M40 junct 7 onto A370 towards Thame. Hotel in right in 2m

Panoramic views from the Sakura restaurant's dining room are part of the attraction to this contemporary hotel in the heart of the Chilterns (handy for the M40, too). Alongside the Oxfordshire views, a golf course is a big draw for those who indulge, with the spa an attraction for one and all. In the restaurant, well-spaced tables are laid with smart modish crockery, with floor-to-ceiling windows and traditional furnishings creating a gently contemporary setting. The appealing menu delivers the likes of caramelised onion and mature cheddar tart with tomato and basil sauce and rocket, followed by braised blade of Oxfordshire beef with mashed potato, baby carrots, creamed spinach, wild mushrooms and red wine jus, and for dessert, strawberry champagne bavarois with ripple ice cream.

Chef Richard Bly **Owner** Paul Gibbons **Times** 6-9.30 Closed Xmas, New Year, D Sun **Prices** Fixed D 3 course £27.50-£35, Starter £5-£9.50, Main £16-£19.50, Dessert £6-£8, Service optional **Wines** 46 bottles over £20, 2 bottles under £20, 10 by glass **Notes** Vegetarian available, Dress restrictions, Smart casual **Seats** 50, Pr/dining room 40 **Parking**

| MURCOTT | Map 11 SP51 |

The Nut Tree Inn

◉◉ Modern European ⬥NOTABLE WINE LIST

Confident cooking in a pretty village inn

☎ 01865 331253
Main St OX5 2RE
e-mail: info@nuttreeinn.co.uk
dir: M40 junct 9. A34 towards Oxford, take 2nd exit for Islip. At Red Lion pub turn left, then 3rd right signposted Murcott

Propping up the bar of this chocolate-box pretty thatched 14th-century inn with a pint of real ale is a mighty inviting prospect, but chef-proprietor Mike North's assured cooking is the real draw at The Nut Tree. Deep in the historic Oxfordshire wetland of Otmoor, the inn stands idyllically in four acres populated by porkers and a donkey, overlooking the village pond; inside are stone walls, gnarled beams, wood-burning stoves, high-backed leather chairs, and upholstered benches in the cosy dining room, plus an airy conservatory extension decorated with modern art. The cooking is unfussy, precise and assured, squeezing every molecule of flavour from ingredients of exemplary - often wild or organic - provenance. Pan-fried terrine of pig's head and black pudding with sauerkraut, piccalilli dressing and a fried quail's egg is a typically gutsy starter; next out, there might be fillet of Cornish cod with oxtail cannelloni, braised leeks and horseradish velouté, and to finish, perhaps Green & Black's chocolate in a fondant with orange jelly, toasted almonds and cardamom ice cream.

Chef Michael North, Mary North **Owner** Michael North, Imogen North **Times** 12-2.30/7-9 Closed Mon, D Sun **Prices** Fixed L 2 course £18, Fixed D 2 course £18, Starter £8.50-£14, Main £17-£27, Dessert £6.50-£8, Service optional, Groups min 6 service 10% **Wines** 118 bottles over £20, 3 bottles under £20, 13 by glass **Notes** Tasting menu available Tue-Sat L & D, Sunday L, Vegetarian available **Seats** 70, Pr/dining room 36 **Children** Portions **Parking** 30

| OXFORD | Map 5 SP50 |

Ashmolean Dining Room

◉ Traditional, European

Good food and city views

☎ 01865 553823
Ashmolean Museum, Beaumont St OX1 2PH
e-mail: ashmolean@benugo.com
dir: Ashmolean Museum, 4th floor, opposite the Randolph Hotel

High on the museum's roof, this relative newcomer is a light and airy space, with a wooden floor, bare tables, and sliding doors giving on to a large terrace for summer dining and great cityscape views. The well-planned menu is built around fresh, seasonal produce, and the kitchen clearly knows what it's doing, sending out a simple but appetising starter of grilled squid marinated in lemon, garlic and smoked paprika, then generously sized lamb rump, accurately cooked, with black olive jus and roast vegetables, and lemon sole meunière. Grazers could choose a platter of seafood - cured herring, smoked salmon, and prawns, also served as a main course - or charcuterie, and a meal could end with a classic example of Paris-Brest.

Chef Alun Roberts **Owner** Benugo **Times** 10-6 Closed Mon, D all week **Prices** Food prices not confirmed for 2013. Please telephone for details **Wines** 8 bottles over £20, 7 bottles under £20, 15 by glass **Notes** Tue-Wed L close 5.30pm, Rooftop bar menu Thu-Fri until late, Sunday L, Vegetarian available **Seats** 100, Pr/dining room 18 **Children** Portions, Menu

---

Gee's Restaurant

◉ Modern European

Well-judged menu in handsome Victorian conservatory

☎ 01865 553540
61 Banbury Rd OX2 6PE
e-mail: info@gees-restaurant.co.uk
dir: N of city centre off A4165, from city centre right onto Banbury Rd, located just past Bevington Rd

The gastronomes of Oxford have loved Gee's for over 20 years, and little wonder when you take in the luminous Victorian conservatory space and colonial chic style of its chequerboard floor tiles, slatted window blinds, Lloyd Loom chairs and tables turned out in their best whites. The place runs as smoothly as clockwork with smart black-and-white clad staff serving upmarket contemporary brasserie food with its roots in classic dishes - stuffed pig's trotters, or rib-eye steak with parsley butter for example. Simple presentation and accurate cooking are hallmarks of ideas such as home-smoked salmon fishcakes served with buttered spinach and chervil beurre blanc, or saddle of rabbit wrapped in Parma ham with runner bean and artichoke salad. Lavender adds its fragrance to a crème brûlée at the end. On Sunday evenings the joint is jumping to the rhythms of live jazz.

Times 12-2.30/5.45-10.30 Closed 25-26 Dec

Jamie's Italian, Oxford

◉ Italian

Jamie does Oxford

☎ 01865 833150
24-26 George St OX1 2AE

Close to Oxford's main shopping drag, this outpost of the burgeoning chain is in a compact site which proves to be a bit of a Tardis. It looks the part, Jamie stylee, with lots of Italian produce used by way of decoration, and a central iron spiral staircase leading down to the main restaurant and its open-plan kitchen, exposed brick walls and colourful grafitti-style decoration. Expect rustic Italian dishes bigged up by Jamie-isms and well-sourced ingredients providing big, honest flavours. Antipasti planks are a good (and sharing) way to start, or try the 'famous' polenta chips, or Sicilian spaghetti fritters. Next up, maybe home-made pasta (wild rabbit tagliolini - slow-cooked ragù, with garlic and herbs, mascarpone and Amalfi lemon), or a main of 'Jamie's favourite' turkey Milanese stuffed with proscuitto and fontina cheese with a fried free-range egg and truffles.

Times noon-11

Save on Hotels. Book at **theAA.com/hotel**

OXFORDSHIRE 403 ENGLAND

Macdonald Randolph

◎◎ Traditional British

Classic Oxford dining experience

☎ 0844 879 9132 & 01865 256400
Beaumont St OX1 2LN
e-mail: foodservice.randolph@macdonald-hotels.co.uk
dir: M40 junct 8, A40 towards Oxford, follow city centre
signs, leads to St Giles, hotel on right

The Randolph is a flag-waving slice of Gothic Victorian
empire pomp that is as much an Oxford landmark as the
Ashmolean Museum opposite. Thanks to its TV
appearances as the watering hole of choice for Colin
Dexter's world-famous detective, Inspector Morse, a visit
to the oponymous bar is de rigueur for a pre-dinner before
you marvel at the grand staircase sweeping aloft from
the lobby, amid a fantasy of vaulted ceilings and oak
panelling. Cut from the same cloth as the grand London
hotels of yesteryear, the high-ceilinged baronial
restaurant is presided over by a maître d' who runs a
tight ship, directing a well-drilled team beneath walls
emblazoned with college shields. In tune with the old-
school vibe, the kitchen delivers British classics done
right, using top-class ingredients treated with care.
Smoked salmon from the trolley, served with mustard,
capers, shallots and crème fraîche is a time-honoured
way to start, followed by juicy slow-roasted pork belly,
which is served with perfect crunchy crackling, poached
apple as a foil to the rich sweetness of the pig, Anna
potato, and pork jus. Raspberry and vanilla pannacotta
with a sesame tuile is a surprisingly delicate way to end
proceedings.

Chef Tom Birks **Owner** Macdonald Hotels
Times 12-2.30/6.30 10 **Prices** Fixed L 2 course fr £21,
Fixed D 3 course fr £34.95, Starter £7.50-£11, Main
£13.50-£27.50, Dessert £7.95-£11.50, Service optional
Wines 100 bottles over £20, 15 by glass **Notes** Pre-
theatre menu 2 course & glass wine £19, Sunday L,
Vegetarian available, Dress restrictions, Smart casual,
Civ Wed 200 **Seats** 90, Pr/dining room 30
Children Portions, Menu **Parking** 50, (Chargeable - pre-
booking essential)

Malmaison Oxford

◎ Modern British & French 🍃

Egalitarian menu in former prison canteen

☎ 01865 268400
Oxford Castle, New Rd OX1 1AY
e-mail: oxford@malmaison.com
dir: M40 junct 9 (signed Oxford/A34). Follow A34 S to
Botley Interchange, then A420 to city centre

Hopefully the nearest you will ever get to a stay at Her
Majesty's pleasure is the Oxford outpost of the stylish
boutique chain. The city's former prison has been taken
into custody by the designers and is now leading a
reformed life as a classy hotel, with luxurious bedrooms
in the cells and a seductive, moodily-lit brasserie in the
old basement canteen. Cast-iron staircases and arched
doorways are an atmospheric reminder of its past, but
the vibe is now pure 21st-century pampering in shades of
chocolate brown and aubergine. The kitchen takes the
route of French brasserie classics given a modern British
spin, and there is no doubting the quality or freshness of
its supplies. Forget foams and fussiness, this is the world
of game terrine with pickles, and French onion soup
gratinée, followed by braised blade of beef and steamed
herb dumpling, or 35-day aged rump steaks straight from
the grill.

Chef Russell Heeley **Owner** MWB **Times** 12-2.30/6-10.30
Prices Tasting menu £45, Starter £5.95-£7.50, Main
£13.95-£24.95, Dessert £5.95-£9.95, Service added but
optional 10%, Groups min 6 service 10%
Wines 120 bottles over £20, 20 bottles under £20, 18 by
glass **Notes** Tasting menu with wine 5 course, pre-theatre
menu available, Sunday L, Vegetarian available, Civ Wed
110 **Seats** 100, Pr/dining room 35 **Children** Portions,
Menu **Parking** Worcester St, Westgate

Mercure Oxford Eastgate Hotel

◎ Modern British

Vibrant brasserie in an historic building

☎ 01865 248695
73 High St OX1 4BE
e-mail: h6668-fb1@accor.com
dir: A40 follow signs to Headington & Oxford city centre,
over Magdalen Bridge, stay in left lane, through lights,
left into Merton St, entrance to car park on left

There's a decidedly contemporary gloss to the High Table
Brasserie & Bar in the 17th-century building that houses
the Eastgate Hotel, which is indeed on the site of the
historic medieval East Gate into the city. It's close to all
the city-centre action these days. Grey banquette seating,
whitewashed walls, white-tiled flooring and bare wooden
tables set the scene, and on the menu is some smart

Mediterranean-influenced food. Start with hand-rolled
paccheri with butternut squash, black truffle emulsion,
sage and almond, follow on with pan-roasted Cornish
bass with braised puy lentils, celeriac and pear
remoulade and orange micro salad or, under a brasserie
classics sections, a burger or steak. Puds might run to
flaming five spice ice cream and apple compôte.

Chef Anthony Pitcher **Owner** MREF Trade Co
Times 12-2.30/6-9.30 **Prices** Fixed L 2 course £10.95,
Tasting menu £55, Starter £4.75-£8.50, Main £9.95-
£17.50, Dessert £3.95-£6.50, Service added but optional
12.5%, Groups min 6 service 12.5% **Wines** 11 bottles
over £20, 8 bottles under £20, 13 by glass **Notes** Tasting
menu 12 course, Veg 10 course £25, 24 hrs notice req,
Sunday L, Vegetarian available, Dress restrictions, Smart
casual **Seats** 70, Pr/dining room 8 **Children** Portions,
Menu **Parking** 40, Parking charges apply

Old Parsonage Restaurant

◎ Traditional British 🍃

Broadly appealing menu in a charming setting

☎ 01865 292305 & 310210
The Old Parsonage Hotel, 1 Banbury Rd OX2 6NN
e-mail: restaurant@oldparsonage-hotel.co.uk
dir: M40 junct 8, A40. Right onto ring road, 1st left into
Banbury Rd. Hotel & restaurant on right just before St
Giles Church

With bags of old-world style, the luxurious 17th-century
Old Parsonage Hotel is close to the University College
Press and Keble, St John and Somerville colleges. If you
don't fancy the alfresco option of the wisteria-clad walled
terrace (live jazz on Wednesday evenings), go for the
bohemian club-like environs of the restaurant. Its dark
red walls are covered in original cartoons, tables are all
dressed up, and the service is young and enthusiastic.
Some of the seasonal British ingredients on the menu
come from the owners' farm nearby. The unfussy, clearly-
focused combinations hit the spot; lobster and saffron
soup, for example, followed by roast chicken with new
season garlic and lemon, or the Old Parsonage steak
sandwich and chips. To finish, custard tart and poached
rhubarb competes with fruit fool and shortbread. A major
refurbishment is planned in 2013.

Chef Alicia Storey **Owner** Jeremy Mogford
Times 12-2/6-10.30 **Prices** Fixed L 2 course £15.95, Fixed
D 3 course £34.50-£44.50, Starter £6.50-£11.95, Main
£13.95-£23.50, Dessert £6.50-£7, Service added but
optional 12.5% **Wines** 42 bottles over £20, 8 bottles
under £20, 26 by glass **Notes** Pre-theatre 2 course
£15.95, 3 course £18.95 5.45-7pm, Sunday L, Vegetarian
available, Civ Wed 65 **Seats** 75, Pr/dining room 16
Children Portions, Menu **Parking** 16, Metered parking in
road opposite

OXFORD *continued*

The Oxford Hotel

Modern British

Innovative cooking in modern hotel restaurant

☎ 01865 489988
Gidstow Rd, Wolvercote Roundabout OX2 8AL
e-mail: oxford@pumahotels.co.uk
dir: A34 Peartree junct, follow signs to A40, take 4th exit at rdbt

A couple of miles from the city centre, The Oxford is a modern hotel with a full range of conference and leisure facilities - and a bright and spacious first-floor restaurant, where smartly dressed staff are friendly and chatty. The menu is a slate of modern ideas, and the kitchen pulls together some intriguing combinations: a terrine of confit duck and cherries with tea-smoked breast and sour cherries, say, followed by stuffed wood pigeon with pea and ham cream and baby vegetables. Fish options may extend to crisply crumbed smoked haddock and spring onion fishcake with properly made tartare sauce, and a beautifully cooked fillet of sea bream with pak choi, citrus potatoes and crisp fennel, tomato chutney adding a good foil to the last component. Among desserts might be dark chocolate truffle torte with caramelised hazelnuts, the plate scattered with sea salt.

Times 7-9.30 Closed L all week

STADHAMPTON   Map 5 SU69

The Crazy Bear

Modern British

Charming 16th-century inn with some fine cooking

☎ 01865 890714
Bear Ln OX44 7UR
e-mail: enquiries@crazybear-stadhampton.co.uk
web: www.crazybeargroup.co.uk
dir: M40 junct 7, A329. In 4m left after petrol station, left into Bear Lane

With a name like that, The Crazy Bear is never going to be an identikit country inn. Accordingly, quirky character runs to the heart of this sprawling set-up in a 16th-century pub, remodelled to combine eclectic design with splendid gardens, an up-tempo vibe and great food, whether it comes from the English or Thai (see separate entry for the latter) side of the culinary fence. Candy-pink and crimson high-backed chairs, buttoned cream leather walls, crystal chandeliers, leopard-print floors, and a novel - if rather worrying - wine storage solution that racks bottles overhead certainly adds up to a setting of eclectic theatricality. A wide-ranging all-day menu of modern dishes covers most bases, and it's all commendably local (as local as meat and veg from the Crazy Bear farm) and seasonal. First out is charred squid pil-pil with home-cured pancetta, coriander and chilli, followed by rack and rump of the Bear's own lamb, served with pan-roasted potato, peas and beans. Pudding brings a bar of salted butter caramel with peanuts and

pistachios, teamed with dark chocolate sorbet and a peanut and popcorn wafer.

Times 12-10

Thai Thai at The Crazy Bear

Modern Thai

Thai cooking in an old coaching inn

☎ 01865 890714
The Crazy Bear, Bear Ln OX44 7UR
e-mail: enquiries@crazybear-stadhampton.co.uk
web: www.crazybeargroup.co.uk
dir: M40 junct 7, A329. In 4m left after petrol station, left into Bear Lane

A 16th-century coaching inn in sleepy Oxfordshire countryside is not the sort of place one might expect to find a Thai restaurant, less still one that wears the costume of a velvet-sheathed Bedouin boudoir. But The Crazy Bear has never been one for toeing the line. The funky scene is set by etched brass and copper tables, a mirror-panelled ceiling, fretwork screens and bronze velvet banquettes, or on a fine day, move out to the oasis and dine to the music of birdsong and running water at a table in the garden. The cooking is an enticing blend of pukka Thai classics and fusion dishes that bring together western and Pan-Asian ideas. Tom yam kung yai is a soup of king prawns, mushrooms, lemongrass, galangal, chillies and lime that falls into the former category, while mains sees crispy sea bream fillets paired with hot-and-sour sauce and Thai basil; a meaty option could be pot-roasted ox cheek with braised lettuce, shiitaki mushrooms, spring onions and roasted garlic. See entry above for the English dining option.

Times 12-3/6-12 Closed L Sun

SWINBROOK   Map 10 SP21

The Swan Inn

Modern British

Historic village inn with locally-sourced ingredients

☎ 01993 823339
OX18 4DY
e-mail: info@theswanswinbrook.co.uk
dir: A40 towards Cheltenham, turn left to Swinbrook

On the borders of Oxfordshire and Gloucestershire, this quintessential village pub, with an apple orchard to the rear and the Windrush River running by, takes the food-side of the operation seriously. It's owned by the Dowager Duchess of Devonshire and there is interesting memorabilia around the place relating to the Mitford sisters, including canvas prints of family portraits. Seasonal ingredients are sourced with care (traceability is a big deal here), and the fine produce turns up in dishes such as plum tomato and mozzarella tartlet with rocket and pesto, followed by confit belly of Cotswold lamb with spring vegetables, capers and mint, or locally-reared Aberdeen Angus steaks served with horseradish cream, green beans and skinny chips.

Times 12-2/7-9 Closed 25-26 Dec

TOOT BALDON   Map 5 SP50

The Mole Inn

Modern European

Big flavours at a top-class dining pub

☎ 01865 340001
OX44 9NG
e-mail: info@themoleinn.com
dir: 5m S of Oxford, restaurant 15 mins from M40 junct 7

The 300-year-old Mole Inn has been transformed into a smartly-attired dining pub that draws foodies on the short drive out from the city centre to the superbly-named hamlet of Toot Baldon. The postcard-pretty honey-stone country pub brings together the best of ancient and modern in a tasteful blend of wood and terracotta floors, bare stone and brick walls, age-worn timbers, chunky rustic tables, leather chairs and chocolate-brown sofas. The cooking has moved up a gear too, delivering dishes of assured, unpretentious modern cooking. Sautéed lamb's kidneys with devilled jus and roasted garlic makes a suitably full-on starter, while mains could be as rooted into the Oxfordshire landscape as slow-braised blade of local beef with parsnip purée, truffled mushrooms and potatoes, or as infused with Mediterranean sunshine as roast cod teamed with Amalfi lemon, and olive oil baked potatoes with soft herbs and spinach. Pudding could be a thumb-sucking treat such as treacle tart with Carnation milk ice cream.

Chef Gary Witchalls **Owner** Gary Witchalls
Times 12-2.30/7-9.30 Closed 25 Dec **Prices** Fixed L 2 course £14.95, Fixed D 3 course £18.95, Starter £5.95-£7.95, Main £13.50-£22.50, Dessert £6.50, Service optional **Wines** 21 bottles over £20, 13 bottles under £20, 8 by glass **Notes** Sunday L, Vegetarian available **Seats** 70 **Children** Portions, Menu **Parking** 40

WALLINGFORD   Map 5 SU68

The Partridge

Modern French

Refined modern cooking in converted pub

☎ 01491 825005
32 St Mary's St OX10 0ET
e-mail: contact@partridge-inn.com
dir: From M40 junct 6, B4009, follow Wallingford signs through Watlington to Benson. A4074 to rdbt. Right through Crowmarsh Gifford to Wallingford

Just away from the centre of the charming town, near the Thames, The Partridge is a gastro-pub of some style, with boldly patterned wallpaper, bare bricks and leather-look sofas. The cooking, based on the classical repertory, is highly crafted and ambitious, as seen in skilfully made and elegantly presented starters of ballottine of quail, with veal sweetbreads, morels, fig compôte and a soft-boiled quail's egg, and seared scallops with caramelised cauliflower mash, pea shoots, Avruga caviar and lemongrass. Main courses can be as modish as sea bass with crispy pig's trotter, roast beetroot and celeriac and as straight and true as pink-roast rump of lamb with a

Save on Hotels. Book at **theAA.com/hotel**

OXFORDSHIRE 405 **ENGLAND**

deeply flavoured jus accompanied by minted pea purée and fondant potato. Properly made soufflés get the thumbs up: hazelnut and Nutella, say, or coconut with a matching mousse and mango sorbet.

Chef José Cau **Owner** José Cau **Times** 12-2.30/6-9.30 Closed D Sun **Prices** Fixed L 2 course fr £13.95, Fixed D 3 course fr £19.95, Starter £7.80-£12, Main £14.50-£22.95, Dessert £6.50, Groups min 6 service 10% **Wines** 85 bottles over £20, 23 bottles under £20, 9 by glass **Notes** Fixed L menu available £10, menu Gourmand, Sunday L, Vegetarian available, Dress restrictions, Smart casual **Seats** 50 **Children** Portions

The Springs Hotel & Golf Club

⚲ Modern British **V** ✋

Gentle country-house cooking and lakeside views

☏ 01491 836687
Wallingford Rd, North Stoke OX10 6BE
e-mail: info@thespringshotel.com
web: www.thespringshotel.com
dir: Edge of village of North Stoke

The Tudor-style timbered façade of this house in the glorious Oxfordshire countryside is actually a faithful Victorian copy. Set in landscaped gardens with a spring-fed lake (hence the name), The Springs Hotel now trades as a tranquil golf-oriented bolt-hole, and its Lakeside Restaurant is looking spruce after a makeover in 2012 brought in bare wooden floors and contemporary hues of beige and deep purple (in honour of a former rock band connection). Gently modernised country-house classics are the order of the day here - perhaps pan-fried pigeon breast with caramelised apple and black pudding, and redcurrant jus, followed by chargrilled rump steak with hand-cut chips, roasted tomato and garlic mayonnaise, or grilled whole Cornish plaice with roasted new potatoes, fine beans, sun-blushed tomatoes, and pesto dressing. End with sticky toffee pudding with treacle ice cream.

Chef Paul Franklin **Owner** Lakeside Restaurant **Times** 12-2/6.30-9.45 **Prices** Fixed L 2 course fr £13.50, Fixed D 3 course fr £27.50, Service optional **Wines** 30 bottles over £20, 21 bottles under £20, 7 by glass **Notes** Sunday L, Vegetarian menu, Dress restrictions, Civ Wed 60 **Seats** 80, Pr/dining room 30 **Children** Portions, Menu **Parking** 150

WITNEY Map 5 SP31

The Restaurant at Witney Lakes Resort

⚲ Modern European ✋

Simple brasserie cooking at an Oxfordshire resort

☏ 01993 893012 & 893000
Downs Rd OX29 0SY
e-mail: restaurant@witney-lakes.co.uk
dir: 2m W of Witney town centre, off B4047 Witney to Burford road

The Resort does spa treatments, golf and weddings, among other things, in a low-slung complex of buildings made from imported Finnish wood. In the restaurant, background jazz murmurs, yuccas stand in tall pots and relaxed staff sashay among the bare-topped tables, while guests take in the views of fountain and fairway. The cooking keeps things simple most of the time, with smoked mackerel and potato salad, pâtés, soups, fishcakes, pork faggots, and sirloin and chips with peppercorn or béarnaise sauces, but Thursday night is Foodie night, when things get a little more enterprising. Roast rump and breast of lamb with peas, onions and wild garlic on a spring menu, for example, followed by variations on rhubarb - millefeuille, ice cream and jelly.

Chef Sean Parker, Owen Little **Owner** Sean Parker **Times** 12-3/6-9 Closed 25 & 31 Dec, 1 Jan, L Sat, D Sun-Mon **Prices** Fixed L 2 course £12-£15, Fixed D 3 course £23-£26, Service optional **Wines** 19 bottles over £20, 19 bottles under £20, 6 by glass **Notes** Themed evenings, Sunday L, Vegetarian available, Civ Wed 50 **Seats** 75 **Children** Portions, Menu **Parking** 400

WOODCOTE Map 5 SU68

Woody Nook at Woodcote

⚲ British, International **V**

International flavours and top-notch Australian wines

☏ 01491 680775
Goring Rd RG8 0SD
e-mail: info@woodynookatwoodcote.co.uk
dir: Opposite village green

A quick glance at the menu shows kangaroo, barramundi, king crab and Pavlova, so there are no prizes for spotting the Aussie connection at this cottage restaurant overlooking the village green and cricket pitch. Named after the owners' award-winning boutique winery in the Margaret River region of Western Australia, whose products feature prominently on the wine list, it is a thoroughly English setting with low beams and a cosy, rustic vibe within, and a delightfully flowery alfresco terrace for fine days. Food-wise, the deal is an eclectic international array of ideas, kicking off, perhaps, with truffle ravioli with vine tomato sauce, herb oil and parmesan shavings, while roast butternut squash, black pudding and juniper berry jus might be the accompaniments to a main course venison loin. The Australian national pudding is Pavlova, so why not go along with the theme - it is served here with Chantilly cream, and kiwi, passionfruit and mango coulis.

Chef Stuart Shepherd **Owner** Jane & Peter Bailey **Times** 12-2.30/7-9.30 Closed Xmas, Mon-Tue, D Sun **Prices** Food prices not confirmed for 2013. Please telephone for details **Wines** 23 bottles over £20, 5 bottles under £20, 8 by glass **Notes** Sunday L, Vegetarian menu **Seats** 50 **Children** Portions **Parking** 25

WOODSTOCK Map 11 SP41

The Feathers Hotel

⚲⚲ Modern British ✋

Bold design and imaginative cooking (and gin)

☏ 01993 812291
Market St OX20 1SX
e-mail: enquiries@feathers.co.uk
web: www.feathers.co.uk
dir: From A44 (Oxford to Woodstock), 1st left after lights. Hotel on left

A feature in the historic Cotswold market town of Woodstock since the 17th century, The Feathers carries itself in a thoroughly modish manner these days, for this is boutique hotel territory, blending the indisputable traditional charms of the old building with a stylish contemporary sheen. The dining room, split into two on quiet nights, has crisp white line-clad tables with silver cutlery and sparkling glassware - a suitable setting for the refined modern British cooking courtesy of the team in the kitchen. Much is made of seasonality and locality in dishes such as confit foie gras (served on a square glass plate if you care for such details) with celeriac, pear, and quince jam, followed by a rustic, meltingly tender Longhorn beef (cooked sous-vide) with shallot pickle and red wine jus. Clementine cheesecake with oatmeal and orange jelly is typical of desserts. The gin bar is worth a visit, with over 100 varieties on offer, or, if you're up to it, there's the 'gin experience' tasting menu, where a different gin is paired with or appears in each of the seven courses.

Chef Kevin Barrett **Owner** Empire Ventures Ltd **Times** 12.30-2/7.10-9.30 **Prices** Fixed L 2 course £39.95-£49.95, Fixed D 3 course £49.95, Service added but optional 10% **Wines** 180+ bottles over £20, 30 bottles under £20, 16 by glass **Notes** Tasting menu available, Sunday L, Vegetarian available, Dress restrictions, No shorts or T-shirts **Seats** 40, Pr/dining room 24 **Children** Portions, Menu **Parking** On street

WOODSTOCK *continued*

Kings Arms Hotel

◉ Modern British

Stylishly revamped Georgian hotel

☎ 01993 813636
19 Market St OX20 1SU
e-mail: stay@kingshotelwoodstock.co.uk
dir: In town centre, on corner of Market St & A44

A stylish contemporary facelift blends seamlessly with the splendid period character of this lovely Georgian hotel right in the thick of Woodstock's bustle. When you have the posh neighbours in Blenheim Palace at the end of the street, you have to dress to impress, and the Atrium restaurant sports a sharp contemporary look: chunky wooden tables and black high-backed chairs sit on a black-and-white chequerboard floor, and there are original artworks and huge antique mirrors with rococo frames. On the menu are familiar combinations of quality ingredients celebrating classic as well as unpretentious modern ideas. You might find mushroom and ham Charlotte with oven-roasted tomatoes alongside a straight-up crayfish cocktail, while mains bring braised beef and onions with bubble-and-squeak as well as baked cod wrapped in bacon with butternut squash purée, parsley duchess potatoes and watercress cream.

Chef Brian Arnold **Owner** David & Sara Sykes
Times 12-2.30/6.30-9.30 **Prices** Starter £4.75-£9.50, Main £8.50-£21.75, Dessert £4.75-£7.75, Service optional, Groups min 10 service 10% **Wines** 20 bottles over £20, 15 bottles under £20, 13 by glass **Notes** Sunday L, Vegetarian available **Seats** 80 **Children** Portions **Parking** On street

Macdonald Bear Hotel

◉◉ Modern European

Accomplished modern cooking in medieval hotel

☎ 0844 879 9143
Park St OX20 1SZ
e-mail: bear@macdonald-hotels.co.uk
dir: M40 junct 9 follow signs for Oxford & Blenheim Palace. A44 to town centre, hotel on left

Woodstock is not without its complement of attractive old buildings, and this creeper-covered hotel is one of them. Inside, evidence of the great age of the property is seen in the beams, stone walls and fireplaces in the traditional-looking dining rooms. The kitchen, though, keeps abreast of matters culinary, producing starters of pan-fried scallops with pancetta and sweet potato purée, and a pressing of flavourful ham with beetroot carpaccio and apple foam. Beef and lamb are reared in Scotland and may turn up as sirloin steak with a rich red wine sauce. Finish with zesty lemon and lime tart. As we go to press, Alan Murchison's 10 in 8 Group are due to revamp the restaurant and add the Bear to their slate of glossy fine-dining establishments.

Times 12.30-2/7-9.30

RUTLAND

CLIPSHAM   Map 11 SK91

The Olive Branch

◉◉ British, European V ✆

Refined modern pub dishes in a charming village inn

☎ 01780 410355
Main St LE15 7SH
e-mail: info@theolivebranchpub.com
dir: 2m from A1 at Stretton junct, 5m N of Stamford

Converted into a pub from a row of three cottages back in the Victorian era, today's Olive Branch satisfies on every level. They serve a fine pint of beer here for a start, plus offer a good range of wines, and even go as far as making their own lemonade and sloe gin. There is equal passion in the delivery of food, which can sort you out for a proper sandwich (minute steak with caramelised onions, perhaps), something traditional such as fish and chips with minted peas and tomato sauce, or a more restauranty dish like honey-roast pork belly with cider fondant. Whatever you eat, the produce is most likely local and, rather like the décor, the presentation has that appealing blend of slick rusticity. And in the true inn tradition, if you want to stay over, there are some charming rooms at your disposal.

Chef Sean Hope **Owner** Sean Hope, Ben Jones
Times 12-2/7-9.30 Closed D 25 Dec **Prices** Fixed L 2 course £16.95, Fixed D 3 course £24.50, Starter £5.50-£10.95, Main £12.95-£21.50, Dessert £4.95-£6.95, Service optional, Groups min 12 service 10%
Wines 40 bottles over £20, 10 bottles under £20, 15 by glass **Notes** Sat afternoon menu available 2.30-5.30, Sunday L, Vegetarian menu **Seats** 45, Pr/dining room 20 **Children** Portions, Menu **Parking** 15

OAKHAM   Map 11 SK80

Barnsdale Lodge Hotel

◉ Modern British

Regionally-based cooking by Rutland Water

☎ 01572 724678
The Avenue, Rutland Water, North Shore LE15 8AH
e-mail: enquiries@barnsdalelodge.co.uk
web: www.barnsdalelodge.co.uk
dir: Turn off A1 at Stamford onto A606 to Oakham. Hotel 5m on right. (2m E of Oakham)

Thomas Noel's family have owned Barnsdale Lodge since 1760, and who can blame them for putting down roots in this splendid spot - it was once part of Exton Park, the seat of the Earls of Gainsborough - on the north shore of Rutland Water. Since 1989, the Lodge has earned a crust as a small-scale, easygoing country hotel with a dinky spa and quietly stylish interior kitted out with old-school squidgy sofas blending with pastel-hued contemporary elegance. The cooking is on the money, too - produce is hauled in from the kitchen garden and farms in the surrounding area to create simple, seasonal menus that wouldn't look out of place in a slick city brasserie. Expect the likes of smoked haddock risotto with a duck egg and rocket followed by roast Grasmere Farm pork chop with sautéed kale and a mixed bean and sausage casserole, or pan-fried hake with leek and prawn hash, mixed greens and pesto.

Chef Steve Conway **Owner** The Hon Thomas Noel
Times 12-2.15/7-9.30 **Prices** Food prices not confirmed for 2013. Please telephone for details **Wines** 45 bottles over £20, 33 bottles under £20, 10 by glass
Notes Vegetarian available **Seats** 120, Pr/dining room 50 **Children** Portions, Menu **Parking** 250

Hambleton Hall

◉◉◉◉ *– see opposite*

Save on Hotels. Book at **theAA.com/hotel**

RUTLAND 407 ENGLAND

Hambleton Hall

Modern British V ⬥NOTABLE WINE LIST

Superb fine-dining in majestic country-house hotel

☎ 01572 756991
Hambleton LE15 8TH
e-mail: hotel@hambletonhall.com
web: www.hambletonhall.com
dir: 8m W of A1 Stamford junct (A606), 3m E of Oakham

The 1970s was a big decade for this one-time Victorian hunting lodge: first off, a reservoir was built on its doorstep in '76, courtesy of Anglian Water, which is now the magnificent Rutland Water Nature Reserve; and Tim and Stefa Hart bought the house in '79 and gave it a new lease of life as a splendid country-house hotel. It is truly a magnificent spot, sitting amid rolling green hills, and surrounded by handsomely manicured gardens. It comes as no surprise that the owners, manager and chef have all clocked up years of service here - who would want to leave? Stefa Hart is responsible for the interior design of the hotel and jolly fabulous it looks too, with fine period details and furniture, and a soothing elegance that fits the house to a T. The two dining rooms are no less glamorous with splendid chandeliers, oil paintings, and tables dressed with reassuring formality, while the service team glides around with charm and confidence. Aaron Patterson has headed up the kitchen since 1992,

and not for one moment has he stood still in that time. The kitchen's output is refined, intelligent and modern, but never fussy or overblown, with wonderful ingredients at the heart of everything, and as such the seasons lead the way. Canapés in the elegant bar is a lovely start to proceedings (beetroot meringue topped with goats' cheese among them, perhaps), while the hotel has its own bakery down the road from whence come the superb breads that pitch up at the table. The langoustines which appear in a first course with braised pork belly and rhubarb are delivered to Hambleton alive from Scotland - a beautifully balanced plate it is too. Cornish crab might come in a salad with potatoes and mango, alongside an ice cream made from the brown meat, or there's a wonderfully light salad made from vegetables from the garden, dressed in a truffle oil vinaigrette. Tronçon of turbot comes with variations of onion - purée, spring onions, bhaji and pannacotta - and two fried quail's eggs in a delightful main course, along with both hollandaise sauce and truffled mash served in accompanying copper dishes and ready to join in at your pleasure. There are fashionable ideas among desserts, too: a terrine of pear and blackberry, for example, is partnered with a doughnut, salted caramel and caramel ice cream. If all of the above is not proof enough of the attention to detail and passion on display here, reading the wine list will confirm that Hambleton is a major player in the UK dining scene, and,

if you need a little help with it, sommelier Dominique Baduel is on hand with plenty of good advice.

Chef Aaron Patterson **Owner** Mr T Hart **Times** 12-2/7-9.30 **Prices** Fixed L 2 course fr £22, Fixed D 3 course £38.50-£47.50, Starter £14.75-£26, Main £34-£39, Dessert £15-£17, Service added but optional 12.5% **Wines** 375 bottles over £20, 10 bottles under £20, 10 by glass **Notes** Tasting menu available, Sunday L, Vegetarian menu, Dress restrictions, Smart dress, no jeans, T-shirts or trainers, Civ Wed 64 **Seats** 60, Pr/dining room 20 **Children** Portions, Menu **Parking** 40

UPPINGHAM
Map 11 SP89

The Lake Isle

◉◉ British, French

Georgian townhouse hotel with confident cooking

☎ 01572 822951
16 High Street East LE15 9PZ
e-mail: info@lakeisle.co.uk
web: www.lakeisle.co.uk
dir: M1 junct 19 to A14 Kettering, at rdbt take A43 signed
Corby and then A6003 to Rockingham/Uppingham.
Continue to pedestrian lights Uppingham, right onto High
St, Lake Isle on right after the Square

Named for W. B. Yeats' *Lake Isle of Innisfree*, the hope is
that visitors will experience a similar feeling of
tranquillity in this Georgian townhouse with rooms in the
lovely market town of Uppingham. On a pleasingly
intimate scale, with a large window looking out onto the
high street, inside there are panelled walls and original
mahogany fittings, plus simply laid, heavy wooden tables
attended by the friendly and efficient service team.
French influences are in evidence on the broadly British
menu, which changes every six weeks to keep flow with
the seasons. There are some smart flavour combinations
on show; take a starter of grilled medallion (well, fillet) of
south coast mackerel with crispy ham, bitter leaves,
sautéed potatoes and a punchy piccalilli dressing. The
quality of the lamb is indisputable in a duo including
pan-roasted rack and medallion of braised shoulder,
served with creamed celeriac, Savoy cabbage and
pancetta. Then, sit back and wait while the dark
chocolate and baby pear fondant pudding (served with
stem ginger ice cream) is cooked to order.

Chef Stuart Mead **Owner** Richard & Janine Burton
Times 12-2.30/7-9 Closed 26 Dec-1 Jan, L Mon, D Sun
Prices Starter £6.75-£7.50, Main £13.50-£17.95, Dessert
£6.25-£7.75, Service optional **Wines** 155 bottles over
£20, 18 bottles under £20, 15 by glass **Notes** Sunday L,
Vegetarian available, Dress restrictions, Smart casual
preferred **Seats** 40, Pr/dining room 16 **Parking** 6, P&D car
park adjacent

WING
Map 11 SK80

Kings Arms Inn & Restaurant

◉◉ Modern British 🍃

Supplier-led hearty cooking in a traditional inn

☎ 01572 737634
13 Top St LE15 8SE
e-mail: info@thekingsarms-wing.co.uk
dir: 1m off A6003, between Oakham & Uppingham

Not many village inns can say that they have their own
smokehouse, produce their own charcuterie, bake the
bread and generally make everything from jams to
chutneys to sauces the hard way, from scratch. Amid the
flagstone floors, low-beamed ceilings and open fires of
the classic rustic interior you may also spot the map
where local suppliers are proudly pinpointed. It all adds
up to a deep commitment to real food at the Kings Arms,
a 17th-century gem in a photogenic village near Rutland
Water. Whether you stay in the bar with the ranks of
splendid real ales and cider, or settle in the relaxed
dining room, you can expect generous, big-hearted
cooking with strong flavours from a kitchen that takes its
work seriously. Home-smoked eel with horseradish potato
salad, rocket and soft-boiled egg shows the no-nonsense
style, while mains bring loin, liver and chipolata of local
venison with juniper fondant, butternut purée and
elderberry jus, or tournedos of hare loin wrapped in the
in-house air-dried ham and teamed with red cabbage,
sautéed potatoes and celeriac purée.

Chef James Goss **Owner** David, Gisa & James Goss
Times 12-2.30/6.30-9 Closed Mon, L Tue (Nov-Apr), D
Sun **Prices** Starter £6-£12.50, Main £9.50-£22, Dessert
£6-£20, Service optional, Groups min 7 service 10%
Wines 20 bottles over £20, 28 bottles under £20, 20 by
glass **Notes** Sunday L, Vegetarian available **Seats** 38, Pr/
dining room 24 **Children** Portions, Menu **Parking** 30

SHROPSHIRE

BRIDGNORTH
Map 10 SO79

Old Vicarage Hotel and Restaurant

◉◉ British, European

**Classic combinations in a conservatory-style hotel
dining room**

☎ 01746 716497
Hallow, Worfield WV15 5JZ
e-mail: admin@oldvicarageworfield.com
dir: Off A454, approx 3.5m NE of Bridgnorth, 5m S of
Telford on A442, follow brown signs

Perfectly positioned, in Worfield, to enjoy the rolling
Shropshire countryside, yet not far from Bridgnorth and
Telford, the Old Vicarage is the kind of hotel that aims to
cover all bases, from business conferences to country
nuptials. An expansive conservatory-style dining room
looking out over the gardens is filled with daylight on
sunny days, and is the setting for cooking that aims for
classic combinations, both old and new. For starters
could be smoked salmon served warm, with rye bread and
horseradish cream, or goats' cheese with baked beetroot,
walnuts and endive. Neck end of local lamb, braised to
tenderness, and served with pearl barley and sweet-and-
sour red cabbage, makes an impressive main course, or
there may be fillet of sea rout with roasted fennel in
tomato vinaigrette. Rhubarb turns up in a dessert with
sweet wine jelly and orange ice cream.

Times 12-2.30/7-9.30 Closed L Mon-Tue, Sat-Sun (by
reservation only), D 24-26 Dec

CHURCH STRETTON
Map 15 SO49

The Pound at Leebotwood

◉ Modern British 🍃

Reworked pub cooking in a thatched 15th-century inn

☎ 01694 751477
Leebotwood SY6 6ND
e-mail: info@thepound.org.uk
dir: On A49, 9m S of Shrewsbury

A thatched country pub on the A49 near Shrewsbury, The
Pound is a former drovers' watering-hole dating from the
Plantagenet era. Inside, the dining room done out in
assertive primary colours with modern artworks is the
uplifting setting for some decent pub cooking inflected
with modern treatments. Gingerbread-crusted smoked
salmon with cucumber and wasabi mayonnaise is
certainly a modern reworking, but mains ply a more
traditional line for whole grilled plaice with garlic butter,
burgers with cheese, bacon and chilli, or 28-day aged
sirloin with chips, a roast flat mushroom and a choice of
sauces. Finish with spiced apple crumble and vanilla ice
cream, or local cheeses with onion and balsamic relish.

Save on Hotels. Book at theAA.com/hotel

SHROPSHIRE 409 ENGLAND

Chef John Williams **Owner** John & Debbie Williams
Times 12-2.30/6-9 Closed Mon, D Sun **Prices** Food prices not confirmed for 2013. Please telephone for details **Wines** 15 bottles over £20, 26 bottles under £20, 9 by glass **Notes** Sunday L, Vegetarian available **Seats** 60 **Children** Portions **Parking** 60

The Studio

🏵 British, French

Homely village restaurant with a local flavour

☎ 01694 722672
59 High St SY6 6BY
e-mail: info@thestudiorestaurant.net
dir: Off A49 to town, left at T-junct onto High St, 300yds on left

A swinging palette sign greets customers at this erstwhile artist's studio on the high street. The arty theme continues indoors in a stylish room of summery yellow and exposed stone walls hung with artworks and ceramic pieces spread around; on mild summer evenings (this is a dinner-only operation) there's a delicious pocket-sized patio garden overlooking the Shropshire hills for alfresco dining. Run with considerable charm by chef-patrons Tony and Sheila Martland, the culinary focus is broadly modern British, unpretentious dishes with plenty of local input, although that doesn't preclude pan-fried scallops as a starter (since Shropshire is not known for its shellfish), served with smoked salmon, and white wine, mustard and cheese velouté. Local Mortimer Forest venison could star in a main course, partnered by red cabbage, pickled pears, and a blackberry and port wine jus. Sheila's warm ginger parkin with poached rhubarb, vanilla ice cream and butterscotch sauce is a fortifying finale.

Chef Tony Martland **Owner** Tony & Sheila Martland
Times 7-9 Closed 2 wks Jan, 1 wk Apr, 1 wk Nov, Sun-Tue, L all week **Prices** Food prices not confirmed for 2013. Please telephone for details **Wines** 13 bottles over £20, 27 bottles under £20, 6 by glass **Notes** Vegetarian available, Dress restrictions, Smart casual **Seats** 34 **Children** Portions **Parking** On street parking available

GRINSHILL   Map 15 SJ52

The Inn at Grinshill

🏵🏵 Modern British 🥄

Village coaching inn with modish menu

☎ 01939 220410 & 07730 066451
High St SY4 3BL
e-mail: info@theinnatgrinshill.co.uk
dir: 7m N of Shrewsbury towards Whitchurch on A49

This particular inn is a Georgian coaching one that now trades as a 21st-century restaurant with rooms near to Shrewsbury in the foodie heartlands of Shropshire. The place throws its arms open to all comers - if you're turning up with muddy boots off the local hills, the pubby Elephant and Castle bar should hit the spot, or the slick Bubbles Bar is the place to start when you're looking for a glass of pre-dinner fizz. In the unstuffy contemporary restaurant, an open hatch lets you keep tabs on the talented young kitchen team as they turn out sophisticated country-pub cooking. The menu lists the components of each dish with no clue to treatments. A starter wraps pheasant confit, prunes and pancetta in a ravioli parcel, teamed with wilted spinach and truffled celeriac purée, while main course serves braised shoulder of lamb with green olive-crumbed loin, goats' cheese tortellini and baby plum tomatoes. It is all inventive stuff, all the way through to a dessert of coconut parfait with caramelised banana and chocolate and pecan macaroon.

Chef Chris Conde, David Brazier **Owner** Kevin & Victoria Brazier **Times** 12-2.30/6.30-9.30 Closed Mon, D Sun **Prices** Fixed L 2 course fr £29.50, Fixed D 3 course fr £35.50, Service optional **Wines** 40 bottles over £20, 5 bottles under £20, 10 by glass **Notes** Sunday L, Vegetarian available **Seats** 80, Pr/dining room 40 **Children** Portions **Parking** 35

HADNALL   Map 15 SJ52

Saracens at Hadnall

🏵🏵 Modern British 🥄

Upbeat cooking at village restaurant with rooms

☎ 01939 210877
Shrewsbury Rd SY4 4AG
e-mail: reception@saracensathadnall.co.uk
dir: M54 onto A5, at junct of A5/A49 take A49 towards Whitchurch. Follow A49 to Hadnall, diagonally opposite church

This charming restaurant with rooms, a Grade II listed Georgian coaching inn, has two dining rooms, a contemporary-looking one incorporating a feature stone fireplace and beams, and a conservatory with a 40-foot-deep well. The kitchen is not short on confidence and technical expertise, turning out starters like smoked haddock fishcake with crabmeat and cress and citrus salad, and warm tea-smoked chicken breast with gingered celeriac remoulade, pak choi and mushrooms. Main courses give plenty of choice, from accurately grilled cod fillet with classic Mornay sauce, leeks and parsley mash, to thyme-roast loin of lamb (from the owners' own farm) with garlicky jus, gratin potatoes and roast root vegetables. Resourcefulness doesn't falter when it comes to puddings either, judging by terrine of iced banana parfait with Bacardi-spiked berry jelly, and blueberry and hazelnut cheesecake with lemon curd sauce.

Chef David Ostle **Owner** Ben & Steve Christie
Times 11.30-2.30/6.30-9.30 Closed 26 Dec-2 Jan, Mon, L Tue, D Sun **Prices** Fixed D 3 course £19.50, Starter £5-£6.50, Main £11.95-£21.50, Dessert £5.10-£5.95, Service optional **Wines** 20 bottles over £20, 22 bottles under £20, 8 by glass **Notes** Sunday L, Vegetarian available, Dress restrictions, Smart casual **Seats** 45 **Children** Portions **Parking** 20

IRONBRIDGE   Map 10 SJ60

Restaurant Severn

🏵🏵 British, French 🥄

Country cooking beside the Ironbridge gorge

☎ 01952 432233
33 High St TF8 7AG
web: www.restaurantsevern.co.uk
dir: Travelling along High St pass Restaurant Severn on right, to mini rdbt, 3rd exit into Waterloo St, continue 50mtrs to car park on left

Eric and Beb Bruce's small neighbourhood restaurant blends in unobtrusively with the terrace of souvenir and tea shops facing Abraham Darby's World Heritage cast iron bridge. Inside, however, sunny yellow walls, bare wooden floors, unclothed tables and high-backed toffee leather chairs make for an intimate brasserie look. The supply lines to local producers are good in these parts, and full advantage is taken of the local larder, supplemented by home-grown organic seasonal materials from their own smallholding. Classical French influences are evident in starters such as a smooth chicken liver and malt whisky parfait served with red onion marmalade and melba toast, while mains plough a similarly simple and unfussy furrow, partnering medallions of Shropshire venison saddle with braised red cabbage, and Cognac and sun-dried cranberry sauce. Puddings are Beb Bruce's domain - perhaps dark Belgian chocolate délice with chocolate cannelloni - or you might be tempted by a platter of Shropshire cheeses served with home-made chutney and Beb's spiced bread.

Chef Eric & Beb Bruce **Owner** Eric & Beb Bruce
Times 12-2/6.30-8.30 Closed BHs, Mon-Tue, L Wed-Sat, D Sun **Prices** Fixed D 3 course £28.95, Service optional, Groups min 8 service 10% **Wines** 15 bottles over £20, 25 bottles under £20, 5 by glass **Notes** Monthly Gourmet evenings, midweek promotion Wed-Thu, Sunday L, Vegetarian available, Dress restrictions, Smart casual **Seats** 30 **Children** Portions **Parking** On street & car park opposite

LUDLOW   Map 10 SO57

La Bécasse

🏵🏵🏵 — *see page 410*

LUDLOW continued

The Clive Bar and Restaurant with Rooms

◉◉ Modern British 🌸

Smart, modish cooking on Robert Clive's former estate

☎ 01584 856565 & 856665
Bromfield SY8 2JR
e-mail: info@theclive.co.uk
web: www.theclive.co.uk
dir: 2m N of Ludlow on A49, near Ludlow Golf Club, racecourse & adjacent to Ludlow food centre

Just off the A49 outside Ludlow, the converted farmhouse stands on an estate that once belonged to Clive of India. Uncovered wood is the modish decorative theme for both floors and tables, while the aubergine and sea-green walls are contrastingly smothered in pictures. Mark Davey arrived in November 2011 to head up the already distinguished culinary operation here, and is clearly well capable of maintaining the technically polished, inventive British cooking for which the place has become noted. Three ways with mackerel - escabèche, céviche and sashimi - is a strong, imaginative opener, gaining extra flash from its accompaniments of warm lime jelly and horseradish dressing. After that bravura prelude, there may be venison Wellington made with tender loin meat encased with lightly cooked foie gras in fine crisp pastry, served with braised red cabbage and puréed parsnip in a rich Madeira jus. Fish might be parsley-crusted brill with black gnocchi and braised chicory in shrimp butter, while desserts go for voguish techniques such as the black cherry milkshake that comes with dark chocolate fondant and white chocolate mousse.

Chef Mark Davey **Owner** Paul & Barbara Brooks **Times** 12-3/6.30-10 Closed 25-26 Dec **Prices** Starter £5.50-£7.50, Main £10.25-£18.95, Dessert £5.25-£6.95, Service optional **Wines** 39 bottles over £20, 31 bottles under £20, 9 by glass **Notes** Sunday L, Vegetarian available **Seats** 90 **Children** Portions **Parking** 80

Dinham Hall Hotel

◉◉ Modern British

Opulent modern British cooking opposite the castle

☎ 01584 876464
By the Castle, Dinham SY8 1EJ
e-mail: info@dinhamhall.com
dir: Town centre, off Market Place, opposite Ludlow Castle

If you're contemplating a pilgrimage to Shropshire's foodie mecca of Ludlow, Dinham Hall is a dapper Georgian house cheek-by-jowl with the ruined medieval castle above the looping River Teme. All of the requisite oak floors, lofty plasterwork ceilings and bay windows are present and correct, but when you step into the glassed-over brasserie, it is fast forward to the contemporary world of clean-cut design and bare wooden tables. Wayne Smith's kitchen team also takes a clean, modern approach, drafting in prime seasonal produce from the local area to shine in a fine-tuned starter of ballottine of salmon, cucumber and crème fraîche. At main course, the unmistakable French accent continues in a loin of lamb with peas and bacon, boulangère potatoes and red wine sauce. Invention and flair continue through to dessert, as witnessed in a luscious trio of caramel parfait, banana bread and chocolate ice cream.

Chef Wayne Smith **Owner** Metzo Hotels Ltd **Times** 12.30-2.30/6.30-9.30 **Prices** Food prices not confirmed for 2013. Please telephone for details **Wines** 98 bottles over £20, 9 bottles under £20, 8 by glass **Seats** 36, Pr/dining room 60 **Parking** 16, On street

---

La Bécasse

LUDLOW   Map 10 SO57

Modern French **V** 🌸

Thrilling modern cooking in charming 17th-century building

☎ 01584 872325
17 Corve St SY8 1DA
e-mail: info@labecasse.co.uk
web: www.labecasse.co.uk
dir: In town centre opposite Feathers Hotel, at bottom of hill

The Ludlow foodie phenomenon is a strange sort of beast: a postcard-pretty market town lost in sleepy Shropshire that suddenly exploded into an epicentre of high-achieving culinary endeavours. The fantastic raw materials available within a 30-mile radius of Ludlow certainly play their part in its unique status, and are enthusiastically embraced by chef-patron Will Holland, who is a keen supporter of the 'Local to Ludlow' movement. Since Holland took the reins of La Bécasse (part of Alan Murchison's group of restaurants, see also L'ortolan in Shinfield, among others), his public profile has opened up to a wider audience, boosted undeniably by telly appearances with the Hairy Bikers and on the *Great British Menu*. The venue - a 17th-century coaching inn - is a warren of interconnecting rooms where understated contemporary design offsets expanses of handsome burnished oak panelling and walls of exposed brick; it is a look that stamps its claim to high-end dining, whilst steering clear of any feeling of starched stuffiness. Holland's approach to cooking is a finely-judged blend of invention and convention, delivering contemporary dishes of great flair based on classical principles. But he's not a one-man band: the whole kitchen team clearly have a passion for their craft, foraging in their breaks for produce that's on the doorstep - wild garlic or mushrooms, perhaps - and they have no fear of hard work. Great care and finesse is evident in a knockout starter of foie gras ballottine served with toasted brioche, cherry chutney and purée, which manages to look as pretty as a picture whilst delivering head-spinning clarity of flavour and texture. A main course of pan-fried halibut is served atop an island of white beans within a circle of silky caramelised onion purée and intensely-flavoured quenelles of mushroom duxelle. After that, it's time for pudding, which works an apple theme involving pain perdu, apple galette, cinnamon crumble, and apple sorbet, all pointed up with a feisty cider reduction syrup. Excellent front-of-house staff make sure that everything runs at just the right pace for maximum satisfaction.

Chef Will Holland **Owner** Alan Murchison Restaurants Ltd **Times** 12-2/7-9.30 Closed Xmas-New Year, Mon, L Tue, D Sun **Prices** Fixed L 2 course £26, Fixed D 3 course £60, Tasting menu £65, Starter £15, Main £30, Dessert £15, Service added but optional 12.5% **Wines** 180 bottles over £20, 4 bottles under £20, 20 by glass **Notes** Tasting menu 7 course, surprise menu 10 course £90, Vegetarian menu, Dress restrictions, Smart casual **Seats** 40 **Children** Portions **Parking** 6

Save on Hotels. Book at **theAA.com/hotel**

SHROPSHIRE 411 **ENGLAND**

The Feathers Hotel

◉ British, European

Modern British cooking in 'the most handsome inn in the world' (official)

☎ 01584 875261
Bull Ring SY8 1AA
e-mail: enquiries@feathersatludlow.co.uk
web: www.feathersatludlow.co.uk
dir: from A49 follow town centre signs to centre. Hotel on left

The intricate timber-framed Jacobean façade of the Feathers is certainly a head-turning piece of woodwork: Pevsner bigs it up in *The Buildings of England*, and according to the *New York Times*, it is 'the most handsome inn in the world'. Luckily there is more to it than a handsome frontage, as the interior lives up to its promise with carved fireplaces, ornate 17th-century plaster ceilings and enough timbers to build a galleon. The restaurant's blackened beams, exposed stone walls and flagstones set the scene for sound contemporary cooking from a kitchen that delivers the goods. The quality of local raw materials is evident in starters such as pheasant and rabbit terrine with apple and celery chutney, while mains could team roast loin of venison with roast root vegetables, sweet potato mash, and a blackberry and red wine reduction. Finish with tarte Tatin with apple sorbet and cinnamon crème anglaise.

Chef Stuart Forman **Owner** Ceney Developments
Times 7-9 Closed L all week **Prices** Fixed L 2 course £32.50, Service optional, Groups min 12 service 10%
Wines 27 bottles over £20, 9 bottles under £20, 10 by glass **Notes** Vegetarian available, Dress restrictions, Smart casual, Civ Wed 80 **Seats** 50, Pr/dining room 30 **Children** Portions, Menu **Parking** 36

Fishmore Hall

◉ ◉ ◉ — *see page 412*

Overton Grange Country House & Restaurant

◉◉ Modern British, French

French-infused cooking and attentive service in Ludlow

☎ 01584 873500
Old Hereford Rd SY8 4AD
e-mail: info@overtongrangehotel.com
dir: M5 junct 5. On B4361 approx 1.5m from Ludlow towards Leominster

This elegant Edwardian house in the Shropshire hills outside Ludlow has a recently built spa, pool and treatment room to further boost the feelgood factor. The dining room looks good too, with its lavender-shaded walls, and chocolate coloured leather chairs at tables draped in floor-length linen, while the cooking is in the capable hands of French chef Christophe Dechaux-Blanc, who puts a modern British spin into dishes rooted in French classics. Burgundy snails could be crusted with parsley and garlic, and matched with parsley gâteau, butternut squash purée, and black garlic cream, while splendid local Mortimer Forest venison loin stars in a main course with creamy Savoy cabbage and oyster mushrooms, and cider jus. Find room to end with a zingy trio of plum bavarois, yuzu jelly and orange ice cream.

Chef Christophe Dechaux-Blanc **Owner** Metzo Hotels Ltd
Times 12-2.30/7-10 **Prices** Food prices not confirmed for 2013. Please telephone for details **Wines** 150 bottles over £20, 20 bottles under £20, 12 by glass **Notes** Pre-theatre meal available from 5.30pm, Sunday L, Vegetarian available, Dress restrictions, Smart casual, Civ Wed 50 **Seats** 40, Pr/dining room 24 **Parking** 50

MARKET DRAYTON Map 15 SJ63

Goldstone Hall

◉◉ Modern British ◉

Georgian manor-house hotel with confident cooking

☎ 01630 661202
Goldstone Rd, Goldstone TF9 2NA
e-mail: enquiries@goldstonehall.com
dir: 4m S of Market Drayton off A529 signed Goldstone Hall Hotel. 4m N of Newport signed from A41

Much of Goldstone Hall is Georgian, though its ancestry has been traced back to medieval times. Set in impressive gardens, off the A259 south of Market Drayton, it is a jewel of a country house, stylishly appointed throughout and featuring original beams and exposed timbers, while antique furnishings and open fires abound, and many rooms, including the Arts and Crafts-style dining room, have beautiful panelled walls. Steven Blackshaw's menus evolve with the seasons, drawing on top-notch kitchen garden produce and meat from a neighbouring farm. His confident modern British cooking shows great technical ability and creativity; tender and juicy scallops served with pickled pear, chorizo and pea purée, for example, and rabbit leg stuffed with thyme mousse, served with seared loin, nasturtium pesto and carrot purée. Cheeses fly the flags proudly for the best

British and Irish artisan produce, or round off with a chocolate and cherry tart.

Chef Steven Blackshaw **Owner** John Cushing & Helen Ward **Times** 11-7-10 **Prices** Fixed L 2 course fr £17, Fixed D 3 course fr £23.50, Starter £6.50-£15, Main £12.50-£30, Dessert £5.50-£8.50, Service included **Wines** 50 bottles over £20, 11 bottles under £20, 14 by glass **Notes** Sunday L, Vegetarian available, Civ Wed 100 **Seats** 60, Pr/dining room 14 **Children** Portions **Parking** 70

Ternhill Farm House & The Cottage Restaurant

◉◉ Modern International ◉

Ambitious cooking in homely Georgian farmhouse

☎ 01630 638984
Ternhill TF9 3PX
e-mail: info@ternhillfarm.co.uk
dir: On junct A53 & A41, archway off A53 to back of property

Mike and Jo Abraham, have been hard at work for the last decade, unleashing a top-to-bottom facelift on their red-brick Georgian farmhouse and giving the place a new lease of life as a smart restaurant with rooms. The dining room occupies the old kitchen, complete with Aga, where they have pulled off a clean-cut modern look, blending original oak beams and pine flooring with leather seats and bare wooden tables, and custard yellow walls hung with mirrors and eclectic art. The cooking takes a hearty, crowd-pleasing approach, relying on the excellent quality of the local and home-grown ingredients for its effect. A complex beetroot medley delivers chilli-spiced beetroot soup with chive cream, chilled beetroot and orange-cured salmon with mustard and lime dressing, and goats' cheese and beetroot bruschetta, while main course is another multi-faceted dish involving pan-fried partridge breast wrapped in honey-cured bacon, slow-braised leg, pheasant confit, rabbit, venison and pigeon with plum jus, spiced red cabbage, thyme dauphinoise potato and quince jelly.

Chef Michael Abraham **Owner** Michael & Joanne Abraham **Times** 6.30-mdnt Closed L all week, D Sun-Mon **Prices** Starter £4.50-£7.25, Main £10.95-£21.95, Dessert £4.95-£7.95, Service optional, Groups min 8 service 10% **Wines** 4 bottles over £20, 20 bottles under £20, 6 by glass **Notes** Sunday L, Vegetarian available, Dress restrictions, Smart casual **Seats** 22, Pr/dining room 14 **Parking** 16

Fishmore Hall

Modern European **V** 🍴

Well-crafted dishes in luxurious boutique hotel

☎ 01584 875148
Fishmore Rd SY8 3DP
e-mail: reception@fishmorehall.co.uk
web: www.fishmorehall.co.uk
dir: A49 from Shrewsbury, follow Ludlow & Bridgnorth signs. 1st left towards Bridgnorth, at next rdbt left onto Fishmore Rd. Hotel 0.5m on right after golf course

The first glimpse of the elegantly proportioned white Georgian property on a hill overlooking the town suggests that this boutique hotel is somewhere special, an impression not dispelled by its smartly and comfortably furnished interior. Flowers and candles reinforce an impression of refinement in the restaurant, which has been extended into a bright orangery with views over fields. David Jaram sources his materials from within a 30-mile radius (apart from seafood, of course, which comes from Brixham and Skye), and has devised a Taste of the Marches menu in support of the short carte. The first impression is one of well-judged flavours; curried pine nuts adding an extra dimension to wood pigeon with cauliflower and apricots, for instance, and accompaniments of goats' curd, star anise-glazed beetroot and red

chard making another starter, of confit salmon, into an appealing whole. Compositions are carefully considered, every component serving a function: sautéed snails for roast loin of lamb, served pink (as requested), with garlic and parmesan pommes purée, and scallop carpaccio for sea bass fillet with tapenade and tomato confit. Breads and extras like canapés are well up to snuff, too, and for some the pudding may well be the high point; perhaps tropical fruit salad with lychee pannacotta, pineapple consommé and coconut sorbet.

Chef David Jaram **Owner** Laura Penman **Times** 12-2.30/7-9.30 **Prices** Fixed L 2 course £20, Fixed D 3 course £49, Tasting menu £59-£69, Service optional, Groups min 10 service 10% **Wines** 94 bottles over £20, 6 bottles under £20, 12 by glass **Notes** Tasting menu 6,9 course, Vegetarian 2,3,6,9 course £30-£60, Sunday L, Vegetarian menu, Dress restrictions, Smart casual, Civ Wed 130 **Seats** 40, Pr/dining room 20 **Children** Portions, Menu **Parking** 36

MUCH WENLOCK   Map 10 SO69

Raven Hotel

◉◉ British, Mediterranean

Ambitious cooking in the home of the Olympic Games (really)

☎ 01952 727251
30 Barrow St TF13 6EN
e-mail: enquiry@ravenhotel.com
dir: 10m SW from Telford on A4169, 12m SE from Shrewsbury. In town centre

Before the Olympic shenanigans in 2012 publicised the fact more widely, not a lot of people knew that the modern games started off in Much Wenlock, when local doctor, William Penny Brookes, organised an Olympian event here in 1850. The 17th-century Raven no doubt played its part in refreshing the athletes back then, and continues the tradition nowadays in a smartly-updated setting. Venerable beams, log fires, and hand-pulled ales make for a cheerfully pubby vibe, while the kitchen hauls in splendid Shropshire produce as the backbone of its appealing repertoire. Sea bass and mullet escabèche might be served with a chilli and vegetable broth, then a sorbet offers breathing space before the main event - perhaps rack of Stottesdon lamb with fondant potato and pea and redcurrant fricassée, or pan-fried venison loin with boulangère potato, and creamed celeriac and bacon. Puddings such as double chocolate cheesecake with raspberry ripple ice cream aim straight at the comfort zone, if you're not tempted towards the splendid local artisan cheeses.

Times 12-2.30/6.45-9.30 Closed 25 Dec

MUNSLOW   Map 10 SO58

Crown Country Inn

◉◉ Modern British ◖

Classy cooking in old village inn

☎ 01584 841205
SY7 9ET
e-mail: info@crowncountryinn.co.uk
dir: On B4368 between Craven Arms & Much Wenlock

A typical old English village coaching inn, the Crown has the usual exposed beams, inglenooks and flagstone floors. No surprises there, then. What elevates the place well above the gastro-pub norm is the quality of the food served in the upstairs restaurant. The kitchen works around a modern English style based on a well-mastered traditional repertoire, sourcing seasonal local produce in the process. Start with home-made bacon and herb black pudding with tomatoes topped with farm bacon, or a crisp fishcake of haddock, leeks and smoked cheese with chilli and tomato jam. Main courses are never over-elaborate, so flavours are clear: mushroom and barley risotto for smoked chicken breast with chorizo and chive sauce, say, and mushy peas and straw potatoes for crisply fried gurnard fillet with balsamic syrup. Summer may see a pudding like roast nectarine with vanilla

pannacotta, the plate streaked with raspberry coulis and dotted with sugared almonds.

Chef Richard Arnold **Owner** Richard & Jane Arnold **Times** 12-2/6.45-8.45 Closed some days during Xmas, Mon, D Sun **Prices** Fixed L 2 course fr £13.50, Fixed D 3 course fr £20, Starter £5.25-£6.75, Main £14.95-£18.75, Dessert £6.50-£9.95, Service optional **Wines** 13 bottles over £20, 29 bottles under £20, 5 by glass **Notes** Sunday L, Vegetarian available **Seats** 65, Pr/dining room 42 **Children** Portions **Parking** 20

NORTON   Map 10 SJ70

The Hundred House Hotel

◉◉ Traditional British, French ◖

Hands-on family hotel where quirky charm meets skilled modern cuisine

☎ 01952 580240
Bridgnorth Rd TF11 9EE
e-mail: reservations@hundredhouse.co.uk
dir: Midway between Telford & Bridgnorth on A442. In village of Norton

There are plenty of old Georgian coaching inns around the UK, but the hands-on family who have run Hundred House for a quarter of a century make this one stand out from the pack with a streak of mild eccentricity. There are stained glass Temperance Hall panels at the front door, and if you want to check in and take full advantage of the restaurant's delights, your bedroom will come with a swing hanging from the oak beams. Despite the quirky style, food is taken seriously; reminders of the local larder come in the shape of baskets of pumpkins and squashes, and bunches of dried herbs are dotted all around the warren of characterful rooms making up the bar, brasserie and main restaurant. Shropshire's superb produce is spiked with a hundred-odd herbs fresh from the kitchen garden and appears in flavour-driven, creative modern ideas; perhaps a platter of home-smoked trout, gravad lax and crab gâteau, grilled mussels and prawn filo, then duck breast with a duck confit and sage pasty and crab apple jelly sauce.

Chef Stuart Phillips **Owner** Mr H Phillips, Mr D Phillips, Mr S G Phillips **Times** 12-2.30/6-9.30 Closed D 25 Dec **Prices** Fixed L 2 course £12-£20, Fixed D 3 course £15-£35, Starter £4.95-£9.95, Main £10.95-£22.95, Dessert £5.95, Service optional, Groups min 7 service 10% **Wines** 18 bottles over £20, 20 bottles under £20, 11 by glass **Notes** Gourmet evenings, Sunday L, Vegetarian available, Civ Wed 120 **Seats** 80, Pr/dining room 34 **Children** Portions, Menu **Parking** 60

OSWESTRY   Map 15 SJ22

Pen-y-Dyffryn Country Hotel

◉◉ Modern British ◖

Splendid views and superb Welsh produce

☎ 01691 653700
Rhydycroesau SY10 7JD
e-mail: stay@peny.co.uk
dir: 3m W of Oswestry on B4580

Sitting atop a hillside on the Welsh border (on the English side), Pen-y-Dyffryn is a fine Georgian rectory with a smart and intimate restaurant. Its position ensures that walkers will be in their element, but there are less strenuous ways to enjoy the glorious views, such as relaxing with a sundowner, or tea and cake, on the hotel's terrace looking across to the Welsh mountains to the west. The restaurant makes the most of what nature provides, too, with huge sash windows, plus elegant features like a marble mantle piece and ornate dresser. Each table is formally laid with a fresh flower, and what's on the menu is dictated by what local (often organic) produce is up to snuff. So you might start with terrine of Shropshire rose veal (welfare friendly), apricot and pistachio nuts with fig and date chutney and toasted soda bread. Next up, best end of Welsh lamb with gratin dauphinoise, ragoût of courgettes, red peppers and tomato, and a thyme jus, finishing with lemon crème brûlée with pressed Granny Smith apples, buttered shortbread and apple sorbet.

Chef David Morris **Owner** MJM & AA Hunter **Times** 6.45-11 Closed 20 Dec-21 Jan, L all week **Prices** Fixed D 3 course £30-£36, Service optional **Wines** 30 bottles over £20, 40 bottles under £20, 3 by glass **Notes** Vegetarian available **Seats** 25 **Children** Portions, Menu **Parking** 18

Wynnstay Hotel

◉◉ Modern European

Supplier-led cooking in an old coaching inn

☎ 01691 655261
Church St SY11 2SZ
e-mail: info@wynnstayhotel.com
web: www.wynnstayhotel.com
dir: In town centre, opposite church

Formerly a coaching inn for the London-to-Holyhead and Liverpool-to-Cardiff routes, this red-brick Georgian building is now home to over 30 bedrooms and a luxurious fitness club. The traditional Four Seasons
continued

OSWESTRY *continued*

restaurant has tables smartly dressed in cream linen with paintings of wine bottles and fruit adorning the walls. Unfussily presented dishes are based on well-sourced ingredients given a modern European spin; thus a generous portion of fresh crab and cucumber cannelloni with coriander, lime and chilli bursts with flavour, and tender roasted saddle of Welsh lamb is accompanied by confit aubergine and tomato, sweetbread beignet and rosemary jus. For those with a sweet tooth, the assiette gourmand's hot chocolate fondant, praline crème brûlée and rhubarb cheesecake will hit the spot.

Times 12-2/7-9.30 Closed 25 Dec

SHIFNAL　　　　Map 10 SJ70

Park House Hotel

◎ Modern European

Modern cooking in singular market town hotel

☎ 01952 460128
Park St TF11 9BA
e-mail: reception@parkhousehotel.net
dir: From M54 J4 take A464 through Shifnal; hotel 200yds after railway bridge

Two 17th-century country houses, one red-brick, one faced with white stucco have been pasted seamlessly together to make Park House, an upmarket venue in a pleasant Shropshire market town. Period oak panelling and ornate plasterwork combine with a dramatic contemporary colour scheme to provide a classy backdrop in the brasserie-style Butlers restaurant. The kitchen doesn't try to reinvent the wheel here, focusing instead on good quality local produce in a repertoire of straightforward modern European ideas. King scallops with pancetta and pea purée might lead the way, followed by rump of lamb served with Puy lentil and root vegetable cassoulet. At the end, local cheeses compete for your attention with crowd-pleasers such as hot chocolate fondant with pistachio ice cream.

Chef Paul Davies **Owner** Andrew Hughes **Times** noon-3/6-10 **Prices** Fixed L 3 course £19.95, Fixed D 4 course £27.50, Starter £6-£9.95, Main £14-£22.95, Dessert £5.50-£7.50, Service optional **Wines** 16 bottles over £20, 14 bottles under £20, 11 by glass **Notes** Sunday L, Vegetarian available, Dress restrictions, Smart casual preferred, Civ Wed 180 **Seats** 50, Pr/dining room 180 **Children** Portions, Menu **Parking** 100

SHREWSBURY　　　　Map 15 SJ41

Albright Hussey Manor Hotel & Restaurant

◎◎ Modern British

Medieval manor with refined contemporary cooking

☎ 01939 290571
Ellesmere Rd, Broad Oak SY4 3AF
e-mail: info@albrighthussey.co.uk
dir: 2.5m N of Shrewsbury on A528, follow signs for Ellesmere

The medieval manor, reached across a stone bridge, is actually a building of two halves: a timber-framed house next to a brick and stone wing. Inside are all the ancient features expected in a property of this age, the restaurant a chintzy, beamed room with a huge inglenook and period memorabilia like helmets and shields. There's nothing old-school about the menus, which list all the suppliers of top-quality materials. Leek and potato broth with three tortellini stuffed with smoked chicken is the sort of ambitious, successful starter to expect in winter, or there may be a blini with crabmeat and grapefruit salad. Loin of local venison, cooked pink, is imaginatively - even daringly - crusted with praline and thyme and accompanied by hazelnut and celeriac purée to make a good balance of flavours and textures. A fish option might be roast fillet of sea bass with orzo pasta and ratatouille, and soufflés should not be overlooked, among them orange and Cointreau with lemon sorbet.

Chef Michel Nijsten **Owner** Franco, Vera & Paul Subbiani **Times** 12-2.15/7-10 **Prices** Fixed L 2 course £15-£20, Fixed D 3 course £25-£40, Starter £6.50-£12, Main £15.50-£35, Dessert £6.50-£8, Service optional, Groups min 6 service 10% **Wines** 53 bottles over £20, 43 bottles under £20, 14 by glass **Notes** Tasting menu available, Sunday L, Vegetarian available, Dress restrictions, No jeans, trainers or T-shirts **Seats** 80, Pr/dining room 40 **Children** Portions **Parking** 100

Drapers Hall

◎◎ Modern, Traditional

Medieval setting for gently contemporary cooking

☎ 01743 344679
10 Saint Mary's Place SY1 1DZ
e-mail: goodfood@drapershallrestaurant.co.uk
dir: From A5191 (St Mary's St) on one-way system into St Mary's Place

One of the oldest buildings in Shrewsbury, Drapers Hall dates back to 1556 and retains enough period detail to impress even the most jaded historian. A 17th-century fireplace, wood panelling and exposed beams are just the start of it, with the restaurant priding itself on being 'a little posh, but not stuffy', and delivering high impact with its medieval floors and oak panels combining well with linen-clad tables and tartan chairs. Don't go thinking the menu is stuck in the past however. What you can expect is some excellent Welsh Marches produce subjected to some gently modish preparations; parfait of

chicken livers, for example, comes with onion marmalade and toasted brioche, followed by Cornish black bream with fish velouté and braised fennel, or slow-roast duckling with Cointreau and capsicum sauce. Less formal dining is available in the Bar & Grill.

Times 11-3.30/6-9.30 Closed D Sun

Lion & Pheasant Hotel

◎◎ British 🕯

Vibrant brasserie cooking in a townhouse hotel

☎ 01743 770345
49-50 Wyle Cop SY1 1XJ
e-mail: info@lionandpheasant.co.uk
web: www.lionandpheasant.co.uk

At the end of 2010, the wraps came off the Lion & Pheasant to reveal a hot-looking contemporary boutique townhouse hotel. The dove-grey façade offers a foretaste of the pared-back setting within: tongue-and-groove-panelled walls, chunky bleached wood tables and blond wood flooring all combine in a minimal look which you might call New England-style beachcomber chic, were it not for areas of bare brick and ancient gnarled beams as a reminder of the venerable age of this historic inn. The cooking works with the setting, delivering modern brasserie-style dishes that deploy British ingredients to telling effect. You might kick off with a skilfully-wrought idea such as pigeon breast partnered with clementine, Medjool date and endive salad, and pistachio dressing, then follow with pan-fried fillet of brill with oxtail tortellini, winter greens and roast garlic sauce, or a tasting plate of Gloucestershire Old Spot pork with mustard mash, sage and sauce soubise, and roasting juices. Close the show with tarte Tatin and brown butter ice cream.

Chef Matthew Strefford **Times** 12-2.30/6-9.30 Closed 25 Dec **Prices** Starter £5.95-£8.50, Main £10.95-£21.95, Dessert £4.95-£9.95, Service optional **Wines** 88 bottles over £20, 18 bottles under £20 **Notes** Early bird menu 2 course £11.95, 3 course £13.95 6-7pm, Sunday L, Vegetarian available, Dress restrictions, Smart casual **Seats** Pr/dining room 45 **Children** Portions, Menu **Parking** 14, NCP opposite

Mad Jack's Restaurant & Bar

◉ Modern British **V**

Modern brasserie food in the town centre

☎ 01743 358870
15 St Mary's St SY1 1EQ
e-mail: info@madjacks.uk.com
dir: In Shrewsbury town centre, on the one-way system, almost opposite St Mary's Church

At the heart of town, MJ's (to its friends) is in a period building but has a thoroughly contemporary vibe, with a seat in its courtyard garden amid the palms more Mediterranean than medieval Shrewsbury. The interior is light and on-trend, decked out with a terracotta-tiled floor, black sparkly marble-topped tables and fashionable high-back chairs, while walls are hung with cartoon sketches of the namesake 'Mad Jack' - a legendary local squire who blew his fortune on boozing and hell-raising (we say blew...). There's nothing risque about the menu though, which is an accomplished roster of modern brasserie dishes fashioned from fresh local produce; Indonesian seafood chowder, for example, followed by sea bass fillet teamed with mango and crab salsa, potato galette, wilted spinach and pea and mint sabayon. To finish, vanilla pod crème brûlée with poached pear and shortbread fits the bill.

Owner Ann & Danny Ditella **Times** 12-10 Closed 25-26 Dec **Prices** Starter £5.95-£7.95, Main £9.95-£17.95, Dessert £5.95-£6.95 **Wines** 30 bottles over £20, 30 bottles under £20, 12 by glass **Notes** Sunday L, Vegetarian menu **Seats** 60, Pr/dining room 30 **Children** Portions **Parking** Town centre

Mytton & Mermaid Hotel

◉ ◉ Modern British **V**

Riverside setting and a true Shropshire flavour

☎ 01743 761220
Atcham SY5 6QG
e-mail: reception@myttonandmermaid.co.uk
web: www.myttonandmermaid.co.uk
dir: Just outside Shrewsbury on B4380 (old A5). Opposite NT Attingham Park

Named after a local reprobate who squandered his fortune, the Mytton & Mermaid is a creeper-clad Georgian coaching inn in a lovely spot near the Atcham Bridge on the banks of the River Severn close to Shrewsbury. The riverside tables are a magnet for a pre-dinner drink on a fine day, before moving into the elegant restaurant, which

has the feel of a relaxed country house with its linen-clothed antique oak tables, gilt mirrors on terracotta walls and bare wooden floors. The kitchen shows ambition, putting together seasonal menus of modern British ideas built on a good showing of local materials. Start, perhaps, with pan-seared scallops with celeriac and truffle purée, warm apple jelly and bacon powder, before considering a venison 'mixed grill' comprising pan-fried loin, faggot, cottage pie, bonbon of fillet, roast beets, parsnip purée, rösti potato and game jus. Sloe gin crème brûlée with damson ice cream, shortbread crumble and blackberries is typical of the vibrantly flavoured desserts.

Chef Adrian Badland **Owner** Mr & Mrs Ditella **Times** 12-2.30/6.30-10 Closed 25 Dec, D 26 Dec, 1 Jan **Prices** Starter £6.45-£7.95, Main £12.95-£19.95, Dessert £5.95-£7.95, Service optional **Wines** 20 bottles over £20, 30 bottles under £20, 12 by glass **Notes** Sunday L, Vegetarian menu, Civ Wed 90 **Seats** 100, Pr/dining room 12 **Children** Portions, Menu **Parking** 80

TELFORD   **Map 10 SJ60**

Best Western Valley Hotel & Chez Maw Restaurant

◉ ◉ Modern British **V**

Modern British food near the Ironbridge

☎ 01952 432247
Buildwas Rd TF8 7DW
e-mail: info@thevalleyhotel.co.uk
dir: M6/M54 from junct 6 take A5223 to Ironbridge for 4m. At mini island right, hotel 80yds on left

The polite chink of teacups has replaced the bedlam of heavy industry in Ironbridge these days, so go with the flow and explore the Coalbrookdale World Heritage area from this lovely Georgian mansion on the banks of the River Severn. The house was the Maws family's reward for their part in the industrial revolution when they kept the Victorian world supplied with lovely ceramic tiles. Updated in a soft-focus contemporary vein with warm tones of peach and caramel, bare wooden floors and tables, and modern art on the walls, the restaurant makes a fine end to a day around Ironbridge's museums. The wide-ranging menu of European-influenced dishes works throughout, thanks to a dedication to well-sourced local ingredients, which appear in a starter of pressed ham hock terrine teamed with black pudding beignets, piccalilli purée and quail's egg. Next up, roast butter-basted chicken with mushroom pâté, swede and potato dauphinoise, butternut squash purée and Madeira jus all comes together a treat, and chocolate brownie with peanut butter ice cream, caramelised peanuts and chocolate sauce ends on a high note.

Chef Barry Workman **Owner** Philip & Leslie Casson **Times** 12-2/7-9.30 Closed 26 Dec-2 Jan, L Sat-Sun **Prices** Fixed D 3 course fr £16.95, Starter £4.95-£7.50, Main £12.95-£22.50, Dessert £6.25, Service optional **Wines** 2 bottles over £20, 27 bottles under £20, 7 by glass **Notes** Vegetarian menu, Dress restrictions, Smart

casual, Civ Wed 120 **Seats** 50, Pr/dining room 30 **Children** Portions, Menu **Parking** 100

Church Farm Guest House

◉ Modern British

Charming service and well-judged menu

☎ 01952 251927
Wrockwardine Village, Wellington TF6 5DG
e-mail: info@churchfarm-shropshire.co.uk

This family-run Georgian farmhouse has four bedrooms and a genuinely homely approach to hospitality. Basil's Restaurant named after the family's obliging Staffordshire bull terrier, takes a flexible approach to proceedings. It's unlicensed - so BYO with a glowing fire in winter and lovely views out over the village and church. Martin Board does all of the cooking and dinner is served dinner-party style. On the regularly-changing menu you'll find lots splendid Shropshire produce supplemented by Brixham fish; start with Jerusalem artichoke soup with confit duck ragoût, followed by fillet of venison with pickled red cabbage, butternut squash purée, toasted walnuts and red wine reduction, and finish in style with apple trifle with cider granita and doughnuts.

Chef Martin Board **Owner** Melanie & Martin Board **Times** 7-close Closed L Mon-Sat, D Sun **Prices** Fixed D 3 course £25, Service optional **Notes** Sunday L, Vegetarian available **Seats** 12, Pr/dining room 18 **Children** Portions **Parking** 10

Hadley Park House

◉ Modern British

Locally-sourced menu in an 18th-century manor

☎ 01952 502684
TF1 6QJ
e-mail: info@hadleypark.co.uk
dir: M54 junct 5, A5 (Rampart Way), at rdbt take A442 towards Hortonwood, over double rdbt, next rdbt take 2nd exit, hotel at end of lane

Thanks to a hefty investment to extend and revamp the Georgian manor house, Hadley Park is looking pretty sharp these days, and is a big hit with those looking for somewhere swanky for their big day. If you're just in the market for a spot of lunch or dinner, though, the conservatory-based restaurant, Dorrells (part of the new extension, so only a couple of years old) is the place to go. There's plenty of natural light, naturally, plus smartly dressed tables and darkwood floors, and a service team who hit the right notes. Expect pleasingly unfussy dishes with the majority of ingredients coming from the region, with a 50-mile target set by the kitchen. Warm cauliflower, leek and Wrekin white cheese tart with a sweet tomato compôte and toasted pine nuts is one way to start, followed perhaps by pan-fried Buttercross Farm pork cutlet with buttery sage mash, black pudding and Madeira jus, with warm black treacle and spice cake with chilled vanilla bean custard and clotted cream to finish.

Times 12-2/6.30-9.30 Closed 25-26 Dec D

SOMERSET

BATH
Map 4 ST76

The Bath Priory Hotel, Restaurant & Spa

⊛⊛⊛ – see opposite

The Cavendish Restaurant

⊛⊛ Modern British ⊛

Ambitious cooking in a lovely townhouse setting

☎ 01225 787960

Dukes Hotel, Great Pulteney St BA2 4DN

e-mail: info@dukesbath.co.uk

dir: M4 junct 18, A46 to Bath, at rdbt right on A4. 4th set of lights turn left (A36), then right into Great Pulteney St. Hotel on left

The Cavendish is part of the classy Dukes Hotel in the heart of Bath's Georgian splendour, but it has the feel of a stand-alone operation thanks to its own separate entrance on the lower-ground floor of the Grade I listed Palladian-style townhouse. The tastefully restrained restaurant is well-lit enough to avoid claustrophobic basement syndrome, and fine weather lets you get out to eat alfresco in the charming secluded walled patio garden. Firmly rooted in classic combinations, the modern cooking is big on seasonal ideas and organic local materials, so loin of local rabbit might be teamed with a pressing of leg meat with smoked ham hock and piccalilli, while mains could deliver an assiette of Langley Chase Farm lamb, comprising confit shoulder, roasted loin and belly, and crispy lamb's tongue with lamb's jus gras; fish gets similarly refined treatment - perhaps roast wild sea bass with langoustine, haricot blanc, monk's beard, violet artichokes and langoustine foam.

Chef Roland Hughes **Owner** Alan Brookes, Michael Bokenham **Times** 12-2/6.30-10 Closed L Mon-Thu **Prices** Fixed L 2 course £12.95-£19.95, Fixed D 3 course £45-£55, Tasting menu £55-£65, Starter £7.50-£9.50, Main £15.50-£24.50, Dessert £6.50-£9.50, Service optional **Wines** 28 bottles over £20, 10 bottles under £20, 16 by glass **Notes** Tasting menu 7 or 9 course, Sunday L, Vegetarian available **Seats** 28, Pr/dining room 16 **Children** Portions, Menu **Parking** On street (with permits)

The Circus Cafe and Restaurant

⊛ Modern British

Attention to detail all day long

☎ 01225 466020

34 Brock St BA1 2LN

e-mail: ali@allgolden.co.uk

dir: From West side of The Circus turn into Brock St, second bldg on right heading towards the Royal Crescent

Bracketed by the great Georgian architectural landmarks of Bath - the eponymous Bath Circus and the iconic Royal Crescent - this trendy venue is rather more posh than its name suggests, with ladies who lunch piling into its classy olive-washed interior to refuel on an eclectic modern British menu of seasonally-driven ideas along the lines of spring nettle and lovage soup with a swirl of truffle cream, and celeriac crisps, or savoury cheddar éclairs filled with twice-baked Bath soft cheese soufflé, and served with roasted vine tomatoes and wild garlic pesto. Turn up for dinner, and a more intimate candlelit mood takes over, and the kitchen sends out starters such as monkfish cheeks with roasted peppers, butter beans, Bath pig chorizo, and paprika and parsley sauce, followed by rack of lamb with rosemary and sweet garlic crust matched with crushed flageolet beans and red wine gravy. Puddings deliver more well-considered flavour combinations - perhaps rhubarb trifle with layers of vanilla sponge and rhubarb purée, jelly and fool served with honeycomb syllabub.

Chef Alison Golden, Adrian Ware, Dicky Simpson **Owner** Alison & Geoffrey Golden **Times** 10-mdnt Closed 2 wks from 24 Dec, Sun **Prices** Fixed L 2 course £10.50-£15.80, Fixed D 3 course £25.10-£28.70, Starter £5.90-£6.90, Main £14.70-£16.30, Dessert £4.50-£5.50, Service optional, Groups min 6 service 10% **Wines** 22 bottles over £20, 8 bottles under £20, 3 by glass **Notes** ALC D, Vegetarian available **Seats** 48, Pr/dining room 32 **Parking** On street, NCP Charlotte St

Combe Grove Manor Hotel

⊛⊛ British, European

Finely tuned country-house cooking

☎ 01225 834644

Brassknocker Hill, Monkton Combe BA2 7HS

e-mail: combegrovemanor@pumahotels.co.uk

dir: Exit A36 at Limpley Stoke onto Brassknocker Hill. Hotel 0.5m up hill on left

Although only three miles from the city centre, this Georgian-built hotel is surrounded by 69 acres of gardens and woodlands and has breathtaking views of the Limpley Stoke Valley. The tastefully fitted-out Georgian Room, its formality cut by friendly and helpful staff, is the main dining room (there's also a brasserie), its ambitious menu showing a kitchen trained in the classical European tradition and respecting seasonality. Starters of gnocchi with a rich sauce of roast plum tomatoes, basil and feta, and pan-fried scallops with barbecued belly pork and roast pumpkin are well judged, followed by successful mains such as roast haunch of venison with red cabbage, parsnip-mashed potatoes, wild mushrooms and juniper berries, or sea bass fillet accompanied by cockles and clams served with boulangère potatoes and ratatouille. Breads and canapés are first-rate and, to finish, dark chocolate fondant is a textbook example, partnered by orange ice cream.

Times 12-2/7-9.30

Jamie's Italian

⊛ Modern Italian

Jamie's winning way with real Italian food

☎ 01225 432340

10 Milsom Place BA1 1BZ

e-mail: bath.office@jamiesitalian.com

dir: M4 junct 18, A46 for 10m, right rdbt take A4 follow signs to city centre.Opposite Jolly's department store

They found a very nice Georgian building to house the Bath outpost of the brand, and inside it feels just as it should chez Jamie: rustic finishes and a wholesome lack of formality and fluff. It covers two floors and is relentlessly busy, so much so that a wait for a table is a probability (bookings are taken for large groups only). This popularity brings a surefire buzz to the place, matched by the energy and enthusiasm of the staff. On the menu is Jamie Oliver's style of rustic Italian food, based around the quality of the ingredients and little in the way of adulteration. Start with planks of excellent cured meats, Italian cheeses, pickles and vegetables, or dive straight into a pasta dish such as wild rabbit tagliolini. Main courses include braised shin of British beef and Jamie's Italian burger; note that side dishes are often necessary.

Chef Eric Bernard **Owner** Jamie's Italian **Times** 12-11 Closed 25-26 Dec **Prices** Food prices not confirmed for 2013. Please telephone for details **Wines** 15 bottles over £20, 11 bottles under £20, 16 by glass **Notes** Vegetarian available **Seats** 180 **Children** Portions, Menu **Parking** Podium car park Walcot St (A3039)

Save on Hotels. Book at **theAA.com/hotel**

SOMERSET 417 **ENGLAND**

The Bath Priory Hotel, Restaurant & Spa

BATH	Map 4 ST76

Modern European

Impeccable modern cooking in a gorgeously decorated house

☎ 01225 331922
Weston Rd BA1 2XT
e-mail: mail@thebathpriory.co.uk
dir: Adjacent to Victoria Park

A short walk from the centre of the city, the Priory is a luxurious retreat for lovers of the country-house style, but which doesn't involve a trek out into the country to find. Its public rooms are gorgeously decorated and furnished in colourful style, with diverting paintings and shelves of books. If that were all, the place would be jewel enough in the regional crown, but a kitchen under the auspices of Michael Caines, executive chef here and at the sibling hotel, Gidleigh Park (see entry, Chagford, Devon), seals the deal. Head chef Sam Moody interprets the Caines style with panache, producing dishes that look impeccably modern in their presentations, but which are founded on sound principles. A starter of caramelised veal sweetbreads is given the gently insistent accompanying flavours of preserved lemon, white asparagus and candied hazelnuts for a thoroughly seductive opener, while a tartare of salmon from Loch Duart gets East Asian treatment, with wasabi cream and a vinaigrette of honey and soy. Appealing, and often hearteningly simple, main courses might feature fine Brixham fish, such as turbot, served with crushed peas and a bacon velouté, or the earthy flavours of roast squab with a fricassée of broad beans and mushrooms and croquette potatoes in a glossily rich Madeira jus. The cheese trolley is tempting indeed, or else stick to the lavishly worked desserts, which may offer a serving of poached strawberries with rice pudding, or see hot prune and Armagnac soufflé offset with the sublime chill of an ice cream composed of the same.

Chef Sam Moody **Owner** Mr A Brownsword
Times 12.30-2.30/6.30-9.30 **Prices** Fixed L 2 course fr £25, Fixed D 3 course fr £75, Tasting menu £90, Service optional, Groups min 10 service 12% **Wines** 466 bottles over £20, 20 bottles under £20, 14 by glass **Notes** Tasting menu D 7 course, Sunday L, Vegetarian available, Dress restrictions, No jeans, T-shirts or trainers, Civ Wed 64 **Seats** 64, Pr/dining room 64 **Children** Portions, Menu **Parking** 40

The Olive Tree at the Queensberry Hotel

BATH	Map 4 ST76

Modern British

Creative modern cooking in a top-drawer hotel

☎ 01225 447928
4-7 Russel St BA1 2QF
e-mail: reservations@olivetreebath.co.uk
web: www.olivetreebath.co.uk
dir: 100mtrs from the Assembly Rooms

Under the guardianship of Laurence and Helen Beere, the Queensberry Hotel's Olive Tree restaurant has established itself firmly as a centre of serious gastronomy in Bath. Four Georgian townhouses have been transformed into a prestigious boutique operation that ticks all the chic style boxes. Its restaurant occupies a series of low-lit interconnecting basement rooms done out in cool neutral tones, with abstract modern art on the walls, and chocolate-brown high-backed leather chairs at white linen tables; on-the-ball, informed service helps to set the mood. Nick Brodie heads up a kitchen team that is turning out some impressive work, calling on an arsenal of top-grade local and seasonal materials to generate vivid flavours, informed here and there by Brodie's Asian travels - as in squab pigeon marinated in yuzu and partnered by a green mango salad and roasted pink peanuts. Next comes a line-up of Bishop Collings pork, which offers the kitchen a chance to show off the technical skills needed to tease perfect textures from slow-cooked belly, cheek, loin, kidney and crackling. Nor is presentation neglected: a dessert of iced meringue and white peach parfait with caramel almonds and peach liqueur paints a vibrant picture on the plate and palate. A superb wine list brings together an eclectic blend of traditional and new styles grouped by flavour types to help with food pairing.

Chef Nick Brodie **Owner** Mr & Mrs Beere **Times** 12-2/7-10 Closed L Mon **Prices** Fixed L 2 course £18.50, Fixed D 3 course £38.50, Starter £10-£13.50, Main £16.50-£26.95, Dessert £9.25-£12, Service added but optional 10%
Wines 320 bottles over £20, 8 bottles under £20, 34 by glass
Notes Sunday L, Vegetarian available **Seats** 60, Pr/dining room 30 **Children** Portions, Menu **Parking** On street pay & display

BATH *continued*

Macdonald Bath Spa Hotel, Vellore Restaurant

◉◉ Traditional British, International

Well-judged menu in grand Georgian hotel

☎ 0844 879 9106
Sydney Rd BA2 6JF
e-mail: sales.bathspa@macdonald-hotels.co.uk
dir: A4 and follow city-centre signs for 1m. At lights turn left towards A36. Turn right after pedestrian crossing then left into Sydney Place. Hotel 200yds on right

Overlooking landscaped gardens, and perfectly placed for exploring the city, the Bath Spa is a grand Georgian mansion with a distinctly elegant finish. The classy (and formal) Vellore Restaurant is in the original ballroom - they partied in style back then - with its high-domed ceiling, pillars and all round stately air. There's also a canopied outdoor terrace. Engaging staff and a helpful sommelier keep things on track. On the menu, the crowd-pleasing and sensibly unfussy dishes have broad appeal, and are not beyond a few bright ideas too; beer battered scampi comes with dipping sauces (sweet chilli and Dijon mustard among them), followed by roast saddle of hare with braised haunch and chicory, or herb risotto with aubergine caviar and basil oil. Finish with dark chocolate pannacotta with a cocoa and almond crumble and toffee ice cream.

Times 12-2/6.15-10 Closed L Mon-Sat

Marlborough Tavern

◉◉ Modern British 🍷

Seasonal cooking and proper beer

☎ 01225 423731
35 Marlborough Buildings BA1 2LY
e-mail: info@marlborough-tavern.com
dir: 200mtrs from W end of Royal Crescent

Just round the corner from Bath's celebrated Royal Crescent, the 18th-century Marlborough Tavern ticks all the right gastro-pub boxes with its rustic-chic stripped floors, sage-green wall panels and church candles on scrubbed tables. And while food is clearly the prime focus, drinkers are as welcome as diners and amply catered for by well-kept local ales and ciders, and an international cast of wines. The food is straightforward, seasonal stuff, with suppliers name-checked on a daily-changing menu that might kick off with rosemary-skewered lamb's kidney with a lamb and Puy lentil casserole, followed by the full-on partnership of fillet steak, braised ox cheek and marrow bone with horseradish and black pudding mash, seasonal greens and cooking juices. Desserts such as spiced Guinness parkin with pear sorbet and salt caramel sauce complete the picture.

Chef Richard Knighting **Owner** Joe Cussens, Justin Sleath **Times** 12-2.30/6-10 Closed 25 Dec, D Sun **Prices** Fixed L 2 course £12, Starter £5.90-£8, Main £10.50-£22.50, Dessert £5.90-£7.50, Service optional, Groups min 6

service 10% **Wines** 43 bottles over £20, 15 bottles under £20, 20 by glass **Notes** Sunday L, Vegetarian available, Dress restrictions, Smart casual **Seats** 60 **Children** Portions **Parking** On street opposite

The Olive Tree at the Queensberry Hotel

◉◉◉ — *see page 417*

Woods Restaurant

◉ Modern British, French

Good bistro cooking in charming setting

☎ 01225 314812 & 422493
9-13 Alfred St BA1 2QX
e-mail: claude@woodsrestaurant.fsnet.co.uk

A firm favourite with the locals and the tourist hordes, Woods has been family-run since 1979, with David Price and his French wife Claudette now training-up the next generation (son and daughter). Occupying the ground floor of some Georgian townhouses, it's set away from the hustle-and-bustle in a quiet cul de sac opposite the Assembly Rooms. Inside the open-plan dining room is packed with large mirrors, horseracing prints and photos, looking every inch the French bistro. Service runs smoothly and the set lunch is particularly good value. The small kitchen team does a good line in straightforward seasonal food with French inclinations; oxtail and thyme rillette with pickled walnuts and gherkins, maybe, followed by fillets of sea bass with vermouth cream sauce, warm cucumber, parsley and smoked tomato.

Times 12-2.30/5.30-10 Closed 25-26 Dec, Sun (open for special request)

Walnut Tree Hotel

◉ Modern British

Enterprising cooking at a small country hotel

☎ 01278 662255
Fore St, North Petherton TA6 6QA
e-mail: reservations@walnuttreehotel.com
dir: M5 junct 24, A38, hotel 1m on right opposite St Mary's Church

At the heart of a thriving village south of Bridgwater, the Walnut Tree is a carefully modernised and extended former 18th-century coaching inn. Now a comfortable hotel, popular with the local business community, it has an elegant restaurant, the Lemon Tree, located in the original building. Here, there is bags of character and charm, with warm blue and lemon décor and some consistently good modern British cooking. With good use of local and seasonal produce, the regularly-changing menu may kick off with duck and chicken terrine with home-made piccalilli and onion loaf, followed by apple and apricot stuffed pork tenderloin with mustard mash and steamed cabbage and bacon, or roast cod with

mussel cream. Leave room for chocolate roulade with vanilla and raspberries.

Chef Luke Nicholson, Debbie Palmer **Owner** Kristine & Stephen Williams **Times** 12-2.30/6.30-9.30 Closed D 25 Dec **Prices** Fixed L 2 course £24-£28, Fixed D 3 course £29-£32, Service optional **Wines** 15 bottles over £20, 17 bottles under £20, 11 by glass **Notes** Fixed L 2 course available at £10 Mon-Fri, Sunday L, Vegetarian available, Civ Wed 100 **Seats** 40, Pr/dining room 100 **Children** Portions **Parking** 70

The Pilgrims

◉ Modern British V 🍷

Husband-and-wife-team serving up fine Somerset produce

☎ 01963 240597
Lovington BA7 7PT
e-mail: jools@thepilgrimsatlovington.co.uk
dir: On B3153, 1.5m E of lights on A37 at Lydford

Hands-on proprietors Sally (front of house) and Jools (at the stoves) Mitchison do just about everything at The Pilgrims, an old stone-built pub with bare beams, flagstoned floors and a log fire crackling away. They describe the place as 'the pub that thinks it's a restaurant with rooms', which is an apt summary, since the focus these days is food, although there's a cosy bar area too. Three dining areas are kitted out in an eclectic, quirky style, part old-school inn, part contemporary shabby-chic with clubby leather sofas, polished darkwood tables, deep green walls and mahogany Venetian blinds. Jools makes everything in-house, so you might be in for a bit of a wait when it's busy, but the results are worth it. Raw materials are emphatically local, often wild or organic, and not fussed over, whether it's 'Pilgrims on Horseback' - seared Lyme Bay scallops with local black pudding - or venison Wellington with mushroom stuffing and red wine sauce. Finishing with artisan cheeses all made within 30 miles and with names like Ogle Shield, Black-Eyed Susan, and Partridge Blue is hard to resist.

Chef Julian Mitchison **Owner** Julian & Sally Mitchison **Times** 12-3/7-11 Closed 2 wks Oct, Mon, L Tue, D Sun **Prices** Starter £5-£10, Main £12-£23, Dessert £5-£9, Service optional **Wines** 26 bottles over £20, 15 bottles under £20, 15 by glass **Notes** Sunday L, Vegetarian menu **Seats** 25 **Children** Portions **Parking** 40

Cricket St Thomas Hotel

◉ Italian

Tuscan specialities in Somerset cider country

☎ 01460 30111
TA20 4DD
e-mail: cricket.sales@bourne-leisure.co.uk

In the buxom embrace of rolling Somerset hills, this porticoed Regency mansion sits in magnificent gardens

Save on Hotels. Book at **theAA.com/hotel**

SOMERSET 419 **ENGLAND**

that the 2nd Baron Bridport lavished a quarter of a million pounds on, including creating a chain of lakes. All of which historical trivia has nothing whatsoever to do with the cuisine of the Tuscan hills, which is the deal in Fenocchi's restaurant. The contemporary venue looks sharp with its darkwood tables, lime and chocolate-hued seats and grey-painted panelled walls, while the kitchen sends out simple classic pasta ideas along the lines of rigatoni alla bolognese, and mains such as prosciutto-wrapped chicken with sage butter, gnocchi, girolle and Italian bean casserole. End sweetly with panettone bread-and-butter pudding with orange zest mascarpone, or the Italian formaggi-board.

Chef Jason Eland **Owner** Bourne Leisure **Times** 6.30-9 **Prices** Food prices not confirmed for 2013. Please telephone for details **Wines** 8 bottles over £20, 6 bottles under £20, 5 by glass **Notes** Vegetarian available, Civ Wed 50 **Seats** 80 **Parking** 200

CHEW MAGNA — Map 4 ST56

The Pony & Trap

◉ Modern British **NEW** ◎

Big-hearted modern food in a country cottage inn

☎ 01275 332627
Knowle Hill BS40 8TQ
e-mail: info@theponyandtrap.co.uk
dir: Take A37 S from Bristol. After Pensford turn right at rdbt onto A368 towards Weston-Super-Mare. In 1.5m right signed Chew Magna & Winford. Pub 1m on right

This 200-year-old country cottage in lush Chew Valley countryside between Bristol and Bath has been transformed into a food-driven inn by chef Josh Eggleton, and is a relaxed and welcoming place. Whether you go for the more traditional wooden tables in the bar, or trade up to linen in the restaurant area, the menu stays the same: punchy food with a big heart, and no purple prose in its description. It is the sort of switched-on, hearty cooking that makes you want to try it all, whether you're starting off with spiced venison faggot with pumpkin purée or crispy skate cheeks with tartare sauce, before pushing on through a main-course stuffed pheasant with cotechino, black cabbage and carrot purée, or whole lemon sole with caper and lime brown shrimp butter. Caramel pannacotta and home-made gingerbread makes a fine finish.

Chef Josh Eggleton **Owner** Josh Eggleton **Times** 12-2.30/7-9.30 Closed Mon **Prices** Tasting menu £45, Starter £5-£7.50, Main £10.50-£22, Dessert £4-£6, Service optional **Wines** 32 bottles over £20, 25 bottles under £20, 15 by glass **Notes** Tasting menu 7 course, Sunday L, Vegetarian available **Seats** 60 **Children** Portions **Parking** 40

CORTON DENHAM — Map 4 ST62

The Queens Arms

◉ Modern British **NEW** ◎

Compelling cooking in a village pub

☎ 01963 220317
DT9 4LR
e-mail: relax@thequeensarms.com
dir: A303 exit Chapel Cross signed South Cadbury & Corton Denham. Follow signs to South Cadbury. Through village, after 0.25m turn left up hill signed Sherborne & Corton Denham. Left at top of hill, pub at end of village on right

In an ancient village on the Somerset-Dorset border, The Queens Arms is a late 18th-century pub overflowing with character. You can have a pork pie and a pint by the open fire in the bar (with its own menu) or a full meal in the adjoining restaurant. Food is a serious preoccupation here, the kitchen's inventive treatments seen in salmon and scallop céviche with pea vinaigrette and pea shoots, then slow-roast pork belly, rich, sticky and delicious, in a pepper and cider glaze served with poached rhubarb and an apple and potato cake. Lamb - loin and rump - is served straightforwardly with potato gratin, baby onions and spinach purée, or go for the seared tuna with seafood, tomato and chilli tagliatelle and a lime and ginger dressing. And who could resist a light, airy, well-risen pistachio soufflé with a pot of chocolate sauce?

Chef Boyd Macintosh, James Cole, Tony Doyle **Owner** Jeanette & Gordon Reid **Times** 12-3/6-10 Closed D 1 Jan **Prices** Fixed L 2 course fr £12.50, Starter £5.50-£7.95, Main £13.50-£18.95, Dessert £5.95-£6.75, Service optional **Wines** 22 bottles over £20, 9 bottles under £20, 19 by glass **Notes** Weekly menu L 2 course, Queen's classic menu L,D £5.95-£11, Sunday L, Vegetarian available **Seats** 40, Pr/dining room 30 **Children** Portions, Menu **Parking**

DULVERTON — Map 3 SS92

Tarr Farm Inn

◉ Modern British ◎

Exmoor riverside inn with appealing brasserie menu

☎ 01643 851507
Tarr Steps, Liscombe TA22 9PY
e-mail: enquiries@tarrfarm.co.uk
dir: 6m NW of Dulverton. Off B3223 signed Tarr Steps, signs to Tarr Farm Inn

Bedded deep in the Barle Valley in the south of Exmoor, this riverside inn is situated not far from the thousand-year-old Tarr Steps, one of the country's surviving clapper bridges (the kind that consist of no more than low stone slabs supported on piers). It's an agreeably remote location, but one handy nonetheless for Exmoor lamb, Devon beef and Cornish seafood, all of which find their way to the dining room. The menu has a brasserie feel, opening with sharing platters of seafood, charcuterie or meze, backed up by smoked mackerel with apple and walnut salad, and main courses such as rack of lamb

with sweetbreads and ratatouille in thyme jus. Ruby beef steaks and chips are a strong lure too. Finish with a lemon threesome of parfait, soufflé and tart.

Chef Paul Webber **Owner** Richard Benn & Judy Carless **Times** 12-3/6.30-12 Closed 1-10 Feb **Prices** Food prices not confirmed for 2013. Please telephone for details **Wines** 53 bottles over £20, 40 bottles under £20, 12 by glass **Notes** Sunday L, Vegetarian available **Seats** 50, Pr/dining room 20 **Children** Portions **Parking** 40

Woods Bar & Dining Room

◉ Modern British, French

Well-judged menu and relaxed vibe

☎ 01398 324007
4 Banks Square TA22 9BU
e-mail: woodsdulverton@hotmail.com
dir: From Tiverton take A396 N. At Machine Cross take B3222 to Dulverton. Establishment adjacent to church

Looking something like a quaint little tea shop on the outside, the abidingly popular neighbourhood venue on the edge of Exmoor is consecrated to both eating and drinking, and doesn't much trouble to draw a strict dividing line between them. Indeed, the line between rusticity and refinement in the cooking itself is also appealingly blurred, and while there may be black plates and triangular plates, they get put down on chunky, unclothed tables in a place warmed by a log fire when needed. Good bistro accents are sounded in a twice-cooked Swiss cheese soufflé, served with fig chutney, walnut dressing and aged balsamic, followed by rump of Exmoor lamb - tender, accurately cooked and flavourful - with a miniature pie, wilted spinach and mash, in thyme-scented juices. To finish, orange pannacotta is of the firm-textured school.

Times 12-2/7-9.30 Closed 25 Dec

EXFORD — Map 3 SS83

Crown Hotel

◉ Modern British ◎

Good cooking in a handsome coaching inn

☎ 01643 831554
Park St TA24 7PP
e-mail: info@crownhotelexmoor.co.uk
dir: From Taunton take A38 to A358. Turn left at B3224 & follow signs to Exford

Amid the gently rolling hills of Exmoor, in the charming village of Exford, the Crown has been doing business for 300 years or so. With three acres of grounds to explore, there's plenty to keep you close by, not least a menu of appealing dishes with a local flavour. Eat in the traditional bar (complete with stag's head) or the handsome dining room and expect well-crafted dishes such as Cornish mussels steamed in cider, followed by a steak from the grill with triple-cooked chips, or fillet of line-caught sea bass with Bombay crushed potatoes, braised fennel, aubergine caviar and curried velouté.

continued

EXFORD *continued*

Apple and raisin crumble with spiced poached pear and cinnamon ice cream brings it all to a comforting close. This is a dog- and horse-friendly establishment.

Chef Olivier Certain **Owner** Mr C Kirkbride & S & D Whittaker **Times** 6.45-9.15 Closed L all week **Prices** Fixed D 3 course £30-£37.50, Service optional **Wines** 25 bottles over £20, 16 bottles under £20, 19 by glass **Notes** Vegetarian available, Dress restrictions, Smart casual, no football shirts or shorts **Seats** 45, Pr/dining room 20 **Children** Portions **Parking** 30

HINTON CHARTERHOUSE — Map 4 ST75

Homewood Park Hotel & Spa

◉◉ British **V**

Bright modern cooking in a grand Georgian house

☎ 01225 723731
Abbey Ln BA2 7TB
e-mail: info@homewoodpark.co.uk
dir: 6m SE of Bath on A36, turn left at 2nd sign for Freshford

Overlooking the Limpley Stoke valley not far from Bath, Homewood is a spiffing country house in the classic mould, with trimly manicured grounds and a dining room that looks out over them. The cooking is broadly contemporary and avoids undue showboating. Smoked ham tortellini with parmesan foam and rocket sounds an Italian note at the outset, as does the outstandingly flavourful beetroot and blue cheese risotto with pea shoots. Rump of local lamb with thyme mash and parsnip purée and pork three ways (loin, belly and ears) are typical of the style. Fish could be a pavé of salmon in saffron-scented mussel and potato broth, and you might finish with the likes of an enthusiastically nutmegged egg custard tart, which boasts superb pastry and offsetting tang from a rhubarb sorbet.

Chef Daniel Maudsley **Owner** Longleat Hotels **Times** 12-1.30/7-9.30 **Prices** Food prices not confirmed for 2013. Please telephone for details **Notes** Sunday L, Vegetarian menu, Dress restrictions, Smart casual, Civ Wed 55 **Seats** 50, Pr/dining room 40 **Children** Portions, Menu **Parking** 40

HOLCOMBE — Map 4 ST64

The Holcombe Inn

◉◉ Traditional French **NEW** ☺

Well-crafted modish cooking at a Somerset inn

☎ 01761 232478
Stratton Rd BA3 5EB
e-mail: bookings@holcombeinn.co.uk
dir: From Bath or Shepton Mallet take A367 (Fosse Way) to Stratton. Follow inn signs

A whitewashed 17th-century listed inn within sight of Downside Abbey, The Holcombe is a proper country refuge, with its panelled interiors, original fireplaces, oak beams and eight guest rooms. There are outdoor tables with

ravishing Somerset views for sunny days, and candlelit intimacy in the dining room for the evenings. The present owners took over in February 2011, and set about putting the place on the map with events nights and a seasonally driven menu that makes the most of good local beef and lamb, and fish from St Ives and Brixham. A good indication of the range might be had from a starter of seared tuna with Thai salad dressed in coconut cream, basil and lime, followed by rack of Elm Farm lamb, cooked pink and served with its crisped sweetbreads, garlicky mash, baby leeks, sautéed trompettes and girolles, Jerusalem artichoke purée and a rosemary jus. That main course may sound fairly busy, but all the flavours show through. Fish receives favourable treatment too, as in roast monkfish tail with mussels, pak choi and apple and vanilla compôte. Good ideas abound, through to desserts such as the plate of lemon variations that incorporates a lemon iced tea granita.

Chef Thomas Scurr **Owner** Julie Berry **Times** 12-2.30/6.30-9 **Prices** Food prices not confirmed for 2013. Please telephone for details **Wines** 27 bottles over £20, 20 bottles under £20, 20 by glass **Notes** Sunday L, Vegetarian available **Seats** 65 **Children** Portions, Menu **Parking** 30

LOWER VOBSTER — Map 4 ST74

The Vobster Inn

◉◉ British, European

Spanish-influenced menus in a country pub

☎ 01373 812920
BA3 5RJ
e-mail: info@vobsterinn.co.uk
dir: 4m W of Frome, between Wells & Leigh upon Mendip

The Vobster is a friendly and welcoming stone-built inn dating from the 17th century surrounded by four acres of rolling countryside. Food is an important part of the operation, with the lively bar serving baguettes, sausage and mash and cheese omelette with chips. A blackboard lists tapas (the chef-proprietor is Spanish) along the lines of chorizo, patatas bravas, and chick pea and beetroot houmus, while a full menu operates in the quieter dining room. Start with onion soup twirled with truffle oil, or seared pigeon breast with white pudding, and go on to tender rib-eye with garlic butter, crisp onion rings and a fried egg, roast sea bass with pesto, or roast chicken breast flavoured with thyme and saffron served with braised red cabbage and truffled potatoes. Finish with a straightforward dessert like crema catalana with orange sorbet, or chocolate mousse.

Times 12-3/6.30-11 Closed 25 Dec, Mon (check at BHs), D Sun

MIDSOMER NORTON — Map 4 ST65

The Moody Goose at The Old Priory

◉◉ Modern British

Stylish modern cooking in ancient priory

☎ 01761 416784 & 410846
Church Square BA3 2HX
e-mail: info@theoldpriory.co.uk
web: www.theoldpriory.co.uk
dir: Along High St, right at lights, right at rdbt, behind St John's Church

Dating from 1152, The Old Priory is one of the oldest properties in the county and has the usual allocation of flagstones, inglenooks and beams. The restaurant, though, has been given a contemporary look while still respecting original features. The kitchen has a modern outlook too, turning its attention to a warm buttery pastry tart of crab, tomato and parmesan topped with rocket pesto, and a labour-intensive plate of wild rabbit and shiitaki terrine with ham knuckle and quince jelly. Ideas are carefully thought out so dishes are a happy marriage of tastes and textures; seen in main courses of pan-fried strips of rib-eye accompanied by oxtail ravioli and wilted spinach, for example, and steamed cold-smoked salmon with scallop mousseline and a potato cake. Breads and incidentals like canapés are consistently impressive, as are puddings like a trio of banana - parfait, tempura and caramelised - with chocolate and butterscotch sauces.

Chef Stephen Shore **Owner** Stephen Shore **Times** 11.30-2/6.30-9 Closed Xmas, New Year, Sun **Prices** Fixed D 3 course £39.50, Service optional, Groups min 8 service 10% **Wines** 81 bottles over £20, 13 bottles under £20, 9 by glass **Notes** Vegetarian available, Dress restrictions, Smart casual **Seats** 34, Pr/dining room 22 **Children** Portions **Parking** 12

Save on Hotels. Book at **theAA.com/hotel**

SOMERSET 421 ENGLAND

MILVERTON
Map 3 ST12

The Globe

◉ Modern British

Modern culinary thinking in a country pub

☎ 01823 400534
Fore St TA4 1JX
e-mail: adele@theglobemilverton.co.uk
dir: M5 junct 26 onto A38, then B3187 to Milverton

The peaceful village setting not far from Taunton is one of the main attractions of this appealing red-brick country pub. Inside is airy and light in the modern way, with lots of white paint and blond wood, and comfortable high-backed chairs at bare-topped tables. The kitchen goes in for up-to-date ideas, bringing on a starter of goats' cheese mousse with a black olive cake and semi-dried tomatoes, and mains such as sea bass with curried lentils in Thai coconut broth, or Creedy Carver duck breast in a spiced plum glaze with Savoy cabbage and apple. Most of your dessert favourites appear at the finishing line: crème brûlée, sticky toffee pudding, tiramisù and the like.

Times 12-3/6-11.30 Closed L Mon, D Sun

OAKHILL
Map 4 ST64

The Oakhill Inn

◉ Modern British **NEW**

Well-judged menu in a country inn

☎ 01749 840442
Fosse Rd BA3 5HU
e-mail: info@theoakhillinn.com
dir: On A367 between Stratton-on-the-Fosse & Shepton Mallet

A country inn on the A367, The Oakhill gazes out over the undulating Mendips, with the village church for company. Inside, the stone interiors presents a mix of sofas and tables in the main bar, where locals knock back Orchard Pig cider and cask ales, and a quieter dining area with unclothed wooden tables and candles and a log fire. The kitchen uses quality regional produce in an uncomplicated way for pub cooking that's a cut above the norm. Tiger prawns dressed in sweet chilli sauce on a crisp salad with coriander fires up the taste buds, as a prelude to a venison steak with dauphinoise and seasonal greens in gin sauce, or roast salmon with Jersey Royals and kale in caper butter. Puddings include apple and pear crumble, bread-and-butter pudding with banana, and a fine, thin-shelled treacle tart served with excellent vanilla ice cream.

Chef Neil Creese **Times** 12-3/6-9 **Prices** Food prices not confirmed for 2013. Please telephone for details

PORLOCK
Map 3 SS84

The Oaks Hotel

◉ Traditional British

Traditional cooking in the Exmoor National Park

☎ 01643 862265
TA24 8ES
e-mail: info@oakshotel.co.uk
dir: At bottom of Dunstersteepe Road, on left on entering Porlock from Minehead

This Edwardian house hotel is the kind of place where the genuine hospitality of the hands-on, husband-and-wife-team who run the place keeps the customers coming back. It helps that it's in a lovely spot, of course, on the outskirts of a village in the Exmoor National Park. The cheery yellow-walled restaurant has panoramic views and a short daily-changing dinner menu of unfussy, traditional dishes, cooked by Anne Riley. There's plenty of local produce and a genuine regional flavour; start with a delicious bacon, mushroom and cheese savoury, moving on to a tender breast of guinea fowl with morels, and finish with a flavoursome banana and ginger ice cream.

Times 7-8 Closed Nov-Mar

SHEPTON MALLET
Map 4 ST64

Charlton House Spa Hotel

◉ Modern British **NEW** ◉

Good cooking in a smart country house

☎ 01749 342008
Charlton Rd BA4 4PR
e-mail: enquiries.charltonhousehotel@bannatyne.co.uk
dir: On A361 towards Frome, 1m from town centre

Owned by *Dragon's Den* star Duncan Bannatyne, Charlton House aims at the corporate market, with business facilities and spa pampering all part of the package, as well as a dining room done in best country-house chintz, with swagged curtains framing a view over the gardens. Service is from a keen young team, who maintain a relaxed atmosphere for a dining experience that draws on local produce for simple but effective dishes with much to commend them, not least the fact that the main ingredient in each case is allowed to shine. A mousse of Cerney Ash goats' cheese is wrapped in wild garlic leaves and accompanied by roast red and yellow peppers for a well-balanced opener, while mains deal in the likes of lightly poached fillets of John Dory with spiced cauliflower fritters and a salad dressed in mint and chilli, and desserts aim for a triumphant final flourish with banana Tatin and rum and raisin ice cream, garnished with caramelised pecans.

Chef Matt Lord **Owner** Bannatyne Fitness Ltd
Times 12-3/7-9.30 **Prices** Fixed L 2 course £13.95, Fixed D 3 course £32.95, Service optional **Wines** 50 bottles over £20, 3 bottles under £20, 8 by glass **Notes** Sunday L, Vegetarian available, Dress restrictions, Smart casual, Civ Wed 120 **Seats** 50, Pr/dining room 18 **Children** Portions, Menu **Parking** 50

Rendezvous Restaurant

◉ Modern British, European **NEW**

Smart old inn with an industrious kitchen

☎ 01749 342058
Thatched Cottage, 63-67 Charlton Rd BA4 5QF
e-mail: david@thatchedcottage.info
dir: 0.6m E of Shepton Mallet, at lights on A361

The Grade II listed Thatched Cottage Inn has the eponymous covering on the roof of its three-and-half-century-old frame. Don't go thinking that inside it is stuck in the past though, with a refurb providing a gently contemporary polish without detracting from the charm of the place - wooden beams and panelling, large stone fireplaces and a neutral colour scheme. The two main dining areas (there's a relaxed bar area too) have well-spaced wooden tables topped with flickering candles, looked over by an engaging service team. Good local produce takes centre stage and just about everything is made in-house; Somerset smokey is a first course consisting of smoked haddock, salmon and cod in a creamy white wine sauce, while main course might be lamb steak with red onion marmalade, potatoes boulangère and seasonal vegetables. For dessert, treacle tart hedges its bets with its accompanying vanilla ice cream and pot of vanilla custard.

Times 12-2.30/6.30-9.30

SOMERTON
Map 4 ST42

The Devonshire Arms

◉ Modern British

Good, honest cooking by the village green

☎ 01458 241271
Long Sutton TA10 9LP
e-mail: mail@thedevonshirearms.com
dir: Off A303 onto A372 at Podimore rdbt. After 4m, left onto B3165, signed Martock and Long Sutton

Set on a picturesque village green, The Devonshire Arms is a Grade II listed former hunting lodge turned restaurant with rooms. A cheery atmosphere awaits whether you're after a pint or a full-blown meal in the restaurant with its modern, muted tones and unclothed tables, or outside in the courtyard or large walled garden. From the locally-sourced and daily-changing menu of well-judged dishes comes the like of roast fillet of bream with horseradish mousse and herb salad, and Quantock duck confit with pearl barley 'risotto'. Finish with a West Country cheeseboard or ginger sticky toffee pudding with Grand Marnier sauce and lime leaf ice cream.

Chef Sasha Matkevich **Owner** Philip & Sheila Mepham **Times** 12-2.30/7-9.30 Closed 25-26 Dec, 1 Jan **Prices** Starter £5.95-£10.50, Main £10.50-£17.95, Dessert £5.75-£8.75, Service optional **Wines** 20 bottles over £20, 10 bottles under £20, 8 by glass **Notes** ALC menu served D, Sunday L, Vegetarian available **Seats** 40 **Children** Portions, Menu **Parking** 6, On street

Ston Easton Park

◉◉ Modern British

Properly memorable cooking at a Palladian manor

☎ 01761 241631
BA3 4DF
e-mail: info@stoneaston.co.uk
dir: A39 from Bath for approx 8m. Onto A37 (Shepton Mallet). Hotel in next village

A splendid snapshot of the early-Georgian Palladian style, Ston Easton is a treat. The 36 acres of grounds include gardens landscaped by Humphry Repton, as well as an 18th-century icehouse and a fountain in a ruined grotto, plus the babbling waters of the River Norr. There's also a Victorian walled kitchen garden that serves the kitchen well with organic fruit and veg, herbs and even edible flowers. You're positively invited to have a wander round, and get some green-fingered tips from the head gardener. It all ends up being transformed into the carefully worked-out menus of the Sorrel dining room, where intense flavours and pin-sharp presentations are the order of the day. A first-course plate bravely teams up poached salmon, Brixham crab, merguez sausage and heritage tomatoes from the garden for a stimulating composition, followed perhaps by a cleverly modulated take on classic French cuisine, as in the lapin aux pruneaux that features the fruit-stuffed saddle with braised lentils and a bubble-and-squeak croquette. Desserts bring on garden berries in the season, perhaps loaded on to a Pavlova and accompanied by a raspberry sorbet.

Times 12-2/7-9.30

Farthings Country House Hotel and Restaurant

◉ Traditional British ☘

Farmhouse hotel with appealingly unfussy cooking

☎ 01823 480664 & 0785 6688128
Village Rd, Hatch Beauchamp TA3 6SG
e-mail: farthingshotel@yahoo.co.uk
dir: M5 junct 25 towards Ilminster, Yeovil, Chard on A358. From A303 towards Taunton & M5. Hatch Beauchamp signed off A358

Originally a 17th-century farmhouse, not far from Taunton, Farthings retains echoes of its former life, in that poultry, pigs and lambs are reared by the owners to supply the kitchens. Three acres of walled garden and orchards also earn their keep, and it all turns up in the high-ceilinged, comfortable dining room, warmed by log-fires in winter. The cooking keeps things simple, the better to showcase that assiduously raised produce, offering a bacon and sage terrine to start, for instance, perhaps followed by Gressingham duck breast with red cabbage and dauphinoise in quince jus, or Lyme Bay king scallops with black pudding and chilli-dressed leaves.

Chocolate marquise with mango sorbet is an appealingly indulgent way to finish.

Chef Vincent Adeline **Owner** John Seeger
Times 12-3/6.30-9.15 **Prices** Fixed L 2 course £22-£29.50, Fixed D 3 course £29-£39, Starter £6.50-£9, Main £16-£25, Dessert £7-£9, Service optional
Wines 48 bottles over £20, 4 bottles under £20, 6 by glass **Notes** Sunday L, Vegetarian available, Civ Wed 50 **Seats** 60, Pr/dining room 24 **Children** Portions **Parking** 25

The Mount Somerset Hotel

◉◉ British

Luxurious cooking in a luxurious hotel

☎ 01823 442500
Henlade TA3 5NB
e-mail: info@mountsomersethotel.co.uk
dir: M5 junct 25, A358 towards Chard/Ilminster; right in Henlade (Stoke St Mary), left at T-junct. Hotel 400yds on right

Sitting in four acres of grounds in an elevated position between the Quantock and Blackdown Hills, The Mount Somerset surely boasts some of the best views in the county. It's an elegant Regency building, full of period features such as high ceilings, a sweeping spiral staircase (unsurprisingly popular for wedding photos), wooden floors and open fireplaces. The restaurant has a similarly traditional look, with muted tones and views out to the terrace, croquet lawn and gardens. The modern British cooking is founded on top-notch seasonal and local produce, and dishes are simply but attractively presented. A spring meal might begin with something delightfully simple like a velouté of English asparagus with a poached hen's egg and asparagus tips, while to follow the whole Brixham day-boat lemon sole with crème fraîche crushed potato, spinach and lemon and herb butter may appeal. Rhubarb pannacotta with poached rhubarb, curd, jelly and lemon sorbet makes a fine finish.

Times 12-2/7-9.30

The Willow Tree Restaurant

◉◉ Modern British ☘

Pin-sharp cooking in a 17th-century townhouse

☎ 01823 352835
3 Tower Ln, Off Tower St TA1 4AR
e-mail: dine@thewillowtreerestaurant.com
dir: 200yds from Taunton bus station

Tucked away down a little lane beside a stream, The Willow Tree is a cosy and intimate sort of restaurant, beamed and tastefully furnished and decorated, with well-chosen artwork on the walls and high-backed chairs at clothed tables. Darren Sherlock applies his distinctively precise, thoughtful cooking style to tip-top produce to give it the maximum impact with the minimum of fuss. Cheddar soufflé is a light, well-risen classic of great flavour balanced by a creamy sauce of walnuts and celery, and another starter, of confit duck gizzard, served with Puy lentils, bacon, smoked celeriac

purée and a pear and quince jelly, impresses for its well-thought-out marriage of flavours and textures. Main courses include pan-fried venison, tender and succulent, served simply with pan-fried root vegetables and contrasting sweet potato purée, and seared hake fillet topped with brandade sauced with chive beurre blanc. Baking skills are evident in breads, and thought and workmanship are behind even straightforward-sounding desserts like Muscovado crème brûlée with spicy fig compôte.

Chef Darren Sherlock **Owner** Darren Sherlock & Rita Rambellas **Times** 6.30-9 Closed Jan, Aug, Sun-Mon, Thu, L all week **Prices** Fixed D 3 course £24.95-£29.95, Service added but optional 10% **Wines** 10 bottles over £20, 25 bottles under £20, 6 by glass **Notes** Vegetarian available, Dress restrictions, Smart casual **Seats** 25 **Parking** 20 yds, 300 spaces

Crown & Victoria

◉ British

Good, honest cooking in a village pub

☎ 01935 823341
14 Farm St BA22 8PZ
e-mail: info@thecrownandvictoria.co.uk
dir: W'bound off A303 follow signs for Tintinhull

Drinkers as well as diners are welcomed at this village pub in pretty, peaceful gardens, with a selection of real ales to choose from. It's a relaxing place, with friendly service and a jolly atmosphere. The kitchen prides itself on its use of free-range and organic produce, much sourced from local farms, and it makes good use of it, producing well-executed dishes of well-matched combinations - nothing too over-elaborate though. A thick slab of goats' cheese coated in almonds, orange and black pepper, served warm and melting with red onion marmalade, is an impressive opener, with perhaps a terrine of pigeon, ham and quail with gooseberry chutney an alternative. Familiar staples like beer-battered haddock with the usual accompaniments can be found among main courses, alongside pan-fried duck breast with Madeira sauce, rösti and spinach. Finish with impeccable vanilla pannacotta with wafer-thin slices of pineapple.

Chef Steven Yates **Owner** Isabel Thomas, Mark Hillyard **Times** 12-2.30/6.30-9.30 Closed D Sun **Prices** Food prices not confirmed for 2013. Please telephone for details **Wines** 20 bottles over £20, 11 bottles under £20, 8 by glass **Notes** Sunday L, Vegetarian available **Seats** 100, Pr/dining room 45 **Children** Portions, Menu **Parking** 50

WELLS   Map 4 ST54

Ancient Gate House Hotel

◉ Italian

Refined Italian cooking opposite the cathedral

☎ 01749 672029
20 Sadler St BA5 2SE
e-mail: info@ancientgatehouse.co.uk
dir: 1st hotel on left on cathedral green

A more quintessentially English scene than the green in front of Wells cathedral's sublime west face is hard to imagine, and you have an unobstructed view of it from the Ancient Gate House Hotel. The hotel itself does not lack for history, as the 15th-century Great West Gate, once part of the city wall, forms part of the building. With its fireplace, black beams, and red lampshades set against white walls, the Rugantino Restaurant may have the look of a tea room, but the kitchen speaks Italian. Under the leadership of the Rossi family, there are good supply lines to authentic materials from Italy, and free-range egg pasta is freshly made in-house. It all adds up to good Italian cooking, all the way from an exemplary risotto of Umbrian black truffle and porcini, through a rich lasagne made with bolognese sauce, buffalo mozzarella, fresh basil, salami and parmesan, to main courses such as parmesan-and-herb-crusted lamb cutlets with onion and garlic rösti, and shallot and redcurrant jus.

Chef Simon Jackson **Owner** Nicholas & Jonathan Rossi **Times** 12-2.30/6-10 Closed 25-29 Dec **Prices** Fixed L 2 course fr £10.90, Fixed D 3 course £25, Starter £5.75-£8.25, Main £12.50-£16.50, Dessert £6, Service added but optional 10% **Wines** 16 bottles over £20, 19 bottles under £20, 8 by glass **Notes** Tasting menu & pre/post cathedral concert menu available, Sunday L, Vegetarian available **Seats** 40, Pr/dining room 20 **Children** Portions **Parking** On street

Best Western Swan Hotel

◉◉ Modern British 🍃

An ancient inn with creative contemporary cooking

☎ 01749 836300
Sadler St BA5 2RX
e-mail: info@swanhotelwells.co.uk
dir: A39, A371, on entering Wells follow signs for Hotels & Deliveries. Hotel on right opposite cathedral

The Swan, in the shadow of the cathedral, has 600 years of history behind it, although restoration and extensions mean guests have all the amenities of a 21st-century hotel. The restaurant is a characterful room, with antiques, panelling, just-so table settings and comfortable upholstered seats. The menus offer much of interest, from teriyaki-grilled salmon fillet with lime-scented new potatoes and red pepper butter, to steak and chips with béarnaise. Top-notch produce is handled confidently, from partridge breast, cooked just right, served with chicory, wild mushrooms and apple jus, to fresh-tasting, well-timed fried halibut fillet with a rich saffron beurre blanc, three mussels, some kohlrabi and

slices of chorizo. Puddings make an impact too: perhaps an assiette of chocolate desserts.

Chef Leigh Say **Owner** Kevin Newton **Times** 12-2/7-9.30 **Prices** Fixed L 2 course fr £12, Fixed D 3 course fr £25.50, Starter £5.50-£8.50, Main £15.50-£28.95, Dessert £6.50-£8, Service optional **Wines** 20 bottles over £20, 16 bottles under £20, 7 by glass **Notes** Sunday L, Vegetarian available, Civ Wed 90 **Seats** 50, Pr/dining room 90 **Children** Portions, Menu **Parking** 25

Goodfellows

◉◉ Mediterranean, European

Seafood and pâtisserie in a restaurant of two halves

☎ 01749 673866
5 Sadler St BA5 2RR
e-mail: goodfellows@btconnect.com
web: www.goodfellowswells.co.uk
dir: Town centre near Market Place

Here is the very image of a 21st-century eatery. Spread over two levels there's an open-plan kitchen on the ground floor (effectively making the whole area a chef's table) big tables and seating for lolling around on upstairs, and next door, a café-pâtisserie where the croissants, pastries, cakes and chocolates can be eaten in or taken away. Apart from all that enticing sweet stuff, fish and seafood are the principal draw, the Brixham boats supplying most of the sea-fresh catch. Start perhaps with scallop ravioli in oyster and lettuce velouté, before moving on to brill with cucumber spaghetti and keta in champagne and dill butter sauce, or sea bass with saffron-braised fennel, Med veg and tapenade. West Country cheeses are a feature, or go for bitter chocolate mousse with hazelnut praline and raspberry sorbet.

Chef Adam Fellows **Owner** Adam & Martine Fellows **Times** 12-2/6.30-9.30 Closed 25-27 Dec, 1,7-20 Jan, Sun-Mon, D Tue **Prices** Fixed L 2 course fr £20, Fixed D 3 course fr £39, Starter £6.50-£14, Main £13.50-£24, Dessert £4-£8, Service optional, Groups min 8 service 8%

Wines 38 bottles over £20, 9 bottles under £20, 11 by glass **Notes** Tasting menu 6 course, Vegetarian available **Seats** 35, Pr/dining room 20 **Children** Portions

The Old Spot

◉◉ European

Superior bistro in the shadow of the cathedral

☎ 01749 689099
12 Sadler St BA5 2SE
e-mail: theoldspotwells@googlemail.com
dir: On entering Wells, follow signs for Hotels & Deliveries. Sadler St leads into High St, Old Spot on left opposite Swan Hotel

We're already off to a flying start with the setting of the Old Spot: a Georgian townhouse in the historic heart of Wells with views of the ornate west façade of the cathedral. Even the name is appetising, conjuring images of unpretentious porcine pleasure, and there's nothing flashy about the relaxed interior, just French oak tables on polished wooden floors and framed menus on the walls. The ethos here is that less is more, so the cooking kicks unnecessary adornment into touch to focus on what counts: top quality ingredients brought together intelligently with a minimum of fuss and maximum flavour. Clearly-focused menus - four choices at each stage - get under way with the likes of potato pancake with mallard, onion confit and Parma ham. This is the kind of food that makes you want it all - whether it is roast brill with mussel cream sauce, cucumber and dill, or an earthy braised pork belly partnered with black pudding, celeriac purée and caramelised pears. Chef-proprietor Ian Bates has a long connection with Gallic cuisine, so you just know that a classic crème brûlée is the way to end.

Chef Ian Bates **Owner** Ian & Clare Bates **Times** 12.30-2.30/7-10.30 Closed 1 wk Xmas, Mon, L Tue, D Sun **Prices** Fixed L 2 course fr £15.50, Starter £5.50-£8.50, Main £12.50-£21, Dessert £6-£7.50, Service optional, Groups min 6 service 10% **Wines** 46 bottles over £20, 10 bottles under £20, 17 by glass **Notes** Sunday L, Vegetarian available **Seats** 50 **Children** Portions **Parking** On street, Market Square

WESTON-SUPER-MARE   Map 4 ST36

The Cove

◉ Modern British 🍃

Stylish seafront dining with a Mediterranean influence

☎ 01934 418217
Marine Lake, Birnbeck Rd BS23 2BX
e-mail: info@the-cove.co.uk
dir: From Grand Pier on Royal Parade N onto Knightstone Rd. Left into Birnbeck Rd. Restaurant on left

Forget images of knotted hankies on the head: Weston-super-Mare's northern seafront has been propelled upmarket by an ongoing programme of redevelopment that has seen an erstwhile bandstand get a new lease of life as this smartly revamped bistro-style restaurant.

continued

WESTON-SUPER-MARE *continued*

Smack on the seafront near Birnbeck Pier, The Cove falls nicely into step with the town's new look. Inside it has all been thought through: the minimal contemporary style - oak floors, white walls, floor-to-ceiling picture windows - could hold its own in any trendy coastal hotspot, while chunky pale wood tables are thoughtfully angled so that everyone gets a sea view. Good quality fish and seafood landed by dayboats in Newlyn and Brixham forms the backbone of a Mediterranean-accented menu which runs a gamut from old favourites like breaded fish with home-made tartare sauce and proper chips, to herb-crusted cod with olive oil mash, mussel and pea velouté. Leave room for an inventive pudding such as steamed ale cake with local beer ice cream and dark Muscovado sauce.

Chef Richard Tudor, Gemma Stacey **Owner** Heath Hardy & Gemma Stacey **Times** 12-6/6-9.30 Closed 25 Dec, Mon, D Sun **Prices** Fixed L 3 course £16.50, Starter £4.50-£8, Main £10.95-£18.95, Dessert £4.50-£5.25, Service optional **Wines** 26 bottles over £20, 21 bottles under £20, 11 by glass **Notes** Sunday L, Vegetarian available **Seats** 65 **Children** Portions, Menu **Parking** On street/car park

---

WINCANTON	Map 4 ST72

Holbrook House

@ @ British, French 🕭

Inventive cooking in a charming country-house setting

☎ 01963 824466
Holbrook BA9 8BS
e-mail: enquiries@holbrookhouse.co.uk
web: www.holbrookhouse.co.uk
dir: From A303 at Wincanton, turn left on A371 towards Castle Cary & Shepton Mallet

On the borders of Somerset, Dorset and Wiltshire, this elegant country-house hotel is in a peaceful rural spot, close to abundant running rivers, lush green hills and woodland. Inside all is traditionally done out, and smartly so, with the comfort factor extending to the convivial and elegant Cedar restaurant and its crisply laid tables. There's an undoubted French-influence to the kitchen's modish output, plus a genuine seasonal flavour. A first-course trio of smoked quail comes with artichoke purée, frisée salad and saffron vinaigrette, or go for the tried-and-true combo of pan-friend scallops with pancetta crisp, cauliflower purée, jazzed up with coriander oil. Main-course rosé-wine poached halibut is served with braised bok choy, clams and mussels, and finished with a champagne and caviar sauce, and for dessert, an assiette of rhubarb with rhubarb custard, sorbet and jelly is a dessert for our times.

Chef Callum O'Doherty **Owner** Mr & Mrs J McGinley **Times** 12.30-2/7-9 Closed L Mon-Thu, D Sun **Prices** Fixed L 2 course fr £14.50, Starter £7.25-£9, Main £17.50-£26.50, Dessert £6.50-£7.95 **Wines** 86 bottles over £20, 20 bottles under £20, 10 by glass **Notes** Sunday L, Vegetarian available, Dress restrictions, Smart casual, Civ Wed 250 **Seats** 70, Pr/dining room 140 **Children** Portions **Parking** 100

Little Barwick House

YEOVIL	Map 4 ST51

Modern European 🍷

Consistently high standards in village restaurant with rooms

☎ 01935 423902
Barwick Village BA22 9TD
e-mail: reservations@barwick7.fsnet.co.uk
dir: Turn off A371 Yeovil to Dorchester opposite Red House rdbt, 0.25m on left

This Georgian dower house is tucked away on a quiet lane in peaceful gardens, while within are wooden floors, open fires, and comfortable sofas - all very inviting. Candlelight and crisp napery set the tone in the restaurant, where staff, led by Emma Ford, go about their business professionally with the minimum of fuss. Tim Ford's confident cooking takes a no bells-and-whistles approach; rather, he turns out disarmingly simple, enjoyably balanced dishes, changing his menus daily depending on availability. Cheese soufflé is served with a spicy ragoût of smoked haddock and mussels, and a deeply flavoured, warm terrine is made with veal sweetbreads and confit pork belly and accompanied by deep-fried leeks and cider and brandy sauce. Pink-roast saddle of roe deer, served with braised red cabbage, beetroot purée and rösti, is considered Tim's tour de force, each element making an impact, while other main courses are equally on the money: perhaps pan-fried fillet of sea bass with champagne sauce, roast fennel and saffron potato. Puddings are as impressively made as what precedes them: try passionfruit tart and sorbet with mango mousse and coconut pannacotta.

Chef Timothy Ford **Owner** Emma & Timothy Ford **Times** 12-2/7-9.30 Closed New Year, 2 wks Jan, Mon, L Tue, D Sun **Prices** Fixed L 2 course £23.95, Fixed D 3 course £43.95, Service optional **Wines** 179 bottles over £20, 21 bottles under £20, 6 by glass **Notes** ALC L 2 course fr £20, 3 course fr £24.95, Vegetarian available **Seats** 40 **Children** Portions **Parking** 25

WOOKEY HOLE   Map 4 ST54

Wookey Hole Inn

@ Modern European

Vibrant cooking in quirky Somerset inn

☎ 01749 676677
High St BA5 1BP
e-mail: mail@wookeyholeinn.com

The beamed exterior of this village inn opposite the eponymous tourist-magnet caves presents an orthodox face to the world, but inside there's a one-off maverick approach to interior décor, with a quirky collection of art and objets referencing the Mediterranean, North Africa and nearby Glastonbury. You may never make it out of the convivial bar unless you approach the arsenal of local ales, ciders and perries, and tongue-twisting, brain-scrambling Belgian brews with caution, which would be a shame as the eclectic menu sings in tune with the setting, referencing the Mediterranean and North Africa in an enticing repertoire. Ham and spinach potato cake with tomato and cardamom chutney, and smoked mayonnaise is a typical starter, while mains could bring on pan-roasted rump of lamb with dauphinoise potato, red onion tarte Tatin and carrot purée. Medjool date and custard tart with a shot glass of rhubarb and Campari jelly is an inventive way to finish.

Chef Adam Kennington **Owner** Richard Davey
Times 12-2.30/7-9.30 Closed 25-26 Dec, D Sun
Prices Starter £6-£8, Main £12.95-£24.60, Dessert £4-£7.95, Service optional **Wines** 15 bottles over £20, 12 bottles under £20, 6 by glass **Notes** Sunday L, Vegetarian available **Seats** 60, Pr/dining room 12 **Children** Portions, Menu **Parking** 12

YEOVIL   Map 4 ST51

Lanes

@@ Modern British

Contemporary brasserie amid boutique splendour

☎ 01935 862555
West Coker BA22 9AJ
e-mail: stay@laneshotel.net
dir: 2m W of Yeovil, on A30 towards Crewkerne

From the outside you'd be forgiven for thinking this Edwardian rectory in the rolling hills of Somerset housed a traditional country-house hotel, but, in fact, behind the trad façade lies a modish boutique hotel with a spa and a conspicuously contemporary brasserie. The coolly minimalist brasserie, with its acres of plate glass and white walls hung with striking modern artworks by local artist John Adam, wouldn't look out of place in a big city. The menu is an appealing blend of traditional comforts and more contemporary ideas, all of which are presented with a 21st-century sheen and suit the brasserie vibe. You might take the more traditional route from moules marinière to a cheeseburger with smoked applewood cheddar and home-made ketchup. Alternatively, there are more creative offerings such as breadcrumbed lamb's sweetbreads with ratatouille, followed by venison steak

with potato puffs and a chilli-chocolate jus. Finish with St Clement's tart with lime syrup and frozen yoghurt or West Country cheeses.

Chef Marcela Morales **Owner** John & Alison Roehrig
Times 12-2.30/7-9.30 Closed L Sat **Prices** Fixed L 2 course fr £14, Starter £4.25-£7, Main £9.50-£16, Dessert £5, Service optional **Wines** 27 bottles over £20, 21 bottles under £20, 10 by glass **Notes** Sunday L, Vegetarian available **Seats** 85, Pr/dining room 40 **Children** Portions **Parking** 65

Little Barwick House

@@@ – see opposite

The Yeovil Court Hotel & Restaurant

@@ Modern European

Modern hotel with stimulating brasserie cooking

☎ 01935 863746
West Coker Rd BA20 2HE
e-mail: unwind@yeovilhotel.com
web: www.yeovilhotel.com
dir: 2.5m W of town centre on A30

On the outskirts of town, the sparkling white Yeovil Court has been kitted out with a modern makeover. It's all expansive, light-filled, airy spaces these days, and is run with a relaxed approach by a young team. The entire ground floor is given over to eating and drinking in one form or another, from the bar where lighter bites are served to the large restaurant with its black-and-white window blinds and elegant table settings. The cooking offers a stimulating version of modern brasserie food, influences drawn from far and wide for the likes of marinated tuna with Thai noodle salad dressed in chilli and sesame oil, followed by fillet of Dorset beef with satisfyingly textured pearl barley risotto and parsnip crisps, or grilled monkfish with red onion couscous and rocket. A classic combination of flavours and temperatures distinguishes a finisher of hot chocolate fondant with pistachio ice cream.

Chef Simon Walford **Owner** Brian Devonport
Times 12-1.45/7-9.30 Closed 26-30 Dec, L Sat
Prices Food prices not confirmed for 2013. Please telephone for details **Wines** 12 bottles over £20, 27 bottles under £20, 8 by glass **Notes** Vegetarian available **Seats** 50, Pr/dining room 80 **Children** Portions **Parking** 65

STAFFORDSHIRE

BURTON UPON TRENT   Map 10 SK22

Three Queens Hotel

@ Modern British

Central location, traditional home comforts

☎ 01283 523800
1 Bridge St DE14 1SY
e-mail: hotel@threequeenshotel.co.uk
dir: On A511, at junct of High St & Bridge St

The Three Queens Hotel dates from 1531 and sits at the centre of town close to the River Trent amid Burton's brewing heritage. Friendly staff make sure everyone gets a warm welcome, and the place exudes an easygoing, lived-in vibe. The relaxed Grill Room has a clubby intimacy with its wood panelling, screens and stained-glass windows that sits well with the kitchen's straightforward traditional cooking. Reliable hands in the kitchen conjure up comfortable mainstream ideas from well-sourced ingredients - seared scallops in garlic butter with salsify purée might appear among starters, while mains can be as simple as chargrilled steaks, braised lamb shank with roasted root vegetables and rosemary jus, or follow a more Mediterranean route by teaming chicken ballottine filled with sun-dried tomatoes with black olive mash and basil cream.

Chef Stuart Robotham **Owner** Three Queens Hotel Ltd
Times 12-9.15/6.15-10 Closed L all week **Prices** Fixed L 2 course £12.95-£14.50, Fixed D 3 course £17.50, Starter £4.95-£7.95, Main £9.95-£17.95, Dessert £4.95, Service optional **Wines** 17 bottles over £20, 18 bottles under £20, 8 by glass **Notes** Gourmet D £39.50, wine tasting evening £19.50, Vegetarian available **Seats** 36, Pr/dining room 60 **Children** Portions, Menu **Parking** 55

LEEK   Map 16 SJ95

Three Horseshoes Inn & Country Hotel

@@ Modern British, Thai V

Thai and modern Brit food in charming country inn

☎ 01538 300296
Buxton Rd, Blackshaw Moor ST13 8TW
e-mail: enquiries@threeshoesinn.co.uk
dir: M6 junct 15 or 16 onto A500. Exit A53 towards Leek. Turn left onto A50 (Burslem)

The setting amid the Staffordshire moorlands, overlooking the Tittesworth reservoir, makes for a fine first impression here, and behind the bucolic creeper-covered frontage of this old inn lies a surprise or two. For on the menu is a mix of Thai and modern British food, all based on a good deal of carefully-sourced regional produce. It is served up in a splendid room, the modish looking brasserie, with its high oak-beamed ceiling and open-to-view kitchen (elsewhere the more trad country inn accoutrements are present and correct). You might start with duck spring roll served with a coriander dip, or terrine of chicken, rabbit and pigeon with fig and cherry chutney - this is not

continued

LEEK *continued*

fusion food, with the two styles of cooking kept distinct. Main-course Penang beef is a fine version, or go for gilt head bream stuffed with langoustine mousse.

Chef Mark & Stephen Kirk **Owner** Bill, Jill, Mark & Stephen Kirk **Times** 6.30-9 Closed 26-30 Dec, 1-2 Jan, Sun, L all week **Prices** Fixed D 3 course £19.95, Starter £5.50-£7.50, Main £10.95-£19.95, Dessert £4.95-£6.75 **Wines** 30 bottles over £20, 50 bottles under £20, 10 by glass **Notes** Tasting menu available, Vegetarian menu, Dress restrictions, Smart casual, Civ Wed 178 **Seats** 50, Pr/dining room 150 **Children** Portions, Menu **Parking** 100

LICHFIELD   Map 10 SK10

Swinfen Hall Hotel

@@ Modern British V ☝

Classy modern cooking in a classic location

☎ 01543 481494
Swinfen WS14 9RE
e-mail: info@swinfenhallhotel.co.uk
web: www.swinfenhallhotel.co.uk
dir: 2m S of Lichfield on A38 between Weeford rdbt & Swinfen rdbt

Swinfen Hall is a neo-classical Georgian manor house that has the look of a costume drama film set, an impression which continues through to the Four Seasons Restaurant, where oak panelling, opulent swagged drapes at sash windows, and linen-clad tables set with shiny silver, Wedgwood china and crystal glasses create a suitably classical setting. The country-house cooking fits the bill, but it shows its mettle with some gently contemporary touches. An emphasis on local-sourcing sees head chef Adam Thomson curing his own meats and smoking his own fish, while the hotel's own walled garden supplies much of the seasonal fruit and vegetables. If you're not up to the full-dress tasting menu, the prix-fixe formula might set off with tortellini of lobster with confit tomatoes and basil purée, then proceed via a classy turf and surf combo of pan-fried John Dory and crisp pork belly matched with a leek tarte fine and pork jus, to conclude exotically with star anise pannacotta with pineapple and pink peppercorn salad and rum sorbet.

Chef Adam Thomson **Owner** Helen & Vic Wiser **Times** 12.30-2.30/7.30-9.30 Closed L Sat, D Sun **Prices** Tasting menu £59, Service optional **Wines** 108 bottles over £20, 9 bottles under £20, 6 by glass **Notes** ALC D 3 course £47.50, Sunday L, Vegetarian menu, Dress restrictions, No trainers or jeans, Civ Wed 120 **Seats** 50, Pr/dining room 20 **Parking** 80

STAFFORD   Map 10 SJ92

The Moat House

@@ Modern British ☝

Confident, creative cooking by a canal

☎ 01785 712217
Lower Penkridge Rd, Acton Trussell ST17 0RJ
e-mail: info@moathouse.co.uk
dir: M6 junct 13 towards Stafford, 1st right to Acton Trussell, hotel by church

This Grade II-listed moated manor house dating back to the 14th century has a lovely waterside location; diners in the Conservatory Restaurant get to watch the narrow boats wend their way along the canal from the comfort of their linen-clad tables, where candles flicker in the evening. The hotel competes in the wedding and business markets, while its restaurant is a hit for its ambitious contemporary cooking. The presence of a tasting menu nails their ambition to the mast (there's a veggie one too), with matching wines available if you wish to go the whole hog. From the à la carte, start with a decidedly modish Jerusalem artichoke velouté with caper and sultana purée, cauliflower beignet and micro coriander, before moving on to a flavoursome slow-cooked blade of beef with Savoy cabbage and bacon, creamed potatoes, chestnut mushrooms, glazed shallots and Guinness sauce. The creative thinking continues at dessert stage, too: banana and caramel parfait, perhaps, with toffee popcorn and bitter chocolate sorbet.

Chef Matthew Davies, James Cracknell **Owner** The Lewis Partnership **Times** 12-2/6.30-9.30 Closed 25 Dec **Prices** Fixed L 2 course £17-£25, Fixed D 3 course £22.95-£30, Starter £8-£12, Main £17-£28, Dessert £8-£9, Service optional **Wines** 94 bottles over £20, 41 bottles under £20, 16 by glass **Notes** Tasting & early doors menu available, Sunday L, Vegetarian available, Dress restrictions, No jeans, Civ Wed 120 **Seats** 120, Pr/dining room 150 **Children** Portions, Menu **Parking** 200

UTTOXETER   Map 10 SK03

Restaurant Gilmore at Strine's Farm

@@ Modern British ☝

Locally-supplied kitchen in a Staffordshire farmhouse

☎ 01889 507100
Beamhurst ST14 5DZ
e-mail: paul@restaurantgilmore.com
web: www.restaurantgilmore.com
dir: 1.5m N of Uttoxeter on A522 to Cheadle. Set 400yds back from road along fenced farm track

Sweep up the long drive to the Gilmore's converted farmhouse restaurant for hearty modern British cooking set in a pretty cottage garden. The house has the anticipated country charm and comforts, with the restaurant divided between a number of intimate ground-floor rooms decorated in warm neutral tones and tables laid with crisp white linen. The kitchen (with Paul Gilmore behind the stove) deals in quality produce, looking to the local Staffordshire larder wherever possible, including the property's own kitchen garden which supplies some of the fresh fruit, veg and herbs. Everything is home-made, while seasonality is a given and attention to detail reigns in dishes underpinned by a classical theme. Poached blade of Staffordshire beef 'bourguignonne' (with onions, mushrooms, bacon and mash), for example, or baked fillet of brill served with a spiced tomato and brown shrimp velouté, and to finish, maybe a signature bread-and-butter pudding with rich vanilla sauce anglaise.

Chef Paul Gilmore **Owner** Paul & Dee Gilmore **Times** 12.30-2/7.30-9 Closed 1 wk Jan, 1 wk Etr, 1 wk Jul, 1 wk Oct, Mon-Tue, L Sat, Wed, D Sun **Prices** Fixed L 2 course £24.50, Fixed D 3 course £30, Service optional, Groups min 8 service 10% **Wines** 35 bottles over £20, 9 bottles under £20, 6 by glass **Notes** Fixed D 5 course £40, Sunday L, Vegetarian available, Dress restrictions, Smart casual **Seats** 24 **Children** Portions **Parking** 12

Save on Hotels. Book at **theAA.com/hotel**

SUFFOLK 427 **ENGLAND**

SUFFOLK

ALDEBURGH
Map 13 TM45

Brudenell Hotel

◎◎ British, European ◎

New England style on the Suffolk coast

☎ 01728 452071
The Parade IP15 5BU
e-mail: info@brudenellhotel.co.uk
web: www.brudenellhotel.co.uk
dir: A12/A1094, on reaching town, turn right at junct into High St. Hotel on seafront adjoining Fort Green car park

Completely refurbished in 2010, this handsome Edwardian seafront hotel almost has its toes in the water. It is a setting that the contemporary brasserie-style restaurant takes full advantage of: light floods the expansive split-level space, which works a classy city-slicker look with pale oak floors, sage-green walls, bare blond-wood tables, and brown leather chairs. With a wall of huge picture windows, it feels almost as if you're eating on the beach, and on fine days you can move a step closer to the sea, out on the splendid terrace. The kitchen's thing is unfussy, modern European food, and with the sea just a pebble's throw away, it's no surprise that local fish is a big player. Start with treacle-cured salmon, matched with cucumber and ginger salad and wasabi cream, and follow that with a whole locally-landed Orford plaice with new potatoes, crayfish and caper beurre noisette. Summer strawberries might be celebrated in an assiette involving shortbread, mousse, pannacotta and ice cream.

Owner TA Hotel Collection **Times** 12-2.30/6.30-9 **Prices** Fixed L 2 course £14, Starter £4.65-£8.95, Main £12.50-£20.95, Dessert £5.95, Service optional **Wines** 91 bottles over £20, 8 bottles under £20, 47 by glass **Notes** Sunday L, Vegetarian available, Dress restrictions, Smart casual **Seats** 100, Pr/dining room 20 **Children** Portions, Menu **Parking** 15, Fort Green car park

152 Aldeburgh

◎ Modern European ◎

Beachside brasserie serving up good local produce

☎ 01728 454594
152 High St IP15 5AX
e-mail: andy.lister@virgin.net
dir: From A12, follow A1094 to Aldeburgh, located next to Tourist Information Centre

Accessed via an archway from the High Street leading to the shingle beach, this bustling brasserie serves up unpretentious dishes in an unbuttoned setting. Stripped wooden floors, pine tables and chairs and fresh flowers suit the seaside mood, helped along by the friendly service. Expect vibrantly fresh and carefully prepared rustic-style stuff along the lines of savoury smoked salmon and dill cheesecake with salmon keta and lemon and cracked pepper dressing, followed by seared scallops with garlic mash, black pudding, crisp pancetta and tomato compôte. Finish with white chocolate truffle tart with raspberry sorbet.

Chef Christopher Selby **Owner** Andrew Lister **Times** 12-3/6-10 Closed 25 Dec **Prices** Starter £5.50-£9.95, Main £9.95-£18.95, Dessert £5.50, Service optional **Wines** 23 bottles over £20, 11 bottles under £20, 9 by glass **Notes** Sunday L, Vegetarian available **Seats** 56 **Children** Portions, Menu **Parking** On street parking on High St & Kings St

Regatta Restaurant

◎ Modern British

Buzzy bistro, local fish the star

☎ 01728 452011
171 High St IP15 5AN
e-mail: rob.mabey@btinternet.com
dir: Middle of High St, town centre

The sea is just a pebble's skim away, so it is only right that super-fresh fish landed on the beach in Aldeburgh is showcased in Robert and Johanna Mabey's cheery bistro. Regatta has been going for two decades, drawing in local foodies with its bright and breezy ambience, stylish seaside-themed decor, and of course, Robert's confident and accurate treatment of splendid locally-sourced raw materials. A blackboard of spanking fresh fish specials bolsters the carte, which might get going with home-smoked prawns with garlic mayonnaise, then continue with Thai-style crayfish with chick pea salad and prawn crackers. Meat eaters could set about confit crispy duck leg with carrot purée and sautéed foie gras, and for pudding, something like a classic vanilla crème brûlée.

Chef Robert Mabey **Owner** Mr & Mrs R Mabey **Times** 12-2/6-10 Closed 24-26 & 31 Dec, 1 Jan, D Sun (Nov-Feb) **Prices** Starter £4-£8, Main £10.50-£19.50, Dessert £4.50-£5.50 **Wines** 6 bottles over £20, 40 bottles under £20, 8 by glass **Notes** Sunday L, Vegetarian available **Seats** 90, Pr/dining room 30 **Children** Portions, Menu **Parking** On street

Wentworth Hotel

◎◎ Modern British ◎

Family-run hotel with impeccable traditional cooking

☎ 01728 452312
Wentworth Rd IP15 5BD
e-mail: stay@wentworth-aldeburgh.co.uk
web: www.wentworth-aldeburgh.com
dir: From A12 take A1094 to Aldeburgh. In Aldeburgh straight on at mini rdbt, turn left at x-roads into Wentworth Rd. Hotel on right

The Wentworth is in a peaceful spot on Aldeburgh's seafront. Its restaurant has claret-coloured walls hung with portraits, a thickly carpeted floor, crisp napery and sea views. The cooking has its roots in the traditional English repertory, with local produce the mainstay: meats from Suffolk farms, fish landed on the beach that morning. There may not be many modern culinary fireworks, but techniques are sound and tried-and-tested combinations mean that dishes hit the spot. Starters range from prawn and crayfish salad with Marie Rose sauce to baked mushrooms in a stilton crust with roast red pepper and rocket salad, while main courses take in perhaps guinea fowl casseroled with root vegetables and bacon, served with mash and kale, beef bourguignon, or beautifully fresh, perfectly grilled Dover sole. A separate seafood listing may offer pan-fried skate wing with caper and lemon butter, and among puddings could be zesty lemon tart.

Chef Tim Keeble **Owner** Wentworth Hotel Ltd, Michael Pritt **Times** 12-2/7-9 **Prices** Fixed L 2 course fr £11, Fixed D 3 course fr £14.90, Service optional **Wines** 40 bottles over £20, 23 bottles under £20, 9 by glass **Notes** Sunday L, Vegetarian available **Seats** 90, Pr/dining room 22 **Children** Portions, Menu **Parking** 33

ALDEBURGH *continued*

White Lion Hotel

◉ British, French ✿

Modern brasserie dining on the Aldeburgh seafront

☎ 01728 452720
Market Cross Place IP15 5BJ
e-mail: info@whitelion.co.uk
web: www.whitelion.co.uk
dir: M25 junct 28 to A12 onto A1094, follow signs to
Aldeburgh at junct on left. Hotel on right

Situated right on the beachfront in the Suffolk festival
town, the White Lion is a sparkling-white edifice, though
lit in dramatic cobalt-blue by night. A refurbishment has
produced a light, contemporary feel to the public rooms,
with informal brasserie dining in a ground-floor, open-
plan venue. Grilled sardines are coated in Meaux mustard
and served with a 'cassoulet' of curried butter beans for
a statement of intent at the start of proceedings, while
main courses extend from steak frîtes and coq au vin
with mash, to spanking-fresh sea bass with a crab and
tomato risotto seasoned with lemon and dill. Local and
continental cheeses come with home-made chutney, and
desserts include tarte Tatin with cinnamon ice cream.

Chef Jason Shaw **Owner** TA Hotels Collection Ltd
Times 12-3/5.30-10 **Prices** Fixed L 2 course £10.50-
£27.45, Fixed D 3 course £14.50-£33.45, Starter £4.95-
£9.95, Main £9.25-£17.50, Dessert £6-£8.50, Service
optional **Wines** 30 bottles over £20, 9 bottles under £20,
13 by glass **Notes** Sunday L, Vegetarian available, Civ
Wed 80 **Seats** 80, Pr/dining room 80 **Children** Portions,
Menu **Parking** 10, On street

| BILDESTON | Map 13 TL94 |

The Bildeston Crown

◉◉◉ – see opposite

| BRANDESTON | Map 13 TM26 |

The Queen's Head Inn

◉ Modern, Traditional British ✿

Superior pub cooking in relaxing village inn

☎ 01728 685307
The Street IP13 7AD
e-mail: thequeensheadinn@btconnect.com
dir: Signed from A1120 at Earl Soham, follow signs to
village, on left hand side

This old red-brick village pub has been decked out in
contemporary style, with comfortable seating in the
spacious interior, where log fires burn in winter and the
atmosphere is informal and relaxed, helped along by
pleasant, efficient staff. Ales from Adnams are on the
pumps, baguettes and traditional pub fare are the deal
at lunchtime, with more gastronomic offerings in the
evening. Typical of the kitchen's output is beer-battered
squid and deep-fried whitebait with tartare sauce, and a
main course of slow-roast belly pork with Cognac-

poached apples, fondant potato, greens and red wine
gravy. Alternatively, start with an assiette of smoked fish
and go on to a pie of local game with herbed mash and
root vegetables. Either way, finish with something like
poached pear and almond tart.

Chef Jerome Dawson, Andrew Logan-Smith **Owner** Oliver
Coote **Times** 12-2/6.30-9 Closed Mon, D Sun
Prices Starter £4.50-£7.95, Main £7.95-£17.50, Dessert
£4.50-£7.95, Service optional **Wines** 10 bottles over £20,
12 bottles under £20, 9 by glass **Notes** Sunday L,
Vegetarian available **Seats** 65 **Children** Portions, Menu
Parking 25, On street

| BURY ST EDMUNDS | Map 13 TL86 |

The Angel Hotel

◉◉ Modern British ✿

Mediterranean menu in creeper-covered hotel

☎ 01284 714000
Angel Hill IP33 1LT
e-mail: staying@theangel.co.uk
dir: Town centre, right from lights at Northgate St

This former Georgian coaching inn on the historic town
square includes Charles Dickens amongst its former
visitors. Covered in deep-green creepers and purple-pink
wisteria, it is a quintessential British inn, albeit at the
grander end of the spectrum. Inside, alongside the period
features, there's a more contemporary tone, nowhere
more so than in its stylish, pine-floored Eaterie
restaurant, with its stunning artworks and views across
the square to the cathedral. Mediterranean-influenced
modern brasserie food is what the kitchen's all about;
Tuscan ribollita or bruschetta with wild mushrooms,
poached egg, parmesan cream and tuile to start,
perhaps. Follow on with roasted pork belly teamed with
walnut and goats' cheese croquettes, cabbage and apple
and celeriac purée. Unashamedly Anglo dishes have their
say too, perhaps delivered in a rhubarb and apple
crumble dessert with crème anglaise.

Chef Simon Barker **Owner** Robert Gough **Times** 12-10
Prices Fixed L 2 course fr £13.95, Starter £5.25-£10.95,
Main £9.95-£27, Dessert £5.25-£9.95, Service added but
optional 10% **Wines** 49 bottles over £20, 21 bottles under
£20, 34 by glass **Notes** Sunday L, Vegetarian available,
Dress restrictions, Smart casual **Seats** 85, Pr/dining room
16 **Children** Portions, Menu **Parking** 20

Best Western Priory Hotel

◉◉ Modern British, International ✿

Adept cooking in characterful old hotel

☎ 01284 766181
Mildenhall Rd IP32 6EH
e-mail: reservations@prioryhotel.co.uk
dir: From A14 take Bury St Edmunds W slip road. Follow
signs to Brandon. At mini-rdbt turn right. Hotel 0.5m on
left

This characterful old building has seen some changes in
its long history. These days its restaurant has been done

out in contemporary style, with a neutral colour scheme,
artwork on the walls, and darkwood tables; it's split into
three areas, with a conservatory overlooking the pretty
gardens. Thai-style fishcakes with sweet chilli sauce
seems like a bit of an interloper on the menu, which is
otherwise a list of familiar British dishes, from four-
cheese and ale rarebit (add on a fried egg and chutney if
you're really hungry) to poached salmon fillet with new
potatoes and sweet-and-sour cucumber salad. Local
produce gets a good showing: ham hock terrine with
piccalilli, tender chargrilled rib-eye steak with stilton
sauce, and, for Sunday lunch, roast leg of lamb with the
usual trimmings.

Chef Darren Rose **Owner** Peter Hobday **Times** 12-2/7-10
Closed L Sat (unless by arrangement) **Prices** Fixed L 2
course £15, Fixed D 3 course £20, Starter £5-£9, Main
£9-£19, Dessert £6-£8, Service added but optional 10%
Wines 18 bottles over £20, 18 bottles under £20, 9 by
glass **Notes** Sunday L, Vegetarian available, Civ Wed 70
Seats 72, Pr/dining room 28 **Children** Portions
Parking 60, On street

Clarice House

◉ Modern European

Well-crafted, modish cooking at a spa retreat

☎ 01284 705550
Horringer Court, Horringer Rd IP29 5PH
e-mail: bury@claricehouse.co.uk
dir: From Bury St Edmunds on A143 towards Horringer
and Haverhill, hotel 1m from town centre on right

Sybaritic spa pampering is the first item on the agenda
for many of the guests at Clarice House. After a
restorative hit of massage and manipulation, followed by
an appetite-stimulating stroll through the splendid
grounds of the Jacobean-style country house, a table
awaits in the smart oak-panelled restaurant, a suitably
sumptuous backdrop for uncomplicated modern European
cooking. Start with goats' cheese pannacotta served with
hot and sour cherry tomatoes, confit pepper and
parmesan tuile, followed by a more substantial minced
venison ragù with horseradish mash, roasted carrots and
parsnips. With that under your belt, you might as well
throw caution to the wind and finish with an orange and
Grand Marnier crème brûlée with clementine jam and
pistachio madeleine.

Chef Steve Winser **Owner** King Family **Times** 12-2/7-9
Closed 25-26 Dec, 1 Jan **Prices** Starter £5-£7, Main £10-
£14, Dessert £6, Service optional **Wines** 11 bottles over
£20, 7 bottles under £20, 15 by glass **Notes** Sunday L,
Vegetarian available, Dress restrictions, Smart casual D,
Civ Wed 100 **Seats** 70, Pr/dining room 20 **Parking** 110

Save on Hotels. Book at **theAA.com/hotel**

SUFFOLK 429 ENGLAND

The Bildeston Crown

Map 13 TL94

Modern British

High-octane cooking in revamped old coaching inn

☎ 01449 740510
104 High St IP7 7EB
e-mail: hayley@thebildestoncrown.co.uk
web: www.thebildestoncrown.com
dir: A12 junct 31. B1070 to Hadleigh, B1115 to Bildeston

Owned by a local businessman and farmer and run by Chris and Hayley Lee, the Crown is a combination of hotel, restaurant and bar, all housed within a 15th-century timbered coaching inn. There's a metropolitan-chic style to the place, with lots of natural features combining with well-chosen (and striking) colours and a choice of dining spaces. Chris is cooking up a storm in the Suffolk countryside, his adventurous dishes based on sound culinary skills, his mixing and matching of ingredients producing satisfyingly cohesive results. Pork belly is happily married with sweet and succulent seared scallops and accompanied by cooked apple, cauliflower and caper berries, and another starter brings on parsley soup subtly garnished with snails, ham and shallots. Produce is often from the owner's farm, game might be shot by Chris himself - breast of teal with confit leg and lentils, say - and other

materials are well sourced: South Coast brill with warm Caesar salad, bacon and anchovies, Suffolk chicken breast (moist, tender and full of flavour), fashionably partnered by langoustines and accompanied by fennel, mushrooms and truffle. Meals can end with a savoury like herring roes on toast, but it would take a strong will to resist chocolate and orange brûlée artfully arranged with Arctic roll, orange sorbet and chocolate fondant. April 2012 saw the opening of Ingrams at The Bildeston Crown, a smartly done-out room with a touch of fine-dining glamour (white linen cloths and all), where Chris Lee serves up his seasonally-changing 'select' menu and eight-course 'Crown Tasting Menu'.

Chef Chris Lee **Owner** Mrs G Buckle, Mr J K Buckle **Times** 12-7/3-10 Closed D 25-26 Dec, 1 Jan **Prices** Fixed L 2 course fr £18, Starter £10-£15, Main £25-£35, Dessert £10-£15, Service optional, Groups min 10 service 12.5% **Wines** 100 bottles over £20, 11 bottles under £20, 11 by glass **Notes** Fixed L Mon-Sat, D 5 course £50, Tasting 8 course, Sunday L, Vegetarian available, Civ Wed 24 **Seats** 100, Pr/dining room 16 **Children** Portions **Parking** 36, Market Sq (overflow)

BURY ST EDMUNDS *continued*

The Leaping Hare Restaurant & Country Store

◉◉ Modern British ☺

Vineyard restaurant with contemporary menu

☎ 01359 250287
Wyken Vineyards, Stanton IP31 2DW
e-mail: info@wykenvineyards.co.uk
dir: 8m NE of Bury St Edmunds, 1m off A143. Follow
brown signs at Ixworth to Wyken Vineyards

It is hard to think of a more appealing way to acquaint
yourself with the foodie delights of Suffolk than to explore
the local wine trail and turn up for lunch (lunch only, take
note) at Wyken Vineyard's Leaping Hare Restaurant. The
1,200-acre estate keeps food miles to an absolute
minimum, supplying game, and meat from its herd of
Red Poll cattle and flock of Shetland sheep, fruit, herbs
and veg from the kitchen garden, and wine from the
seven-acre vineyard, while a farmers' market brings more
to the doorstep every Saturday. The setting is a striking
400-year-old timbered barn with a soaring raftered
ceiling, wood-burning stoves, exposed wall beams,
wooden floors, leaping hare-themed paintings and
tapestries, and large windows opening onto fields and
ancient woodlands. A simple modern approach to cooking
lets the flavours shine through in dishes such as
Ellingham goats' cheese and spinach soufflé with red
onion sauce, followed by Wyken wild rabbit pie with suet
shortcrust pastry, roast potatoes and anise-glazed
carrots.

Chef Jon Ellis **Owner** Kenneth & Carla Carlisle
Times 12-2.30/7-9 Closed 2 wks Xmas, D Sun-Thu
Prices Fixed L 2 course £16.95, Starter £5.95-£7.95,
Main £10.95-£21.95, Dessert £5.95, Service optional,
Groups min 6 service 10% **Wines** 9 bottles over £20,
13 bottles under £20, 22 by glass **Notes** Sunday L,
Vegetarian available **Seats** 55 **Children** Portions
Parking 50

Maison Bleue

◉◉ Modern French ☺

Smart seafood restaurant with a French flavour

☎ 01284 760623
30-31 Churchgate St IP33 1RG
e-mail: info@maisonbleue.co.uk
web: www.maisonbleue.co.uk
dir: A14 junct 43 (Sugar Beet, Central exit) to town
centre. Follow signs to the Abbey Gdns, Churchgate St is
opposite cathedral

Located in a double-fronted former shop in a small side
street close to the cathedral, Maison Bleue specialises in
all things fishy with, as you might have guessed, a French
accent. Modish neutral tones are preferred to the
eponymous blue on the inside and there's a pleasing
contemporary finish to the place. Depending on when
you're here, you might find 'A Month in Provence' menu or
such like in play, plus a 'Formule Rapide' at lunchtime to

supplement the à la carte. Expect well-crafted dishes
with French roots and detailed menu descriptions, plus a
keen eye for presentation on the plate (which come in all
shapes and sizes). Kick off with a classic fish soup or
crab and lobster terrine (wrapped in smoked salmon and
served with a chive whipped cream), before a main
course such as pan-fried skate wing with tarragon beurre
blanc, or turbot with tagliatelle and sorrel sauce. There
are meat options (roasted fillet of Aberdeen Angus with
red wine sauce), and, to finish, crème brûlée might be
flavoured with pistachio nuts.

Chef Pascal Canevet **Owner** Regis Crepy **Times** 12-2/7-9
Closed Jan, 2 wks summer, Sun-Mon **Prices** Fixed L 2
course £17.50, Fixed D 3 course £31.95, Starter £6.95-
£10.95, Main £15.95-£22.50, Dessert £6.95, Service
optional **Wines** 105 bottles over £20, 45 bottles under
£20, 12 by glass **Notes** Vegetarian available, Dress
restrictions, Smart casual recommended **Seats** 65, Pr/
dining room 35 **Children** Portions **Parking** On street

Pea Porridge

◉◉ Modern Bistro

Accomplished modern cooking

☎ 01284 700200
28-29 Cannon St IP33 1JR
e-mail: enquiries@peaporridge.co.uk
dir: Off A14 towards town, in Northgate St turn left into
Cadney Lane. Restaurant opposite Old Cannon Brewery

The name references its location on a square once called
Pea Porridge Green. The one-time bakery has made a
feature of the old bread oven, and the refined-rustic décor
of darkwood floors, darkwood tables and exposed
brickwork fits the bill to a T. There's a sunny-day
courtyard too. The modish cooking is highly accomplished
and suits the bistro-esque vibe, with plenty of local
seasonal produce on offer, and some compelling
combinations and vibrant flavours up for grabs. Start
with chargrilled quid with risotto nero and gremolata,
moving on to raised hare daube with fondant potato,
butternut squash purée, harissa and golden raisins, or
maybe skate wing teamed with French beans, mussels,
capers, almonds and lemon. To finish, tarte Tatin comes
with Calvados cream.

Chef Justin Sharp **Owner** Justin Sharp
Times 12-2.30/6.30-10 Closed 2wks Xmas, 2 wks Sep,
Sun-Mon **Prices** Fixed L 2 course fr £11.95, Fixed D 3
course fr £15.95, Starter £5.95-£8.95, Main £12.95-
£19.95, Dessert £5-£8.50, Service optional
Wines 20 bottles over £20, 17 bottles under £20, 9 by
glass **Notes** Vegetarian available **Seats** 46, Pr/dining
room 20 **Parking** On street

Ravenwood Hall Hotel

◉◉ Modern British ☺

Reliably interesting food in a Tudor building

☎ 01359 270345
Rougham IP30 9JA
e-mail: enquiries@ravenwoodhall.co.uk
dir: 3m E off A14, junct 45. Hotel on left

If you like your country-house hotels to come with plenty
of history, Ravenwood Hall has 500 years under its belt.
Set in seven acres of bucolic Suffolk, the place has been
around since Henry VIII was in the top job, and it is
propped up by carved oak timbers and decorated with
rare 15th-century wall paintings, antiques and huge
inglenooks. With its warm terracotta-hued walls, oak
panelling, tapestry curtains, crisp white linen and soft
candlelight, the dining room is a delight, as is the
kitchen's approach to uniting harmonious flavours and
textures. Ingredients tick all the seasonal and local boxes
- meats and fish are smoked in-house, and fruit and
vegetables are preserved on the premises. A summer
dinner begins with a cocktail of Norfolk crab with
shredded lettuce, cucumber jelly and tomato dressing,
then proceeds to rack of Bildeston lamb with ratatouille,
glazed carrots, sprouting broccoli, rösti and a delicious
jus. Awaiting at the end, roasted peaches and hazelnuts
with rum syrup, hazelnut syrup, vanilla shortbread,
vanilla cream and peach purée.

Chef Shayne Wood **Owner** Craig Jarvis **Times** 12-2/7-9.30
Prices Starter £7.95-£10.50, Main £11.95-£24.95,
Dessert £6.95, Service optional **Wines** 54 bottles over
£20, 32 bottles under £20, 11 by glass **Notes** 7 Cheese
platter £14.50, Indulgent coffees £6.95, Sunday L,
Vegetarian available, Civ Wed 130 **Seats** 50, Pr/dining
room 50 **Children** Portions, Menu **Parking** 150

The White Horse

◉ Modern British

Well-crafted, unfussy cooking in country gastro-pub

☎ 01284 735760 & 07778 996666
Rede Rd, Whepstead IP29 4SS
dir: 5m from Bury St Edmunds, 2m off A143 Bury/
Haverhill

This buttercup-hued village inn has traded up to gastro-
pub status after a stylish facelift in recent years.
Originally a 17th-century farmhouse, the Victorians
added their bits and the interior is now a series of smart
and cosy rooms with a copper-sheathed bar serving
Suffolk ales, and there are exposed beams, a huge
inglenook, country-style tables and chairs, artwork on the
walls, and soothing Farrow & Ball colour schemes. The
food is all about the ingredients, everything is made from
scratch (they make their own sausages too), and it is all
kept simple and seasonal. The blackboard menu might
kick off with jellied ham hock terrine with home-made
piccalilli, followed by slow-braised shoulder of Ickworth
lamb with black olives, fresh herbs and creamy mash.
Desserts take in chocolate truffle torte, or you could go for
a savoury finish with a plate of East Anglian cheeses.

Save on Hotels. Book at **theAA.com/hotel**

SUFFOLK 431 ENGLAND

Chef Dougie Lindsey, Gareth Carter **Owner** Gary & Di Kingshott **Times** 12-2/7-9.30 Closed 25-26 Dec, D Sun **Prices** Fixed L 2 course £12.95, Fixed D 3 course £16.95, Starter £5.95-£9.95, Main £9.95-£15.95, Dessert £5.95, Service optional **Wines** 10 bottles over £20, 16 bottles under £20, 8 by glass **Notes** Fixed L Mon-Fri, Fixed D Mon-Thu, Sunday L, Vegetarian available **Seats** 50, Pr/dining room 25 **Children** Portions **Parking** 30

CAVENDISH   Map 13 TL84

The George

◉ Modern British

Modish cooking in characterful inn

☎ 01787 280248
The Green CO10 8BA
e-mail: thegeorgecavendish@gmail.com
web: www.thecavendishgeorge.co.uk

The whitewashed inn is 16th-century and Grade II listed, though better described as a restaurant with rooms in today's parlance. Its interior is dominated by wood, from the bare tables to the heavy beams that lend the place its character, and the reassuring buzz of kitchen activity in the background reminds you what the main priority is. A Mediterranean-inflected repertoire of modern British dishes is on offer, from the olives and garlic focaccia nibbles to the smoked monkfish with risotto nero, or cod with borlotti beans and pancetta. In between come some less familiar but equally tempting ideas - starters of hickory-smoked venison saddle with truffled beurre noisette and hazelnuts, or breast and leg of partridge with garlic pommes purée and capers - and a meal might end with rice pudding, but a chilled lemon and ginger version with red berries and jelly.

Chef Lewis Bennet **Owner** Lewis Bennet, Bonnie Steel **Times** 12-2/6-9.30 Closed 25 Dec, 1 Jan, D Sun **Prices** Fixed L 2 course £12.50, Fixed D 3 course £15, Starter £5-£8, Main £9-£18.50, Dessert £2-£5.50, Service optional **Wines** 15 bottles over £20, 21 bottles under £20, 12 by glass **Notes** Sunday L, Vegetarian available **Seats** 50 **Children** Portions, Menu **Parking** On street directly outside

CHILLESFORD   Map 13 TM35

The Froize Freehouse Restaurant

◉ British, European

Popular inn with cracking menu

☎ 01394 450282
The Street IP12 3PU
e-mail: dine@froize.co.uk
dir: On B1084 between Woodbridge & Orford

This substantial red-brick gabled property has been converted from a pair of gamekeepers' cottages, and subsequent modernisation has given the interior a smart, contemporary look. Chef-proprietor David Grimwood has racked up quite a reputation, judging by the popularity of the place. His unfussy style - what he calls rustic British and European - deals in top-notch local foodstuffs, with some home-grown. Winter brings on game - perhaps breast of guinea fowl with pumpkin and redcurrants - or there might be roast pork shoulder, with apple sauce, crisp crackling and gravy, exactly as it should be. There's more of a concentration on seafood in summer: baked cod (from just down the road at Orford) on crayfish risotto, for instance. Most starters are cold, with simple exceptions like soup, or pan-fried scallops with bacon, whilst desserts are the business, whether upside-down ginger pudding, or sherry trifle.

Chef David Grimwood **Owner** David Grimwood **Times** 12-2/7 Closed Mon (ex BHs) **Prices** Food prices not confirmed for 2013. Please telephone for details **Wines** 6 bottles over £20, 14 bottles under £20, 14 by glass **Notes** Vegetarian available **Seats** 48, Pr/dining room 20 **Children** Portions **Parking** 40

DUNWICH   Map 13 TM47

The Ship at Dunwich

◉ Modern British ◕

Straightforward British cooking in seaside inn

☎ 01728 648219
St James St IP17 3DT
e-mail: info@shipatdunwich.co.uk
dir: From N: A12, exit at Blythburgh onto B1125, then left to village. Inn at end of road. From S: A12, turn right to Westleton. Follow signs for Dunwich

At the heart of the village (some of which disappeared under the sea centuries ago), The Ship is a nicely pubby series of rooms with flagstone floors, brick walls, open fires and rustic furniture. Food is taken seriously here, with locally-landed fish taking centre stage - fillet of hake, say, in a light, crisp batter, served with proper chips and home-made tartare sauce. Other main courses are along the lines of slow-cooked belly pork with black pudding, sautéed potatoes and spicy gravy, with interesting starters (also served as lighter main courses) extending the range into sardines on toast with home-made tomato sauce, Scotch egg with black pudding and piccalilli, and twice-baked cheese soufflé.

Chef Matthew Last **Owner** Agellus Hotels Ltd **Times** 12-3/6-9 **Prices** Starter £4.95-£7.50, Main £9.50-£17.95, Dessert £4.50-£5.50, Service optional **Wines** 12 bottles over £20, 9 bottles under £20, 6 by glass **Notes** Open all day for food Jul-Aug, Sunday L, Vegetarian available **Seats** 70, Pr/dining room 35 **Children** Portions, Menu **Parking** 20

EYE   Map 13 TM17

Lexington

◉ Modern British

No-nonsense cooking in a charming Suffolk manor

☎ 01379 870326 & 08444 146 524
The Cornwallis Hotel, Rectory Rd, Brome IP23 8AJ
e-mail: reservations.cornwallis@ohiml.com

The tree-lined drive and 23 acres of tranquil grounds - dotted with topiary trees - are really rather impressive. They say first impressions count, and so it is that by the time you've stepped inside the Grade II listed Cornwallis Hotel, you'll probably be anticipating good things to come. A pre-dinner drink in the Tudor Bar with its open fires and beamed ceilings is a pleasing way to begin, before moving through to the classically-furnished Lexington restaurant for some straightforward modern British cooking. Chicken liver and orange pâté with red onion chutney and toasted ciabatta could get the ball rolling, with baked fillet of salmon in a crayfish, white wine and butter sauce with crushed new potatoes for the main event. Save room for the lemon and coconut pannacotta with a berry coulis.

Times 12-3/6-9 Closed L Mon-Sat

FRESSINGFIELD   Map 13 TM27

Fox & Goose Inn

◉◉ Modern British

Village restaurant and bar with modish cooking

☎ 01379 586247
Church Rd IP21 5PB
e-mail: foxandgoose@uk2.net
dir: A140 & B1116 (Stradbroke) left after 6m - in village centre by church

Abutting Fressingfield's medieval church, this one-time timber-framed Tudor guildhall turned local inn - set at the heart of a small chocolate-box village - ticks all the quintessential English boxes. But appearances can be deceiving; inside the place sports a thoroughly pared-back modern look, and, while there's a wealth of character in its old beams and open fires and the bar still serves real ales tapped straight from the barrel, it's much more a restro-pub these days. Accomplished and creative European ideas pepper the kitchen's modern cooking driven by Suffolk's abundant larder. Take lemon sole fillets served with crab and potato tempura, English asparagus, chervil mayo, micro greens and a hazelnut vinaigrette, or perhaps beef bourguignon with horseradish mash, glazed carrots and parsnip purée.

continued

FRESSINGFIELD *continued*

Finish in classic style with vanilla crème brûlée accompanied by an oatmeal tuile and blackcurrant sorbet. The more formal evenings-only restaurant is upstairs, while downstairs there's a smaller dining room in the old lounge as well as the bar area.

Chef P Yaxley, M Wyatt **Owner** Paul Yaxley **Times** 12-2/7-8.30 Closed 25-30 Dec, 2nd wk Jan for 2 weeks, Mon **Prices** Fixed L 2 course fr £14.25, Fixed D 3 course £31-£34, Tasting menu £45, Service optional **Wines** 31 bottles over £20, 23 bottles under £20, 8 by glass **Notes** Tasting menu 8 course, Sunday L, Vegetarian available **Seats** 70, Pr/dining room 35 **Children** Portions **Parking** 15

HINTLESHAM
Map 13 TM04

Hintlesham Hall Hotel

🏵🏵🏵 Modern European

Polished cooking in top-ranking country-house hotel

☎ 01473 652334
IP8 3NS
e-mail: reservations@hintleshamhall.com
web: www.hintleshamhall.com
dir: 4m W of Ipswich on A1071

The hall has its origins in the 16th century, the symmetrically proportioned façade seen today a 1720 addition. Within are all the elements associated with a top-ranking country-house hotel, from antiques to oil paintings, while the main restaurant, the Salon, is as stunningly grand as a room in a stately home or royal palace. The kitchen has its feet firmly on the ground, producing nothing too rarefied or gimmicky, serving grilled fillet of haddock in mussel and clam chowder, and tournedos with braised oxtail and horseradish. Quality materials are evident throughout, seen in starters of venison carpaccio with pickled figs and marinated purple potatoes, and well-timed caramelised scallops with cauliflower puréed with truffle oil sprinkled with Sauternes-soaked sultanas. Fruit is used effectively in puddings: expect roast plum tart scented with star anise with crème fraîche sorbet, or pear and blackberry terrine.

Hintlesham Hall Hotel

Times 12-2.30/7-10 Closed L Sat

INGHAM
Map 13 TL87

The Cadogan Arms

🏵 Traditional British

Well-executed dishes in stylish gastro-pub

☎ 01284 728443
The Street IP31 1NG
e-mail: info@thecadogan.co.uk
dir: A134 4m from Bury St Edmunds

The interior of this former coaching inn has been reworked and spruced up with a stylish décor, subdued lighting, upholstered sofas and chairs and a curved bar dispensing real ales. Flexibility is the name of the game, with grazing boards for snackers and a lunch menu of sandwiches and dishes like local ham, eggs and chips. The kitchen moves up a couple of gears in the evening, its skills and nifty presentation evident in smoked chicken with home-made chorizo and a crisp poached egg, followed by confit shoulder of mutton with fondant potato and root vegetable purée. Seafood gets the modern treatment: battered shrimps cut by sweet chilli jam, and smoked coley fillet in Welsh rarebit with pea velouté and new potatoes.

Chef Ricky Calder **Owner** David Marjoram **Times** 12-2.30/6-9.30 Closed 25-31 Dec **Prices** Starter £5-£6.50, Main £10-£15.50, Dessert £5, Service optional **Wines** 20 bottles over £20, 25 bottles under £20, 12 by glass **Notes** Sunday L, Vegetarian available **Seats** 72 **Children** Portions, Menu **Parking** 39

IPSWICH
Map 13 TM14

Best Western Claydon Country House Hotel

🏵 Modern British V

Modern British cooking close to Ipswich

☎ 01473 830382
16-18 Ipswich Rd, Claydon IP6 0AR
e-mail: enquiries@hotelsipswich.com
dir: A14, junct 52 Claydon exit from rdbt, 300yds on left

Two old village houses were joined seamlessly together to form this friendly, small-scale hotel to the north west of Ipswich. The Victorian-style restaurant overlooks the gardens through a conservatory extension, although the

classic look has been given a gentle update by ditching the cloths on its darkwood tables and adding high-backed leather chairs. Staff are smartly turned out to create a professional, welcoming vibe, and the kitchen draws on splendid locally-sourced produce as the bedrock of its unfussy European-accented modern British dishes. Expect starters along the lines of seafood risotto with rocket and parmesan, while mains could turn up roast rack of lamb with chive mash, wilted greens, and red wine and rosemary glaze. End with a warm Belgian chocolate muffin with chocolate sauce and vanilla ice cream.

Chef Frankie Manners **Owner** Mr Khurram Saeed **Times** 12-2/7-9.30 **Prices** Food prices not confirmed for 2013. Please telephone for details **Wines** 25 bottles under £20, 5 by glass **Notes** Sunday L, Vegetarian menu, Civ Wed 80 **Seats** 40, Pr/dining room 85 **Children** Portions, Menu **Parking** 80

Best Western The Gatehouse Hotel

🏵 Modern British V

Unfussy modern food in Regency-style country house

☎ 01473 741897
799 Old Norwich Rd IP1 6LH
dir: A14 junct 53 take A1156 Ipswich, left at lights onto Norwich road, hotel on left

There's a pleasant juxtaposition of town and country in this handsome Regency country hotel on the fringes of Ipswich. Three acres of immaculately-kept mature gardens provide pleasant pre-dinner strolls before settling into the easygoing ambience of the restaurant, where smart high-backed leather seating and bare darkwood tables add a contemporary note to its elegant period character. The kitchen keeps it simple, relying on quality local produce in a menu of uncomplicated modern ideas, as in a starter that teams garlicky local field mushrooms with stilton, lettuce and pesto, followed by rump of Pelham estate lamb with minted new potatoes, fine green beans and red wine jus. To finish, there's a white and dark chocolate brownie with vanilla ice cream.

Chef Frankie Manners **Owner** Khurram Saeed **Times** 12-2/7-9.30 **Prices** Fixed D 3 course fr £24.95, Service optional **Wines** all bottles under £20, 5 by glass **Notes** Sunday L, Vegetarian menu **Seats** 40 **Children** Portions, Menu **Parking** 30

Mariners

🏵 French, Mediterranean

Honest Gallic fare afloat in Ipswich

☎ 01473 289748
Neptune Quay IP4 1AX
e-mail: info@marinersipswich.co.uk
dir: On Wherry Quay, accessed via Key St. Follow brown tourist signs to waterfront

Moored alongside Neptune Quay at Ipswich Marina, close to the town centre, this floating French brasserie on an old gunboat is a quirky destination to enjoy some good Gallic cuisine. The vessel might date back to 1899 when it was launched in Belgium, but inside it's all shipshape; original brass and woodwork are coupled with chandeliers and candles on the clothed tables, and you can even hear the calls of seagulls while you eat. Go up on deck for an alfresco lunch in the sun, but wherever you choose to eat, look forward to good, honest French food confidently presented. Maroille cheese tart and green leaves, perhaps, or moules marinière, followed by grilled halibut fillet with chive and shrimp sauce, or rabbit hotpot with prune and white wine sauce. To finish, an apple 'tart of Normandy' is served warm with vanilla ice cream.

Times 12-2.30/7-9.30 Closed Jan, Sun-Mon

Salthouse Harbour Hotel, The Eaterie

◎◎ Modern British

Well-executed, modish dishes on the waterfront

☎ 01473 226789
1 Neptune Quay IP4 1AX
e-mail: staying@salthouseharbour.co.uk
dir: A14 junct 53, A1156 to town centre & harbour, off Key St

Converted from a former warehouse, Salthouse Harbour is now every bit a contemporary boutique hotel - brimful of vivid colours and interesting art - and comes set smack on the waterfront overlooking the marina. The Eaterie follows the theme with its leather banquettes, large windows (for those harbour views) and rich red-brick walls dominated by striking artworks and installations. The kitchen concentrates on quality, local and seasonal produce and rightly puts flavour at the heart of everything. There's something of a Mediterranean accent to the menu; wild sea bass fillet, perhaps, served with olive oil mash, caponata and grilled courgettes, or slow-cooked Dingley Dell pork belly teamed with goats' cheese, walnut and sage croquettes, celeriac purée, cabbage and bacon. Desserts follow suit, maybe a glazed lemon tart or Baileys pannacotta with espresso syrup and hazelnut tuile.

Chef Simon Barker, Arron Jackson **Owner** Robert Gough
Times 12-6/6-10 **Prices** Fixed L 2 course £13.95-£17, Starter £5.95-£9.95, Main £13.50-£48.50, Dessert £5.95-£10.50, Service added but optional 10% **Wines** 49 bottles over £20, 21 bottles under £20, 34 by glass **Notes** Sunday L, Vegetarian available **Seats** 70 **Children** Portions, Menu **Parking** 30

IXWORTH   Map 13 TL97

Theobalds Restaurant

◎◎ Modern British

Seasonal country cooking in a Tudor inn

☎ 01359 231707
68 High St IP31 2HJ
dir: 7m from Bury St Edmunds on A143 (Bury to Diss road)

A Tudor inn in a village to the north of Bury St Edmunds, Theobalds could hardly be mistaken for anything else inside, with its abundance of uneven oak timbers,

inglenook fireplace and plain whitewashed walls. Simon Theobald is an assiduous country chef, seeking out the best of seasonal produce, and letting it lead the transformation of his menus through the year. Autumn might bring a salad of shredded Serrano ham with gruyère, Cox's and croûtons in mustard seed vinaigrette, or poached mussels with shallots in cider cream, to start. Game crops up alluringly in the form of roast breast of partridge with golden sultanas in Calvados sauce, or there may be grilled plaice with brown shrimps in chive-strewn white wine butter sauce. Dishes boast well-defined flavours and confident timing, through to a serving of blackberry and apple clafoutis in a crisp pastry shell with apple ice cream.

Chef Simon Theobald **Owner** Simon & Geraldine Theobald
Times 12.15-1.30/7-9 Closed 10 days in Spring/Summer, Mon, L Tue-Thu, Sat, D Sun **Prices** Fixed L 2 course £20.95-£21.95, Fixed D 2 course £24.95-£29.95, Starter £6.95-£8.95, Main £15.95-£19.75, Dessert £6.95-£7.95, Service optional **Wines** 34 bottles over £20, 18 bottles under £20, 7 by glass **Notes** Fixed L menu available Fri, Fixed D midweek & Fri, Sunday L, Vegetarian available **Seats** 42, Pr/dining room 16 **Children** Portions **Parking** On street

KESGRAVE   Map 13 TM24

Milsoms Kesgrave Hall

◎ Modern International ⌘

Relaxed dining in a contemporary setting

☎ 01473 333741
Hall Rd IP5 2PU
e-mail: reception@kesgravehall.com
web: www.kesgravehall.com
dir: A12 N of Ipswich/Woodbridge, rdbt onto B1214

A buzzy bistro is at the culinary heart of Kesgrave Hall, a Georgian mansion in thick woodland just north of Ipswich. Inside, however, a boutique makeover in recent years has reinvented the place as a stylish boutique hotel with a pared-back modern look involving oak floors, pine tables, leather chairs and muted shades of cream and sage; outdoors, there's a spacious terrace with a retractable awning that keeps the place on the boil whatever the weather. The crew in the open kitchen are nicely in tune with the surrounding landscape, serving modern brasserie dishes along the lines of smoked haddock fishcake with a soft boiled egg, pickled cucumber and lemon mustard mayonnaise, followed by braised Dedham Vale beef featherblade with carrot purée, cavolo nero and crispy bone marrow. Wrap it all up with

pineapple tarte Tatin, with coconut sorbet, candied noodles and rum syrup.

Milsoms Kesgrave Hall

Chef Stuart Oliver **Owner** Paul Milsom **Times** 12-9.30
Prices Starter £5.75-£14.95, Main £10.95-£21.50, Dessert £5.95, Service optional **Wines** 80 bottles over £20, 16 bottles under £20, 23 by glass **Notes** Sunday L, Vegetarian available **Seats** 80, Pr/dining room 24 **Children** Portions, Menu **Parking** 150

LAVENHAM   Map 13 TL94

Lavenham Great House Restaurant with Rooms

◎◎ Modern French

Contemporary French cooking in a medieval building

☎ 01787 247431
Market Place CO10 9QZ
e-mail: info@greathouse.co.uk
dir: In Market Place (turn onto Market Lane from High Street)

The Great House, dating from the Middle Ages behind its Georgian façade, is on the market place of this picturesque village (once a centre of the wool trade). Its restaurant, though, is bang up to date (apart from a grand inglenook), with a décor of soft, soothing pastels and a dark wooden floor. The knowledgeable staff tend to be French and the classically-based cooking leans heavily on their native land. Moules marinière could make an appearance, followed by sautéed veal kidneys in orange and Grand Marnier sauce. But the kitchen doesn't toe the line of orthodoxy, producing cod gravad lax marinated in beetroot, served with slaw, then caramelised confit of belly pork with honey and pepper sauce, and steamed monkfish fillet with garlic mousseline and chorizo sauce. Puddings include lemon tart, with orange sorbet, and crémeux au café with Marsala sabayon.

Chef Regis Crepy **Owner** Mr & Mrs Crepy
Times 12-2.30/7-9.30 Closed Jan & 2 wks summer, Mon, L Tue, D Sun **Prices** Fixed L 2 course fr £17.50, Fixed D 3 course fr £31.95, Starter £9-£15, Main £18-£25, Dessert £7, Service optional, Groups min 10 service 10%
Wines 65 bottles over £20, 75 bottles under £20, 10 by glass **Notes** Sunday L, Vegetarian available **Seats** 40, Pr/dining room 15 **Children** Portions **Parking** Market Place

LAVENHAM *continued*

The Swan

◉◉ Modern British V

Modern dining in medieval splendour

☎ 01787 247477
High St CO10 9QA
e-mail: info@theswanatlavenham.co.uk
web: www.theswanatlavenham.co.uk
dir: From Bury St Edmunds take A134 (S) for 6m. Take A1141 to Lavenham

The striking, timber-framed Swan has been welcoming guests since the 15th century and is a splendid example of Elizabethan architecture in this historic market town. Bristling with wonky beams and timbers, ancient brick floors, fine oak panels, inglenook fireplaces and cosy nooks and crannies, it is the quintessential English inn. Choose from classic pub dishes in the characterful bar, which is full of Second World War memorabilia as it often hosted pilots from Lavenham airfield, or head for the atmospheric Gallery restaurant and tuck into modern British dishes beneath soaring barn-style rafters and the impressive minstrels' gallery. Typically, start with confit pig's cheek with lentil and pancetta broth, follow with seared monkfish with mussel and clam chowder, or roast poussin with truffle and wild mushroom risotto, and finish with chocolate fondant plum pudding.

Chef Justin Kett **Owner** Thorpeness & Aldeburgh Hotels Ltd **Times** 12-2.30/7-9.30 **Prices** Fixed L 2 course £16.95, Starter £9, Main £21.95-£25.95, Dessert £6.95-£9.95, Service optional **Wines** 80 bottles over £20, 20 bottles under £20, 14 by glass **Notes** Sunday L, Vegetarian menu, Dress restrictions, No jeans or trainers, Civ Wed 100 **Seats** 90, Pr/dining room 32 **Children** Portions, Menu **Parking** 50

The Black Lion Hotel

◉◉ Modern British **NEW** ✋

Imaginative cooking in Georgian hotel

☎ 01787 312356
Church Walk, The Green CO10 9DN
e-mail: enquiries@blacklionhotel.net
dir: From Bury St Edmunds take A134 to Sudbury. Right onto B1064 to Long Melford. Right onto A1092 to Cavendish. Hotel on village green

Overlooking Long Melford's village green, and with the town's antiques and crafts shops, and the Tudor delights of Melford Hall to explore, the Georgian Black Lion is an inviting prospect. Expect full-flavoured modern British dishes with plenty of flair and imagination. You could keep things casual in the lovely bar, where there's a real fire, water bowl for Rover, views across the green, and tuck into the likes of smoked eel and ham hock Scotch egg with beetroot and apple chutney, followed by caramelised loin of cod with Shetland mussels, spinach, and curry and Sauternes velouté. Otherwise, the more formal Georgian room restaurant with its deep-green walls antiques and oil paintings, opening into a Victorian walled garden, is the setting for similarly clever combinations, as in diver-caught scallops with pig's head, cumin and pickled apple, then perhaps saddle of rabbit with Alsace bacon, violet potatoes, parsnip, prune, and verjus.

Chef Murdo Alex Macritchie **Owner** Craig Jarvis **Times** 12-2/7-9.30 **Prices** Fixed D 4 course fr £45, Tasting menu £60, Starter £7-£11.95, Main £15-£22.50, Dessert £6.95, Service optional **Wines** 53 bottles over £20, 31 bottles under £20, 10 by glass **Notes** Tasting menu must be taken by whole table, Sunday L, Vegetarian available, Civ Wed 55 **Seats** 55, Pr/dining room 26 **Children** Portions, Menu **Parking** 10, On street

---

The Crooked Barn Restaurant

◉◉ Modern European

Locally-based cooking in a thatched barn

☎ 01502 501353
Ivy House Country Hotel, Ivy Ln, Oulton Broad NR33 8HY
e-mail: aa@ivyhousecountryhotel.co.uk
dir: A146 into Ivy Lane

The thatched barn was built around 1800, and is a beautifully atmospheric edifice, complete with creaking floorboards and a welter of skew-whiff heavy beams. Views over pretty gardens and ornamental ponds are a draw, and on summer days, you can sit in the courtyard and get close to nature. The culinary stock-in-trade is modern British and European dishes made with predominantly local prime ingredients, making a virtue of their simplicity and freshness. A densely textured terrine of pork and apricots with a wholegrain mustard dressing is a bold starter, and could be succeeded by crisp-skinned grilled sea bass with beetroot and samphire in hollandaise, or roast rack of lamb with red onions and peas in minted red wine sauce. A version of summer pudding stuffed with raspberries and strawberries is a seasonal treat, and is served with fragrant lavender ice cream.

Chef Martin Whitelock **Owner** Caroline Coe **Times** 12-1.45/7-9.30 Closed 24 Dec-8 Jan **Prices** Starter £4.95-£10.95, Main £12.95-£24.95, Dessert £4.95-£9.95, Service optional **Wines** 18 bottles over £20, 24 bottles under £20, 4 by glass **Notes** Sunday L, Vegetarian available, Dress restrictions, Smart casual, No shorts, Civ Wed 80 **Seats** 45, Pr/dining room 24 **Children** Portions **Parking** 50

The Olde Bull Inn

◉ Modern British ✋

Local produce and appealing modern menus

☎ 01638 711001
The Street, Barton Mills IP28 6AA
e-mail: bookings@bullinn-bartonmills.com
web: www.bullinn-bartonmills.com
dir: Off A11 between Newmarket & Mildenhall, signed Barton Mills. Hotel by Five Ways rdbt

The Old Bull is over 500 years old, a stagecoach archway a reminder of its days as a coaching inn, with the

Save on Hotels. Book at **theAA.com/hotel**

SUFFOLK 435 ENGLAND

restaurant, all designer fabrics and furnishings, very much of the 21st century. The kitchen is dedicated to buying materials locally, from Denham Estate lamb - perhaps roast rump with a red wine and thyme jus, cheesy potato gratin, and leeks with crispy bacon - to artisan cheeses. Such a policy pays off, with dishes noted for their clearly defined flavours, sometimes boosted with a bit of Eastern piquancy; caramelised pork belly in hoi sin with pickled stir-fried vegetables, or prawn risotto with coriander and sweet chilli sauce. There's also the likes of pan-fried sea bass with new potatoes crushed with sun-blush tomatoes and spring onions, sautéed spinach, red pepper coulis and lemon-infused rapeseed oil.

The Olde Bull Inn

Chef Cheryl Hickman, Shaun Jennings, Loic De Coatpont **Owner** Cheryl Hickman & Wayne Starling **Times** 12-9 Closed 25 Dec, **Prices** Starter £6-£7.50, Main £14-£24, Dessert £6-£7, Service optional **Wines** 21 bottles over £20, 15 bottles under £20, 11 by glass **Notes** Sunday L, Vegetarian available **Seats** 60, Pr/dining room 30 **Children** Portions, Menu **Parking** 60

See advert below

MONKS ELEIGH   Map 13 TL94

The Swan Inn

◎◎ British, Mediterranean 🍷

Thatched country pub with clearly-focused menu

☎ 01449 741391
The Street IP7 7AU
e-mail: carol@monkseleigh.com
dir: On B1115 between Sudbury & Hadleigh

The decidedly chocolate box village of Monks Eleigh is home to this attractive 16th-century thatched pub. It matters not if you're after a pint of local real ale, a bar snack or a full-on feed: flexibility is the name of the game. Old beamed ceilings and oak floors await, plus some intelligently unfussy bistro-style cooking which can be taken in any part of the building, including the smart bar. Sound judgement from the kitchen allows the main ingredient (often local) to shine through in the likes of coarse pork rillette with green tomato chutney, or chilled Suffolk asparagus with parmesan flakes and balsamic dressing. Next up, perhaps grilled fillet of turbot with lobster and crayfish sauce, crushed celeriac and new potatoes, and, for dessert, an individual apple pie with vanilla custard.

Chef Nigel Ramsbottom **Owner** Nigel Ramsbottom **Times** 12-2/7-9 Closed 25-26 Dec, Mon (except BHs), D Sun **Prices** Fixed L 2 course £12.75, Fixed D 3 course £12.75-£19.75, Starter £4.95-£8, Main £9.75-£18.75, Dessert fr £5.75, Service optional **Wines** 10 bottles over £20, 30 bottles under £20, 10 by glass **Notes** Sun L winter only, Sunday L, Vegetarian available **Seats** 30, Pr/ dining room 24 **Children** Portions **Parking** 12

NEWMARKET   Map 12 TL66

Bedford Lodge Hotel

◎◎ Modern International 🍷

Inventive cooking near the races

☎ 01638 663175
Bury Rd CB8 7BX
e-mail: info@bedfordlodgehotel.co.uk
dir: From town centre take A1304 towards Bury St Edmunds, hotel 0.5m on left

Equine artworks and a colourful collection of racing silks are a reminder that this Georgian hunting lodge has good form in Newmarket's racing circles. If you're up for a flutter on the gee gees, here's another insider tip: the hotel's three acres of lovely gardens are bordered by the paddocks and training stables, while the hotel itself is a winning blend of period elegance and easygoing informality. The restaurant has been redesigned and relaunched as Squires, and its high ceilings and wall murals make a smartly formal setting for a repertoire that takes in classic as well as more modern ideas. Foie gras custard with spiced duck jelly is as contemporary a dish as you could ask for, while mains could take refuge in the traditions of steaks from the grill or beer-battered haddock with hand-cut chips and tartare sauce; otherwise you might strike out into the realms of slow-roasted Suffolk pork belly with fondant potato, carrot purée, scallops, and fennel and apple salad. To finish, perhaps a modish deconstruction of rhubarb crumble served with crème anglaise gel and apple purée.

Chef James Fairchild **Owner** Review Hotels Ltd **Times** 12-2/7-9.30 Closed L Sat **Prices** Fixed L 2 course £16.50-£21.50, Fixed D 3 course £26.50-£29, Starter £6-£12.50, Main £11-£27, Dessert £6-£11, Service added but optional 10% **Wines** 158 bottles over £20, 8 bottles under £20, 12 by glass **Notes** Sunday L, Vegetarian available, Dress restrictions, No shorts, sandals, vests, Civ Wed 150 **Seats** 47, Pr/dining room 150 **Children** Portions, Menu **Parking** 140

NEWMARKET *continued*

The Rutland Arms Hotel

◉ British, European

Classic bistro cookery in a 17th-century coaching inn

☎ 01638 664251
33 High St CB8 8NB
e-mail: reservations.rutlandarms@ohiml.com
dir: A14 junct 37 onto A142, or M11 junct 9 onto A11 then A1304 - follow signs for town centre

A coaching inn with lots of period charm, The Rutland Arms is at the heart of the action in the racing hotspot of Newmarket. Runners and riders on the menu in the informal, green-carpeted Carriages dining room take in bistro classics, as well as one or two more modern dishes. Start with deep-fried whitebait with lemon mayo, or goats' cheese truffles with balsamic glaze and confit tomatoes, before moving to sea bass on tagliatelle in white wine and shellfish cream, or liver and bacon with creamy mash and sage and onion gravy. Desserts come in a range of sizes, depending on appetite, but feature the comforting likes of poached pear in chocolate sauce, or lemon tart with raspberry compôte.

Chef Raymond Revel **Owner** Oxford Hotels & Inns **Times** 12-2.30/7-9.30 **Prices** Starter £5, Main £8.95-£17.95, Dessert £5, Service optional **Wines** 23 bottles over £20, 19 bottles under £20, 6 by glass **Notes** Sunday L, Vegetarian available **Seats** 50, Pr/dining room 30 **Children** Portions **Parking** 40

Tuddenham Mill

◉◉◉ *— see below*

ORFORD	Map 13 TM45

The Crown & Castle

◉◉ British, International V

Unpretentious cooking in a charming inn by the castle

☎ 01394 450205
IP12 2LJ
e-mail: info@crownandcastle.co.uk
dir: Off A12, on B1084, 9m E of Woodbridge

There has been a hostelry hard by the ruins of Orford's Norman castle for eight centuries, and today's incarnation is a soothing bolt-hole with a warm, friendly atmosphere and vibrantly-flavoured food cooked with skill and presented without undue fuss in the convivial Trinity restaurant. It is hardly surprising that good food is the beating heart of this operation, for food writer, cookbook author and TV presenter Ruth Watson is co-owner and executive chef. Menus offer plentiful choice, with crowd-pleasing, modern focused dishes conjured from quality local, seasonal ingredients, particularly locally-landed fish. Orford-landed skate, for example, might come with brown shrimps, sautéed cucumber and nut-brown butter, whilst rump of Suffolk lamb could arrive with a creamy broad bean sauce and rosemary mash. To finish, perhaps loganberry jam and frangipane tart with proper custard.

Chef Ruth Watson, Nick Thacker **Owner** David & Ruth Watson, Tim Sunderland **Times** 12.15-2.15/7-9.30 Closed L 31 Dec **Prices** Starter £4.95-£12.50, Main £14.95-£25, Dessert £6.95, Service added but optional 10%, Groups min 8 service 10% **Wines** 98+ bottles over £20, 16 bottles under £20, 16 by glass **Notes** Pre-concert supper available (Prior booking essential), Sunday L, Vegetarian menu **Seats** 60, Pr/dining room 10 **Children** Portions, Menu **Parking** 17, Market Sq, on street

SIBTON	Map 13 TM36

Sibton White Horse Inn

◉ Modern European ☺

Classic country pub with impressive modern cooking

☎ 01728 660337
Halesworth Rd IP17 2JJ
e-mail: info@sibtonwhitehorseinn.co.uk

There's not a pool table or bleeping one-armed bandit in sight at the White Horse, a textbook real pub in a picturesque sleepy Suffolk village. The food may be great, but the place hasn't gone all gastro, first and foremost it is the village boozer where locals pop in for a pint and a chat in a true-blue setting dating back to Tudor times, as its raised gallery, blackened beams, huge inglenooks, and ancient floors of recycled Roman tiles all attest. The kitchen deals in unpretentious modern dishes created with a passion that hauls in fish from the nearby Suffolk coast, and meat and game from local farms and shoots,

Tuddenham Mill

NEWMARKET	Map 12 TL66

Modern British

Imaginative modern British cooking in a converted watermill

☎ 01638 713552
High St, Tuddenham St Mary IP28 6SQ
e-mail: info@tuddenhammill.co.uk
dir: M11 junct 9 towards Newmarket, then A14 exit junct 38 in direction of Norwich. Turn right at Herringswell road

The old mill has scrubbed up very well indeed. 'Rustic chic' they call it, which sums up the place perfectly, being both full of original beams and character, but with a contemporary gloss to the fixtures and fittings. And an alluring boutique hotel it doth make. The restaurant is up on the first floor, with the glassed-in top half of the

waterwheel a reminder of the great buildings original function. (Glass inset panels in the floor give views down to the flowing water below, too). But despite the reminders of times gone by, this is a modish feeling space, with a decided lack of pretension, and a menu that features lots of little-seen ingredients, such as pennywort and water mint, and makes use of contemporary cooking techniques. A beautifully smokey main course of river trout, local eel, broad beans, kohlrabi and orpine leaves might precede pork neck carpaccio with crackling and pickled turnip. Precise cooking temperatures might appear on the menu - 40 degrees for organic salmon with brown shrimps, for example - and desserts show no less ambition; witness an egg custard tart with parsnip toffee, pear and nutmeg. The knowledgeable service fits the bill and the wine list is well worth exploring.

Chef Paul Foster **Owner** Agellus Hotels **Times** 12-2.15/6.30-9.15 **Prices** Fixed L 2 course £20, Tasting menu £65, Starter £7.25-£8.50, Main £20.50-£25, Dessert £7.25-£9.75, Service optional **Wines** 56 bottles over £20, 11 by glass **Notes** Tasting menu 8 course, Fixed L 5 course £35, Sunday L, Vegetarian available, Civ Wed 120 **Seats** 54, Pr/dining room 18 **Children** Portions, Menu **Parking** 40

offering among starters seared wood pigeon breast with poached quail's egg and crispy bacon, then fillet of Lowestoft cod with sweet potato fondant, stir-fried vegetables and herb oil, or breast and leg of wild duck teamed with dauphinoise potato, butternut squash purée, braised red cabbage and cherry jus.

Chef Michael McMullan, James Finch **Owner** Neil & Gill Mason **Times** 12-2/6.45-9 Closed Xmas, **Prices** Fixed L 2 course £12, Starter £5.25-£6.50, Main £10.25-£19.50, Dessert £5.50-£8, Service optional **Wines** 12 bottles over £20, 18 bottles under £20, 7 by glass **Notes** Sunday L, Vegetarian available **Seats** 40, Pr/dining room 18 **Children** Portions **Parking** 45

SOUTHWOLD   Map 13 TM57

The Blyth Hotel

◉ Modern British 🕏

Family-run seaside hotel with accomplished cooking

☎ 01502 722632
Station Rd IP18 6AY
e-mail: reception@blythhotel.com
dir: Follow A1095 from the A12, signed Southwold. Hotel on left after bridge

The Blyth ticks all of the contemporary style-led boxes needed to figure among Southwold's on-trend addresses. The beach is just a five-minute stroll away, and stripped pine floors, chunky wooden tables and a switched-on family- and dog-friendly attitude lend the place an appropriately seasidey vibe. Adnams ales are almost de rigueur in the brewery's home manor, so have a pint in the relaxed bar, then move into the classier environs of the contemporary restaurant, for appealing modern ideas built on seasonal and local materials. Expect starters along the lines of pan-fried pigeon breast with bacon, black pudding, soft-boiled quail's egg and celeriac purée, then intelligently composed main courses such as braised Dingley Dell pork belly with apple mashed potato, buttered Savoy cabbage, sage jus and crackling. Sweet treats to finish might run to dark chocolate tart with chocolate sauce, griottine cherries and chocolate brownie ice cream.

Chef Shaun Doig **Owner** Richard & Charlie Ashwell **Times** 12-2/6.30-9 **Prices** Fixed L 2 course £11.95, Fixed D 3 course £27.95, Service optional **Wines** 30 bottles under £20, 2 by glass **Notes** Pre-theatre/Family dining from 5.30 Jul & Aug, Sunday L, Vegetarian available **Seats** 38, Pr/dining room 14 **Children** Portions, Menu **Parking** 8, On street

The Crown

◉ Modern British 🍷 NOTABLE WINE LIST

Buzzy pub and restaurant in the heart of the action

☎ 01502 722275
90 High St IP18 6DP
e-mail: crown.reception@adnams.co.uk
web: www.adnams.co.uk
dir: A12 onto A1095 to Southwold. Hotel on left in High St

Right on the main street in the centre of town, this Adnams' brewery-owned pub, restaurant and wine bar within a hotel has something for everyone. It's informal and lively throughout, whether you're in the pub-brasserie or the restaurant with its scrubbed pine tables. The Adnams wine list is as good as you'd expect with a great selection by the glass. The young and enthusiastic kitchen team turn out some appealing modern, rustic British dishes, with plenty of Mediterranean sunshine along the way, and good quality ingredients at the heart of everything. There might be wild garlic risotto with braised pig's cheek and parmesan; a fantastic chargrilled pork rack with mustard mash, kale, caramelised apple and roasted shallot jus; and smoked haddock and prawn crumble with leeks, fennel and dressed rocket. To bow out in style go for the limoncello and lemon plate.

Times 12-2/6.30-9 Closed 25 Dec

Sutherland House

◉◉ Modern British 🕏

Neighbourhood fish restaurant with diligent sourcing

☎ 01502 724544
56 High St IP18 6DN
e-mail: enquiries@sutherlandhouse.co.uk
web: www.sutherlandhouse.co.uk
dir: A1095 into Southwold, on High St on left after Victoria St

Dating back to the 14th century, this Grade II listed place on Southwold High Street is packed full of fascinating period details - most of the wooden beams come from battle ships used in the battle of Sole Bay, plus there's ornate ceilings, coving and open fireplaces. In contrast

the furniture cuts a contemporary dash - think plain wooden tables and high-backed chairs. Relaxed, casual service helps the buzzy feel, and fish, locally-landed daily, is a big part of the draw. The menu stalks a modern British path, ingredients are sourced with care and food miles get listed alongside each dish. Kick off with goats' cheese pannacotta with walnut pesto, carpaccio of beetroot and rocket, then move on to pan-roasted turbot (served on the bone) with rösti potato and brown shrimp and lemon butter. There are a couple of meat main courses, too, plus desserts such as lemon posset with candied lemon and Chantilly cream.

Chef Jed Tejada **Owner** Peter & Anna Banks **Times** 12-3/7-9.30 Closed 25 Dec, 2 wks Jan, Mon (off season only) **Prices** Food prices not confirmed for 2013. Please telephone for details **Wines** 35 bottles over £20, 15 bottles under £20, 10 by glass **Notes** Sunday L, Vegetarian available **Seats** 50, Pr/dining room 60 **Children** Portions, Menu **Parking** 1, On street

Swan Hotel

◉◉ Modern British 🕏

Smart British cooking at Adnams' flagship hotel

☎ 01502 722186
High St, Market Place IP18 6EG
e-mail: swan.hotel@adnams.co.uk
dir: A1095 to Southwold. Hotel in town centre. Parking via archway to left of building

The Adnams empire has things pretty tied up in Southwold, where it is the seaside town's brewer, main publican, wine merchant and hotelier. Just in front of the brewery, the Swan - a handsome bay-fronted Victorian façade occupying pole position among the boutiques - is the epicentre of operations. Inside, its 17th-century origins are revealed: there are wall panels, genuine 18th-century oil paintings and gilt chandeliers, but time has not stood still, so it is all leavened with smart contemporary styling, particularly in the bar, which was made over in 2010. Afternoon tea in the drawing room is something of a local institution, but don't spoil your appetite for dinner in the smart dining room. As one would hope from a set-up with its roots deep into the local area, provenance of raw materials is emphatically regional, and the cooking is confident, full-flavoured stuff. That old stalwart of seared scallops and black pudding is matched here with celeriac, apple purée and pea shoots, and followed by a big-hearted dish of confit duck leg with bubble-and-squeak, roast parsnips, plum compôte and port jus.

Chef Rory Whelan **Owner** Adnams plc **Times** 12-2.30/7-9.30 **Prices** Fixed L 2 course £15.95, Fixed D 3 course £30, Starter £5-£7.95, Main £14.95-£23, Dessert £5-£7.95, Service optional **Wines** 95 bottles over £20, 19 bottles under £20, 12 by glass **Notes** Pre-theatre picnic hampers & D (summer only), Sunday L, Vegetarian available, Dress restrictions, Smart casual, No jeans, Civ Wed 100 **Seats** 65, Pr/dining room 36 **Children** Portions, Menu **Parking** 42

The Crown

◎ ◎ Modern British

Boutique hotel and village inn in one

☎ 01206 262001
CO6 4SE
e-mail: info@crowninn.net
dir: Stoke-by-Nayland signed from A12 & A134. Hotel in village off B1068 towards Higham

The 16th-century Crown has taken the fashionable boutique route, reinventing the one-time village inn with a stylish modern makeover and the addition of 11 classy bedrooms. There are still plenty of cosy corners to settle into though; whether it's in the beamed bar or the more contemporary dining areas, you'll find snug seats and log fires. Supplies are garnered from Suffolk's bountiful larder, and a daily-changing blackboard reflects the catch landed by local fishing boats working from the Blackwater Estuary; pan-fried mackerel fillets, for example, with pickled beetroot, soft-boiled egg, bacon, horseradish cream and potatoes. The kitchen's confident creative spirit also shows its hand in meat dishes; take roasted rump of lamb with rösti potato, smoked bacon, fresh peas and samphire and a port sauce, or perhaps a chocolate cola cake, teamed with Coca-Cola jelly. It's a perfect spot for Constable aficionados; The Crown lies in a sleepy village above the Stour and Box River valleys in deepest Constable Country with the soaring tower of nearby St Mary's church immortalised in the artist's works.

Chef Dan Hibble **Owner** Richard Sunderland
Times 12-2.30/6-9.30 Closed 25-26 Dec **Prices** Starter £4.65-£6.95, Main £9.95-£18.95, Dessert £4.55-£9.40, Service optional, Groups min 13 service 10%
Wines 16 bottles over £20, 22 bottles under £20, 22 by glass **Notes** Sunday L, Vegetarian available **Seats** 125, Pr/dining room 12 **Children** Portions, Menu **Parking** 49

The Shepherd and Dog

◎ ◎ Modern European

Revitalised village pub with creative cooking

☎ 01449 711361
Forward Green IP14 5HN
e-mail: marybruce@btinternet.com
web: www.theshepherdanddog.com
dir: On A1120 between A14 & A140

The Shepherd and Dog may still be the village inn, but the modern signs outside and Wagyu beef burgers on the menu are a clear hint that it has gone gastro. An open-plan bar leads into the restaurant, and a very chic and contemporary place it is too - all pale wood tables, leather high-backed chairs and unclothed tables, and an unbuttoned yet on-the-ball approach to service. The kitchen mixes pub favourites and daily-changing specials with big-city flavours inspired by Europe and further afield, pitching vibrant crab and salmon spring rolls with chilli crème fraîche and crisp seaweed against mains taking in rump of English lamb with mint and feta cheese couscous and mint jus, or grilled sea bass fillets teamed with butternut squash purée, shallot chutney and apple dressing. Desserts span everything from iced popcorn and caramel parfait with toffee popcorn to Bavarian bread pudding with rum, grated apple and sultanas.

Chef Christopher Bruce & Daniela Bruce
Owner Christopher & Mary Bruce **Times** 12-2/7-11 Closed mid Jan, Mon, D Sun **Prices** Fixed L 2 course £20-£24, Fixed D 3 course £20-£24, Starter £5.50-£8.50, Main £14.50-£19, Dessert £6-£7, Service optional
Wines 28 bottles over £20, 25 bottles under £20, 19 by glass **Notes** Sunday L, Vegetarian available **Seats** 50, Pr/dining room 24 **Children** Portions, Menu **Parking** 35

The Case Restaurant with Rooms

◎ Modern British

Characterful Suffolk inn with a brasserie-style menu

☎ 01787 210483
Further St, Assington CO10 5LD
e-mail: restaurant@thecaserestaurantwithrooms.co.uk
dir: Located on A134 between Sudbury & Colchester. 0.5m past Newton Golf Club

Located in deepest Suffolk countryside, this great little property has bags of character. Dating back to about 1700, the whitewashed country inn used to be a private home and now there are beautiful bedrooms and a cosy little restaurant to attract paying customers. It's a little like eating in someone's front room (in a nice way), with a wood-burning stove, darkwood tables and low ceiling beams. Brasserie cooking is the name of the game and a highlight of the meal may well be the mini-beef Wellington that is a first-course option, but what follows on the daily-changing menu is sure to appeal too - a meaty Dingley dell pork chop and sausage, perhaps, with apple tartlet, jacket potato, green vegetables and Suffolk Aspall cider sauce, or poached fillet of plaice filled with salmon mousse.

Times 12-2/6.30-9 Closed L Mon

Thorpeness Hotel

◎ Modern British **NEW**

Broadly appealing menu at a coastal golf club

☎ 01728 452176
Lakeside Av IP16 4NH
e-mail: manager@thorpeness.co.uk
web: www.thorpeness.co.uk
dir: A1094 towards Aldeburgh, take coast road N for 2m

An especially picturesque 18-hole course is the main outdoor attraction at this 1920s golf club hotel, named after the village it stands in by the Suffolk coast, not far from Aldeburgh. That bizarre looking house on a stalk nearby is the surrealistically disguised water-tower. Picture windows in the hotel serve up panoramic views of the pitching and putting, and there is some unfussy modern British food to accompany. A hot suet pudding of beetroot, red pepper and feta in grain mustard dressing is an unusual curtain-raiser. Mains run the gamut from local cod, which might appear poached on a bed of roasted vine tomatoes, olives and garlic in sorrel butter, to moistly tender Gressingham duck confit with pak choi in kumquat jus. Finish with chocolate and orange ganache torte and cinnamon doughnuts.

Times 12.30-3/7-9.30 Closed L Mon-Sat

Save on Hotels. Book at theAA.com/hotel

SUFFOLK 439 ENGLAND

The Anchor

◉◉ Modern British

Tempting seasonal dishes in a coastal inn

☎ 01502 722112
Main St IP18 6UA
e-mail: info@anchoratwalberswick.com
dir: On entering village The Anchor on right, immediately after MG garage

Mark and Sophie Dorber decamped from The Smoke in 2004 and set about reworking this 1920s Arts and Crafts-style inn facing Walberswick's pebbly beach. The result is an Anchor that is painstakingly restored and brought up to speed for savvy visitors who prefer a more tranquil spot than trendy Southwold just across the River Blyth. On a fine day, alfresco dining on parasol-shaded benches is the way to go, while inside is a cosy beamed cocoon. The kitchen is supplied by the owners' allotment and neighbours' gardens, plus a trusty network of local producers, naturally, and it all translates into hearty contemporary food that eschews jellies and foams in favour of things that have to be bitten, chewed and crunched. A game terrine involving duck confit and pigeon is flavoured with star anise, prune and pistachio, wrapped in pancetta and served with spiced pear, while main-course grilled brill fillet is set on a bed of curly kale and partnered with Puy lentils and chorizo. Each dish is matched with beer and wine recommendations by owners who have a vast knowledge of the subject.

Chef Sophie Dorber **Owner** Sophie & Mark Dorber
Times 11-4/6-11 **Prices** Food prices not confirmed for 2013. Please telephone for details **Wines** 138 bottles over £20, 17 bottles under £20, 20 by glass **Notes** Sunday L, Vegetarian available **Seats** 55, Pr/dining room 26 **Children** Portions, Menu **Parking** 60

The Westleton Crown

◉◉ Modern British V ✪

Vibrant modern cooking in an ancient inn

☎ 01728 648777
The Street IP17 3AD
e-mail: info@westletoncrown.co.uk
dir: A12 N, turn right for Westleton just after Yoxford. Hotel opposite on entering village

This textbook red-brick Suffolk coaching inn may date from the 12th century, but there's nothing archaic about the gastronomic side of the operation. The Crown is still an endearingly cosy local with well-kept real ales, a log fire and ancient beams in the bar, while the modern conservatory restaurant is done out in a clean-cut style with mismatched scrubbed wood tables and a wall of sliding glass doors that opens up to the lovely terraced gardens. The food also keeps its feet planted in the present with some cleverly-honed modern ideas wrought from first-rate local produce. Orford smoked haddock might provide the foundations for a puff pastry tart made with spinach and free-range eggs, ahead of main courses running from steamed halibut with cocotte potatoes, wilted red chard and a vegetable and herb nage, to a more gutsy four-way workout of local Suffolk chicken, in the form of poached breast, roasted thigh, confit leg, and breaded wing with pasta, parsley sauce and braised lettuce.

Chef Richard Bargewell **Owner** Agellus Hotels Ltd
Times 12-2.30/7-9.30 **Prices** Starter £5.50-£7, Main £12.95-£23.25, Dessert £5.75-£9, Service optional **Wines** 29 bottles over £20, 22 bottles under £20, 9 by glass **Notes** Sunday L, Vegetarian menu, Civ Wed 90 **Seats** 85, Pr/dining room 50 **Children** Portions, Menu **Parking** 50

The Crown at Woodbridge

◉◉ Modern European

Distinguished brasserie cooking in a market town

☎ 01394 384242
2 Thoroughfare IP12 1AD
e-mail: info@thecrownatwoodbridge.co.uk
dir: A12 follow signs for Woodbridge onto B1438, after 1.25m from rdbt turn left into Quay Street & hotel on right, approx 100 yds from junct

A complete refurbishment saw The Crown triumphantly reopen for business in 2009, and become one of the prime draws of this attractive riverside market town. It still feels very much an inn, with food served throughout a range of different eating areas, all pervaded by a relaxed, easygoing ambience and a good mix of keen local clientele. The main business is brasserie cooking of genuine flair, based on local materials and mixing culinary ideas to good effect. Start with deep-fried crabcakes served with fennel escabèche dressed in soy, and follow up with roasted sea bass, samphire and lentils in anchovy vinaigrette, or succulently tender ox cheek braised in ale, with cavolo nero and horseradish mash. Desserts to indulge include chocolate brownie with banoffee ice cream, or pear sponge pudding and vanilla-pod custard.

Times 12-2.15/6.15-9 Closed D 25 Dec (available for residents only)

Seckford Hall Hotel

◉◉ Modern European ✪

Castellated Tudor hall with modish menu

☎ 01394 385678
IP13 6NU
e-mail: reception@seckford.co.uk
dir: Hotel signed on A12 (Woodbridge bypass). Do not follow signs for town centre

Approached by a sweeping drive, the imposing Tudor pile of Seckford - with its brick façade, soaring chimneys, carved-oak entrance door and well-preened grounds - is no less impressive than when Queen Elizabeth I held court here. Today, a country-house hotel for the 21st century it maybe, but its interior successfully blends its regal past with modern-day comforts. The main dining room embodies that classical look, with oak panelling, rich tapestries, white linen and rich drapes, while the accomplished kitchen deals in country-house cooking with a modern spin, based on a good deal of local produce. Fillet of East Coast cod, for example, is accompanied by sautéed potatoes, chorizo and spinach, or there might be roast rump of salt marsh lamb teamed with sweet garlic and goats' cheese mash. Desserts continue the classic-with-a-twist trend in the form of glazed citrus tart served with a cinnamon doughnut and raspberry sorbet.

Chef Mark Archer **Owner** Mr & Mrs Bunn
Times 12.30-1.45/7-9.30 Closed 25 Dec, L Mon **Prices** Fixed L 2 course £12.95-£21.95, Fixed D 3 course fr £31.50, Starter £5.95-£8.50, Main £14.50-£24.50, Dessert £4.95-£6.95, Service included **Wines** 40 bottles over £20, 45 bottles under £20, 11 by glass **Notes** Sunday L, Vegetarian available, Dress restrictions, Smart casual, Civ Wed 120 **Seats** 70, Pr/dining room 100 **Children** Portions, Menu **Parking** 100

The Auberge

◉◉ Traditional, International

Well-crafted dishes in a medieval Suffolk inn

☎ 01379 783604
Ipswich Rd IP23 8BZ
e-mail: aubmail@the-auberge.co.uk
dir: 5m S of Diss on A140

Dating back to medieval times, The Auberge has been a public house for many centuries, and its reincarnation as a modern restaurant with rooms doesn't disguise the fact. The ancient beams and panelling and exposed brickwork make an atmospheric setting, whether you're after a cosy corner with a table for two, or a groaning board that will seat 20. As the name would suggest, French influence is in evidence in the cooking, but the kitchen relies solidly on local materials for its deft handling of modern pub food. Start perhaps with partridge and pork rillettes with green tomato and mango chutney, or a sustaining smoked haddock and fennel chowder, before moving to fried calves' liver with quince sauce and onion mash, or one of the speciality rump or rib steaks with garlic and herb butter or pink peppercorn sauce. Puddings go unashamedly for the populist vote, with a concoction of dark chocolate, dried fruits and nuts in coffee and Marsala mascarpone, or ginger trifle with egg nog custard.

Chef John Stenhouse **Owner** John & Dee Stenhouse
Times 12-2/7-9.30 Closed 1-7 Jan, Sun, L Sat-Mon **Prices** Fixed L 2 course £16.95, Fixed D 3 course £19.95, Starter £7.50-£9.50, Main £16.50-£27.90, Dessert £6.90-£8.90, Service optional **Wines** 39 bottles over £20, 11 bottles under £20, 13 by glass **Notes** Vegetarian available **Seats** 60, Pr/dining room 20 **Children** Portions **Parking** 25

YOXFORD — Map 5 TM36

Satis House

@@ Modern British 🌱

Piquant flavours in rural Suffolk

☎ 01728 668418
Main Rd IP17 3EX
e-mail: enquiries@satishouse.co.uk
dir: off A12 between Ipswich & Lowestoft. 9m E Aldeburgh & Snape

Satis House is a Grade II listed building dating from the 18th century with connections to Charles Dickens (it gets a name-check in *Great Expectations*). Today's incarnation has lost none of its period charm and it is decorated in such a way as to enhance the period features without seeming chintzy or dated. The restaurant has a decidedly contemporary sheen to it, with its polished wooden floor, bold red-flowered wallpaper and darkwood, unclothed tables. Carefully-sourced local produce features prominently on the menu, which might take you from chicken liver parfait with onion marmalade to veal cutlet with olive and caper butter, or the more Eastern-inspired pan-fried scallops with crème fraîche and sweet chilli jam to Thai duck leg curry with pickled plums and duck spring roll. For dessert, chocolate mousse comes with a peanut parfait and brittle, while the seasonal celebration of rhubarb brings forth jelly, brûlée and pudding (with ginger).

Chef David Little **Owner** David Little, Kevin Wainwright **Times** 12-3/6.30-11 Closed L Mon-Tue **Prices** Fixed L 2 course £15-£20, Fixed D 3 course £22-£25, Starter £5.75-£10.95, Main £13.95-£22.95, Dessert £4.50-£9.75, Service optional **Wines** 30 bottles over £20, 14 bottles under £20, 10 by glass **Notes** Sunday L, Vegetarian available, Dress restrictions, Smart casual, Civ Wed 50 **Seats** 60, Pr/dining room 30 **Children** Portions **Parking** 25

SURREY

ABINGER HAMMER — Map 6 TQ04

Drakes on the Pond

@@ Modern British

Well-crafted dishes in a classy village restaurant

☎ 01306 731174
Dorking Rd RH5 6SA
dir: On A25 between Dorking & Guildford

On the Dorking Road next to, you've guessed it, a large pond, Drakes looks charmingly old-school and rustic from the outside, but inside it's another story. The ceiling beams are boxed in and painted white to lighten the tone, the walls are a cheery yellow ocre and beechwood chairs are more new school than old; with tables neatly dressed in white linen, it's a smart contemporary setting for some smart and well-judged contemporary cooking. Chef-patron John Morris seeks out high quality ingredients and creates dishes which are based on sound classical principles, but given a satisfying modish sheen. Thus scallops are given the tempura treatment, served with pan-fried squid, chorizo, dressed leaves and orange salad, or there might be twice-baked St Agur cheese soufflé with a sweet pepper relish and parmesan tuiles. Next up, breast of quail comes with its crispy leg, potato and cep dauphinoise, buttered spinach, carrot and cardamom purée and cep sauce, finishing with baked vanilla cheesecake with strawberry ice cream.

Times 12-2/7-10 Closed 2 wks Aug-Sep, Xmas, New Year, BHs, Sun (except Mothering Sun), Mon

BAGSHOT — Map 6 SU96

The Brasserie at Pennyhill Park

@@ Modern British V 🌱

Relaxed brasserie with contemporary cooking

☎ 01276 471774
Pennyhill Park Hotel & Spa, London Rd GU19 5EU
e-mail: enquiries@pennyhillpark.co.uk
dir: M3 junct 3, through Bagshot, left onto A30. 0.5m on right

The Brasserie is the more informal and relaxed alternative to Pennyhill Park's trailblazing Latymer (see entry), a large, bright room, with stone walls, lots of windows overlooking the pool, opposite the huge spa complex. The kitchen puts a fresh spin on the brasserie repertoire, pairing roast fillet of sea bass with confit, squid ink gnocchi, a prawn and ginger 'cigar' and watercress purée, and beef Wellington with Parma ham, smoked potato purée and Madeira jus. Ideas are contemporary without being outlandish, as in successful starters of crab with tuna carpaccio, lime and tomato jelly, caper berries and pea shoots, and roast local quail with a cep and quail consommé. Grilled steaks are options too, and puddings might bring on chocolate fondant with a caramel centre, prettily arranged with raspberry compôte and sorbet.

Chef Ram Jalasutram **Owner** Exclusive Hotels **Times** 12-2.30/6-10 Closed L Sat **Prices** Fixed L 3 course £25, Fixed D 2 course £25, Starter £6.50-£14.50, Main £15.90-£29.99, Dessert £8-£11, Service added but optional 10% **Wines** 130 bottles over £20, 13 by glass **Notes** Fixed D Mon-Sat 2 course before 7pm, Sunday L, Vegetarian menu **Seats** 120, Pr/dining room 30 **Children** Portions, Menu **Parking** 500

Michael Wignall at The Latymer

@@@@@ – *see opposite*

CAMBERLEY — Map 6 SU86

Macdonald Frimley Hall Hotel & Spa

@@ Modern European

Smart modern British cooking in peaceful setting

☎ 0844 879 9110
Lime Av GU15 2BG
e-mail: gm.frimleyhall@macdonald-hotels.co.uk
dir: M3 junct 3, A321 follow Bagshot signs. Through lights, left onto A30 signed Camberley & Basingstoke. To rdbt, 2nd exit onto A325, take 5th right

This ivy-covered manor house surrounded by pretty gardens and unspoilt woodland scrubs up very nicely indeed (perhaps because it was built as the home of the Wright family of Coal Tar soap fame). Today's country-house hotel has been brought up to date with the addition of a spa and health club, but preserves plenty of grand period details such as an oak staircase and panelling. The Linden restaurant is a soothing space where neutral colours and simple table settings set the scene for modish cooking in the vein of roasted oxtail faggots with puy lentils, toasted brioche and red wine jus, followed by fillet of wild brill served with a crab fritter, coriander gnocchi, spinach and coconut cream. Finish on a creative note with a blood orange tart and cardamom ice cream.

Chef Sanobia Cutino **Owner** Macdonald Hotels **Times** 12.30-2/7-9.30 Closed 25 & 26 Dec (eve), L Sat **Prices** Food prices not confirmed for 2013. Please telephone for details **Wines** 50 bottles over £20, 4 bottles under £20, 12 by glass **Notes** Sunday L, Vegetarian available, Dress restrictions, Smart casual **Seats** 70, Pr/dining room 200 **Children** Portions, Menu **Parking** 100

Michael Wignall at The Latymer

BAGSHOT Map 6 SU96

Modern European V NOTABLE WINE LIST

Compelling contemporary cooking in world-class hotel

☎ 01276 471774
Pennyhill Park Hotel & Spa, London Rd GU19 5EU
e-mail: enquiries@pennyhillpark.co.uk
dir: M3 junct 3, through Bagshot, left onto A30. 0.5m on right

The original house, built in the 19th century for a high-flying man of business, remains the heart and soul of the Pennyhill estate, and it's a fair bet you will have stayed in hotel rooms elsewhere that arc smaller than the devilishly swish en suite bathrooms here. The 123 acres of lush and wooded Surrey parkland that surrounds Pennyhill adds to that sense of escape and there is enough going on here to entice even the most reluctant of sybarites - nine-hole golf course, shooting lodge, a gym equipped to the gunnels with all the latest stuff, and a spa that could wash away the troubles from all but perhaps the Greek Finance Minister. And then there is the food. There are a number of eating options (see entry for The Brasserie), but the main attraction, le gros poisson, summo canis...is Michael Wignall at The Latymer. As the five Rosettes attest, this is contemporary cooking of the highest order. The action takes place in a room

with oak panelled walls and stained-glass windows, the space given a high-end contemporary feel with its burnt orange, rust and pale green colour palette. In the kitchen, a dramatic bubble-glass chef's table sits amid onyx walls, a glass mosaic floor, and an LCD screen for close-ups of the action. The service team are top-drawer, too, with nary a step out of place. Michael Wignall's food is creative and majestically-crafted stuff, with modern culinary thinking warmly embraced but never allowed to detract or overwhelm the ingredients (and what ingredients!), whilst presentation is beautiful without being frivolous. An amuse-bouche of an open ravioli with pork loin, crab and bergamot sets the bar about as high as it can go, the flavours and aromas leaving a lasting impression - wow. The technical abilities on show are phenomenal: the attention to detail in a starter of Cotswold white chicken, for example, has the meat poached in an aromatic consommé and served super-thin with its crispy skin, a 'cigar' of smoked eel, ponzu jelly and a horseradish emulsion. Next up, main-course Lakeland roe deer is a superb piece of meat, the loin soft and packed with flavour, served with Hereford snails, parsley cream and salad, sprouting broccoli, bread and bay, or from the 10-course Tasting Menu might be cassoulet of razor and palourde clams with cuttlefish gnocchi, free-range Farnborough quail's egg and

cuttlefish crisp. The skill, craft and creativity continues through to desserts such as iced yuzu mousse with dehydrated yoghurt, Alphonse mango sabayon and coconut sorbet. The breads are all freshly made in the hotel's in-house bakery, including your morning croissant if you're lucky enough to be staying over.

Chef Michael Wignall **Owner** Exclusive Hotels **Times** 12.30-2/7-9.30 Closed 1-14 Jan, Sun-Mon (Open Sun BHs but closed following Tue), L Tue, Sat **Prices** Fixed L 2 course fr £26, Fixed D 3 course fr £60, Tasting menu £60-£82, Service added but optional 12.5% **Wines** 220 bottles over £20, 20 by glass **Notes** Tasting menu L 8 course, D 10 course, Vegetarian menu **Seats** 50, Pr/dining room 30 **Parking** 500

CHIDDINGFOLD — Map 6 SU93

The Swan Inn

◉ British, International

Wide-ranging menus in a former coaching inn

☎ 01428 684688
Petworth Rd GU8 4TY
e-mail: info@theswaninnchiddingfold.com
dir: On A283 Petworth road, towards Chichester

Expect to see lots of exposed brickwork, stripped floors, logs burning, and a comfortable and inviting dining room, with flowers on wooden tables, at this former coaching inn in a quintessential English village. The kitchen turns its hands to a principally British menu with some input from further afield, so roast chicken breast with merguez sausage and white bean cassoulet might appear next to rump of lamb with roast root vegetables, braised red cabbage and red wine jus. An innovative soup could kick things off - perhaps white onion, cider and sage - or go for soused mackerel with potato, cucumber and dill salad. End with a creditable trio of English cheeses or with passionfruit pannacotta with a kick of lime.

Chef Graham Digweed **Owner** Annemaria & Stuart Boomer Davies **Times** 12-3/6.30-10 **Prices** Starter £4.95-£12.25, Main £13-£19.95, Dessert £5-£6, Service optional **Wines** 43 bottles over £20, 10 bottles under £20, 16 by glass **Notes** Sunday L, Vegetarian available, Air con **Seats** 40, Pr/dining room 40 **Children** Portions, Menu **Parking** 35

DORKING — Map 6 TQ14

Mercure Box Hill Burford Bridge Hotel

◉ British, European

Traditionally-based hotel cooking in rural Surrey

☎ 01306 884561
Burford Bridge, Box Hill RH5 6BX
e-mail: h6635@accor.com
dir: M25 junct 9, A245 towards Dorking. Hotel within 5m on A24

At the foot of Box Hill by the River Mole, the Burford Bridge is in a peaceful spot (though not far from the A24), as may be appreciated by those availing themselves of the outdoor pool or the croquet lawn. A beige-hued modern dining room, the Emlyn, is the setting for some gently tweaked, traditionally-based cooking, along the lines of oxtail soup with herb dumplings, grilled haddock with shrimp butter and parsley mash, or breast and cabbage-wrapped confit leg of duck in sloe gin sauce. Interesting ideas for pudding include chocolate and rosemary soufflé with orange biscotti, or praline parfait with wine- and cinnamon-poached pear.

Chef Andrew Barrass **Owner** MREF Ltd **Times** 12-2.30/7-9.30 Closed D Sun **Prices** Fixed L 2 course £20, Fixed D 3 course £27, Starter £6.95-£8.95, Main £17.50-£28.95, Dessert £7.50, Service included **Wines** 39 bottles over £20, 4 bottles under £20, 14 by glass **Notes** Sunday L, Vegetarian available, Civ Wed 200

Seats 70, Pr/dining room 200 **Children** Portions, Menu **Parking** 140

Two To Four

◉◉ Modern European 🍃

Modern cooking in a thriving neighbourhood joint

☎ 01306 889923
2-4 West St RH4 1BL
e-mail: two_to_four@hotmail.com
web: www.twotofourrestaurant.com
dir: M25, exit at Leatherhead junct, follow signs to town centre

This neighbourhood restaurant is a textbook example of its ilk, and the sort of place we'd all like on our patch. It is a buzzy, sprawling venue spread over three floors of a terrace of converted cottages, kitted out in smart-casual mode with undressed tables, and run with the sort of friendly, relaxed vibe where staff greet regulars by name. Blackboards supplement the menu, where uncomplicated modern European-style dishes come to the table with a good-looking contemporary gloss. Seared scallops with fennel purée, bacon crumbs, and a salad of shaved fennel and Granny Smith apple is a typical starter, while mains follow the classic lines of chargrilled 35-day-aged rib of beef with chunky chips, salad and béarnaise sauce, or a grilled whole Dover sole with lemon mash, and buttered and wilted local greens. For pudding, Eton Mess could be made with pink champagne, rhubarb, honeycomb and orange.

Chef Rob Gathercole **Owner** Restaurant 2to4 Ltd **Times** 12-2.30/6.30-10 Closed Xmas, Mon (subject to change) **Prices** Food prices not confirmed for 2013. Please telephone for details **Wines** 35 bottles over £20, 4 bottles under £20, 8 by glass **Notes** Sun L winter only, Vegetarian available **Seats** 70, Pr/dining room 12 **Children** Portions **Parking** West St car park

EGHAM — Map 6 TQ07

The Oak Room at Great Fosters

◉◉◉ *— see opposite*

GODALMING — Map 6 SU94

La Luna

◉◉ Modern Italian 🏅

Stylish modern Italian venue

☎ 01483 414155
10-14 Wharf St GU7 1NN
e-mail: info@lalunarestaurant.co.uk
web: www.lalunarestaurant.co.uk
dir: In town centre, at junct of Wharf St & Flambard Way

Lucky Godalming locals have taken this smart contemporary Italian to their hearts - and who can blame them when it delivers on all counts: great-value lunch menus, charming, knowledgeable service, a modish interior in soothing hues of caramel, chocolate and black, with oak tables, and a well-chosen Italian wine list to support an appealing modern repertoire of southern-leaning dishes. The menu follows the traditional route, starting out with antipasti such as smoked swordfish with shaved fennel, or well-sourced Italian charcuterie - wild boar and pork salami, or prosciutto from free-range Sicilian pigs - then Neapolitan scialatielli pasta with Sicilian fennel seed sausage ragù and smoked scamorza cheese. Main courses could bring rump of local South Downs lamb, meltingly tender (cooked sous-vide), teamed with Umbrian lentils and rosemary jus, while puddings run from a top-class tiramisù to chocolate and hazelnut torta Caprese with salted caramel truffles and crème brûlée ice cream.

Chef Valentino Gentile **Owner** Daniele Drago **Times** 12-2/7-10 Closed 2 wks Aug, BHs, Sun-Mon **Prices** Food prices not confirmed for 2013. Please telephone for details **Wines** 158 bottles over £20, 14 bottles under £20, 8 by glass **Notes** Vegetarian available **Seats** 58, Pr/dining room 24 **Children** Portions **Parking** Public car park behind restaurant

Save on Hotels. Book at **theAA.com/hotel**

SURREY 443 ENGLAND

The Oak Room at Great Fosters

EGHAM Map 6 TQ07

Modern British V 🍷 NOTABLE WINE LIST 🐦

Classy modern cooking in an historic mansion

☎ 01784 433822
Stroude Rd TW20 9UR
e-mail: reception@greatfosters.co.uk
web: www.greatfosters.co.uk
dir: From A30 (Bagshot to Staines), right at lights by Wheatsheaf pub into Christchurch Rd. Straight on at rdbt (pass 2 shop parades on right). Left at lights into Stroude Rd. Hotel 0.75m on right

The historic core of Great Fosters was built in the 16th century as a hunting lodge, then spread its wings and grew into the full-blown magnificence of a manor house. It certainly fits the bill as a 21st-century palace of pleasure too, with its 50 acres of gorgeous gardens fringed by a Saxon moat, and an interior fully laden with oak panelling, stone-mullioned windows and elaborate plasterwork ceilings. Of course it is not all original: tasteful touches of contemporary style lift the house from museum territory into the world of a premier-league country house with oodles of character and a completely modern approach to gastronomy. The Oak Room restaurant typifies the look: an intricate canopy of vaulted oak beams spreads over a subtle décor involving a vibrantly coloured modern

wall tapestry and high-backed cream leather chairs at linen-clothed tables. Head chef Simon Bolsover leads a skilled kitchen brigade along a path of light-touch modern cooking based on materials from local producers - some as local as the house's own estate where honey bees and Middlewhite pigs are kept. His feel for intricacy, balance and turbo-charged flavours shows in a starter partnering seared scallops with warm brawn jelly, pickled clams, creamed shallots and crunchy slices of radish. Next up, rump of Cumbrian lamb is delivered with its sweetbreads, smoked pancetta, sautéed curly kale and creamed carrots, while those in the mood for fish might see salsify, artichoke and pickled trompette mushrooms used to point up the flavours of line-caught sea bass, and calamari. Finally, raspberry Breton tart with white chocolate cream, raspberry jelly and a quenelle of bitter chocolate is a thrilling explosion of flavours and textures.

Chef Simon Bolsover **Owner** Great Fosters (1931) Ltd
Times 12.30-2/7-9.30 Closed L Sat
Prices Fixed D 3 course £42, Starter £13, Main £24, Dessert £11, Service added but optional 12.5%
Wines 285 bottles over £20, 17 by glass
Notes Sunday L, Vegetarian menu, Civ Wed 180 **Seats** 60, Pr/dining room 20 **Children** Portions, Menu
Parking 200

HASLEMERE · Map 6 SU93

Lythe Hill Hotel & Spa

Modern British

Ambitious modern food in the Surrey Hills

☎ 01428 651251
Petworth Rd GU27 3BQ
e-mail: lythe@lythehill.co.uk
dir: 1m E of Haslemere on B2131

With its various buildings, including a swish spa and health set-up, clustered together in 22 acres of beautiful grounds, Lythe Hill has the look of a small hamlet tucked away in the Surrey Hills. Housed within the timbered Tudor building, the classy restaurant is an easy-on-the-eye fusion of 15th-century beams, oak panelling, and a stylish, clean-lined contemporary look. In tune with the setting, the kitchen keeps things modern and inventive, its menu embracing entertaining juxtapositions - terrine of roast quail, potato and Parma ham, served with candied beetroot, spiced lentils and Madeira pearls, while main course employs ricotta gnocchi, pickled grapes, samphire, and crayfish ravioli as a foil to a poached fillet of brill. A creative finale involves date parfait matched with confit orange, poached apple, meringue, and Grand Marnier sorbet. A bar with splendid countryside views, and attentive, clued-up staff complete an impressive package.

Chef Malcolm Campbell **Times** 12-2.30/7-9.30
Prices Fixed L 2 course fr £18, Fixed D 3 course fr £25, Starter £6.50-£8, Main £17.95-£24, Dessert £6.50-£8, Service optional **Wines** 50 bottles over £20, 7 bottles under £20, 7 by glass **Notes** Fixed L all week, Sunday L, Vegetarian available, Dress restrictions, Smart casual, Civ Wed 120 **Seats** 70, Pr/dining room 34
Children Portions **Parking** 65

HORLEY

For restaurant details see Gatwick Airport (London), (Sussex, West)

OCKLEY · Map 6 TQ14

Bryce's Seafood Restaurant & Country Pub

Modern British, Seafood V

Enterprising seafood in a smart country inn

☎ 01306 627430
The Old School House, Stane St RH5 5TH
e-mail: fish@bryces.co.uk
web: www.bryces.co.uk
dir: From M25 junct 9 take A24, then A29. 8m S of Dorking on A29

The inn was at one time a boys' boarding school dating from the mid-18th century, today's bars once classrooms and the beamed restaurant - windows on one side, comfortable high-backed chairs - the gym. The restaurant celebrated its 20th anniversary in 2012, and it's easy to see why it's still going strong: tip-top seafood, cooked just so, and a menu with enough variety to keep even regulars happy. Potted brown shrimps, or grilled sardine fillets with a rocket, orange and hazelnut salad might be precursors to well-planned main courses like seared swordfish steak on warm salade Niçoise, or plaice fillets stuffed with salmon, crab and prawn mousse served on wilted spinach with champagne sauce. A separate bar menu takes in sandwiches and chargrilled steaks as well as the fruits of the sea.

Chef B Bryce, Peter Howard **Owner** Mr W Bryce & Mrs E Bryce **Times** 12-2.30/7-9.30 Closed 25 Dec, 1 Jan, D Sun (Nov & Jan-Feb) **Prices** Food prices not confirmed for 2013. Please telephone for details **Wines** 11 bottles over £20, 19 bottles under £20, 14 by glass **Notes** ALC 2/3 course £29/£34, Fixed 2/3 course £12.50/£16 Sun-Thu, Sunday L, Vegetarian menu **Seats** 50 **Children** Portions **Parking** 35

REDHILL · Map 6 TQ25

Nutfield Priory Hotel & Spa

Modern British V

Creative modern cooking in Gothic country pile

☎ 0845 072 7486 & 01737 824400
Nutfield Rd RH1 4EL
e-mail: nutfieldpriory@handpicked.co.uk
dir: On A25, 1m E of Redhill, off M25 junct 8 or M25 junct 6, follow A25 through Godstone

The priory's architect was inspired by Pugin's Palace of Westminster and designed it in high Gothic style. Renovations have retained the original features of fine wood and stone carvings and panelling and added all the amenities of a modern country-house hotel, including a health club and spa. Cloisters Restaurant, aptly named, is smartly kitted out and gives breathtaking country views from its leaded mullioned windows. The kitchen shows sure-footed techniques, turning out ambitious starters like a terrine of foie gras, ham hock and poached chicken, its richness cut by piccalilli, and pan-fried scallops with parsnip purée, truffles and parsley 'air'. Main courses can be complex too, but ingredients are brought together with culinary good sense: amazingly fresh roast halibut fillet with brandade, mushrooms, cauliflower cream and chicken jus, say, or breast of duck with consommé, confit leg spring roll, parsnip rösti, a pistachio crumb and cherries. Chocoholics could end with a trio of brûlée, mousse and fondant.

Chef Roger Gadsden **Owner** Hand Picked Hotels
Times 12.30-2/7-9.30 Closed L Sat **Prices** Fixed L 2 course fr £20, Fixed D 3 course £40-£50, Starter £8-£13, Main £18-£30, Dessert fr £12, Service optional
Wines 100+ bottles over £20, 18 by glass **Notes** Sunday L, Vegetarian menu, Dress restrictions, Smart casual **Seats** 60, Pr/dining room 60 **Children** Portions, Menu **Parking** 100

Save on Hotels. Book at **theAA.com/hotel**

SURREY 445 ENGLAND

Drake's Restaurant

RIPLEY   Map 6 TQ05

Modern British **V**

Outstanding cooking near the RHS gardens at Wisley

☎ 01483 224777
The Clock House, High St GU23 6AQ
e-mail: info@drakesrestaurant.co.uk
web: www.drakesrestaurant.co.uk
dir: M25 junct 10, A3 towards Guildford. Follow Ripley signs. Restaurant in village centre

Refurbishment at Drake's, in a Georgian property with a distinctive clock hanging above the entrance, has levelled the floor, uncovered beams, created a bar area, and given a more contemporary feel to the place: all very elegant it is too. 'An adventure in flavour is our inspiration', says Steve Drake, an inspiration that manifests itself in a painstakingly assembled, successful starter of two pink, succulent quail breasts served with a slice of foie gras, a scoop of fluffy rhubarb, and a small glass of sweetcorn purée. Menu descriptions - 'blow-torched mackerel, beetroot, avocado and cucumber', for example - are as bald as dishes are complex, but confidence and good judgement mean that each leaves a clear impression on the palate. Take a main course of sea bass: a faultlessly timed fillet is served on a thin layer of braised oxtail, with triangles of three types of beetroot (yellow, red and

purple) nicely arranged on the plate, each retaining a bit of bite, accompanied by caramelised fennel and wild chervil mayonnaise, the whole dish a triumph of flavours, textures and colours. The menus change with the seasons, so expect game in winter: perhaps venison with chestnuts and stilton butter. Breads - and butter, come to that - are excellent, and desserts make an impact on the eye as well as the taste buds, among them dense-tasting chocolate mousse with slices of coriander-infused pear and walnuts.

Chef Steve Drake **Owner** Steve & Serina Drake **Times** 12-2/7-9.30 Closed 2 wks Jan, 2 wks Aug, Sun-Mon, L Tue **Prices** Fixed L 2 course fr £22, Fixed D 3 course fr £60, Service added but optional 12.5% **Wines** 170 bottles over £20, 3 bottles under £20, 8 by glass **Notes** Discovery menu £80, Vegetarian menu **Seats** 40 **Parking** 2

REIGATE | Map 6 TQ25

The Dining Room

◉◉ Modern British V

Smart modern cooking in elegant surroundings

☎ 01737 226650
59a High St RH2 9AE
dir: M25 junct 8/A217 follow one way system into High St, restaurant on left

Tony Tobin set about making The Dining Room a destination restaurant back in 1993, having done a long stint as one of Nico Ladenis's chefs in London. The place eschews rough-and-ready minimalism for an elegant Sunday-supplement look, with lit framed pictures, formally dressed tables and quality glassware. The cooking has moved with the times over the past two decades, bringing in a range of innovative and modern-classic ideas from around the world in true modern British fashion. Proceedings may open with the needle-sharp seasonings of pickled mooli, yuzu dressing and mustard leaves as accompaniments to a fillet of seared tuna, while mains might offer maple-glazed duck breast with confit leg, kumquat jam and Sarladaise potatoes. Monkfish is wrapped in Parma ham and served on a fresh tomato fondue with splots of lemon and basil oil. It's stimulating, clearly defined food, ending with crowd-pleasers such as apple fritters with cinnamon ice cream.

Chef Tony Tobin **Owner** Tony Tobin **Times** 12-2/7-10 Closed Xmas, BHs, L Sat, D Sun **Prices** Fixed L 2 course fr £16.95, Fixed D 3 course fr £24.95, Starter £12.50-£18, Main £22-£35, Dessert £8.95, Service added but optional 12.5% **Wines** 61 bottles over £20, 16 bottles under £20, 10 by glass **Notes** Tasting menu available, Sunday L, Vegetarian menu, Dress restrictions, Smart casual **Seats** 75, Pr/dining room 28 **Children** Portions **Parking** On street, car park

RIPLEY | Map 6 TQ05

Drake's Restaurant

◉◉◉ – see page 445

The Talbot Inn

◉ British

Historic coaching inn with smart contemporary menu

☎ 01483 225188
High St GU23 6BB
e-mail: info.thetalbot@bespokehotels.com
dir: Exit A3 signed Ripley, on left on High St

Proud to have 'provided the stage' for Lord Nelson and Lady Hamilton's affair in 1798, this rather grand one-time Georgian inn has plenty to attract the 21st-century traveller. Real ales and open fires are a draw in the traditional bar, while the restaurant is an altogether more contemporary proposition; think light oak floorboards and tables, sand-blasted brickwork, modish chairs and floor-to-ceiling glass giving a view in the winter and access to the fab terrace and garden in summer. The food fits the bill, with lots of up-to-date ideas and plenty of locally-sourced ingredients on the menu. Toasted rarebit doorstops with confit vine tomatoes and onion marmalade is a rustic opener, moving onto braised oxtail with fondant potato, Savoy cabbage and root vegetable roulade, or the Talbot cheese burger with chunky chips and tomato relish from the classics section. Finish with Talbot Eton Mess with blueberries, crushed meringue, white chocolate and vanilla cream.

Times 12-2.30/6.30-9.30 Closed D Sun (winter only)

STOKE D'ABERNON | Map 6 TQ15

Woodlands Park Hotel

◉◉ Modern European

Formal dining in a grand Victorian country house

☎ 01372 843933
Woodlands Ln KT11 3QB
e-mail: woodlandspark@handpicked.co.uk
dir: A3 exit at Cobham. Through town centre & Stoke D'Abernon, left at garden centre into Woodlands Lane, hotel 0.5m on right

A fortune built on matches allowed Victorian industrialist William Bryant (of Bryant and May fame) to build this red-brick mansion, and simultaneously dispense with the need for his own products to light the gas lamps, by being one of the first houses in the UK to have electric lighting. He picked a lovely spot, set in landscaped gardens and grounds, while the Oak Room restaurant is a period piece, all beautiful oak-panelled walls and splendid coffered oak ceilings, and well-padded leather seats at linen-swathed tables. It all adds up to an impressive scene for some vibrant modern cooking, along the lines of crab ravioli teamed with seared scallops and shellfish bisque, followed by daube of Chanctonbury Estate venison with thyme fondant potato and horseradish cream. Desserts might be as creative as mint and chocolate millefeuille with a white chocolate sorbet shot and chocolate orange bonbon.

Chef Matthew Ashton **Owner** Hand Picked Hotels **Times** 12-2.30/7-9.30 Closed Mon, L Tue-Sat, D Sun **Prices** Fixed D 3 course £47, Service optional **Wines** 125 bottles over £20, 10 by glass **Notes** Sunday L, Vegetarian available, Dress restrictions, No jeans or trainers, Civ Wed 100 **Seats** 35, Pr/dining room 150 **Children** Portions, Menu **Parking** 150

WEYBRIDGE | Map 6 TQ06

Brooklands Hotel

◉ British, European **NEW**

Striking modern hotel where British motor-racing began

☎ 01932 335700
Brooklands Dr KT13 0SL
e-mail: brasserie@brooklandshotelsurrey.com
dir: Telephone for detailed directions

Built on the site of the country's oldest motor-racing circuit, the Brooklands is an architecturally ambitious destination hotel for our times. The interiors manage to combine art deco references with impeccably contemporary styling, as well as a bar that opens out on to the historic racetrack. Linger there for the kinds of uncomplicated cocktails that wowed the twenties crowd (real dry martinis and whisky sours), before sashaying through to the 1907 restaurant, where a moody ambience of charcoal and aubergine prevails. Neatly timed seafood risotto, chicken breast stuffed with Parma ham and taleggio, and pear simmered in Barolo with hazelnuts show Italianate leanings, or go for sautéed tiger prawns with a peanut and green papaya salad, and nam jim dressing. A British path might lead to shepherd's pie with braised red cabbage and honey-roast roots, and banoffee steamed pudding with rum and caramel anglaise.

Times 12.30-2.30/6.30-10

Oatlands Park Hotel

◉ Modern British, French **NEW**

Upmarket dining in Weybridge

☎ 01932 847242
146 Oatland Dr KT13 9HB
e-mail: info@oatlandsparkhotel.com
web: www.oatlandsparkhotel.com
dir: From Weybridge town centre approach Monument Hill, follow road to mini rdbt. 1st left into Oatlands Drive. Hotel 500mtrs on left

The Broadwater Restaurant at Oatlands Park, part of which dates from Henry VIII's reign, is a large, traditional-looking room with ornate ceilings, well-spaced tables and views over the grounds. The cooking has a degree of ambition and elaboration, and the kitchen team displays genuine confidence. Start with foie gras terrine lined with truffle butter and served with duck rillette and warm apple chutney, followed by tournedos sauced with

Save on Hotels. Book at **theAA.com/hotel**

SURREY – SUSSEX, EAST 447 ENGLAND

wild mushrooms, served with oxtail ravioli, rösti and spinach. The food generally follows modern European conventions, but there are also eastern influences at work: a starter of seared scallops with coconut and coriander risotto, Thai cream and mango salsa, for example. Successful desserts include vanilla pannacotta with cinnamon doughnuts and raspberry syrup.

Oatlands Park Hotel

Chef Darren Kimber **Times** 1-3/7-10 Closed L Sat, D Sun **Prices** Fixed L 2 course fr £19.95, Fixed D 3 course fr £24.95, Starter £6.50-£14.95, Main £15-£26.50, Dessert £7.50-£10.50 **Wines** 68 bottles over £20, 3 bottles under £20, 12 by glass **Notes** BBQ on lawn summer, Sunday L, Vegetarian available, Civ Wed 220 **Seats** 100 **Children** Portions, Menu **Parking**

SUSSEX, EAST

ALFRISTON   Map 6 TQ50

Deans Place

◉◉ Modern British

Charming country hotel with confident cooking

☎ 01323 870248
Seaford Rd BN26 5TW
e-mail: mail@deansplacehotel.co.uk
dir: off A27, signed Alfriston & Drusillas Zoo Park. Continue south through village

Originally part of a substantial farming estate, at the beginning of the 20th century Deans Place Hotel came into being. In a lovely spot in the South Downs National Park, with the River Cuckmere flowing by, afternoon tea in the garden is a real treat, as is lunch or dinner on the terrace. Inside, traditional, elegant country-house style rules the roost, with the Harcourts Restaurant benefitting from lovely views and a refined finish. The food chimes with its setting so expect modern British ideas without anything too outlandish; vegetarians are well-looked after, too, with a bespoke menu and two starter options on the à la carte - artichoke and Sussex Blue cheese risotto with walnut and sun-dried tomato pesto and micro basil leaves, or Kent cauliflower and vanilla velouté with goats' cheese beignets, crisp pea shoots and parmesan. For main course, pink-roasted local beef fillet comes with truffle mash, candied beetroot, wilted greens, chestnut mushroom purée and claret jus, while a fish option may be pan-fried sea bass with pea and sorrel scented gnocchi, pancetta and pearl onion broth.

Times 12.30-2.30/6.30-9.30

The Star Alfriston

◉ Modern British

Ancient Sussex inn with unfussy modern food

☎ 01323 870495
High St BN26 5TA
e-mail: bookings@thestaralfriston.co.uk
dir: 2m off A27, at Drusillas rdbt follow Alfriston signs. Hotel on right in centre of High St

Whether you're a walker on the South Downs Way, or just pootling around Sussex in the car, The Star makes a tempting pitstop. On the pretty high street of a chocolate box-pretty Sussex village, the venerable timbered inn has been trading since the 13th century, and was run by the monks of Battle Abbey as a 'Holy House' - the wooden sanctuary post offering instant church protection is still in the bar. It hasn't saved the old place from a spot of updating through the centuries though: the Victorians added their bits, and there's a 1960s extension. The kitchen deals in straightforward ideas built on splendid Sussex ingredients, be it a quail's Scotch egg with tartare sauce, or pork tenderloin with château potatoes, braised red cabbage and celeriac purée. Dessert could be chocolate millefeuille with vanilla crème fraîche.

Chef David Shiers **Owner** Damian Martin & Martin Gobbee **Times** 12-2.30/7-9 Closed L Mon-Sat **Prices** Fixed D 3 course £19.95-£29.95, Service added but optional 10% **Wines** 11 bottles over £20, 18 bottles under £20, 10 by glass **Notes** Sunday L, Vegetarian available, Civ Wed 120 **Seats** 50, Pr/dining room 32 **Children** Portions, Menu **Parking** 35

BATTLE   Map 7 TQ71

Powder Mills Hotel

◉ Modern British V

Appealing modish cooking near the 1066 battlefield

☎ 01424 775511
Powdermill Ln TN33 0SP
e-mail: powdc@aol.com
dir: M25 junct 5, A21 towards Hastings. At St Johns Cross take A2100 to Battle. Pass abbey on right, 1st right into Powdermills Ln. 1m, hotel on right

Just outside Battle in the heart of 1066 country, Powder Mills is a lovely Georgian mansion set in 150 acres of splendid Sussex countryside made up of parkland, lakes and woods. Named after a gunpowder works whose materials helped fight off Napoleon, it now lives out a more tranquil existence, including leisurely dining in the bright and summery Orangery Restaurant. Wicker seats and linen-clothed tables on black and white marble floors, and Italian statuary reinforce the sunny feel, while the kitchen looks to the Sussex larder for the ingredients forming the bedrock of an appealing modern repertoire. You might start with that trusty combo of seared scallops and black pudding, pointed up by Calvados-marinated Cox's apples, then move on to loin of local venison with creamed potato, Savoy cabbage, butternut squash, and Cassis sauce. Finish with a luxurious Valrhona chocolate délice with griottine cherries.

Chef Lee Griffin **Owner** Mrs J Cowpland **Times** 12-2/7-9 **Prices** Fixed L 3 course £18.50-£29.95, Fixed D 3 course £29.50-£42.50, Service added but optional 10%, Groups min 10 service 10% **Wines** 38 bottles over £20, 32 bottles under £20, 4 by glass **Notes** Sunday L, Vegetarian menu, Dress restrictions, Smart casual, no jeans, shorts or T-shirts, Civ Wed 100 **Seats** 90, Pr/dining room 16 **Children** Portions, Menu **Parking** 100

BODIAM   Map 7 TQ72

The Curlew Restaurant

◉◉ Modern British V

Sharply focused modern cooking

☎ 01580 861394 & 861202
Junction Rd TN32 5UY
e-mail: enquiries@thecurlewrestaurant.co.uk
dir: A21 south turn left at Hurst Green signed Bodiam. Restaurant on left at end of road

The white-painted, clapboarded Curlew presents a soothingly old-school façade to the world, the former coaching inn catching the eye with its immaculately kept demeanor. But inside awaits a heady mix of the old and new - this place looks great and make no mistake. Mark and Sara Colley's restaurant successfully melds classic and modish design touches, which meet somewhere on the smart-town, country-chic axis. The mood is suitably relaxed, helped along by a service team who know their onions. Head chef Neil McCue's cooking fits the bill to a T, too, with local and regional produce at the heart of everything, and a desire to keep things relatively simple, thus keeping the integrity of said ingredients. This is smart cooking: intelligent combinations and sound techniques. Pressed goose leg enriched with the liver and served with chutney and toast, and crispy veal tongue with rock salt beetroot and mustard cress are first courses presented with real flair. Next up, perhaps a roasted fillet of sea bass with smoked bacon and potato and rosemary stew, or 'Chop & Chips', which is Jacob's ladder (what the American's call short-rib of beef - the chef has had a spell across the pond), with beef dripping potatoes and pickled cabbage. To finish, a rum-flavoured junket is served with an Eccles cake.

Chef Neil McCue **Owner** Mark & Sara Colley **Times** 12-2.30/6.30-9.30 Closed 2 wks Jan, 1 wk Jun, 1 wk Nov, Mon-Tue **Prices** Fixed L 2 course £18-£19, Starter £7.50-£9.50, Main £12-£22, Dessert £7-£8, Service optional **Wines** 70 bottles over £20, 2 bottles under £20, 19 by glass **Notes** Sunday L, Vegetarian menu **Seats** 64 **Children** Portions **Parking** 16

Chilli Pickle

◉◉ Indian

Vibrant Indian flavours in buzzy venue

☎ 01273 900383
17 Jubilee St BN1 1GE
e-mail: enquiries@thechillipicklebistro.co.uk
web: www.thechillipicklebistro.co.uk
dir: Situated off Church Lane, attached to myhotel
Brighton, opposite Library

The Chilli Pickle has settled into its expansive new venue
on a pedestrianised square in a regenerated part of the
town opposite the city's library, and continues to impress
with its contemporary reworkings of classic Indian
themes. Walls of glass create the impression of eating
outdoors, while the menagerie of Brighton's street life
provides endless entertainment. Done out with chunky
wooden tables, blond-wood floors, and splashes of blue
and yellow to enliven its stripped-out minimalism, the
place still has the unbuttoned relaxed vibe that goes well
with its switched-on menu of authentic regional cooking
tweaked for modern sensibilities. Raw materials are
conscientiously sourced from local producers, and appear
at lunch in pukka Indian street food, including thalis,
dosai, and roti rolls, while dinner produces the likes of
Kerala-style lemon sole, deep-fried with red chilli and
ginger masala and served with green mango chutney,
followed by spiced sea bass, or a platter comprising
Sussex lamb chops in onion paste and cumin, and
venison seekh kebab from a pair of tandoors. Elsewhere,
there may be crispy pork belly vindaloo, or Chennai
seafood stew with king prawns, crab claws, palourde
clams and scallops.

Chef Alun Sperring **Owner** Alun & Dawn Sperring
Times 12-3/6-10.30 Closed 25-26 Dec, 1 Jan, Tue
Prices Fixed D 3 course £25.50, Starter £4.50-£7.95,
Main £8.50-£18.50, Dessert £4.75-£5.95, Service
optional, Groups min 8 service 10% **Wines** 15 bottles

over £20, 14 bottles under £20, 7 by glass **Notes** King
Thali menu daily £13, Sunday L, Vegetarian available, Civ
Wed 130 **Seats** 115 **Children** Portions **Parking** NCP
Church St

The De Vere Grand, Brighton

◉ Modern European **NEW**

Modern classics in the grand old Grand Hotel

☎ 01273 224300 & 224309
King's Rd BN1 2FW
e-mail: reception@grandbrighton.co.uk
dir: On A259 (seafront road between piers) adjacent to
Brighton Centre

The venerable Grand was built during the Italianate
Renaissance revival in the 1860s, and was the tallest
building in Brighton until its upstart next door neighbour
shot up above it 30 years later. It still looks the part, a
stately, creamy edifice that soars above the seafront, all
wrought-iron balconies and Victorian dignity, gazing out
over the skeletal remains of what was once the West Pier.
Alan White is on a mission to put the place on Brighton's
busy culinary map, and has the twin settings of a high-
ceilinged, panelled dining room and glassed-in terrace as
a backdrop. Modern classic dishes are the strategy,
beginning perhaps with sweet local scallops partnered
with pancetta, black pudding and puréed cauliflower, and
continuing with roast breast of local lamb with liver and
smoked bacon, puréed carrots and a creamy caper sauce,
or ink-black lobster risotto with parmesan and purple
shiso. Finish with textbook sticky toffee pudding with ice
cream in a chocolate cup, garnished with a caramelised
date.

Times 12.30-2/7-10 Closed L Sat

Drakes

◉◉ British, French

Chic setting and confident contemporary cooking

☎ 01273 696934
43-44 Marine Pde BN2 1PE
e-mail: therestaurant@drakesofbrighton.com
dir: From A23 at Brighton Pier rdbt. Left into Marine Pde
towards marina. Hotel on left before lights (ornate water
feature at front)

There aren't as many boutique hotels as you might
imagine in Brighton, and certainly none that can match
Drakes for its classy fine-dining restaurant. Overlooking
the sea, the hotel has a prime spot a short stroll from the
centre of the city, and has all the lived-in, bow-fronted
Georgian elegance you might hope for. The restaurant is
down in the basement - so no sea view - but is none the
worse for that, for it gives the smart space a sense of
exclusivity. It feels quite plush with its posh table
settings and well-drilled service team, and is an
appropriate setting for Andrew MacKenzie's refined
contemporary cooking. Start, perhaps, with oxtail ravioli
with beef broth, or wild rabbit terrine enriched with
poached prunes, before main-course fillet of salt pollock
with squid, butter bean and paprika stew, topped with a

crispy quail's egg. The confident Modish European
cooking continues at dessert stage with roasted
pineapple with black pepper and vanilla ice cream.

Chef Andrew MacKenzie **Owner** Andy & Gayle Shearer
Times 12.30-2/7-10 **Prices** Fixed L 2 course £20-£29.95,
Fixed D 3 course £39.95-£48.95, Tasting menu £55-£90,
Service added but optional 12.5% **Wines** 55 bottles over
£20, 14 by glass **Notes** Tasting menu 5 course D (with
wine £90), Sunday L, Vegetarian available, Civ Wed 40
Seats 42, Pr/dining room 12 **Parking** On street

The Foragers

◉ Modern European **NEW** 🍃

A local pub which keeps things local

☎ 01273 733134
3 Stirling Place BN3 3YU
e-mail: info@theforagerspub.co.uk
web: www.theforagerspub.co.uk
dir: A2033 Sackville Rd, left Stirling Place, restaurant
200m on left

Deep in Hove, some distance from the seafront, The
Foragers does what it says on the tin. The aim is to use
as much seasonally-harvested, organic and sustainable
produce as possible, and when local foragers turn up at
the kitchen door with bags of goodies, their wares will
appear on the day's menu. The venue chimes well with
the quirky, laid-back aesthetic prevalent in Brighton &
Hove - a bit shabby-chic, a bit locals' bar - and there's
certainly no pretension or standing on ceremony. A risotto
starter featuring nettles and truffle from the local Sussex
village of Steyning shows the style, followed by a
perfectly-timed steak of yellowfin tuna teamed with
chicory, fennel, fregola, and chilli and ginger dressing;
meatier ideas might offer game ragù with pan-fried
gnocchi, Sussex parmesan and gremolata. For pudding,
an exemplary lemon meringue pie comes with foraged
blackberry ice cream.

Save on Hotels. Book at **theAA.com/hotel**

SUSSEX, EAST 449 ENGLAND

The Foragers

Chef Josh Kitson **Owner** Paul Hutchison **Times** 12-3/6-10 Closed D Sun **Prices** Fixed L 2 course fr £12, Fixed D 2 course fr £12, Starter £5-£7, Main £10-£16, Dessert £5-£8, Service optional, Groups min 6 service 10% **Wines** 10 bottles over £20, 16 bottles under £20, 16 by glass **Notes** Sunday L, Vegetarian available **Seats** 74 **Children** Portions, Menu

The Gingerman Restaurant

◉◉ Modern British

Modern cooking without clichés near seafront

☎ 01273 326688
21A Norfolk Square BN1 2PD
e-mail: info@gingermanrestaurants.com
dir: A23 to Palace Pier rdbt. Turn right onto Kings Rd. At art deco style Embassy building, right into Norfolk Sq

The original venue of Ben McKellar's little Brighton & Hove empire, The Gingerman is tucked away in a former tea-room off the seafront. It's an intimate place, run with the unbuttoned familiarity that Brighton loves, decorated with pictures you may wish to purchase while you're buying the gutsy, well-wrought modern British food. A disinclination to rely on modern clichés produces starters such as lemon-marinated chargrilled cuttlefish with romesco sauce and rocket, and mains like roast guinea fowl with a gruyère croquette, crispy ham, spinach purée and Marsala jus. The fish special is usually worth a gander, supplementing menu offerings such as grilled sea bass with spiced crab gnocchi and puréed courgette in a reduction of Pernod. Dessert can be as inventive as orange and thyme pannacotta with orange and passionfruit sauce, or as satisfyingly old-fangled as tarte Tatin with cinnamon ice cream.

Chef Ben McKellar, Simon Neville Jones **Owner** Ben & Pamela McKellar **Times** 12.30-2/7-10 Closed 2 wks Xmas, Mon **Prices** Fixed L 2 course £15-£30, Fixed D 3 course £35, Service optional, Groups min 6 service 12.5% **Wines** 40 bottles over £20, 11 bottles under £20, 10 by glass **Notes** Sunday L, Vegetarian available **Seats** 32 **Children** Portions

Graze Restaurant

◉◉ Modern British V

Ambitious contemporary cooking and charming Regency décor

☎ 01273 823707
42 Western Rd BN3 1JD
e-mail: info@graze-restaurant.co.uk
dir: Along A2010 Queens Rd, from clock tower head W on B2066 Western Rd. Restaurant on S/side of road just beyond Brunswick Sq

For a city of its size, Brighton & Hove is short of eating establishments with ambition, places that want to create modish plates of food with a fine-dining gloss - Graze is such a place. Among the miscellaneous shops of Western Road, just around the corner from the fabulous Georgian Brunswick Square, the décor takes inspiration from the city's Regency heritage without resorting to pastiche, which amounts to shades of rich reds and gold, lots of mirrors, artful objets and evocative lighting, plus well-spaced, well-dressed tables. The restaurant's name alludes to the tasting menu concept which is one way to go, although three course convention is also on the menu. The kitchen sources with care and duly follows the seasons, with everything including bread made in-house, and a meal takes in amuse-bouche (a shot glass of tomato soup topped with a basil foam, for example) and pre-dessert. First course roast breast of pigeon, perfectly pink and tender, served with hazelnuts, asparagus, meltingly soft onions and morels might precede line-caught sea bass with mussels, clams, cauliflower and coconut purée, white coco beans and samphire, topped with a light curry foam.

Chef Will Stanyer **Owner** Kate Alleston, Neil Mannifield **Times** 12-2/6.30-9.30 Closed 1-4 Jan **Prices** Fixed L 2 course £16-£26, Fixed D 3 course fr £32, Tasting menu £42-£45, Service added but optional 12% **Wines** 44 bottles over £20, 6 bottles under £20, 11 by glass **Notes** Vegetarian tasting menu £42, Tasting menu 7 course, Sunday L, Vegetarian menu, Dress restrictions, Smart casual **Seats** 50, Pr/dining room 24 **Children** Portions

Hotel du Vin Brighton

◉◉ Traditional British, French 🍷

Upmarket bistro cooking off the seafront

☎ 01273 718588
2-6 Ship St BN1 1AD
e-mail: info@brighton.hotelduvin.com
dir: A23 to seafront, at rdbt right, then right onto Middle St, bear right into Ship St, hotel at sea end on right

The Brighton branch of the chain, just off the seafront, has all the expected Francophile touches, its walls adorned with wine and spirit posters and risqué pictures, leather-look banquettes running back to back down the centre, and small wooden tables (easily pushed together by nifty staff for larger groups). A glance at the menu shows that this is more than your average bistro fare, with potted crab with caper berries and egg salad

followed by ox cheek bourguignon alongside chicken terrine and bouillabaisse. The consensus is that the kitchen orders great-quality raw materials, often locally, and treats them with care and respect at the stoves. A simple starter of salmon ballottine with herbed fromage blanc might precede main-course chicken Dijonnaise, moist and full of flavour, with mousseline potatoes. Momentum doesn't falter at the final stretch, with light and tasty pistachio parfait with chocolate ice cream, the plate dotted with thick caramel sauce.

Chef Rob Carr **Times** 12-2/7-10 **Prices** Food prices not confirmed for 2013. Please telephone for details **Wines** 300 bottles over £20, 10 bottles under £20, 12 by glass **Notes** Sunday L, Vegetarian available, Civ Wed 90 **Seats** 100, Pr/dining room 90 **Children** Portions, Menu **Parking** The Lanes NCP

Indian Summer

◉ Indian NEW

A cool venue for hot cuisine

☎ 01273 711001
69 East St BN1 1HQ
e-mail: manager@indian-summer.org.uk
dir: 500yds from Palace Pier

Tucked away on the edge of Brighton's labyrinthine Lanes, this cool modern Indian has built up a strong local following. To celebrate a decade in business, the place got a new look and a reworked menu in 2011, so the décor is contemporary and funky with smart wooden tables and floors and big pictures of Indian street food vendors on the walls, while the cooking offers interesting dishes you would have trouble finding elsewhere in the UK. Rajasthani dishes such as laal maas - tandoori lamb chop served with an earthy tomato, clove, chilli and bayleaf sauce - reflect the head chef's origins, while mains offer ideas such as swordfish narayali, marinated in coconut and mint and served with coriander and curry leaf sauce, or lamb kohlapuri, a robust dish of diced lamb with toasted peanuts, red chillies and coconut. To finish, mango puts an exotic spin on a crème brûlée.

Chef Maharaj Jaswantsingh **Owner** Mikesh Aginlistri, Byron Swales **Times** 12-3/6-10.30 Closed 25-26 Dec, L Mon **Prices** Fixed L 2 course fr £10, Fixed D 3 course fr £26.95, Service added but optional 10%, Groups min 5 service 10% **Wines** 13 bottles over £20, 16 bottles under £20, 5 by glass **Notes** Vegetarian available **Seats** 60 **Children** Portions **Parking** On street, car park

BRIGHTON & HOVE *continued*

Sam's of Brighton

◉ Modern British

Regionally-based cooking just off Kemp Town seafront

☎ 01273 676222
1 Paston Place, Kemp Town BN2 1HA
e-mail: info@samsofbrighton.co.uk
dir: Between Brighton Pier & Marina, close to hospital

After stamping his name on the local foodie scene at his Seven Dials bistro (see entry below), Sam Metcalfe launched his second Brighton operation just back from the Kemp Town seafront, between the pier and marina. The buzzy neighbourhood bistro vibe sits well with Brighton's easygoing mood; the décor is neutral, woody and unfussy, and the straightforward culinary approach keeps things fresh and simple. Working with the best seasonal materials that Sussex and Kent have to offer, the menu might have boudin noir Scotch egg with celeriac remoulade and date and apple chutney, alongside roast juniper-marinated haunch of venison with croquette potatoes and beetroot purée. Dessert could be a traditional number such as steamed treacle pudding with vanilla custard.

Chef Simon Duncan, Sam Metcalfe **Owner** Sam & Lara Metcalfe **Times** 12-3/6-10 Closed Mon, L Tue-Wed, D Sun **Prices** Fixed L 2 course £12, Fixed D 3 course £14, Starter £5-£7, Main £11.50-£19, Dessert £5-£7.50, Service optional, Groups min 6 service 12.5% **Wines** 18 bottles over £20, 10 bottles under £20, 12 by glass **Notes** Fixed menu available L & early evening 6-7pm wk days only, Sunday L, Vegetarian available, Air con **Seats** 52 **Children** Portions, Menu **Parking** On street

Sam's of Sevendials

◉◉ Modern British

Lively cooking in trendy Seven Dials

☎ 01273 885555
1-3 Buckingham Place, Seven Dials BN1 3TD
e-mail: info@samsatsevendials.co.uk
dir: From Brighton station turn right 0.5m up hill, restaurant at Seven Dials rdbt

High ceilings and large windows are all that remain of this brasserie's former incarnation as a bank; it's now decorated in neutral colours, with a darkwood floor, plants in the windows, a large mirror and blackboards listing specials on the walls. The eponymous Sam has devised a broadly-based menu of invigorating ideas, showing influences culled from around the globe: fillet of pollock on creamy Thai-spiced broth, for instance, accompanied by plump mussels and saffron-braised potatoes. Dishes are well considered, a starter of roast pork belly with crispy braised local octopus and creamed celeriac, for example, and roast turbot fillet partnered by confit chicken thigh, truffle-flavoured gnocchi and

sautéed salsify and leek. Puddings are not without a degree of complexity and all the better for it, among them perhaps warm parkin with orange sorbet and pear poached in red wine.

Chef Sam Metcalfe, Stuart Thrasher **Owner** Sam Metcalfe **Times** 12-3/6-10.30 Closed 25-26 Dec **Prices** Fixed L 2 course £12, Fixed D 3 course £14, Starter £6-£8, Main £13-£19, Dessert £5-£7.50, Service optional, Groups min 6 service 12% **Wines** 6 bottles over £20, 8 bottles under £20, 12 by glass **Notes** Fixed menu available L, D 6-7pm Mon-Sat, Sunday L, Vegetarian available, Civ Wed 75 **Seats** 60, Pr/dining room 20 **Children** Portions, Menu **Parking** 5, On street, close to restaurant

Terre à Terre

◉◉ Modern Vegetarian **V**

Ground-breaking vegetarian and vegan cooking

☎ 01273 729051
71 East St BN1 1HQ
e-mail: mail@terreaterre.co.uk
web: www.terreaterre.co.uk
dir: Town centre, close to Brighton Pier & The Lanes

This veggie-vegan trailblazer (strutting its stuff since '93) still pulls in the crowds. The food remains innovative with dazzling flavour combinations and menu descriptions that are lengthy, esoteric and a little confusing. Inspiration comes from across the globe, backpacking its way from the off; an opener of 'arepas chilli candy', for example, which is deep-fried corn cakes rolled in spice dust and served with chilli chelly jelly, avocado and lime hash, chilled pokey gazpacho and a candied chilli. There's no holding back at main's either; perhaps a 'rösti Raj' - crispy fried potato, onion and garlic rösti topped with griddled tandoori halloumi, channa tamarind dhal, coconut, green chilli and curry leaf chutney with deep-fried chick peas, chilli slivers, and dressed with tangy lime and Mumbai mixed spice dust. And all this colourful fun's just a stone's throw from the English seafront, the modern, up-tempo restaurant appropriately decked out in bright tones with staff who

share a passion for the food, while organic and biodynamic wines further enhance credibility.

Chef Dino Pavledis, A Powley, P Taylor **Owner** A Powley & P Taylor **Times** 12-10.30 Closed 25-26 Dec, 1 Jan **Prices** Fixed L 2 course fr £15, Fixed D 3 course fr £30, Starter £4.95-£8.95, Main £13.70-£14.65, Dessert £7.70-£8.10, Service optional, Groups min 6 service 10% **Wines** 31 bottles over £20, 13 bottles under £20, 23 by glass **Notes** Promotional fixed price L & D menus available, Vegetarian menu **Seats** 110 **Children** Portions, Menu **Parking** NCP, on street

EASTBOURNE **Map 6 TV69**

The Grand Hotel, Mirabelle Restaurant

◉◉ Modern, Classic ⬥

Grand seafront hotel with confident cooking

☎ 01323 412345
King Edward's Pde BN21 4EQ
e-mail: reservations@grandeastbourne.com
web: www.grandeastbourne.com
dir: Western end of seafront, 1m from Eastbourne station

If *Downton Abbey* and *Upstairs Downstairs* have engendered a longing for a more elegant past, the wedding cake pomp of Eastbourne's Grand Hotel - the 'White Palace' to its friends - should hit the spot. Built in 1875, the grande dame of the seafront still has a whiff of the past about it that makes it easy to picture its prestigious guests - Winston Churchill, Charlie Chaplin, Elgar, and Debussy, who composed *La Mer* on his hols in 1905. Gastronomes might want to get in the mood with afternoon tea, served in the marble-columned grandeur of the Great Hall, then take a stroll on the prom to work up an appetite for dinner in the fine dining Mirabelle restaurant. Battalions of crisply uniformed staff pushing trolleys certainly add to the old-school trappings, but when the silver cloches are lifted, the plates beneath reveal modern European flavour combinations and textures to keep 21st-century guests sweet. You might be treated to a warm salad of confit duck leg with Japanese-spiced green pea ragoût, followed by slow-cooked navarin of Kent Marsh lamb with potato purée and parsnip crisps. A Thai basil pannacotta with blueberries, lime, strawberries and mint makes a fine finale.

Save on Hotels. Book at **theAA.com/hotel**

SUSSEX, EAST 451 **ENGLAND**

The Grand Hotel, Mirabelle Restaurant

Chef Keith Mitchell, Gerald Roser **Owner** Elite Hotels
Times 12.30-2/7-10 Closed 2-16 Jan, Sun-Mon
Prices Fixed L 3 course fr £21.50, Fixed D 3 course fr £38,
Starter £5-£7.50, Main £7.50-£16, Dessert £5.50, Service
optional, Groups min 6 service 12.5% **Wines** 302 bottles
over £20, 30 bottles under £20, 14 by glass **Notes** Fixed
L/D supplements added to price, Tasting menu 5 course,
Sunday L, Vegetarian available, Dress restrictions, Jacket
or tie for D **Seats** 50 **Parking** 70

Langham Hotel

◉ Modern British

Enticing modern cooking on the seafront

☎ 01323 731451
43-48 Royal Pde BN22 7AH
e-mail: neil@langhamhotel.co.uk
dir: A22 follow signs for seafront Sovereign Centre, take
3rd exit onto Royal Pde. Hotel on corner Royal Pde &
Cambridge Rd

The location of Langham, actually three knocked-through
Victorian houses, must be the envy of many a seaside
hotel, as it's right on the seafront, with expansive views
towards the pier and Beachy Head. And the Conservatory
restaurant is the place to be for some equally uplifting
cooking. Pea soup is enhanced by mint oil, quail's egg
and pea shoots, and carrot emulsion adds an interesting
dimension to seared scallops with fennel and apple
salad. Main courses are no less pleasing, among them
perhaps halibut steak roasted in Parma ham on onion
purée with tomato vinaigrette, and pesto-crusted rack of
lamb with herby potato cake and red pepper compôte.
Vegetarians are well looked after, and among puddings
could be summery peach compôte and matching sponge
cake with lemongrass sorbet.

Chef Michael Titherington **Owner** Neil & Wendy Kirby
Times 12-2.30/6-9.30 **Prices** Fixed L 2 course £10-£18,
Fixed D 3 course £16-£26, Starter £4.25-£8, Main £14-
£21, Dessert £4.25-£8, Service optional **Wines** 4 bottles
over £20, 16 bottles under £20, 18 by glass **Notes** Sunday
L, Vegetarian available **Seats** 24 **Children** Portions, Menu

---

FOREST ROW   Map 6 TQ43

Ashdown Park Hotel & Country Club

◉◉ British, European V   NOTABLE WINE LIST

Grand hotel dining in an upmarket country house

☎ 01342 824988
Wych Cross RH18 5JR
e-mail: reservations@ashdownpark.com
web: www.ashdownpark.com
dir: A264 to East Grinstead, then A22 to Eastbourne. 2m
S of Forest Row at Wych Cross lights. Left to Hartfield,
hotel on right 0.75m

Everything about the swanky Ashdown Park Hotel and
Country Club is done in the high-flown style you would
expect of an upscale Victorian country house: its 186
acres of landscaped gardens and parkland are secluded
in the depths of Ashdown Forest, and there's an 18-hole
golf course and a fitness and spa complex. Gents will
need to pack a jacket and tie, and everyone can expect
old-school formality in the Anderida Restaurant, with
service that delivers all the precision of silver service. On
the plate comes flamboyantly-presented classical cuisine,
glossed up with modern takes on time-honoured ideas
and fashionably-deconstructed dishes; a starter of
smoked haddock fish 'pie', for example, presented in a
Kilner jar with a scallop on top, pea purée, prawn toast
and a tranche of fish terrine. Main course brings roasted
rump of lamb with a pastilla of shoulder teamed with
sweet tomato risotto and pesto, then a final flourish of
brown sugar parfait with banana rice pudding, exotic
foam and honeycomb brings down the curtain.

Chef Andrew Wilson **Owner** Elite Hotels **Times** 12-2/7-10
Prices Fixed L 2 course fr £17.50, Fixed D 3 course fr

£38.50, Tasting menu £82.50, Starter £8-£11, Main
£19.50-£30, Dessert £9-£11, Service optional, Groups
min 6 service 10% **Wines** 362 bottles over £20, 9 by
glass **Notes** Tasting menu 8 course, Sunday L, Vegetarian
menu, Dress restrictions, Jacket or tie for gentlemen after
7pm, Civ Wed 150 **Seats** 120, Pr/dining room 160
Children Portions, Menu **Parking** 120

HASTINGS & ST LEONARDS   Map 7 TQ80

Jali Restaurant

◉ Traditional and Modern Indian

An Indian flavour by the seaside

☎ 01424 457300 & 720188
Chatsworth Hotel, 7-11 Carlisle Pde TN34 1JG
e-mail: info@chatsworthhotel.com
dir: On Hastings seafront, near railway station

The original in a small chain that now includes Crewe
and Blackpool amongst its number, Jali is in the
Chatsworth Hotel, with a prime seafront position close to
the old town and the pier. It's all very civilized inside,
with some Indian artefacts and artworks dotted around
but resisting clichés, with tables smartly dressed in white
linen cloths. The menu also avoids the typical curry house
standards; start, perhaps, with gin-fried chicken, the
meat marinated in the said booze and stir-fried with
fresh herbs, and from the long kebab section there might
be noorani seekh (minced lamb kebab) or salmon sula
(grilled in the tandoor with a lime and herb crust). There's
plenty for vegetarians, too, such as a main-course khumb
kaju curry (mushrooms and cashew nuts in a spicy
tomato, onion and yoghurt gravy) and meat course might
be dal gosht (lamb cooked with lentils).

Times 6.30-11 Closed L all week

LEWES   Map 6 TQ41

Jolly Sportsman

◉ Modern European V

Enterprising cooking in a Sussex country pub

☎ 01273 890400
Chapel Ln, East Chiltington BN7 3BA
e-mail: info@thejollysportsman.com
dir: From Lewes A275, East Grinstead road, left onto the
B2116 Offham, 2nd right into Novington Lane. In approx
1m first left Chapel Lane

Tucked away among the hedgerows and country lanes of
the Sussex hinterland, the Sportsman is a smartly
revamped country pub, which serves quality local ales
and a splendid range of bottled beers to the inhabitants
of East Chiltington (albeit from a very small bar), as well
as offering some enterprising and inventive cooking,
based on Sussex produce, to appeal to a wider
constituency. The broadly-based bill of fare may include
roast veal sweetbread with celeriac remoulade in aged
balsamic to start, followed by butter-roasted pollock in a
bacon and hazelnut crust with confit Jerusalem
artichokes and cockles in beurre noisette. Finishers

continued

LEWES continued

include gypsy tart (a confection of evaporated milk and Muscovado sugar) with frozen yoghurt, or pineapple and coconut sorbet.

Chef Anthony Masters **Owner** Bruce Wass **Times** 12-3/6.30-10 Closed 25 Dec, D Sun **Prices** Fixed L 2 course £13.50, Fixed D 2 course £19.50, Starter £5.75-£9.50, Main £11.85-£19.85, Dessert £5.75-£11.75, Service optional **Wines** 180 bottles over £20, 20 bottles under £20, 13 by glass **Notes** Sunday L, Vegetarian menu, Air con **Seats** 80, Pr/dining room 20 **Children** Portions, Menu **Parking** 35

NEWICK   Map 6 TQ42

Newick Park Hotel & Country Estate

◎◎ Modern European

Classy cooking on a sumptuous Sussex estate

☎ 01825 723633
BN8 4SB
e-mail: bookings@newickpark.co.uk
dir: Exit A272 at Newick Green, 1m, pass church & pub. Turn left, hotel 0.25m on right

Aficionados of the blue-blooded country house idiom will go weak at the knees over Newick Park, a classy, intimate package of plush interiors laden with antiques and an unintimidating, easygoing mood set by personable staff. The handsome Georgian pile sits by the South Downs in 250 acres of parkland and gardens that are not just pretty to look at, but which also earn their keep, providing seasonal fruit, veg, herbs and game for Chris Moore's kitchen team who deliver a refined style of modernised country-house cooking perfectly in keeping with the surroundings. A spring lunch could open with crab salad with chorizo, potato, onion and lemon mayonnaise, then proceed to roast guinea fowl breast with thyme boudin, boulangère potatoes and garlic creamed cabbage. The intelligent Anglo-French polish continues through to desserts such as lime clafoutis with ginger ice cream and pomegranate dressing.

Newick Park Hotel & Country Estate

Chef Chris Moore **Owner** Michael & Virginia Childs **Times** 12-1.45/7-9 Closed 31 Jan **Prices** Fixed L 2 course fr £17.50, Starter £7.25-£9.50, Main £14.50-£24.50, Dessert £6.75-£9.50, Service optional **Wines** 85 bottles over £20, 25 bottles under £20, 9 by glass **Notes** Sunday L, Vegetarian available, Civ Wed 100 **Seats** 40, Pr/dining room 74 **Children** Portions, Menu **Parking** 100

See advert below

RYE   Map 7 TQ92

The George in Rye

◎ Modern Mediterranean

Modern restaurant in historic town

☎ 01797 222114
98 High St TN31 7JT
e-mail: stay@thegeorgeinrye.com
dir: M20 junct 10, then A2070 to Brenzett, then A259 to Rye

The 16th-century George has been transformed from a down-at-heel Tudor pub into a spiffy boutique hotel with a thoroughly modern roll-call of dishes coming out of the kitchen, and splendid wines from Sussex and Kent vineyards to bolster the sense of local terroir. The best bits are still there - beams from an Elizabethan ship, an 18th-century wig store, and the Georgian ballroom - but these are overlaid with a classy contemporary look, as typified in the George Grill, where olive-green walls, bare darkwood tables, buttoned banquettes and funky designer fabrics make a trendy setting for the kitchen's Mediterranean-accented ideas. Full advantage is taken of local supplies from the farms of Sussex and Kent, and the trawlers of Rye Bay, starting with the scallops that could come with cauliflower purée and raisin and caper vinaigrette. Next out, a Barnsley chop of Romney Marsh lamb might be paired with purple sprouting broccoli, and rosemary and anchovy dressing, while desserts supply the simple pleasures of sticky toffee pudding with stem ginger ice cream.

Chef Andy Billings **Owner** Alex & Katie Clarke **Times** 12-3/6.30-9.30 **Prices** Fixed L 2 course fr £13, Starter £7-£11, Main £8-£23, Dessert £6-£7, Service added 7.5% **Wines** 31 bottles over £20, 10 bottles under £20, 12 by glass **Notes** Vegetarian available **Seats** 60, Pr/dining room 100 **Children** Portions, Menu **Parking** On street

Mermaid Inn

◉ British, French **V** ♨

Atmospheric medieval inn with modish menu

☎ 01797 223065
Mermaid St TN31 7EY
e-mail: info@mermaidinn.com
web: www.mermaidinn.com
dir: A259, follow signs to town centre, then into Mermaid St

The delightful Cinque Port is not without its quota of ancient buildings, and this half-timbered inn is certainly one of them, rebuilt in 1420 on cellars going back to 1156. The bar's giant inglenook, with a priest's hole, is not to be missed, and the linenfold-panelled restaurant is an atmospheric room too. The cooking is based on Anglo-French foundations, with dishes in the recognisably contemporary mode, from venison carpaccio with roast beetroot, goats' cheese and basil jelly, to baked salmon fillet with chorizo, Puy lentils, braised fennel and spinach purée. Local ingredients are rigorously sought out: pan-fried Rye Bay scallops in a starter with cauliflower purée, bacon crisps and black pudding, and Cranbrook lamb - slow-roast shoulder, devilled kidneys and fried liver - in a main course with pan juices. Specialities include lobster thermidor and among puddings may be a seasonal assiette of strawberries.

Chef Barry I Smith **Owner** J Blincow & R I Pinwill **Times** 12-2.30/7-9.30 **Prices** Fixed L 2 course £21, Fixed D 3 course £37.50, Starter £7.50-£9.50, Main £34.25-£39.50, Dessert £7, Service added but optional 10% **Wines** 48 bottles over £20, 1 bottle under £20, 15 by glass **Notes** Sunday L, Vegetarian menu, Dress restrictions, Smart casual, no jeans or T-shirts **Seats** 64, Pr/dining room 14 **Children** Portions, Menu **Parking** 26

Webbes at The Fish Café

◉ Modern British

Wide-ranging seafood dishes in converted warehouse

☎ 01797 222226
17 Tower St TN31 7AT
e-mail: info@thefishcafe.com
dir: 100mtrs before Landgate Arch

A red-brick converted warehouse in the centre of town, Webbe's consists of a ground-floor café with an open-plan kitchen and a more formal dining room upstairs. Accurately timed, first-rate seafood, sustainably sourced, is the business, from Shetland mussels simply cooked in white wine with leeks to pan-fried fillet of sea bass with saffron mash and spicy prawns. The wide-ranging menu accommodates most tastes, from bouillabaisse or a shellfish platter to start, to Thai green curry of monkfish, prawns and potatoes, served with a poppadom, or beer-battered cod with chips and mushy peas. Vegetarians and meat-eaters are given a few alternatives, and puddings like cardamom pannacotta, with rhubarb poached and sorbet, do the business.

Chef Paul Webbe, Matthew Drinkwater **Owner** Paul & Rebecca Webbe **Times** 11.30-2.30/6-9.30 Closed 24 Dec-10 Jan **Prices** Starter £6-£12, Main £12-£20, Dessert £6-£7, Service optional **Wines** 49 bottles over £20, 15 bottles under £20, 10 by glass **Notes** Sunday L, Vegetarian available, Dress restrictions, Smart casual **Seats** 52, Pr/dining room 60 **Children** Portions, Menu **Parking** Cinque Port Street

---

TICEHURST　　　　　　　　　　Map 6 TQ63

Dale Hill Hotel & Golf Club

◉ Modern European ♨

Modern European menu in a golfing hotel

☎ 01580 200112
TN5 7DQ
e-mail: info@dalehill.co.uk
dir: M25 junct 5/A21. 5m after Lamberhurst turn right at lights onto B2087 to Flimwell. Hotel 1m on left

Golf is the signature dish at this hotel and country club in a fabulous location high on the Sussex Weald. A duo of 18-hole courses provide the main event, but for starters there are sweeping views over the hills of East Sussex, and side dishes taking in a heated indoor pool and gym. Of the two restaurants, the expansive fine-dining Wealden Restaurant is the star attraction, and it comes - perhaps inevitably - with vistas of the 18th green. Modern European cooking is par for this particular course, and it appears in some adventurous ideas: braised veal and mandarin ravioli teamed with marinated tuna carpaccio and caper berries, followed by fillet of monkfish in a cockle crust with braised pork belly, crab croquette, carrot purée and red pepper salsa. Finish with an apricot crème brûlée.

Chef Mark Carter **Owner** Mr & Mrs Paul Gibbons **Times** 12-2.30/6.30-9 Closed 25 Dec, L Mon-Sat **Prices** Fixed D 3 course £30-£37, Service optional **Wines** 46 bottles over £20, 8 bottles under £20, 7 by glass **Notes** Sunday L, Vegetarian available, Dress restrictions, Smart casual, Civ Wed 120 **Seats** Pr/dining room 24 **Children** Portions, Menu **Parking**

UCKFIELD　　　　　　　　　　Map 6 TQ42

Buxted Park Hotel

◉◉ Modern European **V**

Skilful cooking in a luxurious Georgian manor

☎ 01825 733333
Buxted TN22 4AY
e-mail: buxtedpark@handpicked.co.uk
dir: From A26 (Uckfield bypass) take A272 signed Buxted. Through lights, hotel 1m on right

Built 300 years ago on a fortune made from importing port wine, Buxted Park is still in the business of gastronomic indulgence thanks to the kitchen brigade. Heads of state, and a cast of celebs including Marlon Brando and Gregory Peck have all enjoyed the Georgian manor house's 300 acres of grounds and lavish period interiors; today's visitors, however, dine in an altogether more chic modern setting, done out with purple velour banquettes and curvy fairground waltzer-style booths set against cream walls, and tended to by a team of real pros. The kitchen sends out well-tuned modern dishes of vibrant flavours, which might translate as pan-seared scallops with cauliflower purée, crisp apple and baby herb salad, followed by Buxted Park venison with creamed Savoy cabbage, celeriac rösti and redcurrant jus. Desserts deliver the likes of baked white chocolate tart with coffee and white chocolate sorbet.

Chef Neil Davison **Owner** Hand Picked Hotels **Times** 12-2/7-9.30 **Prices** Fixed L 2 course fr £17.50, Fixed D 3 course £38-£56, Tasting menu £64-£99, Service optional **Wines** 130 bottles over £20, 18 by glass **Notes** Dégustation 7 course with/without wine, Sunday L, Vegetarian menu, Dress restrictions, Smart casual, Civ Wed 120 **Seats** 40, Pr/dining room 120 **Children** Portions, Menu **Parking** 100

East Sussex National Golf Resort & Spa

◉ British, French

Well-executed modern cooking - and golf

☎ 01825 880088
Little Horsted TN22 5ES
e-mail: reception@eastsussexnational.co.uk
dir: M25 junct 6, A22 signed East Grinstead & Eastbourne. Straight on at rdbt junct of A22 & A26 (Little Horsted). At next rdbt right to hotel

The name nails this sprawling, purpose-built operation's colours to the mast. And if it would appear that you must be here for its two obvious core attractions - the fairways of its two championship golf courses and spa pampering treatments - there is a very good third reason to be here, and that is the fine dining on offer in the Pavilion restaurant. The setting is on the minimal end of the contemporary spectrum, and looks through a wall of full-length windows onto the greens and the rolling South Downs countryside. The kitchen has the bountiful produce of Sussex close to hand, which it deploys in appealing ideas along the lines of pan-seared rabbit loin with bacon and leek risotto balls and béarnaise sauce, followed by

continued

UCKFIELD *continued*

roast venison from the estate served with Lyonnaise potatoes, buttered curly kale, broad beans and wild mushroom jus.

Chef Andrew Wiles **Owner** East Sussex National Ltd **Times** 12-2/7-9.30 Closed L Sun **Prices** Fixed L 2 course £15.95-£18.95, Starter £6.50-£8, Main £14-£22, Dessert £6.50-£8, Service optional **Wines** 25 bottles over £20, 17 bottles under £20, 14 by glass **Notes** Sunday L, Vegetarian available, Dress restrictions, Smart casual, Civ Wed 250, Air con **Seats** 90 **Children** Portions, Menu **Parking** 500

Horsted Place

◉ Modern British

Fine food in a striking setting

☎ 01825 750581
Little Horsted TN22 5TS
e-mail: hotel@horstedplace.co.uk
dir: From Uckfield 2m S on A26 towards Lewes

Augustus Pugin designed much of this turreted and crenallated Victorian Gothic fantasy mansion squirrelled away in 1,000 acres of verdant Sussex countryside. You could find serenity in fabulous gardens, or get competitive playing on two championship golf courses, a tennis court and croquet on the lawn. The elegant jade-green restaurant is completely in tune with the elevated tone of the grand house, and there's an extra note of romance when candles are lit for dinner. The kitchen handles the modern British country-house idiom with aplomb, serving up uncontroversial ideas along the lines of slow-roasted belly pork with apple and shallot purée and port jus, ahead of medallions of local venison teamed with spätzle noodles and Scottish girolle mushrooms. Puddings are perennial favourites such as summer pudding with blackberry sauce and thick cream.

Chef Allan Garth **Owner** Perinon Ltd **Times** 12-2/7-9.30 Closed 1st wk Jan, L Sat **Prices** Fixed L 2 course £18.95, Starter £9.50, Main £20, Dessert £8.50, Service optional **Wines** 124 bottles over £20, 2 bottles under £20, 9 by glass **Notes** Sunday L, Vegetarian available, Dress restrictions, No jeans, Civ Wed 100 **Seats** 40, Pr/dining room 80 **Children** Portions **Parking** 50

Map 7 TQ81

The Wild Mushroom Restaurant

◉◉ Modern British

Modern British cooking in a charming converted farmhouse

☎ 01424 751137
Woodgate House, Westfield Ln TN35 4SB
e-mail: info@wildmushroom.co.uk
dir: From A21 towards Hastings, left onto A28 to Westfield. Restaurant 1.5m on left

A converted 19th century farmhouse surrounded by countryside just a short drive from Hastings, Paul and

Rebecca Webbe's restaurant is part of a mini-empire that includes Webbe's at The Fish Café in Rye - see entry - and Rock-a-nore in Hastings Old Town. The restaurant takes up the whole of the ground floor, with a conservatory bar overlooking a small garden at the rear. There are original features like flagged floors and low beams, and a smart country feel to the place, helped along by the friendly service. Sharp contemporary cooking is the name of the game, with ingredients shipped in locally from trusted suppliers and due heed paid to the seasons. There are set lunch, à la carte and tasting menus to choose from, with canapés, an amuse-bouche and home-made breads all part of the package. Pork and wild mushroom rillette served with toasted granary bread and home-made piccalilli is a switched-on starter, with slow-cooked ox cheek with garlic mash and Shiraz jus a hit among main courses.

Chef Paul Webbe, Christopher Weddle **Owner** Mr & Mrs P Webbe **Times** 12-2.30/7-10 Closed 25 Dec, 2 wks at New Year, Mon-Tue, D Sun **Prices** Fixed L 2 course fr £16.95, Tasting menu £35, Starter £6-£9, Main £12-£22, Dessert £6-£7.95, Service optional **Wines** 46 bottles over £20, 33 bottles under £20, 6 by glass **Notes** Tasting menu 6 course, Sunday L, Vegetarian available, Dress restrictions, Smart casual **Seats** 40 **Children** Portions **Parking** 20

Map 6 TQ50

Crossways

◉◉ Modern British

Country-house dining in relaxed restaurant with rooms

☎ 01323 482455
Lewes Rd BN26 5SG
e-mail: stay@crosswayshotel.co.uk
dir: On A27, 2m W of Polegate

Crossways, a Georgian house below the South Downs Way, was at one time the home of Elizabeth David's parents, and foodies can pay their respects to the writer as her grave is a short distance away. A monthly-changing four-course dinner is served in the small and comfortable dining room, with its private party vibe created in part by relaxed service from the proprietors. The well-balanced menu could kick off with seafood pancake, or smoked duck and Asian pear salad, with a soup of the day to follow. Main courses reflect the kitchen's straightforward, uncluttered approach to its output - perhaps game pie in a rich gravy - and sauces and garnishes are well considered: wild mushroom sauce for sautéed loin of local venison, say, mango, ginger and cranberry for roast breast of Gressingham duck, and a maple glaze for pork tenderloin in a parmesan crumb coating.

Chef David Stott **Owner** David Stott, Clive James **Times** 7.30-8.30 Closed 24 Dec-24 Jan, Sun-Mon, L all week **Prices** Fixed D 4 course £38.95, Service optional **Wines** 24 bottles over £20, 15 bottles under £20, 10 by glass **Notes** Vegetarian available **Seats** 24 **Parking** 20

Map 6 TQ21

The Ginger Fox

◉ Modern British

Classy country gastro-pub

☎ 01273 857888
Muddleswood Rd BN6 9EA
e-mail: gingerfox@gingermanrestaurants.com
dir: On A281 at the junction with B2117

Part of a small Brighton-based group (see entry for mothership Gingerman Restaurant), The Ginger Fox is a country pub with the South Downs as its backyard and food very much at its heart. Done out in modern gastro-pub fashion, it blends neutral tones, unclothed oak tables, black tiled floors and enough original features to remind you of the antiquity of the old thatched building. The kitchen deals in up-to-the-minute dishes conjured from locally-sourced ingredients and is not afraid to travel the globe for inspiration. Roasted harissa spring chicken with pea and mint tabouleh, baba ganoush and coriander yoghurt sits alongside pork and cider pie with mash, spring greens and gravy, and to finish, perhaps a tropically influenced passionfruit posset (with mango jelly and coconut tapioca) or crowd-pleasing dark chocolate brownie. There's a garden with views of the Downs too.

Chef Ben McKellar, Caye Nunez **Owner** Ben & Pamela McKellar **Times** 12-2/6-10 Closed 25 Dec **Prices** Fixed L 2 course £12.50, Starter £5-£8.50, Main £11.50-£18.50, Dessert £5-£7.50, Service optional, Groups min 6 service 12.5% **Notes** Fixed L 2 course Mon-Fri until 7pm, Sunday L, Vegetarian available **Seats** 50, Pr/dining room 24 **Children** Portions, Menu **Parking** 60

Map 6 TQ00

The Town House

◉◉ Modern V

Accomplished cooking bang opposite the castle

☎ 01903 883847
65 High St BN18 9AJ
e-mail: enquiries@thetownhouse.co.uk
dir: Follow A27 to Arundel, onto High Street, establishment on left at top of hill

If you're looking for The Town House, just head for Arundel Castle and you're pretty much there. This elegant , three-storey, Grade II listed Regency townhouse perches on the hill right opposite the castle wall, so you can gaze out at the imposing residence of the Duke of Norfolk through the restaurant's large front window. But there's much to admire inside too: look up, and you'll see a marvellously ornate gilt ceiling, dating back to the 16th century and shipped over to West Sussex from Florence. The small, intimate dining room has been brought into the 21st century with high-backed black chairs, contemporary artworks and mirrors with funky striped frames. Chef-patron Lee Williams' food is pretty voguish too - using plenty of local and seasonal ingredients - and what's

Save on Hotels. Book at **theAA.com/hotel**

SUSSEX, WEST 455 **ENGLAND**

more he offers a fashionably good value lunch menu. Start with Thai-spiced butternut squash soup or duck confit and foie gras terrine with fig and apple chutney, and, for a real treat in season, there might be among main courses a dish of expertly cooked fillet of local venison with confit haunch, spinach, dauphinoise and red wine jus. Dessert ends on a high with home-made apple tart with clotted cream.

Chef Lee Williams **Owner** Lee & Kate Williams **Times** 12-2.30/7-9.30 Closed 2 wks Oct, Xmas, 2 wks Feb, Sun-Mon **Prices** Fixed L 2 course fr £15.50, Fixed D 3 course fr £29, Service optional **Wines** 50+ bottles over £20, 6 bottles under £20, 8 by glass **Notes** Vegetarian menu **Seats** 24 **Children** Portions **Parking** On street or nearby car park

---

BOSHAM Map 5 SU80

The Millstream Hotel & Restaurant

@@ Modern British 🕙

Smart, contemporary cooking in a tranquil setting

☎ 01243 573234
Bosham Ln PO18 8HL
e-mail: info@millstreamhotel.com
web: www.millstreamhotel.com
dir: 4m W of Chichester on A259, left at Bosham rdbt. After 0.5m right at T-junct signed to church & quay. Hotel 0.5m on right

It's all very chocolate-boxy around here, with The Millstream occupying a peaceful spot by a stream in the harbourside village. In the charming restaurant, with its country-style décor and smartly dressed tables, there is some modish thinking going on. The menu has plenty of contemporary appeal without pushing the envelope too far. Thus among starters comes wild scallops with cauliflower and almond purée and thin slices of crisp pancetta, or lightly spiced mussel and vegetable chowder with crispy shallots. Next up, breast of guinea fowl might come with braised chestnuts, black trumpet mushrooms, risotto and white truffle oil, and desserts extend to iced cappuccino with hot cinnamon and custard doughnuts, or caramel popcorn ice cream served in a tuile basket.

Chef Neil Hiskey **Owner** The Wild family **Times** 12.30-2/6.30-9 **Prices** Fixed L 2 course fr £20, Fixed D 3 course fr £32.50, Service optional **Wines** 59 bottles over £20, 9 bottles under £20, 13 by glass **Notes** Tasting menu with wine 6 course, Pre-theatre menu, Sunday L, Vegetarian available, Dress restrictions, Smart casual, Civ Wed 75 **Seats** 60, Pr/dining room 14 **Children** Portions, Menu **Parking** 40

BURPHAM Map 6 TQ00

George & Dragon

@ British, French

Classy pub food in atmospheric setting

☎ 01903 883131
BN18 9RR
e-mail: info@gdinn.co.uk
dir: Off A27 1m E of Arundel, signed Burpham, 2.5m pub on left

In a village that dates from Saxon times and stands in the newly formed South Downs National Park, the white-painted George & Dragon is a real pub. It dates from the 17th century and has all the accordant charms, plus a very nice line in rustic British cooking. The beers reflect the terroir - courtesy of the Arundel Brewery who supply everything from Sussex Gold to Pickled Mouse - and wine is given top billing, too, with a good list from Berry Bros & Rudd. The cooking is a few notches above the pub norm and shows plenty of creativity and an eye for good combinations. Golden Cross goats' cheese on anchovy toast is one way to proceed, or there's an Asian flavour with tiger prawns marinated in chilli, lime and garlic, served with Thai noodles. Next up, loin of lamb comes with mint potato 'liquid', red pepper, caramelised aubergine, pine nuts, mint and red wine jus, while Sunday lunch might bring forth roast aged rump with Yorkshire pudding. There are sandwiches, ploughman's and meat and cheese platters at lunchtime.

Times 12-2/7-9 Closed 25 Dec, D Sun

CHICHESTER Map 5 SU80

Comme Ça

@ French

A taste of France close to the Festival Theatre

☎ 01243 788724 & 536307
67 Broyle Rd PO19 6BD
e-mail: comme.ca@commeca.co.uk
dir: On A286 near Festival Theatre

In case the name isn't enough of a clue, the blue-shuttered Georgian inn is the very image of rustic French charm, except it is located rather more conveniently on this side of the Channel, just a short walk from Chichester's Festival Theatre. Chef-patron Michel Navet was born in Normandy and despite spending a quarter of a century at the stoves in Sussex, his culinary heart has never left France. Boosting the already considerable Gallic factor are knowledgeable French staff, and a bilingual menu of old-school French country cooking that cherry picks its way through the country's varied regional cuisines. The good old French concept of terroir is alive and well in the use of local produce, so you can expect to see Selsey crab starring in a tartlet flavoured with saffron and sun-dried tomatoes, served simply with watercress; following this, perhaps slow-cooked leg of Sussex rabbit in a wholegrain mustard and Madeira sauce on a bed of crushed celeriac. Skipping dessert is out of the question

when there is a véritable vanilla crème brûlée up for grabs.

Chef Michel Navet, Mark Howard **Owner** Mr & Mrs Navet **Times** 12-2/6-10.30 Closed Xmas & New Year wks, BHs, Mon, L Tue, D Sun **Prices** Food prices not confirmed for 2013. Please telephone for details **Wines** 60 bottles over £20, 60 bottles under £20, 7 by glass **Notes** Dress restrictions, Smart casual **Seats** 100, Pr/dining room 14 **Children** Portions, Menu **Parking** 46

Croucher's Country Hotel & Restaurant

@@ Modern British V

Imaginative cooking in stylish hotel

☎ 01243 784995 & 07887 744570
Birdham Rd PO20 7EH
e-mail: crouchers@btconnect.com
dir: From A27 Chichester bypass onto A286 towards West Wittering, 2m, hotel on left between Chichester Marina & Dell Quay

Just to the south of Chichester, Croucher's is a classy and comfortable hotel, with a sleek bar and a stylish oak-beamed restaurant looking over green fields. The kitchen devises and serves up some ambitious modern dishes such as starters like crab and leek tartlet with smoked salmon and green olive purée, and smoked chicken and chorizo risotto with pancetta foam and pea shoots. The cooking brings out the best of quality raw materials, to produce well-composed main courses such as pork three ways - crisp belly, braised cheek and roast medallion of fillet - served with mustard sauce, apple purée, creamed shallots and champ, and, among fish offerings, grilled fillet of grey mullet with saffron and chive velouté, olive oil mash and leek fondue. For dessert there may be rich hot chocolate fondant with rhubarb jelly.

Chef N Markey **Owner** Lloyd van Rooyen **Times** 12-2.30/7-9.30 **Prices** Fixed L 2 course £13.50, Fixed D 3 course £26.50, Starter £5.95-£9.75, Main £17.50-£24.50, Dessert £6.25-£8.50, Service optional **Wines** 30 bottles over £20, 20 bottles under £20, 9 by glass **Notes** Pre-theatre menu from 6pm, Sunday L, Vegetarian menu, Civ Wed 75 **Seats** 80, Pr/dining room 22 **Children** Portions, Menu **Parking** 40

CHICHESTER *continued*

Earl of March

◎◎ British ◎

Classy cooking in revamped old pub

☎ 01243 533993 & 783991
Lavant Rd PO18 0BQ
e-mail: info@theearlofmarch.com
dir: On A286, 2m N of Chichester towards Midhurst, on
the corner of Goodwood Estate

The 18th-century pub overlooking Goodwood racecourse
and the South Downs looks like your typical downland
hostelry from the outside, but it has a contemporary
finish within. That's not to say it has lost it pubby
credentials entirely; cool leather sofas and a real fire
await. When you discover that the owner was once
executive chef of The Ritz, it will come as no surprise to
hear that food is the main focus these days. The
restaurant area looks good with its darkwood tables and
swish leather chairs, and during the summer months
there's a seafood and champagne shack in the former
bakehouse. The classical training of the patron is evident
from the bar snacks, via set menus and daily specials, to
the carte. Start with something as à la mode as pan-
seared diver scallops with pork belly, pancetta and apple,
moving on to loin of venison with celeriac dauphinoise,
sweet beetroot ripple and port wine game jus, with a
traditional favourite such as sticky toffee pudding,
butterscotch sauce and vanilla ice cream providing a
satisfying finale.

Chef Giles Thompson **Owner** Giles & Ruth Thompson
Times 12-2.30/5.30-9.30 Closed D Sun **Prices** Fixed L 2
course £18.50, Starter £6.50-£9.50, Main £14.50-£23.50,
Dessert £6.50-£7.50, Service optional, Groups min 11
service 12.5% **Wines** 33 bottles over £20, 16 bottles
under £20, 18 by glass **Notes** Pre-theatre/Early bird menu
2/3 course, Sunday L, Vegetarian available **Seats** 60, Pr/
dining room 12 **Children** Portions, Menu **Parking** 30

Hallidays

◎◎ Modern British ◎

Quality local produce cooked with flair

☎ 01243 575331
Watery Ln, Funtington PO18 9LF
e-mail: hallidaysdinners@aol.com
dir: 4m W of Chichester, on B2146

Hallidays occupies three flint-fronted thatched farm
workers' cottages dating from the 15th century, now split
in two eating areas with a small bar in between.
Everything is made in-house, from breads to petits fours,
and Andy Stephenson has an impressive network of local
suppliers; he buys whole carcasses from neighbouring
farmers and butchers them himself, perhaps turning up
as 21-day aged sirloin steak with wild mushrooms
(gathered by chef) with Madeira and tarragon sauce. A
grounding in the great French traditions is evident in

some dishes - roast duck breast à l'orange with champ,
say, or baked gurnard with scallops and white wine
beurre blanc - with other ideas culled from elsewhere, as
seen in starters of risotto nero with crispy squid, and red
lentil, spinach and coconut soup. Finish with thin apple
tart dusted with cinnamon sugar and served with vanilla
ice cream.

Chef Andrew Stephenson **Owner** Mr A & Mrs J Stephenson
Times 12-2.15/7-10.15 Closed 1 wk Mar, 2 wks Aug,
Mon-Tue, L Sat, D Sun **Prices** Fixed L 2 course £15, Fixed
D 3 course £27.50, Starter £7-£9, Main £17-£20, Dessert
£6.25-£8.50, Service optional **Wines** 54 bottles over £20,
18 bottles under £20, 8 by glass **Notes** Sunday L,
Vegetarian available, Dress restrictions, No shorts
Seats 26, Pr/dining room 12 **Children** Portions
Parking 12

Royal Oak Inn

◎ Modern British

Congenial pub restaurant with an appealing menu

☎ 01243 527434
Pook Ln, East Lavant PO18 0AX
e-mail: info@royaloakeastlavant.co.uk
web: www.royaloakeastlavant.co.uk
dir: From Chichester take A286 towards Midhurst, 2m to
mini rdbt, turn right signed East Lavant. Inn on left

As well as functioning as the village pub, this 200-year-
old inn is a welcoming restaurant, done out in rustic
style, with exposed brick walls, beams, and leather-look
chairs at wooden-topped tables. Contemporary ideas
share the billing with well-established British favourites
like cod and chips with pea purée. Starters can span
game terrine with hedgerow jelly and a well-balanced
dish of grilled plaice with chorizo and baby squid, and
main courses can encompass moist and tasty pork belly
with sage-flavoured rösti and roast apple, and sautéed
fillet of sea bream with tapenade and potatoes crushed
with lemon. Daily specials are listed on boards, and
puddings can run to classics like vanilla crème brûlée or
a crisp pastry tart of dark chocolate with raspberries.

Royal Oak Inn

Chef Steven Ferre **Owner** Charles Ullmann
Times 10-3/6-10.30 Closed 25 Dec **Prices** Fixed L 2
course £16.95, Service optional, Groups min 6 service
10% **Wines** 78 bottles over £20, 15 bottles under £20, 20
by glass **Notes** Pre-theatre menu from 5.30pm, Sunday L,
Vegetarian available **Seats** 55 **Children** Portions
Parking 25

See advert opposite

| CLIMPING | Map 6 SU90 |

Bailiffscourt Hotel & Spa

◎◎ Modern European

Modern European cooking in a grand spa hotel

☎ 01903 723511
BN17 5RW
e-mail: bailiffscourt@hshotels.co.uk
dir: A259, follow Climping Beach signs. Hotel 0.5m on right

When your surname is Guinness, you may well find
yourself with the wherewithal to indulge a folly or two -
hence the creation of Bailiffscourt. When you arrive at this
apparently medieval cluster of buildings in 30 acres of
parkland just back from Climping Beach, the impression
is of having stepped through a time portal to the Middle
Ages, although this was actually an exercise in
architectural salvage on a monumental scale, with the
stone buildings, beamed ceilings and mullioned windows
relocated from sites elsewhere. Naturally these days, the
upscale bolt-hole is happy to pamper you in the glitzy spa
before delivering the restored version of you to the
Tapestry Restaurant. Here, the eponymous wall hangings
are matched with opulent red and gold drapes, a coffered
ceiling and candlelight for a scene of Gothic romance. The
kitchen sends out an impeccably modern European
repertoire built on top-notch materials, as in a starter of
home-made pasta with sautéed baby squid, mussels and
shrimps in dill butter, followed by roast rump of lamb with
a braised lamb and onion faggot, and crisp-baked lemon-
peppered goats' cheese with rosemary and pepper sauce.

Chef Russell Williams **Owner** Pontus & Miranda
Carminger **Times** 12-2/7-9.30 **Prices** Fixed L 2 course
£13.50, Fixed D 3 course fr £49.50, Starter £7.50-£11.95,
Main £16.50-£24.95, Dessert £9.75-£11.75, Service
optional **Wines** 125 bottles over £20, 16 by glass
Notes Sunset pamper package incl 2 course meal & glass
champagne £89, Sunday L, Vegetarian available, Dress
restrictions, Smart casual, no jeans or T-shirts, Civ Wed
75 **Seats** 70, Pr/dining room 70 **Children** Portions, Menu
Parking 80

Save on Hotels. Book at **theAA.com/hotel**

SUSSEX, WEST 457 ENGLAND

Ockenden Manor Hotel & Spa

CUCKFIELD — Map 6 TQ32

Modern French

Refined, modern cooking in Elizabethan manor

☎ 01444 416111
Ockenden Ln RH17 5LD
e-mail: ockenden@hshotels.co.uk
web: www.hshotels.co.uk
dir: A23 towards Brighton. 4.5m left onto B2115 towards Haywards Heath. Cuckfield 3m. Ockenden Lane off High St. Hotel at end

This romantic Elizabethan manor house is a vision of idyllic English charm set in a painterly Sussex landscape sweeping away to the spine of the South Downs. A tiny lane leads from Cuckfield's postcard-perfect high street into Ockenden's nine acres of pretty grounds, where a 19th-century walled garden now houses the latest string to the hotel's bow - a newly-built contemporary spa. Inside, period feel is present in abundance in its wooden panelling and venerable Tudor beams, but the weight of the ages is lightened by cheerful hues of summery yellow, and the excellent staff add to the feeling of friendly welcome. The restaurant has moved from the older part of the hotel to the extended original conservatory, a setting which makes the most of those views across verdant meadows to the Downs. Chef Stephen Crane has been orchestrating proceedings in the kitchen for over a decade, so his supply lines to the finest Sussex produce are well-established as the bedrock of his highly-polished French-accented country-house cooking. His feel for the nit-picking detail and sharp technical skills that raise dishes to a refined level shows in a starter of cod with sesame, contrasted with cauliflower saag curry. Next out, saddle of local Balcombe venison is paired with a pasty of the same meat, and delivered with red cabbage and wild mushrooms, while caramelised lemon tart served with a blackcurrant sorbet is a perennial favourite to end the show. On the wine front, classic French appellations are abundant on a list of serious bottles at equally serious prices.

Chef Stephen Crane **Owner** The Goodman & Carminger family **Times** 12-2/7-9 **Prices** Fixed L 2 course fr £16.50, Tasting menu £75, Service optional, Groups min 10 service 10% **Wines** 207 bottles over £20, 11 by glass **Notes** ALC 3 course £55, Sunday L, Vegetarian available, Dress restrictions, No jeans, T-shirts, Civ Wed 150 **Seats** 70, Pr/dining room 96 **Children** Portions **Parking** 98

CUCKFIELD — Map 6 TQ32

Ockenden Manor Hotel & Spa

◉◉◉ – see page 457

EAST GRINSTEAD — Map 6 TQ33

The Felbridge Hotel & Spa

◉◉ Modern British

Inventive modern food in a spa hotel

☎ 01342 337700
London Rd RH19 2BH
e-mail: info@felbridgehotel.co.uk
web: www.felbridgehotel.co.uk
dir: From W: M23 junct 10, follow signs to A22. From N: M25 junct 6. Hotel on A22 at Felbridge

When you're done with spoiling yourself in the treatment rooms of the classy Felbridge Hotel's spa and slipped a cocktail or two under the belt, it is time to move into the fine dining Anise restaurant and let the kitchen team do their stuff. The venue is glossy, cosseting, and intimately-lit - rather like sinking into a box of posh chocolates with its tones of cream, caramel and rich brown. The kitchen hauls in the best produce from the surrounding counties of Sussex, Surrey and Kent as the building blocks of a French-accented modern menu conceived with oodles of inventive flair and delivered with impressive technical skills. Roast loin of rabbit stars in a starter with piccalilli, cauliflower and watercress. Next comes filet of halibut with crab and scallops, courgette and potato fondant, or confit duck with an anise jus. And to finish, carrot cake alongside ginger and brown sugar parfait, orange jelly and white chocolate mousse.

The Felbridge Hotel & Spa

Chef Kirk Johnson **Owner** New Century, East Grinstead Ltd **Times** 6-10 Closed L all week **Prices** Fixed D 3 course £37.50-£43.50, Service optional **Wines** 64 bottles over £20, 6 bottles under £20, 12 by glass **Notes** Vegetarian available, Civ Wed 200 **Seats** 34, Pr/dining room 20 **Children** Portions, Menu **Parking** 200

See advert below

Gravetye Manor Hotel

◉◉◉ – see opposite

GATWICK AIRPORT (LONDON) — Map 6 TQ24

Langshott Manor

◉◉ Modern European V ✿

Impressive cooking in elegant manor house

☎ 01293 786680
Langshott Ln, Horley RH6 9LN
e-mail: admin@langshottmanor.com
dir: From A23 take Ladbroke Rd, off Chequers rdbt to Langshott, after 0.75m hotel on right

The frenetic environs of Gatwick Airport are not the most obviously fertile ground for finding gastronomic excellence, but rest assured any distractions melt away as you step into this serene timber and herringbone-brickwork Elizabethan manor house set in three acres of landscaped gardens. Its Mulberry Restaurant boosts the feelgood factor further still with a setting of contemporary country-house chic blending with the period charm of oak beams, panelling, and leaded windows. The hotel's kitchen garden pulls its weight in supplying the chefs, along with splendid materials from Sussex and Surrey. The food makes an impact: an up-to-date repertoire of creative and skilfully crafted dishes might open with braised cheek and belly of Sussex White pork with rhubarb and chicory, while main courses could run to loin of venison matched with thyme and Cognac mousseline, cavolo nero, swede and beetroot. Desserts such as Muscovado savarin with coffee, mango and passionfruit are equally refined and impeccably presented.

Chef Phil Dixon **Owner** Peter & Deborah Hinchcliffe **Times** 12-2.30/7-9.30 **Prices** Fixed L 2 course £15-£39, Fixed D 3 course £45, Tasting menu £65-£95, Service added but optional 12.5% **Wines** 120 bottles over £20, 18 by glass **Notes** Sunday L, Vegetarian menu, Dress restrictions, Smart casual, no jeans or shorts **Seats** 55, Pr/dining room 22 **Children** Portions **Parking** 25

Sofitel London Gatwick

◉ British, French

Contemporary and relaxed dining near the airport

☎ 01293 567070

North Terminal RH6 0PH

e-mail: h6204-re@accor.com

dir: M23 junct 9, follow to 2nd rdbt. Hotel straight ahead

The Sofitel's Gatwick outpost flies the flag for good quality food near a UK airport. The striking atrium is home to three restaurants, with La Brasserie given a slick contemporary look with textures of wood and chrome, plus smartly laid linen-clad tables. Seasonal, regionally-sourced ingredients are not the norm when it comes to airport dining, so it's a joy to see them here, and duly flagged on the menu. Start with home-smoked Loch Duart salmon cured in Talisker whisky, and follow on with slow-cooked belly and crispy crackling of Forest of Dean Gloucestershire old spot, served with butter mash, anise-flavoured carrots and Calvados jus, or fillet of Cornish whiting in yeast batter with hand-cut chips, mini pickles and home-made tartare sauce.

Chef David Woods **Owner** S Arora **Times** 6.30-10.30 Closed L all week **Prices** Fixed D 3 course £26.75-£45.55, Starter £6.75-£11.95, Main £17.50-£25.95, Dessert £2.50-£7.65, Service added but optional 12.5% **Wines** 36 bottles over £20, 13 by glass **Notes** Vegetarian available, Dress restrictions, Smart casual **Seats** 70, Pr/dining room 40 **Children** Portions, Menu **Parking** 100

GOODWOOD   Map 6 SU80

The Goodwood Hotel

◉◉ Modern British

Distinctive cooking on the Goodwood Estate

☎ 01243 775537

PO18 0QB

e-mail: reservations@goodwood.com

dir: Off A285, 3m NE of Chichester

The 12,000-acre Goodwood Estate includes a contemporary hotel and country club as well as this light and airy restaurant in an 18th-century coaching inn. The Home Farm, run on organic principles, provides the restaurant with meats and cheeses, the latter perhaps in a soufflé with deconstructed Waldorf salad and red wine syrup. Other starters can be as complex as crab and coronation salad, with crisp apple jelly, melon and meat radish, or as familiar as chicken liver parfait with onion jam. Well-composed main courses are in the modern vein of turbot fillet cooked in chicken jus, accompanied by chicken mousse and popcorn and truffled mash, although there may also be an excellent version of venison Wellington. Expectations are heightened from the off by an amuse-bouche - mushroom velouté, say - and high standards continue into desserts like vanilla crème brûlée with gingerbread ice cream.

Chef Paul Owens **Owner** The Goodwood Estate Company Ltd **Times** 12.30-2.30/6.30-10.30 Closed L Mon-Sat **Prices** Tasting menu fr £55, Starter £5.50-£15, Main £14-£27.95, Dessert £6-£9.95, Service optional **Wines** 63 bottles over £20, 12 by glass **Notes** Sunday L, Vegetarian available, Civ Wed 100 **Seats** 85, Pr/dining room 120 **Children** Portions, Menu **Parking** 150

Gravetye Manor Hotel

EAST GRINSTEAD   Map 6 TQ33

Modern British **NEW** V

Country-house cooking in oak-panelled splendour, with gardens to match

☎ 01342 810567

Vowells Ln, West Hoathly RH19 4LJ

e-mail: info@gravetyemanor.co.uk

dir: From M23 junct 10 take A264 towards East Grinstead. After 2m take B2028 to Haywards Heath. 1m after Turners Hill fork left towards Sharpthorne, immediate 1st left into Vowels Lane

With its combination of heaps of historic charm and high standards of service, not forgetting some seriously good cooking and beautiful gardens with impeccable English horticultural credentials, Gravetye is a country-house hotel which leaves a lasting impression. That impression is likely to be one of comfort and joy. The wood-panelled dining room is brimful of traditional features with all that burnished oak, a real fire and oil paintings, and tables are dressed with all the anticipated fine-dining elegance. When the Sussex climate allows, lunch can be taken in the garden. The plush lounges make a fine introduction - canapés and all - before you head into the dining room. The fixed-price menu delivers all the hoped for little treats one expects in this sort of setting, kicking off with an amuse-bouche such as crab with potato espuma and citrus salad, and a pre-dessert designed to complement your own choice rather than duplicate it. Presentation is good, the quality of the produce high. A first course ballottine of foie gras with pickled girolles, salted grapes, hazelnuts and celeriac demonstrates sound classical technique, whilst main-course loin of deeply flavoured Balcombe venison comes with a superb boudin, turnip gratin, a lusciously smooth butternut purée and sloe gin sauce. Dark Amedei chocolate is given the soufflé treatment with thrilling results, successfully partnered with a mandarin compôte and cream. New owners since 2010 have successfully brought Gravetye back to the top table.

Chef Rupert Gleadou **Owner** Jeremy & Elizabeth Hosking **Times** 12-2/6.30-9.30 **Prices** Fixed L 2 course £22.50, Fixed D 3 course £40, Tasting menu £70-£90, Starter fr £15, Main fr £30, Dessert fr £10, Service added but optional 12.5% **Wines** 300 bottles over £20, 10 by glass **Notes** All day menu 10am-10pm, Sunday L, Vegetarian menu, Dress restrictions, Smart casual, Civ Wed 60 **Seats** 40, Pr/dining room 20 **Children** Portions **Parking** 25

Jeremy's at Borde Hill

⚫ Modern European, Mediterranean ⚫

Confident cooking in idyllic garden setting

☎ 01444 441102
Balcombe Rd RH16 1XP
e-mail: reservations@jeremysrestaurant.com
web: www.jeremysrestaurant.com
dir: 1.5m N of Haywards Heath, 10mins from Gatwick
Airport. From M23 junct 10a take A23 through Balcombe

The enchanting location among the lush splendour of the
Borde Hill gardens is a major plus at chef-patron Jeremy
Ashpool's relaxed country restaurant. The converted
stable block is utterly idyllic when you can bask in the
Sussex sun on the south-facing terrace overlooking a
Victorian walled garden, while indoors, it's a bright and
airy space with smart high-backed leather chairs, wooden
floors and local artists' work on the walls. All in all, a
thoroughly modern place, with cooking to match. The
bounteous Sussex larder (supported by produce from the
walled garden) provides the wherewithal for the rustic,
Mediterranean-inflected repertoire, which might open
with seared squid with roasted peppers, aïoli, and garlic
and parsley dressing, followed by roast loin and braised
belly of Southdown lamb with dauphinoise potato,
Jerusalem artichoke purée, smoked asparagus and mint
jelly. For dessert, new season's rhubarb might get an
outing in a parfait teamed with meringue, celery sorbet,
hazelnut and mint.

Chef Jimmy Gray, Jeremy Ashpool **Owner** Jeremy Ashpool
Times 12-3/7-9.30 Closed after New Year for 7 days,
Mon, D Sun **Prices** Fixed L 2 course fr £15, Fixed D 3
course fr £18, Tasting menu £35-£60, Starter £8.50-£10,
Main £15-£22, Dessert fr £7.50, Service optional, Groups
min 8 service 10% **Wines** 10 by glass **Notes** Tasting
menu 6 course (with wine £60), fixed D midweek, Sunday
L, Vegetarian available **Seats** 55 **Children** Portions
Parking 15, Overspill car park

Restaurant Tristan

⚫⚫ Modern British, French

Inventive cooking in a 500-year-old building

☎ 01403 255688
3 Stan's Way, East St RH12 1HU
e-mail: info@restauranttristan.co.uk

Training with Marco Pierre White is certainly a good
grounding for a rising star of the culinary world, and
Tristan Mason's first solo flight looks the part too: set on
the first-floor of a 16th-century building in old Horsham,
the restaurant has a striking beamed vaulted ceiling,
wall timbers, bare floorboards, and Mondrian-esque slabs
of abstract modern art. The cooking is of-the-moment
stuff, displaying a high level of technical ability and the
nous not to overwork things. The menu eschews
descriptive prose, bringing together eclectic partnerships
along the lines of rabbit and lobster ballotine with leek

and purple potato, or low-temperature treatment of Arctic
char, which is matched with quail's egg, watercress and
truffle. Main courses also aim for big earthy flavours -
monkfish shares a plate with chicken wings, chervil root
and trompette risotto, perhaps, while haunch and saddle
of venison could come with beetroot, chocolate and rose
hip. Puddings offer creative reworkings of old favourites,
such as banana tarte Tatin with lemon sauce and
caramelised walnut and parsley ice cream.

Chef Tristan Mason **Owner** Tristan Mason
Times 12-2.30/6.30-9.30 Closed Sun-Mon **Prices** Fixed L
2 course fr £16, Fixed D 3 course fr £40, Tasting menu
£55-£80, Service added but optional 12.5%
Wines 57 bottles over £20, 2 bottles under £20, 12 by
glass **Notes** Tasting menu 5 course (with wine £80),
Vegetarian available, Dress restrictions, Smart casual
Seats 40

Wabi

⚫⚫ Japanese V

Modern Japanese cuisine, prime British produce

☎ 01403 788140
38 East St RH12 1HL
e-mail: reservations@wabi.co.uk
dir: Corner Penne Rd & East St

In a change of career direction, this Horsham boozer
began a new life as Wabi, a style-driven contemporary
Japanese operation comprising a buzzy cocktail bar, an
open ground-floor grill, where a long counter lets you get
up close to the chefs at work, and up on the first floor, a
more orthodox restaurant. Wherever takes your fancy, the
décor goes for a pared-back minimal Japanese style with
screens of timber and tatami, bare darkwood tables and
luscious shades of chocolate and caramel brown.
Japanese ideas are obviously the kitchen's primary
inspiration, but that doesn't preclude input from a wider
European idiom. Ingredients of unimpeachable pedigree
arrive courtesy of the Japanese Nama Yasai organic farm
in East Sussex, while fish for sushi and sashimi travels a
short way from the south coast. Roasted scallop and foie
gras miso zuke is one way to get going (don't worry about
the language barrier - friendly staff will talk you through
the menu) or crispy soft-shelled crab tempura might
tempt. From the robata grill, there could be tea-smoked
lamb chops hoba-yaki with sweet-and-sour nasu and
miso sauce, or among main courses, grilled Sussex unagi
(freshwater eel) with foie gras, gobo and apple balsamic.

Chef Scott Hallsworth **Owner** Andre Cachia
Times 12-2.30/6-10.30 Closed BH's, Sun-Mon
Prices Fixed L 2 course £8-£17.50, Starter £4-£12.50,
Main £9.75-£19.50, Dessert £6-£6.50, Service added but
optional 12.5% **Wines** 86 bottles over £20, 6 bottles
under £20, 11 by glass **Notes** Fixed L & D 6 course £32-
£55, Vegetarian menu, Dress restrictions, Smart casual,
Air con **Seats** 90, Pr/dining room 12 **Children** Portions,
Menu **Parking** Car park

Camellia Restaurant at South Lodge Hotel

⚫⚫ British V ⚫NOTABLE WINE LIST

Traditional comfort and modern cooking

☎ 01403 891711
Brighton Rd RH13 6PS
e-mail: enquiries@southlodgehotel.co.uk
dir: On A23 left onto B2110. Turn right through Handcross
to A281 junct. Turn left, hotel on right

The very picture of rosy-hued Englishness, this wisteria-
festooned Victorian lodge sits in 90 acres of stunning
gardens with restorative views over the undulating spine
of the South Downs; it is a special delight when the
fabulous collection of magnolias, rhododendrons and rare
orchids is in bloom. Within, the lodge is a plush oasis of
opulent style imparting a sense of well-being that
pervades through to the Camellia Restaurant: ornate oak-
panels and camellia-patterned wallpaper make for an
elegant space here, although gentle design tweaks have
added some contemporary vibrancy to keep it looking
fresh. The kitchen takes a similar old-meets-new
approach: rooted in classic ideas from the French
brasserie repertoire, this is skilful, creative contemporary
cooking that uses ingredients from the splendid Sussex
larder to telling effect. A smoked haddock risotto with
Jerusalem artichoke, quail's eggs and chives precedes a
main course of breast and leg of Gressingham duck
partnered by braised red cabbage, confit potato and
pickled apple. To finish, crispy baklava and pistachio ice
cream lift a well-made crème caramel to a higher plane.
Aficionados of British wine will be delighted by an
impressive listing of Sussex bottles produced within 15
miles of the hotel. (See also entry for The Pass
Restaurant)

Chef Lewis Hamblet **Owner** Exclusive Hotels
Times 12-2.30/7-10 **Prices** Fixed L 2 course £16.50-£45,
Fixed D 3 course £30-£45, Service added but optional
10% **Wines** 250 bottles over £20, 250 by glass
Notes Sunday L, Vegetarian menu **Seats** 75, Pr/dining
room 140 **Children** Portions, Menu **Parking** 200

The Pass Restaurant at South Lodge Hotel

⚫⚫⚫⚫ – *see opposite*

Save on Hotels. Book at **theAA.com/hotel**

SUSSEX, WEST 461 **ENGLAND**

The Pass Restaurant at South Lodge Hotel

British **V** NOTABLE WINE LIST

Ringside seats for cooking that's teeming with excitement

☎ 01403 891711
Brighton Rd RH13 6PS
e-mail: enquiries@southlodgehotel.co.uk
dir: From A23 turn left onto B2110 & then right through Handcross to A281 junct. Turn left hotel, on right

It says a lot about restaurant fashion in the 21st century that the most coveted table in the house might be in the kitchen. South Lodge Hotel has a perfectly standard panelled country-house dining-room, the Camellia (see separate entry), but if your soul chafes under a burdensome surfeit of country-house comfort, head it off at The Pass. Here is where the main action is, quite literally. A row of raised tables and swivel chairs overlooking the kitchens, with plasma screens set in the walls relaying a live feed of the chefs at their chopping and searing, offers the up-close-and-personal touch of realism. If you're expecting a sizzling cauldron of frayed temper, though, think again. Matt Gillan's team don't forget they're in polite company, and the prospect is one of serene creativity, as detailed on the fixed-price menus, which are teeming with excitement. Dinner might start with a vivid pasta dish of beetroot cannelloni garnished with orange and a wonderful horseradish sorbet, prior to chicken leg confit with baby artichokes and chick peas in lemon oil. Fish is handled with care, as when a piece of salmon is rare throughout, accompanied by a salmon version of brandade and a clever contrast of poached peach, and succulent pinkness also distinguishes a serving of duck breast with chervil root, purple carrots and chestnuts. A pre-dessert of pannacotta with soy sauce and popcorn has become something of a signature, while an understanding of the full flavour range of chocolate is on show in a white chocolate mousse with bitter dark chocolate sorbet, sprinkled with blackberries and passionfruit oil. If finances allow, surrender to the whole experience by taking the recommended wine flight, itself a voyage of discovery that may guide you from an improbably stunning Soave to a fortified Rivesaltes Ambré with the chocolate.

Chef Matt Gillan **Owner** Exclusive Hotels **Times** 12-2/7-9 Closed 1st 2 wks Jan, Mon-Tue **Prices** Fixed L 3 course £25, Service added but optional 10% **Wines** 200 bottles over £20, 200 by glass **Notes** Fixed L 5 course £35, 7 course £55, Sunday L, Vegetarian menu **Seats** 22 **Children** Menu **Parking** 200

MIDHURST
Map 6 SU82

Spread Eagle Hotel and Spa

◉◉ British

Up-to-the-minute cooking in a Tudor house

☎ 01730 816911
South St GU29 9NH
e-mail: reservations@spreadeagle-midhurst.com

The Eagle first took flight around 1430, and there are parts of this ancient coaching inn that are truly a step back in time; local lore has it that Elizabeth I stayed here, and the oak panelling and beams, Tudor bread ovens and Flemish stained glass in the atmospheric dining room certainly date from her era. Christmas puddings dangling from the roof beams make a talking point for diners, but there's nothing quirky about what comes out of the kitchen: this is cooking full of modern ideas and punchy flavours - home-smoked salmon, for example, comes with fromage blanc, confit fennel, lemon-scented couscous and Avruga caviar, while local meat is showcased in main courses taking in South Downs venison, served as roast saddle and sausage roll with roasted salsify, or roast loin, confit belly and crispy galette of Sussex pork with champ potatoes, roast organic carrots and roasting juices. Desserts keep the well-judged flavours coming with a chocolate moelleux with pistachio ice cream and caramel sauce.

Chef Nathan Marshall **Owner** The Goodman family
Times 12.30-2/7-9.30 **Prices** Fixed D 3 course fr £35, Starter £5-£10.50, Main £13-£25, Dessert £7-£11, Service optional **Wines** 100 bottles over £20, 20 bottles under £20, 15 by glass **Notes** Sunday L, Vegetarian available, Dress restrictions, Smart casual **Seats** 50, Pr/dining room 12 **Children** Portions, Menu **Parking** 75

PETWORTH
Map 6 SU92

The Leconfield

◉ Modern British **NEW**

Lots of creative energy

☎ 01798 345111
New St GU28 0AS
e-mail: reservations@theleconfield.co.uk

The Leconfield's lively ground-floor restaurant, with its bar and white walls hung with artwork, opens on to a light and airy orangery leading to a cobbled courtyard; there's also a splendidly beamed room upstairs. All sorts of ideas find their way on to the menus, from foie gras parfait with cherry fluid gel and pickled walnuts, to crab salad with pickled daikon, pea shoots and crab mayonnaise. Crab and lobster bisque is a convincing rendition, and may be followed by accurately timed sesame-crusted tuna steak accompanied by ginger-flavoured glass noodles and a blob of wasabi, or herb-coated rack of lamb with white bean purée and tomato and garlic fondue. Good home-made breads come with

dripping, and among interesting puddings may be rhubarb cheesecake with apple sorbet.

Chef David Craig Lewis **Owner** Nicola Jones
Times 12-3/6-9.30 Closed Mon, D Sun **Prices** Fixed L 2 course £15, Fixed D 3 course £30, Starter £8-£10, Main £16-£27, Dessert £7-£9.50, Service added but optional 12% **Wines** 43 bottles over £20, 7 bottles under £20, 7 by glass **Notes** Fixed D early evening, Sunday L, Vegetarian available **Seats** 60, Pr/dining room 30 **Children** Portions, Menu **Parking** On street, car park

ROWHOOK
Map 6 TQ13

The Chequers Inn

◉ British

Ambitious modern cooking in village inn

☎ 01403 790480
RH12 3PY
e-mail: thechequersrowhook@googlemail.com
dir: From Horsham A281 towards Guildford. At rdbt take A29 signed London. In 200mtrs left, follow Rowhook signs

The Chequers is very much a village local, with real ales on handpump, a bar menu along the lines of ciabattas and sausage and mash, and a welcoming atmosphere generated by friendly staff and open fires. It dates from the 15th century, and still has its complement of oak beams and flagstones. The kitchen here is a busy place, making its own bread and black pudding (in a starter with sautéed pigeon breast, beetroot relish and pancetta), and smoking its own salmon. The menu is full of intriguing modern ideas, from risotto of chorizo, peas and manchego cheese to duck confit on creamed potatoes with a dressing of sherry vinegar, shallots and lentils. A fish option may stretch to crisp-skinned pollock fillet with cep velouté, wild mushrooms and spinach, and you could end with coffee pannacotta.

Chef Tim Neal **Owner** Mr & Mrs Neal **Times** 12-2/7-9 Closed 25 Dec, D Sun **Prices** Starter £5.50-£9.75, Main £13.50-£21.50, Dessert £5.75-£8.25, Service optional, Groups min 8 service 10% **Wines** 22 bottles over £20, 29 bottles under £20, 8 by glass **Notes** Sunday L, Vegetarian available **Seats** 40 **Children** Portions **Parking** 40

RUSPER
Map 6 TQ23

Ghyll Manor

◉ Modern British

Traditionally-based cooking in a Tudor manor

☎ 0845 345 3426
High St RH12 4PX
e-mail: reception@ghyllmanor
dir: M23 junct 11, A264 signed Horsham. Continue 3rd rdbt, 3rd exit Faygate, follow signs for Rusper, 2m to village

The timbered Tudor manor sits in 40 acres of sumptuous grounds with the South Downs all around it. This sylvan setting can be enjoyed from a wide terrace that overlooks the lake and gardens, before you move indoors to the modern dining room with its woodblock floor, unclothed tables and white bucket chairs. Fixed-price menus (with supplements for appetisers and pre-desserts) offer engaging, traditionally-inspired brasserie food, perhaps starting with fried scallops, seaweed and pancetta, or confit duck tian dressed in blood orange, before following on with rib-eye steak served with horseradish mash, balsamic shallots and carrot purée, or fish and chips. Puddings include banoffee tart with coffee ice cream.

Chef Alec Mackins **Owner** Civil Service Motoring Association **Times** 12-2/6.30-9 **Prices** Fixed L 2 course £25-£27.50, Service optional **Wines** 7 bottles under £20, 9 by glass **Notes** Sunday L, Vegetarian available, Dress restrictions, Smart casual **Seats** 48, Pr/dining room 40 **Children** Portions **Parking**

SIDLESHAM
Map 5 SZ89

The Crab & Lobster

◉ Modern British

Switched-on modern menu in a waterside restaurant with rooms

☎ 01243 641233
Mill Ln PO20 7NB
e-mail: enquiries@crab-lobster.co.uk
web: www.crab-lobster.co.uk
dir: A27 S onto B2145 towards Selsey. At Sidlesham turn left onto Rookery Ln, continue for 0.75m

The Crab & Lobster may sound (and even look) like a pub, but gone are the days when this 350-year-old, whitewashed inn on the fringes of the Pagham Harbour nature reserve served pints and pork pies. The chic restaurant with rooms ticks all the right boxes for a switched-on contemporary operation - a sleek modern dining area where ancient flagstoned floors and oak beams are offset by chocolate-coloured leather, and cerise, mushroom and sage-green fabrics, and there's a creative modern British menu heaped with local produce. Given the watery setting, expect plenty of piscine pleasures - perhaps a parcel of Selsey crab, crayfish and smoked salmon topped with Avruga caviar, then baked cod loin wrapped in pancetta and matched with cavolo nero, braised potato and tarragon cream. After such light dishes there's always room for pudding, so go for something like deep-fried coconut ice cream with exotic fruit salad.

The Crab & Lobster

Chef Sam Bakose, Malcolm Goble, Simon Haynes **Owner** Sam & Janet Bakose **Times** 12-2.30/6-10 **Prices** Fixed L 2 course £19.50, Starter £6.50-£14.50, Main £15.85-£29, Dessert £6.95-£9.50, Service optional, Groups min 7 service 10% **Wines** 35 bottles over £20, 9 bottles under £20, 20 by glass **Notes** Sunday L, Vegetarian available **Seats** 54 **Children** Portions **Parking** 12

See advert below

TILLINGTON	Map 6 SU92

The Horse Guards Inn

◉ Traditional British 🍷

Skilful cooking near Petworth House

☎ 01798 342332
Upperton Rd GU28 9AF
e-mail: info@thehorseguardsinn.co.uk
dir: On A272, 1m west of Petworth, take road signposted Tillington. Restaurant 500mtrs opposite church

The Horse Guards got its name in the 1840s, when part of the Household Cavalry frequented the place while their horses rested in nearby Petworth Park. It's full of rustic charm, with wooden furniture, the odd chesterfield, oak beams, bric-à-brac and log fires. The menu changes daily, depending on what the kitchen has bought from local farms or dug up from its vegetable garden, and ingredients are treated respectfully with no artifice. Bone marrow on toast with salsa verde is a simple, tasty starter, and may appear alongside salted fish fritters with aïoli. Game pitches up in season - perhaps partridge with root vegetable mash, kale and red wine sauce - with scope extended by something like prawns stir-fried with chilli, garlic and ginger accompanied by potato and aubergine salad. Finish with a British pud like Bakewell tart.

Chef Mark Robinson **Owner** Sam Beard & Michaela Hohrkoua **Times** 12-2.30/6.30-9 **Prices** Starter £5.50-£9.50, Main £9-£21, Dessert £5.50-£12, Service optional, Groups min 12 service 12% **Wines** 42 bottles over £20, 9 bottles under £20, 14 by glass **Notes** Sunday L, Vegetarian available **Seats** 55, Pr/dining room 20 **Children** Portions, Menu **Parking** On street

---

TROTTON	Map 5 SU82

The Keepers Arms

◉ British, Mediterranean 🍷

Upmarket country pub with appealing menu

☎ 01730 813724 & 07506 693088
Love Hill, Terwick Ln GU31 5ER
e-mail: sharonmcgrath198@btinternet.com
dir: A272 towards Petersfield after 5m, restaurant on right just after narrow bridge. From Midhurst follow A272 for 3m, restaurant on left

The Keepers Arms is a gem of an ancient inn tweaked for 21st-century sensibilities. Although it has been opened out and decluttered, the friendly bar hasn't forgotten its roots - it has all the beams, timbers and well-kept real ales you'd hope for, while the stylish dining room goes for an easy-on-the-eye contemporary hunting lodge look involving blond-wood tables, warm colours and funky tartans; outdoors, the lush garden and terrace have plenty of alfresco appeal. Chalkboards offer pubby staples taking in Cumberland sausages with mash and onion gravy, or beer-battered cod with chips, mushy peas and home-made tartare sauce, while the carte deals in simple, seasonal, hearty ideas - game terrine with elderberry jelly, perhaps, then rack of Rother Valley lamb with dauphinoise potatoes, roast vine tomatoes and red wine jus.

Chef Sharon McGrath, James Nelson **Owner** Sharon McGrath **Times** 11-3/6.30-9.30 **Prices** Food prices not confirmed for 2013. Please telephone for details **Wines** 30 bottles over £20, 8 bottles under £20, 8 by glass **Notes** Vegetarian available **Seats** 56, Pr/dining room 8 **Children** Portions **Parking** 25, On street

---

TURNERS HILL — Map 6 TQ33

AG's Grill Room

◉◉ British, French ⊕

Smart country house with creative cooking

☎ 01342 714914

Alexander House Hotel, East St RH10 4QD
e-mail: info@alexanderhouse.co.uk
dir: On B2110 between Turners Hill & East Grinstead; 6m
from M23 junct 10

Alexander House sits in picturesque Sussex countryside
and marries its mansion country-house credentials with
sumptuous bedrooms and a Utopia spa. Reflections
restaurant (see entry below) is the bistro-style option,
whilst AG's Grill is an elegant space with ornate ceiling
and cornices, smartly laid tables and some confident
contemporary cooking supported by the eponymous grill.
Friday and Saturday nights brings forth a tasting menu
(veggies get their own). The grill menu of classic dishes
supplements the à la carte where you'll find dishes such
as butter-poached native lobster with Russet apples,
coral mayonnaise and crab fritters to start, followed by
free-range Fen Place pork and crackling with salt-baked
celeriac, morels and wild garlic. The creativity continues
into desserts like iced lemon curd and hibiscus with
chocolate pancake and marshmallow.

Chef Mark Budd **Owner** Alexander Hotels Ltd
Times 12-2.30/7-9.30 Closed Mon-Tue **Prices** Fixed L 2
course £23.95, Tasting menu £105, Starter £5-£10, Main
£12-£25, Dessert £8-£10, Service added but optional
12.5% **Wines** 130 bottles over £20, 4 bottles under £20,
18 by glass **Notes** Tasting menu with wine 9 course,
Sunday L, Vegetarian available, Dress restrictions, Smart
casual, no trainers or T-shirts **Seats** 34, Pr/dining room
18 **Parking** 100

Reflections at Alexander House

◉ Modern, International

Modern brasserie cooking in an elegant spa hotel

☎ 01342 714914

Alexander House Hotel, East St RH10 4QD
e-mail: admin@alexanderhouse.co.uk
dir: On B2110 between Turners Hill & East Grinstead; 6m
from M23 junct 10

Spa enthusiasts will be delighted by the restorative
facilities at Alexander House but there's also a buzzy
brasserie to lift the spirits still further. The setting is
impressive inside and out: 120 acres of gardens,
woodland and parkland surround a handsome 17th-
century mansion which has had a thoroughly modern
makeover, moving it into boutique territory. New head
chef Mark Budd presides over both the fine dining AG's
Grill Room (see entry above) and the less formal
Reflections. Expect sleek chocolate-coloured leather
banquettes, slate floors and subtle grey and peach tones
on the walls, plus there's a champagne bar and tables in
the courtyard for eating outdoors. Expect confidently
constructed dishes such as baked South Coast scallops
with a Mornay sauce preceding roast white chicken with

Alsace cabbage and glazed onions, finishing with
lemongrass pannacotta with raspberry sorbet and
hazelnut biscotti.

Times 12-3/6.30-10

TYNE & WEAR

GATESHEAD — Map 21 NZ26

Eslington Villa Hotel

◉ Modern British V

Good honest cooking in a 19th-century mansion

☎ 0191 487 6017

8 Station Rd, Low Fell NE9 6DR
e-mail: home@eslingtonvilla.co.uk
dir: off A1(M) exit for Team Valley Trading Estate. Right
at 2nd rdbt along Eastern Av. Left at car show room, hotel
100yds on left

Originally built for a Victorian industrialist, today's hotel
retains bags of features from the period. Surrounded by
two acres of gardens, it's a relaxed place to dine, with a
smart modern country-house look. Choose between the
light-and-airy conservatory or the more traditional mood
of the high-ceilinged restaurant, with its tartan-style
carpet and antler chandeliers. The kitchen takes a
straightforward, modern approach underpinned by a
classical theme and reliance on quality local ingredients.
Think Gressingham duck breast accompanied by
dauphinoise, spinach and a juniper berry sauce, or
perhaps stone bass served up with new potatoes, fine
beans and a lobster reduction. Predominantly nursery-
esque desserts, such as treacle tart, vie with the likes of
a vanilla pannacotta.

Chef Jamie Walsh **Owner** Mr & Mrs N Tulip
Times 12-2/5.30-9.45 Closed 25-26 Dec, 1 Jan, BHs
Prices Fixed L 2 course £13.95-£15.95, Fixed D 3 course
£24.95-£26.95, Service optional **Wines** 23 bottles over
£20, 22 bottles under £20, 8 by glass **Notes** Early bird D
2 or 3 course available 5.30-6.45, Sunday L, Vegetarian
menu **Seats** 80, Pr/dining room 30 **Children** Portions
Parking 30

NEWCASTLE UPON TYNE — Map 21 NZ26

Blackfriars Restaurant

◉ Traditional British ⊕

Confident cooking in an ancient monastic refectory

☎ 0191 261 5945

Friars St NE1 4XN
e-mail: info@blackfriarsrestaurant.co.uk
web: www.blackfriarsrestaurant.co.uk
dir: Take only small cobbled road off Stowell St (China
Town). Blackfriars 100yds on left

This highly atmospheric restaurant lays claim to being
the oldest in the country, originally used as a refectory by
Dominican friars...any advance on AD 1239? Brimful of
medieval charm, with stone walls, venerable timbers,
wood panelling and floors and carved wooden chairs, it's
an evocative space. The food has fast-forwarded the
centuries and comes fashioned from quality local
seasonal produce, with traditional Brit favourites sitting
alongside more contemporary thinking. Take hearty
braised Northumbrian beef shin served with glazed
carrots, red cabbage and horseradish mash, or lighter
North Sea halibut fillet teamed with chicken ballottine,
roasted celeriac and oyster mushrooms. Desserts might
include 'frutours' (medieval beer-battered apple fritters
with Horlicks ice cream) and bread-and-butter pudding
with peanut butter ice cream.

Chef Troy Terrington **Owner** Andy & Sam Hook
Times 12-2.30/5.30-12 Closed Good Fri & BHs, D Sun
Prices Fixed L 2 course £12, Starter £5-£11, Main £9-
£21, Dessert £5-£8, Service added but optional 10%
Wines 26 bottles over £20, 17 bottles under £20, 8 by
glass **Notes** Fixed menu available 5.30-7pm, Sunday L,

Save on Hotels. Book at **theAA.com/hotel**

TYNE & WEAR 465 ENGLAND

Vegetarian available, Civ Wed 50 **Seats** 80, Pr/dining room 50 **Children** Portions, Menu **Parking** Car park next to restaurant

Café 21 Newcastle

Modern British V

Modern bistro and bar by revamped quayside

☎ 0191 222 0755
Trinity Gardens, Quayside NE1 2HH
e-mail: enquiries@cafetwentyone.co.uk
dir: From Grey's Monument, S to Grey St & Dean St towards Quayside, left along the Quayside, 3rd left into Broad Chare. 1st right then 1st left into Trinity Gdns, restaurant on right

Terry Laybourne's glossy Café 21 in the heart of the regenerated quayside quarter remains a stalwart of the city's dynamic eating scene. The dining room looks as sharp as the suits from the law courts opposite who are attracted by its switched-on urban vibe and fashionably curvaceous banquettes, darkwood floors, classy glassware and crisp napery. The food sings in tune with the venue, which means modern British brasserie dishes driven by top-quality local produce. Classic French-based combinations sit cheek by jowl with Spanish, Italian and Asian influences, so crab salad is perked up with apple

and sweet Indian spices, while mains take in braised rabbit with mustard and noodles, or green curry with monkfish cheeks and tiger prawns. Wild Bolivian chocolate ganache with milk chocolate ice cream is a good way to finish.

Chef Chris Dobson **Owner** Terry Laybourne
Times 12-2.30/5.30-10.30 Closed 25-26 Dec, 1 Jan, Etr Mon, D 24 Dec **Prices** Fixed L 2 course fr £16.50, Fixed D 3 course fr £20, Starter £5.50-£14.50, Main £15.50-£29.80, Dessert £6.20-£9.20, Service added but optional 10% **Wines** 78 bottles over £20, 9 bottles under £20, 17 by glass **Notes** Fixed L/D 2/3 course available Mon-Fri D 5.30-7pm, Sunday L, Vegetarian menu **Seats** 90, Pr/dining room 40 **Children** Portions **Parking** NCP/Council

David Kennedy's Food Social

Modern British

Brasserie dining in a stylish commercial art gallery

☎ 0191 260 5411
The Biscuit Factory, 16 Stoddart St, Shieldfield NE2 1AN
e-mail: info@foodsocial.co.uk

The venue formerly known as the Black Door Brasserie may have a new name, but its fans will be relieved to know that the kitchen's ethos stays more or less the

same: the best, freshest - even foraged - local produce is treated simply to deliver cooking that is honest, generous and full of robust flavours. Located in the revived Biscuit Factory - home to Britain's largest art emporium - an arty theme is played out on the walls of the industrial heritage venue, an expansive open-plan space done out with beefy wooden tables, squishy leather chairs and warm colours beneath a lofty warehouse ceiling; friendly staff do their bit in keeping the buzzy, chatty vibe ticking along. Home-made black pudding with wilted greens, crispy onions and mustard dressing is a fine wintery starter; next up, monkfish appears in a more unusual partnership with braised mussels and a root vegetable vinaigrette, before a dessert that neatly contrasts the sharpness of blood orange and rhubarb with a perfectly-made, well-flavoured vanilla pannacotta, and a vanilla sablé biscuit.

Times 12-3/7 10 Closed 25-26 Dec, D Sun

Jesmond Dene House

Modern British, European

Dazzling, innovative food in a splendid Georgian house

☎ 0191 212 3000
Jesmond Dene Rd NE2 2EY
e-mail: info@jesmonddenehouse.co.uk
dir: From city centre follow A167 to junct with A184. Turn right towards Matthew Bank. Turn right into Jesmond Dene Rd

The handsome house, built by Lord Armstrong in the 1820s, was intended to impress and continues to do so in the 21st century - this place has bags of style. He chose a lovely spot, His Lordship, just a short distance from the city but basking in splendid isolation, and it makes the perfect setting for a luxury hotel and restaurant. Inside, elegant original Arts and Crafts features coexist with

well-chosen furniture and fabrics, and the service team ensure that Jesmond Dene maintains its place at the top table. There are two dining areas: the former music room and the light and bright garden room, with its lovely fair-weather terrace. There's a pleasing lack of stuffiness all round, and although it's very smart, there's a genuine sense of bonhomie. Head chef Michael Penaluna takes all the right steps to ensure the produce is second to none, and local where possible, and is adept at letting the flavours speak for themselves. There is refinement, creativity and skill in the execution of dishes, such as a fashionable first course partnership of creel-caught langoustines and roast belly pork, with apple fondant and kohlrabi, or East Coast cockle and clam risotto, with a Laphroaig single malt whisky sauce. Next up, Goosnargh duck comes with gomashio (a Japanese condiment of toasted salted sesame seeds), braised lettuce and orange, and to finish, flavours are once again balanced with precision: rhubarb jelly with vanilla bavarois, for example, with champagne granité and vanilla ice cream.

The excellent wine list gives a good showing by the glass and carafe.

Chef Michael Penaluna **Owner** Peter Candler, Tony Ganley
Times 12-2/7-9.30 **Prices** Fixed L 2 course £16.95-£19.95, Fixed D 3 course fr £28, Starter £13.50-£17.50, Main £15.50-£35, Dessert £4-£10.50, Service added but optional 10% **Wines** 203 bottles over £20, 6 bottles under £20, 17 by glass **Notes** Tasting menu available, Sunday L, Vegetarian available, Dress restrictions, Smart casual, Civ Wed 100 **Seats** 80, Pr/dining room 24 **Children** Portions, Menu **Parking** 64

NEWCASTLE UPON TYNE *continued*

Hotel du Vin Newcastle

◎◎ British, French ♨ 🍴

Stylish urban French bistro dining in designer hotel

☎ 0191 229 2200
Allan House, City Rd NE1 2BE
e-mail: reception.newcastle@hotelduvin.com
dir: A1 junct 65 slip road to A184 Gateshead/Newcastle,
Quayside to City Rd

The Newcastle offshoot of the HdV chain conforms to the
brand's values with its stylish reworking of a character-
laden old building, in this case the red-brick Edwardian
warehouse of the Tyne Tees Steamship Company. The
riverside location puts it in pole position for shopping and
taking in the city's arts and cultural attractions, with
glorious urban landscapes along the Tyne to the iconic
arching bridge as a backdrop. True to house style, the
restaurant sports the trademark retro French bistro look,
while the kitchen hauls in Northumberland's fine produce
as the basis of its please-all modern brasserie repertoire
- slow-cooked duck leg with wild mushrooms and Puy
lentil jus, or roast cod with chorizo, butter beans, chilli
and lemon are typical main course ideas. As is always the
case in a Hotel du Vin, you can bank on a superb wine list
of intelligently-chosen bottles that casts its net wide for
quality drinking, with an expert sommelier on hand.

Chef Stuart Donaldson **Owner** MWB Holdings PLC
Times 12-2/6-10 Closed L 1 Jan, D 25 Dec **Prices** Food
prices not confirmed for 2013. Please telephone for
details **Wines** 370 bottles over £20, 9 bottles under £20,
20 by glass **Notes** Vegetarian available, Civ Wed 80, Air
con **Seats** 86, Pr/dining room 22 **Children** Portions
Parking On street

Jesmond Dene House

◎◎◎ – *see page 465*

Malmaison Newcastle

◎ French, British

Brasserie dining in a quayside setting

☎ 0191 245 5000
Quayside NE1 3DX
e-mail: newcastle@malmaison.com
dir: Follow signs for city centre, then for Quayside/Law
Courts. Hotel 100yds past Law Courts

In a former warehouse on the lively quayside, Newcastle's
'Mal' enjoys a prime location on the River Tyne with views
of the blinking Millennium Bridge. The trendy boutique
hotel chain's set-up works a treat here, with the public
areas decked out in the multi-textural tones of deep reds
and purples. Moody lighting in the bar sets the scene for
a cocktail or something from the impressive wine list,
taken seated at a purple velvet bar stool or tucked away
in a velvet booth. The brasserie is typically relaxed and
informal with the closely-packed tables leading to a
happy hum, especially in the evening. Straightforward
classics make the most of Northumberland's fine larder;

Scotch quail's egg and bacon salad with piccalilli
vinaigrette is one way to start, followed by Herdwick
mutton masala with pilaf rice and naan bread, or, from
the grill, lobster with garlic butter, herb aïoli and fries.
Baked New York cheesecake and blueberries is a fitting
finish.

Times 12-2.30/6-11

Pan Haggerty Restaurant

◎ Modern British **NEW**

Classic British and more in relaxed quayside restaurant

☎ 0191 221 0904
21 Queen St NE1 3UG
e-mail: info@panhaggerty.com

Named after a classic Northumbrian dish, and with an
impeccable Tyneside address, this restaurant off
Newcastle's bustling quayside serves up British classics
with a bit of modish va-va-voom. It's a suitably
unpretentious place, with masculine tones (darkwood
floors and tables, brown leather chairs and banquettes),
chilled-out service, and the gentle beat of background
music. On the menu, there are classics such as beer-
battered fish and thick-cut chips, or something more à la
mode such as a first-course dish of seared scallop with
confit pork cheek, squash fondant and purée. End on a
high with apple and winter berry crumble with Calvados
custard, or a selection of five British cheeses with home-
made chutney.

Chef Kelvin Linstead **Owner** Craig Potts, Mike Morely
Times 12-2.30/5.30-9.30 Closed 25-26 & 31 Dec, 1 Jan,
BHs, D Sun **Prices** Fixed L 2 course £10–£14.95, Fixed D 3
course £17.95, Starter £5.95–£9.50, Main £13.95–£20.50,
Dessert £4.95–£7.95, Service added but optional 10%
Wines 28 bottles over £20, 9 bottles under £20, 7 by
glass **Notes** Fixed D Mon-Fri, 5.30-7pm, Sat 5-6.30pm,
Sunday L, Vegetarian available **Seats** 65
Children Portions **Parking** On street, NCP

Sangreela Indian Restaurant

◎ Indian, Bangladeshi V 🍴

Indian and Bangladeshi cooking in smart venue

☎ 0191 266 2777 & 266 2444
North View House, Front St, Four Lane Ends NE7 7XF
e-mail: managementofsangreela@gmail.com

Converted from old stables, Sangreela still has a high
vaulted ceiling and some exposed brick walls, but the
comfort factor is high with well-spaced tables set with
candles and flowers. The menu sets out the restaurant's
credentials: it serves the traditional cuisines from India
and Bangladesh, with top-quality ingredients either local
or flown in. The long menu (over 200 items) takes in
starters from sas ni machli (herbed and spiced tuna
kebab) to Bengali roast potatoes with spicy chicken tikka,
with main courses running from lamb masala or naram
duck (breast cooked with yoghurt and pistachios
garnished with spiced honey) to chingri saag wala
(prawns cooked with spinach, garlic, ginger, herbs and
spices).

Chef Nazim Khan **Owner** Nazim Khan
Times 12-2/4.30-11.30 Closed L Fri-Sat **Prices** Fixed L 2
course £10–£25, Fixed D 3 course £95, Starter £5.90–
£9.90, Main £8.90-£24.90, Dessert £2.90-£5.90, Service
added but optional 10% **Wines** 22 bottles over £20,
8 bottles under £20 **Notes** Sunday L, Vegetarian menu,
Dress restrictions, No T-shirts **Seats** 135
Children Portions, Menu **Parking** 16

WARWICKSHIRE

ALCESTER   Map 10 SP05

Essence

◎ Modern British

Unfussy cooking in a friendly modern bistro

☎ 01789 762764
50 Birmingham Rd B49 5EP
e-mail: info@eatatessence.co.uk
dir: From town centre towards Birmingham & M42.
Restaurant is opposite Alcester Grammar School

The columned frontage of this former cottage catches the
eye along the main road leading into the small market
town of Alcester, and once inside Essence presents a
clean-cut contemporary look that blends 17th-century
oak beams with modern art on cream walls, and leather
chairs at darkwood tables. The vibe is the relaxed,
friendly bustle of a well-loved neighbourhood eatery with
easygoing, uncomplicated modern cooking to go with the
surroundings. A terrine of pork and local game with
spiced pear chutney has all the advertised flavours
singing in tune, while main-course sea bass is accurately
cooked and matched with a tomato and borlotti bean
'cassoulet'. Finish with warm pineapple tarte Tatin with
coconut sorbet.

Chef Chris Short **Owner** Chris Short **Times** 10-3/6.30-10
Closed Mon, D Sun **Prices** Fixed L 2 course £9.95, Fixed D
3 course £17.50, Starter £5.50–£9.75, Main £11.50-
£19.95, Dessert £6-£8.50, Service optional
Wines 20 bottles over £20, 11 bottles under £20, 5 by
glass **Notes** Fixed price menu L & D Tue-Sat, Sunday L,
Vegetarian available **Seats** 50 **Children** Portions, Menu
Parking 19

ALDERMINSTER   Map 10 SP24

Ettington Park Hotel

◎◎ Traditional British V 🍴

Confident cooking in a grandiose mansion

☎ 01789 450123
CV37 8BU
e-mail: ettingtonpark@handpicked.co.uk
dir: M40 junct 15/A46 towards Stratford-upon-Avon, then
A439 into town centre onto A3400 5m to Shipston. Hotel
0.5m on left

Squirrelled away in 40 acres of parkland and gardens
just a few miles outside Stratford-upon-Avon, and with a
history-steeped interior chock-full of antiques and
artworks, neo-Gothic Ettington Park certainly puts on a

Save on Hotels. Book at theAA.com/hotel

WARWICKSHIRE 467 ENGLAND

grand face. It could be intimidating, but terrific service from keen and chatty staff dispel any hint of stuffiness. Resplendent with family heraldry, the aptly-named Oak Room is the imposing setting for a repertoire of honest, unshouty modern ideas built on sound traditionalist foundations. As an opening gambit, a pressed terrine of confit duck and foie gras with balsamic dressing is right on target, while a pan-seared fillet of wild sea bass is served alongside new potatoes, confit orange fennel and sauce vierge. Just the ticket, too, is a distinguished dessert of Worcestershire pear and almond tart with vanilla sauce and Poire William ice cream.

Chef Gary Lissemore **Owner** Hand Picked Hotels **Times** 12-2/7-9.30 Closed L Mon-Fri **Prices** Food prices not confirmed for 2013. Please telephone for details **Wines** 52 bottles over £20, 6 bottles under £20, 12 by glass **Notes** Sunday L, Vegetarian menu **Seats** 50, Pr/dining room 80 **Children** Portions, Menu **Parking** 80

ANSTY · Map 11 SP48

Macdonald Ansty Hall

🏵 British 🍷

Tried-and-tested modern dishes not far from Stratford

☎ 0844 879 9031
Main Rd CV7 9HZ
e-mail: ansty@macdonald-hotels.co.uk
dir: M6/M69 junct 2 through Ansty village approx 1.5m

The handsome, three-storey, red-brick house standing in eight acres of landscaped greenery is a short hop from the year-round bardolatry at Stratford-on-Avon. It boasts a properly elegant dining room, the Shilton, with crisp linen and ravishing views of Warwickshire through lushly draped windows, where a menu of bright modern dishes is on offer. Pigeon breast with black pudding, toasted pine nuts and watercress could be the preamble to salmon with buttered kale, or braised shoulder of lamb with root veg and mash, and then treacle tart garnished with a roasted fig and clotted cream to conclude. Local cheeses come with red onion and cranberry chutney.

Chef Paul Kitchener **Owner** Macdonald Hotels **Times** 12.30-2.30/6.30-9.30 Closed D 25 Dec **Prices** Food prices not confirmed for 2013. Please telephone for details **Wines** 57 bottles over £20, 3 bottles under £20, 12 by glass **Notes** Sunday L, Vegetarian available, Dress restrictions, Smart casual, Civ Wed 100 **Seats** 60, Pr/dining room 40 **Children** Portions, Menu **Parking** 100

ATHERSTONE · Map 10 SP39

Chapel House Restaurant With Rooms

🏵 British, French 🍷

Elegant surroundings for French-accented cooking

☎ 01827 718949
Friar's Gate CV9 1EY
e-mail: info@chapelhouse.eu
dir: Off Market Sq in Atherstone, behind High St

This gracious 18th-century dower house to the now-demolished Atherstone Hall once put up Florence Nightingale on her visits to its owners who funded her trip to the Crimea. Trading these days as a restaurant with rooms, Chapel House is squirrelled away in a secluded walled garden on the market square, and comes with oodles of period character in its elegant Georgian dining room, where classic French-accented cuisine is the order of the day. Built on soundly-sourced ingredients, and gently updated for contemporary tastes, the menu could open with rabbit and olive terrine with melba toast, then progress to a showing of local Grendon lamb loin in port, orange and redcurrant sauce, or an admirable pairing of turbot and oysters, the former served in a white wine, tomato and herb sauce, and the latter in the form of a gratin, and florentine-style with spinach. Round things off with a sautéed apple and rum-soaked raisin-filled crêpe with sweet cider sauce.

Chef Richard Henry Napper **Owner** Richard & Siobhan Napper **Times** 7-9.30 Closed 24 Dec-3 Jan, Etr wk, late Aug-early Sep, Sun, L unless booked in advance **Prices** Food prices not confirmed for 2013. Please telephone for details **Wines** 61 bottles over £20, 44 bottles under £20, 9 by glass **Notes** Vegetarian available, Dress restrictions, Smart casual **Seats** 24, Pr/dining room 12 **Children** Portions **Parking** On street

HENLEY-IN-ARDEN · Map 10 SP16

The Bluebell

🏵🏵 British **NEW** 🍷

Highly polished cooking in a Tudor coaching inn

☎ 01564 793049
93 High St B95 5AT
e-mail: info@bluebellhenley.co.uk
dir: M4 junct 4, A3400 (Stratford Rd) to Henley-in-Arden

The timbered front of this Tudor coaching inn speaks of its venerability, and although the interiors have been freshened up, the design job hasn't overwhelmed the intrinsic character of the place. The original beams and fireplaces, and the flagstone floor, are all present and correct, the waft of Michael Bublé on the sound system more a matter of taste. The cooking works within the grain of modern British thinking, bringing some very polished classical technique to the broadly-based repertoire. Dishes are cleverly thought out, so that even the relatively familiar can come as a revelation. A slab of duck and green peppercorn terrine offers the contrasts of rich meat, sweet cabbage and sharp peppercorns, offset by the juice of a poached pear accompaniment, the whole

supported by a gently warming honey and mustard dressing. Fish is accurately timed and seasoned, as in the fillet of cod that comes with a razor sharp caper butter sauce. Two servings of local lamb with sweet-and-sour peppers in olive and rosemary jus is the kind of meat dish to expect. At dessert, the Valrhona chocolate brownie with salt caramel, candied pecans and banana ice cream is a surefire bet.

Chef Simon Malin **Owner** Leigh & Duncan Taylor **Times** 12-2.30/6-9.30 Closed Mon, D Sun **Prices** Fixed L 2 course fr £15, Fixed D 3 course fr £18, Starter £5.50-£8, Main £13-£19, Dessert £6-£6.75, Service optional **Wines** 12 bottles over £20, 13 bottles under £20, 12 by glass **Notes** Sunday L, Vegetarian available, Dress restrictions, Smart casual **Seats** 46, Pr/dining room 10 **Children** Portions **Parking** 20

LEA MARSTON · Map 10 SP29

Lea Marston Hotel & Spa

🏵🏵 Modern British

Modern cooking in a golf and spa hotel

☎ 01675 470468
Haunch Ln B76 0BY
e-mail: info@leamarstonhotel.co.uk
web: www.leamarstonhotel.co.uk
dir: From M42 junct 9/A4097 signed Kingsbury Hotel, 2nd turning right into Haunch Lane. Hotel 200yds on right

Handy for all that Brum has to offer, yet feeling away from it all in 54 acres of north Warwickshire countryside, the modern Lea Marston Hotel has a golf course and spa by way of pursuits and a good eating option in the shape of The Adderley Restaurant. Decked out in shades of aubergine and grey, it's a swish, modish space for some breezy contemporary food. Black pudding and bacon terrine, comes with a quail's egg and mesclun salad and makes a fine precursor to shin of beef served with an oxtail faggot, parsley root and truffle mash, or go for duck three ways - confit leg, liver, breast - with braised cabbage and liquorice jus. Finish with a boozy chocolate and vodka parfait partnered with a blood orange sorbet.

Chef Richard Marshall **Owner** Blake Family **Times** 1-3/7-9 Closed L Mon-Sat, D Sun **Prices** Food prices not confirmed for 2013. Please telephone for details **Notes** Sunday L, Vegetarian available, Dress restrictions, Smart casual, Civ Wed 100 **Seats** , Pr/dining room 120 **Children** Portions, Menu **Parking** 220

The Brasserie at Mallory Court

🏵🏵 Modern British V 🖐

The simpler dining option in opulent Mallory Court

☎ 01926 453939 & 330214
Harbury Ln, Bishop's Tachbrook CV33 9QB
e-mail: thebrasserie@mallory.co.uk
web: www.mallory.co.uk
dir: M40 junct 13 N'bound left, left again towards
Bishop's Tachbrook, right onto Harbury Ln after 0.5m.
M40 junct 14 S'bound A452 to Leamington, at 2nd rdbt
left onto Harbury Ln

Mallory Court may be known for its opulent fine-dining in
the main restaurant (see separate entry), but when you
want something more casual and wallet-friendly, The
Brasserie is the place to head for. Inspired by the sleek
lines of art-eco style, it is a thoroughly glammed-up
operation: cool jazz floats around the glossy cocktail bar,
while the dining area works smart tones of coffee and
cream matched with high-backed Lloyd Loom chairs and
blond-wood floors. What the kitchen offers is very much in
tune with modern times: straightforward brasserie
classics tweaked with international accents - perhaps
mackerel kebab teamed with tempura squid and spiced
ratatouille, or confit duck pastilla with roasted pak choi
and sesame dressing. Mains continue the unfussy mood,
delivering pan-roasted pork fillet with prunes, tagliatelle
and Calvados sauce, or pan-fried mullet with smoked eel
risotto, braised chicory and sautéed baby squid. Finish
with something simple such as chocolate mousse with
orange sorbet.

Chef Simon Haigh, Jim Russell **Owner** Sir Peter Rigby
Times 12-2.30/6.30-9.30 Closed D Sun **Prices** Fixed L 2
course fr £15, Starter £4.25-£6.75, Main £12.50-£18.50,
Dessert £5.85, Service optional **Wines** 60 bottles over
£20, 2 bottles under £20, 10 by glass **Notes** Sunday L,
Vegetarian menu, Civ Wed 160 **Seats** 80, Pr/dining room
24 **Children** Portions, Menu **Parking** 100

Mallory Court Hotel

🏵🏵🏵 – *see opposite*

Restaurant 23 & Morgan's Bar

🏵🏵 Modern European 🖐

Imaginative modern dishes in plush new premises

☎ 01926 422422
34 Hamilton Ter CV32 4LY
e-mail: info@restaurant23.co.uk
dir: M40 junct 13 onto A452 towards Leamington Spa.
Follow signs for town centre, just off Holly Walk, next to
police station

Peter Knibb's neighbourhood Leamington eatery has
moved to a new neighbourhood. Plush new premises in a
listed Victorian building are where to find him now (only
about five minutes from the original address, in fact). The
ground-floor dining room with contemporary chandeliers
opens on to a courtyard for open-air dining, while
upstairs a stylish lounge bar, Morgan's, serves up
sophisticated mixology to the cocktail cognoscenti. The
Knibb culinary style, which explores modern British
experimentalism with plenty of freshness and
imagination, has survived the removals intact. Dishes are
built up of many elements into harmonious, workable
compositions, as when a roasted quail to start is spiced
in ras el hanout, along with apricot and pistachio and a
black pudding bonbon. At main course, a swashbuckling
approach to fish finds sea bass partnered with sautéed
chorizo and squid, as well as leeks and white coco beans,
while roasted duck breast comes with smoked onion
purée and a spring roll of the confit leg. Pause for breath
for 20 minutes, and await the creation of a pear and
rosemary tarte Tatin, served with salted caramel mousse
and pear sorbet.

Chef Peter Knibb **Owner** Peter & Antje Knibb, Richard
Steeves **Times** 12-2/6.15-9.45 Closed 25-26 Dec, 1 Jan, D
Sun **Prices** Fixed L 2 course £15, Fixed D 3 course £25,
Tasting menu £60, Starter £8.50-£14, Main £17-£27,
Dessert £7.50-£12, Service optional, Groups min 7 service
10% **Wines** 120 bottles over £20, 14 bottles under £20, 7
by glass **Notes** Sunday L, Vegetarian available **Seats** 65,
Pr/dining room 16 **Parking** On street opposite

Save on Hotels. Book at theAA.com/hotel

WARWICKSHIRE 469 ENGLAND

Mallory Court Hotel

Modern British V ☺

Creative cooking in a creeper-clad mansion

☎ 01926 330214
Harbury Ln, Bishop's Tachbrook CV33 9QB
e-mail: reception@mallory.co.uk
web: www.mallory.co.uk
dir: M40 junct 13 N'bound. Left, left again towards Bishop's Tachbrook. 0.5m, right into Harbury Ln. M40 junct 14 S'bound, A452 for Leamington. At 2nd rdbt left into Harbury Ln

The entrance is certainly impressive: you approach the creeper-clad manor along an immaculate drive to draw up at an apparently ancient manor house with gables and mullioned windows secluded in 10 acres of lovely gardens. But Mallory isn't as old as it looks, as it was built at the dawn of the 20th century for a cotton magnate, and those primped gardens also serve a more utilitarian end, supplying the kitchen with seasonal herbs, fruit and veg. The oak-panelled dining room offers an unquestionably refined setting for the hotel's fine-dining experience, which purrs along like a well-oiled engine thanks to the efforts of a switched-on front-of-house team. Views across the manicured grounds to a backdrop of rolling Warwickshire countryside get even better when fine weather allows

you outdoors to dine on the terrace. The kitchen has honed a highly-polished culinary style which is rather more in touch with the experimental British idiom than the surroundings might suggest. A well-tuned feel for intricacy and contrast, bolstered by the confidence to bring in unusual ingredients shows in, say, ballottine of rabbit with a salad of carrots and brown beech mushrooms, and violet mustard ice cream. Flavours are kept at full throttle in main courses such as roast medallions of pepper-crusted monkfish with basil gnocchi and confit tomato, and meaty ideas that could see braised and rolled shin, textures of shallots, and red wine sauce supporting a pan-roasted fillet of Dexter beef. There is also plenty of skill and artistry at dessert stage - perhaps hot gingerbread soufflé paired with Granny Smith apple sorbet, or an inventive composition of rhubarb and yoghurt cannelloni, pistachio crumble, and Advocaat ice cream. The wine list has something for all occasions, and there's also a less formal brasserie (see separate entry).

Chef Simon Haigh, Andrew Scott
Owner Sir Peter Rigby
Times 12-1.45/6.30-8.45 Closed L Sat
Prices Fixed D 3 course £45-£59.50, Tasting menu £59-£79, Service optional **Wines** 200 bottles over £20, 2 bottles under £20, 12 by glass
Notes Tasting menu 7 course, Sunday

L, Vegetarian menu, Dress restrictions, No jeans or sportswear **Seats** 56, Pr/dining room 14 **Children** Portions, Menu **Parking** 100

The Red Lion

◉ Traditional British

Tip-top Cotswold produce in a charming pub

☎ 01608 684221
Main St, Long Compton CV36 5JJ
e-mail: info@redlion-longcompton.co.uk
dir: 5m S on A3400

The nearby Roll Right Stones and some folklore regarding witches means there's plenty to ponder whilst sipping a pint of real ale at the bar of The Red Lion. Built as a coaching inn way back in 1748, the Grade II listed freehouse has a traditional interior of oak beams and inglenook fireplaces, plus some comfy leather armchairs to sink into. You can eat in the bar or the restaurant area that leads out onto a patio. Daily specials are chalked on the board to subsidise the frequently-changing menu; curried whitebait, mango and spring onion salad comes with minted yoghurt, followed by slow-cooked gammon with bubble-and-squeak, soft-poached egg and mustard hollandaise, with raspberry and toasted hazelnut Pavlova and raspberry sauce to finish. There's a good children's menu too.

Times 12-2.30/6-9

The Arden Hotel

◉◉ Modern British

Smart hotel brasserie opposite the RSC

☎ 01789 298682
Waterside CV37 6BA
e-mail: enquiries@theardenhotelstratford.com
web: www.theardenhotelstratford.com

The riverside location is hard to beat, and having the world-famous RSC Theatre across the road means that there's always real buzz about the Arden's Waterside Brasserie, as visiting luvvies and aficionados of the Bard rub shoulders over a glass of bubbly in the Champagne bar. The hotel has splashed serious money on a chic revamp, turning the Waterside into a thoroughly modern space kitted out with leather tub seats, trendy patterned wallpaper and hues of plum and caramel; seats overlooking the river have year-round attraction, and for balmy months there's an alfresco terrace. The kitchen delivers waves of invention and well-honed technique while keeping an eye to quality local seasonal produce. Crispy breast of Lighthorne lamb is served with its sweetbreads and a slather of olive tapenade and parsley, setting the tone for what is to follow - pan-roasted fillet of cod with vanilla foam arrives with confit fennel, samphire, choucroute and new potatoes, and to finish there's a dark Tanzanian chocolate tart with white chocolate cream and honeycomb.

Times 12-5

Billesley Manor Hotel

◉◉ Modern European

Traditional Anglo-French cooking in Tudor manor house

☎ 01789 279955
Billesley, Alcester B49 6NF
e-mail: billesleymanor@pumahotels.co.uk
dir: M40 junct 15, A46S towards Evesham. Over 3 rdbts, right for Billesley after 2m

Billesley Manor is a charm-laden mellow-stone Tudor mansion dating from Shakespeare's day. Set in 11 acres of well-preened grounds, including a striking topiary garden and fountain, it was built to impress. The panelled, classically appointed Stuart Restaurant fits the quintessential English country-house hotel setting - all carpeted comfort with rich colours and white linen-dressed tables. The kitchen's seasonally-informed menus take an appropriately classic approach, showcasing clean-cut flavours and Anglo-French style with a nod to modern trends and presentation. Go for slow-cooked belly of pork served with mash potato, glazed apples and crisp black pudding, Chantenay carrots and an apple cider jus, or maybe chargrilled breast of free-range chicken with thyme potato pressing, slow-cooked tomato and cracked black peppercorn cream. Finish on a light note with vanilla pannacotta, poached rhubarb, ginger bavarois and shortbread.

Chef Ales Maurer **Owner** Puma Hotels
Times 12.30-2/7-9.30 **Prices** Fixed L 3 course £14.95-£25, Fixed D 3 course fr £39.50, Starter fr £8.75, Main fr £22, Dessert fr £8.75, Service optional **Wines** 39 bottles over £20, 5 bottles under £20, 12 by glass **Notes** Sunday L, Vegetarian available, Dress restrictions, Smart casual, Civ Wed 75 **Seats** 42, Pr/dining room 100
Children Portions, Menu **Parking** 100

The Legacy Falcon Hotel

◉ British

Creative modern cooking in updated old hotel

☎ 0844 411 9005
Chapel St CV37 6HA
e-mail: res-falcon@legacy-hotels.co.uk
dir: M40 junct 15, follow town centre signs towards Barclays Bank on rdbt. Turn into High Street, between Austin Reed & WH Smith. Turn 2nd right into Scholars Lane & right again into hotel

The Falcon, in the town centre not far from the theatre and the river, is a timbered building that blends in well with Stratford's other old properties - if you ignore the modern block built on the back. The old-world theme has been carried through successfully into the restaurant, a richly carpeted room with beams and some exposed-stone walls. The cooking is ambitious enough to please both the eye and the palate (and satisfy the stomach) without resorting to fancy twirls or twists, and it trades in the modern style of terrine of ham hock, chicken and white pudding, served with pickled vegetables, and three crisply fried salmon and cod fishcakes with a chilli dressing. Roast chicken breast, moist and succulent, wrapped in bacon, is an impressive main course, complemented by chorizo, pea and spring onion risotto, with well-made lemon tart to finish.

Times 12.30-2/6-9

Macdonald Alveston Manor

◉ Modern British

Deft modern cooking in an ancient manor-house hotel

☎ 01789 205478
Clopton Bridge CV37 7HP
e-mail: events.alvestonmanor@macdonald-hotels.co.uk
dir: 6m from M40 junct 15, (on edge of town) across Clopton Bridge towards Banbury

Happily, historic Alveston Manor - set in primped grounds with the scent of closely-mown lawns - hasn't lost all its Tudor-house charm since its hotel makeover. The story its cedar tree was the backdrop for the debut performance of *A Midsummer Night's Dream* will excite those drawn to the area in pursuit of things Shakespearean, while the Manor Restaurant does not let the side down with its traditional charms (original oak beams and timbers, mullioned windows and candlelight). Granted it's an old-school setting, but the kitchen's smartly executed British cooking has a decidedly modern spin. Pan-fried wild halibut fillet, for example, comes with shrimp butter, roasted langoustine and new potatoes, and pan-roasted free-range chicken with fondant potato and a chorizo and broad bean casserole.

Chef Paul Harris **Owner** Macdonald Hotels plc
Times 6-9.30 Closed L all week **Prices** Food prices not confirmed for 2013. Please telephone for details
Wines 69 bottles over £20, 15 by glass **Notes** Pre-theatre menu available, Vegetarian available, Civ Wed 140
Seats 110, Pr/dining room 40 **Children** Portions, Menu
Parking 120

Save on Hotels. Book at **theAA.com/hotel**

WARWICKSHIRE 471 **ENGLAND**

Menzies Welcombe Hotel Spa & Golf Course

◉◉ Modern, Traditional

Confident cooking in a grand Victorian house

☎ 01789 295252
Warwick Rd CV37 0NR
e-mail: welcombe@menzieshotels.co.uk
dir: M40 junct 15, A46 towards Stratford-upon-Avon, at rdbt follow signs for A439. Hotel 3m on right

Built in the mid-Victorian era to a Jacobean template, the Welcombe commands over 150 acres of grounds. Kitted out now with modern amenities such as spa treatments and an indoor pool, it's a gratifying hotel package. An expansive dining room with its high ceilings and crisp table napery enjoys appetising views over the lawns, and staff deliver assured, accomplished service. The modern British cooking has acquired a certain complexity over recent years, so that rabbit and black pudding ballottine may be accompanied by pickled baby carrots, raisins, pine nuts and capers, all dressed in extra-virgin olive oil, before braised shoulder, liver and kidney of local hill lamb might come with marquise potato and pea purée in a tomato and marjoram jus, or sea trout with crayfish and mascarpone and caper risotto dressed in lemon oil.

Chef Dean Griffin **Owner** Menzies Hotels
Times 12.30-2/7-9.30 Closed L Sat **Prices** Food prices not confirmed for 2013. Please telephone for details **Wines** 89 bottles over £20, 6 bottles under £20, 22 by glass **Notes** Pre-theatre D menu available from 5.30pm, Sunday L, Vegetarian available, Dress restrictions, Smart casual, no sportswear or ripped jeans **Seats** 70, Pr/dining room 150 **Children** Portions, Menu **Parking** 150

Mercure Shakespeare

◉ British, European

Modish cooking in historic Tudor building

☎ 01789 294997
Chapel St CV37 6ER
e-mail: h6630@accor.com
dir: Follow signs to town centre. Round one-way system, into Bridge St. At rdbt turn left. Hotel 200yds on left

Good for getting in the Tudor mood on a visit to Stratford-upon-Avon, this historic timbered hotel is one of the oldest in town, and wears its age well after a modern spruce-up has juxtaposed a clean-cut contemporary look with its venerable beams. Othello's Brasserie is a contemporary space warmed by the glow of a real fire in winter, with a friendly and relaxed ambience to go with a straightforward European-accented menu. Expect starters along the lines of seared scallops with black pudding, quail's egg and vanilla and apple purée, followed by pan-fried sea bass served with crushed new potatoes, hollandaise sauce and dill. Pudding might offer a play on apple involving compôte, soup, crisp apple tuile and cinnamon mascarpone.

Chef Marc Ward **Owner** Mercure Hotels **Times** 12-10 **Prices** Food prices not confirmed for 2013. Please telephone for details **Wines** 22 bottles over £20, 16 bottles under £20, 15 by glass **Notes** Vegetarian available **Seats** 80, Pr/dining room 90 **Children** Portions, Menu **Parking** 31, NCP nearby

THURLASTON   Map 11 SP47

Draycote Hotel

◉ Modern, International

Modern golf hotel with contemporary cooking

☎ 01788 521800
London Rd CV23 9LF
e-mail: mail@draycotehotel.co.uk
dir: M1 junct 17 onto M45/A45. Hotel 500mtrs on left

The modern Draycote Hotel is any golf buff's dream destination, with its championship 18-hole course right beside the beautiful Draycote Water reservoir. What's more, the hotel offers some good eating in the form of the Papaveri restaurant, a contemporary space with a friendly, relaxed vibe. There's a traditional carvery on Sundays, and during the rest of the week the modern menu offers the likes of smoked haddock fishcake with dressed leaves and a mature cheddar cheese sauce to start, followed by slow-roasted lamb shank with mash, caramelised onion and minted sauce, or pan-fried fillet of black bream with egg noodles and Asian-style dressing. Warm dark chocolate brownie with mint ice cream and lemon tart are typical desserts.

Times 7-9.30

WARWICK   Map 10 SP26

Ardencote Manor Hotel, Country Club & Spa

◉ Modern European

Ambitious cooking by a lake

☎ 01926 843111
The Cumsey, Lye Green Rd CV35 8LT
e-mail: hotel@ardencote.com
web: www.ardencote.com
dir: Off A4189. In Claverdon follow signs for Shrewley & brown tourist signs for Ardencote Manor, approx 1.5m

The Lodge, a short stroll from the hotel itself, is in a splendid location by a lake, with lovely views of the grounds. It's a high-ceilinged room with a stone fireplace, done out in contemporary style, with an unbuttoned atmosphere. A vein of experimentation runs through the cooking, the kitchen producing a starter of smoked beef cheek with watercress pannacotta, potato crisps, pickled onions and onion purée, then seared tuna steak with octopus carpaccio, sautéed squid, pak choi and crisp rice. Good ingredients are put to use, and presentation is a strength, as seen in the likes of goats' cheese mousse served with intense-tasting roast tomatoes dressed with balsamic, and an accurately fried fillet of zander sauced with salsa verde, accompanied by sweet, tender clams in tomato broth.

Times 6-10 Closed L all week ex by request

WELLESBOURNE   Map 10 SP25

Walton Hall

◉◉ British ❀

Contemporary cooking in a grand dining room

☎ 01789 842424
Walton CV35 9HU
dir: A429 through Bradford towards Wellesbourne, right after watermill, follow signs to hotel

Walton Hall is a huge stately pile beside a lake within 65 acres of grounds. The restaurant, overlooking the gardens, can't help but engender a sense of grandeur, with its high ceiling, chandeliers, drapes, crisp napery, and uniformed, obliging staff. The kitchen displays lots of imagination and flair, basing its modern ideas on classical foundations. Salmon terrine with horseradish, celeriac and caviar is an impressively successful starter, as is confit duck and foie gras with smoked duck breast and prune purée. Main courses are as appealing: a plate of pork served simply with squash, capers and sultanas, and well-timed fillet of sea bream partnered by crab mousse, mussels and spinach. The signature passionfruit soufflé with coconut ice cream is on the money.

Chef Darren Long **Times** 7-9.30 **Prices** Food prices not confirmed for 2013. Please telephone for details **Wines** 53 bottles over £20, 7 bottles under £20, 10 by glass **Notes** Vegetarian available, Dress restrictions, Smart casual, Civ Wed 170 **Seats** 60, Pr/dining room 40 **Children** Portions, Menu **Parking** 240

WEST MIDLANDS

BALSALL COMMON   Map 10 SP27

Oak Room

◉ Modern European

Traditional and modern in a 17th-century house

☎ 024 7646 6174
Nailcote Hall Hotel, Nailcote Ln, Berkswell CV7 7DE
e-mail: info@nailcotehall.co.uk
dir: On B4101 towards Tile Hill/Coventry, 10 mins from
NEC/Birmingham Airport

A half-timbered 17th-century house sitting in 15 acres of
Warwickshire, Nailcote Hall became a hotel in 1990. It's a
country house on a human scale, not far from the
Midlands business hubs, and there's a golf course on
hand. The low-ceilinged Oak Room restaurant with its
inglenook fireplace and darkwood tables provides an
atmospheric ambience in the evenings especially, when a
resourceful repertoire of traditional British and more
modern dishes is tried out. You might begin with well-
seasoned asparagus velouté with a parmesan gougère
and hazelnut oil, before tackling tender loin of
venison with spiced caramelised red cabbage and roast
celeriac, finishing with prune and Armagnac soufflé with
Earl Grey ice cream.

Chef Neil Peers, Matthew Wiltshire **Owner** Richard
Cressman **Times** 12-2.30/7-9.30 Closed L Sat
Prices Fixed L 2 course £16.50, Fixed D 3 course £29.50,
Starter £5.50-£8.95, Main £16.95-£29.50, Dessert £5.50-
£15, Service optional **Wines** 80 bottles over £20, 6 bottles
under £20, 8 by glass **Notes** Vegetarian available, Dress
restrictions, Smart casual, no jeans, trainers or T-shirts,
Civ Wed 135 **Seats** 50, Pr/dining room 300
Children Portions, Menu **Parking** 150

BARSTON   Map 10 SP27

The Malt Shovel at Barston

◉◉ Traditional, Modern British

Updated pub food in smart village inn

☎ 01675 443223
Barston Ln B92 0JP
e-mail: themaltshovelatbarston@gmail.com
web: www.themaltshovelatbarston.com
dir: M42 junct 5, take turn towards Knowle. 1st left on
Jacobean Ln, right at T-junct (Hampton Ln). Sharp left
into Barston Ln. Restaurant 0.5m

A charming country pub decked out in the modern way
with light wooden floors and furniture, The Malt Shovel
has an easygoing air which brings in the crowds.
Background music seems entirely in keeping with the
relaxed, buzzy vibe and, depending on the weather, settle
down by the log fire or head out into the rear garden. The
restaurant in a converted barn is the more formal choice,
but loses none of that relaxed bonhomie. Modern pub food
is the thing, with well-thought-through, crowd-pleasing
stuff on the menu, with roasts on Sundays and
inspiration drawn from far and wide. Jamaican-spice
pork ribs to start, perhaps, with sweetcorn and sugared
mango, or seared scallops with butter bean purée,
Clonakilty black pudding and bacon. Next up, there are
sound flavour combinations in a dish of roast pork fillet
with apple cider risotto, Serrano ham and sage, and in a
modish dessert of raspberry and hibiscus flower
cheesecake with pannacotta ice cream. Daily specials are
big on seafood; whole turbot, perhaps, with artichokes,
sun-dried tomatoes and chorizo.

The Malt Shovel at Barston

Chef Maxie Murphy **Owner** Caroline Furby
Times 12-2.30/6-9.30 Closed D Sun **Prices** Starter £5.50-
£8.95, Main £11.95-£20.50, Dessert £5.50-£8, Service
optional, Groups min 6 service 10% **Wines** 13 bottles
over £20, 14 bottles under £20, 10 by glass **Notes** Sunday
L, Vegetarian available **Seats** 40, Pr/dining room 40
Children Portions **Parking**

BIRMINGHAM   Map 10 SP08

Hotel du Vin & Bistro

◉ British, French 🏆 🍽️

Bistro dining in converted former eye hospital

☎ 0121 200 0600
25 Church St B3 2NR
e-mail: info@birmingham.hotelduvin.com
dir: M6 junct 6/A38(M) to city centre, over flyover. Keep
left & exit at St Chads Circus signed Jewellery Quarter. At
lights & rdbt take 1st exit, follow signs for Colmore Row,
opposite cathedral. Right into Church St, across Barwick
St. Hotel on right

This Brummie outpost of the boutique HdV brand - set in
the trendy regenerated Jewellery Quarter - is right at
home in the red-brick Victorian grandeur of the city's
erstwhile eye hospital. Sympathetic remodelling offers
plenty of period detail alongside cool modern styling and
hallmark drinks-led features. Set around a courtyard,
there's a stylish champagne bar, plus, on the lower
ground, a Pub du Vin outlet specialising in local ales
served up in pewter tankards. The trademark bistro
comes with incredibly high ceilings and decorated in
yellow and gold with floorboards, wooden tables and
leather upholstered period chairs. Framed wine-themed
pictures adorn the walls. The Anglo-French cooking is
driven by top-notch local produce on a please-all roster;
think salt cod served with chorizo and white bean stew, or
perhaps braised shoulder of lamb accompanied by rissole
potato, pea purée, sweetbreads and a rosemary jus. The
wine list is once again outstanding.

Chef Mark Nind **Owner** MWB **Times** 12-2/6-10
Prices Starter £4.50-£6.50, Main £13.95-£25, Dessert
£6.75, Service added but optional 10% **Wines** 600 bottles
over £20, 40 bottles under £20, 16 by glass
Notes Vegetarian available **Seats** 85, Pr/dining room 120
Children Portions, Menu **Parking** 20, NCP Livery St

Save on Hotels. Book at **theAA.com/hotel**

WEST MIDLANDS 473 ENGLAND

Loves Restaurant

BIRMINGHAM   Map 10 SP08

Modern British V 🍷NOTABLE WINE LIST 🐧

Starry cooking on the Birmingham waterside

☎ 0121 454 5151
The Glasshouse, Canal Square, Browning St B16 8FL
e-mail: info@loves-restaurant.co.uk
web: www.loves-restaurant.co.uk
dir: Turn off Broad St towards NEC & Sherbourne Wharf then left to Grosvenor St West & right into Sherbourne St, at end take right into Browning St

Steve and Claire Love's trajectory through the fine-dining scene of the Midlands has been little short of astonishing. From early days in Leamington Spa to the present glitzy waterside address in the centre of Birmingham, they have turned heads and dropped jaws along the way. The architecture of the place celebrates today's urge to transparency in everything, with a glass frontage and a huge glass wall overloooking the canal basin. The interior is starkly minimal, its monochrome purity thrown into relief by the bold swirls of modern prints. Tables are elegantly set, and the whole front-of-house, led by Claire Love, radiates a sense of upscale civility. Mr Love's cooking is technically precise, with extreme care being poured into the pinpoint accuracy of each presentation. Dishes achieve a full aesthetic purchase on the senses, visually, aromatically and on the palate, with many of the concepts and techniques of current times used with imagination. A bowl of wild garlic velouté might open a meal, its flavours rich and soft rather than harshly garlicky, its textures gaining from the addition of a coddled egg, the textural range further broadened with salt-and-vinegar crispy rice and deep-fried garlic flowers, for a stunning production. Those unexpected elements, which help to sustain interest throughout a dish, return in a main course of John Dory fillet in its accompaniments of popcorn pork and tiger prawns with leeks, or in a vegetarian dish of braised bulgur wheat with cauliflower, golden raisins and cauliflower milk. Cotswold lamb appears in two servings, the belly as confit cooked for 36 hours, the neck fillet bundled into a roll of cannelloni pasta, alongside garnishes of Paris mushrooms, peas, crispy anchovy, blanched almonds and pea purée for a fabulous array of flavours. Britain's thoroughgoing celebration of rhubarb, which extends over the first half of the year these days, is hard to fault when it forms the basis, as here, for a dessert show that encompasses sticky toffee pudding, a glass of buttermilk pannacotta layered with jelly, crumble and yoghurt, as well as a miniature meringue filled with rhubarb jelly and palm sugar ice cream.

Chef Steve Love **Owner** Steve & Claire Love
Times 12-2.30/7-9.30 Closed 2 wks Xmas & Aug, 1 wk Etr, Sun-Mon **Prices** Fixed L 2 course fr £20, Tasting menu £68, Service added 10% **Wines** 171 bottles over £20, 19 bottles under £20, 20 by glass **Notes** ALC 2 course £38, 3 course £42, Vegetarian menu **Seats** 32, Pr/dining room 8 **Children** Portions **Parking** Brindley Place car park

Purnell's

BIRMINGHAM   Map 10 SP08

Modern British 🍷NOTABLE WINE LIST

Stellar cooking with bags of local pride

☎ 0121 212 9799
55 Cornwall St B3 2DH
e-mail: info@purnellsrestaurant.com
dir: Close to Birmingham Snow Hill railway station and the junction of Church Street

Five years after he moved out of the leafy 'burbs of Edgbaston, Glynn Purnell's chic contemporary restaurant is still in the vanguard of his home city's gastronomic renaissance. You'll find it in a stylishly-converted red-brick Victorian warehouse on a corner site in the financial district; it is a space that is designed with a nod to industrial heritage minimalism, and furnished with creamy yellow leather seats, bare darkwood tables, black slate floors and neutral hues all well-lit by huge windows - a slick look that could hold its own in Mayfair or any of the world's cosmopolitan centres. This is the UK's second city after all, and Purnell makes a fine unofficial ambassador for the revitalised metropolis. His cooking is entirely of-the-moment - creative, full of fun, bursting with entertaining flavours and textures, and it is all underpinned by top-level culinary skills. You could take the budget route in with the keenly-priced lunch menu, getting off the blocks with ballottine of ham hock with pig's trotter nuggets, shallot and parsley salad, and caramelised onion purée, followed by black bream with woodland mushrooms, green mustard, confit potato and chicken jus. Otherwise there's a fixed-price carte, market menu, and the full-on, eight-course tasting menu, all wrought from unstintingly superb ingredients and delivered dressed to thrill. The latter might include monkfish masala with Indian red lentils, pickled carrots, coconut and coriander as a nod to Brum's renowned Asian cuisine, and venison rolled in liquorice charcoal and matched with foie gras, and liquorice and tamarind purée. Puddings are handled with equal skill and inventiveness - a chocolate and passionfruit dome, perhaps, served with warm chocolate, and pineapple sorbet. Discreet, knowledgeable service and a well-chosen French-leaning wine list add to the thrill of it all.

Chef Glynn Purnell **Owner** Glynn Purnell
Times 12-1.30/7-9 Closed Xmas, New Year, 1 wk Etr, 2 wks end Jul-beg Aug, Sun-Mon, L Sat **Prices** Fixed L 2 course £22, Fixed D 3 course £50, Tasting menu £80, Service added but optional 12.5% **Wines** 400 bottles over £20, 17 by glass **Notes** Tasting menu 8 course, wine tasting £65, Vegetarian available, Dress restrictions, Smart casual **Seats** 45, Pr/dining room 10 **Parking** On street, Snow Hill car park nearby

BIRMINGHAM *continued*

Lasan Restaurant

◉ Indian

Exciting contemporary Indian cuisine

☎ 0121 212 3664 & 3665
3-4 Dakota Buildings, James St, St Paul's Square
B3 1SD
e-mail: info@lasan.co.uk
dir: Near city centre, adj to Jewellery Quarter

The Great British Curry has certainly come of age in recent years, and Lasan stands up to be counted among the glossy contemporary new kids on the block. It is in the Jewellery Quarter - a cool postcode these days - and works an appropriately pared-back industrial chic look of bare wood and neutral shades to go with an up-tempo, high-decibel vibe. The kitchen team has the sub-continent's multi-faceted cuisine covered by a team of chefs who know the ins and outs of its regional subtleties, and it all comes to the table prepared with a light contemporary touch and dressed to impress. Afghani lamb sees a tandoor-roasted lamb chop alongside a pattie of minced shoulder and lentils spiced with cinnamon and black cardamom, while nellore chappa delivers pan-fried Lyme Bay monkfish with spiced aubergine and potato pakora, and a sauce of coconut milk infused with curry leaves, mustard seeds and sour tamarind.

Chef Aktar Islam, Gulsher Khan **Owner** Jabbar Khan **Times** 12-2.30/6-11 Closed 25 Dec, L Sat **Prices** Starter £5.95-£12.95, Main £12.95-£25.95, Dessert £4.50-£7.95, Service included, Groups min 5 service 10% **Wines** 17 bottles over £20, 9 bottles under £20, 7 by glass **Notes** Sunday L, Vegetarian available, Dress restrictions, Smart casual, Air con **Seats** 64 **Parking** On street

Loves Restaurant

◉◉◉ – *see page 473*

Malmaison Bar & Brasserie

◉ Traditional, Modern

Buzzy setting for smart brasserie-style cooking

☎ 0121 246 5000
1 Wharfside St, The Mailbox B1 1RD
e-mail: birmingham@malmaison.com
dir: M6 junct 6, follow the A38 (city centre), via Queensway underpass. Left to Paradise Circus, 1st exit Brunel St, right T-junct, Malmaison directly opposite

This cool 'Mal' location is a former Royal Mail sorting office reborn as the Mailbox complex. Images of when Birmingham's canals were the arteries of the city adorn

the walls in the first floor brasserie where unclothed dark wood tables and leather-style banquettes combine to create a fair approximation of a French brasserie. Service manages to be knowledgeable and keep it all bright and breezy, with the sommelier particularly on the ball. Unfussy brasserie-style food is the name of the game; kick off with chicken liver parfait with grape chutney and toasted brioche, follow on with Malmaison fishcake with spinach and parsley sauce, then finish on a comforting note with steamed sponge of the day with custard, cream or ice cream.

Times 12-2.30/6-10.30

Opus Restaurant

◉◉ Modern British

Exhilarating modern cooking in smart modish setting

☎ 0121 200 2323
54 Cornwall St B3 2DE
e-mail: restaurant@opusrestaurant.co.uk
web: www.opusrestaurant.co.uk
dir: Close to Birmingham Snow Hill railway station in the city's business district

Opus is a large, buzzy, modern restaurant done out in cool, contemporary colours, flooded with light from large windows at the front and a skylight at the back. Personable, well-informed staff contribute to the vibe. The kitchen is ingredients-led, with the broadly British menus changing with each session, and it avoids gimmicks and over-elaboration. Delicate pumpkin soup floated with slivers of garlic and thyme is a good opener, or there may be a seared quail on carrot risotto. Among main courses might be whole lemon sole accompanied by a simple lemon and herb butter, and more robust dishes are handled adroitly too - loin of lamb with belly and sweetbreads served with braised salsify and rösti, say. Standards are maintained to the end with desserts along the lines of delicate rum and raisin mousse with dried-

fruit and nut ice cream, or dark chocolate torte with cherries and almond-flavoured Chantilly.

Chef David Colcombe **Owner** Ann Tonks, Irene Allan, David Colcombe **Times** 12-2.45/6-10 Closed between Xmas & New Year, BHs, Sun, L Sat **Prices** Fixed L 3 course £24.50, Fixed D 3 course £19-£24.50, Starter £7.50-£12.50, Main £16-£24, Dessert £6.50-£9.50, Service added but optional 12.5% **Wines** 72 bottles over £20, 3 bottles under £20, 11 by glass **Notes** Chef's tasting menu 6 course, Vegetarian available **Seats** 85, Pr/dining room 24 **Children** Portions, Menu **Parking** On street

Purnell's

◉◉◉ – *see page 473*

Simpsons

◉◉◉ – *see opposite*

Thai Edge Restaurant

◉ Thai

Smart, modish Thai in Brindley Place

☎ 0121 643 3993
7 Oozells Square, Brindley Place B1 2HS
e-mail: birmingham@thaiedge.co.uk
dir: Brindley Place just off Broad St (approx 0.5m from B'ham New Street station)

The Birmingham outpost of this modern Thai restaurant chain (with siblings in Cardiff, Leeds and Bristol) looks smart with its glass partitions, tiled floor, plentiful Thai artefacts and orchids on the tables. Thai music plays in the background (unobtrusively so) and waitresses are dressed in traditional garb. The charming staff can advise about the heat of the dishes and can get them tweaked up or down according to your liking. The expansive menu runs the gamut of set banquets, soups and salads with familiar and not so familiar choices along the way; toro mun khoa pod is sweetcorn cakes with sweet plum sauce (light and packed with flavour) and phed nam makam is pan-fried duck with sweet-and-sour tamarind sauce (tender and sticky). Tago and Woon Ka Ti sees coconut cream with taro, sweetcorn and sago wrapped in pandanus leaf and served with coconut jelly cubes topped with water chestnut jelly.

Times 12-2.30/5.30-11 Closed 25-26 Dec, 1 Jan

Turners

◉◉ Modern French

Classy French-influenced food in suburban Brum

☎ 0121 426 4440
69 High St, Harborne B17 9NS
e-mail: info@turnersrestaurantbirmingham.co.uk

Set in a busy parade of shops on the High Street, Turners is a class act that brings a highly accomplished dining experience to the city's Harborne suburb. Inside is glossily kitted out in the modern manner, with striking logoed mirrors on black and navy blue panelled walls, old quarry-tiled floors and fashionable seating, while well-judged professional service ratchets up the experience factor. The kitchen doesn't disappoint, delivering refined, confident and ambitious modern French cooking conjured from top-notch seasonal ingredients. Whether you plump for the top-drawer tasting menu or good value entry-level fixed-price lunch du jour, the quality doesn't waver. Witness a ballotine of Anjou pigeon served with duck liver, braised cabbage, mushroom purée and truffle jus, or perhaps a pavé of sea bass teamed with new season English asparagus, crushed Jersey Royals, baby gem lettuce and a velouté of oysters. Luxury for two to share comes in the form of Chateaubriand, and to finish there might be apple tarte Tatin, or prune and Armagnac soufflé with Armagnac ice cream.

Chef Richard Turner **Owner** Richard Turner
Times 12-2/7-9.30 Closed Mon-Sun, L Sat **Prices** Fixed L 2 course fr £22, Fixed D 3 course fr £50, Tasting menu £75, Service added but optional 12.5% **Wines** 90 bottles over £20, 17 by glass **Notes** ALC 3 course £60, Menu du Jour D Wed-Thu £37.95, Vegetarian available **Seats** 30 **Parking** 50

The Forest

◉◉ Modern European

Inspired modern cooking in a stylish hotel

☎ 01564 772120
Station Approach, 25 Station Rd B93 8JA
e-mail: info@forest-hotel.com
dir: M42 junct 5, through Knowle right to Dorridge, left before bridge

Once a Victorian railway hotel, nowadays The Forest is a rather chic affair with modern-day boutique credentials and a bar and restaurant at its heart. A white-line-free zone, the restaurant's fashionable banquette seating and chairs stand alongside wooden floors, feature wallpaper and a full-height wine cabinet. The brasserie-style menu is equally of-the-moment, delivering some appealing innovative ideas from quality produce with a broadly modern European accent. Think roasted turbot fillet with leek and mussel velouté and potato foam, and, for dessert, a plum tarte Tatin with cinnamon ice cream and hazelnuts. A range of classic dishes (steak-and-kidney pudding to fish and chips) keeps traditionalists happy.

Chef Dean Grubb **Owner** Gary & Tracy Perkins
Times 12-2.30/6.30-10 Closed 25 Dec, D Sun
Prices Fixed L 2 course £13.45, Fixed D 3 course £15.90, Starter £4.25-£7.50, Main £11.50-£18, Dessert £5.65-£6.50, Service added but optional 10% **Wines** 18 bottles over £20, 26 bottles under £20, 13 by glass **Notes** Fixed L Mon-Sat, D Mon-Fri, Sunday L, Vegetarian available, Civ Wed 130 **Seats** 70, Pr/dining room 150 **Children** Portions, Menu **Parking** 40

Simpsons

Modern European V ♦NOTABLE WINE LIST

Smart, confident cooking in classy Edgbaston favourite

☎ 0121 454 3434
20 Highfield Rd, Edgbaston B15 3DU
e-mail: info@simpsonsrestaurant.co.uk
dir: 1m from city centre, opposite St Georges Church, Edgbaston

The good people of Edgbaston have a gem of a restaurant in their midst, and with four smart bedrooms available, the option to stop over in the borough is always on the cards for the rest of us. It's a smart house, a charming villa of fine proportions, with a glassed-in verandah giving views over the pretty garden. In fact the garden is quite the hotspot when the Brummy sunshine allows, with a meal outside under a parasol a real treat. But no matter if the weather keeps you indoors, for this is a charming setting, with tables dressed up in their best whites, and a service team who know their onions. There are top-notch ingredients at the heart of the kitchen's output, a good deal sourced from these parts, and the menus show genuine creative flair with some Far-Eastern flavours amongst the broadly modern European output. There are classical foundations at the heart of things, though, and nothing feels out of place. Start, perhaps, with squab pigeon with poached kumquats, mouli, dandelion salad and five-spice sauce, before sea bass with artichoke purée, potato gnocchi, cavolo nero and red wine sauce. Cod is salted in-house and might come with samphire, prawns and a seaweed sauce, and to finish, there's evident skill in the making of a chocolate tart with orange and a fabulous cocoa bean ice cream. There's a tasting menu, plus bespoke dishes for vegetarians and children.

Chef Luke Tipping **Owner** Andreas & Alison Antona
Times 12-2.30/7-9.30 Closed BHs, D Sun **Prices** Fixed L 3 course fr £38, Service added but optional 12.5% **Notes** Tasting menu 8 course, Sunday L, Vegetarian menu, Dress restrictions, Smart casual **Seats** 70, Pr/dining room 20 **Children** Portions, Menu **Parking** 12, On street

HOCKLEY HEATH Map 10 SP17

Nuthurst Grange Country House Hotel

⚜️⚜️ British, French

Inventive cooking in classy country-house hotel

☎ 01564 783972
Nuthurst Grange Ln B94 5NL
e-mail: info@nuthurst-grange.co.uk
web: www.nuthurst-grange.com
dir: Off A3400, 0.5m south of Hockley Heath. Turn at sign into Nuthurst Grange Lane

Within acres of woodland, Nuthurst Grange, much extended from its Victorian core, is a stylish country-house hotel. Have a drink in the bar or beside a log fire in the lounge before proceeding to the restaurant, an elegant room with a restful décor, country views and formal and focused service. The kitchen makes everything in-house and assembles menus that cover a wide swath of modern ideas, among them, for instance, a main course of Asian-spiced roast pork with pan-fried squid and seaweed. Among starters, seasonal asparagus comes with a crisp duck egg drizzled with truffle oil, and ballottine of sea trout with cucumber sorbet and horseradish has the welcome addition of crackling. Produce is well chosen, timings are just so, and dishes are properly thought out; fillet of red mullet is given a watercress emulsion and partnered by tasty confit chorizo and shallots, for example. A lot of effort goes into desserts, too, resulting in a first-rate dark chocolate truffle with orange ice cream, honeycomb and popping candy.

Times 12-2/7-9.30 Closed 25-26 Dec, L Sat

See advert opposite

MERIDEN Map 10 SP28

Forest of Arden Marriott Hotel & Country Club

⚜️ Modern British

Good eating at a smart golfing hotel

☎ 01676 522335
Maxstoke Ln CV7 7HR
e-mail: mukesh.kumasi@marriothotels.com

A big hotel with lots going on - golf and spa for a start - the Forest of Arden Marriott is well-positioned for the East Midlands hub, and its Oaks Bar and Grill is a restaurant of note in its own right. There's a bold carpet, leather banquettes, straight-backed chairs and scatter cushions giving it a bright and breezy modish feel, and views over the grounds are an added bonus. On the menu, straightforward grills rub shoulders with more inventive things; a classic combination of warm figs and Parma ham is paired with bucks fizz jelly and sweet saffron syrup, followed perhaps by baked fillet of haddock with a poached egg, curried sauce and sautéed greens. To finish, strawberry Arctic Roll, vanilla pannacotta and compôte is a good bet.

Times 1-2.30/6.30-9.45

Manor Hotel

⚜️⚜️ Modern British, French

Smart modish cooking in a Midlands Manor

☎ 01676 522735
Main Rd CV7 7NH
e-mail: reservations@manorhotelmeriden.co.uk
dir: M42 junct 6, A45 towards Coventry then A452 signed Leamington. At rdbt take B4102 signed Meriden, hotel on left

Handy if you're hitting the National Exhibition Centre, the restaurant at the family-run Manor Hotel in the small village of Meriden has also caught the eye of savvy locals, who come for the classy modish cooking. The large, traditionally-styled Regency Restaurant is hung with paintings depicting English country scenes, and combined with smartly dressed tables laid with sparkling glasses and fresh flowers, it's a charming spot for lunch or dinner. Young and upbeat staff ensure it all ticks along nicely. Modern British cooking is the order of the day; kick off with Loomswood Farm Gressingham duck and wild mushroom terrine with provençale vegetable and celeriac velouté, before moving on to pan-roasted Cornish monkfish with cauliflower, pressed potato and garlic, mussel velouté, cumin-scented carrots and rocket pesto.

Chef Darion Smethurst **Owner** Bracebridge Holdings **Times** 12.30-3/6.30-9.45 Closed L Mon-Sat **Prices** Fixed L 3 course £19.50-£21.50, Fixed D 3 course £21.50-£29, Starter £6.25-£8.95, Main £12.95-£19.95, Dessert £5.25-£5.95, Service optional **Wines** 15 bottles over £20, 20 bottles under £20, 14 by glass **Notes** Sunday L, Vegetarian available, Civ Wed 200 **Seats** 150, Pr/dining room 220 **Children** Portions, Menu **Parking** 180

OLDBURY Map 10 SO98

Saffron Restaurant

⚜️ Modern Indian **NEW**

New-wave Indian cooking in chic surroundings

☎ 0121 552 1752
909 Walverhampton Rd B69 4RR
e-mail: suds_sh@yahoo.co.uk
dir: M5 junct 2. Follow A4123 (S) signs towards Harborne. Restaurant on right

Contemporary Indian cooking is one of the UK's growth areas, and Sudha Saha's pair of restaurants - this, and Saffron Blue in Ashby-de-la-Zouch - represent a particularly vivid example of the genre. A smart, pink-and-black colour scheme and stripped wood floor are the backdrop to some sizzling culinary action. Sea bass in a lightly spiced batter with diced apple and saffron marinade is full of bracing flavours, none of which manages to overwhelm the very fresh fish. Sticking with fish into main courses might lead you to spicy, crisp-skinned fried red mullet with a chick pea and spinach gâteau, accompanied by tomato relish and a cumin and coriander beurre blanc, while Barbary duck breast may be braised and served in a hickory masala sauce. Ras malai in saffron milk are firm textured and garnished with crumbled pistachios, or there's a version of faluda, soft vermicelli in almond milk and rose syrup, topped with vanilla ice cream. Nor do the deeply trad poppadoms and pickle tray let the side down.

Chef Sudha Shankar Saha **Owner** Abdul Rahman & A Momin **Times** 12-2.30/5.30-11 Closed D 25 Dec **Prices** Starter £3.95-£6.95, Main £8.50-£19.95, Dessert £2.95-£3.50, Groups min 10 service 10% **Wines** 11 bottles over £20, 24 bottles under £20, 6 by glass **Notes** Sunday L, Vegetarian available, Dress restrictions, Smart casual, Air con **Children** Portions **Parking** 15

SUTTON COLDFIELD	Map 10 SP19

New Hall Hotel & Spa

@ @ Modern British

Modern fine-dining in historic house

☎ 0121 378 2442 & 08450 727 577
Walmley Rd, Walmley B76 1QX
e-mail: newhall@handpicked.co.uk
web: www.handpickedhotels.co.uk/newhall
dir: On B4148, E of Sutton Coldfield, close to M6 & M42

It is hard to imagine, but before Birmingham's suburban sprawl engulfed the village of Sutton Coldfield, this 800-year-old moat house stood in empty countryside. The hall hasn't actually been 'new' since the 14th century, and does business nowadays as an upmarket operation that on one hand flaunts its age in medieval beams, flagstones, and heraldic crests, and on the other, supplies 21st-century spa pampering with all the bells and whistles, and it is all cushioned from the hurly-burly of modern Brum by 26 acres of fabulous grounds. The Bridge Restaurant is the top-end dining option, where mullioned stained-glass windows blend with a gently modern neutral décor as a setting for cooking whose roots are set in the classics but tweaked for today's tastes with modern techniques and presentation. Expect starters along the lines of smoked eel salad with new potato, red onion and apple, followed by slow-cooked Kentish lamb shoulder partnered with its sweetbreads, Jerusalem artichoke purée, and wholegrain mustard jus.

New Hall Hotel & Spa

Chef Ian Penn **Owner** Hand Picked Hotels **Times** 7-9.30 Closed Mon-Wed, L Thu-Sat **Prices** Fixed D 3 course fr £45, Starter £13-£14, Main £18-£24, Dessert £7-£10, Service optional **Wines** 65 bottles over £20, 14 bottles under £20, 14 by glass **Notes** Sunday L, Vegetarian available, Dress restrictions, Smart casual, no jeans or T-shirts, Civ Wed 75 **Seats** 24, Pr/dining room 14 **Children** Portions, Menu **Parking** 60

WALSALL	Map 10 SP09

Fairlawns Hotel and Spa

@ @ Modern British V

Smart hotel with confident modern cooking

☎ 01922 455122
178 Little Aston Rd, Aldridge WS9 0NU
e-mail: reception@fairlawns.co.uk
web: www.fairlawns.co.uk
dir: Outskirts of Aldridge, 400yds from junction of A452 (Chester Rd) & A454

Well-insulated from the concrete sprawl of Greater Birmingham by nine acres of landscaped gardens, this family-run hotel north of Walsall is in a useful spot for plugging in to the big Midlands cities and the motorway network. The Victorian building at the heart of Fairlawns is smartly updated and extended, and comes with a spa and fitness centre. Completing the attractive package is the kitchen's deft line in modern British cooking, presented on a broad-ranging menu built on well-sourced materials. Things could kick off with Craster smoked haddock fishcakes with prawn and chive beurre blanc, followed by roast rack and confit shoulder of lamb served with fondant potato and roasted root vegetables. To wrap it all up, there may be a home-grown rhubarb soufflé.

continued

WALSALL *continued*

Chef Neil Atkins **Owner** John Pette **Times** 12-2/7-10 Closed 25-26 Dec, 1 Jan, Good Fri, Etr Mon, May Day, BH Mon, L Sat **Prices** Fixed L 2 course £14.50, Fixed D 3 course £32.50, Starter £7.50-£12.50, Main £18.50-£32.50, Dessert £6.95, Service optional **Wines** 36 bottles over £20, 30 bottles under £20, 12 by glass **Notes** Sunday L, Vegetarian menu, Dress restrictions, No jeans, trainers, sports clothing **Seats** 80, Pr/dining room 100 **Children** Portions, Menu **Parking** 120

WOLVERHAMPTON Map 10 SO99

Bilash

🏵 Indian

Classy Bangladeshi and Indian cooking

☎ 01902 427762
2 Cheapside WV1 1TU
e-mail: m@thebilash.co.uk
dir: Opposite Civic Hall & St Peter's Church

Bilash's décor of white walls and red and beige seats at bare wooden tables suggests that this is not a typical high-street curry house, an impression soon corroborated by the modern layout and typography of the menu. What's on offer here is classy, authentic Bangladeshi and Indian cooking of top-quality ingredients. Tandoori king prawns and chicken biryani sound familiar enough, but they jostle for attention with gohst rezala, a spicy lamb dish from Kashmir, murghi xacuti, chicken marinated in ginger and garlic, and lobster chor chori. Starters are an appealing bunch, from accurately cooked prawns in pepper sauce to Lucknow-style roast lamb chop. Accompaniments and relishes are carefully prepared, and to finish there may even be the chance of cherry clafoutis or kheer (a rice pudding).

Chef Sitab Khan **Owner** Sitab Khan **Times** 12-2.30/5.30-10.30 Closed 25-26 Dec, 1 Jan, Sun **Prices** Fixed L 2 course £9.50-£15.90, Fixed D 3 course £19.90-£29.90, Starter £5.90-£12.90, Main £9.90-£28.90, Dessert £4.50-£6.90, Service optional **Wines** 12 bottles over £20, 4 bottles under £20, 5 by glass **Notes** Pre-theatre D, tasting menu with wine, L specials, Vegetarian available, Dress restrictions, No tracksuits & trainers **Seats** 48, Pr/dining room 40 **Children** Portions, Menu **Parking** 15, Civic car park

---

WIGHT, ISLE OF

FRESHWATER Map 5 SZ38

Justin Brown at Farringford

🏵🏵 Modern Irish **NEW**

Clever modern food in a cool setting

☎ 01983 752500
Farringford PO40 9PE
e-mail: contact@farringford.co.uk

Justin Brown's restaurant - his first solo venture as chef-patron - sits in the most southerly part of the Isle of

Wight on a grand estate that was once owned by Lord Tennyson. Housed in a log cabin-style building, the place has a clean-lined, Scandinavian-inspired contemporary look that matches scrubbed pine floors with blond wood tables and chairs, and a domed wood-burning pizza oven as its centrepiece - although this ambitious operation certainly aims higher than just the delicious pizza's. There's a chef's table in the kitchen for those who want to get talked through the dishes as the chefs put together well-wrought and intelligently-conceived modern ideas, and it is all based on excellent local materials and produce from the organic vegetable patch. Locally-shot pigeon is timed to perfection and served with a glossy red wine jus and a three-way presentation of sweetcorn comprising purée, a crisp relish, and dust. Next comes local cod, mussels and crayfish with samphire, and a Thai-style infusion of lemongrass, coriander, lime, ginger and chilli. For dessert, vanilla pannacotta is offset by tangy blood orange granité.

Chef Justin Brown **Owner** Justin Brown, Martin Beasley **Times** 12-2.30/6-9 Closed Jan, Mon, D Sun **Prices** Tasting menu £50-£75, Starter £7.95-£9.95, Main £11.95-£19.95, Dessert £5-£6.50, Service optional **Wines** 29 bottles over £20, 11 bottles under £20, 9 by glass **Notes** Tasting menu 6 course, with matching wine £75, Sunday L **Seats** 40 **Children** Menu **Parking** 100

RYDE Map 5 SZ59

Lakeside Park Hotel

🏵🏵 Modern European V 🏵

Creative cooking in a lakeside setting

☎ 01983 882266
High St PO33 4LJ
e-mail: info@lakesideparkhotel.com
dir: A3054 towards Newport. Hotel on left after crossing Wotton Bridge

The impressive spa and treatment rooms are a big draw to this slick purpose-built hotel in an Area of Outstanding Beauty overlooking a peaceful tidal lake. It's a stylish place with two dining options adding to its attraction - the Bar & Brasserie has a lakeside terrace which is a big hit when the weather plays ball, and the more classical Oyster Room, which has views of the lake in a more formal setting. Isle of Wight produce figures large in a broadly modern European repertoire in the Oyster Room, with lots of up-to-the-minute cooking techniques on show; expect to see foams, espumas and jellies. Start with citrus salmon, which is smoked salmon sausage with potato tartar, pickled cucumber and orange semi-gel and, if you're lucky enough to be here in season, grouse with boudin blanc, swede, bread purée and liquorice foam. The creativity extends to desserts such as chocolate tart soufflé with vanilla ice cream and grue de cacao brittle.

Chef Gary Cooke **Owner** Mr Sheaff **Times** 12-2.30/6.30-9.30 Closed Dec-Jan, Mon-Tue, D Sun **Prices** Food prices not confirmed for 2013. Please telephone for details **Wines** 55 bottles over £20, 15 bottles under £20, 8 by glass **Notes** Sunday L, Vegetarian menu, Civ Wed 120 **Seats** 26, Pr/dining room 10 **Parking** 120

SEAVIEW Map 5 SZ69

Priory Bay Hotel

🏵 Modern

Attractive Regency dining room and creative menu

☎ 01983 613146
Priory Dr PO34 5BU
e-mail: enquiries@priorybay.co.uk
dir: B3330 towards Seaview, through Nettlestone. (Do not follow Seaview turn, but continue 0.5m to hotel sign)

Set within a 70-acre estate of gardens, woodlands and even with its own beach, this sumptuous former Tudor farmhouse is home to the elegant Island Room restaurant. The Regency-style dining room dazzles with murals of local scenery and gilded plasterwork, with floor-to-ceiling windows giving views across to the Solent. The fine-dining menu is based around local seafood, game and a good deal of fresh produce from the gardens and woodlands. Kick off with céviche of mackerel with horseradish pannacotta, pickled garden beetroot salad and beetroot jelly, followed by rump of island lamb with Medjool date purée, crushed pistachio, yeast extract-glazed potatoes and rosemary oil. The Oyster Bar & Grill does a fine line in unadulterated seafood.

Times 12.30-2.15/7-9.30

The Seaview Hotel & Restaurant

🏵 Traditional European **NEW**

Enterprising cooking in a sailing village

☎ 01983 612711
High St PO34 5EX
e-mail: reception@seaviewhotel.co.uk
dir: Take B3330 from Ryde to Seaview, left into Puckpool Hill, follow signs for hotel

The Victorian hotel close to the sea has two dining rooms, one with a traditional look, the other more contemporary with a conservatory; the same menus are served in both. The kitchen majors on the island's produce, with meat, vegetables and eggs provided by its own farm, and, like the dining rooms, the menus span the traditional - fish pie, say, or chargrilled sirloin steak with the usual accompaniments - and more modern ideas like roast sea bass, well timed, served with bouillabaisse sauce, braised fennel and saffron-flavoured potatoes. To start may be straightforward dressed crab, or an unusual pairing of ham hock terrine and monkfish nuggets with caper berry butter, and to finish could come classic Bakewell tart with raspberry jam sauce and raspberry ripple ice cream.

Chef Colby Meredith **Owner** B E F Gardener **Times** 12-2.30/6.30-9.30 Closed 23-27 Dec **Prices** Starter £4.95-£9.95, Main £13.50-£20.50, Dessert £5.95-£8.95, Service optional **Wines** 27 bottles over £20, 9 bottles under £20, 6 by glass **Notes** Sunday L, Vegetarian available **Seats** 70, Pr/dining room 25 **Children** Portions, Menu **Parking** 8

The Hambrough

VENTNOR   Map 5 SZ57

Modern European V 🍷 NOTABLE WINE LIST

Inspirational modern cooking overlooking the sea

☎ 01983 856333
Hambrough Rd PO38 1SQ
e-mail: reservations@robert-thompson.com
web: www.robert-thompson.com
dir: From A3055 follow signs to Ventnor & St Catherine's Church, turn right into Hambrough Rd, restaurant on left

Perched above the esplanade at Ventnor, the Hambrough is a smart Victorian villa turned sybaritic boutique hotel with uplifting views out to sea across the harbour. With Robert Thompson at the culinary helm, however, the place has established itself as the island's premier foodie address. A classy makeover has brought in a light and airy look of neutral refinement to the two front-facing rooms that comprise the restaurant, without detracting from their period character or those watery scenes stretching far beyond the bay windows. Robert Thompson made his name with immaculately-executed, labour-intensive modern French dishes inspired by the surrounding landscape, and here that means splendid produce hauled in from the local farms and fishing boats, as well as further afield. A signature pressing of lightly-smoked eel with foie gras, pork belly and Granny Smith apple served with celeriac remoulade and toasted brioche is typical of the full-throated flavours and rich textures on offer. Next out, roasted loin of New Forest venison might star in a perfectly-judged composition with snails, roast parsley root and field mushroom purée, and garlic and parsley butter. Puddings are equally intelligent combinations such as tarte Tatin of Pink Lady apples matched with cassia ice cream. On the wine front, there's more than ample choice by the glass, and intelligent global coverage by the bottle.

Chef Robert Thompson **Owner** Robert Thompson **Times** 12-1.30/7-9.30 Closed 1.5 wks Apr, 2 wks Nov & Jan, Mon & most Sun **Prices** Fixed L 3 course £32, Service optional **Wines** 177 bottles over £20, 10 by glass **Notes** Tasting menu 4 course £60, 7 course £85, Vegetarian menu, Dress restrictions, Smart casual, No sportswear, Civ Wed 45 **Seats** 45, Pr/dining room 22 **Children** Portions **Parking** On street

VENTNOR   Map 5 SZ57

The Hambrough

@@@ – *see page 479*

The Leconfield

@ Traditional British V ⟡

Hotel with a local flavour and sea views

☎ 01983 852196
85 Leeson Rd, Upper Bonchurch PO38 1PU
e-mail: enquiries@leconfieldhotel.com
dir: Situated Upper Bonchurch on A3055, 1m from
Ventnor, 2m from Shanklin opposite turning, Bonchurch
Shute

There are great views over the English Channel from
inside and out of this ivy-clad hotel up on St Boniface
Down above the village of Bonchurch. The Seascape
Dining Room duly delivers the vista on a plate in the
daylight hours, while the room's traditional charms
should easily satisfy evening guests. There are plenty of
local ingredients on the menu (beef and lobster, for
example), which might take you from sautéed tiger
prawns in garlic butter (served on toasted brioche) to
orange Bakewell tart with Chantilly cream and chocolate
sauce, via some of that local beef - fillet steak, perhaps,
served Wellington style with a port sauce.

Chef Jason Lefley **Owner** Paul & Cheryl Judge
Times 6.30-8 Closed 24-26 Dec, 3 wks Jan, L all week
(except by prior arrangement) **Prices** Fixed D 3 course
£27-£38, Service optional **Wines** 24 bottles over £20,
12 bottles under £20, 13 by glass **Notes** Vegetarian
menu, Dress restrictions, Smart casual **Seats** 26
Parking 14

The Pond Café

@@ Modern Italian

Charming village setting and Italian-inspired menu

☎ 01983 855666 & 856333
Bonchurch Village Rd, Bonchurch PO38 1RG
e-mail: reservations@robert-thompson.com
dir: A3055 to Leeson Rd follow Bonchurch signs until
village turn off

Robert Thompson is an ever-rising culinary star, cooking
up a storm at The Hambrough (see entry). The Pond Café
is his second address on the island and rather than
competing with the fireworks up the road, it is a charming
and understated place, with an equally straight-up and
unfussy approach to its food. The eponymous pond is
across the quiet road and outside tables are a real treat
when the weather allows. The menu blends seasonal and,
more often than not, local ingredients with broadly Italian
preparations, and it's the kind of cooking where flavour is
king. Start with local beef carpaccio with rocket,
parmesan and pine nuts, or a sea bass version with chilli,
marjoram and lemon, before pasta or risotto (in two
different portion sizes) such as linguini with local crab,
spiked with fresh red chillies. Main courses run to

chargrilled leg of island lamb with roasted beetroots,
salsify and braised lentils, or sea bream with a risotto of
clams and cockles and braised fennel.

Chef Robert Thompson **Owner** Robert Thompson
Times 12-2.30/6-9.30 **Prices** Fixed L 3 course £18,
Starter £6-£9, Main £12-£22, Dessert £5-£7, Service
optional **Wines** 19 bottles over £20, 4 bottles under £20,
5 by glass **Notes** Early bird menu 2 course £15, 3 course
£18 6-7pm, Sunday L, Vegetarian available **Seats** 26
Children Portions **Parking** On street

The Royal Hotel

@@ Modern British ⟡

Refined cooking in grand setting

☎ 01983 852186
Belgrave Rd PO38 1JJ
e-mail: enquiries@royalhoteliow.co.uk
dir: On A3055 (coast road) into Ventnor. Follow one-way
system, left at lights into Church St. At top of hill left into
Belgrave Rd, hotel on right

The Royal is a classic slice of Victoriana that slots right
in with the time-warp mood of the Isle of Wight. It sits in
the embrace of lush sub-tropical gardens overlooking the
sea, and sticks to the admirable old-school traditions of
doing things correctly, including a very fine spread for
afternoon tea. Inside, is a classic English scene fully
loaded with fancy plasterwork ceilings, crystal
chandeliers, parquet floors and decorative ironwork; the
dining room is an elegant grande dame too with its
swagged drapes and oil paintings and correctly formal,
but not starchy, service. The kitchen, however, works in a
parallel time zone - that of the 21st century, where meals
might start with Isle of Wight Gallybagger cheese soufflé,
then move on to roast fillet of pollock with crushed
hazelnuts, saffron potatoes, smoked mussels and leeks,
and parsley emulsion. Desserts are equally impressive -
perhaps spiced plum crème brûlée with cinnamon
shortbread.

Chef Alan Staley **Owner** William Bailey
Times 12-1.45/6.45-9 Closed 2 wks Jan or 2 wks Dec, L
Mon-Sat **Prices** Fixed L 2 course fr £15, Fixed D 3 course
fr £40, Tasting menu £50, Service optional
Wines 82 bottles over £20, 6 bottles under £20, 8 by
glass **Notes** Tasting menu 6 course, Sunday L, Vegetarian
available, Dress restrictions, Smart casual, no shorts or
trainers, Civ Wed 125 **Seats** 140, Pr/dining room 40
Children Portions, Menu **Parking** 50

YARMOUTH   Map 5 SZ38

The George Hotel

@@ British, Mediterranean

Refined seasonal cookery on the Solent

☎ 01983 760331
Quay St PO41 0PE
e-mail: res@thegeorge.co.uk
web: www.thegeorge.co.uk
dir: Between castle & pier

The location of this charming hotel could hardly be
bettered, as it's on the water's edge looking over the
Solent, while the bright, conservatory-style brasserie has
views of the castle and manicured lawns to the quay and
pier beyond. The kitchen focuses on the profusion of local
produce, from chicken, in a boudin, served with wings,
parsnip and ginger, to venison (from over the water in the
New Forest) with beetroot, red cabbage and Jerusalem
artichoke. The cooking has its roots in the great French
traditions, brought up to date with contemporary touches,
so sea bass is given the tartare treatment and served
with shiso, lime and beetroot, and pan-fried fillet of cod,
extremely fresh and perfectly cooked, comes with chorizo,
grapefruit and lime Basquaise. A pre-dessert - perhaps
passionfruit sorbet with pineapple jelly - is served before
the real thing, among which could be a light, airy
raspberry soufflé with raspberry custard and a memorable
champagne sorbet.

Chef Liam Finnegan **Owner** John Illsley, Jeremy Willcock
Times 12-3/7-10 **Prices** Fixed L 2 course £17.95-£25,
Starter £6.95-£9.50, Main £15.95-£24, Dessert £6.95-
£7.95, Service optional **Wines** 31 bottles over £20,
12 bottles under £20, 11 by glass **Notes** Sunday L,
Vegetarian available, Dress restrictions, Smart casual
Seats 60, Pr/dining room 20 **Children** Portions, Menu
Parking The Square

Save on Hotels. Book at **theAA.com/hotel**

WILTSHIRE 481 ENGLAND

WILTSHIRE

AMESBURY
Map 5 SU14

Holiday Inn Salisbury - Stonehenge

Modern International **NEW**

Seasonal brasserie cooking near Woodhenge

☎ 0845 241 3535 & 01980 677466
Midsummer Place, Solstice Park SP4 7SQ
e-mail: reservations@hisalisbury-stonehenge.co.uk
dir: Exit A303, follow signs into Solstice Park. Hotel
adjacent to service area

The Salisbury-Stonehenge branch of Holiday Inn is an
alien spacecraft of a building, its copiously windowed
frontage looking out over the surrounding countryside. It's
not far from the ancient henge at Amesbury, hence the
restaurant name, although there is nothing ancient about
either the décor, the muzak or the seasonal brasserie
dishes. Start with a pair of Thai fishcakes, spiced with
chilli and lemongrass, alongside bean sprouts and spring
onion salad, then head west for the likes of sea bass with
roast baby fennel, samphire and red pepper pesto, or
slow-roast honeyed duck breast with braised red cabbage
and redcurrant, and Brussels sprout bubble-and-squeak.
Dark chocolate tart made with 70% cocoa, served with
lime sorbet, will get you nicely revved up for an all-night
summer solstice gathering.

Chef Matthew Bills **Owner** Arman Hotels Ltd **Prices** Fixed
D 3 course fr £18.95, Starter £5.40-£7.95, Main £11.25-
£18.80, Dessert £5.40-£5.60, Service optional
Wines 12 bottles over £20, 12 bottles under £20, 14 by
glass **Notes** Sunday L, Vegetarian available, Air con
Seats 80 **Children** Portions, Menu **Parking**

BRADFORD-ON-AVON
Map 4 ST86

The Three Gables

Modern European **NEW** V

Italian-influenced menu in a venerable greystone inn

☎ 01225 781666
St Margaret St BA15 1DA
e-mail: info@thethreegables.com

The name reflects the trio of architectural eminences that
surmount the façade of this venerable greystone inn not
far from the Silver Street town bridge. It's had an
extensive restoration throughout, with a contemporary
feel to the first-floor dining room, which extends across
the three gable windows, where a mixture of exposed
stonework and washed walls and a wood floor look the
part. The team that runs the place worked together in
Trowbridge before setting up here, and comprises front-
of-house manager Vito Scaduto and head chef Marc
Salmon. While the former proselytises for Italian wines
out front, the latter rustles up some assured, Italian-
influenced cooking out back. An assertive starter might
see arancini rice balls made with chorizo in pesto
dressing, or sweet potato tortellini given crunch with
roasted hazelnuts. Pasta dishes generally are full of to-
the-life authenticity, no more so than in a classic lunch

dish of wild mushroom ravioli dressed in parmesan and
truffle oil, while substantial main dishes in the evening
may encompass seared monkfish with braised lettuce, a
spring roll and bouillabaisse. A light and airy rhubarb
fool with coconut shortbread is a simple but effective
finisher.

Chef Marc Salmon **Owner** Marc Salmon
Times 12-2/6.30-10 Closed 1-12 Jan, Sun-Mon
Prices Fixed L 2 course fr £14, Fixed D 3 course fr £29.50,
Starter £5.50-£12.50, Main £15-£22, Dessert £6.25-
£8.50, Service optional **Wines** 250 bottles over £20,
20 bottles under £20, 16 by glass **Notes** Vegetarian menu
Seats 55 **Children** Portions **Parking** Public car park

The Tollgate Inn

Modern British

Spot-on cooking in 16th-century building

☎ 01225 782326
Ham Green, Holt BA14 6PX
e-mail: alison@tollgateholt.co.uk
web: www.tollgateholt.co.uk
dir: 2m E on B3107, at W end of Holt

The dual face that it presents to the world (half-and-half
stone and whitewash) reflects a little of the various roles
that the Tollgate has served within the community since
the 16th century. Firstly a weaving-shed, then a school,
and - until the 1970s - a cider house, it's now a
thoroughly hospitable country inn with four guest rooms
and the requisite accoutrements of comfy seating and
wood fires in the public rooms. A relaxing dining area
with candles and smartly attired staff aims to put
everybody at their ease, the more so with classically-
based, locally-sourced British cooking. Confit duck leg on
cabbage and bacon with orange and thyme sauce is a
crowd-pleaser, to the extent that it may be taken as
either starter or main. An Arnold Bennett omelette filled
with smoked fish also kicks things off with brio, before
something like Japanese-style sticky pork belly in soy and
ginger with wilted greens and chopped leeks. The
traditional beef Wellington has become something of a
local legend.

The Tollgate Inn

Chef Alexander Venables **Owner** Alexander Venables,
Alison Ward-Baptiste **Times** 11-2.30/5.30-11
Closed 25-26 Dec, 1 Jan, D Sun **Prices** Fixed L 2 course
£15.50, Fixed D 3 course £25.95-£32.95, Starter £5.50-
£12.50, Main £13.50-£21.50, Dessert £6.75-£7.95,
Service optional, Groups min 6 service 10%
Wines 22 bottles over £20, 16 bottles under £20, 9 by
glass **Notes** Sunday L, Vegetarian available **Seats** 60, Pr/
dining room 38 **Children** Portions **Parking** 40

Widbrook Grange

Modern British, French

French-accented brasserie in elegant country house

☎ 01225 864750
Trowbridge Rd, Widbrook BA15 1UH
e-mail: stay@widbrookgrange.com
dir: 1m S of Bradford-on-Avon on A363

Named after the brook that runs through its 11 peaceful
acres, Widbrook Grange was originally built as a model
farm in the early 18th century, and a keen eye can spot
bee bowls built into low walls on both sides of the house.
Sitting on the outskirts of the ancient town of Bradford-
on-Avon, close to the Kennet and Avon Canal, it is run
with a relaxed attitude. The former milking parlour now
houses the revamped French brasserie-inspired dining
room, a sunny setting of cheery pastels and coral-hued
high-backed chairs with a suitably Anglo-French accent
to its culinary output. Seasonal produce from the gardens
bolsters good quality ingredients from local suppliers -
perhaps rillettes of Wiltshire pork shoulder with rhubarb
chutney and melba toast to start, followed by duck leg
confit with Cassis sauce, garlicky green beans, Toulouse
sausage and gratin dauphinoise. The roll-call of desserts
might offer dark chocolate fondant with home-made
clotted cream ice cream and white chocolate sauce.

Chef Phil Carroll **Owner** Peter & Jane Wragg
Times 11.30-2.30/6-11 Closed 24-30 Dec **Prices** Starter
£5-£6.50, Main £12.50-£21.50, Dessert £5.50-£6.50,
Service included **Wines** 20 bottles over £20, 8 bottles
under £20, 8 by glass **Notes** Pre-theatre menu available,
Sunday L, Vegetarian available, Dress restrictions, Smart
casual, Civ Wed 50 **Seats** 45, Pr/dining room 14
Children Portions, Menu **Parking** 50

CALNE
Map 14 ST97

Bowood Hotel, Spa and Golf Resort

◉◉ Modern British V

Estate hotel with confident team in the kitchen

☎ 01249 822228
Derry Hill SN11 9PQ
e-mail: resort@bowood.org
dir: M4 junct 17, 2.5m W of Calne off A4

Newly-built in 2009, the Bowood Hotel delivers the full spa and golfing deal within the 2,000 sprawling acres of the eponymous estate. The classy Shelburne Restaurant takes its architectural inspiration from Robert Adam's 18th-century orangery fronting the nearby stately home, with its sweep of French windows looking over the outdoor terrace to the wooded green slopes of 'Capability' Brown-designed parkland beyond. The setting is slick and contemporary - neutral, earthy hues, darkwood tables, and stripy banquettes - and the grounds out there aren't just for show, since Lord and Lady Lansdowne's four-acre walled garden supplies a cornucopia of seasonal fruit and veg. The kitchen charts a contemporary course, keeping local produce at the heart of things, whether it's a terrine of smoked bacon, chicken and foie gras with Caesar dressing, or main-course best end and shoulder of Poll Dorset lamb accompanied by pea purée, chorizo dauphinoise and rosemary jus. The net has to be cast wider to bring in fish from Cornish day boats - perhaps

turbot fillet with smoked bacon and spring onion risotto with tarragon cream. For dessert, Baileys ganache might be the surprise at the melting heart of a chocolate fondant served with praline ice cream.

Chef Chris Lee **Owner** The Marquis of Lansdowne
Times 7-9.15 Closed L Mon-Sat **Prices** Starter £6.50-£12.50, Main £13.95-£27.50, Dessert £6.50-£9.50, Service optional **Wines** 103 bottles over £20, 5 bottles under £20, 12 by glass **Notes** Sunday L, Vegetarian menu, Dress restrictions, Smart casual, No jeans, Civ Wed 160 **Seats** 50, Pr/dining room 172 **Children** Portions, Menu **Parking** 200

CASTLE COMBE
Map 4 ST87

The Bybrook at the Manor

◉◉◉ – *see below*

COLERNE
Map 4 ST87

The Brasserie

◉ Modern British ☺

Wood-fired brasserie dining next to the spa

☎ 01225 742777
Lucknam Park Hotel & Spa SN14 8AZ
e-mail: brasserie@lucknampark.co.uk
dir: M4 junct 17, A350 towards Chippenham, then A420 towards Bristol for 3m. At Ford left to Colerne, 3m, right at x-rds, entrance on right

Right next door to the spa at Lucknam Park is The Brasserie, set within the walled garden, and enjoying views of the magnificent grounds. Dishes constituting lighter alternatives are flagged throughout the menu for the conscientious, but there's nothing to stop you undoing a morning's detoxing in the old-fashioned way. A wood-burning oven takes centre stage, producing rib-eye and fillet steaks and burgers, as well as roast halibut with aubergine and pine nuts in chilli-citrus dressing. Start with Fowey mussels steamed over cider with Carmarthen ham and a hunk of caramelised onion bread, and build up to white chocolate pannacotta with cinnamon doughnuts, glazed apples and sultanas, and happiness seems assured.

Chef Hywel Jones **Owner** Lucknam Park Hotels Ltd
Times 7.30am-10pm **Prices** Fixed L 2 course fr £19, Starter £7-£9, Main fr £16, Dessert fr £8, Service optional **Notes** Sunday L, Vegetarian available, Air con **Seats** 40 **Children** Portions, Menu **Parking** 80

The Bybrook at The Manor

CASTLE COMBE
Map 4 ST87

Modern British V ◆ NOTABLE WINE LIST

Modern British classics in a medieval manor house

☎ 01249 782206
The Manor House Hotel SN14 7HR
e-mail: enquiries@manorhouse.co.uk
dir: M4 junct 17, follow signs for Castle Combe via Chippenham

The unmolested medieval village of Castle Combe, about 20 minutes' drive out of Bath, is worth the journey all in itself, and has garnered an exalted reputation for itself in period filming. At its heart, The Manor House is a 14th-century edifice, among whose previous occupants was the real-life prototype of Shakespeare's Falstaff. The interiors are furnished with all the panache you would expect of such a grandiose house, with The Bybrook dining room

sporting mullioned windows, muted colours and linen-clad tables. Any lack of vivacity there is made up for by Richard Davies's cooking, which utilises local produce in an enterprising, though not deliberately startling, version of modern British thinking. That might translate as seared scallops with good old cauliflower purée in an agro-dolce dressing, or in more obviously Francophile guise as fine duck foie gras torchon in fig and port reduction with gingerbread. Fish main courses strike out into less familiar territory, as when Cornish turbot arrives with pak choi and a fricassée of ceps, celeriac and pancetta, while meats offer the reassuring likes of loin of rose veal with its sweetbreads in Madeira jus, or slow-cooked shoulder of Downlands lamb with confit shallots, minted peas and a rosemary jus. Salt, curtailed almost by government decree in savoury courses, reliably turns up in desserts these days, usually in the form of the salted caramel that accompanies powerfully rich Valrhona chocolate fondant and crème fraîche ice cream.

Chef Richard Davies **Owner** Exclusive Hotels
Times 12.30-2.30/7-9.30 Closed L Mon **Prices** Fixed L 2 course £25, Fixed D 3 course £60, Service added but optional 12.5% **Wines** 305 bottles over £20, 12 by glass **Notes** Tasting menu 7 course, Sunday L, Vegetarian menu, Dress restrictions, Smart casual, Civ Wed 100 **Seats** 60, Pr/dining room 120 **Children** Portions, Menu **Parking** 100

Save on Hotels. Book at **theAA.com/hotel**

WILTSHIRE 483 ENGLAND

The Park restaurant

COLERNE Map 4 ST87

Modern British V 🍷NOTABLE WINE LIST 🖐

Adventurous cooking in a stately home

☎ 01225 742777
Lucknam Park Hotel & Spa SN14 8AZ
e-mail: reservations@lucknampark.
co.uk
web: www.lucknampark.co.uk
dir: M4 junct 17, A350 to Chippenham,
then A420 towards Bristol for 3m. At
Ford left towards Colerne. In 4m right
into Doncombe Ln, then 300yds on right

Lucknam was built in the late 17th
century by a wealthy cloth merchant,
one James Wallis, who furnished it from
the proceeds of his sideline importing
Virginia tobacco in bulk. It continued to
pass from one well-heeled family to
another down the centuries, only
becoming corporately owned in the
1980s. Sitting serenely in 500 acres of
lush parkland, it's a stately pile indeed,
immaculately kept up within, and
decorated in soothing tones of English
pastoral. The Park restaurant is the
principal dining room, a light elegant
space with chandeliers and swags, but
with none of the panelled stolidity that
can weigh down the atmosphere of
country-house hotels. In any case,
nobody's spirits could droop with Hywel
Jones's cooking on hand. There has
always been a cheering sense of
adventure to his repertoire, which is
modern European in scope, but imbued

with a determination to sidestep many
of the clichés of contemporary dining.
Overtures and beginners are as lightly
and elegantly constructed as the
surroundings, from the cauliflower
pannacotta with salmon as a nibble, to
the hors d'oeuvre of something like
poached lobster with an ingenious
potato mousse, Oscietra and gribiche.
Succeeding dishes gradually build a
sense of substance, as in a main course
of very tender Brecon venison loin with
butternut squash and firm-textured
chestnut cannelloni, sauced with sloe
gin, or another of Cornish brill with
smoked sausage, girolles and Puy
lentils in red wine. Desserts maintain
the momentum with compositions such
as roast pineapple croustillant with rum
and raisin parfait, coconut sorbet and
macadamia caramel, or a crisp-topped
passionfruit cream, with textured
accompaniments in lemongrass, lime
leaf and mango.

Chef Hywel Jones **Owner** Lucknam Park
Hotels Ltd **Times** 1-3/6.30-10
Closed Mon, L Tue-Sat, D Sun
Prices Fixed L 3 course fr £39, Fixed D 3
course fr £70, Service optional
Wines 450 bottles over £20, 15 by glass
Notes Gourmand menu available from
£90, Sunday L, Vegetarian menu, Dress
restrictions, Jacket & tie preferred, no
jeans, leisurewear, Civ Wed 110
Seats 80, Pr/dining room 30
Children Portions, Menu **Parking** 80

COLERNE *continued*

The Park restaurant

🏵🏵🏵 *– see page 483*

See advert opposite

Guyers House Hotel

🏵🏵 Modern European **NEW**

Creative ideas in a traditional country house

☎ 01249 713399
Pickwick SN13 0PS
e-mail: enquiries@guyershouse.com

Set in six acres of lovely English gardens with a tennis court and croquet lawn, Guyers House is a classic country-house hotel that is equally as happy to sort out your wedding or business needs as it is to put you up in serene comfort. When it comes to dining, the kitchen keeps fruitful connections with the local food network, as well as furnishing the larder with fresh, seasonal ingredients from its own vegetable and herb garden. Although the setting is resolutely traditional, the menu can come up with some surprising compositions that work well, as in a starter that sees creamy fennel velouté poured over a roll of smoked salmon with crème fraîche and mixed cress at the table, or an unusual dessert involving spiced chocolate and sweet potato dauphine matched with chestnut ice cream and a dark chocolate pavé. Sandwiched between these delicious ideas, there's a fashionable multi-cut tasting of top-quality local Biddestone pork, consisting of roast belly and fillet, braised shoulder and a full-flavoured faggot matched with caramelised onion purée and crispy shallots.

Chef Gary Gardener, Gareth Johns, James Jones **Owner** Mr & Mrs Hungerford **Times** 12.30-2.30/7-9 Closed 30 Dec-3 Jan, **Prices** Fixed L 2 course £37-£47, Fixed D 3 course £55.50-£70.50, Starter £7.25-£8.25, Main £17-£24.95, Dessert £6.95-£7.95, Service optional **Wines** 42 bottles over £20, 6 bottles under £20, 5 by glass **Notes** Sunday L, Vegetarian available **Seats** 66, Pr/dining room 56 **Children** Portions, Menu **Parking** 60

Jack's Restaurant

🏵 Modern British, Mediterranean 🍃

Top-notch produce treated with respect

☎ 01249 700100
Hartham Park SN13 0RP
e-mail: rsupervisor@harthampark.com
dir: M4 junct 17, 2nd exit signed A350 Poole/
Chippenham, A4 signed Corsham/Bath

It is a pleasure to come across this smart modern restaurant in the lovely grounds of the historic Hartham House estate. The exterior says country house, but inside the décor fast-forwards to the 21st century, with its slick tiled walls and bare wooden tables. The kitchen cuts no corners, sourcing its produce diligently from duly name-checked local suppliers and making just about everything in-house from scratch, including jams, chutneys and ketchup. An unpretentious approach delivers a crowd-pleasing repertoire of traditional and contemporary ideas with a pleasingly domestic ring: take home-cured bresaola with fennel coleslaw and rocket, followed by a duo of Longhorn beef (chargrilled fillet and braised shin) with fondant potato, kale, shallot purée and sautéed wild mushrooms. Desserts can be as homespun as Bakewell tart with vanilla ice cream, or come with a touch of Mediterranean sun, as in an Amalfi lemon polenta cake with lemon and thyme ice cream.

Chef Jamie Hirst **Owner** Jeff Thomas **Times** 12-2.30/7-9 Closed 26 Dec-2 Jan, D Sun-Mon **Prices** Fixed L 2 course £15, Fixed D 3 course fr £19, Starter £5-£7.50, Main £10-£19, Dessert £5, Service optional, Groups min 8 service 10% **Wines** 14 bottles over £20, 13 bottles under £20, 20 by glass **Notes** Early D 3 course Tue-Thu 6.30-7.30pm, Sunday L, Vegetarian available, Air con **Seats** 40, Pr/dining room 170 **Children** Portions **Parking** 200

The Methuen Arms

🏵🏵 British, European 🍃

Gimmick-free modern cookery

☎ 01249 717060
2 High St SN13 0HB
e-mail: info@themethuenarms.com
dir: M4 junct 17 onto A350 towards Chippenham, at rdbt exit onto A4 towards Bath. 1m past lights, at next rdbt turn sharp left onto Pickwick Rd, 0.5m on left

The Methuen Arms is looking good after a classy refurb in 2010 relaunched the place as a contemporary boutique inn and put the handsome porticoed Georgian house back in action at the hub of Corsham village life. Bare elm floorboards, log fires, ancient beams and exposed stone walls all add up to a rustic-chic look, there are hand-pulled real ales at the bar, and the extensive menu of confident up-to-date dishes is just what we like to eat these days. The kitchen has taken a stance against foams and swipes, and promises top-grade local ingredients treated without fuss. Expect the likes of duck, pigeon and pork terrine with Cumberland sauce, followed by slow-roasted Longhorn brisket with butter beans, sauté spinach, and sherry vinegar and caper sauce; fish

fans might find roast monkfish in a Provençal partnership with aubergine ratatouille, olive oil mash and olive dressing. Desserts run to treacle tart with Wiltshire honey and yoghurt ice cream.

Chef Piero Boi **Owner** Still family **Times** 12-3/6-10 **Prices** Fixed L 2 course £15.50, Starter £5.95-£12.50, Main £12.50-£26.50, Dessert £5.50-£7.50, Service included **Wines** 52 bottles over £20, 15 bottles under £20, 14 by glass **Notes** Sunday L, Vegetarian available **Seats** 60, Pr/dining room 20 **Children** Portions, Menu **Parking** 40

The Bear Hotel

🏵🏵 Modern European **NEW**

Contemporary cooking in an elegant hotel

☎ 01380 722444
2-3 Market Place SN10 1HS
e-mail: info@thebearhotel.net
dir: In town centre, follow Market Place signs

There has been a hostelry of one sort or another on this site since medieval times, but The Bear really came up in the world in the 18th century, when the Lawrence family acquired it. They were soon welcoming George III and Queen Charlotte, and the honour-roll of famous names has barely abated since. Its restaurant, Lambtons, is named after a painting by the Lawrences' most famous scion, the portraitist Sir Thomas. It's an elegant space, with smartly clothed tables, polished silver and chandeliers. Adam Harty's cooking plies a popular line, mixing modern European influences with classical technique. Flavour combinations are sharply defined, as in starters of cured salmon with crab mayonnaise and fennel coleslaw, or pressed pig's head, foie gras and apple with thin toast. Some enterprising things are done with fish, in main courses such as brill with lobster ravioli in a shellfish essence and basil syrup. A study in citrus juxtaposes lemon tart, lime posset and grapefruit sorbet, or there may be apple and toffee variations. A fine selection of unpasteurised English farmhouse cheeses looks tempting too.

Chef Adam Harty **Owner** Craneview (Roundway) Ltd **Times** 12-2.30/7-9.30 Closed Mon-Tue, L Wed-Sat, D Sun **Prices** Fixed L 2 course £19, Starter £6.25-£9, Main £14-£26.95, Dessert £6-£9, Service optional **Wines** 28 bottles over £20, 27 bottles under £20, 16 by glass **Notes** Vegetarian available, Dress restrictions, Smart casual **Seats** 50, Pr/dining room 16 **Children** Portions, Menu **Parking**

The Lamb at Hindon

Traditional British

Comforting cooking in an ancient inn

☎ 01747 820573
High St SP3 6DP
e-mail: info@lambathindon.co.uk
dir: M3 junct 8 onto A303. Exit towards Hindon 4m after
Salisbury exit & follow signs to Hindon

In case you are wondering why this 17th-century coaching
inn in deepest Wiltshire has the feel of a Scottish hunting
lodge, that could be because it is owned by the group that
includes Boisdale of Belgravia (see entry) and brings the
same signature Scottish-accented style, including north-
of-the-border ingredients to rub shoulders with produce
sourced from closer to home. Inside, it is all heavy beams,
flagstoned floors, warm red walls, open fires in
inglenooks, and an impressive listing of wines and malts
to promote a convivial ambience. The kitchen deals in
hearty contemporary comforts along the lines of Bury
black pudding served with a poached hen's egg, chorizo,
bacon and mushrooms to start, followed perhaps by pot-
roasted loin of pork with cider and Calvados sauce, apple
purée and crackling, or breast and confit leg of guinea
fowl with sun-dried cranberry and Cognac sauce. A dark
Belgian chocolate and cocoa liqueur torte with crème
fraîche keeps the comfort factor topped up to the end.

Chef Andrzej Piechocki **Owner** Ranald Macdonald
(Boisdale plc) **Times** 12-2.30/7-9.15 **Prices** Starter
£4.50-£12, Main £9.50-£25, Dessert £4-£6.50, Service
added but optional 10% **Wines** 68 bottles over £20,
21 bottles under £20, 9 by glass **Notes** Vegetarian
available **Seats** 52, Pr/dining room 32 **Children** Portions,
Menu **Parking** 16

The Bath Arms at Longleat

Modern, Traditional British

Charming boutique hotel with accomplished cooking

☎ 01985 844308 & 07770 268359
Longleat Estate BA12 7LY
e-mail: enquiries@batharms.co.uk
dir: A36 Warminster. At Cotley Hill rdbt 2nd exit
(Longleat), Cleyhill rdbt 1st exit. Through Hitchcombe
Bottom, right at x-rds. Hotel on the green

A solid-looking stone property covered in creeper, The
Bath Arms is in a peaceful village within the Longleat
Estate. The hotel's aim is to create an atmosphere of
'informality, fun, friendliness and efficiency' and seems
to succeed on all counts, from a welcoming bar with its
own popular menu and local ales on handpump to a
dining room with chandeliers and king-sized candles
where young staff are friendly and eager. Local supplies
are at the heart of the operation, the menu focusing on
game in season: game sausage (actually more akin to
partridge mousse) with deeply flavoured apple jelly,
followed by roast pigeon with wild mushrooms and

braised chicory, say. Dishes are marked by an absence of
fuss and frills but the results hit the spot: duck pudding
with pickled cherries and walnuts, followed by pan-fried
sea bass with brown shrimps and white bean cassoulet,
and, to finish, rhubarb and coconut crumble with coconut
ice cream.

Times 12-2.30/7-9

The Harrow at Little Bedwyn

— see opposite

Compasses Inn

Modern British

Broadly appealing menu in an ancient inn

☎ 01722 714318
SP3 6NB
e-mail: thecompasses@aol.com
dir: Off A30 signed Lower Chicksgrove, 1st left onto
Lagpond Ln, single-track lane to village

Reached via a series of narrow lanes, the Compasses is a
low-slung thatched inn dating from the 14th century, a
charming place with a full quota of beams, standing
timbers, open fires, nooks and crannies and high-backed
wooden booths. It all seems a traditional setting for pub
classics like fish pie, and pork and apple sausages with
mustard mash and shallot jus, but the kitchen also gets
to work on more challenging modern ideas: roast
pheasant breast with shepherd's pie of the leg with pink
peppercorn sauce and mash, or pan-fried sea trout with
roast beetroot and horseradish cream. To start may be a
satisfying terrine of pork, liver and pistachios with
pickled red cabbage and chutney, or seared scallops on
black pudding with bacon, and to cap things off go for
rice pudding with home-made raspberry jam

Chef Dave Cousin, Geoff Mowlem **Owner** Alan & Susie
Stoneham **Times** 12-3/6-11 **Closed** 25-26 Dec, L Mon
(Jan-Mar) **Prices** Starter £5-£8.50, Main £9.50-£17.50,
Dessert £5.50-£6, Service optional **Wines** 10 bottles over
£20, 20 bottles under £20, 8 by glass **Notes** Sunday L,
Vegetarian available **Seats** 50, Pr/dining room 14
Children Portions, Menu **Parking** 35

Best Western Mayfield House Hotel

Modern British V

Well-judged British cooking with a local flavour

☎ 01666 577409
Crudwell SN16 9EW
e-mail: reception@mayfieldhousehotel.co.uk
dir: M4 junct 17, A429 to Cirencester. 3m N of
Malmesbury on right in Crudwell

In a wee village a few miles from Malmesbury, the
Mayfield is in the southern reaches of the Cotswolds and

is handy for the M4. The rambling, stone-built hotel is
furnished in a traditional manner with a restaurant done
out in soothing warm tones with modish leather-look,
high-backed chairs and white linen on the tables. On the
menu, local ingredients get a look in on the roster of well-
judged gently modern British dishes. Start with pan-fried
Cotswold duck livers with black pudding and poached
egg, or home-smoked Cornish mackerel fillets partnered
with an orange salsa, before main-course slow-roasted
Gloucestershire Old Spot pork belly (soft and tender,
excellent crackling) with roast sweet potato and
caramelised apple and cider jus.

Chef Nick Batstone **Owner** Frank & Lynne Segrave-Daly
Times 1-3/6-11 **Prices** Fixed L 2 course £10-£18, Fixed D
3 course £14-£26, Starter £4.50-£7, Main £12.50-£22.50,
Dessert £5-£7, Service optional **Wines** 8 bottles over £20,
16+ bottles under £20, 12 by glass **Notes** 20% discount
for pre-booked D, Sunday L, Vegetarian menu **Seats** 60,
Pr/dining room 30 **Children** Portions, Menu **Parking** 40

Old Bell Hotel

Modern British, French

Nearly eight centuries of service to Malmesbury

☎ 01666 822344
Abbey Row SN16 0BW
e-mail: info@oldbellhotel.com
dir: M4 junct 17, follow A429 north. Left at 1st rdbt. Left
at T-junct. Hotel next to Abbey

Laying claim to being the longest-serving hotel in
England (we're talking 1220 here), the Old Bell's
wisteria-clad, honey-hued Cotswold stone exterior
certainly looks the part. It's an effortlessly charming
place, with a rather grand dining room (high ceilings,
mullioned windows, white linen) that adds a sense of
occasion. But the accomplished kitchen is not stuck in
the past, serving up modern British dishes underpinned
by a classical theme. Interesting flavour combinations
are fashioned from quality produce and delivered with
cheffy presentation; sautéed monkfish, perhaps, served
with cep consommé, oxtail and spinach to open
proceedings, while to follow, rabbit loin might be wrapped
in Parma ham accompanied by rabbit ragout, fondant
potato and carrots. Finish on a light note with Muscat
mousse with almond foam and crème fraîche sorbet.

Chef Jason Drew **Owner** The Old Bell Hotel Ltd
Times 12.15-2/7-9.30 **Closed** D Sun-Mon **Prices** Fixed D
3 course £42.50, Service optional **Wines** 180 bottles over
£20, 5 bottles under £20, 13 by glass **Notes** Sunday L,
Vegetarian available, Dress restrictions, Smart dress
preferred, Civ Wed 90 **Seats** 60, Pr/dining room 48
Children Portions, Menu **Parking** 35

Save on Hotels. Book at **theAA.com/hotel**

WILTSHIRE 487 **ENGLAND**

The Harrow at Little Bedwyn

LITTLE BEDWYN Map 5 SU26

Modern British V NOTABLE WINE LIST

Shining beacon of quality food and wine in a Victorian pub

☎ 01672 870871
SN8 3JP
e-mail: reservations@harrowinn.co.uk
web: www.theharrowatlittlebedwyn.com
dir: Between Marlborough & Hungerford, well signed

The Harrow is a Victorian pub, built of red and grey brick, partly clothed in climbing foliage, not far from the Kennet and Avon canal in rural Wiltshire. Inside has been carefully modernised, with a tawny palette to soothe the senses, original floorboards and tiles retained, the interlinked rooms joined by that familiar fixture of the modern country pub, a double-sided wood-burning stove. If it all sounds pleasantly unremarkable so far, think again. Now in its second decade under the conscientious stewardship of Roger and Sue Jones, the place is a shining beacon of quality. Roger's food celebrates simplicity, with each of the classy components of a dish speaking of itself. Spring's reds and purples arrive in the form of an intense beetroot and rhubarb chutney to accompany Dorstone, a Herefordshire goats' cheese, while poached lobster from the Welsh coast is given an equally vivid carrot jus. The celebrated versatility of pork takes on the guises of belly, fillet and a faggot of Kelmscott, with traditional apple garnishes, or there may be Cornish sea bass with bracing accompaniments of lobster and shrimp tempura. Multi-course tasting menus, including a vegetarian version that essays a culinary tour d'horizon from Morocco, via Italy and India, to exotic England for a dish of Somerset's Tymsboro cheese with truffles and cauliflower. Desserts strike out for distant shores too, when Thai rice pudding comes with marinated lychees, pistachio ice cream and a pine nut tuile, but there could just as easily be bread-and-butter pudding with prunes. It won't be long before you notice that everything on every menu comes with a drink suggestion (usually grape wine, but there's a Japanese plum wine to go with that Thai pudding). Sue Jones's enthusiasm and profound knowledge shine through in what is undoubtedly one of England's premier-league wine lists. You can only feel sorry for the designated driver.

Chef Roger Jones, John Brown
Owner Roger & Sue Jones
Times 12-3/7-11 Closed Xmas & New Year, Sun-Tue **Prices** Fixed L 3 course fr £30, Fixed D 4 course fr £50, Starter £15, Main £28, Dessert £9.50, Service optional **Wines** 900 bottles over £20, 10 bottles under £20, 20 by glass **Notes** Fixed L 3 course & wine £30, Gourmet menu 8 course £75, Vegetarian menu, Dress restrictions, Smart casual **Seats** 34 **Children** Menu **Parking** On street

MALMESBURY *continued*

Whatley Manor

◉◉◉◉ – *see opposite*

Beechfield House Hotel, Restaurant & Gardens

◉ Modern British ✿

Contemporary country-house dining

☎ 01225 703700
Beanacre SN12 7PU
e-mail: reception@beechfieldhouse.co.uk
dir: M4 junct 17, A350 S, bypass Chippenham, towards Melksham. Hotel on left after Beanacre

Externally, Beechfield House is a striking Venetian style late-Victorian country house built of Bath stone, but once inside it is clearly a switched-on operation that stays abreast of the times. An understated contemporary style has lightened up the look in the dining room: ornate period plasterwork sits well alongside a crystal chandelier above a de-cluttered setting of plush burgundy velvet seats, white linen-clad tables and an antique rug on stripped pine floors. Modern sensibilities are also assuaged by creative cooking founded on top-grade local produce - a simple, well-balanced starter involving duck breast 'bresaola', Medjool dates and blood orange might precede a chop and slow-cooked breast of Gloucestershire lamb, partnered by fondant potato, swede and leek. Finish with ginger parkin, marmalade ice cream, golden raisins and spiced syrup.

Chef Paul Horrell **Owner** Chris Whyte **Times** 12-2/7-9 Closed 23-26 Dec, D Sun **Prices** Fixed L 2 course fr £17.50, Starter £5.25-£5.95, Main £16.25-£18.25, Dessert £5-£5.85, Service optional **Wines** 29 bottles over £20, 16 bottles under £20, 5 by glass **Notes** Sunday L, Vegetarian available, Dress restrictions, Smart casual, Civ Wed 70 **Seats** 22, Pr/dining room 20 **Children** Portions, Menu **Parking** 70

The Wheatsheaf at Oaksey

◉◉ Modern British ✿

Intelligent modish food in a lovely pub setting

☎ 01666 577348
Wheatsheaf Ln SN16 9TB
e-mail: info@thewheatsheafatoaksey.co.uk
dir: Off A429 towards Cirencester, near Kemble

Relaxed and informal pub dining is the name of the game at this smart village inn. Inside it has roaring fires and comfy armchairs and the sort of relaxed approach which means you can take the same menu in the more formal restaurant or the traditional bar. The kitchen is in the capable hands of father and son team, Tony and Jack Robson-Burrell, the latter having been trained at The Ritz. The menu reveals sound classical thinking and

judiciously imagined flavour combinations; thus home-smoked salmon salad with pecorino and caper dressing might be followed by Hereford beef shin suet pudding with Savoy cabbage and bacon, and for dessert, a dark chocolate pot is served with hazelnut and chocolate chip cookie. There are also gourmet burgers (The Surfer or New Yorker, perhaps?), and children are well catered for.

Chef Tony Robson-Burrell, Jack Robson-Burrell **Owner** Tony & Holly Robson-Burrell **Times** 12-2/6.30-9.30 Closed Mon, D Sun **Prices** Starter £6.50-£9, Main £13.50-£26.50, Dessert £6.50-£7, Service optional **Wines** 16 bottles over £20, 16 bottles under £20, 10 by glass **Notes** Sunday L, Vegetarian available **Seats** 50, Pr/dining room 8 **Children** Portions, Menu **Parking** 15

The Pear Tree at Purton

◉◉ Modern British

Confident modern cooking in a former vicarage

☎ 01793 772100
Church End SN5 4ED
e-mail: stay@peartreepurton.co.uk
web: www.peartreepurton.co.uk
dir: From M4 junct 16, follow signs to Purton. Turn right at Bestone shop, hotel 0.25m on right

On the outskirts of the Saxon village of Purton, between the Marlborough Downs and the Cotswolds, this Cotswold-stone one-time vicarage has beautiful gardens which extends to wetlands, a wild flower meadow and a 600-vine-strong vineyard. Today's country-house hotel has a conservatory restaurant where local produce is the star of the show on the menu, be it the hotel's own honey for breakfast, pork and eggs from nearby villages and their truly house wine, Cuvée Alix. Bibury trout rillette with confit chicken wings and cucumber salsa verde is a smart, modish starter, followed by the likes of Wiltshire pork tenderloin with black pudding purée, cider vinegar and spring onion mash. Creative puds might take in pistachio cake with burnt orange syrup, Pear Tree honey and lavender ice cream.

Chef Alan Postill **Owner** Francis & Anne Young
Times 12-2/7-9.15 **Prices** Fixed L 2 course fr £15, Fixed D

4 course fr £35.50, Service optional **Wines** 76 bottles over £20, 24 bottles under £20, 11 by glass **Notes** Sunday L, Vegetarian available, Dress restrictions, Smart casual, no shorts **Seats** 50, Pr/dining room 50 **Children** Portions **Parking** 70

The George & Dragon

◉◉ Modern British

Old coaching inn with the focus on seafood

☎ 01380 723053
High St SN10 2PN
e-mail: thegandd@tiscali.co.uk
dir: On A342, 1m from Devizes towards Chippenham

This 16th-century coaching inn specialises in seafood brought up every day from St Mawes in Cornwall. It's a wonderfully atmospheric place with bags of period character, including a Tudor rose carved into one of the ancient beams. You can eat in the small bar or the equally diminutive restaurant, which sports antique rugs on wooden floors and unclothed wooden tables. The food keeps things pleasingly straightforward and it's not entirely about seafood. You might kick off with fishy hors d'oeuvres or salt and pepper chilli squid salad, followed by whole grilled mackerel with anchovy butter, or salmon fillet teriyaki with soy, ginger and spinach. A meaty alternative might be roast rack of lamb with mint pea purée and red wine jus, with the reassuringly named ye olde lemon posset for afters.

Times 12-3/7-11 Closed D Sun

Best Western Red Lion Hotel

◉ Modern European

Contemporary cooking in an 800-year-old inn

☎ 01722 323334
Milford St SP1 2AN
e-mail: reception@the-redlion.co.uk
dir: In city centre close to Guildhall Square

Whether or not the venerable Red Lion really is England's oldest surviving purpose-built hotel is something the historians can argue over, but you'll certainly find little to fault in the atmospheric vibes, ancient wattle-and-daub walls and gnarled beams of the Vine dining room, which is named in honour of the 300-year-old Virginia creeper in the courtyard. Hearty, uncomplicated flavours prevail on a menu of modern European ideas that could get under way with oak-smoked duck breast partnered with foie gras brûlée and apple and radish salad, followed by a main course of confit pork belly with pork and foie gras ballotine, pan-fried pork fillet, roasted pear, mash, choucroute, and mustard cream. At the end, perhaps rhubarb and custard iced parfait with popping candy, raspberry purée and raspberry crumble topping.

Times 12.30-2/6-9.30 Closed L Mon-Sat

Save on Hotels. Book at **theAA.com/hotel**

WILTSHIRE 489 ENGLAND

Whatley Manor

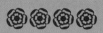

Modern French   NOTABLE WINE LIST

Technically brilliant contemporary French cooking in a luxury spa hotel

☎ 01666 822888
Easton Grey SN16 0RB
e-mail: reservations@whatleymanor.com
web: www.whatleymanor.com
dir: M4 junct 17, follow signs to Malmesbury, continue over 2 rdbts. Follow B4040 & signs for Sherston, hotel 2m on left

Whatley Manor is one of the UK's A-list country-house hotels, a place where absolute attention to detail in every aspect of its operation reigns supreme. There's a real feeling of expectation as the gated entrance swings open into its cobbled courtyards of honey-stone Cotswold buildings. Insulated from the real world by 12 acres of meadows, woodland, and fabulous gardens, Whatley is undeniably special, but there's nothing that jars in its opulent interiors: serious money has been lavished on designing its rambling lounges and it's all effortlessly tasteful. Luxurious La Prairie spa treatments in the Wave Dream Sensory Room and the Camomile Steam Grotto are no doubt poetry to sybaritic ears, but gastronomes will be transported by the prospect of culinary nirvana in the Dining Room, a quietly refined, understated space of unusual pale bamboo wood floors, buttermilk walls, and subtle lighting. After perfecting his craft at stellar establishments such as Pied à

Terre, L'ortolan and Raymond Blanc's Le Manoir aux Quat' Saisons, it should come as no surprise that chef Martin Burge's cooking is driven by the values of the modern French idiom, and a perusal of the menu reveals a cerebral approach to balancing flavours. From the off - an amuse of smoked haddock tartare with compressed cucumber and wasabi ice cream - it is clear that every molecule of flavour is teased out of the ingredients. A signature starter offers a playful take on the classic escargots Bourguignon, setting braised snails in a garlic cassonade with side dishes of intense parsley purée, and red wine sauce infused with veal kidney. Having grabbed your attention with this display of finely-honed technical skills, an elaborately-crafted main course brings delicately-flavoured breasts of roast partridge with Morteau sausage, pearl barley and a crisp samosa of leg meat - a simple-sounding idea that is in fact a virtuoso workout involving mousse, jelly, purée and ballottine of the various elements. An invigorating pre-dessert of banana pannacotta, passionfruit granita and crisp crêpes paves the way for an intriguing finale of black truffle ice cream dressed with lightly-creamed roquefort, deep fried crottin goats' cheese and candied walnuts. This is all ravishingly good-looking food with flavours that show this chef has an innate understanding of what works with what, and luckily there is an expert sommelier at hand to ensure that you drink something that will enhance the experience further still, chosen from a formidable list of modern and classic

bottles from the Old and New worlds. Last but not least, staff work with the same precision that informs the cooking, friendly and knowledgeable and devoid of any starchy formality. The less formal dining venue is Le Mazot, a Swiss chalet-style brasserie with a lovely alfresco patio.

Chef Martin Burge **Owner** Christian Landolt & Alix Landolt **Times** 7-10 Closed Mon-Tues, L all week **Prices** Food prices not confirmed for 2013. Please telephone for details **Wines** 265 bottles over £20, 5 bottles under £20, 18 by glass **Notes** ALC menu £76, tasting menu £96, Vegetarian available, Civ Wed 120 **Seats** 40, Pr/dining room 30 **Children** Portions **Parking** 120

SALISBURY *continued*

Salisbury Seafood & Steakhouse

◉ International

The clue is the name

☎ 01722 417411 & 424110
Milford Hall Hotel, 206 Castle St SP1 3TE
e-mail: reception@milfordhallhotel.com
dir: From A36 at rdbt on Salisbury ring road, right onto Churchill Way East. At St Marks rdbt left onto Churchill Way North to next rdbt, left in Castle St

Just a gentle stroll from Salisbury's historic market square, Milford Hall Hotel is a red-brick Georgian mansion on the outside, with a stylish blend of period elegance and clean-cut contemporary style within. Cream and brown leather high-backed chairs, wooden floors and walls lined with suede and stacked with wine bottles make a stylish setting for a hearty repertoire of surf and turf dishes. Old favourites strike a retro note - perhaps chicken liver and brandy terrine with Cumberland sauce to get things going, followed by a properly aged and chargrilled steak, or slow-braised beef sirloin with roast potatoes, shallots and a blue cheese, port and chive jus. On the surf side, you could go for a whole grilled plaice with crab, lime and ginger stuffing and lemongrass oil or chargrilled salmon steak with dill and lemon butter.

Chef Chris Gilbert **Owner** Simon Hughes **Times** 12-2/6-10 Closed 26 Dec, D 25 Dec **Prices** Fixed L 2 course £9.95, Fixed D 3 course £19.95, Starter £4.95-£8.25, Main £9.95-£24, Dessert £4.95-£6.50, Service optional, Groups min 6 service 10% **Wines** 18 bottles over £20, 18 bottles under £20, 10 by glass **Notes** Sunday L, Vegetarian available, Civ Wed 120 **Seats** 55, Pr/dining room 20 **Children** Portions, Menu **Parking** 60

Stanton Manor Hotel

◉ British, French

Modish cooking in a country house with a history

☎ 01666 837552
SN14 6DQ
dir: M4 junct 17 onto A429 Malmesbury/Cirencester, in 200yds 1st left signed Stanton St Quintin. Hotel entrance on left just after church

The once ancient manor - set in six acres of well-preened grounds - was formerly owned by Elizabeth I's High Treasurer and Chief Minister, Lord Burghley, but after a rebuild in 1840, all that remains of the original are its fireplaces and a dovecote. That said, it doesn't lack character; there are high ceilings and flagstone floors, and the stylishly refurbished Gallery Restaurant looks the part with apricot-washed walls, wooden flooring and artworks by young Asian artists. The kitchen deals in accomplished, classically-rooted modern cooking driven by prime local produce; think braised shoulder of spring lamb served with seared sweetbread, crushed peas, truffled creamed potato and smoked garlic jus, while a fish dish might be fillet of guilt head bream with bubble-and-squeak, carrot purée, baby spinach and a port reduction.

Chef Christopher Box **Owner** Robert David **Times** 12-2.30/7-9 Closed for wedding receptions **Prices** Fixed D 3 course £29.50, Service optional **Wines** 24 bottles over £20, 6 bottles under £20, 4 by glass **Notes** Sunday L, Vegetarian available, Dress restrictions, Smart casual **Seats** 26, Pr/dining room 80 **Children** Portions **Parking**

Chiseldon House Hotel

◉ Modern European

Unfussy cooking in a Regency manor house

☎ 01793 741010
New Rd, Chiseldon SN4 0NE
e-mail: welcome@chiseldonhouse.com
dir: M4, junct 15, A346 signed Marlborough. After 0.5m turn right onto B4500 for 0.25m, hotel on right

Chiseldon is an elegant Regency-era manor house in the Marlborough Downs, in the embrace of beautiful gardens where wedding parties are often to be found roaming. Inside, it is a relaxed and traditional place, with dining taking place in the romantically candlelit Orangery restaurant. A young front-of-house crew makes sure that everyone is at their ease, while the kitchen brigade has an eye for good-quality local produce, which it brings together in uncomplicated, tried-and-true combinations - duck liver parfait with apricot chutney and melba toast being a case in point. No horses will be scared either by a main course of roast chicken breast with fondant potato, crispy pancetta and thyme jus, but it is all nicely-balanced, flavoursome and comforting stuff. Rounding

things off, there may be a bitter chocolate tart with vanilla pannacotta.

Chef Robert Harwood **Owner** Mark & David Pennells **Times** 12-2/7-9 **Prices** Fixed L 2 course £15.95-£19.95, Fixed D 3 course £25.95-£31.95, Service optional **Wines** 13 bottles over £20, 15 bottles under £20, 7 by glass **Notes** Sunday L, Vegetarian available, Civ Wed 85 **Seats** 65, Pr/dining room 25 **Children** Portions **Parking** 85

The Dove Inn

◉ Modern, Traditional

Appealing local inn with good pub grub

☎ 01985 850109
Corton BA12 0SZ
e-mail: info@thedove.co.uk
web: www.thedove.co.uk
dir: A303 off A36, Salisbury to Bath road

The local community is lucky to have the pretty 19th-century Dove Inn in its midst. Whether it's for a pint of real ale, a sandwich or the full three-courses, the traditional country freehouse has bags of charm and plenty of style. There are period features aplenty - flagstone and oak floors, wood-burning stove - and a restaurant with a conservatory that serves up some crowd-pleasing food in a charming and relaxed setting. Start with garden pea and Wiltshire ham soup served with crusty bread, or a cheese fondue with spring dips, followed by the 'Corton classic' (a burger with melted cheese, bacon, red onion marmalade and skinny fries), something from the daily fish board, or a light main course of devilled kidneys on sourdough bread.

Times 12-3/6-11 Closed D Sun

Save on Hotels. Book at **theAA.com/hotel**

WORCESTERSHIRE 491 **ENGLAND**

WORCESTERSHIRE

BEWDLEY   Map 10 SO77

The Mug House Inn

◉ Modern British

Good country-inn cooking alongside the Severn

☎ 01299 402543
12 Severnside North DY12 2EE
e-mail: drew@mughousebewdley.co.uk
web: www.mughousebewdley.co.uk
dir: B4190 to Bewdley. On river, just over bridge on right

Not every dining venue is equipped with a sonorous name, and the Angry Chef restaurant at The Mug House has rather a lot of preconception to overcome, you might think. In fact, it's in a dream location alongside the Severn with a sun terrace and glassed-in patio, the mugs are the kind you drink ale out of, and the chef isn't angry at all, just furiously dedicated. A live lobster tank is a relatively unusual sight these days; overcome any misgivings and you could have one grilled with mustard and paprika cream, garnished with slices of scallop and truffle. At the pubbier end of the spectrum, expect goats' cheese baked in filo with spicy tomato chutney, then flavourful, pink-cooked rump of lamb with roasted shallots and ratatouille in thyme jus, finishing with pannacotta served with chocolate and coffee sauces and amaretti.

Chef Drew Clifford, Zac Birchley **Owner** Drew Clifford
Times 12-2.30/6.30-9 Closed D Sun **Prices** Fixed D 3 course fr £15.95, Starter £3.95-£6.75, Main £12.95-£30, Dessert £5.95-£6.95, Service optional **Wines** 8 bottles over £20, 22 bottles under £20, 10 by glass **Notes** Fixed D Mon-Thu only, Sunday L, Vegetarian available, Dress restrictions, Smart casual **Seats** 26, Pr/dining room 12 **Parking** Car park 100mtrs along river

Royal Forester Country Inn

◉ Modern European

Contemporary dining in medieval inn

☎ 01299 266286
Callow Hill DY14 9XW
e-mail: royalforesterinn@btinternet.com

A sympathetic makeover has brought 21st-century comforts to this 15th-century inn while retaining the best of its venerable features. There's a bar with sofas and a baby grand, and a meandering restaurant full of nooks and crannies, with bare-brick walls and ancient timbers. The menus change daily on the basis of that morning's deliveries, with fish brought up from Cornwall (perhaps grilled tranche of turbot with clams and Parmentier potatoes) and game a speciality in season: perhaps a starter of guinea fowl and tarragon ballottine with pickled carrots and a verjus reduction. Consistently high standards can be seen throughout the wide-ranging menu, from mackerel three ways (pan-seared fillet, spicy tartare and pâté) to monkfish tails roasted with pancetta, served with tomato and herb sauce, or roast duck breast

with a damson gin jus, with chocolate bread-and-butter pudding to finish.

Chef Mark Hammond **Owner** Sean McGahern, Maxine Parker **Times** 12-3/6-9.30 **Prices** Fixed L 2 course £9.99-£11.99, Fixed D 3 course £14.99, Starter £4.95-£9.50, Main £11.50-£18.50, Dessert £4.45-£5.50, Service optional **Wines** 38 bottles over £20, 39 bottles under £20, 6 by glass **Notes** Gourmet menu with 4 glasses of wine £30, Sunday L, Vegetarian available **Seats** 60, Pr/dining room 18 **Children** Portions **Parking** 25

BROADWAY   Map 10 SP03

Dormy House Hotel

◉◉ Modern British

Creative cooking in an impressive Cotswold house

☎ 01386 852711
Willersey Hill WR12 7LF
e-mail: reservations@dormyhouse.co.uk
web: www.dormyhouse.co.uk
dir: 2m E off A44, top of Fish Hill, turn for Saintbury picnic area. After 0.5m left, hotel on left

Dormy House has come a long way since the 17th century, when it was a simple farmhouse in the heart of the Cotswolds. Fast forward to the modern world and the honey-stone hotel above Broadway is a class act, pulling off that elusive trick of being an elegant, smooth-running country house that nonetheless retains the human touch. A tasteful conversion has resulted in a luminous, romantic feel throughout, with high-backed chairs, blond-wood floors, down-lit artwork and sculptures and linen-swathed tables in the understated contemporary dining room. Menu descriptions sound refreshingly simple and display a keen eye to the seasons. The result is imaginative dishes in the contemporary country-house vein, kicking off with a pumpkin crème brûlée topped with a crunchy thyme-flavoured crust, followed by perfectly-judged medallions of venison served enterprisingly with Savoy cabbage and bacon, spinach-filled chocolate ravioli and parsnip crisps. Flavours and seasonings remain clear as a bell all the way through to a dessert line-up of chocolate fondant served with blood orange sorbet and a warm chocolate milkshake.

Chef Paul Napper **Owner** Mrs I Philip-Sorensen
Times 12-2/7-9.30 Closed 24-27 Dec, L Mon-Sat
Prices Fixed L 2 course £19.50, Fixed D 3 course £38, Starter £5.95-£8.95, Main £12.95-£21.95, Dessert £6.95-£8, Service optional **Wines** 70 bottles over £20, 10 bottles under £20, 10 by glass **Notes** Sunday L, Vegetarian

available, Dress restrictions, No jeans **Seats** 80, Pr/dining room 170 **Children** Portions, Menu **Parking** 80

The Lygon Arms

◉◉ Modern British

Majestic Tudor hotel with 21st-century comforts

☎ 01386 852255
High St WR12 7DU
e-mail: info@thelygonarms.co.uk
dir: From Evesham take A44 signed Oxford, 5m. Follow Broadway signs. Hotel on left

The old honey-stoned Lygon has borne witness to a good deal of history over its 500 or so years, not least hosting both Oliver Cromwell and his regal adversary, Charles I. These days a smart and rather luxurious country-house hotel, there is much to remind one of times gone by, not least the impressive great hall, with its barrel-vaulted ceiling and minstrels' gallery, which serves as the main restaurant. It is quite a space, with acres of oak panelling, two giant chandeliers (not trad ones though) and tables set with crisp white linen. And in keeping with the building, the cooking is built on classic foundations with an added touch of 21st-century vitality. An open ravioli first course is packed with wild mushrooms, Italian bacon, chestnuts and lentils, and finished with a deftly judged truffle and black vinegar dressing. Next up, perhaps a fillet of turbot with stir-fried kale and spring onions, and beetroots both roasted and puréed. For dessert, lemon meringue pie with lemon jelly and citrus sorbet is dressed to kill.

Chef Peter Manner **Owner** Puma Hotels
Times 12-2/7-9.30 Closed L Sat **Prices** Fixed L 2 course £19-£22.50, Fixed D 3 course £39-£45, Starter £10.50-£13.50, Main £32-£36, Dessert £10.50-£11, Service optional **Wines** 101 bottles over £20, 16 by glass **Notes** Sunday L, Vegetarian available, Dress restrictions, Smart casual, no jeans, T-shirts or trainers, Civ Wed 100 **Seats** 80, Pr/dining room 110 **Children** Portions, Menu **Parking** 150

BROADWAY *continued*

Russell's

@@ Modern British 🌱

Smart setting for modern cooking

☎ 01386 853555
20 High St WR12 7DT
e-mail: info@russellsofbroadway.co.uk
dir: A44 follow signs to Broadway, restaurant on High St
opposite village green

The pretty village isn't short of mellow Cotswold-stone
properties, and this is one of them, now a stylish,
contemporary-looking restaurant with rooms, where large
glass doors open on to a patio for alfresco dining.
Produce bought locally, with fish from English waters,
means that ingredients are fresh and seasonal, and the
kitchen uses them to put together a wide-ranging menu
that's full of appeal. An orient-inspired starter of crab, as
tempura, spring roll and with coconut and lemongrass
broth, may appear alongside foie gras with Armagnac
prunes and brioche. Main courses show the same sort of
scope, from precisely timed turbot fillet roasted in a herb
crust, served with leek terrine and chervil mousseline, to
a well-composed meat offering of roast breast of chicken
accompanied by crisp prosciutto and cannelloni of leg
confit and sweetbreads.

Chef Damian Clisby **Owner** Andrew Riley
Times 12-2.30/6-9.30 Closed D Sun & BH Mon
Prices Fixed L 2 course £14.95, Fixed D 3 course £17.95-
£22.95, Service optional **Wines** 38 bottles over £20,
12 bottles under £20, 12 by glass **Notes** Sunday L,
Vegetarian available **Seats** 60, Pr/dining room 14
Children Portions **Parking** 7

CHADDESLEY CORBETT   Map 10 SO87

Brockencote Hall Country House Hotel

@@ Modern British **V** 🌱

Vivid modern British dishes amid Victorian splendour

☎ 01562 777876
DY10 4PY
e-mail: info@brockencotehall.com
dir: M5 junct 4 to A38 Bromsgrove, then A448 just outside
village, between Kidderminster & Bromsgrove

A rather grand country manor house in 70 acres, complete
with lake and views of the Malvern Hills, Brockencote Hall
is a compelling exercise in country luxury. The dining
room looks the part, with elegant cutlery and glassware
on formally dressed tables, beneath a frosted-glass
skylight. A kitchen team with quite some pedigree
specialises in inspired modern British dishes with plenty
of vivid flavours and some interesting juxtapositions.
First up might be brown crab bavarois with salmon
rillettes and cucumber, before pan-roasted hake and
choucroute, with onions and nigella seed, or loin of beef
with smoked ox tongue, sprouting broccoli and beetroot.
Dessert might showcase that fashionable citrus,
kalamansi, in the form of a rich curd, with a fromage
blanc sorbet and pine nuts, while the crème brûlée is

made with duck egg, and accompanied by poached
rhubarb and its sorbet.

Chef Adam Brown **Owner** Eden Hotel Collection
Times 12-3/6.45-9.45 **Prices** Fixed L 2 course £22.50,
Fixed D 3 course £39.50-£59.50, Tasting menu £55-£75,
Service optional **Wines** 142 bottles over £20, 8 bottles
under £20, 12 by glass **Notes** Tasting menu L 5 course, D
6 course, Sunday L, Vegetarian menu, Dress restrictions,
Smart dress, Civ Wed 80 **Seats** 80, Pr/dining room 20
Children Portions, Menu **Parking** 60

EVESHAM   Map 10 SP04

The Kings Arms at Cleeve Prior

@ Traditional British **NEW**

British classics in an inviting village inn

☎ 01789 773335
Bidford Rd, Cleeve Prior WR11 8LQ
e-mail: contact@thekingsarmsatcleeveprior.co.uk
dir: M50, M40 between Stratford-upon-Avon & Evesham

In the postcard-pretty village of Cleeve Prior, within
striking distance of Stratford-upon-Avon and the
Cotswolds, hands-on new owners have injected a healthy
shot of contemporary flair to this charming 16th-century
stone-built inn. Inside, there's a proper pubby bar, and in
the dining room ancient oak beams blend with exposed
stone, wooden boards and bare tables. The man at the
stoves is a finalist from BBC's *MasterChef* 2011, who
treats the classic British food in a simple, forthright
manner, whether you go for the keenly-priced fixed-price
menu, or trade up to the carte, where you might get going
with guinea fowl and mushroom terrine served with
gherkins and toast, and follow with slow-cooked duck leg
with mustard croûtons and red wine sauce. Finish with a
plate of local cheeses or something sweet like oven-
roasted caramel bananas with hot chocolate sauce.

Chef Peter Seville **Owner** Peter Seville, Bryan Marshall
Times 12-3/6-9 Closed Mon, D Sun **Prices** Fixed L 2
course £12, Fixed D 3 course £15, Starter £4.95-£6.95,
Main £10.95-£16.95, Dessert £4.95-£7.95, Service
optional **Wines** 13 bottles over £20, 22 bottles under £20,
14 by glass **Notes** Fixed L Tue-Fri 12-3pm & D Tue-Thu
6-9pm, Sunday L, Vegetarian available **Seats** 50
Children Portions **Parking** 20

KIDDERMINSTER   Map 10 SO87

The Granary Hotel & Restaurant

@@ Modern British

Smart seasonal cooking

☎ 01562 777535
Heath Ln, Shenstone DY10 4BS
e-mail: info@granary-hotel.co.uk
web: www.granary-hotel.co.uk
dir: On A450 between Worcester & Stourbridge. 2m from
Kidderminster

Close to the Midlands motorway arteries, yet nicely
located in the countryside on the fringes of Kidderminster,
the boutique-style Granary Hotel boasts its own market
garden to supply the kitchen with the ultimate in low-
mileage fruit and veg. The key players in the kitchen
brigade have worked together for the best party of a
decade and have developed a contemporary style of
cooking that is all about working with the seasons and
bringing great ingredients together in well-considered
compositions. Given that the restaurant is about as far
from the coast as it is possible to be in the UK, the team's
dedication to sourcing fresh fish for the daily fish menu is
impressive, and it is presented without fuss in simple
dishes such as poached turbot with mussels, or pan-
roast monkfish in Cajun spices. Elsewhere, there could be
lambs' kidneys sautéed with mushrooms, bacon and
cream as a curtain-raiser to marinated rump of lamb
with dauphinoise potatoes, roasted root vegetables,
spinach, and redcurrant jus.

Chef Tom Court **Owner** Richard Fletcher
Times 12-2.30/7-11 Closed L Mon, Sat, D Sun
Prices Fixed L 2 course £10.95, Fixed D 3 course £17.95-
£19.95, Starter £5.95-£9.95, Main £14.50-£24.50,
Dessert £5.25-£6.50, Service optional **Wines** 14 bottles
over £20, 24 bottles under £20, 12 by glass **Notes** Sunday
L, Vegetarian available, Civ Wed 200 **Seats** 60, Pr/dining
room 40 **Children** Portions **Parking** 95

Save on Hotels. Book at **theAA.com/hotel**

WORCESTERSHIRE 493 ENGLAND

Stone Manor Hotel

◉ Modern British

Traditional comforts and good, modish eating

☎ 01562 777555
Stone DY10 4PJ
e-mail: enquiries@stonemanorhotel.co.uk
dir: 2.5m from Kidderminster on A448, on right

The restaurant at this rambling property is notable for its standing timbers and ceiling beams; tables are well spaced, some in bays at banquettes, lighting is from ceiling spots and wall lights, and the room has a good vibe. The kitchen steers a course through a largely modern British repertoire, which means that seared scallops are served with black pudding, a purée of fennel, lemon and apple, and monkfish is wrapped in Parma ham and accompanied by lobster foam, saffron mash, roast chicory and pea purée. Dishes are well conceived - witness a crab tian, the plate dotted with horseradish cream and capers - and timings are accurate, as in a roast rump of lamb in herb and mustard crust served just pink along with thyme jus, scallion potatoes, and carrot purée. The kitchen's fond of flambéing, so finish with the theatre of crêpe Suzette.

Chef James McCarroll **Owner** Mr Dunn **Times** 12-2/7-10 **Prices** Fixed L 2 course £13, Fixed D 3 course £26.50, Starter £6.75-£10.95, Main £15.50-£25, Dessert £6.50-£7.50, Service included **Wines** 22 bottles over £20, 23 bottles under £20, 10 by glass **Notes** Sunday L, Vegetarian available, Dress restrictions, No jeans, Civ Wed 150 **Seats** 90 **Children** Portions, Menu **Parking** 400

MALVERN   Map 10 SO74

L'Amuse Bouche Restaurant

◉◉ Traditional French, British ✪

Classic cooking in an attractive country-house hotel

☎ 01684 572427
The Cotford Hotel, 51 Graham Rd WR14 2HU
e-mail: reservations@cotfordhotel.co.uk
dir: From Worcester follow signs to Malvern on A449. Left into Graham Rd signed town centre, hotel on right

Though set in a quintessential English country-house hotel (once the summer residence of the Bishops of Worcester), the restaurant's name gives a clue to the kitchen's classical French roots, though it takes a decidedly progressive focus. Local and organic produce underpins the appealing roster, kicking-off, of course, with a namesake amuse-bouche - perhaps a mini-cup of tomato and basil soup. Apple-cider braised pork belly, set on black pudding with a fresh chestnut mousse crust and Malvern honey and cider sauce, might catch the eye among main courses, while to finish, perhaps a spin on the tarte Tatin theme, with a banana and rosemary version. There are views over the beautiful gardens through the large sash windows of the stylish dining room - formerly the private chapel of the original Gothic Victorian house.

Chef Christopher Morgan **Owner** Christopher & Barbara Morgan **Times** 12-1.30/6-8 Closed L Mon-Sat **Prices** Fixed D 3 course £29.50, Service optional **Wines** 15 bottles over £20, 11 bottles under £20, 6 by glass **Notes** Pre-theatre menu available, Sunday L, Vegetarian available, Dress restrictions, Smart casual **Seats** 40, Pr/dining room 12 **Parking** 15

Colwall Park Hotel

◉◉ Modern British ✪

Excellent modern British cooking in the Malvern Hills

☎ 01684 540000
Walwyn Rd, Colwall WR13 6QG
e-mail: hotel@colwall.com
dir: On B4218, off A449 from Malvern to Ledbury

Tucked beneath the glorious Malvern Hills, this substantial mock-Tudor timbered Edwardian country hotel has a fine pedigree, but is not stuck in an Elgar-themed past. The upmarket Seasons Restaurant provides an elegant backdrop, blending elements of old and new - pale oak panelling offset by vibrantly-coloured modern art, and wrought-iron chandeliers hanging from a vaulted ceiling. Contemporary British trends and an obvious penchant for top-grade local materials form the backbone of an accessible brasserie-style menu. Excellent home-made breads get things off on the right foot, then a crunchy fishcake of cod, haddock and salmon appears with a zesty shallot and tarragon dressing. Next comes herb-crumbed loin of Longdon Marsh lamb with thyme mash, peas, broad beans, in-house dried tomatoes, and a red wine and rosemary sauce, while pudding keeps up standards to the end with a refreshing lemon posset with blueberry sorbet and shortbread.

Chef James Garth **Owner** Mr & Mrs I Nesbitt **Times** 12-2/7-9 Closed L all week (ex by arrangement) **Prices** Fixed L 2 course £16.95, Starter £3.55-£8.25, Main £10.75-£19.95, Dessert £6-£8.75, Service included **Wines** 55 bottles over £20, 19 bottles under £20, 9 by glass **Notes** Sunday L, Vegetarian available **Seats** 40, Pr/dining room 100 **Children** Portions, Menu **Parking** 40

The Cottage in the Wood Hotel

◉◉ Modern British ♠ ✪

Ambitious cooking in charming hotel

☎ 01684 588860
Holywell Rd, Malvern Wells WR14 4LG
e-mail: reception@cottageinthewood.co.uk
web: www.cottageinthewood.co.uk
dir: 3m S of Great Malvern off A449, 500yds N of B4209, on opposite side of road

The Outlook is the aptly named restaurant of the delightful family-run Cottage in the Wood Hotel - a one-time Georgian dower house perched on the side of the Malvern Hills - and it offers a show-stopping 30-mile sweep across the Severn Valley through its huge floor-to-ceiling windows. It's a light and airy space with pale-wood tables and chocolate brown leather upholstered seats. The modern British cooking shows plenty of flair with dishes fashioned from carefully-sourced local produce - to keep the eyes and interest on the plate. Ham, peas and Pommery mustard might appear in a risotto with a red wine jus and parmesan crisp among starters, followed by pan-seared sea bream with crushed potatoes and basil, warm gazpacho of cucumber, roasted peppers and tomatoes. A meaty main course might bright forth marinated saddle of venison with gratin dauphinoise, roots and barley, and juniper and damson jus, and dessert such as a duo of brûlées - vanilla pod and orange and cardamom - brings things to a close. The wine list is exceptional.

Chef Dominic Pattin **Owner** The Pattin Family **Times** 12.30-2/7-9.30 **Prices** Starter £5.45-£10.95, Main £11.95-£23.95, Dessert £2.50-£9.95, Service optional **Wines** 389 bottles over £20, 41 bottles under £20, 14 by glass **Notes** Pre-theatre D from 6pm, Sunday L, Vegetarian available **Seats** 70, Pr/dining room 20 **Children** Portions **Parking** 40

MALVERN *continued*

The Malvern

◉ Modern British **NEW**

Contemporary brasserie dining in the Malvern Hills

☎ 01684 898290
Grovewood Rd WR14 1GD
e-mail: enquiries@themalvernspa.com
dir: A4440 to Malvern. Over 2 rdbts, at 3rd turn left. After 6m, left at rdbt, over 1st rdbt, hotel on right

It's hard to believe that this sleek contemporary spa hotel and restaurant was actually Malvern's first spa resort when it opened in 1910, since the interior has been completely reworked using pared-back modern design fused with period features. The brasserie-style restaurant follows the chic, fresh-looking contemporary aesthetic with scrubbed wood tables, sage-green and mushroom-hued chairs and local artworks on the walls. The cooking fits the surroundings, offering plenty of light and healthy options (given the spa and health club slant) built on a good showing of locally-sourced ingredients. Slow-cooked venison with carrot and cumin purée, and lentil and thyme jus sets the ball rolling, while free-range chicken breast comes with chicken liver, potato fondant, wild mushrooms, onion purée and chicken jus in a well-balanced main course. To finish, there's baked poached pear with hazelnut crumble, and caramel and sea salt ice cream.

Chef Steve Rimmer **Owner** Huw Watson
Times 12-3/7-9.30 **Prices** Fixed L 2 course £12-£14, Fixed D 3 course £28-£33, Starter £5.75-£8.95, Main £12.50-£16.50, Dessert £6-£7.50, Service optional **Wines** 17 bottles over £20, 7 bottles under £20, 9 by glass **Notes** Vegetarian available, Dress restrictions, Smart casual **Seats** 34, Pr/dining room 24 **Parking** 82

| OMBERSLEY | Map 10 SO86 |

The Venture In Restaurant

◉◉ British, French

Forthright flavours in a half-timbered medieval house

☎ 01905 620552
Main Rd WR9 0EW
dir: From Worcester N towards Kidderminster on A449 (approx 5m). Left at Ombersley turn. Restaurant 0.75m on right

Behind the ancient black-and-white façade is a bar with a massive inglenook, beams and exposed brick walls, while the restaurant is a more contemporary space (despite ceiling beams), with comfortable leather-look seats at the tables. The kitchen produces consistently interesting, well-balanced dishes using excellent locally-sourced produce: roast breast of pheasant with game pie and wilted Savoy cabbage, for instance, or confit duck leg and roast breast on sage gnocchi with pickled carrot purée. Components tend to complement or contrast, so seared scallops are partnered by pea and ham fricassée, creamed potato and parsley emulsion, and ham hock, black pudding and pork terrine comes with a toasted

croûton, poached egg and hollandaise. Puddings incline to the classics like crème brûlée and chocolate brownie, an exotic touch added by the likes of coconut and lemon tart with mango ice cream.

Chef Toby Fletcher **Owner** Toby Fletcher
Times 12-2/7-9.30 Closed 25 Dec-1 Jan, 2 wks summer & 2 wks winter, Mon, D Sun **Prices** Fixed L 2 course £24, Fixed D 3 course £38, Service optional **Wines** 40 bottles over £20, 20 bottles under £20, 6 by glass **Notes** Sunday L, Vegetarian available, Dress restrictions, Smart casual **Seats** 32, Pr/dining room 32 **Parking** 15, on street

---

| TENBURY WELLS | Map 10 SO56 |

Cadmore Lodge Hotel & Country Club

◉ British ☺

Rural lakeside setting with trad cooking

☎ 01584 810044
Berrington Green, St Michaels WR15 8TQ
e-mail: reception.cadmore@cadmorelodge.com
dir: Off A4112 from Tenbury Wells to Leominster. 2m from Tenbury Wells, turn right opposite St Michael's Church

Cadmore is a small, modern family-run hotel set in peaceful countryside with the bonus of a nine-hole golf course and stunning lake within its 70-acre grounds. The country-style restaurant is old-school traditional, sporting neatly clothed tables, warm colours and an inglenook fireplace with log-burning stove, plus some great views over the grounds. The food makes use of some local ingredients and suits the mood of the place. Go retro with a classic prawn cocktail opener, and perhaps follow up with chicken Madeira and mash or lightly grilled fillet of plaice accompanied by spinach, new potatoes and hollandaise. To finish, there's nursery dessert heaven with apple crumble and custard or strawberry Bakewell tart.

Chef Christopher Bushell **Owner** Mr & Mrs J Weston
Times 12-2/7-9.15 Closed 25 Dec **Prices** Fixed L 2 course £13-£15, Fixed D 3 course £22-£24.50 **Wines** 3 bottles over £20, 13 bottles under £20, 6 by glass **Notes** Sunday L, Vegetarian available **Seats** 50, Pr/dining room 50 **Children** Portions, Menu **Parking** 100

| UPTON UPON SEVERN | Map 10 SO84 |

White Lion Hotel

◉ Modern British

Historic hotel with contemporary feel and flavour

☎ 01684 592551
21 High St WR8 0HJ
e-mail: info@whitelionhotel.biz
dir: From A422 take A38 towards Tewkesbury. After 8m take B4104 for 1m, after bridge turn left to hotel

At the heart of town life since 1510, the White Lion is rooted into Upton upon Severn's history. Henry Fielding put up here while writing *Tom Jones*, and as the Malvern theatres are just a short drive away, visiting thespians often choose to hole up here while in the area. The place

has pulled off the tricky balancing act of staying in touch with current trends without effacing its immense character, as typified in the Pepperpot Brasserie where a cheerfully-updated look pulls together black timbered walls filled with blocks of yellow ochre, apricot, and terracotta colour with chunky oak tables and high-backed chairs. The menu covers a lot of ground, and it is all unpretentious stuff. Expect hearty, full-on flavours from dishes such as pan-fried wood pigeon breast with grilled white pudding, potato cake and apple jus, followed by roast rump of lamb with a mustard and herb crust, teamed with carrot purée, roasted shallots, and rosemary jus. Desserts conjure up nursery flavours with the likes of apple and blueberry bread-and-butter pudding with home-made custard.

Chef Jon Lear, Richard Thompson **Owner** Mr & Mrs Lear
Times 12-2/7-9.15 Closed 31 Dec-1 Jan, L few days between Xmas & New Year, D 24 Dec **Prices** Fixed L 2 course fr £12.50, Starter £8.25-£9.50, Main £9.95-£21, Dessert £6.45-£7, Service optional **Wines** 2 bottles over £20, 23 bottles under £20, 7 by glass **Notes** Sunday L, Vegetarian available **Seats** 45 **Children** Portions **Parking** 16

| YORKSHIRE, EAST RIDING OF |

| BEVERLEY | Map 17 TA03 |

Beverley Tickton Grange

◉◉ Modern British

Period charm and fine local produce

☎ 01964 543666
Tickton HU17 9SH
e-mail: info@ticktongrange.co.uk
dir: From Beverley take A1035 towards Bridlington. After 3m hotel on left, just past Tickton

Tickton Grange is as English as warm beer and the sound of leather on willow: a Grade II listed Georgian country house in four acres of gardens with plenty of period character. Just the sort of place, then, for celebrating a special occasion in the fine-dining restaurant, which is just the right side of elegant with its Georgian bits, linen-clothed tables and rich, red leather chairs. There's a deft team at work in the kitchen, turning great local ingredients into stunning modern versions of classic dishes. Hot-smoked sea trout with sea purslane and liquorice gets things moving, and while there are drizzles, swirls and jellies aplenty, it all packs plenty of punch, whether it's local sea bass with saffron potatoes, tempura squid rings and bouillabaisse sauce, or a pan-fried steak of venison haunch with damson gin and turnips. To finish, a slate of Yorkshire cheeses is a savoury alternative to something like pistachio and walnut baklava with rosewater ice cream and jelly.

Chef David Nowell **Owner** Mr & Mrs Whymant
Times 12-2/7-9.30 Closed 26 Dec **Prices** Food prices not confirmed for 2013. Please telephone for details **Wines** 33 bottles over £20, 32 bottles under £20, 8 by glass **Notes** Vegetarian available, Civ Wed 150 **Seats** 45, Pr/dining room 20 **Children** Portions, Menu **Parking** 75

The Pipe and Glass Inn

⚫⚫ Modern British Ⓥ ☆ NATIONAL WINE LIST ✋

Superior modern cooking in stylishly modernised country inn

☎ 01430 810246
West End, South Dalton HU17 7PN
e-mail: email@pipeandglass.co.uk
dir: Just off B1248

The Mackenzies have renovated their 15th-century village pub with a great deal of style, now a restaurant with rooms and a proper pubby bar. The restaurant has a modern look, with high-backed chairs at decently spaced wooden tables, leather chesterfields, and copper pans and prints on the walls. James Mackenzie's menus are bursting with appealing modern ideas, from smoked mackerel croquette and tartare with pickled samphire, horseradish and a soft-boiled quail's egg, to breast of guinea fowl with a parcel of the leg, accompanied by sherry cream, Devils on Horseback, curly kale and sautéed potatoes. Top-drawer materials are assembled intelligently; a starter of bresaola of Leven duck with a duck leg rissole, orange and celery perhaps, and a main course of turbot fillet with a monkfish cheek fritter, kale colcannon and braised oxtail and horseradish sauce. Technical expertise is evident throughout, and if dishes are complex they are not overworked, seen in startlingly ingenious desserts like a pudding of dark chocolate, sloe gin and juniper served with damson ripple ice cream.

Chef James Mackenzie **Owner** James & Kate Mackenzie **Times** 12-2/6.30-9.30 Closed 25 Dec, 2 wks Jan, Mon (except BH), D Sun **Prices** Food prices not confirmed for 2013. Please telephone for details **Wines** 71 bottles over £20, 26 bottles under £20, 15 by glass **Notes** Vegetarian menu **Seats** 70, Pr/dining room 26 **Children** Portions, Menu **Parking** 60

WILLERBY   Map 17 TA03

Best Western Willerby Manor Hotel

⚫ Modern European ✋

Extensive brasserie menu in countryside setting

☎ 01482 652616
Well Ln HU10 6ER
e-mail: willerbymanor@bestwestern.co.uk
dir: M62/A63, follow signs for Humber Bridge, then signs for Beverley until Willerby Shopping Park. Hotel signed from rdbt next to McDonald's

Four miles out of Hull, Willerby Manor is a modern spa hotel in the East Yorkshire countryside. Its fine dining goes on in Figs Brasserie, a relaxing room done in avocado and coffee tones, which extends on to a paved outdoor terrace on balmy evenings. An extensive menu of brasserie dishes incorporates some neat ideas, such as a starter of goats' cheese pannacotta with red wine-poached pear and gingerbread, but also features many classic ideas like Whitby scampi and chips, chicken breast with black pudding, chestnuts, sprouts and mash in red wine sauce, and apple and blueberry crumble with vanilla cream.

Chef David Roberts, Ben Olley **Owner** Alexandra Townend **Times** 10am-10pm Closed 25 Dec **Prices** Starter £5.30-£6, Main £5.20-£19, Dessert £4-£4.85, Service optional **Wines** 4 bottles over £20, 10 bottles under £20, 14 by glass **Notes** Sunday L, Vegetarian available **Seats** 40, Pr/dining room 40 **Children** Portions, Menu **Parking** 200

YORKSHIRE, NORTH

ALDWARK   Map 19 SE46

The Aldwark Arms

⚫⚫ Modern **NEW** ✋

Invigorating cooking in the Vale of York

☎ 01347 838324
YO61 1UB
e-mail: enquiries@aldwarkarms.co.uk

This white part-timbered inn in a village in the Vale of York has a traditional bar - a winter fire, bar food, real ales - and a parquet-floored conservatory restaurant with neat, linen-clad tables. The chef's classical training is evident in celeriac remoulade accompanying home-smoked salmon, served with sourdough, and a foie gras and duck terrine flavoured with Grand Marnier - an outstanding example it is too. Well-chosen raw materials pay dividends: local venison is full of gamey flavour, served with a Scotch egg, autumn vegetables and a deeply flavoured thyme and port jus. Dishes are well rounded in the modern manner - spring onion and coriander risotto and smoked salmon accompanying roast sea bass fillet with tartare dressing, for instance - and pastry work is irreproachable in puddings like bitter chocolate tart, well matched by peanut ice cream and salted caramel.

Chef Chris & Nick Hill **Owner** Chris & Nick Hill **Times** 12-2/5-9 Closed Mon, D Sun **Prices** Fixed L 2 course £20-£22.50, Fixed D 3 course £25-£27.50, Starter £5-£8, Main £15-£20, Dessert £5, Service optional **Wines** 5 bottles over £20, 15 bottles under £20, 8 by glass **Notes** Sunday L, Vegetarian available **Seats** 60 **Children** Portions, Menu **Parking** 30

ASENBY   Map 19 SE37

Crab Manor

⚫⚫ Modern British, European ✋

Idiosyncratic restaurant with a strong line in seafood

☎ 01945 577286
Dishforth Rd YO7 3QL
e-mail: enquiries@crabandlobster.co.uk
dir: A1(M) junct 49, on outskirts of village

At first sight, this thatched and creeper-clad Georgian inn could be the template for a classic Yorkshire country pub, although an observant eye might spot the old enamelled advertising signs that are a hint to the Aladdin's cave of esoteric odds and ends that fills the interior with endless visual entertainment. In case the name isn't enough of a clue, fish and seafood is the kitchen's main culinary focus, whether you choose to eat in the sun-trap garden, the airy pavilion, the main restaurant or the convivial bar. The choice is vast, taking in starters such as seared hand-dived scallops with confit belly pork, crisp black pudding, and roast butternut squash cream, or fishcakes of local cod, pollock, and cured fish served with creamed greens and a poached egg. Next up, a chunk of local cod could come with spicy sausage boulangère potatoes, buttered greens and gravy, or you might take a meatier route with the likes of herb-crusted roast rump of Faceby lamb with cumin-roasted carrots, gratin potatoes, rosemary and redcurrant. To finish, go for something like chilled Valrhona chocolate fondant with honeycomb and caramelised banana yoghurt ice cream.

Chef Steve Dean **Owner** Vimac Trading **Times** 12-2.30/7-9.30 **Prices** Fixed L 2 course fr £15.95, Starter £8.50-£12.50, Main £15-£30, Dessert £7.50-£10, Service optional **Wines** 8 bottles over £20, 8 bottles under £20, 8 by glass **Notes** Sunday L, Vegetarian available, Civ Wed 120 **Seats** 85, Pr/dining room 24 **Children** Portions **Parking** 80

AUSTWICK — Map 18 SD76

The Traddock

◎◎ Modern British ✋

Charming hotel with a local flavour

☎ 015242 51224
Settle LA2 8BY
e-mail: info@austwicktraddock.co.uk
web: www.thetraddock.co.uk
dir: From Skipton take A65 towards Kendal, 3m after Settle turn right signed Austwick, cross hump back bridge, hotel 100yds on left

Whether you're in the area to tackle the Three Peaks, amble along Wainwright's route to Crummackdale, or you've something entirely more leisurely in mind, The Traddock is perfectly placed to explore the Yorkshire Dales National Park. The hotel itself is rather handsome, dating from the 1740s, and done out in a traditional yet smart manner. An aperitif in one of the two elegant, antique-filled lounges is a suitably sybaritic beginning, before moving into the dining room with its linen-clad tables and flickering candles in the evening. Organic and local ingredients are central to the kitchen's output, with daily specials bolstering the seasonally-changing carte. The focus is classical, broadly modern British preparations, which means twice-baked soufflé of Whitby crab, or Yorkshire Blue, Brazil and walnut loaf with cranberry coulis and melba toast to start. Next up, roast rack of Mansergh Hall lamb with a quince and rosemary jus, and, to finish, Turkish delight pannacotta with pistachio tuile.

Chef John Pratt **Owner** The Reynolds family
Times 12-2.30/6.30-11 **Prices** Starter £4.95-£6.95, Main £14.95-£19.95, Dessert £5.95-£7.95, Service optional **Wines** 45 bottles over £20, 12 bottles under £20, 16 by glass **Notes** Sunday L, Vegetarian available **Seats** 36, Pr/dining room 16 **Children** Portions, Menu **Parking** 20, On street

BAINBRIDGE — Map 18 SD99

Yorebridge House

◎◎ British, European Ⅴ ✋

Bright, modish cooking in Wensleydale

☎ 01969 652060
DL8 3EE
e-mail: enquiries@yorebridgehouse.co.uk
dir: A648 to Bainbridge. Yorebridge House N of centre on right before river

In a peaceful setting on the edge of the village by the river in Wensleydale, Yorebridge House has been converted into a luxury boutique hotel, with a decently sized restaurant with a boarded floor, upholstered chairs at white-clothed tables, and plenty of light from skylights and a number of windows. The menu (there's a separate one in the bar) is a roll-call of fresh, vibrant ideas. Saddle of rabbit with langoustines, sweet potato purée, asparagus and morels is an unusual take on the surf and turf combination, followed perhaps by a more conventional main course of loin and belly of pork with black pudding and apple sauce, an extra flavour dimension given by walnut jus. Sound materials, high technical skills and an imaginative approach are evident throughout. A starter of smoked duck and foie gras comes not just with rhubarb as a foil but with three ways with the fruit - purée, crisp and pickled - and desserts are as labour-intensive as the rest, judging by ginger pannacotta with poached quince, Poire William jelly and apple and blackberry sorbet.

Chef Aaron Craig **Owner** Damien Fort (GM)
Times 12-2.30/6.30-9.30 **Prices** Fixed D 3 course £44.50, Starter £5.95-£8.95, Main £12.95-£21.95, Dessert £7.50, Service optional, Groups min 12 service 10% **Wines** 75 bottles over £20, 4 bottles under £20, 8 by glass **Notes** Tasting menu can be arranged by reservation, Sunday L, Vegetarian menu, Dress restrictions, Smart casual **Seats** 35, Pr/dining room 12 **Children** Portions, Menu **Parking** 30

BOLTON ABBEY — Map 19 SE05

The Devonshire Arms Country House Hotel & Spa

◎◎◎◎ — *see opposite*

The Devonshire Brasserie & Bar

◎ Modern British **NEW** Ⅴ

Smart brasserie cooking in a top-class country hotel

☎ 01756 710710 & 710441
Bolton Abbey BD23 6AJ
e-mail: res@devonshirehotels.co.uk
dir: On B6160, 250yds N of junct with A59

This is the informal brasserie within The Devonshire Arms (see entry opposite), a room marked out by bright vibrant colours, contemporary artwork, comfortable seating, informal service, and a buzz in the air. The menu runs along modern British brasserie lines; ingredients cut the mustard, and the kitchen knows what it's about, producing starters of tender, crisply battered monkfish tails with a vegetable and noodle salad and sweet chilli, and chicken liver parfait with tangy red onion marmalade. Crowd-pleasing main courses vary from beer-battered haddock, through lamb shank hotpot to fillet of beef Wellington with Madeira sauce, and populist desserts might include sticky toffee pudding and profiteroles.

Chef Dan Field **Owner** The Duke & Duchess of Devonshire **Times** 12-2.30/6-9.30 **Prices** Starter £4.50-£7.95, Main £7.25-£24, Dessert £4.95-£6.25, Service added but optional 12.5% **Wines** 87 bottles over £20, 12 bottles under £20 **Notes** Sunday L, Vegetarian menu, Civ Wed 90 **Seats** 60 **Children** Portions, Menu **Parking** 40

BOROUGHBRIDGE — Map 19 SE36

The Crown Inn

◎ Modern British Ⅴ ✋

Old coaching inn with modish cooking

☎ 01423 322300
Roecliffe YO51 9LY
e-mail: info@crowninnroecliffe.com
dir: A1M junct 48, follow brown sign

The Crown is an old coaching inn which still radiates charm and hospitality within its 16th-century walls, with the hoped for stone-flagged floors, chunky oak beams and roaring log fires all present and correct. It's been revamped with a keen eye by owners Karl and Amanda Mainey, blending traditional and contemporary touches into a pleasing whole. A good deal of local produce finds its way into the kitchen and is turned into brasserie-style dishes which have a regional flavour, and a bit more besides. Start with Whitby crab soup perked up with brandy, or a terrine of local rabbit studded with pickled walnuts and served with Wakefield rhubarb chutney and granary toast. Next up, there might be fish pie, or steak and kidney pie made with local ale, or the more outré spiced monkfish with chilli-spiked Puy lentils and a crab and coriander bhaji.

Chef Darryn Asher **Owner** Karl Mainey
Times 12-3.30/6-11 **Prices** Fixed L 2 course £16.95, Starter £4.95-£8.95, Main £13.95-£16.95, Dessert £5.95-£6.95, Service optional **Wines** 33 bottles over £20, 21 bottles under £20, 19 by glass **Notes** Sunday L, Vegetarian menu, Civ Wed 120 **Seats** 60, Pr/dining room 20 **Children** Portions, Menu **Parking** 30

Save on Hotels. Book at **theAA.com/hotel**

YORKSHIRE, NORTH 497 ENGLAND

The Devonshire Arms Country House Hotel & Spa

BOLTON ABBEY   Map 19 SE05

Modern French **V** ⬥ NOTABLE WINE LIST

Stunning Yorkshire Dales setting for top-flight cooking

☎ 01756 710441 & 718111
BD23 6AJ
e-mail: res@devonshirehotels.co.uk
dir: On B6160 to Bolton Abbey, 250 yds
N of junct with A59 rdbt

The Devonshire Arms has 30,000 acres of prime Yorkshire Dales to call its own, or at least the Duke of Devonshire does, for this magnificent one-time coaching inn dating back to the 17th century is part of his estate (technically it's in trust, but...). It's in an impressive position, surrounded by green rolling hills and close to the famously ruined priory, but the Devonshire has moved with the times - while remaining timeless to some degree - with sympathetic extensions over the centuries. These days it's a luxurious country-house hotel with a swish spa and a restaurant that has put it well and truly on the map. There are roaring log fires, elegant furniture, bags of antiques and grand pictures, plus plush sofas to sink into as you study the menu and bite into canapés. The Burlington Restaurant is the star of the show, where chef Steve Smith delivers food of craft and creativity, making good use of the estate's excellent produce (dining during the game season is a good idea)

and the kitchen garden for herbs, vegetables and fruits. The setting is suitably elegant, with burnished darkwood tables dressed up for the business of fine dining, and the formal, traditionally decorated space watched over by the impeccable service team, including the wonderful sommelier (more of him later). It is jackets for the men, so come prepared. What follows is technically impressive, contemporary cooking, with lots of great ideas and compelling flavours. Things kick off with all the little freebies you might be expecting - perhaps an apple and pork cromesquis and a rather fun grapefruit and basil mojito - and the fabulous breads (baked in-house) come with two butters, including a fabulous seaweed and sea salt version. Hand-dived Orkney scallops are as delightfully fat as they come, cooked perfectly, served with smoked eel, celeriac and apple jelly, with truffle grated over the top at the table. Next up, main-course Hebridean lamb comes in various 'textures', including the slow-cooked shoulder and a superb, flavoursome piece of loin, partnered with goats' cheese bonbon, broccoli purée, tomato, and garlic and rosemary jus, or there's Brixham sea bass with fennel, figs, ceps and red wine. To finish, after the pre-requisite pre-dessert, comes coffee pannacotta and sponge with perfectly judged caramelised milk purée and liqourice ice cream. The wine list of some 2,500 bins is the domain of Nigel Fairclough and

contains some of the best vintages to be found in the country. And note there's a brasserie on site, too (see entry).

Chef Stephen Smith **Owner** Duke & Duchess of Devonshire
Times 12-2.30/7-9.30 Closed Xmas, 3-11 Jan, Mon, L Tue-Sat **Prices** Tasting menu £72, Service added but optional 12.5% **Wines** 2300 bottles over £20, 30 bottles under £20, 12 by glass
Notes ALC menu £65, Tasting menu 6 course, Prestige menu £80, Sunday L, Vegetarian menu, Dress restrictions, Smart dress, no jeans or T-shirts, Civ Wed 90 **Seats** 70, Pr/dining room 90
Children Portions **Parking** 100

BOROUGHBRIDGE *continued*

The Dining Room Restaurant

◉◉ British, French

Assured cooking in stylish neighbourhood restaurant

☎ 01423 326426
20 St James Square YO51 9AR
e-mail: chris@thediningroom.co.uk
web: www.thediningroomonline.co.uk
dir: A1(M), Boroughbridge junct, follow signs to town. Opposite fountain in town square

This self-effacing restaurant in a bow-fronted Queen Anne building would be easy to pass by, but a horde of local fans would tell you the folly of your ways. Once inside there's a definite wow factor to its bright white contemporary looks, and there's a delightful walled terrace for alfresco aperitifs and open-air eating when the weather is up to scratch. Husband-and-wife-team Christopher and Lisa Astley run a tight ship, with Chris at the stoves and Lisa orchestrating front-of-house. Chris's cooking plays it straight, relying on mainstream flavour combinations that let the top-class local materials speak for themselves. Chicken liver parfait, melba toast, gherkins and chutney make reliable bedfellows in a well-flavoured starter, followed by free-range belly pork with black pudding mash, apple compôte and barbecue sauce. There's a classic crème brûlée with blackberries for a finale.

Chef Christopher Astley **Owner** Mr & Mrs C Astley
Times 12-2/7-9.30 Closed 26-28 Dec, 1 Jan, BHs, Mon, L Tue-Sat, D Sun **Prices** Fixed L 2 course £21, Fixed D 3 course £29.95, Starter £7.50, Main £18.50, Dessert £7, Service optional **Wines** 60 bottles over £20, 15 bottles under £20, 9 by glass **Notes** Sunday L, Vegetarian available, Dress restrictions, Smart casual, no T-shirts **Seats** 32 **Children** Portions **Parking** On street/Private on request

BURNSALL Map 19 SE06

The Devonshire Fell

◉◉ Modern British **V**

Classy cooking in a chic Yorkshire conservatory

☎ 01756 729000
BD23 6BT
e-mail: manager@devonshirefell.co.uk
dir: On B6160, 6m from Bolton Abbey rdbt A59 junct

Yes, Wharfedale is a long way from Devonshire, but the name comes from the Duke and Duchess of that name who sprinkled a touch of up-to-date magic over this erstwhile club for Victorian gentlemen mill owners. The Duchess oversaw the reworking of the interior, creating a bright and funky boutique-style restaurant with rooms, done out with bold blocks of vibrant colour, stripy fabrics and contemporary artworks in the bistro and conservatory restaurant. The vibrant style of modern British food fits the setting perfectly, with much use made of local produce, and no lack of technical wizardry in starters such as seared scallops with clear tomato jelly, fennel

purée and caper and shallot dressing. After that, loin of pork might be partnered with vanilla and apple purée, fondant potato, black pudding and cider jus, while desserts stay in the creative zone with the likes of dark chocolate marquise with basil ice cream and fresh raspberries.

Chef Oliver Adams **Owner** Duke & Duchess of Devonshire **Times** 12-2.30/6.30-9.30 **Prices** Starter £6.50-£7.95, Main £13.95-£18.50, Dessert £4.95-£6.95, Service added but optional 12.5% **Wines** 35 bottles over £20, 8 bottles under £20, 11 by glass **Notes** Fixed D 5 course £50, Sunday L, Vegetarian menu, Civ Wed 70 **Seats** 40, Pr/dining room 70 **Children** Portions, Menu **Parking** 40

CRATHORNE Map 19 NZ40

Crathorne Hall Hotel

◉◉ Modern British ◔

Contemporary British style in stately Edwardian hotel

☎ 01642 700398
TS15 0AR
e-mail: crathornehall@handpicked.co.uk
dir: Off A19, 2m E of Yarm. Access to A19 via A66 or A1, Thirsk

A palatial-sized property of mellow stone, with four soaring columns above the front door, Crathorne Hall was built in 1906 as a private residence. The décor and furnishings give the impression of a stately home, a feeling not dispelled in the restaurant, a carpeted room with drapes at tall windows and oil paintings on semi-panelled walls. The kitchen is clearly very much of the 21st century, not hidebound by tradition, although a mixed grill may offer comfort to some. A canapé of beef teriyaki with horseradish is a foretaste of the style to follow. Monkfish tails, beautifully cooked and seasoned, are served on spinach, joined by tender baby squid and sauced with curried mussel broth, and another starter might be venison set off by beetroot, liquorice and horseradish. Timings are spot on and combinations are successful: duck with red cabbage and orange, say, and pan-fried stone bass with delicate garlic risotto and modish parsley foam. Breads are well made, and an expert pastry chef is responsible for light, crumbly pecan pie with honeycomb ice cream.

Chef Mark Brankin **Owner** Hand Picked Hotels **Times** 12.30-2.30/7-9.30 **Prices** Fixed L 2 course £16.50, Fixed D 3 course £30, Starter £10-£14, Main £20-£25, Dessert £9-£12, Service included **Wines** 98 bottles over £20, 18 by glass **Notes** Sunday L, Vegetarian available, Civ Wed 90 **Seats** 45, Pr/dining room 26 **Children** Portions, Menu **Parking** 80

ESCRICK Map 16 SE64

The Parsonage Country House Hotel

◉ Modern British **V**

Victorian-era country house with creative cooking

☎ 01904 728111
York Rd YO19 6LF
e-mail: sales@parsonagehotel.co.uk
dir: From A64 take A19 Selby. Follow to Escrick. Hotel on right of St Helen's Church

This 1940s former parsonage - now country-house hotel - is in six acres of formal gardens and woodlands and retains bags of period features. The smart Lascelles restaurant goes for a more modish vibe, which means pale-wood floors and vibrant colours, while white linen-clad tables make sure it doesn't get out of hand. The kitchen's modern approach fits the surroundings, with admirable emphasis on home-grown, local and seasonal produce and clear-cut flavours. Start with salmon and lobster ravioli served with lemongrass velouté and confit tomatoes, followed on with roast venison loin partnered with celeriac and potato dauphinoise, red wine and garlic purée and a redcurrant jus, and draw to a satisfying close with an assiette including pear terrine with stem ginger mousse, pear jelly and pear sorbet.

Owner P Smith **Times** 12-2/6.30-9 Closed L Sat **Prices** Fixed L 2 course £12.95, Fixed D 3 course £18.95, Starter £5.50-£8.25, Main £15.95-£18.95, Dessert £6.25-£8.50, Service included **Wines** 10 bottles over £20, 10 bottles under £20, 11 by glass **Notes** Sunday L, Vegetarian menu, Dress restrictions, No shorts **Seats** 70, Pr/dining room 40 **Children** Portions, Menu **Parking** 100

GRASSINGTON Map 19 SE06

Grassington House

◉◉ Modern European ◔

Stylish hotel with creative, locally-inspired cooking

☎ 01756 752406
5 The Square BD23 5AQ
e-mail: bookings@grassingtonhousehotel.co.uk
dir: A59 into Grassington, in town square opposite post office

A boutique-style makeover has kitted out the interior of this three-storey Georgian hotel on the cobbled square of a delightful Dales village with dollops of contemporary style. Owners John and Susan Rudden are the hands-on type, and that attitude extends to John's raising his own porkers to ensure that the kitchen is stocked with the best local and seasonal produce he can lay his hands on, and it is all translated into a carefully-considered repertoire of creative modern dishes underpinned by classic French influences. Dinner in the smart '5 The Square' restaurant could kick off with the house's own rare breed pork rillettes with Bramley apple jam, then showcase local pheasant in the form of a pan-fried breast and braised pheasant pie. Fish fans might find turbot as proof that quality ingredients are sourced and handled with aplomb - perhaps poached and served with bacon, wild mushrooms, broad beans and red wine fish jus. Yorkshire rhubarb could get an outing for dessert, in the shape of an assiette involving jelly, sorbet, steamed sponge, pannacotta, confit and crisps.

Chef John Rudden **Owner** Susan & John Rudden **Times** 12-2.30/6-9.30 **Prices** Fixed L 2 course fr £14.50, Starter £4.50-£7.95, Main £11.95-£23, Dessert £5.25-£7.50, Service optional **Wines** 16 bottles over £20, 14 bottles under £20, 12 by glass **Notes** Fixed D 4 course Sun-Tue, £39.50 per couple, Sunday L, Vegetarian available **Seats** 40 **Children** Portions, Menu **Parking**

GUISBOROUGH　　　　　　Map 19 NZ61

Macdonald Gisborough Hall

◉◉ Modern British

Well-crafted dishes in a Victorian country house

☎ 0844 879 9149
Whitby Ln TS14 6PT
e-mail: general.gisboroughhall@macdonald-hotels.co.uk
dir: A171, follow signs for Whitby to Waterfall rdbt then 3rd exit into Whitby Lane, hotel 500yds on right

Only 20 minutes drive out of Middlesbrough, the Hall sits amid rolling grounds and woodland, with a backdrop of the Cleveland Hills. The Chaloner's dining room is named after the family who used to own Gisborough, and is spacious and gently formal, with white-upholstered chairs and unclothed tables, and glass partitions to divide the space. Simple but imaginative modern British menus are also divided - as between seasonal specials and signature dishes. A serving of duck liver pâté and toasted brioche is lifted out of the ordinary by its accompaniments of a cromesquis of the confit leg, shallot salad and orange purée, while that modern classic, monkfish wrapped in Parma ham, is generously partnered with a seared scallop and a well-timed risotto of tomatoes, fennel and basil. Finish with warm chocolate fondant with a properly gooey centre, served with blueberry and lavender compôte and vanilla ice cream.

Times 12.30-2.30/6.30-9.30

HAROME　　　　　　　　Map 19 SE68

The Star Inn

◉◉ Traditional British V ◆NOTABLE WINE LIST ☺

First-class, creative cooking at renowned village inn

☎ 01439 770397
YO62 5JE
e-mail: reservations@thestaratharome.co.uk
dir: From Helmsley take A170 towards Kirkbymoorside, after 0.5m turn right towards Harome. After 1.5m, inn 1st building on right

Andrew and Jacquie Pern have established The Star firmly as a dining destination that should be on the agenda for any self-respecting foodie up in the area of the North York Moors. And there's no denying their energy and enthusiasm for the job: as an alternative to the original low-beamed bar-dining room scented with woodsmoke

from an open fire, and kitted out with oak furniture made by a local craftsman, the Perns have considerably extended the capacity of the postcard-pretty 14th-century thatched longhouse in recent years by adding a new dining area with banquette seating and high-backed leather chairs. There's also a deli opposite, and a sister property, the Pheasant Hotel to keep them busy. Good business acumen, then, but none of it would happen without Andrew Pern's pitch-perfect cooking and unimpeachable commitment to Yorkshire's larder. Grilled black pudding with pan-fried foie gras, Pickering watercress salad, apple and vanilla chutney with a scrumpy reduction is the sort of starter that demonstrates the full-on vibrancy of his flavours. You might continue with a riff on local duck, served as breast, leg, liver, egg and sausage with a baked potato, traditional Yorkshire sauce and soublse cream. Quality is unwavering all the way to a celebration of Yorkshire rhubarb, taking in parkin, ice cream, fool and jelly with a palate-sharpening shot of rhubarb schnapps.

Chef Andrew Pern **Owner** A & J Pern **Times** 11.30-3/6.30-11 Closed 1 Jan, L Mon, D Sun **Prices** Fixed L 2 course £20, Fixed D 3 course £25, Starter £6-£15, Main £17-£27, Dessert £5-£15, Service included **Wines** 105 bottles over £20, 3 bottles under £20, 24 by glass **Notes** Chef's table for 6-8 people, tasting menu 6-8 course, Sunday L, Vegetarian menu **Seats** 70, Pr/dining room 10 **Children** Portions, Menu **Parking** 30

HARROGATE　　　　　　　Map 19 SE35

Hotel du Vin Harrogate

◉◉ British, Mediterranean ◆NOTABLE WINE LIST

Fine food and wine in chic Georgian townhouse setting

☎ 01423 856800
Prospect Place HG1 1LB
e-mail: reception.harrogate@hotelduvin.com
dir: A1(M) junct 47, A59 to Harrogate, follow town centre signs to Prince of Wales rdbt, 3rd exit, remain in right lane. Right at lights into Albert St, right into Prospect Place

This Victorian spa town's tea shops have a long tradition of spoiling its visitors, and the HdV's Harrogate outpost continues the tradition with dollops of 21st-century verve. The operation occupies a sybaritically-converted terrace of eight handsome Georgian townhouses opposite the 200-acre Stray common, and its interior will ring a bell with fans of the brand: style-savvy, unbuttoned luxury rubbing along seamlessly with the 18th-century grandeur of the rooms. The 'vin' part of the equation delivers fine wines at affordable prices to go with the French-influenced bistro-style menu. Terrine of belly pork with crisp black pudding and apple sauce is a typical starter, but it is the superb locally-sourced steaks that grab carnivores' attention at main course stage. On a more fishy note, sea bass fillets are teamed with a deeply-flavoured cauliflower purée and crispy pancetta and to finish, it just has to be a classic crème brûlée.

Times 12-2/6.30-10

Nidd Hall Hotel

◉◉ Modern British V

Culinary thrills in a Yorkshire country house

☎ 01423 771598
Nidd HG3 3BN
dir: A1M junct/A59 follow signs to Knaresborough. Continue through town centre & at Bond End lights turn left, then right onto B6165 signed Ripley & Pateley Bridge. Hotel on right in approx 4m

The Hall was built during the reign of George IV for a Bradford wool merchant keen to display his success, and is a true English country house, down to its mature landscaped grounds, creeper-covered façade and elegant late-Georgian interiors. Of the dining options, the Terrace Restaurant is the prime site, a light room tinged with verdant green décor, with antlered heads on the wall, and views over the gardens. A highly accomplished contemporary repertoire is in the practised hands of a large kitchen brigade, and the attention to detail in dishes such as butternut squash velouté with haricots and rabbit tortellini, laced with sherry, lifts them way above the humdrum. A main course of seared sea bass with more pasta parcels, this time of crab, is full of technical virtuosity, and benefits from accompaniments of fennel purée and a buttery shellfish and tomato sauce, while meats might offer venison saddle with textural contrasts of crispy celeriac, trompettes and sloe gin jelly. Fifteen minutes' wait seems a reasonable request for properly made cherry clafoutis, which comes with pistachio ice cream and Amaretto anglaise.

Chef Jason Wardill **Owner** Bourne Leisure **Times** 6.30-9.30 Closed L Mon-Sat, D Tue-Wed **Prices** Food prices not confirmed for 2013. Please telephone for details **Wines** 20 bottles over £20, 10 bottles under £20, 11 by glass **Notes** Vegetarian menu, Dress restrictions, Smart casual **Seats** 42 **Parking** 300

HARROGATE *continued*

Rudding Park Hotel, Spa & Golf

◉◉ Modern British **V**

A menu devoted to Yorkshire's food heroes

☎ 01423 871350
Follifoot HG3 1JH
e-mail: reservations@ruddingpark.com
web: www.ruddingpark.co.uk
dir: A61 at rdbt with A658 follow signs 'Rudding Park'

Rudding Park Hotel is at the centre of a large complex that includes luxury self-catering lodges with their own spas, a golf course, conference facilities and a traditional pub. The hotel's spacious Clocktower restaurant, accessed via the bar, is distinguished by a striking pink chandelier, and there's a conservatory with a 400-year-old olive tree smack in the middle. A 'food heroes' menu specifies the number of miles each principal ingredient has travelled to reach the table - for example, mussels, leeks and bacon in cider (37 miles), chicken, leek and pearl barley broth with parsley dumplings (20 miles), and so on - and the kitchen's armoury is no less intelligently sourced, with ingredients carried through to satisfying results: ham hock ballottine with peas and mint, then monkfish wrapped in Parma ham with prawns and lemon and thyme risotto, rounded off by summery strawberry savarin with passionfruit sorbet or the choice of European or Yorkshire cheeses.

Chef Eddie Gray **Owner** Simon Mackaness
Times 12-2.30/7-9.30 **Prices** Fixed L 2 course £27.50, Fixed D 3 course £36, Starter £9-£13, Main £20-£28, Dessert £9.50-£16, Service optional **Wines** 86 bottles over £20, 17 by glass **Notes** Sunday L, Vegetarian menu, Civ Wed 180 **Seats** 170, Pr/dining room 16 **Children** Portions, Menu **Parking** 250

Studley Hotel

◉◉ Pacific Rim

Smart hotel restaurant giving culinary tour of Asia

☎ 01423 560425
28 Swan Rd HG1 2SE
e-mail: info@orchidrestaurant.co.uk
dir: Adjacent to Valley Gardens, opposite Mercer Gallery

The Studley Hotel takes in an impressive array of cuisines from China, Indonesia, Japan, Korea, Malaysia, the Philippines, Thailand and Vietnam in a setting as exotic as its Pan-Asian food. Mango and darkwood interiors are

divided by Japanese lattice-style screens, while a large TV screen has all the live webcam action from the kitchen. The extensive menu utilises imported ingredients for added authenticity and knowledgeable staff are on hand to guide you through. Start in Hong Kong with roasted sliced belly pork with a crispy crackling served with a yellow bean and honey dip, before dropping in on the Philippines for tiger prawns cooked with butternut, green beans and coconut milk. Desserts don't disappoint either: Thailand's steamed banana cake cooked in a banana leaf and served with coconut ice cream, for example.

Chef Kenneth Poon **Owner** Bokmun Chan
Times 12-2/6-10 **Prices** Food prices not confirmed for 2013. Please telephone for details **Wines** 13 bottles over £20, 15 bottles under £20, 8 by glass **Notes** Tue D sushi & sashimi, Vegetarian available **Seats** 72, Pr/dining room 20 **Parking** 18

van Zeller

◉◉ Modern British **V** 🍷

First-rate contemporary cooking

☎ 01423 508762
8 Montpellier St HG1 2TQ
e-mail: info@vanzellerrestaurants.co.uk

With his name above the door, Tom van Zeller knows his onions. He's a local lad who has come full circle, starting his culinary journey in good old Betty's Tea Rooms up the road, before busking his way around the world and honing his craft in big names in big cities, before settling back in Harrogate with the backing of David Moore of Pied à Terre fame (see entry, London). The dining room sets out its stall impressively with a classy, understated modern look, all darkwood floors, banquettes, chocolate brown high-backed seats, and abstract artworks to inject a note of pizzazz to the neutral, low-lit tones. He sources his ingredients carefully for maximum local input, but that doesn't exclude seared foie gras from Strasbourg opening the show together with Yorkshire rhubarb, sorrel purée, celery and buckwheat granola. Serious intentions, innovation and technical accomplishment are all present and correct again in main courses such as braised leg and seared loin of local hare supported by swede, sprouts and spätzle, and pickled apple purée. Finish with a dark chocolate marquise with roasted banana sorbet, salted caramel, and peanut sablé.

Chef Tom van Zeller **Owner** Tom van Zeller
Times 12-2/6-10 Closed 1st wk Jan & Aug, Mon, D Sun **Prices** Food prices not confirmed for 2013. Please telephone for details **Wines** 85 bottles over £20, 8 bottles under £20, 9 by glass **Notes** Vegetarian available, Vegetarian menu, Dress restrictions, Smart casual **Seats** 34 **Children** Portions **Parking** Montpellier Hill

The White Hart Hotel

◉◉ British

Modern brasserie dishes in a Georgian landmark

☎ 01423 505681
2 Cold Bath Rd HG2 0NF
e-mail: reception@whitehart.net
web: www.whitehart.net

Not far from the Valley Gardens park, The White Hart is something of a Harrogate landmark, having been a comfortable resort of the discerning traveller since the Georgian era. The old dining room is now a trendy pub called the Fat Badger, while the main eating space is a light room done out in on-trend sandy neutral colours with a checkered pattern in curtains and seating. They call it a Brasserie, the logic of which is revealed at sight of a menu that deals in the likes of grilled scallops with leeks, bacon and cheddar, or oxtail risotto with a crisp-fried quail's egg and horseradish bubbles. An interesting fish offering is goujons of Scarborough woof (a catfish, despite its name) with baby clams in Cullen skink, and there's also a voguish three-way serving of pork - belly, fillet and cheek - seasoned with vanilla and purple sage. Puddings include the regional delicacy, Yorkshire curd tart, dolled up with cinnamon ice cream and blood orange, as well as peanut butter crumble with caramel.

Times 6-10

See advert opposite

WHITE HART

The White Hart Hotel is a landmark in Harrogate's Montpellier Quarter and has been welcoming visitors for over 200 years. It offers a 2 rosette brasserie, tearoom, award winning public house, wedding & conference facilities and comfortable accommodation.

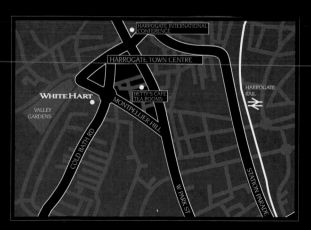

WHITE HART HOTEL
COLD BATH ROAD, HARROGATE HG2 0NF
T. 01423 505681   WWW.WHITEHART.NET

HAWNBY — Map 19 SE58

The Inn at Hawnby

Modern British

Hearty, honest cooking at a welcoming village inn

☎ 01439 798202
YO62 5QS
e-mail: info@innathawnby.co.uk
dir: From the S, A1 to Thirsk & Teeside exit A19/A168 for Scarborough onto A170. 1st left through Felixkirk. Through Boltby into Hawnby

Hawnby is a lovely village with an unspoilt authenticity that attracts hikers and bikers who come to take on the North York Moors National Park, and this stone-built Victorian village inn makes an inviting prospect as a base, thanks to the sincere and friendly owners who make it stand out from the crowd. When it comes to feeding hungry souls in from the great outdoors, the kitchen takes a no-nonsense approach, drawing on quality local ingredients for its gutsy, crowd-pleasing contemporary dishes. You could nurse a pint and eat in the cosy bar, but then you would miss the splendid views and wildlife in the garden that is a backdrop to eating in the old-fashioned elegance of the dining room. Confit of Yorkshire

duck leg served with roasted peppers, chorizo and courgettes and glazed with red onion marmalade is a satisfying starter, followed by a luxurious fish pie filled with halibut, haddock, smoked salmon, trout, crayfish and white wine and leek sauce. Finish with a trio of well-made desserts - strawberry Pavlova, dark chocolate mousse and fruit crumble.

Chef Jason Reeves **Owner** Kathryn & David Young **Times** 12-2/7-9 Closed 25 Dec, L Mon-Tue (limited opening Feb-Mar please phone) **Prices** Fixed L 3 course £10, Starter £4.25-£6.50, Main £10.95-£18.50, Dessert £5.50-£6.50, Service optional **Wines** 19 bottles over £20, 15 bottles under £20, 12 by glass **Notes** Sunday L, Vegetarian available, Civ Wed 35 **Seats** 32, Pr/dining room 30 **Children** Portions, Menu **Parking** 22

HELMSLEY — Map 19 SE68

Black Swan Hotel

Modern British V

Yorkshire boutique inn with modish cooking

☎ 01439 770466
Market Place YO62 5BJ
e-mail: enquiries@blackswan-helmsley.co.uk
web: www.blackswan-helmsley.co.uk
dir: A170 towards Scarborough, on entering Helmsley hotel at end of Market Place, just off mini-rdbt

Cantering through the centuries from Elizabethan to Georgian to Victorian, the Black Swan mixes its historic

Feversham Arms Hotel & Verbena Spa

HELMSLEY — Map 19 SE68

Modern British V

Culinary innovation in a modern spa hotel

☎ 01439 770766
1-8 High St YO62 5AG
e-mail: info@fevershamarmshotel.com
dir: A1 junct 49 follow A168 to Thirsk, take A170 to Helmsley. Turn left at mini rdbt then right, hotel on right past church

On the edge of the North York Moors, the creatively refurbished country house has become a modern spa hotel of character and style. All is as contemporary as can be in the dining room, where modern artworks look down on vibrantly upholstered seating, leather bucket-chairs and smartly dressed tables. Simon Kelly draws on the bounty of what the region's inhabitants consider to be

God's Own Country, with fine seasonal game from the moors, fish from the east coast, and plenty of farm-fresh produce comprising the bulk of the carte and five-course taster menus. A pressing of foie gras with quince and salsify shows a confident way with flavour combinations, followed by a main-course portion of nori-wrapped cod, timed to perfection, accompanied by croque-monsieur and brown shrimps tossed through blanched greens and a delicate grain-mustard sauce. Meats may include lamb rump, poached and roasted, served with violet artichoke and ricotta in brazil nut and lemon jus. A postmodern take on Arctic roll involves spiced cranberry, blood orange and white chocolate, or you might opt to conclude with a chocolate and hazelnut brownie, blitzed up with crème de cacao and Guinness.

Chef Simon Kelly **Times** 12-2/6.30-9.30 **Wines** 215 bottles over £20, 11 by glass **Notes** Tasting menu 5 course, ALC 3 course £45, Sunday L, Vegetarian menu, Dress restrictions, Smart casual, Civ Wed 70 **Seats** 65, Pr/dining room 24 **Children** Portions, Menu **Parking** 35

Save on Hotels. Book at **theAA.com/hotel**

YORKSHIRE, NORTH 503 **ENGLAND**

pedigree with a stylish 21st-century boutique look these days. Smack on the square of this pretty North York Moors village, the tea shop does a roaring trade in Yorkshire's celebrated bakery indulgences, while the elegant Rutland restaurant overlooking the walled garden is the scene for vibrant, thoroughly modern cooking with an unerring eye for splendid local produce. Pithivier of venison is served with 'flavours and textures' of beetroot, horseradish cream, and chocolate and balsamic dressing, and could precede slow-braised featherblade of beef with pommes purées, roasted shallot, baby onions and red wine jus. Poached pear with cinnamon parfait and caramel sauce is a typical finale.

Chef Paul Peters **Owner** John Jameson
Times 12.30-2.30/7-9.30 Closed L Mon-Sat **Prices** Fixed L 2 course £19.95, Fixed D 4 course £33, Service optional **Wines** 165 bottles over £20, 2 bottles under £20, 12 by glass **Notes** Tasting menu 6 course, Sunday L, Vegetarian menu, Dress restrictions, Smart casual, Civ Wed 90 **Seats** 65, Pr/dining room 30 **Children** Portions, Menu **Parking** 40

Feversham Arms Hotel & Verbena Spa

◉◉◉ – see opposite

HETTON	Map 18 SD95

The Angel Inn

◉◉ British ⬤NOTABLE WINE LIST

Well-judged menu in the Dales

☎ 01756 730263
BD23 6LT
e-mail: info@angelhetton.co.uk
dir: 6m N Skipton, follow B6265 towards Grassington, left at duck pond & again at T-junct. The Angel up the hill on right

In a tiny village in the Yorkshire Dales National Park, The Angel is a combination of a beamed bar-brasserie with a buzzing atmosphere and its own menu (food is ordered at the bar) and a calmer restaurant of interconnecting rooms with high-backed upholstered chairs at smartly set tables and waiter service. The well-drilled kitchen brigade maintains consistently high standards even at the busiest times and applies sound techniques to high-quality produce. Dishes are intelligently put together, so chargrilled beef fillet is sauced with girolles and served with seared foie gras, truffle foam, nutmeg-flavoured spinach and fondant potato, and cod suprême comes with chive and lobster butter, caper berries, lentils, spinach and saffron Parmentier potatoes. Lively starters include black pudding with bacon and pear bonbons, mustard jelly, Puy lentil sauce and home-made ketchup, and memorable puddings end a meal in style, with pineapple carpaccio and sorbet with white chocolate mousse, and a taste of apple (sparkling jelly, tarte Tatin and sorbet).

Times 12-2.30/6-10 Closed 25 Dec & 1wk Jan, L Mon-Sat, D Sun

KIRKBY FLEETHAM	Map 19 SE20

The Black Horse

◉◉ Traditional & Modern

Modernised Yorkshire pub fare by the village green

☎ 01609 749010 & 749011
7 Lumley Ln DL7 0SH
e-mail: gm@blackhorsekirkbyfleetham.com
web: www.blackhorsekirkbyfleetham.com
dir: Exit A1 to Kirkby Fleetham, follow restaurant signs

The stone-built pub by a Yorkshire village green has been given a confident but careful modern makeover, its guest rooms full of modern comforts, and a range of regular events - a wine club, fish-and-chip Fridays and weekly quiz nights - to lure in an enthusiastic crowd of supporters. Sleek table surfaces and a muted colour scheme distinguish the stylish dining room, and there's garden seating for drinks and nibbles and the chance to watch a game of quoits. Up-to-date spins on traditional Yorkshire pub fare raise the game, with openers such as salmon cured in malt whisky with honey-mustard dressing, a breakfast salad of black pudding, dry-cured bacon and a poached egg, or a sharing board offering 'bits and bats' of all the starters. Mains include an enterprising version of fish pie, incorporating smoked haddock, mussels and Wensleydale, while signature dishes embrace a textbook take on braised lamb shank with roasted garlic mash, confit roots, redcurrants and rosemary. You'd expect Yorkshire rhubarb to feature strongly in the season, and it does - in the form of a spicy crumble with vanilla ice cream.

Times 12-2.30/5-9

See advert on page 504

KNARESBOROUGH	Map 19 SE35

General Tarleton Inn

◉◉ Modern British ◉

Polished cooking in refined old coaching inn

☎ 01423 340284
Boroughbridge Rd, Ferrensby HG5 0PZ
e-mail: gti@generaltarleton.co.uk
web: www.generaltarleton.co.uk
dir: A1(M) junct 48 at Boroughbridge, take A6055 to Knaresborough. 4m on right

This 18th-century coaching inn, in open countryside, is a characterful place, with low beamed ceilings, rustic walls, log fires and cosy corners. It has a private dining room and separate cocktail bar - sure indicators of its market - as well as a smart restaurant in what was the stable. 'Food with Yorkshire Roots' is emblazoned on the menu, and indeed a taste of Nidderdale salmon (smoked, mousse, and seared with pickled fennel, accompanied by horseradish ice cream) may precede chargrilled fillet of Dales beef with foie gras tortellini and veal consommé. Locally sourced or not, dishes are well rendered and combinations intelligent: chilli-spiced crispy squid on a julienne of peppers and coriander, say, then roast pheasant breast rolled in sage and pancetta accompanied by confit leg, Savoy cabbage, and boulangère potatoes. The kitchen's momentum continues into the final straight, with puddings like chocolate fondant with orange ice cream and mandarin jelly, and classic lemon tart with raspberry sorbet.

Chef John Topham **Owner** John & Claire Topham
Times 12-1.45/5.30-9.15 Closed L Mon-Sat, D Sun, 26 Dec, 1 Jan **Prices** Fixed L 2 course £15, Fixed D 3 course £18.50, Starter £4.95-£10.95, Main £12.50-£27.50, Dessert £5.75-£7.95, Service optional, Groups min 6 service 10% **Wines** 70 bottles over £20, 8 bottles under £20, 11 by glass **Notes** Sunday L, Vegetarian available, Dress restrictions, Smart casual **Seats** 64, Pr/dining room 40 **Children** Portions, Menu **Parking** 40

BLACK HORSE INN

Whether it's 'welcome back' or 'welcome for the first time'
the Black Horse Inn is riding high once again.
Our menu is freshly prepared using locally sourced produce, providing you
with a delicious range of Great British Classic Dishes, all at affordable prices
for the whole family to enjoy.
Hand-pulled ales and a great selection of wines by the glass
are also available for your pleasure.

Our beautiful bedrooms offer you en-suite bed and breakfast from £75 a night.

We hope to welcome you very soon.

Black Horse Inn, Lumley Lane, Kirkby Fleetham, North Yorkshire, DL7 0SH
T 01609 749 010   www.blackhorsekirkbyfleetham.com

Save on Hotels. Book at **theAA.com/hotel**

YORKSHIRE, NORTH 505 **ENGLAND**

MALTON — Map 19 SE77

The Talbot Hotel

◎◎ British **NEW** 🖐

Highly accomplished local cooking from a local chef

☎ 01653 639096
Yorkersgate YO17 7AJ
e-mail: reservations@talbotmalton.co.uk
dir: A46 Malton

The Talbot is a foursquare Yorkshire house that has been in the Naylor-Leyland family since 1739, and they've looked after it well over the centuries, from the landscaped gardens to the light-toned contemporary elegance with which today's hotel is furnished. If localism is a virtue in food sourcing, it's surely all the more so in the provenance of the chef himself, and James Martin was born in Malton, so has Yorkshire blood and Yorkshire pride flowing through him. The style of cooking he delivers (in an executive capacity) rises to the occasion of the smart, sophisticated dining room, where crisp white linen, silver cutlery and formal service play their parts. Modern British thinking is to the fore, with a mix of classical and up-to-date technique brought to bear on the fine ingredients the kitchen has at its disposal. A kind of croquette of lightly smoked kipper starts things off with a flourish, accompanied as it is by seasonal Sand Hutton asparagus and a capery Cambridge butter sauce. That's followed by superb lamb from Terrington, roasted in lavender and hay and partnered by braised shallots, peas and celery cress, with daringly savoury notes creeping into desserts too - dark chocolate fondant with caramel ice cream and black salt praline, for example.

Chef James Martin, Craig Atchinson **Owner** Fitzwilliam Estate **Times** 6.30-9.30 Closed L Mon-Sat **Prices** Fixed L 2 course fr £20, Fixed D 3 course £29-£35, Service optional **Wines** 133 bottles over £20, 4 bottles under £20, 14 by glass **Notes** Sunday L, Vegetarian available, Dress restrictions, No ripped jeans, football shirts, Civ Wed 40 **Seats** 40, Pr/dining room 40 **Children** Portions **Parking** 40

MASHAM — Map 19 SE28

Samuel's at Swinton Park

◎◎◎ – see page 506

Vennell's

◎◎ Modern British

Smart, modish cooking and a new look

☎ 01765 689000
7 Silver St HG4 4DX
e-mail: info@vennellsrestaurant.co.uk
dir: 8m from A1 Masham exit, 10m N of Ripon

An interior makeover in 2012 has produced a stylish aubergine-coloured room (to match the frontage), hung with framed pictures and mirrors, with split-level dining and comfortable sitting-out areas featuring abstract-patterned upholstery. It makes an elegant context for Jon Vennell's appealingly ungimmicky cooking, offered in the form of short menus that draw on Italian and French traditions. A duo of salmon, poached and tartare, comes with beetroot wafers and a lemon dressing as a refreshing opener, while main courses aim for substance in the shape of oxtail and mushroom suet pudding with minute steak and mash, or sea bass with crab tortelloni and tomato concasse in basil oil. A clutch of fine Yorkshire cheeses will prove a strong lure, if you're not in the market for something like a chocolate fondant with passionfruit sorbet.

Chef Jon Vennell **Owner** Jon & Laura Vennell **Times** 12-2/7.15-mdnt Closed 26-29 Dec, 1-14 Jan, 1 wk Sep, BHs, Mon, L Tue-Sat, D Sun **Prices** Fixed D 3 course fr £27.99, Service optional **Wines** 48 bottles over £20, 12 bottles under £20, 11 by glass **Notes** Sunday L, Vegetarian available **Seats** 30, Pr/dining room 16 **Children** Portions **Parking** On street & Market Sq

MIDDLESBROUGH — Map 19 NZ41

Chadwicks Inn

◎◎ Modern British 🖐

Well-judged menus at revamped country inn

☎ 01642 590300
High Ln, Maltby TS8 0BG
e-mail: enquiries@chadwicksinnmaltby.co.uk
dir: A19-A174(W)/A1045, follow signs to Yarm & Maltby, left at the Manor House inn 500yds on left through village

Chadwicks was built in the 19th century and still has the original stone fireplace and beams to show for it. Renovation has given a modern look to the restaurant, candlelit at night, where there are unclothed wooden tables and upholstered banquettes. As well as the carte, a bistro menu operates at lunchtimes (sandwiches also available then) and early evening, ranging from leek and potato soup to confit duck leg with chorizo cassoulet. The carte itself raises the stakes to well-thought-out main courses of breast of guinea fowl, accurately cooked, with truffle stuffing, a pasty of leg confit, and sweet potato, the plate dotted with sultanas, or cod fillet with wild mushrooms, cabbage cooked with pancetta in shallot butter, herb and parmesan gnocchi, and parsley root purée. Good sourcing may bring on a starter of seared Shetland scallops sitting on broad bean risotto along with air-dried ham and a dash of smoked garlic purée, and among desserts could be a celebration of pineapple.

Chef Matthew Roath **Owner** Paul & Bernie Jenkins **Times** 12-2.30/5-9.30 Closed 25 Dec, 1 Jan, Mon, D Sun **Prices** Fixed L 2 course £12.95, Starter £6.50-£9, Main £12.95-£28, Dessert £4.95-£6.50, Service optional, Groups min 8 service 10% **Wines** 41 bottles over £20, 10 bottles under £20, 6 by glass **Notes** Early evening bistro 5-6.30, weekly steak night from £29.95, Sunday L, Vegetarian available **Seats** 47 **Children** Portions, Menu **Parking** 50

OLDSTEAD — Map 19 SE57

The Black Swan at Oldstead

◎◎◎ – see page 506

PICKERING — Map 19 SE78

Fox & Hounds Country Inn

◎ Modern British 🖐

Quality fare in village gastro-pub

☎ 01751 431577
Main St, Sinnington YO62 6SQ
e-mail: fox.houndsinn@btconnect.com
dir: In Sinnington centre, 3m W of Pickering, off A170

The bar is a popular place at this 18th-century inn, originally three separate cottages (count the front doors), with its log burner, settles and beams. Just as popular with diners is the stylish restaurant, where upholstered chairs are pulled up at oak tables. Light lunches run from black pudding with sautéed potatoes, a poached egg and crispy bacon to fish pie, while the kitchen sets out its stall with a more ambitious evening menu. First-course sea bass fillet accompanied by chilli and ginger scallops, stir-fried shiitake mushrooms and Chinese greens might precede beef brisket slowly braised with red wine, bacon and shallots, served with croquette potatoes and roast root vegetables. Diehards could go for a steak with the usual trimmings, and desserts are a satisfying lot, among them perhaps apple and plum crumble with custard.

Chef Mark Caffrey **Owner** Mr & Mrs A Stephens **Times** 12-2/6.30-9 Closed 25-26 Dec **Prices** Starter £4.95-£7.75, Main £9.95-£22.95, Dessert £5.95-£10.95, Service optional **Wines** 21 bottles over £20, 19 bottles under £20, 9 by glass **Notes** Early eve menu 5.30-6.30 Sun-Thu, Sunday L, Vegetarian available, Dress restrictions, Smart casual, No shorts **Seats** 40, Pr/dining room 12 **Children** Portions, Menu **Parking** 35

Samuel's at Swinton Park

MASHAM	Map 19 SE28

Modern British V 🖐

Creative cooking in an imposing ancestral home

☎ 01765 680900
Swinton HG4 4JH
e-mail: enquiries@swintonpark.com
web: www.swintonpark.com
dir: A1 take B6267, from Masham follow brown signs for Swinton Park

As you approach this grand castellated mansion you're more than likely to spot wild deer wandering in its 200 acres of surrounding parkland and gardens, birds of prey flapping through the trees, and llamas roaming in the distance... llamas? Your eyes do not deceive you. The ancestral home of the Cunliffe-Lister family is a mightily impressive residence, with more than a passing resemblance to a castle, and it makes for an impressive country-house hotel. The grand impression continues on the inside - imposing proportions, magnificent period detailing and luxurious fixtures and fittings. And no less so in Samuel's restaurant, where Yorkshireman Simon Crannage cooks up a storm. Simon is a lucky chef, for at his fingertips is the produce from the four-acre walled kitchen garden (and they don't get any bigger than that), plus game from the Swinton Estate. This fine bounty is put to good use in the kitchen. Hand-dived scallops might come in a fashionable pairing with cauliflower (both tempura and purée), with some curry seasoning and Wharfe Valley lemon oil, followed perhaps by roasted loin of Swinton Estate venison with chestnuts, mulled pears, woodland mushrooms and garden greens. For dessert, Granny Smith apples appear as mousse and crisp, alongside bergamot syrup and lemon sorbet, while pear sorbet and spiced pear purée is partnered with gingerbread.

Chef Simon Crannage **Owner** Mr and Mrs Cunliffe-Lister **Times** 12.30-2/7-9.30 Closed L Mon (Only Castle menu in bar) **Prices** Fixed L 2 course £22, Fixed D 4 course £52, Tasting menu £60, Starter £6.25-£8.25, Main £10.95-£15.50, Dessert £6.50-£9.25, Service optional

Wines 85 bottles over £20, 3 bottles under £20, 11 by glass **Notes** Signature tasting menu, Sunday L, Vegetarian menu, Civ Wed 120 **Seats** 60, Pr/dining room 20 **Children** Portions, Menu **Parking** 80

The Black Swan at Oldstead

OLDSTEAD	Map 19 SE57

Modern British V 🖐

Top-notch cooking in charming country inn

☎ 01347 868387
YO61 4BL
e-mail: enquiries@blackswanoldstead.co.uk
web: www.blackswanoldstead.co.uk
dir: A1 junct 49, A168, A19 S (or from York A19 N), then Coxwold, Byland Abbey, Oldstead

In a tiny village in the North York Moors National Park, this 16th-century inn has a traditional bar - flagstones, oak furniture and an open fire - and a stylish restaurant on the first floor, with a beamed ceiling, Persian rugs on the oak floor, and prints on neutral walls. Friendly and unpretentious staff serve the kitchen's output of accurately timed, well-conceived dishes, after a taster of perhaps onion soup. Foie gras is imaginatively teamed with green lentils and onion purée, and scallops are pan-fried, their fresh, sweet flavour complemented by celeriac purée and given a contrast from the subtle saltiness of Parma ham and the sharpness of Granny Smith and capers. The kitchen doesn't stint its efforts with main courses: Hebridean lamb, for instance, comes three ways - roast loin, braised shoulder and confit belly - accompanied by carrot choucroute and pommes Anna, and four slices of flavourful, tender venison are served with a bolognese-style sauce of meat and mushrooms topped with parmesan, deep-fried gnocchi, and butternut squash purée, a resoundingly successful dish. Fish might appear as Japanese-style tuna tartare, followed by sea bass fillet with Jerusalem artichoke risotto, bacon and sprouts, and to finish could be intense chocolate délice with orange sorbet and jelly.

Chef Adam Jackson **Owner** The Banks family **Times** 12-2/6-9 Closed 1 wk Jan, L Mon-Wed **Prices** Fixed L 2 course £20, Fixed D 3 course £25, Tasting menu £60-£98, Starter £9.95-£12.50, Main £18.95-£25.95, Dessert £7.50-£8.95, Service optional **Wines** 113 bottles over £20, 6 bottles under £20, 18 by glass **Notes** Tasting menu 7 course (with wine £98), Sunday L, Vegetarian menu **Seats** 35, Pr/dining room 12 **Children** Portions, Menu **Parking** 25

Save on Hotels. Book at **theAA.com/hotel**

YORKSHIRE, NORTH 507 **ENGLAND**

PICKERING *continued*

The White Swan Inn

Modern British V

Smart market-town inn with well-judged menu

☎ 01751 472288
Market Place YO18 7AA
e-mail: welcome@white-swan.co.uk
dir: Just beyond junct of A169/A170 in Pickering, turn right off A170 into Market Place

Originally a refuelling post for the York to Whitby stagecoach, the centuries-old White Swan hasn't forgotten its pub roots, but neither has it stood still when it comes to embracing the country-chic interior design of today's top-ranking country inns. There's still a cosy bar with well-kept ales and a smart lounge with squashy sofas and log fire. The classy restaurant at the rear ups the ante with its modish country good looks; think ruby red walls, winter fire, stone floors and evening candlelight. Unfussy modern cooking fashioned from good quality seasonal Yorkshire produce (with an admirable eye on food miles) is the kitchen's mantra. Take an opener of Whitby fishcakes served with herbed shrimp salad and tartare, perhaps followed up with slow-cooked belly pork (Plum Pudding breed) matched with sweet red cabbage, brandy apple sauce, mustard mash and crackling.

Chef Darren Clemmit **Owner** The Buchanan family
Times 12-2/6.45-9 **Prices** Starter £5.25-£10.95, Main £12.95-£23.50, Dessert £4.50-£11.95, Service optional **Wines** 73 bottles over £20, 8 bottles under £20, 11 by glass **Notes** Fixed L & D menu on request, Sunday L, Vegetarian menu **Seats** 50, Pr/dining room 18 **Children** Portions, Menu **Parking** 45

PICKHILL   Map 19 SE38

Nags Head Country Inn

Modern British V

Ambitious cooking in country inn

☎ 01845 567391
YO7 4JG
e-mail: reservations@nagsheadpickhill.co.uk
dir: Leave A1 junct 50 (travelling N) onto A6055; junct 51 (travelling S) onto A684, then A6055

In a quiet village just off the A1, The Nags Head is a civilised, welcoming inn, dating from the 17th century. The taproom dispenses real ales and has a separate menu, with the restaurant menu focused on seasonal ingredients, with game prominent in season: seared breast of wood pigeon with apple and blue cheese salad and mustard dressing, say, followed by game pie. New season's asparagus may appear in late spring, with a fried egg and ham shavings, alongside a more exotic starter of tempura king prawns with salt-and-pepper squid, wasabi and pickled ginger. Prime ingredients are sometimes given a surprising twist - foie gras terrine with pease pudding, for instance, in a starter with ham hock, tomato relish and crumbled crackling - and flavours

can be piled up, although the results are normally successful, as when seared loin of lamb with confit breast and sautéed sweetbreads is joined by beetroot risotto, broad bean and lovage stew and nettle purée.

Chef Louie Miller **Owner** Edward & Janet Boynton
Times 12-2/6-9.30 Closed 25 Dec **Prices** Fixed L 2 course fr £15.95, Starter £3-£7.95, Main £9.50-£18.95, Dessert £3.95-£5.95, Service optional **Wines** 30 bottles under £20, 8 by glass **Notes** Fixed L 2,3 course Sun, Sunday L, Vegetarian menu **Seats** 40, Pr/dining room 24 **Children** Portions, Menu **Parking** 50

RICHMOND   Map 19 NZ10

The Frenchgate Restaurant and Hotel

Modern British

Complex cooking in a Georgian townhouse

☎ 01748 822087 & 07921 136362
59-61 Frenchgate DL10 7AE
e-mail: info@thefrenchgate.co.uk
dir: From A1 (Scotch Corner) to Richmond on A6108. After lights, 1st left into Lile Close (leading to Flints Terrace) for hotel car park. Or for front entrance continue to 1st rdbt, left into Dundas St. At T-junct left into Frenchgate

The Frenchgate is a classic Georgian townhouse in the knot of cobbled streets at the heart of old Richmond, done out with a stylish 21st-century cocktail of works by local artists, designer touches and period elegance. Intimate is certainly the right word for the elegant dining room, where bare oak tables - just seven of them - sit on restored foot-wide floorboards, and with such a select audience of diners to cater for, the kitchen can keep a tight rein on the quality and precision of its clever and ambitious contemporary dishes - an opener of black pudding Scotch egg with confit pork belly, apple gel, pancetta and onion shows the style. Yorkshire's fine produce is a strong element of the output too, whether it is roasted cannon of Swaledale lamb with cassoulet, basil mash and rosemary jus, or pan-fried North Sea halibut served with horseradish creamed leeks, cucumber, semi-dried grapes and Gewürztraminer foam. Puddings are equally thoughtful compositions - clotted cream pannacotta, partnered with sticky lemon and poppy seed cake, lemon curd, black olive caramel and pistachio.

Chef Ross Hadley **Owner** David & Luiza Todd
Times 12-2/6-9.30 **Prices** Fixed L 2 course £12-£18, Fixed D 3 course £34-£39, Starter £4.95-£7.95, Main £8.95-£19, Dessert £5.95-£9, Service optional, Groups min 6 service 10% **Wines** 82 bottles over £20, 8 bottles under £20, 9 by glass **Notes** Pre-theatre & tasting menu available, matching wine flights, Sunday L, Vegetarian available, Civ Wed 30 **Seats** 24, Pr/dining room 24 **Children** Portions **Parking** 12

RIPON   Map 19 SE37

The George at Wath

Modern British **NEW**

Revamped country inn with enterprising cooking

☎ 01765 641324
Main St, Wath HG4 5EN
e-mail: reception@georgeatwath.co.uk

The George's traditional bar, with its log-burner and mixture of oak and flagstone floors, leads to the smartly furnished restaurant, where helpful and genuinely friendly staff provide a good level of service. The menu has universal appeal, judging by openers of potted crab with a saffron brioche, and carpaccio with parmesan shavings, and main courses of steak and ale pie, and beer-battered haddock with the usual accompaniments. Presentation is carefully considered - seen in a colourful starter of ham knuckle terrine capped by a fried quail's egg, accompanied by a small jar of piccalilli topped with pea shoots - and quality meats are properly prepared: perfectly roast squab pigeon, tender and full of flavour, with confit leg, sauced with pan juices and served with red cabbage and carrot purées and hash browns.

Times 12-2.30/5.30-9 Closed D Sun **Prices** Fixed L 2 course £13, Groups min 8 service 10% **Notes** Early evening menu 5.30-7pm, Sunday L

The Royal Oak

Modern British

Modernised traditional inn with food to suit

☎ 01765 602284
36 Kirkgate HG4 1PB
e-mail: info@royaloakripon.co.uk
dir: In town centre

With the cathedral, museum and attractions of Ripon's historic centre on the doorstep, as well as a flutter on the gee-gees at the racecourse, or visits to Newby Hall, Fountains Abbey and the Yorkshire Dales, The Royal Oak hardly lacks for attractions. Inside is unexpectedly contemporary after a facelift, giving the place a de-cluttered modern look of wooden floors, open fires and leather sofas. Sensible menus of modern and classic British pub dishes do the rest. Local produce from a network of well-chosen suppliers is used to good effect: potted Bishop Thornton pork with apple chutney, crackling and sourdough toast shows the no-nonsense style, then blade of beef comes with the hearty company of horseradish rösti, spinach, oxtail bourguignon and port jelly. Finally, artisan Yorkshire cheeses run neck and neck with Yorkshire rhubarb crumble and gingerbread ice cream.

Chef Jonathan Murray **Owner** Timothy Taylor & Co Ltd
Times 12-2.30/5.30-9.30 **Prices** Starter £3-£8, Main £9-£18, Dessert £5-£7, Service optional **Wines** 10 bottles over £20, 12 bottles under £20, 10 by glass **Notes** Quarterly seasonal tasting menu, Vegetarian available, Air con **Seats** 50 **Children** Portions, Menu **Parking** 4, Market car park

SCARBOROUGH   Map 17 TA08

Beiderbecke's Hotel

◉ Modern British

Modish hotel brasserie with good food

☎ 01723 365766 & 350349
1-3 The Crescent YO11 2PW
e-mail: info@beiderbeckes.com
dir: In town centre, 200mtrs from railway station

The hotel's upbeat Marmalade's Brasserie follows the jazz theme suggested by the Beiderbecke name (for those non-jazz aficionados, 'Bix' Beiderbecke was a famous American jazz cornetist, pianist and composer). It's a modern and stylish venue all the same, yet still suitably relaxed, with jazz-theme photos donning the walls and a live jazz trio laying down tunes on a Saturday night. The kitchen plays it relatively modern, keeping things simple and fashioned from fresh local produce; fillet of cod, for example, with lemon and caper butter served with new potatoes and green beans, or perhaps a fillet of pork wrapped in pancetta with an accompaniment of creamed potatoes, roast parsnips and a cider jus. For the encore, traditional crème brûlée with shortbread biscuit.

Times 12-2/5.30-9.30

Best Western Ox Pasture Hall Country Hotel

◉◉ Modern British

Confident modern cooking on the North York Moors

☎ 01723 365295
Lady Edith's Dr, Raincliffe Woods YO12 5TD
e-mail: oxpasture.hall@btconnect.com
dir: A171, left onto Lady Edith's Drive, 1.5m, hotel on right

Reclining in 17 acres on the North York Moors, only a couple of miles from Scarborough, the stone-built hall looks more soft-focus Cotswold than most people's idea of rugged Yorkshire. That said, the exposed stone walls and foursquare furnishings inside have a coolly understated air, banishing any sense of chintziness. Pastel-hued walls and a tiled floor lend the Courtyard dining-room the air of a Provençal farmhouse, and the approach of staff is cheeringly friendly. The kitchen marches manfully into the modern British arena, taking on the presentational tricks of today's ambitious cooking (think slate-plates, Kilner jars and squiggles of sauce), but it's all in a good cause, as the results on the palate are strong and convincing. Roast breast and confit leg of quail make a confident starter, alongside a slice of black pudding roulade in honey-mustard dressing, or there might be a labour-intensive, impressive four-way rendition of Whitby crab - as crabcake, sandwich, tian and bisque, served with a blini. Fish and meat combinations are handled with assurance, as when stone bass is teamed with merguez sausage, along with white beans and gnocchi, and themed desserts take on chocolate and orange, orchard fruits and caramel.

Chef Anthony Griffiths **Owner** Lifestyle Hotels Ltd
Times 12-2.30/6.30-9.30 Closed Mon-Tue **Prices** Starter

£7.95-£11.50, Main £15.95-£21.95, Dessert £7.50-£12, Service included **Wines** 60 bottles over £20, 15 bottles under £20, 10 by glass **Notes** Sunday L, Vegetarian available, Dress restrictions, Smart casual **Seats** 50, Pr/dining room 12 **Children** Portions, Menu **Parking** 100

SCAWTON   Map 19 SE58

The Hare Inn

◉ Modern British

Comforting pub food in the Rievaulx Valley

☎ 01845 597769
YO7 2HG
e-mail: info@thehareinn.co.uk
dir: From A170 Sutton Bank take 1st left signed Rievaulx Abbey. Restaurant in 1.5m along road

A visit to the Hare is a true trip back in time. It's a 13th-century inn near Rievaulx Abbey, with uplifting views over the valley, and a cheering rural look inside - floral wallpaper, big fat candles on unclothed tables, a private dining room with beams and lobster-coloured walls. The comforting pub menus are supplemented by daily specials and blackboard lunch options, incorporating a wealth of choice. Start with deep-fried crab beignets and chilli mayonnaise, or that brasserie favourite, smoked haddock with spinach and a poached egg in hollandaise. Main courses offer the chance to showcase some regional meats, such as rack of Dales lamb with Puy lentils and roasted shallots in redcurrant and thyme jus, or there might be fried gilt head bream with provençale vegetables. Round things off with lemon posset or blueberry cheesecake.

Times 12-2/6-9.30 Closed 4 days Feb, Mon, D Sun

SKIPTON   Map 18 SD95

The Bull at Broughton

◉ Traditional British 🍃

Confident, regional cooking in charming village inn

☎ 01756 792065
Broughton BD23 3AE
e-mail: enquiries@thebullatbroughton.com
web: www.thebullatbroughton.com
dir: M65/A6068 (Vivary Way) for 1m, turn left onto A56 (Skipton Rd) for 7m, then right onto A59. Restaurant on right

The Bull is part of a mini empire of four gastro-pubs run by Nigel Haworth and Craig Bancroft of Northcote Manor

(see entry), an enterprise whose praiseworthy aim is to showcase the best of Yorkshire and Lancashire produce in a switched-on, convivial, modern pub ambience. Accordingly, the stone-built Bull has received a smartly contemporary facelift, grafting a light and airy style and casually mis-matched furniture with traditional flagstoned floors and low beamed ceilings. Obliging staff play a key part in the Bull's welcoming vibe, backed up by good beer, and no-nonsense food. A glance at the menu shows a kitchen striving for local and seasonal output - a filo pastry parcel of local seafood with Lancashire cheese fondue to start, followed by a pie of Goosnargh turkey, ham, leek and chestnuts with celeriac mash and Brussels sprouts. Puddings take no prisoners, offering deep comfort in the shape of sticky toffee pudding with vanilla ice cream or blackcurrant Bakewell tart with clotted cream.

The Bull at Broughton

Chef Michael Emminson **Owner** Craig Bancroft & Nigel Haworth **Times** 12-2/5.30-8.30 Closed 25 Dec, Mon (ex BHs) **Prices** Fixed L 2 course £11.50, Fixed D 3 course £15, Starter £4.75-£7.50, Main £10.50-£17.50, Dessert £5-£5.50, Service optional **Wines** 20 bottles over £20, 17 bottles under £20, 5 by glass **Notes** Fixed L & D Tue-Thu only, Sunday L, Vegetarian available **Seats** 101 **Children** Portions, Menu **Parking** 41

See advert opposite

Save on Hotels. Book at **theAA.com/hotel**

YORKSHIRE, NORTH 509 ENGLAND

SNAINTON
Map 17 SE98

The Coachman Inn

◉ Modern British

Updated country inn with quality cooking

☎ 01723 859231
Pickering Road West YO13 9PL
e-mail: info@coachmaninn.co.uk
dir: From A170 between Pickering & Scarborough onto
B1258 (high St) in Stainton

Within a tranquil North York Moors village, this tastefully-
remodelled Georgian inn - once the last staging post
before Scarborough for York mail coaches - serves up a
pleasing blend of old and new. Eat in the bar with its
chunky Arts and Crafts tables, quarry-tiled floor and open
fire, or go for the more sophisticated charm of the New
England-styled Carriages Restaurant, kitted out in sage-
green with linen-swathed tables, period chairs and
original pine flooring. The kitchen's fresh modern ideas
are admirably based around quality seasonal produce
from the local area. Thus supreme of East Coast hake
with roasted and creamed fennel, East Coast mussels,
broad beans and beurre blanc sits alongside Yorkshire
lamb three ways (roasted rump, pressed neck, pan-fried
kidney) with hotpot potatoes, pea purée, trumpets,
creamed kale and pan jus. A classic menu option might
be beer-battered cod.

Chef Greg Wallace **Owner** Taylor Family **Times** 12-9.30
Prices Starter £5.95-£9.95, Main £10.95-£24.95, Dessert
£5.95-£6.95, Service optional **Wines** 11 bottles over £20,
16 bottles under £20, 13 by glass **Notes** Sunday L,
Vegetarian available **Seats** 42, Pr/dining room 12
Children Portions, Menu **Parking** 30

STILLINGTON
Map 19 SE56

The Bay Tree

◉ Traditional, International ✿

Accurate cooking with flair in revamped village inn

☎ 01347 811394
Main St YO61 1JU
e-mail: gm.baytreestillington.com
web: www.baytreestillington.com
dir: A19 into Tollerton Rd (signed Huby, Public
Weighbridge, Sutton Park). In Huby left into Main St, right
into Stillington Rd. 1m, right into Roseberry Ln. 0.5m, left
into Carr Ln (B1363), right into Main St

This whitewashed one-time village inn is these days a
remodelled boutique-style restaurant with rooms, but it
hasn't forgotten its roots. Inside, the modern-rustic vibe
combines a homely bar - with flagstone floor and open
fires - alongside a more intimate, conservatory-style
restaurant. The cooking is based on solid British
foundations, with some modern additions, and keeps
things relatively simple and focussed. Steak and Black
Sheep Ale pie with puff-pastry top hits the spot, or go for
the more modish pork medallions served with toasted
pine nuts, sun-dried tomatoes and saffron vinaigrette.
Steamed syrup sponge might line up alongside a
blueberry sundae at dessert stage.

Chef Rob Chrystal, Toby Wells **Owner** John Sparrow
Times 12-2/6-9 Closed L Mon **Prices** Starter £4.50-£6.25,
Main £8.95-£16.95, Dessert £5.50-£7.50, Service
optional **Wines** 6 bottles over £20, 20 bottles under £20,
6 by glass **Notes** Sunday L, Vegetarian available **Seats** 25
Children Portions, Menu **Parking** On street

See advert opposite

SUTTON-ON-THE-FOREST
Map 19 SE56

The Blackwell Ox Inn

◉ British

Unfussy dining in a picturesque North York village

☎ 01347 810328
Huby Rd YO61 1DT
e-mail: enquiries@blackwelloxinn.co.uk
dir: Off A1237, onto B1363 to Sutton-on-the-Forest. Left
at T-junct, 50yds on right

This characterful village inn is rooted in the appreciation
of fine local produce - its name even commemorates a
legendary Shorthorn Teeswater ox that stood six feet at
the crop before it was delivered to the butcher. Just a
short drive from the city, the Regency-era Blackwell Ox
has five stylish en suite bedrooms that make it a good
rural bolt-hole for exploring York and the North York
Moors; at the end of the day, you'll return to a classic
rustic bar with log fires and chunky tables, and a country-
style restaurant that deals in uncomplicated British
dishes that showcase local and seasonal ingredients. The
menu changes daily and might start with pan-fried
scallops with pancetta, and pea and mint purée, followed
by slow-roasted pork belly with saffron potatoes, sherry
lentils, wild mushrooms and pan juices, while for fish
fans there could be pan-roast cod loin with creamed
cabbage, rösti and herb sauce.

Owner Blackwell Ox Inns (York) Ltd **Times** 12-2/6-9.30
Closed 25 Dec, 1 Jan, D Sun **Prices** Starter £4.95-£6.95,
Main £9.95-£18.95, Dessert £4.95-£6.95, Service
optional **Wines** 36 bottles over £20, 32 bottles under £20,
20 by glass **Notes** Vegetarian available **Seats** 50, Pr/
dining room 20 **Children** Portions, Menu **Parking** 19

Rose & Crown

◉ Modern British

Local meats and game in a rustic village pub

☎ 01347 811333
Main St YO61 1DP
e-mail: mail@rosecrown.co.uk
dir: 8m N of York towards Helmsley on B1363

The village inn not far from York has a reassuringly rustic
feel within, with oak floors and solid wood tables
inspiring confidence. The principal focal points of the
menu are locally-reared and bagged meat, poultry and
game, though fish-lovers need not feel neglected. It all
gets fashioned into modern brasserie-style dishes such
as smoked haddock fishcakes with poached egg, black
pudding, spinach and curry sauce, followed by pan-
roasted chicken breast with chorizo and king prawns in
garlicky white wine cream, or slow-roast pork belly with
horseradish mash and black pepper sauce. The fillet
steaks of 45-day-aged Yorkshire beef are understandably
popular too. A dessert to conjure with is the hot
chocolate-orange meltdown cake.

Times 12-2/6-9.30 Closed 1st wk Jan, Mon, D Sun

The BayTree
Country Pub & Restaurant

The Bay Tree in Stillington enjoys a loyal following amongst clientele from the region, who travel religiously from near and far to this little jewel. We are located just 20 minutes from York in North Yorkshire. Lovingly refurbished throughout, a strong reputation is being developed for great food, including our own South Farm meats, reared and fattened just down the road. Winner of the Flavours of Hambleton Pub and Restaurant of the year 2010, with menu choices using a variety of local produce, whatever you fancy, you can be sure of a very warm welcome and a really delicious meal!

The Bay Tree provides a charming resting spot, ideally placed for those visiting Castle Howard, Walled Gardens at Scampston, Byland Abbey, Sutton Park, Burn Hall, Helmsley and other stately homes and historic sites.

The Bay Tree, Main Street Stillington, York, YO61 1JU
www.baytreestillington.com
Tel: 01347 811 394

Gift Vouchers available, please give us a call for further details.

The Wensleydale Heifer

◉◉ Traditional, International **V**

Top-notch seafood in the heart of the Yorkshire Dales

☎ 01969 622322
Main St DL8 4LS
e-mail: info@wensleydaleheifer.co.uk
dir: On A684 (3m W of Leyburn)

Given the bovine name and the location in the landlocked
Yorkshire Dales, it may come as a surprise that this
whitewashed 17th-century coaching inn is a fish and
seafood specialist, but chef-proprietor David Moss
(formerly of the Crab and Lobster in Asenby - see entry) is
a man who likes to plough his own furrow. The buzzy
set-up operates on two distinctly different levels: the
more casual fish bar, with seagrass matting, rattan
chairs, pale wood tables and pictures of seafaring cows
as a nod to the heifer theme, and a more upmarket
restaurant done out with stylish chocolate leather chairs,
linen-clothed tables and Doug Hyde artwork. The kitchen
team takes an eclectic modern approach to its weekly-
changing menus - fish and chips with posh peas and
tartare sauce is, of course, written in stone, but the
changing cast of unpretentious dishes might include
smoked haddock, chorizo and white onion chowder with
chorizo oil, followed by maple-roast scallops with king
prawn and lobster salad, crispy bacon, pork belly and
shallots.

Chef David Moss **Owner** David & Lewis Moss
Times 12-2.30/6-9.30 **Prices** Food prices not confirmed
for 2013. Please telephone for details **Wines** 68 bottles
over £20, 23 bottles under £20, 14 by glass **Notes** Sunday
L, Vegetarian menu **Seats** 70 **Children** Portions, Menu
Parking 30

The Cliffemount Hotel

◉◉ Modern British ⏁

Pragmatic cooking in a Yorkshire clifftop hotel

☎ 01947 840103
Bank Top Ln, Runswick Bay TS13 5HU
e-mail: info@cliffemounthotel.co.uk
dir: Exit A174, 8m N of Whitby, 1m to end

Perched on the cliffs overlooking Runswick Bay, the hotel
is blissfully insulated from almost any other sound but
the distant plashing of waves below. That imperious view
can be enjoyed from the Pasión dining room, where light
boutique styling meets a country-pub approach to menu
construction, with the day's specials chalked up on the
board. Seafood is a particular lure, from crab spring rolls
in sesame dressing, or roast mackerel with Yorkshire Blue
rarebit and a salad of marinated apricot and red onion, to
mains such as sea trout on brown shrimp and spring
onion risotto. Homely dishes such as steak-and-ale pie
and mash (made with Black Sheep ale) dispel any sense
of pretentiousness, and that local beef might also appear

roasted with a Yorkshire pudding and potatoes done in
duck fat.

Chef David Spencer **Owner** Ian & Carol Rae
Times 12-2.30/6-9 **Prices** Starter £4.95-£11.95, Main
£14.95-£32.95, Dessert £6.75, Service optional
Wines 34 bottles over £20, 16 bottles under £20, 8 by
glass **Notes** Sunday L, Vegetarian available **Seats** 50
Children Portions **Parking** 25

Dunsley Hall

◉ Modern, Traditional **V** ⏁

Accomplished cooking in a striking property

☎ 01947 893437
Dunsley YO21 3TL
e-mail: reception@dunsleyhall.com
dir: 3.5m from Whitby off A171(Teeside road)

The Victorian shipping magnate who built his dream
country home up on the headland above the North
Yorkshire coast clearly wanted inspirational views of the
sea that had made his fortune. Dunsley Hall is an
imposing mansion built with a swagger that says that
this is the house of a gentleman of substance, and the
oak panelling, mullioned and stained-glass windows and
fine plasterwork of the interior hammer the message
home. Of course it's all softened with a gentle modern
touch, and staffed with a professional team, while the
kitchen brigade works with top-class Yorkshire
ingredients to produce an ambitious menu of modern
country-house dishes. To start, perhaps a robust trio of
crispy new season lamb's sweetbreads, breast and
tongue with caramelised cauliflower purée, cumin and
poached apricots. With Whitby's fishing fleet just up the
road, it makes sense to go for a main course of roast
pavé of cod with violet artichoke barigoule, cherry
tomatoes, flowering courgettes, pearl couscous, and
lemon, chilli and brown shrimp vinaigrette.

Chef Graham Hughes **Owner** Mr & Mrs W Ward
Times 12-2/7.30-9.30 **Prices** Food prices not confirmed
for 2013. Please telephone for details **Wines** 10 bottles
over £20, 10 bottles under £20, 10 by glass
Notes Vegetarian menu, Dress restrictions, Smart casual,
no jeans or shorts **Seats** 85, Pr/dining room 30
Children Portions, Menu **Parking** 30

Estbek House

◉◉ Modern British ⬥

Fresh seafood by the sea near Whitby

☎ 01947 893424
East Row, Sandsend YO21 3SU
e-mail: info@estbekhouse.co.uk
web: www.estbekhouse.co.uk
dir: From Whitby follow A174 towards Sandsend. Estbek
House just before bridge

Estbek House, a Grade II listed property built in the mid-
18th century, stands on the beachfront a few miles out of
Whitby. It's a small and comfortable restaurant with
rooms, with a bright and modern dining room with a
wooden floor, a neutral décor and comfortable high-
backed leather-look chairs. Not surprisingly, fish is the
speciality, whatever was landed that morning making its
way on to the daily-changing menu. Fillet of cod, turbot,
halibut - whatever - is simply seared in the pan, offered
with a choice of sauces - perhaps creamy lemon - and
accompanied by fresh seasonal vegetables. Other options
could extend to seafood pie or the extravagance of lobster
thermidor. Seafood in a number of guises goes into
starters - chowder, say, or smoked salmon and crayfish
with seasonal samphire. For meat-eaters there may be
moist and tender local lamb with rhubarb compôte and
steamed vegetables, and you might end with white
chocolate crème brûlée with raspberries.

Times 6-9

See advert opposite

Judges Country House Hotel

◉◉◉ *– see opposite*

Save on Hotels. Book at **theAA.com/hotel**

YORKSHIRE, NORTH 513 ENGLAND

Judges Country House Hotel

YARM Map 19 NZ41

Modern British V

Sharp modern British cooking in a charming Victorian house

☎ 01642 789000
Kirklevington TS15 9LW
e-mail: enquiries@judgeshotel.co.uk
web: www.judgeshotel.co.uk
dir: 1.5m from junct W A19, take A67 towards Kirklevington, hotel 1.5m on left

The approach through mature gardens allows for beguiling peeps through the trees of the charming greystone Victorian country house, which once provided top-notch accommodation for circuit judges doing their rounds. The gardens outside the conservatory dining room are a hive of activity when evening draws on, as rabbits and even the odd fox can be spotted mooching about in search of something for dinner. Ensconced behind glass walls, you'll be rather more securely provided for, courtesy of John Schwarz and his sizeable kitchen team. The style is recognisably contemporary British, with some modern classic combinations mixing it with less familiar ideas on the fixed-price menus. In the former camp, the partnering of scallops with black pudding and cauliflower is seen to good effect, the shellfish themselves seared on one side only for textural contrast. A piece of sea bass is timed to perfection, the skin properly crisped, the moist flesh standing up well to the accompaniments of chorizo, sweetcorn and leek, or there may be English rose veal with pommes purée, morels and sweetbreads. Variations on strawberry are a fitting accompaniment to a cheesecake made with Brillat-Savarin, dressed with aged balsamic, while 'Passion for Pineapple' offers a cocktail, ravioli and frozen soufflé variants of that sunniest of fruits.

Chef John Schwarz **Owner** Mr M Downs
Times 12-2/7-9.30 **Prices** Fixed L 2 course £22.90, Fixed D 4 course £29.50, Starter £10.25-£17.25, Main £31.50-£39.50, Dessert £10.25-£17.25, Service optional
Wines 117 bottles over £20, 45 bottles under £20, 12 by glass **Notes** Early bird menu available, Sunday L, Vegetarian menu, Dress restrictions, Jacket & tie preferred, no jeans or trainers **Seats** 60, Pr/dining room 50 **Children** Portions, Menu **Parking** 110

Cedar Court Grand Hotel & Spa

◉◉ Modern British NEW ◔

Elegant grill restaurant in a renovated Edwardian hotel

☎ 01904 380038
Station Rise YO1 6GD
e-mail: dining@cedarcourtgrand.co.uk
dir: A1 junct 47, A59 signed York, Harrogate &
Knaresborough. In city centre, near station

Overlooking the historic walls of one of northern
England's best-loved cities, the imposing red-brick
Edwardian edifice was given a major makeover, or
'reimagining' as design parlance now has it, in 2010.
Huge windows let in plenty of light, and the principal
restaurant, the Grill Room, is an expansive room done in
today's favoured neutral colours, offset with lemon-yellow
light-fittings, under which smartly dressed tables are set
well apart. A formal service approach is quite in keeping
with the overall tone, and the cooking plies a confident
brasserie line, such as seared pigeon breast, wild
mushroom risotto, or king scallops with black pudding
(home-made) and creamed leeks, to start, followed
ideally by something from the grill, be it a chicken breast,
pork cutlet, or one of the first-rate and carefully timed
steaks. Sauces are at an extra charge. Desserts can be of
the deconstructed variety, as in a tiramisù which consists
of a boozy sponge with whipped mascarpone, cubes of
jelly and coffee sauce.

Chef Martin Henley **Owner** Cedar Court Hotels
Times 12.30-2.30/6.30-10 **Prices** Food prices not
confirmed for 2013. Please telephone for details
Wines 173 bottles over £20, 7 by glass **Notes** Sunday L,
Vegetarian available, Dress restrictions, Smart casual, no
ripped jeans, Civ Wed 120 **Seats** 45, Pr/dining room 32
Children Portions **Parking** NCP Tanner Row

The Churchill Hotel

◉◉ Modern British ◔

Imaginative food and piano music

☎ 01904 644456
65 Bootham YO30 7DQ
e-mail: info@churchillhotel.com
web: www.churchillhotel.com
dir: On A19 (Bootham), W from York Minster, hotel 250yds
on right

The set up is all rather civilised in this Georgian mansion
in its own grounds just a short walk from York Minster.
The Churchill blends the airy elegance of its period
pedigree with the sharp looks of a contemporary boutique
city hotel in a dining room that looks through those vast
arching windows (that the Georgians did so well) into the
garden, where the trees are spangled in fairy-lights.
Laid-back live music floats from a softly-tinkling baby
grand piano as the soundtrack to cooking that hits the
target with its imaginative modern pairings of top-grade
regional produce. Local wood pigeon, for example, is
paired with black pudding bonbons, bitter chocolate and
espresso jelly, while main-course saddle of venison might
share a plate with Morteau sausage, choucroute, parsley
root, and red wine salsify. To finish, duck eggs add extra
oomph to a custard tart served with clementine, apricot,
and vanilla ice cream.

Chef Andrew Carr **Owner** Dennis Dewsnap
Times 11-2.30/5-9.30 **Prices** Fixed D 3 course £27.95,
Service optional **Wines** 43 bottles over £20, 19 bottles
under £20, 6 by glass **Notes** Early bird menu 3 course
daily 5-7pm £17.95, Sunday L, Vegetarian available, Civ
Wed 70 **Seats** 30, Pr/dining room 30 **Children** Portions
Parking 35

Dean Court Hotel

◉ Modern British

High quality ingredients and stunning Minster views

☎ 01904 625082
Duncombe Place YO1 7EF
e-mail: sales@deancourt-york.co.uk
web: www.deancourt-york.co.uk
dir: City centre, directly opposite York Minster

The boutique-style Dean Court Hotel - originally built to
house the clergy of York Minster - makes the most of its
pole position overlooking the Gothic masterpiece. The
window tables at its elegant, contemporary-styled D.C.H
restaurant offer the best views in town to a backing track
of chiming Minster bells. The kitchen makes sterling use
of local seasonal produce in unpretentious, eye-catching
modish dishes. Breast of wild duck, perhaps, served with
duck-leg faggots, smoked potatoes, roasted beetroot and
orange-braised chicory salad, or baked cod accompanied
by fennel bhaji and shellfish consommé. End in similar
vein with an interesting fresh fig and griottine cherry
tarte Tatin with cherry sorbet.

Chef Paul Laidlaw **Owner** Mr B A Cleminson
Times 12.30-2/7-9.30 Closed L 31 Dec, D 25 Dec
Prices Fixed L 2 course £17.50-£20, Starter £6.50-£10,
Main £18.75-£25, Dessert £7.50-£13 **Wines** 62 bottles
over £20, 10 bottles under £20, 17 by glass **Notes** Pre-
theatre menu available, Sunday L, Vegetarian available,
Dress restrictions, No T-Shirts, Civ Wed 50 **Seats** 60, Pr/
dining room 40 **Children** Portions, Menu **Parking** Pay &
display car park nearby

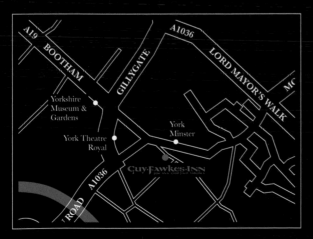

YORK *continued*

The Grange Hotel

◉◉ Modern

Classy brasserie in city-centre hotel

☎ 01904 644744
1 Clifton YO30 6AA
e-mail: info@grangehotel.co.uk
web: www.grangehotel.co.uk
dir: A19 (York/Thirsk road), approx 400yds from city
centre

A short walk from the Minster, The Grange is an elegantly
proportioned townhouse dating from the 1830s. The
interior has all the style and comfort of a country-house
hotel - open fires, deep sofas, antique paintings,
swagged curtains - while the Ivy Brasserie has a more
modish design, the most striking feature a mural of
horseracing. The cooking is a cut above the brasserie
norm, the kitchen clearly a creative and skilful
powerhouse. Pressed ham hock and guinea fowl is vivified
by zingy pineapple chutney, and curried crab goes into a
salad with apple, almonds and cauliflower fritters to
make another lively starter. Braised beef cheeks with
parsnip purée and bourguignon sauce is a gutsy winter
main course, and at other times there may be a lighter
dish of pan-fried salmon fillet with shellfish chowder,
creamed sweetcorn and baby leeks. Grilled steaks are
possibilities, and proceedings can close with lemon and
thyme pannacotta topped with lemon curd, meringue and
blackberry jelly.

Chef Jonathan Elvin **Owner** Jeremy & Vivien Cassel
Times 12.30-2.30/6.30-9.30 Closed L Mon-Sat, D Sun
Prices Starter £5.95-£9.50, Main £14.50-£22.50, Dessert
£5.85-£7.75, Service added but optional 10%
Wines 38 bottles over £20, 8 bottles under £20, 9 by
glass **Notes** Sunday L, Vegetarian available, Civ Wed 75
Seats 60, Pr/dining room 75 **Children** Portions, Menu
Parking 26

Guy Fawkes Inn

◉ Traditional British

Historic city centre inn serving classic British food

☎ 01904 466674
25 High Petergate YO1 7HP
e-mail: reservations@gfyork.com
web: www.gfyork.com

The Gunpowder Plotter was born on this spot in 1570, in
the shadow of York Minster, a fact which adds a frisson
to the pub that has done business here for centuries. It is
a darkly atmospheric, history-steeped den with an interior
akin to stepping into an Old Master painting; recently
restored and scrubbed up, there are roaring log fires, a
timber staircase, wooden floors, gas lighting, cosy nooks
and crannies, and cheerful service that suits the buzzy
vibe. Monthly-changing menus and daily chalkboard
specials follow a hearty modern pub grub course, treating
great local produce with honest, down-to-earth simplicity
- expect hearty main courses such as faggots in rich
gravy with mushy peas and buttery mash, cider-braised
rabbit with tarragon mash, or battered haddock with
mushy peas and proper chips. And for pudding, it's
Yorkshire parkin with butterscotch sauce.

Times 12-3/6-9 Closed D Sun

See advert on page 515

Hotel du Vin York

◉ European, French

Trendy bistro with classic and contemporary ideas

☎ 01904 557350
89 The Mount YO24 1AX
e-mail: info.york@hotelduvin.com
dir: A1036 towards city centre, 6m. Hotel on right through
lights

In keeping with the Hotel du Vin's trademark style, the
York branch occupies a characterful old building - in this
case an elegant early 19th-century property - in the
neighbourhood known as The Mount, close by Micklegate
Bar and the historic city centre. French-style prints, wine-
related paraphernalia, and walls adorned with equine
scenes (the famous racecourse is nearby) work with
textures of slate, bare wood and chocolate leather chairs
in the vibrant bistro, where on-the-ball staff do a
professional job in guiding you through the outstanding
wine list and a crowd-pleasing, French-influenced menu
of classics and straightforward modern ideas. Start with
moules du vin or a dressed crab served with walnut toast,
before something from the grill (rib-eye, perhaps, with
your choice of sauce), or a fish dish along the lines of
roast cod with buttered leeks and salsa verde, and a
classic tarte au citron to finish.

Times 12-2.30/6.30-10.30

The Lamb & Lion

◉ Traditional & Modern British

Good honest cooking in a historic city centre pub

☎ 01904 654112
2-4 High Petergate YO1 7EH
e-mail: reservations@lambandlionyork.com
web: www.lambandlionyork.com

The Lamb & Lion has everything you could reasonably ask
of a historic pub: hand-pulled real ales ranked in a bar
furnished with church pews, bare wooden tables and a
real fire, and skinny corridors leading to the back snugs
and 'Parlour' dining room. If that's not enough, the place
sits in the shadow of York Minster and is quite literally
built into the ancient city walls. The traditional food aims
at all-round satisfaction without messing about with
foams and such, and you can be sure that the quality of
the ingredients is up to scratch. Home-made pies with
mash and real gravy, or fish and chips with mushy peas
and tartare sauce share the honours with, say, hay-baked

continued

Save on Hotels. Book at **theAA.com/hotel**

YORKSHIRE, NORTH 517 ENGLAND

YORK *continued*

chicken breast with sage mash, or pan-fried sea bream with salad Niçoise. Bringing up the rear is a cast of desserts that might run to ginger burnt cream with rhubarb compôte.

The Lamb & Lion

Times 12-3/6-9

See advert on page 517

Melton's Restaurant

◉ Modern British 🍷

Long-running favourite with well-judged menu

☎ 01904 634341

7 Scarcroft Rd YO23 1ND

e-mail: greatfood@meltonsrestaurant.co.uk
web: www.meltonsrestaurant.co.uk
dir: South from centre across Skeldergate Bridge, restaurant opposite Bishopthorpe Road car park

Melton's remains as popular as ever, and it's been going for over 20 years. In a Victorian terrace, it's bright and modern, with mirrors and murals on the walls, a wooden floor, banquettes and unclothed tables - all very unpretentious, with friendly but efficient service. The kitchen conscientiously uses Yorkshire produce, dishes are well thought out and carefully cooked, and the menu of modern ideas offers plenty to enjoy. Typical starters are filo pissaladière with scallops, anchovies, capers and mint, and a dariole of warm chicken liver. Among main courses, a smoked haddock and crabcake is served on soft polenta with leeks, or there might be full-blooded pork trotter, belly and hock with cabbage, boulangère potatoes and Madeira jus. The regional approach extends to cheeses and iced rhubarb sticks with two custards.

Chef Michael Hjort, Calvin Goddard **Owner** Michael & Lucy Hjort **Times** 12-2/5.30-10 Closed 23 Dec-9 Jan, Sun-Mon **Prices** Fixed L 2 course fr £21, Starter £6.50-£9, Main £14.90-£19.50, Dessert £6.30-£7, Service optional **Wines** 117 bottles over £20, 15 bottles under £20, 6 by glass **Notes** Pre-theatre D, early evening 2 course £21, 3 course £25, Vegetarian available **Seats** 30, Pr/dining room 16 **Children** Portions **Parking** Car park opposite

---

Middlethorpe Hall & Spa

◉◉ Modern British 🍷

Elegant modern cooking in Lady Mary Wortley Montagu's old house

☎ 01904 641241

Bishopthorpe Rd, Middlethorpe YO23 2GB

e-mail: info@middlethorpe.com
web: www.middlethorpe.com
dir: A64 exit York West. Follow signs Middlethorpe & racecourse

Middlethorpe, built during the reign of William and Mary, was once the home of the society diarist and orientalist, Lady Mary Wortley Montagu. Twenty acres of lush parkland and garden and a panelled dining room from which to admire it are what we expect from a country-house hotel, and we are not disappointed here. After the colourful chintz of the rest of the house, the restaurant comes as a sober comfort, to which the professionally drilled staff contribute hugely. Nicholas Evans offers a locally-based style of supremely elegant modern cooking. Freshness and big flavour jump out of a starter dish of poached mackerel, served with heritage potato, cucumber jelly and crème fraîche, and pains taken over meat dishes are figured in the 13 hours devoted to roasting a featherblade of Dales beef in parsley and horseradish crust, served with beetroot and shallots and sauced in red wine. Fun breaks out at dessert stage, as it should, when an incredibly rich chocolate délice made with popping candy comes with crunchy popcorn, salt-butter caramel and vanilla ice cream.

Chef Nicholas Evans **Owner** The National Trust **Times** 12.30-2/7-9.45 **Prices** Fixed L 2 course £19.50, Starter £10.50-£13.50, Main £19.50-£28.50, Dessert £7.50-£13, Service included **Wines** 221 bottles over £20, 17 bottles under £20, 9 by glass **Notes** Gourmet 6 course menu £65, with wine £95, Sunday L, Vegetarian available, Dress restrictions, Smart, no trainers, tracksuits or shorts, Civ Wed 56 **Seats** 60, Pr/dining room 56 **Children** Portions **Parking** 70

YORKSHIRE, SOUTH

CHAPELTOWN   Map 16 SK39

Greenhead House

◉ British, European

Accomplished, seasonal cooking

☎ 0114 246 9004

84 Burncross Rd S35 1SF

dir: A629 towards Chapeltown/Huddersfield, straight across 2 rdbts, turn right in 150 yds into Burncross Rd

Dining in this charming restaurant in a 17th-century house out in the Sheffield suburb of Chapeltown is rather like being invited to a friend's place. Peruse the menu in the comfort of the cosy lounge with quirky knitted cushions and warming fireplace, then move into the relaxed dining room which looks through French windows into the pretty walled garden. Chef proprietor Neil Allen has been coming up with the goods at the stoves here for pushing 30 years, while wife Anne takes care of front of house. Expect Mediterranean leanings on the monthly-changing menu - perhaps pappardelle pasta to go with a ragù of hare, tomatoes, white wine, sage and parmesan, followed by a three-way presentation of pork - slow-cooked belly with apple and cider, pork and mushroom Wellington, and meatball with tomatoes, green olives and red wine. Passionfruit might be the theme for dessert, served as cheesecake in a shot glass, as part of a crème brûlée with white chocolate, and as orange and passionfruit jelly.

Chef Neil Allen **Owner** Mr & Mrs N Allen **Times** 12-1/7-9 Closed Xmas-New Year, 2wks Etr, 2wks Aug, Sun-Tue, L Wed-Thu, Sat **Prices** Fixed L 2 course £13.75-£20.25, Fixed D 4 course £46.95-£48.95, Service included **Wines** 30 bottles over £20, 13 bottles under £20, 20 by glass **Notes** ALC L only, Vegetarian available **Seats** 32 **Children** Portions **Parking** 10

ROSSINGTON   Map 16 SK69

Best Western Premier Mount Pleasant Hotel

◉ Modern British

Sound country-house cooking in tip-top hotel

☎ 01302 868696 & 868219

Great North Rd, Rossington DN11 0HW

e-mail: reception@mountpleasant.co.uk
dir: S of Doncaster, adjacent to Robin Hood Airport, on A638 between Bawtry & Doncaster

This smart 18th-century country-house hotel squirrelled away in 100 acres of beautiful woodland feels miles from anywhere, yet it is on the outskirts of Doncaster. While the grand old house is traditional in many aspects of its cosy décor and formal-yet-friendly service, Mount Pleasant comes fully geared for the 21st century with a full complement of glossy spa, leisure and conference facilities. The kitchen takes a broadly modern British line in its well-judged repertoire of comfort-oriented classics. You might get off the blocks with a black pudding Scotch

Save on Hotels. Book at theAA.com/hotel

YORKSHIRE, SOUTH 519 ENGLAND

egg with spiced apple marmalade and watercress ketchup, ahead of braised ox cheek with pommes purée, pancetta and braised shallots, and black truffle jus. For pudding it's back to school with 'jelly and ice cream', although this is a grown-up's take on the theme, comprising pear cider jelly, blackberry ripple ice cream, brioche and cinnamon.

Times 12-2/6.45-9.30 Closed 25 Dec

SHEFFIELD   Map 16 SK38

Copthorne Hotel Sheffield

🏵 Modern European

Contemporary cooking at the home of the Blades

☎ 0114 252 5480
Sheffield United Football Club, Bramall Ln S2 4SU
e-mail: orla.watt@millenniumhotels.co.uk
dir: M1 junct 33, A57 Sheffield, A61 Chesterfield Rd, follow brown tourist signs for Bramall Lane

Although it is tucked away in a quiet corner of Sheffield United's football ground, the 1855 restaurant is a clean-cut contemporary space with no obvious overtones related to the Beautiful Game. Understated and stylish, the setting goes for dark wood tables, neutral, earthy tones, and soft-focus lighting, while the kitchen has created a menu in the modern European mould, built on top-class, often local, ingredients. The menu keeps things accessible, focusing on intuitive combinations of flavour and texture, as seen in a starter that matches confit duck leg with celeriac remoulade, ahead of main-course seared sea bream with moules marinière and crushed new potatoes. And it's straight in the back of the net for dark chocolate tart with honeycomb ice cream.

Chef Marcus Hall **Owner** Millennium Copthorne Group **Times** 12.30-2.30/5.30-10 Closed 24 Dec-4 Jan **Prices** Fixed D 3 course £19.95, Starter £6.25-£11.95, Main £15.95-£29.95, Dessert £5.25-£6.25, Service optional **Wines** 17 bottles over £20, 7 bottles under £20, 12 by glass **Notes** Sunday L, Vegetarian available **Seats** 100, Pr/dining room 300 **Children** Portions, Menu **Parking** 250

The Milestone

🏵 Modern British

Full-on flavours in industrial Sheffield

☎ 0114 272 8327
84 Green Lane at Ball St, Kelham Island S3 8SE
e-mail: bookings@the-milestone.co.uk

This revamped Victorian boozer shouts contemporary gastro-pub loud and clear with its bare wooden floors, mismatched chairs and tables, and hues of peppermint, coffee and cream. And it's not just about easygoing good looks either - the passion for fine produce and devotion to doing things right without cutting corners is all present and correct too: the kitchen hauls in top-class materials from local suppliers (including its own herd of rare-breed pigs) and makes everything in-house from daily-baked organic breads to pasta, ice cream, preserves and ketchup. The results are an undeniable triumph - fuss-free, flavour-driven dishes that are just the sort of thing you want to eat - perhaps home-made black pudding with pickled vegetables and pear and black pudding purée, followed by beef flank with roast garlic mash, broccoli and red wine jus. End with white chocolate pannacotta with blood orange.

Times 12-4/5-10 Closed 25-26 Dec, 1 Jan

Nonnas

🏵 Modern Italian V 🏷NOTABLE WINE LIST

Italian mini-chain with authentic cooking

☎ 0114 268 6166
535-541 Ecclesall Rd S11 8PR
e-mail: info@nonnas.co.uk
dir: From city centre onto Ecclesall Rd, large red building on left

Nonna's is the real deal, serving-up authentic Italian food and drink, from a shot of espresso or glass of prosecco taken at a high stool at the bar, to some full-flavoured home cooking at the table. Blending Yorkshire's best produce with specialist materials from Italy, Nonna's piles on the authenticity still further with its unabashedly Italian service. The place has a charming, relaxed, retro-Italian rusticity about it, with café-style marble-topped tables and olive green walls, while bread, biscotti, pizza, pasta and ice cream are all made daily in-house. The menu opens with the likes of vongole (steamed clams in white wine with garlic butter and chargrilled piadina bread), then pasta such as tagliatelle salsiccia (with eight-hour slow-cooked sausage sauce with tomato, bay leaf and red wine chilli), and secondi of roast rump of Yorkshire lamb with salsa di cipolle. Italian wines and artisan beers sing to the same song sheet.

Chef Jamie Taylor **Owner** Gian Bohian, Maurizio Mori **Times** 12-3.15/5-9.45 Closed 25 Dec, 1 Jan **Prices** Fixed L 2 course fr £18, Fixed D 3 course £24, Starter £4.95-£10, Main £8.95-£37, Dessert £4.95-£12, Service optional, Groups min 6 service 10% **Wines** 73 bottles over £20, 7 bottles under £20, 15 by glass **Notes** Pre-theatre menu available, Vegetarian menu **Seats** 75, Pr/dining room 30 **Children** Portions, Menu **Parking** On street

Rafters Restaurant

🏵🏵 Modern European

Dependable modern cooking in leafy neighbourhood

☎ 0114 230 4819
220 Oakbrook Rd, Nethergreen S11 7ED
e-mail: marcus.lane@tiscali.co.uk
web: www.raftersrestaurant.co.uk
dir: 5 mins from Ecclesall road, Hunters Bar rdbt

Above a corner shop in a leafy suburb of Sheffield, this relaxed neighbourhood restaurant provides an informal and attractive stage for Marcus Lane's contemporary cooking. The place is well known to Sheffield's gastronomes after more than a decade of delivering creative, flavour-driven food in a rustic-chic setting of exposed brickwork and the age-old oak beams that give the place its name. Expect exact, assured cooking that coaxes the maximum intensity from top-quality ingredients, sprinkled with international accents - spiced roast pineapple might turn up to put a new slant on that tried-and-tested duo of pan-fried scallops and black pudding, while main courses run from roast loin of lamb with a modish mini-shepherd's pie, sautéed spring cabbage and bacon, to pan-fried sea bass with crisp calamari and a melon, rocket and raspberry sauce vierge. Leave room for pudding when there's the likes of Valrhona dark chocolate marquise with cinder toffee ice cream and crackle crystals up for grabs.

Chef Marcus Lane, Gareth Ducker **Owner** Marcus Lane **Times** 5-10 Closed 25-26 Dec, 1wk Jan, 2 wks Aug, Sun, Tue, L all week **Prices** Fixed D 3 course £36.95, Service optional, Groups min 8 service 10% **Wines** 20 bottles over £20, 25 bottles under £20, 7 by glass **Notes** Fixed D 2 course with glass wine available Mon-Thu, Vegetarian available, Dress restrictions, Smart casual, no jeans **Seats** 38 **Children** Portions, Menu **Parking** 15

SHEFFIELD *continued*

Staindrop Lodge Hotel

⊛ Modern, Traditional ✿

Far-reaching menus in art-deco-style brasserie

☎ 0114 284 3111
Lane End, Chapeltown S35 3UH
e-mail: info@staindroplodge.co.uk
dir: M1 junct 35, take A629 for 1m, straight over 1st rdbt, right at 2nd rdbt, hotel approx 0.5m on right

Seven miles from the city centre, within easy reach of both the M1 and the Peak District, Staindrop Lodge is a much-extended 19th-century hotel with conference facilities and an art-deco-style, split-level brasserie. The kitchen travels near and far for inspiration, with an eclectic menu running from starters of a simple plate of charcuterie, through seafood salad with garlic butter and crab mayonnaise, to sizzling chicken wings with chilli. Main courses are just as diverse: steak, ale and mushroom pie, say, Szechuan-style duck breast with plum sauce, wok-fried vegetables and deep-fried shrimps, and linguine with crab, tuna and prawns. Finish with a straightforward pudding like chocolate fudge cake, or crème brûlée.

Chef Andrew Roebuck **Owner** David Slade, John Wigfield **Times** 12-9.30 **Prices** Starter £3.95-£6.25, Main £5.25-£18.95, Dessert £4.95, Service optional **Wines** 6 bottles over £20, 33 bottles under £20, 7 by glass **Notes** Sunday L, Vegetarian available, Civ Wed 150 **Seats** 100, Pr/dining room 20 **Children** Portions, Menu **Parking** 60

Whitley Hall Hotel

⊛⊛ Modern British

Imaginative British cooking in a stunning country hotel

☎ 0114 245 4444
Elliott Ln, Grenoside S35 8NR
e-mail: reservations@whitleyhall.com
dir: A61 past football ground, then 2m, right just before Norfolk Arms, left at bottom of hill. Hotel on left

Whitley Hall is a textbook 16th-century ivy-clad country house set in 20 acres of immaculate grounds with lakes and superb gardens. It has stayed abreast of current trends in interior design and dining thanks to a modern facelift, and a restaurant that delivers a style of modernised country cooking perfectly in keeping with the surroundings. The oak panelling and white linen in the dining room may speak of old-school formality, and staff are suitably well-drilled and professionally correct in their ministrations, but what leaves the kitchen is switched-on contemporary cooking, presented in a way that is precise and well-considered, but not at all fussy. The newly-fashionable Scotch egg opens the show, made in this case from confit duck leg, and teamed with mature cheddar soufflé and plum chutney. Next out, a pan-fried fillet of wild sea bass arrives with mussels, steamed spinach dumplings, leeks, and saffron and tomato essence. Bringing down the curtain, an enterprising chocolate and beetroot cake is served with balsamic and raspberry sauce and goats' milk ice cream.

Chef Ian Spivey **Owner** Mr D Broadbent **Times** 12-2/7-9.30 **Prices** Fixed L 3 course £15.95, Starter £6.50-£8.25, Main £20-£28, Dessert £6.95, Service optional **Wines** 50 bottles over £20, 30 bottles under £20, 14 by glass **Notes** Fixed L 1 course £10.95, Sunday L, Vegetarian available, Dress restrictions, Smart casual, Civ Wed 100 **Seats** 80, Pr/dining room 16 **Children** Portions **Parking** 80

WORTLEY   Map 16 SK39

Montagu's at the Wortley Arms

⊛⊛ Modern British V ✿

Up-to-the-minute brasserie food in a Georgian pub

☎ 0114 288 8749
Halifax Rd S35 7DB
e-mail: enquiries@wortley-arms.co.uk
dir: M1 junct 36. Follow Sheffield North signs, right at Tankersley garage, 1m on right

A two-pronged operation consists of the Wortley Arms, a traditional Georgian pub with panelled walls, a jumble of furniture and oak beams, and a more obviously modern urban-style restaurant upstairs that tends only to open at weekends now. The up-to-the-minute brasserie stylings of the menu are on offer throughout, though, so there's no need to miss out on tian of crab, squid and crayfish, or ham hock terrine with piccalilli and saladings, to start, followed by cod with garlic mash and walnut pesto, or a special such as breast of duck with a confit leg croquette, braised cabbage and puréed carrot. Treacle tart comes with cream to anoint it with, or there may be good sharp lemon posset with lavender shortbread.

Chef Andy Gabbitas **Owner** Andy Gabbitas **Times** 12-2.30/5-9 Closed D Sun **Prices** Starter £4.50-£8.50, Main £10.50-£22.50, Dessert £5.95-£8.50, Service optional **Wines** 10 bottles over £20, 19 bottles under £20, 8 by glass **Notes** Sunday L, Vegetarian menu **Seats** 80, Pr/dining room 12 **Children** Portions **Parking** 30

YORKSHIRE, WEST

BINGLEY   Map 19 SE13

Five Rise Locks Hotel & Restaurant

⊛ Modern British

Unfussy cooking in family-run hotel

☎ 01274 565296
Beck Ln BD16 4DD
e-mail: info@five-rise-locks.co.uk
dir: From A650 signed Bingley centre, turn right Park Rd. Beck Lane 300mtrs on left

Built by a successful Victorian businessman in 1875, this one-time mill owner's family home is now a family-run hotel on a pleasingly intimate scale (just nine bedrooms), with a restaurant that's worth knowing about. Done out in a smart manner with high-backed leather chairs, linen-clad tables and a splendid burgundy and cream paint job, it offers views in daylight hours over the garden and Aire Valley. On the menu you'll find some appealing

combinations such as warm goats' cheese and red onion confit served en croûte, or pigeon breast with rocket and beetroot salad to start. Next up, perhaps pan-fried calves' liver with crushed new potatoes, cabbage and onion confit, and, to finish, lemon posset or a selection of British cheeses.

Chef Steven Heaton, Richard Stoyle **Owner** Richard & Margaret Stoyle **Times** 12-2/6.30-9.15 Closed L Mon-Sat, D Sun (ex residents) **Prices** Food prices not confirmed for 2013. Please telephone for details **Wines** 6 bottles over £20, 24 bottles under £20, 10 by glass **Notes** Early bird menu 2 course, Mon-Sat 6.30-7.30pm, Vegetarian available **Seats** 40, Pr/dining room 20 **Children** Portions **Parking** 15

BRADFORD   Map 19 SE13

Prashad

⊛ Indian Vegetarian V

Indian vegetarian food of the highest order

☎ 01274 575893
86 Horton Grange Rd BD7 2DW
e-mail: info@prashad.co.uk
web: www.prashad.co.uk
dir: Follow signs to Bradford University, keep university on right then straight across mini-rdbt & turn left at lights

It may not be the most alluring of premises from the outside, but that does not bother the happy crowds who come here for the Patels' top-notch Indian vegetarian cooking. The one-time launderette is bright and cheerful on the inside, with a menu that takes inspiration from South India, the Gujarat and the Punjab, and proudly name-checks famous vegetarians (Danny de Vito...who knew?). Start with pea kachori, or top-notch samosas, before a spicy uttapam or massala dosa (the 'monster dosa' is just that). Spicing is spot on throughout, breads are cooked to order, and the thali is always a good option. Curries include black channa and potato; chole (chick peas in a tomato and onion sauce); and mushroom palak, with everything annotated as to its suitability for vegans, plus wheat, garlic and onion content.

Chef Kaushy & Minal Patel **Owner** Mohan Patel **Times** 11-3/6-10.30 Closed 25 Dec, Mon **Prices** Food prices not confirmed for 2013. Please telephone for details **Notes** Vegetarian menu **Seats** 40 **Parking** On street

The Black Horse Inn

Clifton Village, Brighouse, West Yorkshire HD6 4HJ
Tel: 01484 713862　**Fax:** 01484 400582
E-mail: mail@blackhorseclifton.co.uk　**Web:** www.blackhorseclifton.co.uk

"The Black Horse Inn is a family owned village Inn, steeped in local history and bubbling with country charm. It is located in Clifton village, which is a real oasis and easily accessible only half a mile from Junction 25 off the M62.

With Passionate Chefs at the kitchen's helm - luscious food is at the heart of the Black Horse Inn, and the seasonal menu, sourced from Yorkshire's ambrosial larder, has won a loyal following, as well as an array of awards.

With two restaurant areas - private dining can be arranged if desired. The self contained function room is suitable for all events and there is a civil ceremony licence for wedding celebrations. There are 21 individually designed boutique bedrooms, perfect for the corporate traveller, or that special secret escape away from it all. The delightful flower filled courtyard is probably the property's best kept secret and yet in the summer months bathed in sunshine it is an idyllic place to relax with your favourite tipple.

With great food comes great drink – cask conditioned ales such as championship bitter from local brewer Timothy Taylor are served and also their own beer – Black Horse Brew, made exclusively for them by a small micro brewery. It has a well stocked bar including over 100 wine bins.

Why not take advantage of The Black Horse Inn Sleep Over Nights and events and enjoy a delicious combination of delectable food, excellent service and first class accommodation. Visit the website for more information www.blackhorseclifton.co.uk"

CLIFTON   Map 16 SE12

Black Horse Inn Restaurant with Rooms

◉ British, Mediterranean

Bold British flavours in a Yorkshire inn

☎ 01484 713862
Westgate HD6 4HJ
e-mail: mail@blackhorseclifton.co.uk
web: www.blackhorseclifton.co.uk
dir: M62 junct 25, Brighouse, follow signs

A quick glance over the menu reveals that the 17th-century Black Horse is a food-oriented pub that takes its output seriously - but that's not to say that you can't drop in for a pint and a warm-up by a real fire in the down-to-earth beamed bar. But when you really want to see what the kitchen can do with top-quality local ingredients, take a seat in the restaurant, where high-backed leather chairs and bare dark wood tables make for a stylish setting, and get started with something like pan-fried scallops with apple purée, crispy Parma ham and red grape sorbet. Main course ideas could include roast fillet and slow-braised shoulder of local pork with caramelised apple terrine and caraway crumble, or pan-fried cod loin with saffron Jersey Royals and red pepper compôte.

Times 12-2.30/5.30-9.30 Closed D 25-26 Dec, 1 Jan

See advert on page 521

HALIFAX   Map 19 SE02

Holdsworth House Hotel

◉◉ Modern British **V** ☙

Secluded manor house with well-crafted cooking

☎ 01422 240024
Holdsworth Rd, Holmfield HX2 9TG
e-mail: info@holdsworthhouse.co.uk
dir: From Halifax take A629 (Keighley road), in 2m right at garage to Holmfield, hotel 1.5m on right

It's little wonder that Holdsworth House is so popular with wedding parties - it really is a fairytale setting in secluded gardens. The oak-panelled rooms and roaring fires will certainly win you over, and the three inter-connecting rooms which make up the restaurant have oodles of period charm too (the building dates back to 1633), with low beams and mullioned windows, plus super views of the gardens. Yorkshire ingredients are much in evidence in traditional British cooking which is not adverse to some contemporary thinking. Start with sautéed black pearl scallops and marinated squid with pea purée and roasted red pepper sabayon, before Holme Farm venison Wellington with buttered spinach, gratin potatoes and juniper jus. Sarsaparilla and peanut butter cheesecake and honeycomb ice cream is a creative finish.

Chef Simon Allott **Owner** Gail Moss, Kim Wynn
Times 12-2/7-9.30 Closed Xmas (open 25-26 Dec L only)
Prices Fixed L 2 course fr £15, Fixed D 3 course fr £19.95, Starter £5.95-£11.95, Main £15.50-£24.50, Dessert fr £7, Service optional, Groups min 10 service 10%
Wines 40 bottles over £20, 32 bottles under £20, 13 by glass **Notes** Tasting menu 5 course, Sunday L, Vegetarian menu, Dress restrictions, Smart casual, No shorts, Civ Wed 120 **Seats** 45, Pr/dining room 120 **Children** Portions, Menu **Parking** 60

Shibden Mill Inn

◉◉ Modern British **V** ☙

Adventurous flavours in renovated corn mill

☎ 01422 365840
Shibden Mill Fold, Shibden HX3 7UL
e-mail: enquiries@shibdenmillinn.com
dir: From A58 into Kell Lane, after 0.5m left into Blake Hill. Inn at bottom of hill on left

Converted from a 17th-century mill, the inn consists of a series of rooms connected by steps and stairs, with a rustic look generated by beams, exposed stone, and mismatched tables and chairs. Service is friendly but polished, and the whole place has a warm, good-humoured atmosphere. The kitchen's a hive of industry, judging by an assiette of pork: potted belly, a miniature pie, and crispy cheek, all accompanied by black pudding bread, beetroot and orange coleslaw, and beetroot chips - and that's just a starter. Another one combines pan-fried scallops with caramelised pistachio crumble and truffle and Jerusalem artichoke. The compositions of dishes may sound far-fetched, but the results are successful; Wellington-style baked salt cod, for instance, comes with spinach and mushrooms, smoked kippers and curried

mussels. Cheeses are all made by Yorkshire artisan producers, or you could end with a plate of banana - crème brûlée, fritter and cake with salted toffee sauce.

Chef Darren Parkinson **Owner** Simon & Caitlin Heaton
Times 12-2/6-9.30 Closed Xmas, D 24-26 Dec, 1 Jan
Prices Fixed L 2 course £12, Starter £5.50-£8.95, Main £17.50-£19.25, Dessert £5.50-£6.50, Service optional
Wines 64 bottles over £20, 24 bottles under £20, 22 by glass **Notes** Sunday L, Vegetarian menu **Seats** 50, Pr/dining room 8 **Children** Portions, Menu **Parking** 60

HAWORTH   Map 19 SE03

Ashmount Country House

◉ Modern British **NEW V**

Confident cooking in the Brontë village

☎ 01535 645726 & 07814 536044
Mytholmes Ln BD22 9EZ
e-mail: info@ashmounthaworth.co.uk
dir: M65 junct 13A Laneshaw Bridge, turn right over moors to Haworth. Turn left after car park on right, 100yds on right

A solid Victorian house with open fires and antique furniture, Ashmount is a short stroll from the Brontës' famous parsonage. Elegantly laid tables set the tone in the dining room, with its views over the hillside. The sensibly short menu, which changes every few days, is well planned to offer plenty of scope, the style set by a well-conceived main course of pan-fried sea bass fillet with tomato velouté, English asparagus, spinach and saffron-flavoured new potatoes. Equally, there may be honey-roast duck breast with blackberry jus, sweet potato dauphinoise and baked vegetables, with starters like a chunky galantine of duck and chicken with fruity marmalade, and puddings tend to the hearty: sticky toffee, say, or apple and raspberry crumble.

Chef Danny Ife **Owner** Ray & Gill Capeling
Times 6.30-8.30 **Prices** Fixed D 3 course fr £25, Starter £4.95-£7.95, Main £14.95-£24.50, Dessert £5.95-£6.75, Service optional **Wines** 13 bottles over £20, 13 bottles under £20, 11 by glass **Notes** L service commences winter 2012, Vegetarian menu, Civ Wed 40 **Seats** 26, Pr/dining room 20 **Parking** On street

Weavers Restaurant with Rooms

◉ Modern British ☙

A local flavour near the Brontë Parsonage

☎ 01535 643822
15 West Ln BD22 8DU
e-mail: weaversltd@btconnect.com
dir: From A629 take B6142 towards Haworth, follow signs for Brontë Parsonage Museum, use museum car park

Weavers is an idiosyncratic gem, fashioned from a group of hand-loom weavers' cottages, and is a longstanding Brontë hometown favourite. There's a shabby-chic, retro, eccentric style here (certainly not minimalist or shy), with literary artefacts, antique mirrors and weavers' cotton-reels dangling here and there within its warm red, stone-built walls and grey flagstone floors. Mismatched dining chairs and solid-wood tables confirm the relaxed vibe, while the cooking turns out unexpectedly sophisticated, reinvented northern-based dishes from local ingredients - many grown on their own allotment. Take slow-cooked Pennine lamb with its accompaniment of Wakefield forced rhubarb and custard crumb meringue with crumble dust for a northern twist, or perhaps sea bass fillets teamed with brown shrimps and wild mushrooms, rösti potato and smoky malt whisky, butter and cream.

Chef Colin & Jane Rushworth, Ross Swinson **Owner** Colin & Jane Rushworth & family **Times** 11.30-2.30/6.30-9.30 Closed 26 Dec-10 Jan, Sun-Mon, L Sat **Prices** Fixed L 2 course fr £15.95, Fixed D 3 course fr £17.95, Starter £5-£8, Main £12.50-£22.50, Dessert £4.50-£6.50, Service optional **Wines** 11 bottles over £20, 32 bottles under £20, 8 by glass **Notes** Vegetarian available, Dress restrictions, Smart casual **Seats** 65 **Children** Portions **Parking** Car park at rear (free 6pm-8am)

HEBDEN BRIDGE   Map 19 SD92

Moyles

◉ Modern European

Confident cooking in stylish small hotel

☎ 01422 845727
6-10 New Rd HX7 8AD
e-mail: enquire@moyles.com
dir: M62 junct 24. A646 Halifax to Burnley through Hebden Bridge. Located in the centre of town opposite marina

A down-at-heel Victorian guesthouse was given a new lease of life in 2008 when the wraps came off to reveal Moyles, a boutique-chic restaurant with rooms. The local arty enclave of Hebden Bridge has taken the place to their hearts, and no wonder: the light-flooded restaurant has a cool, contemporary feel, and a relaxed approach, with local artists' work on the walls set against organic textures of wood and cane, flagstone and pebble flooring, and restful hues of duck-egg blue. The bar is stocked with an impressive arsenal of draught ales to set a convivial mood, and the kitchen takes an unpretentious modern approach, starting with home-made crumpets with goats' cheese, garlic and thyme cream, followed by a simple, well-balanced dish of seared tuna steak on a warm salad of chicory, slow-roasted tomato, green beans and olives, and new potatoes dressed with parsley and capers. These are all good ideas, well executed and rounded off by honest desserts such as vanilla pannacotta with seasonal berry compôte.

Chef Ashley Dibb **Owner** Simon Moyle **Times** 12-3/6-10 **Prices** Fixed L 2 course £16.50, Fixed D 3 course £16.50-£24, Service optional **Wines** 70 bottles over £20, 30 bottles under £20, 10 by glass **Notes** Tasting menu 7 course, Sunday L, Vegetarian available **Seats** 70 **Children** Portions **Parking** NCP opposite

HUDDERSFIELD   Map 16 SE11

315 Bar and Restaurant

◉ Modern **NEW** V

Ambitious city-smart cooking in a reborn Yorkshire pub

☎ 01484 602613
315 Wakefield Rd HD8 0LX
e-mail: info@315barandrestaurant.co.uk
dir: M1 junct 38 to Huddersfield

Out in the sumptuous Yorkshire countryside not far from Huddersfield, 315 is a refurbished pub reborn as a city-smart restaurant and bar, with a fine conservatory room and a chef's table, which is pretty much all bases covered. Chairs upholstered in silver velvet and orchids on the tables make an aspirational statement, as does Jason Neilson's cooking, which is based on industrious in-house production of everything from breads to ice creams, and represents a successful alliance of English ingredients with modern French technique. A tall, thin, twice-cooked goats' cheese soufflé is an architectonic masterwork, and comes with a pecorino salad, the plate squiggled with sun-dried tomato sauce and pesto, while salmon and haddock are fashioned into a sausage that comes with warm potato salad and cauliflower cream. Local lamb gets a good outing, the best end crusted in garlic and rosemary, the liver sautéed, accompanied by fennel and red onion purée, or there might be sea bass with green-lip mussels and saffron potatoes. Desserts such as treacle apple tart with apple crumble ice cream on shortbread are a strength.

Chef Jason J Neilson **Owner** Jason Neilson, Terry Dryden **Times** 12-9 Closed D Sun **Prices** Food prices not confirmed for 2013. Please telephone for details **Wines** 54 bottles over £20, 15 bottles under £20, 18 by glass **Notes** Sunday L, Vegetarian menu, Civ Wed 150 **Seats** 90, Pr/dining room 115 **Children** Portions, Menu **Parking** 97

ILKLEY   Map 19 SE14

Best Western Rombalds Hotel & Restaurant

◉ Modern European ✿

Confident seasonal cooking in charming restaurant

☎ 01943 603201
11 West View, Wells Rd LS29 9JG
e-mail: reception@rombalds.demon.co.uk
dir: From Leeds take A65 to Ilkley. At 3rd main lights turn left & follow signs for Ilkley Moor. At junct take right onto Wells Rd, by HSBC bank. Hotel 600yds on left

Dating from 1835, Rombalds is a charming family-run hotel in a terrace not far from the famous moor, with a restaurant in Wedgwood blue. The kitchen proudly uses as much local produce as it can, with farm-smoked venison (seen in a starter with beetroot and potato salad), locally-reared meats and exclusively Yorkshire cheeses. The cooking displays a high level of skill and aspiration, producing modern-accented starters such as

brandade of Nidderdale smoked fish with grilled asparagus and tomato and caper relish. Well-judged sauces and gravies add depth to main courses, with spring onion pesto for pork fillet wrapped in Serrano ham, served with dauphinoise, and saffron-creamed mussels for sautéed fillet of sea bass, accompanied by braised fennel and leeks. Don't overlook enterprising puddings like steamed vanilla sponge with banana and rum toffee.

Chef Matthew Degregorio **Owner** Colin & Jo Clarkson **Times** 12-2/6.30-9 Closed 31 Dec-9 Jan **Prices** Fixed L 2 course £11.95-£13.90, Fixed D 3 course £21.95-£26.95, Starter £3.95-£5.95, Main £11.95-£18.95, Dessert £6.25-£7.25, Service optional **Wines** 35 bottles over £20, 40 bottles under £20, 6 by glass **Notes** Sunday L, Vegetarian available, Civ Wed 75 **Seats** 34, Pr/dining room 50 **Children** Portions **Parking** 22

Box Tree

◉◉◉ – *see page 524*

LEEDS   Map 19 SE23

Anthony's Restaurant

◉◉◉ – *see page 524*

De Vere Oulton Hall

◉◉ British

Modernised British cooking in a splendid mansion

☎ 0113 282 1000
Rothwell Ln, Oulton LS26 8HN
e-mail: oulton.hall@devere-hotels.com
dir: 2m from M62 junct 30, follow Rothwell signs, then 'Oulton 1m' sign. 1st exit at next 2 rdbts. Hotel on left. Or 1m from M1 junct 44, follow Castleford & Pontefract signs on A639

The De Vere group's Oulton Hall is a magnificent country mansion off the M62 to the south of Leeds. It's the kind of place that's grand enough to have staff swishing about the grounds on golf buggies, though ever mindful not to interrupt the outdoor Shakespeare that goes on in the summer. A stylish contemporary refurbishment has produced dashing interiors, and a strikingly elegant dining room done in black and crimson, with rich fabrics and lots of dark wood, and lighting low enough for an undercover rendezvous. The chosen culinary idiom is modernised classic British, with a fair bit of table side theatre if you don't mind the company, mixing up salads, slicing smoked salmon and carving the Chateaubriand before your very eyes. Baked cod with mushrooms, peas and pea shoots is an example of one of the attractively presented mains, or venison loin with poached pear and cocoa nibs in port. In the season, you could opt for a three-course rhubarb menu.

Times 12.30-2/7-10

Box Tree

British, French

Refined classically-inspired cooking at a Yorkshire landmark restaurant

☎ 01943 608484
35-37 Church St LS29 9DR
e-mail: info@theboxtree.co.uk
dir: On A65 from Leeds through Ilkley, main lights approx 200yds on left

Harold Macmillan was Prime Minister when the Box Tree first opened its doors as a restaurant (1962 since you ask), and the old-stone building - dating back to the 1720s - remains a near iconic Yorkshire dining address. Simon and Rena Gueller took over the reins in the noughties, and have Marco Pierre White as a partner these days (Marco started out here back in the 1980s).

There's a smart, traditional finish to the interior, with lots of well chosen antique furniture, warm colours, large canvases and rich fabrics, and the formal service does not want for Yorkshire hospitality. Simon's cooking is based around sound French classical thinking, which means everything makes sense, each dish is balanced in terms of flavours and textures, and contemporary ideas are embraced with a light touch. A terrine of Périgord foie gras, for example, comes with a salad of smoked eel, Granny Smith apple as purée and jelly and Poilâne toast in a first course of classic flavours, impeccably executed. Next up, main-course tranche of turbot is served with fennel, pommes noisettes, essence of orange and coriander, or there's squab pigeon en vessie with a tian of beetroot and boudin noir, Puy lentils and a jus à la fleur de thyme. Lemon rice pudding with textures of lemon and elderflower jelly is a light and perfectly judged finale.

Chef Mr S Gueller, Mr D Birk **Owner** Mrs R Gueller **Times** 12-2/7-9.30 Closed 27-31 Dec, 1-7 Jan, Mon, L Tue-Thu, D Sun **Prices** Fixed L 3 course £25, Fixed D 3 course £55, Tasting menu £65, Groups min 8 service 10% **Wines** 100+ bottles over £20, 2 bottles under £20, 7 by glass **Notes** Fixed L Fri & Sat only, Sunday L, Vegetarian available, Dress restrictions, Smart dress preferred, Civ Wed 30 **Seats** 50, Pr/dining room 20 **Parking** NCP

Anthony's Restaurant

Modern European

A shining star of the north

☎ 0113 245 5922
19 Boar Ln LS1 6EA
e-mail: anthonys@anthonysrestaurant.co.uk
dir: 500 yds from Leeds Central Station towards The Corn Exchange

Anthony Flinn, card-carrying molecular gastronomist, has been slowly building his foodie Leeds empire with a little help from his family - Piazza by Anthony in the city's historic Corn Exchange and Anthony's Patisserie in the Victoria Quarter to name but two addresses. But fear not, for his flagship restaurant has lost none of its pizzazz. Boar Lane may not be the most chic address in the city, but the smart interior has a decidedly contemporary

sheen with its dark brown leather seating, glass-topped tables and colour-themed artwork; the eating business takes place in the basement restaurant, with the ground-floor bar with its easy-listening jazz making a good first impression. Top-notch produce and contemporary presentation is a given here, with dishes described in a minimalist manner that belies the skill and creativity in the execution. The excellent value lunch menu should not be missed. But whatever time of day you eat, prepare to have your socks blown off. Start with five-spiced pigeon breast with peanuts and rich date purée, before moving onto pork belly with crab croquette, Asian pear and celeriac. A British dessert of poached rhubarb with goats' milk espuma and rosemary is a divine combination of flavours and textures. The tasting menu with accompanying wine flight is available for those wishing to push the boat out.

Chef Anthony Flinn **Owner** Anthony Flinn **Times** 12-2/7-9.30 Closed Xmas-New Year, Sun, Mon **Prices** Tasting menu £65, Service optional **Wines** 110 bottles over £20, 10 bottles under £20, 16 by glass **Notes** Vegetarian available **Seats** 40 **Children** Portions **Parking** NCP 20 yds

Save on Hotels. Book at theAA.com/hotel

YORKSHIRE, WEST 525 ENGLAND

LEEDS *continued*

Jamie's Italian, Leeds

◉ Italian

Vibrant, branded Italian brasserie for all

☎ 0113 322 5400
35 Park Row LS1 5JL

The Leeds city centre branch of the Jamie Oliver empire (over two-dozen of them across the UK) occupies a handsome old bank building with a stylishly reworked interior. The remarkable old marquetry ceiling and huge upstairs windows add grandeur to a simple café-style décor with a bustling upbeat vibe, while racks of quality breads alongside the open-to-view kitchen get you in mind for the business in hand. The menu touts the roll-call of unfussy, colourful, rustic Italian lifestyle food that has inspired millions of TV viewers and cookbook buyers. Get going with planks of cured meat, fish, cheese, or tapas-style plates of crispy squid or stuffed risotto balls, then go for rabbit tagliolini with mascarpone and Amalfi lemon in the pasta department, and steaks, burgers or fritto misto from the mains section. As is usually the case in the chain, the 'walk-in' concept means you will probably have to queue for a table.

Times noon–11

Lounge Leeds

◉ Modern British

Stylish, dynamic modern brasserie in the city centre

☎ 0113 285 5964
St Johns House, Merrion St LS2 8JE
e-mail: info@loungebarandgrill.com

The two Lounges, one in Driffield and this one in the heart of Leeds, are all about unbuttoned, stylish modern dining. Eat and drink cocktails in the pacy ground-floor bar, or head on up to the Terrace, where a menu of dynamic brasserie cooking is on offer, with pre-curtain deals for those on their way to the Grand Theatre. Scallops and pancetta with rocket and watercress might set the ball rolling, while play continues with chargrilled lamb chops with couscous and tzatziki, or roasted duck salad with mango and chorizo. Finish with meringue baskets of fruit, or classic crêpes filled with home-made jam, cream and sugar.

Chef Trevor Bailey **Owner** HRH Group **Times** 12-5/5-9 Closed D Sun **Prices** Fixed D 3 course £14.95, Starter £4.95-£5.95, Main £7.95-£19.50, Dessert £4.95, Service optional **Wines** 12 bottles over £20, 10 bottles under £20, 10 by glass **Notes** Sunday L, Vegetarian available **Seats** 80, Pr/dining room 80 **Children** Portions **Parking** St Johns NCP

Malmaison Leeds

◉ Modern British ✪

Vibrant cooking in stylish city brasserie

☎ 0113 398 1000
1 Swinegate LS1 4AG
e-mail: leeds@malmaison.com
dir: City centre. 5 mins walk from Leeds railway station. On junct 16 of loop road, Sovereign St & Swinegate

In pole position near the waterfront, and close by the intensive retail therapy provided by the city's chic boutiques and department stores, the Leeds outpost of the Mal stable delivers the expected house style of contemporary brasserie dining in a sultry, design-savvy venue. The building is converted from the offices of a bus and tram company and provides an atmospheric basis for a moodily-lit brasserie done out with intimate leather booths, dark wood galore, and a funky glass fireplace beneath a vaulted ceiling. Old friends from the British and European repertoire turn up on a please-all menu that works with the seasons and name-checks its Yorkshire food heroes. Expect the likes of smoked salmon rösti with horseradish cream, followed by venison haunch with roasted beetroot and grain mustard mash, or pan-fried cod with white bean and chorizo cassoulet.

Chef Andrew Lawson **Owner** Malmaison
Times 12-2.30/6.30-9.30 **Prices** Starter £4.95-£9.50, Main £11.50-£24.95, Dessert £1.75-£8.50, Service added but optional 10% **Wines** 90% bottles over £20, 10% bottles under £20, 25 by glass **Notes** Sunday L, Vegetarian available, Civ Wed 80 **Seats** 85, Pr/dining room 12 **Children** Portions, Menu **Parking** Criterion Place car park, Q Park

Nash's

◉ Traditional British, Fish

Traditional fish and chips from a family firm

☎ 0113 285 5961 & 285 5960
Merrion St LS2 8JE
e-mail: nashsfishandchips@hotmail.com
dir: Main Inner Ring Road Leeds, opposite Grand Theatre

The Nash family has been feeding Leeds one way or another since the 1920s, moving to the present venue just round the corner from the Grand Theatre in 1963. Although the approach may have been streamlined for the modern era, the backbone is still fish and chips done in the time-honoured fashion, freshly battered fish from sustainable sources with thick, satisfying chips, cooked in dripping. There are goujons and fishcakes, as well as classic fish pie, assuming you're not in the market for the cod and haddock that are the main business. If you've time for three courses, you might bookend them with smoked salmon and dill crème fraîche, and then either sticky toffee pudding or a helping of Mr Moo's hand-made ice cream from Skipsea.

Chef Jason Buitin **Owner** Don Wilson **Times** 11-8 Closed 25-26 Dec, 1 Jan, D Sun **Prices** Fixed D 2 course £23.90, Starter £3.25-£6.95, Main £6.95-£11.95, Dessert £3.95, Service optional **Wines** 11 bottles under £20, 8 by glass **Notes** Pre-theatre 3 course £11.95, Sunday L, Vegetarian available **Seats** 68, Pr/dining room 50 **Children** Portions, Menu

The New Ellington

◉◉ Modern British **NEW** ✪

Stylish boutique hotel with bold, modish cooking

☎ 0113 204 2150
23-25 York Place LS1 2EY
e-mail: info@thenewellington.com

Named in honour of Duke Ellington, who played in the Leeds music festival back in 1958, there's a touch of New Orleans style to this boutique hotel in the financial district of the city. It's no pastiche, though, so expect a plush setting of rich warm colours, opulent furnishings, and, in the lower-ground floor restaurant, smart velour banquette seating and tables dressed up in crisp white linen. Modern British cooking is the name of the game here, with a Taste of Yorkshire menu focusing on the region's produce and delivering Yorkshire forest mushroom soup with crisp egg and local asparagus, followed by braised rose veal with pickled cabbage, summer girolles, pancetta and creamed mash. From the à la carte (also based on tip-top produce) might come risotto of queenie scallops, clams and spring onion with smoked bacon and herb breadcrumbs, followed by pot-roasted haunch of venison accompanied by a small suet pudding, pickled red cabbage, fresh ceps and roasted pumpkin flavoured with liquorice. Finish with Yorkshire blue cheese or pear and almond tart with liquorice ice cream.

Chef Andrew Brookes **Times** 6.30-10.30 Closed 25-26 Dec, L all week, D Sun **Prices** Fixed D 3 course fr £21.95, Starter £6.95-£11.50, Main £13.95-£21.95, Dessert £6.95-£10.50, Service optional **Notes** Vegetarian available **Seats** 50, Pr/dining room 24 **Children** Portions, Menu **Parking** On street

LEEDS *continued*

Salvo's Restaurant & Salumeria

🌐 Italian

Popular Italian with salumeria (deli-café)

☎ 0113 275 5017 & 275 2752
115 Otley Rd, Headingley LS6 3PX
e-mail: dine@salvos.co.uk
dir: On A660 2m N of city centre

Having been around since 1976 in the buzzy studenty area of Headingley, it's fair to say that the Dammone family-run Salvo's is a Leeds institution, although the salumeria side of the operation, situated a couple of doors away, came along more recently in 2005. It is a deli/café by day (the name comes from the traditional Italian purveyor of salumi - cured meats), and an intimate extension of the original restaurant space in the evening. The whole shebang has a strong local fan base, varying from budget-conscious students dropping in for the top-class pizzas to those with a bit more cash to splash on authentic regional dishes such as Calabrian penne picante Nduje, served with spicy salami, and fennel sausage sauce with fresh pecorino, followed by twice-cooked belly pork in a sweet-and-sour red pepper and caper confit, or roasted chicken thigh rolled and stuffed with Italian sausage, sage and garlic, wrapped in pancetta and served with mushroom sauce and potatoes.

Chef Giuseppe Schirripa, Geppino Dammone **Owner** John & Gip Dammone **Times** 12-2/5.30-10.30 Closed 25-26 Dec, 1 Jan, L BH's **Prices** Fixed L 2 course £11.50, Fixed D 3 course £17.50, Starter £3.95-£8.50, Main £8.50-£21.95, Dessert £5.50-£10.50, Service optional **Wines** 21 bottles over £20, 15 bottles under £20, 6 by glass **Notes** Vegetarian available, Air con **Seats** 88 **Children** Portions, Menu **Parking** On street, Pay & display nearby

Thorpe Park Hotel & Spa

🌐 Modern British

Modern restaurant cooking regional produce

☎ 0113 264 1000
Century Way, Thorpe Park LS15 8ZB
e-mail: thorpepark@shirehotels.com
dir: M1 junct 46, follow signs off rdbt for Thorpe Park

Don't muddle up this classy hotel on the outskirts of Leeds with the brain-scrambling thrills of Thorpe Park in Surrey. Here we're dealing with a relaxed vibe rather than white-knuckle rides, and whether you're in the city for business or a spot of down time, the place hits the spot with its smart contemporary look and state-of-the-art spa and leisure facilities. When it comes to dining, the top-end option offers the cosmopolitan style of a city-centre restaurant with its open-plan, split-level space kitted out with black leather seats, pale-wood flooring and abstract art, and a menu that plays to the crowd via a roll-out of uncomplicated modern ideas. The flexible format lets you open with sharing plates of fish or charcuterie, or you might go for chicken liver parfait with Sauternes jelly and toasted brioche. Main courses run

from chargrilled steaks to salmon fishcakes with fresh tomato and coriander salsa, or simple classics such as rosemary roasted rump of lamb with aubergine and tomato parmigiana.

Times 12-2/6.45-9.30 Closed L Sat & Sun

Town Hall Tavern

🌐 Modern British **NEW**

Superior gastro-pub in city-centre

☎ 0113 244 0765
17 Westgate LS1 2RA
e-mail: info@townhalltavernleeds.co.uk
dir: Located city centre, opposite the Law Courts

This gem of a city-centre pub has something for all comers, with traditional ales on tap, a choice of wines and all-day eating, with a variety of platters and quick bites - pig's cheek Scotch egg, for example - for grazers. Those wanting the full monty won't leave disappointed either, with arresting palate-pleasing starters like crisp curried squid with watermelon and apple salad, and salt beef with beetroot and radish. A policy of sourcing locally from ethical producers pays off, seen in a flavourful plate of Yorkshire pork (roast shoulder, cheek, crisp ears, mock goose pie and Scotch egg, served with sticky red cabbage), slowly cooked Dales lamb shoulder with crisp belly, haricot beans and tartare jus, and battered East Coast haddock fillet with dripping-fried chips. As this is so close to the rhubarb triangle, finish with a trio of the fruit: a yummy pie, poached with yoghurt parfait, and trifle.

Chef Anton Scoones **Owner** Timothy Taylor **Times** 11.30-9 Closed 25-26 Dec, BH Mon **Prices** Starter £1.95-£6.95, Main £5.25-£17.25, Dessert £1.95-£4.95, Service optional **Wines** 4 bottles over £20, 18 bottles under £20, 10 by glass **Notes** Sunday L, Vegetarian available **Seats** 26 **Children** Portions, Menu **Parking** On street at rear

Healds Hall Hotel & Restaurant

🌐 Modern British 🍃

Stimulating medley of styles in 18th-century hotel

☎ 01924 409112
Leeds Rd WF15 6JA
e-mail: enquire@healdshall.co.uk
dir: M1 junct 40, A638. From Dewsbury take A652 signed Bradford. Left at A62. Hotel 50yds on right

Healds Hall, an 18th-century mill owner's mansion, has two dining rooms: a contemporary, vibrantly decorated bistro, and more formal and demure Harringtons Restaurant. The long menu, served in both, has broad appeal, thus, tempura king prawns with tomato and chilli jam and coriander dressing may appear next to fennel and onion bhaji with raita, followed by duck leg confit with cassoulet-type casserole, or beef bourguignon with mash and root vegetables. Homelier dishes have included a simple plate of smoked salmon, and beer-battered

haddock with mushy peas, while puddings can be as inspiring as rhubarb pancakes with ginger ice cream.

Chef Andrew Ward, David Winter **Owner** Mr N B & Mrs T Harrington **Times** 12-2/6-10 Closed 1 Jan, BHs, L Sat, D Sun (ex residents) **Prices** Fixed L 2 course £9.95-£12.95, Fixed D 3 course £18-£23, Starter £4.65-£8.50, Main £11-£24, Dessert £5.95-£6.95, Service optional **Wines** 30 bottles over £20, 20 bottles under £20, 8 by glass **Notes** Sunday L, Vegetarian available, Civ Wed 100 **Seats** 46, Pr/dining room 30 **Children** Portions **Parking** 90

The Olive Branch Restaurant with Rooms

🌐 Modern British

Fine Yorkshire cooking at a Victorian roadside inn

☎ 01484 844487
Manchester Rd HD7 6LU
e-mail: eat@olivebranch.uk.com
dir: On A62 between Slaithwaite & Marsden

A traditional Victorian roadside inn in the heart of the Colne Valley, The Olive Branch is a welcoming rural bolt-hole. Sit outside if weather permits, and drink in the views over the Marston Moor estate and the waters of the recently restored canal, or snuggle indoors by the fire in winter chill. It's all good. Up-to-the-minute brasserie dishes offer a world of satisfaction, based as they are on Yorkshire ingredients in fine fettle. Yorkshire Blue soufflé with roasted chestnuts, spinach and creamed leeks is an example for starters, before poached salmon in crab and lobster cream, or Gressingham duck breast with truffled mash in port and peppercorn sauce. Think chocolate, caramel and toffee at dessert stage, and you won't be disappointed.

Chef Paul Kewley **Owner** Paul Kewley & John Lister **Times** 6.30-9.30 Closed 26 Dec, 1st 2 wks Jan, L Mon-Sat **Prices** Starter £5.95-£9.95, Main £13.95-£25.95, Dessert £6.50-£7.95, Service optional **Wines** 100 bottles over £20, 30 bottles under £20, 16 by glass **Notes** Early menu offers available, Sunday L, Vegetarian available **Seats** 65, Pr/dining room 40 **Children** Portions, Menu **Parking** 20

Chevin Country Park Hotel

🌐 Modern British **NEW**

Appealing modern cooking in lakeside log cabin

☎ 01943 467818
Yorkgate LS21 3NU
e-mail: gm.chevin@crerarhotels.com
dir: A658 towards Harrogate. Left at 1st turn towards Carlton, 2nd left towards Yorkgate

The Chevin Country Park Hotel's Lakeside restaurant stakes its claim to being one of the largest log cabins in the UK. Set in Yorkshire woodland handily close to Leeds-Bradford airport, its 50 acres of grounds encompass

Save on Hotels. Book at **theAA.com/hotel**

YORKSHIRE, WEST 527 ENGLAND

three lakes that provide a haven for wildlife (and anglers). The dining area has a Scandinavian style, split between a deeply-cossetting log-walled area with a mezzanine level, and an extension that offers the best views of the lake through full-length picture windows. The kitchen takes a populist approach on a wide-ranging menu that offers something to put a smile on everyone's face - local smoked venison, for example, served with a caramelised onion scone and beetroot relish. Mains could involve a steak sizzling from the grill, or Scottish scallops sautéed with butter and pancetta lardons, and to finish, a vanilla pannacotta with stewed rhubarb compôte and ginger shortbread.

Times 12-2.30/6-9

PONTEFRACT   Map 16 SE42

Wentbridge House Hotel

◉◉ Modern British V ▲ NOTABLE WINE LIST ✋

Yorkshire-French cooking in a grand country house

☎ 01977 620444
The Great North Rd, Wentbridge WF8 3JJ
e-mail: info@wentbridgehouse.co.uk
web: www.wentbridgehouse.co.uk
dir: 4m S of M62/A1 junct, 0.5m off A1

The stone-built house, which dates from the turn of the 18th century, has been home variously to the Bowes-Lyon and Leatham families (the latter founders of Barclays Bank). Century-old trees add venerable dignity to the grounds, while the Fleur de Lys dining room eschews today's default beige approach for the cheerier tones of rhubarb and custard. It's a fresh and airy atmosphere during the day, which softens to dimmed lighting and crystal candles in the evenings, the better that you may enjoy some of the tableside cooking that has become a feature. Start with crab and hot-smoked salmon with tempura lobster and Bloody Mary mayonnaise, moving on to Gressingham duck breast with duck and spring onion tortellini in hazelnut and truffle dressing, or the beef Diane, a prime piece of Yorkshire fillet with mushrooms, onions and Dijon mustard, flamed up in red wine, brandy and cream. After that, go native with warm Yorkshire parkin and spiced rhubarb, served with Pontefract liquorice ice cream.

Chef Steve Turner **Owner** Mr G Page **Times** 7.15-9.30 Closed L Mon-Sat, D Sun, 25 Dec **Prices** Starter £8.95-£12.95, Main £19.95-£32.95, Dessert £6.95-£9.50, Service optional **Wines** 100 bottles over £20, 30 bottles under £20, 10 by glass **Notes** Sunday L, Vegetarian menu, Civ Wed 130 **Seats** 60, Pr/dining room 24 **Children** Portions **Parking** 100

SHIPLEY   Map 19 SE13

Marriott Hollins Hall Hotel & Country Club

◉ British

Refined cooking in a Victorian hotel

☎ 01274 530053
Hollins Hill, Baildon BD17 7QW
e-mail: mhrs.lbags.frontdesk@marriotthotels.com
dir: From A650 follow signs to Salt Mill. At lights in Shipley take A6038. Hotel 3m on left

Hollins Hall is a good all-rounder, appealing to both business people and tourists, with a pool and spa as well as a golf course by way of R&R, and two restaurants to choose from. The Zest Bar and the dressier Heathcliff's - which occupies the original Victorian drawing room - are the dining options. Don't expect too many wild cards on the menu. The kitchen hits the spot with the likes of chicken liver and orange pâté, served with fruity chutney, or a platter of seafood. Around half a dozen main courses may offer salmon fillet sauced with tomato butter, accompanied by Puy lentils, and honey-glazed duck breast with cherry jus, braised red cabbage and sweet potato purée, and to finish could be rhubarb crumble with custard.

Times 12-2/7-10 Closed L Sat

WAKEFIELD   Map 16 SE32

Waterton Park Hotel

◉ Traditional British V ✋

Sound cooking by a huge lake

☎ 01924 257911
Walton Hall, The Balk, Walton WF2 6PW
e-mail: info@watertonparkhotel.co.uk
dir: 3m SE off B6378. Exit M1 junct 39 towards Wakefield. At 3rd rdbt right for Crofton. At 2nd lights right & follow signs

Locations don't come much more memorable than this Georgian mansion marooned on an island in the middle of a 26-acre lake, with an 18-hole golf course in the wooded parkland all around. An iron footbridge links the castaway to the shore, where you'll find the Bridgewalk restaurant in the hotel's modern, purpose-built annexe. Decorated in restful neutral shades and lined with books, the smart setting suits the contemporary country-house cooking. Ingredients are well-sourced and handled with care in a nice balance of simple and more labour-intensive dishes. Game terrine with beetroot relish and toasted brioche might be one way to get started, while

mains could bring line-caught sea bass with pickled fennel and tarragon cream, or seared duck breast with black cherry confit and gravy. Wind things up with pear and almond frangipane with pear crumble and custard, or go for a savoury finish with a trio of Yorkshire cheeses.

Chef Armstrong Wgabi **Owner** The Kaye family **Times** 7-9.30 **Prices** Food prices not confirmed for 2013. Please telephone for details **Wines** 10 bottles over £20, 50 bottles under £20, 10 by glass **Notes** Vegetarian menu, Dress restrictions, Smart casual, Civ Wed 150 **Seats** 50, Pr/dining room 40 **Children** Portions, Menu **Parking** 150

WETHERBY   Map 16 SE44

Wood Hall Hotel & Spa

◉◉ Modern British ✋

Classy cooking in splendid Georgian country house

☎ 01937 587271
Trip Ln, Linton LS22 4JA
e-mail: woodhall@handpicked.co.uk
dir: From Wetherby take A661 (Harrogate road) N for 0.5m. Left to Sicklinghall/Linton. Cross bridge, left to Linton/Woodhall, right opposite Windmill Inn, 1.25m to hotel (follow brown signs)

The Wood Hall Estate makes a fine first impression as one approaches down the winding driveway, and the 100 or so acres is the source of many of the ingredients served in the restaurant, including a herd of Dexter cattle and vegetables and herbs from the kitchen garden. Built in 1750, the house has splendid Georgian features as well as plenty of contemporary facilities, plus a restaurant that more than does justice to the splendid home-grown (or carefully-sourced) produce. The Georgian Restaurant is packed with period details and is given a contemporary sheen with its modishly chosen colour scheme (natural and neutral) and smartly dressed tables. The cooking is equally of the moment, based around classical principles with a dash of contemporary vigour. Start, perhaps, with mushroom and chestnut ravioli with a ginger mirin broth, or venison carpaccio with a black pudding bonbon and sorrel. Next up, Dales lamb might come with hazelnut gnocchi and pear purée, and to finish, a soufflé may well steal the show (toffee and banana, perhaps, or apricot and yoghurt).

Chef Neal Birtwell **Owner** Hand Picked Hotels **Times** 12-2.30/7-9.30 Closed L Mon-Sat **Prices** Fixed D 3 course £37, Starter £15-£18, Main £19-£28, Dessert fr £8.50, Service optional **Wines** 112 bottles over £20, 2 bottles under £20, 18 by glass **Notes** Sunday L, Vegetarian available, Dress restrictions, Smart casual, no jeans or trainers, Civ Wed 100 **Seats** 40, Pr/dining room 100 **Children** Portions, Menu **Parking** 100

CHANNEL ISLANDS
ALDERNEY

ALDERNEY   Map 24

Braye Beach Hotel

◉ Modern British ⚘

Creative cooking by the beach

☎ 01481 824300
Braye St GY9 3XT
e-mail: reception@brayebeach.com
dir: Follow coast road from airport

With dream-ticket views across the bay and harbour beyond, this large, splendidly multi-gabled hotel sits beside the beautiful white sands of the beach. The restaurant - decked out in natural tones with an understated contemporary vibe - is the place to soak up the magnificent watery vista, while in the summer you can get even closer with a table on the decked terrace. Expect some classy modern cooking to match the surroundings, with local seafood rightly getting a good showing. Pan-roasted sea bass, perhaps, with broad beans, peas, bok choy and clams and a chive butter sauce, or butter-poached whole Alderney lobster with crab ravioli, samphire, lobster cream and Avruga caviar. There are full-on seafood platters, too, plus Gressingham duck breast with pumpkin gnocchi, Morteau sausage, Puy lentils and a Madeira jus. To finish, Manjari chocolate soufflé and white chocolate sorbet rises to the occasion.

Chef Liam Foster **Owner** Healthspan Leisure Ltd
Times 12-2.30/6.30-9.30 Closed Jan-Mar **Prices** Fixed L 2 course £12-£37, Fixed D 3 course £20-£25, Starter £5.50-£9.50, Main £14-£35, Dessert £5.50-£6.60, Service optional **Wines** 59 bottles over £20, 34 bottles under £20, 8 by glass **Notes** Sunday L, Vegetarian available **Seats** 65, Pr/dining room 18 **Children** Portions, Menu **Parking** On street

GUERNSEY

CASTEL   Map 24

Cobo Bay Hotel

◉◉ Traditional European

Superb views and admirable use of local produce

☎ 01481 257102 & 07781 156757
Cobo Coast Rd, Cobo GY5 7HB
e-mail: reservations@cobobayhotel.com
dir: From airport turn right, follow road to W coast at L'Erée. Turn right onto coast road for 3m to Cobo Bay. Hotel on right

Sunset dinners are the thing at this west-facing beachside hotel, whether you are dining alfresco on the beach terrace or indoors in the smart contemporary restaurant. Even if the sun fails to put on its show, the view across the bay is well worth turning up for at any time of day. As you might hope, locally-sourced produce, especially deliveries of seafood from the boats, is at the heart of Euro-accented ideas. A starter of splendid seared scallops comes with wild mushrooms, wilted spinach, and dry vermouth sauce, while pan-fried brill might be matched with sweet Muscat grapes and a champagne and dill cream sauce. Meat is handled deftly too: perhaps rump of lamb from the grill, served with ratatouille, dauphinoise potatoes and port and rosemary jus. Coconut pannacotta with vanilla and pineapple salsa provide a totally tropical finish, or stay at home with local strawberries with Guernsey double cream.

Chef John Chapman **Owner** Mr D & Mrs J Nussbaumer
Times 12-2/6-9.30 Closed 2 Jan-28 Feb **Prices** Fixed L 2 course fr £16.50, Fixed D 3 course £25-£30, Starter £6.95-£9.50, Main £6.95-£37.50, Dessert £6.50-£7.50, Service optional **Wines** 31 bottles over £20, 11 by glass **Notes** Sunday L, Vegetarian available **Seats** 120, Pr/dining room 70 **Children** Portions **Parking** 100

La Grande Mare Hotel Golf & Country Club

◉ Traditional, International

International dining at a popular golf hotel

☎ 01481 256576
The Coast Rd, Vazon Bay GY5 7LL
e-mail: simon@lagrandemare.com
dir: From airport turn right. 5 mins to reach Coast Rd. Turn right again. Hotel 5 min drive

Sitting alongside stunning Vazon Bay on Guernsey's west coast, this purpose-built hotel (opened in the 1970s) is surrounded by 120 acres of peaceful grounds complete with lakes, woodland walks, gardens and an 18-hole golf course. It's a tranquil spot, with relaxed and friendly service and three different dining experiences to choose from, including the main restaurant which is spacious and decorated in a contemporary but sophisticated style. The international menu is based on great Guernsey produce and may take in six iced oysters to start with, served with shallots and a Bloody Mary shot, followed by confit of duck leg with caramelised apple pancake and wild berry jus, or lobster linguini with chilli, garlic and parsley. Vanilla pannacotta with framboise coulis might bring things to a close.

Times 12-2/7-9.30

ST MARTIN   Map 24

The Auberge

◉◉ Modern European

Great sea views and well-judged menu

☎ 01481 238485
Jerbourg Rd GY4 6BH
e-mail: dine@theauberge.gg
web: www.theauberge.gg
dir: End of Jerbourg Rd at Jerbourg Point

Magnificent sea views and exciting modern cooking bring discerning diners to this contemporary and stylish clifftop eatery just a few miles from St Peter Port. On sunny days be sure to arrive early to bag a table on the terrace for a memorable outdoor dining experience. Expect a cosmopolitan, brasserie-style vibe in the minimalist conservatory dining area, where floor-to-ceiling windows frame the glorious view across the bay and neighbouring islands. Tables are unclothed and service is relaxed and efficient, while the imaginative cooking makes sound use of fresh, locally-sourced produce, in particular top-notch island-landed fish and seafood. From the seasonal menu, follow beef carpaccio or scallop tempura with brill with chorizo, mussels and olive broth. Steaks get their own section of the menu, vegetarians are well looked after, and puddings may include vanilla and champagne poached pear with hazelnut financier and thick Guernsey cream.

Chef Daniel Green **Owner** Lapwing Trading Ltd
Times 12-2/7-9.30 Closed 25-26 Dec, D Sun **Prices** Fixed L 2 course £14.95, Fixed D 3 course £18.95, Starter £5.95-£8.95, Main £12.95-£30, Dessert fr £5.95, Service optional **Wines** 19 bottles over £20, 16 bottles under £20,

Save on Hotels. Book at **theAA.com/hotel**

GUERNSEY 529 **ENGLAND**

12 by glass **Notes** Sunday L, Vegetarian available **Seats** 70 **Children** Portions, Menu **Parking** 25

See advert on page 530

La Barbarie Hotel

◉ British, French

Charming spot for excellent local produce

☎ 01481 235217
Saints Rd GY4 6ES
e-mail: reservations@labarbariehotel.com
dir: At lights in St Martin take road to Saints Bay. Hotel on right at end of Saints Rd

The former priory has a charming cottage-feel about it, with the overall impression one of soothing comfort rather than chintz. The name references Barbary Coast pirates, by the way, who reputedly kidnapped a former owner of the building a few hundred years ago. The restaurant is bathed in natural light during the day while candles bring a warm glow in the evening, and a professional service team strike the right balance (there's a cheerful, unpretentious buzz to the place). The cooking is pleasingly to the point - chargrilled steaks (10oz rib-eye, perhaps) come with a choice of sauces, although the local seafood may well steal the show - lobster or brill among them, again with the sauce of your choice (champagne, lemon butter and more). Finish with pear and almond tart with dark chocolate sorbet, Guernsey ice creams or a platter of local cheeses.

Chef Colin Pearson **Owner** La Barbarie Ltd
Times 12 1.45/6 9.30 Closed mid Nov–mid Mar
Prices Food prices not confirmed for 2013. Please telephone for details **Wines** 6 bottles over £20, 16 bottles under £20, 6 by glass **Notes** Early D £8.25, Vegetarian available **Seats** 70 **Children** Portions, Menu **Parking** 60

ST PETER PORT   Map 24

The Absolute End

◉ Mediterranean, International

Fresh seafood in a harbourside cottage

☎ 01481 723822
St Georges Esplanade GY1 2BG
e-mail: the-absolute-end@cwgsy.net
dir: Less than 1m from town centre. N on seafront road towards St Sampson

When you're overlooking the harbour just outside St Peter Port you might hope for spanking-fresh fish and seafood, and this well-loved, unpretentious restaurant in a converted fisherman's cottage duly obliges with its repertoire of Italian-accented classics. Bright white and creamy yellow half-panelled walls hung with colourful artwork combine with pale wooden floors for a crisp modern look, and the Italian chef-proprietor serves up an accessible menu that remains faithful to the island's maritime heritage. A starter of fritto misto or crabcakes with sweet chilli sauce might be followed by a trio of locally-caught monkfish, scallops and brill served with olive oil, capers, fried sage leaves and wilted spinach, or

perhaps lobster linguine. Roast rack of lamb with rosemary sauce is a typical meaty alternative.

Times 12-2.30/6.30-10 Closed Sun

Fermain Valley Hotel

◉◉ Modern European **NEW** V ✍

Brasserie-style dishes in a beautiful Guernsey valley

☎ 01481 235666
Fermain Ln GY1 1ZZ
e-mail: info@fermainvalley.com
dir: From town centre on Fort Rd follow St Martin signs. Fermain Ln on left. Hotel 0.5m on left

The Fermain Valley Hotel is in an utterly delicious part of Guernsey. It's a dazzling-white building up a steep valley road from the beach and bay at St Peter Port, sitting proudly in acres of beautifully tended gardens. The Rock Garden is an expansive, blond-wooded space for drinks and lighter food, while the tile-floored Valley dining room is the fine-dining option, but still retaining the sense of breezy relaxation that pervades the whole place. The culinary style is European brasserie, with French and Italian modes to the fore in dishes that gain strength from their simplicity and the excellence of the raw materials. A starter of breast and croquette of partridge, with plum purée and vanilla oil, shows a willingness to look beyond the usual confines, but there are more classical offerings too - lobster linguine, crab mayonnaise. At main course, the range extends from beef fillet with shallot purée in red wine jus to the likes of seared sea bass with sweet pepper and chilli coulis and pistachio oil. Vegetables are charged extra, but include triple-cooked chips (a banker with that steak, surely?), and desserts aim to spoil you with orange and Grand Marnier iced soufflé with chocolate sauce.

Chef Christopher Vincent **Owner** Vista Hotels Ltd
Times 12-2.30/6.30-9.30 **Prices** Fixed L 2 course £20-£25, Fixed D 3 course £25-£30, Starter £6.50-£8.50, Main £14-£22, Dessert £5.95-£8, Service included **Wines** 40 bottles over £20, 15 bottles under £20, 8 by glass **Notes** Sunday L, Vegetarian menu, Dress restrictions, smart casual, Air con **Seats** 80 **Children** Portions, Menu **Parking** 50

Mora Restaurant & Grill

◉ Traditional European

Quality cooking in old wine cellars by the Marina

☎ 01481 715053
The Quay GY1 2LE
e-mail: eat@mora.gg
dir: Facing Victoria Marina

On the site of 18th-century wine cellars, Mora is two restaurants in one: Little Mora downstairs for a quick meal or light lunch, and upstairs for the full monty in the smart, modern room overlooking the marina. Seafood is a strong suit, from lobster thermidor to pan-fried medallions of monkfish with three scallops, all perfectly timed, served simply on roast red peppers with oregano dressing. The kitchen also has some thoroughly modern

ideas, turning out potted duck with orange and nutmeg butter and rhubarb relish, crabcakes with harissa mayonnaise, venison fillet with a ragoût of the same meat with apricots and chestnuts served with braised red cabbage, and rum and coconut pannacotta with marinated pineapple.

Chef Trevor Baines **Owner** Nello Ciotti
Times 12-2.15/6-10 Closed 25 Dec **Prices** Fixed L 2 course fr £12.50, Fixed D 3 course £13.95-£23.50, Starter £4.75-£9.95, Main £13.50-£25, Dessert £4.95-£7.50, Service optional **Wines** 50 bottles over £20, 18 bottles under £20, 11 by glass **Notes** Fixed D 3 course £13.95 available 6-7pm, Sunday L, Vegetarian available **Seats** 90 **Children** Portions, Menu **Parking** On pier

The Old Government House Hotel

◉◉ Traditional French V 🏅 ✍

Refined cooking in grand harbourside restaurant

☎ 01481 724921
Old Government House Hotel, St Ann's Place GY1 2NU
e-mail: governors@theoghhotel.com
dir: At junct of St Julian's Av & College St

In a stunning location overlooking the old town and harbour, The Old Government House dates back to 1748 and was once the official residence of the Governor of Guernsey. The OGH, as it's affectionately known, has been a hotel since 1857 and the pristine white façade, the classically elegant entrance hall and the intimate, beautifully decorated Governor's fine-dining restaurant are reminders of its illustrious past. Overlooked by photos of former Island governors and surrounded by military memorabilia are just six tables, so be sure to book to experience Clément Baris's innovative and refined classic French cooking. Choose from his weekly seven-course dégustation menu, which is a genuine 'menu surprise' put together using the best of the Island's fresh ingredients, or delve into the regular carte. From the latter, kick off with caramelised veal sweetbreads with parsnip purée and coffee bean foam, then follow with braised turbot with white bean and Spanish sausage cassoulet and thyme reduction. Autumn pear soufflé with honey and cardamom ice cream should round things off in style.

Chef Clément Baris **Owner** Red Carnation Hotels
Times 7-11 Closed 25 & 31 Dec, L all week
Prices Tasting menu £50, Starter £9.50-£14, Main £13.50-£23.50, Dessert £8.50-£12, Service added but optional 10% **Wines** 80 bottles over £20, 2 bottles under £20, 17 by glass **Notes** Tasting menu 7 course, Vegetarian menu, Dress restrictions, Smart casual **Seats** 14 **Parking** 10

the
AUBERGE

bar & restaurant

With unrivalled views, The Auberge offers consistent award winning imaginative cuisine in informal surroundings.

Jerbourg Road, St. Martin, Guernsey.
T. 01481 238485 www.theauberge.gg

Save on Hotels. Book at theAA.com/hotel

GUERNSEY 531 ENGLAND

ST PETER PORT *continued*

Les Rocquettes Hotel

◉ Modern International

Modish cooking in extended former mansion

☎ 01481 722146
Les Gravees GY1 1RN
e-mail: rocquettes@sarniahotels.com
dir: From ferry terminal take 2nd exit at rdbt, through 5 sets of lights. After 5th lights into Les Gravees. Hotel on right opposite church

After a contemporary makeover, the Oak restaurant of the Les Rocquettes hotel on the edge of St Peter Port offers a slick brasserie-style setting for modern European food that is seasonal, locally sourced, and cooked with confidence to tease out well-defined flavours. Start with home-made salmon and parsley fishcake with Provençal tomato compôte and herb oil, then look for locally-caught seafood in mains such as pan-fried black bream fillet with braised leeks, olive-crusted potato, and Chablis beurre blanc. Simple desserts such as baked vanilla cheesecake with fresh berry compôte complete the picture.

Chef Said Acharki, Fernando Gomes **Owner** Mr Sendlhofer **Times** 12.30-2/6.30-9.30 Closed L Mon-Sat **Prices** Fixed L 3 course £18-£25, Fixed D 3 course £23.50-£30, Service optional **Wines** 13 bottles over £20, 51 bottles under £20, 5 by glass **Notes** Sunday L, Vegetarian available, Dress restrictions, Smart casual **Seats** 120, Pr/dining room 50 **Children** Portions, Menu **Parking** 70

ST SAVIOUR   Map 24

The Farmhouse Hotel

◉ Modern British 🍃

Creative cooking in stylishly refurbished hotel

☎ 01481 264181
Route des bas Courtils GY7 9YF
e-mail: enquiries@thefarmhouse.gg
web: www.thefarmhouse.gg
dir: From airport, left to 1st lights, left then left again. Follow for 1.5m around airport perimeter & turn left, hotel on right

Originally a 15th century farmhouse, and one of the island's oldest family-run hotels, today's incarnation blends country-house character with contemporary cool. The summer months offer outdoor dining by the pool, on the terrace, or perhaps in one of the garden gazebos. Top-notch ingredients from Guernsey's abundant larder (the menu proudly guarantees 80%) are competently handled and suitably well dressed. Top-notch fish and seafood are an obvious major player, perhaps featuring pan-fried turbot teamed with truffle-scented purée mousseline, leeks and a Muscat de Beaumes de Venise reduction, while pork (maybe '3 ways' - tenderloin, braised belly and pan-fried haslet) could arrive with spiced apple purée. If chocolate's your bag, finish with a second triple - white chocolate and pistachio mousse, dark chocolate jelly and cocoa cookie.

Chef Robert Birch **Owner** David & Julie Nussbaumer **Times** 12-2.30/6.30-9.30 **Prices** Fixed L 2 course £19.95-£21.50, Fixed D 3 course £24.95-£29.50, Starter £6.95-£9.95, Main £9.95-£27.50, Dessert £5.50-£8.95, Service optional **Wines** 35 bottles over £20, 20 bottles under £20, 12 by glass **Notes** Sunday L, Vegetarian available, Dress restrictions, Smart casual **Seats** 60, Pr/dining room 162 **Children** Portions, Menu **Parking** 80

See advert below

HERM

HERM	Map 24

White House Hotel

◉ Traditional British

Simple cooking and sea views in an island retreat

☎ 01481 722159
GY1 3HR
e-mail: admin@herm-island.com
dir: Close to harbour. Access by regular 20 min boat trip from St Peter Port, Guernsey

Life goes along at a slower pace on Herm, where the only means of transport are bicycles and Shank's pony (the island is a car-free zone). At the White House Hotel you won't even find a phone, TV or clock - such is the owners' determination to make you switch off and leave the stresses of the modern world behind you. That doesn't mean you can totally kick back and relax in the restaurant, mind you: gentlemen are required to wear jackets and/or ties. Every table has a sea view, which helps make the White House a popular dining venue. The sensibly concise menu (boosted by daily fish specials) offers simple dishes with an international flavour, such as crispy confit of duck to start, served with sweet-and-sour vegetable noodles, coriander and iceberg salad and hoi sin dressing. Main-course could be sirloin of beef with sweet potato and celeriac dauphinoise, roasted peppers and a pea and smoked bacon sauce.

Times 12.30-2/7-9 Closed Nov-Apr

JERSEY

GOREY	Map 24

The Moorings Hotel & Restaurant

◉ Traditional **NEW**

Local food on the quayside

☎ 01534 853633
Gorey Pier JE3 6EW
e-mail: reservations@themooringshotel.com
dir: At foot of Mont Orgueil Castle

Smack on Gorey's picturesque harbourfront, the Moorings has a real continental feel with its pavement terrace overlooking the sea and ruins of Mont Orgueil Castle. If you're forced indoors by inclement weather, the front-facing bistro is decked out with colourful art on summery yellow walls, or there's the smart restaurant at the rear, which goes for a more plush style with linen-clad tables and red and grey-striped banquettes. Being rather closer to the French mainland than the UK, and with the smell of the sea in the air, it's no surprise to see Gallic influences underpinning the menu, and plenty of splendid local seafood featuring on it - perhaps a seafood tasting plate or pan-fried scallops with truffled celeriac purée, soy and truffle dressing to get you started. Mains could

continue the piscine theme with pan-fried fillet of brill with chancre crab risotto, baby spinach and herb velouté, or switch over to meaty mode with an immaculately-cooked rack of herb-crusted lamb served with vibrantly fresh peas, asparagus, green beans and watercress, Jersey Royals and rosemary jus. And what better way to end a summer meal than a dish of local strawberries with Jersey cream?

Chef Simon Walker **Owner** Simon & Joanne Walker **Times** 12-2/7-8.30 **Prices** Fixed L 2 course £12.50-£17, Fixed D 4 course £22.50-£25.50, Starter £9.90-£13.25, Main £22-£32, Dessert £6.95-£14, Service optional **Wines** 35 bottles over £20, 24 bottles under £20, 8 by glass **Notes** Sunday L, Vegetarian available, Dress restrictions, Smart casual **Seats** 65, Pr/dining room 35 **Children** Portions, Menu

Sumas

◉◉ Modern British

Inventive cooking and marina views

☎ 01534 853291
Gorey Hill JE3 6ET
e-mail: info@sumasrestaurant.com
web: www.sumasrestaurant.com
dir: From St Helier take A3 E for 5m to Gorey. Before castle take sharp left. Restaurant 100yds up hill on left (look for blue & white blind)

A blue and white colour scheme, with flowers on the tables, gives a fresh, clean feel to this small restaurant overlooking the marina, the views all the more enjoyable from the terrace in warm weather. The kitchen focuses on getting hold of Jersey's seasonal produce and mobilising it along modern British lines. Local scallops are joined by brandade fritters, cauliflower purée, saffron aïoli and herbs to make a vibrant starter of contrasting textures and flavours, and may be offered next to roast quail with rosemary gnocchi, salsify and herb purée. Loin of venison, served with fondant potato, sprouts with chestnuts, poached pear, celeriac purée and a meaty gravy can turn up in colder months, while fish main courses are invariably strong points: perhaps sea bass accompanied by crab croquettes, Savoy cabbage and sauce vierge (a straightforward, attractively presented dish). If choosing a dessert poses too much of a dilemma, go for an assiette of mini puddings.

Chef Daniel Ward **Owner** Mrs Bults & Paul Dufty **Times** 12-2.30/6-9.30 Closed late Dec-mid Jan (approx), D Sun **Prices** Fixed L 2 course fr £17.50, Fixed D 3 course fr £20, Starter £5.75-£12, Main £14.50-£25, Dessert £5.75-£9.75, Service optional, Groups min 10 service 10% **Wines** 38 bottles over £20, 11 bottles under £20, 13 by glass **Notes** Sunday L, Vegetarian available **Seats** 40 **Children** Portions, Menu **Parking** On street

ROZEL	Map 24

Chateau La Chaire

◉◉ Traditional British, French **V** ◐

Quality modern cooking in charming small hotel

☎ 01534 863354
Rozel Bay JE3 6AJ
e-mail: res@chateau-la-chaire.co.uk
dir: From St Helier NE towards Five Oaks, Maufant, then St Martin's Church & Rozel; 1st left in village, hotel 100mtrs

Set in subtropical gardens, La Chaire is a short stroll from the quaint fishing village of Rozel. It dates from Victorian times, and is now a delightful small hotel, comfortable and well appointed, with a rococo-style lounge and a part-panelled restaurant. The kitchen overlays the best traditions of British cooking on the classical French repertoire but adds its own modern European twists. Thus, you could start with duck rillette and smoked breast with cranberry chutney, or scallops wrapped in pancetta with apple and vanilla purée. Likewise, roast fillet of lamb, cooked pink, is served with familiar rosemary-flavoured gravy, accompanied by fondant potato and carrot purée, while pan-fried fillet of locally-landed brill comes with moules à la crème. Puddings make an impact, among them memorable quince crumble with Calvados custard and cinnamon ice cream.

Chef Marcin Ciehomski **Owner** The Hiscox family **Times** 12-2/7-9 **Prices** Fixed L 3 course fr £14.95, Fixed D 3 course fr £36.95, Tasting menu £45-£55, Service added but optional 10% **Wines** 69 bottles over £20, 16 bottles under £20, 7 by glass **Notes** 'Taste of Jersey' Tasting menu with/out wines available, Sunday L, Vegetarian menu, Dress restrictions, Smart casual, Civ Wed 60 **Seats** 60, Pr/dining room 28 **Children** Portions, Menu **Parking** 30

Save on Hotels. Book at **theAA.com/hotel**

JERSEY 533 ENGLAND

Ocean Restaurant at the Atlantic Hotel

❀ ❀ ❀ ❀

Modern British V NOTABLE WINE LIST 🐚

Stunning island location for some scintillating cooking

☎ 01534 744101
Le Mont de la Pulente JE3 8HE
e-mail: info@theatlantichotel.com
web: www.theatlantichotel.com
dir: A13 to Petit Port, turn right into Rue de la Sergente & right again, hotel signed

First opening its doors in 1970, there's a good deal of contemporary glamour about the Atlantic Hotel. The sub-tropical gardens and championship golf course next door help to give it a jet-set feel, which is more than matched by the light and bright, chic interior, and the polished service. The setting above St Ouen's Bay and the vast open beach is rather gorgeous, with the panoramic view as good as any on the island. The Ocean Restaurant has been Mark Jordan's domain since 2004, and the room has a real sense of place, with its white, blue and cream colour scheme, as does the menu, which is packed with wonderful Jersey produce. This is a kitchen which has confidence in its abilities and in the strength of the ingredients at its disposal, whether that's from local growers, producers or fishermen. Jordan leads a team which displays finely tuned technical skills and delivers refined, expertly-crafted

dishes. A starter of langoustines, for example, served on a heart-shaped stone, is three perfectly cooked, fresh-as-a-daisy tails in a dish that bursts with the taste of the sea, the accompanying oyster mayonnaise, Ébéne caviar and anchovy crumbs proving perfect textural foils. Main-course turbot is a fish more than happy in the earthy company of ceps and an oxtail crepinette, alongside garlic-flavoured pommes purée, or there might be honey-roast breast of Gressingham duck, with the leg meat rillettes stuffed into cannelloni, served with peach purée and vanilla jus. Addicts of the cocoa bean will find deep satisfaction in a dessert made with 70% cocoa Guanaja chocolate, or there's all the comforting stickiness of pear tarte Tatin with star anise and vanilla caramel, served with lavender ice cream. With everything from the superlative breads to the petits fours subjected to the same exacting standards, and a wine list that runs to some stellar names without neglecting those who simply want a good choice by the glass, the Ocean Restaurant is a genuine star turn.

Chef Mark Jordan **Owner** Patrick Burke
Times 12.30-2.30/7-10 Closed Jan
Prices Fixed L 2 course £20, Fixed D 3 course £55, Tasting menu £75, Service included **Wines** 468 bottles over £20, 2 bottles under £20, 13 by glass
Notes Fixed ALC 2/3 course £55/£65, Tasting menu 7 course, Sunday L,

Vegetarian menu, Dress restrictions, Smart dress, Civ Wed 80 **Seats** 60, Pr/dining room 20 **Children** Portions, Menu **Parking** 60

ST AUBIN   Map 24

The Boat House

◉ Modern British

Modern cooking with harbourside views

☎ 01534 744226 & 747101
One North Quay JE3 8BS
e-mail: enquiries@theboathousegroup.com
dir: 3m W of St Helier

Walls of glass mean that every table in this buzzy modern venue gets fabulous views of the ranks of yachts moored in St Aubin's busy harbour. In the daytime, the alfresco terrace exerts its own attraction, but you need to head upstairs to the aptly-named Sails Brasserie for a wide-ranging, globally-influenced menu of contemporary crowd pleasers. Fish and seafood are at the forefront of most people's minds in such a watery setting, so locally-dived scallops duly turn up in the company of hazelnuts and coriander butter to set the ball rolling, before a tip-top main course of turbot with creamy mash, crab mayonnaise, and mussel and scallop cream. Nor do carnivores get a raw deal - there could be Spanish-style slow-roasted shoulder of lamb with garlic, mash, and baked tomatoes and courgettes, while dessert brings a simple but effective pairing of vanilla pannacotta with poached plums.

Times 12-2/6-9.30 Closed 25 Dec & Jan, Mon-Tue (Winter), L Wed-Thu & Sat (Winter), D Sun (Winter)

The Salty Dog Bar & Bistro

◉ Modern International V 🕯

Vibrant seafood cooking (and more) by the harbour

☎ 01534 742760
Le Boulevard JE3 8AB
e-mail: info@saltydogbistro.com
web: www.saltydogbistro.com
dir: Walking from centre of St Aubin Village along harbour, approx halfway along, slightly set back

With a seafaring name and location by the harbour-front, it's only right that fish and seafood are a major player on the menu, while the building's former life as a smugglers'

residence adds a little spice. The canopied terrace extends the outdoor season, while inside comes cheerily decked out and supported by engaging staff that lend it the relaxed, friendly air of a family-run Mediterranean outfit. Fresh, locally-sourced island produce is rightly king, with flavour-led dishes given a modern spin. Backpack the globe with pan-roasted salmon with teriyaki and toasted sesame sauce, Asian greens and jasmine rice to sea bass fillet teamed with sautéed greens, Jersey Royals, chorizo and sauce vierge. There are also grilled meats and salads, or hit the spice trail with Keralan fish curry or Delhi buttered chicken.

Chef Damon James Duffy **Owner** Damon & Natalie Duffy **Times** 12.30pm-1.30am Closed 25-26 Dec, 1 Jan, L Tue-Fri (Jan-Mar) **Prices** Fixed L 3 course fr £25, Fixed D 3 course fr £32, Starter £8.45-£9.50, Main £13.50-£30, Dessert £4.95-£6.50, Service optional, Groups min 12 service 10% **Wines** 26 bottles over £20, 16 bottles under £20, 7 by glass **Notes** Sunday L, Vegetarian menu, Dress restrictions, Smart casual **Seats** 60 **Children** Portions, Menu **Parking** Car parks & on street parking nearby

ST BRELADE   Map 24

L'Horizon Hotel & Spa

◉◉ Modern, Traditional

Appealing menu and a touch of luxury on the beach

☎ 01534 743101
La Route de la Baie JE3 8EF
e-mail: lhorizon@handpicked.co.uk
dir: From airport right at rdbt towards St Brelades & Red Houses. Through Red Houses, hotel 300mtrs on right in centre of bay

In a prime spot on one of Jersey's best beaches, L'Horizon dates back to 1850, when it was built by a colonel in the Bengal army. The interior still has the feel of Victorian elegance, overlaid with the trappings of a luxury hotel, including an indoor seawater pool. The Grill is where to head to for some modern takes on the classic British and French repertories, with the kitchen creaming off the best of the island's produce. A platter of top-notch charcuterie with chutney, or a tian of crab and guacamole with Marie Rose salad are typical starters. Among main courses, cod fillet is partnered by garlicky prawns and accompanied by crab butter and crushed potatoes, and roast chicken breast is stuffed with prunes and almonds and served with bubble-and-squeak and chicken jus. Finish with a classic version of lemon tart with raspberry sorbet.

Chef James Whitesmith **Owner** Julia Hands **Times** 6.45-10 Closed Sun-Mon, L all week **Prices** Fixed D 4 course £35-£45.50, Service optional **Notes** Sunday L, Vegetarian available, Dress restrictions, Smart casual, Civ Wed 300 **Seats** 36, Pr/dining room 300 **Children** Portions, Menu **Parking** 50

Hotel La Place

◉ Modern British

Modern bistro cooking near the harbour

☎ 01534 744261 & 748173
Route du Coin, La Haule JE3 8BT
e-mail: andy@hotellaplacejersey.com
dir: Off main St Helier/St Aubin coast road at La Haule Manor (B25). Up hill, 2nd left (to Red Houses), 1st right. Hotel 100mtrs on right

A short walk from St Aubin's harbour, the hotel is a collection of country cottages centred on an original 17th-century farmhouse in a particularly tranquil district of Jersey. Dining goes on in a pale beige and white room known as the Retreat, where modern bistro dishes in a light style are on the menu. Bresaola with fennel slaw, or crab fritters with beetroot and apple salsa, fire the starting gun, and may be followed by the likes of pollock on wilted spinach in parsley sauce, or braised ox cheeks on celeriac purée, served with braised leeks and rosemary roast potatoes. Finish up with lemon tart and blueberry compôte, or a canonical version of Eton Mess.

Chef Roger Holmes **Owner** Mycroft Holdings **Times** 6.30-9 Closed L Sat-Sun **Prices** Food prices not confirmed for 2013. Please telephone for details **Notes** Vegetarian available, Civ Wed 75 **Seats** 76 **Parking** 30

Ocean Restaurant at the Atlantic Hotel

◉◉◉◉ – see page 533

Save on Hotels. Book at theAA.com/hotel

JERSEY 535 ENGLAND

Bohemia Restaurant

Modern European V NOTABLE WINE LIST

Pace-setting contemporary cooking in a smart spa hotel

☎ 01534 880588 & 876500
The Club Hotel & Spa, Green St JE2 4UH
e-mail: bohemia@huggler.com
dir: In town centre. 5 mins walk from main shopping centre

A visit to The Club Hotel & Spa will dispel any misconceptions you might have that Jersey is in some way preserved in aspic or behind the times - this place is as chic and sharp as any slick metropolitan joint, while, thanks to the cooking of Shaun Rankin in the Bohemia Restaurant, you'll always know you are on the island. The hotel has bags of boutique style and the requisite luxurious spa, plus in the swanky Bohemia Bar, somewhere to sip a cocktail or a glass of champagne. The restaurant is a smart space that wears its refinement lightly - high quality finishes in neutral, natural shades, rich leather chairs, and tables laid with crisp white linen - watched over by a professional service team who are entirely up to speed with the menu. Shaun Rankin hails from Yorkshire but has made Jersey his home and it is the produce from the land and waters around the island that informs his food. This passion for things local combines with Rankin's prodigious talent and creative streak to produce dishes of refinement, craft and contemporary dynamism. Flavours pack a punch from the off - an amuse-bouche of butternut squash velouté with goats' cheese beignets, for example - and are acutely judged in a first-course dish where local scallops are given a touch of Indian spicing (lightly curried, roasted and served with a coconut dhal, wonderfully light onion bhajis and a coriander and apple salad). Not only does everything look beautiful on the plate, everything has its place on the plate. Main-course ox cheek is slow-cooked in red wine and comes with deep-fried salt-cod purée, pickled onion 'shells', cod 'popcorn' and sea purslane, whilst local pollock is roasted and teamed with cockles cooked in sherry vinegar and parsley risotto. If you're on the lookout for some luscious Jersey cream, go for the Black Forest gâteau soufflé, a bright idea which comes with Jersey double cream ice cream. There's a mid-week market menu and a good-value set lunch that runs to duck liver parfait with apple and quince purée and toasted brioche followed by grilled fillet of lemon sole with potato croquettes and sauce vierge. The wine list is a cracker, make no mistake.

Chef Shaun Rankin **Owner** Lawrence Huggler **Times** 12-2.30/6.30-10 Closed 24-30 Dec **Prices** Fixed L 2 course £25, Service added but optional 10% **Wines** 180 bottles over £20, 4 bottles under £20, 24 by glass **Notes** Tasting menu 11 course, ALC 3 course £55, Market D menu Mon-Thu, Vegetarian menu, Dress restrictions, Smart casual, Civ Wed 80 **Seats** 60, Pr/dining room 24 **Children** Portions **Parking** 20, Opposite

ST BRELADE *continued*

The Oyster Box

🏵🏵 Modern British 🍃

A beachside setting for spankingly fresh seafood

☎ 01534 743311
St Brelade's Bay JE3 8EF
e-mail: eat@oysterbox.co.uk
dir: on the beach just east of Fishermen's chapel

St Brelade's Bay is one of Jersey's most beautiful spots, and smack in the middle of it, dipping its toes in the sand, is the Oyster Box. It is a luminous space, flooded with light and stylishly kitted out with slate floors, white walls, high-backed wicker chairs at wooden tables, and netted glass floats hanging from the ceiling as a nod to the piscine pleasures that await; in case the vast picture windows don't give a clear enough view of the bay, go alfresco on the beachside terrace. Local fish is the main thrust of the kitchen's culinary endeavours, but that's not to say that dedicated carnivores are sidelined: there are steaks and the likes of roast venison loin with wild mushroom ravioli, warm truffled celeriac remoulade and venison gravy to keep them quiet. But it is the island's seafood that gets star billing here, served without undue fuss or pointless adornments: platters of fruits de mer, crab bisque served with gruyère, aïoli and croûtons, or mains that deliver sautéed brill fillets with squid ink tagliatelle, chorizo, scallops and garlic butter, or line-caught bass with crab ravioli, buttered leeks and creamed shellfish sauce.

Chef Patrick Tweedy **Owner** Jersey Pottery Restaurants **Times** 12-2.30/6-9.30 Closed 25-26 Dec, Mon (Jan-Mar), L Mon, D Sun (winter only) **Prices** Starter £7-£11.50, Main £11.50-£42, Dessert £6.50, Service included **Wines** 47 bottles over £20, 23 bottles under £20, 21 by glass **Notes** Sunday L, Vegetarian available **Seats** 100 **Children** Portions, Menu **Parking** Car park oppposite

ST CLEMENT — Map 24

Green Island Restaurant

🏵 Mediterranean

Great local seafood in bustling beach café

☎ 01534 857787
Green Island JE2 6LS
e-mail: info@greenisland.je

This laid-back beach café and restaurant stakes its claim to the title of most southerly eatery in the British Isles, so kick back and bask in its sun-kissed views over sandy Green Island bay. As you'd hope in this briny location, the emphasis is firmly on fish and shellfish, and the kitchen has the nous to treat them with a light touch to let the freshness and quality do the talking, as in an ultra-simple dish of freshly-landed sole meunière with Jersey potatoes and salad. If it's meat you're after, tarragon-crusted roast rack and braised shank of lamb with boulangère potatoes, garlicky flageolet beans and baby carrots, roasted root vegetables and garlic might be up for grabs, and to finish, a classic crème brûlée with sablé biscuits should strike a suitably Gallic note.

Times 12-3/7-10 Closed 21 Dec-Mar, Mon, D Sun

ST HELIER — Map 24

Bohemia Restaurant

🏵🏵🏵🏵 – *see page 535*

Grand Jersey

🏵🏵🏵 – *see opposite*

Hotel Savoy

🏵 Modern British 🍃

Smart hotel dining room specialising in local seafood

☎ 01534 727521
37 Rouge Bouillon JE2 3ZA
e-mail: info@thesavoy.biz
dir: From airport 1st exit at rdbt. At next rdbt take 2nd exit right, down Beaumont Hill. At bottom turn left, along coast onto dual carriageway. At 3rd lights turn 1st left. Right at end. Remain in right lane, into left lane before hospital. Hotel on left opposite police station

Jersey's version of the iconic name occupies a Victorian manor house on the outskirts of St Helier which has been given a more boutique-style spin by a recent revamp. As you might hope in this island setting, seafood and fish landed on the Jersey coast figure prominently on the menu in the Montana restaurant - a compact but stylish space with service on the correctly formal end of the spectrum. The kitchen plays out well-rehearsed flavour combinations - sautéed seafood in garlic butter, or smoked salmon pâté with horseradish cream and blinis, perhaps, ahead of grilled Jersey plaice with Jersey Royals (what else?), and buttered vegetables. On the meat front there may be roast rack of lamb with dauphinoise potatoes, broccoli purée and thyme jus, and with the French coast so close, it seems right to end with a classic crème brûlée. Note that the Savoy is home to Roberto's Jazz Bar if you like a side order of cool jazz.

Chef Christopher Croize **Owner** Mr J Lora **Times** 7-9.30 Closed L ex by prior arrangement **Prices** Fixed L 3 course £18.95-£25, Fixed D 3 course £25-£28, Starter £7.50-£12.50, Main £11.75-£16.50, Dessert £5.75-£8.50, Service included **Wines** 34 bottles over £20, 13 bottles under £20, 14 by glass **Notes** Sunday L, Vegetarian available, Dress restrictions, Smart dress, Civ Wed 80 **Seats** 36, Pr/dining room 120 **Children** Portions, Menu **Parking** 35

Seasons

🏵 Modern European

Modern cooking in a popular hotel

☎ 01534 726521
Best Western Royal Hotel, 26 David Place JE2 4TD
e-mail: manager@royalhoteljersey.com
dir: Follow signs for Ring Rd, pass Queen Victoria rdbt keep left, left at lights, left into Piersons Rd. Follow one-way system to Cheapside, Rouge Bouillon, at A14 turn to Midvale Rd, hotel on left

The Best Western Royal has been providing accommodation in the heart of St Helier since around 1842, making it possibly the longest established hotel on the island. Much modernisation has taken place in recent years, including in the Seasons restaurant, which has a contemporary but elegant look with its white-linen-clothed tables and black chairs on bare oak floorboards. The cooking is equally of-the-moment, and makes good use of Jersey ingredients on menus that have a true European flavour. A typical dinner might begin with pan-fried quail's breast with potato gallette and port and juniper berry jus, followed by fillets of sea bass with a shellfish risotto, chive beurre blanc and buttered fennel, or saddle of venison with beetroot and salsify. For dessert you could go Italian with tiramisù, or perhaps take a slightly more fusion route with plum fritters with lemon rice pudding.

Times 12.30-2.30/6.30-9 Closed L Mon-Sat

ST PETER — Map 24

Greenhills Country Hotel

🏵 Mediterranean

Contemporary cooking of Jersey's fine produce

☎ 01534 481042
Mont de L'Ecole JE3 7EL
e-mail: reserve@greenhillshotel.com
dir: A1 signed St Peters Valley (A11). 4m, turn right onto E112

It may have its origins in 1674, but Greenhills is a contemporary hotel surrounded by delightful gardens complete with a heated outdoor pool. The kitchen has at its disposal the island's bountiful natural resources and weaves its way around a modern Anglo-Continental repertory, so carpaccio with rocket and parmesan may be followed by poached salmon and scallops on an artichoke and tomato concasse with mussel sauce. Specialities are listed separately (and incur an extra charge): alcohol-infused foie gras and duck terrine with maple-glazed figs, say, grilled lobster, and grilled medallions of beef fillet with black pudding sauce, thyme-flavoured vegetables, a potato gâteau and braised shallots. Dishes can be complex, but careful handling means they succeed, and presentation is a forte, as seen in desserts like sticky toffee pudding on Advocaat custard with vanilla ice cream and a coconut tulip.

Chef Marcin Dudek **Owner** Seymour Hotels **Times** 12.30-2/7-9.30 Closed 23 Dec-14 Feb **Prices** Fixed L 2 course fr £13, Fixed D 3 course fr £28.50, Service added 10% **Wines** 37 bottles over £20, 46 bottles under £20, 8 by glass **Notes** Sunday L, Vegetarian available, Dress restrictions, Smart casual, Civ Wed 60 **Seats** 90, Pr/dining room 40 **Children** Portions, Menu **Parking** 45

Save on Hotels. Book at theAA.com/hotel

JERSEY 537 ENGLAND

Grand Jersey

ST HELIER   Map 24

Modern British

Top-end contemporary cooking in landmark hotel

☎ 01534 722301
The Esplanade JE2 3QA
e-mail: reservations@grandjersey.com
dir: Located on St Helier seafront

The Grand overlooks St Aubin's Bay from its prime position on the esplanade, with the hubbub of St Helier a short distance should you wish to tear yourself away from the five-star luxury on offer here. There's a spa of course, plus the glamorous Champagne Lounge where you've around 100 bottles of bubbly to choose from, and shining brightly among the dining options is the Tassili restaurant. The sleek, contemporary good looks of the hotel are matched in the restaurant, which, following a gentle refurbishment, looks a little lighter than previously, with tables dressed up to the nines. Executive chef Richard Allen rightly puts the quality of the produce at the heart of everything, seeking out the best the island has to offer (which is a plentiful bounty indeed), and constructs some bright modern dishes using acute technical skills and a keen eye for the balancing of flavours and textures. Following the prerequisite amuse-bouche (tuna tartare, perhaps), Jersey scallops take centre stage, with an apple and vanilla purée, eel beignet and scallop essence, or go for the marinated foie gras and smoked Creedy Carver duck with 100% cocoa Indonesian black chocolate, peanut butter and pain d'épice. Everything looks stunning on the plate, every element plays its part. Main-course turbot is a superb piece of fish, served with chancre crab mayonnaise, saffron (nicely judged too), crab essence and coriander shoots, while pistachio and olive cake with chocolate sorbet, macaroon, orange, cocoa and pistachio crumbs makes for a memorable finish. If you can fit in a cheese course, do it, as they are fabulously kept (all British), served with excellent breads and home-made accompaniments such as truffled honey and 'rhubarb and mustard'.

Chef Richard Allen **Owner** BDL Hotels **Times** 12-2.30/7-9.30 Closed Sun-Mon, L Sat-Wed **Prices** Fixed L 3 course £18.95, Fixed D 3 course £49, Service optional **Wines** 250 bottles over £20, 6 bottles under £20, 14 by glass **Notes** Tasting menu 6 course, Chef's surprise menu 9 course, Vegetarian available, Dress restrictions, Smart casual, Civ Wed 150 **Seats** 25 **Parking** 32, NCP

Longueville Manor Hotel

ST SAVIOUR   Map 24

Modern British V

Superior cooking in unique medieval manor

☎ 01534 725501
JE2 7WF
e-mail: info@longuevillemanor.com
dir: From St Helier take A3 to Gorey, hotel 0.75m on left

There's something very special about Longueville Manor, the quintessential country-house hotel. It's surrounded by 17 acres of grounds that include woodland walks, a spectacular rose garden and a lake, and the interior is full of charm and character, with much oak panelling, exposed stone, deep sofas and open fires. Staff are polished, professional, welcoming and friendly. Dinner is taken in one of two rooms, the panelled and beamed Oak Room or the more contemporary Garden Room. Andrew Baird runs a busy kitchen, marshalling fruit, vegetables, herbs and salads from the manor's gardens and glasshouses and buying the best of the island's seafood and farmed produce. Techniques are second to none, and the menus are full of imaginative ideas: stuffing ravioli with lobster, for instance, and partnering it with pineapple compôte and cocoa and lobster sauce. The vogue for streaks of this and foams of that is eschewed in favour of sensible, well-considered combinations. Roast turbot is enhanced by a shallot jus with crisp lardons and accompanied by new season's peas, baby carrots and Jersey Royals, and well-timed grilled fillet of Angus comes with deeply flavoured slowly braised oxtail, mustard and cheese-topped fondant potato. Cheeses are an impressive bunch, hand-picked by Andrew himself, and puddings are irresistible, judging by raspberry soufflé with peach and clotted cream ice cream.

Chef Andrew Baird **Owner** Malcolm Lewis **Times** 12.30-2/7-10 **Prices** Fixed L 2 course fr £22.50, Fixed D 3 course £57.50-£72, Service included **Wines** 300+ bottles over £20, 10 bottles under £20, 23 by glass **Notes** Discovery menu with/without wine £75-£102, Sunday L, Vegetarian menu, Dress restrictions, Smart casual, Civ Wed 40 **Seats** 65, Pr/dining room 22 **Children** Portions, Menu **Parking** 45

ST PETER *continued*

Mark Jordan at the Beach

◉◉ Modern British **NEW** ✑

Simple but stunning food by the St Peter Plage

☎ 01534 780180
La Plage, La Route de la Haule JE3 7YD
e-mail: bookings@markjordanatthebeach.com
dir: A1 W from St Helier, left mini-rdbt towards St Aubins, follow sign 50m on left

The website shows a picture of a solitary table with two chairs actually dug into the sand on the Plage at St Peter, but Mark Jordan - he of the Ocean Restaurant at the Atlantic Hotel (see entry) - isn't quite as much 'at the beach' as that. Nonetheless, the restaurant is right next to the golden sands, with views of the castle and St Aubin harbour. A breezy seaside feel pervades the place, its chunky wood tables and broad-beam flooring offset with pictures of local scenes, and a smart, voguish air distinguishes the cookery. It all sounds beautifully simple, and is in fact, but impresses with depth and quality in all the right places. Crab and sweetcorn risotto dressed in vivid herb oil is a masterpiece of timing and intensity, and continuing the seafood route into mains might turn up an improbably spectacular grilled fillet of plaice with prawn, cockle and caper butter, served with indigenous Jersey Royals. While seafood is thus a strong point, there are pedigree meats too: steak burger with foie gras, rump of lamb with lentils, or the pairing of curried pork loin with mussel marinière. Note the richly yellow pastry (made with incomparable local butter) of a salted chocolate tart before you set about it, its melting filling echoed by good pistachio ice cream.

Chef Mark Jordan, Karl Tarjani **Owner** Mark Jordan, Patrick Burke **Times** 12-2.30/6-9.30 Closed 24 Dec-15 Jan, Mon (winter) **Prices** Fixed L 2 course fr £17.50, Starter £6.50-£12.50, Main £16-£30, Dessert £4.50-£9.50, Service optional **Wines** 49 bottles over £20, 6 bottles under £20, 6 by glass **Notes** Sunday L, Vegetarian available **Seats** 50 **Children** Portions **Parking** 16

ST SAVIOUR   Map 24

Longueville Manor Hotel

◉◉◉ *– see page 537*

SARK

SARK   Map 24

Hotel Petit Champ

◉◉ Modern British **V**

Ambitious cooking featuring the island's produce

☎ 01481 832046 & 07781 132046
GY10 1SF
e-mail: info@hotelpetitchamp.com
dir: Follow signs from the Methodist Chapel

Visiting car-less Sark is like taking a step back in time, an idyllic rural island with wonderful views of the sea and neighbouring islands. This small hotel, with an outdoor pool, offers the choice of eating outside in the pretty garden or in the stylish restaurant. Either way, the cooking is based on produce from the hotel's organic garden and local suppliers. The switched-on menu may open with oak-smoked pigeon, moist and tender, with soft-boiled quail's eggs, tangy pickled vegetables and truffled croûtons. Dishes are long on flavour and short on fuss, such as main courses of roast fillet of veal, cooked pink, with a well-made red wine jus, rich mushroom gratin and dauphinoise, and pan-fried sea bream with a vanilla reduction, sautéed potatoes and broad beans. Pastry work is well up to the mark, if desserts are anything to go by, as in a noteworthy glazed passionfruit tart.

Chef Adrian Graham **Owner** Hotel Petit Champ Ltd **Times** 12-6/6.45-9 **Prices** Food prices not confirmed for 2013. Please telephone for details **Wines** 32 bottles over £20, 11 bottles under £20, 5 by glass **Notes** Sunday L, Vegetarian menu **Seats** 30 **Children** Portions, Menu **Parking** No cars on Sark

---

La Sablonnerie

◉ Modern, Traditional International

Seasonal French-influenced cooking in a car-free zone

☎ 01481 832061
Little Sark GY9 0SD
e-mail: lasablonnerie@cwgsy.net
web: www.lasablonnerie.com
dir: On southern part of island. Horse & carriage transport to hotel

It's as well to be prepared for the fact that there is no motor traffic on Sark, so once you alight from the ferry, you have the option of hiring a bicycle, or - more stylishly - getting into a horse-drawn carriage. Whatever your method of locomotion, the journey to Elizabeth Perrée's white-fronted, 16th-century farmhouse hotel is worth the effort. Log fires and comfy sofas set the welcoming tone, and the oak-beamed dining room opens out to the garden to catch the summer sun. French-influenced seasonal dishes are the order of the day, including monkfish and salmon terrine with vegetable brunoise and roasted yellow pepper dressing, caramelised Barbary duck breast with Sarladaise potatoes in green peppercorn and sage jus, and banana and rum Tatin with vanilla and sultana parfait.

Chef Martin Cross **Owner** Elizabeth Perrée **Times** 12-2.30/7-9.30 Closed mid Oct-Etr **Prices** Fixed L 2 course £24.50, Fixed D 3 course £32.50, Starter £9.80, Main £16.50, Dessert £8.80, Service added 10% **Wines** 31 bottles over £20, 38 bottles under £20, 6 by glass **Notes** Sunday L, Vegetarian available **Seats** 39 **Children** Portions, Menu

"With all food made in-house you can experience an exceptional Isle of Man Restaurant utilising the best local and regional produce and ingredients."

JAR

not JUST ANOTHER RESTAURANT

01624 663553 | www.jar.co.im

ADMIRAL HOTEL Loch Promenade Douglas Isle of Man IM1 2LX

ISLE OF MAN

DOUGLAS   Map 24 SC37

Admiral House Hotel

◉◉ Modern **NEW**

Upmarket dining in grand Victorian hotel

☎ 01624 663553 & 629551
12 Loch Promenade IM1 2LX
e-mail: jar@admiralhouse.com

Admiral House is a grand Victorian pile on Douglas promenade, smartly revamped for urban contemporary tastes, and a favourite destination for the town's movers and shakers. Start in the classy champagne and cocktail JAR bar - JAR being shorthand for Just Another

Restaurant, the tongue in cheek moniker of the main dining area, which should really be preceded by the words 'much more than'. The setting goes for a light and breezy de-cluttered look of pale wooden floors, easy-on-the-eye modern artwork and immaculate table settings on cream linen. The kitchen knows its business, cooking in an unfussy modern manner to produce well-presented dishes, starting with seared scallops teamed with cauliflower purée, pork spring roll and spiced oil, while flash-fried calves' liver comes with crisp black pudding, creamed potato and apple-scented jus. Dessert turns up a perfectly-crafted pear tarte Tatin with vanilla pod ice cream.

Admiral House Hotel

Chef Malcolm Bartolo **Owner** Branwell Ltd
Times 12-2/6-10 Closed 26-30 Dec, L Sat, D Sun
Prices Fixed L 2 course fr £25, Starter £8-£11.95, Main £17.50-£28.50, Dessert £5.95-£16, Service optional
Notes Tasting menu available, Sunday L, Vegetarian available, Dress restrictions, Smart casual
Children Portions **Parking** Free parking opposite

See advert on page 539

Sefton Hotel

◉◉ Modern European

Traditional dining and plenty of tip-top Manx produce

☎ 01624 645500
Harris Promenade IM1 2RW
e-mail: info@seftonhotel.co.im
dir: From sea terminal, hotel 1m along Promenade

You can't miss the Sefton on the seafront at Douglas, with its imposing white-painted Victorian façade. Once inside it's just as striking, particularly when it comes to the beautiful indoor water garden. The elegant public rooms are spacious and comfortable, while the fine-dining Gallery Restaurant has sea views and, as its name suggests, quite a collection of paintings on its golden walls. The kitchen makes everything in-house, and Isle of Man produce features heavily, as in a starter of cumin spiced Manx sea scallops with cauliflower purée, pancetta crisps and truffle salad, and main-course Manx four-bone rack of lamb with colcannon, wilted baby spinach, tomato and tarragon jus. Flambés at the table and old-school dishes like Chateaubriand for two are part of the appeal here, while the traditional theme continues at dessert stage with home-made ice creams in a brandy snap basket vying for your attention with the Manx, English and continental cheese selection complete with grapes, celery, home-made chutney and biscuits.

Times 6-10 Closed L all week

Scotland

Urquhart Castle, Loch Ness

Holiday Inn Aberdeen West

◉ Contemporary Italian **NEW**

Sound Italian cooking in Westhill

☎ 01224 270300
Westhill Dr, Westhill AB32 6TT
e-mail: marc.jones@hiaberdeenwest.co.uk
dir: On A944 in Westhill

Located in a dormitory town to the west of the city, the Holiday Inn offers an unexpectedly authentic Italian restaurant called Luigi's. The chef isn't called Luigi, but does know how to mix well-researched Italian dishes with local Scottish ingredients to create a style of straightforward, neatly presented food that has some undoubted high points. Tuscan-style soft-baked egg with cheese and pancetta, or mussels marinara, might start you off, and be followed by sea bream with gnocchi primavera in garlic cream, accurately timed king prawn tagliatelle with courgette strips, garlic and chilli, or hearty Tuscan meat stew with pork belly, Italian sausage and beans in herb-scented tomato sauce. Finish with tiramisù or sharply flavoured lemon tart.

Times 6.30-9.30 Closed Sun, L all week

Malmaison Aberdeen

◉ Modern British

Cool brasserie with theatre kitchen

☎ 01224 327370
49-53 Queens Rd AB15 4YP
e-mail: info.aberdeen@malmaison.com
dir: A90, 3rd exit onto Queens Rd at 3rd rdbt, hotel on right

The Granite City's outpost of the boutique Malmaison chain has all the buzz, bold colours and sensual textures that you expect from the brand; the industrial-chic interior certainly making a good first impression. Dark wood tables and funky modern tartans make for a sassy, cool setting in the cavernous, moodily-lit Brasserie restaurant; high stools overlook the centrepiece Josper grill, where a busy chorus of chefs turn out fuss-free modern dishes using top-notch Scottish produce. Slow-cooked leg of mutton, perhaps, simply served with pommes purée and black olive sauce, or from the Josper, 28-day aged rib-eye steak, and to finish, tiramisù or jam roly-poly. Great wines are a trademark and you get to walk through a glassed-in wine tunnel with the cellar visible through a glass floor.

Chef Stuart Thomson **Owner** Malmaison
Times 12-2.30/5.30-10.30 Closed D 25 Dec
Prices Starter £5.95-£9.95, Main £11.75-£48, Dessert £5-£5.50, Service added but optional 10%
Wines 161 bottles over £20, 7 bottles under £20, 16 by glass **Notes** Sunday L, Vegetarian available **Seats** 90, Pr/dining room 30 **Children** Portions, Menu **Parking** 50

Maryculter House Hotel

◉ Modern British

Contemporary Scottish dishes by the Dee

☎ 01224 732124
South Deeside Rd, Maryculter AB12 5GB
e-mail: info@maryculterhousehotel.com
dir: Off A90 to S of Aberdeen and onto B9077. Hotel is located 8m on right, 0.5m beyond Lower Deeside Caravan Park

Maryculter House, on the banks of the Dee, has its origins in the 13th century, when it had strong associations with the Knights Templar. The short but balanced dinner menu, served in the stone-walled Priory restaurant in the oldest part of the property, might kick off with a modish starter of foie gras with seared scallops served with rhubarb and lime compôte, chicory and chive salad and balsamic dressing. At main-course stage, well-considered sauces and accompaniments bring out the best of fine Scottish produce: a truffle jus for ballotine of guinea fowl and spinach with swede purée, braised roots and Savoy cabbage, and beetroot coulis for fillet of salmon with pea- and mint-crushed potatoes, pickled cucumber and caramelised shallots. End with dark chocolate and passionfruit brûlée.

Chef Martyn O'Donnell **Owner** James Gilbert **Times** 7-9 Closed L all week **Prices** Starter £5.95-£9, Main £15.95-£27.95, Dessert £6.25-£6.95, Service optional **Wines** 23 bottles over £20, 18 bottles under £20, 3 by glass **Notes** 8 course gourmet menu available Fri-Sun, Sunday L, Vegetarian available, Dress restrictions, Smart casual, no jeans or T-shirts, Civ Wed 225 **Seats** 40, Pr/dining room 18 **Children** Portions **Parking** 150

Mercure Aberdeen Ardoe House Hotel & Spa

◉ Modern European

19th-century hotel with 21st-century cooking

☎ 01224 860600
South Deeside Rd AB12 5YP
e-mail: h6626-dm@accor.com
dir: 4m W of city off B9077

This fine old greystone house does a fine impression of a castle - think soaring towers and grand gables - but it was built as a family home back in the 1870s. Three miles from the city centre and surrounded by 30 acres of grounds, these days it's a smart hotel with a spa and all mod-cons. The overall impression is one of traditional comfort, elegance and even a bit of old-world grandeur. Blair's Restaurant fits the bill with its hand-carved ceilings, tapestry-clad walls, and smartly laid tables. The menu treads a more modish path, going from Cullen skink in salad form or chicken, leek and Arran mustard terrine, to main-course slow-braised pork belly with sour apple purée, braised red cabbage and Vichy carrots.

Chef James Thomson **Owner** Accor
Times 12.30-3.30/6.30-9.30 **Prices** Food prices not confirmed for 2013. Please telephone for details

Wines 16 bottles over £20, 15 bottles under £20, 12 by glass **Notes** Sunday L, Vegetarian available, Civ Wed 400, Air con **Seats** 100, Pr/dining room 25 **Children** Portions, Menu **Parking** 90

Norwood Hall Hotel

◉ Modern British

Victorian mansion showcasing fine Scottish produce

☎ 01224 868951
Garthdee Rd, Cults AB15 9FX
e-mail: info@norwood-hall.co.uk
dir: Off A90, at 1st rdbt cross Bridge of Dee, left at rdbt onto Garthdee Rd (B&Q & Sainsburys on left) continue to hotel sign

Norwood Hall, built in 1881, is a magnificent mansion with the sort of grand interior - ornate fireplaces, an oak staircase, stained-glass windows - that makes the jaw drop. The restaurant is a grand wood-panelled room with tapestries, but the friendly and efficient staff ensure there's no stuffiness, and the menu, built around first-rate seasonal produce, is a list of approachable dishes. Hits have included a starter of Loch Snizort scallops topped with a soft herb crust on a bed of leek and potato ragoût in vermouth cream, and seared Shetland halibut fillet, flavourful and accurately timed, with baby vegetables and chive butter sauce. Carnivores could opt for a salad of roast quail, pickled beetroot and sweet potato, followed by a steak from the grill. All-comers can finish with rice pudding with warm apple compôte and toffee sauce.

Chef Johhny Urquhart **Owner** Monument Leisure **Times** 12-2.30/6.30-9.45 Closed L Mon-Fri **Prices** Fixed L 2 course £24-£45, Service included **Wines** 74 bottles over £20, 12 by glass **Notes** Vegetarian available, Dress restrictions, Smart casual, no T-shirts, Civ Wed 200 **Seats** 40, Pr/dining room 180 **Children** Portions **Parking** 140

The Silver Darling

◉◉ French, Seafood

Interesting ways with superbly fresh seafood

☎ 01224 576229
Pocra Quay, North Pier AB11 5DQ
e-mail: silverdarling@hotmail.co.uk
dir: At Aberdeen Harbour entrance

Reached by a spiral metal staircase, Silver Darling is on the first floor of a crenallated quayside building with floor-to-ceiling windows looking over the harbour out to sea. It gets its name from the local colloquialism for herring, and sure enough this is predominantly a seafood restaurant. The kitchen takes its inspiration from France but exhibits a flexible, contemporary approach to its output. 'Seafood Darling', for instance, is a mixture of fish and shellfish, served with samphire, saffron potatoes, rouille and croûtons, and steamed fillet of lemon sole is wrapped in lettuce and served with shellfish fricassée, seaweed risotto and saffron broth. Dishes can be multi-layered - a starter of pan-fried tiger prawns and bacon comes with curried courgette and fennel salpicon and piperade dressing, a main course of steamed turbot with cockle and seaweed risotto, spring onions, a poached oyster and watercress sauce - but supremely confident handling means results are nothing less than satisfying.

Chef Didier Dejean **Owner** Didier Dejean & Karen Murray **Times** 12-1.45/6.30-10 Closed Xmas-New Year, L Sat, D Sun **Prices** Fixed L 2 course fr £19.50, Starter £8.50-£13.50, Main £16.50-£28.50, Dessert £8.50-£11.50, Service added but optional 10% **Wines** 51 bottles over £20, 5 bottles under £20, 8 by glass **Notes** Vegetarian available **Seats** 50, Pr/dining room 8 **Children** Portions **Parking** On quayside

La Stella

🌸 Modern British **NEW** 🍷

Starry little restaurant in the Adelphi district

☎ 01224 211414 & 07912 666256
28 Adelphi AB11 5BL
e-mail: info@lastella.co.uk
dir: Off Union St

Chris and Lynsey Tonner opened in the Adelphi district of the city in the late 1990s, and have painstakingly established an elevated reputation for their appropriately starry-named restaurant. It's a small, smart place, decorated with framed pictures of the local area, the modishly monochrome look offset with shell-pink napkins. Chris works within defined parameters of simplicity and balance to create some dynamic, carefully crafted and popular dishes. A pairing of pressed ham and apple terrine with Waldorf salad in chive oil is an appealing opener, followed by a main course that matches king scallops with chorizo, pea purée and crisp-fried kale, dressed in white truffle oil. A bells-and-whistles presentation of rabbit offers no fewer than four treatments on one plate, including the rolled saddle and a pastry-clad Wellington. Fish specials and desserts are written up on the board, the latter perhaps including a flawlessly caramelised coffee crème brûlée with cappuccino foam and shortbread.

Chef Chris Tonner, Alan Will **Owner** Beetroot Restaurants Ltd **Times** 12-2.30/5-9.45 Closed 1st 2 wks Jan, Sun **Prices** Fixed L 2 course £9-£18, Fixed D 3 course £40, Service included, Groups min 6 service 10% **Wines** 12 bottles over £20, 6 bottles under £20, 4 by glass **Notes** Vegetarian available **Seats** 37 **Children** Portions **Parking** On street

---

ABERDEENSHIRE

BALLATER   Map 23 NO39

The Auld Kirk

🌸🌸 Traditional 🍷

Modernised Scottish cooking in a converted church

☎ 01339 755762
Braemar Rd AB35 5RQ
e-mail: info@theauldkirk.com
dir: From Braemar on A93, on the right before entering village

A deconsecrated Free Church with soaring spire in the heart of Royal Deeside makes a diverting setting for a contemporary restaurant with rooms. The original features have been treated as sacredly as seems proper, the reverent ambience of Gothic-arched windows and vaulted ceiling offset in the Spirit dining room by twinkling chandeliers and a series of detail studies of the Rolls-Royce Spirit of Ecstasy statuette. Modernist tweaking of venerable tradition also characterises the menus, which run from salmon crêpes in tarragon cream, to mains such as roasted Aberdeenshire beef rump with braised oxtail, served with rumbledethumps (a potato and cabbage dish) and shredded neep, or baked halibut with sautéed leeks and crushed carrots on cardamom-scented tomato concasse. The house pudding is a fruit crumble with shortbread crumb topping served with both custard and ice cream, or there may be chocolate ganache meringue with pear and plum in spiced white wine syrup.

Chef Tony Fuell **Owner** Tony Fuell & Peter Graydon **Times** 12-2/6.30-9 Closed Xmas, Mon, L Tue-Sat, D Sun **Prices** Fixed D 3 course £36.50, Service optional **Wines** 27 bottles over £20, 15 bottles under £20, 6 by glass **Notes** Sunday L, Vegetarian available, Civ Wed 34 **Seats** 26, Pr/dining room 20 **Children** Portions **Parking** 7

Darroch Learg Hotel

🌸🌸🌸 – *see page 544*

The Green Inn

🌸🌸🌸 – *see page 544*

Loch Kinord Hotel

🌸 Modern British 🍷

Imaginative Scottish-focused cooking in Royal Deeside

☎ 01339 885229
Ballater Rd, Dinnet AB34 5JY
e-mail: stay@lochkinord.com
web: www.lochkinord.com
dir: Between Aboyne & Ballater, on A93, in Dinnet

Whether you're drawn to Royal Deeside for rod-and-fly-related activities on the salmon fishing beats of the River Dee, or a malt-tasting tour of the Speyside distilleries, this sturdy family-run Victorian hotel is an ideal spot to finish the day with local bounty on the table. The restaurant is a snug, smartly-updated space of colourful fabrics and rugs on the pale wooden floor, which chimes in tune with the kitchen's French-inflected modern cooking. Great store is set by the provenance of raw materials, much of them local and, where possible, organic. Pan-fried hand-dived scallops with cauliflower purée and caper and apple dressing shows the style, while mains could be roast saddle and confit leg of local rabbit matched with spring cabbage, dauphinoise potato and prune essence. To conclude, there might be glazed lemon tart with clotted cream ice cream and raspberry coulis.

Owner Andrew & Jenny Cox **Times** 6.30-9 Closed L all week **Prices** Food prices not confirmed for 2013. Please telephone for details **Wines** 15 bottles over £20, 15 bottles under £20, 4 by glass **Notes** Vegetarian available, Civ Wed 70 **Seats** 30, Pr/dining room 30 **Children** Portions, Menu **Parking** 20

Darroch Learg Hotel

BALLATER   Map 23 NO39

Modern Scottish

Stunning Dee Valley views and modern Scottish cooking

☎ 01339 755443
56 Braemar Rd AB35 5UX
e-mail: enquiries@darrochlearg.co.uk
dir: On A93 at the W end of village

Family-run for over 40 years, it is easy to imagine why Darroch Learg inspires such loyalty - who would want to leave this fabulously tranquil place on a wooded hillside with views over Ballater and the Dee Valley? The Victorian mansion was built in 1888 and today it is dressed in true country-house style with rich upholstery, antique furniture and oak panelling. The restaurant opens out into a splendid conservatory serving up those views over the valley. The cooking is modern Scottish, with a good showing of ingredients from the region. Dinner kicks off with canapés in the charmingly traditional lounge before moving into the dining room, where an amuse-bouche such as celeriac and truffle soup topped with a puff pastry lid gets the ball rolling. Next up, perhaps a ravioli packed with excellent smoked haddock and partnered with parmesan velouté and sauce vierge, followed by main-course breast of Gressingham duck with black pudding, shallot jam, parsnip purée and olive sauce. Among desserts, lemon tart has just the right amount of zesty sharpness and excellent pastry, or go for Scottish cheeses with oatcakes and digestive biscuits. The Franks run the place with a good deal of charm and efficiency, leading from the front and putting everyone at ease. Finally, the wine list deserves a mention for its democratic fixed mark-up policy and the fact that the bins are extremely well chosen.

Chef John Jeremiah **Owner** The Franks family **Times** 12.30-2/7-9 Closed Xmas, last 3wks Jan, L Mon-Sat **Prices** Fixed L 3 course fr £24, Fixed D 3 course £45-£51, Service included **Wines** 130 bottles over £20, 4

by glass **Notes** Sunday L, Vegetarian available, Dress restrictions, Smart casual **Seats** 48 **Children** Portions, Menu **Parking** 15

The Green Inn

BALLATER   Map 23 NO39

British, French V

Precision cooking bursting with seasonal flavours in a family-run restaurant

☎ 01339 755701
9 Victoria Rd AB35 5QQ
e-mail: info@green-inn.com
web: www.green-inn.com
dir: In village centre

There's rather more grandeur in this old stone house on the church green than the word 'inn' suggests. In the hands of the O'Halloran family, with son Chris at the stoves, the erstwhile temperance hotel runs on a more joyous footing as a charming restaurant with rooms with a good deal of culinary ambition. The public areas are agreeably traditional, with the lived-in feel of a family home; in the lounge, there are squashy sofas to sink into, while the dining room is a cosseting, intimate space done out with scarlet walls hung with bright art, a green tartan carpet to remind you where you are, and blond wood seats at well-spaced linen-clad tables. Chris spent time training chez Raymond Blanc so you can expect finely-honed classical French techniques to underpin his modern ideas, and tip-top local materials at the core of the menu; he's ably assisted by mum, Evelyn, while paterfamilias Trevor orchestrates front-of-house service with confident charisma. Typical of the style is a terrine of guinea fowl, foie gras and smoked ham hock teamed with marinated beetroot, raisin purée, and white port syrup, while slow-braised Aberdeen Angus beef might star in a well-thought-out main course, with a supporting cast of spinach, smoked pommes purées, baby onions, wild mushrooms, foie gras, and red wine jus. Fish dishes might bring a hit of Mediterranean warmth to the table - perhaps wild sea bass with globe artichoke tortellini, carrots, pickling onions, and artichoke vinaigrette. Desserts continue in a similar contemporary vein: bittersweet chocolate cakes with cinnamon ice cream and cookies, for instance.

Chef Chris O'Halloran **Owner** Trevor & Evelyn O'Halloran **Times** 7-9 Closed 2 wks Nov, 2 wks Jan, Sun-Tue, L all week **Prices** Fixed D 3 course fr £42.50, Service optional **Wines** 62 bottles over £20, 1 bottle under £20, 7 by glass **Notes** Vegetarian menu, Dress restrictions, Smart casual **Seats** 30, Pr/dining room 24 **Parking** On street & car park nearby

Save on Hotels. Book at **theAA.com/hotel**

ABERDEENSHIRE 545 | SCOTLAND

BALMEDIE
Map 23 NJ91

Cock & Bull

@ Modern Scottish 🍴

Big flavours at a distinctive country inn

☎ 01358 743249
Ellon Rd, Blairton AB23 8XY
e-mail: info@thecockandbull.co.uk
web: www.thecockandbull.co.uk
dir: 6m N of Aberdeen on A90

A 19th-century coaching inn in a lovely spot close to the coast, the Cock & Bull continues to seduce visitors with its infectiously cosy ambience: nooks, wooden beams and log fire in the lounge, a chic contemporary restaurant hung with artwork by local artists (for sale, if something catches your eye), and a conservatory. The kitchen sets about its work with a serious approach, sourcing its materials locally, and bringing them together in honest, unpretentious, big-hearted dishes along the lines of a tartlet of mushrooms, leeks and Isle of Mull blue cheese with a pine nut and porcini dressing, which could lead on to confit belly of local pork with prune and Armagnac purée, apple and black pudding bonbons and rich jus, or pan-roasted halibut with pommes dauphine, Savoy cabbage and pancetta cream.

Chef Michael Middleton **Owner** Rodger Morrison
Times 10.30-late Closed 26 Dec, 2 Jan **Prices** Starter £4.75-£12.95, Main £10.95-£18.25, Dessert £4.95-£8.50, Service optional **Wines** 13 bottles over £20, 15 bottles under £20, 7 by glass **Notes** Vegetarian available **Seats** 80, Pr/dining room 30 **Children** Portions, Menu

---

BANCHORY
Map 23 NO69

Raemoir House Hotel

@@ Modern, Traditional British **NEW** 🍴

Refined country-house cooking in a Georgian mansion

☎ 01330 824884
Raemoir AB31 4ED
e-mail: hotel@raemoir.com
dir: A93 to Banchory then A980, hotel at x-rds after 2.5m

Handy for Royal Deeside and the Scotch whisky and castle trails, but only half-an-hour's drive from Aberdeen, Raemoir House is a stone-built, early Georgian mansion that's full of character. There's no point in advising you not to miss the 96lb mounted fish above the bar - you can't - and the refurbishment undertaken by the present owners has created a series of comfortable, colourful rooms, among which in pride of place is the velvet-walled dining room, an oval former ballroom hung about with Victorian family portraits and gilt-framed mirrors. The traditional approach results in a fixed-price menu that deals in a gently modernised style of country-house cooking. Expect to start with the likes of goose and chicken liver parfait with brioche, or pigeon breast with black pudding and caramelised onions in juniper jus, before pausing with a bowl of soup, such as pea and smoked ham. A fish option for main might well be pollock served with polenta and wilted greens in a curried mussel velouté, but many will find it hard to resist the generous serving of Scottish beef - roast sirloin and braised featherblade with horseradish mash and woodland mushrooms in Merlot. Scots cheeses are a good bet to finish, but the sweet of tooth will be well rewarded by a slice of sumptuous treacle tart, served with caramel ice cream and citrus syrup.

Chef David Littlewood, John Chomba **Owner** Neil & Julie Rae **Times** 12-2.30/5.30-9.30 **Prices** Food prices not confirmed for 2013. Please telephone for details **Wines** 74 bottles over £20, 5 bottles under £20, 12 by glass **Notes** Tasting menu available, Sunday L, Vegetarian available, Dress restrictions, smart casual, Civ Wed 70 **Seats** 40, Pr/dining room 18 **Children** Portions **Parking** 40

CRATHES
Map 23 NO79

The Milton Restaurant

@ Traditional British 🍴

Accomplished cooking at the gateway to Royal Deeside

☎ 01330 844566 & 844474
AB31 5QH
e-mail: jay@themilton.co.uk
web: www.themilton.co.uk
dir: On the A93, 15m W of Aberdeen, opposite Crathes Castle

Part of a complex of shops, studios and a steam rail museum, The Milton occupies one of a cluster of farm buildings, with a beamed vaulted ceiling, white walls dotted with pictures and tall-backed dining chairs covered in red or blue fabric. The menu kicks off with a list of 'classics' - dishes customers clearly can't live without - running from Cullen skink, through minute steak with chips, to vanilla crème brûlée. Otherwise there are more modern, peppier ideas such as duck rillette with orange compôte, then tender, crisp-skinned chicken breast on a potato pancake with a tasty sauce of mustard and café au lait. End with a trio of rhubarb: crumble, jelly and ice cream.

Chef Bob Miller **Owner** Neil Rae **Times** 9.30am-9.30pm Closed 25 Dec, 1 Jan, D Sun-Tue **Prices** Fixed L 2 course £12-£15, Starter £5-£8, Main £11-£21, Dessert £6-£8, Service optional **Wines** 14 bottles over £20, 17 bottles under £20, 11 by glass **Notes** Sunday L, Vegetarian available, Civ Wed 60 **Seats** 90, Pr/dining room 30 **Children** Portions **Parking** 70

ELLON
Map 23 NJ93

Eat on the Green

@@ Traditional British and Scottish **NEW**

Imaginative cooking opposite the village green

☎ 01651 842337
Udny Green AB41 7RS
e-mail: enquiries@eatonthegreen.co.uk
dir: A920 towards Udny Green/Ellon

The early 19th-century inn was built as a staging post for commercial traffic, overlooking what was once a livestock market, but is now the village green. Situated on the estate of the nearby privately owned castle, it's a smart and warmly welcoming venue with a light-filled restaurant served by a window as broad as an ear-to-ear grin. Classic dishes are built out of impeccable local produce and presented imaginatively. A chunk of baked sea bass dressed in coriander, lime and chilli, with potato salad, makes a bracing opener, and might be succeeded by herb-crusted loin of lamb with a faggot of the shank in brandy cream, alongside peas, broccoli and pancetta and a portion of dauphinoise. Rich sauces are favoured, as in the Chardonnay cream that comes with fried salmon, pommes purée and wilted greens, as well as (an inspired touch, this) small balls of fishcake. The dessert plate of hot chocolate fondant, Baileys pannacotta, passionfruit syllabub meringue sandwich and chocolate ice cream is the all-singing, all-dancing finale.

Chef Craig Wilson **Owner** Craig Wilson, Lindsay Wilson **Times** 12-2/6-9.30 Closed Mon-Tue, L Sat **Prices** Fixed L 2 course £21.95-£24.95, Fixed D 4 course £49-£52, Tasting menu £95-£125, Starter £5.95-£8.95, Main £15.95-£26.95, Dessert £5.95-£10, Service optional **Wines** 59 bottles over £20, 4 bottles under £20, 9 by glass **Notes** Tasting menu 12 course 48hr notice required, Sunday L, Vegetarian available, Civ Wed 70, Air con **Seats** 70, Pr/dining room 28 **Children** Portions **Parking** 7, On street

INVERURIE — Map 23 NJ72

Macdonald Pittodrie House

◉ Modern Scottish **NEW**

Period setting for well-sourced Scottish produce

☎ 0870 194 2111 & 01467 681744
Chapel of Garioch, Pitcaple AB51 5HS
e-mail: pittodrie@macdonald-hotels.co.uk
web: www.macdonald-hotels.com/pittodrie

Parts of this historic hotel, set in extensive grounds in the Aberdeenshire countryside, date back to the 15th century and the interior retains much of its period charm. You can peruse the menu by the real fire in the cosy lounge, or the bar, and then move on to the small, traditionally decorated restaurant, where oil paintings hang on the walls and white linen and candles make sure the tables look up to snuff. Service is suitably formal. Good quality ingredients are a feature of the menus, with suppliers proudly name-checked, and the kitchen's modern Scottish output shows good judgement when it comes to balancing flavours. Start with roast breast of partridge, apricot and pine nut croûte, with apple and Calvados cream, before moving on to roast rack of Scottish lamb with butternut squash and parsnip gratin, Savoy cabbage, kale mousse, and grain mustard jus, or a Scotch steak from the grill.

Times 12-2/7-9

OLDMELDRUM — Map 23 NJ82

Meldrum House Country Hotel & Golf Course

◉◉ Modern British ✱

Lively modern cooking in smart country-house hotel

☎ 01651 872294
AB51 0AE
e-mail: enquiries@meldrumhouse.co.uk
dir: 11m from Aberdeen on A947 (Aberdeen to Banff road)

This golfing hotel now straddles three buildings, the original low-slung property of mellow stone in the baronial style, dating from the 13th century. A sense of luxury pervades the place, with its open fires, high-backed easy chairs and deep sofas, oil paintings and objets, while in the restaurant candlelight is reflected in polished wooden tables under a lofty, intricately corniced ceiling. What's on offer depends on availability: locally-foraged mushrooms, say, in a main course of fillet of cod with oxtail to make a toothsome combination. The kitchen cuts out any gimmicks or frills so flavours are distinct; for example, a starter of rillette and seared loin of rabbit in a meaty jus, offset by sweet pea purée and carrots, while a salad of pickled mooli, apple and watercress is a good foil for glazed mackerel. A modern slant is given to the traditional when loin of local venison and liver is served with beetroot and rosemary gnocchi, and desserts make an impact in the form of a perfectly executed chocolate soufflé with a resonant chocolate sauce and zesty orange sorbet.

Chef David Bruce **Owner** Peter Walker **Times** 12-2/6.30-9 **Prices** Starter £6-£12, Main £12-£30, Dessert £7-£10, Service optional **Wines** 60 bottles over £20, 20 bottles under £20, 8 by glass **Notes** Vegetarian available, Dress restrictions, Smart casual, Civ Wed 150 **Seats** 40, Pr/dining room 16 **Children** Portions, Menu **Parking** 70

PETERHEAD — Map 23 NK14

Buchan Braes Hotel

◉ Modern European ✱

Local produce getting top billing

☎ 01779 871471
Boddam AB42 3AR
e-mail: info@buchanbraes.co.uk
dir: From Aberdeen take A90, follow Peterhead signs. 1st right in Stirling signed Boddam. 50mtrs, 1st right

When it opened in 2008, Buchan Braes quickly acquired a reputation for good food. You could say it has cooking in its roots, as it was once the officers' mess at RAF Buchan, although the building was totally remodelled before its relaunch as a smart and contemporary hotel and restaurant. The open-plan Grill Room has a buzzy vibe and a thoroughly modern look, with its eye-catching chandeliers and open-to-view kitchen. Local produce is the driving force here - meats come from the surrounding area, smoked fish courtesy of the ancient Ugie smokehouse; the individual boats supplying the fish even get a name-check. A seasonal focus means they seek out the best of what's to hand and deliver it on weekly-changing menus of unaffected modern Scottish ideas. Scallops baked with herbs in Silver Birch Moniack wine is a typically appealing starter, while mains could be poached fillet of lemon sole with Boddam crab risotto and Jerusalem artichoke velouté.

Chef Gary Christie, Paul McLean, Michael Watt **Owner** Kenneth Watt, Tony Jackson **Times** 11.45-2.30/6-9.30 **Prices** Food prices not confirmed for 2013. Please telephone for details **Wines** 16 bottles over £20, 16 bottles under £20, 7 by glass **Notes** Sunday L, Vegetarian available, Civ Wed 150 **Seats** 70, Pr/dining room 80 **Children** Portions, Menu **Parking** 100

STONEHAVEN — Map 23 NO88

Carron Art Deco Restaurant

◉ Modern British

Distinctive modern cooking in art deco surroundings

☎ 01569 760460
20 Cameron St AB39 2HS
e-mail: jacki@cleaverhotels.eclipse.co.uk
dir: From Aberdeen, right at town centre lights, 2nd left onto Ann St, right at road end, 3rd building on right

Built in 1937 as a venue for wedding tea dances, this bustling restaurant is a distinctive example of art-deco style. Original features were restored during refurbishment, including a notable mirror etched with a nude surrounded by silver mosaic tiles. The menus are a lively mix of the contemporary and traditional, boosted by a specials board focusing on local seafood: perhaps an indulgent main course of turbot layered with lobster in a citrusy white wine and cream sauce. Deep-fried battered beetroot, with chilli and mango mayonnaise, is a popular starter, while main courses run to pork fillet on a bed of braised red cabbage with apple and Calvados sauce. As this is Scotland, expect to finish with a cheesecake version of cranachan.

Chef Robert Cleaver **Owner** Robert Cleaver **Times** 12-2/6-9.30 Closed 24 Dec-10 Jan, Sun-Mon **Prices** Starter £4.35-£6.95, Main £11.95-£18.25, Dessert £5.95, Service optional **Wines** 7 bottles over £20, 18 bottles under £20, 4 by glass **Notes** Vegetarian available **Seats** 80, Pr/dining room 30 **Children** Portions, Menu **Parking** Town Square

The Tolbooth Restaurant

◉ Modern British

Speciality seafood restaurant overlooking the harbour

☎ 01569 762287
Old Pier, Stonehaven Harbour AB39 2JU
e-mail: enquiries@tolbooth-restaurant.co.uk
dir: 15m S of Aberdeen on A90, located in Stonehaven harbour

Steps up the side of the 400-year-old harbourside stone building (Stonehaven's oldest) lead up to the first-floor restaurant, with its open-plan layout, maritime décor and view over the quay. Seafood is the speciality, from mussels steamed with white wine, shallots and herbs to roast fillet of hake with a Thai-style dressing, accompanied by crab risotto and pak choi hearts. Locally-landed shellfish is a high point, seen in crab soup spiked with dill and sherry, pan-seared scallops, and lobster, lightly grilled with garlic and lemon butter served simply with new potatoes and green vegetables. A few meat and vegetarian dishes are offered - perhaps loin of venison with a port and bitter chocolate sauce - and a handful of desserts may include baked Alaska or treacle tart.

Chef Craig Somers **Owner** J Edward Abbott **Times** 12-4/6-12 Closed 1st 3wks Jan, Sun (Oct-Apr) & Mon **Prices** Fixed L 2 course £15.95, Starter £5.75-£10.95, Main £14.95-£24.95, Dessert £6.25-£7.95, Service optional, Groups min 10 service 10% **Wines** 24 bottles over £20, 8 bottles under £20, 6 by glass **Notes** Sun L May-Sep, Sunday L, Vegetarian available **Seats** 46 **Children** Portions **Parking** Public car park, 100 spaces

Save on Hotels. Book at **theAA.com/hotel**

ANGUS – ARGYLL & BUTE 547 **SCOTLAND**

ANGUS

CARNOUSTIE   Map 21 NO53

Carnoustie Golf Hotel & Spa

British

Fine dining and premium golf course views

☎ 01241 411999
The Links DD7 7JE
e-mail: reservations.carnoustie@ohiml.com
dir: From A92 exit at Upper Victoria junct, follow signs for town centre, then signs for golf course

With fine views across the famous Carnoustie golf links - home to the 136th British Open - the setting of the Dalhousie Restaurant is any golf-lover's dream. The Dalhousie is the only dining option within the modern Carnoustie Golf Hotel, and it's the place to head to for no-nonsense, cooking based on mostly local produce. Start, perhaps, with in-house cured Scottish salmon with horseradish ice cream and beetroot crisp, or crayfish and Orkney crab ravioli with pak choi and beurre blanc. Scottish beef medallions with wild mushroom duxelle, pommes Anna and Madeira, or rock turbot with crab mash, wilted greens and lemon butter sauce might feature among main courses, with dark chocolate torte with popping candy and blackcurrant sorbet for pud.

Times 7-9.30 Closed L all week

INVERKEILOR   Map 23 NO64

Gordon's

❀❀❀ – see below

ARGYLL & BUTE

ARDUAINE   Map 20 NM71

Loch Melfort Hotel

❀❀ Modern British

Culinary panache and wide sea views

☎ 01852 200233
PA34 4XG
e-mail: reception@lochmelfort.co.uk
dir: On A816, midway between Oban & Lochgilphead

The white-painted hotel, in stark contrast to the greenery around it, is in a magnificent position on the shore of Asknish Bay, with views over the loch to the islands of Shuna, Scarba and distant Jura - an outlook shared by the restaurant. Perhaps surprisingly, the kitchen places as much emphasis on meat as on seafood, with most produce, including organic vegetables, sourced from within the county. Classic treatments make the most of ingredients - scallops meunière, langoustines with lemon aïoli, for example - with a contemporary spin given to others - carpaccio of Barbreck beef, fig confiture,

reggiano parmesan and truffle brioche, followed by roast halibut fillet in beurre blanc with crispy ox tongue, squash purée, pak choi, and potato croquettes. Steaks, with a choice of sauces, or lobster, with garlic and parsley butter, are alternatives to the likes of roast loin of venison with bitter chocolate jus. A lot of workmanship goes into puddings like caramelised banana bavarois with Baileys ice cream, whisky-infused custard and a florentine.

Chef David Bell **Owner** Calum & Rachel Ross **Times** 7-9 Closed mid 2 wks Jan, L all week, D Tue-Wed (Nov-Mar) **Prices** Fixed D 4 course £36.95, Starter £7.50-£10.50, Main £19.95-£21.95, Dessert £6.25-£8.95, Service optional **Wines** 25 bottles over £20, 40 bottles under £20, 8 by glass **Notes** Vegetarian available, Dress restrictions, Smart casual, no jeans, Civ Wed 100 **Seats** 60, Pr/dining room 14 **Children** Portions, Menu **Parking** 65

ERISKA   Map 20 NM94

Isle of Eriska

❀❀❀ – see page 548

KILCHRENAN   Map 20 NN02

The Ardanaiseig Hotel

❀❀❀ – see page 549

Gordon's

INVERKEILOR   Map 23 NO64

Modern British

Outstanding cooking in a tiny village

☎ 01241 830364
Main St DD11 5RN
e-mail: gordonsrest@aol.com
dir: From A92 exit at signs for Inverkeilor (between Arbroath & Montrose)

A Victorian house in a tiny village is the location of this small, family-run restaurant. It may look homely enough on the outside, but there's some seriously dynamic cooking going on within. With its beamed ceilings, rugs on the wooden floor, heraldic fabrics and wood-burning stove, it's a suitably smart and atmospheric setting for what follows. And what follows is seasonal local produce of exceptional quality cooked imaginatively to bring out

the natural flavours. Two cuts of the same meat can be used in main courses, adding a further dimension of flavour and texture, so roast Gressingham duck breast is served with confit leg and accompanied by glazed apples, celeriac remoulade and a sauce of honey and black pepper. Combinations are judiciously considered, resulting in well-balanced, clearly defined flavours, as in a starter of mosaic of Loch Duart salmon and dill with a smooth and gentle citrus dressing and apple remoulade, and a main course of pan-fried hake fillet with sauce vierge, a courgette beignet, carrot tagliatelle, and lobster cannelloni. Starters are followed by an intermediate course - perhaps artichoke velouté with smoked bacon and truffle cream - incidentals like breads and canapés are exemplary, and desserts are memorable: perhaps hot Valrhona chocolate pudding with a centre of liquid Drambuie served with orange salad and honeycomb ice cream.

Chef Gordon Watson, Garry Watson **Owner** Gordon & Maria Watson **Times** 12-1.45/7-9 Closed 2 wks Jan, Mon, L Sat, D Sun (in Winter) **Prices** Fixed L 3 course £28, Fixed D 4 course £48, Service optional **Wines** 31 bottles over £20, 13 bottles under £20, 5 by glass **Notes** All bookings essential, Vegetarian available, Dress restrictions, Smart casual **Seats** 24, Pr/dining room 8 **Parking** 6

KILCHRENAN *continued*

Taychreggan Hotel

◉◉ Modern British

Inventive cooking with sublime loch views

☎ 01866 833211 & 833366
PA35 1HQ
e-mail: info@taychregganhotel.co.uk
dir: W from Crianlarich on A85 to Taynuilt, S for 7m on
B845 (single track) to Kilchrenan

Assuming you're not immune to a stunning location,
Taychreggan should make an impression: the 17th-
century low-slung, whitewashed hotel stands in glorious
isolation on a peninsula jutting into Loch Awe, framed by
timeless Highland landscapes - scenery that hasn't
changed since herders swam their cattle across to stay
here when the place was a lowly drovers' inn. A wall of
floor-to-ceiling large arched windows makes sure
everyone gets that view in the restaurant, while the
kitchen delivers the goods with its creative modern fusion
of Scottish and French influences. Much care goes into
the sourcing of ingredients in five-course set dinner
menus, which might begin with a very with-it 14-minute-
cooked duck egg partnered by compressed turnip, brown
bread tart and smoked salmon, then progress via a
Scottish cider vinegar 'soup' with apples, Oban prawns
and oyster, to a main event involving beef with oatmeal,
bacon, baked potato purée and pickled egg whites.
Scottish cheeses are served French-style before dessert,

which could offer sweet pear with iced milk, toast and
honey cream.

Times 7-8.45 Closed 3 Jan-9 Feb

LOCHGILPHEAD　　　　**Map 20 NR88**

Cairnbaan Hotel

◉ British, European

Canal views and local ingredients

☎ 01546 603668
Crinan Canal, Cairnbaan PA31 8SJ
e-mail: info@cairnbaan.com
web: www.cairnbaan.com
dir: From Lochgilphead 2m N to Cairnbaan on A83, hotel
1st on left

At the halfway point of the beautiful nine-mile stretch of
the Crinan Canal connecting Loch Fyne to the Sound Of

Jura, the Cairnbaan has been serving fishermen, walkers
and waterborne traffic since 1801. The restaurant makes
the most of the waterside views of 'Britain's most
beautiful short cut' with its split-level layout, while the
décor has a jaunty nautical edge with its polished brass
handrails, high-backed leather chairs and colourful
artworks, and the whole operation is run with easygoing
charm. As you might hope, the straightforward modern
European menu has a strong line in local fish and
seafood - perhaps grilled sea bass with a Provençal-style
stew of fennel, tomato and black olives, or monkfish
wrapped in Parma ham and stuffed with rosemary pesto;
for fans of local meat, there could be a pie of local game
with chestnuts, mash and vegetables.

Times 12-2.30/6-9.30

Isle of Eriska

ERISKA　　　　**Map 20 NM94**

Modern British Ⅴ 🍷 🌿

Luxurious island retreat with class act in the kitchen

☎ 01631 720371
Benderloch, By Oban PA37 1SD
e-mail: office@eriska-hotel.co.uk
dir: Exit A85 at Connel, onto A828, follow for 4m, then
follow hotel signs from N of Benderloch

Crossing the small bridge onto the 300-acre island brings
a palpable sense of expectation, which is more than met
by the hotel's grand baronial appearance and the top-
drawer facilities on offer. There's a delicious blend of old
and new here, with plenty of period details and features
- lots of fabulous log fires for example - and furniture and
decoration that maintains the sense of grandeur and
occasion whilst showing contemporary good taste. The

restaurant is now under the auspices of Simon McKenzie
and he has hit the ground running. Dinner is served in
the dining room made up of a series of spaces including
a conservatory, each done out with fashionably neutral
tones, splashes of colour coming from creative lighting,
with tables dressed to impress. Simon's cooking matches
the mood of the place perfectly - refined and classy,
maintaining the integrity of the regional produce with a
finger on the pulse of contemporary culinary thinking.
Smoked haddock tortellini - full of rich, smoky flavour
- with fennel and truffle bouillon gets things off to a
flying start, before a first course such as rabbit and
langoustine terrine or cauliflower velouté with Isle of Mull
cheddar beignet. Main-course line-caught west coast
halibut is a superb piece of fish, served with watercress
from the island (in a sauce), braised onion and Parma
ham, and to finish, chocolate parfait comes with the
flavours of coriander (in an ice cream), passionfruit and
banana. Don't let the cheese trolley pass you by if you've

room, and the wine list is a serious piece of work, with an
excellent range by the glass and half bottle.

Chef Simon McKenzie **Owner** Mr Buchanan-Smith
Times 7.30-9 Closed Jan, L all week **Prices** Fixed D 4
course £47, Service optional **Wines** 236 bottles over £20,
60 bottles under £20, 10 by glass **Notes** Vegetarian menu
Seats 50, Pr/dining room 20 **Children** Portions, Menu
Parking 50

The Ardanaiseig Hotel

Modern British V

Wild foods and high comfort in a stunning lochside hotel

☎ 01866 833333
PA35 1HE
e-mail: info@ardanaiseig.com
web: www.ardanaiseig.com
dir: From A85 at Taynuilt onto B845 to Kilchrenan. Left in front of pub (road very narrow) signed 'Ardanaiseig Hotel' & 'No Through Road'. Continue for 3m

The house is a particularly fine example of (just pre-) Victorian architecture. Built by William Burn in aspirant Scottish baronial for a colonel of Clan Campbell, it's reached via seven miles of single-track road, on the shore of Loch Awe facing the peak of Ben Cruachan. The interiors have been sedulously preserved, and are both grandiose and easy on the eye, with enchanting views over the loch from the full-dress dining room. Gary Goldie believes strongly in a cuisine that begins with what is available in the glorious vicinity, from the kitchen garden outwards into the surrounding countryside, from whence come wild berries and garlic, rosehips and wild mushrooms in profusion, and from the waters of the loch. Daily-changing menus of deeply congenial dishes give evidence of the considered approach: a bowl of soup could be something as

seductive as velouté of asparagus with smoked trout and caviar Chantilly, while seafood receives the full works, perhaps pan-roasted John Dory with deep-fried scallop ravioli, purple carrot purée, pak choi and Sauternes sauce. Interesting meat cuts are always a strength, whether braised ox cheek with smoked tongue, mushrooms and watercress, or loin and braised cheek of pork with quince and Brussels sprouts. The subtle combining of flavours goes on into desserts such as a white chocolate and beetroot sandwich with blood orange sorbet, or terrine of russet apples with prune and honey cake and vanilla ice cream. Staff are fully conversant with the menus, and contribute to making Ardanaiseig the complete package.

Chef Gary Goldie **Owner** Bennie Gray
Times 12-2.30/7-11 **Prices** Fixed L 3 course £35, Tasting menu £50, Service optional **Wines** 12 by glass
Notes Tasting menu 6 course, Sunday L, Vegetarian menu, Dress restrictions, Smart casual, Civ Wed 40 **Seats** 38
Children Portions, Menu **Parking** 20

LUSS
Map 20 NS39

Colquhoun's

◉◉ Modern British

Idyllic Loch Lomond location for confident cooking

☎ 01436 860201
The Lodge on Loch Lomond G83 8PA
e-mail: res@loch-lomond.co.uk
web: www.loch-lomond.co.uk
dir: N of Glasgow on A82

It is remarkable but true that you can leave Glasgow behind and be sitting in this lodge on a pine-fringed beach on Loch Lomond in half an hour. The sense of remoteness is enhanced by dense pine forest screening out the cares of the daily grind, and the hotel is designed to revel in the uplifting location; best of all are the ringside views of the iconic lake as seen through a wall of full-length windows from Colquhoun's restaurant. Inside, there's a shipshape Scandi-style décor of pine walls and pillars, but when the climate lets you out onto the decked terrace for alfresco dining, the beachfront position turns into a little slice of heaven. The kitchen walks a line between serving simple comfort-oriented dishes - deep-fried haddock with hand-cut chips, pea purée and home-made tartare sauce, burgers or steaks - and getting more creative with the likes of pan-seared bream with lemon pommes dauphine, braised fennel, wilted greens, and olive and caper dressing. Finish with a straight-up vanilla crème brûlée or Scottish farmhouse cheeses.

Times 12-5/6-9.45

OBAN
Map 20 NM82

Coast

◉◉ Modern

Chic, high street eatery with classy cooking

☎ 01631 569900
104 George St PA34 5NT
e-mail: coastoban@yahoo.co.uk
web: www.coastoban.co.uk
dir: On main street in town centre

Coast retains the imposing original granite façade of the high street bank that it once was before its transformation into a sharp-looking contemporary restaurant. Soothing neutral shades, designer fabrics, abstract art and textures of wood and leather combine in a fashion-conscious décor that is a million miles from the fish-and-chips tone of much of Oban's centre. It all makes a perfect foil for the efforts of a kitchen that has its priorities spot-on, offering contemporary cooking based on super-fresh local fish and shellfish. Oban whisky-smoked salmon is a fine way to start, ahead of pan-fried halibut with crushed new potatoes, pork cheek ravioli, Mediterranean vegetables and olive dressing. If you're in the market for something sweet, hazelnut honeycomb vanilla cheesecake with berry sorbet should provide a satisfactory conclusion.

Chef Richard Fowler **Owner** Richard & Nicola Fowler
Times 12-2/5.30-9.30 Closed 25 Dec, 2 wks Jan, Sun (Nov-Mar), L Sun **Prices** Fixed L 2 course £12.95, Fixed D 3 course £15.95, Starter £4.50-£8.95, Main £13.50-£22.95, Dessert £6.25, Service optional, Groups min 8 service 10% **Wines** 19 bottles over £20, 22 bottles under £20, 5 by glass **Notes** Fixed D available early eve, Vegetarian available **Seats** 46 **Parking** On street

Manor House Hotel

◉ Scottish, European

Modern Scottish food overlooking Oban harbour

☎ 01631 562087
Gallanach Rd PA34 4LS
e-mail: info@manorhouseoban.com
web: www.manorhouseoban.com
dir: follow MacBrayne Ferries signs, pass ferry entrance for hotel on right

The house is a Georgian villa built for the Duke of Argyll during the reign of George III. With panoramic views over Oban harbour, the ground-floor dining room is an elegant space with dark green walls and original paintings on maritime themes. Knowledgeable staff contribute to the professionalism that imbues the place, and a restrained style of modern Scottish cooking is the order of the day. A warm roulade of corn-fed chicken and Stornoway black pudding with sun-dried tomato stuffing and tarragon cream is a gentle opener, and could be succeeded (after intervening soup and sorbet offerings) by well-timed grilled halibut on courgette risotto with tomato confit. Marmalade from the Isle of Kerrera, which you can see across the water, might be used to glaze a peppered duck breast, served with creamed leeks and fennel potatoes, and meals end happily with loose-textured orange crème brûlée, garnished with a pair of pistachio tuiles.

Chef Shaun Squire **Owner** Mr P L Crane
Times 12-2.30/6.45-8.45 Closed 25-26 Dec **Prices** Fixed L 3 course £28, Starter £9.50, Main £16-£22, Dessert £7.50, Service optional **Wines** 23 bottles over £20, 32 bottles under £20, 8 by glass **Notes** Fixed D 5 course £39, Sunday L, Vegetarian available, Dress restrictions, Smart casual, Civ Wed 30 **Seats** 34 **Children** Portions **Parking** 18

PORT APPIN
Map 20 NM94

Airds Hotel and Restaurant

◉◉◉ – see opposite

Save on Hotels. Book at theAA.com/hotel

ARGYLL & BUTE 551 SCOTLAND

The Pierhouse Hotel

@ Modern, International 🍷

Top-notch fish and seafood with stunning views

☎ 01631 730302 & 730622
PA38 4DE
e-mail: reservations@pierhousehotel.co.uk
dir: M8, A82 to Crianlarich & Fort William. At Ballachulish take A828 towards Oban. Turn right in Appin for Port Appin & Lismore Ferry

Hidden away in a quiet corner of Loch Linnhe where the little foot passenger ferry shuttles across to Lismore Island, and wild peaks crowd across the skyline, this relaxed brasserie-style restaurant is a fish and seafood specialist. And it couldn't be in a better place for taking delivery of the necessary raw materials: crabs and lobsters are kept in tip-top condition in creels off the jetty outside, day boats drop off fish at the door, oysters are hand-picked from the Lismore shellfish beds, and mussels and langoustines come from the loch's waters. There's only one thing to do with produce like that: keep it simple - and the kitchen accordingly sends out crabcakes with lime mayonnaise, classic seafood platters, and lobsters or langoustines in garlic butter. If you want to put the chefs through their paces, go for something like sea bass with pistachio and Sauternes sauce, tagliatelle, mushrooms and braised leek rösti, or go meaty with pan-fried venison with gratin dauphinoise, tempura kale, and a port and gooseberry reduction.

Chef Kristian Wilson **Owner** Nicholas & Nicolette Horne **Times** 12.30-2.30/6.30-9.30 Closed 25-26 Dec **Prices** Starter £4.95-£9.95, Main £15.95-£34.95, Dessert £4.95-£9.95, Groups min 10 service 15% **Wines** 10 bottles over £20, 21 bottles under £20, 5 by glass **Notes** Vegetarian available, Civ Wed 100 **Seats** 45, Pr/dining room 20 **Children** Portions, Menu **Parking** 25

STRACHUR	Map 20 NN00

Creggans Inn

@@ Modern British, French 🍷

Locally-sourced cooking on the shore of Loch Fyne

☎ 01369 860279
PA27 8BX
e-mail: info@creggans-inn.co.uk
dir: A82 from Glasgow, at Tarbet take A83 towards Cairndow, left onto A815 to Strachur Or by ferry from Gourock to Dunoon onto A815

Rather more handsome than the word 'inn' might suggest, Creggans is a smart yet homely whitewashed hotel and restaurant on the banks of Loch Fyne. This to-die-for location not only adds an extra level of well-being to proceedings for diners, but also comes in pretty handy for the kitchen's sourcing of spanking fresh fish and seafood, and game from the hills all around. Staff in black and white uniforms, and softly burbling classical music add a refined note to dinner, kicking off with hand-dived Loch Fyne scallops twinned with Stornoway black pudding and served with a sharp citrus butter sauce to cut through the richness. Main-course keeps the big flavours coming - roast loin of venison appears with gratin potatoes, pickled red cabbage, celeriac purée, earthy wild mushrooms and a sticky raspberry vinegar reduction. To conclude, it's showtime with a beautifully presented bitter chocolate tear drop with milk chocolate mousse and boozy griottine cherries.

Chef Gordon Smilie **Owner** The MacLellan family **Times** 7-9 Closed 25-26 Dec, L all week **Prices** Food prices not confirmed for 2013. Please telephone for details **Wines** 32 bottles over £20, 33 bottles under £20, 6 by glass **Notes** Vegetarian available, Dress restrictions, Smart casual, Civ Wed 80 **Seats** 35 **Children** Portions, Menu **Parking** 25

Airds Hotel and Restaurant

PORT APPIN	Map 20 NM94

Modern British V

Delightfully situated hotel with scintillating food

☎ 01631 730236
PA38 4DF
e-mail: airds@airds-hotel.com
dir: On A828 (Oban to Fort William road) follow signs for Port Appin. 2.5m, hotel on left

There is an ineffable beauty to Western Scotland and adjectives such as idyllic and spectacular roll off the tongue all too easily. And if you want to get away from it all, there simply is nowhere better. In a former life, Airds was a ferry inn serving the needs of the local farmers and livestock drovers, but today's incarnation of the 18th-century property is altogether more rarified. There are lovely lounges, spacious, traditionally decorated bedrooms (so you don't have to rush away), and a smart restaurant with wonderful Argyll views and cooking by Robert Macpherson that is both rooted in the landscape and placed among the higher peaks of Scottish contemporary cooking. First-rate regional ingredients play a starring role - the chef is indeed a Scotsman as his name might suggest - and acute technical ability and sound culinary judgement are hallmarks of the refined dishes. Baked Lanark Blue cheese soufflé with beetroot, pickled walnuts and garden leaves looks stunning on the plate and delivers a superb balance of flavours. Seafood is equally well handled, and with such top-notch stuff all around, you might find perfectly timed roasted Mallaig turbot served with lobster, black beluga lentils, carrot gel and chard among main courses. Pudding might bring forth apple tart with Armagnac custard and Agen prune ice cream (great skills on show again here), or that Armagnac and those prunes put to good effect in a soufflé. Canapés, pre-starters and pre-desserts all impress, and the wine list is equally on the money.

Chef Robert Macpherson **Owner** Mr & Mrs S McKivragan **Times** 12-1.45/7.30-9.30 **Prices** Tasting menu £70, Service optional **Wines** 225 bottles over £20, 10 bottles under £20, 12 by glass **Notes** Fixed D 5 course £53, Gourmet 7 course with wine £80, Sunday L, Vegetarian menu, Dress restrictions, Smart casual at D, no jeans/trainers/T-shirts **Seats** 32 **Children** Portions, Menu **Parking** 20

TARBERT LOCH FYNE — Map 20 NR86

Stonefield Castle Hotel

◉ Modern British ◷

Classic Scottish cooking in a Victorian castle

☎ 01880 820836
PA29 6YJ
e-mail: reservations.stonefieldcastle@ohiml.com
dir: From Arrochar follow signs for A83 through Inveraray & Lochgilphead, hotel on left 2m before Tarbert

Finely detailed down to the last crenallation, Stonefield is a hubristic piece of Victorian pastiche, a medieval-effect castle sitting high on the Kintyre peninsula. The décor inside matches the exterior grandiosity, and the views over the water from the wide-screen picture windows in the dining room are a rare old treat. The cooking keeps things relatively simple, opening with a serving of langoustines with shallot and caper hollandaise, and following up with beef in three guises - medallion, burger and mini-pie - served with cauliflower purée strongly spiked with Lanark Blue, all sauced with port, or lobster glazed in Arran mustard and Mull cheddar. Finish with apple, toffee and almond tart with apple syrup and cinnamon ice cream.

Chef Oscar Sinjorgo **Owner** Oxford Hotels & Inns **Times** 12-9 **Prices** Food prices not confirmed for 2013. Please telephone for details **Wines** 23 bottles over £20, 38 bottles under £20, 6 by glass **Notes** Sunday L, Vegetarian available, Dress restrictions, Smart casual, Civ Wed 120 **Seats** 120, Pr/dining room 40 **Children** Portions, Menu **Parking** 65

AYRSHIRE, EAST

SORN — Map 20 NS52

The Sorn Inn

◉◉ Modern British ◷

Contemporary-styled coaching inn with modern cuisine

☎ 01290 551305
35 Main St KA5 6HU
e-mail: craig@sorninn.com
dir: From A77 take A76 to Mauchline. Take B743, 4m to Sorn

This 18th-century coaching inn deep in the Ayrshire countryside may look pubby from the outside, but the unmistakable focus of the operation is food - a fact that the knife and fork logo displayed prominently next to the Sorn Inn's name makes clear. Inside, you're greeted by the smart contemporary look of a dining pub - chocolate-brown leather chairs and funky tartan carpets to remind you where you are. The kitchen sets great store by the provenance of the local produce that forms the bedrock of a reworked menu fusing classic bistro-style dishes with more modern ideas. Whether you prefer the pubby vibe of the Chop House or the chic fine-dining restaurant, expect to kick off with something like a fricassée of Shetland mussels, smoked haddock and leeks, finished with whisky and served with carrot pasta; mains take in everything from contemporary dishes such as roast wood pigeon teamed with millefeuille of Stornoway black pudding, and white beans with pancetta, to 36-day aged Scotch steaks from the grill.

Chef Craig Grant **Owner** The Grant Partnership **Times** 12-2.30/6-9 Closed 2 wks Jan, Mon **Prices** Fixed L 3 course £13.95-£16.95, Starter £4.25-£6.50, Main £9.95-£24.50, Dessert £4.50-£5.95, Service optional, Groups min 8 service 10% **Wines** 49 bottles over £20, 12 bottles under £20, 12 by glass **Notes** Sunday L, Vegetarian available **Seats** 42 **Children** Portions, Menu **Parking** 9

AYRSHIRE, NORTH

DALRY — Map 20 NS24

Braidwoods

◉◉ Modern Scottish

Creative cooking from a gifted husband-and-wife-team

☎ 01294 833544
Drumastle Mill Cottage KA24 4LN
e-mail: keithbraidwood@btconnect.com
dir: 1m from Dalry on Saltcoats road

In a small cottage in the middle of a field near Dalry, Braidwoods is a small, unpretentious restaurant, its two rooms split by a central fireplace, with beams in the low ceilings, close-set tables, an informal, relaxed atmosphere, and young and helpful staff. Dinner, of three or four courses, could open with a well-balanced dish of seared scallops on pea purée along with crispy chicken wings, or perhaps even more modish beetroot-cured gravad lax on beetroot and clementine salad with a potato cake. Main courses impress with their timing and presentation: melt-in-the-mouth roast best end of local lamb on wilted spinach, with a mound of cauliflower purée topped with confit neck fillet and a square of dauphinoise, all complemented by rosemary jus, or grilled turbot fillet crowned with tapenade served on herb risotto and a rich shellfish jus. Canapés make a great introduction to a meal, and puddings impress too, among them Valrhona truffle cake with prune and Armagnac ice cream.

Times 12-1.45/7-9 Closed 25-26 Dec, 1st 3 wks Jan, 1st 2 wks Sep, Mon, L Tue (Sun Etr-Sep), D Sun

AYRSHIRE, SOUTH

AYR — Map 20 NS32

Browne's @ Enterkine

◉◉ Modern British V ◷

Well-crafted contemporary cooking in an elegant 1930s country house

☎ 01292 520580
Enterkine Country House, Annbank KA6 5AL
e-mail: mail@enterkine.com
dir: 5m E of Ayr on B743

An avenue of mature trees leads to the door of Enterkine, a pristine art-deco mansion that is run with the relaxed intimacy of a small-scale family residence rather than the tweedy grandeur of a full-dress country house. The restaurant was renamed Browne's in recent years to go with its new contemporary look, and comes with the extra bonus of uplifting views over the Ayr Valley through vast picture windows. The kitchen takes a suitably contemporary line with its output, sending out well-sourced Scottish produce in dishes bursting with full-on flavours - an Arbroath smokie soufflé backed up by goats' cheese, chorizo and lobster bisque to start, then rump of Borders lamb with mashed potatoes and Toulouse sausage, Provençal vegetables, smoked anchovy and cubes of redcurrant jelly. A line-up of superb Scottish cheeses is one way to finish, or you might opt for something more complex such as Bramley apple crumble parfait with spiced apple pithivier, toffee sauce and shortbread.

Chef Paul Moffat **Owner** Mr Browne **Times** 12-2/7-9 **Prices** Fixed L 2 course fr £16.50, Service optional **Wines** 59 bottles over £20, 4 by glass **Notes** Tasting menu available, Sunday L, Vegetarian menu, Dress restrictions, Smart casual, Civ Wed 200 **Seats** 40, Pr/dining room 14 **Children** Portions, Menu **Parking** 20

Save on Hotels. Book at **theAA.com/hotel**

AYRSHIRE, SOUTH 553 SCOTLAND

Fairfield House Hotel

@@ Modern International

Great views and cooking with broad appeal

☎ 01292 267461
12 Fairfield Rd KA7 2AS
e-mail: reservations@fairfieldhotel.co.uk
web: www.fairfieldhotel.co.uk
dir: From A77 to Ayr South. Follow signs for town centre.
Left into Miller Rd. At lights turn left, then right into
Fairfield Rd

Built as the seaside home of a Glasgow tea merchant
who clearly had an eye for a rapturous view, this Victorian
mansion looks across to the Firth of Clyde and the Isle of
Arran. The owners have brought the old girl gently up to
date with a tasteful, neutral modern look without losing
any of the period charm inherent in its lofty plasterwork
ceilings. In Martin's Bar and Grill - the culinary heart of
the enterprise - you could keep things simple with
something from the grill - a steak, say - or go for Arran
ale-battered haddock and chunky chips, or trade up to
the Rosette menu which has its heart in fine Scottish
produce, as in a simply-cooked trio of scallops, squid and
Tarbet crab. Local game is always a good idea,
particularly when it happens to be Athol Estate venison
Wellington served with spiced red cabbage, parsnip mash
and Madeira sauce. It is all prepared in a positive,
confident style that delivers clear, well-judged flavours,
culminating in a zesty passionfruit baked Alaska with
passionfruit syrup and the textural contrast of praline
crisp.

Chef Liam Murphy **Owner** G Martin **Times** 11am-9.30pm
Prices Starter £4.50-£9.95, Main £9.50-£25.95, Dessert
£4.50-£6.95, Service optional **Wines** 34 bottles over £20,
16 bottles under £20, 6 by glass **Notes** Vegetarian
available, Civ Wed 150 **Seats** 80, Pr/dining room 12
Children Portions, Menu **Parking** 50

See advert below

The Western House Hotel

@@ Modern British

Modern Scottish cooking at Ayr racecourse

☎ 0870 055 5510
2 Craigie Rd KA8 0HA
e-mail: msimpson@ayr-racecourse.co.uk
dir: From Glasgow M77 then A77 towards Ayr. At Whitletts
rdbt take A719 towards town centre

The Ayr racecourse hotel extends over two buildings, a
main house and a courtyard section, which is where most
of the guest rooms are. Well-tended gardens and a patio
area make it a pleasant place on a summer's day in the
Lowlands, and the equestrian theme is given the
thorough airing you would expect in pictures of the
thoroughbred champions of yesteryear on the walls of the
Jockey Club restaurant. Here, the net is cast widely for
culinary influences from hither and yon, hauling in
smoked haddock and tiger prawn gratin with creamed
leeks and gruyère, a version of cassoulet with confit duck
leg, merguez, pancetta and white beans, and steamed
lemon sponge with cardamom anglaise and ginger ice
cream. Look to the grill for steaks of 28-day, dry-aged
prime Scottish beef from the Carrick Hills.

Times 12-2/7-9.30

BALLANTRAE   Map 20 NX08

Glenapp Castle

@@@@ – *see page 554*

TROON   Map 20 NS33

Lochgreen House Hotel

@@@ – *see page 555*

MacCallums of Troon

@ Seafood

Simple, fresh seafood on the harbourside

☎ 01292 319339
The Harbour KA10 6DH

Right on theme, the décor at this harbourside restaurant
delivers exposed brick walls covered in all things boat
and sea related, with unclothed tables perfect for the
business of eating freshly-landed seafood (from the quay
opposite) cooked in an unfussy manner as suits it best.
Start with grilled langoustines with garlic butter, move on
to seared scallops with Stornoway black pudding and a
lemon cream sauce, or fillet of halibut with baked
ratatouille, saffron potatoes and a fish fumet. Puddings
don't dare let the side down; how about a moist dark
chocolate torte paired with a refreshing crème fraîche
sorbet?

Chef Philip Burgess **Owner** John & James MacCallums
Times 12-2.30/6.30-9.30 Closed Xmas, New Year, Mon, D
Sun **Prices** Starter £3.95-£8.95, Main £9.95-£27.50,
Dessert £4.95-£6.95, Service optional, Groups min 12
service 10% **Wines** 9 bottles over £20, 17 bottles under
£20, 4 by glass **Notes** Sunday L **Seats** 43
Children Portions **Parking** 12

Glenapp Castle

Modern British **V** NOTABLE WINE LIST

Splendid Scottish castle with classy and creative cooking

☎ 01465 831212
KA26 0NZ
e-mail: info@glenappcastle.com
dir: S through Ballantrae, cross bridge over River Stinchar, 1st right, castle gates in 1m, use entry system

If you're wondering what to do with your crumbling country seat, take a leaf out of Graham and Fay Cowan's book and turn it into a glorious country-house hotel. Admittedly it took them around seven years, and cost a few bob, but the results are impressive. It's been up-and-running since 2000 and the old girl, built for a coal merchant back in 1870, has surely never looked so good. Admittedly, your own pile might not be able to compete with the location, which is rather special with views over the Irish Sea to Arran and the rock of Ailsa Craig, and it has more than its fair share of towers and turrets, too. And it's surrounded by 36 acres including manicured lawns, an azalea lake, woodland and walled vegetable gardens with restored greenhouses. Once over the threshold, all is in keeping with the grandeur of the building, with plenty of period details (the magnificent panelled entrance hall and staircase, for example) and elegant, traditional furniture raising the comfort factor still further. Oak panels are also a feature in the dining room, with its rich red tones, moody oil paintings and tables dressed for fine dining. The kitchen, headed up by Adam Stokes, lives up to the splendid setting, producing modern Scottish food of class and impact, built on fine regional produce and the fruits of the hotel's kitchen garden. Lunch is a four-course affair, with Scottish cheeses with white truffle honey, grape chutney and salty and sour crispbreads served before dessert in the French manner, whilst dinner is a six-course extravaganza with choices only at main course and dessert stages. An evening meal might begin with smoked mackerel velouté with a mackerel tartar and sorrel, followed by English asparagus if you're lucky enough to be there in season, served perhaps with lamb sweets, morels and Arran mustard vinaigrette. The fish course might be the kitchen's version of a fish pie, with the main course choice between Goosnargh duck (with radish, almonds and rhubarb) or Cairnhill Farm lamb (with gentleman's relish, purple sprouting broccoli and wild garlic). Those wonderful cheeses appear at dinner too, followed by a dessert such as rhubarb crumble soufflé with pink rhubarb sorbet. With delightful service headed up by the owners, and a wine list that is worth more than a moment of your time, Glenapp is a class act.

Chef Adam Stokes **Owner** Graham & Fay Cowan **Times** 12.30-2/7-10
Closed 3 Jan-25 Mar, Xmas **Prices** Fixed L 3 course £39.50, Service optional **Wines** 200 bottles over £20, 9 by glass **Notes** Fixed D 6 course £65, Gourmet D £65, Sunday L, Vegetarian menu, Civ Wed 40 **Seats** 34, Pr/dining room 20 **Children** Portions, Menu **Parking** 20

Lochgreen House Hotel

| TROON | Map 20 NS33 |

Modern Scottish

Modern Scottish cooking in a stunningly restored manor house

☎ 01292 313343
Monktonhill Rd, Southwood KA10 7EN
e-mail: lochgreen@costley-hotels.co.uk
web: www.costley-hotels.co.uk
dir: From A77 follow Prestwick Airport signs, take B749 to Troon, hotel on left, 1m from junct

Rubbing shoulders with the famous Royal Troon golf course, Lochgreen House is a grand seaside mansion in 30 acres of woodlands and immaculately-tended gardens overlooking the Ayrshire coastline. You don't need to have any interest in the action on the venerable links to stay here though, as the main draw is what is going on in the Tapestry restaurant, a sympathetic and expansive extension overlooking the gardens at the rear of the house; beneath a lofty beamed roof hung with vast crystal chandeliers are well-spaced tables dressed in their best whites, and plush tapestry-upholstered seats (the clue is in the name). Led by the owners' son, Andrew Costley, the kitchen team go about their work with fine attention to detail, delivering food that is full of freshness and flavour, backed by well-tuned technical skills and intelligently-composed ideas. All the bits and bobs, from Bloody Mary mousse and salmon

tartare canapés to a crab and carrot cannelloni amuse-bouche, and rhubarb crumble and custard pre-dessert are spot-on, and it is all underpinned by a flag-waving attachment to Scottish produce, whether it's a starter of hand-dived Scottish scallops with apple and ginger purée, and apple caramel, or main courses built on Ayrshire lamb - roast loin and braised leg, perhaps, accompanied by potato pressé, asparagus, broad beans and lamb jus - or medallions of local beef with pommes purée, buttered Savoy cabbage and glazed pearl onions. Clear flavours and textural contrasts continue through to desserts that tread the line between tradition and modern flair; these can be as classic as an apple tarte Tatin with vanilla ice cream and crème anglaise, or as contemporary as Earl Grey soufflé with a lemon 'sugar cube', granola biscuits and milk sorbet.

Chef Andrew Costley, Jordon Annabi **Owner** Mr W Costley **Times** 12-2/7-10 **Prices** Starter £8.95-£11.95, Main £19.95-£22.95, Dessert £6.95-£8.95, Service optional **Wines** 98 bottles over £20, 12 bottles under £20, 10 by glass **Notes** Fixed D 5 course £39.95, Sunday L, Vegetarian available, Dress restrictions, Smart casual, Civ Wed 140 **Seats** 80, Pr/dining room 40 **Children** Portions, Menu **Parking** 70

TROON *continued*

Troon Marine Hotel

✿✿ Modern British

Colourful cooking and fantastic coastal views

☎ 01292 314444

Crosbie Rd KA10 6HE

e-mail: marine@pumahotels.co.uk

dir: A77, A78, A79 onto B749. Hotel on left after golf course

The tripartite, split-level Fairways dining room at the Troon Marine enjoys fantastic views over the Firth of Clyde towards the Isle of Arran; the sunsets are amazing. Formally dressed tables and formally drilled service establish a civilised tone, with colourful artworks on the warm orange walls and a wine store that seems to invite exploration. Equally as colourful as the surroundings is a starter of beetroot-stained mackerel with red onion confit in orange and tomato dressing, seasoned with sesame oil and soy. A brace of pork servings - roast fillet and cider-braised belly - with a long smear of garlic and chive mash makes for an elegant main course, its creamy cider sauce adding to the dish, or there could be salmon with aubergine purée, king scallop and sesame-fried pak choi. The filling of a slice of dark chocolate tart is thickly luxurious, and is partnered with vanilla ice cream and a garnish of orange.

Times 7-9.30 Closed L all week

The James Miller Room

✿✿✿ — see below

Turnberry Resort, Scotland

✿✿ Traditional French 🍽

Classical dining at renowned coastal golf resort

☎ 01655 331000

Maidens Rd KA26 9LT

e-mail: turnberry@luxurycollection.com

dir: From Glasgow take A77, M77 S towards Stranraer, 2m past Kirkoswald, follow signs for A719/Turnberry. Hotel 500mtrs on right

The 1906 Restaurant of this upscale golfing resort is named after the year it opened, so the place has had plenty of time to polish its act to a high gloss. With the wild Ayrshire coast to explore, plus golf (of course) and a state of the art spa, there's plenty to keep you busy before slotting in the genteel custom of afternoon tea. There's no denying the splendour of the 1906 Restaurant, which is somewhat akin to dining inside a vast white wedding cake, and thus an entirely appropriate setting for the output of a kitchen that takes its spiritual inspiration from Escoffier's classics, in a luxury-laden repertoire of old-school classicism. You might as well stick with the theme and start with a torchon of foie gras marinated in

white port and Sauternes and served with poached pear and toasted brioche, then follow that with something from Escoffier's recipe book - perhaps halibut Trouvillaise, the fish pot-roasted with shrimp and mussel salpicon, or beef Diane flambéed with brandy and finished with cream. For more table-side theatre, finish with the indulgence of a Grand Marnier-flambéed crêpe Suzette. See separate entry for the James Miller Room which is also in the hotel.

Chef Justin Galea **Owner** Leisurecorp **Times** 6.30-10 Closed L all week **Prices** Starter £9-£14, Main £17-£34, Dessert £7-£10, Service optional **Wines** 320 bottles over £20, 16 by glass **Notes** Vegetarian available, Dress restrictions, Smart casual **Seats** 120, Pr/dining room 10 **Children** Portions, Menu **Parking** 200

The James Miller Room

Modern V 🏅 NOTABLE WINE LIST 🍽

Imaginative cooking in famous golfing hotel

☎ 01655 331000

Turnberry Resort, Scotland, Maidens Rd KA26 9LT

e-mail: turnberry@luxurycollection.com

dir: From Glasgow take A77/M77 S towards Stranraer, 2m past Kirkoswald, follow signs for A719/Turnberry. Hotel 500mtrs on right

Golf is usually foremost in guests' minds at this luxurious hotel on the fabulous Ayrshire coast, but gastronomes will also find the place worth going out of their way for. The world-famous Turnberry Resort hotel has a trick up its sleeve if you're after that extra touch of exclusivity: the small sanctuary set just off the main 1906 dining room (see separate entry), known as The James Miller Room.

The setting brings together the Edwardian grandeur of high ceilings, ornate plaster cornicing and a grand centrepiece fireplace with the contemporary style of curvy crimson chairs and dark wood, and as there are just 12 diners to cater for, the vibe is more romantic, staff can provide a knowledgeable and more attentive service, and the chef delivers a style of cuisine that is considerably more haute than can be achieved in the busy main dining room. For this select few, the kitchen has an open door policy: head chef Justin Galea is happy to invite you in for a close-up look at the action and to see how sustainably-sourced fish and a cornucopia of first-class materials are used to great effect. Sound of Kilbrannon scallops are matched with the textural interest of crumbed cauliflower and parsley, the subtle hint of garlic flowers and the kick of chilli. Next up, Orkney lamb is showcased in a dish comprising pink loin and crisp belly teamed with earthy artichoke, and rich lamb jus; elsewhere, fish fans might find a turbocharged partnership of pot roast halibut with girolles, bone marrow and pork scratching. The same

high-end technique closes the show with a splendid chocolate and passionfruit soufflé with vanilla ice cream. Presenting the impressive wine list on an iPad is a switched-on quirky detail that adds to the enjoyment.

Chef Justin Galea **Owner** Leisurecorp **Times** 7-9.30 Closed Sun-Mon **Prices** Fixed D 4 course fr £65, Service optional **Wines** 100+ bottles over £20, 26 by glass **Notes** Vegetarian menu, Dress restrictions, Smart casual **Seats** 14, Pr/dining room 10 **Parking** 200

Save on Hotels. Book at **theAA.com/hotel**

DUMFRIES & GALLOWAY 557 | SCOTLAND

DUMFRIES & GALLOWAY

ANNAN — Map 21 NY16

Del Amitri Restaurant

◎ Modern European ◎

Creative cooking in the Borders

☎ 01461 201999
95a High St DG12 6DJ
e-mail: enquiries@del-amitri.co.uk
web: www.del-amitri.co.uk
dir: Located above the Cafe Royal

This first-floor restaurant consists of a long, narrow room with a polished wooden floor, brown leather-look seats at clothed tables, spotlights on the ceiling, and prints of old Annan on the walls; all very charming it is too. The kitchen applies some modern European ideas to the classic traditions - and fine produce - of Scotland, turning out perhaps a tian of white Scottish crabmeal with caper and cucumber pickle, pea shoots and caviar, then a carefully made roulade of wood pigeon, black pudding mousse and ham, served with haggis-flavoured potato and thyme jus. Finnan haddock is served on potato purée with a soft egg and mustard sauce, and among desserts may be traditional rice pudding with apple and cranberry compôte.

Chef Martin Avey **Owner** Martin & Lisa Avey
Times 12-2/6-10 Closed Mon, L Tue-Sat, D Sun (Nov-May)
Prices Starter £4.60-£6.10, Main £12.50-£15.35, Dessert £4.95-£6.50, Service optional **Wines** 9 bottles over £20, 21 bottles under £20, 8 by glass **Notes** Cinema supper offer, Sunday L, Vegetarian available, Air con **Seats** 45 **Children** Portions **Parking** On street, car park

AUCHENCAIRN — Map 21 NX75

Balcary Bay Hotel

◎◎ Modern European

Modern country-house cooking on the Solway coast

☎ 01556 640217 & 640311
Shore Rd DG7 1QZ
e-mail: reservations@balcary-bay-hotel.co.uk
dir: on A711 between Dalbeattie & Kirkcudbright. In Auchencairn follow Balcary signs along shore road for 2m

Named for the beautiful bay whose waters lap on its doorstep, this snow-white hotel on the Solway coast sits in splendid isolation at the end of a single-track lane with uninterrupted views sweeping as far as the distant

Cumbrian peaks. The arty enclave of Kircudbright is nearby, and there is magnificent hiking to be had along the coastline, and when the day is done, the restaurant is ready with an accomplished repertoire of inviting modern European ideas built on the peerless produce of the Dumfries & Galloway region. The area's marine bounty is always at hand, perhaps in a starter of breaded langoustine tails with saffron linguine and sauce antiboise, followed by pan-fried hake fillet with vegetable cannelloni, roast salsify and herb foam. This is prime farming country too, so meatier ideas could be Galloway beef fillet layered between puff pastry with oxtail tongue and veal jus, or loin, braised cheek and belly of pork with pea purée and cider jus. End with dark chocolate marquise with cherry ice cream, or a spread of artisan Scottish cheeses with home-made chutney.

Times 12-2/6.45-7.30 Closed Dec-Jan

GATEHOUSE OF FLEET — Map 20 NX55

Cally Palace Hotel

◎ Traditional

Formal dining on the Solway coast

☎ 01557 814341
Cally Dr DG7 2DL
e-mail: info@callypalace.co.uk
web: www.callypalace.co.uk
dir: From A74(M) take A75, at Gatehouse take B727. Hotel on left

Although golf rules the roost in this Georgian country manor in 150 acres of parkland on the Solway coast, you don't need to have any interest at all in the game to have a great time here. There are hiking and biking trails criss-crossing the area, and every imaginable leisure activity for pampering or punishing yourself in readiness for dinner in the formal restaurant, where that starchy institution of jacket and tie for gentlemen still holds sway. A pianist tinkling away in the background adds a softer note to proceedings as a repertoire of gently-modernised country-house classics built on soundly-sourced Scottish produce gets under way with the likes of chicken, mozzarella and roast pepper terrine with pesto dressing. This might be followed by pan-fried pork fillet with Stornoway black pudding, Bramley apple purée, fondant potato, celeriac purée, and Calvados jus; awaiting at the end, there may be caramelised banana parfait with passionfruit and lime syrup and coconut tuile.

Times 12-1/6.45-9 Closed 3 Jan-early Feb

GRETNA — Map 21 NY36

Smiths at Gretna Green

◎◎ Modern British ◎

Sound modish cooking in smart, contemporary hotel

☎ 01461 337007
Gretna Green DG16 5EA
e-mail: info@smithsgretnagreen.com
dir: From M74 junct 22 follow signs to Old Blacksmith's Shop. Hotel opposite

Smiths brings a touch of modern-day swagger to the self-styled capital of runaway weddings. Next to the famous Old Blacksmith's Shop of old, it's a modern hotel done out in the boutique vogue, with its Chainmail Restaurant (aptly cordoned from the bar-lounge - and those numerous wedding parties - by a namesake curtain) - and comes suited and booted in cosmopolitan style. The kitchen admirably puts its faith in locally-sourced seasonal produce and takes a progressive spin on classical themes; wild halibut teamed with creamed potatoes, marsh samphire and confit beetroot, or perhaps stuffed rabbit leg with smoked ham linguini and peas. Puds keep up the interest, extending to an assiette of rhubarb (parfait, compôte and sorbet) or chocolate fondant (with lavender ice cream).

Chef Stephen Myers **Owner** Alasdair Houston **Times** 12-9.30 Closed 25 Dec **Prices** Fixed L 2 course £15.95-£22, Fixed D 3 course £19.95-£48.50, Starter £6.50-£9.50, Main £14.50-£32, Dessert £6.50-£8.50, Service optional **Notes** Sunday L, Vegetarian available, Civ Wed 150 **Seats** 60, Pr/dining room 18 **Children** Portions, Menu **Parking** 115

KIRKBEAN — Map 21 NX95

Cavens

◎ British, French

Locally-sourced food in a tranquil Galloway setting

☎ 01387 880234
DG2 8AA
e-mail: enquiries@cavens.com
dir: From Kirkbean, follow signs for Cavens

Tucked away in six acres of immaculately kept grounds close by Dumfries and the Galloway Forest Park, Cavens is a good spot to escape the real world for a while. The peaceful lounge features a baby grand and is done out in soothing chintz, while garden views offer a calming backdrop in the dining room. It is all run with old-school homely charm by chef-patron Angus Fordyce, who knows where to get his hands on the best local produce for his straightforward three-course dinners. Choosing from two or three options at each stage, you might begin with pan-fried scallops with lime and vermouth, then follow that with grilled Galloway beef sirloin with red onion and red wine marmalade, or grilled salmon with home-made dill tartare sauce. Finish with excellent regional cheeses from the Loch Arthur estate or a zesty lemon brûlée.

Times 7-8.30 Closed Dec-1 Mar, L all week

MOFFAT   Map 21 NT00

Annandale Arms Hotel

🏵 Modern Scottish 🕸

250-year-old inn serving well-cooked local produce

☎ 01683 220013

High St DG10 9HF

e-mail: reception@annandalearmshotel.co.uk

dir: M74 junct 15/A701. Hotel on west side of central square that forms High St

Still very much a pub and the hub of Moffat life for 250 years, this fine old inn draws loyal locals into the oak-panelled bar for tip-top real ales, decent malt whiskies, and the relaxing atmosphere. Food is also worth more than a passing glance, served at bare darkwood tables with imperial purple velvet seats in a good-looking contemporary venue. Regularly-changing menus make sound use of meat, game and fish sourced from north of the border and dishes are given a modern spin to keep things interesting. Typically, kick off with pan-fried pigeon breast on black pudding with blueberry sauce, then move on to roast monkfish wrapped in Parma ham with a tarragon and dill cream sauce, or venison loin with red wine jus. Finish with raspberry cranachan.

Chef Margaret Tweedie **Owner** Mr & Mrs Tweedie **Times** 12-2/6-8.45 Closed 25-26 Dec **Prices** Fixed D 3 course £30, Starter £3.95-£8.50, Main £10.50-£20, Dessert £4.50-£6.50, Service optional **Wines** 23 bottles over £20, 18 bottles under £20, 4 by glass **Notes** Vegetarian available **Seats** 30, Pr/dining room 50 **Children** Portions, Menu **Parking** 20

Brodies

🏵 Modern British V 🕸

Smart modish cooking in contemporary setting

☎ 01683 222870

Holm St DG10 9EB

e-mail: whatscooking@brodiesofmoffat.co.uk

web: www.brodiesofmoffat.co.uk

dir: M74 junct 15 towards Selkirk, take 2nd right turn

Natural light floods in during the day through its glass frontage, but this restaurant, just off the high street, serves up bright modern food day and night. There's a decidedly modish sheen to the room with its trendy neutral colour scheme, dark wood tables, with little goldfish bowl flower arrangements on the tables and decorative stencils on the walls. A large bar is just the

ticket for pre- or post-prandial drinks. Local ingredients from Dumfries & Galloway pop up in the likes of double-baked cheese soufflé made with mature Lockerbie cheddar, followed by trout and clam chowder with Parmentier potatoes and smoked Ayrshire bacon. There's a decent veggie selection too, including sweetcorn fritters with warm cannellini beans, spinach and tomato, and, for dessert, perhaps apple and custard galette with cinnamon ice cream.

Chef Russell Pearce **Owner** Russell & Danyella Pearce **Times** 10-11 Closed 25-26 Dec, D Wed (Oct-Mar) **Prices** Food prices not confirmed for 2013. Please telephone for details **Wines** 3 bottles over £20, 10 bottles under £20, 6 by glass **Notes** Early door menu available 5.30-7pm, Sunday L, Vegetarian menu **Seats** 40 **Children** Portions **Parking** On street

Hartfell House & The Limetree Restaurant

🏵 Modern British 🕸

Skilful cooking based on local ingredients

☎ 01683 220153

Hartfell Crescent DG10 9AL

e-mail: enquiries@hartfellhouse.co.uk

web: www.hartfellhouse.co.uk

dir: Off High St at war memorial onto Well St & Old Well Rd. Hartfell Crescent on right

The Limetree Restaurant operation in Victorian Hartfell House has a reputation that extends way beyond Moffat and the rolling Dumfriesshire hills. The setting remains true to the house's pedigree, an expansive, bright room with an oak floor, local artwork on the walls, high plasterwork ceilings and fancy chandeliers. The kitchen cooks with flair, sending out dishes that are a happy mix of old and new ideas, and big on local materials. A starter could be straightforward hot-smoked salmon with fresh beetroot and dill mustard sauce, while mains such as confit duck with Sarladaise potatoes, shredded sprouts stir-fried with lemon and spices, and orange and rosemary sauce demonstrate a lively mind in the kitchen. End with orange and Brazil nut torte with dark chocolate sauce and crème fraîche ice cream.

Chef Matt Seddon **Owner** Robert & Mhairi Ash **Times** 12.30-2.30/6.30-9 Closed Xmas, Mon, L Tue-Sat, D Sun **Prices** Fixed L 2 course £18.50, Fixed D 3 course £27.50, Service optional, Groups min 6 service 10% **Wines** 12 bottles over £20, 12 bottles under £20, 5 by glass **Notes** Sun L by arrangement, Vegetarian available **Seats** 26 **Children** Portions **Parking** 6

NEWTON STEWART   Map 20 NX46

Kirroughtree House

🏵🏵 Modern British

Historic Scottish mansion serving up fine Scottish produce

☎ 01671 402141

Minnigaff DG8 6AN

e-mail: info@kirroughtreehouse.co.uk

dir: From A75 take A712, entrance to hotel 300yds on left

This baronial Scottish country mansion on the edge of Galloway Forest Park comes with the ultimate hallmark of authenticity: the great bard Rabbie Burns stayed at the house many times in the late 18th century, and sat on the grand staircase to recite his poetry. Inside, it looks like little has changed since his last visit (in a good way): there are antiques and plush carpets, lofty corniced ceilings, and expanses of wood panelling, and a grand dining room attired in a suitably traditional and formal manner. The kitchen makes the most of splendid Scottish ingredients in its four-course dinner menus, kicking off with tried-and-tested ideas such as game terrine with spiced pear chutney, and progressing via soup (cream of sweet potato and lime, perhaps) to mains of Kirroughtree venison partnered with fondant potato, parsnip purée, roast beetroot and Grand Veneur sauce. You could go for a savoury finish with artisan Scottish cheeses, including Cairnsmore which is made just up the road in Sorbie, or head instead for the sweet comfort of a Baileys pannacotta with roast hazelnuts.

Chef Matthew McWhir **Owner** Mr D McMillan **Times** 12-1.30/7-9 Closed 2 Jan-mid Feb **Prices** Fixed D 4 course £35, Starter £3.50-£6.25, Main £12.75-£17.75, Dessert £3.50-£6.25, Service optional **Wines** 78 bottles over £20, 9 bottles under £20, 5 by glass **Notes** ALC L only, Sunday L, Vegetarian available, Dress restrictions, Smart casual **Seats** 45 **Parking** 50

PORTPATRICK   Map 20 NW95

Knockinaam Lodge

🏵🏵🏵 – *see opposite*

Save on Hotels. Book at theAA.com/hotel

DUMFRIES & GALLOWAY 559 SCOTLAND

SANQUHAR

Map 20 NS70

Blackaddie House Hotel

@@ Modern British

Traditional country-house hotel with engaging modern cooking

☎ 01659 50270

Blackaddie Rd DG4 6JJ

e-mail: ian@blackaddiehotel.co.uk

web: www.blackaddiehotel.co.uk

dir: 300 mtrs off A76 on north side of Sanquhar

It's only a short distance from the main road, but this honey-coloured stone house, once a manse, seems like light years away, set in its own grounds alongside the River Nith. The pint-sized restaurant has artwork by a local artist on its walls, and service is professional but unbuttoned and welcoming. The menu gives a choice of only four items per course, one vegetarian, allowing the kitchen to concentrate its efforts, and the terse descriptions are at odds with the workmanship behind each dish. Parmesan-crusted lamb terrine is served on a salad of baby leeks in a vividly flavoured herb and anchovy dressing, for instance, and may be followed by fillet of halibut poached in vanilla-infused olive oil, served on parmesan gnocchi, with shallots in red wine and pancetta vinaigrette. Dishes are properly thought out, and imaginative touches make flavours sing, as in a starter of grilled mackerel fillet with beetroot purée and goats' cheese in pesto, and in a main course of beef three ways including deep-fried braised shin. Rhubarb from the garden makes a good conclusion: tart, jelly, sorbet, and creamed with ginger.

Blackaddie House Hotel

Chef Ian McAndrew **Owner** Ian McAndrew **Times** 12-2/6.30-9 **Prices** Fixed L 2 course £20.50, Fixed D 3 course £26.50, Starter £5.50-£14.95, Main £16.60-£29.50, Dessert £10.50-£14.50, Service optional **Wines** 61 bottles over £20, 3 bottles under £20, 10 by glass **Notes** Gourmet tasting menu available, Sunday L, Vegetarian available, Civ Wed 25 **Seats** 20, Pr/dining room 20 **Children** Portions, Menu **Parking** 20

See advert on page 560

Knockinaam Lodge

PORTPATRICK

Map 20 NW95

Modern Scottish V ♦ NOTABLE WINE LIST

Well-judged, classically-based cooking in splendid Galloway isolation

☎ 01776 810471

DG9 9AD

e-mail: reservations@knockinaamlodge.com

dir: From A77, follow signs to Portpatrick, follow tourist signs to Knockinaam Lodge

If it's seclusion you're after, few places fit the bill quite like Knockinaam. The rugged Galloway coastline runs away to the horizon from this isolated Victorian hunting lodge in 30 acres of glorious gardens and neatly-trimmed lawns extending to its own pocket-sized private beach. The place is so cut off from the outside world in its own inlet that Eisenhower and Churchill met here in complete security in wartime, and the setting within is still redolent of an oak-panelled gentlemen's club in the well-stocked whisky bar. When you enter the restaurant - a classic country-house scene furnished with antique chairs at linen tables and swagged toile de jouy drapes - you need to reset your clock to Knockinaam's seductively leisurely pace. Dinner takes a four-course, set-menu format, and changes every day, so you can be sure that it is all built on the best the season's larder can offer. Long-serving chef Tony Pierce is key to the kitchen's output, cooking with the maturity to bring together flavours in well-judged harmony, and the confidence to know when to stop and leave well alone. An early spring dinner might begin with chicken and basil sausage with grilled black pudding, crisp pancetta, and a bell pepper and port reduction, then proceed via soup (celeriac, parsley and truffle, perhaps) to a grilled fillet of Luce bay turbot served with a potato crust, creamed spinach, green asparagus, and beetroot beurre noisette. After that, hot pistachio soufflé with double vanilla bean ice cream and chocolate sauce should hit the spot before you slink off for coffee and petits fours in the cosy lounge. Not to be out done by the kitchen, the cellar is stocked by an enthusiastic owner and runs to over 450 bins of seriously good, hand-picked bottles, plus a decent choice by the glass.

Chef Anthony Pierce **Owner** David & Sian Ibbotson **Times** 12.30-2/7-9 **Wines** 335 bottles over £20, 18 bottles under £20, 7 by glass **Notes** Fixed L 4 course £40, D 5 course £58, Sunday L, Vegetarian menu, Dress restrictions, No jeans, Civ Wed 36 **Seats** 32, Pr/dining room 18 **Children** Menu **Parking** 20

STRANRAER   Map 20 NX06

Corsewall Lighthouse Hotel

◉ Modern Scottish V

A unique location for modern Scottish cooking

☎ 01776 853220
Corsewall Point, Kirkcolm DG9 0QG
e-mail: info@lighthousehotel.co.uk
dir: Take A718 from Stranraer to Kirkcolm, then follow
B718 signposted Lighthouse

A long single-track drive leads to the rocky shore and this
lighthouse conversion, which has wonderful sea views
towards Arran and Ailsa Craig. The bedrooms and
restaurant are in what used to be the keeper's
accommodation and stores, the restaurant itself a small
and cosy room with bare wooden tables and a friendly,
relaxed atmosphere. The kitchen deploys Scotland's
larder and in general follows a conventional enough
route, producing starters of game terrine with chutney, or
home-smoked duck breast with orange salad and honey
and mustard dressing, then baked salmon fillet with
Pernod cream topped with Avruga caviar. But the
kitchen's equally at home with Thai-style cured salmon
with raita, following it with Cajun-style loin of lamb with
couscous.

Chef Andrew Downie **Owner** Gordon, Kay & Pamela Ward
Times 12-1.45/7-8.45 **Wines** 30 bottles over £20,
13 bottles under £20, 4 by glass **Notes** Fixed D 5 course
£35-£39.75, Vegetarian menu, Dress restrictions, Smart
casual **Seats** 28 **Children** Portions, Menu

DUNBARTONSHIRE, WEST

BALLOCH   Map 20 NS38

The Cameron Grill

◉ British

Classy grill in grand lochside hotel

☎ 01389 755565
Cameron House on Loch Lomond G83 8QZ
e-mail: reservations@cameronhouse.co.uk
dir: M8 (W) junct 30 for Erskine Bridge. A82 for
Crainlarich. 14m, at rdbt signed Luss, hotel on right

It's not all about steak at The Cameron Grill, but they are
truly exceptional. Take a 320g rib-eye (we're in metric
land here), from Angus-Limousin cattle bred at Cairnhill
Farm in Ayrshire, which is as fully-flavoured and tender
as can be. They're cooked on a Josper grill and the local
stuff is joined by American grain-fed USDA Creekstone
and Casterbridge from Devon. You could skip the red
meat and start with Loch Creran oysters and move onto
roasted Atlantic halibut if you wish. All this in a room
that bristles with club-like masculinity - rich, brown
leather chairs and banquettes, lots of burnished
darkwood, and a huge mural showing how clansmen
entertained back in the day. The hotel is also home to
Martin Wishart at Loch Lomond (see entry).

Times 5.30-9.30 Closed L all week

Martin Wishart at Loch Lomond

◉◉◉ – *see opposite*

CLYDEBANK   Map 20 NS47

Beardmore Hotel

◉ Modern British ☺

Modern and classic mix on the banks of the Clyde

☎ 0141 951 6000
Beardmore St G81 4SA
e-mail: info@beardmore.scot.nhs.uk
dir: M8 junct 19, follow signs for Clydeside Expressway to
Glasgow road, then A814 (Dumbarton road), then follow
Clydebank Business Park signs. Hotel on left

Right on the banks of the Clyde, the Beardmore is a large,
purpose-built modern hotel and conference centre with a
range of dining options, including a bar menu (with
outdoor piazza) and fine-dining restaurant. In the latter,
the modern Scottish cooking comes underpinned by a
classical French theme and shows sound commitment to
local produce, including sustainable fish landed by day-
boats. Pan-seared sea bass fillet, for instance, might be
served with boulangère potatoes, wilted spinach and a
tomato beurre blanc, or go for roast fillet of Gleniffer beef
(from Paisley) with curly kale, Arran mustard mash,
devilled mushroom and shallot jus. Desserts run to warm
plum and frangipane tart with sauce anglaise or spiced
pear pannacotta with pecan and redcurrant compôte.

Chef Iain Ramsay **Owner** NHS **Times** 6.30-10 Closed Sun,
L all week **Prices** Food prices not confirmed for 2013.
Please telephone for details **Wines** 18 bottles over £20,
12 bottles under £20, 12 by glass **Notes** Vegetarian
available, Civ Wed 120, Air con **Seats** 36, Pr/dining room
200 **Children** Menu **Parking** 300

CITY OF DUNDEE

DUNDEE   Map 21 NO43

The Landmark Hotel

Modern British

Contemporary setting for modish and trad food

☎ 01382 641122
Kingsway West DD2 5JT
e-mail: meetings@thelandmarkdundee.co.uk
dir: A90 at Landmark rdbt, west Dundee city centre

The original stone-built baronial mansion bristling with turrets makes an impressive sight, but the Landmark has spread its wings into modern extensions and been brought up to speed with a smart leisure club, spanking new bedrooms and a classy conservatory restaurant. The Garden Room looks into the hotel's lovely grounds and mature gardens from an upmarket setting with linen-swathed tables and moody lighting at dinner. The kitchen steers a crowd-pleasing course with its appealing menus of tried-and-trusted modern ideas. You could encounter turnip soup with haggis croquette, ahead of chargrilled venison loin teamed with braised red cabbage, carrot and parsnip purée, and thyme jus, fish could put in an appearance as a combo of roast monkfish wrapped in Parma ham, served with dauphinoise potato and rosemary jus. Ending it all, there might be iced hazelnut parfait with rhubarb coulis.

Chef Graham Riley **Owner** BDL Management
Times 12-2.30/6.30-9.30 Closed L Mon-Sat **Prices** Fixed L 2 course fr £14.95, Starter £5-£10, Main £12-£20, Dessert £6-£9.50, Service optional **Wines** 26 bottles over £20, 8 bottles under £20, 9 by glass **Notes** Fixed L & D on request only, Sunday L, Vegetarian available, Dress restrictions, Smart casual **Seats** 100, Pr/dining room 50 **Children** Portions, Menu **Parking** 150

CITY OF EDINBURGH

EDINBURGH   Map 21 NT27

Apex City Hotel

Modern

Modern brasserie cooking in a contemporary hotel

☎ 0845 365 0002 & 0131 243 3456
61 Grassmarket EH1 2HJ
e-mail: agua@apexhotels.co.uk
dir: into Lothian Rd at west end of Princes St, 1st left into King Stables Rd. Leads into Grassmarket

A contemporary four-star hotel in the Grassmarket district of the capital, the Apex City is an essay in modern styling. All hard-edged contours within, it has an up-to-the-minute canteen-style restaurant in Agua, where the unclothed tables and banquette seating are the setting for sharply defined, latter-day brasserie cooking. A tripartite terrine is comprised of hot-smoked, cured and poached salmon, dressed in capers and lemon. Mains feature good Scottish meats for the likes of slow-roast breast of lamb with Marag black pudding, pearl barley and an apricot and apple casserole, or there may be baked cod on saffron risotto with garlicky mussels and leek foam. Desserts aim to win over the sweet of tooth with tablet brûlée, hot Nutella fondant, or Malibu parfait and cranberry sorbet with mini-meringues.

Chef James McCann **Owner** Norman Springford
Times 12-2/4-9.45 Closed Xmas **Prices** Fixed L 2 course fr £10.95, Fixed D 3 course £19.95, Starter £5.50-£7.50, Main £15.50-£19.50, Dessert £5.95-£7.95, Service optional **Wines** 9 bottles over £20, 6 bottles under £20, 15 by glass **Notes** Pre-theatre menu available, Sunday L, Vegetarian available, Civ Wed 80 **Seats** 60, Pr/dining room 60 **Children** Menu **Parking** On street & NCP

Martin Wishart at Loch Lomond

BALLOCH   Map 20 NS38

Modern French V ⓘNOTABLE WINE LIST ✋

Refined, intelligent cooking on the shores of Loch Lomond

☎ 01389 722504
Cameron House on Loch Lomond G83 8QZ
e-mail: info@mwlochlomond.co.uk
dir: From A82, follow signs for Loch Lomond. Restaurant 1m after Stoneymullan rdbt on right

On the banks of Loch Lomond (truly as bonnie as they say), Cameron House is a five-star hotel with a good deal of Scottish baronial grandeur and, in the form of Martin Wishart at Loch Lomond, a restaurant run by one of the country's finest chefs (Mr W has bagged four Rosettes at his Leith flagship restaurant). With a delicious heather and tan colour scheme, the restaurant has an air of easy refinement and a charming service team to match, plus tables which are suitably formally dressed and laid with high quality silver and glassware. Wishart's style of cooking, created here by head chef Graeme Cheevers, blends French classical thinking with well-judged creative ideas, features supremely high quality ingredients (with a genuine Scottish flavour), and no flim-flam on the plate. And it all looks beautiful, too. Ballottine of foie gras could teach a textbook a thing or two: perfectly light and topped with salted Marcona almonds and a pear purée to allay any richness. Main-course wild sea bass displays equal technical virtuosity, wrapped as it is in crisp potato and served with outstandingly good roasted langoustines, leek royale and red wine sauce. For dessert, vanilla parfait and caramelised apples continues in the same vein, delivering clear and complementary flavours and textures. There's a tasting menu, plus a vegetarian version which might include a winter truffle risotto among its delights. The wine list - and wine service - is top drawer.

Chef Graeme Cheevers **Owner** Martin Wishart
Times 12-2.30/6.30-10 Closed 25-26 Dec, 1 Jan, Mon-Tue, L Wed-Fri **Prices** Fixed L 3 course £25, Fixed D 3 course £65, Tasting menu £65-£70, Service added but optional 10% **Wines** 190 bottles over £20, 12 by glass **Notes** ALC menu £65, Tasting menu 6 course, Sunday L, Vegetarian menu, Dress restrictions, Smart casual **Seats** 40 **Children** Portions **Parking** 150

EDINBURGH *continued*

Apex International Hotel

◎◎ Modern Scottish

Modern hotel with stunning views of the Castle

☎ 0845 365 0002
31-35 Grassmarket EH1 2HS
e-mail: heights@apexhotels.co.uk
dir: Into Lothian Rd at west end of Princes St, then 1st left into King Stables Rd, leads into Grassmarket

The full-drop windows that constitute one side of the fifth-floor Heights dining room at the Apex International frame stunning views of the Castle, theatrically illuminated on its mound after dark. Here, a fixed-price menu deals in modern European cooking using good Scottish ingredients in stimulating ways. Start perhaps with a two-tone mousse of red and yellow peppers, served with a polenta muffin and a pesto-ish basil and pine nut purée. That might lead on to sea bass and fennel with puréed artichoke and sweet cicely in a sauce of liquorice and red wine, or to braised Scottish beef cheeks with caramelised shallots, salsify crisps and barley. Finish fragrantly with lavender pannacotta, summer berries and sabayon gratin. Cheeses come with beetroot and apple chutney and home-made walnut and fruit bread.

Chef John Newton **Owner** Norman Springford **Times** 6-10 Closed Sun-Mon, Tue (Sep-Jul), Wed (Sep-May), L all week

Prices Fixed D 3 course £35, Service optional **Wines** 16 bottles over £20, 5 bottles under £20, 9 by glass **Notes** Vegetarian available, Civ Wed 100 **Seats** 120 **Children** Menu **Parking** 65

Café Royal

◎ Modern Scottish

Grandly opulent setting in the heart of the city

☎ 0131 556 1884
19 West Register St EH2 2AA
e-mail: info@caferoyal.org.uk
dir: Just off Princes St, close to Waverley Station

The Baroque extravaganza of the Café Royal is a delicious slice of belle époque Paris-meets-Edinburgh. Originally intended as a showroom for the latest fancy Victorian gas and sanitary appliances, it is a time warp space of splendid Doulton ceramic murals, panelled walls, chequerboard floor tiles, stained glass, and ornate plasterwork ceilings. The food, on the other hand, has evolved somewhat: these days the kitchen supports Scottish producers, and takes on board influences from Europe. In the magnificent bar are hand-pumped beers to wash down fresh oysters and haggis and whisky cream pie (served with chips, of course), while a revolving door leads into the restaurant, where tables are dressed in their best white linen and the menu trades up to the likes of smoked Scottish venison with blueberries and red

cabbage, steaks from the chargrill with Arran mustard butter, or a seafood platter for two. Keep things north of the border and finish with a raspberry cranachan.

Times 12-2.30/5-9.30 **Prices** Fixed L 2 course £18-£25, Fixed D 3 course £30-£40, Starter £4.80-£8.15, Main £10.20-£22.75, Dessert £4.40-£6.50, Service added but optional 10% **Wines** 4 bottles over £20, 14 bottles under £20, 8 by glass **Notes** Sunday L, Vegetarian available **Seats** 40 **Children** Portions

Castle Terrace Restaurant

◎◎◎ – *see below*

Channings Bar and Restaurant

◎ Modern British

Fine local produce in townhouse hotel

☎ 0131 274 7465
12-15 South Learmonth Gardens EH4 1EZ
e-mail: food@channings.co.uk
dir: From Princes St follow signs to Forth Bridge (A90), cross Dean Bridge, 4th right into South Learmonth Ave. Follow to bottom of hill and turn right

Channings is an informal, relaxed townhouse hotel carved out of four properties, in one of which Antarctic explorer Sir Ernest Shackleton once lived. It's a comfortable place,

---

Castle Terrace Restaurant

EDINBURGH   **Map 21 NT27**

Scottish, French **V** 🍷 NOTABLE WINE LIST

Refined, intelligent cooking near the castle

☎ 0131 229 1222
33-35 Castle Ter EH1 2EL
e-mail: info@castleterracerestaurant.com
dir: Close Edinburgh Castle, at the bottom of Lady Lawson St on Castle Terrace

French-trained chef-patron Dominic Jack spent years in stellar kitchens across the Channel perfecting his craft before coming home to Edinburgh to set up Castle Terrace in collaboration with his friend Tom Kitchin (see entry, The Kitchin). The two restaurants share a common

culinary direction, summed up by the 'from nature to plate' mantra printed on the carte. They also share a similar aesthetic in their approach to of-the-moment interior design, as the restaurant occupies a Georgian townhouse resplendent with chic contemporary Scottish tweeds and purple-toned fabrics matched with designer wallpapers in earthy hues, dark wood tables, dove-grey walls and an opulent golden ceiling. Since Castle Terrace opened its doors in 2010 it has shot straight into the top flight of Edinburgh's Premier League dining destinations thanks to Jack's elegant and precise cooking and a passion verging on obsession for seasonal Scottish ingredients. There's a clear inclination to impress with earthy ingredients - as in a starter of organic spelt risotto served with crispy ox tongue and veal heart confit, deep-fried flat parsley, dried chorizo and a rich oxtail consommé poured at the table. The game season produces saddle of roe deer from Saltoun Estate partnered with quince tarte Tatin, seared pumpkin, chestnut and pepper sauce, while those looking for the

fruits of the sea could take slow-cooked fillet of monkfish with salt-cod brandade, crisp spaghetti-style potato, and broad beans. It is all perfectly judged and delivered with high-level technical skills that ensure flavours are all maxed out and clearly identifiable, culminating in a dessert of Cox's apples which produces the fruit caramelised and jellied with yoghurt sorbet and apple soup. The cooking is done justice by an intelligently composed wine list, and there's a keenly priced set lunch menu to allow access on a budget.

Chef Dominic Jack **Owner** Dominic Jack **Times** 12-2/6.30-10 Closed Xmas, New Year (subject to change), Sun-Mon **Prices** Fixed L 3 course £24, Starter £11-£16, Main £24-£34, Dessert £7-£10, Service optional, Groups min 8 service 10% **Wines** 260+ bottles over £20, 3 bottles under £20, 17 by glass **Notes** Tasting menu 6 course, Vegetarian menu, Dress restrictions, Smart casual **Seats** 52, Pr/dining room 16 **Children** Portions **Parking** NCP, on street

with the looks and style of a country home, while the restaurant is decorated in dark shades, with soft lighting and candles adding to the atmosphere. A glance at the menu explains why: appealing modern dishes, with the kitchen clearly following the seasons. Pan-fried coley fillet with crushed potatoes, new season's asparagus and hollandaise is a fresh-tasting main course, preceded perhaps by glazed goats' cheese with orange and local beetroot salad. Winter might bring on melt-in-the-mouth braised shin of beef with a red wine reduction, mustard mash and glazed carrots, and among desserts might be caramelised rice pudding with a compôte of local strawberries.

Chef Karen Higgins **Owner** Rakesh Kapoor **Times** 12-10/6-10 Closed Mon, L Tue-Thu, D Sun **Prices** Food prices not confirmed for 2013. Please telephone for details **Wines** 22 bottles over £20, 10 bottles under £20, 7 by glass **Notes** Vegetarian available, Civ Wed 50 **Seats** 40, Pr/dining room 30 **Children** Portions, Menu **Parking** On street, free wknds

Chop Chop

◎ Chinese

The cuisine of north-eastern China in Haymarket

☎ 0131 221 1155
248 Morrison St, Haymarket EH3 8DT
e-mail: info@chop-chop.co.uk
dir: From Haymarket Station, restaurant 150 yds up Morrison St

The cuisine of Dongbei, China's north-eastern region, is the USP here, with the kitchen cooking domestic recipes to gourmet standards without resorting to MSG. Unclothed wooden tables with upholstered chairs give the place the air of a canteen, but staff are friendly and informative, explaining dishes to first-timers. Banquets are a good introduction, the rest of the menu given over to jiao zi (boiled dumplings) or guo tie (fried) with various fillings - beef and chilli, pork with prawn, with dipping sauces - plus lamb with cumin seeds, crisp fish balls in Chinese sauce, and various salads. Flavours are outstanding, cooking is spot on, and as these are Chinese-style tapas, order a selection, get stuck in and have fun - not least with sugar string apple, coated in piping-hot caramel with a dish of iced water for dunking, to set it immediately. A new outlet is now open in Leith (see entry).

Chef Yu Xu Wei **Owner** Jian Wang **Times** 12-2/5.30-10 **Prices** Fixed L 3 course £7.50, Starter £2.30-£5.50, Main £7.70-£10.50, Dessert £2.30-£6.50, Service added but optional 10%, Groups min 5 service 10% **Wines** 12 bottles under £20, 7 by glass **Notes** Unlimited banquet £19.50 (min 2 people), Sunday L, Vegetarian available, Air con **Seats** 60

Chop Chop Leith

◎ Chinese NEW

Chop Chop's tip-top cooking brought to Leith

☎ 0131 553 1818
76 Commercial St, Commercial Quay, Leith EH6 6LX
e-mail: info@chop-chop.co.uk
dir: From Ocean Terminal follow Commercial St for 400 yds

Opposite the Scottish Office in the heart of Leith, this is the younger sister of the original Chop Chop (see entry), with a more upmarket vibe: glass-topped metal tables, red-upholstered chairs, and Chinese fans and prints on the walls. The menus at both are identical, concentrating on the cuisine of Dongbei, and staff are as charming and helpful as they are at Morrison Street. Go for a banquet or order a selection of dishes and create your own beanfeast: prawn, vegetable and chicken boiled and fried dumplings zinging with flavour, tender strips of stir-fried chilli beef, noodles in a sweet-and-sour sauce with crisp battered shreds of tender chicken breast and mushrooms, and aubergine flash-fried with garlic and spring onions. Don't leave without trying the fruit dumplings with vanilla ice cream.

Chef Holl Zhen Hui **Owner** Jian Wang **Times** 12-2/6-10 Closed L Mon-Fri **Prices** Fixed L 3 course £7.50, Starter £2.30-£5.50, Main £7.70-£10.50, Dessert £2.30-£6.50, Service added but optional 10% **Wines** 12 bottles under £20, 7 by glass **Notes** Unlimited banquet £19.50 per person (min 2 people), Vegetarian available **Seats** Pr/dining room 10 **Parking** 50

Dungeon Restaurant

◎◎ Traditional European

Creative cuisine in a truly unique setting

☎ 01875 820153
Dalhousie Castle & Aqueous Spa, Bonnyrigg EH19 3JB
e-mail: info@dalhousiecastle.co.uk
dir: From A720 (Edinburgh bypass) take A7 south, turn right onto B704. Castle 0.5m on right

Dalhousie Castle is a pukka 13th-century fortress in acreages of wooded parkland on the banks of the River Esk, so you know you're in for something a bit special when you're heading for the Dungeon Restaurant. And the reality does not disappoint: the barrel-vaulted chamber comes with a full complement of romantic medieval candlelit vibes and enough weaponry - suits of armour, battleaxes and broadswords - to sort out the French all over again. Mentioning our cross-Channel cousins, the cooking here has its roots in French classicism, and is built on top-class ingredients with plenty of luxury factor. But the kitchen doesn't rely on the one-off setting and posh ingredients for its effect: a spirit of eclectic creativity reworks it all with a clever contemporary spin that might see wild garlic and cream cheese terrine matched with roast plum tomato jelly and Bloody Mary foam, ahead of lavender and honey-glazed pork fillet served with artichoke barigoule and onion textures. To

finish, consider date and walnut soufflé with coffee mocha sauce and honey madeleines.

Chef Francois Graud **Owner** Robert & Gina Parker **Times** 7-10 Closed L all week **Prices** Service optional **Wines** 100 bottles over £20, 23 bottles under £20, 15 by glass **Notes** Fixed D 5 course £45, Sunday L, Vegetarian available, Civ Wed 100 **Seats** 45, Pr/dining room 100 **Children** Portions **Parking** 150

La Favorita

◎ Modern Italian

Authentic pizzas and more

☎ 0131 554 2430 & 555 5564
325-331 Leith Walk EH6 8SA
e-mail: info@la-favorita.com
dir: On A900 from Edinburgh to South Leith

La Favorita is aptly named: it's a popular place, large and bustling, its lively atmosphere helped along by friendly staff. Pizzas from the wood-fired oven are the real McCoy, crisp and light, with a wide choice, from fiorentina, topped with tomato, mozzarella, rocket, parmesan, and slices of sirloin steak, to vegetarian versions. But it would be a mistake to ignore the rest of the carte and its collection of authentic modern Italian dishes. Arancini di riso alla siciliana - balls of rice stuffed with tomato sauce, mince and melting mozzarella - make an excellent starter, to be followed perhaps by pasta, or steamed sole fillet rolled around prawns and asparagus served on sweet pepper sauce with vegetable risotto. Finish in true Italian style with tiramisù or pannacotta.

Chef Japeck Splawski **Owner** Tony Crolla **Times** 12-11 Closed 25 Dec-1 Jan **Prices** Fixed L 2 course £7.25-£10.50, Fixed D 3 course £22-£27, Starter £3-£6.95, Main £7.25-£24.95, Dessert £2.50-£7, Service added but optional 10%, Groups min 10 service 10% **Wines** 15 bottles over £20, 25 bottles under £20, 7 by glass **Notes** Sunday L, Vegetarian available **Seats** 120, Pr/dining room 30 **Children** Portions, Menu **Parking** On street

EDINBURGH *continued*

La Garrigue

◉◉ French, Mediterranean ☆NOTABLE WINE LIST

Charming French bistro in the heart of Edinburgh

☎ 0131 557 3032
31 Jeffrey St EH1 1DH
e-mail: reservations@lagarrigue.co.uk
web: www.lagarrigue.co.uk
dir: Halfway along Royal Mile towards Holyrood Palace, turn left at lights into Jeffrey St

To paraphrase Rupert Brooke, this bustling bistro is a corner of Edinburgh's Old Town that will be forever France. Chef Jean-Michel Gauffre has brought the honest rustic cooking of his native Languedoc into a suitably contemporary rustic interior kitted out with delicious plain wooden tables and chairs hand-made by artist and woodcarver Tim Stead. There are no foams or jellies here, just straight down-the-line authentique French country dishes done properly. The menu is a joy to read - rabbit rillettes with herb and lentil salad, or fish soup with croûtons and rouille to start, and as Gauffre hails from the heartlands of cassoulet, dig into his version of the rich stew of pork, duck, Toulouse sausage and white beans, or go for a slow-cooked stew of beef cheeks in a Provençal sauce of red wine, tomatoes and olives, and finish with a lavender crème brûlée. Garrigue has clearly given Edinburgh's foodies a formula they like as the original Jeffrey St operation has spread its wings into branches in Leith and the New Town.

Chef Jean-Michel Gauffre **Owner** Jean-Michel Gauffre **Times** 12-3/6.30-10.30 Closed 26-27 Dec, 1-2 Jan **Prices** Fixed L 2 course fr £12.50, Fixed D 3 course fr £30, Starter £4.50-£7, Main £12.50-£18.50, Dessert £4.50-£6, Service added but optional 10% **Wines** 24 bottles over £20, 10 bottles under £20, 11 by glass **Notes** Sunday L, Vegetarian available **Seats** 48, Pr/dining room 11 **Children** Portions **Parking** On street, NCP

Hadrian's

◉ Modern Scottish

Classy brasserie in landmark hotel

☎ 0131 557 5000 & 557 2414
The Balmoral Hotel, 1 Princes St EH2 2EQ
e-mail: hadrians.balmoral@roccofortecollection.com
dir: Follow city centre signs. Hotel at E end of Princes St, adjacent to Waverley Station

The more informal dining option of the palatial landmark Balmoral Hotel (see entry for Number One) is a modish, art deco-styled brasserie venue that goes by the name of Hadrian's. Not to be outdone by its highfalutin sibling, it is quite a looker with its walnut floors and palette of violet and lime, while staff turned out smartly in classic long white aprons and black waistcoats add a suitably continental note for its crowd-pleasing menu of European-inflected dishes. Home-cured whisky and honey salmon with fennel salad and rye bread offers plenty of Scottish terroir, as do mains such as haggis, neeps and tatties with braised shallots and whisky cream, or that now classic pairing of seared West Coast scallops with pork belly and butternut squash purée. At the end, perhaps sticky ginger pudding with orange yoghurt ice cream and biscotti.

Times 12-2.30/6.30-10.30

Harvey Nichols Forth Floor Restaurant

◉ Modern, International ☆NOTABLE WINE LIST

City views and modern Scottish cooking

☎ 0131 524 8350
30-34 St Andrew Square EH2 2AD
e-mail: forthfloor.reservations@harveynichols.com
web: www.harveynichols.com
dir: Located on St Andrew Square at the east end of George Street, 2 min walk from Princes Street

Harvey Nic's has a habit of naming its classy restaurants after the floor on which they are found. In the case of the Edinburgh outpost, the name is not further evidence of a decline in national standards of literacy: from its open-plan perch on the store's top floor you get 360-degree views of the Edinburgh cityscape and, of course, the Forth. The kitchen sends out dishes as modish as the glossy clientele who like to take the weight off their Louboutin's after a hard day's shopping. The foodie paradise here comprises the adjacent food hall, brasserie and seafood bar as well as the restaurant, where an excellent chicken liver parfait with apple and pear chutney and toasted sourdough bread leads on to Toulouse sausage with warm potato salad, grain mustard and the contrasting crunch of onion rings. Rounding things off, there may be damson parfait with olive oil and thyme sablé.

Chef Stuart Muir **Owner** Harvey Nichols **Times** 12-3/6-10 Closed 25 Dec, 1 Jan, D Sun-Mon, 24 & 26 Dec, 2 Jan **Prices** Fixed L 2 course £20, Tasting menu £55-£90, Starter £8-£11.50, Main £18-£24, Dessert £8-£10, Service added but optional 10% **Wines** 300 bottles over £20, 2 bottles under £20, 12 by glass **Notes** Tasting menu 6 course (with wine £90), Market L Mon-Fri, Sunday L, Vegetarian available, Air con **Seats** 47, Pr/dining room 14 **Parking** 20

The Honours

◉◉ Modern French **NEW** ⦿

Classic French brasserie food Wishart style

☎ 0131 220 2513
58a North Castle St EH2 3LU
e-mail: info@thehonours.co.uk
dir: In city centre

Opened in 2011, here is the latest side project of Edinburgh's hot-shot chef Martin Wishart. In the heart of the New Town, it aims at the style of a classic French brasserie, a restaurant mode that has long enjoyed great purchase in the Scottish capital. It's split into a large bar area with comfortable seating for informal eating, with restaurant tables on the next level up. Service is impeccably practised and professional, and the kitchen's orientation is modern French food interpreted through quality Scots produce, with accurate, well-honed flavours and eye-catching presentation. Pork and duck rillettes are wonderfully earthy and savoury, accompanied by spiced prune chutney, cornichons and toasted hazelnuts for texture in a bravura starter. Alternatives take in crab Marie Rose, sea bream tartare, and portions of jamón Bellota. Main courses offer grilled steaks, ox cheeks bordelaise or lamb tagine, as well as beautifully expressive fish dishes like sautéed fillets of John Dory with leeks and mussels topped with an evanescent curry foam and sauced with Sauternes. A crème brûlée to finish is boosted with Kirsch and textured with marinated cherries.

Chef Paul Tamburrini **Owner** Martin Wishart **Times** 12-2.30/6-10 Closed Xmas, New Year, Sun-Mon **Prices** Fixed L 3 course £17.50, Fixed D 3 course £19.50, Starter £5.95-£16, Main £11.50-£30, Dessert £6.50-£7.95, Service optional, Groups min 6 service 10% **Wines** 49 bottles over £20, 3 bottles under £20, 19 by glass **Notes** Fixed D Tue-Fri 6-7pm, Vegetarian available **Seats** 65 **Children** Portions, Menu **Parking** On street

Hotel du Vin Edinburgh

⊛ British, French ⊛

Bags of HdV style and sound brasserie cooking

☎ 0131 247 4900
11 Bristo Place EH1 1EZ
e-mail: reception.edinburgh@hotelduvin.com
dir: M8 junct 1, A720 (signed Kilmarnock/W Calder/ Edinburgh W). Right at fork, follow A720 signs, merge onto A720. Take exit signed A703. At rdbt take A702/ Biggar Rd. 3.5m. Right into Lauriston Pl which becomes Forrest Rd. Right at Bedlam Theatre. Hotel on right

The former city asylum is the setting for HdV's Edinburgh outpost. These days the setting is considerably more cheerful thanks to the group's trademark clubby look of well-worn leather seats and woody textures. There's a splendid tartan-clad whisky snug, plus a buzzy mezzanine bar overlooking the bistro, which offers the usual nods to France with its wine-related paraphernalia and hearty, rustic contemporary brasserie cooking that the group specialises in everywhere from Royal Tunbridge Wells to the Scottish capital. An Isle of Mull cheese soufflé is the signature starter, which you might follow with a classic plate of haggis, neeps and tatties, or hake paella.

Chef Matt Powell **Owner** Hotel du Vin & Malmaison
Times 12–2.30/5.30–10.30 Closed D 25 Dec
Prices Starter £5–£7, Main £10.50–£23, Dessert £4–£9, Service added but optional **Wines** 600 bottles over £20, 5 bottles under £20, 12 by glass **Notes** Pre-theatre 2 course with wine £14.50, Sunday L, Vegetarian available **Seats** 82, Pr/dining room 26 **Children** Portions **Parking** NCP

Hotel Missoni Edinburgh

⊛⊛ Italian **NEW** ♦

Modern Italian cucina in a glamorous Royal Mile hotel

☎ 0131 220 6666 & 240 1666
1 George IV Bridge EH1 1AD
e-mail: cucina.edinburgh@hotelmissoni.com

Rosita Missoni's hotel group, which extends from Kuwait to Edinburgh's Royal Mile, is a byword for contemporary grande luxe. Rooms have all the latest technology, the design job is jaw-dropping throughout (you can't miss the gigantic vases that sit in the lobby windows), and the restaurants very much have their own identity, rather than feeling like corporate dining. Here, at Cucina, the dolce vita is enthusiastically celebrated. A light-filled room in busy monochrome patterns, offset by hotly coloured psychedelic abstracts, opens on to a small alfresco area, while a large communal table at the front offers dining with the Italian familial touch. Chef Mattia Camorani is from the Locatelli stable, and offers a robust style of gently modernised Italian cooking that keeps one foot firmly rooted in classic technique. Pasta and risotto showings are very fine: begin with ravioli filled with seasonal pheasant, supported by a strongly savoury rosemary sauce, or a deep-dyed risotto made with radicchio and Montepulciano ripasso wine. Either could

be followed by exemplary calves' liver in a balsamic reduction, accompanied simply by pine nuts, sultanas and spinach, a sublime essay in textural and flavour contrasts. A subtly flavoured rum pannacotta shows all those modern-Britishers how it's done.

Chef Mattia Camorani **Owner** Hotel Missoni
Times 12.30–3/6–10 Closed D 25 Dec **Prices** Fixed L 2 course £14.95, Starter £7–£12, Main £9.50–£26, Dessert £6.50–£13.50, Service optional, Groups min 6 service 12.5% **Wines** 165 bottles over £20, 2 bottles under £20, 14 by glass **Notes** Pre-theatre 2 course £16, 3 course £19 6–7pm, Vegetarian available, Dress restrictions, **Seats** 90, Pr/dining room 40 **Children** Portions

The Howard

⊛ Modern Scottish

Modern Scottish cooking in a swanky hotel

☎ 0131 557 3500
34 Great King St EH3 6QH
e-mail: reception@thehoward.com
dir: E on Queen St, 2nd left, Dundas St. Through 3 lights, right, hotel on left

The Howard is a smart, intimate hotel with extremely personal service (a collection of butlers look after every whim) created from three late-Georgian townhouses in Edinburgh's New Town. Rich fabrics, oil paintings and period furniture create a traditional, luxury feel, and that extends to The Atholl restaurant, which seats just 14 people (booking is a must). Take a pre-dinner drink in the comfort of the drawing room while perusing the modern Scottish menu, before settling down to a meal that might begin with cauliflower and Arran mustard velouté with herb crostini, followed by grilled Highland venison cutlets, root vegetables, roast potatoes and a port glaze. Finish with baked dark chocolate cheesecake with ginger ice cream, or perhaps a more traditional sticky toffee pudding with Madagascan vanilla ice cream and butterscotch sauce.

Times 12–2/6–9.30

Iggs

⊛ Modern ♦

Enterprising modern Spanish cooking in the city centre

☎ 0131 557 8184
15-19 Jeffrey St EH1 1DR
e-mail: info@iggs.co.uk
web: www.iggs.co.uk
dir: In heart of Old Town, 0.5m from castle, just off Royal Mile

Ignacio 'Iggy' Campos has been bringing the taste of the Mediterranean to Edinburgh for almost a quarter of a century, but hasn't let the grass grow under his feet. A revamp in 2011 has produced a new look to the venue and new tweaks to the menu. Contemporary Spanish dishes are built on authentic materials imported from Spain allied with pedigree Scottish produce and are available in small and large portions to suit a modish sharing and grazing format; be prepared to go with the flow, as plates arrive when they are ready. From the robust end of the scale, free-range Iberian pork might appear with pan-seared scallops, braised pig's cheek, olive oil purée and baked baby onions, while morcilla blood pudding and Iberica ham are teamed with Tempranillo-glazed roast partridge. On the seafood side, how about pan-roasted sea bass fillet with fried razor clams and Calasparra rice? End with a classic crema catalana with honeycomb, milk syrup, and lemon ice.

Chef Mark Spence-Ishaq **Owner** Mr I Campos
Times 12–2.30/6–10.30 Closed Sun **Prices** Fixed L 2 course £15, Starter £5.50–£13.95, Main £11–£24.95, Dessert £6–£8, Service added but optional 10% **Wines** 80 bottles over £20, 20 bottles under £20, 18 by glass **Notes** Sunday L, Vegetarian available **Seats** 80, Pr/ dining room 40 **Children** Portions **Parking** On street, NCP

The Kitchin

Scottish, French **V** NOTABLE WINE LIST

Nature-to-plate cooking of a very high order in fashionable Leith

☎ 0131 555 1755
78 Commercial Quay, Leith EH6 6LX
e-mail: info@thekitchin.com
dir: In Leith opposite Scottish Executive building

The once dubious streets of Leith are positively humming with culinary endeavour these days, and standing head and shoulders above the herd is Tom Kitchin's restaurant. The old dockyards lend themselves nicely to urban-chic regeneration projects, and accordingly in 2006, Kitchin and his wife Michaela took an old whisky warehouse as the raw material for their venue. The place was made over again in 2012, and now works a Scotland-meets-Scandinavia look involving modishly neutral tones pointed up with Scottish tweeds, luxurious turquoise velvet, dining chairs upholstered in Burgundy red, and walnut tables. Presiding over it all is a clued-up, courteous, largely French front-of-house team. The kitchen action is laid bare behind a glass screen, and while Kitchin has succumbed to the lure of telly, (naturally there's a cook book of recipes from The Kitchin) he is usually to be seen here at the sharp end of proceedings. Kitchin trained with French super-chefs Alain Ducasse and Pierre Koffmann, so you can be sure that finely-honed French technique lies at the foundations of his cooking, while the 'from nature to plate' ethos is proof that the man is passionate about seasonal Scottish produce. In fact, that is stating things mildly: obsessive might be a more accurate description of an attitude that insists on seafood and game being delivered in shells, scales, fur and feathers so that the chefs can make sure that butchery and preparation are second to none. Kitchin manages to create stunning food that also gets the juices flowing rather than presenting the components as some sort of clever, intellectual exercise; this is inspired, ingredient-led cooking put together with a clear, common-sense vision of what works with what. A budget-friendly set-lunch menu offers an accessible entry route, or if you're going the whole hog, there's a tasting extravaganza that goes by the name of 'Tom's Land and Sea Surprise', and of course a carte to showcase the best of what's in season. You might set out with razor clams, or 'spoots' in the local vernacular, served with diced vegetables, chorizo and lemon confit, but you could also be tempted by the French accent that is evident in crispy pig's ears in a salad accompanying boned and rolled pig's head with roasted Isle of Skye langoustines. A spring main course could deliver wild North Sea turbot roasted on the bone and matched with braised Swiss chard, lemon and croûtons, while two could sign up for saddle of Highland lamb cooked on hay, and partnered with garlic potatoes, 'white kidney', and baby gem lettuce. Desserts bring things to a close without letting up on the full-on flavours: unusual items such as sea buckthorn could appear in a tart served with glazed orange and dark chocolate sorbet, or you could go for a classical dish of chocolate financier with coffee sabayon and ice cream.

Chef Tom Kitchin **Owner** Tom & Michaela Kitchin **Times** 12.15-3/6.45-10 Closed Xmas, New Year, 1st 2wks Jan, Sun-Mon **Prices** Fixed L 3 course £26.50, Tasting menu £70, Starter £16.50-£19, Main £31-£36, Dessert £9.50-£11, Service optional, Groups min 8 service 10% **Wines** 245 bottles over £20, 40 by glass **Notes** Tasting menu 6 course, Vegetarian menu **Seats** 50 **Children** Portions **Parking** 30, On site parking eve only, all day Sat

Save on Hotels. Book at theAA.com/hotel

CITY OF EDINBURGH 567 SCOTLAND

EDINBURGH *continued*

The Indian Cavalry Club

@ Indian

The West End's Indian star

☎ 0131 220 0138
22 Coates Crescent EH3 7AF
e-mail: info@indiancavalryclub.co.uk
dir: Few mins walk from Haymarket Railway Station & the west end of Princes St

Edinburgh's slickest Indian restaurant offers a classy quartet of dining spaces all kitted out in an upmarket modern vein with wooden floors, coffee and cream hues, and tended by well-drilled staff happy to talk you through the menu. As with any restaurant that stands out from the herd, dedication to top-class materials is key to the pan-Indian repertoire on offer here. An impressive regiment of pakora and tandoori classics leads the charge into dishes that span the sub-continent, running the gamut of Kashmiri, Punjabi, Jaipuri, Afghan and Keralan specialities, all with clearly-defined, fresh flavours. Red Fort lamb delivers tender tandoori-cooked meat in a mild sauce of yoghurt and ground almonds - perfect with a side dish of sag makkai (spinach with sweetcorn) or you might go for a blowout seafood banquet comprising tandoori salmon tikka, sea bass chargrilled with mustard seeds, tomato and coriander, and jumbo king prawns curried with spring onions sweetcorn and potatoes.

Chef Muktar Miah, M D Qayum **Owner** Shahid Chowdhury **Times** 12-4/5.30-11.30 **Prices** Fixed L 2 course £5.95, Fixed D 3 course £18.85-£24.85, Starter £4.85-£9.85, Main £9.85-£22.85, Dessert £3.85-£6.50, Service added but optional 10% **Wines** 15 bottles over £20, 16 bottles under £20, 2 by glass **Notes** Vegetarian available **Seats** 120, Pr/dining room 50 **Parking** On street

Kanpai Sushi

@ Japanese **NEW**

On-trend Japanese fast food in the cultural district

☎ 0131 228 1602
8-10 Grindlay St EH3 9AS

Kanpai is the Japanese for 'cheers!', and neatly sums up the hospitable informality of this sushi bar near the Usher Hall and Lyceum Theatre. Split between two rooms, the interiors utilise the light wood tones favoured by such places, with chefs on view chopping and sculpting amid an air of minimalist purity. The expected things are done well, with diamond-bright seasonings, ultra-fresh fish and bags of umami underpinning the menus. Miso soup and squid tempura with dipping sauce kick things off well, there are well-made sticky maki rolls of tuna or crispy chicken and avocado, topped with fish roe, and of course an array of fine sushi and sashimi. Regularly replenished side-plates of hot wasabi dumplings and pickled ginger keep you going, while you wait perhaps for salmon teriyaki or a piece of expertly grilled sirloin. Sake, plum wine and Japanese beers flesh out the drinks list.

Chef Jack Zhang **Times** 12-2.30/5-10.30 Closed Mon **Prices** Starter £4-£15, Main £8-£13, Dessert £3-£4, Service optional **Wines** 5 bottles over £20, 2 bottles under £20, 7 by glass **Notes** Vegetarian available **Seats** 45, Pr/dining room 8 **Children** Portions **Parking** On street

The Kitchin

@@@@ *– see opposite*

Mark Greenaway at No 12 Picardy Place

EDINBURGH   Map 21 NT27

Modern Scottish

Thrilling cooking in the heart of Edinburgh

☎ 0131 557 0952
12 Picardy Place EH1 3JT
e-mail: info@no12picardyplace.com

No. 12 Picardy Place is at the heart of the action, a short amble from Princes Street, and has a restaurant headed up by Mark Greenaway that places it at the forefront of the city's culinary firmament. Behind the handsome Georgian façade you'll find bags of boutique style in the form of a cocktail bar, über-cool bedrooms, a swanky room for the swankiest of events, and a restaurant with exposed stone walls, done-out with colours chosen from the suitably fashionably muted palette. Mark Greenaway gets his name over the door, and rightly so, for he is a talented chef serving up some rather thrilling food. The lunch and early evening menu - the Market Menu - is a bit of a steal for two or three courses, whilst the carte (decent value itself by today's standards) proudly lists the Scottish suppliers. Whilst flavour and texture are to the fore, there is no stinting with the presentation either, as witnessed in an eye-catching first course ham hough (hock to the Sassenachs) and Granny Smith pie, served with seared West Coast scallops, parsley mayonnaise and pickled shallots - a fabulous combination of harmonious flavours and textures. Skate wing is boned and cooked sous-vide, and served up with excellent olive mash, beetroot purée, crispy squid and a brown butter jus that deserves a place on the highest of tables. For dessert, who could resist the jam jar filled with warm rice pudding, rhubarb compôte, vanilla ice cream and rhubarb éspuma?

Times 12-3/5.30-10 Closed Sun

EDINBURGH *continued*

Locanda De Gusti

◉◉ Italian

Neapolitan-accented cooking in the heart of the city

☎ 0131 558 9581
7-11 East London St EH7 4BN
e-mail: info@locandadegusti.com
dir: Corner of Broughton & East London St, 5 min walk from the Playhouse

Neapolitan-inspired food, authentically executed, gives this city centre restaurant an edge when it comes to eating Italian in Edinburgh. It looks nicely contemporary in a clean-lined minimalist sort of way; think terracotta floors, whitewashed walls hung with bright artworks, bare tables and an open-plan kitchen. A new wine and beer cellar is spot on for pre- and post-prandial drinking. There's a good amount of great Scottish seafood on the menu, plus a generous sprinkling of imported Italian ingredients. Start with foccacia topped with cream of salted cod, smoked pancetta and Sardinian pecorino cheese, before a pasta dish such as linguine with plenty of top-notch seafood (langoustines, prawns, squid, mussels and clams). Among secondi might be braised Scottish Borders lamb shank or breaded escalope of swordfish with a sweet Sicilian-style ratatouille, and, to finish, how about tortino ricotta e pere?

Chef Rosario Sartore **Owner** Rosario Sartore, Mario Gagliardini **Times** 12-2.30/5-11 Closed Sun-Mon **Prices** Fixed L 2 course fr £10.95, Fixed D 2 course fr £10.95, Starter £4.95-£9.95, Main £9.95-£17.95, Dessert fr £4.95, Service optional **Wines** 80% bottles over £20, 20% bottles under £20, 7 by glass **Notes** Fixed L 2 course available until 6.30pm & Tue-Sat until 4pm, Vegetarian available **Seats** 60, Pr/dining room 30 **Children** Portions **Parking** On street

Malmaison Edinburgh

◉ British, French

Dockside Mal style

☎ 0131 468 5000
One Tower Place, Leith EH6 7DB
e-mail: edinburgh@malmaison.com
dir: A900 from city centre towards Leith, at end of Leith Walk through 3 lights, left into Tower St. Hotel on right at end of road

Edinburgh's branch of the Mal was the original incarnation, stylishly set in the capital's dynamic Leith development, with views over the water. Dining goes on amid an ambience of retro wood panelling, brown leather upholstery and unclothed tables, a surprisingly clubby feel for what is impeccably contemporary, defiantly simple brasserie food. Moules marinière is a benchmark, its liquor excellent, the mussels fresh and plump, while a main course of braised ox cheek with shallot purée and polenta croûtons brings on well-seasoned, resonantly flavoured meat and good textural contrasts. Blowtorched

crème brûlée is singing with vanilla, and arrives with a spiced madeleine.

Times 12-2.30/6-10.30

Mark Greenaway at No 12 Picardy Place

◉◉◉ *– see page 567*

Marriott Dalmahoy Hotel & Country Club

◉ Modern, Traditional

Georgian manor serving up a genuine Scottish flavour

☎ 0131 333 1845
Kirknewton EH27 8EB
e-mail: mhrs.edigs.frontdesk@marriotthotels.com
dir: Edinburgh City bypass (A720) turn onto A71 towards Livingston, hotel on left in 2m

The Pentland hills enfold this upscale country club in a verdant embrace, yet Edinburgh is close enough for you to see its castle on the skyline. Those with a serious golf habit are kept busy by two courses woven into a thousand acres of wooded parkland, and the glorious Georgian mansion is now kitted out with all the requisite gym and spa action you could ask for as foreplay to dining in the glossy Pentland restaurant. A split-level layout means that everyone gets a piece of the glorious hilly backdrop, while splendid Scottish ingredients take a bow in uncomplicated modern dishes. Pan-fried scallops on cauliflower purée with lemon-dressed pea shoots might precede a delicate fillet of plaice with white wine, mussel and parsley risotto. To finish, Drambuie crème brûlée and shortbread hits the spot.

Chef Alan Matthew **Owner** Marriott Hotels Ltd **Times** 7-10 Closed L all week **Prices** Food prices not confirmed for 2013. Please telephone for details **Wines** 21 bottles over £20, 7 bottles under £20, 11 by glass **Notes** Vegetarian available, Dress restrictions, Smart casual, Civ Wed 300 **Seats** 120, Pr/dining room 16 **Children** Portions, Menu **Parking** 350

North Bridge Brasserie

◉ Modern Scottish ♨

Unique brasserie setting for Scotland's native produce

☎ 0131 622 2900 & 556 5565
The Scotsman, 20 North Bridge EH1 1TR
e-mail: northbridge@tshg.co.uk
web: www.northbridgebrasserie.com
dir: Town centre, next to railway station, 1 min from Royal Mile & 2 mins to Princes St

This landmark Victorian building was home to the Scotsman newspaper for nearly a century before its conversion into a swanky boutique hotel. The grand old baronial property's remodelling combines sheet glass and girders with original walnut panelling, stained-glass windows and a showpiece marble staircase, while the brasserie, once the reception hall, brings contemporary style to the original architecture. Ornate ceilings, marble pillars and a wooden balcony - which runs right around the room - are features, while the kitchen takes a modern approach with focus on quality Scottish seasonal produce. Herb-crusted rack of Scottish lamb is served with potatoes cooked in garlic and cream, flageolet beans and bacon, while smoked Shetland halibut might come with a crayfish and ham hock cassoulet and lobster sauce. From the grill, there is a range of 28-day hung Highland steaks, and to finish, maybe baked Selkirk Bannock Queen of Puddings with Drambuie soaked raisins.

Chef Paul Hart **Owner** The Scotsman Hotel Ltd **Times** 12-2/6-10 **Prices** Starter £6.50-£13.50, Main £13.25-£28.95, Dessert £5.25-£7.50, Service added but optional 10% **Wines** 80 bottles over £20, 12 bottles under £20, 14 by glass **Notes** Pre-theatre menu 5.30-6.30 2/3 courses £17.50/£22.50, Vegetarian available, Dress restrictions, Smart casual, Civ Wed 80 **Seats** 80, Pr/dining room 80 **Children** Portions, Menu **Parking** Station car park

See advert opposite

Save on Hotels. Book at **theAA.com/hotel**

CITY OF EDINBURGH 569 SCOTLAND

Norton House Hotel & Spa

Modern British, French NEW

Enterprising modern cookery away from the city bustle

☎ 0131 333 1275

Ingliston EH28 8LX

e-mail: nortonhouse@handpicked.co.uk

dir: M8 junct 2, off A8, 0.5m past Edinburgh Airport

The intention behind Norton House was always that it would offer respite from the bustle of the capital, ever since it was built in 1840. Modern urban sprawl hasn't encroached on it - it's still a 20-minute drive out of the city - and the sense of tranquillity is undisturbed, for all that the best in modern spa treatments and technology are now available. In the upscale Ushers restaurant, some enterprising modern Scottish cooking is on the menu too, in the more-than-capable hands of Graeme

Shaw. Amid a slightly unassuming ambience of coffee-cream and darkwood, the culinary fireworks burst forth the more radiantly, perhaps nowhere more so than in a bold first course of wild squirrel ravioli with hazelnuts, nettles and baby onions. Nettles are a favoured accompaniment indeed, cropping up again with wild leeks, morels and white asparagus as the partners for a main course of John Dory. The signature dish is a right-royal treatment of Goosnargh duck, which combines the roast breast with confit leg en crépinette, with orange purée and prune sauce. Desserts designed to keep your taste buds on their toes include lime chiboust with roast pineapple and vanilla foam, and there are some excellent Scottish and French cheeses.

Chef Graeme Shaw, Glen Bilins **Owner** Hand Picked Hotels **Times** 7-9.30 Closed Jan, Sun-Tue, L all week **Prices** Tasting menu £65, Starter £6.95-£10.50, Main £16.95-£28.95, Dessert £6.50-£8.95, Service optional **Wines** 150 bottles over £20, 12 by glass **Notes** Tasting menu 8 course, Vegetarian available, Civ Wed 140 **Seats** 22, Pr/dining room 40 **Children** Portions **Parking** 100

EDINBURGH *continued*

Norton House Hotel & Spa

🏵🏵🏵 *– see page 569*

Number One, The Balmoral

🏵🏵🏵 *– see opposite*

Ondine Restaurant

🏵 Seafood **NEW**

Contemporary seafood restaurant with ethical outlook

☎ 0131 226 1888
2 George IV Bridge EH1 1AD
e-mail: enquiries@ondinerestaurant.co.uk

Ondine's central horseshoe-shaped crustacea bar is both a feature in the restaurant and a declaration of intent - this place is about seafood, and top-notch sustainable Scottish seafood at that. Just off the Royal Mile, on George IV Bridge, it's a modish space with great views out over the old town and lots of dark wood and quality fixtures and fittings giving it a pleasing contemporary sheen. Start with rock oysters (Lindisfarne, Maldon, Carlingford), either as they come or cooked (Kilpatrick, perhaps), or salt-and-pepper squid tempura (wonderfully light batter) with a perky Vietnamese sauce. Next up, expect the likes of grilled Native Isle of Mull lobster, or brown shrimp and butternut squash risotto. Steak is an alternative to seafood and desserts extend to coconut pannacotta with mango salsa.

Chef Roy Brett **Times** 12-3/5.30-10 **Prices** Fixed L 2 course £16.95 **Notes** Pre theatre menu 2/3 course

One Square

🏵 British

Modernised British cooking in a grand café

☎ 0131 221 6422
1 Festival Square EH3 9SR
e-mail: info@onesquareedinburgh.co.uk
dir: From west end of Princes St, turn onto Lothian Rd. 1st right at lights onto West Approach Rd. 1st left to the Sheraton Grand Hotel & Spa, restaurant on right

Formerly Santini, this swish place overlooking Festival Square and overlooked by the Castle, was once consecrated to pan-Italian cooking, but is now re-made as a cool café, open from freshly squeezed breakfast juices to evening digestifs, with laid-back brunches, trend-setting lunches and stylish afternoon teas in between. Designer touches, smart panelled walls and bare tables are the setting for classic British dishes that have had the modernising magic wand waved over them. Roasted beetroot served cold and sandwiching sweet

Highland Crowdie cheese with a garnish of toasted pine nuts may be the prelude to hearty beef and lentil cobbler with roasted roots and rosemary dumplings, while puddings include a rhubarb and custard spin that comprises rhubarb sorbet and custard ice cream covered in frozen clotted cream, with chunks of poached rhubarb, crumble and honeycomb.

Chef Malcolm Webster **Owner** Hotel Corporation of Edinburgh **Times** 12-10.30 **Prices** Starter £4.50-£13.50, Main £9.50-£37.50, Dessert £6.50-£9, Service added but optional 10% **Wines** 58 bottles over £20, 12 bottles under £20, 11 by glass **Notes** Sunday L, Vegetarian available, Civ Wed 500 **Seats** 135, Pr/dining room 40 **Children** Menu **Parking** 119

Plumed Horse

🏵🏵🏵 *– see opposite*

Restaurant Martin Wishart

🏵🏵🏵🏵 *– see page 572*

Rhubarb at Prestonfield House

🏵🏵 Traditional British 🍷 👐

Opulent surroundings for high-impact cooking

☎ 0131 225 1333
Priestfield Rd EH16 5UT
e-mail: reservations@prestonfield.com
web: www.rhubarb-restaurant.com
dir: Exit city centre on Nicholson St, onto Dalkeith Rd. At lights turn left into Priestfield Rd. Prestonfield on left

If you were wondering why Rhubarb was chosen as the name for this splendid restaurant, it's because we have the former owner of Prestonfield, Sir Alexander Dick, to thank for bringing the eponymous Asian vegetable to Scotland in 1746. Nowadays, the aristocratic 17th-century mansion earns a crust as the Prestonfield House Hotel, a decadent, theatrical and totally glam destination whose look is the polar opposite of stripped-out minimalism. Rhubarb has serious wow-factor with its Regency rooms done out in darkly opulent shades of blood red and burgundy, and, not wanting to be outfaced by the dramatic surroundings, the kitchen puts on quite a show, sending out dishes with plenty of impact - braised leg, poached loin and croquette of wild Scottish rabbit served with the animal's lunch - carrot and dandelion - as well as prune pumpernickel crumb. Next out, hand-dived scallops are partnered to great effect with cauliflower purée, lovage, chorizo, apple and truffle dressing and confit lemon, and at the end, perhaps a creative dish involving Earl Grey tea-poached pear, Perthshire brambles, wood sorrel sorbet, rice pudding, and yoghurt ice cream.

Rhubarb at Prestonfield House

Chef John McMahon **Owner** James Thomson OBE **Times** 12-2/6.30-10 **Prices** Fixed L 2 course £16.95, Fixed D 3 course £30, Starter £8.95-£18.50, Main £14-£35, Dessert £8-£9.95, Service optional, Groups min 8 service 10% **Wines** 500+ bottles over £20, 12 by glass **Notes** Theatre D 2 course £16.95, Sunday L, Vegetarian available, Civ Wed 500 **Seats** 90, Pr/dining room 500 **Children** Portions **Parking** 200

Save on Hotels. Book at **theAA.com/hotel**

CITY OF EDINBURGH 571 SCOTLAND

Number One, The Balmoral

Modern Scottish V

Smart, confident cooking in an opulent address

☎ 0131 557 6727 & 556 2414
1 Princes St EH2 2EQ
e-mail: numberone@roccofortecollection.com
dir: follow city centre signs. Hotel at E end of Princes St, adjacent to Waverley Station

Number one Princes Street must be the capital's pre-eminent address, so it's entirely fitting that the Balmoral was built here. The hotel is luxuriously furnished and decorated, the spacious Number One restaurant no exception, interior-designed by Olga Polizzi, with an abundance of artwork on red-lacquered walls, deep carpets, comfortable gold seating at large, well-spaced tables, and a profusion of courteous staff. Jeff Bland's cooking is based on the classical French repertoire, but his individual style makes him difficult to pigeonhole, pairing, for example, the depth of oxtail in a starter with foie gras, bittersweet orange and sherry jelly, and the crunch of Macadamia nuts. Dinner starts with a variety of tempting canapés, before, say, scallops with Iberico ham and sweet-and-sour and puréed apple, topped with crackling-like crisp chorizo. Produce is top-drawer stuff, of course, and technical skills are never in doubt, seen in main courses of rib of beef cooked in hay, accompanied by truffle, marrowbone and tarragon-flavoured spelt, and Dover sole, with a langoustine wrapped in crisp angel-hair noodles, confit fennel, couscous and a first-class sauce Choron. A pre-dessert - say, intense caramel mousse with grapefruit sorbet and mango - is as ambitious as what comes next, perhaps a pretty plate of light Baileys cream, coffee granita topped with chocolate ganache, and coffee mousse, all garnished with thin sticks of chocolate.

Chef Jeff Bland, Billy Boyter **Owner** Rocco Forte Collection **Times** 6.30-10 Closed 1st 2 wks Jan, L all week **Prices** Fixed D 3 course fr £64, Tasting menu £70, Service optional, Groups min 6 service 10% **Wines** 350 bottles over £20, 8 by glass **Notes** Tasting menu 8 course, Vegetarian menu, Dress restrictions, Smart casual preferred, Civ Wed 60 **Seats** 50, Pr/dining room 50 **Children** Portions **Parking** NCP: Greenside/St James Centre

Plumed Horse

Modern European V

Consistently imaginative contemporary cuisine near the Leith dockland

☎ 0131 554 5556 & 05601 123266
50-54 Henderson St, Leith EH6 6DE
e-mail: plumedhorse@aol.com
web: www.plumedhorse.co.uk
dir: From city centre N on Leith Walk, left into Great Junction St & 1st right into Henderson St. Restaurant 200mtrs on right

The green frontage on a corner on the way to the Leith dockland hides an irregularly shaped, understated room with a mixture of figurative and abstract modern artworks and high-class tableware. It's here that Tony Borthwick produces some of the capital's most consistently imaginative contemporary cuisine. There are strong French influences at work, and an unintimidated approach to complexity, but dishes never feel crowded or incoherent, and are always high on impact. A forgivable recourse to modish formats may see things arriving on slate slabs, one component in a glass, or else piled in precarious-looking stacks, but the underlying principles are not hard to locate. A tian of white crabmeat is given the tropical treatment with pineapple salsa and a passionfruit dressing, while an earthier start might be made with rabbit and wood pigeon terrine bound in Alsace bacon, served with brioche and raisins. Main courses are multi-layered creations, perhaps bringing together roast monkfish and langoustines in saffron, with a smoked haddock and brown shrimp croquette, in shellfish sauce for a glorious maritime assemblage, while meats might see two servings of veal - roast loin and braised breast - alongside its kidney and bacon, with wild leeks, garlic and spinach in a veal stock jus. Reinventions turn desserts into voyages of discovery, as when rum baba is given a rhubarb and ginger makeover, with ginger ice cream, or a trendy trifle is fashioned from the components of Piña Colada. Fine farmhouse cheeses are served with home-made oatcakes and membrillo.

Chef Tony Borthwick **Owner** The Company of The Plumed Horse Ltd **Times** 12-3.30/7-11.30 Closed Xmas, New Year, 2 wks Summer, 1 wk Etr, Sun-Mon **Prices** Tasting menu £65, Service optional, Groups min 6 service 10% **Wines** 290 bottles over £20, 16 by glass **Notes** Fixed L 5 course £26.50, D 5 course £55, Tasting menu 8 course, Vegetarian menu **Seats** 40 **Parking** On street

Restaurant Martin Wishart

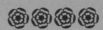

Modern French **V** NOTABLE WINE LIST

Reference-point Scottish address for outstanding contemporary food

☎ 0131 553 3557
54 The Shore, Leith EH6 6RA
e-mail: info@martin-wishart.co.uk
dir: off the A199

Martin Wishart's eponymous Leith operation still sets the benchmark for eating in Edinburgh - you might expand that accolade to embrace all of Scotland. In the dozen years since he led the charge from the thriving enclave of modish bars and restaurants in the revitalised docklands area, the man has not let the grass grow under his feet. A brasserie in Edinburgh, The Honours, opened in July 2011, boosting a portfolio that encompasses the restaurant on Loch Lomond, Cameron House (see entry), as well as a cookery school. Nor has the mothership been left to languish or rest on its laurels: refurbished at the start of 2012, the brightened-up décor exudes the sort of understated class that befits a venue of this standing, without distracting attention from the culinary pyrotechnics. The menu talks the terse language of any self-respecting A-lister, so irreproachably attentive staff (one for every two diners, no less) are intelligently briefed on what is actually happening with the bare list of ingredients that announces each dish. Read it carefully and reflect that each intelligently-conceived dish reveals a deep understanding of how ingredients interact, without needing to resort to empty gestures and snake-oil gimmickry for effect - although there are some off-the-wall ideas that turn out to be triumphs of culinary judgement. Scottish produce of the finest order underpins it all, but the modern French accent is unmistakable, and unsurprising, when you consider that Wishart's formative years were spent with the Roux family, Marco Pierre White and stellar French super-chef Marc Meneau, among others of a Gallic-influenced persuasion. Ultimately, what separates these rarefied practitioners of high culinary art from the mere technicians is their ability to make every advertised flavour come to life and sing in tune with its companions on the plate. Beetroot and horseradish macaroons make the palate stand to attention for a starter of roasted Isle of Mull scallops with chopped braised pigs' trotters, brought into sharp perspective with a Chardonnay vinaigrette and the accompanying flavours of artichoke and potatoes. Main courses ratchet up the intensity with a robust breast of grouse 'au foie gras' earthily partnered with red cabbage, chervil root, bitter cocoa sauce, and a crunchy walnut and feta topping. All the stops are pulled out for fish too, in dishes that might see wild sea bass wrapped in potato supported by poached scallops, bone marrow and smoked celeriac jus. In comparison, puddings such as a sublime clementine soufflé with mango sorbet and passionfruit cream sound almost prosaic, but the level of artistry and technical skill is always of the highest order. France is, perhaps inevitably, where the wine list's compass points, but there is much, much more to enthrall from the rest of the globe, and it doesn't all come as a shock to the pocket.

Chef Martin Wishart, Joe Taggart **Owner** Martin Wishart **Times** 12-2/6.30-10 Closed 25-26 Dec, 1 Jan, 2 wks Jan, Sun-Mon **Prices** Fixed L 3 course fr £28.50, Fixed D 3 course fr £65, Tasting menu £70, Service optional, Groups min 6 service 10% **Wines** 200+ bottles over £20, 14 by glass **Notes** Tasting menu 6 course, Vegetarian menu, Dress restrictions, Smart casual **Seats** 50, Pr/dining room 10 **Children** Portions **Parking** On street

Save on Hotels. Book at **theAA.com/hotel**

CITY OF EDINBURGH 573 **SCOTLAND**

EDINBURGH *continued*

The Royal Terrace Hotel

@ British

Inventive brasserie cooking in a Georgian townhouse

☎ 0131 557 3222 & 524 5030
18 Royal Ter EH7 5AQ
e-mail: restaurant@royalterracehotel.co.uk
dir: A8 to city centre, follow one-way system, left into
Charlotte Sq. At end right into Queens St. Left at rdbt. At
next island right into London Rd, right into Blenheim
Place leading to Royal Terrace

A Georgian townhouse hotel on the eponymous terrace,
with relaxing views of the surrounding gardens, this
place has Edinburgh stamped all the way through it. With
outdoor tables as well as a fittingly elegant dining room,
all possible weather options are covered. Unclothed
tables and a menu of brasserie-style dishes give
indication of the hang-loose approach, but there is a real
streak of inventiveness in the cooking too. Marie Rose
prawns and white crabmeat are fashioned into a tower,
and stuck with a parmesan wafer, ready for you to
demolish it, or there could be cabbage-wrapped pig's
cheek with cauliflower purée, mushrooms and watercress
for a thoroughly robust starter. Mains might see sea
bream partnered with artichoke barigoule and pea purée,
and proceedings end satisfyingly with the house wild
berry and chocolate cake, served with passionfruit and
mango sorbet and warm chocolate sauce.

Chef Gregor Kazmierczak **Owner** Prima Hotels
Times 5-9.30 Closed L all week **Prices** Food prices not
confirmed for 2013. Please telephone for details
Wines 48 bottles over £20, 8 bottles under £20
Notes Pre-theatre menu 2,3 course 5-7pm daily,
Vegetarian available, Civ Wed 70 **Seats** 36, Pr/dining
room 10 **Children** Portions, Menu **Parking** On street
(metered)

The Sheep Heid

@ British **NEW V**

Hearty dining in the city's oldest pub

☎ 0131 661 7974
43-45 The Causeway EH15 3QA
e-mail: enquire@thesheepheidedinburgh.co.uk

Edinburgh's oldest pub has been in the business of
supplying good food and drink to the residents of
Duddingston village since 1360. On the edge of Holyrood
Park, it is a convivial watering hole with a traditional
skittle alley and relaxed, shabby-chic décor of olive-green
painted panelling, traditional pews and mismatched
antique chairs at bare wooden tables. Whether you eat in
the pubby setting downstairs or go up a level to the
eclectically-furnished first-floor restaurant, expect robust,
unpretentious food with generous portions, clear flavours
and sound ingredients. The local specialities once served
here - from which the pub perhaps gets its name - were
sheep's head broth and singed sheep's head, but for now
the sheep's head is off the menu: instead you might get
going with Rannochmoor smoked beef with roasted

beetroot and horseradish cream, followed with grilled
venison steak with dauphinoise potatoes and a cranberry,
pear and port reduction, and, to finish, Belgian chocolate
brownie with vanilla ice cream.

Chef Antonio Lopez **Times** 12-10 **Prices** Fixed L 2 course
fr £12.99, Fixed D 3 course fr £15.99, Starter £3.95-
£8.95, Main £10.95-£18.95, Dessert £3.95-£5.50, Service
optional **Wines** 6 bottles over £20, 12 bottles under £20,
12 by glass **Notes** Sunday L, Vegetarian menu **Seats** 140
Children Portions **Parking** 16, On street, NCP

Stac Polly

@ Scottish

City centre cellar with Franco-Scottish flavour

☎ 0131 556 2231
29-33 Dublin St EH3 6NL
e-mail: bookings@stacpolly.com
dir: On corner of Albany St & Dublin St

In the New Town area of Edinburgh, Stac Polly occupies a
labyrinthine cellar and serves up Scottish dishes with the
twang of a French accent. Housed in a 200-year-old
building, the place has loads of character thanks to stone
floors, bare brick walls, linen-clad tables, and there's
even a small outside courtyard if you fancy a bit of
alfresco eating. The well-judged cooking sees some
interesting flavour combinations and a few firm
favourites such as haggis filo pastry parcels stay on the
menu by popular demand. Start perhaps with queen
scallops grilled in the shell and topped with a smoked
salmon and citrus butter, followed by a multi-component
main course such as suprême of halibut with a parsley
crust, citrus and dill mash, broccoli and creamy curry
sauce with fresh mussels. There's another branch in St
Mary's Street.

Chef Andre Stanislas **Owner** Roger Coulthard
Times 12-2/6-10 Closed L Sat-Sun **Prices** Fixed L 2
course fr £13.95, Starter £6.95-£8.25, Main £15.95-
£22.95, Dessert £6.75-£8.25, Service added but optional
10% **Wines** 40+ bottles over £20, 12 bottles under £20, 8
by glass **Notes** Pre-theatre menu 2 course £18, 3 course
£23, Vegetarian available **Seats** 100, Pr/dining room 54
Children Portions **Parking** On street - after 5.30pm

The Stockbridge Restaurant

@@ Modern European ◐

Spirited flavours in distinctive surroundings

☎ 0131 226 6766
54 Saint Stephen St EH3 5AL
e-mail: jane@thestockbridgerestaurant.com
web: www.thestockbridgerestaurant.com
dir: From A90 towards city centre, left Craigleith Rd
B900, 2nd exit at rdbt B900, straight on to Kerr St, turn
left onto Saint Stephen St

The Stockbridge occupies the basement of a large
Georgian property in the area it takes its name from. It's
at the same time dramatic and cosy, with large still lifes
and mirrors hanging on the dark walls and clever lighting
adding a cosseting glow to the white-clothed tables and
gold-upholstered seats. The menu delivers a broadly
European range of full-bodied flavours showcasing
seasonal Scottish produce. Start with seared scallops
with crisp pork belly, black pudding, parsnip purée and
cider vinegar syrup, or a fun mini version of cod, chips
and tartare sauce. Pork belly may crop up again in a
gutsy main course with cheeks and crispy ear, served
with creamed potato, Puy lentils and apple purée, the
kitchen pulling off another winner with the unlikely but
successful blend of seared sea bass and crispy squid
with roast beetroot, chorizo, and sautéed Pink Fir Apple
potatoes.

Chef Jason Gallagher **Owner** Jason Gallagher & Jane
Walker **Times** 7-9.30 Closed 1st 2 wks Jan after New
Year, Mon, L all week (open on request only) **Prices** Fixed
L 2 course fr £14.95, Fixed D 3 course fr £23.95, Starter
£6.95-£11.95, Main £17.95-£23.95, Dessert £4.95-£7.95,
Service optional, Groups min 6 service 10%
Wines 34 bottles over £20, 19 bottles under £20, 5 by
glass **Notes** Pre-theatre Aug only, open L only on request
min 6 people, Vegetarian available **Seats** 40
Children Portions **Parking** On street

21212

@@@ *– see page 574*

EDINBURGH *continued*

The Witchery by the Castle

Traditional Scottish

Confident Scottish cooking in magnificent surroundings

☎ 0131 225 5613
Castlehill, The Royal Mile EH1 2NF
e-mail: mail@thewitchery.com
web: www.thewitchery.com
dir: Top of Royal Mile at gates of Edinburgh Castle

This place is the real deal. Where so many strive for individuality by adding 'boutique' character, The Witchery is as strikingly unique, intriguing and lavish as they come. The higgledy piggledy collection of 16th-century buildings in the old town right by the castle has a slate of glamorous rooms and a restaurant that really takes the biscuit. The two dining rooms (Witchery and Secret Garden) leave a lasting impression: the former with its fabulous oak panelling and tapestries, the latter with its ornately painted ceiling and French windows onto a secluded terrace with great views. On the menu is some smart Scottish cooking, rooted in tradition but with a contemporary sheen. Haggis, neeps and tatties is blended into a chicken mousse to begin, followed by a seafood platter, slow-cooked monkfish with an Asian broth, or steamed saddle of rabbit served with a suet pudding filled with braised shoulder and kidney.

The Witchery by the Castle

Chef Douglas Roberts **Owner** James Thomson
Times 12-4/5.30-11.30 Closed 25 Dec **Prices** Fixed L 2 course £15.95, Fixed D 3 course £30, Starter £8.50-£13.50, Main £16-£39, Dessert £8-£9, Service optional
Wines 800 bottles over £20, 12 by glass **Notes** Pre & post theatre supper 2 course £15.95, Sunday L, Vegetarian available **Seats** 110, Pr/dining room 60

BANKNOCK Map 21 NS77

Glenskirlie House and Castle

Modern British

Inventive Scottish cuisine in a castle setting

☎ 01324 840201
Kilsyth Rd FK4 1UF
e-mail: macaloneys@glenskirliehouse.com
web: www.glenskirliehouse.com
dir: Follow A803 signed Kilsyth/Bonnybridge, at T-junct turn right. Hotel 1m on right

With a snazzy look that is boutique rather than baronial, Glenskirlie sits in splendid landscaped gardens and parkland next to the imposing white castle. The Edwardian country-house is a well-run, switched-on

21212

EDINBURGH Map 21 NT27

Modern French

Bold and dynamic cooking from unique talent

☎ 0131 523 1030 & 0845 222 1212
3 Royal Ter EH7 5AB
e-mail: reservation@21212restaurant.co.uk
dir: Calton Hill, city centre

The name lays out the culinary concept of Paul Kitching's much talked-about Edinburgh venue: the menu format offers up to five courses - choose from two starters, two mains, two desserts with small-but-perfectly-formed morsels in between. And there you have it: 21212 - unless, that is, you turn up for lunch when the kitchen lets you field a more conventional 1-1-1 formation (you can go for three to five courses depending on your appetite and budget). As the unorthodox name suggests, Kitching's cooking is exciting, artful, complex, even confrontational stuff that defies easy classification. But more of that later. The venue is a splendid townhouse in a smart Edinburgh postcode, with four cool boutique-style bedrooms (numbered 1, 2, 12 and 21, of course). Its high-ceilinged Georgian dining room is done out with the original fancy plasterwork and a deluxe designer assemblage of curvaceous banquettes, muslin-draped walls, and giant moths on a chocolate-brown carpet. Patterned glass partitions the diners and the kitchen, where Kitching - unlike many a big-name chef - is hard at it with his battalion-strength team every day. And so to the cooking, which is best described as belonging to the avante-garde school, with its intense hits of flavour and textural contrasts delivering a sustained assault on the senses (in a very good way). Fortunately, Kitching has the razor-sharp technical skills needed to keep his deep well of fizzing creativity on track, and deliver maverick ideas that are endlessly entertaining. Dish descriptions are lengthy, providing a hell of a lot more detail than is the norm these days; 'sea bass blanc bread and popcorn' is the opening headline of a first course, for example, which first-and-foremost consists of a spectacular piece of fish, cooked perfectly, plus a fab king prawn, and 'all things white' - cauliflower and cardamom, shimeji mushrooms, confit of onion, jumbo butterbean, celeriac and white asparagus, curried popcorn, macadamia nuts, crispy bean sprouts, soy sauce mayonnaise and bread sauce. What may be rather a lot to take in when written on the page makes a whole lot more sense on the plate (and palate), the flavours, textures and visual appeal leaving no doubt that you're in safe hands. Next up, 'steak & kidney, chips and beans, horseradish, watercress', the beef a superb piece of fillet, the kidney actually being the bean variety (he's playing with your mind, keep strong), with watercress and horseradish cream, white button mushroom purée, chestnuts, toasted crumpets, smoked bacon, exotic mushrooms and morels - a compelling plate of food. A dessert of 'banana and peach assiette summer trifle' is a lesson in the balance of tastes, and just to prove that quality runs from top to bottom, the breads are superb and the cheese is a fine selection (British, French and Spanish) kept in perfect condition. Kitching's partner Katie O'Brien directs service with immense charm.

Chef Paul Kitching **Owner** P Kitching, K O'Brien, J Revle
Times 12-1.45/6.45-9.30 Closed 2 wks Jan, 2 wks summer, Tue-Sat **Prices** Fixed L 3 course fr £28, Service optional
Wines 200 bottles over £20, 5 by glass **Notes** Fixed L 4 course £38, 5 course £52, 5 course D £68, Vegetarian available
Seats 36, Pr/dining room 10 **Parking** On street

Save on Hotels. Book at **theAA.com/hotel**

FALKIRK – FIFE 575 SCOTLAND

operation with two dining options serving up creative modern Scottish cuisine. The Grill does what it says on the tin, serving straight-up Scottish steaks, salmon and simple crowd pleasers in a funky setting with kaleidoscopic stained-glass windows, otherwise the fine-dining restaurant offers a more intimate vibe and a décor that sets plushly upholstered high-backed chairs against dramatic designer wallpapers. The kitchen uses carefully-sourced Scottish ingredients brought together in a well-conceived carte or set menus, which could open with pan-roasted wood pigeon paired with Jerusalem artichoke purée and a port reduction with wild mushrooms and shaved truffle, then follow with steamed Scottish beef pudding with red onion gravy, skirlie and vegetables. For dessert, perhaps a zesty finale of lemon cream macaroon with lemon jelly and lemon curd ice cream.

Times 12-2/6-9.30 Closed 26-27 Dec, 1-4 Jan, D Mon

FIFE

ANSTRUTHER Map 21 NO50

The Cellar

◉◉◉ – *see below*

CUPAR Map 21 NO31

Ostlers Close Restaurant

◉◉ Modern British V 🕯

Fabulous seasonal produce and skilled hand in the kitchen

☎ 01334 655574
Bonnygate KY15 4BU
dir: In small lane off main street, A91

Down a narrow alley just off the main street, this one-time scullery of a 17th-century Temperance hotel has been a favoured foodie bolt-hole since 1981. That's when James (Jimmy) and Amanda Graham bought the place, and their passion and dedication has put it well and truly on the map. With red-painted walls and linen-clad tables, it's an intimate space (just 26 covers), which is watched over by Amanda with a good deal of charm and

enthusiasm. Jimmy's pleasingly concise, hand-written menus make the most of fruit, veg and herbs from the restaurant's garden (and polytunnel), and at the right time of year he can be found gathering wild mushrooms from the local woods. Seasonal Scottish produce takes centre stage, and you might spot an occasional Spanish influence amid the well-crafted modern repertoire. Dishes are packed with flavour, never over worked, with the ingredients given room to shine. Start, perhaps, with roast breast of Perthshire partridge with Stornoway black pudding mash and pork belly confit, before moving on to fillet of wild Scottish halibut (perfectly cooked) served with Pittenweem prawns, winter greens and saffron sauce. Vanilla pannacotta with a compôte of fruits, damson gin coulis and damson sorbet makes a fine and refreshing finale.

Chef James Graham **Owner** James & Amanda Graham **Times** 12.15-1.30/7-9.30 Closed 25-26 Dec, 1-2 Jan, 2 wks Oct, 2 wks Apr, Sun-Mon, L Tue-Fri **Prices** Starter £5.95-£12.50, Main £13-£24, Dessert £6.75-£7.75, Service optional **Wines** 60 bottles over £20, 31 bottles under £20, 6 by glass **Notes** Fixed D 3 course only available Tue-Fri, Nov-May £28.50, Vegetarian menu **Seats** 26 **Children** Portions **Parking** On street, public car park

The Cellar

ANSTRUTHER Map 21 NO50

Seafood

Romantic old smokery turned classy seafood restaurant

☎ 01333 310378
24 East Green KY10 3AA
dir: Behind Scottish Fisheries Museum

The dedication, commitment and passion required to run a restaurant at this level for nearly 30 years is phenomenal. Chef-proprietor Peter Jukes has cracked open a lot of lobsters, filleted a lot of halibut, and kept The Cellar at the front of the list of top Scottish seafood restaurants all this time. Rumour has it that retirement is on the cards, so head on down soon before it's too late. It's the perfect spot to get hold of prime seafood: right by the harbour, down a pretty cobbled courtyard near the

Scottish Fisheries Museum. The 17th-century house has bags of period charm, which in buildings from that period means low ceilings, wooden beams, exposed stone walls, and real fires; add to that, burnished dark wood tables and quality glassware and cutlery, and the stage is set for some first-class seafood, cooked with skill, restraint and a sure hand. Cured salmon is served as a first-course trio (oak-smoked, gravad lax - made in-house - and hot smoked), served with leaves dressed with dill and sweet mustard dressing, or go for the East Neuk smoked fish stew. There's non-fishy stuff, too, such as risotto of celeriac, apple, walnuts and goats' cheese. Main-course brings forth the likes of half a local lobster with seared scallops and herb and garlic butter, or pesto-crusted cod with pak choi, basil mash and balsamic dressing. There are a couple of meat main courses, plus desserts such as classic crème brûlée.

Chef Peter Jukes **Owner** Susan & Peter Jukes **Times** 12.30-1.30/6.30-9.30 Closed Xmas, Sun (also Mon winter), L Mon-Tue **Prices** Fixed L 2 course £19.50, Fixed D 3 course fr £37.50, Service optional **Wines** 300 bottles over £20, 20 bottles under £20, 5 by glass **Seats** 38 **Children** Portions **Parking** On street

---

DUNFERMLINE — Map 21 NT08

Pitfirrane Hotel

◉ Modern, Traditional

Top-notch Scottish ingredients given due respect

☎ 01383 736132
27 Main St, Crossford KY12 8NJ
e-mail: reception@pitfirranehotel.co.uk
dir: A994 Dunfermline, Crossford is 2nd village from rdbt, hotel is on right after traffic lights

In case you hadn't picked up on the golfing vibe, the 40 golf courses that lie within a 45-minute drive of this family-run hotel are given due prominence in the artworks on the wood-panelled walls of the hotel's Fairways restaurant (the clue is also in the name). It is an easygoing venue done out with unchallenging traditional colours and unclothed darkwood tables, while friendly staff keep everything cheerfully down to earth. The flag-waving menu quite rightly puts top-class Scottish ingredients at the heart of matters, sending out unfussy ideas such as a north-of-the-border take on samosas - filled with haggis, neeps and tatties, and served with whisky sauce - followed perhaps by a classic rib-eye from the grill, or pan-fried sea bass teamed with saffron risotto and salsa verde. Awaiting at the end, there may be Drambuie and vanilla crème brûlée with home-made shortbread.

Times 12-2.30/6-9

ELIE — Map 21 NO40

Sangsters

◉◉ Modern British

Modern Scottish cooking on the village high street

☎ 01333 331001
51 High St KY9 1BZ
dir: From St Andrews on A917 take B9131 to Anstruther, right at rdbt onto A917 to Elie. (11m from St Andrews)

Bruce and Jackie Sangster set up shop plumb in the middle of the main street of this unassuming Fife village, and set about wowing the locals with finely-crafted modern Scottish cooking that showcases plenty of local produce, including apples and herbs from the back garden. It all takes place in a smart dining room hung with landscape pictures, and furnished with crisply dressed tables and high-backed chairs. Dinner follows a four-course, fixed-price format, kicking off perhaps with seared Ross-shire scallops in a Thai-fragrant dressing of chilli, ginger, galangal and lemongrass, before an intermediate fish course, which could be steamed stuffed Loch Duart salmon, teamed with Arbroath smokie and Finnan haddock, in Sauternes and ginger sauce. Main course might be pork two ways, braised cheek and fillet stuffed with black pudding and apricot, with fennel, cabbage and braising juices, while mango and white chocolate parfait with tropical fruits and a sesame and poppy seed biscuit brings things to a close in style.

Chef Bruce R & Jacqueline Sangster **Owner** Bruce & Jacqueline Sangster **Times** 12.30-1.30/7-8.30 Closed 25-26 Dec, Jan, 1st wk Nov, Mon (also Tue winter), L Tue-Sat, D Sun **Prices** Fixed L 3 course £27.50, Fixed D 3 course fr £39.50, Service optional **Wines** 45 bottles over £20, 2 bottles under £20, 8 by glass **Notes** Vegetarian options must be pre-ordered, Sunday L, Vegetarian available, Dress restrictions, Smart casual **Seats** 28 **Parking** On street

---

PEAT INN — Map 21 NO40

The Peat Inn

◉◉◉ – *see below*

ST ANDREWS — Map 21 NO51

Esperante at Fairmont St Andrews

◉◉ Modern European

Mediterranean flavour at a coastal golf resort

☎ 01334 837000
KY16 8PN
e-mail: standrews.scotland@fairmont.com
dir: 1.5m outside St Andrews on A917 towards Crail

The sprawling Fairmont resort stands in 520 acres in a grand coastal setting. There are all the facilities you could wish for, including golf, massages, and a butler to

---

The Peat Inn

PEAT INN — Map 21 NO40

Modern British 🍴

Virtuoso skills in village institution

☎ 01334 840206
KY15 5LH
e-mail: stay@thepeatinn.co.uk
web: www.thepeatinn.co.uk
dir: At junction of B940/B941, 6m SW of St Andrews

A whitewashed cottagey former coaching inn in a tiny village is the setting of the Smeddles' small-scale restaurant. A welcoming lounge with a log fire and beamed ceiling leads on to three small dining rooms, where a décor of muted, natural tones helps create a relaxing atmosphere, backed up by staff who are friendly, confident and knowledgeable. The style is classically based but noticeably modern, seen in a starter of carpaccio of scallops served with pumpkin purée, spring

onions, hazelnuts and bacon dressing. Materials are carefully sourced and thoughtfully handled, and while dishes can be complex they are never showy or fussy. Cannelloni of lobster and scallops, the pasta with a slight bite, is served with creamed kohlrabi and a gentle shellfish velouté, and could be followed by tender, flavoursome daube of pork with braised white beans, roast turnips, apple and onion purée, crispy sage and crackling (a cohesive dish indeed), while caper and raisin dressing adds interest to seared hake with poached scallops. Presentation throughout is as attractive as you would expect, culminating in a pudding like compôte of mango, passionfruit and pineapple together with coconut parfait, lychee sorbet and chocolate ganache.

Chef Geoffrey Smeddle **Owner** Geoffrey & Katherine Smeddle **Times** 12.30-2/7-9 Closed 25-26 Dec, 1-14 Jan, Sun-Mon **Prices** Fixed L 3 course £19, Fixed D 3 course £40, Starter £8-£18, Main £12-£28, Dessert £8-£12, Service optional **Wines** 350 bottles over £20, 3 bottles under £20, 16 by glass **Notes** Tasting menu 6 course D, Vegetarian available **Seats** 40, Pr/dining room 14 **Parking** 24

run your bath for you, as well as the Esperante dining room, named after a classic racing car. Done in autumnal hues of terracotta, brown and olive, it's a relaxing venue for cooking that makes a virtue of healthy eating. A terrine of smoked salmon and caper butter is fruitily garnished with poached apple and peach jelly, and there's mango purée with the duck rillettes. Mediterranean influences waft over mains such as cod with chorizo fricassée, sun-blush tomatoes and beans, while a winning pasta combination offers goats' cheese cannelloni with sweet potato tortellini in sauce vierge. Finish with a dark chocolate and Frangelico mousse with praline ice cream, perhaps with a glass of Muscat de Beaumes-de-Venise.

Chef David Andrews **Owner** Apollo European Real Estate **Times** 6.30 10 Closed Seasonal, L all week, D Mon-Tue **Prices** Fixed D 3 course £49.50, Tasting menu £40-£60, Service optional **Wines** 115 bottles over £20, 1 bottle under £20, 6 by glass **Notes** Tasting menu 6 course, Vegetarian available, Dress restrictions, Semi formal, no denim, trainers or shorts, Civ Wed 300, Air con **Seats** 60, Pr/dining room 80 **Parking** 250

The Inn at Lathones

◉◉ Modern European

Imaginative cooking in a characterful coaching inn

☎ 01334 840494
Largoward KY9 1JE
e-mail: innatlathones.com
dir: 5m SW of St Andrews on A915. In 0.5m before Largoward on left, just after hidden dip

Yes, it is possible to stay in St Andrews and largely avoid mention of the 'G' word if the action on the historic links is not your bag. Of course, golfers are more than welcome at this stylishly updated, 400-year-old drovers' inn tucked away among the back roads, but there's also a thriving live music scene and assured modern cooking in its cosy restaurant. The décor blends whitewashed walls, bare stone fireplaces and contemporary artworks with new oak tables, while friendly service bolsters the feeling of all-over well being. The kitchen has taken a simpler tack with its output recently, but you can be sure that locally-sourced materials are still at the heart of an imaginative repertoire taking in the likes of Dunsyre Blue crème brûlée, followed by the deep comfort of slow-cooked ox cheek with foie gras ravioli and Chantenay carrots, or hand-dived scallops matched with salt-cod brandade and stuffed pequillo peppers.

Chef Ewan Keane **Owner** Mr N White
Times 12-2.30/6-9.30 Closed 26 Dec, 1st 2 wks Jan **Prices** Starter £4.50-£8.50, Main £13.50-£22, Dessert £5.95-£7.50, Service optional **Wines** 89 bottles over £20, 13 bottles under £20, 5 by glass **Notes** Sunday L,

Vegetarian available, Dress restrictions, Smart casual, Civ Wed 40 **Seats** 40, Pr/dining room 40 **Children** Portions, Menu **Parking** 35

Nahm-Jim & the L'Orient Lounge

◉ Japanese, Thai

The flavours of Thailand in the town centre

☎ 01334 470000 & 474000
60-62 Market St KY16 9NT
e-mail: manager@nahm-jim.co.uk

Nahm-Jim is a popular family-run Thai restaurant over two floors, often full, in the town centre, with red and white walls, a wooden floor and some South-East Asian decorations. Produce is flown in weekly from Bangkok, the cooking is consistently of a high standard, and presentation is ever attractive. After a starter like spicy fishcakes, move on to a curry (lamb massaman, perhaps, slowly braised with shallots and potatoes in a gentle sauce), Thai-style local scallops, pan-fried in a garlic, oyster and miso sauce served with a spicy dip, and end with a deep-fried banana in coconut and honey with coconut ice cream. The long menu of authentic dishes gives plenty of scope and includes a selection from Japan as well as around half a dozen banquets.

Chef Bunonerd Mayoo, Bee Mitchell **Owner** Sandy & Bee Mitchell **Times** 12-5/5-10 Closed 25-26 Dec, 1 Jan **Prices** Food prices not confirmed for 2013. Please telephone for details **Notes** Vegetarian available, Air con **Seats** 85, Pr/dining room 8 **Children** Portions

Road Hole Restaurant

British ▮ NOTABLE WINE LIST ◉

High-achieving Scottish cooking on the Fife coast

☎ 01334 474371
The Old Course Hotel, Golf Resort & Spa KY16 9SP
e-mail: reservations@oldcoursehotel.co.uk
dir: M90 junct 8 then A91 to St Andrews

The imposing Old Course Hotel towers above the iconic greens of quite possibly the most famous golf course in the world, with the 17th hole, or 'Road Hole', on its doorstep. That's where The Road Hole Restaurant gets its name and there is no denying the views through the full-drop windows deliver all that you might hope for: a perfect view over the green across to the beautiful Fife coastline. This is the fine-dining option within the hotel and it delivers visual impact on the plate as well as

through those windows. The room is formally dressed in warm masculine tones with tables draped in white linen, while an open-to-view kitchen helps give it a pleasingly contemporary feel. Modern Scottish cooking is the thing and that includes careful sourcing of high quality regional produce, with sustainability and traceability as touchstones. Start, perhaps, with an East Neuk crab formed into a tower and flavoured with sorrel, or a Balgrove Farm beef carpaccio with parmesan. The simple things are done extremely well here, with attention to detail evident throughout a meal, and there's usually a twist to elevate dishes into three-Rosette territory. Craigtoun Estate rabbit might appear among main courses, with boulangère potatoes and carrot purée, whilst Gigha halibut is a possible fish option, served with roasted garlic risotto. Orange tart with liquorice ice cream is a nicely judged dessert, or go for Scottish cheeses with chutney. The serious wine list confirms the Road Hole's position as a serious player.

Chef Ross Marshall **Owner** Kohler Company
Times 12-2.30/7-10 Closed Jan **Prices** Fixed L 3 course fr £16.50, Fixed D 3 course fr £35, Starter £6-£12, Main £12-£22, Dessert £6-£8, Service optional **Wines** 400 bottles over £20, 11 by glass **Notes** Sunday L, Vegetarian available, Dress restrictions, Smart, no jeans/ trainers, collared shirt req, Civ Wed 260 **Seats** 70, Pr/ dining room 16 **Parking** 100

ST ANDREWS *continued*

Road Hole Restaurant

@@@ – *see page 577*

Rocca Grill

@@@ – *see below*

Rufflets Country House

@@ British, European

Daily-changing menus in smart country-house hotel

☎ 01334 472594
Strathkinness Low Rd KY16 9TX
e-mail: reservations@rufflets.co.uk
web: www.rufflets.co.uk
dir: 1.5m W of St Andrews on B939

Rufflets is an impressive turreted mansion, its white façade covered in creepers, standing in 10 acres (the flower garden is well worth a stroll). Its restaurant is a spacious, elegant and calming room, looking over the grounds, with faux wood panelling, deep terracotta walls hung with prints, and upholstered seats at formally set tables. The menu has much that catches the eye, from smoked salmon, prawn and dill roulade, served with herby crème fraîche and roast cherry tomatoes, to pavé of venison with blackcurrant jus, caramelised red cabbage, and potato gratin. Dishes can be as reassuring as chicken and apricot terrine with Cumberland sauce, and chargrilled rib-eye with Café de Paris butter, although the repertoire extends to Thai-style salmon fillet sauced with salsa verde, served with steamed pak choi and crushed potatoes, before the comfort of Eton Mess.

Chef David Kinnes **Owner** Ann Murray-Smith
Times 12.30-2.30/7-9.30 Closed L Mon-Sat **Prices** Fixed L 2 course £11-£15, Fixed D 3 course £35-£40, Service optional, Groups min 20 service 10% **Wines** 88 bottles over £20, 18 bottles under £20, 9 by glass **Notes** Sunday L, Vegetarian available, Dress restrictions, Smart casual, Civ Wed 150 **Seats** 60, Pr/dining room 130 **Children** Portions, Menu **Parking** 50

Russell Hotel

@ Scottish, International

Scottish-influenced menus in small townhouse hotel

☎ 01334 473447
26 The Scores KY16 9AS
e-mail: enquiries@russellhotelstandrews.co.uk
web: www.russellhotelstandrews.co.uk
dir: From A91 left at 2nd rdbt into Golf Place, right in 200yds into The Scores, hotel in 300yds on left

A two-minute stroll from the breakfast table to the first tee of the Old Course, the world-famous cradle of golf, coupled with spectacular views over St Andrews Bay, make this family-run Victorian townhouse an attractive prospect. And when you have finished with the mashies and niblicks, or had a bit of fun recreating the slow-mo running scene from *Chariots of Fire* along the endless sands, there's imaginative Scottish cooking to round off the day in the cosy candlelit restaurant. Ham hock and confit duck terrine with home-made piccalilli is a dependable starter, then local materials come into play in a main course such as roast saddle of Highland venison with glazed pear, apricot and honey stuffing and red wine jus. The addition of egg nog makes for an interesting take on pannacotta, served with, what else, shortbread biscuit.

Times 12-2/6.30-9.30 Closed Xmas

Rocca Grill

ST ANDREWS   Map 21 NO51

Italian, Scottish **V**

Smart, modish food overlooking the Royal and Ancient

☎ 0844 879 9136
Macdonald Rusacks Hotel, The Links KY16 9JQ
e-mail: info@roccagrill.com
web: www.roccagrill.com
dir: M90 junct 8, A91 to St Andrews. Turn left onto Golf Place, then right onto the links

The grill has a unique location looking over the 18th fairway of the Old Course and West Sands beach (where some scenes of *Chariots of Fire* were shot). It's a spacious room, with high ceilings, big feature lights, drapes and a chic décor, but friendly and relaxed staff dispel any suspicion of stuffiness. 'Classical Scottish cooking with a creative Italian twist' is the restaurant's mantra, so langoustines from Pittenweem (just around the coast) go into agnolotti served with crisp pork belly, Jerusalem artichoke purée and shellfish emulsion to make a memorable starter, and halibut fillet is wrapped in lardo, poached, and accompanied by pappardelle verde, vegetable minestrone and confit tomato. There are pastas and risottos, too, perhaps a lobster tagliolini served with the butter-poached claw and a vanilla and basil foam. Meats are handled just as confidently, a main course of Scottish lamb - loin, shoulder and belly - served with cauliflower and Mull cheddar purée, braised baby gem and sauce Reform, and the curtain might be brought down with lemon tart with orange sorbet, or an excellent dark chocolate ganache with an accompanying banana parfait, peanut purée amd rum jelly (a winning combination).

Chef Scott Davies **Owner** APSP Restaurants Ltd
Times 6.30-9.30 Closed L all week, D Sun (Oct-Mar)
Prices Fixed D 3 course £27.50-£45, Starter £7.95-£12.50, Main £15.95-£29.50, Dessert £6.95-£8.95, Service optional, Groups min 8 service 10% **Wines** 52 bottles over £20, 2 bottles under £20, 10 by glass **Notes** Tasting menu available, Vegetarian available, Vegetarian menu, Dress restrictions, Smart casual, Civ Wed 40 **Seats** 80, Pr/dining room 34 **Children** Portions, Menu **Parking** 23

Sands Grill

◉ Steak & Seafood ◔

Locally-inspired brasserie-style cooking

☎ 01334 474371 & 468228
The Old Course Hotel, Golf Resort & Spa KY16 9SP
e-mail: reservations@oldcoursehotel.co.uk
dir: M90 junct 8 then A91 to St Andrews

The Old Course has a range of dining options in its favour, plus quite possibly the most famous golf course in the world on its doorstep. It's a luxurious five-star affair and Sands Grill, as the name suggests, is the informal (relatively speaking) dining venue, done out with lots of black leather and darkwood, and looked over by a slick and unstuffy service team. From the Josper grill come excellent locally-sourced meats (10oz Scotch Black Isle rib-eye, 8oz flat iron, and whole baby chicken, perhaps), whilst among fish main courses might be roast wild Shetland pollock with chorizo, mussels and borlotti bean chowder. Finish with a warm hazelnut brownie with praline ice cream.

Chef Simon Whitley, Sean McGinley **Owner** Kohler Company **Times** 6-10 Closed L all week **Prices** Fixed L 3 course £15-£40, Service optional **Wines** 60 bottles over £20, 11 by glass **Notes** Sunday L, Vegetarian available, Dress restrictions, Smart casual, Civ Wed 260 **Seats** 75, Pr/dining room 40 **Children** Portions, Menu **Parking** 100

The Seafood Restaurant

◉◉ Modern Seafood ❶ NOTABLE WINE LIST

Racy contemporary fish cookery on the coast

☎ 01334 479475
Bruce Embankment KY16 9AB
e-mail: standrews@theseafoodrestaurant.com
dir: On A917 turn left along Golf Place

From unassuming beginnings in a former fishermen's pub in St Monans in the 1990s, the Seafood spread its wings and arrived at this perch on the St Andrews coast nearly a decade ago. Glass-walled on all sides, cantilevered out at one end over the embankment, so that you can watch the four seasons that often go by in a day on the east coast, it's a suitably dramatic environment for the racy, contemporary fish cookery that's on offer. Smoked haddock rarebit is a popular starter, chunks of fine fish in rich rarebit on sliced baguette, possibly coming with creamed leeks and pancetta, while crab from East Neuk is not merely dressed, but tricked out too with avocado espuma, confit tomato and sweetcorn sorbet. An in-betweenie at dinner - smoked salmon terrine, or half-a-dozen oysters with shallot vinegar and Bloody Mary - precedes a main such as crisp-skinned sea trout with sun-dried tomato linguini, tapenade and basil. Desserts have got it going on, in the form of complicated assemblages like apple and cinnamon pannacotta, cinnamon and almond crumble, caramel custard and apple sorbet.

Chef Colin Fleming **Owner** Tim Butler
Times 12-2.30/6.30-10 Closed 25-26 Dec, 1 Jan
Prices Fixed L 2 course £22, Fixed D 3 course £45, Service

optional **Wines** 180 bottles over £20, 5 bottles under £20, 12 by glass **Notes** Express L menu 2 course £12.95, Vegetarian available **Seats** 60 **Children** Portions **Parking** 50mtrs away

---

ST MONANS   **Map 21 NO50**

Craig Millar @ 16 West End

◉◉ Modern Scottish, Seafood ❶ NOTABLE WINE LIST

Eclectic cooking with sweeping harbour views

☎ 01333 730327
16 West End KY10 2BX
e-mail: craigmillar@16westend.com
dir: Take A959 from St Andrews to Anstruther, then W on A917 through Pittenweem. In St Monans to harbour then right

Sweeping views of the harbour in what was a former fisherman's cottage make for a neat blend of the dramatic and the homely at a seafood-specialising restaurant on the peaceful Fife coast. The well-spaced tables are washed with oodles of natural light during the day, and the informal tone of service enhances the chilled out vibe. Craig Millar incorporates elements from East Asian and European cooking into his short, enticing menus. Meals might open with a bowl of Thai coconut broth with squid 'chorizo', spring onion and chilli, or gravad lax with pickled beetroot, radish and a quail's egg. Following an intermediate course, which may be jarlsberg cheese tart with red onion confit, there's usually a choice of two fish and one meat, the former perhaps coley with Puy lentils, Chantenay carrots, cauliflower purée and curry oil, the latter roast pork loin with a mini-cottage pie and buttered cabbage in sage jus. Trendy flavour combinations see lemon polenta cake matched with Earl Grey sorbet for dessert, or there could be a pistachio soufflé with lime and fromage frais ice cream.

Chef Craig Millar **Owner** Craig Millar
Times 12.30-2/6.30-9 Closed 25-26 Dec, 1-2 Jan, 2 wks Jan, Mon-Tue **Prices** Fixed L 2 course £22, Fixed D 3 course £26-£40, Tasting menu £55, Service optional **Wines** All bottles over £20, 6 by glass **Notes** Tasting menu available, Sunday L, Vegetarian available **Seats** 35, Pr/dining room 25 **Children** Portions **Parking** 10

CITY OF GLASGOW

GLASGOW   **Map 20 NS56**

Blythswood Square

◉◉ Modern British ◔

Contemporary and classic cooking in former automobile headquarters

☎ 0141 248 8888
11 Blythswood Square G2 4AD
e-mail: reserve@blythswoodsquare.com

This luxurious townhouse spa hotel dates from 1821 and was once the HQ of the Royal Scottish Automobile Club. A painstaking restoration has delivered all the marbled and corniced grandeur you can handle, pointed up with a

generous hit of contemporary boutique style. Cocktails in the palatial Salon Lounge amid the forest of fluted columns topped with gilt capitals are a fine idea before you totter along to the restaurant in the erstwhile ballroom, where a stylish décor works a blend of period splendour and ultra-modern, bare dark wood tables, herringbone parquet floors, and scarlet tasselled lightshades with images of vintage cars as a nod to the building's heritage. The cooking displays a nicely inventive dynamic, delivering feisty contemporary dishes alongside comforting classics. Shetland cod with smoked egg yolk, ratte potatoes, soft herbs and clam juices is an opening gambit from the contemporary camp, while mains run from Josper-grilled Scottish steaks and lobster to confit sea trout with razor clam and citrus juices.

Chef Derek Donaldson **Owner** Peter Taylor
Times 12-2.30/6-10 **Prices** Food prices not confirmed for 2013. Please telephone for details **Notes** Sunday L **Seats** 120, Pr/dining room 80 **Children** Menu **Parking** On street

La Bonne Auberge

◉ French, Mediterranean

A touch of Parisian style in Glasgow

☎ 0141 352 8310
Holiday Inn Theatreland, 161 West Nile St G1 2RL
e-mail: info@higlasgow.com
dir: M8 junct 16, follow signs for Royal Concert Hall, hotel opposite

The menu and Parisian brasserie-style setting might scream Gallic through and through, but the menu at this smart restaurant in the Holiday Inn at the heart of Glasgow's Theatreland displays a rather more widely-ranging international remit. Going along with the French theme, a rich chicken liver pâté flavoured with garlic and port and served with red onion marmalade and toasted brioche hits all the right cross-channel buttons, while a well-constructed main course delivers a fillet of sea bass with peas, wilted lettuce and herb-crushed potatoes with white wine and chive cream. The choice extends its global reach to the likes of Thai-spiced pork belly, or Moroccan spiced chicken with white bean and chorizo stew. Puddings aim squarely at the comfort zone - sticky toffee pudding with vanilla ice cream, or a rhubarb and yoghurt mousse with ginger ice cream.

Times 12-2.15/5-10

GLASGOW *continued*

Brian Maule at Chardon d'Or

French V

Classical cooking in classy city-centre venue

☎ 0141 248 3801
176 West Regent St G2 4RL
e-mail: info@brianmaule.com
dir: 10 minute walk from Glasgow central station

His name is over the door, and unlike many absentee chefs, Brian Maule has spent the last decade (after a stint as head chef of Le Gavroche, no less) working in the kitchen of his city-centre Victorian townhouse restaurant. As the name might suggest, Chardon d'Or deals in contemporary French cuisine allied to top-grade Scottish produce, served in a modishly neutral setting of suede and leather banquettes, high-backed chairs, wooden floors, cream walls and glass panels. Pan-fried scallops might be accompanied by spätzle, chorizo and beetroot essence as a curtain-raiser, while mains could bring on braised Scottish beef cheek with rich red wine sauce and seasonal vegetables. At dessert, expect classics such as vanilla crème brûlée or apple tarte Tatin with vanilla ice cream and butterscotch sauce.

Chef Brian Maule **Owner** Brian Maule at Chardon d`Or **Times** 12-3/5-10 Closed 25-26 Dec, 1-2 Jan, 1 wk Jan, BHs, Sun **Prices** Fixed L 2 course £17, Fixed D 3 course £20.50, Starter £6.75-£12.75, Main £22-£26.50, Dessert £8.75-£12.50, Service optional, Groups min 8 service 10% **Wines** 170 bottles over £20, 2 bottles under £20, 9 by glass **Notes** Tasting menu 6 course, Pre-theatre 5-6.30, Vegetarian menu, Dress restrictions, Smart casual **Seats** 90, Pr/dining room 60 **Children** Portions **Parking** On street (metered)

Cail Bruich

Modern European **NEW**

Distinctive Scots cuisine with Scandinavian influences

☎ 0141 334 6265
752 Great Western Rd G12 8QX
e-mail: info@cailbruich.co.uk

Opposite the Botanical Gardens, the brothers Charalambous aim to bring a resourceful and distinctive style of new Scottish cuisine to a city not short of good restaurants. Influences from the French culinary lexicon may be familiar enough, but a Scandinavian streak (chef Chris has worked in Europe's chilly north) is altogether rarer. Preservation techniques such as pickling are on show in the carrot garnish that comes with pigeon breast and goats' curd to start. Small producers and suppliers are the mainstays of the kitchen, which imbues the dishes with both quality and character. Crisp-skinned Scrabster hake with bashed ratte potatoes, samphire and hollandaise is a satisfying main course, or there may be Perthshire mallard with pumpkin purée and ceps in a spicy jus. A soft chocolate brownie barely cooked past cookie dough texture is inspiringly teamed with candied walnuts, alcoholic cherries and rich vanilla ice cream for a visually appealing dish.

Chef Chris Charalambous **Owner** Paul & Chris Charalambous **Times** 12-2.30/5.30-9.30 Closed Xmas, New Year, 1 wk summer, 1 wk winter, Mon **Prices** Fixed L 2 course £14.95-£17.95, Fixed D 3 course £17.95-£20.95, Starter £6.95-£9.50, Main £16.50-£28.50, Dessert £6.50-£6.95, Service optional, Groups min 6 service 10% **Wines** 33 bottles over £20, 7 bottles under £20, 16 by glass **Notes** Tasting menu Fri-Sat, Sunday L, Vegetarian available, Air con **Seats** 48 **Children** Portions, Menu **Parking** On street

Gamba

Scottish, Seafood

Vibrant fish and seafood in the West End

☎ 0141 572 0899
225a West George St G2 2ND
e-mail: info@gamba.co.uk
dir: On the corner of West Campbell St & West George St, close to Blythswood Sq

Down in the basement - but none the worse for that - of a Georgian townhouse in the fashionable West End, Gamba is a perennial favourite with a stellar reputation for top-notch seafood. Its popularity is also a testament to its friendly approach to service. The clean-cut contemporary

---

Hotel du Vin at One Devonshire Gardens

GLASGOW   Map 20 NS56

French, European

Well judged, creative cooking in an elegant townhouse hotel

☎ 0141 339 2001
1 Devonshire Gardens G12 0UX
e-mail: bistro.odg@hotelduvin.com
dir: M8 junct 17, follow signs for A82 after 1.5m turn left into Hyndland Rd

Hotel du Vin have a knack of picking good buildings for their portfolio of boutique hotels, and at One Devonshire Gardens they have found a match made in heaven. The address has long been a player in the Glasgow dining scene, and now, as part of the HdV Group, it has maintained its culinary aspirations. The row of porticoed Georgian townhouses makes for an appealing hotel, with lots of period charm and done out in the group's favoured blend of old and new, with bags of good taste. The Bistro - as the restaurant is styled in line with other HdVs - is a rather grand room with burnished oak panelling, smartly dressed tables and bold food-related prints on the walls. And what comes out of the kitchen is a cut above. There's plenty of fine Scottish produce on the menu and dishes have a decidedly French-inflected, modish sheen to them: a starter of ravioli of wild mushrooms, for example, comes with cocoa bean foam and white spring truffles. Next up, perhaps pan-fried Tarbert halibut with a Scottish shellfish and saffron cream broth, or 28-day aged Cairnhill Farm steaks from the grill, and to finish, mango soufflé is a sterling version, served with lime and coconut coulis. The wine list is brimful of interesting things and the sommelier is on hand to ease you through it if you so wish.

Chef Darin Campbell **Owner** MWB/Hotel Du Vin **Times** 12-2.30/6-10 Closed L Sat **Prices** Fixed L 2 course £19.95, Fixed D 3 course £24.95, Tasting menu £69, Starter £9.95-£13.95, Main £17-£29.95, Dessert £9-£12, Service added but optional 10% **Wines** 600 bottles over £20, 12 bottles under £20, 12 by glass **Notes** Tasting menu 6 course, Sunday L, Vegetarian available, Dress restrictions, Smart casual, Civ Wed 70 **Seats** 78, Pr/dining room 70 **Children** Portions **Parking**

interior takes in terracotta tiled or boarded floors, pale wooden tables, fashionable seating and plenty of piscine references in its fish-themed artwork. The kitchen draws on Mediterranean and Asian influences and is passionate about sourcing the best seasonal produce from the Scottish larder, with fish from sustainable stocks cooked with simplicity and flair. The menu takes in a classic combo of grilled or pan-fried lemon sole with browned lemon and parsley butter, to the Med-inspired red mullet with chorizo peperonata and chick peas, and the Asian flavours of whole line-caught sea bass teriyaki with wasabi and fragrant rice.

Chef Derek Marshall **Owner** Mr D Marshall **Times** 12-2.30/5-10.30 Closed 25-26 Dec, 1st wk Jan, L Sun **Prices** Fixed L 2 course £16.95, Fixed D 3 course £19.95, Starter £7.50-£14.50, Main £15.50-£25, Dessert £4.95-£8.95, Service optional, Groups min 6 service 12.5% **Wines** 60 bottles over £20, 8 bottles under £20, 8 by glass **Notes** Pre-theatre menu, 3 course market menu for 2 incl wine £50, Vegetarian available **Seats** 66 **Parking** On street

Hotel du Vin at One Devonshire Gardens

◉◉◉ – **see opposite**

Ian Brown Food & Drink

◉ Modern Scottish **NEW**

Impressive modern Scottish cooking in Giffnock

☎ 0141 638 8422
55 Eastwood Mains Rd G46 6PW
e-mail: ian@ianbrownrestaurant.co.uk

Ian Brown was head chef at Ubiquitous Chip (see entry) for many years before finally opening his own restaurant in Giffnock. It's a friendly, family-run place, with much light wood in evidence, splashes of colour brought to the neutral décor by red lampshades and works by local artists on the walls. Dishes can sound deceptively simple, but they are big on flavour, as seen in a starter of melt-in-the-mouth pig's cheek with smooth Madeira sauce and herbed polenta, and main-course collops of venison, their richness cut by sweet-and-sour bramble sauce, nicely accompanied by celeriac purée, kale and sesame potatoes. Produce is of the first order, and the menus of contemporary ideas give plenty to consider, including a couple of fish options (baked sea bass fillet with clapshot and lemon hollandaise, perhaps). Don't miss out on a pudding like chocolate and ginger fondant with satsuma sauce.

Chef Ian Brown **Owner** Ian & Sheila Brown **Times** 12-2/5.30-9.30 Closed Mon **Notes** Fixed L/D 2/3 course £11-£14.40 (except Fri-Sat)

Jamie's Italian, Glasgow

◉ Italian

Jamie's Glasgow branch, vast, authentic and buzzing

☎ 0141 404 2690
1 George Square G1 1HL
e-mail: glasgow@jamiesitalian.com
dir: On the corner of Hanover St, opposite the Millennium Hotel

Jamie's Glasgow branch occupies the ground floor and basement of the old GPO building, the former a huge open-plan space with a high ceiling and a view into the hectic kitchen; the smaller downstairs area (just as atmospheric) hosts the bar. Despite its vast size, you may have to queue. Start with some antipasti - a board of meats, cheeses, pickles and salad, say - or a special like ricotta and parmesan fritters with chilli and tomato sauce, then go on to breadcrumbed turkey escalope stuffed with fontina and prosciutto topped with a soft-fried egg and truffle shavings. The polenta chips, flavoured with rosemary and parmesan, are worth a punt, as are puddings like tiramisù. Top-quality ingredients are authentically Italian and well-drilled staff are as enthusiastic as the man himself.

Times 12-11 Closed 25-26 Dec

Malmaison Glasgow

◉ Modern French, Scottish ◉

Reliable brasserie food in a former church

☎ 0141 572 1000
278 West George St G2 4LL
e-mail: glasgow@malmaison.com
dir: From George Square take St.Vincent St to Pitt St. Hotel on corner with West George St

It would break the mould if the Glasgow outpost of this boutique hotel group was housed in an ordinary building - it isn't. It was once a Greek Orthodox church and, once you've left the bar to descend the spiral staircase, the brasserie is to be found in the original crypt. Vaulted ceilings, a dark, tactile colour scheme and candlelight ensure bags of atmosphere. The eclectic menu is packed with comfort food, perfect for the jaded corporate diner, alongside more refined ideas. Classic starters might include coquille St Jacques, or cock-a-leekie, before main courses such as the Mal salmon fishcake with spinach and parsley sauce, or half a roast Normandy chicken with broad beans and morels. To finish, cherry clafoutis hits the spot.

Chef Colin Manson **Owner** Malmaison Hotels Ltd **Times** 12-2.30/5.30-10.30 **Prices** Fixed L 2 course fr £14.50, Fixed D 3 course fr £16.50, Starter £4.95-£7.95, Main £11.95-£25, Dessert £5.95, Service added 10%, Groups min 10 service 10% **Wines** 160 bottles over £20, 10 bottles under £20, 20 by glass **Notes** Pre-theatre menu available, Vegetarian available, Civ Wed 40 **Seats** 85, Pr/dining room 12 **Children** Portions, Menu **Parking** Q Park Waterloo St

Menzies Glasgow

◉ British, European **NEW**

Brasserie cooking in a chic city-centre hotel

☎ 0141 222 2929 & 270 2323
27 Washington St G3 8AZ
e-mail: philip.mellow@menzieshotels.co.uk
dir: M8 junct 19 for SECC & follow signs for Broomielaw. Left at lights

Built on the site of a former rice mill, Menzies is a chic city-centre hotel full of bright contemporary design. Low ceilings are a feature in the public rooms, with the main dining room an elegant space done in lemon and cream, softly lit and attentively run. Perky modern European brasserie food is the order of the day, with dishes coming simply and neatly presented. A pairing of seared pork belly and tiger prawns with apple mousse might get the ball rolling, while mains deliver the likes of smoked haddock with parsley mash and grain mustard cream sauce, or haggis-stuffed chicken breast with whisky sauce. Good textural contrasts are on show in a finale of apple crumble tart with salted caramel ice cream.

Times 12-2/7-9.30

Number Sixteen

◉ Modern International **NEW**

Buzzy neighbourhood venue

☎ 0141 339 2544 & 07957 423615
16 Byres Rd G11 5JY
dir: 2 mins walk from Kelvinhall tube station, at bottom of Byres Rd

This tiny neighbourhood restaurant on Glasgow's vibrant Byres Road has a strong local following who appreciate its unbuttoned approach and the kitchen's creative mission. It is an elbow-to-elbow sort of space with a pocket-sized downstairs area, and a mini-mezzanine above, all decorated with colourful artwork, and kept ticking over by casually dressed, on-the-ball staff. The chefs beavering away in the open-to-view kitchen aren't scared to experiment with novel flavour combinations, so a starter might bring together a galette of Jerusalem artichoke purée with roast beetroot, figs, crumbled feta, sumac and roast onion vinaigrette. Next up, braised pork belly is served with crackling, piccalilli, pumpkin and sage gratin, apple purée and red wine sauce. Pudding delivers an exotic combo of passionfruit and coconut tart with passionfruit ice cream.

Chef Gerard Mulholland **Owner** Gerard Mulholland, Joel Pomfret **Times** 12-2.30/5.30-9.30 **Prices** Fixed L 2 course £10.95, Fixed D 3 course £12.95-£15.95, Starter £4.95-£7.50, Main £13.95-£17.50, Dessert £6.75, Service optional **Wines** 20 bottles over £20, 13 bottles under £20 **Notes** Sunday L, Vegetarian available **Seats** 36, Pr/dining room 17 **Children** Portions **Parking** On street

GLASGOW *continued*

La Parmigiana

◉◉ Italian, Mediterranean

West End Italian institution

☎ 0141 334 0686
447 Great Western Rd, Kelvinbridge G12 8HH
e-mail: sgiovannazzi@btclick.com
web: www.laparmigiana.co.uk
dir: Next to Kelvinbridge underground

Coming up to its 35th birthday, La Parmigiana has earned its place as a Glasgow institution. Family-run, the small restaurant with its warm red walls, smartly dressed tables, and equally well turned-out staff, garners a loyal following for its traditional Italian cooking. The place is not preserved in aspic, though, and there is a nicely restrained modish influence to the menu, with the fine Scottish ingredients allowed to shine. Excellent home-made pasta is a good place to start, perhaps flavoursome lobster ravioli with a cream and basil sauce. Roast fillet of venison comes with a rich Brunello, porcini and Italian sausage ragù, plus a polenta croûton - a wonderful, hearty plate of food - while an elegantly put-together Calvados crème brûlée with apple confit and apple crumble ice cream makes a memorable finish.

Chef Peppino Camilli **Owner** Sandro & Stefano Giovanazzi
Times 12-2.30/5.30-10.30 Closed 25-26 Dec, 1 Jan
Prices Fixed L 2 course £15.90, Fixed D 3 course £18.25, Starter £5.40-£11.50, Main £13.25-£25.65, Dessert £5.90-£7.50, Service optional **Wines** 50 bottles over £20, 7 bottles under £20 **Notes** Pre-theatre 2 course £16.10, 3 course £18.25 5.30-7.30pm, Sunday L, Vegetarian available **Seats** 50 **Children** Portions **Parking** On street

RESTAURANT OF THE YEAR FOR SCOTLAND

Rogano

◉◉ Scottish, Seafood **NEW V**

Modern cooking with a sense of occasion in an art deco masterpiece

☎ 0141 248 4055
11 Exchange Place G1 3AN
e-mail: info@roganoglasgow.com

The Exchange Place quarter of Glasgow may be home to the city's thriving café culture, but Rogano is no mere parvenu. Having opened in 1935, at the time the Cunard liner Queen Mary was being built on the Clyde, it, could teach the skinny-latte brigade a thing or two. The art-deco styling, captured at its most lustrous in the bar, brings a sense of bygone sophistication to the place, a vision of grand living reinforced by the presence of bowls of chilled champagne. The service approach is reassuringly formal and the kitchen, while definably modern in its orientation, manages to imbue most dishes with a sense of occasion. A partnership of scallops with bacon-wrapped black pudding in shallot-dressed watercress is handled with delicacy, but delivers big flavour punch, while the haggis comes with foie gras and a potato rösti, with a dressing of red onion marmalade. Fish dishes are generous in their scope, taking in grilled sea bass with a smoked haddock fishcake in mussel and saffron cream, while a main course of rabbit offers moist and tender meat, wrapped in Parma ham, accompanied by earthy beech mushrooms and a sweet garlic jus.

Chef Andy Cumming **Owner** Lynnet Leisure
Times 12-2.30/6-10.30 Closed 1 Jan **Prices** Fixed L 2 course £16.50, Fixed D 3 course £40-£45, Tasting menu £40-£75, Starter £6.50-£12, Main £19.50-£30.95, Dessert £6.95-£7.95, Service added but optional 12.5%
Wines 100 bottles over £20, 6 bottles under £20, 14 by glass **Notes** Tasting menu 4 course, Sunday L, Vegetarian menu, Dress restrictions, Smart casual **Seats** 70, Pr/dining room 16 **Children** Portions **Parking** NCP car parks

Shish Mahal

◉ Modern Indian, European

Long-standing Indian in a quiet part of the city

☎ 0141 339 8256
60-68 Park Rd G4 9JF
e-mail: reservations@shishmahal.co.uk
web: www.shishmahal.co.uk
dir: From M8/A8 take exit towards Dumbarton. On Great Western Rd 1st left into Park Rd

Since the '60s, generations of Glaswegian curry aficionados have beaten a path to the Shish Mahal, a Kelvinbridge institution that inspires a following as loyal as Celtic and Rangers. And no wonder: service is friendly and knowledgeable, and there's a smart modern feel to its warm Asian colour scheme, leather seating and linen-clad tables that make it stand out from the high-street curry-house pack. Classic Indian cooking comes in many forms and the extensive menu explores its multitude of regional variations, taking in the usual suspects from the Madras, dopiaza and dansak departments, but broadening its remit to cover an intriguing listing of stuff you are less likely to have heard of. Start in time-honoured style with a kebab - perhaps a murgh swatti kofta comprising minced chicken with mint and coriander, then head down south for a garlic nashilee, a South Indian dish of chicken with heaps of garlic in a tomato-based sauce with sun-dried chillis. Pukka roti and naan breads are, of course, freshly baked and fine examples of their ilk.

Chef Mr I Humayun **Owner** Ali A Aslam, Nasim Ahmed
Times 12-2/5-11 Closed 25 Dec, L Sun **Prices** Food prices not confirmed for 2013. Please telephone for details

Wines 3 bottles over £20, 13 bottles under £20, 1 by glass **Notes** Fixed L 4 course, Vegetarian available **Seats** 95, Pr/dining room 14 **Children** Portions **Parking** Side street, Underground station car park

Stravaigin

◉◉ Modern International

Popular eatery with creative, multi-national flavour

☎ 0141 334 2665
28-30 Gibson St, Kelvinbridge G12 8NX
e-mail: stravaigin@btinternet.com
web: www.stravaigin.com
dir: Next to Glasgow University. 200yds from Kelvinbridge underground

'Think global, eat local' is the mantra of this contemporary Glasgow stalwart. Set against a backdrop of rough stone walls, beams, reclaimed and reinvented pieces of modern art and eclectic objets spread over two floors of café-bar and a basement restaurant, the cooking is consistently imaginative and full of flavour thanks to a kitchen that makes full use of Scotland's larder. Ideas are pressed into service from all over the world - from sticky Korean pork cheek with brown rice cake and kimchee, to haggis, mashed neeps and tatties to start, followed by Pentland pheasant Kiev with poppy seed and horseradish rösti and pickled cabbage, or Scottish seafood in a deep south marriage with sweet potato and bell pepper gumbo and okra tempura. Desserts keep up the globetrotting approach - perhaps kaffir lime and lemongrass arancini with coconut pannacotta, and mango and chilli salad.

Save on Hotels. Book at **theAA.com/hotel**

CITY OF GLASGOW 583 SCOTLAND

Stravaigin

Chef Doug Lindsay **Owner** Colin Clydesdale, Carol Wright **Times** 5-11 Closed 25 Dec, 1 Jan, L Mon-Fri **Prices** Fixed L 2 course £10-£11.95, Fixed D 3 course £15.95, Starter £3.65-£6.95, Main £8.95-£22.95, Dessert £4.65-£6.95, Service optional **Wines** 34 bottles over £20, 13 bottles under £20, 23 by glass **Notes** Pre-theatre menu 2 £13.95, 3 course £15.95, Sunday L, Vegetarian available **Seats** 50, Pr/dining room 50 **Children** Portions, Menu **Parking** On street, car park 100yds

See advert on page 584

Ubiquitous Chip

◎◎ Scottish

Iconic address for modern Scottish cooking

☎ 0141 334 5007
12 Ashton Ln G12 8SJ
e-mail: mail@ubiquitouschip.co.uk
web: www.ubiquitouschip.co.uk
dir: In West End, off Byres Rd. Adjacent to Hillhead underground station

In business for over 40 years, this West End institution is still propelled onwards by the urge to show off the best of Scotland's produce. The Chip is a true one-off, a hive of lively conversation, art and fine dining tucked away down a cobbled alley. Inside it's a warren of four dining areas, including a brasserie, and the in-demand courtyard and mezzanine beneath a glassed-over roof, as well as a trio of bars. All around are sprawling colourful murals in what might politely be called the naïve style, but there's no doubting the professionalism of what leaves the kitchen. The cooking takes a broad sweep through Scottish themes with plenty of imagination evident in ideas such as seared Galloway venison loin with mustard and apple tarte Tatin, and chive purée, or pistachio-dusted Islay scallops with pickled apple purée and crisp pork belly. At main course stage, a stuffing of Brazil nut and sultana could add depth to pan-fried breast and confit leg of guinea fowl, while roast halibut might be partnered with parsnip rösti and crisps, and watercress and spinach sauce. Go for a savoury finish with artisan Scottish cheeses, or rum crème caramel with raisin purée and treacle ice cream.

Ubiquitous Chip

Chef Andrew Mitchell **Owner** Colin Clydesdale **Times** 12-2.30/5-11 Closed 25 Dec, 1 Jan **Prices** Fixed L 2 course fr £15.95, Fixed D 3 course fr £39.95, Service optional **Wines** 306 bottles over £20, 19 bottles under £20, 27 by glass **Notes** Pre-theatre 2 course fr £15.95, 3 course £19.95 5-6.30pm, Sunday L, Vegetarian available, Civ Wed 60 **Seats** 100, Pr/dining room 45 **Children** Portions, Menu **Parking** Lilybank Gardens (50mtrs)

See advert on page 584

Urban Bar and Brasserie

◎ Modern British, French

Updated brasserie fare in an ex-bank

☎ 0141 248 5636
23-25 St Vincent Place G1 2DT
e-mail: info@urbanbrasserie.co.uk
dir: In city centre between George Sq & Buchanan St

Climb the small set of stairs, pass the champagne bar and enter the spacious dining room, where the décor, leather-look banquettes and booths, black-clad staff wearing long white aprons, and the bustle are all reminiscent of a Parisian brasserie. The menu runs to Serrano ham with borlotti beans, marinated artichokes and parmesan and steamed fillets of plaice with chorizo, fennel and sticky rice. The kitchen knows its stuff, producing smooth, rich foie gras and chicken liver parfait cut by Oxford sauce, then accurately cooked crisp-fried salmon fillet on a velvety, buttery lemon and vanilla sauce accompanied by crabmeat and truffled new potatoes. Francophiles will be pleased to see boeuf bourguignon, served with parsnip champ, and who could resist a jam jar filled with popcorn-flavoured pannacotta topped with salted caramel?

Chef David Clunas **Owner** Alan Tomkins **Times** noon-10 Closed 25-26 Dec, 1-2 Jan **Prices** Fixed L 2 course £16.95, Starter £6.50-£12, Main £11.50-£28.95, Dessert £5.50-£7.50, Service optional, Groups min 6 service 10% **Wines** 40 bottles over £20, 20 bottles under £20, 13 by glass **Notes** Fixed D menu available, Sunday L, Vegetarian available **Seats** 110, Pr/dining room 20 **Children** Portions **Parking** NCP West Nile St

La Vallée Blanche

◎ French NEW

French bistro cooking in a Glasgow ski lodge

☎ 0141 334 3333
360 Byres Rd G12 8AW
e-mail: enquiries@lavalleeblanche.com

A bustling venue in the West End, this place is named after one of the ski districts in the Haute-Savoie. With its log cabin walls, rustic tables and piles of freshly chopped wood, it certainly looks the part, even if the crisp virgin snow may be lacking. It makes an original and welcoming ambience for some straightforwardly conceived modern bistro cooking, taking peasanty French culinary influence as its touchstone. Start with a salad of smoked mackerel with a remoulade of beetroot, celeriac and apple, dressed in horseradish cream, and continue with fried sea bass on ham hock and butter bean cassoulet, topped with anchoïade and hedged about with curly kale and herbed crumbs. Classic steak frites with roast garlic and a buttery sauce of red wine and shallots is an obvious crowd pleaser, as is a subtly anise-laced version of crème brûlée with shortbread.

Chef David Maxwell **Times** 12-2.15/5.30-9.45 Closed 25 Dec, 1 Jan, Mon **Prices** Fixed L 2 course £14.95, Starter £4.95-£10.95, Main £11.95-£27.95, Dessert £5.95-£7.95, Service optional, Groups min 8 service 10% **Wines** 37 bottles over £20, 2 bottles under £20, 8 by glass **Notes** Sunday L, Vegetarian available, Air con **Seats** 78 **Children** Portions

GLASGOW *continued*

Wee Lochan

🌸 Modern Scottish **NEW**

Polished modern Scottish cooking in the West End

☎ 0141 338 6606
340 Crow Rd, Broomhill G11 7HT
e-mail: eat@an-lochan.com

Whether you watch the world go by from one of the outside tables on the street depends on the Glasgow weather, but it's lovely inside too, with its white walls hung with bright artwork and white leather-look chairs at wooden tables. You can just pop in for a coffee, but this restaurant and café deals in intelligently worked, bright, modern cooking, so it's worth staying around to eat. Chicken liver parfait sounds ordinary enough, but here it's served on a slate with pickled plums, and sautéed scallops and chorizo are accompanied by chilli, lime and herb butter. Among main courses, grilled fillet of hake, moist and succulent, comes atop a tower of crushed potatoes and green vegetables, surrounded by rich red wine sauce, and you might finish with something like saffron-poached pear served with a financier and clotted cream ice cream.

Chef Rupert Staniforth **Owner** Aisla & Rupert Staniforth **Times** 12-3/5-10 Closed 25 Dec, 1-2 Jan **Prices** Fixed L 2 course fr £10.95, Fixed D 3 course fr £15.95, Starter £3.50-£8, Main £8-£17.50, Dessert £4-£6.90, Service optional, Groups min 8 service 10% **Wines** 12 bottles over £20, 13 bottles under £20, 13 by glass **Notes** Pre-theatre set menu available, Sunday L, Vegetarian available **Seats** 50 **Children** Portions **Parking** On street (no charge)

HIGHLAND

ACHILTIBUIE   Map 22 NC00

The Summer Isles Hotel

🌸🌸 Modern British **V**

Tranquil surroundings, superb sea views and top class Scottish ingredients

☎ 01854 622282
IV26 2YG
e-mail: info@summerisleshotel.co.uk
dir: 10m N of Ullapool. Left off A835 onto single track road. 15m to Achiltibuie. Hotel 100yds after post office on left

This remote hideaway will stay with you forever - and for all the right reasons. After negotiating miles of single-track roads on the remote Coigach peninsula in Scotland's far north west, the Summer Isles come into view, and perched above the coastline, Terry and Irina Mackay's classy bolt-hole takes in the view across the islands to the Hebrides beyond. Inside, the ambience is upmarket, refined, but totally unstuffy - it has to be with the great outdoors all around waiting to be explored with wellies and the dog. Despite the out-of-the-way location, the kitchen here impressively sources 80% of its

materials from within a 30-mile radius, and what great ingredients they are: seafood is all landed locally, a local smokehouse supplies its fine wares, the Achiltibuie gardens across the road sort out herbs and salads, and bread is all baked in-house. Five-course dinners kick off to sunset over the isles if you're lucky; starting, perhaps, with a filo parcel of monkfish with lime and ginger, ahead of grilled breast of quail on wilted spinach with mushroom purée. The main event could offer saddle of Summer Isles Shetland lamb with bubble-and-squeak rösti, roasted garlic and rosemary, then the dessert trolley trundles around, before a superb array of Scottish cheeses brings down the curtain.

Chef Chris Firth-Bernard **Owner** Terry Mackay **Times** 12.30-2/8 Closed mid Oct-Etr **Prices** Food prices not confirmed for 2013. Please telephone for details **Wines** 4 by glass **Notes** Fixed D 5 course, Vegetarian menu **Seats** 28 **Children** Portions **Parking** 15

BOAT OF GARTEN   Map 23 NH91

Boat Hotel

🌸🌸 Modern Scottish

Modern bistro classics in a majestic Cairngorm setting

☎ 01479 831258
Deshar Rd PH24 3BH
e-mail: info@boathotel.co.uk
dir: Turn off A9 N of Aviemore onto A95. Follow signs to Boat of Garten

In such a traditional-looking Scottish country hotel in the heart of the Cairngorms, you might be forgiven for expecting the full-monty formal approach to dining. But its panelled Boat Bistro has moved with the times and gone all refreshingly unbuttoned and chilled, with unclothed wooden tables, tealights and relaxed service. Quality local and seasonal produce underpins the kitchen's well-presented modernised bistro repertoire; think hand-dived scallops teamed with butternut squash purée and crispy pancetta, or loin of Speyside venison with skirlie potato cake, Chantenay carrots and juniper jus. To finish, go for saffron and orange frangipane tart with vanilla ice cream or fresh raspberry cranachan pepped-up with toasted oatmeal and whisky cream. (Lighter options - classic Caesar salad to fish and chips - are available in the adjoining bar.)

Chef Sachin Kumar **Owner** Mr J Erasmus & Mr R Drummond **Times** 12-3/5-9 Closed Dec-Feb (bookings only) **Prices** Fixed L 2 course £9.95-£19.95, Fixed D 3 course £14.95-£29.95, Starter £6.95-£10.95, Main £10.95-£29.95, Dessert £5.95-£10.95 **Wines** 40 bottles over £20, 6 bottles under £20, 8 by glass **Notes** Early bird menu available daily, Sunday L, Vegetarian available **Seats** 70, Pr/dining room 40 **Children** Portions, Menu **Parking** 36

BRACHLA   Map 23 NH53

Loch Ness Lodge

🌸🌸 French, Scottish

Modern Highland cooking overlooking Loch Ness

☎ 01456 459469
Loch Ness-Side IV3 8LA
e-mail: escape@loch-ness-lodge.com
web: www.loch-ness-lodge.com
dir: A9 onto A82 Fort William/Loch Ness Rd. On right after Clansman Hotel

This stylish modern restaurant with rooms is a luxurious retreat, but top of the pile of its many attractions is the unforgettable location perched atop lovely grounds dropping steeply down to the western flank of Loch Ness. The interior is upliftingly colourful with the best tables in the rose-pink dining room those by the large picture windows with unobstructed views of the Loch. The Franco-Scottish five-course dinner menus should grab your attention more than any hope of spotting the loch's most famous wildlife. From start to finish, the quality of Scottish ingredients is obvious, whether it's locally-foraged ground elder in a velouté with extra virgin olive oil, or St Kilda crab with croûtons and tomato dressing. Main course could be pan-fried wild halibut with potato scales, creamed celeriac, caramelised shallots and soya beans, or a duo of Highland beef. Cheeses arrive French-style before pudding, which could bring caramelised brioche with roasted plums and orange and olive oil sorbet.

Chef Ross Fraser, Chris Leisk **Owner** Scott & Iona Sutherland **Times** 7-11 Closed 1st 2 wks Jan, L all week **Prices** Fixed D 3 course £32.50-£42.50, Service optional **Wines** 38 bottles over £20, 4 by glass **Notes** Vegetarian available, Dress restrictions, Smart casual, no jeans, Civ Wed 24 **Seats** 14 **Parking** 10

BRORA
Map 23 NC90

Royal Marine Hotel, Restaurant & Spa

◉ Modern Scottish V

Traditional Highland hotel with reliable cooking

☎ 01408 621252
Golf Rd KW9 6QS
e-mail: info@royalmarinebrora.com
dir: off A9 in village towards beach & golf course

It's no surprise that this smartly refurbished Edwardian country-house hotel does good service as a 19th hole, with Brora's renowned golf links on the doorstep. Lorimer's Restaurant - the hotel's fine-dining option - is the nattily traditional setting for dinner, formally attired in blue-themed Scottish baronial style, carpeted for comfort, with heavy tartan drapes and white linen-dressed tables. The kitchen keeps things intelligently simple, allowing quality produce from the local Scottish larder to shine in hearty portions. West Coast haddock, perhaps, lightly grilled with lemon and simply served with sautéed garden vegetables and new potatoes, or saddle of Highland venison accompanied by crunchy champ (studded with toasted seeds), roasted root vegetables and a rich port and red wine jus.

Chef Steven Oglesby **Owner** Duncraggie Ltd
Times 12-2/6.30-8.45 Closed L (pre booking only)
Prices Food prices not confirmed for 2013. Please telephone for details **Wines** 35 bottles over £20, 35 bottles under £20, 10 by glass **Notes** Vegetarian menu, Civ Wed 60 **Seats** 50, Pr/dining room 12 **Children** Portions, Menu **Parking** 40

DORNOCH
Map 23 NH78

Dornoch Castle Hotel

◉ Modern Scottish ☺

Traditionally-based cooking in a medieval castle hotel

☎ 01862 810216
Castle St IV25 3SD
e-mail: enquiries@dornochcastlehotel.com
dir: 2m N of Dornoch Bridge on A9, turn right to Dornoch. Hotel in village centre opp Cathedral

The medieval Highland seaside town of Dornoch is no unassuming hamlet. Facing each other across the market square are the 12th-century cathedral and the 15th-century castle, the latter now an idiosyncratic hotel with appealing walled gardens, overlooked by a plush, comfortable dining room with conservatory extension. Locally-informed, traditionally-based Scottish dishes add to the cheer, offering a duo of crab claw and langoustine with citrus salad dressed in herb oil to begin, and then seared loin of venison with juniper-spiked potato cake and port jus. Finish with a dessert trio, comprised of coffee-chocolate mousse, tarte Tatin and almond pannacotta.

Chef Mikael Helies **Owner** Colin Thompson
Times 12-3/6-9.30 Closed 25-26 Dec, 2nd wk Jan
Prices Fixed L 2 course £12, Fixed D 3 course £32.50, Starter £6.50-£7.95, Main £15.50-£20.50, Dessert £7-£8.50, Service optional **Wines** 25 bottles over £20, 22 bottles under £20, 6 by glass **Notes** Early D special menu, Sunday L, Vegetarian available **Seats** 75, Pr/dining room 25 **Children** Portions, Menu **Parking** 12, On street (free)

FORT AUGUSTUS
Map 23 NH30

Inchnacardoch Lodge Hotel

◉ Modern Scottish

Unfussy, produce-led cooking beside Loch Ness

☎ 01456 450900
Inchnacardoch Bay PH32 4BL
e-mail: info@inchhotel.com
web: www.inchhotel.com
dir: From Fort Augustus towards Inverness on A82

On the banks of Loch Ness, this 150-year-old former hunting lodge is now a traditionally done out country-house hotel with a lot going for it. Affectionately known as the Inch, it has smart bedrooms and, in the form of the Yard, a restaurant with fabulous views. Original polished floors, high ceilings and local artwork (for sale) set the scene, whilst well-laid tables and leather chairs crank up the comfort factor. Good quality local ingredients figure large in the slate of unfussy dishes; start, perhaps, with haggis, neaps and tatties, before moving on to oven-baked fillet of haddock with baby potatoes, red onion, courgettes and a creamy fish sauce, finishing with a four-layer chocolate cake served with

---

The Inch Hotel
Fort Augustus, Inverness-shire, PH32 4BL
Tel: 01456 450900 Fax: 01320 366248 www.inchhotel.com

The Inch Hotel, Fort Augustus is a beautiful country house hotel and hunting lodge on the banks of Loch Ness with tons of traditional character and a Scottish welcome so warm and friendly that you'll never want to leave.

All our well-equipped, comfortable, rooms come complete with WiFi, telephones, hair-dryers, tea and coffee making facilities and flat-screen TV's with Free View. All rooms are en-suite and many rooms also enjoy stunning views over Loch Ness, including our romantic bridal suite which comes complete with a beautiful 4 poster bed.

We are a family friendly hotel and have two suites with connecting rooms at the Inch that are ideal for families. Children under 5 also eat for free in the restaurant.

Dining is a real pleasure at the Inch. Our AA award-winning restaurant, The Yard, serves a superb Scottish menu using locally sourced produce that is prepared fresh every day, whilst the relaxing bar and lounge has an open log fire and over 60 malt whiskies to choose from.

Whether you're looking for a relaxing holiday or something more adventurous, the Inch provides the perfect base to explore the beautiful Great Glen and Loch Ness area. Scenic Urquhart Castle is just 20 minutes away by car, whilst Fort Augustus village centre is walking distance from the hotel and is the base for a number of Loch Ness cruises and trips along the Caledonian Canal.

For the more active amongst our guests, we have a number of stunning walks that start right outside our front door, and our friendly and knowledgeable staff are happy to advise on the wealth of local activities in the area and can arrange walking, climbing, rafting, horse-riding and golfing trips for guests, as well as cruises on Loch Ness. We also have mountain bike and boat hire available directly from the hotel and have our own mooring rights on the Loch.

For guests wishing to do a real Grand Tour of the Highlands and Islands, you'll find that the Inch makes the perfect holiday destination. We're only a 45 minute drive from both Inverness, the capital of the Highlands on the East Coast and also Fort William on the West Coast which is regarded as the Outdoor Capital of Britain. Further afield Kyle of Lochalsh and the Isle of Skye can be reached within a few short hours, as can the Cairngorms National Park. Private minibus tours of many of these areas can be arranged for guests by the hotel.

The Inch provides everything you need from a Loch Ness hotel to make your holiday in the Highlands an unforgettable experience. Our stunning backdrop, professional staff, award winning restaurant and flexible approach also make us the ideal venue for weddings, meetings, touring groups, reunions and festive breaks with family and friends.

Whatever your needs, the Inch Hotel can be assured to leave you feeling Highland Happy.

Save on Hotels. Book at **theAA.com/hotel**

HIGHLAND 587 SCOTLAND

caramel ice cream. It's worth noting that the bar lounge is home to 60 malt whiskies.

Inchnacardoch Lodge Hotel

Chef Paul Draper **Times** 12-4/7.30-10 **Prices** Fixed L 2 course £13-£15, Fixed D 3 course £22-£30, Starter £3.95-£5.95, Main £13.95-£21.95, Dessert £4.95-£6.95, Service added but optional 12.5% **Wines** 4 bottles over £20, 4 bottles under £20, 3 by glass **Notes** Vegetarian available, Civ Wed 35 **Seats** 24, Pr/dining room 6 **Children** Portions **Parking** 15

See advert opposite

The Lovat, Loch Ness

@@ Modern British **NEW** V ⟡

Distinguished contemporary cooking at the southern end of Loch Ness

☎ 01456 459250 & 0845 450 1100
Loch Ness PH32 4DU
e-mail: info@thelovat.com
web: www.thelovat.com
dir: On A82 between Fort William & Inverness

Lurking at the southern tip of mystery-shrouded Loch Ness, The Lovat is a Victorian house that still boasts part of the original wall of Fort Augustus in its grounds. Views from the hotel are as sumptuous as only the Highlands can offer, while inside has all the comfy sofas, wood fires, white linen and flickering candles you could hope for. Staff are extremely knowledgeable about the food, and have that precarious balance between formality and good cheer off to a fine art. The Scottish larder provides prime materials for the smart, seasonal cookery in which Sean

Kelly is bounteously gifted. Poached oysters with saffron linguine, chorizo and cucumber is a distinguished opener, as is the circular slice of confit duck and foie gras terrine, served on a bed of crumbled gingerbread and pickled apple. Fish is accurately and respectfully treated, as when a herb-crusted tranche of halibut turns up with a cannelloni roll of stewed beef shin, alongside sprouting broccoli and its purée, chanterelles and horseradish foam. Nerveless counterpointing of sweet and savoury elements lifts a dessert such as chocolate fondant, clementine cream, chocolate sorbet and salty black olive purée into the big league.

The Lovat, Loch Ness

Chef Sean Kelly **Owner** Caroline Gregory **Times** 7-9 Closed Nov-Mar, Sun-Mon, L all week **Prices** Fixed D 4 course £45-£55, Service optional **Wines** 24 bottles over £20, 10 bottles under £20, 6 by glass **Notes** Vegetarian menu, Civ Wed 120 **Seats** 24, Pr/dining room 50 **Parking** 30

See advert below

FORT WILLIAM — Map 22 NN17

Inverlochy Castle Hotel

◉◉◉ – see below

Lime Tree Hotel & Restaurant

◉◉ Modern Scottish

Modern Scottish cooking at the foot of Ben Nevis

☎ 01397 701806
The Old Manse, Achintore Rd PH33 6RQ
e-mail: info@limetreefortwilliam.co.uk
web: www.limetreefortwilliam.co.uk
dir: On the A82 on entering Fort William

At the foot of Ben Nevis overlooking Loch Linnhe, the former manse is now a combination of hotel, restaurant and art gallery. Artists' works are displayed on the neutral-coloured walls of the small, relaxed restaurant, where unclothed tables are simply laid and enhanced by candlelight. The menus are well considered, and dishes are distinctly flavoured and founded on good Scottish produce; Ayrshire belly pork, for example, slowly roasted and served with Stornoway black pudding, braised red cabbage and mustard jus, and fillet of salmon from the loch, accompanied by mussel and leek broth and crushed potatoes. Starters are inspired by the classics, which means haggis, neeps and tatties with whisky sauce, and Cullen skink. Among eye-catching desserts may be coconut and lemon verbena parfait with coconut sponge and passionfruit sauce, and a rhubarb and ginger version of cranachan.

Lime Tree Hotel & Restaurant

Chef John Wilson **Owner** David Wilson & Charlotte Wright
Times 6-9 Closed 24-26 Dec, L all week **Prices** Fixed D 3 course fr £29.95, Service optional **Wines** 35 bottles over £20, 7 bottles under £20, 10 by glass **Notes** Vegetarian available, Civ Wed 50 **Seats** 30 **Children** Portions **Parking** 10

Moorings Hotel

◉ Modern European

Popular Highland hotel with accomplished cooking

☎ 01397 772797
Banavie PH33 7LY
e-mail: reservations@moorings-fortwilliam.co.uk
web: www.moorings-fortwilliam.co.uk
dir: From A82 take A830 W for 1m. 1st right over Caledonian Canal on B8004, signed Banavie

There is no lack of Highland entertainment at this peaceful hotel on the Caledonian Canal. On the sedate side, you could watch boats stepping up the flight of locks known as Neptune's Staircase on the canal as it leaves Loch Linnhe, or wave at the Jacobite train as it chuffs by on its way to the fishing port of Mallaig; in more active mode, try hiking in the steps of World War II commandos who trained in the Great Glen. When the

Inverlochy Castle Hotel

FORT WILLIAM — Map 22 NN17

Modern British V

Stunningly situated and luxurious country-house hotel

☎ 01397 702177
Torlundy PH33 6SN
e-mail: info@inverlochy.co.uk
dir: 3m N of Fort William on A82, just past Golf Club, N towards Inverness

It would be a hard heart indeed that did not melt at the sight of this grand Victorian building by its own loch in the foothills of Ben Nevis. Built by the first Lord Abinger as a family home, it has been a hotel since the end of the 1960s, and its grandeur and scale is well suited to the country-house hotel form. Queen Victoria described it as 'one of the loveliest and most romantic spots'. Enough said. Traditional décor and luxuriant furnishings make for a cosseting and comfortable setting, and to maintain the impeccable royal connections, the furniture in the three dining rooms was a gift from the King of Norway. Note, gents, that jacket and tie are expected. The fixed-price menu offers up refined contemporary food, starting perhaps with caramelised scallops with lettuce risotto and smoked bacon espuma, the first course followed by a soup (Jerusalem artichoke and salsify, maybe). Next up, a main course such as crispy breast of Gressingham duck with magret cabbage, confit garlic and beetroot and, for dessert, hot Cassis soufflé with glazed lemon tart. Incidentals such as excellent breads and creative amuse-bouche hit the spot.

Chef Philip Carnegie **Owner** Inverlochy Hotel Ltd
Times 12.30-1.45/6.30-10 **Prices** Fixed L 2 course £28, Fixed D 4 course £67, Service added but optional **Wines** 295 bottles over £20, 11 by glass **Notes** Vegetarian menu, Dress restrictions, Jacket & tie for D, Civ Wed 80 **Seats** 40, Pr/dining room 20 **Children** Portions, Menu **Parking** 20

day's activities are done, Moorings is a welcoming, traditional place to return to, with the beamed Neptune's restaurant serving unfussy modern Scottish dishes. Local seafood and game star in a menu that might get going with moules marinière, followed by rib-eye of Highland beef cooked in Madeira, with parsley mash, mustard sauce and buttered beans, or roast rump of lamb with buttered cabbage, fondant potato and garlic and rosemary jus. Finish with white chocolate pannacotta with orange brandy jelly and a ginger cookie.

Chef Paul Smith **Owner** Mr S Leitch **Times** 7-9.30 Closed 24-26 Dec, L all week **Prices** Fixed D 3 course fr £30, Starter £3.40 £5.95, Main £10.95 £18.45, Dessert £4.65-£5.95, Service optional **Wines** 17 bottles over £20, 28 bottles under £20, 7 by glass **Notes** Vegetarian available, Dress restrictions, Smart casual, Civ Wed 120 **Seats** 60, Pr/dining room 120 **Children** Portions **Parking** 50

FOYERS   Map 23 NH42

Craigdarroch House

◉ British **NEW** ☺

Skilled Scottish cooking in Loch Ness country house

☎ 01456 486400
IV2 6XU
e-mail: info@hotel-loch-ness.co.uk
dir: Take B862 from either end of the Loch, then B852 signed Foyers

Traditional dark oak panelling, high corniced ceilings and crackling log fires are all part of the Highland appeal at Craigdarroch. The house is tucked away in a forest near the Falls of Foyers, and basks in splendid views down to the wild east bank of Loch Ness, which form the backdrop to dining in the romantic candlelit restaurant. Chef-proprietor Martin Donnelly mans the stoves single-handed, cooking everything from scratch in daily-changing set dinner menus that work within the modern British idiom. Elegantly-presented dishes start out with black pudding with sautéed mushrooms and brioche topped with a poached egg and pointed up with a subtly spicy sherry and Tabasco sauce. Next up, fillet of Highland beef is served simply with creamed cabbage and pepperoni, intricately-carved carrots and swede, and roast potatoes. Skilled execution is also the hallmark of a well-crafted apple tart and a punchy apple sorbet.

Chef Martin Donnelly **Owner** Martin & Elinor Donnelly **Times** 8 **Prices** Fixed D 4 course fr £36.50, Service optional **Wines** 40 bottles over £20, 6 bottles under £20, 4 by glass **Notes** Vegetarian available, Civ Wed 30 **Seats** 20 **Children** Portions **Parking** 30

GLENFINNAN   Map 22 NM98

The Prince's House

◉◉ Modern British ☺

Warm hospitality and confident cooking

☎ 01397 722246
PH37 4LT
e-mail: princeshouse@glenfinnan.co.uk
dir: From Fort William N on A82 for 2m. Turn left on to A830 Mallaig Rd for 15m to hotel

Not far from the breathtakingly beautiful spot where, in 1745, Bonnie Prince Charlie raised the last rebel army ever to be mustered on British soil (don't miss the enclosed stone monument), the white-fronted hotel certainly has location going for it. It also has warmth and hospitality too, all the more welcome when you're miles from anywhere, and the white-painted dining room, complete with log-fire and framed pictures of an assortment of ladies, is the setting for confident cooking that capitalises on the respective bounties of the hill country and the coastal waters. A seared fillet of sea bass is accompanied by provençale sunshine in the forms of roast peppers, aubergine fondant, salted lemon and herbs, while mains may offer the signature loin of hill lamb with a baked mushroom in green peppercorn jus, or a classy trio of Moidart venison medallion, loin of rabbit and breast of wood pigeon with their separate garnishes. Consistent finishers include chocolate and banana parfait with rum syrup.

Chef Kicron Kelly **Owner** Kieron & Ina Kelly **Times** 7-9 Closed Xmas, Jan-Feb, Low season - booking only, L all week **Prices** Fixed D 3 course £30-£35, Starter £7-£12, Main £18-£25, Dessert £7-£9, Service included **Wines** 70 bottles over £20, 12 bottles under £20, 8 by glass **Notes** Vegetarian available **Seats** 30 **Children** Portions **Parking** 18

INVERGARRY   Map 22 NH30

Glengarry Castle Hotel

◉ Scottish, International

Country-house comfort food by Loch Oich

☎ 01809 501254
PH35 4HW
e-mail: castle@glengarry.net
dir: 1m S of Invergarry on A82

Peering through dense woodland cloaking the hillsides above Loch Oich, and with the ruins of Invergarry Castle in its grounds, this grand Victorian mansion was built for the Ellice family, who got rich in the Canada fur and logging trades. Glengarry is a classic small-scale country

---

house, replete with the traditional comfort of tartans, chintz and antlers on the walls, and Victorian period charm in the classy dining room. Daily-changing dinner menus keep things traditional and uncomplicated - locally-smoked venison with cherry tomato and quail's egg salad to start, followed by roast loin of lamb with garlic-roasted vegetables and port wine jus. Given the setting, the finale just has to be a luxurious cranachan, with the requisite raspberries, Drambuie, honey-flavoured cream and toasted oatmeal all present and correct.

Times 12-1.45/7-8.30 Closed mid Nov-mid Mar, L all week

INVERGORDON   Map 23 NH76

Kincraig Castle Hotel

◉ French, British **V** ☺

Scottish fine dining in a splendid castle setting

☎ 01349 852587
IV18 0LF
e-mail: info@kincraig-castle-hotel.co.uk
dir: Off A9, past Alness towards Tain. Hotel is 0.25m on left past church

When you're a laird, you want an impressive base of operations, thus the former seat of the Mackenzie clan is a suitably Baronial castle complete with mini turrets and gables and heavenly views over the Cromarty Firth and Black Isle. Inside, it looks the part too - this is a house of some magnificence, but it is run with a hands-on style. The vibe continues in the romantically candlelit restaurant, where the scene is set by a centrepiece stone hearth, cherry-red walls and tables draped in pristine white linen. Excellent local produce takes a starring role in a modern Franco-Scottish repertoire that might get going with smoked ham hock terrine with confit cherry tomatoes and melba toasts, then proceed to fillets of sea bass served with mussel and saffron broth, baby potatoes and braised fennel.

Chef Denis MacKay **Owner** Kevin Wickman **Times** 12.30-2/6.45-9 **Prices** Fixed L 2 course £12.95-£20, Starter £4.25-£7.25, Main £8.95-£18.25, Dessert £3.25-£5.95, Service optional **Wines** 29 bottles over £20, 23 bottles under £20, 4 by glass **Notes** Fixed D 7 course £40, Sunday L, Vegetarian menu, Dress restrictions, Smart casual, Civ Wed 50 **Seats** 30, Pr/dining room 50 **Children** Portions, Menu **Parking** 40

Abstract Restaurant & Bar

Rosettes not confirmed at time of going to press – see below

Bunchrew House Hotel

◉◉ Modern, Traditional

A touch of Scottish baronial splendour

☎ 01463 234917
Bunchrew IV3 8TA
e-mail: welcome@bunchrewhousehotel.com
dir: 3m W of Inverness on A862 towards Beauly

With 400 years of history to its name, Bunchrew is a baronial-style country-house hotel in a glorious position on the banks of Beauly Firth. Spires rise into the Highland sky, 20 acres of gardens and woodlands await to be explored, and the sunsets over the distant hills may well leave a lasting impression. The dining room, resplendent with its wood-panelled walls, old portraits and smartly laid tables, serves up some excellent Scottish produce, including the harvest of the hotel's own gardens. Slices of salt-roasted duck might come in a first course with caramelised red onion tartlet and a sloe gin sauce, followed by local salmon with a Savoy cabbage parcel and shellfish sauce, or go for breast and thigh of guinea fowl with Stornoway black pudding. To finish, pannacotta gets perked up with blueberry and orange.

Times 12-1.45/7-9 Closed 23-26 Dec

Culloden House Hotel

◉◉ Modern British

Historic mansion with a locally-inspired menu

☎ 01463 790461
Culloden IV2 7BZ
e-mail: info@cullodenhouse.co.uk
dir: From A96 left turn at junction of Balloch, Culloden, Smithton. 2m, hotel on right

Set on the edge of the Culloden battlefield, the historic, three-storey Palladian building is an impressive sight with its creeper-covered façade and vast grounds. Inside is no less impressive. The restaurant has neck-achingly high ceilings from which hangs a large crystal chandelier, plus a plethora of fine antiques adds an air of grandeur commensurate with elaborately engraved red walls and carved stone. Tables feature a splash of the official Culloden tartan. Formal service also manages to be engaging as well as knowledgeable. A strong presence of local, seasonal produce, bolsters the imaginative menu. A pressing of confit guinea fowl with fine bean and celeriac salad and pickled vegetables works a treat, as does a balanced main-course seared fillet of Scottish salmon with a shellfish and vanilla risotto and lemon beurre blanc. Finish with poached pear alongside pear pannacotta, Sauternes jelly and caramel ice cream.

Chef Michael Simpson **Owner** Culloden House Ltd
Times 12.30-2/7-9 Closed 25-26 Dec **Prices** Food prices not confirmed for 2013. Please telephone for details **Wines** 76 bottles over £20, 9 bottles under £20, 8 by glass **Notes** Vegetarian available, Dress restrictions, Smart casual, Civ Wed 95 **Seats** 50, Pr/dining room 17 **Children** Portions **Parking** 50

Loch Ness Country House Hotel

◉◉ Modern British ⌖

Ambitious country-house cooking in former shooting lodge

☎ 01463 230512
Loch Ness Rd IV3 8JN
e-mail: info@lochnesscountryhousehotel.co.uk
dir: On A82 (S), 1m from Inverness town boundary

On the outskirts of Inverness, with great views over the city, this small country-house hotel, built in 1710, has bags of charm. Six acres of gardens, a cosy lounge with an open fire, an intimate restaurant and engaging staff all contribute to the appeal. The dinner menu offers a handful of dishes at each course, kicking off perhaps with oxtail risotto topped with a duck egg, or that

Abstract Restaurant & Bar

Rosettes not confirmed at time of going to press

Modern French

Riverside setting for imaginative cooking

☎ 01463 223777
Glenmoriston Town House Hotel, 20 Ness Bank IV2 4SF
e-mail: reception@glenmoristontownhouse.com
web: www.glenmoristontownhouse.com
dir: 2 mins from city centre, on river opposite theatre

The Glenmoriston is a swish hotel with an awful lot of good things going on. There's a Piano Bar with over 250 malt whiskies for a start, plus local beers, wines and cocktails, and a brasserie called Contrast which has tables right by the River Ness. The star of the show, though, is the Abstract Restaurant, which has a new head chef in the kitchen as we go to press. It's a thoroughly contemporary kind of place, featuring a chef's table where you can tuck into the tasting menu right in the heart of the action, and a good deal of effort is put into sourcing high quality Scottish produce for the broadly modern French output. Start with seared hand-dived West Coast scallops with a celeriac and white truffle purée, or mixed beetroot salad with goats' cheese 'snow', parmesan and leaves, followed by roasted rack and braised shoulder of new season Ross-shire lamb partnered with aubergine purée, fondant potato and balsamic jus. Desserts are an inventive bunch – how about lemon sherbet, lemon meringue ice cream, candied lemon and tarragon pesto syrup?

Times 6-10 Closed 26-28 Dec, Sun-Mon, L all week

fashionable pairing of scallops and belly pork, here served with black pudding and pea purée. Main courses can sound complicated, but the kitchen's lightness of touch manages to bring things together, as in halibut fillet with langoustines in a lobster and bacon vinaigrette with spinach and saffron-flavoured potatoes, or protein-rich venison (loin and fillet) with a rabbit leg, chicken and truffle mousse and a rich gravy. Rhubarb soufflé is worth waiting for.

Chef Chris Crombie **Owner** Loch Ness Hospitality Ltd **Times** 12-2.30/6-9 **Prices** Fixed L 2 course £12.95-£15.95, Starter £4.95-£10.50, Main £14.95-£22.50, Dessert £5.95-£8.50, Service optional **Wines** 19 bottles over £20, 12 bottles under £20, 9 by glass **Notes** Sunday L, Vegetarian available, Civ Wed 150 **Seats** 42, Pr/dining room 14 **Children** Portions, Menu **Parking** 50

The New Drumossie Hotel

@@ @ Modern Scottish

Confident, seasonal cooking at an art deco hotel

☎ 01463 236451
Old Perth Rd IV2 5BE
e-mail: stay@drumossiehotel.co.uk
web: www.drumossiehotel.co.uk
dir: From A9 follow signs for Culloden Battlefield, hotel on left after 1m

Just a short drive from Inverness, the Drumossie is a delightful place, an immaculately-white art deco beauty in acres of well-tended grounds framed all around by the Scottish Highlands. Its charm is due in no small part to the staff who treat guests with engaging politeness and feed them with high-class Scottish cuisine in the Grill Room. The quality of the raw materials shines out in a starter of hand-dived scallops teamed with Stornoway black pudding, cauliflower purée and a crispy shard of Parma ham, while mains bring on perfectly-timed honey-roast Gressingham duck with fondant potato, red cabbage and star anise jus. If something sizzling from the grill appeals, the meat delivered is impeccable Scottish rib-eye and sirloin steaks, with a choice of sauces that includes Arran mustard or whisky cream. Form stays true to the end with superb regional cheeses, or an intense dark chocolate ganache balanced by the counterpoint of orange sorbet, and kumquat and ginger compôte.

Chef Kenny McMillan **Owner** Ness Valley Leisure **Times** 12.30-2/7-9.30 **Prices** Food prices not confirmed for 2013. Please telephone for details **Wines** 2 bottles over £20, 2 bottles under £20, 13 by glass

Notes Vegetarian available, Civ Wed 400 **Seats** 90, Pr/dining room 30 **Children** Portions, Menu **Parking** 200

Rocpool

@@ Modern European

Riverside setting and smart modern cooking

☎ 01463 717274
1 Ness Walk IV3 5NE
e-mail: info@rocpoolrestaurant.com
web: www.rocpoolrestaurant.com
dir: On W bank of River Ness close to the Eden Court Theatre

On a corner site overlooking the River Ness, with windows on two sides, Rocpool has a cool, contemporary look, with lots of wood and a décor of natural tones. The kitchen picks up ideas from around the globe, so the menu is a crowd-pleaser, with everything from Cullen skink to fillets of sea bream steamed with spring onions, ginger and soy served with a crisp oriental salad and coriander-scented jasmine rice. Techniques are sound and presentation a forte: intensely flavoured chicken liver parfait is plated alongside thin fingers of toasted brioche with a small spoonful of home-made mango chutney, and three collops of roast venison loin, melt-in-the-mouth tender, are wrapped in Parma ham and served on top of rounds of black pudding and accompanied by a pool of parsnip purée topped with potatoes sautéed with mushrooms, garlic and thyme. Well-tried desserts run to vanilla crème brûlée and lemon meringue pie.

Chef Steven Devlin **Owner** Steven Devlin **Times** 12-2.30/5.45-10 Closed 25-26 Dec, 1-3 Jan, Sun (Oct-Jun), L Sun **Prices** Fixed L 2 course £13.95, Fixed D 2 course £15.95, Starter £3.95-£9.95, Main £11.95-£22.95, Dessert £5.95, Service optional **Wines** 42 bottles over £20, 4 bottles under £20, 13 by glass **Notes** Early D 2 course £13.95 5.45-6.45pm, Vegetarian available **Seats** 55 **Children** Portions **Parking** On street

---

KINGUSSIE　　　　　　　　Map 23 NH70

The Cross at Kingussie

@@ @ – *see page 592*

KYLE OF LOCHALSH　　　　　Map 22 NG72

The Waterside Seafood Restaurant

@ Modern, Traditional Seafood

Popular fish restaurant in the old railway waiting room

☎ 01599 534813
Railway Station Buildings, Station Rd IV40 8AE
e-mail: seafoodrestaurant@btinternet.com
dir: Off A87

Located in the old railway station waiting room, with original carved British Rail chairs (you weren't expecting Rennie Mackintosh, were you?), the nautical-hued blue and yellow restaurant is simple and informal. Fish and seafood specials are the name of the game, the menu updated as items sell out, the staff doing their efficient best to cope with the press of business. Among the popular dishes are lightly spiced crabcakes with red pepper and coriander salsa, smoked mackerel with sour cream and dill, and mains such as fat scallops complete with their roe, fried in herb butter and served in the shell with rice, red Thai seafood curry replete with hot spice and coconut milk, and the all-important seafood platters with salads and dips. Finish straightforwardly with a chunky and nutty chocolate brownie, served with vanilla ice cream.

Times 11-3/5-9.30 Closed end Oct-beginning Mar, Sun (please phone to confirm opening hrs), L Sat

---

LOCHINVER　　　　　　　　Map 22 NC02

Inver Lodge Hotel

@@ Traditional French V

Refined country cooking and breathtaking sea views

☎ 01571 844496
IV27 4LU
e-mail: stay@inverlodge.com
dir: A835 to Lochinver, left at village hall, private road for 0.5m

From its hillside location, the hotel looks down on to the fishing village and across the sea to the distant outline of the Western Isles; a stunning view shared by large windows in two sides of the restaurant. As if anyone needed reminding that Albert Roux, he of Le Gavroche fame (see entry, London), is involved in the place, the Chez Roux logo is stamped on everything, from butter dish to plates. Resolutely French cuisine may be expected under the circumstances - and, indeed, potatoes may be turned and soufflé suissesse may be among starters - but this is hearty country cooking, albeit with the refinements of the 21st century. Seared scallops with apple purée, pork belly and maple beurre blanc has good balance of

continued

LOCHINVER *continued*

flavours and textures, an alternative perhaps to smoked duck and leek terrine. Fish is a strength, inevitably, four well-timed varieties going into a daily special with diced tomato adding a dash of colour to tasty saffron sauce. Winter might see 12-hour-braised local beef cheek with lardons, served with glazed carrots and creamed potato.

Chef Albert Roux, Lee Pattie **Owner** Robin Vestey **Times** 12-6/7-9.15 Closed Nov-Mar, **Prices** Fixed D 3 course fr £42.50, Service added 10% **Wines** 62 bottles over £20, 6 by glass **Notes** Fixed L 4 course from £16.50, Vegetarian menu, Civ Wed 40 **Seats** 50 **Children** Portions, Menu **Parking** 30

MUIR OF ORD	Map 23 NH55

Ord House Hotel

⊛ Modern British

Comforting bistro cooking in a 17th-century house

☎ 01463 870492
Ord Dr IV6 7UH
e-mail: admin@ord-house.co.uk
dir: off A9 at Tore rdbt onto A832. 5m, through Muir of Ord. Left towards Ullapool (A832). Hotel 0.5m on left

A Stuart country house in its own expansive and manicured gardens not far from Inverness, Ord House is popular among local anglers and country sports people.

Log fires and a snug bar make a comforting scene in winter, and the first-floor dining room is small enough to feel intimate, with views over the grounds. Residents may make the acquaintance of the lady ghost who stalks the place after dark. A vegetable garden supplies much of the kitchen's fresh produce, and local suppliers the bulk of the rest. The culinary style is modern bistro, starting with the likes of tempura king prawns and sweet chilli dip, or foie gras with baked egg, and then going on to well-judged baked halibut in dill hollandaise, or Highland pheasant with crumble-topped leeks and mushrooms. Finish with defiantly textbook crème brûlée.

Chef Eliza Allen **Owner** Eliza & John Allen **Times** 7-9 Closed Nov-end Feb **Prices** Starter £5-£10.50, Main £12-£22, Dessert £4.95-£7.95, Service included **Wines** 14 bottles over £20, 18 bottles under £20, 4 by glass **Notes** Vegetarian available **Seats** 26 **Children** Portions **Parking** 24

NAIRN	Map 23 NH85

Boath House

⊛⊛⊛⊛ — *see opposite*

Golf View Hotel & Leisure Club

⊛ Traditional

Fine Scottish produce and sea views

☎ 01667 452301
Seabank Rd IV12 4HD
e-mail: golfview@crerarhotels.com
dir: Off A96 into Seabank Rd & continue to end

The hotel could just as well be named 'Sea View', as it has wonderful views over the Moray Firth, with access to long sandy beaches, the picture windows in the restaurant giving the same magical vista. There's a lot to recommend on a menu that's built on Scotland's bounty, from goats' cheese vol-au-vent to smoked haddock and langoustine chowder. The kitchen tends to favour a traditional approach, seen in a quenelle of salmon, and a main course of pavé of lamb with roast garlic and rosemary. There's no better way to finish than with cranachan with shortbread.

Times 6.45-9 Closed L Mon-Sat

The Cross at Kingussie

KINGUSSIE	Map 23 NH70

Modern Scottish 🏅NOTABLE WINE LIST 🐓

Sophisticated modern cooking in charming restaurant with rooms

☎ 01540 661166
Tweed Mill Brae, Ardbroilach Rd PH21 1LB
e-mail: relax@thecross.co.uk
dir: From lights in Kingussie centre along Ardbroilach Rd, 300yds left onto Tweed Mill Brae

Built as a water-powered tweed mill in the late 19th century, The Cross is surrounded by four acres of riverside grounds with an abundance of wildlife to spot. Drinks are served out on the terrace in summer, in one of the lounges in winter, and dinner is taken in the stone-walled, beamed restaurant, a warm and welcoming room with well-oiled, personable service. The format is a

set-price menu of three courses, with an appetiser to activate the taste buds (perhaps Jerusalem artichoke soup). Menus change daily and choice is restricted to two items per course, allowing the kitchen to select and concentrate on whatever ingredients are at their very best. Among successful starters has been salt-and-pepper squid, perfectly cooked, an added dimension given by anchovy and Riesling jelly. Conscientious sourcing pays off, seen in another starter of baked boudin of Rothiemurchus roe deer with beetroot, pickled apple and caramelised walnuts. Main courses can be complex without being overwrought; Trossachs wild boar, perhaps, served as seared loin, braised neck and slow-roast belly, all incredibly tender, with the sharpness of mustard fruits and the sweetness of vin santo. The fish option might be roast monkfish with caper and lemon dressing and herb gnocchi, and pudding may bring on a light, crumbly tart of pear and butterscotch with caramel ice cream and contrasting salted caramel. As we went to press we

learned the Youngs are planning to sell. Check theAA.com for the latest information.

Chef Becca Henderson, David Young **Owner** David & Katie Young **Times** 7-8.30 Closed Xmas & Jan (ex New Year), Sun-Mon, L all week **Prices** Fixed D 4 course £50, Service included, Groups min 6 service 10% **Wines** 200 bottles over £20, 20 bottles under £20, 4 by glass **Notes** L for large parties by arrangement, Vegetarian available **Seats** 20 **Parking** 12

Save on Hotels. Book at **theAA.com/hotel**

HIGHLAND 593 SCOTLAND

Boath House

NAIRN	Map 23 NH85

Modern British V

Small luxury country-house hotel with an outstanding restaurant

☎ 01667 454896
Auldearn IV12 5TE
e-mail: wendy@boath-house.com
dir: 2m E of Nairn on A96 (Inverness to Aberdeen road)

Don and Wendy Matheson's beautiful Regency mansion is a true labour of love. It is hard to imagine nowadays as you crunch along the immaculate gravel drive to the pillared Palladian façade designed by the celebrated architect Archibald Simpson, but the place was in a sorry state before they came to the rescue in the early 1990s. Now fully restored, Boath House has all the right ingredients for a world-class, small-scale country-house hotel. It helps that Wendy Matheson is a garden designer, so the 20 acres of grounds are now a sight worth seeing in their own right, taking in woodland, wildflower meadows, sweeps of lawn, and streams feeding an ornamental lake speckled with swans, wild geese and ducks, and stocked with trout. As food is what we're dealing with here, it's worth noting that the gardens earn their keep - particularly the orchard and Victorian walled garden, which supply the kitchen with organic fruits, herbs and vegetables, and there are bee hives for

honey. Inside, there's not a detail out of place in lounges that seem lifted straight from the pages of a glossy interiors magazine, and the artily-inclined will appreciate the fact that Boath is designated an art gallery, so there are works of 30 or so Scottish artists adorning the walls throughout, as well as sculptures in the gardens. A passionate believer in slow food and organic cooking, chef Charlie Lockley has been with the hotel since it opened its doors, so has long-established relationships with suppliers of impeccable materials that can't be plucked from the hotel's gardens or foraged from the woods. The result is food that is fizzing with freshness and flavour, bolstered by razor-sharp technique, spot-on timing and meticulous attention to detail from start to finish. Six-course, no-choice menus change daily, and unwind at a leisurely pace in an elegantly-proportioned, candlelit dining room, where French windows look across the gardens to the lake. Tersely-worded descriptions give no clue as to the deep, intelligently-combined flavours in each dish. Following the seasons beadily, you might set out with a soup of onion squash, seeds and oil, and note that with a maximum of 28 diners to cater for, quality control is second to none, as an intriguing array of dishes unfolds, from rabbit with oatmeal, bacon and pear, via salmon crème fraîche and caviar, to Speyside lamb with white

beans, crosnes and tongue. Cheese - Bonnet goats' cheese with crispbreads, for example - comes, French-style, before dessert, which might be a fine specimen of ginger cake with dates and chestnut.

Chef Charles Lockley **Owner** Mr & Mrs D Matheson **Times** 12.30-1.15/7-7.30 **Prices** Fixed L 2 course £24, Service included **Wines** 145 bottles over £20, 9 by glass **Notes** Fixed D 6 course £70, Sunday L, Vegetarian menu, Dress restrictions, Smart casual, no shorts/T-shirts/jeans, Civ Wed 32 **Seats** 28, Pr/dining room 8 **Children** Portions **Parking** 25

NAIRN *continued*

Newton Hotel

◉ Traditional European

Successful modern cooking in baronial-style hotel

☎ 01667 453144
Inverness Rd IV12 4RX
e-mail: salesnewton@ohiml.com
dir: A96 from Inverness to Nairn. In Nairn hotel signed on left

Newton Hotel was built in the 17th century in Scottish baronial style, complete with crenallated tower and turrets, although it's been much extended to accommodate conferences for hundreds of delegates. Catering for large numbers does not mean that the cooking here is in any way institutional; high levels of ambition, technical skill and thoughtfulness are clear throughout a meal. Seared scallops, with pressed pork cheek and a bisque reduction, is an up-to-the-minute starter, and could be followed by roast venison loin and braised oxtail with juniper sauce, vegetable boulangère, creamed parsnips and choucroute, or seared fillet of sea bream with salsa verde, avocado mousse and asparagus and watercress risotto. Key lime pie with strawberry sorbet may be among puddings.

Times 12-2.30/6-9 Closed Xmas & New Year

Grants at Craigellachie

◉ Modern Scottish

Well-crafted cooking in charming setting

☎ 01599 511331
Craigellachie, Ratagan IV40 8HP
e-mail: info@housebytheloch.co.uk
dir: A87 to Glenelg, 1st right to Ratagan opposite the Youth Hostel sign

A great little restaurant with rooms in a splendid location just off the main road to Skye, Grants is run by a hands-on husband-and-wife-team. There are (perhaps unsurprisingly in this neck of the woods) superb views from the white-painted house (over Loch Duich as it happens, across to the Five Sisters of Kintail mountains). The conservatory restaurant has just four tables so booking is advisable to say the least. It's a charming and elegant place to eat, with tables laid with crisp white linen and fresh flowers. Co-owner Liz Taylor runs front of house with relaxed charm while hubby Tony works his magic in the kitchen, championing local producers as he goes. Warm mousse of Loch Hourn queen scallops with Corran Red Velvet crab and squat lobster bisque is a beautifully flavoured first course, followed perhaps by braised tongue of Highland beef with glazed baby onions and an Amontillado sherry and rosemary reduction. To finish, a pear poached in mulled wine comes with banana crème caramel and mascarpone, almond and Amaretto ice cream.

Chef Tony Taylor **Owner** Tony & Liz Taylor **Times** 7-11 Closed Dec-mid Feb, L all week, D Sun, Mon **Prices** Starter £6-£10, Main £15-£20, Dessert £7-£10, Service optional **Wines** 57 bottles over £20, 11 bottles under £20, 7 by glass **Notes** Restaurant open only by reservation, Vegetarian available **Seats** 12 **Children** Portions

Tigh an Eilean Hotel Restaurant

◉◉ Modern Scottish

Imaginative cooking with loch views

☎ 01520 755251
IV54 8XN
e-mail: tighaneilean@keme.co.uk
dir: From A896 follow signs for Shieldaig. Hotel in village centre on water's edge

In a charming village on the shore of Loch Torridon, Tigh an Eilean Hotel has a small and intimate restaurant, its green walls hung with colourful posters, with fabulous sea views, (so window seats are at a premium). Locally-landed seafood runs like a rich seam through the daily-changing menu, perhaps as a straightforward starter of potted shrimps, and a main course of well-timed fillet of salmon on fettuccine with saffron sauce. Imaginative ideas are culled globally, so a taster of sopa de guisantes (spicy pea soup) may precede tricolore salad, to be followed by tender duck breast roasted with plums on a ginger, honey and soy sauce accompanied by pak choi and spicy sautéed potatoes. Local game pops up in season - perhaps as quail with grapes - and dinner ends strongly with a pudding like classic cherry clafoutis.

Times 7-9 Closed end Oct-mid Mar (except private booking), L all week

Russell's at Smiddy House

◉◉ Modern Scottish

Seasonal cooking amid elegant pastoral surroundings

☎ 01397 712335
Roy Bridge Rd PH34 4EU
e-mail: enquiry@smiddyhouse.com
dir: In village centre, 9m N of Fort William, on A82 towards Inverness

The low-roofed white building stands on a corner on the main road through the village, in front of a cottage that was once the village blacksmith's (hence 'Smiddy'). It's a gentle, pastoral setting with elegant country décor, and serves as a fine backdrop for Glen Russell's modish seasonal Scottish cooking. A salad of warm figs with caramelised pecans and avocado ice cream offers nice contrasts of texture and temperature, and ushers in main courses built around pedigree raw materials. Grilled hake in smoked haddock chowder is a robustly satisfying fish dish, while saddle of Highland venison comes with pancetta, Puy lentils and mushrooms in red wine jus.

Piquant flavours at dessert stage are mobilised for rhubarb cheesecake or lemon and fennel tart.

Chef Glen Russell **Owner** Glen Russell, Robert Bryson **Times** 6-9 Closed 2 days a week (Nov-Apr), L Mon-Sat **Prices** Food prices not confirmed for 2013. Please telephone for details **Wines** 31 bottles over £20, 8 bottles under £20, 5 by glass **Notes** Sunday L, Vegetarian available, Dress restrictions, Smart casual **Seats** 38 **Children** Portions, Menu **Parking** 15

Kilcamb Lodge Hotel & Restaurant

◉◉ Modern European, Scottish

Idyllically situated lodge with skilful cooking

☎ 01967 402257
PH36 4HY
e-mail: enquiries@kilcamblodge.co.uk
web: www.kilcamblodge.co.uk
dir: Take Corran ferry off A82. Follow A861 to Strontian. 1st left over bridge after village

It takes effort to get to Kilcamb Lodge out on the remote Ardnamurchan Pensinsula, but when you arrive the rewards are more than ample. The setting in 22 acres of lochside meadows and woodland on the wild shores of Loch Sunart, with the mountains all around, is one that stays with you forever, while the elegant house is run with easygoing, unpretentious charm. As an escape from the daily grind, it can't be beaten, and with views like this you need to try to bag a window table in the restaurant, where intelligent contemporary country-house cooking showcases top-class local produce. Game and shellfish, often sourced from local estates and fishing boats, is a particular focus - perhaps Oban Bay scallops and Orkney crabcake with oriental dressing as an opener, while main course partners twice-cooked belly of Tamworth pork with spinach, salsify, mushroom tortellini and crackling. At the end, a fine plum crumble and pear frangipane tart is served with home-made vanilla ice cream.

Times 12-1.30/7.30-9.30 Closed 1 Jan-1 Feb

Save on Hotels. Book at **theAA.com/hotel**

HIGHLAND 595 SCOTLAND

TAIN
Map 23 NH78

The Glenmorangie Highland Home at Cadboll

◉◉ British, French 🌸

Fine dining in Highland hideaway

☎ 01862 871671
Cadboll, Fearn IV20 1XP
e-mail: relax@glenmorangie.co.uk
web: www.theglenmorangiehouse.com
dir: N on A9, at Nigg Rdbt turn right onto B9175 (before Tain) & follow signs for hotel

By any standards the setting is pretty impressive: a T-shaped house next to the ruins of a 13th-century castle in its own grounds with a private beach on the Dornoch Firth. Furnishings and decorations are of a particularly

high standard, and there's a dinner party vibe in the evening with guests seated at a long oak table set with candles, flowers and crystal. The meal is a no-choice four-course event, a sorbet following the second, with the menu changing daily. The kitchen needs to look no further than the locality for top Highland produce, with fruit, vegetables and herbs grown in the hotel's two walled gardens. A typical starter is foie gras terrine with pear chutney, followed perhaps by lobster with mango and avocado salsa and apricot and plum sauce. Main courses show a good balance of flavours - roast loin of roe deer with black pudding sauce, Puy lentils and an apple and beetroot galette, say with a prettily presented pudding like passionfruit and chocolate tart with coffee and chocolate ice cream and orange sauce to round things off.

Chef David Graham, Ross Sutherland
Owner Glenmorangie Ltd **Times** 8 Closed L except by prior arrangement **Prices** Food prices not confirmed for 2013. Please telephone for details **Wines** 38 bottles over £20, 5 bottles under £20, 15 by glass **Notes** Vegetarian available, Dress restrictions, Smart casual, no jeans or T-shirts, Civ Wed 26 **Seats** 30, Pr/dining room 12 **Parking** 60

THURSO
Map 23 ND16

Forss House Hotel

◉◉ Modern Scottish 🌸

Confident cooking in Georgian country-house hotel

☎ 01847 861201
Forss KW14 7XY
e-mail: anne@forsshousehotel.co.uk
web: www.forsshousehotel.co.uk
dir: On A836, 5m outside Thurso

Built as a private home in 1810, Forss House is surrounded by 20 acres of woodland and overlooks the river from which it takes its name; small wonder, then, that it's a popular base for anglers and game sportsmen. The restaurant is a high-ceilinged room with large portraits and an elegant fireplace; seats are comfortable, with shoulder-height backs, and staff add to a sense of well-being. Modern Scottish cooking is the name of the game, and dishes demonstrate that a confident, experienced team is at the stoves. A starter of scallop and lobster raviolo comes with the pasta on a bed of spinach, the shellfish on top in a rich bisque, all the flavours working in harmony. There could also be a soup - perhaps sweetcorn - followed by roast medallions of venison, cooked pink, sitting on roast salsify with a mini pie of minced meat and a dollop of beetroot fondant, with monkfish with crushed potatoes and olives a fishy

continued

The Torridon Restaurant

TORRIDON
Map 22 NG95

British, French V 🍷 NOTABLE WINE LIST

A piece of loch-side Highland luxury

☎ 01445 791242
IV22 2EY
e-mail: info@thetorridon.com
dir: From Inverness take A9 N, follow signs to Ullapool (A835). At Garve take A832 to Kinlochewe; take A896 to Torridon. Do not turn off to Torridon Village. Hotel on right after Annat

It takes effort to get to this magnificent turreted Victorian shooting lodge at the head of a sea loch in the remote western Highlands - unless of course you go for the helicopter option. But when you arrive, the view more than compensates for the time spent on the final 10 miles of long-and-winding single-track road. There may

not quite be a piper to welcome you, but the scene is as quintessentially Scottish as you could reasonably ask for, with 58 acres of wooded grounds and lochside rambles to blow away the cobwebs. Inside, the scene is a stylish and harmonious meeting of period features and contemporary designer input. Fans of a wee dram will boggle in anticipation at the whisky bar's arsenal of over 350 malts, in fact why not ape the European habit, and treat the water of life as an aperitif before moving into the restaurant? The setting, in two interconnecting dining rooms, is suitably grand: that splendid view is spread before you, and there are acres of clubby oak panelling, fancy plasterwork ceilings and crisp white linen on the tables; staff are knowledgeable about food and wine and keep everything moving forward at a well-orchestrated pace. Driving it all is the skilled modern cooking of chef 'Bruno' Birkbeck, who relies on classical techniques and close-to-hand ingredients for his five-course table d'hôte dinner menus. The performance begins with canapés - mini cod and chips in a paper cone, perhaps - then

proceeds to butternut squash and sage risotto with a crispy quail's egg, ahead of pan-fried Loch Ewe scallops with caramelised cauliflower purée and caper chicken jus. A well-conceived main course teams roast saddle of Applecross venison with black pudding ravioli, creamed cabbage, beetroot purée and juniper jus. After a pre-dessert, the curtain comes down with a dessert of glazed banana, banana bread, peanut ice cream, and peanut cannelloni.

Chef Jason 'Bruno' Birkbeck **Owner** Daniel & Rohaise Rose-Bristow **Times** 12-2/7-9 Closed 2 Jan for 5 wks, L all week **Prices** Fixed D 3 course £25-£45, Service optional **Wines** 156 bottles over £20, 27 bottles under £20, 8 by glass **Notes** Fixed D 5 course £55, Vegetarian menu, Dress restrictions, No jeans or trainers, Civ Wed 42 **Seats** 38, Pr/dining room 16 **Children** Portions, Menu **Parking** 20

THURSO *continued*

alternative. To finish, a perfectly made, intensely flavoured banana soufflé is served with rum and raisin ice cream.

Chef Gary Stevenson **Owner** Ian & Sabine Richards **Times** 7-9 Closed 23 Dec-4 Jan, L all week **Prices** Starter £5.95-£6.95, Main £19.95-£24.50, Dessert £6.50-£6.95, Service optional **Wines** 23 bottles over £20, 5 bottles under £20, 2 by glass **Notes** Vegetarian available **Seats** 26, Pr/dining room 14 **Children** Portions **Parking** 14

TORRIDON   Map 22 NG95

The Torridon Restaurant

⊛⊛⊛ – *see page 595*

INVERCLYDE

KILMACOLM   Map 20 NS37

Windyhill Restaurant

⊛ Modern British V

Engaging Scottish bistro food

☎ 01505 872613

4 St James Ter, Lochwinnoch Rd PA13 4HB
e-mail: matthewscobey@hotmail.co.uk
dir: From Glasgow Airport, A737 take Bridge of Weir exit. Onto A761 to Kilmacolm. Left into High Street

The name of this engaging little bistro, housed in former shop premises on Kilmacolm's main street, pays homage to the town's L-shaped, white-fronted Charles Rennie Mackintosh house, built in 1900. Inside is pleasantly cosy, with fairy-lights and candles to soften the scene, comfortable chairs and friendly staff. The background clatter of a busy kitchen adds to the homeliness of it all. Fresh seasonal produce informs the gently modern menus, producing a starter of West Calder haggis and pancetta beignets in horseradish batter on root vegetable champ, a complicated idea that comes off well. Main courses take in Shetland salmon fillet on smoked haddock and spinach risotto, and well-rendered rump of lamb with sweet-braised red cabbage, in a jus incorporating Puy lentils and chorizo. Finish with baked lemon and white chocolate cheesecake with blueberry compôte.

Chef Matthew Scobey **Owner** Matthew Scobey & Careen McLean **Times** 6-10 Closed Xmas-New Year, last wk Jul, 1st wk Aug, Sun-Mon, L all week **Prices** Fixed D 3 course £20-£21, Starter £4.95-£6.95, Main £9.95-£20.95, Dessert £5.95-£6.95 **Wines** 18 bottles over £20, 8 bottles under £20, 6 by glass **Notes** Sunday L, Vegetarian menu **Seats** 45 **Children** Portions, Menu **Parking** On street, car park opposite

LANARKSHIRE, NORTH

CUMBERNAULD   Map 21 NS77

The Westerwood House & Golf Resort

⊛ Modern Scottish

Confident modern cooking and top-drawer service

☎ 01236 457171

1 St Andrews Dr, Westerwood G68 0EW
e-mail: stewartgoldie@qhotels.co.uk
dir: A80 junct signed Dullatur, from junct follow signs for hotel

Westerwood House is a stylish contemporary golf and spa-oriented hotel in extensive grounds overlooking the Campsie Hills, yet only a 15-minute drive from the bright lights of Glasgow city centre. On the food front, Fleming's Restaurant fits the bill with its clean-cut modern look, all darkwood tables and seats upholstered in warm hues of tangerine and sage-green, while a switched-on professional team make sure it all goes with a swing. The kitchen follows a broadly modern Scottish path, enlivened with a splash of well-considered creativity here and there. Pan-fried scallops with chorizo and sweetcorn salsa and sweetcorn purée is a typical starter, while mains might run to roast rump of Perthshire lamb with Provençal vegetables, pan juices and pesto. To round things off, an irresistibly Scottish Irn Bru baked Alaska should hit the spot.

Times 6-9.30 Closed Sun-Mon, L all week

LANARKSHIRE, SOUTH

EAST KILBRIDE   Map 20 NS65

Macdonald Crutherland House

⊛⊛ British ☺

Elegant hotel dining room with accomplished cooking

☎ 01355 577000

Strathaven Rd G75 0QZ
e-mail: general.crutherland@macdonald-hotels.co.uk
dir: Follow A726 signed Strathaven, straight over Torrance rdbt, hotel on left after 250yds

A large white building in 37 peaceful acres, the original Crutherland House was built in 1705. The restaurant provides a suitably elegant backdrop for dinner, with its panelled walls hung with paintings and comfortable chairs at highly polished tables. The menu spells out the sources of the kitchen's raw materials - outdoor-reared free-range pork (perhaps belly with confit cheeks, fondant potato and kale), traceable beef from Scottish herds (grilled steaks with a choice of sauces), potatoes from a Northumberland farm, and so on. Dishes are thoughtfully integrated, with palate-pleasing results; grilled fillet of salmon with a lobster and langoustine reduction and saffron potatoes, or pan-fried chicken breast with garlic jus, roast salsify and Swiss chard. Starters span smoked salmon with capers, shallots and horseradish cream, and black pudding with pancetta, apple and a poached egg, and desserts might run to crème brûlée.

Chef Phillip Reilly **Owner** Macdonald Hotels **Times** 7-9 Closed L all week **Prices** Starter £6.50-£9.95, Main £16.25-£24.50, Dessert £6.50-£8.95, Service optional **Wines** 53 bottles over £20, 11 bottles under £20, 15 by glass **Notes** Vegetarian available, Dress restrictions, Smart dress, Civ Wed 300 **Seats** 80, Pr/dining room 300 **Children** Portions, Menu **Parking** 200

STRATHAVEN   Map 20 NS74

Rissons at Springvale

⊛ Modern Scottish V ☺

Uncomplicated modern Scottish cooking

☎ 01357 520234 & 521131

18 Lethame Rd ML10 6AD
e-mail: info@rissons.co.uk
dir: M74 junct 8, A71, through Stonehouse to Strathaven

Overlooking Strathaven Park, the Baxters' restaurant with rooms occupies a Victorian merchant's house, with dining divided between the restaurant or conservatory. Scott Baxter runs a tight ship, making bread and pasta in-house, and offering a clean-cut style of uncomplicated modern Scottish cooking. Rillettes of salmon with smoked salmon and potato salad is a satisfying starter, and could be the prelude to shoulder of lamb with barley risotto and rosemary gravy, or the signature Finnan haddock with leek sauce and mash, topped with a poached egg. Desserts are of the naughty-but-nice variety, including dark chocolate terrine with roast banana and caramel sauce, and there's home-made tablet on hand to round things off.

Chef Scott Baxter **Owner** Scott & Anne Baxter **Times** 12-2.30/6-9.30 Closed New Year, 1 wk Jan, 1st wk Jul, Mon-Tue, L Wed-Fri, D Sun **Prices** Fixed L 2 course £15.95, Fixed D 3 course £17.95, Starter £4.25-£10, Main £9.95-£22, Dessert £4.75-£6, Service optional **Wines** 13 bottles over £20, 23 bottles under £20, 6 by glass **Notes** Early evening menu Wed-Fri, Sunday L, Vegetarian available, Vegetarian menu **Seats** 40 **Children** Portions, Menu **Parking** 10

LOTHIAN, EAST

ABERLADY   Map 21 NT47

Ducks of Kilspindie

◎◎ Modern British **NEW**

Inventive modern cooking in smart restaurant with rooms

☎ 01875 870682
EH32 0RE
e-mail: kilspindie@ducks.co.uk

After moving out from his city-slicker restaurant in Edinburgh to the high street of the East Lothian village of Aberlady, Malcolm Duck has a winning formula at his smart restaurant with rooms. The décor in the cosy ten-table Ducks Restaurant references the local golf courses and also gives a nod to the duck theme in its eclectic mix of objets and artworks, while the kitchen team works a modern British vein to deliver inventive dishes of excellent quality. Much care goes into the sourcing of ingredients to produce an impressive understated warm salad starter involving roasted beetroot, alexander stem, goats' cheese bonbons and hazelnut dressing, followed by fillet of wild sea bass teamed with artichoke purée, alexander leaves, samphire, wild leeks, and saffron and pea risotto, or local pheasant with spiced red cabbage, bread sauce, Parmentier potatoes and star anise jus. As a finale, dark chocolate fondant with iced chocolate parfait and raspberry sorbet delivers the advertised flavours loud and clear. Donald's Bar Bistro serves up real ale and whisky (over 50) alongside the likes of sandwiches and 40-day aged steaks.

Times 12-3/5-9.30

GULLANE   Map 21 NT48

La Potinière

◎◎ Modern British ✋

Long-running gastronomic landmark with loyal following

☎ 01620 843214
Main St EH31 2AA
dir: 5m from North Berwick on A198

A modest-looking, intimate high-street restaurant that put Gullane on the gastronomic map a generation ago, the Potinière is done out in a fetching shade of raspberry, both outside and in. Essentially a two-handed operation, in which both partners cook and occasionally serve, it's the very model of a small fine-dining operation, as its band of regulars attests. Clearly not all the out-of-towners are here for the Muirfield golf nearby. An array of local suppliers is credited on menus that offer a pair of choices at each stage. Proceedings might open with a cheddar soufflé teamed with a tomato tart, alongside rocket and pesto, to be followed at dinner by an intervening soup, perhaps Thai-style coconut with poached scallops. The fish or meat choice at main could be between halibut, braised and served with sole and smoked salmon mousse and chive mash in saffron sauce, or fine Scotch beef, the fillet poached and then seared, alongside dauphinoise, in red wine and shallot sauce. A world of sweet satisfaction arrives in the shape of gooey-centred chocolate moelleux with a poached pear, caramel sauce and vanilla ice cream, and there are thoroughbred Scottish cheeses too.

Chef Mary Runciman, Keith Marley **Owner** Mary Runciman **Times** 12.30-1.30/7-8.30 Closed Xmas, Jan, BHs, Mon-Tue, D Sun (Oct-May) **Prices** Fixed L 2 course £19.50, Fixed D 4 course fr £43, Service optional **Wines** 39 bottles over £20, 8 bottles under £20, 5 by glass **Notes** Sunday L, Vegetarian available, Dress restrictions, Smart casual **Seats** 24 **Children** Portions **Parking** 10

NORTH BERWICK   Map 21 NT58

Macdonald Marine Hotel & Spa

◎◎ European ✋

Impressive Victorian pile with confident cooking

☎ 01620 897300
Cromwell Rd EH39 4LZ
e-mail: sales.marine@macdonald-hotels.co.uk
dir: from A198 turn into Hamilton Rd at lights then 2nd right

The views over the Firth of Forth and the East Lothian golf course give the Marine Hotel a sense of place - this is the east coast of Scotland and no mistake. The house is of 19th-century provenance, with all the expected Grade II listed grandeur, and its restaurant, named after the man at the stoves (John Paul McLachlan), serves up plenty of fine Scottish produce. The dining room is done out in rich, warming colours, with panelling and traditional portraits on the walls, but the dark wood tables remain clothless and the service keeps things suitably friendly and relaxed. John Paul is up to speed with contemporary culinary goings on, while his food shows respect for classical thinking. Ravioli filled with salmon and lobster and finished with lobster bisque is one way to start, or try the chef's modish take on the Arbroath smokie. Next up, perhaps slowly-braised Scottish beef cheeks with creamed potatoes and rosemary jus, and, to finish, hot chocolate fondant might come with griottine cherries and milk sorbet.

Chef John Paul McLachlan **Owner** Donald Macdonald **Times** 12.30-2.30/6.30-9.30 **Prices** Fixed D 3 course £35, Starter £5.50-£9, Main £12.50-£29.50, Dessert £7-£9, Service optional **Wines** 80 bottles over £20, 40 bottles under £20, 12 by glass **Notes** Sunday L, Vegetarian available, Dress restrictions, Smart casual, Civ Wed 150 **Seats** 80, Pr/dining room 20 **Children** Portions, Menu **Parking** 50

LOTHIAN, WEST

LINLITHGOW   Map 21 NS97

Champany Inn

◎◎ Traditional British

Upmarket steakhouse in a characterful old mill

☎ 01506 834532 & 834388
Champany Corner EH49 7LU
e-mail: reception@champany.com
dir: 2m NE of Linlithgow. From M9 (N) junct 3, at top of slip road turn right. Champany 500yds on right

The Champany Inn deals in the polar opposite of fussy, faddy food and sticks to what it knows best: this is the destination of choice for fans of properly-hung, expertly-butchered and chargrilled slabs of Class-A meat. The rambling cluster of buildings dates from the 16th century, and focuses on the main circular restaurant, which was once a horse-powered flour mill. The place has a baronial charm, with candle-lit burnished wooden tables, and oil paintings on bare-stone walls beneath a vaulted roof. Loch Gruinart oysters or hot-smoked salmon or cod from the Champany smokepot are a good way to get going, or you might opt for Brechin black pudding fried in a skillet with potato and apple rösti and red onion marmalade. But this is a mecca for beef, so the main event offers up your favourite cut - T-bone, porterhouse, rib-eye, Chateaubriand and all points in between - whacks it on a charcoal grill, and delivers the result timed to perfection. Quality of the raw materials is second to none, and consequently expensive. If you're on a budget, go for the more wallet-friendly Chop and Ale House.

Chef C Davidson, D Gibson, R Gilfillan **Owner** Mr & Mrs C Davidson **Times** 12.30-2/7-10 Closed 25-26 Dec, 1-2 Jan, Sun, L Sat **Prices** Food prices not confirmed for 2013. Please telephone for details **Wines** 650 bottles over £20, 8 bottles under £20, 8 by glass **Notes** Vegetarian available, Dress restrictions, Smart casual, no jeans or T-shirts **Seats** 50, Pr/dining room 30 **Parking** 50

LINLITHGOW *continued*

Livingston's Restaurant

◉◉ Modern European Ⅴ

Modern European cookery at a family-run place

☎ 01506 846565
52 High St EH49 7AE
e-mail: contact@livingstons-restaurant.co.uk
web: www.livingstons-restaurant.co.uk
dir: On high street opposite old post office

The family-run restaurant on the busy high street is imbued with just the right kind of homely feel. Candlelit tables in the original building are a welcoming proposition in the evenings, while the patio extension looking over the garden with its frolicking rabbits makes the most of fine days. The culinary style is trend-conscious modern European, drawing Mediterranean influences in to cast their warmth over chilly northern climes. Confit chicken and smoked pancetta terrine with pickled veg and prune purée might be the opener to good Scottish beef or lamb, the latter manifesting as loin and shoulder, with an array of today's soft textures - pea purée, carrot jelly and new potato fondant - in rosemary jus. A pre-dessert intervenes before the likes of passionfruit parfait with roasted pineapple, a grenadine pannacotta and mango jelly.

Chef Max Hogg **Owner** The Livingston Family **Times** 12-2.30/6-9.30 Closed 1 wk Jun, 1 wk Oct, 2 wks Jan, Sun-Mon (ex Mothering Sun) **Prices** Fixed L 2 course fr £16.95, Fixed D 3 course fr £39.95, Service optional, Groups min 8 service 10% **Wines** 37 bottles over £20, 24 bottles under £20, 6 by glass **Notes** Vegetarian menu, Dress restrictions, Smart casual **Seats** 60, Pr/dining room 15 **Children** Portions **Parking** NCP Linlithgow Cross, on street

---

The Tower

◉ Traditional British 🍴

Good Scottish fare in Queen Mary's old place

☎ 0844 879 9043
Macdonald Houstoun House EH52 6JS
e-mail: houstoun@macdonald-hotels.co.uk
dir: M8 junct 3 follow Broxburn signs, straight over rdbt then at mini-rdbt turn right towards Uphall, hotel 1m on right

It is easy to get into the Highland mood at the Macdonald Houstoun House hotel: the white-painted 16th-century house comes fully loaded with stag's heads, tartans, open fires and clubby chesterfields, and was once home to the doomed Mary, Queen of Scots. Climb an atmospheric staircase up the tower to a quartet of romantic and stylish dining rooms with panelled and burgundy-painted walls, bare wooden tables and open fires. Scottish produce underpins the kitchen's modern country-house cooking, so expect the likes of Cullen skink soup or haggis, neeps and tatties among starters, while mains take in classic grilled steaks, or rump of Borders lamb with stovie potatoes, barley and rosemary. The Saltire-waving repertoire closes with desserts such as Dundee pudding with butterscotch sauce or Clootie dumpling.

Chef David Murray, Jeremy Wares **Owner** Macdonald Hotels **Times** 6.30-9.30 Closed L all week **Prices** Starter £6.95-£9, Main £14.95-£22, Dessert £5-£14.95, Service optional **Wines** 74 bottles over £20, 16 bottles under £20, 13 by glass **Notes** Sunday L, Vegetarian available, Dress restrictions, Smart casual, no jeans or trainers **Seats** 65, Pr/dining room 30 **Children** Portions, Menu **Parking** 200

The Sun Inn

◉ Modern British 🍴

Winning menus in a popular gastro-pub

☎ 0131 663 2456 & 663 1534
Lothian Bridge EH22 4TR
e-mail: thesuninn@live.co.uk
dir: Opposite Newbattle Viaduct on the A7 near Eskbank

Looking for a classy country pub with rooms close to Edinburgh, then look no further than the Sun Inn, AA Scottish Pub of the Year 2011, situated eight miles south off the A7. Chef-patron Craig Minto spruced up the old building in 2009, maintaining the oak beams, panelling and crackling log fires, yet adding boutique rooms, modern creature comforts and a quirky décor. Menus champion local producers, with many named on the menu or the chalkboard in the bar, and offer a mix of classic comfort food and more innovative modern British ideas. Razor clams with crayfish, chorizo and confit lime with a lemon caper dressing, for example, followed by beer-battered Pittenweem haddock with hand-cut chips and

mushy peas, or roast duck with gooseberry compôte, confit duck wontons and stir-fry greens. For pudding, try the sharp and creamy limoncello tiramisù with amaretti biscuits.

Chef Ian & Craig Minto **Owner** Bernadette McCarron **Times** 12-2/6-9 **Prices** Food prices not confirmed for 2013. Please telephone for details **Wines** 27 bottles over £20, 24 bottles under £20, 33 by glass **Notes** Vegetarian available, Dress restrictions, Smart casual **Seats** 90 **Children** Portions **Parking** 125

Archiestown Hotel

◉ Modern British

Assured cooking in a small village hotel

☎ 01340 810218
AB38 7QL
e-mail: jah@archiestownhotel.co.uk
dir: Turn off A95 onto B9102 at Craigellachie

Archiestown, long a draw for salmon fishers on the Spey, is a lovely village on the Whisky Trail, and this small stone-built hotel, cosy and inviting, has been standing here for over 200 years. The bright, contemporary restaurant has a friendly feel, with artwork hanging on the walls, its regularly-changing menu boosted by daily specials. Local produce forms the core of the operation: venison, for instance, is carefully seared rare and served with sweet potato dauphinoise, roast roots and a modish beetroot and port jus. Among the handful of other main courses may be herb-crusted cod fillet on pea mash with shellfish cream. Sound technique means that twice-baked crab and lemon soufflé topped with cheddar, served as a starter, is a precisely cooked, fluffy version, while a trio of desserts brings on a light pear and plum pudding, velvety treacle tart, and sticky toffee pudding with custard.

Chef Robert Aspden **Owner** Alan & Jane Hunter **Times** 12-2/7-9 Closed Xmas, 3 Jan-10 Feb **Prices** Fixed L 2 course £13.50-£15, Fixed D 3 course £29.50-£32.50, Service optional, Groups min 10 service 10% **Wines** 24 bottles over £20, 11 bottles under £20, 6 by glass **Notes** Sunday L, Vegetarian available, Dress restrictions, Smart casual **Seats** 35, Pr/dining room 16 **Children** Portions **Parking** 30

Craigellachie Hotel

◉ Traditional Scottish

Modern Scottish cooking in whisky country

☎ 01340 881204
Victoria St AB38 9SR
e-mail: reservations.craigellachie@ohiml.com
dir: 12m S of Elgin, in village centre

The white-fronted Victorian hotel, not far from Elgin in the heart of Speyside, is a destination both for weary

Save on Hotels. Book at **theAA.com/hotel**

MORAY – PERTH & KINROSS 599 SCOTLAND

travellers and for lovers of the malted grain, which appears in no fewer than 700 manifestations in the Quaich Bar. In the Ben Aigan dining room, meanwhile, a modern Scottish agenda is pursued, with confident and consistent results. Fixed-price menus might open with a salmon array comprised of beetroot-cured gravad lax, home-smoked rillettes, pannacotta and a rose of smoked salmon, garnished with keta roe, to be followed by breast of duck with a pithiviers of the leg, creamed cabbage and a purée of carrot and ginger. Rounding it all off comes a wine-poached pear garnished with crushed hazelnuts and ginger ice cream cranachan.

Times 12-2/6-9

PERTH & KINROSS

AUCHTERARDER   Map 21 NN91

Andrew Fairlie @ Gleneagles

◉◉◉◉ – *see page 600*

The Strathearn

◉◉ British, French

Classical cooking in a grand but intimate dining room

☎ 01764 694270
The Gleneagles Hotel PH3 1NF
e-mail: resort.sales@gleneagles.com
web: www.gleneagles.com
dir: Off A9 at exit for A823 follow signs for Gleneagles Hotel

Elsewhere in the sprawling Gleneagles Hotel (see also Andrew Fairlie), The Strathearn dining room is a more mainstream experience, though one that has been given a refurbishment in the interests of a slightly more intimate atmosphere. That said, the art deco grandeur of the surroundings, from the moulded ceilings to the table lights, are still something to see, and the tableside labours of carving smoked salmon and setting fire to various items retain their allure. Sixes of oysters and dollops of caviar are the high-rolling ways to start, and the Franco-Scottish remit of the kitchen is ably fulfilled in the pairing of a clootie dumpling with foie gras in ginger wine. Mains bring on lobster thermidor, whole Dover soles, and a range of grilled meats, and also rack of lamb with boulangère potatoes in olive and thyme jus. At dessert stage, chocoholics can get stuck into the Valrhona menu, while the rest gravitate towards something like classic tarte Tatin, served with Calvados anglaise and clotted cream ice cream.

Times 12.30-2.30/7-10 Closed L Mon-Sat

COMRIE   Map 21 NN72

Royal Hotel

◉ Traditional British

Luxury small hotel with confident cooking

☎ 01764 679200
Melville Square PH6 2DN
e-mail: reception@royalhotel.co.uk
dir: In main square, 7m from Crieff, on A85

The Royal, at one time a coaching inn, is a small luxury hotel, its two dining rooms linked by double doors, the more traditional restaurant decorated with patterned wallpaper hung with numerous pictures. The menus may not hold too many surprises, but the kitchen is conscientious about sourcing fresh local produce, timing and seasoning are spot on, and presentation is a strength. Devilled lamb's kidneys could precede sea bass fillet atop curly kale in prawn butter sauce with new potatoes, or moist, crisp-skinned pan-fried chicken breast with a good Madeira and mushroom sauce and truffle-scented mash. Meals end happily enough with desserts like bread-and-butter pudding or hot chocolate fondant, both served with vanilla ice cream.

Chef David Milsom **Owner** The Milsom family
Times 12-2/6.30-9 Closed 25-26 Dec **Prices** Fixed D 3 course fr £29.50, Starter £4.85-£7.75, Main £7.95-£22.50, Dessert £5.95, Service optional **Wines** 46 bottles over £20, 47 bottles under £20, 7 by glass **Notes** Sunday L, Vegetarian available **Seats** 60 **Children** Portions **Parking** 25

FORTINGALL   Map 20 NN74

Fortingall Hotel

◉◉ Modern Scottish

Well-balanced menu in Arts and Crafts village

☎ 01887 830367 & 830368
PH15 2NQ
e-mail: enquiries@fortingall.com
dir: B846 from Aberfeldy for 6m, left signed Fortingall for 3m. Hotel in village centre

Fortingall Hotel, near Loch Tay with views down Glen Lyon, is a solidly built property, and within is a lounge bar that serves pub-style food and a choice of two dining rooms, one in Arts and Craft style, the other slightly less formal; staff are knowledgeable and approachable throughout. Set dinners offer a trio of choices at each course, the kitchen utilising as much local produce as it can; Perthshire lamb, for example, as a main course of pink-roast loin with thyme jus, creamed cabbage, artichoke purée and pommes en cocotte. Meals might kick off with a platter of smoked salmon, quail's eggs and Avruga caviar adding touches of luxury, or foie gras and game terrine complemented by Sauternes jelly, Cumberland sauce and poached figs. Fish is well handled, judging by pan-fried fillet of halibut served on

two balls of saffron-flavoured noodles with caviar butter and pak choi. Go for cranachan if offered - the real thing, served with whisky jelly.

Times 12-2/6.30-9

GLENFARG   Map 21 NO11

The Famous Bein Inn

◉ Modern British

Traditional inn serving up good Scottish food

☎ 01577 830216
PH2 9PY
e-mail: enquiries@beininn.com
web: www.beininn.com
dir: 2m N of Glenfarg, on the intersection of A912 & B996

Once a grand Georgian manor house and old drovers' inn in a wooded glen just off the M90 south of Perth, the Bein has joined the ranks of the gastro brigade, offering admirably fuss-free Scottish cooking with a side order of hearty Scottish welcome. It's a cheery, traditional place with a Saltire flapping from the flagpole and tartan on the floor of the lounge bar, and whether you choose to eat in the bistro or the Balvaird restaurant, the kitchen deploys top-class local and seasonal produce as the basis of an unpretentious menu. Work your way through the likes of pan-roasted loin of pork with apple purée, black pudding tempura and real ale sauce, or lamb rump steak with pommes Anna, baby veg, pea purée and pan juices. To finish, consider sticky toffee pudding with rich toffee sauce, or keep things savoury with Scottish cheeses served with oatcakes and chutney.

Chef Jian Bin Yo **Owner** John & Alan MacGregor
Times 12-9 Closed 25 Dec **Prices** Food prices not confirmed for 2013. Please telephone for details
Wines 8 bottles over £20, 14 bottles under £20, 5 by glass **Notes** Vegetarian available **Seats** 65
Children Portions, Menu **Parking** 27

Andrew Fairlie @ Gleneagles

AUCHTERARDER   Map 21 NN91

Modern French V  NOTABLE WINE LIST

France meets Scotland in luxurious Perthshire hotel

☎ 01764 694267
The Gleneagles Hotel PH3 1NF
e-mail: reservations@andrewfairlie.
co.uk
web: www.andrewfairlie.co.uk
dir: From A9 take Gleneagles exit, hotel in 1m

Gleneagles is a behemoth of a five-star hotel whose reputation well and truly precedes it. There is a chance, however, thanks to the prodigious talents of Andrew Fairlie, that it is no longer simply golf which springs to mind at the mention of its name. For despite the three championship golf courses, luxurious spa facilities and 850 acres of precious Perthshire countryside, the cooking of Andrew Fairlie grabs the headlines. He won the first ever Roux scholarship aged just 20, then went on to work under French super-chef Michel Guérard in Gascony, and accordingly French classical thinking runs deep in his restaurant. It all takes place in a cosseting room, moodily lit, with extravagant floor-to-ceiling silk drapes, deep-brown panelled walls, stylish banquettes emblazoned with the house's leaf motif, and original artworks by Archie Frost. The service meets the high-end expectations with its professional, slick and confident manner. If you've unanimity on your table, the menus du marché and dégustation give the opportunity to submit safely to the will of the kitchen, the former taking you perhaps from pressed confit pork with alexanders cream, black pudding and walnut crumble, via fillet of red mullet with squid, chorizo and saffron broth, to hot almond praline coullant with black treacle ice cream (six courses in all; eight for the dégustation). Produce is brought up from Rungis market on the outskirts of Paris and combines with first-class materials from Scotland in dishes of compelling refinement and craft. On the carte, a tripartite of Scottish shellfish (crab, langoustines and scallop) comes with winter vegetables and shellfish broth in a dish which sings in perfect harmony, or go for the unctuous caramelised veal sweetbreads and slow-cooked cheek, any richness relieved by the accompanying lemon peel. Main-course loin of Highland roe deer with pommes dauphine and confit pear shows the depth of affection for French culinary ways, likewise the selection of cheeses which comes before pud. The technical skills in the kitchen are very much in evidence at dessert stage, whether it is in a pear and almond tart with poached pear and quince sorbet, or hot lime soufflé with lychee sorbet and guava sauce. The wine list is big and smart, with an expert sommelier on hand to aid navigation.

Chef Andrew Fairlie **Owner** Andrew Fairlie **Times** 6.30-10 Closed 24-25 Dec, 3 wks Jan, Sun, L all week
Wines 350 bottles over £20, 12 by glass **Notes** ALC 3 course £85, 6 course Degustation £125/Du Marché £95, Vegetarian menu, Dress restrictions, Smart casual **Seats** 54 **Parking** 300

KENMORE   Map 21 NN74

Taymouth Restaurant

◉ Traditional Scottish

Modish Scottish cooking with glorious Tay views

☎ 01887 830205
Kenmore Hotel, The Square PH15 2NU
e-mail: reception@kenmorehotel.co.uk
dir: off A9 at Ballinluig onto A827, through Aberfeldy to Kenmore, hotel in village centre

Three of the four walls in the Taymouth are floor-to-ceiling windows giving unparalleled views over the Tay as it flows under the 1774 bridge. Tables, unclothed, are set with slate place mats, and candles and uplighters create a romantic atmosphere in the evening. The kitchen handles impeccable regional ingredients confidently and accurately and works around a perceptibly modern Scottish repertory, from venison and cranberry sausages in a broth of Puy lentils and vegetables to baked fillet of salmon on leek sauce. Chicken liver pâté with cranberry and port compôte, served with home-made oatcakes, may precede tender collops of venison on pickled red cabbage with redcurrant and bramble jus, and, to finish, an ice cream version of cranachan with shortbread hits the spot. Before leaving, take a look at the poem Burns scribbled on the chimney breast in the lounge.

Chef Spencer Barrie **Owner** Kenmore Estates Ltd
Times 12-6/6-9.30 **Prices** Starter £3.75-£9.95, Main £12.95-£24.95, Dessert £6-£8, Service optional **Wines** 17 bottles over £20, 30 bottles under £20, 13 by glass **Notes** Vegetarian available, Civ Wed 70 **Seats** 140, Pr/dining room 65 **Children** Portions, Menu **Parking** 40

KILLIECRANKIE   Map 23 NN96

Killiecrankie House Hotel

◉◉ Modern British V ✋

Satisfying country-house cooking in tranquil Perthshire

☎ 01796 473220
PH16 5LG
e-mail: enquiries@killiecrankiehotel.co.uk
dir: off A9 at Pitlochry, hotel 3m along B8079 on right

At this friendly small-scale hotel by the River Garry at the gateway to the Pass of Killiecrankie, tranquillity and space are part of the draw. It's a comfy, non-pretentious country house with lovely landscaped gardens all around, and period character inside, particularly in the romantic, candlelit, tartan-splashed dining room where a keen front-of-house team ensures everything ticks along at the right pace. The cooking keeps to established Franco-Scottish principles and serves up plenty of materials from local farmers, sea lochs and the kitchen garden. Fresh fish and seafood is always on offer - perhaps seared scallops with chorizo risotto, crispy Parma ham and chive oil, ahead of crispy-skinned sea bass fillets with potato Provençale, courgette ribbons and pesto dressing. Meats are well sourced too: pan-fried fillet of Highland venison, perhaps, teamed with dauphinoise potatoes, turnip fondant, braised red cabbage and sloe gin jus. End with

a dark chocolate and salted caramel tartlet with stem ginger ice cream.

Chef Mark Easton **Owner** Henrietta Fergusson
Times 6.30-8.30 Closed Jan-Feb, L all week **Prices** Fixed D 4 course £42, Service optional, Groups min 10 service 10% **Wines** 72 bottles over £20, 10 bottles under £20, 7 by glass **Notes** Pre-theatre menu from 6.15pm Mon-Sat, Sunday L, Vegetarian menu, Dress restrictions, No shorts **Seats** 30, Pr/dining room 12 **Children** Portions, Menu **Parking** 20

KINCLAVEN   Map 21 NO13

Ballathie House Hotel

◉◉ Classic V

Modern country-house cooking at the threshold of the Highlands

☎ 01250 883268
PH1 4QN
e-mail: info@ballathiehousehotel.com
dir: From A9, 2m N of Perth, take B9099 through Stanley & follow signs, or from A93 at Beech Hedge follow signs for Ballathie, 2.5m

The Glasgow to Aberdeen train used to deliver anglers to this turreted Scottish mansion by the River Tay, and although Ballathie is still a prime spot for the rod and line brigade, you don't need to dangle your fly into frigid waters to enjoy a stay here. The gastronomically inclined will appreciate the elegant buttercup-hued restaurant, and a kitchen team that takes native produce - much of it from the surrounding estate - as its starting point. Cooking is unapologetically in the tried-and-tested modern country-house idiom, and succeeds thanks to its superb ingredients and refusal to veer off course into faddish trends. Judicious balance and luxury touches combine in a starter of confit duck croustillant with seared foie gras, macerated apricots and carrot and orange purée, ahead of loin and truffled haunch of Sutherland venison with thyme rösti, red wine salsify, celeriac purée and praline sauce. Dessert wraps things up with a melting chocolate fondant with cherry compôte and pistachio ice cream.

Chef Scott Scorer **Owner** John Milligan **Times** 12.30-2/7-9 **Prices** Fixed L 2 course fr £19.50, Fixed D 3 course £43.50, Service optional **Wines** 140 bottles over £20, 20 bottles under £20, 14 by glass **Notes** Sunday L, Vegetarian menu **Seats** 60, Pr/dining room 35 **Children** Portions **Parking** 100

KINLOCH RANNOCH   Map 23 NN65

Dunalastair Hotel

◉ Modern British

Modern Scottish cooking in a tranquil country retreat

☎ 01882 632323
PH16 5PW
e-mail: info@dunalastair.co.uk
dir: From Pitlochry N, take B8019 to Tummel Bridge then B846 to Kinloch Rannoch

The stone-built Perthshire hotel is a tranquil bolt-hole, in which you will feel agreeably cocooned from the hurly-burly of urban life. Its interiors are all about venerable panelling and swagged curtains, with the elegant Schiehallion dining room at the centre of the operation. Here, a gentle style of country-house modern Scottish is practised, bringing on confit belly pork with pea pannacotta and an apple beignet to start, as a prelude to catch of the day, which may be seared and served with a lightly spiced clam casserole and samphire, or Perthshire beef daube with spinach, salsify and puréed caramelised carrot. Keep those taste buds alert for desserts that might add a pineapple and pink peppercorn salsa to traditional rice pudding.

Times 12-2.30/6.30-9

KINROSS   Map 21 NO10

The Green Hotel

◉ Modern European

Regional produce in a Perthshire golfing hotel

☎ 01577 863467
2 The Muirs KY13 8AS
e-mail: reservations@green-hotel.com
dir: M90 junct 6 follow Kinross signs, onto A922 for hotel

The green in the name is a reference to the hotel's two golf courses. What was once a modest 18th-century coaching inn has mushroomed into a sprawling golf and leisure resort with a spa and health club, curling rink, and five dining venues in a 5,000-acre estate on the shores of Loch Leven. Basil's Grill Room is the fine-dining option, where excellent regional produce is pressed into service in modern European dishes such as pan-seared scallops with parmesan spätzle, followed by venison loin and liver with dauphinoise potato. End with a warm chocolate fondant with white chocolate and almond milk.

Chef James Downes **Owner** Sir David Montgomery
Times 6.30-9.30 Closed L all week **Prices** Fixed D 3 course £25-£30, Service optional, Groups min 8 service 8% **Wines** 40 bottles over £20, 14 bottles under £20, 6 by glass **Notes** Vegetarian available, Dress restrictions, Smart casual **Seats** 90, Pr/dining room 22 **Children** Portions **Parking** 80

MUTHILL Map 21 NN81

Barley Bree Restaurant with Rooms

◉◉ Modern Scottish

Well-crafted contempory cooking

☎ 01764 681451
6 Willoughby St PH5 2AB
e-mail: info@barleybree.com
dir: A9 onto A822 in centre of Muthill

Barley Bree is a smart restaurant with rooms in a quiet conservation village, just a mile from the magnificent Drummond Castle Gardens. A one-time coaching inn dating from the 18th-century, it oozes spruced up rustic charm these days, with candles and flowers on scrubbed wooden tables, stone walls adorned with original artwork, old beams and boarded floors, and a double-sided wood burning stove that pumps out heat in the main dining room. Expect a cosy, informal atmosphere and good modish cooking with a distinct Gallic twist from Fabrice Bouteloup, the French chef-patron. Top-notch local ingredients are well sourced and traditional and contemporary techniques combine to good effect. A starter of succulent red mullet with a crisp fennel salad and rich, anchovy-infused caper dressing might precede melt-in-the-mouth slow-cooked blade of Aberdeen Angus with wild mushroom gratin, Jerusalem artichoke purée, roseval potatoes and black pepper jus. Round off with a simple, beautifully caramelised apple tarte Tatin.

Chef Fabrice Bouteloup **Owner** Fabrice & Alison Bouteloup **Times** 12-2/6-9 Closed mid Feb-early Mar, 2 wks Oct, Xmas, Mon-Tue **Prices** Starter £5.50-£11, Main £16.50-£23.50, Dessert £5.50-£8, Service included **Wines** 53 bottles over £20, 19 bottles under £20, 10 by glass **Notes** Sunday L, Vegetarian available **Seats** 35 **Children** Portions, Menu **Parking** 12

PERTH Map 21 NO12

Deans@Let's Eat

◉◉ Modern Scottish

Skilled modern Scottish cooking in smart setting

☎ 01738 643377
77-79 Kinnoull St PH1 5EZ
e-mail: deans@letseatperth.co.uk
web: www.letseatperth.co.uk
dir: On corner of Kinnoull St & Atholl St, close to North Inch & cinema

Husband-and-wife-team Willie and Margo Deans continue to run their down-to-earth restaurant near Perth centre with affable professionalism that has garnered a loyal fan base. Willie Deans' confident cooking shows clear French-influenced pedigree after years spent in some of Scotland's most prestigious kitchens, and he displays it in a repertoire of vibrant modern Scottish dishes. The setting is a warm and stylish blend of burgundy and terracotta with linen-clad tables, service is relaxed and knowledgeable, and the show might get going with a flag-waving dish of twice-baked cheddar soufflé with spicy haggis, whisky and cream sauce, then proceed to robust ideas such as loin of local venison with rosemary butternut squash purée, dauphinoise potato, roast onions, and cinnamon and red wine sauce; fish might get an outing as John Dory with lemon thyme couscous, corn kernels, samphire, wild mushrooms and cream. Desserts are reliably indulgent - perhaps white chocolate crème brûlée with Cointreau ice cream, candied orange and toasted marshmallows.

Chef Willie Deans **Owner** Mr & Mrs W Deans **Times** 12-3/6-10 Closed 1st 2 wks Jan, Sun-Mon **Prices** Fixed L 2 course £12.50, Fixed D 3 course £18.95-£22.95, Starter £4.95-£9.50, Main £12.95-£20, Dessert £2-£8.95, Service optional **Wines** 45 bottles over £20, 22 bottles under £20, 14 by glass **Notes** Sunday L, Vegetarian available, Dress restrictions, Smart casual **Seats** 70 **Children** Portions **Parking** Multi-storey car park (100 yds)

Murrayshall House Hotel

◉◉ Modern British ✿

Polished cooking amid the rolling Lowland acres

☎ 01738 551171
New Scone PH2 7PH
e-mail: info@murrayshall.co.uk
dir: From Perth A94 (Coupar Angus) turn right signed Murrayshall before New Scone

With a brace of 18-hole courses woven into its densely-wooded 350-acre estate, it's fair to say that most of Murrayshall's guests have golf in mind, but there are other attractions too, not least the fine dining to be had in its Old Masters restaurant. Bag a window table to soak up the views which stretch all the way to the city of Perth, and take in the leaded windows, original artworks and faultlessly elegant tone of the room. Menus bang the drum for Scottish produce and offer much to please traditionalists, plus a few creative flourishes to assuage modern tastes. The fatty richness of a duck liver pâté is offset with the acid twang of tart gooseberries and smoked bacon salad, while main course brings layers of pork belly and black pudding atop crushed apple purée spiked with Calvados and served with Savoy cabbage, mushrooms and rich jus. Puddings take refuge in classily-tweaked old favourites - cherry Bakewell tart with cherry ice cream and a shot glass of cranberry punch, for example.

Chef Craig Jackson **Owner** Old Scone Ltd **Times** 12-2.30/7-9.45 Closed 26 Dec, L Sat- Mon **Prices** Fixed L 3 course £18.95, Fixed D 3 course £28.50, Starter £4.95-£5.75, Main £12.95-£19.95, Dessert £5-£6.95, Service optional **Wines** 30 bottles over £20, 20 bottles under £20, 8 by glass **Notes** Sunday L, Vegetarian available, Civ Wed 130 **Seats** 55, Pr/dining room 40 **Children** Portions, Menu **Parking** 120

The New County Hotel

◉◉ Modern British ✿

Modish cooking in city-centre boutique hotel

☎ 01738 623355
22-30 County Place PH2 8EE
e-mail: enquiries@newcountyhotel.com
web: www.opusone-restaurant.co.uk
dir: A9 junct 11, Perth. Follow signs for town centre. Hotel on right after library

The boutique New County Hotel sits smack in Perth centre next to the Bell Library, handy for business lunches or checking out the cultural side of Perth on trips to the theatre, concert hall and galleries. The smart white façade opens into a clean-cut minimal space with a cool, cosmopolitan ambience, and on the food front there's a please-all approach in Café 22, and the cheerful, pubby bar-bistro. If you have something more ambitious in mind, head for the Opus One restaurant, where sharp technique and a lively imagination are brought to bear on top-class materials from Perthshire's larder. A menu of bang up-to-date ideas might see a racy composition of sea bass fillet with scallop boudin, carrot purée and citrus emulsion, followed by rump of local lamb teamed with goats' cheese pommes purée, black olives, wild garlic and lamb jus. Desserts keep the good ideas on stream - perhaps a blood orange workout that delivers the fruit as posset, jelly, sorbet and sablé biscuit.

Chef Rory Lovie **Owner** Mr Owen Boyle, Mrs Sarah Boyle **Times** 12-2/6.30-9 Closed Sun-Mon **Prices** Fixed L 2 course £14-£19, Fixed D 3 course £30, Service optional **Wines** 50 bottles over £20, 14 bottles under £20, 10 by glass **Notes** Early bird menu available, Vegetarian available **Seats** 48 **Children** Portions **Parking** 10, plus opposite on street

The North Port Restaurant

◉ British, International

Modern bistro cooking in the cultural district

☎ 01738 580867
8 North Port PH1 5LU
e-mail: thenorthport@mail.com
dir: In town centre behind concert hall & museum

Set in the heart of Perth's cultural district, near the concert hall and museum, as well as the historic Fair Maid's House, the stone-built house that is now North Port dates from the 1770s. Bare wood floors and tables establish an informal, pubby ambience, and the cooking is squarely in the modern bistro mould. A good value pre-theatre dinner menu is a reliable draw, but if you've more time, consider crab, tomato and avocado tian bound with garlic mayonnaise, followed by confit duck leg with truffle-oiled celeriac mash and pearl onion gravy, or piri-piri mackerel fillets with sauce gribiche. A vegetarian main might be sweetcorn and cheddar polenta cakes with mushroom crumble.

Chef Kevin Joubert **Owner** Kevin Joubert, Aleksandra Trzcinska **Times** 12-2.30/5-9 Closed 1st 2wks Jan, Sun-Mon, L Tue-Thu **Prices** Fixed L 2 course £11.95-£18.95, Fixed D 2 course £13.95-£24.95, Starter £4.25-£7.95, Main £9.95-£19.95, Dessert £4.95-£7.95, Service optional **Wines** 3 bottles over £20, 16 bottles under £20, 6 by glass **Notes** Pre-theatre menu daily 5-6.30pm, Vegetarian available **Seats** 55, Pr/dining room 20 **Children** Portions, Menu **Parking** On street, car park Kinnoull St

63 @ Parklands

◉◉ Modern European V

Smart contemporary cooking in a chic hotel

☎ 01738 622451
Parklands Hotel, St Leonards Bank PH2 8EB
e-mail: info@63atparklandshotel.com
dir: Adjacent to Perth station, overlooking South Inch Park

What was the Acanthus Restaurant at this smart hotel near the river has come under the creative aegis of Graeme Pallister, whose 63 Tay Street (see entry) is another of the city's gastronomic attractions. The same style of technically adept, well-focused cooking is on offer in the contemporary restaurant space here, which includes an outdoor patio and a small mezzanine. Fixed-

price menus with choices of two at the principal stages are the business, opening perhaps with Loch Nevis langoustine fricassée with shimeji mushrooms and penne. A soup is interposed before the main-course alternatives of Kirriemuir lamb rump crusted in olives and pine nuts, with tomato, basil and garlic, or salmon roasted in Hebridean salt and herbs with smoked salmon noodles in salmon roe butter sauce. Cheeses are followed by creative desserts such as rhubarb burnt cream with a salty ginger ice cream doughnut.

Chef Graeme Pallister **Owner** Scott & Penny Edwards **Times** 7-9 Closed Tue-Wed, L all week **Prices** Fixed D 4 course £35, Service optional, Groups min 8 service 10% **Wines** 32 bottles over £20, 18 bottles under £20, 8 by glass **Notes** Vegetarian menu, Civ Wed 30 **Seats** 32, Pr/dining room 22 **Children** Portions **Parking** 25

63 Tay Street

◉◉ Modern Scottish V ✦ NOTABLE WINE LIST ✿

Local, honest cooking by the River Tay

☎ 01738 441451
63 Tay St PH2 8NN
e-mail: info@63taystreet.com
dir: In town centre, on river

This easygoing contemporary restaurant in the historic riverside heart of Perth has a strong local following who agree wholeheartedly with chef-patron and local lad Graeme Pallister's 'local, honest, simple' mantra. He knows where to track down the best regional produce and how to treat it in an unfussy manner for maximum effect, whether you're there for a busy lunch with the Tay as a backdrop, or for a more leisurely and sophisticated date with dinner. The setting is a high-ceilinged dining room of unshouty neutral elegance jazzed up by a changing cast of artwork on the walls, with service ably orchestrated by switched-on staff. Scottish game pie with port and a roquefort, chicory and walnut salad is one way to start, while main course could be ox cheek with braised pearl barley, crispy veal sweetbread, aged parmesan and winter truffle. Finish with classic crème brûlée with 'cat's tongues' (langues de chat) biscuits and tiramisù ice cream.

Chef Graeme Pallister **Owner** Scott & Penny Edwards, Graeme Pallister **Times** 12-2/6.30-9 Closed Xmas, New Year, 1st wk Jul, Sun-Mon **Prices** Fixed L 2 course fr £18, Fixed D 2 course fr £24, Fixed D 4 course £37, Service optional, Groups min 8 service 10% **Wines** 248 bottles over £20, 7 by glass **Notes** Fixed D 4 course £25, 5 course £35-£39 Tue-Fri, Vegetarian menu **Seats** 38 **Children** Portions **Parking** On street

---

PITLOCHRY　　　　　　　　　　**Map 23 NN95**

Green Park Hotel

◉ British

Family-run country-house hotel

☎ 01796 473248
Clunie Bridge Rd PH16 5JY
e-mail: bookings@thegreenpark.co.uk
dir: Turn off A9 at Pitlochry, follow signs for 0.25m through town, turn left at Clunie Bridge Rd

Uplifting views over Loch Faskally are a big plus at this family-run country house in the Southern Highlands. Inside, it is the sort of traditional operation that immediately puts you at ease with its relaxed ambience, and charming service from two generations of the McMenemie family. Just as important is the classic Scottish country-house cooking, served in the tranquil, claret and honey-hued dining room. The four-course dinner menus offer an impressive hike through the best produce the surrounding landscape can offer, from a starter of home-smoked chicken breast with feta cheese, crispy bacon and walnut dressing to a main course of roast pork fillet with thyme mousse and chorizo and white bean cassoulet. For dessert, perhaps warm marmalade pudding and a Drambuie crème anglaise.

Times 12-2/6.30-8.30

Knockendarroch House Hotel

◉ Traditional British

Luxury small hotel with sophisticated dining

☎ 01796 473473
Higher Oakfield PH16 5HT
e-mail: bookings@knockendarroch.co.uk
dir: On entering town from Perth, 1st right (East Moulin Road) after railway bridge, then 2nd left, last hotel on left

Knockendarroch, on a hill overlooking the busy town but only a five-minute stroll away, has accommodation and attentive and friendly staff, while its restaurant, with its ornate cornices and ceiling roses, is a destination in its own right. The menu may kick off with haggis and clapshot with whisky jus, or a pretty dish of crab with a light tomato mousse topped with a seared scallop, accompanied by lime crème fraîche. Good materials are well handled as in succulent roast chicken breast with a cheese topping, potato and cress salad, and mustard jus, or baked plaice fillet with parsley butter, crushed potatoes, and spinach with bacon. Among puddings might be profiteroles with marshmallows in hot chocolate and whisky sauce.

Chef Robert McKillop **Owner** Liz Martin & Elaine Muldoon **Times** 5.30-8.30 Closed mid Nov-mid Jan, L all week **Prices** Starter £4.25-£6.95, Main £10.95-£22.95, Dessert £5.95-£7.95, Service optional **Wines** 40 bottles over £20, 8 bottles under £20, 5 by glass **Notes** Pre-theatre D Jun-Oct, Vegetarian available, Dress restrictions, Smart casual **Seats** 24 **Parking** 12

ST FILLANS
Map 20 NN62

The Four Seasons Hotel

◉◉ Modern British V

Breathtaking loch views and appealing modern cooking

☎ 01764 685333
Lochside PH6 2NF
e-mail: info@thefourseasonshotel.co.uk
dir: From Perth take A85 W, through Crieff & Comrie. Hotel at west end of village

Perched on the edge of Loch Earn, The Four Seasons has breathtaking south-westerly views over the water and wooded hills. The hotel dates from the 19th century, with additions and modifications made over the years to meet modern sensibilities. The Meall Reamhar restaurant is a spacious room, with colourful fabric chairs at rectangular and circular tables and a display of artwork (for sale) on neutral-coloured walls - and that spectacle of the loch. The kitchen takes full advantage of Scotland's natural larder, and its cooking makes an impact with its sharply modern combinations. A pavé of salmon wrapped in ham, on a sorrel and lemon balm potato cake, surrounded by braised fennel and a Bloody Mary nage is typical of main courses. Starters can range from smoked duck with apple chutney and red wine jelly to crab and mussel risotto, and winning desserts have included pear and honey frangipane tart with whisky-soaked prunes and custard lightly flavoured with tarragon.

Chef Mathew Martin **Owner** Andrew Low
Times 12-2.30/6-9.30 Closed Jan-Feb & some wkdays Mar, Nov & Dec **Prices** Food prices not confirmed for 2013. Please telephone for details **Wines** 71 bottles over £20, 29 bottles under £20, 8 by glass **Notes** Vegetarian menu, Dress restrictions, No jeans or trainers, Civ Wed 80 **Seats** 40, Pr/dining room 20 **Children** Portions, Menu **Parking** 30

RENFREWSHIRE, EAST

UPLAWMOOR
Map 10 NS45

Uplawmoor Hotel

◉ Modern Scottish 🍃

Good cooking in a Georgian coaching inn

☎ 01505 850565
66 Neilston Rd G78 4AF
e-mail: info@uplawmoor.co.uk
dir: M77 junct 2, A736 signed Barrhead & Irvine. Hotel 4m beyond Barrhead

Many of Britain's coaching inns saw unofficial service in the past as staging-posts for smugglers, and this Georgian hostelry was smack on the route from the Ayrshire coast to Glasgow. What was its stable-block, complete with copper-canopied fireplace surmounted with quotations from Robert Burns, is now a weekend dining room with darkwood tables, a small wood-fired stove and many good pictures. A homely style of Scots bistro cooking, built around fine local meats and fresh fish, provides plenty to satisfy. Cullen skink is a properly pungent, smoky, creamy version with good bite from leek, potato and celery, while mains run the gamut from pink-cooked haunch of Highland venison with dauphinoise in redcurrant jus, to poached sole, cheddar-glazed leeks and chive mash. The toffee pudding has all the stickiness one could wish for from butterscotch sauce, as well as a scoop of smooth vanilla ice cream.

Chef Paul Brady **Owner** Stuart & Emma Peacock
Times 12-3/6-9.30 Closed 26 Dec, 1 Jan, L Mon-Sat **Prices** Fixed L 2 course £15.50-£16.50, Fixed D 3 course £19.50-£25, Starter £4.50-£8.95, Main £10.95-£23.95, Dessert £5.25-£6, Service optional **Wines** 5 bottles over £20, 15 bottles under £20, 8 by glass **Notes** Early evening menu available 5.30-7pm Sun-Fri, Sunday L, Vegetarian available, Dress restrictions, Smart casual **Seats** 30 **Children** Portions, Menu **Parking** 40

SCOTTISH BORDERS

EDDLESTON
Map 21 NT24

The Horseshoe Inn

◉◉ Modern Scottish ⬛

Inventive Scottish cooking in an old smithy

☎ 01721 730225
Edinburgh Rd EH45 8QP
e-mail: reservations@horseshoeinn.co.uk
web: www.horseshoeinn.co.uk
dir: On A703, 5m N of Peebles

The name is an acknowledgement of the fact that these premises, near Peebles in the border country, once housed a smithy. Now a stylishly decorated restaurant (and-bistro) with rooms, the fine dining arm of the operation is done in gold and mustard, with modern artworks and elegant table-settings complete with outsized stemware. Professional service avoids any OTT flummery, and the menus ply an inventive version of modern Scottish cooking that naturally makes much use of fine local meats and seasonal produce. Braised cuttlefish is subtly spiked with chilli and appears with squid-inked cauliflower purée, a pea casserole and sea beets, and more braising is applied to a main-course duo of belly and cheek of Hawick pork, whilst sea bass is pan-fried and comes with creamed Swiss chard and braised leeks, confit tomato and persillade. Good dessert thinking sees a rectangular slab of chocolate financier offset with vanilla biscuit crumbs and coconut cremeux, accompanied by an assertive passionfruit sorbet.

Chef Riad Peerbux **Owner** Border Steelwork Structures Ltd
Times 12-2.30/7-9 Closed 2 wks Jan, Mon, D Sun **Prices** Fixed L 2 course £17.50, Fixed D 3 course £40, Service optional, Groups min 8 service 10% **Wines** 100 bottles over £20, 12 bottles under £20, 12 by glass **Notes** Tasting menu available, Sunday L, Vegetarian available, Dress restrictions, Smart casual **Seats** 40 **Children** Menu **Parking** 20

KELSO
Map 21 NT73

The Cobbles Inn

◉ British, Pacific Rim 🍃

Appealing menu in cheerful pubby setting

☎ 01573 223548
7 Bowmont St TD5 7JH
e-mail: info@thecobblesinn.co.uk
dir: A6089 from Edinburgh, turn right at rdbt into Bowmont Rd. Restaurant in 0.3m

Located in a pretty cobbled area just behind Kelso's town square, this cracking little pub is the brewery tap for the Tempest Brewery, a craft brewery set up in the town in 2010. Expect to find a cosy beamed bar brimming with atmosphere, with a blazing winter log fire, regular quizzes and live music and tip-top ales, and a comfortable and convivial dining area. It may look and feel like a proper pub but food is taken seriously, too, the eclectic menu combining gastro-pub classics with modern European

Save on Hotels. Book at **theAA.com/hotel**

SCOTTISH BORDERS 605 SCOTLAND

dishes. Typically, tuck into deep-fried squid with lime mayonnaise followed by roast saddle of roe deer with mini venison Wellington, dauphinoise and port jus, and rhubarb and almond tart with whisky, honey and oatmeal ice cream.

Chef Gavin Meiklejohn **Owner** Annika & Gavin Meiklejohn **Times** 12-2/6-9 Closed 25-26 Dec, Mon **Prices** Fixed D 3 course £22.95-£29.95, Starter £4-£7.50, Main £9.95-£22, Dessert £4.75-£6.75, Service optional, Groups min 10 service 10% **Wines** 8 bottles over £20, 17 bottles under £20, 7 by glass **Notes** Sunday L, Vegetarian available **Seats** 35, Pr/dining room 30 **Children** Portions, Menu **Parking** Behind restaurant

The Roxburghe Hotel & Golf Course

◉ Modern British ✿

Modern country-house style in a stately hotel

☎ 01573 450331
TD5 8JZ
e-mail: hotel@roxburghe.net
web: www.roxburghe-hotel.com
dir: From A68, 1m N of Jedburgh, take A698 for 5m to Heiton

This substantial turreted mansion near the River Teviot is on an estate that includes a championship golf course and shooting and fishing rights. High ceilings, open fires, expensive fabrics and antiques mark out the ducal interior, and formal service prevails in the bay-windowed dining room. Good-quality materials, much of them from the estate - wild mushrooms in a risotto with parmesan crisps and truffle oil, say - form a solid base for the kitchen to work with in a modern country-house style. Smoked goats' cheese adds some oomph to watercress soup scattered with pumpkin seeds, an alternative to roast quail with crispy Parma ham and a salad of Jersey Royals and asparagus topped with a poached quail's egg. Sauces and accompaniments are effective partners in main courses: date purée for loin of venison, accompanied by rösti, celeriac and wild mushrooms, for instance. The short dessert list may include banana parfait with glazed fruit and caramel.

Chef Neville Merrdu **Owner** Duke of Roxburghe **Times** 12.30-2/7-9.30 **Prices** Fixed L 2 course £15-£20, Fixed D 3 course £37.50-£42.50, Starter £8.50-£14, Main £21-£35, Dessert £8-£14, Service optional **Wines** 80 bottles over £20, 8 bottles under £20, 10 by glass **Notes** Sunday L, Vegetarian available, Dress restrictions, No jeans, trainers or T-shirts, Civ Wed 64 **Seats** 40, Pr/dining room 16 **Children** Portions, Menu **Parking** 150

The Black Bull

◉ Modern Scottish **NEW**

Inventive Scottish pub cooking in the border country

☎ 01578 722208
Market Place TD2 6SR
e-mail: enquiries@blackbull-lauder.com

A white-fronted Georgian inn, The Black Bull is a proper local, with regulars drinking cask ales in the Harness Room bar, and an eating area of bare floorboards and tables with paper napkins, where the hands-on service sees everybody pitching in at busy times. Victor Garcia has honed a well-crafted version of modern Scottish pub food for this appealing setting, mixing some new ideas in with the beef casseroles, fish and chips, and sticky toffee pudding. A filo-pastry leek and goats' cheese tart with pea shoots and balsamic reduction is a starter to make you sit up and take notice, while a Spanish note creeps into crisp-skinned cod fillet with butter beans and chorizo in a delicately sharp lemon cream sauce. There's always something new to do to crème brûlée, and here it appears under a layer of vanilla-soaked bread, the crème itself boosted with Amaretto, or there might be banana meringue with mandarin sauce and honeycomb.

Times 12-2.30/5-9 **Notes** Sunday L **Children** Menu

Cringletie House

French **V**

Intelligent and refined cooking in baronial-style country house

☎ 01721 725750
Edinburgh Rd EH45 8PL
e-mail: enquiries@cringletie.com
web: www.cringletie.com
dir: 2.5m N of Peebles on A703

A fine example of a Scottish baronial mansion, built in 1861, Cringletie has turrets and gables aplenty and makes a good first impression. The 28-acres of grounds only add to its appeal and the sense of splendid isolation, whilst the décor is as smart and traditional as you might expect given the setting. There's bags of period charm here, not least in the first-floor restaurant with its ornately painted ceiling and period detailing, plus richly burnished darkwood tables dressed up for fine dining. The kitchen is in the hands of Patrick Bardoulet, and experienced hands they are too, with a classical French flavour and lots of excellent Scottish ingredients on the menu. There is a nicely retrained modernism on display too, with no lack of ambition and ideas, but a pleasing lack of overworking of that splendid produce. Things get off to a magnificent start with canapés such as aubergine caviar with beetroot jelly and venison en croûte with candied orange peel, plus top-notch home-baked breads (pancetta and onion, perhaps). A first-course serves up roasted scallop with duck (a richly unctuous bonbon) and a counter-pointing hit of piccalilli, plus cucumber and radish. Next up, crispy lamb served with its sweetbread, scented with orange and sage and a crab and curry sauce, or tail and cheek of monkfish - superb quality fish, perfectly cooked - in a clever partnership with sauerkraut and apple and buttery cider sauce. This is well-judged, refined and intelligent cooking, with flavour combinations thought through to the nth degree. To finish, the BFG is a deconstructed Black Forest gâteau which looks wonderful on the plate and gets all the flavours and textures spot on. All this and engaging and effective service too.

Chef Patrick Bardoulet **Owner** Jacob & Johanna van Houdt **Times** 12.30-2.30/6.30-9 Closed 2-23 Jan **Prices** Fixed L 2 course fr £15.95, Fixed D 3 course fr £33, Tasting menu £55-£90, Starter £8.50-£10.50, Main £21-£25, Dessert £9-£11.50, Service optional **Wines** 99 bottles over £20, 6 bottles under £20, 8 by glass **Notes** Sunday L, Vegetarian menu, Dress restrictions, Smart casual, no jeans or trainers, Civ Wed 60 **Seats** 60, Pr/dining room 14 **Children** Portions, Menu **Parking** 30

MELROSE
Map 21 NT53

Burt's Hotel

Modern Scottish

Contemporary cooking at an old favourite

☎ 01896 822285
Market Square TD6 9PL
e-mail: enquiries@burtshotel.co.uk
web: www.burtshotel.co.uk
dir: A6091, 2m from A68, 3m S of Earlston. Hotel in market square

Burt's, on the attractive 18th-century Market Square, manages successfully to combine the roles of hotel, bar and restaurant, as it has done for years. The restaurant itself is a stylish room, with high-backed chairs, crisp napery and a paean to sports in its hunting, fishing and shooting theme; it also has strong rugby links with the town's club. The kitchen moves with the times, laying its own inventive take on Scottish materials. Crisp belly pork comes with squid marinated in red wine, balsamic onions and apples, and well-timed fried halibut is served with gooey pancetta sauce, shallot purée, salsify in red wine, and wilted kale. A tian of beetroot and goats' cheese mousse, accompanied by apple compôte, beetroot jelly and pickled shallots, sounds thoroughly cosmopolitan, and, as this is Scotland, expect accurately roast venison with a game boudin, shallots, Savoy cabbage and parsnip purée. Finish with rum crème brûlée with caramelised bananas, chocolate fondant and banana sorbet.

Chef Trevor Williams **Owner** The Henderson family **Times** 12-2/7-9 Closed 26 Dec, 3-8 Jan, L Mon-Fri **Prices** Food prices not confirmed for 2013. Please telephone for details **Wines** 40 bottles over £20, 18 bottles under £20, 8 by glass **Notes** Vegetarian available, Dress restrictions, Jacket & tie preferred **Seats** 50, Pr/dining room 25 **Children** Portions **Parking** 40

PEEBLES
Map 21 NT24

Cringletie House

– see page 605

Renwicks

British

Modish cooking and ravishing country views

☎ 0844 879 9024 & 01896 833600
Macdonald Cardrona Hotel, Golf & Country Club, Cardrona Mains EH45 8NE
e-mail: general.cardrona@macdonald-hotels.co.uk
dir: From Edinburgh on A701 signed Penicuik/Peebles. Then A703, at 1st rdbt beside garage turn left onto A72, hotel 3m on right

Part of the Macdonald group, the Cardrona is a classy modern hotel that has most bases covered: it is on the banks of the Tweed, so fishing is sorted, and golf is taken care of by the 18-hole course. All around are the rolling Borders hills, perfect for biking and hiking, or if that is all too outdoorsy to contemplate, you can get pampered in the glossy spa. Nor is dining neglected: from its vantage point on the second-floor, Renwicks restaurant provides outstanding views to go with a well-thought-out repertoire of uncomplicated modern dishes, running from seared peppered tuna loin with couscous, and coriander and lime butter sauce, to mains along the lines of braised shoulder of Highland lamb with roast root vegetables and garlic mash, or grilled fillet of cod with spring onion and pancetta crust, braised leeks and herb mash. To finish, perhaps rhubarb and ginger crumble tart with crème anglaise.

Chef Ivor Clark **Owner** Macdonald Hotels **Times** 12.30-2/6.30-9.45 **Prices** Fixed L 2 course £12.50-£25, Fixed D 3 course £18-£30, Starter £5.50-£7.95, Main £6-£17.75, Dessert £5.50-£8.50, Service optional **Wines** 54 bottles over £20, 6 bottles under £20, 18 by glass **Notes** Vegetarian available, Dress restrictions, Smart casual, no jeans or T-shirts, Civ Wed 200 **Seats** 70, Pr/dining room 200 **Children** Portions, Menu **Parking** 200

ST BOSWELLS
Map 21 NT53

The Tweed Restaurant

Modern Scottish

Exciting modern cooking and superb river views

☎ 01835 822261
Dryburgh Abbey Hotel TD6 0RQ
e-mail: enquiries@dryburgh.co.uk
dir: From A68 to St Boswells. Take B6404 for 2m. Take B6356 for about 2m to hotel.

With the atmospheric ruins of Dryburgh Abbey on one side, and the salmon fishing mecca of the River Tweed on the other, this Victorian baronial mansion turned country-house hotel is an impossibly romantic spot. Insulated from the outside world by a 10-acre estate, which provides a goodly chunk of the kitchen's wants from an expansive walled garden, the house's Tweed Restaurant features high ceilings with fancy plasterwork and ornate chandeliers as a backdrop to modern Scottish food that is nicely in tune with the surrounding landscape. Ballottine of local pheasant with pine nuts, pea shoots and red onion might pave the way for roast rump of Aberdeen Angus beef with braised oxtail, thyme, beetroot, risotto

and jus. Finally, rhubarb from the garden might appear with gingerbread in an inventive take on a trifle.

Chef Peter Snelgar **Owner** Dryburgh Abbey Hotel Limited **Times** 7-9 Closed L all week **Prices** Service optional **Wines** 52 bottles over £20, 28 bottles under £20, 11 by glass **Notes** Fixed D 5 course £35, Vegetarian available, Dress restrictions, No sportswear, Civ Wed 120 **Seats** 78, Pr/dining room 40 **Children** Portions, Menu **Parking** 50

STIRLING

ABERFOYLE
Map 20 NN50

Macdonald Forest Hills Hotel & Resort

Modern British

Modern cooking in a happening resort hotel

☎ 0844 879 9057 & 01877 389500
Kinlochard FK8 3TL
e-mail: forest-hills@macdonald-hotels.co.uk

Whether you're here to roam the Trossachs, soak up the fabulous views of Loch Ard, de-stress in the spa, get pumped up with the plentiful indoor and outdoor sports facilities, or do a bit of everything, the friendly team at Forest Hills will make sure that it all goes with a swing. When you're done with the day's activities, the classy restaurant provides a relaxed and informal setting for unchallenging modern cooking built on solid French-accented foundations. The kitchen's commitment to well-sourced ingredients is impressive, starting, say, with a fillet of seared sea trout with potato and horseradish compôte and aïoli, and continuing through to main-course ideas such as poached organic salmon and wild halibut matched with saffron and shellfish broth. To finish, expect orange crème brûlée with white wine-poached pear or Scottish cheeses with home-made chutney and oatcakes.

Times 7-9.30

Roman Camp Country House Hotel

Modern French v

Ritzy luxury and immaculate modern cooking

☎ 01877 330003
FK17 8BG
e-mail: mail@romancamphotel.co.uk
web: www.romancamphotel.co.uk
dir: N on A84 through Callander, Main St turn left at East End into drive

In 20 acres, Roman Camp was built in 1625 as a hunting lodge and became a hotel in 1939, since when it has been one of Scotland's foremost country-house retreats. Rooms are sumptuously furnished and decorated, with yards of swagged drapes at the windows, plush soft furnishings, open fires, ornate moulded ceilings, and a grand oval dining room softly lit by candles in the evening. Given the surroundings, it's no surprise to find a menu dripping with luxuries, from roast foie gras with a fig tart and Muscovado jelly, but there's the more humble spinach soup, too, albeit pepped up by an oyster beignet and caviar cream. The cooking is rooted in the classics and pairings are well-timed; top-quality beef fillet, perhaps, with wild mushrooms, a croûton of foie gras and a rich, creamy truffle velouté. The kitchen moves with the times, too: pheasant breast is modishly and attractively plated with beetroot purée and Madeira butter, and pork fillet

comes with confit belly, apples, calvados and mustard sauce. Freebies arrive thick and fast, from haggis bonbons to a pre-dessert of apple jelly with yoghurt foam. Dessert confirms the kitchen's high ambition, technical expertise and eye for detail: subtly flavoured lemon tart, in a thin pastry case, for example, with creamy coconut ice cream and pistachio syrup.

Chef Ian McNaught **Owner** Eric Brown **Times** 12-2/7-9 **Prices** Fixed L 3 course £29-£32.50, Fixed D 4 course £49-£54, Starter £19-£24, Main £28-£37, Dessert £14-£18, Service optional
Wines 210 bottles over £20, 16 by glass
Notes Tasting menu 4 course dishes change daily, Sunday L, Vegetarian menu, Dress restrictions, Smart casual, Civ Wed 150 **Seats** 120, Pr/dining room 36 **Children** Portions **Parking** 80

CALLANDER — Map 20 NN60

Callander Meadows

Modern British

Flavour-focussed cooking in charming restaurant with rooms

☎ 01877 330181
24 Main St FK17 8BB
e-mail: mail@callandermeadows.co.uk
web: www.callandermeadows.co.uk
dir: M9 junct 10, A84 for 15m, restaurant 1m in village on left past lights

The Parkes' restaurant with rooms - within a charming Georgian townhouse at the centre of town - has the bonus of a sun-trap garden for a spot of dining alfresco. Inside, the intimate dining room is a light-filled, unpretentious kind of place, with bare-wood floors and undressed tables, crimson walls and fresh flowers. Both proprietors are chefs and have cooked at top restaurants, including the Gleneagles Hotel, but the cooking here takes a much simpler approach than any grand hotel dining, with fresh quality local seasonal produce, simplicity and flavour doing the talking. Roast rump of lamb, for example, is teamed with couscous, ratatouille and a rosemary jus, or go for pan-fried salmon with roasted garlic mash, spinach and citrus segments. Steak lovers will be drawn to the likes of grilled Scottish sirloin with horseradish mash, red onion marmalade and thyme sauce.

Chef Nick & Susannah Parkes **Owner** Nick & Susannah Parkes **Times** 12-2.30/6-9 Closed 25-26 Dec, Tue-Wed **Prices** Fixed L 2 course £8.95-£12.95, Starter £4.50-£6.95, Main £11.50-£26.95, Dessert £5.95-£7.95 **Wines** 15 bottles over £20, 17 bottles under £20, 8 by glass **Notes** Sunday L, Vegetarian available **Seats** 40, Pr/dining room 16 **Children** Portions **Parking** 4, 80 yds council car park

Roman Camp Country House Hotel

— see page 607

CRIANLARICH — Map 20 NN32

The Crianlarich Hotel

Modern Scotiish

Simple, accurate cooking in smartly refurbished hotel

☎ 01838 300272
FK20 8RW
e-mail: info@crianlarich-hotel.co.uk
dir: At junct of A85 Oban & Fort William to Perth and A82 Glasgow road, in Crianlarich

The whitewashed Crianlarich Hotel stands at a crossroads by the railway in a village that makes a handy base for exploring Loch Lomond and Glencoe, as well as taking on the West Highland Way. Outside are classic elemental Highland vistas; inside, Victorian oak panelling and period charm are made over with a stylish contemporary look. The Highland Lounge restaurant is an airy conservatory-style venue, where the simple cooking exerts its own attraction in an appealing version of modern Scottish food with plenty of input from local ingredients. An opener of haggis and clapshot drizzled in whisky sauce is a case in point, while main courses could bring on pan-fried venison with redcurrant jus and Lyonnaise potatoes, or citrus-crusted cod with steamed spinach and tomato butter. Stick with the Scottish theme and finish with a classic cranachan made with whisky-infused cream and fresh raspberries.

Chef Stephen Banks **Owner** Byrne Ventures Ltd **Times** 12-5/5-9.30 **Prices** Starter £3.95-£7.95, Main £9.95-£21.95, Dessert £5.95-£7.95, Service optional **Wines** 1 bottle over £20, 11 bottles under £20, 5 by glass **Notes** Sunday L, Vegetarian available, Civ Wed 100 **Seats** 70, Pr/dining room 50 **Children** Portions, Menu **Parking** 50

PORT OF MENTEITH — Map 20 NN50

The Lake of Menteith Hotel

Modern Scottish **NEW**

Breathtaking settings and modern Scottish food

☎ 01877 385258
FK8 3RA
e-mail: enquiries@lake-hotel.com
dir: M9 junct 10, A84. At Blairdrummond take A873. Left onto A81 to Port of Menteith. Left onto B8034, hotel 200yds on right

As its name suggests, this hotel close to Loch Lomond makes the most of its idyllic lakeside location. The original 19th-century house has been expanded and takes its decorative inspiration from the muted tones of New England lakeside hotels, making good use of local stone and timber. The restaurant is housed in a conservatory looking out to the stunningly romantic lake (you might see an otter if you're lucky), whilst inside large wooden geese swoop from the ceiling and nautical ornaments are dotted about the place. Contemporary techniques are favoured by the team in the kitchen, the modern Scottish cooking serving up the likes of Stornoway haggis and neep cake with goats' cheese dauphinoise as a first

course. Next up, Perthshire Red-Legged partridge 'Smokehead', pan-roasted breasts with buttered leeks, rösti potato and 'Smokehead' malt cream. Finish with a Scottish cheese selection or iced cranachan parfait with fresh berries and shortbread.

Chef Mark De Freitas **Owner** Ian Fleming **Times** 12-2.30/6.30-9.30 **Prices** Starter £6.80-£10.95, Main £14.95-£24.65, Dessert £5.95-£10.95, Service optional **Wines** 40 bottles over £20, 4 bottles under £20, 8 by glass **Notes** Sunday L, Vegetarian available, Civ Wed 50 **Seats** 50, Pr/dining room 18 **Children** Portions, Menu **Parking** 40

STRATHYRE — Map 20 NN51

Creagan House

French, Scottish

17th-century Trossachs farmhouse with good food

☎ 01877 384638
FK18 8ND
e-mail: eatandstay@creaganhouse.co.uk
dir: 0.25m N of village, off A84

Gordon and Cherry Gunn's long-established restaurant with rooms stands at the head of Loch Lubnaig, surrounded by mountains, rivers and forests, with free access to peaceful walks and wonderful views. The converted 17th-century farmhouse is well worth seeking out for Gordon's bold, classically-inspired French dishes, served at large wooden tables in the impressive dining room with its stripped floors, grand open fireplace and fabulous views. Cooking is well executed and sourcing of top-notch local produce is a priority and reflected on the sensibly short yet well balanced dinner menu. Herbs and vegetables come from the garden and local small-holdings, while meat is all reared on Perthshire farms. Typically, begin with breast of grouse with boudin of leg and compôte liver, served with apple and smoked bacon, then follow with John Dory with puréed plum chutney and a scallop and mussel sauce. To finish, try the steamed butterscotch and pecan pudding with Macallan whisky sauce.

Chef Gordon Gunn **Owner** Gordon & Cherry Gunn **Times** 7.30-8.30 Closed 6-22 Nov, Xmas, 16 Jan-8 Mar, Wed-Thu, L all week (ex parties) **Prices** Fixed D 3 course fr £32.50, Service optional **Wines** 60 bottles over £20, 8 bottles under £20, 7 by glass **Notes** Vegetarian available, Dress restrictions, Smart casual **Seats** 15, Pr/dining room 6 **Children** Portions **Parking** 15

SCOTTISH ISLANDS
ARRAN, ISLE OF

BRODICK   Map 20 NS03

Kilmichael Country House Hotel

◉◉ Modern British 🌿

Refined cooking in stylish country-house hotel

☎ 01770 302219
Glen Cloy KA27 8BY
e-mail: enquiries@kilmichael.com
dir: Turn right on leaving ferry terminal, through Brodick
& left at golf club. Follow brown sign. Continue past
church & onto private drive

Sitting in four acres of lovely gardens just a few minutes'
drive from the Brodick ferry, Kilmichael lays claim to
being the oldest house on the Isle of Arran, but rather
than its history, what grabs the attention these days is
its impeccably tasteful interior furnished with antiques,
artworks and china. The foodie action in this refined
small-scale country house goes on in a delicious dining
room with claret walls, plush golden fabrics and gilt-
framed mirrors. Four-course dinners are wrought from
peerless Scottish produce, including fruit, vegetables and
herbs from the garden and estate, and eggs from their
own chickens and ducks. Things get under way with
canapés, followed by a starter such as smoked salmon
and prawn cheesecake with a salad of herbs and flowers,
then sorbet - lemon and lavender, say - before roast
Gressingham duck breast stuffed with wild rice, walnuts
and raspberries. To finish, perhaps lemon berry tart with
gin and lemon honeycomb jelly, and home-made Cassis
Ice cream.

Chef Antony Butterworth **Owner** G Botterill & A
Butterworth **Times** 7-8.30 Closed Nov-Mar, Tue, L all
week **Prices** Fixed D 4 course £45, Service optional
Wines 32 bottles over £20, 23 bottles under £20, 3 by
glass **Notes** Vegetarian available, Dress restrictions,
Smart casual, no T-shirts or bare feet **Seats** 18
Parking 12

HARRIS, ISLE OF

SCARISTA (SGARASTA BHEAG)   Map 22 NG09

Scarista House

◉◉ Modern Scottish 🌿

Modern Scottish cooking and stunning sea views

☎ 01859 550238
HS3 3HX
e-mail: timandpatricia@scaristahouse.com
dir: On A859 15m S of Tarbert

When you head for the Isle of Harris, the idea is usually to
get away from it all, and the remoteness and beauty
boxes are certainly ticked at this Georgian manse. Jaw-
dropping views are of a three-mile-long white beach and
the Atlantic, and within is a civilised, soothing, TV-free
space with antiques, open fires in the library and drawing

room, and a great CD collection to set the mood. The
island's bounty is the star of the show in the two elegant
dining rooms - seafood tends to feature prominently, and
there is lamb, beef and game, all full of freshness and
flavour, and backed by accurate timings and attention to
detail. Dinner menus are no-choice affairs that could kick
off with porcini risotto with grilled breast of quail,
followed by Stornoway-landed monkfish tail wrapped in
smoked Argyll ham roasted with lemon, saffron and basil,
and served with broccoli, pea and mint purée. Dessert -
perhaps chocolate truffle with coffee ice cream and
raspberry coulis - precedes a finale of Scottish farmhouse
cheeses.

Chef Tim Martin **Owner** Tim & Patricia Martin
Times 7.30-8 Closed 25 Dec, Jan-Feb, L all week
Prices Fixed D 3 course £43, Service optional
Wines 59 bottles over £20, 10 bottles under £20, 37 by
glass **Notes** Vegetarian available, Civ Wed 40 **Seats** 20,
Pr/dining room 14 **Children** Portions, Menu **Parking** 10

TARBERT (TAIRBEART)   Map 22 NB10

Hotel Hebrides

◉ Scottish

A thoroughly Scottish menu with views to match

☎ 01859 502364
Pier Rd HS3 3DG
e-mail: stay@hotel-hebrides.com

Right beside the Tarbert ferry terminal, this modern
boutique hotel is a great base for exploring the Hebridean
islands. As you might imagine, the views from here
across the pier and out to sea - with the hills of Harris in
the opposite direction - are stunning, hence proprietors
Angus and Chirsty Macleod have gone for an understated,
simple look inside The Pierhouse Restaurant so as not to
compete with that fantastic vista. Food is served pretty
much all day, with coffees and home-made cakes
available in the morning and a lounge bar menu served
throughout the afternoon. In the evening, the carte brims
with local and seasonal produce, offering the likes of
hand-dived Harris scallops with mango salsa and
caramelised pineapple to start with, followed by local
smoked haddock with chive mash, a poached egg and
cheese sauce. The Harris cranachan with vanilla
shortbread makes a suitably Scottish finale.

Times 12-4/5-9

MULL, ISLE OF

TOBERMORY   Map 22 NM55

Highland Cottage

◉◉ Modern Scottish, International

Hospitable island hotel with locally-sourced menu

☎ 01688 302030
24 Breadalbane St PA75 6PD
e-mail: davidandjo@highlandcottage.co.uk
web: www.highlandcottage.co.uk
dir: Opposite fire station. Main St up Back Brae, turn at
top by White House. Follow road to right, left at next
junct into Breadalbane St

David and Jo Currie's small-scale hotel and restaurant
couldn't be better placed for hauling in the freshest fish
and seafood imaginable, as it lies just a few minutes'
stroll from the colourful Tobermory waterfront. There's a
bit more to the operation than the word 'cottage' might
suggest but it is nonetheless a cosy, welcoming place
crammed with interesting art and objets. The dedication
to local sourcing is admirable, and the materials are
brought together in well-conceived and well-balanced
dishes that run the gamut from crabcakes with mixed
leaves and chilli caper sauce, to mains such as roast
halibut fillet with boulangère potatoes, and leek and
smoked mussel cream sauce. Carnivores are not sent
away unhappy - roast loin and braised shoulder of lamb
with dauphinoise potato and redcurrant and rosemary
gravy might be on the cards, and to finish there may be
chocolate and orange truffle torte.

Times 7-9 Closed Nov-Mar, L all week

ORKNEY ISLANDS

ST MARGARET'S HOPE   Map 24 ND49

The Creel Restaurant with Rooms

◉◉ British

First-class cooking of outstanding produce

☎ 01856 831311
The Creel, Front Rd KW17 2SL
e-mail: creelorkney@btinternet.com
dir: A961 into village, on seafront

The cream-painted house in the quiet village overlooking the bay looks modest enough, while inside is an unassuming stone-floored dining room with bare wooden tables, a stove and local artwork on the walls - and on the cards is the highly accomplished cooking from Alan Craigie. What marks out his cooking is his professional, imaginative handling of top-rate Orcadian produce, from the island's new potatoes via seafood to seaweed-feeding North Ronaldsay mutton, which might appear in a pithivier with parsnip purée and barley gravy alongside another successful starter of crab salad, with apple mayonnaise, avocado salsa and pickled cucumber. Main courses are never too elaborate, so flavours are clearly defined: pan-fried scallops with steamed halibut and braised lentils, say, or slowly braised beef brisket with onion marmalade and glazed carrots. Less familiar but sustainable varieties of fish also find their way on to the menu - seared wolf fish, for example, with spinach and roast courgettes.

Chef Alan Craigie **Owner** Alan & Joyce Craigie
Times 7-8.30 Closed mid Oct-Apr, Mon-Tue, L all week
Prices Food prices not confirmed for 2013. Please telephone for details **Wines** 14 bottles over £20, 8 bottles under £20, 2 by glass **Notes** Vegetarian available
Seats 20, Pr/dining room 12 **Children** Portions
Parking 10

SKYE, ISLE OF

COLBOST   Map 22 NG24

The Three Chimneys

◉◉◉ – *see opposite*

ISLEORNSAY   Map 22 NG71

Duisdale House Hotel

◉◉ Modern

Modern Scottish cooking in remotest southern Skye

☎ 01471 833202
Sleat IV43 8QW
e-mail: info@duisdale.com
web: www.duisdale.com
dir: 7m N of Armadale ferry & 12m S of Skye Bridge on A851

Overlooking the mournful beauty of the Sound of Sleat at the southern tip of Skye, the conservatory dining room has the best seats in the house for sunset-washed mountain views. And when the weather draws a veil over nature's splendour, the darkly intimate interior room is a stylish setting with its red arched walls, cream high-backed chairs and views over the garden. The cooking reflects the surrounding landscapes with its unchallenging modern compositions - scallops are hand dived from the wine-dark waters that lay before your eyes, then sautéed with precision to capture their sweetness, and served with with pimento relish, smoked vine tomato and butter sauce. Moving on, roast loin of venison is matched with mash, carrots, spinach and juniper jus, and to close the show, there's banana tarte Tatin with vanilla ice cream and orange syrup.

Duisdale House Hotel

Chef George McCallum **Owner** K Gunn & A Gracie
Times 12-2.30/6.30-9 **Prices** Food prices not confirmed for 2013. Please telephone for details **Wines** 55 bottles over £20, 8 bottles under £20, 9 by glass
Notes Vegetarian available, Dress restrictions, Smart casual, Civ Wed 60 **Seats** 50 **Children** Portions
Parking 30

See advert below

Save on Hotels. Book at **theAA.com/hotel**

SKYE, ISLE OF 611 SCOTLAND

The Three Chimneys

COLBOST   Map 22 NG24

Modern Scottish

Matchless produce immaculately cooked in a wild, romantic setting

☎ 01470 511258
IV55 8ZT
e-mail: eatandstay@threechimneys.co.uk
web: www.threechimneys.co.uk
dir: 5m W of Dunvegan take B884 signed Glendale. On left beside loch

There is no building more synonymous with the Inner Hebrides, and Skye in particular, than a crofter's cottage, and today the two that form The Three Chimneys are as rooted in the terroir as they ever were. For Eddie and Shirley Spear's restaurant with rooms is so much a part of this wild and beautiful landscape it is hard to imagine life around here without it. In fact, it is so magically remote you're unlikely to be heading this way without a reservation secured and maybe even your bags packed (there are six bedrooms in the house next door). And in this splendid setting, the cooking of Michael Smith has made The Three Chimneys one of the top dining experiences in the country. What appears on the plate - and the plate may well be a piece of slate - is beautifully crafted, creative modern Scottish stuff, made using the fabulous and abundant natural larder at his disposal. The unfettered rusticity of the restaurant fits well with the surrounding rugged landscape, with exposed stone walls, low beams and open fireplaces combining with richly burnished darkwood tables and designer chairs, and well chosen original artworks. It looks the part for some divertingly confident and compelling food. First contact is made with canapés, amuse and bread that set the bar exceedingly high; that amuse-bouche ('a wee taste'), for example, might be a rabbit and prune broth with a fabulous depth of flavour. The fixed-price menu changes every day and showcases the lamb, beef and venison reared on the island's hills, the herbs and vegetables grown in its crofts and gardens, and the pick of whatever is landed fresh that day from the sea. Slow-cooked blade and crispy tongue of Black Isle beef, for example, comes in an exceptional first course, the meat as tender as can be, served with Jerusalem artichokes and delicate sage soubise, the richness of the meat cut with pickled onions and walnuts. Main-course Gigha halibut gets a hazelnut crust and comes with two perfectly cooked scallops, split-pea purée and a chicory, apple and orange salad. Every dish manages to maintain the integrity of the produce, and flavours and textures are judged to a tee. For dessert, dark chocolate and Amaretto délice comes with blaeberries (foraged that very day) dipped in white chocolate and Issy's crème fraîche. Another good reason to stay the night is to have the chance to do justice to the magnificent wine list.

Chef Michael Smith **Owner** Eddie & Shirley Spear
Times 12.15-1.45/6.15-9.45
Closed 6-21 Jan, L Sun & Nov-Mar
Prices Food prices not confirmed for 2013. Please telephone for details
Wines 180 bottles over £20
Notes Tasting menu 7 course, Vegetarian available, Dress restrictions, Smart casual preferred **Seats** 40, Pr/dining room 12

Kinloch Lodge

French, Scottish V

Majestic setting for bravura Scottish cooking

☎ 01471 833214 & 833333
Sleat IV43 8QY
e-mail: reservations@kinloch-lodge.co.uk
web: www.kinloch-lodge.co.uk
dir: 1m off main road, 6m S of Broadford on A851, 10m N of Armadale

The Hebridean fastness of Kinloch is the ancestral home of the 34th High Chief of Clan Donald, which is as rarefied a claim as any entry in the Guide can make. Portraits of illustrious antecedents stare down benignly in oils, and an air of unruffled calm is the prevailing tone, as well it might be, given the remote splendour of the setting. Lady Claire Macdonald has long been a name to conjure with in Scots gastronomy and she still gives cookery demonstrations in her own kitchen here. Clearly, head chef Marcello Tully has a lot to live up to, but rises to the mark with a bravura style of French-inflected modern cooking that owes much to the surroundings. A tranche of salmon opens an evening in fine style; gently steamed with dill, it sits amid leeks and crisped beetroot for a bracing start. Main courses can be as complex as the beginners are straightforward, as when a roast quail is stuffed with honeyed

roast vegetable mousse, and served with wilted spinach in a deep-flavoured sweetcorn velouté. If you're sticking with fish, try rolled Mallaig skate wings with deep-fried red pepper gnocchi and Drumfearn mussels in caper and parsley sauce. The freshness and precision are what distinguish these dishes. At dessert stage, you might return to the simplicity approach with an exceptionally intense lemon tart in vanilla pastry. Scottish and French cheeses are from the top drawer, and may well be offered in interesting presentations themselves, such as the serving of Strathdon Blue with prune and orange mousse, Perthshire honey jelly and poached pear in cinnamon syrup.

Chef Marcello Tully **Owner** Lord & Lady Macdonald **Times** 12-2.30/6.30-9 **Prices** Fixed L 2 course £29.99, Fixed D 3 course £60, Service optional **Wines** 200 bottles over £20, 16 by glass **Notes** Tasting menu available, Sunday L, Vegetarian menu **Seats** 40, Pr/dining room 20 **Children** Portions **Parking** 20

Save on Hotels. Book at **theAA.com/hotel**

SKYE, ISLE OF 613 **SCOTLAND**

ISLEORNSAY *continued*

Hotel Eilean Iarmain

◉◉ Traditional Scottish

Stunning views and accomplished Scottish cooking

☎ 01471 833332
IV43 8QR
e-mail: hotel@eileaniarmain.co.uk
dir: Mallaig & cross by ferry to Armadale, 8m to hotel or via Kyle of Lochalsh

This whitewashed 19th-century hotel sticks to Highland tradition right down to its tartan carpets, stag antlers and golden eagle in the hall. The waves of the Sound of Sleat lap almost at the doorstep and views sweep across the Isle Ornsay lighthouse to the mainland hills - dramatic scenery that is best taken in at leisure from the romantic wood-panelled restaurant. A pre-dinner snifter by the log fire in the lounge is a good plan, before you cast an eye over the menu, at which point it becomes abundantly clear that you're in for a treat courtesy of the excellent produce from local estates and seafood landed at the old stone pier just outside. The location might be remote, but the kitchen stays in touch with what's happening in the modern world; expect confident, creative ideas such as perhaps potted squat lobster with garlic focaccia and orbost leaves to start, then a pan-seared fillet of Eilean Iarmain estate venison with garlic and white truffle mash, braised red cabbage, celeriac fondant and red wine jus, and prune and honey cake with lemongrass granita to round it all off.

Times 12-2.30/6.30-8.45

Kinloch Lodge

◉◉◉ — *see opposite*

Toravaig House Hotel

◉◉ Modern Scottish ☐

Plush island retreat with modern Scottish cooking

☎ 01471 820200
Knock Bay IV44 8RE
e-mail: info@skyehotel.co.uk
web: www.skyehotel.co.uk
dir: From Skye Bridge, left at Broadford onto A851, hotel 11m on left. Or from ferry at Armadale take A851, hotel 6m on right

What is now the Toravaig House Hotel was in something of a sorry state when the present owners took it under their wing in 2003, and set about laying on the TLC. Its location, overlooking the Sound of Sleat in southern Skye, demanded nothing less. Amid the gentle Hebridean wildness, it's now a welcoming retreat, with plush smartly finished interiors and a candlelit dining room, the Islay, that looks out over the gardens and the distant hills. Dinner comes in the form of a short menu of three choices each for first course and main, with a sorbet in

between. A highly polished version of modern Scottish cooking draws on local seafood for a starter of lobster and crab tortellini with fennel and apple in a light bisque, served with radish and confit tomato, and a main course of cod fillet in mussel broth with cauliflower beignets, beetroot and samphire. Meatier appetites may be lured by rack of Highland lamb with a fricassée of Savoy cabbage and carrot, butternut squash and onion jam. The concluding choice of savoury or sweet is between Scottish and European artisan cheeses with oatcakes, or something like warm walnut and banana bread with a cinnamon and caramel doughnut and marmalade ice cream.

Toravaig House Hotel

Chef Chris Coombe **Owner** Anne Gracie & Ken Gunn **Times** 12.30-2.30/6.30-9.30 **Prices** Fixed D 2 course £16-£30, Fixed D 4 course £48, Service optional **Wines** 48 bottles over £20, 20 bottles under £20, 6 by glass **Notes** Sunday L, Vegetarian available, Dress restrictions, Smart casual **Seats** 25 **Children** Portions **Parking** 20

See advert below

Cuillin Hills Hotel

⊛⊛ Modern Scottish

Creative dining and breathtaking views

☎ 01478 612003
IV51 9QU
e-mail: info@cuillinhills-hotel-skye.co.uk
web: www.cuillinhills-hotel-skye.co.uk
dir: 0.25m N of Portree on A855

Views surely don't come much better than this: looking out across Portree Bay, the Sound of Raasay and the cockscomb crags of the Cuillin Mountain range, this former hunting lodge in 15 acres of mature grounds is in a truly stunning location. And if you book a table in its very aptly named 'The View' restaurant, you can gaze at that breathtakingly beautiful panorama to your heart's content. The split-level room is decked out in classic ivory and white tones, with regularly-changing works by local artists adding splashes of colour. First-class West Coast materials are given a chance to shine on the European-accented modern menu, as in a starter of hand-dived Loch Sligachan scallops with crispy deep-fried pork belly, wasabi purée, tomato and caper salsa. Chicken three

ways - haggis stuffed breast, confit leg, chicken mousse and whisky cream - leaves us in no doubt we're in Scotland, and there could be a 'deconstructed cranachan' for dessert.

Chef Chris Donaldson **Owner** Wickman Hotels
Times 6.30-9 Closed L all week **Prices** Food prices not confirmed for 2013. Please telephone for details
Wines 11 bottles under £20, 8 by glass **Notes** Sunday L, Vegetarian available, Civ Wed 60 **Seats** 40
Children Portions, Menu **Parking**

Skeabost Country House

⊛ British V

Country-house cooking in a lochside hunting lodge

☎ 01470 532202 & 0844 4146572
IV51 9NP
e-mail: manager.skeabost@ohiml.com
dir: Follow A87 over Skye Bridge to Portree then Uig. Left onto A850, Skeabost on right

A bright white hotel by the edge of Loch Snizort, Skeabost was built by the Macdonald clan as a hunting lodge. They

certainly knew how to pick a spot. The tranquil expanses of Skye are all around, and the modern lochside golf course must be one of the most picturesque in Scotland. Dining goes on in a formal panelled room with starched linen and good tableware, the menus offering a wide choice of assured country-house cooking. Start with locally-landed langoustines in garlic mayonnaise, or crab tian with home-grown baby chard, before going on to chicken breast with parsley mash and broccoli tempura in whisky cream, or wonderful Scottish salmon with pea purée and courgette julienne in caper beurre blanc. For pudding, there's gingerbread sponge with caramel sauce and whisky marmalade ice cream.

Chef James Cosgrove **Owner** Oxford Hotels & Inns
Times 12-3/6-8.45 **Prices** Fixed L 2 course £9-£20, Starter £50-£9.50, Main £15-£25, Dessert £5-£8.50, Service optional **Wines** 25 bottles over £20, 18 bottles under £20, 6 by glass **Notes** Tasting menus available, Sunday L, Vegetarian menu, Dress restrictions, Smart casual, Civ Wed 120 **Seats** 40, Pr/dining room 80
Children Portions, Menu **Parking** 30

Ullinish Country Lodge

Modern French V 🍃

Electrifying cooking in a Skye hideaway

☎ 01470 572214
IV56 8FD
e-mail: ullinish@theisleofskye.co.uk
web: www.theisleofskye.co.uk
dir: 9m S of Dunvegan on A863

The breathtaking views alone make the journey to this white-painted hotel worthwhile, with lochs on three sides and the rugged beauty of the Black Cuillins and MacLeod's Tables. The interior is comfortingly traditional, with tartan used in moderation in the panelled restaurant, where service is relaxed, friendly and polished. A daily 'link van' collects meat, seafood and garden produce from a network of the island's small

suppliers and delivers them to the kitchen, where Craig Halliday works his wizardry. Dishes sound convoluted, but Halliday shows considerable talent when it comes to the art of balancing flavours. Take a starter of poached quail breast which arrives perfectly cooked, with a crisp samosa of rich-tasting confit leg, together with a port and plum reduction, crisp nuggets of bread sauce, lightly pickled shimeji mushrooms and orange butter, all beautifully presented and working in harmony. Langoustine grilled with garlic butter and parsley, served with leaves, herbs and flowers, is as straight and true as they come. Among main courses, three slices of melt-in-the-mouth venison comes with beetroot and apple risotto, with sprinkles of pomegranate vinaigrette, and four firm blocks of balsamic jelly arranged around the plate - another resounding success. The fish alternative (just two main courses are offered) might be fillet of turbot with crepinette of oxtail, red wine vinaigrette and pommes purée. Extras like canapés are not only plentiful but

exemplary, as are puddings, among which is a stunning blueberry soufflé with ripple ice cream.

Chef Craig Halliday **Owner** Brian & Pam Howard
Times 7.30-8.30 Closed mid Dec-Jan, L all week
Prices Fixed D 4 course £49.50, Service optional
Wines 77 bottles over £20, 3 bottles under £20, 22 by glass **Notes** Vegetarian menu, Dress restrictions, Smart casual, No T-shirts **Seats** 22 **Parking** 10

Save on Hotels. Book at **theAA.com/hotel**

SKYE, ISLE OF 615 SCOTLAND

STAFFIN　　　　　　　Map 22 NG46

Flodigarry Country House Hotel

◉ Modern Scottish

Stunning views and local produce

☎ 01470 552203
IV51 9HZ
e-mail: info@flodigarry.co.uk
dir: Take A855 from Portree, through Staffin, N to
Flodigarry, signed on right

In an elevated position in the far North of Skye, Flodigarry
may well look like a castle but was originally a hunting
lodge and has a rich history - Flora MacDonald, Bonnie
Prince Charlie's mistress, settled in the cottage behind
the hotel after helping him evade capture in the Jacobite
rebellion (you know the song). On a clear night in the
dining room you can see right across the water to the
Torridon Mountains and Gairloch. As you don't need much
else to accompany those views, the room is simply
decorated with local artwork depicting scenes from the
island. Staff get into the spirit by wearing Highland
dress. Good use of local, seasonal produce characterises
the modish output; a multi-dimensional seared scallop
dish, for example, with black pudding, butternut squash
purée and reduced shellfish broth could lead to herb-
crusted rack of Highland lamb with garlic mash and a
sweet pepper and mint jus. Finish with iced cranachan
with wild berry coulis and Flodigarry shortbread.

Times 12-2.30/7-9.30 Closed Nov & Jan, L Mon-Sat

The Glenview

◉◉ British, French 🍃

Skilled cooking with local ingredients

☎ 01470 562248
Culnacnoc IV51 9JH
e-mail: enquiries@glenviewskye.co.uk
dir: 12m N of Portree on A855, 4m S of Staffin

On the wild Trotternish Peninsula in the north of the Isle
of Skye, where snow-dusted peaks march across the
skyline, this delightful whitewashed restaurant with
rooms certainly lives up to its name. Housed in a
Victorian croft that was once the Culnacnoc village shop,
it now deals in unpretentious modern cooking built on
splendid materials, many of which have travelled but a
short distance from producers and fishermen on the
island. These prime ingredients are then handled with
due confidence and care, as in a simple but perfectly-
executed starter of braised and glazed Staffin pork belly
with pickled carrot salad and sweet chilli dressing. Next
out, the venison from MacLeod's Table - a hill range near
the hotel - couldn't be more local, and it appears with
roast garlic and rosemary sauce, gratin potatoes and
spring greens. A chocolate fudge tart with crème fraîche
sorbet and sugared macadamia nuts ends on a note of
splendid indulgence.

Chef Simon Wallwork **Owner** Kirsty Faulds **Times** 7 8.30
Closed Jan, 8 Feb, Sun-Mon, L all week **Prices** Fixed D 3
course £35, Service optional **Wines** 10 bottles over £20,
10 bottles under £20, 4 by glass **Notes** Vegetarian
available **Seats** 22 **Children** Portions **Parking** 12

STEIN　　　　　　　Map 22 NG25

Loch Bay Seafood Restaurant

◉ British Seafood 🍃

Pleasingly straightforward seafood cookery by the bay

☎ 01470 592235
MacLeod Ter IV55 8GA
e-mail: lochbay@gmail.com
dir: 4m off A850 by B886

A show-stopping location - secreted away in unruffled
silence in one of a straddle of former 18th-century
fishermen's cottages on the loch shore - this homely little
nautical-themed restaurant is a fish-and-seafood lovers'
nirvana. In summer there's the whiff of sea air through
the open door, or you can perch on a table outside, while
the vibe is friendly and informal. Expect intelligently
simple cooking where freshness and local provenance are
king (check-out the blackboard for the day's catch);
grilled Isle of Gigha halibut, perhaps, seasoned with an
emulsion of olive oil and fresh citrus juice, or maybe
collops of monkfish with herb and garlic butter, or whole
young turbot. Apple and plum crumble might be among
desserts.

Chef David Wilkinson **Owner** David & Alison Wilkinson
Times 12-2/6-9 Closed Nov-Etr, Sun-Mon **Prices** Starter
£4-£10.50, Main £12.50-£22, Dessert £5.40, Service
optional, Groups min 7 service 10% **Wines** 24 bottles
over £20, 13 bottles under £20, 6 by glass
Notes Blackboard choices, child portions L, veg menu on
request, Vegetarian available **Seats** 23 **Parking** 6

STRUAN　　　　　　　Map 22 NG33

Ullinish Country Lodge

◉◉◉ *– see opposite*

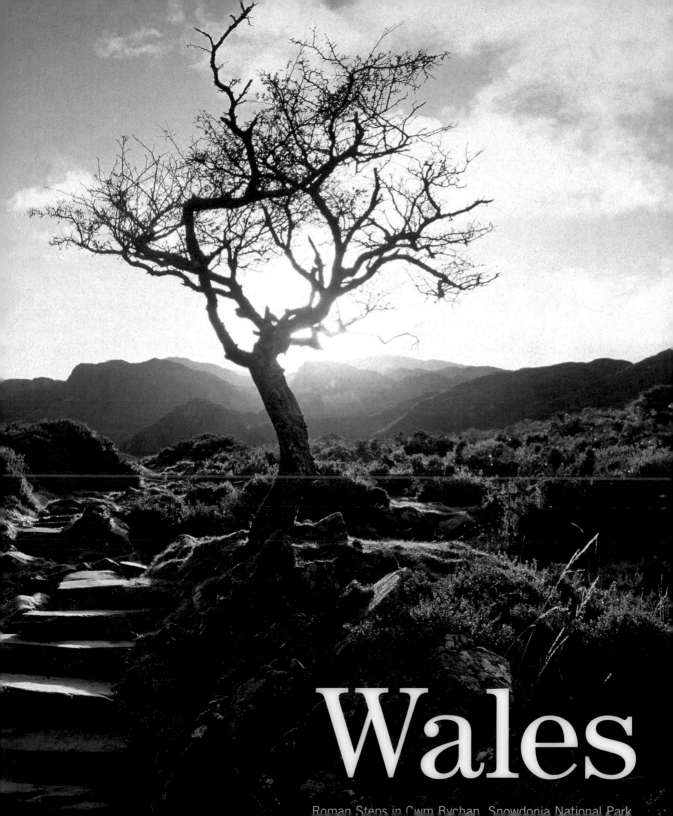

Wales

Roman Steps in Cwm Bychan, Snowdonia National Park

ANGLESEY, ISLE OF

BEAUMARIS   Map 14 SH67

Bishopsgate House Hotel

⊛ Traditional Welsh

Bistro cookery on the Beaumaris waterfront

☎ 01248 810302
54 Castle St LL58 8BB
e-mail: hazel@bishopsgatehotel.co.uk
web: www.bishopsgatehotel.co.uk
dir: from Menai Bridge onto A545 to Beaumaris. Hotel on left in main street

The Georgian townhouse done in minty green, outside and in, looks out from the Beaumaris waterfront over the Menai Strait. It's a cheering place all round, through to the dining room at the back, where stained-glass windows give the impression of looking out over the mainland. Simple bistro dishes are capably rendered, starting with a duo of black and white puddings and Carmarthen ham for a meaty starter, or a parcel of smoked salmon and white crabmeat for something from the sea. Well-sauced fish main courses may include halibut, richly served with mushrooms in tarragon and Pernod, or there might also be loin of lamb on crushed new potatoes in port and redcurrant jus. Finish with pecan tart and vanilla ice cream.

Times 12.30-2.30/6.30-9.30 Closed L Mon-Sat

Ye Olde Bulls Head Inn

⊛⊛ Modern British

Creative modern British dishes in a medieval inn

☎ 01248 810329
Castle St LL58 8AP
e-mail: info@bullsheadinn.co.uk
web: www.bullsheadinn.co.uk
dir: Town centre, main street

History seeps from the pores of the originally 15th-century inn in the shadow of Beaumaris Castle. Not only did Parliamentary forces requisition the place during the Civil War but, once that hoo-ha was settled, it began to boast a steady stream of less belligerent illustrious patrons, including Dr Samuel Johnson and Charles Dickens. Its flagship dining room is the Loft, so called because it was once the hayloft serving the stables, the ancient beams extending over a strikingly contemporary space done in beige, with swirly-patterned walls and smartly clothed tables. A lot of imaginative work goes into the modern British dishes, which are comprised of a multiplicity of premium Welsh ingredients. Start with a seared Anglesey king scallop, partnered with curried mussels, a crab fritter and langoustines in lemon hollandaise, before turning to excellent Welsh beef fillet, which comes with salt beef and potato hash and girolles in mustard jus, or steamed black bream with lemon polenta, feta ravioli, fennel, sugar snaps and pak choi. The creative juxtapositions persist through to desserts such as roast peanut cake with lemon pannacotta, burnt mango and cardamom meringue.

Chef Hefin Roberts **Owner** D Robertson, K Rothwell
Times 7-9.30 Closed 25-26 Dec, 1 Jan, Sun-Mon, L all

week **Prices** Fixed D 3 course £42.50, Service optional **Wines** 82 bottles over £20, 12 bottles under £20, 4 by glass **Notes** Vegetarian available **Seats** 45 **Parking** 10

BRIDGEND

BRIDGEND   Map 9 SS97

Bokhara Brasserie

⊛ Mediterranean, Indian V

Indian and Mediterranean dishes in a classy country-house hotel

☎ 01656 720212
Court Colman Manor, Pen-y-Fai CF31 4NG
e-mail: experience@court-colman-manor.com
dir: M4 junct 36/A4063 in direction of Maesteg, after lights take 1st exit at rdbt to Bridgend continue under motorway, take next right & follow hotel signs

It's not often that you come across an Indian restaurant in a Welsh country-house hotel, but then again the Bokhara Brasserie is far from your average high street curry house. If the warm glow of the terracotta and ochre interior brings to mind a more Mediterranean setting, that is a clue to the culinary direction of the kitchen's efforts, since the menu is a one-off hybrid, split between 'Indian' and 'Mediterranean' dishes. On the exotic side, you might meet up with old sub-continental friends such as seekh kebabs followed by a Punjabi rara gosht - lamb with a cast of Indian spices. If curry just isn't ringing your bell, go Mediterranean with something along the lines of pan-fried monkfish in herbs and butter sauce, or a fashionably retro duck with honey, orange and Cointreau sauce.

Chef Sarvesh Jadon, Tulsi Kandel, Ganga Kandel **Owner** Sanjeev Bhagotra **Times** 7-10 Closed 25 Dec, L all week **Prices** Starter £2.30-£9.95, Main £4.25-£10.95, Dessert £3.95, Service optional **Wines** 4 bottles over £20, 14 bottles under £20, 3 by glass **Notes** All you can eat buffet Sun-Mon, Vegetarian menu, Civ Wed 120 **Seats** 65, Pr/dining room 120 **Children** Portions, Menu **Parking** 100

CARDIFF

CARDIFF   Map 9 ST17

Bully's

⊛ French, European

Lively modern dishes in relaxed restaurant

☎ 029 2022 1905
5 Romilly Crescent CF11 9NP
e-mail: info@bullysrestaurant.co.uk
dir: 5mins from city centre

'Shabby chic, eclectic' is the self-styled description of Bully's: walls crammed with pictures, gilt mirrors and framed restaurant menus and bills, wooden tables, Persian rugs on the floor and books everywhere. The kitchen takes its inspiration from France, adding some modern European and Asian touches, and depends on local produce with some imports - foie gras, for instance,

Save on Hotels. Book at **theAA.com/hotel**

CARDIFF 619 **WALES**

fried and served with rhubarb compôte and sake dressing as a starter. Or there may be pickled herring with fennel and apple salad and beetroot dressing, followed by chargrilled beef fillet, accurately cooked, with port jus, kale and dauphinoise, or seared loin of yellowfin tuna with green pepper sauce, braised fennel and confit potatoes. Finish with pear tarte Tatin with pear drop ice cream.

Chef Gareth Farr **Owner** Russell Bullimore **Times** 12-2/7-9 Closed Mon-Tue, D Sun **Prices** Fixed L 2 course £14, Starter £5-£9.50, Main £13-£25, Dessert £6-£9.50, Service added but optional 10% **Wines** 42 bottles over £20, 5 bottles under £20, 9 by glass **Notes** Gourmet menu 7 course, 8 wines bi monthly £77, Sunday L, Vegetarian available **Seats** 40 **Children** Portions **Parking** On street

Cardiff Marriott Hotel

◉ British, French

A little corner of France in the Welsh capital

☎ 029 2078 5872 & 2039 9944
Mill Ln CF10 1EZ
dir: M4 junct 29, A48M E follow signs city centre & Cardiff Bay. 3m, right into Mill Lane

The split-level Brasserie Centrale restaurant of this smart city-centre hotel does just what it says on the tin: the concept is an updated take on a classic French brasserie kitted out with a sharp-looking décor of white-tiled and wood floors, unclothed dark wood tables, and squidgy, tobacco-brown leather banquettes. There's a buzzy, unbuttoned vibe that suits the unpretentious carte and daily-changing table d'hôte menus, which might set out with classics such as onion soup or snails with garlic butter, and progress to Toulouse sausages with creamed potatoes, crisp onions, and red wine and thyme jus, or grilled rib-eye steak with fries, garlic mushrooms and Provençal tomato. Puddings stick resolutely to the Gallic theme - try prune and almond tart with Armagnac cream.

Chef Anthony Barnes **Owner** Marriott International **Times** 12.30-2.30/6-10 Closed D Sun **Prices** Fixed L 2 course £9.75, Fixed D 3 course £19.50, Starter £5.25-£9.75, Main £10.75-£23.50, Dessert £6.50-£8.75, Service optional **Wines** 34 bottles over £20, 12 by glass **Notes** Pre-concert D 2 course £15.75, 3 course £19.50, Sunday L, Vegetarian available, Civ Wed 150 **Seats** 120 **Children** Portions, Menu **Parking** 140

Copthorne Hotel Cardiff-Caerdydd

◉ Traditional

Confident cooking on the outskirts of Cardiff

☎ 029 2059 9100
Copthorne Way, Culverhouse Cross CF5 6DH
e-mail: sales.cardiff@millenniumhotels.co.uk
dir: M4 junct 33 take A4232 (Culverhouse Cross), 4th exit at rdbt (A48), 1st left

The sprawling contemporary Copthorne Hotel is surrounded by a business and shopping park and whichever of those two pursuits brings you to the area, the Copthorne has a surprise up its sleeve - its Raglans Restaurant. The richly panelled room overlooks a small lake and is the setting for some smart, wide-reaching contemporary cooking. There's a grill and classics section if you want to keep things nice and simple - 28-day aged rib-eye, perhaps, or smoked haddock and salmon fishcake - or you can branch out into the likes of foie gras and chicken liver parfait with pear and apple chutney and toasted brioche, followed by pan-fried fillets of bream served with langoustine, sweet potato and chick pea ragoût and aïoli. This is a kitchen team who bake their own bread and, for dessert, might flavour a crème brûlée with Tia Maria.

Chef Damien Pondevie **Owner** Millennium & Copthorne Hotels **Times** 12.30-2/6.30-9.45 **Prices** Food prices not confirmed for 2013. Please telephone for details **Wines** 25 bottles over £20, 10 bottles under £20, 12 by glass **Notes** Sunday L, Vegetarian available, Dress restrictions, Smart casual, Civ Wed 200 **Seats** 100, Pr/dining room 220 **Children** Portions, Menu **Parking** 225

The Parc Hotel, Cardiff

◉◉ Modern Welsh NOTABLE WINE LIST

Exhilarating cooking in remodelled Victorian hotel

☎ 0871 376 9011 & 029 2078 5593
Park Place CF10 3UD
e-mail: restaurant-cardiff@thistle.co.uk
dir: M4 junct 29, A48, 4th exit signed City Centre/A470. At rdbt 2nd exit signed City Centre/A470

The Parc is now a chic but casual city-centre hub in which to relax and chill out over a drink, and its restaurant, The Social, is a thoroughly contemporary venue. See-through floor-to-ceiling shelves divide the room up, seating is banquettes and upholstered seats, tables are unclothed, and clever lighting creates the right mood. Seriously good food is the attraction here, the menu suitably of the moment. Expect pork faggots with mash and root vegetables, and a brochette of curried whelks with a ragoût of black beans and tripe among starters. Well-conceived main courses, drawing on fine Welsh produce, are full of clearly defined, often robust flavours: fillet of Anglesey sea bass partnered by cod brandade with squid ink and braised leeks, say, or salt brisket with braised oxtail, sautéed calves' liver, parsnip purée and crisps and garlic-flavoured kale. Puddings are no less appealing: try mango bavarois with chilli and lime syrup and coconut tapioca for example.

Chef Iain Inman **Owner** Curzon Hotel Ltd **Times** 12-2/6-9.30 **Prices** Fixed L 2 course £12.50, Fixed D 3 course £19.95, Starter £6.50-£8, Main £14.50-£19.50, Dessert £6-£9.50, Service optional **Wines** 106 bottles over £20, 10 by glass **Notes** Tasting menu available, Sunday L, Vegetarian available, Dress restrictions, Smart casual **Seats** 80, Pr/dining room 14 **Children** Portions, Menu **Parking** 50

CARDIFF *continued*

The Thai House Restaurant

◉ Thai **V**

Top Thai cooking in the centre of the city

☎ 029 2038 7404
3-5 Guildford Crescent, Churchill Way CF10 2HJ
e-mail: info@thaihouse.biz
web: www.thaihouse.biz
dir: At junct of Newport Rd & Queen St turn left past
Queen St station, before lights turn left into Guildford
Crescent

Right in the heart of Cardiff, Thai House pulls in the
punters keen to get a hit of the flavours of south-east
Asia. The staff certainly look the part in their national
costumes and what comes out of the kitchen is cooked
with a sure hand. Ingredients that are not available in
Wales are flown in from Bangkok for that touch of
authenticity. Try bor bia - crispy pancakes filled with
vermicelli, pork and Thai mushrooms - or yam talay
seafood salad, before the house speciality, hor moak
(salmon and broccoli marinated in red curry paste and
steamed in banana leaves), or gai pat bai krapow
(chicken with Thai basil and chilli). End with 'Eastern
Promise' - home-made lemongrass and green tea ice
creams.

Chef Sujan Klingson **Owner** Noi & Arlene Ramasut
Times 12-2.30/5.30-10.30 Closed Xmas, 1 Jan, Sun
Prices Fixed L 2 course fr £10.95, Fixed D 3 course fr £27,
Starter £5.50-£12.50, Main £9.50-£18.95, Dessert £4.95-
£7.95, Service optional, Groups min 8 service 10%
Wines 34 bottles over £20, 16 bottles under £20, 16 by
glass **Notes** Vegetarian menu, Dress restrictions, Smart
casual **Seats** 130, Pr/dining room 20 **Parking** On street,
NCP opposite

See advert on page 619

Woods Brasserie

◉◉ Modern European 🍷

Modern brasserie fare in trendy Cardiff Bay

☎ 029 2049 2400
Pilotage Building, Stuart St CF10 5BW
e-mail: woods@knifeandforkfood.co.uk
dir: In heart of Cardiff Bay. From M4 junct 33 towards
Cardiff Bay, large stone building on right

Near the Welsh Assembly in Cardiff Bay, Woods is housed
in the 19th-century Pilotage Building, with picture
windows looking over the water. It has the look of a
thoroughly 21st-century restaurant, with its grey-tiled
floor, lime-green banquettes, and bare light wood tables.
The kitchen works closely with farms, butchers and other
suppliers, so quality and seasonality are its stock-in-
trade, and produces menus brimful with imaginative,
appealing dishes. Start with smoked eel, egg and cress
tart, or a playful 'breakfast' of boudin noir, bacon,
mushrooms, quail's egg and Bloody Mary ketchup, before
well-timed pan-fried cod fillet on a bed of baby onions,
peas and carrots, served with beetroot tartare. Southern
Europe is the inspiration for some dishes - for example,
roast cured salmon fillet in olive oil emulsion with
panzanella salad and squid ink - and meals end
memorably with a dessert like vanilla and coconut
pannacotta served in a jam jar topped with mango
sorbet.

Chef Wesley Hammond **Owner** Knife & Fork Food Ltd
Times 12-2/5.30-10 Closed 25-26 Dec & 1 Jan, D Sun
(Sep-May) **Prices** Fixed L 2 course £13-£30, Fixed D 3
course £20, Starter £4-£9, Main £9-£22.50, Dessert
£4.50-£6, Service optional, Groups min 6 service 10%
Wines 35 bottles over £20, 25 bottles under £20, 20 by
glass **Notes** Fixed L & D Mon-Sat, Sunday L, Vegetarian
available **Seats** 90, Pr/dining room 40 **Children** Portions,
Menu **Parking** Multi-storey car park opposite

The Cors Restaurant

◉◉ Modern

Charming restaurant in Dylan Thomas country

☎ 01994 427219
Newbridge Rd SA33 4SH
e-mail: nickpriestland@hotmail.com
dir: A40 from Carmarthen, left at St Clears & 4m to
Laugharne

Chef-proprietor Nick Priestland has taken a lovely
Victorian rectory and transformed it into a one-off,
idiosyncratic restaurant with rooms. Just off Laugharne's
main street in Dylan Thomas country, the trees, shrubs,
ponds, and modern sculptures in the magical bog garden

('cors' is Welsh for bog) are unmissable when lit up at
night, while the moody interior has a gothic edge with its
deep claret-hued walls, wrought-iron seats and stained-
glass windows; an atmospheric setting for unaffected,
precise cooking that trumpets the virtues of excellent
local ingredients. Full-on flavours are more important
here than fancy presentation, thus smoked haddock
brûlée certainly grabs the attention at the start of a
summer's dinner, before roast rack of Welsh lamb arrives
with the punchy flavours of a rosemary and garlic crust,
dauphinoise potatoes and caramelised onion gravy, and
it all ends happily with a summer fruit Pavlova.

Times 7-9.30 Closed 25 Dec, Sun-Wed

The Plough Inn

◉ Modern International 🍷

Broad menu in friendly roadside hotel

☎ 01558 823431
Rhosmaen SA19 6NP
e-mail: info@ploughrhosmaen.com
dir: On A40 1m N of Llandeilo towards Llandovery. From
M4 onto A483 at Pont Abraham

The Plough may sound like a pub, but it has morphed into
a smartly-updated small hotel and restaurant overlooking
the Towy Valley on the edge of the Brecon Beacons
National Park. Whether you go for the convivial bar or
stylish dining room, there's a please-all menu built on
tip-top ingredients sourced from Welsh suppliers, taking
in everything from old favourites - steaks from the grill,
or crisp belly pork with black pudding, caramelised apple,
buttered mash and cider jus, say - to more ambitious,
modern ideas along the lines of crayfish and prawn ravioli
with seafood bouillabaisse and chervil foam, followed by
braised shoulder of Welsh lamb with goats' cheese tarte
Tatin and Madeira sauce.

Chef Steven Hodson **Owner** Andrew Roberts
Times 11.30-3.30/5.30-9.30 Closed 26 Dec **Prices** Fixed
L 2 course £12.75, Fixed D 3 course fr £19, Service
optional **Wines** 15 bottles over £20, 28 bottles under £20,
7 by glass **Notes** Sunday L, Vegetarian available, Civ Wed
140 **Seats** 190, Pr/dining room 35 **Children** Portions,
Menu **Parking** 70

Save on Hotels. Book at **theAA.com/hotel**

CARMARTHENSHIRE – CEREDIGION 621 | WALES

LLANELLI
Map 8 SN50

RESTAURANT OF THE YEAR FOR WALES

Sosban Restaurant

◎◎ British, French **NEW**

Dockside brasserie dining in a local landmark

☎ 01554 270020
The Pumphouse, North Dock SA15 2LF
e-mail: ian@sosbanrestaurant.com
web: www.sosbanrestaurant.com

The Victorian building that once provided hydraulic power for Llanelli's docks has been revitalised as an industrial-chic powerhouse on the local gastronomic scene. The 90-foot-high castellated stone tower is a local landmark, which makes it easy enough to find; once inside, the setting is certainly impressive with walls of arched glass windows looking out to sea, Welsh slate floors, and classy bare wooden tables beneath the exposed industrial skeleton of the heritage building. At work inside an open-to-view kitchen, the team at the stoves turns out a French-accented brasserie-style repertoire with a broad appeal and maximum input from local suppliers and producers all over Wales. A signature starter of crab lasagne shows the unfussy style, followed by hearty crowd-pleasers along the lines of breast and confit leg of Barbary duck with Puy lentils and red wine sauce, or braised Brecon venison with red cabbage and celeriac purée. To finish, the Welsh cheeseboard is hard to overlook, otherwise prune and Armagnac parfait makes a grown-up pudding.

Chef Sian Rees **Times** 12-2.45/6-9.45 Closed D Sun
Prices Fixed L 2 course £15, Fixed D 3 course £18, Starter £5.50-£15, Main £14-£21, Dessert £4.50-£8, Service included **Wines** 53 bottles over £20, 9 bottles under £20, 14 by glass **Notes** Fixed D available until 6.45pm, Sunday L, Vegetarian available **Seats** 100, Pr/dining room 20 **Children** Portions **Parking** 40

NANTGAREDIG
Map 8 SN42

Y Polyn

◎◎ Modern British ✿

Locally inspired cooking in a country pub

☎ 01267 290000
SA32 7LH
e-mail: ypolyn@hotmail.com
dir: Follow brown tourist signs to National Botanic Gardens, Y Polyn signed from rdbt in front of gardens

The Mansons' welcoming country pub makes no bones about its unpretentiousness. The service approach is friendly, chatty and informal, the place is furnished in true rustic style with bare wood tables, and the happy buzz of customers is testimony to the success of the cooking. There is no desire to innovate for its own sake, just reliable local ingredients cooked with bravura. Start with fried mackerel, served with vegetable slaw in blood orange and ginger dressing, and follow up with a shepherd's pie made with duck, served with celeriac, parsnip and parmesan mash, or a restorative vegetable tagine with a dressing of coriander yoghurt. Favourite puddings such as knickerbocker glory with flavours of chocolate and orange, or plum frangipane tart served warm, will send everyone home happy. Home-baked bread and mineral water are included in the menu price.

Chef Susan Manson **Owner** Mark & Susan Manson
Times 12-2/7-9 Closed Mon, D Sun **Prices** Fixed L 2 course fr £12, Fixed D 3 course £30, Starter £5-£7.50, Main £10-£16.50, Dessert £6, Service optional **Wines** 20 bottles over £20, 31 bottles under £20, 9 by glass **Notes** ALC prices for L only, Sunday L, Vegetarian available **Seats** 40 **Children** Portions **Parking** 25

CEREDIGION

ABERAERON
Map 8 SN46

Ty Mawr Mansion

◎◎ Modern British, Welsh ✿

Food from within 10 miles of a handsome Georgian mansion

☎ 01570 470033
Cilcennin SA48 8DB
e-mail: info@tymawrmansion.co.uk
dir: 4m from Aberaeron on A482 to Lampeter road

In a lofty position above the Aeron Valley, this stone-built Georgian mansion is tucked away in 12 acres of gorgeous grounds. Inside, it is an authentically-restored gem right down to its heritage colour schemes - sunny yellows lighten the feel, while lavender walls combine with darkwood floors and blue and white Regency-striped chairs at bare wooden tables in the rather splendid restaurant. Lots of hotels go on about their organic and local ingredients, but in this case it is not empty bluster: most of the materials come from within a 10-mile radius, including organic produce from Cilcennin village's farms on the doorstep, while the coast (four miles distant) supplies the fishy stuff. Start, perhaps, with seared Cardigan Bay scallops with cauliflower risotto, chorizo and tempura caper berries, then move on via a sorbet, to pan-seared fillet and confit belly of local pork served with crackling, parsnip purée and pan juices. For pudding there may be duck egg tart with garden rhubarb in the form of compôte and sorbet.

Chef Geraint Morgan **Owner** Martin & Catherine McAlpine
Times 7-9 Closed 26 Dec-7 Jan, Sun, L all week
Prices Starter £5.95-£10.95, Main £17.95-£24.95, Dessert £5.50-£9.95, Service optional **Wines** 23 bottles over £20, 13 bottles under £20, 6 by glass **Notes** ALC 5 course available, Vegetarian available, Dress restrictions, Smart casual, Civ Wed 35 **Seats** 35, Pr/dining room 12 **Parking** 20

EGLWYS FACH
Map 14 SN69

Ynyshir Hall

◎◎◎ – *see page 622*

LAMPETER
Map 8 SN54

The Falcondale Hotel & Restaurant
@@ Modern British V 🖐

Fine Welsh produce cooked in a lovely rural setting

☎ 01570 422910
Falcondale Dr SA48 7RX
e-mail: info@thefalcondale.co.uk
dir: 1m from Lampeter take A482 to Cardigan, turn right at petrol station, follow for 0.75m

Built on a Victorian banking fortune, this handsome Italianate mansion stands in 14 acres of grounds ensconced in lovely mid-Wales countryside. The Falcondale earns its living as an easygoing country-house hotel these days, with a classy dining room gently updated to assuage contemporary sensibilities - rugs on wooden floors, unclothed darkwood tables set against period features, and a relaxed and friendly ambience. Local hills and valleys and the nearby coastline supply the lion's share of the kitchen's raw materials for menus of broadly modern British ideas - Cardigan Bay lobster and crab, perhaps, served simply with tagliatelle and saffron sauce, followed by a winter season main course of roast loin of Pembrokeshire venison with braised red cabbage, caramelised walnuts and quince purée. For those who fancy fish, there could be a duo of salmon and sea bass served with wilted spinach, dauphinoise potatoes, artichoke 'textures' and shellfish bisque. At the end, Welsh cheeses are delivered with home-made chutney and oatcakes, and finely-crafted desserts could extend to a peppermint custard tart with bitter chocolate mousse, candyfloss and coconut sorbet.

Chef Michael Green, Andy Beaumont **Owner** Chris & Lisa Hutton **Times** 12-2/6.30-9 **Prices** Fixed L 2 course £15-£25, Fixed D 3 course fr £39, Starter fr £7, Dessert fr £6.50, Service optional, Groups min 8 service 10% **Wines** 71 bottles over £20, 11 bottles under £20, 16 by glass **Notes** Tasting menu 7 course (pre-booked), Sunday L, Vegetarian menu, Dress restrictions, Smart casual, no shorts **Seats** 36, Pr/dining room 20 **Children** Portions **Parking** 60

CONWY

ABERGELE
Map 14 SH97

The Kinmel Arms
@@ Modern Welsh 🖐

Refined, rustic food in an idyllic setting

☎ 01745 832207
The Village, St George LL22 9BP
e-mail: info@thekinmelarms.co.uk
dir: From A55 junct 24a to St George. E on A55, junct 25. 1st left to Rhuddlan, then 1st right into St George. Take 2nd right

As you enter the Kinmel Arms the friendly greeting from staff tells you that this is a restaurant with rooms (and very swish, boutique-style rooms they are too) rather than a simple pub. Originally an 18th-century sandstone-built coaching inn, the location is a secluded hamlet on the North Wales coast; inside, the bar is warmly lit and welcoming, with real ales on tap and fine wines by the glass, while the conservatory dining room is decorated with the owner's striking mountain-themed artworks in a setting that is both atmospheric and stylish. The kitchen has a real passion for regional ingredients and the intelligence not to mess about with them. Quail is served off the bone with thyme rösti and pear and vanilla purée before pan-seared black sea bream, which gets a lively accompaniment of fennel and potato cake, Menai mussel

Ynyshir Hall

EGLWYS FACH
Map 14 SN69

Modern British 🖐

Vibrant modern cooking in a charming country house

☎ 01654 781209
SY20 8TA
e-mail: ynyshir@relaischateaux.com
dir: On A487, 6m S of Machynlleth

It's quite a story. Joan and Rob Reen bought this delightful manor house back in 1989 and created one of the UK's most divertingly appealing country-house hotels. They operated it with full-on passion until 2006, when they sold it to von Essen Hotels, but stayed on to run the place. Following the collapse of von Essen, Joan and Rob managed to buy it back from the administrators. Phew. They've already started to spruce up this much-loved hotel and they've recruited a bright new chef in the form of Paul Croasdale. There's no change to the stunning setting, of course - the surrounding mountains, Dovey Estuary and 14 acres of tranquil grounds making it the archetypal escape from the world. It's all very splendid inside, with comfortable lounges filled with big comfy sofas, Rob's impressive original paintings hanging on the walls, and an elegant dining room suitably dressed for the occasion. Consider the menu in the lounge and nibble on creative canapés (the playfully described 'cheese on toast', perhaps) before moving through for a lunch or dinner based on sparkling seasonal Welsh produce, including the fruits of the kitchen garden. The new man at the stove delivers smart, contemporary dishes with bags of good ideas, acute technical ability and a keen eye for a good-looking plate of food. Start with 50 degree olive oil-poached tuna loin with a tomato consommé pouring forth from within its crumbed olive casing, plus ketchup and salsa verde and a poached quail's egg - there's a lot going on, but the flavours hit home and the technique is indisputable. Next up, first-rate Rhug Estate organic pork (the loin beautifully pink and tender) comes with apple sauce, tonka beans, a nutty ravioli and shrimp noisette, and for dessert, hazelnut, pistachio and chocolate mousse is enlivened by its accompanying chilli fromage blanc sorbet. All is well with the world.

Chef Paul Croasdale **Owner** Rob & Joan Reen **Times** 12.30-2/7-9 **Prices** Fixed L 2 course £25, Tasting menu £90, Service optional **Wines** 250 bottles over £20, 3 bottles under £20, 25 by glass **Notes** Tasting menu 9 course, Fixed D 5 course £72.50, Sunday L, Vegetarian available, Dress restrictions, No jeans, beachwear shorts or trainers, Civ Wed 28 **Seats** 30, Pr/dining room 16 **Children** Portions **Parking** 15

fritters, courgettes Parisiennes, and beetroot and orange salsa. The Welsh theme concludes with bara brith apple Charlotte with treacle toffee ice cream.

Chef Gwyn Roberts **Owner** Tim & Lynn Watson **Times** 12-3/6.30-9.30 Closed 25 Dec, 1-2 Jan, Sun-Mon **Prices** Starter £4.50-£9.50, Main £14.50-£26.95, Dessert £5.95-£6.75, Service optional **Wines** 87 bottles over £20, 20 bottles under £20, 20 by glass **Notes** Vegetarian available **Seats** 70 **Children** Portions, Menu **Parking** 60

BETWS-Y-COED   Map 14 SH75

Craig-y-Dderwen Riverside Hotel & Restaurant

@ Traditional, International ♨

Idyllic riverside setting for fine Welsh ingredients

☎ 01690 710293
LL24 0AS
e-mail: info@snowdoniahotel.com
dir: A5 to Betws-y-Coed, cross Waterloo Bridge, take 1st left

Elgar was a great fan of the peace and seclusion he found at this half-timbered Victorian country-house hotel tucked away at the end of a tree-lined drive in well-maintained gardens on the River Conwy - a view that is opened up to the max by a wall of glass in the dining room. The kitchen is clearly passionate about the produce from this landscape, growing vegetables, herbs and fruit in the extensive kitchen garden, and sourcing the rest from local and Welsh suppliers. Gently contemporary ideas take their cue from Europe and further afield, starting with Conwy crab cake with chive, rocket and warm potato salad, and proceeding to slow-braised neck of Conwy Valley lamb with roast vegetables and fondant potatoes. An apple tarte fine is as good as it should be to finish.

Chef Paul Goosey **Owner** Martin Carpenter **Times** 12.30-5/6.30-9 Closed 2 Jan-1 Feb, **Prices** Fixed D 3 course £32.50-£37, Service optional **Wines** 52 bottles over £20, 40 bottles under £20, 4 by glass **Notes** Sunday L, Vegetarian available, Dress restrictions, Smart casual, Civ Wed 125 **Seats** 82, Pr/dining room 40 **Children** Portions, Menu **Parking** 50

Llugwy River Restaurant @ Royal Oak Hotel

@ Modern British, Welsh ♨

Former coaching inn with modish menu

☎ 01690 710219
Holyhead Rd LL24 0AY
e-mail: royaloakmail@btopenworld.com
web: www.royaloakhotel.net
dir: on A5 in town centre, next to St Mary's church

The Royal Oak Hotel will never lack for custom in the tourist honeypot of Betws-y-Coed, where ambling day-trippers and hardy hikers fresh off the peaks of Snowdonia are all in need of refuelling. After a thorough facelift, the Victorian coaching inn sports a smart contemporary interior that has also given the Llugwy River Restaurant a swish new look involving cappuccino walls, crystal chandeliers, LED wall panels and bare blond-wood tables. The kitchen takes a suitably modern Welsh line with top-grade local materials - perhaps ballottine of local pheasant with spinach and walnut mousse and red onion marmalade to start, followed by Welsh lamb starring as a half rump, rillettes of slow-cooked shoulder, and a lamb and mint shortcrust pie teamed with leek dauphinoise potatoes. Welsh cheeses with bara brith fruitcake make a savoury alternative to puddings such as rich dark chocolate terrine with amaretti biscuits and pistachio.

Chef Dylan Edwards **Owner** Royal Oak Hotel Ltd **Times** 12-3/6.30-9 Closed 25-26 Dec, Mon-Tue, L Wed-Sat, D Sun **Prices** Fixed L 2 course fr £12.50, Starter £5.25-£10.95, Main £14.75-£27.50, Dessert £5.25-£6.95, Service optional **Wines** 19 bottles over £20, 32 bottles under £20, 11 by glass **Notes** Sunday L, Vegetarian available, Dress restrictions, Smart casual, no jeans, shorts or T-shirts, Civ Wed 60 **Seats** 60, Pr/dining room 20 **Children** Portions, Menu **Parking** 100

Tan-y-Foel Country House

@@@ – see page 624

CONWY   Map 14 SH77

Castle Hotel Conwy

@@ British, International ♨

Fine Welsh produce in local landmark

☎ 01492 582800
High St LL32 8DB
e-mail: mail@castlewales.co.uk
web: www.castlewales.co.uk
dir: A55 junct 18, follow town centre signs, cross estuary (castle on left). Right then left at mini-rdbts onto one-way system. Right at Town Wall Gate, right onto Berry St then High St

The Castle Hotel is not hard to find as its Victorian bell-gabled façade of local green granite and red Ruabon bricks is a Conwy landmark. Built on the site of a Cistercian abbey, it has been around since the castle was built, and has played host to many a passing luminary since the 15th century. Top-class Welsh produce is the name of the game in Dawsons restaurant, named after painter and illustrator John Dawson-Watson whose works are spread liberally around the hotel. A recent revamp has added a smart contemporary sheen to the venue, while the kitchen works in a modern British vein, delivering a daytime menu of 'dipyn bach' (little bits) for grazing and sharing, while the wide-ranging main menu takes in the likes of pan-roasted breast and confit leg of pheasant matched with a casserole of venison sausage and Puy lentils, or oven-baked cod with smoked haddock fishcake, buttered spinach, tempura baby leeks, and parsley and chorizo sauce.

Chef Graham Tinsley, Andrew Nelson **Owner** Lavin Family & Graham Tinsley **Times** 12-10 Closed D 25 Dec **Prices** Starter £5.75-£9.50, Main £13.95-£24.50, Dessert £4.50-£6.95, Service added but optional 10% **Wines** 19 bottles over £20, 12 bottles under £20, 16 by glass **Notes** Small plates menu spring & summer, Sunday L, Vegetarian available **Seats** 70 **Children** Portions, Menu **Parking** 36

Tan-y-Foel Country House

BETWS-Y-COED　　　Map 14 SH75

Modern British

First-class cooking in stylish small hotel

☎ 01690 710507
Capel Garmon LL26 0RE
e-mail: enquiries@tyfhotel.co.uk
dir: A5 onto A470; 2m N towards Llanrwst, then turning for Capel Garmon. Country House on left 1m before village

Its location could hardly be bettered: high on a hill above picture-postcard Betws-y-Coed, Tan-y-Foel has magnificent views of the Conwy Valley and the Snowdonia range. It may be a 17th-century stone farmhouse, but the Pitmans have transformed the interior into a stylishly contemporary space where modern artwork provides a talking point. Dinner is restricted to two choices per course, which suits the scale of the operation (the dining room seats only about a dozen people) and allows Janet Pitman to concentrate on her own highly individual, self-assured cooking style. Beautifully cooked fillet of lemon sole, in a light crunchy coating of poppy seeds, served on parsnip purée with a buttery curry sauce, is a fine, well-rounded starter, competing for attention with perhaps baked courgettes stuffed with beef and tomato under a smoked rarebit topping. Dishes impress with their technical precision and well-considered flavour combinations, seen in a main course of crisp-skinned duck breast with tender leg confit and poached sausage, accompanied by fondant potato, black kale, butternut squash purée, red wine sauce, and a modish clementine foam adding tartness. The alternative main course is normally fish: perhaps baked local wild sea bass fillet with pea risotto topped with crisp pea shoots and a rich red wine sauce. Janet's fine-tuned abilities and attention to presentation carry into desserts like custard tart with roast plums.

Chef Janet Pitman **Owner** Mr & Mrs P Pitman **Times** 7.30 Closed Dec-Jan, L all week, D Sun-Mon **Prices** Fixed D 3 course £49, Service optional **Wines** 70 bottles over £20, 6 by glass **Notes** Dress restrictions, No jeans, trainers, tracksuits, walking boots **Seats** 10 **Parking** 14

Bodysgallen Hall and Spa

LLANDUDNO　　　Map 14 SH78

Modern British V

Classy country-house cooking in a splendid mansion

☎ 01492 584466
LL30 1RS
e-mail: info@bodysgallen.com
web: www.bodysgallen.com
dir: A55 junct 19, A470 towards Llandudno. Hotel 2m on right

Magnificent Bodysgallen is one of those stately country homes that you feel should be owned by the National Trust, which has in fact been the case since 2008. Perched on a rise, the 17th-century hall is framed within 200 acres of parkland, rose gardens and geometrically precise parterres. The view is none too shabby either, sweeping across the skyline to Snowdonia, Conwy Castle and the Isle of Anglesey. With expectations raised skywards, you enter through the door into a genteel world of antiques, oil paintings, dark oak panelling and stone mullioned windows. Yet this is no starchy country house, thanks largely to the efforts of the staff who strike all the right notes - obliging, courteous and always on the ball. So you might say that there is rather a sense of occasion building by the time you get to the dining room. Happily, head chef Michael Cheetham, who has taken over the culinary reins after a decade in Bodysgallen's kitchen, continues to produce the light, fresh, seasonal cuisine that is the house's trademark. Top class Welsh materials are married with virtuoso classic French technique, beginning with a posh surf and turf duo of hand-dived scallops with Oakwood Park pork belly, golden raisins and caramelised cauliflower. Next up, an immaculate fillet of hake is poached and thoughtfully brought together with carrot and vanilla purée, roasted carrots and girolles. To end, a visually-stunning dessert keeps up the impetus with an assemblage of confit banana, cinder toffee espuma and bitter chocolate mousse. If you're in the mood for something less high toned, the Bistro 1620 in the old coach house offers more casual dining.

Chef Michael Cheetham **Owner** The National Trust **Times** 12.30-1.45/7-9.30 Closed Mon (winter), L Mon **Prices** Fixed L 2 course fr £19.50, Service included **Wines** 100 bottles over £20, 30 bottles under £20, 8 by glass **Notes** Pre-theatre D available, Tasting menu on request, Sunday L, Vegetarian menu, Dress restrictions, Smart casual, no trainers/T-shirts/tracksuits **Seats** 60, Pr/dining room 40 **Children** Portions **Parking** 40

Save on Hotels. Book at **theAA.com/hotel**

CONWY 625 **WALES**

CONWY *continued*

The Groes Inn

Traditional British

Traditional pub food in Wales's first licensed house

☎ 01492 650545
Tyn-y-Groes LL32 8TN
e-mail: reception@groesinn.com
dir: On B5106, 3m from Conwy

Set amid the hills of north Wales, overlooking the Conwy estuary, the white-fronted Groes (Cross) became, in the 16th century, the first licensed house in Wales, a tradition that it maintains with full honours in the 21st, with a comfortable bar in which to sink a jar or three of local ale. Some eye-catching collections are on show too, including military headgear and old cooking utensils, although there's nothing old-hat about the food presentation. The menu serves up sound country-pub fare, going from smoked mackerel and potato salad in mustard dressing, to corned beef hash, chicken curry, and prime Welsh beef fillet with all the trimmings. What better way to finish than with reassuringly boozy sherry trifle?

Chef Lewis Williams, D Kapin **Owner** Dawn & Justin Humphreys **Times** 12-2.15/6.30-9 **Prices** Starter £5.20-£8.95, Main £9.75-£28.20, Dessert £5.75-£8.25, Service optional, Groups min 8 service 10% **Wines** 12 bottles over £20, 27 bottles under £20, 16 by glass **Notes** Vegetarian available, Dress restrictions, Smart casual **Seats** 100, Pr/dining room 20 **Children** Portions **Parking** 100

DEGANWY   Map 14 SH77

Quay Hotel & Spa

Modern European

Appealing modern cooking and wonderful estuary views

☎ 01492 564100 & 564165
Deganwy Quay LL31 9DJ
e-mail: reservations@quayhotel.com
dir: M56, A494, A55 junct 18, straight across 2 rdbts. At lights bear left into The Quay. Hotel/Restaurant on right

From its location right on the edge of the water, this smart hotel has awesome views over the Conwy estuary to the ruined castle beyond. Bag a table on the terrace in good weather or take in the same incredible views from the stylish first-floor restaurant. The kitchen uses good locally sourced materials, from Menai mussels, cooked in a pot with a choice of sauce, to Black beef from Anglesey, seen in a number of grilled steaks with Café de Paris butter. Dishes are in the modern mould, taking in warm goats' cheese pannacotta with tomato sorbet, then salmon fillet with haricot bean and chorizo cassoulet, or twice-cooked belly pork with apple chutney, creamy onions and rösti. Top off a meal with an enterprising pudding like raspberry tart soufflé with lemon sorbet.

Chef Sue Leacy **Owner** Exclusive Hotels
Times 12-3/6.30-9.30 **Prices** Food prices not confirmed

for 2013. Please telephone for details **Wines** 76 bottles over £20, 18 bottles under £20, 19 by glass **Notes** Sunday L, Vegetarian available, Civ Wed 180 **Seats** 120, Pr/dining room 40 **Children** Portions, Menu **Parking** 110

LLANDUDNO   Map 14 SH78

Bodysgallen Hall and Spa

⊛⊛⊛ – *see opposite*

Empire Hotel

Modern British

Appealing brasserie dishes in a majestic Victorian hotel

☎ 01492 860555
Church Walks LL30 2HE
e-mail: reservations@empirehotel.co.uk
web: www.empirehotel.co.uk
dir: From Chester, A55 junct 19 for Llandudno. Follow signs to Promenade, turn right at war memorial & left at rdbt. Hotel 100yds on right

Britannia still ruled the waves when the Empire Hotel set up shop in the Edwardian era, and its grandiose pedimented and pillared entrance speaks of a bygone age of imperial confidence. Run by the same family since 1946, the majestic Llandudno landmark is done out in period style with swagged drapes and chandeliers, while the Watkins Restaurant - named after the wine merchant's business that once occupied the premises - works an art-deco-inspired look to go with its crowd-pleasing repertoire of modern brasserie dishes. Start out with something like grilled black pudding with crispy smoked bacon and wholegrain mustard and port sauce, and follow with the comfort of braised lamb shank with rosemary jus and crushed root vegetables, or grilled monkfish with spinach and bacon salad.

Chef Michael Waddy, Larry Mustisya **Owner** Len & Elizabeth Maddocks **Times** 12.30-2/6.30-9.30 Closed 22-30 Dec, L Mon-Sat **Prices** Fixed L 3 course £15.50, Fixed D 4 course £22.50, Service optional **Wines** 19 bottles over £20, 30 bottles under £20, 10 by glass **Notes** Fixed L Sun only, Sunday L, Vegetarian available, Dress restrictions, Smart casual **Seats** 110 **Children** Portions, Menu **Parking** 44, On street

Imperial Hotel

Modern, Traditional British

Contemporary cooking on the seafront

☎ 01492 877466
The Promenade LL30 1AP
e-mail: reception@theimperial.co.uk
web: www.theimperial.co.uk
dir: A470 to Llandudno

Built with all the confidence of the Victorian era, the wedding cake stucco façade of the Imperial is a landmark on Llandudno's seafront. Dine out on the terrace when weather allows and you have a splendid backdrop of Llandudno Bay, a view which remains constant indoors, seen through the huge picture windows of Chantrey's Restaurant. Freshness and care distinguish the cooking, with a nice balance of simple and more highly-worked dishes, and a full complement of Welsh produce proudly featuring from the off; perhaps céviche of local trout fillet served with crisp fennel and watercress salad, cucumber jelly and dill dressing, followed by slow-braised shoulder of Welsh lamb wrapped in Italian ham, with seasonal veg flavoured with rosemary and port, fondant potato, and a bonus lamb cutlet with pea purée.

Chef Arwel Jones, Joanne Williams **Owner** Greenclose Ltd **Times** 12.30-3/6.30-9.30 **Prices** Fixed L 2 course £20-£25, Starter £6.50-£8.50, Main £18.50-£25, Dessert £6.50-£8.50, Service optional **Wines** 39 bottles over £20, 23 bottles under £20, 19 by glass **Notes** Sunday L, Vegetarian available, Dress restrictions, Smart casual **Seats** 150, Pr/dining room 30 **Children** Portions, Menu **Parking** 20, Promenade pay & display 10-4pm

LLANDUDNO continued

The Lilly Restaurant with Rooms

@ Modern, Traditional British ✪

Ambitious cooking and sea views

☎ 01492 876513
West Pde LL30 2BD
e-mail: thelilly@live.co.uk
dir: Just off A546 at Llandudno, follow signs for the Pier, beach front on right

There are several windows at this seafront restaurant, decorated dramatically in white and black, which means that most tables have a sea view. Dishes, served with aplomb by friendly staff, are based on modern Anglo-European ideas, from roast rabbit loin with cottage pie of shoulder, pancetta and a quail's egg, to well-timed fried sea bass fillet with tender, juicy scallops, tomato salsa and asparagus. Starters range from the robust flavours of braised ox cheek ravioli with root vegetables and beetroot emulsion to the refinement of crab with lobster jelly and fennel cream. Puddings can be as inventive as Pimm's trifle, and liquorice pannacotta.

Chef Phillip Ashe, Jonathon Goodman **Owner** Roxanne & Phillip Ashe **Times** 12-3/6-9 **Closed** Mon, L Tue-Sat, D Sun-Mon **Prices** Fixed D 3 course fr £26.95, Service included **Wines** 75 bottles over £20, 29 bottles under £20, 15 by glass **Notes** Sunday L, Vegetarian available, Dress restrictions, Smart **Seats** 35 **Children** Portions, Menu **Parking** unlimited

Osborne House

@ Modern British

All-day brasserie menu on the promenade

☎ 01492 860330
17 North Pde LL30 2LP
e-mail: sales@osbornehouse.co.uk
web: www.osbornehouse.co.uk
dir: A55 at junct 19, follow signs for Llandudno then Promenade, at War Memorial turn right, Osborne House on left opposite entrance to pier

Smack on the seafront promenade, this grand townhouse hotel is luxuriously and romantically decorated. The dining room is a real show-stopper, where beautifully restored period features abound; think Roman pillars, large paintings, opulent drapes, gilt mirrors and dazzling statement chandeliers. So, in these opulent surroundings - formally decked out in white-linen dressed tables and with uniformed staff - you might not ordinarily expect a more relaxed café/brasserie-style operation. But here it is. The long, all-day, please-all menu offers bags of choice whatever the time of day; from a sandwich and bakery menu to more substantial things like grilled sea bass on bacon creamed cabbage, or braised lamb shank with crushed root vegetables and rosemary jus. To finish, retro desserts like treacle tart or sherry trifle hit the spot.

Chef Michael Waddy, Tim McAll **Owner** Len & Elizabeth Maddocks **Times** 10.30-10 **Closed** 22-30 Dec **Prices** Fixed L 2 course £10.50, Fixed D 3 course £19.95, Starter

£4.05-£7.25, Main £8.95-£18.05, Dessert £3.70-£4.70, Service optional, Groups min 12 service 10% **Wines** 19 bottles over £20, 30 bottles under £20, 8 by glass **Notes** Pre-theatre menu 5pm, Sunday L, Vegetarian available, Dress restrictions, Smart casual **Seats** 70, Pr/dining room 24 **Children** Portions **Parking** 6, On street

St Tudno Hotel and Restaurant

@ Modern British

Brasserie-style cooking on the Llandudno seafront

☎ 01492 874411
The Promenade LL30 2LP
e-mail: sttudnohotel@btinternet.com
web: www.st-tudno.co.uk
dir: On Promenade towards pier, hotel opposite pier entrance

Alice Liddell, she for whom Lewis Carroll once made up Wonderland, stayed here when she was a little girl, and the place has never forgotten its association with her. The dining room offers a trompe l'oeil seaside mural for those who aren't facing the windows, and able to take in succulent views of the real thing. The kitchen turns out modern brasserie food of obvious appeal, with good prime ingredients evident in the shape of Conwy mussel and smoked bacon chowder made with white wine, pot-roast guinea fowl in a coq au vin treatment, with wild mushrooms and shallots in Burgundy jus, and dark chocolate fondant with coffee ice cream.

Chef Andrew Foster **Owner** Mr Bland
Times 12.30-2/6.30-9.30 **Prices** Fixed L 2 course £15, Starter £6.95-£9.95, Main £16.95-£25.95, Dessert £5.95-£6.95, Service optional **Wines** 155 bottles over £20, 16 bottles under £20, 12 by glass **Notes** Pre-theatre menu available, Sunday L, Vegetarian available, Dress restrictions, Smart casual, no shorts, tracksuits or jeans, Civ Wed 70 **Seats** 60 **Children** Portions, Menu **Parking** 9, On street

Terrace Restaurant, St George's Hotel

@ Modern, Traditional

Patriotic Welsh cooking in a grand seafront hotel

☎ 01492 877544 & 862184
The Promenade LL30 2LG
e-mail: info@stgeorgeswales.co.uk
dir: A55, exit at Glan Conwy for Llandudno. A470 follow signs for seafront (distinctive tower identifies hotel)

Llandudno's prom is the place to be for splendid sunsets and sweeping views across the bay, and St George's Hotel sits centre stage among a grand line-up of seafront buildings. The place is a timeless slice of Victorian wedding cake pomp, whose terrace is the place to be on balmy days, although the floor-to-ceiling windows of the eponymous restaurant allow you to enjoy the same views when the weather isn't playing ball. Balancing trends with tradition, the kitchen brings together excellent local ingredients with confident simplicity: crab, saffron and chilli risotto cake with aïoli is a typical starter, while main courses could see thyme-roasted rump of lamb served with creamed root vegetables and roasted garlic, or monkfish starring in a casserole with shallots, white beans, saffron and tomato. Desserts conclude in a similar vein, perhaps warm bara brith-and-butter pudding with almond sabayon and Penderyn ice cream.

Times 12-2.30/6.30-9.30

Plas Meanan Country House

@@ Traditional British

Wonderful views and country-house cooking

☎ 01492 660232
Meanan LL26 0YR
e-mail: caroline.burt@btconnect.com
dir: On A470 between Glan Conwy & Llanrwst

At 300 feet above the Conwy Valley, this Edwardian manor gives stunning views over the river and Snowdonia National Park. The whole property has been traditionally decorated, and the restaurant, candlelit at night, is no exception with its country-house good looks. The kitchen knows its market and generally follows a traditional route, from herb-crusted scallops with smoked salmon and tartare sauce, or venison carpaccio with morels, parmesan and truffle cream, to pannacotta, or chocolate and orange mousse. Ingredients are chosen and cooked with care: pheasant casseroled with girolles, bacon, potatoes, and prunes, say, or roast fillet of sea bass well matched by its accompaniments of broad beans, peas, wild mushrooms, baby potatoes and vermouth sauce.

Chef Jason Stock **Owner** James & Caroline Burt **Times** 12-2.30/6-9 **Closed** Mon, D Sun **Prices** Fixed L 2 course £16-£20, Starter £5.50-£7.75, Main £15.95-£22.95, Dessert £5.50, Service optional **Wines** 25 bottles over £20, 26 bottles under £20, 6 by glass **Notes** Sunday L, Vegetarian available, Dress restrictions, No shorts or vests **Seats** 30, Pr/dining room 40 **Children** Portions **Parking** 60

DENBIGHSHIRE

LLANDRILLO   Map 15 SJ03

Tyddyn Llan Restaurant

◉◉ Modern British V

Contemporary flavours in a charmingly pastoral restaurant with rooms

☎ 01490 440264
LL21 0ST
e-mail: mail@tyddynllan.co.uk
web: www.tyddynllan.co.uk
dir: Take B4401 from Corwen to Llandrillo. Restaurant on right leaving village

Tyddyn Llan, dating from the Georgian period, is set in three acres of peaceful landscaped grounds surrounded by the Berwyn Mountains. The restaurant is a grand room, done out in country-house style, richly decorated, the walls hung with prints of the area and menus gathered on the owners' travels. The cooking is a convincing rendition of classical skills and up-to-date flavours, from stuffed pig's trotter with piccalilli and a chicory and watercress salad to the luxury of lobster with the counterpoint of lime, ginger and coriander butter. Main courses can be as full-flavoured as ox cheeks braised in red wine, or laverbread butter accompanying sea bass fillet, with perhaps roast chicken breast with a potato pancake and wild mushrooms as an alternative. Prune and Armagnac tart seems to be a signature pudding, well-kept farmhouse cheeses from Neal's Yard a tempting alternative.

Chef Bryan Webb **Owner** Susan & Bryan Webb
Times 12.30-2/7-9.30 Closed last 2 wks Jan, L Mon-Thu
Prices Fixed L 2 course fr £19.50, Fixed D 3 course fr £55, Tasting menu £75, Starter £9-£16, Main £20-£28, Dessert £8, Service optional **Wines** 200 bottles over £20, 14 by glass **Notes** Tasting menu 8 course, Sunday L, Vegetarian menu, Civ Wed 40 **Seats** 40, Pr/dining room 30 **Children** Portions, Menu **Parking** 20

RHYL   Map 14 SJ08

Barratt's at Ty'n Rhyl

◉◉ British, French ⊙

Exuberant traditional cooking in Rhyl's oldest house

☎ 01745 344138
167 Vale Rd LL18 2PH
e-mail: ebarratt5@aol.com
dir: From A55 take Rhyl exit onto A525. Continue past Rhuddlan Castle, supermarket, petrol station, 0.25m on right

David and Elvira Barratt are hands-on owners in the best sort of way - at the stove, front-of-house (David the former, Elvira the latter) and their passion for the place runs right through. It's a lovely old building   the oldest parts dating from the 1670s - although the conservatory adds a more contemporary perspective (eat here or in the traditionally done-out dining room). David writes the menu by hand, with four or so choices at each course, and the fruits of the one-acre walled garden - alongside judiciously-sourced local stuff - loom large in the Welsh and French-inspired dishes. Start with asparagus soup or roast mackerel with a mustard and sherry sauce, moving on to fillet of cod with air-dried ham, or sirloin of beef with caramelised onions and truffle jus. Rhubarb from the kitchen garden stars in a glazed tart with rhubarb ice cream.

Chef David Barratt **Owner** David Barratt
Times 12-2.30/7.30-9 Closed 26 Dec, 1 wk holiday, L Mon-Sat (ex private bkgs) **Prices** Starter £7, Main £25, Dessert £7, Service optional **Wines** 3 bottles over £20, 18 bottles under £20, 4 by glass **Notes** Sunday L, Vegetarian available, Dress restrictions, Smart casual **Seats** 24, Pr/dining room 16 **Children** Portions **Parking** 20

GWYNEDD

ABERSOCH   Map 14 SH32

Porth Tocyn Hotel

◉◉ Modern British

Well-established country-house with first-class cooking

☎ 01758 713303
Bwlch Tocyn LL53 7BU
e-mail: bookings@porthtocyn.fsnet.co.uk
web: www.porthtocynhotel.co.uk
dir: 2m S of Abersoch, through Sarn Bach & Bwlch Tocyn. Follow brown signs

There's a certain sense of continuity and polish that hotels only acquire after being in the same ownership for many years, and Porth Tocyn certainly fits that bill, having been run by the Fletcher-Brewer family for 64 years. Converted originally from a terrace of lead miners' cottages with wide-screen views over Cardigan Bay, it is a comfy, relaxed, and unstuffy small-scale country house with homely antique-filled lounges and a smart restaurant, where large picture windows open up the unforgettable views across the bay to the peaks of Snowdonia. The kitchen cooks up a confident repertoire of traditional and more modern dishes led by judiciously-sourced local, seasonal produce. Home-smoked salmon risotto with parmesan and lemon oil is a typical opener, followed by pan-fried fillet of Welsh beef with boulangère potatoes, confit root vegetables, broccoli and stilton purée, and oxtail jus. Finish with a retro Black Forest Arctic Roll with griottine sorbet and blackcurrant jelly.

Chef L Fletcher-Brewer, A Mancini **Owner** The Fletcher-Brewer Family **Times** 12.15-2.30/7.30-9 Closed mid Nov, 2 wks before Etr, occasional low season, L Mon-Sat **Prices** Fixed D 3 course £43.50, Service included **Wines** 76 bottles over £20, 23 bottles under £20, 6 by glass **Notes** Sunday L, Vegetarian available, Dress restrictions, Smart casual preferred **Seats** 50 **Children** Portions

CAERNARFON Map 14 SH46

Rhiwafallen Restaurant with Rooms

◉◉ Modern British

Local, seasonal food in a converted farmhouse

☎ 01286 830172
Rhiwafallen, Llandwrog LL54 5SW
e-mail: robandkate@rhiwafallen.co.uk
dir: A487 from Caernarfon, A499 restaurant 1m on left

Renovated in boutique style using the natural textures of slate and wood, this converted farmhouse in two acres of gardens is just the place to hole up and switch off. The countryside all around is uplifting, there are views across to the Llyn Peninsula, and chef-patron Rob John and his wife Kate run the whole show with easygoing hospitality - just as they have done for the last 20-odd years. Rob's cooking brings together excellent local materials with flair and imagination, and it all takes place in a charming conservatory restaurant with pale wooden tables, modern art on the walls, and a backdrop of fine sunsets over the coast when the weather plays ball. Three-course, fixed-price menus follow the seasons and offer half a dozen choices at each stage - perhaps spiced, home-cured salmon with celeriac and toasted cumin salad to start, then fillet of Welsh Black beef in a crust of crushed pepper and mustard with tomato and thyme confit and a stack of potato and onion. Finish with eggy bara brith with roasted nectarines and cinnamon ice cream.

Times 12.30-7 Closed 25-26 Dec, 1-2 Jan, Mon, L Tue-Sat, D Sun

Seiont Manor Hotel

◉◉ Modern British V

Bright cooking in an old manor-house dining hall

☎ 01286 673366
Llanrug LL55 2AQ
e-mail: seiontmanor@handpicked.co.uk
dir: From Bangor follow signs for Caernarfon. Leave Caernarfon on A4086. Hotel 3m on left

Set in 150 acres of parkland with the peaks of Snowdonia all around, and the Isle of Anglesey nearby, Seiont Manor has grown up from its roots as a stone-built Georgian farmstead into a slickly-run, upmarket hotel. The fine-dining Llwyn y Brain restaurant occupies the old dining hall of the manor, and makes a suitably refined setting of contemporary neutral hues, and high-backed leather chairs at well-spaced, linen-clad tables. The kitchen brings together well-sourced local produce in a repertoire that blends contemporary and classic ideas starting, perhaps, with a fashionable pairing of diver-caught scallops and crispy chicken wings served with wild rice and saffron foam, followed by a robust main-course duo of roasted salt cod with sticky oxtail, winter vegetables and garden parsley. For pudding, how about a hit of the Med from pistachio and olive oil cake with almond ice cream and orange jelly?

Chef Andrew Sheridan **Owner** Hand Picked Hotels
Times 12-2/7-9.30 **Prices** Fixed D 3 course £30, Starter £7.50-£10.50, Main £17.50-£24, Dessert £7-£11, Service optional **Wines** 104 bottles over £20, 2 bottles under £20, 18 by glass **Notes** Sunday L, Vegetarian menu, Dress restrictions, Smart casual, Civ Wed 100 **Seats** 55, Pr/dining room 30 **Children** Portions, Menu **Parking** 60

CRICCIETH Map 14 SH53

Bron Eifion Country House Hotel

◉ Modern British ☺

Elegant country-house hotel in stunning setting

☎ 01766 522385
LL52 0SA
e-mail: enquiries@broneifion.co.uk
dir: A497, between Porthmadog & Pwllheli

Set in lovely landscaped gardens with uplifting views over Snowdonia and the coastline of the Lleyn Peninsula, Bron Eifion is a small-scale Victorian country-house in the classic vein. Inside, its period features have survived unscathed, and include the impressive Great Hall with a minstrels' gallery as a perfect spot for aperitifs. The Orangery Restaurant offers panoramic views as a backdrop to a repertoire of modern ideas. Driven by well-sourced ingredients - top-class fish and shellfish from nearby Pwllheli, and locally-reared beef and lamb - and unfussy execution, the kitchen sends out a wide-ranging menu that might start with Tyddyn Mawr pork belly teamed with pan-seared scallops, caramelised apple purée and rosemary jus, then proceed to fillet of Welsh Black beef with blue cheese rösti, wilted spinach with nutmeg, root vegetables and wild mushroom jus.

Chef Matthew Philips **Owner** John & Mary Heenan
Times 12-2/6.30-9 **Prices** Fixed L 2 course £11.95-£16.95, Starter £6.45-£9.95, Main £16.95-£24.95, Dessert £6.95-£7.95, Service included **Wines** 37 bottles over £20, 26 bottles under £20, 6 by glass **Notes** Gourmand menu 8 course £55, Sunday L, Vegetarian available, Dress restrictions, No jeans, T-shirts, Civ Wed 150 **Seats** 150, Pr/dining room 24 **Children** Portions, Menu **Parking** 50

DOLGELLAU Map 14 SH71

Bwyty Mawddach Restaurant

◉ Modern British **NEW**

Confident modern British cooking in barn conversion

☎ 01341 424020
Pen Y Garnedd, Llanelltyd LL40 2TA
e-mail: enquiries@mawddach.com
dir: A470 Llanelltyd to A496 Barmouth, restaurant 0.2m on left after primary school

Ifan Dunn has transformed an old granite barn on his family farm into a restaurant. Now you might be picturing a chintzy farmhouse bistro with flowery tablecloths and walls adorned with farming implements, but nothing could be further from the truth. The conversion is modern, simple and clean lined, whilst respecting the nature of the building, and the only cheese here is a fine selection of Welsh favourites served with oat biscuits and home-made pear and Bramley apple fruit cheese. Spread over two floors, there are exposed beams in the vaulted ceiling upstairs, slate floors on the ground floor, and a glass frontage that gives views over the Mawddach Estuary and Cader Idris (the second highest mountain in Wales). It will come as no surprise in such a pastoral setting that local and home-grown produce figures large on a menu packed with well considered dishes. Pressed Bala pork to start, perhaps, with grilled sourdough bread (home-made), lemon and quick pickled onions, followed by pan-fried salted hake with butter beans, slow-cooked tomato and balsamic sauce and salsa verde, with hot vanilla rice pudding or those cheeses to finish.

Chef Ifan Dunn **Owner** Roger, Will & Ifan Dunn
Times 12-2.30/6-9.30 Closed 26 Dec, 1 wk Jan, 2 wks Nov, 1 wk Apr, Mon-Tue, D Sun **Prices** Starter £5-£7, Main £11-£18, Dessert £5-£6.50, Service optional **Wines** 16 bottles over £20, 14 bottles under £20, 7 by glass **Notes** Fixed L only Sun, Vegetarian available, Civ Wed 100 **Seats** 75 **Children** Menu **Parking** 20

Penmaenuchaf Hall Hotel

◉ Modern British

Modern British cooking in a Snowdonia garden room

☎ 01341 422129
Penmaenpool LL40 1YB
e-mail: relax@penhall.co.uk
dir: From A470 take A493 (Tywyn/Fairbourne), entrance 1.5m on left by sign for Penmaenpool

The 'treats of Penmaenpool' were hymned in verse by the Victorian poet Gerard Manley Hopkins, and undoubtedly the said treats must include this handsome greystone Hall. A slate-floored dining room, Llygaid yr Haul, looking out on to the gardens is particularly appealing on a candlelit evening, and is the setting for some lightly Gallic-toned modern British cooking that emphasises flavour and texture contrasts in suave presentations. Make a start with Llandudno smoked salmon dressed with red onion, capers, gherkins and lemon. Mains bring on Black beef and Bala lamb, but also Coed y Brenin venison Wellington, served with braised red cabbage in redcurrant and juniper jus, while the attractively light desserts may feature rhubarb bavarois with matching sorbet and nougat croûtons in ginger syrup.

Chef J Pilkington, T Reeve **Owner** Mark Watson, Lorraine Fielding **Times** 12-2/7-9.30 **Prices** Fixed L 2 course fr £16.50, Fixed D 4 course fr £42.50, Starter £8-£10.50, Main £24-£27.50, Dessert £8-£10.50, Service optional **Wines** 112 bottles over £20, 13 bottles under £20, 6 by glass **Notes** Sunday L, Vegetarian available, Dress restrictions, Smart casual, no jeans or T-shirts, Civ Wed 50 **Seats** 36, Pr/dining room 20 **Children** Portions, Menu **Parking** 36

PORTHMADOG   Map 14 SH53

Royal Sportsman Hotel

◉◉ Modern British ☺

Innovative cooking in friendly old coaching inn

☎ 01766 512015
131 High St LL49 9HB
e-mail: enquiries@royalsportsman.co.uk
dir: At rdbt junct of A497 & A487

It might have been built as a coaching inn in 1862, but this unpretentious family-run hotel has been thoroughly updated. The stone and slate fireplaces are still in place in the lounge and bar (great places for a pre-prandial snifter) and renovation uncovered the original darkwood floor in the restaurant, now done out in pastel shades. The kitchen is committed to fresh Welsh produce and displays a sense of adventure without straying too far off the beaten track. Perfectly roast scallops are joined in a starter by cauliflower three ways (couscous, purée and tempura), and carpaccio comes with 'corned beef' and a purée of celeriac and horseradish. Main courses can seem a tad more traditional: fillet of beef with potato terrine, kale and mushroom purée, roast partridge with a game faggot, swede and carrots. Desserts show a high level of skill and imagination: limoncello tart, say, or chocolate fondant, its richness cut by ginger and tangerine ice cream.

Chef Dan Owen **Owner** L Naudi **Times** 12-2.30/6-9 **Prices** Food prices not confirmed for 2013. Please telephone for details **Wines** 7 bottles over £20, 16 bottles under £20, 11 by glass **Notes** Vegetarian available, Dress restrictions, Smart casual **Seats** 50 **Children** Portions, Menu **Parking** 17, On street

PORTMEIRION   Map 14 SH53

Castell Deudraeth

◉ Modern British ☺

Stylish dining in the North Wales fantasy village

☎ 01766 772400
LL48 6ER
e-mail: castell@portmeirion-village.com
dir: Off A487 at Minffordd. Between Porthmadog & Penrhyndeudraeth

This pocket-sized Gothic castle is a classic slice of Victorian folly sat happily alongside Sir Clough Williams-Ellis' show-stopping Italianate fantasy village of Portmeirion. However, the real shock comes once you're inside, with a seriously stylish modern makeover revealed - think textures of Welsh oak and slate, pine tables and blue leather high-backed chairs - delivering an unexpectedly, in-vogue brasserie-style restaurant. The kitchen garden supplies much of the veg, while the local Welsh hillsides and waters of the Lleyn Peninsula and the Menai Straits take care of meat and seafood for a menu of modern European focus. Sea bass is served with shellfish and saffron risotto, while slow-braised Welsh lamb Henry might come with minted mash, caramelised red onion and lamb jus. There's a range of Welsh steaks,

too, or whole lobster from the grill, while desserts extend to rhubarb crumble, sticky toffee pudding and floating islands.

Chef Peter Hedd Williams **Owner** Portmeirion Ltd **Times** 12-2.30/6.30-9.30 Closed 7 Jan-7 Feb **Prices** Food prices not confirmed for 2013. Please telephone for details **Wines** 20 bottles over £20, 15 bottles under £20, 8 by glass **Notes** Vegetarian available **Seats** 80, Pr/dining room 40 **Children** Portions, Menu **Parking** 40

The Hotel Portmeirion

◉◉ Modern Welsh

Modern Welsh cooking and sea views

☎ 01766 770000 & 772324
Minffordd LL48 6ET
e-mail: hotel@portmeirion-village.com
dir: Off A487 at Minffordd

The hotel is at the foot of the unique village Italianate, close to the shore, looking over the estuary to Snowdonia beyond. It's a striking place, filled with antiques and artwork, the curvilinear restaurant, sharing that sea view, decorated in shades of blue and green. Dishes are well executed and nicely presented without being too flashy. Pan-fried lamb's kidneys appear as a starter with bacon, garlic mash and rich Madeira sauce, and main courses could see pan-fried turbot served up with a cannelloni of crab and an orange and cardamon sauce, or protein-rich lamb cutlets, shoulder and liver with braised potatoes. Finish with an excellent citrus financier with accompanying caramelised blood oranges and crème fraîche sorbet.

Chef Steven Roberts **Owner** Portmeirion Ltd **Times** 12-2.30/6.30-9.30 Closed 2 wks Nov **Prices** Fixed L 2 course £18.50, Fixed D 3 course £25-£38, Starter £7-£10.95, Main £17-£30, Dessert £7-£11, Service optional **Wines** 120 bottles over £20, 10 bottles under £20, 17 by glass **Notes** Concert meal packages available, Sunday L, Vegetarian available, Civ Wed 120 **Seats** 100, Pr/dining room 36 **Children** Portions, Menu **Parking** 130

PWLLHELI   Map 14 SH33

Plas Bodegroes

◉◉ Modern British

First-rate cooking in a small-scale country house

☎ 01758 612363
Nefyn Rd LL53 5TH
e-mail: gunna@bodegroes.co.uk
dir: On A497, 1m W of Pwllheli

Husband and wife Chris and Gunna Chown have been running Plas Bodegroes as a restaurant with rooms since 1986. It's easy to see why the business has been going strong for so long: the white-painted Georgian manor is full of charm and surrounded by stunning gardens brimming with beautiful flowers. Add to that some luxuriously furnished accommodation, a friendly vibe, and top-notch cooking from Chris in the modern but elegant restaurant decorated with colourful artworks, and all the

bases are covered. Chris diligently sources ingredients for his modern British menus from local suppliers, with some herbs, fruits and vegetables picked fresh from the garden, and everything (including the excellent breads) is made in-house. Flavour combinations are well-considered, as in a starter of crispy smoked pork cheek with black pudding, Scotch egg and spiced lentil dressing. Fabulous Welsh mountain lamb turns up in a main-course roast rump with slow-cooked shoulder cake, pea sausage and mint jus, and you can bet that the grilled fillet of hake (on a bed of spinach with tomato and garlic casserole) will be sustainably sourced. For dessert it could be a toss up between lemon curd parfait with Eton Mess, or plum tart with plum ripple ice cream.

Times 12.30-2.30/7-9.30 Closed Dec-Feb, Mon, L Tue-Sat, D Sun

MONMOUTHSHIRE

ABERGAVENNY   Map 9 SO21

Angel Hotel

◉ Modern, Traditional

Old coaching inn with broadly, appealing menu

☎ 01873 857121
15 Cross St NP7 5EN
e-mail: mail@angelabergavenny.com
dir: From A40 & A465 junct follow town centre signs, S of Abergavenny, past rail & bus stations

In its heyday a staging post on the Fishguard to London route, this Georgian hotel is still a refuge for travellers, although nowadays a good proportion of its patrons will have come here to dine. Eating in the popular bar is an option, while the menu in the restaurant, with its well-spaced neat tables under the chandeliers, follows a modern brasserie format - even down to moules et frites. Thai fishcake with spicy mayonnaise, followed by seared scallops with chorizo, gnocchi and red pepper sauce, and steak sandwich with chips show the diversity on offer, while desserts can stretch to pannacotta with grilled pineapple, or crème brûlée.

Chef David Hill **Owner** Caradog Hotels Ltd **Times** 12-2.30/7-10 Closed 25 Dec, D 24-30 Dec **Prices** Starter £5.90-£8.90, Main £9.90-£22, Dessert £4.90-£6.80, Service optional **Wines** 72 bottles over £20, 17 bottles under £20, 10 by glass **Notes** Pre-theatre menu 2 course & coffee £15, Sunday L, Vegetarian available, Civ Wed 120 **Seats** 80, Pr/dining room 120 **Children** Portions, Menu **Parking** 30

ABERGAVENNY *continued*

The Foxhunter

◉◉ Modern British ⬛ 🖐

Carefully-sourced ingredients cooked with flair

☎ 01873 881101
Nantyderry NP7 9DN
e-mail: info@thefoxhunter.com
dir: Just off A4042 between Usk & Abergavenny

Fans of good honest food will be pleased to find an absence of foams, espumas and look-at-me prestidigitation in Matt Tebbutt's cooking. The setting is an unassuming stationmaster's house in a quiet hamlet on the fringes of the Brecon Beacons, and as Matt is no stranger to the world of telly, he has created a photogenic dining room of wooden and Welsh stone floors, food-related paintings on cream walls, gleaming glassware on smart clothed tables, and a centrepiece log fire. Amiable service further ups the feelgood factor, and at the heart of it all is a clear love for local produce treated with the minimum of faff. The influence of mentors including Marco Pierre White is clear in sharp technique and eye-catching presentation of each dish. Hereford beef bolognese arrives in a lasagne format with lashings of parmesan grated over the top, while splendid fresh John Dory and sea trout are accompanied by a mussel bourride with spinach, samphire and broad beans. The excellent wine list has a global reach and something to please all pockets and palates.

Chef Matt Tebbutt **Owner** Lisa & Matt Tebbutt
Times 12-2.30/7-9.30 Closed Xmas, 1 Jan, BHs, Mon, D Sun **Prices** Fixed L 2 course fr £20.95, Starter £7.25-£10.25, Main £14.50-£20.50, Dessert £6.25-£8.25, Service optional, Groups min 8 service 10%
Wines 40 bottles over £20, 20 bottles under £20, 5 by glass **Notes** Sunday L, Vegetarian available **Seats** 50, Pr/dining room 30 **Children** Portions **Parking** 25

The Hardwick

◉◉ Modern British ⬛

Top-notch rustic cooking in revamped country pub

☎ 01873 854220
Old Raglan Rd NP7 9AA
e-mail: info@thehardwick.co.uk

After a journey of many years taking him through a long rollcall of A-list kitchens, Stephen Terry is now winning hordes of admirers in his whitewashed pub (now with rooms) just outside Abergavenny. The Hardwick is a deceptively unassuming place, certainly more restaurant than pub these days, although the look is more upmarket rustic-chic, with its wooden and quarry-tiled floors, low black beams and unclothed tables. There's also a new extension with a more contemporary brasserie vibe. There's nothing revolutionary about Stephen's cooking: no fireworks or chasing the next ephemeral trend, just back-to-basics, intelligent stuff based on stunning ingredients brought together in combinations aiming for deep satisfaction. The menu covers a lot of ground from Middle White pork and venison meatballs with toasted

sourdough, and Italian greens, chilli and garlic, to Black Mountain smoked salmon and olive oil-poached salmon with beetroot, horseradish, potatoes, capers and watercress. Mains could bring an assiette of local beef comprising grilled fillet, oxtail suet pudding, rib burger with creamed mushrooms and onion rings, braised shin with confit shallots and sauce bordelaise. If you've space left, there could be panettone bread-and-butter pudding brûlée for afters.

Times 12-3/6.30-10 Closed 25 Dec, D Sun Jan-Etr

Llansantffraed Court Hotel

◉◉ Modern British ⬛ 🖐

Good views and accomplished cooking

☎ 01873 840678
Old Raglan Rd, Llanvihangel Gobion, Clytha NP7 9BA
e-mail: reception@llch.co.uk
web: www.llch.co.uk
dir: M4 junct 24/A449 to Raglan. At rdbt take last exit to Clytha. Hotel on right in 4.5m

The wild beauty of the Brecon Beacons makes a memorable backdrop to this elegant Georgian mansion in 20 acres of landscaped grounds on the edge of the Usk Valley. Plushly-decorated lounges and blazing log fires in winter provide the requisite country-house comforts within, and friendly, unobtrusive staff add to the sense of luxury. The restaurant, in the oldest part of the house, goes for a surprisingly contemporary contrast, with its high-backed chairs, and church candles on smartly-laid tables beneath a black-beamed ceiling. The kitchen is ideally placed to access prime materials from Monmouthshire's army of small artisan producers, which are put to effective use in unfussy dishes prepared with good technical skill. Expect well-considered combinations delivered in good-looking modern presentations - perhaps air-dried Welsh Longhorn beef teamed with shaved Caerphilly cheese, rocket and lemon, followed by roast loin and rib of local lamb with spring greens, creamed potato and cawl jus, or if you're in the mood for fish, maybe fillet of sea bream partnered with squid, lime and chilli tagliatelle, roast carrots and fennel and crushed potatoes. Round it off with milk chocolate and almond brownie with Baileys ice cream.

Chef Jim Hamilton **Owner** Mike Morgan **Times** 12-2/7-9 **Prices** Fixed L 2 course £14.50, Fixed D 3 course £27.50, Tasting menu £65, Starter £4.75-£9.95, Main £13.95-£26.50, Dessert £5.50-£8.95, Service optional **Wines** 94 bottles over £20, 21 bottles under £20, 94 by glass **Notes** Tasting menu 7 course with matched wines, Sunday L, Vegetarian available **Seats** 50, Pr/dining room 35 **Children** Portions, Menu **Parking** 300

Restaurant 1861

◉◉ Modern British 🖐

Charming country setting and confident cooking

☎ 0845 388 1861 & 01873 821297
Cross Ash NP7 8PB
web: www.18-61.co.uk
dir: On B4521, 9m from Abergavenny, 15m from Ross-on-Wye, on outskirts of Cross Ash

Under the stewardship of Simon and Kate King, this restaurant in the hamlet of Cross Ash near Abergavenny has become a force to be reckoned with on the Monmouthshire foodie scene. The Victorian building (no prizes for guessing in what year it was built) was once a pub, and has been thoroughly made over with a clean-lined, gently contemporary look involving black beams, stone walls, and Welsh slate place mats on bare wooden tables. Simon's cooking certainly makes an impact as he brings his sound classical technique to bear on pedigree local ingredients. Tortellini of braised lamb could arrive with black olives and capers, or there might be a duo of smoked and confit goose with sweet-and-sour cherries to start. Main courses again give those quality meats and fish star billing, whether in fricassée of pheasant with grain mustard, or fillet of brill poached in red wine, while honey and lavender pannacotta with mulled pear makes a splendid finale.

Chef Simon King **Owner** Simon & Kate King
Times 12-2/7-9 Closed 1st 2 wks Jan, Mon, D Sun **Prices** Fixed L 2 course fr £19, Fixed D 3 course fr £34, Starter £8-£13.50, Main £19-£23, Dessert £7-£8.50, Service optional **Wines** 49 bottles over £20, 10 bottles under £20, 7 by glass **Notes** Tasting menu 7 course, Sunday L, Vegetarian available **Seats** 40 **Children** Portions **Parking** 20

Walnut Tree Inn

◉◉◉ — *see opposite*

Save on Hotels. Book at **theAA.com/hotel**

MONMOUTHSHIRE 631 WALES

Walnut Tree Inn

Modern British 🍷 NOTABLE WINE LIST

Blissfully unfussy and focused cooking by Shaun Hill

☎ 01873 852797
Llandewi Skirrid NP7 8AW
e-mail: mail@thewalnuttreeinn.com
web: www.thewalnuttreeinn.com
dir: 3m NE of Abergavenny on B4521

After moving on from the Merchant House in Ludlow in 2005, Shaun Hill has settled in as joint owner and chef at the resurrected Walnut Tree - and he really is the chef, cooking at the stoves with his select brigade most days of the week. For those unfamiliar with the history of this iconic whitewashed inn in a pretty hamlet near the south Wales foodie magnet of Abergavenny, its glory days ran for 30 years under Franco and Ann Taruschio before it fell on hard times, so it is heartening that Hill has succeeded in restoring the place to its former glory and is moving it ever onwards. Shaun Hill has never been one for chasing ephemeral culinary fads and trends, preferring to keep it real, pulling together the best ingredients he can lay his hands on and unleashing his formidable, seemingly effortless technical skills on making it all look deceptively simple. The food is the star here; the venue, by the way, is charmingly unstuffy, easygoing and done out with darkwood tables, plain

walls, and exuberant sprays of flowers, and the waiting staff are knowledgeable and friendly. The cooking references Hill's unpretentious style at the Merchant House - straight-talking stuff such as a spectacular piece of sea trout with a punchy saffron sauce and watercress, while main courses could offer a fortifying cassoulet of goose, pork and smoked sausage or a rack of lamb with spring vegetable stew, which may sound pedestrian, but delivers flavours to knock your socks off. Awaiting at the end is a virtuoso version of apricot tart served with almond ice cream. There's no faffing about with wine service either, no topping up or trying to talk you into trading up to pricy bottles, although the list is full of good things, with plenty available by the glass or a 35cl carafe.

Chef Shaun Hill **Owner** Shaun Hill, William Griffiths **Times** 12-2.30/7-10 Closed 1 wk Xmas, Sun-Mon **Prices** Starter £8-£15, Main £15-£25, Dessert £7, Service optional **Wines** 70 bottles over £20, 2 bottles under £20, 8 by glass **Notes** Vegetarian available **Seats** 70, Pr/dining room 26 **Children** Portions, Menu **Parking** 30

CHEPSTOW Map 4 ST59

St Pierre, A Marriott Hotel & Country Club

◉ Modern British **NEW**

Classic cooking in upscale 14th-century manor

☎ 01291 625261

St Pierre Park NP16 6YA

e-mail: mhrs.cwigs.frontdesk@marriotthotels.com
dir: M48 junct 2, A466 for Chepstow. At next rdbt 1st exit signed Caerwent A48. Hotel approx 2m on left

A 14th-century manor with turrets and battlements set in 400 acres of buxom South Wales hill country near Chepstow, the upmarket Marriott St Pierre Hotel does country-house splendour with knobs on. With its own course, golf is naturally high on the agenda for many guests, but there's also the full complement of leisure and fitness facilities you'd expect in a hotel of this standing. In keeping with the hotel's blend of ancient and modern, Morgan's restaurant works a clean-lined contemporary look to go with its simple, please-all modern repertoire. Pea and ham risotto with crisp pancetta and chives is a well-made starter, then comes rump of lamb, given the unusual - but not unwelcome-treatment of oak smoking, and served with gratin dauphinoise, Chantenay carrots and rosemary jus. An exemplary vanilla crème brûlée ends on a high note.

Times 1-3/7-10

LLANGYBI Map 9 ST39

The White Hart Village Inn

◉◉ Modern British

Impressive gastro-pub cooking in a smart village inn

☎ 01633 450258 & 07748 114838

Old Usk Rd NP15 1NP

e-mail: enquiries@thewhitehartvillageinn.com
dir: M4 junct 25 onto B4596 Caerleon road, through town centre on High St, straight over rdbt onto Usk Rd continue to Llangybi

Rich in history and atmosphere, the handsomely revamped 16th-century White Hart is the hub of Llangybi and stands close to the Roman settlement of Caerleon in the beautiful Usk Valley. The traditional bar has low-slung windows, black-painted beams and a blazing fire in the grand inglenook fireplace, while the more contemporary dining areas are the setting for some top-notch gastro-pub food. Regional produce is supplemented by fish deliveries from Brixham, and it all finds its way on to the enticing modern British menus and daily-changing blackboards. Cooking is accurate with good, well-balanced flavours and presentation is simple with no flowery garnishes. Well-seasoned leek and potato soup may get the ball rolling, followed by a moist, well-cooked bream served on an oblong piece of slate with crushed parsnip, sweet-tasting beetroot and orange chicory. A light apple trifle served with refreshing cider granité

rounds off the meal nicely. The individual mini-loaves of bread are spot-on - great texture and flavour.

Chef Adam & Liam Whittle **Owner** Michael Bates
Times 12-3/6-10 Closed Mon (ex BHs), D Sun
Prices Fixed L 2 course £14.95-£17.95, Fixed D 3 course £18.95, Tasting menu £45, Starter £5.95-£9.50, Main £12.50-£21, Dessert £5.50-£8.50, Service optional **Wines** 20 bottles over £20, 16 bottles under £20, 13 by glass **Notes** Fixed D Tue-Thu, Tasting menu 6 course Tue-Sat, Sunday L, Vegetarian available **Seats** 46, Pr/dining room 36 **Children** Portions, Menu **Parking** 30

MONMOUTH Map 10 SO51

The Inn at Penallt

◉ Modern British **NEW** 🖐

Straightforward, honest cooking in the Wye Valley

☎ 01600 772765

Penallt NP25 4SE

e-mail: enquiries@theinnatpenallt.co.uk

Slate floors, ceiling beams, lots of wooden furniture, a fireplace in the bar and a jolly atmosphere throughout - all nicely traditional and reassuring in a 17th-century inn in a tiny village in the Wye Valley. The food is the draw here, its appeal due to good-quality materials treated straightforwardly, so belly pork is breadcrumbed, fried and served with herby leaf salad and mustard dressing, and ham is roasted in honey and served with chips, a duck egg and caper mayonnaise. Fish gets a fair showing - perhaps accurately grilled sea bass fillet, from Anglesey, with simple beurre blanc, buttery new potatoes and a warm salad of asparagus and curly endive - and well-presented desserts might extend to chocolate pannacotta spiked with rosemary accompanied by stewed plums.

Chef Peter Hullsman **Owner** Andrew & Jackie Murphy
Times 12-2.30/6-9 Closed Mon, L Tue **Prices** Fixed L 2 course £13.95, Starter £5.95-£9.75, Main £9.95-£19.95, Dessert £6.25, Service optional **Wines** 20 bottles over £20, 15 bottles under £20, 8 by glass **Notes** Sunday L, Vegetarian available **Seats** 28, Pr/dining room 28 **Children** Portions, Menu

RAGLAN Map 9 SO40

The Beaufort Arms Coaching Inn & Brasserie

◉ Modern British 🖐

Historic Welsh Marches inn with modern food

☎ 01291 690412

High St NP15 2DY

e-mail: enquiries@beaufortraglan.co.uk
dir: M4 junct 24 (Newport/Abergavenny), north on A449 to junct with A40, 1 min from turning to Abergavenny

In a world of constant change it is reassuring to see a place such as The Beaufort Arms, which is still serving Raglan after four centuries. The years have seen roundhead soldiers drop by for a flagon of ale, Prime

Ministers staying to fish on the Wye and the Usk, and in the 21st century, the Beaufort Arms now lures diners with great locally-sourced food. The old place has brushed up nicely after a stylish modern facelift, hanging on to its characterful slate floors, venerable beams and wood panelling, while the slick Brasserie restaurant looks the part with its tones of cappuccino, cream and cerise and designer Lloyd loom chairs at unclothed darkwood tables. Modern British food fits the setting to a T - perhaps Grand Marnier-glazed pigeon breast with red onion marmalade to start, then venison loin with roasted beetroot, celeriac and potato gratin and juniper berry jus.

Chef Paul Webber, Alex Mobsby **Owner** Eliot & Jana Lewis
Times 12-3/6-10 Closed 25 Dec **Prices** Fixed L 2 course £12.95, Fixed D 3 course fr £15.95, Service optional **Wines** 10 bottles over £20, 25 bottles under £20, 12 by glass **Notes** Sunday L, Vegetarian available **Seats** 60, Pr/dining room 26 **Children** Menu **Parking** 30

ROCKFIELD Map 9 SO41

The Stonemill & Steppes Farm Cottages

◉◉ Modern British, International 🖐

Clearly-focused cooking in a 16th-century cider mill

☎ 01600 716273

NP25 5SW

e-mail: enquiries@thestonemill.co.uk
dir: A48 to Monmouth, B4233 to Rockfield. 2.6m from Monmouth town centre

A 16th-century cider mill is the focal point of an operation that offers self-catering cottages, as well as an accomplished restaurant, a short distance from Monmouth. Oak timbering and vaulted ceilings speak of the age of the place, while the simple wooden tables and well-wrought pan-European food bring it all up to date. Start with home-cured salmon, served with potato and dill salad and horseradish crème fraîche, before a main course as straightforward but effective as grilled cod with crushed new potatoes in tomato and herb velouté, or roast pork tenderloin in red wine jus. Blackberry crème brûlée with shortbread is one of the sweet alternatives to a slate of Welsh cheeses with oatcakes and chutney.

Chef Carl Hammett, Richard Bryan **Owner** Mrs M L Decloedt **Times** 12-2/6-9 Closed 25-26 Dec, 2 wks Jan, Mon, D Sun **Prices** Fixed L 2 course £14.95, Fixed D 3 course £20.95, Starter £5.95-£8.75, Main £15.95-£23.95, Dessert £5.95, Service optional **Wines** 15 bottles over £20, 28 bottles under £20, 8 by glass **Notes** Sunday L, Vegetarian available **Seats** 56, Pr/dining room 12 **Children** Portions **Parking** 40

Save on Hotels. Book at **theAA.com/hotel**

MONMOUTHSHIRE 633 **WALES**

SKENFRITH Map 9 SO42

The Bell at Skenfrith

◉◉ Modern British ⚑ 🍷

Impeccable ingredients and modern ideas

☎ 01600 750235
NP7 8UH
e-mail: enquiries@skenfrith.co.uk
dir: N of Monmouth on A466 for 4m. Left on B4521
towards Abergavenny, 3m on left

The Bell, dating from the 17th century, is in a beautifully rural setting in the Monnow Valley. Slate floors, beams, pews, a log fire in the bar, and rustic wooden tables and varying styles of chairs in the restaurant are what to expect - plus an ambitious menu with plenty of scope. What stands out is the quality of the ingredients - fruit and veg from the organic garden, seafood from Skye and Dartmouth, with suppliers specified on the menu - all treated with know-how and imagination. Beetroot-cured salmon with Gewürztraminer jelly and a potato pancake, or game terrine partnered by poached quince and fig compôte are thoroughly modern starters. Roast sea bass in a rich shellfish sauce with smoked garlic and lemon purée may be among mains, or roast rib of beef, its accompaniments revealing a hard-working kitchen: shallot tarte Tatin, oxtail faggot, pommes Sarladaise, winter greens and Madeira jus. Puddings can be labour-intensive too; marmalade soufflé, for instance, with whisky ice cream.

Chef Kristian Greenwell **Owner** Mr & Mrs W Hutchings
Times 12-2.30/7-9.30 Closed last wk Jan, 1st wk Feb, Tue (Nov-Mar) **Prices** Fixed L 2 course £22, Fixed D 3 course £26, Starter £6-£11, Main £15-£20, Dessert £7, Service optional **Wines** 254 bottles over £20, 34 bottles under £20, 16 by glass **Notes** Sunday L, Vegetarian available, Dress restrictions, Smart casual **Seats** 60, Pr/dining room 40 **Children** Portions, Menu **Parking** 35

USK Map 9 SO30

Newbridge on Usk

◉◉ Traditional British 🍷

Polished contemporary cooking in a riverside setting

☎ 01633 451000 & 410262
Tredunnock NP15 1LY
e-mail: newbridgeonusk@celtic-manor.com
web: www.newbridgeonusk.co.uk
dir: A449 to Usk exit through town & turn left after bridge through Llangiby. After approx 1m Cwrt Bleddyn Hotel is on the right, turn left opposite hotel up the lane. Drive through village of Tredunnock, down hill, inn on banks of River Usk

Sitting on a bend of the Usk, behind its well-tended riverbank gardens, the hotel is in a beguiling spot indeed. On a summer evening, birds swoop and fish jump, the bucolic clarity of the light is crying out for a latter-day Constable or Turner to do it justice, and the polished, attentive service in the beamed and bare-floored dining room is exactly what we want of a country inn. Great efforts are made to invest traditional pub dining with a sheen of contemporary professionalism. That's clear from the opening serving of ham hock with its little pot of piccalilli and tiny Scotch egg, which turns out to be a quail's egg encased in black pudding. Hard to resist are the copiously laden local fish market platters for two to share, comprised of scallops in the shell, crisp-fried squid, mackerel escabèche and more, a high-rolling way of leading into mains such as Preseli Blue Mountain lamb rump in herb and garlic crust, which comes with earthy kohlrabi gratin, roasted baby vine tomatoes and olives in a deeply intense jus. Dessert can be as light as perry jelly with a bouquet of summer fruits, elderflower ice cream and a lime tuile, or as traditional as Bramley apple shortbread crumble.

Chef Justin Llewelyn **Owner** The Celtic Manor Resort
Times 12-2.30/7-10 **Prices** Fixed L 2 course £14.95, Starter £7.50-£25, Main £15.95-£48.50, Dessert £5.95-£10.50, Service optional **Wines** 21 bottles over £20, 10 bottles under £20, 9 by glass **Notes** Sunday L, Vegetarian available **Seats** 90, Pr/dining room 16 **Children** Portions, Menu

---

Raglan Arms

◉ Modern British ⚑ 🍷

Unpretentious atmosphere and good, honest food

☎ 01291 690800
Llandenny NP15 1DL
e-mail: theraglanarms@gmail.com
dir: M4 junct 24. Turn off A449 towards Usk, then immediately right towards Llandenny

This flint-built pub traded up from a local boozer to lure in diners with a winning combo of great locally-sourced food and a relaxed, informal ambience. It is in a peaceful Monmouthshire village, and if you're into the pubby side of things, there's a cosy feel to the flagstoned bar serving well-kept real ales, but it's clear that culinary matters are what drives the place these days, the action focused in the conservatory extension. Taking its spiritual inspiration from France and Italy, and its ingredients from the surrounding area, the kitchen delivers snappy crowd-pleasers such as traditional Welsh lamb broth 'cawl', or local goose rillettes with home-made chutney to start, then mains such as locally-farmed pork and smoked paprika meatballs in tomato sauce with bucatini and manchego cheese. Finish with Valrhona chocolate and orange fool.

Chef Giles A Cunliffe **Owner** Giles A Cunliffe
Times 12-2.30/7-9.30 Closed 25-26 Dec, Mon, D Sun
Prices Fixed L 2 course £15.50-£18, Starter £6-£7.50, Main £14-£20, Dessert £5-£8.50, Service optional
Wines 41 bottles over £20, 13 bottles under £20, 12 by glass **Notes** Sunday L, Vegetarian available **Seats** 65 **Children** Portions **Parking** 20

USK *continued*

Three Salmons Hotel

◎◎ Modern Welsh

Widely appealing menus in revamped old coaching inn

☎ 01291 672133
Bridge St NP15 1RY
e-mail: general@threesalmons.co.uk
web: www.threesalmons.co.uk
dir: M4 junct 24/A449, 1st exit signed Usk. On entering
town hotel on main road

The hotel, a Grade II listed former coaching inn, is bang
in the centre of the charming market town. Renovation
and upgrading have been carried out sympathetically and
have brought a high level of refinement and comfort to
the property. The restaurant has been done out in a
cappuccino colour scheme, with a beamed ceiling, local
prints on the walls and a stone fireplace adding
character. The menu lists the kitchen's 'trusted
suppliers', all in the vicinity, with beef from the Usk
Valley and vegetables from the hotel's garden. Dishes are
well composed and skilfully executed, from roast
partridge with bubble-and-squeak, sprouts, bacon and
chestnuts, to pan-fried monkfish with curried mussel
sauce, crushed potatoes and pak choi. A nod may be
made to the traditional - cod and chips, say - but ideas
tend to the modish, with starters of crab custard with
pickled cucumber and soda bread and, as a finale,
deconstructed lemon meringue pie with basil custard is
an alternative to spotted dick with whisky ice cream.

Chef James Bumpass **Owner** T Strong, B Dean, P Clarke, J
Bumpass **Times** 12-2.30/6.30-9.30 **Prices** Starter £6.50-
£9, Main £11.50-£26.50, Dessert £6-£7.50, Service
optional **Wines** 67 bottles over £20, 36 bottles under £20,
13 by glass **Notes** Sunday L, Vegetarian available, Civ
Wed 100 **Seats** 55, Pr/dining room 22 **Children** Portions,
Menu **Parking** 40

WHITEBROOK   **Map 4 SO50**

The Crown at Whitebrook

◎◎◎ *– see opposite*

NEWPORT

NEWPORT   **Map 9 ST38**

Le Patio at the Manor House

◎ Modern French

French country cooking in a Welsh golf resort

☎ 01633 413000
**The Celtic Manor Resort, The Manor House, Coldra
Woods NP18 1HQ**
e-mail: bookings@celtic-manor.com
web: www.celtic-manor.com
dir: M4 junct 24, B4237 towards Newport. Hotel 1st on
right

If you're splashing out on a golfing week at the sprawling
Celtic Manor Resort, you can ring the changes by eating
in a different venue every day you're there. Tucked away
in the historic part of the old manor house, Le Patio is the
place to head for when you need a hit of hearty French
country cooking, served in an informal glass-roofed
extension done out with bare blond-wood tables and
wicker seats. Starters are as simple as onion soup with
croûtons and gruyère, or confit pork terrine with almonds,
herbs and sweet garlic served with plum and ginger
chutney and onion bread, while mains take in regional
classics such as beef bourguignon with mash,
bouillabaisse with rouille and toasted garlic bread, and
Alsatian chicken slow-cooked in Riesling with cream,
lardons, mushrooms and served with sweet potato purée.
End with cinnamon and apple bavarois with apple sorbet.

Chef Mikael le Cuziat **Owner** Celtic Manor Resort
Times 6.30-10 Closed L all week **Prices** Food prices not
confirmed for 2013. Please telephone for details
Notes Sunday L, Vegetarian available, Civ Wed 100, Air
con **Seats** 65, Pr/dining room 20 **Children** Portions, Menu
Parking 400

Rafters

◎ Modern British

Grill classics at the 19th hole

☎ 01633 413000
The Celtic Manor Resort, Coldra Woods NP18 1HQ
e-mail: bookings@celtic-manor.com
web: www.celtic-manor.com
dir: M4 junct 24, B4237 towards Newport. Hotel 1st on
right

The upmarket golf-centric Celtic Manor Resort offers a
huge spread of eating venues, but golfers who fancy
eating without having to miss the action can get the best
of both worlds in Rafters grill, where the Ryder Cup
course fills the view outside the window. The restaurant is
striking in its own right, with soaring cedar wood beams
climbing high to the ceiling, and a smart contemporary
look. The kitchen's main culinary building blocks come
from Welsh suppliers, but also cast the net a bit wider for
starters such as Severn and Wye smoked salmon with
Sakura cress and honey, mustard and dill sauce. At the
heart of things is prime Welsh beef - not the national
rugby team, but rib-eye, sirloin, fillet, or - pushing the
boat out - a Chateaubriand for two, served with triple-
cooked chips, watercress and classic sauces. End with
crème brûlée with cardamom-spiced oranges, or an
updated take on sherry trifle.

Chef Simon Searle **Owner** Celtic Manor Resort
Times 12-2.30/6-10 Closed D Mon-Wed (Oct-Mar)
Prices Food prices not confirmed for 2013. Please
telephone for details **Wines** 34 bottles over £20, 1 bottle
under £20, 6 by glass **Notes** Sunday L, Vegetarian
available, Dress restrictions, Smart casual, no trainers or
flip-flops, Civ Wed 100 **Seats** 80, Pr/dining room 96
Children Portions **Parking** 115

Terry M at The Celtic Manor Resort

◎◎◎ *– see opposite*

Save on Hotels. Book at **theAA.com/hotel**

NEWPORT 635 WALES

The Crown at Whitebrook

WHITEBROOK	Map 4 SO50

Modern British V ♦NOTABLE WINE LIST

Modern metropolitan cooking in the Wye Valley

☎ 01600 860254
NP25 4TX
e-mail: info@crownatwhitebrook.co.uk
web: www.crownatwhitebrook.co.uk
dir: From Monmouth take B4293 towards Trellech, in 2.7m left towards Whitebrook, continue for 2m

The setting, in the densely-wooded Wye Valley near to Tintern Abbey, may be Welsh through and through, but The Crown seems to model its modus operandi on the classic upmarket French country auberge. Originally a drovers' inn dating from the 17th century, its venerable beams are the only clue to the building's age once you're inside. A well-drilled team of staff get things off on the right foot with aperitifs served at leather sofas in the cosy lounge area,

then it is time to move through to the classy dining room, a modern space of soft-focus coffee and cream hues, with original artwork on the walls. The kitchen here is firing on all cylinders under head chef James Sommerin, who has taken The Crown on an ever-upwards trajectory into the top handful of Welsh restaurants. Rock-solid technical abilities are the foundations of a dazzling repertoire of modern ideas, marked by flavours that are never less than fascinating - take grey mullet, which appears in the company of smoked eel wrapped with lemon and crème fraîche in a light cannelloni, avocado purée and a wild leaf salad dressed with shiso. Fresh flavours and razor-sharp timing are to the fore in a main course of poached and roasted sea bass with langoustines, artichoke and butternut squash, while those seeking more robust things might find a nose-to-tail treatment of woodland pork with five spices, date and broccoli. A dessert described tersely as 'rhubarb, vanilla, lemon' delivers rhubarb as a consommé and poached within ravioli parcels, partnered with vanilla cream and lemon crumbs. The cellar is amply stocked with a globe-trotting list that covers all bases.

Chef James Sommerin **Owner** The Crown Hotels & Restaurants Ltd **Times** 12-2/7-9.30 Closed 2 wks Xmas, New Year **Prices** Fixed L 2 course fr £29.50, Fixed D 3 course £55, Service optional, Groups min 8 service 12.5% **Wines** 200+ bottles over £20, 10 bottles under £20, 10 by glass **Notes** Tasting menu 6 or 9 course, Sunday L, Vegetarian menu, Dress restrictions, Smart casual, no T-shirts, shorts or sandals **Seats** 30, Pr/dining room 12 **Parking** 20

Terry M at The Celtic Manor Resort

NEWPORT	Map 9 ST38

Modern British ♦NOTABLE WINE LIST 🍽

Flagship resort restaurant with creative Welsh cooking

☎ 01633 413000
Coldra Woods NP18 1HQ
e-mail: thecrown@celtic-manor.com
web: www.crown.celtic-manor.com
dir: From M4 junct 24 take B4237 towards Newport, turn right after 300yds

Hospitality on an epic scale is the name of the game at the luxurious Celtic Manor Resort, whether you are here for a leisure splurge in the spa and health club, suited and booted for a corporate event, or up for the golf (the Twenty Ten course was designed for the Ryder Cup tournament of that year). Terry M is the relaunched flagship dining venue. It is a triumph of glossy

contemporary design with its darkwood flooring, space age blue and gold lighting, crystal bead chandeliers, and high-backed leather chairs at linen-clad tables. As you would hope, the kitchen headed up by Tim McDougall takes a serious approach to its work, delivering refined, high-gloss dishes with full-on, clearly delineated flavours. The bounty of Wales is treated with due respect in a repertoire that has its feet solidly in the classics, but doesn't shy from reworking it all with well-judged flair. A richly indulgent first course might be torchon of duck liver cooked in port and served with an ultra-thin walnut wafer, followed by tenderloin and rump of woodland pork (wonderful flavour) with black pudding and choucroute. To finish; bitter chocolate mousse looks (and tastes) a treat with its accompanying basil sorbet and blood oranges. The heavyweight wine list takes an entertaining global tour of the world's prestigious vineyards.

Chef Tim McDougall **Owner** Celtic Manor Resort **Times** 12-2.30/7-9.30 Closed 1-14 Jan, Mon **Prices** Fixed L 2 course £14.95, Fixed D 3 course £49.50, Tasting menu £70, Service optional, Groups min 8 service 10% **Wines** 242 bottles over £20, 12 by glass **Notes** Tasting

menu 6 course, Sunday L, Vegetarian available, Dress restrictions, Smart casual **Seats** 50, Pr/dining room 12 **Children** Portions **Parking** 100

PEMBROKESHIRE

HAVERFORDWEST — Map 8 SM91

Wolfscastle Country Hotel

◉ Modern British ✇

Appealing menu in peaceful country hotel

☎ 01437 741225
Wolf's Castle SA62 5LZ
e-mail: info@wolfscastle.com
web: www.wolfscastle.com
dir: From Haverfordwest take A40 towards Fishguard.
Hotel in centre of Wolf's Castle

This ancient stone-built hotel sits on a promontory above
the confluence of two rivers in lush Pembrokeshire
countryside, and is still known locally as Allt-yr-Afon ('Hill
by the River') which is not only an accurate description of
its location, but also has a nice ring as the name for its
restaurant. The setting is smart, with high-backed dark
brown leather chairs at unclothed wooden tables, and if
you fancy a more casual setting, the same menu is served
in the convivial bar. The kitchen keeps things
straightforward, hauling in quality local supplies for its
unfussy repertoire, starting with the likes of pan-fried
local sea bass with a laverbread, chilli, ginger and basil
sauce. Mains can be as simple as a sirloin of local Welsh
Black steak with triple-cooked chips, portobello
mushrooms and classic sauces, or might seek inspiration
from further afield with a lemon and chicken tagine with
couscous and Moroccan salad. Puddings revert to local
mode with a bara brith pain perdu served with roasted
plums and maple syrup ice cream.

Chef Owen Hall **Owner** Mr A Stirling **Times** 12-2/6.30-9
Closed 24-26 Dec **Prices** Fixed L 2 course £15.50, Fixed D
3 course £21.95, Service optional **Wines** 33 bottles over
£20, 15 bottles under £20, 9 by glass **Notes** Sunday L,
Vegetarian available **Seats** 55, Pr/dining room 32
Children Portions, Menu **Parking** 75

NARBERTH — Map 8 SN11

The Grove

◉◉ Modern British ⬩NOTABLE ✇

**Elegant restaurant with rooms making the most of its
kitchen garden**

☎ 01834 860915
Molleston SA67 8BX
e-mail: info@thegrove-narberth.co.uk
dir: From A40, take A478 to Narberth. Continue past
castle & Herons Brook, turn right bottom of hill

Surrounded by 24 acres of hillside meadows and
beautiful flower gardens, this elegant 18th-century
country house has been lovingly restored and transformed
into a unique and very intimate restaurant with rooms.
Unlike many, this stylish venue cleverly combines a quirky
modern décor with period features without losing the
historic charm and character of the building. Neither
boutique nor country house chintz, interiors blend a
sumptuous Arts and Crafts style with tasteful colours,
fine fabrics and ever-changing exhibitions of artwork.
Using fruit, salads, herbs and vegetables from the
kitchen garden and top-notch produce from local
suppliers, the cooking is innovative modish stuff, with
classic French and Welsh influences. Dishes evolve with
the seasons and you might expect to find on the weekly-
changing menus the likes of mackerel with carrot, apple,
beetroot, horseradish and scurvy grass for starters,
followed by roast loin and glazed neck fillet of Preseli
Bluestone lamb with carrot mousse, garlic mash and a
rich lamb jus. Finish with a light and full-flavoured
Penderyn whisky parfait with oat crumble and raspberry
sorbet. Dinner is served the main dining room with its
wood-panelled walls and Georgian window frames and
real log fire, while breakfast and lunch is taken in the
gold and cream Garden Room with its conservatory style
roof and windows.

Chef Duncan Barham **Owner** Neil Kedward & Zoe Agar
Times 12-2.30/6-9.30 **Prices** Fixed L 2 course £15, Fixed
D 3 course £45, Tasting menu £65, Service optional
Wines 260 bottles over £20, 8 bottles under £20, 17 by
glass **Notes** Tasting menu 6 course, Sunday L, Vegetarian
available **Seats** 55, Pr/dining room 25 **Children** Portions,
Menu **Parking** 42

NEWPORT — Map 8 SN03

Llys Meddyg

◉◉ British ✇

Accomplished cooking in a former coaching inn

☎ 01239 820008 & 821050
East St SA42 0SY
e-mail: contact@llysmeddyg.com
dir: A487 to Newport, located on the Main Street, through
the centre of town

Llys Meddyg is easy to spot in the centre of Newport, a
village a few miles from Fishguard within the
Pembrokeshire Coast National Park. It used to be a
coaching inn and is now a comfortable, smartly done out

restaurant with rooms. There's a stone-walled cellar bar
with a wood-burner, a compact and elegant restaurant
and a lovely garden for pre-dinner drinks. The kitchen
takes great pains to buy local produce, from sustainable
sources whenever possible, or goes foraging; thus a salad
of pennywort, wild sorrel and beetroot to partner home-
smoked salmon. Main courses are praiseworthy for their
lack of gimmickry and for their precision: roast rump of
Preseli lamb, served pink, with boulangère potatoes and
parsnip purée flavoured with cumin, or fillet of hake
poached in olive oil accompanied by mushroom macaroni.
Seasonality applies to puddings too, with blackcurrant
soufflé and Eton Mess coming on the menu in summer.

Chef James Oakley **Owner** Ed & Louise Sykes
Times 12-2/6.30-9 Closed Sun-Mon, L all week (excl
summer L kitchen garden) **Prices** Fixed D 3 course
£29.50-£35, Service optional **Wines** 35 bottles over £20,
12 bottles under £20, 4 by glass **Notes** A la carte
available Apr-Oct, restricted menu other months,
Vegetarian available, Civ Wed 40 **Seats** 30, Pr/dining
room 14 **Parking** 8, On street

PEMBROKE — Map 8 SM90

Best Western Lamphey Court Hotel & Spa

◉ Modern British **NEW**

Local approach at a grandiose Georgian villa

☎ 01646 672273
Lamphey SA71 5NT
e-mail: info@lampheycourt.co.uk

Lamphey Court is a grandiose Georgian villa, complete
with massive portico entrance, standing in extensive
grounds amid the Pembrokeshire Coast National Park.
Relaunched on the world as a contemporary spa hotel, it
loses nothing of its august dignity, although the main
dining now goes on in a conservatory extension with
marble-topped tables and views of the gardens from
three sides. Localism is the watchword, with Black beef,
salt marsh lamb and pork from local farms, Cardigan Bay
fish and seafood from the dayboats at Milford, and a
plethora of Welsh cheeses all on hand. The menus don't
try anything too daring, but keep the focus on quality and
simplicity, producing a rarebit starter into which smoked
haddock has been productively inveigled. Main courses
run to maple-glazed salmon dressed in curry oil, and
pan-roasted venison with Lyonnaise potatoes and puréed
butternut squash in port jus. Hazelnut praline brings
texture to crème brûlée.

Times 6.15-10

The Shed

◉ Traditional British, Mediterranean 🍷

Spanking-fresh seafood on the harbour

☎ 01348 831518
SA62 5BN
e-mail: caroline@theshedporthgain.co.uk
web: www.theshedporthgain.co.uk
dir: 7m from St David's. Off A40

The Shed is right on the harbour of this tiny village within the Pembrokeshire Coast National Park. It's a friendly, relaxed and informal place, simply decorated and furnished, with fish and shellfish delivered daily the main business. Timings are spot on, whatever the cooking medium, and sauces and seasonings are a well-considered match for the main component, with nothing too elaborate. Start with prawns simply fried in butter with lots of garlic and parsley, or cockle chowder, and progress to seafood stew with rouille, or whole sea bream baked en papillote with lemon, garlic and thyme. Beer-battered fillets are options too, chips or colcannon are the accompaniments, and you can end with a simple dessert like rhubarb crumble with custard.

Chef Viv Folan, Rob Jones **Owner** Rob & Caroline Jones **Times** 12-3/6.30-5 Closed Nov-Apr open only wknds (except half term & Xmas hols), D Tue (off peak) **Prices** Starter £4.95-£8.50, Main £9.50-£19.50, Dessert £3.50-£6.95, Service optional **Wines** 14 bottles over £20, 12 bottles under £20, 7 by glass **Notes** Sunday L, Vegetarian available **Seats** 60 **Children** Portions **Parking** On village street

Cwtch

◉ Modern British 🍷

The taste of Wales in the smallest city

☎ 01437 720491
22 High St SA62 6SD
e-mail: info@cwtchrestaurant.co.uk
dir: A487 St Davids, restaurant on left before Cross Square

If your Welsh isn't up to scratch, the name is pronounced 'cutsh' and it has all the cosseting connotations of hug, snug, and cosy. The restaurant lives up to its name as far as the ambience goes, with three small dining rooms spread over two floors, and done out with the pared-back simplicity of whitewashed stone walls, sturdy cross-beams and a mini-library of foodie books for diners to leaf through. The cooking takes a similarly restrained approach, leaving peerless Pembrokeshire produce to do the talking without unwelcome interference from trendy ideas or foams and froths. It's clearly a formula that works, as the local following is loyal and keen for more: the place now opens for lunch, when soul-soothing Welsh lamb cawl, full of the goodness of cabbage, onion, carrot and swede, is served with Caerfai cheddar and granary bread. Turn up in the evening, and you might trade up to pan-fried sea bass with sauce vierge, cockles and samphire, and round things off with puddings that fly the Welsh dragon - sticky toffee bara brith pudding with vanilla ice cream, or dark chocolate Merlyn liqueur torte with berry compôte and raspberry sorbet.

Chef Andy Holcroft **Owner** Rachael Copley **Times** 12-2.30/6-9.30 Closed 25-26 Dec, Sun-Mon (Nov-Mar) **Prices** Starter £5-£7.50, Main £13.50-£19.50, Dessert £5.50-£7, Service optional **Wines** 15 bottles over £20, 15 bottles under £20, 8 by glass **Notes** Sunday L, Vegetarian available **Seats** 50 **Children** Portions, Menu **Parking** On street

Warpool Court Hotel

◉◉ Modern British

Assured modern Welsh cooking on the beautiful St David's peninsula

☎ 01437 720300
SA62 6BN
e-mail: info@warpoolcourthotel.com
web: www.warpoolcourthotel.com
dir: From Cross Sq in centre of St David's, left by HSBC bank into Goat St, at fork follow hotel signs

Fans of world-class coastal locations should schedule in a trip to this Victorian house in the heart of the Pembrokeshire Coast National Park, since it basks in outstanding views over St Bride's Bay. Built in 1870 to house the St David's Cathedral school boarders, the hotel also has a vast collection of 3,000 decorative tiles, which are well worth checking out, as is the confident modern cooking. Local and seasonal materials are a bedrock of the tersely-worded menu, so a summer outing starts with a Pant-Ysgawn goats' cheese croquette with beetroot,

walnuts and truffle oil, followed by rump of salt marsh lamb teamed with glazed carrots, pearl barley, dauphinoise potatoes, and garlic and rosemary jus. With the sea so close, it is only right that fish gets a good showing - wild sea bass, perhaps, with samphire, cockles, squid and Amalfi lemon, while dessert produces a wildflower honey parfait with Pembrokeshire strawberries and honeycomb.

Chef Stuart Wills **Owner** Peter Trier **Times** 12-1.45/6.45-9.15 Closed Nov **Prices** Fixed L 2 course fr £21, Fixed D 3 course £43.50-£53.50, Service included **Wines** 120 bottles over £20, 9 bottles under £20, 4 by glass **Notes** Sunday L, Vegetarian available **Seats** 50, Pr/dining room 22 **Children** Portions, Menu **Parking** 100

St Brides Spa Hotel

◉ Modern British **NEW**

Pleasingly unfussy food and fabulous sea views

☎ 01834 812304
St Brides Hill SA69 9NH
e-mail: reservations@stbridesspahotel.com
dir: A478 onto B4310 to Saundersfoot. Hotel above harbour

Built to make the very best of the views out across Saundersfoot harbour and Carmarthen Bay, this spa hotel is a good option in fair weather or foul. There is the spa for a start, to sooth the mind and body, and in the form of the Cliff Restaurant, a dining option that delivers some classic dishes based on high quality regional produce. There's also a bar (the Gallery) with its own menu, and a terrace that is the hot ticket in warmer months. The genuinely charming and friendly staff are also a big part of the hotel's appeal. In the Cliff Restaurant, you might start with Welsh beef in carpaccio form, marinated in lime, coriander and chilli, before main-course breast of Gressingham duck with wild garlic mash, finishing with orange and cinnamon crème brûlée served with a lemon tuile, or go for the Welsh cheeses.

Chef Toby Goodwin **Owner** Andrew & Lindsey Evans **Times** 11-6.30 **Prices** Starter £6.50-£7.50, Main £16-£23, Dessert £6.25-£7.25, Service optional **Wines** 100 bottles over £20, 25 bottles under £20, 14 by glass **Notes** All day Gallery menu, L all day from 11am, Sunday L, Vegetarian available, Dress restrictions, Smart dress **Seats** 100, Pr/dining room 50 **Children** Portions, Menu **Parking** 60

POWYS

BRECON · Map 9 SO02

WINNER OF THE WINE AWARD FOR WALES

The Felin Fach Griffin

◉◉ British 🏅 🐾

Top dining and quality drinking in a rural Brecon pub

☎ 01874 620111
Felin Fach LD3 0UB
e-mail: enquiries@felinfachgriffin.co.uk
dir: 3.5m N of Brecon on A470. Large terracotta building on left, on edge of village

Although the Griffin treats its real ales with due respect, the level of refinement in this country inn in a tiny Brecon village places it more in the category of a restaurant than a pub. It is, though, a welcoming place that won't turn up its nose if you pitch up with the dog after a walk on the hills, and the interior is an equally cosseting chintz-free zone with its deep sofas, smell of woodsmoke, glowing Aga, painted stone walls and floors of wood and Welsh slate. When it comes to the fresh and local mantra, the organically certified kitchen garden puts the team ahead of the game, while a solid network of local suppliers takes care of the rest. A starter of oak-roasted salmon fishcakes with lemon mayonnaise and cucumber relish shows the style, then comes rack of Welsh lamb with garlic pommes purée, crushed peas and kale from the garden. For afters, creamed vanilla rice pudding with caramelised pistachios and butterscotch hits the spot. A compelling idiosyncratic wine list has much of interest and offers heaps of choice by the glass.

Chef Ross Bruce **Owner** Charles Inkin, Edmund Inkin **Times** 12.30-2.30/6-9 Closed 24-25 Dec, few days Jan **Prices** Fixed L 2 course £16.50, Fixed D 3 course £27, Starter £7-£8.50, Main £14.50-£19.50, Dessert £5.50-£9, Service optional **Wines** 100 bottles over £20, 30 bottles under £20, 20 by glass **Notes** Vegan menu available, contact in advance special dietary req, Sunday L, Vegetarian available **Seats** 45, Pr/dining room 20 **Children** Portions, Menu **Parking** 60

Peterstone Court

◉◉ Modern British, European 🐾

Excellent local food on the edge of the Brecon Beacons

☎ 01874 665387
Brecon Rd, Llanhamlach LD3 7YB
e-mail: info@peterstone-court.com
dir: 1m from Brecon on A40 to Abergavenny

Peterstone Court is impressive on several levels. The handsome Georgian house overlooks the River Usk beneath the brooding peak of Pen-y-Fan in the Brecon Beacons National Park, a perfect location for hiking with our four-legged friends, who are made equally welcome as their owners. Inside, the place is a class act, blending eclectic contemporary style with period elegance; there's

a lovely pocket-sized spa to de-stress in, and a classy pared-back contemporary restaurant with unclothed antique tables, oak floors and white walls. The team behind this polished modern country-house operation are passionate about food, starting with a thoroughly local approach that keeps food miles to a minimum - meat and poultry are bred just seven miles up the road at the family's Glaisfer farm - and handled with skill to produce intelligently-considered juxtapositions of flavour and texture. Chicken terrine might appear with pickled wild mushrooms and carrots, carrot purée and pea cress salad, then rump and braised shoulder of lamb from the family farm is teamed with garlic mash, parsnip and rosemary purée, roasted parsnip, and mint jus.

Chef Sean Gerrard, Kelvin Parry **Owner** Jessica & Glyn Bridgeman, Sean Gerrard **Times** 12-2.30/7-9.30 **Prices** Fixed L 2 course fr £12, Starter £5-£9, Main £14-£19, Dessert £6.50-£8.95, Service optional **Wines** 30 bottles over £20, 31 bottles under £20, 12 by glass **Notes** 7 mile menu with wine available, using local produce, Sunday L, Vegetarian available **Seats** 45, Pr/dining room 120 **Children** Portions, Menu **Parking** 40

CAERSWS · Map 15 SO09

The Talkhouse

◉◉ British, European

Friendly service and hearty portions in a cosy pub

☎ 01686 688919
Ty Siarad, Pontdolgoch SY17 5JE
e-mail: info@talkhouse.co.uk
web: www.talkhouse.co.uk
dir: 1.5m W of Caersws on A470 (Machynlleth road)

This whitewashed 17th-century inn with welcoming staff is bursting with character and personal touches. At the heart of it all is a homely bar warmed by a log burner, which is a deservedly popular place to eat; otherwise head for one of the bare wooden tables in the beamed restaurant, or if you really hit it lucky with the weather, carry on through the French windows to dine in the secluded garden. The chef-patron is a staunch advocate of Welsh seasonal bounty, showcased on daily-updated blackboards. The food plays to the crowd with hearty ideas such as duck liver pâté infused with port and served with caramelised red onion chutney, followed by the simplicity of local lamb rump served with creamed potatoes and pan juices. Fish might appear in the guise of organic Shetland salmon with sweet pea risotto, while puddings deliver the timeless pleasures of vanilla crème brûlée or Eton Mess.

Chef Stephen Garratt **Owner** Stephen & Jackie Garratt **Times** 12-2/6.30-8.45 Closed 24-26 Dec, Mon-Tue (only open for group booking of 15 or more), L Wed-Sat **Prices** Starter £4.95-£7.95, Main £11.95-£22, Dessert £5.95-£6.95, Service optional **Wines** 20 bottles over £20, 20 bottles under £20, 8 by glass **Notes** Vegetarian available, Dress restrictions, Smart casual **Seats** 40 **Children** Portions **Parking** 40

CRICKHOWELL · Map 9 SO21

The Bear Hotel

◉ Modern British

Convivial dining in a thriving 15th-century village inn

☎ 01873 810408
High St NP8 1BW
e-mail: bearhotel@aol.com
dir: Town centre, off A40 (Brecon road). 6m from Abergavenny

If you're tired of village inns that have inflicted identikit contemporary makeovers on their venerable heritage, head for The Bear which has been the heart and soul of its village community between Abergavenny and the Brecon Beacons since 1432. Its enduring appeal is due to its custodians, the Hindmarsh family, who have run the place for over 30 years without being blown around in the ephemeral winds of fashion. Just look inside: what's not to like about flagstoned floors, cosy log fires, venerable oak beams and stone walls? And the kitchen only has to look to the hills, valleys and rivers all around for the supplies that are the backbone of its unpretentious modern comfort food repertoire. Evergreen ideas such as platters of smoked salmon and trout from the Black Mountains served with lemon and tarragon dressing, or chicken liver and Cognac parfait with red onion marmalade lead on to mains starring slow-braised Welsh lamb shank with spring onion mash and braising juices, or slow-roasted belly pork with colcannon, black pudding, and cider cream reduction.

Chef Matthew Voyle **Owner** Mrs J Hindmarsh, Stephen Hindmarsh **Times** 12-2/7-9.30 Closed 25 Dec, Mon, L Tue-Sat, D Sun **Prices** Food prices not confirmed for 2013. Please telephone for details **Wines** 47 bottles over £20, 22 bottles under £20, 10 by glass **Notes** Vegetarian available, Dress restrictions, Smart casual **Seats** 60, Pr/dining room 30 **Children** Portions, Menu **Parking** 40

Manor Hotel

◉ Modern British 🐾

Local produce and stunning mountain views

☎ 01873 810212
Brecon Rd NP8 1SE
e-mail: info@manorhotel.co.uk
dir: On A40, 0.5m from Crickhowell

Sitting at the foot of the dramatic Black Mountains in a lovely valley, the family-owned Manor Hotel is within fabulous walking country. But whatever's on your mind, this is a great place to get your hands on some good local produce turned into appealing contemporary dishes. A good proportion of the meat served comes from the family farm seven miles down the road, and what they don't produce themselves is sourced with due diligence. The dining room has an unfussy bistro vibe, with its bare oak tables and views out onto the terrace and hills beyond. The presentation of the food is equally unfussy and gently modish, with the likes of confit of duck leg with potato salad and red onion marmalade or Cromer crab and coriander soufflé to start. Main-course pan-fried cannon and confit shoulder of Breconshire lamb is typical of main courses, and, to finish, local cheeses are an appealing savoury option. Same owners as Peterstone Court (see entry).

Chef Glyn Bridgeman **Owner** Glyn & Jessica Bridgeman, Sean Gerrard **Times** 12-2.30/6-9.30 **Prices** Fixed L 2 course £12, Starter £4.95-£8.95, Main £7.95-£18.95, Dessert £4.50-£7.25, Service optional **Wines** 32 bottles over £20, 15 bottles under £20, 17 by glass **Notes** Sunday L, Vegetarian available **Seats** 54, Pr/dining room 26 **Children** Portions, Menu **Parking** 200

HAY-ON-WYE   Map 9 SO24

The Old Black Lion

◉ Traditional British

Traditional cookery in historic inn

☎ 01497 820841
26 Lion St HR3 5AD
e-mail: info@oldblacklion.co.uk
dir: 1m off A438. From TIC car park turn right along Oxford Rd, pass NatWest Bank, next left (Lion St), hotel 20yds on right

Perfectly placed to absorb at least some of the international literati who throng the town during its annual Book Festival, the whitewashed 17th-century inn on a corner is yet another of those places in which Oliver Cromwell once took refuge on his way to victory over the Royalists. Dining is offered in both restaurant and bar areas, and is cosily informal throughout. Traditional dishes with a modernised look are the strong suit, whether for halibut with sautéed potatoes and sweet chilli dressing, or rack of Welsh lamb on leek-flecked mash in port sauce. Bookending those might be crab baked in the shell with spring onion and chilli and gratinated with brie, and lusciously textured chocolate torte with vanilla ice cream, garnished with red fruits.

Times 12-2/6.30-9 Closed 24-26 Dec

KNIGHTON   Map 9 SO27

Milebrook House Hotel

◉◉ Modern, Traditional V ☺

Quality British food on the Welsh-English border

☎ 01547 528632
Milebrook LD7 1LT
e-mail: hotel@milebrookhouse.co.uk
web: www.milebrookhouse.co.uk
dir: 2m E of Knighton on A4113 (Ludlow)

When the legendary explorer and travel writer Sir Wilfred Thesiger took time out from crossing Arabia's Empty Quarter on a camel, he returned home to this handsome 18th-century Marches mansion in the Teme Valley. The riotously colourful gardens must have been balm to his soul, and are not merely decorative, since they supply the kitchen with heaps of fresh, seasonal fruit, veg and herbs. The kitchen delivers deceptively-simple and well-balanced modern British country-house dishes that impress with their light touch and flavour combos. Rhubarb and mustard seed sauce might be used as a sharpening foil for a pan-fried fillet of Cornish mackerel, while main courses could see rump of local Welsh lamb in a time-honoured partnership with dauphinoise potatoes, spring cabbage, creamed leeks and rosemary juice. Desserts such as garden rhubarb and ginger crème brûlée hit the spot, or there are artisan cheeses from both sides of the border.

Chef Amy Lewis **Owner** Mr & Mrs R T Marsden **Times** 12-2/7-9 Closed Mon **Prices** Fixed L 2 course fr £15.95, Starter £5.25-£7.25, Main £16.75-£19.75, Dessert £6.50-£6.75, Service optional **Wines** 40 bottles over £20, 25 bottles under £20, 8 by glass **Notes** Sunday L, Vegetarian menu **Seats** 40, Pr/dining room 16 **Children** Portions **Parking** 24

LLANDRINDOD WELLS   Map 9 SO06

The Metropole

◉ Modern British V

Stylish spa hotel with sound modern cooking

☎ 01597 823700
Temple St LD1 5DY
e-mail: info@metropole.co.uk
dir: In centre of town off A483, car park at rear

The emerald green hexagonal turrets of the Metropole have been a landmark since the height of the Victorian vogue for taking the waters in spa towns, and incredibly,

the hotel has been in the hands of the same family since Queen Victoria was on the throne. In the Radnor restaurant, however, there's a rather more contemporary approach, both in the décor of tobacco-hued leather high-backed chairs at white linen-clad tables, and in what leaves the kitchen. The chefs haul in the best locally-farmed Welsh lamb, Black beef, game, cheeses, and are to be seen foraging the local woods when ceps and chanterelles are in season. A sensibly concise menu offers the likes of ham hock and chestnut terrine with caramelised onion marmalade, and pursues the unpretentious theme on through main courses like confit Welsh White belly pork with bashed apple and butter beans, pak choi and Asian broth, to conclude with the comforts of sticky date pudding with toffee sauce and vanilla ice cream.

Chef Nick Edwards **Owner** Justin Baird-Murray **Times** 12.30-1.45/7-9.30 **Prices** Starter £4.95-£6.10, Main £14.95-£20, Dessert £4.95-£5.95, Service included **Wines** 30 bottles over £20, 23 bottles under £20, 9 by glass **Notes** Sunday L, Vegetarian menu **Seats** 200, Pr/dining room 250 **Children** Portions, Menu **Parking** 150

LLANFYLLIN   Map 15 SJ11

Seeds

◉ Modern British

Accurate cooking in an intimate, relaxed setting

☎ 01691 648604
5-6 Penybryn Cottages, High St SY22 5AP
dir: In village centre. Take A490 N from Welshpool, follow signs to Llanfyllin

Run by an amiable husband and wife and their cheery and personable front-of-house team, Seeds is a totally chilled little bistro in a 500-year-old terrace. Artworks and eclectic travel souvenirs decorate the low-beamed, slate-floored dining room, and cool jazz is the soundtrack to chef proprietor Mark Seager's full-flavoured and unpretentious classic bistro dishes. Starters can be as simple as grilled goats' cheese salad with sweet chilli sauce, while mains could take in rack of Welsh lamb with a Dijon mustard and herb crust, or grilled sea bass fillet with tagliolini and rich tomato sauce. Puddings aim for the classic comforts of treacle tart or sticky toffee pudding with cream, ice cream or custard.

Chef Mark Seager **Owner** Felicity Seager, Mark Seager **Times** 11-2.15/7-8.30 Closed 25 Dec, Late May BH, 1 wk Oct, Sun-Mon (Sun-Wed winter) **Prices** Fixed D 3 course £27.50-£30.45, Starter £4.50-£6.95, Main £9.95-£18.95, Dessert £4.95-£6.95, Service optional **Wines** 35 bottles over £20, 60 bottles under £20, 3 by glass **Notes** Pre-music festival menu Jun-Jul, Vegetarian available **Seats** 20 **Children** Portions **Parking** Free town car park, on street

LLANGAMMARCH WELLS   Map 9 SN94

The Lake Country House & Spa

@@ Modern British 🌱

Classy modern cooking in a relaxing country house

☎ 01591 620202 & 620474
LD4 4BS
e-mail: info@lakecountryhouse.co.uk
dir: W from Builth Wells on A483 to Garth (approx 6m).
Left for Llangammarch Wells, follow hotel signs

Within easy reach of the rugged wildness of the Brecon Beacons, amid peaceful countryside, this handsome country-house hotel dates back to the 1840s, where it started life as a hunting and fishing lodge. Now you can take advantage of its impressive acreage to play golf on the 9-hole course, fish in the lake or river, or simply cut loose in the spa (which is in a separate building). The traditional-looking fine-dining restaurant has bags of period charm (and lovely views over the garden in daylight hours), with summery pastel colours, well-spaced and impeccably dressed tables and a wood burner in the fireplace. The service team treads with a light step adding to the soothing atmosphere. The accurate cooking of seasonal produce characterises the intelligent modern British output; fillet of brill, perhaps, with a tomato pressing and balsamic dressing, before main-course breast of duck (perfectly pink) with roast salsify, braised cabbage, dauphine potatoes, chargrilled plums and star anise sauce. Finish with fig tarte Tatin with vanilla ice cream and caramel sauce.

Chef Russell Stach **Owner** Jean Pierre & Jan Mifsud
Times 12.30-2.30/7-9 **Prices** Fixed L 2 course £17.50,
Fixed D 4 course £38.50, Service optional
Wines 300 bottles over £20, 11 by glass **Notes** Sunday L,
Vegetarian available, Dress restrictions, Smart casual,
Civ Wed 100 **Seats** 80, Pr/dining room 70
Children Portions **Parking** 40

LLANGATTOCK   Map 9 SO21

The Old Rectory Country Hotel & Golf Club

@ British

Golfing hotel with locally-sourced menu

☎ 01873 810373
NP8 1PH
e-mail: oldrectoryhotel@live.com
dir: Opposite Shell garage in Crickhowell turn down hill, signed Llangattock. Cross bridge, turn left & immediately right into Llangattock village. Pass Horseshoe Inn on right & after 60mtrs turn right into narrow lane between houses. Follow lane past Church, hotel on right

Dating back to the 16th century, The Old Rectory certainly has a peaceful and picturesque location - a backdrop of rolling hills and gardens - and with its own golf course in situ, it's got even broader appeal. From the dining room you can gaze out across the grounds through the feature window, but all is perfectly charming inside too, with its

smartly laid tables. Unfussy, broadly modern British cooking is the thing here, utilising lots of locally-sourced ingredients. Start with game terrine with walnut chutney, moving on to braised confit of Welsh lamb with herb mash and red wine glaze, or 'posh fish and chips' (fillets of sole in tempura batter), and end with the nicely judged sharpness of lemon tart with liquorice ice cream.

Times 12-2/6-9.30

LLANWDDYN   Map 15 SJ01

Lake Vyrnwy Hotel & Spa

@ Modern British

Interesting menus, breathtaking views

☎ 01691 870692
Lake Vyrnwy SY10 0LY
e-mail: info@lakevyrnwyhotel.co.uk
web: www.lakevyrnwy.com
dir: on A4393, 200yds past dam turn sharp right into drive

This stylishly converted Victorian sporting lodge is in a superb spot above the eponymous lake. For the breathtaking view, try to bag a window seat in the conservatory-style restaurant, a long room divided by a sliding door. The frequently-changing menus showcase Welsh produce, which the kitchen treats with skill and accuracy. Starters hit the mark, from lightly pickled mackerel on a bed of leaves with saffron aïoli to chicken and wild mushroom terrine with pineapple chutney. Main courses can vary from traditional roast loin of lamb, served unusually with herby confit, accompanied by mash and Savoy cabbage, to medallions of monkfish marinated in yoghurt, chilli and lime, served with leek dauphinoise and fennel purée. Puddings like runny-centred baked chocolate fondant with vanilla ice cream maintain standards to the end.

Chef David Thompson **Owner** The Bisiker family
Times 12-2/6.45-9.15 **Prices** Food prices not confirmed for 2013. Please telephone for details **Wines** 50 bottles over £20, 30 bottles under £20, 10 by glass **Notes** Sunday L, Vegetarian available, Dress restrictions, Smart casual preferred, Civ Wed 220 **Seats** 85, Pr/dining room 220 **Children** Portions **Parking** 80

LLANWRTYD WELLS   Map 9 SN84

Carlton Riverside

@@ Modern British 🌱

Creative cooking in family-run riverside restaurant

☎ 01591 610248
Irfon Crescent LD5 4SP
e-mail: info@carltonriverside.com
dir: In town centre beside bridge

Its name is a bit of a giveaway: this small restaurant is beside the River Irfon running through the village. The restaurant's large windows let in plenty of light, while at night, when the beige-patterned curtains are closed, the lighting level is pitched to create an intimate feel in the elegantly decorated room. An amuse-bouche of leek and potato soup can get things off to a resounding start before chicken and pork terrine with plum chutney, or a plate of charcuterie with a textbook version of celeriac remoulade. The kitchen's clearly well versed in the classical repertory, and technical skills are evident too in a main course of Dover sole with salmon mousse, chive beurre blanc and crushed potatoes. While some dishes can appear busy, a steady nerve keeps them balanced and flavours pull together, not apart, as in partridge breast on cabbage and bacon, served with a venison noisette, and game pie in a ramekin under a pastry lid, all accompanied by port and game jus and dauphinoise. Finish with a trio of rhubarb: jelly, fool and crumble.

Chef Mary Ann Gilchrist **Owner** Dr & Mrs Gilchrist
Times 7-9 Closed Sun, L all week **Prices** Fixed D 3 course £27.50-£43.50, Service optional **Wines** 60 bottles over £20, 15 bottles under £20, 4 by glass **Notes** Vegetarian available **Seats** 20 **Children** Portions, Menu **Parking** Car park opposite

Lasswade Country House

@@ Modern British 🌱

Organic focus in an Edwardian country house

☎ 01591 610515
Station Rd LD5 4RW
e-mail: info@lasswadehotel.co.uk
dir: On A483, follow signs for station, opposite Spar shop, adjacent to tourist info office, 400yds on right before station

Run with great charm by owners Roger and Emma Stevens, this grand Edwardian house sits at the edge of the Victorian spa town with 360-degree views of the Cambrian Mountains and Brecon Beacons. It's a soothing spot, and when you add the chef-proprietor's skilled modern Welsh cooking into the deal, the whole package is an inviting prospect. After pre-dinner drinks in the homely lounge, it all takes place in a traditional-style dining room kitted out with burnished mahogany furniture. Driven by a passion for sourcing organic and sustainable produce from Wales and the Marches area, Roger keeps combinations straightforward, timings accurate, and interweaves flavours intelligently. Expect daily-changing dinner menus to get going with home-smoked trout fillets matched with potato and radish salad, and lemon and thyme oil, followed, perhaps, by a plate of that splendid Cambrian mountain lamb, comprising roast rump, braised breast and sautéed kidneys in grain mustard and tomato sauce with leek soufflé and Madeira wine reduction.

Chef Roger Stevens **Owner** Roger & Emma Stevens **Times** 7.30-9.30 Closed 25 Dec, L all week **Prices** Fixed D 3 course £34-£36, Service optional **Wines** 9 bottles over £20, 17 bottles under £20, 2 by glass **Notes** Vegetarian available, Dress restrictions, Smart casual **Seats** 20, Pr/ dining room 20 **Parking** 6

LLYSWEN   Map 9 SO13

Llangoed Hall

@ @ Traditional, European

Traditional cooking in an impressive house

☎ 01874 754525
LD3 0YP
e-mail: enquiries@llangoedhall.co.uk
dir: On A470, 2m from Llyswen towards Builth Wells

An impressive old pile dating from 1632, Llangoed sits in the lush green embrace of the Wye Valley. There are seven acres of fabulous landscaped gardens to roam, or if you're up to the challenge, the nearby Black Mountains offer more testing hikes. It is a grand house with some parts going back to the early Stuart era, and others, such as the sweeping pillared gallery, added by Clough Williams-Ellis (of Portmeirion fame) just before the Great War. The dining room is light and elegant in shades of duck egg-blue, and tables are draped decorously with floor-length floral chintz beneath white linen. In such a setting you don't expect the kitchen to upset the apple cart with wild experimentation, and the team duly serves up a gently-updated, well-balanced repertoire with local produce well to the fore - especially in the 'Taste of Wales' menu, which might set out with goats' cheese pannacotta with pineapple jam, balsamic reduction and walnuts. Mains could produce braised shank of Welsh lamb with dauphinoise potato, and mint and red onion gravy, and for dessert, perhaps warm apple tart with espresso crème brûlée and vanilla sauce.

Chef Sean Ballington **Times** 12.30-2/7-9 **Prices** Fixed L 3 course £25, Fixed D 4 course £30-£45, Service optional **Wines** 100+ bottles over £20, 7 by glass **Notes** Sunday L, Vegetarian available, Dress restrictions, Smart dress, Civ Wed 90 **Seats** 40, Pr/dining room 80 **Children** Portions

MONTGOMERY   Map 15 SO29

The Dragon

@ Modern, Traditional

Appealing bistro cooking in a timbered inn

☎ 01686 668359
Market Square SY15 6PA
e-mail: reception@dragonhotel.com
dir: Behind town hall

With its striking black-and-white timbered frontage and an interior dating back to the mid-1600s, there is plenty to catch the eye at this old coaching inn set on the town square. The homely, split-level dining room boasts ancient black timbers and a slate fireplace, and service is friendly and efficient from welcoming staff. The cooking style is traditional British, with accurately cooked and simply presented dishes making good use of locally-sourced ingredients. Choose from the short table d'hôte of reliable bistro favourites, or look to the carte for home-made stilton soup, followed by slow-cooked Welsh lamb shank with roasted garlic mash and Cumberland sauce, with traditional sticky toffee pudding to finish.

Chef Matthew Evans **Owner** M & S Michaels **Times** 12-2/7-9 **Prices** Fixed L 3 course £26.25, Fixed D 3 course £26.25, Starter £4.75-£6.50, Main £12.25-£25.50, Dessert £4.35-£5.60, Service optional **Wines** 7 bottles over £20, 43 bottles under £20, 12 by glass **Notes** Sunday L, Vegetarian available **Seats** 42, Pr/dining room 50 **Children** Portions **Parking** 20

RHONDDA CYNON TAFF

MISKIN   Map 9 ST08

Miskin Manor Country Hotel

@ @ Modern, Traditional British V

Inventive modern British cooking in tranquil setting

☎ 01443 224204
Pendoylan Rd CF72 8ND
e-mail: info@miskin-manor.co.uk
dir: M4 junct 34, exit onto A4119, signed Llantrisant, hotel 300yds on left

The modern world seems a long way off from Miskin Manor's 22 acres of grounds with renowned colourful gardens, yet Cardiff and the M4 are close to hand. Steeped in history, the house nevertheless keeps step with the times with the requisite spa and pampering facilities, and contemporary cooking in the romantic Meisgyn restaurant, where curvy wrought iron seats, oak panelling and swagged-back gauzy curtains add an atmospheric Gothic edge to proceedings. The kitchen takes a serious approach to its work, growing vegetables and herbs in the gardens, and turning out top-notch bread, cake and desserts from its in-house pastry section. You might start with an inventive idea involving hare ballottine served with its liver, sugar snap peas, truffle, shallot emulsion and garlic purée, then proceed to pan-fried duck breast served with sweet potato purée, braised red cabbage, cherry compôte and sloe gin jus.

Fish gets equally creative treatment - perhaps sea bass with vanilla mash, sautéed langoustines, tomatoes and a fish velouté. Dessert might be an invigorating combo of lime pannacotta with mango and pineapple sorbet, and an oat and coconut biscuit sprinkled with popping candy.

Chef Mark Beck **Owner** Mr & Mrs Rosenberg **Times** 12-2.30/6-10 Closed D 25-26 Dec **Prices** Fixed L 2 course £15.95, Fixed D 3 course £19.25, Starter £7.50-£8.25, Main £19-£26.50, Dessert £6.85, Service optional **Wines** 34 bottles over £20, 6 bottles under £20, 12 by glass **Notes** Sunday L, Vegetarian menu, Dress restrictions, Smart casual, Civ Wed 130 **Seats** 50, Pr/ dining room 30 **Children** Portions, Menu **Parking** 200

PONTYCLUN   Map 9 ST08

La Luna

@ Modern International

Relaxed bistro dining

☎ 01443 239600
79-81 Talbot Rd, Talbot Green CF72 8AE
e-mail: info@la-lunarestaurant.com
dir: M4 junct 34, follow signs for Llantrisant, turn left at 2nd lights

Opposite the retail park in the village of Talbot Green - a prime spot for pulling in the punters at lunchtime - La Luna is a relaxed place with some good food on offer. When the weather allows, there are some tables on the street for that continental vibe. Inside, there's a pleasing lack of pretention, a modish bistro look, and a contented buzz about the place. On the menu, expect a broad range of European ideas and some local ingredients; thus you might start with seafood risotto or a sharing platter of continental meats (with onion marmalade, olives and various breads). Next up, perhaps a rump steak from the grill (21-day matured from the Usk Valley), or pan-fried sea bass with warm crab Niçoise and Spanish-style coriander sauce, and finish with Eton Mess or tiramisù.

Times 12-2.30/7-10.30 Closed 24 Dec, 1 Jan & BHs, Mon, L Sat, D Sun

PONTYPRIDD
Map 9 ST08

Llechwen Hall Hotel

◉ Modern Welsh V

Scenic, historical setting for unfussy cooking

☎ 01443 742050
Llanfabon CF37 4HP
e-mail: reservations@llechwenhall.co.uk
dir: A470 Cardiff

In six acres of grounds, perched atop a hill with exemplary views out across the valley, it's easy to see why Llechwen Hall is such a big hit with the wedding parties - there's even a permanent marquee in the grounds. The fine-dining restaurant is a draw by itself and is housed in the traditional 17th-century beamed longhouse, where well-appointed tables are laid with crisp white linen. Wedding parties aside, don't expect floweriness to the cooking here: carefully-sourced ingredients are the star of the show in straightforward, modish dishes. Start with pan-fried sea bass with rocket, parmesan and cherry tomato compôte, before moving on to roast supreme of chicken with a tomato, tarragon and roast shallot sauce, and a fondant potato. End with all the comfort of the nursery in the form of sticky toffee pudding.

Chef Matthew Eales **Owner** Ramish Gor **Times** 12-2/7-9 **Prices** Starter £4.95-£6.95, Main £10.95-£23.45, Dessert £3.95-£5.95, Service optional **Wines** 10 bottles over £20, 4 bottles under £20, 4 by glass **Notes** Sunday L, Vegetarian menu, Dress restrictions, Smart casual, Civ Wed 80 **Seats** 35, Pr/dining room 300 **Parking** 100

SWANSEA

LLANRHIDIAN
Map 8 SS49

The Welcome to Town

◉◉ British, French

Fine locally-based cooking on the Gower Peninsula

☎ 01792 390015
SA3 1EH
e-mail: enquiries@thewelcometotown.co.uk
web: www.thewelcometotown.co.uk
dir: 8m from Swansea on B4231. M4 junct 47 towards Gowerton. From Gowerton take B4295

Llanrhidian is more of a sleepy village than a 'town', but let's not quibble about the name, as this cosy little country bistro is most definitely welcoming, and couldn't be better placed to source Gower's remarkable bounty. Chef-patron Ian Bennett can call on salt marsh lamb, splendid pork and beef, and super-fresh fish and seafood which turns up practically on the doorstep as the foundations for his French-accented menus of pleasingly uncomplicated contemporary ideas. For the lowest food miles and maximum seasonality, a spring menu could open with the new season's Gower asparagus with a poached egg, chive beurre blanc and crispy pancetta, followed by slow-braised shoulder and roast rack of lamb teamed with pea purée, glazed spring vegetables, Maxime potatoes and garlic beignet. Fish could be sea bass with

crushed new potatoes, artichoke barigoule and sauce légère, and to finish, perhaps orange crème caramel with orange and Grand Marnier salad.

Times 12-2/7-9.30 Closed 25-26 Dec, 1 Jan, 1 wk Oct, Mon, D Sun

PARKMILL
Map 8 SS58

Maes-Yr-Haf Restaurant with Rooms

◉ Modern British ◐

Imaginatively cooked Welsh produce

☎ 01792 371000
SA3 2EH
e-mail: enquiries@maes-yr-haf.com
dir: On A4118

In a picturesque Gower village, five minutes from Three Cliffs Bay, Maes-Yr-Haf is a boutique restaurant with rooms, with a design-led modern dining room with relaxed and friendly staff. The menu is as contemporary as the surroundings, from duck 'ham' with duck liver arancini, partnered by beetroot and cranberry compôte, to pavé of cod in a parsley crust with sausage and bean cassoulet and laverbread. Local produce forms the bedrock of the operation, and the kitchen gets the most out of flavour combinations, with Penrhiw Farm duck in ravioli, given an exotic lift with pak choi, star anise and orange, followed by dry-aged local rib-eye steak with oxtail pudding and caramelised shallots.

Chef Ben Griffiths **Owner** Patty Ford **Times** 12-2/7-9 Closed 2 wks Jan, Mon, D Sun **Prices** Fixed L 2 course fr £16.95, Starter £6.25-£8.45, Main £14.80-£23, Dessert £6.75, Service optional **Wines** 8 bottles over £20, 23 bottles under £20, 5 by glass **Notes** Tasting menu available some evenings, Sunday L, Vegetarian available **Seats** 44 **Children** Portions **Parking** 20

REYNOLDSTON
Map 8 SS48

Fairyhill

◉◉ Modern British V ▲NOTABLE WINE LIST ◐

Elegant country-house hotel with real local flavour

☎ 01792 390139
SA3 1BS
e-mail: postbox@fairyhill.net
dir: M4 junct 47, take A483 then A484 to Llanelli, Gower, Gowerton. At Gowerton follow B4295 for approx 10m

For a restorative retreat, this lovely 18th-century country house is hard to beat. In the heart of Gower, Fairyhill has bags of style in an interior kitted out in the hybrid of old and new that defines a modern country house. And with just eight bedrooms, its 24 acres of delightful grounds with mature woodland, a lake and trout stream mean you won't have difficulty shaking off the other guests. Better still, you don't need to head off into the wilds to look for dinner, as the best table for miles around is right here. The kitchen stocks its larder with Welsh Black beef, salt marsh lamb, Penclawdd cockles and fresh fish, most of which comes from a ten-mile radius around Gower.

Simple, fresh and local are the watchwords of the modern Welsh menu; for the least food miles, open with Gower crab with chilli and apple, toast, rocket and endives, and follow with loin, rib and sweetbread of Cefn Stylle salt marsh lamb matched with spring greens, mash and cawl jus. Round it off with chocolate brownie, coffee pannacotta and milk ice cream.

Chef Paul Davies, Neil Hollis **Owner** Mr Hetherington, Mr Davies **Times** 12-2/7-9 Closed 26 Dec, 1-25 Jan **Prices** Fixed L 2 course £20, Fixed D 3 course £45, Service optional **Wines** 400 bottles over £20, 50 bottles under £20, 10 by glass **Notes** Sunday L, Vegetarian menu, Civ Wed 40 **Seats** 60, Pr/dining room 40 **Children** Portions **Parking** 45

SWANSEA
Map 9 SS69

The Dragon Hotel

◉ Modern European

A touch of modern style in the heart of Swansea

☎ 01792 657100 & 657159
Kingsway Circle SA1 5LS
e-mail: enquiries@dragon-hotel.co.uk
web: www.dragon-hotel.co.uk
dir: M4 junct 42, A483 follow signs for city centre A4067. After lights at Sainsbury's right onto The Strand then left into Kings Ln. Hotel straight ahead

The Dragon is breathing fire after a megabucks renovation has brought everything up to full contemporary spec, making the most of its location in the thick of Swansea's town centre action. The buzzy Dragon Brasserie is in pole position for watching the world go by: ringside seats look through floor-to-ceiling windows onto the high street in a thoroughly modern venue with exposed industrial ducting and spotlights above bare darkwood tables and pale wooden floors. The cooking is well-focused and in tune with the setting, offering straightforward modern European dishes built from local produce; keenly-priced two or three-course dinner menus could get going with smooth chicken liver parfait with pear and ginger chutney, then move on to confit belly pork with pork and apple sausage and spring onion mash. Dessert might be saffron and vanilla crème brûlée with chocolate shortbread.

Chef Steve Williams **Owner** Dragon Hotel Ltd **Times** 12-2.30/6-9.30 **Prices** Food prices not confirmed for 2013. Please telephone for details **Wines** 17 bottles over £20, 21 bottles under £20, 12 by glass **Notes** Tasting menu & pre-theatre menu by reservation only, Sunday L,

Vegetarian available **Seats** 65, Pr/dining room 80 **Children** Menu **Parking** 50

Hanson at the Chelsea Restaurant

◎◎ Modern Welsh, French

Modern bistro-style fare in relaxed restaurant

☎ 01792 464068
17 St Mary St SA1 3LH
e-mail: andrew_hanson@live.co.uk
dir: In small lane between St Mary Church & Wine St

Lemon-coloured walls give a fresh feel to this small restaurant in a terrace on a narrow city-centre side street. Banquettes and high-backed wooden chairs with padded seats, clothed tables, a board listing seafood specials, and friendly uniformed staff all add to the appeal. The weekly-changing menu is a roll-call of contemporary British and French bistro-style dishes, from fishcake with pommes allumette and tartare sauce to duck rillette with cornichons. Seafood is a forte and receives inventive treatment, partnering pan-fried scallops with a cockle and laverbread crumble and parmesan and rocket. Elsewhere, shoulder of local lamb is slowly cooked French-style with navarin of vegetables, served with mash, and veal rump is simmered in Madeira with mushrooms and accompanied by potato gratin. Desserts are a familiar enough bunch, among them chocolate tart with clotted cream.

Chef Andrew Hanson, Gareth Sillman **Owner** Andrew & Michelle Hanson **Times** 12-2/7-10 Closed 25-26 Dec, BHs, Sun **Prices** Food prices not confirmed for 2013. Please telephone for details **Wines** 20 bottles over £20, 20 bottles under £20, 8 by glass **Notes** Vegetarian available, Dress restrictions, Smart casual **Seats** 50, Pr/dining room 20 **Children** Portions, Menu

VALE OF GLAMORGAN

HENSOL   Map 9 ST07

Vale Grill

◎ Modern British

Welsh resort hotel with local flavour

☎ 01443 667800
Vale Hotel, Golf & Spa Resort, Hensol Park CF72 8JY
e-mail: sales@vale-hotel.com
dir: M4 junct 34, exit signed Pendoylan, turn 1st right twice, then 1st left before white house on bend. Hotel on right

This plush contemporary resort hotel sprawls in 650 glorious acres of countryside just a short hop from Cardiff and the Glamorgan coast. As well as a brace of golf courses, it boasts the largest spa in Wales, and the modern bistro-style Vale Grill, a clean-lined space with bare dark wood tables, views of the action out on the greens and fairways and - more to the point - an open-to-view kitchen to watch the chefs doing their stuff. And that stuff translates as a straightforward modern European repertoire, with plenty of input from Welsh produce, starting, perhaps, with a layered terrine of

chicken and ham hock served with red onion marmalade, toasted rye bread and gribiche sauce, followed by a pairing of pork tenderloin and pork and sage faggots, with carrot and potato rösti, parsnip purée, and mace and tomato sauce.

Chef Daniel James **Owner** Leekes Family **Times** 7-11 Closed L all week **Prices** Food prices not confirmed for 2013. Please telephone for details **Notes** Vegetarian available, Dress restrictions, Smart casual, Civ Wed 500 **Seats** 80, Pr/dining room 500 **Children** Menu **Parking** 500

LLANTWIT MAJOR   Map 9 SS96

Illtud's 216

◎ Modern Welsh

Good brasserie cooking in a medieval malthouse

☎ 01446 793800
Church St CF61 1SB
e-mail: info@illtuds216.co.uk

There's a hint of the medieval hall in the main dining area at Illtud's, with its sky-high pointed ceiling, rustic furniture and flagstone floor scattered with rugs. The place was a malthouse back in the 16th century, and the namesake St Illtud himself is reputed to have once brewed beer here. On the menu, chef-patron Georg Fuchs takes a modern approach driven by the best produce from the Welsh larder. From the land, perhaps roasted leg of Black Mountain lamb with roast potatoes and rich bouquet of seasonal veg, while dessert might feature a nod to Georg's Austrian heritage, with a signature Austrian apple strudel served with custard or vanilla ice cream.

Chef Georg Fuchs **Owner** Georg & Einar Fuchs **Times** 12-2.30/6-9.30 Closed Mon, D Sun **Prices** Fixed L 2 course £9.50, Fixed D 3 course £15.50, Starter £4.75-£8.50, Main £11.25-£15.50, Dessert £4.25-£6.50, Service optional **Wines** 11 bottles over £20, 15 bottles under £20, 7 by glass **Notes** Fixed menu available L Tue-Fri, D Tue-Thu, Sunday L, Vegetarian available **Seats** 65, Pr/dining room 12 **Children** Portions, Menu **Parking** Town Hall car park

WREXHAM

LLANARMON DYFFRYN CEIRIOG   Map 15 SJ13

The Hand at Llanarmon

◎ Modern British

Well-executed country-pub food in the Ceiriog Valley

☎ 01691 600666
Ceiriog Valley LL20 7LD
e-mail: reception@thehandhotel.co.uk
dir: Leave A5 at Chirk onto B4500 signed Ceiriog Valley, continue for 11m

If you're looking for a traditional country inn with a voluble, friendly ambience and classy cooking in the Ceiriog Valley, talk to the Hand. The surrounding landscape of moor and mountain makes a haunting backdrop to the simple but well-executed pub dishes on offer. A plate of crab from the Llyn peninsula combines fresh white and brown meat, a crab and ginger bhaji and a filo parcel of crab and tiger prawn. Then it's grilled mackerel with smoked salmon and pea shoot salad, topped with a poached egg, or slow-braised lamb shoulder in redcurrant and lamb jus. Banana fritters with berry compôte and honey makes a fitting finale.

Chef Grant Mulholland **Owner** Gaynor & Martin De Luchi **Times** 12-2.20/6.30-8.45 Closed 25 Dec **Prices** Fixed L 2 course £15-£17, Starter £5-£7, Main £12-£20, Dessert £5-£5.75, Service optional **Wines** 5 bottles over £20, 19 bottles under £20, 4 by glass **Notes** Sunday L, Vegetarian available **Seats** 40 **Children** Portions **Parking** 15

West Arms

◎ British, French

Traditional cooking in an ancient inn

☎ 01691 600665 & 600612
LL20 7LD
e-mail: info@thewestarms.co.uk
dir: Exit A483 (A5) at Chirk (mid-way between Oswestry & Llangollen). Follow signs for Ceiriog Valley (B4500), 11m

The West Arms has been standing in the foothills of the Berwyn Mountains since 1570, and with its slate-flagged floors, exposed beams and inglenook fireplaces, it's easy to imagine the drovers dropping in for some good food and good cheer on their way back from the market in the inn's early days. Produce from trusted local suppliers informs the largely traditional menu, thus an evening meal might kick off with the chef's watercress, leek and home-grown Jerusalem artichoke soup finished with cream and herb croûtons. Medallions of Welsh beef fillet with wild mushrooms, dauphinoise potato and a Burgundy sauce could be on the cards for the main event, while an iced lemon and ginger semi-fredo layered with biscuit shows that the chef has no lack of ambition when it comes to dessert stage.

Times 12-2/7-9 Closed L Mon-Sat

Northern Ireland

Giants Causeway, County Antrim

NORTHERN IRELAND
CO ANTRIM

BALLYMENA · Map 1 D5

Galgorm Resort & Spa

◉◉ International V

Modish cooking by the river

☎ 028 2588 1001
136 Fenaghy Rd, Galgorm BT42 1EA
e-mail: info@galgorm.com
web: www.galgorm.com
dir: A26 Ballymena, follow signs to hotel

Luxurious rooms, swanky spa and posh conference facilities are just part of the draw at Galgorm. The upscale country hotel stands in 163 acres of parkland with the River Maine flowing through, and is quite a destination for dining these days, thanks to the efforts of Chris Bell who heads up the team at the River Room Restaurant - so named because you get fabulous views over the river via the floor-to-ceiling windows. The kitchen delivers waves of invention and well-tuned technique without a dewy-eyed glance backwards to the old school country-house idiom. True to contemporary style, the menu (which reads rather like a shopping list) might open with ballottine of rabbit and black pudding with leeks, English mustard, rhubarb, ginger and carrots. After that, perhaps fillet of beef with braised ox cheek, beetroot, horseradish, fondant potatoes, thyme and Madeira, or fish in the form of roast halibut fillet with potato rösti, braised peas and lettuce, smoked bacon, mint and olive oil.

Chef Chris Bell **Owner** Nicholas & Paul Hill
Times 12-2.30/6.30-9.30 Closed Mon-Tue, L Wed-Sat
Prices Fixed L 3 course £24-£28, Fixed D 3 course £35-£45, Starter £7-£9, Main £24-£28, Dessert £6-£9, Service added but optional 10% **Wines** 43 bottles over £20, 3 bottles under £20, 6 by glass **Notes** Taste of Antrim menu 6, 8 course £45-£55, Sunday L, Vegetarian menu, Civ Wed 250 **Seats** 50, Pr/dining room 14
Children Portions **Parking** 200

BUSHMILLS · Map 1 C6

Bushmills Inn Hotel

◉ Traditional

Locally-based cooking near the Giant's Causeway

☎ 028 2073 3000 & 2073 2339
9 Dunluce Rd BT57 8QG
e-mail: mail@bushmillsinn.com
dir: 2m from Giant's Causeway on A2 in Bushmills after crossing river

Whether you're an aficionado of Irish whiskey on a pilgrimage to the eponymous distillery or en-route to the iconic Giant's Causeway, this 17th-century coaching inn is a refuge of welcome hospitality. Seated snugly in intimate wooden booths, all is busy, convivial and good natured, while the kitchen hauls in the best locally-landed fish, and meat and game from nearby estates, then subjects it all to straightforward modern treatments. Dundrum Bay mussels come tossed in white wine and chive cream, then topside of venison appears in the robust company of glazed beetroot, roasted garlic, black pudding sausage and crème de Cassis foam. You could finish with chocolate tart filled with dark chocolate ganache and chocolate mousse with candied orange ice cream.

Times 12-9.30

CARNLOUGH · Map 1 D6

Frances Anne Restaurant

◉ Traditional ☜

Traditional cooking on the Antrim coast

☎ 028 2888 5255
Londonderry Arms Hotel, 20 Harbour Rd BT44 0EU
e-mail: lda@glensofantrim.com
dir: 14m N of Larne on Causeway coastal route

Completed in 1848 as a coaching inn commissioned by Frances Anne Tempest, Marchioness of Londonderry, the stately black-and-white hotel is in a little seaside village on the Antrim Coast road. Her memory is honoured in the name of the pretty dining room with its shell-pink walls and elegant table settings, where a thorough-going traditionalism informs the capably rendered menus. A Glenarm salmon fishcake or red onion and Irish brie tartlet with fig relish and pesto might get things going, before pork fillet with wholegrain mustard mash and creamed cabbage, or duck breast with celeriac purée in redcurrant jus. Finish with well-turned-out lemon tart. If ever dinner feels like a long way off, note that high tea in the late afternoon is a daily fixture.

Chef Manus Jamison **Owner** Frank O'Neill **Times** 12-3/5-9 Closed 25 Dec, **Prices** Food prices not confirmed for 2013. Please telephone for details **Wines** 6 bottles over £20, 23 bottles under £20 **Notes** Vegetarian available, Civ Wed 150 **Seats** 50, Pr/dining room 30
Children Portions, Menu **Parking** 50

BELFAST

BELFAST · Map 1 D5

Beatrice Kennedy

◉ Modern, Traditional

Modern bistro food in the university district

☎ 028 9020 2290
44 University Rd BT7 1NJ
e-mail: reservations@beatricekennedy.co.uk
dir: Adjacent to Queens University

Ring the doorbell to be admitted to this distinctive restaurant in the heart of the university district. Inside, it feels a little like a private home, and the service approach is appropriately unfussy too. Jim McCarthy tries out some novel ideas in what is essentially a bistro culinary idiom, serving up scallop carpaccio with crabmeat, puréed basil and red pepper jam to start, followed up by Fermanagh dry-aged rib-eye with potato rösti, mushroom duxelle and red wine onions, or roast haddock in a sustaining broth of mussels, cockles and smoked haddock, alongside fennel and tomato salsa. Dessert brings on ginger pannacotta with poached pear.

Times 12.30-3/5-10.30 Closed 24-26 Dec, 1 Jan, Etr, Mon, L Mon-Sat

Cayenne

◉ Modern International V

Buzzy atmosphere and cooking with a global flavour

☎ 028 9033 1532
7 Ascot House, Shaftesbury Square BT2 7DB
e-mail: belinda@cayenne-restaurant.co.uk
dir: Top of Great Victoria St

As the red-hot name suggests, the food at Cayenne - chef Paul Rankin (as seen on TV) and wife Jeanne's flagship restaurant - does not lack oomph. Backpacking the globe for influences while incorporating well-sourced Irish ingredients, the kitchen puts together something of a fusion showstopper. Take lemon and almond panko-breaded hake, for instance, partnered with lime chilli lentils, wasabi potato salad and sauce gribiche. European flavours have their say too, perhaps pork belly and cheek teamed with a saffron and tomato risotto, while a homely sticky toffee pudding dessert might come in the more straight-laced company of clotted cream ice cream. The large, buzzy, voguish space looks the part, too, with vivid earthy colours predominating and artworks (by locally-born artist Peter Anderson) suitably innovative and interactive alongside groovy lighting and co-ordinated music.

Chef Paul Rankin **Owner** Paul & Jeanne Rankin
Times 12-2.15/5-late Closed 25-26 Dec, Etr Mon, May Day BH, 12-13 Jul, Mon-Tue, L Wed **Prices** Food prices not confirmed for 2013. Please telephone for details **Wines** 400 bottles over £20, 12 bottles under £20, 15 by glass **Notes** Vegetarian menu **Seats** 150, Pr/dining room 16 **Children** Portions **Parking** On street, NCP

Save on Hotels. Book at **theAA.com/hotel**

BELFAST 647 **IRELAND**

Deanes at Queens

⚜ Modern European, Irish **NEW**

Buzzy brasserie dining near the university

☎ 028 9038 2111
1 College Gardens BT9 6BQ
e-mail: deanesatqueens@michaeldeane.co.uk

Part of Michael Deane's Belfast gastro-empire, this bright and buzzy bar and grill operation is located on College Gardens in the university quarter. The luminous space makes the most of its leafy surrounds overlooking the Botanic Gardens with a wall of full-length windows, while friendly service and a crowd-pleasing menu of brasserie staples all add to the upbeat vibe. The bar runs most of the length of the venue, and you can see the chefs behind it putting together starters ranging from a classic chicken liver and foie gras pâté with pear chutney to salt-and-chilli squid with garlic mayo, chilli and sesame. Next up, crisp Lissara duck leg is teamed with duck croquettes, sweet potato and saffron purée and Madeira jus, and to finish, go for orange crème brûlée with shortbread.

Chef Chris Fearon **Times** 12-3/5.30 **Notes** Prix fixe menu 3 course £15 Mon-Thu 5.30-7, Sunday L

Deanes Restaurant

⚜⚜⚜ – *see below*

James Street South Restaurant & Bar

⚜⚜ Modern European ✋

Confident modern cooking in the city centre

☎ 028 9043 4310
21 James Street South BT2 7GA
e-mail: info@jamesstreetsouth.co.uk
dir: Located between Brunswick St & Bedford St

This Belfast city centre restaurant has slick urban style in spades, opting for a minimal contemporary look involving abstract art on white walls and dark brown leather seats on a blond-wood floor. The man directing the action at the sharp end is Niall McKenna who learned his trade under the sort of chefs who go by just one name - Marco and Nico - and now ploughs his own furrow, deploying well-honed French techniques in a blend of classical and contemporary ideas. Seared scallops come with smoked haddock brandade, chorizo and tomato chutney, ahead of Portvoe pheasant teamed with wild mushroom fricassée and piccolo parsnips. The signature '*Great British Menu*' dessert is right on the money, an inventive confection of rhubarb and strawberry jelly with lavender ice cream and 'yellow man' - the local term for honeycomb.

Chef Niall McKenna, Stephen Toman **Owner** Niall & Joanne McKenna **Times** 12-2.45/5.45-10.45 Closed 25-26 Dec, 1 Jan, Etr Sun & Mon, 12-15 Jul, Sun **Prices** Fixed L 2 course £14.95, Fixed D 3 course £18.95, Tasting menu £55, Starter £4.50-£10.50, Main £14.50-£21, Dessert £5.50-£8.50, Service optional, Groups min 5

service 10% **Wines** 90 bottles over £20, 6 bottles under £20, 8 by glass **Notes** Pre-theatre menu Mon-Sat 2/3 course, Vegetarian available **Seats** 60, Pr/dining room 40 **Children** Portions **Parking** On street

Malmaison Belfast

⚜ French

Confident Anglo-French brasserie cooking

☎ 028 9022 0200 & 9022 0201
34-38 Victoria St BT1 3GH
e-mail: belfast@malmaison.com
dir: M1 along Westlink to Grosvenor Rd. Follow city centre signs. Pass City Hall on right, turn left onto Victoria St. Hotel on right

The Malmaison hotel group has been extremely resourceful when it comes to finding places to pitch camp, and in Belfast a former seed warehouse is the chosen setting. Boutique design gives the venue as much idiosyncratic class as the rest of the chain has, offering a mixture of wall-mounted objets and boldly striped upholstery in the Brasserie. Head chef Ip Wai oversees a confident version of the Anglo-French brasserie idiom, from a high-impact smoked ham hock and foie gras terrine with spiced apple chutney, through tender and unctuous duck confit with garlic potatoes and pickled girolles, to a warming wintry dessert of creamy rice pudding with mulled cherries.

Times 12-2.30/6-12.30

Deanes Restaurant

⚜⚜⚜

BELFAST   Map 1 D5

Modern French, Irish V 🍷 ✋

Classy and confident cooking chez Michael Deane

☎ 028 9033 1134
36-40 Howard St BT1 6PF
e-mail: info@michaeldeane.co.uk
dir: At rear of City Hall. Howard St on left opposite Spires building

With his name and considerable reputation behind a number of outlets in Belfast, Michael Deane has helped raise the culinary stakes in the city. It was here in Howard Street where the foundations of that reputation were cemented, and today's restaurant is still a gastronomic powerhouse of national reputation. It's a pleasingly egalitarian space, not overly posh, but not unsophisticated either, with smartly laid, linen-dressed

tables, blond-wood floor and rich vermillion-coloured walls. It's a suitably sharply-focused setting for some fine contemporary cooking, which has at its core excellent regional produce that arrives on the plate with its integrity intact. The concepts are not fanciful, simply focused on flavour and executed with a high degree of skill. A clear quail broth, for example, comes with the roasted bird, porcini mushrooms and quail's egg, or there might be pan-fried Strangford scallops in a modish pairing with slow-cooked pork and apple purée. Next up, perhaps, roast Fermanagh chicken with a cauliflower and asparagus tarte fine and black pudding dauphinoise, or the gloriously soft and melting 12-hour braised shin of beef with roasted vegetables, bone marrow and red wine. To finish, pear and chocolate come together in a mousse, served with the fruit in sorbet and caramelised form, and the textural addition of macadamia nuts. Supporting the carte is a stupendously good value prix fixe, plus a tasting menu should you choose to come along for the

ride. Deanes Seafood Bar is also at this address if you fancy local lobster with chips and salad and the like.

Chef Michael Deane, Simon Toye **Owner** Michael Deane **Times** 12-3/5.30-10 Closed 25 Dec, BHs, Sun **Prices** Fixed L 2 course £14.95, Service added but optional 10% **Wines** 99 bottles over £20, 8 bottles under £20, 9 by glass **Notes** Vegetarian menu **Seats** 80, Pr/dining room 50 **Children** Portions, Menu **Parking** On street (after 6pm), car park Clarence St

BELFAST *continued*

Malone Lodge Hotel

◉ Modern European Ⓥ ✋

International flavours at stylish hotel

☎ 028 9038 8000
60 Eglantine Av, Malone Rd BT9 6DY
e-mail: info@malonelodgehotel.com
dir: At hospital rdbt exit towards Bouchar Rd, left at 1st rdbt, right at lights at top, then 1st left

Green Door is the informal, relaxed and friendly restaurant within the stylish Malone Lodge Hotel, which has been converted from a row of townhouses a few minutes from the centre. Over two levels, it's a comfortable room with high-backed chairs and crisply clothed tables. The broad-based menu caters to all comers, ranging from dry-aged sirloin steak with the usual accompaniments, through five spice-flavoured duck breast with spicy plums and Asian slaw to fish pie. Start perhaps with seafood chowder, served in a Belfast bap, or goats' cheese and cranberry soufflé and end with a comforting pudding like cheesecake or apple and berry crumble.

Chef Dean Butler **Owner** Brian & Mary Macklin
Times 12.30-3/5-10 Closed L Mon-Sat, D Sun
Prices Starter £3.50-£7, Main £8-£20, Dessert £5, Service optional **Wines** 10 bottles over £20, 14 bottles under £20, 6 by glass **Notes** Sunday L, Vegetarian menu, Civ Wed 130 **Seats** 60, Pr/dining room 50
Children Portions, Menu **Parking** 40, On street

The Merchant Hotel

◉ Modern European

Modern Franco-Irish cooking in a former bank

☎ 028 9023 4888
16 Skipper St, Cathedral Quarter BT1 2DZ
e-mail: thegreatroom@merchanthotel.com
dir: In city centre, 2nd left at Albert clock onto Waring St. Hotel on left

You may think you've seen everything that converted Victorian bank buildings have to offer in the modern hospitality lark, but until you've been to The Merchant, you haven't quite. At the centre of a hotel that comes with all the city furbelows (nightclub, champagne lounge, hydrotherapy pool) is a masterpiece of a restaurant, truly a Great Room which ascends in gilt plasterwork to hovering celestial cherubs and a vast glass cupola. It also features a well-wrought, broadly-based menu of modern Irish cooking with French overlays, the latter appearing in a starter of egg meurette, a poached egg in red wine sauce with lardons and mushrooms. Elsewhere, it's smoked haddock ballotine with pickled beetroot in onion seed beurre blanc, and venison en croûte with truffled mash in Cassis jus, finishing with cinnamon pear Tatin and candied walnut ice cream.

Chef John Paul Leake **Owner** The Merchant Hotel
Times 12-2.30/6-10 Closed L Sat **Prices** Fixed L 2 course £18.50-£26.50, Fixed D 3 course £26.50-£31.50, Tasting

menu £65-£85, Starter £6.50-£11, Main £19.50-£28.50, Dessert £8.50-£12.50, Service added but optional 10% **Wines** 157 bottles over £20, 13 by glass **Notes** Pre-theatre 2 course £18.50, 3 course £22.50, Sunday L, Vegetarian available, Dress restrictions, Smart casual, Civ Wed 120 **Seats** 85, Pr/dining room 18
Children Portions, Menu **Parking** On street

Shu

◉◉ Modern European ✋

Contemporary Irish cooking with a buzz

☎ 028 9038 1655
253-255 Lisburn Rd BT9 7EN
e-mail: eat@shu-restaurant.com
dir: From city centre take Lisburn Rd (lower end). Restaurant in 1m, on corner of Windsor Avenue

A terrace of whitewashed Victorian houses in the fashionable Lisburn shopping district of Belfast is the setting for this sleek modern restaurant. The name might hint at something Oriental, but this Shu is named after the Egyptian God of atmosphere, who seems pleased by what is going on and has obligingly breathed a real buzz into the air of the breezy, open-plan venue. An open-to-view kitchen throws its culinary theatre and enticing smells into the mix as the chefs turn out some real treats in a repertoire of Irish-accented modern European dishes. Expect well-conceived ideas such as crispy pork cromesquis with Jerusalem artichoke purée and hazelnuts, followed by Clandeboye wood pigeon scented with lapsang souchong tea, beetroot, celeriac purée, kale and purple carrots. To close the show, only the finest Amedei chocolate will do for a finale of chocolate mousse with hazelnuts and banana cream.

Chef Brian McCann **Owner** Alan Reid **Times** 12-2.30/6-10 Closed 25-26 Dec, 1 Jan, 12-13 Jul, Sun **Prices** Fixed L 2 course £13.25, Fixed D 3 course £28-£30.50, Starter £4.50-£9, Main £12.50-£21.25, Dessert £5.75-£6.75, Service optional, Groups min 6 service 10%
Wines 57 bottles over £20, 12 bottles under £20, 19 by glass **Notes** Supper menu Mon-Fri 5.30-6.30, 1course £9.50, Vegetarian available **Seats** 100, Pr/dining room 24 **Children** Portions, Menu **Parking** 4, On street

BANGOR Map 1 D5

Lewis at The Old Inn

◉◉ Modern European

Revamped restaurant in historic Old Inn

☎ 028 9185 3255
15 Main St, Crawfordsburn BT19 1JH
e-mail: info@theoldinn.com
web: www.theoldinn.com
dir: From Belfast along A2, past Belfast City Airport. Contine past Holywood & Belfast Folk & Transport museum. 2m after museum left at lights onto B20 for 1.2m

The Old Inn certainly lives up to its name, as the oldest thatched part of the sprawling building dates from the dawn of the 17th century. A roll-call of famous writers and poets as well as the usual motley crew of smugglers has frequented the place over the years, but none has dined as well as its 21st-century guests in the smartly-refurbished Lewis restaurant. Named after author C. S. Lewis who hung out with his literary pals in the 1950s, the contemporary bistro-style venue centres on a state-of-the-art, open-to-view kitchen, where slithery fresh seafood from the local ports of Strangford and Portavogie, as well as impeccably-sourced Irish meat and game, are subjected to straightforward modern European treatments. The cooking is assured, and peppered with bold flavours - perhaps foie gras with caramelised apples and marzipan sauce to start, followed by pork loin with apple and Clonakilty black pudding, Parmentier potatoes and cider jus. Simple and delicious desserts might include lemon-iced gingerbread with toffee sauce.

Chef Gavin Murphy **Owner** Danny, Paul & Garvan Rice **Times** 12-3/7-9.30 Closed 25 Dec, **Prices** Fixed L 2 course £8.95, Fixed D 3 course £30, Service optional **Wines** 24 bottles over £20, 25 bottles under £20, 10 by glass **Notes** Sunday L, Vegetarian available **Seats** 134, Pr/dining room 25 **Children** Portions, Menu **Parking** 80

Mourne Seafood Bar

◉ Seafood ☙

Vibrant fish restaurant 30 minutes from Belfast

☎ 028 4375 1377
10 Main St BT33 0LU
e-mail: bob@mourneseafood.com
dir: On main road from Belfast to The Mournes, on village main street

The name of this famous seafood joint says it all really - set in a handsome Georgian building in a pretty fishing village, it comes with the Mourne Mountains as a backdrop and seafood centre stage. Inside there's none of that big-city cool, just an easygoing, relaxed kind of place with wooden floors and chunky wooden tables buoyed up by vibrant artwork, smiley staff and a warm, buzzy atmosphere. Straightforward fish and shellfish dishes that allow sea-fresh produce (and local organic veg) to shine is the key to success here, with the kitchen even garnering oysters and mussels from its own beds. Expect Mourne seafood chowder perhaps, modish hake fillet with chick pea and chorizo, or monkfish with avocado salsa, while for the traditionalists, fish 'n' chips with mushy peas.

Chef Wayne Carville **Owner** Bob & Joanne McCoubrey
Times 12.30-9.30 Closed 25 Dec, Mon-Thu (winter)
Prices Fixed D 3 course £26.50, Starter £4.50-£6.50, Main £9-£16, Dessert £4.50, Service optional, Groups min 6 service 10% **Wines** 18 bottles over £20, 22 bottles under £20, 5 by glass **Notes** Fixed D menu Sat only, Sunday L, Vegetarian available **Seats** 75, Pr/dining room 20 **Children** Portions, Menu **Parking** On street

The Catalina Restaurant, Lough Erne Resort

◉◉ Modern, Traditional

Great Irish produce in golfer's paradise

☎ 028 6632 3230
Lough Erne Resort, Belleek Rd BT93 7ED
e-mail: info@lougherneresort.com
dir: A46 from Enniskillen towards Donegal, hotel in 3m

This vast and luxurious, purpose-built golfing hotel guarantees panoramic views, located on its own 60-acre peninsula jutting into the lough. It's a golfer's haven, with one of its two championship courses designed by Nick Faldo. The Catalina is the fine-dining option here, named after the famous seaplanes that were based on the lough during the Second World War and commemorated in framed photos on the walls. It's an expansive space sporting a classic look and formal vibe, with vaulted ceilings and views of the course and water through its arched windows. Home-grown chef Noel McMeel's menus showcase quality seasonal produce from the local larder in creative dishes underpinned by classical foundations. Think pan-fried breast of Lissara duck with mixed bean cassoulet, marinated cherries, beetroot, parsnip purée and red wine jus, or perhaps roast fillet of Irish hake with citrus-infused lentils, confit carrot and Madeira Jus. Otherwise, try the signature 'Lough Erne mixed grill' and perhaps an apple duo finish - bavarois and tarte Tatin with vanilla ice cream.

Times 1-2.30/6.30 Closed L Mon-Sat

Manor House Country Hotel

◉◉ Irish

Creative Irish cookery in a majestic house

☎ 028 6862 2200
Killadeas BT94 1NY
e-mail: info@manorhousecountryhotel.com
web: www.manorhousecountryhotel.com
dir: On B82, 7m N of Enniskillen

The Victorian colonel who rebuilt this centuries-old manor house on the shores of Lower Lough Erne in 1860 clearly had his heart in Italy, as he shipped over a team of Italian craftsmen to do the job, and also grafted on a squat Italianate tower. There are more contemporary additions too, so the whole caboodle adds up to an imposing pile with the full-works weddings and conferencing, spa and leisure package to cater for all comers. Uniformed staff are friendly and welcoming enough to strip away any hint of starch, and foster a relaxed ambience in the fine dining Belleek restaurant, a luminous space with splendid views of Lough Erne through vast picture windows. The kitchen's philosophy keeps menus true to the region and the seasons, giving a modern spin to intelligently-conceived dishes - perhaps port-marinated Irish venison carpaccio with celeriac remoulade, pickled girolles and parmesan shavings, then following that by teaming lemon-glazed sweetbreads and kale colcannon cake with roast rack of Fermanagh spring lamb. Fish-fanciers might find roast monkfish with buttered samphire, grilled pancetta, and tomato and clam ragoût.

Owner Manor House Country Hotel Ltd
Times 12.30-3/6-10 Closed L Mon-Fri **Prices** Fixed L 2 course fr £14.50, Fixed D 4 course fr £28, Starter £5.50-£8, Main £18-£25, Dessert £5.50-£7.50, Service optional **Wines** 40 bottles over £20, 25 bottles under £20 **Notes** Sunday L, Vegetarian available, Dress restrictions, Smart casual, Civ Wed 350 **Seats** 90, Pr/dining room 350 **Children** Portions, Menu **Parking** 300

CO LONDONDERRY

CASTLEDAWSON   Map 1 C5

The Inn Castledawson

◉◉ Modern Irish

Creative cooking in Seamus Heaney's birth place

☎ 028 7946 9777
47 Main St BT45 8AA
e-mail: info@theinncastledawson.com
dir: Castledawson rdbt, from Belfast take 3rd exit, from Londonderry take 1st exit

The custard-yellow inn at the heart of Castledawson village was brought into the world of contemporary design with a classy makeover in 2009, transforming its restaurant into a glossy new look. Beneath its high, blond-wood beamed ceilings are chocolate and cream leather high-backed chairs at linen-clad tables, a centrepiece fireplace resplendent in gold designer wallpaper, cream walls hung with photos of Castledawson in the old days, and a large rear window looking across the decking terrace to the River Moyola. The kitchen makes the most of fine regionally-sourced produce in creative modern ideas - perhaps breast of local estate wood pigeon teamed with a croquette of confit leg, onion purée and Clonakilty black pudding, while mains extend to a boozy dish of perry-poached pheasant with mulled wine cabbage and walnuts; fishy ideas might offer pan-fried skate wing with caper and orange butter and parsley gnocchi.

Chef Roland Graham **Owner** Paula Sturges **Times** 12-8.30 Closed 25-26 Dec, 1 wk Jan, **Prices** Fixed L 2 course £14-£16, Fixed D 3 course £18-£25, Tasting menu £60, Starter £6.25-£8.50, Main £14-£21.50, Dessert £4.95-£6.50, Service included **Wines** 8+ bottles over £20, 12+ bottles under £20, 5 by glass **Notes** Gourmet menu £45-£65, Sunday L, Vegetarian available, Civ Wed 40 **Seats** 80, Pr/dining room 12 **Parking** 8, On street

LIMAVADY   Map 1 C6

The Lime Tree

◉ Traditional Mediterranean 🍃

Long-running neighbourhood restaurant showcasing the pick of the province

☎ 028 7776 4300
60 Catherine St BT49 9DB
e-mail: info@limetreerest.com
dir: Enter Limavady from Derry side. Restaurant on right on small slip road

Named after the linden - or lime - trees planted in Limavady in honour of local lad William Massey's landing the top job as PM in New Zealand, Stanley and Maria Matthews's immensely pleasing neighbourhood restaurant is intimate, cosy and impeccably run by Maria's hands-on approach out front, and firmly in touch when it comes to the food on the plate. Menus are updated daily to serve up the best of what Northern Ireland has to offer, particularly in the realm of freshly-landed fish and seafood, which could put in an appearance as the perennially popular Malin Head crabcakes in balsamic syrup, followed by pan-fried turbot with fresh asparagus and chive cream sauce; meat-eaters can expect confit duck with potato bread and red wine sauce. At the end, Aghadowey honey turns up in an iced parfait with a crystallised ginger cookie.

Chef Stanley Matthews **Owner** Mr & Mrs S Matthews **Times** 6-9 Closed 25-26 Dec, 12 Jul, Sun-Mon, L all week (except by prior arrangement) **Prices** Fixed D 3 course fr £17.95, Starter £4.70-£7.95, Main £15.50-£23.50, Dessert £5.50-£6.95, Service optional **Wines** 15 bottles over £20, 25 bottles under £20, 5 by glass **Notes** Early bird menu 2-3 course Tue-Fri 6-7pm, Vegetarian available **Seats** 30 **Children** Portions, Menu **Parking** 15, On street

Roe Park Resort

◉ Modern

Traditional dining in a relaxed resort hotel

☎ 028 7772 2222
BT49 9LB
e-mail: reservations@roeparkresort.com
dir: On A6 (Londonderry-Limavady road), 0.5m from Limavady. 8m from Derry airport

Built as a country mansion in the 18th century, surrounded by 150 acres of grounds beside the River Roe, Roe Park has been extended in recent years into a vast modern golfing and leisure resort. Just one of several dining options at Roe Park, Greens Restaurant is a stylish, split-level space offering mostly traditional cooking with the odd modern twist. Start, perhaps, with confit duck rillette with toasted sourdough, beetroot and orange relish, moving on to fillet of Irish beef with potato croquette, confit garlic, button mushrooms and jus, or grilled salmon supreme with oriental noodles and a ginger and soy dressing. If cheesecake is your thing, there's a daily-changing selection of flavours, or you may want to go down the comfort route with the steamed banana and ginger pudding with fresh cream and sauce anglaise.

Times 12-3/6.30-9

Republic of Ireland

Malahide Castle

REPUBLIC OF IRELAND
CO CARLOW

TULLOW Map 1 C3

Mount Wolseley Hotel, Spa & Country Club

◉ Modern European **V**

Intriguing modern dining at a luxury golfing hotel

☎ 059 9180100 & 9151674
e-mail: info@mountwolseley.ie
dir: N7 from Dublin. In Naas, take N9 towards Carlow. In Castledermot left for Tullow

The 200-acre country estate once owned by Frederick Wolseley, of car making renown, is now a splendiferous golf resort with all of the spa and leisure bells and whistles you can imagine. The championship course attracts golfers from all over the world, so the hotel's main restaurant duly serves up a wide-ranging repertoire of modern European ideas on a menu spiked with dishes with supplementary charges. Fine local materials are to the fore - seared Kilmore scallops, say, teamed with hot cacao, potato popcorn and hollandaise sauce, while mains could see Cajun-spiced Slaney Valley lamb served with rosemary fondant potatoes, asparagus, celeriac purée and minted yoghurt. Finish with pineapple beignet, crispy sweet tagliatelle, and pineapple and coconut cappuccino.

Chef David Cuddihy, Ronnie Wolf **Owner** The Morrissey Family **Times** 12.30-2.30/6-9.30 Closed 24-26 Dec, L Mon-Sat **Prices** Food prices not confirmed for 2013. Please telephone for details **Wines** 56 bottles over €20, 6 by glass **Notes** Sunday L, Vegetarian menu **Seats** 150, Pr/dining room 40 **Children** Portions, Menu **Parking** 500

CO CAVAN

CAVAN Map 1 C4

Cavan Crystal Hotel

◉◉ Modern

Innovative cooking in contemporary hotel

☎ 049 4360600
Dublin Rd
e-mail: info@cavancrystalhotel.com
dir: Approach Cavan on N3, straight over rdbt, hotel immediately on left

As you might expect, Ireland's second oldest crystal manufacturer can afford to be lavish in the use of its products in the striking contemporary hotel sharing the same site as its factory. Sure, there are dark wood tables and leather chairs, but it is the crystal chandeliers, glasses and dishes all gleaming away in the glossy Opus One restaurant that catches the eye. The food chimes in tune with the setting: confident and creative, the kitchen reworking classic dishes, making liberal use of foams and savoury jellies, and sending it all out looking as pretty as a picture on slates, designer plates, and in shot

glasses. Confit duck leg served with lightly pickled red cabbage and duck jus is a simple concept that works well, while main-course sea bass is partnered with purée and confit salsify, garden peas and creamed potato with fresh basil. Dessert is a pleasing textural play on iced banana parfait with peanut ice cream, candied hazelnuts and cubes of caramelised banana bread. It all comes punctuated by a well-made amuse-bouche (Carrigbyrne goats' cheese pannacotta with blackcurrant gel), a mini '99' ice cream pre-dessert, and splendid petits fours to demonstrate sharp technical skills.

Times 12.30-3.30/6-10 Closed 24-25 Dec

VIRGINIA Map 1 C4

The Park Hotel

◉ European, International

Classical cooking on a vast private estate

☎ 049 8546100
Virginia Park
e-mail: info@parkhotelvirginia.com
dir: exit N3 in Virginia onto R194. Hotel 500yds on left

Built in the 18th-century as the Marquis of Headfort's summer residence, this intimate small-scale country house is hidden away in 100 acres of estate with garden walks and loch fishing to help keep you occupied and work up an appetite for dinner. The Marquis dining room is an elegant affair with period plasterwork, high ceilings, striped walls, swagged curtains and oceans of space between tables; proceedings are kept ticking over at a well-judged pace by a hugely experienced front-of-house team. Food-wise, expect classic country-house cooking based on judiciously-sourced local and seasonal ingredients. Dinner might get going with a terrine of Irish bacon pointed up with Granny Smith purée, pickled vegetables, and Pommery mustard dressing, and proceed to braised lamb shank with carrot and cumin purée, fondant potato, and rosemary and garlic jus.

Times 12.30-3.30/6.30-9.30 Closed Jan, Xmas, Mon, L Tue-Sat, D Sun

CO CLARE

BALLYVAUGHAN Map 1 B3

Gregans Castle

◉◉◉ – *see opposite*

DOOLIN Map 1 B3

Cullinan's Seafood Restaurant & Guest House

◉ Modern French ◔

Seafood and more besides the river

☎ 065 7074183
e-mail: cullinans@eircom.net
dir: Located in Doolin town centre R479

The lovely conservatory restaurant of this welcoming traditional guest house in the village of Doolin overlooks the Aille River - a charming setting, but it is chef-proprietor James Cullinan's skilful French-influenced modern cooking that is the showstopper here. Cream leather seating and linen-clad tables in the intimate dining room make for a smart setting, and there are cracking sunsets to go with dinner at the right time of year. Carol Cullinan takes care of front of house, while James delivers local produce - particularly freshly-landed fish and seafood - in thoughtful dishes of full-on, clear flavours. A platter of prawns, salmon, cod and monkfish is one way to start the show - otherwise go for something like seafood chowder, before going on to butter-roasted hake wrapped in Parma ham, with lemon and herbs, roast tomatoes and smoked paprika.

Chef James Cullinan **Owner** James & Carol Cullinan **Times** 6-9 Closed Nov-Etr, Sun, Wed, L all week **Prices** Fixed D 3 course €29.50, Starter €6-€9.50, Main €20-€27, Dessert €6.75, Service optional, Groups min 8 service 10% **Notes** Vegetarian available **Seats** 24 **Children** Portions **Parking** 20

ENNIS Map 1 B3

Temple Gate Hotel

◉ Modern International

Modern bistro cooking in a former convent

☎ 065 6823300
The Square
e-mail: info@templegatehotel.com
dir: Exit N18 onto Tulla Rd for 0.25m, hotel on left

The Sisters of Mercy having relocated to a new home nearby in 1995, their Victorian convent not far from the cobbled town centre became a modern hotel, with a pub called Preachers and a dining room named Legends. That latter is a three-part room with big windows and plenty of natural daylight, where modern bistro cooking is the order of the day. Fried garlic mushrooms, or a smoked chicken salad start things off, with follow-ups of salmon darne and pea purée in smoked salmon and dill cream sauce, or nutty pork (an escalope coated in nutty breadcrumbs with colcannon in apple and cider sauce). Finish with an ice cream meringue nest and dark chocolate mousse, or lemon cheesecake.

Times 12.30-2.30/5.30-9.30 Closed 25-26 Dec

Save on Hotels. Book at **theAA.com/hotel**

CO CLARE 653 **IRELAND**

Moy House

◉◉ Modern French V ✋
- -
Modern cooking and fabulous sea views

☎ 065 7082800
e-mail: moyhouse@eircom.net
dir: Located 1km from Lahinch on the Miltown Malbay road

Moy House looks spruce with its whitewashed 18th-century Italianate tower lording it over picturesque Lahinch Bay. The small-scale country house stands in 15 acres of grounds with mature woodlands and a river to stroll along, while a classy contemporary makeover has added a dollop of up-to-date style to the period elegance of its interior. The conservatory restaurant is easy on the eye with its burnished wooden floors and cream-jacketed high-backed chairs at romantically candlelit linen-clothed tables, while a floor-to-ceiling wall of windows makes the most of the fabulous sea views. The wealth of excellent ingredients available locally means that the kitchen is never lost for inspiration when composing its menus of modern French ideas, so you might see smoked salmon from the Burren area adding interest to potato-filled agnolotti pasta with sauce soubise and spring onions. Next up, local beef could be partnered with potato millefeuille, mushroom duxelles, confit garlic, wilted spinach and sauce Bordelaise, before almond cake with lemon curd and meringue closes the show.

Chef Gerard O'Connor **Owner** Antoin O'Looney
Times 7-8.30 Closed Jan-Mar, Nov-Dec, Sun-Mon (off peak) **Wines** 25 bottles over €20, 4 by glass **Notes** Fixed D 5 course €55 (reservation req), Vegetarian menu, Dress restrictions, Smart casual **Seats** 35, Pr/dining room 22 **Children** Portions, Menu **Parking** 50

Sheedy's Country House Hotel

◉◉ Modern Irish
- -
Flavour-led cooking in small rural hotel

☎ 065 7074026
e-mail: info@sheedys.com
dir: 20m from Ennis on N87

In the centre of the village, not far from the coast, Sheedy's is a small country-house hotel named after its hands-on proprietors. John Sheedy is passionate about his supplies, buying organic meat from local producers, fish landed at nearby Doolin, and growing his own herbs and vegetables, the last going into a 'cannelloni' of summer varieties for a main course of baked fillets of the catch of the day with bouillabaisse sauce. His cooking is marked by the clarity of flavours of his materials, with a lack of fuss and flummery; confit duck leg bolstered by celeriac salad and pickled plums, for example, and seared scallops by a simple red pepper sauce spiked with sherry, ahead of pan-fried duck breast and roast leg, served pink, with a gingery jus, plums and butternut

squash. Desserts follow the established route of sticky toffee pudding, and lemon posset with raspberry sorbet.

Times 6.45-8.30 Closed mid Oct-mid Mar, 1 day a week Mar-Apr

Dromoland Castle

◉◉ Traditional Irish, European V
- -
Classical haute cuisine in a spectacular castle

☎ 061 368144
e-mail: sales@dromoland.ie
dir: From Ennis take N18, follow signs for Shannon/Limerick. 7m follow Quin. Newmarket-on-Fergus sign. Hotel 0.5m. From Shannon take N18 towards Ennis

The spectacular castle with its turrets and ramparts makes a memorable setting for a top-notch country hotel. Layers of luxury await inside, scarcely more so than in the flagship Earl of Thomond dining room, where oak panelling, intricate plasterwork and antiques confer a sense of historic lustre on proceedings. Formal service is fully in keeping, and the cooking tacks to classical haute cuisine, based on local materials, including game from the surrounding estate, presented with a high degree of polish. A cabbage-wrapped terrine of confit duck, foie gras and celeriac comes with prune and Armagnac chutney and slices of toasted country loaf to set the tone,

continued

Gregans Castle

Modern European

Outstanding contemporary food at a little house in the Burren

☎ 065 7077005
e-mail: stay@gregans.ie
dir: On N67, 3.5m S of Ballyvaughan

The unshowy, low-slung 18th-century manor house at the foot of Corkscrew Hill isn't really a castle - that would be the towered building opposite, which was once the ancestral seat of the Princes of the Burren. The hotel that has usurped its title is hunkered down amid the blasted lunar limestone landscape of the Burren region of West Ireland, and its almost anonymous exterior conceals a luxurious bolt-hole filled with antiques and period Georgian elegance. Dining goes on in a romantic and

refined room where picture windows open onto a view across the gardens to Galway Bay; candlelight flickers in the evening, and as the summer sun sets, diners are treated to an eerie light show as the dying rays ignite the grey limestone rocks. But aside from the wonders of nature, you're here for the cooking - not that you'd have much idea of the technical dexterity and meticulously-sourced ingredients that await from a reading of the menu, which restricts itself to a mere listing of the components of each dish without any elucidation as to cooking methods. Be assured, however, that the kitchen has strong supply lines to local artisan suppliers, and a spot of foraging in woodland and coast will add further interest. An unmistakably modern approach sees Liscanor Bay lobster meat served in a bowl, with chicken and lobster jus poured over at the table, and paired with a crispy chicken wing lollipop, crystal-clear jellied cubes and silky purée of Granny Smith apple, and a cannelloni-style tube of celeriac filled with truffled celeriac remoulade. Next up, loin of wild rabbit is wrapped in

Serrano ham, cooked sous-vide for maximum tenderness, then crisped on the outside and matched with smoky carrot purée and a purée of wild garlic plucked from the gardens. And it doesn't stop there: there's also a quenelle of braised shoulder meat flavoured with herbs and sweet onion, caramelised shallots and crispy discs of deep-fried potato. At dessert, an assemblage of 'banana, caramel, coffee, salted peanut, chocolate' is no less creative. All the peripheral appetisers, pre-desserts and petits fours that you take as read with this style of dining are equally labour intensive, intelligently conceived and deeply flavoured.

Chef David Hurley **Owner** Simon Haden
Times 12.30-2/6-9 Closed mid Nov-mid Feb, L all week (served in bar only) **Prices** Fixed L 2 course €21, Fixed D 3 course €50, Service included **Wines** 100 bottles over €20, 14 by glass **Notes** Fixed menu D 6 course €69, Vegetarian available, Dress restrictions, Smart casual, no shorts, Civ Wed 65 **Seats** 50, Pr/dining room 36 **Children** Portions, Menu **Parking** 20

NEWMARKET-ON-FERGUS *continued*

and may be followed by halibut with mussels, baby gem, French beans and tomato in chive sauce, or beautifully timed roast pheasant breasts with root vegetable ragoût and parsnip purée in truffled game jus. A dessert soufflé is given real lift by the combining of raspberry and lime in its filling, and offset by gently rich vanilla ice cream.

Chef David McCann **Owner** Dromoland Castle Holdings Ltd **Times** 7-10 Closed 24-27 Dec, L all week **Prices** Fixed L 3 course €40, Fixed D 4 course €50, Starter €15-€19, Main €35-€38, Dessert €10-€15, Service added 15% **Wines** 10 bottles under €20, 10 by glass **Notes** Vegetarian menu, Dress restrictions, Smart dress, no jeans, shorts or T-shirts, Civ Wed 140 **Seats** 80, Pr/dining room 40 **Children** Portions, Menu **Parking** 140

CO CORK

BALLYCOTTON
Map 1 C2

Bayview Hotel

◉◉ Modern Irish, French V

Imaginative contemporary cooking and sea views

☎ 021 4646746
e-mail: res@thebayviewhotel.com
web: www.thebayviewhotel.com
dir: At Castlemartyr on N25 (Cork-Waterford road) turn onto R632 to Garryvoe, then follow signs for Shanagarry & Ballycotton

On its clifftop above the bay, this large white hotel lives up to its name, with sweeping coastal views, and lots of window tables in the restaurant to make the most of it. The kitchen is fastidious about the provenance of its raw materials, with local farmers delivering meats as they reach their prime, and seafood landed at the pier at the end of the road. A starter of beautifully presented prawns, fresh that morning, set around two ravioli of gazpacho jelly, with tomato fondue drizzled with tapenade and saffron aïoli is a modish opener, or there could be roast belly pork with sauce soubise and prunes in a port reduction. Main courses demonstrate imaginative, modern ideas, such as roast cod fillet with violet-flavoured carrots braised in mirin with carrot and ginger 'air', while desserts could bring on a refreshing mixture of fruits, jellies and mousses, attractively arranged on a black slate, with a sprinkle of sherbet on the side.

Chef Ciaran Scully **Owner** John & Carmel O'Brien **Times** 1-3/7-9 Closed Nov-Apr, L Mon-Sat **Prices** Food prices not confirmed for 2013. Please telephone for

details **Wines** 28 bottles over €20, 7 by glass **Notes** Vegetarian menu, Dress restrictions, Smart casual **Seats** 65, Pr/dining room 30 **Children** Portions, Menu **Parking** 40

BALLYLICKEY
Map 1 B2

Sea View House

◉◉ Traditional V 🍴

Polished cooking in smart country-house hotel

☎ 027 50073
e-mail: info@seaviewhousehotel.com
web: www.seaviewhousehotel.com
dir: 3m N of Bantry towards Glengarriff, 70yds off main road, N71

An elegant country-house retreat on Bantry Bay, Sea View House is in delightfully colourful gardens giving glimpses of the sea between the trees (even better views from some of the bedrooms), with the restaurant taking up three charming rooms, one a conservatory. There's plenty of seafood among main courses, normally grilled, poached or baked and served with a classic sauce - suprême of cod Mornay, say, or grilled fillets of plaice with tartare sauce - accompanied by seasonal vegetables. Top-class ingredients are treated with restraint in a first course light and luscious scallop mousse, topped with a creamy sauce hinting of vermouth, and a main course duckling (all meats are local and 'can be traced from farm to fork') roasted until pink and tender, stuffed with a tasty mix of potato, herbs and sultanas, and given a port and orange sauce.

Chef Eleanor O'Donavon **Owner** Kathleen O'Sullivan **Times** 12.30-1.45/7-9.30 Closed Nov-Mar, L Mon-Sat **Prices** Fixed L 3 course €30, Starter €7.50-€10, Main €22.50-€30, Dessert €5.50, Service included, Groups min 10 service 10% **Wines** 40 bottles over €20, 8 bottles under €20, 10 by glass **Notes** Sunday L, Vegetarian menu, Dress restrictions, Smart casual, Civ Wed 75 **Seats** 50 **Children** Portions, Menu

BALTIMORE
Map 1 B1

Rolfs Country House

◉ French, European **NEW** V 🍴

Continental classics in a heavenly spot

☎ 028 20289
e-mail: info@rolfscountryhouse.com
dir: Into Baltimore, sharp left, follow restaurant signs, up hill

The Haffner family have been in business here since 1979, and who could blame them for staying put when you see the location. Set in beautiful sub-tropical gardens, the stone-built restaurant has world-class views overlooking Baltimore Harbour to Roaringwater Bay and Carbery's 100 islands. Johannes Haffner is the current incumbent at the stoves, and he runs the restaurant with his sister Frederica, bringing a dedication to the job that ensures produce is locally grown, reared and caught, organic whenever possible, and pastries and breads are all home-baked. The beamed restaurant provides a cosy and informal setting for a classic European repertoire: king scallops flambéed in Cognac come simply with salad leaves from the garden, while monkfish gets an equally fuss-free treatment: medallions poached in white wine and butter and served with chive and white wine sauce. End with a properly buttery caramelised apple tarte Tatin.

Chef Johannes Haffner **Owner** Johannes Haffner **Times** 6-9.30 Closed Xmas, Mon-Tue (winter) **Prices** Fixed D 3 course €29.50-€35, Starter €4.50-€13, Main €18-€29, Dessert €6, Service included **Wines** 30 bottles over €20, 3 bottles under €20, 12 by glass **Notes** Sunday L, Vegetarian menu, Dress restrictions, **Seats** 50 **Children** Portions, Menu **Parking** 45

Save on Hotels. Book at **theAA.com/hotel**

CO CORK 655 | IRELAND

BLARNEY
Map 1 B2

Blarney Golf Resort

◉ Modern Irish

Modern Irish cookery near the Blarney Stone

☎ 021 4384477
Kerry Rd, Tower
e-mail: reservations@blarneygolfresort.com
dir: Exit N20 for Blarney, 4km to Tower, turn right onto Old Kerry Rd. Hotel 2km on right

Not far from the town where tourists throng to kiss the famous Blarney Stone, the homonymous golf and spa hotel stands rather grandly in 170 acres. The Inniscarra dining room is a split-level space, next door to Cormac's Bar, with large windows framing views of the sun setting over the surrounding hills. Modern Irish cooking draws influences from around the world, perhaps for a stir-fry of Barbary duck and vegetable strips, spiked with ginger and chilli and piled on to a herb pancake, ahead of baked whole sea bass with caramelised chicory in caper and parsley butter, or pork chop topped with aubergine, courgette and melted brie in cider jus. To finish, passionfruit pannacotta turns up neatly capped with crumbled white chocolate and accompanied by cherry purée.

Times 6-8.45 Closed 24-25 Dec, L all week

CASTLEMARTYR
Map 1 C2

Castlemartyr Resort

◉ Modern Irish

Fine dining in elegant surroundings

☎ 021 4219000
e-mail: reception@castlemartyrresort.ie
dir: N25 from Cork City, located between Midleton and Youghal

Once the home of Sir Walter Raleigh, this refurbished 18th-century manor house stands beside the ruins of an 800-year-old castle in 320 acres of farmland and mature parkland. A thriving sporting and leisure hotel, replete with health club, spa and golf course, it offers informal eating in the Knights Bar and formal fine dining at smart tables in the elegant Bell restaurant. The modern Irish cooking makes the most of the fabulous ingredients sourced from the surrounding countryside and uncomplicated dishes are kept simple to allow the natural flavours to shine through. This translates to pepper-crusted tuna loin with aubergine chutney, beef fillet with spinach and garlic purée, carrot fondant and béarnaise, and apple tarte Tatin with blackberry compôte.

Chef Kevin Burke **Owner** Ophelia Partnership
Times 6.30-10 Closed Sun (Nov-Mar), L all week
Prices Fixed D 4 course €62.50, Starter €12.50, Main €30, Dessert fr €12.50, Service optional
Wines 300 bottles over €20, 12 by glass **Notes** Vegetarian available, Dress restrictions, Smart dress, no jeans or T-shirts **Seats** 65, Pr/dining room 180 **Children** Portions, Menu

CLONAKILTY
Map 1 B2

Inchydoney Island Lodge & Spa

◉◉ Modern Mediterranean

Fine West Cork ingredients in a glorious coastal setting

☎ 023 8833143
Inchydoney
e-mail: reservations@inchydoneyisland.com
dir: From Cork take N71 following West Cork signs. Through Innishannon, Bandon & Clonakilty, then follow signs for Inchydoney Island

Bracketed by heavenly beaches and undisturbed views of the Atlantic, this luxurious contemporary resort hotel is reached by a causeway from the mainland, which adds further to the sense of exclusivity. When you want to spoil yourself with a bit of me-time, the operation has the full-dress package of sybaritic spa treatments, an impeccably stylish interior that ticks all the boxes for style slaves, and for gastronomes, the Gulfstream Restaurant is the top-end dining option. It is a chic, contemporary space basking in fabulous ocean views to go with its repertoire of French and Mediterranean-accented dishes. A fair few guests are here to firm up and detox, so the kitchen puts a lightened-up spin on things, making plentiful use of West Cork's splendid fresh local seafood and organic materials. You might open with crab, prawn and lobster with marinated courgette, celeriac carpaccio and chilled lobster bisque, then move on to roast cannon, leg, and crisp-fried loin of local lamb teamed with sweetbread hotpot, smoked aubergine, red pepper, and rosemary jus, and abandon restraint altogether for a finale of hot chocolate fondant with white chocolate sauce and a dark chocolate marquise.

Chef Adam Medcalf **Owner** Des O'Dowd **Times** 6.30-9.30 Closed 24-25 Dec **Notes** Fixed D 5 course €58, Vegetarian available, Dress restrictions, Smart casual **Seats** 80, Pr/dining room 250 **Children** Portions, Menu **Parking** 200

CORK
Map 1 B2

Maryborough Hotel & Spa

◉ Modern International V

Traditional and modern in a 300-year-old country house

☎ 021 4365555
Maryborough Hill
e-mail: info@maryborough.ie
dir: From Jack Lynch Tunnel take 2nd exit signed Douglas. Right at 1st rdbt, follow Rochestown road to fingerpost rdbt. Left, hotel on left 0.5m up hill

The 300-year-old country house near Cork stands in 14 acres of luxurious grounds and woodland, full of rare plant species and with a magnificent display of rhododendrons. It has been brought thoroughly up-to-date inside, with the promisingly named Zings restaurant featuring a walk-in wine cellar on the lower of its two levels. A congenial mix of traditional and modern thinking is in evidence from the kitchen, which delivers some well-rendered, satisfying dishes. Panko-crumbed fishcakes of salmon and cod, blended with tarragon and wholegrain mustard, served with wilted spinach and sorrel cream, get things off to a good savoury start. Main courses might see lamb in two presentations - roast rack and braised shank - with canny accompaniments of roast red and yellow peppers, citrus-spiked onion compôte and a rosemary jus. Finish with passionfruit crème brûlée and macadamia cookies.

Chef Gerry Allen **Owner** Dan O'Sullivan
Times 12.30-2.30/6.30-10 Closed 24-26 Dec, Mon-Thu, L Fri-Sat, D Sun **Prices** Fixed L 2 course €20-€25, Fixed D 3 course fr €35, Starter €5.50-€8.95, Main €15.50-€27, Dessert €5.95-€7.95, Service optional, Groups min 10 service 10% **Wines** 44 bottles over €20, 11 bottles under €20, 4 by glass **Notes** Sunday L, Vegetarian menu, Dress restrictions, Smart casual **Seats** 120, Pr/dining room 60 **Children** Portions, Menu **Parking** 300

DURRUS
Map 1 B2

Blairscove House & Restaurant

◉◉ Modern, International

Local produce in magnificent converted stables

☎ 027 61127
e-mail: mail@blairscove.ie
dir: R591 from Durrus to Crookhaven, in 1.5m restaurant on right through blue gate

This Georgian manor house with uplifting views over Dunmanus Bay hides a real treat in the stylishly converted stables and outbuildings. Bare stone walls hung with vivid contemporary art soar upwards to a crystal chandelier suspended from a church-like beamed ceiling, making for a memorable setting in which to explore the local larder. Fresh, local and seasonal are buzz words, and the kitchen doesn't need to worry about food miles as the materials all come from nearby ports or the surrounding hills. It's a case of helping yourself to starters from the buffet - perhaps duck rillettes or spiced calves' tongue - before perfectly caramelised lambs' kidneys with Dijon mustard-spiked garlicky spinach, or a well-hung rib-eye cooked before your eyes on the beech wood grill. Dessert reverts to the help-yourself format, so go for something like a classic crème brûlée or pannacotta with strawberry compôte.

Chef Ronald Klötzer **Owner** P & S De Mey **Times** 6.30-9.30 Closed Nov-17 Mar, Sun-Mon, L all week **Prices** Fixed D 3 course fr €58, Service optional, Groups min 8 service 10% **Notes** Vegetarian available, Dress restrictions, Smart casual, Civ Wed 30 **Seats** 75, Pr/dining room 48 **Children** Portions **Parking** 30

GARRYVOE
Map 1 C2

Garryvoe Hotel

Modern Irish

Modern Irish cooking in a grand seafront hotel

☎ 021 4646718
Ballycotton Bay, Castlemartyr
e-mail: res@garryvoehotel.com
web: www.garryvoehotel.com
dir: From N25 at Castlemartyr (Cork-Rosslare road) take R632 to Garryvoe

Right on the seafront overlooking Ballycotton Bay, the Garryvoe is something of a local institution, but one that has moved with the times, modernising and aggrandising in the process. The high-ceilinged dining room naturally makes the most of those Cork coastal views, with well-spaced tables set with high-class accoutrements. The cooking might be described as modern Irish, but with no inhibitions about featuring retro dishes too. Start with crab croquette with chilli jam, citrus crab millefeuille and celeriac in wild mushroom bisque, moving onto a classic main course such as roast rump of local lamb with creamed cabbage and root veg in red wine reduction. The finale could be chocolate fondant with pistachio ice cream and raspberry coulis.

Chef Kevin O'Sullivan **Owner** O'Brien Family
Times 1-2.30/6.30-8.45 Closed 24-25 Dec, L Mon-Sat **Prices** Fixed L 3 course fr €27, Fixed D 3 course fr €32, Starter €6-€10, Main €21-€28, Dessert €7, Service optional **Wines** 70 bottles over €20, 4 bottles under €20, 6 by glass **Notes** Sunday L, Vegetarian available **Seats** 80, Pr/dining room 45 **Children** Portions, Menu **Parking** 100

GOLEEN
Map 1 A1

The Heron's Cove

Traditional Irish

Unbroken sea views, super-fresh seafood and more

☎ 028 35225
The Harbour
e-mail: suehill@eircom.net
dir: In Goleen village, turn left to harbour

Head for the most south-westerly tip of the country where the beam of the Fastnet Rock lighthouse scans the Atlantic at Mizen Head, and pull in at this charming rustic restaurant with rooms in Goleen Harbour. In summer, it is a magical spot when you can eat out to sublime sea views on the balcony overlooking the tiny inlet, and the menu offers a roll-call of fabulous local seafood and meats prepared with forthright simplicity. Starters might include crabcakes with wasabi mayonnaise, while variety is ensured at main course stage by seared Dunmanus Bay scallops with creamy smoked bacon sauce or pan-fried John Dory with balsamic butter alongside local lamb chops with rosemary jus. Sticky toffee pudding with vanilla ice cream wraps things up on a comforting note.

Chef Irene Coughlan **Owner** Sue Hill **Times** 7-9.30 Closed Xmas, Oct-Mar only open for pre-bookings, L all week (ex private functions) **Prices** Fixed D 4 course €27.50-€34, Starter €5.50-€14, Main €17.50-€29.95, Dessert €6.95-€8.50, Service optional **Wines** 23 bottles over €20, 16 bottles under €20, 2 by glass **Notes** Vegetarian available **Seats** 30 **Children** Portions, Menu **Parking** 10

GOUGANE BARRA
Map 1 B2

Gougane Barra Hotel

Irish, French

Traditional country-house cooking in lakeside setting

☎ 026 47069
e-mail: info@gouganebarrahotel.com
dir: Off R584 between N22 at Macroom & N71 at Bantry. Take Keimaneigh junct for hotel

Its magical lakeside setting in the mountains of County Cork is one of the powerful draws of the Gougane Barra, and so is the warmly friendly approach with which the place is run. The owner's collection of photographs of the environs during the winter months is worth a peek, and the locally supplied menus of classic country-house cooking exercise their own allure. You might start with a serving of the legendary Clonakilty black pudding with apples and bacon, or a salad of smoked salmon and prawns dressed in honey and Dijon, before moving to grilled halibut on spicy roast veg with red pepper relish, and finishing up with richly flavoured crème caramel garnished with redcurrants.

Chef Katy Lucey, Rudy Parsooramen **Owner** Neil & Katy Lucey **Times** 12.30-2.30/6-8.30 Closed 20 Oct-10 Apr, winter, L Mon-Sat (ex group bookings) **Prices** Fixed L 2 course €21.45, Fixed D 3 course €26.95, Starter €6-€7.75, Main €22.50-€24.50, Dessert €6.50, Service optional **Wines** 10 bottles over €20, 44 bottles under €20, 6 by glass **Notes** Pre-theatre menu 3 course €26.95, Sunday L, Vegetarian available, Civ Wed 40 **Seats** 70 **Children** Portions, Menu **Parking** 40

KINSALE
Map 1 B2

Carlton Hotel Kinsale

European V

Modern cooking in a stunning contemporary hotel

☎ 021 4706000
Rathmore Rd
e-mail: reservations.kinsale@carlton.ie
dir: Before Kinsale turn left signed Charles Fort. 3kms, hotel on left

The strikingly modern Kinsale Carlton makes quite a design statement with its frontage of glass, wood and stone, and is set in a remarkable location with dreamy views over Oysterhaven Bay and the headland. From its first-floor elevation, the Rockpool Restaurant surveys that sweeping panorama through a wall of glass, and there are tables out on the terrace for balmy days. The look inside is bright and contemporary, but it is the novelty of cooking on hot volcanic rocks that brings in the diners - a culinary method from the dawn of time, but in these surroundings it makes for an irresistible piece of restaurant theatre. As well as the DIY approach to cooking your West Cork beef, duck breast, scallops, prawns, or tuna on the hot rocks, you could take the more orthodox route, starting perhaps with baked crab and prawn gratin with toasted focaccia, followed by roast fillet and belly of Kilbrittan pork with swede purée and cider jus, and iced rhubarb soufflé with cinnamon crumble topping and Bramley apple and orange purée to finish.

Chef Aidano Driscoll **Owner** Carlton Hotels
Times 12-2.30/6.30-9.30 Closed Xmas, **Prices** Fixed D 3 course €30, Starter €5.50-€8.50, Main €14.95-€19.95, Dessert €6.50-€7.50, Service optional **Wines** 30 bottles over €20, 2 bottles under €20 **Notes** Sunday L, Vegetarian menu, Civ Wed 209 **Seats** 90, Pr/dining room 15 **Children** Portions, Menu **Parking** 100

The White House

Traditional, International

Traditional and modern Irish cooking in a gastronomic hub

☎ 021 4772125
Pearse St, The Glen
e-mail: whitehse@indigo.ie
dir: located town centre

The White House has been in the hospitality game since the mid-19th century, and occupies a prime site in the centre of a town that holds a renowned Gourmet Festival every autumn. That means there's plenty to live up to in the gastronomic stakes, and the kitchen here rises to the occasion with a resourceful repertoire of modern Irish dishes that draws inspiration from far and wide, but is also a dab hand at Irish stews, fish pies and the like. Baked cod fillet is coated in Cajun spices for a satisfying main course, accompanied by ratatouille topped with melted cheese. Local mussels make a fine starter, with a creamy dressing of white wine, garlic and lemongrass, and favourite puddings take in apple and cinnamon crumble with well-churned vanilla ice cream, or passionfruit and mango cheesecake.

Chef Martin El Sahen **Owner** Michael Frawley
Times 12-10 Closed 25 Dec, **Prices** Food prices not confirmed for 2013. Please telephone for details **Wines** 24 bottles over €20, 2 bottles under €20, 9 by glass **Notes** Vegetarian available **Seats** 45 **Children** Portions, Menu **Parking** Car park at rear of building

MALLOW　　　　　　　　　　　　　Map 1 B2

Springfort Hall Country House Hotel

◉ Modern Irish **NEW** ☙

Modern dining in a Georgian country house

☎ 022 21278 & 30620
e-mail: stay@springfort-hall.com
dir: N20 onto R581 at Two Pot House, hotel 500mtrs on right

The kitchen team in this immaculately-preserved Georgian country house certainly aren't scared of a bit of domestic hard graft: no corners are cut here - meat and fish is smoked in-house and everything is made from scratch from fresh, judiciously-sourced local produce. The setting for all of this laudable culinary endeavour is the palatial Lime Tree Restaurant, where all the detail of the original ornate plasterwork is picked out in gold paint, and a crystal chandelier hangs above pristine white linen-clothed tables on polished timber flooring. The kitchen deals in a broadly modern Irish style of cookery, sending out ideas such as black pudding and glazed pork belly with pickled leeks, apple purée and cider jelly, followed by seared wild venison with butternut squash purée, Savoy cabbage, pickled mushrooms and candied pumpkin seeds.

Chef Bryan McCarthy **Owner** The Walsh Family
Times 12-6/6-9.30 Closed 25-26 Dec, **Prices** Fixed L 2 course €22.50-€25.50, Fixed D 3 course €25-€26.95, Starter €7-€10, Main €23-€27, Dessert €7.75, Service optional **Wines** 4 bottles under €20, 38 by glass **Notes** Sunday L, Vegetarian available, Civ Wed 300 **Seats** 60, Pr/dining room 40 **Children** Portions, Menu **Parking** 250

SHANAGARRY　　　　　　　　　　Map 1 C2

Ballymaloe House

◉◉ Traditional ⬥ NOTABLE WINE LIST ☙

Fabulous food in a classic country-house setting

☎ 021 4652531
e-mail: res@ballymaloe.ie
dir: From R630 at Whitegate rdbt, left onto R631, left onto Cloyne. Continue for 2m on Ballycotton Rd

The concept of sourcing local, seasonal produce is taken to extremes at Ballymaloe, where most of what turns up on your plate comes from the 400 acres of their East Cork estate, which includes 100 acres of organic farm, and pretty walled gardens that supply herbs, fruit and vegetables. The Allen family have followed the ethos of taking the best regional ingredients and treating them simply and with respect for 40 years - long before it became fashionable to trumpet such credentials - and it is all served up in four traditional dining rooms. The daily menus are driven by what the chefs bring in from the garden and what has been landed by the boats at Ballycotton, so you might find roast hake with chilli, parsley and garlic oil alongside locally-smoked salmon rillettes with pickled cucumber, then raise the comfort rating further still with slow-roast free-range pork with

Bramley apple sauce and roast Jerusalem artichokes, or an equally unfussy pairing of grilled cod and lobster with wild watercress relish and leek Julienne.

Chef Jason Fahey **Owner** The Allen family
Times 1-1.30/7-9.30 Closed Xmas & 2 wks Jan, **Prices** Fixed L 3 course €37.50, Starter €10-€25, Main €40-€45, Dessert €10-€15, Service optional **Wines** 300 bottles over €20, 12 by glass **Notes** Fixed D 5 course €70-€75, Pre-concert menu from €45, Sunday L, Vegetarian available, Dress restrictions, Smart casual, no jeans or T-shirts, Civ Wed 120 **Seats** 110, Pr/dining room 50 **Children** Portions, Menu **Parking** 100

YOUGHAL　　　　　　　　　　　　Map 1 C2

Ahernes

◉ Traditional Irish, European ☙

Bracingly fresh fish and seafood in a family-run hotel

☎ 024 92424
163 North Main St
e-mail: ahernes@eircom.net

The Fitzgibbon family has been running this townhouse hotel within the historic walled port since 1923, and may be presumed to know a thing or two about hospitality. The warmth and cheer don't disappoint, and there is an infectious feeling of informality in the snug, but vibrantly buzzy dining room. Prime fish and seafood cookery is the priority, with plentiful supplies from Ballycotton Bay to enrich the menu choice. Seared scallops with bacon and spinach are bracingly fresh, to the extent of not needing quite so much of the creamy vermouth sauce they come with, and mains might offer monkfish on crab risotto with excellent tomato salsa, or grilled hake with mango and avocado salsa. If you're not into fish, a fillet steak or chicken breast may suffice, while the signature dessert is the coffee meringue roulade, which incorporates chewy as well as crunchy passages, as well as a centre of whipped cream marbled with ristretto.

Chef David Fitzgibbon **Owner** John & David Fitzgibbon
Times 6-9.30 Closed 24-27 Dec, L all week (open by arrangement) **Prices** Fixed D 3 course €30-€40, Starter €5-€15, Main €20-€35, Dessert €7.50, Service optional **Notes** Vegetarian available, Dress restrictions, Smart casual **Seats** 60, Pr/dining room 12 **Children** Portions, Menu **Parking** 20

CO DONEGAL

DONEGAL　　　　　　　　　　　　Map 1 B5

Harvey's Point Country Hotel

◉◉ Modern, European ☙

High-impact cooking in a soothing lakeside location

☎ 074 9722208
Lough Eske
e-mail: stay@harveyspoint.com
dir: From Donegal 2m towards Lifford, left at Harvey's Point sign, follow signs, take 3 right turns to hotel gates

It's hard to imagine that just 20 years ago, Harvey's Point was nothing more than a tumbledown cottage. Fast forward to 2012 and the Swiss family Gysling's vision has resulted in the sprawling upmarket hotel complex that now stands by the shores of Lough Eske in the Donegal Hills. It was the heavenly setting that brought the Gyslings here, and the restaurant capitalises on those splendid lough views through a wall of full-length windows. The food is modern, inventive and seasonal, hitting all the right buttons with its exemplary local and organic ingredients. A starter of, say, roast monkfish with braised oxtail tortellini, bone marrow custard and caramelised onion sets the full-flavoured tone, then mains might see breast and pressed leg of duck sharing a plate with turnip and vanilla purée, poached rhubarb, spring cabbage and duck gravy. Lemon tart with crème fraîche ice cream and candied lemon makes for a zesty finale.

Chef Paul Montgomery **Owner** Marc & Deirdre Gysling
Times 6.30-9.30 Closed Sun-Thu (Nov-Apr), Wed (Jun-Oct), L all week **Prices** Fixed D 3 course €45-€50, Starter €12, Main €24-€32, Dessert €9, Service optional **Wines** 60 bottles over €20, 14 bottles under €20, 14 by glass **Notes** Sunday L, Vegetarian available, Dress restrictions, Smart casual, Civ Wed 220 **Seats** 108 **Children** Portions **Parking** 200

DUNFANAGHY　　　　　　　　　　Map 1 C6

Arnolds Hotel

◉ Traditional

Sea views and an Irish flavour

☎ 074 9136208
Main St
e-mail: enquiries@arnoldshotel.com
dir: On N56 from Letterkenny, hotel on left entering the village

The family-run Arnolds Hotel has been in business for 90 years, and it's not hard to understand its perennial popularity. It stands in Donegal's windswept Sheephaven Bay in a perfect spot for riding along the coast and surfing the Atlantic rollers, and once inside, there's the timeless hospitality of peat fires and a sincere welcome. The Seascapes dining room basks in sweeping views of Killahoey beach and Horn Head - a panorama that puts you in the mood for freshly-landed fish, which the unfussy

continued

DUNFANAGHY *continued*

menu is happy to supply. Local crab claws tossed in garlic and coriander butter should get things off to a flying start, then you might follow with baked monkfish wrapped in prosciutto and teamed with red pepper coulis, or griddled Irish pork fillet with Savoy cabbage and sticky shallot sauce.

Times 5-9.30

DUNKINEELY
Map 1 B5

Castle Murray House and Restaurant

◉ Traditional, Modern French ◔

Seafood-led menus, prime produce and ravishing sea views

☎ 074 9737022
St Johns Point
e-mail: info@castlemurray.com
dir: From Donegal take N56 towards Killybegs. 1st left at end of Dunkineely village

Castle Murray's beamed and flagstoned restaurant, with an open fire, has a view to die for: it looks over the Atlantic and the floodlit ruins of McSwyne's Castle. The French-flavoured menu majors on seafood, from a salad of pan-fried squid and crab with pickled fennel and horseradish mayonnaise, through prawns and monkfish in garlic butter topped with mozzarella, to poached turbot fillet with saffron and mussel risotto and bouillabaisse sauce. In winter, when seafood is less plentiful, more meat dishes appear: perhaps chicken risotto, then roast fillet of local lamb with a garlicky potato fritter, basil purée and red wine jus. At all times, expect something like lemon crème brûlée to finish.

Chef Remy Dupuy **Owner** Marguerite Howley **Times** 1.30-3.30/6.30-9.30 Closed Mon-Tue, also Wed-Thu (low season), L Wed-Sat **Prices** Fixed D 4 course €47-€52, Service added but optional 10%, Groups min 10 service 10% **Wines** 36 bottles over €20, 5 by glass **Notes** Fixed L 4 course €32, Sunday L, Vegetarian available, Civ Wed 80 **Seats** 80, Pr/dining room 40 **Children** Menu **Parking** 30

LETTERKENNY
Map 1 C5

Radisson Blu Hotel Letterkenny

◉ Modern Seafood

Unpretentious cooking in a modern hotel

☎ 074 9194444
Paddy Harte Rd
e-mail: info.letterkenny@radissonblu.com
web: www.radissonblu.ie/hotel-letterkenny
dir: N14 into Letterkenny. At Polestar Rdbt take 1st exit, to hotel

The contemporary-styled hotel in Ireland's far northwest is a bright and airy building with plenty of glass, and a modern dining option in the TriBeCa Brasserie, named after the trendy area of New York City. Light wood cladding and unclothed tables create a laid-back ambience, and the menus offer an expansive choice of simple, unpretentious dishes. Start with baked St Kevin brie wrapped in Parma ham on orange and rocket salad with cranberry chutney, as a prelude to honey-roast half a duck with sweet potato mash and a red onion tart, or seafood pie topped with parmesan mash. Key lime and chocolate pie is a typical dessert.

Chef Collette Langan **Owner** Paul Byrne **Times** 12.30-3.30/6-9.30 Closed L Mon-Sat **Prices** Fixed L 2 course fr €17.95, Fixed D 3 course fr €24.50, Starter €4.50-€8, Main €12.95-€19.95, Dessert €5.95-€8.95, Service optional **Wines** 14 bottles over €20, 4 bottles under €20, 5 by glass **Notes** Early bird menu 6-7pm €19.95, Fixed L 2,3 course Sun only, Sunday L, Vegetarian available, Civ Wed 600 **Seats** 120, Pr/dining room 320 **Children** Portions, Menu **Parking** 150

RATHMULLAN
Map 1 C6

Rathmullan House

◉◉ Modern Irish

Charming country hotel with contemporary cooking

☎ 074 9158188
e-mail: info@rathmullanhouse.com
dir: R245 Letterkenny to Ramelton, over bridge right onto R247 to Rathmullan. On entering village turn at Mace shop through village gates. Hotel on right

Rathmullan is an elegant Regency-era mansion in wooded grounds overlooking Lough Swilly, and just a short stroll from a two-mile golden sand beach. Run by the second generation of the Wheeler family, who celebrated 50 years in business as a country-house hotel in 2012, the whole operation has a well-established feel and ticks along with discreet charm. The Weeping Elm restaurant is housed in a modern extension with a tented ceiling, wooden floors and views through the trees to the Lough. Chef Kelan McMichael runs an industrious kitchen supporting local artisan suppliers, and raiding the hotel's Victorian walled garden for seasonal organic fruit, salad and herbs. Mackerel caught a few hours previously from the lough appears seared and teamed with wild garlic tapenade, a punchy horseradish and rhubarb compôte, and pickled beetroot, while main course stars Rathmullan lamb from a neighbouring farm - roast loin, rolled breast and a breadcrumbed croquette of braised neck, to be precise - served with a ragoût of morels and sweet garlic, olive oil mash and rosemary jus. To finish, there's a delicate rhubarb treacle tart with praline ice cream.

Times 7.30-8.45 Closed Jan-mid Feb

DUBLIN

DUBLIN Map 1 D4

Castleknock Hotel & Country Club

◉ European, International

Contemporary dining in country club setting

☎ 01 6406300
Porterstown Rd, Castleknock
e-mail: info@chcc.ie
web: www.castleknockhotel.com
dir: M50 exit 3 to Castleknock village, left at Myos junct &
follow signs. From airport/Blanch exit, left, right, right
again into Castleknock. At Myos pub left, right at x-rds,
follow signs

When the All Blacks rugby team are on tour in this
hemisphere they hole up at this glossy contemporary
country club hotel to wash off the mud and relax with a
spot of pampering and beauty therapy between tussles on
the pitch. Although it is just 15 minutes from Dublin city
centre, it feels surprisingly rural - perhaps because it sits
surrounded by its own 18-hole golf course. A slew of bars,
a brasserie and the Park Restaurant cover all of the
eating and drinking bases, the latter being a modern
bistro and steak house with views of the club-swinging
action as a backdrop. Using plenty of Irish produce, the
kitchen keeps things modern, upbeat and uncomplicated
- perhaps warm grilled smoked duck breast with saffron
and pea risotto, and parmesan mousse, ahead of
chargrilled slabs of 21-day-aged Irish beef; for something
less primordial, yet equally full-flavoured, there may be
slow-roasted pork belly with Clonakilty black pudding,
pan-fried scallops, creamy celeriac, and Calvados jus.
Fine Irish cheeses are the alternative to desserts like
chocolate bread pudding with vanilla and bourbon ice cream.

Owner FBD Group **Times** 12.30-3/5.30-10
Closed 24-26 Dec, **Prices** Food prices not confirmed for
2013. Please telephone for details **Wines** 41 bottles over
€20, 12 by glass **Notes** Fixed 4 course D 2 people &
includes wine, Sunday L, Vegetarian available, Civ Wed
120 **Seats** 65, Pr/dining room 400 **Children** Portions,
Menu **Parking** 200

The Cellar Restaurant

◉◉ Modern Irish **NEW** ⏱

Smart cooking of fine local produce

☎ 01 6030600
Merrion Hotel, Upper Merrion St
e-mail: info@merrionhotel.com
dir: Top Upper Merrion Street, opp Government buildings

The Merrion Hotel's Cellar Restaurant (see also
Restaurant Patrick Guilbaud) may have no natural light,
but it's a bright room under its vaulted ceiling, with lots
of nooks and crannies and top-end fittings and
furnishings. The kitchen bases its cooking on indigenous
ingredients and promotes local and artisan producers
whenever possible, seen in imaginative starters like
confit of Galway salmon with horseradish and potato
salad, pickled cucumber and cucumber gel, and

saddleback pork and pistachio terrine with fig chutney, a
cherry and balsamic treacle adding another flavour
dimension. Main courses pull some punches too, without
being overwrought or fussy: meltingly tender veal liver
with rich onion gravy laced with red wine, accompanied
by bacon and buttery mash, say, or roast skate wing with
lemon and brown shrimp beurre noisette and garlicky
spinach. Cheeses are Irish, with ingredients in some
puddings coming from wilder shores: a smooth light
soufflé of exotic fruits, for instance, with mango ice
cream and coconut liqueur-infused custard.

Chef Ed Cooney **Times** 12.30-2/6-10 Closed L Sat
Prices Fixed L 2 course fr €20, Fixed D 3 course fr €29.95,
Starter €7.50-€10, Main €20-€35, Dessert €8-€12,
Service optional **Notes** Vegetarian available, Dress
restrictions, Smart casual, Civ Wed 55 **Children** Portions,
Menu **Parking** Merrion Square

The Clarence

◉◉ Irish, French

Grand hotel brasserie dining by the Liffey

☎ 01 4070813 & 4070800
6-8 Wellington Quay
e-mail: tearoom@theclarence.ie
dir: from O'Connell Bridge, W along Quays, through 1st
lights (at Ha'penny Bridge) hotel 500mtrs on left

Owned by U2's Bono and The Edge, The Clarence is a
Victorian hotel in the heart of the Irish capital on the
Liffey. Refurbished to a state of contemporary elegance,
its premier dining space is the modestly named Tea
Room, a majestic, tall-windowed room that looks out
towards the cultural entrepot of Temple Bar. A minstrels'
gallery looks down on oak tables set with modern cutlery
and sparkling glassware, and the modern Irish brasserie
cooking on offer chimes in with the mood of the moment.
A slice of buttery-crusted seafood quiche stuffed with
lemon sole, mussels and crab is served on red pepper
sauce with saladings, and might be followed by rack of
lamb with grilled Mediterranean veg and olive and mint
jus, or grilled tuna with stir-fried noodles in wasabi
butter. The desserts - lemon tart, vanilla cheesecake,
pistachio crème brûlée - know how to please a crowd as
unerringly as U2 themselves do.

Chef Mathieu Melin **Owner** Bono, The Edge & Quinlan
Private **Times** 12-5/5-10.30 **Prices** Food prices not
confirmed for 2013. Please telephone for details
Wines 36 bottles over €20, 3 bottles under €20, 8 by
glass **Notes** Sunday L, Vegetarian available, Dress
restrictions, Smart casual, Civ Wed 40 **Seats** 85, Pr/
dining room 130 **Children** Portions, Menu **Parking** 5

Crowne Plaza Dublin Northwood

◉ Asian, International **NEW**

Fusion food and more in modern hotel

☎ 01 8628888
Northwood Park, Santry Demesne, Santry
e-mail: info@crowneplazadublin.ie
dir: M50 junct 4, left into Northwood Park, 1km, hotel on
left

In a quiet location on the edge of Northwood Park, 10
minutes from the airport, the Crowne Plaza is a modern
hotel, its restaurant a bright and airy space, overlooking
the courtyard gardens. The kitchen takes its inspiration
from the techniques and flavours of Asia and the Pacific
Rim, with crisp duck spring roll with an Asian-style salad
and yoghurt and chilli dressing to start, followed by
chicken stir-fried with noodles and vegetables sauced
with coconut green curry. But this is no style slave, so
asparagus and Parma ham with a poached egg and
hollandaise may appear before roast halibut fillet with
tapenade and a casserole of haricot beans, chorizo and
red peppers, with lemon tart for pudding.

Chef Logan Inwin **Owner** Tifco Ltd **Times** 12-2.30/6-10.30
Closed 25 Dec, L Sat **Prices** Food prices not confirmed for
2013. Please telephone for details **Wines** 34 bottles over
€20, 22 bottles under €20, 23 by glass **Notes** Dress
restrictions, Smart dress, Civ Wed 100 **Seats** 156, Pr/
dining room 15 **Children** Portions, Menu **Parking** 360

Crowne Plaza Hotel

◉ Italian **NEW**

Italian dining in funky modern venue

☎ 01 8977777
The Blanchardstown Centre
e-mail: info@cpireland.crowneplaza.com
dir: M50 junct 6 (Blanchardstown)

The Blanchardstown branch of the Crowne Plaza empire
fits the bill, whether you're suited and booted for
business, or dropping by to refuel after a hit of retail
therapy in the shops and boutiques of the nearby
Blanchardstown Centre. The Forchetta restaurant works a
loud and proud contemporary look with bold floral
wallpaper and bare dark wood tables - it's a buzzy, breezy
setting that suits the crowd-pleasing modern Italian
menu. The usual suspects from the world of pizza and
pasta are all present and correct, or you might ignore
convention and start with a fish soup involving mussels,
clams, prawns, salmon and cod in a tomato and white
wine broth, and follow with a chargrilled Irish steak, or
lamb shank roasted in red wine, garlic and rosemary.
Puddings are Italian classics - pannacotta or tiramisù,
for example.

Chef Jason Hayde **Owner** Tifco Hotels **Times** 6-9.30
Closed 24-25 Dec, **Prices** Fixed L 2 course €19.95-€35,
Fixed D 3 course €24.95-€45, Starter €4-€11.50, Main
€8.95-€24.95, Dessert €6, Service optional
Wines 16 bottles over €20, 4 bottles under €20, 6 by glass
Notes Vegetarian available, Civ Wed 400 **Seats** 100, Pr/
dining room 45 **Children** Portions, Menu **Parking** 200

Restaurant Patrick Guilbaud

Modern French V

Outstanding French cooking at the pre-eminent Dublin address

☎ 01 6764192
Merrion Hotel, 21 Upper Merrion St
e-mail: info@
restaurantpatrickguilbaud.ie
web: www.restaurantpatrickguilbaud.ie
dir: Opposite government buildings, next to Merrion Hotel

After celebrating 30 years at the top of Dublin's gastronomic game, it is a good time to look at what exactly it is that keeps Patrick Guilbaud's restaurant in its apparently unassailable position as the outstanding address in the Irish capital. The setting, amid the elegant Georgian splendour of the upscale Merrion Hotel, certainly raises expectations sky-high: all around are bold contemporary abstract canvasses by Irish artists including Dublin-born Sean Scully, set beneath a minimally white-painted, barrel-vaulted ceiling. Diners receive a personal welcome from M. Guilbaud before settling into the hushed environs of the dining room, where a polished team of staff preside in an ambience of correctly polite formality. Guillaume Lebrun is the man in the kitchen in charge of carrying forward the house's reputation for high-end culinary achievement and his starting point is impeccable sourcing of

the best Irish country produce, since he knows that without first-rate materials you cannot achieve top-quality results. The cooking is obsessively intricate stuff which requires top-level technical skills to balance the multi-faceted flavours and textures that define the inventive contemporary repertoire. Finely crafted ideas get things off to a good start - perhaps croquettes of suckling pig teamed with fried quail's egg, foie gras, pancetta and red pepper mostardo, while half a dozen of Carlingford's finest oysters are given a deeply layered lift by the addition of shallots, ginger, Oriental-style dressing and a coriander and lime salad. Intelligent and intriguing contrasts of taste and texture continue to inform main courses - a jus of salsify, clam and hazelnut to counterpoint a pancetta-wrapped fillet of monkfish being a case in point, or a new spin could be brought to a fillet of Wicklow lamb by the mellow-spiced, North African warmth of aubergine purée and pickle, harissa and cumin. Desserts continue the theme of exploring ingredients and extracting contrasting textures while turbo-charging flavours, for instance Poire William soufflé with pear sorbet and warm Guanaja espuma, or roast spiced pineapple with pineapple sorbet, almond milk, lemon jelly and pink praline. All of this is bolstered by memorable crisp-baked breads, including tomato and fennel, and traditional brown soda bread, exemplary

amuses and petits fours, and an outstanding wine list of serious producers from France and far beyond.

Chef Guillaume Lebrun **Owner** Patrick Guilbaud **Times** 12.30-2.15/7.30-10.15 Closed 25 Dec, 1st wk Jan, Sun-Mon **Prices** Fixed L 2 course €38, Fixed D 4 course €90, Service optional **Wines** 1000 bottles over €20, 12 by glass **Notes** A la carte menu 2 course €85, 3 course €105, 4 course €130, Vegetarian menu, Dress restrictions, Smart casual **Seats** 80, Pr/dining room 25 **Children** Portions **Parking** Parking in square

Save on Hotels. Book at **theAA.com/hotel**

DUBLIN 661 **IRELAND**

DUBLIN *continued*

Finnstown Country House Hotel

◉ Traditional European

Accomplished cooking in 18th-century manor hotel

☎ 01 6010700

Newcastle Rd

e-mail: edwina@finnstown-hotel.ie

dir: N4 S/bound exit 4, left on slip road straight across rdbt & lights. Hotel on left

This creeper-hung 18th-century hotel, a portico over the front door, is on a 45-acre estate but is only a half-hour from the city centre. Its Peacock restaurant is a handsome room for dining, offering honest-to-goodness cooking of fine ingredients from a menu that doesn't try to change the world. Mango and chilli salsa, for grilled duck and spring roll sausage, is about as exotic as things get, with tian of crab and prawns Marie Rose more typical. Crabmeat may turn up again in a main course as a partner for baked fillet of sea trout in a herb crust with shellfish and brandy bisque, an alternative to seared peppered duck breast with mushroom and basil cream and sautéed spinach. End with a straightforward dessert, such as lemon tart or chocolate mousse.

Chef Steve McPhillips **Owner** Finnstown Country House Hotel **Times** 12.30-2.30/7-9.30 Closed 24-26 Dec, D Sun **Prices** Fixed L 3 course €23-€30, Fixed D 4 course €30-€40, Starter €8-€12, Main €16-€26, Dessert €6-€8 **Wines** 20 bottles over €20, 1 bottle under €20, 5 by glass **Notes** Fri D, Dine out €58 for 2 people, incl bottle wine, Sunday L, Vegetarian available, Dress restrictions, Smart casual, Civ Wed 180 **Seats** 150 **Children** Portions, Menu **Parking** 300

Restaurant Patrick Guilbaud

◉◉◉◉ – *see opposite*

The Shelbourne Dublin, a Renaissance Hotel

◉◉ Irish, European ◐

Grand hotel with top-notch steak and seafood

☎ 01 6634500

27 St Stephen's Green

e-mail: eamonn.casey@marriott.com

dir: M1 to city centre, along Parnell St to O'Connell St towards Trinity College, 3rd right into Kildare St, hotel on left

The Victorian builders of the Shelbourne set out to impress with this neo-classical Grand Hotel on St Stephen's Green in the heart of Dublin. Lavishly restored to its former glory, it is a splendid sight as soon as you're through the doors with its domed stained-glass ceiling and sweeping staircase. It is fast forward to a more contemporary clubby look in the Saddle Room restaurant, however, where leather banquettes, dark oak walls and curtained booths with buttoned bronze leather dividing screens set an opulent and intimate stage for tucking into oysters, steaks and seafood dishes. Classic brasserie staples are all built on materials of peerless provenance, whether it is a starter of pan-seared Dublin Bay prawns with artichoke, and shellfish sabayon, or prime Irish beef from the grill. Otherwise, go for Wicklow venison loin with braised red cabbage and Chinese leaves, or if you're up for fish, there could be seared halibut fillet with a buttered broth of root vegetables and kale. To finish, it has to be a classic crème brûlée with a palmier biscuit.

Chef Garry Hughes **Owner** Renaissance Hotels **Times** 12.30-2.30/6-10.30 **Prices** Fixed L 2 course fr €21, Fixed D 3 course fr €27.95, Starter €7.95-€19, Main €22.95-€35.95, Dessert fr €8.95, Service optional **Wines** 100+ bottles over €20, 12 by glass **Notes** Daily pre-theatre menu 2-3 course available 6-7pm, Sunday L, Vegetarian available, Dress restrictions, No sports wear, Civ Wed 300 **Seats** 120, Pr/dining room 20 **Children** Portions, Menu **Parking** Valet parking

Stillorgan Park Hotel

◉ Traditional Mediterranean, International ◐

Striking-looking restaurant with ambitious cooking

☎ 01 2001800

Stillorgan Rd

e-mail: info@stillorganpark.com

dir: On N11 follow signs for Wexford, pass RTE studios on left, through next 5 sets of lights. Hotel on left

Moody lighting and intimate alcoves combine with funky floral fabrics, vibrant colours and modern art in the upmarket Stillorgan Park Hotel's Purple Sage restaurant. As you might expect in such a contemporary setting, the cooking takes a distinctly modern tack, serving up an eclectic output of dishes that can be as simple as smoked haddock, leek and potato chowder, or as labour intensive as a main course of grilled corn-fed chicken stuffed with sun-dried tomato pesto, wrapped in Parma ham, and served with potato gnocchi and herb sauce. Fish dishes might see pan-fried sea bass fillet teamed

with pak choi, parmesan polenta, citrus fruit segments, and chilli and lime butter, while artisan Irish cheeses offer a savoury alternative to comfort-oriented desserts such as apple and blackberry crumble with vanilla ice cream.

Chef Enda Dunne **Owner** Des Pettitt **Times** 12.30-3/5.45-10.15 Closed 25 Dec, L Sat, D Sun **Prices** Fixed L 2 course fr €19.25, Service optional **Wines** 12 bottles over €20, 10 bottles under €20, 14 by glass **Notes** Early bird menu 2 course €21, 3 course €25, Sunday L, Vegetarian available, Civ Wed 120 **Seats** 100, Pr/dining room 60 **Children** Portions, Menu **Parking** 300

The Westbury Hotel

◉ Modern International **NEW** ◐

Smart Dublin hotel with confident team in the kitchen

☎ 01 6791122

Grafton St

e-mail: westbury@doylecollection.com

dir: Adjacent to Grafton St, half way between Trinity College & St Stephen's Green

This prestigious city-centre hotel has a fine-dining restaurant that sets it apart from some of the opposition. Recently treated to a swanky refurbishment, it's certainly a luxurious and stylish address these days. Wilde, the restaurant, has a bust of the said writer and poet with the references continuing into the artworks dotted around the place. Well-spaced tables, in what's essentially a modern grill restaurant, are set with crisp white napery, sparkling silver and glassware, and the service suits the mood. Plenty of good Irish produce is on the menu with the well-crafted dishes including the likes of a first-course pan-fried fillet of sea bass with ravioli of spinach and chorizo, dressed with a roast red pepper and basil cream, followed by glazed Silver Hill duck breast with a tian of wilted baby spinach, caramelised red onion and swede, sweet potato barrels and honey and ginger jus. Finish with a passionfruit and coconut parfait with champagne jelly. The wine list has a good selection of organic bottles and plenty by the half bottle and glass.

Chef John Nagle **Owner** The Doyle Collection **Times** 6.30-10.30 Closed Sun-Mon, L all week **Prices** Fixed D 3 course €35-€46, Starter €8-€16, Main €21-€45, Dessert €8-€11, Service optional **Wines** 130 bottles over €20 **Notes** Vegetarian available, Civ Wed 80 **Seats** 95 **Children** Portions, Menu

CO DUBLIN

KILLINEY   Map 1 D4

Fitzpatrick Castle Hotel

◉ Traditional, International

Fine dining overlooking Dublin Bay

☎ 01 2305400
e-mail: info@fitzpatricks.com
dir: From Dun Laoghaire port turn left, on coast road right at lights, left at next lights. Follow to Dalkey, right at Ivory pub, immediate left, up hill, hotel at top

The sweeping views across Dublin Bay from this grand 18th-century pile atop Killiney Hill are worth driving the nine miles out of Dublin for in their own right, but it's worth factoring in a pitstop at the hotel's classy fine-dining restaurant PJ's while you're there. Crystal chandeliers and well-spaced tables dressed in crisp linen create a sense of occasion for tackling the wide-ranging menu of skilfully-cooked seasonal dishes built on excellent local ingredients. You might start with plum tomato and roasted pepper soup with fresh ricotta and basil croûton, and follow with rack of lamb with a mustard and pistachio crust, mint mash, and red wine jus. Finish with luscious black cherry crêpes with Cognac ice cream.

Times 12.30-2.30/6-10 Closed 25 Dec, Mon, Tue, L Wed-Sat, D Sun

CO GALWAY

BARNA   Map 1 B3

The Twelve

◉◉ Modern Irish ≣NOTABLE WINE LIST ✋

Top-drawer local produce in boutique hotel

☎ 091 597000
Barna Village
e-mail: west@thetwelvehotel.ie
dir: Coast road Barna village, 10 mins from Galway

'True to the region, true to the season' is the kitchen's mantra at this design-led first-floor restaurant in a boutique hotel. The menu lists seasonal produce and the proximity of the sea means fish is spankingly fresh - roast sea trout, perhaps, with a poached oyster reduction - and good quality local meats run to rack of lamb with a croquette of shoulder, served with spinach and cumin-spiced carrots, or seared fillet steak on organic kale and parsnips, with truffle chips and béarnaise butter. To start may be smoked rabbit loin with warm potato salad and carrot velouté, or fish soup, with a collection of Irish cheeses competing with rhubarb soup with custard ice cream to finish.

Chef Martin O'Donnell **Owner** Fergus O'Halloran
Times 1-4/6-10 Closed Mon-Tue, L Wed-Fri **Prices** Fixed L 2 course €20-€22, Fixed D 3 course €25-€29, Starter €6-€12, Main €18-€32, Dessert €6-€9, Service optional **Wines** 500 bottles over €20, 18 bottles under €20, 37 by glass **Notes** Gourmet menu 5 course with wine, wine tutorials, Sunday L, Vegetarian available, Dress restrictions, Smart casual, Civ Wed 100 **Seats** 94, Pr/dining room 100 **Children** Portions, Menu **Parking** 120

CASHEL   Map 1 A4

Cashel House

◉◉ Traditional **V** ✋

A heavenly location and top-notch regional produce

☎ 095 31001
e-mail: res@cashel-house-hotel.com
dir: S of N59. 1m W of Recess

The McEvilly family have run Victorian Cashel House as a gracious, old-school country-house hotel since 1968, and anyone who visits their 50 acres of splendid gardens running down to the private beach at the head of Cashel Bay will appreciate why they've stayed put. When it comes to gastronomic matters, the setting is a sunny split-level restaurant done out in a traditional manner with antiques and artworks, and a commodious conservatory extension. With wild Connemara landscapes all around, you should easily work up an appetite to do justice to the kitchen's repertoire of French-inflected classic dishes. The fishermen out in the bay, backed up by Connemara's lakes, rivers and hillsides, furnish the essentials for straight-talking food - steamed Cleggan mussels are spiked with coconut milk, lemongrass and chilli, while pheasant breasts are casseroled with red wine, bacon and walnuts and served with crushed potatoes, braised red cabbage, sautéed leeks and roast beets. For pudding, a pannacotta is set with carrageen moss foraged from the shore outside the hotel, and served with a winter berry compôte.

Chef Arturo Tillo, John O'Toole **Owner** Kay McEvilly & family **Times** 12.30-2.30/6.30-9 Closed 2 Jan-2 Feb, **Prices** Fixed L 2 course €25-€35, Fixed D 3 course €35-€40, Starter €6-€12.75, Main €16.95-€38, Dessert €9.50, Service added 12.5% **Wines** 90 bottles over €20, 4 bottles under €20, 5 by glass **Notes** Sunday L, Vegetarian menu, Dress restrictions, Smart casual, Civ Wed 80 **Seats** 70, Pr/dining room 20 **Children** Portions, Menu **Parking** 30

CLIFDEN   Map 1 A4

Abbeyglen Castle Hotel

◉ French, International

Fresh local produce in a charming old property

☎ 095 21201
Sky Rd
e-mail: info@abbeyglen.ie
dir: N59 from Galway towards Clifden. Hotel 1km from Clifden on Sky Rd

The crenallated Victorian fantasy of Abbeyglen Castle basks in views sweeping from Connemara's Twelve Bens mountains to the shores of Clifden Bay. Ensconced in 12 acres of lovely grounds, it is just a five-minute walk from the bustle and cosy pubs of Clifden village, but you might find it hard to drag yourself away from its classic country-house comforts. In the restaurant at dinner, the décor is bold and bright with artworks on cherry-red walls, crystal chandeliers, and a pianist tinkles away on a grand piano. Expect classic cooking built on excellent local materials. As you'd hope, given the closeness to the briny, fish and seafood makes a good showing - fresh oysters, seafood chowder, or poached salmon with hollandaise - while meat could turn up as slow-roasted suckling pig teamed with braised belly pork, apple chutney, celeriac crisps and a grain mustard reduction. Puddings finish slap in the comfort zone with the likes of chocolate bread-and-butter pudding or rhubarb crumble with crème anglaise.

Chef Kevin Conroy **Owner** Paul Hughes **Times** 7-9 Closed 6 -31 Jan, L all week **Prices** Fixed D 3 course €43-€48, Starter €6.50-€10.95, Main €19.95-€21.50, Dessert €7, Service added 12.5% **Wines** 50 bottles over €20, 8 by glass **Notes** Vegetarian available **Seats** 75 **Parking** 40

GALWAY   Map 1 B3/4

Ardilaun Hotel & Leisure Club

◉ Modern International

Contemporary cooking in a quietly set hotel

☎ 091 521433
Taylor's Hill
e-mail: info@theardilaunhotel.ie
dir: 1m from city centre, towards Salthill on west side of city, near Galway Bay

In a quiet spot on the outskirts of the city towards Galway Bay, The Ardilaun Hotel has been built up around a 19th-century property, with the restaurant looking out on its five acres of grounds. The kitchen takes a European-wide stance, with starters along the lines of smoked haddock and potato cake on spinach with sauce vierge and pickled cucumber, and a salad of crisp pancetta, radish, peas and mozzarella with coriander and green pepper dressing. Well-chosen ingredients go into main courses too: a medley of Galway Bay seafood with a ragoût of sweetcorn, fennel and spring onions and truffle and chive cream, and roast bacon-wrapped chicken breast stuffed with sage and onions on cauliflower purée with mushroom sauce. Lemon meringue pie with berry compôte is a good way to end.

Chef David O'Donnell **Owner** John Ryan
Times 1-2.30/6.30-9.15 Closed 23-27 Dec, L Mon-Sat **Prices** Fixed L 2 course €14.50, Fixed D 3 course €29.50, Service added 10% **Wines** 62 bottles over €20, 9 bottles under €20, 9 by glass **Notes** Sunday L, Vegetarian available, Dress restrictions, Smart casual, Civ Wed 650 **Seats** 180, Pr/dining room 380 **Children** Portions, Menu **Parking** 300

The G Hotel

◎◎ Modern French **NEW**

Ultra-modern cooking in a hotel setting to match

☎ 091 865200
Wellpark, Dublin Rd
e-mail: info@theg.ie

Gigi's restaurant on the ground floor of the ultra-modern town centre hotel looks every inch a 21st-century dining experience. Designed in the main by society milliner Philip Treacy (note the hat-related prints on the walls), it's a riot of dayglo-coloured seats in a sepulchrally lit space with subdued spotlights and candles. Modern Euro-cuisine is the order of the day, with artistically presented dishes appearing on a range of eccentrically shaped plates. A beautifully rendered pearl barley risotto topped with local black pudding and a couple of seared Clew Bay scallops, surrounded by a ribbon of beurre blanc, is a confident opener, followed perhaps by seared breast of crisp-skinned duck, accompanied by a cauliflower fritter and a combined purée of celeriac and sweet potato eased into a hollowed-out fondant potato, with two dressings - one of hazelnut oil, the other a deeply glossy port-based jus. A dish from the Sea section of the menu might be grilled turbot in a spicy mussel and clam broth, garnished with a crisp-textured abalone and beetroot 'tagliatelle'. The architectural complexity of dishes continues through to spectacular desserts such as the banana bavarois.

Chef Bcgis Hervioux **Owner** Edward Haters **Times** 1-3/6-9 Closed 23-26 Dec, L Mon-Sat **Prices** Fixed L 2 course fr €25, Fixed D 3 course fr €55, Starter €7.50-€15, Main €18-€29.50, Dessert €8.50-€10, Service included **Wines** 60 bottles over €20, 14 by glass **Notes** Seasonal menu Mon-Thu 6-7 pm 2,3 course €29.50-€36, Sunday L, Vegetarian available, Civ Wed 100 **Seats** 90 **Children** Portions, Menu **Parking** 200

Park House Hotel & The Park Restaurant

◎ Modern Irish, International ◔

Appealing menu in bustling city-centre hotel

☎ 091 564924
Forster St, Eyre Square
e-mail: parkhousehotel@eircom.net

Standing just off the city's Eyre Square and built of striking pink granite, Park House has been offering high standards of food and accommodation for well over 35 years. Its celebrated Park Restaurant - where paintings of old Galway help keep the past alive - fairly bustles at lunchtime and mellows in the evening. Endearing classical design - in reds and golds with banquette seating and chairs and closely-set tables - suits the surroundings, likewise the traditional-inspired cooking is classically underpinned, while making good use of traceable local ingredients on a menu with broad appeal. Orange- and honey-glazed breast of duckling with a peppercorn sauce, for instance, or prime fillet steak au

poivre to Dublin Bay prawns thermidor. Finish with profiteroles, apple pie or Pavlova.

Chef Robert O'Keefe, Martin Keane **Owner** Eamon Doyle, Kitty Carr **Times** 12-3/6-10 Closed 24-26 Dec **Prices** Fixed L 2 course €15-€30, Fixed D 3 course €32.50-€39.95, Starter €5.65-€12.25, Main €12.50-€28.25, Service optional **Wines** 27 bottles over €20, 56 bottles under €20, 4 by glass **Notes** Early evening menu €32.75, Sunday L, Vegetarian available **Seats** 145, Pr/dining room 45 **Children** Portions, Menu **Parking** 40, Adjacent to hotel

RECESS (SRAITH SALACH)   Map 1 A4

Lough Inagh Lodge

◎ Irish, French

Spectacular scenery and Irish country-house cooking

☎ 095 34706 & 34694
Inagh Valley
e-mail: inagh@iol.ie
dir: From Galway take N344. After 3.5m hotel on right

Right on the shores of Lough Inagh, with Connemara's wild mountains all around, this 19th-century fishing lodge will melt the heart of anyone with an eye for beautiful landscapes. You can fill the daylight hours with fishing the lake and hiking around the Inagh Valley, before returning to the comfy country house for a pre-dinner snifter by an open fire in the lounge or the oak-panelled bar. Top-drawer native ingredients form the cornerstones of the kitchen's efforts, which aim for all-round satisfaction with the likes of smoked salmon with walnuts and raspberry vinaigrette preceding equally straightforward main courses - perhaps roast duck with French beans and cherry sauce, lobster from the lough, or Irish fillet steak with braised red cabbage and onion jus. Finish with Irish artisan cheeses or classic profiteroles with vanilla cream and chocolate sauce.

Times 7-8.45 Closed mid Dec-mid Mar

CO KERRY

CAHERDANIEL (CATHAIR DÓNALL)   Map 1 A2

Derrynane Hotel

◎ Irish, European

Straightforward cooking amid stunning coastal scenery

☎ 066 9475136
e-mail: info@derrynane.com

From its clifftop location amid the magnificent scenery of the Ring of Kerry, the Derrynane has breathtaking coastal views over Kenmare Bay. It's an excellent place for a hotel-based family holiday, with a number of sports facilities and a heated outdoor pool, as well as good for exploring this beautiful area, with the restaurant, where huge windows give those wide sea views, an ideal spot for admiring the sunset. The best of the locality's prime produce finds its way on to the menus, which are clearly devised with the hotel's residents in mind: smoked salmon and cream cheese roulade, or feta, olive and

tomato salad with croûtons, ahead of roast sirloin with bordelaise sauce, or baked fillet of hake with tomato and chive butter. Crowd-pleasing desserts include banoffee pie.

Times 7-9 Closed Oct-mid Apr

DINGLE (AN DAINGEAN)   Map 1 A2

Gormans Clifftop House & Restaurant

◎ Modern, Traditional **NEW** ◔

Clifftop cracker with splendid local produce

☎ 066 9155162 & 083 0033133
Glaise Bheag, Ballydavid (Baile na nGall)
e-mail: info@gormans-clifftophouse.com
dir: R559 to An Mhulrloch, turn right at T-junct, N for 3km

Simplicity is the key to this delightful restaurant with rooms out on the north-western tip of the Dingle Peninsula. The stone-built house perches on the clifftops above Smerwick harbour; this is about as far west as you can expect to eat in Europe, so there's nothing to get in the way of the dining room's sweeping views across the Atlantic. The Gorman family have owned the house since the 18th century, which might explain why chef-proprietor Vincent Gorman has an innate passion for sourcing as much as possible of his materials from the local farms and ports. Produce as spanking fresh as this doesn't need to be messed with, so the menu is appropriately to the point, offering five choices at each stage. You might start with Annascaul black pudding served with traditional potato cakes, glazed apples and grain mustard sauce, and follow with Dingle Bay prawns stir-fried with vegetables, herbs, garlic and white wine, or a Moroccan-style tajine of West Kerry lamb. To finish, there could be stewed rhubarb from the garden topped with a buttery walnut crumble and served with vanilla ice cream.

Chef Vincent Gorman **Owner** Sile & Vincent Gorman **Times** 7-8 Closed Oct-Mar, Sun, L all week **Prices** Fixed D 3 course €35-€45, Starter €6.50-€15.50, Main €17.50-€32.50, Dessert €6.50-€9.50, Service optional **Notes** Vegetarian available **Seats** 30 **Children** Portions **Parking** 25

KENMARE Map 1 B2

La Cascade

◉◉ Modern European V

Waterfall views and striking modern cooking

☎ 06466 41600
Sheen Falls Lodge
e-mail: info@sheenfallslodge.ie
dir: From Kenmare take N71 to Glengarriff. Take 1st left after suspension bridge. 1m from Kenmare

Surrounded by 300 acres of woodland and gardens, Sheen Falls Lodge, once the summer home of the Marquis of Lansdowne, is perched on a high promontory over Kenmare Bay. La Cascade is the name of its restaurant, a light, split-level, high-ceilinged room of some grandeur, and it's aptly named, with picture windows overlooking the falls (floodlit at night). The menus are as sophisticated as the surroundings would suggest, the enthusiastic kitchen working around a modern European repertoire. Lobster with truffle cream and asparagus salad makes a luxurious starter, contrasting with the full-on flavours of glazed sweetbreads with apple chutney. Main courses are never too complicated, so roast loin of lamb is accompanied by sun-dried tomato jus, broad beans, sautéed artichokes and marjoram-spiked potatoes, and sea bass fillet in a light beurre blanc comes with cucumber sautéed with dill, grilled potatoes and a prawn and pancetta 'hedgehog'. A champagne sorbet may appear after the starter, and meals might end with a variation on a theme of raspberries or chocolate, the latter with blackberry sorbet and hazelnut ice cream.

Chef Heiko Riebandt **Owner** Sheen Falls Estate Ltd
Times 7-9.30 Closed 2 Jan-1 Feb, L all week
Prices Starter €9.50-€18, Main €25.50-€34.50, Dessert €9-€13.50, Service optional **Wines** 793 bottles over €20, 6 bottles under €20, 16 by glass **Notes** Tasting menu available, Vegetarian menu, Dress restrictions, Smart casual (jacket), no jeans or T-shirts, Civ Wed 150
Seats 120, Pr/dining room 40 **Children** Portions, Menu
Parking 75

KILLARNEY Map 1 B2

Cahernane House Hotel

◉◉ Modern European, International

Modern country-house cooking in a tranquil setting

☎ 06466 31895
Muckross Rd
e-mail: info@cahernane.com
dir: From Killarney follow signs for Kenmare, then from Muckross Rd over bridge. Hotel signed on right. Hotel 1m from town centre

On its own private estate on the edge of the Killarney National Park, Cahernane House was once the seat of the Earls of Pembroke. Approached via a long avenue of trees, it's in a beautiful, secluded setting, yet it's only a 10-minute walk to the town centre. Inside, the house shows its 17th-century credentials with original fireplaces, ornate ceilings and ancestral oil portraits. The traditional style continues into the Herbert Room restaurant, an elegant space with sparkling silverware on the tables, crisp napery and a view of the lake and immaculately-kept grounds. Menu descriptions may sound simple, but this belies the attention to detail and sharp technique employed by head chef David Norris and his team. Slow-roasted breast of pork, Sneem black pudding, spiced apple purée and red wine jus might feature among starters, followed by poached fillet of sea bass with Chinese leaves, jasmine rice, tomato and cumin. Desserts continue the modern country-house theme - perhaps chocolate tart with passionfruit sorbet and roasted bananas.

Times 12-14.30/7-9.30 Closed Jan-Feb, L all week ex by arrangement

Killeen House Hotel

◉ Modern International

Tried-and-true cooking in a homely hotel

☎ 06466 31711 & 087 284 3814
Aghadoe, Lakes of Killarney
e-mail: charming@indigo.ie
dir: 4m from Killarney town centre, in Aghadoe, just off Dingle Road

This charming little red-and-white hotel stands in pretty gardens on the edge of honeypot Killarney, handy for sightseeing, hiking, or golfing on the local courses. The family-run vibe makes for a relaxed stay, and the kitchen's uncomplicated style of country-house cooking is a further bonus. Head chef Paul O'Gorman has been at the culinary helm since the 1990s so knows where to get his hands on the best local produce to deliver menus that might kick off with lemon, dill and caper-infused rillettes of fresh and smoked salmon with cucumber relish, before proceeding to mains like pan-seared monkfish medallions with sun-dried tomato and black olive crushed potatoes, and fresh crab béarnaise. For afters, how about a luscious pecan and chocolate fudge pudding with chocolate and marshmallow sauce and vanilla ice cream?

Times 6.30-9.30 Closed 20 Oct-20 Apr, L all week

Save on Hotels. Book at **theAA.com/hotel**

CO KERRY – CO KILDARE 665 | IRELAND

The Lake Hotel

◉ Traditional European ◉

Lough views and wide-ranging menus

☎ 064 6631035
On the Shore, Muckross Rd
e-mail: info@lakehotel.com
web: www.lakehotelkillarney.com
dir: 2 km from town centre on N71 Muckross Rd

The luxury hotel, on the shore of Lough Lein, might be on a grand scale, but staff are personable and friendly. The Castlelough Restaurant has wonderful views over the lough to the mountains beyond, and an ambitious menu with some international touches. The kitchen uses mostly local produce, Annascaul black pudding in a starter with potato, onion marmalade, a poached quail's egg and hollandaise, for example, and black sole fillet is given the tempura treatment served with mango and radish salad, lemon mayonnaise and chilli jam. Well-composed main courses have included a summery dish of seared sea trout with marjoram-crushed peas, broad beans and samphire and tomato confit; note gluten-free and healthier options are flagged on the menu, one of which is not rich chocolate délice with hazelnut ice cream and passionfruit cream.

Chef Paul O'Connor **Owner** The Huggard Family
Times 12-4.30/6.30-9 Closed Dec-Jan, L all week
Prices Fixed L 2 course €18-€22, Fixed D 3 course €25-€35, Starter €5-€12, Main €18-€25, Dessert €8-€12, Service optional **Wines** 61 bottles over €20, 5 by glass
Notes Signature tasting menu available, Sunday L, Vegetarian available, Civ Wed 150 **Seats** 90, Pr/dining room 120 **Children** Portions, Menu **Parking** 150

See advert opposite

KILLORGLIN | Map 1 A2

Carrig House Country House & Restaurant

◉ Modern Irish, European

Fine dining with expansive lough views

☎ 066 9769100
Caragh Lake
e-mail: info@carrighouse.com

Carrig is a lovingly restored Victorian country manor in acres of colourful woodland gardens with views across Caragh Lake to the Kerry Mountains. Inside, the genteel house is done out in period style, with turf fires sizzling in cosy, chintzy lounges, while the dining room is the very image of 19th-century chic, all William Morris wallpapers, swagged curtains, polished floorboards, and formally laid tables. The cooking, on the other hand, takes a more up-to-date approach, lining up superb local ingredients and sending them to finishing school: crab could get a modish three-way treatment as ravioli, soup and pasty, and might be followed by Skeganore duck breast with vanilla and lime potato purée, and sweet port and brandy jus. For dessert, maybe prune and Armagnac crème brûlée.

Times 7-9

TRALEE | Map 1 A2

Ballyseede Castle

◉ Traditional European **NEW**

Appealing food in a historic castle

☎ 066 7125799
e-mail: info@ballyseedecastle.com
dir: On N21 just after N21/N22 junct

Crenallated and turreted, and with a pedigree dating back to the 1590s, Ballyseede certainly delivers the full-dress stately home experience. With its deep green walls, heavy swagged-back drapes, crystal chandelier and gilt-framed oil paintings, the fine-dining O'Connell Restaurant makes a suitably plush setting for food that calls on top-class Irish materials for its crowd-pleasing menus, which essay a broad sweep from pan-fried tiger prawns with garlic butter as a simple opener, to a main course that sees roast suprême of chicken partnered with Irish cider velouté, foie gras risotto and white truffle oil. For fish fans, there could be roast loin of cod with mussel, chorizo, black olive and roast tomato cream sauce, and comfort-oriented desserts such as sticky toffee pudding with butterscotch sauce and vanilla ice cream will help to fill any holes.

Owner Marnie & Rory O'Sullivan **Times** 12.30-2.30/7-9 Closed Jan-3 Mar, L Mon-Sat **Prices** Fixed L 3 course fr €28.95, Fixed D 3 course fr €35 **Wines** 4 by glass
Notes Sunday L, Vegetarian available, Civ Wed 130 **Seats** 40, Pr/dining room 70 **Children** Portions, Menu **Parking** 180

CO KILDARE

NAAS | Map 1 D4

Virginia Restaurant at Maudlins House Hotel

◉◉ Modern French

Modish menus in comfortable country-house hotel

☎ 045 896999
Dublin Rd
e-mail: info@maudlinshousehotel.ie
dir: Exit N7 approaching large globe, at rdbt head towards Naas, restaurant 200mtrs on right

Beautiful and sensitive restoration and updating has brought all the creature comforts and décor of a modern-day country-house hotel to Maudlins, a creeper-swathed one-time Victorian residence on the edge of town. The Virginia Restaurant - a series of four elegant rooms at the front of the house - perfectly fits with the new image, where the kitchen's accomplished, clear-flavoured well-dressed modern Irish-French cooking - conjured from prime seasonal produce - takes centre stage. Expect the likes of roast duck breast accompanied by fondant potato, parsnip purée and parsnip cone, and a spinach and thyme jus, or for a lighter touch, perhaps pan-seared sea bass fillet with buttered spring cabbage and chive and vegetable velouté. Finish in flamboyant style with a Kahlua pannacotta, Amaretto jelly, orange tuile and honeycomb.

Times 12.30-9.30

STRAFFAN | Map 1 C/D4

Barberstown Castle

◉◉ Irish, French ◉

Classic cooking in a 13th-century castle

☎ 01 6288157
e-mail: info@barberstowncastle.ie
dir: R406, follow signs for Barberstown

Close to Dublin city centre and the airport, Barberstown Castle presents a fascinating timeline running through eight centuries of history from its 13th-century crenallated tower to wings added by Elizabethan and Victorian inhabitants, which now house the elegant dining rooms. You can take oodles of period character as read: amid walls hung with tapestries, wooden and flagstoned floors, and throne-like wooden chairs at candlelit, linen-clad tables, dinner is always a bit special, and staff make sure it all ticks along in a smooth and professional manner. Classical country-house influences are to the fore - the man directing the culinary action is French, after all - in a repertoire built on prime local materials and a pitch-perfect grasp of how flavours and textures work together. Expect main courses such as chargrilled Irish beef fillet with fondant potato, baby spinach, celeriac purée and foie gras sauce, or wild sea bass matched with scallops, fennel compôte, vine tomatoes, and star anise cream. Bringing up the rear are
continued

STRAFFAN *continued*

desserts that might include buttermilk pannacotta with Irish rhubarb compôte and jelly.

Chef Bertrand Malabat **Owner** Kenneth Healy
Times 7.30-10 Closed 24-26 Dec, Jan, Sun-Thu, L all week **Prices** Fixed D 3 course €45, Tasting menu €65, Service optional **Wines** 4 by glass **Notes** Tasting menu 6 course, Vegetarian available, Civ Wed 200 **Seats** 120, Pr/dining room 65 **Parking** 200

CO KILKENNY

KILKENNY   Map 1 C3

Riverside Restaurant

⚜ Modern, Traditional

Historic castle setting for ambitious cooking

☎ 056 7723388
Kilkenny River Court Hotel, The Bridge, John St
e-mail: info@rivercourthotel.com
dir: In town centre, opposite castle

The Kilkenny River Court Hotel is superlatively placed on the bank of the River Nore. Its Riverside Restaurant overlooks the illuminated battlements and towers of 12th-century Kilkenny Castle through large windows - it's a splendid spot. An elaborate international menu features something for all tastes, be they for potted freshwater baby shrimps and crabmeat scented with dill and lime wrapped in smoked salmon, with caperberry and lime dressing, or a main-course breast of chicken with a squash and feta stuffing. Or even dessert of individual rustic Orange Pippin tarte Tatin topped with home-made gingerbread ice cream and Grand Marnier soaked apricots.

Chef Gerrard Dunne **Owner** Xavier McAuliffe
Times 12.30-3/6-9.30 Closed Xmas, L Mon-Sat, D Sun
Prices Fixed D 3 course fr €29.50, Service optional
Wines 37 bottles over €20, 2 bottles under €20, 4 by glass **Notes** Fixed price D 2 course €29.50, Vegetarian available, Civ Wed 260 **Seats** 80 **Children** Portions, Menu **Parking** 120

THOMASTOWN   Map 1 C3

Kendals

⚜ Modern

A taste of France beside the golf course

☎ 056 7773000
Mount Juliet Hotel
e-mail: info@mountjuliet.ie
dir: Just outside Thomastown S on N9

The name might not have a cross-Channel ring to it, but French brasserie classics are the name of the game at Kendals, which is the more casual venue at the swanky 18th-century Mount Juliet Hotel. Housed in the estate's converted stables - now the golf clubhouse - the setting is light and airy in the day, looking over the fairways through large windows, and more romantic when it is candlelit for dinner. Top-class local ingredients underpin the repertoire of French brasserie classics, which could kick off with salade Lyonnaise, beef carpaccio, or salt-cod brandade with marinated cherry tomatoes and curly endive, ahead of local Slaney lamb, slow-cooked for 15 hours and served with pommes Anna, Chantenay carrots and peas, and thyme jus. Finish with banana tarte Tatin with home-made rum and raisin ice cream. If you want to trade up on another visit, the posh option is the Lady Helen Restaurant (see entry below).

Chef Cormac Rowe **Owner** Mount Juliet **Times** 6-9.30 Closed Mon & Wed (seasonal) **Wines** 54 bottles over €20, 10 by glass **Notes** Early bird menu 6-7pm 3 course €25, Vegetarian available, Civ Wed 160 **Seats** 70 **Children** Portions, Menu **Parking** 200

The Lady Helen Restaurant

⚜⚜⚜ *– see below*

The Lady Helen Restaurant

  ⚜⚜⚜

THOMASTOWN   Map 1 C3

Modern Irish **V**

Innovative seasonal cooking in a Georgian manor

☎ 056 7773000
Mount Juliet Hotel
e-mail: info@mountjuliet.ie
dir: M7 from Dublin, N9 towards Waterford, exit at junct 9/Danesfort for hotel

The Mount Juliet Hotel is an 18th-century manor house of great opulence, full of original plaster mouldings and deep windows overlooking the 1,500 acres of parkland in which it stands. It's a grand backdrop for some innovative cooking, based on local seasonal supplies, including the kitchen's own herb garden, and which is seen to its best effect in the full-dress Lady Helen dining room. Presentations are creative and minutely detailed, and yet nothing feels overworked. Three slices of Duncannon lobster, wrapped in nori and topped with dried coral and salt flakes, sit on a jellied tomato consommé, accompanied by a quenelle of rich lobster mayonnaise. That expressive opener may be followed by a trio of servings of Gloucestershire Old Spot pork: seared loin, shredded confit shoulder mixed with apple on an open raviolo, and a mosaic of lightly caramelised belly with black pudding - the unifying factor a wonderful glossy veal jus sweetened with apple. A summer treat to finish might be a fragile buttermilk pannacotta surrounded by strawberries in Kirsch, strawberry jelly and a silky strawberry sorbet, dressed in strawberry consommé poured on at the table.

Chef Cormac Rowe **Owner** Kileen Investments
Times 6.30-9.45 Closed L all week, D Sun, Tue
Prices Tasting menu €65, Service optional
Wines 125 bottles over €20, 18 bottles under €20, 10 by glass **Notes** Fixed D 4 course, Tasting menu 8 course, Vegetarian menu, Dress restrictions, No jeans or T-shirts, Civ Wed 100 **Seats** 60, Pr/dining room 80 **Children** Portions, Menu **Parking** 200

CO LEITRIM

MOHILL   Map 1 C4

Lough Rynn Castle

◉ Modern, Traditional Irish V ✪

Contemporary flavours in a peaceful location

☎ 071 9632700
e-mail: enquiries@loughrynn.ie
dir: N4 (Dublin to Sligo), hotel 8km off N4 & 2km from
Mohill

Beside the lough, with a golf course in its 300-acre
grounds, Lough Rynn Castle is quite a pile, the ancestral
seat of the Earl of Leitrim. The Sandstone Restaurant is
in a separate building, a strikingly decorated room
featuring stripped sandstone (hence the name, of course)
and tall-backed upholstered dining chairs. The
enterprising menu bursts with appealing ideas, from
starters such as an assiette of smoked seafood (trout
cheesecake, salmon and curry roulade, and haddock
velouté) to main courses like cannon of lamb wrapped in
spinach mousse, accompanied by garlic pannacotta,
sautéed mushrooms and noodles, and pan-fried Dover
sole with caper butter, culminating in puddings like
banana tarte Tatin with caramel ice cream.

Chef Clare O'Leary **Owner** Hanly Group **Times** 12-6-9.30
Closed L Mon-Sat **Prices** Fixed L 3 course €27-€32, Fixed
D 4 course €42-€55, Starter €7.25-€15.50, Main €21.50-
€75, Dessert €8.95-€16, Service optional **Wines** all
bottles over €20, 12 by glass **Notes** Sunday L, Vegetarian
menu, Civ Wed 350 **Seats** 90, Pr/dining room 10
Children Portions, Menu

CO LIMERICK

ADARE   Map 1 B3

Dunraven Arms

◉◉ International ✪

Classical and modern thinking in a seductive hotel

☎ 061 605900
Main St
e-mail: reservations@dunravenhotel.com
dir: N18 from Limerick, change to N21

This thatched one-time coaching inn in a chocolate-box-
pretty village is these days an intimate country-house
hotel imbued with Irish cosiness and charm. It's a lovely
setting, seducing with its well-preened gardens and the
Maigue Restaurant, which offers an endearingly
traditional vibe across a series of rooms kitted out in
deep crimson with sparkling crystal chandeliers and crisp
white linen. The cooking sits comfortably with the
country-house theme, balancing the classical and the
more modish with standout quality regional produce.
Rump of spring lamb is served with crushed pea and
mint, roast garlic, fondant potato and lamb jus, while a
vegetarian alternative might be Bluebell Falls goats'
cheese strudel teamed with baby spinach, sun-dried
tomato, orzo pasta and balsamic vinaigrette. Finish in

traditional vogue with Queen of Puddings or Baileys
cheesecake.

Chef David Hayes **Owner** Bryan & Louis Murphy
Times 12.30-2.30/7-9.30 Closed Xmas, L Mon-Sat, D
24-26 Dec **Prices** Food prices not confirmed for 2013.
Please telephone for details **Wines** 25 bottles over €20,
25 bottles under €20, 6 by glass **Notes** Vegetarian
available, Dress restrictions, Smart casual **Seats** 80, Pr/
dining room 30 **Children** Portions **Parking** 60

LIMERICK   Map 1 B3

Carlton Castletroy Park Hotel

◉ Modern Irish

Welcoming modern hotel serving Irish produce

☎ 061 335566
Dublin Rd
e-mail: events.castletroy@carlton.ie
dir: On Dublin road, 3km from city, opposite University of
Limerick

The modern four-star Carlton Castletroy Park Hotel on the
outskirts of Limerick sits next to the university campus -
just cross a bridge over the Shannon and you're off into
133 hectares of wooded parkland to walk up an appetite.
In the smart McLaughlin's Restaurant, full-length
windows on two sides flood the space with light, and
uniformed staff keep things light-hearted and chatty. The
kitchen tacks a modern course underpinned by clear
French influences and plenty of produce from rather
closer to home - a formula that could see local scallops
teamed with rare breed pork belly, sweet pea foam and a
yuzu and truffle vinaigrette, followed by another surf and
turf duo such as saddle of rabbit and Dublin bay prawns
with Serrano ham, Biarritz potato with wilted spinach and
smoked garlic beurre blanc. Irish Munster cheeses could
round off the show, unless you fancy something homely
and sweet - maybe warm treacle tart with vanilla bean
ice cream and custard.

Chef Gavin Horgan **Owner** Carlton Hotel Group
Times 12.30-3/6.30-9 Closed Xmas, Mon-Wed, L Thu-Sat,
D Sun **Prices** Fixed L 2 course fr €19.50, Fixed D 3 course
fr €25, Service optional **Wines** 10 bottles over €20,
1 bottle under €20, 10 by glass **Notes** Pre-theatre 2
course incl wine €59 for 2, L 3 course Sun, Vegetarian
available, Civ Wed 300 **Seats** 80, Pr/dining room 120
Children Portions, Menu **Parking** 100

Limerick Strand Hotel

◉ Modern International **NEW**

River views and comforting food

☎ 061 421800 & 421870
Ennis St
e-mail: info@strandlimerick.ie
dir: On the Shannon side of Sorsfield Bridge, on River
Shannon

The aptly-named River Restaurant of the spanking-new
contemporary Limerick Strand Hotel is the place to head
for dining with the best views in town. Floor-to-ceiling
glass walls mean everyone gets a view of the Shannon
flowing by to go with a well-prepared and presented
repertoire of straightforward modern European food.
There's an abundance of splendid raw materials in these
parts, and they find their way into dishes such as beef
carpaccio with rocket, parmesan, horseradish crisp and
citrus vinaigrette, while mains run to mixed grills, steaks
or herb-crusted rack of new season Kerry lamb with
fondant potato, carrot gratin, and red wine jus. For
pudding, perhaps a refreshing lemon vacherin with
raspberry sauce.

Chef Tom Flavin **Times** 12-3/6-10 **Prices** Fixed D 4 course
fr €27, Starter €4.95-€8.50, Main €14.95-€29.95, Dessert
€4.95-€8, Service optional **Wines** 35 bottles over €20,
4 bottles under €20, 4 by glass **Notes** Early bird menu 2
course €19.95, 3 course €24.95, Sunday L, Vegetarian
available, Civ Wed 400 **Seats** 180, Pr/dining room 450
Children Portions, Menu **Parking** 200

CO LOUTH

CARLINGFORD   Map 1 D4

Ghan House

◉◉ Modern Irish ✪

Ambitious modern cooking in a country-house setting

☎ 042 9373682
e-mail: info@ghanhouse.com
web: www.ghanhouse.com
dir: M1 junct 18 signed Carlingford, 5mtrs on left after
50kph speed sign

Just a hop skip and a jump, or 50 metres if you prefer
precision, from medieval Carlingford's town gate, 18th-
century Ghan House is a charming family-run operation
set in secluded walled gardens, with delightful views of
the Mourne Mountains and Carlingford Lough. The dining

continued

CARLINGFORD *continued*

room basks in these views as well as a soothing ambience, orchestrated ably by pleasant and professional staff. If you're keen on the concept of terroir, try this for size: herbs are picked fresh from the garden, fish and shellfish come courtesy of the lough, and lamb and beef are reared on the surrounding hills, and everything is made in-house. Menus cover a lot of ground, starting with the likes of millefeuille of wood pigeon with woodland mushroom fricassée, and wholegrain apple and mustard jus, and on through mains starring Cooley lamb - hay-cooked rack partnered by crisp-fried breast, carrot fondant and purée, mint jelly and jus. For dessert there might be pear tarte Tatin with fennel ice cream and Amaretto sabayon.

Chef Robert Read **Owner** Joyce & Paul Carroll **Times** 1-6-11 Closed 24-26 & 31 Dec, 1-2 Jan, 1 day a week (varies), L Mon-Sat (open most Sun or by arrangement) **Prices** Fixed L 3 course €25, Fixed D 3 course fr €40, Tasting menu €27.50, Service optional **Wines** 59 bottles over €20, 13 by glass **Notes** Tasting menu 6 course Mon-Thu 5.30-8.30, Sunday L, Vegetarian available, Civ Wed 45 **Seats** 50, Pr/dining room 34 **Children** Portions **Parking** 24

CO MAYO

BALLINA   Map 1 B4

Belleek Castle

🏵 Traditional **NEW** V 🍴

Special occasion dining in historic castle

☎ 096 22400 & 21878
Belleek
e-mail: info@belleekcastle.com

This pocket-sized stately home certainly looks castle-like, but it is actually a Victorian folly whose dainty 19th-century gables and skinny turrets wouldn't put up much of a fight if shots were fired in anger. In fact, the only popping noises to be heard are caused by the opening of champagne bottles at one of the many weddings taking place. Inside, oak panelling, coffered ceilings, chandeliers, and crimson walls hung with tapestries make for a suitably faux-medieval baronial setting in the dining room, where well-sourced ingredients form the building blocks of a straightforward country-house menu. Boneless roasted quail with sage stuffing and a rosemary reduction could start the show - and a show it indeed is, if you go for the 'Drunken Bullock' signature dish, a slab of local beef fillet impaled on an antique Spanish sabre and flambéed theatrically at the table with Jameson's whiskey, then served with roasted root vegetables and pepper jus.

Chef Stephen Lenahan **Owner** Paul Marshal Doran **Times** 1-6/5.30-9.30 Closed Xmas & Jan, **Prices** Fixed L 3 course €38-€65.50, Starter €8.90-€12.90, Main €18.90-€32.50, Dessert €8.90-€12.50, Service optional **Wines** 47 bottles over €20, 4 bottles under €20, 5 by glass **Notes** Early bird menu 3 course €28, Gourmet menu €65.50, Vegetarian menu, Civ Wed 200 **Seats** 55, Pr/dining room 30 **Children** Portions, Menu **Parking** 90

Mount Falcon Estate

🏵🏵 Traditional French, International 🍴

Polished cooking using exemplary local materials

☎ 096 74472
Mount Falcon Country House, Foxford Rd
e-mail: info@mountfalcon.com
dir: On N26, 6m from Foxford & 3m from Ballina. Hotel on left

On the banks of the River Moy, the Mount Falcon is a splendidly baronial-looking pile sitting in its own 100-acre estate, and in its Kitchen Restaurant, it has a dining address that elevates it above the country-house norm. It will come as no surprise that the restaurant is in the old kitchen and pantry of this grand old house, and it is done out with a good degree of style, with linen-clad tables and food-related prints on the walls. Head chef Philippe Farineau hails from France and has a passion for cooking - in a mostly French classical style - with local and regional ingredients. The wares of small-scale and artisan producers and suppliers are bolstered by home-grown stuff (from the kitchen's own poly-tunnel). Start, perhaps, with an assiette of local seafood which includes salmon rillette, glazed oyster, gravad lax and a crab beignet, and move on to loin of venison served with a venison sausage, leek and cep tart, celeriac and cauliflower purée, finished with a game jus. End in fine style with a stunningly presented plate dedicated to the pear: poached in saffron syrup, in a tart with almond, and a light pear mousse.

Chef Philippe Farineau **Owner** Alan Maloney **Times** 6.30-9 Closed Xmas, L Mon-Sat **Prices** Fixed L 2 course €28.50, Starter €8-€13, Main €19-€29, Dessert €7.50-€13, Service optional **Wines** 140 bottles over €20, 6 bottles under €20, 12 by glass **Notes** Fixed L 5 course €49-€55, Sunday L, Vegetarian available, Dress restrictions, Smart dress **Seats** 70, Pr/dining room 30 **Children** Portions, Menu **Parking** 100

The Pier Restaurant

🏵🏵 Modern

Modern cooking in a striking venue

☎ 096 23500
The Ice House Hotel, The Quay Rd
e-mail: chill@theicehouse.ie

As its name suggests, The Ice House Hotel was built in the Victorian period as a chilled warehouse for storing fish, now a designer-led hotel for the 21st century. The back of The Pier occupies part of the original building, while the front is in a boxy-looking modernist space of glass and timber dramatically sited on the River Moy with views over to the woods opposite. Prime ingredients are to the fore - Atlantic brown trout, say, Connemara hill lamb (infused with liquorice, braised and served with fennel jam, new season's peas and broad beans, and pommes Anna) - and with-it ideas litter the menu. Seafood figures large; a mini version of fish and chips to start, say, or sautéed Dublin Bay prawns with squid ink fettuccine. Main-course fillet of beef comes with its cocoa-braised cheek and an oxtail croquette, served with smoked potato purée and sauce bordelaise.

Times 12-6.30-10.30 Closed 24-27 Dec

CONG   Map 1 B4

The George V Dining Room

🏵🏵 Traditional European, International V 🍴

Impeccable cooking in magnificent castle

☎ 094 9546003
Ashford Castle
e-mail: ashford@ashford.ie
dir: In Cross, turn left at church onto R345 signed Cong. Turn left at hotel sign & continue through castle gates

The huge castle by the lough certainly makes an impression. It was once the Guinness family estate, which accounts for its opulent interior, with the restaurant, a splendid room with chandeliers and panelling, specially designed for George V's visit. Dinner here is an occasion, with formal service (though staff are friendly enough), a roast of the day - perhaps rack of pork - still carved from a trolley, for example. Pedigree produce can be expected, including luxuries - foie gras three ways in a starter, and as an accompaniment to seared beef fillet with truffled potatoes - and techniques are razor-sharp: reed-roasted rack of lamb, cooked perfectly pink. Elsewhere, the menu covers quite a span, with go-ahead starters such as roast quail with apricot, tonka bean and whiskey stuffing and toffee dressing, preceding fillet of cod with black pudding crumble and apple chutney, then chocolate soufflé.

Chef Stefan Matz **Owner** Edward Holdings **Times** 7-9.30 Closed L all week **Prices** Fixed L 3 course €39, Fixed D 4 course €67, Starter €12-€19, Main €26-€32, Dessert €10-€12, Service added 15% **Wines** 600 bottles over €20, 12 by glass **Notes** Vegetarian menu, Dress restrictions, Jacket & tie, Civ Wed 166 **Seats** 166, Pr/dining room 44 **Children** Portions, Menu **Parking** 115

Save on Hotels. Book at **theAA.com/hotel**

CO MAYO 669 **IRELAND**

Mulranny Park Hotel

◉ Modern V ♨

Local produce and dramatic Atlantic views

☎ 098 36000
e-mail: info@mulrannyparkhotel.ie
web: www.mulrannyparkhotel.ie
dir: R311 from Castlebar to Newport onto N59. Hotel on
right

This smart modern restaurant in a refurbished Victorian
railway hotel benefits from breathtaking views across
Clew Bay and out to sea. Unsurprisingly window tables
are worth their weight in gold while professional service
is underpinned by a genuine friendliness. Classically-
based cooking lets its hair down in the presentation
stakes but make no mistake, this is sound cooking using
well-sourced, local ingredients. You might be offered
chilled Irish Cashel Blue cheese and Guinness parfait,
tomato and mint chutney and pickled pear, followed by a
perfectly cooked baked suprême of organic Clare Island
salmon, crab and chive orzo, aubergine caviar and cep
jus. Honey and yoghurt pannacotta is a delicate finale.

Chef Ollie O'Regan **Owner** Tom Bohan & Tom Duggan
Times 12-4/6.30-9 Closed Jan, **Prices** Food prices not
confirmed for 2013. Please telephone for details
Wines 38 bottles over €20, 7 bottles under €20, 4 by
glass **Notes** Sunday L, Vegetarian menu, Civ Wed 100
Seats 100, Pr/dining room 50 **Children** Portions, Menu
Parking 200

Bluewave Restaurant

◉ Modern European ♨

Sea views and imaginatively treated local produce

☎ 098 29000
Carlton Atlantic Coast Hotel, The Quay
e-mail: info@atlanticcoasthotel.com
dir: From Westport take coast road towards Louisburgh
for 1m. Hotel on harbour on left

Careful restoration has brought an 18th-century mill into
a boutique hotel. It's on the harbour looking over Clew
Bay, the Bluewave Restaurant placed on the top floor to
give the best sea views. There's plenty of exemplary
seafood in evidence: starters of crab tian with chilli
mayonnaise, or seared scallops with white pudding and
cumin-infused carrot purée, then salmon and smoked
haddock in a risotto flavoured with lemongrass and
chives. Elsewhere may be baked goats' cheese with
Parma ham and balsamic-dressed strawberries, and
chargrilled beef fillet with blue cheese fondant potato
and Portobello mushrooms, with, capping things off, fruit
pannacotta, or apple meringue pie with vanilla ice cream.

Chef John Elannelly **Owner** Carlton Hotel Group
Times 6.30-9.15 Closed 20-27 Dec, L all week
Prices Fixed D 3 course €39, Starter €6.95-€10.95, Main
€19.95-€27.95, Dessert €7.95-€9.95, Service optional
Wines 12 bottles over €20, 14 bottles under €20, 12 by
glass **Notes** Early bird menu available 6.30-7.30pm,
Sunday L, Vegetarian available, Civ Wed 140 **Seats** 85,
Pr/dining room 140 **Children** Portions, Menu **Parking** 80

Hotel Westport Leisure, Spa & Conference

◉ Irish, European NEW ♨

Exemplary local produce at riverside hotel

☎ 098 25122
Newport Rd
e-mail: reservations@hotelwestport.ie
web: www.hotelwestport.ie
dir: N5 to Westport. Right at end of Castlebar St, 1st right
before bridge, right at lights, left before church. Follow to
end of street

The restaurant at this large hotel in seven acres is a
spacious room overlooking the Carrowbeg River, with
plush carpets and seating under an ornate ceiling. The
kitchen works in tandem with its providers to use what is
best from each season, seen in pink roast leg of lamb,
carved to order, with a well-flavoured red wine and
rosemary jus, with sweet carrots, red cabbage and
colcannon, and grilled fillet of locally-landed hake with a
simple beurre blanc. Among starters, confit duck leg,
meltingly tender, is plated on creamy celeriac mash with
contrasting bitter orange sauce, and a trio of local oysters
are baked in a herb crust. For pudding, go for 'very berry'
trifle with mascarpone custard, or crème brûlée.

Chef Stephen Fitzmaurice **Owner** Cathal Hughes
Times 1-2.30/6-9.30 **Prices** Fixed L 3 course €21.50,
Fixed D 4 course fr €32.50, Starter €4.50-€5.80, Main
€17.50-€19.50, Dessert €4.50-€5.75, Service optional
Wines 37 bottles over €20, 10 by glass **Notes** Sunday L,
Vegetarian available, Civ Wed 200 **Seats** 120
Children Portions, Menu **Parking** 220

Knockranny House Hotel

◉◉ Modern International

Fresh culinary ideas in a luxurious hotel setting

☎ 098 28600
e-mail: info@khh.ie
dir: On N5 (Dublin to Castlebar road), hotel on left before
entering Westport

Opening in the 1990s in a splendidly tranquil setting on
the west coast, Knockranny enjoys commanding views of
the mountain pilgrimage site of Croagh Patrick and the
many-islanded Clew Bay. Its split-level dining room, La
Fougère, takes full advantage of this seductive setting,
with elegant furnishings and appointments and
confident, formally attired staff. The kitchen works
seasonally to produce appealingly presented modern
dishes. Langoustines from the Bay outside the windows
turn up with a fine tortellini of earthy mushrooms in an
accurately seasoned seafood bisque with chervil jelly.
Next up could be roast pork tenderloin wrapped in caul,
served with a thin cigar of black pudding encased in filo,
sharply pickled sauerkraut, parsnip purée and an apple
paste. Similar contrasts of sweet and sour are mobilised
for a dessert of parfait and purée of rhubarb, served with
buttery shortbread, rich vanilla anglaise and a rapidly
vanishing yoghurt foam.

Times 6.30-9.30 Closed Xmas, L Mon-Sat (open selected
Sun)

CO MEATH

KILMESSAN
Map 1 D5

The Station House Hotel

◉ European, Mediterranean

Country-house dishes in a former railway station

☎ 046 9025239
e-mail: info@stationhousehotel.ie
dir: From Dublin N3 junct 6 to Dunshaughlin, R125 to Kilmessan

No passenger trains have puffed along the disappeared line from Dublin to Kilmessan since the 1940s, although the town's railway station lives on as a characterful hotel set in 12 acres of landscaped gardens. The old station master's office and waiting rooms now house the Signal Restaurant, a spruce traditional venue with linen-clothed tables and elegant country-house charm. The kitchen takes an eclectic approach, catering to a strong local fan base who come for a wide-ranging repertoire of comforting classics. Kick off with a creamy wild mushrooms risotto served with crushed pine nuts, pesto, and shaved parmesan, and follow that with herb and olive oil-marinated chicken suprême with roasted red pepper stuffing, sautéed celery, and cranberry jus. Great pastry skills are worth travelling for, displayed here in a deep dish apple pie with almonds and crème anglaise.

Chef David Mulvihill **Owner** Chris & Thelma Slattery **Times** 12.30-4.30/5-10.30 **Prices** Fixed L 3 course €12.95-€19.95, Fixed D 3 course €26.95, Starter €5.95-€8.95, Main €17.50-€26.95, Dessert €5.95, Service optional **Wines** 43 bottles over €20, 3 bottles under €20, 6 by glass **Notes** Fixed D 5 course €24.95-€44.95, Sunday L, Vegetarian available, Civ Wed 180 **Seats** 90, Pr/dining room 180 **Children** Portions, Menu **Parking** 200

SLANE
Map 1 D4

Tankardstown

◉ Modern, Irish **NEW** ☺

Modern Irish cooking in a classy rustic setting

☎ 041 9824621
e-mail: info@tankardstown.ie
dir: N51 (Navan to Slane road), turn directly opposite main entrance to Slane Castle, signed Kells. Continue for 5km

At the heart of the Tankardstown estate is a handsome Georgian manor house and the stylishly rustic Brabazon restaurant, housed in a converted stone outbuilding. In fine weather, the lavender-scented garden terrace is an irresistible spot for alfresco dining, or through the French doors, the dining room features a central hearth, flagstoned floors and exposed stone walls. The kitchen hauls in ingredients from the walled organic gardens and the estate's flock of hens, as well as top-class local and seasonal materials from a trusty network of suppliers, and treats them simply in classic combinations given a modern spin - Scotch egg is made with shredded wild rabbit, and served with broad beans and peas, while a main-course assiette of pork delivers roast loin, braised cheek, beech-smoked belly, orange-glazed sticky rib, and local black pudding served with pork and Calvados jus. A dessert of strawberry and rhubarb trifle evokes childhood picnic memories with its accompaniment of home-made lemonade with a straw.

Chef Richard Luckey **Owner** Patricia & Brian Conroy **Times** 12-4/6-9 Closed 3 days Xmas, Mon-Tue, L Wed-Sat **Prices** Starter €8-€9.50, Main €20-€27, Dessert €7-€9.50, Service optional **Wines** 33 bottles over €20, 9 by glass **Notes** Fixed 3 course menu available for groups over 10 €35 pp, Sunday L, Vegetarian available, Civ Wed 50 **Seats** 70, Pr/dining room 50 **Children** Portions, Menu

CO MONAGHAN

CARRICKMACROSS
Map 1 C4

Restaurant at Nuremore

◉◉◉ – see opposite

GLASLOUGH
Map 1 C5

Snaffles

◉◉ Modern Irish **NEW**

Modern country-house cooking in splendid isolation

☎ 047 88100
The Lodge, Castle Leslie Estate
e-mail: info@castleleslie.com
dir: M1 junct 14 N Belfast signed Ardee/Derry. Follow N2 Derry Monaghan bypass, then N12 to Armagh for 2m, left N185 to Glaslough

The Castle Leslie Estate extends over 1,000 acres, and both the castle and The Lodge are separate country-house hotels within the estate. Snaffles, in the latter, is a large, stylish restaurant where a glass wall gives country views, and a baby grand piano adds to the atmosphere. The kitchen keeps its finger on the pulse of culinary trends, turning its hands to crab salad with citrus fruit and herb salad, and duck confit with pickled girolles and pear chutney. Among main courses, Fermanagh Saddleback pork comes as glazed rib, rolled roasted fillet and black pudding with Parmentier potatoes and sauerkraut, with an Armagh cider sauce and sultanas, and pan-fried halibut is fashionably partnered by bean and chorizo cassoulet. Finish with a lemon tartlet with Italian meringue and blackberry puree - beautifully presented and bursting with vibrant flavours.

Chef Andrew Bradley **Owner** Samantha Leslie **Times** 6-9.30 Closed various, L all week **Prices** Fixed D 4 course €45-€55, Service optional **Wines** 68 bottles over €20, 10 by glass **Notes** Tasting menu available, Vegetarian available **Seats** 110, Pr/dining room 50 **Children** Portions, Menu **Parking** 200

Save on Hotels. Book at **theAA.com/hotel**

CO MONAGHAN 671 IRELAND

Restaurant at Nuremore

Modern French v NOTABLE WINE LIST

Creative cooking at first-class country house

☎ 042 9661438
Nuremore Hotel
e-mail: info@nuremore.com
web: www.nuremore.com
dir: M1 junct 14, N2. Hotel 3km S of Carrickmacross

In that sweet spot about an hour's drive from both Dublin and Belfast, this classic country-house hotel in the rolling Monaghan countryside is the perfect upscale bolt-hole for anyone who's up for a bit of downtime in the luxurious spa, or simply ambling about in its acres of parkland. But for many, the name of the game at Nuremore is golf: thanks to its A-list championship course in the backyard. Quite apart from the pampering and putting, there is also serious gastronomy going on in the restaurant, a classically-styled venue with a split-level layout that gives everyone fine views across the gardens and lake; a confident and thoroughly professional front-of-house team keeps it all moving along with smiling efficiency. After more than a decade at the culinary helm, head chef Ray McArdle has moved on to pastures new, leaving a crack team who have all served stints in top London kitchens to carry on the good work. The style is

underscored by classical French techniques, backed by a kitchen tooled up with all the cutting edge technology of a 21st-century operation. What turns up on the table is creative and of-the-moment, often involving fashionable treatments such as sous-vide cooking and low-temperature poaching. Expert butchery and bakery is all done in-house, and attention to detail is meticulous. A brace of perfectly-roasted herb and garlic-marinaded quail breasts opens the show, supported by a deep-fried fritter of leg meat and black pudding, caramelised shallots and roasting juices. Next comes a roast fillet of line-caught halibut atop a purée of fennel with Sauternes, and Sauternes butter sauce, or go for a sautéed rack of Cooley Mountain lamb with shallot soubise, roast silverskin onions, onion 'snow' and red wine jus. Finally, a rich and buttery almond financier filled with diced pear is teamed with pear poached in sauvignon blanc syrup.

Chef Kevin Crossan **Owner** Gilhooly Family **Times** 12.30-2.30/6.30-9.45 Closed L Mon-Sat **Prices** Starter €5-€13.50, Main €19.50-€26.50, Dessert €7.50, Service optional
Wines 153 bottles over €20, 18 by glass
Notes Prestige menu €80, Sunday L, Vegetarian menu, Civ Wed 300
Seats 120, Pr/dining room 50
Children Portions, Menu **Parking** 200

CO SLIGO

SLIGO
Map 1 B5

The Glasshouse

◉ Modern V

Modern Irish brasserie cooking

☎ 071 9194300
Swan Point
e-mail: info@theglasshouse.ie
dir: N4 to Sligo town. Continue through rdbt, on entering relief road take 2nd turning on right, continue to Wine Street, Hotel on left on Hyde Bridge

Rising majestically above the River Garravogue in the city centre, the hotel is kitted out in impeccable modern taste, with lots of glass, simmering blocks of primary colour (including a café-bar in lipstick-crimson) and a light, spacious restaurant with smart table settings and chairs in alternating red and yellow. The modern Irish brasserie food delivers some palpable hits, from accurately timed smoked haddock risotto topped with a poached egg, through breast and confit leg of duck on braised red cabbage with a boldly assertive chocolate and port sauce, or fillet of cod with Killybegs crab on red pepper coulis, to cinnamon-scented crème brûlée.

Chef Enda Delaney **Owner** Michael O'Heir, Ronnie Grenoey **Times** 12-5/6.30-9.30 Closed 25 Dec, **Prices** Food prices not confirmed for 2013. Please telephone for details **Wines** 34 bottles over €20, 8 bottles under €20, 8 by glass **Notes** Sunday L, Vegetarian menu, Dress restrictions, Smart casual, Civ Wed 120 **Seats** 108, Pr/dining room 140 **Children** Portions, Menu **Parking** 160

Radisson Blu Hotel & Spa Sligo

◉ Modern Irish

Classy hotel serving top-grade local produce

☎ 071 9140008 & 9192400
Rosses Point Rd, Ballincar
e-mail: info.sligo@radissonblu.com
dir: From N4 into Sligo to main bridge. Take R291 on left. Hotel 1.5m on right

Named after a castle once owned by Lord Mountbatten, the Classiebawn Restaurant is the culinary focus of this clean-cut modern hotel. Although the décor is faultlessly upmarket, it is the breathtaking views of Sligo Bay and Knockhaven Mountain that immediately grab your attention. The kitchen stays abreast of modern trends and serves up contemporary, internationally-inspired food made with fresh, seasonal, locally-sourced ingredients. Fussy embellishments are kicked into touch here in tried-and-tested stalwarts such as seared scallops with Clonakilty black pudding, creamed potatoes and chive butter sauce, or rump of Connemara lamb with braised Puy lentils teamed with confit garlic and thyme jus. Flavours are on the money to the end - a Classiebawn lemon tart made with an unstinting hand on the lemon zest, served with lime curd.

Chef Joe Shannon **Owner** Radisson Blu **Times** 6-10 **Prices** Fixed D 3 course €25-€34, Starter €6-€9, Main €16-€28, Dessert €6 **Wines** 15 bottles over €20, 4 bottles under €20, 7 by glass **Notes** Seasonal early bird menu, Vegetarian available, Civ Wed 450 **Seats** 120, Pr/dining room 60 **Children** Portions, Menu **Parking** 600

CO TIPPERARY

THURLES
Map 1 C3

Inch House Country House & Restaurant

◉ Irish NEW ⊘

Splendid ingredients cooked simply in Georgian manor

☎ 0504 51348
e-mail: mairin@inchhouse.ie
dir: 6.5km NE of Thurles on R498

Inch House is a lovingly restored Georgian manor house at the heart of a working farm run with hands-on charm by the Egan family. Provenance of food is key here: if it's not local, seasonal, organic or sourced from an artisan producer, it doesn't make it onto the table, and the Inch House own-label black pudding and range of preserves and chutneys are renowned in these parts. The setting for dinner is a classically elegant claret and gold-hued dining room with polished wood floors and white linen on the tables. When the raw materials are as good as we have here, you don't need to gild the lily, so the kitchen treats them with simple, accurately-cooked care in classic dishes that could see the celebrated black pudding appearing in a tartlet with red onion marmalade and Knockdrinna goats' cheese, followed by roast belly of locally-farmed pork served with creamed cabbage, apple sauce and red wine jus.

Chef John Barry **Owner** John & Nora Egan **Times** 6-9.15 Closed Xmas, Sun-Mon, L all week **Prices** Fixed D 3 course fr €35, Starter €9-€13, Main €20-€32, Dessert €8-€12, Service optional **Wines** 4 by glass **Notes** Early bird 5 course D menu, Vegetarian available, Dress restrictions, Smart casual, Civ Wed 30 **Seats** 50 **Children** Portions **Parking** 50

CO WATERFORD

ARDMORE
Map 1 C2

The House

◉◉◉ – see opposite

WATERFORD
Map 1 C2

Faithlegg House Hotel

◉ Modern Irish, French ⊘

Country-house cooking in a historic Waterford hotel

☎ 051 382000
Faithlegg
e-mail: liammoran@fhh.ie
dir: From Waterford follow Dunmore East Rd then Cheekpoint Rd

The present house arose in the 1780s, after Cromwell's ravages in Ireland had gifted the original property to the Bolton family. For a large part of the 20th century, it was a monastic novitiate, with the modern hotel opening in 1998. Overlooking the gardens, the Roseville dining room, with its high ceilings, is fashioned from a pair of original drawing rooms, with a conservatory extension to boot. Modern country-house cooking in a fixed-price format is what to expect, with smoked salmon and guacamole tian and tomato and apple salsa to start, leading to lamb shank Cajun-style with chick peas, bulgar and spiced tomato sauce, or poached haddock with honey-roast parsnips in grain mustard sauce, topped with a poached egg. Finish with crème brûlée, enriched with Tia Maria and served with poppy seed biscuits.

Chef Jenny Flynn **Owner** Tower Hotel Group **Times** 1-2.30/6-9.30 Closed 25 Dec, L pre-book only **Prices** Fixed L 3 course €28.50, Fixed D 4 course €49, Service optional **Wines** 52 bottles over €20, 8 by glass **Notes** Twilight menu 6-7.30 wine & dine €79 per couple, Sunday L, Vegetarian available, Dress restrictions, Smart casual, Civ Wed 200 **Seats** 86, Pr/dining room 50 **Children** Portions, Menu **Parking** 120

The House

Modern Irish v 🍲

Thrilling cooking at the sea's edge

☎ 024 87800 & 87803
The Cliff House Hotel
e-mail: info@thecliffhousehotel.com
web: www.thecliffhousehotel.com
dir: N25 to Ardmore. Hotel at the end of
village via The Middle Road

Built into the cliffs of Ardmore Bay - a
couple more feet and it would be in the
water - the hotel has dramatic sea
views, and a speedboat to whisk guests
away to picnics on secluded beaches.
The architects chose a number of
natural materials for the interior, among
them slate, granite and wood, but it
feels more comfortable than a shrine to
modernism, not least in the bar and
restaurant, which both look out to sea
over a terrace. Quite where Martijn
Kajuiter gets inspiration is difficult to
judge, but he produces extraordinarily
creative, complex dishes; even reading
the menu takes some concentration.
Take a starter of three perfectly seared
scallops; they come dusted with dried
coral powder, served with textures of
cauliflower - grilled, pickled, purée -
along with borage jelly, cubes of
carrageen, lightly blanched samphire
(both from the seashore below) and wild
flowers, a triumph of flavours, colours
and textures. Another tour de force, and
just as prettily arranged, is a main

course of meltingly tender loin of veal
with herb stuffing, slowly poached, then
quickly seared, accompanied by
delicious saffron-flavoured gnocchi,
sweetbread croquettes and deep-fried
courgette flowers in a light tempura.
Fish gets similar treatments: sea bass
fillet with brandade cannelloni, crab
porridge, leeks and two sauces, a red
wine syrup and fish jus. If dishes
haven't already induced oohs and ahs,
then inventive desserts like a theme on
peach certainly will.

Chef Martijn Kajuiter **Owner** Valshan
Ltd **Times** 6.30-10 Closed Xmas, Sun-
Mon (occasional Tue), L all week
Prices Fixed D 3 course €68, Tasting
menu €95, Service included
Wines 120 bottles over €20, 12 by glass
Notes Tasting menu available, Sunday
L, Vegetarian menu **Seats** 64, Pr/dining
room 20 **Children** Portions **Parking** 30

WATERFORD *continued*

Waterford Castle Hotel and Golf Resort

◉◉ French, European ✪

Traditional setting for confident, modish cooking

☎ 051 878203
The Island
e-mail: info@waterfordcastle.com
dir: From city centre turn onto Dunmore East Rd, 1.5m, past hospital, 0.5m left after lights, ferry at bottom of road

Set on its own private 300-acre island accessed by a ferry, Waterford Castle is a charming traditionally-decorated hotel with the added attraction of a golf course and the Munster Dining Room. Here, men are encouraged to wear jackets. There's a resident pianist adding further to the old-school atmosphere generated by the oak-panelled walls and ornate ceiling. The modish Irish cooking is underpinned with French classical thinking, the daily-changing menu making the most of the local larder. Start perhaps with Sally Barnes' smoked haddock in a risotto with fennel, tarragon, parmesan shavings and herb oil, before a soup or sorbet (carrot and coriander or apple respectively). For the main event might come peppered haunch of wild Wicklow venison with celeriac purée, red cabbage, oxtail croquette and beetroot jus, and to finish, a perfectly wobbly vanilla pannacotta with poached champagne rhubarb, almond crumble and green tea and pickled ginger sorbet.

Chef Michael Quinn **Owner** Munster Dining Room
Times 6.30-9 Closed Xmas, early Jan, L all week
Prices Fixed D 4 course €62.50, Service added but optional 10% **Wines** 50+ bottles over €20, 8 by glass
Notes Early bird menu 5.30-7, Vegetarian available, Dress restrictions, Jacket or shirt required for D, Civ Wed 100 **Seats** 50, Pr/dining room 30 **Children** Portions, Menu **Parking** 200

CO WEXFORD

GOREY   Map 1 D3

Ashdown Park Hotel

◉ Mediterranean, European

Straightforward cooking in an elegant setting

☎ 053 9480500
Station Rd
e-mail: info@ashdownparkhotel.com
dir: On approach to Gorey town take N11 from Dublin. Take left signed for Courtown. Hotel on left

The popular Ashdown Park Hotel is just a short stroll from the town centre in Gorey, and its Rowan Tree Restaurant attracts both overnight guests and locals alike with its accomplished traditional cooking. Located on the first floor, it's an elegant space, with tables spilling out onto a terrace for alfresco dining when the weather allows. The menu changes daily and makes good use of quality, often local, ingredients. There could be cream of celeriac and apple soup with a selection of breads to start, or golden

fried brie with Ballymaloe relish and green leaves. Braised shank of Wexford lamb with sweet potato purée, roast garlic and thyme jus makes a fine main course, while dessert could be a tricky choice between mango cheesecake or warm Bakewell tart with vanilla custard.

Chef David Crossoir **Owner** Thomas & Patrick Redmond
Times 12.30-3/5.30-9 Closed 24-26 Dec, L Mon-Fri
Prices Food prices not confirmed for 2013. Please telephone for details **Wines** 4 by glass **Notes** Sunday L, Vegetarian available, Dress restrictions, Smart casual, Civ Wed 400 **Seats** 104, Pr/dining room 100 **Children** Portions, Menu **Parking** 150

Marlfield House

◉◉ Classical ✪

Grand hotel dining in the heart of Wexford

☎ 053 9421124
Courtown Rd
e-mail: info@marlfieldhouse.ie
dir: N11 junct 23, follow signs to Courtown. Turn left for Gorey at Courtown Road Rdbt, hotel 1m on the left

There's a more democratic system in place since the times when the Earls of Courtown held grand house parties in their opulent Regency era Wexford home. These days, anyone with the price of dinner to hand can buy into Marlfield's luxurious country-house experience, sipping cocktails in the library before taking a seat in one of the series of dining rooms leading onto the elegant conservatory. Lovely murals and mirrors interspersed with huge windows opening onto immaculate gardens, and well-polished service help create a sense of occasion for the kitchen's confidently-cooked contemporary dishes. The kitchen garden furnishes seasonal herbs, fruit and vegetables to bolster supplies of local fish and meat, which are put to good use in Mediterranean-accented ideas such as spiced vegetable couscous in filo pastry with houmous, and coriander and chilli gremolata, followed by grilled brill with sauté baby fennel, creamed potato and dill beurre blanc.

Chef Ruadhan Furlong **Owner** The Bowe Family
Times 12.30-2.30/7-9 Closed Xmas, Jan-Feb, Mon-Tue (Mar-Apr, Nov-Dec), L Mon-Sat **Prices** Fixed L 2 course fr €22, Fixed D 3 course fr €43, Service added 5% **Wines** 200 bottles over €20, 20 bottles under €20, 10 by glass **Notes** Fixed D 5 course €64, Sunday L, Vegetarian available, Dress restrictions, Smart dress, no jeans, Civ Wed 140 **Seats** 80, Pr/dining room 50 **Children** Portions, Menu **Parking** 100

Seafield Golf & Spa Hotel

◉ Modern European **NEW**

Contemporary cooking in a modern spa hotel

☎ 053 942 4000
Ballymoney
e-mail: reservations@seafieldhotel.com

A contemporary, Italian-designed hotel on the shore at Ballymoney, less than an hour's drive out of Dublin, caters for modern tastes, in the familiar spectrum from fairways to massage-tables, with some fine dining in the intervals between. A nine-foot-high bronze female centaur stands guard over the dining room, where lighting and music levels are kept soft, and the décor is in fashionable black, from the marble walls to the chandeliers. The modern European cooking makes all the right noises, starting with a rectangular plate of salmon variations - poached, confit, lime-cured with dill, and a smoked salmon crème brûlée - followed by more variations on a theme, this time of aubergine, with seared best end of Wicklow lamb, served with a single roasted polenta chip and air-dried cherry tomatoes, finished at the table with a reduced lamb jus.

Times 12.30-3/6.30-9.30

ROSSLARE   Map 1 D2

Beaches

◉ Traditional European

Beachside resort hotel with modern cooking

☎ 053 9132114
Kelly's Resort Hotel & Spa
e-mail: info@kellys.ie

The Beaches restaurant is aptly named, as it sits on five miles of golden sands in Rosslare. The Kelly family have run their resort hotel since 1895 - why move when you can work in a setting like this? - and the venue is set up to capitalise on the views, bathed in light through good-sized windows, and with restful pastel hues, white linen on the tables, and a mini gallery of original artworks on the walls. Local produce is as good as it gets, and the kitchen has the experience and confidence to treat it all simply and let the sheer quality do the talking in simple contemporary dishes. Confit duck arrives in an unfussy combo with spiced pears and baked plums with five spice, while local goose is roasted and pointed up with chestnut stuffing, braised ham, caramelised pear and glazed pearl onions. Yoghurt and lime pannacotta with raspberry sorbet provides a refreshing finale.

Times 1-2/7.30-9 Closed mid Dec-mid Feb

La Marine Bistro

◉ Modern

Bistro-style cooking at a smart seaside resort hotel

☎ 053 9132114
Kelly's Resort Hotel & Spa
e-mail: info@kellys.ie

The more casual stand-alone restaurant of Kelly's Resort Hotel is an easygoing venue with views of the chefs at work in the open kitchen. The shipshape French bistro theme suits the beachside setting to a T, as does its menu of classic Gallic bistro fare, which is all built on the eminently solid foundations of spanking fresh local produce. Top-class fish and seafood comes but a short way from Kilmore Quay to be treated simply and sent out in ideas such as monkfish medallions with warm saffron and garlic mayonnaise, or scallops with creamy spiced Puy lentils and coconut crème fraîche. Meat eaters are not sent home hungry either - there may be roast rack of lamb with gratin dauphinoise and redcurrant sauce, and to finish, pear, chocolate and almond pithivier or well-chosen local cheeses. (See entry above for another dining option.)

Times 12.30-2/6.30-9

CO WICKLOW

ENNISKERRY   Map 1 D3

Gordon Ramsay at The Ritz Carlton Powerscourt

◉◉ Modern European V

Ramsay-style fine dining in a hidden Palladian hotel

☎ 01 2748888
Powerscourt Estate
e-mail: powerscourtgordonramsay@ritzcarlton.com
dir: N11 to R117 Enniskerry, follow signs for Powerscourt Gardens

Crouched beneath thick woodland on the east coast, the hotel looks a little as though it's hiding from the outside world, which is a fair approximation of the mood that the Ritz Carlton empire has attempted to create here. Within the Palladian mansion, it's possible to sit in state by full-drop windows, or take your table in the light, white, spacious Gordon Ramsay dining room. The menu is written with admirable concision, but what turns up on the plate is all flash and panache, underpinned by fantastic materials such as daisy-fresh seafood, Wicklow lamb, organic pork and pedigree Irish cheeses. A cold lobster starter is traditionally served with potato salad, plum tomatoes and basil, or there might be west Cork scallops with broad beans, girolles and pea shoots. Next along could be duck breast with Savoy and baby beetroot, served with a little cottage pie, with classic French pâtisserie to conclude - nougat glacé with cherry compôte and a pistachio tuile, perhaps, or raspberry vacherin with matching sorbet.

Chef Peter Byrne **Owner** Treasury Holdings
Times 1-2.30/6-10 Closed Mon, L Tue-Fri **Prices** Food prices not confirmed for 2013. Please telephone for details **Wines** 200 bottles over €20, 15 by glass **Notes** Vegetarian menu **Seats** 120, Pr/dining room 24 **Children** Portions, Menu

MACREDDIN   Map 1 D3

BrookLodge & Wells Spa

◉◉ Modern Irish ☺

Dramatic dining venue, organic and wild food

☎ 0402 36444
e-mail: info@brooklodge.com
web: www.brooklodge.com
dir: N11 to Rathnew, R752 to Rathdrum, R753 to Aughrim, follow signs to Macreddin Village

The Strawberry Tree is the foodie destination at the swanky country-house retreat of the BrookLodge hotel at the purpose-built Macreddin Village - comprising an 18-hole golf course and spa, a pub and brewery, café, bakery, smokehouse, and Italian restaurant. In a strikingly opulent setting, The Strawberry Tree (dinner-only) spreads through three grand, moodily Gothic rooms with mirrored ceilings reflecting twinkling modern chandeliers, bare burnished mahogany tables, and gilt-framed mirrors on midnight-blue walls. Given its status as Ireland's first certified organic restaurant, provenance of seasonal ingredients is king; so if it's not wild it's sourced from certified organic producers, with herbs and soft fruit grown in the estate's own walled garden. The kitchen shows its skill in dishes like seared wild mallard breast served with parsnip mash, red onion jam and rosemary sauce, or pan-fried wild John Dory teamed with swiss chard and saffron cream. To finish, gingerbread with apple compôte, honey-vanilla cream and hazelnut tuile.

Chef Tim Daly, Evan Doyle **Owner** The Doyle Family
Times 7-9.30 Closed varies, check web, L all week **Wines** 100 bottles over €20, 21 by glass **Notes** Fixed D 5 course €65-€95, Vegetarian available, Dress restrictions, Smart casual, Civ Wed 120 **Seats** 120, Pr/dining room 50 **Children** Portions **Parking** 200

RATHNEW   Map 1 D3

Hunter's Hotel

◉ Traditional

Well-judged Irish cooking in the Wicklow countryside

☎ 0404 40106
e-mail: reception@hunters.ie
dir: N11 exit at Wicklow/Rathnew junct. 1st left onto R761. Restaurant 0.25m before village

Maybe someone should inform the Guinness World Records people that this coaching inn set in lovely gardens on the banks of the River Vartry has been run by five generations of the same family since 1825. And its heritage shows in an old school approach that delivers courteous, chatty service in a delightful primrose-yellow-walled dining room, and honest-to-goodness traditional Irish cooking that leaves pedigree local produce to speak for itself in accurately-cooked dishes such as butter-poached grey mullet with chilli and garlic beurre blanc, or chargrilled beef fillet with spring onion and mushroom velouté. Before that, you might begin with pan-fried foie gras with fresh strawberry relish, and wind things up with toffee, pecan and hazelnut roulade.

Times 12.45-3/7.30-9 Closed 3 days Xmas

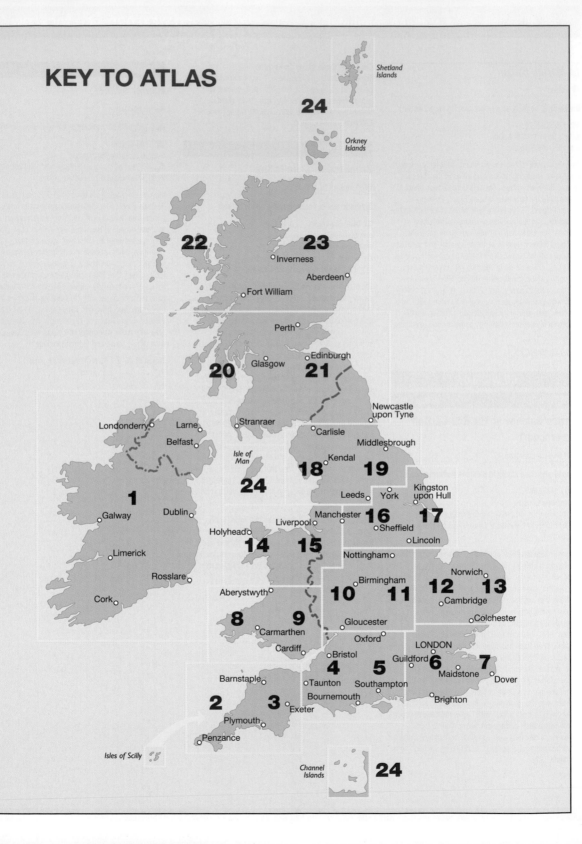

KEY TO ATLAS

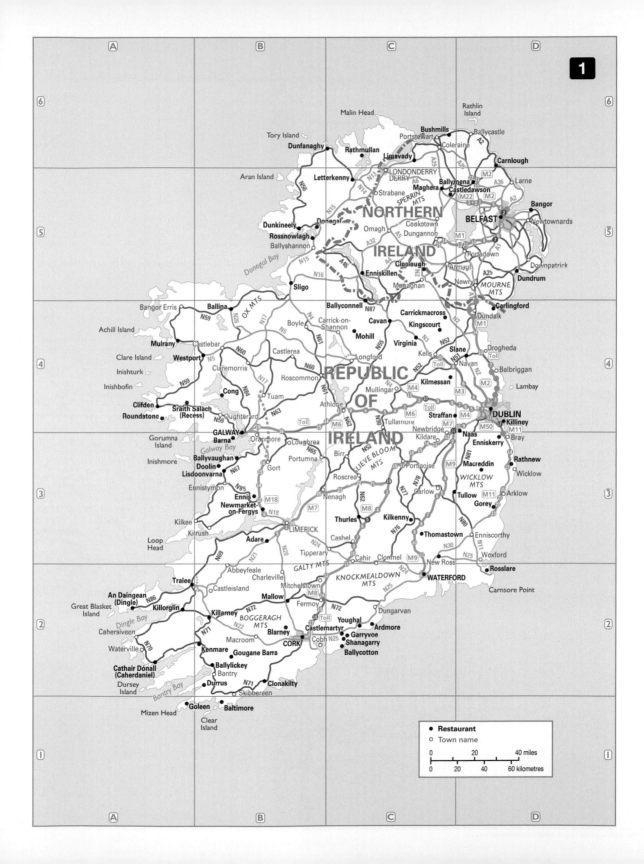

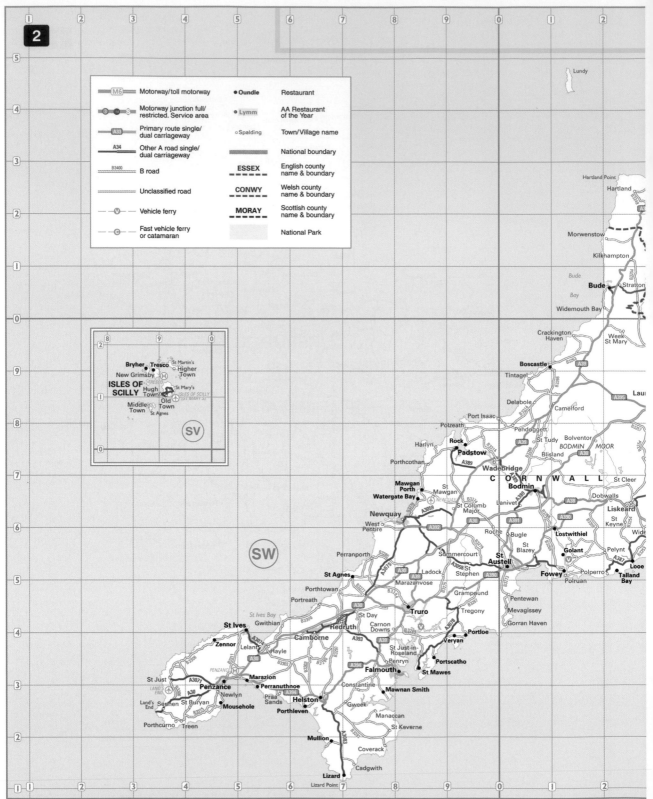

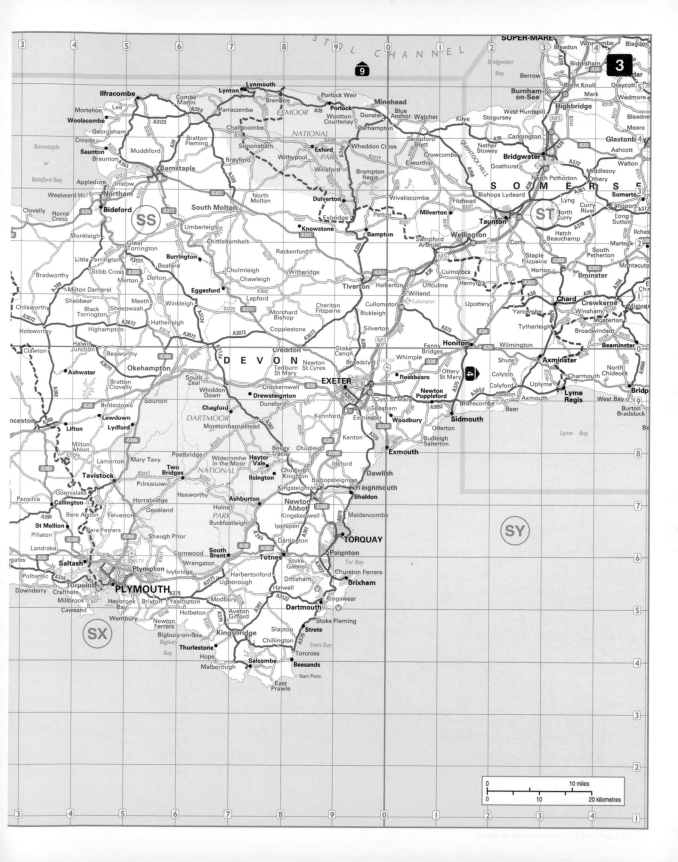

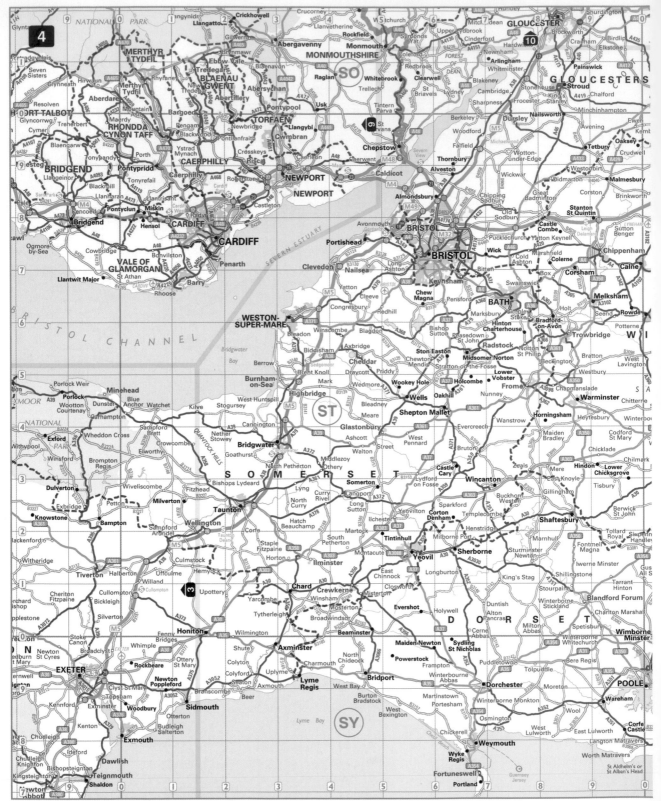

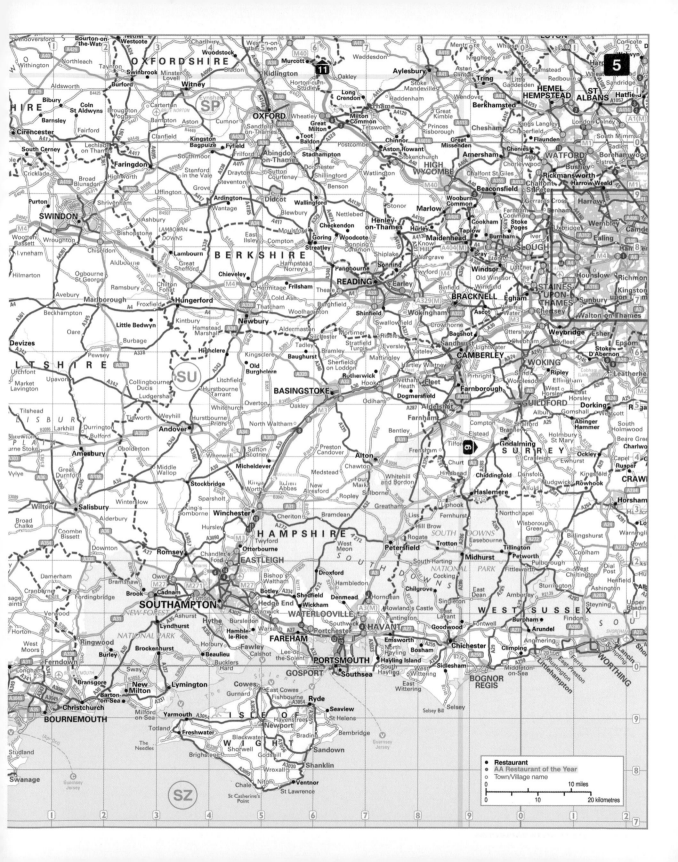

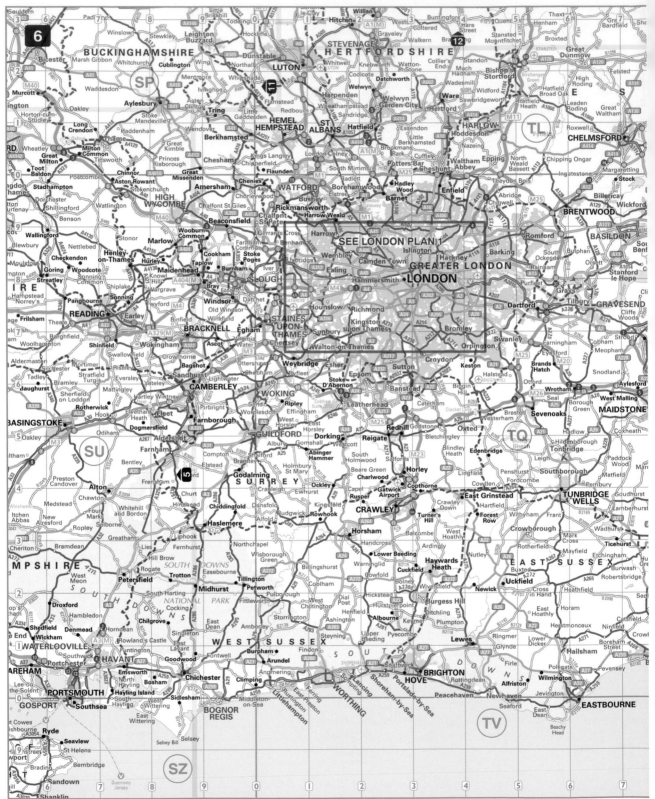

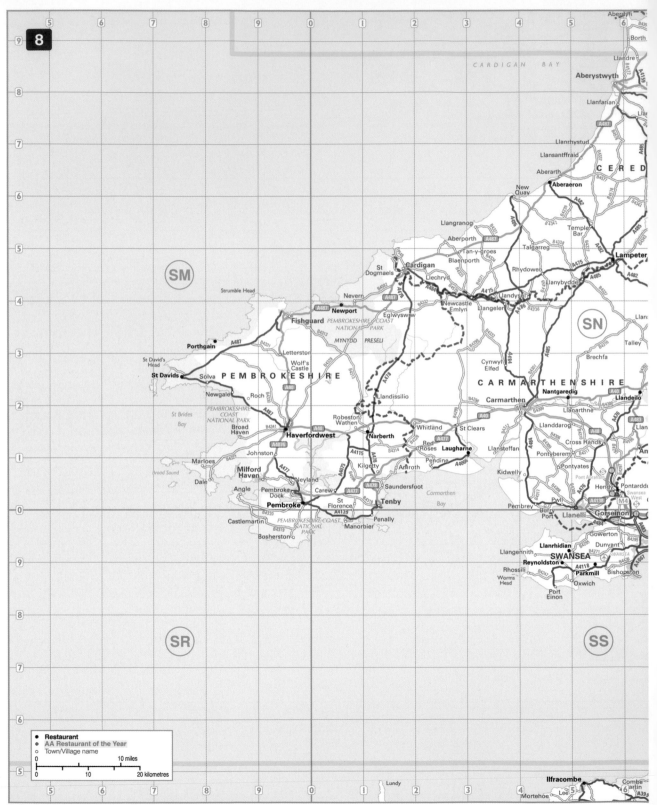

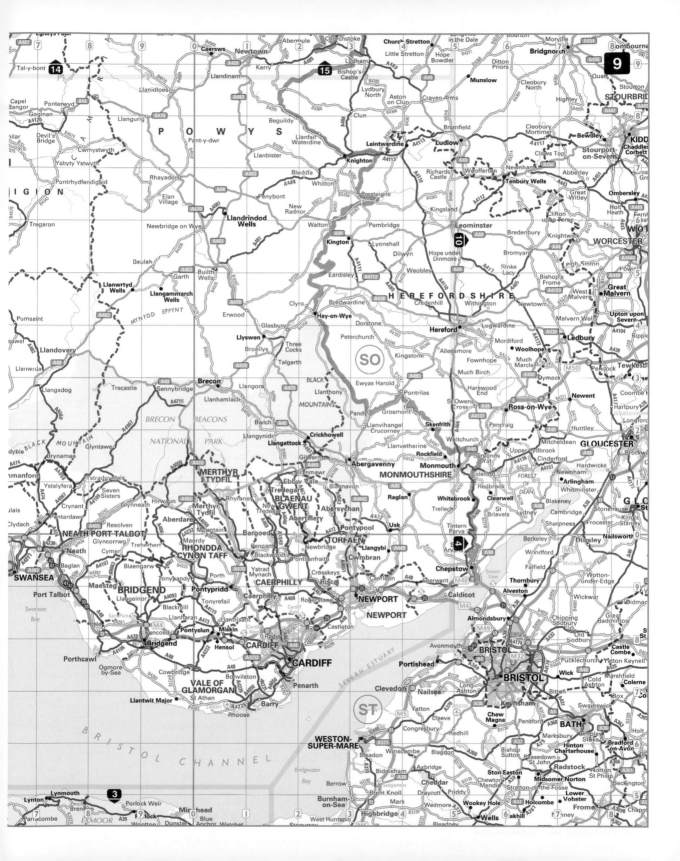

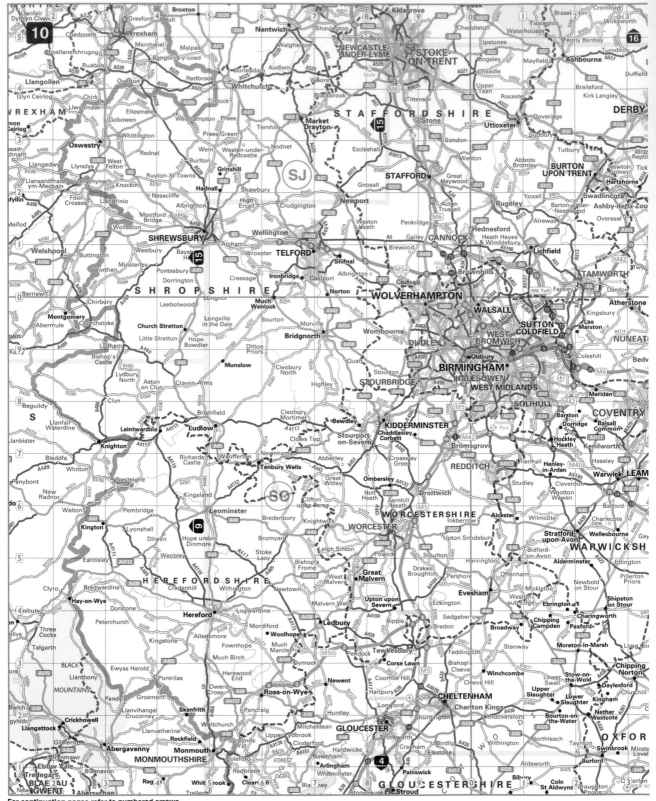

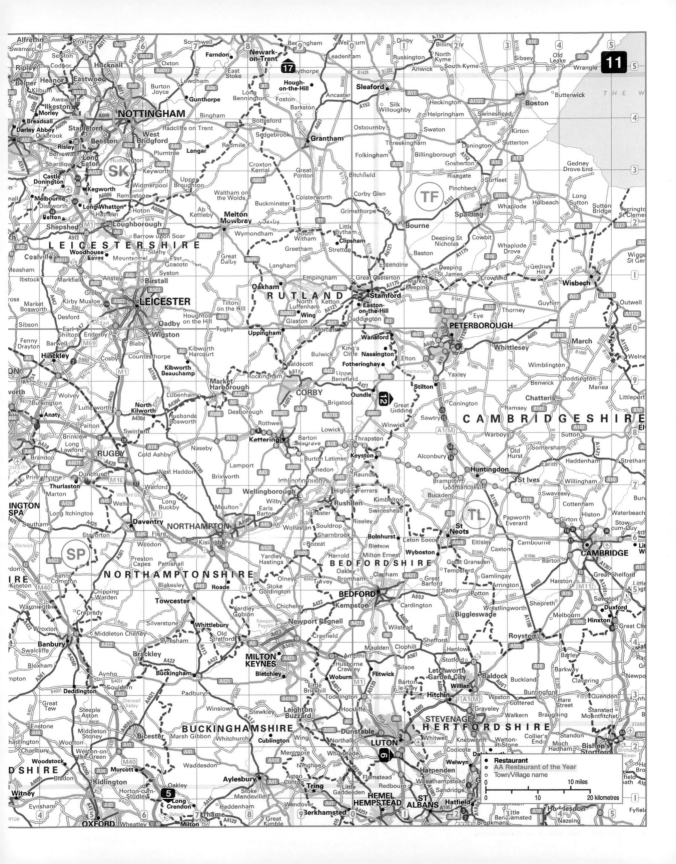

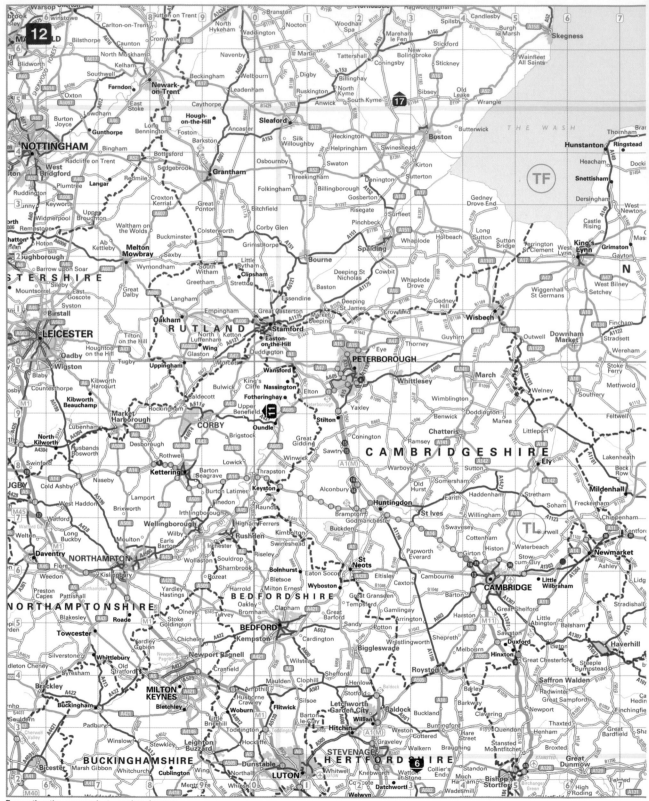

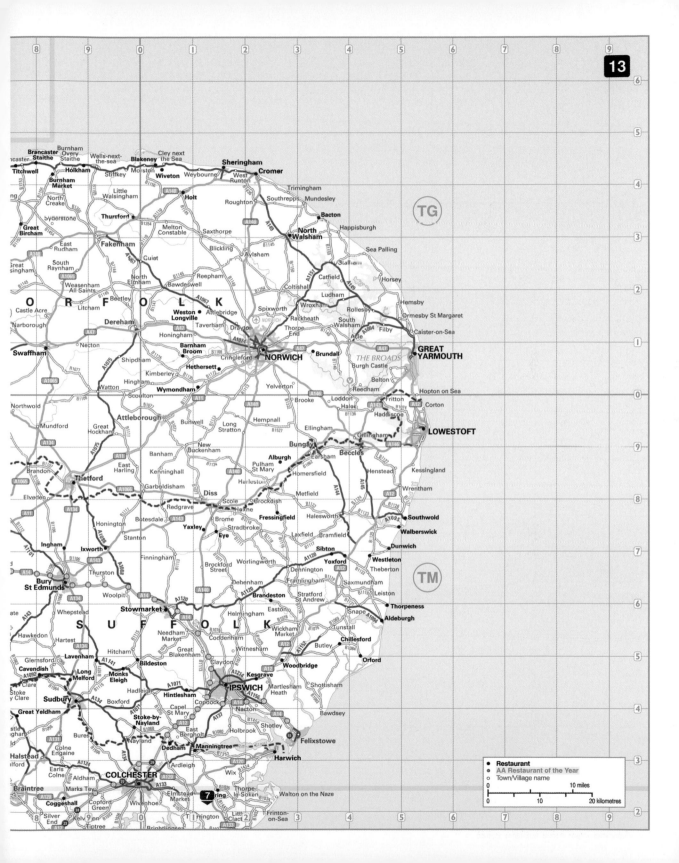

ISLE OF
ANGLESEY

Cemaes

Amlwch

Llanerchymedd

Holyhead

Treaddur Bay

Holy
Island

Rhosneigr

Aberffraw

Newborough

Llanfachraeth

Llangefni

Benllech

Red
Wharf Bay

Llangoed

Pentraeth

Llanfair
P G

Menai
Bridge

Bangor

Beaumaris

Llanfairfechan

Penmaenmawr

Llandudno

Deganwy

Conwy

Rhôs-
on-Sea

Colwyn Bay

Llanddulas

Llansanffraid
Glan Conwy

Betws-yn-Rhos

Rhyl

Abergele

Y Felinheli

Caernarfon

Bontnewydd

Caernarfon
Bay

Llandwrog

Clynnog-fawr

Llanaelhaearn

Morfa Nefyn

Nefyn

Sarn

Bodfuan

LLEYN

PENINSULA

Aberdaron

Y Rhiw

Bardsey
Island

Pwllheli

Llanbedrog

Abersoch

Criccieth

Borth-y-Gest

Porthmadog

Portmeirion

Tremadog

Llanystumdwy

Penygroes

Penrhyndeudraeth

Penmorfa

Talsarnau

Trawsfynydd

Harlech

Llanbedr

Dyffryn Ardudwy

Tal-y-bont

Barmouth

Fairbourne

Llwyngwril

Bryncrug

Tywyn

Aberdyfi

Borth

Tal-y-bont

Llandre

Aberystwyth

Capel
Bangor

Ganllwyd

Dolgellau

Pennal

Machynlleth

Eglwys Fach

Ponterwyd

Llanrug

Llanberis

Llanllechid

Bethesda

Tal-y-Bont

Llanwnda

Rhyd-Ddu

Beddgelert

SH

Dolwyddelan

Capel Curig

Betws-y-Coed

Penmachno

Blaenau Ffestiniog

Ffestiniog

Moelwyn

Maentwrog

GWYNEDD

Llanuwchllyn

NATIONAL

PARK

Dinas-Mawddwy

Mallwyd

Corris

Cemmaes
Road

Llangadfan

Llanbrynmair

Carno

SN

CARDIGAN   BAY

CONWY

Tal-y-Cafn

Trefriw

Llanrwst

Llanfairfechan

Llangernyw

Llanfair
Talhaiarn

Llansannan

Bylchau

Pentrefoelas

Cerrigydrudion

Y Maerd

Bala

SNOWDONIA

MOUNTAIN

9

For continuation pages refer to numbered arrows

Restaurant
AA Restaurant of the Year
Town/Village name

0   10 miles
0   10   20 kilometres

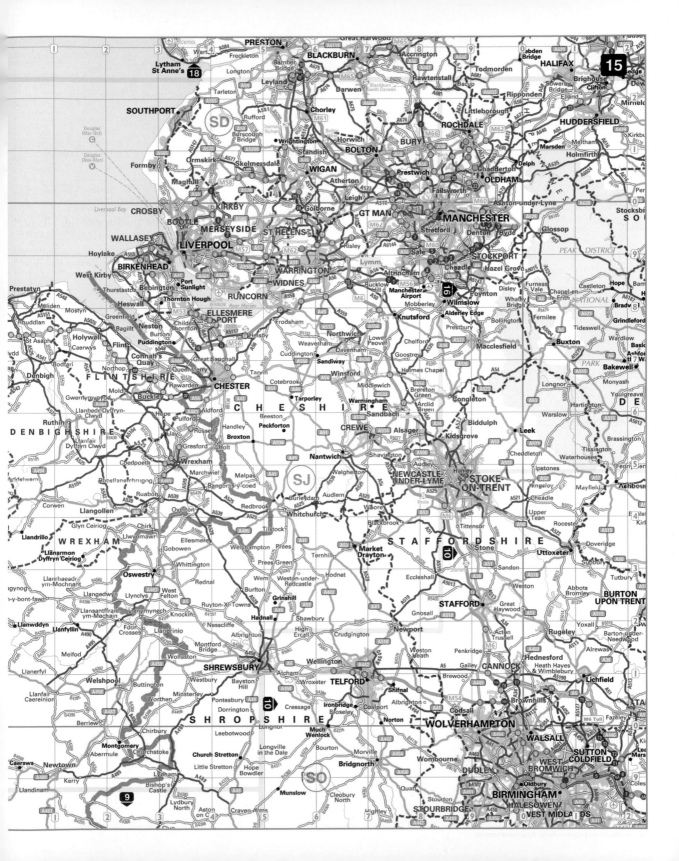

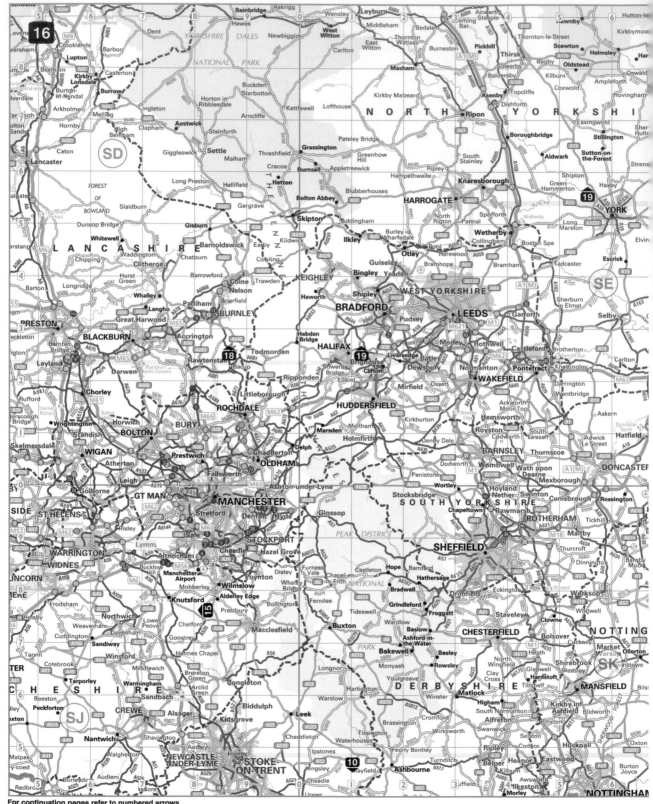

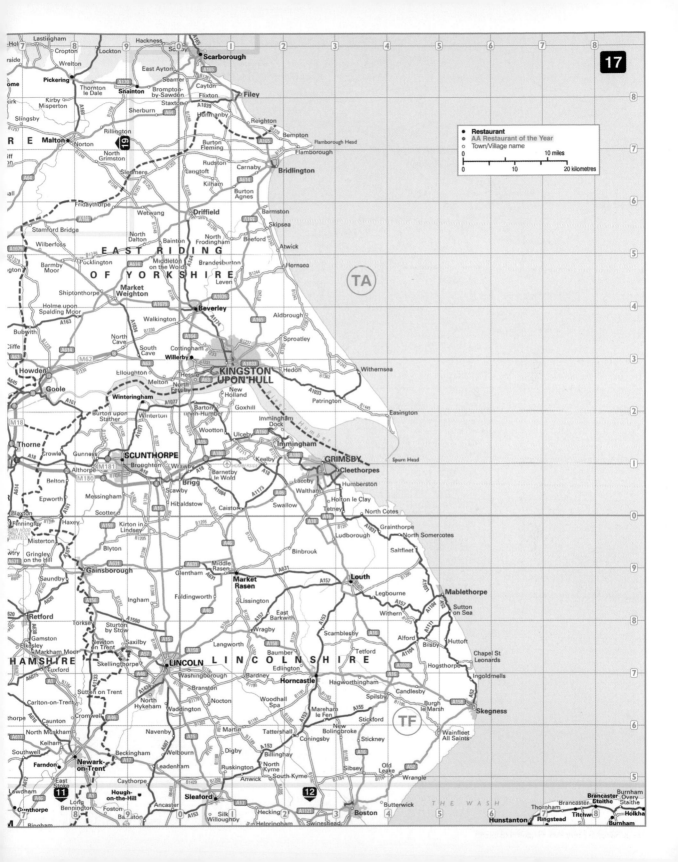

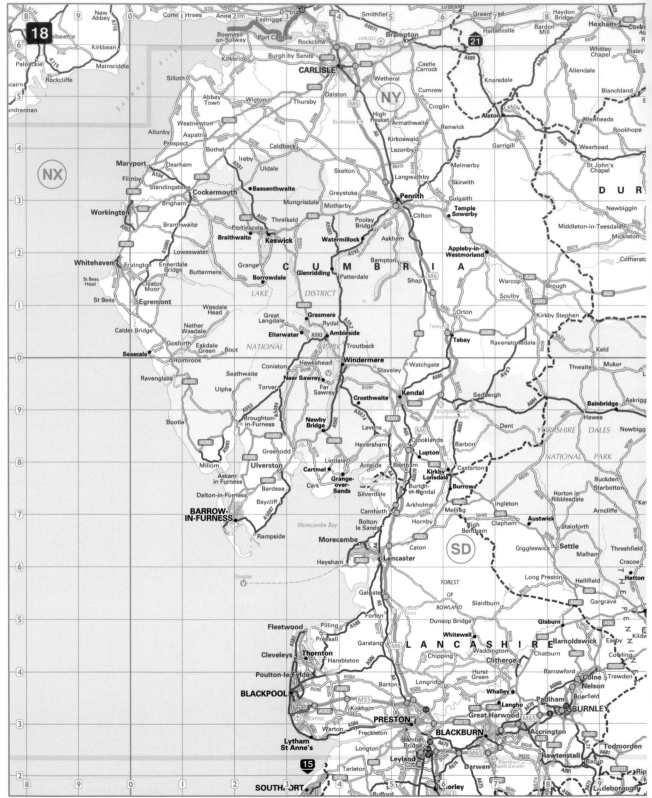

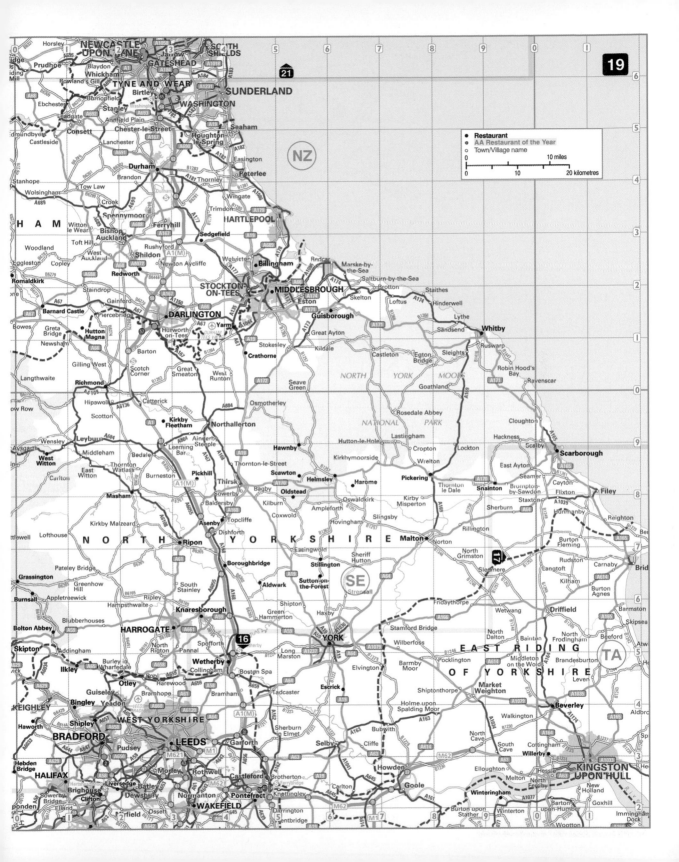

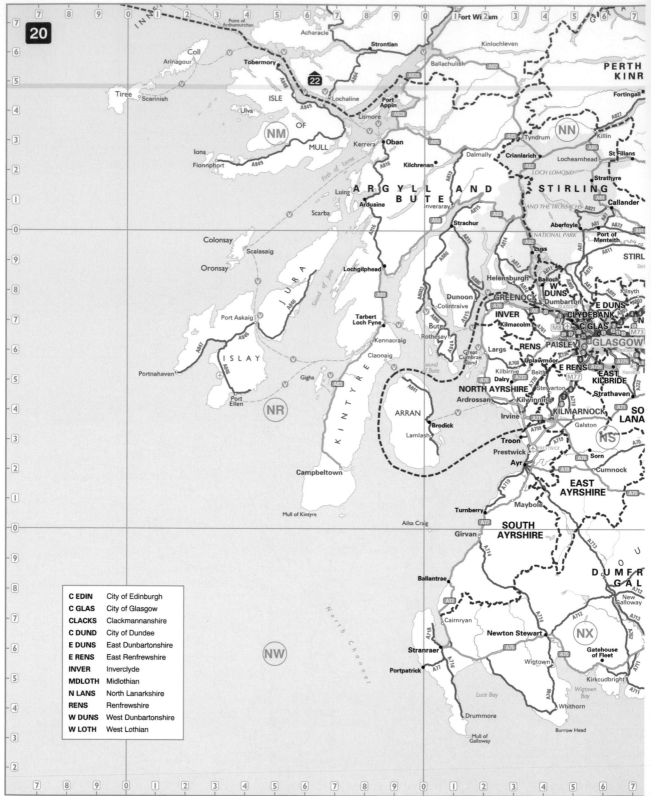

C EDIN   City of Edinburgh
C GLAS   City of Glasgow
CLACKS   Clackmannanshire
C DUND   City of Dundee
E DUNS   East Dunbartonshire
E RENS   East Renfrewshire
INVER   Inverclyde
MDLOTH   Midlothian
N LANS   North Lanarkshire
RENS   Renfrewshire
W DUNS   West Dunbartonshire
W LOTH   West Lothian

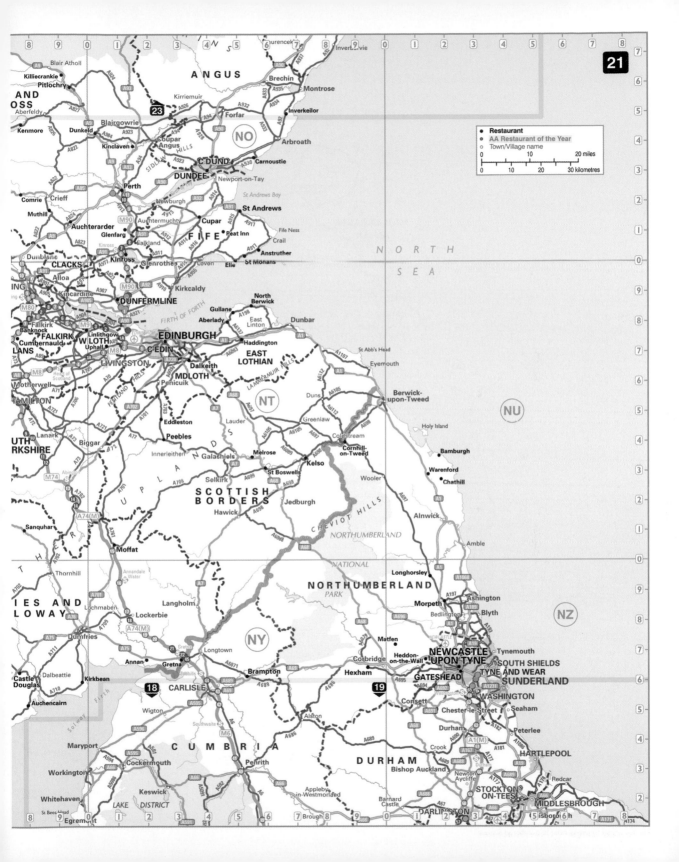

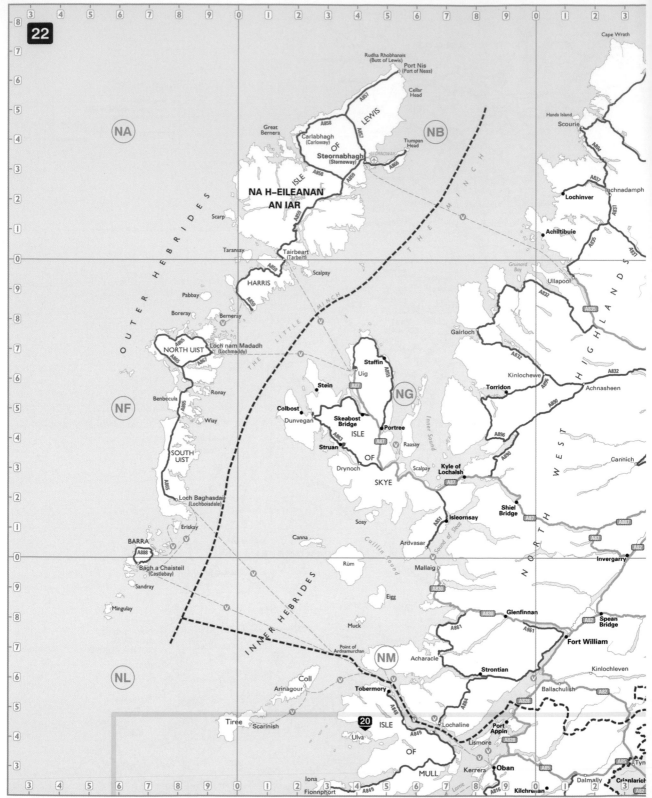

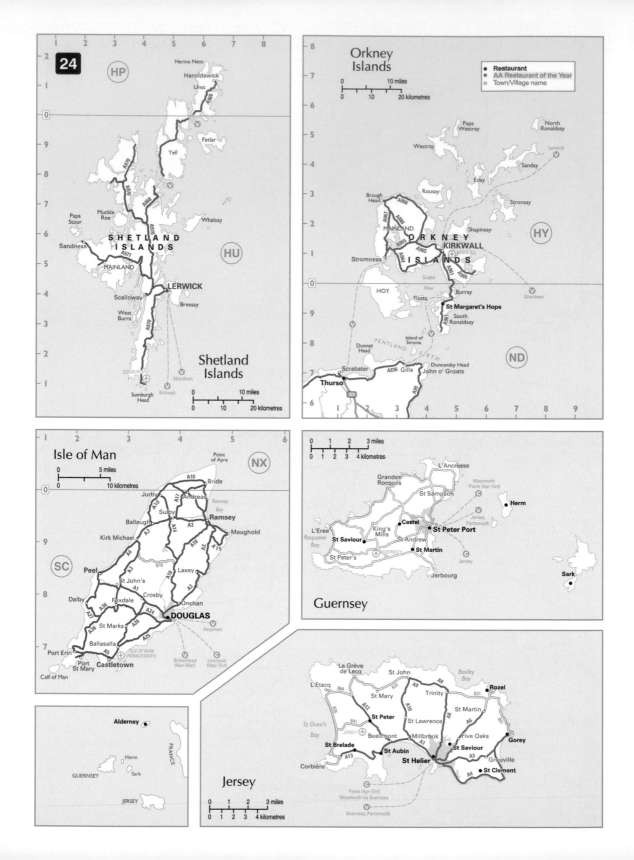

Save on Hotels. Book at theAA.com/hotel

INDEX 701 ENGLAND

Index of Restaurants

Save on Hotels. Book at **theAA.com/hotel**

INDEX 705 ENGLAND

Save on Hotels. Book at **theAA.com/hotel**

INDEX 707 ENGLAND

Save on Hotels. Book at theAA.com/hotel

INDEX 711 ENGLAND

Save on Hotels. Book at theAA.com/hotel

INDEX 713 ENGLAND

Acknowledgments

The Automobile Association would like to thank the following photographers, companies and picture libraries for their assistance in the preparation of this book.

Abbreviations for the picture credits are as follows – (t) top; (b) bottom; (c) centre; (l) left; (r) right; (AA) AA World Travel Library.

England Opener AA/Tom Mackie; London Opener AA/James Tims; Scotland Opener AA/Jonathan Smith; Wales Opener AA/Harry Williams; Northern Ireland Opener AA/Christopher Hill; Republic of Ireland Opener AA/AA; 001b Courtesy The Tom Aikens Restaurant; 002l Martin Thomas Photography/Alamy; 003tl keith morris/Alamy; 005b AA/Neil Setchfield; 007tr Courtesy Pollen Street Social; 008/009l VIEW Pictures Ltd/Alamy; 011tl Photoshot; 012bl Courtesy The Hand & Flowers/Nikki English; 013tr Getty Images; 014tl Courtesy Pierre Koffmann; 015bl Courtesy Pierre Koffmann; 016tl Courtesy Tony Briggs; 017 Courtesy Tony Briggs; 018l Courtesy The Church Green British Grill; 018r Courtesy Dinner by Heston Blumenthal; 019l Courtesy Rogand; 019r Courtesy Sosban Restaurant; 020 Courtesy Chewton Glen Restaurant; 022tr Courtesy L'Etranger; 023l Courtesy L'Etranger; 023c Courtesy Castle Terrace; 023r Courtesy The Felin Fach Griffin; 024 Courtesy The Pig in Brockenhurst; 027t Courtesy The Tom Aikens Restaurant; 028t Courtesy Pollen Street Social; 028b Courtesy Pollen Street Social; 030c Courtesy Chewton Glen Restaurant; 031tl Courtesy Roganic; 031cl Courtesy Roganic; 031bl Courtesy Roganic; 032/033l Courtesy Neal Haynes; 034bl Courtesy Ashley Palmer-Watts; 035tr Courtesy Neal Haynes

Every effort has been made to trace the copyright holders, and we apologise in advance for any unintentional omissions or errors. We would be pleased to apply any corrections in a following edition of this publication.

Readers' Report Form

Please send this form to:–
Editor, The Restaurant Guide,
Lifestyle Guides,
AA Media,
Fanum House,
Basingstoke RG21 4EA

e-mail: lifestyleguides@theAA.com

Please use this form to recommend any restaurant you have visited, whether it is in the guide or not currently listed. Feedback from readers helps us to keep our guide accurate and up to date. Please note, however, that if you have a complaint to make during your visit, we strongly recommend that you discuss the matter with the restaurant management there and then, so that they have a chance to put things right before your visit is spoilt.

Please note that the AA does not undertake to arbitrate between you and the restaurant management, or to obtain compensation or engage in protracted correspondence.

Date

Your name (BLOCK CAPITALS)

Your address (BLOCK CAPITALS)

Post code

E-mail address

Restaurant name and address: (if you are recommending a new restaurant please enclose a menu or note the dishes that you ate.)

Comments

(please attach a separate sheet if necessary)

Please tick here ☐ if you DO NOT wish to receive details of AA offers or products

PTO

Readers' Report Form *continued*

Have you bought this guide before?   ☐ YES   ☐ NO

Please list any other similar guides that you use regularly

What do you find most useful about The AA Restaurant Guide?

Please answer these questions to help us make improvements to the guide:

What are your main reasons for visiting restaurants? (tick all that apply)

Business entertaining ☐   Business travel ☐   Trying famous restaurants ☐   Family celebrations ☐

Leisure travel ☐   Trying new food ☐   Enjoying not having to cook yourself ☐

To eat food you couldn't cook yourself ☐   Because I enjoy eating out regularly ☐

Other (please state)

How often do you visit a restaurant for lunch or dinner? (tick one choice)

Once a week ☐   Once a fortnight ☐   Once a month ☐   Less than once a month ☐

Other (please state)

Do you use the location atlas?   ☐ YES   ☐ NO

Do you generally agree with the Rosette ratings at the restaurants you visit in the guide?
(If not please give examples)

Who is your favourite chef?

Which is your favourite restaurant?

Which type of cuisine is your first choice e.g. French?

Which of these factors is the most important when choosing a restaurant? (tick one choice)

Price ☐   Service ☐   Location ☐   Type of food ☐

Awards/ratings ☐   Decor/surroundings ☐

Other (please state)

What elements of the guide do you find most useful when choosing a restaurant? (tick all that apply)

Description ☐   Photo ☐   Rosette rating ☐   Price ☐

Other (please state)